Preface

For almost a year I've worked on this book, putting countless demonstration programs on paper and developing new subject matter. I wanted to present my readers with EVERYTHING they'd need to know about system programming on the PC, but this is an impossible task. The PC world is affected by what science has long recognized as one of the basic principles of evolution: the differentiation of sub-systems.

We cannot know everything, whether the subject is politics, science or PC system programming. There are simply too many subjects in a state of permanent flux. Think about PC hardware. Ten years ago we had a clear definition of a PC: a system with an 8088 processor, a hastily designed bus system, a simple ROM-BIOS, one disk drive, 256K of RAM at most, and a Monochrome Display Adapter for displaying text. Today, the term "PC" refers to a set of hardware and software standards, on which an almost infinite number of products are based, in almost infinite complexity.

The Protected mode available on high end Intel processors is one of the major subjects of this decade, and you'll find a chapter that discusses Protected mode in this book. This book also features other subjects of great interest to the software developer: DOS Version 5.0, network programming, and even Microsoft Windows.

I wrote this book with the idea of addressing system programming from the angle of everyday work on the PC. For this reason, some subjects aren't covered as exhaustively as others. You'll find general information on hard drives, the realtime clock and the parallel interface.

If you've read my first book, *PC System Programming*, you'll notice that this book is organized differently. This should help you find subject matter faster. Above all, you'll notice that hardware and BIOS programming has been redistributed.

Last but not least, I thank all who were involved with this book, especially the Product Development Department at Data Becker and Abacus.

Michael Tischer   February 1992

PC INTERN

SYSTEM PROGRAMMING

The Encyclopedia of
DOS Programming Know How

By Michael Tischer

 **Abacus**
A Data Becker Book

Printed in U.S.A.
10 9 8 7 6 5 4 3 2 1

Copyright © 1994, 1993, 1992   Abacus
     5370 52nd Street, S.E.
     Grand Rapids, MI 49512

Copyright © 1993, 1992   DATA BECKER GmbH
     Merowingerstrasse 30
     4000 Duesseldorf, Germany

Every effort has been made to ensure complete and accurate information concerning the material presented in this book. However, Abacus can neither guarantee nor be held legally responsible for any mistakes in printing or faulty instructions contained in this book. The authors always appreciate receiving notice of any errors or misprints.

This book contains trade names and trademarks of many companies and products. Any mention of these names or trademarks in this book are not intended to either convey endorsement or other associations with this book.

PC-DOS, IBM PC, XT, AT, PS/2, OS/2 and PC-BASIC are trademarks or registered trademarks of International Business Machines Corporation. Ventura Publisher is a trademark or registered trademark of Xerox Corporation. GEM and CP/M are trademarks or registered trademarks of Digital Research Corporation. Microsoft Works, Microsoft Quick C, Microsoft Windows, MS-DOS, XENIX and GW-BASIC are trademarks or registered trademarks of Microsoft Corporation. Lotus 1-2-3 is a trademark or registered trademark of Lotus Development Corporation. dBASE is a registered trademark of Ashton-Tate, Inc. Sidekick, Turbo C and Turbo Pascal are trademarks or registered trademarks of Borland International. UNIX is a registered trademark of Bell Laboratories. Mickey Mouse is a registered trademark of Walt Disney Corporation.

```
Library of Congress Cataloging-in-Publication Data
Tischer, Michael, 1953-
    PC intern / Michael Tischer.
        p.  cm.
    Includes index.
    ISBN 1-55755-145-6 : $59.95
    1. Microcomputers.  I. Title.
QA76.5.T545  1992                              92-7362
004.165--dc20                                  CIP
```

Printer in USA

10 9 8 7 6 5 4

Table of Contents

Chapter 1

System Programming Basics

In the first part of this book we'll discuss the fundamentals of system programming. We'll talk about the purpose of, the methods and tools used in system programming. We'll also explain the PC's basic structure and the interaction between hardware, BIOS, and DOS.

1.1 What's System Programming?

If you asked beginning PC users or programmers for their definition of system programming, you'd probably receive different answers. Some users think system programming is a programming technique that converts a problem into a finished program. Others think system programming means developing programs for one particular computer system.

Application programming vs. system programming

Although both answers are incorrect, the second is more accurate than the first. The most accurate description of system programming can be derived from the term *application programming*. This type of programming refers to information management and presentation within a program. This involves arranging this information into lists, etc., and processing this information. The algorithms used for this are system independent and can be defined for almost any computer.

The way that this information is passed to a program, and the way that the information is displayed or printed are system dependent. System programming controls any hardware that sends information to, or receives information from, the computer. However, since this information must be processed, developing programs for PCs requires both application programming and system programming.

Programming hardware requires the interaction of system programming, DOS, and the ROM-BIOS (more on this later).

1.2 The Three-Layer Model

One of the most important tasks of system programming involves accessing the PC hardware. However, the access doesn't have to occur immediately, with the program turning directly to the hardware, which is similar to accessing the processor on a video card. Instead, the program can use the ROM-BIOS and DOS to negotiate hardware access. The ROM-BIOS and DOS are software interfaces, which were created specifically for hardware management.

Advantages of the DOS and BIOS interfaces

The greatest advantage of using DOS or BIOS is that a program doesn't have to communicate with the hardware on its own. Instead, it calls a ROM-BIOS routine that performs the required task. After the task is completed, the ROM-BIOS returns status information to the program as needed. This saves the programmer a lot of work, because calling one of these functions is faster than directly accessing the hardware.

There's another advantage to using these interfaces. The ROM-BIOS and DOS function interfaces keep a program isolated from the physical properties of the hardware. This is very important because monochrome graphic cards, such as the MDA and Hercules cards, must be programmed differently from color graphic cards, such as the CGA, EGA, VGA, and Super VGA. If you want a program to support all of these cards, you must implement individual routines for each card, which is very time-consuming. The ROM-BIOS functions used for video output are adapted to the resident video card, so the program can call these functions without having to adapt to the video card type.

ROM-BIOS

As the following illustration shows, the ROM-BIOS can be viewed as a layer overlapping the hardware. The BIOS offers functions for accessing the following devices:

- Video cards
- RAM (extended memory)
- Diskettes
- Hard drives
- Serial ports
- Parallel ports
- Keyboard
- Battery-operated realtime clock

Although you can bypass the ROM-BIOS and directly access the hardware, generally you should use the ROM-BIOS functions because they are standardized and can be found in every PC. The ROM-BIOS, as its name indicates, is in a ROM component on the computer's motherboard. The moment you switch on your computer, the ROM-BIOS is available (see Chapter 3 for more information).

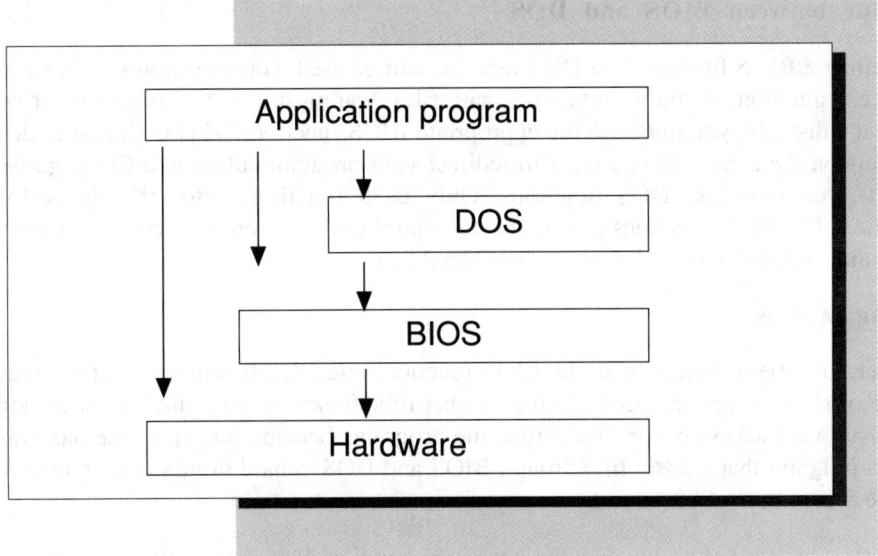

The three-layer-model

DOS interface

Along with BIOS, DOS provides functions for accessing the hardware. However, since DOS views hardware as logical devices instead of physical devices, DOS functions handle hardware differently. For example, the ROM-BIOS views disk drives as groups of tracks and sectors, but DOS views these drives as groups of files and directories. If you want to view the first thousand characters of a file, first you must tell the ROM-BIOS the location of the file on the drive. With DOS functions, you simply instruct DOS to open a file on drive A:, C:, or whatever device, and display the first thousand characters of this file.

Access often occurs through BIOS functions used by DOS. However, sometimes DOS also accesses hardware directly, but you don't have to worry about this when you call a DOS function.

Which functions should you use?

Later in this chapter we'll show you how to call DOS and BIOS functions. Before doing this, however, we must determine which hardware access to use. We have the option of direct hardware programming, calling BIOS functions, and calling DOS functions.

First, you don't always have a choice between direct hardware programming, and BIOS and DOS functions. Many tasks aren't supported by the BIOS or DOS functions. For example, if you want your video card to draw circles or lines, you won't find the appropriate functions in DOS or the BIOS. You must use direct hardware programming or purchase a commercial software library that contains this program code.

Choosing between BIOS and DOS

When either a BIOS function or a DOS function can be used, your decision should be based on the current situation. If you want to work with files, you must use DOS functions. If you want to format a diskette, you must use the appropriate BIOS functions. This is similar to displaying characters on the screen. If you want to redirect your program output to a file (e.g., with DIR >list.txt), you must use DOS functions. Only DOS functions automatically perform this redirection. The BIOS functions provide better control of the screen (e.g., cursor placement). So, the situation determines which function you should use.

Slowing access

However, in some instances, both the BIOS functions and DOS functions are at a disadvantage because of slow execution speed. As the number of software layers, which must be negotiated before hardware access occurs, increases, the programs become longer. If the hardware must access a program that reads a file through BIOS and DOS, a hard drive's data transfer rate can decrease a maximum of 80 percent.

This problem is caused by the way the layers are handled. Before the call can be passed to the next level, parameters must be converted, information must be loaded from internal tables, and buffer contents must be copied. The time needed for this passage is called *overhead*. So, as overhead increases, so does the programmer's work.

As a result, when maximum execution speed is required and direct hardware programming is relatively simple, programmers often use direct access instead of the BIOS and DOS. The best example of this is character output in text mode. Almost all commercial applications choose the most direct path to the hardware because BIOS and DOS output functions are too slow and inflexible. Direct video card access in text mode is quite easy (refer to Chapter 4 for more information), although graphic mode output offers more challenges.

Later in this chapter you'll learn how to call the DOS and BIOS functions and how to directly access the hardware of the PC.

1.3 Basics of PC Hardware

In this section we'll examine some of the basic concepts of PC architecture, which lead all the way to the system programming level. Knowing something about the hardware will make it easier to understand some of the programming problems discussed later in this book.

1.3.1 Birth of the PC

When the PC appeared on the market, much of what PC users take for granted today was inconceivable. The concept of having a flexible computer on a desktop wasn't new; companies much smaller than IBM had already introduced similar computers. IBM had just completed work on its System/23 DataMaster. However, the DataMaster was equipped with an 8085 8-bit processor from Intel, which was outdated. In 1980, the 16-bit processor was introduced and IBM began planning a new, revolutionary machine.

Choosing a processor

The 8086 and 8088 processors from Intel were the first representatives of the new 16-bit processors. Both had 16-bit registers. This meant that they could access 1 megabyte memory addresses instead of the old 64K memory addresses. A megabyte was an unimaginable amount of memory in 1980, just as 1 gigabyte of RAM is still unimaginable to many today.

Another reason developers were anxious to use the 8086 and 8088 processors was that many support chips already existed. Obviously this saved a lot of development time. Also, both processors were supported by an operating system and an implementation of the BASIC language, which was developed by Microsoft Corporation.

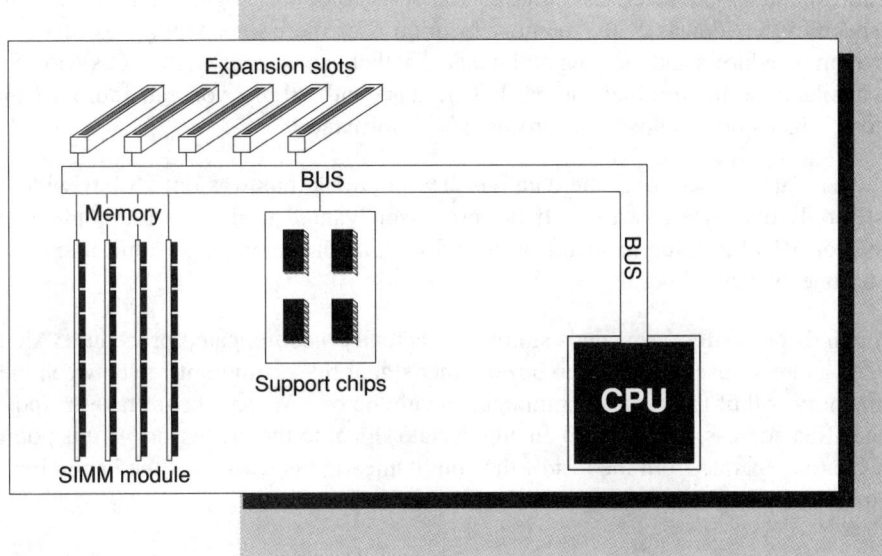

Block diagram of a PC's hardware

The developers chose the 8088 over the 8086 because, while the 8088 worked on a 16-bit basis internally, it only communicated with the outside world using an 8-bit data bus. Since the 8-bit DataMaster data bus already existed, the 8088 was the obvious choice.

This bus connects the motherboard of the PC, where the processor and its support chips are resident, to the memory and the expansion boards, which are plugged into the expansion slots.

1.3.2 The Bus

Although the bus is vital to the operation of the computer system, the development of the PC bus represents one of the darkest moments in the history of the PC. Although IBM tried to create an open system and publish all technical information, it neglected to document the exact sequence of the bus signals, probably assuming that no one would need or want this information.

However, the openness of the PC and the option of easily adding expansion boards and more hardware added to the PC's success on the market. Many users quickly took advantage of this, buying IBM expansion boards and third-party compatible boards. The PC has its entire data and address bus on the outside; the bus connects to RAM, the various expansion boards, and some support chips.

Operating the PC bus

The bus is basically a cable with 62 lines, from which data are loaded into memory by the processor, and through which data can be transported to the processor.

The bus consists of the data bus and the address bus. When memory is accessed, the processor puts the address of the desired memory location on the address bus, with the individual lines indicating a binary character. Each line can be only a 0 or a 1. Together, the lines form a number that specifies the address of the memory location. The more lines that are available, the greater the maximum address and the greater the memory that can be addressed in this way. Twenty lines were available on the original address bus because with 20 bits you can address 1 megabyte of memory, which corresponds to the processor's performance.

The actual data are sent over the data bus. The first data bus was only 8 bits wide, so it could transfer only one byte at a time. If the processor wanted to discard the contents of a 16-bit register or a 16-bit value in memory, it had to split the register or value into two bytes and transfer one byte at a time.

Although theoretically this sounds simple, it's actually a complicated procedure. Along with the data and address buses, almost two dozen other signal lines communicate between the processor and memory. All of the boards communicate with the bus. When a board takes responsibility for the specified address, it must send an appropriate signal to the processor. At this point, all of the other boards separate from the rest of the communication and wait for the beginning of the next data transfer cycle.

Using expansion boards always leads to problems. This usually occurs when two boards claim the same address range or there are overlapping address ranges. The DIP switches on these boards let you specify the address range. One board must be reconfigured to avoid conflict with the other board.

As a system programmer, you'll never encounter bus signals. Actually, bus performance usually isn't important to system programming.

The bus signal timing is very important to expansion board manufacturers. Their products must follow this protocol in order to function in the PC. However, this is the protocol that IBM never published. So, the manufacturers must measure the signal sequences by using existing cards and then imitate those cards.

AT bus

In 1991, the IEEE (Institute of Electrical and Electronic Engineers) submitted an international standard for the AT bus. The PC bus was limited by its 8-bit width. When the AT appeared on the market, it included a 16-bit bus that was compatible with the older bus. That's why the old PC 8-bit boards can be used with the new 16-bit boards in one device. Obviously, the 16-bit boards are much faster because they can transfer the same data in half the time it would take an 8-bit board.

The address bus was expanded to 24 bits, so the AT can address 16 megabytes of memory. Also, higher clock signal speed increased bus transfer time. From 4.77 MHz on the PC, the AT speed increased to 8 MHz. However, that's as fast as the AT address bus can handle information, even though processor speeds are quickly approaching the 50 MHz limit. As a result, the bus is a bottleneck, through which the data will never be transferred quickly enough between memory and the processor. Modern hard drives have a higher data transfer rate than the bus.

Wait state

The *wait state* signals found in some expansion boards give slow boards more time to deliver data to the processor.

This is also one reason why the classic AT bus resulted in more powerful successors like the Micro Channel bus and the EISA bus, which haven't been very successful on the market for other reasons. At first there wasn't a generic name for the AT bus. However, when competition appeared on the market, the bus was assigned the name Industry Standard Architecture bus, or ISA bus.

Problems with 16-bit boards on the AT bus

Since most of the modern 386s and 486s have an ISA bus, many problems in the PC can be traced to this bus. For example, the coexistence of 8-bit and 16-bit expansion boards within a PC causes problems as long as the address range for which these boards are responsible is located within any area of 128K. The problem starts at the beginning of a data transfer, when a 16-bit board has to signal from a control line that it can take a 16-bit word from the bus and, unlike an 8-bit board, doesn't depend on the transfer being split into two bytes.

However, the board must send this signal when it cannot even be aware that the address on the data bus is intended for it and requires an answer. Of the 24 address lines that carry the desired address, only lines A17 to A23 have been correctly initialized up to this point. This means that the board only recognizes bits 17 to 23. These bits cover a complete 128K region, regardless of what might follow in address bits 0 to 16. So for the moment, the board only knows whether the memory address is located in the 0K—127K region, the 128K—255K region, etc.

If the 16-bit board sends the signal for a 16-bit transfer at this moment, it's speaking for all other boards within this region. They experience this in the next moment, because after address bits 0 to 16 have arrived on the bus, the intended board will be determined. If it really is the 16-bit board, no problems occur. However, if an 8-bit board was intended, the 16-bit board will simply separate from the rest of the transfer, leaving the 8-bit board by itself. However, the 8-bit board won't be able to manage the transfer because it's only set for 8-bit transfers. So, the expansion board cannot accept the data as sent.

1.3.3 Support Chips

Developers supplied the processor with some additional chips to handle tasks that the processor cannot handle on its own. These support chips, which are also called controllers because they control a part of the hardware for the processor, perform many tasks. This enables the processor to concentrate on other tasks.

The following are descriptions of these support chips and the chips initially selected by IBM. If a support chip is programmable, we'll indicate this later in the book.

DMA controller (8237)

DMA is an abbreviation for Direct Memory Access. This technique transfers data directly to memory by using a device (e.g., a hard drive). This method seems to work much faster than the normal method, in which the processor prompts the hardware for each word or byte and then sends the word or byte to memory. Actually, the DMA controller's advantages are evident only with slow processors because the DMA is linked to the bus speed.

Modern processors, which work more than five times as fast as their bus, barely benefit from DMA transfer because the DMA controller in the PC is obsolete. Because of this, the DMA controller cannot even be used for one of the most interesting areas of programming, which is moving large amounts of data from conventional RAM to video RAM (RAM on the video card). This chip is still found in all PCs even though it isn't used for its original purpose, which is data transfer between disk drives and memory. ATs have two DMA controllers.

The PC is equipped with DRAM (dynamic RAM) instead of SRAM (static RAM). DRAMs lose their contents unless the system continually refreshes the RAM. The DMA controllers in AT systems, instead of the processors, perform this RAM refresh.

Interrupt controller (8259)

The interrupt controller is important for controlling external devices, such as the keyboard, hard drive, or serial port. Usually the processor must repeatedly prompt a device, such as the keyboard, in short intervals to react immediately to user input and pass this input to the program currently being executed. However, this continual prompting, also called *polling*, wastes processor time because the user doesn't press a key as often as the processor polls the keyboard. However, the less often the processor prompts the keyboard, the longer it takes until a program notices that a key has been pressed. This obviously defeats the purpose, since the system is supposed to react promptly.

Hardware interrupt

The PC takes another route. Instead of the processor repeatedly prompting the devices, the devices report activity to the processor. This is an example of a *hardware interrupt*, because at that exact moment the processor interrupts the execution of the current program to execute an *interrupt handler*. This interrupt handler is a small routine, usually provided by the BIOS, that deals with the event that triggered the interrupt. After the routine ends, the processor continues executing the interrupted program as though nothing happened. This means that the processor is called only when something actually happens.

However, the process of triggering an interrupt, halting program execution, and calling the interrupt handler takes a long time. Expansion board and support chip interrupt requests are sent to the interrupt handler first, instead of to the processor. The PC has several interrupt lines, each connected to a device. Each of these devices could trigger an interrupt over its line simultaneously.

Because the processor can only process one interrupt at a time, priorities must be defined so that the incoming interrupt requests are handled according to their priority. The interrupt controller is responsible for determining priority.

The interrupt controller in a PC/XT can process up to eight interrupt sources, which enables it to handle eight interrupt requests simultaneously. Since this isn't sufficient for an AT, two interrupt controllers are coupled on the AT. Together they can process up to 15 interrupt requests simultaneously. For more information about hardware interrupts, refer to Section 1.6.3.

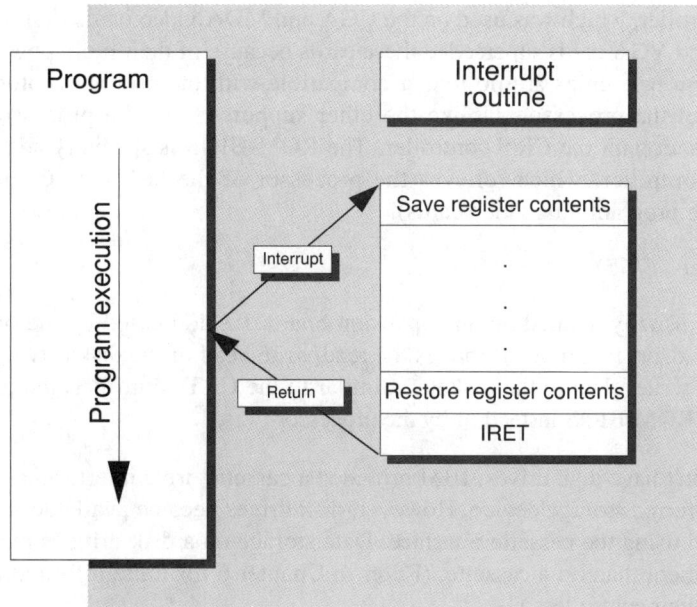

Interrupting a program through an interrupt

Programmable peripheral interface (8255)

This chip connects the processor to peripheral devices, such as the keyboard and speaker. It acts only as a mediator, which is used by the processor to pass given signals to the desired device. (Refer to Chapter 13 for more information on this chip and how it's used to make musical sounds.)

The clock (8248)

If the microprocessor is the brain of the computer, then the clock could be considered the heart of the computer. This heart beats several million times a second (about 14.3 MHz) and paces the microprocessor and the other chips in the system. Since almost none of the chips operate at such high frequencies, each support chip modifies the clock frequency to its own requirements.

The timer (8253)

The timer chip can be used as a counter and timekeeper. This chip transmits constant electrical pulses from one of its output pins. The frequency of these pulses can be programmed as needed, and each output pin can have its own frequency. Each output pin leads to another component. One line goes to the audio speaker and another to the interrupt controller. The line to the interrupt controller triggers interrupt 8 at every pulse, which advances the timer count.

CRT controller (6845)

Unlike the chips we've discussed so far, the CRT (Cathode Ray Tube) controller is separate from the PC's motherboard (main circuit board). This chip is located on the video card, which is mounted in one of the computer's expansion slots. Originally the controller was a Motorola 6845 model controller, which was used on the CGA and MDA video cards first released by IBM. The later EGA and VGA cards superseded these cards because of their more powerful processors. Even though these new chips are no longer compatible with the original Motorola controllers, this doesn't affect the processor. Unlike the other support chips, the processor doesn't come directly into contact with the CRT controller. The ROM-BIOS is specially adapted to working with the CRT controller, which relieves the processor of the task (see Chapter 4 for more information about programming video cards).

Disk controller (765)

This chip is also usually located on an expansion board. It's addressed by the operating system and controls disk drive functions. It moves the read/write head of the disk drive, reads data from the diskette, and writes data to the diskette. Similar to the CRT controller, the disk controller is addressed by the ROM-BIOS instead of by the processor.

The first PCs didn't have disk drives. IBM provided a cassette drive interface, assuming that this would be the preferred storage device. However, disk drives became available shortly afterward, and IBM stopped using the cassette interface. Data storage on a disk drive is much safer, faster, and more convenient than on a cassette. (Refer to Chapter 6 for more information on diskettes, hard drives, and their controllers.)

The math coprocessors (8087/80287/80387)

The 8088, 80286, or 80386 aren't capable of performing floating point arithmetic operations directly. A socket on the motherboard of the PC can be used to add a special math coprocessor. Each of the Intel 8088's successors have a matching coprocessor. A coprocessor can significantly increase the execution speed of certain software (e.g., CAD programs). However, coprocessors aren't widely used because they are expensive.

We won't discuss programming a coprocessor in this book because this involves normal assembly language processing instead of system programming. (Refer to Chapter 14 for more information about coprocessors.)

1.3.4 Memory Layout

The first PCs were equipped with 16K of memory, which could be upgraded to as much as 64K on the motherboard. IBM also sold memory expansion boards containing 64K of memory, which could be inserted in one of the five expansion slots. You could install up to three of these boards, upgrading your PC to 256K of memory. In 1981, this was considered a lot of memory.

The PC developers defined a memory layout that allowed RAM expansion to 640K. Along with the RAM expansion, they also planned for additional video RAM, additional ROM-BIOS, and some ROM expansions in the 1 megabyte address space of the 8088 processor.

Whether RAM or ROM is in a given memory location doesn't matter to the processor, except that ROM locations cannot be written. The processor can also address memory locations that don't exist physically. Although the processor can manage up to 1 megabyte of memory, this doesn't guarantee that a RAM or ROM component exists behind every memory address.

As the following illustration shows, this memory layout is based on 64K segments because the 8088 and its successors manage memory in blocks of this size (more on this in Chapter 12). Sixteen of these blocks comprise an address space of 1 megabyte.

Block	Address	Contents
	■ Division of PC RAM ■	
15	F000:0000 – F000:FFFF	ROM-BIOS
14	E000:0000 – E000:FFFF	Free for ROM cartridges
13	D000:0000 – D000:FFFF	Free for ROM cartridges
12	C000:0000 – C000:FFFF	additional ROM-BIOS
11	B000:0000 – B000:FFFF	Video RAM
10	A000:0000 – A000:FFFF	Additional video RAM (EGA/VGA)
9	9000:0000 – 9000:FFFF	RAM from 576K to 640K
8	8000:0000 – 8000:FFFF	RAM from 512K to 576K
7	7000:0000 – 7000:FFFF	RAM from 448K to 512K
6	6000:0000 – 6000:FFFF	RAM from 384K to 448K
4	5000:0000 – 5000:FFFF	RAM from 320K to 384K
5	4000:0000 – 4000:FFFF	RAM from 256K to 320K
3	3000:0000 – 3000:FFFF	RAM from 192K to 256K
2	2000:0000 – 2000:FFFF	RAM from 128K to 192K
1	1000:0000 – 1000:FFFF	RAM from 64K to 128K
0	0000:0000 – 0000:FFFF	RAM from 0K to 64K

The first 10 memory segments are reserved for conventional memory, limiting its size to 640K. Memory segment 0 is important because it contains important data and operating system routines.

Memory segment A follows conventional memory. This segment indicates an EGA or VGA card and contains additional video RAM for generating the various graphics modes supported by these cards.

Memory segment B is reserved for a Monochrome Display Adapter (MDA) or Color/Graphics Adapter (CGA). They share the same segment of video RAM. The monochrome card uses the lower 32K and the color card uses the upper 32K. Each video card only uses as much memory as it needs for the display. The MDA uses 4K while the CGA card uses 16K.

The next memory segment contains ROM beginning at segment C. Some computers store the BIOS routines that aren't part of the original BIOS kernel at this location. For example, the XT uses these routines for hard drive support. Since this location isn't completely utilized, this memory range may be used later to store BIOS routines supporting hardware extensions.

ROM cartridges

Segments D and E were originally reserved for ROM cartridges, but they were never properly used. Today this range is used either for additional RAM or EMS memory (see Chapter 12 for more information).

Segment F contains the actual BIOS routines, the original system loader, and the ROM BASIC available on early PCs.

Following this memory layout

The PC hardware isn't limited to any particular memory layout, including IBM's. However, IBM set the standard with its first PC, and suppliers still follow this standard. This usually affects software because the BIOS and DOS have adapted to the locations of certain memory areas (e.g., video RAM). Every software product on the market also complies with IBM's memory structure.

1.3.5 After the PC

Although the original IBM PC wasn't the last development in the PC world, it did establish a series of basic concepts, including the BIOS functions, the memory layout, and the interaction between the processor and the support chips.

However, the XT and the AT brought a few small changes to these concepts. The XT, released in 1983, had the first hard drive with a 10 megabyte capacity. This upgrade barely affected the total system, except that the C segment was given an additional hard drive ROM, which added some ROM-BIOS functions for hard drive access.

The AT

The AT (Advanced Technology) computer was released in 1984, only one year after the XT. The most significant improvement involved the processor because developers used the Intel 80286 instead of the 8088. This processor finally gave the PC a 16-bit data bus. So, memory accesses no longer had to be divided into two bytes, as long as the memory and expansion board cooperated. Also, the address lines of the bus were increased from 20 to 24 bits because the 80286 could manage 24-bit addresses, which allowed it to address a memory range of 16 megabytes.

Disk drives

The AT doubled the hard drive capacity to 20 megabytes and introduced the 5.25" HD (high density) disk drive with a capacity of 1.2 megabytes. This disk drive is still used today. Also, the AT had a battery operated realtime clock, which finally made it possible for the clock to continue running even after the computer was switched off. The AT also increased the number of DMA controllers and interrupt controllers to two each.

A few new ROM-BIOS functions, such as functions for accessing the battery operated realtime clock, supported the new hardware.

Although the AT provided many improvements, it signaled the beginning of a trend that favors the current version instead of creating solutions for future upgrades. For example, "downward compatibility" in protected mode (an operating mode that separated the 80286 from its predecessors) wasn't widely used until the 80386 and Windows 3.0 were introduced.

When the 80286 appeared, preparations hadn't been made for protected mode. DOS, BIOS, and software avoided supporting this mode. Users continued working in real mode, in which the 80286 acts like a glorified 8088, performing at a fraction of its total capacity. Unfortunately, this is still happening today; real mode will probably be used until the switch to Windows NT and OS/2.

PS/2

After the AT, IBM attempted to set another standard with its PS/2 systems. These systems were successful mainly because of an improved bus system called the Micro-Channel Architecture (MCA). However, IBM kept the architecture of the new bus secret. It provided the information needed for building expansion cards only to hardware manufacturers that paid the licensing fees. This resulted in a limited supply of expansion boards for a system that wouldn't accept any AT boards. ISA boards cannot be used in systems with an MCA bus because the MCA bus has an entirely different line capacity.

No standards after the AT

Many companies began offering less expensive (and sometimes better) alternatives to the AT and PS/2. Companies like Compaq, which released laptop computers and an AT that had an 80386 processor, kept PC technology moving forward.

However, no company could fill the gap that was left by IBM when it dropped in the market. Once the PC market became fragmented, none of the companies had the power to define new hardware/software standards and push them onto the market. After a few years, committees met to set hardware standards (e.g., the Super VGA standard) that improved system and software compatibility.

After the AT, a new PC based on the ISA bus wasn't defined. So, systems with 80386 or 80486 processors are still generically referred to as ATs because they're based on the technology introduced by IBM when the AT was released.

1.4 The Processor

You don't have to become a professional assembly language programmer in order to understand system programming. You can also use high level languages, such as BASIC, Pascal, or C, for system programming. However, you must understand some concepts of the processor that are important in system programming. These concepts, which overlap into high level language programs, include the processor register, memory addressing, interrupts, and hardware access.

Although these principles haven't changed much since the 8088 was introduced, this chip is in its fifth generation and has capabilities that were unheard of ten years ago. However, these changes relate to the processor's speed instead of its fundamental concept.

1.4.1 The PC's Brain

Let's discuss the family of Intel PC processors. The *microprocessor* is the brain of the PC. It understands a limited number of assembly language instructions and processes or executes programs in this assembly language. These instructions are very simple and can't be compared to commands in *high level* languages, such as BASIC, Pascal, or C. Commands in these languages must be translated into numerous assembly language instructions that the PC's microprocessor can then execute. For example, displaying text with the BASIC PRINT statement requires the equivalent of several hundred assembly language instructions.

Assembly language instructions are different for each microprocessor used in different computers. The terms Z-80, 6502, or 8088 assembly language (or machine language) refer to the microprocessor being programmed.

Intel's 80xx series

The PC has its own family of microprocessor chips, which were designed by the Intel Corporation. The following figure shows the Intel 80xx family tree. Your PC may contain an 8086, an 8088 (used in the PC/XT), an 80186, an 80286 (used in the AT), or even an 80386 microprocessor. The first generation of this group (the 8086) was developed in 1978. The successors of the 8086 were different from the original chip. The 8088 is actually a step backward because it has the same internal structure and instructions of the 8086, but is slower than the 8086. The reason for this is that the 8086 transfers 16 bits (2 bytes) between memory and the microprocessor simultaneously. The 8088 is slower since it transfers only 8 bits (1 byte) at a time.

The other microprocessors of this family are improved versions of the 8086. The 80186 provides auxiliary functions. The 80286 has additional registers and extended addressing capabilities. However, the 80286's greatest innovation is protected mode (see Chapter 33 for more information). DOS doesn't support protected mode.

The 80386 followed the 80286, and is considered the standard beginner's processor. This processor has advanced protected mode and 32-bit registers. Like protected mode, DOS doesn't support these registers. The 80386 includes SX and DX versions, which differ in clock frequency and data bus width. The SX works with a 16-bit data bus, while the DX can transfer an entire 32-bit word at one time.

The 80486 (often called the "i486" by Intel) is considered the most advanced processor. It differs from the 80386 because it includes the 80387 mathematical coprocessor, a code cache, and faster processing of many assembly language instructions. However, the 80486 also maintains downward compatibility with the 8086.

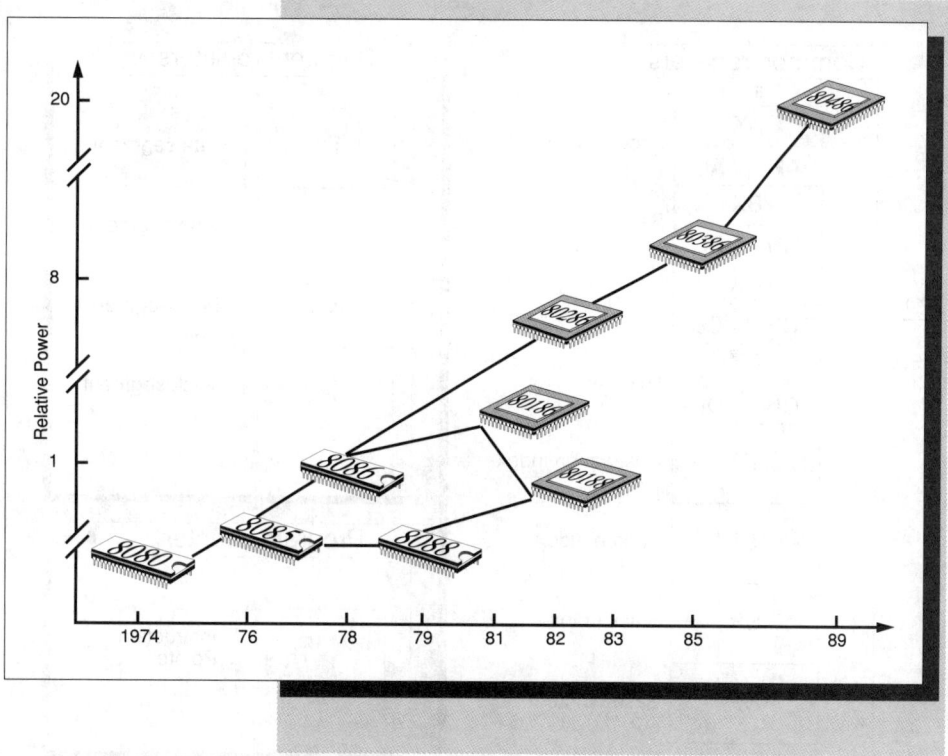

The Intel 80xx processor family

1.4.2 Processor Registers

Registers are memory locations within the processor itself, instead of in RAM. These registers can be accessed much faster than RAM. Registers are also specialized memory locations. The processor performs arithmetic and logical operations using its registers.

The processor registers are important for system programming because the flow of information between a program and the DOS and BIOS functions that call this program occurs through these registers.

From a system programming viewpoint, nothing has changed in registers since the 8086. This is because the BIOS and DOS were developed in connection with this processor, so they only support this processor's 16-bit registers. The 32-bit registers of an 80386 and i486 cannot be used in system programming under DOS. We'll discuss only 8088 registers, which apply to all later chips.

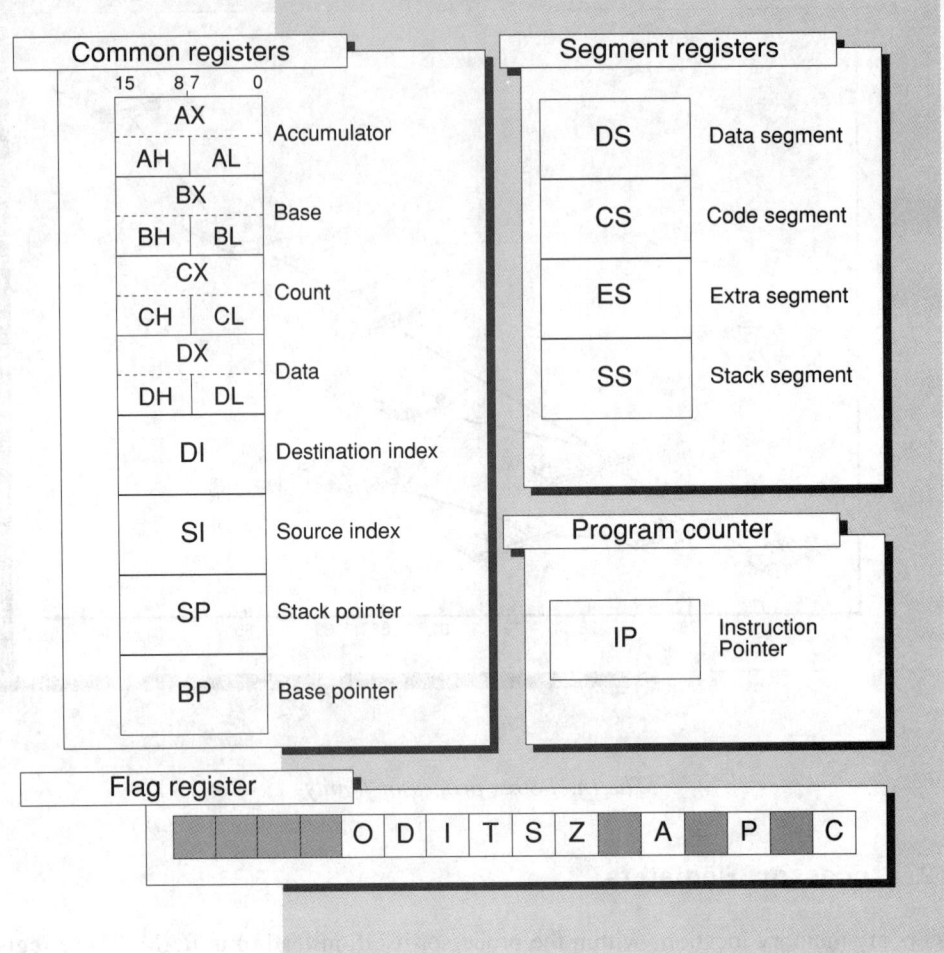

8088 registers

All registers are 16 bits (2 bytes) in size. If all 16 bits of a register contain a 1, the result, which is the decimal number 65535, is the largest number that can be represented within 16 bits. So, a register can contain any value from 0 to 65535 (FFFFH or 1111111111111111b).

Register groupings

As the previous figure shows, registers are divided into four groups: common registers, segment registers, the program counter, and the flag register. The different register assignments are designed to duplicate the way in which a program processes data, which is the basic task of a microprocessor.

The disk operating system and the routines stored in ROM use the common registers extensively, especially the AX, BX, CX, and DX registers. The contents of these registers tell DOS what tasks it should perform and which data to use for execution.

These registers are affected mainly by mathematical (addition, subtraction, etc.) and input/output instructions. They are assigned a special position within the registers of the 8088 because they can be separated into two 8-bit (1 byte) registers. Each common register usually contains three registers: a single 16-bit register and two smaller 8-bit registers.

Common registers

The common registers are important for calling DOS and BIOS functions and are used to pass parameters to a particular function that needs these parameters for execution. These registers are also influenced by mathematical operations (addition, subtraction, etc.), which are the central focus of all software activities at processor level. Registers AX, BX, CX, and DX have a special position within this set of registers, because they can be divided into two 8-bit registers. This means that each of these registers consists of three registers, one big 16-bit register and two small 8-bit registers.

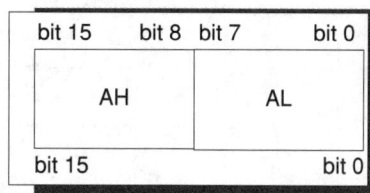

AX register

The registers have H (high) and L (low) designators. So, the 16-bit AX register may be divided into an 8-bit AH and an 8-bit AL register. The H and the L register designators occur in such a way that the L register contains the lower 8 bits (bit 0 through 7) of the X register, and the H register contains the higher 8 bits (bits 8 through 15) of the X register. The AH register consists of bits 8-15 and the AL register consists of bits 0-7 of the AX register.

However, the three registers cannot be considered independent of each other. For example, if bit 3 of the AH register is changed, then the value of bit 11 of the AX register also changes automatically. The values change in both the AH and the AX registers. The value of the AL register remains constant since it is made of bits 0-7 of the AX register (bit 11 of the AX register doesn't belong to it). This connection between the AX, the AH, and the AL register is also valid for all other common registers and can be expressed mathematically.

You can determine the value of the X register from the values of the H and the L registers, and vice versa. To calculate the value of the X register, multiply the value of the H register by 256 and add the value of the L register.

> **Example:** The value of the CH register is 10 and the value of the CL register is 118. The value of the CX register results from CH*256+CL, which is 10*256+118 = 2678.

Specifying register CH or CL, you can read or write an 8-bit data item from or to any memory location. Specifying register CX, you can read or write a 16-bit data item from or to a memory location.

Along with common registers, segment registers and the flag register are an important part of system programming.

Flag register

The flag register communicates between consecutive assembly language instructions by storing the status of mathematical and logical operations. For example, after using the carry flag to add two 16-bit registers, a program can determine whether the result is greater than 65535, and thus present it as a 32-bit number. The sign, zero, and overflow bits perform similar tasks and can be used after two registers have been compared to establish whether the value of the first register is greater than, less than, or equal to the value of the second register.

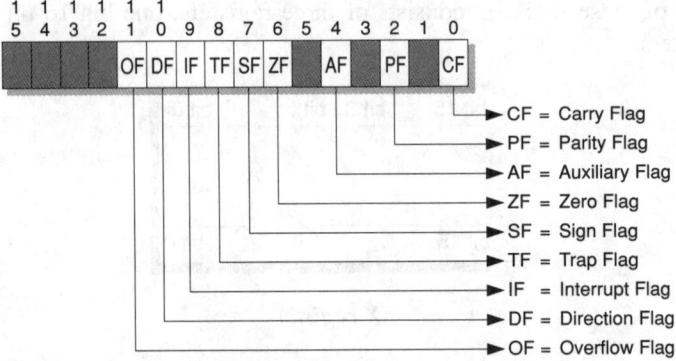

Flags of the flag register

Only the carry flag and zero flag are important for system programming from high level languages. Most DOS and BIOS functions use these flags to indicate errors for insufficient memory or unknown filenames (see Chapter 2 for information on accessing these flags from high level languages).

1.4.3 Memory Addresses

How the processor generates memory addresses is especially important for system programming, because you must constantly pass buffer addresses to a DOS or BIOS function. In these instances, you must understand what the processor is doing. The 8088 and its descendants use a complicated procedure. So that you'll understand this procedure, we'll discuss the origins of the 8086.

One of the design goals of the 8088 was to provide an instruction set that was superior to the earlier 8-bit microprocessors (6502, Z80, etc.). Another goal was to provide easy access to more than 64K of memory. This was important because increasing processor capabilities allows programmers to write more complex applications, which require more memory. The designers of the 8088 increased the memory capacity or *address space* of the microprocessor (more than 16 times) to one megabyte.

Address register

The number of memory locations that a processor can access depends on the width of the *address register*. Since every memory location is accessed by specifying a unique number or *address*, the maximum value contained in the address register determines the address space. Earlier microprocessors used a 16-bit address register, which enables users to access addresses from 0 to 65535. This corresponds to the 64K memory capacity of these processors.

To address one megabyte of memory, the address register must be at least 20 bits wide. At the time the 8088 was developed, it was impossible to use a 20-bit address register, so the designers used an alternate way to achieve the 20-bit width. The contents of two different 16-bit numbers are used to form the 20-bit address.

Segment register

One of these 16-bit numbers is contained in a *segment register*. The 8088 has four segment registers. The second number is contained in another register or in a memory location. To form a 20-bit number, the contents of the segment register are shifted left by 4 bits (thereby multiplying the value by 16) and the second number is added to the first.

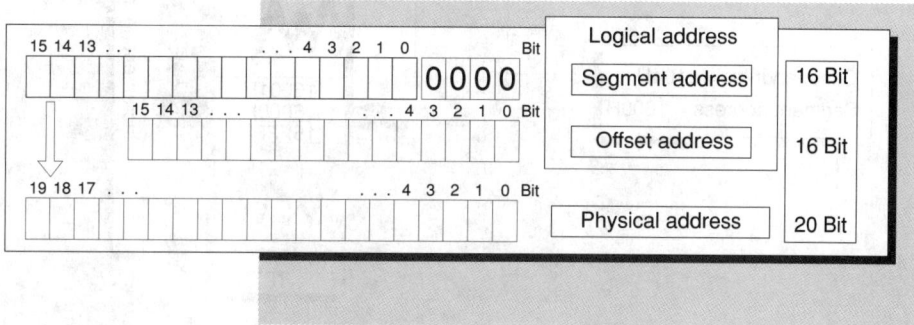

Structure of memory address from segment and offset addresses

Segment and offset addresses

These addresses are the *segment address* and the *offset address*. The segment address, which is formed by a segment register, indicates the start of a segment of memory. When the address is created, the offset address is added to the segment address. The offset address indicates the number of the memory location within the segment whose beginning was defined by the segment register. Since the offset address cannot be larger than 16 bits, a segment cannot be larger than 65,535 bytes (64K).

Let's assume that the offset address is always 0 and the segment address is also 0 at first. In this case, you receive the address of memory location 0. If the segment address is increased to 1, you receive the address of memory location 1 instead of memory location 16. This happens because the segment address is multiplied by 16 when addresses are formed.

If you continue incrementing the segment address, you'll receive memory addresses of 32, 48, 64, etc., if the offset address continues to be 0. According to this principle, the maximum memory address is 1 megabyte when the segment address reaches 65535 (FFFFH), which is its maximum value. However, if you keep the segment address constant and increment the offset address instead, the segment address will quickly become the base address for a memory segment from which you can reach a total of 65,536 different memory locations. Each memory segment contains 64K. The offset address represents the distance of the desired memory locations from the beginning of the segment.

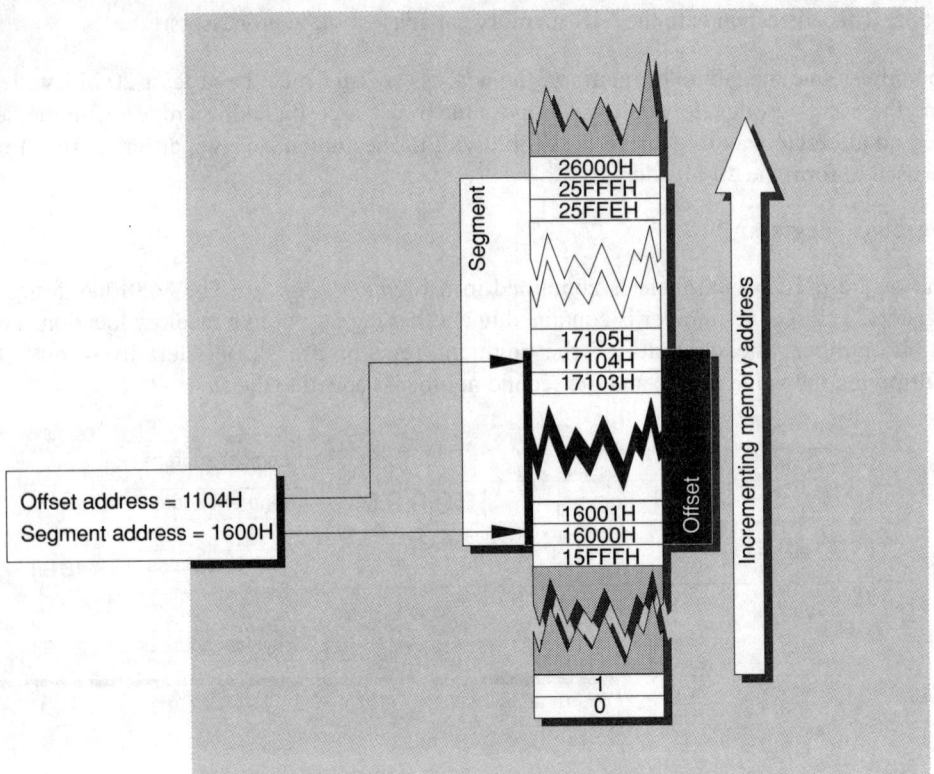

Tasks performed by the segment and offset addresses

Although the individual memory segments are only 16 bytes apart, they contain 64K. So they obviously overlap in memory. Because of this, a memory address, such as 130, can be represented in various ways by using segment and offset addresses. For example, you could specify 0 as the segment address and 130 as the offset address. It's also possible to specify 1 as the segment address and 114 as the offset address or 2 as the segment address and 98 as the offset address, etc.

These overlapping segments are actually easy to use. When you specify an address you can choose the combination of segment address and offset address yourself. You must obtain the desired address by multiplying the segment address by 16 and adding the offset address to it; everything else is unimportant.

A segment cannot start at every one of the million or so memory locations. Multiplying the segment register by 16 always produces a segment address that is divisible by 16. For example, it's not possible for a segment to begin at memory location 22.

Segmented address

The *segmented address* results from the combined segment and offset addresses. This segmented address specifies the exact number of the memory location that should be accessed. Unlike the segmented address, the segment and the offset addresses are *relative addresses* or *relative offsets*.

Combining the segment and offset addresses requires special notation to indicate a memory location's address. This notation consists of the segment address, in four-digit hexadecimal format, followed by a colon, and the offset address in four-digit hexadecimal format. For example, in this notation a memory location with a segment address of 2000H and an offset address of AF3H would appear as "2000:0AF3". Because of this notation, you can omit the H suffix from hexadecimal numbers.

The segment register for program execution

The 8088 contains four segment registers, which are important for the execution of an assembly language program. These registers contain the basic structure of any program, which consists of a set of instructions (code). Variables and data items are also processed by the program. A structured program keeps the code and data separate from each other while they reside in memory. Assigning code and data their own segments conveniently separates them. These segment registers are as follows:

CS   The CS (Code Segment) register uses the IP (Instruction Pointer) register as the offset address. Then it determines the address at which the next assembly language instruction is located. The IP is also called the Program Counter. When the processor executes the current instruction, the IP register is automatically incremented to point to the next assembly language instruction. This ensures that the instructions are executed in the proper order.

DS   Like the CS register, the DS (Data Segment) register contains the segment address of the data that the program accesses (writing or reading data to or from memory). The offset address is added to the content of the DS register and may be contained in another register or may be contained as part of the current instruction.

SS   The SS (Stack Segment) register specifies the starting address of the *stack*. The stack acts as temporary storage space for some assembly language programs. It allows fast storage and retrieval of data for various instructions. For example, when the CALL instruction is executed, the processor places the return address on the stack. The SS register and either the SP or BP registers form the address that is pushed onto the stack.

When accessing the stack, address generation occurs from the SS register in conjunction with the SP or BP register.

ES   The last segment register is the ES (Extra Segment) register. It's used by some assembly language instructions to address more than 64K of data or to transfer data between two different segments of memory.

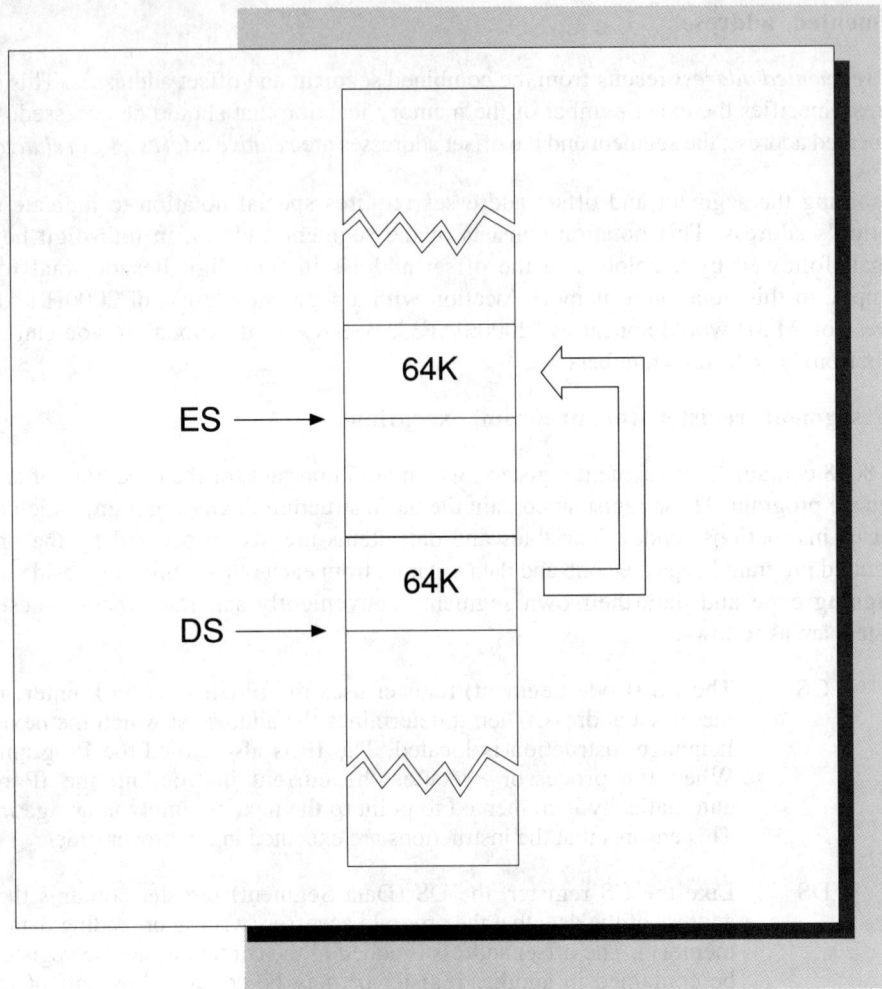

Copying of Memory Areas with the help of DS and ES Segment Addresses

With the help of the ES register, however, it's possible to leave the DS register on the memory segment of the source area while referencing the target area using the ES memory segment. The 8088 and its descendants even have assembly language instructions that can copy an entire buffer by assuming, before their execution, that the segment address of the start area has been loaded into the DS register and the segment address of the target area has been loaded into the ES register.

To copy, the instructions also need the start of both areas within their memory segments. They expect the start of the source area in the SI register and the start of the target area in the DI register. Expressed in the notation introduced earlier, these instructions copy data from DS:SI to ES:DI.

Overlapping segments

As the following illustration shows, two segment registers can specify areas of memory that overlap or are completely different from each other. Usually a program doesn't require a full 64K segment for storing code or data. So, you can conserve memory by overlapping the segments. For example, you can store data, which immediately follows the program code, by setting the DS and CS registers accordingly.

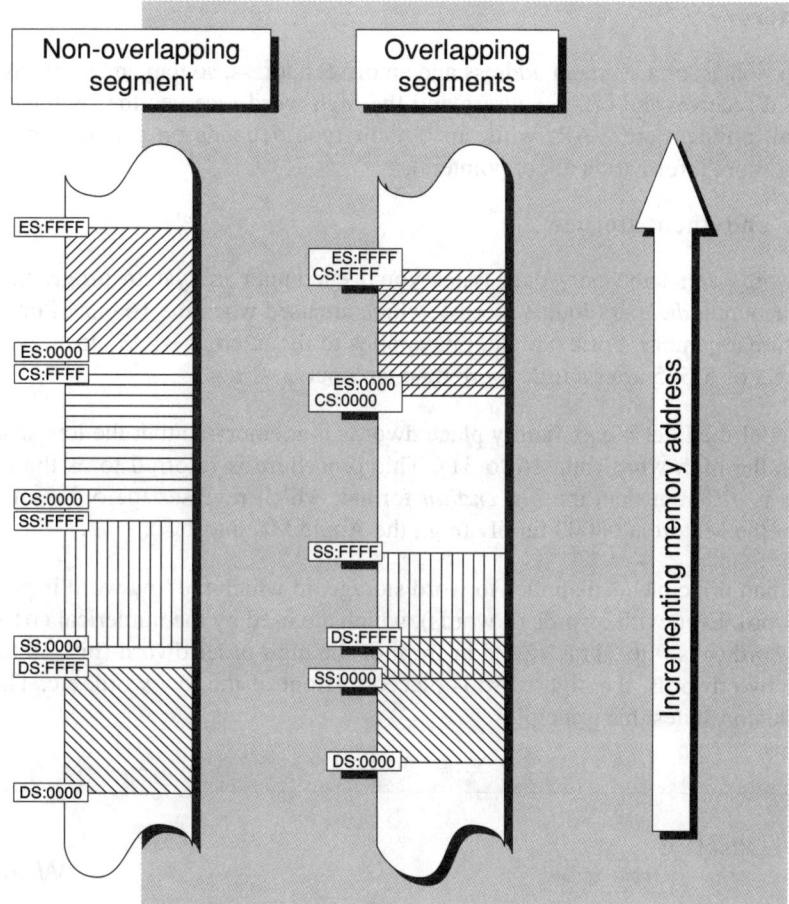

Overlapping and non-overlapping segments

NEAR and FAR pointers

The numbers we've been calling memory addresses are called *pointers* in high level languages. A pointer in the Pascal or C language receives the addresses of the objects referenced by the pointers. If these addresses change location in memory, the pointers also change. The two types of pointers are NEAR pointers and FAR pointers.

NEAR pointers

NEAR pointers specify the offset address of an object and are only 16 bits wide. Memory cannot be accessed without a segment address. So the compiler prepares the segment address, which it automatically loads, to the appropriate segment register when accessing the object. Because of this, NEAR pointer access is only possible for variables within the 64K segment created by the compiler.

FAR pointers

FAR pointers consist of a segment address and an offset address, so they are saved as two words. The low word receives the offset address and the high word receives the segment address. In Turbo Pascal, pointers are VAR, while in C their type depends on the memory model (see Chapter 2 for more information about pointers).

Data types and their storage

Bytes and words aren't the only data types you'll encounter in system programming. You'll frequently encounter *dwords* (double words), which are used when the 16 bits of one word aren't enough to store a number. For example, this applies to the internal BIOS clock, which exceeds the 16-bit level of 65535 after a little more than ten hours.

The members of the Intel 80xxx family place dwords in memory so that the low word (bits 0 to 15) precedes the high word (bits 16 to 31). This procedure is referred to as the *little endian* format. This is different than the *big endian* format, which reverses the order and is used by processors of the Motorola 68000 family (e.g., the Apple Macintosh®).

The little endian principle also applies to word storage, in which the low word is placed in front of the high word. Even with qwords (4 words), which are used by the numerical coprocessor, the low-order dword (bits 0 to 31) is stored in front of the high-order dword (bits 32 to 63). Then, within these two dwords, the high word is placed in front of the low word, etc. The following illustration demonstrates this principle:

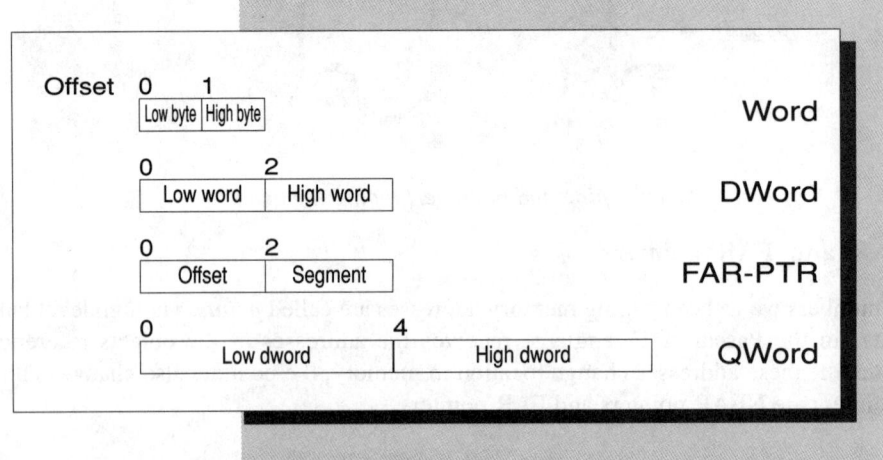

Storage of different data types in little endian format

1.5 Ports

Ports represent interfaces between the processor and the other system hardware. A port is similar to an 8-bit-wide data input or output connected to a specific piece of hardware. It has an assigned address with values ranging from 0 to 65,535.

The processor uses the data bus and address bus to communicate with the ports. If the processor needs to access a port, it transmits a port control signal. This signal instructs the other hardware that the processor wants to access a port instead of RAM.

Although ports have addresses that are also assigned to memory locations in RAM, these addresses aren't related to the memory locations. The port address is placed on the lowest 16 bits of the address bus. This instructs the system to transfer the eight bits of information on the data bus to the proper port. The hardware connected with this port receives the data and responds accordingly.

The 80(x)xx processor series has two instructions that control this process from within a program. The IN instruction sends data from the processor to a port; and the OUT instruction transfers data from a port into the processor.

Each hardware device is responsible for an area of port addresses. For this reason, conflicts between expansion boards that allocate the same port address area often occur. So, most expansion boards have DIP switches for setting the port address to which the board will respond. This helps avoid conflicts with other boards.

Standardizing port addresses

The system can set the port address of a certain hardware device. Since this address isn't a constant value, port addressing is similar for the PC, XT, and AT. Although there are only a few differences between the PC and XT, there are many differences between the PC and AT.

The following table shows the port addresses of individual chips in each system.

Component	PC/XT	AT
DMA controller (8237A-5)	000-00F	000-01F
Interrupt controller (8259A)	020-021	020-03F
Timer	040-043	040-05F
Programmable Peripheral Interface (PPI 8255A-5)	060-063	none
Keyboard (8042)	none	060-06F
Realtime clock (MC146818)	none	070-07F
DMA page register	080-083	080-09F
Interrupt controller 2 (8259A)	none	0A0-0BF
DMA controller 2 (8237A-5)	none	0C0-0DF
Math coprocessor	none	0F0-0F1
Math coprocessor	none	0F8-0FF
Hard drive controller	320-32F	1F0-1F8
Game port (joysticks)	200-20F	200-207
Expansion unit	210-217	none
Interface for second parallel printer	none	278-27E
Second serial interface	2F8-2FF	2F8-2FF
Prototype card	300-31F	300-31F
Network card	none	360-36F
Interface for first parallel printer	378-37E	378-37E
Monochrome Display Adapter and parallel interface	3B0-3BE	3B0-3BE
Color/Graphics Adapter	3D0-3DE	3D0-3DE
Disk controller	3F0-3F7	3F0-3F7
First serial interface	3F8-3FF	3F8-3FF

1.6 Interrupts

In Section 1.3.3 we explained that interrupts are mechanisms that force the processor to briefly interrupt the current program and execute an interrupt handler. However, this is only one aspect of interrupts. They are also important for controlling the hardware, and act as the main form of communication between a program and the BIOS and DOS functions.

1.6.1 Software Interrupts

Software interrupts call a program, with a special assembly language instruction, to execute a DOS, BIOS, or EMS function. The program execution isn't really interrupted; the processor views the called function as a subroutine. After the subroutine executes, the processor continues with the calling program.

To call a DOS or BIOS function using a software interrupt, only the number of the interrupt, from which the routine can be reached, is needed. The caller doesn't even need to know the address of the routine in memory. These routines are standardized. So, regardless of your DOS version, you know that by calling interrupt 21H you can access DOS functions.

The processor calls the interrupt handler using the interrupt vector table, from which the processor takes the addresses of the desired function. The processor uses the interrupt number as an index to this table. The table is set during system bootup so that the various interrupt vectors point to the ROM-BIOS.

This illustrates the advantage of using interrupts. A PC manufacturer who wants to produce an IBM compatible PC cannot copy the entire ROM-BIOS from IBM. However, the manufacturer is allowed to implement the same functions in its ROM-BIOS, even if the BIOS functions are coded differently from within. So, the BIOS functions are called using the same interrupts that IBM uses and expect parameters in the same processor registers. But the routines that provide the functions are organized differently than the routines provided by IBM.

However, these aren't the only advantages of using interrupts. We'll discuss interrupts in more detail in Chapter 2. First, let's look at the interrupt vector table, which represents the key to calling the interrupts.

1.6.2 Interrupt Vector Table

So far we've discussed a single interrupt and a single interrupt routine. Actually, the 8088 has 256 possible interrupts numbered from 0 to 255.

Each interrupt has an associated *interrupt routine* to handle the particular condition. To organize the 256 interrupts, the starting addresses of the corresponding interrupt routines are arranged in the *interrupt vector table*.

When an interrupt occurs, the processor automatically retrieves the starting address of the interrupt routine from the interrupt vector table.

The starting address of each interrupt routine is specified in the table in terms of the offset address and segment address. Both addresses are 16 bits (2 bytes) wide. So each table entry occupies 4 bytes. The total length of the table is 256*4 or 1024 bytes (1K).

Because the interrupt vector table is in RAM, any program can change it. However, TSR programs and device drivers use the table the most. (See Chapter 32 for more information.)

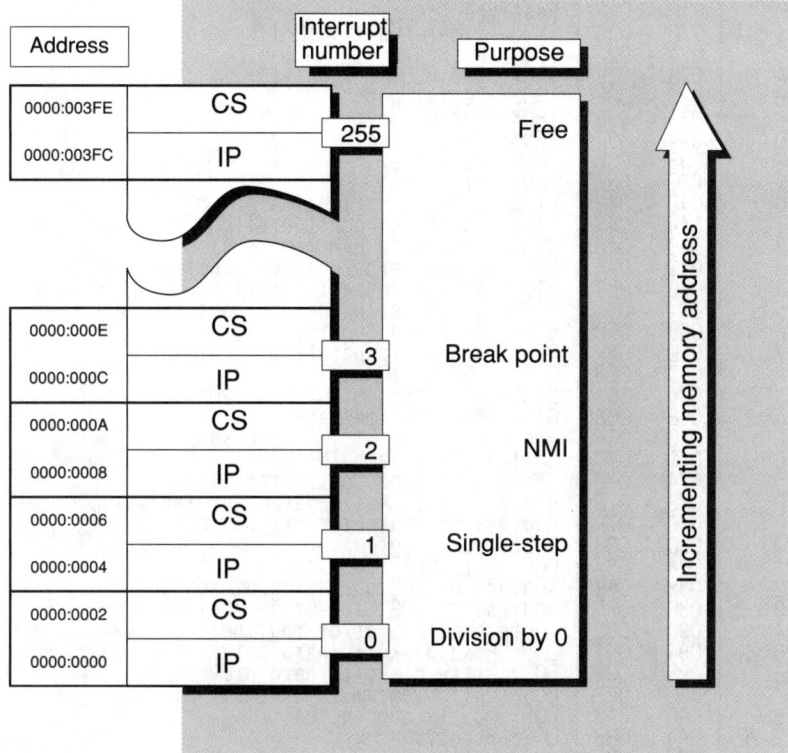

Interrupt vector table

The following table shows the addresses of the various interrupt vectors, as well as the utilities from which they can be reached. This layout applies to all PCs and is an essential component of the PC standard. A program that uses these interrupts will find these utilities on all PCs. Most of these interrupts and their functions are mentioned throughout this book.

Many of these interrupt vectors are only allocated when the corresponding hardware has also been installed. For example, this applies to interrupt 33H (mouse driver functions) and interrupt 5CH (network functions).

The term "reserved" indicates that the interrupt is called by a certain system component (usually DOS), but the interrupt's use was never documented. In other words, we know who is using it, but we don't know why.

No. *	Address*	Purpose
00	000 – 003	Processor: Division by zero
01	004 – 007	Processor: Single step
02	008 – 00B	Processor: NMI (Error in RAM chip)
03	00C – 00F	Processor: Breakpoint reached
04	010 – 013	Processor: Numeric overflow
05	014 – 017	Hardcopy
06	018 – 01B	Unknown instruction (80286 only)
07	01D – 01F	Reserved
08	020 – 023	IRQ0: Timer (Call 18.2 times/sec.)
09	024 – 027	IRQ1: Keyboard
0A	028 – 02B	IRQ2: 2nd 8259 (AT only)
0B	02C – 02F	IRQ3: Serial port 2
0C	030 – 033	IRQ4: Serial port 1
0D	034 – 037	IRQ5: Hard drive
0E	038 – 03B	IRQ6: Diskette
0F	03C – 03F	IRQ7: Printer
10	040 – 043	BIOS: Video functions
11	044 – 047	BIOS: Determine configuration
12	048 – 04B	BIOS: Determine RAM memory size
13	04C – 04F	BIOS: Diskette/hard drive functions
14	050 – 053	BIOS: Access to serial port
15	054 – 057	BIOS: Cassettes/extended function
16	058 – 05B	BIOS: Keyboard inquiry
17	05C – 05F	BIOS: Access to parallel printer
18	060 – 063	Call ROM BASIC
19	064 – 067	BIOS: Boot system (Ctrl+Alt+Del)
1A	068 – 06B	BIOS: Prompt time/date
1B	06C – 06F	Break key (not Ctrl–C) pressed
1C	070 – 073	Called after each INT 08
1D	074 – 077	Address of video parameter table
1E	078 – 07B	Address of diskette parameter table
1F	07C – 07F	Address of character bit pattern
20	080 – 083	DOS: Quit program
21	084 – 087	DOS: Call DOS function
22	088 – 08B	Address of DOS quit program routine
23	08C – 08F	Address of DOS Ctrl-Break routine
24	090 – 093	Address of DOS error routine
25	094 – 097	DOS: Read diskette/hard drive
26	098 – 09B	DOS: Write diskette/hard drive
27	09C – 09F	DOS: Quit program, stay resident
28	0A0 – 0A3	DOS: DOS is unoccupied
29-2E	0A4 – 0BB	DOS: Reserved
2F	0BC – 0BF	DOS: Multiplexer
30-32	0C0 – 0CB	DOS: Reserved
33	0CC – 0CF	Mouse driver functions
34-40	0D0 – 0FF	DOS: Reserved
41	104 – 107	Address of hard drive table 1
42-45	108 – 117	Reserved
46	118 – 11B	Address of hard drive table 2
47-49	11C – 127	Can be used by programs
4A	128 – 12B	Alarm time reached (AT only)
4B-5B	12C – 16F	Free: can be used by programs
5C	170 – 173	NETBIOS functions
5D-66	174 – 19B	Free: can be used by programs
67	19C – 19F	EMS memory manager functions
68-6F	1A0 – 1BF	Free: can be used by programs
70	1C0 – 1C3	IRQ08: Realtime clock (AT only)
71	1C4 – 1C7	IRQ09: (AT only)
72	1C8 – 1CB	IRQ10: (AT only)

No.*	Address*	Purpose
73	1CC – 1CF	IRQ11: (AT only)
74	1D0 – 1D3	IRQ12: (AT only)
75	1D4 – 1D7	IRQ13: 80287 NMI (AT only)
76	1D8 – 1DB	IRQ14: Hard drive (AT only)
77	1DC – 1DF	IRQ15: (AT only)
78–7F	1E0 – 1FF	Reserved
80–F0	200 – 3C3	Used within the BASIC interpreter
F1–FF	3C4 – 3CF	Reserved

*= All addresses and numbers in hexadecimal notation

General overview of interrupts

1.6.3 Hardware Interrupts

Hardware interrupts are produced by various hardware components and passed, by the interrupt controller, to the processor. In this section we'll explain the steps involved in this process and the differences between PC/XTs and ATs.

PC/XT hardware interrupts

Hardware interrupts 8 to 15 are called by the interrupt controller. Up to eight devices (interrupt sources) can be connected to the PC interrupt controller, using interrupt lines IRQ0 to IRQ7. The device on line IRQ0 has the highest priority, while the device connected with IRQ7 has the lowest priority. For example, if two interrupt requests arrive on lines IRQ3 and IRQ5, IRQ3 is addressed first. The number of the interrupt results from adding 8 to the IRQ number. In this case, it would be interrupt 11.

Disabling hardware interrupts

It's possible for a program to prevent the execution of hardware interrupts. This is useful when program execution shouldn't be interrupted. The processor will release a hardware interrupt, upon request from the interrupt controller, only if the interrupt flag is set in the processor's flag register. If the software has cleared the flag, the interrupt controller won't receive the requested interrupt.

You can also block single interrupts by programming the interrupt mask register in the interrupt controller.

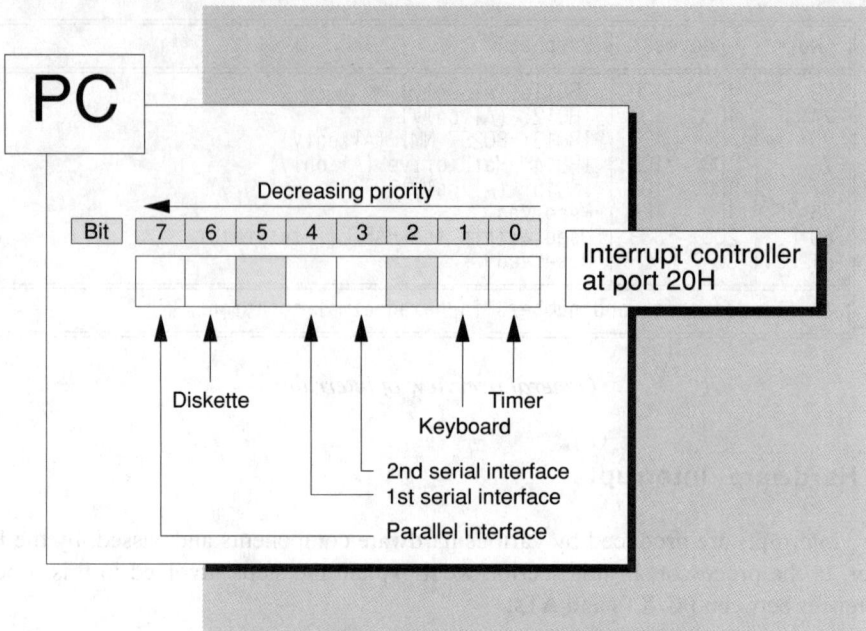

PC interrupt requests and priorities

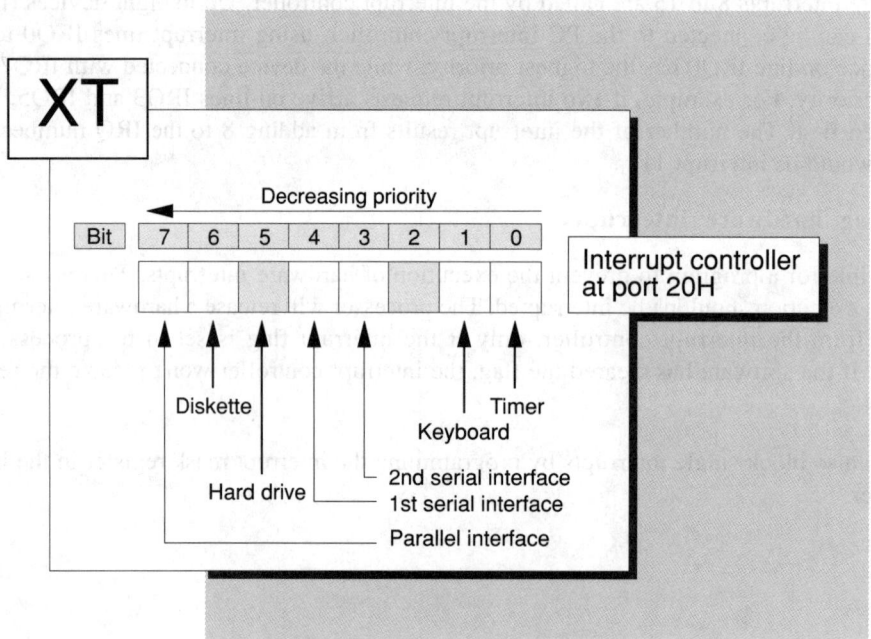

XT interrupt requests and priorities

AT hardware interrupts

ATs have two 8259 interrupt controllers, which provide 16 interrupt sources. The eight additional interrupts are labeled IRQ08 to IRQ15. When an interrupt request addresses the second interrupt controller, it emulates an IRQ2 from the first interrupt controller. All the interrupt requests of the second interrupt controller are assigned a higher priority than lines IRQ4 to IRQ7 of the first interrupt controller.

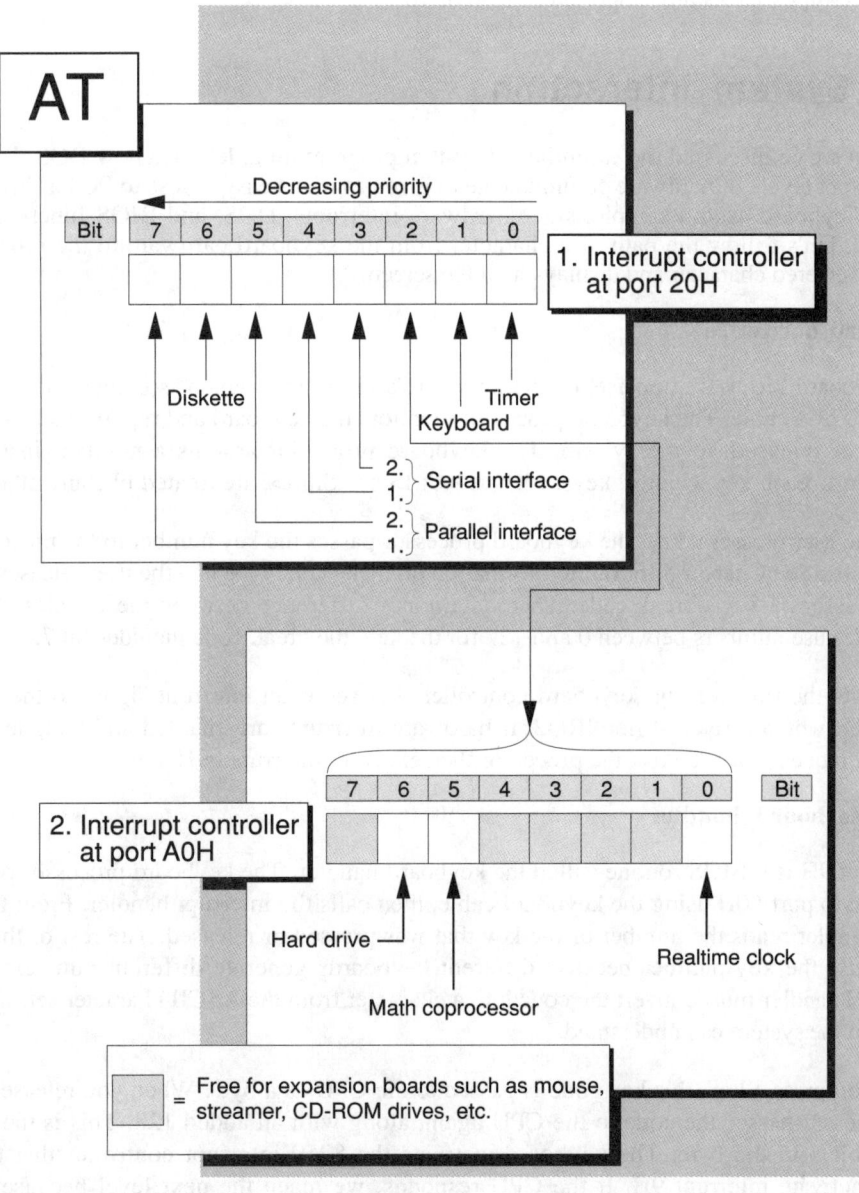

AT interrupts and priorities

If a request for IRQ2 is granted, the interrupt handler of interrupt 10 is executed. This interrupt handler first reads some of the registers of the second interrupt controller to determine the number of the IRQ. Based on the IRQ number, one of interrupts 70H to 77H is called as a software interrupt. It doesn't matter that the call was actually initiated by the hardware because the device is waiting for execution of "its" interrupt handler.

However, as a result of this procedure, the IRQ2 is unavailable to the first interrupt controller. So 15 interrupt sources are supported instead of 16.

1.7   System Interaction

Now that we've discussed the essentials of system programming, let's see how DOS, BIOS, and the different levels of hardware communicate to give programs easy access to PC hardware. We'll use the keyboard as an example, since hardware interrupts, DOS, and BIOS functions are all involved. Let's follow the path of a character from the keyboard hardware to the program that reads the entered character and displays it on the screen.

Keyboard hardware

The keyboard hardware consists of the keyboard's processor, which is connected to the PC's processor by a cable. The keyboard processor monitors the keyboard and reports each key, that is pressed or released, to the system. The keyboard processor assigns a number, instead of a character, to each key. Control keys, such as <Ctrl> or <Shift>, are treated like any other key.

When the user presses a key, the keyboard processor passes the key number to the processor as a make code. (See Chapter 5 for more information on make codes.) When the user releases the key, the processor passes a break code. There is a minor difference between these codes. Although both codes use numbers between 0 and 127 for the key, the break code includes bit 7.

To initiate the transfer, the keyboard controller first sends an interrupt signal to the interrupt controller, which arrives at line IRQ2. If hardware interrupts are enabled and a higher priority interrupt request doesn't exist, the processor then executes interrupt 09H.

BIOS keyboard handler

Interrupt 09H is a BIOS routine called the keyboard handler. The keyboard processor passes the key code to port 60H using the keyboard cable, then calls the interrupt handler. From there, the BIOS handler reads the number of the key that was pressed or released. The rest of the system cannot use the key number because different keyboards generate different numbers. So, the keyboard handler must convert the code into a character from the ASCII character set, which is a form that the system can understand.

When you press a key, this key code is passed to the CPU as a byte. When you release the key, the processor passes the code to the CPU again, along with an added 128. This is the same as setting bit 7 in the byte. The keyboard instructs the 8259 interrupt controller that the CPU should activate interrupt 9H. If the CPU responds, we reach the next level because a BIOS routine is controlled through interrupt 9H. While this routine is being called, the keyboard processor sends the key code to port 60H of the main circuit board using the asynchronous transmission protocol. The BIOS routine checks this port and obtains the number of the depressed or released key. This routine then generates an ASCII code from this key code.

This task is more complicated than it first appears because the BIOS routine must test for a control key, such as <Shift> or <Alt>. Depending on the key or combination of keys, either a normal ASCII code or an extended keyboard code may be required. The extended key codes include any keys that don't input characters (e.g., cursor keys).

Keyboard buffer

Once BIOS determines the correct code, this code is passed to the 16-byte BIOS keyboard buffer, which is located in the lower area of RAM. If it's full, the routine sounds a beep that informs the user of an overflow in the keyboard buffer. The processor returns to the other tasks that were in progress before the call to interrupt 09H.

BIOS keyboard interrupt

The next level, BIOS interrupt 16H, reads the character in the keyboard buffer and makes it available to a program. This interrupt includes three BIOS routines for reading characters, as well as the keyboard status (e.g., which control keys were pressed), from the keyboard buffer. These routines can be called with an INT assembly language instruction.

DOS level

The keyboard's device driver routines represent the DOS level. These DOS routines read a character from the keyboard and store the character in a buffer using the BIOS functions from interrupt 16H. In some instances, the DOS routines may clear the BIOS keyboard buffer. If the system uses the extended keyboard driver ANSI.SYS, this keyboard driver can translate certain codes (e.g., function key 1) into other codes or strings. For example, it's possible to program the <F10> key to display the DIR command on the screen. Although, theoretically, you can call device driver functions from within a program, DOS functions usually address these functions.

DOS is the highest level you can go. Here you'll find the keyboard access functions in DOS interrupt 21H. These functions call the driver functions, transmit the results, and perform many other tasks. For example, characters and strings can be read and displayed directly on the screen until the user presses the <Enter> key. These strings are called by a program and complete a long process.

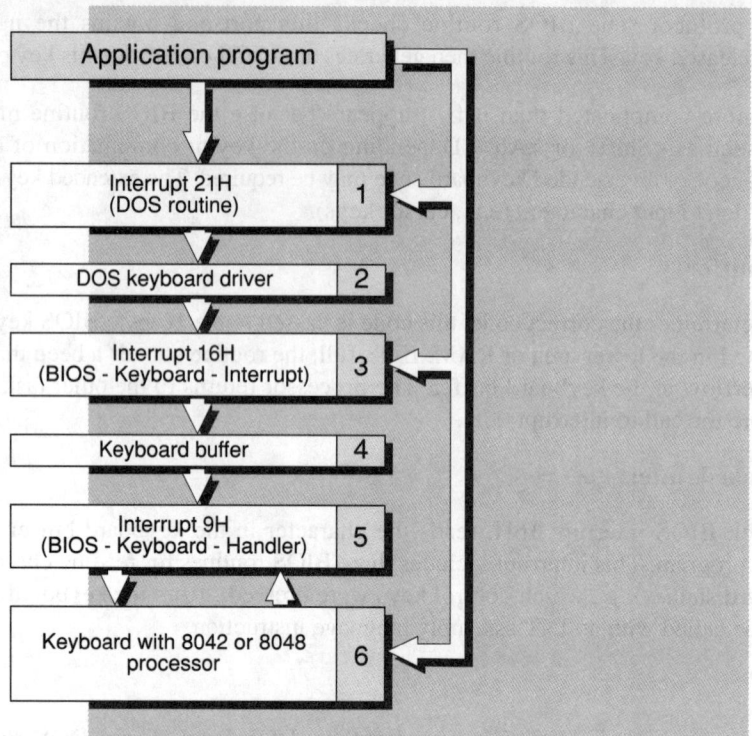

Keyboard access using the three-layer model

Chapter 2

System Programming in Practice

Now that you know some fundamentals, we can look at the practical side of system programming: program development in BASIC, Pascal, and C. Each language has its own commands, procedures, and functions for addressing memory, reading ports, or calling interrupts.

2.1 QuickBASIC

BASIC isn't the best language to use for system programming because it's more limited than Pascal or C. However, system programming in BASIC is possible even if you cannot do everything that you can in Pascal or C. For example, BASIC doesn't have direct pointer access. In this book, you'll find fewer demonstration programs in BASIC than in Pascal and C. We included any programs that could be translated into BASIC.

The BASIC demonstration programs listed in this book run under the QuickBASIC interpreter Version 4.5. Most of these programs require that you run the QuickBASIC environment while loading a library named QB.LIB:

```
QB /L QB
```

> **Note:** These programs don't run under Microsoft's QBasic interpreter (QBasic isn't able to call interrupts).

2.1.1 QuickBASIC Data Types

When you call interrupt functions, you must be familiar with the processor data types. Interrupt functions are written in assembly language and no other data types are available at that level of programming. So, if you want to perform system programming in QuickBASIC, you must copy the QuickBASIC data types to the data types of the processor. The following table shows which types correspond:

QuickBASIC Type	Stored as
String * 1 Integer Long	BYTE WORD DWORD

Unlike Pascal and C (the char type), QuickBASIC doesn't recognize single characters. The String * 1 type compensates for this limitation. String * 1 is a string the length of a byte. The QuickBASIC compiler views this string in memory as a single byte.

However, it's more difficult to operate one of these strings than a normal byte. The reason for this is that a numeric value can only be loaded into a variable declared in this way using the CHR$() function, as the following example shows:

```
DIM byte AS STRING * 1
byte = CHR$(5)      'This is O.K.          - Program runs if you enter this
byte = 5            'Error: Type mismatch  - Program does not run
```

You can derive the value of such a byte only by using the ASC function:

```
DIM byte AS STRING * 1
byte = CHR$(13)
IF ASC(byte) = 13 THEN PRINT 13    'This is O.K.          - Program runs if you
                                   '                        enter this
IF byte = 13 THEN PRINT 13         'Error: Type mismatch - Program does not run
```

Working with the integer and long data types is also difficult if you use them to reproduce words and dwords. QuickBASIC views the highest bit as the type of number (positive or negative) and views the number as negative when that bit is set.

For example, if you receive a word after the interrupt call and bit 15 is set in this word (indicating that the value is greater than 32768), QuickBASIC views the number as negative. The same problem occurs with dwords, only less frequently. (A number with bit 31 set is much larger than you'd normally see in system programming.)

You can manage integer types by converting them into floating point numbers with a function. Check the sign bit, make the conversion, and continue processing. The following MakeWord function listed appears under different names, such as GetWord, in some of the BASIC demonstration programs listed in this book:

```
FUNCTION MakeWord& (ANum AS INTEGER)

IF ANum < 0 THEN
   MakeWord = 65536& + ANum
ELSE
   MakeWord = ANum
END IF
END FUNCTION
```

You pass the integer, which may have a set bit 15, to the function. The function returns a positive long data type because the function assumes that bit 31 specifies the sign.

Strings

Most DOS and BIOS functions expect strings as a sequence of bytes containing the ASCII codes of the individual characters and terminated by a null byte (a byte consisting of the value 0). System programming books often call this type of string an ASCIIZ (ASCII-Zero) string.

BASIC stores strings in a different format, from which you must distinguish between variable length strings and fixed length strings. System programming always uses fixed length strings because it's easier to calculate their addresses in memory than variable length strings. You need the string addresses to pass them to a DOS or BIOS function (more on this later).

If you declare a string of fixed length in your programs, QuickBASIC reserves that many bytes of the string. The following reserves 20 bytes, whose contents are undefined:

```
DIM S as STRING * 20
```

Adding the following loads the contents of the array S in these 20 bytes, padding the remainder of the allocated string with spaces:

```
S = "PC Intern"
```

Adding the null byte to create an ASCIIZ string requires special handling. We need a WHILE...WEND loop to locate the last character of the string, then we must add the null byte to the string using the MID$ statement:

```
DIM S AS STRING * 20
DIM I AS INTEGER

S = ""
INPUT "Please enter a string"; s

I = LEN(S) - 1
WHILE (I > 0) AND (MID$(S, I, 1) = "")
  I = I - 1
WEND
IF I = 0 THEN I = 1
MID$(S, I) = CHR$(0)
```

However, if you know the string and don't want the user to enter it, you can include the null byte in the string allocation:

```
S = "PC Intern" + CHR$(0)
```

Structures and arrays

Similar to applications and other programs, DOS and the BIOS manage much information using structures and arrays. The following table shows an example of a structure returned to the caller by DOS. This information occurs when you browse through directories looking for files.

Addr.	Contents	Type
■ Directory entry structure as returned by DOS functions 4EH and 4FH ■		
00H	Reserved	21 bytes
15H	Attribute byte of the file	1 byte
16H	Time of last modification	1 word
18H	Date of last modification	1 word
1AH	File size	1 dword
1EH	Filename and extension separated by a period but without a path specification (ends with a null byte)	13 bytes
■ Length: 43 bytes		

The following program listing excerpt shows how this structure can be recreated in QuickBASIC (you'll find this structure in the DIRB.BAS program discussed later in this book):

```
TYPE DirStruct
   Reserved AS STRING * 21
   Attrib AS STRING * 1
   Time AS INTEGER
   Date AS INTEGER
   Size AS LONG
   DatName AS STRING * 13
END TYPE
```

As you can see, the Reserved element at the beginning of the DirStruct structure is represented by a fixed length string. This is the easiest way to reserve a specific number of bytes.

The rest of the elements in the DirStruct structure refer to the various components of the DOS structure in their data types. Bytes are reproduced as String * 1, words as INTEGERs, and dwords as LONGs. The names of the individual fields are unimportant. You can choose any name you want because the names don't affect the structure. Obtaining a correct reproduction of the structure is all that matters.

Accessing bit fields

In structures, fields often represent bit fields, in which individual bits or groups of bits have a specific meaning. The attribute byte in the previous directory structure also represents a bit field. As the following illustration shows, each single bit represents a certain file attribute. For example, a bit might provide information about whether the file is write/protected, is a system file, or not a file at all (a subdirectory). You must know how to read the individual bits.

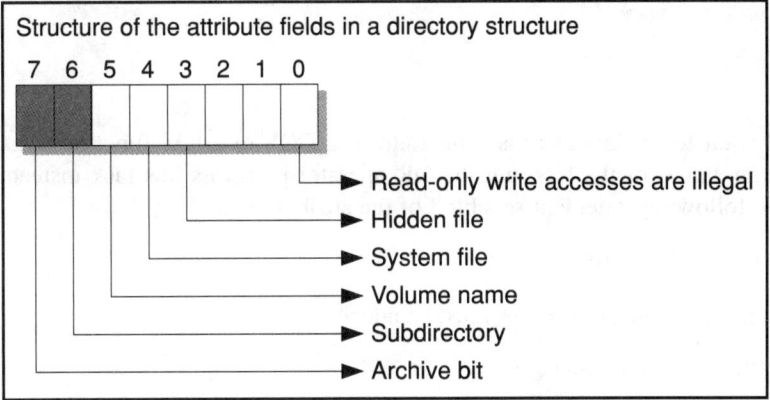

If you want to read a certain bit, first you must know its value. You know that bit 0 has a value of 1, bit 1 a value of 2, bit 2 a value of 4 and so on, until you reach bit 7, which has a value of 128. To determine whether you're dealing with a subdirectory, you must use the value of bit 4, which is 16.

You want to set all the attribute byte's other bits to 0. From there you can then determine whether bit 4 is set. The AND operator masks all bits not in the AND mask. The following expression unsets all bits except bit 4 (bit 4 = 16):

```
AttributeByte AND 16
```

If bit 4 is set, a result of 16 is returned. Otherwise, the result is 0.

We can apply this expression using IF...THEN...ELSE:

```
IF ( ( AttributeByte AND 16 ) <> 0 ) THEN
     'If the result <> 0 it's a subdirectory
ELSE
     'If the result = 0 there's no subdirectory
ENDIF
```

Unfortunately, checking more than one bit at a time complicates this process. The values of the different bits must be added together. For example, suppose that you want to determine whether the file is both hidden and a system file. The corresponding flags are stored in bits 1 and 2, and have a value of 6 when added together. The following expression returns the contents of both bits:

```
AttributeByte AND 6
```

This time, however, the expression used in the previous example cannot be directly applied to this example:

```
( AttributeByte AND 6 ) <> 0
```

This expression is already TRUE if one of the two bits is set and the result of the AND operation doesn't equal 0. However, if you want to know whether both flags were set, you must modify the process to something similar to the following:

```
IF ( ( AttributeByte AND 6 ) = 6 ) THEN
```

```
        'Hidden and System
    ELSE
        'Not Hidden, not System
    ENDIF
```

Often you'll want to set bits to pass a bit field to a DOS or BIOS function. Again, the main focus is on the values of the bits, but the OR operator performs this task instead of the AND operator. The following statement sets bit 3 of the attribute byte:

```
    AttributeByte = AttributeByte OR 8
```

Again, to set multiple bits, the values must be added:

```
    AttributeByte = AttributeByte OR ( 8 + 16 )
```

Both of these expressions set the desired bit to 1. Suppose that you want to set a bit to 0. To do this, use an AND operation in a different arrangement to mask the bit you want set to 0. According to the laws of binary logic, you must then invert the value using the NOT operator in order to achieve the desired result. To set bit 5 to 0, use the following statement:

```
    AttributeByte = AttributeByte AND NOT(32)
```

Once again, you can mask more than one bit at a time using the following:

```
    AttributeByte = AttributeByte AND NOT( 32 + 8 );
```

However, bit fields don't always consist of separate bits. Often they are comprised of bit groups, whose individual bits form a certain value when added together. An example of this is the date field in the directory entry of a file. This field contains three bit groups that specify the day, month, and year the particular file was created or last modified. So, to analyze this information, you must determine the value the three bit groups represent instead of checking the status of given bits.

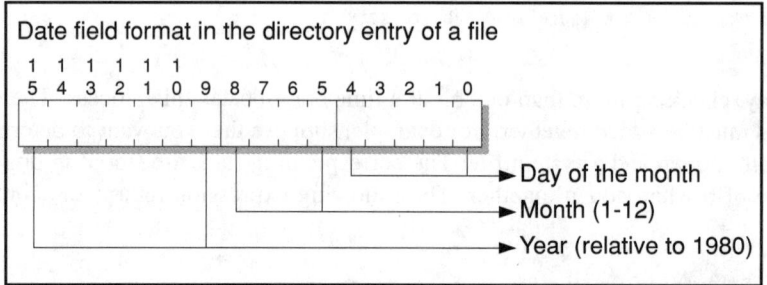

You can easily determine the day by using the described procedure with an AND operator:

```
    Day = DateField AND ( 1 + 2 + 4 + 8 )
```

When you want to determine the month, the AND operation is no longer sufficient because the isolated bit group must also be shifted to the right by five bits to obtain the number of the month. In BASIC, the only way to do this is by dividing the value by 2 raised exponentially by the number of bit positions (by which the value is to be shifted to the right). You can determine the month and the year by using the following statements:

```
Month = ( DateField AND ( 32 + 64 + 128 + 256 ) ) \ 32  '2^5 power = 32
Year = ( DateField AND ( 512+1024+2048+4096+8192+16384+32768 ) ) \ 512
```

However, you'll encounter problems again, at least with the second statement, because of the sign bit. This is why you should use the MakeWord function described earlier in this section:

```
Year = ( MakeWord(DateField) AND 65024& \ 512
```

To shift bits to the left instead of to the right, use multiplication instead of division. For example, the following will make a DateField out of a given day, month, and year:

```
DateField = Day + ( Month * 32 ) + ( Year * 512 )
```

2.1.2 Calling Interrupts from QuickBASIC

The QuickBASIC QB.QLB quick library provides the INTERRUPT and INTERRUPTX statements for calling software interrupts. You can call all 256 Intel processor interrupts with these statements. To access this library, you must start QuickBASIC with the /L QB switch.

INTERRUPT and INTERRUPTX can also access interrupt 21H, which lets you call the DOS API (DOS Application Program Interface) functions. There are more than 200 of these functions, which refer to functions provided by DOS applications.

The QB.BI include file lets you access DOS API functions. You must include this file in your programs by using the following:

```
REM $INCLUDE: 'QB.BI'
```

The syntax for both statements is:

```
CALL INTERRUPT(Interruptnum, InReg, OutReg)
CALL INTERRUPTX(Interruptnum, InReg, OutReg)
```

Accessing the processor registers

The InReg and OutReg parameters used by the INTERRUPT statement are of type RegType, which represents a structure defined within QB.BI. The RegType structure makes the various processor registers available to a BASIC program. From the InReg structure, the INTERRUPT command loads the processor registers with the specified values from the InReg structure. After the interrupt call, the OutReg structure contains the contents of the processor registers.

From the definition of RegType you may conclude that the different variables within this structure reflect the processor registers of the same name.

```
TYPE RegType
     ax AS INTEGER
     bx AS INTEGER
     CX AS INTEGER
     dx AS INTEGER
     bp AS INTEGER
     si AS INTEGER
     di AS INTEGER
  flags AS INTEGER
END TYPE
```

41

RegType accesses only the 16-bit registers instead of the 8-bit registers. So, to access an 8-bit register, you must use a 16-bit register. For example, the following lines load the value 1BH (&h1B) into the AH register by multiplying that register's value by 256, and then moving the value eight bit positions to the left:

```
DIM Regs AS RegType
Regs.AX = &h1B * 256
CALL INTERRUPT( &hxyz, Regs, Regs )    'The result of the interrupt call
```

However, this also sets AL to 0. If you don't want this to happen, set the desired value with OR:

```
DIM Regs AS RegType
Regs.AX = Regs.AX OR ( &h1B * 256 )
CALL INTERRUPT( &hxyz, Regs, Regs )    'The result of the interrupt call
```

Write the desired value to the AX register (and ensure that the AH register is empty) to access the AL register. However, if there is already a value in AH, you should use the OR operator to avoid destroying the contents of AH.

```
DIM Regs AS RegType
Regs.AX = &h1B                         'Load AL with 1BH (&h1B), assume AH = 0
Regs.AX = Regs.AX OR &h1B              'AH remains unchanged
CALL INTERRUPT( &hxyz, Regs, Regs )    'The result of the interrupt call
```

You could also use the same principle with all the other general registers. For example, it's just as easy to determine the contents of the various 8-bit registers after an interrupt call. If you're interested in the high byte, simply divide the contents of the 16-bit register by 256. If you're interested in the low byte, you can mask the high byte with an AND operator.

```
DIM Regs AS RegType
CALL INTERRUPT( &hxyz, Regs, Regs )    'Interrupt call (replace &hxyz with
                                       'the interrupt of your choice
PRINT "AH = "; MakeWord(Regs.AX) \ 256
PRINT "AL = "; Regs.AX AND &HFF
```

Including the segment register

Maybe you've already noticed that the segment register is ignored in RegType. Numerous DOS and BIOS functions expect parameters in the DS and ES segment registers or return information to these registers. Because of this, there is a command called INTERRUPTX, which works exactly like INTERRUPT except that it works with structures of the RegTypeX type. Although RegTypeX is similar in structure to RegType, it also contains two fields for the ES and DS registers.

```
TYPE RegTypeX
    ax AS INTEGER
    bx AS INTEGER
    CX AS INTEGER
    dx AS INTEGER
    bp AS INTEGER
    si AS INTEGER
    di AS INTEGER
 flags AS INTEGER
    ds AS INTEGER
    es AS INTEGER
END TYPE
```

Reading the flags in the flag register

In many cases, the flag registers can also return information to the calling program. DOS functions extensively use the carry flag, which is set after the function is called and when the function call fails.

You can also access the various processor flags after calling INTERRUPT or INTERRUPTX using the FLAGS variable in the OutReg structure. You can calculate the contents of each flag using an AND operator, with the value of the flag, as the following table shows:

Flag	Bit Pos.	Value
Carry	0	1
Parity	2	4
Auxiliary	4	16
Zero	6	64
Sign	7	128
Overflow	11	2048

So, a test for the carry flag could look like the following:

```
DIM Regs AS RegType
CALL INTERRUPT( &hxyz, Regs, Regs )     'The interrupt call
IF ( Regs.Flags AND 1 ) <> 0 THEN PRINT "Error"
```

2.1.3 Buffers and QuickBASIC

Many functions expect pointers to buffers when they are called. The functions either take information from the buffers or place information in the buffers (e.g., file contents). These pointers are always FAR; they consist of a segment address and an offset address. This FAR pointer data can be anywhere in memory, not necessarily in the current program's memory segment.

Passing pointers to interrupt functions

DOS function 09H is an example of a function that takes pointers. This function displays a string on the screen beginning at the current cursor position. Like all DOS functions, it expects the function number in the AH register and the address of the buffer containing the string to be displayed in the DS:DX register pair. DS takes the segment address of the buffer, and DX takes the offset address.

Although creating a string is easy in QuickBASIC, you may also want to know how to pass the buffer address. QuickBASIC provides the VARSEG and VARPTR functions, which supply the segment and offset addresses of the specified variable. The following program demonstrates how to use these functions with DOS function 09H (&H09) as an example. Unlike other DOS functions, function 09H looks for a $ character, instead of a null byte, at the end of the buffer.

```
'9HDEMOB.BAS

'$INCLUDE: 'QB.BI'              'Include file for interrupt call

DIM S AS STRING * 20
```

```
DIM RegsX AS RegTypeX

CLS
S = "PC Intern" + "$"
RegsX.AX = &H900                        'Function number 09H
RegsX.DS = VARSEG(s)                    'Segment address
RegsX.DX = VARPTR(s)                    'Offset address
CALL InterruptX(&H21, RegsX, RegsX)
```

Receiving pointers from interrupt functions

The following program calls DOS function 1BH, which returns a pointer in the DS:BX register pair. This pointer points to a byte containing the media code of the current drive. DOS uses the media code to describe the different types of drives, with codes between F0H and FFH. The value F8H (248) characterizes all types of hard drives.

Since QuickBASIC doesn't recognize FAR pointers, you must use the PEEK() command to read the media ID. Although this command can be used to read the contents of any memory location, it accepts only one offset address and always accesses the "current" segment. Fortunately, you can define this segment with the help of the DEF SEG command, as the following program demonstrates.

```
'MEDIAIDB.BAS

'$INCLUDE: 'QB.BI'                      'Include file for interrupt call

DIM RegsX AS RegTypeX
DIM MediaID AS INTEGER

CLS
RegsX.AX = &H1B00                       'Function number
CALL interruptx(&H21, RegsX, RegsX)
DEF SEG = RegsX.DS                      'Define segment
MediaID = PEEK(RegsX.BX)                'Read media ID
PRINT "Media ID = "; MediaID
```

2.2 Turbo Pascal

Our discussion of Pascal in this book is based on Borland's Turbo Pascal. Although Turbo Pascal compatible Pascal compilers (e.g., Pascal+™ from Stony Brook Software) are available, we'll concentrate on Turbo Pascal. All the demonstration programs in this book were developed using Turbo Pascal Version 6.0.

Since the demonstration programs in this book illustrate system programming, we omitted all the OOP (Object Oriented Programming) enhancements that are available in Turbo. Once you understand the logic of each demonstration program, you can add any extras, such as OOP objects, to suit your own needs.

2.2.1 Turbo Pascal Data Types

Similar to other compilers, Turbo Pascal's data types mostly correspond with processor data types, which allow fast and easy processing. The following table shows how Turbo Pascal stores the different data types:

Pascal Type	Stored as
CHAR	BYTE
BYTE	BYTE
BOOLEAN	BYTE
INTEGER	WORD
WORD	WORD
LONGINT	DWORD
POINTER	DWORD

In Turbo Pascal, pointers are always FAR, regardless of whether they point at data or are procedural pointers, which refer to program code.

Strings

Most DOS and BIOS functions expect strings as a sequence of bytes, containing the ASCII codes of the individual characters, and terminated by a null byte (a byte consisting of the value 0). In system programming, this type of string is called an ASCIIZ (ASCII-Zero) string.

Pascal also saves a string as a sequence of bytes, with each byte representing the ASCII codes of the characters. However, unlike ASCIIZ strings, the first byte indicates the string's length, instead of the string null byte at the end of the string. Although this method is more practical for processing strings, it's incompatible with DOS and BIOS functions.

The following program listing demonstrates how Pascal strings can be easily converted into ASCIIZ strings by simply adding a null byte. However, when passing such a string to a DOS or BIOS function using its address, you must specify the address of the first character (string[1]), instead of the address of the length byte (string[0]). We'll discuss this in detail after the program listing.

```
{* ASZDEMO.PAS *}

program ASZDemo;

var ASCIIZ : string[100];
    i : integer;

begin
  write ( 'String: ' );
  readln( ASCIIZ );
  ASCIIZ := ASCIIZ + chr(0);
  for i := 0 to ord( ASCIIZ[0] ) do
    begin
      write( i:2, '   ', ord( ASCIIZ[i] ):3 );
      if ( ASCIIZ[i] > ' ' ) then
        write( '   ', ASCIIZ[i] );
      writeln;
    end;
end.
```

The following shows the screen output that's created by the previous program after it's compiled and called. The program prompted the user for a string. After the user typed the string and pressed <Enter>, the program added a null byte and displayed the string on the screen, including the length byte and null byte.

```
┌─────────────────────────────────────────────────────────────┐
│ ┌───────────────────────────────────────────────────────────┐│
│ │ String: ASCIIZ string        <---- Prompt and input       ││
│ │    0     14                  <---- Length byte            ││
│ │    1     65   A                                           ││
│ │    2     83   S                                           ││
│ │    3     67   C                                           ││
│ │    4     73   I                                           ││
│ │    5     73   I                                           ││
│ │    6     90   Z                                           ││
│ │    7     32                                               ││
│ │    8    115   s                                           ││
│ │    9    116   t                                           ││
│ │   10    114   r                                           ││
│ │   11    105   i                                           ││
│ │   12    110   n                                           ││
│ │   13    103   g                                           ││
│ │   14      0                  <---- Added null byte        ││
│ └───────────────────────────────────────────────────────────┘│
└─────────────────────────────────────────────────────────────┘
```

Output of the ASZDEMO program

Structures and arrays

Similar to applications and other programs, DOS and the BIOS manage much information using structures and arrays. The most important factor lies in the compiler's creating the information in the sequence specified, aligning each field on a word boundary. Although Turbo Pascal has a compiler directive for aligning data (the {A$} directive), this directive usually doesn't work on structures and arrays.

The following table shows an example of a structure returned to the caller by DOS.

■ Directory entry structure as returned by DOS functions 4EH and 4FH ■		
Addr.	**Contents**	**Type**
00H	Reserved	21 bytes
15H	Attribute byte of the file	1 byte
16H	Time of last modification	1 word
18H	Date of last modification	1 word
1AH	File size	1 dword
1EH	Filename and extension separated by a period but without a path specification (ends with a null byte)	13 bytes
■ Length: 43 bytes		

The following program listing excerpt shows how this structure can be recreated in Pascal (you'll find this structure in the DIRP1.PAS program discussed later in this book):

```
type DirBufTyp = record     { Data structures of functions 4EH and 4FH }
                Reserved : array [1..21] of char;
                Attr     : byte;
                Time     : integer;
                Date     : integer;
```

```
Size       : longint;
Name       : array [1..13] of char
end;
```

As you can see, the Reserved element at the beginning of the DOS structure is represented by an array. This can be either a char or byte array. The fields within this structure must have the same offset address, which means that these elements are the same distance from the beginning of the structure as in the DOS structure.

The rest of the elements in the DirBufType structure refer to the various components of the DOS structure in their data types. Bytes are reproduced as bytes, words as integers, and dwords as longints. The individual field names are unimportant. You can choose any name you want because the names don't affect the structure. Obtaining a correct reproduction of the structure is all that matters.

Accessing bit fields

In structures, fields often represent bit fields, in which individual bits or groups of bits have a specific meaning. The attribute byte in the previous directory structure also represents a bit field. As the following illustration shows, each single bit represents a certain file attribute. For example, a bit may provide information about whether the file is write/protected, is a system file, or not a file at all (a subdirectory). You must know how to read the individual bits.

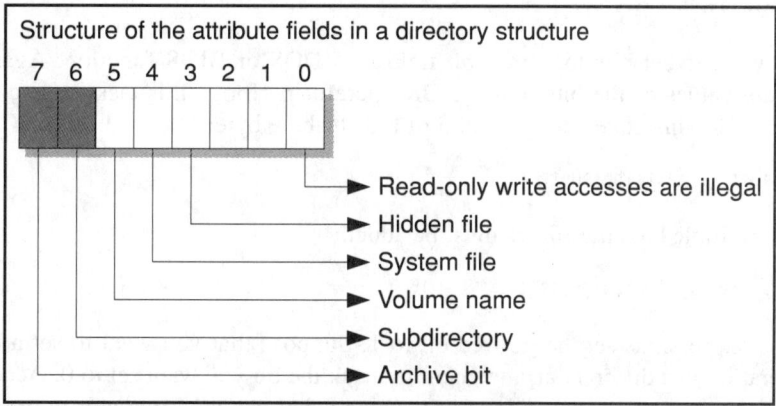

If you want to read a certain bit, first you must know its value. You know that bit 0 has a value of 1, bit 1 a value of 2, bit 2 a value of 4, and so on until you reach bit 7, which has a value of 128. To determine whether you're dealing with a subdirectory, you must use the value of bit 4, which is 16.

You want to set all the attribute byte's other bits to 0. From there you can then determine whether bit 4 is set. The AND operator masks all bits not in the AND mask. The following expression unsets all bits except bit 4 (bit 4 = 16):

```
AttributeByte and 16
```

If bit 4 is set, a result of 16 is returned. Otherwise, the result is 0.

This expression can be used as follows within an if loop:

```
If AttributeByte and 16 <> 0 then
  { If the result <> 0 it's a subdirectory }
else
  { If the result = 0 there's no subdirectory }
```

Checking more than one bit at a time complicates this process. The values of the different bits must be added together. For example, suppose that you want to determine whether the file is both hidden and a system file. The corresponding flags are stored in bits 1 and 2, and have a value of 6 when added together. The following expression returns the contents of both bits:

```
AttributeByte and 6
```

This time, however, the expression used in the previous example cannot be directly applied to this example:

```
AttributeByte and 6 <> 0
```

This expression is already TRUE if one of the two bits is set and the result of the AND operation doesn't equal 0. However, if you want to know whether both flags were set, you must modify the process to something similar to the following:

```
If AttributeByte and 6 = 6 then
  { Hidden and System }
else
  { not Hidden, not System }
```

Often you'll want to set bits to pass a bit field to a DOS or BIOS function. Again, the main focus is on the values of the bits, but the OR operator performs this task instead of the AND operator. The following statement sets bit 3 of the attribute byte:

```
AttributeByte := AttributeByte or 8;
```

Again, to set multiple bits, the values must be added:

```
AttributeByte := AttributeByte or ( 8 + 16 );
```

Both of these expressions set the desired bit to 1. Suppose that you want to set a bit to 0. Use an AND operation in a different arrangement to mask the bit you want set to 0. According to the laws of binary logic, you must then invert the value using the NOT operator in order to achieve the desired result. To set bit 5 to 0, use the following statement:

```
AttributeByte := AttributeByte and not( 32 );
```

Once again, you can mask more than one bit at a time using the following:

```
AttributeByte := AttributeByte and not( 32 + 8 );
```

However, bit fields don't always consist of separate bits. Often they are comprised of bit groups, whose individual bits form a certain value when added together. An example of this is the date field in the directory entry of a file. This field contains three bit groups that specify the day, month, and the year the particular file was created or last modified. So, to analyze this information, you must determine the value the three bit groups represent instead of checking the status of given bits.

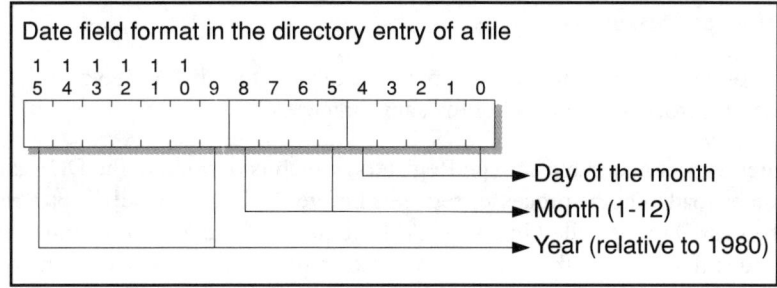

You can easily determine the day by using the described procedure with an AND operator:

```
Day := DateField and ( 1 + 2 + 4 + 8 );
```

When you want to determine the month, the AND operation is no longer sufficient because the isolated bit group must also be shifted to the right by five bits to obtain the number of the month. The SHR operator in Turbo Pascal shifts an expression to the right by any number of bits. You can determine the month and the year by using the following statements:

```
Month := ( DateField and ( 32 + 64 + 128 + 256 ) ) shr 5;
Year := ( DateField and ( 512+1024+2048+4096+8192+16384+32768 ) shr 9;
```

The SHL operator, which is the opposite of the SHR operator, shifts a value to the left bit by bit. For example, you can use this operator to create a date field from a given day, month, and year:

```
DateField := Day + ( Month shl 5 ) + ( Year shl 9 );
```

2.2.2 Calling Interrupts from Turbo Pascal

Turbo Pascal provides the Intr and MsDos procedures, which are defined in the DOS unit. This unit also contains some type and constant declarations that are needed for calling types and constants.

The syntax for Intr is as follows:

```
Intr(InterruptNumber : byte, Regs : Registers);
```

The InterruptNumber parameter specifies the number of the interrupt to be called. Since every value between 0 and 255 is accepted for this parameter, you can call all available interrupts, including hardware interrupts.

The MsDos procedure is a special form of the Intr procedure. You can call it the same way you call Intr:

```
MsDos(Regs : Registers);
```

Notice that unlike Intr, MsDos doesn't have an InterruptNumber parameter. MsDos accesses interrupt 21H, which lets you call the DOS API (DOS Application Program Interface) functions. There are over 200 of these functions, which refer to functions provided by DOS applications.

Accessing the processor registers

As you may conclude from the definition of RegType, the different variables within this structure reflect the processor registers of the same name.

Both procedures expect a variable of type Registers, which is defined in the DOS unit. Registers accepts the values loaded in the processor registers before the interrupt call. Then these values are supposed to be passed to the called interrupt. After returning from MsDos or Intr, these variables contain the values that were in the various processor registers after the called interrupt function ends.

To simplify register addressing, Registers provides a variant record, in which the registers are listed with their normal names. Registers is defined as follows in the DOS unit:

```
type Registers = record
                   case integer of
                     0 : (AX, BX, CX, DX, BP, SI, DI, DS, ES, Flags : word);
                     1 : (AL, AH, BL, BH, CL , CH, DL, DH : byte);
                 end;
```

The 16-bit processor registers AX to ES are represented by the word variables of the same name. The 8-bit processor registers AL to DH are represented by variables of type byte.

The divisions of 8-bit and 16-bit registers into half registers results in overlapping between both register groups in memory (i.e., two 8-bit variables overlap the corresponding 16-bit variable). So, AL and AH share the same memory space as AX; BL and BH share the same memory space of BX. This also applies to the CL/CH and DL/DH variables.

Notice the order in which 8-bit registers are specified. This order must mirror the format in which the 16-bit register is placed in memory above them. Since, in memory, the low byte of a word precedes the high byte, the L register must be declared before the corresponding H register.

If Regs is a variable of type Registers, you can easily address the single processor registers by the different components of this variable:

- Regs.ax,
- Regs.bx,
- Regs.cx,
- Regs.ah,
- Regs.dl, etc.

To pass the value D3H to the DL register during an interrupt call, do the following:

```
Regs.DL := $D3;
```

Before calling an interrupt using Intr or MsDos, load the registers, which are used by the function you'll call, with the information you want passed to the function. The interrupt ignores all registers except those on which it directly relies.

Reading the flags in the flag register

In many cases, the flag registers can also return information to the calling program. DOS functions extensively use the carry flag, which is set after the function is called and when the function call fails.

To simplify checking the flags, the DOS unit defines different constants, which reflect the bit values of the processor flags:

Constant	Bit Pos.	Bit Value
FCarry	0	1
FParity	2	4
FAuxiliary	4	16
FZero	6	64
FSign	7	128
FOverflow	11	2048

You can use an AND operator to check whether one of these bits is set. The following expression sets the Boolean variable to TRUE when the carry flag is set.

```
Error := ( ( Regs.Flags and FCarry ) <> 0 );
```

2.2.3 Buffers and Turbo Pascal

Many functions expect pointers to buffers when they're called. The functions either take information from or place information in the buffers (e.g., file contents). These pointers are always FAR; they consist of a segment address and an offset address. This FAR pointer data can be anywhere in memory, not necessarily in the current program's memory segment.

Passing pointers to interrupt functions

DOS function 09H is an example of a function that takes pointers. This function displays a string on the screen, beginning at the current cursor position. Like all DOS functions, it expects the function number in the AH register and the address of the buffer containing the string to be displayed in the DS:DX register pair. DS takes the segment address of the buffer and DX takes the offset address.

Although creating a string in Pascal is easy, you may also want to know how to pass the buffer address. Turbo Pascal provides the Seg() and Ofs() functions, which supply the segment and offset addresses of any memory object. It doesn't matter whether you're working with a local or global variable or a typed constant.

The following program demonstrates how to use these functions with DOS function 09H ($09) as an example. The program uses DOS function 09H to display the string from the Message variable on the screen. Unlike other DOS functions, function 09H looks for a $ character, instead of a null byte, at the end of the buffer.

```
'9HDEMOP.PAS

program 9HDemoP;
```

```
uses DOS;

var Regs    : Registers;
    Message : string[20];

begin
  Message := 'DOSPrint' + '$';

  Regs.AH := $09;
  Regs.DS := seg( Message[1] );
  Regs.DX := ofs( Message[1] );
  MsDos( regs );
end.
```

Receiving pointers from interrupt functions

The following program calls DOS function 1BH, which returns a pointer in the DS:BX register pair. This pointer points to a byte containing the media code of the current drive. DOS uses the media code to describe the different types of drives, with codes between F0H and FFH. The value F8H (248) characterizes all types of hard drives.

To determine the media ID from the returned pointer, the MediaPtr type is defined as a pointer to a byte at the beginning of the program. Since pointers are always FAR in Turbo Pascal, you can be certain that you've created a FAR pointer. The program defines MP as a variable of this type. After calling the DOS $1B function, the program loads MP with the returned pointer from the register pair DS:BX. The program uses Turbo Pascal's Ptr function to do this. This function receives a segment and offset address and forms a generic pointer from them.

This pointer can be used to access the referenced information as in any normal pointer operation. The Writeln statement at the end of the program demonstrates this.

```
{* MEDIAIDP.PAS      *}

program MediaIdP;

uses Dos;                                { Add Dos unit }

type MediaPtr = ^byte;                   { Create a byte pointer }

var Regs : Registers;        { Processor registers for interrupt call }
    MP   : MediaPtr;               { Variable for media pointer }

begin
  Regs.AH := $1B;                   { Pass 1BH to AH register }
  MsDos( Regs );                    { Call DOS interrupt 1BH }
  MP := ptr( Regs.DS, Regs.BX );         { Read pointer }
  writeln( 'Media ID = ', MP^ );       { Display media ID }
end.
```

Accessing memory with Mem, MemW, and MemL

Turbo Pascal has three predefined arrays, called Mem, MemW, and MemL, that are used to access bytes, words, and longints (dwords). A special syntax is used to access these arrays within brackets and the segment address is separated from the offset address by a colon.

You could have accessed the media ID using the following in the MEDIAIDP.PAS program:

```
mem[ Regs.DX : Regs.BX ];
```

When accessing multiple pointers, Mem, MemW, and MemL will need a more complex syntax than the one previously shown.

2.2.4 Port Access in Turbo Pascal

Turbo Pascal recognizes PC ports as a predefined array. However, Turbo Pascal also supports two arrays for port access: Port (for 8-bit ports) and PortW (for 16-bit ports). PortW allows you to send 16-bit values to ports, while Port only accepts 8-bit values. The array you select will depend on the expansion board or support chip you want to access. If the board or chip is 16-bits, you can use PortW; otherwise, you must use Port for access.

You can read information from ports and write information to ports using normal array syntax. For example, both of the following statements dump the contents of port 3C4H, which is part of the graphics controller on an EGA/VGA card:

```
XByte := port[ $3C4 ];
XWord := portw[ $3C4 ];
```

The following statements allow you to send a byte or word just as easily:

```
port[ $3C4 ] := XByte;
portw[ $3C4 ] := XWord;
```

Examples of these statements are located in Chapter 4.

2.3 The C Language

Unlike Pascal, the market for C compilers is characterized by the rivalry between Microsoft and Borland. Both companies have several products on the market: Microsoft QuickC and Microsoft C 6.0, Borland Turbo C++ and Borland C++. Both C++ compilers preserve the compatibility with the standard (Turbo C) implementation.

The C programs in this book can be compiled under all the compilers we just named, although some warning messages may appear on the screen. All of the programs were compiled under Microsoft C 6.00, with warning levels changed as needed. We also test-compiled programs using Borland's Turbo C++ and the default settings of the Turbo C++ environment.

These programs are affected by the differences between the libraries found in the Microsoft and Borland compilers. Because of this, some programs contain constructs like the following, which is taken from the DIRC2.C demonstration program listed later in this book. The differences between the two libraries are intercepted by defining macros.

```
#ifdef __TURBOC__                          /* Turbo C Compiler? */
   #define DIRSTRUCT            struct ffblk
   #define FINDFIRST( path, buf, attr )  findfirst( path, buf, attr )
   #define FINDNEXT( buf )      findnext( buf )
   #define NAME                 ff_name
   #define ATTRIBUTE            ff_attrib
   #define TIME                 ff_ftime
```

```
         #define DATE                       ff_fdate
         #define SIZE                       ff_fsize
       #else                                            /* No --> Microsoft C */
         #define DIRSTRUCT                  struct find_t
         #define FINDFIRST( path, buf, attr )  _dos_findfirst(path, attr, buf)
         #define FINDNEXT( buf )            _dos_findnext( buf )
         #define NAME                       name
         #define ATTRIBUTE                  attrib
         #define TIME                       wr_time
         #define DATE                       wr_date
         #define SIZE                       size
       #endif
```

Since the demonstration programs in this book illustrate system programming, we omitted all the OOP (Object Oriented Programming) enhancements available in Turbo C++. Once you see the logic of each demonstration program, you can add any extras, such as OOP objects, to suit your own needs.

2.3.1 C Data Types

Like all compilers, the C data types mainly correspond with processor data types, which allows fast and easy processing. The following table shows how various C compilers store the different data types:

C Type	Stored as
unsigned char	BYTE
char	BYTE
int	WORD
unsigned int	WORD
near *void	WORD
long	DWORD
far *void	DWORD

Since C doesn't have a byte type or word type, you'll find typedef functions, similar to the following, at the beginning of many of the C programs in this book:

```
   typedef unsigned char BYTE;
   typedef unsigned int WORD;
```

These lines define the two types that are very important to system programming.

In C, the memory model that's used governs the use of NEAR and FAR pointers. The programs in this book were developed using the SMALL memory model. So they work exclusively with NEAR pointers. When FAR pointers are needed for system programming, the far modifier is used in the variable declaration:

```
   int far *p;      /* P is a FAR pointer */
```

We found that Microsoft QuickC doesn't like working with FAR pointers while the Options/Compiler Flags/Pointer Check option is enabled. Disable this option to avoid problems while executing the demonstration programs from this book.

Strings

Most DOS and BIOS functions expect strings as a sequence of bytes, containing the ASCII codes of the individual characters, and terminated by a null byte (a byte consisting of the value 0). In system programming, this type of string is called an ASCIIZ (ASCII-Zero) string. Since C stores strings in ASCIIZ format, they don't have to be converted.

Structures and arrays

Similar to applications and other programs, DOS and the BIOS manage much information using structures and arrays. The most important factor lies in the compiler's creating the information in the sequence specified, aligning each field on a word boundary.

All C compilers are familiar with compiler directives that can influence this structure. Microsoft C compilers support the /Zp directive, which ensures that the fields within structures aren't separated. Borland compilers have an option called Word alignment in the Options/Compiler.../Code generation... dialog box within the integrated development environment. Ensure that this option is disabled; otherwise the compiler will separate the fields.

The following table shows an example of a structure returned to the caller by DOS:

■ Directory entry structure as returned by DOS functions 4EH and 4FH ■		
Addr.	Contents	Type
00H	Reserved	21 bytes
15H	Attribute byte of the file	1 byte
16H	Time of last modification	1 word
18H	Date of last modification	1 word
1AH	File size	1 dword
1EH	Filename and extension separated by a period but without a path specification (ends with a null byte)	13 bytes
■ Length: 43 bytes		

The following excerpt from a program listing (DIRC1.C) described later in this book demonstrates how this structure can be reproduced in C.

```
typedef unsigned char BYTE;                       /* Create a byte */
typedef struct {            /* DIR structure for functions 4EH and 4FH */
            BYTE          Reserved[21];
            BYTE          Attribute;
            unsigned int  Time;
            unsigned int  Date;
            unsigned long Size;
            char          Name[13];
            } DIRSTRUCT;
```

As you can see, the Reserved element at the beginning of the DOS structure is represented by an array. You can use either a CHAR array or BYTE array. The various fields within the C structure must have the same offset addresses so that they are the same distance from the beginning of the structure as in the DOS structure.

The remaining elements in the DIRSTRUCT structure correspond to the various components of the DOS structure in reference to their data types. Bytes are reproduced as bytes, words as unsigned ints, and dwords as unsigned longs. The names of the individual fields are unimportant. Since the names don't affect the structure, you can choose any name you want. Obtaining a correct reproduction of the structure is all that matters.

Accessing bit fields

In structures, fields often represent bit fields, in which individual bits or groups of bits have a specific meaning. The attribute byte in the previous directory structure also represents a bit field. As the following illustration shows, each single bit represents a certain file attribute. For example, a bit may provide information about whether the file is write/protected, is a system file, or not a file at all (a subdirectory). You must know how to read the individual bits.

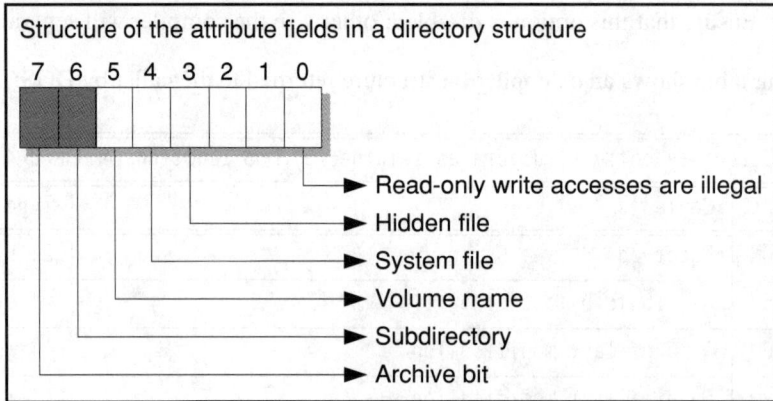

If you want to read a specific bit, first you must know its value. You know that bit 0 has a value of 1, bit 1 a value of 2, bit 2 a value of 4, and so on until you reach bit 7, which has a value of 128. To determine whether you're working with a subdirectory, you must use the value of bit 4, which is 16.

You want to set all the attribute byte's other bits to 0. From there you can then determine whether bit 4 is set. The AND operator (the & character in C) masks all bits that aren't in the AND mask. The following expression unsets all bits except bit 4 (bit 4 = 16):

```
AttributeByte & 16
```

If bit 4 is set, a result of 16 is returned. Otherwise, the result is 0.

This expression can be used, as follows, within an if loop:

```
if ( ( AttributeByte & 16 ) != 0 )
   /* If the result <>0 it's a subdirectory */
else
   /* If the result = 0 there's no subdirectory */
```

Checking more than one bit at a time complicates this process. The values of the different bits must be added together. For example, suppose that you want to determine whether the file is both hidden and a system file. The corresponding flags are stored in bits 1 and 2, and have a value of 6 when added together. The following expression returns the contents of both bits:

```
AttributeByte & 6
```

This time, however, the expression used in the previous example cannot be directly applied to this example:

```
( AttributeByte & 6 ) != 0
```

This expression is already TRUE if one of the two bits is set and the result of the AND operation doesn't equal 0. However, if you want to know whether both flags were set, you must modify the process to something similar to the following:

```
If ( ( AttributeByte & 6 ) == 6 )
   /* Hidden and System */
else
   /* Not Hidden, Not System ) */
```

Frequently you'll want to set bits to pass a bit field to a DOS or BIOS function. Again, the main focus is on the values of the bits, but the OR operator (the | character in C), instead of the AND operator, performs this task. The following statement sets bit 3 of the attribute byte:

```
AttributeByte = AttributeByte | 8;
AttributeByte |= 8; /* Abbreviated version */
```

Again, to set multiple bits, the values must be added:

```
AttributeByte = AttributeByte | ( 8 + 16 );
```

Both of these expressions set the desired bit to 1. Suppose that you want to set a bit to 0. Use an AND operation in a different arrangement to mask the bit you want set to 0. According to the laws of binary logic, you must then invert the value using the NOT operator (the ! character in C) to achieve the desired result. To set bit 5 to 0, use the following statement:

```
AttributeByte = AttributeByte & !32;
```

Once again, you can mask more than one bit at a time using the following statement:

```
AttributeByte = AttributeByte & !( 32 + 8 );
```

However, bit fields don't always consist of separate bits. Often they are comprised of bit groups, whose individual bits form a certain value when added together. An example of this is the date field in the directory entry of a file. This field contains three bit groups that specify the day, month, and year the particular file was created or last modified. So, to analyze this information, you must determine the value the three bits represent instead of checking the status of the given bits.

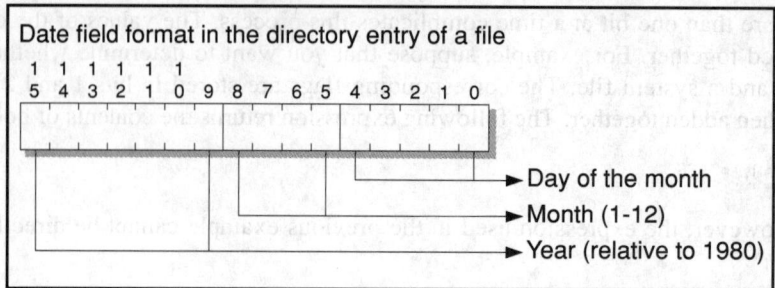

Date field format in the directory entry of a file

You can easily determine the day by using the described procedure with an AND operator:

```
Day = DateField & ( 1 + 2 + 4 + 8 );
```

However, when determining the month, the AND operation is no longer sufficient because the isolated bit group must also be shifted to the right by five bits to get the number of the month. In C, the >> operator shifts an expression to the right by any number of bits. You can determine the month and the year by using the following statements:

```
Month = ( DateField & ( 32 + 64 + 128 + 256 ) ) >> 5;
Year = ( DateField & ( 512+1024+2048+4096+8192+16384+32768 ) ) >> 9;
```

The << operator, which is the opposite of the >> operator, shifts a value to the left bit by bit. For example, you can use this operator to create a date field from a given day, month, and year:

```
DateField = Day + ( Month << 5 ) + ( Year << 9 );
```

2.3.2 Calling Interrupts from C

Both Borland and Microsoft compilers provide the int86(), int86x(), intdos(), and intdosx() functions for calling software interrupts. While the int86() and int86x() functions can call all 256 interrupts of the Intel processor, the intdos() and intdosx() functions direct their attention to interrupt 21H (0x21), which lets you call the DOS API (DOS Application Program Interface) functions. There are over 200 of these functions, which refer to functions provided by DOS applications.

The declarations of these functions are in the DOS.H include files of both compilers, which must be linked to a C program in order to work with these functions. These declarations are as follows:

```
int intdos(union REGS *inregs, union REGS *outregs);
int intdosx(union REGS *inregs, union REGS *outregs, struct SREGS *sreg);
int int86(int, union REGS *inregs, union REGS *outregs);
int int86x(int, union REGS *inregs, union REGS *outregs, struct SREGS *sreg);
```

Accessing processor registers

All four procedures expect pointers to structures of type REGS, while the two functions that end with "x" expect a variable of type SREGS. These are structures that reproduce the processor registers.

From the first passed structure (inregs), the functions load the various processor registers before the interrupt call, while they load the contents of the processor registers in the second passed structure (outregs) after the call.

To make it easier to address both the 8-bit and the 16-bit registers, REGS represents a union in which two structures of WORDREGS and BYTEREGS type can be placed on top of each other:

```
union REGS {
            struct WORDREGS x;
            struct BYTEREGS h;
            };

struct WORDREGS {
                unsigned int ax;
                unsigned int bx;
                unsigned int cx;
                unsigned int dx;
                unsigned int si;
                unsigned int di;
                unsigned int cflag;
                };

struct BYTEREGS {
                unsigned char al, ah;
                unsigned char bl, bh;
                unsigned char cl, ch;
                unsigned char dl, dh;
                };
```

The 16-bit processor registers AX to ES are represented by the unsigned int variables of the same name in the WORDREGS structure. The 8-bit processor registers AL to DH are represented by the variables in the BYTEREGS structure.

The variant record applies to the 8-bit registers, which are as important as the 16-bit registers for carrying information during the interrupt call. Dividing the 8-bit and 16-bit registers into two variants results in an overlapping of both register sets in memory, with two 8-bit variables overlapping "their" 16-bit variable. So, AL and AH share the same memory space as AX; BL, and BH share the same memory space of BX. This also applies to the CL/CH and DL/DH variables.

Notice the order in which 8-bit registers are specified. This order must mirror the format in which the 16-bit register is placed in memory above them. Since, in memory, the low byte of a word precedes the high byte, the L register must be declared before the corresponding H register.

If pregs is a variable of the REGS type, you can easily address the processor registers from the various components of this variable:

- pregs.x.ax,
- pregs.x.bx,
- pregs.x.cx,
- pregs.h.ah,
- pregs.h.dl, etc.

If you want to pass the value D3H (0xD3) to the DL register during an interrupt call, do the following:

```
pregs.h.dl = 0xD3;
```

Before calling an interrupt using Intr or MsDos, load the registers, which are used by the function you'll call, with the information you want passed to the function. The interrupt ignores all other registers except those on which it directly relies.

Including the segment register

As the definitions of BYTEREGS and WORDREGS show, these structures ignore the various segment registers and duplicate only the general registers. This occurs because segment registers aren't needed in most function calls. If a function call requires a segment register, use the int86x() and intdosx() functions, which expect a pointer to a variable of the SREGS type, as well as two pointers to variables of the REGS type. The two functions load the various segment registers from this variable before the interrupt call, and save their contents there after the interrupt call.

Here's the definition of SREGS:

```
struct SREGS {
            unsigned int es;
            unsigned int cs;
            unsigned int ss;
            unsigned int ds;
            };
```

Reading the flags in the flag register

In many cases, the flag registers can also return information to the calling program. DOS functions extensively use the carry flag, which is set after the function is called and when the function call fails.

To simplify checking the flags, the WORDREGS structure contains a field named CFLAG, which is loaded with the contents of the carry flag after a function call. This field shows a value of 1 if the carry flag is set and a value of 0 if it isn't set. Before the function call, the contents of this variable are ignored because the carry flag isn't important for working with interrupt functions until after the interrupt call.

The following program excerpt shows that after the interrupt call it's easy to determine whether the carry flag is set. This program also demonstrates that it's definitely possible to specify a single variable for the inregs and outregs parameters, which will be loaded before the interrupt call with the desired parameters, and accept the contents of the processor register afterwards.

```
#include <dos.h>

void test( void )
{
union REGS pregs;
pregs.h.ah = 0x13;          /* Function number */
pregs.h.dl = 0;             /* Any value */
intdos( &pregs, &pregs );
if ( pregs.x.cflag )
    ;                       /* Carry flag set */
else
    ;                       /* Carry flag unset */
}
```

However, you'll encounter problems if you want to read other flags because some BIOS functions use the zero flag for returning information. In these instances, you can't accomplish anything on Microsoft compilers with the int...() functions. However, the developers at Borland were clever enough to expand the WORDSREG structure by a FLAGS variable, which reflects the contents of the entire flag register after the function call.

```
struct WORDREGS {                    /* Borland only! */
            unsigned int ax, bx, cx, dx, si, di, cflag, flags;
            };
```

With Borland compilers, you can determine whether one of the flags is set in the flag register. This is done after calling an int...() function through a binary combination of the flags variable with the value of the particular flag.

The following are the values of the various processor flags:

Constant	Bit Pos.	Bit Value
Carry	0	1
Parity	2	4
Auxiliary	4	16
Zero	6	64
Sign	7	128
Overflow	11	2048

2.3.3 Buffers and the C Language

Many functions expect pointers to buffers when they're called. The functions either take information from the buffers or place information in the buffers (e.g., file contents). These pointers are always FAR; they consist of a segment address and an offset address. This FAR pointer data can be anywhere in memory; it doesn't have to be in the current program's memory segment.

Passing pointers to interrupt functions

DOS function 09H (0x09) is an example of a function that takes pointers. This function displays a string on the screen beginning at the current cursor position. Like all DOS functions, it expects the function number in the AH register and the address of the buffer containing the string to be displayed in the DS:DX register pair. DS takes the segment address of the buffer, and DX takes the offset address.

Although creating a string is easy in C, you may also want to know how to pass the buffer address. At first this may seem quite simple because both the Borland and the Microsoft compilers define two macros named FP_SEG() and FP_OFF(), which help determine a segment and offset address. However, because these manufacturers define FP_OFF() and FP_SEG() differently, there are some problems:

Borland:

```
#define FP_SEG(fp) ((unsigned)(void _seg *)(void far *)(fp))
#define FP_OFF(fp) ((unsigned)(fp))
```

Microsoft:

```
#define FP_SEG(fp) (*((unsigned _far *)&(fp)+1))
#define FP_OFF(fp) (*((unsigned _far *)&(fp)))
```

Although the Borland definition's macros can contain the variables whose segment or offset addresses you want to determine, the Microsoft macros must be passed a FAR pointer that refers to the appropriate variable.

The following programs also show the differences. Both programs use DOS function 09H (0x09) to display the string from the Message variable on the screen. Unlike other DOS functions, function 09H looks for a $ character, instead of a null byte, at the end of the buffer. The Borland version is as follows:

```
/*************** 9HDEMOBC.C ******************/

#include <dos.h>              /* Borland Version */

void main( void )
{
 union REGS pregs;
 struct SREGS sregs;
 char Message[20] = "PC Intern$";

 pregs.h.ah = 0x09;
 sregs.ds = FP_SEG( Message );    /* Get the var. */
 pregs.x.dx = FP_OFF( Message ); /* addresses    */
 intdosx( &pregs, &pregs, &sregs );
}
```

As you can see, the FP_SEG() and FP_OFF() functions specify the address at which the message can be found. However, the Microsoft version of the same program requires a FAR pointer that points to the string:

```
/*************** 9HDEMOMC.C *********************/
#include <dos.h>                  /* Microsoft Version */

void main( void )
{
 union REGS pregs;
 struct SREGS sregs;
 char Message[20] = "PC Intern$";
 void far *mesptr = Message; /* FAR pntr to string */

 pregs.h.ah = 0x09;
 sregs.ds = FP_SEG( mesptr );    /* Pass address to */
 pregs.x.dx = FP_OFF( mesptr ); /* FAR pointer     */
 intdosx( &pregs, &pregs, &sregs );
}
```

Receiving pointers from interrupt functions

The following program calls DOS function 1BH (0x1B), which returns a pointer in the DS:BX register pair. This pointer points to a byte containing the media code of the current drive. DOS uses the media code to describe the different types of drives, with codes between F0H (0xF0) and FFH (0xFF). The value F8H (248) characterizes all types of hard drives.

A FAR pointer, from which the media ID can be read, must be generated. Borland implementations of C provide the MK_FP() macro defined in the DOS.H include file. This macro expects two parameters describing the segment and offset addresses to which the desired pointer should refer. This pointer results from this macro and the void far type *.

Although the Microsoft compilers don't define this type of macro, you could easily make your own MK_FP, as shown in the following program listing. MK_FP is defined here, in case it hasn't already been defined by the include files.

After the interrupt call, a FAR pointer is formed by MK_FP() and assigned the mp variable. In the printf() call at the end of the program, this pointer "de-references" the media ID so that it can be displayed on the screen.

```
/******************* M E D I A I D C . C *********************/

#include <dos.h>
#include <stdio.h>

#ifndef MK_FP                          /* Macro MK_FP already defined */
  #define MK_FP(seg,ofs) ((void far *) ((unsigned long) (seg)<<16|(ofs)))
#endif

void main( void )
{
  union REGS pregs;
  struct SREGS sregs;
  unsigned char far *mp;

  pregs.h.ah = 0x1B;
  intdosx( &pregs, &pregs, &sregs );
  mp = MK_FP( sregs.ds, pregs.x.bx );
  printf( "Media ID = %d\n ", *mp );
}
```

If you examine the definition of the MK_FP() macro, you'll notice that it's quite simple despite the many parentheses and keywords. Within the definition, the segment is cast into a long type, shifted to the left by 16 bits and the offset address is then set in the lower 16 bits of the resulting new long type. The result corresponds exactly to the desired FAR pointer in its composition, so it only has to be accessed by a cast.

2.3.4 Port Access in C

Both the Microsoft and Borland compilers offer various functions for accessing ports. However, they have different names and are declared in different include files. Borland has its declarations in DOS.H, while Microsoft has its declarations in CONIO.H.

The following figure shows the different routines and declarations of the two compiler manufacturers:

Microsoft: Include file <conio.h>

```
int      inp( unsigned port );
unsigned inpw( unsigned port );
int      outp( unsigned port, int databyte );
unsigned outpw( unsigned port, unsigned dataword );
```

Borland: Include file <dos.h>

```
int           inport (int __portid);
unsigned char inportb(int __portid);
void          outport (int __portid, int __value);
void          outportb(int __portid, unsigned char __value);

#define inp(portid)    inportb(portid)
#define outp(portid,v) outportb(portid,v)
```

As you can see, theoretically the same functions are available from both manufacturers. Each has two functions for reading and writing to ports; one is for 8-bit ports and one is for 16-bit ports.

The Borland compiler demonstrates some cooperation with Microsoft with its inp() and outp() macros, which the Borland functions copied from the names of the two Microsoft functions. Unfortunately, Borland did this only for the two 8-bit functions. However, it's easy to do the same for the two 16-bit functions within a program:

```
#ifdef __TURBOC__                          /* Compiling with Turbo C? */
   #define inpw(portid)    inport(portid)
   #define outpw(portid,v) outport(portid,v)
#endif
```

This enables you to use the names of the Microsoft functions in your programs even if you're working with a Borland compiler. For example, the following statements read the contents of port 3C4H (0x3C4), which is part of the graphics controller on an EGA/VGA card:

```
XByte = inp( 0x3C4 );
XWord = inpw( 0x3C4 );
```

The following statements allow you to send a byte or word just as easily:

```
outp( 0x3C4, XByte );
outpw( 0x3C4 XWord );
```

You'll find examples of these statements in Chapter 4.

Chapter 3

The BIOS

Most users associate the term *operating system* with DOS. However, DOS isn't the only operating system on a PC. Before hard drives became standard equipment, the PC searched the BIOS (Basic Input/Output System) for the basic input and output routines needed for communicating between software and hardware. The BIOS can be found on a ROM chip, which is usually placed on the PC's main circuit board. The BIOS is accessed every time you switch on your PC.

This BIOS contains all the essential routines needed by the PC for communication between hardware and peripheral devices. These routines include instructions for handling screen output, printed output, fonts, date, and time.

Why the BIOS is important

Since these routine calls are standardized, the programmer doesn't have to fit programs to one particular PC hardware configuration. This means you can develop a program on one PC or compatible, and run it on another compatible PC without errors, even though neither the hardware nor the individual BIOS routines are completely compatible.

The BIOS is an integral part of the PC. It doesn't matter whether a system contains a 20 megabyte hard drive or a 20 gigabyte hard drive or whether the system is made by IBM or a smaller manufacturer, the BIOS hard drive functions are identical in both instances.

This hardware independent concept is mainly responsible for the PC's popularity. It enables computer manufacturers to develop PCs that aren't identical to a true IBM PC, but can still run popular software. Except for additions to accommodate the AT system, few changes have been made to the BIOS since the PC's introduction on the market.

Over a dozen companies manufacture BIOS chips. (These companies include AMI, Phoenix, Award, and Quadtel.) Although there are differences in each BIOS, they all perform the same essential tasks.

3.1 The BIOS Standard

Let's begin with the basics of BIOS: How it works, its ground level functions, and how it contributes to starting a PC when you switch on your computer.

IBM defined the types of different BIOS functions and parameters needed in a PC. There are 256 BIOS interrupts, which are divided into functions. This provides a wider selection than that provided by one function per interrupt. These functions provide the communication with the hardware. The following table displays the different BIOS interrupts. BIOS views some interrupts as variables, such as video and hard drive functions. (We'll discuss these in more detail later.)

Number	Meaning
10H	Video card access
11H	Configuration test
12H	RAM test
13H	BIOS disk functions
14H	Serial interface functions
15H	Cassette and extended AT functions
16H	Keyboard functions
17H	Parallel interface functions
1AH	Date/time/realtime clock functions

BIOS architecture

The BIOS itself is located in PC ROM, which makes it resident even after the computer has been switched off. It's stored very high in the processor's address space. The ROM chip that contains the BIOS code is always located in the highest area of memory segment F000H. The exact starting location of BIOS varies depending on the BIOS, the system, and sometimes the memory capacity. For example, the original IBM BIOS started at offset address E000H, while Phoenix BIOS may start at offset address C000H.

The starting point of the BIOS ROM varies with the size of the BIOS ROM. It usually ends at the last memory location of the F segment, at offset address FFFFH. This is the last memory address accessible to Intel processors running in real mode.

Some manufacturers add little extras to their BIOS designs so that they can beat their competition. For example, VGA cards often bypass ROM-BIOS. These cards include such features as shadow RAM, hard drive parameters, independent setup, and password protection. Let's examine these items individually.

Shadow RAM

Shadow RAM is hidden at the same memory addresses as ROM-BIOS. Since double memory allocation isn't permitted in RAM, the ROM-BIOS keeps this shadow RAM hidden from the operating system and applications. Many BIOS systems copy their ROM-BIOS code to shadow RAM, from which BIOS data is accessed. This generally improves execution speed in the PC, because the shadow RAM data bus is 16 bits wide, and the ROM-BIOS data bus is only 8 bits wide. NEAT chips from Chips&Technologies support shadow RAM.

Hard drive parameters

BIOS often has trouble communicating with the many hard drives on the market. This problem is caused by the different type numbers assigned to each hard drive. Before BIOS can communicate with a hard drive, it must know the number of tracks and sectors available, the number of sectors per track, and other hard drive data.

The original solution to this problem was a table of hard drives from which the user could select the drive information using a SETUP program. This information would then be passed to the ROM-BIOS. However, because of the numerous hard drives currently on the market, this solution has become obsolete. Instead, with the SETUP program, the user can manually enter the hard drive parameters. This information is then passed to battery operated RAM (sometimes called CMOS) for access from BIOS.

SETUP

The SETUP program enables the user to configure elements of the ROM-BIOS according to his/her own needs. These elements include date, time, and drive types. Some BIOS systems offer the option of configuring part of RAM as expanded memory, if the PC supports EMS. Laptop computers include an option for blanking LCD screens and disabling hard drives after a period of keyboard inactivity. This saves battery power on the laptop.

Most SETUP programs support adjustments to the processor's timer frequency. The user can make this adjustment by holding the <Alt> key, and pressing the <+> and <-> keys on the numeric keypad.

Password entry

ROM-BIOS is the best place to include password protection. Password access can then be requested before the system starts, and before DOS is loaded. Many BIOS manufacturers permit password entry through the SETUP program. The password is then stored in battery operated RAM (CMOS) or on the hard drive.

3.2 POST

Program execution in a computer based on the Intel 8088 (or one of its successors) starts after the computer is switched on at memory location F000:FFF0. This memory location is part of the ROM-BIOS and contains a jump instruction to a BIOS routine, which takes system testing and hardware component initialization. This routine is called the POST (Power-On Self-Test).

The tests

The POST consists of many tests for checking onboard PC hardware (the processor, memory, the interrupt controller, DMA, etc.), as well as the ability to initialize expansion cards (e.g., video cards). If an error occurs during these tests, the POST displays an error message or error number on the screen and instructs the computer to beep.

The following table shows the different tests performed by the POST and the sequence in which these tests are executed. This sequence isn't absolute and can change depending on the manufacturer.

- Function check of CPU (coprocessor, real mode, protected mode, etc.).
- BIOS ROM checksum
- CMOS RAM (battery operated RAM) checksum
- Test/initialize DMA controller
- Test/initialize keyboard controller
- Check first 64K of RAM
- Test/initialize interrupt controller
- Test/initialize cache controller (AT only)

First the POST tests individual functions of the processor, its registers, and some instructions. If an error occurs during this test, the system stops without displaying an error message (since the processor is defective, screen display would be impossible). If the processor passes the test, a checksum is computed for each of the BIOS ROM's contents and compared with the various ROMs to determine whether a defect exists there. Each chip on the main circuit board (such as the 8259 interrupt controller, the 8237 DMA controller, and the RAM chips) undergoes tests and initialization.

- Video controller
- RAM above 64K
- Serial and parallel interfaces
- Disk and hard drive controllers

Peripheral testing

After determining that the main circuit board is fully functional, the POST tests the peripherals (keyboard, disk drives, etc.). In addition to these hardware related tasks, the BIOS variables and the interrupt vector table must be initialized.

Searching for ROM extensions

Once these tests are completed, the search for ROM extensions begins. These ROM extensions originate either from the main circuit board or an expansion card, and augment or replace onboard BIOS functions. For example, EGA, VGA, and Super VGA cards have their own BIOS functions to replace the old BIOS interrupt 10H, which was designed specifically for handling MDA and CGA cards. Also, SCSI controllers, which are used for controlling hard drives, don't use BIOS disk interrupt 13H.

The POST tests for ROM extensions by checking offset 00H and 01H in the memory range allocated for BIOS functions. If the contents of these two bytes are 55H and AAH respectively, a BIOS extension exists. Offset 02H indicates the size of the ROM module in blocks of 512 bytes. The module's initialization routine begins at offset 03H.

Initialization of ROM Module		
Offset	Contents	Type
00H	ID byte #1 (55H)	1 byte
01H	ID byte #2 (AAH)	1 byte
02H	Module length in 512-byte blocks	1 byte
	Initialization routine	....

ROM modules

These ROM modules have the option of replacing existing BIOS routines with their own routines, and integrating these new routines with the system. The module routines must be placed in memory ranges specifically allocated for such routines.

C000H:0000H - C000H:7FFFH: EGA and VGA BIOS extensions

This range is usually reserved for the BIOS extensions provided by EGA, VGA, and Super VGA cards. BIOS divides this range into 2K increments because most extensions accept this division.

C000H:8000H - D000H:FFFFH: Hard drive extensions

This range is usually reserved for the BIOS extensions provided by many hard disk controllers. BIOS divides this range into 2K increments. The D segment of this range (D000H:0000H - D000H:FFFFH) is often used for the page frame by EMS cards. If an EMS card is being used, this range is unavailable for ROM extensions.

E000H:0000H - E000H:FFFFH: Miscellaneous

This range is reserved for BIOS systems that require more memory than is provided by memory segment F. Few BIOS extensions recognize this range.

After POST

Once ROM initialization ends, the boot process directly applying to BIOS also ends. Interrupt 19H, known as the *bootstrap loade*r, tries to load some form of the basic operating system on startup or on system reset (when you press the <Alt><Ctrl><Delete> key combination), from a predetermined place on the diskette.

This bootstrap process may fail for various reasons:

- There is no disk in the disk drive.

- There is a non system disk in the drive (the DOS files are not available on the diskette). If this occurs, the bootstrap routine attempts to find the routine on the other disk drives connected to the PC, or on a predetermined location on an existing hard disk.

If the system still cannot find the bootable system disk, there are two other reasons that may be causing the problem:

- Some older systems switch to *ROM BASIC*, a BASIC interpreter stored in PC ROM directly beneath the BIOS, starting at memory location F000H:6000H. Newer PCs display a message on the screen requesting that the user insert a system diskette and press a key.

- BIOS doesn't care what operating system it loads, so it may attempt to load a non-DOS operating system if one exists on the disk. This makes it possible to load other operating systems, such as XENIX.

3.3 Determining BIOS Version

Next to the BIOS code and some static variables (e.g., the hard drive parameter table), you'll find information describing the BIOS brand and the type of PC. You can access this information.

The previous section described memory location F000H:FFF0H in conjunction with the system startup and POST. Usually a 5-byte-long jump instruction to the POST routine can be found at this location. After this instruction, an additional 11 bytes are available (to F000:FFFF) in the ROM chip, which are normally used to store the BIOS version or release date.

You can examine the contents of these memory locations to determine which BIOS version your PC uses. Call the DEBUG program from the DOS prompt:

```
debug
```

Enter the following line to display the bytes at the end of the ROM-BIOS (the character following the memory location is a lowercase "l", not the number "1"):

```
d f000:fff0 l 10
```

The next line displays the contents of this memory location as a hexadecimal number; the characters to the right of the hex display are the corresponding ASCII codes. Day, month, and year appear as two digits separated by "/" characters.

```
C>debug
-d f000:fff0 1 10
F000:FFF0  EA 5B E0 00 F0 30 32 2F-30 36 2F 38 36 00 FC 00   [...02/06/86...
-q
C>_
```

BIOS date display in DEBUG

Determining the PC Type

Certain BIOS functions are used more for model identification than for BIOS version identification. They indicate the type of PC being used. They also indicate when the BIOS has additional functions (e.g., AT BIOS is better equipped than the PC and XT BIOS). These extra functions essentially handle string output on the screen, realtime clock access (standard on the AT), and additional RAM beyond the 1 megabyte memory limit (also standard on the AT).

A program that calls these functions must first ensure that the computer being used is actually an AT, and that the functions addressed are available. The programmer can use the model identification byte located in the last memory location of the ROM-BIOS at address F000:FFFE. This byte can contain the following codes:

Model identification byte codes	
Code	Meaning
FCH	AT
FEH FBH	XT
FFH	PC

Note: These values aren't entirely accurate. Many PC/XT compatibles indicate completely different values in the model identification byte. Use the following guideline: A model identification byte of FCH identifies an AT; any other number indicates a PC/XT.

Only IBM computers have guaranteed reliable model identification numbers at memory location F000:FFFE. This may not apply to compatible computers because the BIOS varies slightly with each manufacturer. Refer to Chapter 14 for more information on determining processor types.

3.4 BIOS Variables

The preceding sections described different BIOS interrupts and their functions. These functions require a segment of memory for storing variables and data. For this reason, the BIOS reserves over 256 bytes of memory, starting at address 0040H:0000H, for storing internal variables. This range is called the *BIOS variable range* or *BIOS variable segment*.

This memory range's allocation is standardized because many DOS programs directly access the BIOS variables and BIOS manufacturers don't provide alternate ways of accessing these variables. This standardization refers to the BIOS variables developed for the PC and PC/XT models, which stands in this range up to offset address 0071H. Memory beyond this point is used by EGA and VGA cards, as well as AT and PS/2 systems. The contents change after 0071H depending on the BIOS, PC type, and video card available.

The following list describes the individual variables, their purposes, and addresses. The address indicated is the offset address of segment address 0040H. For example, a variable with the offset address 10H has the address 0040H:0010H or 10H.

00H   Serial interface port addresses   4 words   INT 14H

During the POST (Power On Self Test), a BIOS routine determines the configuration of its PC. Among other things, this routine determines the number of installed serial (RS-232) interfaces. These interface numbers are stored as four words in memory. Each word represents one of the four cards that can be installed for asynchronous data transmission. First the low byte is stored, followed by the high byte. Since few PCs have four serial cards at their disposal, the words that represent a missing card contain the value 0.

08H   Parallel interface port addresses   4 words   INT 17H

During the POST (Power On Self Test), a BIOS routine determines the configuration of its PC. Among other things, it determines the number of installed parallel interfaces. These card numbers are stored as four words in memory. Each word represents one of the four cards that can be installed for parallel data transmission. First the low byte is stored, followed by the high byte. Since few PCs have four parallel cards at their disposal, the words that represent a missing card contain the value 0.

10H   Configuration   1 word   INT 11H

This word represents the hardware configuration of the PC as called through BIOS interrupt 11H. Similar to the previous two words, this configuration is determined during the booting process. The purposes of individual bits of this word are standardized for the PC and the XT, but can differ in other computers.

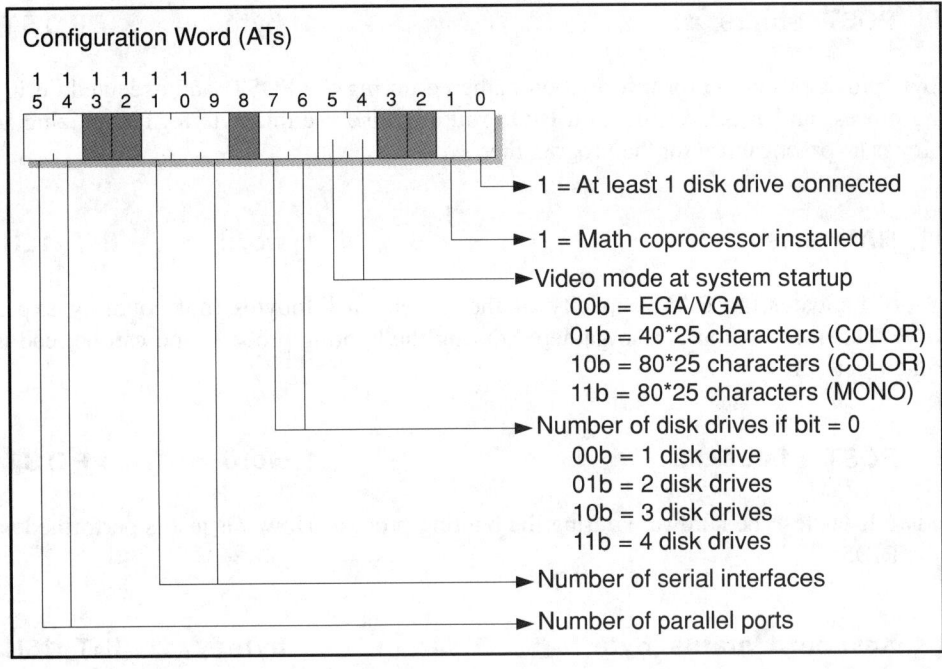

Configuration Word (ATs)

1 = At least 1 disk drive connected

1 = Math coprocessor installed

Video mode at system startup
00b = EGA/VGA
01b = 40*25 characters (COLOR)
10b = 80*25 characters (COLOR)
11b = 80*25 characters (MONO)

Number of disk drives if bit = 0
00b = 1 disk drive
01b = 2 disk drives
10b = 3 disk drives
11b = 4 disk drives

Number of serial interfaces

Number of parallel ports

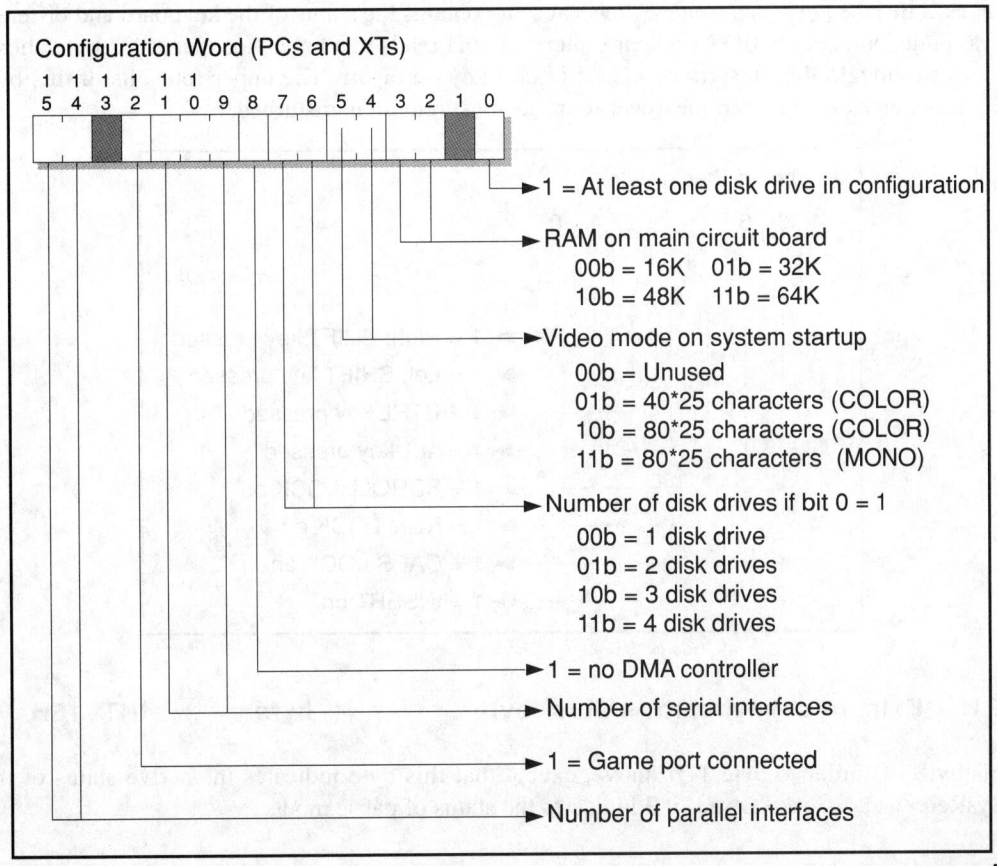

Configuration Word (PCs and XTs)

1 = At least one disk drive in configuration

RAM on main circuit board
00b = 16K   01b = 32K
10b = 48K   11b = 64K

Video mode on system startup
00b = Unused
01b = 40*25 characters (COLOR)
10b = 80*25 characters (COLOR)
11b = 80*25 characters (MONO)

Number of disk drives if bit 0 = 1
00b = 1 disk drive
01b = 2 disk drives
10b = 3 disk drives
11b = 4 disk drives

1 = no DMA controller

Number of serial interfaces

1 = Game port connected

Number of parallel interfaces

12H   POST status #1   **1 byte**   **POST**

This byte provides storage for information gathered during the POST, and executed during the booting process and after a warm start. BIOS routines also use this byte for recognizing active keys. It has no practical use for the programmer.

13H   RAM size   **1 word**   **INT 12H**

This word indicates the RAM capacity of the system in kilobytes (not counting expanded memory). This information is also gathered during the booting process, and can be read using BIOS interrupt 12H.

15H   POST status #2   **1 word**   **POST**

These two bytes test the hardware during the booting process. How this test is performed varies with the BIOS.

17H   Keyboard status byte   **1 byte**   **INT 16H**

This is called the *keyboard status byte* because it contains the status of the keyboard and different keys. Function 02H of BIOS keyboard interrupt 16H reads this byte. Accessing this byte allows the user to toggle the <Insert> or <Caps Lock> key on or off. The upper four bits of this byte may be changed by the user; the lower four bits must remain undisturbed.

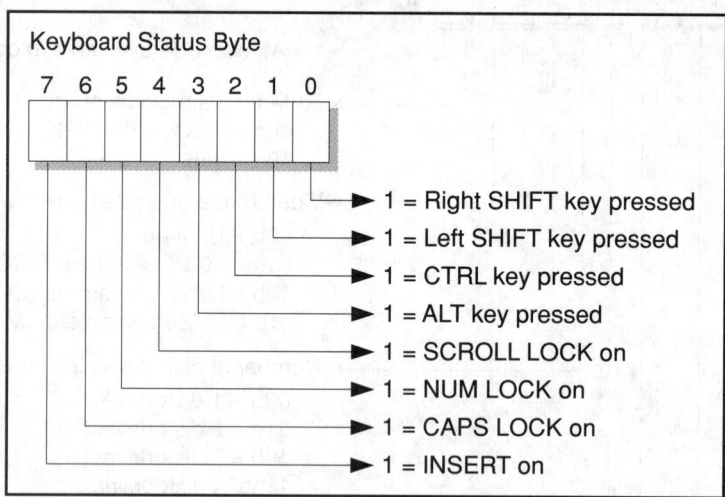

18H   Extended keyboard status byte   **1 byte**   **INT 16H**

This byte is similar to byte 17H above, except that this byte indicates the active status of the <SysReq> and <Break> keys. Bit 3 indicates the status of pause mode.

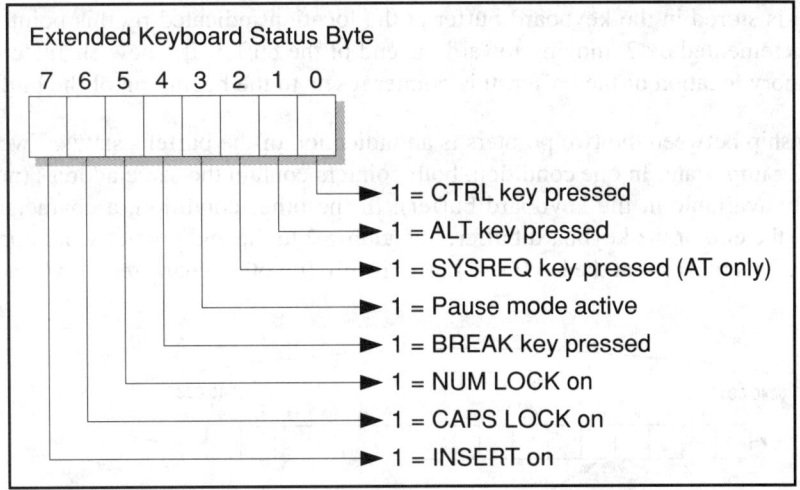

19H   ASCII code entry   1 byte   INT 16H

This byte isn't used in older systems. Newer systems use this byte for storing ASCII codes produced from the numeric keypad and the <Alt> key.

1AH   Next character in keyboard buffer   1 word   INT 16H

This word contains the offset address of the next character to be read in the keyboard buffer (see also 1EH).

1CH   Last character in keyboard buffer   1 word   INT 16H

This word contains the offset address of the last character in the keyboard buffer (see also 1EH).

1EH   Keyboard buffer   16 words   INT 16H

These 16 words contain the actual keyboard buffer. Since every character stored in the keyboard buffer requires 2 bytes, its 32-byte capacity provides space for a maximum of 16 characters. For a normal ASCII character, the buffer stores the ASCII code and then the character's *scan code* (the number of the key that generated the ASCII character). If the character in the keyboard buffer uses an extended code (e.g., a cursor key), then the first byte contains the value 0 and the second byte contains the extended key code.

The computer constantly reads characters from the keyboard buffer. If the buffer isn't full, characters can be added. The address of the next character to be read from the keyboard buffer is stored in the word at offset address 001AH. When a character is read, the character moves 2 bytes toward the end of the buffer in memory. When a character was read from the last memory location of the buffer, this pointer resets to the beginning of the buffer. This also applies to the pointer in offset address 001CH, which indicates the end of the keyboard buffer. If you add a new character, it is stored in the keyboard buffer at the location indicated by this pointer. Then the pointer is incremented by 2, moving toward the end of the buffer. If a new character is stored at the last memory location of the buffer, this pointer resets to the beginning of the buffer.

The relationship between the two pointers is an indication of the buffer's status. Two conditions are especially important. In one condition, both pointers contain the same address (no characters are currently available in the keyboard buffer). In the other condition, a character should be appended to the end of the keyboard buffer, but adding 2 to the end pointer would point it to the start pointer. This means that the keyboard buffer is full, (no other characters can be accepted).

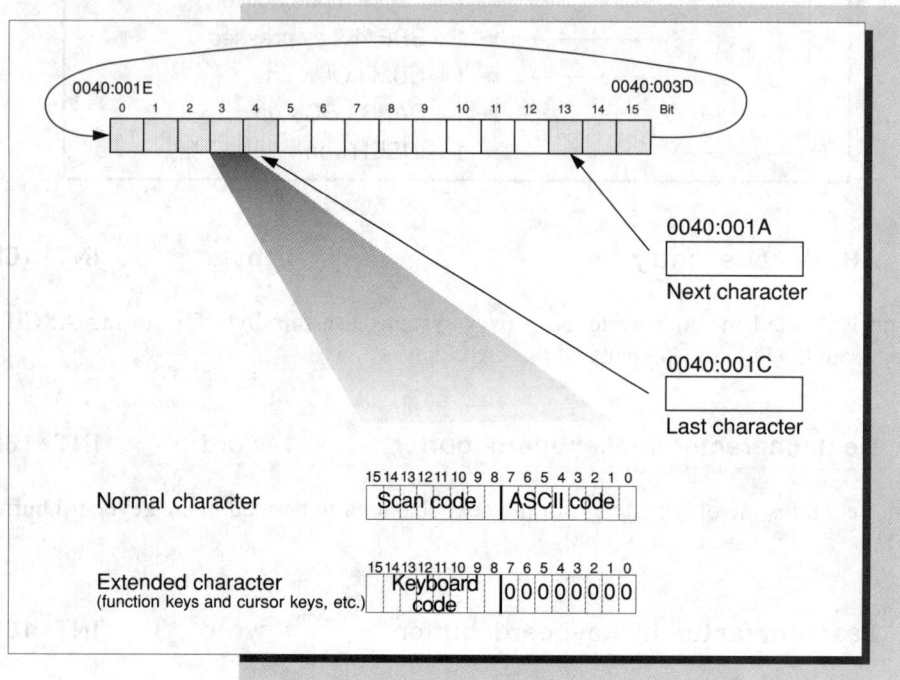

Keyboard buffer with start, end pointers and ring buffer

3EH Disk drive recalibration   1 byte   INT 13H

The lowest four bits correspond to the number of installed PC disk drives specified by BIOS (you can use a maximum of four drives). These bytes also indicate whether the connected drives must be calibrated. Usually this is necessary after an error occurs during read, write, or search access. Bit 7 is set to 1 when a disk drive releases the disk hardware interrupt.

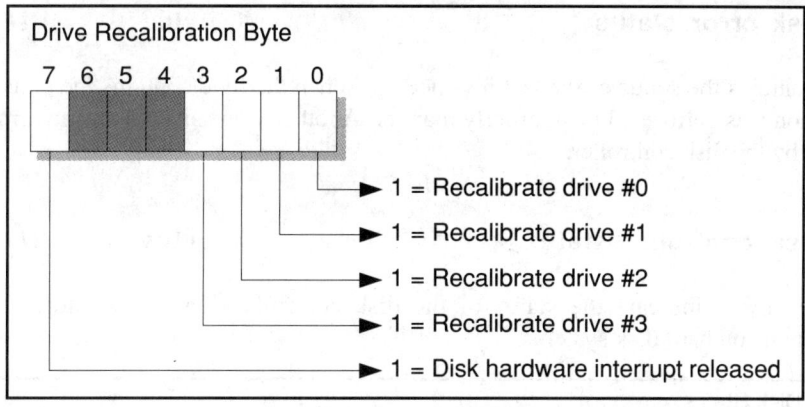

3FH   Disk drive motor status   1 byte   INT 13H

The four lower bits of this byte indicate whether the current disk drive motor is running. A 1 in the corresponding bit indicates this. Bit 7 is always set during write access or formatting, and unset during read access or a search.

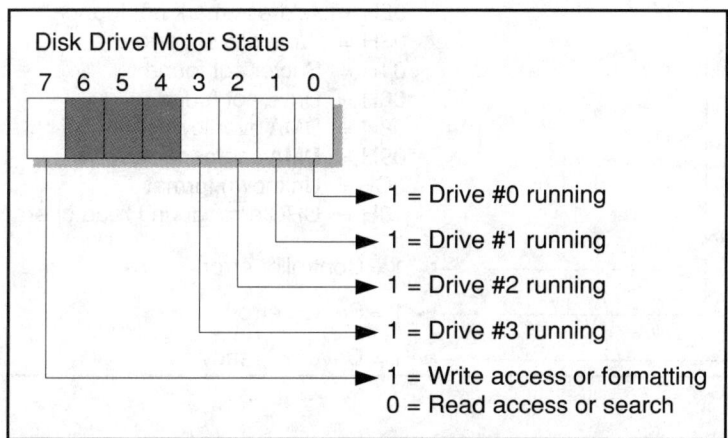

40H   Disk drive motor timer   1 byte   INT 13H

This byte contains a numerical value that indicates the number of calls made to the timer (interrupt 08H) until a disk drive motor switches off. Since BIOS can only access one disk drive at a time, this value refers to the last drive that was accessed. Following access to this drive, BIOS places the value 37 (25H) into this register, indicating a duration of about two seconds. During each timer interrupt (which occurs about 18.2 times per second), the value in this byte is decremented by 1. When it finally reaches 0, the disk motor is switched off. This occurs after about two seconds.

41H   Disk error status   **1 byte**   **INT 13H**

This byte contains the status of the last disk access. When the byte contains the value 0, the last disk operation was performed in an orderly manner. Another value signals that an error code was transmitted by the disk controller.

42H   Disk controller status   **7 bytes**   **INT 13H**

These seven bytes indicate the status of the disk controller. They also indicate hard disk controller status on hard disk systems.

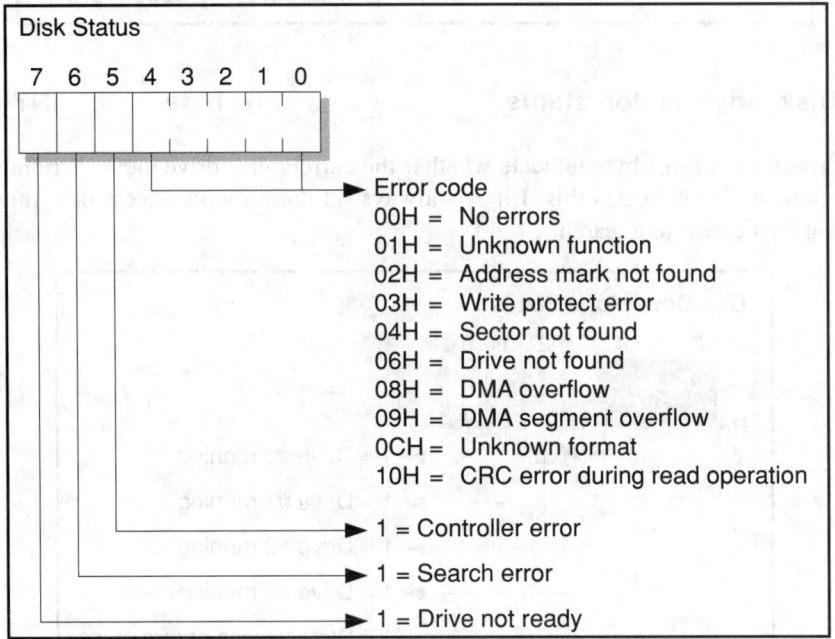

```
Disk Status

 7  6  5  4  3  2  1  0

                           ► Error code
                             00H =  No errors
                             01H =  Unknown function
                             02H =  Address mark not found
                             03H =  Write protect error
                             04H =  Sector not found
                             06H =  Drive not found
                             08H =  DMA overflow
                             09H =  DMA segment overflow
                             0CH =  Unknown format
                             10H =  CRC error during read operation

                           ► 1 = Controller error
                           ► 1 = Search error
                           ► 1 = Drive not ready
```

49H   Current video mode   **1 byte**   **INT 10H**

This byte contains the current video mode as reported by the BIOS. This is the same value indicated when the user activates a video mode through function 0H of BIOS video interrupt 10H.

4AH   Number of screen columns   **1 word**   **INT 10H**

This word contains the number of text columns per display line in the current display mode.

4CH   Screen page size   1 word   INT 10H

This word contains the number of bytes required for the display of a screen page in the current display mode, as reported by the BIOS. In the 80x25 character text mode, this is 4,000 bytes.

4EH   Offset address of current screen page   1 word   INT 10H

This word contains the address of the current screen page now on the monitor, relative to the beginning of video RAM.

50H   Cursor position in eight screen pages   8 words   INT 10H

These 8 words contain the current cursor position for each screen page. BIOS can control a maximum of 8 screen pages and reserves two bytes for each screen page. The low byte indicates the screen column, and the high byte indicates the screen line.

60H   Starting line of screen cursor   1 byte   INT 10H

This byte contains the starting line of the blinking cursor, which can have values ranging from 0 to 7 (color card) or from 0 to 14 (monochrome card). Changing the contents of this byte doesn't change the cursor's appearance, because first it must be transmitted by BIOS to the video controller.

61H   Ending line of screen cursor   1 byte   INT 10H

This byte contains the ending line of the blinking cursor, which can have values ranging from 0 to 7 (color card) or from 0 to 14 (monochrome card). Changing the contents of this byte doesn't change the cursor's appearance, since it must first be transmitted by BIOS to the video controller.

62H   Current screen page number   1 byte   INT 10H

This byte contains the number of the currently displayed screen page.

63H   Port address of video controller   1 word   INT 10H

This word contains the address of the video card port. If a PC contains several video cards, the value stored will be the address of the currently active video card's port. This address is 3B4H in monochrome video cards, and 3D4H on CGA, EGA, and VGA video cards.

65H   Mode selector register contents   1 byte   INT 10H

The contents of a video controller card's mode selector determines the current video mode. The current value is stored in this memory location.

66H   Palette register contents   1 byte   INT 10H

A color card in medium-resolution CGA compatible graphic mode can display 320x200 pixels in four different colors. This byte indicates the currently active color palette.

67H   Miscellaneous   5 bytes   POST

The early PC BIOS versions could use a cassette recorder for data storage. Those early versions of BIOS used these five bytes for cassette access when storing data. XT and AT models, which don't have this interface, use these memory locations for other purposes.

6CH   Timer   1 dword   INT 1AH

These four bytes act as a 32-bit counter for both BIOS and DOS. The counter is incremented by 1 on each of the 18.2 timer interrupts per second. This permits time measurement and time display. The value of this counter can be read and set with BIOS interrupt 1AH. If 24 hours have elapsed, it resets to 0 and counts up from there.

70H   24-hour flag   1 byte   INT 1AH

This byte contains a 0 when the timer routine is between 0 and 24 hours. Byte 70H changes to 1 when the time counter routine exceeds its 24-hour limit. If the BIOS timer interrupt 1AH is used to set the time, this byte resets to 0.

71H   CTRL-Break flag   1 byte   INT 16H

This byte indicates whether or not a keyboard interrupt occurs after the user presses <Ctrl><C> or <Ctrl><Break>. If bit 7 of this byte contains the value 1, a keyboard interrupt has occurred.

XT BIOS variables

The hardware configurations of the XT permit the introduction of additional variables. The following is a list of BIOS variables found in the XT and AT.

72H   POST test   1 word   POST

During the POST, a reset command is sent to the keyboard controller, whether a cold or warm start has occurred. For the duration of this reset, this location assumes the value 1234H. No memory test occurs when a warm start is executed.

74H   Last hard drive operation (AT)   1 byte   INT 13H

This byte indicates the status of the last hard drive operation.

```
01H: Function not available, or invalid drive specification
02H: Address marker not found
04H: Sector not found
05H: Controller reset error
07H: Controller initialization error
09H: DMA transfer error: Segment overflow
0AH: Bad sector
0BH: Bad track
0DH: Invalid number of sectors in track
0EH: Address mark not found
0FH: DMA overflow
10H: Read error
11H: Corrected ECC read error
20H: Controller defect
40H: Seek failed
80H: Drive time out
AAH: Drive not ready
CCH: Write error
```

75H   Number of hard drives (AT)   1 byte   INT 13H

This byte indicates the number of hard drives connected to the system.

76H   Hard drive control byte (AT)   1 byte   INT 13H

This byte controls the hard drive from BIOS interrupt 13H. Its exact purpose is unknown.

77H   Hard drive port (AT)   1 byte   INT 17H

This byte contains the base address of the hard drive controller.

78H   Parallel interface time out counter   4 bytes   INT 14H

These 4 bytes correspond to the time out counters for the four parallel interfaces. Each byte indicates the number of times a parallel time out error occurs.

7CH   Serial interface time out counter   4 bytes   INT 16H

These 4 bytes correspond to the time out counters for the four serial interfaces. Each byte indicates the number of times a serial time out error occurs.

80H   Keyboard buffer starting address (AT)   1 word   INT 16H

This word contains the beginning of the keyboard buffer as the offset address to segment address 0040H. Since the keyboard buffer normally starts at address 0040H:001EH, this memory location usually contains the value 1EH.

82H   Keyboard buffer ending address (AT)   1 word   INT 10H

This word contains the end of the keyboard buffer as the offset address to the segment address 0040H.

84H   Number of screen lines (EGA/VGA)   1 byte   INT 10H

This byte contains the number of screen lines being used by the EGA or VGA card.

85H   Character height (EGA/VGA)   1 word   INT 10H

This byte indicates EGA/VGA character height in pixels, as well as the number of visible text lines.

87H   EGA/VGA status range (EGA/VGA)   4 bytes   INT 10H

These 4 bytes indicate the status of the EGA or VGA card.

8BH   Disk drive/hard drive parameters (PS/2) 11 bytes   INT 13H

These bytes describe PS/2 disk drive and hard drive information.

96H   MF II status (AT)   1 byte   INT 16H

This byte indicates the status of an MF II model keyboard. Bit 4 of this byte indicates whether the system includes an MF II American (101-key) or European (102-key) keyboard. Applications that use the additional keys found on the MF II keyboard (e.g., <F11> and <F12>) check 96H and adjust to the keyboard.

97H   LED status (AT)   1 byte   INT 16H

This byte indicates the status of the keyboard LEDs. MF II keyboards include three LEDs, which correspond to the three toggled keyboard modes (Num Lock, Caps Lock, and Scroll Lock). Function 02H returns keyboard status without reading characters from the keyboard.

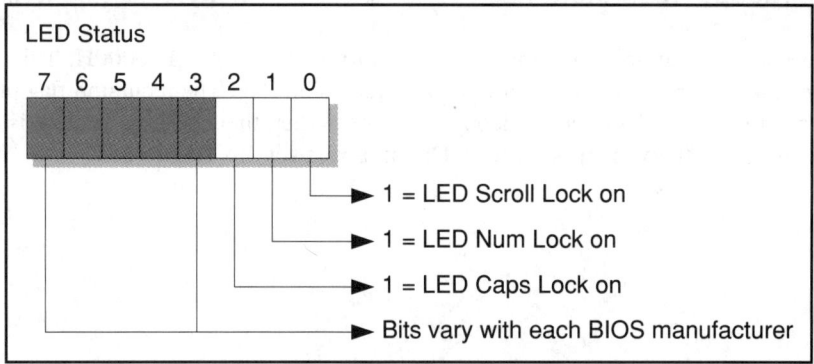

98H   Wait flag pointer (AT)   1 dword   INT 15H

You can define a BYTE variable whose bit 7 will be set to 1 after a specific amount of time has elapsed (see the description of interrupt 15H, function 83H in the Appendices for more information). The address of the BYTE variable is stored at this location in the BIOS variable segment.

9CH   Timer (AT)   1 dword   INT 15H

This dword represents the variable in which the timer duration can be placed before passing the duration to the caller (see the descriptions of interrupt 15H, functions 83H and 86H in the Appendices for more information).

A0H   Wait status (AT)   1 byte   INT 15H

This variable states whether the system is waiting, and whether interrupt 15H, function 86H is active.

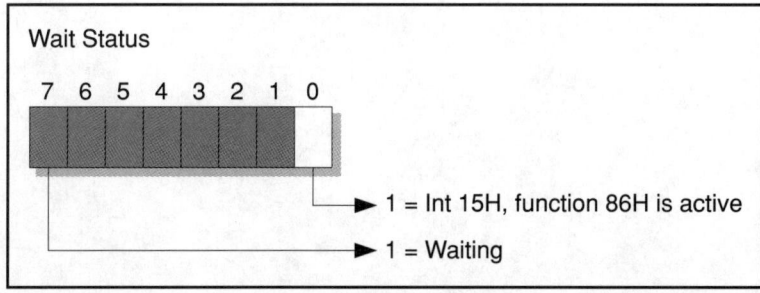

A1H   Reserved   95 bytes   ---------

This range is reserved for BIOS extensions and programs.

100H Hardcopy recursion flag   1 byte   INT 05H

All PC types have a variable in common, at memory location 0050H:0000H. This location is used by the hardcopy routine (interrupt 05H) as a recursion flag. The recursion flag prevents the user from printing more than one hardcopy at a time. When the hardcopy routine is executing, this flag is set to 1; otherwise it is set to 0. Output errors set this flag to 255.

Chapter 4

Video Cards

Since there are several graphic standards (MDA, CGA, EGA, VGA, and Hercules), a single standard hasn't been established for video cards. Even the new Super VGA and TIGA card types don't have a single standard. We'll describe all these video graphic cards in this chapter.

4.1 History and Highlights

Let's begin with an overview of the history of the different video standards used in PCs. Significant advancements have been made in two areas of computer hardware technology. Processor speeds have increased and video cards have been improved. The video card improvements have resulted in higher resolutions and a larger spectrum of colors.

A few years ago, advancements in video cards dramatically improved the capabilities and performance of video displays. The original idea was to take the burden of drawing lines and figures away from the 80x86 processor.

As you probably already know, graphical user interfaces have become the preferred way to interact with the computer. Therefore, video technology has become even more important because software places more demands on the processor. If the application seems to operate quickly, the video card is probably sharing some of the work with the 80x86 processor. Intelligent graphic cards, such as the 8514/A and TIGA, perform especially well in these situations. (We'll discuss these cards later.)

In the following sections we'll discuss the history of hardware development and describe the highlights of various types of video cards.

Monochrome Display Adapter (MDA)

Besides the CGA card, the IBM Monochrome Display Adapter, or MDA, is the oldest graphics adapter available for the PC. The MDA was the standard when IBM released the first PCs in 1981.

The MDA card supports only one operating mode. This is a text mode consisting of 80 screen columns and 25 screen rows. Unlike other graphics cards, the MDA contains very little video RAM. So, it can store only one screen page in RAM.

Although this card cannot display graphics, many users preferred the MDA over the CGA card because it was the only alternative at the time. Compared to CGA, the MDA actually has a higher screen resolution, which reduces eye-strain.

Few PCs use MDA cards today and IBM stopped manufacturing them years ago. The Hercules Graphics Card (HGC) has replaced the MDA. The Hercules card has all the attributes of the MDA but can also display graphics.

Color/Graphics Adapter (CGA)

The CGA (Color/Graphics Adapter) standard was also introduced in 1981. This card, which can display graphics, offered users an alternative to the MDA card.

Users who could afford a CGA card could actually save money. Instead of using a monitor, these users could connect a standard television set to a special connector on the CGA card. Also, a CGA card can produce RGB output, in which electrical lines send different signals for the colors red, green, and blue. However, the CGA graphics quality wasn't as good as the MDA's because of the larger three color pixels that were generated.

Similar to the MDA card, the CGA card also has a text mode consisting of 80 columns and 25 rows. The individual characters are based on a smaller pixel matrix. However, a CGA card can also display graphics with a resolution of 320x200 pixels, in four colors. Color suppressed mode produces graphics with a resolution of 600x200 pixels, in only two colors.

Although CGA and MDA differ, they are based upon the same video controller (the Motorola MC6485).

Hercules Graphics Card (HGC)

A year after the PC was introduced, a company called Hercules released a new graphics card that immediately made them famous. The Hercules Graphics Card (HGC), which is based on the Motorola MC6485, is completely MDA compatible. This card can display two 720x348 graphic screen pages. The Hercules card combines the readability of the MDA card and the graphic output of the CGA card. However, it also has the resolution to display high quality graphics and text.

The Hercules card is still considered the standard among monochrome graphics cards. Whenever monochrome cards must be used instead of the more popular color cards, the Hercules card is used. Although today only a few firms manufacture CGA or MDA cards, many firms produce Hercules Graphics Cards.

Unfortunately both the original HGC and its clones have a flaw. Since IBM won't support third party video cards, Hercules cards have incomplete BIOS support. However, the system tolerates Hercules cards because they are compatible with the old MDA card and because of ROM BIOS support in text mode.

When discussing the graphics mode on this card, you must remember that it doesn't support BIOS. This applies to graphics mode initialization and screen pixel access. This isn't actually a problem because the BIOS would only slow down screen display. As you'll see in this chapter, it's easy to access Hercules pixel information.

Since the Hercules Graphics Card represents a fixed standard in the ever-changing PC market, the card has undergone the miniaturization applied to many PC components. While the first Hercules cards required a full card's length and 40 ICs, newer Hercules cards now require half a card and use as few as 10 ICs. Some of these cards also include a parallel printer interface.

Although the Hercules Corporation has manufactured new video cards (the Hercules Graphics Card Plus and the Hercules InColor Card), they haven't achieved the success of the original Hercules Graphics Card. However, the recently released TIGA card may change this. (We'll discuss TIGA in more detail later in this chapter).

Enhanced Graphics Adapter (EGA)

After the release of the Hercules Graphics Card, IBM tried to design a card to replace the CGA card and surpass the capabilities of the Hercules card. The result was the EGA (Enhanced Graphics Adapter), which was released in 1985.

Due to the numerous technological advances that occurred between 1981 and 1985, the EGA started a minor revolution in PC computing. Since the EGA was more powerful than the CGA and MDA cards combined, it set a new standard for screen resolution and price. This card placed high resolution graphics in a price range most users could afford.

The EGA card has its own video modes, as well as fully compatible MDA and CGA modes. This is useful for programs that support multiple video modes. Because of its ability to display monochrome graphics on a monochrome monitor, the EGA is similar to the Hercules card. The EGA card was the first graphics card for the PC that could handle both monochrome and color screens.

The EGA is most effective when it's combined with an EGA monitor. This monitor is similar to a CGA monitor except that the graphics mode resolution is much higher (640x350 pixels) and more color options are available (16 colors at a time, from a total palette of 64 colors). Also, the EGA card contains increased video RAM (some EGA cards can hold up to 256K of video RAM) for displaying different graphic screen pages.

Instead of the MC6845 video controller, the EGA card uses highly integrated VLSI chips for handling video display. All screen information is stored in video RAM, which makes this standard dramatically different from earlier methods.

Because of its smaller pixel size, the EGA's screen resolution is sharper than the CGA's resolution. Also, the EGA offers more options for generating custom fonts than the earlier cards.

The EGA card also gives users the power needed to create computer animation and other applications, such as arcade-style games.

Unlike MDA and CGA cards, the EGA isn't supported by the IBM ROM BIOS. So, the EGA has its own ROM BIOS. The EGA ROM BIOS replaces the original BIOS and allows access to all the features of the EGA card.

As the EGA became more popular, manufacturers began developing compatible cards with additional video modes, which weren't supported by many programs. Even though IBM sued manufacturers for marketing EGA compatible cards, it couldn't stop the flow of compatible cards from the Far East.

Many EGA cards are still being used although VGA cards have replaced EGA cards as the standard for video display. However, many VGA cards include EGA modes.

Video Graphics Array (VGA)

The VGA (Video Graphics Array) card was released in 1987, which was the same year IBM introduced its PS/2 systems. This card combines new technology and the features found in the EGA card. So, it maintains compatibility with all predecessors, and offers more colors, higher resolution, and better text display.

Although today most VGA cards are inexpensive, the monitor needed for VGA graphics is expensive. Although users may not want to view VGA display in monochrome, many computer systems are equipped with only VGA monochrome monitors.

The VGA standard was originally designed for IBM's PS/2 machines and the Micro Channel bus. However, since many manufacturers sell VGA cards for the ISA bus, almost any system can use a VGA card.

The VGA's advantages over EGA is its higher integration density and an entire control logic that's packed into a single chip. Unlike the EGA card, the VGA card sends analog color signals to its monitor instead of digital signals. This means that VGA cards can generate more than 260,000 different colors when modes 2, 4, 16, or 256 are active.

The highest resolution VGA mode provides 640x480 pixels, with either 2, 4, or 16 colors, depending on the mode selected. The extended 320x200 pixel mode is more versatile, offering up to 256 colors on the screen at a time. Higher resolution or more colors means that some video RAM will be needed to handle screen information. So, VGA cards frequently contain a minimum of 256K of video RAM; this can easily be increased to 512K.

Like an EGA card, a VGA card has its own BIOS, which replaces the standard BIOS video output functions. The VGA hardware is often downwardly compatible with EGA BIOS. So, all the programs intended for the EGA BIOS will also operate without problems under the VGA card.

Third party VGA cards encounter the same problems faced by the EGA cards (added video modes and different color capabilities). Although it may be tempting for the system programmer to use one of these additional modes or color sets, we'll concentrate on standard VGA modes in this book.

An extended VGA standard will make it possible to standardize the extended video modes with access to any program.

Super VGA

Super VGA cards have the same hardware as normal VGA cards, but they display pixels faster, in more colors, and with higher resolutions than their predecessors. These cards support all VGA modes.

While a normal VGA card can display 256 colors in 320x200 mode, Super VGA cards can display the same amount of colors in three other modes (640x200, 640x350, and 640x480 pixels). Other graphics modes can display 800x600 and 1024x768 pixels on a compatible VGA or multiscan monitor, if sufficient video RAM is available.

Again, different manufacturers have added their own extended modes and hardware registers to Super VGA cards. The largest VGA chip manufacturers (Tseng, Paradise, and Video Seven) formed a consortium, called Video Electronic Standard Association (VESA). Its goal was to present a standard for Super VGA modes and video BIOS that was based on the chips developed by these three manufacturers. TSR programs can be used to add the new BIOS functions to older Super VGA cards.

Unfortunately, this consortium wasn't formed until 1990, so a lot of time passed before the VESA standard became effective. Until then, every program had to directly access the hardware of different Super VGA cards in order to use the extended VGA modes.

Memory Controller Gate Array (MCGA)

While VGA cards were designed for the IBM's upscale PS/2 models, the MCGA (Memory Controller Gate Array) cards were designed for the lower end PS/2 machines. This card was intended to replace almost every previous standard.

The MCGA's text mode, which is similar to the CGA card's, provides a 80x24 character display. The foreground and background colors can be selected from a 16 color palette. Unlike the CGA card, the MCGA's palette can be selected from a group of 262,000 colors (similar to VGA). The MCGA's vertical resolution in text mode is 400 pixels rather than 200 pixels, which provides a higher quality display.

For a hybrid, the MCGA card handles various graphics modes. In addition to two VGA compatible modes, the MCGA supports both CGA modes (320x200 and 640x200 pixels). Because the card uses a vertical resolution of 400 pixels, the vertical pixels in the CGA modes are doubled. Otherwise, the image on the screen would appear in only half its height.

A major disadvantage of the VGA modes on this card is the color selection. Although the MCGA can display the necessary VGA resolution, the card is limited in its color palette because of the small amount of video RAM that's available (only 64K).

MCGA cards are so named because they will operate only on Micro Channel systems. This means that only low end PS/2 systems can use the MCGA.

8514/A

Still trying to set video standards, IBM presented a successor to the VGA standard in 1987. This card, ambiguously named the 8514/A, caused a revolution in video cards. While earlier video controllers relied upon the main processor for information (i.e., they were "dumb" controllers), this video card had its own processor.

With this feature, graphics functions could be delegated to the graphics processor on the card, instead of requiring the PC's 80x86 processor to calculate these functions. So the graphics are drawn from the video card itself, which frees the PC's processor for other tasks.

So far, the 8514/A hasn't been able to replace the VGA. This may have been caused by poor development and marketing decisions. For instance, this graphic standard was intended for only the PS/2 models and Micro Channel. This immediately reduced the market share. Also, IBM kept the technical details of this card confidential, so third party manufacturers couldn't build compatible copies of the card. This strategy is quite different from IBM's earlier "open system" attitude. Finally, this video card requires a software interface developed by IBM, which developers have avoided. Although this software interface is powerful, sometimes it hinders the hardware's performance. Consequently, the 8514/A has a small following.

Even if the 8514/A was modified to work on the ISA bus and the Chips&Technologies 8514/A compatible chip set was added, we don't think this standard's acceptance would be increased. However, Texas Instruments has developed a fairly intelligent graphics card for the ISA bus, at a relatively low price, that doesn't require special monitors.

Texas Instruments Graphics Architecture (TIGA)

The technology needed to produce intelligent and programmable video cards has been available for years. However, the Texas Instruments 34010 and Intel 82786 processors combine this technology into single chips. The TI 34010 and its successor, the TI 34020, are among the most popular graphics processors.

Remember that the idea behind the 8514/A was to offload the PC's processor by building a graphics board that was capable of performing, for example, ray tracing and mirroring. The graphics board had to be backwardly compatible with the VGA modes.

Although the various cards have different resolutions and programming requirements, Texas Instruments developed the TIGA (Texas Instruments Graphics Architecture) standard, along with a unified software interface. TIGA describes a group of functions that can be accessed from a high level language program to control the graphics processor.

Many TIGA-based cards are now available, including one manufactured by the Hercules Corporation.

Running Microsoft Windows in TIGA mode demonstrates the effectiveness of this card. TIGA redraws the Windows screen five times faster than a normal VGA card. It's obviously time for programmable video cards, and, as the 1990s progress, we'll be seeing more of them. For now, TIGA is the most likely replacement for VGA and Super VGA cards.

4.2 The Video BIOS

The PC's ROM BIOS performs many actions for different screen display tasks. These actions are grouped as functions of interrupt 10H (video interrupt functions). Although there are other interrupt 10H functions, we'll discuss only the video BIOS functions.

In this section, we'll describe the video BIOS functions, how you can access them, and why direct access to video hardware is usually the best method.

The video BIOS and its extensions

Originally, the functions of interrupt 10H applied only to MDA and CGA cards. These functions also support Hercules cards in text mode because the Hercules cards are fully compatible with the MDA standard.

The original BIOS doesn't support EGA and VGA cards or their extended features in text and graphics modes. So, EGA and VGA cards include their own BIOS extensions on a ROM chip. These extensions are enabled when you boot the system.

This set of BIOS extensions interact with interrupt 10H to add EGA and VGA functions to the existing BIOS. Although they contain the same extensions, the EGA BIOS has fewer capabilities than the VGA BIOS. EGA and VGA cards are manufactured by numerous manufacturers, but they have the same BIOS extensions as IBM's EGA and VGA cards. Only a few cards are incompatible with these functions.

Some top-of-the-line PCs are packaged with VGA cards directly on the motherboard. In these instances, the VGA and EGA BIOS functions are added to the ROM BIOS, which eliminates the extensions. However, this doesn't change how the cards are programmed.

Speed and BIOS functions

Using the video BIOS functions isn't the only way to handle tasks such as positioning the cursor or drawing characters on the screen. The DOS screen output functions and any BIOS functions used for direct video hardware programming can also be used. If listed according to effectiveness, the BIOS functions would be located between the DOS functions and direct hardware programming. These functions are used when execution speed, compatibility, device independence, and flexibility are important to program development.

The DOS functions offer the most device independence because the output can be sent to the screen, the printer, or a disk as a file. However, DOS functions execute slowly and aren't very flexible.

Direct hardware programming provides the highest possible execution speed and flexibility because the programmer has absolute control over execution. However, direct hardware programming is extremely hardware dependent. For example, a character output routine written for a CGA won't work when on an MDA.

The BIOS functions aren't as fast as direct access routines, but they will work with the currently installed video card. So, the programmer doesn't have to make a distinction between cards; the BIOS always performs the tasks.

You may be wondering why the BIOS functions are slower than direct hardware access. There are two reasons for this. First, the mechanism used to call these BIOS functions is slow. Second, the call to an interrupt takes much longer than a routine within a program. All BIOS routines use this latest technique, called the interrupt programmer.

Many video cards are 8-bit cards, which slow down access to the ROM BIOS. Remember that 80286, 80386, and 80486 processors "think" in 16-bit and 32-bit units. If you consider that the PC must execute every assembly language instruction in the BIOS routines as an 8-bit instruction, you can see why the routines are so slow.

With many PCs, you can relocate their ROM BIOS to a range of RAM between video RAM and the 1 Meg memory limit, called shadow ROM. This makes the BIOS routines run considerably faster since the processor can make 16 and 32-bit accesses. However, the disadvantages of direct hardware programming also apply in this instance.

While the BIOS functions perform many useful services, most PC applications use a combination of BIOS functions and direct access routines, especially for fast screen output in text and graphics modes. Control tasks, such as video mode initialization, text cursor placement, and screen page selection should be handled by the BIOS.

The video BIOS services

In this section we'll describe the most important control functions and the services used in text output. We'll discuss other functions in later chapters and in the Appendix.

Let's begin with an overview of the different services available from the BIOS video interrupts and their sub-functions.

```
┌─────────────────────────────────────────────────────────────────────┐
│    Video BIOS functions and support from EGA, VGA and standard BIOS   │
├──────┬──────────────────────────────────────────────────────┬─────────┤
│ No.  │ Meaning                                              │ BIOS*   │
├──────┼──────────────────────────────────────────────────────┼─────────┤
│ 00H  │ Determine video mode                                 │ SEV     │
│ 01H  │ Define cursor size                                   │ SEV     │
│ 02H  │ Set cursor position                                  │ SEV     │
│ 03H  │ Read cursor position                                 │ SEV     │
│ 04H  │ Read light pen                                        │ SEV     │
│ 05H  │ Define current screen page                           │ SEV     │
│ 06H  │ Scroll screen up                                     │ SEV     │
│ 07H  │ Scroll screen down                                   │ SEV     │
│ 08H  │ Read character and attribute                         │ SEV     │
│ 09H  │ Write character and attribute                        │ SEV     │
│ 0AH  │ Write character to cursor position                   │ SEV     │
│ 0BH  │ Set color palette for graphics mode                  │ SEV     │
│ 0CH  │ Set screen pixel in graphics mode                    │ SEV     │
│ 0DH  │ Read screen pixel in graphics mode                   │ SEV     │
│ 0EH  │ Terminal character output                            │ SEV     │
│ 0FH  │ Determine video mode                                 │ SEV     │
│ 10H  │ EGA/VGA color options                                │ EV      │
│ 11H  │ Character generator access                           │ EV      │
│ 12H  │ Set/read video configuration                         │ EV      │
│ 13H  │ Write string (AT only)                               │ SEV     │
│ 14H  │ Reserved                                             │ ---     │
│ 15H  │ Reserved                                             │ ---     │
│ 16H  │ Reserved                                             │ ---     │
│ 17H  │ Reserved                                             │ ---     │
│ 18H  │ Reserved                                             │ ---     │
│ 19H  │ Reserved                                             │ ---     │
│ 1BH  │ Toggle between video cards                           │ V       │
│ 1CH  │ Save/restore video card status                       │ V       │
├──────┴──────────────────────────────────────────────────────┴─────────┤
│ *S = Standard BIOS      E = EGA BIOS      V = VGA BIOS                 │
└─────────────────────────────────────────────────────────────────────┘
```

The first step in calling these functions is to load the AH register with the function number. If a sub-function exists, this number is loaded into the AL register. However, there are exceptions to this rule, which are indicated throughout this book. One exception to the rule are the functions that alter the contents of the registers because most functions usually change registers.

Selecting character and background colors

Some character display functions expect foreground and background colors from the caller. Some video cards have separate systems for setting foreground and background colors. Unfortunately, monochrome and color video cards determine these colors differently. In both cases, each character has a color or attribute byte divided into two nibbles. The least significant nibble (bits 0-3) defines the foreground color, while the most significant nibble (bits 4-7) defines the background color.

MDA cards divide the nibbles into bits for foreground intensity and character blinking, as shown below:

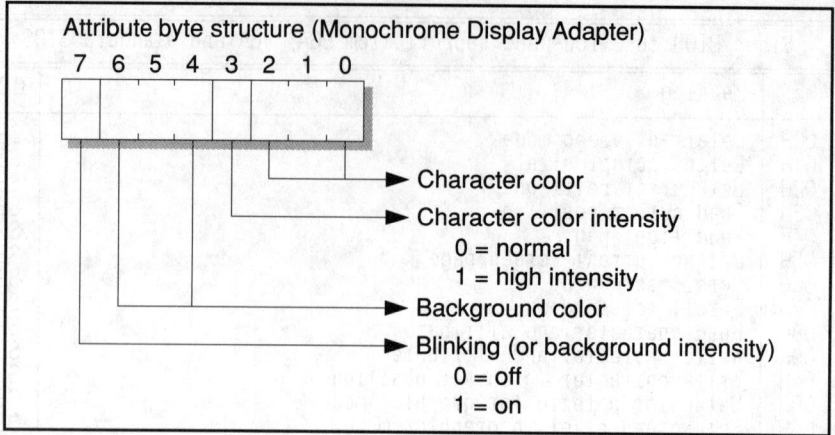

The following illustration shows how the intensity bits for foreground and background colors interact through bit combinations:

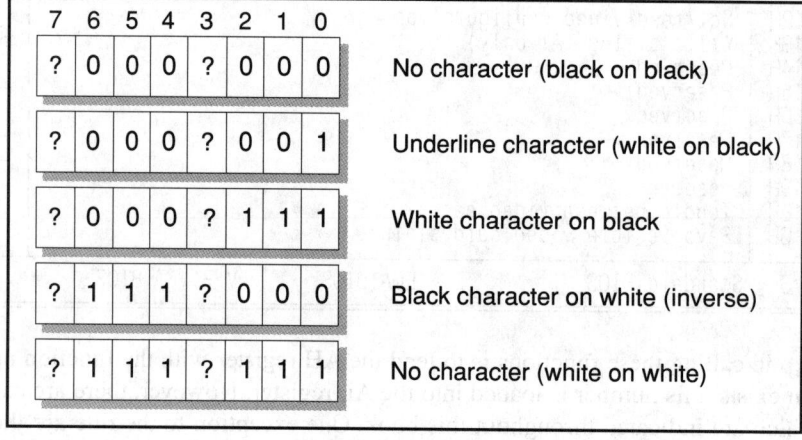

Character and background color combinations (MDA)

Frequently selected monochrome video card colors are 07H (light text on dark background) and 70H (dark text on a light background). These codes also work with color cards for color combinations such as light gray on black and black on light gray.

Selecting 0 or 7 as text or background color changes the status of bit 7 in the attribute byte. This byte determines whether the character blinks or the background appears in high intensity color. The following shows the structure of the color attribute bytes.

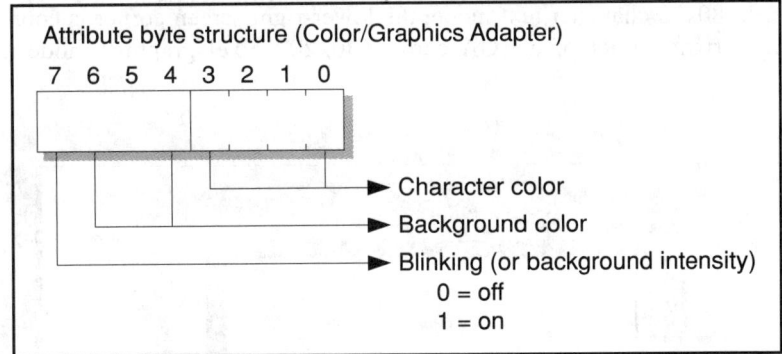

The color card lets you specify colors for foreground and background from a palette of 16 colors. The following shows the structure of the color palette.

Color/Graphics Adapter color palette			
Decimal	Hex	Bin	Color
0	00H	0000(b)	Black
1	01H	0001(b)	Blue
2	02H	0010(b)	Green
3	03H	0011(b)	Cyan
4	04H	0100(b)	Red
5	05H	0101(b)	Purple
6	06H	0110(b)	Brown
7	07H	0111(b)	Light gray
8	08H	1000(b)	Dark gray
9	09H	1001(b)	Light blue
10	0AH	1010(b)	Light green
11	0BH	1011(b)	Light cyan
12	0CH	1100(b)	Light red
13	0DH	1101(b)	Light purple
14	0EH	1110(b)	Yellow
15	0FH	1111(b)	White

The ASCII character set

The PC uses a character set based on 256 symbols, numerals, letters, and special characters. Many of these special characters are foreign language characters, mathematical symbols, and linedrawing characters.

For more information and examples of these characters, refer to the Appendix. We've included a complete ASCII table which displays these codes.

The screen coordinate system

Many BIOS functions require screen coordinates as a parameter. These coordinates specify the location on the screen where you want to display the character. You must understand this coordinate system before you can call many of the functions.

Whether in text or graphics mode, the origin of this coordinate system is the upper-left corner of the screen. Moving to the right increments the X-coordinate, while moving down increments the

Y-coordinate. In 80x25 character text mode, the lower-right screen corner is coordinate 79/24, while the lower-right corner of a CGA card's 640x200 pixel graphics mode is coordinate 639/199.

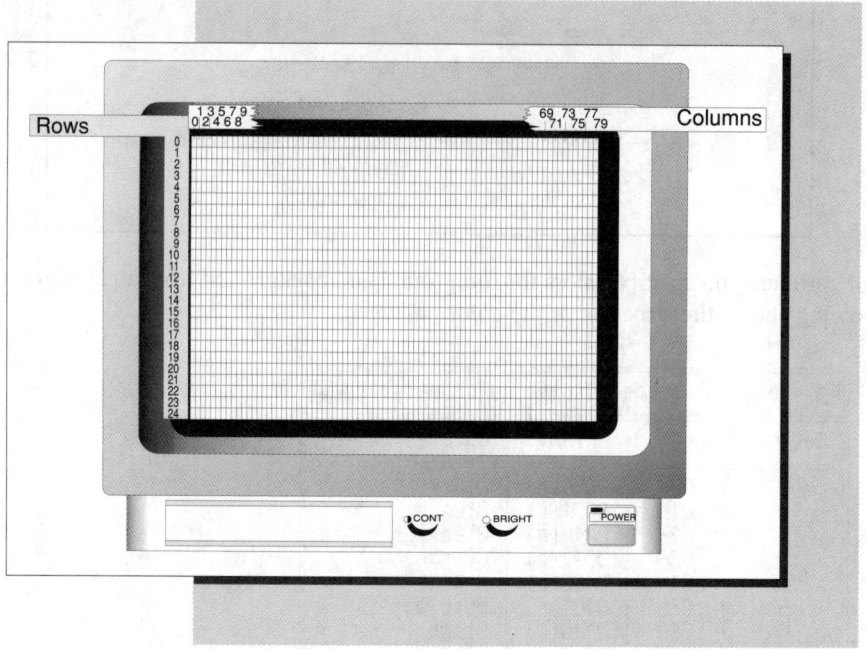

Screen row and column numbering

Initializing a video mode

Using function 00H initializes the video mode of a graphics card. Placing 00H in the AH register and a sub-function code in the AL register initializes the standard video mode in text or graphics mode (except graphics mode on the Hercules card).

Initializing a video mode assumes that the corresponding video card is installed. If you initialize a video card or mode that doesn't exist, the system may crash.

When you call function 00H, the contents of video RAM are cleared and the selected video mode is initialized. The contents can be retained on EGA and VGA cards by adding 128 to the mode number (i.e., by setting bit 7 in the mode number). Calling function 00H in this way keeps the contents of video RAM intact and displays these contents on the screen after initialization.

You can immediately set 80x25 character text mode as active when a program starts. This is mode 7 on MDAs and mode 3 on CGAs. You don't need to call function 00H when you want your program to operate in 80x25 text mode.

Function 0FH reads the current video mode. Call this function by passing 0FH in the AH register. After you call the function, the AL register returns a value. Use the table previously listed to determine the currently active video mode.

The number of columns per screen line is returned in the AH register (if this mode is a text mode). The number of current screen pages, if applicable, is returned in the BH register.

```
┌────────────────────────────────────────────────────────────────────┐
│        Video mode sub-functions from video BIOS function 00H        │
├──────┬──────────────────────────────────────────────────────┬───────┤
│ Code │ Mode                                                 │ Card  │
├──────┼──────────────────────────────────────────────────────┼───────┤
│ 00H  │ 40x25 character text, 16 colors, no color display    │ CEV   │
│ 01H  │ 40x25 character text, 16 colors                      │ CEV   │
│ 02H  │ 80x25 character text, 16 colors, no color display    │ CEV   │
│ 03H  │ 80x25 character text, 16 colors                      │ CEV   │
│ 04H  │ 320x200 pixel graphics, 4 colors                     │ CEV   │
│ 05H  │ 320x200 pixel graphics, 4 colors, no color display   │ CEV   │
│ 06H  │ 640x200 pixel graphics, 2 colors                     │ CEV   │
│ 07H  │ 80x25 character text, mono                           │ MHE*  │
│ 08H- │ Reserved                                             │ ───── │
│ 0CH  │ Reserved                                             │ ───── │
│ 0DH  │ 320x200 pixel graphics, 16 colors                    │ EV    │
│ 0EH  │ 640x200 pixel graphics, 16 colors                    │ EV    │
│ 0FH  │ 640x350 pixel graphics, mono                         │ E*    │
│ 10H  │ 640x350 pixel graphics, 16 colors                    │ EV    │
│ 11H  │ 640x480 pixel graphics, 2 colors                     │ V     │
│ 12H  │ 640x480 pixel graphics, 16 colors                    │ V     │
│ 13H  │ 320x200 pixel graphics, 256 colors                   │ V     │
├──────┴──────────────────────────────────────────────────────┴───────┤
│  * EGA card on MDA monitor                                           │
│    M = MDA     H = Hercules     C = CGA     E = EGA     V = VGA       │
└────────────────────────────────────────────────────────────────────┘
```

Programming the text cursor

In text mode, every video card from MDA to VGA has a blinking cursor. This cursor indicates the current input or output position. The video BIOS controls both the appearance and screen position of this cursor.

Function 02H handles cursor positioning. Place the function number (02H) in the AH register. Place the row where you want to locate the cursor in the DH register and place the column where you want to locate the cursor in the DL register. Also, place the number of the screen page, at which you want the cursor located, in the BH register. This is applicable only if each page has its own cursor available. The blinking cursor only appears when the value in the BH register corresponds to the current screen page.

This function call determines the next location at which screen input and output will occur. Refer to the Appendix for more information about this function.

Function 03H reads the current cursor position in a specified screen page and returns this position to the program that called the function. Place the function number (03H) in the AL register and the screen page that should be read in the BH register. This function returns the cursor position in the CH register (starting pixel line of the cursor) and the Cl register (ending pixel line of the cursor), instead of the actual position.

To understand these values, remember that a character in text mode on a color card is eight pixels high, and that a character in text mode on a monochrome card is 14 pixels high (not screen rows). These values tell the programmer where the blinking cursor begins and ends.

These values also provide information about the height of the character matrix, from which you can determine the sizes of the characters. Since the CGA card generates characters that are eight pixels high, the starting and ending lines should be from 0 to 7. Since a Hercules and an MDA card generate characters that are 14 pixels high, the cursor values range from 0 to 13. The EGA and VGA cards use even higher values, but the CGA measurement of 0 to 7 is used here. The actual character matrix can be recalculated from these values.

Greater values for the starting and ending lines can occur when the cursor disappears from the screen.

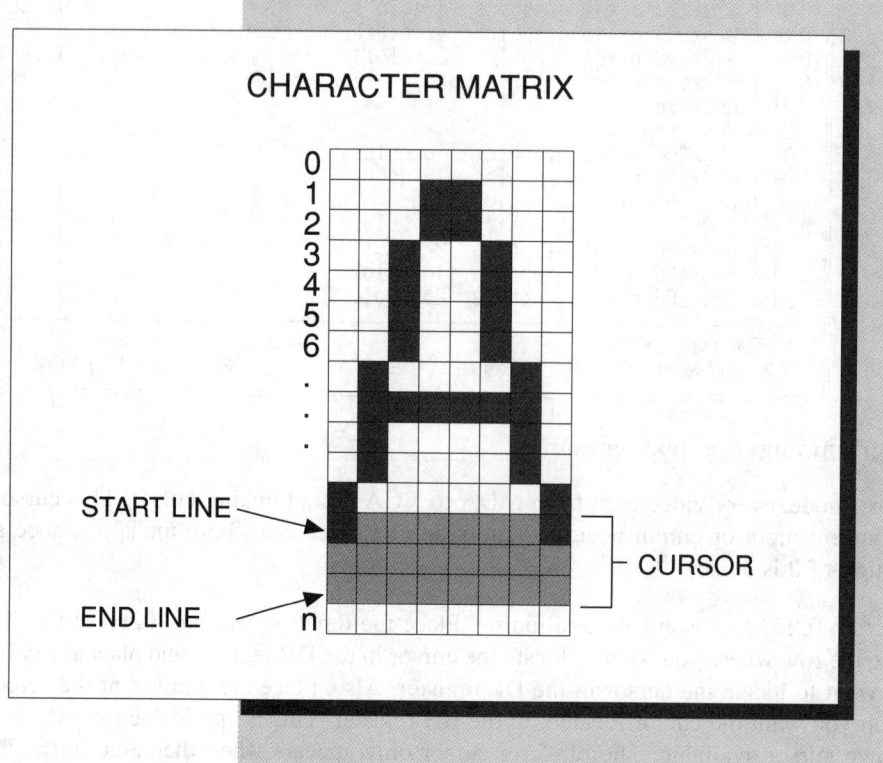

Starting and ending line of a text cursor

Function 01H defines the appearance of the cursor. To do this, place 1 in the AH register, the starting line in the CH register, and the ending line in the CL register. Be sure that the starting line is less than or equal to the ending line; otherwise the cursor will no longer be visible.

Selecting the screen page

Although we've mentioned the current screen page, we haven't explained how to activate a screen page. Function 05H of the video BIOS performs this task. Place the value 05H in the AH register, and the number of the screen page you want activated in the AL register. The screen page number will vary depending on the number of pages available in the video card. For example, since the MDA has only one page, calling this function for an MDA card is useless. The following values apply to the video cards that support multiple screen pages, along with their video modes:

```
┌─────────────────────────────────────────────────┐
│  Number of available screen pages,              │
│  dependent on video card and video mode         │
├───────┬────────────┬────────────┬───────────────┤
│ Mode  │ Resolution │ Card       │ Pages         │
├───────┼────────────┼────────────┼───────────────┤
│   7   │  80x25     │ MDA/Hercules│  1           │
│  0/1  │  40x25     │ CGA        │  8            │
│  2/3  │  80x25     │ CGA        │  4            │
│  0/1  │  40x25     │ EGA/VGA    │ 16            │
│  2/3  │  80x25     │ EGA/VGA    │  8            │
└───────┴────────────┴────────────┴───────────────┘
```

Screen page numbering always begins at 0. So, an EGA or VGA card in mode 2 can access screen pages 0 to 7.

Character output and BIOS

The video BIOS contains various character output functions. Each function handles control codes differently. These control codes consist of ASCII codes 7, 8, 10, and 13. Although the IBM system views them as normal characters, data processing history considers these characters text controls:

```
┌─────────────────────────────────────────────────────────────┐
│  PC ASCII control characters                                 │
├────────────┬────────────┬───────────────────────────────────┤
│ ASCII code │ Name       │ Purpose                           │
├────────────┼────────────┼───────────────────────────────────┤
│     7      │ Bell       │ Sounds beep                       │
│     8      │ Backspace  │ Deletes character left of cursor and moves │
│            │            │ cursor right one character        │
│    10      │ Linefeed   │ Moves cursor to next line         │
│    13      │ Carriage   │ Moves cursor to beginning of      │
│            │ Return     │ current line                      │
└────────────┴────────────┴───────────────────────────────────┘
```

Some functions view these codes as normal ASCII characters and display them as such. Other functions execute the controls specified by these codes. For example, code 7 instructs the computer to sound a beep. The function you select determines the actions performed by these codes.

Remember that all text output functions operate in both text mode and graphics mode. Character output in graphics mode isn't directly accessible because a character set isn't available. However, BIOS compensates for this limitation by setting the ASCII character patterns as graphic pixels. While the character patterns for ASCII codes 0 to 127 are already stored in ROM, codes 128 to 255 are taken from a table in RAM, which is installed by the GRAFTABL command from MS-DOS.

BIOS removes the address of this table as a FAR pointer (you'll find the table starting at 0000:007C). Although these memory addresses lie within the interrupt vector table, interrupt 1FH, which normally uses this address, cannot be used.

The condition that stores this table in RAM enables you to design your own table. With a user-defined table, special characters, which aren't found in the standard character table, can be displayed on the screen. Each character requires eight bytes. The first eight bytes in the table define ASCII code 128, the second eight bytes define ASCII code 129, etc. Each byte represents the bit pattern for one of the eight lines used in each character. Bit 0 represents the right border of each character matrix, while bit 7 represents the left border of each character matrix. If a bit is set as 1, the corresponding pixel appears on the screen.

Although functions 09H and 0AH both display characters, there is a difference between them. Function 0AH displays the character in the color established for that position on the screen and function 09H displays the color (the attribute) set by the character itself. After character output, both functions keep the cursor at the same cursor position so the next call of either function places character output at that same location.

Function 02H moves the cursor to the next screen position.

Both functions interpret control codes as normal characters and display these characters as such. Place the function number in the AH register and the ASCII code you want displayed in the AL register. The BH register contains the screen page, on which the character should be displayed (where applicable). The CX register contains a number that indicates how often the output should follow. This enables you to display a single character several times in one function call. If the character in the AL register should be displayed only once, the CX register should contain the value 1.

Because of an error in BIOS, the repeat factor during the call of this function in graphics mode should be limited to the maximum number of characters that can be displayed in one line.

Function 09H passes the character and its color. Place the character color number in the BL register.

Both functions have a disadvantage. The cursor remains at the same cursor position, unlike function 0EH, which increments the cursor to the next screen position. It simulates a terminal; this process is often referred to as the TTY (teletype) routine. Calling function 0EH displays the character and increments the cursor to the next character. If the cursor reaches the end of a screen line, the cursor jumps to the beginning of the next screen line.

If the cursor reaches the lower-right corner of the screen (column 79, line 24), the entire contents of the screen scroll up one line, and the cursor moves to the first column of line 24.

Unlike functions 09H and 0AH, the TTY function handles the control codes as control codes instead of as normal ASCII characters. The TTY function displays the character in the color previously defined for that screen location. This function applies only to text mode. In graphics mode, the TTY function must have the character color stored in the BL register.

Place the function number 0EH in the AH register, the code you want displayed in the AL register, and the screen page, in which the character should be displayed, in the BH register.

String output

When the AT was introduced, the video BIOS included a new function (13H), which was also found in the BIOS versions included on EGA and VGA cards. This function displays a character string on the screen with a single function call.

Place the function number in the AH register, and the screen page to be displayed in the BH register. Place the starting position of the string in the DH register (row) and the DL register (column). The CX register should contain the number of characters to be displayed in the string.

The AL register contents define one of four available modes, in which the string can be displayed. Modes 0 and 1 specify the format in the first screen page and modes 2 and 3 specify the format in other screen pages. Modes 0 and 1 contain only the characters to be displayed, but modes 2 and 3 include both characters and attribute bytes for each character. The BL registers should contain the attribute bytes for all characters. Whatever buffers are allocated, the ES:BP register pair must contain a FAR pointer to the buffer.

Modes 2 and 3 contain two bytes (character byte and attribute byte) for every character in the string. So, a string that's four characters long actually contains eight characters. However, the CX register should contain the number 4 (i.e., the number of bytes in the actual string). There's another difference between modes 0 and 2 and modes 1 and 3. After screen output in modes 1 and 3, the cursor moves to the next screen position so BIOS output continues at this point. However, in modes 0 and 2, the cursor position isn't updated.

Reading characters from the screen

While functions 09H, 0AH, and 0EH display characters, function 08H reads characters currently on the screen. The function senses which character is at a particular screen position, and which attribute applies to that character. Place the function number in the AH register and the screen page number in the BH register. The screen position is the current cursor position.

Although the character code can be read directly from video RAM in text mode, in graphics mode, the character pattern at the current cursor position must be compared with all available character patterns. However, since this doesn't always work, you shouldn't rely on this function in graphics mode.

The function returns the attribute (color) in the AH register and returns the ASCII code of the character in the AL register.

Screen scrolling

In the description of the TTY output function (0EH) we mentioned that the screen scrolls (moves up) when the cursor reaches the last column and line on the screen.

Function 0EH executes an internal call to function 06H to perform the scrolling. Function 06H scrolls the screen area one or more lines up, displaying a blank space at the bottom of the screen. Only the currently displayed screen page is affected by this operation. Place the function number 06H in the AH register, and the number of lines you want scrolled in the AL register. If you place a value of 0 in this register, instead of being scrolled, the line(s) will be filled with spaces. In this case, the BH register contains the color you want assigned to the blank line(s). The CH, CL, DH, and DL registers define the screen range.

CH	Upper-left window corner (line)
CL	Upper-left window corner (column)
DH	Lower-right window corner (line)
DL	Lower-right window corner (column)

Function 07H scrolls the screen window down rather than up. The same parameters are used for function 07H and function 06H.

Demonstration programs

The following programs demonstrate how to use the BIOS video interrupt functions that are available from higher level languages. In Pascal and C, you'll find that using BIOS display functions works much faster than the standard procedures and functions, which use the slower DOS functions, that are included in these languages.

Advantage

An advantage of accessing BIOS video interrupt functions instead of using onboard graphics commands in higher level languages is that the BIOS function can be accessed at any time.

Disadvantage

However, there is a disadvantage to using BIOS functions for screen output. The higher level language display commands can accept numeric variables, which are then converted to ASCII characters. These higher level commands can format the variables according to decimal places (or a certain degree of precision) and then display them. However, if numeric variables are displayed using the BIOS functions, first they must be converted into a character string that must be transferred to the BIOS output function. Obviously, this procedure is very time-consuming.

Both programs operate the same way. Each fills the screen with continuous characters from the PC character set, then opens two windows in which two arrows move up and down. You'll understand how this was done and how it will actually appear on the screen, after you've studied the program codes. The programs limit their access to one screen page because of incompatibility problems that could occur between monochrome and color cards. Also, they don't present subroutines, functions, or procedures for calling the BIOS graphics functions.

Once you understand this section you should be able to add the missing functions and even write a short demonstration program of your own. Using the BIOS video interrupt ensures that the computer won't crash and that you won't encounter serious problems.

The individual functions and procedures of the following two programs are fully documented and should be self-explanatory. These programs look similar because the procedures, functions, and variables have the same names.

Pascal listing: VIDEOP.PAS

```
{*****************************************************************}
{*                      V I D E O P                             *}
{*-------------------------------------------------------------*}
{*    Task      : Makes functions available based on the BIOS   *}
{*                video interrupt not provided by Pascal.       *}
{*-------------------------------------------------------------*}
{*    Author    : Michael Tischer                               *}
{*    Developed on  : 07/10/87                                  *}
{*    Last update   : 02/18/92                                  *}
{*****************************************************************}

program VIDEOP;
```

```
Uses Crt, Dos;                          { Add DOS and CRT units }

const NORMAL    = $07;      { Definition of character attribute }
      BOLD      = $0f;      { in relation to a Monochrome       }
      INVERS    = $70;      { Display Adapter                   }
      UNDERLINE = $01;
      BLINK     = $80;

type  TextTyp = string[80];

var  i,                      { Loop variable for the main program }
     j,
     k,
     l  : integer;
```

```
       IString : string[2];              { Accepts number of arrows }

{*************************************************************}
{* GETVIDEOMODE: Reads current video mode and parameters.    *}
{* Input      : None                                         *}
{* Output     : Variables receive values after procedure call *}
{*************************************************************}

procedure GetVideoMode(var VideoMode, { Number of current video mode }
                           Number,     { Number of columns per line }
                           Page : integer); { Current screen page }

var Regs : Registers;         { Register variables for interrupt call }

begin
  Regs.ah := $0F;                          { Function number }
  intr($10, Regs);                 { Call BIOS video interrupt }
  VideoMode := Regs.al;               { Number of video mode }
  Number := Regs.ah;          { Number of characters per line }
  Page := Regs.bh;         { Number of the current screen page }
end;


{*************************************************************}
{* SETCURSORTYPE: Defines the appearance of the blinking cursor. *}
{* Input      : See below                                    *}
{* Output     : None                                         *}
{* Info       : Parameters can be from 0 to 13 for a Monochrome *}
{*               Display Adapter, and from 0 to 7 for a color card. *}
{*************************************************************}

procedure SetCursorType(Beginline,    { Beginning line of the cursor }
                        Endl  : integer); { End line of the cursor }

var Regs : Registers;       { Register variable for the interrupt call }

begin
  Regs.ah := 1;                            { Function number }
  Regs.ch := Beginline;                    { Beginning and }
  Regs.cl := Endl;                         { End line }
  intr($10, Regs);                 { Call BIOS video interrupt }
end;


{*************************************************************}
{* SETCURSORPOS: Defines cursor position during screen page display. *}
{* Input      : See below                                    *}
{* Output     : None                                         *}
{* Info       : The cursor position changes only when this    *}
{*               procedure is called, if the current screen page is *}
{*               indicated.                                   *}
{*************************************************************}

procedure SetCursorPos(Page,       { Screen page containing cursor }
                       Column,         { New cursor column }
                       CRow  : integer);   { New cursor row }

var Regs : Registers;        { Register variable for the interrupt }

begin
  Regs.ah := 2;                         { Function number }
  Regs.bh := Page;                         { Screen page }
  Regs.dh := CRow;                    { Display coordinates }
  Regs.dl := Column;
  intr($10, Regs);               { Call BIOS video interrupt }
end;
```

```
{*************************************************************}
{* GETCURSORPOS: Gets the cursor's position, starting and ending *}
{*               lines.                                       *}
{* Input      : See below                                    *}
{* Output     : Variables contain values after procedure call *}
{* Info       : Start and end cursor lines are independent of the *}
{*               screen page.                                 *}
{*************************************************************}

procedure GetCursorPos(Page : integer;        { The screen page }
                       var Column,            { Cursor column }
                           CRow,              { Cursor row }
                           Beginline,  { Start line of the cursor }
                           Endl : integer); { End line of the cursor }

var Regs : Registers;        { Register variables for the interrupt }

begin
  Regs.ah := 3;                         { Function number }
  Regs.bh := Page;                         { Screen page }
  intr($10, Regs);               { Call BIOS video interrupt }
  Column := Regs.dl;              { Read function results }
  CRow := Regs.dh;                 { from these registers }
  Beginline := Regs.ch;            { and store in proper }
  Endl := Regs.cl;                 { variables }
end;


{*************************************************************}
{* SETSCREENPAGE : Sets the screen page for output on the monitor. *}
{* Input       : See below                                   *}
{* Output      : None                                        *}
{*************************************************************}

procedure SetScreenPage(Page : integer);     { The new screen page }

var Regs : Registers;        { Register variables for interrupt call }

begin
  Regs.ah := 5;              { Function number and screen page }
  Regs.al := Page;                         { Screen page }
  intr($10, Regs);               { Call BIOS video interrupt }
end;


{*************************************************************}
{* SCROLLUP: Scrolls a display area by one or more           *}
{*           lines up or erases it.                          *}
{* Input    : See below                                      *}
{* Output   : None                                           *}
{* Info     : If number 0 is passed, the display area        *}
{*            is filled with spaces                          *}
{*************************************************************}

procedure ScrollUp(Number,        { Number of lines to be scrolled }
                   COLOR,     { Attribute for the blank lines created }
                   ColumnUL,     { Column in the upper-left corner }
                   CRowUL,          { Row in the upper-left corner }
                   ColumnLR,     { Column in the lower-right corner }
                   CRowLR : integer); { Row in the lower-right corner }

var Regs : Registers;        { Register variables for interrupt call }

begin
  Regs.ah := 6;                   { Function number and number }
```

```
Regs.al := Number;
Regs.bh := COLOR;                          { Color of empty line(s) }
Regs.ch := CRowUL;                                      { Upper-left }
Regs.cl := ColumnUL;                                   { coordinates }
Regs.dh := CRowLR;                                     { Lower-right }
Regs.dl := ColumnLR;                                   { coordinates }
Intr($10,Regs);                         { Call BIOS video interrupt }
end;


{*****************************************************************}
{* SCROLLDOWN: Scrolls a display area by one or more            *}
{*             lines down or erases it.                          *}
{* Input   : See below                                          *}
{* Output  : None                                               *}
{* Info    : If number 0 is passed, the display area            *}
{*           is filled with spaces.                             *}
{*****************************************************************}

procedure ScrollDown(Number,          { Number of lines to be scrolled }
                COLOR, { Attribute for the blank line(s) created }
                ColumnUL,        { Column in the upper-left corner }
                CRowUL,             { Row in the upper-left corner }
                ColumnLR,        { Column in the lower-right corner }
                CRowLR : integer);   { Row in lower-right corner }

var Regs : Registers;      { Register variables for interrupt call }

begin
Regs.ah := 7;                       { Function number and number }
Regs.al := Number;
Regs.bh := COLOR;                        { Color of blank line(s) }
Regs.ch := CRowUL;                                    { Upper-left }
Regs.cl := ColumnUL;                                 { coordinates }
Regs.dh := CRowLR;                                   { Lower-right }
Regs.dl := ColumnLR;                                 { coordinates }
Intr($10, Regs);                      { Call BIOS video interrupt }
end;


{*****************************************************************}
{* GETCHAR: Reads a character including attribute from an indicated *}
{*          position in a screen page.                          *}
{* Input  : See below                                           *}
{* Output : See below                                           *}
{*****************************************************************}

procedure GetChar(Page,                      { Screen page accessed }
                Column,                         { Screen column }
                SRow    : integer;              { Screen row }
                var Character : char;           { Character }
                var COLOR   : integer);         { Its attribute }

var Regs : Registers;      { Register variables for interrupt call }
    CurColumn,                              { Current column }
    CurCRow,                                { Current row }
    CurPage,                                { Current screen page }
    Dummy   : integer;           { Stores unnecessary variables }

begin
GetVideoMode(Dummy, Dummy, CurPage);       { Get current screen page }
GetCursorPos(CurPage, CurColumn, CurCRow, { Get cursor position in }
            Dummy, Dummy);                 { the current screen page }
SetCursorPos(Page, Column, SRow);          { Set cursor position }

Regs.ah := 8;        { Get function number for char. and attribute }
```

```
Regs.bh := Page;                               { Screen page }
Intr($10,Regs);                       { Invoke DOS registers }
Character := chr(Regs.al);             { ASCII character code }
COLOR := Regs.ah;                      { Character attribute }
SetCursorPos(CurPage, CurColumn, CurCRow);{ Set old cursor position }
end;


{*****************************************************************}
{* WRITECHAR: Writes a character with indicated color to the    *}
{*            current cursor position in the screen page.       *}
{* Input   : See below                                          *}
{* Output  : None                                               *}
{* Info    : During execution, control characters (CRLF) are    *}
{*           handled as control characters.                     *}
{*****************************************************************}

procedure WriteChar(Page    : integer;      { Screen page for writing }
                Character : char;           { ASCII character code }
                COLOR   : integer);            { Its attribute }

var Regs : Registers;      { Register variables for interrupt call }

begin
Regs.ah := 9;
Regs.al := ord(Character);   { Function number and character code }
Regs.bh := Page;                               { Screen page }
Regs.bl := COLOR;                              { Display color }
Regs.cx := 1;                 { Display character only once }
Intr($10,Regs);                     { Call BIOS video interrupt }
end;


{*****************************************************************}
{* WRITETEXT: Writes a string starting at an indicated position in *}
{*            a screen page.                                    *}
{* Input   : See below                                          *}
{* Output  : None                                               *}
{* Info    : During execution, control characters (CRLF) are    *}
{*           handled as control characters. If display goes past *}
{*           the last screen line, the display scrolls up.      *}
{*****************************************************************}

procedure WriteText(Page,                   { Screen page for output }
                Column,         { Column, from which output starts }
                SRow,            { Line, from which output starts }
                COLOR : integer;     { Color for all characters }
                Text  : TextTyp);           { Text for output }

var Regs : Registers;      { Register variables for interrupt call }
    Counter : integer;                       { Loop counter }

begin
SetCursorPos(Page, Column, SRow);                     { Set cursor }

for Counter := 1 to length(Text) do          { Process characters }
  begin                                      { in sequence       }
    WriteChar(Page, ' ', COLOR);   { Color at the current position }
    Regs.ah := 14;
    Regs.al := ord(Text[Counter]);   { Function number and character }
    Regs.bh := Page;                               { Screen page }
    Intr($10,Regs);                     { Call BIOS video interrupt }
  end;
end;


{*****************************************************************}
```

```
{**                    MAIN PROGRAM                    **}
{***********************************************************************}

begin
clrscr;                                      { Clear screen }
for i := 1 to 24 do                          { Do rows 1 to 24 }
 for j := 0 to 79 do                         { Do all columns }
  begin
   SetCursorPos(0, j, i);                    { Position cursor }
   WriteChar(0, chr(i*80+j and 255), NORMAL); { Write a character }
  end;
ScrollDown(0, NORMAL, 5, 8, 19, 22);         { Clear window 1 }
WriteText(0, 5, 8, INVERS, '   Window 1   ');
ScrollDown(0, NORMAL, 60, 2, 74, 16);        { Clear window 2 }
WriteText(0, 60, 2, INVERS, '   Window 2   ');
WriteText(0, 24, 12, INVERS or BLINK, ' >>>      PC   INTERN      <<<
');
WriteText(0, 0, 0, INVERS, '              -->    <-- arrows remain'+
                 'ing in sequence                     ');
for i := 49 downto 0 do                      { Draw a total of 50 arrows }
 begin
  str(i:2, IString);                         { Convert i to ASCII string }
  WriteText(0, 20, 0, INVERS, IString);
  j := 1;                                    { Every arrow consists of 16 lines }
  while j <= 15 do
   begin
    k := 0;
    while k < j do                           { Create a line for an arrow }
     begin
      SetCursorPos(0, 12-(j shr 1)+k, 9);    { Arrow window 1 }
      WriteChar(0, '*', BOLD);
      SetCursorPos(0, 67-(j shr 1)+k, 16);   { Arrow window 2 }
      WriteChar(0, '*', BOLD);
      k := succ(k);
     end;
    ScrollDown(1, NORMAL, 5, 9, 19, 22);     { Scroll window 1 }
    ScrollUp(1, NORMAL, 60, 3, 74, 16);      { Scroll window 2 }
    for l := 0 to 8000 do                    { Delay loop }
     ;
    j := j+2;
   end;
 end;
clrscr;                                      { Clear screen }
end.
```

C listing: VIDEOC.C

```
/*********************************************************************/
/*                      V I D E O C                      */
/*-------------------------------------------------------------------*/
/*    Task       : Makes functions available based on the BIOS       */
/*                 video interrupt not provided by C.                */
/*-------------------------------------------------------------------*/
/*    Author     : Michael Tischer                                   */
/*    Developed on : 08/13/87                                        */
/*    Last update  : 02/18/92                                        */
/*-------------------------------------------------------------------*/
/*    (MICROSOFT C)                                                  */
/*    Compilation  : cl /AS videoc.c                                 */
/*    Call         : VIDEOC                                          */
/*-------------------------------------------------------------------*/
/*    (BORLAND TURBO C)                                              */
/*    Compilation  : through the RUN command on the menu bar         */
/*********************************************************************/

#include <dos.h>                             /* Add include files */
#include <io.h>

#define NORMAL      0x07    /* Definition of a character attribute */
#define BOLD        0x0F    /* in relation to a Monochrome         */
#define INVERS      0x70    /* Display Adapter                     */
#define UNDERLINE   0x01
#define BLINK       0x80

/*********************************************************************/
/* GETVIDEOMODE: Reads current video mode and parameters.            */
/* Input        : None                                               */
/* Output       : See below                                          */
/*********************************************************************/

void GetVideoMode(VideoMode, Number, Page)
int *VideoMode;                      /* Number of current video mode */
int *Number;                         /* Number of columns per line */
int *Page;                           /* Current screen page */

{
 union REGS Register;       /* Register variables for interrupt call */

 Register.h.ah = 15;                        /* Function number */
 int86(0x10, &Register, &Register);         /* Call interrupt 10H */
 *VideoMode = Register.h.al;                /* Number of video mode */
 *Number = Register.h.ah;           /* Number of characters per line */
 *Page = Register.h.bh;             /* Number of current screen page */
}


/*********************************************************************/
/* SETCURSORTYPE: Defines the appearance of the blinking cursor.     */
/* Input        : See below                                          */
/* Output       : None                                               */
/* Info         : Parameters can be from 0 to 13 for a Monochrome    */
/*                Display Adapter, and from 0 to 7 for a color card.  */
/*********************************************************************/

void SetCursorType(Beginline, Endl)
int Beginline;                       /* Beginning line of the cursor */
int Endl;                            /* End line of the cursor */

{
 union REGS Register;       /* Register variables for interrupt call */
```

```
Register.h.ah = 1;                               /* Function number */
Register.h.ch = Beginline;          /* Beginning line of cursor */
Register.h.cl = Endl;                  /* End line of cursor */
int86(0x10, &Register, &Register);        /* Call interrupt 10H */
}


/*****************************************************************/
/* SETCURSORPOS: Defines cursor position during screen page display. */
/* Input      : See below                                        */
/* Output     : None                                             */
/* Info       : The cursor position changes only when this       */
/*              procedure is called, if the current screen page is */
/*              indicated.                                        */
/*****************************************************************/

void SetCursorPos(Page, Column, CRow)
int Page;                           /* Screen page containing cursor */
int Column;                              /* New cursor column */
int CRow;                                /* New cursor row */

{
  union REGS Register;       /* Register variables for interrupt call */

  Register.h.ah = 2;                               /* Function number */
  Register.h.bh = Page;                        /* Screen page */
  Register.h.dh = CRow;                        /* Screen row */
  Register.h.dl = Column;                      /* Screen column */
  int86(0x10, &Register, &Register);        /* Call interrupt 10H */
}


/*****************************************************************/
/* GETCURSORPOS: Gets the cursor's position, starting and ending */
/*               lines.                                          */
/* Input      : None                                            */
/* Output     : See below                                       */
/*****************************************************************/

void GetCursorPos(Page, Column, CRow, Beginline, Endl)
int Page;                           /* Number of screen page */
int *Column;                              /* Cursor column */
int *CRow;                                /* Cursor row */
int *Beginline;                     /* Start line of the cursor */
int *Endl;                          /* End line of the cursor */

{
  union REGS Register;       /* Register variables for interrupt call */

  Register.h.ah = 3;                               /* Function number */
  Register.h.bh = Page;                        /* Screen page */
  int86(0x10, &Register, &Register);        /* Call interrupt 10H */
  *Column = Register.h.dl;              /* Read function results */
  *CRow = Register.h.dh;                /* from these registers */
  *Beginline = Register.h.ch;          /* and store in proper */
  *Endl = Register.h.cl;               /* variables */
}


/*****************************************************************/
/* SETSCREENPAGE: Sets the screen page for output on the monitor. */
/* Input       : See below                                      */
/* Output      : None                                           */
/*****************************************************************/

void SetScreenPage(Page)
```

```
int Page;                           /* Number of the new screen page */
{
  union REGS Register;       /* Register variables for interrupt call */

  Register.h.ah = 5;                               /* Function number */
  Register.h.al = Page;                        /* Screen page */
  int86(0x10, &Register, &Register);        /* Call interrupt 10H */
}

/*****************************************************************/
/* SCROLLUP: Scrolls a screen area up one or several            */
/*           lines or erases it.                                */
/* Input    : See below                                         */
/* Output   : None                                              */
/* Info     : If number 0 is passed, the screen area            */
/*            is filled with spaces.                            */
/*****************************************************************/

void ScrollUp(Number, Color, ColumnUL, CRowUL, ColumnLR, CRowLR)
int Number;                         /* Number of lines to be scrolled */
int Color;                 /* Color or attribute for the blank lines */
int ColumnUL;                       /* Column in upper-left corner */
int CRowUL;                            /* Row in upper-left corner */
int ColumnLR;                       /* Column in lower-right corner */
int CRowLR;                            /* Row in lower-right corner */

{
  union REGS Register;       /* Register variables for interrupt call */

  Register.h.ah = 6;                               /* Function number */
  Register.h.al = Number;                      /* Number of lines */
  Register.h.bh = Color;               /* Color of blank line(s) */
  Register.h.ch = CRowUL;              /* Set coordinates of the */
  Register.h.cl = ColumnUL;            /* window to be scrolled */
  Register.h.dh = CRowLR;              /* or erased */
  Register.h.dl = ColumnLR;
  int86(0x10, &Register, &Register);        /* Call interrupt 10H */
}


/*****************************************************************/
/* SCROLLDOWN: Scrolls a screen area by one or more             */
/*             lines down or erases it.                         */
/* Input    : See below                                         */
/* Output   : None                                              */
/* Info     : If number 0 is passed, the screen area            */
/*            is filled with spaces.                            */
/*****************************************************************/

void ScrollDown(Number, Color, ColumnUL, CRowUL, ColumnLR, CRowLR)
int Number;                         /* Number of lines to be scrolled */
int Color;                 /* Color or attribute for the blank lines */
int ColumnUL;                       /* Column in upper-left corner */
int CRowUL;                            /* Row in upper-left corner */
int ColumnLR;                       /* Column in lower-right corner */
int CRowLR;                            /* Row in lower-right corner */

{
  union REGS Register;       /* Register variables for interrupt call */

  Register.h.ah = 7;                               /* Function number */
  Register.h.al = Number;                      /* Number of lines */
  Register.h.bh = Color;               /* Color of blank line(s) */
  Register.h.ch = CRowUL;              /* Set coordinates for the */
```

106

```
Register.h.cl = ColumnUL;            /* window to be scrolled */
Register.h.dh = CRowLR;              /* or erased             */
Register.h.dl = ColumnLR;
   int86(0x10, &Register, &Register);       /* Call interrupt 10H */
}


/***********************************************************************/
/* GETCHAR: Reads a character including attribute from an indicated   */
/*          position in a screen page.                               */
/* Input  : See below                                                */
/* Output : See below                                                */
/***********************************************************************/

void GetChar(Page, Column, SRow, Character, Color)
int Page;                            /* Screen page accessed */
int Column;                          /* Screen column */
int SRow;                            /* Screen row */
char *Character;                     /* Character at this position */
int *Color;                          /* Its attribute byte (color) */

{
   union REGS Register;       /* Register variables for interrupt call */
   int Dummy;                       /* Stores unnecessary variables */
   int CurPage;                     /* Current screen page */
   int CurCRow;                     /* Current row */
   int CurColumn;                   /* Current column */

   GetVideoMode(&Dummy, &Dummy, &CurPage); /* Get current screen page */
   GetCursorPos(&CurPage, &CurColumn, &CurCRow,   /* Get current */
                &Dummy, &Dummy);                   /* cursor position */
   SetCursorPos(Page, Column, SRow);            /* Set cursor */
   Register.h.ah = 8;                           /* Function number */
   Register.h.bh = Page;                        /* Screen page */
   int86(0x10, &Register, &Register);   /* Call interrupt 10H */
   *Character = Register.h.al;      /* Read results from the */
   *Color = Register.h.ah;          /* registers and assign */
   SetCursorPos(CurPage, CurColumn, CurCRow);  /* Set old cursor pos. */
}


/***********************************************************************/
/* WRITECHAR: Writes a character with indicated color to the         */
/*            current cursor position in the screen page.            */
/* Input  : See below                                                */
/* Output : None                                                     */
/***********************************************************************/

void WriteChar(Page, Character, Color)
int Page;                            /* Screen page for writing */
char Character;                      /* ASCII character code */
int Color;                           /* Its attribute or color */

{
   union REGS Register;       /* Register variables for interrupt call */

   Register.h.ah = 9;                           /* Function number */
   Register.h.al = Character;                    /* Character code */
   Register.h.bh = Page;                         /* Screen page */
   Register.h.bl = Color;                        /* Character color */
   Register.x.cx = 1;               /* Display character only once */
   int86(0x10, &Register, &Register);   /* Call interrupt 10H */
}


/***********************************************************************/
/* WRITETEXT: Writes a string starting at a specific screen position.*/
```

```
/* Input   : See below                                               */
/* Output  : None                                                    */
/* Info    : Text is a pointer to a character vector which contains  */
/*           the text to be output and is terminated                 */
/*           with a '\0' character.                                  */
/***********************************************************************/

void WriteText(Page, Column, SRow, Color, Text)
int Page;                            /* Screen page for output */
int Column;                          /* Column for output */
int SRow;                            /* Row for output */
int Color;                           /* Color for all characters */
char *Text;                          /* Text for output */

{
   union REGS Register;       /* Register variables for interrupt call */

   SetCursorPos(Page, Column, SRow);            /* Set cursor */
   while (*Text)                    /* Process text up to '\0' character */
   {
      WriteChar(Page, ' ', Color);              /* Character color */
      Register.h.ah = 14;                       /* Function number */
      Register.h.bh = Page;                     /* Screen page */
      Register.h.al = *Text++;                  /* Character */
      int86(0x10, &Register, &Register);        /* Call interrupt */
   }
}


/***********************************************************************/
/* CLEARSCREEN: Clears the 80x25 text screen.                        */
/* Input    : None                                                   */
/* Output   : None                                                   */
/***********************************************************************/

void ClearScreen()

{
   int CurPage;                     /* Current screen page */
   int Dummy;                       /* Dummy variable */

   ScrollUp(0, NORMAL, 0, 0, 79, 24);           /* Clear screen */
   GetVideoMode(&Dummy, &Dummy, &CurPage); /* Get current screen page */
   SetCursorPos(CurPage, 0, 0);                 /* Set cursor */
}


/***********************************************************************/
/**                     MAIN PROGRAM                               **/
/***********************************************************************/

void main()

{
   int i, j, k, l;                           /* Loop variables */
   char Arrows[3];        /* accepts number of arrows as ASCII string */

   ClearScreen();                               /* Clear screen */
   for (i = 1; i < 25; i++)                     /* Process all rows */
      for (j = 0; j < 80; j++)                  /* Process all columns */
      {
         SetCursorPos(0, j, i);                 /* Position cursor */
         WriteChar(0, i*80+j&255, NORMAL);      /* Write characters */
      }
   ScrollDown(0, NORMAL, 5, 8, 19, 22);         /* Clear window 1 */
   WriteText(0, 5, 8, INVERS, "  Window 1  ");
```

107

```
ScrollDown(0, NORMAL, 60, 2, 74, 16);          /* Clear window 2 */        SetCursorPos(0, 12-(j>>1)+k, 9);            /* Arrow window 1 */
WriteText(0, 60, 2, INVERS, "   Window 2   ");                             WriteChar(0, '*', BOLD);
WriteText(0, 24, 12, INVERS | BLINK, " >>>     PC   INTERN    <<<          SetCursorPos(0, 67-(j>>1)+k, 16);           /* Arrow window 2 */
");                                                                        WriteChar(0, '*', BOLD);
WriteText(0, 0, 0, INVERS, "                  -->  <-- arrows remain");     }
WriteText(0, 40, 0, INVERS,"ing in sequence               ");            ScrollDown(1, NORMAL, 5, 9, 19, 22);          /* Scroll window 1 down */
for (i = 49; i >= 0 ; i--)                      /* Draw 50 arrows */      ScrollUp(1, NORMAL, 60, 3, 74, 16);           /* Scroll window 2 up */
{                                                                         for (l = 0; l < 4000 ; l++)                   /* Wait loop */
  sprintf(Arrows, "%2d", i);   /* Convert number of arrows to ASCII */      ;
  WriteText(0, 20, 0, INVERS, Arrows);          /* and output */          }
  for (j = 1; j < 16; j+= 2)   /* Every arrow consists of 16 lines */   }
  {                                                                     ClearScreen();                                  /* Clear screen */
    for (k = 0; k < j; k++)        /* Create a line for an arrow */     }
    {
```

4.3 Determining Video Card Type

Whenever you want to access the video card hardware or use a BIOS function that's only available in special versions of the BIOS, first you must ensure that the card is actually installed in the system. If you don't do this, the image that appears on the screen may look different than what you expected.

If the program is supposed to be compatible with all types of cards, it's especially important that it recognize the type of video card that's installed, while still directly accessing video hardware. The output routines need this information in order to use the special properties of the given card effectively.

Remember that the PC can have both a monochrome video card (MDA, HGC, or EGA with a monochrome monitor) and a color video card (EGA, VGA, or CGA) installed. However, only one of the cards can be active at a time.

Combinations - PC video cards	VGA	EGA	HGC	CGA	MDA
VGA			■		■
EGA			■	■	
HGC	■	■		■	
CGA		■	■		■
MDA	■	■		■	

We must determine which video cards are installed. BIOS or DOS functions cannot be used to do this and variables cannot be read. So, we must write an assembly language routine that checks for the existence of different video cards.

Refer to the documentation for the various cards. Manufacturers usually include a procedure for determining whether their card is being used. It's important to keep the test specific (i.e., it doesn't return a positive result if a certain type of video card isn't installed). This is difficult to do with EGA and VGA cards, which can emulate CGA or MDA cards with the appropriate monitor, and are difficult to distinguish from true CGA or MDA cards.

However, not all registers can be described and read in this case. Registers 14 and 15, which determine the address of the blinking cursor, don't cause any problems.

All the tests we present are located at the end of this section in the form of two assembly language programs. These programs are intended to be used with C and Pascal programs. The functions place the type of video card installed and the type of monitor connected to it into an array. The function is passed a pointer to this array. If two video cards are installed, their order in the array indicates which one is active.

The following cards can be detected by t e assembly language routine:

- MDA cards
- CGA cards
- HGC cards
- EGA cards
- VGA cards

Since the assembly language routine checks for the existence of a specific video card, there is a separate subroutine for each type of card. The name of the subroutine is the same as the video card for which it tests. For example, these routines could be called TEST_EGA, TEST_VGA, etc.

Although these tests can be called sequentially, certain tests can be excluded if you know that they would return a negative result. For example, this applies to the CGA test if an EGA or VGA card has already been detected and is connected to a high resolution color monitor. Since a CGA card cannot be installed along with this type of card, you don't need to test for it.

A flag for each test determines whether the test will be performed. Before the first test (the VGA test), all the flags are set to 1 so all the tests will be performed sequentially. During the testing, certain flags can be set to 0 so the corresponding tests won't be performed.

VGA test

The tests begin with the VGA test. A special function in the VGA BIOS, sub-function 00H of function 1AH, returns the information needed by the assembly language routine. The information is available only if a VGA card and a VGA BIOS are installed. This is the case if the value 1AH is found in the AL register after the call. If the test routine encounters a different value there, the VGA test will be terminated and the other tests will be performed. This indicates that a VGA card is <u>not</u> installed.

Based on this information, the sequence of both entries is exchanged in the last step of the assembler routine.

After this function is called, the BL register contains a special device code for the active video card and the BH register contains a code for the inactive card. The following codes can occur:

```
┌─────────────────────────────────────────────────┐
│  Return Code of Function 00H of Function 1AH      │
│  ┌──────┬──────────────────────────────────────┐ │
│  │ Code │ Meaning                              │ │
│  ├──────┼──────────────────────────────────────┤ │
│  │ 00H  │ No video card                        │ │
│  │ 01H  │ MDA card/monochrome monitor          │ │
│  │ 02H  │ CGA card/color monitor               │ │
│  │ 03H  │ Reserved                             │ │
│  │ 04H  │ EGA card/high resolution monitor     │ │
│  │ 05H  │ EGA card/monochrome monitor          │ │
│  │ 06H  │ Reserved                             │ │
│  │ 07H  │ VGA card/analog monochrome monitor   │ │
│  │ 08H  │ VGA card/analog color monitor        │ │
│  └──────┴──────────────────────────────────────┘ │
└─────────────────────────────────────────────────┘
```

These codes are separated into values for the video card and the monitor connected to it, and loaded into the array whose address is passed to the assembly language routine. Since this routine already has information about both video cards, the following tests don't have to be performed. However, the routine executes the monochrome test if the functions discover a monochrome card, because it cannot distinguish between an MDA and HGC card.

EGA test

After the VGA test, the EGA test is performed only if the VGA test was unsuccessful, and, consequently, the EGA flag wasn't cleared. This test uses a function that's found only in the EGA BIOS, called sub-function 10H of function 12H. If an EGA card isn't installed and this function isn't available, the value 10H will still be found in the BL register after the function call. In this case, the EGA test ends.

If an EGA card is installed, the CL register will contain the settings of the DIP switches on the EGA card after the call. These switches indicate which type of monitor is connected. They are converted to the monitor codes the assembly language routine uses and placed in the array along with the code for the EGA card. The CGA or monochrome test flag is cleared, depending on the type of monitor connected. The EGA routine ends.

CGA test

If the CGA flag hasn't been cleared by the previous tests, the CGA test follows the EGA test. As with the monochrome test, there aren't any special BIOS functions that can be used and we must check for the presence of the appropriate hardware. In both routines this is done by calling the routine TEST_6845, which tests to determine whether the 6845 video controller found on these cards is at the specified port address. On a CGA card this is port address 3D4H, which is passed to the routine TEST_6845.

The only way to test the existence of the CRTC at a given port address is to write some value (other than 0) to one of the CRTC registers and then read it back immediately. If the value read matches the value written, then the CRTC and, therefore, the video card are present.

Before writing a value into a CRTC register, you should remember that these registers have a major impact on the makeup of the video signals. So, carelessly accessing them can not only thoroughly confuse the CRTC, but also harm the monitor. Registers 00H to 09H cannot be used for this test, so only registers 0AH to 0FH are available. All these registers affect the screen contents. We can use registers 0AH and 0BH, which control the starting and ending lines of the cursor.

The assembly language routine first reads the contents of register 0AH before it loads any value into this register. After a short pause so the CRTC can react to the output, the contents of this register are read back. Before the value read is compared to the original value, the old value is first written back into the register so the screen is disturbed as little as possible. If the comparison is positive, then a CRTC is present and so is the video card (CGA in this case). The CGA routine responds by loading the code for a color monitor into the array because this is the only type of monitor that can be used with a CGA card.

Monochrome test

The last test is the monochrome test, which also checks for the existence of a CRTC; except this time port address 3B4H is checked. If it finds a CRTC there, then a monochrome card is installed and we must determine whether it's an MDA or HGC card. The status registers of the two cards, at port address 3BAH, are used to determine this. Since bit 7 of this register is meaningless on the MDA card, its value is undefined. However, it contains a 1 on an HGC card whenever the electron beam is returning across the screen. Since this isn't permanent and occurs only at intervals of about two milliseconds, the contents of this bit constantly alternate between 0 and 1.

Hercules

The test routine first reads the contents of this register and masks out bits 0 to 6. The resulting value is used in a maximum of 32768 loop passes, in which the value is read again and compared with the original value. If the value changes, which means that the state of bit 7 changes, then an HGC card is probably installed. If this bit doesn't change over the course of 32768 loop passes, then an MDA card is being used.

Again, we place the appropriate code for the video card in the array. The monitor code is also set to monochrome, since this is the only monitor that can be connected to an MDA card or an HGC card.

Primary and secondary video systems

The tests are now complete. Next we must determine which card is active (primary) and which is inactive (secondary). If the outcome of the VGA test was positive, we can skip this because the VGA BIOS routine determines the active card automatically.

In other instances, we can determine the active video card from the current video mode, which can be read with the help of function 0FH of the BIOS video interrupt. If the value seven is returned, then the 80x25 text mode of the monochrome card is active. All the other modes indicate that a CGA, EGA, or VGA card is active. This information is used to exchange the order of the two entries in the array if it doesn't match the actual situation.

The assembly language routine returns control to the calling program.

Here we include C and Pascal programs that call the function GetVIOS from the assembly language module and demonstrate how GetVIOS works.

Pascal listing: VIOSP.PAS

```
{****************************************************************}
{*                        V I O S P                            *}
{*------------------------------------------------------------*}
{*  Task        : Returns the type of video card installed.   *}
{*------------------------------------------------------------*}
{*  Author      : Michael Tischer                             *}
{*  Developed on : 10/02/88                                    *}
{*  Last update  : 02/18/92                                    *}
{****************************************************************}

program VIOSP;


{$L viospa}                         { Link assembler module }

const NO_VIOS  = 0;                        { No video card }
      VGA      = 1;                         { VGA card }
      EGA      = 2;                         { EGA card }
      MDA      = 3;             { Monochrome Display Adapter }
      HGC      = 4;              { Hercules Graphics Card }
      CGA      = 5;               { Color Graphics Adapter }

      NO_MON     = 0;                        { No monitor }
      MONO       = 1;               { Monochrome monitor }
      COLOR      = 2;                     { Color monitor }
      EGA_HIRES  = 3;             { High-resolution monitor }
      ANLG_MONO  = 4;             { Monochrome analog monitor }
      ANLG_COLOR = 5;                { Color analog monitor }

type Vios = record        { Describes video card and attached monitor }
              VCard,
              Monitor : byte;
            end;
     ViosPtr = ^Vios;                  { Pointer to a VIOS structure }

procedure GetVios( vp : ViosPtr ) ; external ;

var VidSys : array[1..2] of Vios; { Array containing video structures }


{****************************************************************}
{* PrintSys: Gives information about a video system.          *}
{* Input   : - VCARD: Code number of the video card           *}
{*           - MON  : Code number of the attached monitor     *}
{* Output  : None                                             *}
{****************************************************************}

procedure PrintSys( VCard, Mon : byte );

begin
  write(' ');
  case VCard of
    NO_VIOS : write('Unknown');              { For "other" code }
    VGA : write('VGA');
    EGA : write('EGA');
    MDA : write('MDA');
    CGA : write('CGA');
    HGC : write('HGC');
  end;
  write(' card/ ');
  case Mon of
    MONO    : writeln('monochrome monitor');
    COLOR   : writeln('color monitor');
    EGA_HIRES  : writeln('high-resolution monitor');
    ANLG_MONO  : writeln('monochrome analog monitor');
    ANLG_COLOR : writeln('color analog monitor');
  end;
end;

{****************************************************************}
{**                    MAIN  PROGRAM                         **}
{****************************************************************}

begin
  GetVios( @VidSys );              { Check installed video card }
  writeln('VIOSP  -  (c) 1988, 1992 by Michael Tischer');
  write('Primary video system: ');
  PrintSys( VidSys[1].VCard, VidSys[1].Monitor );
  if VidSys[2].VCard <> NO_VIOS then { Second video system installed? }
    begin                                              { Yes }
      write('Secondary video system:');
      PrintSys( VidSys[2].VCard, VidSys[2].Monitor );
    end;
end.
```

Assembler listing: VIOSPA.ASM

```
;***************************************************************;
;*                    V I O S P A                           *;
;*-------------------------------------------------------------*;
;*    Task        : Creates a function for determining the type *;
;*                  of video card installed on a system. This  *;
;*                  routine must be assembled into an OBJ file, *;
;*                  then linked to a Turbo Pascal program.     *;
;*-------------------------------------------------------------*;
;*    Author      : Michael Tischer                           *;
;*    Developed on : 10/02/88                                 *;
;*    Last update  : 02/18/92                                 *;
;*-------------------------------------------------------------*;
;*    Assembly     : MASM VIOSPA;                             *;
;*                   ... Link to a Turbo Pascal program        *;
;*                   using the {$L VIOSPA} compiler directive  *;
;***************************************************************;

;== Constants for the VIOS structure ================================

                              ;Video card constants
NO_VIOS   = 0                 ;No video card/unrecognized card
VGA       = 1                 ;VGA card
EGA       = 2                 ;EGA card
MDA       = 3                 ;Monochrome Display Adapter
HGC       = 4                 ;Hercules Graphics Card
CGA       = 5                 ;Color Graphics Adapter

                              ;Monitor constants
NO_MON    = 0                 ;No monitor/unrecognized code
MONO      = 1                 ;Monochrome monitor
COLOR     = 2                 ;Color Monitor
EGA_HIRES = 3                 ;High-resolution/multisync monitor
ANLG_MONO = 4                 ;Monochrome analog monitor
ANLG_COLOR = 5                ;Analog color monitor

;== Data segment ====================================================

DATA   segment word public       ;Turbo data segment

DATA   ends

;== Code segment ====================================================

CODE      segment byte public    ;Turbo code segment

          assume cs:CODE, ds:DATA

public    getvios

;-- Initialized global variables must be placed in the code segment ---

vios_tab  equ this word

          ;-- Conversion table for supplying return values of VGA ---
          ;-- BIOS function 1AH, sub-function 00H            ---

          db NO_VIOS, NO_MON    ;No video card
          db MDA   , MONO       ;MDA card/monochrome monitor
          db CGA   , COLOR      ;CGA card/color monitor
          db ?     , ?          ;Code 3 unused
          db EGA   , EGA_HIRES  ;EGA card/hi-res monitor
          db EGA   , MONO       ;EGA card/monochrome monitor
```

```
          db ?     , ?          ;Code 6 unused
          db VGA   , ANLG_MONO  ;VGA card/analog mono monitor
          db VGA   , ANLG_COLOR ;VGA card/analog color monitor

ega_dips  equ this byte

          ;-- Conversion table for EGA card DIP switches -----

          db COLOR, EGA_HIRES, MONO
          db COLOR, EGA_HIRES, MONO

;---------------------------------------------------------------------
;-- GETVIOS: Determines type(s) of installed video card(s) -----------
;-- Pascal call : GetVios ( vp : ViosPtr ); external;
;-- Declaration : Type Vios = record VCard, Monitor: byte;
;-- Return Value: None

getvios   proc near

sframe    struc                  ;Stack access structure
cga_possi db ?                   ;Local variables
ega_possi db ?                   ;Local variables
mono_possi db ?                  ;Local variables
bptr      dw ?                   ;BPTR
ret_adr   dw ?                   ;Return address of calling program
vp        dd ?                   ;Pointer to first VIOS structure
sframe    ends                   ;End of structure

frame     equ [ bp - cga_possi ] ;Address elements of structure

          push bp                ;Push BP onto stack
          sub sp,3               ;Allocate memory for local variables
          mov bp,sp              ;Move SP to BP

          mov frame.cga_possi,1  ;Is it a CGA?
          mov frame.ega_possi,1  ;Is it an EGA?
          mov frame.mono_possi,1 ;Is it an MDA or HGC?

          mov di,word ptr frame.vp  ;Get offset addr. of structure
          mov word ptr [di],NO_VIOS  ;No video system or unknown
          mov word ptr [di+2],NO_VIOS ;system found

          call test_vga          ;Test for VGA card
          cmp frame.ega_possi,0  ;Or is it an EGA card?
          je gv1                 ;No --> Go to CGA test

          call test_ega          ;Test for EGA card
gv1:      cmp frame.cga_possi,0  ;Or is it a CGA card?
          je gv2                 ;No --> Go to MDA/HGC test

          call test_cga          ;Test for CGA card
gv2:      cmp frame.mono_possi,0 ;Or is it an MDA or HGC card?
          je gv3                 ;No --> End tests

          call test_mono         ;Test for MDA/HGC card

          ;-- Determine video configuration --------------------------

gv3:      cmp byte ptr [di],VGA  ;VGA card?
          je gvi_end             ;Yes --> Active card indicated
          cmp byte ptr [di+2],VGA ;VGA card part of secondary system?
          je gvi_end             ;Yes --> Active card indicated

          mov ah,0Fh             ;Determine video mode using
```

```
        int  10h              ;BIOS video interrupt

        and  al,7             ;Only modes 0-7 are of interest
        cmp  al,7             ;Mono card active?
        jne  gv4              ;No --> CGA or EGA mode

;-- MDA, HGC or EGA card (mono) currently active -----------

        cmp  byte ptr [di+1],MONO ;Mono monitor in first structure?
        je   gvi_end          ;Yes --> Sequence O.K.
        jmp  short switch     ;No --> Switch sequence

;-- CGA or EGA card currently active ----------------------

gv4:    cmp  byte ptr [di+1],MONO ;Mono monitor in first structure?
        jne  gvi_end          ;No -->Sequence O.K.

switch: mov  ax,[di]          ;Get contents of first structure
        xchg ax,[di+2]        ;Switch with second structure
        mov  [di],ax

gvi_end: add  sp,3            ;Add local variables from stack
        pop  bp               ;Pop BP off of stack
        ret  4                ;Clear variables off of stack;
                              ;Return to Turbo
getvios endp


;----------------------------------------------------------
;-- TEST_VGA: Determines whether a VGA card is installed

test_vga  proc near

        mov  ax,1a00h         ;Function 1AH, sub-function 00H
        int  10h              ;Call VGA-BIOS
        cmp  al,1ah           ;Function supported?
        jne  tvga_end         ;No --> End routine

        ;-- If function is supported, BL contains the code of the --
        ;-- active video system, while BH contains the code of   --
        ;-- the inactive video system                            --

        mov  cx,bx            ;Move result to CX
        xor  bh,bh            ;Set BH to 0
        or   ch,ch            ;Only one video system?
        je   tvga_1           ;Yes --> Display first system's code

        ;-- Convert code of second system -------------------------

        mov  bl,ch            ;Move second system's code to BL
        add  bl,bl            ;Add offset to table
        mov  ax,vios_tab[bx]  ;Get code from table and move into
        mov  [di+2],ax        ;caller's structure
        mov  bl,cl            ;Move first system's code into BL

        ;-- Convert code of second system -------------------------

tvga_1: add  bl,bl            ;Add offset to table
        mov  ax,vios_tab[bx]  ;Get code from table
        mov  [di],ax          ;and move into caller's structure

        mov  frame.cga_possi,0 ;CGA test fail?
        mov  frame.ega_possi,0 ;CGA test fail?
        mov  frame.mono_possi,0 ;Test for mono
```

```
        mov  bx,di            ;Address of active structure
        cmp  byte ptr [bx],MDA ;Monochrome system online?
        je   do_tmono         ;Yes --> Execute MDA/HGC test

        add  bx,2             ;Address of inactive structure
        cmp  byte ptr [bx],MDA ;Monochrome system online?
        jne  tvga_end         ;No --> End routine

do_tmono: mov  word ptr [bx],0 ;Emulate if this system
                              ;isn't available
        mov  frame.mono_possi,1;Execute monochrome test

tvga_end: ret                 ;Return to caller

test_vga  endp

;----------------------------------------------------------
;-- TEST_EGA: Determine whether an EGA card is installed

test_ega  proc near

        mov  ah,12h           ;Function 12H
        mov  bl,10h           ;Sub-function 10H
        int  10h              ;Call EGA-BIOS
        cmp  bl,10h           ;Is this function supported?
        je   tega_end         ;No --> End routine

        ;-- If the function IS supported, CL contains the    ---
        ;-- EGA card DIP switch settings                     ---

        mov  bl,cl            ;Move DIP switches to BL
        shr  bl,1            ;Shift one position to the right
        xor  bh,bh            ;Index high byte to 0
        mov  ah,ega_dips[bx]  ;Get element from table
        mov  al,EGA           ;Is it an EGA card?
        call found_it         ;Transfer data to the vector

        cmp  ah,MONO          ;Mono monitor connected?
        je   is_mono          ;Yes --> Not MDA or HGC

        mov  frame.cga_possi,0 ;No CGA card possible
        jmp  short tega_end   ;End routine

is_mono: mov  frame.mono_possi,0;EGA can either emulate MDA or HGC,
                              ;if mono monitor is attached

tega_end: ret                 ;Back to caller

test_ega  endp

;----------------------------------------------------------
;-- TEST_CGA: Determines whether a CGA card is installed

test_cga  proc near

        mov  dx,3D4h          ;Port addr. of CGA's CRTC addr. reg.
        call test_6845        ;Test for installed 6845 CRTC
        jc   tega_end         ;No --> End test

        mov  al,CGA           ;Yes --> CGA installed
        mov  ah,COLOR         ;CGA uses color monitor
        jmp  found_it         ;Transfer data to vector

test_cga  endp
```

```
;-------------------------------------------------------------------
;-- TEST_MONO: Checks for MDA or HGC card

test_mono  proc near

           mov   dx,3B4h         ;Port addr. of MONO's CRTC addr. reg.
           call  test_6845        ;Test for installed 6845 CRTC
           jc    tega_end         ;No --> End test

           ;-- Monochrome video card installed -----------------------
           ;--
           mov   dl,0BAh          ;MONO status port at 3BAH
           in    al,dx            ;Read status port
           and   al,80h           ;Separate bit 7 and
           mov   ah,al            ;move to AH

           ;-- If the contents of bit 7 in the status port change   ---
           ;-- during the following readings, it is handled as an   ---
           ;-- HGC                                                   ---

           mov   cx,8000h         ;Maximum 32768 loop executions
test_hgc:  in    al,dx            ;Read status port
           and   al,80h           ;Isolate bit 7
           cmp   al,ah            ;Contents changed?
           jne   is_hgc           ;Bit 7 = 1 --> HGC
           loop  test_hgc         ;Continue

           mov   al,MDA           ;Bit 7 <> 1 --> MDA
           jmp   set_mono         ;Set parameters

is_hgc:    mov   al,HGC           ;Bit 7 = 1 --> HGC
set_mono:  mov   ah,MONO          ;MDA and HGC set as mono screen
           jmp   found_it         ;Set parameters

test_mono  endp

;-------------------------------------------------------------------
;-- TEST_6845: Returns set carry flag if 6845 doesn't lie in the
;--            port address in DX

test_6845  proc near

           mov   al,0Ah           ;Register 0AH
           out   dx,al            ;Register number in CRTC address reg.
           inc   dx               ;DX now in CRTC data register

           in    al,dx            ;Get contents of register 0AH
           mov   ah,al            ;and move to AH

           mov   al,4Fh           ;Any value
           out   dx,al            ;Write to register 0AH

           mov   cx,100           ;Short wait loop to which
waitforit: loop  waitforit        ;6845 can react

           in    al,dx            ;Read contents of register 0AH
           xchg  al,ah            ;Exchange Ah and AL
           out   dx,al            ;Send value

           cmp   ah,4Fh           ;Written value been read?
           je    t6845_end        ;Yes --> End test

           stc                    ;No --> Set carry flag

t6845_end: ret                    ;Back to caller

test_6845  endp

;-------------------------------------------------------------------
;-- FOUND_IT: Transfers type of video card to AL and type of     ----
;--          monitor in AH in the video vector                   ----

found_it   proc near

           mov   bx,di            ;Address of active structure
           cmp   word ptr [bx],0  ;Video system already  onboard?
           je    set_data         ;No --> Data in  active structure

           add   bx,2             ;Yes --> Inactive structure address

set_data:  mov   [bx],ax          ;Place data in structure
           ret                    ;Back to caller

found_it   endp

;-------------------------------------------------------------------

code       ends                   ;End of code segment
           end                    ;End of program
```

115

C listing: VIOSC.C

```
/*********************************************************************/
/*                         V I O S C                              */
/*------------------------------------------------------------------*/
/*   Task        : Determines the type of video card and monitor    */
/*                 installed in the system.                         */
/*------------------------------------------------------------------*/
/*   Author      : Michael Tischer                                  */
/*   Developed on : 10/02/88                                        */
/*   Last update  : 02/18/92                                        */
/*------------------------------------------------------------------*/
/*   (MICROSOFT C)                                                  */
/*   Compilation  : CL /AS /c VIOSC.C                               */
/*                  LINK VIOSC VIOSCA;                              */
/*   Call         : VIOSC                                          */
/*------------------------------------------------------------------*/
/*   (BORLAND TURBO C)                                             */
/*   Compilation  : Create project file made of the following:     */
/*                  VIOSC                                          */
/*                  VIOSCA.OBJ                                     */
/*   Info         : Some cards may return errors or "unknown"      */
/*********************************************************************/

/*== Declarations of external functions ============================*/

extern void get_vios( struct vios * );

/*== Type defs =====================================================*/

typedef unsigned char BYTE;               /* Create a byte */

/*== Structures ====================================================*/

struct vios {              /* Describe video card and attached monitor */
             BYTE vcard,
                  monitor;
            };

/*== Constants =====================================================*/

/*-- Constants for the video card ----------------------------------*/

#define NO_VIOS    0                   /* No video card */
#define VGA        1                   /* VGA card */
#define EGA        2                   /* EGA card */
#define MDA        3           /* Monochrome Display Adapter */
#define HGC        4            /* Hercules Graphics Card */
#define CGA        5           /* Color Graphics Adapter */

/*-- Constants for monitor type ------------------------------------*/

#define NO_MON     0                   /* No monitor */
#define MONO       1            /* Monochrome monitor */
#define COLOR      2                 /* Color monitor */
#define EGA_HIRES  3        /* High-res/multisync monitor */
#define ANLG_MONO  4         /* Analog monochrome monitor */
#define ANLG_COLOR 5             /* Analog color monitor */

/*********************************************************************/
/**                    MAIN PROGRAM                               **/
/*********************************************************************/

void main()
{
static char *vcnames[] = {          /* Pointer to the video card name */
                "VGA",
                "EGA",
                "MDA",
                "HGC",
                "CGA"
                };

static char *monnames[] = {   /* Pointer to the monitor type's name */
                 "monochrome monitor",
                 "color monitor",
                 "high-res/multisync monitor",
                 "analog monochrome monitor",
                 "analog color monitor"
                 };

struct vios vsys[2];                      /* Vector for GET_VIOS */

get_vios( vsys );                       /* Determine video system */
printf("\nVIOSC (c) 1988, 1992 by Michael Tischer\n\n");
printf("Primary video system:   %s card/ %s\n",
      vcnames[vsys[0].vcard-1], monnames[vsys[0].monitor-1]);
if ( vsys[1].vcard != NO_VIOS ) /* Is there secondary video system? */
  printf("Secondary video system: %s card/ %s\n",
        vcnames[vsys[1].vcard-1], monnames[vsys[1].monitor-1]);
}
```

Assembler listing: VIOSCA.ASM

```
;************************************************************;
;*                     V I O S C A                        *;
;*--------------------------------------------------------*;
;*   Task       : Creates a function for determining video *;
;*                adapter and monitor type, when linked with *;
;*                a C program.                             *;
;*--------------------------------------------------------*;
;*   Author     : Michael Tischer                          *;
;*   Developed on : 10/02/88                               *;
;*   Last update : 02/18/92                                *;
;*--------------------------------------------------------*;
;*   Assembly    : MASM VIOSCA;                            *;
;*                ... link to a C program                  *;
;************************************************************;

;== Constants for VIOS structure =========================

                          ;Video card constants
NO_VIOS   = 0             ;No video card
VGA       = 1             ;VGA card
EGA       = 2             ;EGA card
MDA       = 3             ;Monochrome Display Adapter
HGC       = 4             ;Hercules Graphics Card
CGA       = 5             ;Color Graphics Adapter


                          ;Monitor constants
NO_MON    = 0             ;No monitor
MONO      = 1             ;Monochrome monitor
COLOR     = 2             ;Color monitor
EGA_HIRES = 3             ;High-resolution or multisync monitor
ANLG_MONO = 4             ;Analog monochrome monitor
ANLG_COLOR = 5            ;Analog color monitor

;== Segment declarations for the C program ===============

IGROUP group _text        ;Addition to program segment
DGROUP group const,_bss, _data  ;Addition to data segment
      assume CS:IGROUP, DS:DGROUP, ES:DGROUP, SS:DGROUP

CONST segment word public 'CONST';This segment includes all read-only
CONST ends                ;constants


_BSS  segment word public 'BSS'   ;This segment includes all
_BSS  ends                ;un-initialized static variables

_DATA segment word public 'DATA' ;Data segment

vios_tab  equ this byte

          ;-- Conversion table for return values of function 1AH, ----
          ;-- sub-function 00H of the VGA-BIOS              ----

          db NO_VIOS, NO_MON    ;No video card
          db MDA   , MONO       ;MDA card and monochrome monitor
          db CGA   , COLOR      ;CGA card and color monitor
          db ?     , ?          ;Code 3 unused
          db EGA   , EGA_HIRES  ;EGA card and hi-res monitor
          db EGA   , MONO       ;EGA card and monochrome monitor
          db ?     , ?          ;Code 6 unused
          db VGA   , ANLG_MONO  ;VGA card and analog mono monitor
          db VGA   , ANLG_COLOR ;VGA card and analog color monitor
```

```
ega_dips  equ this byte

          ;-- Conversion table for EGA card DIP switch settings ------

          db COLOR, EGA_HIRES, MONO
          db COLOR, EGA_HIRES, MONO

_DATA ends

;== Program ===============================================

_TEXT segment byte public 'CODE' ;Program segment

public    _get_vios

;---------------------------------------------------------
;-- GET_VIOS: Determines types of installed video cards ---------
;-- Call from C : void get_vios( struct vios *vp );
;-- Declaration : struct vios { BYTE vcard, monitor; };
;-- Return value: none
;-- Info        : This example uses function in SMALL memory model

_get_vios proc near

sframe    struc               ;Stack access structure
cga_possi db ?                ;Local variable
ega_possi db ?                ;Local variable
mono_possi db ?               ;Local variable
bptr      dw ?                ;Take BP
ret_adr   dw ?                ;Return address to caller
vp        dw ?                ;Pointer to first VIOS structure
sframe    ends                ;End of structure

frame     equ [ bp - cga_possi ] ;Address elements of the structure

          push bp             ;Push BP onto stack
          sub  sp,3           ;Allocate space for local variables
          mov  bp,sp          ;Transfer SP to BP
          push di             ;Push DI onto stack

          mov  frame.cga_possi,1 ;Could be CGA
          mov  frame.ega_possi,1 ;Could be EGA
          mov  frame.mono_possi,1;Could be MDA or HGC

          mov  di,frame.vp    ;Get offset address of structure
          mov  word ptr [di],NO_VIOS   ;Still no video
          mov  word ptr [di+2],NO_VIOS ; system found

          call test_vga       ;Test for VGA card
          cmp  frame.ega_possi,0 ;EGA card still possible?
          je   gv1            ;No --> Test for CGA

          call test_ega       ;Test for EGA card
gv1:      cmp  frame.cga_possi,0 ;CGA card still possible
          je   gv2            ;No --> Test for MDA/HGC

          call test_cga       ;Test for CGA card
gv2:      cmp  frame.mono_possi,0;MDA or HGC card still possible?
          je   gv3            ;No --> End tests

          call test_mono      ;Test for MDA/HGC cards
```

117

```
              ;-- Determine active video card --------------------------

gv3:     cmp  byte ptr [di],VGA ;VGA card active?
         je   gvi_end          ;Yes --> Active card determined
         cmp  byte ptr [di+2],VGA ;VGA card as secondary system?
         je   gvi_end          ;Yes --> Active card determined

         mov  ah,0Fh           ;Determine active video mode using
         int  10h              ;BIOS video interrupt

         and  al,7             ;Only modes 0-7 are of interest
         cmp  al,7             ;Monochrome card active?
         jne  gv4              ;NO, in CGA  or EGA mode

         ;-- MDA, HGC, or EGA card (mono) is active -----------------

         cmp  byte ptr [di+1],MONO ;Mono monitor in first structure?
         je   gvi_end          ;Yes --> Sequence O.K.
         jmp  short switch     ;NO, Change sequence

         ;-- CGA or EGA card currently active -----------------------

gv4:     cmp  byte ptr [di+1],MONO ;Mono monitor in first structure?
         jne  gvi_end          ;No --> Sequence O.K.

switch:  mov  ax,[di]          ;Get contents of first structure
         xchg ax,[di+2]        ;Exchange with second structure
         mov  [di],ax

gvi_end: pop  di               ;Get DI from stack
         add  sp,3             ;Get local variables from stack
         pop  bp               ;Get BP from stack
         ret                   ;Return to C program

_get_vios  endp

;-------------------------------------------------------------------------
;-- TEST_VGA: Determines whether a VGA card is installed

test_vga   proc near

         mov  ax,1a00h         ;Function 1AH, sub-function 00H
         int  10h              ;calls VGA-BIOS
         cmp  al,1ah           ;Is this function supported?
         jne  tvga_end         ;No --> End routine

         ;-- If function is supported, BH contains the active video -
         ;-- system code; BH contains the inactive video sys. code  -

         mov  cx,bx            ;Move result to CX
         xor  bh,bh            ;Set BH to 0
         or   ch,ch            ;Just one video system?
         je   tvga_1           ;Yes --> Convey first system's code

         ;-- Convert code of second system --------------------------

         mov  bl,ch            ;Move second system code to BL
         add  bl,bl            ;Add offset to table
         mov  ax,offset DGROUP:vios_tab[bx] ;Get code from table and
         mov  [di+2],ax        ;place in caller's structure
         mov  bl,cl            ;Move first system's codes to BL

         ;-- Convert code of first system ---------------------------
```

```
tvga_1:  add  bl,bl            ;Add offset to table
         mov  ax,offset DGROUP:vios_tab[bx] ;Get code from table and
         mov  [di],ax          ;place in caller's structure

         mov  frame.cga_possi,0 ;CGA test failed
         mov  frame.ega_possi,0 ;EGA test failed
         mov  frame.mono_possi,0 ;MONO still needs testing

         mov  bx,di            ;Address of active structure
         cmp  byte ptr [bx],MDA ;Monochrome system available?
         je   do_tmono         ;Yes --> Execute MDA/HGC test

         add  bx,2             ;Address of inactive structure
         cmp  byte ptr [bx],MDA ;Monochrome system available?
         jne  tvga_end         ;No --> End routine

do_tmono: mov word ptr [bx],0  ;Pretend that this system
                               ;is still unavailable
         mov  frame.mono_possi,1 ;Execute monochrome test

tvga_end: ret                  ;Back to caller

test_vga   endp

;-------------------------------------------------------------------------
;-- TEST_EGA: Determines whether an EGA card is installed

test_ega   proc near

         mov  ah,12h           ;Function 12H
         mov  bl,10h           ;Sub-function 10H
         int  10h              ;Call EGA-BIOS
         cmp  bl,10h           ;Is the function supported?
         je   tega_end         ;No --> End routine

         ;-- When this function is supported, CL contains the EGA ---
         ;-- card's DIP switch settings                           ---

         mov  al,cl            ;Move DIP switch settings to AL
         shr  al,1             ;Shift one position to the right
         mov  bx,offset DGROUP:ega_dips ;Offset address of table
         xlat                  ;Move element AL from table to AL
         mov  ah,al            ;Move monitor type to AH
         mov  al,EGA           ;It's an EGA card
         call found_it         ;Move data to vector

         cmp  ah,MONO          ;Connected to monochrome monitor?
         je   is_mono          ;Yes --> not MDA or HGC

         mov  frame.cga_possi,0 ;Cannot be a CGA card
         jmp  short tega_end   ;End routine

is_mono: mov  frame.mono_possi,0;If EGA card is connected to a mono
                               ;monitor, it can be installed as
                               ;either an HGC or MDA

tega_end: ret                  ;Back to caller

test_ega   endp

;-------------------------------------------------------------------------
;-- TEST_CGA: Determines whether a CGA card is installed

test_cga   proc near
```

```
        mov  dx,3D4h       ;CGA tests port addr. of CRTC addr.    test_6845  proc near
        call test_6845     ;reg., to see if 6845 is installed
        jc   tega_end      ;No --> End test                              mov  al,0Ah       ;Register 10
                                                                         out  dx,al        ;Register number of CRTC address reg.
        mov  al,CGA        ;Yes --> CGA is installed                     inc  dx           ;DX now in CRTC data register
        mov  ah,COLOR      ;CGA has color monitor attached
        jmp  found_it      ;Transfer data to vector                      in   al,dx        ;Get contents of register 10
                                                                         mov  ah,al        ;and move to AH
test_cga  endp
                                                                         mov  al,4Fh       ;Any value
                                                                         out  dx,al        ;Write to register 10
;-------------------------------------------------------------
;-- TEST_MONO: Checks for the existence of an MDA or HGC card             mov  cx,100       ;Short delay loop--gives 6845 time
                                                              waitforit: loop waitforit    ; to react
test_mono  proc near
                                                                         in   al,dx        ;Read contents of register 10
        mov  dx,3B4h       ;Check port address of CRTC addr. reg          xchg al,ah        ;Exchange AH and AL
        call test_6845     ;with MONO to see if there's a 6845            out  dx,al        ;Send old value
                           ;installed
        jc   tega_end      ;No --> End test                              cmp  ah,4Fh       ;Written value read?
                                                                         je   t6845_end    ;Yes --> End test
        ;-- If there is a monochrome video card installed, the -----
        ;-- following determines whether it's an MDA or an HGC -----      stc               ;No --> Set carry flag

        mov  dl,0BAh       ;Read MONO status port using 3BAH   t6845_end: ret               ;Back from caller
        in   al,dx         ;
        and  al,80h        ;Check bit 7 only and               test_6845  endp
        mov  ah,al         ;move to AH

        ;-- If contents of bit 7 change during one of the following   ;-------------------------------------------------------------
        ;-- readings, the card is handled as an HGC -----             ;-- FOUND_IT: Transfers video card type to AL and monitor type to ----
                                                                     ;--          AH in the video vector                           ----
        mov  cx,8000h      ;Maximum of 32768 loop executions
test_hgc: in  al,dx        ;Read status port                   found_it   proc near
        and  al,80h        ;Check bit 7 only
        cmp  al,ah         ;Contents changed?                          mov bx,di           ;Address of active structure
        jne  is_hgc        ;Bit 7 = 1 --> HGC                          cmp word ptr [bx],0 ;Video system already onboard?
        loop test_hgc      ;Continue loop                             je  set_data        ;No --> Data in active structure

        mov  al,MDA        ;Bit 7 <> 1 --> MDA                         add bx,2            ;Yes --> Inactive structure address
        jmp  set_mono      ;Set parameters
                                                              set_data: mov [bx],ax         ;Place data in structure
is_hgc:  mov  al,HGC       ;Bit 7 = 1 --> is HGC                        ret                 ;Back to caller
set_mono: mov  ah,MONO     ;MDA/HGC on mono monitor
        jmp  found_it      ;Set parameters                    found_it   endp

test_mono  endp
                                                              ;-------------------------------------------------------------
;-------------------------------------------------------------  _text    ends              ;End of code segment
;-- TEST_6845: Sets carry flag if no 6845 exists in port address of DX   end                ;End of program
```

4.4 Anatomy of a Video Card

Regardless of whether a card is an old MDA or the newest Super VGA card, all video cards operate under the same principles. Before we discuss each video standard in detail, we'll look at the general design of video cards. You'll learn how a monitor generates a video image and how to control the CRT controller. We'll also discuss the CRT controller's registers.

This section also contains information about video RAM and how you can use it for creating a video image. In addition, you'll learn the basics of video RAM programming.

Getting to the screen

The character generator first accesses video RAM and reads each characters individually. It uses a character pattern table to construct the bitmap that will later form the character on the screen. The attribute controller also receives information about the display attributes (color, underlining, reverse, etc.) of the character from the video RAM.

Both the character generator and the attribute controller prepare this information and send it to the signal controller. This controller converts the information to the appropriate signals, which are sent to the monitor. The signal controller itself is controlled by the CRT controller, which is the central point of video card operations. Besides the monitor and the video RAM, this CRT controller is one of the most important components of a video system. We'll discuss all these components in detail.

The monitor

The monitor is the device on which the video data is displayed. Unlike the video card, the monitor is a "dumb" device. This means that it has no memory and cannot be programmed. All monitors used with PCs are *raster-scan devices*, in which the picture consists of many small dots arranged in a rectangular pattern or raster.

When forming the picture, the electron beam of the picture tube touches each individual dot and illuminates it if it's supposed to be visible on the screen. This is done by switching on the electron beam as it passes over this dot, which causes a phosphor particle on the picture tube to light up.

Color monitors

While monochrome monitors need only one electron beam to create a picture, color monitors use three beams that scan the screen simultaneously. Here a screen pixel consists of three phosphor particles in the basic colors of light: red, green, and blue. Each color has a matching electron beam. Any color in the spectrum can be created by combining these three colors and varying their intensities.

However, since an ionized phosphor particle emits light for only a very brief period of time, the entire screen must be scanned many times per second to create the illusion of a stationary picture. PC monitors perform this task between 50 and 70 times per second. This repeated re-scanning is called the *refresh rate*. Generally, the quality of the picture improves as the refresh rate increases.

Each new screen image begins in the upper-left corner of the screen. From there, the electron beam moves to the right along the first raster line. When it reaches the end of this line, the electron beam moves back to the start of the next line down, similar to pressing the <Return> key on a typewriter. The electron beam then scans the second raster line, at the end of which it moves to the start of the next raster line, etc. Once it reaches the bottom of the screen, the electron beam returns to the upper-left corner of the screen and the process starts over again. The following illustration shows the path of the electron beam.

Remember the the video card, and not the monitor, controls the movement of the electron beam.

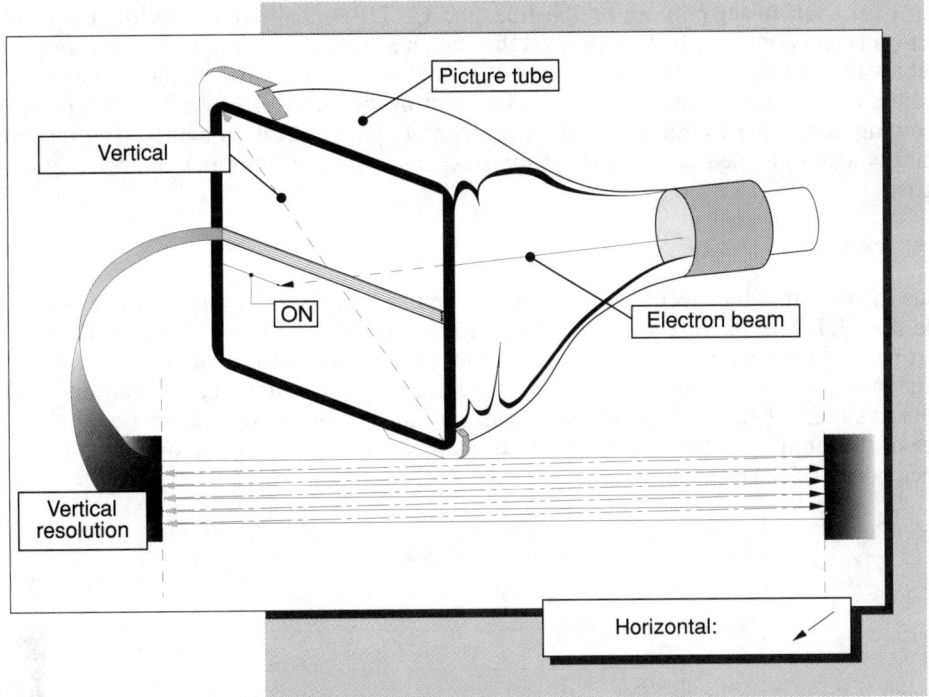

Electron beam scan movement

The resolution of the monitor naturally controls the number of raster lines and columns, which the electron beam scans when creating a display. So, a monitor that has only 200 raster lines of 640 raster columns each cannot handle the high resolutions of an EGA card at 640x350 pixels. The monitor types used with a PC generally have the following resolutions:

■ Resolution on different monitor types ■		
Monitor	Raster lines	Raster columns
MDA/Hercules	350	720
CGA	200	640
EGA	350	640
VGA*	350	640
Super VGA*	600	800
Multisync	Variable, up to 800	Variable, up to 1200
*Available in monochrome and color versions		

The CRT controller

The CRT controller or CRTC is the heart of a video card. It controls the operation of the video card and generates the signals the monitor needs to create the image. Its tasks also include controlling light pens, generating the cursor, and controlling the video RAM.

To inform the monitor of the next raster line, the CRTC sends a display enable signal at the start of each line. This signal activates the electron beam. While the beam moves from left to

121

right over each raster column of the line, the CRTC controls the individual signals for the electron beam(s) so the pixels appear on the screen as desired. At the end of the line, the CRTC disables the display enable signal so the electron beam's return to the next raster line doesn't produce a visible line on the screen. The electron beam is directed to the left edge of the following raster line by the output of a horizontal synchronization signal. The display enable signal is again enabled at the start of the next raster line and the generation of the next line begins.

Overscan

Since the time that the electron beam needs to return to the start of the next line is less than the time the CRTC needs to receive and prepare new information from the video RAM, there is a short pause. However, the electron beam cannot be stopped, so *overscan* occurs, which is visible as the left and right borders of the actual screen contents. Although this is an undesirable side effect, it's useful because it prevents the edges of the screen contents from being hidden by the edge of the monitor. If the electron beam is enabled while it's traveling over this border, a color screen border can be created.

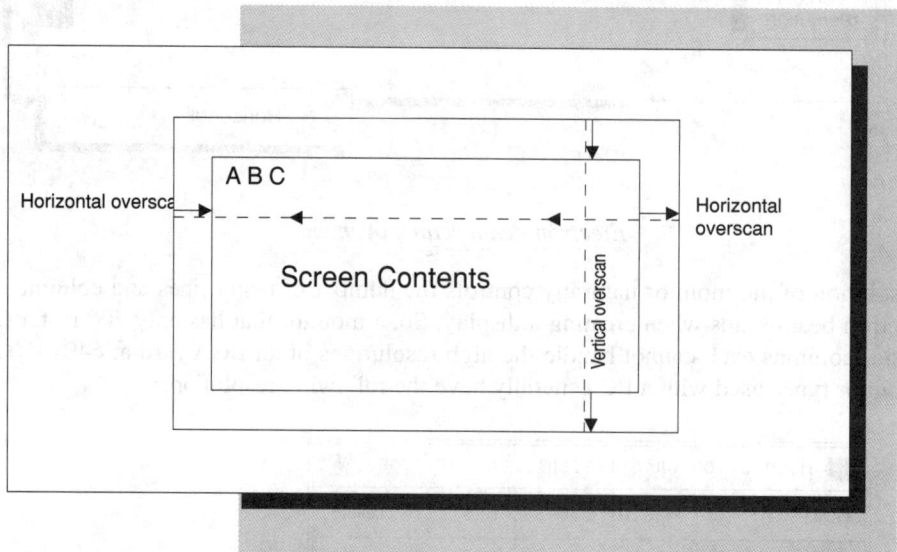

Rasters and overscan on a screen

Once the electron beam reaches the end of the last raster line, the display enable signal is disabled, and a vertical synchronization signal is sent. The electron beam returns to the upper-left corner of the screen. Again the display enable signal is re-enabled and scanning begins again.

Pause and overscan

As with the horizontal electron beam return, a pause occurs. This pause is displayed in the form of overscan, which creates a vertical screen border.

The registers of the CRT controller

The timing of individual signals varies depending on the video mode. For this reason, the CRTC has numerous registers that describe the signal outputs and their timing. The structure of these registers and how they are programmed will be discussed in the remainder of this section. Many of these registers originate from the registers of the 6845 video controller from Motorola. This controller is used in the MDA, CGA, and Hercules graphics cards. The EGA and VGA cards use a special VLSI (very large scale integration) chip as a CRTC, and its registers are slightly more complicated. The techniques described here are intended as general descriptions for all video cards.

Motorola 6845 video controller registers		
Register	Meaning	Access
0CH	Starting address of screen page (high byte)	Write
0DH	Starting address of screen page (low byte)	Write
0EH	Character address of blinking screen cursor (high byte)	Read / Write
0FH	Character address of blinking screen cursor (low byte)	Read / Write
10H	Light pen position (high byte)	Read
11H	Light pen position (low byte)	Read

These registers, like all the other registers on the video card, are accessed using I/O ports with the assembly language instructions IN and OUT. Instead of being accessed directly from the address space of the processor, the registers of the CRTC are accessed through a special address register. The number of the desired CRTC register is written to the port corresponding to this address register. Then the contents of this register can be read into a special data register with the IN assembly language instruction. If a value must be written to the addressed register, it must be transferred to the data register with the OUT instruction. Then the CRTC automatically places it in the desired register. Although these two registers are actually found at successive port addresses, these addresses vary among video cards.

Monochrome video card port addresses are 3B4H and 3B5H, and color card port addresses are 3D4H and 3D5H.

Throughout this chapter we've included tables to describe the contents of individual CRTC registers under the various video modes. The following example shows how the contents of these registers are calculated and how the individual registers are related to each other. If you try some of these calculations with your calculator or PC, you'll notice that some of them do not work out evenly. But since the registers of the CRTC hold only integer values, they will be rounded up or down.

The basis for the various calculations are the bandwidth and the horizontal and vertical scan rates of a monitor. As the following table shows, MDA, CG, and Hercules cards operate with a single bandwidth, while EGA and VGA cards have two or more different bandwidths. Although Super VGA cards use normal VGA bands, they can operate with more bandwidths.

Bandwidths and scan rates of different video cards				
Video card	Resolution	Bandwidth	Vertical scan rate	Horizontal scan rate
MDA	720 x 350	16.257 MHz	50 Hz*	18.43 KHz*
CGA	640 x 200	14.318 MHz	60 Hz	15.75 KHz
HGC	640 x 200	14.318 MHz	50 Hz	18.43 KHz
EGA	640 x 350 640 x 200 720 x 350	16.257 MHz 14.318 MHz 16.257 MHz	60 Hz 60 Hz 50 Hz	21.85 KHz 15.75 KHz 18.43 KHz
VGA	640 x 350 640 x 200 720 x 480	16.257 MHz 14.318 MHz 28.000 MHz	60 Hz 60 Hz 70 Hz	21.85 KHz 15.75 KHz 31.50 KHz
*MHz=Megahertz, KHz=Kilohertz, Hz=Hertz				

The bandwidths in the previous table specify the number of points that the electron beam scans per second. This is also called the point or dot rate. The vertical scan rate specifies the number of screen refreshes per second, while the horizontal scan rate refers to the number of raster lines that the electron beam scans per second.

Starting with these values, let's practice calculating the individual CRTC register values for the 80x25 character text mode on a CGA card.

Occasionally you can determine the number of bands supported by a video card by looking at the circuitry of the card. The video card needs a quartz crystal for each bandwidth and for keeping the CRT controller as accurate as possible. You can easily identify the crystal components on the board by looking for a component or set of components that are silver instead of black. The timing rate should be printed on these crystals.

If you want to look at the Hercules card's graphics mode, you can activate it by directly accessing the different CRTC registers. Function 00H initializes these registers. However, it's interesting to look at the different values that apply to each CRTC register, such as the values needed to produce 80x25 character text mode on a CGA card.

Since a CGA card has an 8x8 character matrix, a screen resolution of 80x25 characters corresponds to a "graphic" resolution of 640x200 pixels. This mode amounts to a bandwidth of 14.318 MHz, a screen refresh frequency of 60 Hz, and a horizontal scan rate of 15.740 KHz.

To obtain the number of pixels (screen dots) per raster line, divide the bandwidth by the horizontal scan rate.

```
    Bandwidth                    14.318 MHz
  ÷ Horizontal scan rate         15.570 KHz
  -------------------------------------------------
    Pixels per line              919
```

Since the CRTC registers usually refer to the number of characters instead of pixels, this value must be converted to the number of characters per line. This is done by dividing the number of pixels per line by the width of the character matrix. On the CGA card this is eight pixels.

```
      Pixels per line        919
  ÷   Pixels per character      8
  ---------------------------------------------
      Characters per line    114
```

This value, decremented by one, is placed in the first register of the CRTC and specifies the total number of characters per line. In the second register we load the number of characters that will actually be displayed per line. The 80x25 character text mode usually provides 80 characters.

The difference between the total and the number of characters actually displayed per line is the number of characters that can be displayed between the horizontal return and the overscan. In this instance, the difference is 34 characters.

The duration of the horizontal beam return must be entered in the fourth register of the CRTC. This register stores the number of characters that could be displayed during this time, rather than the actual time duration. The monitor specifications define this instead of the video card itself. Usually this number is between 5% and 15% of the total number of characters per line. A color monitor uses exactly ten characters.

This leaves 24 characters for the overscan (the horizontal screen border). The third CRTC register specifies how these characters are divided between the left and right screen borders. This register specifies the number of character positions that will be scanned before the horizontal beam return occurs. The BIOS specifies the value 90 here, or after ten characters have been displayed for the screen borders. The remaining 14 characters are placed at the start of the next line and form the left screen border.

The calculations for the vertical data, the number of vertical lines, the position of the vertical synchronization signal, etc., follow a similar scheme. The first calculation is the number of raster lines per screen. This results from the division of the number of lines displayed per second by the number of screen refreshes per second:

```
      Pixels per line        919
  ÷   Pixels per character      8
  ---------------------------------------------
      Characters per line    114
      Horizontal scan rate   15.750 KHz
  ÷   Screen refreshes        60    Hz
  ---------------------------------------------
      Raster lines           262
```

Since the characters in CGA text mode are eight pixels high by eight pixels wide, again we divide by eight to obtain the number of text lines per screen:

```
      Raster lines           262
  ÷   Pixels per character      8
  ---------------------------------------------
      Lines per screen        32
```

This result must be decremented by 1 and loaded into the fifth CRTC register (resulting in 7). The seventh register receives the number of lines to be displayed per screen (25). Seven lines less are displayed on the screen. So after overscan, the vertical rescan occurs after the 28th line.

The character height must be decremented by one and loaded into CRTC register 9. The decrement result is 7 in this example. This value also determines the range for the values loaded into registers 0AH and 0BH. They specify the first and last raster lines of the screen cursor. The cursor position is determined by the contents of registers 0EH and 0FH. They refer to the distance of the character from the upper-left corner of the screen, instead of line and column. This value is calculated by multiplying the cursor line by the number of columns per line and then adding the cursor column. The high byte of the result must be loaded into register 0EH and the low byte in register 0FH.

Structure of a video card

The CRT controller provides many tasks for screen design, but these tasks cannot work on their own. A video card consists of additional function levels which interact with the CRT controller. The following illustration shows the block diagram of a video card.

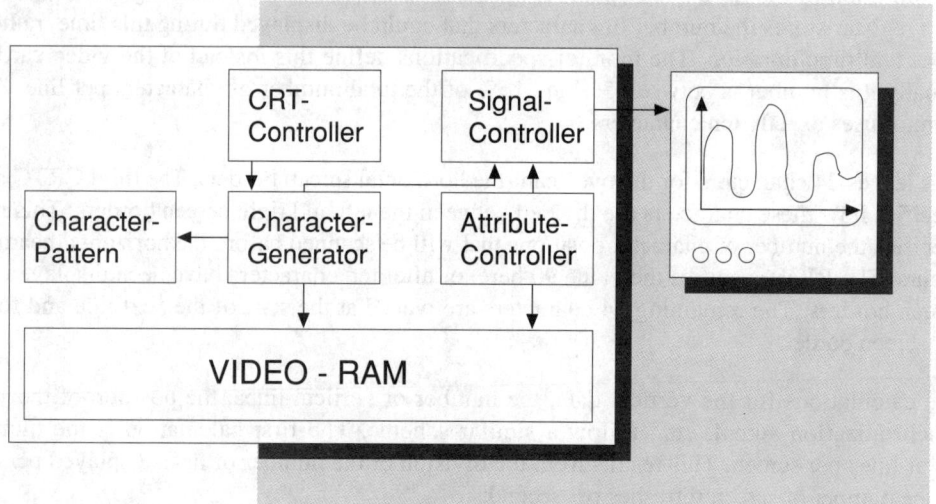

Block diagram of a video card

The video RAM is the most important starting point for creating a graphic. Video RAM is a memory range directly connected to the video card (more on this later). When the video card operates in text mode, video RAM contains the ASCII character codes and the character colors, while in graphic mode, video RAM is used to store individual pixels and the number of bits needed for colors.

Video RAM accessed the character generator and attribute controller from text mode. First, an instruction from the CRT controller loads a character from video RAM and generates the character from pixels. A ROM chip containing all the character patterns found in the ASCII character set converts the patterns into table form. The result of this conversion is then passed directly to the signal controller, which is driven by the CRT controller. This signal controller instructs the lines in the monitor cable to display the character pattern.

The signal controller and attribute controller prepare for output. In text mode, the CRT controller is responsible for conveying the character color and reading the signal controller. Although other orders aren't needed for graphics mode, the alternate structure of video RAM must be remembered.

If you look at an early video card, you'll see that it's easy to visually divide it into function units. One reason this is possible is because of the different ICs scattered around the card. Because of advances in miniaturization, almost all components in modern video cards can be packed into a single IC. This applies to EGA and VGA cards, which have a more complicated design than older cards, but still closely match the previous block diagram.

In the following sections we'll present detailed information about the design of specific video cards.

4.4.1 Video RAM

Video RAM is a location common to all video cards (from MDA to Super VGA), whether in text mode or graphics mode. Before you can directly program a graphics card (i.e., communicate with the card's ROM BIOS), you must know the design and position of video RAM. While video RAM is organized differently in different video cards when in graphics mode, the structure is virtually identical for all video cards in text mode.

In this section you'll learn about video RAM organization in different graphics modes. You'll find descriptions of different video cards, as well as how to set and read different graphics modes.

Video RAM in the PC's address space

You may already know that a PC's RAM doesn't always have to be on the motherboard; it can also exist on an expansion card. Video cards often use this expansion RAM as address space and video RAM.

Although the video cards themselves are established, the video RAM found in a PC's address range isn't completely flexible. Much of this space is already committed to other tasks. Remember that the early PCs had to store RAM, ROM, and any system extensions into one megabyte. Video cards only need memory segments A and B, starting at segment addresses A000H and B000H, which requires only 64K.

In order for the user to utilize these features, both a monochrome card and color card must be running simultaneously. The B segment would be divided into two equal parts. Monochrome video cards (i.e., MDA and Hercules) use video RAM in the range B000:0000 to B000:7FFF. Color cards (i.e., CGA, EGA, and VGA) use video RAM starting at B800:0000.

The locations of video RAM in EGA and VGA cards isn't always clear. For example, an MDA monitor can be connected to an EGA card, and the EGA card will then emulate an MDA card. Then video RAM begins at B000H (which would also apply to an MDA) instead of B800H. The case is similar with VGA cards. You cannot connect an MDA monitor to a VGA card, but you can run a VGA monitor from the MDA. In either case, the video RAM begins at B000H.

However, a video card won't always use the entire 32K that's allocated for it. So, the MDA card uses only the first 4K of video RAM, the CGA card uses the first 16K (one half of the available address range), and the Hercules card uses 32K and may extend into the second half of the B segment. The range beginning at B800:0000 acts as the second screen page. Changing DIP switches on the video card may be required, if range B800:0000 is being used by a color card.

Also, EGA and VGA cards use a large portion of video RAM. Generally, these cards use up to 256K of video RAM; most of the first 32K of the B segment is used frequently. Section 4.8.2 demonstrates how to access the remaining portion of video RAM.

Addressing video RAM

Since video RAM is part of the PC's normal address space, usually it can be accessed just like normal RAM. The entire video RAM can be read with a screen refresh rate of 70 times per second by different components of the video card, which generates a video image.

While this access isn't possible during an application or during ROM BIOS access, most video cards include options for avoiding memory conflict while accessing video RAM. The only exception is the older IBM CGA cards, which required some foresight in ROM BIOS or program access. (We'll discuss this in more detail in Section 4.7.)

Video RAM structure in text mode

Most programs operate in text mode. However, some characters can be written directly to video RAM, regardless of the type of video card installed. Many programs, such as Lotus 1-2-3 and dBASE IV, use this option, with the help of equivalent BIOS functions.

At the end of this section you'll find programs in Pascal and C. Both programs demonstrate direct access to video RAM in text mode. You could improve the speed even more by writing the code in assembly language. However, the routines are already quite fast.

To understand how these routines work, you'll need a visual idea of how video RAM works, as demonstrated in the figure on the next page.

As you can see from the illustration, in video RAM each screen position is represented as two bytes. The ASCII code of the character to be displayed is placed in the first of these two bytes (the one with the even address). By using eight bits per character code, a maximum of 256 characters can be displayed. See Section 4.2 for more information on the PC character set.

The attribute byte (which defines the appearance of the character on the screen) follows the ASCII code. The attribute byte always appears at the odd offset address. The attribute controller subdivides this byte into two nibbles. The most significant nibble (bits 4 to 7) contains the character background and the least significant nibble (bits 0 to 3) describes the character foreground. These nibbles contain two values between 0 and 15, depending on the type of monitor involved. A color monitor (CGA or EGA) can display up to 16 possible colors on the screen. Each character has its own foreground and background.

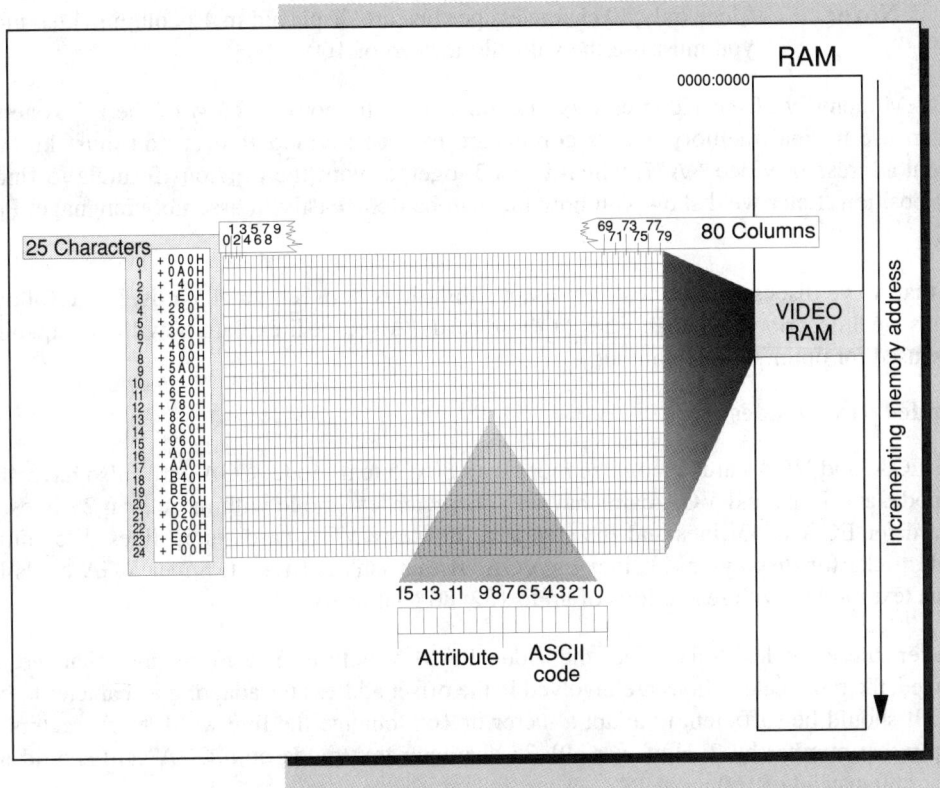

Normal video RAM structure in text mode

Character organization in video RAM

To access video RAM, you must know how the individual characters are organized within this memory. This organization is similar to character display on the screen.

The first character on the screen (the character in the upper-left corner) is also the first character in video RAM, located at offset position 0000H. The next character to the right is located at offset position 0002H. All 80 characters of the first screen line follow in this manner. Since each screen character requires two bytes of memory, each line occupies 160 bytes of RAM. The first character of the second screen line follows the last character of the first line, etc.

Finding character locations in video RAM

You can easily find the starting address of a line within video RAM by multiplying the line number (starting with zero) by 160. To get from the beginning of the line to a character within the line, the distance of the character from the start of the line must be added to this value. Since each character requires two bytes, this is done by simply multiplying the column number (also starting at zero) by two. Add both products together to obtain the offset position of the character in the video RAM. These calculations can be combined into a single formula:

```
Offset_position(row, column) = row * 160 + column * 2
```

129

Note: Since only 40 characters per line are displayed in 40-column video modes, you must use the value 80 instead of 160.

The RAM memory of the video card is integrated into the normal RAM of the PC system, so you can use normal memory access commands to access video RAM. You must know the segment address of video RAM, which is used together with the previous formula to find the offset position. Later we'll show you how this can be done easily in assembly language, Pascal and C.

Now that we've discussed the most important similarities between video cards, in the following sections we'll describe the capabilities of these cards. Also, we'll explain how these capabilities can be used for optimal screen output.

Extended text modes

CGA, EGA, and VGA cards recognize more than 80x25 text mode. CGA cards also have 40x25 text mode, and EGA and VGA cards have 80 character text mode with more than 25 lines. The standard for EGA is 43 lines and the standard for many VGA cards is 50 lines. We can also include tricks for displaying 43 lines on VGA. If that isn't sufficient, Super VGA cards have various text modes, with resolutions of up to 132x80 characters.

However, these modes don't affect the video RAM structure. The more lines that we want displayed, the more calculations are involved in the offset address for adapting a character to video RAM. It should be sufficient to adapt a factor of 160, change the line width to characters, and multiply that number by 2. However, 40x25 character text mode on a CGA card should use a factor of 80 instead of 160.

Occasionally, you won't have to program the video card. For example, a program run from DOS will usually start in 80x25 character text mode.

Access to different screen pages

As we mentioned earlier, Hercules, CGA, EGA, and VGA cards support multiple screen pages because video RAM offers much space for allocating a video page. To access multiple screen pages, you must take the formula discussed earlier and add the respective page to the offset address and starting offset.

We can organize the different screen pages in 40x25 text mode in 4K (4096 byte) units. Since a single screen page occupies 4000 bytes (80*25*2), 96 bytes are unused and ready for other applications.

The offset formula for screen pages and 80x25 text mode is similar to the following:

```
Offset_position(column, row) = row * 160 + column * 2 + page * 4096
```

The first screen page contains a value of 0.

Since the screen pages will be placed in 2K units, 40x25 text mode requires a factor of 2048 instead of 4096. If you're working with EGA and VGA text modes of 43 or 50 lines, then you must use a factor of 8K.

Demonstration programs

The following programs implement the above formula as a routine to transmit a string directly from video RAM to the screen. This is a small example, as many applications use multiple routines for direct video RAM access. These routines can include coloration of a screen range, storing screen contents in a window and restoring these contents later.

The three programs in BASIC, Pascal and C contain the same general components, but you'll notice that there are some major differences in the way these programs are coded because of language differences.

You'll find the display routine itself, as well as an initialization routine for accessing the segment address of video RAM. The program determines whether a monochrome card or color card is installed in the system, by examining one of the BIOS variables (see Chapter 3). So at first glance, the video RAM segment address doesn't seem to have anything to do with it, because it contains the address of the CRTC address register. Upon closer examination, however, you will notice a direct connection between these two bits of information:

On monochrome cards this register is always located at port address 3B4H, and the video RAM is always at segment address B000H. This connection between the port address of the address register and the segment address of the video RAM also applies to color cards, where the address register of the CRTC is always found at port address 3D4H and the video RAM is at segment address B800H. By determining the port address of the CRTC data register then, you find a statement about the segment address of the video RAM at the same time. Once you have determined this address, it is placed in a global variable and the initialization routine ends.

Along with this routine, all three programs have the actual output routine, which uses the segment address previously determined to access the video RAM. On top of that, the routine determines the start address of the screen page being displayed on the screen every time it is called. This is supposed to guarantee that the output also appears on the screen and is not redirected to a screen page that doesn't get displayed on the screen. The routine also uses a variable from the BIOS variable area. The variable CRT_START is located at the address 0040:004E and registers the offset address of the displayed screen page relative to the first screen page at offset address 0000H.

After determining this address, the video RAM can finally be accessed. However, if this is done within the program, it is dependent on the particular language to a great extent. Let's take a look at the programs.

The BASIC implementation

The BASIC version of this program performs the required task. The execution of this program is slow, because of the alternative means of display. However, this program is a good example of how BASIC can take full advantage of the 80x86 memory system. DEF SEG, PEEK and POKE perform much of this memory access.

While DEF SEG always defines the segment address of the "current" 64K segment, PEEK and POKE lets you read the contents of a byte (PEEK) and write new contents to a byte (POKE). The InitDPrint routine uses this technique to define the current segment as the BIOS variable segment. After defining the segment, two PEEK commands read the port address of the CRTC address register, and changes the contents of the VSeg variable to the segment address of video RAM.

Once the current video RAM segment is defined, the offset address of video RAM must be defined as well. From this address the program takes the screen page from the BIOS variable range and adds this page to the offset of the display position within video RAM. The row coordinates (the ScRow% variable) are multiplied by 160, and the column coordinates (the Column% variable) are multiplied by 2.

BASIC listing: DVIB.BAS

```
'*********************************************************
'*                      DVIB                            *
'*-------------------------------------------------------*
'* Task       : Demonstrates direct access to video RAM. *
'*-------------------------------------------------------*
'* Author     : Michael Tischer                          *
'* Developed on : 05/06/91                               *
'* Last update  : 02/05/92                               *
'*********************************************************

DECLARE SUB InitDPrint ()
DECLARE SUB Demo ()
DECLARE SUB DPrint (Column%, ScRow%, DColr%, StrOut AS STRING)


CONST NORMAL = &H7              'Define character attributes
CONST HIINT = &HF                 'on monochrome video card
CONST INVERSE = &H70
CONST UNDERSCORED = &H1
CONST BLINKING = &H80

CONST BLACK = &H0          'Color attributes on color video card
CONST BLUE = &H1
CONST GREEN = &H2
CONST CYAN = &H3
CONST RED = &H4
CONST VIOLET = &H5
CONST BROWN = &H6
CONST LGHTGRAY = &H7
CONST DARKGRAY = &H8
CONST LGHTBLUE = &H9
CONST LGHTGREEN = &HA
CONST LGHTCYAN = &HB
CONST LGHTRED = &HC
CONST LGHTVIOLET = &HD
CONST YELLOW = &HE
CONST WHITE = &HF

DIM SHARED VSeg AS LONG         'Segment address of video RAM

CALL InitDPrint               'Initialize DPrint information
CALL Demo                           'Demonstrate DPrint
END

'*********************************************************
'* Demo    : Demonstrates DPrint routine.               *
'* Input   : None                                       *
'* Output  : None                                       *
'*********************************************************
SUB Demo

DIM Column AS INTEGER                      'Display column
```

```
DIM ScRow AS INTEGER                       'Display row
DIM DColr AS INTEGER                        'Display attribute

RANDOMIZE TIMER                    'Initialize random generator

IF VSeg = &HB800 THEN               'Color adapter connected?
  CLS                                       'Clear screen
  CALL DPrint(22, 0, WHITE, " DVIB - (c) 1988, 92 by Michael Tischer ")
  DO
    Column = INT(76 * RND)              'Select random columns
    ScRow = INT(22 * RND) + 1             'Select random rows
    DColr = INT(14 * RND) + 1             'Select random color
    CALL DPrint(Column, ScRow, DColr, "█")        'Display block
  LOOP UNTIL INKEY$ <> ""       'Repeat until user presses a key
ELSE                             'Monochrome adapter connected
  CLS                                       'Clear screen
  CALL DPrint(22, 0, INVERSE, " DVIB - (c) 1988, 92 by Michael Tischer ")
  DO
    Column = INT(76 * RND)               'Select random column
    ScRow = INT(22 * RND) + 1              'Select random row
    SELECT CASE INT(4 * RND)     'Select random character attribute
      CASE 0
        DColr = NORMAL
      CASE 1
        DColr = HIINT
      CASE 2
        DColr = INVERSE
      CASE 3
        DColr = BLINKING OR INVERSE             'For maximum
visibility
    END SELECT
    CALL DPrint(Column, ScRow, DColr, "█")        'Display block
  LOOP UNTIL INKEY$ <> ""       'Repeat until user presses a key
END IF
END SUB


'*********************************************************
'* DPrint  : Writes a string directly to video RAM.     *
'* Input   :  - Column : The display column             *
'*            - ScRow  : The display row                *
'*            - DColr  : Character color (attribute)     *
'*            - StrOut : The string to be displayed      *
'* Output  : None                                       *
'*********************************************************
SUB DPrint (Column%, ScRow%, DColr%, StrOut AS STRING)

DIM Offset AS INTEGER          'Offset address of char. should be poked
DIM Counter AS INTEGER                        'Loop counter

DEF SEG = &H40              'Segment address of BIOS variable range
Offset = PEEK(&H4E) + PEEK(&H4F) * 256    'Get starting address of page
Offset = Offset + ScRow% * 160 + Column% * 2  'Offset address: 1st char.
```

```
DEF SEG = VSeg                       'Segment address of video RAM
FOR Counter = 1 TO LEN(StrOut)                   'Execute string
  POKE Offset, ASC(MID$(StrOut, Counter, 1))  'ASCII code in video RAM
  POKE Offset + 1, DColr%                    'Color in video RAM
  Offset = Offset + 2                 'Set offset to next character
NEXT
END SUB


'*******************************************************************
'* InitDPrint : Gets the segment address for DPrint.          *
'* Input      : None                                          *
'* Output     : The segment address of video RAM through the VSeg  *
```

```
'*          global variable                                   *
'*******************************************************************
SUB InitDPrint

DEF SEG = &H40            'Segment address: BIOS variable register
IF PEEK(&H63) + PEEK(&H64) * 256 = &H3B4 THEN     'Monochrome adapter?
  VSeg = &HB000                              'Video RAM at 8000:0000
ELSE                                              'Color adapter?
  VSeg = &HB800                              'Video RAM at B800:0000
END IF
END SUB
```

The Pascal implementation

The ABSOLUTE statement and assembler routines allow Turbo Pascal to handle video RAM as a normal variable. Turbo Pascal provides a simpler method of doing this.

Turbo Pascal's MEM and MEMW functions allow Turbo to access memory ranges with known offset and segment addresses outside the Turbo Pascal data segment MEM handles bytes, while MEMW handles words. The two arrays are virtual (i.e., they don't really exist) and cover the entire memory range.

Values can be read from and written to these arrays, using the following syntax:

```
MEMW[ Segmentaddr. : Offsetaddr. ] := Expression
```

or

```
Variable := MEMW[ Segmentaddr. : Offsetaddr. ]
```

We use the MEM array in a display procedure which takes converted ASCII characters and a constant attribute. The DPrint procedure uses the MEMW array, as one 16-bit access on a 16-bit PC runs much more quickly than two consecutive 8-bit accesses on the same machine.

The MEMW array in DPrint takes the video RAM segment address from the VSeg variable initialized at the beginning of the program in the InitDPrint procedure. This procedure checks the contents of the BIOS variable contained in the port address of the CRTC address register. This is declared like other BIOS variables, called from within DPrint. Turbo's ABSOLUTE function prepares both variables, then handles them as global variables.

During DPrint's access to video RAM, the screen page number and coordinates are taken from the offset address of the MEMW array. From this information, the row coordinates are multiplied by 160, and the column coordinates are multiplied by 2. The string being processed is incremented by 2, shifting the paired ASCII attribute bytes to the right.

The Write statement and corresponding procedures write the text to the screen, provided the Crt unit is linked to the program, and provided that DIRECTVIDEO is not set to FALSE.

Pascal listing: DVIP.PAS

```
{*****************************************************************}
{*                        D V I P                              *}
{*-------------------------------------------------------------*}
{*   Task     : Demonstrates direct access to video RAM.       *}
{*-------------------------------------------------------------*}
{*   Author   : Michael Tischer                                *}
{*   Developed on : 01/02/87                                   *}
{*   Last update  : 02/26/92                                   *}
{*****************************************************************}

program DVIP;

Uses Crt, Dos;                          { Add CRT and DOS units }

const NORMAL      = $07;        { Define character attributes }
      HIINT       = $0f;        { on monochrome video card   }
      INVERSE     = $70;
      UNDERSCORED = $01;
      BLINKING    = $80;

      BLACK       = $00;   { Color attributes on color video card }
      BLUE        = $01;
      GREEN       = $02;
      CYAN        = $03;
      RED         = $04;
      VIOLET      = $05;
      BROWN       = $06;
      LGHTGRAY    = $07;
      DARKGRAY    = $01;
      LGHTBLUE    = $09;
      LGHTGREEN   = $0A;
      LGHTCYAN    = $0B;
      LGHTRED     = $0C;
      LGHTVIOLET  = $0D;
      YELLOW      = $0E;
      WHITE       = $0F;

type TextType = string[80];

var VSeg : word;               { Segment address of video RAM }

{*****************************************************************}
{* InitDPrint: Gets the segment address for DPrint.            *}
{* Input   : None                                              *}
{* Output  : None                                              *}
{*****************************************************************}

procedure InitDPrint;

var CRTC_PORT : word absolute $0040:0063;  { Seg.addr.: BIOS var.reg. }

begin
  if CRTC_PORT = $3B4 then             { Monochrome adapter? }
    VSeg := $B000               { Yes --> Video RAM at B000:0000 }
  else                        { No --> Must be a color adapter }
    VSeg := $B800;                 { Video RAM at B800:0000 }
end;

{*****************************************************************}
{* DPrint: Writes a string directly to video RAM.             *}
```

```
{* Input   : - COLUMN: The display column                     *}
{*           - SCROW: The display row                         *}
{*           - DCOLR : Character color (attribute)            *}
{*           - STROUT: The string to be displayed            *}
{* Output  : None                                             *}
{*****************************************************************}

procedure DPrint( Column, SCRow, DColr : byte; StrOut : TextType);

var PAGE_OFS  : word absolute $0040:$004E;{ Seg. addr: BIOS var. reg. }
    Offset    : word;          { Pointer to current display position }
    i, j      : byte;                       { Loop counter }
    Attribute : word;                     { Display attribute }

begin
  Offset := SCRow * 160 + Column * 2 + PAGE_OFS;
  Attribute := DColr shl 8;  { High byte for word access to video RAM }
  i := length( StrOut );                { Get string length }
  for j:=1 to i do                      { Execute string }
    begin                { Apply next character attribute to video RAM }
      memw[VSeg:Offset] := Attribute or ord( StrOut[j] );
      Offset := Offset + 2;      { Set to next ASCII attribute pair }
    end;
end;

{*****************************************************************}
{* Demo: Demonstrates DPrint routine.                         *}
{* Input   : None                                             *}
{* Output  : None                                             *}
{*****************************************************************}

procedure demo;

var Column,                           { Current display position }
    SCRow,
    DColr  : integer;

begin
  TextBackGround( BLACK );                   { Black background }
  ClrScr;                                    { Clear screen }
  DPrint( 22, 0, WHITE, 'DVIP - (c) 1988, 1992 by Michael Tischer');
  Randomize;                       { Initialize reandom generator }
  while not KeyPressed do       { Repeat until user presses a key }
    begin
      Column := Random( 76 );          { Column, row and color }
      SCRow := Random( 22 ) + 1;       { Select random factors }
      DColr := Random( 14 ) + 1;
      DPrint( Column, SCRow,   DColr, '██'); { Display block }
      DPrint( Column, SCRow+1, DColr, '██');
    end;
  ClrScr;                                    { Clear screen }
end;

{*****************************************************************}
{**                    MAIN PROGRAM                          **}
{*****************************************************************}

begin
  InitDPrint;                     { Initialize DPrint display }
  Demo;                           { Demonstrate DPrint }
end.
```

The C implementation

This is the neatest of the three solutions, because the video RAM is treated as a normal variable. First, the VELB structure is defined, which describes the ASCII attribute pair as found in the video RAM. A new data type called VP is formed as pointers to this structure. It is important that these be FAR type pointers, since these structures are within the video RAM, placing them outside of the C data segment. It is impossible to reach them in smaller memory models with their NEAR addressing without explicitly specifying the command word FAR.

The VPTR global variable within the INIT_DPRINT initialization routine is created as a pointer to the first ASCII attribute pair in page 0 of the video RAM. Within the actual output routine, it serves the DPRINT function as a basis for addressing the characters within the video RAM.

The LPTR pointer is loaded in the DPRINT output function with the address of the passed output position in the screen. First, the pointer is loaded with the contents of the VPTR global variable, with the offset address of the displayed screen page (from the variables in the BIOS region) being added to it.

Don't forget that the LPTR pointer must first be cast in a BYTE pointer, since the contents of the BIOS variables don't refer to the VELB structure, but rather to Byte. Without the appropriate CAST operator, the C compiler would generate a code that multiplied the contents of the BIOS variables by the length of the VELB structure (2 bytes) before the addition, giving us the wrong result.

The actual output position, transmitted to the DPRINT function in the form of a Y- and an X-coordinate, must be added to the pointer. The video RAM is viewed as a kind of vector, whose 2000 components consist of the VELP structure. Since you have already determined the base address of this vector in LPTR, all that's left is to determine the index in this vector. Multiply the X-coordinate times 80 (columns per line) and then add the Y-coordinate. As an end result, you get a pointer to the output position in the video RAM, which can be treated like any other C pointer.

This pointer executes the specified string by pointing to the next VELB structure on each loop run. On each execution of the loop, the next ASCII attribute pair is placed in video RAM. The DPRINT function writes the ASCII code and character color to the specified string. This process repeats until the last character in the string is reached.

C listing: DVIC.C

```
/******************************************************************/
/*                         D V I C                             */
/*------------------------------------------------------------*/
/*  Task        : Demonstrates direct access to video RAM.     */
/*------------------------------------------------------------*/
/*  Author      : Michael Tischer                              */
/*  Developed on : 10/01/88                                    */
/*  Last update  : 02/26/92                                    */
/*------------------------------------------------------------*/
/*  (MICROSOFT C)                                              */
/*  Compilation : CL /AS /WO DVIC.C                            */
/*  Call        : DVIC                                         */
/*------------------------------------------------------------*/
/*  (BORLAND TURBO C)                                          */
/*  Compilation  : Use Run command (no project file needed)    */
/******************************************************************/

/*== Add include files =======================================*/

#include <dos.h>
#include <stdlib.h>
#include <string.h>
#include <stdarg.h>
#include <bios.h>

/*== Type definitions ========================================*/

typedef unsigned char BYTE;              /* Create a byte */
```

```
typedef struct velb far * VP;        /* VP = FAR pointer to video RAM */
typedef BYTE BOOL;                   /* like BOOLEAN in Pascal */

/*== Structures =======================================================*/

struct velb {                 /* Describes a screen position as 2 bytes */
          BYTE zeichen,                 /* ASCII code */
               attribut;               /* Corresponding attribute */
          };

/*== Macros ===========================================================*/

/*-- MK_FP creates a FAR pointer to an object ----------------------*/
/*-- from a segment address and offset address ---------------------*/

#ifndef MK_FP                         /* MK_FP still not defined? */
#define MK_FP(seg, ofs) ((void far *) ((unsigned long) (seg)<<16|(ofs)))
#endif

#define COLOR(VG, HG) ((VG << 3) + HG)

/*== Constants ========================================================*/

#define TRUE   1              /* Constants for working with BOOL */
#define FALSE  0

/*-- The following constants return pointers to BIOS ---------------*/
/*-- variables at segment address 0x40               ---------------*/

#define CRT_START ((unsigned far *) MK_FP(0x40, 0x4E)
#define ADDR_6845 ((unsigned far *) MK_FP(0x40, 0x63)

#define NORMAL       0x07      /* Define character attributes */
#define HIINT        0x0f      /* for monochrome video card   */
#define INVERSE      0x70
#define UNDERSCORED  0x01
#define BLINKING     0x80

#define BLACK        0x00      /* Color attributes for color card */
#define BLUE         0x01
#define GREEN        0x02
#define CYAN         0x03
#define RED          0x04
#define VIOLET       0x05
#define BROWN        0x06
#define LGHTGRAY     0x07
#define DARKGRAY     0x01
#define LGHTBLUE     0x09
#define LGHTGREEN    0x0A
#define LGHTCYAN     0x0B
#define LGHTRED      0x0C
#define LGHTVIOLET   0x0D
#define YELLOW       0x0E
#define WHITE        0x0F

/*== Global variables =================================================*/

VP vptr;              /* Pointer to first character in video RAM */

/********************************************************************
*  Function      : D P R I N T                                     *
**----------------------------------------------------------------**
*  Task          : Writes a string directly to video RAM.         *
*                                                                  *
```

```
*  Input parameters : - COLUMN   = The display column             *
*                     - SCROW    = The display row                *
*                     - DCOLR    = Character color (attribute)     *
*                     - STROUT   = The string to be displayed     *
*  Return values  : None                                          *
********************************************************************/

void dprint(BYTE column, BYTE scrow, BYTE dcolr, char * string)

{
  register VP lptr;                /* Floating pointer to video RAM */
  register BYTE i;                 /* Points to number of characters */

  /*-- Set pointer to display position in video RAM ---------------*/
  lptr = (VP) ((BYTE far *) vptr + *CRT_START) + scrow * 80 + column;
  for (i=0 ; *string ; ++lptr, ++i)          /* Execute string */
  {
    lptr->zeichen = *(string++);       /* Character in video RAM */
    lptr->attribut = dcolr;            /* Set character attribute */
  }
}

/********************************************************************
*  Function      : I N I T _ D P R I N T                           *
**----------------------------------------------------------------**
*  Task          : Gets the segment address for DPrint.           *
*  Input parameters : None                                        *
*  Return values  : None                                          *
*  Info          : Segment address is stored in VPTR.             *
********************************************************************/

void init_dprint( void )
{
  vptr = (VP) MK_FP( (*ADDR_6845 == 0x3B4) ? 0xB000 : 0xB800, 0 );
}

/********************************************************************
*  Function      : C L S                                           *
**----------------------------------------------------------------**
*  Task          : Clears screen with help from DPrint.           *
*                                                                  *
*  Input parameters : CCOLR    = Character attribute              *
*  Return values  : None                                          *
********************************************************************/

void cls( BYTE ccolr )

{
  static char blankline[] =
    "                                                              " \
    "                                                              ";
  register BYTE i;                              /* Loop counter */

  for (i=0; i<24; ++i)                    /* Execute individial lines */
    dprint(0, i, ccolr, blankline);          /* Display blank line */
}

/********************************************************************
*  Function      : N O K E Y                                       *
**----------------------------------------------------------------**
*  Task          : Checks for a keypress.                         *
*  Input parameters : None                                        *
*  Return values  : TRUE when a key is pressed, otherwise FALSE.  *
********************************************************************/
```

```
BOOL nokey( void )


{
#ifdef __TURBOC__                        /* Turbo C used for compiling? */
 return( bioskey( 1 ) == 0 );      /* Yes --> Read keyboard using BIOS */
#else                                     /* No --> Microsoft C used */
 return( _bios_keybrd( _KEYBRD_READY ) == 0 );   /* Read using BIOS */
#endif
}


/**************************************************************/
/**                    MAIN PROGRAM                        **/
/**************************************************************/

void main()
{
 BYTE firstcol,                 /* Color for first square on screen */
      dcolr,                                   /* Current color */
      column,                          /* Current screen position */
      scrow;
```

```
 init_dprint();                    /* Get segment address of video RAM */
 cls( COLOR(BLACK, GREEN) );                   /* Clear the screen */
 dprint(22, 0, WHITE, "DVIC  - (c) 1988, 1992 by Michael Tischer");
 firstcol = BLACK;                        /* Start with basic BLACK */
 while( nokey() )                  /* Repeat until user presses a key */
 {
   if (++firstcol > WHITE)                    /* Last color found? */
    firstcol = BLUE;                  /* Yes --> Continue with BLUE */
   dcolr = firstcol;             /* Place first color on the screen */

   /*-- Fill the screen with squares --------------------------------*/

   for ( column=0; column < 80; column += 4)
    for (scrow=1; scrow < 24; scrow += 2)
     {
      dprint( column, scrow,   dcolr, "███");
      dprint( column, scrow+1, dcolr, "███");
      dcolr = ++dcolr & 15;
     }
 }
}
```

4.5 The IBM Monochrome Display Adapter (MDA)

The IBM Monochrome Display Adapter, or MDA, is probably the oldest video card. This card is based on the Motorola 6845 video controller, which is an intelligent peripheral chip. The 6845 controller constructs a display by generating the proper signals for the monitor from video RAM.

This card is excellent for text display because of its 9x14 character matrix, which permits high resolution character display. The format of this matrix is unusual since a character generator containing the bit pattern of each character can only produce characters that are 8 pixels wide. Characters from the IBM character set may not connect with each other (e.g., using box characters to draw a box). A circuit on the graphics card avoids this problem by copying the eighth pixel of the line into the ninth pixel for any characters whose ASCII codes are between B0H and DFH. This enables the horizontal box drawing characters to connect.

The character generator requires one byte for each screen line: one bit per pixel, eight bits per line. Each character requires 14 bytes. The complete character set has a memory requirement of almost 4K, which is stored in a ROM chip on the card. For some reason the card has an 8K ROM, so the second bank of 4K remains unused.

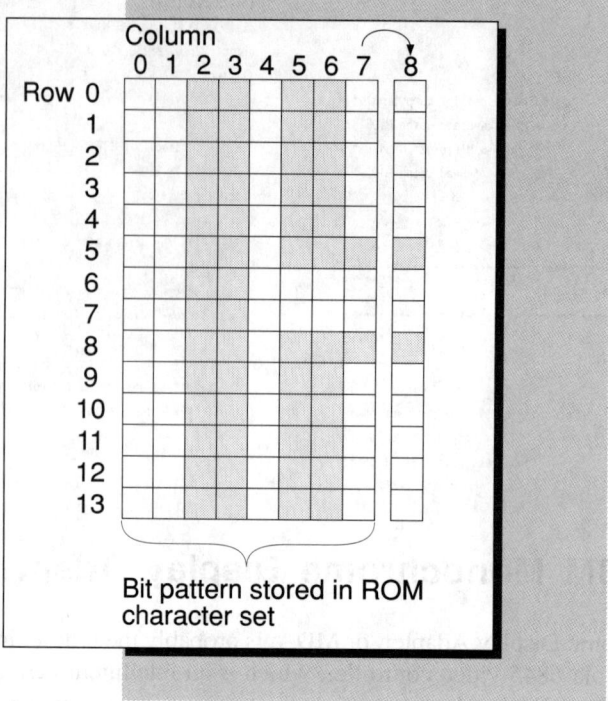

Monochrome Display Adapter—9x14 character matrix

Video RAM on the MDA

The video RAM of the card starts at address B000:0000 and extends over 4K (4,096 bytes). Since the screen display only has space for 2,000 characters and requires only 4,000 bytes of memory for those characters, the unused 96 bytes at the end of video RAM are available for other applications.

The following figure shows the meanings of the different values representing the attribute byte:

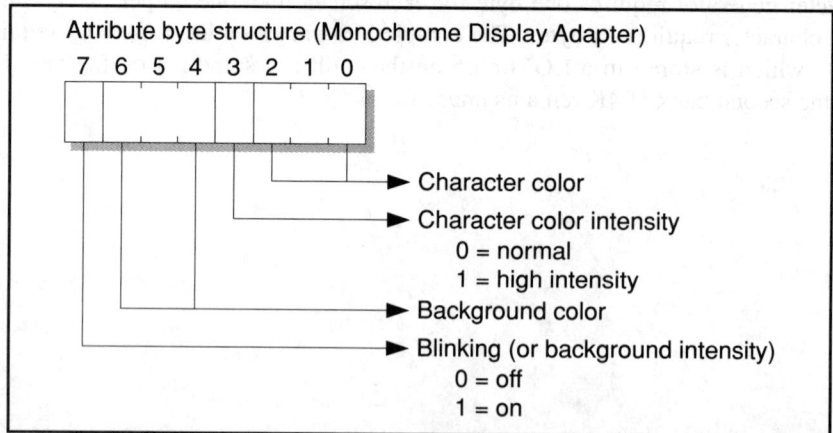

Any combination of bits can be loaded into this byte. However, the MDA only accepts the following combinations:

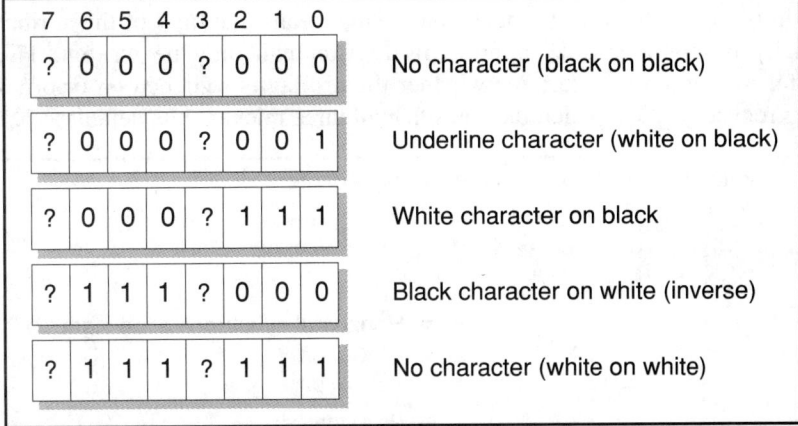

7	6	5	4	3	2	1	0	
?	0	0	0	?	0	0	0	No character (black on black)
?	0	0	0	?	0	0	1	Underline character (white on black)
?	0	0	0	?	1	1	1	White character on black
?	1	1	1	?	0	0	0	Black character on white (inverse)
?	1	1	1	?	1	1	1	No character (white on white)

Character and background color combinations (MDA)

Besides these bit combinations, bits 3 and 7 of the attribute byte can be set or unset. Bit 3 defines the intensity of the foreground display. When this bit is set, the characters appear in higher intensity. Bit 7's purpose varies with the contents of the control registers (more on this later). For now, all you need to know is that bit 7 can either enable blinking characters or enable an intensity matching the background color.

The control register and the status register are also available for monochrome cards.

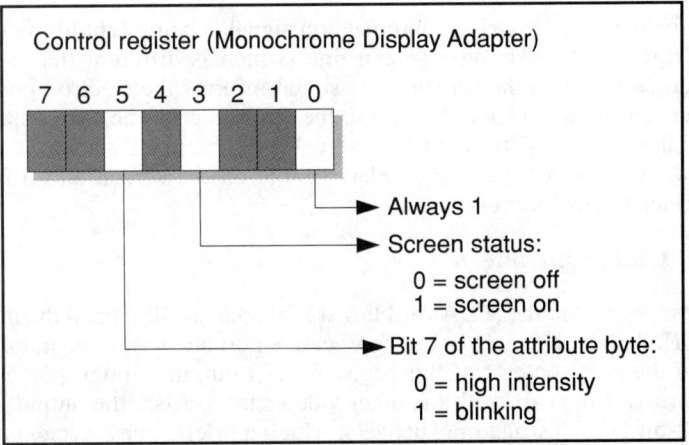

Control register (Monochrome Display Adapter)

7	6	5	4	3	2	1	0

➤ Always 1
➤ Screen status:
  0 = screen off
  1 = screen on
➤ Bit 7 of the attribute byte:
  0 = high intensity
  1 = blinking

MDA control register

The control register, which is located at port 3B8H, controls the monochrome display adapter's various functions. As the following figure shows, only bits 0, 3, and 5 are important. Bit 0 controls the resolution on the card. Although the card only supports one resolution (80x25 characters), this bit must be set to 1 during system initialization. Otherwise, the computer goes into an infinite wait loop. Bit 3 controls the creation of a visible display on the monitor. If bit 3 is set to 0, the screen is black and the blinking cursor disappears. If bit 3 is set to 1, the display returns to the screen. Bit 5 has a similar function. If bit 7 in the attribute byte of the character is set to 1, it enables blinking characters. If bit 7 contains the value 0, the character appears, unblinking, in front of a light background color. This means that bit 7 of the attribute byte acts as an intensity bit for the background. This register can only be written. This makes it impossible for a program to determine whether the display is switched on or off. The normal value for this register is 29H, which indicates that all three relevant bits default to 1.

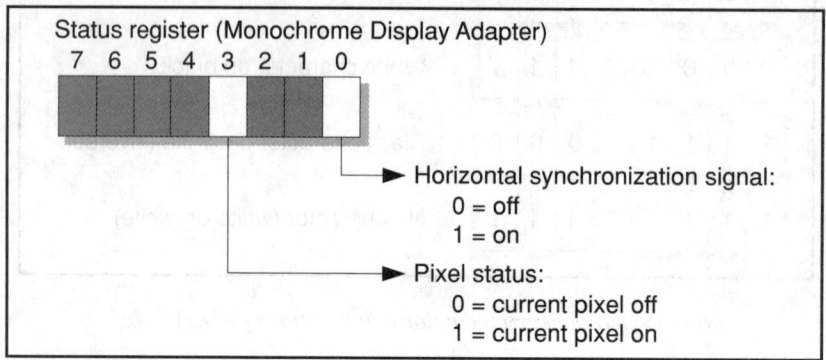

MDA status register

Only bits 0 and 3 are used in the status register; all the other bits must contain the value 1. Unlike the control register, programs can read this register, but register contents cannot be changed by program code.

Horizontal synchronization

Bit 0 indicates whether a horizontal synchronization signal is being sent to the screen. The video card sends this signal after creating a screen line (which is different than a text line, which consists of 14 screen lines) on the screen. This signal informs the electron gun, which "draws" the picture on the screen, that it should return to the left border of the current screen line. In this case, the bit has the value 1. Bit 3 contains the value of the pixel where the electron beam is currently located. A 1 signals that the pixel is visible on the screen and 0 indicates that the screen remains black at this location.

Accessing the CRT controller

The 6845's address register in the MDA card lies at port address 3B4H and the data register lies at port address 3B5H. Although these exist as consecutive port addresses, the number of registers to be addressed and the new contents of this register aren't output through port 3B4H by a 16-bit OUT instruction (this is the case with the other video cards). Also, the output must follow with the help of two 8-bit OUT instructions, between which a brief (5 or 6 cycles) pause is added to give the CRTC a chance to react to the output in the address register. Within an assembly language program, this pause executes, and, after the OUT instruction, is followed by a jump instruction.

```
JMP $+2
```

The transfer of program execution to the instructions that follow takes some time, but doesn't change the actual program execution. This time can be used by the CRTC to prepare access to the desired register.

Programming the CRTC register on this card consists of the starting and ending line of the blinking cursor and its position on the screen. These tasks can be easily accomplished using the function 10H sub-functions from the BIOS interrupts. This keeps hardware calls to a minimum.

If you want to juggle CRTC registers and create different displays, such as an 81 column or 26 line screen, you can do this by manipulating CRTC registers in the MDA card while in 80x25 text mode.

Reg.	Meaning	Content
	CRTC registers in 80x25 text mode (Monochrome Display Adapter)	
00H	Total horizontal character	97
01H	Display horizontal character	80
02H	Horizontal synchronization signal after ...char	82
03H	Duration of horiz. synchronization signal in char.	15
04H	Total vertical character	25
05H	Adjust vertical character	6
06H	Display vertical character	25
07H	Vertical synchronization signal after ...char	25
08H	Interlace mode	2
09H	Number of scan lines per screen line	13
0AH	Starting line of blinking screen cursor	11
0BH	Ending line of blinking screen cursor	12
0CH	Starting address of displayed screen page (high byte)	0
0DH	Starting address of displayed screen page (low byte)	0
0EH	Character addr. of blinking screen cursor (high byte)	0
0FH	Character addr. of blinking screen cursor (low byte)	0
10H	Light pen position (high byte)	*
11H	Light pen position (low byte)	*
	*not available on MDA	

The following program utilizes all the Monochrome Display Adapter's capabilities. It was written in assembly language. The individual routines are completely documented and require no additional explanation. The demonstration program that's built into the listing demonstrates some practical ways to use the individual routines.

Assembler listing: VMONO.ASM

```
;****************************************************************;
;*                      V M O N O                             *;
;*------------------------------------------------------------*;
;*   Task       : Makes some elementary functions available for *;
;*                access to the monochrome display screen.     *;
;*------------------------------------------------------------*;
;*   Info       : All functions subdivide the screen          *;
;*                into columns 0 to 79 and lines 0 to 24       *;
;*------------------------------------------------------------*;
;*   Author     : Michael Tischer                             *;
;*   Developed on : 8/11/87                                   *;
;*   Last update : 3/02/92                                    *;
;*------------------------------------------------------------*;
;*   Assembly    : MASM VMONO;                                *;
;*                LINK VMONO;                                  *;
;*------------------------------------------------------------*;
;*   Call        : VMONO                                      *;
;****************************************************************;

;== Constants ======================================

CONTROL_REG = 03B8h        ;Control register port address
ADDRESS_6845 = 04B4h       ;6845 address register
DATA_6845   = 03B5h        ;6845 data register
VIO_SEG     = 0B000h       ;Segment address of video RAM

CUR_START  = 10            ;Register # CRTC: Starting cursor line
CUR_END    = 11            ;Register # CRTC: Ending cursor line
CURPOS_HI  = 14            ;Register # CRTC: Cursor pos. high byte
CURPOS_LO  = 15            ;Register # CRTC: Cursor pos. low byte

DELAY      = 20000         ;Counter for delay loop

;== Stack ======================================================

stack      segment para stack    ;Definition of stack segment

           dw 256 dup (?)         ;256-word stack

stack      ends                   ;End of stack segment

;== Data =======================================================

data       segment para 'DATA'   ;Define data segment

;== the Data for the Demo-Program =============================

str1  db "a",0
str2  db " >PC INTERN< ",0
str3  db "   window 1   ",0
str4  db "   window 2   ",0
str5  db "          the program is stopped by "
      db " pressing a Key....          ",0
```

```
initm   db 13,10,"VMONO (c) 1987 by Michael Tischer",13,10,13,10
        db "This demonstration program only runs with "
        db " a monochrome",13,10,"display card. If your PC "
        db "has another type of display card,",13,10
        db "please enter <s> to stop the "
        db " program.",13,10,"Otherwise press any "
        db "key to start ",13,10
        db "the program ...",13,10,"$"


;== Data ================================================================

linen   dw  0*160,1*160,2*160 ;Start addresses of the lines as
        dw  3*160,4*160,5*160 ;offset addresses in the video RAM
        dw  6*160,7*160,8*160
        dw  9*160,10*160,11*160,12*160,13*160,14*160,15*160,16*160
        dw  17*160,18*160,19*160,20*160,21*160,22*160,23*160,24*160


data    ends                        ;End of data segment

;== Code =========================================================

code    segment para 'CODE'     ;Definition of the CODE segment

        assume cs:code, ds:data, es:data, ss:stack

;== this is the Demo-Program ===================================

demo    proc far

        mov ax,data             ;Get segment address of data segment
        mov ds,ax               ;and load into DS
        mov es,ax               ;as well as ES

        ;-- Display initial msg./wait for input ----------------

        mov ah,9                ;String output function
        mov dx,offset initm     ;Address of initial message
        int 21h                 ;Call DOS interrupt 21H

        xor ah,ah               ;Get function number for key
        int 16h                 ;Call BIOS keyboard interrupt
        cmp al,"s"              ;was <s> entered?
        je  ende                ;YES --> end program
        cmp al,"S"              ;was <S> entered?
        jne startdemo           ;NO --> start demo

ende:   mov ax,4c00h            ;Function number for program end
        int 21h                 ;Call DOS interrupt 21H

startdemo label near
        mov cx,0d00h            ;Enable full cursor
        call cdef
        call cls                ;Clear screen

        ;-- Fill screen with ASCII characters -------------

        xor di,di               ;Start in upper left corner
        mov si,offset str1      ;Offset address of string1
        mov cx,2000             ;2,000 characters fit on the screen
        mov al,07h              ;white letters on black background
demo1:  call print              ;Display string
        inc str1                ;Increment character in test string
        jne demo2               ;NUL code suppressed
```

```
        inc str1
demo2:  loop demo1              ;Repeat output

        ;-- Create window 1 and window 2 ----------

        mov bx,0508h            ;Upper left corner of window 1
        mov dx,1316h            ;Lower right corner of window 1
        mov ah,07h              ;White letters, black background
        call clear              ;Clear window 1
        mov bx,3C02h            ;Upper left corner of window 2
        mov dx,4A10h            ;Lower right corner window 2
        call clear              ;Clear window 2
        mov bx,0508h            ;Upper left corner of window 1
        call calo               ;Convert to offset address
        mov si,offset str3      ;Offset address string 3
        mov ah,70h              ;Black characters, white background
        call print              ;Display string 3
        mov bx,3C02h            ;Upper left corner of window 2
        call calo               ;Convert to offset address
        mov si,offset str4      ;Offset address string 4
        call print              ;Display string 4
        xor di,di               ;Upper left display corner
        mov si,offset str5      ;Offset address string 5
        call print              ;Display string 5

        ;-- Display program logo --------------------------------

        mov bx,1E0Ch            ;Column 30, line 12
        call calo               ;Convert offset address
        mov si,offset str2      ;Offset address string 2
        mov ah,0F0h             ;Inverse blinking
        call print              ;Display string 2

        ;-- Fill window with arrows -----------------------------

        xor ch,ch               ;high-byte of the counter to 0
arrow:  mov bl,1                ;Asterisk
arrow0: push bx                 ;Push BX on the stack
        mov di,offset str3      ;Draw arrow line in string 3
        mov cl,15               ;Total of 15 characters in a line
        sub cl,bl               ;Calculate number of spaces
        shr cl,1                ;Divide by 2 (for left half)
        or  cl,cl               ;No blanks ?
        je  arrow1              ;YES --> ARROW1
        mov al," "             
        rep stosb               ;Draw blanks in string 3
arrow1: mov cl,bl               ;Number of asterisks in counter
        mov al,"*"
        rep stosb               ;Draw stars in string 3
        mov cl,15               ;Total of 15 characters in a line
        sub cl,bl               ;Calculate number of blanks
        shr cl,1                ;Divide by 2 (for right half)
        or  cl,cl               ;No blanks?
        je  arrow2              ;YES --> ARROW2
        mov al," "
        rep stosb               ;Draw blanks in string 3
arrow2: mov bx,0509h            ;below the first line of window 1
        call calo               ;Convert to offset address
        mov si,offset str3      ;Offset address string 3
        mov ah,07h              ;White characters, black background
        call print              ;Display string 3
        mov bx,3C10h            ;into the lowest line of window 2
        call calo               ;Convert offset address
        call print              ;Display string 3
```

```
                ;-- Brief pause ----------------------------------

        mov   cx,DELAY          ;Loop counter
waitlp: loop waitlp             ;Count loop to 0

                ;-- Scroll window 1 line down ----------------------

        mov   bx,0509h          ;Upper left corner of window 1
        mov   dx,1316h          ;Lower right corner window 1
        mov   cl,1              ;Scroll down
        call scrolldn           ;one line

                ;-- Scroll window 2 one line up --------------------

        mov   bx,3C03h          ;Upper left corner window 2
        mov   dx,4A10h          ;Lower right corner window 2
        call scrollup           ;Scroll up

                ;-- Was a key pressed? (end program) ----------------

        mov   ah,1              ;Function number for testing key
        int   16h              ;Call BIOS keyboard interrupt
        jne   end_it           ;Keypress -> goto end of program

                ;-- NO, display next arrow -------------------------

        pop   bx               ;Pop BX from stack again
        add   bl,2             ;2 more stars in next line
        cmp   bl,17            ;Reached 17 ?
        jne   arrow0           ;NO --> next arrow
        jmp   arrow            ;No key --> next arrow

                ;-- Get ready to end program

end_it: xor   ah,ah             ;Get function number for key
        int   16h              ;Call BIOS keyboard interrupt
        mov   cx,0D0Ch         ;Restore normal cursor
        call cdef
        call cls               ;Clear screen
        jmp   ende             ;Go to end of program

demo    endp

;== Functions ====================================================

;-- SOFF: switches the display off ------------------------
;-- Input   : none
;-- Output  : none
;-- register : AX and DX are changed

SOFF    proc near

        mov   dx,CONTROL_REG    ;Address of display control register
        in    al,dx            ;read its content
        and   al,11110111b     ;bit 3 = 0: display off
        out   dx,al            ;set new value (display off)

        ret                    ;back to caller

SOFF    endp

;-- SON: switches the display on --------------------------
;-- Input   : none
```

```
;-- Output   : none
;-- register : AX and DX are changed

SON     proc near

        mov   dx,CONTROL_REG    ;Address of display control register
        in    al,dx            ;Read its content
        or    al,8             ;Bit 3 = 1: display on
        out   dx,al            ;Set new value (display on)
        ret                    ;Back to caller

SON     endp

;-- CDEF: sets the start and end line of the cursor -------------
;-- Input   : CL = Start line
;--           CH = End line
;-- Output  : none
;-- register : AX and DX are changed
cdef    proc near

        mov   al,CUR_START     ;Register 10: start line
        mov   ah,cl            ;Start line to AH
        call setvk             ;Transmit to video controller
        mov   al,CUR_END       ;Register 11: end line
        mov   ah,ch            ;End line to AH
        jmp   short setvk      ;Transmit to video controller

cdef    endp

;-- SETBLINK: sets the blinking display cursor --------------------
;-- Input    : DI = offset address of the cursor
;-- Output   : none
;-- register : BX, AX and DX are changed

setblink  proc near

        mov   bx,di            ;Transmit offset to BX
        mov   al,CURPOS_HI     ;Register 15:high byte of cursor
offset
        mov   ah,bh            ;high-byte of the offset
        call setvk             ;Transmit to video controller
        mov   al,CURPOS_LO     ;Register 15:Low byte of cursor offset
        mov   ah,bl            ;Low byte of the offset

                ;-- SETVK is called automatically ------------------------

setblink  endp

;-SETVK: sets a byte in one of the registers of the video controller --
;-- Input   : AL = number of the register
;--           AH = new content of the register
;-- Output  : none
;-- register : DX and AL are changed

setvk   proc near

        mov   dx,ADDRESS_6845  ;Address of the index register
        out   dx,al            ;Send number of the register
        jmp   short $+2        ;Small I/O pause
        inc   dx               ;Address of the index register
        mov   al,ah            ;Content to AL
        out   dx,al            ;Set new content
        ret                    ;Back to caller
```

```
setvk     endp


;-- GETVK: reads a byte from one register of the video controllers -
;-- Input   : AL = number of the register
;-- Output  : AL = content of the register
;-- register : DX and AL are changed

getvk     proc near

          mov   dx,ADDRESS_6845    ;Address of the index register
          out   dx,al              ;Send number of the register
          jmp short $+2
          inc   dx                 ;Address of the index register
          in    al,dx              ;Read content to AL
          ret                      ;Back to caller

getvk     endp

;-- SCROLLUP: scrolls a window up by N lines ----------------
;-- Input   :    BL = line upper left
;--              BH = column upper left
;--              DL = line lower right
;--              DH = column lower right
;--              CL = number of lines to scroll
;-- Output  : none
;-- register : only FLAGS are changed
;-- Info    :  the display lines released are erased

scrollup  proc near

          cld                      ;Increment on string instructions

          push ax                  ;Push all changed registers on the
          push bx                  ;stack
          push di                  ;In this case the sequence
          push si                  ;must be observed!

          push bx                  ;These three registers are restored
          push cx                  ;from the stack before ending
          push dx
          sub  dl,bl               ;Calculate the number of lines
          inc  dl
          sub  dl,cl               ;Deduct number of lines scrolled
          sub  dh,bh               ;Calculate number of columns
          inc  dh
          call calo                ;Convert upper left in offset
          mov  si,di               ;Record Address in SI
          add  bl,cl               ;First line in scrolled window
          call calo                ;Convert first line to offset
          xchg si,di               ;Exchange SI and DI
          push ds                  ;Store segment register on
          push es                  ;the stack
          mov  ax,VIO_SEG          ;Segment address of the video RAM
          mov  ds,ax               ;to DS
          mov  es,ax               ;and ES
sup1:     mov  ax,di               ;Record DI in AX
          mov  bx,si               ;Record SI in BX
          mov  cl,dh               ;Number of column in counter
          rep movsw                ;Move a line
          mov  di,ax               ;Restore DI from AX
          mov  si,bx               ;Restore SI from BX
          add  di,160              ;Set next line
          add  si,160
          dec  dl                  ;Processed all lines ?
```

```
          jne  sup1                ;NO --> move another line
          pop  es                  ;Get segment register from
          pop  ds                  ;stack
          pop  dx                  ;Get lower right corner
          pop  cx                  ;Read number of lines
          pop  bx                  ;Get upper left corner
          mov  bl,dl               ;Lower line to BL
          sub  bl,cl               ;Deduct number of lines
          inc  bl
          mov  ah,07h              ;Color : black on white
          call clear               ;Erase lines freed

          pop  si                  ;CX and DX have already
          pop  di                  ;been read
          pop  bx
          pop  ax

          ret                      ;Back to caller

scrollup  endp

;-- SCROLLDN: scrolls a window down N lines ---------------
;-- Input   :    BL = line upper left
;--              BH = column upper left
;--              DL = line lower right
;--              DH = column lower right
;--              CL = number of lines to scroll
;-- Output  :  none
;-- register : only FLAGS are changed
;-- Info    :  display lines released are erased

scrolldn  proc near

          cld                      ;Increment on string instructions

          push ax                  ;Store all changed registers on the
          push bx                  ;stack
          push di                  ;In this case the sequence
          push si                  ;must be observed !

          push bx                  ;These three registers are returned
          push cx                  ;from the stack before the end
          push dx                  ;of the routine

          sub  dh,bh               ;Calculate the number of the column
          inc  dh
          mov  al,bl               ;Record line upper left in AL
          mov  bl,dl               ;Line upper right to line upper left
          call calo                ;Convert upper left into offset
          mov  si,di               ;Record address in SI
          sub  bl,cl               ;Deduct number of lines to scroll
          call calo                ;Convert upper left in offset
          xchg si,di               ;Exchange SI and DI
          sub  dl,al               ;Calculate number of lines
          inc  dl                  ;Deduct number
          sub  dl,cl               ;of lines to be scrolled
          push ds                  ;Push segment register onto stack
          push es
          mov  ax,VIO_SEG          ;Segment address of video RAM
          mov  ds,ax               ;to DS
          mov  es,ax               ;and ES
sdn1:     mov  ax,di               ;Move DI to AX
          mov  bx,si               ;Move SI to BX
          mov  cl,dh               ;Number column in counter
```

```
        rep movsw              ;Scroll one line               mov  cx,VIO_SEG        ;Segment address of the video RAM
        mov  di,ax             ;Get DI from AX                mov  es,cx             ; to ES
        mov  si,bx             ;Restore SI from BX            xor  ch,ch             ;high-bytes of the counter to 0
        sub  di,160            ;Set next line                 mov  al," "             ;Space character
        sub  si,160                                   clear1: mov  si,di             ;Move DI to SI
        dec  dl                ;All lines processed ?         mov  cl,dh             ;Number of column in counter
        jne  sdn1              ;NO --> scroll another line    rep  stosw             ;Store space character
        pop  es                ;Get segment register from     mov  di,si             ;Restore DI from SI
        pop  ds                ;stack                         add  di,160            ;Set in next line
        pop  dx                ;Return lower right corner     dec  dl                ;All lines processed ?
        pop  cx                ;Return number of lines        jne  clear1            ;NO --> erase another line
        pop  bx                ;Return upper left corner
        mov  dl,bl             ;Upper line to DL              pop  es                ;Restore registers from
        add  dl,cl             ;Add number of lines           pop  di                ;stack
        dec  dl                                               pop  si
        mov  ah,07h            ;Color : black on white        pop  dx
        call clear             ;Erase lines which were released pop cx
                                                              ret                    ;Back to caller
        pop  si                ;CX and DX are
        pop  di                ; already returned     clear   endp
        pop  bx
        pop  ax                                       ;-- PRINT: outputs a string on the Display --------------------
                                                      ;-- Input    : AH = Attribute/color
        ret                    ;Back to caller        ;--            DI = offset address of the first character
                                                      ;--            SI = offset address of the string to DS
scrolldn endp                                         ;-- Output   : DI points behind the last character output
                                                      ;-- register : AL, DI and FLAGS are changed
;-- CLS: Clear the complete screen ------------------------------  ;-- Info  : the string must be terminated with a NUL-character.
;-- Input  : none                                     ;--          other control characters are not recognized
;-- Output : none
;-- register : only FLAGS are changed                 print   proc near

cls     proc near                                             cld                    ;Increment on string instructions
                                                              push si                ;Store SI, DX and ES on the stack
        mov  ah,07h            ;Color is white on black        push es
        xor  bx,bx             ;Upper left is (0/0)            push dx
        mov  dx,4F18h          ;Lower right is (79/24)         mov  dx,VIO_SEG        ;Segment address of the video RAM
                                                              mov  es,dx             ;First to DX and then to ES
        ;-- Execute Clear --------------------------------------   jmp  print1            ;YES --> Output finished

cls     endp                                          print0: stosw                  ;Store attribute and color in V-RAM
                                                      print1: lodsb                  ;Get next character from the string
;-- CLEAR: fills a designated display with space characters ----   or   al,al             ;Is it NUL
;-- Input  : AH = Attribute/color                             jne  print0            ;NO --> output
;--          BL = line upper left
;--          BH = column upper left                   printe: pop  dx                ;Get SI, DX and ES back from stack
;--          DL = line lower right                            pop  es
;--          DH = column lower right                          pop  si
;-- Output : none                                             ret                    ;Back to caller
;-- register : only FLAGS are changed
                                                      print   endp
clear   proc near
                                                      ;- CALO: converts line and column into offset address ----------------
        cld                    ;Increment on string instructions  ;-- Input   : BL = line
        push cx                ;Store all registers which    ;--            BH = column
        push dx                ;are changed on the stack      ;-- Output   : DI = the offset address
        push si                                               ;-- Registers: DI and FLAGS are changed
        push di
        push es                                       calo    proc near
        sub  dl,bl             ;Calculate number of lines
        inc  dl                                               push ax                ;Store AX on the stack
        sub  dh,bh             ;Calculate number of columns   push bx                ;Store BX on the stack
        inc  dh
        call calo              ;Offset address of upper left corner  shl  bx,1              ;Column and line times 2
```

```
mov   al,bh          ;Column to AL                                    ret                    ;Back to caller
xor   bh,bh          ;Get high-byte
mov   di,[linen+bx]  ;Offset address of the line          calo   endp
xor   ah,ah          ;high-byte for column offset
add   di,ax          ;Add line- and column offset         ;== End ================================================


pop   bx             ;Get BX from stack again             code   ends               ;End of the CODE segment
pop   ax             ;Get AX from stack again             end demo                   ;Start program execution w/ demo
```

4.6 The Hercules Graphics Card (HGC)

In 1982, only a year after the IBM PC was released, Hercules Computer Technology made their contribution to the PC market by releasing the Hercules Graphics Card or HGC. Until then, only two video systems existed for the IBM: the MDA card for reading only text and the CGA for graphics display and fuzzy text. The Hercules card was intended for excellent text and graphics display. This card can drive a normal monochrome monitor in 80x25 text mode, with a 720x348 pixel graphics mode. The Hercules Graphics Card was an immediate success.

Non-BIOS support

Since the IBM BIOS supports only the MDA and CGA cards, the Hercules card isn't supported by BIOS. This doesn't present a problem in text mode because the Hercules text mode is completely compatible with the MDA card. However, this non-support is noticeable in graphics mode because in this mode BIOS functions cannot set or read pixels. In this chapter you'll find some assembly language routines that solve these problems.

Video RAM on a Hercules Graphics Card

The Hercules card contains 64K of RAM, allowing it to operate in a memory intensive graphic mode. This RAM can be divided into two screen pages. Each of the two pages is 32K in length, and can comprise either a text page requiring only 4K, or a graphic page. The first screen page lies in the address range from B000:0000 to B000:7FFF. The second screen page follows, lying in the range from B000:8000 to B000:FFFF. Since this range matches those normally used by color video cards (CGA, EGA and VGA), this range can be adjusted by setting the DIP switches on the card. You can reconfigure the card to provide only one screen page.

Unlike the MDA card, you can communicate with the configuration register through port 3BFH. You can write to this port, but you cannot read from it. This register has two bits (0 and 1). Bit 0 specifies whether graphic mode is enabled (1) or disabled (0). Bit 1 specifies whether the second screen page is available (0 if not, 1 if so).

To avoid conflicts with other video cards (color cards) both bits must be set to 0 so a graphic won't be displayed and the second screen page won't be used. If you want a program with these features to continue accessing the card, the control register must be changed accordingly.

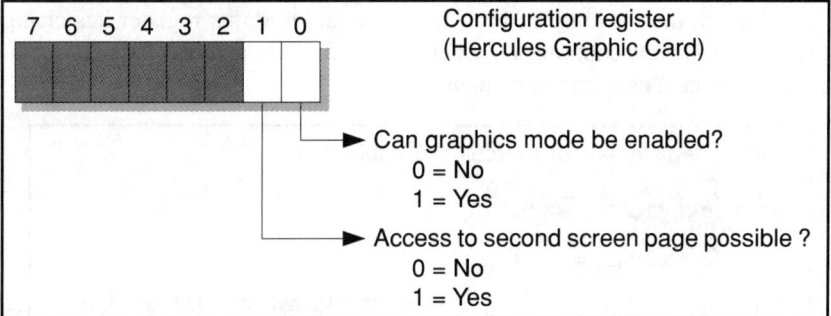

The control register of the Hercules card differs from the control register of the MDA, which we discussed in the previous section.

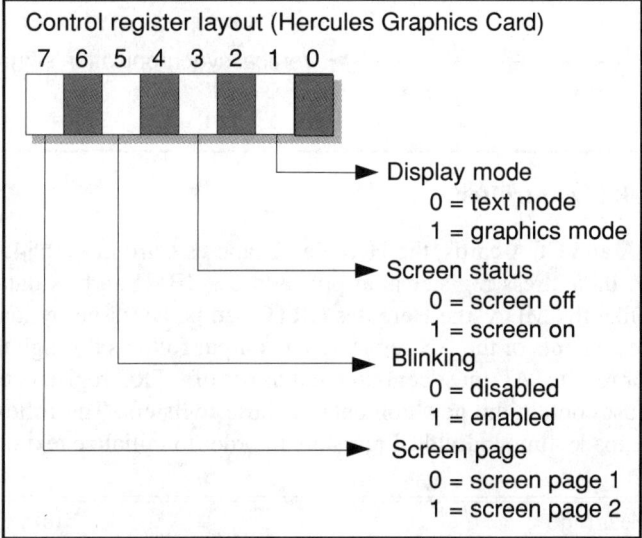

Unlike the IBM monochrome display adapter, bit 0 is unused and doesn't have to be set to 1 during the system boot. Bit 1 determines text or graphics mode; a 0 in bit 1 enables text mode, while a 1 in bit 1 enables graphics mode. As you'll see in the following examples, changing these bits isn't sufficient for switching between text and graphics modes. The internal registers of the 6845 must also be reset. During this process, the screen display must be switched off to prevent the 6845 from creating garbage during its reprogramming.

The Hercules card has a seventh bit in this register. The contents of this bit determine which of the two screen pages appear on the screen. If this bit is 0, the first screen page appears and if it is 1, the second screen page appears. The user can write to or read from either page at any time. You can only write to this register; if you try to read this register, the value FFH is returned. Because of this, it's impossible to switch off the display simply by reading the contents of the status register and erasing bit 3, regardless of the display mode and the screen page selected.

Unfortunately, the control register cannot be read. This means that you won't know the card's current mode or when the card has initialized itself. This is a serious problem in TSR programs.

Unlike the MDA card, the meaning of bit 7 in the Hercules status register has changed. In the Hercules card this bit always contains a 0 when the 6845 sends a vertical synchronization signal to the screen, to generate a new screen structure.

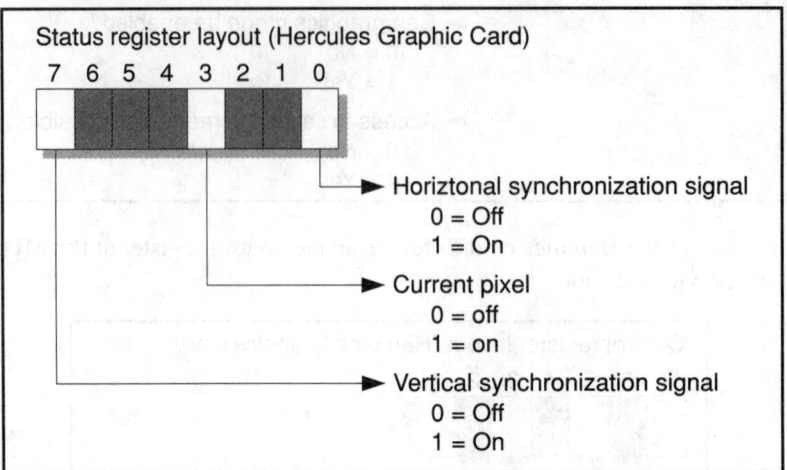

Status register layout (Hercules Graphic Card)

7 6 5 4 3 2 1 0

Horiztonal synchronization signal
0 = Off
1 = On

Current pixel
0 = off
1 = on

Vertical synchronization signal
0 = Off
1 = On

The Hercules CRT controller

Similar to the MDA and CGA cards, the Hercules Graphics Card has a 6845 CRT controller as its main processor. Its address register is at port address 3B4H and its data register is at port address 3B5H. Unlike the MDA, the Hercules CRTC can be accessed by loading a 16-bit OUT instruction with the contents of the AX register. The output follows through the address register, where the processor register AL must contain the number of CTRC registers to be addressed, and the AH register must contain the new contents of these registers. The following table lists the values that must be loaded into individual registers in order to initialize text or graphics mode.

No.	Meaning	Text	Graphics
0H	Total horizontal character	97	53
1H	Horizontal character displayed	80	45
2H	Horiz. synchronization signal after character	82	46
3H	Horiz. synchronization signal width	15	7
4H	Total vertical character	25	91
5H	Vertical character justified	6	2
6H	Vertical character displayed	25	87
7H	Vert. synchronization signal after character	25	87
8H	Interlace mode	2	2
9H	Number of scan lines per line	13	3
AH	Starting line of blinking cursor	11	0
BH	Ending line of the blinking cursors	12	0
CH	High byte of screen page starting address	0	0
DH	Low byte of screen page starting address	0	0
EH	High byte of blinking cursor char. address	0	0
FH	Low byte of blinking cursor char. address	0	0
10H	Light pen position (high byte)	?	?
11H	Light pen position (low byte)	?	?

? = depends on light pen's position

Starting and programming graphics mode

You cannot switch to graphics mode using BIOS, although text mode automatically starts on bootup through the BIOS.

As we mentioned earlier, the Hercules card in graphics mode provides 348x720 resolution. Each pixel on the screen corresponds to one bit in the video RAM. If the corresponding bit contains the value 1, the dot is visible on the screen; otherwise it remains hidden. The following figure shows the arrangement of video RAM in graphics mode.

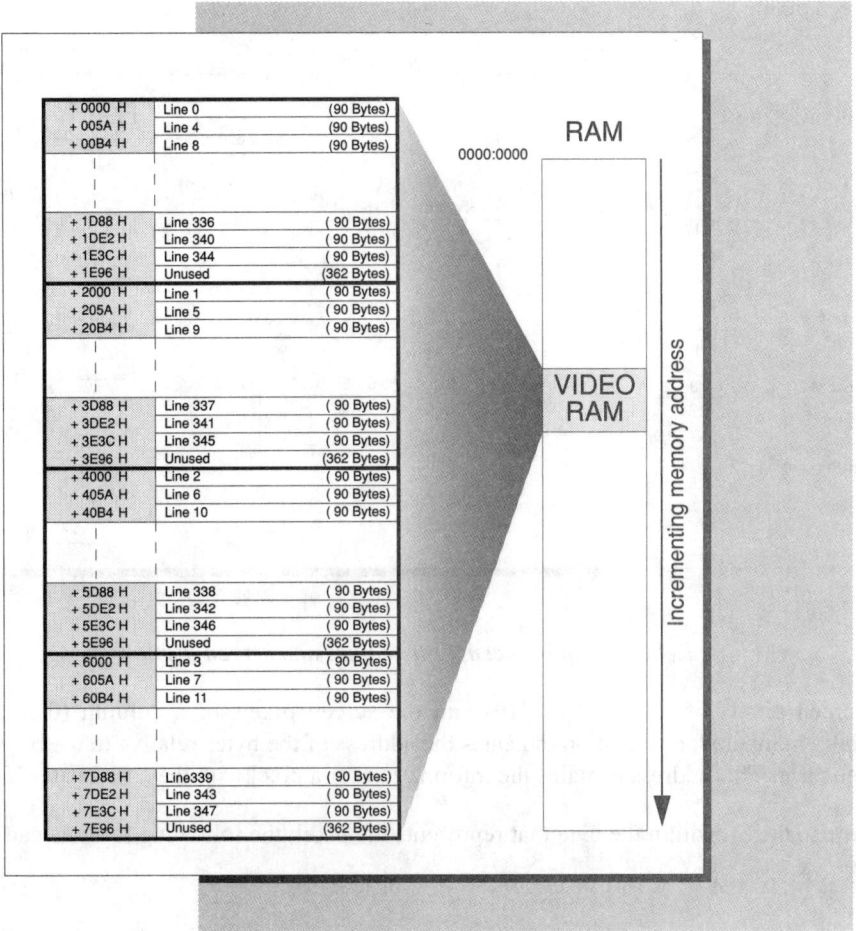

Arrangement of video RAM in graphics mode

The bit patterns of the individual lines in the video RAM aren't arranged sequentially. Instead, the 32K of video RAM is divided into four 8K blocks. The first block contains the bit pattern for any lines divisible by 4 (0, 4, 8, 12, etc.). The second block contains the bit patterns for lines 1, 5, 9, 13, etc. The third block contains the bit patterns for lines 2, 6, 10, 14, etc., and the last block contains lines 3, 7, 11, 15, etc.

When the 6845 generates a display, it obtains information for screen line zero from the first data block and screen line one from the second data block, etc. After it has obtained the contents of the third screen line from the fourth data block, it accesses the first data block again for the structure of the fourth line. Each line requires 90 bytes within the individual data blocks and each pixel requires a bit (720 pixels divided by 8 bits (per byte) equals 90). The first 90 bytes in the first memory area provide the bit pattern for screen line zero, and the next 90 bytes provide the bit pattern for the fourth screen line. The zero byte of one of these 90-byte sets represents the first eight columns of a screen line (columns 0-8). The first byte represents columns 8-15, etc. Within one of these bytes, bit 7 corresponds to the left screen pixel and bit 0 corresponds to the right screen pixel.

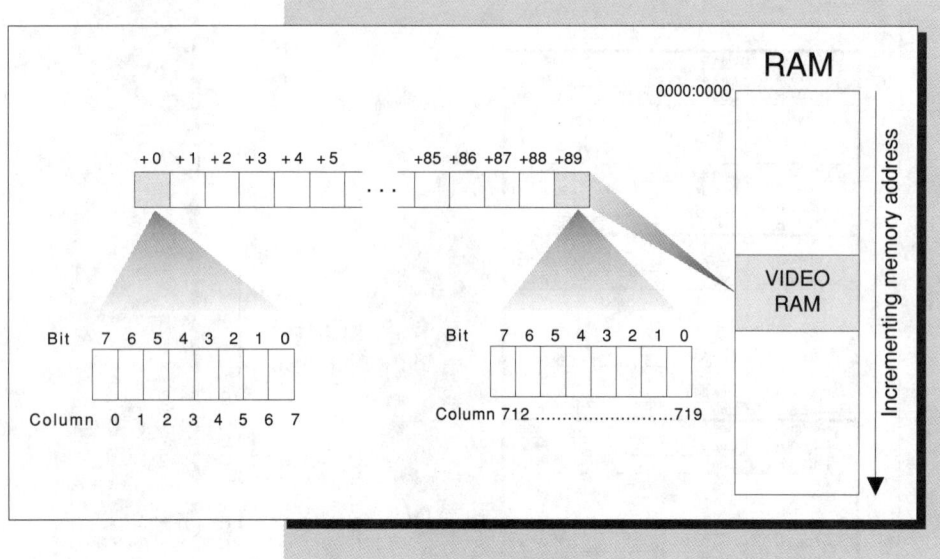

Relationship between 90-byte lines and screen display

If the screen pixels of a line (0 to 719) and the screen pixels of a column (0 to 347) are sequentially numbered, an equation indicates the address of the bytes relative to the beginning of the screen page. This address contains the information for a pixel with the coordinates X/Y.

To determine the bit within the byte that represents the pixel, the following formula can be used:

```
Address = 2000H * (Y mod 4) + 90 * int(Y/4) + int(X/8)
```

In order to send the number of desired bits within this byte, use the following formula:

```
Bitnumber = 7 - (X mod 8)
```

The following program demonstrates the capabilities of the Hercules Graphics Card. The individual routines within this program differ from the routines in the Monochrome Display Adapter demo program from the previous section. The routines here enable access to both screen pages and support the Hercules graphics mode.

Assembler listing: VHERC.ASM

```
;*****************************************************************;
;*                        V H E R C                            *;
;*-------------------------------------------------------------*;
;*   Task       : Makes a basic function available for         *;
;*                access to the Hercules Graphics Card.        *;
;*-------------------------------------------------------------*;
;*   Info       : All functions partition the screen display   *;
;*                into columns  0-79 and lines 0-24 (text mode)*;
;*                & columns 0-719 and lines 0-347 (graphic mode)*;
;*-------------------------------------------------------------*;
;*   Author     : Michael Tischer                              *;
;*   Developed on : 08/11/89                                   *;
;*   Last update  : 03/02/92                                   *;
;*-------------------------------------------------------------*;
;*   Assembly   : MASM VHERC;                                  *;
;*                LINK VHERC;                                   *;
;*-------------------------------------------------------------*;
;*   Call       : VHERC                                        *;
;*****************************************************************;


;== Constants ====================================================

CONTROL_REG  = 03B8h              ;Control register port address
ADDRESS_6845 = 03B4h              ;6845 address register
DATA_6845    = 03B5h              ;6845 data register
CONFIG_REG   = 03BFh              ;Configuration register
VIO_SEG      = 0B000h             ;Video RAM segment address
CUR_START    = 10                 ;Reg. # for CRTC: Start cursor line
CUR_END      = 11                 ;Reg. # for CRTC: End cursor line
CURPOS_HI    = 14                 ;Reg. # for CRTC: Cursor pos hi byte
CURPOS_LO    = 15                 ;Reg. # for CRTC: Cursor pos lo byte

DELAY        = 20000              ;Count for delay loop

;== Macros =======================================================

setmode   macro modus            ;Set control register

          mov  dx,CONTROL_REG     ;Screen control register address
          mov  al,modus           ;Put new mode in AL register
          out  dx,al              ;Send mode to control register

          endm

setvk     macro                   ;Write value to CRTC registers
                                  ;Input: AL = register number
                                  ;       AH = Value for register

          mov  dx,ADDRESS_6845    ;Index register address
          out  dx,ax              ;Display register number and new value

          endm

;== Stack ========================================================

stack     segment para stack      ;Definition of stack segment

          dw 256 dup (?)          ;Stack is 256 words in size

stack     ends                    ;End of stack segment

;== Data =========================================================
```

```
data      segment para 'DATA'     ;Define data segment

;== Data needed for demo program ==============================

initm     db 13,10, "VHERC (c) 1987 by Michael Tischer",13,10,13,10
          db "This demonstration program runs only with "
          db " a HERCULES",13,10,"graphics card. If your PC "
          db "has another type of display card, ",13,10
          db "please input an >s< to stop the "
          db " program.",13,10,"Otherwise please press any "
          db "key to start the ",13,10
          db "program ...",13,10,"$"

str1      db 1,17,16,2,7,0
str2      db 2,16,17,1,7,0

domes     db 13,10
          db "This program creates a short graphic demo ",13,10
          db "and a text demo. Pressing a key during the",13,10
          db "demo ends the program.",13,10
          db "Press a key to start the program...",13,10,"$"

;== Table of line offset addresses =========================

lines     dw  0*160,1*160,2*160 ;Beginning addresses of the lines as
          dw  3*160,4*160,5*160 ;offset addresses in video RAM
          dw  6*160,7*160,8*160
          dw  9*160,10*160,11*160,12*160,13*160,14*160,15*160,16*160
          dw  17*160,18*160,19*160,20*160,21*160,22*160,23*160,24*160

grafikt   db 35h, 2Dh, 2Eh, 07h, 5Bh, 02h ;Register values for the
          db 57h, 57h, 02h, 03h, 00h, 00h ;graphic mode

textt     db 61h, 50h, 52h, 0Fh, 19h, 06h ;Register values for the
          db 19h, 19h, 02h, 0Dh, 0Bh, 0Ch ;text mode

data      ends                    ;End of data segment

;== Code segment =========================================

code      segment para 'CODE'     ;Definition of the code segment

          org 100h

          assume cs:code, ds:data, es:data, ss:stack

;== this is only the Demo-Program ==============================

demo      proc far

          mov  ax,data            ;Get segment address of data segment
          mov  ds,ax              ;Load into DS
          mov  es,ax              ;and ES

          ;-- Opening msg., wait for input --------------------

          mov  ah,9               ;Output function number for string
          mov  dx,offset initm    ;address of the message
          int  21h                ;Call DOS interrupt

          xor  ah,ah              ;Get function number for key
          int  16h                ;Call BIOS keyboard interrupt
          cmp  al,"s"             ;Was <s> entered?
```

```
            je    ende           ;YES--> End program              xor  ah,ah          ;Wait for function nr. for key
            cmp   al,"S"          ;Was <S> entered?                int  16h            ;Call BIOS keyboard interrupt
            jne   startdemo       ;NO --> Start demo
                                                                   ;-- Initialize text mode ---------------------------
ende:       mov   ax,4C00h        ;Function number - end program
            int   21h             ;Call DOS interrupt 21(h)        call text           ;Switch on text mode
                                                                   mov  cx,0d00h       ;Switch on full cursor
startdemo label near                                               call cdef
            mov   ah,9            ;Output function number for string call cls           ;Clear screen
            mov   dx,offset domes ;address of the message
            int   21h             ;Call DOS interrupt              ;-- Display strings in display page 0 ---------------

            xor   ah,ah           ;Get function number for key     xor  bx,bx          ;Start in upper left display corner
            int   16h             ;Call BIOS keyboard interrupt    call calo           ;Convert to offset address
                                                                   mov  si,offset str1 ;Offset address of string1
            ;-- Initialize graphic mode ----------------------     mov  cx,16*25       ;The string is 5 characters long
                                                            demo1:  call print          ;Output string
            mov   al,11b          ;Graphic and page 2 possible     loop demo1
            call  config          ;Configure
            xor   bp,bp           ;Access display page 0           ;-- Display strings in display page 1 ---------------
            call  grafik          ;Switch to graphic mode
            xor   al,al                                            inc  bp             ;Process display page 1
            call  cgr             ;Erase graphic page 0            xor  bx,bx          ;Start in the upper left corner
            xor   bx,bx           ;Begin in the upper left         call calo           ;Convert to offset address
            xor   dx,dx           ;Display corner                  mov  si,offset str2 ;Offset address of string1
            mov   ax,347          ;Vertical pixels                 mov  cx,16*25       ;string is 5 characters long
            mov   cx,719          ;Horizontal pixels       demo2:  call print          ;Output string
gr1:        push  cx              ;Push horizontal pixels on stack loop demo2
            mov   cx,ax           ;Vertical pixels in counter
            push  ax              ;Push vertical pixels on stack demo3: setmode 10001000b ;Display text page 1
gr2:        call  spix            ;Set pixel
            inc   dx              ;Increment line                  ;-- short Pause ------------------------------------
            loop  gr2             ;Draw line                       mov  cx,DELAY       ;Load counter
            pop   ax              ;Get vert. pixels from stack pause: loop pause         ;Count to 65,536
            sub   ax,3            ;next line 3 pixels less
            pop   cx              ;Get horiz. pixels from stack    setmode 00001000b   ;Display page 0
            push  cx              ;Store horizontal pixels
            push  ax              ;Push vertical pixels on stack   ;-- short pause ------------------------------------
gr3:        call  spix            ;Set pixel                       mov  cx,DELAY       ;Load counter
            inc   bx              ;Increment column         pause1: loop pause1        ;Count to 65,536
            loop  gr3             ;Draw line
            pop   ax              ;Get vertical pixels from stack  mov  ah,1           ;Test function nr. for key
            pop   cx              ;Get horizontal pixels from stack int  16h            ;Call BIOS-keyboard-Interrupt
            sub   cx,6            ;Next line 6 pixels less         je   demo3          ;No key --> continue
            push  cx              ;Record horizontal pixels
            mov   cx,ax           ;Vertical pixels in counter      xor  ah,ah          ;Get function number for key
            push  ax              ;Note vertical pixels on stack   int  16h            ;Call BIOS-keyboard-Interrupt
gr4:        call  spix            ;Set pixel
            dec   dx              ;Decrement line                  mov  bp,0           ;Display page 1
            loop  gr4             ;Draw line                       call cls            ;Clear screen
            pop   ax              ;Get vertical pixels from stack  mov  cx,0D0ch       ;Restore normal cursor
            sub   ax,3            ;Next line 3 pixels less         call cdef
            pop   cx              ;Get horizontal pixels from stack call cls            ;Clear screen
            push  cx              ;Record horizontal pixels        jmp  ende           ;End program
            push  ax              ;Record vertical pixels on stack
gr5:        call  spix            ;Set pixel                demo   endp
            dec   bx              ;Increment column
            loop  gr5             ;Draw line                       ;== The actual functions follow =========================
            pop   ax              ;Get vertical pixels from stack
            pop   cx              ;Get horizontal pixels from stack ;-- CONFIG: configures the HERCULES card ----------------
            sub   cx,6            ;Next line 6 pixels less         ;-- Input    : AL : bit 0 = 0 : Only text presentation possible
            cmp   ax,5            ;Is the vertical line longer than 5 ;--               1 : also graphic presentation possible
            ja    gr1             ;YES --> continue                ;--        bit 1 = 0 : RAM for display page 2 off
                                                                   ;--               1 : RAM for display page 2 on
```

```
;-- Output  : none
;-- Register : AX and DX are changed

config    proc near

          mov  dx,CONFIG_REG    ;Address of configuration register
          out  dx,al            ;Set new value
          ret                   ;Back to caller

config    endp

;-- TEXT: switches the text presentation on --------------------------
;-- Input  : none
;-- Output  : none
;-- Register : AX and DX are changed

text      proc near

          mov  si,offset textt  ;Offset address of the register-table
          mov  bl,00100000b     ;Display page 0,text mode,blinking
          jmp  short vcprog      ;Program video-controller again

text      endp

;-- GRAFIK: switches on the graphic mode ------- ----------------------
;-- Input  : none
;-- Output  : none
;-- Register : AX and DX are changed

grafik    proc near

          mov  si,offset grafikt ;Offset address of the register-table
          mov  bl,00000010b     ;Display page 0, graphic mode

grafik    endp

;-- VCPROG: programs the video controller -----------------------------
;-- Input  :  SI = address of a register-table
;--           BL = value for display-control-register
;-- Output  : none
;-- register : AX, SI, BH, DX and FLAGS are changed

vcprog    proc near

          setmode bl            ;Bit 3 = 0: display off

          mov  cx,12            ;12 registers are set
          xor  bh,bh            ;Start with register 0
vcp1:     lodsb                 ;Get register value from the table
          mov  ah,al            ;Register value to AH
          mov  al,bh            ;Number of the register to AL
          setvk                 ;Transmit value to the controller
          inc  bh               ;Address next register
          loop vcp1             ;Set additional registers

          or   bl,8             ;Bit 3 = 1: display on
          setmode bl            ;Set new mode
          ret                   ;Back to caller

vcprog    endp

;-- cDEF: sets the start and end line of the cursor--------------------
;-- Input  : cL = start line
;--          cH = end line
```

```
;-- Output  : none
;-- register : AX and DX are changed

cdef      proc near

          mov  al,CUR_START     ;Register 10: start line
          mov  ah,cl            ;Start line to AH
          setvk                 ;Transmit to video-controller
          mov  al,CUR_END       ;Register 11: Endline
          mov  ah,ch            ;End line to AH
          setvk                 ;Transmit to video-controller
          ret

cdef      endp

;-- SETBLINK : sets the blinking display cursor -----------------------
;-- Input    : DI = offset address of the cursor
;-- Output   : none
;-- register : BX, AX and DX are changed

setblink  proc near

          mov  bx,di            ;Transmit offset to BX
          mov  al,CURPOS_HI     ;Register 15:Hi Byte of cursor offset
          mov  ah,bh            ;HI byte of the offset
          setvk                 ;Transmit to video-controller
          mov  al,CURPOS_LO     ;Register 15:Lo-Byte of cursor offset
          mov  ah,bl            ;Lo byte of the offset
          setvk                 ;Transmit to CRTC
          ret

setblink  endp

;-- GETVK    : reads a byte from one register of the video-controller -
;-- Input    : AL = number of the register
;-- Output   : AL = content of the register
;-- register : DX and AL are changed

getvk     proc near

          mov  dx,ADDRESS_6845  ;Address of the index register
          out  dx,al            ;Send number of the register
          jmp  $+2              ;Short io pause
          inc  dx               ;Address of the index register
          in   al,dx            ;Read content to AL
          ret                   ;Back to caller

getvk     endp

;-- SCROLLUp: scrolls a window by N lines upward ----------------------
;-- Input  :  BL = line upper left
;--           BH = column upper left
;--           DL = line lower right
;--           DH = column lower right
;--           CL = number of the lines to be scrolled
;--         : BP = number of the display page (0 or 1)
;-- Output  : none
;-- register : only FLAGS are changed
;-- Info    : the display lines released are erased

scrollup  proc near

          cld                   ;Increment for string instructions
          push ax               ;Store all changed registers
```

```
        push bx             ;on the stack
        push di             ;In this case the sequence
        push si             ;must be followed !

        push bx             ;These three registers are returned
        push cx             ;from the stack before
        push dx             ;the end of the routine
        sub  dl,bl          ;Calculate number of lines
        inc  dl             ;Deduct number
        sub  dl,cl          ;of lines to be scrolled
        sub  dh,bh          ;Calculate number of columns
        inc  dh
        call calo           ;Convert upper left in offset
        mov  si,di          ;Note address in SI
        add  bl,cl          ;First line in scrolled window
        call calo           ;Convert first line in offset
        xchg si,di          ;Exchange SI and DI
        push ds             ;Store segment register
        push es             ;on the stack
        mov  ax,VIO_SEG     ;Segment address of the video RAM
        mov  ds,ax          ;to DS
        mov  es,ax          ;and ES
sup1:   mov  ax,di          ;Note DI in AX
        mov  bx,si          ;Note SI in BX
        mov  cl,dh          ;Number of columns in counter
        rep  movsw          ;Move a line
        mov  di,ax          ;Restore DI from AX
        mov  si,bx          ;Restore SI from BX
        add  di,160         ;Set next line
        add  si,160
        dec  dl             ;Processed all lines ?
        jne  sup1           ;NO --> move another line
        pop  es             ;Get segment register from
        pop  ds             ;stack
        pop  dx             ;Get lower right corner
        pop  cx             ;Get number of lines
        pop  bx             ;Get upper left corner
        mov  bl,dl          ;Lower line to BL
        sub  bl,cl          ;Deduct number of lines
        inc  bl
        mov  ah,07h         ;Color : black on white
        call clear          ;Erase liberated lines

        pop  si             ;CX and DX have been brought back
        pop  di             ;already
        pop  bx
        pop  ax

        ret                 ;Back to caller

scrollup endp

;-- SCROLLDN: scroll a Window by N lines upwards ----------------------
;-- Input    : BL = line upper left
;--            BH = column upper left
;--            DL = line lower right
;--            DH = column lower right
;--            CL = number of the lines to be scrolled
;--            BP = number of the display page (0 or 1)
;-- Output   : none
;-- register : only FLAGS are changed
;-- Info     : released lines are deleted

scrolldn proc near

        cld                 ;Increment on string instructions

        push ax             ;Secure all changed registers on the
        push bx             ;stack
        push di             ;In this case the sequence must
        push si             ;be followed!

        push bx             ;These three registers are
        push cx             ;returned from the stack before the
        push dx             ;end of the routine

        sub  dh,bh          ;Calculate number of columns
        inc  dh
        mov  al,bl          ;Record line upper left in AL
        mov  bl,dl          ;Line lower right top lower left
        call calo           ;Convert upper left in offset
        mov  si,di          ;Note address in SI
        sub  bl,cl          ;Deduct number of chars to scroll
        call calo           ;Convert upper left in offset
        xchg si,di          ;Exchange SI and DI
        sub  dl,al          ;Calculate number of lines
        inc  dl
        sub  dl,cl          ;Deduct number of lines to scroll
        push ds             ;Store segment register on the
        push es             ;stack
        mov  ax,VIO_SEG     ;Segment address of the video RAM
        mov  ds,ax          ;to DS
        mov  es,ax          ;and ES
sdn1:   mov  ax,di          ;Record DI in AX
        mov  bx,si          ;Record SI in BX
        mov  cl,dh          ;Number of columns in counter
        rep  movsw          ;Move a line
        mov  di,ax          ;Restore DI from AX
        mov  si,bx          ;Restore SI from BX
        sub  di,160         ;Set next line
        sub  si,160
        dec  dl             ;All lines processed ?
        jne  sdn1           ;NO --> move another line
        pop  es             ;Get segment register from
        pop  ds             ;stack
        pop  dx             ;Get lower right corner
        pop  cx             ;Get number of lines
        pop  bx             ;Get upper left corner
        mov  dl,bl          ;Upper line to DL
        add  dl,cl          ;Add number of lines
        dec  dl
        mov  ah,07h         ;Color : black on white
        call clear          ;Erase liberated lines

        pop  si             ;CX and DX have already
        pop  di             ;been read
        pop  bx
        pop  ax

        ret                 ;Back to caller

scrolldn endp

;-- cLS: clear the whole screen ---------------------------------------
;-- Input    : BP = number of the display page (0 or 1)
;-- Output   : none
;-- register : only FLAGS are changed
```

```
cls     proc near

        mov   ah,07h          ;Color is white on black
        xor   bx,bx           ;Upper left is (0/0)
        mov   dx,4F18h        ;Lower right is (79/24)

        ;-- perform clear -------------------------------------

cls     endp

;-- CLEAR: fills a designated display area with space character -------
;-- Input    : AH = Attribute/color
;--            BL = line upper left
;--            BH = column upper left
;--            DL = line lower right
;--            DH = column lower right
;--            BP = number of the display page (0 or 1)
;-- Output   : none
;-- register : only FLAGS are changed

clear   proc near

        cld                   ;Increment on string instructions
        push  cx              ;Secure all changed
        push  dx              ;registers on the stack
        push  si
        push  di
        push  es
        sub   dl,bl           ;Calculate number of lines
        inc   dl
        sub   dh,bh           ;Calculate number of columns
        inc   dh
        call  calo            ;Offset address of upper left corner
        mov   cx,VIO_SEG      ;Segment address of the video RAM
        mov   es,cx           ;to ES
        xor   ch,ch           ;Hi byte of the counter to 0
        mov   al," "          ;Space character
clear1: mov   si,di           ;Note DI in SI
        mov   cl,dh           ;Number of columns in counter
        rep   stosw           ;Store space character
        mov   di,si           ;Restore DI from SI
        add   di,160          ;Set next line
        dec   dl              ;All lines processed ?
        jne   clear1          ;NO --> erase another line

        pop   es              ;Get secured registers
        pop   di              ;from the stack
        pop   si
        pop   dx
        pop   cx
        ret                   ;Back to caller

clear   endp

;-- PRINT: outputs a string on the display --------------------------
;-- Input    : AH = attribute/color
;--            DI = offset address of the first character
;--            SI = offset address of the strings to DS
;--            BP = number of the display page (0 or 1)
;-- Output   : DI points behind the last character to be output
;-- register : AL, DI and FLAGS are changed
;-- Info     : the string must be terminated with NUL-character.
;--            other control characters are not recognized
```

```
print   proc near

        cld                   ;Increment on string instructions
        push  si              ;SI, DX and ES to the stack
        push  es
        push  dx
        mov   dx,VIO_SEG      ;First segment address of video RAM
        mov   es,dx           ;to DX and then to ES
        jmp   print1          ;Get first character from string
print0: stosw                 ;Store attribute and color in V-RAM
print1: lodsb                 ;Get next character from the string
        or    al,al           ;Is it NUL
        jne   print0          ;NO --> output

printe: pop   dx              ;Get SI, DX and ES from stack again
        pop   es
        pop   si
        ret                   ;Back to caller

print   endp

;-- cALO: converts line and column into offset address ----------------
;-- Input    : BL = line
;--            BH = column
;--            Bp = number of the display page (0 or 1)
;-- Output   : DI = offset address
;-- register : DI and FLAGS are changed

calo    proc near

        push  ax              ;Record AX on the stack
        push  bx              ;Record BX on the stack

        shl   bx,1            ;Column and line times 2
        mov   al,bh           ;Column to AL
        xor   bh,bh           ;Hi byte
        mov   di,[lines+bx]   ;Get offset address of the line
        xor   ah,ah           ;Hi byte for column offset
        add   di,ax           ;Add lines- and column offset
        or    bp,bp           ;Display page 0?
        je    caloe           ;YES --> address ok

        add   di,8000h        ;Add 32 KB for display page 1

caloe:  pop   bx              ;Get BX from stack again
        pop   ax              ;Get AX from the stack again
        ret                   ;Back to caller

calo    endp

;-- CGR: clear the complete graphic screen ----------------------------
;-- Input    : BP = number of the display page (0 or 1)
;--            AL = 00(h) : erase all pixels
;--                 FF(h) : set all pixels
;-- Output   : none
;-- register : AH, BX, cX, DI and FLAGS are changed

cgr     proc near

        push  es              ;Record ES on the stack
        cbw                   ;Expand AL to AH
        xor   di,di           ;Offset address in video RAM
        mov   bx,VIO_SEG      ;Segment address display page 0
        or    bp,bp           ;Erase page 1?
```

```
            je    cgr1              ;NO --> erase page 0          mov  ax,dx         ;Move line to AX
                                                                 shr  ax,1          ;Shift line right 2 times
            add   bx,0800h          ;Segment address display page 1   shr  ax,1     ;This divides by four
                                                                 mov  cl,90         ;The factor is 90
   cgr1:    mov   es,bx             ;Segment address to segment register   mul  cl   ;Multiply line by 90
            mov   cx,4000h          ;A page is 16K-words          and  dx,11b        ;AND all bits except for 0 and 1
            rep   stosw             ;Fill page                    mov  cl,3          ;3 shifts
            pop   es                ;Get ES from stack            ror  dx,cl         ;Rotate right  (* 2000(h))
            ret                     ;Back to caller               mov  di,bx         ;Column to DI
                                                                 mov  cl,3          ;3 shifts
   cgr      endp                                                  shr  di,cl         ;divide by 8
                                                                 add  di,ax         ;+ 90 * int(line/4)
   ;-- SPIX: sets a pixel in the graphic display -----------------   add  di,dx     ;+ 2000(h) * (line mod 4)
   ;-- Input    : BP = number of the display page (0 or 1)       mov  cl,7          ;Maximum of 7 moves
   ;--            BX = column (0 to 719)                          and  bx,7          ;Column mod 8
   ;--            DX = line  (0 to 347)                           sub  cl,bl         ;7 - column mod 8
   ;-- Output   : none                                           mov  ah,1          ;Determine bit value of the pixels
   ;-- register : AX, DI and FLAGS are changed                   shl  ah,cl
                                                                 mov  al,es:[di]    ;Get 8 pixels
   spix     proc near                                            or   al,ah         ;Set pixel
                                                                 mov  es:[di],al    ;Write 8 pixels ;
            push  es                ;Store ES on the stack
            push  bx                ;Store BX on the stack        pop  dx            ;Get DX from stack
            push  cx                ;Store cX on the stack        pop  cx            ;Get cX from stack
            push  dx                ;Store DX on the stack        pop  bx            ;Get BX from stack
                                                                 pop  es            ;Get ES from stack
            xor   di,di             ;Offset address in video RAM   ret               ;Back to caller
            mov   cx,VIO_SEG        ;Segment address display page 0
            or    bp,bp             ;Access page 1 ?             spix     endp
            je    spix1             ;NO --> access page 0        ;== End ==================================================

            mov   cx,0800h          ;Segment address display page 1   code     ends      ;End of the code segment
                                                                      end demo
   spix1:   mov   es,cx             ;Segment address in segment register
```

4.7 The IBM Color/Graphics Adapter (CGA)

Similar to the MDA card, the CGA card was introduced in the early days of the PC. It was the standard for graphics output for many years until the EGA card replaced it. Unlike any other card, you cannot access the video RAM without the help of the CRT controller, without causing grainy pictures or snow.

CGA text modes

The CGA card recognizes two text modes, which comprise 40x25 characters and 80x25 characters. In reference to the video BIOS initialization function, these modes are assigned codes 1 (40x25) and 3 (80x25). These modes include two variants, which let you select the foreground and background colors from a palette of 16 colors. BIOS modes 0 (40x25) and 2 (80x25) send no color signal to the monitor, where the color codes are automatically converted to gray scales.

Each 80x25 text page requires 4,000 bytes of video RAM. 16K allows a total of four text pages. The first page starts at address B800:0000, the second at B800:1000, the third at B800:2000, and the last at B800:3000. The 40x25 mode allows storage of eight screen pages because, in this mode, each screen page only requires 2,000 bytes. The first screen page starts at address B800:0000, the second at B800:0800, and the third at B800:1000.

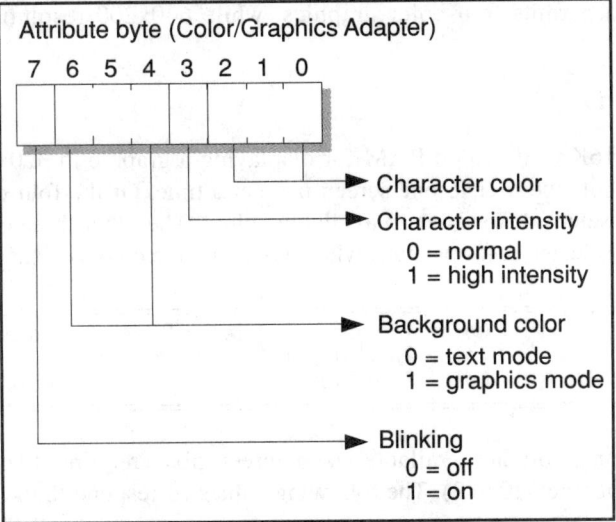

Attribute bytes

The lower four bits of the attribute byte indicate one of the 16 available colors. The meanings of the upper four bits depend on whether blinking is active. If it's active, bits 4 to 6 indicate the background color (taken from one of the first eight colors of the color palette), while bit 7 determines whether the characters blink. If blinking is disabled, bits 4 to 7 indicate the background color (taken from one of the 16 available colors).

```
┌──────────────────────────────────────────────────┐
│ Color/Graphics Adapter color palette               │
│ ┌────────────────────────────────────────────────┐ │
│ │ Dec.    Hex.    Binary     Color name           │ │
│ │  0      00H     0000(b)     Black                │ │
│ │  1      01H     0001(b)     Blue                 │ │
│ │  2      02H     0010(b)     Green                │ │
│ │  3      03H     0011(b)     Cyan                 │ │
│ │  4      04H     0100(b)     Red                  │ │
│ │  5      05H     0101(b)     Magenta              │ │
│ │  6      06H     0110(b)     Brown                │ │
│ │  7      07H     0111(b)     Light gray           │ │
│ │  8      08H     1000(b)     Dark gray            │ │
│ │  9      09H     1001(b)     Light blue           │ │
│ │ 10      0AH     1010(b)     Light green          │ │
│ │ 11      0BH     1011(b)     Light cyan           │ │
│ │ 12      0CH     1100(b)     Light red            │ │
│ │ 13      0DH     1101(b)     Light magenta        │ │
│ │ 14      0EH     1110(b)     Yellow               │ │
│ │ 15      0FH     1111(b)     White                │ │
│ └────────────────────────────────────────────────┘ │
└──────────────────────────────────────────────────┘
```

Graphics modes

The CGA supports three different graphics modes, of which only two are normally used. The *color-suppressed* mode displays 160x100 pixels with 16 colors. The 6845 supports this resolution, but the rest of the hardware doesn't offer color-suppressed mode support. The remaining two graphic modes have resolutions of 320x200 and 640x200 respectively. The

320x200 resolution permits four-color graphics, while 640x200 resolution only allows two colors.

320x200 resolution

The CGA uses all 16K of its video RAM for displaying a graphic in 320x200 resolution with four colors. This limits the user to one screen page at a time. Of the four colors permitted, the background can be selected from the 16 available colors. The other three colors originate from one of the two user-selected color palettes, which contain three colors each.

```
Palette 1:        Color 1: Cyan    Palette 2:        Color 1: Green
                  Color 2: Violet                    Color 2: Red
                  Color 3: White                     Color 3: Yellow
```

Since a total of four colors are available, each screen pixel requires two bits. Four bits can represent the color numbers (0 to 3). The following values correspond to the various colors:

```
0 │   00(b) = freely selectable background color
1 │   01(b) = color 1 of the selected palette
2 │   10(b) = color 2 of the selected palette
3 │   11(b) = color 3 of the selected palette
```

The video RAM assignment in this mode is similar to that of the Hercules card during graphics display. The individual graphic lines are stored in two different blocks of memory. The first block, which begins at address B800:0000, contains the even lines (0, 2, 4...); the second block, which begins at B800:2000, contains odd lines (1,3,5).

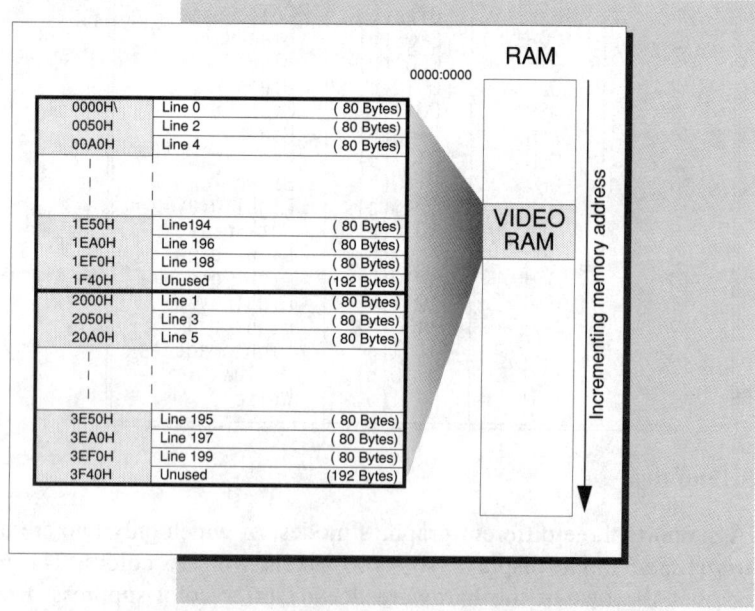

Arrangement of video RAM in graphics mode (blocking)

The desired palette can be accessed either by direct programming of the color selection registers or by calling a special BIOS function (interrupt 10H, function 0BH, sub-function 01H). Load the AH register with the function number (0BH), the BH register with the sub-function (01H), and the BL register with the number of the desired palette (0 or 1).

Each graphic line within the two blocks requires 80 bytes, since the 320 pixels in a line are coded into four pixels to a byte. The first byte in a graphic line (an 80-byte series) corresponds to the first four dots of the graphic on the screen. Bits 7 and 8 contain the color information for the leftmost pixel, while bits 0 and 1 contain the color information for the rightmost pixel of the byte.

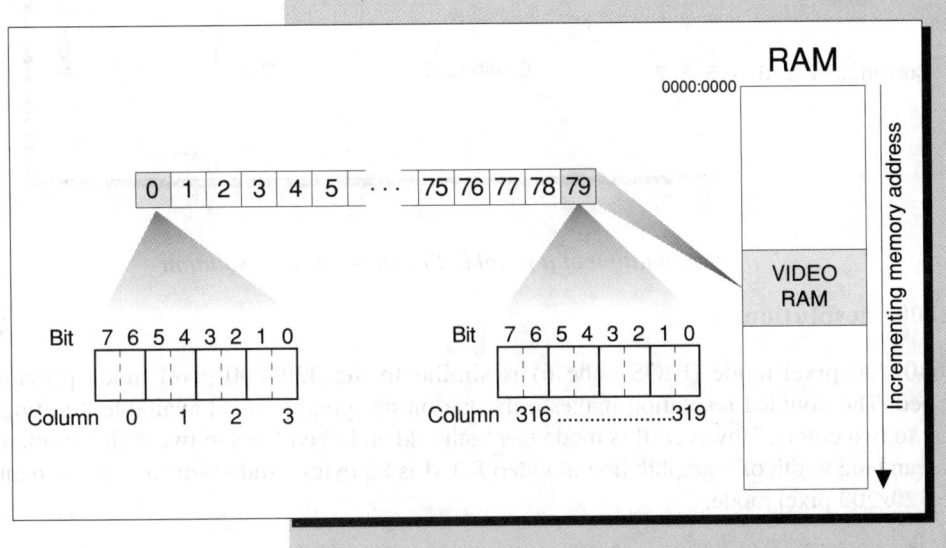

Representation of a graphic line in 320x200 resolution

With this information, you can derive a formula for determining the byte in video RAM, similar to the Hercules card. This byte is relative to the starting address of the screen page, which contains the color information for a pixel. The screen column (0—319) is designated as X and the screen line (0—199) as Y:

```
Address = 2000H * (Y mod 2) + 80 * int(Y/2) + int(X/4)
```

To determine the number of the two bits within this byte that represents the pixel, use the following formula:

```
Bit number = 6 - 2 * (X mod 4)
```

For example, if this formula returns 4, the color information for the dot is coded into bits 4 and 5.

320x200 pixel graphics mode can also suppress the color signal, converting colors to gray scales using mode code 5.

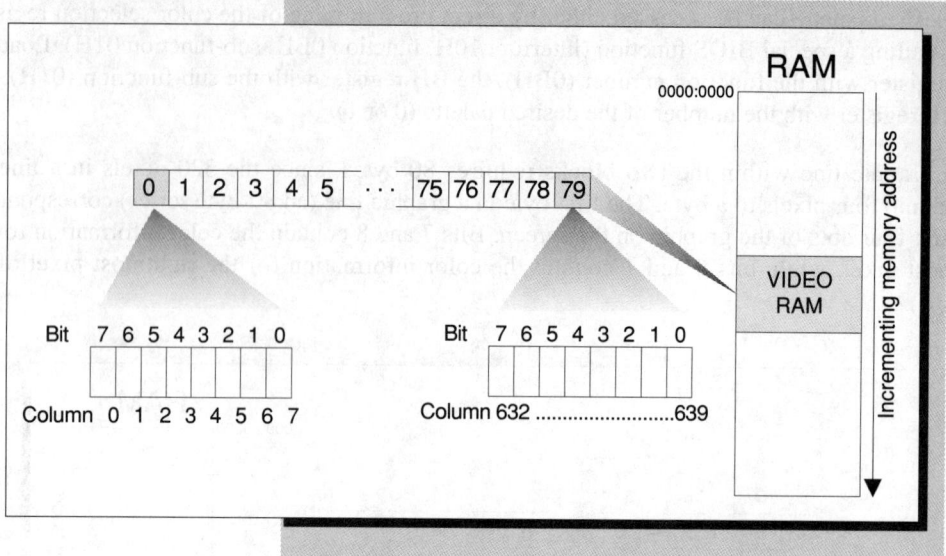

Representation of a graphic line in 640x200 resolution

640x200 resolution

The 640x200 pixel mode (BIOS code 6) is similar to the 320x200 pixel mode previously described. The doubled resolution makes only one bit per graphic pixel available, limiting the display to two colors. However, this mode has both odd and open lines in two different memory blocks, and the width of a graphic line in video RAM is 80 bytes. Addressing a pixel is identical to the 320x200 pixel mode.

```
Address = 2000H * (Y mod 2) + 80 * int(Y/2) + int(X/8)
Bit_number = 7 - (X mod 8)
```

CGA registers

The CGA has a mode selection register at address 3D8H, which is comparable with the control register of the monochrome display adapter. You can write to this register but you cannot read it.

Pixels that represent bits with values of 0 appear in this mode as black pixels. However, if a bit is set, the corresponding pixel appears on the screen as coded in one of the bottom four bits of the color selection register (more on this register later).

The desired color can be implemented without direct programming by using a video BIOS function (interrupt 10H, function 0BH, sub-function 00H). Place the function number (0BH) in the AH register, the sub-function (00H) in the BH register, and the color (0 to 15) in the BL register.

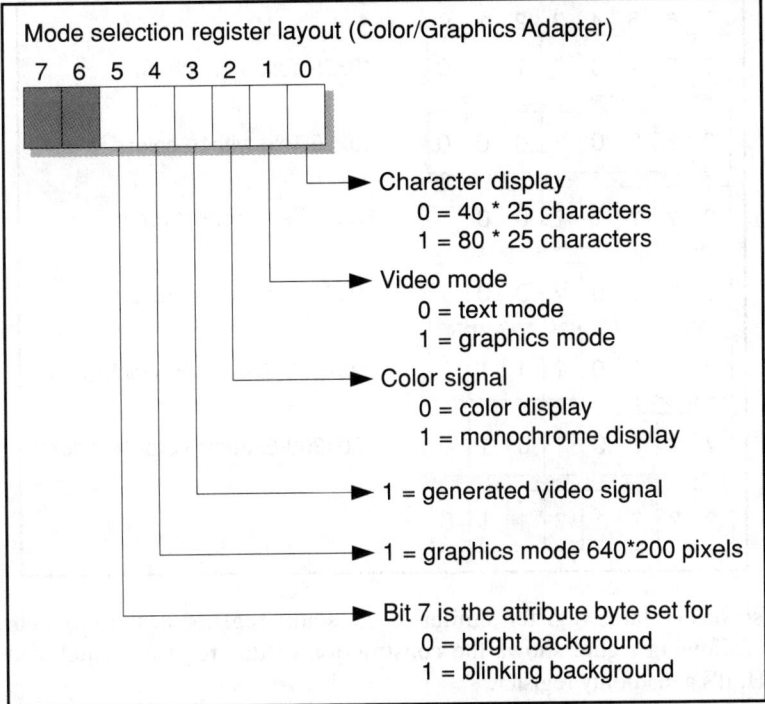

Mode selection register layout (Color/Graphics Adapter)

7 6 5 4 3 2 1 0

Character display
0 = 40 * 25 characters
1 = 80 * 25 characters

Video mode
0 = text mode
1 = graphics mode

Color signal
0 = color display
1 = monochrome display

1 = generated video signal

1 = graphics mode 640*200 pixels

Bit 7 is the attribute byte set for
0 = bright background
1 = blinking background

Bit layout

Bit 0 of this register determines the text mode display of 80 or 40 columns per line. A 1 in bit 0 displays 80 columns, while a 0 in bit 0 displays 40 columns.

The status of bit 1 switches the CGA from text mode to the 320x200 bit-mapped graphics mode. A 1 in this register selects graphics mode, while a 0 selects text mode.

Bit 2 is useful if you want to use your CGA with a monochrome monitor. If this bit contains the value 1, the 6845 suppresses the color signal, displaying monochrome mode only.

Bit 3 is responsible for creating screens. If this bit contains the value 0, the screen remains black. This suppression is useful when changing between display modes; it prevents sudden signals, which could cause damage, from reaching the monitor.

Bit 4 enables and disables 640x200 bitmapped graphics mode. A 1 in bit 4 enables this mode, while a 0 disables it.

Bit 5 has the same significance as in the monochrome card. If it contains a 0, blinking stops and bit 7 returns one of the 16 available background colors. This bit contains a default value of 1, which causes blinking characters.

The various text or graphics modes and the color or monochrome display can be selected in these modes with this register. Bits 0, 1, 2, and 4 are used for this. The following table shows how these bits must be programmed to obtain certain modes:

7	6	5	4	3	2	1	0	
?	?	?	0	?	1	0	0	40x25 Text monochrome
?	?	?	0	?	0	0	0	40x25 Text with 16 colors
?	?	?	1	?	0	0	1	80x25 Text monochrome
?	?	?	0	?	0	0	1	80x25 Text with 16 colors
?	?	?	0	?	1	1	0	320x200 Graphic monochrome
?	?	?	0	?	0	1	0	320x200 Graphic color (4 colors)
?	?	?	1	?	1	1	0	

The CGA also has a status register similar to the status register in the monochrome display adapter. The following figure shows the construction of this register, which can be found at address 3DAH. It's a read-only register.

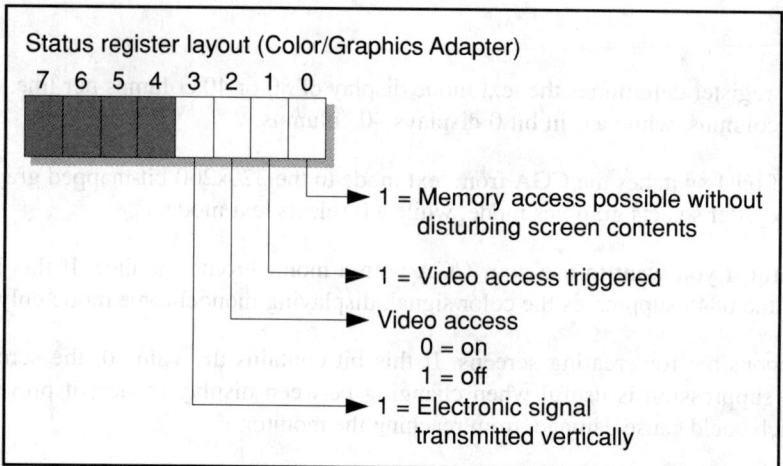

Bit 0 of this register always contains the value 1 when the 6845 sends a horizontal synchronization signal to the monitor. This signal is transmitted when the creation of a line ends and the CRT's electron beam reaches the end of the screen line. The electron beam then jumps back to the left corner of the screen line. This bit is significant because the CGA doesn't always allow data reading or writing within video RAM.

Flickering and the CGA

Flickering occurs because the 6845 must continuously access video RAM in order to read its contents for screen display. If a program tries to transmit data to video RAM, problems can arise when the 6845 accesses video RAM simultaneously. The result of this memory conflict is an occasional flickering on the screen.

To avoid this problem, you should only access video RAM when the 6845 isn't accessing it. This only occurs when a horizontal synchronization signal travels to the screen because it needs some time until the electron beam has executed this instruction. Therefore, the status register must be read before every video RAM access on a CGA. This process must be repeated until bit 0 contains the value 1. When this happens, a maximum of two bytes can then be transmitted to video RAM.

Demonstration program

The program at the end of this section demonstrates how this process works. This delay in video RAM access doesn't occur with monochrome cards because they are equipped with special hardware logic and fast RAM chips. This is also true of most of the newer model color cards. Before waiting for the horizontal synchronization signal, which results in a delay of the display output, the user should try direct access to video RAM to test the color card's reaction time.

If many accesses to video RAM occur within a short period of time (e.g., scrolling the screen), the electron beam doesn't respond fast enough. The screen should be switched off using bit 3 of the mode selection register. This prevents the 6845 from accessing video RAM, which allows unlimited user access to video RAM. When data transfer ends, the screen can be switched on again. BIOS uses this method during scrolling, which results in the flickering "strobe effect".

Color selection register

The color selection register is located at address 3D9H. This register is write-only (cannot be read).

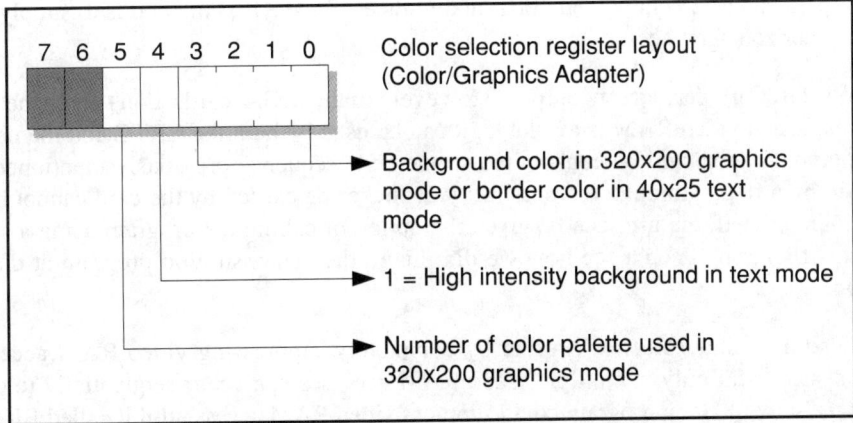

The meanings of the individual bits in this register depend on the display mode. Text mode uses the lowest four bits for assigning the background color from the 16 available colors. In 320x200

graphics mode, these four bits indicate the color of all pixels represented by the bit combination 00(b) (background color).

Synchronizing screen access

To minimize flickering, the CRT controller and video RAM must be synchronized. Bit 0 in the CGA card's status register helps you do this. If bit 0 contains a value of 1, the electron beam is performing a horizontal scan. If pixels aren't currently being displayed on the screen, the CRT controller isn't accessing video RAM. So, it can place a program in video RAM undisturbed.

To use this mechanism, every CGA access to video RAM should start with a short code sequence, consisting of two loops, and end when the CRTC performs a horizontal rescan. The first loop reads the contents of the status register as long as a horizontal rescan doesn't occur (i.e., bit 0 contains 0). If this condition occurs, the second loop, which reads the contents of the status register, executes. This continues until bit 0 contains 1 and the system performs a horizontal rescan.

At first this procedure may seem very complicated. Although it's not immediately clear why the first loop waits for a horizontal rescan, it's important to know what happens when the rescan occurs. This loop ensures that the second loop ends at the beginning of a horizontal retrace. If the first loop failed, then the second loop would end before it was supposed to end. However, then a conflict with the CRTC may occur during video RAM access.

Linking this routine doesn't guarantee access to video RAM because when the horizontal retrace ends, the video RAM access ends about 4 microseconds later. How many bytes can be transferred between video RAM and the processor in that time depends on the processor speed and other factors, such as data bus width. Let's see how this works on a basic PC with a system timer of 4.77 MHz. Exactly two bytes (an ASCII character and its attribute) can be transferred during the horizontal retrace.

In addition to horizontal retrace, you can also use the 7 millisecond pause during vertical retrace to access video RAM. Up to 800 bytes can be transferred during this period. However, vertical retraces are much less frequent than horizontal retraces. So, the best method is to simply transfer data during horizontal retraces.

Both procedures hinder screen output. However, many CGA cards don't even need these procedures. When video RAM is available, it can be used by both the CRTC and the processor. Your program code should be constructed so the code sequence previously mentioned can be suppressed by a flag. Although the possibility of flickering caused by the card cannot be tested by the program itself, the user can be given the option of calling the program using a switch to control this flickering. You'll see how we did this in the demonstration program at the end of this section.

We can also minimize screen flickering by completely suppressing video RAM access. This method is successful only if multiple video RAM accesses can occur sequentially (e.g., when scrolling the screen). So, a program could suppress video RAM access until it called BIOS video interrupt functions 06H (scroll up) or 07H (scroll down). To realize this, bit 3 of the mode select register would have to be switched off before the access, and switched on after the access. The result is a "strobe effect" that occurs during scrolling or other functions.

Bit 5 selects the color palette for 320x200 mode. If this bit contains the value 1, the first color palette (cyan, violet, white) is selected. A value of 0 selects the second color palette (green, yellow, red).

The CGA card's CRT controller

The CGA card uses the 6845 CRT controller from Motorola (see Section 4.4 for more information on this controller). This controller accesses the 18 internal registers exactly like the MDA card, using two consecutive 8-bit OUT instructions. A single 16-bit OUT instruction (used in Hercules cards) isn't permitted. Unlike the MDA, the CGA's registers are at port address 3D4H and 3D5H. The following table shows the contents of the CRT register in different display modes:

CGA CRTC register contents in 40x25 text mode (Txt1), 80x25 text mode (Txt2) and graphics mode (Grfx)				
Reg.	Meaning	Txt1	Txt2	Grfx
0H	Horiz. character total	56	113	56
1H	Horiz. characters displayed	40	80	40
2H	Horiz. synchronization signal to	45	90	45
3H	Horiz. synchronization signal in chars.	10	10	10
4H	Vert. character total	31	31	127
5H	Vert. characters justified	6	6	6
6H	Vert. characters displayed	25	25	100
7H	Vert. synchronization signal to chars.	28	28	112
8H	Interlace mode	2	2	2
9H	Number of scan lines per line	7	7	1
AH	Starting line of blinking cursor	6	6	6
BH	Ending line of blinking cursor	7	7	7
CH	Screen page starting address (high byte)	0	0	0
DH	Screen page starting address (low byte)	0	0	0
EH	Cursor character address (high byte)	0	0	0
FH	Cursor character address (low byte)	0	0	0
10H	Light pen position (high byte)	?	?	?
11H	Light pen position (low byte)	?	?	?
? = depends on light pen's position				

These registers are useful because they define the position and appearance of the cursor on the screen. In Section 4.1 we described how to program these registers. The CGA adds registers 0CH and 0DH. These registers indicate the start of the video page, that must be displayed on the screen, as offset of the beginning of the 16K RAM on the card (B800:0000), divided by 2. Register 0CH contains the most significant 8 bits of this offset, while register 0DH contains the least significant 8 bits. Usually both registers contain the value 0, displaying the first screen page (beginning at the address B800:0000) on the screen. To display the first screen page, which begins at location B800:1000 in the 80x25 text mode, the value 1000H divided by 2 (800H) must be entered in both registers.

The following demonstration program accesses the Color/Graphics Adapter. The only significant difference between this program and the previous programs is that the video controller can synchronize video RAM access and screen construction. This is necessary on all video cards where direct access to video RAM causes a flickering on the screen. The WAIT constant, defined directly after the program header, switches synchronization on or off. Its contents decide during the assembly of the program, whether to assemble the program lines for synchronization listed in the source listing. Since these lines would slow down the screen considerably, they should be included only if it's absolutely necessary.

Assembler listing: VCOL.ASM

```
;********************************************************************;
;*                          V C O L                               *;
;*----------------------------------------------------------------*;
;*   Task       : Makes some basic functions available for        *;
;*                access to the Color Graphics Adapter (CGA).      *;
;*----------------------------------------------------------------*;
;*   Info       : All functions subdivide the screen              *;
;*                into  columns 0 to 79 and lines 0 to 24          *;
;*                in text mode and into  columns 0 to 719 and      *;
;*                the lines 0 to 347 in graphic mode.              *;
;*                the 40 column text mode is not supported !       *;
;*                A high resolution graphic screen should appear*;
;*                first, followed by a text screen. If the high   *;
;*                res screen doesn't appear, try running the       *;
;*                program a few times in succession.               *;
;*----------------------------------------------------------------*;
;*   Author     : Michael Tischer                                 *;
;*   Developed on : 08/13/87                                       *;
;*   Last update : 03/02/92                                        *;
;*----------------------------------------------------------------*;
;*   Assembly    : MASM VCOL;                                      *;
;*                LINK VCOL;                                       *;
;*----------------------------------------------------------------*;
;*   Call        : VCOL                                            *;
;********************************************************************;

;== Constants ===================================================

CONTROL_REG  = 03D8h          ;Control register port address
CCHOICE_REG  = 03D9h          ;Color select register port address
ADDRESS_6845 = 03D4h          ;6845 address register
DATA_6845    = 03D5h          ;6845 data register
VIO_SEG      = 0B800h         ;Video RAM segment address
CUR_START    = 10             ;Reg # for CRTC: Cursor start line
CUR_END      = 11             ;Reg # for CTRC: Cursor end line
CURPG_HI     = 12             ;Page address (high byte)
CURPG_LO     = 13             ;Page address (low byte)
CURPOS_HI    = 14             ;Reg # for CRTC: Cursor pos high byte
CURPOS_LO    = 15             ;Reg # for CRTC: Cursor pos low byte
DELAY        = 20000          ;Counter for delay loop

;== Macros ======================================================

;-- SETMODE : Macro for configuring screen control register ---------

setmode  macro modus

         mov  dx,CONTROL_REG   ;Address of the display control
register
         mov  al,modus         ;New mode into the AL register
         out  dx,al            ;Send mode to control register

         endm

;-- WAITRET: waits until display is completed -----------------------

waitret  macro
```

```
         local  wr1            ;Local label

         mov  dx,3DAh          ;Address of the display status
register
wr1:     in   al,dx            ;Get content
         test al,8             ;Vertical retrace?
         je   wr1              ;No --> waitforit

         endm

;== Stack =======================================================

stack    segment para stack    ;Definition of stack segment

         dw 256 dup (?)         ;256-word stack

stack    ends                   ;End of stack segment

;== Data ========================================================

data     segment para 'DATA'    ;Definition of data segment

;== Data required for demo program =======================================

initm    db 13,10
         db "VCOL (c) 1988,1989 by Michael Tischer "
         db 13,10,13,10
         db "This demo program only runs with a Color/Graphics",13,10
         db "Adapter ( CGA ).  If your PC uses another type of",13,10
         db "video card press the <s> key to stop the program.",13,10
         db "Press any other key to start the program...",13,10,"$"

str1     db 1,0

;== Table of offset addresses of line beginnings =====================
lines    dw  0*160, 1*160, 2*160 ;start addresses of the lines as
         dw  3*160, 4*160, 5*160 ;offset addresses in the video RAM
         dw  6*160, 7*160, 8*160
         dw  9*160,10*160,11*160,12*160,13*160,14*160,15*160,16*160
         dw 17*160,18*160,19*160,20*160,21*160,22*160,23*160,24*160

graphict db 38h, 28h, 2Dh, 0Ah, 7Fh, 06h  ;register values for the
         db 64h, 70h, 02h, 01h, 06h, 07h  ;graphic-modes

textt    db 71h, 50h, 5Ah, 0Ah, 1Fh, 06h  ;register values for the
         db 19h, 1Ch, 02h, 07h, 06h, 07h  ;graphic modes

waitforit db 0                   ;TRUE (<>0) when caller uses the
                                 ;/F switch

data     ends                    ;End of data segment

;== Code ========================================================

code     segment para 'CODE'     ;Definition of the CODE segment
         assume cs:code, ds:data, es:data, ss:stack

;== This is only the Demo-Program =======================================
```

```
demo      proc far

          ;-- Look for /F from DOS prompt ------------------------

          mov  cl,ds:128       ;Get number of bytes from prompt
          or   cl,cl           ;No parameters given?
          je   switch1         ;No --> Ignore
          mov  bx,129          ;BX points to first byte in prompt
          mov  ch,bh           ;Set loop high byte to 0

switch:   cmp  [bx],"F/"       ;Switch in this position?
          je   switch1         ;Yes --> Switch found
          cmp  [bx],"f/"       ;Switch in this position?
          je   switch1         ;Yes --> Switch found
          inc  bl              ;Set BX to next character
          loop switch          ;Check next character

switch1:  mov  ax,data         ;Get segment addr. of data segment
          mov  ds,ax           ;and load into DS
          mov  es,ax           ;and ES

          mov  waitforit,cl    ;Set WAIT flag

          ;-- Display init message and wait for input -------------

          mov  ah,9            ;Function number for string display
          mov  dx,offset initm ;Address of initial message
          int  21h             ;Call DOS interrupt 21H

          xor  ah,ah           ;Function number: get key
          int  16h             ;Call BIOS keyboard interrupt
          cmp  al,"s"          ;<s> key pressed?
          je   ende            ;Yes --> End program
          cmp  al,"S"          ;<S> key pressed?
          jne  startdemo       ;No --> Start demo

ende:     mov  ax,4C00h        ;Function number: End program
          int  21h             ;Call DOS interrupt 21H

startdemo label near
          call grafhi          ;switch on 320x200 pixel graphics
          xor  al,al
          call cgr             ;Clear graphic display

          xor  bx,bx           ;Column 0
          xor  dx,dx           ;Line 0
          mov  ax,199          ;Pixels-vertical
          mov  cx,639          ;Pixels-horizontal
gr1:      push cx              ;Record horizontal pixels
          mov  cx,ax           ;Vertical pixels to counter
          push ax              ;Record vertical pixels on the stack
          mov  al,1
gr2:      call pixhi           ;Set pixel
          inc  dx              ;Increment line
          loop gr2             ;Draw line
          pop  ax              ;Get vertical pixels from the stack
          sub  ax,3            ;Next line 3 pixels less
          pop  cx              ;Get horizontal pixels from the stack
          push cx              ;Record horizontal pixels
          push ax              ;Record vertical pixels on the stack
          mov  al,1
gr3:      call pixhi           ;Set pixel
          inc  bx              ;Increment column
```

```
          loop gr3             ;Draw line
          pop  ax              ;Get vertical pixels from stack
          pop  cx              ;Get horizontal pixels from stack
          sub  cx,6            ;Next line 6 pixels less
          push cx              ;Record horizontal pixels
          mov  cx,ax           ;Vertical pixels to counter
          push ax              ;Record vertical pixels on the stack
          mov  al,1
gr4:      call pixhi           ;Set pixel
          dec  dx              ;Decrement line
          loop gr4             ;Draw line
          pop  ax              ;Get vertical pixels from stack
          sub  ax,3            ;Next line 3 pixels less
          pop  cx              ;Get horizontal pixels from stack
          push cx              ;Record horizontal pixels
          push ax              ;Record vertical pixels on the stack
          mov  al,1
gr5:      call pixhi           ;Set pixel
          dec  bx              ;Increment column
          loop gr5             ;Draw line
          pop  ax              ;Get vertical pixels from the stack
          pop  cx              ;Get horizontal pixels from the stack
          sub  cx,6            ;Next line 6 pixels less
          cmp  ax,5            ;Is the vertical line longer than 5
          ja   gr1             ;YES--> continue

          xor  ah,ah           ;Wait for function number of key wait
          int  16h             ;Call BIOS keyboard interrupt

          call text            ;Switch on 80x25 character text mode
          xor  bp,bp           ;Process screen page 0 first
demo1:    mov  al,30h          ;ASCII code "0"
          or   ax,bp           ;Convert page number to ASCII
          mov  str1,al         ;Store in string
          call setcol          ;Set color
          call setpage         ;Activate screen page in BP
          call cls             ;Clear screen page
          xor  bx,bx           ;Begin in the upper left
          call calo            ;Screen corner with output
          mov  cx,2000         ;A page contains 2,000 characters
          xor  ah,ah           ;Start with color code 0
          mov  si,offset str1  ;Offset address of string 1
demo2:    inc  ah              ;Increment color value
          call print           ;Output string 1
          loop demo2           ;Repeat until screen is full

          xor  ah,ah           ;Wait for key
          int  16h             ;Call BIOS keyboard interrupt
          inc  bp              ;Increment page number
          cmp  bp,4            ;All 4 pages processed ?
          jne  demo1           ;No --> then next page

          xor  bp,bp           ;Activate page 0 again
          call setpage
          jmp  ende
demo      endp                 ;Goto program end

;== The actual functions follow ==============================

;-- TEXT: switches the text display on ----------------------------
;-- Input   : none
;-- Output  : none
;-- Register : AX, SI, BH, DX and FLAGS are changed
```

```
text    proc near

        mov  si,offset textt    ;Offset address of the register table
        mov  bl,00100001b       ;80x25 text mode,blinking
        jmp  short vcprog        ;Program video controller again

text    endp

;-- GRAFHI: switches the 640*200 pixel graphic mode on ----------------
;-- Input  : none
;-- Output : none
;-- Register : AX, SI, BH, DX and FLAGS are changed

grafhi  proc near

        mov  bl,00010010b       ;Graphic mode with 640x200 pixels
        jmp  short graphic       ;Program video controller again

grafhi  endp

;-- GRAFLO: switches the 320x200 pixel graphic mode on ----------------
;-- Input  : none
;-- Output : none
;-- Register : AX, SI, BH, DX and FLAGS are changed

graflo  proc near

        mov  bl,00100010b       ;Graphic mode with 320x200 pixels
graphic: mov si,offset graphict ;Offset address of the register
table

graflo  endp

;-- VCPROG: programs the video controller ----------------------------
;-- Input  : SI = Address of a register table
;--          BL = Value for display control register
;-- Output : none
;-- Register : AX, SI, BH, DX and FLAGS are changed

vcprog  proc near

        setmode bl              ;Bit 3 = 0: screen off

        mov  cx,12              ;12 registers are set
        xor  bh,bh              ;Start with register 0
vcp1:   lodsb                   ;Get register value from table
        mov  ah,al              ;Register value to AH
        mov  al,bh              ;Number of the register to AL
        call setvk              ;Transmit value to controller
        inc  bh                 ;Address next register
        loop vcp1               ;Set additional registers

        or   bl,8               ;Bit 3 = 1: screen on
        setmode bl              ;Set new mode
        ret                     ;Back to caller

vcprog  endp

;-- SETCOL : Sets the color of the display frame and Background -----
;-- Input  : AL = color value
;-- Output : none
;-- register : AX and DX are changed
;-- Info   : in text mode the lowest 4 bits indicate the frame color
;--          in graphic mode the lowest 4 bits indicate the frame
```

```
;--          and background color, bit 5 selects the color palette

setcol  proc near

        mov  dx,CCHOICE_REG     ;Address of the color selection
register
        out  dx,al              ;Output color value
        ret                     ;Back to caller

setcol  endp

;-- CDEF   : sets the start  and end line of the cursor --------------
;-- Input  : CL = start line
;--          CH = end line
;-- Output : none
;-- register : AX and DX are changed

cdef    proc near

        mov  al,CUR_START       ;Register 10: start line
        mov  ah,cl              ;Start line to AH
        call setvk              ;Transmit to video controller
        mov  al,CUR_END         ;Register 11: end line
        mov  ah,ch              ;End line to AH
        jmp  short setvk        ;Transmit to video controller

cdef    endp

;-- SETPAGE : sets the screen page ----------------------------------
;-- Input  : BP = Number of the screen page (0 to 3)
;-- Output : none
;-- register : BX, AX, CX and DX are changed
;-- Info   : in the Graphic modes the first screen page has the
;--          number 0, the second the number 2

setpage proc near

        mov  bx,bp              ;Screen page to BX
        mov  cl,5               ;Multiply by 2,048
        ror  bx,cl
        mov  al,CURPG_HI        ;Register 12: High byte page address
        mov  ah,bh              ;High byte of the screen page to AH
        call setvk              ;Transmit to video controller
        mov  al,CURPG_LO        ;Register 13: Low byte page address
        mov  ah,bl              ;Low byte of the screen page to AH
        jmp  short setvk        ;Transmit to video controller

setpage endp

;-- SETBLINK : sets the blinking cursor -----------------------------
;-- Input  : DI = Offset address of the cursor
;-- Output : none
;-- register : BX, AX and DX are changed

setblink proc near

        mov  bx,di              ;Move offset to BX
        mov  al,CURPOS_HI       ;High byte of the cursor offset
        mov  ah,bh              ;High byte of the offset
        call setvk              ;Transmit to video controller
        mov  al,CURPOS_LO       ;Low byte of the cursor offset
        mov  ah,bl              ;Low byte of the offset

        ;-- SETVK is called automatically ---------------------------
```

```
setblink  endp

;-- SETVK    : sets a byte in one register of the video controller ----
;-- Input    : AL = Number of the register
;--            AH = new content of the register
;-- Output   : none
;-- register : DX and AL are changed

setvk     proc near

          mov   dx,ADDRESS_6845    ;Address of the index register
          out   dx,al             ;Send number of the register
          jmp   short $+2         ;Short I/O pause
          inc   dx                ;Address of the index register
          mov   al,ah             ;Content to AL
          out   dx,al             ;Set new content
          ret                     ;Back to caller

setvk     endp

;-- GETVK    : gets a byte from one register of the video controller -
;-- Input    : AL = Number of the register
;-- Output   : AL = Contents of register
;-- register : DX and AL are changed

getvk     proc near

          mov   dx,ADDRESS_6845    ;Address of the index register
          out   dx,al             ;Send number of the register
          inc   dx                ;Index register address
          jmp   short $+2         ;Short io pause
          in    al,dx             ;Set new contents
          ret                     ;Back to caller

getvk     endp

;-- SCROLLUP: scrolls a window N lines upward ------------------------
;-- Input    : BL = line upper left
;--            BH = column upper left
;--            DL = line below right
;--            DH = column below right
;--            CL = Number of lines, to be scrolled
;--            : BP = Number of the screen page (0 to 3)
;-- Output   : none
;-- register : only FLAGS are changed
;-- Info     : the display lines liberated are cleared

scrollup  proc near

          cld                     ;On string commands count up

          push  ax                ;All changed registers to the
          push  bx                ;Secure stack
          push  di                ;In this case the sequence
          push  si                ;must be observed !

          push  bx                ;These three registers are returned
          push  cx                ;before the end of the routine
          push  dx                ;From the stack
          sub   dl,bl             ;Calculate the number of lines
          inc   dl
          sub   dl,cl             ;Subtract number of lines to be
scrolled
```

```
          sub   bh,dh             ;Calculate number of columns
          inc   dh
          call  calo              ;Convert upper left in offset
          mov   si,di             ;Record address in SI
          add   bl,cl             ;First line in scrolled window
          call  calo              ;Convert first line in offset
          xchg  si,di             ;Exchange SI and DI

          cmp   waitforit,0       ;Flicker suppressed?
          je    sup0              ;No --> SUP0

waitret                          ;Yes -->Wait for retrace
          setmode 00100101b       ;Disable screen

sup0:     push  ds                ;Store segment register
          push  es                ;On the stack
          mov   ax,VIO_SEG        ;Segment address of the video RAM
          mov   ds,ax             ;To DS
          mov   es,ax             ;And ES

sup1:     mov   ax,di             ;Record DI in AX
          mov   bx,si             ;Record SI in BX
          mov   cl,dh             ;Number of columns in counter
          rep movsw               ;Move a line
          mov   di,ax             ;Restore DI from AX
          mov   si,bx             ;Restore SI from BX
          add   di,160            ;Set next line
          add   si,160
          dec   dl                ;processed all lines ?
          jne   sup1              ;No --> move another line

          pop   es                ;Get segment register from
          pop   ds                ;Stack

          cmp   waitforit,0       ;Flickering suppressed?
          je    sup2              ;No --> SUP2

          setmode 00101101b       ;Yes --> Enable screen

sup2:     pop   dx                ;Get lower right corner back
          pop   cx                ;Return number of lines
          pop   bx                ;Return upper left corner
          mov   bl,dl             ;Lower line to BL
          sub   bl,cl             ;Subtract number of lines
          inc   bl
          mov   ah,07h            ;Color : black on white
          call  clear             ;Clear lines

          pop   si                ;CX and DX have already been
          pop   di                ;Restored
          pop   bx
          pop   ax

          ret                     ;Back to caller

scrollup  endp

;-- SCROLLDN: scrolls a window N lines down --------------------------
;-- Input    : BL = line upper left
;--            BH = column upper left
;--            DL = line below right
;--            DH = column below right
;--            CL = number of lines to be scrolled
;--            : BP = number of the screen page (0 to 3)
```

169

```
;-- Output   : none                                      sdn2:    pop  dx              ;Get lower right corner
;-- register : only FLAGS are changed                             pop  cx              ;Return number of lines
;-- Info     : the display lines liberated are cleared            pop  bx              ;Return upper left corner
                                                                  mov  dl,bl           ;upper line to DL
scrolldn proc near                                                add  dl,cl           ;Add number of lines
                                                                  dec  dl
         cld                  ;On string commands count up        mov  ah,07h          ;Color : black on white
                                                                  call clear           ;Erase liberated lines
         push ax              ;Record all changed registers
         push bx              ;On the stack                       pop  si              ;CX and DX have already been
         push di              ;In this case the sequence          pop  di              ;Returned
         push si              ;Must be observed !                 pop  bx
                                                                  pop  ax
         push bx              ;These three registers are returned
         push cx              ;From the stack before the end      ret                  ;Back to caller
         push dx              ;Of the routine
                                                         scrolldn endp
         sub  dh,bh           ;Calculate the number of columns
         inc  dh                                         ;-- CLS: Clear the screen completely ----------------------------------
         mov  al,bl           ;Record line upper left in AL   ;-- Input   : BP = number of the screen page (0 or 1)
         mov  bl,dl           ;Line below right to line below left ;-- Output  : none
         call calo            ;Convert upper left in offset   ;-- register : only FLAGS are changed
         mov  si,di           ;Record address in SI
         sub  bl,cl           ;Subtract number of characters to cls     proc near
scroll
         call calo            ;Convert upper left in offset       mov  ah,07h          ;Color is white on black
         xchg si,di           ;Exchange SI and DI                 xor  bx,bx           ;upper left is (0/0)
         sub  dl,al           ;Calculate number of lines          mov  dx,4F18h        ;Lower right is (79/24)
         inc  dl
         sub  dl,cl           ;Subtract number of lines to be     ;-- Execute Clear --------------------------------------
scrolled
                                                         cls     endp
         cmp  waitforit,0     ;Flicker suppressed?
         je   sdn0            ;No --> SDNO                ;-- CLEAR: fills a designated display area with space characters ------
                                                         ;-- Input    : AH = attribute/color
         waitret              ;Yes --> Wait for retrace   ;--           BL = line upper left
         setmode 00100101b    ;Disable screen             ;--           BH = column upper left
                                                         ;--           DL = line below right
sdn0:    push ds              ;Store segment register on the ;--       DH = column below right
         push es              ;Stack                      ;--           BP = number of the screen page (0 to 3)
         mov  ax,VIO_SEG      ;Segment address of the video RAM ;-- Output : none
         mov  ds,ax           ;To DS                      ;-- register : only FLAGS are changed
         mov  es,ax           ;and ES
                                                         clear   proc near
sdn1:    mov  ax,di           ;Record DI in AX
         mov  bx,si           ;Record SI in BX                    cld                  ;On string commands count up
         mov  cl,dh           ;Number of columns in counter       push cx              ;Store all register which are
         rep movsw            ;Move a line                        push dx              ;Changed on the stack
         mov  di,ax           ;Restore DI from AX                 push si
         mov  si,bx           ;Restore SI from BX                 push di
         sub  di,160          ;Set into next line                 push es
         sub  si,160                                              sub  dl,bl           ;Calculate number of lines
         dec  dl              ;processed all lines ?              inc  dl
         jne  sdn1            ;No --> move another line           sub  dh,bh           ;Calculate number of columns
                                                                  inc  dh
         pop  es              ;Return segment register from       call calo            ;Offset address of the upper left
         pop  ds              ;Stack                      corner
                                                                  mov  cx,VIO_SEG      ;Segment address of the video RAM
         cmp  waitforit,0     ;Flicker suppressed?                mov  es,cx           ;To ES
         je   sdn2            ;No --> SDN2                        xor  ch,ch           ;High bytes of the counter to 0
                                                                  mov  al," "          ;Space character
         setmode 00101101b    ;Yes --> Enable screen
                                                                  cmp  waitforit,0     ;Flickering suppressed?
                                                                  je   clear1          ;No --> CLEAR1
```

```
            push dx                 ;Store DX on the stack
            waitret                 ;Retrace wait
            setmode 00100101b       ;Switch screen off
            pop  dx                 ;Return DX from the stack

clear1:     mov  si,di              ;Record DI in SI
            mov  cl,dh              ;Number columns in counter
            rep stosw               ;Store space character
            mov  di,si              ;Return DI from SI
            add  di,160             ;Set in next line
            dec  dl                 ;All lines processed ?
            jne  clear1             ;No --> erase another line

            cmp  waitforit,0        ;Flicker suppressed?
            je   clear2             ;No --> CLEAR2

            setmode 00101101b       ;Enable screen

clear2:     pop  es                 ;Get registers from
            pop  di                 ;Stack again
            pop  si
            pop  dx
            pop  cx
            ret                     ;Back to caller

clear       endp

;-- PRINT: outputs a string on the screen -----------------------------
;-- Input  : AH = attribute/color
;--          DI = offset address of the first character
;--          SI = offset address of the strings to DS
;--          BP = number of the screen page (0 to 3)
;-- Output : DI points behind the last character output
;-- register : AL, DI and FLAGS are changed
;-- Info   : the string must be terminated by a NUL-character.
;--          other control characters are not recognized

print       proc near

            cld                     ;On string commands count up
            push si                 ;Store SI, DX and ES on the stack
            push es
            push cx
            push dx
            mov  dx,VIO_SEG         ;Segment address of the video RAM
            mov  cl,waitforit       ;Get WAITFORIT flag
            mov  es,dx              ;First to DX and then to ES

            jmp  short print3       ;Get character and display it

print1      label near

            or   cl,cl              ;Flicker suppressed?
            je   print2             ;No --> PRINT2

            push ax                 ;Record characters and color
            mov  dx,3DAh            ;Address of the display-status-
register
hr1:        in   al,dx             ;Get content
            test al,1              ;Horizontal retrace?
            jne  hr1               ;No --> wait
            cli                    ;permit no further interrupts
hr2:        in   al,dx             ;Get content
```

```
            test al,1              ;Horizontal retrace?
            je   hr2               ;Yes --> wait
            pop  ax                ;Restore characters and color
            sti                    ;Do not suppress Interrupts any more

print2:     stosw                  ;Store attribute and color in V-RAM
print3:     lodsb                  ;Get next character from the string
            or   al,al             ;Is it NUL
            jne  print1            ;No --> output

printe:     pop  dx                ;Get SI, DX, CX and ES from stack
            pop  cx
            pop  es
            pop  si
            ret                    ;Back to caller

print       endp

;-- CALO: Converts line and column into offset address ----------------
;-- Input  : BL = line
;--          BH = column
;--          BP = number of the screen page (0 to 3)
;-- Output : DI = the offset address
;-- register : DI and FLAGS are changed

calo        proc near

            push ax                ;Secure AX on the stack
            push bx                ;Secure BX on the stack

            shl  bx,1              ;Column and line times 2
            mov  al,bh             ;Column to AL
            xor  bh,bh             ;High byte
            mov  di,[lines+bx]     ;Get offset address of the line
            xor  ah,ah             ;HI byte for column offset
            add  di,ax             ;Add line and column offset
            mov  bx,bp             ;Screen page to BX
            mov  cl,4              ;Multiply by 4,096
            ror  bx,cl
            add  di,bx             ;Add beginning of screen page to
offset
            pop  bx                ;Restore BX from stack
            pop  ax                ;Restore AX from stack
            ret                    ;Back to caller

calo        endp

;-- CGR: Erase the complete Graphic display ---------------------------
;-- Input  : AL = 00H : erase all pixels
;--               FFH : set all pixels
;-- Output : none
;-- register : AH, BX, CX, DI and FLAGS are changed
;-- Info   : this Function erases the Graphic display in both
;--          Graphic modes

cgr         proc near

            push es                ;Store ES on the stack
            cbw                    ;Expand AL to AH
            xor  di,di             ;Offset address in video RAM
            mov  bx,VIO_SEG        ;Segment address screen page
            mov  es,bx             ;Segment address into segment register
            mov  cx,2000h          ;One page is 8KB words
            rep stosw              ;Fill page
```

171

```
        pop   es              ;Return ES from stack
        ret                   ;Back to caller

cgr     endp

;-- PIXLO: sets a pixel in the 320*200 pixel graphic mode -------------
;-- Input  :   BP = number of the screen page (0 or 1)
;--            BX = column (0 to 319)
;--            DX = line  (0 to 199)
;--            AL = color of the pixels (0 to 3)
;-- Output : none
;-- register : AX, DI and FLAGS are changed

pixlo   proc near

        push  ax              ;Secure AX on the stack
        push  bx              ;Note BX on the stack
        push  cx              ;Store CX on the stack
        mov   cl,7
        mov   ah,bl           ;Transmit column to AH
        and   ah,11b          ;Column mod 4
        shl   ah,1            ;Column * 2
        sub   cl,ah           ;7 - 2 * (column mod 4)
        mov   ah,11           ;Bit value
        shl   ax,cl           ;Move to pixel position
        not   ah              ;Reverse AH
        shr   bx,1            ;Divide BX by 4 by shifting
        shr   bx,1            ;Right twice
        jmp   short spix      ;Set pixel

pixlo   endp

;-- PIXHI: sets a pixel in the 640*200 pixel graphic mode -------------
;-- Input  :   BP = number of the screen page (0 or 1)
;--            BX = column (0 to 639)
;--            DX = line  (0 to 199)
;--            AL = color of the pixels (0 or 1)
;-- Output : none
;-- register : AX, DI and FLAGS are changed

pixhi   proc near

        push  ax              ;Store AX on the stack
        push  bx              ;Note BX on the stack
        push  cx              ;Note CX on the stack
        mov   cl,7
        mov   ah,bl           ;Transmit column to AH
        and   ah,111b         ;Column mod 8
        sub   cl,ah           ;7 - column mod 8
        mov   ah,1            ;Bit value
        shl   ax,cl           ;Move pixel position
        not   ah              ;Reverse AH
        mov   cl,3            ;3 shifts
        shr   bx,cl           ;Divide BX by 8

        ;-- set pixel -------------------------------------------------
pixhi   endp

;-- SPIX: sets a pixel in the graphic display --------------------------
;-- Input   : BX = column offset
;--           DX = line  (0 to 199)
;--           AH = Value to cancel old Bits
;--           AL = new Bit value
;-- Output  : none
```

```
;-- register : AX, DI and FLAGS are changed

spix    proc near

        push  es              ;Secure ES on the stack
        push  dx              ;Secure DX on the stack
        push  ax              ;Secure AX on the stack

        xor   di,di           ;Offset address in video RAM
        mov   cx,VIO_SEG      ;Segment address screen page
        mov   es,cx           ;Segment address into segment register
        mov   ax,dx           ;Move line to AX
        shr   ax,1            ;Divide line by 2
        mov   cl,80           ;The factor is 90
        mul   cl              ;Multiply line by 80
        and   dx,1            ;Line mod 2
        mov   cl,3            ;3 shifts
        ror   dx,cl           ;Rotate right (* 2000H)
        mov   di,ax           ;80 * int(line/2)
        add   di,dx           ;+ 2000H * (line mod 4)
        add   di,bx           ;Add column offset
        pop   ax              ;Return AX from stack
        mov   bl,es:[di]      ;Get pixel
        and   bl,ah           ;Erase Bits
        or    bl,al           ;Add pixel
        mov   es:[di],bl      ;write pixel back

        pop   dx              ;Return DX from stack
        pop   es              ;Return ES from stack
        pop   cx              ;Return CX from stack
        pop   bx              ;Return BX from stack
        pop   ax              ;Return AX from stack

        ret                   ;Back to caller

spix    endp
;== end ================================================================
code    ends                  ;End of the code segment
        end demo
```

4.8 EGA and VGA Cards

In this section we'll discuss the features of EGA and VGA cards that separate them from their predecessors. The most important feature in text output is the ability to work with different fonts (refer to Section 4.8.2). We'll discuss both the 16 color and 256 color VGA graphics modes and some tricks you can use to double VGA resolution in 256 color mode.

Although IBM set the standards with its original EGA and VGA cards, the newer cards from third party manufacturers surpass the performance and capabilities of the originals. While all cards adhere to IBM standards, there still isn't a standard for the expanded modes with resolutions up to 1024x768 pixels. So, each manufacturer has its own idea of what works best. We'll discuss this in more detail later in this book, try to find some common features, and suggest some ways you can use them.

The complexity of EGA/VGA cards makes the direct programming of different controllers and registers more complicated. Programming becomes even more involved when manufacturers don't adhere to the standards set by IBM. As you'll see in this section, you won't always have to rely on direct programming to fully utilize these cards. Instead, programming can access the special functions supported by the special EGA/VGA BIOS.

In Section 4.8.9 we'll discuss sprites because EGA and VGA cards can be used in animation programming.

Some of the subsections describe how individual registers are programmed for performing certain tasks. The last section summarizes all standard functions of the EGA and VGA registers. This section also includes a listing of expanded EGA and VGA BIOS functions. Before programming a register, check references to ensure that the appropriate EGA/VGA BIOS function actually exists.

4.8.1 Monitors and Cards

The kind of monitor used can significantly affect the performance of an EGA or VGA card. If your video card's capabilities exceed the physical capabilities of your monitor, you won't get the 800x600 resolution and billions of colors that may have been advertised. You'll need a more sophisticated monitor to utilize all the capabilities of your video card.

This applies to all the applications using your EGA or VGA card. Matching the capabilities of the video card and monitor is extremely important.

First you must determine whether the monitor is color or monochrome. There are several possibilities with EGA and VGA cards.

EGA monitors

An EGA card may be connected to a CGA, EGA, multisync, or monochrome MDA monitor. Depending on the type of monitor connected, the card behaves like either a normal EGA card or like an expanded MDA card. Switching between these modes affects the internal registers of the EGA card and video RAM. In monochrome mode, video RAM begins at B000H instead of B800H. Also, the attribute bytes of the characters in video RAM are interpreted in monochrome

173

mode as they are with an MDA card. The CRT controller's index and data registers change to conform to the MDA standard.

Since an EGA card connected to a monochrome monitor behaves like an MDA card, we won't discuss this configuration in detail. When we mention an EGA card, we're referring to an EGA card with a high resolution monitor attached. This is usually the case because many EGA compatible cards don't even support monochrome monitors, even though the original IBM EGA card offered such support. Compatible cards work only with EGA or multisync monitors.

Another accessory that has almost vanished is the IBM EGA card with 64K of video RAM. These cards could be expanded to 128K, 192K, and 256K. All newer EGA cards include 256K of RAM as standard equipment and we assume this standard configuration in the following sections.

VGA monitors

VGA cards operate differently. A VGA card can be connected to a monochrome monitor, but it must be an analog monochrome VGA monitor instead of a simple MDA monitor. Although analog VGA monitors cost less than color VGA monitors, they can still use the high resolution VGA modes.

An analog VGA monitor isn't able to produce the entire VGA palette of 256 colors because it can display only 64 shades of gray. Usually this won't make a difference as long as you avoid colors that differ slightly in green components. Analog VGA monochrome monitors ignore the red and blue components of the RGB signal and use only the green component.

One advantage the monochrome VGA monitor has over its color counterpart is that the VGA card can be switched into a monochrome mode, in which it behaves like a very powerful MDA card. Just as with the EGA card, the video RAM begins at B000H instead of B800H, and the addresses of the various registers conform to the MDA standard.

You can switch modes on the card using the MODE MONO and MODE CO80 DOS commands, or by using function 00H of the BIOS video interrupt. Only video mode 07H (which is also used by the MDA card) gives you monochrome operation. All other modes enable color operation on a VGA card.

The following table summarizes which monitors can display which EGA and VGA video modes:

EGA/VGA card video modes		Monitor		
Code	Mode	MONO	CGA	EGA/VGA
00H	40x25 character text, 16 colors		■	■
01H	40x25 character text, 16 colors		■	■
02H	80x25 character text, 16 colors		■	■
03H	80x25 character text, 16 colors		■	■
04H	320x200 pixel graphics, 4 colors		■	■
05H	320x200 pixel graphics, 4 colors		■	■
06H	640x200 pixel graphics, 2 colors		■	■
07H	80x25 characters, monochrome	■		
0DH	320x200 pixel graphics, 16 colors			■
0EH	640x200 pixel graphics, 16 colors			■
0FH	640x350 pixel graphics, monochrome	■		
10H	640x350 pixel graphics, 16 colors+			■
11H	640x480 pixel graphics, 2 colors			■*
12H	640x480 pixel graphics, 16 colors			■*
13H	320x200 pixel graphics, 256 colors			■*

```
* only possible with VGA card
+ EGA cards with only 64K of RAM can only display 4 colors
```

Throughout this section we assume that your VGA card has already been switched to color mode for the demonstration program. For EGA cards, we'll always assume 256K of RAM and an EGA or a multisync monitor are being used.

Identifying EGA and VGA cards

If your programs use features that are unique to EGA or VGA cards and the performance depends on a certain monitor type, then your programs should include a query routine that checks for the required hardware before proceeding.

Our routine, called IsEgaVga, is listed as a function in both the C and Pascal versions of the demonstration program. The routine calls two BIOS functions that are found only in EGA and VGA cards. One of these functions immediately determines whether you have an EGA/VGA card or an older card (from MDA to CGA). The function fails if the card is a CGA or an MDA (i.e., the function doesn't exist on these cards).

The other function is available only on the VGA card, which then lets you distinguish between EGA and VGA. This is function 1AH, which has two sub-functions. We're interested in sub-function 00H, which returns information on active and passive video cards.

Active and passive video cards refer to a PC that may have a second video card, such as an MDA or a Hercules card, installed in addition to a VGA card. However, this doesn't apply to most PS/2 models because MDA or Hercules cards aren't available for the MCA bus on these systems.

When you call the 1AH function with the function number in the AH register and the sub-function number in the AL register, you can tell by the contents of the AL register if the function is supported by the BIOS and if a VGA card is installed. A normal BIOS will simply leave the value 00H unchanged in the AL register, indicating that the requested function isn't supported. The VGA BIOS loads the function number 1AH in the AL register to acknowledge the function call. The code returned to the BL register indicates the active video card and the code returned to the BH register indicates the passive video card. These codes are described in the following table:

Code	Meaning
00H	No video card
01H	MDA card with MDA monitor
02H	CGA card with CGA monitor
03H	reserved
04H	EGA card with EGA color monitor
05H	EGA card with MDA monitor
06H	reserved
07H	VGA card with analog monochrome monitor
08H	VGA card with analog color monitor
09H	reserved
0AH	MCGA with CGA card
0BH	MCGA with analog monochrome monitor
0CH	MCGA with analog color monitor

If the call to function 1AH fails, then we assume that a VGA card doesn't exist. In the next step, we check for an EGA card. Sub-function 10H of function 12H is supported only by EGA cards. Unlike many other BIOS functions, the sub-function number is passed in the BL register instead of the AL register. If the sub-function number 10H remains in this register after the function call, the system contains an EGA card.

The contents of the BH register indicate if the EGA card is connected to an MDA or EGA color monitor. The value of this register is 1 for MDA and 0 for EGA. Also, the contents of the BL register indicates how much RAM is available, as indicated by the following table:

Code	EGA Video RAM
00H	64K
01H	128K
02H	192K
03H	256K

The demonstration programs ISEVP.PAS and ISEVC.C each contain an IsEgaVga function and demonstrate its use within a program. You'll also find other slightly modified versions of this function in other demonstration programs later in this section.

Pascal listing: ISEVP.PAS

```
{**********************************************************
*                  I S E V P . P A S                      *
**--------------------------------------------------------**
*  Task         : Tests for an active EGA or VGA card.    *
**--------------------------------------------------------**
*  Author       : Michael Tischer                         *
*  Developed on  : 08/05/90                               *
*  Last update   : 02/26/92                               *
**********************************************************}

Program IsEgaVgaP;

uses DOS;                                  { Add Dos unit }

{-- Type declarations -------------------------------------}

type VCARD = ( EGA_MONO, EGA_COLOR, VGA_MONO, VGA_COLOR, NEITHERNOR );

{**********************************************************
*  IsEgaVga : Determines whether an EGA or a VGA card is installed.  *
**--------------------------------------------------------**
*  Input   : None                                         *
*  Output  : Video card type of type VCARD                *
**********************************************************}

function IsEgaVga : VCARD;

var Regs : Registers;       { Processor registers for interrupt call }

begin
  Regs.AX := $1a00;             { Function 1AH applies to VGA only }
  Intr( $10, Regs );
  if ( Regs.AL = $1a ) then          { Is the function available? }
    case Regs.BL of                       { Yes --> Pass code }
        4 : IsEgaVga := EGA_COLOR;
        5 : IsEgaVga := EGA_MONO;
        7 : IsEgaVga := VGA_MONO;
        8 : IsEgaVga := VGA_COLOR;
      else IsEgaVga := NEITHERNOR;
    end
  else                          { Not a VGA, but it may be an EGA }
    begin
      Regs.ah := $12;                     { Call function 12H, }
      Regs.bl := $10;                     { sub-function 10H   }
      intr($10, Regs);                     { Call video BIOS }
      if ( Regs.bl <> $10 ) then              { EGA card? }
        begin                    { Yes --> Then which monitor? }
          if Regs.BH = 0 then IsEgaVga := EGA_COLOR
                         else IsEgaVga := EGA_MONO;
        end
      else IsEgaVga := NEITHERNOR;
    end;
end;

{**********************************************************}
{**              M A I N   P R O G R A M                **}
{**********************************************************}

begin
  writeln( 'ISEVP - (c) 1990, 1992 by Michael Tischer'#13#10 );
  case IsEgaVga of
    NEITHERNOR : writeln( 'The active video card is ' +
                                'neither EGA nor VGA');

    EGA_MONO   : writeln( 'This is an EGA card with an MDA monitor');

    EGA_COLOR  : writeln( 'This is an EGA card with an EGA or '+
                                'multiscan monitor' );

    VGA_MONO   : writeln( 'This is a VGA card with an analog ' +
                                'monochrome monitor');

    VGA_COLOR  : writeln( 'This is a VGA card with a VGA or '+
                                'multiscan monitor' );
  end;
end.
```

C listing: ISEVC.C

```
/****************************************************************
*                         I S E V C . C                        *
**------------------------------------------------------------**
* Task            : Tests for an active EGA or VGA card.       *
**------------------------------------------------------------**
* Author          : Michael Tischer                            *
* Developed on    : 08/06/90                                   *
* Last update     : 02/26/92                                   *
**------------------------------------------------------- --**
* (MICROSOFT C)                                                *
* Compilation     : CL /AS isevc.c                             *
**------------------------------------------------------------**
* (BORLAND TURBO C)                                            *
* Compilation     : Use the integrated development environment *
**------------------------------------------------------------**
* Call            : isevc                                      *
****************************************************************/

#include <dos.h>                        /* Add include files */
#include <stdarg.h>
#include <stdio.h>

/*-- Constants -----------------------------------------------*/

#define EGA_MONO  0                     /* EGA and MDA monitor */
#define EGA_COLOR 1                     /* EGA and EGA monitor */
#define VGA_MONO  2          /* VGA and analog monochrome monitor */
#define VGA_COLOR 3              /* VGA and VGA monitor */
#define NEITHERNOR 4                    /* No VGA, no EGA */

/*-- Type declarations ---------------------------------------*/

typedef unsigned char BYTE;

/****************************************************************
* IsEgaVga : Determines whether an EGA or a VGA card is installed. *
**------------------------------------------------------------**
* Input   : None                                               *
* Output  : Taken from constants EGA_MONO, EGA_COLOR, etc.     *
****************************************************************/

BYTE IsEgaVga( void )
{
 union REGS Regs;        /* Processor registers for interrupt call */

 Regs.x.ax = 0x1a00;            /* Function 1AH applies to VGA only */
 int86( 0x10, &Regs, &Regs );
 if ( Regs.h.al == 0x1a )          /* Is the function available? */
   switch ( Regs.h.bl )            /* Yes --> Pass code */
   {
    case  4 : return EGA_COLOR;
    case  5 : return EGA_MONO;
    case  7 : return VGA_MONO;
    case  8 : return VGA_COLOR;
    default : return NEITHERNOR;
   }
 else                             /* Not a VGA, but it may be an EGA */
 {
   Regs.h.ah = 0x12;                        /* Call function 12H, */
   Regs.h.bl = 0x10;                        /* sub-function 10H   */
   int86(0x10, &Regs, &Regs );              /* Call video BIOS */
   if ( Regs.h.bl != 0x10 )                 /* EGA? */
    return Regs.h.bh == 0 ? EGA_COLOR : EGA_MONO;   /* Yes */
   else                                     /* No */
    return NEITHERNOR;
 }
}

/****************************************************************
*                     M A I N   P R O G R A M                  *
****************************************************************/

void main( void )
{
 printf( "ISEVP  -  (c) 1990, 1992 by Michael Tischer\n\n" );
 switch ( IsEgaVga() )
 {
   case NEITHERNOR :
     printf( "The active video card is neither EGA nor VGA");
     break;

   case EGA_MONO :
     printf( "This is an EGA card with an MDA monitor" );
     break;

   case EGA_COLOR :
     printf( "This is an EGA card with an EGA or " \
             "multiscan monitor" );
     break;

   case VGA_MONO :
     printf( "This is a VGA card with an analog monochrome monitor");
     break;

   case VGA_COLOR :
     printf( "This is a VGA card with a VGA or " \
             "multiscan monitor" );
 }
 printf( "\n\n" );
}
```

4.8.2 Selecting and Programming Fonts

Unlike earlier video cards, EGA and VGA cards aren't limited to the fonts present in the ROM chips on the card. Instead, they use a powerful character generator that relates the characters in an area of the video RAM to the corresponding bitmaps used to display the characters. In this section we'll discuss the structure of the character table and explain how to use it.

Loading and defining fonts with the BIOS

The expanded EGA and VGA BIOS has several functions that allow you to manipulate character tables. There are more than a dozen sub-functions available through function 11H of the BIOS video interrupt. As usual, you must place the function number in the AH register and the sub-function number in the AL register when making the call.

In addition to working with predefined character tables, these functions also allow you to load your own character tables, display a character table on screen, or switch between different character tables. The predefined character tables are stored in a ROM chip on the EGA or VGA card and copied from there to a portion of the video RAM. The character generator then accesses the information about the appearance of certain characters.

EGA cards have only two fonts in ROM and VGA cards have three fonts. The third font on the VGA card can be activated through the BIOS.

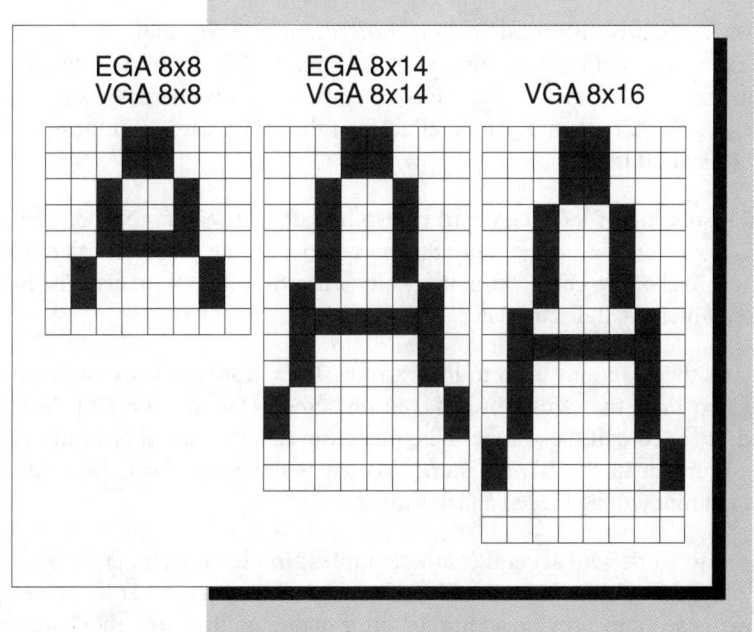

Character structure within a matrix

The structure of the video fonts is different than the fonts that are used on a printer. The difference lies in the size of the characters (i.e., the matrix size on which the characters are based). The EGA card normally uses an 8x14 pixel matrix for the first ROM font. The second ROM font uses a smaller matrix that squeezes the characters into an 8x8 pixel box. The pixels remain the same size, although the font changes in size. Since this means that the characters in the 8x8 matrix are smaller and harder to read, you may be wondering why you would select a smaller font.

A smaller font occupies less space on the screen, which enables you to display more characters. The 8x8 font lets you display 43 lines of text instead of the usual 25, allowing you to display more information on a single screen.

The number of text lines actually depends on the vertical resolution of the EGA card, which is always 350 pixels in text mode. From the calculations listed below, we see there are actually 43.75 lines available on the screen. But since displaying 3/4 of a line isn't possible, the number is rounded down to 43.

```
EGA vertical resolution:    350 pixels      350 pixels
Character matrix height:  ÷ 14 pixels     ÷  8 pixels
                          -----------     -----------
Number of text lines :      25 lines      43.75 lines
```

The horizontal resolutions for the two character matrices are the same. The EGA card always contains 640 pixels per line. Since each character matrix is 8 pixels wide, there are 80 characters per line.

The VGA card is slightly different in both horizontal and vertical resolution. The vertical resolution in text mode is 400 pixels instead of 350 pixels. So, the normal text screen of 80x25 characters is obtained with a special VGA character matrix. This character matrix has a height of 16 pixels. The two EGA fonts are also available on the VGA card, and these fonts permit text resolutions of 28 and 50 lines.

The horizontal resolution of the VGA card is also higher with 720 pixels per line instead of 640 pixels per line. However, we still get only 80 characters per line in VGA text modes because the horizontal dimensions of the character matrices increase from 8 to 9 pixels. The ninth pixel has a special purpose, which we'll discuss later.

First, let's discuss the functions used to load a font. These functions also automatically specify the number of text lines that will be displayed on screen. The numbers of these functions are 11H, 12H, and 14H. To call these functions, place the function number in the AX register and an additional argument in the BL register. This gives the number of the character table into which the selected font will be loaded and activated.

If you don't want to work with several character tables simultaneously, enter a value of 0 for the first character table. EGA cards can use values from 0 to 3, and VGA cards can use values from 0 to 7. The following sections provide additional information on the different character tables.

```
Sub-function    Matrix    EGA lines...VGA lines
    11H          8x14         25          28
    12H          8x8          43          50
    14H          8x16        (n.a.)       25
```

These functions always load a certain font and then set the registers of the video card to display the corresponding number of text lines. It's also possible to simply load a font into a character table. If you want to work with a character table other than the one currently active, this won't affect the screen display because the font isn't activated and the number of text lines doesn't change. Calling this function is identical to the three functions we just described except for the contents of the registers.

Sub-function	Matrix	EGA	VGA
1H	8x14	√	√
2H	8x8	√	√
4H	8x16		√

You aren't limited to the character tables stored in ROM; the BIOS also lets you load your own fonts. You can leave certain characters undefined or select different fonts, just as you can with a printer.

One feature allows you to set the character height from 1 to 32 pixels. The number of lines of text displayed on the screen is set accordingly. However, remember that characters less than 6 pixels high can't be read on the screen. Characters greater than 16 pixels high are easy to read, but this limits the number of lines you can display on screen simultaneously. Generally character heights should be from 8 to 16 pixels; otherwise an unusual looking screen display may be produced.

The BIOS lets you specify any number as the character height. Place the character height in the BH register when calling function 10H.

The character width cannot be altered in any way; it remains fixed at 8 pixels for EGA mode and 9 for VGA mode.

You can also select any character table for your font. The character table number is loaded in the BL register. The CX register is passed the number of characters to be loaded. This allows you to load only selected characters, if desired. In the DX register, you're expected to enter the ASCII code of the first character you want to load. This may be a number from 0 to 255.

The BIOS retrieves the pixel pattern data for the characters from a buffer. This buffer must be created and initialized by the function caller. The address of the buffer is expected as a FAR pointer in the ES:BP register pair.

As the previous figure shows, the buffer must have an entry for each character to be defined. The size of the entry in bytes corresponds to the character height. For example, if an 8x12 matrix has been defined, each buffer entry consists of 12 bytes. The total buffer size is then 12 times the number of characters to be defined, since the entries follow each other. The first entry has the offset address of 0000H. The data for the first character is found here, followed by the data for subsequent characters.

Within each entry, each byte represents the pixel pattern for one pixel line of the character. The bytes correspond to lines in ascending order from the first to the last line of the character. Within each byte, the individual bits indicate the status of each pixel in the line, from left to right. If the bit's set, then the corresponding pixel is displayed using the text foreground color. If the bit's off, then the pixel is displayed in the background color.

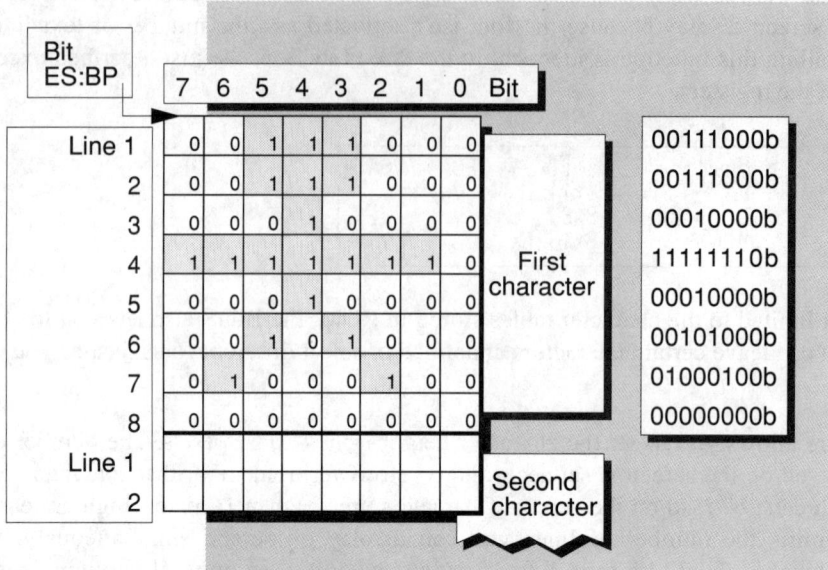

Buffer structure expected by function 10H

Sub-function 00H works the same as 10H. This function loads the given character definition in a character table, but doesn't activate the font or change the number of text lines on the screen. Function 00H corresponds to function 10H just as we saw functions 01H, 02H, and 04H correspond to 11H, 12H, and 14H.

When using characters and fonts that you've designed, don't forget that they can be displayed only on your screen. Your printer won't be able to reproduce them. So, don't be surprised if your printer uses a completely different font if you try to print a screen displaying a custom font.

Changing from 9 pixel to 8 pixel display

The following program is an example of user-defined fonts applied to company logos and compound characters. However, this program has a problem with VGA cards because of the width of the characters. With an EGA card, each character has an actual width of 8 pixels. VGA characters are 9 pixels wide. This produces horizontal screen resolutions of 640 (EGA) and 720 (VGA).

You're probably wondering why there is a ninth pixel when the standard ROM fonts, as well as any font you can load with the BIOS, are 8 pixels wide. The ninth pixel is usually left blank. The only exceptions are characters with ASCII codes between C0H and DFH. This range contains various characters used for drawing frames and borders. These characters must be connected, without any space between them, in order to create unbroken horizontal lines. So, these characters simply copy the eighth pixel to the ninth to fill the empty space.

By adding the ninth pixel, VGA achieves higher resolution even though only 8 of the pixels are coded. This is possible because EGA actually uses only seven of the eight pixels. The eighth remains empty to ensure spacing between characters. VGA can use eight pixels and leave the ninth free.

As long as you define individual characters that have spaces between them, this characteristic of the VGA card doesn't usually cause any problems. But if you want to create a logo or a compound character (with two or more characters joined together), you'll encounter problems because you cannot control the ninth pixel. To work with such a font, you must sacrifice the additional resolution of the 9 pixel mode and use one of the normal 8 pixel modes as they are used with the EGA card.

This mode change involves several registers of the VGA card. Unfortunately, not all of these can be addressed through the BIOS. Some must be programmed directly. First we'll discuss the miscellaneous output register. This register can be read using port address 3CCH and written using port address 3C2H. It contains two bits (bits 2 and 3) that set the VGA clock, which in turn determines the horizontal resolution.

In normal text mode, the VGA card runs at 28.322 MHz with 720 pixels per line. The frequency with 640 pixels per line is 25.175. This is the resolution we want in order to create a screen with 80 characters per line using 8 pixel characters. To switch your VGA card to the desired 640 pixel mode, we must modify bits 2 and 3 and then return the new register values. However, since the characters in VGA fonts are nine pixels wide, we must also switch to a character width of 8 pixels.

This is done by changing the contents of the clocking mode register. This register is part of the sequencer controller and cannot be directly addressed like the miscellaneous output register. Before and after the sequencer controller register is accessed, it is reset using its reset register. This is done before a sequencer register, such as the clocking register, can be changed. Bit 0 of the clocking register is responsible for the character width.

The last step is to modify the horizontal pel panning register. We've already encountered this register in a description of smooth scrolling. After switching to the 8 pixel width, this register is loaded with the value 0. This moves the picture one pixel to the left. If you don't do this, the first pixel column on the screen would flicker. We don't have to access this register directly, since there is a BIOS function available.

The three steps required to change from a 9 pixel character width to an 8 pixel character can also be reversed in order to revert to 9 pixel width. Simply switch the horizontal resolution back to 720 in the miscellaneous output register and set the character width back to 9 pixels in the clocking mode register. Don't forget to set the horizontal pel panning register back to 8 so the first pixel column is visible again.

If you want to know the exact structure of these registers, refer to the end of this chapter. You'll find detailed descriptions of all EGA and VGA registers. The demonstration program in the following section contains a routine for executing these changes.

Logos

Now let's discuss creating logos. Logos are an attractive way to introduce your software on screen. They give your software a professional look. For example, a logo, instead of a simple copyright message, can be displayed on the screen. However, it's difficult to create an interesting logo using only the standard characters available in the normal ASCII set. But both the EGA and VGA cards allow you to change the appearance of individual characters. Remember that if you have a VGA card, you must reduce the character width to 8 pixels.

Usually, you need more than one character to create an interesting logo. Each character consists of 128 pixels on a VGA card (8x16) and only 112 on an EGA card (8x14). We'll explain how you can create logos by combining several characters into complex patterns.

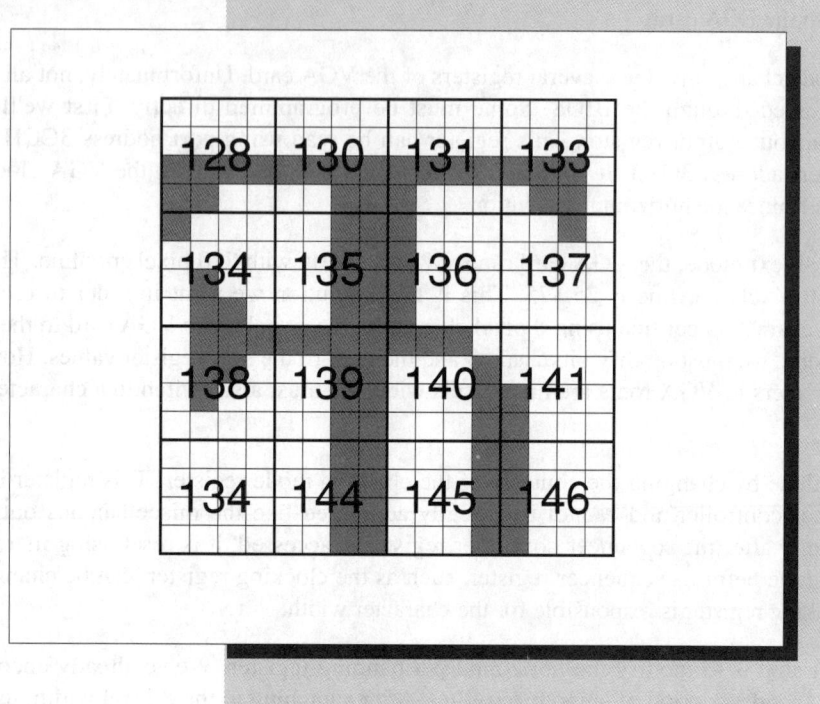

Logos from compound characters

Combining characters to create logos provides more pixels to work with and allows you to create a larger logo, which in turn demands more detail. However, you shouldn't use too many characters in your logo. Otherwise, you may lose too many useful characters from the ASCII character set. Also, you should ensure that all the characters continue to appear correctly so subsequent text is readable. Remember that to create the logo, we're redefining only a few characters instead of the entire font.

You should select characters that aren't used elsewhere in your program. Characters with ASCII codes less than 32, the foreign language characters, and characters with ASCII codes greater than 224 are good choices. Depending on which characters your program needs, up to 100 characters are usually available for creating a logo. This allows you to create a 10x10 character logo with a resolution of more than 12,000 pixels.

We've included an ASCII table in the Appendix which displays the possible choices. You'll see examples of the ASCII codes, including those described above, in this ASCII table.

To help you create your own logos, we've included the LOGO program in both C (LOGOC.C) and Pascal (LOGOP.P) versions. The main feature of each program is a function called BuildLogo, which is responsible for the structure of the logo and for displaying it on screen. Data about the desired position of the logo on screen, the logo's height in pixels, its color, and the string array that defines how the logo looks is required by this function.

In this array, each string represents one pixel line of the logo. Each character in the string represents a pixel in the line. If the character for a certain pixel is a space, then this pixel is blank. If any other character is used, the pixel is set. Although this method of storing the information for creating the logo uses a lot of memory, it also allows you to edit the appearance of the logo in the source code easily, without using a special editor. Also, since the logo's width is taken directly from the length of the string array, it doesn't have to be passed as an extra parameter.

Depending on the size of the logo and the video card that's installed (EGA or VGA), BuildLogo calculates the number of characters required and defines the pixel patterns for each individual logo character using sub-functions 00H and 10H of the BIOS video interrupt (previously described). If the logo doesn't completely fill the rectangle reserved for it, it is centered within it.

BuildLogo uses the foreign language characters to create logos. These are the characters with ASCII codes from 128 to 167; this provides a total of 39 characters. You can easily modify the BuildLogo function so you can also use other ASCII characters.

This function also switches the VGA character width from 9 pixels to 8 pixels. The IsEgaVga function determines whether the current system has a VGA card. The SetCharWidth function makes the switch. The steps required to switch the character width were previously described.

BuildLogo defaults to character heights of 14 pixels on EGA cards and 16 pixels on VGA cards. The normal fonts are used, which produces a screen resolution of 25 lines by 80 columns. If you want to use BuildLogo in a program that uses a smaller font (resulting in better screen resolution), then you must change the value of the CharHeight variable in the LOGO programs. If you use a smaller font, remember that you'll need more characters to create the same logo because each character will have fewer pixels in its height.

If you no longer need a logo, the ResetLogo function can restore all the characters of the original font and set the character width back to 9 pixels for VGA systems.

Both of the LOGO demonstration programs use the BuildLogo function to create a small logo and display it on the screen. The ASCII character set is displayed in the portion of the screen above the logo. The characters that were redefined to form the logo will be highlighted with a different color. This allows you to see each redefined character and how they fit together like the pieces of a puzzle to form the logo.

The Pascal version LOGOP.PAS doesn't require any assembler routines, but the LOGOCA.ASM assembly language module supports the C version LOGOC.C. This assembly language module supplies character definition information because the BIOS function that defines characters cannot access character information in the BP register using the int86() C input function. The defchar routine in the assembler module handles character definition.

Pascal listing: LOGOP.PAS

```pascal
{****************************************************************
*                      L O G O P . P A S                        *
**------------------------------------------------------------**
*  Task       : Demonstrates custom character definition for EGA *
*               and VGA cards, for use as a logo design.        *
**------------------------------------------------------------**
*  Author     : Michael Tischer                                 *
*  Developed on : 08/05/90                                      *
*  Last update  : 02/21/92                                      *
****************************************************************}

Program Logop;

uses DOS, CRT;

{-- Constants ------------------------------------------------}

const EGAVGA_SEQUENCER = $3C4;    { Sequencer address/data port }
      EGAVGA_MONCTR    = $3D4;         { Monitor controller }
      EGAVGA_GRAPHCTR  = $3CE;{ Graphics controller address/data port }
      EV_STATC         = $3DA;    { EGA/VGA color status register }
      EV_STATM         = $3BA;    { EGA/VGA mono status register }
      EV_ATTR          = $3C0;    { EGA/VGA color attribute controller }

{-- Type declarations ----------------------------------------}

type CRDTYPE = ( EGA, VGA, NEITHERNOR );

procedure CLI; inline( $FA );             { Disable interrupts }
procedure STI; inline( $FB );             { Enable interrupts }

{****************************************************************
*  SetCharWidth: Sets VGA character width to 8 or 9 pixels.     *
**------------------------------------------------------------**
*  Input   : HWIDTH = Character width (8 or 9)                  *
****************************************************************}

procedure SetCharWidth( hwidth : byte );

var Regs : Registers;      { Processor registers for interrupt call }
    x    : byte;                 { Value for misc. output reg. }

begin
  if ( hwidth = 8 ) then Regs.BX := $0001  { BH = horiz. direction }
                    else Regs.BX := $0800;  { BL = seq. reg. value }

  x := port[ $3CC ] and not(4+8);          { Toggle horizontal }
  if ( hwidth = 9 ) then                    { resolution from }
    x := x or 4;                            { 720 to 640 pixels }
  port[ $3C2 ] := x;

  CLI;                    { Toggle sequencer from 8 to 9 pixels }
  portw[ EGAVGA_SEQUENCER ] := $0100;
  portw[ EGAVGA_SEQUENCER ] := $01 + Regs.BL shl 8;
  portw[ EGAVGA_SEQUENCER ] := $0300;
  STI;

  Regs.AX := $1000;             { Change screen configuration }
  Regs.BL := $13;
  intr( $10, Regs );
end;

{****************************************************************
```

```pascal
*  IsEgaVga : Determines whether an EGA or a VGA card is installed. *
**------------------------------------------------------------**
*  Input    : None                                              *
*  Output   : EGA, VGA or NEITHERNOR                            *
****************************************************************}
function IsEgaVga : CRDTYPE;

var Regs : Registers;       { Processor registers for interrupt call }

begin
  Regs.AX := $1a00;               { Function 1AH applies only to VGA }
  Intr( $10, Regs );
  if ( Regs.AL = $1a ) then          { Is the function available? }
    IsEgaVga := VGA
  else
    begin
      Regs.ah := $12;                    { Call function 12H, }
      Regs.bl := $10;                    { sub-function 10H }
      intr($10, Regs);                   { Call video BIOS }
      if ( Regs.bl <> $10 ) then IsEgaVga := EGA
                            else IsEgaVga := NEITHERNOR;
    end;
end;

{****************************************************************
*  BuildLogo : Draws a logo on the screen using custom characters *
*              based on existing ASCII characters.              *
**------------------------------------------------------------**
*  Input  : COLUMN = Starting column of logo (1-80)             *
*           LGROW  = Starting row of logo (1-25)                *
*           DEPTH  = Number of logo scan lines                  *
*           OPCOL  = Logo output color                          *
*           BUF    = String array containing character patterns for *
*                    logo                                       *
*  Info   : - The Test procedure demonstrates how the logo buffer *
*             works.                                            *
*           - The logo is displayed centered in a block         *
*             of characters.                                    *
****************************************************************}

procedure BuildLogo( column, lgrow, depth, opcol : byte; var buf );

type BYTEAR = array[0..10000] of byte;          { Byte array for }
     BARPTR = ^BYTEAR;                           { logo buffer }

const MAX_CHAR = 32;      { Maximum number of redefinable characters }

const UseChars : array[1..MAX_CHAR] of byte =    { Redefinable chars. }
      ( 128, 130, 131, 133, 134, 135, 136, 137, 138, 139,
        140, 141, 143, 144, 145, 146, 147, 149, 150, 151,
        152, 155, 156, 157, 158, 159, 160, 161, 162, 163,
        164, 165 );

var Regs     : Registers;   { Processor registers for interrupt call }
    videoc   : CRDTYPE;            { Type of video card installed }
    chardef  : array[0..15] of byte; { Bit pattern of one character }
    charheight,                 { Number of scan lines per character }
    i, j, k, l,                        { Loop variables }
    bmask,               { Bit mask for generating a scan line }
    swidth,                            { String width }
    index,              { Index for executing the UseChars array }
    dx,                      { Logo block width (text columns) }
    dy,                       { Logo block depth (text rows) }
    leftb,                       { Left border in pixels }
    rightb,                       { Right border in pixels }
```

```
        topb,                               { Top border in pixels }
        bttmb     : byte;                    { Bottom border in pixels }
        bptr      : barptr;                  { For addressing logo buffer }

{-- IsSet function: Checks for set logo pixels -----------------------}

function IsSet( lgrow, column : byte ) : boolean;

begin
    if ( lgrow < topb ) or ( lgrow > bttmb ) or      { Pixel outside }
       ( column < leftb ) or ( column > rightb ) then  { border?        }
       IsSet := false                        { Yes --> Don't set it }
    else                                     { No --> Pass to logo buffer }
       IsSet := bptr^[ (lgrow-topb)*(swidth+1) + 1 + (column-leftb) ] <> 32;
end;

{-- Main procedure --------------------------------------------------}

begin
    videoc := IsEgaVga;                      { Check for video card }
    case videoc of
       NEITHERNOR :
          begin
             writeln( 'Warning: No EGA or VGA card found' );
             exit;
          end;

       EGA        :
          charheight := 14;                  { EGA: 14 scan lines per character }

       VGA        :
          begin                              { VGA }
             SetCharWidth( 8 );              { Set char. width to 8 pixels }
             charheight := 16;               { 16 scan lines per character }
          end;
    end;

    bptr := @buf;                            { Set pointer to logo buffer }
    swidth := bptr^[0];                      { Get string length and logo width }
    dx := ( swidth + 7 ) div 8;              { Compute number of characters needed }
    dy := ( depth + charheight - 1 ) div charheight;
    if ( dx*dy > MAX_CHAR ) then
       writeln( 'Error: Logo in BuildLogo too large' )
    else
       begin
          topb  := ( dy*charheight-depth ) div 2;    { Compute border }
          bttmb := depth + topb - 1;
          leftb := ( dx*8-swidth ) div 2;
          rightb := swidth + leftb - 1;

          TextColor( opcol and 15 );         { Set display color }
          TextBackGround( opcol shr 4 );
          index := 1;                        { Get first character from UseChar array }
          for i := 0 to dy-1 do              { Execute text rows }
             begin
                GotoXY( column, lgrow + i );
                for j := 1 to dx do          { Execute text characters }
                   begin
                      write( chr( UseChars[ index ] ) );  { Display character }

                      {-- Compute new character pattern for the char --------}

                      for k := 0 to charheight-1 do   { Execute scan lines }
                         begin
```

```
                            bmask := 0;                      { Bit mask orig. 0 }
                            for l := 0 to 7 do{ Each character is 8 pixels wide }
                               begin
                                  bmask := bmask shl 1;       { Move mask left }
                                  if IsSet( i*charheight+k, (j-1)*8+l ) then
                                     bmask := bmask or 1;     { Set pixel in logo }
                               end;
                            chardef[ k ] := bmask;{ Bit pattern in char. buffer }
                         end;
                      Regs.AX := $1100;          { Call BIOS video interrupt, }
                      Regs.BH := charheight;     { function 10H, sub-function }
                      Regs.BL := 0;              { 00H to specify new        }
                      Regs.CX := 1;              { character pattern         }
                      Regs.DX := UseChars[ index ];
                      Regs.ES := seg( chardef );
                      Regs.BP := ofs( chardef );
                      intr( $10, Regs );

                      inc( index );          { Get next character from UseChar }
                   end;
             end;
       end;
end;

{******************************************************************
* ResetLogo : Reloads original character definitions.            *
**--------------------------------------------------------------**
* Input   : None                                                 *
******************************************************************}
procedure ResetLogo;

var Regs      : Registers;   { Processor registers for interrupt call }

begin
   case IsEgaVga of
      EGA  : begin
                Regs.AX := $1101;              { Load new 8x14 font }
                Regs.BL := 0;
                intr( $10, Regs );
             end;

      VGA  : begin
                SetCharWidth( 9 );             { Set char. width to 9 pixels }
                Regs.AX := $1104;              { Load new 8x16 font }
                Regs.BL := 0;
                intr( $10, Regs );
             end;
   end;
end;

{******************************************************************
* Test : Demonstrates the BuildLogo procedure.                   *
**--------------------------------------------------------------**
* Input   : None                                                 *
******************************************************************}
procedure Test;

const MyLogo : array[1..32] of string[38] =
              ( '                    **                    ',
                '                  ****                    ',
                '                  ****                    ',
                '                    **                    ',
```

187

```
                           ****                    ',
                           ****                    ',
          '*******************************         ',
          '*******************************         ',
          '***              ****          ***',
          '**               ****           **',
          '                 ****             *'
          '                 ****
          '                 ****
          '         *******  ****  *******
          '         ****  **** ****  ****
          '         ****  *********  ****
          '         ****    ******    ****
          '         ****     ****     ****
          '         ****     ****     ****
          '         ****     ****     ****
          '         ****     ****     ****
          '         ****     ****     ****
          '         ****     ****     ****
          '         ****     ****     ****
          '         ****     ****     ****
          '         ****     ****     ****     ' );
```

```pascal
var ch : char;
    i  : byte;


const NewDef : set of char = [ #128, #130, #131, #133..#141, #143..#147,
                               #149..#152, #155..#165 ];


begin
 TextBackGround( BLACK );
 ClrScr;
 GotoXY( 1, 1 );
 for i := 0 to 255 do             { Display entire character set }
   begin
      if ( chr(i) in NewDef ) then TextColor( WHITE )
                        else TextColor( YELLOW );

      GotoXY( i mod 13 * 6 + 2, i div 13 + 1 );
      write( i:3 , ':' );
      if ( i <> 13 ) and ( i <> 10 ) and ( i <> 7 ) then
        write( chr( i ) );
   end;


 GotoXY( 23, 22 );
 write( 'LOGOP  -  (c) 1992 by Michael Tischer' );
 BuildLogo( 61, 21, 32, CYAN shl 4 + WHITE, MyLogo );  { Build logo }
 ch := ReadKey;                                   { Wait for a key }
 ResetLogo;                                         { Clear logo }
 ClrScr;
 GotoXY( 1, 1 );
end;


{************************************************************}
{**                 M A I N   P R O G R A M             **}
{************************************************************}
begin
 Test;
end.
```

C listing: LOGOC.C

```c
/**************************************************************
*                    L O G O C . C                          *
**----------------------------------------------------------**
* Task        : Demonstrates custom character definition for *
*               EGA and VGA cards, for use as a logo design. *
**----------------------------------------------------------**
* Author      : Michael Tischer                              *
* Developed on : 08/06/90                                    *
* Last update : 03/02/92                                     *
**----------------------------------------------------------**
* (MICROSOFT C)                                              *
* Compilation : CL /AS /c /WO LOGOC.C                        *
*               LINK LOGOC LOGOCA;                           *
**----------------------------------------------------------**
* (BORLAND TURBO C)                                          *
* Compilation : Create a project file containing the following: *
*               LOGOC.C                                      *
*               LOGOCA.OBJ                                   *
**----------------------------------------------------------**
* Call        : LOGOC                                        *
**************************************************************/

#include <dos.h>                        /* Add include files */
#include <stdarg.h>
#include <stdio.h>
#include <string.h>
#include <conio.h>


#ifdef __TURBOC__                     /* Compiling with Turbo C? */
  #define CLI()         disable()
  #define STI()         enable()
  #define outpw( p, w ) outport( p, w )
  #ifndef inp
    #define outp( p, b )  outportb( p, b )
    #define inp( p )      inportb( p )
  #endif
#else                               /* No --> QuickC 2.0 or MSC */
  #include <conio.h>
  #define MK_FP(seg,ofs) ((void far *)\
                         (((unsigned long)(seg) << 16) | (ofs)))
  #define CLI()         _disable()
  #define STI()         _enable()
#endif


#define EGA       0                      /* Card types */
#define VGA       1
#define NEITHERNOR 2


#define EGAVGA_SEQUENCER 0x3C4     /* Sequencer address/data port */
#define EGAVGA_MONCTR    0x3D4         /* Monitor controller */
#define EGAVGA_GRAPHCTR  0x3CE/* Graphics controller addr./data port */


/*-- Type declarations -------------------------------------*/

typedef unsigned char BYTE;

extern void defchar( BYTE ascii, BYTE table, BYTE height, /*Assembler*/
                     BYTE numchar, void far * buf );       /*routine */


/**************************************************************
* SetCursor : Specifies screen cursor position.             *
**----------------------------------------------------------**
* Input parameters : CURCOL = New cursor column (0-79)       *
```

```
*                     CURROW = New cursor row (0-24)              *
* Return values   : None                                         *
******************************************************************/
void SetCursor( BYTE curcol, BYTE curow )
{
  union REGS regs;                      /* Processor regs. for interrupt call */

  regs.h.ah = 2;                          /* Function number: Set cursor */
  regs.h.bh = 0;                             /* Access screen page 0 */
  regs.h.dh = curow;                                  /* Set row */
  regs.h.dl = curcol;                              /* Set column */
  int86(0x10, &regs, &regs);            /* Call BIOS video interrupt */
}


/******************************************************************
* PrintfAt : Displays a formatted string anywhere on the screen.  *
**--------------------------------------------------------------**
* Input parameters: COLUMN = Column                               *
*                   SCROW  = Row                                  *
*                   CHCOL  = Character attribute                  *
*                   STRING = Pointer to string                    *
* Return values   : None                                          *
* Info            : This function should only be called if the    *
*                   system running this program contains an EGA card*
*                   or a VGA card.                                 *
******************************************************************/
void PrintfAt( BYTE column, BYTE scrow, BYTE chcol, char * string, ... )
{
  va_list parameter;              /* Parameter list for VA_... macros */
  char outbufr[255],                   /* Buffer for formatted string */
       *outptr;
  BYTE far *vptr;                          /* Pointer to video RAM */

  va_start( parameter, string );            /* Convert parameters */
  vsprintf( outbufr, string, parameter );            /* Format */

  vptr = (BYTE far *) MK_FP( 0xB800, column*2+scrow*160 );

  for ( outptr = outbufr; *outptr ; )         /* Execute string */
  {
    *vptr++ = *(outptr++);        /* Write character to video RAM */
    *vptr++ = chcol;              /* Write attribute to video RAM */
  }
}


/******************************************************************
* ClrScr: Clears the screen.                                      *
**--------------------------------------------------------------**
* Input parameters: CHATT  = Character attribute                  *
* Return values   : None                                          *
******************************************************************/
void ClrScr( BYTE chatt )
{
  BYTE far *vptr;                          /* Pointer to video RAM */
  int  count = 2000;           /* Number of characters to be cleared */

  vptr = (BYTE far *) MK_FP( 0xB800, 0 );  /* Set pointer to video RAM */

  for ( ; count--; )                        /* Execute video RAM */
  {
    *vptr++ = ' ';                /* Write character to video RAM */
    *vptr++ = chatt;              /* Write attribute to video RAM */
  }
}
```

```
/******************************************************************
* SetCharWidth: Sets VGA character width to 8 or 9 pixels.        *
**--------------------------------------------------------------**
* Input    : HWIDTH = Character width (8 or 9)                    *
******************************************************************/
void SetCharWidth( BYTE hwidth )
{
  union REGS Regs;        /* Processor registers for interrupt call */
  unsigned char x;                  /* Value for misc. output reg. */

  Regs.x.bx = ( hwidth == 8 ) ? 0x0001 : 0x0800;

  x = inp( 0x3CC ) & (255-12);             /* Toggle horizontal */
  if ( hwidth == 9 )                       /* resolution from   */
    x |= 4;                                /* 720 to 640 pixels */
  outp( 0x3C2, x );

  CLI();                        /* Toggle sequencer from 8 to 9 pixels */
  outpw( EGAVGA_SEQUENCER, 0x0100 );
  outpw( EGAVGA_SEQUENCER, 0x01 + ( Regs.h.bl << 8 ) );
  outpw( EGAVGA_SEQUENCER, 0x0300 );
  STI();

  Regs.x.ax = 0x1000;         /* Change horizontal screen position */
  Regs.h.bl = 0x13;
  int86( 0x10, &Regs, &Regs );
}


/******************************************************************
* IsEgaVga : Determines whether an EGA or a VGA card is installed. *
**--------------------------------------------------------------**
* Input    : None                                                 *
* Output   : EGA, VGA or NEITHERNOR                               *
******************************************************************/
BYTE IsEgaVga( void )
{
  union REGS Regs;        /* Processor registers for interrupt call */

  Regs.x.ax = 0x1a00;         /* Function 1AH applies to VGA only */
  int86( 0x10, &Regs, &Regs );
  if ( Regs.h.al == 0x1a )         /* Is the function available? */
    return VGA;
  else
  {
    Regs.h.ah = 0x12;                        /* Call function 12H, */
    Regs.h.bl = 0x10;                        /* sub-function 10H   */
    int86(0x10, &Regs, &Regs );              /* Call video BIOS */
    return ( Regs.h.bl != 0x10 ) ? EGA : NEITHERNOR;
  }
}


/******************************************************************
* BuildLogo : Draws a logo on the screen using custom characters  *
*             based on existing ASCII characters.                 *
**--------------------------------------------------------------**
* Input   : COLUMN = Starting column of logo (1-80)               *
*           SLROW  = Starting row of logo (1-25)                  *
*           DEPTH  = Number of logo scan lines                    *
*           OPCOL  = Logo output color                            *
*           BUFP   = Pointer to strings containing character      *
*                    patterns for logo                            *
* Info    : - The TEST function demonstrates how the logo buffer  *
*             works.                                              *
```

```
*              - The logo is displayed centered in a block        *
*                 of characters.                                   *
************************************************************************/
void BuildLogo( BYTE column, BYTE slrow, BYTE depth,
                BYTE opcol, char **bufp )
{
#define MAX_CHAR 32        /* Maximum number of redefinable characters */

static BYTE UseChars[MAX_CHAR] =              /* Redefinable chars. */
               { 128, 130, 131, 133, 134, 135, 136, 137, 138, 139,
                 140, 141, 143, 144, 145, 146, 147, 149, 150, 151,
                 152, 155, 156, 157, 158, 159, 160, 161, 162, 163,
                 164, 165 };

BYTE     videoc;               /* Type of video card installed */
BYTE     chardef[16],          /* Bit pattern of one character */
         charheight,           /* Number of scan lines per character */
         i, j, k, l,                    /* Loop variables */
         bmask,                /* Bit mask for generating a scan line */
         swidth,                        /* String width */
         index,          /* Index for executing the UseChars array */
         dx,                    /* Logo block width (text columns) */
         dy,                    /* Logo block depth (text rows) */
         lcolumn,                       /* Current column */
         lcurow,                        /* Current row */
         leftb,                 /* Left border in pixels */
         rightb,                /* Right border in pixels */
         topb,                  /* Top border in pixels */
         bttmb;                 /* Bottom border in pixels */

videoc = IsEgaVga();                    /* Check for video card */
switch ( videoc )
{
  case NEITHERNOR :
    printf( "Warning: No EGA or VGA card found\n" );
    return;

  case EGA      :
    charheight = 14;            /* EGA: 14 scan lines per character */
    break;

  case VGA      :
    SetCharWidth( 8 );          /* Set char. width to 8 pixels */
    charheight = 16;            /* 16 scan lines per character */
    break;
}

swidth = strlen( *bufp );       /* Get string length and logo width */
dx = ( swidth + 7 ) / 8;        /* Compute number of characters needed */
dy = ( depth + charheight - 1 ) / charheight;
if ( dx*dy > MAX_CHAR )
printf( "Error: Logo in BuildLogo too large\n" );
else
{
  topb = ( dy*charheight-depth ) / 2;        /* Compute border */
  bttmb = depth + topb - 1;
  leftb = ( dx*8-swidth ) / 2;
  rightb = swidth + leftb - 1;

  for ( index = 0, i = 0; i < dy; ++i )
  {                                     /* Execute text rows */
    for (j = 0; j < dx; ++j, ++index )  /* Execute text columns */
    {
      PrintfAt( column+j, slrow+i, opcol,       /* Display character */
```

```
                        "%c", UseChars[ index ] );

      /*-- Compute new character pattern for the character ---------*/
      for ( k = 0; k < charheight; ++ k )       /* Execute scan lines */
      {
        bmask = 0;                              /* Bit mask orig. 0 */
        for ( l = 0; l <= 7; ++l )      /* Each char. is 8 pixels wide */
        {
          bmask <<= 1;                          /* Move mask left */
          lcurow = i * charheight + k;
          lcolumn = j * 8 + l;

          if ( lcurow>=topb  && lcurow<=bttmb &&    /* Pixel out */
               lcolumn>=leftb && lcolumn<=rightb )   /* of border? */
            if ( *(*(bufp+lcurow-topb)+lcolumn-leftb) != ' ' )
              bmask |= 1;                       /* Set pixel in logo */
        }
        chardef[ k ] = bmask;           /* Bit pattern in char. buffer */
      }
      defchar( UseChars[ index ], 0, charheight, 1, chardef );
    }
  }
}
}


/************************************************************************
* ResetLogo : Reloads original character definitions.                 *
**--------------------------------------------------------------------**
* Input   : None                                                      *
************************************************************************/
void ResetLogo( void )
{
union REGS Regs;            /* Processor registers for interrupt call */

switch ( IsEgaVga() )
{
  case EGA :
    Regs.x.ax = 0x1101;                         /* Load new 8x14 font */
    Regs.h.bl = 0;
    int86( 0x10, &Regs, &Regs );
    break;

  case VGA :
    SetCharWidth( 9 );                  /* Set char. width to 9 pixels */
    Regs.x.ax = 0x1104;                         /* Load new 8x16 font */
    Regs.h.bl = 0;
    int86( 0x10, &Regs, &Regs );
}
}


/************************************************************************
* Test : Demonstrates BuildLogo.                                      *
**--------------------------------------------------------------------**
* Input   : None                                                      *
************************************************************************/
void Test( void )
{
static char *MyLogo[32] =
               { "               **               ",
                 "              ****              ",
                 "              ****              ",
                 "               **               ",
```

```
            "                                    ",
            "                                    ",
            "               ****                 ",
            "               ****                 ",
            "************************************",
            "************************************",
            "***            ****            ***",
            "**             ****             **",
            "*              ****              *",
            "               ****                 ",
            "               ****                 ",
            "      ********      ********      ",
            "      ****  ****  ****  ****  ****  ",
            "      ****  ********  ****        ",
            "      ****  ******  ****        ",
            "      ****  ****  ****        ",
            "      ****  ****  ****        ",
            "      ****  ****  ****        ",
            "      ****  ****  ****        ",
            "      ****  ****  ****        ",
            "      ****  ****  ****        ",
            "      ****  ****  ****        ",
            "      ****  ****  ****        ",
            "      ****  ****  ****        ",
            "      ****  ****  ****     " };

int i, j;
BYTE opcol;

static BYTE NewDef[MAX_CHAR] =         /* Chars. to be redefined */
           { 128, 130, 131, 133, 134, 135, 136, 137, 138, 139,
             140, 141, 143, 144, 145, 146, 147, 149, 150, 151,
             152, 155, 156, 157, 158, 159, 160, 161, 162, 163,
             164, 165 };

ClrScr( 0 );
for ( i = 0; i < 256; ++i )          /* Display entire character set */
{
  for ( j = 0; j < MAX_CHAR; ++ j )  /* Should chars be redefined? */
  {
    if ( NewDef[ j ] == i )          /* Corresponding chars? */
      break;                         /* Yes --> Exit loop */
  }
  opcol = ( j < MAX_CHAR ) ? 15 : 14;

  PrintfAt( (i % 13) * 6 + 1, i / 13, opcol, "%3d:%c", i, i );
}

PrintfAt( 22, 22, 14, "LOGOC  -  (c) 1992 by Michael Tischer" );
BuildLogo( 60, 21, 32, 0x3F, MyLogo );      /* Build logo */
getch();
ResetLogo();                                /* Reset logo */
ClrScr( 15 );
SetCursor( 0, 0 );
}
/*********************************************************************
 * M A I N   P R O G R A M                                          *
 *********************************************************************/
void main( void )
{
  Test();
}
```

Assembler listing: LOGOCA.ASM

```
;*******************************************************************;
;*                    L O G O C A . A S M                         *;
;*---------------------------------------------------------------*;
;*   Task        : Creates a function for redefining existing    *;
;*                 characters on EGA and VGA cards.              *;
;*---------------------------------------------------------------*;
;*   Author      : Michael Tischer                               *;
;*   Developed on : 08/07/90                                     *;
;*   Last update  : 02/21/92                                     *;
;*---------------------------------------------------------------*;
;*   Assembly    : TASM -mx LOGOCA   or     MASM -mx LOGOCA;     *;
;*******************************************************************;

          DOSSEG               ;Arrange segment
          .MODEL SMALL, C      ;Link object code to a C program
                               ;using SMALL memory model


;== Code ===========================================================

          .CODE

;-- DEFCHAR: Specifies character pattern for EGA/VGA characters
;-- Declaration in C : void defchar( BYTE ascii, BYTE table, BYTE height
;--                               BYTE numchar, void far * buf );
;-- Input        : ASCII   = Number of first redefinable character
;--                TABLE   = Number of font table
;--                HEIGHT  = Character height in scan lines
;--                NUMCHAR = Number of characters
;--                BUF     = FAR pointer to buffer
;-- Output   : None

defchar   proc ascii:byte, table:byte, height:byte, \
               numchar:byte, buf:dword

          mov  ax,1100h        ;Call function 11H, sub-function 00H
          mov  bh,height       ;Load parameters into
          mov  bl,table        ;appropriate registers
          mov  dl,ascii
          xor  dh,dh
          mov  cl,numchar
          mov  ch,dh

          push bp              ;Push BP onto stack
          les  bp,buf
          int  10h             ;Call BIOS video interrupt
          pop  bp              ;Pop BP off of stack

          ret                  ;Return to caller

defchar   endp

;== End ============================================================

          end
```

Character table structure and location

You don't need to worry about the structure and location of character tables as long as you use only the BIOS to access them. However, occasionally you'll have to access them directly. Let's examine when this occurs and see how to access character definitions directly from character tables by using BIOS functions.

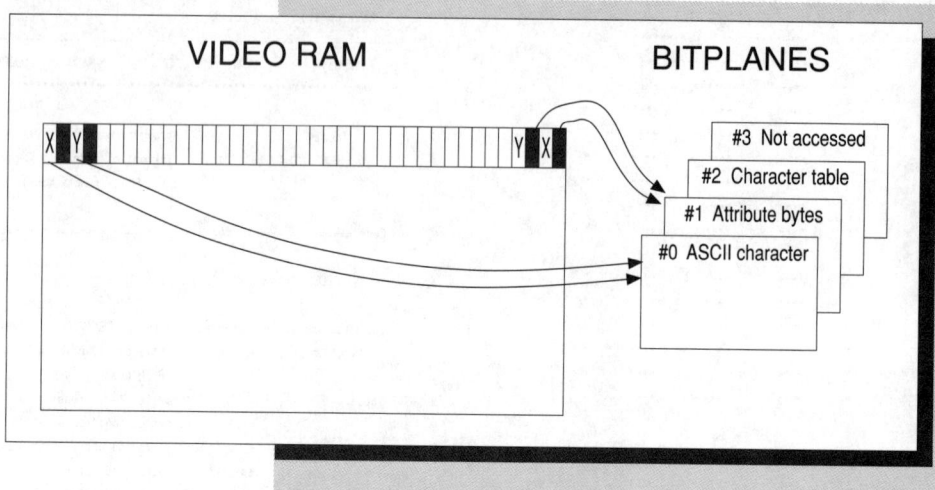

Using bitplanes in text mode

We'll begin by studying the structure of the video RAM on EGA and VGA cards. In Section 4.8.5 we note that EGA and VGA cards divide their video RAM into four large areas called *bitplanes*. These areas serve different purposes in text and graphics modes. A fully populated video card (with 256K) allocates 64K per bitplane.

The first two bitplanes (0 and 1) contain character codes and attribute bytes in text mode. The ASCII character codes are stored in bitplane 0. Accessing the video RAM above B800H at an even offset address is directed to this bitplane. Accessing the video RAM at an odd offset address is directed to bitplane 1, which contains the attribute bytes.

The other bitplanes are also used in text mode. EGA and VGA cards normally use the third bitplane for the character table. In a fully populated video card, each bitplane has 64K of RAM. Since each character table requires 8K, this allows you to store 8 different character tables. But only the VGA card fully utilizes this bitplane. Since the EGA card uses only four character tables, 32K of memory remains unused.

EGA Offset		VGA Offset	
	Unused		Character table #7
E000H		E000H	
	Character table #3		Character table #3
C000H		C000H	
	Unused		Character table #6
A000H		A000H	
	Character table #2		Character table #2
8000H		8000H	
	Unused		Character table #5
6000H		6000H	
	Character table #1		Character table #1
4000H		4000H	
	Unused		Character table #4
2000H		2000H	
	Character table #0		Character table #0
0000H		0000H	

Location of character tables within bitplane 2

Each character table needs 8K because 32 bytes are reserved for each of the 256 characters (32 x 256 = 8192 bytes, or 8K). Remember that 32 pixels is also the maximum character height for EGA and VGA fonts. The character tables are organized for the maximum font size. If a smaller font is used, then the extra bytes at the end of each entry simply remain unused.

The bytes that are used are coded in connection with the BIOS functions for character definitions. Each byte represents the bit pattern for one pixel line of the character. The individual bits in each byte indicate whether the corresponding pixel is on or off. You can easily determine the starting address for a specific character or a pixel line within a character if you know the starting address for the character table. Simply multiply the ASCII code number for the character by 32, then add the starting address for the table and the number of the desired pixel line.

Before accessing a character table, we must perform one more step. Since direct access to bitplane 2 isn't allowed, its contents must first be loaded into memory, from which it can be accessed from segment address A000H. Unfortunately, a BIOS function doesn't do this. So, again we must program the EGA and VGA registers.

Specifically, we'll be working with various registers of the sequencer and graphics controllers. Registers 2 and 4 of the sequencer controller are known as the map mask register and the memory mode register. The first register determines which bitplane is accessed. Each bit in this register represents a bitplane. In this case, we want bit 2 to be set for bitplane number 2. All other bits should be cleared. This ensures that only bitplane 2 is accessed.

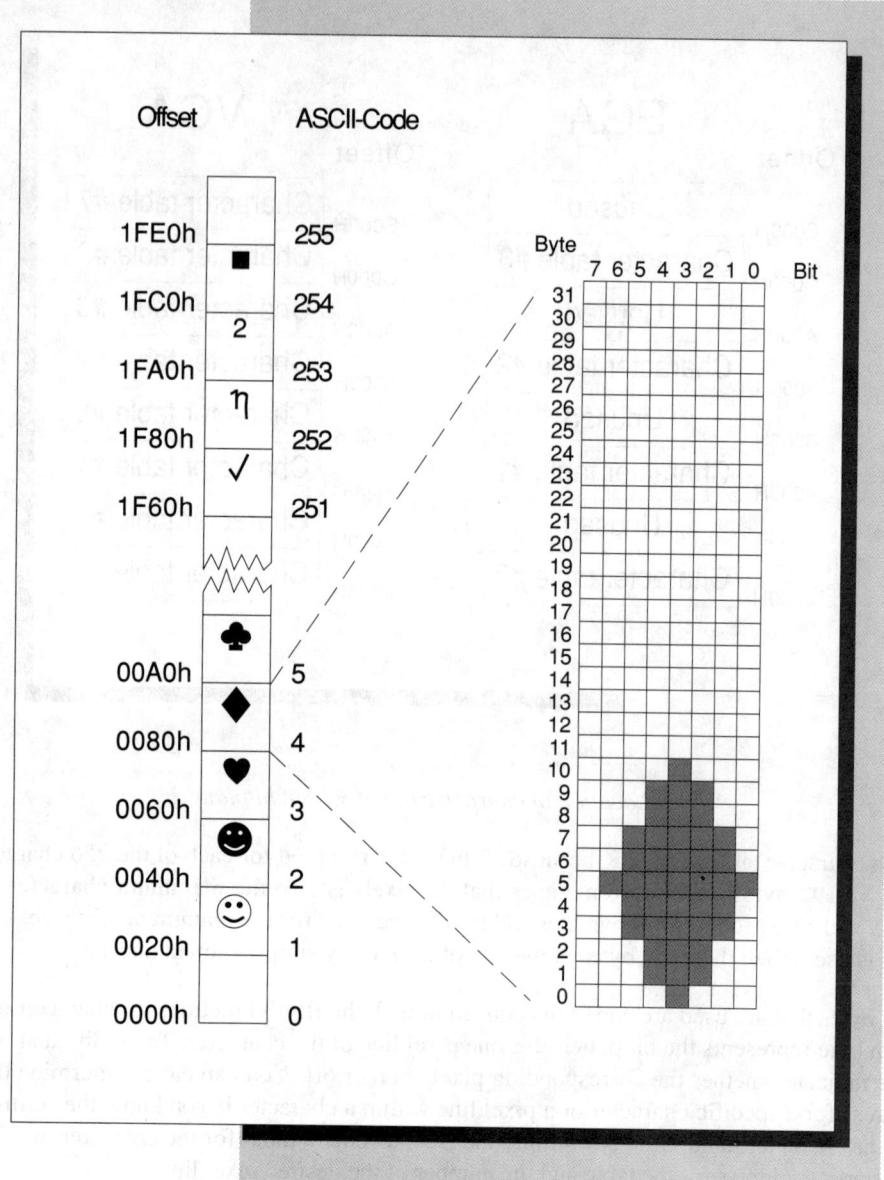

Character table structure

To ensure that only the bitplanes indicated in the map mask register are accessed, you must also load the value 7 in the memory mode register. In normal text modes, this register contains the value 3. This means that when the B800H video RAM is accessed, all even memory addresses (ASCII codes) go to bitplane 0, and all odd memory addresses (attribute codes) go to bitplane 1. Changing the value to 7 changes the memory addressing method.

We must also reset the sequencer registers by accessing the reset register, just as we did when changing from a 9 pixel to an 8 pixel character width. So before accessing the map mask and memory mode registers, we load the value 1 and the value 3 in the reset register.

A reset isn't required to access the graphics controller registers. We need to manipulate registers 4, 5, and 6 to access bitplane 2. These are known as the read map select register, the graphics mode register, and the miscellaneous register.

The read map select register is loaded with the value of the bitplane we want to read (2, in this case). This means that read access to the video RAM is also directed to bitplane 2. The graphics mode register requires a value of 0. This is accomplished by simply clearing bit 4, since all other bits pertain only to graphics mode. Clearing this bit ensures that the odd and even memory addresses won't be split into different bitplanes.

This information is repeated in bit 1 of the miscellaneous register. We're also interested in bits 2 and 3 of this register. These bits indicate where we can find the video RAM and where the bitplanes should be stored. In text mode, the video RAM is located at segment address B800H and extends for 32K. Bitplane 2 begins at segment address A000H, allowing access to the entire 64K.

Setting up the registers in this way destroys the normal text mode settings. So, now you're able to access bitplane 2, but you can no longer access the normal video RAM at B800H. Any character output that occurs during access to bitplane 2 is ignored by the video RAM. The picture on your screen appears unchanged because the video card can directly access the video RAM internally.

Remember that in order for your program or the BIOS to access the video RAM again, you must reset of the registers to their original values. The following table shows the proper register values for access to bitplane 2 and for access to video RAM at B800H:

Register	Bitplane	Video RAM
Map mask register (sequencer controller)	04H	03H
Memory mode register (sequencer controller)	07H	03H
Read map select register (graphics controller)	02H	00H
Graphics mode register (graphics controller)	00H	10H
Miscellaneous registers (graphics controller)	04H	0EH

The demonstration program MIKADO (listed later in this chapter) contains two routines used for toggling access between video RAM and bitplane 2. Also, at the end of this chapter, you'll find additional information about the registers we just discussed.

Switching between fonts: 512 different characters simultaneously

We've seen that bitplane 2 can store four different fonts on an EGA card and eight different fonts on a VGA card, and that BIOS access isn't limited to the first font. Now we must determine how to switch between fonts in order to display the desired one on the screen. We must use register number 4 (the character map select register) of the sequencer controller. This register is responsible for selecting the current character table, as the following figure shows:

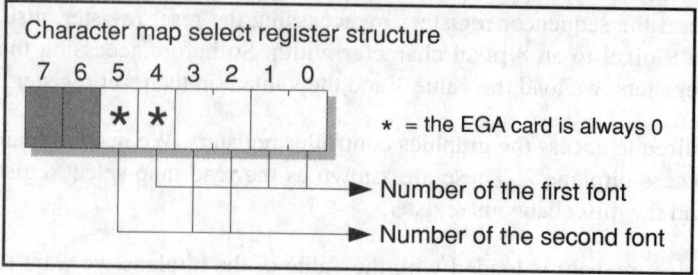

As you can see, the character map select register works with two fonts instead of only one. The order of the bits that specify the two fonts is confusing. Instead of using three consecutive bits to identify the font, each font has a group of two bits and one additional bit that's separate from the other two. The single bit is the highest bit of the group. The reason for this can be traced back to the development of EGA and VGA cards. Since EGA cards have only four fonts, they only need to represent the numbers 0 through 3, which can be done with 2 bits.

VGA cards have eight available fonts, so we need to represent the values 0 through 7. To maintain compatibility, the VGA card was developed to imitate the original two bit configuration of the EGA card. A single extra bit was then added to accommodate the extra fonts. Since this extra bit was never used in the EGA card, it doesn't interfere with its operations.

The fonts listed in the previous figure are called first font and second font. However, this doesn't represent a hierarchical relationship. Instead, this is what gives the EGA and VGA cards the ability to display 512 characters on the screen simultaneously, unlike their predecessors, which can display only 256 characters. You may be wondering how to select characters from one of these fonts. Since there are only 256 ASCII codes, this isn't the answer.

At first, you might think that the attribute byte for a character doesn't have enough space for this kind of information. The two nibbles of this byte select a background and a foreground color for the character. However, this is the key to working with 512 characters simultaneously. The highest bit of the foreground color (bit 3 in the attribute byte) is used to select the first or second font.

If this bit is set to 0, then the foreground color is less than 8 and the video card will use the corresponding character from the first font. If this bit is set, then a foreground color greater than or equal to 8 is indicated and the character is taken from the second font.

Although the user may not notice, a distinction is always made between the first and second font. This is because the same font is specified twice in the character map select register. Once two numbers are entered in this register, the difference between the fonts immediately becomes apparent on the screen.

Access this register if you want to display two fonts on the screen simultaneously or if you just want to switch to another font. You can produce some very interesting visual effects by simply switching between two fonts in your application.

You don't have to program the character map select register directly because the video BIOS uses sub-function 03H of function 11H to do this. This sub-function expects the two function numbers in the AH and the AL registers. When sub-function 03H is called, an additional parameter must be passed to the BL register. This parameter is the value that you want to load in the character map select register to indicate a desired font. The following section contains an example of how this function is used. This example uses the second font to create a graphic window within a text screen.

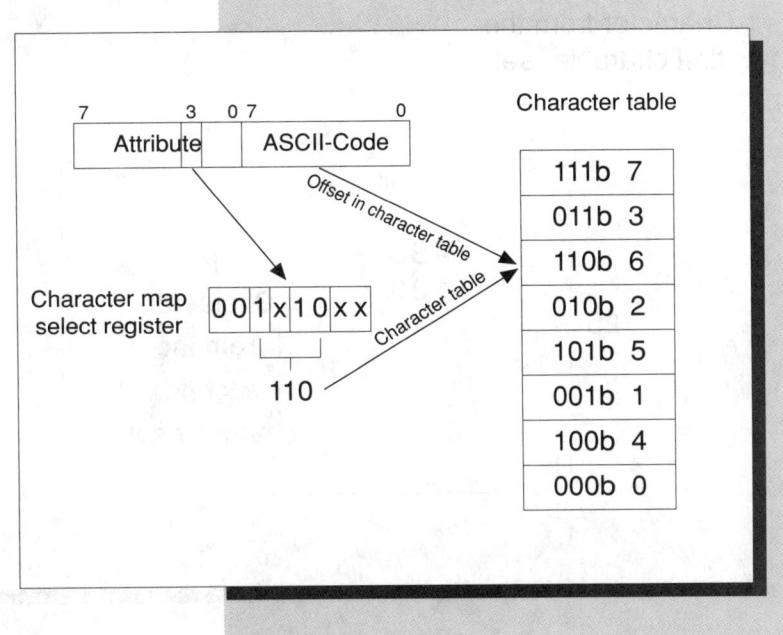

Selecting fonts from the character map select register and attribute byte

One problem you may encounter when using a second font is that the characters of the second font may appear lighter on screen. This occurs because bit 3 of the attribute byte is set, which results in a foreground color number of 8 or greater being used for characters of the second font. This problem can easily be solved by simply changing the palette registers to set foreground colors 8-15 equal to those assigned to 0-7.

Since the BIOS has many functions for handling this type of manipulation, this operation can easily be performed. Although this limits the number of foreground colors to eight, few programs would use that many foreground colors simultaneously. You could program the palette registers yourself to obtain additional colors if necessary.

A graphics window in text mode

Suppose that instead of displaying 512 characters, you need mathematical symbols or other special characters. There's an alternative to using the character select map register. Instead, you can use the second font to create a graphics window in your text screen. Then you can display small graphics or images without switching to the more complicated graphics mode.

The technique for creating a graphics window is similar to the technique for creating a logo. Simply piece together a number of specially defined characters to form the desired image. Each character from the second font appears once in the graphics window. This is important because it

197

limits the size of the graphics window to 256 characters. The resulting block may be as large as 16x16 characters, but you aren't limited to any particular shape of window.

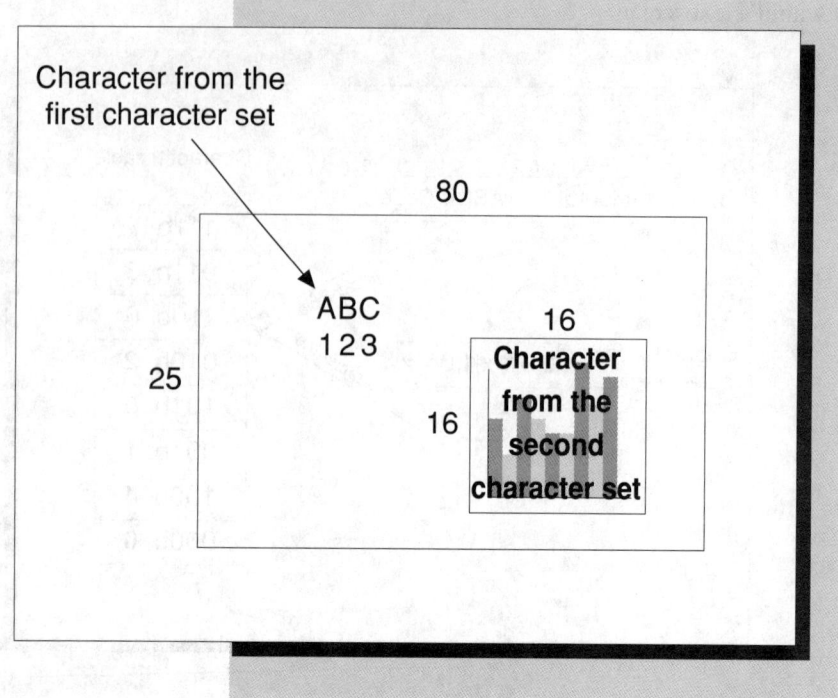

Graphics window structure in text mode

The second font is considered an array of individual pixels relating to coordinates within the graphics window. To set or clear a pixel within the graphics window, first you must calculate which character contains the appropriate pixel. The pixel position is determined relative to the upper-left corner of the character. The pixel is then set or cleared in the bit pattern for the character in the character table.

For example, suppose that a VGA character comprises 16 pixel lines, each consisting of eight pixels. If we take the lower-left corner of the screen as the point of origin for our graphics window, then all pixels with X-coordinates less than 8 and Y-coordinates less than 16 are considered part of the first character, which is in the lower-left corner of the graphics window. As the previous figure indicates, this character is always ASCII code 0. The number of each character in our window remains fixed.

The next step calculates which pixel line within the character we want to manipulate. This structure is the same as that found in the character table. So, a pixel with a Y-coordinate of 15 would be in the top pixel line of the character with ASCII code 0 and a pixel with a Y-coordinate of 0 would be in the bottom line of the character. This enables us to easily calculate the location of any pixel.

The final step determines the location of the desired pixel within the pixel line. The bit positions of the pixels are numbered 7 to 0 from left to right. By knowing the character number, pixel line, and bit number, any pixel can be switched on or off by passing the corresponding information to the character table in video RAM.

Redefining an entire character every time you want to set or clear a single pixel may seem inefficient. However, if you're using the BIOS functions for defining characters, there's no alternative. Also, since these functions aren't very fast, you'll notice problems when you want to process pixels in rapid succession (e.g., when drawing a line). For these reasons, both programs presented in this section access bitplane 2 directly. This allows you to manipulate the graphics window effectively.

Unfortunately, there is a problem with VGA because of the ninth pixel. We've already encountered this problem while using the LOGO program. As you may remember, the ninth pixel always remains blank, so we must limit the VGA character width to 8 pixels so the characters will flow together smoothly and without an empty space between them. We described the procedure for changing VGA character width from 9 pixels to 8 pixels earlier in this chapter.

The demonstration program discussed in this section is called MIKADO. Again, we've included both Pascal (MIKADO.PAS) and C (MIKADO.C) versions. The highlight of these programs is a routine called InitGraphArea, which configures the graphics window. The programs also include a routine called SetPixel, which allows you to set or delete individual pixels. This routine acts as the basis of the Line function, which draws a line within the graphics window.

The InitGraphArea procedure accepts data about the location of the graphics window, its size, and the colors to be used. You can also select the font number that you want to use to create the graphics window. The maximum X and Y coordinates are calculated from the character resolution and the window's size. These values are then stored in the xmax and ymax global variables.

Bitplane 2 is accessed using the procedure we previously described (in the GetFontAccess routine). The ReleaseFontAccess function performs the opposite task; it restores access to the video RAM at B800H. These routines aren't called very often because "snow" appears on your screen while they are executing.

The SelectMaps procedure is also important to the MIKADO program. This routine enters the desired fonts in the character map select register, using the BIOS function we described earlier. This prevents direct hardware access to the video card. Bypassing hardware access makes the program more compatible with all types of VGA cards because different manufacturers may assign different uses to the registers.

Several procedures in the MIKADO programs use the BIOS to program the palette registers. Any element of the 16 color palette can be changed, the entire palette can be redefined, or the current contents of the palette can be queried. The procedures that set the colors for the text and graphics windows are called SetPalCol, SetPalAry, GetPalCol, and GelPalAry.

When considering colors for the graphics window, remember that color must be assigned by character instead of by pixel, which is possible in graphics mode. A character consists of 14x8 pixels with EGA and 16x8 pixels with VGA. Usually it's best to assign one background color and one foreground color to the graphics window.

But the MIKADO programs do something entirely different. These programs assign a successive color code to each character in the graphics window. This gives the illusion of gradually changing bands of color.

These two programs also clarify the order in which the various routines must be called. First, IsEgaVga determines whether an EGA card or VGA card is available. Only then can the graphics window be opened with InitGraphArea. Before the window can be accessed, GetFontAccess must be called. Then you can draw lines or pictures within the window using SetPixel.

If you want to send text to the screen, you must call ReleaseFontAccess first, then call GetFontAccess again to return to graphics output. ClearGraphArea clears the graphics window, then restores access to video RAM and the default font (font 0).

MIKADO fills the screen around the graphics window with ASCII characters, showing the complete ASCII character set is still available with the graphics window in place.

The MIKADO programs contain of the tools you'll need to work with a graphics window in text mode. After studying the listing, you'll be able to modify or expand these routines according to your own needs. Having a graphics window open in the middle of a text screen can be very useful. Now you can add this feature to your own applications.

Pascal listing: MIKADOP.PAS

```
{*********************************************************
* M I K A D O P : Demonstrates 512 character mode on EGA & VGA color *
*                 systems: Displays graphics within text mode.       *
*                 This program runs in VGA color mode only. If you   *
*                 are running a VGA mono system, switch your card to *
*                 VGA color mode before running this program.        *
**---------------------------------------------------------------**
* Author        : Michael Tischer                                  *
* Developed on  : 04/02/90                                         *
* Last update   : 02/12/92                                         *
*********************************************************}

program MikadoP;

uses DOS, CRT;                          { Add DOS and CRT units }

{-- Constants ---------------------------------------------}

const EGAVGA_SEQUENCER = $3C4;      { Sequencer address/data port }
      EGAVGA_MONCTR    = $3D4;          { Monitor controller }
      EGAVGA_GRAPHCTR  = $3CE;{ Graphics controller address/data port }
      CHAR_WIDTH       = 8;
      CHAR_BYTES       = 32;
      MIKADOS          = 5;  { Number of mikados drawn simultaneously }

{-- Type declarations ------------------------------------}

type VEL      = record            { Describes character attribute }
                  case boolean of   { combination in video RAM    }
                    true  : ( Chractr, ChAttrib : byte );
                    false : ( Contnt            : word );
                end;
     VPTR     = ^VEL;              { Pointer to a character/attribute }
     VELARRAY = array [1..25,1..80] of VEL;    { Video RAM array }
     VELARPTR = ^VELARRAY;                { Pointer to video RAM }
```

```
     FONT  = array[0..255,0..CHAR_BYTES-1] of byte;    { Font array }
     FPTR  = ^font;                          { Pointer to a font }

     PALARY = array[ 1..16] of BYTE;       { Palette register array }

{-- Global variables ----------------------------------------}

const vioptr : VELARPTR = ptr( $B800, $0000 ); { Pointer to video RAM }

var CharHeight,
    lenx     : byte;        { Width of graphic window in characters }
    xmax,             { Max. pixel coordinates of graphic window }
    ymax     : integer;
    fontptr  : fptr;                 { Pointer to graphic font }

procedure CLI; inline( $FA );
procedure STI; inline( $FB );

{*********************************************************
* IsEgaVga : Determines whether an EGA or a VGA card is installed,   *
*            then places the number of scan lines per character in   *
*            the CharHeight global variable.                         *
**---------------------------------------------------------------**
* Input    : None                                                  *
* Output   : TRUE if EGA or VGA card, otherwise FALSE              *
*********************************************************}

function IsEgaVga : boolean;

var Regs : Registers;       { Processor registers for interrupt call }

begin
  Regs.AX := $1a00;                { Function 1AH applies to VGA only }
  Intr( $10, Regs );
```

```
  if ( Regs.AL = $1a ) then          { Is the function available? }
    begin
      IsEgaVGa := TRUE;
      CharHeight := 16;                        { 16 scan lines }
    end
  else
    begin
      Regs.ah := $12;                  { Call function 12H, }
      Regs.bl := $10;                  { sub-function 10H }
      intr($10, Regs);                     { Call video BIOS }
      IsEgaVga := ( Regs.bl <> $10 );
      CharHeight := 14;                        { 14 scan lines }
    end;
end;
```

```
{*****************************************************************
* SetCharWidth: Sets VGA character width to 8 or 9 pixels.      *
**-----------------------------------------------------------**
* Input   : HWIDTH = Character width (8 or 9)                   *
*****************************************************************}
```

```
procedure SetCharWidth( hwidth : byte );

var Regs : Registers;       { Processor registers for interrupt call }
    x    : byte;                      { Value for misc. output reg. }

begin
  if ( hwidth = 8 ) then Regs.BX := $0001   { BH = horiz. direction }
                    else Regs.BX := $0800;   { BL = seq. reg. value }

  x := port[ $3CC ] and not(4+8);          { Toggle horizontal }
  if ( hwidth = 9 ) then                    { resolution from   }
    x := x or 4;                            { 720 to 640 pixels }
  port[ $3C2 ] := x;

  CLI;                  { Toggle sequencer from 8 to 9 pixels }
  portw[ EGAVGA_SEQUENCER ] := $0100;
  portw[ EGAVGA_SEQUENCER ] := $01 + Regs.BL shl 8;
  portw[ EGAVGA_SEQUENCER ] := $0300;
  STI;

  Regs.AX := $1000;              { Change screen configuration }
  Regs.BL := $13;
  intr( $10, Regs );
end;
```

```
{*****************************************************************
* SelectMaps : Selects fonts, with the selection depending on bit 3  *
*              of the attribute byte.                           *
**-----------------------------------------------------------**
* Input   : MAP0 = Number of first font    ( bit 3 = 0 )       *
*           MAP1 = Number of second font   ( bit 3 = 1 )       *
* Info    : EGA cards can select fonts 0-3,                     *
*           VGA cards can select fonts 0-7.                     *
*****************************************************************}
```

```
procedure SelectMaps( map0, map1 : byte );

var Regs : Registers;      { Processor registers for interrupt call }

begin
  Regs.AX := $1103;                { Program font map select register }
  Regs.BL := ( ( map0 and 3 ) + ( map0 and 4 ) shl 2 ) +
             ( ( map1 and 3 ) shl 2 + ( map1 and 4 ) shl 3 );
```

```
  Intr( $10, Regs );        { Call BIOS function 11H, sub-function 03H }
end;
```

```
{*****************************************************************
* GetFontAccess: Enables direct access to the second memory map in  *
*                which the font is stored at address A000:0000.  *
**-----------------------------------------------------------**
* Input   : None                                                *
* Info    : After calling this procedure you cannot access video RAM *
*           at B800:0000.                                       *
*****************************************************************}
```

```
procedure GetFontAccess;

const SeqRegs : array[1..4] of word = ( $0100, $0402, $0704, $0300 );
      GCRegs  : array[1..3] of word = ( $0204, $0005, $0406 );

var i : byte;                                    { Loop counter }

begin
  CLI;
  for i := 1 to 4 do          { Load different sequencer registers }
    portw[ EGAVGA_SEQUENCER ] := SeqRegs[ i ];

  for i := 1 to 3 do          { Load graphics controller registers }
    portw[ EGAVGA_GRAPHCTR ] := GCRegs[ i ];
  STI;
end;
```

```
{*****************************************************************
* ReleaseFontAccess: Releases access to video RAM at B800:0000, but  *
*                    fonts in memory page #2 remain blocked.    *
**-----------------------------------------------------------**
* Input   : None                                                *
*****************************************************************}
```

```
procedure ReleaseFontAccess;

const SeqRegs : array[1..4] of word = ( $0100, $0302, $0304, $0300 );
      GCRegs  : array[1..3] of word = ( $0004, $1005, $0E06 );

var i : byte;                                    { Loop counter }

begin
  for i := 1 to 4 do          { Load different sequencer registers }
    portw[ EGAVGA_SEQUENCER ] := SeqRegs[ i ];
  for i := 1 to 3 do          { Load graphics controller registers }
    portw[ EGAVGA_GRAPHCTR ] := GCRegs[ i ];
end;
```

```
{*****************************************************************
* ClearGraphArea: Clears the graphic area in which the character *
*                 patterns of stored characters are set to 0.   *
**-----------------------------------------------------------**
* Input   : None                                                *
*****************************************************************}
```

```
procedure ClearGraphArea;

var exchars,                          { Characters to be executed }
    chrow   : byte;      { Row within the corresponding character }

begin
  for exchars := 0 to 255 do                    { Loop characters }
```

```pascal
     for chrow := 0 to CharHeight-1 do           { Loop rows }
       fontptr^[ exchars, chrow ] := 0;          { & set to 0 }
end;


{**********************************************************
 *  InitGraphArea: Initializes a screen area for graphic display.  *
 **------------------------------------------------------**
 *  Input   : X     = Starting column of area (1-80)           *
 *            Y     = Starting row of area (1-25)              *
 *            XLEN  = Area width in characters                 *
 *            YLEN  = Area height in characters                *
 *            MAP   = Number of the graphic font              *
 *            GACOL = Graphic area color (0-7 or FFH)          *
 *  Info    : If a color value of FFH exists, the system generates an  *
 *            appropriate color code needed for the mikado effect.     *
 **********************************************************}

procedure InitGraphArea( x, y, xlen, ylen, map, gacol : byte );

var column, chrow : integer;                    { Loop variables }
    ccode        : byte;                        { Floating character code }

begin
  if ( xlen * ylen > 256 ) then                 { Range too large? }
    writeln( 'Error: Area larger than the 256-character maximum' )
  else
    begin
      if ( CharHeight = 16 ) then               { VGA? }
        SetCharWidth( 8 );                      { Yes --> Set character width }
      SelectMaps( 0, map );                     { Select font }
      xmax := xlen*CHAR_WIDTH;                   { Compute max. pixel coordinates }
      ymax := ylen*CharHeight;
      lenx := xlen;
      fontptr := ptr( $A000, map * $4000 );     { Pointer to graphic map }
      GetFontAccess;                            { Enable font access }
      ClearGraphArea;                           { Clear font }
      ReleaseFontAccess;                        { Enable video RAM access }

      {-- Fill graphic area with character codes ---------------------}

      ccode := 0;
      for chrow := ylen-1 downto 0 do           { Rows from bottom to top }
        for column := 0 to xlen-1 do            { Columns from left to right }
          begin                                 { Set character code and attribute }
            vioptr^[chrow+y,column+x].Chractr := ccode;
            if ( gacol = $ff ) then
              vioptr^[chrow+y,column+x].ChAttrib := ccode mod 6 + 1 + 8
            else
              vioptr^[chrow+y,column+x].ChAttrib := gacol or $08;
            inc( ccode );                       { Next character code }
          end;
    end;
end;


{**********************************************************
 *  CloseGraphArea: Closes graphic area.               *
 **------------------------------------------------------**
 *  Input   : None                                     *
 **********************************************************}

procedure CloseGraphArea;

begin
  ReleaseFontAccess;                            { Release access to video RAM }
```

```pascal
      SelectMaps( 0, 0 );                       { Always display font 0 }
      if ( CharHeight = 16 ) then               { VGA? }
        SetCharWidth( 9 );                      { Yes --> Set character width }
end;


{**********************************************************
 *  SetPixel: Sets or unsets a pixel in the graphic window.   *
 **------------------------------------------------------**
 *  Input   : X,Y   = Pixel coordinates (0-...)               *
 *            ON    = TRUE to set, FALSE to unset             *
 **********************************************************}

procedure SetPixel( x, y : integer; on : boolean );

var charnum,                                    { Code for character at coordinates }
    line    : byte;                             { Pixel line in the character }

begin
  if ( x < xmax ) and ( y < ymax ) then         { Coordinates O.K.? }
    begin                                       { Yes --> Compute character no. and line }
      charnum := ((x div CHAR_WIDTH) + (y div CharHeight * lenx));
      line    := CharHeight - ( y mod CharHeight ) - 1;
      if on then                                { Set or unset character? }
        fontptr^[charnum, line] := fontptr^[charnum, line] or
          1 shl (CHAR_WIDTH - 1 - ( x mod CHAR_WIDTH ) )
      else
        fontptr^[charnum, line] := fontptr^[charnum, line] and
          not( 1 shl (CHAR_WIDTH - 1 - ( x mod CHAR_WIDTH ) ) );
    end;
end;


{**********************************************************
 *  Line: Draws a line within the graphic window, using the Bresenham  *
 *        algorithm.                                    *
 **------------------------------------------------------**
 *  Input   : X1, Y1 = Starting coordinates (0 - ...)         *
 *            X2, Y2 = Ending coordinates                     *
 *            ON     = TRUE to set pixel, FALSE to unset pixel *
 **********************************************************}

procedure Line( x1, y1, x2, y2 : integer; on : boolean );

var d, dx, dy,
    aincr, bincr,
    xincr, yincr,
    x, y               : integer;

{-- Procedure for swapping two integer variables ----------------------}

procedure SwapInt( var i1, i2: integer );

var dummy : integer;

begin
  dummy := i2;
  i2    := i1;
  i1    := dummy;
end;

{-- Main procedure ---------------------------------------------------}

begin
  if ( abs(x2-x1) < abs(y2-y1) ) then           { X- or Y-axis overflow? }
    begin                                       { Check Y-axes }
```

```
if ( y1 > y2 ) then                        { y1 > y2? }
  begin
    SwapInt( x1, x2 );            { Yes --> Swap X1 with X2 }
    SwapInt( y1, y2 );            {         and Y1 with Y2 }
  end;

if ( x2 > x1 ) then xincr := 1    { Set X-axis increment }
               else xincr := -1;

dy := y2 - y1;
dx := abs( x2-x1 );
d  := 2 * dx - dy;
aincr := 2 * (dx - dy);
bincr := 2 * dx;
x := x1;
y := y1;

SetPixel( x, y, on );                    { Set first pixel }
for y:=y1+1 to y2 do             { Execute line on Y-axes }
  begin
    if ( d >= 0 ) then
      begin
        inc( x, xincr );
        inc( d, aincr );
      end
    else
      inc( d, bincr );
    SetPixel( x, y, on );
  end;
end
else                                       { Check X-axes }
begin
  if ( x1 > x2 ) then                          { x1 > x2? }
    begin
      SwapInt( x1, x2 );        { Yes --> Swap X1 with X2 }
      SwapInt( y1, y2 );        {         and Y1 with Y2 }
    end;

  if ( y2 > y1 ) then yincr := 1    { Set Y-axis increment }
                 else yincr := -1;

  dx := x2 - x1;
  dy := abs( y2-y1 );
  d  := 2 * dy - dx;
  aincr := 2 * (dy - dx);
  bincr := 2 * dy;
  x := x1;
  y := y1;

  SetPixel( x, y, on );                  { Set first pixel }
  for x:=x1+1 to x2 do           { Execute line on X-axes }
    begin
      if ( d >= 0 ) then
        begin
          inc( y, yincr );
          inc( d, aincr );
        end
      else
        inc( d, bincr );
      SetPixel( x, y, on );
    end;
  end;
end;
```

```
{*********************************************************
* SetPalCol: Defines a color from the 16-part color palette or the *
*            screen border (overscan) color.             *
**-----------------------------------------------------**
* Input   : RegNr = Palette register number (0-15) or 16 for the  *
*                   overscan color                       *
*           Col   = Color value from 0 to 15             *
*********************************************************}

procedure SetPalCol( RegNr : byte; Col : byte );

var Regs  : Registers;      { Processor registers for interrupt call }

begin
  Regs.AX := $1000;         { Video function 10H, sub-function 00H }
  Regs.BH := Col;                            { Color value }
  Regs.BL := RegNr;      { Register number of attribute controller }
  intr( $10, Regs );              { Call BIOS video interrupt }
end;


{*********************************************************
* SetPalAry: Installs a new 16-color palette without changing the *
*            screen border color.                        *
**-----------------------------------------------------**
* Input   : NewCol = Palette array of type PALARY        *
*********************************************************}

procedure SetPalAry( NewCol : PALARY );

var i : byte;                              { Loop counter }

begin
  for i := 1 to 16 do          { Execute 16 entries in array }
    SetPalCol( i-1, NewCol[ i ] );    { Set corresponding colors }
end;


{*********************************************************
* GetPalCol: Gets the contents of a palette register.    *
**-----------------------------------------------------**
* Input   : RegNr = Palette register number (0-15) or 16 for the  *
*                   overscan color                       *
* Output  : Color value                                  *
* Info    : Alternate included for EGA cards, which do not support *
*           interrupt 10H, function 10H, sub-function 07H. *
*********************************************************}

function GetPalCol( RegNr : byte ) : byte;

var Regs  : Registers;      { Processor registers for interrupt call }

begin
  if ( CharHeight = 14 ) then                    { EGA card? }
    GetPalCol := RegNr       { Yes --> Cannot read palette registers }
  else                                           { No --> VGA }
    begin
      Regs.AX := $1007;      { Video function 10H, sub-function 07H }
      Regs.BL := RegNr;    { Register number of attribute controller }
      intr( $10, Regs );           { Call BIOS video interrupt }
      GetPalCol := Regs.BH;     { Palette register contents are here }
    end;
end;


{*********************************************************
* GetPalAry: Gets contents of 16-color palette registers and places *
```

```
*          these contents in an array for the caller.           *
**----------------------------------------------------------------**
* Input   : ColAry = Palette array of type PALARY, into which colors *
*                    are placed                                  *
*********************************************************************}

procedure GetPalAry( var ColAry : PALARY );

var i : byte;                              { Loop counter }

begin
  for i := 1 to 16 do                  { Execute 16 entries in array }
    ColAry[ i ] := GetPalCol( i-1 );   { Set corresponding colors }
end;


{*********************************************************************
* Mikado: Applies the procedures and functions in this program.   *
**----------------------------------------------------------------**
* Input   : None                                                  *
*********************************************************************}

procedure Mikado;

type lcoor = record                    { Get coordinates of a line }
             x1, y1,
             x2, y2 : integer;
             end;

const NewCols : PALARY =
       ( {--------- Normal text character colors ----------------}
         BLACK,                        { Formerly...   black }
         BLUE,                         {               blue }
         GREEN,                        {               green }
         RED,                          {               cyan }
         CYAN,                         {               red }
         MAGENTA,                      {               magenta }
         YELLOW,                       {               brown }
         WHITE,                        {               light gray }
         {------------- Graphic colors ---------------------------}
         LIGHTBLUE,                    { Formerly  dark gray }
         LIGHTGREEN,                   {               light blue }
         LIGHTRED,                     {               light green }
         LIGHTCYAN,                    {               light cyan }
         LIGHTMAGENTA,                 {               light red }
         BLUE,                         {               light magenta }
         YELLOW,                       {               yellow }
         WHITE );                      {               white }

var i,                                 { Loop counter }
    first,                             { Array index of most recent mikado }
    last   : integer;                  { Array index of oldest mikado }
    clear  : boolean;                  { Clear mikados }
    lar    : array[1..MIKADOS] of lcoor;  { Mikado array }
    OldCols: PALARY;                   { Get old colors }

begin
  GetPalAry( OldCols );                { Get old colors }
  SetPalAry( NewCols );                { Install new color palette }
  TextColor( 7 );
  TextBackGround( 1 );
  ClrScr;                              { Clear screen }
  GotoXY(1,1);                         { Fill with characters }
  for i:=1 to 25*80-1 do              { from default font }
  write( chr(32 + i mod 224) );
```

```
{-- Initialize graphic area and generate mikados --------------------}

  GotoXY(27,6);
  TextColor( 7 );
  TextBackGround( 3 );
  write('      M I K A D O      ' );
  GotoXY(27,6);
  InitGraphArea( 27, 7, 25, 10, 1,  $FF );
  GetFontAccess;                       { Get access to font }

  clear := false;                      { No mikados cleared yet }
  first := 1;                          { Start with first array position }
  last := 1;
  repeat                               { Mikado loop }
    if first = MIKADOS+1 then first := 1;     { Wraparound? }
    lar[first].x1 := random( xmax-1 );       { Create mikado }
    lar[first].x2 := random( xmax-1 );
    lar[first].y1 := random( ymax-1 );
    lar[first].y2 := random( ymax-1 );
    line( lar[first].x1, lar[first].y1,       { and draw it }
          lar[first].x2, lar[first].y2, true );
    inc( first );                            { Next Mikado }
    if first = MIKADOS+1 then clear := true;  { Already clear? }
    if clear then                            { Clear now? }
      begin                                  { Yes }
        line( lar[last].x1, lar[last].y1,
              lar[last].x2, lar[last].y2, false );
        inc( last );                         { Clear next Mikado }
        if last = MIKADOS+1 then last := 1;
      end;
  until keypressed;                    { Repeat until user presses a key }

  {-- End program -----------------------------------------------------}

  CloseGraphArea;
  SetPalAry( OldCols );                { Restore old color palette }
  GotoXY(1, 25 );
  TextColor( 7 );
  TextBackGround( 0 );
  ClrEol;
  writeln( 'System has reverted to old font.');
end;


{*********************************************************************
*               M A I N   P R O G R A M                          *
*********************************************************************}

begin
  if IsEgaVga then     { Is there an EGA or a VGA card installed? }
    Mikado                          { Yes --> Execute demo }
  else                 { No --> Program cannot be started }
    writeln( 'Warning: No EGA or VGA card found' );
end.
```

C listing: MIKADOC.C

```
/***************************************************************
*                     M I K A D O C . C                       *
**-----------------------------------------------------------**
* Task        : Demonstrates 512 character mode on EGA & VGA color *
*               systems: Displays graphics within text mode.  *
*               This program runs in VGA color mode only. If you *
*               are running a VGA mono system, switch your card to *
*               VGA color mode before running this program.   *
**-----------------------------------------------------------**
* Author      : Michael Tischer                               *
* Developed on : 04/02/90                                     *
* Last update  : 02/12/92                                     *
***************************************************************/


/*-- Define constants and add include files ------------------*/

#include <dos.h>                          /* Add include files */
#include <stdarg.h>
#include <stdlib.h>
#include <stdio.h>
#include <conio.h>

#ifdef __TURBOC__                     /* Compiling with Turbo C? */
  #define CLI()        disable()
  #define STI()        enable()
  #define outpw( p, w ) outport( p, w )
  #ifndef inp
    #define outp( p, b )  outportb( p, b )
    #define inp( p )      inportb( p )
  #endif
#else                        /* No --> Then QuickC 2.0 or MSC */
  #include <conio.h>
  #define random(x)      (rand() % ( x + 1 ))
  #define MK_FP(seg,ofs) ((void far *)\
                         (((unsigned long)(seg) << 16) | (ofs)))
  #define CLI()          _disable()
  #define STI()          _enable()
#endif

#define EGAVGA_SEQUENCER 0x3C4      /* Sequencer address/data port */
#define EGAVGA_MONCTR    0x3D4            /* Monitor controller */
#define EGAVGA_GRAPHCTR  0x3CE /* Graphics controller addr./data port*/

#define CHAR_WIDTH      8
#define CHAR_BYTES      32
#define MIKADOS         5 /* Number of mikados drawn simultaneously */

#define TRUE  ( 0 == 0 )
#define FALSE ( 0 == 1 )

#define BLACK        0x00          /* Color attributes */
#define BLUE         0x01
#define GREEN        0x02
#define CYAN         0x03
#define RED          0x04
#define MAGENTA      0x05
#define BROWN        0x06
#define LIGHTGRAY    0x07
#define GRAY         0x01
#define LIGHTBLUE    0x09
#define LIGHTGREEN   0x0A
#define LIGHTCYAN    0x0B
```

```
#define LIGHTRED     0x0C
#define LIGHTMAGENTA 0x0D
#define YELLOW       0x0E
#define WHITE        0x0F

/*-- Type declarations ---------------------------------------*/

typedef unsigned char BYTE;
typedef BYTE BOOL;

typedef BYTE PALARY[16];                /* Palette register array */

/*-- Global variables ----------------------------------------*/

BYTE far *vioptr = (BYTE far *) 0xb8000000,  /* Pointer to video RAM */
         far *fontptr;                  /* Pointer to graphic font */

BYTE CharHeight,
     lenx;             /* Width of graphic window in characters */
int  xmax,             /* Max. pixel coordinates of graphic window */
     ymax;


/***************************************************************
* IsEgaVga : Determines whether an EGA or VGA card is installed. *
**-----------------------------------------------------------**
* Input   : None                                              *
* Output  : EGA, VGA or NEITHER                               *
***************************************************************/

BYTE IsEgaVga( void )
{
 union REGS Regs;        /* Processor registers for interrupt call */

 Regs.x.ax = 0x1a00;           /* Function 1AH applies to VGA only */
 int86( 0x10, &Regs, &Regs );
 if ( Regs.x.al == 0x1a )        /* Is the function available? */
  {                                      /* Yes --> It's VGA */
   CharHeight = 16;                       /* VGA character height */
   return 1;
  }
 else
  {
   CharHeight = 14;                       /* EGA character height */
   Regs.h.ah = 0x12;                      /* Call function 12H, */
   Regs.h.bl = 0x10;                      /* sub-function 10H */
   int86(0x10, &Regs, &Regs );            /* Call video BIOS */
   return Regs.h.bl != 0x10;
  }
}


/***************************************************************
* SetCursor : Specifies screen cursor position.               *
**-----------------------------------------------------------**
* Input parameters : CURCOL = New cursor column (0-79)         *
*                    CUROW  = New cursor row (0-24)            *
* Return value     : None                                     *
***************************************************************/

void SetCursor( BYTE curcol, BYTE curow )
{
 union REGS regs;        /* Processor registers for interrupt call */

 regs.h.ah = 2;                   /* Function number: Set cursor */
 regs.h.bh = 0;                        /* Access screen page 0 */
```

```
regs.h.dh = curow;                              /* Set row */
regs.h.dl = curcol;                             /* Set column */
int86(0x10, &regs, &regs);                      /* Call BIOS video interrupt */
}


/****************************************************************
 * PrintfAt : Displays a formatted string anywhere on the screen. *
 **------------------------------------------------------------**
 * Input  : COLUMN = Column                                       *
 *          SCROW  = Row                                          *
 *          CHCOL  = Character attribute                          *
 *          STRING = Pointer to string                           *
 * Output : None                                                 *
 * Info   : This function should only be called if the system running *
 *          this program contains an EGA card or a VGA card.     *
 ****************************************************************/

void PrintfAt( BYTE column, BYTE scrow, BYTE chcol, char * string, ... )
{
 va_list parameter;             /* Parameter list for VA_... macros */
 char outbufr[255],             /* Buffer for formatted string */
      *outptr;
 BYTE far *vptr;                /* Pointer to video RAM */

 va_start( parameter, string );          /* Convert parameters */
 vsprintf( outbufr, string, parameter ); /* Format */

 vptr = (BYTE far *) MK_FP( 0xB800, column*2+scrow*160 );

 for ( outptr = outbufr; *outptr ; )     /* Execute string */
  {
   *vptr++ = *(outptr++);       /* Write character to video RAM */
   *vptr++ = chcol;             /* Write attribute to video RAM */
  }
}


/****************************************************************
 * ClrScr: Clears the screen.                                    *
 **------------------------------------------------------------**
 * Input parameters : CHATT = Character attribute                *
 * Return value     : None                                       *
 ****************************************************************/

void ClrScr( BYTE chatt )
{
 BYTE far *vptr;                        /* Pointer to video RAM */
 int  count = 2000;             /* Number of characters to be cleared */

 vptr = (BYTE far *) MK_FP( 0xB800, 0 ); /* Set pointer to video RAM */

 for ( ; count--; )                     /* Execute video RAM */
  {
   *vptr++ = ' ';               /* Write character to video RAM */
   *vptr++ = chatt;             /* Write attribute to video RAM */
  }
}


/****************************************************************
 * SetCharWidth: Sets VGA character width to 8 or 9 pixels.      *
 **------------------------------------------------------------**
 * Input  : HWIDTH = Character width (8 or 9)                    *
 ****************************************************************/

void SetCharWidth( BYTE hwidth )
```

```
{
 union REGS Regs;           /* Processor registers for interrupt call */
 unsigned char x;                       /* Value for misc. output reg. */

 Regs.x.bx = ( hwidth == 8 ) ? 0x0001 : 0x0800;

 x = inp( 0x3CC ) & (255-12);           /* Toggle horizontal */
 if ( hwidth == 9 )                     /* resolution from    */
  x |= 4;                               /* 720 to 640 pixels */
 outp( 0x3C2, x);

 CLI();                         /* Toggle sequencer from 8 to 9 pixels */
 outpw( EGAVGA_SEQUENCER, 0x0100 );
 outpw( EGAVGA_SEQUENCER, 0x01 + ( Regs.h.bl << 8 ) );
 outpw( EGAVGA_SEQUENCER, 0x0300 );
 STI();

 Regs.x.ax = 0x1000;            /* Change horizontal screen position */
 Regs.h.bl = 0x13;
 int86( 0x10, &Regs, &Regs );
}


/****************************************************************
 * SelectMaps : Selects fonts, with the selection depending on bit 3 *
 *              of the attribute byte.                           *
 **------------------------------------------------------------**
 * Input  : MAP0 = Number of first font          (Bit 3 = 0 )   *
 *          MAP1 = Number of second font         (Bit 3 = 1 )   *
 * Info   : EGA cards can select fonts 0-3,                      *
 *          VGA cards can select fonts 0-7.                      *
 ****************************************************************/

void SelectMaps( BYTE map0, BYTE map1)
{
 union REGS Regs;           /* Processor registers for interrupt call */

 Regs.x.ax = 0x1103;            /* Program font map select register */
 Regs.h.bl = ( map0 & 3 ) + ( ( map0 & 4 ) << 2 ) +
             ( ( map1 & 3 ) << 2 ) + ( ( map1 & 4 ) << 3 );
 int86( 0x10, &Regs, &Regs ); /* Call function 11H, sub-function 03H */
}


/****************************************************************
 * GetFontAccess: Enables direct access to the second memory map in *
 *              which the font is stored at address A000:0000.  *
 **------------------------------------------------------------**
 * Input  : None                                                 *
 * Info   : After calling this procedure you cannot access video RAM *
 *          at B800:0000.                                        *
 ****************************************************************/

void GetFontAccess( void )
{
 static unsigned SeqRegs[4] = { 0x0100, 0x0402, 0x0704, 0x0300 },
                 GCRegs[3]  = { 0x0204, 0x0005, 0x0006 };
 BYTE i;                                        /* Loop counter */

 CLI();                                 /* Disable interrupts */

 for ( i=0; i<4; ++i )          /* Load different sequencer registers */
  outpw( EGAVGA_SEQUENCER, SeqRegs[ i ] );

 for ( i=0; i<3; ++i )          /* Load graphics controller registers */
  outpw( EGAVGA_GRAPHCTR, GCRegs[ i ] );
```

```
    STI();                           /* Enable interrupts */
}


/************************************************************************
*  ReleaseFontAccess: Releases access to video RAM at B800:0000, but   *
*                     fonts in memory page #2 remain blocked.          *
**--------------------------------------------------------------------**
*  Input   : None                                                      *
************************************************************************/

void ReleaseFontAccess( void )
{
  static unsigned SeqRegs[4] = { 0x0100, 0x0302, 0x0304, 0x0300 },
                  GCRegs[3] = { 0x0004, 0x1005, 0x0E06 };
  BYTE i;                            /* Loop counter */

  CLI();                             /* Disable interrupts */

  for ( i=0; i<4; ++i )             /* Load different sequencer registers */
    outpw( EGAVGA_SEQUENCER, SeqRegs[ i ] );

  for ( i=0; i<3; ++i )             /* Load graphics controller registers */
    outpw( EGAVGA_GRAPHCTR, GCRegs[ i ] );

  STI();                             /* Enable interrupts */
}


/************************************************************************
*  ClearGraphArea: Clears the graphic area in which the character      *
*                  patterns of stored characters are set to 0.         *
**--------------------------------------------------------------------**
*  Input   : None                                                      *
************************************************************************/

void ClearGraphArea( void )
{
  int exchars,                       /* Characters to be executed */
      chrow;                         /* Row within the corresponding character */

  for ( exchars = 0; exchars < 256; ++exchars )   /* Loop characters */
    for ( chrow = 0; chrow < CharHeight; ++ chrow )   /* Loop rows */
      *(fontptr+exchars*CHAR_BYTES+chrow) = 0;        /* & set to 0 */
}


/************************************************************************
*  InitGraphArea: Initializes a screen area for graphic display.       *
**--------------------------------------------------------------------**
*  Input   : X     = Starting column of area (1-80)                    *
*            Y     = Starting row of area (1-25)                       *
*            XLEN  = Area width in characters                          *
*            YLEN  = Area height in characters                         *
*            MAP   = Number of the graphic font                        *
*            GACOL = Graphic area color (0-7 or FFH)                   *
*  Info    : If a color value of 0xFF exists, the system generates an  *
*            appropriate color code needed for the mikado effect.      *
************************************************************************/

void InitGraphArea( BYTE x, BYTE y, BYTE xlen, BYTE ylen, BYTE map,
                    BYTE gacol )
{
  unsigned offset;                   /* Offset in video RAM */
  int     column, chrow;             /* Loop variables */
  BYTE    ccode;                     /* Floating character code */
```

```
  if ( xlen * ylen > 256 )                    /* Range too large? */
    printf( "Error: Area larger than the 256-character maximum\n" );
  else
  {
    if ( CharHeight == 16 )                   /* VGA? */
      SetCharWidth( 8 );                      /* Yes --> Set character width */
    SelectMaps( 0, map );                     /* Select font */
    xmax = xlen*CHAR_WIDTH;          /* Compute max. pixel coordinates */
    ymax = ylen*CharHeight;
    lenx = xlen;
    fontptr = MK_FP( 0xA000, map * 0x4000 );/* Pointer to graphic map */
    GetFontAccess();                          /* Enable font access */
    ClearGraphArea();                         /* Clear font */
    ReleaseFontAccess();                      /* Enable video RAM access */

    /*-- Fill graphic area with character codes ----------------------*/

    ccode = 0;
    for ( chrow = ylen-1; chrow >= 0; --chrow )        /* Loop rows */
      for ( column = 0; column < xlen; ++column )      /* Loop columns */
      {                                /* Set character code and attribute */
        offset = ((chrow+y)*80+column+x) << 1;  /* Offset in video RAM */
        *(vioptr+offset) = ccode;               /* Write character */
        *(vioptr+offset+1) = ( gacol == 0xff ) ? ( ccode % 6 ) + 1 + 8
                                               : gacol | 0x08;
        ++ccode;                                /* Next character code */
      }
  }
}


/************************************************************************
*  CloseGraphArea: Closes graphic area.                                *
**--------------------------------------------------------------------**
*  Input   : None                                                      *
************************************************************************/

void CloseGraphArea( void )
{
  ReleaseFontAccess();               /* Release access to video RAM */
  SelectMaps( 0, 0 );                /* Always display font 0 */
  if ( CharHeight == 16 )            /* VGA? */
    SetCharWidth( 9 );               /* Yes --> Set character width */
}


/************************************************************************
*  SetPixel: Sets or unsets a pixel in the graphic window.             *
**--------------------------------------------------------------------**
*  Input   : X,Y   = Pixel coordinates (0-...)                         *
*            ON    = TRUE to set, FALSE to unset                       *
************************************************************************/

void SetPixel( int x, int y, BOOL on )
{
  BYTE charnum,                      /* Code for character at coordinates */
       linenr,                       /* Pixel line in the character */
       far *bptr;

  if ( ( x < xmax ) && ( y < ymax ) )          /* Coordinates O.K.? */
  {                            /* Yes --> Compute character no. and line */
    charnum = ((x / CHAR_WIDTH) + (y / CharHeight * lenx));
    linenr = CharHeight - ( y % CharHeight ) - 1;
    bptr = fontptr + charnum * CHAR_BYTES + linenr;
    if ( on )                          /* Set or unset character? */
```

```c
    *bptr = *bptr | ( 1 << (CHAR_WIDTH - 1 - ( x % CHAR_WIDTH ) ) );
  else
    *bptr = *bptr & !( 1 << (CHAR_WIDTH - 1 - ( x % CHAR_WIDTH ) ) );
  }
}

/*********************************************************************
* Line: Draws a line within the graphic window, using the Bresenham *
*       algorithm.                                                   *
**------------------------------------------------------------------*
* Input   : X1, Y1 = Starting coordinates (0 - ...)                  *
*           X2, Y2 = Ending coordinates                              *
*           ON     = TRUE to set pixel, FALSE to unset pixel         *
*********************************************************************/

/*-- Function for swapping two integer variables --------------------*/

void SwapInt( int *i1, int *i2 )
{
 int dummy;

 dummy = *i2;
 *i2   = *i1;
 *i1   = dummy;
}

/*-- Main function --------------------------------------------------*/

void Line( int x1, int y1, int x2, int y2, BOOL on )
{
 int d, dx, dy,
     aincr, bincr,
     xincr, yincr,
     x, y;

 if ( abs(x2-x1) < abs(y2-y1) )       /* X- or Y-axis overflow? */
  {                                          /* Check Y-axes */
   if ( y1 > y2 )                            /* y1 > y2? */
    {
     SwapInt( &x1, &x2 );            /* Yes --> Swap X1 with X2 */
     SwapInt( &y1, &y2 );            /*         and Y1 with Y2  */
    }

   xincr = ( x2 > x1 ) ? 1 : -1;           /* Set X-axis increment */

   dy = y2 - y1;
   dx = abs( x2-x1 );
   d  = 2 * dx - dy;
   aincr = 2 * (dx - dy);
   bincr = 2 * dx;
   x = x1;
   y = y1;

   SetPixel( x, y, on );                    /* Set first pixel */
   for (y=y1+1; y<= y2; ++y )          /* Execute line on Y-axes */
    {
     if ( d >= 0 )
      {
       x += xincr;
       d += aincr;
      }
     else
       d += bincr;
     SetPixel( x, y, on );
    }
  }
 else                                     /* Check X-axes */
  {
   if ( x1 > x2 )                            /* x1 > x2? */
    {
     SwapInt( &x1, &x2 );            /* Yes --> Swap X1 with X2 */
     SwapInt( &y1, &y2 );            /*         and Y1 with Y2  */
    }

   yincr = ( y2 > y1 ) ? 1 : -1;           /* Set Y-axis increment */

   dx = x2 - x1;
   dy = abs( y2-y1 );
   d  = 2 * dy - dx;
   aincr = 2 * (dy - dx);
   bincr = 2 * dy;
   x = x1;
   y = y1;

   SetPixel( x, y, on );                    /* Set first pixel */
   for (x=x1+1; x<=x2; ++x )           /* Execute line on X-axes */
    {
     if ( d >= 0 )
      {
       y += yincr;
       d += aincr;
      }
     else
       d += bincr;
     SetPixel( x, y, on );
    }
  }
}

/*********************************************************************
* SetPalCol: Defines a color from the 16-part color palette or the  *
*            screen border (overscan) color.                        *
**-----------------------------------------------------------------**
* Input   : RegNr = Palette register number (0-15) or 16 for the    *
*                   overscan color                                  *
*           Col   = Color value from 0 to 15                        *
*********************************************************************/

void SetPalCol( BYTE RegNr, BYTE Col )
{
 union REGS Regs;        /* Processor registers for interrupt call */

 Regs.x.ax = 0x1000;         /* Video function 10H, sub-function 00H */
 Regs.h.bh = Col;                              /* Color value */
 Regs.h.bl = RegNr;      /* Register number of attribute controller */
 int86( 0x10, &Regs, &Regs );          /* Call BIOS video interrupt */
}

/*********************************************************************
* SetPalAry: Installs a new 16-color palette without changing the   *
*            screen border color.                                   *
**-----------------------------------------------------------------**
* Input   : NewColPtr = Palette array of type PALARY                *
*********************************************************************/

void SetPalAry( BYTE *NewColPtr )
{
 BYTE i;                                      /* Loop counter */
```

```
for (i = 0; i < 16; ++i )          /* Execute 16 entries in array */
  SetPalCol( i, NewColPtr[i] );        /* Set corresponding colors */
}


/********************************************************************
* GetPalCol: Gets the contents of a palette register.              *
**----------------------------------------------------------------**
* Input    : RegNr = Palette register number (0-15) or 16 for the  *
*                    overscan color                                *
* Output   : Color value                                           *
* Info     : Alternate method included for EGA cards, which do not *
*            support interrupt 10H, function 10H, sub-function 07H. *
********************************************************************/

BYTE GetPalCol( BYTE RegNr )
{
  union REGS Regs;         /* Processor registers for interrupt call */

  if ( CharHeight == 14 )                          /* EGA card? */
    return RegNr;          /* Yes --> Cannot read palette registers */
  else                                          /* No --> VGA */
  {
    Regs.x.ax = 0x1007;      /* Video function 10h, sub-function 07H */
    Regs.h.bl = RegNr;    /* Register number of attribute controller */
    int86( 0x10, &Regs, &Regs );   /* Call BIOS video interrupt */
    return Regs.h.bh;        /* Palette register contents are here */
  }
}


/********************************************************************
* GetPalAry: Gets contents of 16-color palette registers and places *
*            these contents in an array for the caller.            *
**----------------------------------------------------------------**
* Input    : ColAryPtr = Palette array of type PALARY, into which  *
*                        colors are placed                         *
********************************************************************/

void GetPalAry( BYTE *ColAryPtr )
{
  BYTE i;                                    /* Loop counter */

  for (i = 0; i < 16; ++i )          /* Execute 16 entries in array */
    ColAryPtr[i] = GetPalCol( i );       /* Set corresponding colors */
}


/********************************************************************
* Mikado: Applies the functions in this program.                   *
**----------------------------------------------------------------**
* Input    : None                                                  *
********************************************************************/

void Mikado( void )
{
  typedef struct {                  /* Get coordinates of a line */
            int x1, y1,
                x2, y2;
          } LINIE;

  static PALARY NewCols =
         { /*------------ Normal text character colors --------------*/
           BLACK,                          /* Formerly... black */
           BLUE,                           /*            blue */
           GREEN,                          /*            green */
```

```
           RED,                            /*            cyan */
           CYAN,                           /*            red */
           MAGENTA,                        /*            magenta */
           YELLOW,                         /*            brown */
           WHITE,                          /*            light gray */
           /*------------- Graphic colors --------------------------*/
           LIGHTBLUE,                     /* Formerly dark gray */
           LIGHTGREEN,                     /*            light blue */
           LIGHTRED,                       /*            light green */
           LIGHTCYAN,                      /*            light cyan */
           LIGHTMAGENTA,                   /*            light red */
           BLUE,                           /*            light magenta */
           YELLOW,                         /*            yellow */
           WHITE };                        /*            white */

  int   i, j,                             /* Loop counter */
        first,               /* Array index of most recent mikado */
        last;                /* Array index of oldest mikado */
  BOOL  clear;                            /* Clear mikados */
  LINIE lar[MIKADOS];                     /* Mikado array */
  PALARY OldCols;                         /* Get old colors */

  GetPalAry( OldCols );                   /* Get old colors */
  SetPalAry( NewCols );             /* Install new color palette */
  /*TextColor( 7 );
  TextBackGround( 1 );
  GotoXY(1,1); */                         /* Move */
  ClrScr( 0x07 );                    /* Clear screen and    */
  for (i=0; i<25; ++i )              /* fill with characters */
    for (j=0; j<80; ++j )
      PrintfAt( j, i, 0x07, "%c", 32 + (((int) i*80+j) % 224) );

  /*-- Initialize graphic area and generate mikados ------------------*/

  PrintfAt( 27,6, 0x70, "      M I K A D O      " );
  SetCursor(27,6);
  InitGraphArea( 27, 7, 25, 10, 1, 0xFF );
  GetFontAccess();                        /* Get access to font */

  clear = FALSE;                   /* No mikados cleared yet */
  first = 0;                /* Start with first array position */
  last = 0;
  do
  {                                       /* Mikado loop */
    if (first == MIKADOS )                /* Wraparound? */
      first = 0;
    lar[first].x1 = random( xmax-1 );     /* Create mikado */
    lar[first].x2 = random( xmax-1 );     /*    ...    */
    lar[first].y1 = random( ymax-1 );     /*    ...    */
    lar[first].y2 = random( ymax-1 );     /*    ...    */
    Line( lar[first].x1, lar[first].y1,   /* and draw it */
          lar[first].x2, lar[first].y2, TRUE );
    if ( ++first == MIKADOS )             /* Already clear? */
      clear = TRUE;
    if ( clear )                          /* Clear now? */
    {                                     /* Yes */
      Line( lar[last].x1, lar[last].y1,
            lar[last].x2, lar[last].y2, FALSE );
      if ( ++last == MIKADOS )
        last = 0;
    }
  }
  while (!kbhit());              /* Repeat until user presses a key */
  getch();                    /* Remove key from keyboard buffer */
```

```
                                                        *            M A I N   P R O G R A M            *
/*-- End program ----------------------------------------*/       **************************************************************************/

CloseGraphArea();                                       void main()
SetPalAry( OldCols );          /* Restore old color palette */    {
SetCursor(0,24);                                          if ( IsEgaVga() )      /* Is there an EGA or a VGA card installed? */
printf( "\nSystem has reverted to old font.\n" );          Mikado();                         /* Yes --> Execute demo */
}                                                          else                    /* No --> Program cannot be started */
                                                            printf( "Warning: No EGA or VGA card found" );
/**********************************************************         }
```

Fonts for graphics mode

Character tables also display characters in EGA and VGA graphics modes by using the corresponding BIOS functions. Since it's already being used to store pixel information for the graphics screen, bitplane 2 won't be available for storing character tables in graphics mode.

So, the pixel pattern for each character must be passed to the BIOS. This can be done either directly from the ROM chip or from a RAM buffer. However, you must determine which font to access.

If you don't tell the BIOS which font you want to use, it defaults to the font enabled for 80x25 character text mode. EGA cards default to the 8x14 font and VGA cards default to the 8x16 font. To determine the number of text lines that will fit on the graphics screen, divide the vertical resolution by the pixel height of a character. Dividing the character width (8) by the horizontal resolution determines the number of characters per line.

You don't have to use the default font for text output in graphics mode. The BIOS allows you to access any font available in ROM. To do this, use sub-functions 22H, 23H, and 24H of video BIOS function 11H. The system documentation indicates that in addition to the function numbers in the AL and AH registers, you must also pass two other items of information in the BL and DL registers. Based on our experiences with the original IBM cards, the information passed in these registers doesn't affect text output in graphics mode and can be ignored. You only need the function numbers in order to call these functions.

Sub-function.	Matrix	EGA	VGA
22H	8x14	█	█
23H	8x8	█	█
24H	8x16	(n.a.)	█

You can also use sub-function 21H to load your own character table for graphics mode. This character table must include all 256 characters. This call requires the function numbers in the AH and AL registers, and the individual character height in the CX register. As with all other BIOS functions used to define characters, this function requires a pointer to the character table in the ES:BP register pair. The structure of this pointer corresponds to that of the character table pointers used by sub-functions 00H and 10H.

4.8.3 Smooth Scrolling

Prior to EGA and VGA, it was impossible to create a smoothly moving picture with video cards. It was possible to scroll one character at a time in a single direction in text mode. But to scroll in graphics mode, you had to recopy the entire video RAM, even if you only wanted to move the screen by one pixel. This was one of the reasons why the PC lagged so far behind other computers in pixel animation.

EGA and VGA cards offer some relief. The video hardware on these cards contains the ability to move the screen pixel by pixel, and perform *smooth scrolling*. This made the first convincing animated graphics possible on the PC, and opened new horizons in text mode.

Smooth scrolling using the pel panning register

In the EGA and VGA cards, two registers are used to move the screen display pixel by pixel. These two registers control different parts of the video hardware, but they work together to perform basically the same task, which is setting the screen origin (the horizontal and vertical starting points of the screen).

The vertical pel panning register is part of the CRT controller, and the horizontal pel panning register is part of the attribute controller.

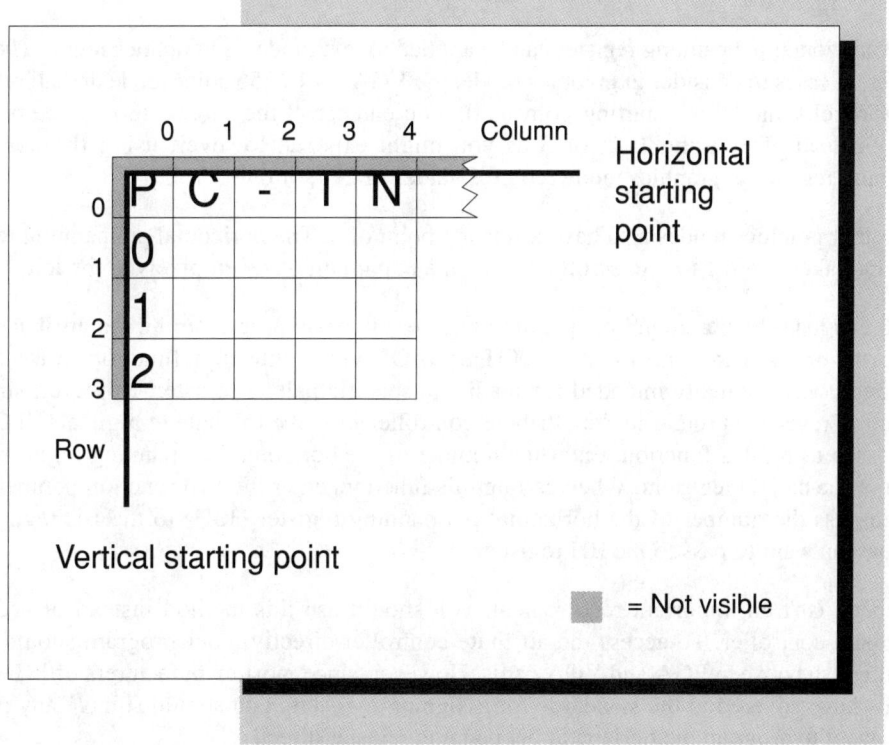

Horizontal scrolling

First let's look at the horizontal pel panning register. In its normal state, this register contains a value of either 0 or 8. These values indicate the character width in text mode, ensuring the correct horizontal proportions in characters.

A value of 8 is the default setting for all video modes with a character width of nine pixels. This applies to the VGA card and the EGA card when emulating an MDA card (i.e., when the EGA is attached to a monochrome monitor). The default value for an EGA card attached to a color monitor is 0.

Incrementing the value in the horizontal pel panning register moves the contents of the entire screen to the left, pixel by pixel. For an EGA card with color monitor, the values would be 1, 2, 3, etc. The larger the number, the further to the left the screen scrolls. The maximum value is 7, which scrolls the screen the width of one entire character. You cannot use the horizontal pel panning register to scroll more than the width of one character.

This procedure works differently for VGA cards and EGA cards in MDA emulation mode. As we previously mentioned, the default value is 8. The numbers 0 to 7 perform scrolling to the right.

Unlike left scrolling, you must begin with the maximum number (7) and decrement the value to 0. With VGA cards and EGA cards with MDA monitors, you can skip up to a value of 8 for the final step.

The horizontal pel panning register can be applied to text mode and graphics mode. There are two different cases to consider in graphics mode: the VGA card's 256 color mode and all other modes. In 256 color mode, the starting point is 0. You can scroll the screen up to three pixels to the left, instead of entering 1, 2, or 3 as you might expect. However, using the horizontal pel panning register in graphics mode requires values of 2, 4, or 6 to scroll.

All other graphics modes also have a starting point of 0. The horizontal pel panning register will accept values from 1 to 7 to scroll the screen a maximum of seven pixels to the left.

You can load the horizontal pel panning register either by programming the attribute controller directly or by using sub-function 00H of BIOS video interrupt function 10H. This BIOS function was originally intended for loading a specific palette register. However, since the pel panning register is found in the attribute controller just like the palette registers, it can also be accessed using this function. Enter the number of the horizontal pel panning register instead of one of the palette registers. When calling this function, enter the two function numbers as usual. Then pass the number of the horizontal pel panning register (13H) to the BL register and the value you want to pass to the BH register.

If speed isn't an important requirement, you should use this method instead of accessing the attribute controller. To access the attribute controller directly, your program should be able to distinguish between EGA and VGA cards. However, since most manufacturers of EGA and VGA cards have adhered to the standards for assigning registers, you shouldn't have any problems if you want to program the horizontal pel panning register directly.

If you prefer the direct route, first the number of the horizontal pel panning register (13H) must be passed to the combined data/index register of the attribute controller at port address 3C0H. When doing this, remember to set bit 5 in this register. This bit enables and disables the attribute controller. If this bit isn't set, the attribute controller remains disabled and the screen will be black.

After sending value 33H (register number 13H plus bit 5) to port 3C0H, you can pass the new value that should be placed in the horizontal pel panning register. This value is the pixel counter that controls the degree of screen scrolling.

Vertical scrolling

Vertical scrolling using the vertical pel panning register is less complicated because the starting point is always 0, regardless of the mode or video card type. Any value greater than 0 scrolls the screen the corresponding number of pixels up, and any value less than 0 scrolls the screen down. In the normal 80x25 character text mode, the maximum values for vertical scrolling are 13 for EGA and 15 for VGA.

In graphics mode, the vertical pel panning register accepts values from 0 to 31, where 31 (not 0) is the starting point. Any smaller value moves the screen the corresponding number of pixels down. If you want to scroll up, set the starting point from 31 to the minimum scroll value, then increment that value.

To scroll down in text mode, the procedure is the same as horizontal scrolling to the right. Start with the highest value and decrement the value until you reach the starting point.

The vertical pel panning register must be accessed directly using the CRT controller; there are no BIOS functions available. First pass vertical pel panning register number (08H) to the CRT controller's index register.

The port address of this index register depends on the video card's current operating mode. In color mode, the port address is 3D4H. In monochrome mode, it is 3B4H. The data register, which immediately follows the index register, must be loaded with the new value for the vertical pel panning register. Instead of two 8-bit operations, you can perform a single 16-bit operation and load both the index and data registers simultaneously.

In practice, the pel panning registers are rarely used for scrolling the screen. A developer usually wants to scroll continuously instead of one character at a time. You could scroll the screen in this way, reset the pel panning registers to their starting points, move the entire contents of video RAM, and repeat the procedure to obtain continuous scrolling. However, moving the characters in video RAM takes too much time, and results in a slower execution time.

The technique described in the following paragraphs is usually preferable. It involves moving the screen display's point of origin and changing the line length in video RAM.

Moving the screen origin and changing the line length in video RAM

One way to scroll the screen contents up by one text line is to move the contents of the video RAM up by 160 bytes (160 bytes is equivalent to one line in 80x25 character text mode). You could also simply increment the starting address of the current screen page by 160 bytes. The CRT controller will begin the display with what was originally the second line when the screen is repainted. Regardless of which method you use, the result is the same to the user.

Instead of moving everything in the video RAM, it's much easier, from a programmer's point of view, to change the contents of the CRT controller registers and move the starting address of the current screen page. This same register also allows you to jump directly from one screen page to another. This method also stores the lines you've scrolled past in video RAM so they can be recalled later.

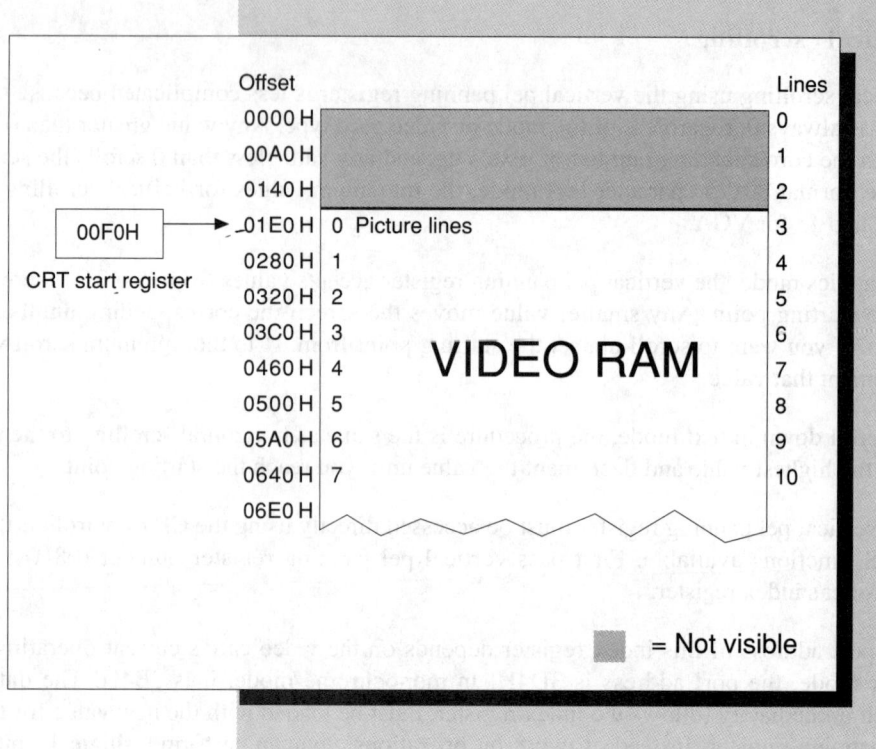

Moving the screen origin by changing the starting address

Changing the starting address of the video RAM is similar to using your arrow keys to scroll to different pages of a document in a word processing program. Instead of using arrow keys, we use the CRT starting registers. And instead of the text in a document, we're scrolling the contents of the video RAM.

The numbers of the two registers we use are 0CH and 0DH. These registers contain the starting address of the portion of the video RAM that's currently visible on the screen. These registers cannot be reached directly using the BIOS, so again we must program the CRT controller directly. You should remember two important points when doing this. First, the starting address is given in the form of a 16-bit offset address with its high byte in register 0CH and its low byte in register 0DH. The order is reversed from what you would normally expect because the high byte appears before the low byte. Also, this offset is counted in words rather than bytes, so you must divide by two before writing the address to the register.

You can easily scroll vertically by accessing the pel panning register and changing the screen origin. However, this method has some unpleasant surprises if you try to use it to scroll horizontally. For example, suppose that you scroll one character to the left and then increment the starting address from 0000H to 0002H.

The character from the second column of the first line is now in the first column. But the first character from the second line now appears in the last column of the first line, and so on down the screen. This is known as *character wrapping*.

Character wrapping when moving the screen origin

The character wrapping problem is related to video RAM organization; this problem can't be solved using the CRT start registers. Fortunately, we don't have to move the entire contents of the video RAM. The CRT controller has another register called the offset register. This register stores the length of a text line in video RAM. The normal value for this register is 80 words, which corresponds to a line length of 160 bytes.

Increasing this value doesn't instruct your system to display more characters per line on the screen. Instead, the CRT controller's internal address counter increments to make more room per line in the video RAM. For example, if you placed a value of 82 (52H) in this register instead of the normal value of 80 (50H), then each line in video RAM would contain 82 characters. Only the first 80 are visible on the screen until you scroll. Once you scroll, the last two characters in the line become visible and the first two characters move beyond the left border of the screen.

The offset register (register 13H in the CRT controller) is 8 bits wide. So, it can accommodate line lengths of up to 255 characters, which gives each line a length of 510 bytes in video RAM.

Remember this when you're addressing a certain line within the video RAM. Before, you would always multiply by 160 to access a certain line. Now, you must multiply by 510, 320, or whatever the video RAM line length is at the time. In all cases, this number will be twice the number of characters per video RAM line.

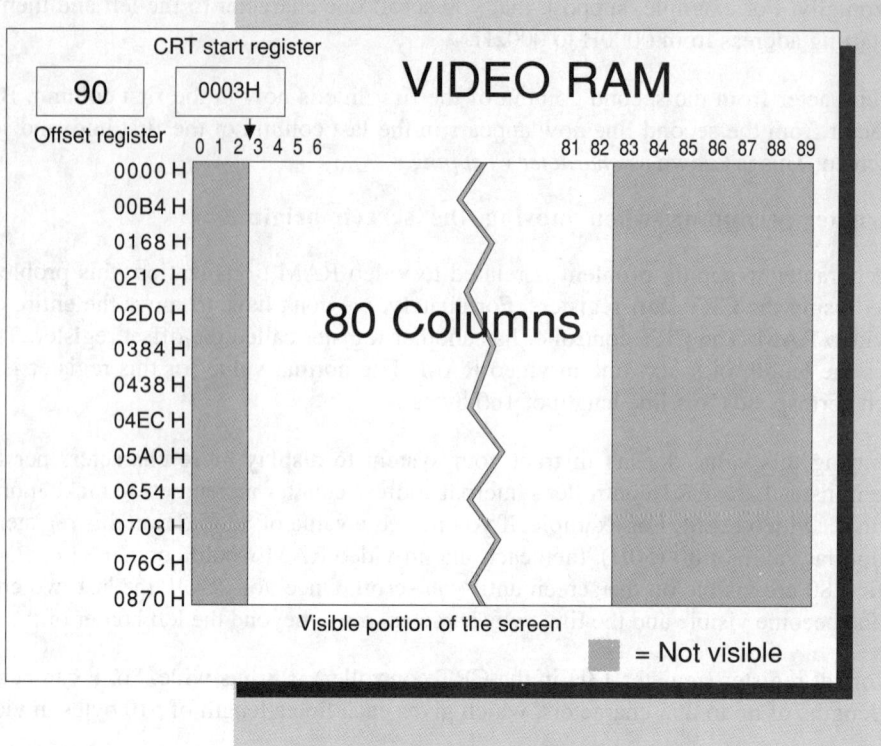

CRT start register

| 90 | 0003H |

Offset register

VIDEO RAM

0 1 2 3 4 5 6   81 82 83 84 85 86 87 88 89

0000 H
00B4 H
0168 H
021C H
02D0 H
0384 H
0438 H
04EC H
05A0 H
0654 H
0708 H
076C H
0870 H

80 Columns

Visible portion of the screen

■ = Not visible

Scrolling the screen by increasing line length in the offset register

Once you've increased the internal line length using the offset register, you can easily scroll the screen by using the pel panning register and changing the screen origin. Another important point to consider when scrolling (both vertically and horizontally) is the synchronization of events. If you aren't careful with synchronization, the result on the screen may be completely different from what you had intended.

Synchronization with the CRT controller

Scrolling the screen by manipulating the pel panning register and screen origin must always be coordinated with the CRT controller. First, the pel panning register should be accessed only during vertical synchronization of the electron beam (i.e., when visual information isn't being sent to the screen). This ensures that the changes to these registers won't affect any parts of the screen that are created with different values in these registers.

If the pel panning register and the CRT start register must be programmed simultaneously (e.g., to return the pel panning register to its starting value and to move the screen origin), then you must be very careful. While the changes to the pel panning register are taken into account immediately as the next screen is built, the change to the CRT start register takes longer to process.

This occurs because a program usually hesitates after starting vertical synchronization, even if the hesitation is only a fraction of a second. The hesitation occurs because of querying the vertical synchronization. This query is usually done using bit 3 of the input status register, which shows the vertical synchronization status. It's on during synchronization and off at all other times. The query takes place in a program loop that constantly checks the status, and the hesitation occurs because the assembly language instructions in this query need some time to execute. The delay is worse if you program in a high level language, in which the query code will be even slower.

Once the program recognizes the vertical synchronization, it may already be a fraction of a second into its execution, and the CRT controller may have already loaded the starting address for the next screen refresh from the CRT start register. So, any change to the contents of this register won't be considered until the subsequent screen refresh.

Changes to the pel panning register take effect with the next screen refresh. This results in internal inconsistencies that are visible on screen. To avoid these problems, you must follow a specific procedure when programming the pel panning register and the CRT start register simultaneously.

This procedure uses input status register 1 to wait for a vertical synchronization to start and finish. Then the new screen origin is loaded in the proper register of the CRT controller. This won't disturb the next screen refresh because the CRT controller has already loaded the screen origin address into its internal address counter before the screen refresh, and doesn't have to access the register again.

Now, wait for the screen to regenerate and for the next vertical synchronization. After this event, you can program the pel panning register. The change to this register is then taken into account with the next screen refresh. Now we can be sure that the address of the new screen origin is correctly loaded into the internal address counter for this screen refresh as well.

Algorithms for setting the pel panning register and CRT start register

Waiting for the vertical synchronization also synchronizes your program with the video frequency of the video card, regardless of the CPU speed. This is very useful, especially with games. If you continuously call the routine for setting the pel panning register and the CRT start register, you can move the screen contents by a few pixels each time the picture regenerates. This involves 50 to 70 movements per second, depending on whether you have an EGA or VGA card. Since the human eye cannot follow so many rapid changes, it interprets this as smooth animation.

Scrolling in text mode

The following programs (SOFTSCRP.PAS and SOFTSCRC.C) are examples of this combined control of the pel panning register and the CRT start register. Each program scrolls text printed in a large font, from right to left across the screen.

These programs are based on two routines called ShowScrlText and SetOrigin. ShowScrlText takes the text to be displayed and stores it in the video RAM in such a way that it's not completely visible at once. The program divides the text into three sections, each 216 characters long by 25 characters high. Each section uses 10800 bytes (or a total of 32400 bytes), leaving only 368 bytes of video RAM unused.

After the text is placed in video RAM, ShowScrlText begins the display. The SetOrigin procedure is important because it sets the starting point for the screen. The section of text, the starting row and column, and the number of pixels to move must be specified. The number of pixels is entered directly in the pel panning register. The number of the text section and the starting column and row are linked to a starting address of the visible screen and loaded in the CRT start register.

First SetOrigin is called from within ShowScrlText using constant values for the starting column and row. Only the pixel counter increments to create the horizontal movement. Then when the maximum value for the horizontal pixel counter is reached, the counter resets to 0 or 8, and the starting column increments.

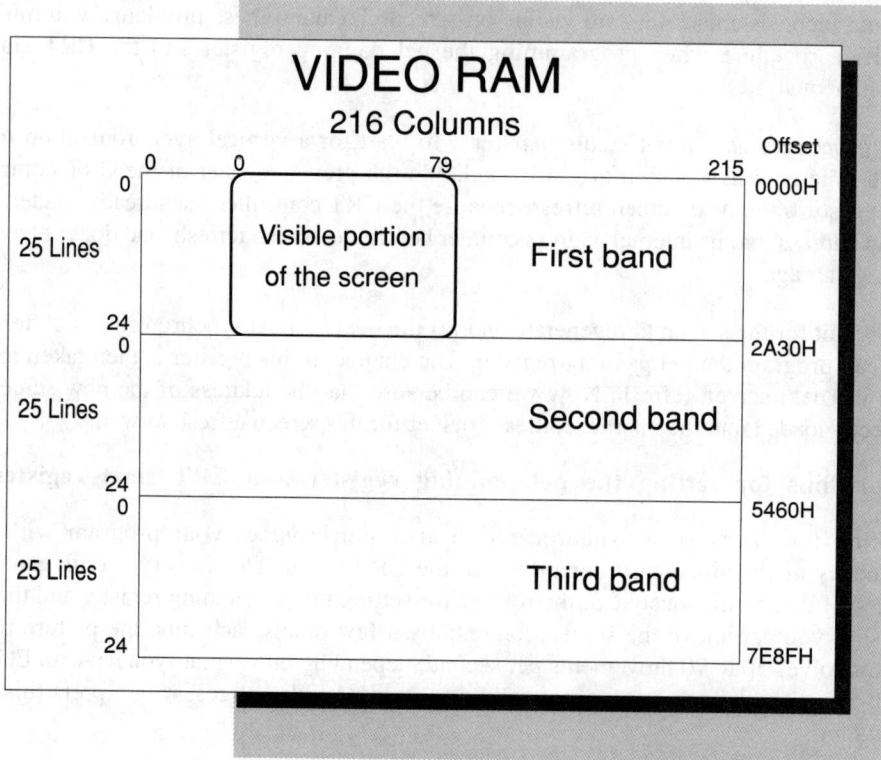

Partitioning video RAM in SOFTSCRP.PAS and SOFTSCRC.C

The SOFTSCRP.PAS and SOFTSCRC.C programs allow the user to control the scrolling speed. The differences in character width between EGA and VGA are also taken into account. To control this, the ShowScrlText routine accepts two parameters. One parameter is used for the scrolling speed and the other is used for the video card type. Speed is determined by selecting either the FAST, MEDIUM, or SLOW constant and the video card type is determined by entering either EGA or VGA.

While the screen origin is being moved in ShowScrlText, these two constants are converted to an index in the array step table. This table is declared within the routine. Depending on the speed and video card type, a series of values for the horizontal pixel counter is selected. The value 255 indicates the end of each row of values in the array, which means that scrolling continues in the next column.

Different scrolling speeds are obtained with different intervals in the value of the horizontal pixel counter. In SLOW mode, each pixel in each character is scrolled. In MEDIUM mode, every other pixel is skipped, which doubles the scrolling speed. The speed is doubled again for FAST mode, in which only two pixels in each character are scrolled.

The value 216 indicates the limit for incrementing the starting column. This value refers to the last column in a section. The program must switch to the next section of text and start again with column one. But since the contents of the last screen in the previous text section can no longer be scrolled left off the screen, the next section must begin with the same characters found at the end of the previous section. This allows you to program a completely smooth transition between sections of text.

The speed at which the user can comfortably read the characters that are scrolling by depends mostly on the character width. The PrintChar routine is responsible for building the characters in video RAM. The arguments PrintChar requires are the character code, and the column number and text section number where the character should appear. The row number is given by the constant STARTR, so it doesn't have to be passed again. The routine obtains the bit pattern for the characters from the 8x14 pixel font, which is included in ROM on both EGA and VGA cards. This font is accessed using sub-function 30H of BIOS video interrupt function 11H.

This routine is also the reason why the C version of this program requires the small assembler routine called SOFTSCCA.ASM. The BIOS function previously mentioned returns information to the BP register, which cannot be accessed by normal C interrupt functions.

PrintChar sends the 8x14 character matrix to the screen by mapping each pixel in the pattern to a character position on the screen. This means that one character will occupy 8 screen columns and 14 screen rows. So, one section of the text contains 27 characters (216/8). Any 10 characters (80/8) are visible at a time. However, remember that the second and third sections of the text must repeat the last screen of the previous section. This means that sections 2 and 3 can only contain 17 new characters instead of 27. Therefore, the total number of characters that can be loaded in video RAM is 61 (27 + 17 + 17).

Pascal listing: SOFTSCRP.PAS

```
{*********************************************************************
* SoftScrp : Demonstrates soft scrolling on EGA and VGA cards.      *
**-----------------------------------------------------------------**
* Author       : Michael Tischer                                    *
* Developed on  : 01/23/90                                          *
* Last update   : 02/20/92                                          *
*********************************************************************}

program SoftScrp;

uses dos,                              { Add units }
     crt;

const SLOW    = 1;         { Speed constant for ShowScrlText() }
      MEDIUM  = 2;
      FAST    = 3;
```

```
const PCOLR    = $5E;            { Yellow from lilac palette }
      PCOLR1   = $5F;            { White from lilac palette }
      CWIDTH   = 8;              { Character width in pixels }
      CHEIGHT  = 14;        { Character height in scan lines }
      COLUMNS  = 216;        { Columns per row in video RAM }
      BANDSIZE = 10800;                       { Band size }
      BANDNUM  = 3;                       { Number of bands }
      MAXLEN   = 61;         { Maximum number of characters }
      STARTR   = 6;       { Starting character row on screen }

      CrtAttr   = $3C0;   { CRT attribute controller register }
      CrtStatus = $3da;                      { Status port }
      CrtAdr    = $3d4;             { Monitor address port }

type VRAM = array[1..BANDNUM, 1..25, 1..COLUMNS] of word;  { Video RAM }
     VPTR = ^VRAM;                       { Pointer to video RAM }
```

```
var vp        : vptr;                        { Pointer to video RAM }

type CRDTYPE = ( EGA, VGA, NEITHERNOR );         { Video card type }

procedure CLI; inline( $FA );               { Disable interrupts }
procedure STI; inline( $FB );               { Enable interrupts }

{*****************************************************************
* SetOrigin : Specifies the visible part of video RAM for       *
*             programming the video controller.                 *
**-----------------------------------------------------------**
* Input   :  BAND    = Number of band to be displayed (1-5)     *
*            COLUMN, = Number of columns and rows displayed in the *
*            SCROW     upper-left corner of the screen (origin=0/0) *
*            PIXX,   = Pixel offsets                             *
*            PIXY                                                *
*****************************************************************}

procedure SetOrigin( band, column, scrow, pixx, pixy : byte );

var offset : integer;               { Offset of video RAM start }
ch : char;

begin
  offset := ( BANDSIZE div 2 ) * (band-1) + scrow * COLUMNS + column;

  {-- Execute vertical rescan and wait for end -----------------------}

  repeat until port[CrtStatus] and 8 = 8;
  repeat until port[CrtStatus] and 8 = 0;

  {-- Write offset for start of video RAM to registers 0CH and 0DH, }
  {-- after ensuring that next screen layout is valid             }

  CLI;                                   { Disable interrupts }
  portw[ CrtAdr ] := hi( offset ) shl 8 + $0c;
  portw[ CrtAdr ] := lo( offset ) shl 8 + $0d;
  STI;

  {-- While waiting for next rescan, write new    -------------------}
  {-- pixel offset and set up new starting address -----------------}

  repeat until port[CrtStatus] and 8 = 8;

  {-- Write pixel offsets in register 08H or   --------------------}
  {-- register 13H of the attribute controller -------------------}

  CLI;
  portw[ CrtAdr ] := pixy shl 8 + $08;
  port[ CrtAttr ] := $13 or $20;         { Access attribute  }
  port[ CrtAttr ] := pixx;               { controller by bytes }
  STI;                                   { Enable interrupts }

                                         { ch := readkey; }
end;

{*****************************************************************
* PrintChar : Creates a character within the visible range of   *
*             video RAM.                                        *
**-----------------------------------------------------------**
* Input   :  THECHAR = Character to be created                  *
*            BAND    = Band number (0-4)                        *
*            COLUMN  = Column in video RAM at which the column   *
```

```
*            should begin                                       *
* Info   :  The character can be moved in the visible range of  *
*           the screen by calling SmoothLeft.                   *
*           The character is created from a 14x8 matrix, based on *
*           the EGA/VGA ROM font.                                *
*****************************************************************}

procedure PrintChar( thechar : char; band, column : byte );

type FDEF = array[0..255,1..14] of byte;           { Font array }
     TPTR = ^FDEF;                             { Pointer to font }

var Regs : Registers;          { Registers for interrupt call }
    ch   : char;                         { Character pixels }
    i, k;                                { Loop counter }
    BMask : byte;          { Bit mask for character design }

const fptr : TPTR = NIL;                  { Pointer to ROM font }

begin
  if fptr = NIL then               { Pointer to font already set? }
    begin                                          { No }
      Regs.AH := $11;              { Call video BIOS function }
      Regs.AL := $30;              {  11H, sub-function 30H  }
      Regs.BH := 2;                { Get pointer to 8x14 font }
      intr( $10, Regs );
      fptr := ptr( Regs.ES, Regs.BP );           { Set pointers }
    end;

  {-- Generate character line by line -----------------------------}

  for i := 1 to CHEIGHT do
    begin
      BMask := fptr^[ord(thechar),i]; { Get bit pattern for one line }
      for k := 1 to CWIDTH do            { Set individual bits }
        begin
          if BMask and 128 = 128 then ch := #219      { Set pixel }
                           else ch := #32;     { Unset pixel }
          vp^[band, STARTR+i, (column-1)*CWIDTH+k] :=
                              ord(ch) + PCOLR shl 8;
          BMask := BMask shl 1;              { Process next bit }
        end;
    end;
end;

{*****************************************************************
* IsEgaVga : Determines whether an EGA or a VGA card is installed. *
**-----------------------------------------------------------**
* Input   : None                                                *
* Output  : EGA, VGA or NEITHERNOR                              *
*****************************************************************}

function IsEgaVga : CRDTYPE;

var Regs : Registers;       { Processor registers for interrupt call }

begin
  Regs.AX := $1a00;           { Function 1AH applies to VGA only }
  Intr( $10, Regs );
  if ( Regs.AL = $1a ) then            { Is the function available? }
    IsEgaVga := VGA
  else
    begin
      Regs.ah := $12;                       { Call function 12H, }
```

```
      Regs.bl := $10;                        { sub-function 10H  }      Regs.AL := $01;                           { Sub-function number }
      intr($10, Regs);                       { Call video BIOS }        Regs.BH := PCOLR shr 4;                       { border color }
      if ( Regs.bl <> $10 ) then IsEgaVga := EGA                        intr( $10, Regs );
                      else IsEgaVga := NEITHERNOR;
   end;                                                                 {-- Place number of columns per row in video RAM from COLUMNS ------}
end;
                                                                        portw[ CrtAdr ] := ( COLUMNS div 2 ) shl 8 + $13;

{*****************************************************************       {-- Place scrolling text in video RAM ----------------------------}
* ShowScrstext : Scrolls text on the screen.                   *
**_____**       if length( stext ) > MAXLEN then len := MAXLEN
* Input   : STEXT = String of text for scrolling              *                        else len := length( stext );
*           SPEED = Scroll speed (see SLOW, FAST constants)   *         column := 1;
*           VC    = Video card type (EGA or VGA)              *         band   := 1;
*****************************************************************}       index  := 1;
                                                                        while ( index <= len ) do
procedure ShowScrlText( stext : string; speed : byte; vc : crdtype );     begin
                                                                            PrintChar( stext[index], band, column );      { Draw characters }
var band,                                    { Current band }              inc( column );                           { in next column  }
    column,                                  { Current column }            inc( index );                       { Process next character }
    index,                          { Index to string to be created }     if ( column > ( COLUMNS div CWIDTH ) ) then    { Band change? }
    len,                            { Length of text to be displayed }       begin                                             { Yes }
    i, k : integer;                          { Loop counter }                  column := 1;                         { Restart in column 1 }
    step,                                    { Increment }                     inc( band );                              { Next band }
    uplimit : byte;                 { Number of loop executions }             dec( index, ( 80 div CWIDTH ) );  { Character one page back }
    Regs : Registers;           { Processor registers for interrupt call }   end
                                                                          end;
const steptable : array [EGA..VGA,1..3,1..10] of byte =
        (                                                               {-- Move scroll text from right to left on the screen -------------}
          (                          { EGA step values }
           ( 0,  1,  2,  3,  4,  5,  6,  7, 255, 255 ),                 column := 0;                    { Start in column 0 with band 1 }
           ( 0,  2,  4,  6, 255, 255, 255, 255, 255, 255 ),            band   := 1;
           ( 0,  4, 255, 255, 255, 255, 255, 255, 255, 255 )          for i := 1 to (len-( 80 div CWIDTH )) * CWIDTH do
          ),                                                             begin
          (                          { VGA step values }                    k := 1;
           ( 8,  0,  1,  2,  3,  4,  5,  6,  7, 255 ),                      while ( steptable[vc, speed, k] <> 255 ) do
           ( 8,  2,  5, 255, 255, 255, 255, 255, 255, 255 ),                 begin
           ( 8,  3, 255, 255, 255, 255, 255, 255, 255, 255 )                   SetOrigin( band, column, 0, steptable[vc, speed, k], 0 );
          )                                                                    inc( k );
        );                                                                    end;

begin                                                                       inc( column );                             { Next column }
   vp := ptr( $B800, $0000 );              { Set pointer to video RAM }      if ( column = COLUMNS - 80 ) then           { Band change? }
                                                                              begin                                             { Yes }
{-- Fill entire video RAM with blank spaces ------------------------}           column := 0;                        { Restart in column 0 }
                                                                                inc( band );                         { Increment band }
   for index := 1 to BANDNUM do                                               end
    for i := 1 to 25 do                                                    end;
     for k := 1 to COLUMNS do
       vp^[ index, i, k ] := PCOLR shl 8 + 32;                          {-- Revert to 80 characters per row in video RAM ------------------}

{-- Draw horizontal bands ------------------------------------------}   portw[ CrtAdr ] := 40 shl 8 + $13;

   for k := 1 to BANDNUM do                                             {-- Reset border colors ------------------------------------------}
    for i := 1 to COLUMNS do
      begin                                                             Regs.AH := $10;              { Function number: Set border color }
        vp^[ k, STARTR-2, i ] := ord(' ') + PCOLR1 shl 8;              Regs.AL := $01;                     { Sub-function number }
        vp^[ k, STARTR + CHEIGHT + 2, i ] := ord(' ') + PCOLR1 shl 8;  Regs.BH := 0;                           { Black border }
      end;                                                              intr( $10, Regs );

   gotoxy( 1, 1 );           { Remove cursor when scrolling the screen }   if ( vc = EGA ) then                       { Revert to default }
                                                                            SetOrigin( 1, 0, 0, 0, 0 )                     { for EGA }
{-- Set screen border color ---------------------------------------}    else
                                                                            SetOrigin( 1, 0, 0, 8, 0 );                    { for VGA }
   Regs.AH := $10;           { Function number: Set screen border color }
```

221

```
  ClrScr;
end;


{[*****************************************************]
{**                 M A I N   P R O G R A M        **}
{[*****************************************************]

var  ch : char; i : integer;
     vc : crdtype;

begin
  vc := IsEgaVga;                        { Get video card type }
  if vc = EGA then halt;
  if ( vc = NEITHERNOR ) then
    begin
      writeln( 'SOFSCRP - (c) 1992 by Michael Tischer' );
      writeln( #13#10'Warning: No EGA or VGA card found');
    end
  else
    ShowScrlText( '++ PC Intern..........Published by Abacus ++'+
                  '                     ', FAST, vc );
  while keypressed do
    ch := readkey;

end.
```

C listing: SOFTSCRC.C

```
/*******************************************************************
*                    S O F T S C R C . C                          *
**---------------------------------------------------------------**
* Task          : Demonstrates soft scrolling on EGA & VGA cards. *
**---------------------------------------------------------------**
* Author        : Michael Tischer                                 *
* Developed on   : 08/26/90                                        *
* Last update    : 02/21/92                                        *
**---------------------------------------------------------------**
* (MICROSOFT C)                                                   *
* Compilation    : CL /AS /c /WO softscrc.c                        *
*                  LINK softscrc softscca;                         *
**---------------------------------------------------------------**
* (BORLAND TURBO C)                                               *
* Compilation    : Create a project file containing the following: *
*                       softscrc.c                                *
*                       softscca.obj                              *
**---------------------------------------------------------------**
* Call          : softscrc                                        *
*******************************************************************/

#include <dos.h>                            /* Add include files */
#include <stdarg.h>
#include <string.h>
#include <stdio.h>

#ifdef __TURBOC__                    /* Compiling with Turbo C? */
  #define CLI()        disable()
  #define STI()        enable()
  #define outpw( p, w ) outport( p, w )
  #ifndef inp
    #define outp( p, b ) outportb( p, b )
    #define inp( p )     inportb( p )
  #endif
#else                               /* No --> QuickC 2.0 or MSC */
  #include <conio.h>
  #define MK_FP(seg,ofs) ((void far *)\
                          (((unsigned long)(seg) << 16) | (ofs)))
  #define CLI()        _disable()
  #define STI()        _enable()
#endif

#define FAST      2          /* Speed constant for ShowScrlText() */
#define MEDIUM    1
#define SLOW      0

#define PCOLR     0x5E                /* Yellow from lilac palette */
#define PCOLR1    0x5F                 /* White from lilac palette */
#define CWIDTH    8                   /* Character width in pixels */
#define CHEIGHT   14             /* Character height in scan lines */
#define COLUMNS   216            /* Columns per row in video RAM */
#define BANDSIZE  10800                            /* Band size */
#define BANDNUM   3                           /* Number of bands */
#define MAXLEN    61           /* Maximum number of characters */
#define STARTR    5             /* Starting character row on screen */

#define CrtAttr   0x3C0     /* CRT attribute controller register */
#define CrtStatus 0x3da                         /* Status port */
#define CrtAdr    0x3d4                   /* Monitor address port */

#define TRUE      ( 0 == 0 )
#define FALSE     ( 0 == 1 )
```

```
#define EGA         0                          /* Card types */
#define VGA         1
#define NEITHERNOR  2

typedef unsigned char BYTE;                    /* Create a BYTE */
typedef unsigned int WORD;                     /* Create a WORD */
typedef BYTE BOOL;

typedef WORD VRAM[BANDNUM][25][COLUMNS];       /* Video RAM definition */
typedef VRAM far *VPTR;                        /* FAR pointer to video RAM */

typedef BYTE FDEF[256][14];                    /* Font array */
typedef FDEF far *TPTR;                        /* Pointer to font */

/*-- External functions ------------------------------------------*/

extern void far * getfontptr( void );          /* Assembler function */

/*-- Global variables --------------------------------------------*/

VPTR vp;                                        /* Pointer to video RAM */

/****************************************************************
 * SetOrigin : Specifies the visible part of video RAM for      *
 *             programming the video controller.                *
 **------------------------------------------------------------**
 * Input  :  BAND   = Number of band to be displayed (1-5)      *
 *           COLUMN, = Number of columns and rows displayed in the  *
 *           SCROW     upper-left corner of the screen (origin=0/0) *
 *           PIXX,   = Pixel offsets                            *
 *           PIXY                                               *
 * Output :  None                                               *
 ****************************************************************/

void SetOrigin( BYTE band, BYTE column, BYTE scrow,
                BYTE pixx, BYTE pixy)
{
 int offset;                                    /* Offset of video RAM start */

 offset = ( BANDSIZE >> 1 ) * band + scrow * COLUMNS + column;

 /*- Execute vertical rescan and wait for end -----------------------*/

 while ( !(( inp(CrtStatus) & 8 ) == 8 ))
  ;
 while ( !(( inp(CrtStatus) & 8 ) == 0 ))
  ;

 /* Write offset for start of video RAM to registers 0CH and 0DH,  */
 /* after ensuring that next screen layout is valid                */

 CLI();                                         /* Disable interrupts */
 outpw( CrtAdr, ( offset & 0xFF00 ) + 0x0c );
 outpw( CrtAdr, ( (BYTE) offset << 8 ) + 0x0d );
 STI();                                         /* Enable interrupts */

 /*- While waiting for next rescan, write new pixel offset ----------*/
 /*- and set up new starting address                      ----------*/

 while ( !(( inp( CrtStatus ) & 8 ) == 8 ))
  ;

 /*- Write pixel offsets in register 08H or  ------------------------*/
```

```
 /*- register 13H of the attribute controller -----------------------*/

 CLI();                                         /* Disable interrupts */
 outpw( CrtAdr, ( pixy << 8 ) + 0x08 );
 outp( CrtAttr, 0x13 | 0x20 );
 outp( CrtAttr, pixx );
 STI();                                         /* Enable interrupts */
}

/****************************************************************
 * PrintChar : Creates a character within the visible range of  *
 *             video RAM.                                        *
 **------------------------------------------------------------**
 * Input  :  THECHAR = Character to be created                  *
 *           BAND    = Band number (0-4)                        *
 *           COLUMN  = Column in video RAM at which the column  *
 *                     should begin                             *
 * Info   :  The character can be moved in the visible range of *
 *           the screen by calling SmoothLeft.                  *
 *           The character is created from a 14x8 matrix, based on *
 *           the EGA/VGA ROM font.                              *
 ****************************************************************/

void PrintChar( char thechar, BYTE band, BYTE column )
{
 char ch;                                       /* Character pixels */
 BYTE i, k,                                      /* Loop counter */
      BMask;                                     /* Bit mask for character design */
 static TPTR fptr = (TPTR) 0;                    /* Pointer to ROM font */

 if ( fptr == (TPTR) 0 )                         /* Pointer to font already set? */
  fptr = getfontptr();                           /* No --> Get assembly language function */

 /*- Generate character line by line --------------------------------*/

 for ( i = 0; i < CHEIGHT; ++i )
 {
  BMask = (*fptr)[thechar][i];                   /* Get bit pattern for one line */
  for ( k = 0; k < CWIDTH; ++k )                 /* Set individual bits */
  {
   ch = ( BMask & 128 ) ? 219 : 32;
   (*vp)[band][STARTR+i][column*CWIDTH+k] = (BYTE) ch+( PCOLR << 8 );
   BMask <<= 1;                                  /* Process next bit */
  }
 }
}

/****************************************************************
 * IsEgaVga : Determines whether an EGA or a VGA card is installed.  *
 **------------------------------------------------------------**
 * Input  : None                                                *
 * Output : EGA, VGA or NEITHERNOR                              *
 ****************************************************************/

BYTE IsEgaVga( void )
{
 union REGS Regs;                                /* Processor registers for interrupt call */

 Regs.x.ax = 0x1a00;                             /* Function 1AH applies to VGA only */
 int86( 0x10, &Regs, &Regs );
 if ( Regs.h.al == 0x1a )                        /* Is the function available? */
  return VGA;
 else
  {
```

```
     Regs.h.ah = 0x12;                      /* Call function 12H, */
     Regs.h.bl = 0x10;                      /* sub-function 10H   */
     int86(0x10, &Regs, &Regs );            /* Call video BIOS */
     return ( Regs.h.bl != 0x10 ) ? EGA : NEITHERNOR;
    }
  }

/************************************************************************
 * ShowScrlText : Scrolls text on the screen.                          *
 **--------------------------------------------------------------------**
 * Input   : STEXT = String of text for scrolling                      *
 *           SPEED = Scroll speed (SLOW, MEDIUM or FAST)               *
 *           VC    = Video card type (EGA or VGA)                      *
 ************************************************************************/

void ShowScrlText( char * stext, BYTE speed, BYTE vc )
{
  int    band,                             /* Current band */
         column,                           /* Current column */
         index,                 /* Index to string to be created */
         len,                   /* Length of text to be displayed */
         i, k,                             /* Loop counter */
         pixx;                         /* Horizontal pan value */
  WORD far *wptr;                    /* Pointer to video RAM loop */
  union REGS Regs;          /* Processor registers for interrupt call */

  static BYTE steptable[2][3][10] =
              {
                {                              /* EGA step values */
                  { 0,  1,  2,  3,  4,  5,  6,  7, 255, 255 },
                  { 0,  2,  4,  6, 255, 255, 255, 255, 255, 255 },
                  { 0,  4, 255, 255, 255, 255, 255, 255, 255, 255 }
                },
                {                              /* VGA step values */
                  { 8,  0,  1,  2,  3,  4,  5,  6,  7, 255 },
                  { 8,  2,  5, 255, 255, 255, 255, 255, 255, 255 },
                  { 8,  3, 255, 255, 255, 255, 255, 255, 255, 255 }
                }
              };

  vp = MK_FP( 0xB800, 0x0000 );         /* Set pointer to video RAM */

/*- Fill entire video RAM with blank spaces ------------------------*/

  for ( index = 0; index < BANDNUM; ++index )
   for ( i = 0; i < 25; ++i )
    for ( k = 0; k < COLUMNS; ++k )
     (*vp)[index][ i ][ k ] = ( PCOLR << 8 ) + 32;

/*- Draw horizontal bands ------------------------------------------*/

  for ( k = 0; k < BANDNUM; ++k )
   for ( i = 0; i < COLUMNS; ++i )
    {
     (*vp)[ k ][ STARTR-2 ][ i ] = (BYTE) '' + ( PCOLR1 << 8 );
     (*vp)[ k ][ STARTR + CHEIGHT + 2][ i ] = (BYTE) '' + ( PCOLR1 << 8
);
    }

/*- Remove blinking cursor from the screen -------------------------*/

  Regs.h.ah = 0x02;                /* Function number: Set cursor */
  Regs.h.bh = 0;                              /* Screen page */
  Regs.x.dx = 0;                              /* coordinates */
```

```
  int86( 0x10, &Regs, &Regs );

/*- Set screen border color ----------------------------------------*/

  Regs.h.ah = 0x10;                /* Function number: Set border color */
  Regs.h.al = 0x01;                        /* Sub-function number */
  Regs.h.bh = PCOLR >> 4;                      /* Border color */
  int86( 0x10, &Regs, &Regs );

/*- Place number of columns per row in video RAM from columns ------*/

  outpw( CrtAdr, ( ( COLUMNS >> 1 ) << 8 ) + 0x13 );

/*-- Place scrolling text in video RAM -----------------------------*/

  if ( ( len = strlen( stext ) ) > MAXLEN )      /* String too long? */
   *(stext + ( len = MAXLEN )) = '\0';           /* Yes --> Truncate */

  for ( column = band = index = 0; index < len; )
  {
   PrintChar( *(stext+index++), band, column++ ); /* Draw characters */
   if ( column >= COLUMNS / CWIDTH )            /* Band change? */
    {                                            /* Yes */
     column = 0;                                 /* Restart in column 1 */
     ++band;                                     /* Next band */
     index -= 80 / CWIDTH;                /* Character one page back */
    }
  }

/*-- Move scroll text from right to left on the screen ------------*/

  for ( column = band = 0 , i = (len - ( 80 / CWIDTH )) * CWIDTH;
        i > 0;
        --i )
  {
   for ( k = 0; ( pixx = steptable[vc][speed][k]) != 255 ; ++k )
    SetOrigin( band, column, 0, pixx, 0 );

   if ( ++column == COLUMNS - 80 )               /* Band change? */
    {                                            /* Yes */
     column = 0;                                 /* Restart in column 0 */
     ++band;                                     /* Increment band */
    }
  }

/*- Revert to 80 characters per row in video RAM -------------------*/

  outpw( CrtAdr, ( 40 << 8 ) + 0x13 );

  SetOrigin( 0, 0, 0, 8, 0 );                    /* Revert to default */

/*- Return cursor to the screen ------------------------------------*/

  Regs.h.ah = 0x02;                /* Function number: Set cursor */
  Regs.h.bh = 0;                              /* Screen page */
  Regs.x.dx = 0;                              /* coordinates */
  int86( 0x10, &Regs, &Regs );

/*- Reset border colors --------------------------------------------*/

  Regs.h.ah = 0x10;                /* Function number: Set border color */
  Regs.h.al = 0x01;                        /* Sub-function number */
  Regs.h.bh = 0;                              /* Black border */
  int86( 0x10, &Regs, &Regs );
```

```
/*-- Clear screen --------------------------------------------*/

for ( wptr = (WORD far *) vp, i = 80*25; i-- ; )
  *wptr++ = 0x0720;
}

/***************************************************************/
/**              M A I N   P R O G R A M                     **/
/***************************************************************/

void main( void )
{
  BYTE vc;                            /* Get video card type */

  if ( ( vc = IsEgaVga() ) == NEITHERNOR )
   printf( "SOFTSCRC - (c) 1992 by Michael Tischer\n" \
           "Warning: No EGA or VGA card found\n" );
  else
   ShowScrlText( "++ PC Intern...........Published by Abacus ++" \
           "          ", FAST, vc );
}
```

Assembler listing: SOFTSCCA.ASM

```
;****************************************************************;
;*                  S O F T S C C A . A S M                  *;
;*------------------------------------------------------------*;
;*   Task        : Creates a function used by SOFTSCRC.C for  *;
;*                 implementing a pointer to the EGA/VGA      *;
;*                 8x14 font table.                           *;
;*------------------------------------------------------------*;
;*   Author      : Michael Tischer                            *;
;*   Developed on : 08/23/90                                  *;
;*   Last update  : 02/21/92                                  *;
;*------------------------------------------------------------*;
;*   Assembly    : MASM /mx SOFTSCCA;   or  TASM -mx SOFTSCCA *;
;*                 ... link to SOFTSCRC.C                     *;
;****************************************************************;

IGROUP group _text               ;Program segment
DGROUP group const,_bss, _data   ;Data segment
       assume CS:IGROUP, DS:DGROUP, ES:DGROUP, SS:DGROUP

CONST  segment word public 'CONST';This segment handles all
CONST  ends                       ;readable constants

_BSS   segment word public 'BSS'  ;This segment handles all uninitial-
_BSS   ends                       ;ized static variables

_DATA  segment word public 'DATA' ;This segment handles all initialized
                                  ;global and static variables

_DATA  ends

;== Program ===================================================

_TEXT  segment byte public 'CODE' ;Program segment

public _getfontptr               ;Function accessible from other
                                 ;programs

;-- GETFONTPTR: Returns FAR pointer to the 8x14 font table -----------
;-- Declaration : void far * getfontptr( void )

_getfontptr proc near

       push bp              ;Push BP onto stack

       mov  ax,1130h        ;Load register for function call
       mov  bh,2
       int  10h             ;Call BIOS video interrupt

       mov  dx,es           ;Move ES:BP to DX:AX
       mov  ax,bp

       pop  bp              ;Pop BP from stack

       ret                  ;Return to caller

_getfontptr endp            ;End of procedure

;== End =======================================================

_text  ends                 ;End program segment
       end                  ;End program
```

225

4.8.4 Disabling the Screen

Occasionally the screen display of your video card must be disabled. Screen saver programs do this to prevent the screen image from burning into your monitor. The EGA and VGA cards offer capabilities for disabling screen display, which we'll discuss in this section. Specifically, we'll look at the attribute controller, its role in generating the video picture, and how this can be used to disable the screen display.

The attribute controller's role

The four basic control components in EGA and VGA cards are the CRT controller, the graphics controller, the attribute controller, and the sequencer controller. The attribute controller assigns color information to the picture. If its operation is interrupted, then no color information will reach the screen, and the result is a black screen.

It's much easier to interrupt the attribute controller than the other controllers found on EGA and VGA cards. When bit number 5 in the index register is set to 0, the attribute controller is switched off and color information doesn't reach the screen.

This bit is only significant to the attribute controller. To the other controllers, the index register only accepts the number of the register being addressed. The reason for the difference in the attribute controller involves the palette register (the attribute registers most frequently addressed). Before accessing a palette register, the attribute controller must be temporarily stopped. Since accessing a palette register requires access to an index register anyway, it makes sense to put the bit used for suspending the attribute controller in the index register also. And since there are only 21 registers available to the attribute controller, only bits 0 to 4 of the index register are needed for accepting a register number.

However, before we can disable the attribute controller by clearing bit 5, we must first read the CRT controller's status register. This makes the attribute controller reset effective and must be done before enabling or disabling the attribute controller.

Demonstration programs

The programs VONOFFP.PAS and VONOFFC.C demonstrate how to enable or disable the screen display using the attribute controller. First these programs check to ensure that the system is using an EGA or VGA card. If it isn't, an error message is displayed and the program ends.

If an EGA or VGA card is found, a different message is displayed. The user is given five seconds to read this message, then the ScrOff routine disables the screen display.

The ScrOff routine starts by reading the status register of the CRT controller. To make this routine work with both color and monochrome monitors, a double reset occurs: once using the monochrome address of the status register (3BAH) and once using the color address (3DAH). This won't cause any problems, since only one of these two ports will be used.

Next, the value 0 is written to the attribute controller's index register at port address 3C0H, bit 5 is set to 0, and attribute controller activity is suspended. The screen display goes black.

The ScrOn routine executes after the user has pressed a key. This routine writes the value 20H to the attribute controller's index register. This activates the controller again and enables screen display.

Pascal listing: VONOFFP.PAS

```
{****************************************************************
*                    V O N O F F P . P A S                     *
**------------------------------------------------------------**
* Task        : Demonstrates video display enable and disable on *
*               EGA and VGA cards.                             *
**------------------------------------------------------------**
* Author      : Michael Tischer                                *
* Developed on : 08/05/90                                      *
* Last update  : 02/18/92                                      *
****************************************************************}

program VOnOffP;

uses DOS, CRT;                          { Add CRT and DOS units }

{-- Constants -------------------------------------------------}

const EV_STATC   = $3DA;      { EGA/VGA color status register }
      EV_STATM   = $3BA;      { EGA/VGA mono status register }
      EV_ATTR    = $3C0;      { EGA/VGA attribute controller }

procedure CLI; inline( $FA );           { Disable interrupts }
procedure STI; inline( $FB );           { Enable interrupts }

{****************************************************************
* ScrOff : Disables the EGA/VGA screen.                        *
**------------------------------------------------------------**
* Input   : None                                               *
****************************************************************}

procedure ScrOff;

var dummy : BYTE;       { Dummy variable for register contents }

begin
 cli;                                  { Disable interrupts }
 dummy := port[EV_STATC];        { Reset color status reg }
 dummy := port[EV_STATM];        { Reset mono status reg }
 port[EV_ATTR] := $00;           { Mask bit 5 from access }
                                 {      to CRT controller  }
 sti;                            { Enable interrupts }
end;

{****************************************************************
* ScrOn : Enables the EGA/VGA screen.                          *
**------------------------------------------------------------**
* Input   : None                                               *
****************************************************************}

procedure ScrOn;

var dummy : BYTE;       { Dummy variable for register contents }

begin
 cli;                                  { Disable interrupts }
 dummy := port[EV_STATC];        { Reset color status reg }
 dummy := port[EV_STATM];        { Reset mono status reg }
 port[EV_ATTR] := $20;           { Set bit 5 for access }
                                 {      to CRT controller }
 sti;                            { Enable interrupts }
end;

{****************************************************************
* IsEgaVga : Determines whether an EGA or a VGA card is installed. *
**------------------------------------------------------------**
* Input    : None                                             *
* Output   : TRUE if EGA or VGA card, otherwise FALSE         *
****************************************************************}

function IsEgaVga : boolean;

var Regs : Registers;       { Processor registers for interrupt call }

begin
 Regs.AX := $1a00;              { Function 1AH applies to VGA only }
 Intr( $10, Regs );
 if ( Regs.AL = $1a ) then       { Is the function available? }
   IsEgaVga := TRUE
 else
   begin
     Regs.ah := $12;                        { Call function 12H, }
     Regs.bl := $10;                        { sub-function 10H   }
     intr($10, Regs);                       { Call video BIOS }
     IsEgaVga := ( Regs.bl <> $10 );
   end;
end;

{****************************************************************}
{**                 M A I N   P R O G R A M              **}
{****************************************************************}

var ch : char;                                { Get a key }

begin
 ClrScr;
 writeln( 'VONOFFP  -  (c) 1992 by Michael Tischer'#13#10 );
 if IsEgaVga then                      { EGA or VGA card? }
   begin                               { Yes --> Do it }
     writeln( 'ATTENTION: Screen will go black in five seconds. ' );
     writeln( 'Press any key to enable screen again. ' );
     Delay( 5000 );                            { Wait five seconds }
     while KeyPressed do   { Purge all keys from the keyboard buffer }
       ch := ReadKey;
     ScrOff;                                        { Screen off }
     ch := ReadKey;                            { Wait for a key }
     ScrOn;                                         { Screen on }
     writeln ( #13#10#10 + 'End program' );
   end
 else                                  { No --> No EGA or VGA }
   writeln( 'Warning: No EGA or VGA card found' );
end.
```

C listing: VONOFFC.C

```
/*****************************************************************
*                    V O N O F F C . C                          *
**-------------------------------------------------------------**
*  Task          : Demonstrates video display enable and disable *
*                  on EGA and VGA cards.                         *
**-------------------------------------------------------------**
*  Author        : Michael Tischer                              *
*  Developed on  : 08/26/90                                     *
*  Last update on : 02/18/92                                    *
**-------------------------------------------------------------**
*  (MICROSOFT C)                                                *
*  Compilation    : CL /AS vonoffc.c                            *
**-------------------------------------------------------------**
*  (BORLAND TURBO C)                                            *
*  Compilation    : Use the integrated development environment  *
*****************************************************************/

#include <dos.h>                         /* Add include files */
#include <conio.h>
#include <stdio.h>

#ifdef __TURBOC__                  /* Compiling with Turbo C? */
  #define CLI()        disable()
  #define STI()        enable()
  #define outpw( p, w ) outport( p, w )
  #ifndef inp
    #define outp( p, b )  outportb( p, b )
    #define inp( p )      inportb( p )
  #endif
#else                              /* No --> With Quick C or MSC */
  #include <conio.h>
  #define MK_FP(seg,ofs) ((void far *)\
                        (((unsigned long)(seg) << 16) | (ofs)))
  #define CLI()        _disable()
  #define STI()        _enable()
#endif

/*-- Constants -------------------------------------------------*/

#define EV_STATC 0x3DA          /* EGA/VGA color status register */
#define EV_STATM 0x3BA          /* EGA/VGA mono status register */
#define EV_ATTR  0x3C0          /* EGA/VGA attribute controller */

/*****************************************************************
*  ScrOff : Disables the EGA/VGA screen.                        *
**-------------------------------------------------------------**
*  Input  : None                                                *
*****************************************************************/

void ScrOff( void )
{
 CLI();                                /* Disable interrupts */
 inp( EV_STATC );                      /* Reset color status reg */
 inp( EV_STATM );                      /* Reset mono status reg */
 outp( EV_ATTR, 0x00 );                /* Mask bit 5 from access */
                                       /* to CRT controller     */
 STI();                                /* Enable interrupts */
}

/*****************************************************************
*  ScrOn : Enables the EGA/VGA screen.                          *
**-------------------------------------------------------------**
*  Input  : None                                                *
*****************************************************************/

void ScrOn( void )
{
 CLI();                                /* Disable interrupts */
 inp( EV_STATC );                      /* Reset color status reg */
 inp( EV_STATM );                      /* Reset mono status reg */
 outp( EV_ATTR, 0x20 );                /* Set bit 5 for access */
                                       /* to CRT controller     */
 STI();                                /* Enable interrupts */
}

/*****************************************************************
*  IsEgaVga : Determines whether an EGA or VGA card is installed. *
**-------------------------------------------------------------**
*  Input  : None                                                *
*  Output : TRUE if EGA or VGA card, otherwise FALSE            *
*****************************************************************/

int IsEgaVga( void )
{
 union REGS Regs;             /* Processor registers for interrupt call */

 Regs.x.ax = 0x1a00;          /* Function 1AH applies to VGA only */
 int86( 0x10, &Regs, &Regs );
 if ( Regs.h.al == 0x1a )        /* Is the function available? */
  return 1;
 else
  {
   Regs.h.ah = 0x12;                    /* Call function 12H, */
   Regs.h.bl = 0x10;                    /* sub-function 10H   */
   int86(0x10, &Regs, &Regs);           /* Call video BIOS */
   return ( Regs.h.bl != 0x10 );
  }
}

/*****************************************************************
*  Delay : BIOS induced time delay.                            *
**-------------------------------------------------------------**
*  Input  : Delay in seconds                                    *
*  Output : None                                                *
*****************************************************************/

void Delay( int pauslen )
{
 unsigned int tico_hi,                      /* Time counter */
              tico_lo,
              ticks;
 union REGS   inregs,                       /* Processor registers */
              outregs;

 ticks = pauslen * 182 / 10;
 inregs.h.ah = 0;               /* Function 00H = Read counter */
 int86( 0x1a, &inregs, &outregs );          /* Get and store time */
 tico_hi = outregs.x.cx;
 tico_lo = outregs.x.dx;

 while ( ticks )                /* Repeat until ticks = 0 */
  {
   int86( 0x1a, &inregs, &outregs );             /* Get time */

   /*-- New tick occurred? ------------------------------------*/
```

```
  if ( tico_hi != outregs.x.cx  ||  tico_lo != outregs.x.dx )
  {                                                    /* Yes */
    tico_hi = outregs.x.cx;          /* Store new counter value */
    tico_lo = outregs.x.dx;
    --ticks;                    /* Decrement number of remaining ticks */
  }
 }
}

/*********************************************************************/
/**                M A I N   P R O G R A M                        **/
/*********************************************************************/

void main( void )                              /* Get a key */
{
  int i;                                       /* Loop counter */

  for ( i=0; i<25; ++i )                        /* Clear screen */
```

```
    printf( "\n" );

  printf( "VONOFFC  -  (c) 1992 by Michael Tischer\n\n" );
  if ( IsEgaVga() )                             /* EGA or VGA card? */
  {                                             /* Yes --> Do it */
    printf( "ATTENTION: Screen will go black in five seconds.\n"\
            "Press any key to enable screen again." );
    Delay( 5 );                                 /* Wait five seconds */
    while ( kbhit() )      /* Purge all keys from the keyboard buffer */
      getch();
    ScrOff();                                   /* Screen off */
    getch();                                    /* Wait for a key */
    ScrOn();                                    /* Screen on */
    printf( "\n\n\nEnd program\n" );
  }
  else                                          /* No --> No EGA or VGA */
    printf( "Warning: No EGA or VGA card found\n" );
}
```

4.8.5 Understanding Bitplanes

The technological progress of PC video cards has produced higher resolutions and increasing numbers of colors. As resolution increases, so does the amount of video RAM required. As the need to display more colors increases, more than one bit is needed to represent each pixel. For example, VGA cards with 256 colors require 8 bits per pixel. As a result, almost all EGA and VGA cards manufactured today include 256K of RAM as standard equipment. Depending on the video mode and the number of screen pages stored, this memory is often used to capacity.

Although the 64K limitation of early video cards no longer exits, we can't continue to add more video RAM. Remember that PCs are limited to 1 megabyte of addressable memory. In this section, we'll discuss how the PC's addressable memory handles the 256K of video RAM and how this affects programming EGA and VGA cards.

Dividing video RAM into bitplanes

In the total addressable memory of the PC, only segments A (from A000:0000) and B (from B000:0000) are available to the video card. Segment B is already reserved for the video RAM in MDA, CGA, and Hercules cards. So, only segment A can be used for EGA and VGA cards. This means that the developers of the first EGA card had to address 256K of video RAM in a 64K area.

The solution resulted in the development of bitplanes, which divide the video RAM of EGA and VGA cards into equal sections. On a card with 256K of video RAM, each bitplane has 64K that is completely addressable using memory segment A, starting at A000:0000. If your video card has less video RAM, such as the first EGA cards that had only 64K, then each bitplane is correspondingly smaller.

This memory addressing technique, which was developed in 1984, is valid for all EGA and VGA cards. This includes the Super VGA card, although the addressing is used in a slightly expanded form (more on this later).

Latch registers

Use different bitplanes in text modes only if you want to use more than one font simultaneously. Bitplanes are always used when graphics modes are active. Pixel information is spread out among the bitplanes in various ways for different modes. Regardless of this, EGA and VGA cards manage communications between the processor and video RAM using four 8-bit registers known as the latch registers. Each latch register corresponds to one of the four bitplanes.

Latch registers cannot be directly accessed by programs. If a program wants to access a byte in video RAM, then the four latch registers receive this byte from the four corresponding bitplanes using the same offset address. For example, if the offset address is 9, then the tenth byte (byte 0 is the first) from the first bitplane will be loaded into the first latch register, the tenth byte from the second bitplane will be loaded into the second latch register, and so on for the third and fourth.

The same procedure is used for a write access to video RAM. The contents of the four latch registers are written to the corresponding bitplanes at the specified offset address.

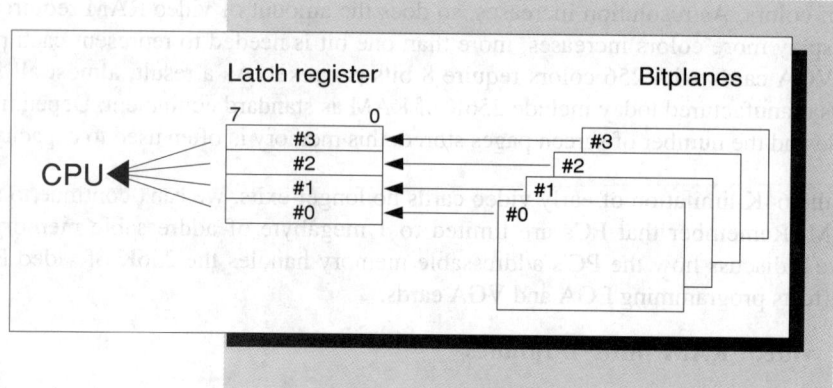

Video RAM access-loading the four latch registers

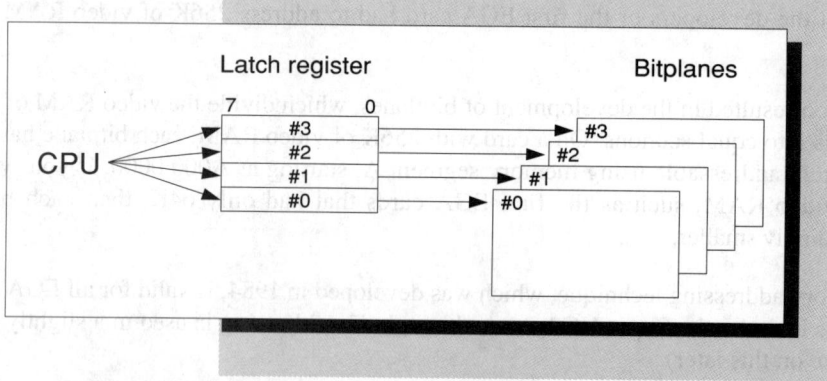

Video RAM access-writing the four latch registers

This process involves more than simply reading or writing to the latch register. A read access of video RAM must result in a byte being sent to the processor and a write access must result in a byte being transferred from the processor to the video RAM.

However, during a read access, only one byte can be sent to the processor at a time. So, we must determine which of the four bytes in the latch registers is sent. This also applies to writing to video RAM because four different bytes (one for each bitplane) must be transferred from the processor.

The graphics controller's role in graphics programming

The answer to all of these questions comes from the nine registers of the graphics controller, which is an important component of every EGA and VGA card. These registers determine how and where all read and write accesses to the video RAM occur. This applies not only to the different graphics modes, but also to the text modes. You may frequently use these registers in graphics programming by assigning them different values, depending on the desired operation. However, this isn't the case in text mode.

In text mode, during initialization of the mode through the BIOS, the various registers are set so that additional accesses aren't necessary after initialization. However, all input and output to or from the video RAM in text mode is conducted through the four latch registers, even if this process is transparent for a program.

The nine registers of the graphics controller for the EGA card and their defaults:

Reg	Meaning	Default
00H	Set / Reset	00H
01H	Enable Set / Reset	00H
02H	Color Compare	00H
03H	Function Select / Data Rotate	00H
04H	Read Map Select	00H
05H	Mode	00H
06H	Miscellaneous	various
07H	Color Don't Care	0FH
08H	Bit Mask	FFH

Programming the registers of the graphics controller is similar to accessing the CRTC register of the Hercules graphics card. These registers can also be used on other controllers of an EGA and VGA card. Port address 3CEH has an address register, in which the number of the register within the graphics controller that's being accessed must be loaded first. The value for this register can then be output to the data register next to the address register, which has a port address of 3CFH.

However, access to these two ports doesn't have to be separate. Instead, you can use a 16-bit OUT command on the address register. The AX register sent to this port in the course of the machine language command, OUT DX,AX must contain the register number in the AL register and the value to be loaded for this register in the AH register.

Although values can be loaded in the individual registers of the graphics controller in this way, a read access is only possible with VGA cards; you cannot read these registers on EGA cards.

The mode register, number 5, is important to the graphics controller during read and write accesses to the video RAM. This register sets one of two read modes and one of three write modes. These modes affect read or write accesses to the video RAM. The other registers are only accessories, which specify given parameters depending on the set read and write mode.

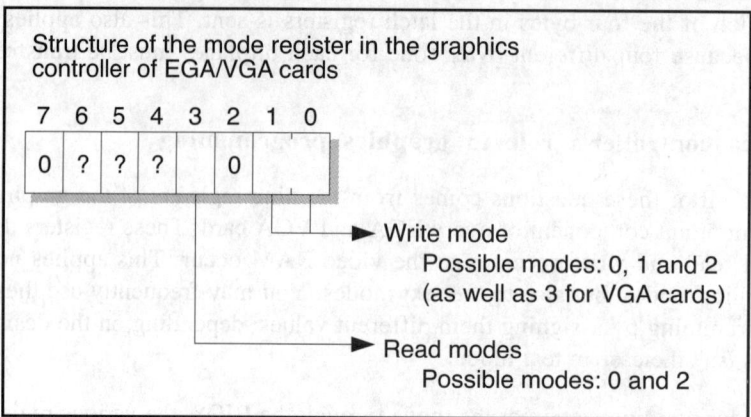

In the following sections we'll discuss how the various read and write modes operate, their tasks, and how other registers of the graphics controller affect these modes. However, you will quickly realize that you need to use only a few of these modes because the other modes are too difficult to use.

Read mode 0

Read mode 0 gives a program the option of reading a byte from a specific bitplane. This is practical, for example when a part of the video RAM must be saved, for which purpose the four bitplanes are executed sequentially in a loop and the desired area from each bitplane is loaded and placed in main memory.

During a read access to the video RAM in read mode 0 all four latch registers are loaded with the addressed byte of their plane. However, only one of these four bytes gets by its latch register and reaches the CPU. Which bitplane the byte comes from is determined by the contents of the read map select register, which is number 4 within the graphics controller.

Only the lower two bits in this register are allocated. These two bits decide on the number of the latch register, whose contents can advance up to the CPU. When programming this register, ensure that the first bitplane is set to 0 (i.e., don't set it to 1 if you want to access the first bitplane).

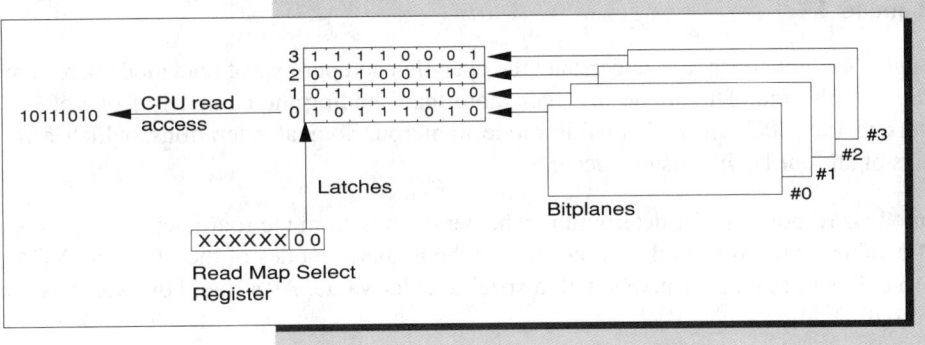

Read access to the video RAM in read mode 0

The following sequence of assembly commands demonstrates how read mode 0 is used. The first 8K from the second bitplane are loaded into the main memory. First read mode 0 is set and then the read map select register is loaded with the value 1 so the second bitplane can be read. With the help of the assembly command REP MOVSB, the first 8K are then loaded byte by byte from the video RAM and copied to a buffer.

```
mov ax,ds              ;ES:DI to target buffer
mov es,ax
mov di,offset buffer
mov ax,0A000h          ;DS:SI to starting address of bitplane
mov ds,ax              ;in video RAM
xor si,si
mov cx,8*1024          ;Copy 8K

mov dx,3CEh            ;Address graphics controller
mov ax,0005h          ;Write read mode 0 in mode register
out dx,ax             ;
mov ax,0104h          ;Write 1 (plane number in read map
out dx,ax             ;register

rep movsb             ;Copy 8K
```

After studying the assembly sequence, you may think that you could speed up the copying process by simply copying 4096 words instead of 8192 bytes. To do this you would have to convert REP MOVSB to REP MOVSW and load the CX register with 4096 instead of 8192. This would work for copying memory areas within the main memory. However, in this case, it would result in some unpleasant consequences.

Because 16-bit accesses aren't possible in video RAM, the CPU would first execute two read accesses at byte level before executing the write access. The second read access would overwrite the results of the first read access within the latch register before these results could even reach the CPU. As a result, in the target buffer, you would find only words whose low and high byte have the same value. Only the high byte would correspond to the actual contents of the video RAM. For this reason, 16-bit read accesses to video RAM should be avoided in all forms on EGA and VGA cards.

Read mode 1

Although it's relatively easy to understand the operation and purpose of read mode 0, read mode 1 is more complicated. This mode involves more than sending the contents of one of the latch registers to the CPU. Instead, in this mode numerous logical operations, which affect the contents of all four latch registers, occur.

This mode is responsible for determining whether the bits from the four latch registers contain a specific value. Later, this mode can be used in the graphics modes of the EGA and VGA cards with 16 colors to search for pixels with a specific color value. As a rule, however, this mode is rarely used.

After the four latch registers are loaded, eight groups, each consisting of four bits, are formed. The four bits occupying an identical bit position within the four different latch registers are located in one group. For example, all the bits at bit position 0 are in one group, all the bits from bit position 1 are in another group, etc.

Each of these eight groups of four bits is now compared with the value from the color compare register, which was loaded into this register before the read access. The result of this comparison determines the byte that is sent to the CPU as the result of the read operation.

All the bits, whose group showed the value from the color compare register, are set to 1, while the other bits contain the value 0. So, after the read access, it's possible to determine not only whether one of the groups corresponded to the value from the color compare register, but also which groups correspond.

Although it may be difficult to believe, this isn't the entire process. Actually, the Color Don't Care register is also involved. Only when this register contains the value 00001111b are the various groups of four bits completely compared with the comparison value from the Color Compare register. Each of the lower four bits in the Color Don't Care register represents one of the four bitplanes: bit 0 for the first, bit 1 for the second, etc. Only if one of these bits contains the value 1 is the corresponding bitplane also included in this comparison of the four bit groups with the value from the Color Compare register.

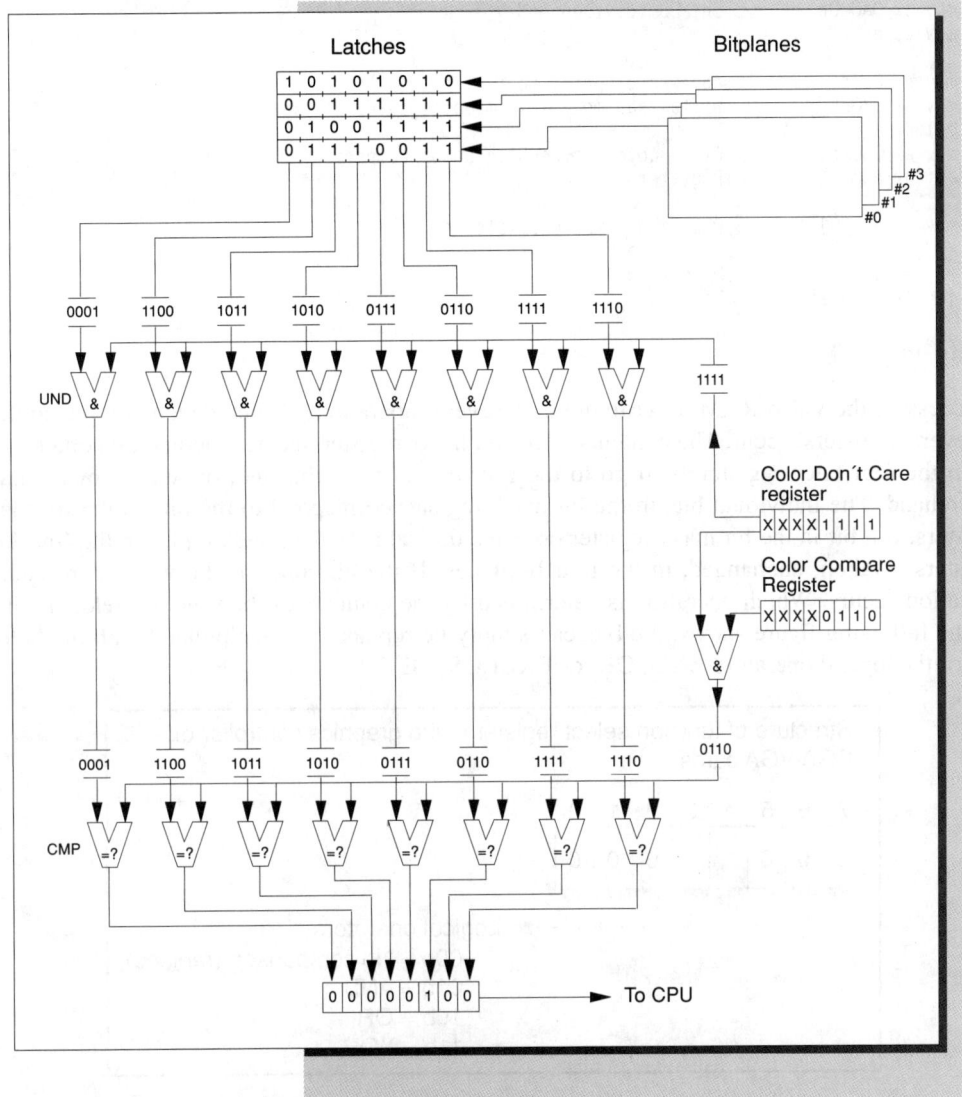

Read access to the video RAM in read mode 1

However, if the value is 0, it's as if the value from this bitplane matches the corresponding bit from the Color Compare register in all eight groups. So, specifying the value 0 in the Color Don't Care Register always returns the value 11111111b to the CPU, regardless of the contents of the four latch registers and Color Compare register. This is possible because the eight groups are no longer compared with the comparison value. Instead, all the groups are considered to be appropriate.

The following assembly sequence demonstrates the use of read mode 1. This assembly sequence establishes which of the groups of four, from the first byte in the four bitplanes in video RAM, has the value 5. The Color Don't Care register isn't explicitly programmed, because it's assumed that its default value is 00001111b. So, all the bitplanes will be included in the comparison.

```
        mov ax,0A000h        ;Set ES to video RAM
        mov es,ax

        mov dx,3CEh          ;Address graphics controller
        mov ax,0805h         ;Write read mode 1 in mode register
        out dx,ax
        mov ax,0502h         ;Write color value 5 in color compare
        out dx,ax            ;Register

        mov al,es:[0]        ;Read and compare pixels,
                             ;return result in AX
        or  al,al            ;No bit to 1?
        je  AllUnequal       ;No
```

Write mode 0

In accessing the video RAM in write mode 0, several operations, which depend on the contents of several registers, occur. The contents of the bit mask register decide whether the contents of a bit in the four latch registers will go to the four bitplanes unchanged, or will be manipulated beforehand. The individual bits in the bit mask register correspond to the bits in the four latch registers. If a bit in the bit mask register contains the value 0, the matching bit in the four latch registers is taken, unchanged, in the four bitplanes. If the bit contains the value 1 instead, an operation occurs. Which operation is determined by the contents of the function select register. As the following figure shows, the bits can simply be replaced or manipulated with the help of one of the logical operators AND, OR, or EXCLUSIVE OR.

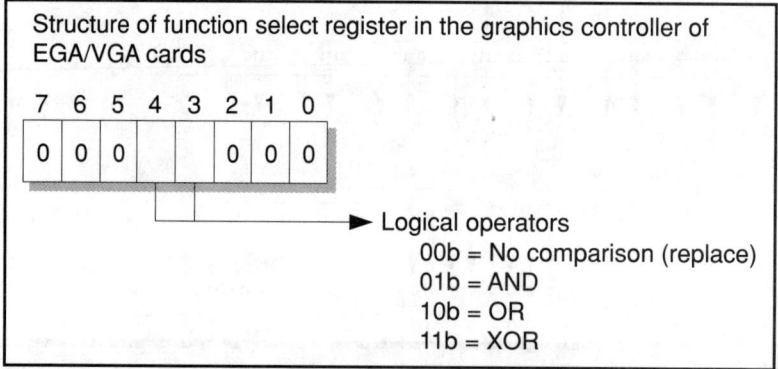

The contents of the Enable Set/Reset register determine what will be the partner of these bits in the operation. If the lower four bits each contain the value 1, the operation takes place through the contents of the lower 4 bits of the Set/Reset register. Each of these bits is used in the operation with the four bits of a bit position from the four latch registers, whose type is described by the contents of the function select register.

All of the bits to be manipulated from latch register 0 are then linked with bit 0 of the Set/Reset register by the selected operator. In the same way, all the bits to be manipulated from latch registers 1, 2, and 3 are linked with bits 1, 2, and 3 from the Set/Reset register. The CPU byte, which is transferred to the graphics controller during a write access, is unimportant here. The write access is reduced to a trigger, which cannot have any direct influence on the contents of the latch register (or the bitplanes).

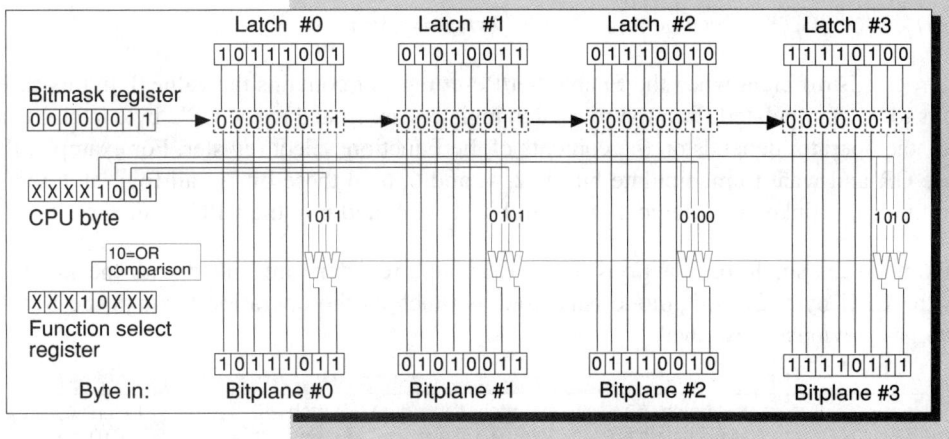

Write mode 0 when the Enable Set/Reset register contains the value 00001111b

The following assembly language sequence assigns code 1011b to the group of four with bit 2 from the first byte in the video RAM, without disturbing the contents of the other groups. As you'll see in the next section, this is a technique that's frequently used in setting pixels in the 16 color graphics modes of EGA and VGA cards.

Since the color of the other groups of four shouldn't be changed, their contents are first loaded into the latch register through a read access to the video RAM. Which of the various read modes is active is unimportant. After all, the value returned to the processor is not important; it simply fills the latch register.

Since only the group of four at bit position 2 must be manipulated, and the other groups return to the bitplanes unchanged, the value 00000100b (04H) is loaded into the bit mask register first. Then, the value 0 is written in the Function Select register because the bits to be manipulated should be replaced by a new bit combination. After that, the color for the group of four at bit position 2 (1011b = 0BH) is loaded into the Set/Reset register.

To remove the color from this register when writing to the video RAM, write the value 1111b (0FH) to the Enable Set/Reset register as the last access to the register of the graphics controller. Then execute the write access to the video RAM, in which the transferred processor byte is unimportant.

```
mov ax,0A000h      ;Video RAM segment address
mov ds,ax          ; to DS
mov al,ds:[0]      ;Load byte 0 in latch register
mov dx,3CEh        ;Address graphics controller
mov ax,0005h       ;Read mode 0, write mode 0
out dx,ax          ; to mode register
mov al,03h         ;Write 0 to function select
out dx,ax          ;register
mov ax,0408h       ;Write bit masks in bit mask register
out dx,ax
mov ax,0B00h       ;Write new color value to
out dx,ax          ;Set/Reset register
mov ax,0F01h       ;Write 1111b to Enable Set/Reset
```

```
out dx,ax            ;register
mov ds:[0],al        ;Manipulate & return latch register
```

This process is different when the Enable Set/Reset register contains the value 0. In this case, all the bits to be manipulated from the four latch registers are linked to the CPU byte latch by latch. Again, the operator depends on the contents of the Function Select register. For example, if you choose OR and want to manipulate bits 1, 2, 4, and 6, then these bits in all four latch registers are individually linked by a logical OR with bits 1, 2, 4, and 6 in the CPU byte.

In this mode the single bit positions in the four latch registers are linked with the same value from the CPU byte. So, this mode isn't used as much as the operation through the Set/Reset register, as previously described.

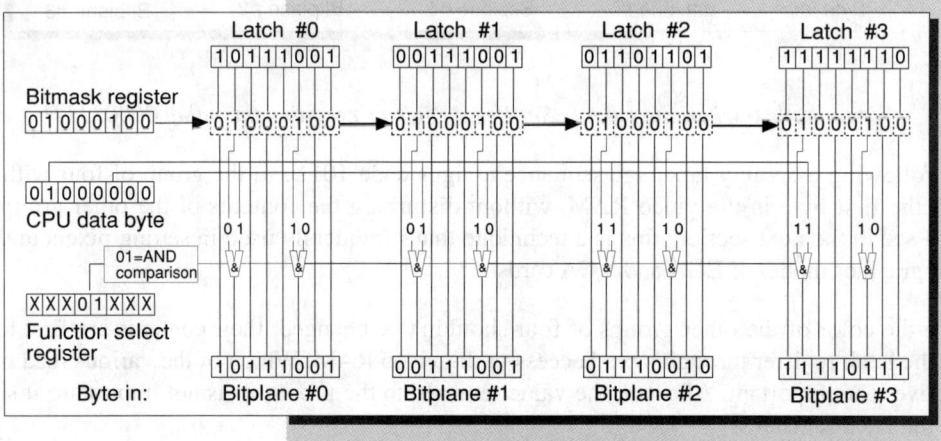

Write mode 0, when the Enable Set/Reset register contains the value 00000000b

Write mode 1

Compared to the complex operations in write mode 0, write mode 1 seems very simple. The contents of the various registers of the graphics controller and the passed CPU byte are no longer important here, since the contents of the four latch registers are written to the specified offset address within the four bitplanes in unchanged form.

For example, it makes sense to use this write mode to copy a specific area from the video RAM to another area. Simply run this area in the video RAM, fill the contents of the four latches through a read access in any read mode, and then write the latch register to video RAM through a write access in write mode 1. This allows you to copy four bytes at a time, which saves a lot of time.

```
mov ax,0A000h        ;Segment address of video RAM
mov ds,ax            ; to DS and ES
mov es,ax
mov si,0000h         ;Source begins at 0000H
mov di,0200h         ;Target begins at 0200H
mov cx,100h          ;Copy 256 bytes
cld                  ;Increment on string inst.
```

```
mov dx,3CEh          ;Address graphics controller
mov ax,0105h         ;Read mode 0, Write mode 1
out dx,ax            ; to mode register

rep movsb            ;Copy all four bitplanes
```

Write mode 2

Write mode 2 is like a combination of the different modes in write mode 0. Like write mode 0, in write mode 2, the bit mask register decides which bits are sent unchanged to the latch registers and which ones are to be manipulated.

The linking mode recorded in the Function Select register determines the manner in which the single bits are manipulated. Regardless of the contents of the Enable Set/Reset register, the lower 4 bits of the CPU byte are linked with the latch registers within write mode 2. Bit 0 of the CPU byte is linked with all bits in latch register 0 that are to be manipulated. The same applies for CPU bits 1, 2 and 3, which are linked individually with all the bits in latch registers 1, 2 and 3.

This mode is well-suited for setting the color of single pixels in 16 color graphics mode on EGA and VGA cards. While this is also possible in write mode 0, the appropriate assembly sequence is shorter in write mode 2, since neither the Enable Set/Reset register nor the Set/Reset register must be programmed.

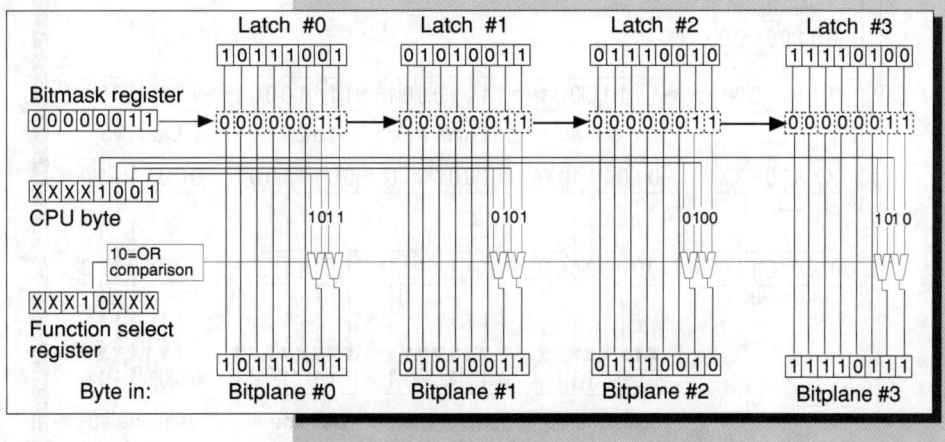

Write access to the video RAM in write mode 2

Here's the same example for write mode 2:

```
mov ax,0A000h        ;Segment address of video RAM
mov ds,ax            ; to DS
mov al,ds:[0]        ;Load byte 0 to latch register
mov dx,3CEh          ;Address graphics controller
mov ax,0205h         ;Write read mode 0, write mode 2
out dx,ax            ; to mode register
mov ax,0003h         ;Write REPLACE mode (0) to
out dx,ax            ; function select register
mov ax,0408h         ;Write bit mask to bit mask register
out dx,ax
```

```
mov byte ptr ds:[O],OBh ;New color value in video RAM
```

Write mode 3

In addition to the three write modes of the EGA card, the developers of the VGA card added a fourth mode. This mode is selected in the same way as the others; enter the corresponding mode number in the mode register of the graphics controller.

During a read access to video RAM in this mode, the four low bits from the set/reset register must first be coupled with the bits from the four latch registers. Unlike write mode 0, the contents of the enable set/reset register are included in this operation. However, the type of coupling is determined by the Function select register as usual.

In this mode, a logical AND combines the CPU byte with the contents of the bit mask register. The result then determines which bits from the latch registers are written to the bitplanes unchanged and which are taken as the combination of the set/reset register and the latch bits. The CPU byte is helping in the task that the bit mask register performs alone in modes 0 and 2.

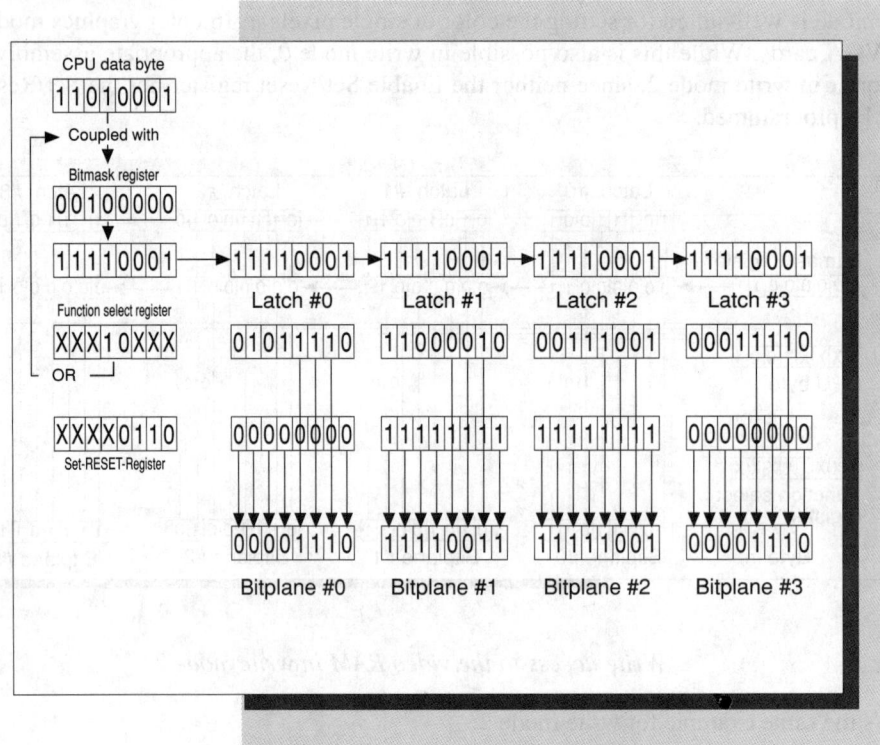

Write access to video RAM in write mode 3

We haven't found a meaningful application for this mode yet. So, we couldn't provide a practical example.

The map mask register

Another register we'll discuss is the map mask register of the sequencer controller. With it, individual bitplanes can be locked to prevent reading or writing them. This is useful when you want to manipulate the contents of only one specific bitplane.

Each bitplane's status is represented in this register by the four low bits. Each bit corresponds to a bitplane. The bit must be set to 1 to allow access to the corresponding bitplane.

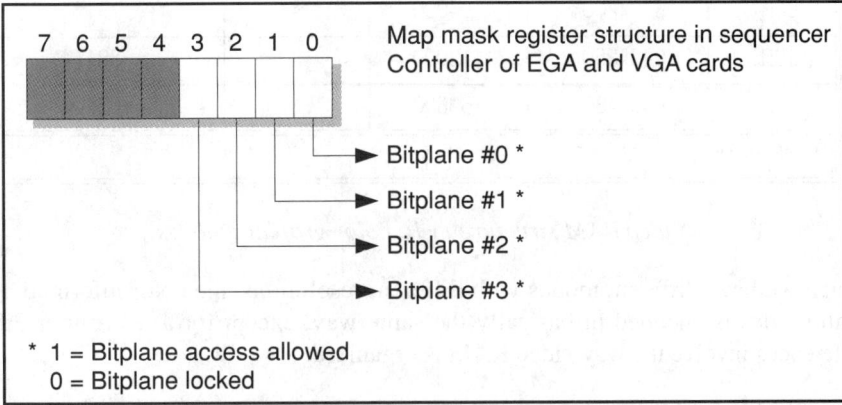

The following sections describe how to implement the various read and write modes to perform tasks such as setting and querying pixels in graphics modes or copying areas of the screen from video RAM to main memory.

4.8.6 The 16 Color EGA and VGA Graphics Modes

The most important feature of EGA and VGA cards is the 16 color graphics modes. These modes are available with resolutions from 320x200 to 640x350 pixels. For those used to working with the four colors of the CGA card, the 16 color modes are a definite improvement. Although EGA and VGA are still far from the ultimate goal of photographic quality screen displays, which would require approximately 16 million colors, the color graphics modes are a start.

Why multiple 16 color graphics modes?

The development of PC video cards includes a steady progression of higher resolutions with more colors. Why then would the EGA card want to include two lower resolution 16 color graphics modes in addition to the high resolution 640x350 mode? As you'll see in the following table, the lower resolution modes require less memory per screen page. This allows more pages to be stored in video RAM simultaneously. In many user applications, a greater number of screen pages in video RAM may be more important than higher resolution. One example of this is sprite programming, which is discussed in Section 4.8.9. This section also explains how the remaining video RAM can be used.

As the following table shows, the 16 color graphics modes are also fully supported by the VGA card. The VGA card also has an additional 640x480 mode. Even though this resolution is exceeded on the Super VGA card, it remains the highest resolution mode for the standard VGA card and has been widely used by many applications.

The EGA and VGA 16 color graphics modes				
Mode	Resolution	Memory	Pages	Remaining bytes
0DH	320x200	32000	8	6144
0EH	640x200	64000	4	6144
10H	640x350	112000	2	38144
12H*	640x480	153600	1	108544
*VGA only				

Video RAM structure in 16 color graphics modes

Even though we have different modes with different resolutions, the color information for each pixel in all modes is encoded in basically the same way, except for a few minor differences. These differences involve the way video RAM is organized.

Each byte of video RAM contains color information for eight consecutive pixels in the same pixel line of the screen. This means that each pixel is represented by one bit. In the 16 color modes this isn't sufficient because each pixel needs four bits to identify the color. These bits are obtained by using one bit from each of the four bitplanes, as shown in the following figure.

Let's look at a practical example. The first eight pixels in the upper-left corner of the screen are represented by the four bytes found at offset address 0000H in each of the four bitplanes. The four bits required to encode the color information are obtained by combining the bits at the same bit position in the first byte of each bitplane. The procedure creates eight groups of four bits, each of which determines the color of a single pixel.

The bit from bitplane 0 becomes bit 0 of the color code. The bit from bitplane 1 is bit 1 of the color code, and so on for bits 2 and 3. The color code is then interpreted as a color, just as with the CGA card: black (0), blue (1), green (2), etc.

In Section 8.5.8 we discussed how the division of video RAM into bitplanes works in the various read and write modes. The same groups of four bits are at work with the read and write modes, accessing individual pixels using the latch registers in 16 color graphics modes.

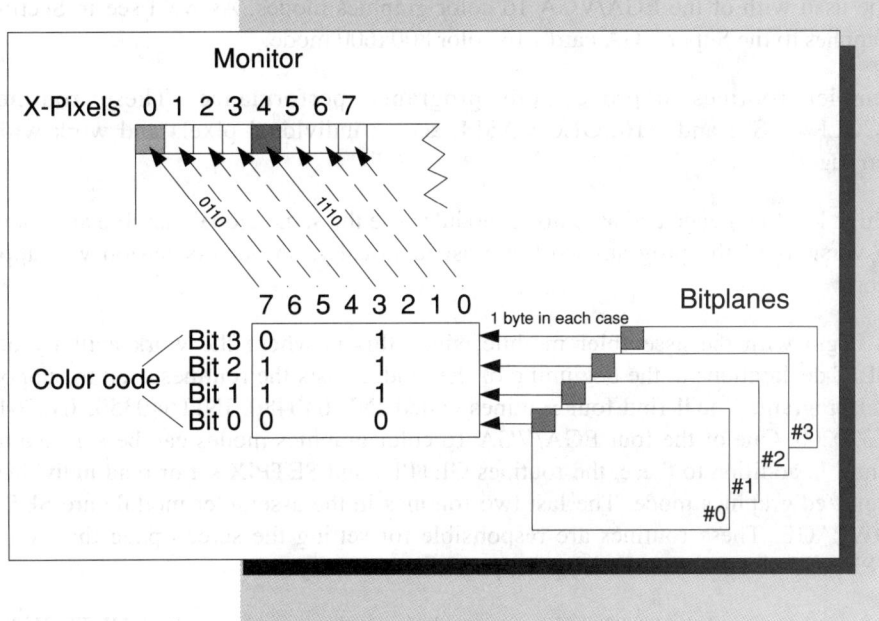

Structure of video RAM in EGA and VGA 16 color graphics modes

In addition to the structure of each byte, the order in which these bytes are stored in video RAM is an important aspect of programming the graphics modes. EGA and VGA cards use a very simple procedure for this in the 16 color modes. Starting at offset address 0000H (the start of video RAM), each pixel line is represented by a certain number of consecutive bytes. For graphics modes with a horizontal resolution of 640 pixels, this is 80 bytes. Mode 0DH (320x200) uses 40 bytes per pixel line.

Pixel lines follow one another sequentially in memory, so you can use the following formula to calculate the offset address of the byte that contains any given pixel:

```
Offset = Y * (horizontal_resolution / 8 ) + int( X / 8)
```

The byte found at this address contains information for eight consecutive pixels. To find the specific bit that contains the color information for the desired pixel, use the following formula:

```
Bit = 7 - (X mod 8)
```

The difference between the various 16 color graphics modes lies in the length of a graphic line in RAM, the number of lines per screen, and the amount of memory required per screen page instead of in how the color information is encoded. This information must be considered when programming each of the various graphics modes.

Accessing individual pixels in 16 color graphics modes

The following demonstration programs show how these formulas are used to access individual pixels through read and write modes. The programs, named V16COLP.PAS and V16COLC.C, can be used with of the EGA/VGA 16 color graphics modes. As we'll see in Section 4.9, this also applies to the Super VGA card's 16 color 800x600 mode.

Assembler routines improve both programs' performance. These routines, called V16COLPA.ASM and V16COLCA.ASM, access individual pixels and work with different screen pages.

The high level language and assembler modules use the same global variable and routine names. Both versions of the program work almost identically, so our discussion will apply to both versions.

Let's begin with the assembler module, since this is where the work actually occurs. The PUBLIC declarations at the beginning of the module lists the routines used to support the C or Pascal program. You'll find four routines called INIT640480, INIT640350, INIT640200, and INIT320200. One of the four EGA/VGA 16 color graphics modes can be selected using these routines. In addition to these, the routines GETPIX and SETPIX set or read individual pixels in the selected graphics mode. The last two routines in the assembler module are SETPAGE and SHOWPAGE. These routines are responsible for setting the screen page that is accessed by GETPIX and SETPIX and selecting the page that is displayed.

The assembler module for the C program has another routine called GETFONTPTR. This routine actually has nothing to do with graphics programming. It simply returns a pointer to the 8x8 font stored in the EGA/VGA ROM chip. This pointer is required by the C or Pascal module to display characters on screen in graphics mode. The Pascal version of the program gets this pointer without using an assembler routine, so GETFONTPTR isn't used in V16COLPA.ASM.

The INIT routines for initializing the graphics mode perform two basic tasks. First, function 00H of the BIOS video interrupt sets the desired video mode and clears the screen. Then three global variables are declared for use in accessing individual pixels and screen pages.

The three variables are VIO_SEG, LNWIDTH, and PAGEOFS. The first variable, VIO_SEG, stores the segment address of video RAM. This variable also represents the current screen page because the offset of the current screen page is included in this segment address. This means that SETPIX and GETPIX don't have to consider the starting address of the current screen page when addressing a pixel; the segment address in VIO_SEG already reflects this information.

For example, in 640x200 pixel graphics mode, each screen page requires 64,000 bytes, which is spread across the four bitplanes. This means that a new screen page starts every 8000 bytes within a bitplane. In hexadecimal mode, this interval is 1F40H bytes.

The first screen page begins at A000:0000, the second at A000:1F40, the third at A000:3E80, the fourth at A000:5DC0, etc. Using the segment address, the first pages starts at A000:0000, the second at A1F4:0000, the third at A3E8:0000, and the fourth at A5DC:0000.

You must take the screen size into account before calculating the start of each screen page for each video mode. The INIT routines store this information in the global variable PAGEOFS, which represents the offset address divided by 16. This division allows easy merging with the segment address.

The global variable LNWIDTH calculates individual pixel addresses. It stores the width of a single pixel line in bytes. This value is plugged into the "horizontal_resolution / 8" expression in the equation previously listed.

With the information stored in the global variables VIO_SEG and LNWIDTH, routines such as SETPIX and SHOWPAGE can perform their tasks. With SETPIX and GETPIX, the screen coordinates specified by the caller are converted into an offset address for accessing video RAM. This is done by multiplying the Y-coordinate by LNWIDTH, dividing the X-coordinate by eight, and adding the two results.

Then the bit position of the desired pixel is calculated from the X-coordinate. In addition to the MOD operation in the equation previously listed, the assembler instruction AND is used to ignore all but the three lowest bits of the X-coordinate. This performs the same task as a MOD operation with 8, but runs faster.

Until now, GETPIX and SETPIX are identical in their execution. With SETPIX, the next step is to convert the bit position into a bit mask, which is needed later to access the pixel using write mode 2. This is done by shifting the value 1 to the left by the number of the bit position. For example, by using bit position 4 you would end up with the value 0010000(b).

This value is then loaded into both the bit mask register of the graphics controller and the mode register for write mode 2 and read mode 0. Next, the segment address of the video RAM, including the offset address of the current screen page, is loaded in the ES register so video RAM is addressable.

Although we're going to set the pixel without reading it, the next step is to load the byte that contains the pixel to be accessed. The value passed to the CPU is actually meaningless. The purpose of this operation is only to load the four latch registers with the four bitplane bytes that contain the color code for the pixel we want to access. The pixel color is then set by writing the desired color code to video RAM.

According to write mode 2, the EGA or VGA card then writes this bit value in all the latch register groups of four that have a value of 1 in the corresponding bit position of the bit mask register. In our case, this applies only to the bit position of the pixel we're accessing, so all other groups of four remain unaffected by the write access. In the four bitplane bytes, only the four bits that determine the pixel we're accessing are changed in the write operation that automatically follows.

This completes the task of SETPIX. Before returning to the caller, however, the changed graphics controller registers are set back to their default values. This should always be done whenever these registers are manipulated so the next routine that uses them can assume that they contain the default values. This allows you to change only the appropriate registers; the others can be left with their default values.

The same applies to GETPIX. However, here only one register of the graphics controller must be programmed. This is the read map register. At the end of the routine, this register is set back to its default value. It's more difficult for GETPIX to read a pixel than for SETPIX to set one. Unfortunately, there is no corresponding read mode in the EGA and VGA cards, so GETPIX must manage with read mode 0.

This mode returns only one byte per read access of the video RAM. This byte comes from the bitplane indicated by the number in the read map register of the graphics controller. So, GETPIX must run through a loop four times, reading a byte from one of the four bitplanes each time. Before this bit can be read, GETPIX programs the read map register within the loop.

Access proceeds from bitplane 3 to bitplane 2, bitplane 1, and finally bitplane 0. At the end of the loop, the read map register is loaded again with its default value of 0.

Within the loop, the color of the desired pixel is represented using the four bytes read. All the bits in each byte that don't apply to the desired pixel are hidden using a previously defined bit mask. The result is a byte with either only one bit set or with none. The latter case indicates that the corresponding bit from the color code of the pixel wasn't set in the bitplane currently being processed.

The status of this bit is obtained by executing the NEG instruction after all other bits have been blanked out with the bit mask. The result of this instruction is that the status of the bit not affected by the bit mask is reflected in bit 7 of the register. If the isolated color bit was set, then bit 7 of this register is set after the NEG operation. Similarly, bit 7 is off if the corresponding color bit isn't set.

The bit 7 obtained in this way is moved from the BH register to the BL register with the ROL instruction. This operation is executed four times. With each execution of the loop, the previous result is moved one place to the left to a lower position. This results in the color of the desired pixel loaded in the lower four bits of the BL register.

This is why it's important to process the bitplanes from number 3 to number 0. If you switched this, you would end up inverting the color code.

This is how GETPIX returns the actual color code of the selected pixel. This method works, even if it's slower and more complicated than the procedure for setting a pixel.

The SETPAGE and GETPAGE routines are much simpler than SETPIX and GETPIX. This is especially true for SETPAGE, which sets the current page number in video RAM. SETPIX and GETPIX operate within this routine. SETPAGE works by multiplying the screen page number by the page length as stored in the PAGEOFS variable. The base segment address of A000H is added and the result is stored in the global variable VIO_SEG.

All subsequent calls of SETPIX and GETPIX are then based on this screen page. Remember that a screen page isn't displayed on screen simply by selecting it with SETPAGE. This enables you to select a page in the background and work on it with SETPIX and GETPIX while a different page is displayed.

SHOWPAGE actually displays a page. SHOWPAGE accepts a page number as input, and begins by converting this page number into an offset address in video RAM. This operation also multiplies the value of PAGEOFS by the page number. This time, however, the result is also multiplied by 16, because the value in PAGEOFS is a segment address and not an offset address as is required here.

To display a screen page on screen, the offset address of the screen origin is loaded into two registers of the CRT controller. Theoretically, you can load any value you want in these registers. However, for the display to be understandable, the screen origin and the starting address(es) used by routines, such as SETPIX and GETPIX, must be specified. So, the page number is also multiplied by PAGEOFS here.

From the assembler modules V16COLPA.ASM and V16COLCA.ASM we move on to the main program modules, from which the routines previously described are called. Both programs can work in all EGA and VGA 16 color graphics modes, as long as the mode is set before the program is compiled.

In the declaration of constants, we find a constant called MODUS, which must be assigned a value of A320200, A640200, A640350, or A640480. These values indicate the various graphics modes.

At runtime, the main program uses the IsEgaVga function to determine if the mode indicated by the value of VMODE can be initialized. For the 640x480 mode, this means that a VGA card must be installed. All other modes will run with either VGA or EGA.

If the installed video card passes this test, the global variables MAXX, MAXY, and PAGES are loaded with values that depend on the selected video mode. These variables indicate the maximum X-coordinates and Y-coordinates on the screen, and the total number of screen pages available.

This information is very important for the DEMO routine, which is called next. DEMO uses the various assembler module routines for running through each screen page in a loop, defining each page with SETPAGE, using each page in conjunction with SETPIX and GETPIX, and finally displaying each page with SHOWPAGE. Finally (also within the loop), the COLORBOX, DRAWAXIS, and GRFXPRINT or GRFXPRINTF (in the C version) routines are called to fill the screen.

COLORBOX essentially draws a box filled with lines drawn by the LINE routine. LINE is based on the Bresenham algorithm that draws lines without complicated floating point mathematics. Each pixel in the line is drawn with SETPIX.

Because of the way it works, this routine isn't very fast. However, it is intentionally written in the high level language instead of assembly language. Of course, you can rewrite this routine in assembly language. To do so, you need routines for filling areas, drawing circles and polygons, etc. You'll quickly realize that this requires a lot of work. We didn't think that the added performance was worth the extra programming effort, so the C and Pascal LINE routines are suitable for demonstration purposes. In addition to LINE, the GRFXPRINT and GRFXPRINTF functions also use SETPIX. These routines print letters and numbers in graphics modes. Each character is read pixel by pixel from the 8x8 ROM resident font and transferred to video RAM using SETPIX.

Although it's not extremely fast, this program demonstrates how assembler routines can be used in the EGA/VGA 16 color graphics modes. The routines in this demo program serve as a starting point for your own 16 color graphics programs.

Pascal listing: V16COLP.PAS

```
{***********************************************************
*                    V 1 6 C O L P . P A S                 *
**-------------------------------------------------------**
*  Task      : Demonstrates programming in EGA and VGA graphic *
*              modes using 16 colors. This program requires    *
*              the V16COLPA.ASM assembly language module.      *
**-------------------------------------------------------**
*  Author    : MICHAEL TISCHER                             *
*  Developed on : 12/20/90                                 *
*  Last update  : 01/14/91                                 *
***********************************************************}

program V16COLP;

uses dos, crt;

{-- Type declarations ------------------------------------}

type BPTR = ^byte;

{-- External references to the assembler routines --------------------}

{$L v16colpa}                         { Link assembler module }

procedure init640480; external;
procedure init640350; external;
procedure init320200; external;
procedure init640200; external;
procedure setpix( x, y : integer; pcolor : byte ); external;
function getpix( x, y: integer ) : byte ; external;
procedure setpage( page : integer ); external;
procedure showpage( page : integer ); external;

{-- Constants --------------------------------------------}

const A320200 = 1;               { Possible resolutions and modes }
      A640200 = 2;
      A640350 = 3;
      A640480 = 4;

      VMODE   = A640350;         { Specify constants for desired mode }
                                 { here                             }

{-- Type declarations ------------------------------------}

type VCARD = ( EGA, VGA, NEITHERNOR ); { Type of installed video card }

{-- Global variables -------------------------------------}

var MaxX,                        { Maximum X- and Y-coordinates }
    MaxY : integer;
    Pages : byte;                { Number of screen pages }

{***********************************************************
*  IsEgaVga : Determines whether an EGA or a VGA card is installed. *
**-------------------------------------------------------**
*  Input   : None                                         *
*  Output  : TRUE if EGA or VGA card, otherwise FALSE     *
***********************************************************}

function IsEgaVga : VCARD;
```

```
var Regs : Registers;         { Processor registers for interrupt call }

begin
  Regs.AX := $1a00;              { Function 1AH applies only to VGA }
  Intr( $10, Regs );
  if ( Regs.AL = $1a ) then           { Function available? }
    IsEgaVga := VGA
  else
    begin
      Regs.ah := $12;                 { Call function 12h, }
      Regs.bl := $10;                 { sub-function 10h }
      intr($10, Regs);                { Call video BIOS }
      if ( Regs.bl <> $10 ) then IsEgaVga := EGA
                            else IsEgaVga := NEITHERNOR;
    end;
end;

{***********************************************************
*  PrintChar : Writes a character to the screen while in graphic mode.*
**-------------------------------------------------------**
*  Input    :  THECHAR = Character to be written          *
*              X, Y    = X- and Y-coordinates of upper-left corner *
*              FG      = Foreground color                 *
*              BK      = Background color                  *
*  Info     : Character is created in an 8x8 matrix, based on the *
*             8x8 ROM font.                               *
***********************************************************}

procedure PrintChar( thechar : char; x, y : integer; fg, bk : byte );

type FDEF = array[0..255,0..7] of byte;      { Font array }
     TPTR = ^FDEF;                            { Pointer to font }

var Regs  : Registers;              { Registers for interrupt call }
    ch    : char;                   { Individual pixels in character }
    i, k,                           { Loop counter }
    BMask : byte;                   { Bit mask for character design }

const fptr : TPTR = NIL;            { Pointer to font in ROM }

begin
  if fptr = NIL then              { Pointer to font already set? }
    begin                         { No }
      Regs.AH := $11;             { Call video BIOS function 11H, }
      Regs.AL := $30;             { sub-function 30H }
      Regs.BH := 3;               { Get pointer to 8x8 font }
      intr( $10, Regs );
      fptr := ptr( Regs.ES, Regs.BP );      { Set pointers }
    end;

  if ( bk = 255 ) then            { Drawing transparent characters? }
    for i := 0 to 7 do            { Yes --> Set foreground pixels only }
      begin
        BMask := fptr^[ord(thechar),i];  { Get bit pattern for a line }
        for k := 0 to 7 do
          begin
            if ( BMask and 128 <> 0 ) then      { Pixel set? }
              setpix( x+k, y+i, fg );           { Yes }
            BMask := BMask shl 1;
          end;
      end
  else                            { No --> Consider background as well }
    for i := 0 to 7 do                       { Execute lines }
      begin
```

```
  BMask := fptr^[ord(thechar),i];{ Get bit pattern for one line }
  for k := 0 to 7 do
    begin
      if ( BMask and 128 <> 0 ) then          { Foreground? }
        setpix( x+k, y+i, fg )                         { Yes }
      else
        setpix( x+k, y+i, bk );          { No --> Background }
      BMask := BMask shl 1;
    end;
  end;
end;


{************************************************************
* Line: Draws a line based on the Bresenham algorithm.      *
**--------------------------------------------------------**
* Input    : X1, Y1 = Starting coordinates (0 - ...)        *
*            X2, Y2 = Ending coordinates                    *
*            LPCOL  = Color of the line pixels              *
************************************************************}

procedure Line( x1, y1, x2, y2 : integer; lpcol : byte );

var d, dx, dy,
    aincr, bincr,
    xincr, yincr,
    x, y                : integer;

{-- Procedure for swapping two integer variables --------------------}

procedure SwapInt( var i1, i2: integer );

var dummy : integer;

begin
  dummy := i2;
  i2    := i1;
  i1    := dummy;
end;

{-- Main procedure -----------------------------------------------}

begin
  if ( abs(x2-x1) < abs(y2-y1) ) then     { X- or Y-axis overflow? }
    begin                                        { Check Y-axis }
      if ( y1 > y2 ) then                            { y1 > y2? }
        begin
          SwapInt( x1, x2 );            { Yes -->   swap X1 with Y1 }
          SwapInt( y1, y2 );            {            and Y1 with Y2 }
        end;

      if ( x2 > x1 ) then xincr := 1       { Set X-axis increment }
                     else xincr := -1;

      dy := y2 - y1;
      dx := abs( x2-x1 );
      d  := 2 * dx - dy;
      aincr := 2 * (dx - dy);
      bincr := 2 * dx;
      x := x1;
      y := y1;

      setpix( x, y, lpcol );                       { Set first pixel }
      for y:=y1+1 to y2 do               { Execute line on Y-axes }
        begin
```

```
          if ( d >= 0 ) then
            begin
              inc( x, xincr );
              inc( d, aincr );
            end
          else
            inc( d, bincr );
          setpix( x, y, lpcol );
        end;
    end
  else                                           { Check X-axes }
    begin
      if ( x1 > x2 ) then                            { x1 > x2? }
        begin
          SwapInt( x1, x2 );           { Yes --> swap X1 with X2 }
          SwapInt( y1, y2 );           {          and Y1 with Y2 }
        end;

      if ( y2 > y1 ) then yincr := 1        { Set Y-axis increment }
                     else yincr := -1;

      dx := x2 - x1;
      dy := abs( y2-y1 );
      d  := 2 * dy - dx;
      aincr := 2 * (dy - dx);
      bincr := 2 * dy;
      x := x1;
      y := y1;

      setpix( x, y, lpcol );                       { Set first pixel }
      for x:=x1+1 to x2 do              { Execute line on X-axes }
        begin
          if ( d >= 0 ) then
            begin
              inc( y, yincr );
              inc( d, aincr );
            end
          else
            inc( d, bincr );
          setpix( x, y, lpcol );
        end;
    end;
end;


{************************************************************
* GrfxPrint: Displays a formatted string on the graphic screen. *
**--------------------------------------------------------**
* Input    : X, Y  = Starting coordinates (0 - . . . .)     *
*            FG    = Foreground color                       *
*            BK    = Background color (255 = transparent)   *
*            STRING = String with format information        *
************************************************************}

procedure GrfxPrint( x, y : integer; fg, bk : byte; strt : string );

var i : integer;                               { Loop counter }

begin
  for i:=1 to length( strt ) do
    begin
      printchar( strt[i], x, y, fg, bk );   { Display using PrintChar }
      inc( x, 8 );                  { Move X to next character position }
    end;
end;
```

```
{*****************************************************************
* ColorBox: Draws a rectangle and fills it with a line pattern. *
**-------------------------------------------------------------**
* Input   : X1, Y1 = Upper-left coordinates of window          *
*           X2, Y2 = Lower-right coordinates of window          *
*           COLMAX = Greatest color value                       *
* Info    : Line colors are selected in a cycle of 0-COLMAX     *
*****************************************************************}

procedure ColorBox( x1, y1, x2, y2 : integer; colmax : byte );

var x, y,                              { Loop counter }
    sx, sy : integer;                  { Exit point for last color loop }

begin
  Line( x1, y1, x1, y2, 15 );                  { Draw border }
  Line( x1, y2, x2, y2, 15 );
  Line( x2, y2, x2, y1, 15 );
  Line( x2, y1, x1, y1, 15 );

  for y := y2-1 downto y1+1 do         { Bottom left to right border }
    Line( x1+1, y2-1, x2-1, y, y mod colmax );

  for y := y2-1 downto y1+1 do         { Bottom right to left border }
    Line( x2-1, y2-1, x1+1, y, y mod colmax );

  {-- From center of box to top border --------------------------------}

  sx := x1+ (x2-x1) div 2;
  sy := y1+ (y2-y1) div 2;
  for x := x1+1 to x2-1 do
    Line( sx, sy, x, y1+1, x mod colmax );
end;

{*****************************************************************
* DrawAxis: Draws axes from left and top borders on the screen. *
**-------------------------------------------------------------**
* Input   : STEPX = Increment for X-axis                        *
*           STEPY = Increment for Y-axis                        *
*           FG    = Foreground color                            *
*           BK    = Background color (255 = transparent)        *
*****************************************************************}

procedure DrawAxis( stepx, stepy : integer; fg, bk : byte );

var x, y    : integer;                 { Loop coordinates }
    ordinate : string[3];

begin
  Line( 0, 0, MAXX, 0, fg );                   { Draw X-axis }
  Line( 0, 0, 0, MAXY, fg );                   { Draw Y-axis }

  x := stepx;                                  { Scale X-axis }
  while ( x < MAXX ) do
    begin
      Line( x, 0, x, 5, fg );
      str( x, ordinate );
      if ( x < 100 ) then
        GrfxPrint( x - 8 , 8, fg, bk, ordinate )
      else
        GrfxPrint( x - 12, 8, fg, bk, ordinate );
      inc( x, stepx );
    end;
```

```
      y := stepy;                              { Scale Y-axis }
  while ( y < MAXY ) do
    begin
      Line( 0, y, 5, y, fg );
      str( y:3, ordinate );
      GrfxPrint( 8, y-4, fg, bk, ordinate );
      inc( y, stepy );
    end;
end;

{*****************************************************************
* Demo: Demonstrates the functions and procedures in this module. *
**-------------------------------------------------------------**
* Input   : None                                               *
*****************************************************************}

procedure Demo;

const PAUSE = 100;                 { Pause counter in milliseconds }

var pgcount : byte;                            { Page counter }

begin
  for pgcount := 1 to Pages do
    begin
      setpage( pgcount-1 );                    { Process page }
      showpage( pgcount-1 );                   { Process page }
      ColorBox( 50+pgcount*2, 40, MaxX-50+pgcount*2, MaxY-40, 16 );
      DrawAxis( 30, 20, 15, 255 );             { Draw axes }
      GrfxPrint( 46, MAXY-10, 15, 255,
                 'V16COLP  - (c) by Michael Tischer' );
    end;

  {-- Display graphic pages in sequences --------------------------}

  for pgcount := 0 to 50 do                    { 50 executions }
    begin
      showpage( pgcount mod Pages );           { Display page }
      delay( PAUSE );                          { Brief pause }
    end;
end;

{-------------------------------------------------------------------}
{--             M A I N   P R O G R A M                         ---}
{-------------------------------------------------------------------}

begin
  writeln( 'V16COLP.PAS  - (c) 1992 by Michael Tischer'#13#10 );
  if ( VMODE = A640480 ) then              { VGA mode selected? }
    begin
      if ( IsEgaVga <> VGA ) then          { VGA card installed? }
        begin                              { No }
          writeln( 'This program requires a VGA card');
          exit;                            { End program }
        end
      else             { Yes --> initialize mode and set parameters }
        begin                              { 640x480 pixels }
          MaxX := 639;
          MaxY := 479;
          Pages := 1;
          init640480;
        end;
    end
```

```
else                          { Must be one of the EGA modes }
begin
  if ( IsEgaVga = NEITHERNOR ) then    { No EGA or VGA card? }
    begin                                          { No }
      writeln( 'This program requires an EGA card');
      exit;                             { End program }
    end
  else              { Yes --> initialize mode and set parameters }
    case VMODE of
      A320200 : begin                { 320x200 pixels }
                  MaxX := 319;
                  MaxY := 199;
                  Pages := 8;
                  init320200;
                end;
      A640200 : begin                { 640x200 pixels }
                  MaxX := 639;
                  MaxY := 199;
                  Pages := 4;
                  init640200;
                end;
      A640350 : begin                { 640x350 pixels }
                  MaxX := 639;
                  MaxY := 349;
                  Pages := 2;
                  init640350;
                end;
    end;
  end;

Demo;                             { Execute demo }
repeat until keypressed;          { wait for key }
Textmode( C080 );                 { Shift into text mode }
end.
```

Assembler listing: V16COLPA.ASM

```
;****************************************************************;
;*                    V 1 6 C O L P A . A S M               *;
;*------------------------------------------------------------*;
;*   Task        : Contains various routines for operating in *;
;*                 EGA and VGA graphics mode in 16 colors     *;
;*------------------------------------------------------------*;
;*   Author      : MICHAEL TISCHER                            *;
;*   Developed on : 12/05/90                                  *;
;*   Last update  : 01/14/92                                  *;
;*------------------------------------------------------------*;
;*   Assembly    : MASM V16COLPA.ASM; or TASM V16COLPA.ASM    *;
;****************************************************************;

;== Constants ================================================

SC_INDEX      = 3c4h        ;Index register for sequencer ctrl.
SC_MAP_MASK   = 2           ;Number of map mask register
SC_MEM_MODE   = 4           ;Number of memory mode register

GC_INDEX      = 3ceh        ;Index register for graphics ctrl.
GC_FN_SELECT  = 3           ;Number of function select reg.
GC_READ_MAP   = 4           ;Number of read map register
GC_GRAPH_MODE = 5           ;Number of graphics mode register
GC_MISCELL    = 6           ;Number of miscellaneous register
GC_BIT_MASK   = 8           ;Number of bit mask register

CRTC_INDEX    = 3d4h        ;Index register for CRT controller
CC_MAX_SCAN   = 9           ;Number of maximum scan line reg.
CC_START_HI   = 0Ch         ;Number of high start register
CC_UNDERLINE  = 14h         ;Number of underline register
CC_MODE_CTRL  = 17h         ;Number of mode control register

DAC_WRITE_ADR = 3C8h        ;DAC write address
DAC_READ_ADR  = 3C7h        ;DAC read address
DAC_DATA      = 3C9h        ;DAC data register

VERT_RESCAN   = 3DAh        ;Input status register #1

;== Data segment =============================================

DATA    segment word public    ;Must be initialized during runtime

vio_seg   dw (?)            ;Video segment with current page
lnwidth   dw (?)            ;Width of a pixel line in bytes
pageofs   dw (?)            ;Page offset in the segment address

DATA    ends

;== Program ==================================================

CODE    segment byte public    ;Program segment

        assume cs:code, ds:data

;-- Public declarations --------------------------------------

public   init640480          ;Initialize 640x480 mode
public   init640350          ;Initialize 640x350 mode
public   init640200          ;Initialize 640x200 mode
public   init320200          ;Initialize 320x200 mode
public   setpix              ;Set pixel
public   getpix              ;Get pixel color
```

```
public    showpage              ;Display page O or 1
public    setpage               ;Set page for setpix and getpix

;-----------------------------------------------------------------
;-- INIT640350: Initializes 640x350 EGA graphics mode for 16 colors
;-- Call from TP:  init640350;

init640350 proc near

          mov    al,10h         ;Set mode 10H
          mov    cx,28000 / 16  ;Page offset

init16:   mov    bx,640/8        ;Line width

init:     mov    lnwidth,bx     ;Save line width
          mov    pageofs,cx     ;Store page offset for segment addr.

          xor    ah,ah          ;Call function OOH for setting
          int    10h            ;mode

          mov    vio_seg,0A000h ;Set segment address of video RAM
          ret                   ;Return to caller

init640350 endp                 ;End of procedure

;-----------------------------------------------------------------
;-- INIT640480: Initializes 640x480 VGA graphics mode with 16 colors
;-- Call from TP:  init640480;

init640480 proc near

          mov    al,12h         ;Set mode 12H

          ;-- Page offset unimportant, since only one page
          ;-- can be displayed

          jmp    init16

init640480 endp                 ;End of procedure

;-----------------------------------------------------------------
;-- INIT640200: Initializes 640x200 EGA graphics mode with 16 colors
;-- Call from TP:  init640200;

init640200 proc near

          mov    al,OEh         ;Set OEH mode
          mov    bx,640/8        ;Line width
          mov    cx,( 64000 / 4 ) / 16 ;Page offset
          jmp    init16

init640200 endp                 ;End of procedure

;-----------------------------------------------------------------
;-- INIT320200: Initializes 320*200 pixel mode
;-- Call from TP: init320200;

init320200 proc near

          mov    al,ODh         ;Set ODH mode
          mov    bx,320/8        ;Line width
          mov    cx,( 32000 / 4 ) / 16 ;Page offset
          jmp    init
```

```
init320200 endp                 ;End of procedure

;-----------------------------------------------------------------
;-- SETPIX: Changes a pixel to a certain color
;-- Call from TP: setpix( x , y : integer; pcolor : byte );

setpix    proc near

sframe    struc                 ;Structure for stack access
bpO       dw ?                  ;Gets BP
ret_adrO  dw ?                  ;Return address to caller
pcolor    dw ?                  ;Color
yO        dw ?                  ;Y-coordinate
xO        dw ?                  ;X-coordinate
sframe    ends                  ;End of structure

frame     equ [ bp - bpO ]      ;Addresses structure elements

          push   bp             ;Prepare for addressing
          mov    bp,sp          ; through BP register

          ;-- First compute offset in video RAM and shift value ------

          mov    ax,frame.yO    ;Load Y-coordinate
          mov    dx,lnwidth     ;Multiply by line width
          mul    dx
          mov    bx,frame.xO    ;Load X-coordinate
          mov    cl,bl          ;Store Lo byte for shift calculation

          shr    bx,1           ;Divide X-coordinates by eight
          shr    bx,1
          shr    bx,1
          add    bx,ax          ;add offset from multiplication to it

          and    cl,7           ;Compute bit mask from X-coordinates
          xor    cl,7
          mov    ah,1
          shl    ah,cl

          mov    dx,GC_INDEX    ;Access to graphics controller
          mov    al,GC_BIT_MASK ;Write bit mask to bit mask
          out    dx,ax          ;register

          mov    ax,(02h shl 8) + GC_GRAPH_MODE;Set write mode 2 &
          out    dx,ax                        ;read mode O

          mov    ax,vio_seg     ;Set ES to video RAM
          mov    es,ax          ;

          mov    al,es:[bx]        ;Load latch register
          mov    al,byte ptr frame.pcolor ;Load pixel color and
          mov    es:[bx],al        ;write back to latch reg.

          ;-- Set default values in various registers of the graphics
          ;-- controller that have been changed

          mov    ax,(OFFh shl 8 ) + GC_BIT_MASK
          out    dx,ax

          mov    ax,(OOh shl 8) + GC_GRAPH_MODE
          out    dx,ax

          pop    bp
          ret    6              ;Return to caller, remove
```

```
                          ;arguments from stack

setpix    endp            ;End of procedure


;-------------------------------------------------------------------
;-- GETPIX: Returns a pixel color
;-- Call from TP: x := getpix( x , y : integer );

getpix    proc near

sframe1   struc           ;Structure for stack access
bp1       dw ?            ;Gets BP
ret_adr1  dw ?            ;Return address to caller
y1        dw ?            ;Y-coordinate
x1        dw ?            ;X-coordinate
sframe1   ends            ;End of structure

frame     equ [ bp - bp1 ]   ;Addresses structure elements

          push bp         ;Prepare for parameter addressing
          mov  bp,sp      ; through BP register

          ;-- First compute offset in video RAM and shift value ------

          mov  ax,frame.y1    ;Load Y-coordinates
          mov  dx,lnwidth     ;multiply times line width
          mul  dx
          mov  si,frame.x1    ;Load X-coordinates
          mov  cx,si          ;Store shift calculation

          shr  si,1           ;Divide X-coordinate by eight
          shr  si,1
          shr  si,1
          add  si,ax          ;Add offset from multiplication to it

          and  cl,7           ;Compute bit mask from X-coordinate
          xor  cl,7
          mov  ch,1
          shl  ch,cl

          mov  ax,vio_seg     ;Set ES to video RAM
          mov  es,ax          ;

          mov  dx,GC_INDEX    ;Load graphics controller index
          mov  ax,(3 shl 8)+ GC_READ_MAP   ;First read
          xor  bl,bl                       ;plane #3

gp1:      out  dx,ax          ;Load read map register
          mov  bh,es:[si]     ;Load value from latch register
          and  bh,ch          ;Leave only desired pixels
          neg  bh             ;Set bit 7 according to pixel
          rol  bx,1           ;Rotate bit 7 from BH to bit 1 in BL

          dec  ah             ;Process next bitplane
          jge  gp1            ;>= 0? --> Continue

          mov  al,bl          ;Function result to AL

          pop  bp
          ret  4              ;Return to caller, remove
                              ;arguments from stack

getpix    endp            ;End of procedure
```

```
;-------------------------------------------------------------------
;-- SETPAGE: Sets page for access from setpix and getpix
;-- Call from TP: setpage( page : byte );

setpage   proc near

          pop  cx         ;Pop return address from stack
          pop  ax         ;Pop argument from stack

          push cx         ;Push return address back
          mul  pageofs    ;Multiply page number by page offset

          add  ax,0A000h  ;Add base segment address to it.
          mov  vio_seg,ax ;Store new segment address

          ret             ;Return to caller, argument already
                          ;removed from stack

setpage   endp            ;End of procedure

;-------------------------------------------------------------------
;-- SHOWPAGE: Display one of the two screen pages
;-- Call from TP: showpage( page : byte );

showpage  proc near

          pop  cx         ;Pop return address from stack
          pop  ax         ;Pop argument from stack

          push cx         ;Push only return address
          mul  pageofs    ;Multiply page number by page offset
          mov  cl,4       ;Multiply all of it by 16
          shl  ax,cl

          mov  bl,al      ;Store Lo byte

          mov  dx,CRTC_INDEX   ;Address CRT controller
          mov  al,CC_START_HI  ;Move register number
          out  dx,ax
          inc  al              ;Now output Lo byte
          mov  ah,bl
          out  dx,ax

          ;-- Wait to return to starting screen design ---------------

          mov  dx,VERT_RESCAN  ;Wait for end of
sp3:      in   al,dx           ;vertical rescan
          test al,8
          jne  sp3

sp4:      in   al,dx           ;Go to start of rescan
          test al,8
          je   sp4

          ret                  ;Return to caller

showpage  endp            ;End of procedure

;== End =========================================================

CODE      ends            ;End of code segment
          end             ;End of program
```

C listing: V16COLC.C

```
/*********************************************************************
*                      V 1 6 C O L C . C                            *
**-----------------------------------------------------------------**
*  Task          : Demonstrates programming in EGA and VGA graphic  *
*                  modes using 16 colors. This program requires     *
*                  the V16COLCA.ASM assembly language module.       *
**-----------------------------------------------------------------**
*  Author        : Michael Tischer                                  *
*  Developed on  : 12/20/90                                         *
*  Last update   : 02/29/92                                         *
**-----------------------------------------------------------------**
*  Memory model  : SMALL                                            *
**-----------------------------------------------------------------**
*  (MICROSOFT C)                                                    *
*  Compilation   : CL /AS /c /WO v16colc.c                          *
*                  LINK v16colc.c v16colca;                         *
**-----------------------------------------------------------------**
*  (BORLAND TURBO C)                                                *
*  Compilation   : Create a project file containing the following:  *
*                     v16colc.c                                     *
*                     v16colca.obj                                  *
**-----------------------------------------------------------------**
*  Call          : v16colc                                          *
**-----------------------------------------------------------------**
*  Info          : Turbo C warning "Unreachable code ... " is not   *
*                  an error.                                         *
*********************************************************************/

#include <dos.h>
#include <stdarg.h>
#include <stdlib.h>
#include <io.h>
#include <stdio.h>
#include <conio.h>

/*-- Type declarations --------------------------------------------*/

typedef unsigned char BYTE;

/*-- External references to the assembler routines ---------------*/

extern void init320200( void );
extern void init640480( void );
extern void init640350( void );
extern void init640200( void );
extern void setpix( int x, int y, unsigned char pcolor);
extern BYTE getpix( int x, int y );
extern void setpage( int page );
extern void showpage( int page );
extern void far * getfontptr( void );

/*-- Constants ----------------------------------------------------*/

#define A320200  1            /* Possible resolutions and modes */
#define A640200  2
#define A640350  3
#define A640480  4

#define VMODE    A640350      /* Specify constants for desired mode */

#define EGA      0
#define VGA      1            /* Card types */
```

```
#define NEITHERNOR 2

/*- Global variables ----------------------------------------------*/

int  MaxX,                    /* Maximum X- and Y-coordinates */
     MaxY;
BYTE Pages;                   /* Number of screen pages */

/*********************************************************************
*  IsEgaVga : Determines whether an EGA or a VGA card is installed.  *
**-----------------------------------------------------------------**
*  Input   : None                                                   *
*  Output  : EGA, VGA or NEITHERNOR                                 *
*********************************************************************/

BYTE IsEgaVga( void )
{
 union REGS Regs;         /* Processor registers for interrupt call */

 Regs.x.ax = 0x1a00;             /* Function 1AH applies only to VGA */
 int86( 0x10, &Regs, &Regs );
 if ( Regs.h.al == 0x1a )            /* Funotion available? */
  return VGA;
 else
  {
   Regs.h.ah = 0x12;                 /* Call function 12H, */
   Regs.h.bl = 0x10;                 /* sub-function 10H */
   int86(0x10, &Regs, &Regs );       /* Call video BIOS */
   return (BYTE) (( Regs.h.bl != 0x10 ) ? EGA : NEITHERNOR);
  }
}


/*********************************************************************
*  PrintChar : Writes a character to the screen while in graphic mode.*
**-----------------------------------------------------------------**
*  Input   :   THECHAR = Character to be written                    *
*              X, Y    = X- and Y-coordinates of upper-left corner  *
*              FG      = Foreground color                           *
*              BK      = Background color                           *
*  Info    : Character is created in an 8x8 matrix, based on the    *
*            8x8 ROM font.                                          *
*********************************************************************/

void PrintChar( char thechar, int x, int y, BYTE fg, BYTE bk )
{
 typedef BYTE FDEF[256][8];                   /* Font array */
 typedef FDEF far *TPTR;                       /* Pointer to font */

 BYTE        i, k,                             /* Loop counter */
             BMask;              /* Bit mask for character design */

 static TPTR fptr = (TPTR) 0;        /* Pointer to font in ROM */

 if ( fptr == (TPTR) 0 )             /* Pointer to font already set? */
  fptr = getfontptr();              /* No --> Use assembler function */

 /*- Draw character pixel by pixel ------------------------------*/

 if ( bk == 255 )               /* Drawing transparent characters? */
  for ( i = 0; i < 8; ++i )     /* Yes --> Set foreground pixels only */
   {
    BMask = (*fptr)[thechar][i];     /* Get bit pattern for a line */
    for ( k = 0; k < 8; ++k, BMask <<= 1 )      /* Execute columns */
     if ( BMask & 128 )                          /* Pixel set? */
```

```
        setpix( x+k, y+i, fg );                        /* Yes */
      }
    else                                     /* No --> Set every pixel */
      for ( i = 0;  i < 8;  ++i )                       /* Execute lines */
      {
        BMask = (*fptr)[thechar][i];     /* Get bit pattern for one line */
        for ( k = 0;  k < 8;  ++k, BMask <<= 1 )         /* Execute columns */
          setpix( x+k, y+i, ( BMask & 128 ) ? fg : bk );
      }
  }


/*******************************************************************
 * Line: Draws a line based on the Bresenham algorithm.           *
 **---------------------------------------------------------------**
 * Input   : X1, Y1 = Starting coordinates (0 - ...)              *
 *           X2, Y2 = Ending coordinates                          *
 *           LPCOL  = Color of the line pixels                    *
 *******************************************************************/

/*-- Function for swapping two integer variables --------------------*/

void SwapInt( int *i1, int *i2 )
{
  int dummy;

  dummy = *i2;
  *i2   = *i1;
  *i1   = dummy;
}

/*-- Main section of function ---------------------------------*/

void Line( int x1, int y1, int x2, int y2, BYTE lpcol )
{
  int d, dx, dy,
      aincr, bincr,
      xincr, yincr,
      x, y;

  if ( abs(x2-x1) < abs(y2-y1) )            /* X- or Y-axis overflow? */
  {                                          /* Check Y-axes */
    if ( y1 > y2 )                           /* y1 > y2? */
    {
      SwapInt( &x1, &x2 );                  /* Yes --> Swap X1 with X2 */
      SwapInt( &y1, &y2 );                  /*         and Y1 with Y2  */
    }

    xincr = ( x2 > x1 ) ?  1 : -1;          /* Set X-axis increment */

    dy = y2 - y1;
    dx = abs( x2-x1 );
    d  = 2 * dx - dy;
    aincr = 2 * (dx - dy);
    bincr = 2 * dx;
    x = x1;
    y = y1;

    setpix( x, y, lpcol );                   /* Set first pixel */
    for (y=y1+1; y<= y2; ++y )              /* Execute line on Y-axes */
    {
      if ( d >= 0 )
      {
        x += xincr;
        d += aincr;
```

```
      }
    else
      d += bincr;
      setpix(x, y, lpcol);
    }
  }
else                                     /* Check X-axes */
  {
    if ( x1 > x2 )                           /* x1 > x2? */
    {
      SwapInt( &x1, &x2 );                  /* Yes --> Swap X1 with X2 */
      SwapInt( &y1, &y2 );                  /*         and Y1 with Y2  */
    }

    yincr = ( y2 > y1 ) ? 1 : -1;           /* Set Y-axis increment */

    dx = x2 - x1;
    dy = abs( y2-y1 );
    d  = 2 * dy - dx;
    aincr = 2 * (dy - dx);
    bincr = 2 * dy;
    x = x1;
    y = y1;

    setpix(x, y, lpcol);                     /* Set first pixel */
    for (x=x1+1; x<=x2; ++x )               /* Execute line on X-axes */
    {
      if ( d >= 0 )
      {
        y += yincr;
        d += aincr;
      }
    else
      d += bincr;
      setpix(x, y, lpcol);
    }
  }
}

/*******************************************************************
 * GrfxPrintf: Displays a formatted string on the graphic screen. *
 **---------------------------------------------------------------**
 * Input   : X, Y   = Starting coordinates (0 - ...)              *
 *           FG     = Foreground color                            *
 *           BK     = Background color (255 = transparent)        *
 *           STRING = String with format information              *
 *           ...    = Arguments are similar to printf             *
 *******************************************************************/

void GrfxPrintf( int x, int y, BYTE fg, BYTE bk, char * string, ... )
{
  va_list parameter;                  /* Parameter list for VA_... macros */
  char stngbuf[255],                  /* Buffer for formatted string */
       *cp;

  va_start( parameter, string );                /* Convert parameters */
  vsprintf( stngbuf, string, parameter );       /* Format */
  for ( cp = stngbuf; *cp; ++cp, x+= 8 )   /* Display formatted */
    PrintChar( *cp, x, y, fg, bk );        /* string using PrintChar */
}

/*******************************************************************
 * ColorBox: Draws a rectangle and fills it with a line pattern.  *
 **---------------------------------------------------------------**
```

```
 *  Input    : X1, Y1 = Upper-left coordinates of window       *
 *             X2, Y2 = Lower-right coordinates of window       *
 *             COLMAX = Greatest color value                    *
 *  Info     : Line colors are selected in a cycle of 0-COLMAX  *
 *************************************************************/

void ColorBox( int x1, int y1, int x2, int y2, int colmax )
{
 int x, y,                              /* Loop variables */
     sx, sy;                            /* Exit point for last color loop */

 Line( x1, y1, x1, y2, 15 );                    /* Draw border */
 Line( x1, y2, x2, y2, 15 );
 Line( x2, y2, x2, y1, 15 );
 Line( x2, y1, x1, y1, 15 );

 for ( y = y2-1; y > y1; --y )          /* Bottom left to right border */
  Line( x1+1, y2-1, x2-1, y, (BYTE) (y % colmax) );

 for ( y = y2-1; y > y1; --y )          /* Bottom right to left border */
  Line( x2-1, y2-1, x1+1, y, (BYTE) (y % colmax) );

 /*-- From center of box to top border -------------------------------*/

 for ( x=x1+1, sx=x1+(x2-x1)/2, sy=y1+(y2-y1)/ 2; x < x2; ++x )
  Line( sx, sy, x, y1+1, (BYTE) (x % colmax) );
}


/*************************************************************
 *  DrawAxis: Draws axes from left and top borders on the screen.  *
 **-----------------------------------------------------------**
 *  Input    : XSTEP = Increment for X-axis                     *
 *             YSTEP = Increment for Y-axis                     *
 *             FG    = Foreground color                         *
 *             BK    = Background color (255 = transparent)     *
 *************************************************************/

void DrawAxis( int stepx, int stepy, BYTE fg, BYTE bk )
{
 int x, y;                              /* Loop coordinates */

 Line( 0, 0, MaxX, 0, fg );                     /* Draw X-axis */
 Line( 0, 0, 0, MaxY, fg );                     /* Draw Y-axis */

 for ( x = stepx; x < MaxX; x += stepx )        /* Scale X-axis */
  {
   Line( x, 0, x, 5, fg );
   GrfxPrintf( x < 100 ? x - 8 : x - 12, 8, fg, bk, "%d", x );
  }

 for ( y = stepy; y < MaxY; y += stepy )        /* Scale Y-axis */
  {
   Line( 0, y, 5, y, fg );
   GrfxPrintf( 8, y-4, fg, bk, "%3d", y );
  }
}


/*************************************************************
 *  Demo: Demonstrates the functions and procedures in this module.  *
 *************************************************************/

void Demo( void )
{
#define PAUSE 100000          /* Pause counter - varies with system */
```

```
 int x;                                 /* Coordinate counter */
 BYTE pgcount;                          /* Page counter */
 long delay;                            /* Pause counter */

 for ( pgcount = 1; pgcount <= Pages; ++pgcount )
  {
   setpage( pgcount-1 );                        /* Process page */
   showpage( pgcount-1 );                       /* Process page */
   ColorBox( 50+pgcount*2, 40, MaxX-50+pgcount*2, MaxY-40, 16 );
   DrawAxis( 30, 20, 15, 255 );                 /* Draw axes */
   GrfxPrintf( 46, MaxY-10, 15, 255,
               "V16COLC  -  (c) by Michael Tischer" );
  }

 /*-- Display graphic pages in sequences --------------------------*/

 for ( x = 0; x < 50; ++x )                      /* 50 executions */
  {
   showpage( x % Pages );                       /* Display page */
   for ( delay = 1; delay < PAUSE; ++delay )    /* Brief pause */
    ;
  }
}


/*************************************************************
 /***            M A I N   P R O G R A M            ***/
 /*************************************************************/

void main( void )
{
 union REGS regs;

 printf( "V16COLC.C  -  (c) 1990, 92 by Michael Tischer\n\n" );
 if ( VMODE == A640480 )                /* VGA mode selected? */
  {                                             /* Yes */
   if ( IsEgaVga() != VGA )             /* VGA card installed? */
    {                                           /* No */
     printf( "This program requires VGA 640x480 mode\n" );
     exit(1);                                   /* End program */
    }
   else                 /* Yes --> Initialize mode and set parameters */
    {
     MaxX = 639;
     MaxY = 479;
     Pages = 1;
     init640480();
    }
  }
 else                                   /* Must be in an EGA mode */
  {
   if ( IsEgaVga() == NEITHERNOR )      /* Neither EGA nor VGA card? */
    {                                           /* No */
     printf( "This program requires an EGA or a VGA card\n" );
     exit(1);                                   /* End program */
    }
   else                 /* Yes --> Initialize mode and set parameters */
    switch( VMODE )
     {
      case A320200 : {                          /* 320x200 pixels */
               MaxX = 319;
               MaxY = 199;
               Pages = 8;
               init320200();
```

```
                break;
                }
      case A640200 : {                          /* 640x200 pixels */
                MaxX = 639;
                MaxY = 199;
                Pages = 4;
                init640200();
                break;
                }
      case A640350 : {                          /* 640x350 pixels */
                MaxX = 639;
                MaxY = 349;
                Pages = 2;
                init640350();
                }
      }
  }

  Demo();
  getch();                                   /* Wait for a key */
  regs.x.ax = 0x0003;                        /* Shift into text mode */
  int86( 0x10, &regs, &regs );
}
```

Assembler listing: **V16COLCA.ASM**

```asm
;****************************************************************;
;*                                                            *;
;*                 V 1 6 C O L C A . A S M                     *;
;*------------------------------------------------------------*;
;*   Task        : Contains various routines for operating in *;
;*                 EGA and VGA graphics modes in 16 colors.   *;
;*------------------------------------------------------------*;
;*   Author      : Michael Tischer                            *;
;*   Developed on : 12/05/90                                  *;
;*   Last update : 02/27/92                                   *;
;*------------------------------------------------------------*;
;*   Memory model : SMALL                                     *;
;*------------------------------------------------------------*;
;*   Assembly    : MASM /mx V16COLCA.ASM;  or  TASM -mx V16COLCA *;
;****************************************************************;


IGROUP group _text               ;Program segment
DGROUP group const,_bss, _data    ;Data segment
       assume CS:IGROUP, DS:DGROUP, ES:DGROUP, SS:DGROUP


CONST  segment word public 'CONST';Readable constants
CONST  ends


_BSS   segment word public 'BSS'  ;Un-initialized static variables
_BSS   ends


_DATA  segment word public 'DATA' ;Initialized global and static vars.

_DATA  ends


;== Constants =============================================================


SC_INDEX       = 3c4h            ;Index register for sequencer ctrl.
SC_MAP_MASK    = 2               ;Number of map mask register
SC_MEM_MODE    = 4               ;Number of memory mode register


GC_INDEX       = 3ceh            ;Index register for graphics ctrl.
GC_FN_SELECT   = 3               ;Number of function select reg.
GC_READ_MAP    = 4               ;Number of read map register
GC_GRAPH_MODE  = 5               ;Number of graphics mode register
GC_MISCELL     = 6               ;Number of miscellaneous register
GC_BIT_MASK    = 8               ;Number of bit mask register


CRTC_INDEX     = 3d4h            ;Index register for CRT controller
CC_MAX_SCAN    = 9               ;Number of maximum scan line reg.
CC_START_HI    = 0Ch             ;Number of high start register
CC_UNDERLINE   = 14h             ;Number of underline register
CC_MODE_CTRL   = 17h             ;Number of mode control register


DAC_WRITE_ADR  = 3C8h            ;DAC write address
DAC_READ_ADR   = 3C7h            ;DAC read address
DAC_DATA       = 3C9h            ;DAC data register


VERT_RESCAN    = 3DAh            ;Input status register #1


PIXX           = 640             ;Horizontal resolution


;== Data ==================================================================


_DATA  segment word public 'DATA'


vio_seg   dw 0A000h              ;Video segment with current page
lnwidth   dw 0                   ;Width of a pixel line in bytes
```

```
pageofs   dw 0                ;Page offset in the segment address

_DATA ends

;== Program ========================================================

_TEXT  segment byte public 'CODE' ;Program segment

;-- Public declarations -----------------------------------------

public  _init640350         ;Initialize 640x350 mode
public  _init640480         ;Initialize 640x480 mode
public  _init640200         ;Initialize 640x200 mode
public  _init320200         ;Initialize 320x200 mode
public  _setpix             ;Set pixel
public  _getpix             ;Get pixel color
public  _showpage           ;Display page 0 or 1
public  _setpage            ;Set page for setpix or getpix
public  _getfontptr         ;Get pointer to 8x8 font

;-----------------------------------------------------------------
;-- INIT640350: Initializes 640x350 EGA graphics mode with 16 colors.
;-- Declaration : void init640350( void );

_init640350 proc near

        mov   al,10h         ;Set mode 10H
        mov   cx,28000 / 16  ;Page offset

init16: mov   bx,640/8       ;Line width

init:   mov   lnwidth,bx     ;Save line width
        mov   pageofs,cx     ;Store page offset for segment addr.

        xor   ah,ah          ;Call function 00H for setting
        int   10h            ;mode

        ret                  ;Return to caller

_init640350 endp            ;End of procedure

;-----------------------------------------------------------------
;-- INIT640480: Initializes 640x480 VGA graphics mode with 16 colors.
;-- Declaration : void init640480( void );

_init640480 proc near

        mov   al,12h         ;Set mode 12H

        ;-- Page offset unimportant, since only one page
        ;-- can be displayed

        jmp   init16

_init640480 endp            ;End of procedure

;-----------------------------------------------------------------
;-- INIT640200: Initializes 640x200 EGA graphics mode with 16 colors.
;-- Declaration : void init640200( void );

_init640200 proc near

        mov   al,0Eh         ;Set mode 0EH
        mov   cx,( 64000 / 4 ) / 16 ;Page offset
```

```
        jmp   init16

_init640200 endp            ;End of procedure

;-----------------------------------------------------------------
;-- INIT320200: Initializes 320x200 EGA graphics mode with 16 colors.
;-- Declaration : void init320200( void );

_init320200 proc near

        mov   al,0Dh         ;Set mode 0DH
        mov   bx,320/8       ;Line width
        mov   cx,( 32000 / 4 ) / 16 ;Page offset
        jmp   init

_init320200 endp            ;End of procedure

;-- SETPIX: Changes a pixel to a certain color -----------------------
;-- Declaration : void setpix( int x, int y, unsigned char pcolor );

_setpix   proc near

sframe    struc              ;Structure for stack access
bp0       dw ?               ;Gets BP
ret_adr0  dw ?               ;Return address to caller
x0        dw ?               ;X-coordinate
y0        dw ?               ;Y-coordinate
pcolor    dw ?               ;Color
sframe    ends               ;End of structure

frame     equ [ bp - bp0 ]   ;Addresses structure elements

        push  bp             ;Prepare for addressing
        mov   bp,sp          ; through BP register

        ;-- First compute offset in video RAM and shift value ------

        mov   ax,frame.y0    ;Load Y-coordinate
        mov   dx,lnwidth     ;Multiply by line width
        mul   dx
        mov   bx,frame.x0    ;Load X-coordinate
        mov   cl,bl          ;Store low byte for shift calculation

        shr   bx,1           ;Divide X-coordinate by eight
        shr   bx,1
        shr   bx,1
        add   bx,ax          ;Add offset from multiplication

        and   cl,7           ;Compute bit mask from X-coordinates
        xor   cl,7
        mov   ah,1
        shl   ah,cl

        mov   dx,GC_INDEX    ;Access to graphics controller
        mov   al,GC_BIT_MASK ;Write bit mask to bit mask
        out   dx,ax          ;register

        mov   ax,(02h shl 8) + GC_GRAPH_MODE;Set write mode 2 &
        out   dx,ax                        ;read mode 0

        mov   ax,vio_seg     ;Set ES to video RAM
        mov   es,ax
```

```
        mov   al,es:[bx]              ;Load latch register
        mov   al,byte ptr frame.pcolor ;Load pixel color and
        mov   es:[bx],al             ;write back to latch register


        ;-- Set default values in various registers of the graphics
        ;-- controller that have been changed

        mov   ax,(0FFh shl 8 ) + GC_BIT_MASK
        out   dx,ax

        mov   ax,(00h shl 8) + GC_GRAPH_MODE
        out   dx,ax


        pop   bp
        ret                          ;Return to caller

_setpix endp                         ;End of procedure


;-- GETPIX: Returns a pixel color -------------------------------------
;-- Declaration : unsigned char getpix( int x, int y );


_getpix proc near

sframe1  struc                       ;Structure for stack access
bp1      dw ?                        ;Gets BP
ret_adr1 dw ?                        ;Return address to caller
x1       dw ?                        ;X-coordinate
y1       dw ?                        ;Y-coordinate
sframe1  ends                        ;End of structure

frame    equ [ bp - bp1 ]           ;Addresses structure elements

        push  bp                     ;Prepare for addressing
        mov   bp,sp                  ; through BP register


        push  si

        ;-- First compute offset in video RAM and shift value ------

        mov   ax,frame.y1            ;Load Y-coordinate
        mov   dx,lnwidth             ;Multiple by line width
        mul   dx
        mov   si,frame.x1            ;Load X-coordinate
        mov   cx,si                  ;Store shift calculation

        shr   si,1                   ;Divide X-coordinate by eight
        shr   si,1
        shr   si,1
        add   si,ax                  ;Add offset from multiplication

        and   cl,7                   ;Compute bit mask from X-coordinate
        xor   cl,7
        mov   ch,1
        shl   ch,cl

        mov   ax,vio_seg             ;Set ES to video RAM
        mov   es,ax

        mov   dx,GC_INDEX            ;Access to graphics controller
        mov   ax,(3 shl 8)+ GC_READ_MAP   ;Read plane #3
        xor   bl,bl                  ;first
gp1:    out   dx,ax                  ;Load read map register
        mov   bh,es:[si]             ;Load value from latch register
```

```
        and   bh,ch                  ;Leave only desired pixels
        neg   bh                     ;Set bit 7 according to pixel
        rol   bx,1                   ;Rotate bit 7 from BH to bit 1 in BL

        dec   ah                     ;Process next bitplane
        jge   gp1                    ;>= 0? --> Continue

        mov   al,bl                  ;Function result to AL

        pop   si
        pop   bp
        ret                          ;Return to caller

_getpix endp                         ;End of procedure

;-- SETPAGE: Sets page for access from setpix and getpix --------------
;-- Declaration : void setpage( int page );

_setpage  proc near

        pop   cx                     ;Pop return address from stack
        pop   ax                     ;Pop argument from stack

        push  ax                     ;Push these onto stack
        push  cx

        mul   pageofs                ;Multiple page number and page offset

        add   ax,0A000h              ;Add base segment address
        mov   vio_seg,ax             ;Store new segment address

        ret                          ;Return to caller, remove
                                     ;arguments from stack

_setpage  endp                       ;End of procedure

;-- SHOWPAGE: Display one of the two screen pages --------------------
;-- Declaration : void showpage( int page );

_showpage proc near

        pop   cx                     ;Pop return address from stack
        pop   ax                     ;Pop argument from stack

        push  ax                     ;Push these onto stack
        push  cx

        mul   pageofs                ;Multiply page number and page offset
        mov   cl,4                   ;Multiply all by 16
        shl   ax,cl

        mov   bl,al                  ;Store low byte

        mov   dx,CRTC_INDEX          ;Address CRT controller
        mov   al,CC_START_HI         ;Display high byte
        out   dx,ax
        inc   al                     ;Display low byte
        mov   ah,bl
        out   dx,ax

        ;-- Wait for start of screen design ------------------------

        mov   dx,VERT_RESCAN         ;Wait for end of vertical rescan
sp3:    in    al,dx
        test  al,8
```

```
          jne    sp3                                           mov    ax,1130h        ;Load register for function call
                                                               mov    bh,3
sp4:      in     al,dx          ;Wait for start of rescan      int    10h             ;Call BIOS video interrupt
          test   al,8
          je     sp4                                           mov    dx,es           ;Return pointer ES:BP in DX:AX
                                                               mov    ax,bp
          ret                   ;Return to caller
                                                               pop    bp              ;Pop BP from stack
_showpage endp                  ;End of procedure              ret                    ;Return to caller

;-- GETFONTPTR: Returns FAR pointer to the 8x8 font table ------------    _getfontptr endp              ;End of procedure
;-- Declaration : void far * getfontptr( void )
                                                               ;== End ==========================================================
_getfontptr proc near
                                                               _text   ends                  ;End of program segment
          push   bp             ;Store BP                              end                    ;End program
```

4.8.7 The VGA 256 Color Graphics Modes

One of the biggest advantages of the VGA card over its predecessor, the EGA card, is its ability to display 256 different colors on the screen simultaneously. This group of 256 is selected from a palette of 262,000 colors. This was a milestone in the development of PC graphics.

But the 256 color mode has a resolution of only 320x200 pixels, which is much less than the 640x480 high resolution 16 color mode. However, display quality is based on more than resolution. For example, it can also be based on the wide variety of colors in this mode.

This section discusses how to select this graphics mode, address individual pixels, and increase the actual resolution.

Setting the 256 color mode and addressing pixels

To programmers, the 256 color mode with a resolution of 320x200 pixels is the easiest VGA graphics mode to use. This is especially evident in the way the pixels are addressed. Pixel addressing is similar to text mode access in some ways.

Before we can access any pixels, we must enable this mode. You can use function 00H of the BIOS video interrupt to do this. The number for this mode (13H) is passed in the AL register and function number 00H is passed in the AH register. These are the only requirements for setting 256 color graphics mode. This single operation also sets the graphics controller's read and write modes and the corresponding registers. This prepares the video card for access to the 320x200 pixels.

The four bitplanes that were so bothersome in the 16 color graphics modes aren't used; 256 color mode uses a much simpler video RAM organization. Each pixel is represented in video RAM by a single byte, just as in text mode. This byte represents the color as a value between 0 and 255. This color value acts as a direct index to the DAC color table, from which the actual color representing the pixel on screen is taken.

Since a single byte describes each pixel, a screen line consists of 320 contiguous bytes in video RAM. These bytes represent pixels in a row, from left to right. As in text mode, each succeeding line (row) begins immediately after the end of the previous line in the video RAM. So the offset address of a pixel is calculated from its screen coordinates as follows:

```
Offset = y * 320 + x
```

All pixels are therefore located within the 64K segment of video RAM that begins at segment address A000H in this mode. This makes it easy to access every pixel.

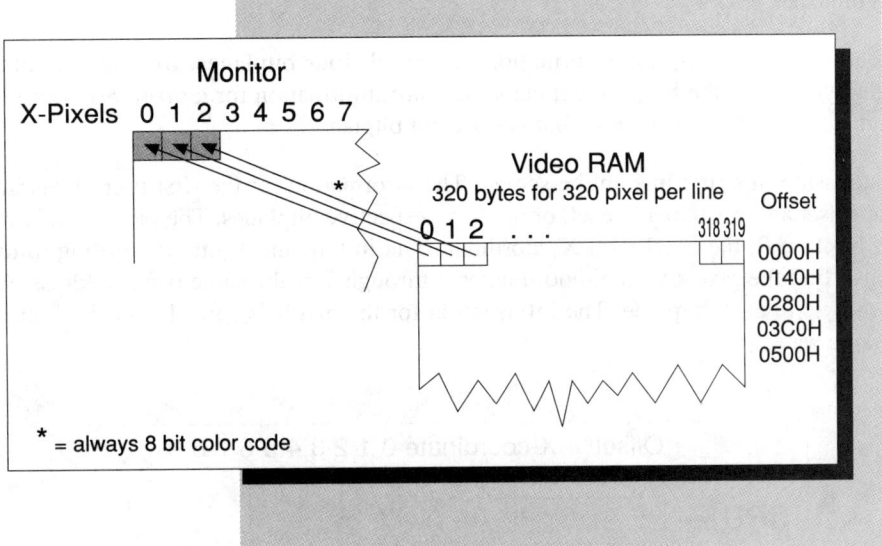

Video RAM structure 320x200 pixel 256 color graphics mode

Since it's easy to access any pixel in this mode, a special demo program isn't required. However, there's another reason for not including a demo program. Since each pixel is represented by one byte, this only requires 320x200 bytes, or 64K. In a fully populated VGA card, this leaves 192K of unused video RAM.

So, why can't we simply include three additional screen pages in the remaining video RAM? Although this is theoretically possible, the video RAM structure previously described won't allow it. This may have something to do with the MCGA card, which is related to the VGA card. The MCGA card has the same 256 color mode that the VGA card uses, but it's limited to 64K of video RAM (i.e., one screen page). Perhaps IBM wanted to maintain compatibility between the two cards in this mode.

Four graphic pages in one

To overcome this limitation, you can use a few tricks to store and access four graphics pages in video RAM while in VGA 256 color graphics mode.

In order to manage four graphics pages in the 256 color mode, you must understand how pixel information can be divided among bitplanes. As in text mode, the contiguous video RAM model beginning at A000H is only an illusion that's created to make it easier for the programmer to address individual pixels.

The pixels are actually managed in four bitplanes, just as we saw earlier, using the Chain4 mode. This mode is an extension of the odd/even mode that the VGA card uses in text mode to move information from video RAM to bitplanes 0 and 1.

In this mode, the lower two bits of a specific offset address determine the number of the bitplane to which the value is sent. These two bits are then internally set to 0 and are used as the offset address to access the selected bitplane. Three bytes remain unused between each occupied byte in each bitplane.

Instead of distributing this information among all four bitplanes, like the 16 color modes, a single byte within the bitplane contains the color information for a pixel. So, four pixels can be found at the same offset address, but in different bitplanes.

Let's consider the first line on the screen. The information for the first four pixels in this line is set at offset address 000H in each of the four respective bitplanes. The pixel with X-coordinate 0 is in bitplane 0, the pixel with X-coordinate 1 is in bitplane 1, etc. According to this scheme, we also find the pixels with X-coordinates 4 through 7 at the same offset address, which is the fourth byte in each bitplane. The information for the pixels is spread over the four bitplanes in the same way.

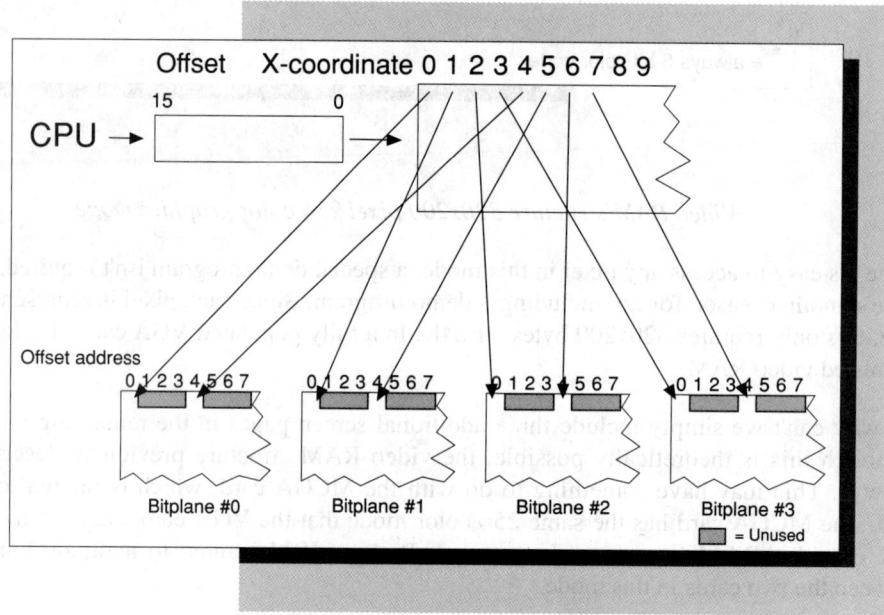

Video information storage—256 color mode, 320x200 pixel resolution

Since the 64,000 bytes needed to store 320*200 pixels are spread out across the four bitplanes, only 16K of each bitplane is actually used. However, there still isn't room for additional screen pages in video RAM. This occurs because the bytes are stored across the entire bitplane with permanent "gaps" of three bytes between each byte that's actually used.

To store more than one page in the video RAM at a time, we must have a way to move the occupied bytes closer together so we don't waste three bytes for every byte used. To do this, you must reprogram several VGA registers.

However, to do this, we must omit Chain4 mode. This means that we must write the color information to the various bitplanes "by hand". The demonstration programs V3220C.C, V3220P.PAS, V3220CA.ASM, and V3220PA.ASM control VGA 320x200 pixel graphics mode. The assembler modules contain various routines for initializing video mode and accessing individual pixels. They are specially developed to be called from the accompanying high level language module.

Both programs use the init320200 assembler routine to configure the 320x200 256 color graphics mode that allows four screen pages in video RAM.

This operation begins by setting the video mode as usual with BIOS function 13H. Then the routine changes the registers that are needed to restructure the video RAM according to our needs.

The first step is to switch off the Chain4 and the odd/even modes. This activates a sort of linear mode, which means that the offset addresses aren't grouped into bitplanes when video RAM is accessed. This affects read and write access to video RAM only from the CPU's point of view. To the CRT controller, nothing has changed yet.

The CRT controller must be informed that the color bytes in the bitplanes are adjacent, rather than spaced in four byte intervals. Next, we switch from doubleword to byte mode, which means that word mode must also be disabled. The program listings document the registers involved with each change. Refer to the end of this chapter for detailed descriptions of the EGA and VGA registers.

After completing this operation, the CRT controller views video RAM as follows:

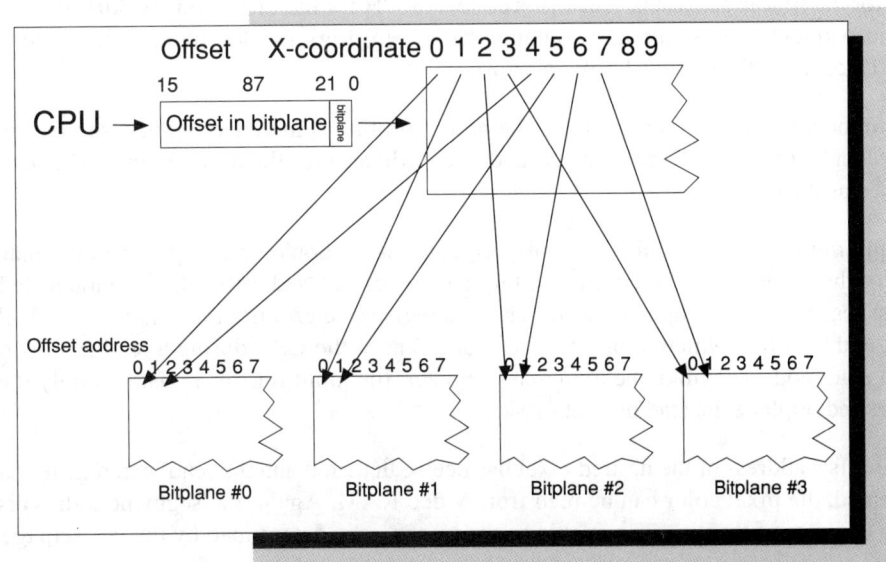

Altered 320x200 pixel mode as seen by the CRT controller

Now, since only the first 16K in each bitplane are occupied, it's possible to store three additional screen pages in the video RAM. The first screen page begins at offset address 0000H in each bitplane, the second at 4000H, the third at 8000H, and the fourth at C000H.

In this mode, it's more difficult to address each pixel because all the pixels aren't available in the 64K of video RAM at A000H. Each bitplane is addressed individually. The setpix routine in the assembler modules performs this task. It expects the X- and Y-coordinates and the pixel color as its arguments.

Setpix starts by creating the offset required to access the desired pixel. According to the new video RAM structure, each bitplane represents 80 pixels instead of 320. So, we begin by multiplying the Y-coordinate by 80. Then, the X-coordinate is divided by four because there are still four consecutive pixels located at each offset address. The sum of these two calculations can then be used to access the proper bitplane.

The number of the bitplane to be accessed is taken from the two lowest bits of the X-coordinate. These two bits represent the number of bits that the value 1 is moved to the left in order to create the bit mask for the map mask register. After this bit mask is passed to the proper register, all subsequent write accesses are addressed to the correct bitplane.

The offset address previously calculated is then used to access the desired pixel and assign the given color to it. Now, all we have to do is determine how the different screen pages are selected.

Instead of being selected by setpix, the screen page is selected by a previous call to setpage. The setpage routine determines the screen page, to which all subsequent calls of setpix will apply. Another setpage call is required to change the page.

The current page is passed to setpix using the segment address stored in the vio_seg variable. This variable stores the video RAM segment address of the page selected by setpage. This is A000H for the first page, A400H for the second, A800H for the third, and AC00H for the fourth. Since the segment address already contains the screen origin, it doesn't have to be considered again in calculating the offset address in setpix.

To determine the color of a given pixel, the getpix routine is included in the assembler module. The arguments for this routine are the X- and Y-coordinates for the desired pixel. The pixel color is returned as the result.

The getpix routine works similar to setpix, except that we don't have to program the map mask register of the sequencer to determine the bitplane to be accessed. Instead, we're interested in the read map register of the graphics controller. This register determines the contents of which latch register, and therefore which bitplane, is read and sent to the CPU during a read access to video RAM in read mode 1. Unlike the map mask register, the input for this register is only the value of the desired bitplane, instead of a bit mask.

After the offset address of the desired pixel has been calculated and the read map register has been programmed, the pixel color can be read from video RAM. Again, the segment address is taken from the contents of the vio_seg variable so the screen page determined by the last setpage call is used.

One more routine is needed to display the selected page on screen. This is the showpage routine. Its argument is the number of the page to be displayed. Showpage then sends the desired page to the screen by loading the offset address 0000H, 4000H, 8000H, or C000H in the starting register of the CRT controller.

The demo program shows what you can do with the routines in the assembler module. Each of the four screen pages is loaded with a very similar pixel pattern, consisting of a coordinate grid, a copyright message, and an object drawn with various lines. These lines use a series of colors with color numbers from 0 to n.

The ColorBox routine draws this object. The variable n represents the upper limit of the color number. This is set to 16 on page 0, 64 on page 1, 128 on page 2, and 256 on page 3. ColorBox uses a routine called Line to draw the various lines. This routine accesses setpix from the assembler module to draw lines according to the Bresenham algorithm.

The four different screens are identical except for minor details. The main program quickly switches between them to create interesting optical effects.

Pascal listing: V3220P.PAS

```
{*****************************************************************
*                                                               *
*                    V 3 2 2 0 P . P A S                        *
**-----------------------------------------------------------**
*  Task          : Demonstrates programming in 320x200 VGA      *
*                  graphic mode, using 256 colors and four screen *
*                  pages. This program requires the V3220PA.ASM   *
*                  assembly language module.                    *
**-----------------------------------------------------------**
*  Author        : Michael Tischer                             *
*  Developed on  : 09/08/90                                    *
*  Last update   : 02/13/92                                    *
*****************************************************************}

program V3220P;

uses dos, crt;


{-- Type declarations ----------------------------------------}

type BPTR = ^byte;

{-- External references to the assembler routines ------------}

{$L v3220pa}                        { Link assembler module }

procedure init320200; external;
procedure setpix( x, y : integer; pcolor : byte ); external;
function  getpix( x, y: integer ) : byte ; external;
procedure setpage( page : byte ); external;
procedure showpage( page : byte ); external;


{-- Constants ------------------------------------------------}

const MAXX = 319;                   { Maximum X- and Y-coordinates }
      MAXY = 199;

{*****************************************************************
*  IsVga : Determines whether a VGA card is installed.         *
**-----------------------------------------------------------**
```

```
*  Input   : None                                              *
*  Output  : TRUE or FALSE                                     *
*****************************************************************}

function IsVga : boolean;

var Regs : Registers;       { Processor registers for interrupt call }

begin
  Regs.AX := $1a00;                 { Function 1AH applies to VGA only }
  Intr( $10, Regs );
  IsVga := ( Regs.AL = $1a );
end;


{*****************************************************************
*  PrintChar : Writes a character to the screen while in graphic mode.*
**-----------------------------------------------------------**
*  Input   :    THECHAR = Character to be written              *
*               X, Y    = X- and Y-coordinates of upper-left corner *
*               FG      = Foreground color                     *
*               BK      = Background color                     *
*  Info    : Character is created in an 8x8 matrix, based on the *
*               8x8 ROM font.                                  *
*****************************************************************}

procedure PrintChar( thechar : char; x, y : integer; fg, bk : byte );

type FDEF = array[0..255,0..7] of byte;         { Font array }
     TPTR = ^FDEF;                              { Pointer to font }

var Regs  : Registers;              { Registers for interrupt call }
    ch    : char;                   { Individual pixels in character }
    i, k,                           { Loop counter }
    BMask : byte;                   { Bit mask for character design }

const fptr : TPTR = NIL;            { Pointer to font in ROM }

begin
  if fptr = NIL then                { Pointer to font already set? }
```

```pascal
  begin                                { No }
    Regs.AH := $11;                    { Call video BIOS function 11H, }
    Regs.AL := $30;                    { sub-function 30H             }
    Regs.BH := 3;                      { Get pointer to 8x8 font }
    intr( $10, Regs );
    fptr := ptr( Regs.ES, Regs.BP );            { Set pointers }
  end;

  if ( bk = 255 ) then                 { Drawing transparent characters? }
    for i := 0 to 7 do                 { Yes --> Set foreground pixels only }
      begin
        BMask := fptr^[ord(thechar),i];{ Get bit pattern for one line }
        for k := 0 to 7 do
          begin
            if ( BMask and 128 <> 0 ) then       { Pixel set? }
              setpix( x+k, y+i, fg );            { Yes }
            BMask := BMask shl 1;
          end;
      end
  else                           { No --> Consider background as well }
    for i := 0 to 7 do                 { Execute lines }
      begin
        BMask := fptr^[ord(thechar),i];{ Get bit pattern for one line }
        for k := 0 to 7 do
          begin
            if ( BMask and 128 <> 0 ) then       { Foreground? }
              setpix( x+k, y+i, fg )             { Yes }
            else
              setpix( x+k, y+i, bk );   { No --> Background }
            BMask := BMask shl 1;
          end;
      end;
end;

{*******************************************************************
* Line: Draws a line based on the Bresenham algorithm.            *
**-------------------------------------------------------------**
* Input   : X1, Y1 = Starting coordinates (0 - ...)              *
*           X2, Y2 = Ending coordinates                          *
*           LPCOL  = Color of line pixels                        *
*******************************************************************}

procedure Line( x1, y1, x2, y2 : integer; lpcol : byte );

var d, dx, dy,
    aincr, bincr,
    xincr, yincr,
    x, y                : integer;

{-- Procedure for swapping two integer variables ---------------------}

procedure SwapInt( var i1, i2: integer );

var dummy : integer;

begin
  dummy := i2;
  i2    := i1;
  i1    := dummy;
end;

{-- Main procedure ----------------------------------------}

begin
```

```pascal
  if ( abs(x2-x1) < abs(y2-y1) ) then        { X- or Y-axis overflow? }
    begin                                    { Check Y-axis }
      if ( y1 > y2 ) then                    { y1 > y2? }
        begin
          SwapInt( x1, x2 );         { Yes --> Swap X1 with X2 }
          SwapInt( y1, y2 );         {         and Y1 with Y2 }
        end;

      if ( x2 > x1 ) then xincr := 1         { Set X-axis increment }
                     else xincr := -1;

      dy := y2 - y1;
      dx := abs( x2-x1 );
      d  := 2 * dx - dy;
      aincr := 2 * (dx - dy);
      bincr := 2 * dx;
      x := x1;
      y := y1;

      setpix( x, y, lpcol );                 { Set first pixel }
      for y:=y1+1 to y2 do             { Execute line on Y-axes }
        begin
          if ( d >= 0 ) then
            begin
              inc( x, xincr );
              inc( d, aincr );
            end
          else
            inc( d, bincr );
          setpix( x, y, lpcol);
        end;
    end
  else                                 { Check X-axes }
    begin
      if ( x1 > x2 ) then                    { x1 > x2? }
        begin
          SwapInt( x1, x2 );         { Yes --> Swap X1 with X2 }
          SwapInt( y1, y2 );         {         and Y1 with Y2 }
        end;

      if ( y2 > y1 ) then yincr := 1         { Set Y-axis increment }
                     else yincr := -1;

      dx := x2 - x1;
      dy := abs( y2-y1 );
      d  := 2 * dy - dx;
      aincr := 2 * (dy - dx);
      bincr := 2 * dy;
      x := x1;
      y := y1;

      setpix( x, y, lpcol );                 { Set first pixel }
      for x:=x1+1 to x2 do             { Execute line on X-axes }
        begin
          if ( d >= 0 ) then
            begin
              inc( y, yincr );
              inc( d, aincr );
            end
          else
            inc( d, bincr );
          setpix( x, y, lpcol );
        end;
    end;
end;
```

```
end;

{*****************************************************************
* GrfxPrint: Displays a formatted string on the graphic screen. *
**-------------------------------------------------------------**
* Input   : X, Y  = Starting coordinates (0 - ...)              *
*           FG    = Foreground color                            *
*           BK    = Background color (255 = transparent)        *
*           STRING = String with format information             *
*****************************************************************}

procedure GrfxPrint( x, y : integer; fg, bk : byte; strt : string );

var i : integer;                          { Loop counter }

begin
 for i:=1 to length( strt ) do
   begin
     printchar( strt[i], x, y, fg, bk );   { Display using PrintChar }
     inc( x, 8 );                          { Move X to next character position }
   end;
end;

{*****************************************************************
* ColorBox: Draws a rectangle and fills it with a line pattern. *
**-------------------------------------------------------------**
* Input   : X1, Y1 = Upper-left coordinates of window           *
*           X2, Y2 = Lower-right coordinates of window          *
*           COLMAX = Greatest color value                       *
* Info    : Line colors are selected in a cycle of 0-COLMAX.    *
*****************************************************************}

procedure ColorBox( x1, y1, x2, y2 : integer; colmax : byte );

var x, y,                                 { Loop counter }
    sx, sy : integer;                     { Exit point for last color loop }

begin
 Line( x1, y1, x1, y2, 15 );              { Draw border }
 Line( x1, y2, x2, y2, 15 );
 Line( x2, y2, x2, y1, 15 );
 Line( x2, y1, x1, y1, 15 );

 for y := y2-1 downto y1+1 do             { Bottom left to right border }
   Line( x1+1, y2-1, x2-1, y, y mod colmax );

 for y := y2-1 downto y1+1 do             { Bottom right to left border }
   Line( x2-1, y2-1, x1+1, y, y mod colmax );

 {-- From center of box to top border ---------------------------------}

 sx := x1+ (x2-x1) div 2;
 sy := y1+ (y2-y1) div 2;
 for x := x1+1 to x2-1 do
   Line( sx, sy, x, y1+1, x mod colmax );
end;

{*****************************************************************
* DrawAxis: Draws axes from left and top borders on the screen. *
**-------------------------------------------------------------**
* Input   : XSTEP = Increment for X-axis                        *
*           YSTEP = Increment for Y-axis                        *
*           FG    = Foreground color                            *
*           BK    = Background color (255 = transparent)        *
*****************************************************************}

procedure DrawAxis( stepx, stepy : integer; fg, bk : byte );

var x, y    : integer;                    { Loop coordinates }
    lpcoords : string[3];

begin
 Line( 0, 0, MAXX, 0, fg );               { Draw X-axis }
 Line( 0, 0, 0, MAXY, fg );               { Draw Y-axis }

 x := stepx;                              { Scale X-axis }
 while ( x < MAXX ) do
   begin
     Line( x, 0, x, 5, fg );
     str( x, lpcoords );
     if ( x < 100 ) then
       GrfxPrint( x - 8 , 8, fg, bk, lpcoords )
     else
       GrfxPrint( x - 12, 8, fg, bk, lpcoords );
     inc( x, stepx );
   end;

 y := stepy;                              { Scale Y-axis }
 while ( y < MAXY ) do
   begin
     Line( 0, y, 5, y, fg );
     str( y:3, lpcoords );
     GrfxPrint( 8, y-4, fg, bk, lpcoords );
     inc( y, stepy );
   end;
end;

{*****************************************************************
* Demo: Demonstrates the functions and procedures in this module. *
**-------------------------------------------------------------**
* Input   : None                                               *
*****************************************************************}

procedure Demo;

const PAUSE = 100;                        { Pause counter in milliseconds }

var page : byte;                          { Page counter }

begin
 for page := 0 to 4 do
   begin
     setpage( page );                     { Process page }
     ColorBox( 80, 25, 308, 175, ( page + 1 ) * 16 );  { Paint box }
     DrawAxis( 30, 20, 15, 255 );         { Draw axes }
     GrfxPrint( 46, MAXY-10, 15, 255,
             'V3220P  - (c) by Michael Tischer' );
   end;

 {-- Display four graphic pages in sequences---------------------------}

 for page := 0 to 50 do                   { 50 executions }
   begin
     showpage( page mod 4 );              { Display page }
     delay( PAUSE );                      { Brief pause }
   end;
end;
```

```
{**************************************************************
*                 M A I N   P R O G R A M                     *
**************************************************************}

begin
  if IsVga then                    { VGA card installed? }
    begin                          { Yes --> Go ahead }
      init320200;                  { Initialize graphic mode }
      Demo;
      repeat until keypressed;
      Textmode( C080 );            { Shift into text mode }
    end
  else
    writeln( 'V3220P  -  (c) 1992 by Michael Tischer'#13#10#10 +
             'This program requires a VGA card', #13#10);
end.
```

Assembler listing: V3220PA.ASM

```
;*****************************************************************;
;*                    V 3 2 2 0 P A . A S M                     *;
;*-------------------------------------------------------------*;
;*     Task       : Contains routines for operating in         *;
;*                  320x200 256 color mode on a VGA card.       *;
;*-------------------------------------------------------------*;
;*     Author     : Michael Tischer                            *;
;*     Developed on : 09/05/90                                 *;
;*     Last update : 02/13/92                                  *;
;*-------------------------------------------------------------*;
;*     Assembly   : MASM /mx V3220PA;    or    TASM -mx V3220PA *;
;*                  ... Link to V3220P.PAS                      *;
;*****************************************************************;

;== Constants =================================================

SC_INDEX      = 3c4h          ;Index register for sequencer ctrl.
SC_MAP_MASK   = 2             ;Number of map mask register
SC_MEM_MODE   = 4             ;Number of memory mode register

GC_INDEX      = 3ceh          ;Index register for graphics ctrl.
GC_READ_MAP   = 4             ;Number of read map register
GC_GRAPH_MODE = 5             ;Number of graphics mode register
GC_MISCELL    = 6             ;Number of miscellaneous register

CRTC_INDEX    = 3d4h          ;Index register for CRT controllers
CC_MAX_SCAN   = 9             ;Number of maximum scan line reg.
CC_START_HI   = 0Ch           ;Number of high start register
CC_UNDERLINE  = 14h           ;Number of underline register
CC_MODE_CTRL  = 17h           ;Number of mode control register

DAC_WRITE_ADR = 3C8h          ;DAC write address
DAC_READ_ADR  = 3C7h          ;DAC read address
DAC_DATA      = 3C9h          ;DAC data register

VERT_RESCAN   = 3DAh          ;Input status register #1

PIXX          = 320           ;Horizontal resolution

;== Data segment ==============================================

DATA    segment word public

vio_seg    dw (?)             ;Video segment with current page
                              ;must be initialized during runtime

DATA    ends

;== Program ===================================================

CODE    segment byte public   ;Program segment

        assume cs:code, ds:data

;-- Public declarations ---------------------------------------

public    init320200          ;Initialize 320x200 mode
public    setpix              ;Set pixel
public    getpix              ;Get pixel color
public    showpage            ;Display page 0 or 1
public    setpage             ;Set page for setpix and getpix
```

```
;-------------------------------------------------------------------
;-- INIT320200: Initializes 320x200 pixel mode
;-- Call from TP: init320200;

init320200 proc near

           ;-- Sets mode 13H, since BIOS uses this mostly for
           ;-- initialization.

           mov   ax,0013h        ;Set normal mode 13H
           int   10h

           mov   dx,GC_INDEX      ;Memory division
           mov   al,GC_GRAPH_MODE ;Disable bit 4 of
           out   dx,al            ;graphic mode register
           inc   dx               ;in graphics controller
           in    al,dx
           and   al,11101111b
           out   dx,al
           dec   dx

           mov   al,GC_MISCELL    ;And change bit 1
           out   dx,al            ;in the miscellaneous
           inc   dx               ;register
           in    al,dx
           and   al,11111101b
           out   dx,al

           mov   dx,SC_INDEX      ;Modify memory mode register in
           mov   al,SC_MEM_MODE   ;sequencer controller so no further
           out   dx,al            ;address division follows in
           inc   dx               ;bitplanes, and set the bitplane
           in    al,dx            ;currently in the
           and   al,11110111b     ;bit mask register
           or    al,4
           out   dx,al

           mov   ax,0A000h        ;Fill all four bitplanes with color
           mov   vio_seg,ax       ;code 00H and clear the screen
           mov   es,ax
           xor   di,di
           mov   ax,di
           mov   cx,8000h
           rep   stosw

           mov   dx,CRTC_INDEX    ;Set double word mode using bit 6
           mov   al,CC_UNDERLINE  ;in underline register of
           out   dx,al            ;CRT controller
           inc   dx
           in    al,dx
           and   al,10111111b
           out   dx,al
           dec   dx

           mov   al,CC_MODE_CTRL  ;Using bit 6 in mode control reg.
           out   dx,al            ;of CRT controller, change
           inc   dx               ;from word mode to byte mode
           in    al,dx
           or    al,01000000b
           out   dx,al

           ret                    ;Return to caller

init320200 endp                   ;End of procedure
```

```
;-------------------------------------------------------------------
;-- SETPIX: Changes a pixel to a specific color
;-- Call from TP: setpix( x , y : integer; pcolor : byte );

setpix     proc near

sframe     struc                  ;Structure for stack access
bp0        dw ?                   ;Gets BP
ret_adr0   dw ?                   ;Return address to caller
pcolor     dw ?                   ;Color
y0         dw ?                   ;Y-coordinate
x0         dw ?                   ;X-coordinate
sframe     ends                   ;End of structure

frame      equ [ bp - bp0 ]       ;Address structure elements

           push  bp               ;Prepare for parameter addressing
           mov   bp,sp            ;through BP register

           mov   ax,PIXX / 4      ;Compute offset in video RAM
           mul   frame.y0         ;and pass to DI
           mov   cx,frame.x0
           mov   bx,cx
           shr   bx,1
           shr   bx,1
           add   ax,bx
           mov   di,ax

           and   cl,3             ;Compute bit mask for map to be
           mov   ah,1             ;addressed, move to AH
           shl   ah,cl
           mov   al,SC_MAP_MASK   ;Register number to AL
           mov   dx,SC_INDEX      ;Load sequencer index address
           out   dx,ax            ;Load bit mask register

           mov   ax,vio_seg       ;Set ES to video RAM
           mov   es,ax
           mov   al,byte ptr frame.pcolor  ;Load pixel color and
           stosb                  ;write to selected bitmap

           pop   bp               ;Get registers from stack

           ret   6                ;Return to caller, remove
                                  ;arguments from stack

setpix     endp                   ;End of procedure
```

```
;-------------------------------------------------------------------
;-- GETPIX: Returns a pixel color
;-- Call from TP: x := getpix( x , y : integer );

getpix     proc near

sframe1    struc                  ;Structure for stack access
bp1        dw ?                   ;Gets BP
ret_adr1   dw ?                   ;Return address to caller
y1         dw ?                   ;Y-coordinate
x1         dw ?                   ;X-coordinate
sframe1    ends                   ;End of structure

frame      equ [ bp - bp1 ]       ;Address structure elements

           push  bp               ;Prepare for parameter addressing
```

```
        mov   bp,sp           ;through BP register

        mov   ax,PIXX / 4     ;Compute offset in video RAM
        mul   frame.y1        ;and pass to SI
        mov   si,frame.x1
        mov   cx,si
        shr   si,1
        shr   si,1
        add   si,ax

        and   cl,3            ;Compute bit mask for map to be
        mov   ah,cl           ;addressed in AH
        mov   al,GC_READ_MAP  ;Move register number to AL
        mov   dx,GC_INDEX     ;Load graphics controller index
        out   dx,ax           ;Load Read Map register

        mov   ax,vio_seg      ;Set ES to video RAM
        mov   es,ax
        mov   al,es:[si]      ;Load pixel color

        pop   bp             ;Pop register from stack

        ret   4              ;Return to caller, remove
                             ;arguments from stack

getpix  endp                 ;End of procedure
;--------------------------------------------------------------------
;-- SETPAGE: Sets page for access from setpix and getpix
;-- Call from TP: setpage( page : byte );

setpage proc near

        pop   bx             ;Pop return address from stack
        pop   cx             ;Pop argument from stack

        push  cx             ;Push these back on
        push  bx

        mov   al,4           ;High byte seg. addr = page * 4 + A0H
        mul   cl
        or    al,0A0h

        mov   byte ptr vio_seg + 1,al ;Move new segment address

        ret   2              ;Return to caller, remove
                             ;arguments from stack

setpage endp                 ;End of procedure
;--------------------------------------------------------------------
;-- SHOWPAGE: Display one of the two screen pages
;-- Call from TP: showpage( page : byte );

showpage proc near

        pop   bx             ;Pop return address from stack
        pop   cx             ;Pop argument from stack

        push  cx             ;Push these back in
        push  bx

        mov   al,64          ;High byte of offset = page * 64
        mul   cl
        mov   ah,al          ;Move high byte of offset to AH

;-- Load new starting address -------------------------------

        mov   dx,CRTC_INDEX  ;Address CRT controller
        mov   al,CC_START_HI ;Move register number
        out   dx,ax          ;to AL and exit

;-- Wait to return to starting screen design ---------------

        mov   dx,VERT_RESCAN ;Wait for end of
sp3:    in    al,dx          ;vertical rescan
        test  al,8
        jne   sp3

sp4:    in    al,dx          ;Go to start of rescan
        test  al,8
        je    sp4

        ret   2              ;Return to caller, remove
                             ;arguments from stack

showpage endp                ;End of procedure
;== End ==========================================================

CODE    ends                 ;End of code segment
        end                  ;End program
```

C listing: V3220C.C

```
/****************************************************************
*                  V 3 2 2 0 C . C                             *
**------------------------------------------------------------**
* Task          : Demonstrates programming in 320x200 VGA      *
*                 graphic mode, using 256 colors and four screen *
*                 pages. This program requires the V3220CA.ASM *
*                 assembly language module.                    *
**------------------------------------------------------------**
* Author        : Michael Tischer                             *
* Developed on  : 09/04/90                                     *
* Last update   : 02/14/92                                     *
**------------------------------------------------------------**
* Memory model  : SMALL                                        *
**------------------------------------------------------------**
* (MICROSOFT C)                                                *
* Compilation   : CL /AS /c V3220C.C                           *
*                : LINK V3220C V3220CA;                        *
**------------------------------------------------------------**
* (BORLAND TURBO C)                                            *
* Compilation   : Create a project file using the following:   *
*                    v3220c.c                                  *
*                    v3220ca.obj                               *
**------------------------------------------------------------**
* Call          : v3220c                                       *
****************************************************************/

#include <dos.h>
#include <stdarg.h>
#include <stdlib.h>
#include <stdio.h>
#include <conio.h>

/*-- Type declarations ----------------------------------------*/

typedef unsigned char BYTE;

/*-- External references to the assembler routines -----------------*/

extern void init320200( void );
extern void setpix( int x, int y, unsigned char pcolor);
extern BYTE getpix( int x, int y );
extern void setpage( BYTE page );
extern void showpage( BYTE page );
extern void far * getfontptr( void );

/*-- Constants ------------------------------------------------*/

#define MAXX 319                     /* Maximum X- and Y-coordinates */
#define MAXY 199

/****************************************************************
* IsVga: Determines whether a VGA card is installed.           *
**------------------------------------------------------------**
* Input   : None                                               *
* Output  : 0  If no VGA exists, otherwise < 0                 *
****************************************************************/

BYTE IsVga( void )
{
 union REGS Regs;          /* Processor registers for interrupt call */

 Regs.x.ax = 0x1a00;              /* Function 1AH applies to VGA only */
```

```
 int86( 0x10, &Regs, &Regs );
 return ( Regs.h.al == 0x1a );          /* Is the function available? */
}

/****************************************************************
* PrintChar : Writes a character to the screen while in graphic mode.*
**------------------------------------------------------------**
* Input    : THECHAR = Character to be written                 *
*            x, y    = X- and Y-coordinates of upper-left corner *
*            FG      = Foreground color                        *
*            BK      = Background color                        *
* Info     : Character is created in an 8x8 matrix, based on the *
*            8x8 ROM font.                                     *
****************************************************************/

void PrintChar( char thechar, int x, int y, BYTE FG, BYTE BK )
{
 typedef BYTE FDEF[256][8];                /* Font definition */
 typedef FDEF far *TPTR;                   /* Pointer to font */

 BYTE       i, k,                          /* Loop counter */
            BMask;                  /* Bit mask for character design */

 static TPTR fptr = (TPTR) 0;          /* Pointer to font in ROM */

 if ( fptr == (TPTR) 0 )          /* Pointer to font already set? */
  fptr = getfontptr();   /* No --> Use the assembler function to load */

 /*- Generate character pixel by pixel ------------------------------*/

 if ( BK == 255 )                 /* Drawing transparent characters? */
  for ( i = 0; i < 8; ++i )     /* Yes --> Set foreground pixels only */
  {
   BMask = (*fptr)[thechar][i];      /* Get bit pattern for one line */
   for ( k = 0; k < 8; ++k, BMask <<= 1 )        /* Execute column */
    if ( BMask & 128 )                            /* Pixel set? */
     setpix( x+k, y+i, FG );                      /* Yes */
  }
 else                    /* No --> Consider background as well */
  for ( i = 0; i < 8; ++i )                       /* Execute lines */
  {
   BMask = (*fptr)[thechar][i];      /* Get bit pattern for one line */
   for ( k = 0; k < 8; ++k, BMask <<= 1 )        /* Execute columns */
    setpix( x+k, y+i, ( BMask & 128 ) ? FG : BK );
  }
}

/****************************************************************
* Line: Draws a line based on the Bresenham algorithm.         *
**------------------------------------------------------------**
* Input   : X1, Y1 = Starting coordinates (0 - ...)            *
*           X2, Y2 = Ending coordinates                        *
*           LPCOL  = Color of line pixels                      *
****************************************************************/

/*-- Function for swapping two integer variables -------------------*/

void SwapInt( int *i1, int *i2 )
{
 int dummy;

 dummy = *i2;
 *i2   = *i1;
 *i1   = dummy;
```

```
}

/*-- Main part of function ------------------------------------*/

void Line( int x1, int y1, int x2, int y2, BYTE pcolor )
{
 int d, dx, dy,
     aincr, bincr,
     xincr, yincr,
     x, y;

 if ( abs(x2-x1) < abs(y2-y1) )          /* X- or Y-axis overflow? */
  {                                      /* Check Y-axis */
   if ( y1 > y2 )                        /* y1 > y2? */
    {
     SwapInt( &x1, &x2 );                /* Yes --> Swap X1 with X2 */
     SwapInt( &y1, &y2 );                /*         and Y1 with Y2 */
    }

   xincr = ( x2 > x1 ) ? 1 : -1;         /* Set X-axis increment */

   dy = y2 - y1;
   dx = abs( x2-x1 );
   d  = 2 * dx - dy;
   aincr = 2 * (dx - dy);
   bincr = 2 * dx;
   x = x1;
   y = y1;

   setpix( x, y, pcolor );               /* Set first pixel */
   for (y=y1+1; y<= y2; ++y )            /* Execute line on Y-axes */
    {
     if ( d >= 0 )
      {
       x += xincr;
       d += aincr;
      }
     else
      d += bincr;
     setpix(x, y, pcolor);
    }
  }
 else                                    /* Check X-axes */
  {
   if ( x1 > x2 )                        /* x1 > x2? */
    {
     SwapInt( &x1, &x2 );                /* Yes --> Swap X1 with X2 */
     SwapInt( &y1, &y2 );                /*         and Y1 with Y2 */
    }

   yincr = ( y2 > y1 ) ? 1 : -1;         /* Set Y-axis increment */

   dx = x2 - x1;
   dy = abs( y2-y1 );
   d  = 2 * dy - dx;
   aincr = 2 * (dy - dx);
   bincr = 2 * dy;
   x = x1;
   y = y1;

   setpix(x, y, pcolor);                 /* Set first pixel */
   for (x=x1+1; x<=x2; ++x )             /* Execute line on X-axes */
    {
     if ( d >= 0 )
```

```
     {
      y += yincr;
      d += aincr;
     }
    else
     d += bincr;
    setpix(x, y, pcolor);
   }
 }
}

/****************************************************************
* GrfxPrintf: Displays a formatted string on the graphic screen. *
**------------------------------------------------------------**
* Input   : X, Y   = Starting coordinates (0 - ...)             *
*           FG     = Foreground color                           *
*           BK     = Background color (255 = transparent)       *
*           STRING = String with format information             *
*           ...    = Arguments similar to printf                *
****************************************************************/

void GrfxPrintf( int x, int y, BYTE FG, BYTE BK, char * string, ... )
{
 va_list parameter;                  /* Parameter list for VA_... macros */
 char stngbuf[255],                  /* Buffer for formatted string */
      *cp;

 va_start( parameter, string );              /* Convert parameter */
 vsprintf( stngbuf, string, parameter );          /* Format */
 for ( cp = stngbuf; *cp; ++cp, x+= 8 )       /* Formatted string */
  PrintChar( *cp, x, y, FG, BK );          /* Display using PrintChar */
}

/****************************************************************
* ColorBox: Draws a rectangle and fills it with a line pattern. *
**------------------------------------------------------------**
* Input   : X1, Y1 = Upper-left coordinates of window          *
*           X2, Y2 = Lower-right coordinates of window          *
*           COLMAX = Greatest color value                       *
* Info    : Line colors are selected in a cycle of O-COLMAX.    *
****************************************************************/

void ColorBox( int x1, int y1, int x2, int y2, int colmax )
{
 int x, y,                               /* Loop variables */
     sx, sy;                         /* Exit point for last color loop */

 Line( x1, y1, x1, y2, 15 );                 /* Draw border */
 Line( x1, y2, x2, y2, 15 );
 Line( x2, y2, x2, y1, 15 );
 Line( x2, y1, x1, y1, 15 );

 for ( y = y2-1; y > y1; --y )         /* Bottom left to right border */
  Line( x1+1, y2-1, x2-1, y, y % colmax );

 for ( y = y2-1; y > y1; --y )         /* Bottom right to left border */
  Line( x2-1, y2-1, x1+1, y, y % colmax );

 /*-- From center of box to top border ---------------------------*/

 for ( x=x1+1, sx=x1+(x2-x1)/2, sy=y1+(y2-y1)/ 2; x < x2; ++x )
  Line( sx, sy, x, y1+1, x % colmax );
}
```

```
/*************************************************************************
* DrawAxis: Draws axes from left and top borders on the screen.        *
**---------------------------------------------------------------------**
* Input   : XSTEP = Increment for X-axis                               *
*           YSTEP = Increment for Y-axis                               *
*           FG    = Foreground color                                   *
*           BK    = Background color (255 = transparent)               *
*************************************************************************/

void DrawAxis( int stepx, int stepy, BYTE FG, BYTE BK )
{
 int x, y;                               /* Loop coordinates */

 Line( 0, 0, MAXX, 0, FG );                      /* Draw X-axis */
 Line( 0, 0, 0, MAXY, FG );                      /* Draw Y-axis */

 for ( x = stepx; x < MAXX; x += stepx )         /* Scale X-axis */
  {
   Line( x, 0, x, 5, FG );
   GrfxPrintf( x < 100 ? x - 8 : x - 12, 8, FG, BK, "%d", x );
  }

 for ( y = stepy; y < MAXY; y += stepy )         /* Scale Y-axis */
  {
   Line( 0, y, 5, y, FG );
   GrfxPrintf( 8, y-4, FG, BK, "%3d", y );
  }
}


/*************************************************************************
* Demo: Demonstrates the functions in this module.                     *
*************************************************************************/


void Demo( void )
{
 #define PAUSE 100000            /* Pause amount, varies with system */

 int x;                                 /* Coordinate counter */
 BYTE page;                             /* Page counter */
 long delay;                            /* Pause counter */

 for ( page = 0; page < 4; ++page )
  {
   setpage( page );                             /* Process page */
   ColorBox( 80, 25, 308, 175, ( page + 1 ) * 16 );  /* Paint box */
   DrawAxis( 30, 20, 15, 255 );                 /* Draw axes */
   GrfxPrintf( 46, MAXY-10, 15, 255,
            "V3220C  -  (c) by Michael Tischer" );
  }

 /*-- Display four graphic pages in sequence -----------------------*/

 for ( x = 1; x < 50; ++x )                      /* 50 executions */
  {
   showpage( x % 4 );                           /* Display page */
   for ( delay = 1; delay < PAUSE; ++delay )    /* Brief pause */
    ;
  }
}


/*************************************************************************/
/**                  M A I N   P R O G R A M                          **/
/*************************************************************************/
```

```
void main( void )
{
 union REGS regs;

 if ( IsVga() )                         /* VGA card installed? */
  {                                     /* Yes --> Go ahead */
   init320200();                        /* Initialize graphic mode */
   Demo();
   getch();                             /* Wait for a key */
   regs.x.ax = 0x0003;                  /* Shift into text mode */
   int86( 0x10, &regs, &regs );
  }
 else
  printf( "V3220C  -  (c) 1992 by Michael Tischer\n\n"\
        "This program requires a VGA card\n\n" );
}
```

273

Assembler listing: V3220CA.ASM

```
;*****************************************************************;
;*                    V 3 2 2 0 C A . A S M                     *;
;*-------------------------------------------------------------*;
;*   Task        : Contains routines for operating in          *;
;*                 320x200 256 color mode on a VGA card.        *;
;*-------------------------------------------------------------*;
;*   Author      : Michael Tischer                             *;
;*   Developed on : 09/05/90                                    *;
;*   Last update  : 02/13/92                                    *;
;*-------------------------------------------------------------*;
;*   Assembly     : MASM /mx V3220CA;    or   TASM -mx V3220CA  *;
;*                  ... Link to V3220C.C                        *;
;*****************************************************************;


IGROUP group _text              ;Program segment
DGROUP group const,_bss, _data  ;Data segment
       assume CS:IGROUP, DS:DGROUP, ES:DGROUP, SS:DGROUP


CONST  segment word public 'CONST';This segment handles all
CONST  ends                       ;readable constants


_BSS   segment word public 'BSS'  ;This segment handles all uninitial-
_BSS   ends                       ;ized static variables


_DATA  segment word public 'DATA' ;This segment handles all initialized
                                  ;global and static variables


_DATA  ends


;== Constants =============================================


SC_INDEX      = 3c4h          ;Index register for sequencer ctrl.
SC_MAP_MASK   = 2             ;Number of map mask register
SC_MEM_MODE   = 4             ;Number of memory mode register

GC_INDEX      = 3ceh          ;Index register for graphics ctrl.
GC_READ_MAP   = 4             ;Number of read map register
GC_GRAPH_MODE = 5             ;Number of graphics mode register
GC_MISCELL    = 6             ;Number of miscellaneous register


CRTC_INDEX    = 3d4h          ;Index register for CRT controller
CC_MAX_SCAN   = 9             ;Number of maximum scan line reg.
CC_START_HI   = 0Ch           ;Number of high start register
CC_UNDERLINE  = 14h           ;Number of underline register
CC_MODE_CTRL  = 17h           ;Number of mode control register


DAC_WRITE_ADR = 3C8h          ;DAC write address
DAC_READ_ADR  = 3C7h          ;DAC read address
DAC_DATA      = 3C9h          ;DAC data register

VERT_RESCAN   = 3DAh          ;Input status register #1

PIXX          = 320           ;Horizontal resolution


;== Data ===================================================


_DATA  segment word public 'DATA'

vio_seg   dw 0a000h           ;Video segment with current page


_DATA  ends
```

```
;== Program ===============================================

_TEXT  segment byte public 'CODE' ;Program segment

;-- Public declarations ------------------------------------

public    _init320200              ;Initialize 320x200 mode
public    _setpix                  ;Set pixel
public    _getpix                  ;Get pixel color
public    _showpage                ;Display page 0 or 1
public    _setpage                 ;Set page for setpix and getpix
public    _getfontptr              ;Return pointer to 8x8 font

;-- INIT320200: Initializes 320x200 pixel mode -------------------
;-- Declaration : void init320200( void );

_init320200 proc near

          ;-- Sets mode 13H, since BIOS uses this mostly for
          ;-- initialization.

          mov    ax,0013h      ;Set normal mode 13H
          int    10h

          mov    dx,GC_INDEX      ;Memory division
          mov    al,GC_GRAPH_MODE ;Disable bit 4 of
          out    dx,al            ;graphics mode register in
          inc    dx               ;graphics controller
          in     al,dx
          and    al,11101111b
          out    dx,al
          dec    dx

          mov    al,GC_MISCELL    ;And change bit 1
          out    dx,al            ;in the miscellaneous
          inc    dx               ;register
          in     al,dx
          and    al,11111101b
          out    dx,al

          mov    dx,SC_INDEX      ;Modify memory mode register in
          mov    al,SC_MEM_MODE   ;sequencer controller so no further
          out    dx,al            ;address division follows in
          inc    dx               ;bitplanes, and set the bitplane
          in     al,dx            ;currently in the
          and    al,11110111b     ;bit mask register
          or     al,4
          out    dx,al

          mov    ax,vio_seg       ;Fill all four bitplanes with color
          mov    es,ax            ;code 00H and clear the screen
          xor    di,di
          mov    ax,di
          mov    cx,8000h
          rep    stosw

          mov    dx,CRTC_INDEX    ;Set double word mode using bit 6
          mov    al,CC_UNDERLINE  ;in underline register of
          out    dx,al            ;CRT controller
          inc    dx
          in     al,dx
          and    al,10111111b
          out    dx,al
          dec    dx
```

```
        mov   al,CC_MODE_CTRL  ;Using bit 6 in mode control reg.
        out   dx,al            ;of CRT controller, change
        inc   dx               ;from word mode to byte mode
        in    al,dx
        or    al,01000000b
        out   dx,al

        ret                    ;Return to caller

_init320200 endp              ;End of procedure

;-- SETPIX: Changes a pixel to a specific color ----------------------
;-- Declaration : void setpix( int x, int y, unsigned char pcolor );

_setpix proc near

sframe  struc                 ;Structure for stack access
bp0     dw ?                  ;Gets BP
ret_adr0 dw ?                 ;Return address to caller
x0      dw ?                  ;X-coordinate
y0      dw ?                  ;Y-coordinate
pcolor  dw ?                  ;Color
sframe  ends                  ;End of structure

frame   equ [ bp - bp0 ]      ;Address structure elements

        push  bp              ;Prepare for parameter addressing
        mov   bp,sp           ;through BP register

        push  di              ;Push DI onto stack

        mov   ax,PIXX / 4     ;Compute offset in video RAM
        mul   frame.y0        ;and pass to DI
        mov   cx,frame.x0
        mov   bx,cx
        shr   bx,1
        shr   bx,1
        add   ax,bx
        mov   di,ax

        and   cl,3            ;Compute bit mask for map to be
        mov   ah,1            ;addressed, move to AH
        shl   ah,cl
        mov   al,SC_MAP_MASK  ;Register number to AL
        mov   dx,SC_INDEX     ;Load sequencer index address
        out   dx,ax           ;Load bit mask register

        mov   ax,vio_seg      ;Set ES to video RAM
        mov   es,ax
        mov   al,byte ptr frame.pcolor ;Load pixel color and.
        stosb                 ;write to selected bitmap

        pop   di              ;Get registers from stack
        pop   bp

        ret                   ;Return to caller

_setpix endp                  ;End of procedure

;-- GETPIX: Returns a pixel color ------------------------------------
;-- Declaration : unsigned char getpix( int x, int y );

_getpix proc near
```

```
sframe1  struc                ;Structure for stack access
bp1      dw ?                 ;Gets BP
ret_adr1 dw ?                 ;Return address to caller
x1       dw ?                 ;X-coordinate
y1       dw ?                 ;Y-coordinate
sframe1  ends                 ;End of structure

frame    equ [ bp - bp1 ]     ;Address structure elements

         push  bp             ;Prepare for parameter addressing
         mov   bp,sp          ; through BP register

         push  si             ;Push SI onto stack

         mov   ax,PIXX / 4    ;Compute offset in video RAM
         mul   frame.y1       ;and pass to SI
         mov   si,frame.x1
         mov   cx,si
         shr   si,1
         shr   si,1
         add   si,ax

         and   cl,3           ;Compute bit mask for map to be
         mov   ah,cl          ;addressed, move to AH
         mov   al,GC_READ_MAP ;Register number to AL
         mov   dx,GC_INDEX     ;Load graphics controller index
         out   dx,ax          ;Load read map register

         mov   ax,vio_seg     ;Set ES to video RAM
         mov   es,ax
         mov   al,es:[si]     ;Load pixel color

         pop   si             ;Get registers from stack
         pop   bp

         ret                  ;Return to caller

_getpix  endp                 ;End of procedure

;-- SETPAGE: Sets page for access from setpix and getpix -------------
;-- Declaration : void setpage( unsigned char page );

_setpage proc near

         pop   bx             ;Pop return address from stack
         pop   cx             ;Pop argument from stack

         push  cx             ;Push these back on
         push  bx

         mov   al,4           ;High byte seg. addr = page * 4 + A0H
         mul   cl
         or    al,0A0h
         mov   byte ptr vio_seg + 1,al ;Move new segment address

         ret                  ;Return to caller

_setpage endp                 ;End of procedure

;-- SHOWPAGE: Display one of the two screen pages --------------------
;-- Declaration : void showpage( unsigned char page );
```

```
_showpage  proc near                                                       ret                      ;Return to caller

           pop   bx          ;Pop return address from stack
           pop   cx          ;Pop argument from stack         _showpage  endp                      ;End of procedure

           push  cx          ;Push these back on             ;-- GETFONTPTR: Returns FAR pointer to 8x8 font table ----------------
           push  bx                                          ;-- Declaration : void far * getfontptr( void )

           mov   al,64        ;High byte of offset = page * 64  _getfontptr proc near
           mul   cl
           mov   ah,al        ;Move high byte of offset to AH      push  bp              ;Push BP onto stack

           ;-- Load new starting address -----------------------------         mov   ax,1130h        ;Get register for function call
                                                                   mov   bh,3
           mov   dx,CRTC_INDEX  ;Address CRT controller            int   10h             ;Call BIOS video interrupt
           mov   al,CC_START_HI ;Move register number
           out   dx,ax          ;to AL and exit                    mov   dx,es            ;Pointer ES:BP returned in DX:AX
                                                                   mov   ax,bp
           ;-- Wait to return to starting screen design ---------------
                                                                   pop   bp              ;Pop BP from stack
           mov   dx,VERT_RESCAN  ;Wait for end of                  ret                   ;Return to caller
sp3:       in    al,dx           ;vertical rescan
           test  al,8                                       _getfontptr endp                     ;End of procedure
           jne   sp3
                                                            ;== End =======================================================
sp4:       in    al,dx           ;Go to start of rescan
           test  al,8                                       _text   ends                         ;End program segment
           je    sp4                                                end                           ;End program
```

320x400 pixels with two screen pages

Although the 256 colors of the 320x200 mode are impressive, the resolution of this mode doesn't compare well with that of other VGA graphics modes. , the highest of the standard VGA modes, uses almost five times as many pixels on screen. Although the numerous colors of the 256 color mode give the impression of higher resolution, just as with a television, it still would be nice to have more pixels with which to work.

When you consider that a single screen page requires only 64K of video RAM in this mode, you may start to wonder if it isn't possible to use more memory per screen page and increase the number of pixels per page. As we'll see later, the VGA card can be programmed to display 400 pixel lines per screen instead of 200. Actually, this is easy to do because the 320x200 mode doesn't actually use 200 horizontal pixel lines.

Even in the 320x200 pixel mode, the VGA card actually has 400 horizontal lines on screen. Since the lines are joined in pairs, it appears as if only 200 lines are on the screen. So, instead of having to double the number of lines, we must simply address each pixel line separately.

The CRT registers responsible for the horizontal and vertical timing don't have to be reprogrammed to change the 320x200 mode to 320x400. Although this results in a rather unusual ratio between the horizontal and vertical axes, the doubled resolution makes this a problem we can tolerate.

The 128,000 pixels in a single screen cannot all be addressed in the usual way. This would require 128K of video RAM, which is too much for the Chain4 mode. So, we use the same method described in the last section to address the pixels in this mode. Each screen page requires

128K, so there is enough room for two pages in video RAM. For most applications, this is sufficient.

Two demonstration programs, called V3240C.C and V3240P.PAS, show you how graphics programming works in this mode. These programs are very similar to the ones discussed in the previous subsection. Each program also uses an assembler module (V3240CA.ASM and V3240PA.ASM). Compared to those previously presented, these modules needed only slight modifications. These changes reflect the differences between the 320x200 and 320x400 modes and are discussed after the program listings.

Pascal listing: V3240P.PAS

```
{*******************************************************************
*                                                                 *
*                    V 3 2 4 0 P . P A S                          *
**---------------------------------------------------------------**
*                                                                 *
*  Task        : Demonstrates programming in 320x400 VGA          *
*                graphic mode, using 256 colors and four screen   *
*                pages. This program requires the V3240PA.ASM      *
*                assembly language module.                        *
**---------------------------------------------------------------**
*                                                                 *
*  Author      : Michael Tischer                                  *
*  Developed on : 09/08/90                                        *
*  Last update  : 02/24/92                                        *
*******************************************************************}

program V3240P;

uses dos, crt;

{-- Type declarations ------------------------------------------}

type BPTR = ^byte;

{-- External references to the assembler routines --------------}

{$L v3240pa}                          { Link assembler module }

procedure init320400; external;
procedure setpix( x, y : integer; pcolor : byte ); external;
function getpix( x, y : integer ) : byte ; external;
procedure setpage( page : byte ); external;
procedure showpage( page : byte ); external;

{-- Constants --------------------------------------------------}

const MAXX = 319;                     { Maximum X- and Y-coordinates }
      MAXY = 399;

{*******************************************************************
*  IsVga : Determines whether a VGA card is installed.            *
**---------------------------------------------------------------**
*  Input  : None                                                  *
*  Output : TRUE or FALSE                                         *
*******************************************************************}

function IsVga : boolean;

var Regs : Registers;      { Processor registers for interrupt call }

begin
  Regs.AX := $1a00;        { Function 1AH applies to VGA only }
  Intr( $10, Regs );
  IsVga := ( Regs.AL = $1a );
end;

{*******************************************************************
*  PrintChar : Writes a character to the screen while in graphic mode.*
**---------------------------------------------------------------**
*  Input   :    THECHAR = Character to be written                 *
*               X, Y    = X- and Y-coordinates of upper-left corner *
*               FG      = Foreground color                        *
*               BK      = Background color                        *
*  Info    : Character is created in an 8x8 matrix, based on the  *
*            8x8 ROM font.                                         *
*******************************************************************}

procedure PrintChar( thechar : char; x, y : integer; fg, bk : byte );

type FDEF = array[0..255,0..7] of byte;          { Font array }
     TPTR = ^FDEF;                                { Pointer to font }

var Regs : Registers;           { Registers for interrupt call }
    ch   : char;                { Individual pixels in character }
    i, k,                       { Loop counter }
    BMask : byte;               { Bit mask for character design }

const fptr : TPTR = NIL;                { Pointer to font in ROM }

begin
  if fptr = NIL then            { Pointer to font already set? }
    begin                       { No }
      Regs.AH := $11;           { Call video BIOS function 11H, }
      Regs.AL := $30;           { sub-function 30H            }
      Regs.BH := 3;             { Get pointer to 8x8 font }
      intr( $10, Regs );
      fptr := ptr( Regs.ES, Regs.BP );      { Set pointers }
    end;

  if ( bk = 255 ) then          { Drawing transparent characters? }
    for i := 0 to 7 do          { Yes --> Set foreground pixels only }
      begin
        BMask := fptr^[ord(thechar),i];{ Get bit pattern for one line }
        for k := 0 to 7 do
          begin
            if ( BMask and 128 <> 0 ) then       { Pixel set? }
              setpix( x+k, y+i, fg );            { Yes }
            BMask := BMask shl 1;
          end;
      end
  else                          { No --> Consider background as well }
```

```
    for i := 0 to 7 do                        { Execute lines }
      begin
        BMask := fptr^[ord(thechar),i];{ Get bit pattern for one line }
        for k := 0 to 7 do
          begin
            if ( BMask and 128 <> 0 ) then          { Foreground? }
              setpix( x+k, y+i, fg )                      { Yes }
            else
              setpix( x+k, y+i, bk );          { No --> Background }
            BMask := BMask shl 1;
          end;
      end;
end;


{*********************************************************************
* Line: Draws a line based on the Bresenham algorithm.             *
**----------------------------------------------------------------**
* Input   : X1, Y1 = Starting coordinates (0 - ...)               *
*           X2, Y2 = Ending coordinates                           *
*           LPCOL = Color of line pixels                          *
*********************************************************************}

procedure Line( x1, y1, x2, y2 : integer; lpcol : byte );

var d, dx, dy,
    aincr, bincr,
    xincr, yincr,
    x, y                    : integer;

{-- Procedure for swapping two integer variables --------------------}

procedure SwapInt( var i1, i2: integer );

var dummy : integer;

begin
  dummy := i2;
  i2    := i1;
  i1    := dummy;
end;

{-- Main procedure -------------------------------------------------}

begin
  if ( abs(x2-x1) < abs(y2-y1) ) then        { X- or Y-axis overflow? }
    begin                                       { Check Y-axis }
      if ( y1 > y2 ) then                          { y1 > y2? }
        begin
          SwapInt( x1, x2 );                 { Yes --> Swap X1 with X2 }
          SwapInt( y1, y2 );                 {         and Y1 with Y2 }
        end;

      if ( x2 > x1 ) then xincr := 1        { Set X-axis increment }
                     else xincr := -1;

      dy := y2 - y1;
      dx := abs( x2-x1 );
      d  := 2 * dx - dy;
      aincr := 2 * (dx - dy);
      bincr := 2 * dx;
      x := x1;
      y := y1;

      setpix( x, y, lpcol );                     { Set first pixel }
```

```
    for y:=y1+1 to y2 do                    { Execute line on Y-axes }
      begin
        if ( d >= 0 ) then
          begin
            inc( x, xincr );
            inc( d, aincr );
          end
        else
          inc( d, bincr );
        setpix( x, y, lpcol);
      end;
  end
else                                              { Check X-axes }
  begin
    if ( x1 > x2 ) then                          { x1 > x2? }
      begin
        SwapInt( x1, x2 );                 { Yes --> Swap X1 with X2 }
        SwapInt( y1, y2 );                 {         and Y1 with Y2 }
      end;

    if ( y2 > y1 ) then yincr := 1        { Set Y-axis increment }
                   else yincr := -1;

    dx := x2 - x1;
    dy := abs( y2-y1 );
    d  := 2 * dy - dx;
    aincr := 2 * (dy - dx);
    bincr := 2 * dy;
    x := x1;
    y := y1;

    setpix( x, y, lpcol );                     { Set first pixel }
    for x:=x1+1 to x2 do                    { Execute line on X-axes }
      begin
        if ( d >= 0 ) then
          begin
            inc( y, yincr );
            inc( d, aincr );
          end
        else
          inc( d, bincr );
        setpix( x, y, lpcol );
      end;
  end;
end;


{*********************************************************************
* GrfxPrint: Displays a formatted string on the graphic screen.    *
**----------------------------------------------------------------**
* Input   : X, Y  = Starting coordinates (0 - ...)                *
*           FG    = Foreground color                              *
*           BK    = Background color (255 = transparent)          *
*           STRING = String with format information               *
*********************************************************************}

procedure GrfxPrint( x, y : integer; fg, bk : byte; strt : string );

var i : integer;                                     { Loop counter }

begin
  for i:=1 to length( strt ) do
    begin
      printchar( strt[i], x, y, fg, bk );   { Display using PrintChar }
      inc( x, 8 );                  { Move X to next character position }
```

```
    end;
  end;

{**********************************************************************
* ColorBox: Draws a rectangle and fills it with a line pattern.      *
**------------------------------------------------------------------**
* Input   : X1, Y1 = Upper-left coordinates of window               *
*           X2, Y2 = Lower-right coordinates of window              *
*           COLMAX = Greatest color value                           *
* Info    : Line colors are selected in a cycle of 0-COLMAX.        *
**********************************************************************}

procedure ColorBox( x1, y1, x2, y2 : integer; colmax : byte );

var x, y,                              { Loop counter }
    sx, sy : integer;                  { Exit point for last color loop }

begin
  Line( x1, y1, x1, y2, 15 );                    { Draw border }
  Line( x1, y2, x2, y2, 15 );
  Line( x2, y2, x2, y1, 15 );
  Line( x2, y1, x1, y1, 15 );

  for y := y2-1 downto y1+1 do          { Bottom left to right border }
    Line( x1+1, y2-1, x2-1, y, y mod colmax );

  for y := y2-1 downto y1+1 do          { Bottom right to left border }
    Line( x2-1, y2-1, x1+1, y, y mod colmax );

  {-- From center of box to top border --------------------------------}

  sx := x1+ (x2-x1) div 2;
  sy := y1+ (y2-y1) div 2;
  for x := x1+1 to x2-1 do
    Line( sx, sy, x, y1+1, x mod colmax );
end;

{**********************************************************************
* DrawAxis: Draws axes from left and top borders on the screen.      *
**------------------------------------------------------------------**
* Input   : XSTEP = Increment for X-axis                            *
*           YSTEP = Increment for Y-axis                            *
*           FG    = Foreground color                                *
*           BK    = Background color (255 = transparent)            *
**********************************************************************}

procedure DrawAxis( stepx, stepy : integer; fg, bk : byte );

var x, y    : integer;                 { Loop coordinates }
    lpcoords : string[3];

begin
  Line( 0, 0, MAXX, 0, fg );                     { Draw X-axis }
  Line( 0, 0, 0, MAXY, fg );                     { Draw Y-axis }

  x := stepx;                                    { Scale X-axis }
  while ( x < MAXX ) do
    begin
      Line( x, 0, x, 5, fg );
      str( x, lpcoords );
      if ( x < 100 ) then
        GrfxPrint( x - 8 , 8, fg, bk, lpcoords )
      else
        GrfxPrint( x - 12, 8, fg, bk, lpcoords );
```

```
      inc( x, stepx );
    end;

  y := stepy;                                    { Scale Y-axis }
  while ( y < MAXY ) do
    begin
      Line( 0, y, 5, y, fg );
      str( y:3, lpcoords );
      GrfxPrint( 8, y-4, fg, bk, lpcoords );
      inc( y, stepy );
    end;
end;

{**********************************************************************
* Demo: Demonstrates the functions and procedures in this module.    *
**------------------------------------------------------------------**
* Input   : None                                                     *
**********************************************************************}

procedure Demo;

const PAUSE = 100;                  { Pause counter in milliseconds }

var page : byte;                                 { Page counter }

begin

  ColorBox( 80, 50, 308, 350, 16 ); { Paint box }
  DrawAxis( 30, 40, 15, 255 ); { Draw axes }
  GrfxPrint( 46, MAXY-10, 15, 255, 'V3240P  -  (c) by Michael Tischer');

  setpage( 1 );                                  { Process page 1 }
  ColorBox( 80, 50, 308, 350, 255 );             { Paint box }
  DrawAxis( 30, 40, 15, 255 );                   { Draw axes }
  GrfxPrint( 46, MAXY-10, 15, 255, 'V3240P  -  (c) by Michael Tischer' );

  {-- Display four graphic pages in sequences-------------------------}

  for page := 0 to 50 do                         { 50 executions }
    begin
      showpage( page mod 2 );                    { Display page }
      delay( PAUSE );                            { Brief pause }
    end;
end;

{**********************************************************************
*                   M A I N   P R O G R A M                          *
**********************************************************************}

begin
  if IsVga then                      { VGA card installed? }
    begin                            { Yes --> Go ahead }
      init320400;                    { Initialize graphic mode }
      Demo;
      repeat until keypressed;
      Textmode( C080 );              { Shift into text mode }
    end
  else
    writeln( 'V3240P  -  (c) 1992 by Michael Tischer'#13#10#10 +
             'This program requires a VGA card', #13#10);
end.
```

Assembler listing: V3240PA.ASM

```
;*****************************************************************;
;*                   V 3 2 4 0 P A . A S M                      *;
;*-------------------------------------------------------------*;
;*   Task       : Contains routines for operating in 320x400   *;
;*                256 color mode on a VGA card.                *;
;*-------------------------------------------------------------*;
;*   Author     : Michael Tischer                              *;
;*   Developed on : 09/05/90                                   *;
;*   Last update : 02/24/92                                    *;
;*-------------------------------------------------------------*;
;*   Assembly    : MASM /mx V3240PA;   or   TASM -mx V3240PA   *;
;*                ... link to V3240P.PAS                       *;
;*****************************************************************;

;== Constants ===============================================

SC_INDEX      = 3c4h      ;Index register for sequencer ctrl.
SC_MAP_MASK   = 2         ;Number of map mask register
SC_MEM_MODE   = 4         ;Number of memory mode register

GC_INDEX      = 3ceh      ;Index register for graphics ctrl.
GC_READ_MAP   = 4         ;Number of read map register
GC_GRAPH_MODE = 5         ;Number of graphics mode register
GC_MISCELL    = 6         ;Number of miscellaneous register

CRTC_INDEX    = 3d4h      ;Index register for CRT controllers
CC_MAX_SCAN   = 9         ;Number of maximum scan line reg.
CC_START_HI   = 0Ch       ;Number of high start register
CC_UNDERLINE  = 14h       ;Number of underline register
CC_MODE_CTRL  = 17h       ;Number of mode control register

DAC_WRITE_ADR = 3C8h      ;DAC write address
DAC_READ_ADR  = 3C7h      ;DAC read address
DAC_DATA      = 3C9h      ;DAC data register

VERT_RESCAN   = 3DAh      ;Input status register #1

PIXX          = 320       ;Horizontal resolution

;== Data segment =============================================

DATA   segment word public

vio_seg   dw (?)          ;Video segment with current page
                          ;must be initialized during runtime

DATA   ends

;== Program ==================================================

CODE   segment byte public   ;Program segment

       assume cs:code, ds:data

;-- Public declarations ------------------------------------

public   init320400      ;Initialize 320x400 mode
public   setpix          ;Set pixel
public   getpix          ;Get pixel color
public   showpage        ;Display page 0 or 1
public   setpage         ;Set page for setpix and getpix
```

```
;-------------------------------------------------------------
;-- INIT320400: Initializes 320x400 pixel mode
;-- Call from TP: init320400;

init320400 proc near

       ;-- Sets mode 13H, since BIOS uses this mostly for
       ;-- initialization.

       mov   ax,0013h        ;Set normal mode 13H
       int   10h

       mov   dx,GC_INDEX     ;Memory division
       mov   al,GC_GRAPH_MODE ;Disable bit 4 of
       out   dx,al           ;graphic mode register
       inc   dx              ;in graphics controller
       in    al,dx
       and   al,11101111b
       out   dx,al
       dec   dx

       mov   al,GC_MISCELL   ;And change bit 1
       out   dx,al           ;in the miscellaneous
       inc   dx              ;register
       in    al,dx
       and   al,11111101b
       out   dx,al

       mov   dx,SC_INDEX     ;Modify memory mode register in
       mov   al,SC_MEM_MODE  ;sequencer controller so no further
       out   dx,al           ;address division follows in
       inc   dx              ;bitplanes, and set the bitplane
       in    al,dx           ;currently in the
       and   al,11110111b    ;bit mask register
       or    al,4
       out   dx,al

       mov   ax,0A000h       ;Fill all four bitplanes with color
       mov   vio_seg,ax      ;code 00H and clear the screen
       mov   es,ax
       xor   di,di
       mov   ax,di
       mov   cx,8000h
       rep   stosw

       mov   dx,CRTC_INDEX   ;Double pixel rows in maximum
       mov   al,CC_MAX_SCAN  ;scan line register of the CRT
       out   dx,al           ;controller by disabling bit 7,
       inc   dx              ;while setting bits 0-4 to 1 to
       in    al,dx           ;change the character
       and   al,01110000b    ;height
       out   dx,al
       dec   dx              ;Return DX to CRT index register

       mov   al,CC_UNDERLINE ;Set double word mode using bit 6
       out   dx,al           ;in underline register of
       inc   dx              ;CRT controller
       in    al,dx
       and   al,10111111b
       out   dx,al
       dec   dx

       mov   al,CC_MODE_CTRL ;Using bit 6 of mode control reg.
       out   dx,al           ;of CRT controller, change
```

```
        inc   dx              ;from word mode to byte mode
        in    al,dx
        or    al,01000000b
        out   dx,al

        ret                   ;Return to caller

init320400 endp              ;End of procedure

;-------------------------------------------------------------------
;-- SETPIX: Changes a pixel to a specific color
;-- Call from TP: setpix( x , y : integer; pcolor : byte );

setpix    proc near

sframe    struc               ;Structure for stack access
bp0       dw ?                ;Gets BP
ret_adr0  dw ?                ;Return address to caller
pcolor    dw ?                ;Color
y0        dw ?                ;Y-coordinate
x0        dw ?                ;X-coordinate
sframe    ends                ;End of structure

frame     equ [ bp - bp0 ]    ;Address structure elements

        push  bp              ;Prepare for parameter addressing
        mov   bp,sp           ; through BP register

        mov   ax,PIXX / 4     ;Compute offset in video RAM
        mul   frame.y0        ; and pass to DI
        mov   cx,frame.x0
        mov   bx,cx
        shr   bx,1
        shr   bx,1
        add   ax,bx
        mov   di,ax

        and   cl,3            ;Compute bit mask for map to be
        mov   ah,1            ; addressed, move to AH
        shl   ah,cl
        mov   al,SC_MAP_MASK  ;Register number to AL
        mov   dx,SC_INDEX     ;Load sequencer index address
        out   dx,ax           ;Load bit mask register

        mov   ax,vio_seg      ;Set ES to video RAM
        mov   es,ax
        mov   al,byte ptr frame.pcolor  ;Load pixel color and
        stosb                 ;write to selected bitmap

        pop   bp              ;Get registers from stack

        ret   6              ;Return to caller, remove
                              ;arguments from stack

setpix    endp               ;End of procedure

;-------------------------------------------------------------------
;-- GETPIX: Returns a pixel color
;-- Call from TP: x := getpix( x , y : integer );

getpix    proc near

sframe1   struc               ;Structure for stack access
bp1       dw ?                ;Gets BP
```

```
ret_adr1  dw ?                ;Return address to caller
y1        dw ?                ;Y-coordinate
x1        dw ?                ;X-coordinate
sframe1   ends                ;End of structure

frame     equ [ bp - bp1 ]    ;Address structure elements

        push  bp              ;Prepare for parameter addressing
        mov   bp,sp           ; through BP register

        mov   ax,PIXX / 4     ;Compute offset in video RAM
        mul   frame.y1        ; and pass to SI
        mov   si,frame.x1
        mov   cx,si
        shr   si,1
        shr   si,1
        add   si,ax

        and   cl,3            ;Compute bit mask for map to be
        mov   ah,cl           ; addressed in AH
        mov   al,GC_READ_MAP  ;Move register number to AL
        mov   dx,GC_INDEX     ;Load graphics controller index
        out   dx,ax           ;Load Read Map register

        mov   ax,vio_seg      ;Set ES to video RAM
        mov   es,ax
        mov   al,es:[si]      ;Load pixel color

        pop   bp              ;Pop register from stack

        ret   4              ;Return to caller, remove
                              ;arguments from stack

getpix    endp               ;End of procedure

;-------------------------------------------------------------------
;-- SETPAGE: Sets page for access from setpix and getpix
;-- Call from TP: setpage( page : byte );

setpage   proc near

        pop   ax             ;Pop return address from stack
        pop   cx             ;Pop argument from stack

        push  ax             ;Push this back on

        mov   bl,0a0h        ;Check for page 0
        or    cl,cl          ;Is this page 0?
        je    sp1            ;Yes --> Store segment address

        mov   bl,0a8h        ;No --> Page 1

sp1:    mov   byte ptr vio_seg + 1,bl ;Move new segment address

        ret                  ;Return to caller, remove
                              ;arguments from stack

setpage   endp               ;End of procedure

;-------------------------------------------------------------------
;-- SHOWPAGE: Display one of the two screen pages
;-- Call from TP: showpage( page : byte );

showpage  proc near
```

```asm
        pop     bx              ;Pop return address from stack
        pop     ax              ;Pop argument from stack

        push    bx              ;Push these back in

        or      al,al           ;Is this page 0?
        je      sp2             ;Yes --> Number is also
                                ;        high-byte of offset

        mov     al,80h          ;No --> Page 1 with offset 8000H

sp2:    mov     dx,CRTC_INDEX   ;Address CRT controller
        mov     ah,al           ;Move high byte of offset to AH
        mov     al,CC_START_HI  ;Move register number to AL
        out     dx,ax           ;and exit

        ;-- Wait to return to starting screen design ---------------

        mov     dx,VERT_RESCAN  ;Wait for end of
sp3:    in      al,dx           ;vertical rescan
        test    al,8
        jne     sp3

sp4:    in      al,dx           ;Go to start of rescan
        test    al,8
        je      sp4

        ret                     ;Return to caller, remove
                                ;arguments from stack

showpage endp                   ;End of procedure

;== End =============================================================

CODE    ends                    ;End of code segment
        end                     ;End program
```

C listing: V3240C.C

```c
/*******************************************************************
*                       V 3 2 4 0 C . C                           *
**---------------------------------------------------------------**
* Task          : Demonstrates programming in 320x400 VGA         *
*                 graphic mode, using 256 colors and four screen  *
*                 pages. This program requires the V3240CA.ASM    *
*                 assembly language module.                       *
**---------------------------------------------------------------**
* Author        : Michael Tischer                                 *
* Developed on  : 09/04/90                                        *
* Last update   : 02/26/92                                        *
**---------------------------------------------------------------**
* Memory model  : SMALL                                           *
**---------------------------------------------------------------**
* (MICROSOFT C)                                                   *
* Compilation   : CL /AS /c /WO V3240C.C                          *
*               : LINK V3240C V3240CA;                            *
**---------------------------------------------------------------**
* (BORLAND TURBO C)                                               *
* Compilation   : Create a project file using the following:      *
*                    v3240c.c                                      *
*                    v3240ca.obj                                   *
**---------------------------------------------------------------**
* Call          : v3240c                                          *
*******************************************************************/

#include <dos.h>
#include <stdarg.h>
#include <stdlib.h>
#include <stdio.h>
#include <conio.h>

/*-- Type declarations -------------------------------------------*/

typedef unsigned char BYTE;

/*-- External references to the assembler routines ---------------*/

extern void init320400( void );
extern void setpix( int x, int y, unsigned char pcolor);
extern BYTE getpix( int x, int y );
extern void setpage( BYTE page );
extern void showpage( BYTE page );
extern void far * getfontptr( void );

/*-- Constants ---------------------------------------------------*/

#define MAXX 319                        /* Maximum X- and Y-coordinates */
#define MAXY 399

/*******************************************************************
* IsVga: Determines whether a VGA card is installed.              *
**---------------------------------------------------------------**
* Input  : None                                                   *
* Output : 0  If no VGA exists, otherwise < 0                     *
*******************************************************************/

BYTE IsVga( void )
{
union REGS Regs;            /* Processor registers for interrupt call */

Regs.x.ax = 0x1a00;              /* Function 1AH applies to VGA only */
```

```
   int86( 0x10, &Regs, &Regs );
   return ( Regs.h.al == 0x1a );          /* Is the function available? */
}


/************************************************************
 * PrintChar : Writes a character to the screen while in graphic mode.*
 **------------------------------------------------------------**
 * Input    :  THECHAR = Character to be written             *
 *             x, y    = X- and Y-coordinates of upper-left corner *
 *             FG      = Foreground color                    *
 *             BK      = Background color                    *
 * Info     : Character is created in an 8x8 matrix, based on the *
 *            8x8 ROM font.                                   *
 ************************************************************/

void PrintChar( char thechar, int x, int y, BYTE FG, BYTE BK )
{
 typedef BYTE FDEF[256][8];                /* Font definition */
 typedef FDEF far *TPTR;                   /* Pointer to font */

 BYTE        i, k,                         /* Loop counter */
             BMask;                        /* Bit mask for character design */

 static TPTR fptr = (TPTR) 0;              /* Pointer to font in ROM */

 if ( fptr == (TPTR) 0 )                   /* Pointer to font already set? */
   fptr = getfontptr();  /* No --> Use the assembler function to load */

 /*- Generate character pixel by pixel -------------------------*/

 if ( BK == 255 )                          /* Drawing transparent characters? */
   for ( i = 0; i < 8; ++i )     /* Yes --> Set foreground pixels only */
   {
     BMask = (*fptr)[thechar][i];          /* Get bit pattern for one line */
     for ( k = 0; k < 8; ++k, BMask <<= 1 )     /* Execute column */
       if ( BMask & 128 )                   /* Pixel set? */
         setpix( x+k, y+i, FG );            /* Yes */
   }
 else                          /* No --> Consider background as well */
   for ( i = 0; i < 8; ++i )                /* Execute lines */
   {
     BMask = (*fptr)[thechar][i];     /* Get bit pattern for one line */
     for ( k = 0; k < 8; ++k, BMask <<= 1 )     /* Execute columns */
       setpix( x+k, y+i, ( BMask & 128 ) ? FG : BK );
   }
}


/************************************************************
 * Line: Draws a line based on the Bresenham algorithm.     *
 **------------------------------------------------------------**
 * Input    : X1, Y1 = Starting coordinates (0 - ...)       *
 *            X2, Y2 = Ending coordinates                    *
 *            LPCOL  = Color of line pixels                  *
 ************************************************************/

/*-- Function for swapping two integer variables --------------------*/

void SwapInt( int *i1, int *i2 )
{
 int dummy;

 dummy = *i2;
 *i2   = *i1;
 *i1   = dummy;
```

```
}

/*-- Main part of function -------------------------------------*/

void Line( int x1, int y1, int x2, int y2, BYTE pcolor )
{
 int d, dx, dy,
     aincr, bincr,
     xincr, yincr,
     x, y;

 if ( abs(x2-x1) < abs(y2-y1) )            /* X- or Y-axis overflow? */
 {                                          /* Check Y-axis */
   if ( y1 > y2 )                           /* y1 > y2? */
   {
     SwapInt( &x1, &x2 );                   /* Yes --> Swap X1 with X2 */
     SwapInt( &y1, &y2 );                   /*         and Y1 with Y2 */
   }

   xincr = ( x2 > x1 ) ? 1 : -1;            /* Set X-axis increment */

   dy = y2 - y1;
   dx = abs( x2-x1 );
   d  = 2 * dx - dy;
   aincr = 2 * (dx - dy);
   bincr = 2 * dx;
   x = x1;
   y = y1;

   setpix( x, y, pcolor );                  /* Set first pixel */
   for (y=y1+1; y<= y2; ++y )           /* Execute line on Y-axes */
   {
     if ( d >= 0 )
     {
       x += xincr;
       d += aincr;
     }
     else
       d += bincr;
     setpix(x, y, pcolor);
   }
 }
 else                                        /* Check X-axes */
 {
   if ( x1 > x2 )                            /* x1 > x2? */
   {
     SwapInt( &x1, &x2 );                    /* Yes --> Swap X1 with X2 */
     SwapInt( &y1, &y2 );                    /*         and Y1 with Y2 */
   }

   yincr = ( y2 > y1 ) ? 1 : -1;            /* Set Y-axis increment */

   dx = x2 - x1;
   dy = abs( y2-y1 );
   d  = 2 * dy - dx;
   aincr = 2 * (dy - dx);
   bincr = 2 * dy;
   x = x1;
   y = y1;

   setpix(x, y, pcolor);                     /* Set first pixel */
   for (x=x1+1; x<=x2; ++x )            /* Execute line on X-axes */
   {
     if ( d >= 0 )
```

```
    {
    y += yincr;
    d += aincr;
    }
  else
    d += bincr;
  setpix(x, y, pcolor);
  }
 }
}


/****************************************************************
* GrfxPrintf: Displays a formatted string on the graphic screen. *
**--------------------------------------------------------------**
* Input   : X, Y  = Starting coordinates (0 - ...)              *
*           FG    = Foreground color                            *
*           BK    = Background color (255 = transparent)        *
*           STRING = String with format information             *
*           ...    = Arguments similar to printf                *
****************************************************************/

void GrfxPrintf( int x, int y, BYTE FG, BYTE BK, char * string, ... )
{
 va_list parameter;            /* Parameter list for VA_... macros */
 char stngbuf[255],            /* Buffer for formatted string */
      *cp;

 va_start( parameter, string );           /* Convert parameter */
 vsprintf( stngbuf, string, parameter );       /* Format */
 for ( cp = stngbuf; *cp; ++cp, x+= 8 )    /* Formatted string */
   PrintChar( *cp, x, y, FG, BK );     /* Display using PrintChar */
}


/****************************************************************
* ColorBox: Draws a rectangle and fills it with a line pattern. *
**--------------------------------------------------------------**
* Input   : X1, Y1 = Upper-left coordinates of window           *
*           X2, Y2 = Lower-right coordinates of window          *
*           COLMAX = Greatest color value                       *
* Info    : Line colors are selected in a cycle of 0-COLMAX.    *
****************************************************************/

void ColorBox( int x1, int y1, int x2, int y2, int colmax )
{
 int x, y,                     /* Loop variables */
     sx, sy;                   /* Exit point for last color loop */

 Line( x1, y1, x1, y2, 15 );             /* Draw border */
 Line( x1, y2, x2, y2, 15 );
 Line( x2, y2, x2, y1, 15 );
 Line( x2, y1, x1, y1, 15 );

 for ( y = y2-1; y > y1; --y )    /* Bottom left to right border */
  Line( x1+1, y2-1, x2-1, y, y % colmax );

 for ( y = y2-1; y > y1; --y )    /* Bottom right to left border */
  Line( x2-1, y2-1, x1+1, y, y % colmax );

 /*-- From center of box to top border -----------------------*/

 for ( x=x1+1, sx=x1+(x2-x1)/2, sy=y1+(y2-y1)/ 2; x < x2; ++x )
  Line( sx, sy, x, y1+1, x % colmax );
}
```

```
/****************************************************************
* DrawAxis: Draws axes from left and top borders on the screen. *
**--------------------------------------------------------------**
* Input   : XSTEP = Increment for X-axis                        *
*           YSTEP = Increment for Y-axis                        *
*           FG    = Foreground color                            *
*           BK    = Background color (255 = transparent)        *
****************************************************************/

void DrawAxis( int stepx, int stepy, BYTE FG, BYTE BK )
{
 int x, y;                     /* Loop coordinates */

 Line( 0, 0, MAXX, 0, FG );              /* Draw X-axis */
 Line( 0, 0, 0, MAXY, FG );              /* Draw Y-axis */

 for ( x = stepx; x < MAXX; x += stepx )    /* Scale X-axis */
  {
   Line( x, 0, x, 5, FG );
   GrfxPrintf( x < 100 ? x - 8 : x - 12, 8, FG, BK, "%d", x );
  }

 for ( y = stepy; y < MAXY; y += stepy )    /* Scale Y-axis */
  {
   Line( 0, y, 5, y, FG );
   GrfxPrintf( 8, y-4, FG, BK, "%3d", y );
  }
}


/****************************************************************
* Demo: Demonstrates the functions in this module.             *
****************************************************************/

void Demo( void )
{
#define PAUSE 100000          /* Pause amount, varies with system */

 int x;                       /* Coordinate counter */
 long delay;                  /* Pause counter */

 ColorBox( 80, 50, 308, 350, 16 );            /* Paint box */
 DrawAxis( 30, 40, 15, 255 );            /* Draw axes */
 GrfxPrintf( 46, MAXY-10, 15, 255,
          "V3240C  - (c) by Michael Tischer");

 setpage( 1 );                       /* Process page */
 ColorBox( 80, 50, 308, 350, 255 );           /* Paint box */
 DrawAxis( 30, 40, 15, 255 );            /* Draw axes */
 GrfxPrintf( 46, MAXY-10, 15, 255,
          "V3240C  - (c) by Michael Tischer" );


 /*-- Display four graphic pages in sequence -----------------*/

 for ( x = 0; x < 50; ++x )              /* 50 executions */
  {
   showpage( x % 2 );                    /* Display page */
   for ( delay = 1; delay < PAUSE; ++delay )    /* Brief pause */
    ;
  }
}


/****************************************************************
/**             M A I N   P R O G R A M                     **/
```

```
/**************************************************************************/

void main( void )
{
 union REGS regs;

 if ( IsVga() )                             /* VGA card installed? */
  {                                         /* Yes --> Go ahead */
   init320400();                      /* Initialize graphic mode */
   Demo();
   getch();                                 /* Wait for a key */
   regs.x.ax = 0x0003;                /* Shift into text mode */
   int86( 0x10, &regs, &regs );
  }
 else
  printf( "V3240C  -  (c) 1992 by Michael Tischer\n\n"\
          "This program requires a VGA card\n\n" );

}
```

Assembler listing: V3240CA.ASM

```
;***************************************************************************;
;*                    V 3 2 4 0 C A . A S M                               *;
;*-----------------------------------------------------------------------*;
;*    Task        : Contains routines for operating in                   *;
;*                   320x400 256 color mode on a VGA card.               *;
;*-----------------------------------------------------------------------*;
;*    Author      : Michael Tischer                                      *;
;*    Developed on : 09/05/90                                            *;
;*    Last update  : 02/24/92                                            *;
;*-----------------------------------------------------------------------*;
;*    Assembly    : MASM /mx V3240CA;     or     TASM -mx V3240CA         *;
;*                   ... Link to V3240C.C                                 *;
;***************************************************************************;

IGROUP group _text                ;Program segment
DGROUP group const,_bss, _data    ;Data segment
       assume CS:IGROUP, DS:DGROUP, ES:DGROUP, SS:DGROUP

CONST  segment word public 'CONST';This segment handles all
CONST  ends                       ;readable constants

_BSS   segment word public 'BSS'  ;This segment handles all uninitial-
_BSS   ends                       ;ized static variables

_DATA  segment word public 'DATA' ;This segment handles all initialized
                                  ;global and static variables

_DATA  ends

;== Constants =============================================================

SC_INDEX       = 3c4h             ;Index register for sequencer ctrl.
SC_MAP_MASK     = 2               ;Number of map mask register
SC_MEM_MODE     = 4               ;Number of memory mode register

GC_INDEX       = 3ceh             ;Index register for graphics ctrl.
GC_READ_MAP     = 4               ;Number of read map register
GC_GRAPH_MODE   = 5               ;Number of graphics mode register
GC_MISCELL      = 6               ;Number of miscellaneous register

CRTC_INDEX     = 3d4h             ;Index register for CRT controller
CC_MAX_SCAN     = 9               ;Number of maximum scan line reg.
CC_START_HI     = 0Ch             ;Number of high start register
CC_UNDERLINE    = 14h             ;Number of underline register
CC_MODE_CTRL    = 17h             ;Number of mode control register

PIXX           = 320              ;Horizontal resolution

VERT_RESCAN    = 3DAh             ;Input status register #1

;== Data =================================================================

_DATA  segment word public 'DATA'

vio_seg    dw 0a000h              ;Video segment with current page

_DATA  ends

;== Program ==============================================================

_TEXT  segment byte public 'CODE' ;Program segment
```

```
;-- Public declarations ---------------------------------------------

public    _init320400       ;Initialize 320x400 mode
public    _setpix           ;Set pixel
public    _getpix           ;Get pixel color
public    _showpage         ;Display page 0 or 1
public    _setpage          ;Set page for setpix and getpix
public    _getfontptr       ;Return pointer to 8x8 font

;-- INIT320400: Initializes 320x400 pixel mode ----------------------
;-- Declaration : void init320400( void );

_init320400 proc near

          ;-- Sets mode 13H, since BIOS uses this mostly for
          ;-- initialization.

          mov   ax,0013h        ;Set normal mode 13H
          int   10h

          mov   dx,GC_INDEX     ;Memory division
          mov   al,GC_GRAPH_MODE ;Disable bit 4 of
          out   dx,al           ;graphics mode register in
          inc   dx              ;graphics controller
          in    al,dx
          and   al,11101111b
          out   dx,al
          dec   dx

          mov   al,GC_MISCELL   ;And change bit 1
          out   dx,al           ;in the miscellaneous
          inc   dx              ;register
          in    al,dx
          and   al,11111101b
          out   dx,al

          mov   dx,SC_INDEX     ;Modify memory mode register in
          mov   al,SC_MEM_MODE  ;sequencer controller so no further
          out   dx,al           ;address division follows in
          inc   dx              ;bitplanes, and set the bitplane
          in    al,dx           ;currently in the
          and   al,11110111b    ;bit mask register
          or    al,4
          out   dx,al

          mov   ax,vio_seg      ;Fill all four bitplanes with color
          mov   es,ax           ;code 00H and clear the screen
          xor   di,di
          mov   ax,di
          mov   cx,8000h
          rep   stosw

          mov   dx,CRTC_INDEX   ;Double pixel rows in maximum
          mov   al,CC_MAX_SCAN  ;scan lines register of the CRT
          out   dx,al           ;controller by disabling bit 7,
          inc   dx              ;while setting bits 0-4 to 1 to
          in    al,dx           ;change the character
          and   al,01110000b    ;height
          out   dx,al
          dec   dx              ;Return DX to CRT index register

          mov   al,CC_UNDERLINE ;in underline register of
          out   dx,al           ;CRT controller
          inc   dx
```

```
          in    al,dx
          and   al,10111111b
          out   dx,al
          dec   dx

          mov   al,CC_MODE_CTRL ;Using bit 6 in mode control reg.
          out   dx,al           ;of CRT controller, change
          inc   dx              ;from word mode to byte mode
          in    al,dx
          or    al,01000000b
          out   dx,al

          ret                   ;Return to caller

_init320400 endp              ;End of procedure

;-- SETPIX: Changes a pixel to a specific color ---------------------
;-- Declaration : void setpix( int x, int y, unsigned char pcolor );

_setpix   proc near

sframe    struc               ;Structure for stack access
bp0       dw ?                ;Gets BP
ret_adr0  dw ?                ;Return address to caller
x0        dw ?                ;X-coordinate
y0        dw ?                ;Y-coordinate
pcolor    dw ?                ;Color
sframe    ends                ;End of structure

frame     equ [ bp - bp0 ]    ;Address structure elements

          push  bp            ;Prepare for parameter addressing
          mov   bp,sp         ;through BP register

          push  di

          mov   ax,PIXX / 4   ;Compute offset in video RAM
          mul   frame.y0      ;and pass to DI
          mov   cx,frame.x0
          mov   bx,cx
          shr   bx,1
          shr   bx,1
          add   ax,bx
          mov   di,ax

          and   cl,3          ;Compute bit mask for map to be
          mov   ah,1          ;addressed, move to AH
          shl   ah,cl
          mov   al,SC_MAP_MASK ;Register number to AL
          mov   dx,SC_INDEX    ;Load sequencer index address
          out   dx,ax          ;Load bit mask register

          mov   ax,vio_seg     ;Set ES to video RAM
          mov   es,ax
          mov   al,byte ptr frame.pcolor ;Load pixel color and
          stosb                ;write to selected bitmap

          pop   di
          pop   bp             ;Pop registers from stack

          ret                  ;Return to caller

_setpix   endp                 ;End of procedure
```

```
;-- GETPIX: Returns a pixel color -------------------------------------
;-- Declaration : unsigned char getpix( int x, int y );

_getpix      proc near

sframe1      struc                     ;Structure for stack access
bp1          dw ?                      ;Gets BP
ret_adr1     dw ?                      ;Return address to caller
x1           dw ?                      ;X-coordinate
y1           dw ?                      ;Y-coordinate
sframe1      ends                      ;End of structure

frame        equ [ bp - bp1 ]          ;Address structure elements

             push  bp                  ;Prepare for parameter addressing
             mov   bp,sp               ; through BP register

             push  si                  ;Push SI onto stack

             mov   ax,PIXX / 4         ;Compute offset in video RAM
             mul   frame.y1            ;and pass to SI
             mov   si,frame.x1
             mov   cx,si
             shr   si,1
             shr   si,1
             add   si,ax

             and   cl,3                ;Compute bit mask for map to be
             mov   ah,cl               ;addressed, move to AH
             mov   al,GC_READ_MAP      ;Register number to AL
             mov   dx,GC_INDEX         ;Load graphics controller index
             out   dx,ax               ;Load read map register

             mov   ax,vio_seg          ;Set ES to video RAM
             mov   es,ax
             mov   al,es:[si]          ;Load pixel color

             pop   si                  ;Get registers from stack
             pop   bp

             ret                       ;Return to caller

_getpix      endp                      ;End of procedure

;-- SETPAGE: Sets page for access from setpix and getpix --------------
;-- Declaration : void setpage( unsigned char page );

_setpage     proc near

             pop   bx                  ;Pop return address from stack
             pop   ax                  ;Pop argument from stack

             push  ax                  ;Push these back on
             push  bx

             mov   bl,0a0h             ;Get out of page 0
             or    al,al               ;Is this page 0?
             je    sp1                 ;Yes --> Store segment address

             mov   bl,0a8h             ;No --> Page 1

sp1:         mov   byte ptr vio_seg + 1,bl ;Move new segment address

             ret                       ;Return to caller
```

```
_setpage     endp                      ;End of procedure

;-- SHOWPAGE: Display one of the two screen pages ---------------------
;-- Declaration : void showpage( unsigned char page );

_showpage    proc near

             pop   bx                  ;Pop return address from stack
             pop   ax                  ;Pop argument from stack

             push  ax                  ;Push these back on
             push  bx

             or    al,al               ;Is this page 0?
             je    sp2                 ;Yes --> Number = high byte of offset

             mov   al,80h              ;No --> Page 1, with offset 8000H

sp2:         mov   dx,CRTC_INDEX       ;Address CRT controller
             mov   ah,al               ;Move high byte of offset to AL
             mov   al,CC_START_HI      ;Move register number
             out   dx,ax               ;to AL and exit

             ;-- Wait to return to starting screen design ---------------

             mov   dx,VERT_RESCAN      ;Wait for end of
sp3:         in    al,dx               ;vertical rescan
             test  al,8
             jne   sp3

sp4:         in    al,dx               ;Go to start of rescan
             test  al,8
             je    sp4

             ret                       ;Return to caller

_showpage    endp                      ;End of procedure

;-- GETFONTPTR: Returns FAR pointer to 8x8 font table -----------------
;-- Declaration : void far * getfontptr( void )

_getfontptr  proc near

             push  bp                  ;Push BP onto stack

             mov   ax,1130h            ;Get register for function call
             mov   bh,3
             int   10h                 ;Call BIOS video interrupt

             mov   dx,es               ;Pointer ES:BP returned in DX:AX
             mov   ax,bp

             pop   bp                  ;Pop BP from stack
             ret                       ;Return to caller

_getfontptr  endp                      ;End of procedure

;== End ===============================================================

_text        ends                      ;End program segment
             end                       ;End program
```

One difference is immediately noticeable. The init320200 routine has been replaced with a routine called init320400. The routine itself has changed very little. Video mode 13H is still initialized using the BIOS. The linear mode for addressing video RAM is selected, and doubleword mode is replaced with byte mode.

A new step in the routine is the access to the maximum scan line register of the CRT controller. Two changes occur: the bits that indicate the number of pixel lines and the character height. The 200 line bit is disabled so all 400 lines are displayed. The other bit must be set from 1 to 0 to indicate that each pixel line will be processed individually instead of in groups of two.

These are the only changes required to switch from 320x200 mode to 320x400 mode.

The change in screen resolution also affects the setpage and showpage assembler routines. These routines are changed to reflect the new screen page size. Also, the second (and last) screen page now begins at 8000H instead of 4000H.

Surprisingly, setpix and getpix don't have to be changed at all. The line length remains the same and the lines are still stored contiguously in video RAM. Now there are twice as many lines as before, and they can be accessed by the correspondingly greater Y-coordinates.

The main programs are also similar. A coordinate grid is drawn on screen along with a copyright message. A box filled with colored lines appears below this.

You can immediately tell there are 400 pixel lines on screen by looking at the coordinate grid. You can also tell that more than one screen page is in memory because of the interesting effects that result from quickly switching the two pages.

Finally, we should mention that some (not all) VGA cards have another 256 color mode, with a resolution of 360x480 pixels. This mode exceeds the limit of 128K per screen page, so only one page can be stored in video RAM at a time.

For these reasons we won't discuss this mode in detail. The practical resolution limit of the VGA card with 256 colors lies with the 320x400 mode. If you really need greater resolution in a 256 color mode, you should consider using the Super VGA card, which offers higher resolution modes as a standard feature.

4.8.8 Freely Selectable Colors

An important difference between the EGA/VGA cards and their predecessors is the ability to work with more than just the 16 basic colors. The EGA card has 64 colors from which to choose and the color palette of the VGA card exceeds 262,000 different colors. Of course, not every available color can be displayed on screen at one time. Depending on which text or graphics mode you're using, you'll be limited to a set of 16 or 256 colors that can be used at any given time.

What are palette registers?

The 16 palette registers are part of the attribute controller. These registers are important for the color display in all text and graphics modes with 16 or fewer colors. When the CRT controller is building a screen, it receives the color information for a given pixel as a value between 0 and 15. This value is used as an index into the palette register table. The color information is taken from the index palette register and sent directly to the monitor by the EGA card.

This process shows how the EGA and VGA cards still have a strong connection between the different color codes and the colors that appear on the screen, similar to the earlier video cards. So the programmer has the option of freely selecting the colors that should appear on the screen. This global color selection must occur without changing the contents of video RAM. For example, if all pixels in 640x350 pixel graphics mode were black and a program abruptly changed these pixels to another color, changing the palette register contents from 0 to another value is all that's needed.

As long as you allow for the palette registers, VGA and EGA color selection isn't different than CGA color selection. The color values are identical to CGA after initializing the palette registers by calling BIOS video interrupt function 00H. The palette registers can then be controlled using the sub-functions of BIOS video interrupt 10H, function 12H, after video mode initialization using function 00H.

To call this function, place the function number 12H in the AH register and the sub-function number (31H) in the BL register. The AL register, which normally contains the sub-function number, is used here to determine whether or not the palette registers are automatically initialized. If this register contains a value of 1, the palette registers aren't initialized with each subsequent call of function 00H. A value of 0 switches on the automatic initialization feature.

With this feature switched on, you can use the expanded color capabilities of the EGA and VGA cards by programming the palette registers. Before doing this, you must understand the structure of the palette registers. With an EGA card and an EGA or multisync monitor, the individual bits in a palette register directly correspond to the different monitor leads that encode the colors. The basic colors red, green, and blue (RGB) each have two leads available. One represents a brighter, more intense display and the other is for a normal display. This makes a total of six bits involved in color programming, which allows for a maximum of 64 (2^6) colors; 16 of these colors can be loaded in the 16 palette registers at a time.

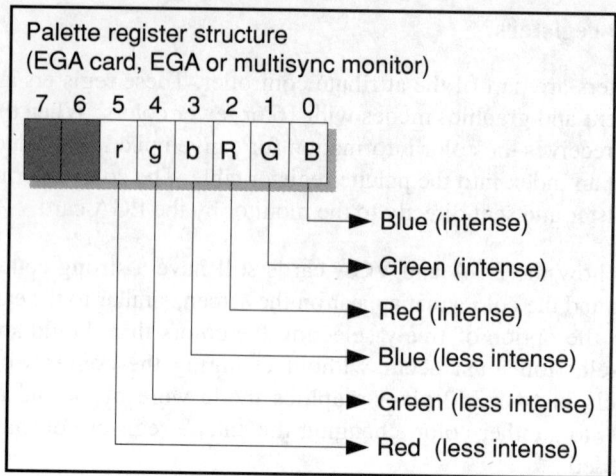

The attribute controller's color plane enable register plays a vital role in color selection and the palette registers. Before every access to one of the 16 palette registers, the EGA/VGA video controller executes a logical AND between the color index and the lower four bits of this register. Generally, this operation is transparent because the lower four bits of the color plane enable register contain a default value of 1111(b). The AND operation with the color index doesn't change the value and the desired color appears on screen.

This is quite different if the value in the color plane enable register changes. For example, if a value of 0111(b) is stored in the color plane enable register, the AND operation with the color value would result in the highest bit from the color value being switched off. This means that all pixels (or characters) with color codes from 8 to 15 would be reassigned to color codes from 0 to 7. Actually, this capability is seldom used and the default value of the color plane enable register is rarely changed.

The DAC color table

The palette register contents can be passed directly from the EGA card to the monitor, through the monitor cable's six color leads. However, this is impossible with the VGA card. The VGA card produces an analog signal for the monitor, which works under a completely different premise.

So, the contents of the VGA card's 16 palette registers are added to the *DAC color table* before color information can be sent to the monitor. DAC is an abbreviation for *Digital to Analog Converter*. As the name suggests, this table converts the digital color information from the palette registers to an analog signal that the monitor can understand.

The DAC color table has 256 registers, each of which stores the information for one color selected from the total VGA palette of over 262,000 colors. This impressive number of colors is a result of 18-bit color coding ($2^{18} = 262,144$). Each entry in the DAC color table consists of three 6-bit color values: one each for the red, green, and blue color components.

To select a register in the DAC color table, the video controller interprets the contents of the palette register as an index to the DAC color table instead of as a color value. The following figure shows how the contents of several other registers determine various ways of organizing the DAC color table into groups.

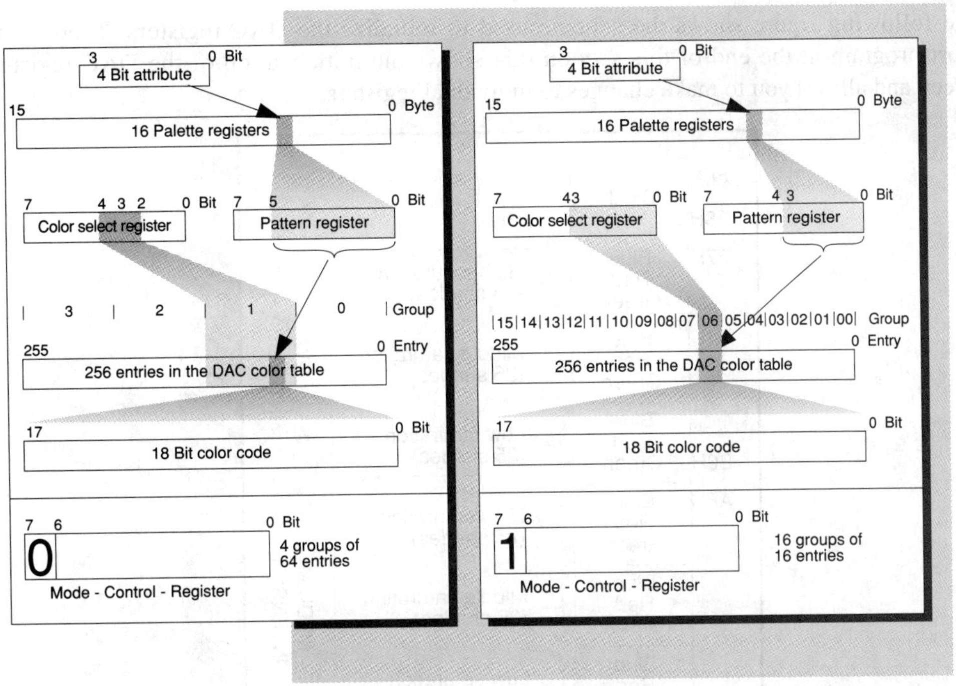

Creating color codes with the VGA card

The mode control register of the video controller plays an important part in this process. If this register contains the value 0, then the index to the DAC color table is created from bits 0 through 5 of the corresponding palette register and bits 2 and 3 of the color select register. This means that the DAC color table is divided into four groups of 64 consecutive registers and that bits 2 and 3 of the color select register determine which of the four groups is currently active.

Things are somewhat different if bit 7 from the mode control register contains a value of 1. In this case, the DAC color table is divided into 16 groups of 16 consecutive registers. The index to the table is then created from bits 0 through 3 of the palette register and bits 0 through 3 from the color select register. Again, the value from the palette register is an index and the value in the color select register determines the currently active group in the DAC color table.

This type of coding can create fast and continuous color changes for entire groups of characters or pixels on screen. To do this, load the color groups of the DAC color table with series of colors that have increasing or decreasing intensities. Then simply change the current DAC color group using the color select register.

To emulate default CGA colors, the VGA card is initialized so the 16 palette registers point to the first 16 registers of the DAC color table. These registers in the DAC color table are loaded with the color information for the standard CGA colors from black (0) to white (15). The other DAC color table registers aren't set when a text mode is initialized with video BIOS function

00H. In a graphics mode, all 256 registers of the DAC color table are initialized as long as the initialization isn't switched off by sub-function 31H of function 12H.

The following figure shows the scheme used to initialize the DAC registers. There is also a short program at the end of this section that shows the initialization of the DAC registers on screen and allows you to make changes to individual registers.

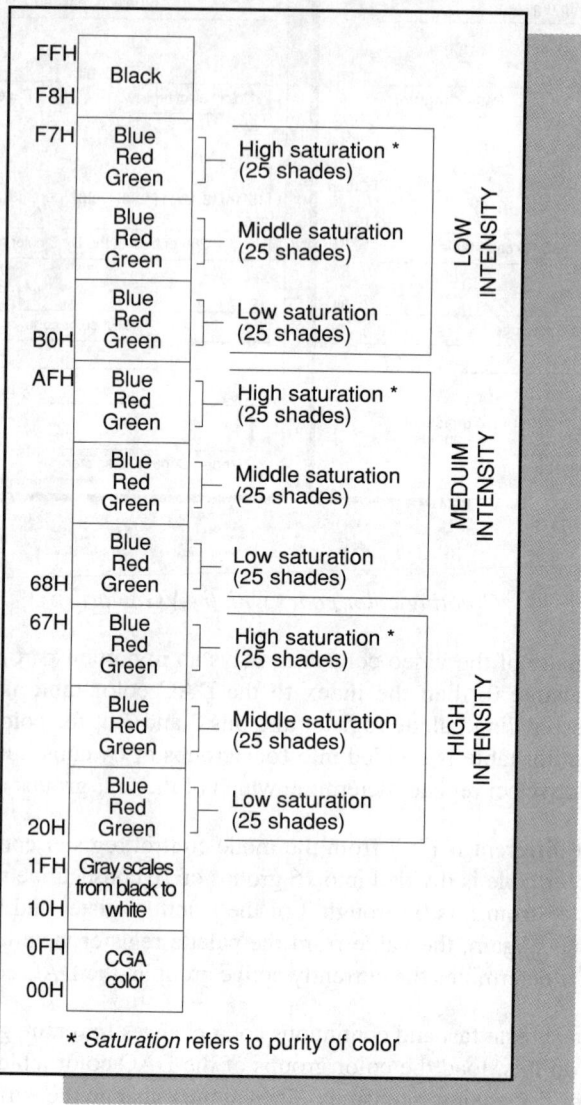

Initialization of 256 DAC color table registers
(VGA graphics modes)

The palette registers themselves are the actual color sources in text and 16 color graphics modes. In the 256 color modes of the VGA card, however, this scheme would require 256 different palette registers. This is why the palette registers store index values to the DAC color table in these modes.

The 256 entries in the DAC color table determine the 256 different colors that can be displayed on the screen at any one time. So, programming the palette registers directly in these modes won't have the desired effect on the screen colors.

Setting colors using the BIOS

The expanded EGA/VGA BIOS has several functions for manipulating the contents of the palette registers and the DAC registers. The other register of the attribute controller can also be set. These tasks are accomplished with sub-functions of function 10H of the BIOS video interrupt. When calling one of these sub-functions, load function number 10H into the AH register, and place the sub-function number in the AL register.

The first of these sub-functions is 00H, which enables you to load any color value into one of the 16 palette registers. To call this sub-function, load function number 10H into the AH register and the sub-function number 00H into the AL register. Also, load the palette register number (00H-0FH) into the BH register and the color number into the BL register.

The register number passed to this sub-function isn't checked. So, you can also use it to access the overscan register, which is found immediately after the last palette register. Since this register determines the color of the screen frame and background color in the CGA compatible graphics modes, it also has its own sub-function (01H).

Since there are only two or three raster lines available for a screen frame, you should only use black as a background color, especially for the EGA text modes. Also, the contents of the overscan register are meaningless when a monochrome monitor is attached.

To call this function for accessing the overscan register, load the function number 10H into the AH register, and sub-function number 01H into the AL register. Load the screen border color into the BH register. This is passed to the overscan register when the function is called.

Sub-function 02H loads both the palette registers and the overscan register in one operation. In addition to the usual function number and sub-function number, load the 17-byte address of a table that contains values for all 17 registers (16 palette registers plus the overscan register) into the ES:DX register pair. When the function executes, the 17 values from this table are loaded into the 17 registers.

Even though we have two functions for changing the contents of the palette registers, the expanded EGA BIOS doesn't have any functions for reading the contents of these registers. The EGA card doesn't allow the contents of the attribute controller registers (and almost all other registers) to be read. This situation worsens when working with TSR programs because they aren't able to restore the palette registers to their original contents when the interrupted program is reactivated.

Many programs solve this problem by diverting the results of sub-functions 00H and 02H to a custom routine that stores the values in the palette registers before writing new values. This method doesn't work, however, if you attempt to bypass the BIOS functions and program the palette registers directly. So, you should always use the BIOS functions, even though Section 4.8.10 shows you how to manipulate the palette registers directly.

The last sub-function of function 10H in the expanded EGA BIOS defines the meaning of bit 7 in the attribute byte of a character in text mode. Just as with the CGA and MDA cards, this bit can be used with the EGA/CGA card to make a character blink or to display a character with an intense background color. The CGA and MDA cards require direct programming to define the meaning of this bit, but the EGA/VGA BIOS has a special function (sub-function 03H of function 10H).

Place the function number (10H) in the AH register and the sub-function number (03H) in the AL register. The BL register specifies the degree of intensity. Loading 0 into this register produces a high intensity background color, and 1 enables character blinking when bit 7 of the attribute byte is set.

Other sub-functions of the expanded VGA BIOS

The VGA BIOS video interrupt has some functions that aren't included in the EGA BIOS. These apply to the DAC color table and palette register reading. Unlike the EGA card, the VGA card can easily read palette register contents. This also applies to several other registers that are inaccessible on the EGA card.

The contents of the DAC color registers can be modified with sub-function 10H. Place the function number (10H) in the AH register and the sub-function number (10H) in the AL register. Also, place the number of the desired DAC color register (0 - 255 [00H - FFH]) in the BX register and the desired color code in the CH, CL, and DH registers. 18-bit VGA color codes consist of three 6-bit components, one for each color component (red, green, and blue). Like many of the other sub-functions we'll describe, 10H expects the red component in DH, the green component in CH, and the blue component in DL. Only the first six bits (0 - 5) are significant.

The DH, DL, and CL registers are also used by sub-function 15H to return the contents of a DAC color register. Place the function number (10H) in the AH register and the sub-function number (15H) in the AL register. Also, place the DAC color register number in the BX register.

Sub-function 12H loads a number of DAC color registers in one operation. The BX register expects the number of the first DAC color register to be loaded and the CX register expects the total number of registers to load. Instead of processor registers, a buffer is used to pass the new values for the given DAC color registers. The address of this buffer is loaded in the ES:DX register pair. Each DAC color register receives three consecutive bytes from this buffer. In each group of three bytes, the first byte provides the green component, the second byte provides the red component, and the third byte provides the blue component.

Sub-function 17H allows you to read the contents of a range of DAC color registers. The number of the first register to read is loaded in the BX register and the total number of registers is loaded in the CX register. The VGA BIOS then copies the contents of these registers to the buffer with the segment and offset address specified in the ES:DX register pair. The structure of this buffer is the same as that described for sub-function 12H. Remember that each register from the DAC color table contains three bytes instead of one, so be sure that you have a large enough buffer.

You can determine the way the DAC color table is organized and which color group is active with sub-function 13H. This sub-function has two sub-functions of its own. If this function is passed the value 0 in the BL register, then bit 0 of the BH register is copied to bit 7 of the mode control register of the VGA controller and the DAC color table is divided into 4 or 16 groups. If the BL register contains the value 1, then the content of the BH register is copied to the color select register and the active color group of the DAC color table is selected.

The contents of these two registers can be determined by calling sub-function 1AH. After this function call, the BL register contains the contents of bit 7 of the mode control register and the BH register contains the contents of the color select register.

There is also a sub-function for converting the color codes of the DAC color table to gray scales. This is sub-function 1BH. This is helpful for displaying a black and white picture on a color VGA monitor. If you have a monochrome VGA monitor, the conversion of colors to gray scales takes place in the monitor itself.

To use sub-function 1BH, load the first register number into the BX register and the total number of registers to convert into the CX register. The actual conversion, or *gray scale summing*, is done by weighting each color component to obtain a gray scale value between 0 (black) and 1 (white). The color component values are weighted so the red component is 30% of the final gray scale value, the green component is 59%, and the blue component is 11%.

In addition to the selective conversion of the certain DAC registers to gray scales, you can use sub-function 33H of BIOS function 12H to convert the contents of the entire table. Before calling the BIOS video interrupt, the sub-function number is loaded in the AL register and the function number is loaded in the AH register as usual. In this case, the AL register determines whether the conversion occurs. A value of 0 tells the BIOS to convert the color values to gray scales. A value of 1 leaves the color values intact.

In addition to the sub-functions for manipulating the DAC color table, the VGA BIOS also has several sub-functions for reading the palette registers using function number 10H.

Sub-function 07H reads the contents of any palette register. The number of the desired palette register is loaded in the BL register, and its contents are returned to the BH register. The contents of the overscan register are also read with this sub-function, but the BIOS has also dedicated sub-functions 08H for this purpose. Just as with sub-function 07H, the result is returned to the BH register.

Sub-function 09H returns a copy of the contents of all 16 palette registers and the overscan register. This sub-function writes the contents of these registers to a 17-byte buffer. The segment address of this buffer is loaded into the ES register when the sub-function is called, and the offset address is loaded into the DX register.

Demonstration programs

The BIOS functions make it easy to set the available colors. It's more difficult to select from these colors the actual colors your program will display on screen for a given character or pixel. This is especially true for the VGA card. The EGA card is limited to a choice of 64 colors, but the VGA's palette of 256 simultaneous colors makes this process more complicated. So, we'll conclude this section with a demo program called VDAC. The companion diskette for this book contains C and Pascal versions of this program called VDACC.C and VDACP.PAS.

The program works in the VGA 256 color graphics mode with a resolution of 320x400 pixels. The assembly language modules V3240PA.ASM and V3240CA.ASM, which were described in Section 4.8.7, are also used. Other routines, which you may remember from previous chapters, such as ISVGA, LINE, and GRAFXPRINT, are also used.

The heart of the program consists of the routines SETDAC, GETDAC, and DEMO. SETDAC and GETDAC are ports to sub-functions 12H and 17H of function 10H. They read and write any number of DAC color registers. The DEMO routine frequently uses these to load all the DAC registers and allows you to read or change the contents of individual registers.

On screen, you'll see a collection of 256 color blocks that are arranged in a square. Each color block consists of pixels of a certain color. The block in the upper-left corner starts with color value 0. The next block to the right uses color value 1, and its neighbor uses color value 2, and etc. to the lower-right block, which uses color value 255.

In this way, all 256 colors in the DAC color table are displayed on screen. First you'll see the colors that the BIOS automatically assigns when the graphics mode is initialized. In addition to the actual colors, the program also displays the numerical data for the color in the status line. When the program begins, the numbers of the red, green, and blue color components for the upper-left color block will be displayed. You can then use the arrow keys to view the color component values for the other color blocks.

As you scroll through the color values, you'll notice that the current color block is indicated by a white frame. The copyright message across the top of the screen will also be displayed in the color of the current color block. At first you cannot see the copyright message because it's initialized with the color black.

To change the color of the copyright message, it is initialized with color code 255, which starts out as black. Then, each time you move the cursor, the color of the current block is copied to DAC color register number 255. This means that the color of the lower-right color block and the color of the copyright message change with each cursor movement.

The program also allows you to change the red, green, and blue components for the current color block with the <R>, <G>, and <B> keys. Pressing one of these keys increments the value of the corresponding color component by one. The change is reflected immediately in the color of the color block, the color of the copyright message, and the contents of the status line. To decrease the value of a color component, hold down the <Shift> key while pressing the corresponding letter. You can also press <Space> to return a color to its original value.

Press the <Enter> key to end the program. The program restores the original color table and returns you to text mode.

Pascal listing: VDACP.PAS

```
{****************************************************            * Author      : MICHAEL TISCHER        *
*                                                  *            * Developed on : 01/02/91              *
*                V D A C P . P A S                 *            * Last update  : 03/03/92              *
**----------------------------------------------**            ****************************************************}
* Task         : Demonstrates programming of the DAC color *
*                register graphics mode of the VGA card, using *      program VDACP;
*                256 colors. This program requires the V3240PA. *
*                ASM assembly language module.     *            uses dos, crt;
**----------------------------------------------**
```

```
{-- Type declarations ------------------------------------------}

type DACREG = record                  { Describes a DAC register }
              case integer of
                0 : ( Red, Green, Blue : BYTE );{RGB color components}
                1 : ( RGB : array[ 1..3 ] of BYTE );
              end;
     DACARRAY = array [0..255] of DACREG;     { Complete DAC table }

{-- External references to the assembler routines --------------------}

{$L v3240pa}                            { Link assembler module }

procedure init320400; external;
procedure setpix( x, y : integer; pcolor : byte ); external;
function getpix( x, y: integer ) : byte ; external;
procedure setpage( page : byte ); external;
procedure showpage( page : byte ); external;

{-- Constants ---------------------------------------------------}

const MAXX = 319;                      { Maximum X- and Y-coordinates }
      MAXY = 399;

      BWIDTH  = 10;               { Width of a color block in pixels }
      BHEIGHT = 20;               { Height of a color block in pixels }
      SPACING = 2;                     { Distance between the blocks }
      TOWIDTH = 16 * BWIDTH + ( 15 * SPACING );    { Total width }
      TOHEIGHT = 16 * BHEIGHT + ( 15 * SPACING );  { Total height }
      STARTX = ( MAXX - TOWIDTH ) div 2;   { Upper left block corner }
      STARTY = ( MAXY - TOHEIGHT ) div 2;

{*********************************************************************
* IsVga : Determines whether a VGA card is installed.              *
**---------------------------------------------------------------**
* Input   : None                                                   *
* Output  : TRUE or FALSE                                          *
*********************************************************************}

function IsVga : boolean;

var Regs : Registers;        { Processor registers for interrupt call }

begin
  Regs.AX := $1a00;              { Function 1AH applies to VGA only }
  Intr( $10, Regs );
  IsVga := ( Regs.AL = $1a );
end;

{*********************************************************************
* PrintChar : Writes a character to the screen while in graphic mode.*
**---------------------------------------------------------------**
* Input    :   THECHAR = Character to be written                   *
*              X, Y     = X- and Y-coordinates of upper-left corner *
*              FG       = Foreground color                         *
*              BK       = Background color                         *
* Info     : Character is created in an 8x8 matrix, based on the   *
*              8x8 ROM font.                                        *
*********************************************************************}

procedure PrintChar( thechar : char; x, y : integer; fg, bk : byte );

type FDEF = array[0..255,0..7] of byte;        { Font array }
```

```
TPTR = ^FDEF;                          { Pointer to font }

var Regs  : Registers;            { Registers for interrupt call }
    ch    : char;           { Individual pixels in character }
    i, k,                          { Loop counter }
    BMask : byte;           { Bit mask for character design }

const fptr : TPTR = NIL;             { Pointer to font in ROM }

begin
  if fptr = NIL then                { Pointer to font already set? }
    begin                                       { No }
      Regs.AH := $11;             { Call video BIOS function 11H, }
      Regs.AL := $30;             { sub-function 30H             }
      Regs.BH := 3;                     { Get pointer to 8x8 font }
      intr( $10, Regs );
      fptr := ptr( Regs.ES, Regs.BP );        { Set pointers }
    end;

  if ( bk = 255 ) then             { Drawing transparent characters? }
    for i := 0 to 7 do          { Yes --> Set foreground pixels only }
      begin
        BMask := fptr^[ord(thechar),i];{ Get bit pattern for one line }
        for k := 0 to 7 do
          begin
            if ( BMask and 128 <> 0 ) then         { Pixel set? }
              setpix( x+k, y+i, fg );                   { Yes }
            BMask := BMask shl 1;
          end;
      end
  else                      { No --> Consider background as well }
    for i := 0 to 7 do                        { Execute lines }
      begin
        BMask := fptr^[ord(thechar),i];{ Get bit pattern for one line }
        for k := 0 to 7 do
          begin
            if ( BMask and 128 <> 0 ) then        { Foreground? }
              setpix( x+k, y+i, fg )                     { Yes }
            else
              setpix( x+k, y+i, bk );        { No --> Background }
            BMask := BMask shl 1;
          end;
      end;
end;

{*********************************************************************
* Line: Draws a line based on the Bresenham algorithm.             *
**---------------------------------------------------------------**
* Input    : X1, Y1 = Starting coordinates (0 - ...)              *
*            X2, Y2 = Ending coordinates                          *
*            LPCOL  = Color of line pixels                        *
*********************************************************************}

procedure Line( x1, y1, x2, y2 : integer; lpcol : byte );

var d, dx, dy,
    aincr, bincr,
    xincr, yincr,
    x, y                : integer;

{-- Procedure for swapping two integer variables --------------------}

procedure SwapInt( var i1, i2: integer );
```

```
var dummy : integer;


begin
  dummy := i2;
  i2    := i1;
  i1    := dummy;
end;


{-- Main procedure -------------------------------------------------}


begin
  if ( abs(x2-x1) < abs(y2-y1) ) then       { X- or Y-axis overflow? }
    begin                                         { Check Y-axis }
      if ( y1 > y2 ) then                              { y1 > y2? }
        begin
          SwapInt( x1, x2 );              { Yes --> Swap X1 with X2 }
          SwapInt( y1, y2 );              {         and Y1 with Y2  }
        end;

      if ( x2 > x1 ) then xincr := 1         { Set X-axis increment }
                     else xincr := -1;

      dy := y2 - y1;
      dx := abs( x2-x1 );
      d  := 2 * dx - dy;
      aincr := 2 * (dx - dy);
      bincr := 2 * dx;
      x := x1;
      y := y1;

      setpix( x, y, lpcol );                       { Set first pixel }
      for y:=y1+1 to y2 do               { Execute line on Y-axes }
        begin
          if ( d >= 0 ) then
            begin
              inc( x, xincr );
              inc( d, aincr );
            end
          else
            inc( d, bincr );
          setpix( x, y, lpcol );
        end;
    end
  else                                            { Check X-axes }
    begin
      if ( x1 > x2 ) then                              { x1 > x2? }
        begin
          SwapInt( x1, x2 );              { Yes --> Swap X1 with X2 }
          SwapInt( y1, y2 );              {         and Y1 with Y2  }
        end;

      if ( y2 > y1 ) then yincr := 1         { Set Y-axis increment }
                     else yincr := -1;

      dx := x2 - x1;
      dy := abs( y2-y1 );
      d  := 2 * dy - dx;
      aincr := 2 * (dy - dx);
      bincr := 2 * dy;
      x := x1;
      y := y1;

      setpix( x, y, lpcol );                       { Set first pixel }
      for x:=x1+1 to x2 do               { Execute line on X-axes }
```

```
      begin
        if ( d >= 0 ) then
          begin
            inc( y, yincr );
            inc( d, aincr );
          end
        else
          inc( d, bincr );
        setpix( x, y, lpcol );
      end;
    end;
end;


{***************************************************************
* GrfxPrint: Displays a formatted string on the graphic screen. *
**-----------------------------------------------------------**
* Input  : X, Y  = Starting coordinates (0 - ...)              *
*          FG    = Foreground color                            *
*          BK    = Background color (255 = transparent)        *
*          STRING = String with format information             *
***************************************************************}

procedure GrfxPrint( x, y : integer; fg, bk : byte; strt : string );

var i : integer;                                 { Loop counter }

begin
  for i:=1 to length( strt ) do
    begin
      printchar( strt[i], x, y, fg, bk );   { Display using PrintChar }
      inc( x, 8 );                   { Move X to next character position }
    end;
end;


{***************************************************************
* GetDac: Gets the contents of a specific number of DAC registers. *
**-----------------------------------------------------------**
* Input   : FIRST = Number of first DAC register (0-255)        *
*           NUM   = Number of DAC registers                     *
*           BUF   = Buffer, in which the contents of the DAC    *
*                   registers are to be loaded. It must be a    *
*                   DACREG type variable or an array of this type. *
* Info    : The passed buffer must have three bytes reserved for *
*           DAC register, in which the red, green and blue parts *
*           of each color are recorded.                         *
***************************************************************}

procedure GetDac( First, Num : integer; var Buf );

var Regs : Registers;      { Processor registers for interrupt call }

begin
  Regs.AX := $1017;                { Function and sub-function number }
  Regs.BX := First;                    { Number of first DAC register }
  Regs.CX := Num;                { Number of registers to be loaded }
  Regs.ES := seg( Buf );                    { Load pointers to buffer }
  Regs.DX := ofs( Buf );
  intr( $10, Regs );                        { Call BIOS video interrupt }
end;


{***************************************************************
* SetDac: Loads a specific number of DAC registers             *
**-----------------------------------------------------------**
* Input   : FIRST = Number of first DAC register (0-255)        *
```

```
*          NUM    = Number of DAC registers                    *
*          BUF    = Buffer, from which the contents of the DAC  *
*                   registers are to be taken. Must be a variable *
*                   of DACREG type or an array of this type.    *
*  Info   : See GetDac                                          *
 ***************************************************************}

procedure SetDac( First, Num : integer; var Buf );

var Regs : Registers;          { Processor registers for interrupt call }

begin
  Regs.AX := $1012;            { Function and sub-function number }
  Regs.BX := First;            { Number of first DAC register }
  Regs.CX := Num;              { Number of registers to be loaded }
  Regs.ES := seg( Buf );       { Load pointer to buffer }
  Regs.DX := ofs( Buf );
  intr( $10, Regs );           { Call BIOS video interrupt }
end;


{***************************************************************
* PrintDac: Displays the contents of a DAC register on the screen *
*           and sets the color in the DAC register 255.         *
**-----------------------------------------------------------**
* Input   : DREG  = DAC register                                *
*           NO    = The number of this register                 *
*           COLOR = Output color                                 *
***************************************************************}

procedure PrintDac( DReg : DACREG; No, Color : BYTE );

var nrstr,                     { String for register number }
    rstr,                      { String for red part }
    gstr,                      { String for green part }
    bstr : string[3];          { String for blue part }

begin
  SetDac( 255, 1, DReg );      { Color in DAC register 255 }
  str( No : 3, nrstr );        { Convert colors and numbers to strings }
  str( DReg.Red : 2, rstr );
  str( DReg.Green : 2, gstr );
  str( DReg.Blue : 2, bstr );
  GrfxPrint( 60, MAXY-10, Color, 0, 'DAC:' + nrstr + '  R:' + rstr +
                                    '  G:' + gstr + '  B:' + bstr);
end;


{***************************************************************
* Frame   : Draws a frame around one of the color boxes         *
**-----------------------------------------------------------**
* Input   : X     = X-coordinate of color box (0-15)            *
*           Y     = Y-coordinate of color box (0-15)            *
*           COLOR = Color of border                             *
* Info    : Line thickness is one pixel, regardless of distance *
*           of color boxes.                                     *
***************************************************************}

procedure Surround( X, Y, Color : BYTE );

var sx, sy,                    { Upper-left corner of frame }
    ex, ey : integer;          { Lower-right corner of frame }

begin
  sx := STARTX + X * (BWIDTH + SPACING) - 1;  { Compute corner }
  ex := sx + BWIDTH + 1;                       { coordinates of frame }
```

```
  sy := STARTY + Y * (BHEIGHT + SPACING) - 1;
  ey := sy + BHEIGHT + 1;
  Line( sx, sy, ex, sy, Color );              { Draw frame }
  Line( ex, sy, ex, ey, Color );
  Line( ex, ey, sx, ey, Color );
  Line( sx, ey, sx, sy, Color );
end;


{***************************************************************
* ChangeDacReg: Changes the contents of a DAC register in memory *
*               and in the DAC table of the video card and then  *
*               displays them on the screen.                     *
**-----------------------------------------------------------**
* Input   : DREG  = DAC register to be changed                  *
*           NO    = Number of DAC register                      *
*           COMP  = Number of components to be changed (1-3)    *
*                   1 = Red, 2 = Green, 3 = Blue                 *
*           INCR  = Increment for these components              *
***************************************************************}

procedure ChangeDacReg( var DReg : DACREG; No, Comp : BYTE;
                        Incr : integer );

begin
  inc( DReg.RGB[ Comp ], Incr );      { Increment components }
  if DReg.RGB[ Comp ] > 63 then       { Greater than 63? }
    DReg.RGB[ Comp ] := 0;            { Yes, set to zero }
  SetDac( No, 1, DReg );              { Load DAC register }
  PrintDac( DReg, No, 15 );           { Output new contents }
end;


{***************************************************************
* Demo: Demonstrates the programming of the DAC register and the *
*       color model of the VGA card.                            *
**-----------------------------------------------------------**
* Input   : None                                                *
***************************************************************}

procedure Demo;

var x,  y,
    ix, jx,
    iy, jy,
    k,  f  : integer;                 { Loop counter }
    ch     : char;                    { Key }
    dacbuf : DACARRAY;                { Array with complete DAC table }
    DReg   : DACREG;                  { Current DAC register }

begin
  {-- Create screen --------------------------------------------}

  SetPage( 0 );                       { Process page 0 }
  ShowPage( 0 );                      { Display page 0 }
  GetDac( 0, 256, dacbuf );           { Load complete DAC table }

  GrfxPrint( 10, 0, 255, 0,
             'VDACP  -  (c) 1992 by Michael Tischer' );

  {-- Create block out of 16x16 color boxes --------------------}

  iy := STARTY;                       { Starting point on the screen }
  jy := STARTY + BHEIGHT - 1;
  f := 0;
  for y := 0 to 15 do                 { Execute 16 block lines }
```

```pascal
  begin
    ix := STARTX;
    jx := STARTX + BWIDTH - 1;
    for x := 0 to 15 do              { Execute 16 block columns }
      begin
        for k := iy to jy do  { Make block out of individual lines }
          Line( ix, k, jx, k, f );
        inc( ix, BWIDTH + SPACING );            { Next block right }
        inc( jx, BWIDTH + SPACING );
        inc( f );                   { Increment color for next block }
      end;
    inc( iy, BHEIGHT + SPACING );    { Output position for next }
    inc( jy, BHEIGHT + SPACING );    { block line              }
  end;

{-- Read user input and respond to it ---------------------------------}

ix := 0;                 { Begin in upper-left corner with the color 0 }
iy := 0;
jx := 0;
jy := 0;
k := 0;
GetDac( 0, 1, DReg );                          { Get color 0 }
Surround( 0, 0, 15 );                          { Frame color box }
PrintDac( DReg, 0, 15 );                       { and output contents }
repeat
  ch := ReadKey;                               { Read key }
  if ( ch <> #0 ) then                  { Not an extended key? }
    case ch of                          { No, evaluate }
      'r' : ChangeDacReg( DReg, k, 1, +1 );    { r = Red   + }
      'g' : ChangeDacReg( DReg, k, 2, +1 );    { g = Green + }
      'b' : ChangeDacReg( DReg, k, 3, +1 );    { b = Blue  + }
      'R' : ChangeDacReg( DReg, k, 1, -1 );    { R = Red   - }
      'G' : ChangeDacReg( DReg, k, 2, -1 );    { G = Green - }
      'B' : ChangeDacReg( DReg, k, 3, -1 );    { B = Blue  - }
      ' ' : begin                 { Space = Set original value }
              DReg := dacbuf[ k ];
              ChangeDacReg( DReg, k, 1, 0 );
            end;
    end
  else                                    { Extended key code }
    case ReadKey of
      #72 : if ( iy = 0 ) then                       { Cursor up }
              jy := 15
            else
              jy := iy - 1;

      #80 : if ( iy = 15 ) then                      { Cursor down }
              jy := 0
            else
              jy := iy + 1;

      #75 : if ( ix = 0  ) then                      { Cursor left }
              jx := 15
            else
              jx := ix - 1;

      #77 : if ( ix = 15 ) then                      { Cursor right }
              jx := 0
            else
              jx := ix + 1;
    end;

  if ( ix <> jx ) or ( iy <> jy ) then     { New cursor position? }
      begin                                        { Yes }
        Surround( ix, iy, 0 );       { Fade out frame in old position }
        Surround( jx, jy, 15 );      { Draw frame around new position }
        ix := jx;                          { Store new color box }
        iy := jy;
        k := iy*16+ix;               { Compute number of new box }
        GetDac( k, 1, DReg );              { Load DAC register }
        PrintDac( DReg, k, 15 );           { and output         }
      end;
  until ch = #13;                    { Repeat until RETURN is pressed }

  SetDac( 0, 256, dacbuf );                  { Restore DAC table }
end;

{*********************************************************************}
{****           M A I N   P R O G R A M                  ****}
{*********************************************************************}

begin
  if IsVga then                            { VGA card installed? }
    begin                                  { Yes --> Go ahead }
      init320400;                          { Initialize graphic mode }
      Demo;
      Textmode( CO80 );                    { Shift into text mode }
    end
  else
    writeln( 'VDACP  -  (c) 1992 by Michael Tischer'#13#10#10 +
             'This program requires a VGA card'#13#10 );
end.
```

C listing: VDACC.C

```
/********************************************************************
*                        V D A C C . C                            *
**---------------------------------------------------------------**
*  Task         : Demonstrates programming of the DAC color       *
*                 register in 256 color graphics mode of the      *
*                 VGA card. This program requires the V3240CA.ASM *
*                 assembly language module.                       *
**---------------------------------------------------------------**
*  Author       : MICHAEL TISCHER                                 *
*  Developed on : 01/02/91                                        *
*  Last update  : 01/14/91                                        *
**---------------------------------------------------------------**
*  Memory model : SMALL                                           *
**---------------------------------------------------------------**
*  (MICROSOFT C)                                                  *
*  Compilation  : CL /AS /c /WO vdacc.c                           *
*                 LINK vdacc v3240ca;                             *
**---------------------------------------------------------------**
*  (BORLAND TURBO C)                                              *
*  Compilation  : Create a project file using the following:      *
*                         vdacc.c                                 *
*                         v3240ca.obj                             *
**---------------------------------------------------------------**
*  Call         : vdacc                                           *
**---------------------------------------------------------------**
*  Info         : Message "Structure passed by value ..." in      *
*                 Turbo C is not an error!                        *
********************************************************************/

#include <dos.h>
#include <stdarg.h>
#include <stdlib.h>
#include <stdio.h>
#include <conio.h>

/*-- Type declarations -------------------------------------------*/

typedef unsigned char BYTE;                    /* We create a BYTE */

typedef union {                           /* Describes a DAC register */
              struct { BYTE Red, Green, Blue; } b;
              BYTE RGB[3];
              } DACREG;
typedef DACREG DACARRAY[256];                  /* Complete DAC table */

/*-- External references to the assembler routines ---------------*/

extern void init320400( void );
extern void setpix( int x, int y, unsigned char pcolor);
extern BYTE getpix( int x, int y );
extern void setpage( BYTE page );
extern void showpage( BYTE page );
extern void far * getfontptr( void );

/*-- Constants ---------------------------------------------------*/

#define MAXX 319                  /* Maximum X- and Y-coordinates */
#define MAXY 399

#define BWIDTH 10             /* Width of a color block in pixels */
#define BHEIGHT  20          /* Height of a color block in pixels */
#define SPACING 2                /* Distance between the blocks */
```

```
#define TOWIDTH ( 16 * BWIDTH + ( 15 * SPACING ) )   /* Total width */
#define TOHEIGHT ( 16 * BHEIGHT + ( 15 * SPACING ) )/* Total height */
#define STARTX  ( MAXX - TOWIDTH ) / 2 /* Upper left corner of block */
#define STARTY  ( MAXY - TOHEIGHT ) / 2

/********************************************************************
*  IsVga: Determines whether a VGA card is installed.             *
**---------------------------------------------------------------**
*  Input   : None                                                 *
*  Output  : 0, if no VGA exists, otherwise < 0                   *
********************************************************************/

BYTE IsVga( void )
{
  union REGS Regs;          /* Processor registers for Interrupt call */

  Regs.x.ax = 0x1a00;              /* Function 1AH applies to VGA only */
  int86( 0x10, &Regs, &Regs );
  return (BYTE) ( Regs.h.al == 0x1a );  /* Is the function available? */
}

/********************************************************************
*  PrintChar : Writes a character to the screen while in graphic mode.*
**---------------------------------------------------------------**
*  Input   :  THECHAR = Character to be written                   *
*             x, y    = X- and Y-coordinates of upper-left corner *
*             FG      = Foreground color                          *
*             BK      = Background color                          *
*  Info    : Character is created in an 8x8 matrix, based on the  *
*            8x8 ROM font.                                         *
********************************************************************/

void PrintChar( char thechar, int x, int y, BYTE fg, BYTE bk )
{
  typedef BYTE FDEF[256][8];                    /* Font definition */
  typedef FDEF far *TPTR;                        /* Pointer to font */

  BYTE       i, k,                              /* Loop counter */
             BMask;                      /* Bit mask for character design */

  static TPTR fptr = (TPTR) 0;              /* Pointer to font in ROM */

  if ( fptr == (TPTR) 0 )              /* Pointer to font already set? */
    fptr = getfontptr();      /* No --> Use the assembly function to load */

  /*- Generate character, pixel by pixel -------------------------*/

  if ( bk == 255 )                 /* Drawing transparent characters? */
    for ( i = 0; i < 8; ++i )      /* Yes --> Set foreground pixels only */
    {
      BMask = (*fptr)[thechar][i];    /* Get bit pattern for one line */
      for ( k = 0; k < 8; ++k, BMask <<= 1 )       /* Execute columns */
        if ( BMask & 128 )                         /* Pixel set? */
          setpix( x+k, y+i, fg );                  /* Yes */
    }
  else                             /* No consider background as well */
    for ( i = 0; i < 8; ++i )                      /* Execute lines */
    {
      BMask = (*fptr)[thechar][i];    /* Get bit pattern for one line */
      for ( k = 0; k < 8; ++k, BMask <<= 1 )       /* Execute columns */
        setpix( x+k, y+i, ( BMask & 128 ) ? fg : bk );
    }
}
```

```
/*************************************************************
* Line: Draws a line based on the Bresenham algorithm       *
*-----------------------------------------------------------*
* Input  : X1, Y1 = Starting coordinates (0 - ...)          *
*          X2, Y2 = Ending coordinates                      *
*          LPCOL  = Color of line pixels                    *
*************************************************************/

/*-- Function for swapping two integer variables --------------------*/

void SwapInt( int *i1, int *i2 )
{
 int dummy;

 dummy = *i2;
 *i2   = *i1;
 *i1   = dummy;
}

/*-- Main part of function ------------------------------------*/

void Line( int x1, int y1, int x2, int y2, BYTE lpcol )
{
 int d, dx, dy,
     aincr, bincr,
     xincr, yincr,
     x, y;

 if ( abs(x2-x1) < abs(y2-y1) )          /* X- or Y-axis overflow? */
  {                                      /* Check Y-axis */
   if ( y1 > y2 )                        /* y1 > y2? */
    {
     SwapInt( &x1, &x2 );                /* Yes --> Swap X1 with Y1 */
     SwapInt( &y1, &y2 );                /*     and Y1 with Y2 */
    }

   xincr = ( x2 > x1 ) ? 1 : -1;         /* Set X-axis increment */

   dy = y2 - y1;
   dx = abs( x2-x1 );
   d  = 2 * dx - dy;
   aincr = 2 * (dx - dy);
   bincr = 2 * dx;
   x = x1;
   y = y1;

   setpix( x, y, lpcol );                       /* Set first pixel */
   for (y=y1+1; y<= y2; ++y )            /* Execute line on Y-axes */
    {
     if ( d >= 0 )
      {
       x += xincr;
       d += aincr;
      }
     else
      d += bincr;
     setpix(x, y, lpcol);
    }
  }
 else                                    /* Check X-axes */
  {
   if ( x1 > x2 )                        /* x1 > x2? */
    {
     SwapInt( &x1, &x2 );                /* Yes --> Swap X1 with X2 */
     SwapInt( &y1, &y2 );               /*      and Y1 with Y2 */
    }

   yincr = ( y2 > y1 ) ? 1 : -1;        /* Set Y-axis increment */

   dx = x2 - x1;
   dy = abs( y2-y1 );
   d  = 2 * dy - dx;
   aincr = 2 * (dy - dx);
   bincr = 2 * dy;
   x = x1;
   y = y1;

   setpix(x, y, lpcol);                         /* Set first pixel */
   for (x=x1+1; x<=x2; ++x )             /* Execute line on X-axes */
    {
     if ( d >= 0 )
      {
       y += yincr;
       d += aincr;
      }
     else
       d += bincr;
     setpix(x, y, lpcol);
    }
  }
}

/*************************************************************
* GrfxPrintf: Displays a formatted string on the graphic screen. *
* Input  : X, Y   = Starting coordinates (0 - ...)          *
*          FG     = Foreground color                        *
*          BK     = Background color (255 = transparent)    *
*          STRING = String with format information          *
*          ...    = Arguments similar to printf             *
*************************************************************/

void GrafPrintf( int x, int y, BYTE fg, BYTE bk, char * string, ... )
{
 va_list parameter;             /* Parameter list for VA_... Macros */
 char stngbuf[255],                     /* Buffer for formatted string */
      *cp;

 va_start( parameter, string );                 /* Convert parameter */
 vsprintf( stngbuf, string, parameter );        /* Format */
 for ( cp = stngbuf; *cp; ++cp, x+= 8 )         /* Formatted string */
   PrintChar( *cp, x, y, fg, bk );      /* Display using PrintChar */
}

/*************************************************************
* GetDac: Gets the contents of a specific number of DAC registers *
*-----------------------------------------------------------**
* Input  : FIRST = Number of first DAC register (0-255)     *
*          NUM   = Number of DAC register                   *
*          BUFP  = Pointer to the buffer, in which the contents *
*                  of the DAC are to be loaded. It must be a DACREG *
*                  type variable or an array of this type.  *
* Info   : The passed buffer must have three reserved for DAC *
*          register, in which the red, green and blue parts of *
*          each color are recorded.                         *
*************************************************************/

void GetDac( int First, int Num, void far *BufP )
{
```

```
  union REGS Regs;              /* Processor register for interrupt call */
  struct SREGS SRegs;                       /* Segment register */

  Regs.x.ax = 0x1017;                /* Function and sub-function no. */
  Regs.x.bx = First;           /* Number of the first DAC register */
  Regs.x.cx = Num;              /* Number of register to be loaded */
  Regs.x.dx = FP_OFF( BufP );
  SRegs.es = FP_SEG( BufP );              /* Load pointer to buffer */
  int86x( 0x10, &Regs, &Regs, &SRegs );  /* Call BIOS video interrupt */
}


/***********************************************************************
 * SetDac: Loads a specific number of DAC registers                    *
 **-------------------------------------------------------------------**
 * Input   : FIRST = Number of the first DAC register (0-255)          *
 *           NUM   = Number of the DAC register                        *
 *           BUFP  = Pointer to the buffer, from which various         *
 *                   DAC registers are to be loaded. It must be        *
 *                   DACREG type variable or an array of this type.    *
 * Info    : See GetDac()                                              *
 ***********************************************************************/

void SetDac( int First, int Num, void far *BufP )
{
  union REGS Regs;           /* Processor registers for interrupt call */
  struct SREGS SRegs;                       /* Segment register */

  Regs.x.ax = 0x1012;                /* Function and sub-function no. */
  Regs.x.bx = First;           /* Number of the first DAC register */
  Regs.x.cx = Num;              /* Number of register to be loaded */
  Regs.x.dx = FP_OFF( BufP );
  SRegs.es = FP_SEG( BufP );              /* Load pointer to the buffer */
  int86x( 0x10, &Regs, &Regs, &SRegs );  /* Call BIOS video interrupt */
}


/***********************************************************************
 * PrintDac: Displays the contents of a DAC register on the screen     *
 *           and sets the color in DAC register 255                    *
 **-------------------------------------------------------------------**
 * Input   : DREG  = DAC register                                      *
 *           NO    = The number of this register                       *
 *           COLOR = Display color                                     *
 ***********************************************************************/

void PrintDac( DACREG DReg, BYTE No, BYTE Color )
{
  SetDac( 255, 1, &DReg );            /* Color in DAC register 255 */
  GrafPrintf( 60, MAXY-10, Color, 0, "DAC:%3d R:%2d G:%2d B:%2d",
              No, DReg.b.Red, DReg.b.Green, DReg.b.Blue);
}


/***********************************************************************
 * Frame   : Draws a frame around one of the color boxes               *
 **-------------------------------------------------------------------**
 * Input   : X     = X-coordinates of the color box (0-15)             *
 *           Y     = Y-coordinates of the color box (0-15)             *
 *           COLOR = Color of the frame                                *
 * Info    : The line thickness is one pixel, regardless of            *
 *           the distance of the color boxes.                          *
 ***********************************************************************/

void Surround( int x, int y, BYTE Color )
{
  int sx, sy,                  /* Upper-left corner of frame */
```

```
      ex, ey;                         /* Lower-right corner of frame */

  /*-- Compute corner coordinates of the frame -----------------------*/

  ex = ( sx = STARTX + x * (BWIDTH + SPACING) - 1 ) + BWIDTH + 1;
  ey = ( sy = STARTY + y * (BHEIGHT + SPACING) - 1 ) + BHEIGHT + 1;

  Line( sx, sy, ex, sy, Color );              /* Draw frame */
  Line( ex, sy, ex, ey, Color );
  Line( ex, ey, sx, ey, Color );
  Line( sx, ey, sx, sy, Color );
}


/***********************************************************************
 * ChangeDacReg: Changes the contents of a DAC register in memory      *
 *               and in the DAC table of the video card and then       *
 *               displays the contents on the screen.                  *
 **-------------------------------------------------------------------**
 * Input   : DREGP = Pointer to DAC register to be changed             *
 *           NO    = Number of DAC register                            *
 *           COMP  = Number of component to be changed (0-2)           *
 *                   0 = Red, 1 == Green, 2 == Blue                     *
 *           INCR  = Increment for these components                    *
 ***********************************************************************/

void ChangeDacReg( DACREG *DRegP, BYTE No, BYTE Comp, BYTE Incr )
{
  if ( ( DRegP->RGB[ Comp ] += Incr ) > 63 )  /* Increment components */
    DRegP->RGB[ Comp ] = 0;                   /* > 63: Set to zero */
  SetDac( No, 1, DRegP );                      /* Load DAC register */
  PrintDac( *DRegP, No, 15 );                  /* Display new contents */
}


/***********************************************************************
 * Demo: Demonstrates the programming of the DAC register and the      *
 *       color model of the VGA card                                   *
 **-------------------------------------------------------------------**
 * Input   : None                                                      *
 ***********************************************************************/

void Demo( void )
{
  int    x,  y,
         ix, jx,
         iy, jy,
         k,  f;                              /* Loop counter */
  char   ch;                                 /* Key */
  DACARRAY dacbuf;                /* Array with complete DAC table */
  DACREG   DReg;                  /* The current DAC register */

  /*-- Generate screen -----------------------------------------------*/

  setpage( 0 );                              /* Process page 0 */
  showpage( 0 );                             /* Display page 0 */
  GetDac( 0, 256, dacbuf );          /* Load complete DAC table */

  GrafPrintf( 10, 0, 255, 0,
              "VDACC - (c) 1991, 1992 by M. Tischer" );

  /*-- Make the block out of 16x16 color boxes -----------------------*/

  iy = STARTY;                     /* Starting point on the screen */
  jy = STARTY + BHEIGHT - 1;
  f  = 0;
```

```
for ( y = 0; y < 16; ++y )           /* Execute the 16 block lines */
 {
  ix = STARTX;
  jx = STARTX + BWIDTH - 1;
  for ( x = 0; x < 16; ++x )          /* Execute the 16 block columns */
   {
    for ( k = iy; k <= jy; ++k )    /* Make block from single lines */
      Line( ix, k, jx, k, (BYTE) f );
    ix += BWIDTH + SPACING;          /* Next block right */
    jx += BWIDTH + SPACING;
    ++f;                          /* Increment color for the next block */
   }
  iy += BHEIGHT + SPACING;             /* Starting pos. for next
*/
  jy += BHEIGHT + SPACING;             /* block line
*/
 }

 /*-- Read user input and respond to it -----------------------------*/

 ix = 0;                   /* Start in upper-left corner with color 0 */
 iy = 0;
 jx = 0;
 jy = 0;
 k = 0;
 GetDac( 0, 1, &DReg );                        /* Get color 0 */
 Surround( 0, 0, 15 );              /* Draw frame around color box */
 PrintDac( DReg, 0, 15 );                 /* and display contents */
 do
 {
   ch = (char) getch();                      /* Read key */
   if ( ch )                         /* Not an extended key? */
    switch ( ch )                    /* No, evaluate */
     {
       case 'r' : ChangeDacReg( &DReg, (BYTE) k, 0, +1 ); /* r = Red + */
                  break;
       case 'g' : ChangeDacReg( &DReg, (BYTE) k, 1, +1 ); /* g = Green
+*/
                  break;
       case 'b' : ChangeDacReg( &DReg, (BYTE) k, 2, +1 ); /* b = Blue +*/
                  break;
       case 'R' : ChangeDacReg( &DReg, (BYTE) k, 0, -1 ); /* R = Red - */
                  break;
       case 'G' : ChangeDacReg( &DReg, (BYTE) k, 1, -1 ); /* G = Green
-*/
                  break;
       case 'B' : ChangeDacReg( &DReg, (BYTE) k, 2, -1 ); /* B = Blue -*/
                  break;
       case ' ' : {                      /* Space = Set original value */
                  DReg = dacbuf[ k ];
                  ChangeDacReg( &DReg, (BYTE) k, 1, 0 );
                  break;
                  }
     }
   else                         /* Extended keyboard code */
    switch ( getch() )
     {
       case 72 : if ( iy == 0 )                   /* Cursor up */
                   jy = 15;
                 else
                   jy = iy - 1;
                 break;

       case 80 : if ( iy == 15 )                  /* Cursor down */
                   jy = 0;
                 else
                   jy = iy + 1;
                 break;

       case 75 : if ( ix == 0 )                   /* Cursor left */
                   jx = 15;
                 else
                   jx = ix - 1;
                 break;

       case 77 : if ( ix == 15 )                  /* Cursor right */
                   jx = 0;
                 else
                   jx = ix + 1;
     }

   if ( ix != jx || iy != jy )            /* New cursor position? */
    {                                        /* Yes */
     Surround( ix, iy, 0 );         /* Mask frame in old position */
     Surround( jx, jy, 15 );        /* Draw frame around new position */
     ix = jx;                              /* Store new color box */
     iy = jy;
     k = iy*16+ix;                       /* Compute number of new box */
     GetDac( k, 1, &DReg );              /* Load DAC register */
     PrintDac( DReg, (BYTE) k, 15 );      /* and display       */
    }
 }
 while ( ch != 13 );            /* Repeat until RETURN is pressed */

 SetDac( 0, 256, dacbuf );                /* Restore DAC table */
}

/*---------------------------------------------------------------------*/
/*--            M A I N   P R O G R A M            --*/
/*---------------------------------------------------------------------*/

void main( void )
{
 union REGS regs;

 if ( IsVga() )                         /* VGA card installed? */
  {                                        /* Yes, go ahead */
   init320400();                         /* Initialize graphics mode */
   Demo();
   regs.x.ax = 0x0003;                    /* Shift into text mode */
   int86( 0x10, &regs, &regs );
  }
 else
  printf( "VDACC - (c) 1991 by MICHAEL TISCHER\n\nAttention! This "\
          "program requires a VGA card.\n\n" );
}
```

4.8.9 Sprites

Nothing dazzles computer users more than slick graphics. Whether it's a PacMan® character zipping across the screen, a starship defending its homeworld from evil invaders, or a dinosaur emerging from the jungle, good graphics and animation always catch the user's attention. But behind every successful animation lie dozens of hours of development. This is especially true for PC software development because most home based PCs contain video hardware that has limited capabilities for graphics programming. So, a lot of coding must be done from scratch.

In this section, we'll show you how to create convincing graphics on the PC in spite of these limitations. The technique involves using sprites, which are graphics objects that are used in almost all computer games and many animation applications.

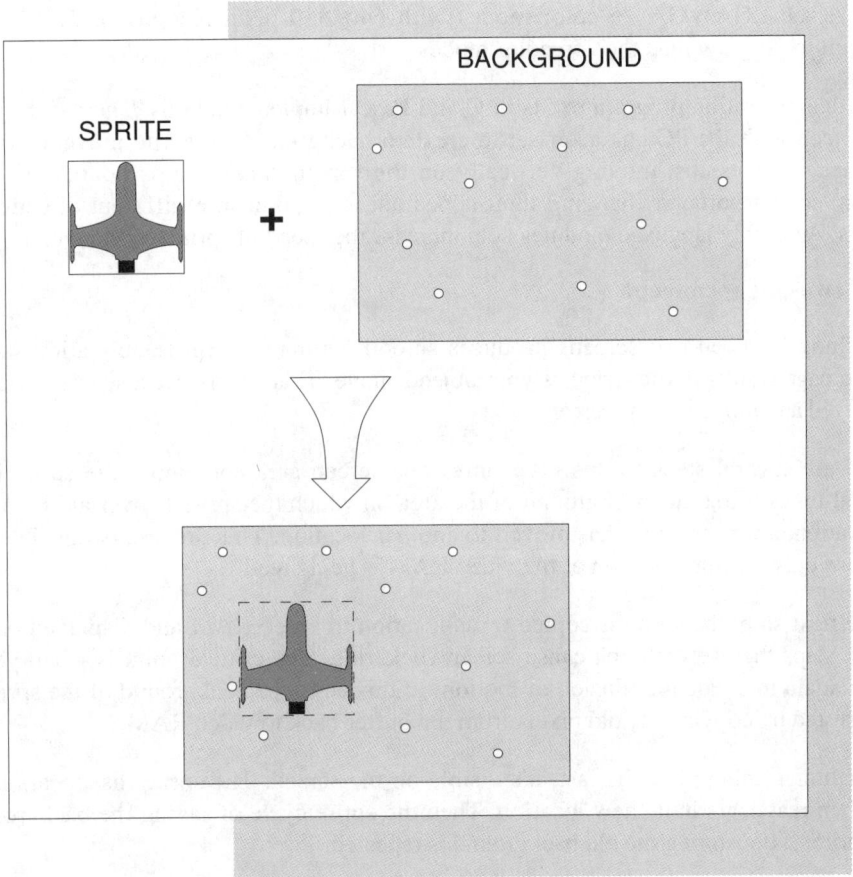

Transparent sprite display

What are sprites?

A sprite is a rectangular block of pixels grouped together to form an object. You can then move this object across the screen. The colors used must be selected carefully. Many programmers assign a single color to the object and then assign the screen background color to all the pixels in the sprite block that don't represent the object itself. Although this simplifies development, it limits your animation options.

In addition to the basic image represented by the sprite, you should also be able to replace it with another image while the program is running. For example, the basic image may be a starship, but the second image may be an exploding starship.

Programming an application then involves coordinating the movement of sprites on the screen to create the desired animation. We won't discuss that here, but we'll cover all the routines you'll need for basic sprite programming. These include routines for sprite definition, movement, removal, and image change.

The demonstration programs show examples of sprite programming on EGA and VGA cards. First, we'll look at the two VGA 256 color modes described in Section 4.8.7. Then, we'll explore the EGA/VGA 16 color modes with 640x350 pixel resolution. This mode is more difficult to program than the 256 color modes.

Each demonstration program exists in C and Pascal implementations. They all begin by filling the screen with the PC character set to create a background for sprite movements. Six sprites appear as spaceships, moving vertically on the screen. These ships bounce off the top and bottom screen borders, changing their appearances to point in a different direction when this occurs. Assembly language modules help increase the speed of sprite movement.

The two-page concept

Switching between two screens produces smooth animation. Sprite animation with only one screen page results in flickering as your objects move. This occurs because of the way sprites are displayed and moved on the screen.

There are several steps to this procedure. The screen area containing the sprite is processed several times. First, the background of the area on which the sprite is overlaid is saved for later restoration, after the sprite has moved to another location. This process is invisible to the user, because only a certain portion of the video RAM is being read.

In the next step, the sprite is copied to its location in video RAM and displayed on the screen. These steps themselves don't cause screen flickering. The critical point is when you move the sprite again to create the illusion of motion. In this case, the background of the sprite must first be restored by copying the old pixels from the buffer back to video RAM.

Even though this process is fast, it's visible on the screen. The sprite disappears momentarily and then reappears in its new location. Then the entire cycle of saving the background, writing the sprite, and restoring the old background is repeated.

The flickering effect cannot be avoided if you're working with only a single screen page. This is why we use two screen pages when programming sprites; this allows you to switch smoothly between screens. The processing always occurs on the hidden screen. When the processing is complete, the next scene in the animation is displayed and the cycle begins again.

The need for two screens also explains why we don't use the high resolution 640x480 VGA mode. A single screen page in this mode requires 150K, leaving only 106K. So, we limit the resolution to 640x350 in the EGA and VGA 16 color modes. This mode is adequate for most games, which are the most common applications for sprites.

Regardless of the video mode and how we choose to write sprites in video RAM and store their old backgrounds, there are certain universal problems that we must address when programming with sprites. The solutions to these problems are similar in both the C and Pascal versions of the demonstration programs. So, we'll discuss common aspects of the two versions before viewing the differences. These occur primarily in the modules that address video RAM, which is organized differently for the various graphics modes. These modules can be modified so the demonstration programs work with other types of video cards, or even in the graphics modes of the Super VGA card.

Structure of the sprite programs

The sprite demo begins by determining the video card type. Next, a routine named DEMO is called from the main program or the MAIN() function. The DEMO routine fills screen pages 0 and 1 with characters from the PC character set using the GRAFXPRINTF (C version) and PRINTCHAR (Pascal version) routines (see Sections 4.8.6 and 4.8.7 for descriptions of these routines). These routines in turn access assembler modules, such as V3220CA.ASM and V3240PA.ASM to enable various video modes (see Section 4.8.7). The assembler modules contain routines for reading and writing pixels, switching between and displaying screen pages, and initializing a specific graphics mode.

After the characters form the background for the sprite display, a copyright message appears in the middle of the screen. Then the COMPILESPRITE routine defines the sprites.

The sprites aren't actually created by COMPILESPRITE. A routine called CREATESPRITE later creates the sprites in each program.

A string array conveys the appearance of a sprite. The COMPILESPRITE routine converts this array to a binary format that is later used to display the sprite on the screen. COMPILESPRITE begins by creating a bit pattern that can later be assigned to a number of sprites. COMPILESPRITE accepts a different number of parameters, depending on the version of the program. The first two parameters are always the same, however. The first parameter contains the string array that describes the appearance of the sprite, and the second parameter contains the number of strings in the array.

This second parameter also defines the height of the sprite. A sprite can have a height ranging from one to hundreds of pixels. Each pixel line is represented by one string in the array. The first string is the top line of the sprite, the next string is the second line from the top, etc.

Each character in a string represents a pixel. Since a sprite is a rectangular object, all strings in the string array have identical widths. So it's unnecessary to pass the width of the sprite, since this can be obtained from the width of the first string in the array.

The following is an example of how a sprite may be coded in a C array:

```
static char *STARSHIPUP[20] =
          { "                    AA                   ",
            "                   AAAA                  ",
            "                   AAAA                  ",
            "                    AA                   ",
            "                  GGBBGG                 ",
            "                 GBBCCBBG                ",
            "                GBBBCCBBBG               ",
            "               GBBBBBBBBBBG              ",
            "               GBBBBBBBBBBG              ",
            " G             GBBBBBBBBBBBG          G ",
            "GCG           GGDBBBBBBBBBBBDGG       GCG",
            "GCG    GGBBBDBBB  BBBDBBBG    GCG",
            "GCBGGGBBBBBDBB       BBDBBBBBGGGBCG",
            "GCBBBBBBBBBBBDB      BDBBBBBBBBBBBCG",
            "BBBBBBBBBBBBDB BB BDBBBBBBBBBBBB",
            "GGCBBBBBBBBDBBBBBBBBBBBDBBBBBBBCG ",
            " GGCCBBBDDDDDDDDDDDDDDBBBCCG       ",
            " GGBBDDDDDGGGGGDDDDDDDBBG         ",
            " GDDDDGGG     GGGDDDDG          ",
            " DDDD         DDDD         " };
```

The sprite demonstration programs were intended for use with color monitors, so each pixel must have a color associated with it instead of a simple "on/off" status. The programs read the @ character as black (color code 0), A as blue (color code 1), B as green (color code 2), and so on.

Pixels that aren't associated with the sprite appear in the background color (blank spaces).

The COMPILESPRITE routine always returns a pointer to a structure of type SPLOOK, which is placed on the heap by the COMPILESPRITE routine. This structure contains all the important information needed about the sprite. Sprite creation requires this structure in the following steps. After COMPILESPRITE is finished, the string array initially used to define the sprite is no longer needed.

Two types of sprites are defined within the programs. They are represented by the string arrays STARSHIPUP and STARSHIPDOWN. One sprite displays the ship going up, and the other displays it going down. Using the pointer to the SPLOOK structure, the sprites are generated within a program loop.

The SPRNUM constant controls the number of times the loop is processed, which is set to a value of 6 in each demonstration program. Each time the loop is processed, a new sprite is created with a call to the CREATESPRITE routine. If you want to experiment with the program, you can easily set this constant to a higher value to create more sprites on the screen. The sprites will be crowded closer and closer together until they overlap. This will cause problems with your display, since these demonstration programs aren't written to handle collisions between sprites.

When experimenting with the number of sprites displayed on screen, you'll notice that the sprite movement suddenly becomes jerky and hesitant. Reduce the number of sprites by one until smooth movement returns. The number of sprites that can be smoothly processed depends on the processor speed and graphics card type in your system. The reason for this problem will become clear as we discuss sprite movement in more detail.

The CREATESPRITE routine creates sprites through recursive calls. The first parameter required by this routine is the pointer to the sprite description, as returned by COMPILESPRITE. This is how the size and appearance of the sprite are defined. The rest of the parameters passed to CREATESPRITE depend on the sprite program, and will be discussed along with the individual details of each program as we encounter these details.

In all the sprite demonstration programs, the CREATESPRITE routine returns a pointer to a structure of type SPID. This structure stores all the relevant data for the sprite that was just created. This information includes the pointer to the appearance of the sprite, its current position in both screen pages, and other information that will vary with the program version. This data structure is also placed on the heap, just as with COMPILESPRITE.

The loop used to create sprites also determines their initial position on screen and the speed at which they will move. This information is generated by a random number function. The speed of movement in the X direction is always set to 0 in the local variable DX, which ensures that the sprites will move only up or down, but never right or left. When experimenting with these programs, you may want to set this variable to a value other than 0 and watch what happens to the sprites.

The pointer to the sprite (or its SPID structure) and its speed of movement are stored in a local variable called SPRITES. This variable is a simple array.

The SETSPRITE procedure displays the sprite on the screen. The first parameter required is the pointer to the sprite description that was returned by CREATESPRITE. Then the X- and Y-coordinates for the sprite in screen page 0 are passed, followed by the X- and Y-coordinates in screen page 1.

The two coordinate pairs are passed separately because they cannot be identical. This is the basis of the two-page concept. If the sprite were located at the same position in both screen pages, it would not appear to move at all when you switch pages. The speed of the sprite's movement is determined by the distance between the sprite's positions in the two screen pages.

Independent movement

Imagine a sprite that you want to move vertically on the screen from the top edge (Y-coordinate = 0) to the bottom edge. Each time the screen is redrawn, the sprite moves down by one pixel.

We can initialize the program with the sprite at Y-coordinate 0 in the first screen page and at Y-coordinate 1 in the second page. Then when the display switches from page 0 to page 1, the sprite appears to move down one pixel.

Now, while screen page 1 is being displayed, the sprite in screen page 0 is moved to a new location. The new location will be two pixels below its original position, so when screen page 0 reappears, the sprite appears at Y-coordinate 2 (one pixel below its previously displayed position). This means that if you want the sprite to appear to move by a certain number of pixels when each new screen is drawn, you must move it by twice as many pixels when internally building a new screen page.

The same is true for changes in the X-coordinate to make your object move horizontally as well.

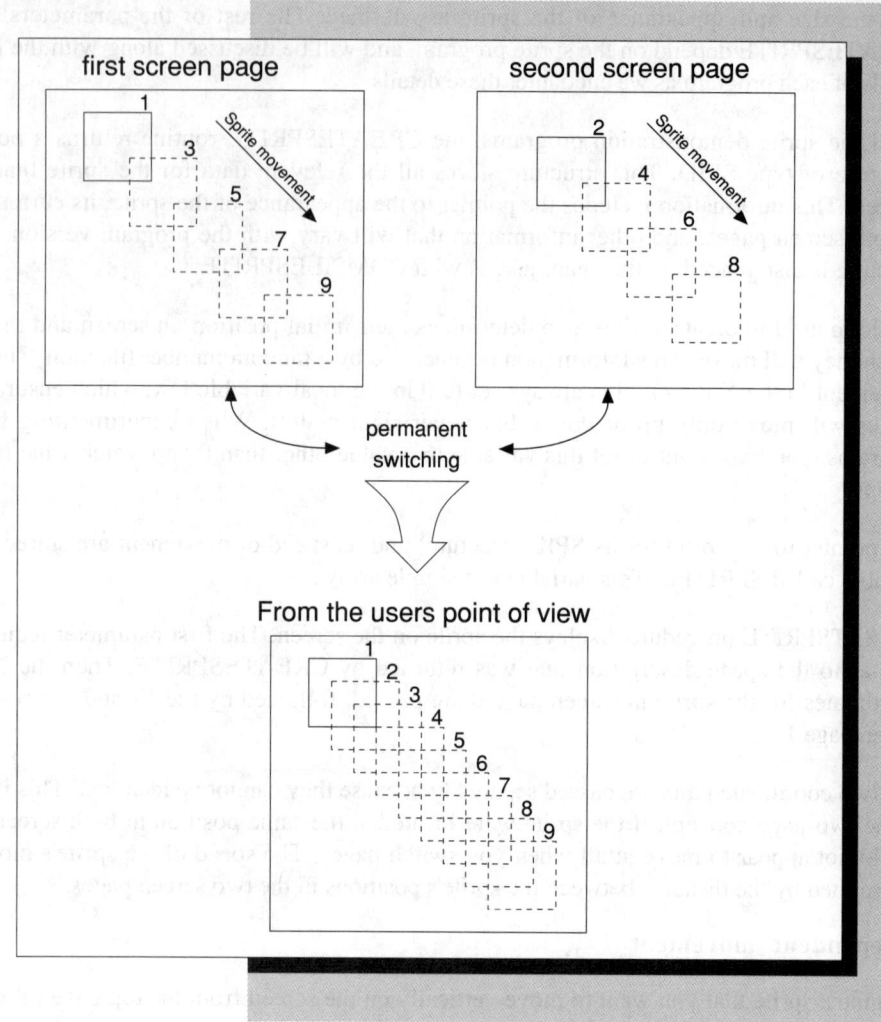

first screen page

second screen page

Sprite movement

Sprite movement

permanent
switching

From the users point of view

Sprite display and movement in the two screen pages

After the sprites are created and initially displayed, a loop processes their movements until the user presses any key on the keyboard. Inside the loop, the program constantly switches between the two screen pages and the sprite is moved on the screen page that isn't displayed.

This is accomplished with the MOVESPRITE function. This is one of the few sprite routines that appears unchanged in all the sprite demonstration programs. That is because this routine is based on the lower level routines that reflect the actual differences between the programs.

The arguments for this routine are a pointer to the sprite description, the page number in which you want to move the sprite, and the number of pixels to move in the X- and Y-directions. The current sprite position and the movement increment ("speed") calculate the new position. Collisions with the edge of the screen are also taken into consideration. If the new sprite position is different from the old position, the movement executes.

The RESTORESPRITEBG routine deletes the sprite from its current position by restoring the background. The background of the sprite's new location is stored in a buffer using the GETSPRITEBG routine. Finally, the sprite itself is copied to its new location using the PRINTSPRITE routine.

The result of the MOVESPRITE function is a byte that reflects any collisions with the edge of the screen. The constants OUT_LEFT, OUT_TOP, OUT_RIGHT, OUT_BOTTOM, and OUT_NO can determine whether any collisions have occurred.

The DEMO routine also uses the information in this byte. Remember that when the sprite collides with the edge of the screen, it changes its appearance as well as its direction. This keeps the nose of the ship pointing in the correct direction.

The execution speed of the sprite movement loop within DEMO (and the speed of the sprite on screen) varies with your processor's speed, your video card, and the bus that connects the two. The frequency of your screen picture also makes a difference, because the rate at which screen pages are changed to create movement must be synchronized with the picture frequency.

A query loop within the assembler routine SHOWPAGE handles this. SHOWPAGE returns to its caller after a screen redraw has begun. The new screen page is selected and displayed only after this occurs. This prevents the caller of the SHOWPAGE routine from accessing a screen page that is still visible for a short time because the next screen redraw hasn't begun yet.

Because of this, it's possible that up to 1/50 of a second is lost, depending on the picture frequency and whether SHOWPAGE is called immediately after a screen redraw has begun. Once you've accumulated a certain number of sprites on the screen, it starts taking too long to switch screen pages. This shows up on the screen as a hesitation in the movement of the sprites.

The speed at which the sprites appear to move is determined by the number of pixels the sprite moves each time the movement loop is processed. There are practical limits here. If you move the sprite too far in a single screen change, it will appear to jump and the impression of fluid movement is lost. The speed with which your system can process the movement loop is also a determining factor.

To limit these problems, the most important routines that connect the program and the video card are written in assembly language. These assembler routines are called by the routines GETVIDEO and PUTVIDEO, which in turn are called by high level language routines, such as PRINTSPRITE, GETSPRITEBG, and RESTORESPRITEBG.

PUTVIDEO and GETVIDEO store an area of the screen in a buffer or fill a screen area with a pixel pattern that has already been stored in a buffer. These routines are used by PRINTSPRITE, GETSPRITEBG and RESTORESPRITEBG to display a sprite on screen, save a background area, and restore a background area.

The assembly language routines called by GETVIDEO and PUTVIDEO differ significantly depending on the graphics mode being used. In the next section, we'll focus on these routines when we discuss the differences caused by the various graphics modes.

We'll start with the VGA 256 color modes. This mode isn't available on the EGA card, but the program is actually simpler in this mode than in the 16 color modes. A discussion of the 640x350 pixel mode for both EGA and VGA appears at the end of this section.

Sprites with 320x200 pixels and 256 colors

Graphics programming requires many compromises. For example, although the 320*200 pixel mode with 256 colors has low resolution, the numerous colors and the ability to program with four screen pages can be great advantages for many applications. Even though only two screen pages are needed to animate with sprites, the other 128K of video RAM can be used to store screen backgrounds and bit patterns for sprites.

This is not just a matter of using less of the main memory. Keeping this information in video RAM can significantly increase the execution speed of your program. Remember that only one byte can be passed from the bitplanes to main memory at once, so this also taxes the system bus. Such limitations are removed if you move these memory areas around exclusively within video RAM.

Not only can we avoid I/O operations between the CPU and the video card over the system bus, but we can also enable four bytes to be copied using the four latch registers of the VGA card at once with a single MOVSB command. The REP MOVSB assembly language instruction allows an entire graphics line to be copied in one operation. This is a sufficient reason to put the unused portion of the video RAM to work doing things besides storing complete screen pages. Unfortunately, there is a problem with this procedure, as we'll see later.

First let's discuss the programs. In the C version, the modules S3220C.C, S3220CA.ASM, and V3220CA.ASM generate sprites in the 320x200 pixel 256 color mode. We've already seen V3220CA.ASM in Section 4.8.7. S3220C.C. and S3220CA.ASM are new. S3220C.C contains the C routines COMPILESPRITE through GETVIDEO, which we've already discussed.

The assembly language module 3220CA.ASM contains only the BLOCKMOVE routine, which moves a rectangular block of pixels within video RAM. The Pascal version isn't much different. The modules are called S3220P.PAS, S3220PA.ASM, and V3220PA.ASM. V3220PA.ASM was also discussed in Section 4.8.7.

Storing sprite information in video RAM itself allows us to move this information quickly to different locations. But the structure of video RAM in the 320x200 pixel mode imposes certain limitations on your program. The width of each sprite must always be rounded to a multiple of four. This is because four pixels (i.e., four bytes) are always copied simultaneously using the four latch registers.

If the sprite width isn't a multiple of four, then you would always have to ensure that you copied only the bytes belonging to the current line. This means one or more latch registers would have to be excluded from the copy operation of the last group of bytes in a line. We always round the width of each sprite to a multiple of four, if only to save some development time.

There's another issue involved in those multiples of four. If the information for the sprite's appearance begins at an X-coordinate that is a multiple of four, then it can only be copied to another X-coordinate that is a multiple of four. A sprite starting at X-coordinate 0 can only be copied to coordinates such as 4, 8, 96, 224, etc., but never to coordinates such as 1, 2, 5, 13, or

182. This is simply because any read access to the video RAM in 320x200 pixel mode must begin with an X-coordinate that is a multiple of four. You must do this if you want to use all four latch registers together. The same is true if you would like to write data with all four latch registers in one operation.

There is only one way to move the copies of the four latch registers one pixel to the right, to X-coordinates such as 1, 2, or 25. You cannot simply move the contents from one latch register to the next. For example, you cannot move latch register 0 to latch register 1, or latch register 1 to 2, or 2 to 3, etc. Likewise, you cannot save the contents of latch register 3 and write it to latch register 0 as part of the next copy operation. However, it's possible to mask latch register 0 before the write operation, so its contents aren't copied to an X-coordinate in video RAM that is divisible by four.

Even this last possibility would require too much effort. So instead of this, we simply store four copies of the sprite with the first one starting at an X-coordinate that is a multiple of four. The second copy is stored starting with the next pixel to the right. This keeps the far left pixel column of the sprite unused. For now, this column takes on the background color and is seen as transparent.

The third and fourth sprites are stored in the same way, with two or three pixel columns remaining transparent.

Sprite definition in video RAM: 320x200 pixel mode with 256 colors

Before a sprite can be displayed on the screen, a sprite must first be moved to an X-coordinate that is divisible by four. The difference between the starting X-coordinate and the target X-coordinate equals the number of empty columns at the start of the sprite. This also gives the number that identifies the sprite to be copied. The following formula can be used:

```
TargetX =  int(X / 4) * 4
       [or] X and not(4)
 Sprite  = X - int(X / 4) * 4
       [or] X and 3
```

However, the problem of the transparent pixel columns still exists. As long as you use the four latch registers together and copy in groups of four pixels, the complete sprite is copied exactly as it was stored and the blank columns will remain blank. So before the write operation we must use the map mask register of the sequencer controller to mask the latch registers that would otherwise be overwritten with background pixels.

Since there is a different latch register for each group of sprite pixels, the map mask register must be specially programmed for each case before writing to the latch registers. This is done using a value calculated while the sprite description was being compiled with COMPILESPRITE. This value is passed to the BLOCKMOVE routine as part of an array.

Although this makes the procedure more complicated, it's unavoidable if you want to store the sprites directly in video RAM. Fortunately, this is only required when writing the sprite itself. It's not necessary to program the map mask register when saving or restoring a sprite background.

This method of storing sprites in video RAM and copying them as part of an array containing values for the map mask register plays a major role in the S3220C.C and S3220P.PAS modules, as well as the BLOCKMOVE procedure used in the S3220CA.ASM and S3220PA.ASM assembly language modules.

This starts with the COMPILESPRITE routine. The string array that defines the sprite and the sprite's height are the first two parameters passed to this routine. There are four others. The first of these specifies the screen page that is used to store the sprite description. Since pages 0 and 1 are being used for the display, this must be either 2 or 3.

The next parameter is the pixel line in which the sprite definition will begin. This can be any value from 0 to 200 (the sprite height). Be careful not to overlap sprite descriptions in video RAM.

Within the given line, the four copies of the sprite are stored right next to one another. You can actually see what this looks like by displaying the screen page with SHOWPAGE after compiling the sprite with COMPILESPRITE in the DEMO routine.

The next parameter for COMPILESPRITE is a character that represents the smallest color value in the string array used to define the sprite. Usually, you use the letter 'A' for this. Of course, you can also use lowercase letters or numbers to code the pixel colors within the string array, in which case you would enter 'a' or '0' for this parameter.

The last parameter also handles pixel colors. It gives the color number assigned to the sprite pixel with the smallest color code ('A', 'a', or '0'). This defines the meanings of all the other characters in the string array, since 'B', 'b', or '1' corresponds to the next color value in the palette.

In this way, more than 128 colors can also be reached without using foreign or special characters in your string array. Regardless of the values in the last two parameters, an empty space always represents a transparent pixel. When the sprite is displayed, the transparent pixel turns to the background color.

COMPILESPRITE uses the information passed to it to build the sprite four times in the given page, as previously described. Background pixels are assigned color code 255 so they can be distinguished from the non-transparent pixels in what follows.

Next, the four sprites are processed again to fill the array that is later used to program the map mask register when BLOCKMOVE is called. The memory for this array is allocated on the heap. Each pixel in the four sprites gets a nibble containing the corresponding value for the map mask register.

The pointer to this array is stored in the sprite description (SPLOOK) along with all other relevant information. A pointer to this structure is returned to the calling routine.

CREATESPRITE also requires more information. In addition to the obligatory pointer to the sprite description, the locations of the two areas in video RAM used to store sprite backgrounds from screen pages 0 and 1 must be passed. This requires the screen page (2 or 3) and the X- and Y-coordinates. Remember that you need an area twice as wide as the sprite area itself. This is because the two buffers from both page 0 and page 1 are stored next to each other.

Once a sprite is created with this procedure, you can use the SETSPRITE routine to display it on screen and MOVESPRITE to animate it. PRINTSPRITE, GETSPRITEBG, and RESTORESPRITEBG support the BLOCKMOVE assembly language routine.

BLOCKMOVE expects a number of parameters, including the starting coordinates of the source and target areas. These locations are represented by the combination of the screen page plus the X- and Y-coordinates. The width and height of the rectangular block are also required. Finally, BLOCKMOVE receives a pointer to the array that contains the values for programming the map mask register.

If all pixels in the rectangular sprite should be copied regardless of the background pixels, then the array isn't required. You can pass a NULL pointer for this parameter. In the Pascal version, this is represented by the predefined NIL constant, and in the C version by the NOBIT MASK constant.

If BLOCKMOVE encounters a NULL pointer, it copies an entire pixel line from the specified area in one move. This is much faster than the normal copy routine, in which the map mask register is programmed before each four byte transfer.

In either case, write mode 1 is set before the copy loop begins. Only this mode allows simultaneous transfer of the latch registers' contents to the four bitplanes. The routine restores the original write mode and ends.

Sprite programs using the 256 color 320x200 pixel graphics mode run faster than the other demonstration programs in this section because they can use video RAM for storing sprite descriptions and sprite backgrounds. Unfortunately, a screen resolution that is lower than what PC users are accustomed to is used. We believe that if 256 colors are needed, the 320x400 pixel mode is better, even in spite of the slower speed of execution.

Before we discuss the other graphics modes, here are the listings for the sprite demonstration programs using 320x200 pixel mode.

Pascal listing: S3220P.PAS

```
{******************************************************
*                S 3 2 2 0 P . P A S                  *
**--------------------------------------------------**
* Task        : Demonstrates sprites in 320x200 VGA graphic  *
*                mode, using 256 colors and four screen pages. *
*                This program requires the assembly language   *
*                modules V3220PA.ASM and S3220PA.ASM.          *
**--------------------------------------------------**
* Author      : Michael Tischer                       *
* Developed on : 09/12/90                             *
* Last update  : 02/12/92                             *
******************************************************}

program S3220P;

uses dos, crt;

{-- External references to the assembler routines -------------------}

{$L v3220pa}                          { Link assembler module }
```

```
procedure init320200; external;
procedure setpix( x, y : integer; pcolor : byte ); external;
function  getpix( x, y: integer ) : byte ; external;
procedure setpage( page : byte ); external;
procedure showpage( page : byte ); external;

{$L s3220pa}                          { Link assembler module }

procedure blockmove( frompage : byte; fromx, fromy : integer;
                     topage : byte; tox, toy : integer;
                     pwidth, pheight: byte; bmskp : pointer ); external;

{-- Constants ---------------------------------------------------------}

const MAXX = 319;                    { Maximum X- and Y-coordinates }
      MAXY = 199;

      OUT_LEFT   = 1;    { For collision documentation in SpriteMove() }
      OUT_TOP    = 2;
      OUT_RIGHT  = 4;
      OUT_BOTTOM = 8;
      OUT_NO     = 0;                { None }
```

```
{-- Type declarations -------------------------------------------}

type SPLOOK = record                          { Sprite design }
              twidth,                          { Total width }
              theight,                  { Height in pixel lines }
              ppage,                      { Placed in page ... }
              msklen : byte;                  { Entry length }
              bmskp  : pointer;          { Pointer to bit mask }
              pxlin  : integer;     { Pixel lines for sprite }
              end;                          { in its page }
       SPLP = ^SPLOOK;                { Pointer to sprite design }

       SPID = record                        { Sprite descriptor }
              bkgpage :byte;              { Background page }
              x, y : array [0..1] of integer;{ Coordinates: pp. 0 & 1 }
              bkx, bky : integer;          { Background buffer }
              splookp : SPLP;        { Pointer to sprite design }
              end;
       SPIP = ^SPID;              { Pointer to sprite descriptor }

       BYTEAR = array[0..10000] of byte;       { Addressing }
       BARPTR = ^BYTEAR;                    { different buffers }

       PTRREC = record         { For pointer or LONGINTS analysis }
              ofs,
              seg : word;
              end;

{********************************************************************
*  IsVga : Determines whether a VGA card is installed.             *
**----------------------------------------------------------------**
*  Input   : None                                                  *
*  Output  : TRUE or FALSE                                         *
********************************************************************}

function IsVga : boolean;

var Regs : Registers;      { Processor registers for interrupt call }

begin
  Regs.AX := $1a00;          { Function 1AH applies to VGA only }
  Intr( $10, Regs );
  IsVga := ( Regs.AL = $1a );
end;

{********************************************************************
*  PrintChar : Writes a character to the screen while in graphic mode.*
**----------------------------------------------------------------**
*  Input   :   THECHAR = Character to be written                   *
*              x, y    = X- and Y-coordinates of upper-left corner *
*              FG      = Foreground color                          *
*              BK      = Background color                          *
*  Info    : Character is created in an 8x8 matrix, based on the   *
*            8x8 ROM font.                                         *
********************************************************************}

procedure PrintChar( thechar : char; x, y : integer; fg, bk : byte );

type FDEF = array[0..255,0..7] of byte;        { Font array }
     TPTR = ^FDEF;                          { Pointer to font }

var Regs  : Registers;      { Registers for interrupt call }
    ch    : char;           { Individual pixels in character }
    i, k,                             { Loop counter }
```

```
    BMask : byte;              { Bit mask for character design }

const fptr : TPTR = NIL;           { Pointer to font in ROM }

begin
  if fptr = NIL then            { Pointer to font already set? }
    begin                                   { No }
      Regs.AH := $11;          { Call video BIOS function 11H, }
      Regs.AL := $30;             { sub-function 30H }
      Regs.BH := 3;              { Get pointer to 8x8 font }
      intr( $10, Regs );
      fptr := ptr( Regs.ES, Regs.BP );        { Set pointers }
    end;

  if ( bk = 255 ) then          { Drawing transparent characters? }
    for i := 0 to 7 do        { Yes --> Set foreground pixels only }
      begin
        BMask := fptr^[ord(thechar),i];{ Get bit pattern for one line }
        for k := 0 to 7 do
          begin
            if ( BMask and 128 <> 0 ) then       { Pixel set? }
              setpix( x+k, y+i, fg );              { Yes }
            BMask := BMask shl 1;
          end;
      end
  else                    { No --> Consider background as well }
    for i := 0 to 7 do              { Execute lines }
      begin
        BMask := fptr^[ord(thechar),i];{ Get bit pattern for one line }
        for k := 0 to 7 do
          begin
            if ( BMask and 128 <> 0 ) then       { Foreground? }
              setpix( x+k, y+i, fg )              { Yes }
            else
              setpix( x+k, y+i, bk );        { No --> Background }
            BMask := BMask shl 1;
          end;
      end;
end;


{********************************************************************
*  PrintString: Writes a string to the screen in graphics mode.   *
**----------------------------------------------------------------**
*  Input   :   X, Y    = X- and Y-coordinates of upper left-corner *
*              FG      = Foreground color                          *
*              BK      = Background color                          *
*              TSTR    = String to be displayed                   *
*  Info    : The characters are designed around an 8x8 matrix, based *
*            on the 8x8 ROM font.                                  *
********************************************************************}

procedure PrintString( x, y : integer; fg, bk : byte; tstr : string );

var i : integer;                            { Loop counter }

begin
  for i := 1 to length( tstr ) do           { Execute string }
    begin
      PrintChar( tstr[i], x, y, fg, bk );    { and display it }
      inc( x, 8 );              { Increment output position }
    end;
end;
```

```
{*************************************************************************
* Line: Draws a line based on the Bresenham algorithm.                  *
**---------------------------------------------------------------------**
* Input   : X1, Y1 = Starting coordinates (0 - ...)                     *
*           X2, Y2 = Ending coordinates                                 *
*           LPCOL  = Color of line pixels                               *
*************************************************************************}

procedure Line( x1, y1, x2, y2 : integer; lpcol : byte );

var d, dx, dy,
    aincr, bincr,
    xincr, yincr,
    x, y                : integer;

{-- Procedure for swapping two integer variables ----------------------}

procedure SwapInt( var i1, i2: integer );

var dummy : integer;

begin
  dummy := i2;
  i2    := i1;
  i1    := dummy;
end;

{-- Main procedure ----------------------------------------------------}

begin
  if ( abs(x2-x1) < abs(y2-y1) ) then    { X- or Y-axis overflow? }
    begin                                { Check Y-axes }
      if ( y1 > y2 ) then                { y1 > y2? }
        begin
          SwapInt( x1, x2 );             { Yes --> Swap X1 with X2 }
          SwapInt( y1, y2 );             {         and Y1 with Y2 }
        end;

      if ( x2 > x1 ) then xincr := 1     { Set X-axis increment }
                     else xincr := -1;

      dy := y2 - y1;
      dx := abs( x2-x1 );
      d  := 2 * dx - dy;
      aincr := 2 * (dx - dy);
      bincr := 2 * dx;
      x := x1;
      y := y1;

      setpix( x, y, lpcol );             { Set first pixel }
      for y:=y1+1 to y2 do               { Execute line on Y-axes }
        begin
          if ( d >= 0 ) then
            begin
              inc( x, xincr );
              inc( d, aincr );
            end
          else
            inc( d, bincr );
          setpix( x, y, lpcol );
        end;
    end
  else                                   { Check X-axes }
    begin

      if ( x1 > x2 ) then                { x1 > x2? }
        begin
          SwapInt( x1, x2 );             { Yes --> Swap X1 with X2 }
          SwapInt( y1, y2 );             {         and Y1 with Y2 }
        end;

      if ( y2 > y1 ) then yincr := 1     { Set Y-axis increment }
                     else yincr := -1;

      dx := x2 - x1;
      dy := abs( y2-y1 );
      d  := 2 * dy - dx;
      aincr := 2 * (dy - dx);
      bincr := 2 * dy;
      x := x1;
      y := y1;

      setpix( x, y, lpcol );             { Set first pixel }
      for x:=x1+1 to x2 do               { Execute line on X-axes }
        begin
          if ( d >= 0 ) then
            begin
              inc( y, yincr );
              inc( d, aincr );
            end
          else
            inc( d, bincr );
          setpix( x, y, lpcol );
        end;
    end;
end;

{*************************************************************************
* GrfxPrint: Displays a formatted string on the graphic screen.        *
**---------------------------------------------------------------------**
* Input   : X, Y   = Starting coordinates (0 - ...)                     *
*           FG     = Foreground color                                   *
*           BK     = Background color (255 = transparent)               *
*           STRING = String with format information                     *
*************************************************************************}

procedure GrfxPrint( x, y : integer; fg, bk : byte; strt : string );

var i : integer;                         { Loop counter }

begin
  for i:=1 to length( strt ) do
    begin
      printchar( strt[i], x, y, fg, bk );  { Display using PrintChar }
      inc( x, 8 );                       { Move X to next character position }
    end;
end;

{*************************************************************************
* CreateSprite: Creates a sprite based on a user-defined               *
*               pixel pattern.                                          *
**---------------------------------------------------------------------**
* Input   : SPLOOKP = Pointer to data structure from CompileSprite      *
*           BKGPAGE = Screen page in which sprite background should      *
*                     be stored                                         *
*           BKX,    = bkgpage coordinates at which sprite background     *
*           BKY       is stored                                         *
* Output  : Pointer to created sprite structure                         *
* Info    : The sprite background requires two areas the same size      *
```

```
*             as the corresponding sprite.              *
*************************************************************************)

function CreateSprite( splookp : SPLP; bkgpage : byte;
                       bkx, bky : integer           ) : SPIP;

var spidp : SPIP;              { Pointer to created sprite structure }

begin
  new( spidp );               { Allocate memory for sprite descriptor }
  spidp^.splookp := splookp;            { Pass data to the }
  spidp^.bkgpage := bkgpage;            { sprite structure }
  spidp^.bkx := bkx;
  spidp^.bky := bky;

  CreateSprite := spidp;     { Return pointer to the sprite structure }
end;

(*************************************************************************
* CompileSprite: Creates a sprite's pixel and bit patterns, based on *
*                the sprite's definition at runtime.                 *
**---------------------------------------------------------------------**
* Input   : BUFP    = Pointer to array contains string pointers      *
*                     controlling sprite's pattern                   *
*           SHEIGHT = Sprite height (and number of strings needed)   *
*           GPAGE   = Graphic page for sprite design                 *
*           Y       = Pixel lines needed for sprite                  *
*           FB      = ASCII characters for the smallest color        *
*           FGCOLOR = First color code for FB                        *
* Info    : Sprite structure of pixel lines starts at left margin.   *
*************************************************************************)

function CompileSprite( var buf; sheight, gpage : byte;
                        y : integer; fb : char; fgcolor : byte ) : SPLP;

type BYPTR = ^byte;                      { Pointer to a byte }

var  swidth,                             { String width }
     c,                    { Get character from c sprite array }
     cvcolor,                    { Converted color of a pixel }
     i, k, l,                          { Loop variables }
     pixc,           { Pixel counter for creating the bit mask }
     pixm    : byte;                     { Pixel mask }
     spacing,      { Spacing from start of sprite to start of sprite }
     lx, ly : integer;              { Floating coordinates }
     splookp : SPLP;      { Pointer to created sprite structure }
     lspb    : BYPTR;     { Floating pointer in sprite buffer }
     bptr    : barptr;    { Addresses buffer with graphic }

begin
{-- Create SpriteLook structure and fill with data ------------------}

new( splookp );
bptr := @buf;                        { Set pointer to logo buffer }
swidth := bptr^[0];    { Get string length and determine logo width }
spacing := ( ( swidth + 3 + 3 ) div 4 ) * 4;
splookp^.twidth := spacing;
splookp^.msklen := (spacing*sheight+7) div 8;
getmem( splookp^.bmskp, splookp^.msklen * 4 );
splookp^.theight := sheight;
splookp^.pxlin  := y;
splookp^.ppage  := gpage;

{-- Fill sprite background in home page with ----------------------}
```

```
{-- codes for transparent character background ---------------------}

setpage( gpage );                         { Set page for drawing }
lx := 4 * spacing - 1;
for ly:=y+sheight-1 downto y do
  Line( 0, ly, lx, ly, 255 );

{-- Draw four matching sprites in the home page --------------------}

lx := 0;                          { Start at left border of line }
for l := 1 to 4 do                        { Draw sprite four times }
  begin
    for i := 0 to sheight-1 do                    { Execute rows }
      for k := 0 to swidth-1 do              { Execute columns }
        begin
          c := bptr^[i*(swidth+1)+k+1];           { Get color }
          if ( c = 32 ) then              { Background pixel? }
            setpix( lx+k, y+i, 255 )   { Yes --> Set color code 255 }
          else                 { No --> Set color code as given }
            setpix( lx+k, y+i, fgcolor+(c-ord(fb)) );
          end;
      inc( lx, spacing+1 );             { Increment design column }
  end;

{-- Execute the four sprites and create bit masks ------------------}
{-- for copying the sprites into the bitplanes    ------------------}

pixm := 0;
pixc := 0;
lx := 0;
for l := 0 to 3 do
  begin
    lspb := splookp^.bmskp;
    inc( PTRREC( lspb ).ofs, splookp^.msklen * l );

    for i := 0 to sheight-1 do
      for k := 0 to spacing-1 do
        begin
          pixm := pixm shr 1;      { Shift pixel mask 1 bit right }
          if ( getpix( lx+k, y+i) <> 255 ) then{ Background pixel? }
            pixm := pixm or 128;        { No --> Set bit for mask }
          inc( pixc, 1 );
          if ( pixc = 8 ) then    { Eight pixels already handled? }
            begin        { Yes --> Place bit mask in sprite buffer }
              lspb^ := pixm;
              inc( PTRREC( lspb ).ofs, 1 );
              pixc := 0;            { Set pixel counter and mask to 0 }
              pixm := 0;
            end;
        end;

    if ( pixc <> 0 ) then          { Last nibble still not in buffer? }
      begin                          { No --> Move high nibble to }
        lspb^ := pixm shr 4;         { low nibble and store them }
        pixc := 0;                   { Set pixel counter and mask to 0 }
        pixm := 0;
      end;

    inc( lx, spacing );            { LX to start of next sprite }
  end;

  CompileSprite := splookp;        { Return pointer to sprite buffer }
end;
```

```
{*******************************************************************
* PrintSprite : Displays sprite in a specified page.              *
**-----------------------------------------------------------------**
* Input   : SPIDP  = Pointer to the sprite structure              *
*           SPRPAGE = Page in which sprite should be drawn (0 or 1) *
*******************************************************************}

procedure PrintSprite( spidp : SPIP; sprpage : byte );

var twidth  : byte;                    { Total width of sprite }
    x       : integer;          { X-coordinate of sprite in its page }
    splookp : SPLP;              { Pointer to sprite's appearance }

begin
  splookp := spidp^.splookp;
  twidth  := splookp^.twidth;
  x       := spidp^.x[sprpage];
  blockmove( splookp^.ppage, twidth * (x mod 4), splookp^.pxlin,
sprpage,
            x and not(3), spidp^.y[sprpage], twidth, splookp^.theight,
            @BARPTR(splookp^.bmskp)^[(x mod 4) * splookp^.msklen] );
end;

{*******************************************************************
* GetSpriteBg: Gets a sprite background and specifies the position. *
**-----------------------------------------------------------------**
* Input   : SPIDP   = Pointer to the sprite structure             *
*           SPRPAGE = Page from which background should be taken   *
*                     (0 or 1)                                     *
*******************************************************************}

procedure GetSpriteBg( spidp : SPIP; sprpage : BYTE );

var splookp : SPLP;              { Pointer to sprite graphic }

begin
  splookp := spidp^.splookp;
  blockmove( sprpage, spidp^.x[sprpage], spidp^.y[sprpage],
            spidp^.bkgpage, spidp^.bkx + ( splookp^.twidth * sprpage ),
            spidp^.bky, splookp^.twidth, splookp^.theight, NIL );
end;

{*******************************************************************
* RestoreSpriteBg: Restores sprite background from original graphic *
*                  page.                                          *
**-----------------------------------------------------------------**
* Input   : SPIDP =  Pointer to the sprite structure              *
*           SPRPAGE = Page from which background should be copied  *
*                     (0 or 1)                                     *
*******************************************************************}

procedure RestoreSpriteBg( spidp : SPIP; sprpage : BYTE );

var splookp : SPLP;    { Pointer to sprite graphic }

begin
  splookp := spidp^.splookp;
  blockmove( spidp^.bkgpage, spidp^.bkx + ( splookp^.twidth * sprpage ),
            spidp^.bky, sprpage, spidp^.x[sprpage], spidp^.y[sprpage],
            splookp^.twidth, splookp^.theight, NIL );
end;

{*******************************************************************
* MoveSprite: Copy sprite within background to original graphic page.*
```

```
**-----------------------------------------------------------------**
* Input   : SPIDP  = Pointer to the sprite structure              *
*           SPRPAGE= Page to which the background should be copied  *
*                    (0 or 1)                                      *
*           DELTAX = Movement counter in X-                        *
*           DELTAY   and Y-directions                             *
* Output  : Collision marker (see OUT_ constants)                 *
*******************************************************************}

function MoveSprite( spidp : SPIP; sprpage : byte;
                     deltax, deltay : integer    ) : byte;

var newx, newy : integer;              { New sprite coordinates }
    out        : byte;         { Display collision with border }

begin
{-- Move X-coordinates and test for border collision ----------------}

  newx := spidp^.x[sprpage] + deltax;
  if ( newx < 0 ) then
    begin
      newx := 0 - deltax - spidp^.x[sprpage];
      out := OUT_LEFT;
    end
  else
    if ( newx > MAXX - spidp^.splookp^.twidth ) then
      begin
        newx := (2*(MAXX+1))-newx-2*(spidp^.splookp^.twidth);
        out := OUT_RIGHT;
      end
    else
      out := OUT_NO;

{-- Move Y-coordinates and test for border collision ----------------}

  newy := spidp^.y[sprpage] + deltay;              { Top border? }
  if ( newy < 0 ) then
    begin                         { Yes --> Deltay must be negative }
      newy := 0 - deltay - spidp^.y[sprpage];
      out := out or OUT_TOP;
    end
  else
    if ( newy + spidp^.splookp^.theight > MAXY+1 ) then    { Bottom? }
      begin                         { Yes --> Deltay must be positive }
        newy := (2*(MAXY+1))-newy-2*(spidp^.splookp^.theight);
        out := out or OUT_BOTTOM;
      end;

{-- Set new position only if different from old position ------------}

  if ( newx <> spidp^.x[sprpage] ) or ( newy <> spidp^.y[sprpage] ) then
    begin                                 { If there's a new position }
      RestoreSpriteBg( spidp, sprpage );  { then reset background and }
      spidp^.x[sprpage] := newx;          { store new coordinates    }
      spidp^.y[sprpage] := newy;
      GetSpriteBg( spidp, sprpage );              { Get new background }
      PrintSprite( spidp, sprpage );    { Draw sprite in specified page }
    end;

  MoveSprite := out;
end;

{*******************************************************************
* SetSprite: Sets sprite at a specific position.                  *
```

```
**-------------------------------------------------------------**
*  Input  : SPIDP = Pointer to the sprite structure          *
*           x0, y0 = Sprite coordinates for page 0           *
*           x1, y1 = Sprite coordinates for page 1           *
*  Info   : This function call should be made the first time that *
*           MoveSprite() is called.                          *
*****************************************************************}

procedure SetSprite( spidp : SPIP; x0, y0, x1, y1 : integer );

begin
  spidp^.x[0] := x0;              { Store coordinates in sprite structure }
  spidp^.x[1] := x1;
  spidp^.y[0] := y0;
  spidp^.y[1] := y1;

  GetSpriteBg( spidp, 0 );                   { Get sprite backgrounds }
  GetSpriteBg( spidp, 1 );                   { in pages 0 and 1      }
  PrintSprite( spidp, 0 );                      { Draw sprite in }
  PrintSprite( spidp, 1 );                      { pages 1 and 0 }
end;


{*****************************************************************
*  RemoveSprite: Removes a sprite from its current position and makes *
*                it invisible.                               *
**-------------------------------------------------------------**
*  Input  : SPIDP = Pointer to the sprite structure          *
*  Info   : After calling this function the SetSprite() function *
*           must be called before the sprite can be moved using the *
*           MoveSprite() function.                           *
*****************************************************************}

procedure RemoveSprite( spidp : SPIP );

begin
  RestoreSpriteBg( spidp, 0 );             { Reset sprite backgrounds }
  RestoreSpriteBg( spidp, 1 );             { in pages 0 and 1        }
end;


{*****************************************************************
*  Demo: Demonstrates these functions.                       *
*****************************************************************}

procedure Demo;

const StarShipUp :array [1..20] of string[32] =
                ( '         AA             ',
                  '         AAAA           ',
                  '         AAAA           ',
                  '         AA             ',
                  '        GGBBGG          ',
                  '       GBBCCBBG         ',
                  '       GBBBCCBBG        ',
                  '      GBBBBBBBBBG       ',
                  '      GBBBBBBBBBG       ',
                  ' G    GBBBBBBBBBBBG    G ',
                  'GCG   GGDBBBBBBBBBDGG   GCG',
                  'GCG   GGBBBBDBBB BBBDBBBBGG   GCG',
                  'GCBGGGBBBBBDBB  BBDBBBBBBGGGBCG',
                  'GCBBBBBBBBBBDB  BDBBBBBBBBBCG',
                  'BBBBBBBBBBBBBDB BB BDBBBBBBBBBBBBBB',
                  'GGCBBBBBBBDBBBBBBBBBBDBBBBBBBBBCG',
                  ' GGCCBBBBDDDDDDDDDDDDDBBBCCG',
                  ' GGBBDDDDDGGGGDDDDDBBG',
```

```
         '   GDDDDGGG     GGGDDDDG     ',
         '   DDDD         DDDD      ' );

const StarShipDown :array [1..20] of string[32] =
         ( '   DDDD         DDDD      ',
           '   GDDDDGGG     GGGDDDDG     ',
           ' GGBBDDDDDGGGGDDDDDBBG    ',
           ' GGCCBBBDDDDDDDDDDDDDBBBCCG   ',
           'GGCBBBBBBBDBBBBBBBBBBDBBBBBBBBBCG ',
           'BBBBBBBBBBBBBDB BB BDBBBBBBBBBBBBBB',
           'GCBBBBBBBBBBDB  BDBBBBBBBBBCG',
           'GCBGGGBBBBBDBB  BBDBBBBBBGGGBCG',
           'GCG   GGBBBDBBB BBBDBBBBGG   GCG',
           'GCG   GGDBBBBBBBBBDGG   GCG',
           ' G    GBBBBBBBBBBBG    G ',
           '      GBBBBBBBBBG       ',
           '      GBBBBBBBBBG       ',
           '       GBBBCCBBG        ',
           '       GBBCCBBG         ',
           '        GGBBGG          ',
           '         AA             ',
           '         AAAA           ',
           '         AAAA           ',
           '         AA             ' );

SPRNUM = 6;                              { Number of sprites }
CWIDTH = 37;          { Width of copyright message in characters }
CHEIGHT = 6;                        { Message height in rows }
SX    = (MAXX-(CWIDTH*8)) div 2;        { Starting X-coordinate }
SY    = (MAXY-(CHEIGHT*8)) div 2;       { Starting Y-coordinate }

type SPRITE = record                    { For sprite management }
                spidp : SPIP;           { Pointer to sprite ID }
                deltax,             { X-movement for pages 0 and 1 }
                deltay : array [0..1] of integer;    { Y-movement }
              end;

var sprites   : array [1..sprnum] of SPRITE;
    page,                                   { Current page }
    lc,                        { Character for screen design }
    out       : byte;           { Get flags for page collision }
    x, y, i,                               { Loop counter }
    dx, dy    : integer;                  { Movement value }
    starshipupp,
    starshipdnp : SPLP;                    { Sprite pointer }
    ch        : char;
begin

  Randomize;                { Initialize random number generator }

{-- Fill the first two graphic pages with characters --------------}

  for page := 0 to 1 do
    begin
      setpage( page );
      lc := 0;
      y := 0;
      while ( y < 200-8 ) do
        begin
          x := 0;
          while ( x < 320-8 ) do
            begin
              PrintChar( chr(lc and 127), x, y, lc mod 255, 0 );
```

```
          inc( lc );
          inc( x, 8 );
        end;
      inc( y, 12 );
    end;

{-- Display copyright message ----------------------------------}

  Line( SX-1, SY-1, SX+CWIDTH*8, SY-1, 15 );
  Line( SX+CWIDTH*8, SY-1, SX+CWIDTH*8, SY+CHEIGHT*8,15 );
  Line( SX+CWIDTH*8, SY+CHEIGHT*8, SX-1, SY+CHEIGHT*8, 15 );
  Line( SX-1, SY+CHEIGHT*8, SX-1, SY-1, 15 );
  PrintString( SX, SY,    15, 4,
                                            '              ' );
  PrintString( SX, SY+8,  15, 4,
               ' *S3220P.PAS - (c) 1992  M. Tischer* ' );
  PrintString( SX, SY+16, 15, 4,
               '                                     ' );
  PrintString( SX, SY+24, 15, 4,
               '     Sprite demo for 320x200 mode    ' );
  PrintString( SX, SY+32, 15, 4,
               '            on VGA cards             ' );
  PrintString( SX, SY+40, 15, 4,
               '                                     ' );

end;

{-- Create patterns for the different sprites ----------------------}

starshipupp := CompileSprite( StarShipUp,   20, 2, 0, 'A', 1 );
starshipdnp := CompileSprite( StarShipDown, 20, 2, 40, 'A', 1 );

{-- Create different sprites -----------------------------------------}
for i := 1 to SPRNUM do
  begin
    sprites[ i ].spidp := CreateSprite( starshipupp, 3, (i mod 3)*100,
                                        (i div 3) * 30 );
    repeat                        { Select movement values for sprites }
      dx := 0;
      dy := random(8) - 4;
    until ( dx <> 0 ) or ( dy <> 0 );

    sprites[ i ].deltax[0] := dx * 2;
    sprites[ i ].deltay[0] := dy * 2;
    sprites[ i ].deltax[1] := dx * 2;
    sprites[ i ].deltay[1] := dy * 2;

    x := ( (320 div SPRNUM) * (i-1) ) + ((320 div SPRNUM) - 40) div 2 ;
    y := random( 200 - 40 );
    SetSprite( sprites[ i ].spidp, x, y, x - dx, y - dy );
  end;

{-- Move sprites and bounce them off the page borders --------------}

page := 1;                                  { Start with page 1 }
while ( not keypressed ) do      { Press a key to end the loop }
  begin
    showpage( 1 - page );                   { Display other page }

    for i := 1 to sprnum do                 { Execute sprites }
      begin             { Move sprite and check for page collision }
        out := MoveSprite( sprites[i].spidp, page,
                           sprites[i].deltax[page],
                           sprites[i].deltay[page] );
        if ( ( out and OUT_TOP ) <> 0 ) or { Top/bottom collision? }
           ( ( out and OUT_BOTTOM ) <> 0 ) then
          begin
          { Yes --> Change direction of movement and sprite graphic }
            sprites[i].deltay[page] := -sprites[i].deltay[page];
            if ( ( out and OUT_TOP ) <> 0 ) then
              sprites[i].spidp^.splookp := starshipdnp
            else
              sprites[i].spidp^.splookp := starshipupp;
          end;
        if ( ( out and OUT_LEFT ) <> 0 ) or { Left/right collision? }
           ( ( out and OUT_RIGHT ) <> 0 ) then
          sprites[i].deltax[page] := -sprites[i].deltax[page];
      end;
    page := (page+1) and 1;                 { Toggle between 1 and 0 }
  end;
  ch := readkey;                 { Remove key from keyboard buffer }
end;

{************************************************************************
*                   M A I N   P R O G R A M                         *
************************************************************************}

begin
  if ( IsVga ) then                         { VGA card installed? }
    begin                                   { Yes --> Go ahead }
      init320200;                           { Initialize graphic mode }
      Demo;
      Textmode( C080 );                     { Shift into text mode }
    end
  else
    writeln( 'S3220P.PAS  -  (c) 1990 by Michael Tischer'#13#10#10 +
             'This program requires a VGA card'#13#10 );
end.
```

Assembler listing: S3220PA.ASM

```
;*********************************************************;
;*                                                       *;
;*                 S 3 2 2 0 P A . A S M                 *;
;*-------------------------------------------------------*;
;*   Task      : Contains routines for generating sprites in *;
;*               320x200 256 color mode on a VGA card.   *;
;*-------------------------------------------------------*;
;*   Author    : Michael Tischer                         *;
;*   Developed on : 09/08/90                             *;
;*   Last update  : 02/13/92                             *;
;*-------------------------------------------------------*;
;*   Assembly   : MASM /mx S3220PA;    or    TASM -mx S3220PA *;
;*               ... Link to S3220P.PAS                  *;
;*********************************************************;


;== Constants ===============================================

SC_INDEX       = 3c4h          ;Index register for sequencer ctrl.
SC_MAP_MASK    = 2             ;Number of map mask register
SC_MEM_MODE    = 4             ;Number of memory mode register

GC_INDEX       = 3ceh          ;Index register for graphics ctrl.
GC_GRAPH_MODE  = 5             ;Number of graphic mode register

VERT_RESCAN    = 3DAh          ;Input status register #1
PIXX           = 320           ;Horizontal resolution

;== Data segment ===========================================

DATA    segment word public

DATA    ends

;== Program =================================================

CODE    segment byte public   ;Program segment

                assume cs:code, ds:data

;-- Public declarations -------------------------------------

public    blockmove

;-----------------------------------------------------------
;-- BLOCKMOVE: Moves a group of pixels in video RAM
;-- Call from TP: blockmove( frompage : byte; fromx, fromy : integer;
;--                          topage : byte; tox, toy : integer;
;--                          pwidth, pheight: byte; bmskp : pointer );

blockmove  proc near

sframe4    struc             ;Structure for stack access
bp4        dw ?              ;Gets BP
additive   dw ?              ;Local variable
restc      dw ?
movec      dw ?
ret_adr4   dw ?              ;Return address from caller
bmskp      dd ?              ;Pointer to buffer with bit mask
pheight    dw ?              ;Pixel height
pwidth     dw ?              ;Pixel width
toy        dw ?              ;To Y-coordinate
tox        dw ?              ;To X-coordinate
topage     dw ?              ;To page
fromy      dw ?              ;From Y-coordinate
fromx      dw ?              ;From X-coordinate
frompage   dw ?              ;From page
sframe4    ends              ;End structure

frame      equ [ bp - bp4 ]  ;Addresses structure elements

           sub  sp,6         ;6 bytes for local variables

           push bp           ;Prepare BP register for
           mov  bp,sp        ;addressing parameters

           push ds
           cld               ;Increment on string instructions

           mov  dx,GC_INDEX  ;Get current write mode and
           mov  al,GC_GRAPH_MODE ;initialize write mode 1
           out  dx,al
           inc  dx
           in   al,dx
           push ax           ;Push current mode onto stack
           and  al,not 3
           or   al,1
           out  dx,al

           mov  al,4         ;Move DS to start of FROM page
           mov  cl,byte ptr frame.frompage
           mul  cl
           or   al,0A0h
           xchg ah,al
           mov  ds,ax

           mov  al,4         ;Move ES to start of TO page
           mov  cl,byte ptr frame.topage
           mul  cl
           or   al,0A0h
           xchg ah,al
           mov  es,ax

           mov  ax,PIXX / 4  ;Move SI to FROM starting position
           mul  frame.fromy
           mov  si,frame.fromx
           shr  si,1
           shr  si,1
           add  si,ax

           mov  ax,PIXX / 4  ;Move DI to TO position
           mul  frame.toy
           mov  di,frame.tox
           shr  di,1
           shr  di,1
           add  di,ax

           mov  dh,byte ptr frame.pheight ;DH = Pixel lines
           mov  dl,byte ptr frame.pwidth  ;DL = Bytes
           shr  dl,1
           shr  dl,1

           mov  bx,PIXX / 4  ;Move BX as offset to next line
           sub  bl,dl
           xor  ch,ch        ;High byte of counter is always 0
           cmp  word ptr frame.bmskp+2,0 ;No background?
           jne  mt2          ;None, use other copy routine
```

```
            push  dx                ;Push DX onto stack              add   si,frame.additive ;SI to next line
            mov   dx,SC_INDEX       ;Get bitplane access            dec   byte ptr frame.restc ;Still more lines?
            mov   ah,0Fh                                            jne   mt3                  ;Yes --> Continue
            mov   al,SC_MAP_MASK
            out   dx,ax                                     mtend:  mov   dx,GC_INDEX          ;Revert to old
            pop   dx                ;Pop DX                         pop   ax                   ;write mode
                                                                    mov   ah,al
                                                                    mov   al,GC_GRAPH_MODE
            ;-- Copy routine for all four bitplanes,                out   dx,ax
            ;-- without checking the background
                                                                    pop   ds
mt1:        mov   cl,dl             ;Number of bytes to CL          pop   bp

            rep movsb               ;Copy lines                     add   sp,6                 ;Add SP to local variables
            add   di,bx             ;DI and                         ret   20                   ;On return remove parameters
            add   si,bx             ;SI in next line                                           ;from stack
            dec   dh                ;Still more lines?
            jne   mt1               ;Yes --> continue       blockmove endp
            jmp short mtend         ;No --> Get out of routine
                                                            ;== End ================================================================
            ;-- Copy routine for individual bitplanes using
            ;-- the specified bit mask arrays               CODE  ends                         ;End of code segment
                                                                  end                          ;End program
mt2:        mov   byte ptr frame.restc,dh ;First specify variables
            mov   byte ptr frame.movec,dl ;placed in local variables
            mov   frame.additive,bx        ;on the stack

            mov   al,SC_MAP_MASK    ;Address permanent
            mov   dx,SC_INDEX       ;Map mask register
            out   dx,al
            inc   dx                ;Increment DX on data register

            push  ds
            lds   bx,frame.bmskp    ;BX is pointer to bit mask array
            mov   al,[bx]           ;Load first byte
            xor   ah,ah             ;Start with an even byte
            pop   ds

mt3:        mov   cl,byte ptr frame.movec ;Move number of bytes to CL

mt4:        out   dx,al             ;Set bit mask
            movsb                   ;Copy 4 bytes

            inc   ah                ;Increment odd/even counter
            test  ah,1              ;Odd again?
            jne   mt5               ;Yes --> Move nibble

            ;-- Get next byte from buffer on every even byte -----------

            inc   bx                ;BX to next bit mask byte
            push  ds
            mov   ds,word ptr frame.bmskp+2
            mov   al,[bx]           ;Load next byte
            pop   ds
            loop  mt4               ;Next four latches
            jmp   short mt6

mt5:        shr   al,1              ;Get odd byte bit mask from
            shr   al,1              ;low nibble
            shr   al,1
            shr   al,1
            loop  mt4               ;Next four latches

mt6:        add   di,frame.additive ;Add DI and
```

C listing: S3220C.C

```
/*******************************************************************
*                        S 3 2 2 0 C . C                          *
**---------------------------------------------------------------**
*  Task          : Demonstrates sprites in 320x200 VGA graphic    *
*                  mode, using 256 colors and four screen pages.  *
*                  This program requires the assembly language    *
*                  modules V3220CA.ASM and S3220CA.ASM.           *
**---------------------------------------------------------------**
*  Author        : Michael Tischer                                *
*  Developed on  : 09/09/90                                       *
*  Last update   : 02/17/92                                       *
**---------------------------------------------------------------**
*  Memory model  : SMALL                                          *
**---------------------------------------------------------------**
*  (MICROSOFT C)                                                  *
*  Compilation   : CL /AS /c /WO s3220c.c                         *
*                  LINK s3220c v3220ca s3220ca;                   *
**---------------------------------------------------------------**
*  (BORLAND TURBO C)                                              *
*  Compilation   : Create a project file containing the following:*
*                        s3220c.c                                 *
*                        v3220ca.obj                              *
*                        s3220ca.obj                              *
**---------------------------------------------------------------**
*  Call          : s3220c                                         *
*******************************************************************/

#include <dos.h>
#include <stdarg.h>
#include <stdio.h>
#include <string.h>
#include <stdlib.h>
#include <conio.h>

/*-- Compiler-dependent declarations ------------------------------*/

#ifdef __TURBOC__
  #include <alloc.h>
#else
  #include <malloc.h>
  #define random(x) ( rand() % (x+1) )        /* Random function */
#endif

/*-- Type declarations --------------------------------------------*/

typedef unsigned char BYTE;

typedef struct {                              /* Sprite design */
           BYTE twidth,                       /* Total width */
                theight,                      /* Height in pixel lines */
                ppage,                        /* Placed in page ... */
                *bmskp,                       /* Pointer to bit mask */
                msklen;                       /* Entry length */
           int  pxlin;                        /* Pixel lines for sprite */
         } SPLOOK;                            /* in its page        */

typedef struct {                              /* Sprite descriptor (ID) */
           BYTE bkgpage;                       /* Background page */
           int  x[2], y[2],                   /* Coordinates: pp. 0 & 1 */
                bkx, bky;                      /* Background buffer */
           SPLOOK * splookp;                   /* Pointer to sprite design */
         } SPID;
```

```
/*-- External references to assembler routines --------------------*/

extern void init320200( void );
extern void setpix( int x, int y, unsigned char pcolor);
extern BYTE getpix( int x, int y );
extern void setpage( BYTE page );
extern void showpage( BYTE page );
extern void far * getfontptr( void );
extern void waitvsync( void );
extern void blockmove( BYTE frompage, int fromx, int fromy,
                       BYTE topage, int tox, int toy,
                       BYTE pwidth, BYTE pheight, BYTE *bmskp );

/*-- Constants ----------------------------------------------------*/

#define NOBITMASK (BYTE *) 0

#define MAXX 319                    /* Maximum X- and Y-coordinates */
#define MAXY 199

#define OUT_LEFT   1  /* For collision documentation in SpriteMove() */
#define OUT_TOP    2
#define OUT_RIGHT  4
#define OUT_BOTTOM 8
#define OUT_NO     0                            /* None */

/*******************************************************************
*  IsVga: Determines whether a VGA card is installed.             *
**---------------------------------------------------------------**
*  Input   : None                                                 *
*  Output  : 0 if no VGA exists, otherwise <0                     *
*******************************************************************/

BYTE IsVga( void )
{
 union REGS Regs;          /* Processor registers for interrupt call */

 Regs.x.ax = 0x1a00;              /* Function 1AH applies to VGA only */
 int86( 0x10, &Regs, &Regs );
 return ( Regs.h.al == 0x1a );         /* Is this function available? */
}

/*******************************************************************
*  Line: Draws a line based on the Bresenham algorithm.           *
**---------------------------------------------------------------**
*  Input   : X1, Y1 = Starting coordinates (0 - ...)              *
*            X2, Y2 = Ending coordinates                          *
*            PCOLOR = Color of line pixels                        *
*******************************************************************/

/*-- Function for swapping two integer variables ------------------*/

void SwapInt( int *i1, int *i2 )
{
 int dummy;

 dummy = *i2;
 *i2   = *i1;
 *i1   = dummy;
}

/*-- Main part of function ----------------------------------------*/
```

```
void Line( int x1, int y1, int x2, int y2, BYTE pcolor )
{
int d, dx, dy,
    aincr, bincr,
    xincr, yincr,
    x, y;

if ( abs(x2-x1) < abs(y2-y1) )          /* X- or Y-axis overflow? */
 {                                       /* Check Y-axis */
 if ( y1 > y2 )                          /* y1 > y2? */
  {
  SwapInt( &x1, &x2 );                   /* Yes --> Swap X1 with X2 */
  SwapInt( &y1, &y2 );                   /*           and Y1 with Y2 */
  }

 xincr = ( x2 > x1 ) ?  1 : -1;          /* Set X-axis increment */

 dy = y2 - y1;
 dx = abs( x2-x1 );
 d = 2 * dx - dy;
 aincr = 2 * (dx - dy);
 bincr = 2 * dx;
 x = x1;
 y = y1;

 setpix( x, y, pcolor );                 /* Set first pixel */
 for (y=y1+1; y<= y2; ++y )              /* Execute line on Y-axes */
  {
   if ( d >= 0 )
    {
    x += xincr;
    d += aincr;
    }
   else
    d += bincr;
    setpix(x, y, pcolor);
  }
 }
else                                     /* Check X-axis */
 {
 if ( x1 > x2 )                          /* x1 > x2? */
  {
  SwapInt( &x1, &x2 );                   /* Yes --> Swap X1 with X2 */
  SwapInt( &y1, &y2 );                   /*           and Y1 with Y2 */
  }

 yincr = ( y2 > y1 ) ? 1 : -1;           /* Set Y-axis increment */

 dx = x2 - x1;
 dy = abs( y2-y1 );
 d  = 2 * dy - dx;
 aincr = 2 * (dy - dx);
 bincr = 2 * dy;
 x = x1;
 y = y1;

 setpix(x, y, pcolor);                   /* Set first pixel */
 for (x=x1+1; x<=x2; ++x )               /* Execute line on X-axes */
  {
   if ( d >= 0 )
    {
    y += yincr;
    d += aincr;
    }
```

```
   else
    d += bincr;
    setpix(x, y, pcolor);
  }
 }
}

/***********************************************************************
* PrintChar : Writes a character to the screen while in graphic mode.*
**-------------------------------------------------------------------**
* Input   : THECHAR = Character to be written                        *
*           X, Y    = X- and Y-coordinates of upper-left corner      *
*           FG      = Foreground color                               *
*           BK      = Background color                               *
* Info    : Character is created in an 8x8 matrix, based on the      *
*           8x8 ROM font.                                            *
************************************************************************/

void PrintChar( char thechar, int x, int y, BYTE fg, BYTE bk )
{
typedef BYTE FDEF[256][8];                /* Font array */
typedef FDEF far *TPTR;                   /* Pointer to font */

BYTE      i, k,                           /* Loop counter */
          BMask;                          /* Bit mask for character design */

static TPTR fptr = (TPTR) 0;              /* Pointer to font in ROM */

if ( fptr == (TPTR) 0 )                   /* Pointer to font already set? */
 fptr = getfontptr();    /* No --> Use the assembler function to load */

/*- Generate character pixel by pixel -------------------------------*/

if ( bk == 255 )                          /* Drawing transparent characters? */
 for ( i = 0; i < 8; ++i )      /* Yes --> Set foreground pixels only */
  {
  BMask = (*fptr)[thechar][i];            /* Get bit pattern for one line */
  for ( k = 0; k < 8; ++k, BMask <<= 1 )  /* Execute column */
   if ( BMask & 128 )                     /* Pixel set? */
    setpix( x+k, y+i, fg );               /* Yes */
  }
else                                /* No --> Consider background as well */
 for ( i = 0; i < 8; ++i )                /* Execute lines */
  {
  BMask = (*fptr)[thechar][i];            /* Get bit pattern for one line */
  for ( k = 0; k < 8; ++k, BMask <<= 1 )  /* Execute columns */
   setpix( x+k, y+i, ( BMask & 128 ) ? fg : bk );
  }
}

/***********************************************************************
* GrfxPrintf: Displays a formatted string on the graphic screen.     *
*-------------------------------------------------------------------*
* Input   : X, Y   = Starting coordinates (0 - ...)                  *
*           FG     = Foreground color                                *
*           BK     = Background color (255 = transparent)            *
*           STRING = String with format information                  *
*           ...    = Arguments similar to printf                     *
************************************************************************/

void GrfxPrintf( int x, int y, BYTE fg, BYTE bk, char * string, ... )
{
va_list parameter;                        /* Parameter list for VA_... macros */
char stngbuf[255],                        /* Buffer for formatted string */
```

325

```
                            *cp;

    va_start( parameter, string );              /* Convert parameter */
    vsprintf( stngbuf, string, parameter );              /* Format */
    for ( cp = stngbuf; *cp; ++cp, x+= 8 )        /* Formatted string */
      PrintChar( *cp, x, y, fg, bk );      /* Display using PrintChar */
}


/**********************************************************************
 *  CreateSprite: Creates a sprite based on a user-defined           *
 *                pixel pattern.                                      *
 **------------------------------------------------------------------**
 *  Input   : SPLOOKP = Pointer the data structure from CompileSprite()*
 *            BKGPAGE = Screen page in which sprite background should *
 *                      be stored                                    *
 *            BKX,    = bkpage coordinates at which sprite background *
 *            BKY       is stored                                    *
 *  Output  : Pointer to created sprite structure                    *
 *  Info    : The sprite background requires two areas the same size *
 *            as the corresponding sprite.                           *
 **********************************************************************/

SPID *CreateSprite( SPLOOK *splookp, BYTE bkgpage, int bkx, int bky )
{
    SPID *spidp;            /* Pointer to created sprite structure */

    spidp = (SPID *) malloc( sizeof(SPID) );  /* Allocate sprite struc. */
    spidp->splookp = splookp;              /* Pass data to the */
    spidp->bkgpage = bkgpage;              /* sprite structure */
    spidp->bkx = bkx;
    spidp->bky = bky;

    return spidp;            /* Return pointer to the sprite structure */
}


/**********************************************************************
 *  CompileSprite: Creates a sprite's pixel and bit patterns, based on *
 *                 the sprite's definition at runtime.               *
 **------------------------------------------------------------------**
 *  Input  : BUFP    = Pointer to array contains string pointers     *
 *                     controlling sprite's pattern                  *
 *           SHEIGHT = Sprite height (and number of strings needed)  *
 *           GPAGE   = Graphic page for sprite design                *
 *           Y       = Pixel lines needed for sprite                 *
 *           FB      = ASCII characters for the smallest color       *
 *           FGCOLOR = First color code for FB                       *
 *  Info   : Sprite structure of pixel lines starts at left margin.  *
 **********************************************************************/

SPLOOK *CompileSprite( char **bufp, BYTE sheight, BYTE gpage, BYTE y,
                       char fb, BYTE fgcolor )
{
    BYTE  swidth,                           /* String width */
          c,                   /* Get character from c sprite array */
          i, k, l,            /* Loop variables */
          pixc,             /* Pixel counter for creating the bit mask */
          pixm,                        /* Pixel mask */
          *lspb;             /* Floating pointer in sprite buffer */
    int   spacing,  /* Spacing from start of sprite to start of sprite */
          lx, ly;                   /* Floating coordinates */
    SPLOOK *splookp;              /* Pointer to created sprite structure */

/*-- Create SpriteLook structure and fill with data ----------------*/

    splookp = (SPLOOK *) malloc( sizeof(SPLOOK) );
    swidth = strlen( *bufp );
    splookp->twidth = spacing = ( ( swidth + 3 + 3 ) / 4 ) * 4;
    splookp->bmskp = (BYTE *) malloc( (spacing*sheight+7)/8*4 );
    splookp->theight = sheight;
    splookp->pxlin = y;
    splookp->ppage = gpage;
    splookp->msklen = (spacing*sheight+7)/8;

/*-- Fill sprite background in  home page  with --------------------*/
/*-- codes for transparent character background --------------------*/

    setpage( gpage );                       /* Set page for drawing sprite */
    for ( ly = y + sheight-1, lx = 4 * spacing - 1; ly >= (int) y; --ly)
      Line( 0, ly, lx, ly, 255 );

/*-- Draw four matching sprites in the home page -------------------*/

    for ( l = 0, lx = 0; l < 4; ++l, lx+=spacing+1 )
      for ( i = 0; i < sheight; ++i )
        for ( k = 0; k < swidth; ++k )
          setpix( lx+k, y+i, ( c = *(*(bufp+i)+k) == ' ' ? 255
                                                    : fgcolor+(c-fb));

/*-- Execute the four sprites and create bit masks -----------------*/
/*-- for copying the sprites into the bitplanes      -----------------*/

    for ( l = pixm = pixc = 0, lx = 0; l < 4; ++l, lx+=spacing )
    {
      lspb = splookp->bmskp + splookp->msklen * l;
      for ( i = 0; i < sheight; ++i )
        for ( k = 0; k < spacing; ++k )
        {
          pixm >>= 1;                      /* Shift pixel mask 1 bit right */
          if ( getpix( lx+k, y+i ) != 255 )        /* Background pixel? */
            pixm |= 128;                    /* No --> Set bit for mask */
          if ( ++pixc == 8 )               /* Eight pixels already handled? */
          {                        /* Yes --> Place bit mask in sprite buffer */
            *lspb++ = pixm;
            pixc = pixm = 0;                /* Set pixel counter and mask to 0 */
          }
        }
        if ( pixc )                       /* Last nibble still not in buffer? */
        {                                 /* No --> Move high nibble to */
          *lspb = pixm >> 4;              /* low nibble and store them */
          pixc = pixm = 0;                /* Set pixel counter and mask to 0 */
        }
    }
    return splookp;                       /* Return pointer to sprite buffer */
}


/**********************************************************************
 *  PrintSprite : Displays sprite in a specified page.               *
 **------------------------------------------------------------------**
 *  Input  : SPIDP   = Pointer to the sprite structure               *
 *           SPRPAGE = Page in which sprite should be drawn (0 or 1)  *
 **********************************************************************/

void PrintSprite( register SPID *spidp, BYTE sprpage )
{
    BYTE twidth;                            /* Total width of sprite */
    int  x;                       /* X-coordinate of sprite in its page */
    SPLOOK *splookp;                        /* Pointer to sprite's appearance */
```

```
twidth = (splookp = spidp->splookp)->twidth;
x = spidp->x[sprpage];
blockmove( splookp->ppage, twidth * (x % 4), splookp->pxlin, sprpage,
           x & ~3, spidp->y[sprpage], twidth, splookp->theight,
           splookp->bmskp + (x % 4) * splookp->msklen );
}


/************************************************************************
* GetSpriteBg: Gets a sprite background and specifies the position.    *
**--------------------------------------------------------------------**
* Input   : SPIDP    = Pointer to the sprite structure                 *
*           SPRPAGE = Page from which the background should be taken *
*                     (0 or 1)                                         *
************************************************************************/

void GetSpriteBg( register SPID *spidp, BYTE sprpage )
{
SPLOOK *splookp;                        /* Pointer to sprite graphic */

splookp = spidp->splookp;
blockmove( sprpage, spidp->x[sprpage], spidp->y[sprpage],
           spidp->bkgpage, spidp->bkx + ( splookp->twidth * sprpage ),
           spidp->bky, splookp->twidth, splookp->theight, NOBITMASK );
}


/************************************************************************
* RestoreSpriteBg: Restores sprite background from original graphic    *
*                  page.                                               *
**--------------------------------------------------------------------**
* Input   : SPIDP    = Pointer to the sprite structure                 *
*           SPRPAGE = Page from which the background should be copied*
*                     (0 or 1)                                         *
************************************************************************/

void RestoreSpriteBg( register SPID *spidp, BYTE sprpage )
{
SPLOOK *splookp;                        /* Pointer to sprite graphic */

splookp = spidp->splookp;
blockmove( spidp->bkgpage, spidp->bkx + ( splookp->twidth * sprpage ),
           spidp->bky, sprpage, spidp->x[sprpage], spidp->y[sprpage],
           splookp->twidth, splookp->theight, NOBITMASK );
}


/************************************************************************
* MoveSprite: Copy sprite within background to original graphic page.*
**--------------------------------------------------------------------**
* Input   : SPIDP    = Pointer to the sprite structure                 *
*           SPRPAGE = Page to which the background should be copied    *
*                     (0 or 1)                                         *
*           DELTAX  = Movement counter in X-                           *
*           DELTAY     and Y-directions                                *
* Output  : Collision marker (see OUT_ constants)                      *
************************************************************************/

BYTE MoveSprite( SPID *spidp, BYTE sprpage, int deltax, int deltay )
{
int newx, newy;                         /* New sprite coordinates */
BYTE out;                          /* Display collision with border */

/*-- Move X-coordinates and test for border collision --------------*/

if ( ( newx = spidp->x[sprpage] + deltax ) < 0 )
  {
```

```
    newx = 0 - deltax - spidp->x[sprpage];
    out = OUT_LEFT;
  }
else
  if ( newx > 319 - spidp->splookp->twidth )
    {
    newx = 640-newx-2*(spidp->splookp->twidth);
    out = OUT_RIGHT;
    }
  else
    out = OUT_NO;

/*-- Move Y-coordinates and test for border collision --------------*/

if ( ( newy = spidp->y[sprpage] + deltay ) < 0 )     /* Top border? */
  {                                     /* Yes --> Deltay must be negative */
    newy = 0 - deltay - spidp->y[sprpage];
    out |= OUT_TOP;
  }
else
  if ( newy + spidp->splookp->theight > 199+1  )   /* Bottom border? */
    {                                  /* Yes --> Deltay must be positive */
    newy = 400-newy-2*(spidp->splookp->theight);
    out |= OUT_BOTTOM;
    }

/*-- Set new position only if different from old position ----------*/

if ( newx != spidp->x[sprpage] || newy != spidp->y[sprpage] )
  {                                   /* If there's a new position */
    RestoreSpriteBg( spidp, sprpage );    /* then reset background and */
    spidp->x[sprpage] = newx;            /* store new coordinates    */
    spidp->y[sprpage] = newy;
    GetSpriteBg( spidp, sprpage );             /* Get new background */
    PrintSprite( spidp, sprpage );   /* Draw sprite in specified page */
  }
return out;
}


/************************************************************************
* SetSprite: Sets sprite at a specific position.                       *
**--------------------------------------------------------------------**
* Input   : SPIDP = Pointer to the sprite structure                    *
*           x0, y0 = Sprite coordinates for page 0                     *
*           x1, y1 = Sprite coordinates for page 1                     *
* Info    : This function call should be made the first time that      *
*           MoveSprite() is called.                                    *
************************************************************************/

void SetSprite( SPID *spidp, int x0, int y0, int x1, int y1 )
{
spidp->x[0] = x0;               /* Store coordinates in sprite structure */
spidp->x[1] = x1;
spidp->y[0] = y0;
spidp->y[1] = y1;

GetSpriteBg( spidp, 0 );                    /* Get sprite backgrounds */
GetSpriteBg( spidp, 1 );                    /* in pages 0 and 1      */
PrintSprite( spidp, 0 );                         /* Draw sprite in */
PrintSprite( spidp, 1 );                         /* pages 0 and 1 */
}


/************************************************************************
* RemoveSprite: Removes a sprite from its current position and makes *
```

```
*              it invisible.                    *                      "         AA          " };
**---------------------------------------------**
*  Input   : SPIDP = Pointer to the sprite structure  *    #define SPRNUM 6                      /* Number of sprites */
*  Info    : After calling this function the SetSprite() function  *  #define CWIDTH 38      /* Width of copyright message in characters */
*            must be called before the sprite can be moved using the  *  #define CHEIGHT  6              /* Message height in rows */
*            MoveSprite() function.              *    #define SX    (MAXX-(CWIDTH*8)) / 2   /* Starting X-coordinate */
***********************************************/           #define SY    (MAXY-(CHEIGHT*8)) / 2   /* Starting Y-coordinate */

void RemoveSprite( SPID *spidp )                          struct {                        /* For sprite management */
{                                                             SPID  *spidp;                /* Pointer to sprite ID */
  RestoreSpriteBg( spidp, 0 );      /* Reset sprite backgrounds */     int  deltax[2],          /* X-movement for pages 0 and 1 */
  RestoreSpriteBg( spidp, 1 );      /* in pages 0 and 1    */             deltay[2];         /* Y-movement for pages 0 and 1 */
}                                                         } sprites[ SPRNUM ];
                                                        BYTE   page,                          /* Current page */
                                                               out;                   /* Get flags for page collision */
/**********************************************            int    x, y, i,                       /* Loop counter */
* Demo: Demonstrates these functions.          *                 dx, dy;                /* Movement value */
***********************************************/           char   lc;
                                                          SPLOOK *starshipupp, *starshipdnp;    /* Sprite pointer */
void Demo( void )
{                                                         srand( *(long far *) 0x0040006c );    /* Initialize random */
  static char *StarShipUp[20] =                                                                /* number generator */
            { "             AA          ",
              "            AAAA         ",            /*-- Fill the first two graphic pages with characters --------------*/
              "            AAAA         ",
              "             AA          ",            for ( page = 0; page < 2; ++ page )
              "           GGBBGG        ",            {
              "          GBBCCBBG       ",              setpage( page );
              "          GBBCCBBBG      ",              for ( lc = 0, y = 0; y < 200-8; y += 12 )
              "          GBBBBBBBBBG    ",                for ( x = 0; x < 320-8; x += 8 )
              "          GBBBBBBBBBG    ",                  GrfxPrintf( x, y, lc % 255, 255, "%c", lc++ & 127 );
              " G    GBBBBBBBBBBBG   G ",
              "GCG   GGDBBBBBBBBBDGG  GCG",          /*-- Display copyright message --------------------------------*/
              "GCG   GGBBBBBBBB BBBDBBBGG  GCG",
              "GCBGGGBBBBBBBDBB   BBDBBBBBGGGBCG",    Line( SX-1, SY-1, SX+CWIDTH*8, SY-1, 15 );
              "GCBBBBBBBBBBBDB   BBDBBBBBBBCG",       Line( SX+CWIDTH*8, SY-1, SX+CWIDTH*8, SY+CHEIGHT*8,15 );
              "BBBBBBBBBBBBDB BB BDBBBBBBBBBBB",      Line( SX+CWIDTH*8, SY+CHEIGHT*8, SX-1, SY+CHEIGHT*8, 15 );
              "GGCBBBBBBBDBBBBBBBBBDBBBBBBCG ",       Line( SX-1, SY+CHEIGHT*8, SX-1, SY-1, 15 );
              "  GGCCBBDDDDDDDDDDDDDDDBBCCG  ",       GrfxPrintf( SX, SY,   15, 4,
              "   GGBBDDDDGGGGGDDDDDDBBG  ",                      "                            " );
              "   GDDDDGGG   GGGDDDDG  ",            GrfxPrintf( SX, SY+8, 15, 4,
              "   DDDD        DDDD    " };                       " S3220C.C (c) 1992 by Michael Tischer " );
                                                      GrfxPrintf( SX, SY+16, 15, 4,
                                                                  "                            " );
  static char *StarShipDown[20] =                       GrfxPrintf( SX, SY+24, 15, 4,
            {                                                       "    Sprite demo for 320x200 mode     " );
              "   DDDD        DDDD    ",              GrfxPrintf( SX, SY+32, 15, 4,
              " GDDDDGGG   GGGDDDDG  ",                          "          on VGA cards          " );
              " GGBBDDDDDDGGGGGDDDDDDDBBG  ",          GrfxPrintf( SX, SY+40, 15, 4,
              " GGCCBBDDDDDDDDDDDDDDDDBBCCG  ",                    "                            " );
              "GGCBBBBBBBBBDBBBBBBBBBDBBBBBBBCG ",  }
              "BBBBBBBBBBBBBDB BB BDBBBBBBBBBBB",
              "GCBBBBBBBBBBBDB   BBDBBBBBBBBCG",    /*-- Create patterns for the different sprites --------------------*/
              "GCBGGGBBBBBBBDBB   BBDBBBBBGGGBCG",
              "GCG   GGBBBBBBBB BBBDBBBGG  GCG",    starshipupp = CompileSprite( StarShipUp,   20, 2, 0, 'A', 1 );
              "GCG   GGDBBBBBBBBBDGG  GCG",          starshipdnp = CompileSprite( StarShipDown, 20, 2, 40, 'A', 1 );
              " G    GBBBBBBBBBBBG   G ",
              "          GBBBBBBBBBG    ",           /*-- Create different sprites -----------------------------------*/
              "          GBBBBBBBBBG    ",
              "          GBBBCCBBBG     ",           for ( i = 0; i < SPRNUM ; ++ i )
              "          GBBCCBBG       ",           {
              "           GGBBGG        ",             sprites[ i ].spidp = CreateSprite( starshipupp, 3, ( i % 3 ) * 100,
              "             AA          ",                                                 (i / 3) * 30 );
              "            AAAA         ",             do                   /* Select movement value for sprites */
              "            AAAA         ",
```

```
          {
            dx = 0;
            dy = random(8) - 4;
          }
        while ( dx==0 && dy==0 );

        sprites[ i ].deltax[0] = sprites[ i ].deltax[1] = dx * 2;
        sprites[ i ].deltay[0] = sprites[ i ].deltay[1] = dy * 2;

        x = ( 320 / SPRNUM * i ) + (320 / SPRNUM - 40) / 2 ;
        y = random( 200 - 40 );
        SetSprite( sprites[ i ].spidp, x, y, x - dx, y - dy );
      }

    /*-- Move sprites and bounce them off the page borders -------------*/

    page = 1;                               /* Start with page 1 */
    while ( !kbhit() )                      /* Press a key to end the loop */
    {
      showpage( 1 - page );                 /* Display other page */

      for ( i = 0; i < SPRNUM; ++ i )       /* Execute sprites */
      {                                     /* Move sprite and check for page collision */
        out = MoveSprite( sprites[i].spidp, page, sprites[i].deltax[page],
                          sprites[i].deltay[page] );
        if ( out & OUT_TOP || out & OUT_BOTTOM )    /* Top/bottom */
                                                    /* collision? */
        {   /* Yes --> Change direction of movement and sprite graphic */
          sprites[i].deltay[page] = 0 - sprites[i].deltay[page];
          sprites[i].spidp->splookp = ( out & OUT_TOP ) ? starshipdnp
                                                        : starshipupp;
        }
        if ( out & OUT_LEFT || out & OUT_RIGHT )
          sprites[i].deltax[page] = 0 - sprites[i].deltax[page];
      }
      page = (page+1) & 1;                  /* Toggle between 1 and 0 */
    }
  }

/************************************************************************/
/**             M A I N   P R O G R A M                               **/
/************************************************************************/

void main( void )
{
  union REGS regs;

  if ( IsVga() )                           /* VGA card installed? */
  {                                        /* Yes --> Go ahead */
    init320200();                          /* Initialize graphic mode */
    Demo();
    getch();                               /* Wait for a key */
    regs.x.ax = 0x0003;                    /* Shift into text mode */
    int86( 0x10, &regs, &regs );
  }
  else
    printf( "S3220C.C - (c) 1992 by Michael Tischer\n\n"\
            "This program requires a VGA card\n\n" );
}
```

Assembler listing: S3220CA.ASM

```
;***********************************************************************;
;*                     S 3 2 2 0 C A . A S M                          *;
;*-------------------------------------------------------------------*;
;*   Task         : Contains routines for generating sprites in      *;
;*                   320x200 256 color mode on a VGA card.            *;
;*-------------------------------------------------------------------*;
;*   Author       : Michael Tischer                                  *;
;*   Developed on : 09/05/90                                         *;
;*   Last update  : 02/17/92                                         *;
;*-------------------------------------------------------------------*;
;*   Assembly     : MASM /mx S3220CA;    or    TASM -mx S3220CA       *;
;*                  ... Link to S3220C.C                             *;
;***********************************************************************;

IGROUP group _text                ;Program segment
DGROUP group const,_bss, _data    ;Data segment
       assume CS:IGROUP, DS:DGROUP, ES:DGROUP, SS:DGROUP

CONST  segment word public 'CONST';This segment handles all
CONST  ends                       ;readable constants

_BSS   segment word public 'BSS'  ;This segment handles all uninitial-
_BSS   ends                       ;ized static variables

_DATA  segment word public 'DATA' ;This segment handles all initialized
                                  ;global and static variables

_DATA  ends

;== Constants =========================================================

SC_INDEX      = 3c4h              ;Index register for sequencer ctrl.
SC_MAP_MASK   = 2                 ;Number of map mask register
SC_MEM_MODE   = 4                 ;Number of memory mode register

GC_INDEX      = 3ceh              ;Index register for graphics ctrl.
GC_GRAPH_MODE = 5                 ;Number of graphic mode register

VERT_RESCAN   = 3DAh              ;Input status register #1
PIXX          = 320               ;Horizontal resolution
;== Programm ==========================================================

_TEXT  segment byte public 'CODE' ;Program segment

;-- Public declarations -----------------------------------------------

public   _blockmove

;-- BLOCKMOVE: Moves a group of pixels in video RAM -------------------
;-- Declaration : void blockmove( unsigned char frompage, int fromx,
;--                               int fromy, unsigned char topage,
;--                               int tox, int toy, BYTE pwidth,
;--                               byte pheight, byte *bmskp );

_blockmove proc near

sframe4    struc                  ;Structure for stack access
bp4        dw ?                   ;Gets BP
additive   dw ?                   ;Local variable
restc      dw ?
movec      dw ?
dataseg    dw ?
```

```
ret_adr4   dw ?              ;Return address from caller        mov    dl,byte ptr frame.pwidth  ;DL = Bytes
frompage   dw ?              ;From page                         shr    dl,1
fromx      dw ?              ;From X-coordinate                 shr    dl,1
fromy      dw ?              ;From Y-coordinate
topage     dw ?              ;To page                           mov    bx,PIXX / 4        ;Move BX as offset to next line
tox        dw ?              ;To X-coordinate                   sub    bl,dl
toy        dw ?              ;To Y-coordinate                   xor    ch,ch              ;High byte of counter is always 0
pwidth     dw ?              ;Pixel width                       cmp    frame.bmskp,0      ;No background?
pheight    dw ?              ;Pixel height                      jne    mt2                ;None, use other copy routine
bmskp      dw ?              ;Pointer to buffer with bit mask
sframe4    ends              ;End structure                     push   dx                 ;Push DX onto stack
                                                                mov    dx,SC_INDEX        ;Get bitplane access
frame      equ [ bp - bp4 ]  ;Addresses structure elements      mov    ah,0Fh
                                                                mov    al,SC_MAP_MASK
           sub   sp,8        ;8 bytes for local variables       out    dx,ax
                                                                pop    dx                 ;Pop DX
           push  bp          ;Prepare BP register for
           mov   bp,sp       ;addressing parameters      ;-- Copy routine for all four bitplanes,
                                                         ;-- without checking the background
           push  ds
           push  si                                     mt1:    mov    cl,dl              ;Number of bytes to CL
           push  di
                                                                rep movsb                 ;Copy lines
           mov   frame.dataseg,ds                                add    di,bx             ;DI and
                                                                add    si,bx             ;SI in next line
           mov   dx,GC_INDEX        ;Get current write mode and dec    dh                ;Still more lines?
           mov   al,GC_GRAPH_MODE   ;initialize write mode 1    jne    mt1               ;Yes --> Continue
           out   dx,al                                          jmp short mtend           ;No --> Get out of routine
           inc   dx
           in    al,dx                                   ;-- Copy routine for individual bitplanes using
           push  ax          ;Push current mode onto stack ;-- the specified bit mask arrays
           and   al,not 3
           or    al,1                                    mt2:    mov    byte ptr frame.restc,dh  ;First specify variables
           out   dx,al                                           mov    byte ptr frame.movec,dl  ;placed in local variables
                                                                 mov    frame.additive,bx        ;on the stack
           mov   al,4        ;Move DS to start of FROM page
           mov   cl,byte ptr frame.frompage                     mov    al,SC_MAP_MASK     ;Address permanent
           mul   cl                                             mov    dx,SC_INDEX        ;Map mask register
           or    al,0A0h                                        out    dx,al
           xchg  ah,al                                          inc    dx                 ;Increment DX on data register
           mov   ds,ax
                                                                mov    bx,frame.bmskp     ;BX is pointer to bit mask array
           mov   al,4        ;Move ES to start of TO page       push   ds
           mov   cl,byte ptr frame.topage                       mov    ds,frame.dataseg
           mul   cl                                             mov    al,[bx]            ;Load first byte
           or    al,0A0h                                        xor    ah,ah              ;Start with an even byte
           xchg  ah,al                                          pop    ds
           mov   es,ax
                                                         mt3:    mov    cl,byte ptr frame.movec  ;Move number of bytes to CL
           mov   ax,PIXX / 4 ;Move SI to FROM starting position
           mul   frame.fromy                             mt4:    out    dx,al              ;Set bit mask
           mov   si,frame.fromx                                  movsb                     ;Copy 4 bytes
           shr   si,1
           shr   si,1                                            inc    ah                ;Increment odd/even counter
           add   si,ax                                          test   ah,1              ;Odd again?
                                                                jne    mt5               ;Yes --> Move nibble
           mov   ax,PIXX / 4 ;Move DI to TO position
           mul   frame.toy                               ;-- Get next byte from buffer on every even byte -----------
           mov   di,frame.tox
           shr   di,1                                            inc    bx                ;BX to next bit mask byte
           shr   di,1                                           push   ds
           add   di,ax                                          mov    ds,frame.dataseg
                                                                mov    al,[bx]            ;Load next byte
           mov   dh,byte ptr frame.pheight ;DH = Pixel lines     pop    ds
```

```
        loop   mt4          ;Next four latches              mov   al,GC_GRAPH_MODE
        jmp    short mt6                                     out   dx,ax

mt5:    shr    al,1         ;Get odd byte bit mask from     pop   di
        shr    al,1         ;low nibble                     pop   si
        shr    al,1                                         pop   ds
        shr    al,1                                         pop   bp
        loop   mt4          ;Next four latches
                                                            add   sp,8        ;Clear local variables
mt6:    add    di,frame.additive ;Add DI and                ret
        add    si,frame.additive ;SI to next line
        dec    byte ptr frame.restc ;Still more lines?     _blockmove endp
        jne    mt3          ;Yes --> Continue
                                                           ; == End ================================================================
mtend:  mov    dx,GC_INDEX  ;Revert to old
        pop    ax           ;write mode                    _text   ends                    ;End of program segment
        mov    ah,al                                               end                     ;End of assembler source
```

Sprites in 320x400 pixel mode with 256 colors

When using the higher resolution 320x400 pixel graphics mode, we must sacrifice the advantage of sprite background and sprite description storage in video RAM. Instead, we must move this information from conventional memory to video RAM. These routines take longer to execute than those used to copy structures directly within the video RAM, but the user shouldn't notice the change in speed.

However, this mode simplifies creating and displaying sprites because the transfer from conventional RAM to video RAM occurs one byte at a time. We can also remove our artificial limitation of making sprite widths divisible by four and the need for maintaining four copies of each sprite. So, a sprite of any width can be copied to any X-coordinate. Also, this mode eliminates the need for the map mask register.

The different method for storing sprite information and for moving the information to video RAM can be seen in the sprite modules required for programming in this mode. These are S3240C.C, S3240CA.ASM, and V3240CA.ASM in the C version, and S3240P.PAS, S3240PA.ASM, and V3240PA.ASM in the Pascal version.

The PUTVIDEO and GETVIDEO routines used by the modules previously listed contain the interface between conventional RAM and video RAM. GETVIDEO transfers the contents of a rectangular screen area from video RAM to conventional RAM, as in cases where you would save a sprite background to a buffer. PUTVIDEO then restores an area saved by GETVIDEO from the conventional RAM buffer to a specified location in video RAM.

These routines are based on two routines called COPYBUF2PLANE and COPYPLANE2BUF from the S3240CA.ASM and S3240PA.ASM assembly language modules. These routines transfer a rectangular area of pixels either from a specified bitplane to conventional RAM or from conventional RAM to a bitplane.

The four bitplanes, used to store pixels in all 256 color modes, are each handled separately. This is why these routines are called four times when they are used within GETVIDEO or PUTVIDEO. This works faster than trying to take four pixels (one from each bitplane) in a single move, in which case the read map register of the graphics controller or the map mask register of the sequencer controller would also have to be programmed before each move. Using the method previously described, these registers need to be programmed only once with each COPYBUF2PLANE or COPYPLANE2BUF call, because these routines access only one bitplane at a time.

GETVIDEO and PUTVIDEO are able to work with rectangular blocks of any width, not just multiples of four. So, the areas to be processed within each bitplane may not always be the same width. Imagine a GETVIDEO call where you want to load an area from video RAM with a width that extends from the X-coordinates 0 to 6. In this area, each pixel line has two pixels from the first bitplane (at X-coordinates 0 and 4), two pixels from the second bitplane (at 1 and 5), and two pixels from the third (at 2 and 6). The fourth bitplane therefore contains only one pixel, the one at X-coordinate 3.

Since GETVIDEO is called separately for each bitplane, the routine must keep track of how many pixels are involved and other information that is needed when GETVIDEO is recalled. This information is stored in a data block allocated on the heap by GETVIDEO when it is called. A pointer to this data block is passed back to the caller.

The data block is of type PIXBUF, which begins with an array of four pointers that point to the four buffers that contain the screen areas represented by the four bitplanes. This is followed by another array with four entries that indicate the number of pixels per bitplane. The last entry in this structure is the height of the screen area or the number of pixel lines.

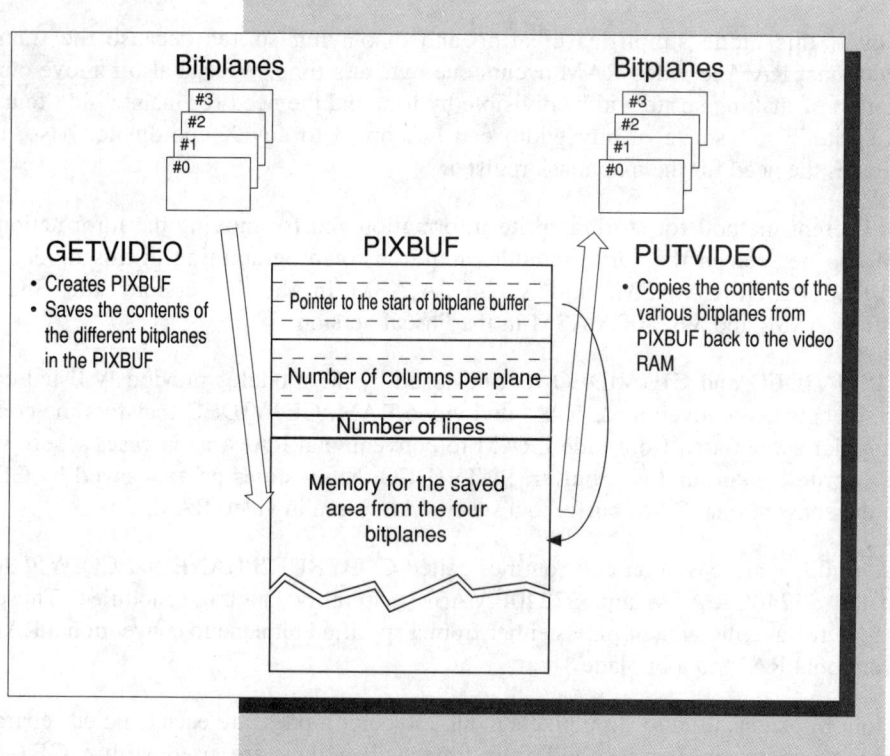

Saving screen areas with GETVIDEO and PUTVIDEO in this mode

The screen area's height is the last entry in the PIXBUF structure. GETVIDEO places the buffer, which stores the pixel information from the individual bitplanes, after this structure. Space for this additional buffer is created when GETVIDEO allocates the PIXBUF buffer. The buffer size required for the information from the four bitplanes is added directly to the size of the PIXBUF structure. The result is a block of memory containing the PIXBUF structure, followed by the pixel information from the four bitplanes as loaded by COPYPLANE2VIDEO.

GETVIDEO returns a pointer to its caller, pointing to the pixel buffer. This pointer can then be passed on to subsequent PUTVIDEO calls. This allows the saved screen area to be copied to any position in video RAM, as often as desired.

The GETVIDEO function serves another purpose. If GETVIDEO is passed a pointer as its last parameter with a value other than NIL (in Pascal) or the ALLOCBUF constant (in C), then the information is loaded into an existing buffer (indicated by the pointer) that was created in a previous call to GETVIDEO. This saves time by allowing you to reuse buffers without having to create a new buffer on the heap each time you call GETVIDEO. When doing this, you must be sure that the new screen area to be saved fits within the existing buffer.

The sprite demo programs for the 320x400 pixel mode use this feature for tasks such as saving a sprite background. This works because the size of a given sprite, and consequently the size of its background, remains constant, so the pixel buffer needs to be allocated only once.

GETVIDEO and PUTVIDEO aren't only used for saving and restoring sprite backgrounds. These routines also compile the sprite description in COMPILESPRITE. Using the information in the string array that defines the sprite, this routine builds the sprite at screen coordinates 0/0 in the specified screen page (the screen page is passed as a parameter).

Then the area occupied by the sprite is simply copied to a pixel buffer by calling GETVIDEO. Any time you want to display the pixel on screen, simply pass this pixel buffer to the PUTVIDEO routine, with the screen page and the desired coordinates. The pointer to the pixel buffer is stored under the name PIXBP in the SPLOOK structure.

Sprite backgrounds are handled in a similar way. The CREATESPRITE routine uses GETVIDEO to create two pixel buffers of the same size as the corresponding sprite. The first buffer stores the sprite background from the first screen page and the other buffer stores the background from the second page. The pointers to these two pixel buffers are stored in an array called HGPTR within a structure of type SPID. CREATESPRITE configures this structure for identifying and working with sprites.

The pixel buffers for the sprite description and the two background areas are then used by routines such as PRINTSPRITE, GETSPRITEBG, and RESTORESPRITEBG, to display the sprite and save or restore its background. You'll see that these routines are simpler than those from the sprite demonstration programs for 320x200 pixel mode.

We haven't explained how background pixels are handled yet. The PUTVIDEO routine uses a Boolean variable called BG. This variable is passed on to the assembler routine COPYBUF2PLANE to determine whether the background should be taken into consideration when copying the buffer to each bitplane.

If this parameter contains the value TRUE, then COPYBUF2PLANE checks each byte to determine whether it represents a background pixel when copying the contents of the specified buffer to video RAM. Background pixels are assigned color code 255. This color code was assigned, within the CREATESPRITE routine, to all pixels represented by a space in the string array. If COPYBUF2PLANE encounters such a pixel, it skips it and doesn't write its color to video RAM. The routine then continues with the next pixel in the buffer.

This represents a rather simple solution to the problem of background pixels, even if it does add some time to the copy procedure between main memory and video RAM. However, the added time isn't really noticeable to the user.

Now we've covered the major points in the 320*400 pixel sprite programs. If you need additional information about how these demo programs work, the listings are fully documented.

Pascal listing: S3240P.PAS

```
{**********************************************************          {-- Constants ----------------------------------------------------}
*               S 3 2 4 0 P . P A S               *
**--------------------------------------------------------**          const MAXX = 319;                    { Maximum X- and Y-coordinates }
* Task          : Demonstrates sprites in 320x400 VGA graphic  *            MAXY = 399;
*                 mode, using 256 colors and four screen pages. *
*                 This program requires the assembly language  *            OUT_LEFT   = 1;  { For collision documentation in SpriteMove() }
*                 modules V3240PA.ASM and S3240PA.ASM.          *            OUT_TOP    = 2;
**--------------------------------------------------------**            OUT_RIGHT  = 4;
* Author        : Michael Tischer                              *            OUT_BOTTOM = 8;
* Developed on   : 09/12/90                                     *            OUT_NO     = 0;                              { None }
* Last update    : 02/26/92                                     *
**********************************************************}          {-- Type declarations -----------------------------------------------}

program S3240P;                                                     type PIXBUF = record          { Information for GetVideo and PutVideo }
                                                                              bitptr : array[0..3] of pointer;  { Ptr. to bitplanes }
uses dos, crt;                                                                byprod : array[0..3] of byte;   { Num. ranges to copy }
                                                                              rhght  : byte;                    { Number of rows }
{-- External references from assembler routines ----------------------}        {-- Here follow bytes from the bitplanes -------------}
                                                                              end;
{$L v3240pa}                               { Add assembler module }      PIXPTR = ^PIXBUF;                         { Pointer to a pixel buffer }

procedure init320400; external;                                     SPLOOK = record                               { Sprite design }
procedure setpix( x, y : integer; pcolor : byte ); external;                 twidth,                                { Total width }
function getpix( x, y: integer ) : byte; external;                           theight : byte;                        { Height in pixel lines }
procedure setpage( page : byte ); external;                                  pixbp   : PIXPTR;                      { Pointer to pixel block }
procedure showpage( page : byte ); external;                                 end;                                   { for allocating sprite }
                                                                    SPLP = ^SPLOOK;                             { Pointer to sprite design }
{$L s3240pa}                               { Add assembler module }
                                                                    SPID = record                              { Sprite descriptor (ID) }
procedure CopyPlane2Buf( bufptr : pointer;                                   splookp : SPLP;                       { Pointer to sprite design }
                  page   : byte;                                             x, y    : array [0..1] of integer;{ Coordinates: pp 0&1 }
                  fromx,                                                     bgptr   : array [0..1] of PIXPTR;     { Pointer to back- }
                  fromy  : integer;                                          end;                                   { ground buffer }
                  rwidth,                                             SPIP = ^SPID;                            { Pointer to sprite descriptor }
                  rheight : byte    ); external;
                                                                    PTRREC = record              { For pointer or LONGINTS analysis }
procedure CopyBuf2Plane( bufptr : pointer;                                   ofs,
                  page   : byte;                                             seg : word;
                  tox,                                                       end;
                  toy    : integer;
                  rwidth,                                             BYTEAR = array[0..10000] of byte;          { Addressing }
                  rheight : byte;                                    BARPTR = ^BYTEAR;                          { different buffers }
                  bg      : boolean ); external;
                                                                    {**********************************************************
```

```
*  IsVga : Determines whether a VGA card is installed.          *
**----------------------------------------------------------------**
*  Input   :  None                                              *
*  Output  :  TRUE or FALSE                                     *
*****************************************************************}

function IsVga : boolean;

var Regs : Registers;        { Processor registers for interrupt call }

begin
  Regs.AX := $1a00;            { Function 1AH applies only to VGA }
  Intr( $10, Regs );
  IsVga := ( Regs.AL = $1a );
end;


{*****************************************************************
*  PrintChar : Writes a character to the screen while in graphic mode.*
**----------------------------------------------------------------**
*  Input    :  THECHAR = Character to be written                *
*              x, y    = X- and Y-coordinates of upper-left corner  *
*              FG      = Foreground color                       *
*              BK      = Background color                       *
*  Info     :  Character is created in an 8x8 matrix, based on the  *
*              8x8 ROM font.                                     *
*****************************************************************}

procedure PrintChar( thechar : char; x, y : integer; fg, bk : byte );

type FDEF = array[0..255,0..7] of byte;          { Font array }
     TPTR = ^FDEF;                                { Pointer to font }

var Regs  : Registers;           { Registers for interrupt call }
    ch    : char;                { Individual pixels in character }
    i, k,                        { Loop counter }
    BMask : byte;                { Bit mask for character design }

const fptr : TPTR = NIL;              { Pointer to font in ROM }

begin
  if fptr = NIL then             { Pointer to font already set? }
    begin                        { No }
      Regs.AH := $11;            { Call video BIOS function }
      Regs.AL := $30;            { 11H, sub-function 30H }
      Regs.BH := 3;              { Get pointer to 8x8 font }
      intr( $10, Regs );
      fptr := ptr( Regs.ES, Regs.BP );     { Set pointers }
    end;

  if ( bk = 255 ) then           { Drawing transparent characters? }
    for i := 0 to 7 do           { Yes --> Set foreground pixels only }
      begin
        BMask := fptr^[ord(thechar),i];{ Get bit pattern for one line }
        for k := 0 to 7 do
          begin
            if ( BMask and 128 <> 0 ) then       { Pixel set? }
              setpix( x+k, y+i, fg );            { Yes }
            BMask := BMask shl 1;
          end;
      end
  else                           { No --> Consider background as well }
    for i := 0 to 7 do           { Execute lines }
      begin
        BMask := fptr^[ord(thechar),i];{ Get bit pattern for one line }
```

```
        for k := 0 to 7 do
          begin
            if ( BMask and 128 <> 0 ) then        { Foreground? }
              setpix( x+k, y+i, fg )              { Yes }
            else
              setpix( x+k, y+i, bk );      { No --> Background }
            BMask := BMask shl 1;
          end;
      end;
end;

{*****************************************************************
*  PrintString: Writes a string to the screen in graphics mode.  *
**----------------------------------------------------------------**
*  Input   :  X, Y   = X- and Y-coordinates of upper-left corner  *
*             FG     = Foreground color                         *
*             BK     = Background color                         *
*             TSTR   = String to be displayed                   *
*  Info    :  The characters are designed around an 8x8 matrix, based  *
*             on the 8x8 ROM font.                              *
*****************************************************************}

procedure PrintString( x, y : integer; fg, bk : byte; tstr : string );

var i : integer;                             { Loop counter }

begin
  for i := 1 to length( tstr ) do            { Execute string }
    begin
      PrintChar( tstr[i], x, y, fg, bk );       { and display it }
      inc( x, 8 );                    { Increment output position }
    end;
end;

{*****************************************************************
*  Line: Draws a line based on the Bresenham algorithm.          *
**----------------------------------------------------------------**
*  Input   :  X1, Y1 = Starting coordinates (0 - ...)           *
*             X2, Y2 = Ending coordinates                       *
*             LPCOL  = Color of line pixels                     *
*****************************************************************}

procedure Line( x1, y1, x2, y2 : integer; lpcol : byte );

var d, dx, dy,
    aincr, bincr,
    xincr, yincr,
    x, y            : integer;

{-- Procedure for swapping two integer variables --------------------}

procedure SwapInt( var i1, i2: integer );

var dummy : integer;

begin
  dummy := i2;
  i2    := i1;
  i1    := dummy;
end;

{-- Main procedure -------------------------------------------------}

begin
```

```
if ( abs(x2-x1) < abs(y2-y1) ) then      { X- or Y-axis overflow? }
  begin                                   { Check Y-axes }
    if ( y1 > y2 ) then                          { y1 > y2? }
      begin
        SwapInt( x1, x2 );              { Yes --> Swap X1 with X2 }
        SwapInt( y1, y2 );              {          and Y1 with Y2 }
      end;

    if ( x2 > x1 ) then xincr := 1        { Set X-axis increment }
                   else xincr := -1;

    dy := y2 - y1;
    dx := abs( x2-x1 );
    d  := 2 * dx - dy;
    aincr := 2 * (dx - dy);
    bincr := 2 * dx;
    x := x1;
    y := y1;

    setpix( x, y, lpcol );                     { Set first pixel }
    for y:=y1+1 to y2 do                  { Execute line on Y-axes }
      begin
        if ( d >= 0 ) then
          begin
            inc( x, xincr );
            inc( d, aincr );
          end
        else
          inc( d, bincr );
        setpix( x, y, lpcol );
      end;
  end
else                                           { Check X-axes }
  begin
    if ( x1 > x2 ) then                          { x1 > x2? }
      begin
        SwapInt( x1, x2 );              { Yes --> Swap X1 with X2 }
        SwapInt( y1, y2 );              {          and Y1 with Y2 }
      end;

    if ( y2 > y1 ) then yincr := 1        { Set X-axis increment }
                   else yincr := -1;

    dx := x2 - x1;
    dy := abs( y2-y1 );
    d  := 2 * dy - dx;
    aincr := 2 * (dy - dx);
    bincr := 2 * dy;
    x := x1;
    y := y1;

    setpix( x, y, lpcol );                     { Set first pixel }
    for x:=x1+1 to x2 do                  { Execute line on X-axes }
      begin
        if ( d >= 0 ) then
          begin
            inc( y, yincr );
            inc( d, aincr );
          end
        else
          inc( d, bincr );
        setpix( x, y, lpcol );
      end;
  end;
end;
```

```
end;

{*********************************************************************
* GrfxPrint: Displays a formatted string on the graphic screen.     *
**-----------------------------------------------------------------**
* Input   : X, Y   = Starting coordinates (0 - ...)                 *
*           fg     = Foreground color                               *
*           bk     = Background color (255 = transparent)           *
*           STRING = String with format information                 *
*********************************************************************}

procedure GrfxPrint( x, y : integer; fg, bk : byte; strt : string );

var i : integer;                                    { Loop counter }

begin
  for i:=1 to length( strt ) do
    begin
      printchar( strt[i], x, y, fg, bk );   { Display using PrintChar }
      inc( x, 8 );                  { Move X to next character position }
    end;
end;

{*********************************************************************
* GetVideo: Places contents of a rectangular range of video RAM     *
*           in a buffer.                                            *
**-----------------------------------------------------------------**
* Input   : PAGE   = Screen page (0 or 1)                          *
*           X1, Y1 = Starting coordinates                          *
*           WRANGE = Width of rectangular range in pixels          *
*           HRANGE = Height of rectangular range in pixels         *
*           BUFPTR = Pointer to pixel buffer into which            *
*                    information should be allocated               *
* Output  : Pointer to allocated pixel buffer with contents of     *
*           specified range                                        *
* Info    : If the BUFPTR parameter contains nothing, a new pixel  *
*           buffer is allocated and returned on the heap. This buffer*
*           can be re-created on each call, provided the previous   *
*           contents are no longer needed, and provided the size    *
*           of the rectangular range remains unchanged.            *
*********************************************************************}

function GetVideo( page : byte; x1, y1 : integer;
                   wrange, hrange : byte; bufptr : PIXPTR ) : PIXPTR;

var i,                                              { Loop counter }
    curplane,                          { Currently processed bitplane }
    sb,                            { Bitplane at starting coordinates }
    eb,                              { Bitplane at ending coordinates }
    b,                                { Number of bytes per bitplane }
    am  : byte;    { Number of bytes in center of both groups of four }
    rptr : pointer;                                 { Offset counter }

begin
  if ( bufptr = NIL ) then                { No buffer passed on call? }
    getmem( bufptr, sizeof( PIXBUF ) + wrange*hrange ); { No --> Alloc}

  {-- Compute number of bytes per bitplane ----------------------------}

  am := ( ( (x1+wrange-1) and not(3) ) - { Number of bytes in center }
          ( x1+4) and not(3) ) ) div 4;
  sb := x1 mod 4;                              { Starting bitplane }
  eb := (x1+wrange-1) mod 4;                     { Ending bitplane }
```

```
rptr := ptr( seg(bufptr^), ofs(bufptr^) + sizeof( PIXBUF ));

{-- Execute four bitplanes -------------------------------------}

for i:=0 to 3 do
  begin
    curplane := (sb+i) mod 4;
    b := am;                    { Base number of bytes to be copied }
    if ( curplane >= sb ) then  { Also in starting block of four? }
      inc( b );                 { Yes --> Add a byte to this bitplane }
    if ( curplane <= eb ) then  { Also in ending block of four? }
      inc( b );                 { Yes --> Add a byte to this bitplane }
    bufptr^.bitptr[i] := rptr;  { Place pointer at start of buffer }
    bufptr^.byprod[i] := b;     { Place number in buffer }
    CopyPlane2Buf( rptr, page, x1+i,        { Get contents }
                   y1, b, hrange );         { of bitplane }
    inc( PTRREC(rptr).ofs, b * hrange );    { Set pointer to next }
  end;                          { bitplane in buffer }


  bufptr^.rhght := hrange;                  { Store height }

  GetVideo := bufptr;           { Return buffer pointer to caller }
end;


{**************************************************************
 * PutVideo: Writes contents of a rectangular screen range generated *
 *           by GetVideo to video RAM.                        *
 **---------------------------------------------------------**
 * Input   : BUFPTR = Pointer to pixel buffer from GetVideo   *
 *           PAGE   = Screen page (0 or 1)                     *
 *           X1, Y1 = Starting coordinates                     *
 *           BG     = Should background pixels (color code 255) not *
 *                    be written to video RAM                  *
 * Info    : Pixel buffer is not cleared by this procedure; use the *
 *           FreePixBuf for this purpose.                      *
 **************************************************************}

procedure PutVideo( bufptr : PIXPTR; page : byte; x1, y1 : integer;
                    bg     : boolean );

var curplane,                   { Currently executed bitplane }
    hrange : byte;

begin
  hrange := bufptr^.rhght;                  { Range height }
  for curplane:=0 to 3 do                   { Execute four bitplanes }
    CopyBuf2Plane( bufptr^.bitptr[curplane], page, x1+curplane,
                   y1, bufptr^.byprod[curplane], hrange, bg );
end;

{**************************************************************
 * FreePixBuf: Clears a pixel buffer previously allocated by Heap. *
 **---------------------------------------------------------**
 * Input   : BUFPTR = Pointer to pixel buffer                 *
 *           WRANGE = Width of rectangular range of pixels    *
 *           HRANGE = Height of rectangular range of pixels   *
 **************************************************************}

procedure FreePixBuf( bufptr : PIXPTR; wrange, hrange : byte );

begin
  freemem( bufptr, sizeof( PIXBUF ) + wrange*hrange );
end;
```

```
{**************************************************************
 * CreateSprite: Creates a sprite based on a user-defined      *
 *               pixel pattern.                                *
 **---------------------------------------------------------**
 * Input   : SPLOOKP = Pointer to data structure from CompileSprite *
 * Output  : Pointer to created sprite structure               *
 **************************************************************}

function CreateSprite( splookp : SPLP ) : SPIP;

var spidp : SPIP;               { Pointer to created sprite structure }

begin
  new( spidp );                 { Allocate memory for sprite descriptor }
  spidp^.splookp := splookp;              { Pass data to the }
                                          { sprite structure }
  {- Create two background buffers, for storing range from video RAM -}

  spidp^.bgptr[0] := GetVideo( 0, 0, 0, splookp^.twidth,
                               splookp^.theight, NIL );
  spidp^.bgptr[1] := GetVideo( 0, 0, 0, splookp^.twidth,
                               splookp^.theight, NIL );
  CreateSprite := spidp;        { Return pointer to sprite structure }
end;


{**************************************************************
 * CompileSprite: Creates a sprite's pixel and bit patterns, based on *
 *                the sprite's definition at runtime.         *
 **---------------------------------------------------------**
 * Input   : BUFP    = Pointer to array containing string pointers *
 *                     controlling sprite's pattern           *
 *           SHEIGHT = Sprite height (and number of strings needed) *
 *           GPAGE   = Graphic page for sprite design         *
 *           FB      = ASCII character for the smallest color *
 *           FGCOLOR = First color code for FB                *
 * Info    : Sprite structure of pixel lines starts at left margin. *
 **************************************************************}

function CompileSprite( var buf; sheight, gpage : byte;
                        fb : char; fgcolor : byte ) : SPLP;

type BYPTR = ^byte;                         { Pointer to a byte }

var swidth,                                 { String width }
    c,                          { Get character from c sprite array }
    cvcolor,                    { Converted color of a pixel }
    i, k, l : byte;             { Loop variables }
    splookp : SPLP;             { Pointer to created sprite structure }
    bptr    : barptr;           { Addresses buffer with graphic }
    pbptr   : PIXPTR;           { Get sprite background }

begin
  {-- Create SpriteLook structure and fill with data ---------------}

  new( splookp );
  bptr := @buf;                 { Set pointer to logo buffer }
  swidth := bptr^[0];   { Get string length and determine logo width }
  splookp^.twidth  := swidth;
  splookp^.theight := sheight;


  {-- Place sprite in page at 0/0 ------------------------------------}

  setpage( gpage );             { Set page for drawing }
  pbptr := GetVideo( gpage, 0, 0, swidth, sheight, nil ); { Get bkgd. }
```

337

```
  for i := 0 to sheight-1 do                      { Execute rows }
    for k := 0 to swidth-1 do                   { Execute columns }
      begin
        c := bptr^[i*(swidth+1)+k+1];                { Get pixels }
        if ( c = 32 ) then                         { Background? }
          setpix( k, i, 255 )             { Yes --> Color code = 255 }
        else                          { No --> Maintain color code }
          setpix( k, i, fgcolor+(c-ord(fb)) );
      end;

  {-- Get sprite in buffer and restore background --------------------}

  splookp^.pixbp := GetVideo( gpage, 0, 0, swidth, sheight, NIL );
  PutVideo( pbptr, gpage, 0, 0, false );
  FreePixBuf( pbptr, swidth, sheight );            { Free buffer }

  CompileSprite := splookp;       { Return pointer to sprite buffer }
end;


{**********************************************************
 * PrintSprite : Displays sprite in a specified page.     *
 **------------------------------------------------------**
 * Input  :  SPIDP   = Pointer to the sprite structure    *
 *           SPRPAGE = Page in which sprite should be drawn (0 or 1) *
 **********************************************************}

procedure PrintSprite( spidp : SPIP; sprpage : byte );

begin
  PutVideo( spidp^.splookp^.pixbp,
            sprpage, spidp^.x[sprpage], spidp^.y[sprpage], true );
end;


{**********************************************************
 * GetSpriteBg: Gets a sprite background and specifies the position. *
 **------------------------------------------------------**
 * Input  : SPIDP   = Pointer to the sprite structure     *
 *          SPRPAGE = Page from which the background should be taken *
 *                    (0 or 1)                             *
 **********************************************************}

procedure GetSpriteBg( spidp : SPIP; sprpage : BYTE );

var dummy : PIXPTR;

begin
  dummy := GetVideo( sprpage, spidp^.x[sprpage],  spidp^.y[sprpage],
                     spidp^.splookp^.twidth, spidp^.splookp^.theight,
                     spidp^.bgptr[sprpage] );
end;


{**********************************************************
 * RestoreSpriteBg: Restores sprite background from original graphic *
 *                  page.                                 *
 **------------------------------------------------------**
 * Input   : SPIDP =  Pointer to the sprite structure     *
 *           SPRPAGE = Page from which background should be copied *
 *                    (0 or 1)                             *
 **********************************************************}

procedure RestoreSpriteBg( spidp : SPIP; sprpage : BYTE );

begin
```

```
  PutVideo( spidp^.bgptr[sprpage], sprpage,
            spidp^.x[sprpage],  spidp^.y[sprpage], false );
end;


{**********************************************************
 * MoveSprite: Copy sprite within background to original graphic page.*
 **------------------------------------------------------**
 * Input  : SPIDP  = Pointer to the sprite structure      *
 *          SPRPAGE= Page to which the background should be copied *
 *                 (0 or 1)                               *
 *          DELTAX = Movement counter in X-               *
 *          DELTAY   and Y-directions                     *
 * Output  : Collision marker (see OUT_ constants)        *
 **********************************************************}

function MoveSprite( spidp : SPIP; sprpage : byte;
                     deltax, deltay : integer   ) : byte;

var newx, newy : integer;             { New sprite coordinates }
    out        : byte;         { Display collision with border }

begin
  {-- Move X-coordinates and test for border collision ----------------}

  newx := spidp^.x[sprpage] + deltax;
  if ( newx  < 0 ) then
    begin
      newx := 0 - deltax - spidp^.x[sprpage];
      out := OUT_LEFT;
    end
  else
    if ( newx > MAXX - spidp^.splookp^.twidth ) then
      begin
        newx := (2*(MAXX+1))-newx-2*(spidp^.splookp^.twidth);
        out := OUT_RIGHT;
      end
  else
    out := OUT_NO;

  {-- Move Y-coordinates and test for border collision ----------------}

  newy := spidp^.y[sprpage] + deltay;            { Top border? }
  if ( newy < 0 ) then
    begin                          { Yes --> Deltay must be negative }
      newy := 0 - deltay - spidp^.y[sprpage];
      out := out or OUT_TOP;
    end
  else
    if ( newy + spidp^.splookp^.theight > MAXY+1  ) then    { Bottom? }
      begin                         { Yes --> Deltay must be positive }
        newy := (2*(MAXY+1))-newy-2*(spidp^.splookp^.theight);
        out := out or OUT_BOTTOM;
      end;

  {-- Set new position only if different from old position ------------}

  if ( newx <> spidp^.x[sprpage] ) or  ( newy <> spidp^.y[sprpage] ) then
    begin                               { If there's a new position }
      RestoreSpriteBg( spidp, sprpage );  { reset background and store }
      spidp^.x[sprpage] := newx;            { new coordinates        }
      spidp^.y[sprpage] := newy;
      GetSpriteBg( spidp, sprpage );             { Get new background }
      PrintSprite( spidp, sprpage );   { Draw sprite in specified page }
    end;
```

```
  MoveSprite := out;
end;


{**********************************************************************
 *  SetSprite: Sets sprite at a specific position.                    *
 **------------------------------------------------------------------**
 *  Input    : SPIDP = Pointer to the sprite structure               *
 *             x0, y0 = Sprite coordinates for page 0                 *
 *             x1, y1 = Sprite coordinates for page 1                 *
 *  Info     : This function call should be made the first time that  *
 *             MoveSprite() is called.                                *
 **********************************************************************}

procedure SetSprite( spidp : SPIP; x0, y0, x1, y1 : integer );

begin
  spidp^.x[0] := x0;          { Store coordinates in sprite structure }
  spidp^.x[1] := x1;
  spidp^.y[0] := y0;
  spidp^.y[1] := y1;

  GetSpriteBg( spidp, 0 );                  { Get sprite backgrounds }
  GetSpriteBg( spidp, 1 );                  { in pages 0 and 1       }
  PrintSprite( spidp, 0 );                     { Draw sprite in }
  PrintSprite( spidp, 1 );                     { pages 0 and 1  }
end;


{**********************************************************************
 *  Demo: Demonstrates these functions.                               *
 **********************************************************************}

procedure Demo;

const StarShipUp :array [1..20] of string[32] =
                 ( '             AA             ',
                   '            AAAA            ',
                   '            AAAA            ',
                   '             AA             ',
                   '           GGBBGG           ',
                   '          GBBCCBBG          ',
                   '         GBBBCCBBBG         ',
                   '         GBBBBBBBBBG        ',
                   '         GBBBBBBBBBBG       ',
                   ' G      GBBBBBBBBBBBBG    G ',
                   'GCG     GGDBBBBBBBBBBBDGG  GCG',
                   'GCG   GGBBBBBBB  BBBDBBBGG  GCG',
                   'GCBGGGBBBBBBDBB    BBDBBBBBBGGGBCG',
                   'GCBBBBBBBBBBBDB    BDBBBBBBBBBCG',
                   'BBBBBBBBBBBBDB BB BDBBBBBBBBBBBB',
                   'GGCBBBBBBBBDBBBBBBBBBBDBBBBBBBCG ',
                   ' GGCCBBBDDDDDDDDDDDDDDDBBBCCG ',
                   '   GGBBDDDDDGGGGGGDDDDDDBBG ',
                   '     GDDDDDGGG   GGGDDDDDG ',
                   '       DDDD        DDDD    ' );

const StarShipDown :array [1..20] of string[32] =
                 ( '      DDDD        DDDD      ',
                   '     GDDDDDGGG   GGGDDDDDG  ',
                   '   GGBBDDDDDGGGGGGDDDDDDBBG ',
                   ' GGCCBBBDDDDDDDDDDDDDDDBBBCCG ',
                   'GGCBBBBBBBBDBBBBBBBBBBDBBBBBBBCG ',
                   'BBBBBBBBBBBBDB BB BDBBBBBBBBBBBB',
                   'GCBBBBBBBBBBBDB    BDBBBBBBBBBCG',
```

```
'GCBGGGBBBBBBDBB    BBDBBBBBBGGGBCG',
'GCG   GGBBBBBBB  BBBDBBBGG  GCG',
'GCG     GGDBBBBBBBBBBBDGG  GCG',
' G      GBBBBBBBBBBBBG    G ',
'         GBBBBBBBBBBG       ',
'         GBBBBBBBBBG        ',
'          GBBBCCBBBG        ',
'           GBBCCBBG         ',
'            GGBBGG          ',
'             AA             ',
'            AAAA            ',
'            AAAA            ',
'             AA             ' );

SPRNUM = 6;                              { Number of sprites }
CWIDTH = 37;          { Width of copyright message in characters }
CHEIGHT = 6;                        { Message height in rows }
SX     = (MAXX-(CWIDTH*8)) div 2;      { Starting X-coordinate }
SY     = (MAXY-(CHEIGHT*8)) div 2;     { Starting Y-coordinate }

type SPRITE = record                   { For sprite management }
                spidp : SPIP;          { Pointer to sprite ID }
                deltax,                { X-movement for pages 0 and 1 }
                deltay : array [0..1] of integer;   { Y-movement }
              end;

var sprites    : array [1..sprnum] of SPRITE;
    page,                              { Current page }
    lc,                      { Character for screen design }
    out        : byte;       { Get flags for page collision }
    x, y, i,                           { Loop counter }
    dx, dy     : integer;              { Movement value }
    starshipupp,
    starshipdnp : SPLP;                { Sprite pointer }
    ch          : char;
begin

  Randomize;              { Initialize random number generator }

  {-- Create patterns for the different sprites ----------------------}

  starshipupp := CompileSprite( StarShipUp,   20, 0, 'A', 1 );
  starshipdnp := CompileSprite( StarShipDown, 20, 0, 'A', 1 );

  {-- Fill the first two graphic pages with characters ---------------}

  for page := 0 to 1 do
    begin
      setpage( page );
      lc := 0;
      y := 0;
      while ( y < (MAXY+1)-8 ) do
        begin
          x := 0;
          while ( x < (MAXX+1)-8 ) do
            begin
              PrintChar( chr(lc and 127), x, y, lc mod 255, 0 );
              inc( lc );
              inc( x, 8 );
            end;
          inc( y, 12 );
        end;
    end;

  {-- Display copyright message ------------------------------------}
```

339

```
        Line( SX-1, SY-1, SX+CWIDTH*8, SY-1, 15 );
        Line( SX+CWIDTH*8, SY-1, SX+CWIDTH*8, SY+CHEIGHT*8,15 );
        Line( SX+CWIDTH*8, SY+CHEIGHT*8, SX-1, SY+CHEIGHT*8, 15 );
        Line( SX-1, SY+CHEIGHT*8, SX-1, SY-1, 15 );
        PrintString( SX, SY,      15, 4,
                                                      '   ' );
        PrintString( SX, SY+8,   15, 4,
                      ' * S3240P.PAS - (c) 1992 M. Tischer* ' );
        PrintString( SX, SY+16, 15, 4,
                                                      '   ' );
        PrintString( SX, SY+24, 15, 4,
                      '     Sprite demo for 320x400 mode   ' );
        PrintString( SX, SY+32, 15, 4,
                      '              on VGA cards          ' );
        PrintString( SX, SY+40, 15, 4,
                      '                                    ' );

    end;

{-- Create different sprites ---------------------------------------}

for i := 1 to SPRNUM do
  begin
    sprites[ i ].spidp := CreateSprite( starshipupp );
    repeat                    { Select movement values for sprites }
      dx := 0;
      dy := random(10) - 5;
    until ( dx <> 0 ) or ( dy <> 0 );

    sprites[ i ].deltax[0] := dx * 2;
    sprites[ i ].deltay[0] := dy * 2;
    sprites[ i ].deltax[1] := dx * 2;
    sprites[ i ].deltay[1] := dy * 2;

    x := ( (320 div SPRNUM) * (i-1) ) + ((320 div SPRNUM)-40) div 2;
    y := random( 200 - 40 );
    SetSprite( sprites[ i ].spidp, x, y, x - dx, y - dy );
  end;

{-- Move sprites and bounce them off the page borders --------------}

page := 1;                              { Start with page 1 }
while ( not keypressed ) do          { Press a key to end the loop }
  begin
    showpage( 1 - page );                { Display other page }

    for i := 1 to sprnum do              { Execute sprites }
      begin            { Move sprite and check for page collision }
        out := MoveSprite( sprites[i].spidp, page,
                           sprites[i].deltax[page],
                           sprites[i].deltay[page] );
        if ( ( out and OUT_TOP ) <> 0 ) or { Top/bottom collision? }
           ( ( out and OUT_BOTTOM ) <> 0 ) then
          begin
          { Yes --> Change direction of movement and sprite graphic }

            sprites[i].deltay[page] := -sprites[i].deltay[page];
            if ( ( out and OUT_TOP ) <> 0 ) then
              sprites[i].spidp^.splookp := starshipdnp
            else
              sprites[i].spidp^.splookp := starshipupp;
          end;
        if ( ( out and OUT_LEFT ) <> 0 ) or { Left/right collision? }
           ( ( out and OUT_RIGHT ) <> 0 ) then
```

```
            sprites[i].deltax[page] := -sprites[i].deltax[page];
      end;
    page := (page+1) and 1;               { Toggle between 1 and 0 }
  end;

  ch := readkey;                          { Wait for a key }
end;

{******************************************************************
*                  M A I N   P R O G R A M                       *
******************************************************************}

begin
  if ( IsVga ) then                       { VGA card installed? }
    begin                                 { Yes --> Go ahead }
      init320400;                  { Initialize graphic mode }
      Demo;
      Textmode( CO80 );                   { Shift into text mode }
    end
  else
    writeln( 'S3240P.PAS  -  (c) 1992 by Michael Tischer'#13#10#10 +
             'This program requires a VGA card'#13#10 );
end.
```

Assembler listing: S3240PA.ASM

```
;***************************************************************;
;*                    S 3 2 4 0 P A . A S M                   *;
;*-----------------------------------------------------------*;
;*   Task        : Contains routines for generating sprites in *;
;*                 320x400 256 color mode on a VGA card.       *;
;*-----------------------------------------------------------*;
;*   Author      : Michael Tischer                            *;
;*   Developed on : 09/08/90                                   *;
;*   Last update  : 02/26/92                                   *;
;*-----------------------------------------------------------*;
;*   Assembly     : MASM /mx S3240PA;   or   TASM -mx S3240PA *;
;*                  ... link to S3240P.PAS                     *;
;***************************************************************;


;== Constants ===============================================

SC_INDEX     = 3c4h        ;Index register for sequencer ctrl.
SC_MAP_MASK  = 2           ;Number of map mask register
SC_MEM_MODE  = 4           ;Number of memory mode register

GC_INDEX     = 3ceh        ;Index register for graphics ctrl.
GC_READ_MAP  = 4           ;Number of read map register

PIXX         = 320         ;Horizontal resolution

;== Data segment ============================================

DATA    segment word public

DATA    ends

;== Program =================================================

CODE    segment byte public      ;Program segment

        assume cs:code, ds:data

;-- Public declarations ------------------------------------

public    copybuf2plane
public    copyplane2buf


;-----------------------------------------------------------
;-- CopyBuf2Plane: Copies buffer contents to rectangular bitplane range
;-- Call from TP : CopyBuf2Plane( bufptr   : pointer;
;--                               topage   : byte;
;--                               tox,
;--                               toy      : integer;
;--                               rwidth,
;--                               rheight  : byte;
;--                               bg       : bool );

copybuf2plane proc near

sfr0      struc          ;Structure for stack access
bp0       dw ?           ;Gets BP
ret_adr0  dw ?           ;Return address from caller
bg        dw ?           ;Background
rheight0  dw ?           ;Range height
rwidth0   dw ?           ;Range width
toy       dw ?           ;To Y-coordinate
tox       dw ?           ;To X-coordinate
```

```
topage    dw ?              ;To page
bufptr0   dd ?              ;Buffer pointer
sfr0      ends              ;End structure

fr        equ [ bp - bp0 ]       ;Addr. of structure elements
bfr       equ byte ptr [ bp - bp0 ] ;Addr. of stack elements as bytes

          push bp              ;Prepare BP register for
          mov  bp,sp           ;addressing parameters

          push ds
          cld                  ;Increment on string instructions

;-- Compute segment address for video RAM access -----

          mov  ah,0A0h         ;Move ES to start of T0 page
          cmp  bfr.topage,0    ;Page 0?
          je   cv0             ;Yes --> AL is O.K.

          mov  ah,0A8h         ;No --> Page 1 from A800H

cv0:      xor  al,al           ;Low byte always null
          mov  es,ax

;-- Compute offset for target position in page -------

          mov  ax,PIXX / 4     ;Move DI to target of T0 page
          mul  fr.toy
          mov  di,fr.tox
          mov  cx,di           ;Store X-coordinate for plane range
          shr  di,1
          shr  di,1
          add  di,ax

;-- Configure bitplane to be addressed ---------------

          mov  ah,1            ;Configure plane number
          and  cl,3            ;as a bit mask
          shl  ah,cl
          mov  dx,SC_INDEX     ;Store access to bitplane
          mov  al,SC_MAP_MASK  ; to be processed
          out  dx,ax

;-- Load copy loop counter --------------------------

          mov  dh,bfr.rheight0 ;DH = Rows
          mov  dl,bfr.rwidth0  ;DL = Bytes
          mov  bx,PIXX / 4     ;BX as offset to next row
          sub  bl,dl
          xor  ch,ch           ;Counter high byte is always 0

          lds  si,fr.bufptr0   ;Set DS:SI to buffer

          cmp  bfr.bg,0        ;Ignore background?
          jne  cv2             ;Yes --> Alternate copy routine

          ;-- Copy routine for bitplane, without background support --

cv1:      mov  cl,dl           ;Number of bytes to CL

          rep  movsb           ;Copy row
          add  di,bx           ;Add DI to next row
          dec  dh              ;One row remaining?
          jne  cv1             ;Yes --> Continue
```

```
              jmp    short cvend    ;No --> Copy entire buffer

              ;-- Copy routine for individual bitplanes using buffer

cv2:          mov    cl,dl          ;Number of bytes to CL

cv3:          lodsb                 ;Load byte from buffer
              cmp    al,255         ;Background byte?
              je     cv5            ;Yes --> Exclude from copy
              stosb                 ;No --> Place in video RAM
              loop   cv3            ;Process next page

cv4:          ;-- Switch video RAM pointer to next row ------------------

              add    di,bx          ;Add DI to next row
              dec    dh             ;One row remaining?
              jne    cv2            ;Yes --> Continue
              jmp    short cvend    ;No --> Copy entire buffer

cv5:          ;-- Background byte, do not include in copy ---------------

              inc    di             ;This byte not described in video RAM
              loop   cv3            ;Byte remaining in this row?
              jmp    cv4            ;No --> Process next row

cvend:        pop    ds
              pop    bp

              ret    16             ;Return to caller, remove
                                    ;parameters from stack
copybuf2plane endp

;-------------------------------------------------------------------
;-- CopyPlane2Buf: Copies rectangular bitplane range to a buffer
;-- Call from C : CopyPlane2Buf( bufptr  : pointer;
;--                              frompage : byte;
;--                              fromx,
;--                              fromy    : integer;
;--                              rwidth,
;--                              rheight  : byte );

copyplane2buf proc near

sfr1      struc                 ;Structure for stack access
bp1       dw ?                  ;Gets BP
ret_adr1  dw ?                  ;Return address from caller
rheight1  dw ?                  ;Range height in pixel rows
rwidth1   dw ?                  ;Range width in pixels
fromy     dw ?                  ;From Y-coordinate
fromx     dw ?                  ;From X-coordinate
frompage  dw ?                  ;From page
bufptr1   dd ?                  ;Buffer pointer
sfr1      ends                  ;End structure

fr        equ [ bp - bp1 ]      ;Addr. of structure elements
bfr       equ byte ptr [ bp - bp1 ] ;Addr. of stack elements as bytes

          push   bp             ;Prepare BP register for
          mov    bp,sp          ;parameter addressing

          push   ds

          ;-- Compute segment address for video RAM access -----
```

```
              mov    ah,0A0h        ;Move ES to start of FROM page
              cmp    bfr.frompage,0 ;Page 0?
              je     cc0            ;Yes --> AL is O.K.

              mov    ah,0A8h        ;No --> Page 1 from A800H

cc0:          xor    al,al          ;Low byte always null
              mov    ds,ax

              ;-- Compute offset of page to be read ----------------

              mov    ax,PIXX / 4    ;Move SI to target of FROM
              mul    fr.fromy
              mov    si,fr.fromx
              mov    cx,si          ;Move coordinates to CX
              shr    si,1
              shr    si,1
              add    si,ax

              ;-- Configure bitplane to be addressed ---------------

              and    cl,3           ;Compute bit mask for map to be
              mov    ah,cl          ;addressed in AH
              mov    al,GC_READ_MAP ;Move AL to register number
              mov    dx,GC_INDEX    ;Load index to graphics controller
              out    dx,ax          ;Load read map register

              ;-- Load copy loop counter ---------------------------

              mov    dh,bfr.rheight1 ;DH = Rows
              mov    dl,bfr.rwidth1  ;DL = Bytes
              mov    bx,PIXX / 4     ;BX as offset to next row
              sub    bl,dl
              xor    ch,ch           ;Counter high byte is always 0

              les    di,fr.bufptr1   ;Set ES:DI to buffer

              ;-- Copy routine for bitplane, without background support --

cc1:          mov    cl,dl          ;Number of bytes to CL

              rep movsb             ;Copy row
              add    si,bx          ;Add SI to next row
              dec    dh             ;One row remaining?
              jne    cc1            ;Yes --> Continue

              pop    ds
              pop    bp

              ret    14

copyplane2buf endp

;== End ==========================================================

CODE      ends                  ;End code segment
          end                   ;End program
```

C listing: S3240C.C

```
/***************************************************************
*                      S 3 2 4 0 C . C                         *
**-----------------------------------------------------------**
* Task          : Demonstrates sprites in 320x400 VGA graphic  *
*                 mode using 256 colors and two screen pages.  *
*                 This program requires the assembly language  *
*                 modules V3240CA.ASM and S3240CA.ASM.         *
**-----------------------------------------------------------**
* Author        : Michael Tischer                             *
* Developed on   : 09/09/90                                   *
* Last update on : 02/27/92                                   *
**-----------------------------------------------------------**
* Memory model  : SMALL                                       *
**-----------------------------------------------------------**
* (MICROSOFT C)                                               *
* Compilation   : CL /AS /c /W0 s3240c.c                      *
*                 LINK s3240c v3240ca s3240ca;                *
*-----------------------------------------------------------**
* (BORLAND TURBO C)                                           *
* Compilation   : Create a project file containing the following: *
*                 s3240c.c                                     *
*                 v3240ca.obj                                  *
*                 s3240ca.obj                                  *
**-----------------------------------------------------------**
* Call          : s3240c                                      *
***************************************************************/

#include <dos.h>
#include <stdarg.h>
#include <stdio.h>
#include <string.h>
#include <stdlib.h>
#include <conio.h>

/*-- Compiler dependent declarations -------------------------------*/

#ifdef __TURBOC__
  #include <alloc.h>
#else
  #include <malloc.h>
  #define random(x) ( rand() % (x+1) )      /* Random function */
#endif

/*-- Type declarations ---------------------------------------*/

typedef unsigned char BYTE;
typedef BYTE BOOL;

typedef struct {        /* Pixel buffer for GetVideo() and PutVideo() */
          BYTE *bitptr[4],     /* Pointer to bitplanes */
               byprod[4],      /* Number of bytes to be copied */
               rhght;          /* Number of rows */
          /*-- Here follow bytes from the bitplanes -----------*/
        } PIXBUF;
typedef PIXBUF *PIXPTR;        /* Pointer to a pixel buffer */

typedef struct {                     /* Sprite design */
          BYTE   twidth,             /* Total width */
                 theight;            /* Height in pixel lines */
          PIXPTR pixbp;              /* Pointer to pixel block */
        } SPLOOK;
```

```
typedef struct {                    /* Sprite descriptor (ID) */
          SPLOOK *splookp;          /* Pointer to sprite design */
          int    x[2], y[2];        /* Coordinates: pp 0&1 */
          PIXPTR hgptr[2];          /* Pointer to background buffer */
        } SPID;

/*-- External references to assembler routines ----------------------*/

extern void init320400( void );
extern void setpix( int x, int y, unsigned char pcolor);
extern BYTE getpix( int x, int y );
extern void setpage( BYTE page );
extern void showpage( BYTE page );
extern void far * getfontptr( void );

extern void copybuf2plane( BYTE *bufptr, BYTE page,
                           int tox, int toy, BYTE rwidth,
                           BYTE rheight, BOOL bg );
extern void copyplane2buf( BYTE *bufptr, BYTE page,
                           int fromx, int fromy, BYTE rwidth,
                           BYTE rheight );

/*-- Constants ------------------------------------------------*/

#define TRUE  ( 0 == 0 )
#define FALSE ( 0 == 1 )

#define MAXX 319                     /* Maximum X- and Y-coordinates */
#define MAXY 399

#define OUT_LEFT   1    /* For collision documentation in SpriteMove() */
#define OUT_TOP    2
#define OUT_RIGHT  4
#define OUT_BOTTOM 8
#define OUT_NO     0                                    /* None */

#define ALLOCBUF ((PIXPTR) 0)       /* GetVideo(): Allocate buffer */

/***************************************************************
* IsVga : Determines whether a VGA card is installed.         *
**-----------------------------------------------------------**
* Input  :  None                                              *
* Output :  0 if no VGA card exists, otherwise <> 0           *
***************************************************************/

BYTE IsVga( void )
{
 union REGS Regs;        /* Processor registers for interrupt call */

 Regs.x.ax = 0x1a00;                 /* Function 1AH applies to VGA only */
 int86( 0x10, &Regs, &Regs );
 return (BYTE) ( Regs.h.al == 0x1a ); /* Is the function available? */
}

/***************************************************************
* Line: Draws a line based on the Bresenham algorithm.        *
**-----------------------------------------------------------**
* Input   : X1, Y1 = Starting coordinates (0 - ...)           *
*           X2, Y2 = Ending coordinates                       *
*           LPCOL  = Color of line pixels                     *
***************************************************************/

/*-- Function for swapping two integer variables --------------------*/
```

```
void SwapInt( int *i1, int *i2 )
{
 int dummy;

 dummy = *i2;
 *i2  = *i1;
 *i1  = dummy;
}


/*-- Main function -------------------------------------------------*/

void Line( int x1, int y1, int x2, int y2, BYTE lpcol )
{
 int d, dx, dy,
    aincr, bincr,
    xincr, yincr,
    x, y;

 if ( abs(x2-x1) < abs(y2-y1) )        /* X- or Y-axis overflow? */
  {                                    /* Check Y-axes */
   if ( y1 > y2 )                      /* y1 > y2? */
    {
     SwapInt( &x1, &x2 );              /* Yes --> Swap X1 with X2 */
     SwapInt( &y1, &y2 );             /*         and Y1 with Y2  */
    }

   xincr = ( x2 > x1 ) ? 1 : -1;       /* Set X-axis increment */

   dy = y2 - y1;
   dx = abs( x2-x1 );
   d  = 2 * dx - dy;
   aincr = 2 * (dx - dy);
   bincr = 2 * dx;
   x = x1;
   y = y1;

   setpix( x, y, lpcol );                      /* Set first pixel */
   for (y=y1+1; y<= y2; ++y )         /* Execute line on Y-axes */
    {
     if ( d >= 0 )
      {
       x += xincr;
       d += aincr;
      }
     else
       d += bincr;
      setpix(x, y, lpcol);
    }
  }
 else                                  /* Check X-axes */
  {
   if ( x1 > x2 )                      /* x1 > x2? */
    {
     SwapInt( &x1, &x2 );             /* Yes --> Swap X1 with X2 */
     SwapInt( &y1, &y2 );             /*         and Y1 with Y2  */
    }

   yincr = ( y2 > y1 ) ? 1 : -1;      /* Set X-axis increment */

   dx = x2 - x1;
   dy = abs( y2-y1 );
   d  = 2 * dy - dx;
   aincr = 2 * (dy - dx);
   bincr = 2 * dy;
```

```
   x = x1;
   y = y1;

   setpix(x, y, lpcol);                         /* Set first pixel */
   for (x=x1+1; x<=x2; ++x )           /* Execute line on X-axes */
    {
     if ( d >= 0 )
      {
       y += yincr;
       d += aincr;
      }
     else
       d += bincr;
      setpix(x, y, lpcol);
    }
  }
}


/**********************************************************************
* PrintChar : Writes a character to the screen while in graphic mode.*
**--------------------------------------------------------------------**
* Input   :   THECHAR = Character to be written                      *
*             x, y    = X- and Y-coordinates of upper-left corner    *
*             FG      = Foreground color                             *
*             BK      = Background color                             *
* Info    : Character is created in an 8x8 matrix, based on the      *
*             8x8 ROM font.                                          *
**********************************************************************/

void PrintChar( char thechar, int x, int y, BYTE fg, BYTE bk )
{
 typedef BYTE FDEF[256][8];                       /* Font array */
 typedef FDEF far *TPTR;                          /* Pointer to font */

 BYTE      i, k,                                  /* Loop counter */
           BMask;               /* Bit mask for character design */

 static TPTR fptr = (TPTR) 0;             /* Pointer to font in ROM */

 if ( fptr == (TPTR) 0 )          /* Pointer to font already set? */
   fptr = getfontptr();   /* No --> Use the assembler function to load */

 /*- Generate character pixel by pixel -------------------------------*/

 if ( bk == 255 )                /* Drawing transparent characters? */
  for ( i = 0; i < 8; ++i )      /* Yes --> Set foreground pixels only */
   {
    BMask = (*fptr)[thechar][i];      /* Get bit pattern for one line */
    for ( k = 0; k < 8; ++k, BMask <<= 1 )       /* Execute columns */
     if ( BMask & 128 )                          /* Pixel set? */
       setpix( x+k, y+i, fg );                   /* Yes */
   }
 else                            /* No --> Consider background */
  for ( i = 0; i < 8; ++i )                    /* Execute lines */
   {
    BMask = (*fptr)[thechar][i];      /* Get bit pattern for one line */
    for ( k = 0; k < 8; ++k, BMask <<= 1 )       /* Execute columns */
     setpix( x+k, y+i, ( BMask & 128 ) ? fg : bk );
   }
}


/**********************************************************************
* GrfxPrintf: Displays a formatted string on the graphic screen.    *
* Input    : X, Y  = Starting coordinates (0 - ...)                 *
```

```
*       FG     = Foreground color              *
*       BK     = Background color (255 = transparent)  *
*       STRING = String with format information  *
*       ...    = Arguments similar to printf     *
*********************************************************/

void GrfxPrintf( int x, int y, BYTE fg, BYTE bk, char * string, ... )
{
  va_list parameter;            /* Parameter list for VA_... macros */
  char stngbuf[255],            /* Buffer for formatted string */
       *cp;

  va_start( parameter, string );         /* Convert parameter */
  vsprintf( stngbuf, string, parameter );      /* Format */
  for ( cp = stngbuf; *cp; ++cp, x+= 8 )  /* Formatted string */
    PrintChar( *cp, x, y, fg, bk );   /* Display using PrintChar */
}


/***********************************************************
* GetVideo: Places contents of a rectangular range of video RAM  *
*           in a buffer.                                  *
**-------------------------------------------------------**
* Input  : PAGE   = Screen page (0 or 1)                  *
*          X1, Y1 = Starting coordinates                  *
*          WRANGE = Width of rectangular range in pixels  *
*          HRANGE = Height of rectangular range in pixels *
*          BUFPTR = Pointer to pixel buffer into which    *
*                   information should be allocated       *
* Output : Pointer to allocated pixel buffer with contents of *
*          specified range                               *
* Info   : If the BUFPTR parameter contains nothing, a new pixel *
*          buffer is allocated and returned on the heap. This buffer* 
*          can be re-created on each call, provided the previous *
*          contents are no longer needed, and provided the size *
*          of the rectangular range remains unchanged.    *
***********************************************************/

PIXPTR GetVideo( BYTE page, int x1, int y1, BYTE wrange, BYTE hrange,
                 PIXPTR bufptr )
{
  BYTE i,                       /* Loop counter */
       curplane,                /* Currently processed bitplane */
       sb,                      /* Bitplane at starting coordinates */
       eb,                      /* Bitplane at ending coordinates */
       b,                       /* Number of bytes per bitplane */
       am;          /* Number of bytes in center of both groups of four */
  BYTE *rptr;                   /* Pointer for bitplane position in buffer */

  if ( bufptr == ALLOCBUF )              /* No buffer passed on call? */
    bufptr = malloc( sizeof( PIXBUF ) + wrange*hrange ); /* No-> Alloc */

  /*-- Compute number of bytes per bitplane -----------------*/

  am = (BYTE) ( ( (x1+wrange-1) & ~3 ) - /* Number of bytes in center */
                ( (x1+4) & ~3 ) ) >> 2;
  sb = (BYTE) (x1 % 4);                /* Starting bitplane */
  eb = (BYTE) ((x1+wrange-1) % 4);         /* Ending bitplane */

  rptr = (BYTE *) bufptr + sizeof( PIXBUF );

  /*-- Execute four bitplanes -----------------------------*/

  for ( i=0; i<4; ++i )
  {
```

```
    curplane = (sb+i) % 4;
    b = am;                      /* Base number of bytes to be copied */
    if ( curplane >= sb )          /* Also in starting block of four? */
      ++b;                       /* Yes --> Add a byte to this bitplane */
    if ( curplane <= eb )          /* Also in ending block of four? */
      ++b;                       /* Yes --> Add a byte to this bitplane */
    bufptr->bitptr[i] = rptr;    /* Place pointer at start of buffer */
    bufptr->byprod[i] = b;            /* Place number in buffer */
    copyplane2buf( rptr, page, x1+1,           /* Get contents */
                   y1, b, hrange );            /* of bitplane */
    rptr += (b * hrange);                    /* Set pointer to next */
  };                                         /* bitplane in buffer */

  bufptr->rhght = hrange;                      /* Store height */

  return bufptr;                    /* Return buffer pointer to caller */
}


/***********************************************************
* PutVideo: Writes contents of a rectangular screen range generated *
*           by GetVideo to video RAM.                    *
**-------------------------------------------------------**
* Input  : BUFPTR = Pointer to pixel buffer from GetVideo *
*          PAGE   = Screen page (0 or 1)                  *
*          X1, Y1 = Starting coordinates                  *
*          BG     = Should background pixels (color code 255) not *
*                   be written to video RAM              *
* Info   : Pixel buffer is not cleared by this procedure; use the *
*          FreePixBuf for this purpose.                  *
***********************************************************/

void PutVideo( PIXPTR bufptr, BYTE page, int x1, int y1, BOOL bg )
{
  BYTE curplane,                /* Currently executed bitplane */
       hrange;

  hrange = bufptr->rhght;                  /* Range height */
  for ( curplane=0; curplane<4; ++curplane )/* Execute four bitplanes */
    copybuf2plane( bufptr->bitptr[curplane], page, x1+curplane,
                   y1, bufptr->byprod[curplane], hrange, bg );
}


/***********************************************************
* FreePixBuf: Clears a pixel buffer previously allocated by Heap. *
**-------------------------------------------------------**
* Input  : BUFPTR = Pointer to pixel buffer              *
***********************************************************/

void FreePixBuf( PIXPTR bufptr )
{
  free( bufptr );
}


/***********************************************************
* CreateSprite: Creates a sprite based on a user-defined *
*               pixel pattern.                           *
**-------------------------------------------------------**
* Input  : SPLOOKP = Pointer to data structure from CompileSprite *
* Output : Pointer to created sprite structure           *
***********************************************************/

SPID *CreateSprite( SPLOOK *splookp )
{
  SPID *spidp;               /* Pointer to created sprite structure */
```

```
spidp = (SPID *) malloc( sizeof(SPID) ); /* Allocate spr. structure */
spidp->splookp = splookp;                    /* Pass data to the */
                                             /* sprite structure */


/*- Create two background buffers, for storing range from video RAM -*/

spidp->hgptr[0] = GetVideo( 0, 0, 0, splookp->twidth,
                            splookp->theight, ALLOCBUF );
spidp->hgptr[1] = GetVideo( 0, 0, 0, splookp->twidth,
                            splookp->theight, ALLOCBUF );
return spidp;             /* Return pointer to sprite structure */
}


/**********************************************************************
* CompileSprite: Creates a sprite's pixel and bit patterns, based on *
*                the sprite's definition at runtime.                 *
**------------------------------------------------------------------**
* Input    : BUFP    = Pointer to array containing string pointers   *
*                      controlling sprite's pattern                  *
*            SHEIGHT = Sprite height (and number of strings needed)  *
*            GPAGE   = Graphic page for sprite design                *
*            FB      = ASCII character for the smallest color        *
*            FGCOLOR = First color code for FB                       *
* Info     : Sprite structure of pixel lines starts at left margin.  *
**********************************************************************/

SPLOOK *CompileSprite( char **bufp, BYTE sheight, BYTE gpage,
                       char fb, BYTE fgcolor )
{
BYTE    swidth,                        /* String width */
        c,                  /* Get character from c sprite array */
        i, k;               /* Loop variables */
SPLOOK *splookp;            /* Pointer to create sprite structure */
PIXPTR  pbptr;             /* Get temporary sprite background */

/*-- Create SpriteLook structure and fill with data ----------------*/

splookp = (SPLOOK *) malloc( sizeof(SPLOOK) );
swidth = (BYTE) strlen( *bufp );
splookp->twidth = swidth;
splookp->theight = sheight;

/*-- Place sprite in page at 0/0 -----------------------------------*/

setpage( gpage );                      /* Set page for drawing */
showpage( gpage );
pbptr = GetVideo( gpage, 0, 0, swidth, sheight, ALLOCBUF );/* Bkgd. */

for (i = 0; i < sheight; ++i )                /* Execute rows */
  for ( k = 0; k < swidth; ++k )             /* Execute columns */
    {
    c = *(*(bufp+i)+k);
    setpix( k, i, (BYTE) (c == ' ' ? 255 : fgcolor+(c-fb)));
    }

/*-- Get sprite in buffer and restore background --------------------*/

splookp->pixbp = GetVideo( gpage, 0, 0, swidth, sheight, ALLOCBUF );
PutVideo( pbptr, gpage, 0, 0, FALSE );
FreePixBuf( pbptr );                     /* Free buffer */

return splookp;             /* Return pointer to sprite buffer */
}
```

```
/**********************************************************************
* PrintSprite : Displays sprite in a specified page.                 *
**------------------------------------------------------------------**
* Input   : SPIDP   = Pointer to the sprite structure                *
*           SPRPAGE = Page in which sprite should be drawn (0 or 1)   *
**********************************************************************/

void PrintSprite( register SPID *spidp, BYTE sprpage )
{
 PutVideo( spidp->splookp->pixbp,
           sprpage, spidp->x[sprpage], spidp->y[sprpage], TRUE );
}


/**********************************************************************
* GetSpriteBg: Gets a sprite background and specifies the position.  *
**------------------------------------------------------------------**
* Input   : SPIDP   = Pointer to the sprite structure                *
*           SPRPAGE = Page from which the background should be taken  *
*                     (0 or 1)                                        *
**********************************************************************/

void GetSpriteBg( register SPID *spidp, BYTE sprpage )
{
 GetVideo( sprpage, spidp->x[sprpage],  spidp->y[sprpage],
           spidp->splookp->twidth, spidp->splookp->theight,
           spidp->hgptr[sprpage] );
}


/**********************************************************************
* RestoreSpriteBg: Restores sprite background from original graphic  *
*                  page.                                             *
**------------------------------------------------------------------**
* Input   : SPIDP   =  Pointer to the sprite structure               *
*           SPRPAGE = Page from which background should be copied     *
*                     (0 or 1)                                        *
**********************************************************************/

void RestoreSpriteBg( register SPID *spidp, BYTE sprpage )
{
 PutVideo( spidp->hgptr[sprpage], sprpage,
           spidp->x[sprpage], spidp->y[sprpage], FALSE );
}


/**********************************************************************
* MoveSprite: Copy sprite within background to original graphic page.*
**------------------------------------------------------------------**
* Input   : SPIDP   = Pointer to the sprite structure                *
*           SPRPAGE = Page to which the background should be copied   *
*                     (0 or 1)                                        *
*           DELTAX  = Movement counter in X-                         *
*           DELTAY    and Y-directions                               *
* Output  : Collision marker (see OUT_ constants)                    *
**********************************************************************/

BYTE MoveSprite( SPID *spidp, BYTE sprpage, int deltax, int deltay )
{
int newx, newy;                        /* New sprite coordinates */
BYTE out;                              /* Display collision with border */

/*-- Move X-coordinates and test for border collision --------------*/

if ( ( newx = spidp->x[sprpage] + deltax ) < 0 )
  {
```

```
    newx = 0 - deltax - spidp->x[sprpage];
    out = OUT_LEFT;
    }
else
  if ( newx > MAXX - spidp->splookp->twidth )
    {
    newx = (2*(MAXX+1))-newx-2*(spidp->splookp->twidth);
    out = OUT_RIGHT;
    }
  else
    out = OUT_NO;


/*-- Move Y-coordinates and test for border collision --------------*/

if ( ( newy = spidp->y[sprpage] + deltay ) < 0 )     /* Top border? */
  {                                        /* Yes --> Deltay must be negative */
  newy = 0 - deltay - spidp->y[sprpage];
  out |= OUT_TOP;
  }
else
  if ( newy + spidp->splookp->theight > MAXY+1 )          /* Bottom? */
    {                                  /* Yes --> Deltay must be positive */
    newy = (2*(MAXY+1))-newy-2*(spidp->splookp->theight);
    out |= OUT_BOTTOM;
    }


/*-- Set new position only if different from old position ----------*/

if ( newx != spidp->x[sprpage] || newy != spidp->y[sprpage] )
  {                                     /* If there's a new position */
  RestoreSpriteBg( spidp, sprpage );   /* reset background and store */
  spidp->x[sprpage] = newx;            /* new coordinates            */
  spidp->y[sprpage] = newy;
  GetSpriteBg( spidp, sprpage );            /* Get new background */
  PrintSprite( spidp, sprpage );     /* Draw sprite in specified page */
  }
return out;
}


/*******************************************************************
* SetSprite: Sets sprite at a specific position.                  *
**-------------------------------------------------------------**
* Input  : SPIDP = Pointer to the sprite structure               *
*          x0, y0 = Sprite coordinates for page 0                 *
*          x1, y1 = Sprite coordinates for page 1                 *
* Info   : This function call should be made the first time that  *
*          MoveSprite() is called.                                *
*******************************************************************/

void SetSprite( SPID *spidp, int x0, int y0, int x1, int y1 )
{
  spidp->x[0] = x0;          /* Store coordinates in sprite structure */
  spidp->x[1] = x1;
  spidp->y[0] = y0;
  spidp->y[1] = y1;

  GetSpriteBg( spidp, 0 );           /* Get sprite backgrounds */
  GetSpriteBg( spidp, 1 );           /* in pages 0 and 1       */
  PrintSprite( spidp, 0 );                /* Draw sprite in */
  PrintSprite( spidp, 1 );                /* pages 0 and 1  */
}


/*******************************************************************
* RemoveSprite: Removes a sprite from its current position and makes *
```

```
*            it invisible.                                        *
**------------------------------------------------------------**
* Input  : SPIDP = Pointer to the sprite structure               *
* Info   : After calling this function the SetSprite() function  *
*          must be called before the sprite can be moved using the *
*          MoveSprite() function.                                 *
*******************************************************************/

void RemoveSprite( SPID *spidp )
{
  RestoreSpriteBg( spidp, 0 );          /* Reset sprite backgrounds */
  RestoreSpriteBg( spidp, 1 );          /* in pages 0 and 1         */
}


/*******************************************************************
* Demo: Demonstrates these functions.                            *
*******************************************************************/

void Demo( void )
{
  static char *StarShipUp[20] =
    { "               AA               ",
      "              AAAA              ",
      "              AAAA              ",
      "               AA               ",
      "             GGBBGG             ",
      "            GBBCCBBG            ",
      "           GBBBCCBBBG           ",
      "           GBBBBBBBBBG          ",
      "           GBBBBBBBBBG          ",
      " G         GBBBBBBBBBBBG       G ",
      "GCG       GGDBBBBBBBBBBDGG    GCG",
      "GCG     GGBBBBDBBB  BBBDBBBGG GCG",
      "GCBGGGBBBBBBBBDBB   BBDBBBBBGGBCG",
      "GCBBBBBBBBBBBBDB   BDBBBBBBBBBBCG",
      "BBBBBBBBBBBBBDB BB BDBBBBBBBBBBBB",
      "GGCBBBBBBBBBBDBBBBBBBBBBBDBBBBBBCG",
      "  GGCCBBBDDDDDDDDDDDDDDDBBBCCG   ",
      "  GGBBDDDDGGGGGDDDDDDBBG         ",
      "  GDDDDGG       GGGDDDDG         ",
      "   DDDD           DDDD          " };


  static char *StarShipDown[20] =
    {
      "   DDDD           DDDD          ",
      "  GDDDDGG       GGGDDDDG         ",
      "  GGBBDDDDDGGGGGGDDDDDDDBBG      ",
      "  GGCCBBBDDDDDDDDDDDDDDDDBBBCCG  ",
      "GGCBBBBBBBBDBBBBBBBBBBBDBBBBBBCG ",
      "BBBBBBBBBBBBBDB BB BDBBBBBBBBBBBB",
      "GCBBBBBBBBBBDB   BDBBBBBBBBBBCG",
      "GCBGGGBBBBBBDBB   BBDBBBBBGGBCG",
      "GCG     GGBBBDBBB  BBBDBBBBGG GCG",
      "GCG       GGDBBBBBBBBBBDGG    GCG",
      " G         GBBBBBBBBBBBG       G ",
      "           GBBBBBBBBBBBG          ",
      "           GBBBBBBBBBBBG          ",
      "           GBBBCCBBBG           ",
      "            GBBCCBBG            ",
      "             GGBBGG             ",
      "               AA               ",
      "              AAAA              ",
      "              AAAA              ",
```

```
                    "            AA            "  );

#define SPRNUM 6                              /* Number of sprites */
#define CWIDTH 38            /* Width of copyright message in characters */
#define CHEIGHT 6                            /* Message height in rows */
#define SX      (MAXX-(CWIDTH*8)) / 2         /* Starting X-coordinate */
#define SY      (MAXY-(CHEIGHT*8)) / 2        /* Starting Y-coordinate */

struct {                                  /* For sprite management */
        SPID *spidp;                       /* Pointer to sprite ID */
        int deltax[2],                     /* X-movement for pages 0 and 1 */
            deltay[2];                     /* Y-movement for pages 0 and 1 */
        } sprites[ SPRNUM ];
BYTE  page,                                /* Current page */
      out;                          /* Get flags for page collision */
int   x, y, i,                             /* Loop counter */
      dx, dy;                              /* Movement value */
char  lc;
SPLOOK *starshipupp, *starshipdnp;         /* Sprite pointer */

srand( *(int far *) 0x0040006cl );     /* Initialize random numbers */

/*-- Create patterns for the different sprites ---------------------*/

starshipupp = CompileSprite( StarShipUp,   20, 0, 'A', 1 );
starshipdnp = CompileSprite( StarShipDown, 20, 40, 'A', 1 );

/*-- Fill the first two graphic pages with characters --------------*/

for ( page = 0; page < 2; ++ page )
  {
  setpage( page );
  for ( lc = 0, y = 0; y < (MAXY+1)-8; y += 12 )
    for ( x = 0; x < (MAXX+1)-8; x += 8 )
      GrfxPrintf( x, y, lc % 255, 255, "%c", lc++ & 127 );

  /*-- Display copyright message -----------------------------------*/

  Line( SX-1, SY-1, SX+CWIDTH*8, SY-1, 15 );
  Line( SX+CWIDTH*8, SY-1, SX+CWIDTH*8, SY+CHEIGHT*8,15 );
  Line( SX+CWIDTH*8, SY+CHEIGHT*8, SX-1, SY+CHEIGHT*8, 15 );
  Line( SX-1, SY+CHEIGHT*8, SX-1, SY-1, 15 );
  GrfxPrintf( SX, SY,     15, 4,
                "                                    "  );
  GrfxPrintf( SX, SY+8,   15, 4,
                " S3240C.C (c) 1992 by Michael Tischer "  );
  GrfxPrintf( SX, SY+16,  15, 4,
                "                                    "  );
  GrfxPrintf( SX, SY+24,  15, 4,
                "     Sprite demo for 320x400 mode    "  );
  GrfxPrintf( SX, SY+32,  15, 4,
                "            on VGA cards             "  );
  GrfxPrintf( SX, SY+40,  15, 4,
                "                                    "  );
  }

/*-- Create different sprites --------------------------------------*/

for ( i = 0; i < SPRNUM ; ++ i )
  {
  sprites[ i ].spidp = CreateSprite( starshipupp );
  do                            /* Select movement value for sprites */
    {
    dx = 0;
```

```
    dy = random(8) - 4;
    }
  while ( dx==0  &&  dy==0 );

  sprites[ i ].deltax[0] = sprites[ i ].deltax[1] = dx * 2;
  sprites[ i ].deltay[0] = sprites[ i ].deltay[1] = dy * 2;

  x = ( 320 / SPRNUM * i ) + (320 / SPRNUM - 40) / 2 ;
  y = random( (MAXY+1) - 40 );
  SetSprite( sprites[ i ].spidp, x, y, x - dx, y - dy );
  }

/*-- Move sprites and bounce them off the page borders -------------*/

page = 1;                                   /* Start with page 1 */
while ( !kbhit() )               /* Press a key to end the loop */
  {
  showpage( (BYTE) (1 - page) );         /* Display other page */

  for ( i = 0; i < SPRNUM; ++ i )            /* Execute sprites */
    {                    /* Move sprite and check for page collision */
    out = MoveSprite( sprites[i].spidp, page, sprites[i].deltax[page],
                      sprites[i].deltay[page] );
    if ( out & OUT_TOP  ||  out & OUT_BOTTOM )    /* Top/bottom */
                                                 /* collision? */
      {  /* Yes --> Change direction of movement and sprite graphic */
      sprites[i].deltay[page] = 0 - sprites[i].deltay[page];
      sprites[i].spidp->splookp = ( out & OUT_TOP ) ? starshipdnp
                                                    : starshipupp;
      }
    if ( out & OUT_LEFT  ||  out & OUT_RIGHT )
      sprites[i].deltax[page] = 0 - sprites[i].deltax[page];
    }
  page = (page+1) & 1;                  /* Toggle between 1 and 0 */
  }
}

/*********************************************************************/
/***                 M A I N   P R O G R A M              ***/
/*********************************************************************/

void main( void )
{
union REGS regs;

if ( IsVga() )                           /* VGA card installed? */
  {                                      /* Yes --> Go ahead */
  init320400();                          /* Initialize graphic mode */
  Demo();
  getch();                               /* Wait for a key */
  regs.x.ax = 0x0003;                    /* Shift into text mode */
  int86( 0x10, &regs, &regs );
  }
else
  printf( "S3240C.C - (c) 1992 by Michael Tischer\n\n "\
          "This program requires a VGA card\n\n" );
}
```

Assembler listing: S3240CA.ASM

```
;*******************************************************************;
;*                  S 3 2 4 0 C A . A S M                        *;
;*---------------------------------------------------------------*;
;*    Task        : Contains routines for generating sprites in  *;
;*                  320x400 256 color mode on a VGA card.         *;
;*---------------------------------------------------------------*;
;*    Author      : Michael Tischer                              *;
;*    Developed on : 09/08/90                                     *;
;*    Last update  : 02/26/92                                     *;
;*---------------------------------------------------------------*;
;*    Assembly     : MASM /mx S3240CA;   or   TASM -mx S3240CA   *;
;*                   ... link to S3240C.C                         *;
;*******************************************************************;

IGROUP group _text               ;Program segment
DGROUP group const, _bss, _data  ;Data segment
       assume CS:IGROUP, DS:DGROUP, ES:DGROUP, SS:DGROUP

CONST  segment word public 'CONST';All readable constants
CONST  ends


_BSS   segment word public 'BSS'  ;All uninitialized static vars.
_BSS   ends


_DATA  segment word public 'DATA' ;All initialized global & static
                                  ;variables
_DATA  ends


; == Constants =============================================

SC_INDEX    = 3c4h             ;Index register for sequencer ctrl.
SC_MAP_MASK = 2                ;Number of map mask register
SC_MEM_MODE = 4                ;Number of memory mode register

GC_INDEX    = 3ceh             ;Index register for graphics ctrl.
GC_READ_MAP = 4                ;Number of read map register

PIXX        = 320             ;Horizontal resolution

; == Program ===============================================

_TEXT  segment byte public 'CODE';Program segment

;-- Public declarations ------------------------------------

public    _copybuf2plane
public    _copyplane2buf


;----------------------------------------------------------
;-- CopyBuf2Plane: Copies buffer contents to rectangular bitplane range
;-- Call from C  : CopyBuf2Plane( byte *bufptr,
;--                               byte topage,
;--                               int tox,
;--                               int toy,
;--                               byte rwidth,
;--                               byte rheight,
;--                               bool bg );

_copybuf2plane proc near

sfr0        struc             ;Structure for stack access
bp0         dw ?              ;Gets BP
```

```
ret_adr0    dw ?              ;Return address from caller
bufptr0     dw ?              ;Buffer pointer
topage      dw ?              ;To page
tox         dw ?              ;To X-coordinate
toy         dw ?              ;To Y-coordinate
rwidth0     dw ?              ;Range width
rheight0    dw ?              ;Range height
bg          dw ?              ;Background
sfr0        ends              ;End structure

fr          equ [ bp - bp0 ]      ;Addr. of structure elements
bfr         equ byte ptr [ bp - bp0 ] ;Addr. of stack elements as bytes

            push  bp                ;Prepare BP register for
            mov   bp,sp             ;addressing parameters
            push  di
            push  si

;-- Compute segment address for video RAM access -----------

            mov   ah,0A0h          ;Move ES to start of TO page
            cmp   bfr.topage,0     ;Page 0?
            je    cv0              ;Yes --> AL is O.K.

            mov   ah,0A8h          ;No --> Page 1 from A800H

cv0:        xor   al,al           ;Low byte always null
            mov   es,ax

;-- Compute offset for target position in page -------------

            mov   ax,PIXX / 4     ;Move DI to target of TO page
            mul   fr.toy
            mov   di,fr.tox
            mov   cx,di           ;Store X-coordinate for plane range
            shr   di,1
            shr   di,1
            add   di,ax

;-- Configure bitplane to be addressed ---------------------

            mov   ah,1            ;Configure plane number
            and   cl,3           ;as a bit mask
            shl   ah,cl
            mov   dx,SC_INDEX     ;Store access to bitplane
            mov   al,SC_MAP_MASK  ; to be processed
            out   dx,ax

;-- Load copy loop counter --------------------------------

            mov   dh,bfr.rheight0 ;DH = Rows
            mov   dl,bfr.rwidth0  ;DL = Bytes
            mov   bx,PIXX / 4     ;BX as offset to next row
            sub   bl,dl
            xor   ch,ch          ;Counter high byte is always 0

            mov   si,fr.bufptr0   ;Set DS:SI to buffer

            cmp   bfr.bg,0       ;Ignore background?
            jne   cv2            ;Yes --> Alternate copy routine

;-- Copy routine for bitplane, without background support --

cv1:        mov   cl,dl          ;Number of bytes to CL
```

```
        rep movsb              ;Copy row
        add   di,bx            ;Add DI to next row
        dec   dh              ;One row remaining?
        jne   cv1             ;Yes --> Continue

        jmp   short cvend      ;No --> Copy entire buffer

        ;-- Copy routine for individual bitplanes using buffer -----

cv2:    mov   cl,dl            ;Number of bytes to CL

cv3:    lodsb                  ;Load byte from buffer
        cmp   al,255           ;Background byte?
        je    cv5             ;Yes --> Exclude from copy
        stosb                  ;No --> Place in video RAM
        loop  cv3              ;Process next page

cv4:    ;-- Switch video RAM pointer to next row -------------------

        add   di,bx            ;Add DI to next row
        dec   dh              ;One row remaining?
        jne   cv2             ;Yes --> Continue
        jmp   short cvend      ;No --> Copy entire buffer

cv5:    ;-- Background byte, do not include in copy ----------------

        inc   di               ;This byte not described in video RAM
        loop  cv3              ;Byte remaining in this row?
        jmp   cv4              ;No --> Process next row

cvend:  pop   si
        pop   di
        pop   bp

        ret                    ;Return to caller, remove
                               ;parameters from stack
_copybuf2plane endp

;--------------------------------------------------------------
;-- CopyPlane2Buf: Copies rectangular bitplane range to a buffer
;-- Call from C : CopyPlane2Buf( byte *bufptr,
;--                              byte frompage,
;--                              int fromx,
;--                              int fromy,
;--                              byte rwidth,
;--                              byte rheight );

_copyplane2buf proc near

sfr1    struc                  ;Structure for stack access
bp1     dw ?                   ;Gets BP
ret_adr1 dw ?                  ;Return address from caller
bufptr1 dw ?                   ;Buffer pointer
frompage dw ?                  ;From page
fromx   dw ?                   ;From X-coordinate
fromy   dw ?                   ;From Y-coordinate
rwidth1 dw ?                   ;Range width in pixels
rheight1 dw ?                  ;Range height in pixel rows
sfr1    ends                   ;End structure

fr      equ [ bp - bp1 ]       ;Addr. of structure elements
bfr     equ byte ptr [ bp - bp1 ] ;Addr. of stack elements as bytes
```

```
        push  bp               ;Prepare BP register for
        mov   bp,sp            ;parameter addressing
        push  di
        push  si
        push  ds
        push  ds

        ;-- Compute segment address for video RAM access -----------
        mov   ah,0A0h          ;Move ES to start of FROM page
        cmp   bfr.frompage,0   ;Page 0?
        je    cc0             ;Yes --> AL is O.K.

        mov   ah,0A8h          ;No --> Page 1 from A800H

cc0:    xor   al,al            ;Low byte always null
        mov   ds,ax

        ;-- Compute offset of page to be read ----------------------
        mov   ax,PIXX / 4      ;Move SI to target of FROM
        mul   fr.fromy
        mov   si,fr.fromx
        mov   cx,si            ;Move coordinates to CX
        shr   si,1
        shr   si,1
        add   si,ax

        ;-- Configure bitplane to be addressed ---------------------
        and   cl,3             ;Compute bit mask for map to be
        mov   ah,cl            ;addressed in AH
        mov   al,GC_READ_MAP   ;Move AL to register number
        mov   dx,GC_INDEX      ;Load index to graphics controller
        out   dx,ax            ;Load read map register

        ;-- Load copy loop counter -------------------------------
        mov   dh,bfr.rheight1  ;DH = Rows
        mov   dl,bfr.rwidth1   ;DL = Bytes
        mov   bx,PIXX / 4      ;BX as offset to next row
        sub   bl,dl
        xor   ch,ch            ;Counter high byte is always 0

        pop   es
        mov   di,fr.bufptr1    ;Set ES:DI to buffer

        ;-- Copy routine for bitplane, without background support --
cc1:    mov   cl,dl            ;Number of bytes to CL

        rep movsb              ;Copy row
        add   si,bx            ;Add SI to next row
        dec   dh              ;One row remaining?
        jne   cc1             ;Yes --> Continue

        pop   ds
        pop   si
        pop   di
        pop   bp

        ret

_copyplane2buf endp
;== End ==========================================================
_text   ends                   ;End code segment
        end                    ;End program
```

Sprites in EGA and VGA 640x350 16 color graphics modes

If you'd rather have higher resolution at the expense of fewer colors, then you should use 16 color 640x350 pixel mode. Another advantage of this mode is that it's compatible with both EGA and VGA cards. The 640x480 pixel VGA mode cannot be used for sprite programming because it doesn't allow two screen pages to be stored in video RAM simultaneously.

The 640x350 pixel mode uses only 219K of the available 256K of video RAM for screen page storage. So 38,144 bytes remain; these bytes can be used for more than 76,000 additional pixels in a 640x120 pixel block. This extra video RAM can be used to store sprite descriptions and sprite backgrounds, as we did in the 320x200 pixel mode demonstration programs.

Depending on the number of sprites you define and the number of sprites actually displayed on screen, this extra video RAM can be used up rather quickly. As we'll see later, the main reason for this is that you must maintain eight copies of each sprite description instead of four.

Because of this potential limitation, the sprite demonstration programs in 640x350 pixel mode store their sprite descriptions and sprite backgrounds in conventional RAM. Although this is the same method used in the 320x400 pixel mode, the sprite creation and data transfer routines in these programs are quite different from the 320x400 mode programs.

The main reason for this is that the video RAM is organized in a completely different way for 16 color modes than for 256 color modes. Previously we saw that eight pixels are represented by a single byte in 16 color modes, as opposed to one pixel per byte in 256 color modes. But one bit isn't sufficient for representing a color code between 0 and 15. This is why the video RAM is organized into bitplanes, allowing the group of four corresponding bytes from each bitplane to define the color information for all eight pixels.

Organizing video RAM into bitplanes can make accessing a specific pixel slow and awkward. This affects the routines found in the S6435C.C (C version) and S6435P.PAS (Pascal version) modules, which display sprites on screen in the 640x350 pixel mode.

The sprite widths are rounded to multiples of eight pixels. If you don't do this, you must isolate only those desired bits from the last byte, save them, and then write them back to ensure that only those bits belonging to the sprite are copied. This also applies to programming the map mask register, which is an alternative method for allowing sprites of any width.

This rounding is done internally and is transparent to routines, such as COMPILESPRITE, CREATESPRITE, and MOVESPRITE. The fact that eight copies of the sprite description are kept is also transparent. Eight copies are required because of a problem similar to that found in 320x200 pixel mode.

For example, if the binary coding of a sprite description begins in bit 7 of the first byte, it can be copied only to a screen area with an X-coordinate that is a multiple of eight if you want the description to remain unchanged. If you copy to any screen area that starts at an X-coordinate whose value mod 8 is unequal to zero, you must then shift all bits to the right by a value equal to the result of the mod 8 operation. This would actually take too much time to execute.

351

So, the COMPILESPRITE routine used in S6435C.C and S6435P.PAS creates eight copies of each sprite description, where each copy is shifted one bit to the right. Whenever you must move a sprite to a certain screen position, simply select the copy that matches the desired X-coordinate.

The eight copies of a given sprite description are stored in the form of a pixel buffer. Just as we saw in the 320x400 pixel demonstrations, the sprite description is built in video RAM and then loaded into a pixel buffer with GETVIDEO. Unlike the 320x400 mode, however, this operation is repeated eight times instead of four. This requires much space in conventional RAM.

For example, imagine a sprite consisting of 20x30 pixels, which is a small object for such a high resolution screen mode. After you increase the width by seven pixels and round the width off to make it a multiple of eight, the result is 32 pixels:

```
int( ( 20 + 7 + 7 ) / 8 ) * 8 = 32
```

Each pixel requires four bits, so this sprite requires 16 bytes per pixel line. This amount multiplied by 20 equals 640 bytes for the pixel buffer, not including the status information in PIXBUF. This must be repeated eight times for each sprite description, which increases the number to 5K. When we include the two background buffers required for each sprite, we must add another 1K to the total.

An AND buffer must also be created for each sprite description. This makes the background transparent so the sprite doesn't appear as a rectangular block on the screen. Because of the way video RAM is organized in this mode, this isn't a simple task. It requires a three step process repeated for each byte to write a sprite to video RAM. This process involves loading the byte to be processed, programming the bit mask register to affect only the desired pixels, and finally writing the value.

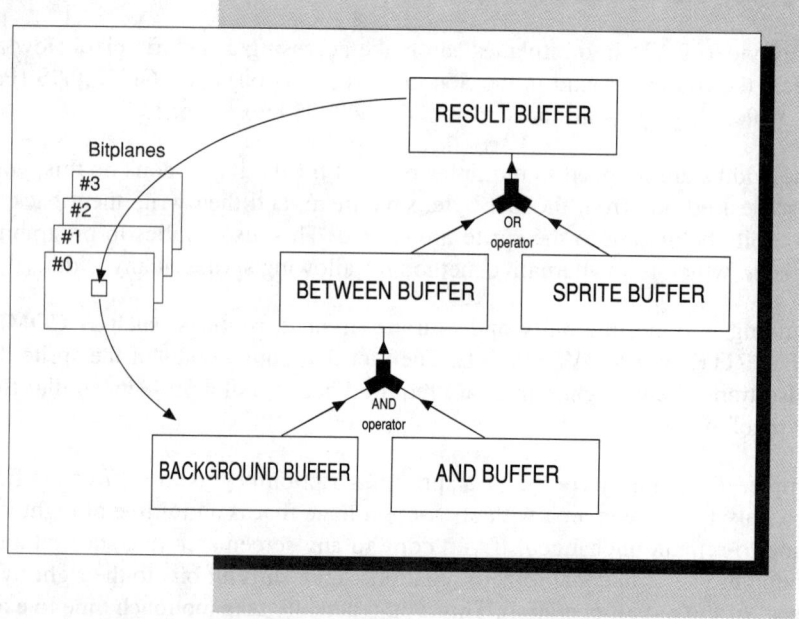

Sprite backgrounds, sprite definition, and the AND buffer

Since the previous process would take too long to execute, you should use another method. Remember that the sprite background is already available before we write the sprite to its new location. This means that we can merge the buffers containing the sprite description and the background information. This creates the desired pattern of background pixels and pixels before we access video RAM. This process results in the bytes that we actually want to write to video RAM, without having to mask certain bits.

This process involves taking the contents of the background buffer and changing only those bits that don't correspond to background pixels in the sprite description. This leaves the background pixels undisturbed and overwrites all other pixels with pixels from the sprite. This is accomplished with the AND mask.

Imagine a byte from the sprite description and the eight pixels it describes. Suppose that in this byte, the last pixel (represented by bit 7) should be transparent or part of the background. The AND mask for this byte would have all bits set to 0 except for bit 7, which would be set to 1. Then, when merging the buffers, the background byte combines with the corresponding byte from the AND buffer using a logical AND operation.

The result is that only the background bit, bit 7, remains unchanged. All other bits are set to 0. In the next step of the process, the result is combined with the corresponding byte from the sprite description using a logical OR operator. This byte contains a 0 in all bit positions that represent transparent background pixels. All other bits contain values that make up part of the four bit color code for a sprite pixel.

The result of this operation is that all pixels needed to display the sprite are changed to the colors given in the sprite description and all background pixels remain unchanged.

This entire operation must be repeated for each bitplane. The AND mask is always the same, however, since the bit positions that represent sprite pixels and background pixels are the same for all bitplanes. The size of the AND buffer in bytes, which is only good for one of the eight copies of the sprite description, is:

```
width * height / 8
```

The AND buffers for each sprite description are created with COMPILESPRITE, in the same way as the sprite descriptions themselves. As the sprite array is processed, a 1 is placed in each bit that describes a transparent background pixel. A 0 represents a sprite pixel that overwrites its background.

The S6435CA.ASM and S6435PA.ASM assembly language modules perform the combination of the sprite background, the sprite description, and the AND buffer. This routine is called MERGEANDCOPYBUF2VIDEO. As its name suggests, this routine merges the necessary buffers to create the desired pixel pattern and copies the buffers from conventional RAM to video RAM. Actually, these operations are done in parallel, byte by byte. First a byte from the three buffers is merged, then it's copied to video RAM; the process continues with the next byte.

This entire process repeated four times in MERGEANDCOPYBUF2VIDEO for each of the four bitplanes. This also applies to the COPYBUF2VIDEO and COPYVIDEO2BUF assembly language routines, which appear instead of the COPYBUF2PLANE and COPYVIDEO2PLANE routines, which are found in the assembler module used in 320x400 pixel mode.

These routines can process all four bitplanes automatically because the width of the screen area is limited to multiples of eight in this mode. So, it's unnecessary for the calling routine to specify the number of bytes to process. So COPYVIDEO2BUF copies the given screen area from all four bitplanes to the specified buffer and COPYBUF2VIDEO copies the specified buffer's contents to all four bitplanes.

This concludes our discussion of conceptual differences in the 640x350 mode sprite demonstration programs. Many features have been documented in the earlier programs in this chapter.

The following 640x350 sprite demonstration programs are listed. These listings are fully documented. Sprites

Pascal listing: S6435P.PAS

```
{***********************************************************
*                   S 6 4 3 5 P . P A S                    *
**-------------------------------------------------------**
*  Task          : Demonstrates the work with sprites in the *
*                  640x350 EGA and VGA graphic modes, using 16 *
*                  colors and two screen pages. This program *
*                  requires assembler routines from modules *
*                  V16COLPA.ASM and S6435PA.ASM.           *
*                                                          *
**-------------------------------------------------------**
*  Author        : MICHAEL TISCHER                         *
*  Developed on   : 12/05/90                               *
*  Last update    : 01/04/91                               *
***********************************************************}

program S6435P;

uses dos, crt;

{-- External references to the assembler routines --------------------}

{$L v16colpa}                            { Link assembler module }

procedure init640350; external;
procedure setpix( x, y : integer; pcolor : byte ); external;
function  getpix( x, y: integer ) : byte ; external;
procedure setpage( page : integer ); external;
procedure showpage( page : integer ); external;

{$L s6435pa}                             { Link assembler module }

procedure CopyVideo2Buf( bufptr  : pointer;
                         page    : byte;
                         fromx,
                         fromy   : integer;
                         rwidth,
                         rheight : byte    ); external;

procedure CopyBuf2Video( bufptr  : pointer;
                         page    : byte;
                         tox,
                         toy     : integer;
                         rwidth,
                         rheight : byte ); external;

procedure MergeAndCopyBuf2Video( spribufptr,
                                 hgbufptr,
                                 andbufptr : pointer;
                                 page      : byte;
                                 tox,
                                 toy       : integer;
                                 rwidth,
                                 rheight   : byte ); external;

{-- Constants ------------------------------------------------------}

const MAXX = 639;                        { Maximum X- and Y-coordinates }
      MAXY = 349;

      OUT_LEFT   = 1;   { For collision documentation in SpriteMove() }
      OUT_TOP    = 2;
      OUT_RIGHT  = 4;
      OUT_BOTTOM = 8;
      OUT_NO     = 0;                                        { None }

{-- Type declarations ----------------------------------------------}

type PIXBUF = record          { Information for GetVideo and PutVideo }
                widthbytes,                { Width of area in bytes }
                numrows  : byte;                   { Number of rows }
                pixblen: integer;          { Length of pixel buffer }
                pixbptr: pointer;          { Pointer to the pixel buffer }
              end;
     PIXPTR = ^PIXBUF;                      { Pointer to a pixel buffer }

     SPLOOK = record                                 { Sprite design }
                twidth,                                { Total width }
                theight : byte;               { Height in pixel rows }
                bmskp   : array [0..7] of pointer;{ Ptr to AND buffer }
                pixmp   : array [0..7] of PIXPTR; { Ptr to pixel def. }
              end;                          { its page was discarded   }
     SPLP = ^SPLOOK;                               { Pointer to design }

     SPID = record                           { Sprite descriptor (ID) }
              splookp : SPLP;                     { Pointer to design }
              x, y    : array [0..1] of integer;{ Coordinates: pp.0&1 }
              hgptr   : array [0..1] of PIXPTR;  { Pointer to back-  }
            end;                               { ground buffer      }
     SPIP = ^SPID;               { Pointer to sprite descriptor }

     BYTEAR = array[0..10000] of byte;         { Addressing       }
     BARPTR = ^BYTEAR;                        { different buffers }
```

```
     VCARD = ( EGA, VGA, NEITHERNOR );


{*********************************************************
 * IsEgaVga : Determines whether EGA or VGA card is installed.  *
 **------------------------------------------------------------**
 * Input   : None                                              *
 * Output  : EGA, VGA or NEITHERNOR                            *
 *********************************************************}

function IsEgaVga : VCARD;

var Regs : Registers;           { Processor register for interrupt call }

begin
  Regs.AX := $1a00;               { Function 1AH applies to VGA only }
  Intr( $10, Regs );
  if ( Regs.AL = $1a ) then                { Function available? }
    IsEgaVga := VGA
  else
    begin
      Regs.ah := $12;                   { Call function 12H, }
      Regs.bl := $10;                   { sub-function 10H  }
      intr($10, Regs);                       { Call video BIOS }
      if ( Regs.bl <> $10 ) then IsEgaVga := EGA
                          else IsEgaVga := NEITHERNOR;

    end;
end;


{*********************************************************
 * PrintChar : Writes a character to the screen while in graphic mode.*
 **------------------------------------------------------------**
 * Input   :    THECHAR = Character to be written            *
 *             x, y    = X- and Y-coordinates of upper left corner *
 *             FG      = Foreground color                    *
 *             BK      = Background color                    *
 * Info    : Character is created in an 8x8 matrix, based on the *
 *             8x8 ROM font.                                  *
 *********************************************************}

procedure PrintChar( thechar : char; x, y : integer; fg, bk : byte );

type FDEF = array[0..255,0..7] of byte;      { Font array }
     TPTR = ^FDEF;                           { Pointer to font }

var Regs  : Registers;            { Registers for interrupt call }
    ch    : char;               { Individual pixels in character }
    i, k,                              { Loop counter }
    BMask : byte;               { Bit mask for character design }

const fptr : TPTR = NIL;           { Pointer to font in ROM }

begin
  if fptr = NIL then              { Pointer to font already set? }
    begin                                      { No }
      Regs.AH := $11;             { Call video BIOS function 11H, }
      Regs.AL := $30;                 { sub-function $30        }
      Regs.BH := 3;                   { Get pointer to 8x8 font }
      intr( $10, Regs );
      fptr := ptr( Regs.ES, Regs.BP );            { Set pointers }
    end;

  if ( bk = 255 ) then            { Drawing transparent characters? }
    for i := 0 to 7 do            { Yes --> Set foreground pixels only }
      begin
```

```
        BMask := fptr^[ord(thechar),i];{ Get bit pattern for one line }
        for k := 0 to 7 do
          begin
            if ( BMask and 128 <> 0 ) then           { Pixel set? }
              setpix( x+k, y+i, fg );                   { Yes }
            BMask := BMask shl 1;
          end;
      end;
  else                        { No --> consider background as well }
    for i := 0 to 7 do                         { Execute lines }
      begin
        BMask := fptr^[ord(thechar),i];{ Get bit pattern for one line }
        for k := 0 to 7 do
          begin
            if ( BMask and 128 <> 0 ) then           { Foreground? }
              setpix( x+k, y+i, fg )                    { Yes }
            else
              setpix( x+k, y+i, bk );          { No --> Background }
            BMask := BMask shl 1;
          end;
      end;
end;


{*********************************************************
 * PrintString: Writes a string to the screen in graphics mode.   *
 **------------------------------------------------------------**
 * Input   :  x, y    = X- and Y-coordinates of upper left-corner *
 *            FG      = Foreground color                     *
 *            BK      = Background color                     *
 *            TSTR    = String to be displayed               *
 * Info    : The characters are designed around an 8x8 matrix, based *
 *            on the 8x8 ROM font.                           *
 *********************************************************}

procedure PrintString( x, y : integer; fg, bk : byte; tstr : string );

var i : integer;                           { Loop counter }

begin
  for i := 1 to length( tstr ) do            { Execute string }
    begin
      PrintChar( tstr[i], x, y, fg, bk );          { and display it }
      inc( x, 8 );                      { Increment output position }
    end;
end;


{*********************************************************
 * Line: Draws a line based on the Bresenham algorithm.          *
 **------------------------------------------------------------**
 * Input   : X1, Y1 = Starting coordinates  (0 - ...)         *
 *           X2, Y2 = Ending coordinates                     *
 *           LPCOL  = Color of line pixels                   *
 *********************************************************}

procedure Line( x1, y1, x2, y2 : integer; lpcol : byte );

var d, dx, dy,
    aincr, bincr,
    xincr, yincr,
    x, y                   : integer;

{-- Procedure for swapping two integer variables ---------------------}

procedure SwapInt( var i1, i2: integer );
```

```
var dummy : integer;

begin
  dummy := i2;
  i2    := i1;
  i1    := dummy;
end,

{-- Main procedure ------------------------------------------------}

begin
  if ( abs(x2-x1) < abs(y2-y1) ) then      { X- or Y-axis overflow? }
    begin                                    { Check Y-axes }
      if ( y1 > y2 ) then                           { y1 > y2? }
        begin
          SwapInt( x1, x2 );           { Yes --> Swap X1 with X2 }
          SwapInt( y1, y2 );           {          and Y1 with Y2 }
        end;

      if ( x2 > x1 ) then xincr := 1       { Set X-axis increment }
                     else xincr := -1;

      dy := y2 - y1;
      dx := abs( x2-x1 );
      d  := 2 * dx - dy;
      aincr := 2 * (dx - dy);
      bincr := 2 * dx;
      x := x1;
      y := y1;

      setpix( x, y, lpcol );                      { Set first pixel }
      for y:=y1+1 to y2 do             { Execute line on Y-axes }
        begin
          if ( d >= 0 ) then
            begin
              inc( x, xincr );
              inc( d, aincr );
            end
          else
            inc( d, bincr );
          setpix( x, y, lpcol );
        end;
    end
  else                                              { Check X-axes }
    begin
      if ( x1 > x2 ) then                            { x1 > x2? }
        begin
          SwapInt( x1, x2 );           { Yes --> Swap X1 with X2 }
          SwapInt( y1, y2 );           {          and Y1 with Y2 }
        end;

      if ( y2 > y1 ) then yincr := 1       { Set Y-axis increment }
                     else yincr := -1;

      dx := x2 - x1;
      dy := abs( y2-y1 );
      d  := 2 * dy - dx;
      aincr := 2 * (dy - dx);
      bincr := 2 * dy;
      x := x1;
      y := y1;

      setpix( x, y, lpcol );                      { Set first pixel }
```

```
      for x:=x1+1 to x2 do                 { Execute line on X-axes }
        begin
          if ( d >= 0 ) then
            begin
              inc( y, yincr );
              inc( d, aincr );
            end
          else
            inc( d, bincr );
          setpix( x, y, lpcol );
        end;
    end;
end;

{***********************************************************************
* GetVideo: Gets the contents of a rectangular range from the video   *
*           RAM and puts them in a buffer                             *
**-----------------------------------------------------------------**
* Input   : PAGE   = Screen page (0 or 1)                            *
*           X1, Y1 = Starting coordinates                            *
*           WRANGE = Width of the rectangular range in pixels        *
*           HRANGE = Height of rectangular range in pixels           *
*           BUFPTR = Pointer to pixel buffer, in which the inform-   *
*                    ation is to be placed                           *
* Output  : Pointer to created pixel buffer with the contents of     *
*           the specified area                                       *
* Info    : If the value NIL is passed for the BUFPTR parameter,     *
*           a new pixel buffer is allocated via the heap and         *
*           returned. This buffer can be specified again for a new   *
*           call, unless the previous contents are still required    *
*           and the size of the rectangular area remains unchanged   *
*           compared to the preceding call.                          *
*           The specified area must begin at an X-coordinate that    *
*           can be divided by eight and extend over a multiple of    *
*           eight pixels.                                            *
***********************************************************************}

function GetVideo( page : byte; x1, y1 : integer;
                   wrange, hrange : byte; bufptr : PIXPTR ) : PIXPTR;

begin
  if ( bufptr = NIL ) then               { No buffer passed during call? }
    begin                                         { No, create one }
      new( bufptr );                          { Create pixel buffer }
      getmem( bufptr^.pixbptr, (wrange*hrange) div 2 );{ Alloc. px.b. }
      bufptr^.numrows := hrange;         { Height of buffer in lines }
      bufptr^.widthbytes := wrange div 8;  { Width of a line in bytes }
      bufptr^.pixblen := (wrange*hrange) div 2; {Total len. of buffer }
    end;

  CopyVideo2Buf( bufptr^.pixbptr, page, x1, y1, wrange div 8, hrange );
  GetVideo := bufptr;             { Returns pointer and buffer to caller }
end;

{***********************************************************************
* PutVideo: Writes the contents of a rectangular area of the screen   *
*           previously saved by GetVideo back to the video RAM        *
**-----------------------------------------------------------------**
* Input   : BUFPTR = Pointer to pixel buffer returned during         *
*                    previous call for GetVideo                      *
*           PAGE   = Screen page (0 or 1)                            *
*           X1, Y1 = Starting coordinates                            *
* Info    : This procedure does not delete the pixel buffer. The     *
*           FreePixBuf procedure must be called for this.            *
```

```
*       The specified X-coordinate must be a multiple of eight!    *
*****************************************************************}

procedure PutVideo( bufptr : PIXPTR; page : byte; x1, y1 : integer );

begin
  CopyBuf2Video( bufptr^.pixptr, page, x1, y1,
                 bufptr^.widthbytes, bufptr^.numrows );
end;


{*****************************************************************
* FreePixBuf: Deletes a pixel buffer, which was allocated previously *
*            via the heap when GetVideo was called.                  *
**----------------------------------------------------------------**
* Input    : BUFPTR = Pointer to pixel buffer returned during        *
*                     previous call for GetVideo                     *
*****************************************************************}

procedure FreePixBuf( bufptr : PIXPTR );

begin
  freemem( bufptr^.pixptr, bufptr^.pixblen );
  dispose( bufptr );
end;


{*****************************************************************
* CreateSprite: Creates a sprite based on a user-defined          *
*               pixel pattern.                                    *
**----------------------------------------------------------------**
* Input    : SPLOOKP = Pointer to data structure from CompileSprite *
* Output   : Pointer to created sprite structure                    *
*****************************************************************}

function CreateSprite( splookp : SPLP ) : SPIP;

var spidp : SPIP;              { Pointer to created sprite structure }

begin
  new( spidp );              { Allocate memory for sprite descriptor }
  spidp^.splookp := splookp;              { Pass data to the }
                                          { sprite structure }
  {-- Create two background buffers by saving a large enough area }
                              { from the video RAM via GetVideo }

  spidp^.hgptr[0] := GetVideo( 0, 0, 0, splookp^.twidth,
                               splookp^.theight, NIL );
  spidp^.hgptr[1] := GetVideo( 0, 0, 0, splookp^.twidth,
                               splookp^.theight, NIL );
  CreateSprite := spidp;     { Return pointer to the sprite structure }
end;


{*****************************************************************
* CompileSprite: Creates a sprite's pixel and bit patterns, based on *
*                the sprite's definition at runtime.                 *
**----------------------------------------------------------------**
* Input    : BUFP    = Pointer to array contains string pointers     *
*                      controlling sprite's pattern                  *
*            SHEIGHT = Sprite height (and number of strings needed)  *
* Info     : In passed sprite pattern, a space stands for a back-    *
*            ground pixel, the A stands for the color code 0, B for  *
*            1, C for 2 etc.                                         *
*****************************************************************}

function CompileSprite( var buf; sheight : byte ) : SPLP;
```

```
type BYPTR  = ^byte;                      { Pointer to a byte }

var stwidth,                              { String width }
    spwidth,                              { Sprite width }
    c,                          { get character from c sprite array }
    i, k, l, y,                           { Loop variables }
    andc,                    { Pixel counter for creating the bit mask }
    andm     : byte;                      { Pixel mask }
    andindex : integer;              { Index in AND buffer }
    splookp  : SPLP;          { Pointer to created sprite structure }
    lspb     : BYPTR;         { Floating pointer in sprite buffer }
    andp,                                 { Pointer to AND buffer }
    bptr     : BARPTR;        { Addresses buffer with graphic }
    tpix     : PIXPTR;        { Pointer to temporary pixel buffer }

{-- Sub-procedure AndBufInit: Initializes an AND-Buffer --------------}

procedure AndBufInit( bufp : BARPTR );

begin
  andp := bufp;                        { Note pointer to buffer }
  andindex := 0;                 { Start at beginning of buffer }
  andm := 0;                             { First bit mask is 0 }
  andc := 0;                       { Still no bit in first byte }
end;

{-- Sub-procedure AndBufAppendBit: Add a bit to the AND buffer -------}

procedure AndBufAppendBit( bit : byte );

begin
  andm := andm or bit;                { Set bit in bit position 0 }
  if andc = 7 then                          { Byte full now? }
    begin                                            { Yes }
      andp^[andindex] := andm;         { Place byte in buffer }
      inc( andindex );                   { address next byte }
      andm := 0;                         { Bit mask back to 0 }
      andc := 0;           { Continue in next byte with first bit }
    end
  else                                { Byte is not yet full }
    begin
      inc( andc );                    { One more bit processed }
      andm := andm shl 1;                   { Shift bit mask }
    end;
end;

{-- Sub-procedure AndBufEnd: Close AND buffer -----------------------}

procedure AndBufEnd;

begin
  if ( andc <> 0 ) then             { Last byte not yet full? }
    andp^[andindex] := andm shl (7 - andc);        { No, close }
end;

begin
  {-- Create Sprite-Look structure and fill with data ---------------}

  new( splookp );
  bptr := @buf;                        { Set pointer to logo buffer }
  stwidth := bptr^[0];   { Get string length and determine log width }
  spwidth := ( ( stwidth + 7 + 7 ) div 8 ) * 8;     { Total width }
  splookp^.twidth := spwidth;          { Note width and height }
```

```
splookp^.theight := sheight;

setpage( 1 );                          { Draw sprites in page 1 }
showpage( 0 );                         { but display page 0 }
tpix := GetVideo( 1, 0, 0, spwidth, sheight, NIL ); { Note backgrnd }

{-- Draw and code sprite eight times -------------------------------}

for 1 := 0 to 7 do
  begin                    { First fill background with black pixels }
    for y := 0 to sheight-1 do
      Line( 0, y, spwidth-1, y, 0 );

    {-- Create and initialize memory for AND buffer ----------------}

    getmem( splookp^.bmskp[ 1 ], (spwidth*sheight) div 8 );
    AndBufInit( splookp^.bmskp[ 1 ] );

    for i := 0 to sheight-1 do                      { Execute lines }
      begin
        for y := 1 to l do       { Create AND bits for left margins }
          AndBufAppendBit( 1 );

        for k := 0 to stwidth-1 do              { Execute columns }
          begin
            c := bptr^[i*(stwidth+1)+k+1];           { Get color }
            if ( c = 32 ) then              { Background pixel? }
              begin                    { Yes --> set color code 0 }
                setpix( k+l, i, 0 );
                AndBufAppendBit( 1 );      { Background pixel stays }
              end
            else                       { No, set color code as given }
              begin
                setpix( k+l, i, c-ord('@') );
                AndBufAppendBit( 0 );      { Mask background pixel }
              end;
          end;
        for y := spwidth-stwidth-l downto 1 do   { Add AND bits for }
          AndBufAppendBit( 1 );                  { the right margin }
      end;
    AndBufEnd;                               { Close AND buffer }

    {-- Get sprite's pixel pattern from video RAM ------------------}
    splookp^.pixmp[ 1 ] := GetVideo( 1, 0, 0, spwidth, sheight, nil );

  end;                             { Draw next of eight sprites }

  PutVideo( tpix, 1, 0, 0 );        { Restore sprite background in }
  FreePixBuf( tpix );               { page 1 and delete buffer }

  CompileSprite := splookp;       { Return pointer to sprite buffer }
end;

{**************************************************************
 * PrintSprite : Displays sprite in a specified page          *
 **----------------------------------------------------------**
 * Input   : SPIDP   = Pointer to the sprite structure        *
 *           SPRPAGE = Page in which sprite should be drawn (0 or 1) *
 **************************************************************}

procedure PrintSprite( spidp : SPIP; sprpage : byte );

var x : integer;                       { X-coordinate of sprite }
```

```
begin
  x := spidp^.x[sprpage];
  MergeAndCopyBuf2Video( spidp^.splookp^.pixmp[x mod 8]^.pixbptr,
                         spidp^.hgptr[sprpage]^.pixbptr,
                         spidp^.splookp^.bmskp[x mod 8],
                         sprpage,
                         x and not(7),
                         spidp^.y[sprpage],
                         spidp^.splookp^.twidth div 8,
                         spidp^.splookp^.theight );
end;

{**************************************************************
 * GetSpriteBg: Gets a sprite background and specifies the position. *
 **----------------------------------------------------------**
 * Input   : SPIDP  = Pointer to the sprite structure          *
 *           SPRPAGE = Page from which the background should be taken *
 *                  (0 or 1)                                    *
 **************************************************************}

procedure GetSpriteBg( spidp : SPIP; sprpage : BYTE );

var dummy : PIXPTR;

begin
  dummy := GetVideo( sprpage, spidp^.x[sprpage] and not(7),
spidp^.y[sprpage],
                     spidp^.splookp^.twidth, spidp^.splookp^.theight,
                     spidp^.hgptr[sprpage] );
end;

{**************************************************************
 * RestoreSpriteBg: Restores sprite background from original graphic *
 *                 page.                                        *
 **----------------------------------------------------------**
 * Input   : SPIDP  = Pointer to the sprite structure          *
 *           SPRPAGE = Page from which background should be copied *
 *                  (0 or 1)                                    *
 **************************************************************}

procedure RestoreSpriteBg( spidp : SPIP; sprpage : BYTE );

begin
  PutVideo( spidp^.hgptr[sprpage], sprpage,
            spidp^.x[sprpage] and not(7), spidp^.y[sprpage] );
end;

{**************************************************************
 * MoveSprite: Copy sprite within background to original graphic page.*
 **----------------------------------------------------------**
 * Input   : SPIDP  = Pointer to the sprite structure          *
 *           SPRPAGE= Page to which the background should be copied *
 *                  (0 or 1)                                    *
 *           DELTAX = Movement counter in X-                    *
 *           DELTAY   and Y-directions                          *
 * Output  : Collision marker (See OUT_ constants)             *
 **************************************************************}

function MoveSprite( spidp : SPIP; sprpage : byte;
                     deltax, delay : integer   ) : byte;

var newx, newy : integer;                { New sprite coordinates }
    out        : byte;               { Display collision with border }
```

```
begin
{-- Move X-coordinates and test for border collision ----------------}

newx := spidp^.x[sprpage] + deltax;
if ( newx  < 0 ) then
  begin
    newx := 0 - deltax - spidp^.x[sprpage];
    out := OUT_LEFT;
  end
else
  if ( newx > MAXX - spidp^.splookp^.twidth ) then
    begin
      newx := (2*(MAXX+1))-newx-2*(spidp^.splookp^.twidth);
      out := OUT_RIGHT;
    end
  else
    out := OUT_NO;

{-- Move Y-coordinates and test for border collision ----------------}

newy := spidp^.y[sprpage] + deltay;           { Top border? }
if ( newy < 0 ) then                          { Top border? }
  begin                              { Yes --> Deltay must be negative }
    newy := 0 - deltay - spidp^.y[sprpage];
    out := out or OUT_TOP;
  end
else
  if ( newy + spidp^.splookp^.theight > MAXY+1 ) then    { Bottom? }
    begin                            { Yes --> Deltay must be positive }
      newy := (2*(MAXY+1))-newy-2*(spidp^.splookp^.theight);
      out := out or OUT_BOTTOM;
    end;

{-- Set new position only if different from old position ------------}

if ( newx <> spidp^.x[sprpage] ) or ( newy <> spidp^.y[sprpage] ) then
  begin                                    { If there's a new position }
    RestoreSpriteBg( spidp, sprpage );     { then reset background and }
    spidp^.x[sprpage] := newx;             { store new coordinates     }
    spidp^.y[sprpage] := newy;
    GetSpriteBg( spidp, sprpage );            { Get new background }
    PrintSprite( spidp, sprpage );   { Draw sprite in specified page }
  end;

MoveSprite := out;
end;

{*************************************************************************
* SetSprite: Sets sprite at a specific position.                        *
**---------------------------------------------------------------------**
* Input    : SPIDP  = Pointer to the sprite structure                   *
*            x0, y0 = Sprite coordinates for page 0                     *
*            x1, y1 = Sprite coordinates for page 1                     *
* Info     : This function call should be made the first time that      *
*            MoveSprite() is called                                     *
*************************************************************************}

procedure SetSprite( spidp : SPIP; x0, y0, x1, y1 : integer );

begin
spidp^.x[0] := x0;            { Store coordinates in sprite structure }
spidp^.x[1] := x1;
spidp^.y[0] := y0;
spidp^.y[1] := y1;
```

```
GetSpriteBg( spidp, 0 );               { Get sprite backgrounds }
GetSpriteBg( spidp, 1 );               {   in pages 0 and 1     }
PrintSprite( spidp, 0 );               {      Draw sprite in    }
PrintSprite( spidp, 1 );               {     pages 1 and 0      }
end;


{*************************************************************************
* Demo: Demonstrates these functions.                                   *
*************************************************************************}

procedure Demo;

const StarShipUp :array [1..20] of string[32] =
         ( '             AA                 ',
           '            AAAA                ',
           '            AAAA                ',
           '             AA                 ',
           '           GGBBGG               ',
           '          GBBCCBBG              ',
           '          GBBBCCBBBG            ',
           '         GBBBBBBBBBBG           ',
           '         GBBBBBBBBBBG           ',
           ' G       GBBBBBBBBBBBBG       G ',
           'GCG     GGDBBBBBBBBBBBDGG     GCG',
           'GCG    GGBBBDBBBB  BBBDBBBGG    GCG',
           'GCBGGGBBBBBBDBB     BBDBBBBBBGGGBCG',
           'GCBBBBBBBBBBDB       BDBBBBBBBBBBCG',
           'BBBBBBBBBBBBBDB  BB  BDBBBBBBBBBBBBB',
           'GGCBBBBBBBBDBBBBBBBBBBBDBBBBBBBCG',
           ' GGCBBBDDDDDDDDDDDDDDDBBCCG     ',
           '  GGBBDDDDDGGGGGDDDDDDBBG       ',
           '   GDDDDGGG     GGGDDDDG        ',
           '    DDDD           DDDD       ' );


const StarShipDown :array [1..20] of string[32] =
         ( '    DDDD           DDDD         ',
           '   GDDDDGGG     GGGDDDDG        ',
           '  GGBBDDDDDGGGGGDDDDDDBBG       ',
           ' GGCBBBDDDDDDDDDDDDDDDBBCCG     ',
           'GGCBBBBBBBBDBBBBBBBBBBBDBBBBBBBCG',
           'BBBBBBBBBBBBBDB  BB  BDBBBBBBBBBBBBB',
           'GCBBBBBBBBBBDB       BDBBBBBBBBBBCG',
           'GCBGGGBBBBBBDBB     BBDBBBBBBGGGBCG',
           'GCG    GGBBBDBBBB  BBBDBBBGG    GCG',
           'GCG     GGDBBBBBBBBBBBDGG     GCG',
           ' G       GBBBBBBBBBBBBG       G ',
           '         GBBBBBBBBBBG           ',
           '         GBBBBBBBBBBG           ',
           '          GBBBCCBBBG            ',
           '          GBBCCBBG              ',
           '           GGBBGG               ',
           '             AA                 ',
           '            AAAA                ',
           '            AAAA                ',
           '             AA                 ' );

SPRNUM = 6;                                { Number of sprites }
CWIDTH = 42;           { Width of copyright message in characters }
CHEIGHT = 6;                             { Message height in rows }
SX     = (MAXX-(CWIDTH*8)) div 2;        { Starting X-coordinate }
SY     = (MAXY-(CHEIGHT*8)) div 2;       { Starting Y-coordinate }

type SPRITE = record                     { For sprite management }
```

359

```
                spidp : SPIP;                     { Pointer to sprite Id }
                deltax,                { X-movement for pages 0 and 1 }
                deltay : array [0..1] of integer;       { Y-movement }
              end;


var sprites    : array [1..SPRNUM] of SPRITE;
    page,                                          { Current page }
    lc,                                  { Character for screen design }
    out     : byte;                    { Get flags for page collision }
    x, y, i,                                       { Loop counter }
    dx, dy    : integer;                           { Movement value }
    starshipupp,
    starshipdnp : SPLP;                            { Sprite pointer }
    ch        : char;

begin
  Randomize;                           { Initialize random number generator }

  {-- Create patterns for the different sprites ----------------------}
  starshipupp := CompileSprite( StarShipUp,   20 );
  starshipdnp := CompileSprite( StarShipDown, 20 );


  {-- Fill the first two graphic pages with characters ---------------}
  for page := 0 to 1 do
    begin
      setpage( page );
      showpage( page );
      lc := 0;
      y := 0;
      while ( y < (MAXY+1)-8 ) do
        begin
          x := 0;
          while ( x < (MAXX+1)-8 ) do
            begin
              PrintChar( chr(lc and 127), x, y, lc and 15, 0 );
              inc( lc );
              inc( x, 8 );
            end;
          inc( y, 12 );
        end;

      {-- Display copyright message -----------------------------}
      Line( SX-1, SY-1, SX+CWIDTH*8, SY-1, 15 );
      Line( SX+CWIDTH*8, SY-1, SX+CWIDTH*8, SY+CHEIGHT*8,15 );
      Line( SX+CWIDTH*8, SY+CHEIGHT*8, SX-1, SY+CHEIGHT*8, 15 );
      Line( SX-1, SY+CHEIGHT*8, SX-1, SY-1, 15 );
      PrintString( SX, SY,    15, 4,
                    '                                   ' );
      PrintString( SX, SY+8,   15, 4,
                   ' S6435P.PAS - (c) 1992 by Michael Tischer ' );
      PrintString( SX, SY+16, 15, 4,
                    '                                   ' );
      PrintString( SX, SY+24, 15, 4,
                    '      Sprite demo for 640x350 mode     ' );
      PrintString( SX, SY+32, 15, 4,
                    '          on EGA and VGA cards         ' );
      PrintString( SX, SY+40, 15, 4,
                    '                                   ' );
    end;

  {-- Create different sprites ---------------------------------------}
  for i := 1 to SPRNUM do
    begin
      sprites[ i ].spidp := CreateSprite( starshipupp );
```

```
      repeat                    { Select movement values for sprites }
        dx := 0;
        dy := random(10) - 5;
      until ( dx <> 0 ) or ( dy <> 0 );

      sprites[ i ].deltax[0] := dx * 2;
      sprites[ i ].deltay[0] := dy * 2;
      sprites[ i ].deltax[1] := dx * 2;
      sprites[ i ].deltay[1] := dy * 2;

      x := ( ((MAXX+1) div SPRNUM) * (i-1) )
           + (((MAXX+1) div SPRNUM)-40) div 2;
      y := random( (MAXY+1) - 40 );
      SetSprite( sprites[ i ].spidp, x, y, x - dx, y - dy );
    end;


{-- Move sprites and bounce them off the page borders --------------}

  page := 1;                                    { Start with page 1 }
  while ( not keypressed ) do        { Press a key to end the loop }
    begin
      showpage( 1-page );                       { Display other page }
      { ch := readkey; }             { Remove key from keyboard buffer }
      for i := 1 to SPRNUM do              { Execute sprites }
        begin                 { Move sprite and check for page collision }
          out := MoveSprite( sprites[i].spidp, page,
                             sprites[i].deltax[page],
                             sprites[i].deltay[page] );
          if ( ( out and OUT_TOP ) <> 0 ) or { Top/bottom collision? }
             ( ( out and OUT_BOTTOM ) <> 0 ) then
            begin
              {-- Yes --> Change direction of movement ---------------}
              {---------- and change sprite graphic -----------------}

              sprites[i].deltay[page] := -sprites[i].deltay[page];
              if ( ( out and OUT_TOP ) <> 0 ) then
                sprites[i].spidp^.splookp := starshipdnp
              else
                sprites[i].spidp^.splookp := starshipupp;
            end;
          if ( ( out and OUT_LEFT ) <> 0 ) or { Left/right collision? }
             ( ( out and OUT_RIGHT ) <> 0 ) then
            sprites[i].deltax[page] := -sprites[i].deltax[page];
        end;
      page := (page+1) and 1;          { Toggle between 1 and 0 }
    end;
  ch := readkey;                 { Remove key from keyboard buffer }
end;


{-------------------------------------------------------------------}
{--             M A I N   P R O G R A M            ----}
{-------------------------------------------------------------------}

begin
  if ( IsEgaVga <> NEITHERNOR ) then    { EGA or VGA card installed? }
    begin                               { Yes --> Go ahead }
      init640350;                       { Initialize graphic mode }
      Demo;
      Textmode( CO80 );                 { Shift into text mode }
    end
  else
    writeln( 'S6435P.PAS - (c) 1992 by Michael Tischer'#13#10#10 +
             'This program requires an EGA or a VGA card'#13#10 );
end.
```

Assembler listing: S6435PA.ASM

```
;******************************************************************;
;*                  S 6 4 3 5 P A . A S M                         *;
;*--------------------------------------------------------------*;
;*  Task        : Contains routines for generating sprites in    *;
;*                640x350 pixel graphic mode on an EGA and VGA    *;
;*                card.                                           *;
;*--------------------------------------------------------------*;
;*  Author      : MICHAEL TISCHER                                 *;
;*  Developed on : 12/08/90                                       *;
;*  Last update  : 01/14/91                                       *;
;*--------------------------------------------------------------*;
;*  Assembly    : MASM /mx S6435PA;    or    TASM -mx S6435PA     *;
;*                ... Link to S6435P.PAS                          *;
;******************************************************************;

;== Constants ===================================================

SC_INDEX      = 3c4h          ;Index register for sequencer ctrl.
SC_MAP_MASK   = 2             ;Number of map mask register
SC_MEM_MODE   = 4             ;Number of memory mode register

GC_INDEX      = 3ceh          ;Index register for graphics ctrl.
GC_READ_MAP   = 4             ;Number of read map register
GC_BIT_MASK   = 8             ;Number of bit mask register

PIXX          = 640           ;Horizontal resolution

;== Data segment ================================================

DATA    segment word public
DATA    ends

;== Program =====================================================

CODE        segment byte public    ;Program segment

            assume cs:code, ds:data

;-- Public declarations -----------------------------------------
public      copybuf2video
public      mergeandcopybuf2video
public      copyvideo2buf


;----------------------------------------------------------------
;-- CopyBuf2Video: Copies the contents of a rectangular area from the
;--               video RAM that were saved by CopyVideo2Buf back to
;--               video RAM
;-- Call from TP : CopyBuf2Plane( bufptr  : pointer;
;--                               topage  : byte;
;--                               tox,
;--                               toy     : integer;
;--                               rwidth,
;--                               rheight : byte );
;-- Info        : See CopyVideo2Buf
copybuf2video proc near


sfr0    struc                 ;Structure for stack access
bp0     dw ?                  ;Gets BP
stofs0  dw ?                  ;Loc. var.: Start offset in video RAM
ret_adr0 dw ?                 ;Return address from caller
rheight0 dw ?                 ;Height of range
rwidth0  dw ?                 ;Width
toy     dw ?                  ;To Y-coordinate
tox     dw ?                  ;To X-coordinate
topage  dw ?                  ;To page
bufptr0 dd ?                  ;Pointer to buffer
sfr0    ends                  ;End structure

fr      equ [ bp - bp0 ]       ;Addresses structure elements
bfr     equ byte ptr [ bp - bp0 ] ;Addresses stack element as byte

        sub   sp,2            ;Space for local variables

        push  bp             ;Prepare BP register for
        mov   bp,sp          ;addressing parameters

        push  ds

        cld                  ;Increment on string instructions

;-- Calculate segment address for access to video RAM ------

        mov   ax,0A000h      ;Move ES to start of TO page
        cmp   bfr.topage,0   ;Page 0?
        je    cv0            ;Yes --> AL already ok

        mov   ax,0A6D6h      ;No --> page 1 of A6D6H

cv0:    mov   es,ax

;-- Calculate offset for target position in page -----------

        mov   ax,PIXX / 8    ;AX to target position FROM
        mul   fr.toy
        mov   bx,fr.tox
        shr   bx,1
        shr   bx,1
        shr   bx,1
        add   bx,ax
        mov   fr.stofs0,bx   ;Store start offset in local variable

        lds   si,fr.bufptr0  ;Set DS:SI on the buffer

;-- Load counter for the copying loop ----------------------

        mov   dl,bfr.rwidth0 ;DL = Bytes
        mov   bx,PIXX / 8    ;BX as offset to next line
        sub   bl,dl
        xor   ch,ch          ;High byte of counter is always 0

;-- Set addressable bitplane -------------------------------

        mov   ah,1           ;Load plane number as bit mask
        mov   al,SC_MAP_MASK ;Register number to AL

cv1:    mov   dx,SC_INDEX    ;Open access to plane for
        out   dx,ax          ;processing

        ;-- Copy routine for a bitplane
        ;-- without checking the background

        mov   di,fr.stofs0   ;DI to startoffset
        mov   dh,bfr.rheight0 ;DH = Lines
        mov   dl,bfr.rwidth0 ;DL = Bytes

cv2:    mov   cl,dl          ;Number of bytes to CL
```

361

```
        rep movsb              ;Copy lines
        add   di,bx            ;DI in next line
        dec   dh              ;Another line?
        jne   cv2             ;Yes ---> Continue

        shl   ah,1            ;Shift to next plane
        test  ah,16           ;All planes processed?
        je    cv1             ;No --> Continue with next plane

        mov   ax,(0Fh shl 8)+ SC_MAP_MASK   ;Allow access to
        mov   dx,SC_INDEX              ;all bitplanes
        out   dx,ax

        pop   ds             ;Retrieve DS and BP
        pop   bp

        add   sp,2           ;Add SP to local variables
        ret   14             ;On return remove parameters
                             ;from stack
copybuf2video endp

;-------------------------------------------------------------------
;-- MergeAndCopyBuf2Video: A bit mask links the contents of a back-
;--                        ground buffer to the contents of a sprite
;--                        buffer and copies the result to video RAM
;-- Call from TP : MergeAndCopyBuf2Video( spribufptr,
;--                                       hgbufptr,
;--                                       andbufptr : pointer;
;--                                       page      : byte;
;--                                       tox,
;--                                       toy       : integer;
;--                                       rwidth,
;--                                       rheight   : byte );
;-- Info        : See CopyVideo2Buf
mergeandcopybuf2video proc near

sfr2         struc              ;Structure for stack access
bp2          dw ?               ;Gets BP
andptr2      dd ?               ;Local var: Pointer in AND buffer
stofs2       dw ?               ;Local var: Startoffset in video RAM
ret_adr2     dw ?               ;Return address from caller
rheight2     dw ?               ;Height of range
rwidth2      dw ?               ;Width
toy2         dw ?               ;To Y-coordinate
tox2         dw ?               ;To X-coordinate
topage2      dw ?               ;To page
andbufptr    dd ?               ;Pointer to AND buffer
hgbufptr     dd ?               ;Pointer to background buffer
spribufptr   dd ?               ;Pointer to sprite buffer
sfr2         ends               ;Ends structure

fr           equ [ bp - bp2 ]   ;Addresses structure elements
bfr          equ byte ptr [ bp - bp2 ] ;Addresses stack element as byte

        sub   sp,6           ;Space for local variables

        push  bp             ;Prepare BP register for
        mov   bp,sp          ;addressing parameters

        push  ds

        cld                  ;Increment on string instructions
```

```
;-- Calculate segment address for access to video RAM ------

        mov   ax,0A000h        ;Move ES to start of TO page
        cmp   bfr.topage2,0   ;Page 0?
        je    cm0            ;Yes --> AL already O.K.

        mov   ax,0A6D6h       ;No --> page 1 of A6D6H

cm0:    mov   es,ax

;-- Calculate offset for target position in page -----------

        mov   ax,PIXX / 8     ;AX to target position FROM
        mul   fr.toy2
        mov   bx,fr.tox2
        shr   bx,1
        shr   bx,1
        shr   bx,1
        add   bx,ax
        mov   fr.stofs2,bx    ;Store start offset in local variable

;-- Load counter for the copying loop ----------------------

        mov   dl,bfr.rwidth2   ;DL = Bytes
        mov   bx,PIXX / 8     ;BX as offset to next line
        sub   bl,dl
        xor   ch,ch          ;High byte of counter is always 0

        mov   ax,word ptr fr.andbufptr+2 ;Copy segment address of
        mov   word ptr fr.andptr2+2,ax   ;AND pointer to local var.

;-- Set addressable bitplane -------------------------------

        mov   ah,1           ;Load plane number as bit mask

cm1:    mov   al,SC_MAP_MASK  ;Register number to AL
        mov   dx,SC_INDEX    ;Open access to plane for
        out   dx,ax          ;processing

;-- Copy routine for a bitplane
;-- without checking the background

        mov   dx,word ptr fr.andbufptr  ;Copy offset address of
        mov   word ptr fr.andptr2,dx    ;AND pointer to local var.
        mov   di,fr.stofs2   ;DI to start offset
        mov   dh,bfr.rheight2 ;DH = Lines
        mov   dl,bfr.rwidth2  ;DL = Bytes

cm2:    mov   cl,dl          ;Number of bytes to CL

cm3:    lds   si,fr.hgbufptr  ;Load pointer to background buffer
        lodsb                ;Load byte from background buffer
        mov   word ptr fr.hgbufptr,si ;Save incr. offset

        lds   si,fr.andptr2   ;Load pointer in AND buffer
        and   al,[si]        ;Link background to AND mask
        inc   si             ;Increment offset in AND buffer
        mov   word ptr fr.andptr2,si  ;and save

        lds   si,fr.spribufptr ;Load pointer to sprite buffer
        or    al,[si]        ;OR byte from sprite buffer
        inc   si             ;Increment byte in sprite buffer
        mov   word ptr fr.spribufptr,si  ;and save
```

```
        stosb                   ;Write byte to video RAM
        loop  cm3               ;Process next byte

        add   di,bx             ;DI in next line
        dec   dh                ;Another line?
        jne   cm2               ;Yes ---> Continue

        shl   ah,1              ;Switch to next plane
        test  ah,16             ;All planes processed?
        je    cm1               ;No --> Continue with next plane

        mov   ax,(0Fh shl 8)+ SC_MAP_MASK   ;Allow access to all
        mov   dx,SC_INDEX                   ;bitplanes
        out   dx,ax

        pop   ds                ;Retrieve DS and BP
        pop   bp

        add   sp,6             ;Add SP to local variables
        ret   22              ;On return remove parameters
                              ; from stack
mergeandcopybuf2video endp


;-----------------------------------------------------------------
;-- CopyVideo2Buf: Copies a rectangular range from the video RAM to
;--                a buffer
;-- Call from TP : CopyVideo2Buf( bufptr : pointer;
;--                               frompage: byte;
;--                               fromx,
;--                               fromy   : integer;
;--                               rwidth,
;--                               rheight : byte );
;-- Info       : In this version of the routine, the area to be
;--              copied must begin at a pixel column that can be
;--              divided by eight and extend over a multiple of
;--              eight pixels.
;--              RWIDTH refers to the number of bytes per line
;--              of a bit plane!
copyvideo2buf proc near

sfr1     struc               ;Structure for stack access
bp1      dw ?                ;Gets BP
stofs1   dw ?                ;Local var: Start offset in video RAM
ret_adr1 dw ?                ;Return address from caller
rheight1 dw ?                ;Pixel line height
rwidth1  dw ?                ;Pixel width of area
fromy    dw ?                ;From Y-coordinate
fromx    dw ?                ;From X-coordinate
frompage dw ?                ;From page
bufptr1  dd ?                ;Pointer to buffer
sfr1     ends                ;Ends structure

fr       equ [ bp - bp1 ]        ;Addresses structure elements
bfr      equ byte ptr [ bp - bp1 ] ;Addresses stack element as byte

        sub   sp,2             ;Space for local variables

        push  bp               ;Prepare BP register for
        mov   bp,sp            ;addressing parameters

        push  ds
        cld                    ;Increment on string instructions

;-- Calculate segment address for access to video RAM ------
```

```
        mov   ax,0A000h        ;Move ES start of FROM page
        cmp   bfr.frompage,0   ;Page 0?
        je    cc0              ;Yes --> AL already ok

        mov   ax,0A6D6h        ;No --> page 1 of A6D6H

cc0:    mov   ds,ax

;-- Form offset in page to be read ------------------------

        mov   ax,PIXX / 8      ;Move AX to target position FROM
        mul   fr.fromy
        mov   bx,fr.fromx
        shr   bx,1
        shr   bx,1
        shr   bx,1
        add   bx,ax
        mov   fr.stofs1,bx    ;Store start offset in local variable

        les   di,fr.bufptr1   ;Set ES:DI on the buffer

;-- Load counter for the copy loop ------------------------

        mov   dl,bfr.rwidth1  ;DL = Bytes
        mov   bx,PIXX / 8     ;BX as offset for next line
        sub   bl,dl
        xor   ch,ch           ;High byte of counter is always 0

;-- Set addressable bitplane -------------------------------

        xor   ah,ah           ;Begin with plane #0
        mov   al,GC_READ_MAP  ;Register number to AL

cc1:    mov   dx,GC_INDEX     ;Load index address of graphic ctrl.
        out   dx,ax           ;Load read map register

;-- Copy routine for a bitplane
;-- without checking the background

        mov   dh,bfr.rheight1 ;DH = Lines
        mov   dl,bfr.rwidth1  ;DL = Bytes
        mov   si,fr.stofs1    ;Load start offset to SI

cc2:    mov   cl,dl           ;Number of bytes to CL
        rep movsb             ;Copy lines
        add   si,bx           ;SI in next line
        dec   dh              ;Another line?
        jne   cc2             ;Yes --> Continue

        inc   ah              ;Switch to next plane
        cmp   ah,4            ;All planes processed?
        jne   cc1             ;No --> Continue with next plane

        pop   ds              ;Retrieve DS and BP
        pop   bp

        add   sp,2            ;Add SP to local variables
        ret   14             ;On return remove parameters
                             ; from stack
copyvideo2buf endp
;== End ==========================================================
CODE    ends                 ;End of code segment
        end                  ;End of program
```

363

C listing: S6435C.C

```
/******************************************************************
*                     S 6 4 3 5 C . C                            *
**--------------------------------------------------------------**
*  Task        : Demonstrates sprites in 640x350 EGA and VGA     *
*                graphic modes, using 16 colors and two screen   *
*                pages. This program requires assembler routines *
*                from modules V16COLCA.ASM and S6435CA.ASM.       *
**--------------------------------------------------------------**
*  Author      : Michael Tischer                                 *
*  Developed on : 12/05/90                                       *
*  Last update  : 03/02/92                                       *
**--------------------------------------------------------------**
*  Memory model : SMALL                                          *
*                                                                *
*  (MICROSOFT C)                                                 *
*  Compilation  : CL /AS /c WO s6435c.c                          *
*                 LINK s6435c s6435ca v16colca;                  *
**--------------------------------------------------------------**
*  (BORLAND TURBO C)                                             *
*  Compilation  : Create a project file containing the following: *
*                  s6435c.c                                       *
*                  v16colca.obj                                   *
*                  s6435ca.obj                                    *
**--------------------------------------------------------------**
*  Call         : s6435c                                         *
******************************************************************/

#include <dos.h>
#include <stdarg.h>
#include <stdio.h>
#include <string.h>
#include <stdlib.h>
#include <conio.h>

/*-- Compiler-dependent declarations -----------------------------*/

#ifdef __TURBOC__
  #include <alloc.h>
#else
  #include <malloc.h>
  #define random(x) ( rand() % (x+1) )        /* Random function */
#endif

/*-- Type declarations -------------------------------------------*/

typedef unsigned char BYTE;
typedef BYTE BOOL;

typedef struct {        /* Pixel buffer for GetVideo() and PutVideo() */
                BYTE widthbytes,          /* Range width in bytes */
                     numrows;             /* Number of rows */
                int pixblen;              /* Length of pixel buffer */
                void *pixbptr;            /* Pointer to pixel buffer */
               } PIXBUF;
typedef PIXBUF *PIXPTR;                    /* Pointer to a pixel buffer */

typedef struct {                          /* Sprite design */
                BYTE  twidth,             /* Total width */
                      theight;            /* Height in pixel rows */
                void  *bmskp[8];          /* Ptr to bit mask for AND */
                PIXPTR pixmp[8];          /* Pointer to pixel definition */
               } SPLOOK;
```

```
typedef struct {                     /* Sprite descriptor (ID) */
                SPLOOK *splookp;         /* Pointer to design */
                int   x[2], y[2];    /* Coordinates in pages 0 and 1 */
                PIXPTR hgptr[2];      /* Pointer to background buffer */
               } SPID;

typedef struct {                         /* Describes a bit field */
                BYTE *fieldptr,   /* Pointer to buffer with bit field */
                     *curptr,  /* Pointer to currently processed byte */
                     curbit,  /* Currently processed bit in cur. byte */
                     curbyte;            /* Current byte value */
               }
                BITFIELD;
typedef BITFIELD *BFPTR;              /* Pointer to a bit field */

/*-- External references to assembler routines ----------------------*/

extern void init640350( void );
extern void setpix( int x, int y, unsigned char pcolor);
extern BYTE getpix( int x, int y );
extern void setpage( int page );
extern void showpage( int page );
extern void far * getfontptr( void );

extern void copybuf2video( BYTE *bufptr, BYTE page,
                           int tox, int toy, BYTE rwidth,
                           BYTE rheight );
extern void copyvideo2buf( BYTE *bufptr, BYTE page,
                           int fromx, int fromy, BYTE rwidth,
                           BYTE rheight );
extern void mergeandcopybuf2video( void * spribufptr, void * hgbufptr,
                                   void * andbufptr, BYTE page,
                                   int tox, int toy,
                                   BYTE rwidth, BYTE rheight );

/*-- Constants ---------------------------------------------------*/

#define TRUE  ( 0 == 0 )
#define FALSE ( 0 == 1 )

#define MAXX 639                        /* Maximum X- and Y-coordinates */
#define MAXY 349

#define OUT_LEFT   1  /* For collision documentation in SpriteMove() */
#define OUT_TOP    2
#define OUT_RIGHT  4
#define OUT_BOTTOM 8
#define OUT_NO     0                            /* None */

#define EGA        0                            /* Card types */
#define VGA        1
#define NEITHERNOR 2

#define ALLOCBUF ((PIXPTR) 0)     /* GetVideo(): Allocate buffer */

/******************************************************************
*  IsEgaVga : Determines whether EGA or VGA card is installed.    *
**--------------------------------------------------------------**
*  Input  : None                                                 *
*  Output : EGA, VGA or NEITHERNOR                               *
******************************************************************/

BYTE IsEgaVga( void )
```

```
{
  union REGS Regs;          /* Processor registers for interrupt call */

  Regs.x.ax = 0x1a00;              /* Function 1AH applies to VGA only */
  int86( 0x10, &Regs, &Regs );
  if ( Regs.h.al == 0x1a )                   /* Function available? */
   return VGA;
  else
   {
    Regs.h.ah = 0x12;                        /* Call function 12H, */
    Regs.h.bl = 0x10;                        /* sub-function 10H   */
    int86(0x10, &Regs, &Regs );                /* Call video BIOS */
    return (BYTE) (( Regs.h.bl != 0x10 ) ? EGA : NEITHERNOR);
   }
}


/**********************************************************************
 * Line: Draws a line based on the Bresenham algorithm.              *
 **------------------------------------------------------------------**
 * Input   : X1, Y1 = Starting coordinates (0 - ...)                 *
 *           X2, Y2 = Ending coordinates                             *
 *           LPCOL  = Color of line pixels                           *
 **********************************************************************/

/*-- Function for swapping two integer variables --------------------*/

void SwapInt( int *i1, int *i2 )
{
  int dummy;

  dummy = *i2;
  *i2   = *i1;
  *i1   = dummy;
}


/*-- Main section of function ---------------------------------------*/

void Line( int x1, int y1, int x2, int y2, BYTE lpcol )
{
  int d, dx, dy,
      aincr, bincr,
      xincr, yincr,
      x, y;

  if ( abs(x2-x1) < abs(y2-y1) )      /* X- or Y-axis overflow? */
   {                                        /* Check Y-axes */
    if ( y1 > y2 )                          /* y1 > y2? */
     {
      SwapInt( &x1, &x2 );                  /* Yes --> Swap X1 with X2 */
      SwapInt( &y1, &y2 );                  /*          and Y1 with Y2  */
     }

    xincr = ( x2 > x1 ) ? 1 : -1;           /* Set X-axis increment */

    dy = y2 - y1;
    dx = abs( x2-x1 );
    d  = 2 * dx - dy;
    aincr = 2 * (dx - dy);
    bincr = 2 * dx;
    x = x1;
    y = y1;

    setpix( x, y, lpcol );                  /* Set first pixel */
    for (y=y1+1; y<= y2; ++y )              /* Execute line on Y-axes */
```

```
   {
    if ( d >= 0 )
     {
      x += xincr;
      d += aincr;
     }
    else
     d += bincr;
    setpix(x, y, lpcol);
   }
  }
 else                                       /* Check X-axes */
  {
   if ( x1 > x2 )                           /* x1 > x2? */
    {
     SwapInt( &x1, &x2 );                   /* Yes --> Swap X1 with X2 */
     SwapInt( &y1, &y2 );                   /*          and Y1 with Y2  */
    }

   yincr = ( y2 > y1 ) ? 1 : -1;            /* Set Y-axis increment */

   dx = x2 - x1;
   dy = abs( y2-y1 );
   d  = 2 * dy - dx;
   aincr = 2 * (dy - dx);
   bincr = 2 * dy;
   x = x1;
   y = y1;

   setpix(x, y, lpcol);                     /* Set first pixel */
   for (x=x1+1; x<=x2; ++x )                /* Execute line on X-axes */
    {
     if ( d >= 0 )
      {
       y += yincr;
       d += aincr;
      }
     else
      d += bincr;
     setpix(x, y, lpcol);
    }
  }
}


/**********************************************************************
 * PrintChar : Writes a character to the screen while in graphic mode.*
 **------------------------------------------------------------------**
 * Input   : THECHAR = Character to be written                       *
 *           X, Y    = X- and Y-coordinates of upper-left corner     *
 *           FG      = Foreground color                              *
 *           BK      = Background color                              *
 * Info    : Character is created in an 8x8 matrix, based on the     *
 *           8x8 ROM font.                                           *
 **********************************************************************/

void PrintChar( char thechar, int x, int y, BYTE fg, BYTE bk )
{
  typedef BYTE FDEF[256][8];                /* Font array */
  typedef FDEF far *TPTR;                   /* Pointer to font */

  BYTE    i, k,                             /* Loop counter */
          BMask;                            /* Bit mask for character design */

  static TPTR fptr = (TPTR) 0;              /* Pointer to font in ROM */
```

```
  if ( fptr == (TPTR) 0 )         /* Pointer to font already set ? */
    fptr = getfontptr();                  /* No --> Get pointer */

/*- Create character pixel by pixel ----------------------------------*/

  if ( bk == 255 )                /* Drawing transparent characters? */
    for ( i = 0; i < 8; ++i )     /* Yes --> Set foreground pixels only */
    {
      BMask = (*fptr)[thechar][i];      /* Get bit pattern for one line */
      for ( k = 0; k < 8; ++k, BMask <<= 1 )    /* Execute columns */
        if ( BMask & 128 )                      /* Pixel set? */
          setpix( x+k, y+i, fg );                       /* Yes */
    }
  else                            /* No --> Set every pixel */
    for ( i = 0; i < 8; ++i )                   /* Execute lines */
    {
      BMask = (*fptr)[thechar][i];      /* Get bit pattern for one line */
      for ( k = 0; k < 8; ++k, BMask <<= 1 )    /* Execute columns */
        setpix( x+k, y+i, ( BMask & 128 ) ? fg : bk );
    }
}


/*********************************************************************
* GrfxPrintf: Displays a formatted string in the graphic screen.   *
* Input    : X, Y  = Starting coordinates (0 - ...)                 *
*            fg    = Foreground color                               *
*            bk    = Background color (255 = transparent)           *
*            STRING = String with formatting information            *
*            ...   = arguments are similar to printf                *
*********************************************************************/

void GrfxPrintf( int x, int y, BYTE fg, BYTE bk, char * string, ... )
{
  va_list parameter;              /* Parameter list for VA_... macros */
  char stngbuf[255],                    /* Buffer for formatted string */
       *cp;

  va_start( parameter, string );        /* Convert parameters */
  vsprintf( stngbuf, string, parameter );       /* Format */
  for ( cp = stngbuf; *cp; ++cp, x+= 8 )  /* Display formatted */
    PrintChar( *cp, x, y, fg, bk );       /* string using PrintChar */
}


/*********************************************************************
* GetVideo: Gets the contents of a rectangular range from video RAM *
*           and puts them in a buffer.                              *
**-----------------------------------------------------------------**
* Input    : PAGE  = Screen page (0 or 1)                           *
*            X1, Y1 = Starting coordinates                          *
*            WRANGE = Width of the rectangular range in pixels      *
*            HRANGE = Height of rectangular range in pixels         *
*            BUFPTR = Pointer to pixel buffer, in which the inform- *
*                     ation is to be placed                        *
* Output   : Pointer to created pixel buffer with the contents of the *
*            specified range                                        *
* Info     : If the BUFPTR parameter passes the ALLOCBUF value, a new *
*            pixel buffer is allocated using the heap, then returned. *
*            This buffer can be specified again for a new call.      *
*            unless the previous contents are still required and the *
*            size of the rectangular area remains unchanged compared *
*            to the preceding call.                                 *
*            The specified area must begin at an X-coordinate that  *
*            can be divided by eight and extend over a multiple of  *
```

```
*            eight pixels.                                          *
*********************************************************************/

PIXPTR GetVideo( BYTE page, int x1, int y1, BYTE wrange, BYTE hrange,
                 PIXPTR bufptr )
{
  if ( bufptr == ALLOCBUF )       /* No buffer passed during call? */
  {                                       /* No --> Create one */
    bufptr = malloc( sizeof( PIXBUF ) );        /* Create pixel buffer */
    bufptr->pixbptr = malloc( (wrange*hrange) / 2 );  /* Alloc. px.b. */
    bufptr->numrows = hrange;           /* Height of buffer in lines */
    bufptr->widthbytes = wrange / 8;    /* Width of a line in bytes */
    bufptr->pixblen = (wrange*hrange) / 2;  /* Total length of buffer */
  }

  copyvideo2buf( bufptr->pixbptr, page, x1, y1, wrange / 8, hrange );
  return bufptr;                 /* Return pointer and buffer to caller */
}


/*********************************************************************
* PutVideo: Writes the contents of a rectangular area of the screen *
*           previously saved by GetVideo back to the video RAM.    *
**-----------------------------------------------------------------**
* Input    : BUFPTR = Pointer to pixel buffer returned during       *
*                     previous call for GetVideo                    *
*            PAGE  = Screen page (0 or 1)                            *
*            X1, Y1 = Starting coordinates                          *
* Info     : This procedure does not delete the pixel buffer. The   *
*            FreePixBuf procedure must be called for this.           *
*            The specified X-coordinate must be a multiple of eight! *
*********************************************************************/

void PutVideo( PIXPTR bufptr, BYTE page, int x1, int y1 )
{
  copybuf2video( bufptr->pixbptr, page, x1, y1,
                 bufptr->widthbytes, bufptr->numrows );
}


/*********************************************************************
* FreePixBuf: Clears a pixel buffer allocated by the heap when      *
*             GetVideo was called.                                  *
**-----------------------------------------------------------------**
* Input    : BUFPTR = Pointer to pixel buffer returned during       *
*                     previous call for GetVideo                    *
*********************************************************************/

void FreePixBuf( PIXPTR bufptr )
{
  free( bufptr->pixbptr );
  free( bufptr );
}


/*********************************************************************
* CreateSprite: Creates a sprite based on a user-defined            *
*               pixel pattern.                                      *
**-----------------------------------------------------------------**
* Input    : SPLOOKP = Pointer to data structure from CompileSprite() *
* Output   : Pointer to created sprite structure                    *
* Info     : Sprite backgrounds comprise two adjacent areas the same *
*            size as the sprites.                                   *
*********************************************************************/

SPID *CreateSprite( SPLOOK *splookp )
{
```

```
SPID *spidp;                    /* Pointer to created sprite structure */

spidp = (SPID *) malloc( sizeof(SPID) );  /* Allocate sprite struc. */
spidp->splookp = splookp;                    /* Pass data to the */
                                             /* sprite structure */
/*- Create two background buffers by saving a large enough area ---*/
/*- from video RAM using GetVideo                             ---*/

spidp->hgptr[0] = GetVideo( 0, 0, 0, splookp->twidth,
                            splookp->theight, ALLOCBUF );
spidp->hgptr[1] = GetVideo( 0, 0, 0, splookp->twidth,
                            splookp->theight, ALLOCBUF );
return spidp;              /* Return pointer to the sprite structure */
}


/*****************************************************************
* BfInit: Creates bit field.                                    *
**-------------------------------------------------------------**
* Input   : NUMBIT = Number of bits to be found in the bit field *
* Output  : Pointer to bit field descriptor                      *
*****************************************************************/

BFPTR BfInit( int NumBit )
{
 BFPTR bfptr;                   /* Pointer to created descriptor */

 bfptr = malloc( sizeof( BITFIELD ) );        /* Create descriptor */

 /*-- Create and initialize bit field --------------------------*/

 bfptr->fieldptr = bfptr->curptr = malloc( ( NumBit + 7 ) / 8 );
 bfptr->curbit = bfptr->curbyte = 0;

 return bfptr;                  /* Return  descriptor pointer */
}


/*****************************************************************
* BfAppendBit: Appends a bit to a bit field.                    *
**-------------------------------------------------------------**
* Input   : BFID = Pointer to the bit field descriptor, returned by *
*                  the call to BfInit()                          *
*           BIT  = Values of bits to be appended (0 or 1)        *
* Output  : None                                                 *
*****************************************************************/

void BfAppendBit( BFPTR bfid, BYTE bit )
{
 bfid->curbyte |= bit;              /* Add bit at bit position 0 */
 if ( bfid->curbit == 7 )           /* Byte already full? */
 {                                  /* Yes */
  *(bfid->curptr++) = bfid->curbyte;    /* Place byte in buffer */
  bfid->curbyte = bfid->curbit = 0;     /* Bit mask reverts to 0 */
 }
 else                               /* Byte still not full */
 {
  ++bfid->curbit;                       /* Process another bit */
  bfid->curbyte <<= 1;                  /* Shift bit mask */
 }
}


/*****************************************************************
* BfEnd : Ends bit field processing, clears descriptor without  *
*         clearing the bit field.                               *
**-------------------------------------------------------------**
```

```
* Input   : BFID = Pointer to the bit field descriptor returned *
*                  after a call to BfInit()                      *
* Output  : Pointer to the bit field whose buffer can be released by *
*           FREE().                                              *
*****************************************************************/

void *BfEnd( BFPTR bfid )
{
 void *retptr;                      /* Pointer to bit field */

 if ( bfid->curbit )                /* Last byte still not full? */
  *bfid->curptr = bfid->curbyte << (7 - bfid->curbit );/*No --> Close*/

 retptr = bfid->fieldptr;           /* Store pointer to bit field */
 free( bfid );                      /* Free descriptor */

 return retptr;                     /* Return pointer to bit field */
}


/*****************************************************************
* CompileSprite: Creates a sprite's pixel and bit patterns, based on *
*                the sprite's definition at runtime.            *
**-------------------------------------------------------------**
* Input   : BUFP    = Pointer to array contains string pointers  *
*                     controlling sprite's pattern               *
*           SHEIGHT = Sprite height and number of strings needed *
* Info    : In passed sprite pattern, a space represents a background*
*           pixel, the A represents color code 0, B represents 1,*
*           1, C represents 2, etc.                              *
*****************************************************************/

SPLOOK *CompileSprite( char **bufp, BYTE sheight )
{
 BYTE  stwidth,                     /* String width */
       spwidth,                     /* Sprite width */
       c,                           /* Get character from c sprite array */
       i, k, l, y;                  /* Loop variables */
 SPLOOK *splookp;             /* Pointer to created sprite structure */
 PIXPTR tpix;                 /* Get sprite background temporarily */
 BFPTR  bfptr;                /* Pointer to bit field descriptor */

 /*-- Create SpriteLook structure and fill with data ---------------*/

 splookp = (SPLOOK *) malloc( sizeof(SPLOOK) );
 stwidth = (BYTE) strlen( *bufp );  /* String length and logo width */
 spwidth = ( ( stwidth + 7 + 7 ) / 8 ) * 8;      /* Total width */
 splookp->twidth = spwidth;
 splookp->theight = sheight;

 setpage( 1 );                      /* Draw sprites in page 1 */
 showpage( 0 );                     /* but show page 0 */

 tpix = GetVideo( 1, 0, 0, spwidth, sheight, ALLOCBUF );/* Store bkg */

 /*-- Draw and code sprite eight times -----------------------------*/

 for (l = 0; l < 8; ++l )
 {                                  /* Fill background with black pixels */
  for ( y = 0; y < sheight; ++y )
   Line( 0, y, spwidth-1, y, 0 );

  bfptr = BfInit( spwidth*sheight ); /* Alloc. mem. for AND buffer */

  for ( i = 0; i < sheight ; ++i )          /* Execute lines */
```

```
      {
        for ( y = 1; y; --y )              /* Create AND bits for left border */
          BfAppendBit( bfptr, 1 );

        for ( k = 0; k < stwidth; ++k )          /* Execute columns */
        {
          if ( ( c = *(*(bufp+i)+k) ) == 32 )     /* Background pixel? */
          {                                      /* Yes --> Color code 0 */
            setpix( k+1, i, 0 );
            BfAppendBit( bfptr, 1 );    /* Background pixel remaining? */
          }
          else                        /* No --> Color code as specified */
          {
            setpix( k+1, i, c-64 );
            BfAppendBit( bfptr, 0 );        /* Mask background pixels */
          }
        }

        for ( y = spwidth-stwidth-1; y ; --y )  /* Append AND bits for */
          BfAppendBit( bfptr, 1 );              /* right border        */
      }
      splookp->bmskp[ 1 ] = BfEnd( bfptr );

      /*-- Get sprite pixel pattern from video RAM ---------------------*/
      splookp->pixmp[ 1 ] = GetVideo( 1, 0, 0, spwidth, sheight, ALLOCBUF
);
   }                                   /* Design first of eight sprites */

   PutVideo( tpix, 1, 0, 0 );          /* Restore sprite background in */
   FreePixBuf( tpix );                 /* page 1 and clear buffer      */

   return splookp;                     /* Return pointer to sprite buffer */
}

/****************************************************************
* PrintSprite : Displays sprite in a specified page.           *
**-----------------------------------------------------------**
* Input   : SPIDP   = Pointer to the sprite structure          *
*           SPRPAGE = Page in which sprite should be drawn (0 or 1) *
****************************************************************/

void PrintSprite( register SPID *spidp, BYTE sprpage )
{
   int x;                             /* X-coordinate of sprite */

   x = spidp->x[sprpage];
   mergeandcopybuf2video( spidp->splookp->pixmp[x % 8]->pixbptr,
                          spidp->hgptr[sprpage]->pixbptr,
                          spidp->splookp->bmskp[x % 8],
                          sprpage,
                          x & (~7),
                          spidp->y[sprpage],
                          spidp->splookp->twidth / 8,
                          spidp->splookp->theight );
}

/****************************************************************
* GetSpriteBg: Gets sprite background and specifies the position. *
**-----------------------------------------------------------**
* Input   : SPIDP   = Pointer to the sprite structure          *
*           SPRPAGE = Page from which background should be copied *
*                     (0 or 1)                                  *
****************************************************************/
```

```
void GetSpriteBg( register SPID *spidp, BYTE sprpage )
{
   GetVideo( sprpage, spidp->x[sprpage] & (~7),  spidp->y[sprpage],
             spidp->splookp->twidth, spidp->splookp->theight,
             spidp->hgptr[sprpage] );
}

/****************************************************************
* RestoreSpriteBg: Restores sprite background from original graphic *
*                  page.                                        *
**-----------------------------------------------------------**
* Input   : SPIDP   = Pointer to the sprite structure          *
*           SPRPAGE = Page from which background should be copied *
*                     (0 or 1)                                  *
****************************************************************/

void RestoreSpriteBg( register SPID *spidp, BYTE sprpage )
{
   PutVideo( spidp->hgptr[sprpage], sprpage,
             spidp->x[sprpage] & (~7), spidp->y[sprpage] );
}

/****************************************************************
* MoveSprite: Copies sprite in background to original graphic page. *
**-----------------------------------------------------------**
* Input   : SPIDP   = Pointer to the sprite structure          *
*           SPRPAGE = Page to which the background should be copied *
*                     (0 or 1)                                  *
*           DELTAX  = Movement counter in X-                    *
*           DELTAY    and Y-directions                          *
* Output  : Collision marker (see OUT_ constants)              *
****************************************************************/

BYTE MoveSprite( SPID *spidp, BYTE sprpage, int deltax, int deltay )
{
   int newx, newy;                    /* New sprite coordinates */
   BYTE out;                          /* Display collision with border */

   /*-- X-coordinates and test for border collision -------------------*/

   if ( ( newx = spidp->x[sprpage] + deltax ) < 0 )
   {
     newx = 0 - deltax - spidp->x[sprpage];
     out = OUT_LEFT;
   }
   else
     if ( newx > MAXX - spidp->splookp->twidth )
     {
       newx = (2*(MAXX+1))-newx-2*(spidp->splookp->twidth);
       out = OUT_RIGHT;
     }
     else
       out = OUT_NO;

   /*-- Y-coordinates and test for border collision -------------------*/

   if ( ( newy = spidp->y[sprpage] + deltay ) < 0 )     /* Top border? */
   {                                      /* Yes --> Deltay must be negative */
     newy = 0 - deltay - spidp->y[sprpage];
     out |= OUT_TOP;
   }
   else
     if ( newy + spidp->splookp->theight > MAXY+1  )  /* Bottom border? */
     {                                      /* Yes --> Deltay must be positive */
```

```
    newy = (2*(MAXY+1))-newy-2*(spidp->splookp->theight);
    out |= OUT_BOTTOM;
    }

/*-- Set new position only if different from old position ----------*/

if ( newx != spidp->x[sprpage] || newy != spidp->y[sprpage] )
  {                                          /* If there's a new position */
  RestoreSpriteBg( spidp, sprpage );   /* then reset background and */
  spidp->x[sprpage] = newx;                  /* store new coordinates   */
  spidp->y[sprpage] = newy;
  GetSpriteBg( spidp, sprpage );             /* Get new background */
  PrintSprite( spidp, sprpage );   /* Draw sprite in specified page */
  }
return out;
}

/***********************************************************************
* SetSprite: Sets sprite at a specific position.                      *
**-------------------------------------------------------------------**
* Input   : SPIDP = Pointer to the sprite structure                   *
*           x0, y0 = Sprite coordinates for page 0                    *
*           x1, y1 = Sprite coordinates for page 1                    *
* Info    : This function call should be made the first time that     *
*           MoveSprite() is called.                                   *
***********************************************************************/

void SetSprite( SPID *spidp, int x0, int y0, int x1, int y1 )
{
spidp->x[0] = x0;           /* Store coordinates in sprite structure */
spidp->x[1] = x1;
spidp->y[0] = y0;
spidp->y[1] = y1;

GetSpriteBg( spidp, 0 );            /* Get sprite backgrounds */
GetSpriteBg( spidp, 1 );            /* in pages 0 and 1       */
PrintSprite( spidp, 0 );                /* Draw sprite in */
PrintSprite( spidp, 1 );                /* pages 1 and 0  */
}

/***********************************************************************
* RemoveSprite: Removes a sprite from its current position, making    *
*               it invisible.                                         *
**-------------------------------------------------------------------**
* Input   : SPIDP = Pointer to the sprite structure                   *
* Info    : After this function call the SetSprite() function must be *
*           called before the sprite can be moved using MoveSprite(). *
***********************************************************************/

void RemoveSprite( SPID *spidp )
{
RestoreSpriteBg( spidp, 0 );        /* Restore sprite background */
RestoreSpriteBg( spidp, 1 );        /* in pages 0 and 1          */
}

/***********************************************************************
* Demo: Demonstrates these functions.                                 *
***********************************************************************/

void Demo( void )
{
static char *StarShipUp[20] =
                    { "            AA          ",
                      "            AAAA        ",
```

```
            "            AAAA          ",
            "            AA            ",
            "           GGBBGG         ",
            "          GBBCCBBG        ",
            "          GBBBCCBBBG      ",
            "         GBBBBBBBBBBG     ",
            "         GBBBBBBBBBBG     ",
            " G       GBBBBBBBBBBBG       G ",
            "GCG      GGDBBBBBBBBBBDGG      GCG",
            "GCG     GGBBBBDBBB  BBBBDBBGG     GCG",
            "GCBGGGBBBBBBBDBB    BBDBBBBBGGGBBGGBCG",
            "GCBBBBBBBBBBBBBDB    BDBBBBBBBBBBBBBCG",
            "BBBBBBBBBBBBBDB  BB  BDBBBBBBBBBBBBBB",
            "GGCBBBBBBBBBDBBBBBBBBBBBDBBBBBBBCG ",
            " GGCCBBBDDDDDDDDDDDDDDDBBBCCG   ",
            "  GGBBDDDDDGGGGGDDDDDDBBG   ",
            "    GDDDDGGG    GGGDDDDDG    ",
            "    DDDD          DDDD     " };

static char *StarShipDown[20] =
                    {
            "    DDDD          DDDD     ",
            "    GDDDDGGG    GGGDDDDDG    ",
            "  GGBBDDDDDGGGGGDDDDDDBBG   ",
            " GGCCBBBDDDDDDDDDDDDDDDBBBCCG   ",
            "GGCBBBBBBBBBDBBBBBBBBBBBDBBBBBBBCG ",
            "BBBBBBBBBBBBBDB  BB  BDBBBBBBBBBBBBBB",
            "GCBBBBBBBBBBBBBDB    BDBBBBBBBBBBBBBCG",
            "GCBGGGBBBBBBBDBB    BBDBBBBBGGGBBGGBCG",
            "GCG     GGBBBBDBBB  BBBBDBBGG     GCG",
            "GCG      GGDBBBBBBBBBBDGG      GCG",
            " G       GBBBBBBBBBBBG       G ",
            "         GBBBBBBBBBBG     ",
            "         GBBBBBBBBBBG     ",
            "          GBBBCCBBBG      ",
            "          GBBCCBBG        ",
            "           GGBBGG         ",
            "            AA            ",
            "            AAAA          ",
            "            AAAA          ",
            "            AA            " };

#define SPRNUM 6                          /* Number of sprites */
#define CWIDTH 42       /* Width of copyright message in characters */
#define CHEIGHT  6                              /* Height in rows */
#define SX      (MAXX-(CWIDTH*8)) / 2    /* Starting X-coordinate */
#define SY      (MAXY-(CHEIGHT*8)) / 2   /* Starting Y-coordinate */

struct {                                   /* For sprite management */
        SPID *spidp;                       /* Pointer to sprite ID */
        int deltax[2],             /* X-movement for pages 0 and 1 */
            deltay[2];             /* Y-movement for pages 0 and 1 */
        } sprites[ SPRNUM ];
BYTE  page,                                       /* Current page */
      out;                        /* Get flags for page collision */
int   x, y, i,                                    /* Loop counter */
      dx, dy;                                     /* Movement value */
char  lc;
SPLOOK *starshipupp, *starshipdnp;             /* Pointer to sprites */

srand( *(int far *) 0x0040006cl );   /* Initialize random generator */

/*-- Create patterns for the different sprites ---------------------*/
```

369

```
starshipupp = CompileSprite( StarShipUp,   20 );
starshipdnp = CompileSprite( StarShipDown, 20 );

/*-- Fill the first two graphic pages with characters --------------*/

for ( page = 0; page < 2; ++ page )
{
  setpage( page );
  showpage( page );
  for ( lc = 0, y = 0; y < (MAXY+1)-8; y += 12 )
    for ( x = 0; x < (MAXX+1)-8; x += 8 )
      GrfxPrintf( x, y, lc & 15, 255, "%c", lc++ & 127 );

  /*-- Display copyright message ------------------------------------*/

  Line( SX-1, SY-1, SX+CWIDTH*8, SY-1, 15 );
  Line( SX+CWIDTH*8, SY-1, SX+CWIDTH*8, SY+CHEIGHT*8, 15 );
  Line( SX+CWIDTH*8, SY+CHEIGHT*8, SX-1, SY+CHEIGHT*8, 15 );
  Line( SX-1, SY+CHEIGHT*8, SX-1, SY-1, 15 );
  GrfxPrintf( SX, SY,    15, 4,
              "                                        " );
  GrfxPrintf( SX, SY+8,  15, 4,
              " S6435C.C  -  (c) 1992 by Michael Tischer " );
  GrfxPrintf( SX, SY+16, 15, 4,
              "                                        " );
  GrfxPrintf( SX, SY+24, 15, 4,
              "      Sprite demo for 640x350 mode      " );
  GrfxPrintf( SX, SY+32, 15, 4,
              "           on EGA and VGA cards         " );
  GrfxPrintf( SX, SY+40, 15, 4,
              "                                        " );
}

/*-- Create sprites -------------------------------------------------*/

for ( i = 0; i < SPRNUM ; ++ i)
{
  sprites[ i ].spidp = CreateSprite( starshipupp );
  do                       /* Select movement values for sprites */
  {
    dx = 0;
    dy = random(8) - 4;
  }
  while ( dx==0  &&  dy==0 );

  sprites[ i ].deltax[0] = sprites[ i ].deltax[1] = dx * 2;
  sprites[ i ].deltay[0] = sprites[ i ].deltay[1] = dy * 2;

  x = ( MAXX / SPRNUM * i ) + (MAXX / SPRNUM - 40) / 2 ;
  y = random( (MAXY+1) - 40 );
  SetSprite( sprites[ i ].spidp, x, y, x - dx, y - dy );
}

/*-- Move sprites and bounce them off the page borders -------------*/

page = 1;                            /* Start with page 1 */
while ( !kbhit() )               /* Press a key to end the loop */
{
  showpage( (BYTE) (1 - page) );       /* Display other page */

  for ( i = 0; i < SPRNUM; ++ i)          /* Execute sprites */
  {                    /* Move sprite and check for page collision */
    out = MoveSprite( sprites[i].spidp, page, sprites[i].deltax[page],
                      sprites[i].deltay[page] );
    if ( out & OUT_TOP || out & OUT_BOTTOM )   /*T/B collision?*/
    { /* Yes --> Change direction and sprite graphic ------------ */
      sprites[i].deltay[page] = 0 - sprites[i].deltay[page];
      sprites[i].spidp->splookp = ( out & OUT_TOP ) ? starshipdnp
                                                    : starshipupp;
    }
    if ( out & OUT_LEFT || out & OUT_RIGHT )
      sprites[i].deltax[page] = 0 - sprites[i].deltax[page];
  }
  page = (page+1) & 1;                    /* Toggle between 1 and 0 */
}
}

/***********************************************************************/
/***                 M A I N   P R O G R A M                 ***/
/***********************************************************************/

void main( void )
{
  union REGS regs;

  if ( IsEgaVga() != NEITHERNOR )     /* EGA or VGA card installed? */
  {                                    /* Yes --> Go ahead */
    init640350();                      /* Initialize graphic mode */
    Demo();
    getch();                                    /* Wait for a key */
    regs.x.ax = 0x0003;                    /* Shift to text mode */
    int86( 0x10, &regs, &regs );
  }
  else
    printf( "S6435C.C - (c) 1992 by Michael Tischer\n\n"\
            "This program requires an EGA or a VGA card\n\n" );
}
```

Assembler listing: S6435CA.ASM

```
;****************************************************;
;*                 S6435CA.ASM                     *;
;*------------------------------------------------- *;
;*  Task       : Contains routines for generating sprites in *;
;*               640x350 mode on EGA or VGA cards.  *;
;*------------------------------------------------- *;
;*  Author     : Michael Tischer                    *;
;*  Developed on : 09/08/90                         *;
;*  Last update  : 02/26/92                         *;
;*------------------------------------------------- *;
;*  Memory model : SMALL                            *;
;*------------------------------------------------- *;
;*  Assembly    : MASM /mx S6435CA;   or   TASM -mx S6435CA *;
;*               ... Link to S6435C.C               *;
;****************************************************;

IGROUP group _text               ;Program segment
DGROUP group const, _bss, _data  ;Data segment
       assume CS:IGROUP, DS:DGROUP, ES:DGROUP, SS:DGROUP

CONST  segment word public 'CONST';All readable constants
CONST  ends

_BSS   segment word public 'BSS'  ;All uninitialized static vars.
_BSS   ends

_DATA  segment word public 'DATA' ;All initialized global & static
                                  ;variables
_DATA  ends

;== Constants ============================================
SC_INDEX     = 3c4h          ;Index register for sequencer ctrl.
SC_MAP_MASK  = 2             ;Number of map mask register
SC_MEM_MODE  = 4             ;Number of memory mode register

GC_INDEX     = 3ceh          ;Index register for graphics ctrl.
GC_READ_MAP  = 4             ;Number of read map register
GC_BIT_MASK  = 8             ;Number of bit mask register

PIXX         = 640           ;Horizontal resolution

;== Program ==============================================
_TEXT  segment byte public 'CODE';Program segment

;-- Public declarations -----------------------------------

public    _copybuf2video
public    _mergeandcopybuf2video
public    _copyvideo2buf

;---------------------------------------------------------
;-- CopyBuf2Video: Copies a rectangular range from video RAM
;-- Declaration: CopyBuf2Plane( byte *bufptr,
;--                             byte topage,
;--                             int  tox,
;--                             int  toy,
;--                             byte rwidth,
;--                             byte rheight );
_copybuf2video proc near

sfr0      struc              ;Structure for stack access
bp0       dw ?               ;Gets BP
```

```
stofs0    dw ?              ;Local var.: Starting offset in video
RAM
ret_adr0  dw ?              ;Return address to caller
bufptr0   dw ?              ;Buffer pointer
topage    dw ?              ;To page
tox       dw ?              ;To X-coordinate
toy       dw ?              ;To Y-coordinate
rwidth0   dw ?              ;Range width
rheight0  dw ?              ;Range height
sfr0      ends              ;End of structure

fr        equ [ bp - bp0 ]  ;Addr. of structure elements
bfr       equ byte ptr [ bp - bp0 ];Addr. of stack elements as bytes
          sub  sp,2         ;Space for local variables

          push bp           ;Prepare BP register for
          mov  bp,sp        ;addressing parameters
          push si           ;Store SI and DI
          push di

;-- Compute segment address for video RAM access -----------
          mov  ah,0A0h      ;Move ES to start of TO page
          cmp  bfr.topage,0 ;Page 0?
          je   cv0          ;Yes --> AL is O.K.

          mov  ax,0A6D6h    ;No --> Page 1 from A6D6H

cv0:      mov  es,ax

;-- Compute offset for target position in page -------------
          mov  ax,PIXX / 8  ;Move AX to TO position
          mul  fr.toy
          mov  bx,fr.tox
          shr  bx,1
          shr  bx,1
          shr  bx,1
          add  bx,ax
          mov  fr.stofs0,bx ;Store starting offset in local vars.

          mov  si,fr.bufptr0 ;Set DS:SI to buffer

;-- Load copy loop counter --------------------------------
          mov  dl,bfr.rwidth0 ;DL = Bytes
          mov  bx,PIXX / 8  ;BX as offset to next row
          sub  bl,dl
          xor  ch,ch        ;Counter high byte is always 0

;-- Prepare bitplane to be addressed ----------------------
          mov  ah,1         ;Load plane number as bit mask
          mov  al,SC_MAP_MASK ;Move register no. to AL

cv1:      mov  dx,SC_INDEX  ;End access to
          out  dx,ax        ;plane

;-- Bitplane copy routine, ignore background --------------
          mov  di,fr.stofs0 ;Move DI to starting offset
          mov  dh,bfr.rheight0 ;DH = Lines
          mov  dl,bfr.rwidth0 ;DL = Bytes

cv2:      mov  cl,dl        ;Move number of bytes to CL

          rep  movsb        ;Copy line
          add  di,bx        ;Add DI to next line
          dec  dh           ;One line remaining?
```

371

```
            jne     cv2             ;Yes --> Continue                      cmp     bfr.topage2,0   ;Page 0?
                                                                           je      cm0             ;Yes --> AL already O.K.
            shl     ah,1            ;Toggle to next plane
            test    ah,16           ;All planes processed?                 mov     ax,0A6D6h       ;No --> page 1 of A6D6H
            je      cv1             ;No --> Process next plane
                                                                   cm0:    mov     es,ax
            mov     ax,(0Fh shl 8)+ SC_MAP_MASK ;Enable access to
            mov     dx,SC_INDEX                 ;all bitplanes     ;-- Computer offset for target position in page -------------
            out     dx,ax                                                  mov     ax,PIXX / 8     ;Move AX to FROM target position
                                                                           mul     fr.toy2
            pop     di              ;Pop DI and SI from stack              mov     bx,fr.tox2
            pop     si                                                     shr     bx,1
            pop     bp              ;Pop BP from stack                     shr     bx,1
                                                                           shr     bx,1
            add     sp,2            ;Remove local variables                add     bx,ax
            ret                     ;Return to caller                      mov     fr.stofs2,bx    ;Store starting offset in local vars.

                                                                   ;-- Load counter for copy loop -----------------------------
_copybuf2video endp                                                        mov     dl,bfr.rwidth2  ;DL = Bytes
                                                                           mov     bx,PIXX / 8     ;BX as offset to next line
;-----------------------------------------------------------------         sub     bl,dl
;-- MergeAndCopyBuf2Video: A bit mask links the contents of a back-        xor     ch,ch           ;High byte of counter is always 0
;--             ground buffer to the contents of a sprite
;--             buffer and copies the result to video RAM         ;-- Configure bitplane to be addressed --------------------
;-- Declaration : MergeAndCopyBuf2Video( void * spribufptr,                mov     ah,1            ;Load plane number as bit mask
;--                                      void * hgbufptr,
;--                                      void * andbufptr,         cm1:    mov     al,SC_MAP_MASK  ;Move register number to AL
;--                                      BYTE page,                        mov     dx,SC_INDEX     ;Open access to plane for
;--                                      int  tox,                         out     dx,ax           ;processing
;--                                      int  toy,
;--                                      BYTE rwidth,             ;-- Copy routine for a bitplane without --------------------
;--                                      BYTE rheight );          ;-- checking the background
;-- Info        : see CopyVideo2Buf                                        mov     dx,fr.andbufptr ;Copy offset address of AND
_mergeandcopybuf2video proc near                                           mov     fr.andptr2,dx   ;pointer to local variable
                                                                           mov     di,fr.stofs2    ;DI to start offset
sfr2        struc               ;Structure for stack access                mov     dh,bfr.rheight2 ;DH = Lines
bp2         dw ?                ;Gets BP                                    mov     dl,bfr.rwidth2  ;DL = Bytes
andptr2     dw ?                ;Local var.: Pointer in AND buffer
stofs2      dw ?                ;Local var.: Starting offset in video cm2:  mov     cl,dl           ;Number of bytes to CL
RAM
ret_adr2    dw ?                ;Return address to caller          cm3:    mov     si,fr.hgbufptr  ;Load pointer to background buffer
spribufptr  dw ?                ;Pointer to sprite buffer                  lodsb                   ;Load byte from background buffer
hgbufptr    dw ?                ;Pointer to background buffer              mov     fr.hgbufptr,si  ;Store incremented offset
andbufptr   dw ?                ;Pointer to AND buffer
topage2     dw ?                ;To page                                   mov     si,fr.andptr2   ;Load pointer in AND buffer
tox2        dw ?                ;To X-coordinate                           and     al,[si]         ;Link background and AND mask
toy2        dw ?                ;To Y-coordinate                           inc     si              ;Increment offset in AND buffer
rwidth2     dw ?                ;Range width                               mov     fr.andptr2,si   ;and save
rheight2    dw ?                ;Range height
sfr2        ends                ;End of structure                          mov     si,fr.spribufptr ;Load pointer to sprite buffer
                                                                           or      al,[si]         ;OR byte from sprite buffer
fr          equ [ bp - bp2 ]      ;Addresses structure elements            inc     si              ;Increment offset in sprite buffer
bfr         equ byte ptr [ bp - bp2 ] ;Addresses stack element as byte     mov     fr.spribufptr,si ;and save

            sub     sp,4            ;Space for local variables             stosb                   ;Write byte to video RAM
                                                                           loop    cm3             ;Process next byte
            push    bp              ;Prepare BP register for
            mov     bp,sp           ;addressing parameters                 add     di,bx           ;DI in next line
                                                                           dec     dh              ;Another line?
            push    ds              ;Store DS                              jne     cm2             ;Yes --> Continue
            push    si              ;Store SI and DI
            push    di                                                     shl     ah,1            ;Switch to next plane
                                                                           test    ah,16           ;All planes processed?
;-- Calculate segment address for access to video RAM ------                je      cm1             ;No --> Continue with next plane
            mov     ax,0A000h       ;Move ES to start of T0 page
```

```
        mov    ax,(0Fh shl 8)+ SC_MAP_MASK  ;Allow access to
        mov    dx,SC_INDEX                  ;all bitplanes
        out    dx,ax

        pop    di                  ;Pop DI and SI from stack
        pop    si
        pop    ds                  ;Pop DS from stack
        pop    bp

        add    sp,4                ;Remove local variables
        ret                        ;Return to caller

_mergeandcopybuf2video endp

;----------------------------------------------------------------------
;-- CopyVideo2Buf: Copies a rectangular range from video RAM to
;--                a buffer
;-- Declaration : CopyPlane2Buf( byte *bufptr,
;--                              byte frompage,
;--                              int fromx,
;--                              int fromy,
;--                              byte rwidth,
;--                              byte rheight );
;-- Info        : In this version of the routine, the area to be
;--               copied must begin at a pixel column that can be
;--               divided by eight and extend over a multiple of
;--               eight pixels.
;--               RWIDTH refers to the number of bytes per line
;--               on a bitplane.
_copyvideo2buf proc near

sfr1     struc              ;Structure for stack access
bp1      dw ?               ;Gets BP
stofs1   dw ?               ;Local var.: Starting offset in video
RAM
ret_adr1 dw ?               ;Return address to caller
bufptr1  dw ?               ;Buffer pointer
frompage dw ?               ;From page
fromx    dw ?               ;From X-coordinate
fromy    dw ?               ;From Y-coordinate
rwidth1  dw ?               ;Range width of range in pixels
rheight1 dw ?               ;Range height in pixel lines
sfr1     ends               ;End of structure

fr       equ [ bp - bp1 ]        ;Addresses structure elements
bfr      equ byte ptr [ bp - bp1 ] ;Addresses stack element as byte

        sub    sp,2                ;Space for local variables

        push   bp                  ;Prepare BP register for
        mov    bp,sp               ;addressing parameters

        push   ds                  ;Store DS
        push   si                  ;Push SI and DI onto stack
        push   di

        push   ds                  ;Prepare ES for buffer access
        pop    es                  ;with DS

;-- Calculate segment address for access to video RAM ------
        mov    ax,0A000h           ;Move ES start of FROM page
        cmp    bfr.frompage,0      ;Page 0?
        je     cc0                 ;Yes --> AL is O.K.
```

```
        mov    ax,0A6D6h           ;No --> Page 1 of A6D6H
cc0:    mov    ds,ax

;-- Form offset in page to be read -----------------------
        mov    ax,PIXX / 8         ;Move AX to target position FROM
        mul    fr.fromy
        mov    bx,fr.fromx
        shr    bx,1
        shr    bx,1
        shr    bx,1
        add    bx,ax
        mov    fr.stofs1,bx        ;Store start offset in local variable

        mov    di,fr.bufptr1       ;Set ES:DI to buffer

;-- Load counter for copy loop ------------------------
        mov    dl,bfr.rwidth1      ;DL = Bytes
        mov    bx,PIXX / 8         ;BX as offset to next line
        sub    bl,dl
        xor    ch,ch               ;High byte of counter is always 0

;-- Set addressable bitplane ------------------------------
        xor    ah,ah               ;Begin with plane #0
        mov    al,GC_READ_MAP      ;Register number to AL
cc1:    mov    dx,GC_INDEX         ;Load index address of graphic ctrl.
        out    dx,ax               ;Load read map register

;-- Copy routine for a bitplane without checking -----------
;-- background
        mov    dh,bfr.rheight1     ;DH = Lines
        mov    dl,bfr.rwidth1      ;DL = Bytes
        mov    si,fr.stofs1        ;Load starting offset to SI

cc2:    mov    cl,dl               ;Number of bytes to CL

        rep movsb                  ;Copy line
        add    si,bx               ;SI in next line
        dec    dh                  ;Another line?
        jne    cc2                 ;Yes --> Continue

        inc    ah                  ;Switch to next plane
        cmp    ah,4                ;All planes processed?
        jne    cc1                 ;No --> Continue with next plane

        pop    di                  ;Pop DI and SI from stack
        pop    si
        pop    ds                  ;Pop DS from stack

        pop    bp

        add    sp,2                ;Remove local variables
        ret                        ;Return to caller

_copyvideo2buf endp

;== End ========================================================
_text    ends               ;End of program segment
         end                 ;End program
```

4.8.10   EGA and VGA Card Registers

EGA and VGA cards are based on several different controllers that share the work of generating a video signal. These are the CRT controller, the attribute controller, the graphics controller, the sequencer controller, and the digital to analog controller (DAC), which is found only on VGA cards. In addition to these, EGA and VGA cards use several general registers. We'll discuss these controllers and registers in this section.

Originally, you could actually see which component on the card was responsible for which function because each was performed by a different chip. However, because of advancements in computer chip technology, all functions are now handled by one or two integrated controller chips.

In many instances, these integrated chips perform functions and graphics modes that far exceed the original EGA/VGA standard. To maintain compatibility, however, the register assignments are kept as similar to the original IBM EGA and VGA registers as possible. You'll find the registers described in this section on almost all EGA/VGA cards. Any registers that have different functions in EGA and VGA cards are discussed in detail.

This section doesn't cover registers that don't follow the EGA/VGA standard. Once we look past standard EGA and VGA functions and registers, standards don't exist. For example, there are no register standards for Super EGA or Super VGA. The three most popular Super VGA cards differ significantly in register assignments and expanded functions.

The registers we'll examine here show how many options haven't been explored yet in the expanded EGA/VGA BIOS.

Warning

Some registers shouldn't be changed. The most important of these are the CRT controller registers that manage the video signal and synchronize horizontal and vertical rescans. The ways these registers interact are very complex and improper programming could cause monitor damage.

There are many other bits and registers that you can manipulate without problems. However, you should be careful because sometimes there are small but important differences between the EGA and VGA cards. We'll document these differences in this section when possible.

General registers

In addition to the special controller registers, other EGA and VGA registers transfer more general information, which is used in the operation of the card. These are known as the *general registers*.

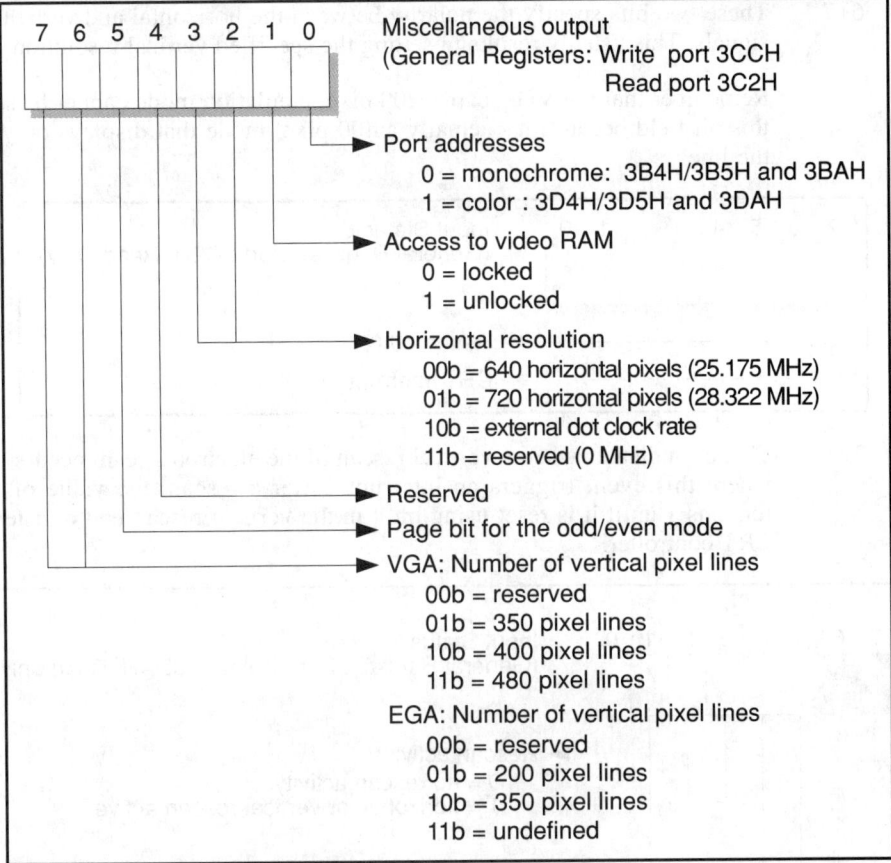

```
7  6  5  4  3  2  1  0      Miscellaneous output
                           (General Registers: Write port 3CCH
                                               Read port 3C2H
```

Port addresses
    0 = monochrome: 3B4H/3B5H and 3BAH
    1 = color : 3D4H/3D5H and 3DAH

Access to video RAM
    0 = locked
    1 = unlocked

Horizontal resolution
    00b = 640 horizontal pixels (25.175 MHz)
    01b = 720 horizontal pixels (28.322 MHz)
    10b = external dot clock rate
    11b = reserved (0 MHz)

Reserved

Page bit for the odd/even mode

VGA: Number of vertical pixel lines
    00b = reserved
    01b = 350 pixel lines
    10b = 400 pixel lines
    11b = 480 pixel lines

EGA: Number of vertical pixel lines
    00b = reserved
    01b = 200 pixel lines
    10b = 350 pixel lines
    11b = undefined

0   For MDA card emulation, this bit specifies the port address of the CRT data
        and index registers, and the input status register 1. These registers normally
        occupy ports 3D4H/3D5H and 3DAH, but this allows you to switch them to
        3B4H/3B5H and 3BAH.

2+3   This bit field selects the active clock. This also specifies the horizontal
        resolution of a pixel line because the dot clock rate is directly related to the
        number of pixels that can be displayed.

        The dot clock rate of 0 MHz is reserved because it may only be used during a
        reset of the VGA card.

        A reset using the sequencer's reset register must always be executed
        immediately after changing this register.

5   In the Odd/Even video modes (0, 1, 2, 3, and 7), this bit acts as the low bit for
        memory access. It determines whether odd or even addresses will be accessed in
        each bitplane. If this bit is 1 (default), then all bytes at even offset addresses
        are accessed. If it is 0, then odd addresses are accessed.

        This bit loses its meaning if bit 1 in register 6 of the graphics controller sets
        chain mode, or if bit 3 in register 4 of the sequencer controller sets chain4
        mode.

                                                                                    375

6+7   These two bits specify the polarity between the horizontal and vertical rescan signals. This usually results in setting the specified vertical resolution.

Remember that the VGA card's 200 pixel emulation mode cannot be set using this bit field because it's actually a 400 pixel mode that displays only half of the lines.

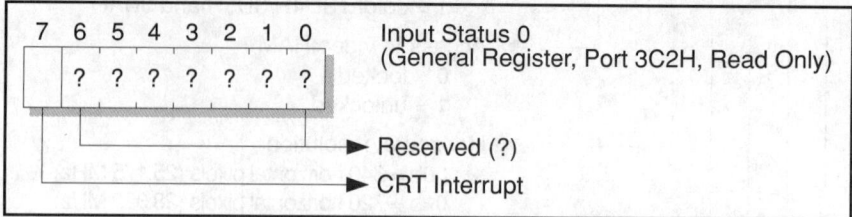

7   This bit indicates when a vertical rescan of the electron stream occurs in cases where this event triggers an interrupt. After a rescan, the value of this bit remains 1 until it is reset using bit 4 in the vertical rescan end register of the CRT controller.

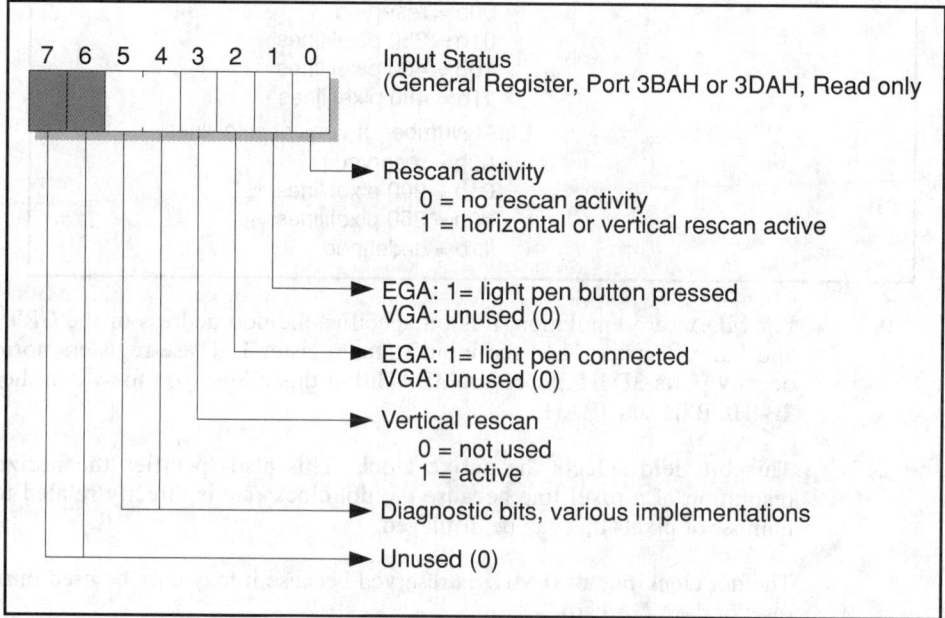

1+2   These bits act as the light pen port on the EGA card. They aren't used on the VGA card. Bit 2 indicates the presence of a light pen, and bit 1 indicates whether the button has been pressed. The position of the light pen can be read using registers 10H and 11H of the CRT controller.

3   This bit indicates the vertical rescan status, which allows a program to determine when certain register changes can safely be made.

CRT controller

The CRT controller is responsible for the picture displayed on your screen. It generates video signals for the monitor using the electron stream generated by the picture tube. It contains a number of registers that manage the timing of the electron stream's horizontal and vertical rescans.

Programmers usually aren't interested in these registers because the interactions between them are very complex. So, programming them should be left to the BIOS, which handles this automatically when you switch video modes. Registers, such as the offset register or the line compare register, are more useful to programmers. These can be used to create special video effects that aren't accessible using the BIOS. The following is an overview of the 25 CRT controller registers:

Nr.	Register Name
00H	Horizontal Total
01H	Horizontal Display End
02H	Start Horizontal Blanking
03H	End Horizontal Blanking
04H	Start Horizontal Rescan
05H	End Horizontal Rescan
06H	Vertical Total
07H	Overflow
08H	Vertical Pel Panning
09H	Maximum Scan Line
0AH	Cursor Start
0BH	Cursor End
0CH	Start Address High
0DH	Start Address Low
0EH	Cursor Location High
0FH	Cursor Location Low
10H	Start Vertical Rescan
11H	End Vertical Rescan
10H	Light Pen Low (EGA only)
11H	Light Pen High (EGA only)
12H	Vertical Display End
13H	Offset
14H	Underline Location
15H	Start Vertical Blank
16H	End Vertical Blank
17H	Mode Control
18H	Line Compare

The CRT controller registers are addressed by an index register and a data register, which are located at port addresses 3D4H and 3D5H when the EGA or VGA card is in color mode. If the card is in monochrome mode, these registers are accessed at port addresses 3B4H and 3B5H.

As usual, the register number must be written to the index register prior to access. With a read access, the contents of the specified register can then be read in the data register. This doesn't apply to most of the registers on the EGA card, however. Only the two light pen registers can be read on this card; all other registers are write-only. All of these VGA registers can be read.

You can write to the index and data registers in a single 16-bit operation during a read access. The value for the index register must be in the low byte and the value for the data register must be in the high byte.

Once you've placed the register number in the index register, it remains valid for subsequent read or write operations. So, you don't have to enter the register number each time if you perform several consecutive operations on the same register.

Remember that the first eight registers of the CRT controller on VGA cards can only be written if bit 7 in register 11H is set to 0. The BIOS will generally set this value to 1, prohibiting access to the first eight CRT registers.

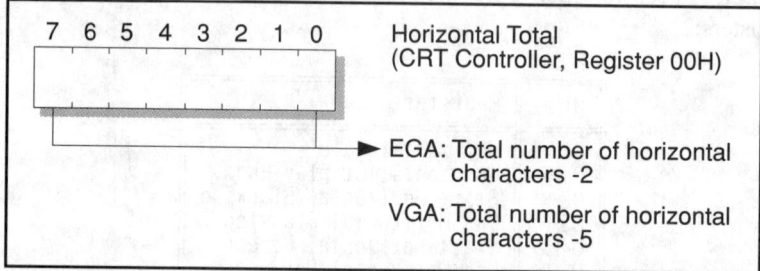

0-7   This specifies the total number of "characters" per screen line. The term "character" indicates an actual ASCII character in text mode. In graphics mode, "character" refers to a group of eight pixels. The total number of characters is calculated as the quotient of the bandwidth and the horizontal scan rate divided by the number of pixels per "character".

On an EGA card, the value in this register must be the number of total characters minus 2. For a VGA card, it's the total number minus 5.

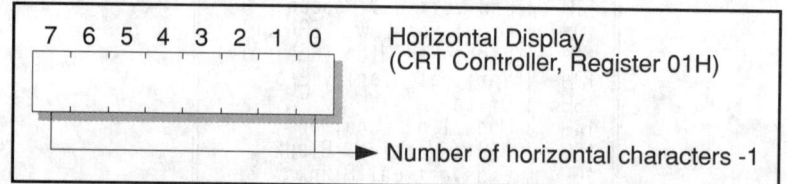

0-7   This register specifies the actual number of horizontal "characters". The value in this register must be reduced by 1 with both EGA and VGA cards.

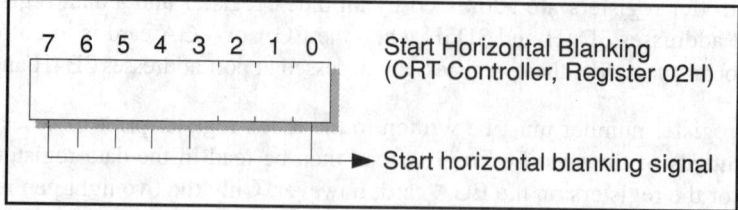

0-7   When the horizontal blanking signal starts, no more characters will be output because the electron stream from the picture tube has been shut off. Once again, the value is given in units of "characters." The first character at the left of the screen is assigned the number 0.

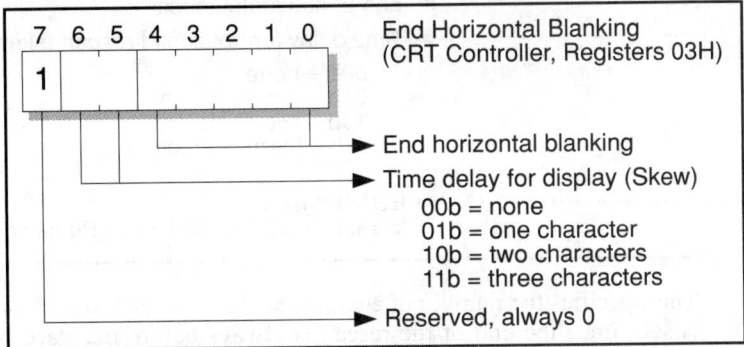

0-7   The end of the horizontal blanking is also described in terms of "characters." The first character output at the left of the screen is counted as 0. The end of the horizontal blanking always occurs before the start, so a maximum of six bits instead of eight are required. The sixth bit is in the end horizontal rescan register, which is number 05H in the CRT controller.

The value in this register is calculated as the sum of the values from the horizontal blanking register and the width of the horizontal blanking in "characters."

5+6   In certain instances, it may be necessary to build in a time delay (skew) in order to give the CRT controller enough time to read a character and its attributes from video RAM and then generate the corresponding pixel pattern with the character generator. The EGA card typically requires a skew of one character, but this usually isn't necessary with a VGA card.

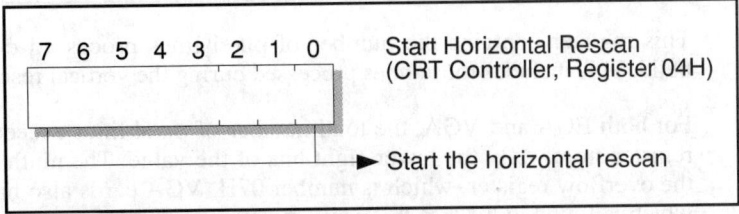

0-7   This register determines the "character" that triggers the rescan. This is used to center the picture horizontally.

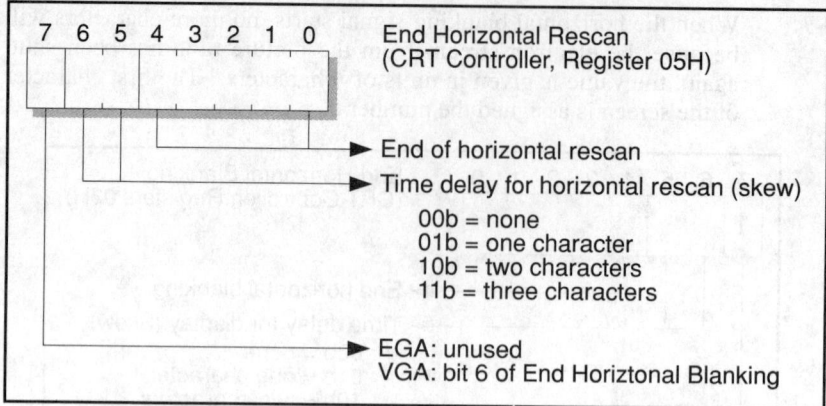

0-4   This specifies the number of characters where the end of the horizontal rescan is set. Since the end of the rescan is always before the start, only 5 bits are needed to code it. The units are again given in "characters".

5+6   A skew, or time delay, can set for the end of the horizontal rescan just as for the end of the horizontal blanking. Since the skew will vary from card to card, you should never change these bits.

7   This bit is an expansion of bits 0 through 4 of the end horizontal blanking register. It's the highest bit of the group.

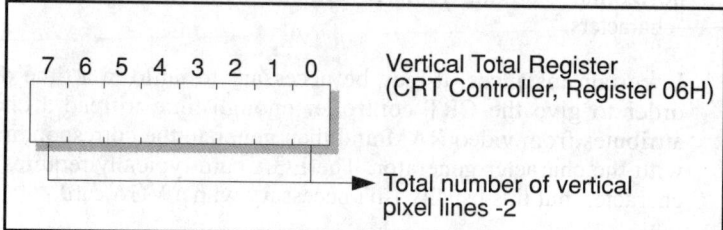

0-7   This register contains the number of pixel lines processed during a screen build. This includes those lines processed during the vertical rescan.

For both EGA and VGA, the total number of pixel lines exceeds 256, so this register stores only the lower eight bits of the value. The ninth bit is found in the overflow register, which is number 07H. VGA cards also have a tenth bit, which is found in bit 5 of this same register.

For both EGA and VGA cards, the value in this register must always be the actual total number of lines minus two.

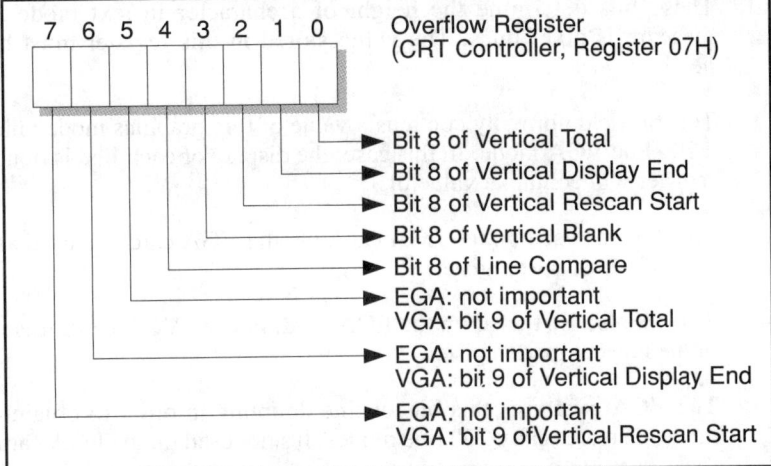

EGA and VGA cards need an overflow register because the number of vertical pixel lines exceeds 256 and therefore cannot be represented in a single eight bit register. The extra bit is kept in the overflow register for the registers that need nine bits.

Additional overflow bits for the VGA card are stored in the maximum scan line register (index number 09H).

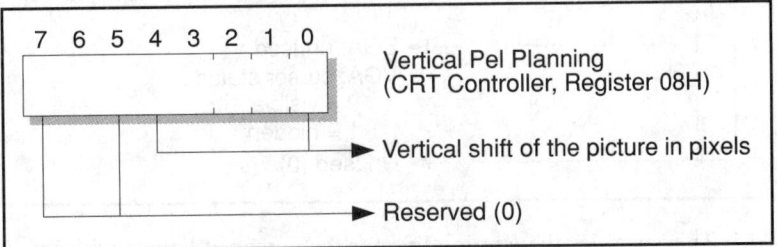

0-4   These bits can be used to create smooth vertical scrolling by moving the entire picture up by a specified number of pixels. A value of 0 represents the normal picture location. Larger values indicate a corresponding upward shift.

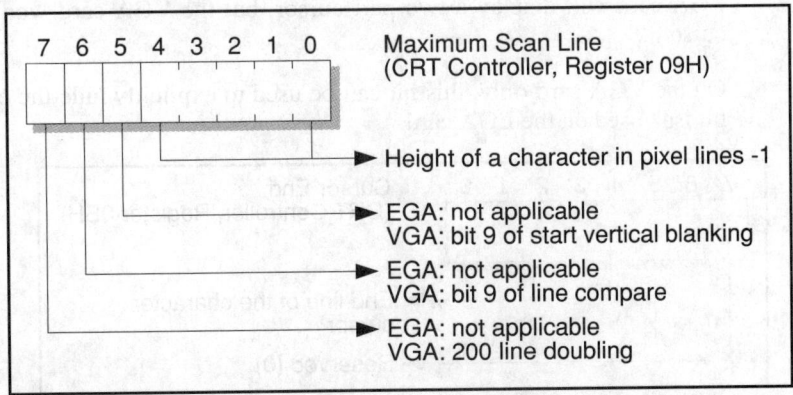

0-4   These bits determine the height of a character in text mode. The unit of measure is pixel lines. The value stored in this register must be the actual height minus 1.

         This bit field normally contains a value of 0 in graphics mode unless it's using a 200 line VGA mode. In this case, the display of each line is doubled and this register will contain a value of 1.

5   This bit isn't used on the EGA card. On the VGA card, it's used as bit 9 of the vertical blank start register.

6   This bit also isn't used on the EGA card. For the VGA card, it is used as bit 9 of the line compare register.

7   The VGA card uses this bit for line doubling in order to obtain 400 lines in modes that are really 200 line modes. It's not used on the EGA card.

         Caution: Do not change this bit in conjunction with the programming of any registers involved in the vertical timing of the screen build.

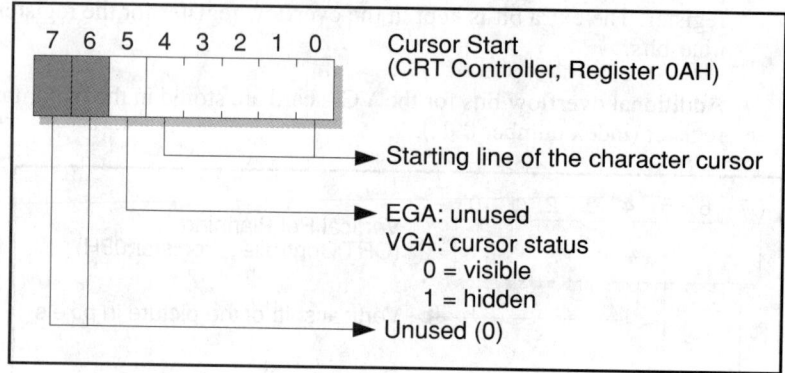

0-4   This specifies the starting line for the cursor; it begins with line 0. It can be a value from 0 to 31. If this value exceeds the actual character height, then the cursor will not be visible on screen.

         If the starting line is greater than the end line (CRT register 0BH), then the EGA card will display a two-part cursor, but the VGA card won't display a cursor.

5   On the VGA card only, this bit can be used to explicitly hide the cursor. This bit isn't used on the EGA card.

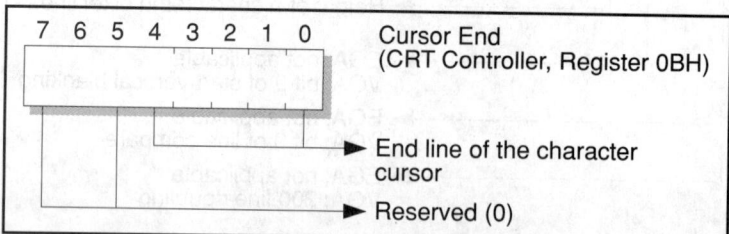

0-4   This bit field contains the last pixel line of the cursor. This value can also be from 0 to 31, but it may not exceed the character height.

If the end line is less than the starting line (CRT register 0AH), then a two-part cursor will appear on an EGA card, and a cursor won't appear on a VGA card.

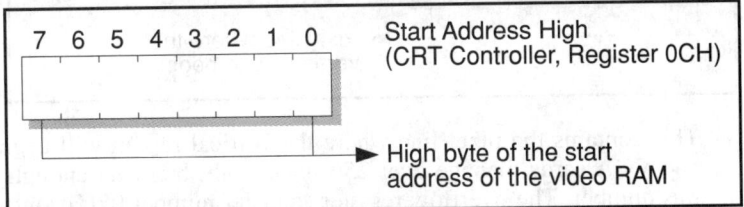

0-7   Together with register 0DH, this register represents the offset address at which the CRT controller will start to read the screen contents from the video RAM. This is the same as the start of the current screen page in video RAM. In odd/even mode, this value must be the actual offset value divided by two. In chain4 mode, it's the actual offset divided by four.

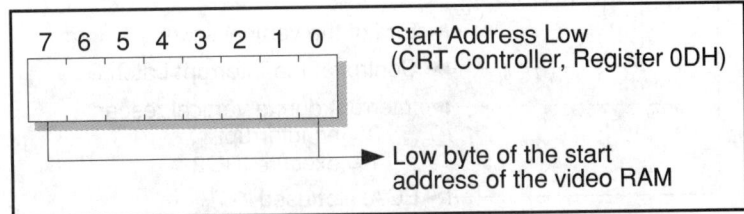

0-7   This register contains the low byte of the start address of the current screen page in video RAM. See also register 0CH.

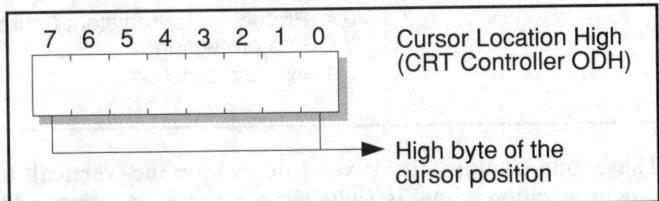

0-7   This register defines the current cursor position as an offset in the current screen page. The address given in this register must be the actual address divided by two. The high byte of the address is stored in this register and the low byte is stored in the next register.

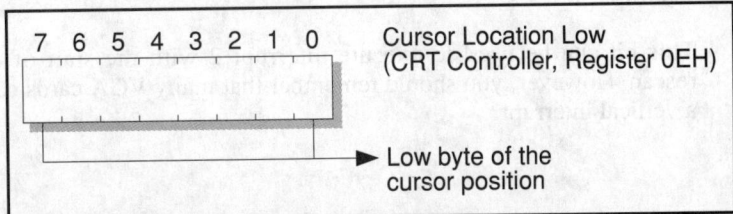

0-7   This register contains the low byte of the cursor position in the current screen page. See also register 0DH.

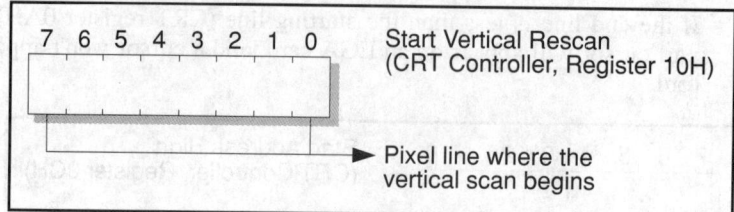

0-7   This contains the pixel line where the vertical rescan will begin. Since EGA and VGA cards manage over 256 lines, eight bits isn't enough room to store this number. The overflow register (register number 07H) contains a ninth bit and tenth bit (for VGA cards).

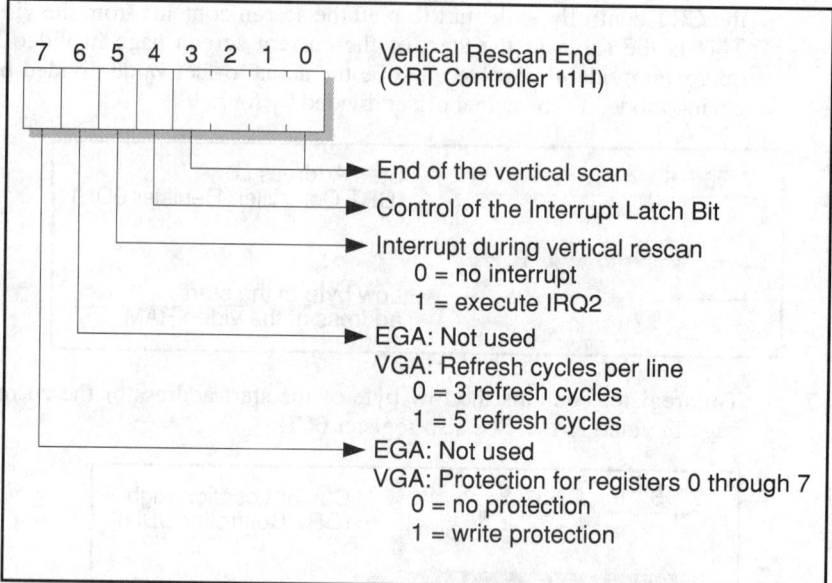

0-3   These bits contain the pixel line where the vertical rescan ends. The synchronization signal is switched off and a new screen build begins. Only four bits are used for this value, so the maximum line number is 15.

4   When a vertical interrupt is executed, bit 7 of the input status register is set to 1 to indicate the start of the vertical rescan. The interrupt bit remains active until it is reset by a value of 1 in this bit, which prohibits a new vertical interrupt.

5   This bit can be used to execute interrupt 2 with the start of every vertical rescan. However, you should remember that many VGA cards cannot generate a vertical interrupt.

6   Only VGA cards are able to change the refresh cycles per line from 3 to 5. Since this requires more time for each refresh of the video RAM, the VGA card operates with a smaller line frequency, which allows the use of monitors that cannot work with the normal VGA line frequency.

7   This bit locks and unlocks access to the first eight registers of the CRT controller on the VGA card. If this bit is set, these registers can be read but not written.

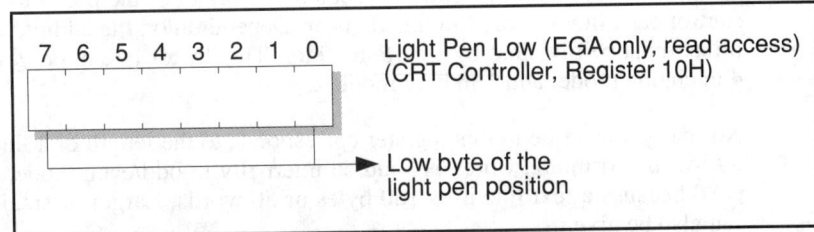

0-7   As we've already seen, the EGA card handles register 10H differently for read and write accesses. During a write access, it contains the start of the vertical rescan. With a read access, it returns the low byte of the current light pen position. As with the cursor position, this value represents the low byte of this address divided by two.

VGA cards, which don't support the use of a light pen, return the contents of the vertical rescan start register during a write access.

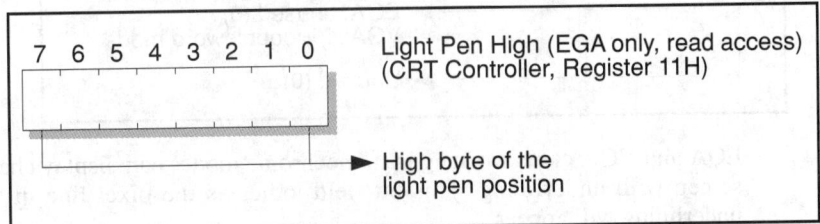

0-7   On EGA cards, this register returns the high byte of the light pen position with a read access. See also the description of register 10H.

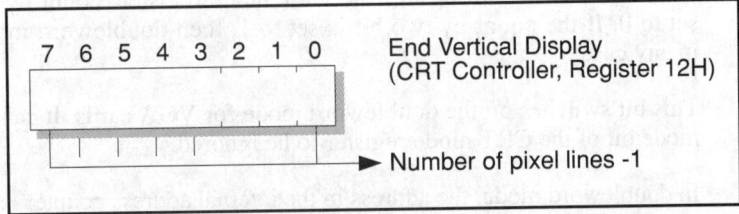

0-7   This register sets the number of the last pixel line in the screen build. This must be a nine bit number for EGA screens and a ten bit number for VGA. The additional bits required are found in the overflow register 07H.

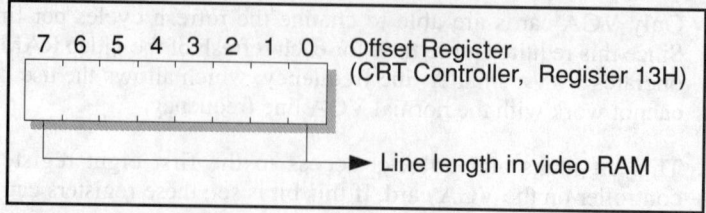

0-7   The offset that the CRT controller adds to the offset of the previous line at the start of each line is stored in this register. Depending on the address mode, this offset must be divisible by a certain factor. This factor is 2 in odd/even mode, 4 in chain4 mode, and 1 in byte mode.

Normally, the value in this register corresponds to the length of a line in video RAM. In text mode, which is handled internally in odd/even mode, this value is 80 because a text line uses 160 bytes or 80 words. Larger or smaller values can also be given.

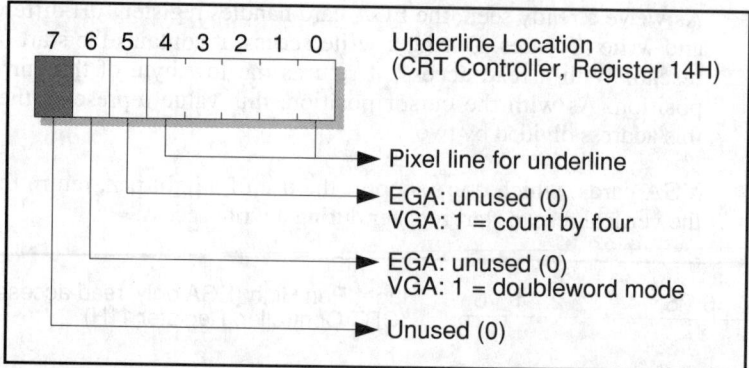

0-4   EGA and VGA cards working in monochrome modes can display characters on screen with underlining. This bit field indicates the pixel line in which the underlining will appear.

5   For VGA cards only, this bit determines whether the internal address counter will be incremented with every fourth tick of the character clock. If so, this bit must be set to 1 and bit 3 of the CRT mode register (count by two) must be set to 0. If the count by two bit is set to 1, then doubleword mode is ignored in any case.

6   This bit switches on the doubleword mode for VGA cards. It causes the access mode bit of the CRT mode register to be ignored.

In doubleword mode, the address in the internal address counter is pushed up by two bits during the screen build. This moves bits 14 and 15 to bit positions 0 and 1. As long as the address counter is less than 4000H, all memory locations between 0000H and FFFCH where modulo 4 = 0 are addressed.

If the internal address counter reaches a value between 4000H and 7FFFH, then all memory locations between 0001H and FFFDH where modulo 4 = 1 are addressed. The same is true for the regions 8000H - BFFFH and C000H -

FFFFH. The memory locations are then addressed where modulo 4 = 2 and 3, respectively.

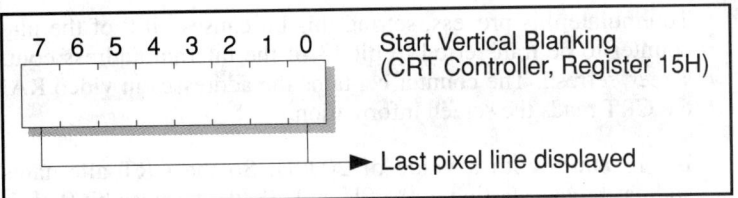

0-7   This register contains the number of the last pixel line plus 1. The ninth bit required for EGA and VGA cards is found in the overflow register (number 07H).

VGA cards require a tenth bit, which is found in the maximum scan line register (register number 09H).

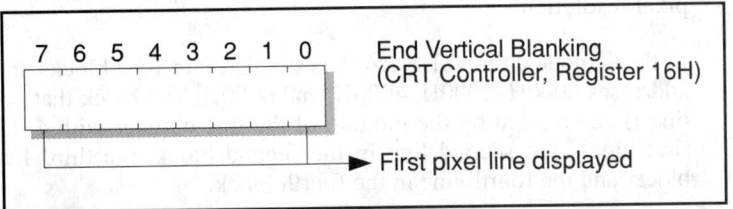

0-7   This register contains the number of the first pixel line. When this line number is reached, the vertical blanking signal is switched off again so a new screen build can begin.

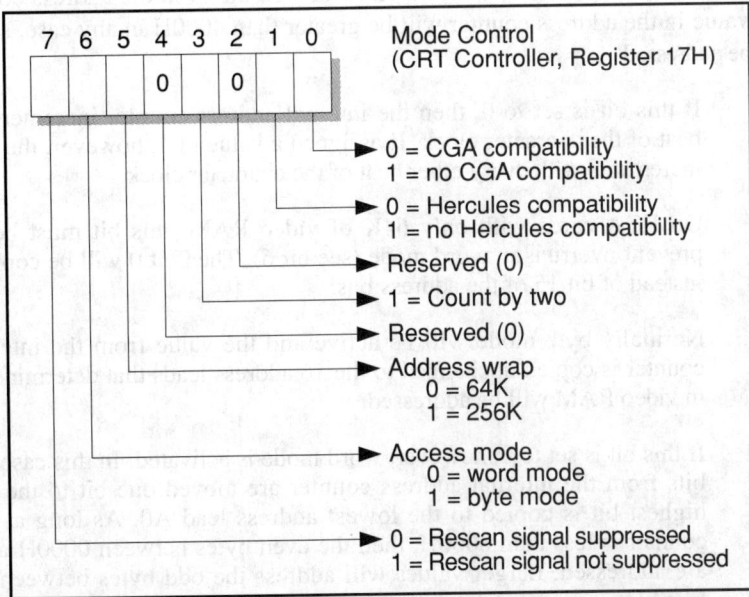

0   If a program sets this bit to 0, other registers can be set to emulate the CGA four color 320*200 pixel mode and CGA video RAM structure. The video RAM is divided into two blocks starting at offset addresses 0000H and 2000H.

The first block contains the even-numbered lines and the second block contains the odd-numbered lines.

To emulate this process, setting this bit causes bit 0 of the internal row scan counter to be transferred to bit 13 of the internal address counter during the screen refresh. The counter contains the addresses in video RAM from which the CRT reads the screen information.

Bit 13 starts with a value of 2000H. So the CRT alternates between the address blocks starting at 0000H and 2000H, because bit 0 of the internal row scan counter alternates between 0 and 1. A requirement for this is that the character height must be set to two by entering a value of 1 in the maximum scan line register.

1 This bit is an extension of bit 0. It must be set to 0 when emulating a foreign video mode that divides the video RAM into four blocks. This includes the Hercules graphics card and other CGA modes with 16 colors and 320*400 pixel resolution.

  In these modes, the video RAM is divided into four blocks starting at offset addresses 0000H, 2000H, 4000H, and 6000H. The block that contains a given line is determined by the modulo of the line number with 4. Line 0 is in the first block, the second line in the second block, the third line in the third block, and the fourth line in the fourth block.

To emulate this structure, a procedure similar to that used with bit 0 copies bit 1 of the internal row scan counter to bit 14 of the internal address counter. Before doing this, you must be sure that the character height has been set to four in the maximum scan line register. This ensures that bit 1 of the row scan counter will have a value of 1 so bit 14 in the address counter will be set to 1. The value in the address counter will be greater than 4000H in any case, so blocks two and three can be addressed.

3 If this bit is set to 0, then the internal address counter increments with each beat of the character clock. If assigned a value of 1, however, the counter only increments with every other beat of the character clock.

5 On EGA cards with only 64K of video RAM, this bit must be set to 0 to prevent overruns in word mode (see bit 6). Then bit 0 will be copied to bit 13, instead of bit 15 of the address bus.

6 Normally byte mode will be active and the value from the internal address counter is copied unchanged to the 16 address leads that determine which byte in video RAM will be addressed.

  If this bit is set to 0, however, word mode is activated. In this case, the address bits from the internal address counter are moved one bit to the left and the highest bit is copied to the lowest address lead A0. As long as the address counter is less than 8000H, then the even bytes between 0000H and 0FFFEH are addressed. Larger values will address the odd bytes between 0001H and FFFFH.

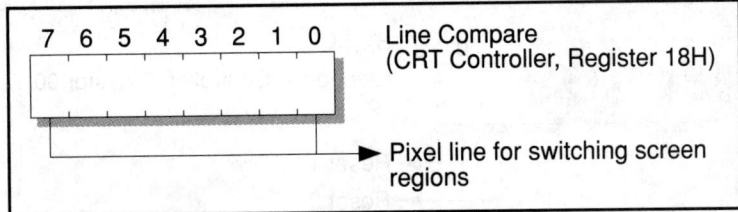

0-7   This register can be used to divide the screen into two different regions in video RAM. The value stored in this register represents the line number where the first region ends and the second begins. When this line is reached, the CRT controller sets the internal offset address for querying screen information from video RAM back to 0.

When a new screen refresh begins, the screen region with the addresses indicated in CRT registers 0CH and 0DH is displayed.

Since both EGA and VGA cards are able to display more than 256 lines on screen, eight bits isn't sufficient to represent the line number. A ninth bit is stored in the overflow register (07). A tenth bit is stored for VGA cards in the maximum scan line register (09).

Sequencer controller

The registers of the sequencer controller are accessed in the usual way using a data register and an index register. The index register is located at port address 3C4H. This is immediately followed by the data register, which is located at port address 3C5H.

As opposed to the other EGA and VGA controllers, the sequencer controller handles a number of miscellaneous tasks and cannot be easily categorized. Its responsibilities range from video RAM memory access and the management of bitplanes to selecting the currently active character table. It's also responsible for refreshing the video RAM.

The sequencer controller on EGA and VGA cards has five different registers, as shown in the following table. Remember that the contents of the register can only be read with VGA cards. This isn't possible with an EGA card.

Nr.	Register Name
00H	Reset
01H	Clocking Mode
02H	Map Mask
03H	Character Map Select
04H	Memory Mode

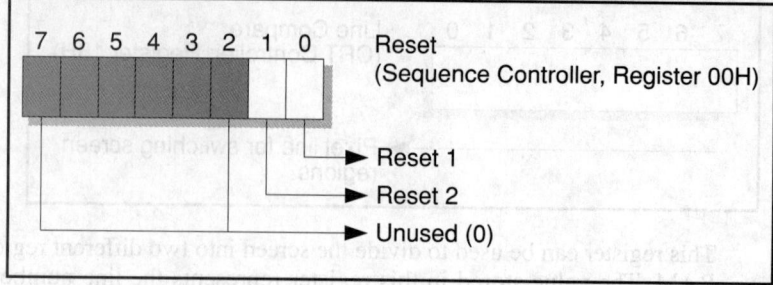

0   This bit usually contains a value of 1. It can be set to 0 to execute a sequencer controller reset, which ends its activity. This ends the generation of horizontal and vertical synchronization signals, causing the screen to go black. Also, the character map select register is set to 0 and the video RAM refresh is switched off. To avoid losing the contents of the video RAM, this bit should be set back to 1 after a maximum of 20 or 30 microseconds. This brings the sequencer controller back to life.

A reset of the sequencer controller is required prior to programming bits 0 and 3 of the clocking mode register of the sequencer controller, as well as bits 2 and 3 of the miscellaneous output register.

1   This bit is also used to reset the sequencer controller, except that it doesn't also reset the character map select register. So, you can use this bit instead bit 0 to reset the sequencer controller, but both bits 0 and 1 must be set back to 1 for the sequencer controller to be able to continue its work.

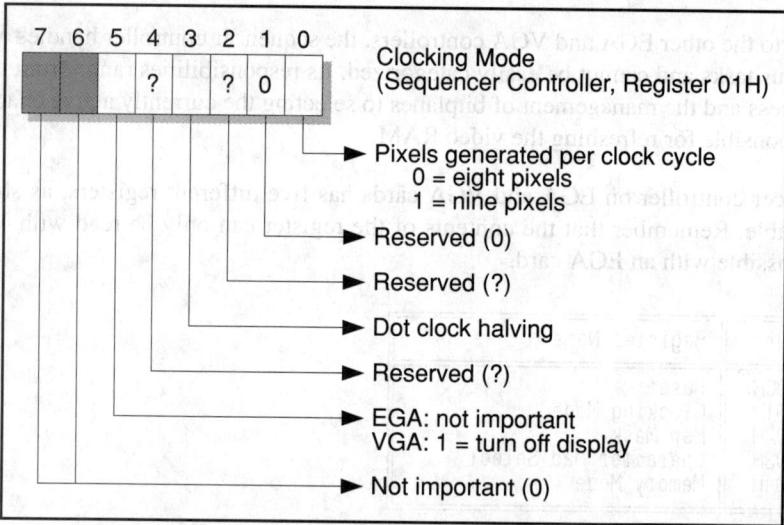

0   This bit sets the number of horizontal pixels that are generated by the CRT controller during each clock cycle. In the graphics modes and with the color text modes of the EGA card, this is always eight. For VGA text modes and for the use of an MDA monitor with an EGA card, this bit must be set to 1 in order to generate nine pixels per clock cycle.

3   Setting this bit to 1 results in halving the dot clock rate. This happens automatically when the BIOS is used to switch on the 320*200 pixel mode for CGA emulation. This bit will be 0 for all other modes (including the 320*200 256 color mode).

5   On a VGA card, setting this bit to 1 will switch off the video signal. This makes the screen go black and allows the CPU unlimited access to the video RAM.

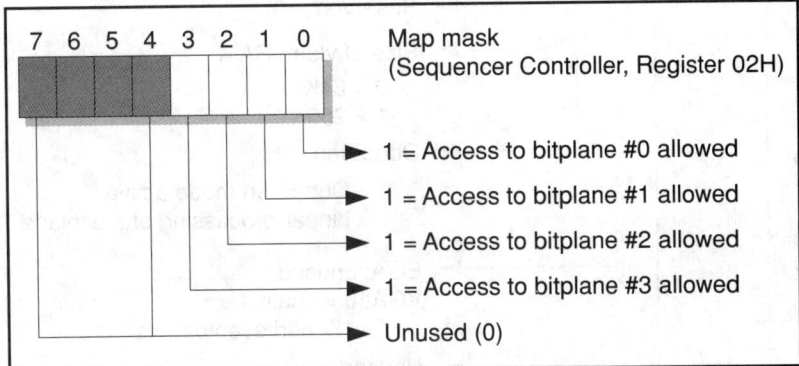

0-3   Each of these bits either blocks or enables access to a bitplane. This is important for accessing the video RAM with the various read and write modes. During a read access, the status of this bit determines whether a byte in the bitplane should be filled with the contents of the corresponding latch register. Conversely, during a read access, this bit determines whether the byte in question should be copied from the bitplane to the latch register or if the contents of the latch register should remain unchanged.

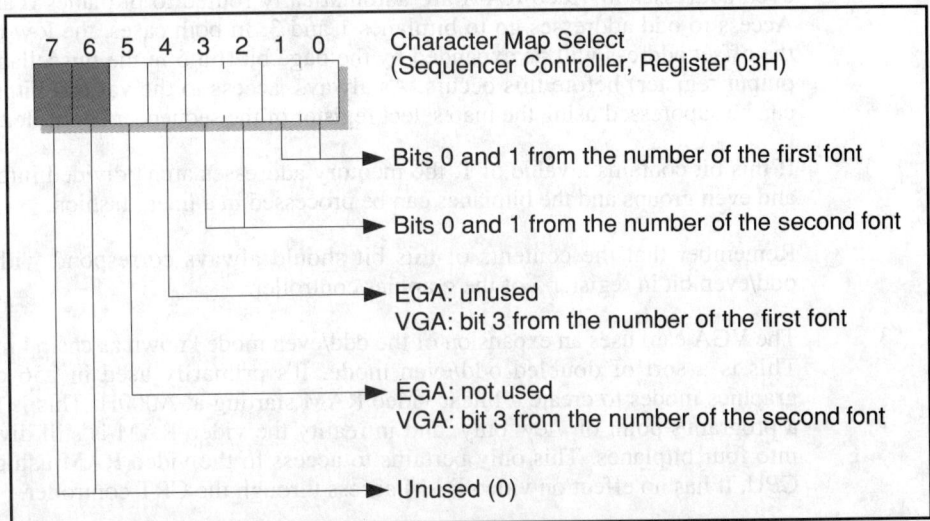

0+1+4 These bits determine the number of the character table that will be used for all characters that have a value of 0 for bit 3 in their attribute byte. Bit 4 isn't used on EGA cards, so font selection is limited to numbers 0 - 3. Bit 4 is used on VGA cards to allow the selection of font numbers from 0 - 7.

2+3+5 These bits determine the number of the character table that will be used for all characters where bit 3 in the attribute byte is set to 1. Again, the third bit (bit 5) is only needed for VGA cards.

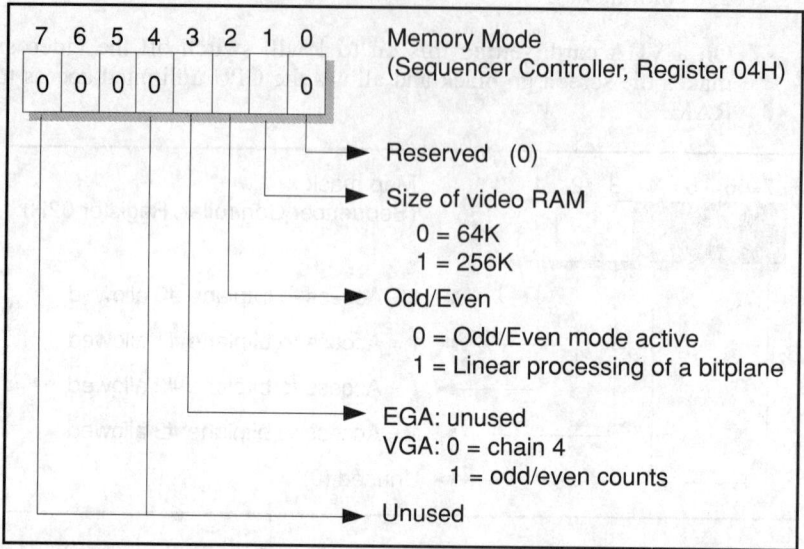

1 This bit applies only to EGA cards because all VGA cards come with 256K of video RAM. You can also safely assume that few, if any, EGA cards with only 64K are still being used.

2 This bit is used to set the division of odd and even memory addresses into different bitplanes. This is known as odd/even mode. In this mode, access to even addresses in video RAM are automatically routed to bitplanes 0 and 2. Access to odd addresses go to bitplanes 1 and 3. In both cases, the low bit of the offset address will be expanded by the page bit (bit 5 in the miscellaneous output register) before this occurs. As always, access to the various bitplanes can be suppressed using the map select register of the sequencer controller.

If this bit contains a value of 1, the memory addresses aren't divided into odd and even groups and the bitplanes can be processed in a linear fashion.

Remember that the contents of this bit should always correspond with the odd/even bit in register 5 of the graphics controller.

3 The VGA card uses an expansion of the odd/even mode known as chain4 mode. This is a sort of doubled odd/even mode. It's primarily used in 256 color graphics modes to create a linear video RAM starting at A000H. This is from a program's point of view only, and in reality the video RAM is still divided into four bitplanes. This only pertains to access to the video RAM using the CPU. It has no effect on video RAM access through the CRT controller.

As with odd/even mode, access to the video RAM is based on the addresses of memory locations within one of the four bitplanes. The two low bits of the offset address are masked (set to 0) so only locations within the bitplanes that are divisible by four can be accessed. The number of the bitplane to be accessed is determined by the value of two bits that were masked, which is the same as modulo 4 of the offset address.

A bitplane can be accessed only if it's freed using the map mask register of the sequencer controller.

If chain4 mode is active, the bits used to control the odd/even mode are ignored. They become valid again when chain4 mode is switched off.

Attribute controller

The attribute controller prepares the color signals for the screen. It manages the palette registers and the other registers needed for generating color signals.

The registers of the attribute controller are accessed using a combined address and data register. The register located at port address 3C0H is used for write operations. For read operations, which are only possible on the VGA card, the register at port address 3C1H is used.

To access an attribute register, first the number of the desired register must be written to port 3C0H or 3C1H. With a read operation, the result can then be read directly from port 3C1H. For a write operation, the new contents of the register must be sent using port 3C0H.

For read access to a register, the combined index and data register at port address 3C1H requires only the register number. The register for write operations requires an additional bit to determine the status of the attribute controller. If this bit is set to 0, then the connection between the attribute controller and the CRT controller is broken and the screen will become black or whatever color is contained in the overscan register of the attribute controller. Separate color signals for the characters or pixels on screen will no longer be produced.

The attribute controller on an EGA card has 20 different registers. The VGA card has these plus one additional register. The assignments for some of the registers differ between EGA and VGA cards because VGA cards require the use of the DAC color table to generate color signals. EGA cards don't have the DAC color table.

As with the sequencer controller, the registers can only be read on a VGA card. These same registers on an EGA card are write-only.

Nr.	Register Name
00H-0FH	Palette Register
10H	Mode Control
11H	Overscan Color
12H	Color Plane Enable
13H	Horizontal Pel Penning
14H	Color Select (VGA only)

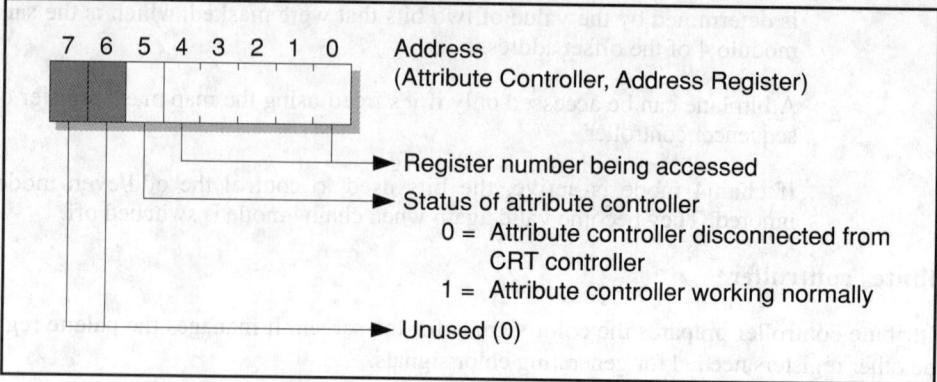

0-4   These bits address the various registers of the attribute controller. This is done in the same way as with other EGA and VGA controllers.

5   If this bit contains 1, the attribute controller works normally. If it contains 0, then the attribute controller is disconnected from the CRT controller, which causes the screen to go black or to become the color stored in the overscan register.

        This is the only time when the palette registers can be accessed directly by the CPU to be read or written.

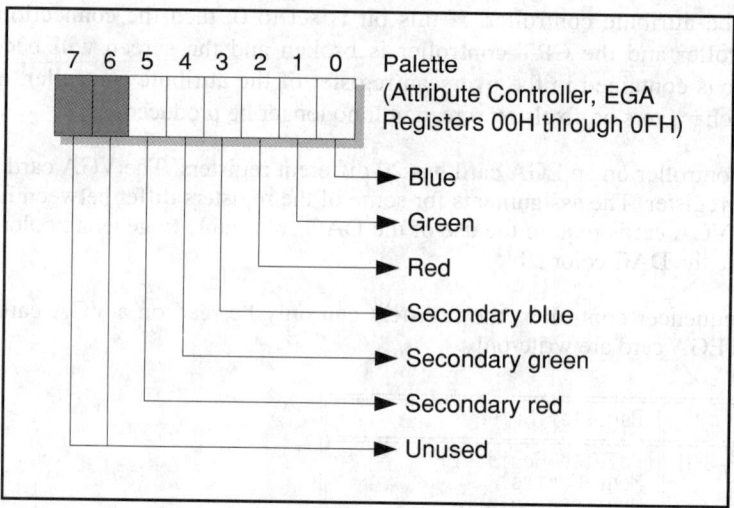

0-5   On an EGA card, the 16 palette registers contain actual 6-bit color codes. This allows for 64 different colors.

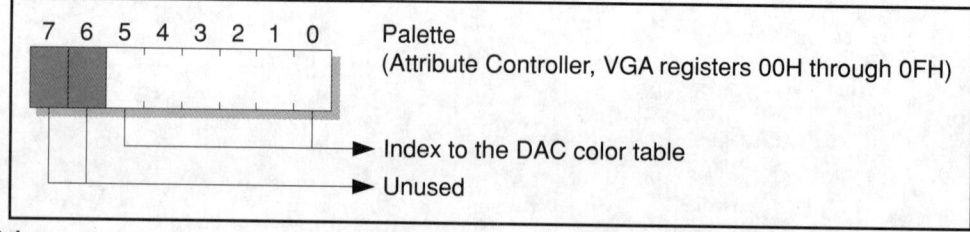

0-5   On a VGA card, a palette register stores an index to the DAC color table instead of an actual color code. The attribute controller uses this index value to load the color assigned to a character or pixel from the DAC color table and send the appropriate color signal to the monitor.

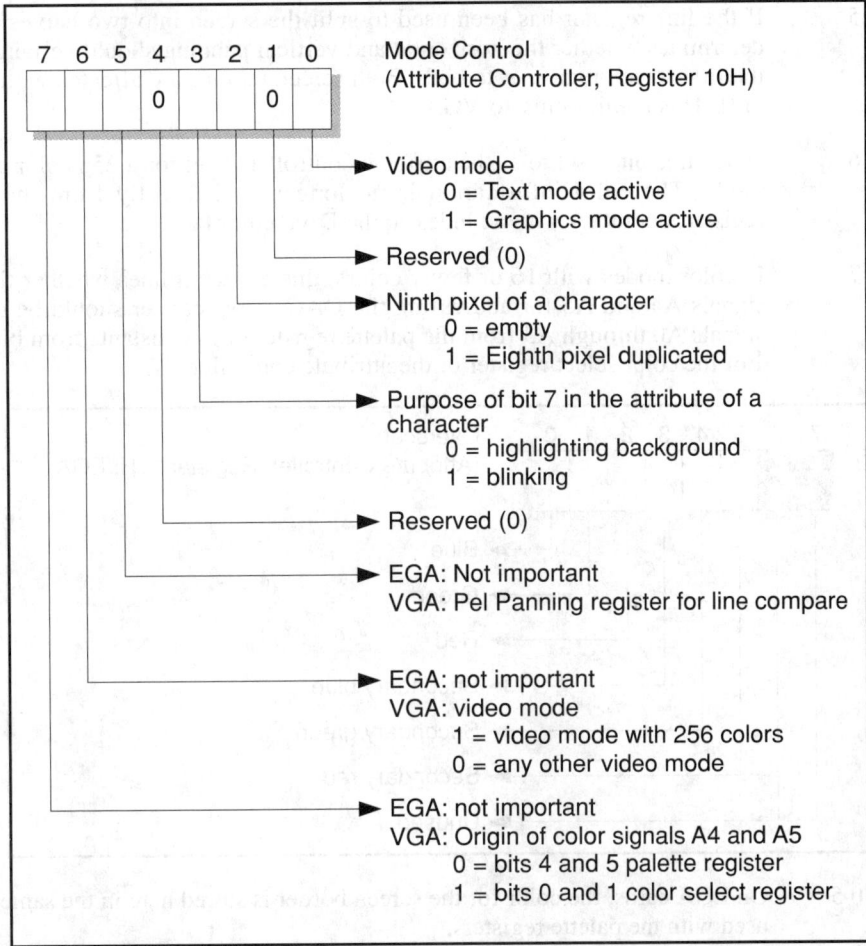

0   This bit is used to tell the attribute controller whether a text mode or a graphics mode is active.

2   This bit is only meaningful for text modes that use a nine pixel character width. This bit determines the meaning of the ninth pixel. The character tables in ROM only store eight pixels per line for each character.

    If this bit is 0, then the ninth pixel remains empty. This creates a space of one pixel between two subsequent characters. If this bit is set to 1, then the contents of this pixel is determined on a character by character basis. If the character is a special border or frame character (ASCII codes between C0H and DFH), then the contents of the eighth pixel are copied to the ninth. The ninth pixel remains empty with all other characters.

3	When this bit is set to 1, a cursor will appear in text mode. The cursor will remain visible for 16 screen generations and then invisible for the next 16. Depending on the frequency of the screen regenerations, this results in a cursor that blinks every 1/3 to 1/4 second.
5	If the line register has been used to split the screen into two halves, this bit determines whether the horizontal and vertical panning should pertain to only the first screen region or to both. Both screen regions are affected with a value of 0. This applies only to VGA.
6	When this bit is set to 1, the attribute controller is set for a 256 color graphics mode. The color information is no longer read directly from the palette register, but rather with an index to the DAC color table.
7	In color modes with 16 or fewer colors, this bit determines whether the color signals A4 and A5 for addressing the DAC color register should be taken as signals A0 through A3 from the palette register or as constants from bits 0 and 1 of the color select register of the attribute controller.

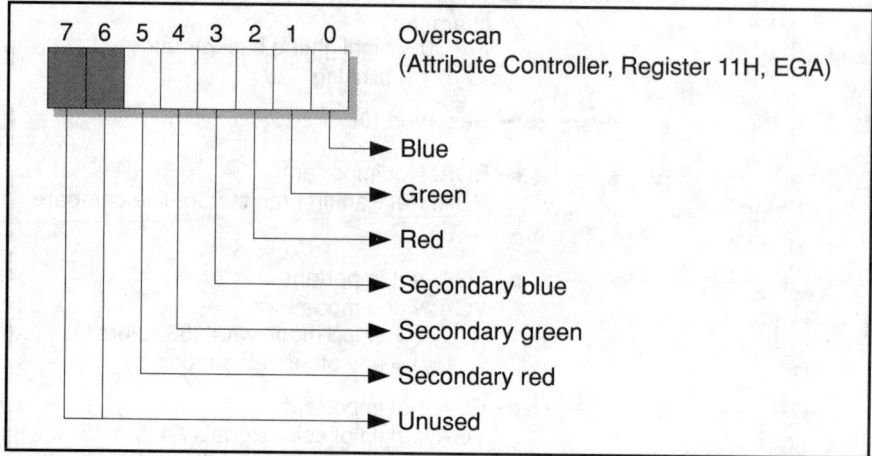

0-5	On EGA cards, the color for the screen border is stored here in the same format used with the palette registers.

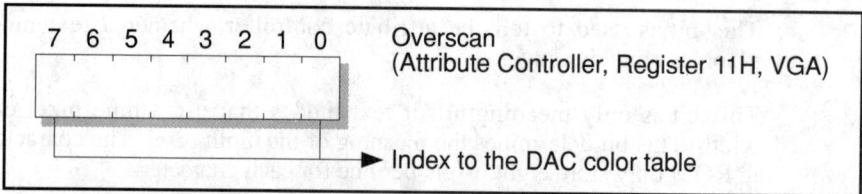

0-7	On a VGA card, the frame color is selected from the DAC color table. Any of the 256 colors in the table can be accessed using this register.

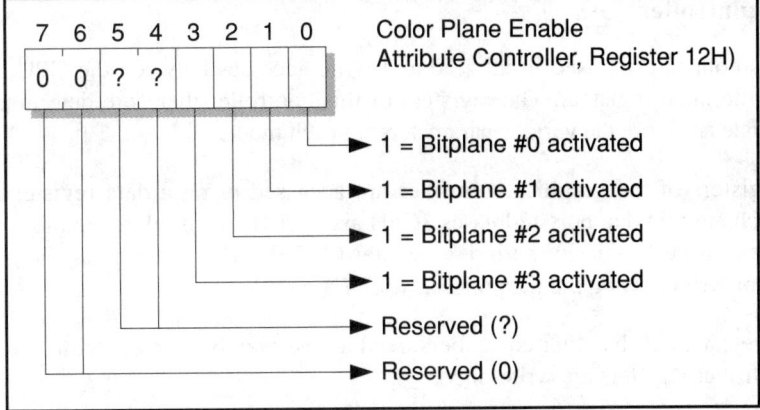

0-3   The four bits in this bit field turn each bitplane on and off for the transfer of color information from the video RAM to the attribute controller. This can be used together with programming the palette or DAC color registers to exclude certain pixels from being displayed.

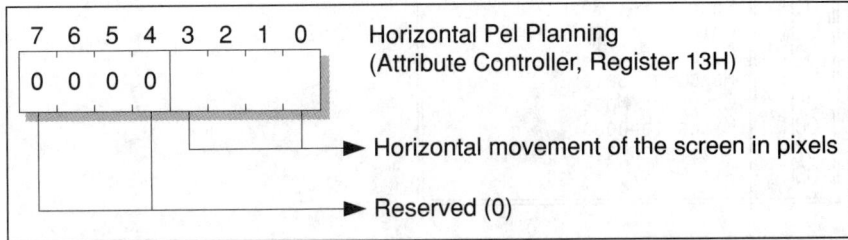

0-3   This is where the counter for horizontal pel panning is stored. This value is used when moving the visible screen display to the left (see also Section 8.3).

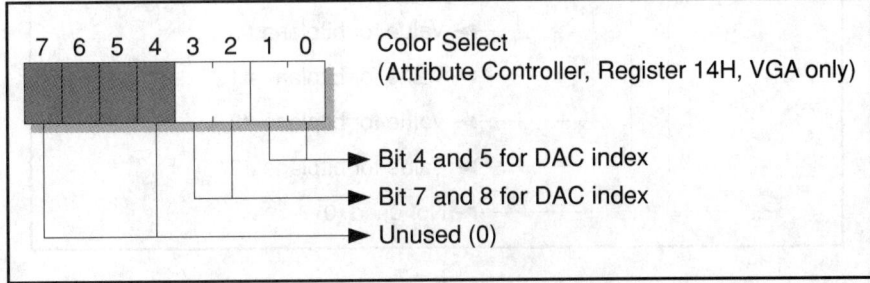

0+1   These two bits are used as bits 4 and 5 of the DAC index number when bit 7 in the mode control register of the attribute controller is set. They then replace bits 4 and 5 from the corresponding palette register.

2+3   These two bits are bits 6 and 7 of the DAC color table index in all graphics modes with less than 256 colors, regardless of the contents of other registers or bit fields.

Graphics controller

The graphics controller is used in all read and write accesses between the CPU and the video RAM using the latch registers. The registers of this controller therefore determine the current read/write mode and store the various parameters for each mode.

The nine registers of the graphics controller are accessed using a data register and an index register, which are found at port addresses 3CFH and 3CEH. As usual, the number of the desired register must first be loaded in the index register (3CEH). This determines the index that will then be read or written using the data register (3CFH).

As with the registers of the other controllers, read access is only possible with VGA cards. EGA graphics controller registers are write-only.

The following is an overview of the graphics controller registers:

Nr.	Register Name
00H	Set/Reset
01H	Enable Set/Reset
02H	Color Compare
03H	Function Select
04H	Read Map Select
05H	Graphics Mode
06H	Miscellaneous
07H	Color Don't Care
08H	Bit Mask

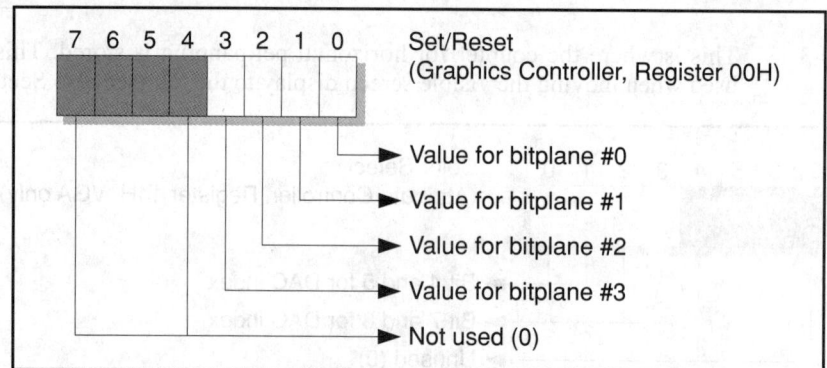

| 0-3 | These bits are used for video RAM access in write mode 0. They determine the value to be written to bit 8 in each bitplane if the source for this bit has been selected as the set/reset register. The source for bit 8 is determined by the enable set/reset register (number 02H). |

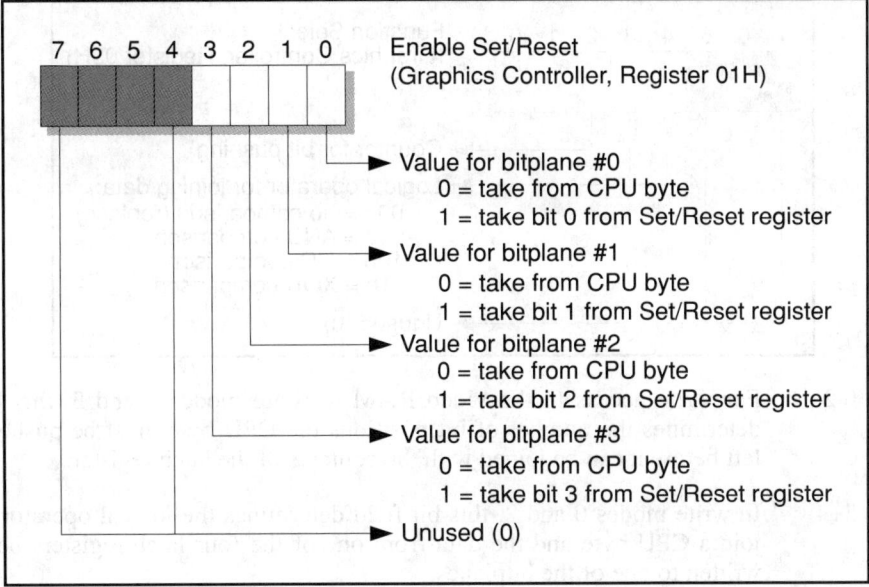

0-3   When working with write mode 0, these bits determine whether the value of bit 8 in the bitplane being accessed should be taken from the CPU byte or from the set-/reset register (number 00H).

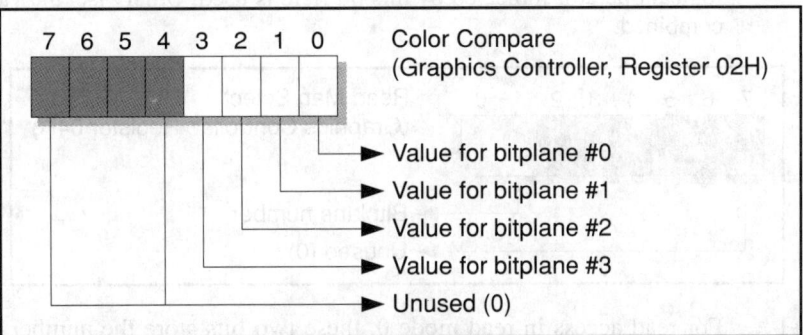

0-3   These bits are important for read access to the video RAM in read mode 1. In this mode, the four bytes read from the four video RAM bitplanes are organized into eight groups of four bits, each of which represents the color of one pixel. The eight resulting color codes are compared individually with the contents of this register and the result of this comparison is sent to the CPU.

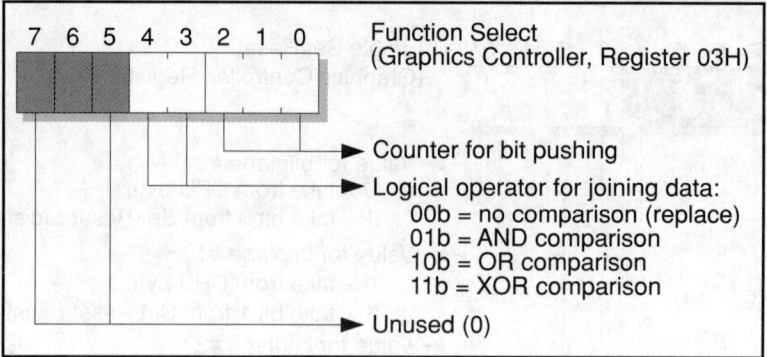

0-2   For write access to the video RAM in write modes 0 and 3, this bit field determines the number of bit positions the CPU byte must be pushed to the left before it can be joined with the contents of the latch register.

3+4   In write modes 0 and 2, this bit field determines the logical operator used to join a CPU byte and the data from one of the four latch registers before it's written to one of the bitplanes.

         The four bits in the bit mask register which correspond to the four latch registers determine whether the CPU byte and latch register will be combined. If the corresponding bit from the bit mask register has a value of 1, then the logical operator indicated by this bit field is used. Otherwise, the values are not combined.

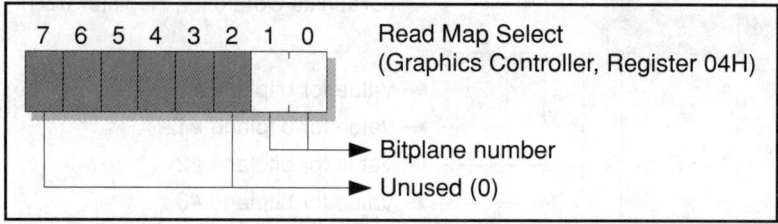

0+1   For read access in read mode 0, these two bits store the number of the latch register (which is the same as the number of the associated bitplane) that will be copied to the CPU. Read accesses in read mode 1 and chain4 mode are not affected.

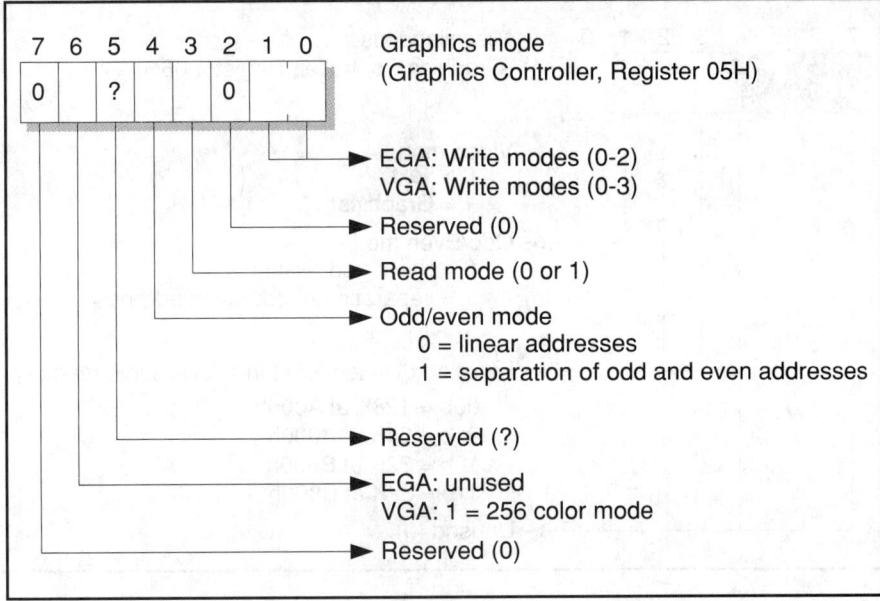

Graphics mode
(Graphics Controller, Register 05H)

EGA: Write modes (0-2)
VGA: Write modes (0-3)

Reserved (0)

Read mode (0 or 1)

Odd/even mode
0 = linear addresses
1 = separation of odd and even addresses

Reserved (?)

EGA: unused
VGA: 1 = 256 color mode

Reserved (0)

0+1   These bits store the number of the write mode used for write access to the video RAM, regardless of the current video mode.

2   This bit stores the number of the currently active video mode.

3   This bit tells the graphics controller whether an odd/even mode is active or if the bitplanes are to be addressed in a linear fashion. This bit must be loaded with the same value found in bit 2 of the memory mode register of the sequencer controller.

5   For VGA, this bit indicates whether a 256 color mode is active. If it is, the graphics controller must use a different method for passing color information on to the attribute controller.

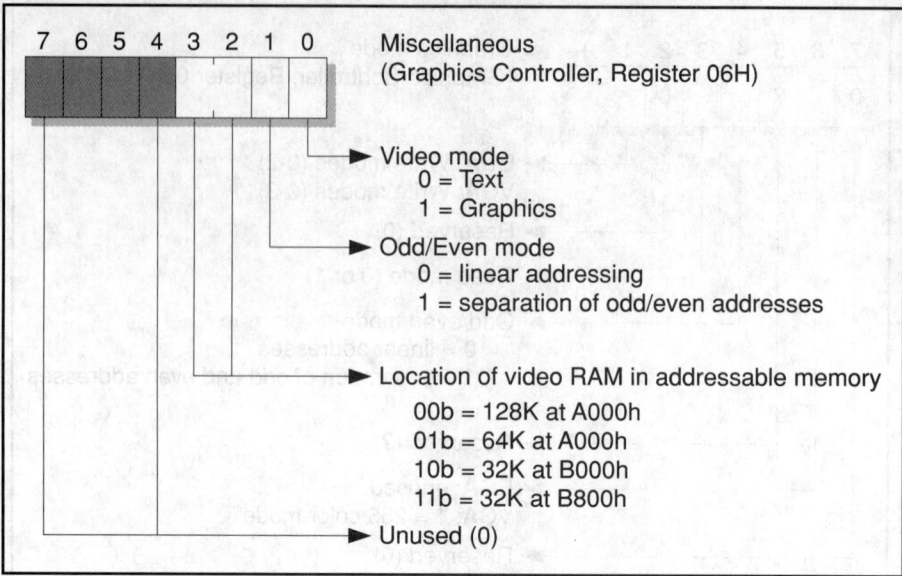

0   This bit indicates whether a text or graphics mode is currently active. This is so the graphics controller will know whether to use the internal latch registers for converting ASCII codes into pixel patterns for text modes.

1   This bit also indicates whether an odd/even mode is active or if linear addressing of the bitplanes is being used.

2+3 This bit field determines where the video RAM will be located in the processor's addressable memory. The BIOS sets this value correctly depending on the video mode and the type of monitor being used.

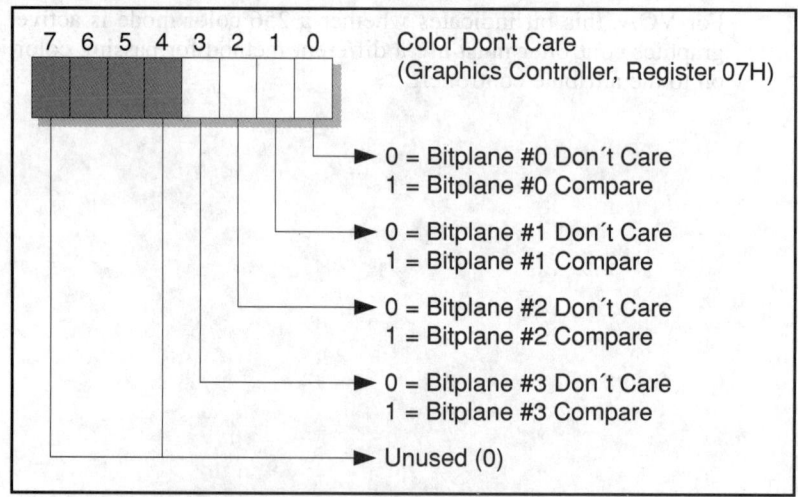

0-3 These bits are important for read accesses to the video RAM in read mode 1. They indicate which bitplanes will be included in the color comparison.

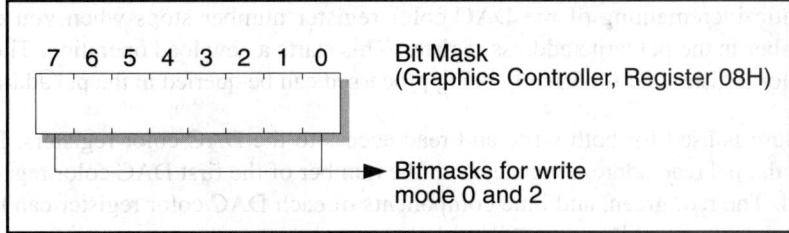

0-7   For write access to the video RAM in write modes 0 and 2, these bits determine which bits from a given bitplane should be written unchanged to the corresponding latch register and which must first be combined with other data (from the CPU or the set/reset register) using the function select register. This happens in all four latch registers to those bits for which the corresponding bit in this register is set to 1.

Digital to Analog Converter (DAC)

The DAC is found only on VGA cards. Its job is to convert the digital color values into analog color signals for the monitor. The DAC is the last step in color generation for VGA. Each palette register contains an index to one of the 256 color registers in the DAC.

A DAC color register consists of 18 bits: six bits for each of the basic colors red, green, and blue (RGB). This allows for 262,144 different colors.

The color registers of the DAC are accessed using the registers listed in the following table. Unlike other EGA and VGA controllers, a single port address is used instead of separate index and data registers.

Port	Register Name
3C8H	Pel Write Address
3C7H	Pel Read Address
3C7H	DAC State
3C9H	Pel Data
3C6H	Pel Mask

To write to one of the DAC color registers, first you must enter its number (0 - 255) in the pel write address register. Then send the data for the new color to the pel data register. The pel data register is only eight bits wide and cannot receive all 18 bits needed to define a color at once. Therefore, the six bits of the red color component are sent first, followed by the six green bits, and finally the six blue bits.

Within a program, usually all 256 DAC color registers (or at least a good number of them), instead of only one or two, are loaded. So, the value in the pel write address register is automatically incremented after the data for the three color components has been sent to the pel data register. This allows you to proceed directly with the color components for the next DAC color register without having to access the pel write address register again.

The automatic incrementing of the DAC color register number stops when you enter a new register number in the pel write address register. This starts a new load operation. The number of the DAC color register that is currently being processed can be queried in the pel address register.

This procedure is used for both write and read access to the DAC color registers. For reading, simply load the pel read address register with the number of the first DAC color register that you want to read. The red, green, and blue components of each DAC color register can then be read from the pel data register. There must be a slight pause between the three read accesses to the pel data register. In an assembler program, this can be done with a jump to the next command.

As previously described, the contents of the pel read address register are also incremented after the contents of the current DAC color register have been read.

The attribute controller has no access to the DAC color registers while they are being read or written. So, the display must be switched off during this time so a blizzard doesn't appear on screen.

Here are the descriptions of each DAC register:

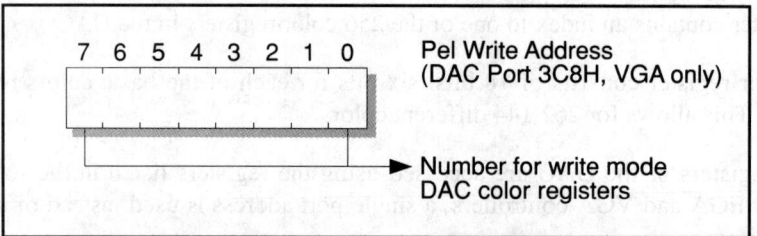

7-0   This register stores the number of the DAC color register that is to be written. The value from the pel data register is copied to this DAC color register in the next step of the write operation. This value is automatically incremented so all (or a large portion) of the DAC color registers can be loaded without having to access this register again.

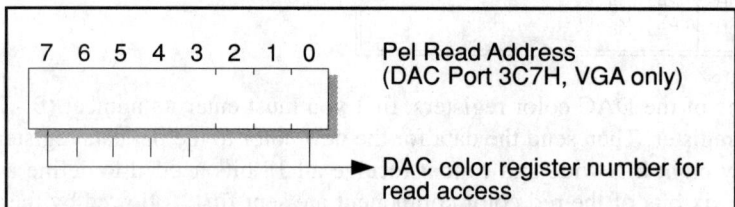

0-7   This register stores the number of the DAC color register that is to be read. The color component values from the DAC color register can be read from the pel data register in the next step of the read operation. This value is also automatically incremented.

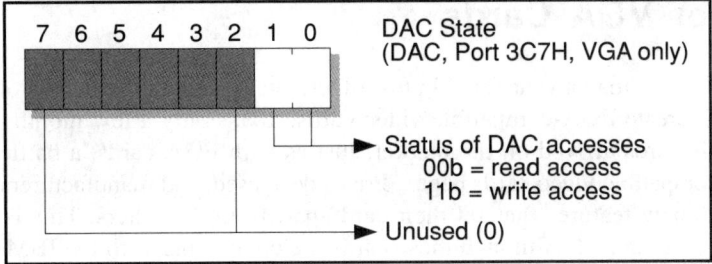

1+2   These bits indicate whether the DAC is currently in read or write mode.

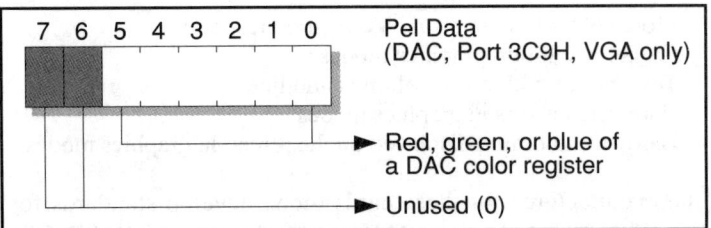

During a write operation on one of the DAC color registers, this register must be loaded with the three color components in sequence: first red, then green, and finally blue. Each color component requires only six bits, so it is the lower six bits that are actually copied to the DAC color register.

During a read access to a DAC color register, this register will first have the six bits of the red, then the green, and finally the blue color components available for querying.

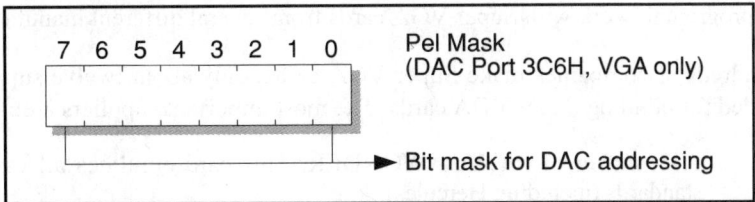

0-7   If the attribute controller wants to read the contents of a DAC color register while generating colors during a screen refresh, the contents of this register must be combined with the number of the desired DAC color register using a logical AND operator. When animating, for example, this allows you to create entire color groups using certain DAC color registers at a low level.

Normally, this register contains the value FFH, so accesses to the DAC color registers aren't changed.

4.9 Super VGA Cards

Although it took more than a year for chip manufacturers to unlock the secrets of the IBM VLSI chips in order to create EGA-compatible video cards, it was only a few months before the first VGA-compatible cards arrived on the market. Just as with EGA cards, a battle for the market share of VGA-compatible video cards began. Prices decreased, and manufacturers were pressured to come up with new features that set their card apart from the others. This is how the Super VGA cards were developed. Although these cards are compatible with the IBM VGA standard, they use many hardware registers that aren't defined in this standard to provide extra features and performance. Some of the enhanced capabilities of Super VGA are:

- More colors in the normal VGA graphics modes
- Higher resolution graphics modes
- Text modes with more columns and lines
- Hardware cursors in graphics modes
- Hardware zooming displayed on the screen in graphics modes

Unfortunately, the manufacturers of these cards didn't develop standards for these advanced features. With a standard, these features could be accessed from the ROM-BIOS. As developers of the expanded capabilities of Super VGA cards know, one program won't work the same way with two different cards. So, to ensure that a program will run with all Super VGA cards, separate routines, which are designed to meet each card's requirements, must be created.

In this section we'll discuss some important aspects of Super VGA cards. Instead of discussing the numerous cards that are available, we'll end this section with a description of the VESA Super VGA Standard. This standard was created in 1990 by the major manufacturers of Super VGA cards in an attempt to create a practical tool for Super VGA programming. This standard enables your program to work with Super VGA cards from several different manufacturers.

Although hundreds of companies make Super VGA cards, only about twelve suppliers provide the chips needed for building Super VGA cards. The most important suppliers are:

- ATI, maker of the VGAWONDER. This card emulates all earlier graphics standards (including Hercules).
- Chips & Technologies, maker of the NEAT chip set.
- Genoa, the company that actually uses the name "SuperVGA" on its Super VGA line of cards.
- Headland (also known as VideoSeven).
- Tseng (probably the leading manufacturer), makers of the ET30000 and ET4000 VGA chips, which are found in numerous VGA cards.
- Paradise, a division of Western Digital, makers of hard drives and other mass storage systems.

Even though there are only six major manufacturers of VGA and Super VGA chip sets, the differences between Super VGA cards aren't limited to the use of six different chip sets. Nearly every chip set allows a card manufacturer some freedom in mode selection and addressing BIOS functions.

Super VGA text modes

Of all the various Super VGA text modes, the 25 line by 132 column mode that's supported by many cards is one of the most interesting. There are also other text modes that have 132 columns and higher numbers of lines.

Several 80 and 100 column modes, with varying numbers of lines, are also supported. The highest resolution text mode supports 160 columns and 50 lines. Whether you can read any of the characters on the screen is another matter.

Here's a sampling of some of the text modes available on various Super VGA cards:

Expanded text modes of various Super VGA cards	
Columns	Rows
80	30
80	34
80	43
80	60
100	37
100	43
100	60
100	75
132	25
132	28
132	30
132	43
132	44
132	50
160	50

Generally all of these text modes can be initialized with function 00H of the BIOS video interrupt, but different cards may have different code numbers for each mode. This is unfortunate because the video RAM in these modes is structured as it is in the normal text modes. This would make it possible to use the expanded modes simply by setting a wider line length in video RAM.

If you want your DOS programs to have flexible screen resolution, you should use the functions of the VESA BIOS. Or, you can let the user decide. Some configuration programs allow the user to set the screen resolution at the DOS level. Then the user can simply pass the screen resolution, as a parameter, to the program when starting it from DOS or enter the value in a configuration file that the program reads after it starts.

Super VGA graphics modes

Super VGA graphic modes also offer a wide variety. The standard VGA modes are supported with more colors, for example 256 instead of only 16. However, there are new graphics modes with higher resolutions, up to 1024x768 pixels.

Unfortunately these higher resolutions are slower. For example, a 640x480 pixel mode uses about 300,000 pixels and an 800x480 mode uses almost 500,000. The processor still must process each pixel, which prevents it from performing other tasks. This is why many Windows users prefer the old standard VGA 640x480 pixel mode. The Super VGA modes simply take too long to paint the screen.

In addition to modes with resolutions like 720x396 or 960x720, the same three modes are included on almost all Super VGA cards:

- 640x400 pixels with 256 colors
- 800x600 pixels with 16 or 256 colors
- 1024x768 pixels with 16 colors

The following table shows that these modes represent only a portion of the various Super VGA graphics modes available on different cards:

Expanded graphic modes of various Super VGA cards			
Resolution	Colors.	Pixels	Memory
512x480	256	245,760	256K
640x400	256	256,000	256K
640x480	256	307,200	512K
720x396	16	285,120	256K
720x512	16	368,640	256K
720x512	256	368,640	512K
720x540	16	388,800	256K
720x540	256	388,800	512K
752x410	16	308,320	256K
800x600	16	480,000	256K
800x600	256	480,000	512K
960x720	16	691,200	512K
1024x768	16	786,432	512K
1024x768	256	786,432	1 Meg

Regardless of which graphics modes a Super VGA card supports, a given mode can be used only if the proper monitor and sufficient video RAM are available. A normal fixed-frequency VGA monitor is sufficient for the 640x480 modes, but the higher resolution modes require a multisync monitor. When you reach resolutions as high as 1024x768, you'll need an XL monitor. This is a special kind of multisync monitor that's often used with CAD/CAM applications. A resolution of 1024x768 would represent the lower end of its capabilities.

Structure of the video RAM in Super VGA modes

When you look at all of the Super VGA graphics modes, they can be divided into modes that use either 16 or 256 colors, just like the standard VGA graphics modes. In both cases, the structure of the video RAM is the same as in the related standard VGA modes. This means that the color of a pixel is determined by four bits from the four bitplanes in the 16 color modes. The 256 color modes use an entire byte to define the color of a pixel. The address of a pixel is the result of multiplying the line number by the line length and adding the column number. The only difference between these modes and the standard VGA modes is the length of each line in video RAM. This makes each screen page longer, which results in a higher resolution.

However, a problem arises. Any mode that requires more than 256K per screen page cannot use standard methods for accessing video RAM. In the 16 color modes, the 64K segment starting at A000:0000 can be used to address only 256K of video RAM using the four bitplanes. This situation is even worse with the 256 color modes. These have only 64K available, even though Section 4.8.7 shows a way to address the entire 256K.

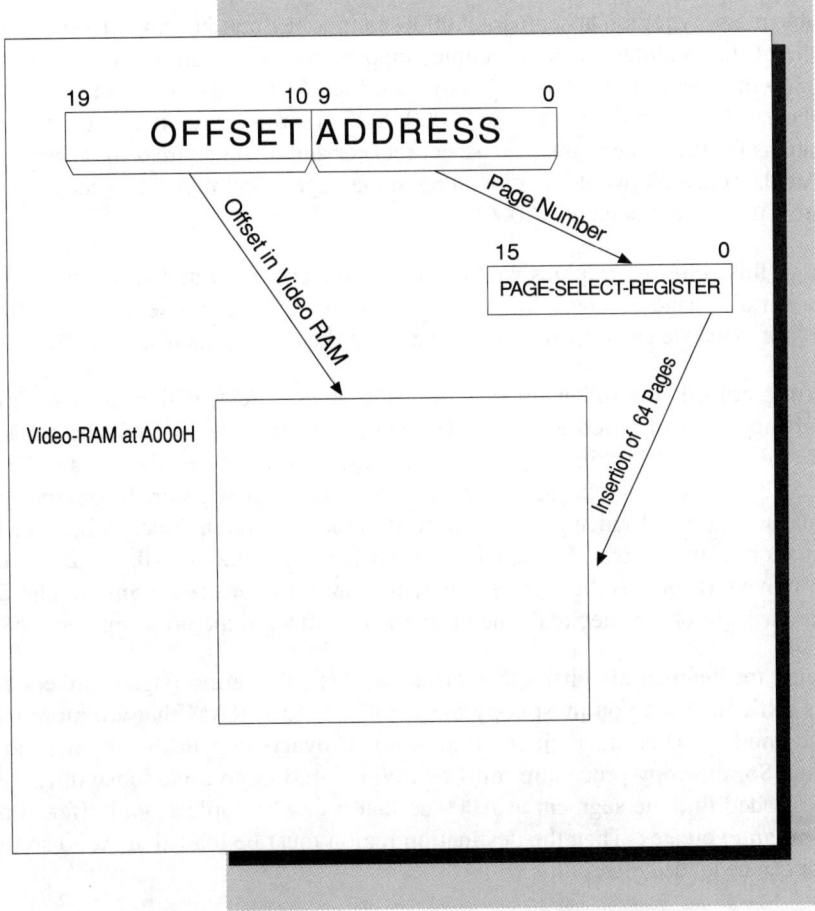

*The 64K limit at A000:0000 is unavoidable for all graphics modes
that need to address more than 256K of video RAM*

For this reason, all Super VGA cards use a mechanism that allows the entire video RAM of the card to be addressed using the memory segment at A000H. Unfortunately, this access can only occur in 64K chunks for 256 color modes, or in 256K chunks for 16 color modes. Various cards use different hardware registers to make a piece of the video RAM available at A000H. These registers aren't found on standard VGA cards. The same mechanism manages EMS memory (see Chapter 12 for more information).

Copy a section of video RAM to the 64K window at A000:0000 by dividing the offset address into page and offset components. This process doesn't simplify the routines to set or read a pixel, because you now must know which 64K memory window, as well as the offset in video RAM, in order to access the desired byte. You also must remember that your 64K window can be moved only in certain increments (*granularities*), such as 1K, 2K, 4K, 8K, etc. You can also think of the video RAM as being divided into "pages" under this scheme. The page size corresponds to the granularity of the 64K window. If you choose 1K, then the 64K window at A000H will have 64 pages. The number of the first page is set by a hardware register called the page select register.

The visible memory region at segment A000H cannot begin at just any offset address. It must be a multiple of the granularity. For example, suppose that you want to access the address 65539 (64K + 3) with a granularity of 1K. You would load 64 into the page select register. Then you could access the desired location at A000:0003. In this case, there are 63 other possible combinations for the value in the page select register and offset address for accessing the segment A000. Another example would be to load 63 in the page select register to access the byte at 1024 + 3 relative to memory segment A000H.

Because of this scheme, graphics routines must convert offset addresses in video RAM to the combination of a page number plus the offset relative to memory segment A000H. This isn't a difficult task, once we consider the binary nature of these components.

The starting point is the offset for access to the video RAM, which must be 20 bits wide to address 1 megabyte of video RAM. If it's only 512K, then 19 bits will be sufficient. For our example, we'll assume 20 bits. If you're using a granularity of 1K, then this offset must always be divided by 1024 to obtain the value for the page select register. In binary terms, "divide" always means that the dividend must be moved to the right the number of bits needed for binary representation of the divisor. Since 1K corresponds to a value of 2^{10}, the 20 bit offset address must be moved 10 bits to the right in order to obtain the desired number. The digits that are moved to the right of the "decimal" then become the offset in memory segment A000H.

The paging mechanism also has other tasks besides calculating page numbers and offsets. It becomes difficult when you must copy pieces of the video RAM that are more than 64K apart from one another. This makes it impossible to fit everything in the segment at A000 at the same time. So, the copy procedure must be divided into three time-consuming steps. First, the source is loaded into the segment at A000 so that it can be copied to a buffer in main memory that the program creates. Then the destination region must be loaded at A000 so the contents of the buffer can be loaded there.

This type of operation is fairly common, especially with animation applications. So, many Super VGA cards divide the memory segment at A000H into two 32K blocks, each of which has its own page select register. This allows the segment at A000H to handle two different regions of video RAM simultaneously. The regions can then be copied directly via the video RAM without having to use a buffer.

There are also no Super VGA standards for the process that controls page switching. Different cards use different registers and different granularities in segment A000H. Also, you cannot assume that all cards divide the A000H segment into two paging regions.

This causes a lot of problems for any programmer who wants to use a Super VGA mode that requires more than 256K. So it's obvious why the manufacturers of some programs, such as AutoCAD or Windows, let the card manufacturers develop software drivers for their products.

However, the VESA standard represents a solution to this problem. This standard represents a hardware independent interface for programming Super VGA modes. We'll discuss the VESA standard in Section 4.9.1.

Doing it yourself

If, in spite of all the problems that may occur, you still want to write a program using a Super VGA graphics mode, you should use the 800x600 pixel mode with 16 colors for several reasons. This mode is available on almost every Super VGA card, and it requires only 256K of video RAM. This eliminates having to program the page select register and will ensure that all Super VGA cards, regardless of how much memory they have, will be able to use your program. This mode will also allow you to use a lot of the routines that we've already seen work with the standard VGA 16 color modes.

Demonstration programs

We'll demonstrate how to do this in the following programs. The Pascal (V8060P.PAS) and C (V8060C.C) versions are based on routines from Section 4.8.6. Initializing the 800x600 mode, and setting or querying pixels are all accomplished with the various assembler routines found in the modules V8060CA.ASM and V8060PA.ASM.

The initialization routine INIT800600 performs the most difficult task. This routine must determine which code number the 800x600 pixel graphics mode uses on the installed video card. One way the routine can do this is by trying different code numbers until it finds one the BIOS accepts. There is a kind of array within the assembler program that stores six code numbers that are often used to identify the 800x600 pixel graphics mode. This array is called MODENO.

The most widely used code numbers are first put in the array. These code numbers are 6AH, 58H, and 29H. The code numbers 54H, 16H, and 79H are also in the array, but these are less common. We encountered these codes frequently while testing various Super VGA cards. They should work for most of the Super VGA cards on the market. If you find a particular card with a different code, you can easily add this code number to the MODENO array.

The INIT800600 routine recognizes the proper code number after it uses one of the codes to successfully initialize a graphics mode with function 00H of the video BIOS. Function 0FH of the video BIOS is used to return the code number of the currently active video mode. If this code number doesn't match the code number the program sent to initialize the mode, then the desired mode wasn't initialized and another code must be tried.

As long as the call to function 0FH doesn't return a match of the code number, the INIT800600 routine will continue to run through the array. This occurs until a code is accepted by the BIOS or until all codes in the array have been tried. In this case, the routine returns a value of 0 to its caller in the C version, or a value of FALSE in the Pascal version. If the mode could be successfully initialized, however, the C version returns 1 and the Pascal version returns TRUE.

According to our tests, this method can be used to set the proper video mode with several different Super VGA cards. However, this method isn't completely foolproof; the entire process can fall apart if the video card uses one of the codes in the MODENO array for a video mode other than the 16 color 800x600 pixel mode. In this case, the INIT800600 routine will return a value of 1 or TRUE, but the rest of the program won't work properly because a different video mode than expected will be functioning. However, this didn't occur in any of our tests, so this doesn't seem likely.

Pascal listing: V8060P.PAS

```
{*****************************************************************
*             V 8 0 6 0 P . P A S                              *
**-------------------------------------------------------------**
* Task         : Demonstrates programming in 800x600 pixel     *
*                graphics mode of Super VGA cards with 16 colors.*
*                This program requires the V8060PA.ASM assembly  *
*                language module.                              *
**-------------------------------------------------------------**
* Author       : Michael Tischer                              *
* Developed on  : 01/14/91                                     *
* Last update   : 03/03/92                                     *
*****************************************************************}

program V8060P;

uses dos, crt;

{-- Type declarations ----------------------------------------}

type BPTR = ^byte;

{-- External references to the assembler routines ------------}

{$L v8060pa}                          { Link assembler module }

function  init800600 : boolean; external;
procedure setpix( x, y : integer; pcolor : byte ); external;
function  getpix( x, y: integer ) : byte ; external;

{-- Constants ------------------------------------------------}

const MAXX    = 799;                  { Maximum X- and Y-coordinates }
      MAXY    = 599;
      NUMLINES = 2500;                        { Number of lines }
      XSPACING = 40;              { Distance of line box from margin }
      YSPACING = 30;
      X1      = ( 2 * XSPACING );         { Coordinates of line box }
      Y1      = ( 2 * YSPACING );
      X2      = ( MAXX-XSPACING );
      Y2      = ( MAXY-YSPACING );

{*****************************************************************
* IsVga : Determines whether a VGA card is installed.          *
**-------------------------------------------------------------**
* Input    : None                                             *
* Output   : TRUE or FALSE                                    *
*****************************************************************}

function IsVga : boolean;

var Regs : Registers;          { Processor registers for interrupt call }

begin
  Regs.AX := $1a00;                  { Function 1AH applies to VGA only }
  Intr( $10, Regs );
  IsVga := ( Regs.AL = $1a );
end;

{*****************************************************************
* PrintChar : Writes a character to the screen while in graphic mode.*
**-------------------------------------------------------------**
* Input    :    THECHAR = Character to be written             *
*               x, y    = X- and Y-coordinates of upper-left corner *
*               FG      = Foreground color                    *
*               BK      = Background color                    *
* Info     : Character is created in an 8x8 matrix, based on the *
*            8x8 ROM font.                                     *
*****************************************************************}

procedure PrintChar( thechar : char; x, y : integer; fg, bk : byte );

type FDEF = array[0..255,0..7] of byte;          { Font array }
     TPTR = ^FDEF;                               { Pointer to font }

var Regs  : Registers;                 { Registers for interrupt call }
    ch    : char;                { Individual pixels in character }
    i, k,                                   { Loop counter }
    BMask : byte;             { Bit mask for character design }

const fptr : TPTR = NIL;                       { Pointer to font in ROM }

begin
  if fptr = NIL then                { Pointer to font already set? }
    begin                                         { No }
      Regs.AH := $11;               { Call video BIOS function 11H, }
      Regs.AL := $30;                     { sub-function 30H        }
      Regs.BH := 3;                     { Get pointer to 8x8 font }
      intr( $10, Regs );
      fptr := ptr( Regs.ES, Regs.BP );           { Set pointers }
    end;
```

```
if ( bk = 255 ) then              { Drawing transparent characters? }
   for i := 0 to 7 do             { Yes --> Set foreground pixels only }
      begin
         BMask := fptr^[ord(thechar),i];{ Get bit pattern for one line }
         for k := 0 to 7 do
            begin
               if ( BMask and 128 <> 0 ) then        { Pixel set? }
                  setpix( x+k, y+i, fg );                    { Yes }
               BMask := BMask shl 1;
            end;
      end
else                              { No --> consider background as well }
   for i := 0 to 7 do             { Execute lines }
      begin
         BMask := fptr^[ord(thechar),i];{ Get bit pattern for one line }
         for k := 0 to 7 do
            begin
               if ( BMask and 128 <> 0 ) then        { Foreground? }
                  setpix( x+k, y+i, fg )                     { Yes }
               else
                  setpix( x+k, y+i, bk );    { No --> Background }
               BMask := BMask shl 1;
            end;
      end;
end;


{*********************************************************************
* Line: Draws a line based on the Bresenham algorithm.             *
**-----------------------------------------------------------------**
* Input   : X1, Y1 = Starting coordinates (0 - ...)               *
*           X2, Y2 = Ending coordinates                           *
*           LPCOL  = Color of line pixels                         *
*********************************************************************}


procedure Line( x1, y1, x2, y2 : integer; lpcol : byte );

var d, dx, dy,
    aincr, bincr,
    xincr, yincr,
    x, y                : integer;

{-- Procedure for swapping two integer variables ----------------------}


procedure SwapInt( var i1, i2: integer );

var dummy : integer;

begin
   dummy := i2;
   i2    := i1;
   i1    := dummy;
end;


{-- Main procedure ----------------------------------------------}

begin
   if ( abs(x2-x1) < abs(y2-y1) ) then    { X- or Y-axis overflow? }
      begin                                { Check Y-axis }
         if ( y1 > y2 ) then                      { y1 > y2? }
            begin
               SwapInt( x1, x2 );    { Yes --> Swap X1 with X2 }
               SwapInt( y1, y2 );    {          and Y1 with Y2 }
            end;
```

```
         if ( x2 > x1 ) then xincr := 1    { Set X-axis increment }
                        else xincr := -1;

         dy := y2 - y1;
         dx := abs( x2-x1 );
         d  := 2 * dx - dy;
         aincr := 2 * (dx - dy);
         bincr := 2 * dx;
         x := x1;
         y := y1;

         setpix( x, y, lpcol );               { Set first pixel }
         for y:=y1+1 to y2 do           { Execute line on Y-axes }
            begin
               if ( d >= 0 ) then
                  begin
                     inc( x, xincr );
                     inc( d, aincr );
                  end
               else
                  inc( d, bincr );
               setpix( x, y, lpcol );
            end;
      end
   else                                    { Check X-axes }
      begin
         if ( x1 > x2 ) then                       { x1 > x2? }
            begin
               SwapInt( x1, x2 );    { Yes --> Swap X1 with X2 }
               SwapInt( y1, y2 );    {          and Y1 with Y2 }
            end;

         if ( y2 > y1 ) then yincr := 1    { Set Y-axis increment }
                        else yincr := -1;

         dx := x2 - x1;
         dy := abs( y2-y1 );
         d  := 2 * dy - dx;
         aincr := 2 * (dy - dx);
         bincr := 2 * dy;
         x := x1;
         y := y1;

         setpix( x, y, lpcol );               { Set first pixel }
         for x:=x1+1 to x2 do           { Execute line on X-axes }
            begin
               if ( d >= 0 ) then
                  begin
                     inc( y, yincr );
                     inc( d, aincr );
                  end
               else
                  inc( d, bincr );
               setpix( x, y, lpcol );
            end;
      end;
end;


{*********************************************************************
* GrfxPrint: Displays a formatted string on the graphic screen.   *
**-----------------------------------------------------------------**
* Input   : X, Y  = Starting coordinates (0 - ...)                *
*           FG    = Foreground color                              *
```

```
*          BK     = Background color (255 = transparent)        *
*          STRING = String with format information              *
***************************************************************}

procedure GrfxPrint( x, y : integer; fg, bk : byte; strt : string );

var i : integer;                              { Loop counter }

begin
 for i:=1 to length( strt ) do
   begin
     printchar( strt[i], x, y, fg, bk );   { Display using PrintChar }
     inc( x, 8 );                     { Move X to next character position }
   end;
end;


{*************************************************************
* DrawAxis: Draws axes from left and top borders on the screen.  *
**---------------------------------------------------------------**
* Input  : STEPX = Increment for X-axis                         *
*          STEPY = Increment for Y-axis                         *
*          FG    = Foreground color                             *
*          BK    = Background color (255 = transparent)         *
***************************************************************}

procedure DrawAxis( stepx, stepy : integer; fg, bk : byte );

var x, y    : integer;                     { Loop coordinates }
    ordinate : string[3];

begin
Line( 0, 0, MAXX, 0, fg );                 { Draw X-axis }
Line( 0, 0, 0, MAXY, fg );                 { Draw Y-axis }

x := stepx;                                { Scale X-axis }
while ( x < MAXX ) do
  begin
    Line( x, 0, x, 5, fg );
    str( x, ordinate );
    if ( x < 100 ) then
      GrfxPrint( x - 8 , 8, fg, bk, ordinate )
    else
      GrfxPrint( x - 12, 8, fg, bk, ordinate );
    inc( x, stepx );
  end;

y := stepy;                                { Scale Y-axis }
while ( y < MAXY ) do
  begin
    Line( 0, y, 5, y, fg );
    str( y:3, ordinate );
    GrfxPrint( 8, y-4, fg, bk, ordinate );
    inc( y, stepy );
  end;
end;


{*************************************************************
* Demo: Demonstrates the functions and procedures in this module.  *
**---------------------------------------------------------------**
* Input  : None                                               *
***************************************************************}

procedure Demo;
```

```
var i : integer;                              { Loop counter }

begin
  Randomize;                    { Set random number generator in motion }
  DrawAxis( 30, 20, 15, 255 );                    { Draw axes }
  GrfxPrint( X1, MAXY-10, 15, 255,
           'V8060P.PAS  -  (c) by Michael Tischer' );

  Line( X1, Y1, X1, Y2, 15 );           { Draw border around line box }
  Line( X1, Y2, X2, Y2, 15 );
  Line( X2, Y2, X2, Y1, 15 );
  Line( X2, Y1, X1, Y1, 15 );

  {-- Create random lines within line box ----------------------------}

  for i := 1 to NUMLINES do
    Line( random( X2 - X1 - 1 ) + X1 + 1,
         random( Y2 - Y1 - 1 ) + Y1 + 1,
         random( X2 - X1 - 1 ) + X1 + 1,
         random( Y2 - Y1 - 1 ) + Y1 + 1,
         i mod 16 );
end;


{---------------------------------------------------------------}
{--            M A I N   P R O G R A M               ----}
{---------------------------------------------------------------}

begin
  writeln( 'V8060P.PAS  - (c) 1992 by Michael Tischer'#13#10 );
  if IsVga then                         { VGA card installed? }
    begin      { Yes --> but can graphics mode also be initialized? }
      if init800600 then
        begin                                     { Mode O.K. }
          Demo;                              { Execute Demo }
          repeat until keypressed;             { Wait for key }
          Textmode( C080 );              { Shift into text mode }
        end
      else
        writeln( '800x600 mode could not be initialized!' );
    end
  else
    writeln( 'This program requires a VGA card', + #13#10);
end.
```

Assembler listing: V8060PA.ASM

```
;****************************************************************;
;*                V 8 0 6 0 P A . A S M                       *;
;*------------------------------------------------------------*;
;*  Task      : Contains routines for operating in 800x600    *;
;*              graphics mode on a Super VGA card with 16     *;
;*              colors.                                        *;
;*------------------------------------------------------------*;
;*  Author    : MICHAEL TISCHER                               *;
;*  Developed on  : 01/14/91                                  *;
;*  Last update   : 01/14/91                                  *;
;*------------------------------------------------------------*;
;*  Assembly  : MASM /mx V8060PA;    or    TASM -mx V8060PA   *;
;*              ... Link to V8060P.PAS                        *;
;****************************************************************;


;== Constants =================================================

GC_INDEX      = 3ceh         ;Index register for graphics ctrl.
GC_READ_MAP   = 4            ;Number of read map register
GC_BIT_MASK   = 8            ;Number of bit mask register
GC_GRAPH_MODE = 5            ;Number of graphics mode register

;== Data segment ==============================================

DATA   segment word public   ;Must be initialized during runtime
DATA   ends

;== Program ===================================================

CODE       segment byte public    ;Program segment

           assume cs:code, ds:data

;-- Public declarations ---------------------------------------

public     init800600        ;Initialize 800x600 mode
public     setpix            ;Set pixel
public     getpix            ;Get pixel color

;-- Data in code segment --------------------------------------

           ;-- Code number of 800x600 mode for
           ;-- different Super VGA cards

modeno     db 6Ah, 58h, 29h, 54h, 16h, 79h
modenoend  equ this byte


;--------------------------------------------------------------
;-- INIT800600: Initializes 800x600 Super VGA graphics mode
;--             with 16 colors
;-- Call from TP: function init800600 : boolean;
;-- Return value: TRUE = Mode was initialized, FALSE = Error

init800600 proc near

           ;-- Try all modes from MODENO table, until
           ;-- BIOS accepts a mode

           mov  si,offset modeno  ;Begin with first mode from table
it1:       xor  ah,ah             ;Function 00H: Initialize mode
           mov  al,cs:[si]        ;Load code number from table
           int  10h               ;Initialize mode
```

```
           mov  ah,0fh            ;Function OFH: Read mode
           int  10h
           cmp  al,cs:[si]        ;Mode set?
           je   it2               ;Yes --> O.K.

           ;-- Wrong code number, choose next one from table ----------

           inc  si                ;SI to next code number
           cmp  si,offset modenoend ;Execute entire table?
           jne  it1               ;No --> Play it again, Sam

           mov  al,0              ;Yes --> End function with error
           ret                    ;Return to caller

it2:       ;-- Mode was initialized ------------------------------------

           mov  al,1              ;All O.K.
           ret                    ;Return to caller

init800600 endp                   ;End of procedure

;--------------------------------------------------------------
;-- SETPIX: Changes a pixel to a specific color
;-- Call from TP: setpix( x , y : integer; pcolor : byte );

setpix     proc near

sframe     struc                  ;Structure for stack access
bp0        dw ?                   ;Gets BP
ret_adr0   dw ?                   ;Return address to caller
pcolor     dw ?                   ;Color
y0         dw ?                   ;Y-coordinate
x0         dw ?                   ;X-coordinate
sframe     ends                   ;End of structure

frame      equ [ bp - bp0 ]       ;Address structure elements

           push bp                ;Prepare for parameter addressing
           mov  bp,sp             ; through BP register

           ;-- First compute offset in video RAM and shift value ------

           mov  ax,frame.y0       ;Load Y-coordinate
           mov  dx,800 / 8        ;Multiply by line width
           mul  dx
           mov  bx,frame.x0       ;Load X-coordinate
           mov  cl,bl             ;Store low byte for shift computation

           shr  bx,1              ;Divide X-coordinate by eight
           shr  bx,1
           shr  bx,1
           add  bx,ax             ;Add offset from multiplication to it

           and  cl,7              ;Compute bit mask from X-coordinate
           xor  cl,7
           mov  ah,1
           shl  ah,cl

           mov  dx,GC_INDEX       ;Access to graphics controller
           mov  al,GC_BIT_MASK    ;Write bit mask in bit mask
           out  dx,ax             ;register

           mov  ax,(02h shl 8) + GC_GRAPH_MODE ;Set write mode 2 &
           out  dx,ax                          ;read mode 0
```

415

```
        mov   ax,0A000h      ;Segment address of video RAM          xor   bl,bl                     ;plane #3
        mov   es,ax          ; to ES
                                                            gp1:    out   dx,ax             ;Load read map register
        mov   al,es:[bx]             ;Load latch register          mov   bh,es:[si]        ;Load value from latch register
        mov   al,byte ptr frame.pcolor ;Load pixel color           and   bh,ch            ;Leave only desired pixels
        mov   es:[bx],al            ;write back to latch reg.        neg   bh              ;Set bit 7 according to pixel
                                                                    rol   bx,1             ;Bit 7 from BH to Bit 1 in BL red.
        ;-- Set default values in different registers of graphics
        ;-- controller that have been changed                       dec   ah              ;Process next bit plane
                                                                    jge   gp1              ;> or = Null? ---> Continue
        mov   ax,(0FFh shl 8 ) + GC_BIT_MASK
        out   dx,ax                                                 mov   al,bl            ;Function result to AL

        mov   ax,(00h shl 8) + GC_GRAPH_MODE                        pop   bp
        out   dx,ax                                                 ret   4                ;Return to caller, remove
                                                                                           ;arguments from stack
        pop   bp
        ret   6                      ;Return to caller, remove  getpix    endp                       ;End of procedure
                                     ;arguments from stack
                                                            ;== End ================================================================
setpix    endp                  ;End of procedure

;---------------------------------------------------------------  CODE    ends                 ;End of code segment
;-- GETPIX: Returns a pixel color                                  end                 ;End of program
;-- Call from TP: x := getpix( x , y : integer );

getpix    proc near

sframe1   struc                  ;Structure for stack access
bp1       dw ?                   ;Gets BP
ret_adr1  dw ?                   ;Return address to caller
y1        dw ?                   ;Y-coordinate
x1        dw ?                   ;X-coordinate
sframe1   ends                   ;End of structure

frame     equ [ bp – bp1 ]      ;Address structure elements

        push  bp               ;Prepare for parameter addressing
        mov   bp,sp            ;through BP register

        ;-- First computer offset in video RAM and shift value -----

        mov   ax,frame.y1      ;Load Y-coordinate
        mov   dx,800 / 8       ;Multiply by line width
        mul   dx
        mov   si,frame.x1      ;Load X-coordinate
        mov   cx,si            ;Store for shift computation

        shr   si,1             ;Divide X-coordinate by eight
        shr   si,1
        shr   si,1
        add   si,ax            ;Add offset from multiplication to it

        and   cl,7            ;Compute bit mask from X-coordinate
        xor   cl,7
        mov   ch,1
        shl   ch,cl

        mov   ax,0A000h       ;Segment address of video RAM
        mov   es,ax           ; to ES

        mov   dx,GC_INDEX     ;Access to graphics controller
        mov   ax,(3 shl 8)+ GC_READ_MAP   ;First read out
```

C listing: V8060C.C

```
/***************************************************
*                 V 8 0 6 0 C . C                  *
**------------------------------------------------**
* Task         : Demonstrates programming in 800x600 graphics *
*                mode on Super VGA cards with 16 colors. This  *
*                program requires V8060CA.ASM assembly          *
*                language module.                               *
**------------------------------------------------**
* Author       : MICHAEL TISCHER                   *
* Developed on  : 01/14/91                          *
* Last update   : 01/14/91                          *
**------------------------------------------------**
* (MICROSOFT C)                                     *
* Compilation                                       *
*                                                   *
**------------------------------------------------**
* (BORLAND TURBO C)                                 *
* Compilation   : Create a project file using the following: *
*                 v8060c.c                          *
*                 v8060ca.obj                       *
**------------------------------------------------**
* Call          : v8060c                            *
***************************************************/

#include <dos.h>
#include <stdarg.h>
#include <stdlib.h>
#include <io.h>
#include <stdio.h>
#include <conio.h>

/*-- Type declarations -----------------------------*/

typedef unsigned char BYTE;

/*-- External references to the assembler routines ------------------*/

extern int  init800600( void );
extern void setpix( int x, int y, unsigned char pcolor);
extern BYTE getpix( int x, int y );
extern void far * getfontptr( void );

/*-- Compiler-dependent declarations ---------------------------*/

#ifndef __TURBOC__
  #define random(x) ( rand() % (x+1) )       /* Random function */
#endif

/*-- Constants -------------------------------------*/

#define MAXX     799           /* Maximum X- and Y-coordinates */
#define MAXY     599
#define NUMLINES 2500                        /* Number of lines */
#define XSPACING 40           /* Distance of line box from border */
#define YSPACING 30
#define X1       ( 2 * XSPACING )   /* Coordinates of the line box */
#define Y1       ( 2 * YSPACING )
#define X2       ( MAXX-XSPACING )
#define Y2       ( MAXY-YSPACING )
#define XRAND    random( X2 - X1 - 1 ) + X1 + 1      /* Random */
```

```
#define YRAND    random( Y2 - Y1 - 1 ) + Y1 + 1      /* coordinates */

/***************************************************
* IsVga: Determines whether a VGA card is installed.          *
**------------------------------------------------**
* Input  : None                                    *
* Output : 0, if no VGA exists, otherwise < 0       *
***************************************************/

BYTE IsVga( void )
{
 union REGS Regs;           /* Processor registers for interrupt call */

 Regs.x.ax = 0x1a00;              /* Function 1AH applies to VGA only */
 int86( 0x10, &Regs, &Regs );
 return (BYTE) ( Regs.h.al == 0x1a );   /* Is the function available? */
}

/***************************************************
* PrintChar : Writes a character to the screen while in graphic mode.*
**------------------------------------------------**
* Input  :   THECHAR = Character to be written      *
*            x, y    = X- and Y-coordinates of upper-left corner *
*            FG      = Foreground color             *
*            BK      = Background color             *
* Info   : Character is created in an 8x8 matrix based on the *
*          8x8 ROM font.                            *
***************************************************/

void PrintChar( char thechar, int x, int y, BYTE fg, BYTE bk )
{
 typedef BYTE FDEF[256][8];                    /* Font definition */
 typedef FDEF far *TPTR;                        /* Pointer to font */

 BYTE     i, k,                               /* Loop counter */
          BMask;                  /* Bit mask for character design */

 static TPTR fptr = (TPTR) 0;         /* Pointer to font in ROM */

 if ( fptr == (TPTR) 0 )            /* Pointer to font already set? */
   fptr = getfontptr();   /*No --> Use the assembler function to load */

 /*- Generate character pixel by pixel -----------------------*/

 if ( bk == 255 )                  /* Drawing transparent characters? */
   for ( i = 0; i < 8; ++i )    /* Yes --> Set foreground pixels only */
   {
     BMask = (*fptr)[thechar][i];      /* Get bit pattern for one line */
     for ( k = 0; k < 8; ++k, BMask <<= 1 )    /* Execute columns */
       if ( BMask & 128 )                       /* Pixel set? */
         setpix( x+k, y+i, fg );                 /* Yes */
   }
 else                        /* No --> Consider background as well */
   for ( i = 0; i < 8; ++i )                   /* Execute lines */
   {
     BMask = (*fptr)[thechar][i];      /* Get bit pattern for one line */
     for ( k = 0; k < 8; ++k, BMask <<= 1 )    /* Execute columns */
       setpix( x+k, y+i, ( BMask & 128 ) ? fg : bk );
   }
}

/***************************************************
* Line: Draws a line based on the Bresenham algorithm.        *
**------------------------------------------------**
```

417

```
*   Input    : X1, Y1 = Starting coordinates (0 - ...)         *
*             X2, Y2 = Ending coordinates                      *
*             LPCOL  = Color of line pixels                    *
*********************************************************************/

/*-- Function for swapping two integer variables --------------------*/

void SwapInt( int *i1, int *i2 )
{
 int dummy;

 dummy = *i2;
 *i2   = *i1;
 *i1   = dummy;
}

/*-- Main part of function -------------------------------------------*/

void Line( int x1, int y1, int x2, int y2, BYTE lpcol )
{
 int d, dx, dy,
     aincr, bincr,
     xincr, yincr,
     x, y;

 if ( abs(x2-x1) < abs(y2-y1) )         /* X- or Y-axis overflow? */
  {                                     /* Check Y-axis */
   if ( y1 > y2 )                       /* y1 > y2? */
    {
     SwapInt( &x1, &x2 );               /* Yes --> Swap X1 with X2 */
     SwapInt( &y1, &y2 );               /*         and Y1 with Y2 */
    }

   xincr = ( x2 > x1 ) ? 1 : -1;        /* Set X-axis increment */

   dy = y2 - y1;
   dx = abs( x2-x1 );
   d = 2 * dx - dy;
   aincr = 2 * (dx - dy);
   bincr = 2 * dx;
   x = x1;
   y = y1;

   setpix( x, y, lpcol );               /* Set first pixel */
   for (y=y1+1; y<= y2; ++y )           /* Execute line on Y-axes */
    {
     if ( d >= 0 )
      {
       x += xincr;
       d += aincr;
      }
     else
       d += bincr;
     setpix(x, y, lpcol);
    }
  }
 else                                   /* Check X-axes */
  {
   if ( x1 > x2 )                       /* x1 > x2? */
    {
     SwapInt( &x1, &x2 );               /* Yes --> Swap X1 with X2 */
     SwapInt( &y1, &y2 );               /*         and Y1 with Y2 */
    }
```

```
   yincr = ( y2 > y1 ) ? 1 : -1;        /* Set Y-axis increment */

   dx = x2 - x1;
   dy = abs( y2-y1 );
   d = 2 * dy - dx;
   aincr = 2 * (dy - dx);
   bincr = 2 * dy;
   x = x1;
   y = y1;

   setpix(x, y, lpcol);                 /* Set first pixel */
   for (x=x1+1; x<=x2; ++x )            /* Execute line on X-axes */
    {
     if ( d >= 0 )
      {
       y += yincr;
       d += aincr;
      }
     else
       d += bincr;
     setpix(x, y, lpcol);
    }
  }
}

/*********************************************************************
* GrfxPrintf: Displays a formatted string on the graphic screen.   *
*-------------------------------------------------------------------*
* Input   : X, Y  = Starting coordinates (0 - ...)                 *
*           FG    = Foreground color                               *
*           BK    = Background color (255 = transparent)           *
*           STRING = String with format information                *
*           ...   = Arguments similar to printf                    *
*********************************************************************/

void GrfxPrintf( int x, int y, BYTE fg, BYTE bk, char * string, ... )
{
 va_list parameter;                     /* Parameter list for VA_... macros */
 char stngptr[255],                     /* Buffer for formatted string */
      *cp;

 va_start( parameter, string );         /* Convert parameter */
 vsprintf( stngptr, string, parameter ); /* Format */
 for ( cp = stngptr; *cp; ++cp, x+= 8 ) /* Formatted string */
   PrintChar( *cp, x, y, fg, bk );      /* Display using PrintChar */
}

/*********************************************************************
* DrawAxis: Draws axes from the left and top borders on the screen. *
*-------------------------------------------------------------------*
* Input   : STEPX = Increment for X-axis                           *
*           STEPY = Increment for Y-axis                           *
*           FG    = Foreground color                               *
*           BK    = Background color (255 = transparent)           *
*********************************************************************/

void DrawAxis( int stepx, int stepy, BYTE fg, BYTE bk )
{
 int x, y;                              /* Loop coordinates */

 Line( 0, 0, MAXX, 0, fg );            /* Draw X-axis */
 Line( 0, 0, 0, MAXY, fg );            /* Draw Y-axis */

 for ( x = stepx; x < MAXX; x += stepx ) /* Scale X-axis */
```

```
{
 Line( x, 0, x, 5, fg );
 GrfxPrintf( x < 100 ? x - 8 : x - 12, 8, fg, bk, "%d", x );
 }


 for ( y = stepy; y < MAXY; y += stepy )          /* Scale Y-axis */
 {
  Line( 0, y, 5, y, fg );
  GrfxPrintf( 8, y-4, fg, bk, "%3d", y );
  }
 }


/***********************************************************
* Demo: Demonstrates the functions in this module.         *
***********************************************************/

void Demo( void )
{
 int i;                                      /* Loop counter */

 DrawAxis( 30, 20, 15, 255 );                      /* Draw axes */

 GrfxPrintf( X1, MAXY-10, 15, 255,
             "V8060C.C  -  (c) by Michael Tischer" );

 Line( X1, Y1, X1, Y2, 15 );    /* Draws a frame around the line box */
 Line( X1, Y2, X2, Y2, 15 );
 Line( X2, Y2, X2, Y1, 15 );
 Line( X2, Y1, X1, Y1, 15 );

 /*-- Create random lines within the line box ----------------------*/

 for ( i = NUMLINES; i > 0 ; --i )
  Line( XRAND, YRAND, XRAND, YRAND, (BYTE) (i % 16) );
 }


/*************************************************************/
/**                  M A I N   P R O G R A M            ***/
/*************************************************************/

void main( void )
{
 union REGS regs;

 printf( "V8060C.C  - (c) 1992 by Michael Tischer\n\n" );
 if ( IsVga() )                         /* VGA card installed? */
  {                      /* Yes, but can the mode also be initialized? */
   if ( init800600() )
    {                                            /* Mode O.K. */
     Demo();                                  /* Execute demo */
     getch();                                /* Wait for a key */
     regs.x.ax = 0x0003;                 /* Shift into text mode */
     int86( 0x10, &regs, &regs );
    }
   else
    {
     printf( "Attention: 800x600 mode could not be initialized\n" );
     exit( 1 );
    }
  }
 else
  {                                       /* No, no VGA card */
   printf( "This program requires a VGA card\n" );
   exit(1);                                /* End program */
  }
 }
```

Assembler listing: V8060CA.ASM

```
;***********************************************************;
;*                 V 8 0 6 0 C A . A S M                  *;
;*-------------------------------------------------------*;
;*   Task      : Contains various routines for operating in  *;
;*               800x600 graphics mode on a Super VGA card   *;
;*               with 16 colors                             *;
;*-------------------------------------------------------*;
;*   Author    : MICHAEL TISCHER                           *;
;*   Developed on  : 01/14/91                              *;
;*   Last update   : 03/03/92                              *;
;*-------------------------------------------------------*;
;*   Memory model : SMALL                                 *;
;*-------------------------------------------------------*;
;*   Assembly   : MASM /mx V8060CA    or    TASM -mx V8060CA *;
;***********************************************************;


IGROUP group _text              ;Program segment
DGROUP group const,_bss, _data  ;Data segment
       assume CS:IGROUP, DS:DGROUP, ES:DGROUP, SS:DGROUP

CONST segment word public 'CONST';This segment handles all
CONST ends                       ;readable constants

_BSS  segment word public 'BSS'  ;This segment handles all uninitial-
_BSS  ends                       ;ized static variables

_DATA segment word public 'DATA' ;This segment handles all initialized
                                 ;global and static variables
_DATA ends


;== Constants =============================================

GC_INDEX    = 3ceh          ;Index register of graphics ctrl.
GC_READ_MAP = 4             ;Number of read map register
GC_BIT_MASK = 8             ;Number of bit mask register
GC_GRAPH_MODE = 5           ;Number of graphics mode register

;== Data =================================================

_DATA  segment word public 'DATA'

              ;-- Code number for 800x600 mode for different
              ;-- Super VGA cards

modeno    db 6Ah, 58h, 29h, 54h, 16h, 79h
modenoend equ this byte

_DATA ends

;== Program =============================================

_TEXT segment byte public 'CODE' ;Program segment

;-- Public declarations ---------------------------------

public  _init800600            ;Initialize 800x600 mode
public  _setpix                ;Set pixel
public  _getpix                ;Get pixel color
public  _getfontptr            ;Return pointer to 8x8 font

;-------------------------------------------------------
;-- INIT800600: Initializes 800x600 Super VGA graphics mode
```

```
;--            with 16 colors
;-- Declaration : int init800600( void );
;-- Return value: 1 = Mode was initialized, O = Error


_init800600 proc near


        ;-- Try all modes from the modeno table, until BIOS
        ;-- accepts a mode

        mov  si,offset modeno  ;Start with first mode from table
it1:    xor  ah,ah             ;Function OOH: Initialize mode
        mov  al,[si]           ;Load code number from table
        int  10h               ;Initialize mode
        mov  ah,Ofh            ;Function OFH: Read mode
        int  10h
        cmp  al,[si]           ;Has mode been set?
        je   it2               ;Yes --> O.K.


        ;-- Wrong code number, select next from table --------------

        inc  si                ;SI to next code number
        cmp  si,offset modenoend ;Execute entire table?
        jne  it1               ;No --> Play it again, Sam

        xor  ax,ax             ;Yes --> End function with error
        ret                    ;Return to caller

it2:    ;-- Mode was initialized ----------------------------------

        mov  ax,1              ;All O.K.
        ret                    ;Return to caller

_init800600 endp             ;End of procedure

;-- SETPIX: Changes a pixel to a specific color -----------------------
;-- Declaration : void setpix( int x, int y, unsigned char pcolor );

_setpix   proc near

sframe    struc              ;Structure for stack access
bp0       dw ?               ;Gets BP
ret_adr0  dw ?               ;Return address to caller
x0        dw ?               ;X-coordinate
y0        dw ?               ;Y-coordinate
pcolor    dw ?               ;Color
sframe    ends               ;End of structure

frame     equ [ bp - bp0 ]   ;Address structure elements

          push bp            ;Prepare for parameter addressing
          mov  bp,sp         ; through BP register


          ;-- First computer offset in video RAM and shift value -----

          mov  ax,frame.y0   ;Load Y-coordinate
          mov  dx,800/8      ;Multiply by line width
          mul  dx
          mov  bx,frame.x0   ;Load X-coordinate
          mov  cl,bl         ;Store low byte for shift computation

          shr  bx,1          ;Divide X-coordinate by eight
          shr  bx,1
          shr  bx,1
          add  bx,ax         ;Add offset from multiplication to it
```

```
        and  cl,7            ;Compute bit mask from X-coordinate
        xor  cl,7
        mov  ah,1
        shl  ah,cl

        mov  dx,GC_INDEX     ;Access to graphics controller
        mov  al,GC_BIT_MASK  ;Write bit mask to bit mask
        out  dx,ax           ; register

        mov  ax,(02h shl 8) + GC_GRAPH_MODE;Set write mode 2 &
        out  dx,ax                         ; read mode 0

        mov  ax,0A000h       ;Segment address of video RAM
        mov  es,ax           ; to ES

        mov  al,es:[bx]          ;Load latch register
        mov  al,byte ptr frame.pcolor ;Load pixel color
        mov  es:[bx],al          ;Write back to latch reg.

        ;-- Set default values in the different registers of
        ;-- graphics controller that have been changed

        mov  ax,(0FFh shl 8 ) + GC_BIT_MASK
        out  dx,ax

        mov  ax,(00h shl 8) + GC_GRAPH_MODE
        out  dx,ax

        pop  bp
        ret                  ;Return to caller

_setpix   endp              ;End of procedure

;-- GETPIX: Returns a pixel color -------------------------------------
;-- Declaration : unsigned char getpix( int x, int y );

_getpix   proc near

sframe1   struc              ;Structure for stack access
bp1       dw ?               ;Gets BP
ret_adr1  dw ?               ;Return address to caller
x1        dw ?               ;X-coordinate
y1        dw ?               ;Y-coordinate
sframe1   ends               ;End of structure

frame     equ [ bp - bp1 ]   ;Address structure elements

          push bp            ;Prepare for parameter addressing
          mov  bp,sp         ; through BP register

          push si

          ;-- First compute offset in video RAM and shift value ------

          mov  ax,frame.y1   ;Load Y-coordinate
          mov  dx,800 / 8    ;Multiply by line width
          mul  dx
          mov  si,frame.x1   ;Load X-coordinate
          mov  cx,si         ;Store for shift computation

          shr  si,1          ;Divide X-coordinate by eight
          shr  si,1
          shr  si,1
```

```
        add    si,ax          ;Add offset from multiplication to it           ret                      ;Return to caller

        and    cl,7           ;Compute bit mask from X-coordinate      _getpix    endp              ;End of procedure
        xor    cl,7
        mov    ch,1                                                    ;-- GETFONTPTR: Returns FAR pointer to 8x8 font table -----------------
        shl    ch,cl                                                  ;-- Declaration : void far * getfontptr( void )

        mov    ax,0A000h      ;Segment address of video RAM     _getfontptr proc near
        mov    es,ax          ; to ES
                                                                          push   bp            ;Push BP onto stack
        mov    dx,GC_INDEX    ;Access to graphics controller
        mov    ax,(3 shl 8)+ GC_READ_MAP  ;First read                   mov    ax,1130h      ;Get register for function call
        xor    bl,bl                   ;plane #3                         mov    bh,3
                                                                          int    10h           ;Call BIOS video interrupt
gp1:    out    dx,ax          ;Specify bit plane to be read
        mov    bh,es:[si]     ;Load value from latch register            mov    dx,es         ;Pointer ES:BP returned in DX:AX
        and    bh,ch          ;Leave only desired pixel                  mov    ax,bp
        neg    bh             ;Set bit 7 according to pixel
        rol    bx,1           ;Bit 7 from BH to bit 1 in BL red.         pop    bp            ;Pop BP from stack
                                                                          ret                  ;Return to caller
        dec    ah             ;Process next bit plane
        jge    gp1            ;> or = 0? ---> Continue           _getfontptr endp            ;End of procedure

        mov    al,bl          ;Function result to AL            ;== End ================================================================

        pop    si                                               _text   ends              ;End program segment
        pop    bp                                                       end               ;End program
```

4.9.1 The VESA Standard

The history of the PC has shown hardware manufacturers how the lack of standards can hurt business. Without standardization, manufacturers can develop features that give their products advantages over the competition. However, a video card that has great features but cannot work with any programs is useless. Software developers aren't going to risk developing products that will work only on one manufacturer's video card. This has been the case in the Super VGA market. Manufacturers are offering different cards with different features and no standard methods for addressing video RAM or using the hardware registers. The result is that software developers have been very reluctant to produce programs that use the expanded Super VGA modes. The card manufacturers must therefore deliver software drivers for their cards so that at least some programs can utilize the additional modes.

In an attempt to solve this problem, several VGA manufacturers established the VESA committee (Video Electronic Standards Association) in 1989. ATI, Chips & Technologies, Everex, Genoa, Intel, Phoenix Technologies, Orchid, Paradise, Video Seven, and many other companies are part of this association.

This committee's goal was to develop a BIOS expansion that would give programmers hardware independent access to the Super VGA features found on many manufacturers' cards. This BIOS expansion, called the VESA standard, was released in 1990. The BIOS expansion described by this standard will be incorporated in the expanded VGA-BIOS found in the ROM chips on these manufacturers' cards. There will be software drivers for older cards. These drivers will be run as TSR programs in order to add the VESA functions to the existing BIOS. For the first time, this will give programmers the freedom to develop applications that work with many Super VGA cards, without having to consider the various hardware differences.

The VESA standard graphics modes

First, the VESA committee members had to decide which graphics modes to support. Obviously each manufacturer wanted their own modes in the standard. After some compromise, they came up with a list of nine modes, which are listed in the following table.

Code numbers were assigned to the graphics modes so that the VESA BIOS could identify them the same way the normal VGA BIOS does. Codes over 100H (256) were selected, however, because the individual manufacturers had already used many of the codes under 100H for their own special modes. So, Super VGA modes are represented with 16 bit codes under the VESA standard. The one exception to this is the 16 color 800x600 pixel mode, which many manufacturers had already assigned the code 6AH. The VESA standard keeps this code for this mode, and supports it as one of the expanded VESA modes.

The VESA BIOS Graphics Modes			
Code	Resolution	Colors	Memory*
100H	640x 400	256	256K
101H	640x 480	256	512K
102H	800x 600	16	256K
103H	800x 600	256	512K
104H	1024x 768	16	512K
105H	1024x 768	256	1 Meg
106H	1280x1024	16	1 Meg
107H	1280x1024	256	1.25 Meg
6AH	800x 600	16	256K

* This number is given in increments of 256, 512, or 1024K, and does represent the actual memory needed for a single screen page.

Calling the VESA BIOS functions

The VESA BIOS functions can be accessed with the BIOS video interrupt 10H, just as the normal functions of the VGA BIOS. There are six subfunctions under function 4FH. Before the function call, the function number 4FH must be placed in the AH register and the desired subfunction number (0 - 5) must be placed in the AL register.

The VESA BIOS Functions	
No.	Description
00H	Query capabilities of Super VGA card
01H	Query identifying information for a certain mode
02H	Set a VESA mode
03H	Query current video mode
04H	Save/restore status of the Super VGA card
05H	Set/query access window to video RAM

The AH and AL registers are also used to read the results of the function after it has been called. If the VESA BIOS functions are supported by the installed video card, then the value 4FH will be returned to the AL register. The AH register receives a status code. A value of 0 indicates that the function was successfully executed and a value of 1 indicates that something went wrong. All other return values (01H - 0FFH) are reserved, but should be handled as error messages if they are encountered. The contents of the registers other than AH and AL aren't changed by these function calls, unless they are used to return specific information.

Usually it isn't necessary to query the contents of the AH and AL registers after every VESA function call to check for errors. But you should always check the results returned to the AH and AL registers after your first VESA function call to ensure that the VESA functions are supported by the installed video card.

Checking a Super VGA card's capabilities

Although the VESA standard provides an interface to the most important video modes of the new Super VGA cards, there is no guarantee that a particular card will support all of the VESA modes. So, at run time (before working with any of the VESA functions), you must call subfunction 00H so that the capabilities of the installed Super VGA card can be queried. For this function call, the function and subfunction numbers are expected in the AH and AL registers, respectively. A FAR pointer to a 256K buffer is also expected in the ES:DI register pair. Subfunction 00H stores information about the capabilities of the installed Super VGA card in this buffer.

Structure of the Subfunction 00H Buffer		
Ofs.	Contents	Type
00H	VESA Signature ("VESA")	4 BYTE
04H	VESA Version, main version number	1 BYTE
05H	VESA Version, secondary version number	1 BYTE
06H	FAR pointer to an ASCII string containing the name of the card manufacturer	1 DWORD
0AH	Flag that indicates the capabilities of the card currently not used, therefore 0000h.	1 DWORD
0EH	FAR pointer to the list of code numbers for the supported video modes	1 DWORD

The most important information for the programmer is obtained via the last pointer in this table. This points to a list of the code numbers, for the video modes, supported by the installed card. This list may be either in the ROM-BIOS of the card or in main memory. It consists of several words. Each word indicates the number of a supported mode. Both the standard VESA modes and the manufacturer's custom modes are listed. The manufacturer's own modes can be easily distinguished from the VESA modes because their code numbers are less than 100H, and therefore contain a value of 00H in the high byte of the corresponding entry in this list.

This list can be a different length for each card, depending on the modes it supports and how much RAM it has. The end of the list is indicated by a word containing the value FFFFH, which doesn't represent any video mode.

Reading a specific video mode

Just knowing that a certain mode exists doesn't mean that you can use this mode. Subfunction 01H is used to query all the information needed to program a given video mode. The function and subfunction numbers are expected in registers AH and AL, respectively. Also, the number of the appropriate mode must be passed in the CX register. This number must correspond to one of the entries in the list that is queried with subfunction 00H. The ES:DI register pair expects a pointer to a buffer that will store this information. This buffer must be able to store 29 bytes.

The subfunction 00H mode list includes both the VESA modes and the manufacturer's own modes. This allows you to use subfunction 01H to retrieve information about the expanded Super VGA text modes as well as the standard VESA modes.

The following figure shows the structure of the information as it's entered in the buffer by subfunction 01H.

Structure of the subfunction 01H buffer		
Ofs.	Contents	Type
00H	Mode flag, see below	1 word
02H	Flags for the first access window, see below	1 byte
03H	Flags for the second access window, see below	1 byte
04H	Granularity of the two access windows, in K,	1 word
06H	Size of the two access windows, in K	1 word
08H	Segment address of the first access window	1 word
0AH	Segment address of the second access window	1 word
0CH	FAR pointer to routine for setting the visible region in the two access windows	1 dword
10H	Number of bytes required by each pixel line in video RAM word	1 byte
Optional information, see mode flag		
12H	X resolution in pixels/character	1 word
14H	Y resolution in pixels/character	1 word
16H	Width of character matrix in pixels	1 byte
17H	Height of character matrix in pixels	1 byte
18H	Number of bitplanes	1 byte
19H	Number of bits per screen pixel	1 byte
1AH	Number of memory blocks	1 byte
1BH	Memory model	1 byte
1CH	Size of memory blocks in K	1 byte

The mode flag (the first bit field in the block) provides information on the queried mode. As shown in the following figure, the mode flag indicates if the mode is a text or graphics mode, if color is supported, if text can be output with the BIOS functions, and, most importantly, if this mode can even be used with the available monitor and memory.

It's also important to determine whether the information in the optional fields of the data block are filled. These fields contain important information for working with a given video mode. This information is usually available.

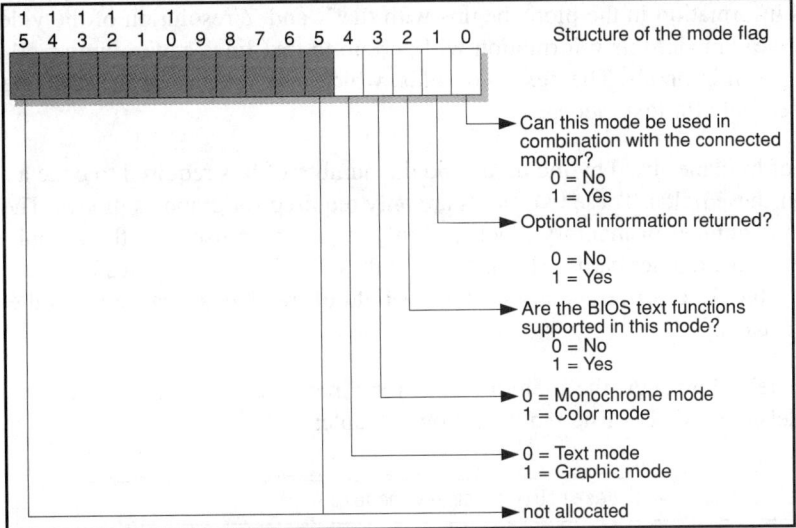

Structure of the mode flag

Can this mode be used in combination with the connected monitor?
0 = No
1 = Yes

Optional information returned?

0 = No
1 = Yes

Are the BIOS text functions supported in this mode?
0 = No
1 = Yes

0 = Monochrome mode
1 = Color mode

0 = Text mode
1 = Graphic mode

not allocated

The two flags that describe the access windows to the video RAM are also represented by bit fields. Since not all Super VGA cards have two access windows, these flags must be used to determine whether a second window is available. Also, these flags will indicate which window is for reading and which is for writing.

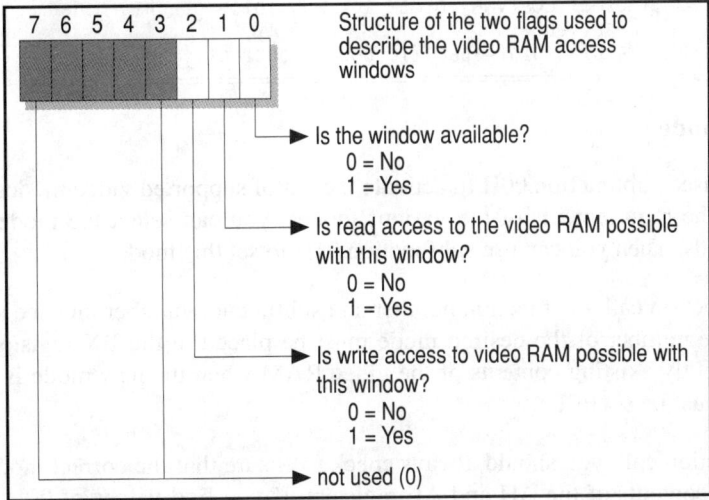

Structure of the two flags used to describe the video RAM access windows

Is the window available?
0 = No
1 = Yes

Is read access to the video RAM possible with this window?
0 = No
1 = Yes

Is write access to video RAM possible with this window?
0 = No
1 = Yes

not used (0)

In addition to the flags that describe the video RAM access windows, some other important information about using the access windows is also given in the subfunction 01H data block. This includes the segment addresses of the two access windows. Obviously the entry for the second window is only valid if the second window actually exists. The size and the granularity of the two windows are also given. Remember that the granularity is the interval with which the window can be "moved" through the video RAM.

The VESA-BIOS has a routine for moving the window through video RAM. This routine protects programmers from the incompatibilities between different Super VGA cards. You'll find more information about this routine when we discuss subfunction 05H at the end of this section.

The optional information in the block begins with the X and Y resolution of the video mode. If the mode is a text mode, this information will pertain to text lines and columns; otherwise, the resolution is given in pixels. The next two fields, which give the size of the character matrix in pixels, are used only for text modes.

The number of bitplanes used by the mode and the number of bits required to code a single pixel are listed after these fields. These two fields are only required for graphics modes. The next field, which gives the number of memory blocks, is only required for use with the graphics modes of CGA and Hercules graphics cards. This is because these cards store graphics lines in video RAM using memory blocks of different sizes. The last field of the data structure gives the size of the memory block used.

Prior to this field, however, the memory used for direct access to video RAM is given. The memory models are coded as listed in the following table:

Valid codes for describing memory models	
No.	Description
00H	Text mode
01H	CGA format, 2 or 4 memory blocks
02H	Hercules format with 4 memory blocks
03H	Normal EGA/VGA format for 16 color graphics modes
04H	Compact format – 2 pixels (4 bits each) per byte
05H	Normal EGA/VGA format for 256 color graphic modes
06H–0FH	Reserved
10H–FFH	Manufacturer-specific codes, currently unused

Setting a mode

Once you've used subfunction 00H to activate the list of supported video modes and subfunction 01H to read the requirements of the various modes, you can select the mode that meets your program's needs. Then you can use subfunction 01H to set this mode.

Before the function call, the function number and subfunction number must be supplied as usual. Also, the code number of the desired mode must be placed in the BX register. If you want to keep the currently existing contents of the video RAM when the new mode is set, bit 15 of the BX register must be set to 1.

After the function call, you should always check to ensure that the correct mode was set. To do this, read the contents of the AH and AL registers. If you find values of 00H in AH and 4FH, then the mode was successfully set.

Subfunction 03H can be used to query the current video mode. This function call doesn't require any arguments besides the function and subfunction numbers. After the function has run, the number of the current video mode can be read from the BX register. As usual, values greater than 100H are for the standard VESA modes, and values less than 100H are for standard VGA or manufacturer-specific modes.

Saving and restoring a setup

When TSR programs such as SideKick are activated, they must save the current setup of the video card before they can switch to the mode they will use. Also, these programs must be able to restore the contents of the screen to its original state. Some of the video RAM must be saved in order to accomplish this. This is very difficult to do with Super VGA cards. So, the VESA standard has three sub-subfunctions under subfunction 04H that help a program manage these tasks.

Subfunction 00H must be called before the current video card setup is saved because this function indicates how much memory is needed in order to save this information. In addition to the function and subfunction numbers, this function also requires the value 00H (sub-subfunction number) in the DL register. In the CX register, a bit field, which describes the components of the video card setup that must be saved, is needed. The structure of this bit field is shown in the following figure.

The entire contents of the video RAM don't have to be saved. Only the portion overwritten by the TSR program must be saved. For example, a TSR program that switches from a graphics mode to a text mode must save only the first 4K of video RAM, which will be overwritten for displaying text. It's not necessary to save the entire graphics screen, which could take up to 1 megabyte of memory.

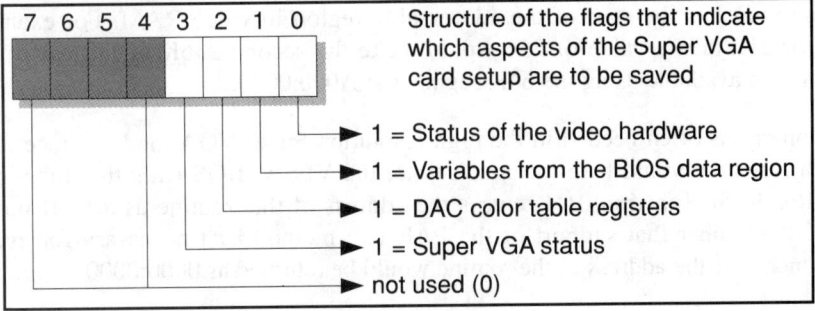

As a result, sub-subfunction 00H returns the number of 64 byte blocks, which are needed to save the indicated status information, to the BX register. The calling routine must prepare a buffer to store this information. The size of the buffer to create is 64 * BX bytes.

Once a program has created this buffer, the setup can be saved with sub-subfunction 01H. This function call requires three parameters in the processor registers in addition to the function and subfunction numbers. The DL register expects the sub-subfunction number 01H. The CX register must contain a bit field that describes which components of the setup should be saved, as we saw with sub-subfunction 00H. It's important that this bit field doesn't contain more components than that of the 00H sub-subfunction call; otherwise the buffer may not be large enough.

The address of the buffer itself must be passed to sub-subfunction 01H as a FAR pointer in the ES:BX register pair.

The same registers are used to restore the saved setup. This is done with a call to sub-subfunction 02H. For this function call, the sub-subfunction number is placed in the DL register. The CX register again must contain a bit field with the components of the setup to be restored and the ES:BX register pair must contain a FAR pointer to the buffer with the stored information.

Moving the access window

Since the entire video RAM can be accessed via the 64K segment at A000:0000, you can easily work with Super VGA modes that use less than 256K of memory per screen page. This process becomes more complicated when more than 256K must be addressed, which applies to most of the modes we're discussing. In these instances, you muse use access windows. These windows allow you to use the 64K segment at A000:0000 (together with the four bitplanes) to access a total of 256K of video RAM simultaneously. Earlier we saw that setting the access window involves programming registers that aren't standardized in Super VGA cards.

The VESA-BIOS solves this problem by providing subfunction 05H. This function is used to set up the access window independent of the hardware on your Super VGA card. In addition to the function and subfunction numbers, this function call requires the value 00H in the BH register and the number of the access window (either 0 or 1) in the BL register. Remember that the second access window can be moved only if the subfunction 01H call has indicated that the installed video card actually has a second access window.

The last parameter is placed in the DX register. This is related to the granularity of the access window and indicates the start of the addressable region in video RAM. For example, if the granularity is 1K, then a value of 256 would make the second 256K of the video RAM on a Super VGA card available using the 64K segment at A000:0000.

This function call is often needed in the high resolution Super VGA modes. Since calling it as an interrupt function would take too much time, the VESA-BIOS calls this function directly with a FAR call. Subfunction 01H returns the address of this routine as a FAR pointer in its data block. Remember that support of the FAR call method isn't necessary for every VESA BIOS, in which case the address of the routine would be returned as 0000:0000.

But if subfunction 05H is available as a FAR call routine, then you should definitely call it if you're concerned with your program's execution speed. One difference between the FAR call and the interrupt call is that the FAR call doesn't return a status code to the AX register. This method still reserves the ability to change the contents of the AX and DX registers during a function call.

Subfunction 05H can also determine the position of the access window in video RAM. To call the function in this way, you must start with the function number and subfunction number as usual. The value 1 must also be entered in the BH register. As a result, the DX register will contain the location of the window, in relation to its granularity.

4.10 Programming TIGA Cards

New graphics standards for PCs usually include higher resolutions, more colors, or simply a clearer picture. Although the 800x600 pixel mode of the Super VGA card is slowly becoming more accepted, it still has one problem. These cards take a long time to display graphics. However, the TIGA (Texas Instruments Graphics Adapter) standard uses its own processor for graphics output, which decreases the amount of work performed by the main processor.

The TIGA standard is a software interface between an application and a graphics card based on a TI34010 or TI34020 graphics processor. As with the 80x86 processor, assembly language must be used. Instead of arithmetic or program control, however, we're interested in drawing lines, circles, and polygons. Distributing the processing in this way can free the 80x86 of the work of calculating the pixels in a line and then placing them in video RAM. This significantly speeds up program execution.

Texas Instruments had four goals when they developed the TIGA standard:

- Faster applications
- Easy to use
- Potential for expansion
- Hardware independence

Applications developed according to the TIGA standard using corresponding video cards should run considerably faster. The TIGA interface was developed as a simple and fast way for the 80x86 and graphics processor to communicate.

C and TIGA

To simplify using the capabilities of the TIGA standard, several basic functions were included in C. These C functions are compatible with the various Microsoft C tools, so you can use QuickC as your development environment for TIGA applications.

If an application needs graphics functions not covered by the TIGA standard functions, the developer can always develop a TIGA expansion in C, assembly language, or a combination of both. This expansion can then be loaded into a TIGA-compatible video card at runtime and used.

The TIGA functions aren't bound to certain limitations, such as the screen resolution or the number of colors, because the 34010 allows for the development of new types of graphics cards. In this respect, the TIGA functions are similar to the graphics functions of a program such as Windows, which are also hardware-independent.

Hardware, software, and TIGA

A TIGA system will have both hardware and software components. The hardware is a TIGA-compatible video card, which will be based on a 34010 graphics processor. The various software components are found on the TIGA card in the PC's RAM or in the TIGA application itself.

The first component is the Application Interface (AI). This provides high level language routines for calling the various TIGA tasks. The AI routines are linked directly to your executable program just like regular library routines. These routines are independent of the type of TIGA card installed because they don't access the hardware themselves.

This task is handled by the Communication Driver (CD). This program is located under the name TIGACD.EXE. It must be called and started as a TSR program prior to the start of the TIGA-compatible application. The CD is then called during the execution of the application via a predefined interrupt (usually 7FFH) to complete the connection with the hardware. Since the CD represents the hardware-dependent portion of the interface, it must be delivered with their specific TIGA card.

The Graphics Manager (GM) can also be found on the hardware along with the CD. This runs as a program in the RAM of the TIGA card. Its most important tasks are accepting commands and queries from the Communication Manager and ensuring that certain graphics functions are available (the so-called core primitives). In addition, the GM is also responsible for initializing the card and managing its memory.

While this handler is comparable to the ROM-BIOS of an EGA or VGA card, it isn't located in the ROM chip of a TIGA card. A special program is required to load it into the TIGA RAM. Because of this, we can't discuss any specific TIGA programs in this section. It's only possible to program a TIGA card by using special development tools, which we'll discuss later. Unlike other video cards, you can't simply place a TIGA card in your computer and start developing software.

You can add to the basic functions of the Graphics Manager with functions called *extended primitives*. The TIGA standard itself provides several of these functions, which are delivered as loadable modules with the TIGA card. These routines are similar to the dynamic link libraries of Windows and OS/2. They are only loaded when a program needs them and calls them at run time.

Also, your applications can load and use their own extended primitives. Generally, extended primitives aren't assembler routines that address the graphics processor themselves. Instead, they are usually macro functions that are used to combine various core primitives into more useful and powerful functions. This also helps to increase the speed of your screen output, since your application must make only one TIGA call, instead of several, in order to get the Graphics Manager to execute a desired task with the TIGA hardware.

To prevent an application from starting a new TIGA call before the current one is finished, the TIGA card uses several command buffers. These buffers store calls to the Graphics Manager so that they can be processed in the order in which they were received. This also leads to a significant performance increase for TIGA-compatible applications.

This is especially true when a TIGA card is used in connection with a graphical user interface. The Hercules TIGA card already has a Windows driver available, which increases the speed of screen output for the average Windows application.

TIGA programmers can use almost 140 functions. Approximately one-third of these functions are extended primitives, which means that they can only be used after the corresponding modules have been loaded. These functions can be divided into 14 groups. The group called Graphics

Output Functions consists of only extended primitives. All other groups contain a mixture of core and extended primitives.

The following is a brief summary of the different function groups:

Graphics system initialization functions

This group contains all functions that affect the initialization of the TIGA card or the TIGA interface. For example, the set_videomode function is needed in order for a TIGA-compatible application to begin work with the TIGA card. This group also contains the function install_primitives, which is used for loading the extended TIGA functions. All functions used to query the TIGA status are also in this group.

Clear functions

The functions of this group are used to clear portions of the screen or video RAM. This includes functions such as clear_frame_buffer, clear_page, and clear_screen.

Graphics attribute control functions

This group contains functions that define or query the numerous attributes required for character operations. This includes the foreground and background colors, the clipping region, the coordinate origin, the fill pattern for polygons, and the transparency of pixels.

Palette functions

The functions in this group affect the color palette. These are all core primitive functions. With these, the current palette can be initialized or read. You can also address an individual palette entry. The get_nearest_color function is also interesting. It can be used to find the palette entry that most closely matches a certain color.

Graphics output functions

Drawing and painting are handled by the functions of this group. They can be used to draw and fill points, lines, ellipses, and rectangles. There are various functions for selecting different fill patterns, as we are used to seeing with various draw and paint programs.

Poly drawing functions

This function group is similar to the Graphics Output Functions except that it affects polygons.

Pixel array functions

The blitter capabilities of the 34010 are contained in these functions. They are used to move, exchange, or change the size of rectangular blocks of pixels (e.g., a Windows application window) within video RAM.

Text functions

This group of functions works with fonts and character strings. Some of these functions are core primitives and some are extended. They can be used to load and activate a font, and then use the font to display characters on screen. They also allow you to query information on the current font and set attributes for character output with a given font.

Cursor functions

The functions of this group are used to manage the graphics cursor. In addition to positioning the cursor, you can also use these functions to change its appearance.

Graphics utility functions

These are miscellaneous functions that include the library functions of a high-level language compiler. This includes functions, such as wait_scan and page_flip, which are useful for animation.

Pointer-based memory management functions

The TIGA interface also supports functions that allow the TIGA memory or portions of it to be managed like a heap. C relies heavily on heap management, so functions such as gsp_malloc, gsp_free, and gsp_realloc support all of your work with the TIGA card functions.

Communication functions

These functions are used whenever the TIGA card and the PC or the 34010 and one of its coprocessors have to exchange data.

Extensibility functions

These functions are used with the extended primitives for tasks such as loading, removing, or replacing so-called relocatable load modules.

Texas Instruments has three developer's packages to support the creation of TIGA compatible hardware and software. The packages have various capabilities and prices.

The least expensive option is the Driver Developer's Kit (DDK). Software developers should select this kit to create applications that need only the TIGA interface for screen output. This package contains a lot of documentation and a software interface used in conjunction with a Microsoft C compiler. The package includes examples of finished TIGA software drivers, such as the source code of the TIGA driver for AutoCAD Version 9. This package sells for less than $500.

The Software Developer's Kit (SDK) provides TIGA graphics functions and additional extended primitives for over $1000. It includes the complete DDK, an assembler for the 34010 processor, a C compiler, and other tools for creating programs for this processor. With this kit you can perform tasks such as loading your own fractal generator directly in the TIGA card or creating a ray tracing algorithm for the card.

If you also want to develop TIGA-compatible hardware you'll need the Software Porting Kit (SPK), which costs approximately $15,000. This kit includes not only the DDK and SDK, but also the complete TIGA source code, which you can modify for your own 34010 hardware. A Windows driver and a license to develop and sell TIGA-compatible graphics cards is also included.

Since TIGA is well-designed and completely documented, it's a standard that should last for years. We believe that TIGA will become the graphics standard of the 1990's because it provides the needed support for advancements in graphical user interfaces.

Chapter 5

Keyboard Programming

The keyboard is one device that you are always concerned with in DOS programming. Since the keyboard is your computer's main input device, it's at the heart of most applications. TSR programs wouldn't even be possible without the keyboard.

TSR programs use the keyboard differently than normal applications. Usually, a program simply queries the keyboard to determine what keys the user has pressed. However, even this simple task can be filled with hidden complications. For example, the meaning of many keys are changed by the status of the <Caps Lock>, <Num Lock>, and <Scroll Lock> keys. Other keys, such as the function keys and the cursor keys, change the meaning of a key press without changing the visible characters on the screen.

However, this can easily be managed, as we'll explain in Section 5.2. Unfortunately this process becomes more complicated with TSR and ISR routines that capture keyboard entry before the entry can reach the application. We'll explain how to do this in Section 5.3.

In Section 5.4 we'll show you how to program the keyboard directly. We'll also examine how a program can effect the way the keyboard functions. For example, you can change the key repeat speed or turn on and off the keyboard LEDs.

5.1 Keyboard Programming Basics

In Chapter 2 we examined the relationship between the hardware, DOS, and the BIOS using the keyboard as our example. In this section we'll discuss this topic in more detail.

5.1.1 Keyboard to Program

When the user presses a key on the keyboard, an electrical impulse, which identifies the location of the key, is generated. This signal is handled by the keyboard processor, which is located inside the keyboard itself. Generally this processor is an Intel 8048 chip or an equivalent from another manufacturer. On AT class computers the communication is handled by an Intel 8042 chip. With this chip, ATs are capable of bi-directional communication between the keyboard and CPU. The earlier PC's and PC/XT's do not have this bi-directional communication capability.

Converting the scan code

The keyboard processor converts the electrical impulse indicating the key position into a number called a *scan code*. There is no relationship between the scan code and the character printed on the key that was pressed or the function that the key represents in the currently running program.

The keyboard processor passes the scan code to the computer. On an AT, the keyboard controller accepts the scan code. This transfer is done serially, since the cable that connects the keyboard and the computer has only one data line. This communication is synchronous, unlike the asynchronous communication found on a PC's serial port. Synchronous communication is achieved by using a clock line and the data line. The clock line transmits a timing signal by continuously switching from hi to lo (1 to 0). The transmission of the individual bits of the scan code are synchronized to this pulse.

If several keys are pressed simultaneously, the keyboard processor stores them in an internal buffer. The buffer usually has enough space for 10 keystrokes. However, you don't have to worry about this buffer becoming full because the data passes to the CPU much faster than a user can type.

Make and break codes

Scan codes are also generated when the user releases a key. This tells the system whether a key is still being pressed or has already been released. This is very important because it's the only way your computer can correctly interpret the situation when more than one key is pressed at once. Without this capability, you wouldn't be able to perform certain tasks, such as typing uppercase letters or rebooting your computer with <Ctrl><Alt><Delete>.

Your system uses make codes and break codes to distinguish the scan codes for keys that have been pressed ("make") and keys that have been released ("break"). The only difference is that bit 7 is set for a break code.

This leads to two important consequences. First, break codes are always greater than 128 and make codes are always less than 128. Second, a PC keyboard cannot have more than 128 keys; otherwise the make codes would overlap the break codes.

The most obvious example of when more than one key must be pressed simultaneously is to type an uppercase letter. For example, to type an uppercase "A", the user presses and holds the right <Shift> key, then presses <A>. The keyboard controller passes the make code for the <Shift> key (36H), then the make code for the <A> key (1EH) to the computer.

Since the system hasn't received a break code for the <Shift> key yet, it recognizes that both keys are being pressed simultaneously and generates an uppercase character instead of a lowercase one.

The ROM-BIOS keyboard handler

How does the processor receive these scan codes? The hardware interrupt IRQ1 is executed each time the keyboard sends a make code or a break code to the computer. This in turn calls interrupt 09H. This *keyboard handler* routine receives the make and break codes and converts them to the corresponding ASCII character codes, which can then be read by the application currently running (more on this later).

Many other tasks must be performed before the program can read the keyboard. First, the keyboard handler must read the make or break code from the keyboard using an I/O port. The address of this port is 60H for all PC systems. This port reads only make and break codes. The keyboard handler evaluates the codes and determines whether a character has been entered.

As we saw in our uppercase "A" example, not all keystrokes result in characters that are visible on the screen. The keyboard handler generated a character only after receiving the make code for the "A". A character wasn't generated when the make code for the <Shift> key was received. Think of entering the ASCII code for a character using the <Alt> key and the numeric keypad. In this instance, several keys are pressed and released before a character appears on screen.

Once the keyboard handler recognizes the character that was entered, it converts that character to a code that the currently running application can understand. The scan codes themselves are unusable, because different keyboards use different sets of scan codes, although most sets are similar.

Scan code/ASCII code conversion

Therefore, scan codes are converted to ASCII codes, which are standard on all computers. Although the normal ASCII character set consists of 128 characters, PCs use an *extended ASCII character set*, which contains 256 characters. A listing of this character set can be found in the Appendices.

The converted ASCII character isn't passed directly to the application. First it's stored in a buffer. The structure of this buffer and the way it works are described in Section 5.2.3.

Now the keyboard handler has completed its work. The application can then read the characters from the keyboard buffer and process them. The ROM-BIOS interrupt 16H has several functions available for this purpose (refer to Section 5.2.3 for more information).

Using foreign language keyboards

You should know one more thing about the keyboard handler. Although the ROM-BIOS defines which handler to use, DOS can replace this handler with another program. The handler in the ROM-BIOS is configured for the American keyboard by default.

To use characters of other languages (such as Ä, Ö, Ü, etc.), you can install another keyboard driver in your AUTOEXEC.BAT file. Installing another keyboard driver on your system will prove that, regardless of the characters printed on your keyboard, the software converts the scan codes to ASCII codes, which determines what characters appear on the screen.

5.1.2 PC Keyboards

Various types of keyboards are available for PCs, but there are really only three standard keyboards. These keyboards were originally introduced by IBM. Although they are standard keyboards, their appearance can vary. This is because these keyboards are designed in many different languages, so the keys can be located in different places and contain different symbols. However, the number of keys and the scan codes they produce are standardized.

Remember, the symbols printed on the keys don't always apply to what occurs inside the keyboard. The following figure shows examples of the standard PC keyboards:

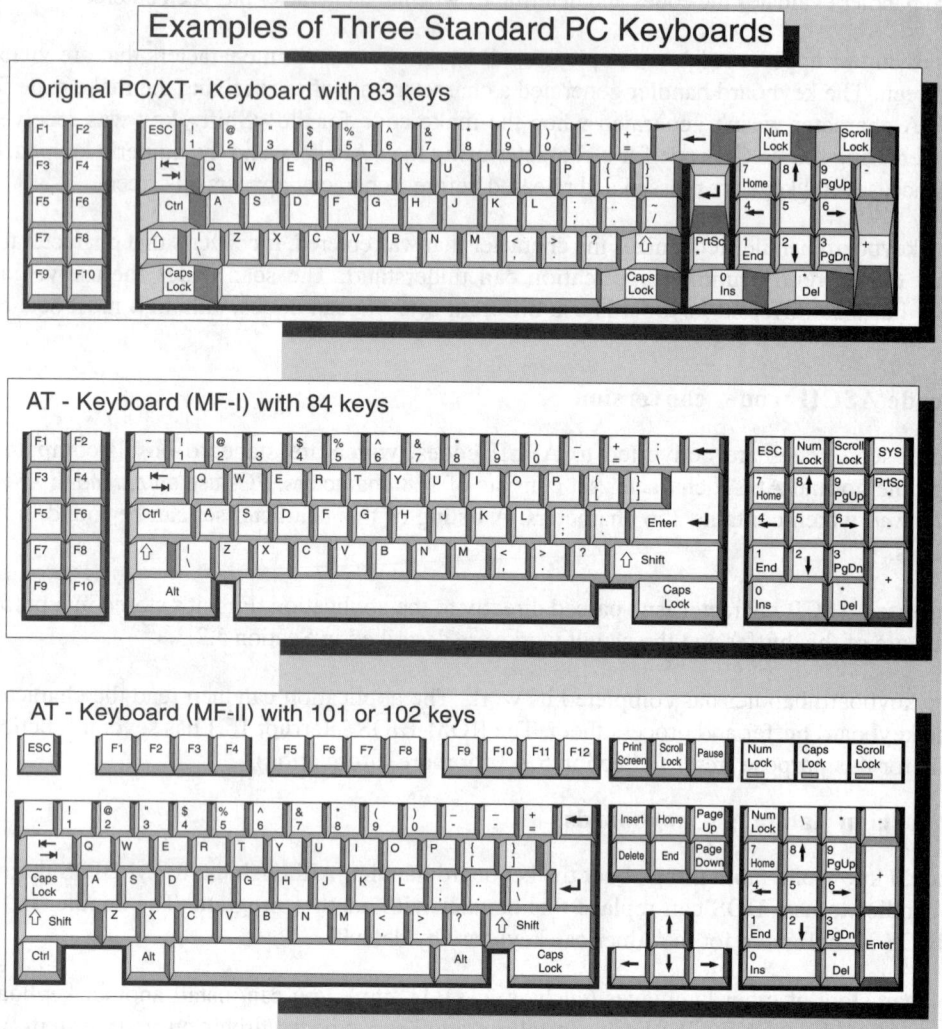

Examples of Three Standard PC Keyboards

Original PC/XT - Keyboard with 83 keys

AT - Keyboard (MF-I) with 84 keys

AT - Keyboard (MF-II) with 101 or 102 keys

PC/XT and AT keyboards

The PC was first introduced with the PC/XT keyboard, which has 83 keys. This keyboard's design has small <Enter> and <Shift> keys, which were difficult to use.

The AT keyboard, which has 84 keys, solved this problem. The <Enter> key and the two <Shift> keys were larger so you could easily find them, even when typing very quickly. However, since the keyboard itself wasn't larger, some other keys had to be smaller. The <Num

Lock>, <Scroll Lock>, and keypad <+> keys became smaller because they aren't used as frequently as the <Shift keys>.

The <Sys> key (later called the <Sys Req> key) was also added to the keyboard. This key was intended to be used as a function key for calling operating system functions or TSR programs, but developers never really adopted it.

The MF-II keyboard

This keyboard evolved from the MF-I keyboard, which was developed for PCs and XTs but wasn't very popular. Many of the MF-II's features have become keyboard standards:

- A group of dedicated cursor keys that are separate from the numeric keypad.
- Function keys at the top of the keyboard.
- <F11> and <F12> function keys.
- <Alt> keys at the bottom of the keyboard for easier access.
- Three LEDs to indicate the status of the <Num Lock>, <Caps Lock>, and <Scroll Lock> keys.

There are two versions of the MF-II keyboard. The US version has 101 keys and the European version has 102. This allows an additional letter key to be added next to the left <Shift> key.

Software (keyboard drivers in particular) can recognize an MF-II keyboard. When checked, the MF-II responds with a corresponding identification code. The other two keyboard types don't have this capability.

Laptop and notebook keyboards

With the introduction of laptop and notebook computers, various types of keyboards and keyboard layouts have appeared. Although this can be very confusing, these keyboards usually emulate one of the three major PC standards previously described. This is accomplished either by emulating the standard scan codes within the keyboard or by converting non-standard scan codes to standard ASCII codes with the keyboard handler. However, this solution isn't used frequently because it also requires changes to the keyboard driver.

Depending on licensing agreements, manufacturers can often modify keyboard drivers. However, the manufacturer may discover that many TSR programs won't work properly with their keyboard. This can occur because TSR programs generally read the keyboard at the lowest level, which is the scan codes themselves.

Keyboards and mouse emulation

Keyboards with mouse capabilities have recently become available. These include trackballs, special mouse pads, or separate cursor keys that emulate mouse movements. As a programmer, you do not have to worry about any differences in these devices because they work with the standard mouse interface as described in Chapter 9.

5.2 Accessing the Keyboard from the BIOS

Interrupt 16H provides three functions to read the keyboard and keyboard status. The BIOS keyboard functions are very limited; there are no BIOS functions for removing characters from the keyboard buffer or renaming keys. DOS functions can perform these operations.

5.2.1 Interrupt 16H Functions

The following functions are available to BIOS interrupt 16H:

Function 00H: **Read keyboard**

Interrupt 16H usually receives a call when a program expects user input of one or more characters. If a character was already entered before the function call, this character is removed from the keyboard buffer and is passed to the calling program. If the keyboard buffer is empty, function 00H waits until a character is input and then returns to the calling program. The caller can determine the character or activate a key by examining the contents of the AL and the AH registers.

Control codes

As you already know, any ASCII code can be entered from the keyboard using the <Alt> key and the keys of the numeric keypad. However, it's also possible to use the <Ctrl> key. When used with other keys, this key can enter ASCII codes smaller than code number 32. The figure on the next page shows which keys can be accessed.

ASCII

If the AL register contains a value other than 00H, it contains the ASCII code of the character. The AH register contains the scan code of the active key. The code in the AL register corresponds to the ASCII codes for character output on the screen. Some differences occur in the control keys:

```
┌─────────────────────────────────────────────────────────────────────┐
│ ASCII control codes on PCs                                           │
├──────┬───────────────────────────────────┬──────┬───────────────────┤
│ Code │ Meaning                           │ Code │ Char.             │
│  8   │ Backspace                         │ BS   │                   │
│  9   │ Tab                               │ TAB  │                   │
│  10  │ Linefeed (Ctrl + Enter)           │ LF   │ XXX               │
│  13  │ Carriage Return                   │ CR   │                   │
│  27  │ Escape                            │ ESC  │                   │
└──────┴───────────────────────────────────┴──────┴───────────────────┘
```

ASCII codes 8, 9, 10, 13, and 27 have special meanings. This makes it difficult to use them as text characters. For example, the small left arrow character is ASCII code 27. However, most programs interpret ASCII code 27 as an escape command rather than a request to enter this character.

ENtering control codes in Edit
CTRL + P   *for Esc*
alt + 012 (on Num Pad)   *for Pg Break*

Dec	Symbol	Kboard codes
	mpty (ll)	Ctrl+2
	☺	Ctrl+A
		Ctrl+B
		Ctrl+C
		Ctrl+D
		Ctrl+E
		Ctrl+F
		Ctrl+G
		Ctrl+H, Backspace Shift+Backspace
		Ctrl+I
	LF	Ctrl+J Ctrl+↵
11	♂	Ctrl+K
12	♀	Ctrl+L
13	♪ CR	Ctrl+M,↵, Shift+↵
14	♫	Ctrl+N
15	✧	Ctrl+O

Dec	Symbol	Kboard codes
16	►	Ctrl+P
17	◄	Ctrl+Q
18	↕	Ctrl+R
19	‼	Ctrl+S
20	¶	Ctrl+T
21	§	Ctrl+U
22	▬	Ctrl+V
23	↨	Ctrl+W
24	↑	Ctrl+X
25	↓	Ctrl+Y
26	→	Ctrl+Z
27	← ESC	Ctrl+[, ESC, Shift+ESC, Ctrl+ESC
28	∟	Ctrl+\
29	↔	Ctrl+]
30	▲	Ctrl+6
31	▼	Ctrl+ -
32	Space	Space key, Shift+Space, Ctrl+Space, Alt+Space

Character input with the <Ctrl> key

To avoid this problem in your programs, define a key, such as <F1>, that must be pressed before one of these special characters is entered. Then you must ensure that your program saves the last keystroke. So, if <Esc>, <Enter>, or <Tab> is pressed, simply check to see whether the previous keystroke was <F1>. If it was, the keystroke should be interpreted as a text character instead of a control character.

Extended keyboard codes

In addition to the ASCII codes, the BIOS functions also support the *extended keyboard codes*. The 256 characters of the PC ASCII character set include certain control characters, such as <Tab>, <Enter>, and <Esc>, but not function keys and cursor keys.

So, the codes for these keys are returned according to a slightly different process, which utilizes ASCII code 0. The real information, the extended keyboard code, is found in the AH register. This is where you would normally find the scan code for the key.

If your program finds the value 00H in the AL register after calling function 00H or 01H of BIOS interrupt 16H, the keyboard code will be found in the AH register. With this method, an additional 256 character codes can be used. The following table lists the extended keyboard codes that can be read with functions 00H and 01H. Key combinations that aren't found in this table, such as all combinations of <Ctrl> + <Shift> + a letter key, aren't recognized by the BIOS and don't have their own keyboard codes.

Extended key codes		
Code (hex)	Code (dec)	Key(s)
0FH	15	Shift + Tab
10H	16	Alt + Q (2nd keyboard series)
11H	17	Alt + W
12H	18	Alt + E
13H	19	Alt + R
14H	20	Alt + T
15H	21	Alt + Y
16H	22	Alt + U
17H	23	Alt + I
18H	24	Alt + O
19H	25	Alt + P
1EH	30	Alt + A (3rd keyboard series)
1FH	31	Alt + S
20H	32	Alt + D
21H	33	Alt + F
22H	34	Alt + G
23H	35	Alt + H
24H	36	Alt + J
25H	37	Alt + K
26H	38	Alt + L
2CH	44	Alt + Z (4th keyboard series)
2DH	45	Alt + X
2EH	46	Alt + C
2FH	47	Alt + V
30H	48	Alt + B
31H	49	Alt + N
32H	50	Alt + M
3BH	59	F1
3CH	60	F2
3DH	61	F3
3EH	62	F4
3FH	63	F5
40H	64	F6
41H	65	F7
42H	66	F8
43H	67	F9
44H	68	F10

Extended key codes		
Code (hex)	Code (dec)	Key(s)
47H	71	Home
48H	72	Cursor Up
49H	73	Page Up
4BH	75	Cursor Left
4DH	77	Cursor Right
50H	80	Cursor Down
51H	81	Page Down
52H	82	Insert
53H	83	Delete
54H	84	Shift + F1
55H	85	Shift + F2
56H	86	Shift + F3
57H	87	Shift + F4
58H	88	Shift + F5
59H	89	Shift + F6
5AH	90	Shift + F7
5BH	91	Shift + F8
5CH	92	Shift + F9
5DH	93	Shift + F10
5EH	94	Ctrl + F1
5FH	95	Ctrl + F2
60H	96	Ctrl + F3
61H	97	Ctrl + F4
62H	98	Ctrl + F5
63H	99	Ctrl + F6
64H	100	Ctrl + F7
65H	101	Ctrl + F8
66H	102	Ctrl + F9
67H	103	Ctrl + F10
68H	104	Alt + F1
69H	105	Alt + F2
6AH	106	Alt + F3
6BH	107	Alt + F4
6CH	108	Alt + F5
6DH	109	Alt + F6
6EH	110	Alt + F7
6FH	111	Alt + F8
70H	112	Alt + F9
71H	113	Alt + F10
73H	115	Ctrl + Cursor Left
74H	116	Ctrl + Cursor Right
75H	117	Ctrl + End
76H	118	Ctrl + Page Down
77H	119	Ctrl + Home
78H	120	Alt + 1 (1st keyboard series)
79H	121	Alt + 2
7AH	122	Alt + 3
7BH	123	Alt + 4
7CH	124	Alt + 5
7DH	125	Alt + 6
7EH	126	Alt + 7
7FH	127	Alt + 8
80H	128	Alt + 9
81H	129	Alt + 0
82H	130	Alt +
83H	131	Alt + '

Keystroke combinations not included in this table cannot be read by the BIOS keyboard functions because they don't create keyboard codes. This applies to the function keys and to combinations of keys, such as <Ctrl>, <Alt>, and <Shift>. Some DOS programs can interpret these keys because they have their own keyboard interrupt handlers that can be programmed to interpret any desired keystroke combinations.

BIOS-proof keys

Some key combinations cannot be read by BIOS as key codes because they execute commands. For example, activating the <PrtSc> or <Print> key calls BIOS interrupt 5H. This starts a routine that copies the current screen display to a printer, to produce a hardcopy.

The <Ctrl><Num Lock> keys stop the system completely until the user presses another key. The keyboard buffer ignores the <Ctrl><Num Lock> keys and the next key pressed, so programs cannot read these keys.

Pressing the <Ctrl><Break> key combination calls interrupt 1BH. Usually the current program stops and returns to DOS. To prevent this from happening, direct this interrupt to a routine, within the application, that continues program execution even if this routine consists only of a single IRET assembly language instruction.

ATs and a few advanced PC/XTs contain the <Sys Req> key. When this key is pressed, interrupt 15H is called by passing the value 8500H to the AX register. When the user releases the key, the AX register then receives the value 8501H. The value 85H in the AH register represents the function number of interrupt 15H. When DOS is first started, function 85H of the BIOS interrupt 15H performs only an IRET instruction; pressing the <Sys Req> key has no visible result. To use this key in your program, you can include your own handler for interrupt 15H and route this function call to this handler.

Function 01H: Read keyboard

Function 01H also reads the keyboard. However, unlike function 00H, function 01H leaves the preceding character in the keyboard buffer. Repeated calls to function 01H or function 00H re-read the keyboard. Place the value 01H in the AH register to call function 01H.

Unlike function 00H, after the function call, function 01H immediately informs the calling program, with the zero flag, whether or not a character is available. If the zero flag equals 1, a character isn't available. If the zero flag is 0, the AL and AH registers contain information about the activated key. As in function 00H, the AL register contains the value 00H if the user activated an extended key and a value unequal to 00H if the user pressed a "normal" key. The AH register contains the scan codes of normal keys; extended keys place their codes in the AH register.

Function 02H: Read control keys

Function 02H has a different task. This function reads the status of certain control keys and conditions (e.g., <Insert>). Place the number 02H in the AH register to call the function. The keyboard status can be found in the AL register after the function call.

For example, if bit 3 is set, the user is holding down the <Alt> key. If bit 6 is set, then the <Caps Lock> key is on and the user is typing in uppercase mode.

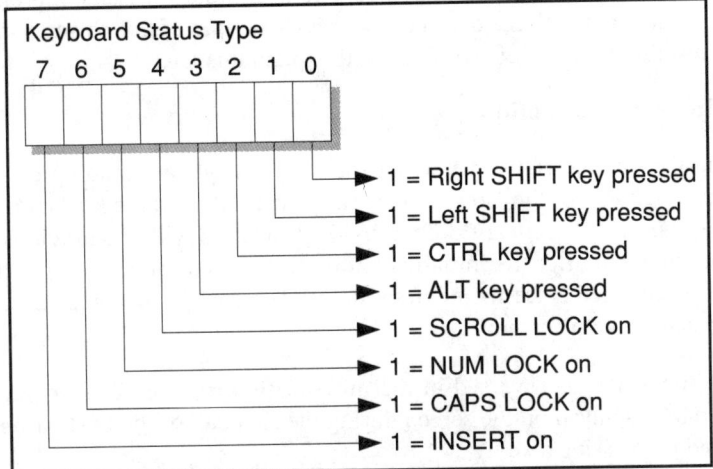

Notice that the keyboard status byte is different depending on the left and right <Shift> keys, but not between the two different <Alt> and <Ctrl> keys of the MF-II keyboard. This is because both the keyboard status byte and the BIOS keyboard function 02H were developed with the first PCs, before the MF-II keyboard even existed.

The keyboard status byte is often used by TSR programs to detect when the hotkeys that activate the program are pressed. For more information on this subject, refer to Chapter 32, which discusses TSR programming.

Demonstration programs

The following programs demonstrate the various functions of the BIOS keyboard interrupts we've discussed. The four programs can be divided into two groups. The first three programs are written in the higher level languages used throughout this book. They call the various functions of BIOS keyboard interrupts for their own uses. The fourth program is an assembly language program. It modifies the BIOS keyboard interrupt functions and processing, and acts as a resident program that can be accessed at a keypress.

Checking key status

The higher level programs provide a subroutine or a function for reading characters from the keyboard. This by itself isn't special because these languages have their own instructions that perform the same task. The important feature of the function is that it accepts other tasks in addition to reading characters. It displays the status of the keyboard functions <Insert>, <Caps Lock>, and <Num Lock> in the upper-right corner of the screen. This is especially useful for XT and PC owners because most keyboards don't indicate the key status. AT keyboards and some XT keyboards provide light emitting diodes (LED) that indicate the status of these keys. Otherwise, you never really know whether the <Insert> or <Caps Lock> mode is on.

Each program begins with a routine that reads the status of the keyboard functions through function 02H of BIOS keyboard interrupt 16H. Since the program only uses the <Insert>, <Caps

Lock>, and <Num Lock> modes, the program only views the three highest level bits in the keyboard status byte. Based on this status byte, a flag initializes for every keyboard function. These flags indicate the status of one of these functions or modes within the program. The status is reversed when compared with the current mode. For example, if the <Insert> mode is switched off, the flag corresponding changes to OFF. We'll explain this later.

Calling the interrupt function

After initializing the internal flags, the actual routine for keyboard reading can be called. This routine also uses function 2 of the BIOS keyboard interrupt to read the keyboard function status. Then it compares the current status of each individual function with the previous status stored in a flag. During its first call after the initialization routine, it determines whether the status of all three functions has changed since its previous status. The change in status causes the routine to display the new status on the screen.

This explains why the flag is reversed in the initialization routine. This enables the keyboard function status to be displayed on the screen during the first call of the keyboard routines instead of after it changed by pressing a key.

Now the routine performs its actual task, which is reading the keyboard. It uses function 01H of the BIOS keyboard interrupt to detect whether a key is available in the keyboard buffer of BIOS. If a key isn't available, the program jumps to the beginning of the routine and reads the keyboard function status again. This creates a loop that runs until a keypress occurs. This loop ensures that any status change is documented immediately on the screen.

Reading the keys

If a character appears in the BIOS keyboard buffer, the loop terminates and BIOS keyboard interrupt function 02H reads the key. The last step of this routine tests for an extended key code. The program adds 256 to the code to inform the calling routine that an extended key code is received. Then control returns to the calling routine.

This routine reads characters from the keyboard and displays them on the screen. This process repeats until the user presses a certain key. If the user presses the <Num Lock>, <Caps Lock>, or <Insert> key, the screen immediately displays the result.

This type of centralized keyboard routine can be used in other programs for additional tasks. For example, with the help of this routine, a macro conversion can change one key into a string of characters. Another application could display help text on the screen when the user presses a certain key. Lotus 1-2-3® and dBASE® use this method for displaying help screens.

Note: A small problem occurs with keyboard flag output. Since displaying keyboard flags on the screen changes the cursor's position, subsequent screen output from the program occurs at unexpected locations. These can disrupt the screen display. To avoid this problem, the keyboard routine must determine the current cursor position before the keyboard flag display. Then the routine must restore the cursor position to its previous value after displaying keyboard status.

A similar problem occurs with the color. The flag output assumes a certain color and the original color must be restored after the output. The problem is that none of the three languages has a command to determine the current color. In Pascal programs for keyboard reading, only a special procedure can set the color by recording the colors in a variable and setting it with a command. With these variables, the keyboard routine restores the current color after the individual flags are displayed.

BASIC listing: KEYB.BAS

```
'********************************************************************
'*                         KEYB                                    *
'------------------------------------------------------------------
'* Task    : Makes a function available which reads a character from *
'*           the keyboard. The status of the INSERT, CAPS LOCK and  *
'*           NUM LOCK keys is displayed on the screen.              *
'------------------------------------------------------------------
'* Author        : Michael Tischer                                 *
'* Developed on  : 06/09/91                                        *
'* Last update   : 01/20/92                                        *
'********************************************************************
'
DECLARE SUB PrintInverse (Text AS STRING)
DECLARE SUB WriteChar (KChar AS INTEGER, CColor AS INTEGER)
DECLARE FUNCTION GetPage% ()
DECLARE SUB Inikey ()
DECLARE FUNCTION NegFlag% (Flag%, FlagReg%, Col%, Row%, Text AS STRING)
DECLARE FUNCTION GetKey% ()

'$INCLUDE: 'QB.BI'        'Include file contains register declarations

CONST TRUE = -1                            'Define the truth
CONST FALSE = NOT TRUE

CONST FZ = 1                               'Display row in the flag
CONST FS = 65                              'Display column in the flag

'-- BIOS keyboard status bits ------------------------------
CONST SCRL = 16                            'SCROLL LOCK bit
CONST NUML = 32                            'NUM LOCK bit
CONST CAPL = 64                            'CAPS LOCK bit
CONST INS = 128                            'INSERT bit

'-- Codes of some keys, returned (e.g., by GETKEY) ----------------
CONST BEL = 7                              'Bell character code
CONST BS = 8                               'Backspace key code
CONST TB = 9                               'Tab key code
CONST LF = 10                              'Linefeed key code
CONST CR = 13                              'Carriage return code
CONST ESC = 27                             'Escape key code
CONST F1 = 315                             'Function keys
CONST F2 = 316
CONST F3 = 317
CONST F4 = 318
CONST F5 = 319
CONST F6 = 320
CONST F7 = 321
CONST F8 = 322
CONST F9 = 323
CONST F10 = 324
CONST CUP = 328                            'Cursor up
CONST CLEFT = 331                          'Cursor left
CONST CRIGHT = 333                         'Cursor right
```

```
CONST CDOWN = 329                          'Cursor down

'-- Global variables ------------------------------------------
DIM SHARED Insert AS INTEGER               'INSERT key status
DIM SHARED Caps   AS INTEGER               'CAPS LOCK key status
DIM SHARED Num    AS INTEGER               'NUM LOCK key status

'-- Main program --------
DIM CKey AS INTEGER                        'Get ASCII code for a key

Inikey                                     'Initialize keyboard flag
CLS                                        'Clear screen
PRINT "KEYB  (C) 1987, 91 by MICHAEL TISCHER"
PRINT
PRINT "You can type some characters and change the status of the";
PRINT "INSERT, CAPS and NUM modes. The upper-right corner of the"
PRINT "screen documents the changes to these keys.";
PRINT "Press <Enter> or <F1> to end the program. ";
PRINT : PRINT "Type text here: ";
DO                                         'Input loop
   CKey = GetKey                           'Read key
   IF CKey < 256 THEN                      'No extended key code?
      PRINT (CHR$(CKey));                  'Display character
   END IF
LOOP UNTIL (CKey = CR) OR (CKey = F1)      'Repeat until the user
                                           ' presses <F1> or <CR>
END

'********************************************************************
'* GetKey : Reads a character and displays flag status.            *
'* Input  : None                                                   *
'* Output : Code of captured key:                                  *
'*              < 256 : Normal key code.                           *
'*              >= 256 : Extended key code.                        *
'********************************************************************
'
FUNCTION GetKey%

DIM Reg AS RegType                         'Processor registers for interrupt call

DO
   Reg.ax = &H200                  'Read function number for keyboard status
   CALL INTERRUPT(&H16, Reg, Reg)          'Call BIOS keyboard interrupt

   '-- Pass new flag status -----------------------------------------
   Insert = NegFlag(Insert, ((Reg.ax MOD 256) AND INS), FS + 9, FZ, "INS")
   Caps = NegFlag(Caps, ((Reg.ax MOD 256) AND CAPL), FS + 3, FZ, " CAPS ")
   Num = NegFlag(Num, ((Reg.ax MOD 256) AND NUML), FS, FZ, "NUM")

   Reg.ax = &H100                          'Character function number ready?
   CALL INTERRUPT(&H16, Reg, Reg)          'Call BIOS keyboard interrupt
   IF (Reg.flags AND 64) = 0 THEN          'Keys are ready
      Reg.ax = &H0                         'Read function number for key
      CALL INTERRUPT(&H16, Reg, Reg)       'Call BIOS keyboard interrupt
      IF (Reg.ax MOD 256) = 0 THEN         'Is it an extended key?
```

447

```
    GetKey = (Reg.ax \ 256) OR &H100      'Yes --> An extended key
  ELSE                                    'No --> Not an extended key
    GetKey = (Reg.ax MOD 256)
  END IF
  EXIT DO                                              'End loop
  END IF
LOOP                                      'Repeat until key captured
END FUNCTION


'*******************************************************************
'* GetPage : Gets the current page.                               *
'* Input   : None                                                 *
'* Output  : The current screen page.                             *
'*******************************************************************
'
FUNCTION GetPage%

DIM Register AS RegType         'Processor registers for interrupt call

Register.ax = &H1500                      'AH = Function number
CALL INTERRUPT(&H10, Register, Register)  'Call BIOS interrupt
GetPage = Register.bx \ 256       'Register.BH returns screen page

END FUNCTION


'*******************************************************************
'* IniKey  : Initializes the keyboard flags.                      *
'* Input   : None                                                 *
'* Output  : None                                                 *
'* Info    : The keyboard flags change when pressed or released,  *
'*           based on information passed by the GetKey function.   *
'*******************************************************************
SUB Inikey

SHARED Insert AS INTEGER                         'INSERT key status
SHARED Caps   AS INTEGER                      'CAPS LOCK key status
SHARED Num    AS INTEGER                       'NUM LOCK key status

DIM Register AS RegType          'Processor registers for interrupt call

Register.ax = &H200              'Read function number for keyboard status
CALL INTERRUPT(&H16, Register, Register)  'Call BIOS keyboard interrupt

IF (Register.ax AND INS) THEN                    'Set INSERT flag
  Insert = FALSE
ELSE
  Insert = TRUE
END IF

IF (Register.ax AND CAPL) THEN                 'Set CAPS LOCK flag
  Caps = FALSE
ELSE
  Caps = TRUE
END IF

IF (Register.ax AND NUML) THEN                  'Set NUM LOCK flag
  Num = FALSE
ELSE
  Num = TRUE
END IF

END SUB


'*******************************************************************
```

```
'* NegFlag : Negates flag and displays corresponding text.        *
'* Input   : See below                                            *
'* Output  : New flag status (True = on, False = off ).           *
'*******************************************************************
FUNCTION NegFlag% (Flag%, FlagReg%, Col%, Row%, Text AS STRING)

DIM CurRow AS INTEGER                    'Stores the current cursor position
DIM CurCol AS INTEGER                    'Stores the current cursor position

'-- Test for change in status --------------

IF Flag% AND (FlagReg% = 0) OR (NOT Flag%) AND (FlagReg% <> 0) THEN
  CurRow = CSRLIN                                 'Yes: Set current row
  CurCol = POS(0)                             'Set current column
  LOCATE Row%, Col%                 'Cursor in position for flag names
  IF FlagReg% = 0 THEN                              'If flag is out
    NegFlag = FALSE                    'Result of function: Flag off
    PRINT SPACE$(LEN(Text))                    'Clear flag display
  ELSE                                                  'Flag is on
    NegFlag% = TRUE                     'Result of function: Flag on
    PrintInverse (Text)                          'Display flag name
  END IF
  LOCATE CurRow, CurCol                    'Restore old cursor position
ELSE                                            'Unchanged status
  NegFlag% = Flag%                     'Return remaining flag status
END IF

END FUNCTION


'*******************************************************************
'* PrintInverse: Writes inverse video string to the current screen *
'*               page, in the current position.                    *
'* Input   : See below                                            *
'* Output  : None                                                 *
'*******************************************************************
SUB PrintInverse (Text AS STRING)

CONST INVERS = &H70                     'Attribute byte for inverse display
DIM Counter AS INTEGER                               'Loop counter

FOR Counter = 1 TO LEN(Text)                 'Display all text characters
  CALL WriteChar(ASC(MID$(Text, Counter, 1)), INVERS)
  LOCATE CSRLIN, POS(0) + 1             'Indent cursor one position
NEXT

END SUB


'*******************************************************************
'* WriteChar : Writes a character with specified attributes to the *
'*             current screen page, in the current position.       *
'* Input   : See below                                            *
'* Output  : None                                                 *
'*******************************************************************
SUB WriteChar (KChar AS INTEGER, CColor AS INTEGER)

DIM Register AS RegType          'Processor registers for interrupt call

Register.ax = &H9 * 256 + KChar      'AH = Funct. No: Write character
                                     'AL = ASCII code of character
Register.bx = GetPage * 256 + CColor 'BH = Curr. screen pg; BL = CColor
Register.cx = 1                          'Display characters once
CALL INTERRUPT(&H10, Register, Register)     'Call BIOS interrupt

END SUB
```

Pascal listing: **KEYP.PAS**

```
{****************************************************************}
{*                      K E Y P                            *}
{*--------------------------------------------------------------*}
{*    Task       : Makes a function available for reading a    *}
{*                 character from the keyboard. The upper-right *}
{*                 corner of the screen lists the status of     *}
{*                 INSERT, CAPS LOCK and NUM LOCK.              *}
{*--------------------------------------------------------------*}
{*    Author     : Michael Tischer                             *}
{*    Developed on : 07/08/87                                  *}
{*    Last update  : 01/21/92                                  *}
{****************************************************************}

program KEYP;


Uses  Crt,Dos;                          { Add Crt and Dos units }

{$V-}                            { Suppresses string length check }

type FlagText = string[6];      { Used for passing the flag name }


const FR   = 1;             { Row in which flags are displayed }
      FC   = 65;            { Column in which flags are displayed }
      FlagFore = 0;            { Foreground color of flags }
      FlagBck  = 7;            { Background color of flags }

      {** BIOS keyboard status bits ************************}
      SCRL = 16;                       { SCROLL LOCK bit }
      NUML = 32;                       { NUM LOCK bit }
      CAPL = 64;                       { CAPS LOCK bit }
      INS  = 128;                      { INSERT bit }
      {** Codes of some keys as presented by GETKEY ****************}
      BEL   = 7;               { Bell character code }
      BS    = 8;               { Backspace character code }
      TAB   = 9;               { Tab character code }
      LF    = 10;              { Linefeed code }
      CR    = 13;              { Carriage return code }
      ESC   = 27;              { Escape character code }
      F1    = 315;                     { F1 key }
      F2    = 316;                     { F2 key }
      F3    = 317;                     { F3 key }
      F4    = 318;                     { F4 key }
      F5    = 319;                     { F5 key }
      F6    = 320;                     { F6 key }
      F7    = 321;                     { F7 key }
      F8    = 322;                     { F8 key }
      F9    = 323;                     { F9 key }
      F10   = 324;                     { F10 key }
      CUP   = 328;                     { Cursor up }
      CLEFT = 331;                     { Cursor left }
      CRIGHT = 333;                    { Cursor right }
      CDOWN  = 328;                    { Cursor down }

var Insert,                            { INSERT flag status }
    Num,                               { NUM flag status }
    Caps  : boolean;                   { CAPS flag status }
    ForeColor,                         { Current foreground color }
    BckColor,                          { Current background color }
    key    : integer;                  { Code of key read }
```

```
{****************************************************************}
{* NEGFLAG: Negates flag and displays text.                *}
{* Input : See below                                       *}
{* Output : The new flag status (TRUE = on, FALSE = off).  *}
{****************************************************************}

function NegFlag(Flag   : boolean;        { The last flag status }
                 FlagReg,            { Current flag status (0 = off) }
                 Column,                  { Column for flag names }
                 Crow  : integer;         { Row for flag names }
                 Text  : FlagText) : boolean;       { Flag names }

var CurCrow,                              { Current row }
    CurColumn : integer;                  { Current column }

begin
  if (Flag and (FlagReg = 0)) or          { Test for change }
     (not(Flag) and (FlagReg <> 0)) then   { to flag status }
    begin                                    { Yes }
      CurCrow := WhereY;                   { Store current row }
      CurColumn := WhereX;                 { Store current column }
      gotoxy(Column, Crow);           { Cursor to flag name position }
      if FlagReg = 0 then                  { Is flag reset? }
        begin                              { Yes }
          NegFlag := false;      { Result of the function : Flag off }
          textcolor(Black);            { Foreground color is black }
          textbackground(Black);       { Background color is black }
        end
      else
        begin                              { Flag is now on }
          NegFlag:=true;         { Result of the function : Flag on }
          textcolor(FlagFore);     { Foreground color is FLAGFORE }
          textbackground(FlagBck); { Background color is FLAGBCK }
        end;
      write(Text);                       { Display flag name }
      gotoxy(CurColumn, CurCrow);     { Restore old cursor position }
      textcolor(ForeColor);        { Restore old foreground color }
      textbackground(BckColor);    { Restore old background color }
    end
  else
    NegFlag := Flag             { Flag status remains unchanged }
end;


{****************************************************************}
{* GETKEY: Reads a character and displays flag status.     *}
{* Input  : None                                           *}
{* Output : Key code -  < 256 : Normal key.                *}
{*                      >= 256 : Extended key.             *}
{****************************************************************}

function Getkey : integer;

var Regs : Registers;       { Register variable for interrupt call }
    keyRec  : boolean;       { Indicates if key already received }

begin
  keyRec := false;                        { No key received }
  repeat
    Regs.ah := $2;          { Function number: keyboard status }
    intr($16, Regs);                { Call BIOS keyboard interrupt }

    {** Adjust flags to new status ***********************}
    Insert := NegFlag(Insert, Regs.al and INS, FC+9, FR, 'INSERT');
    Caps := NegFlag(Caps, Regs.al and CAPL, FC+3, FR, ' CAPS ');
```

```
    Num := NegFlag(Num, Regs.al and NUML, FC, FR, 'NUM');
    Regs.ah := $1;                  { Function number: Character ready? }
    intr($16, Regs);                { Call BIOS keyboard interrupt }
    if (Regs.flags and FZero = 0) then
      begin
       KeyRec := true;
       Regs.ah := 0;
       intr($16, Regs);
       if (Regs.al = 0)                        { Is zero flag set? }
        then Getkey := Regs.ah or $100                  { Yes }
        else Getkey := Regs.al;                          { No }
       end;
    until keyRec;                   { Repeat until a key is received }
  end;


{*********************************************************************}
{* INIKEY: Initializes keyboard flags.                             *}
{* Input  : None                                                   *}
{* Output : None                                                   *}
{* Info   : The keyboard flags are inverted from the current status. *}
{*          The next call to GETKEY displays current flag status.  *}
{*********************************************************************}


procedure Inikey;

var Regs : Registers;          { Register variable for interrupt call }

begin
  Regs.ah := $2;           { Read function number for keyboard status }
  intr($16, Regs);                  { call BIOS keyboard interrupt }
  if (Regs.al and INS <> 0) then Insert := false      { INSERT flag }
                        else Insert := true;          { set }
  if (Regs.al and CAPL <> 0) then Caps   := false     { CAPS flag }
                        else Caps   := true;          { set }
  if (Regs.al and NUML <> 0) then Num    := false     { NUM flag }
                        else Num    := true           { set }
end;


{*********************************************************************}
{* SCOLOR: Sets foreground and background colors for display.      *}
{* Input  : See below                                              *}
{* Output : None                                                   *}
{* Var.   : Color is stored in the FORECOLOR and BCKCOLOR          *}
{*          global variables.                                      *}
{* Info   : This procedure must be called for setting the color    *}
{*          so that after the output of the keyboard flag status,  *}
{*          the current text color can be restored,                *}
{*          since in TURBO no functions exist for sensing          *}
{*          this color.                                            *}
{*********************************************************************}


procedure Scolor(Foreground, Background : integer);

begin
  ForeColor := Foreground;               { Store foreground color }
  BckColor := Background;                 { Store background color }
  textcolor(Foreground);                 { Store foreground color }
  textbackground(Background)             { Store background color }
end;


{*********************************************************************}
{*                      MAIN PROGRAM                               *}
{*********************************************************************}
```

```
begin
  Inikey;                         { Initialize keyboard flags }
  Scolor(7,0);                    { Color is white on black }
  clrscr;                         { Clear screen }
  writeln(#13#10'KEYP (c) 1987, 92 by Michael Tischer');
  writeln(#13#10'You can type some characters and change the status');
  writeln('of the INSERT, CAPS and NUM modes. The upper-right corner');
  writeln('of the screen documents the changes to these keys.');
  writeln('Press <Enter> or <F1> to end the program.');
  write(#13#10'Type text here: ');
  repeat                          { Input loop }
   key := Getkey;                 { Get key }
   if (key < 256) then write(chr(key))    { Output (if normal) }
  until (key = 13) or (key = F1);         { Repeat until F1 or CR }
  writeln;
end.
```

C listing: KEYC.C

```
/*********************************************************/
/*                      K E Y C                          */
/*-------------------------------------------------------*/
/*    Task    : Makes a function available for reading a character */
/*              from the keyboard. The upper-right corner of the   */
/*              screen lists the status of INSERT, CAPS LOCK and    */
/*              NUM LOCK.                                 */
/*-------------------------------------------------------*/
/*    Author       : Michael Tischer                     */
/*    Developed on : 08/13/87                            */
/*    Last update  : 01/21/92                            */
/*-------------------------------------------------------*/
/*    Memory model : SMALL                               */
/*********************************************************/

/*== Add include files ================================*/

#include <dos.h>
#include <bios.h>
#include <stdio.h>

/*== Type definitions =================================*/

typedef unsigned char BYTE;            /* Create a byte */

/*== Macros ===========================================*/

#ifdef __TURBOC__                      /* Definitions for TURBO C */

   #define GetKbKey()     ( bioskey( 0 ) )
   #define GetKbReady()   ( bioskey( 1 ) != 0 )
   #define GetKbStatus()  ( bioskey( 2 ) )

#else                                  /* Definitions for Microsoft C Compiler */

   #define GetKbKey()     ( _bios_keybrd( _KEYBRD_READ ) )
   #define GetKbReady()   ( _bios_keybrd( _KEYBRD_READY ) != 0 )
   #define GetKbStatus()  ( _bios_keybrd( _KEYBRD_SHIFTSTATUS ) )

#endif

/*== Constants ========================================*/

/*-- Bit layout in BIOS keyboard status --------------------------*/

#define SCRL  16                       /* SCROLL LOCK bit */
#define NUML  32                       /* NUM LOCK bit */
#define CAPL  64                       /* CAPS LOCK bit */
#define INS   128                      /* INSERT bit */

#define TRUE  ( 0 == 0 )               /* Constants make reading the */
#define FALSE ( 0 == 1 )               /* program code easier */

#define FR    0    /* Row in which the flags should be displayed */
#define FC    65   /* Column in which the flags should be displayed */
#define FlagColour 0x70  /* Black characters on white background */

/*-- Codes of some keys as returned by GETKEY() ----------------*/
#define BEL   7                        /* Bell character code */
#define BS    8                        /* Backspace key code */
#define TAB   9                        /* Tab key code */
#define LF    10                       /* Linefeed key code */
```

```
#define CR    13                       /* Carriage return code */
#define ESC   27                       /*        Escape key code */
#define F1    315                      /*        Function keys */
#define F2    316
#define F3    317
#define F4    318
#define F5    319
#define F6    320
#define F7    321
#define F8    322
#define F9    323
#define F10   324
#define CUP   328                      /*        Cursor keys */
#define CLEFT 331
#define CRIGHT 333
#define CDOWN 328

/*== Global variables ================================*/

BYTE Insert,                           /* INSERT flag status */
     Num,                              /* NUM flag status */
     Caps;                             /* CAPS flag status */

/*********************************************************/
/* GETPAGE : Gets the current screen page.               */
/* Input   : None                                        */
/* Output  : See below                                   */
/*********************************************************/

BYTE GetPage( void )
{
 union REGS Register;       /* Register variables for interrupt call */

 Register.h.ah = 15;                    /* Function number */
 int86(0x10, &Register, &Register);     /* Call interrupt 10H */
 return(Register.h.bh);                 /* Current screen page number */
}

/*********************************************************/
/* SETPOS: Sets the cursor position in the current screen page. */
/* Input  : ScCol = New cursor column                    */
/*          ScRow = New cursor row                       */
/* Output : None                                         */
/* Info   : The screen cursor may change when you call this */
/*          function if the current screen page is the specified */
/*          screen page.                                 */
/*********************************************************/

void SetPos(BYTE ScCol, BYTE ScRow)
{
 union REGS Register;       /* Register variables for interrupt call */

 Register.h.ah = 2;                     /* Function number */
 Register.h.bh = GetPage();             /* Screen page */
 Register.h.dh = ScRow;                 /* Screen row */
 Register.h.dl = ScCol;                 /* Screen column */
 int86(0x10, &Register, &Register);     /* Call interrupt 10H */
}

/*********************************************************/
/* GETPOS: Gets the cursor position in the current screen page. */
/* Input  : None                                         */
/* Output : - ScCol = Pointer to variable containing current column */
/*            ScRow = Pointer to variable containing current row   */
```

```
/********************************************************/

void GetPos(BYTE * ScCol, BYTE * ScRow)
{
  union REGS Register;        /* Register variables for interrupt call */

  Register.h.ah = 3;                          /* Function number */
  Register.h.bh = GetPage();                  /* Screen page */
  int86(0x10, &Register, &Register);      /* Call interrupt 10H */
  *ScCol = Register.h.dl;              /* Read function result */
  *ScRow = Register.h.dh;              /*   from the registers */
}


/********************************************************/
/* WRITECHAR: Writes a character with attribute to the current  */
/*            cursor position in the current screen page.       */
/* Input  : - CharCode = ASCII code of character to be displayed */
/*          - CAttr    = Character attribute                     */
/* Output : None                                                */
/********************************************************/

void WriteChar(char CharCode, BYTE CAttr)
{
  union REGS Register;        /* Register variables for interrupt call */

  Register.h.ah = 9;                          /* Function number */
  Register.h.al = CharCode;           /* Character to be displayed */
  Register.h.bh = GetPage();                  /* Screen page */
  Register.h.bl = CAttr;          /* Color of char. to be displayed */
  Register.x.cx = 1;                  /* Display character once */
  int86(0x10, &Register, &Register);      /* Call interrupt 10H */
}


/********************************************************/
/* WRITETEXT: Writes a character with constant color to a specific */
/*            position within the current screen page.          */
/* Input  : - ScCol = Display column                            */
/*          - ScRow = Display row                               */
/*          - TEXT  = Pointer to the string to be displayed     */
/*          - CAttr = Attribute for character to be displayed   */
/* Output : None                                                */
/* Info   : Text is a pointer to a character vector, which contains */
/*          the text to be displayed, terminated with '\0'.     */
/********************************************************/

void WriteText(BYTE ScCol, BYTE ScRow, char *Text, BYTE CAttr)
{
  union REGS InRegister,      /* Register variables for interrupt call */
             OutRegister;

  SetPos(ScCol, ScRow);                       /* Place cursor */
  InRegister.h.ah = 14;                       /* Function number */
  InRegister.h.bh = GetPage();                /* Screen page */
  while (*Text)                       /* Display text until '\0' */
  {
    WriteChar(' ', CAttr);              /* Write character color */
    InRegister.h.al = *Text++;          /* for character        */
    int86(0x10, &InRegister, &OutRegister);     /* Call interrupt */
  }
}


/********************************************************/
/* CLS: Clear current screen page                               */
/* Input  : None                                                */
```

```
/* Output : None                                                */
/********************************************************/

void Cls( void )
{
  union REGS Register;        /* Register variables for interrupt call */

  Register.h.ah = 6;                  /* Function number: Scroll Up */
  Register.h.al = 0;                          /* 0 = Clear */
  Register.h.bh = 7;          /* White text on black background */
  Register.x.cx = 0;                  /* Upper-left corner of screen */
  Register.h.dh = 24;                 /* Coordinates of lower- */
  Register.h.dl = 79;                 /* right corner of screen */
  int86(0x10, &Register, &Register);      /* Call BIOS video interrupt */
}


/********************************************************/
/* NEGFLAG: Negates flag and displays corresponding text.       */
/* Input  : FLAG    = Last flag status                          */
/*          FLAGREG = Current flag status (0 = off)             */
/*          ScCol   = Screen column for flag names              */
/*          ScRow   = Screen row for flag names                 */
/*          TEXT    = Flag name                                 */
/* Output : New flag status (TRUE = on, FALSE = off)            */
/********************************************************/

BYTE NegFlag(BYTE Flag, unsigned int FlagReg,
             BYTE ScCol, BYTE ScRow, char * Text)
{
  BYTE CurScRow,                              /*  Current row */
       CurScCol;                              /*  Current column */

  if (!(Flag == (FlagReg != 0)))      /* Has flag been changed? */
  {                                           /* Yes */
    GetPos(&CurScCol, &CurScRow);       /* Get current cursor position */
    WriteText(ScCol, ScRow, Text, (BYTE) ((Flag) ? 0 : FlagColour));
    SetPos(CurScCol, CurScRow);         /* Set old cursor position */
    return(Flag ^1);                    /* Change flag bit 0 */
  }
  else return(Flag);                  /* Change back to old status */
}


/********************************************************/
/* GETKEY: Reads a character and displays flag status.          */
/* Input  : None                                                */
/* Output : Code of captured key:                               */
/*          < 256 : normal key                                  */
/*          >= 256 : extended keycode                           */
/********************************************************/

unsigned int GetKey( void )
{
  int RcKey,                                  /* The received key */
      Status;                                 /* Keyboard status */

  do
  {
    Status = GetKbStatus();             /* Read keyboard status */
    Insert = NegFlag(Insert, Status & INS, FC+9, FR, "INSERT");
    Caps = NegFlag(Caps, Status & CAPL, FC+3, FR, " CAPS ");
    Num = NegFlag(Num, Status & NUML, FC, FR, "NUM");
  }
  while ( !GetKbReady() );             /* Repeat until key is ready */
```

```
  RcKey = GetKbKey();                                 /* Get key */
  return ((RcKey & 255) == 0) ? (RcKey >> 8) + 256 : RcKey & 255;
}


/**********************************************************************/
/* INIKEY: Initializes keyboard flags.                              */
/* Input   : None                                                   */
/* Output  : None                                                   */
/* Info    : The keyboard flags change to their opposite status.    */
/*           The GETKEY function then changes them to their current */
/*           status on the next call.                               */
/**********************************************************************/

void IniKey( void )
{
  int Status;                            /* Keyboard status */

  Status = GetKbStatus();                /* Read keyboard status */
  Insert = (Status & INS) ? FALSE : TRUE;   /* Change current */
  Caps  = (Status & CAPL)? FALSE : TRUE;    /*        status */
  Num   = (Status & NUML) ? FALSE : TRUE;   /*     as needed */
}


/**********************************************************************/
/**                    MAIN PROGRAM                               **/
```

```
/**********************************************************************/

void main( void )
{
  unsigned int AKey;

  Cls();                                      /* Clear screen */
  SetPos(0,0);        /* Move cursor to upper-left corner of screen */
  printf("KEYC - (c) 1987, 92 by Michael Tischer\n\n");
  printf("You can type some character and change the status of the\n");
  printf("INSERT, CAPS and NUM modes. The upper-right corner of the\n");
  printf("screen documents the changes to these keys.\n");
  printf("Press <Enter> or <F1> to end the program. \n\n");
  printf("Type text here: ");
  IniKey();                                /* Initialize keyboard flags */
  do
    {
    if ((AKey = GetKey()) < 256)              /* Read the key */
      printf("%c", (char) AKey);             /* Display (if normal) */
    }
  while (!(AKey == CR || AKey == F1));      /* Repeat until user presses */
                                           /*            <Enter> or <F1> */
  printf("\n");
}
```

5.2.2 Reading MF-II Keyboards

The <F11> and <F12> function keys aren't included in the listing of extended keyboard codes. There is a good reason for this because these keys cannot be read with functions 00H and 01H. The developers of the ROM-BIOS intentionally excluded these keys from being processed by functions 00H and 01H to maintain compatibility.

The keyboard handler writes the scan codes for these keys to the keyboard buffer, just like any other keystroke. But functions 00H and 01H simply ignore them and proceed as if the keyboard buffer is empty.

New BIOS functions

Three new BIOS functions detect these codes. These functions were introduced with the AT and can now be found in almost every ROM-BIOS. Also, if these functions are excluded from the ROM-BIOS, DOS Versions 3.3 and up implement these functions with the DOS keyboard driver KEYB.

These new functions are assigned the numbers 10H, 11H, and 12H. The way these functions are called and work is similar to functions 00H, 01H, and 02H. Function 12H is slightly different from 02H in function results; we'll discuss this difference later.

The new keyboard codes

The differences between 00H and 01H and their counterparts 10H and 11H involve the codes that are returned. This applies almost exclusively to extended keyboard codes that represent keys that aren't found on the PC/XT and AT keyboards or key combinations (such as <Ctrl>+<Tab>, <Ctrl>+<Cursor Up>, or <Alt>+<Esc>) that aren't supported by these keyboards.

The following table lists the keys and key combinations that return different codes with functions 00H/01H and 10H/11H (all codes are in hexadecimal notation):

Extended key combinations when calling BIOS functions 10H/11H								
Function keys			with Shift		with Ctrl		with Alt	
	Old AH/AL	New AH/AL	Old AH/AL	New AH/AL	Old AH/AL	New AH/AL	Old AH/AL	New AH/AL
F11	----	85/00	----	87/00	----	89/00	----	8B/00
F12	----	86/00	----	88/00	----	8A/00	----	8C/00
Gray cursor keys in separate cursor block			with Shift		with Ctrl		with Alt	
	Old AH/AL	New AH/AL	Old AH/AL	New AH/AL	Old AH/AL	New AH/AL	Old AH/AL	New AH/AL
Home	47/00	47/E0	47/00	47/E0	77/00	77/E0	------	97/00
Cursor Up	48/00	48/E0	48/00	48/E0	-----	8D/E0	-----	98/00
Page Up	49/00	49/E0	49/00	49/E0	84/00	84/E0	-----	99/00
Cursor Left	4B/00	4B/E0	4B/00	4B/E0	73/00	73/E0	-----	9B/00
Cursor Right	4D/00	4D/E0	4D/00	4D/E0	74/00	74/E0	-----	9D/00
End	4F/00	4F/E0	4F/00	4F/E0	75/00	75/E0	-----	9F/00
Cursor Down	50/00	50/E0	50/00	50/E0	-----	91/E0	-----	A0/00
Page Down	51/00	51/E0	51/00	51/E0	76/00	76/E0	-----	A1/00
Insert	52/00	52/E0	52/00	52/E0	-----	92/E0	-----	A2/00
Delete	53/00	53/E0	53/00	53/E0	-----	93/E0	-----	A3/00
Other gray keys			with Shift		with Ctrl		with Alt	
	Old AH/AL	New AH/AL	Old AH/AL	New AH/AL	Old AH/AL	New AH/AL	Old AH/AL	New AH/AL
/	35/2F	E0/2F	-----	E0/2F	-----	95/00	-----	A4/00
*	37/2A	37/2A	-----	37/2A	-----	96/00	-----	37/00
-	4A/2D	4A/2D	-----	4A/2D	-----	8E/00	-----	4A/00
+	4E/2B	4E/2B	-----	4E/2B	-----	90/00	-----	4E/00
Enter	1C/0D	E0/0D	-----	E0/0D	-----	E0/0A	-----	A6/00
Additional combinations of white keys			with Shift		with Ctrl		with Alt	
	Old AH/AL	New AH/AL	Old AH/AL	New AH/AL	Old AH/AL	New AH/AL	Old AH/AL	New AH/AL
Tab					-----	94/00	-----	A5/00
5 on keypad					-----	8F/00		
white Cursor Up					-----	8D/00		
white Cursor Down					-----	91/00		
white Insert					-----	92/00		
white Delete					-----	93/00		
Escape							-----	01/00
Backspace							-----	0E/00
Tab							-----	A5/00
[							-----	1A/00
]							-----	1B/00
Enter							-----	1C/00
;							-----	27/00
`							-----	28/00
`							-----	29/00
\							-----	2B/00
,							-----	33/00
.							-----	34/00
/							-----	35/00

The codes for the gray cursor keys have been changed. This was done to distinguish them from the cursor keys of the numeric keypad. The gray cursor keys return ASCII code E0H, instead of 00H, to the AL register. When using BIOS functions 10H and 11H, you must have your programs look for ASCII code E0H as well as 00H to be able to read all extended keyboard codes.

If you're only interested in reading the <F11> and <F12> function keys and don't want to distinguish between the white and gray cursor keys, you can save yourself some work by changing ASCII code E0H to 00H after it's received. This enables you to handle both sets of cursor keys in the same way.

The new status functions

Functions 10H and 11H are identical to their original counterparts, but function 12H differs slightly from 02H in the returned result. In addition to the keyboard status byte, this function returns other information in the AH register. This extra information is known as the extended keyboard status byte. Although this is also a BIOS variable, it's only managed on systems with an MF-II keyboard.

Like the normal keyboard status byte, this byte also contains information on the current status of the various toggle keys. But it also provides the status of both the left and right <Alt> and <Ctrl> keys. The normal keyboard status byte doesn't allow you to read these separately.

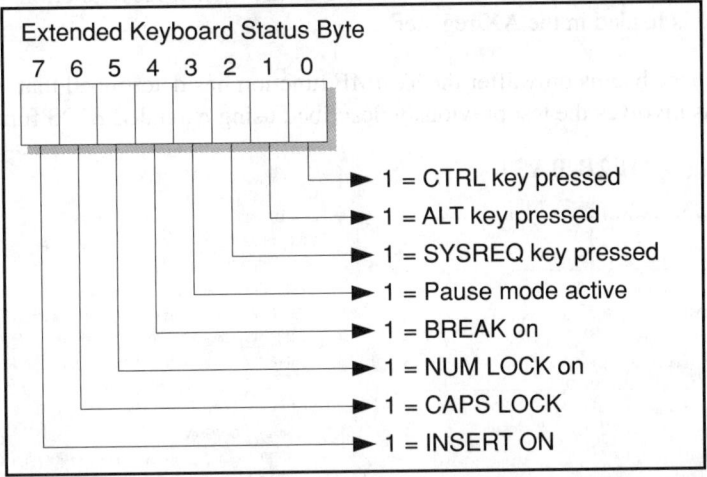

Are these functions available?

As we mentioned earlier, most BIOS manufacturers now include the extended BIOS keyboard functions or they are provided by DOS 3.3 and higher. However, you can't assume that they will be available on all systems.

Because of this, any program that wants to use these functions should first determine whether they are available. This isn't easy to do because no ROM-BIOS function can provide this information.

So you must use a trick. This consists of calling function 12H with the values 12H in the AH register and 00H in the AL register. If the value 1200H is found in the AX register after the function call, you can then be sure that function 12H, and therefore the other extended BIOS functions, are unavailable on the system.

This trick relies on an unwritten law of the ROM-BIOS, Under this "law", when an unknown function is called, the function call will end immediately, and the contents of the AX register (the function and sub-function numbers) will be returned to the caller unchanged.

Demonstration programs

The following demonstration programs listed will demonstrate how easily this test can be implemented in your program code. These implementations in BASIC, Pascal, and C perform only one task; they read the keyboard using BIOS function 10H and display ASCII and scan codes entered at the keyboard. The output is in hexadecimal format so you can compare the values with the previous table.

These programs display the codes produced by the extra keys and key combinations available on the MF-II keyboard. This continues until the user presses the <Esc> key to end the program.

You can easily compare the extended BIOS functions with the normal functions. First, read a few codes with the extended function. Then switch the program to BIOS function 00H and press the same keys again. Simply change the line of code in the GetMFKey function where the BIOS function number is loaded in the AX register.

The keyboard query begins only after the TestMF function has determined that an MF keyboard is available. This involves the test previously described using extended BIOS function 12H.

BASIC listing: MF2B.BAS

```
'*********************************************************
'*                    M F 2 B                          *
'-------------------------------------------------------
'*  Task:       Demonstrates keyboard reading MF-II keyboards.  *
'*              QuickBASIC and the QB.LIB must be loaded using  *
'*              QB /L QB                                 *
'*              before loading and running this file.    *
'-------------------------------------------------------
'*  Author     : Michael Tischer                        *
'*  Developed on : 01/01/92                             *
'*  Last update  : 01/28/92                             *
'*********************************************************

'$INCLUDE: 'QB.BI'          'Include file contains register declarations

DECLARE FUNCTION MakeWord! (WNum AS INTEGER)
DECLARE FUNCTION HexByte$ (bval AS INTEGER)
DECLARE FUNCTION GetMFKey% ()
DECLARE FUNCTION TestMF% ()

CONST TRUE = -1                              'Define the truth
CONST FALSE = NOT TRUE

'-- Main program ---------------------------------------

DIM pdkey AS INTEGER
DIM CR AS STRING
```

```
CLS
CR = CHR$(13)
PRINT "MF2B  -  (c) 1992 by Michael Tischer"; CR
IF TestMF THEN
   PRINT "BIOS functions implemented for MF-II keyboards."
   PRINT CR + CR + "Press any key or combination to display ";
   PRINT "key codes." + CR + CR
   PRINT "Press <Esc> to end the program." + CR

   DO                                                   'Input loop
      pdkey = GetMFKey                                  'Get key
      PRINT "Scan : "; HexByte(MakeWord(pdkey) / 256); "  ";
      PRINT "ASCII: "; HexByte(pdkey AND 255);
      IF ((pdkey AND 255) = &HE0) AND ((pdkey / 256) <> 0) THEN
         PRINT "  <---- MF-II key"
      ELSE
         PRINT
      END IF
   LOOP UNTIL (pdkey = &H11B)          'Repeat until user presses <ESC>
   PRINT CR
ELSE
   PRINT "No BIOS extensions available for MF-II keyboards!"
END IF
END

'*********************************************************
'* GetMFKey  : Reads a key using extended keyboard function 10H.  *
'* Input   : None                                       *
```

```
'* Output  : The returned keycode               *
'****************************************************************

FUNCTION GetMFKey%

DIM reg AS RegType            'Processor registers for interrupt call

reg.ax = &H1000              'Extended read function for MF-II keyboards
CALL INTERRUPT(&H16, reg, reg)      'Call BIOS keyboard interrupt
GetMFKey% = reg.ax                  'Return keycode

END FUNCTION


'****************************************************************
'* HexByte : Changes a byte into a two-digit hex string.      *
'* Input   : BVAL = Byte to be converted                      *
'* Output  : Two-digit hex string                             *
'****************************************************************

FUNCTION HexByte$ (bval AS INTEGER)

IF bval < 16 THEN                           'One digit?
  HexByte$ = "0" + HEX$(bval)        'Yes --> First digit = "0"
ELSE                                 'No --> Make two digits
  HexByte$ = HEX$(bval)
END IF
END FUNCTION


'****************************************************************
'* Makeword : Makes a long number from an integer, to avoid getting *
'*            a negative result during bit manipulations performed  *
'*            through integer division.                       *
'* Input    : Integer number                                  *
'* Output   : Bit pattern compatible long number              *
'****************************************************************

FUNCTION MakeWord! (WNum AS INTEGER)

IF WNum < 0 THEN
  MakeWord = 65536! + WNum
ELSE
  MakeWord = WNum
END IF

END FUNCTION


'****************************************************************
'* TestMF: Tests whether the extended BIOS functions for reading the *
'*         MF-II keyboard are available.                      *
'* Input   : None                                             *
'* Output  : TRUE if the functions are available, otherwise FALSE *
'****************************************************************

FUNCTION TestMF%

DIM reg AS RegType            'Processor registers for interrupt call

reg.ax = &H1200              'Extended status function for MF-II keyboards
CALL INTERRUPT(&H16, reg, reg)      'Call BIOS keyboard interrupt
PRINT HEX$(reg.ax)
TestMF% = (reg.ax <> &H1200)        'AX =1200H : Function absent

END FUNCTION
```

Pascal listing: MF2P.PAS

```
{****************************************************************}
{*                      M F 2 P                              *}
{*------------------------------------------------------------*}
{*    Task        : Demonstrates key read from MF-II keyboards. *}
{*------------------------------------------------------------*}
{*    Author      : Michael Tischer                          *}
{*    Developed on : 01/28/92                                 *}
{*    Last update  : 01/28/92                                 *}
{****************************************************************}

program MF2P;

uses Dos, Crt;                        { Add DOS and CRT units }

const CR = #13#10;                    { Carriage Return & Linefeed }


{****************************************************************}
{* HexByte : Changes a byte into a two-digit hex string.      *}
{* Input   : BVAL = Byte to be converted                      *}
{* Output  : Two-digit hex string                             *}
{****************************************************************}

function HexByte( bval : byte ) : string;

const HexDigits : array [0..15] of char = '0123456789ABCDEF';

var dummy : string[2];                        { Get string }

begin
  dummy[0] := chr(2);           { String consists of two characters }
  dummy[1] := HexDigits[ bval shr 4 ];          { Convert both }
  dummy[2] := HexDigits[ bval and $0F ];        { nibbles to hex }
  HexByte := dummy;
end;


{****************************************************************}
{* TestMF: Tests whether the extended BIOS functions for reading the *}
{*         MF-II keyboard are available.                      *}
{* Input   : None                                             *}
{* Output  : TRUE if the functions are available, otherwise FALSE *}
{****************************************************************}

function TestMF : boolean;

var Regs : Registers;       { Processor registers for interrupt call }

begin
  Regs.AX := $1200;    { Extended status function for MF-II keyboards }
  intr( $16, Regs );
  TestMF := ( Regs.AX <> $1200 );        { AX=1200 : Function absent }
end;


{****************************************************************}
{* GetMFKey : Reads a key using extended keyboard function 10H. *}
{* Input   : None                                             *}
{* Output  : The returned keycode                             *}
{****************************************************************}

function GetMFKey : word;

var Regs : Registers;       { Processor registers for interrupt call }
```

```
begin
  Regs.AH := $10;        { Extended read function for MF-II keyboards }
  intr( $16, Regs );
  GetMFKey := Regs.AX;                      { Return keycode }
end;


{*****************************************************************}
{*                    M A I N   P R O G R A M                   *}
{*****************************************************************}


var pdkey : word;


begin
  clrscr;
  writeln( 'MF2P  -  (c) 1992 by Michael Tischer' + CR );
  if ( TestMF ) then
    begin
      writeln( 'BIOS functions implemented for ' +
               'MF-II keyboards.' + CR + CR + 'Press any key '+
               'or combination to display key codes.' + CR + CR +
               'Press <Esc> to end the program.' + CR );

      repeat                                   { Input loop }
        pdkey := GetMFKey;                        { Get key }
        write( 'Scan : ', HexByte(hi(pdkey)), ' ',
               'ASCII: ', HexByte(lo(pdkey)) );
        if ( (lo(pdkey) = $E0) and (hi(pdkey) <> 0) ) then
          write( ' <---- MF-II key' );
        writeln;
      until ( pdkey = $011b );     { Repeat until user presses <ESC> }
      writeln( CR );
    end
  else
    writeln( 'No BIOS extensions available for MF-II keyboards!');
end.
```

C listing: MF2C.C

```
/***************************************************************/
/*                        M F 2 C                            */
/**-----------------------------------------------------------**/
/*   Task:        : Demonstrates key read from MF-II keyboards. */
/**-----------------------------------------------------------**/
/*   Author       : Michael Tischer                           */
/*   Developed on : 01/01/92                                  */
/*   Last update  : 01/28/92                                  */
/***************************************************************/

/*== Add include files ======================================*/

#include <stdio.h>
#include <dos.h>

/*== Type definitions =======================================*/

typedef unsigned char BYTE;                 /* Create a byte */
typedef unsigned int WORD;

/*== Constants ==============================================*/

#define TRUE  ( 0 == 0 )            /* Constants make reading */
#define FALSE ( 0 == 1 )           /* program code easier    */

/*== Screen routines (Microsoft C) ==========================*/

#ifndef __TURBOC__                          /* Microsoft C? */

  /***********************************************************/
  /* Gotoxy     : Places cursor.                            */
  /* Input      : Cursor coordinates                        */
  /* Output     : None                                      */
  /***********************************************************/

  void gotoxy( int x, int y )
  {
    union REGS regs;       /* Register variables for interrupt call */

    regs.h.ah = 0x02;        /* Function number for interrupt call */
    regs.h.bh = 0;                               /* Color */
    regs.h.dh = y - 1;
    regs.h.dl = x - 1;
    int86( 0x10, &regs, &regs );              /* Interrupt call */
  }


  /***********************************************************/
  /* clrscr     : Clears the screen.                        */
  /* Input      : None                                      */
  /* Output     : None                                      */
  /***********************************************************/

  void clrscr( void )
  {
    union REGS regs;       /* Register variables for interrupt call */

    regs.h.ah = 0x07;          /* Function number for interrupt call */
    regs.h.al = 0x00;
    regs.h.ch = 0;
    regs.h.cl = 0;
    regs.h.dh = 24;
    regs.h.dl = 79;
```

```
   int86( 0x10, &regs, &regs );              /* Interrupt call */
   gotoxy( 1, 1 );                           /* Set cursor */
  }

#endif

/**************************************************************/
/* HexByte : Changes a byte into a two-digit hex string.      */
/* Input   : BVAL = Byte to be converted                      */
/* Output  : Two-digit hex string                             */
/**************************************************************/

char *HexByte( BYTE bval )
{
 char HexDigits[16] = "0123456789ABCDEF";
 static char dummy[3] = "00";

 dummy[0] = HexDigits[ bval >> 4 ];           /* Convert both  */
 dummy[1] = HexDigits[ bval & 0x0F ];         /* nibbles to hex */
 return dummy;
}

/**************************************************************/
/* TestMF: Tests whether the extended BIOS functions for reading the */
/*         MF-II keyboard are available.                      */
/* Input   : None                                             */
/* Output  : TRUE if the functions are available, otherwise FALSE */
/**************************************************************/

int TestMF( void )
{
 union REGS regs;             /* Register variables for interrupt call */

 regs.x.ax = 0x1200; /* Extended status function for MF-II keyboards */
 int86( 0x16, &regs, &regs );
 return ( regs.x.ax != 0x1200 );     /* AX=0x1200 : Function absent */
}

/**************************************************************/
/* GetMFKey : Reads a key using extended keyboard function 10H. */
/* Input   : None                                             */
/* Output  : The returned keycode                             */
```

```
/**************************************************************/
WORD GetMFKey( void )
{
 union REGS regs;          /* Register variables for interrupt call */

 regs.h.ah = 0x10;      /* Extended read function for MF-II keyboards */
 int86( 0x16, &regs, &regs );
 return regs.x.ax;                          /* Return keycode */
}

/**************************************************************/
/*                M A I N   P R O G R A M                     */
/**************************************************************/

void main( void )
{
 WORD pdkey;

 clrscr();
 printf( "MF2C  -  (c) 1992 by Michael Tischer\n\n" );
 if ( TestMF() )
  {
   printf( "BIOS functions implemented for MF-II keyboards.\n\n" \
           "Press any key or combination to display key codes.\n\n" \
           "Press <Esc> to end the program.\n\n" );

   do                                        /* Input loop */
    {
     pdkey = GetMFKey();                      /* Get key */
     printf( "Scan : %s ", HexByte((BYTE) (pdkey >> 8)) );
     printf( "ASCII: %s", HexByte((BYTE) (pdkey & 255)) );
     if ( ((pdkey & 255) == 0xe0) && ((pdkey & 65280 ) != 0 ) )
      printf( " <---- MF-II key" );
     printf( "\n" );
    }
   while ( pdkey != 0x011b );       /* Repeat until user presses <ESC> */
   printf( "\n\n" );
  }
 else
   printf( "No BIOS extensions available for MF-II keyboards!");
}
```

5.2.3 The BIOS Keyboard Interrupt Variables

The BIOS has eight variables in its variable segment for managing the keyboard and communication between the keyboard interrupt handler (interrupt 09H) and the BIOS keyboard functions (interrupt 16H). These are listed in the following table. These variables are useful for TSR programs that change the way the keyboard interrupts work. Even normal programs can find ways to manipulate these variables, as we'll see at the end of this section.

You should be already familiar with two of these variables: the keyboard status byte and the extended keyboard status byte. These two bytes are returned when calling functions 02H and 12H of interrupt 16H.

Offset address 19H is a byte used when entering ASCII codes with the <Alt> key and numeric keypad. When the number keys are pressed, the code entered is stored in this byte.

BIOS Variables For Keyboard Management		
Offset	Meaning	Type
17H	Keyboard status	1 byte
18H	Extended keyboard status	1 byte
19H	Code for ASCII input	1 byte
1AH	Next character in keyboard buffer	1 word
1CH	Last character in keyboard buffer	1 word
1EH	Keyboard buffer	16 words
80H	Start address of keyboard buffer	1 word
82H	End address of keyboard buffer	1 word

Managing the keyboard buffer

The three variables that follow at offset addresses 1AH, 1CH, and 1EH manage the keyboard buffer. This is where the keyboard interrupt handler (interrupt 09H) stores keystrokes so applications can read them using the BIOS keyboard interrupt (16H).

Before you can understand the significance of the first two variables, you must know that the keyboard buffer is structured as a ring buffer. This kind of buffer is used when characters will be written to the buffer and read from it asynchronously (i.e., not within a specific time span). At first, it may seem that storing characters in sequence (the first character in the first position, the second character in the second position, etc.) is the best way to structure such a buffer. When a character is read, it's taken from the first position and all the other characters move up.

Although this method works, it generates unnecessary work for the processor because each time a character is read, all the characters in the buffer must be moved. So, the ring buffer uses two pointers. One pointer indicates the position from which the next character will be read and the other indicates the position where the next new character will be written.

With this method, the pointers move instead of the entire contents of the buffer. Initially, both pointers point to the beginning of the buffer. They move toward the end of the buffer with every read and write access. When the pointers reach the end of the buffer, they are reset to the beginning of the buffer. The ring buffer's name comes from this circular pointer movement.

For example, suppose that the offset address of the next character to be read from the keyboard buffer is 1AH. Once the character is read, the pointer moves two bytes towards the end of the buffer. Each character in the keyboard buffer requires two bytes: one byte for the ASCII code and one byte for the scan code. If the last location in the buffer was read, the pointer is set to the beginning of the buffer.

The same happens with the pointer at 1CH, which points to the position following the last character in the buffer. If the user presses another key, the key is stored at this location. The pointer then moves two bytes towards the end of the buffer. If the new keystroke was stored in the last word of the buffer, this pointer is reset to the beginning of the buffer.

The relationship between the two pointers indicates the buffer's status. Two conditions are important:

1.) If both pointers have the same value, this indicates an empty keyboard buffer.

2.) If the end pointer tries to occupy the same space as the starting pointer, this indicates a full keyboard buffer.

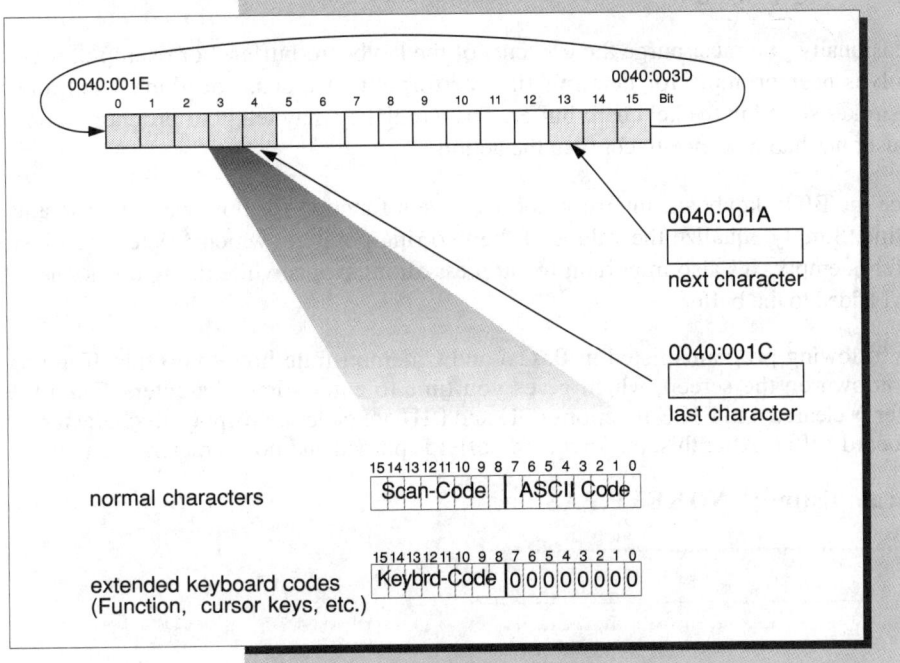

Implementing the keyboard ring buffer and pointers

The BIOS keyboard buffer comprises 32 bytes. Since each character requires two bytes, the buffer can hold up to 16 characters.

With a normal ASCII character, the ASCII code is stored first, followed by the scan code. For extended keyboard codes, the ASCII code will be 0 because the actual character code is in the subsequent byte.

Keyboard buffer location

The concept of the two ring buffer pointers suggests that this is a "mobile" buffer and that its location should be determined by the values of the pointers. However, the keyboard buffer is always located at offset address 1EH. Actually, this was the reason why the two ring buffer was designed; the two pointers would allow the size and location of the keyboard buffer to change as needed.

However, by the time these two variables were introduced with the modified BIOS of the first ATs, there were already numerous TSR programs that expected to find the keyboard buffer in a fixed location at offset address 1EH. So, the original idea never had a chance to be implemented.

Demonstration programs

The following programs, which are in BASIC, Pascal, and C, demonstrate how to manipulate the BIOS variables. These programs use a function that's very important to basic keyboard programming: purging the contents of the keyboard buffer.

Occasionally you must purge the contents of the keyboard buffer. For example, if your program involves user prompts for deleting files or formatting disks, you don't want any accidental keystrokes stored in the keyboard buffer. The wrong key may tell your program to proceed before the user has had a chance to confirm the action.

Since the BIOS keyboard interrupt doesn't have a function for this, we must use a user-defined routine. Simply equalize the values of the two ring pointers, which creates the illusion that the buffer is empty. It's also important to suppress all interrupts while doing this so new keystrokes aren't added to the buffer.

The following programs listed in Pascal and C demonstrate how to do this. They begin with a countdown on the screen, which gives you time to enter some characters. Then the keyboard buffer is cleared and BIOS functions 00H and 01H are called to display all characters found in the keyboard buffer. After this, the keyboard buffer is purged and no characters exist.

Pascal listing: NOKEYP.PAS

```
{**********************************************************}
{*                    N O K E Y P                        *}
{*------------------------------------------------------- *}
{*   Task       : Demonstrates clearing the keyboard buffer.  *}
{*              This is useful for protecting the user from   *}
{*              accidental keystrokes during an important     *}
{*              command (e.g., deleting files).          *}
{*------------------------------------------------------- *}
{*   Author     : Michael Tischer                        *}
{*   Developed on : 01/01/92                             *}
{*   Last update  : 02/10/92                             *}
{**********************************************************}

program NoKeyP;

uses Crt;                              (* Add CRT unit *)


{**********************************************************}
{* ClearKbBuffer : Clears the contents of the keyboard buffer.  *}
{* Input   : None                                        *}
{* Output  : None                                        *}
{**********************************************************}

procedure ClearKbBuffer;

begin
  inline( $fa );              { CLI: Disable hardware interrupts }
  memw[$40:$1A] := memw[$40:$1C];   { No more characters in buffer }
  inline( $fb );              { STI: Enable hardware interrupts }
end;


{**********************************************************}
{*            M A I N   P R O G R A M                    *}
{**********************************************************}

var i,                                 { Loop counter }
    ccount : integer;          { Number of character in keyboard buffer }
    kch    : char;                               { Get keys }

begin
  clrscr;
  writeln( 'NOKEYP  - (c) 1992 by Michael Tischer' );
  writeln;
  writeln( 'Keyboard buffer purged when counter reaches 0.' );
  writeln;

  ClearKbBuffer;                       { Clear the buffer }

  for i := 10 downto 0 do             { Give user time to }
    begin                             { press some keys   }
      writeln( i:5 );
      delay( 750 );
    end;

  {-- Display characters still in keyboard buffer -------------------}

  ccount := 0;                         { No more characters }
  writeln;
  writeln;
  writeln( 'Characters in keyboard buffer :' );

  while KeyPressed do         { Any more characters in keyboard buffer? }
    begin                             { Yes --> Read and display }
      kch := ReadKey;
      write( '   ', ord(kch):5 );      { Display code only first }
      if ord(kch) > 32 then                      { Code > 32? }
        write ( '(', kch, ')' );  { Yes --> Display character as well }
      writeln;
      inc( ccount );                   { More than one character found }
    end;
  if ccount = 0 then                   { Out of characters? }
    writeln( '(None)' );                       { Done }
  writeln;
end.
```

C listing: NOKEYC.C

```c
/*********************************************************/
/*                      N O K E Y C                    */
/*-----------------------------------------------------*/
/*    Task       : Demonstrates clearing the keyboard buffer. */
/*                 This is useful for protecting the user from */
/*                 accidental keystrokes during an important */
/*                 command (e.g., deleting files).     */
/*-----------------------------------------------------*/
/*    Author     : Michael Tischer                     */
/*    Developed on  : 01/01/92                          */
/*    Last update   : 01/28/92                          */
/*********************************************************/

#include <stdio.h>
#include <dos.h>
#include <bios.h>

/*== Macros =============================================*/

#ifndef MK_FP                   /* If MK_FP hasn't been defined, do so */
 #define MK_FP(seg,ofs) \
   ((void far *) (((unsigned long)(seg) << 16) | (unsigned)(ofs)))
#endif

#ifdef __TURBOC__               /* Definitions for TURBO C */

  #define GetKbKey()      ( bioskey( 0 ) )
  #define GetKbReady()    ( bioskey( 1 ) != 0 )
  #define GetBiosTime(x)  ( x = biostime( 0, NULL ) )
  #define CLI()           ( disable() )
  #define STI()           ( enable() )

#else                           /* Definitions for Microsoft C Compiler */

  #define GetKbKey()      ( _bios_keybrd( _KEYBRD_READ ) )
  #define GetKbReady()    ( _bios_keybrd( _KEYBRD_READY ) != 0 )
  #define GetBiosTime(x)  ( _bios_timeofday( _TIME_GETCLOCK, &x ) )
  #define CLI()           ( _disable() )
  #define STI()           ( _enable() )

#endif

/*== Screen routines for Microsoft C ===================*/

#ifndef __TURBOC__                          /* Microsoft C? */

  /*********************************************************/
  /* Gotoxy    : Places the cursor.                      */
  /* Input     : Cursor coordinates.                     */
  /* Output    : None                                    */
  /*********************************************************/

  void gotoxy( int x, int y )
  {
    union REGS regs;                    /* Registers for interrupt call */

    regs.h.ah = 0x02;               /* Function number for interrupt call */
    regs.h.bh = 0;                      /* Color */
    regs.h.dh = y - 1;
    regs.h.dl = x - 1;
    int86( 0x10, &regs, &regs );            /* Interrupt call */
  }

  /*********************************************************/
  /* Clrscr    : Clears the screen.                      */
  /* Input     : None                                    */
  /* Output    : None                                    */
  /*********************************************************/

  void clrscr( void )
  {
    union REGS regs;                    /* Registers for interrupt call */

    regs.h.ah = 0x07;               /* Function number for interrupt call */
    regs.h.al = 0x00;
    regs.h.ch = 0;
    regs.h.cl = 0;
    regs.h.dh = 24;
    regs.h.dl = 79;
    int86( 0x10, &regs, &regs );            /* Interrupt call */
    gotoxy( 1, 1 );                         /* Set cursor */
  }

#endif

/*********************************************************/
/* Delay: Halt program execution for a specific time.  */
/* Input    : PAUSE = Length of time interval in ticks */
/* Output   : None                                     */
/* Info     : One tick = 1/18.2 seconds                */
/*********************************************************/

void delay( unsigned int pause )
{
  long curtime,                         /* Current time.. */
       targtime;                        /* to target time */

  if ( pause )                          /* Pause not 0? */
  {                                     /* No */
    GetBiosTime( targtime );
    targtime += (long) pause;           /* Count to target time */

    do                          /* Delay loop - get current time */
      GetBiosTime( curtime );
    while ( curtime <= targtime );          /* Time elapsed? */
  }                                     /* Yes --> End function */
}

/*********************************************************/
/* ClearKbBuffer : Clears the contents of the keyboard buffer. */
/* Input   : None                                      */
/* Output  : None                                      */
/*********************************************************/

void ClearKbBuffer( void )
{
  CLI();                        /* CLI: Disable hardware interrupts */
  *(int far *) MK_FP(0x40,0x1a) =    /* No more characters in buffer */
  *(int far *) MK_FP(0x40,0x1C);
  STI();                        /* STI: Enable hardware interrupts */
}

/*********************************************************/
/*                  M A I N   P R O G R A M            */
/*********************************************************/
```

```
void main( void )
{
  int        i,                          /* Loop counter */
             ccount;      /* Number of character in keyboard buffer */
  unsigned char ch;                       /* Get keys */

  clrscr();
  printf( "NOKEYC - (c) 1992 by Michael Tischer\n\n" );
  printf( "Keyboard buffer purged when counter reaches 0.\n\n" );

  for ( i = 10; i; --i )                  /* Give user time to */
  {                                        /* press some keys */
    printf( "%5d", i );
    delay( 13 );                           /* Pause for .75 seconds */
  }

/* ClearKbBuffer();  */                    /* Clear the buffer */

/*-- Display characters still in keyboard buffer --------------------*/
```

```
  ccount = 0;                              /* No more characters */
  printf( "\n\nCharacters in keyboard buffer :\n" );

  while GetKbReady()      /* Any more characters in keyboard buffer? */
  {                                        /* Yes --> Read and display */
    ch = GetKbKey();
    printf( "  %3d  ", (int) ch );        /* Display code only first */
    if ( (int) ch > 32 )                   /* Code > 32? */
      printf ( "(%c)", ch );        /* Yes --> Display character as well */
    printf("\n");
    ++ccount;                              /* More than one character found */
  }

  if ( ccount == 0 )                       /* Out of characters? */
    printf( "(None)\n" );                  /* Done */
  printf( "\n" );
}
```

BASIC implementation

Since interrupt suppression is more difficult in BASIC, in this version of the program a different method of clearing the keyboard buffer is used. This process calls BIOS functions 01H and 00H sequentially in a loop until the 01H function call indicates that no more characters are in the buffer.

BASIC listing: NOKEYB.BAS

```
'*********************************************************
'*                   N O K E Y B                       *
'-------------------------------------------------------
'*  Task         : Demonstrates clearing the keyboard buffer. *
'*                 This is useful for protecting the user from *
'*                 accidental keystrokes during an important   *
'*                 command (e.g., deleting files).             *
'-------------------------------------------------------
'*  Author       : Michael Tischer                     *
'*  Developed on  : 01/01/92                            *
'*  Last update   : 01/28/92                            *
'*********************************************************
'-- Main program ---------------------------------------

DIM i AS INTEGER                          'Loop counter

CLS
PRINT ("NOKEYB  - (c) 1992 by Michael Tischer")
PRINT
PRINT ("Keyboard buffer purged when counter reaches 0.")
PRINT

FOR i = 10 TO 0 STEP -1                   'Give user time to
  PRINT i; "    "                         ' press some keys
  SLEEP 1
NEXT

'ClearKbBuffer                            'Clear the buffer

'--- Display characters still in keyboard buffer ----------------------

ccount = 0                                'No more characters
PRINT
```

```
PRINT
PRINT ("Characters in keyboard buffer :")

DO                              'Any more characters in keyboard buffer?
  a$ = INKEY$
  IF a$ <> "" THEN
    FOR i = 1 TO LEN(a$)
      PRINT "  "; ASC(MID$(a$, i, 1)),      'Display code only first
      IF ASC(MID$(a$, i, 1)) > 32 THEN                 'Code > 32?
        PRINT "("; MID$(a$, i, 1); ")"; 'Yes --> Display character also
      END IF
      PRINT
      ccount = ccount + 1               'More than one character found
    NEXT
  END IF
LOOP WHILE a$ <> ""

IF ccount = 0 THEN                        'Out of characters?
  PRINT ("(None)")                              'Done
END IF
PRINT

END

'*********************************************************************
'*  ClearKbBuffer : Clears the contents of the keyboard buffer.     *
'*  Input    : None                                                 *
'*  Output   : None                                                 *
'*********************************************************************
SUB ClearKbBuffer

DO          'Get character from keyboard buffer until buffer is empty
LOOP WHILE INKEY$ <> ""

END SUB
```

5.2.4 Scan Codes

Although the ASCII character set and the extended keyboard codes are standardized, scan codes vary depending on the keyboard. All three keyboard standards work with a different set of scan codes. This is shown in the following two figures, which list the scan codes for the PC/XT and AT keyboards.

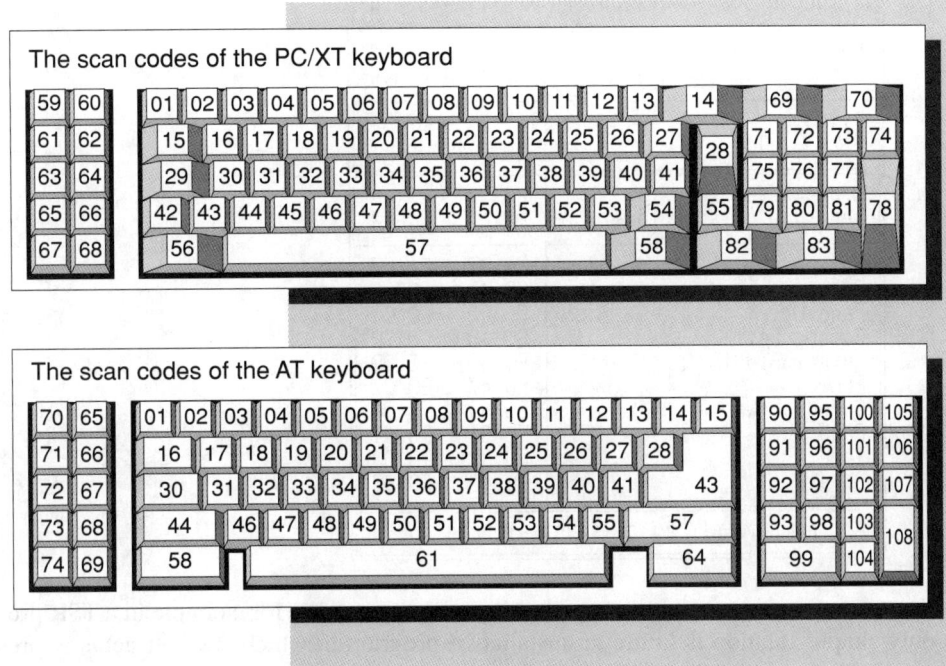

PC/XT and AT scan codes

You cannot always be sure that the break code is the scan code plus 80H. For example, the AT keyboard sends two bytes when a key is released: F0H for a break code, and then the key's scan code. However, the AT keyboard controller handles such incompatibilities. Anything sent through port 60H to the keyboard driver is converted to the normal format.

MF-II extended scan codes

Because of the AT keyboard controller, the MF-II keyboard also returns the same scan codes at port 60H as the AT keyboard, even though they are slightly extended. The MF-II supports three scan code sets that are different from any previous keyboards.

The following illustration lists the additional MF-II keyboard scan codes. A byte containing the value E0H precedes each code. This byte indicates an extended scan code that must be handled in a special way. This is because most of the scan codes are already reserved, and would otherwise be interpreted incorrectly.

In this instance, the break code equals the make code plus 80H and the initial E0H isn't changed. For the cursor keys of the gray cursor block that are used in combination with the <Shift> key,

465

the <Shift> key must first be suppressed. So, the break code for the <Shift> key is sent before this scan code.

For the left <Shift> key, the prefix of this make code is E0H AAH and the prefix of the break code is E0H D2H. For the right <Shift> key, the make code is E0H B6H and the break code is E0H D2H.

Extended Scan Codes on the MF-II Keyboard		
Function keys	Make	Break
F11	57	D7
F12	58	D8
Gray cursor keys in separate cursor block	Make	Break
Home	E0 47	E0 C7
Cursor Up	E0 48	E0 C8
Page Up	E0 49	E0 C9
Cursor Left	E0 4B	E0 CB
Cursor Right	E0 4D	E0 CD
End	E0 47	E0 C7
Cursor Down	E0 50	E0 D0
Page Down	E0 51	E0 D1
Insert	E0 52	E0 D2
Delete	E0 53	E0 D3
All numbers are in hexadecimal notation		

You'll encounter a problem when programming with scan codes, for example in a TSR program. The only simple solution is to use an installation program in which the user actually press the hotkey combinations to be used. Then the program can store the appropriate scan codes. Unless absolutely necessary, don't program with scan codes. Instead, you should use ASCII codes or extended keyboard codes.

Although The scan codes generated by your keyboard or keyboard controller can be listed with the program described in the following section.

5.3   The Keyboard Interrupt Handler

The keyboard is the target of many special programs. Macro recorders, utilities for increasing the size of the keyboard buffer, special keyboard drivers, and TSR programs activated by special hotkeys all affect the operation of the keyboard with their own interrupt handlers.

Depending on the application, these interrupt handlers replace either BIOS keyboard interrupt 09H or 16H. This section contains examples of both types of programs (refer to Chapter 32 for detailed information about TSR programs).

5.3.1 Accessing BIOS Keyboard Interrupt 16H

If you want to extend or change the operations of one of the BIOS keyboard interrupts, simply redirect the interrupt to the interrupt handler within your program. Then when the interrupt executes, your own routine will be called. By doing this, you can insert new functions or redirect functions 00H and 01H to 10H and 11H. This is useful in all high level language programs, in which keyboard reading capabilities are based on various library routines.

Often, these routines simply use functions 00H and 01H of the BIOS keyboard interrupt, blocking the user from reading the <F11> and <F12> keys of the MF-II keyboard. But if you reroute these function calls to the extended functions that support MF-II, you can avoid having to write an extra routine to handle keyboard reading.

A macro utility

The MACROKEY.ASM program is a short macro utility written in assembly language. When you run the executable program from the system prompt, it remains resident in memory until you press the hotkey combination. This version of the program displays the text, "PC Intern published by Abacus" when you press <Alt><N>. You can easily modify the program to display other text by using any other hotkey combination or even by adding multiple macros.

A new BIOS keyboard interrupt handler

The heart of the MACROKEY.ASM program is a new interrupt handler for BIOS keyboard interrupt 16H. We'll discuss this new BIOS keyboard interrupt handler in detail. This handler, which is a routine called NEWI16, is located at the beginning of the program.

At the start of this routine, the STI assembly language instruction enables hardware interrupts. (It's unnecessary to disable interrupts in this program.)

The JMP instruction following the STI checks for an existing MACROKEY program in memory. The "MT" bytes indicate this.

NI1 reads the function number passed in the AH register. The program is only responsible for functions 00H, 01H, 10H, and 11H. Functions 02H and 12H are sent to the old BIOS handler, whose address was stored when the program was started. So, the new handler modifies the old handler instead of completely replacing it.

If a call to one of the desired functions is discovered, the program execution branches to one of two locations, depending on the function required: label FCT0 for 00H or 10H, or FCT1 for 01H or 11H. The functions paired in each group can be handled identically because they both perform the same tasks. In either case, the program checks to see whether the macro has already been called.

If a macro hasn't been called, the new function must determine whether the macro hotkey has been pressed. The specified function is called for the old handler, which returns the function to the AX register if a key has been pressed. The key is compared with the main hotkey code (stored in the MKEY variable at the beginning of the program). The default hotkey is 3100H (<Alt><N>).

The new handler returns the result of the old handler to the caller if the hotkey isn't found. Notice that the function call to 01H or 11H doesn't end with an IRET assembly language instruction. This would also retrieve the flag register from the stack, which was stored there as part of the calling INT instruction. This in turn would change the zero flag's contents, which indicates the availability of a key. The call ends with the VAR RET 2 instruction, which executes a FAR return to the caller just like IRET, but clears the flag register (2 bytes) from the stack without loading it.

If the hotkey is found, the program begins execution. All subsequent calls to 00H/10H or 01H/11H return a character from the macro buffer, instead of calling the old handler to get a keystroke from the keyboard buffer. This can be located using the MSTART variable, which can contain as many characters as you like. The MEND label must also be available. This indicates the offset address where macro playback ends. When this is reached, the old handler functions are called again and keystrokes are taken from the keyboard buffer.

The macro buffer contains only the ASCII character codes, not the scan codes. The value 0 is always returned as the scan code since most programs ignore this value.

Although this saves a lot of work when defining the macro text, it also makes using the extended keyboard codes in the macro text impossible. If necessary, you can always load both the ASCII code and the scan code in the macro buffer so both will be returned to the caller.

Assembler listing: MACROKEY.ASM

```
;*******************************************************;
;*                                                     *;
;*                     M A C R O K E Y                 *;
;*                                                     *;
;*-----------------------------------------------------*;
;*  Task         : Demonstrates the definition of macro keys by *;
;*                 programming a custom handler using BIOS *;
;*                 keyboard interrupt 16H.              *;
;*-----------------------------------------------------*;
;*  Author       : Michael Tischer                     *;
;*  Developed on : 01/03/92                            *;
;*  Last update  : 01/29/92                            *;
;*-----------------------------------------------------*;
;*  Assembly     : MASM MACROKEY                       *;
;*                 LINK MACROKEY                        *;
;*                 EXE2BIN MACROKEY MACROKEY.COM        *;
;*                                                     *;
;*                 or                                  *;
;*                                                     *;
;*                 TASM MACROKEY                        *;
;*                 TLINK /T MACROKEY                    *;
;*-----------------------------------------------------*;
;*  Call         : MACROKEY                            *;
;*******************************************************;

;== Program begins here ================================

code    segment para 'CODE'    ;Define CODE segment

        org 100h

        assume cs:code, ds:code, es:code, ss:code

start:  jmp mcinit             ;Call initialization routine

;== Data (keep in memory) ==============================


olderint  equ this dword       ;Old interrupt vector 16H
intoldoff dw (?)               ;Offset address interrupt vector 16H
intoldseg dw (?)               ;Segment address interrupt vector 16H

mkey      dw 3100h             ;Macro keys: ALT + N
mstart    db "'PC Intern' published by Abacus"
                               ;Macro text
mend      equ this byte

mofs      dw 0FFFFh            ;Pointer to next character from the
                               ;macro text

;== New BIOS keyboard interrupt 16H (keep in memory) ===================

newi16    proc far

          assume cs:code, ds:nothing, es:nothing, ss:nothing

          sti                  ;Re-enable interrupts
          jmp short ni1

          db "MT"              ;Program identifier

ni1:      ;-- First determine whether the new handler applies to the
          ;-- function being called

          or  ah,ah            ;Function 00H or 10H?
          je  fct0
          cmp ah,10h
          je  fct0

          cmp ah,01h           ;Function 01H or 11H?
          je  fct1
          cmp ah,11h
          je  fct1
```

```
              jmp  cs:[olderint]      ;If not, then let function be
                                      ;called by older handler


fct0:    ;-- Function 00H/10H ------------------------------------

              cmp  mofs,offset mend   ;Macro already duplicated?
              jae  check0             ;No --> Check for key

              ;-- If macro is already duplicated, get next key -----------

fct0p:   push bx                      ;Change BX
              mov  bx,mofs            ;Yes --> Pass next character
              mov  al,cs:[bx]         ;Load ASCII code
              xor  ah,ah              ;0 as scan code
              inc  mofs               ;MOFS to next character
              pop  bx                 ;Pop BX from stack

niret0:  iret                        ;Return to caller

check0:  ;-- Check whether macro keys were pressed ------------------

              pushf                   ;Call old handler
              call cs:[olderint]
              cmp  ax,mkey            ;Macro keys pressed?
              jne  niret0             ;No --> Return to caller

              ;-- Macro keys detected, play the macro --------------------

              mov  mofs,offset mstart ;Macro pointer to start of macro
              jmp  fct0p              ;Return first character

fct1:    ;-- Function 01H/11H ------------------------------------

              cmp  mofs,offset mend   ;Macro already duplicated?
              jae  check1             ;No --> Check for key

              ;-- Macro already duplicated, get next character -----------

fct1p:   push bx                      ;Change BX
              mov  bx,mofs            ;Yes --> Pass next character
              mov  al,cs:[bx]         ;Load ASCII code
              xor  ah,ah              ;0 as scan code
              pop  bx                 ;Pop BX from stack
              cmp  ah,1               ;Zero flag at 0: Key available

niret1:  ret 2                        ;Return to caller, but
                                      ;pop flags from stack

check1:  ;-- Check whether macro key has been pressed ---------------

              pushf                   ;Call old handler
              call cs:[olderint]
              je   niret1             ;No keys in keyboard buffer

              cmp  ax,mkey            ;Macro keys pressed?
              je   check1a            ;Yes --> Play macro

              cmp  ax,0               ;Zero flag at 0: Character available
              ret 2                   ;Return to caller, but
                                      ;pop flags from stack

check1a: ;-- Macro key implemented, play macro ----------------------
```

```
              xor  ah,ah             ;Remove macro keys first
              pushf
              call cs:[olderint]

              mov  mofs,offset mstart ;Move macro pointer to start
              jmp  fct1p             ;Get first character

newi16   endp

;== End of memory resident section ======================================

instend  equ this byte

;== Data (can be overwritten by DOS) ===================================

installm db "MACROKEY -  (c) 1992 by Michael Tischer", 13, 10, 13, 10
              db "MACROKEY now installed."
              db 13,10, "Call MACROKEY again to de-install.", 13, 10, "$"

removepg db "MACROKEY de-installed.", 13, 10, "$"

;== Program (can be overwritten by DOS) =================================

mcinit   label near                ;Initialization

              assume cs:code, ds:code, es:code, ss:code

              ;-- First determine whether program is already installed ----

              mov  ax,3516h          ;Get contents of interrupt vector 16H
              int  21h               ;Call DOS function
              cmp  word ptr es:[bx+3],"TM" ;Test for MACROKEY
              jne  mcinstall         ;Not installed --> Do it now

              ;-- If program is already installed, stop and remove it  ----
              ;-- from memory

              mov  dx,es:intoldoff   ;Offset address of interrupt 16H
              mov  ax,es:intoldseg   ;Segment address of interrupt 16H
              mov  ds,ax             ;Move to DS
              mov  ax,2516h          ;Put contents of interrupt vector
              int  21h               ;16H in old routine

              ;-- Release memory allocated for old MACROKEY ---------------

              mov  bx,es             ;Mark segment address of program
              mov  es,es:[2Ch]       ;Get environment seg. addr. from PSP
              mov  ah,49h            ;Release old
              int  21h               ;environment memory

              mov  es,bx             ;Memory for old MACROKEY
              mov  ah,49h            ;Release using DOS
              int  21h               ;function 49H

              push cs                ;Store CS on stack
              pop  ds                ;Pop DS from stack

              mov  ah,09h            ;Message: Program removed
              mov  dx,offset removepg
              int  21h

              mov  ax,4C00h          ;End program in normal manner
              int  21h
```

```
mcinstall:  ;-- Install the program --------------------------------         ;-- data need be resident

        mov  intoldseg,es      ;Pass segment and offset addresses        mov  dx,offset instend  ;Compute the number of 16-byte
        mov  intoldoff,bx      ;of interrupt vector 16H                  add  dx,15              ;paragraphs into which the
                                                                         mov  cl,4               ;program should be inserted
        mov  dx,offset newi16  ;Offset addr.: New interrupt routine      shr  dx,cl
        mov  ax,2516h          ;Hide contents of interrupt vector        mov  ax,3100h           ;End program with end code 0
        int  21h               ;16H in its own routine                   int  21h                ;(O.K.) but keep resident

        mov  dx,offset installm ;Message: Program installed     ;== End ==========================================================
        mov  ah,09h            ;Display function number for string
        int  21h               ;Call DOS function                code    ends                   ;End of CODE segment
                                                                         end  start
        ;-- PSP, new interrupt routine and corresponding ------------
```

5.3.2 Redirecting Keyboard Hardware Interrupts

If you want to access the keyboard at its lowest level, you must capture and redirect keyboard hardware interrupt 90H. We suggest using the existing handler since writing a completely new keyboard handler is a difficult task (refer to the KEYB.COM program using DEBUG).

Capturing scan codes

The GETSCAN.ASM program is a normal transient program that displays scan codes. It lets you view the scan codes of your keyboard on screen before they are actually routed to the keyboard handler. In this way, you can obtain the two byte make code sequences of the <F11> and <F12> function keys and the gray cursor keys, which are otherwise masked by the software.

Running the program in normal operating mode displays only make codes. If you start GETSCAN from the system prompt with the /R switch, break codes will also be displayed.

The main section of this program is the new interrupt handler for keyboard interrupt 09H, which executes each time the user presses or releases a key. The make or break code is received through port 60H and stored in the program's internal scan code buffer (the SCANBUF variable). It's managed as a ring buffer with two pointers, just like the BIOS keyboard buffer. These pointers are called SCANNEXT and SCANLAST.

After the scan codes are stored, the program reverts to the old interrupt handler. The address of this handler was noted at the start of the program. This processes the keystrokes in the usual way and stores them in the keyboard buffer.

This is important because the keyboard buffer contents are read within the program using BIOS functions 01H and 00H until the user presses the <Enter> key. Once <Enter> is pressed, the program ends. Otherwise, the main program continues to read the internal scan code buffer between two BIOS calls. Whatever the new interrupt handler stores in the scan code buffer is immediately read by the main program and removed. The scan codes and break codes aren't lost until the program displays them on the screen.

This program enables you to read the scan codes that your keyboard uses and check for any differences from the standards. You may find some differences on the less expensive imported keyboards, but these differences usually involve seldom used key combinations.

Assembler listing: GETSCAN.ASM

```
;*********************************************************;
;*                    G E T S C A N                     *;
;*-----------------------------------------------------*;
;*   Task        : Displays keyboard scan codes before they can *;
;*                 be filtered and changed by a keyboard driver. *;
;*-----------------------------------------------------*;
;*   Author      : Michael Tischer                      *;
;*   Developed on : 12/08/90                            *;
;*   Last update : 01/29/92                             *;
;*-----------------------------------------------------*;
;*   Assembly     : MASM GETSCAN                        *;
;*                  LINK GETSCAN                        *;
;*                  EXE2BIN GETSCAN GETSCAN.COM         *;
;*                                                      *;
;*                  or                                  *;
;*                                                      *;
;*                  TASM GETSCAN                        *;
;*                  TLINK /T GETSCAN                    *;
;*-----------------------------------------------------*;
;*   Call        : GETSCAN                              *;
;*********************************************************;

;== Constants and structures ===============================

INT_CTR  = 20h               ;Interrupt controller port
EOI      = 20h               ;End of interrupt instruction
KB_PORT  = 60h               ;Keyboard port

;== Program starts here ===============================

code     segment para 'CODE'  ;Define CODE segment

         org 100h

         assume cs:code, ds:code, es:code, ss:code

start:   jmp getscan          ;Jump to actual start of program

;== Data ===============================================

int9_ptr equ this dword       ;Old interrupt vector  9H
int9_ofs dw 0                 ;Offset address of old handler
int9_seg dw 0                 ;Segment address of old handler

allscan  db 0                 ;Display release codes as well?

scanbuf  db 32 dup (0)        ;Scan code buffer
scanend  equ this byte

scannext dw offset scanbuf    ;Next character in scan buffer
scanlast dw offset scanbuf    ;Last character in scan buffer

copyr    db  "GETSCAN - (c) 1990, 92 by MICHAEL TISCHER", 13, 10, 13, 10
         db  "Press any key to see its scan code, ", 13, 10
         db  "or press <Enter> to end the program. "
         db  13, 10, 13, 10, "$"

hexdigits db "0123456789ABCDEF" ;Digits converted to hex numbers

scanmes  db  "Scan code: "    ;Scan code message
scandec  db  "000 ("
scanhex  db  "xx)", 13, 10, "$"
```

```
;== Program code =========================================

getscan: mov  ah,09h          ;Display copyright message
         mov  dx,offset copyr
         int  21h

         ;-- /R switch instructs program to display all codes --------

         cmp  word ptr ds:[130], "R" * 256 + "/"
         je   gsall
         cmp  word ptr ds:[130], "r" * 256 + "/"
         jne  gsnall

gsall:   mov  allscan,1        ;Display release codes as well

gsnall:  ;-- Install new keyboard interrupt handler ------------------

         mov  ax,3509h        ;Get contents of interrupt vector 9H
         int  21h             ;Call DOS interrupt
         mov  int9_seg,es     ;Pass segment and offset addresses
         mov  int9_ofs,bx     ;of interrupt vector 9H

         mov  dx,offset newi9 ;Offset addr. New interrupt routine
         mov  ax,2509h        ;Place interrupt vector 9H
         int  21h             ;in its own routine

gs1:     ;-- Read loop -----------------------------------------

         mov  ah,01h          ;Determine whether a
         int  16h             ;key is ready
         je   gs2             ;No --> GS2

         xor  ah,ah           ;Yes --> Read character
         int  16h
         cmp  al,13           ;Character = <Enter>?
         je   gs4             ;Yes --> End program

gs2:     mov  di,scannext     ;Move pointer to next scan code
         cmp  di,scanlast     ;Buffer empty?
         je   gs1             ;Yes --> Back to start of loop

;== Convert scan code to ASCII and display it ===============

         mov  word ptr scandec, 32 shl 8 + 32
         mov  byte ptr scandec+2, 32

         mov  si,offset scandec+2;Make SI the last number in buffer
         mov  al,[di]         ;Load scan code into AL
         mov  bl,10           ;Divisor is always 10

gs3:     xor  ah,ah           ;Divide high byte by 10
         div  bl              ;Divide AX by 10
         or   ah,'0'          ;Change AH to ASCII format
         mov  [si],ah         ;Place in buffer
         dec  si              ;Address next character
         or   al,al           ;Remainder from division?
         jne  gs3             ;Yes --> Next digit

         ;-- Display code in hexadecimal format ----------------------

         mov  bx,offset hexdigits ;Move BX to table with hex numbers
         mov  al,[di]         ;Isolate low nibble of scan code
         and  al,15
```

```
        xlat                    ;Get hex number from table         new19    proc far
        mov  ah,al              ;Change low digit into high byte
                                                                   assume cs:code, ds:nothing, es:nothing, ss:nothing
        mov  al,[di]            ;Isolate high nibble of scan code
        mov  cl,4                                                          push ax                  ;Push AX onto stack
        shr  al,cl                                                         in   al,KB_PORT          ;Get scan code from keyboard port
        xlat                    ;Get hex number from table
                                                                          cmp  al,128              ;Release code?
        mov  word ptr scanhex,ax ;Place both digits in buffer             jb   19marks             ;No --> Mark it

        ;-- Advance pointer in scan buffer                                 cmp  allscan,0           ;Yes --> Marked?
                                                                          je   19end               ;No --> Return
        inc  di
        cmp  di,offset scanend  ;Overflow?                        19marks: ;-- Place scan code in buffer -----------------------------
        jne  gsnowrap           ;No --> Mark it
                                                                          push di                  ;Push DI onto stack
        mov  di,offset scanbuf  ;Yes --> Back to the start                mov  di,scanlast         ;Move DI to next buffer position
                                                                          mov  cs:[di],al          ;Place scan code at that location
gsnowrap: mov  scannext,di      ;Mark next character position             inc  di                  ;Increment DI to next position
                                                                          cmp  di,offset scanend   ;Overflow?
        ;-- Display message -----------------------------------            jne  19nowrap            ;No ---> Mark it

        mov  ah,09h             ;Display string                           mov  di,offset scanbuf   ;Yes --> Go to beginning
        mov  dx,offset scanmes
        int  21h                                                  19nowrap: mov  scanlast,di        ;Mark next character position
                                                                          pop  di                  ;Pop DI from stack
        jmp  gs1                ;Jump to start of loop
                                                                  19end:   pop  ax                  ;Pass scan code to old
gs4:    ;-- Prepare end of program -----------------------------           jmp  [int9_ptr]          ;keyboard handler

        lds  dx,int9_ptr        ;Back to installing old          new19    endp
        mov  ax,2509h           ;keyboard interrupt handler
        int  21h                                                  ;== End ========================================================

        mov  ax,4C00h           ;Everything is O.K., end program  code     ends                     ;End of CODE segment
        int  21h                                                          end  start

;== Interrupt handler 09H (keyboard) =================================
```

5.4 Programming the Keyboard Controller

The keyboard is an independent unit in the PC system, and has its own microprocessor and memory. The processor informs the system when a key is pressed or released. It does this by sending the system a scan code when a key is pressed or released. In both cases, the key is indicated by a code, which depends on the position of the key. These scan codes aren't related to the ASCII or extended keyboard codes to which the system later converts from the keypresses.

Communication with the system is performed over two bi-directional lines using a synchronous serial communications protocol. In addition to the actual data line used to transfer the individual bits, the clock line synchronizes the periodic transmission of signals. Transfers are made in one-byte increments, whereby a stop bit is transmitted first (with the value 0), followed by the eight data bits, beginning with the least significant bit. A parity bit, calculated using odd parity, follows the eighth data bit. Byte transfer then concludes with a stop bit, which forms the eleventh bit of the transfer. At both ends of the communications line (i.e., in the PC and in the keyboard itself) are devices that convert the signals on the data line to bytes and back again.

Although all types of PCs use this form of communication, we must distinguish between PC/XT and AT models. These systems use different processors as keyboard controllers. The Intel 8048 used in PC and XT keyboards is a relatively "dumb" device, which can only send scan codes to the system. However, the 8042 processor used in AT, 80386, and 80486 keyboards can do much more. With this processor, the communication between the system and the keyboard becomes more complex, and the system can even control parts of the keyboard.

For the keyboard, the basis of this communication is represented by a status register, and input and output buffers. The buffers transfer:

- Keyboard codes that correspond to pressing or releasing a key.

- Data that the system requests from the keyboard.

These buffers can be accessed at port 60H on the AT.

The input buffer can be written at port 60H as well as port 64H. The port that is used depends on the type of information to be transferred. If the system wants to send a command code to the keyboard, the code must be sent to port 60H, while the corresponding data byte must be sent to port 64H. Both end up in the keyboard input buffer, but a flag in the status register indicates whether a command byte (port 64H) or a data byte (port 60H) is involved.

In addition to this flag, bits 0 and 1 of the keyboard status register are especially important for communication with the keyboard. Bit 0 indicates the status of the output buffer. If this bit is 1, then the output buffer of the keyboard contains information that hasn't been read from port 60H yet. Reading from this port will automatically set this bit back to 0, indicating there is no longer a character in the output buffer.

Bit 1 of the status register is always set whenever the system has placed a character in the input buffer, before this character is processed by the keyboard. Nothing should be written to the keyboard input buffer unless this bit is equal to 0, which indicates that the input buffer is empty.

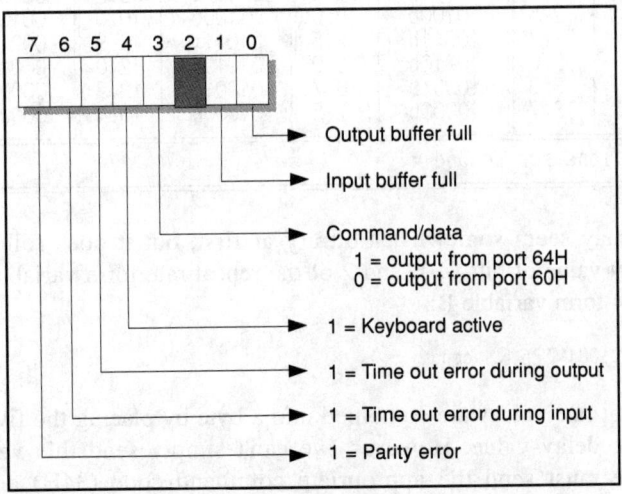

5.4.1 Typematic Rate

Of the various commands that a system can send to the keyboard, two are important to applications because they also play a role outside a keyboard interrupt handler. The first of these commands sets the typematic (repeat) rate of the keyboard. This is the number of make codes per second that the keyboard will send to the system when a key is pressed and held down. It can be between two and 30 codes per second. To prevent the keys from repeating unintentionally, this repeat function doesn't begin until after a certain delay. This delay time can be set by the user and is encoded in binary as follows:

Coding for AT keyboard delay rate	
Code	Delay rate
00b	1/4 second
01b	1/2 second
10b	1/4 second
11b	1 second

The keyboard will observe these times with a tolerance of 20%.

The repeat rate is also encoded in binary. The following table shows the relationship between the repeat (typematic) rate and the number of repetitions per second.

Typematic rate codes for the AT keyboard							
Code	RPS*	Code	RPS	Code	RPS	Code	RPS
11111b	2.0	10111b	4.0	01111b	8.0	00111b	16.0
11110b	2.1	10110b	4.3	01110b	8.6	00110b	17.1
11101b	2.3	10101b	4.6	01101b	9.2	00101b	18.5
11100b	2.5	10100b	5.0	01100b	10.0	00100b	20.0
11011b	2.7	10011b	5.5	01011b	10.9	00011b	21.8
11010b	3.0	10010b	6.0	01010b	12.0	00010b	24.0
11001b	3.3	10001b	6.7	01001b	13.3	00001b	26.7
11000b	3.7	10000b	7.5	01000b	15.0	00000b	30.0
*Repetitions per second							

This relationship may seem somewhat arbitrary at first, but it does follow a mathematical formula. The binary value of bits 0, 1, and 2 of the repeat rate form variable A, and the binary value of bits 3 and 4 form variable B:

$$(8 + A) * 2^B * 0.00417 * 1/second$$

The delay and repeat rate values are combined into a byte by placing the five bits of the repeat rate in front of the delay value. However, we can't simply send this value straight to the keyboard. First we must send the appropriate command code (34H) and then the repeat parameters. Both bytes must be sent to port 60H, but we cannot send them with an OUT instruction. We must use a transmission protocol that includes reading the keyboard status, and which also accounts for the possibility that the transfer might not work the first time. Since we must do this for both bytes, we should write a subroutine to do it. The structure of this subroutine is shown in the following flowchart.

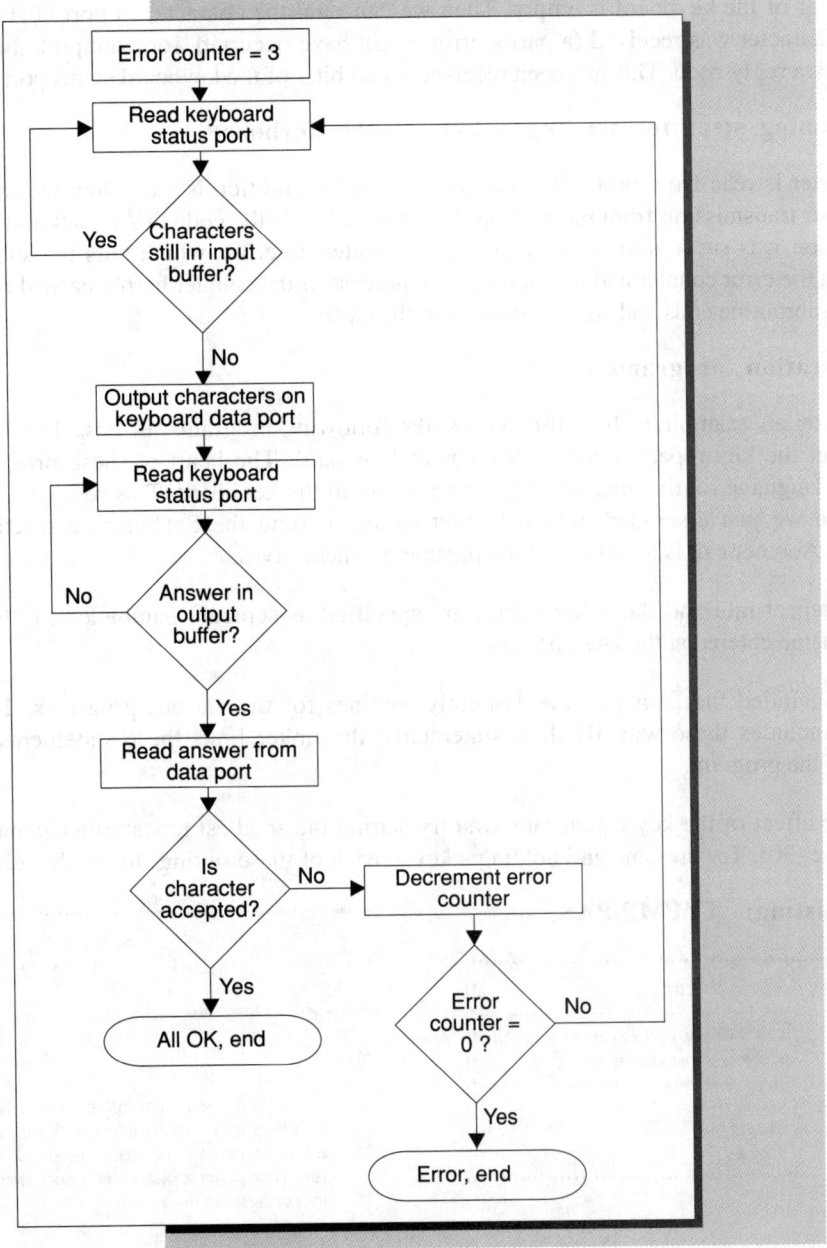

Program flowchart—byte transfer from keyboard

Sending bytes to the keyboard

First we load an error counter that allows the routine to try to send the byte three times before an error is returned. Then the keyboard status port is read in a loop until bit 0 is cleared and the input buffer of the keyboard is empty. Then we can send the character to port 60H. To ensure that the character was received (a parity error might have occurred, for example), the keyboard sends back a reply code. This has been received when bit 1 of the keyboard status port is set.

Programming steps for sending a byte to the keyboard

This register is read from port 64H in a loop until this condition is met. Now we can read the reply to our transmission from the keyboard data port. If it is the code 0FAH (acknowledge), the transmission was successful. Any other code indicates an error, which tells the subroutine to decrement the error counter and repeat the entire process, if the counter hasn't reached zero. In this case, the subroutine ends and signals an error to the caller.

Demonstration programs

To give you an example of how this works, the following programs, in Pascal and C, can be used to set the key repeat parameters on your keyboard. The heart of these programs is an assembly language routine that sends the parameters to the keyboard. This routine contains the subroutine we just discussed, which is first called to send the SetTypm instruction to the keyboard. Another call is used to send the parameters themselves.

The key repeat rate and the delay values are specified as separate parameters, following the program name entered at the DOS prompt.

We also included the listing of the assembly routines for the various programs. The Pascal program includes these with INLINE statements; the linker links these statements to the C version of the program.

To see the effect of the key repeat rate, first try setting the smallest repeat rate (0) and then the highest rate (30). Try pressing and holding a key at each of these settings to see the results.

Pascal listing: TYPMP.PAS

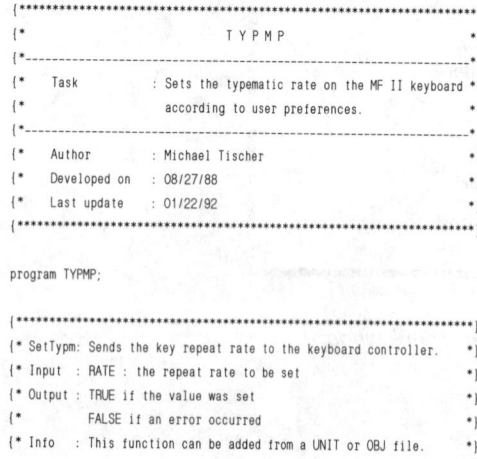

```
{************************************************************}
{*                        T Y P M P                        *}
{*-------------------------------------------------------- *}
{*  Task       : Sets the typematic rate on the MF II keyboard *}
{*               according to user preferences.            *}
{*-------------------------------------------------------- *}
{*  Author     : Michael Tischer                           *}
{*  Developed on : 08/27/88                                *}
{*  Last update : 01/22/92                                 *}
{************************************************************}

program TYPMP;

{************************************************************}
{* SetTypm: Sends the key repeat rate to the keyboard controller. *}
{* Input  : RATE : the repeat rate to be set               *}
{* Output : TRUE if the value was set                      *}
{*          FALSE if an error occurred                     *}
{* Info   : This function can be added from a UNIT or OBJ file. *}
```

```
{************************************************************}

{$F+}                          { This function uses the FAR call model }

function SetTypm( Rate : byte ) : boolean;

begin
  inline(
     $32/$D2/$B4/$F3/$FA/$E8/$13/$00/$75/$0A/$8A/$66/$06/$E8/
     $0B/$00/$75/$02/$FE/$C2/$FB/$88/$56/$FF/$EB/$27/$90/$51/
     $53/$B3/$03/$33/$C9/$E4/$64/$A8/$02/$E0/$FA/$8A/$C4/$E6/
     $60/$E4/$64/$A8/$01/$E1/$FA/$E4/$60/$3C/$FA/$74/$07/$FE/
     $CB/$75/$E6/$80/$CB/$01/$5B/$59/$C3
  );
end;

{$F-}

{************************************************************}
{**                    MAIN PROGRAM                      **}
{************************************************************}
```

```
var Delay,                         { Stores the delay }
    Speed,                         { Stores the key repeat rate }
    Fpos1,
    FPos2  : integer;       { Error position in string conversion }
    ParErr : boolean;              { Error in parameter passing }

begin
  writeln(#13#10,'TYPMP  -  (c) 1988, 92 by MICHAEL TISCHER');
  ParErr := true;                  { Assume error in parameters }
  if ParamCount = 2 then           { Were 2 parameters passed? }
    begin                                                { Yes }
      val(ParamStr(1), Delay, FPos1);  { First parameter to integer }
      val(ParamStr(2), Speed, FPos2);  { Second parameter to integer }
      if ((FPos1=0) and (FPos2=0)) then     { Error in conversion? }
        if ((Delay < 4) and (Speed <32)) then  { No --> Value O.K.? }
          ParErr := false;            { Yes --> Parameters are O.K. }
    end;
  if ( ParErr ) then               { Are parameters O.K.? }
    begin                                                { No }
      writeln('Syntax: TYPMP       delay     key_repeat_rate');
      writeln('                          ',#30,'            ',#30);
      writeln('                          |                |');
      writeln('             ┌─────────────┐ ┌─────────────────────┐');
      writeln('             |  0 : 1/4 second  | | 0 : 30.0 reps/sec |');
      writeln('             |  1 : 1/2 second  | | 1 : 26.7 reps/sec |');
      writeln('             |  2 : 3/4 second  | | 2 : 24.0 reps/sec |');
      writeln('             |  3 : 1 second    | | 3 : 21.8 reps/sec |');
      writeln('             ├──────────────┤ |         .           |');
      writeln('             | all values +-20% |         .           |');
      writeln('             └──────────────┘ |         .           |');
      writeln('                              | 28 :  2.5 reps/sec |');
      writeln('                              | 29 :  2.3 reps/sec |');
      writeln('                              | 30 :  2.1 reps/sec |');
      writeln('                              | 31 :  2.0 reps/sec |');
      writeln('                              └─────────────────────┘');
    end
  else                             { The parameters are O.K. }
  begin
    if (SetTypm( (Delay shl 5) + Speed )) then  { Set key repeat rate }
      writeln('The keyboard repeat rate was set.')
    else
      writeln('ERROR accessing the keyboard controller.');
  end;
end.
```

Assembler listing: TYPMPA.ASM

```
;******************************************************************;
;*                      T Y P M P A                             *;
;*--------------------------------------------------------------*;
;*   Task       : Assembler routine for use with a Turbo Pascal *;
;*                program, which sets the key repeat rate of    *;
;*                the MF II keyboard.                           *;
;*--------------------------------------------------------------*;
;*   Author     : Michael Tischer                               *;
;*   Developed on : 08/27/88                                    *;
;*   Last update  : 01/22/92                                    *;
;*--------------------------------------------------------------*;
;*   Assembly    : MASM TYPMPA;                                 *;
;*                 LINK TYPMPA;                                 *;
;*                 EXE2BIN TYPMPA TYPMPA.BIN                    *;
;*                 ... convert to INLINE statements             *;
;******************************************************************;

;== Constants =================================================

KB_STATUS_P   equ 64h           ;Keyboard status port
KB_DATA_P     equ 60h           ;Keyboard data port

OB_FULL       equ 1             ;Bit 0 in the keyboard status port
                                ;A character in the output buffer

IB_FULL       equ 2             ;Bit 1 in the keyboard status port
                                ;A character in the input buffer

ACK_SIGNAL    equ 0fah          ;Keyboard acknowledge signal
SET_TYPEM     equ 0f3h          ;Set key repeat code

MAX_TRY       equ 3             ;Number of retries

;== Program code =================================================

code     segment para 'CODE'    ;Define CODE segment

         org   100h

         assume cs:code, ds:code, ss:code, es:code


;------------------------------------------------------------------
;-- SET_TYPM: Determines the key repeat rate to be sent to the -------
;--          keyboard controller.
;-- Info  : Set up as a NEAR call
set_typm   proc near              ;GW expects FAR procedures

sframe0    struc                  ;Stack access structure
bp0        dw  ?                  ;Store BP
ret_adr0   dd  ?                  ;Return address to the caller
                                  ;(FAR address)
trate0     dw  ?                  ;Address of the var with the rep rate
sframe0    ends                   ;End of the structure

frame      equ [ bp - bp0 ]       ;Address structure elements

                                  ;Turbo executes the following
;          push bp                ;Push BP onto the stack
;          mov  bp,sp             ;Move SP to BP

           xor  dl,dl             ;Assume transfer failed
           mov  ah,SET_TYPEM      ;Set command code for key rep rate
           cli                    ;Disable interrupts
```

```
        call send_kb          ;Send to the controller
        jne  error            ;Error? Yes --> Error

        mov  ah,byte ptr frame.trate0  ;Get TYPRATE variable addr.
        call send_kb          ;Send to the controller
        jne  error            ;Error? Yes --> Error

        inc  dl               ;Everything O.K., return TRUE

error:  sti                   ;Enable interrupts
        mov  [bp-1],dl        ;Put error static there
        pop  bp               ;Pop BP off of stack
        jmp  ende             ;Return to Turbo Pascal
set_typm endp


;-------------------------------------------------------------------
;-- SEND_KB: Sends a byte to the keyboard controller ---------------
;-- Input    : AH = the byte to be sent
;-- Output   : Zero flag=0: Error
;--            Zero flag=1: O.K.
;-- Registers: AX and FLAGS are affected
;-- Info     : this routine is intended for use only within this
;--            module

send_kb  proc near

        push cx               ;Push all registers used in this
        push bx               ;routine onto the stack

        mov  bl,MAX_TRY       ;Maximum of MAX_TRY retries

        ;-- Wait until the controller is ready to receive data ------

skb_1:  xor  cx,cx            ;Maximum of 65536 loop passes
skb_2:  in   al,KB_STATUS_P   ;Read contents of the status port
        test al,IB_FULL       ;Still a char. in the input buffer?
        loopne skb_2          ;yes --> SKB_2

        ;-- Send character to the controller -----------------------

        mov  al,ah            ;Get character in AL
        out  KB_DATA_P,al     ;Send character to the data port
skb_3:  in   al,KB_STATUS_P   ;Read contents of the status port
        test al,OB_FULL       ;Answer in the output buffer?
        loope skb_3           ;No --> SKB_3

        ;-- Get reply from controller and evaluate -----------------

        in   al,KB_DATA_P     ;Read reply from data port
        cmp  al,ACK_SIGNAL    ;Was the character accepted?
        je   skb_end          ;Yes --> Everything O.K.

        ;-- The character was not accepted -------------------------

        dec  bl               ;Decrement error counter
        jne  skb_2            ;Retries left?
                              ;Yes --> SKB_2

        or   bl,1             ;NO --> Set zero flag to 0,
                              ;indicating an error

skb_end: pop bx               ;Pop registers off of stack
        pop  cx
        ret                   ;Return to caller
```

```
send_kb  endp

;----------------------------------------------------------------
ende         label near
;== End =========================================================

code     ends                 ;End code segment
         end set_typm
```

C listing: TYPMC.C

```
/*************************************************************/
/*                      T Y P M C                        */
/*-----------------------------------------------------------*/
/*  Task        : Sets the typematic rate on the MF II keyboard */
/*                according to user preferences.             */
/*-----------------------------------------------------------*/
/*  Author      : Michael Tischer                          */
/*  Developed on : 08/28/88                                */
/*  Last update  : 01/21/92                                */
/*-----------------------------------------------------------*/
/*  Memory model : SMALL                                   */
/*-----------------------------------------------------------*/
/*  Modules      : TYPMC.C + TYPMCA.ASM                    */
/*  Info         : Microsoft C requires separate compiling and */
/*                 linking:                                 */
/*                 CL /AS /c TYPMC.C                        */
/*                 LINK TYPMC TYPMCA;                       */
/*                 If you omit the /c switch, Microsoft C will */
/*                 give an 'unresolved external' error.     */
/*************************************************************/

/*== Add include files ==================================*/

#include <stdlib.h>
#include <stdio.h>

/*== Type definitions ===================================*/

typedef unsigned char byte;             /* Create a byte */
typedef byte bool;                  /* Specify TRUE or FALSE */

/*== Constants ==========================================*/

#define TRUE  ( 1 == 1 )            /* Needed when working with BOOL */
#define FALSE ( 0 == 1 )

/*== Link external functions from the assembly language module ======*/

extern bool set_typm( byte trate );     /* Set the typematic rate */

/*************************************************************/
/**                 MAIN PROGRAM                         **/
/*************************************************************/

void main(int argc, char *argv[] )
{
 int delay,                      /* Stores the specified delay */
     speed;                      /* Stores the specified repeat rate */

 printf("\nTYPMC  -  (c) 1988, 92 by MICHAEL TISCHER\n");
 if (argc!=3 || ( (delay = atoi(argv[1]))<0 || delay>3 ) ||
              ( (speed = atoi(argv[2]))<0 || speed>31 ))
   {                            /* Illegal parameters were passed */
    printf("Syntax: TYPMC    delay    key_repeat_rate\n");
    printf("                  \x1e              \x1e\n");
    printf("                   |              |\n");
    printf("        ┌──────────────┐ ┌──────────────────────┐\n");
    printf("        ‖ 0 : 1/4 second ‖ ‖ 0 : 30.0 reps/sec. ‖\n");
    printf("        ‖ 1 : 1/2 second ‖ ‖ 1 : 26.7 reps/sec. ‖\n");
    printf("        ‖ 2 : 3/4 second ‖ ‖ 2 : 24.0 reps/sec. ‖\n");
    printf("        ‖ 3 : 1   second ‖ ‖ 3 : 21.8 reps/sec. ‖\n");
    printf("        ‖────────────────‖ ‖                    ‖\n");
    printf("        ‖ All values +-20%% ‖ ‖                  ‖\n");
    printf("        └────────────────┘ ‖                    ‖\n");
    printf("                           ‖ 28 :  2.5 reps/sec. ‖\n");
    printf("                           ‖ 29 :  2.3 reps/sec. ‖\n");
    printf("                           ‖ 30 :  2.1 reps/sec. ‖\n");
    printf("                           ‖ 31 :  2.0 reps/sec. ‖\n");
    printf("                           └────────────────────┘\n");
   }
 else                                /* The parameters are O.K. */
  {
   if (set_typm( (byte) ((delay << 5) + speed )))   /* Set typematic */
    printf("Typematic rate now set.\n");
   else
    printf("Keyboard controller access error.\n");
  }
}
```

Assembler listing: TYPMCA.ASM

```
;***************************************************************.
;*                     T Y P M C A                          *;
;*-----------------------------------------------------------*;
;*  Description : Assembler routine for setting the key repeat *;
;*                rate on an AT keyboard. For linking with a   *;
;*                C program.                                   *;
;*-----------------------------------------------------------*;
;*  Author      : Michael Tischer                            *;
;*  Developed on : 08/27/88                                  *;
;*  Last update  : 01/22/92                                  *;
;*-----------------------------------------------------------*;
;*  Assembly    : MASM TYPMCA;                               *;
;*                ... link with a C program                  *;
;***************************************************************.


;== Constants ===============================================

KB_STATUS_P  equ 64h          ;Keyboard status port
KB_DATA_P    equ 60h          ;Keyboard data port

OB_FULL      equ 1            ;Bit 0 in keyboard status port
                              ;A character in the output buffer
IB_FULL      equ 2            ;Bit 1 in the keyboard status port
                              ;A character in the input buffer

ACK_SIGNAL   equ 0fah         ;Keyboard acknowledge signal
SET_TYPEM    equ 0f3h         ;Set typematic rate code

MAX_TRY      equ 3            ;Number of retries allowed

;== Segment declarations for the C program =====================

IGROUP group _text            ;Combination of the program segments
DGROUP group const,_bss, _data ;Combination of the data segments
       assume CS:IGROUP, DS:DGROUP, ES:DGROUP, SS:DGROUP

CONST  segment word public 'CONST';This segment stores all of the
CONST  ends                   ;read-only constants

_BSS   segment word public 'BSS' ;This segment stores all of the
_BSS   ends                   ;uninitialized static variables

_DATA  segment word public 'DATA' ;This segment stores all of the ini-
                              ;tialized global and static variables
_DATA  ends

;== Program =================================================

_TEXT  segment byte public 'CODE' ;CODE segment

public   _set_typm
;------------------------------------------------------------
;-- SET_TYPM: Sends the key repeat rate to the keyboard controller ----
;-- Call from C : bool set_typm( byte trate );
;-- Return value: TRUE if the repeat rate was set
;--               FALSE if an error occurred

_set_typm  proc near

sframe0    struc              ;Structure for accessing the stack
bp0        dw ?               ;Stores BP
ret_adr0   dw ?               ;Return address to caller
```

```
trate0     dw ?               ;Repeat rate to be set
sframe0    ends               ;End of structure

frame      equ [ bp - bp0 ]   ;Address structure elements

           push bp            ;Push BP onto the stack
           mov  bp,sp         ;Move SP to BP

           xor  dx,dx         ;Assume transfer fails
           mov  ah,SET_TYPEM  ;Set command code for rep rate
           cli                ;Disable interrupts
           call send_kb       ;Send to the controller
           jne  error         ;Error? Yes --> Error routine

           mov  ah,byte ptr frame.trate0
                              ;Get key repeat rate
           call send_kb       ;Send to the controller
           jne  error         ;Error? Yes --> Error routine

           inc  dl            ;Everything O.K., return TRUE

error:     sti                ;Enable interrupts
           mov  ax,dx         ;Return value to AX
           pop  bp            ;Pop BP from the stack
           ret                ;Return to the C program

_set_typm  endp


;------------------------------------------------------------
;-- SEND_KB: Sends a byte to the keyboard controller ------------------
;-- Input    : AH = the byte to be sent
;-- Output   : Zero flag=0: Error
;--                  Zero flag=1: O.K.
;-- Registers: AX and FLAGS are affected
;-- Info     : This routine is to be called only within the module

send_kb    proc near

           push cx            ;Push all registers changed by
           push bx            ;in this routine onto the stack

           mov  bl,MAX_TRY    ;Maximum of MAX_TRY retries

           ;-- Wait until the controller is ready to receive data ------

skb_1:     xor  cx,cx         ;Maximum of 65536 loop passes
skb_2:     in   al,KB_STATUS_P ;Read contents of status port
           test al,IB_FULL    ;Still a char in the input buffer?
           loopne skb_2       ;Yes --> SKB_2

           ;-- Send character to the controller ------------------------

           mov  al,ah         ;Get character in AL
           out  KB_DATA_P,al  ;Send character to the data port
skb_3:     in   al,KB_STATUS_P ;Read contents of the status port
           test al,OB_FULL    ;Reply in output buffer?
           loope skb_3        ;No --> SKB_3

           ;-- Get and process reply from controller -------------------

           in   al,KB_DATA_P  ;Read reply from data port
           cmp  al,ACK_SIGNAL ;Was the character accepted?
           je   skb_end       ;Yes --> Everything O.K.
```

```
    ;-- The character was not accepted -------------------------        pop  cx
                                                                        ret                ;Return to caller

    dec  bl               ;Decrement error counter
    jne  skb_2            ;Still retries left?                  send_kb  endp
                          ;Yes --> SKB_2
                                                                ;-------------------------------------------------
    or   bl,1             ;No --> Set zero flag to 0 to
                          ;      indicate the error            _text    ends              ;End code segment
                                                                        end               ;End program
skb_end: pop  bx          ;Pop registers from the stack
```

5.4.2 LEDs

We can use this same method to switch the LEDs on the AT keyboard on and off. The corresponding instruction code is number 0EDH, and is called the Set/Reset Mode Indicators instruction.

After this command code has been successfully transmitted, the keyboard waits for a byte that reflects the status of the three LEDs. One bit in this byte represents one of the three LEDs, which is switched on when the corresponding bit is set.

Bit Number	LED
0	Scroll Lock
1	Num Lock
2	Caps Lock
3-7	Unused

Setting and resetting these bits is useful only when the keyboard mode, which they indicate, is enabled or disabled.

These modes are managed in the BIOS instead of the keyboard. For example, the keyboard doesn't automatically convert all of the letters to uppercase in <Caps Lock> mode. The keyboard can only associate a key with a virtual key number instead of a specific character. This key number is then converted to an ASCII or extended keyboard code by the BIOS. Obviously this also applies to the <Caps Lock> key, which simply sends a scan code to the computer when it's pressed. The BIOS assigns the <Caps Lock> function to this key by setting an internal flag that marks this mode as active, then sends the Set/Reset Mode Indicators instruction to the keyboard to switch on the appropriate LED.

Although these keyboard modes are usually enabled and disabled by the user pressing the corresponding keys, it may be useful to set a mode from within a program. This applies to keyboards that have separate cursor keys and a numerical keypad, for example. Since most keyboards can only enter numbers when Num Lock mode is on, it makes sense to set this mode automatically when the system is started.

To do this we simply set the appropriate BIOS flag and then switch on the corresponding LED on the keyboard to inform the user that this mode has been activated.

In practice, a program simply must set the appropriate BIOS mode, since the BIOS automatically controls the keyboard LEDs. Whenever one of the functions of the BIOS keyboard interrupt is called, the BIOS checks to see whether the status of the LEDs matches the keyboard status, as indicated in an internal variable. If an inconsistency is found, the BIOS automatically sets the LEDs to the status given in the keyboard status flag.

Since the position of this flag in the BIOS variable segment and the meaning of the individual bits is completely documented (see Chapter 3), we can easily change these modes.

The following programs in BASIC, Pascal, and C offer routines that can enable or disable the individual modes. Although PCs and XTs have corresponding LEDs, these programs won't work or change the modes without changing the status of the LEDs on a PC or XT keyboard. This is because these keyboards are equipped with an 8048 processor, which doesn't offer the ability to manage the LEDs. The fact that these LEDs do switch on and off according to the modes isn't related to the BIOS and is handled directly by the keyboard.

BASIC listing: LEDB.BAS

```
'****************************************************************
'*                            LEDB                             *
'*------------------------------------------------------------*
'*  Task        : Sets the various bits in the BIOS keyboard   *
'*                flag, causing the LEDs on the AT keyboard to *
'*                flash.                                        *
'*                QuickBASIC and the QB.LIB must be loaded using*
'*                QB /L QB                                      *
'*                before loading and running this file.        *
'*------------------------------------------------------------*
'*  Author      : Michael Tischer                              *
'*  Developed on : 06/08/91                                    *
'*  Last update  : 01/20/92                                    *
'****************************************************************

DECLARE SUB SetFlag (Flag AS INTEGER)
DECLARE SUB Delay (Pause AS INTEGER)
DECLARE SUB ClrFlag (Flag AS INTEGER)

'$INCLUDE: 'QB.BI'                       'Include register declarations

CONST SCRL = 16                          'SCROLL LOCK bit
CONST NUML = 32                          'NUM LOCK bit
CONST CAPL = 64                          'CAPS LOCK bit

DIM Counter AS INTEGER                   'Loop counter

CLS                                      'Clear screen
PRINT " LEDB  -  (c) 1988, 92 by Michael Tischer"
PRINT
PRINT " Look at the LEDs on your keyboard"

FOR Counter = 1 TO 10                    'Run through the loop 10 times
   SetFlag (CAPL)                        'Turn CAPS on
   Delay (100)                           'Wait 100 milliseconds
   ClrFlag (CAPL)                        'Turn CAPS off again
   SetFlag (NUML)                        'Turn NUM LOCK on
   Delay (100)                           'Wait 100 milliseconds
   ClrFlag (NUML)                        'NUM LOCK off again
   SetFlag (SCRL)                        'Turn SCROLL LOCK on
   Delay (100)                           'Wait 100 milliseconds
   ClrFlag (SCRL)                        'Turn SCROLL LOCK off again
NEXT

FOR Counter = 1 TO 10                    'Run through the loop 10 times
   SetFlag (CAPL OR SCRL OR NUML)        'Turn all three flags on
   Delay (500)                           'Wait 500 milliseconds
   ClrFlag (CAPL OR SCRL OR NUML)        'Turn all three flags off
   Delay (500)                           'Wait 500 milliseconds
NEXT
END

'****************************************************************
'*  ClrFLAG : Clears a flag in the BIOS status byte.           *
'*  Input   : The flag to be cleared (see constants)           *
'*  Output  : None                                             *
'****************************************************************

SUB ClrFlag (Flag AS INTEGER)

DIM Register AS RegType                  'Processor registers

DEF SEG = &H40          'Segment address of BIOS keyboard status byte
POKE &H17, (PEEK(&H17) AND (NOT Flag))   'Clear keyboard status byte
Register.ax = 1 * 256          'AH = Function number: Character ready?
CALL INTERRUPT(&H16, Register, Register)  'Call BIOS keyboard interrupt

END SUB

'****************************************************************
'*  Delay   : Wait a certain length of time in milliseconds.   *
'*  Input   : PAUSE = The number of milliseconds to wait.      *
'*  Output  : None                                             *
'****************************************************************

SUB Delay (Pause AS INTEGER)

DIM Register AS RegType          'Processor registers for interrupt
DIM Time AS LONG                         'Get the target time value

Register.ax = 0                          'Function no.: Read time counter
CALL INTERRUPT(&H1A, Register, Register)   'Call BIOS timer interrupt
Time = Register.dx + (Register.cx * 32768)        'Compute target
Time = Time + (Pause * 18 + ((Pause * 2) / 10)) / 1000 '  time value
DO
   CALL INTERRUPT(&H1A, Register, Register)  'Call timer interrupt until
LOOP WHILE (Register.dx + (Register.cx * 32768)) <= Time  'time elapses

END SUB

'****************************************************************
'*  SETFLAG : Sets a flag in the BIOS status byte.             *
'*  Input   : The flag to be set (see constants).              *
```

```
'*  Output  : None                                            *
'*************************************************************************
'
SUB SetFlag (Flag AS INTEGER)

DIM Register AS RegType     'Processor registers for interrupt call

DEF SEG = &H40              'Segment address of BIOS keyboard status byte
POKE &H17, (PEEK(&H17) OR Flag)             'OR status byte flag
Register.ax = 1 * 256       'AH = Function number: Character ready?
CALL INTERRUPT(&H16, Register, Register)  'Call BIOS keyboard interrupt

END SUB
```

Pascal listing: LEDP.PAS

```
{*************************************************************************}
{*                       L E D P                                       *}
{*---------------------------------------------------------------------*}
{*    Task         : Sets the various bits in the BIOS keyboard         *}
{*                   status byte, causing the LEDs on the MF II         *}
{*                   keyboard flash.                                    *}
{*---------------------------------------------------------------------*}
{*    Author       : Michael Tischer                                   *}
{*    Developed on  : 08/16/88                                          *}
{*    Last update  : 01/23/92                                          *}
{*************************************************************************}

program LEDP;

uses CRT,                               { Add the CRT and DOS units }
     DOS;

const SCRL = 16;                               { Scroll Lock bit }
      NUML = 32;                                  { Num Lock bit }
      CAPL = 64;                                 { Caps Lock bit }
      INS  = 128;                                   { Insert bit }


{*************************************************************************}
{* SETFLAG: Sets one of the flags in the BIOS keyboard status byte.    *}
{* Input : The flag to be set (see constants)                          *}
{* Output : None                                                       *}
{*************************************************************************}

procedure SetFlag(Flag : byte);

var BiosTSByte : byte absolute $0040:$0017;   { BIOS kbd. status byte }
    Regs       : Registers;  { Processor registers for interrupt call }

begin
  BiosTSByte := BiosTSByte or Flag;  { Mask out the corresponding bit }
  Regs.AH := 1;                      { Function no.: Character ready? }
  intr($16, Regs);                      { Call BIOS keyboard interrupt }
end;


{*************************************************************************}
{* CLRFLAG: clears one of the flags in the BIOS keyboard status byte.*}
{* Input   : the flag to be cleared (see constants)                    *}
{* Output : none                                                       *}
{*************************************************************************}

procedure ClrFlag(Flag : byte);

var BiosTSByte : byte absolute $0040:$0017;   { BIOS kbd. status byte }
    Regs       : Registers;  { Processor registers for interrupt call }

begin
  BiosTSByte := BiosTSByte and ( not Flag );           { mask out bit }
  Regs.AH := 1;                      { Function no.: character ready? }
  intr($16, Regs);                      { Call BIOS keyboard interrupt }
end;


{*************************************************************************}
{**                        MAIN PROGRAM                              **}
{*************************************************************************}

var counter : integer;
```

```
begin
  writeln('LEDP  -  (c) 1988 by Michael Tischer');
  writeln(#13,#10, 'Watch the LEDs on your keyboard');

  for counter:=1 to 10 do          { Run through the loop 10 times }
    begin
      SetFlag( CAPL);                         { Enable CAPS }
      Delay( 100 );                  { Wait 100 milliseconds }
      ClrFlag( CAPL );                       { Disable CAPS }
      SetFlag( NUML);                         { Enable NUM }
      Delay( 100 );                  { Wait 100 milliseconds }
      ClrFlag( NUML );                       { Disable NUM }
      SetFlag( SCRL);                    { Enable SCROLL LOCK }
      Delay( 100 );                  { Wait 100 milliseconds }
      ClrFlag( SCRL );                  { Disable SCROLL LOCK }
    end;

  for counter:=1 to 10 do          { Run through loop 10 times }
    begin
      SetFlag(CAPL or SCRL or NUML);     { All three flags on }
      Delay( 500 );                  { Wait 500 milliseconds }
      ClrFlag(CAPL or SCRL or NUML);    { All flags off again }
      Delay( 500 );                  { Wait 500 milliseconds }
    end;
end.
```

C listing: LEDC.C

```c
/********************************************************************/
/*                        L E D C                                *)
/*----------------------------------------------------------------*/
/*  Task       : Sets the various bits in the BIOS keyboard       */
/*               flag, causing the LEDs on the AT keyboard to     */
/*               flash.                                           */
/*----------------------------------------------------------------*/
/*  Author     : Michael Tischer                                  */
/*  Developed on : 08/22/88                                       */
/*  Last update  : 01/20/92                                       */
/*----------------------------------------------------------------*/
/*  Memory model : SMALL                                          */
/********************************************************************/

/*== Add include files ============================================*/

#include <stdio.h>
#include <dos.h>
#include <bios.h>

/*== Macros =======================================================*/

#ifndef MK_FP                        /* Was MK_FP already defined? */
#define MK_FP(seg, ofs) ((void far *)\
                                   ((unsigned long) (seg)<<16|(ofs)))
#endif

/*-- BIOS_KBF creates a pointer to the BIOS keyboard flag ----------*/

#define BIOS_KBF ((unsigned far *) MK_FP(0x40, 0x17))

#define TICKS(ms) ((ms*10+549) / 550 )    /* Convert millis. to ticks */

/*== Constants ====================================================*/

#define SCRL  16                              /* SCROLL LOCK bit */
#define NUML  32                                 /* NUM LOCK bit */
#define CAPL  64                                /* CAPS LOCK bit */
#define INS  128                                    /* INSERT bit */

#ifdef __TURBOC__                     /* Definitions for TURBO C */
  #define GetBiosTime(x)   ( x = biostime( 0, NULL ) )
#else                          /* Definitions for Microsoft C Compiler */
  #define GetBiosTime(x)    ( _bios_timeofday( _TIME_GETCLOCK, &x) )
#endif

/********************************************************************/
/*  Delay:  Waits a certain length of time.                       */
/*  Input    : PAUSE = The number of ticks to wait.               */
/*  Output   : None                                               */
/*  Info     : One tick = 1/18.2 seconds                          */
/********************************************************************/

void delay( unsigned int pause )
{
  long curtime,                              /* Current time */
       trgttime;                             /* Target time */

  if ( pause )                          /* Pause not equal to 0? */
    {                                                    /* No */
      GetBiosTime( trgttime );
      trgttime += (long) pause;              /* Target time elapsed */
```

```
  do                              /* Wait loop, get current time */
    GetBiosTime( curtime );
  while ( curtime < trgttime );              /* Time elapsed? */
  }                                    /* Yes --> End function */
}


/************************************************************************
* Function        : S E T _ F L A G                      *
**-------------------------------------------------------------------**
* Description      : Sets individual bits or flags in the BIOS    *
*                    keyboard flag.                               *
* Input parameters : FLAG = The bit or flag to be set.            *
* Return value     : None                                         *
*************************************************************************/

void set_flag( unsigned flag )
{
  union REGS regs;              /* Store the processor registers */

  *BIOS_KBF |= flag;    /* Set the specified bits in the keyboard flag */
  regs.h.ah = 1;               /* Function no.: Character ready? */
  int86(0x16, &regs, &regs);        /* Call BIOS keyboard interrupt */
}


/************************************************************************
* Function        : C L R _ F L A G                      *
**-------------------------------------------------------------------**
* Description      : Clears bits or flags in BIOS keyboard flag.   *
* Input parameters : FLAG = Bit or flag to be cleared.            *
* Return value     : None                                         *
*************************************************************************/

void clr_flag( unsigned flag )
{
  union REGS regs;              /* Store the processor registers */

  *BIOS_KBF &= ~flag;          /* Mask bits in BIOS keyboard flag */
  regs.h.ah = 1;               /* Function no.: Character ready? */
  int86(0x16, &regs, &regs);        /* Call BIOS keyboard interrupt */
}


/************************************************************************/
/**                   MAIN PROGRAM                        **/
/************************************************************************/

void main()
{
  unsigned i;                              /* Loop counter */

  printf( "LEDC - (c) 1988, 92 by Michael Tischer\n\n");
  printf( "Watch the LEDs on your keyboard!\n");

  for (i=0; i<10; ++i)          /* Run through the loop 10 times */
  {
    set_flag( CAPL );                       /* Turn CAPS on */
    delay( TICKS(100) );            /* Wait 100 milliseconds */
    clr_flag( CAPL );                /* Turn CAPS off again */
    set_flag( NUML);                  /* Turn NUM LOCK on */
    delay( TICKS(100) );            /* Wait 100 milliseconds */
    clr_flag( NUML );                 /* Turn NUM off again */
    set_flag( SCRL);              /* Turn SCROLL LOCK on */
    delay( TICKS(100) );            /* Wait 100 milliseconds */
    clr_flag( SCRL );          /* Turn SCROLL LOCK off again */
  }

  for (i=0; i<10; ++i)          /* Run through the loop 10 times */
  {
    set_flag(CAPL | SCRL | NUML);          /* All three flags on */
    delay( TICKS(500) );            /* Wait 500 milliseconds */
    clr_flag(CAPL | SCRL | NUML);         /* All three flags off */
    delay( TICKS(500) );            /* Wait 500 milliseconds */
  }
}
```

485

Chapter 6

Diskettes and Hard Drives

The main purpose of the BIOS routines is to perform low-level functions on behalf of DOS. For example, BIOS routines can physically format the surface of a floppy diskette or access the sectors of a hard drive. DOS, however, remains the master controller for these processes. Most applications perform disk drive operations at the DOS level instead of the BIOS level. However, there are exceptions. For example, disk utilities, such as PC Tools or Norton Utilities, access the disk drive at the BIOS level. But generally these specialized programs are rare.

In this chapter we'll show you how to access the disk drives using the BIOS functions. Since all disk controllers aren't programmed identically, we won't be programming the disk controller directly. Most of the functions that you can perform at the disk controller level can also be performed at the BIOS level. It's worth using the BIOS functions in order to avoid hardware-dependent disk controller programming.

In addition to BIOS functions, we'll also discuss a few topics related to the hard drive. We'll explain the different types of hard drive controllers and see how hard drives record data.

We'll end the chapter with a discussion of hard drive partitioning, which lets the user divide the hard drive into several logical drives.

6.1 Floppy Diskette and Hard Drive Structure

Let's begin with a look at the common characteristics of floppy diskettes and hard drives. Floppy diskettes and hard drives have similar structures, which is indicated by the number of BIOS functions that apply to both. If you think of a floppy diskette as a two-dimensional version of a hard drive, the similarities are even more apparent.

Floppy diskette structure

A floppy diskette consists of individual tracks, which are arranged as concentric circles at equal intervals over the surface of the diskette's magnetic media. These tracks are labeled from 0 to N; N represents the total number of sectors minus 1 and varies depending on the format. The outermost track is always numbered 0, the next track is numbered 1, etc. This process continues to the innermost track.

Each track is subdivided into a fixed number of sectors. Each sector holds the same amount of data. Sectors are numbered from 1 to N; N represents the number of sectors per track. The maximum number of sectors in a track depends on the type of floppy disk drive and the diskette's format.

Each sector contains 512 bytes and is the smallest amount of data that a program can access. In other words, you must read or write a complete sector at a time. It isn't possible to read or write a single byte from the diskette.

The data in each sector is recorded using either an FM or MFM technique. These are the same recording methods used in hard drives (refer to Sections 6.6.1 and 6.6.2 for more information). As a programmer, you don't have to worry about these details in order to access the data from the disk drive.

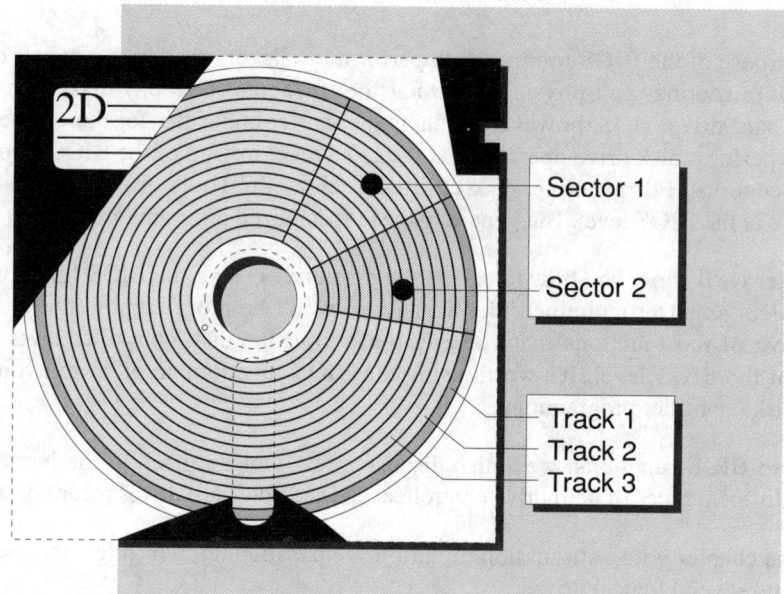

Structure of a 5.25" diskette

Use the following formula to calculate the capacity of a floppy diskette:

```
Sectors * tracks_per_sector * 512 [bytes per sector]
```

Remember that the above formula is for a single side of a diskette. If the floppy disk drive has two read/write heads (like most recent floppy drives), you must double this value. DOS refers to these sides of a diskette as side 0 and side 1.

The number of sectors per track also affects the data transfer rate. The data transfer rate is the speed of the floppy disk drive electronics and its controller. With a constant rotation speed of 300 revolutions a minute, the more bits per time unit that pass by the read/write head, and the more sectors can be written to a track.

Hard drive structure

Since a hard drive rotates ten times faster than a floppy diskette, its data transfer rate is at least ten times higher than a floppy diskette's. The data transfer rate increases by a second power of ten, because modern 3.5" hard drives can store almost 100 sectors per track.

These characteristics don't change the fundamental structure of a hard drive. Think of a hard drive as a group of magnetic plates stacked on top of each other. Each magnetic plate is similar to a floppy diskette; it has two sides, is divided into tracks, and each track is subdivided into sectors. Above the surface of each side of the plate is a read/write head that accesses the data. The plates are aligned so that track 0 on one of the plates is exactly above track 0 of another plate.

A read/write arm links all the read/write heads together. To access a particular track on one of the plates, the arm moves all of the read/write heads to the specific track. Since this arrangement requires only a single positioning mechanism (the read/write arm), it simplifies the design and lowers the cost of the hard drive. However, with this arrangement, all of the read/write heads must be moved to access data on a different track. So, to read data on track 1 of one plate, then data on track 50 of a different plate, and finally data on track 1 of the first plate again, the entire read/write arm must be moved twice. Positioning the arm like this requires a significant amount of time compared to the data transfer time.

To minimize the time needed to access data, you should prevent the data from being spread across multiple tracks. One way to optimize access time to a group of data is to write that data sequentially on a single track. If the data doesn't fit on a single track, then write in on the same track of a different plate. By doing this, the read/write arm doesn't need to be moved. Instead, only the appropriate read/write head needs to be selected in order to read the desired data. Selecting (changing) heads is much faster than physically moving a mechanical read/write arm to change tracks.

The term *cylinder* is used to describe the multiple plates stacked on top of each other. A cylinder refers to all tracks that have the same track number, but are located on different disk plates.

6.2 Disk Drives and Diskette Formats

Before describing the diskette BIOS routines, let's review the various diskette formats. This format is affected by size and density. PC diskettes come in either 5.25" or 3.5" sizes. Each size is either single, double, or high density.

5.25" floppy disk drives and diskettes

Although DOS is able to use the 8" floppy disk drive, this size was never really implemented. The 8" floppy disk drive was simply too large to fit into most PC's. The 5.25" floppy disk drive became the first PC standard floppy. Even today, more than 10 years later, the 5.25" drive is still standard equipment for many PCs. The 5.25" drive supports *double density* diskettes. This term distinguishes the diskettes from the *single density* diskettes that had been used in earlier microcomputers.

A single density diskette has four sectors per track and 40 sectors on each side. This amounts to a capacity of 80K per side or 160K for floppy disk drives with two read/write heads. With 125 kilobits per second, its data transfer rate was rather slow compared to today's standards.

The double density diskette doubles the number of sectors per track to eight, while retaining the number of tracks per side (40). So, the capacity of the diskette is increased to 160K for a single-sided floppy disk drive and 320K for a double-sided floppy disk drive. The data transfer rate also doubles, yielding 250 kilobits per second.

This 320K format was short-lived. Eight sectors doesn't quite fill up a track on double density diskette. So, there is still room for a ninth sector. Adding an extra sector to each track increases the capacity to 360K. This became the standard double density format, which is still widely used.

When the IBM/AT computer was introduced, a new format was also introduced. The new format, called high density, gives the 5-1/4" floppy diskette a capacity of 1.2 Meg. The number of sectors per track was increased to 15 and the number of tracks per side was doubled to 80. As with double density diskettes, both sides of the diskette are used for this high density format.

Theoretically it's possible to have 16 sectors on each track. But for practical considerations, developers settled on the 15 sectors per track arrangement to ensure a reliable floppy disk drive. High capacity floppy disk drives rotate at 360 RPM.

5.25" diskette formats					
Label	Drive	Sectors per Track	Tracks per side	Capacity	Data transfer rate
Double Density	PC/XT	8	40	160/320K	250 KBit/s
Double Density	PC/XT	9	40	80/360K	250 KBit/s
High Density	AT	15	0	1.2 Meg	500 KBit/s

Instead of the 40 tracks used by the double density format, the high density format squeezes 80 tracks onto a diskette. So standard double density floppy disk drives cannot read or write this format. Only newer model MF (multi-function) drives are capable of reading and writing this format. A MF drive also adjusts to the standard double density format, which makes it possible to read and write standard 360K diskettes. In MF drives, the data transfer rate can be adjusted and the rotational speed can be reduced to the normal speed of 300 revolutions a minute.

However, the higher number of sectors per track means that earlier PC and XT floppy disk drives cannot read or write to these high density diskettes. These drives cannot achieve the necessary data transfer rate of 500 kilobits per second because they cannot be designed or configured for the task.

Increasing the recording capacity from double density to high density isn't simply a matter of drive electronics. It's also a question of the "granulation" of the magnetic material on the diskette. The smaller the single magnetic particles, the more information can be recorded on a given surface. This is also the reason why double density diskettes can never be formatted error free in AT disk drives at 1.2 Meg; the granulation on those diskettes is simply too coarse.

While it may be possible to format a double density diskette at high density, these diskettes can usually be read only on the PC on which they were formatted. Other PCs will simply give you read errors, making it almost impossible to use the diskette. This is caused by the variances in the positioning of the read/write heads on different floppy disk drives.

The differences between read/write head positioning may only amount to fractions of a millimeter. A single track may actually be wider than the read/write head, allowing the head to be positioned within the track's range. Even allowing for variances in track size, this allows the head to correctly read the information.

However, this causes problems when re-formatting a standard double density diskette using a high density drive, because the high density drive's formatting capabilities may cause problems when a PC/XT double density drive attempts to read the newly formatted disks. The smaller read/write tolerances may cause track skipping and read errors.

Something similar occurs if you try to format a high density diskette in a double density floppy disk drive. Usually this is also doomed to failure or results in read errors on other drives. So, purchasing expensive HD (High Density) diskettes for your PC or XT disk drives isn't necessarily a good idea.

3.5" floppy disk drives and diskettes

Although 5.25" floppy disk drives are still widely used, they are being replaced by the smaller 3.25" floppy disk drives. These smaller drives first became popular on the laptop computers. Nowadays 3.5" floppy disk drives are also used on most desktop PCs. The 3.5" diskettes are preferred because of their convenient size and the sturdiness of their rigid plastic case. The magnetic surface of a 3.5" diskette is covered by a sliding metal door to protect the data from damage by dust and dirt particles.

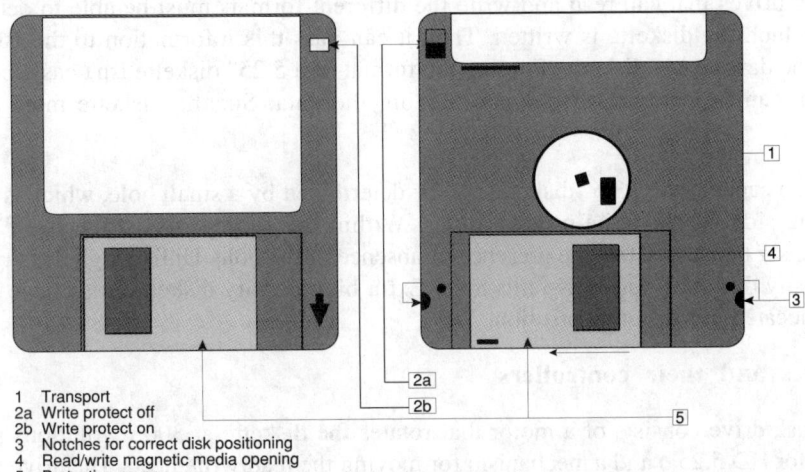

1 Transport
2a Write protect off
2b Write protect on
3 Notches for correct disk positioning
4 Read/write magnetic media opening
5 Protective cover

Structure of a 3.5" diskette

The 3.5" floppy disk drives record data in either double density or high density. Double density has a capacity of 720K, with 9 sectors on a track and 80 tracks on each side of the diskette. A

3.5" diskette has a considerably higher track density than a 5.25" diskette, especially since the diameter of the magnetic media is much smaller.

The original 3.5" floppy disk drives have a double density format with a capacity of 720K. The newer 3.5" floppy disk drives have a 1.44 Meg capacity. A 1.44 Meg floppy disk drive is now the standard in 3.5" drives today. It also has 80 tracks per side, but has 18 sectors per track. This also doubles the data transfer rate, which makes it impossible to use these diskettes in the double density 3.5" floppy disk drives of earlier PCs and XTs.

A 3.5" high density floppy disk drive performs like a 5.25" MF floppy disk drive in that it can adjust to reading, writing, and formatting double density diskettes.

3.5" diskette formats					
Type	Drive	Sectors per Track	Tracks per side	Capacity	Data transfer rate
Double Density	PC/XT	9	80	720K	250 KBit/s
High Density	AT	18	80	1.44 Meg	500 KBit/s
Extra High Density	AT	36	80	2.88 Meg	1 MBit/s

Recently, a new 3.5" format was introduced. Diskettes using this format have a capacity of 2.88 Meg. This format is called extra high density (ED). ED diskettes have double the number of sectors (36) and can only be read by the new ED floppy disk drives. Like HD drives, ED floppy disk drives are also downwardly compatible. This means that they are able to process both double density and high density diskette formats.

Floppy disk drives that can read and write the different formats must be able to determine the format in which the diskette is written. Then it can pass this information to the BIOS before accessing the data on the diskette. Finding the format of a 5.25" diskette isn't easy, because this information can be determined only by reading the data. So, the diskette must already be formatted.

However, the capacity of a 3.5" diskette can be determined by a small hole, which is located on the opposite side of the write-protect slider. Within the floppy disk drive itself is a light-sensitive sensor that can detect the presence or absence of the hole. Unlike high density diskettes, double density diskettes don't have this hole. Extra high density diskettes also have a hole, but the hole is located in a different position.

Disk drives and their controllers

A floppy disk drive consists of a motor that rotates the diskette at 300 revolutions per minute (360 RPM for HD 5.25") and a mechanism for moving the read/write head. The drive also has an electronic component, called a data separator. The data separator converts a voltage into a binary data stream as the read/write head passes over the surface of the diskette.

The floppy drive is controlled by a separate diskette controller, which is either part of the computer's motherboard or on an I/O card in one of the computer's expansion slots.

The main functions of the diskette controller are performed by an NEC µPD765 or a similar chip from another manufacturer. Only NEC chips or NEC compatible chips are able to work with the ROM-BIOS. After all, it's the ROM-BIOS that uses this chip to control access to the floppy disk drive.

Although it's possible to adapt the ROM-BIOS to work with another diskette controller, most manufacturers of ROM-BIOS systems use the established standard of the NEC µPD765.

However, this standard causes problems with the new ED floppy disk drives. These drives have twice the track capacity (36 instead of 18 sectors) and the twice the data transfer rate. But both parameters are unknown to the BIOS. A ROM extension on the controller card can be used to avoid these limitations. The ROM extension wedges itself into the ROM-BIOS when DOS is first started. Then it manages all access to these floppy disk drives. Since the ROM extension is intended to be used only in real mode, it cannot be used if the computer is running protected mode.

Operating systems such as UNIX or OS/2 run in protected mode. These systems rely on the diskette controller to handle all of the details of accessing the drives. So, they'll fail with new floppy disk drives unless special device drivers are written into the operating system. Hopefully a BIOS standard for the new ED drives will be developed soon, making ROM extensions unnecessary. Since Windows will be taking over more of the BIOS tasks in the future, this problem will become more prevalent for PC users.

6.3 Accessing Floppy Disk Drives with the BIOS

There is a complete set of BIOS functions that access floppy disk drives. Interrupt 13H is used to call these functions. This interrupt is also an interface to the hard drive utilities of the BIOS. Wherever possible, similar floppy and hard drive functions share an identical function number. To differentiate between the drives, the drive specification is passed to the function in the DL register.

For floppy disk drives, either the value 0 (for drive A:) or 1 (for drive B:) is used. A few disk controllers support four floppy drives by providing a BIOS extension that also accepts the values 2 and 3 for the other two floppy disk drives. Hard drives are specified by the values 80H and 81H.

As in several other cases, you must distinguish between the PC/XT-BIOS and the AT-BIOS. For example, there are a few BIOS functions that are specific to MF floppy disk drives.

The following table lists the diskette functions of the BIOS interrupt 13H:

Diskette functions of the BIOS interrupt 13H			
No.	Tasks	PC/XT	AT
00H	Reset	Yes	Yes
01H	Read status	Yes	Yes
02H	Read	Yes	Yes
03H	Write	Yes	Yes
04H	Verify	Yes	Yes
05H	Format	Yes	Yes
08H	Request Format	Yes	Yes
15H	Define drive type	No	Yes
16H	Detect diskette change	No	Yes
17H	Determine diskette format	No	Yes
18H	Determine diskette format	No	Yes

Notice that functions 17H and 18H have the same task. This isn't an error. Function 18H was introduced for the 3.5" HD drives. The older function 17H isn't capable of supporting the drive, so it was replaced by a new function. We'll discuss this in more detail later.

Drive Status

These BIOS functions also have another similarity. They return a status or error code. This status code is returned to the caller in the AH register. A non-zero value and a set carry flag indicate an error.

Status and error codes of the BIOS diskette functions	
Code	Meaning
00H	No error
01H	Illegal function number
02H	Address marking not found
03H	Attempt to write to write-protected diskette
04H	Addressed sector not found
06H	Diskette was changed
08H	DMA overflow
09H	Data transfer past the segment limit
10H	Read error
20H	Diskette controller error
40H	Track not found
80H	Time out error, drives does not respond

You can also determine the diskette status through function 01H. Simply pass function number 01H in the AH register and the drive specification value in the DL register. After the function call, the drive status is returned to you in the AH register.

Resetting the floppy disk drive

After an error you must reset the floppy disk drive. To do this, use function 00H. Pass function number 00H in the AH register and the drive specification value in the DL register. After the function call, the current drive status is returned to you in the AH register.

It doesn't matter whether you pass 0 or 1 as the drive specification; all of the floppy disk drives will be reset. Remember that the value in the DL register isn't ignored. Entering a value greater than 80H resets the hard drives.

Prompt for the drive type

A program needs to know the type and format of a floppy disk drive in order to use it. You can use the 08H and 15H functions to determine this information. Function 08H, which is found in the PC/XT-BIOS, is used to distinguish between the different floppy and diskette formats. Pass function number 08H in the AH register and the drive specification in the DL register. The following illustration shows the information that's returned.

Any error code is returned in the AH register with the carry flag set. By using this function, you can determine whether a given drive is installed to demonstrate, for example, that a second, third, or even fourth drive is present.

| Information returned by the 08H function ||
Register	Information
BL	Drive Type 01H = 5.25", 360K 02H = 5.25", 1.2 Meg 03H = 3.5", 720K 04H = 3.5", 1.44 Meg
DH	Maximum number of sides (always 1)
CH	Maximum number of tracks
CL	Maximum number of sectors
ES:DI	Pointers to DDPT

The value in the BL register is especially important. This value not only reveals the floppy disk drive type (3.5" or 5.25"), but also shows the diskette format (DD or HD). However, this value doesn't necessarily describe the format of the diskette that is located in the drive; it describes only the highest possible density.

This information is taken from the CMOS-RAM, in which this information is stored when the computer is originally setup. The Drive Type value is standardized, but doesn't yet include the new ED 3.5" drives. However, in the future these new types will most likely appear under Drive Type 05H.

Even though the number of sectors, tracks, and heads can be derived from the Drive Type value, this information is also specified explicitly in the CH/CL, DH/DL registers.

The DDPT, which is referenced by the pointer in the register pair ES:DI, is the Disk Drive Parameter Table. This table contains a parameter that the BIOS needs for programming the diskette controller. You'll find a description of this table later on in this chapter.

Function 15H has a different purpose. This function is only supported by ATs and their FM drives. Unlike PC/XT floppy disk drives, these drives are able to detect when a diskette has been changed. This feature is important for programs that depend on the presence of a specific diskette. This is true especially for DOS, which reads the FAT table before it accesses a diskette to determine which sectors of the diskette are occupied and which sectors are still unused.

If the diskette is changed without DOS knowing about it, DOS may continue to use the contents of the original diskette's allocation table (FAT) and may inadvertently overwrite and/or destroy data on the newly inserted diskette. However, if the same diskette is reinserted into the floppy, DOS won't have to reread the FAT again.

Function 15H of the BIOS helps determine whether a diskette has been replaced. Pass function number 15H in the AH register and the drive specification in the DL register. After the function call, the following information is returned:

```
┌─────────────────────────────────────────────────────────────┐
│              Drive codes of function 15H                     │
├───────────┬─────────────────────────────────────────────────┤
│ Code      │ Meaning                                          │
├───────────┼─────────────────────────────────────────────────┤
│ AH = 00H  │ Drive not present                                │
│ AH = 01H  │ Disk drive, does not recognize diskette changes  │
│ AH = 02H  │ Disk drive, recognizes diskette changes          │
│ AH = 03H  │ Hard drive                                       │
└───────────┴─────────────────────────────────────────────────┘
```

Reading diskette sectors

Reading diskette sectors is one of the most basic tasks that the BIOS performs. Function 02H reads diskette sectors. Remember that this function can read several sectors through a single call if they're on same track and contiguous.

Pass the following parameters to function 02H:

```
┌─────────────────────────────────────────────────────────────┐
│           Register when calling function 02H                 │
├───────────┬─────────────────────────────────────────────────┤
│ AL        │ Number of sectors to be read                     │
│ DL        │ Drive specification value                        │
│ DH        │ Side (0 or 1)                                    │
│ CL        │ Sector number (1 to N )                          │
│ CH        │ Track number (0 to N-1)                          │
│ ES:BX     │ Address of the buffer for the data to be read    │
└───────────┴─────────────────────────────────────────────────┘
```

Remember that the data isn't transferred to a fixed memory location. Instead, the address of a buffer is passed in the register pair ES:BX. Register ES contains the segment address of the buffer and register BX contains the buffer's offset address.

After the function call, the error status is returned in the AH register and the number of read sectors read is returned in the AL register. If the carry flag is set, it signals an error.

If you're using an MF drive, you can use a trick to determine the format of a diskette. By trying to read a diskette with a sector greater than 9, you can determine whether a diskette is DD or HD. Since the maximum number of sectors per track on a DD diskette is 9, function 15H will return a disk status error. The track number isn't important, but it should be less than 40.

If a disk status error is returned, don't immediately abort the operation. You should repeat all read, write, and format operations at least three times before you give up and assume there is a "real" error. Often an operation fails the first time, but succeeds when you try it a second or third time. Perhaps the read/write head wasn't positioned properly the first time or the floppy drive wasn't synchronized to the electronics yet (see Section 6.6).

In cases of errors, you don't have to worry about the validity of the data because the drive uses parity checking to ensure that the data in each sector is correct.

Writing diskette sectors

Function 03H is used to write to individual sectors. The parameters are passed as follows:

```
┌─────────────────────────────────────────────────────────────┐
│          Register when calling function 03H                  │
├──────────┬──────────────────────────────────────────────────┤
│ AL       │ Number of sectors to be written                  │
│ DL       │ Drive specification value                        │
│ DH       │ Side (0 or 1)                                    │
│ CL       │ Sector number (1 to N )                          │
│ CH       │ Track number (0 to N-1)                          │
│ AL       │ Number of sectors to be read                     │
│ ES:BX    │ Pointer to the buffer containing the data        │
└──────────┴──────────────────────────────────────────────────┘
```

Remember that the buffer, to which the ES:BX register pair points, must contain the data to be written to the diskette.

Verifying diskette sectors

Function 04H tests whether data have been correctly transferred to the diskette. The data in the memory aren't compared with the data on the diskette. Instead, a CRC value is used to determine whether the data was transferred correctly. CRC, which is an abbreviation for "Cyclical Redundancy Check", is a very reliable procedure for verifying accuracy. This procedure combines the values of each byte within the sector with a checksum through a complicated mathematical formula.

Since most disk drives are very reliable, most programmers consider this routine to be unnecessary and don't use it. DOS uses this function when writing data only if the DOS VERIFY ON command is active.

The parameters for function 04H are the same as for function 02H and 03H except that a buffer address isn't required.

Formatting individual tracks on a diskette

Function 07H is used to format an entire diskette. But it's also possible to format individual tracks on a diskette. To do this, first use function 18H to tell the BIOS which format to use. The function number 18H is passed in the AH register, the drive specification value in the DL register, the number of tracks in the CH register, and the number of sectors per track in the CL register. After the function call, the carry flag signals that the specified format is supported by the floppy disk drive. In this case, the register pair ES:DI is a pointer to DDPT, which is required for subsequent formatting functions.

We'll describe the DDPT in more detail later. For now, remember that the pointer must be passed to interrupt vector 1EH, in which the BIOS keeps a pointer to the current DDPT.

497

After function 07H sets the desired format and the DDPT pointer is passed to interrupt vector 1EH, you can start the actual formatting process.

To do this, use function 05H. This function formats a complete track. Although you can format individual sectors with 128, 256, 512, or even 1024 bytes per sector, only a 512 byte format can be used under DOS. This is because DOS supports only this size sector.

To use function 05H, pass the drive specification value in the DL register, the diskette side in the DH register, the number of sectors per track in the AL register, and the track number in the CH register (0 through 39 or 0 through 79).

```
┌─────────────────────────────────────────────────────┐
│        Register when calling function 05H            │
├───────────┬─────────────────────────────────────────┤
│   AL      │  Number of sectors in the track          │
│   DL      │  Number of the drive                     │
│   CH      │  Number of the track                     │
│   DH      │  Side (0 or 1)                            │
│   ES:BX   │  Pointer to format table                 │
└───────────┴─────────────────────────────────────────┘
```

You'll see that the ES:BX register pair points to a "format table". This table represents the formatting attributes. This an array of 4-byte entries (one for each sector to be formatted):

```
┌─────────────────────────────────────────────────────┐
│        ES:BX register pair "format table"            │
├───────────┬─────────────────────────────────────────┤
│  Offset   │  Meaning                                 │
├───────────┼─────────────────────────────────────────┤
│    0      │  Track to be formatted                   │
│    1      │  Diskette side (always 0 for one-sided diskettes): │
│           │         0 = Front side                   │
│           │         1 = Back side                    │
│    2      │  Number of the sector                    │
│    3      │  Number of bytes in this sector          │
│    0      │         0 = 128 bytes                    │
│    0      │         1 = 256 bytes                    │
│    0      │         2 = 512 bytes                    │
│    0      │         3 = 1024 bytes                   │
└───────────┴─────────────────────────────────────────┘
```

Even though the track number and diskette side is passed to function 05H, it must be repeated in the table. The sectors are physically created in the same sequence as the table entries. So it's possible to format the first entry as sector number 1 and the second entry as sector number 7. The logical sector number is recorded in the header of each sector on the diskette, so that the floppy disk drive can later identify the sector being searched for.

Since the BIOS doesn't define the logical sector numbers, you can change the *interleaving*. Generally only hard drives use interleaving, as we'll see in Section 6.7. Since interleaving doesn't have any advantages for floppy diskettes, you should number the sectors consecutively when you create the format table.

The number of bytes per sector don't have to be identical either, since these numbers are defined explicitly for each sector in the table. You can change the number of bytes per sector to develop a form of copy protection, for example. We'll soon see how this is done.

A sample program at the end of this chapter shows how to format diskettes using functions 18H and 05H.

Disk Drive Parameter Table

To program the diskette controller, the BIOS needs the physical formatting information described above and some additional information. We've already introduced you to the Disk Drive Parameter Table (DDPT).

The ROM BIOS contains a table for every drive and supported diskette format. Also, you can define your own DDPT, since the BIOS always references the current DDPT via a FAR pointer, which is contained in the memory locations in which the interrupt vector 1EH is usually found. Since neither DOS nor the PC hardware use interrupt 1EH, you can change the contents of these memory locations.

Actually DOS creates its own DDPT. This DOS DDPT is designed to speed up access to the diskette.

The table is 11 bytes in size, as shown by the following figure. Not all of the parameters can be changed. However, the entries that are marked with an asterisk may be changed.

Structure of the Disk Drive Parameter Table		
Offset	Meaning	Type
*00H	Step rate and head unload time	1 BYTE
*01H	Head load time	1 BYTE
*02H	Post run-time of diskette motor	1 BYTE
03H	Sector size	1 BYTE
04H	Sectors per track	1 BYTE
05H	Length of GAP3 when reading/writing	1 BYTE
06H	DTL (Data Length)	1 BYTE
07H	Length of GAP3 when formatting	1 BYTE
*08H	Fill character for formatting	1 BYTE
*09H	Head settle time	1 BYTE
*0AH	Time to run up of diskette motor	1 BYTE

The first field of the DDPT table actually has two sub-fields: the step rate (bits 4-7) and the head unload time (bits 0-3). The step rate describes the time that the controller has to move the read/write head from one track to another. This value is represented as milliseconds, with the value 0FH representing 1 ms, 0EH representing 2 ms, 0DH representing 3 ms, etc. The head unload time describes the time that the read/write head has to lift up off of the surface of the diskette, for example when changing tracks. It's specified as a factor of 16 ms. The default value 0FH (240 ms) is extremely conservative and can usually be lowered.

The second field is also two sub-fields: the head load time (bits 1-7) and the DMA flag (bit 0). The head load time is the time that the read/write head has to settle to the surface of a track. This value is expressed as a factor of 2 ms. In accessing a diskette, it's usually necessary to wait much longer for the diskette motor to reach its required speed. So it's common to specify a very low value (1 or 2) for the head load time.

The DMA flag is represented by bit 0. This flag must always be set to 0.

The third field is the post run-time of the diskette motor after a diskette operation. This is the period of time that elapses until the diskette motor is switched off when no other diskette operations are being performed. Because it takes a relatively long time to get the motor running, it shouldn't be switched off immediately after each diskette access. This value is related to a cycle of approximately 18 ticks per second (1 tick is approximately 55 ms). So a value of 18 represents a post run-time of about one second. The default value is 25H, which is approximately two seconds.

The forth field specifies the number of bytes per sector that can be used in a read or write operation. This corresponds to the values for formatting a sector, so it usually contains the value 3 for 512 bytes per sector. To read or write to sectors with different sector sizes, you must first enter the appropriate value in this field.

The next field at offset address 04H is the maximum number of sectors per track, which depends on the selected diskette format.

The next three fields refer to the coding and decoding of sector information, which is stored on the diskette along with the actual data. You should never tamper with these values.

However, the field at offset address 08H can be changed. This field contains the ASCII code of the fill character to be used when the diskette is being formatted. During formatting, as the sectors are created, they are also given a fixed contents. The default fill character is a division sign (ASCII code 246).

The next field contains the head settle time. After the read/write head travels from one track to another, a short delay is needed to allow the vibrations from this movement to subside. Only then can the read/write head perform the subsequent data access properly. The value in this field represents a delay in milliseconds. The default value is 25 ms.

The last field in the DDPT specifies the time it takes for the diskette motor to attain its operating speed. The value in this field is a factor of 1/8 seconds. While DOS defaults to a value of 1/4 second, the BIOS equivalent is 1/2 second.

Demonstration programs

Changing the various values in the DDPT won't produce performance miracles. However, you'll probably want to experiment with it. We've developed two small programs in Pascal and C to set the various parameters of the current DDPT. However, the programs won't change all of the parameters because this would be too dangerous.

The two programs, DDPTP.PAS and DDPTC.C, both work according to the same principle. You call both programs from the DOS command line without specifying any parameters. Each program displays the contents of the current DDPT (the DDPT of the last accessed disk drive). To address a certain disk drive, use the DIR command before the DDPTP or DDPTC program.

```
DDPTP  -  (c) 1992 by Michael Tischer
Allows users defined changes to current DDPT

DDPT contents
Step rate          (SR): $0D

Head unload time   (HU): $0F
Head loa dtime     (HL): $01
Head settle time   (HS): $0F

Motor postrun time (MP): $25
Motor startup time (MS): $00
```

DDPTP and DDPTC programs display the contents of the Disk Drive Parameter Table

You can change the contents of a DDPT field by typing the command with the appropriate parameter. The parameter is a two-letter code (the code that appears on the screen when the fields are displayed), followed by a colon, and then followed by a two digit hexadecimal number that represents the new value.

For example, if you type the following command:

```
DDPTP MA:04 SR:08
```

the starting time of the diskette motor is set to one-half second and the step rate is lowered to 8 ms.

This command will work only if the DDPT is in memory, not the one in the ROM-BIOS. Each program will indicate whether you're trying to change the contents of the ROM.

Listing: DDPTP.PAS

```pascal
{*****************************************************}
{*                 D D P T P . P A S               *}
{*-------------------------------------------------*}
{*  Task       : Enables selective changing of individual *}
{*               values in the disk drive parameter table. *}
{*-------------------------------------------------*}
{*  Author     : Michael Tischer                   *}
{*  Developed on : 08/22/91                         *}
{*  Last update  : 03/04/92                         *}
{*****************************************************}

program DDPTP;

Uses Crt, Dos;                        { Add Crt and Dos units }

type DDPT_T   = array[ 0..10 ] of byte; { Structure for the DDPT }
     DDPT_PTR = ^DDPT_T;                { Pointer to the DDPT }

var  DDPT : DDPT_PTR;                   { Pointer to the DDPT }
```

```pascal
{*****************************************************}
{* byte_hex : Changes a byte to a HEX number.      *}
{* Input    : Number to be changed                 *}
{* Output   : Number as a hex string               *}
{*****************************************************}

function byte_hex( rnum : byte ) : string;

{-- Change a numeral from 0 - 15 to 0H - FH ----------------}

function h_numeral( numeral : byte ) : char;

begin
  if ( numeral >= 10 ) then          { Numeral >= 10 then A - F }
    h_numeral := chr( 55 + numeral )
  else                               { No, decimal numeral }
    h_numeral := chr( 48 + numeral );
end;

begin
  byte_hex := '$' + h_numeral( rnum div 16 ) + h_numeral( rnum mod 16 );
end;
```

```
{***************************************************************}
{* hex_byte : Changes a hex string to a byte.                 *}
{* Input    : Hex string to be changed                        *}
{* Output   : Number                                          *}
{***************************************************************}

function hex_byte( hex : string ) : byte;

{-- Change hex numeral 0H - FH to 0 - 15 -------------------}

function d_numeral( numeral : char ) : byte;

begin
  if ( numeral >= 'A' ) and ( numeral <= 'F' ) then
    d_numeral := ord( numeral ) - 55
  else                                    { No, decimal number }
    d_numeral := ord( numeral ) - 48;
end;

begin
  if ( hex[ 1 ] = '$' ) then
    delete( hex, 1, 1 );
  if length( hex ) = 1 then
    hex := '0' + hex;
  hex_byte := d_numeral( hex[ 1 ] ) * 16 + d_numeral( hex[ 2 ] );
end;

{***************************************************************}
{* RAM_DDPT : Test whether DDPT is in RAM or in ROM.          *}
{* Input    : None                                            *}
{* Output   : TRUE if DDPT is in RAM                          *}
{* Info     : The function writes a value to the DDPT, reads it *}
{*            out again, in this way determining whether the value*}
{*            could be changed, since the DDPT is in RAM.      *}
{***************************************************************}

function RAM_DDPT : boolean;

var buffer : byte;        { Memory for current value of the DDPT }

begin
  buffer := DDPT^[ 0 ];                { Save value of the DDPT }
  DDPT^[ 0 ] := not buffer;                   { Invert value }
  RAM_DDPT := ( DDPT^[ 0 ] = not buffer );  { Evaluate write test }
  DDPT^[ 0 ] := buffer                     { Restore old value }
end;

{***************************************************************}
{* DisplayValues: Displays values of the DDPT.                *}
{* Input     : None                                           *}
{* Output    : None                                           *}
{***************************************************************}

procedure DisplayValues;

begin
  writeln( 'Step rate          (SR): ',
             byte_hex( DDPT^[ 0 ] shr 4 ) );
  writeln( #13#10'Head unload time  (HU): ',
             byte_hex( DDPT^[ 0 ] and $F ) );
  writeln( 'Head load time    (HL): ',
             byte_hex( DDPT^[ 1 ] shr 1 ) );
  writeln( 'Head settle time  (HS): ',
```

```
             byte_hex( DDPT^[ 9 ] ) );
  writeln( #13#10'Motor postrun time (MP): ',
             byte_hex( DDPT^[ 2 ] ) );
  writeln( 'Motor startup time (MS): ',
             byte_hex( DDPT^[ 10 ] ) );
end;

{***************************************************************}
{* NewValues: Sets new values of the DDPT.                    *}
{* Input    : None                                            *}
{* Output   : None                                            *}
{***************************************************************}

procedure NewValues;

var i,j      : byte;                        { Loop counter }
    PCh      : string[ 2 ];        { Parameter to be changed }
    NewV     : byte;                { New value to be set }
    AuxiValue : byte;         { Auxiliary value to be saved }
    CmdPar   : string[ 6 ];        { Command line parameter }

begin
  {-- Loop    : Execute all parameters ----------------------}

  for i := 1 to Paramcount do
  begin
    CmdPar := paramstr( i );              { Get parameter }
    for j := 1 to length( CmdPar ) do   { Command in upper-case }
      CmdPar[ j ] := upcase( CmdPar[ j ] );
    PCh := copy( CmdPar, 1, 2 );       { Value to be changed }
    delete( CmdPar, 1, 3 );       { Determine new value }
    NewV := hex_byte( CmdPar );
    if ( PCh = 'SR' ) then                   { Step rate? }
    begin
      NewV := NewV shl 4;            { Value in upper nibble }
      AuxiValue := DDPT^[ 0 ] and $0F;       { Lower nibble }
      DDPT^[ 0 ] := NewV or AuxiValue;         { Save value }
    end
    else if ( PCh = 'HU' ) then           { Head unload time? }
    begin
      NewV := NewV and $0F;     { Only value in lower nibble }
      AuxiValue := DDPT^[ 0 ] and $F0;       { Upper nibble }
      DDPT^[ 0 ] := NewV or AuxiValue;         { Save value }
    end
    else if ( PCh = 'HL' ) then            { Head load time? }
      DDPT^[ 1 ] := NewV shl 1       { Save balue in bit 1 - 7 }
    else if ( PCh = 'HS' ) then            { Head settle time? }
      DDPT^[ 9 ] := NewV                     { Save value }
    else if ( PCh = 'MP' ) then         { Motor post run time? }
      DDPT^[ 2 ] := NewV                     { Save value }
    else if ( PCh = 'MS' ) then          { Motor starting time? }
      DDPT^[ 10 ] := NewV;                   { Save value }
  end;
end;

{***************************************************************}
{*                    MAIN PROGRAM                            *}
{***************************************************************}

begin
  ClrScr;                              { Clear screen }
  writeln( 'DDPTP  -  (c) 1992 by Michael Tischer' );
  writeln( 'Allows user defined changes to current DDPT' );
```

```
GetIntVec( $1E, pointer( DDPT ) );          { Get pointer to DDPT }

if ( RAM_DDPT ) then          { DDPT in RAM, can be changed? }
  begin
    if ( Paramcount > 0 ) then                      { Set values? }
      begin
        NewValues;                     { Yes, set new values }
        writeln( #13#10#10'New DDPT contents:');
        DisplayValues;          { Display new values of DDPT }
        exit;
      end;
  end
else
  writeln( 'Disk drive parameter table in ROM - cannot be changed' );

writeln( #13#10'DDPT contents:');
DisplayValues;                    { Display old values of DDPT }
end.
```

Listing: DDPTC.C

```c
/********************************************************************/
/*                      D D P T C . C                       */
/*------------------------------------------------------------------*/
/*   Task        : Enables selective modification of single   */
/*                 values in the disk drive parameter table.  */
/*------------------------------------------------------------------*/
/*   Author      : Michael Tischer                            */
/*   Developed on : 08/22/91                                  */
/*   Last update  : 03/04/92                                  */
/*------------------------------------------------------------------*/
/*   Memory model  : SMALL                                    */
/*------------------------------------------------------------------*/
/********************************************************************/

/*== Add include files ==========================================*/

#include <dos.h>
#include <stdio.h>
#include <stdlib.h>
#include <io.h>
#include <string.h>

/*== Macros =====================================================*/

#ifdef MK_FP                    /* Macro MK_FP already defined? */
  #undef MK_FP                          /* Yes --> delete macro */
#endif

#define MK_FP(seg,ofs) ((void far *) ((unsigned long) (seg)<<16|( ofs)))

/*== Type definitions ===========================================*/

typedef unsigned char byte;                /* Data type byte */
typedef byte DDPT_Typ[ 11 ];               /* Field for a DDPT */

/********************************************************************/
/* upcase       : Converts a letter to upper-case.            */
/* Input        : Letter                                      */
/* Output       : Uppercase letter                            */
/********************************************************************/

byte upcase( byte letter )
{
  if ( ( letter > 0x60 ) && ( letter < 0x7B ) )      /* Convert? */
    return( letter & 0xDF );              /* Yes --> Mask bit */
  else
    return( letter);            /* No --> Return unchanged */
}

/********************************************************************/
/* D_Numeral : Converts a hexadecimal numeral to a decimal value. */
/* Input    : Hexadecimal numeral                             */
/* Output   : Number                                          */
/********************************************************************/

byte D_Numeral( char Hex )
{
  if ( ( Hex >= 0x41 ) && ( Hex <= 0x46 ) )          /* A - F? */
    return( Hex - 55 );                            /* Yes */
  else
    return( Hex ) - 48;                    /* No --> 0..9 */
}
```

503

```
/***************************************************************/
/* hex_byte : Converts a hex string to a byte.                 */
/* Input    : See below                                        */
/* Output   : Number                                           */
/***************************************************************/

byte hex_byte( char *hex )          /* Hex string to be converted */
{
 if ( hex[ 1 ] == 0x58 )          /* Test for X then number 0x.. */
   hex += 2;                      /* Pointer to first numeral */
 return( ( D_Numeral( *hex ) << 4 ) | D_Numeral( hex[ 1 ] ) );
}


/***************************************************************/
/* GetIntVec: Gets an interrupt vector.                        */
/* Input    : NUMBER = Interrupt number                        */
/* Output   : Interrupt vector                                 */
/***************************************************************/

void far *GetIntVec( int Number )
{
 return( *( ( void far * far * ) MK_FP( 0, Number * 4 ) ) );
}


/***************************************************************/
/* RAM_DDPT : Tests whether DDPT is in RAM or in ROM.          */
/* Input    : DDPT = FAR pointer to DDPT variable              */
/* Output   : TRUE, if DDPT is in RAM                          */
/* Info     : The function writes a value in the DDPT, reads   */
/*            it out again and checks whether the value        */
/*            was written, meaning the DDPT is located in RAM. */
/***************************************************************/

int RAM_DDPT( DDPT_Typ far *DDPT )          /* Pointer to DDPT */
{
 byte buffer;           /* Memory for current value of the DDPT */
 int Flag;              /* Memory for return value */

 buffer = *DDPT[ 0 ];                    /* Save value of DDPT */
 *DDPT[ 0 ] = buffer ^ 0xFF;             /* Invert value */
 Flag = ( *DDPT[ 0 ] == ( buffer ^0xFF ) );
 *DDPT[ 0 ] = buffer;                    /* Restore old value */
 return( Flag );                         /* Return value */
}


/***************************************************************/
/* DisplayValues: Displays values of the DDPT                  */
/* Input      : DDPT = FAR pointer to DDPT variable            */
/* Output     : None                                           */
/***************************************************************/

void DisplayValues( DDPT_Typ far *DDPT )      /* Pointer to DDPT */
{
 printf( "Step rate            (SR): 0x%02x\n\n",
         ( *DDPT )[ 0 ] >> 4 );
 printf( "Head unload time     (HU): 0x%02x\n",
         ( *DDPT )[ 0 ] & 0x0f );
 printf( "Head load time       (HL): 0x%02x\n",
         ( *DDPT )[ 1 ] >> 1 );
 printf( "Head settle time   (HS): 0x%02x\n\n", ( * DDPT )[ 9 ] );
 printf( "Motor postrun time   (MP): 0x%02x\n", ( *DDPT )[ 2 ] );
 printf( "Motor startup time   (MS): 0x%02x\n", ( *DDPT )[ 10 ] );
}
```

```
/***************************************************************/
/* NewValues: Set new values of the DDPT.                      */
/* Input    : See below                                        */
/* Output   : None                                             */
/***************************************************************/

void NewValues( int NumCmd,              /* Number of commands */
                char *CmdFd[],           /* Field with commands */
                DDPT_Typ far *DDPT )     /* Pointer to DDPT */
{
 int i, j;                               /* Loop counter */
 char PCh[ 4 ],                          /* Parameter to be changed */
      CmdPar[ 8 ];                       /* Command line parameter */
 byte NewV,                              /* New value to be set */
      AuxiValue;                         /* Auxiliary value to be be saved */

 /*-- Loop: Execute all parameters --------------------------------*/

 for ( i = 1; i < NumCmd; i++ )
 {
  strcpy( CmdPar, CmdFd[ i ] );          /* Get parameters */
  j = 0;
  while ( CmdPar[ j ] != 0 )
   CmdPar[ j++ ] = upcase( CmdPar[ j ] );

  PCh[ 0 ] = CmdPar[ 0 ];                /* Parameter to be set */
  PCh[ 1 ] = CmdPar[ 1 ];
  PCh[ 2 ] = 0;
  NewV = hex_byte( &CmdPar[ 3 ] );       /* Value to be set */
  if ( !strcmp( PCh, "SR" ) )            /* Step rate? */
   {
    NewV = NewV << 4;                    /* Value in upper nibble */
    AuxiValue = ( *DDPT )[ 0 ] & 0x0F;   /* Read lower nibble */
    ( *DDPT )[ 0 ] = NewV | AuxiValue;   /* Write value */
   }
  else if ( !strcmp( PCh, "HU" ) )       /* Head unload time? */
   {
    NewV = NewV & 0x0F;                  /* Value in lower nibble */
    AuxiValue = ( *DDPT )[ 0 ] & 0xF0;   /* Read upper nibble */
    ( *DDPT )[ 0 ] = NewV | AuxiValue;   /* Write value */
   }
  else if ( !strcmp( PCh, "HL" ) )       /* Head load time? */
   ( *DDPT )[ 1 ] = NewV << 1;           /* Save value in bit 1 - 7 */
  else if ( !strcmp( PCh, "HS" ) )       /* Head settle time? */
   ( *DDPT )[ 9 ] = NewV;                /* Save value */
  else if ( !strcmp( PCh, "MP" ) )       /* Motor postrun time */
   ( *DDPT )[ 2 ] = NewV;                /* Save value */
  else if ( !strcmp( PCh, "MS" ) )       /* Motor starting time */
   ( *DDPT )[ 10 ] = NewV;               /* Save value */
 }
}


/***************************************************************/
/*                  MAIN PROGRAM                               */
/***************************************************************/

void main( int argc, char *argv[] )
{
 DDPT_Typ far *DDPT;               /* Pointer to the current DDPT */

 printf( "DDPTC  -  (c) 1992 by Michael Tischer\n" );
 printf( "Allows user defined changed to current DDPT\n" );
```

```
DDPT = GetIntVec( 0x1E );           /* Get pointer to the DDPT */          exit( 0 );
if ( RAM_DDPT )                /* DDPT is in RAM, can be changed? */          }
{                                                                         }
  if ( argc > 1 )                      /* Set values? */          else                    /* DDPT is in ROM, changes not possible */
  {                                                                   printf( "Disk drive parameter table in ROM - cannot be changed\n" );
    NewValues( argc, argv, DDPT );         /* Set new values */      printf( "\nContents of DDPT:\n" );
    printf( "\n\nNew DDPT contents:\n" );                             DisplayValues( DDPT );         /* Display old values of the DDPT */
    DisplayValues( DDPT );      /* Display new values of the DDPT */  }
```

Do it yourself formatting

Programmers usually don't have to write data directly to or read data directly from a diskette using the BIOS. Generally, your application programs will be working with files. For this purpose, it's better to use the DOS functions.

However, when you're formatting diskettes you must call various BIOS functions.

The following programs, one in Pascal and the other in C, perform this task. These programs are replacements for the DOS FORMAT program. Similar to FORMAT, these programs not only format the diskette, but also create the various data structures that DOS expects. Among these are the boot sector, the root directory of the diskette, which is initially empty, and the FAT. For more information about these data structures and the general structure of mass storage systems under DOS, refer to Chapter 26.

The programs are called DFP.PAS and DFC.C. They can process all known DOS formats (360/1200 on 5.25" diskettes and 720/1140 on 3.5" diskettes). Use the following model to call them:

```
        DFP Drive   Format   [ NV ]
             |         |        |
             |         |        |
 A: or B:    |         |        |
             |         |        |
   360, 720, 1200, 1440|        |
                       |        |
            NV = No Verify      |
```

Since both programs are based on the same algorithm and work with the same data types and constants, we'll discuss them together.

Within the main program, the first argument of the DOS command line is analyzed. It's assumed that this argument will be the drive identifier (letter). This value is converted into the drive number (0 or 1). Next, the format of the drive is determined by using the GetDriveType procedure. To do this, we use function 08H of the BIOS disk interrupt, which returns a type code between 0 and 4. Within the program, this code is represented by the respective constants NO_DRIVE, DD_525, HD_525, DD_35, and HD_35.

The older model PCs and XTs don't support function 08H. In this case, the carry flag is set after the function call to indicate an error. The program then defaults to a DD 5.25" drive that supports only a 360K format.

After GetDriveType() confirms that the specified drive exists, the program then determines the logical and physical formatting parameters through the GetFormatParameter function. The format specified in the command line is passed to GetFormatParameter as a string along with the type code and two variables of type PhysDataType and LogDataType. You can see the organization of the two data structures in the Pascal version:

```
type DdptType = array[ 0..10 ] of byte;           { Structure for DDPT }
     DdptPtr = ^DdptType;                            { Pointer to DDPT }

     PhysDataType = record             { physical format parameters }
       Seiten,                       { desired side number of diskette }
       Spuren,                            { Number of tracks per side }
       sektoren : byte;                  { Number of sectors per track }
       DDPT     : DdptPtr;     { Pointer to Disk Drive Parameter Table }
     end;

     LogDataType = record                     { DOS format parameters }
       Media,                                    { Media-Byte }
       Cluster,                     { Number of sectors per cluster }
       FAT,                          { Number of sectors for the FAT }
       RootSize : byte;              { Entries in the root directory }
     end;

     SpurBufType = array[ 1..18, 1..512 ] of byte;    { Buffer for track }
```

PhysDataType contains the physical parameters needed for formatting. These are the number of sides, the tracks per side, and the number of sectors per track. Also, a pointer to the DDPT is stored here because both programs work with their own "private" DDPTs to speed up the formatting.

While the information in PhysDataType is needed for physical formatting, the information in LogDataType is needed for *logical formatting*, which applies to using different DOS data structures. That's why the DOS media ID, the number of sectors per cluster, the size of the FAT in sectors, and the number of entries in the root directory are recorded here.

The variables of type PhysDataType and LogDataType within GetFormatParameter are initialized with a series of typed constants (or STATIC variables in C), in which the necessary information for all supported formats is recorded. These constants, which are called DDPT_360, LOG_1200, or PHYS_720, can be identified quickly when looking through the listings.

Before the procedure copies the parameters to the passed variables, it checks to determine whether the format specified in the command line is a valid one for the drive. The procedure displays the results of this test to the caller as its return value, which is FALSE if drive and format aren't valid.

After these checks, program execution continues by calling DiskPrepare. This procedure uses BIOS function 18H.

Function 18H returns a pointer to the DDPT to the caller. The DDPT is part of the selected format. This pointer is ignored by the two programs, however, because a different DDPT is used by FormatGetParameter().

After DiskPrepare, the address of this DDPT is stored in the interrupt vector for interrupt 1EH. Remember that the contents of this vector are first saved so that the original DDPT address can be restored later.

Formatting then occurs using the PhysicalFormat function. The third parameter of the DOS command line indicates whether to verify the tracks.

When formatting, PhysicalFormat uses the FormatTrack procedure to format one track at a time. FormatTrack calls the BIOS disk function 05H in a nested loop for tracks 0 to N; it formats side 0 first and then side 1 of each track. Obviously, it's also possible to format the entire first side and then the entire second side. However, this would take much longer because the read/write head would have to travel over the entire diskette twice. With this method, the drive is constantly switching between head 0 and head 1, but the formatting is performed much faster than moving the read/write arm from track to track.

After FormatTrack, PhysicalFormat calls the VerifyTrack procedure to determine the validity of the data (i.e., whether the contents of a sector and the corresponding CRC checksum match). This is performed only if FALSE is returned for the VERIFY parameter.

VerifyTrack, like FormatTrack and WriteTrack, which we haven't discussed yet, is simply a procedure name for the corresponding BIOS function. If the BIOS reports an error, this call is repeated several times before a "real" error indication is finally returned to the caller. The maximum number of attempts is determined by the MaxVersuch constant, which is defined at the beginning of the listings. By setting this constant to one, both versions of the program will frequently report an unsuccessful format because errors occur more often than you might think.

Now let's return to the main program. If the diskette was perfectly formatted with PhysicalFormat, then the last processing step begins. This step involves logically formatting the drive using LogicalFormat. As we already mentioned, in this step the different data structures that DOS needs for managing files are written to the diskette. We discuss this in detail in Chapter 26.

One interesting structure is the boot sector, which must be written to the diskette if it is to contain the DOS operating system. The contents of the boot sector are defined at the beginning of the program in the BootMaske variable. You'll find the details about the data and the small machine language program in Chapter 26. But you should know the meaning of the BootMes variable, which immediately follows the boot sector. This variable contains the string that appears on the screen when the computer is booted. It's written to the diskette with the boot sector.

You can alter the contents of this string. For example, you can add your own name or the name of your company so that it appears on the screen when you boot the computer from the diskette. However, remember that the end of the sector is indicated by a byte with the value 00H.

The end of LogicalFormat is essentially the end of program execution, because nothing happens in the main program except writing the status message. Here are the listings of DFP.PAS and DFC.C:

Listing: DFP.PAS

```
{*****************************************************}
{*                  D F P . P A S                    *}
{*---------------------------------------------------*}
{*   Task       : Formats 3.5" and 5.25" diskettes   *}
{*---------------------------------------------------*}
{*   Author     : Michael Tischer                    *}
{*   Developed on : 08/23/91                         *}
{*   Last update : 03/03/92                          *}
{*****************************************************}

program DFP;

Uses Dos;                          { Add Crt and Dos units }

{-- Constants ---------------------------------------}

const NO_DRIVE   = 0;                      { No drive }
      DD_525     = 1;              { Drive: 5.25" DD }
      HD_525     = 2;              { Drive: 5.25" HD }
      DD_35      = 3;              { Drive: 3.5" DD }
      HD_35      = 4;              { Drive: 3.5" HD }
      MaxNumTries = 5;            { Maximum number of tries }

{-- Type declarations -------------------------------}

type DdptType = array[ 0..10 ] of byte;   { Structure for DDPT }
     DdptPtr = ^DdptType;                  { Pointer to DDPT }

     PhysDataType = record        { Physical format parameters }
       DSides,              { Desired number of sides for diskette }
       STrax,                      { Number of tracks per side }
       TSectors : byte;            { Number of sectors per track }
       DDPT     : DdptPtr   { Pointer to disk drive parameter table }
     end;

     LogDataType = record         { DOS format parameters }
       Media,                             { Media byte }
       Cluster,               { Number sectors per cluster }
       FAT,                     { Number sectors for the FAT }
       RootSize : byte;       { Entries in the root directory }
     end;

     TrackBfType = array[ 1..18, 1..512 ] of byte;  { Buffer for track }

{-- Initialized global variables --------------------}

const {-- Predefined tables for the individual formats ------------}

      {-- Defaults for the BOOT sector with load program ----------}

      BootMask  : array[ 1..102 ] of byte =
                  ( $EB, $35,            { 0000   JMP 0037  }
                    $90,                 { 0002   NOP       }
                    {-- Data of the BPB ------------------------}

                    $50, $43, $49, $4E, $54, $45, $52, $4E,
                    $00, $00, $00, $01, $00, $00, $00, $00,
                    $00, $00, $00, $00, $00, $00, $00, $00,
                    $00, $00, $00, $00, $00, $00, $00, $00,
                    $00, $00, $00, $00, $00, $00, $00, $00,
                    $00, $00, $00, $00, $00, $00, $00, $00,
```

```
                    $00, $00, $00, $00,

                    {-- Actual load program ----------------------}

                    $FA,              { 0037   CLI          }
                    $B8, $30, $00,     { 0038   MOV  AX,0030 }
                    $8E, $D0,          { 003B   MOV  SS,AX   }
                    $BC, $FC, $00,     { 003D   MOV  SP,00FC }
                    $FB,               { 0040   STI          }
                    $0E,               { 0041   PUSH CS      }
                    $1F,               { 0042   POP  DS      }
                    $BE, $66, $7C,     { 0043   MOV  SI,7C66 }
                    $B4, $0E,          { 0046   MOV  AH,0E   }
                    $FC,               { 0048   CLD          }
                    $AC,               { 0049   LODSB        }
                    $0A, $C0,          { 004A   OR   AL,AL   }
                    $74, $04,          { 004C   JZ   0052    }
                    $CD, $10,          { 004E   INT  10      }
                    $EB, $F7,          { 0050   JMP  0049    }
                    $B4, $01,          { 0052   MOV  AH,01   }
                    $CD, $16,          { 0054   INT  16      }
                    $74, $06,          { 0056   JZ   005E    }
                    $B4, $00,          { 0058   MOV  AH,00   }
                    $CD, $16,          { 005A   INT  16      }
                    $EB, $F4,          { 005C   JMP  0052    }
                    $B4, $00,          { 005E   MOV  AH,00   }
                    $CD, $16,          { 0060   INT  16      }
                    $33, $D2,          { 0062   XOR  DX,DX   }
                    $CD, $19 );        { 0064   INT  19      }

      BootMes : string =
      #13#10'DFP  -  (C) 1992 by Michael Tischer'+ #13#10 +
      #13#10'Defective diskette or non-system diskette'#13#10 +
      'Please change diskettes and press any key . . .' +
      #13#10;

{-- Non-initialized global variables -----------------------------}

var CurDrive    : byte;   { Number of drive to be formatted 0, 1 }
    CurDriveType : byte;               { Current disk drive type }
    PData       : PhysDataType;   { Physical format information }
    LData       : LogDataType;    { Logical format information }
    POldDDPT    : pointer;            { Pointer to old DDPT }
    OK          : boolean;         { Flag for program flow }
    ExitCode    : word;      { Return value to calling process }
    Param       : string;      { for evaluation of command line }

{*****************************************************************}
{* GetDriveType : Gets disk drive type.                        *}
{* Input        : DRIVE = Drive number (0, 1 etc.)             *}
{* Output       : Drive code as constant (DD_525, HD_525 etc.) *}
{*****************************************************************}

function GetDriveType( Drive : byte ) : byte;

var Regs    : Registers; { Processor registers for interrupt call }

begin
  Regs.ah := $08;              { Function: Determine drive type }
  Regs.dl := Drive;                         { Drive number }
  intr( $13, Regs );                   { Call BIOS interrupt }
  if ( Regs.flags and fcarry = 0 ) then {Call completed without error?}
    GetDriveType := Regs.bl               { Drive type }
  else
```

```
      GetDriveType := DD_525;        { Function 08H of interrupt does }
end;                                 { not exist => Computer type = XT }


{*****************************************************************}
{* ResetDisk    : Disk reset on all drives.                    *}
{* Input        : None                                         *}
{* Output       : None                                         *}
{* Info         : Regardless of drive number loaded in DL, reset *}
{*                 executed on all drives.                     *}
{*****************************************************************}

procedure DiskReset;

var Regs : Registers;       { Processor registers for interrupt call }

begin
  with Regs do
    begin
      ah := $00;            { Function number for interrupt call }
      dl := 0;                     { Drive a: (see Info) }
    end;
  intr( $13, Regs );                     { Interrupt call }
end;


{*****************************************************************}
{* GetFormatParameter: Determines the logical and physical      *}
{*                      parameters necessary for formatting.    *}
{* Input        : FORMSTRING = Desired capacity as string       *}
{*                             "360", "1200", "720", "1440"     *}
{*                DRIVETYPE  = Drive code as returned from       *}
{*                             GetDriveType                      *}
{*                PDATA      = Loaded by procedure with the      *}
{*                             specifications of the physical    *}
{*                             format                            *}
{*                LDATA      = Like PDATA, only DOS specs        *}
{* Output       : TRUE, if the format is possible, otherwise FALSE *}
{* Info         : New formats can be added by extending this    *}
{*                 procedure                                     *}
{*****************************************************************}

function GetFormatParameter(   FormString : string;
                               DriveType : byte;
                           var PData     : PhysDataType;
                           var LData     : LogDataType ) : boolean;

const DDPT_360  : DdptType = ( $DF, $02, $25, $02, $09, $2A,
                               $FF, $50, $F6, $0F, $08 );
      DDPT_1200 : DdptType = ( $DF, $02, $25, $02, $0F, $1B,
                               $FF, $54, $F6, $0F, $08 );
      DDPT_720  : DdptType = ( $DF, $02, $25, $02, $09, $2A,
                               $FF, $50, $F6, $0F, $08 );
      DDPT_1440 : DdptType = ( $DF, $02, $25, $02, $12, $1B,
                               $FF, $6C, $F6, $0F, $08 );

      LOG_360   : LogDataType = ( Media : $FD; Cluster : 2;
                              FAT  : 2;   RootSize : $70 );
      LOG_1200  : LogDataType = ( Media : $F9; Cluster : 1;
                              FAT  : 7;   RootSize : $E0 );
      LOG_720   : LogDataType = ( Media : $F9; Cluster : 2;
                              FAT  : 3;   RootSize : $70 );
      LOG_1440  : LogDataType = ( Media : $F0; Cluster : 1;
                              FAT  : 9;   RootSize : $E0 );


      PHYS_360  : PhysDataType = ( DSides  : 2; STrax : 40;
                                   TSectors :  9; DDPT  : @DDPT_360 );
      PHYS_1200 : PhysDataType = ( DSides  : 2; STrax : 80;
                                   TSectors : 15; DDPT  : @DDPT_1200);
      PHYS_1440 : PhysDataType = ( DSides  : 2; STrax : 80;
                                   TSectors : 18; DDPT  : @DDPT_1440);
      PHYS_720  : PhysDataType = ( DSides  : 2; STrax : 80;
                                   TSectors :  9; DDPT  : @DDPT_720 );

begin
  if ( FormString = '1200' ) then            { 1.2 Meg on 5.25"? }
    if ( DriveType = HD_525 ) then  { Format compatible with drive? }
      begin                              { Yes, set parameter }
        PData := PHYS_1200;
        LData := LOG_1200;
        GetFormatParameter := true;          { End without error }
      end
    else
      GetFormatParameter := false  { Drive and format incompatible }
  else if ( FormString = '360' ) then            { 360K? }
    if ( DriveType = HD_525 ) or ( DriveType = DD_525 ) then
      begin        { Format and drive compatible, set parameter }
        PData := PHYS_360;
        LData := LOG_360;
        GetFormatParameter := true;          { End without error }
      end
    else
      GetFormatParameter := false  { Drive and format incompatible }
  else if ( FormString = '1440' ) then       { 1.44 Meg on 3.5"? }
    if ( DriveType = HD_35 ) then  { Format compatible with drive? }
      begin                              { Yes, set parameters }
        PData := PHYS_1440;
        LData := LOG_1440;
        GetFormatParameter := true;          { End without error }
      end
    else
      GetFormatParameter := false  { Drive and format incompatible }
  else if ( FormString = '720' ) then        { 720K on 3.5"? }
    if ( DriveType = HD_35 ) or ( DriveType = DD_35 ) then
      begin          { Format and drive compatible, set parameters }
        PData := PHYS_720;
        LData := LOG_720;
        GetFormatParameter := true;          { End without error }
      end
    else
      GetFormatParameter := false  { Drive and format incompatible }
  else
    GetFormatParameter := false;         { Invalid format specified }
end;


{*****************************************************************}
{* DiskPrepare  : Prepare drive, set data transfer rate.        *}
{* Input        : DRIVE = Drive number                          *}
{*                PDATA = Physical parameters                   *}
{* Output       : None                                          *}
{*****************************************************************}

procedure DiskPrepare( Drive : byte; PData : PhysDataType );

var Regs : Registers;    { Processor registers for interrupt call }

begin
  {-- Set media type for format call ----------------------------}

  with Regs do
```

```
    begin
      ah := $18;                  { Function number for interrupt call }
      ch := PData.STrax - 1;            { Number of tracks per side }
      cl := PData.TSectors;           { Number of sectors per track }
      dl := Drive;                            { Drive number }
    end;
  intr( $13, Regs );                             { Interrupt call }
end;


{******************************************************************}
{* FormatTrack  : Formats a track.                               *}
{* Input        : See below                                      *}
{* Output       : Error status                                   *}
{******************************************************************}

function Formattrack( DriveNum,          { The disk drive number }
                          SideNum,              { The side number }
                          TrackF,             { Track to be formatted }
                          SecPTr  : byte ) : byte;{ Sectors per track }

type FormatTyp = record
                    DTrack, DSideNum, DCounter, DLength : byte;
                 end;

var Regs      : Registers;  { Processor registers for interrupt cal }
    DataField : array[ 1..18 ] of FormatTyp;  { Maximum 18 sectors }
    Counter   : byte;                             { Loop counter }
    Attempts  : byte;                       { Maximum number of tries }

begin
  for Counter := 1 to SecPTr do
    with DataField[ Counter ] do
      begin
        DTrack := TrackF;                        { Track number }
        DSideNum := SideNum;                    { Diskette side }
        DCounter := Counter;                    { Sector number }
        DLength := 2;          { Number of bytes per sector (512) }
      end;
  Attempts := MaxNumTries;             { Set maximum number of tries }
  repeat
    with Regs do
      begin
        ah := 5;            { Function number for interrupt call }
        al := SecPTr;          { Number of sectors for one track }
        es := Seg( DataField );            { Address of data field }
        bx := Ofs( DataField );             { to register es:bx    }
        dh := SideNum;                            { Side number }
        dl := DriveNum;                          { Drive number }
        ch := TrackF;                            { Track number }
      end;
    intr( $13, Regs );                   { Call BIOS interrupt }
    if ( Regs.flags and fcarry = 1 ) then             { Error? }
      DiskReset;             { Yes --> Disk reset before next try }
    dec( Attempts );
  until ( Regs.flags and fcarry = 0 ) or ( Attempts = 0 );
  Formattrack := Regs.ah;                    { Read error status }
end;


{******************************************************************}
{* VerifyTrack  : Verify track                                   *}
{* Input        : Drive, side, track, sector number              *}
{* Output       : Error code (0=OK)                              *}
{******************************************************************}
```

```
function VerifyTrack( DriveNum, SideNum, TrackF, TSectors : byte ) : byte;

var Attempts    : byte;                   { Maximum number of tries }
    Regs        : Registers;  { Processor registers for interrupt call }
    TrackBuffer : TrackBtType;              { Memory for a track }

begin
  Attempts := MaxNumTries;             { Set maximum number of tries }
  repeat
    with Regs do
      begin
        ah := $04;            { Function number for interrupt call }
        al := TSectors;          { Number of sectors per track }
        ch := TrackF;                            { Track number }
        cl := 1;                              { Start at sector 1 }
        dl := DriveNum;                          { Drive number }
        dh := SideNum;                            { Side number }
        es := Seg( TrackBuffer );           { Address for buffer }
        bx := Ofs( TrackBuffer );
      end;
    intr( $13, Regs );                   { Call BIOS interrupt }
    if ( Regs.flags and fcarry = 1 ) then             { Error? }
      DiskReset;             { Yes --> Disk reset before next try }
    dec( Attempts );
  until ( Regs.flags and fcarry = 0 ) or ( Attempts = 0 );
  VerifyTrack := Regs.ah;
end;


{******************************************************************}
{* WriteTrack   : Write track                                    *}
{* Input        : Drive, side, track, start sector, number, data *}
{* Output       : Error code (0=OK)                              *}
{******************************************************************}

function WriteTrack(    DriveNum, SideNum, TrackF,
                        Start, SecPTr          : byte;
                            var Buffer ) : byte;

var Attempts : byte;                      { Maximum number of tries }
    Regs     : Registers; { Processor registers for interrupt call }

begin
  Attempts := MaxNumTries;             { Set maximum number of tries }
  repeat
    with Regs do
      begin
        ah := $03;            { Function number for interrupt call }
        al := SecPTr;          { Number of sectors per track }
        ch := TrackF;                            { Track number }
        cl := Start;                            { Start at sector 1 }
        dl := DriveNum;                          { Drive number }
        dh := SideNum;                            { Side number }
        es := Seg( Buffer );               { Address for buffer }
        bx := Ofs( Buffer );
      end;
    intr( $13, Regs );                   { Call BIOS interrupt }
    if ( Regs.flags and fcarry = 1 ) then             { Error? }
      DiskReset;             { Yes --> Disk reset before next try }
    dec( Attempts );
  until ( Regs.flags and fcarry = 0 ) or ( Attempts = 0 );
  WriteTrack := Regs.ah;
end;


{******************************************************************}
```

```
{* PhysicalFormat: Physical formatting of the diskette (Division  *}
{*                 into tracks, sectors).                         *}
{* Input       : DRIVE = Drive code                               *}
{*               PDATA = Physical parameters                      *}
{*               VERIFY = TRUE, If verify is to be executed       *}
{* Output      : FALSE if error, otherwise TRUE                   *}
{****************************************************************}

function PhysicalFormat( Drive  : byte;
                         PData  : PhysDataType;
                         Verify : boolean ) : boolean;

var Attempts : byte;                      { Maximum number of tries }
    Regs     : Registers; { Processor registers for interrupt call }
    TrackF,                                     { Current track }
    SideNum,                                     { Current side }
    Stat     : byte;                { Return value of called functions }

begin
  {-- Format a diskette track by track -----------------------------}

  for TrackF := 0 to PData.STrax - 1 do       { Execute all tracks }
    for SideNum := 0 to PData.DSides - 1 do    { Execute all sides }
      begin
        Write( #13'Track: ', TrackF: 2, '  Side: ', SideNum: 2 );
        {-- A maximum of 5 tries to format a track ----------------}

        Attempts := MaxNumTries;     { Set maximum number of tries }
        repeat
          Stat := FormatTrack( Drive, SideNum, TrackF, PData.TSectors );
          if ( Stat = 3 ) then       { Diskette write/protected? }
            begin
              PhysicalFormat := false;  { End procedure with error }
              WriteLn( #13'Diskette is write/protected' );
              exit;                           { End procedure }
            end;
          if ( Stat = 0 ) and Verify then
            Stat := VerifyTrack( Drive, SideNum, TrackF, PData.TSectors );
          dec( Attempts );
          if ( Stat > 0 ) then                { Format unsuccessful }
            DiskReset;
        until ( Stat = 0 ) or ( Attempts = 0 );
        if ( Stat > 0 )  then              { Error during formatting }
          begin
            PhysicalFormat := false;   { End procedure with error }
            WriteLn( #13'Track defective       ' );
            exit;                           { End procedure }
          end;
      end;
  PhysicalFormat := true;         { Procedure ended without error }
end;

{*****************************************************************}
{* LogicalFormat : Logical formatting of diskette (Writing boot  *}
{*                 sector, FAT and root directory)               *}
{* Input       : DRIVE = Drive number                            *}
{*               PDATA = Physical formatting information          *}
{*               LDATA = Logical formatting information           *}
{* Output      : TRUE, if no error occurs                        *}
{*****************************************************************}

function LogicalFormat( Drive : byte;
                        PData : PhysDataType;
```

```
                        LData : LogDataType ) : boolean;

var Stat         : byte;          { Feedback of called functions }
    TotalNoSectors : word;           { Total number of sectors }
    i            : byte;                   { Loop counter }
    CurSector,
    CurSide,
    CurTrack     : byte;
    SecPTr       : integer;   { Number of tracks to be written }
    TrackBuffer  : TrackBfType;          { Memory for a track }

begin
  fillchar( TrackBuffer, word( PData.TSectors ) * 512, 0 );{ Empty buf}

  {-- Bootsector: Fixed part ------------------------------------}

  move( BootMask, TrackBuffer, 102 );     { Copy boot sector mask }
  move( BootMes[1], TrackBuffer[ 1, 103 ],     { Copy boot texts }
        ord(BootMes[0]) );
  TrackBuffer[ 1, 511 ] := $55;        { End marker of boot sector }
  TrackBuffer[ 1, 512 ] := $AA;

  {-- Bootsector: Variable part ---------------------------------}

  TotalNoSectors := PData.STrax * PData.TSectors * Pdata.DSides;
  TrackBuffer[ 1, 14 ] := LData.Cluster;        { Cluster size }
  TrackBuffer[ 1, 18 ] := LData.RootSize; { Num. entries in root dir. }
  TrackBuffer[ 1, 20 ] := lo( TotalNoSectors );{ Total number sectors }
  TrackBuffer[ 1, 21 ] := hi( TotalNoSectors );{ on the diskette }
  TrackBuffer[ 1, 22 ] := LData.Media;        { Media descriptor }
  TrackBuffer[ 1, 23 ] := LData.FAT;          { Size of FAT }
  TrackBuffer[ 1, 25 ] := PData.TSectors;     { Sectors per track }
  TrackBuffer[ 1, 27 ] := PData.DSides;       { Number of sides }

  {-- Make FAT and FAT copy (Contents 00)------------------------}

  TrackBuffer[ 2, 1 ] := LData.Media;         { Create 1st FAT }
  TrackBuffer[ 2, 2 ] := $FF;
  TrackBuffer[ 2, 3 ] := $FF;
  TrackBuffer[ LData.FAT + 2, 1 ] := LData.Media; { Create 2nd FAT }
  TrackBuffer[ LData.FAT + 2, 2 ] := $FF;
  TrackBuffer[ LData.FAT + 2, 3 ] := $FF;

  {-- Write boot sector and FAT ---------------------------------}

  Stat := WriteTrack( Drive, 0, 0, 1, PData.TSectors, TrackBuffer );
  if Stat <> 0 then
    LogicalFormat := FALSE

  {-- No error, write root directory ----------------------------}

  else
    begin
      fillchar( TrackBuffer, 512, 0 );          { Empty sector }
      CurSector := PData.TSectors;  { Write first track completely }
      CurTrack := 0;                          { Current track }
      CurSide := 0;                           { Current side }

      {-- Determine number of remaining sectors and write ---------}

      SecPTr := LData.FAT * 2 + ( LData.Rootsize * 32 div 512 ) +
                1 - PData.TSectors;

      i := 1;
```

```
    repeat
      inc( CurSector );                          { Next sector }
      if ( CurSector > PData.TSectors ) then     { Track ended? }
        begin
          CurSector := 1;                         { Continue with sector 1 }
          inc( CurSide );                              { Next side? }
          if ( CurSide = PData.DSides ) then   { Side 2 already? }
            begin
              CurSide := 0;                       { Back to side 0 }
              inc( CurTrack );
            end;
        end;
      Stat := WriteTrack( Drive, CurSide, CurTrack,
                          CurSector, 1, TrackBuffer );
      inc( i );
    until ( i > SecPTr ) or ( Stat <> 0 );
    LogicalFormat := ( Stat = 0 )
  end;
end;

{*******************************************************************}
{*                       MAIN PROGRAM                             *}
{*******************************************************************}

begin
  WriteLn( 'DFP  -  (c) 1992 by Michael Tischer'#13#10 );
  if paramcount > 1 then                  { Parameters specified? }
    begin { Yes, evaluate }
      Param := paramstr( 1 );  { Determine drive ( 0 = a:, 1 = b: ) }
      CurDrive := ord( upcase( Param[ 1 ] ) ) - 65;
      CurDriveType := GetDriveType( CurDrive );{ Type of current driv }
      if ( CurDriveType > 0 ) then            { Drive available? }
        begin                { Yes --> Program can be continued }
          if GetFormatParameter( paramstr( 2 ), CurDriveType,
                                 PData, LData) then
            begin                 { Format and drive are compatible }
              DiskPrepare( CurDrive, PData );
              GetIntVec( $1E, POldDDPT );        { Store old DDPT }
              SetIntVec( $1E, PData.DDPT );       { Set new DDPT }

              Param := paramstr( 3 );
              ok := PhysicalFormat( CurDrive, PData,
                                    upcase( Param[ 1 ] ) <> 'N' );
              if ok then
                begin
                  Write( #13'Write boot sector and FAT        ' );
                  ok := LogicalFormat( CurDrive, PData, LData )
                end;

              {-- Evaluation of formatting process ----------------}

              if ok then
                begin
                  WriteLn( #13'Formatting OK                ' );
                  ExitCode := 0;
                end
              else
                begin
                  WriteLn( #13'Error - format cancelled' );
                  ExitCode := 1;
                end;
              SetIntVec( $1E, POldDDPT );      { Restore old DDPT }
            end
          else
```

```
            begin
              WriteLn( 'This drive does not support that format' );
              ExitCode := 2;     { Return value to calling process }
            end
          end
        else
          begin
            WriteLn( 'The specified disk drive does not exist');
            ExitCode := 3;         { Return value to calling process }
          end
      end
    else
      begin
        writeln( 'Syntax: DFP Drive Format [ NV ]' );
        writeln( '            |        |       |' );
        writeln( '          __|____    |       |' );
        writeln( '          A: or B:   |       |' );
        writeln( '          _____|___     |' );
        writeln( '          360, 720, 1200, 1440 |' );
        writeln( '                         ____|__' );
        writeln( '                         NV = No verify' );
        ExitCode := 4;         { Return value to calling process }
      end;
    Halt( ExitCode );
end.
```

Listing: DFC.C

```
/****************************************************************/
/*                   D F C . C                               */
/*------------------------------------------------------------*/
/*   Tasks      : Formats 3.5" and 5.25" diskettes           */
/*------------------------------------------------------------*/
/*   Author     : Michael Tischer                            */
/*   Developed on : 08/28/91                                 */
/*   Last update : 01/26/92                                  */
/*------------------------------------------------------------*/
/*   Memory model : SMALL                                    */
/*------------------------------------------------------------
/*   Attention   : Use the following when compiling in Microsoft */
/*                 C: CL /AS /Gs DFC.C                        */
/****************************************************************/

/*== Link include files ======================================*/

#include <dos.h>
#include <stdio.h>
#include <string.h>

/*== Macros =================================================*/

#ifdef MK_FP                       /* Macro MK_FP already defined? */
  #undef MK_FP                     /* Yes, then delete macro */
#endif

#define MK_FP(seg,ofs) ((void far *) ((unsigned long) (seg)<<16|( ofs)))
#define LO( aval ) ( ( BYTE ) ( aval & 0xFF ) )
#define HI( aval ) ( ( BYTE ) ( aval >> 8 ) )
#define SEG( p ) ( ( unsigned int ) ( ( ( long ) p ) >> 16 ) )
#define OFS( p ) ( ( unsigned int ) ( p ) )

/*== Constants ===============================================*/

#define NOPE        0x4E                        /* N for No */
#define NO_DRIVE    0              /* Drive does not exist */
#define DD_525      1              /* Drive: 5.25" DD */
#define HD_525      2              /* Drive: 5.25" HD */
#define DD_35       3              /* Drive: 3.5" DD */
#define HD_35       4              /* Drive: 3.5" HD */

#define MAXNUMTRIES 5              /* Maximum number of tries */

#define TRUE        ( 0 == 0 )     /* Constants, making it easy */
#define FALSE       ( 1 == 0 )     /* to read the program text */

/*== Typedefs ================================================*/

typedef unsigned char BYTE;                /* Data type byte */

typedef BYTE DDPTType[ 11 ];               /* Field for a DDPT */
typedef DDPTType *DDPTPTR;                  /* Pointer to a DDPT */

typedef struct {                 /* Physical format parameters */
                BYTE    DSides,            /* Number of sides */
                        STrax,             /* Tracks per side */
                        TSectors;          /* Sectors per track */
                DDPTPTR DDPT;              /* Pointer to DDPTR */
               } PhysDataType;

typedef struct {                 /* Logical format parameters */
```

```
                BYTE Media;                /* Media byte */
                BYTE Cluster;      /* Number of sectors per cluster */
                BYTE FAT;          /* Number of sectors for the FAT */
                BYTE BootSize;     /* Entries in the root directory */
               } LogDataType;

typedef BYTE TrackBfType[ 18 ][ 512 ];     /* Memory for a track */

/*== Global variables =======================================*/

/*-- Non variable part of the BOOT sector --------------------*/

BYTE BootMask[ 102 ] =
     { 0xEB, 0x35,       /* 0000    JMP 0037        */
       0x90,             /* 0002    NOP             */
       /*-- Data of BPB -----------------------------*/

       0x50, 0x43, 0x49, 0x4E, 0x54, 0x45, 0x52, 0x4E,
       0x00, 0x00, 0x00, 0x01, 0x00, 0x00, 0x00, 0x00,
       0x00, 0x00, 0x00, 0x00, 0x00, 0x00, 0x00, 0x00,
       0x00, 0x00, 0x00, 0x00, 0x00, 0x00, 0x00, 0x00,
       0x00, 0x00, 0x00, 0x00, 0x00, 0x00, 0x00, 0x00,
       0x00, 0x00, 0x00, 0x00, 0x00, 0x00, 0x00, 0x00,
       0x00, 0x00, 0x00, 0x00,

       /*-- Actual loading program --------------------*/

       0xFA,             /* 0037    CLI             */
       0xB8, 0x30, 0x00, /* 0038    MOV   AX,0030    */
       0x8E, 0xD0,       /* 003B    MOV   SS,AX      */
       0xBC, 0xFC, 0x00, /* 003D    MOV   SP,0OFC    */
       0xFB,             /* 0040    STI             */
       0x0E,             /* 0041    PUSH  CS         */
       0x1F,             /* 0042    POP   DS         */
       0xBE, 0x66, 0x7C, /* 0043    MOV   SI,7C66    */
       0xB4, 0x0E,       /* 0046    MOV   AH,0E      */
       0xFC,             /* 0048    CLD             */
       0xAC,             /* 0049    LODSB           */
       0x0A, 0xC0,       /* 004A    OR    AL,AL      */
       0x74, 0x04,       /* 004C    JZ    0052       */
       0xCD, 0x10,       /* 004E    INT   10         */
       0xEB, 0xF7,       /* 0050    JMP   0049       */
       0xB4, 0x01,       /* 0052    MOV   AH,01      */
       0xCD, 0x16,       /* 0054    INT   16         */
       0x74, 0x06,       /* 0056    JZ    005E       */
       0xB4, 0x00,       /* 0058    MOV   AH,00      */
       0xCD, 0x16,       /* 005A    INT   16         */
       0xEB, 0xF4,       /* 005C    JMP   0052       */
       0xB4, 0x00,       /* 005E    MOV   AH,00      */
       0xCD, 0x16,       /* 0060    INT   16         */
       0x33, 0xD2,       /* 0062    XOR   DX,DX      */
       0xCD, 0x19 };     /* 0064    INT   19         */

char BootMes[] =
  "\nDFC  -  (C) 1992 by Michael Tischer\n\n" \
  "Defective diskette or non-system diskette\n" \
  "Please change diskettes and press any key . . .\n\n";

/****************************************************************/
/* upcase     : Converts lower-case letters to upper-case letters.*/
/* Input      : Letter                                        */
/* Output     : Uppercase letter                              */
/****************************************************************/
```

```
char upcase( char letter )
{
  if ( ( letter > 0x60 ) && ( letter < 0x7B ) )      /* Convert? */
    return (unsigned char) letter & 0xDF;            /* Yes, mask bit */
  else
    return letter;                                   /* No, return unchanged */
}


/********************************************************************/
/* GetIntVec: Gets an interrupt vector.                           */
/* Input    : NUMBER = Interrupt number                           */
/* Output   : Interrupt vector                                    */
/********************************************************************/

void far *GetIntVec( int Number )
{
  return( *( ( void far * far * ) MK_FP( 0, Number * 4 ) ) );
}


/********************************************************************/
/* SetIntVec: Sets an interrupt vector.                           */
/* Input    : NUMBER = Interrupt number                           */
/*            POINTER = Interrupt vector                          */
/* Output   : None                                               */
/********************************************************************/

void SetIntVec( int Number, void far *Pointer )
{
  *( ( void far * far * ) MK_FP( 0, Number * 4 ) ) = Pointer;
}


/********************************************************************/
/* GetDriveType : Determines the disk drive type.                */
/* Input        : DRIVE = Drive number (0, 1 etc.)               */
/* Output       : Drive code as constants (DD_525, HD_525 etc.)  */
/********************************************************************/

BYTE GetDriveType( BYTE Drive )
{
  union REGS regs;         /* Processor registers for interrupt call */

  regs.h.ah = 0x08;              /* Function: Determine drive type */
  regs.h.dl = Drive;                          /* Drive number */
  int86( 0x13, &regs, &regs );           /* Call BIOS interrupt */
  if ( regs.x.cflag )                       /* Error in call? */
    return( DD_525 );       /* Fct. 0x08 does not exist => 360K XT */
  else
    return( regs.h.bl );                     /* Drive type */
}


/********************************************************************/
/* ResetDisk : Disk reset on all drives.                         */
/* Input     : None                                              */
/* Output    : None                                              */
/* Info      : Reset executed on all drives, regardless of drive */
/*             number loaded in DD                               */
/********************************************************************/

void DiskReset( void )
{
  union REGS regs;      /* Processor registers for interrupt call */

  regs.h.ah = 0x00;       /* Function number for interrupt call */
  regs.h.dl = 0;                          /* Drive a: (see Info) */
```

```
  int86( 0x13, &regs, &regs );               /* Interrupt call */
}

/********************************************************************/
/* GetFormatParamter: Determines the logical and physical parameters */
/*                    necessary for formatting.                   */
/* Input    : FORMSTRING = Pointer to string with format         */
/*                         "360", "720", "1200", "1440"          */
/*            DRIVETYPE = Drive code, as supplied by GetDriveType() */
/*            PDATAP    = Pointer to structure that gets physical */
/*                        format parameters                      */
/*            LDATAP    = Pointer to structure that gets logical  */
/*                        format parameters                      */
/* Output   : TRUE, if format is possible, otherwise FALSE       */
/* Info     : New formats can be added by expanding this procedure */
/********************************************************************/

BYTE GetFormatParameter( char      *FormString,
                         BYTE          DriveType,
                         PhysDataType *PDataP,
                         LogDataType  *LDataP )

{
  static DDPTType DDPT_360  = { 0xDF, 0x02, 0x25, 0x02, 0x09, 0x2A,
                               0xFF, 0x50, 0xF6, 0x0F, 0x08 };
  static DDPTType DDPT_1200 = { 0xDF, 0x02, 0x25, 0x02, 0x0F, 0x1B,
                               0xFF, 0x54, 0xF6, 0x0F, 0x08 };
  static DDPTType DDPT_1440 = { 0xDF, 0x02, 0x25, 0x02, 0x12, 0x1B,
                               0xFF, 0x6C, 0xF6, 0x0F, 0x08 };
  static DDPTType DDPT_720  = { 0xDF, 0x02, 0x25, 0x02, 0x09, 0x2A,
                               0xFF, 0x50, 0xF6, 0x0F, 0x08 };

  static LogDataType LOG_360  = { 0xFD, 2, 2, 0x70 };
  static LogDataType LOG_1200 = { 0xF9, 1, 7, 0xE0 };
  static LogDataType LOG_720  = { 0xF9, 2, 3, 0x70 };
  static LogDataType LOG_1440 = { 0xF0, 1, 9, 0xE0 };

  static PhysDataType PHYS_360  = { 2, 40,  9, &DDPT_360 };
  static PhysDataType PHYS_1200 = { 2, 80, 15, &DDPT_1200 };
  static PhysDataType PHYS_720  = { 2, 80,  9, &DDPT_720 };
  static PhysDataType PHYS_1440 = { 2, 80, 18, &DDPT_1440 };

/*-- Take format from string and fill passed structures with  -----*/
/*-- data                                                     -----*/

  if ( strcmp( FormString, "1200" ) == 0 )     /* 1.2 Meg on 5.25"? */
    if ( DriveType == HD_525 )     /* Format compatible with drive? */
    {
      memcpy( PDataP, &PHYS_1200, sizeof( PhysDataType ) );
      memcpy( LDataP, &LOG_1200, sizeof ( LogDataType ) );
      return TRUE;                            /* End without error */
    }
    else
      return( FALSE );          /* Drive and format incompatible */
  else if ( strcmp( FormString, "360" ) == 0 )        /* 360K? */
    if ( ( DriveType == HD_525 ) || ( DriveType == DD_525 ) )
    {                /* Format and drive compatible, set parameters */
      memcpy( PDataP, &PHYS_360, sizeof( PhysDataType ) );
      memcpy( LDataP, &LOG_360, sizeof ( LogDataType ) );
      return TRUE;                            /* End without error */
    }
    else
      return( FALSE );          /* Drive and format incompatible */
  else if ( strcmp( FormString, "1440" ) == 0 ) /* 1.44 Meg on 3.5"? */
```

```
if ( DriveType == HD_35 )      /* Format compatible with drive? */
{                    /* Format and drive compatible, set parameters */
  memcpy ( PDataP, &PHYS_1440, sizeof( PhysDataType ) );
  memcpy ( LDataP, &LOG_1440, sizeof ( LogDataType ) );
  return TRUE;                           /* End without error */
}
else
  return( FALSE );               /* Drive and format incompatible */
else if ( strcmp( FormString, "720" ) == 0 )      /* 720K on 3.5"? */
  if ( ( DriveType == HD_35 ) || ( DriveType == DD_35 ) )
  {                   /* Format and drive compatible, set parameters */
    memcpy ( PDataP, &PHYS_720, sizeof( PhysDataType ) );
    memcpy ( LDataP, &LOG_720, sizeof ( LogDataType ) );
    return TRUE;                         /* End without error */
  }
  else
    return FALSE;                /* Drive and format incompatible */
else
  return FALSE;                 /* Invalid format specified */
}

/***********************************************************************/
/* DiskPrepare: Prepare drive, set data transfer rate.           */
/* Input    : DRIVE = Drive number                               */
/*            PDATA = Table with physical parameters             */
/* Output   : None                                               */
/***********************************************************************/

void DiskPrepare( BYTE Drive, PhysDataType PData )
{
  union REGS regs;        /* Processor registers for interrupt call */

  /*-- Set media type for formatting call -------------------------*/

  regs.h.ah = 0x18;         /* Function number for interrupt call */
  regs.h.ch = PData.STrax - 1;   /* Number of tracks per side */
  regs.h.cl = PData.TSectors;   /* Number of sectors per track */
  regs.h.dl = Drive;                        /* Drive number */
  int86( 0x13, &regs, &regs );              /* Interrupt call */
}

/***********************************************************************/
/* FormatTrack: Formats a track.                                 */
/* Input    : See below                                          */
/* Output   : Error status                                       */
/***********************************************************************/

BYTE FormatTrack( BYTE DriveNum,              /* The drive number */
                  BYTE SideNum,               /* The side number */
                  BYTE TrackF,                /* The track */
                  BYTE SecPTr )   /* Number of sectors for this track */

{
  struct FormatTyp {       /* Sector information for the BIOS */
             BYTE DTrackF, DSideNum, DCounter, DLength;
           };

  BYTE          attempts;   /* Number of tries for interrupt call */
  BYTE          Counter;                  /* Loop counter */
  struct FormatTyp DataField[ 18 ];       /* Maximum 18 sectors */
  void far *     dfp = DataField;      /* Pointer to data field */
  union REGS     regs;   /* Processor registers for interrupt call */
  struct SREGS   sregs;               /* Segment registers */
```

```
  for ( Counter = 0; Counter < SecPTr; Counter++ )
  {
    DataField[ Counter ].DTrackF = TrackF;
    DataField[ Counter ].DSideNum = SideNum;
    DataField[ Counter ].DCounter = Counter + 1;
    DataField[ Counter ].DLength = 2;     /* 512 bytes per sector */
  }

  attempts = MAXNUMTRIES;         /* Set maximum number of tries */
  do
  {
    regs.h.ah = 5;        /* Function number for interrupt call */
    regs.h.al = SecPTr;       /* Number of sectors for a track */
    regs.x.bx = OFS( dfp );            /* Offset addr. of buffer */
    sregs.es = SEG( dfp );                 /* Segment addr. */
    regs.h.dh = SideNum;                   /* Side number */
    regs.h.dl = DriveNum;                  /* Drive number */
    regs.h.ch = TrackF;                    /* Track number */
    int86x( 0x13, &regs, &regs, &sregs );  /* Call BIOS interrupt */
    if ( regs.x.cflag )                    /* Error? */
      DiskReset();
  }
  while ( ( --attempts != 0 ) && ( regs.x.cflag ) );
  return( regs.h.ah );               /* Read error status */
}

/***********************************************************************/
/* VerifyTrack: Verify track.                                    */
/* Input    : See below                                          */
/* Output   : Error status                                       */
/***********************************************************************/

BYTE VerifyTrack( BYTE DriveNum,              /* Drive number */
                  BYTE SideNum,               /* Side number */
                  BYTE TrackF,                /* Track number */
                  BYTE TSectors )   /* Number of sectors per track */

{
  BYTE          attempts;   /* Number of tries for interrupt call */
  union REGS    regs;    /* Processor registers for interrupt call */
  struct SREGS  sregs;  /* Proc. registers for extended interrupt call */
  TrackBfType   sbuf;                    /* Track buffer */
  void far      *sbptr = sbuf;   /* FAR pointer to track buffer */

  attempts = MAXNUMTRIES;         /* Set maximum number of tries */
  do
  {
    regs.h.ah = 0x04;      /* Function number for interrupt call */
    regs.h.al = TSectors;      /* Number of sectors per track */
    regs.h.ch = TrackF;                    /* Track number */
    regs.h.cl = 1;                     /* Start at sector 1 */
    regs.h.dl = DriveNum;                  /* Drive number */
    regs.h.dh = SideNum;                   /* Side number */
    regs.x.bx = OFS( sbptr );          /* Offset addr. of buffer */
    sregs.es = SEG( sbptr );               /* Segment addr. */
    int86x( 0x13, &regs, &regs, &sregs );  /* Call BIOS interrupt */
    if ( regs.x.cflag )                    /* Error? */
      DiskReset();
  }
  while ( ( --attempts != 0 ) && ( regs.x.cflag ) );
  return( regs.h.ah );               /* Read out error status */
}

/***********************************************************************/
```

```
/* WriteTrack: Write track.                               */
/* Input     : See below                                  */
/* Output    : Error code (0=OK)                          */
/****************************************************************/

BYTE WriteTrack( BYTE DriveNum,              /* Drive number */
                 BYTE SideNum,               /* Side number */
                 BYTE TrackF,                /* Track number */
                 BYTE Start,                 /* Start at sector */
                 BYTE TSectors,    /* Number of sectors per track */
                 void far *DaPtr )           /* Pointer to data field */

{
  BYTE attempts;           /* Number of tries for interrupt call */
  union REGS regs;         /* Processor registers for interrupt call */
  struct SREGS sregs;  /* Proc. registers for extended interrupt call */

  attempts = MAXNUMTRIES;          /* Set maximum number of tries */
  do
  {
    regs.h.ah = 0x03;      /* Function number for interrupt call */
    regs.h.al = TSectors;          /* Number of sectors per track */
    regs.h.ch = TrackF;                     /* Track number */
    regs.h.cl = Start;              /* Start at sector */
    regs.h.dl = DriveNum;                   /* Drive number */
    regs.h.dh = SideNum;                    /* Side number */
    regs.x.bx = OFS( DaPtr );       /* Offset addr. of buffer */
    sregs.es = SEG( DaPtr );                /* Segment addr. */
    int86x( 0x13, &regs, &regs, &sregs );   /* Call BIOS interrupt */
    if ( regs.x.cflag )                     /* Error? */
      DiskReset();
  }
  while ( ( --attempts != 0 ) && ( regs.x.cflag ) );
  return( regs.h.ah );              /* Read out error status */
}


/****************************************************************/
/* PhysicalFormat: Physical formatting of diskette (division into */
/*                 tracks, sectors).                        */
/* Input     : See below                                    */
/* Output    : Formatting ended without errors              */
/****************************************************************/

BYTE PhysicalFormat( BYTE     Drive,         /* Drive number */
                     PhysDataType PData,      /* Physical parameters */
                     BYTE     Verify )        /* Flag for Verify */

{
  union REGS regs;         /* Processor registers for interrupt call */
  BYTE     attempts,       /* Number of tries for interrupt call */
           TrackF,                 /* Loop counter: current track */
           SideNum,                /* Loop counter: current side */
           Status;                 /* Return value of the called functions */

/*-- Format diskette track by track -----------------------*/

  for ( TrackF = 0; TrackF < PData.STrax; TrackF++ )
  for ( SideNum = 0; SideNum < PData.DSides; SideNum++ )
  {
    printf( "\rTrack: %d  Side: %d", TrackF, SideNum );
    /*-- Maximum of 5 tries to format a track --------------------*/

    attempts = MAXNUMTRIES;        /* Set maximum number of tries */
    do
```

```
    {
      Status = FormatTrack( Drive, SideNum, TrackF, PData.TSectors );
      if ( Status == 3 )           /* Diskette write/protected? */
      {
          printf( "\rDiskette is write/protected \n" );
          return FALSE;            /* End procedure with error
*/
      }
      if ( Status == 0 && Verify )
        Status = VerifyTrack( Drive, SideNum, TrackF, PData.TSectors );
      if ( Status > 0 )            /* Formatting unsuccessful */
        DiskReset();
    }
    while ( ( --attempts != 0 ) && ( Status != 0 ) );
    if ( Status > 0 )                       /* Error in formatting */
    {
      printf( "\rTrack defective          \n" );
      return FALSE;                /* End procedure with error */
    }
  }
  return TRUE;                     /* Procedure ends without error */
}


/****************************************************************/
/* LogicalFormat : Logical formatting of diskette (writing boot   */
/*                 sectors, FAT and root directory).        */
/* Input     : See below                                    */
/* Output    : TRUE, if no error occurs                     */
/****************************************************************/

BYTE LogicalFormat( BYTE Drive,              /* Drive number */
                    PhysDataType PData,      /* Physical parameters */
                    LogDataType LData )      /* Physical parameters */

{
  BYTE       i,                              /* Loop counter */
             CurSector,
             CurSide,
             CurTrack,
             Status;
  int        TotalSectors,         /* Total number of sectors */
             SecPTr;               /* Number of sectors to be written */
  TrackBfType TrakBuffer;                    /* Gets a complete track */

  memset( TrakBuffer, 0, (int) PData.TSectors * 512 ); /* Empty track */

/*-- Boot sector: fixed part ------------------------------*/

  memcpy( TrakBuffer, BootMask, 102 );  /* Copy boot sector mask */
  memcpy( &TrakBuffer[ 0 ][ 102 ], BootMes, sizeof( BootMes ) );
  TrakBuffer[ 0 ][ 510 ] = 0x55;        /* End marker of boot sector */
  TrakBuffer[ 0 ][ 511 ] = 0xAA;

/*-- Boot sector: variable part ---------------------------*/

  TotalSectors = (int) PData.STrax * (int) PData.TSectors *
                 (int) PData.DSides;   /* Total number of sectors */
  TrakBuffer[ 0 ][ 13 ] = LData.Cluster;         /* Cluster size */
  TrakBuffer[ 0 ][ 17 ] = LData.RootSize;/* Number entries in root dr */
  TrakBuffer[ 0 ][ 19 ] = LO( TotalSectors );
  TrakBuffer[ 0 ][ 20 ] = HI( TotalSectors );
  TrakBuffer[ 0 ][ 21 ] = LData.Media;  /* Media descriptor */
  TrakBuffer[ 0 ][ 22 ] = LData.FAT;             /* Size of FAT */
  TrakBuffer[ 0 ][ 24 ] = PData.TSectors;  /* Sectors per track */
```

```
TrakBuffer[ 0 ][ 26 ] = PData.DSides;          /* Number of sides */

/*-- Create FAT and FAT copy ------------------------------------*/

TrakBuffer[ 1 ][ 0 ] = LData.Media;            /* Create 1st FAT */
TrakBuffer[ 1 ][ 1 ] = 0xFF;
TrakBuffer[ 1 ][ 2 ] = 0xFF;
TrakBuffer[ LData.FAT + 1 ][ 0 ] = LData.Media;    /* Create 2nd FAT */
TrakBuffer[ LData.FAT + 1 ][ 1 ] = 0xFF;
TrakBuffer[ LData.FAT + 1 ][ 2 ] = 0xFF;

/*-- Write boot sector and FAT ----------------------------------*/

Status = WriteTrack( Drive, 0, 0, 1, PData.TSectors, TrakBuffer );
if ( Status )                                  /* Error writing? */
 return FALSE;                                 /* Yes, return error */

/*-- Write root directory ---------------------------------------*/

memset( TrakBuffer, 0, 512 );                  /* Empty sector */
CurSector = PData.TSectors;     /* First track completely written */
CurTrack = 0;                                  /* Current track */
CurSide = 0;                                   /* Current side */

/*-- Determine remaining number of sectors and write ------------*/

SecPTr = LData.FAT * 2 + (LData.RootSize*32/512) + 1-PData.TSectors;

for ( i = 1; i <= SecPTr; i++ )
 {
  if ( ++CurSector > PData.TSectors )          /* End of track? */
   {
    CurSector = 1;                             /* Continue with sector 1 */
    if ( ++CurSide == PData.DSides )           /* 2nd side already? */
     {
      CurSide = 0;                             /* Back to side 0 */
      CurTrack++;
     }
   }
  Status = WriteTrack( Drive, CurSide, CurTrack,
                       CurSector, 1, TrakBuffer );
  if ( Status )                                /* Error? */
   break;                      /* Yes, leave FOR loop prematurely */
 }
return ( Status == 0 );
}

/*****************************************************************/
/*                    MAIN PROGRAM                        */
/*****************************************************************/

int main( argc, argv )

int argc;               /* Number of arguments in the command line */
char *argv[];                          /* Field with parameters */

{
  BYTE        CurDrive;         /* Number of drive to be formatted */
  BYTE        CurDriveType;             /* Current disk drive type */
  PhysDataType PData;              /* Physical format parameters */
  LogDataType LData;               /* Logical format parameters */
  void far    *POldDDPT;               /* Pointer to old DDPT */
  char        *Param;          /* For evaluating the command line */
  BYTE        ok;                  /* Flag for program flow */
```

```
int       ExitCode;

printf( "DFC - (c) 1992 by Michael Tischer\n\n" );

/*-- Evaluate command line --------------------------------------*/

if ( argc > 1 )                              /* Parameters specified? */
 {                                           /* Yes */
  Param = argv[ 1 ];       /* Determine drive ( 0 = a:, 1 = b: ) */
  CurDrive = upcase( Param[ 0 ] ) - 65;
  CurDriveType = GetDriveType( CurDrive );   /* Current drive type */
  if ( CurDriveType > 0 )                     /* Drive exist? */
   if ( GetFormatParameter( argv[ 2 ], CurDriveType, &PData, &LData ))
    {
     DiskPrepare( CurDrive, PData );
     POldDDPT = GetIntVec( 0x1E );           /* Store old DDPT */
     SetIntVec( 0x1E, PData.DDPT );          /* Set new DDPT */

     Param = argv[ 3 ];
     if ( ok = PhysicalFormat( CurDrive, PData,
            (BYTE) ( upcase( Param[ 0 ] ) != 'N' ) ) )
      {
       printf( "\rWrite boot sector and FAT          \n" );
       ok = LogicalFormat( CurDrive, PData, LData );
      }

     /*-- Evaluation of formatting process --------------------*/
     if ( ok )
      {
       printf( "\rFormatting OK                       \n" );
       ExitCode = 0;              /* Program ended successfully */
      }
     else
      {
       printf( "\rError - format cancelled            \n");
       ExitCode = 1;        /* Formatting cancelled with error */
      }
     SetIntVec( 0x1E, POldDDPT );            /* Restore old DDPT */
    }
   else
    {
     printf( "This drive does not support that format\n" );
     ExitCode = 2;        /* Drive and format not compatible */
    }
  else
   {
    printf( "The specified disk drive does not exist\n" );
    ExitCode = 3;                        /* Drive does not exist */
   }
 }
else
 {
  printf( "Call:   DFP Drive Format [ NV ]\n" );
  printf( "                                \n" );
  printf( "             _____           \n" );
  printf( "           A: or  B:            \n" );
  printf( "        _____         \n" );
  printf( "        360, 720, 1200, 1440    \n" );
  printf( "                      _____\n" );
  printf( "                      NV = no Verify\n" );
  ExitCode = 4;                            /* Wrong call */
 }
return( ExitCode );              /* End program with return value */
}
```

6.4 Accessing the Hard Drives with the BIOS

In this section we'll describe the BIOS functions for accessing hard drives. However, before we begin, we must warn you about experimenting with these functions. Unlike a floppy disk drive, in which you can insert an unused diskette for testing, a hard drive cannot be tested in this way. Using write and format functions carelessly can lead to irreparable data loss. Because of the structure DOS imposes on a hard drive, destroying one sector can cause all files and directories to disappear because DOS may no longer know where they are on the hard disk.

So, if you would like to "test" the BIOS functions, be sure to make a complete backup of your entire hard drive beforehand, or use another computer, if available. This is the only way you can avoid data loss, because even the most elaborate hard drive utility may not be able to help you.

The BIOS hard drive interrupt

As we already mentioned, the hard drive shares interrupt 13H with the floppy disk drives. Although the functions for the hard drive and the floppy disk drives are identical, the BIOS controls the hard drive differently than the floppy disk drive. For this reason, the BIOS contains a module for controlling the hard drive and a separate one for controlling the floppy disk drives.

When interrupt 13H is called, the device number in the DL register determines whether a floppy or hard drive is being addressed. A value of 80H represents the first hard drive, while 81H represents the second hard drive. It's not possible to address more than two hard drives via the BIOS.

The functions of the hard drive BIOS have existed since the introduction of the XT. The original PC BIOS didn't have them. In 1981 no one thought of putting hard drives in microcomputers. When the AT and PS/2 model from IBM was introduced, some additional functions were added, as the following table shows:

Function	Task	Origin
00H	Reset	XT
01H	Read status	XT
02H	Read	XT
03H	Write	XT
04H	Verify	XT
05H	Format	XT
08H	Check format	XT
09H	Adapt to foreign drives	XT
0AH	Extended read	XT
0BH	Extended write	XT
0CH	Move read/write head	XT
0DH	Reset	XT
0EH	Controller read test	only PS/2
0FH	Controller write test	only PS/2
10H	Drive ready?	XT
11H	Recalibrate drive	XT
12H	Controller RAM test	only PS/2
13H	Drive test	only PS/2
14H	Controller diagnostic	XT
15H	Determine drive type	AT

Normal application programs don't usually access the hard drive through the BIOS. We'll describe only the most important functions in this section. You can find more information in the Appendix of this book, in which all of the functions are described.

Status code

The hard drive functions use the carry flag to indicate an error. If the carry flag is set, then an error has occurred and the error status code is returned in the AH register.

The codes have the following meanings:

Error codes when calling BIOS Disk Interrupt 13h for accessing the hard drive	
Code	Meaning
00h	No error
01h	Function number or drive not permitted
02h	Address not found
04h	Addressed sector not found
05h	Error on controller reset
07h	Error during controller initialization
09h	DMA transmission error. Segment border exceeded.
0Ah	Defective sector
10h	Read error
11h	Read error corrected by ECC
20h	Controller defect
40h	Search operation failed
80h	Time out, unit not responding
AAh	Unit not ready
CCh	Write error

When one of these error occurs (except for error 1), you should first reset the drive and retry the function. Usually, the operation will then be successful.

If error 11H is returned after a read function, the data isn't necessarily invalid. Actually, this status code indicates that a read error was detected, but was able to be corrected using an ECC (Error Correction Code) algorithm. This procedure is similar to the CRC procedure used by floppy disk drives. The individual bytes of a sector are calculated through a complicated mathematical formula. The resulting sum is written to the sector on the hard disk as four additional bytes. If a read error is detected, it can usually be corrected by using the ECC.

Using the hard drive functions

The hard drive functions also use registers for passing parameters. The function number is passed in the AH register. When the hard drive number must be identified, its value is passed in the DL register. The value 80H always represents the first hard drive, and 81H represents the second hard drive. The number of the read/write head and the side (0 or 1) are passed in the DH register.

The CH register specifies the cylinder number. Since you can represent only 256 cylinders with this 8-bit register and the hard drive of an XT has more than 306 cylinders, this register alone cannot specify the cylinder number. For this reason, bits 6 and 7 of the CL register are "appended" to the value in the CH register to determine the cylinder number. They form bits 8 and 9 of the cylinder number, so that a maximum of 1024 cylinders (numbered 0 to 1023) can be addressed. Bits 0 to 5 of the CL register specify the sector number (1 to 17 per cylinder). If more than one sector is being accessed at the same time, the AL register specifies the number of sectors. In read and write operations you must also specify the address of a buffer, from which the data is written or to which the data are transferred. In this case, the ES register indicates the segment address and the BX register indicates the offset address of the buffer.

Resetting the hard drive controller

One function that doesn't require all of the parameters is function 00H, which, like function 0DH, resets the controller. For example, after an error occurs, this function is routinely performed before the next data access. The only parameter needed is the hard drive number that is passed in the DL register.

Determining the status of the hard drive

Using function 01H, you can determine the status of the hard drive. Again, the drive number whose status is being checked is passed in the DL register.

Reading hard drive sectors

Function 02H reads one or more sectors of the hard drive. On each call to this function, you can read a maximum of 128 sectors. Perhaps you're wondering why the maximum is 128 instead of 256 sectors. The hard disk controller uses DMA capability to transfer data between the computer's memory and the hard drive. However, the DMA components can transfer a maximum of 64K of data at one time. This is equivalent to 128 sectors (64K = 128 sectors * 512 bytes/sector). Another restriction is that the DMA components can transfer data only within a single memory segment. So, the read/write buffer is usually aligned to the start of a memory segment. Remember that the ES:BX register pair point to the buffer. In this case, the ES register will point to the start of this segment and the BX register will have a zero offset.

When you use function 02H to read more than one sector per call, the sectors are read in the following order: First, the sectors in the specified cylinder and side are read in ascending order (by sector number). When the end of the cylinder is reached, the first sector on the same cylinder, but on the next head, is read. Sectors on the next cylinder aren't read until after the last head in the same cylinder is reached and there are sectors remaining to be read.

Writing hard drive sectors

Function 03H is used to write one or more sectors to the hard drive. This function is similar to function 02H except that the data is written from the buffer to the hard drive. For a description of this function, refer to the one above.

Verifying hard drive sectors

Function 04H verifies the sectors of a cylinder. However, the data on the hard drive is compared with the ECC value instead of the data in memory (which is why it isn't necessary to specify a buffer address in ES:BX). The number of sectors to be verified is specified in the AL register.

Formatting the hard drive cylinders

A hard drive must be formatted before it can be used. Function 05H performs this task. This function is similar to the function for formatting a floppy diskette. The address of a buffer is passed in the ES:BX register pair. This buffer must be 512 bytes in size, even though only the first 34 bytes are used.

The buffer consists of two one-byte entries for each of the 17 sectors to be formatted. The first byte indicates whether the sector is good or bad. Before calling this function, we assume that each sector is good. So we store a zero value here. The second byte is the logical sector number.

Bytes 1 and 2 of the table are used when the first physical sector of the cylinder is formatted. Bytes 3 and 4 are used when the second physical sector is formatted, etc. So, while the physical sequence is fixed, the logical sequence of sectors is defined by the two bytes of a sector specification in this table.

The most obvious way to format the hard drive is to assign a sector's physical sector number to each logical sector. However, a technique called *sector interleaving* is actually used to speed up hard disk performance. We'll discuss sector interleaving in more detail in Section 6.7.

The first byte of each table entry may contain the value 00H, which indicates that the sector is good, or 80H, which indicates that the sector is bad. During formatting, this byte is transferred to the sector marker that indicates that DOS shouldn't use this sector to store data.

Determining the hard drive parameters

Unlike floppy diskettes, hard drives don't have uniform characteristics. For some programs, it's important to know the hard drive's parameters. To do this, use function 08H to pass the hard drive number in the DL register.

After calling the function, the DL register contains the number of hard drives connected to the controller. The value returned may be 0, 1, or 2. The DH register contains the number of read/write heads. Since this value is relative to 0, a value of 7 means that there are 8 heads. The number of cylinders is returned both in the CL register (bits 0-7) and the two upper bits of the CH register (bits 8 and 9). Again, this value is relative to 0. Finally, the number of sectors per track is returned in the lower 6 bits of the CH register. This specifies the number of sectors per track, but is relative to 1, not 0.

Initializing a "foreign" hard drive

The BIOS in each computer already contains the specifications for various hard drives. This makes it easy to select the hard drive specifications during SETUP. However, suppose that the specifications for a particular hard drive aren't in the BIOS. There's another way to make the drive's specifications known to the BIOS. First a table containing the specifications is constructed. Then the address of the table is stored at interrupt 41H or interrupt 46H, depending on whether hard drive 0 or hard drive 1 is being initialized. The format of the table is predefined by BIOS and describes the characteristics of the hard drive.

Finally, function 09H, which initializes the controller with the new hard drive specifications, is called. The drive number (80H or 81H) is passed in the DL register. Usually the device driver provided by the hard drive manufacturer manages this function.

Extended hard drive sector read/write

Functions 0AH and 0BH are similar to the read and write functions 02H and 03H. However, one difference is that, in addition to the 512 bytes of data per sector that's transferred, the four ECC bytes at the end of each sector are also transferred. Since each sector is 516 bytes instead of 512 bytes, the maximum number of sectors that can be read or written at a time is 127 sectors, while functions 02H and 03H can handle 128 sectors.

Function 10H tests whether the hard drive, whose number is passed in the DL register, is ready to execute commands. If the carry flag is set to indicate that the drive isn't ready, then the AH register will contain the error code.

Recalibrating the hard drive

Function 0BH is used to recalibrate the hard drive. After the function call, this function returns the error status along with the drive number in the DL register.

Self test of the hard drive controller

Function 14H is used to perform a self test. If the controller passes the test, the carry flag will be reset.

The final hard drive interrupt function is 15H, which is available only on ATs, not XTs. This interrupt returns the drive type. The drive number (80H or 81H) is passed in the DL register. If the drive isn't available, a value of 0 is returned in the AH register. A value of 1 or 2 indicates a floppy disk drive. A value of 3 indicates a hard drive. In this case, registers CX and DX contain the number of sectors on this hard drive. The two registers form a 32 bit number, with the CX register containing the high-order byte and the DX register containing the low-order byte.

6.5 Hard Drives and Their Controllers

The advancements in hard drive technology are related to four types of controllers: ST506, ESDI, SCSI, and IDE. The format, in which the data are saved on the hard drive, not only depends on the controller, but also on the data transfer rate between the computer and the hard drive.

The following table shows the maximum data transfer rates that are possible with the different controllers. However, these are theoretical maximum values that not only are seldom attained, but also are affected by other factors. Imagine a set of data on its way from the hard drive to be displayed on the screen (e.g., when you load a document into a word processor). In addition to the controller, the program must interface with many levels: the BIOS, the DOS, the application program, and perhaps one ore more TSRs.

Another factor that affects the data transfer rate is the speed of the bus. This limits the speed of hard drive controllers because it still operates at 8 MHz, even though the speed of the CPU has reached a maximum of 50 MHz. So, any published values quickly diminishes to about a fifth by the time the data actually appears.

Maximum data transfer rates of the various PC hard drive controllers	
Controller	Maximum Data Transfer Rate
ST506	1 Meg per second
ESDI	2.5 Meg per second
IDE	4 Meg per second
SCSI	5 Meg per second

In the following sections, we'll introduce you to the various hard drive controllers, examine their structure, and describe their advantages and disadvantages. The role of the BIOS is also discussed.

6.5.1 ST506 Controller

The first hard drives that were widely accepted in the PC world were developed for the ST506 and compatible controllers. As its name indicates, this controller originated from the Seagate company, which is an important hard drive manufacturer.

Even today, ST506 controllers are still the most widely used controllers, even though new hard drives usually are equipped with IDE controllers. Generally, hard drives designed for hookup to an ST506 controller are identified by the label "MFM/RLL". These letters refer to the two recording methods by which the controllers save data on the hard drive. Usually you can use DIP switches to set the format the controller uses. The RLL format is preferred because it provides higher hard drive capacity. (Refer to Section 6.6 for more information.)

Because of its wide distribution, the ST506 controller has set different standards in hardware control systems, partly because the BIOS conforms to this controller type. The effects of this are evident today. For example, IDE and ESDI controllers are (and must be) compatible with ST506 controllers in various ways. We'll discuss this in more detail later.

The hardware

In the ST506 standard, the hard drive and controller are two separate components. The controller is on a separate card and occupies one of the PC's expansion slots.

A controller can usually manage two hard drives. Two types of cables connect the controller to each hard drive. Each hard drive connects to the controller with its own 20-pin data cable. If both hard drives are installed, they share the 34-pin control cable. The control cable sends electrical signals to the hard drive to select the desired read/write heads, search for the desired cylinder, etc. Data to be read from or written to the hard drive is transferred over the data cable in serial and analog mode.

The controller can convert the digital information on a cylinder into bit strings. The information on magnetic media exists as values of 0 or 1. The controller can reverse the digital values as needed; this process is called *flux reversal*.

The data transfer rate can be as high as 5 megabits/second using MFM recording and 7.5 megabits/second using RLL recording. Since the control information still must be "filtered out" from the stream of data, the effective transfer rate of useful data is considerably lower. Even so, MFM controllers can process .5 megabytes per second and RLL controller can even process 0.75 megabytes per second. However, usually these theoretical values ignore factors such as head select time, cylinder seek time, etc., and assume that you'll read contiguous sectors. We'll discuss this in more detail in the section on interleaving.

The higher transfer rate of RLL controllers is a result of a more efficient recording scheme. You'll see that more sectors can be written to each track using RLL. MFM drives can write 17 sectors on a track, but RLL drives can fit 26 sectors on each track. In both formats, the rotational speed of the drive is 3600 RPM.

When the XT first appeared, the only controller available was the ST506. As a result, the new hard drive functions of the ROM-BIOS were developed specifically for this controller. These hard drive functions have imposed rigid limitations on PC manufacturers. For example, the number of drives is limited to two, the maximum number of cylinders to 1204, the maximum number of sectors per track to 63, and the maximum number of heads to 16. Also, the sector size is fixed at 512 bytes. When combined with all the other factors, the maximum capacity of a drive is 504 Meg.

To overcome these limitations, some hard drive controllers "trick" the system into believing there are two hard drives, which are actually on the same drive. This makes it possible to have a hard drive with a capacity of up to 1 gigabyte. However, an ST506 controller is too slow for a drive with such enormous capacity. So, it isn't practical to connect such large hard drives to systems with ST506-type controllers. Because of this, the ST506-type controller will gradually disappear in the coming years.

6.5.2 ESDI Controllers

The ESDI controller was developed after the ST506 controller. ESDI, which is an acronym for "Enhanced Small Devices Interface", is found in many IBM PS/2 models. This controller represents an advancement of the ST506 model. Generally, ESDI controllers are compatible with the ST506 and can be used in computers whose BIOS is programmed to support only ST506 controllers.

Unlike the ST506, ESDI doesn't transfer every flux reversal serially to the controller via the data line. Instead, part of the decoding logic, called the *data separator*, is already on the hard drive. The data separator prepares the data read from the hard drive and transfers only the useful data, in digital form, to the controller.

Because the controller and the data separator work in parallel, the transfer rate can be as high as 10 megabits/second. This represents only a doubling of the transfer rate of an MFM ST506 drive. However, this is accompanied by another performance enhancement. ESDI controllers usually have a sector buffer that makes an interleave factor of 1:1 possible. What does this mean? An ST506 drive with an interleave factor of six requires six full revolutions in order to transfer the contents of an entire track. With an interleave factor of three, this same drive still requires three full revolutions to transfer the contents of an entire track. However, an ESDI can perform the same task in a single revolution. This results in increasing the access speed by a factor of three to six.

Also, some ESDI systems can reach a transfer rate of 15, 20, and even 24 megabits per second. However, such controllers are rare and usually quite expensive. So most ESDI controllers work with 10 megabits.

The data separator isn't the only intelligent component on an ESDI system. An ESDI hard drive also stores information about its physical format and the addresses of defective sectors and can send this information to the controller. Then the controller can perform its own SETUP, which is a task that a user has to do with ST506 drives.

The BIOS and ESDI controllers

The hard drive information is then stored in the CMOS RAM of an AT. The BIOS must know the parameters of the hard drive and pass this information to the DOS device driver.

Because the ESDI controller can request this information from the hard drive, the information in the BIOS doesn't have to match the actual characteristics of the drive. Often this discrepancy cannot be avoided, because each BIOS knows only a limited number of hard drive types and their specifications.

You'll encounter problems on an ST506-type hard drive if the installed drive doesn't appear in the BIOS list. In this case, you must select a drive, from the list, whose specifications most closely match those of the installed drive. This often means "wasting" some of the drive capacity. You must select a BIOS entry for a drive with fewer cylinders, tracks, or heads. Otherwise the system might try to access sectors that don't even exist on the installed drive, which results in an error.

Another problem is when the BIOS doesn't have a hard drive type that works with the same number of sectors per track. Then you must select a BIOS entry for a drive with the next smallest sector size, which means wasting valuable sectors in every track on the drive and increasing the number of unused sectors to an undesirable level.

With ST506 drives, this isn't a problem because they only work with 17 or 26 sectors, depending on the recording method. However, ESDI drives have 34 or 36 sectors per track. So, if the BIOS contains entries for drives with only 26 sectors, then you might end up wasting one-third of your expensive hard drive capacity.

Fortunately, most ESDI controllers can avoid this problem. The BIOS entry for a drive with a slightly smaller capacity than the ESDI hard drive is selected during SETUP. Since ESDI hard drives can send their specifications to the ESDI controller, the controller knows the physical characteristics of the drive. Using a special feature called *sector translation*, the ESDI controller converts the BIOS logical drive specifications into the hard drive physical specifications. The conversion takes slightly longer, but ensures that the ESDI hard drive can be used with almost any BIOS entry without wasting a lot of its capacity.

The ability to perform this conversion depends entirely on the ESDI controller. Some controllers support only certain BIOS entries, while others are more flexible and can accept any format. This is also an advantage if an ESDI drive encounters the limits imposed by the BIOS hard drive functions, for example, an ESDI drive with more than 1024 cylinders. Instead of wasting the cylinders above 1024, the controller simulates a greater number of sectors per track. Although the ESDI drive may have only 34 tracks per sector, it can pretend to have up to 63 tracks per sector. The ESDI controller then translates a logical cylinder/sector/head specification to the hard drive's physical specification.

6.5.3 SCSI

The SCSI (pronounced "scuzzy") standard, isn't really a hard drive interface. Instead, it's a way to connect up to eight entirely different devices to a PC. Besides hard drives, you can connect tape backup streamers, CD-ROM drives, or scanners to a SCSI interface.

Unlike other hard drive controller standards, the SCSI (Small Computer System Interface) isn't found only in PCs, but also on many 68000 systems (Macintosh and Atari ST) and large workstations. One reason for its appeal is that you can easily couple and uncouple devices from the SCSI interface because the devices communicate with the controller through a bus that's separate from the PC bus.

Both the SCSI line specifications and the SCSI commands to control the devices are standardized. SCSI devices can be easily exchanged between different systems; only the SCSI controller must be matched to the host computer system.

The SCSI bus, which links different SCSI devices together, is usually a cable with an 80-pin plug. The bus allows 8-bit parallel data transfer. A new version, called SCSI II, allows 16-bit parallel data transfer, but isn't widely used yet.

Manufacturers of SCSI controllers like to tempt their customers by quoting data transfer rates of 4 or 5 Meg per second. Actually, these rates aren't possible. While the SCSI controller can handle these high data transfer rates, the hard drive connected to it cannot. So, you can expect a data transfer rate of between 1.5 and 2 Meg per second, unless you purchase an expensive EISA controller, which can manage 2.5 Meg per second.

SCSI drives continue the trend started by ESDI drives by integrating much of the control circuitry directly on the hard drive. Actually, this must be done with this system, because the controller must remain device-independent and not concern itself with the specific characteristics and features of a hard drive.

Shorter paths aren't the only advantage provided by the close proximity of the hard drive and its control circuitry. This also makes it easier to trick the controller into using a certain disk format that doesn't really exist. Like an ESDI controller, the SCSI controller asks the attached devices for its specification when the system starts and passes this information to the requester.

SCSI systems depend on their own built in BIOS. From a software standpoint, SCSI systems don't support the ST506 standard of the ROM-BIOS. The original functions of the BIOS Disk Interrupt are replaced by the SCSI BIOS. Unfortunately, the SCSI BIOS isn't useful in protected mode, in which "operating environments" such as Novell or OS/2 access the disk directly and often support only the ST506 standard. This requires a specific device driver, which may not be available for the particular operating environment. This is one of the biggest disadvantages of the SCSI interface.

However, if you have the required driver, the hard drive specifications are automatic. To install a new SCSI drive, simply connect it to the bus. The SCSI controller handles the rest by using the correct "driver ware".

6.5.4 IDE

The new star of hard drive controllers is the (Intelligent Drive Electronics) interface. The IDE interface is found in almost every new PC. Its development started in 1984, when PC manufacturer Compaq asked Western Digital to develop an ST506-compatible controller that would fit on the hard drive to save space.

Using an IDE drive provides a hard drive and a controller in one. A single 40-pin cable combines the functions of a data cable and a control cable and connects the IDE drive directly to the system bus.

This is also where IDE drives get their nickname; sometimes they're called "AT Bus Drives". But IDE drives aren't limited to ATs with their 16 bit data buses. You can also use IDE drives on an 8-bit XT bus.

Many PCs have a connector for an IDE cable directly on the motherboard. With other PC's you must use a small expansion slot board, which then connects to the IDE cable.

Combining the drive and controller gives the IDE some of the same advantages of the SCSI controllers. Among these are the ability to emulate any drive format and track caching, in which the drive reads an entire track and keeps the data in an internal cache buffer until it's needed. IDE drives can operate with an interleave factor of 1:1, which provides faster access. IDE combines the advantages of the other three standards; it's flexible like SCSI, fast like ESDI, and is compatible to the ST506 standard so it can be connected to most PC systems easily.

Also, IDE drives have a very low power consumption, so they're ideal for laptops and notebooks.

Many IDE drives have special commands for working with laptops and notebooks. For example, these commands can put the notebook computer "to sleep", which minimizes power consumption. These commands are generally used in connection with special drivers or a BIOS that's adapted to work with IDE drives. From the BIOS' point of view, IDE drives behave like normal ST506 controllers, making it easy to integrate them into existing systems.

New standards are being defined for IDE drives. In the near future we'll most likely see new BIOS systems supporting IDE drives directly. Then PC makers can fully use the extended features offered by these drives, which go unused in many of today's systems.

6.5.5 From the Controller to the Memory

Regardless of the speed of the hard drive and the controller, the way in which the data is transferred by the controller to the memory determines the effective speed of a controller-hard drive combination. Four different methods can be used to do this:

- Programmed I/O (PIO)
- Memory Mapped I/O
- DMA
- Busmaster DMA

Programmed I/O

With programmed I/O, the different controller I/O ports manage both the drive commands and the transfer of the data between the controller and the main memory. If you use programmed I/O, you'll use the IN and OUT machine language instructions. This means that every byte or word must be channeled through the CPU.

Here, the data transfer rate is limited by the speed of the PC bus and the performance of the CPU. While the ISA bus allows a maximum transfer rate of 5.33 Meg per second (16-bit rate), this rate is unattainable with any of today's CPUs. With fast 386's or 486's, the data transfer rate is limited to about 3 or 4 Meg and can be attained only with very fast and expensive hard drives.

Memory Mapped I/O

The CPU can process data from a disk controller even faster if it stores them in a fixed memory region. The segment located above the video RAM is generally used for this purpose. Data in a program's memory area can be transferred faster using MOV instructions. This is faster than accessing the I/O ports with IN and OUT.

Even by using memory mapped I/O, today's speedy CPUs can request data faster than the controller is capable of transferring. The controller can never reach the theoretical maximum value of 8 Meg per second. It can't even reach 5 to 6 Meg per second.

DMA

DMA (Direct Memory Access) transfer is more widely known than the first two methods. Using DMA, a device (hard drive, floppy disk drive, CD-ROM, etc.) can transfer data directly to the computer's memory. The CPU is bypassed. To use DMA, a program only needs to tell the DMA controller how many bytes should be transferred from one location to another. This makes DMA seem like the best method for transferring data.

However, the DMA controller in the PC is inflexible and slow. In fact, it's so slow that Programmed I/O is faster on 386 and 486 systems. The DMA controller operates at 4 MHz on the AT or later systems even though it worked at 4.77 MHz on earlier PCs. So, DMA transfer is faster than Programmed I/O only on PCs. Using DMA, the data transfer rate is limited to about 2 Meg per second.

For this reason, the DMA method is no longer used on most modern hard drives, even though many hard drives do support this method in addition to Programmed I/O.

Busmaster DMA

Busmaster DMA is another form of direct memory access, but isn't related to the DMA circuitry on the motherboard of the computer. Using this method, the hard drive controller disconnects the CPU from the bus and transfers data to memory on its own using its own Busmaster DMA controller. Transfer rates of up to 8 Meg per second are possible. Unfortunately, this feature increases the price of the controller. Busmaster DMA is generally used only with very powerful SCSI controllers.

Protected mode

The methods of DMA transfer are limited to real mode programs. Without special intervention, DMA cannot be used in protected or virtual mode. How virtual memory management is performed by the CPUs memory management unit (MMU) is responsible for this limitation. The MMU maps a program's virtual memory addresses into real physical memory addresses.

A protected or virtual mode program doesn't realize this, because it's never aware of the physical addresses; it works only with virtual addresses. When this program wants to perform a DMA transfer, it passes a virtual address to the DMA chip. However, because the MMU isn't involved in the DMA transfer, it cannot map this virtual address into a physical address. As a result, the data is transferred to a different memory area. The system will soon crash because important memory areas are overwritten.

This is a characteristic of protected mode operating systems, such as Windows and OS/2. However, this also occurs in Virtual 86 mode using DOS if the EMM386.EXE device driver is used to emulate expanded memory. EMM386.EXE depends on the virtual memory management of the processor.

The solution is to "watch" the DMA controller. Do this in protected mode to control all of the I/O ports. In Windows, for example, a virtual control monitor in the background is installed to watch the programming of the DMA controller via the BIOS or another program. This monitor converts the actual physical addresses before they are written to the register of the DMA controller.

6.6 Recording Information on the Hard Drive

To understand how information is written on a hard drive, you must first forget the concept of binary coding. Zeros and ones aren't stored on the magnetic surface of a hard drive. It's impossible to represent these two states as "magnetized" and "not magnetized".

Why isn't this possible? If you try to represent data as sequences of magnetized and non-magnetized particles, the read head of the hard drive wouldn't be able to keep the individual magnetic particles separate. So, it wouldn't be able to distinguish between three or five zeros.

One way to avoid this problem is by knowing the length of a magnetic particle and the elapsed time for each magnetic signal. In other words, you need a kind of clock that indicates, with each tick, that it's time for a new bit.

However, the constant period of time for a cycle cannot be clearly defined because of various factors. For example, the rotational speed of the hard drive may vary slightly. But a bigger factor is that a single magnetic particle can never be magnetized; only a group of magnetic particles, whose number isn't always constant, can be magnetized.

It is possible, however, to record flux reversals, which are short passages between non-magnetized particles and magnetized particles. The reversals in flux create an electrical pulse in the hard drive's read head. This pulse is then passed to the electronic circuitry, where it is used to decode the stored information as zeros and ones.

This coding and decoding of binary information has always been important to hardware developers The number of flux reversals that can be recorded per square inch on a hard drive is limited. This limit depends on the composition of the magnetic material, the gap of the read/write head, its sensitivity, etc. Anyone who can find ways to record more zeros and ones on the hard drive with an equal number of flux reversals will lead the competition in higher and higher disk capacities.

6.6.1 FM Method

The simplest way to encode zeros and ones to a magnetic surface is to record a flux reversal for each one-bit and omit a flux reversal for each zero-bit. However, you'll encounter a problem when you want to record a long series of zeros. In this instance, you must omit many flux reversals to represent the string of zeros. This would confuse the controller that depends on flux reversals to keep in sync with the data on the hard drive.

To avoid this problem, a clock signal is written onto the drive along with the data. Using the FM (Frequency Modulation) recording technique, a one-bit might be recorded as two consecutive flux reversals and a zero-bit recorded as a flux reversal followed by no flux reversal. In both cases, the initial flux reversal represents the timing signal. The data bit is then modulated "between" the timing signal (second flux reversal for one-bit and no flux reversal for zero-bit).

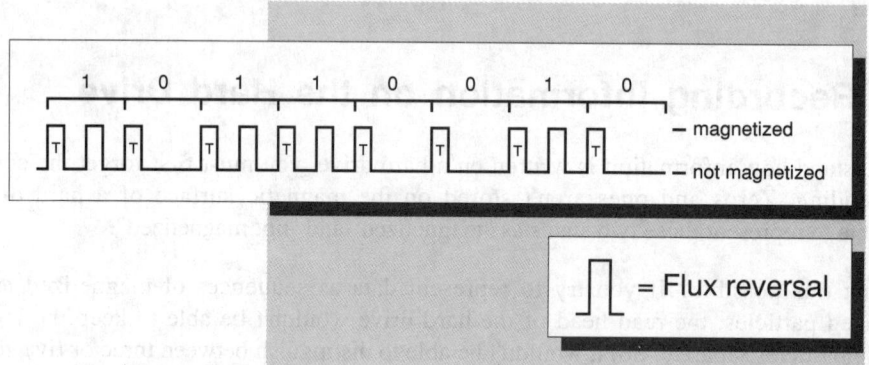

The FM method of recording

Although this method is simple and inexpensive, it has one major disadvantage. Each data bit requires two flux reversals, which reduces the potential disk capacity by half.

6.6.2 MFM Method

To reduce the number of flux reversals of the FM method and thereby increase the density at which information can be recorded, another encoding technique is used. This technique is called MFM (Modified FM). Basically, the data is encoded as follows:

Code table for the MFM	
Data bit value	Encoded as:
1 0 following another 0-bit 0 following another 1-bit	Flux reversal Flux reversal followed by no flux reversal No flux reversal followed by no flux reversal

With this method, the timing signal is also used to store data. Both zero-bits and one-bits are recorded using only a single flux reversal. Longer sequences of zeros and ones appear as a continuous sequence of flux reversals.

This encoding method requires improved control circuitry so that the hard drive can synchronize with the normal sequence of timing flux reversals for longer sequences of zeros.

The only problem is when a one is followed by a zero, which requires a flux reversal to the normal timing position. The time between the flux reversal of the one and that of the zero amounts to only half the normal interval between two flux reversals. However, this won't work because the shortest interval between two flux reversals cannot be shorter; otherwise the electronic circuitry would no longer be able to keep up. Therefore, a flux reversal isn't stored for a zero that follows a one.

The next flux reversal comes after one and a half times the time for a flux change (bit combination 100b) or even after twice the time (bit combination 101b). The following illustration demonstrates this.

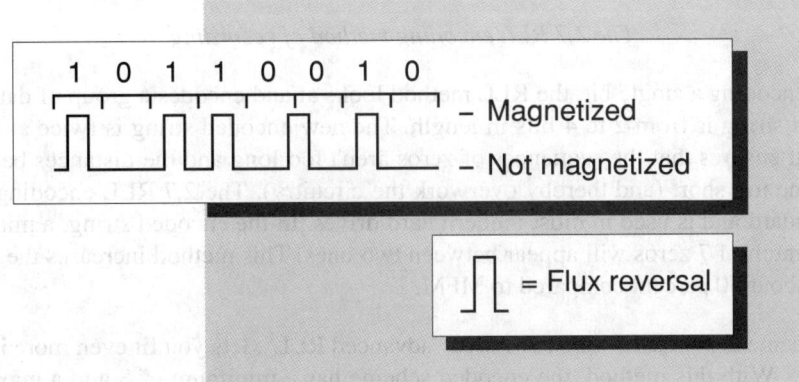

The MFM method of recording

6.6.3 RLL Method

Another encoding method, called RLL (Run Length Limited), packs up to 50 percent more information on the disk than MFM.

In RLL, ones are stored as flux reversals; zeros are stored as the absence of flux reversals. A timing signal isn't recorded. The hard drive circuitry itself supplies the timing reference. However, even with a very constant rotation of the hard drive and improvements in the read head and its electronic circuitry, this is possible only if there aren't too many zeros between two ones. With each zero, the time to the next flux reversal increases, and along with it, the possibility that the hard drive controller will lose its beat.

However, the ones cannot follow each other too rapidly. Otherwise, the controller may not be able to keep pace.

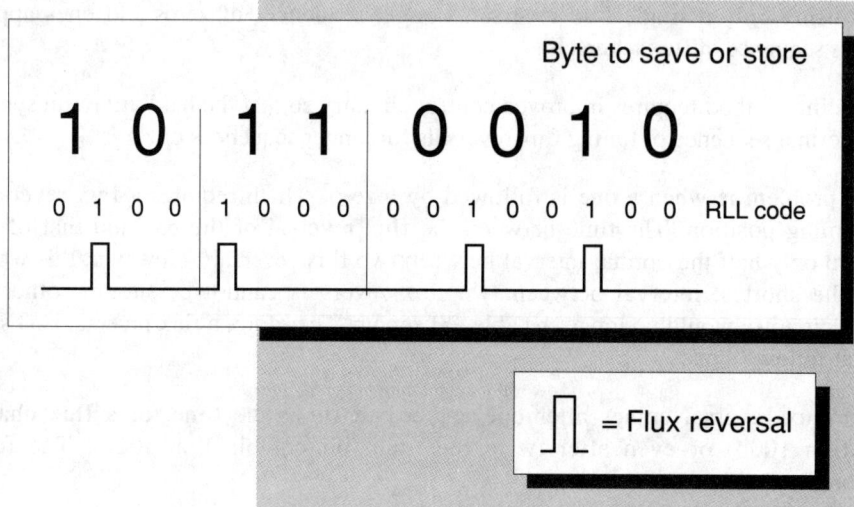

The 2,7 RLL encoding method of recording

Instead of encoding a single bit, the RLL method looks at and encodes a group of data bits. This group or bit string is from 2 to 4 bits in length. The new encoded string is twice as long as the original, but ensures that the sequences of zeros aren't too long and the distances between ones don't become too short (and thereby overwork the circuitry). The 2,7 RLL encoding scheme is today's standard and is used in most modern hard drives. In the encoded string, a minimum of 2 and a maximum of 7 zeros will appear between two ones. This method increases the capacity of a drive by about 50 percent compared to MFM.

Another scheme is 3,9 RLL, which is called "advanced RLL", lets you fit even more information on the drive. With this method, the encoded scheme has a minimum of 3 and a maximum of 9 zeros between two ones.

The following table shows the encoding scheme for 2,7 RLL. At first, you may think that a byte such as 00000001b cannot be encoded. However, don't forget that, on this level, you're working with sectors instead of single bytes. So, it's even possible to encode a byte, such as 00000001b, by including the bits of the following byte in the coding.

Code table for the RLL 2.7	
Bit pattern:	Encoded as:
000	000100
10	0100
010	100100
0010	00100100
11	1000
011	001000
001	00001000

The only problem in coding occurs with the last byte of a sector because this method needs the following byte. This problem is solved by simply using a byte from the hard drive controller. The excess bits are simply truncated so that the last byte of a sector is correctly decoded.

6.7   Hard Drive Advancements

One of the remarkable achievements in PC computers has been the "smaller, faster, cheaper" advancements in hard drive technology. For instance:

- Access times in the top performance models have decreased from over thirty milliseconds to about ten milliseconds.

- Maximum storage capacities have increased by several hundred megabytes. Hard drives with a capacity of more than 1 gigabyte are now common.

- 1 Meg of hard drive capacity costs less than ten dollars.

The hard drive's performance and capabilities has increased because of the optimization in recording and playback techniques. In this section we'll discuss some of these techniques.

6.7.1 The Interleave

Today hard drive controllers are so fast that they can read an entire track even when only the data in a single sector is requested. So, when the data in the next sector is needed, the hard drive controller doesn't have to read the next sector. Instead, it can take the data from the controller's internal buffer. This significantly speeds up data access.

Most ST506 controllers have only an internal sector buffer (with a capacity to store the contents of exactly one sector), so only the newer controller types (SCSI, ESDI, and IDE) are track buffer compatible. Also, the sector buffer cannot be reused until the last byte of the previous sector is passed to the CPU. So, additional time is required until the next sector passes under the read head.

The data in the subsequent sector cannot be read until the sector passes under the read head again; this requires almost an entire revolution of the hard drive. This process continues with each sector, noticeably reducing the speed of disk access. To minimize this delay, *interleaving* is used to spread the logical sectors across the track.

By interleaving the logical sectors, the controller has enough time to process and transfer the data in one sector before the next logical sector passes under the read head. This avoids the rotational delay of having to wait for a complete revolution before the sector can be read.

Interleaving is measured by the *interleave factor*. This value is the number of sectors by which the logical sector number was shifted, compared to the physical sector number. The original XT hard drive uses an interleave factor of 1:6, while the AT uses an interleave factor of 1:3. However, the interleave factor of the AT hard drive can be reduced to 1:2, which increases the access speed.

Today, interleave factors of 1:1 are common, which means that there is no interleaving at all.

However, an interleave of 1:6 requires that five physical sectors be skipped before the next logical sector can be read. An interleave of 1:3 requests that two physical sectors be skipped. The following illustration presents the logical arrangement of sectors on a track with 17 sectors:

Interleaving in the first XT and AT hard drives from IBM			
AT		XT	
Physical sectors	Logical sectors	Physical sectors	Logical sectors
1	1	1	1
2	7	2	4
3	13	3	7
4	2	4	10
5	8	5	13
6	14	6	16
7	3	7	2
8	9	8	5
9	15	9	8
10	4	10	11
11	10	11	14
12	16	12	17
13	5	13	3
14	11	14	6
15	17	15	9
16	6	16	12
17	12	17	15

Despite the advantages of this method, the best interleave is actually no interleave at all. Without an interleave, an entire track be read within a hard drive revolution. However, two, three, or even more revolutions would be needed with interleaving, depending on the interleave factor.

Setting the interleave

Set the interleave in the "low-level-format" of the hard drive, which creates the address labels and sector numbers on the surface on an unused hard drive.

Because the logical sector number of a single sector is determined by the low-level-formatting program, it's possible to shift the sectors. Many hard disk utilities will prompt you for the desired interleave factor. If you select a "bad" value, your hard drive may slow down when loading programs or accessing files.

Even if you do select a "bad" interleave factor, you can still eliminate the problem later. You can use a program, such as the Norton Utilities, to do this. Such programs determine the optimum interleave factor and then execute the appropriate low-level-format for you. This usually takes just a few minutes.

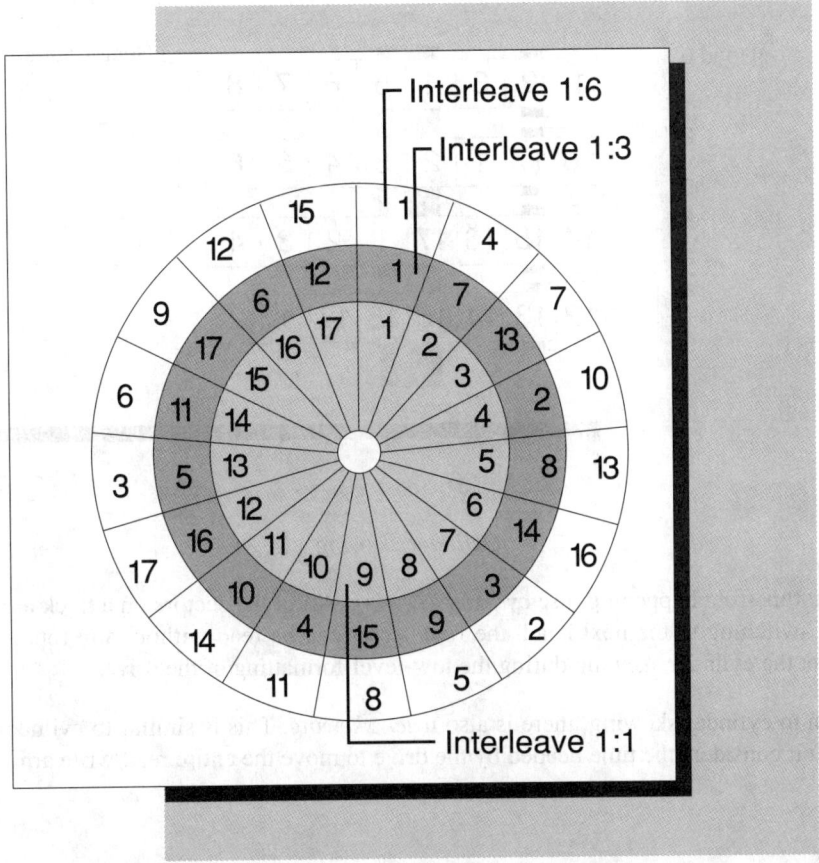

Different interleave factors and their influence on the formatting of a track

You may think that this type of utility will lead to data loss because the program is "tampering" with the hard drive. However, as long as the program is error-free, you shouldn't loose any data. Since these programs work below DOS level, DOS is completely unaffected by the changes. Remember, DOS doesn't know the origin of a sector which it reads or writes. So, as long as the data are read before a track is reformatted and written back, DOS believes that nothing has changed.

6.7.2 Track and Cylinder Skewing

Carefully selecting an interleaving factor significantly increases hard disk performance. After the data from one track is read, data, which is in same cylinder but the following head, are usually accessed. As the controller switches the read/write head, the hard drive continues to rotate. After reading the last sector on the track, the first sector on the next head has already passed the read/write head. So you must wait almost an entire revolution.

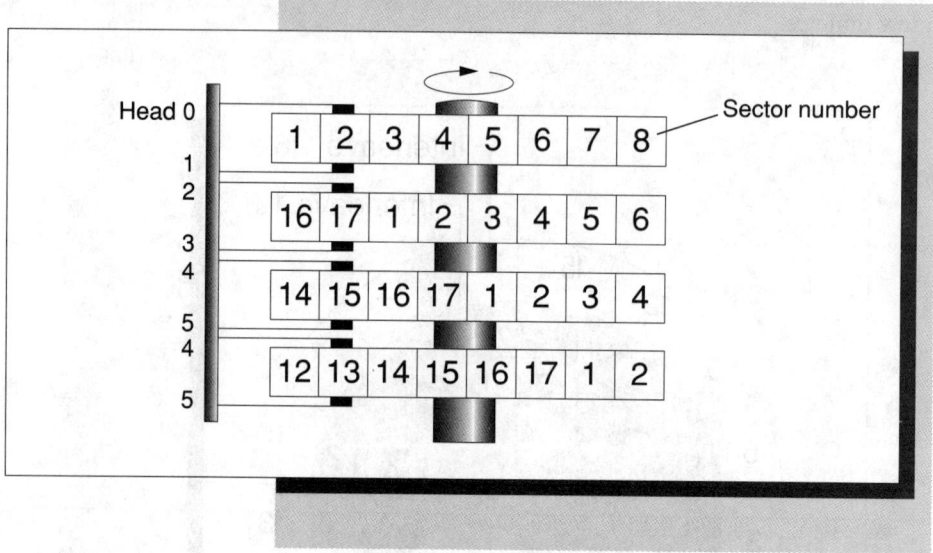

Cylinder skewing

To prevent this from happening, use *cylinder skewing*. All of the sectors on a track are shifted so that, after switching to the next head, the first sector can be read without any rotational delay. You can set the cylinder skewing during the low-level-formatting of the drive.

In addition to cylinder skewing, there is also *track skewing*. This is similar to cylinder skewing, except that it considers the time needed by the drive to move the entire read/write arm to the next track.

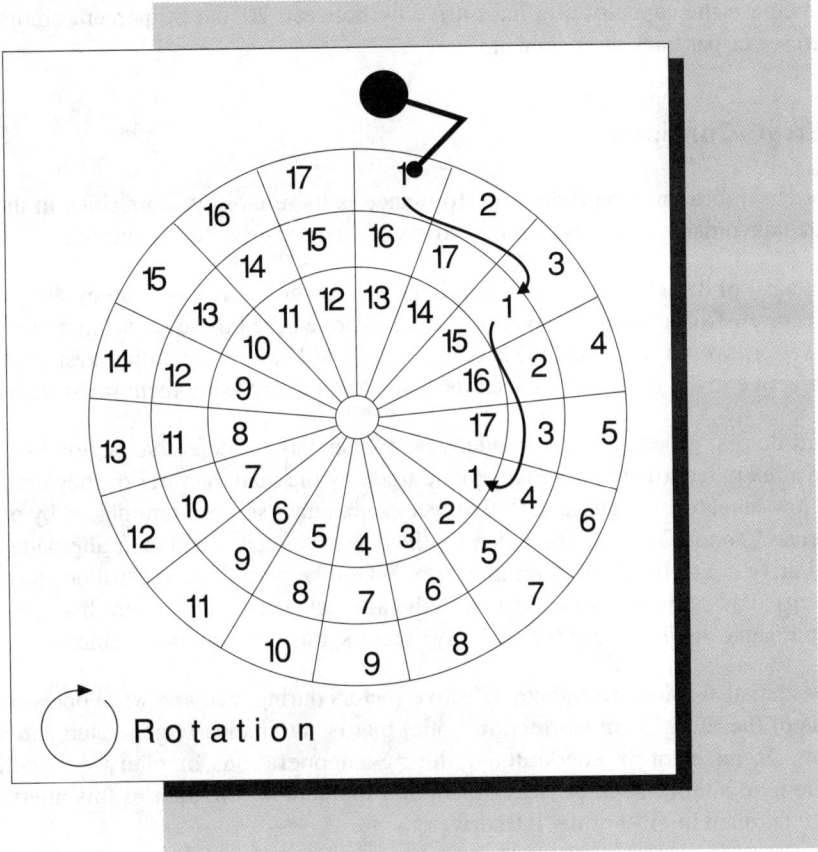

Track skewing with an interleave of 1:1

6.7.3 Multiple Zone Recording

One way to increase the capacity of a hard drive is to format more sectors on the outer tracks. Since they have a larger circumference, the outer tracks have more space than the inner tracks. With ST506 controllers, the number of sectors per track was fixed and limited by the capacity of the innermost (shortest) track.

With modern SCSI and IDE disks, which only simulate the number of heads, tracks, and sectors, it's possible to format individual tracks with a different number of sectors. These controllers and drives translate a logical head, cylinder, and sector number to a physical head, cylinder, and sector number. So, it's possible to vary the number of sectors on outer tracks.

This places a greater demand on the controller circuitry and the read/write head. In the same (rotational) time, more sectors must be read or written to the outer tracks than on the inner track. So, while the length of the flux reversal decreases, the number of data bits to be read or written increases.

This can increase the capacity of a hard drive by between 20 and 50 percent compared to the usual, fixed sector per track arrangement.

6.7.4 Error Correction

One important indicator of hard drive performance is its reliability. Impurities in the magnetic material are unavoidable and cause some sections of the hard drive to be unusable.

In the past, a list of defective sectors were printed on the hard drive case as they were detected by the manufacturer. During the low-level format, the user entered these sector numbers so that the operating system would recognize these defective areas. Then the operating system would mark them as defective in the FAT (File Allocation Table) and avoid using them for storing data.

Newer hard drives, especially IDE models, no longer have a defective sector list. Either the sectors are already recorded on a separate data track by the manufacturer or they are recognized during the low-level format. These defective sectors are either skipped or replaced by other sectors from "alternate" areas. The tables that identify the defective sectors and their alternates are passed to the hard drive controller during initialization. When the hard drive controller tries to access a sector identified as defective, it can switch to the alternate sector. Although this slows access to such a sector, since there are very few defective sectors, this is hardly noticeable.

Many drives are also able to recognize defective sectors during read and write operations. This is the purpose of the ECC (Error Correction Code) that is automatically generated and saved with each sector. If an error is encountered during an operation, in many cases the data is reconstructed, an alternate sector is assigned, and the data is rewritten to this alternate sector. This feature is found in most of the IDE drives.

6.7.5 Other Hard Drive Components

A hard drive contains more than just the data bit information. When a sector is formatted, an entire set of information is also written so that the hard drive correctly recognizes and reads data. Although the format of this information is different depending on the controller, the information itself is the same (e.g., the cylinder number, the sector number, and the error correction code).

Each sector begins with a series of thirteen synchronization bytes with the value 00H (SYNC field). This bit pattern results in a constant series of flux reversals that help the controller synchronize itself to the sector.

Following this is the ID field, which identifies the sector. The cylinder, head, and sector numbers are recorded here (CH/S fields). This information starts with a special ID byte (ID field) and ends with a two byte error code that's used to check the validity of the information (CRCID field).

Next is a gap, which gives the controller a break before the start of the data field. The controller needs this break to read the information from the ID field in order to determine whether this is the desired sector. The gap also lets the controller resynchronize itself.

The actual data field follows. The data field also has an ID byte (AM field) at the start, which is for identification. The 512 data bytes (DATA field) are next. The data field ends with two

538

correction bytes (ECC-DATA field) that the controller uses to determine whether the data is valid.

The sector ends with another gap to give the controller time to check the correction bytes. Here the gap contains bytes with the value 4EH. So the sector's total length is 570 bytes.

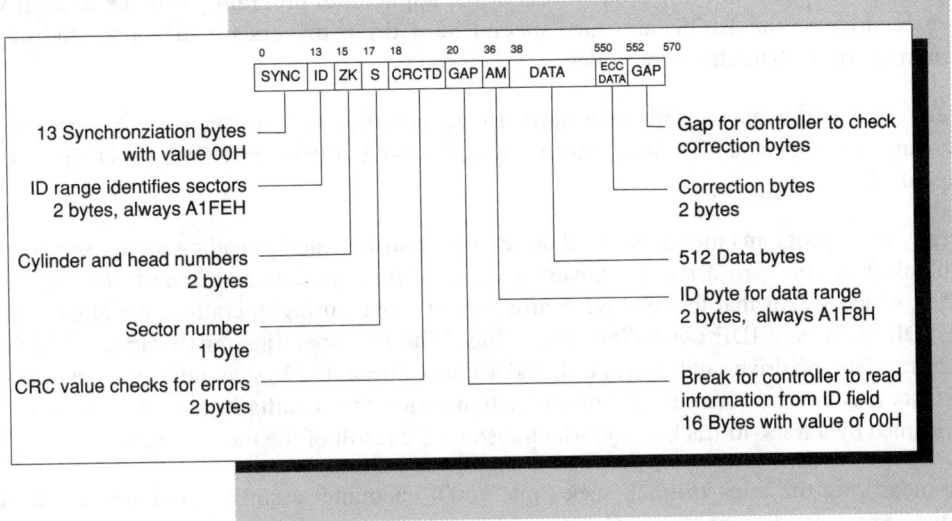

Sector format created by an ST506-type controller

Extra tracks

Hard driveA hard drive also contains other "reserved" areas. For example, there are *servo tracks*, which are used by the hard drive's electronic circuitry to synchronize itself to the data clock. This is especially important when used with RLL controllers and drives.

Some drives also contain "reserved" or "alternate" tracks. These tracks are unknown even to the BIOS. The area on a reserved track is used as a replacement for defective sectors.

Finally, there is the *park area*. When the computer is switched off, the read/write heads "land" or settle on the surface of the park area. If the read/write head lands on a track containing data, that data might be destroyed or damaged. The park area contains no data and is a safe area that cannot be scratched or otherwise damaged by the read/write heads.

6.7.6 Access Times

A hard drive's performance is measured by its access speed. Hardware manufacturers often claim that their hard drives have access speeds of 10 or 30 milliseconds. This value represents the average seek time between two file accesses.

Most manufacturers also use track-to-track seek time and maximum seek time to express hard drive speed. The track-to-track seek time is the time needed to move the read/write head from one cylinder to the next. The maximum seek time is the time needed to move the read/write arm from the first cylinder to the last cylinder of the drive.

Although these factors have an important effect on how a hard drive accesses a file at the DOS level, there are other important factors. For example, a hard drive with extremely fast specification is useless unless the controller can keep pace with it. Also, a hard drive could be so fragmented that the read/write arm is constantly jumping back and forth between different cylinders to access data. So, performance must also be measured according to the time that a read or write request spends at the various levels of the application program, at the DOS level with its device drivers, the BIOS, and any special hard drive drivers up to and including the programming of the hard drive controller.

To verify the performance data of a hard drive manufacturer, you can use a performance measuring program, such as SystemInfo from Norton Utilities or CORETEST from Core International.

Generally these programs measure a hard drive's data transfer rate by reading the largest possible data block from the hard drive. However, the size of this block is restricted to one complete cylinder, which means that the read/write arm doesn't move during operation. We already know that ESDI, SCSI, and IDE controllers often "hide" the true specifications from the BIOS and instead translate the drive's cylinder, head, and sector values into physical ones. So, the results of these tests may not be accurate. A controller translation that results in a track change is also accompanied by a track-to-track delay, which distorts the result of the measurements.

When measuring the track-to-track seek time, you'll encounter a similar problem. To do this, read two sectors in adjacent tracks. However, the controller translation of these two sectors may not result in a track change, which produces an unrealistic zero track-to-track seek time.

Cache controllers and cache programs

The results of these measurements are especially suspicious when cache programs are used. At the software level, disk cache programs, such as SMARTDRV or PCKwik, can have a major effect on disk drive performance. These cache programs hook into the BIOS hard drive interrupt and intercept the read and write calls of the application programs and the device drivers of DOS.

When an application program wants to read data from a hard drive, the cache program intercepts the read request , passes the read request to the hard drive controller in the usual way, saves the data that was read in its cache buffer, and then passes the data back to the application program.

Depending on the size of the cache buffer, numerous sectors are read into and saved in the buffer. When the application wants to read more data, the cache program again intercepts the request and examines its buffers to see if the data is still in the cache. If it is, the data is immediately passed back to the application without another hard drive operation. As you can imagine, this speeds up access tremendously and can greatly affect the disk drive performance measurements.

In order to maintain accurate measurements, you can write a program to check the BIOS disk interrupt 13H. If it's still pointing to the ROM BIOS, then a cache program isn't active. If it's not, then you can request that the user remove or disable the cache program until the measurements are completed.

Another type of disk cache is one that is part of the hard drive controller. This is a hardware disk cache and doesn't use any BIOS interrupts. Instead, the cacheing is performed at the hardware level and is invisible to normal performance measurement software.

6.8   Hard Drive Partitions

If you've ever installed a hard drive or added an operating system, such as XENIX or OS/2, then you've used the DOS FDISK command. This command is used to partition the hard drive. A hard drive must be partitioned when you want to logically divide the hard drive into separate volumes or when you want to install more than one operating system on the same hard drive.

Formatting process

To prepare a hard disk to be used by an operating system, you must perform three tasks.

First you must perform a *low-level format*. When you do this, you are organizing the drive into cylinders, tracks, and sectors by writing the appropriate address markers onto the drive surface. The address markers are later used by the controller to identify the specific sectors.

In the early days of the PC, the DOS DEBUG command was used to perform a low-level format. Today, low-level formatting is no longer complicated because most hard drive manufacturers provide programs that perform this task.

Partitioning the hard drive

Next, you must partition the hard drive. There are two reasons why this is necessary. First, it enables you to install multiple operating systems, such as DOS and XENIX, on a single drive. Partitioning a hard drive into separate areas lets each of the operating systems manage its disk space without the conflicts caused by different file structures.

The other reason for partitioning a hard drive is to be able to use the additional capacity of larger drives. The original XT had a hard drive with a 10 Meg capacity. Then drives with 40 and 80 Meg capacities appeared. Early versions of DOS were able to manage hard drive capacities of only 32 Meg. But this limitation was addressed by DOS 3.3. Now the 32 Meg maximum capacity applied only to a partition. DOS 3.3 allows one primary partition with a 32 Meg maximum and an extended partition that can be divided into as many as 23 logical devices (drives C: through Z:). Each of these logical devices can hold up to 32 Meg, which makes the entire hard drive capacity 768 Meg.

DOS 4.0 goes even farther, supporting drives with a maximum capacity up to 2 gigabytes. Nevertheless, many users continue to partition the hard drive into logical drives, because they would rather work with multiple drives than one large drive and several hundred or even several thousand files.

While the primary partition must be located within the first 32 Megs of the hard drive, the extended partition can be located anywhere. FDISK refers to these partitions as "PRI DOS" and "EXT DOS".

Partition sector

The *partition sector* is the structure that all versions of DOS use to define a hard drive's partitions. When you run the FDISK program for the first time, it creates the partition sector in the hard drive's first sector (cylinder 0, head 0, sector 1).

The BIOS first loads the partition sector, instead of the DOS boot sector, after the system is started or reset. The partition sector is loaded into memory at address 0000:7C00, if there are no diskettes in drive A:.

If the BIOS finds the values 55H, AAH, in the last two bytes of the partition sector's 512 total bytes, it considers the sector to be executable and starts executing the program at the first byte of the sector. Otherwise, the BIOS displays an error message and either starts ROM-BASIC or goes into a continuous loop, depending on the version of BIOS and the manufacturer.

Addr.	Contents	Type
■ Structure of the partition sector of a hard drive ■		
+000h	Partition code	Code
+1BEh	1. Entry in the partition table	16 BYTE
+1CEh	2. Entry in the partition table	16 BYTE
+1DEh	3. Entry in the partition table	16 BYTE
+1EEh	4. Entry in the partition table	16 BYTE
+1FEh	ID code (AA55h), which identifies the partition sector as such	2 BYTE
■ Length: 200h (512 Bytes) ■		

This program recognizes and starts the active partition's operating system. To do this, it must load the operating system's boot sector and pass control to the program within that boot sector. Since the later's program code must also be loaded at memory address 0000:7C00, the code from the partition sector is moved to the memory address 0000:0600 first, to make room for the boot sector.

Partition table

The program in the partition sector must be able to find the boot sector for the active partition. For this, it uses the *partition table*. This table is located at offset 1BEH of the partition sector.

Each entry in the partition table is 16 bytes. The table is located at the end of the partition sector, leaving enough room for 4 entries. So the number of partitions is limited to 4. To accommodate more than four partitions, some hard drive manufacturers use a special configuration program that relocates and enlarges the partition table and adapts the partition sector code to use this relocated table.

Sometimes the partition sector code is changed to allow you to boot any of the installed operating systems on the hard drive. This makes it easy to choose which of the operating systems should run when the computer is first started.

The partition table has the following layout:

```
┌─────────────────────────────────────────────────────────────┐
│ ■ Structure of an entry in the partition table  ▓▓▓▓▓▓      │
├──────┬──────────────────────────────────────────┬───────────┤
│ Addr.│ Contents                                 │ Type      │
├──────┼──────────────────────────────────────────┼───────────┤
│ +00h │ Partition status                         │ 1 BYTE    │
│      │    00h = inactive                        │           │
│      │    80h = Boot-Partition                  │           │
├──────┼──────────────────────────────────────────┼───────────┤
│ +01h │ Read/write head, with which the partition│ 1 BYTE    │
│      │ begins                                   │           │
├──────┼──────────────────────────────────────────┼───────────┤
│ +02h │ sector and cylinder, with which the      │ 1 WORD    │
│      │ partition begins                         │           │
├──────┼──────────────────────────────────────────┼───────────┤
│ +04h │ Partition type                           │ 1 BYTE    │
│      │    00h = Entry not allocated             │           │
│      │    01h = DOS with 12-Bit-FAT (primary    │           │
│      │          Part.)                          │           │
│      │    02h = XENIX                           │           │
│      │    03h = XENIX                           │           │
│      │    04h = DOS with 16-Bit-FAT (primary    │           │
│      │          Part.)                          │           │
│      │    05h = extended DOS-Partition (DOS 3.3)│           │
│      │    06h = DOS-4.0 partition with more     │           │
│      │          than 32 Megs                    │           │
│      │    DBh = Concurrent DOS                  │           │
│      │ Other codes possible in combination with │           │
│      │ other operating systems or special driver│           │
│      │ software.                                │           │
├──────┼──────────────────────────────────────────┼───────────┤
│ +05h │ Read/write head, with which the partition│ 1 BYTE    │
│      │ ends                                     │           │
├──────┼──────────────────────────────────────────┼───────────┤
│ +06h │ sector and cylinder, with which the      │ 1 WORD    │
│      │ partition ends                           │           │
├──────┼──────────────────────────────────────────┼───────────┤
│ +08h │ Removal of first sector of the partition │ 1 DWORD   │
│      │ (Boot-sector) of partition sector in     │           │
│      │ sectors                                  │           │
├──────┼──────────────────────────────────────────┼───────────┤
│ +0Ch │ Number of sectors in this partition      │ 1 DWORD   │
├──────┴──────────────────────────────────────────┴───────────┤
│ ■ Length: 10h (16 Bytes)  ▓▓▓▓▓▓▓▓▓▓▓▓                      │
└─────────────────────────────────────────────────────────────┘
```

Starting the boot partition

The first field of each partition table entry indicates whether a partition is active. A value of 00H indicates that partition isn't active; a value 80H indicates that partition is active and should be booted. If the partition sector program detects that more than one partition is active or that none of the partitions are active, it aborts the booting process, displays an error message, and waits in a continuous loop. You can exit this loop only by resetting.

When the partition sector program recognizes the active partition, is uses the next two fields to determine the location of this partition on the hard drive. The sector and cylinder numbers are expressed exactly as BIOS interrupt 13H (Diskette/Hard drive), including bits 6 and 7 of the sector number, which represent bits 8 and 9 of the cylinder number. At this point, BIOS interrupt 13H and its functions are the only way to access the hard drive. The DOS functions aren't available because DOS hasn't been booted yet.

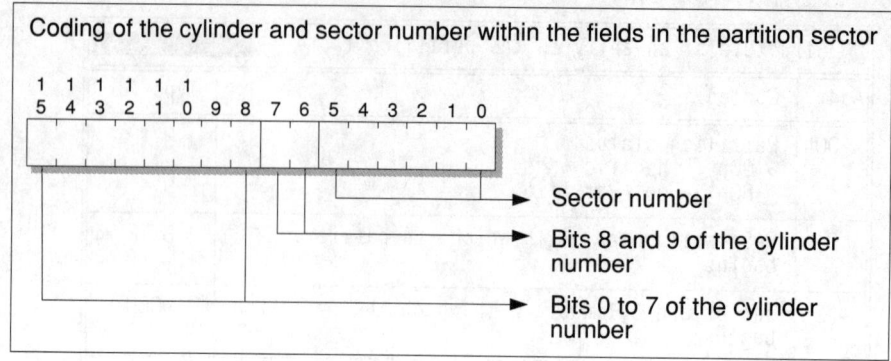

Other information in the partition table

The partition table also contains additional information. For example, each entry has a field that describes the operating system for that partition. The above figure shows the types that are supported.

In addition to the partition's starting sector, another field contains the partition's ending sector, expressed as cylinder, head, and sector numbers.

There are two additional fields for each table entry. The first is the total number of sectors within the partition. The last is the distance of a partition's boot sector from the partition sector, counted in sectors.

Remember that the first partition on a drive usually begins in the first sector of track 0, head 1. In other words, almost an entire track is "wasted" because the partition sector occupies only one sector on track 0, head 0.

Structure of the extended partition under DOS

DOS 3.3 allows you to define one primary and one extended partition on a hard drive. FDISK builds the partition sector and partition table to identify the partitions, but doesn't write the program code into the partition sector.

The partition table has two entries. The first entry is for the first logical device of the extended partition and a partition type (value 1 or 4 that indicates a DOS partition with 12-bit or 16-bit FAT). The second entry is for the next logical device within the extended partition, is one exists.

To support other logical devices, this structure is repeated for each additional device. This results in a chained list that continues until the "partition type" field, in the second table entry of the partition table of the partition sector of an extended partition, contains has a zero value.

6.8.1 Examining the Partition Structure

You can use the following programs to examine the partition structures of a hard drive. One is written in Pascal and the other in C. The programs display the contents of the partition sectors and the extended partitions (if there are any) from the hard drive. By default, they access the first

hard drive, number 0, but you can also specify a different number (1, 2, 3, etc.) when running
the programs to examine a different hard drive.

Listing: FIXPARTP.PAS

```
{**********************************************************}
{*               F I X P A R T P . P A S            *}
{*--------------------------------------------------------*}
{*  Task        : Displays hard disk partitioning.        *}
{*--------------------------------------------------------*}
{*  Author      : Michael Tischer                         *}
{*  Developed on : 04/26/89                               *}
{*  Last update  : 02/12/92                               *}
{*--------------------------------------------------------*}
{*  Call        : FIXPARTP [ Drive_number ]               *}
{*               Default is drive 0 (C:)                  *}
{**********************************************************}

uses Dos;                             { Add DOS unit }

{== Type declarations ====================================}

type SecPos   = record      { Describes a sector position }
                  Head : byte;            { Read/write head }
                  SecCyl : word;   { Sector and cylinder number }
                end;

     PartEntry = record            { Partition table entry }
                   Status  : byte;      { Partition status }
                   StartSec : SecPos;        { First sector }
                   PartTyp : byte;        { Partition type }
                   EndSec  : SecPos;          { Last sector }
                   SecOfs  : longint;   { Offset of boot sector }
                   SecNum  : longint;   { Number of sectors }
                 end;

     PartSec   = record       { Describes partition sector }
                   BootCode  : array [0..$1BD] of byte;
                   PartTable : array [1..4] of PartEntry;
                   IdCode    : word;           { $AA55 }
                 end;

{**********************************************************}
{*  ReadPartSec : Reads a partition sector from the hard drive.  *}
{*--------------------------------------------------------*}
{*  Input  : - DS    : BIOS code for drive (80H, 81H, etc.)  *}
{*           - Head   : Number of read/write heads        *}
{*           - SctCyl : Sector/cylinder numbers in BIOS format *}
{*           - Buf    : Buffer to which sector is passed   *}
{**********************************************************}

function ReadPartSec( DS, Head : byte;
                      SctCyl    : word;
                      var Buf   : PartSec ) : boolean;

var Regs : Registers;   { Processor registers for interrupt call }

begin
  Regs.AX := $0201;    { Funct. no.: READ for first sector }
  Regs.DL := DS;                  { Pass other parameters }
  Regs.DH := Head;                { to their respective   }
  Regs.CX := SctCyl;              { registers            }
  Regs.ES := seg( Buf );
```

```
  Regs.BX := ofs( Buf );
  Intr( $13, Regs );                  { Call hard drive interrupt }
  ReadPartSec := ( Regs.Flags and 1 ) = 0;    { Carry flag = error }
end;

{**********************************************************}
{*  GetSecCyl: Gets the combined sector/cylinder coding of the BIOS  *}
{*             sector and cylinder number.               *}
{*--------------------------------------------------------*}
{*  Input  : SctCyl   : Value to be decoded               *}
{*           Sector   : Sector variable reference         *}
{*           Cylinder : Cylinder variable reference       *}
{**********************************************************}

procedure GetSecCyl( SctCyl : word; var Sector, Cylinder : integer );

begin
  Sector   := SctCyl and 63;            { Mask bits 6 and 7 }
  Cylinder := hi( SctCyl ) + ( lo( SctCyl ) and 192 ) shl 2;
end;

{**********************************************************}
{*  ShowPartition: Displays hard drive partitioning on the screen.*}
{*--------------------------------------------------------*}
{*  Input  : DS : Number of the corresponding hard drive  *}
{**********************************************************}

procedure ShowPartition( ds : byte );

var Head     : byte;             { Head of current partition }
    SecCyl   : byte;     { Sector and cylinder of current partition }
    ParSec   : PartSec;          { Current partition sector }
    Entry    : byte;                    { Loop counter }
    Sector,                          { Get sector and   }
    Cylinder : integer;              { cylinder number }
    Regs     : Registers;     { Processor registers for interrupt call }

begin
  writeln;
  ds := ds + $80;            { Prepare drive number for BIOS }
  if ReadPartSec( ds, 0, 1, ParSec ) then   { Read partition sector }
    begin                          { Sector could be read }
      Regs.AH := 8;               { Funct. no.: Read drive ID }
      Regs.DL := ds;
      Intr( $13, Regs );          { Call hard drive interrupt }
      GetSecCyl( Regs.CX, Sector, Cylinder );
      writeln('╔═══════════════════════════'+
              '═════════════════╗');
      writeln('║ Drive ', ds-$80, ':  ', Regs.DH+1:2,
              ' heads, ', Cylinder:5, ' cylinders, ',
              Sector:3, ' sectors           ║');
      writeln('║ Partition Table in Partition Sector     '+
              '                 ║');
      writeln('╠═══════════════════════════'+
              '═════════════════╣');
      writeln('║   |    |          |          |  Start  |'+
              '   End   |Dis.from |  ║');
      writeln('║No|Boot|Type        |Head Cyl. Sec.|'+
              'Head Cyl. Sec.|Boot Sec.| Total ║');
      writeln('╠═══════════════════════════'+
              '═════════════════╣');
```

```pascal
    for Entry:=1 to 4 do                    { Show entries }
      with ParSec.PartTable[ Entry ] do
        begin
        write('|| ', Entry, '|');
        if Status = $80 then write (' Y ')
                            else write (' N ');
        write('|');
        case PartTyp of                  { Compute partition type }
          $00        : write('Not allocated      ');
          $01        : write('DOS, 12-bit FAT    ');
          $02 or $03 : write('XENIX              ');
          '$04       : write('DOS, 16-bit FAT    ');
          $05        : write('DOS, ext. partition');
          $06        : write('DOS 4.0 > 32 MB    ');
          $DB        : write('Concurrent DOS     ');
          else        write('Unknown   (',PartTyp:3,')    ');
        end;
        GetSecCyl( StartSec.SecCyl, Sector, Cylinder );
        write('|', StartSec.Head:2,' ',Cylinder:5,' ',Sector:3 );
        GetSecCyl( EndSec.SecCyl, Sector, Cylinder );
        write(' |', EndSec.Head:2,' ',Cylinder:5,' ',Sector:3 );
        writeln(' | ', SecOfs:7,'|', SecNum:7,'||');
        end;
      writeln('|└─────────────────────────┘'+
              '─────────────────────┘'#13#10);
    end
  else
    writeln('Error during boot sector access');
end;


{*****************************************************************
*                    M A I N   P R O G R A M                    *
*****************************************************************}

var DS,                             { Variables for hard }
    ErrArg   : integer;             { drive arguments    }
begin
  writeln( #13#10'                      FIXPARTP - (c)',
           ' 1989, 92 by MICHAEL TISCHER         ' );
  DS := 0;                          { Default is first hard drive }
  if ParamCount = 1 then            { User entered different argument? }
    begin                                            { Yes }
    val( ParamStr(1), DS, ErrArg ); { Convert ASCII to decimal }
    if ErrArg <> 0 then             { Error during conversion? }
      begin                                          { Yes }
      writeln(#13#10'Invalid drive number');
      exit;                                    { End program }
      end;
    end;
  ShowPartition( DS );              { Display partition sector }
end.
```

Listing: FIXPARTC.C

```c
/***************************************************************/
/*                                                           */
/*                    F I X P A R T C . C                    */
/*-----------------------------------------------------------*/
/*   Task        : Displays hard disk partitioning.         */
/*-----------------------------------------------------------*/
/*   Author      : Michael Tischer                           */
/*   Developed on : 04/26/89                                 */
/*   Last update  : 02/12/92                                 */
/*-----------------------------------------------------------*/
/*   Memory model  : SMALL                                   */
/*-----------------------------------------------------------*/
/*   Call        : FIXPARTC [ Drive_number ]                 */
/*                 Default is drive 0 (C:)                   */
/***************************************************************/

#include <dos.h>
#include <string.h>
#include <stdlib.h>
#include <stdio.h>

/*== Constants ===============================================*/

#define TRUE  ( 1 == 1 )
#define FALSE ( 1 == 0 )

/*== Macros ==================================================*/

#define HI(x) ( *((BYTE *) (&x)+1) )  /* Returns high byte of word */
#define LO(x) ( *((BYTE *) &x) )      /* Returns low byte of word */

/*== Type declarations =======================================*/

typedef unsigned char BYTE;
typedef unsigned int WORD;

typedef struct {                    /* Describes a sector position */
          BYTE Kopf;                /* Read/write head */
          WORD SecZyl;              /* Sector and cylinder number */
        } SECPOS;

typedef struct {                            /* Partition table entry */
          BYTE          Status;     /* Partition status */
          SECPOS        StartSec;   /* First sector */
          BYTE          PartTyp;    /* Partition type */
          SECPOS        EndSec;     /* Last sector */
          unsigned long SecOfs;     /* Offset of boot sector */
          unsigned long SecAnz;     /* Number of sectors */
        } PARTENTRY;

typedef struct {                    /* Describes partition sector */
          BYTE      BootCode[ 0x1BE ];
          PARTENTRY PartTable[ 4 ];
          WORD      IdCode;                  /* 0xAA55 */
        } PARTSEC;

typedef PARTSEC far *PARSPTR;   /* Ptr. to partition sector in memory */

/***************************************************************/
/*   ReadPartSec : Reads a partition sector from the hard drive.  */
/*   Input  : - DS     : BIOS code for drive (0x80, 0x81, etc.)   */
/*            - Head   : Number of read/write heads              */
/*            - SctCyl : Sector/cylinder numbers in BIOS format  */
```

```
/*          - Buf   : Buffer to which sector is passed      */
/* Output : TRUE if sector can be read without errors,      */
/*           otherwise FALSE                                 */
/************************************************************/

BYTE ReadPartSec( BYTE Laufwerk, BYTE Kopf, WORD SekZyl, PARSPTR Buf )

{
   union REGS   Regs;       /* Processor registers for interrupt call */
   struct SREGS SRegs;

   Regs.x.ax = 0x0201;        /* Funct. no.: READ for first sector */
   Regs.h.dl = Laufwerk;           /* Pass other parameters */
   Regs.h.dh = Kopf;              /* to their respective */
   Regs.x.cx = SekZyl;                  /* registers */
   Regs.x.bx = FP_OFF( Buf );
   SRegs.es  = FP_SEG( Buf );

   int86x( 0x13, &Regs, &Regs, &SRegs );  /* Call hard drive interrupt */
   return !Regs.x.cflag;
}

/************************************************************/
/* GetSecZyl: Gets the combined sector/cylinder coding of the BIOS */
/*            sector and cylinder number.                   */
/* Input  : SekZyl   : Value to be decoded                  */
/*          Sektor   : Sector variable reference            */
/*          Zylinder : Cylinder variable reference          */
/* Output : None                                            */
/************************************************************/

void GetSecZyl( WORD SekZyl, int *Sektor, int *Zylinder )

{
   *Sektor   = SekZyl & 63;                /* Mask bits 6 and 7 */
   *Zylinder = HI(SekZyl) + ( ( (WORD) LO(SekZyl) & 192 ) << 2 );
}

/************************************************************/
/* ShowPartition: Displays hard drive partitioning on the screen.*/
/* Input  : DS : Number of the corresponding hard drive (0, 1, etc.)*/
/* Output : None                                            */
/************************************************************/

void ShowPartition( BYTE LW )
{
#define AP ( ParSec.PartTable[ Entry ] )

   BYTE       Kopf,             /* Head of current partition */
              Entry;              /* Loop counter */
   int        Sektor,           /* Get sector and */
              Zylinder;          /* cylinder number */
   PARTSEC    ParSec;           /* Current partition sector */
   union REGS Regs;       /* Processor registers for interrupt call */

   printf("\n");
   LW |= 0x80;                  /* Prepare drive number for BIOS */
   if ( ReadPartSec( LW, 0, 1, &ParSec ) )   /* Read partition sector */
   {                              /* Sector could be read */
      Regs.h.ah = 8;              /* Funct. no.: Read drive ID */
      Regs.h.dl = LW;
      int86( 0x13, &Regs, &Regs );   /* Call hard drive interrupt */
      GetSecZyl( Regs.x.cx, &Sektor, &Zylinder );
      printf( "╔
```

```
═══════════════════════╗\n");
      printf( "║ Drive %2d:    %2d Heads %4d"
              " Cylinders %3d Sectors         ║\n",
              LW-0x80, Regs.h.dh+1, Zylinder, Sektor );
      printf( "║ Partition table in Partition Sector            ║\n");
      printf( "╠
              ═══════════════════════╣\n");
      printf( "║ │   │      │             │ Start      "
              "   End    │Dist fm│  ║\n");
      printf( "║Nr│Boot│Typ           │Head Cyl. Sec │"
              "Head Cyl. Sec │BootSec│Total ║\n");
      printf( "╠
              ═══════════════════════╣\n");

/*-- Get partition table ------------------------------------*/
      for ( Entry=0; Entry < 4; ++Entry )
      {
         printf( "║ %d│", Entry );
         if ( AP.Status == 0x80 )            /* Partition active? */
            printf(" Yes");
         else
            printf(" No ");
         printf("│");
         switch( AP.PartTyp )             /* Compute partition type */
         {
            case 0x00 : printf( "Not allocated    " );
                             break;
            case 0x01 : printf( "DOS, 12-bit FAT  " );
                             break;
            case 0x02 :
            case 0x03 : printf( "XENIX            " );
                             break;
            case 0x04 : printf( "DOS, 16-bit FAT  " );
                             break;
            case 0x05 : printf( "DOS, ext. partition" );
                             break;
            case 0x06 : printf( "DOS 4.0 > 32 MB  " );
                             break;
            case 0xDB : printf( "Concurrent DOS   " );
                             break;
            default   : printf( "Unknown (%3d)    ",
                                 ParSec.PartTable[ Entry ].PartTyp );
         }

/*-- Get physical and logical parameters --------------------*/
         GetSecZyl( AP.StartSec.SecZyl, &Sektor, &Zylinder );
         printf( "│%2d %5d  %3d ", AP.StartSec.Kopf, Zylinder, Sektor );
         GetSecZyl( AP.EndSec.SecZyl, &Sektor, &Zylinder );
         printf( "│%2d %5d  %3d ", AP.EndSec.Kopf, Zylinder, Sektor );
         printf( "│%6lu │%6lu ║\n", AP.SecOfs, AP.SecAnz );
      }
      printf( "╚
              ═══════════════════════╝\n" );

   }
   else
      printf("Error during boot sector access\n");
}

/*************************************************************
*                     M A I N   P R O G R A M               *
**************************************************************/

int main( int argc, char *argv[] )
{
```

```
int Laufwerk;

printf( "\n██████████████████ FIXPARTC - (c)"
       " 1989, 92 by MICHAEL TISCHER ██ \n" );
Laufwerk = 0;                        /* Default is first hard drive */
if ( argc == 2 )            /* User entered different argument? */
 {                                               /* Yes */
  Laufwerk = atoi ( argv[1] );
  if ( Laufwerk == 0 && *argv[1] != '0' )
   {
    printf("\nInvalid drive number!");
    return( 1 );                               /* End program */
   }
 }
ShowPartition( (BYTE) Laufwerk );     /* Display partition sector */
return( 0 );
}
```

Listing: FIXPARTB.BAS

```
'**********************************************************************
'*                                                                    *
'*                      FIXPARTB.BAS                                   *
'*------------------------------------------------------------------- *
'*  Task           : Displays hard disk partitioning.                 *
'*------------------------------------------------------------------- *
'*  Author         : Michael Tischer                                  *
'*  Developed on   : 05/21/91                                         *
'*  Last update    : 02/06/92                                         *
'*------------------------------------------------------------------- *
'*  Call           : FIXPARTB [Drive_number]                          *
'*                   Default is drive 0 (C:)                          *
'**********************************************************************

DECLARE SUB GetSecCyl (SecCyl AS LONG, Sector AS INTEGER, Cylinder AS
INTEGER)
DECLARE FUNCTION ReadPartSec% (ds%, Head%, SecCyl%, PartiEntry() AS ANY)
DECLARE SUB Showpartition (ds AS INTEGER)
DECLARE FUNCTION MLNG& (TNum AS INTEGER)


'$INCLUDE: 'QB.BI'                    'Add include file for interrupt call


CONST TRUE = -1                                    'Define the truth
CONST FALSE = NOT TRUE


TYPE SecPos                              'Describes a sector position
     Head AS INTEGER                            'Read-write head
     SecCyl AS LONG                         'Sector and cylinder number
END TYPE


TYPE PartEntry                           'Partition table entry
     Status AS INTEGER                          'Partition status
     StartSec AS SecPos                         'First sector
     PartType AS INTEGER                        'Partition type
     EndSec AS SecPos                           'Last sector
     SecOfs AS LONG                       'Offset of boot sector
     SecNum AS LONG                       'Number of sectors
END TYPE


DIM HarDrive AS INTEGER                 'Variable for hard drive argument

CLS
PRINT " FIXPARTB - (C)";
PRINT " 1991, 92 by Michael Tischer "
HarDrive = 0                               'Default is first hard drive
IF COMMAND$ <> "" THEN                      'User entered different argument
   HarDrive = VAL(COMMAND$)                 'Convert ASCII to decimal
END IF
CALL Showpartition(HarDrive)               'Display partition sector
END


'**********************************************************************
'* GetSecCyl : Gets the combined sector/cylinder coding of the BIOS  *
'*             sector and cylinder number.                           *
'* Input   : Sector variable in BIOS coding                          *
'* Output  : References to sector and cylinder variables             *
'**********************************************************************
SUB GetSecCyl (SecCyl AS LONG, Sector AS INTEGER, Cylinder AS INTEGER)

Sector = SecCyl AND 63                        'Mask bits 6 and 7
Cylinder = SecCyl \ 256 + ((SecCyl MOD 256) AND 192) * 4
END SUB


'**********************************************************************
```

```
'*  MLNG    : Converts an integer to its representative long value. *
'*  Input   : Integer value                                         *
'*  Output  : The long number containing corresponding register data *
'*********************************************************************
FUNCTION MLNG& (TNum AS INTEGER)

IF TNum >= 0 THEN                          'Bit 16 unset
  MLNG = TNum                      'Integer corresponds to register contents
ELSE                                       'Bit 16 set
  MLNG = 65536 + TNum              'This value corresponds to register contents
END IF

END FUNCTION

'*********************************************************************
'*  ReadPartSec : Reads a partition sector from the hard drive.     *
'*  Input     : DS       = Drive code                               *
'*              Head     = Number of read/write heads               *
'*              SecCyl   = Sector/cylinder numbers in BIOS format   *
'*  Output n  : PartEntry() = The 4 partition sector tables         *
'*********************************************************************
FUNCTION ReadPartSec% (ds%, Head%, SecCyl%, PrtnEntry() AS PartEntry)

DIM Register AS RegTypeX       'Processor registers for interrupt call
DIM PartSector AS STRING * 512            'Get partition sector
DIM IdCode AS LONG                        'Get partition ID code
DIM i AS INTEGER                          'Loop counter
DIM j AS INTEGER                          'Loop counter

Register.ax = &H201                 'Funct. no.: READ for first sector
Register.cx = SecCyl%               'Sector and cylinder of current partition
Register.dx = Head% * 256 + ds%           ' Head and drive number
Register.es = VARSEG(PartSector)    'Partition sector segment address
Register.bx = VARPTR(PartSector)    'Partition sector offset address
CALL INTERRUPTX(&H13, Register, Register)  'Call hard drive interrupt
DEF SEG = VARSEG(PartSector)    'Set segment address for PEEK command
Pointer = VARPTR(PartSector) + &H1BD 'Pointer to first partition entry
offset = 0                          'Offset of first partition entry
FOR i = 1 TO 4                            'Read all 4 partition entries
  PrtnEntry(i).Status = PEEK(Pointer + offset + 1)
  PrtnEntry(i).StartSec.Head = PEEK(Pointer + offset + 2)
  PrtnEntry(i).StartSec.SecCyl = PEEK(Pointer + offset + 4) * 256& +
PEEK(Pointer + offset + 3)
  PrtnEntry(i).PartType = PEEK(Pointer + offset + 5)
  PrtnEntry(i).EndSec.Head = PEEK(Pointer + offset + 6)
  PrtnEntry(i).EndSec.SecCyl = PEEK(Pointer + offset + 8) * 256& +
PEEK(Pointer + offset + 7)
  PrtnEntry(i).SecOfs = 0
  FOR j = 0 TO 3
    PrtnEntry(i).SecOfs = PrtnEntry(i).SecOfs * 256& + PEEK(Pointer +
offset + 12 - j)
  NEXT
  PrtnEntry(i).SecNum = 0
  FOR j = 0 TO 3
    PrtnEntry(i).SecNum = PrtnEntry(i).SecNum * 256& + PEEK(Pointer +
offset + 16 - j)
  NEXT
  offset = offset + 16         'Set offset of next partition entry
NEXT
IdCode = PEEK(Pointer + offset + 2) * 256& + PEEK(Pointer + offset + 1)
IF (Register.flags AND 1) = 0 THEN
  ReadPartSec = TRUE
END IF
```

```
END FUNCTION

'*********************************************************************
'*  ShowPartition : Displays hard drive partitioning on the screen. *
'*  Input       : Number of the corresponding hard drive            *
'*  Output      : None                                              *
'*********************************************************************
SUB Showpartition (ds AS INTEGER)

DIM Head AS INTEGER                     'Head of current partition
DIM SecCyl AS INTEGER      'Sector and cylinder of current partition
DIM Entry AS INTEGER                       'Loop counter
DIM Sector AS INTEGER                      'Sector number
DIM Cylinder AS INTEGER                    'Cylinder number
DIM PartiEntry(4) AS PartEntry          'Current partition entry
DIM Register AS RegTypeX      'Processor registers for interrupt call

PRINT ;
ds = ds + &H80                      'Prepare drive number for BIOS
IF ReadPartSec(ds, 0, 1, PartiEntry()) THEN  'Read partition sector
  Register.ax = &H800             ' AH = Funct. no: Read drive ID
  Register.dx = ds                          'Drive number
  CALL INTERRUPTX(&H13, Register, Register)  'Call hard drive interrupt
  CALL GetSecCyl(MLNG(Register.cx), Sector, Cylinder) 'Get sec./cyl. #s
  PRINT "";
  PRINT ""
  PRINT USING " Drive  #: ## heads, "; ds – &H80; Register.dx \ 256 + 1;
  PRINT USING "##### cylinders, "; Cylinder;
  PRINT USING "### sectors                "; Sector
  PRINT " Partition Table in Partition Sector       ";
  PRINT "                            "
  PRINT "";
  PRINT ""
  PRINT "                        Start     ";
  PRINT "    End    Dis.from        "
  PRINT "NoBootType              Head ";
  PRINT "Cyl. Sec.Head Cyl. Sec.Boot Sec.  Total  "
  PRINT "";
  PRINT ""
  FOR Entry = 1 TO 4                          'Show entries
    PRINT USING "##"; Entry;
    IF PartiEntry(Entry).Status = &H80 THEN
      PRINT " Y  ";
    ELSE
      PRINT " N  ";
    END IF
    SELECT CASE PartiEntry(Entry).PartType
      CASE 0
              PRINT "Not allocated       ";
      CASE 1
              PRINT "DOS, 12-bit FAT     ";
      CASE 2 OR 3
              PRINT "Xenix             ";
      CASE 4
              PRINT "DOS, 16-bit FAT     ";
      CASE 5
              PRINT "DOS, ext. partition ";
      CASE 6
              PRINT "DOS 4.0 > 32 Meg    ";
      CASE &HDB
              PRINT "Concurrent DOS      ";
      CASE ELSE
              PRINT USING "Unknown     (###) ";
PartiEntry(Entry).PartType
```

```
      END SELECT
      CALL GetSecCyl(PartiEntry(Entry).StartSec.SecCyl, Sector, Cylinder)
      PRINT USING "### ###  "; PartiEntry(Entry).StartSec.Head; Cylinder;
      PRINT USING "### "; Sector;
      CALL GetSecCyl(PartiEntry(Entry).EndSec.SecCyl, Sector, Cylinder)
      PRINT USING "### ####  ### "; PartiEntry(Entry).EndSec.Head;
Cylinder; Sector;

      PRINT USING " ####### "; PartiEntry(Entry).SecOfs;
      PRINT USING " ####### "; PartiEntry(Entry).SecNum
   NEXT
   PRINT "";
   PRINT ""
ELSE
  PRINT "Error during boot sector access"
END IF

END SUB
```

Chapter 7

The Parallel Port

There are three ways to access the parallel port: direct hardware programming, through the ROM-BIOS, or with DOS function calls. In this chapter we'll discuss direct programming and using ROM-BIOS functions to access the parallel port. Section 7.1 describes the BIOS functions used in printing. The ROM-BIOS functions offer an advantage over equivalent DOS functions because they allow better control over printer status. DOS immediately fails when a printer triggers the critical error interrupt, but BIOS offers other options.

Section 7.2 describes direct programming of the parallel port. We'll show you how to connect two computers through their parallel ports and transfer data quickly between these computers using a file transfer program.

7.1 Accessing the Parallel Port from the BIOS

BIOS interrupt 17H is reserved exclusively for communication with the parallel port. Most users call interrupt 17H the BIOS printer interrupt, although other peripheral devices could also be connected to this port.

The BIOS printer interrupt

A maximum of three different parallel ports can be connected to the PC (refer to Section 7.2 for more information). Interrupt 17H provides three different functions for addressing these ports. These functions perform three specialized tasks and can control all three parallel ports.

Function	Task
00H	Display characters
01H	Initialize printer
02H	Request printer status

About these functions

These functions are superior to the equivalent DOS functions in the choice of the addressed port. The DOS functions only control the first parallel port (PRN or LPT1). The three BIOS functions are more flexible in this respect and, when you call them, expect to find the number of the parallel port to be addressed in the DX register. You can specify values of 0, 1, and 2 for the ports: 0 corresponds to LPT1, 1 corresponds to LPT2, and 2 corresponds to LPT3.

Printer status

These functions have something else in common besides being passed the port number. After being called, each function returns the current printer status in the AH register. The bits of this status byte convey information about whether the printer is currently busy, still has paper, or has encountered an error while receiving characters. This status is very important to the communication with the parallel port.

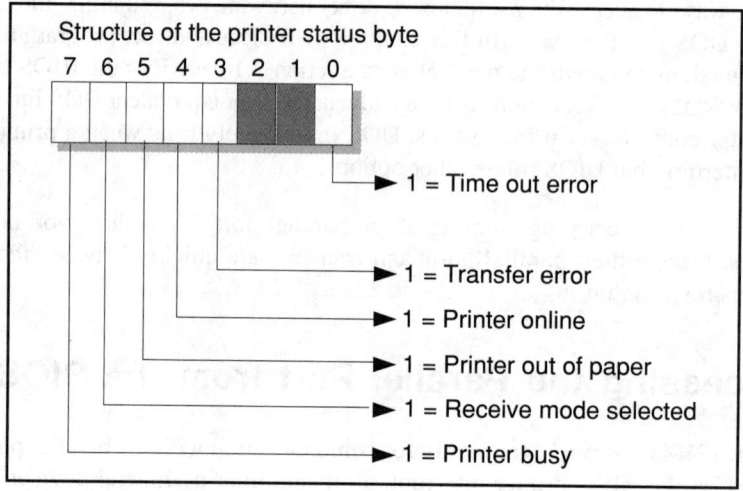

Time out error

A time out error, signaled by bit 0 of the status byte, always occurs when the BIOS attempts to send data to the printer over a certain period of time and the printer is BUSY (bit 7=0) or not accepting the data. This frequently happens because a parallel port can send up to 100,000 characters per second, but none of the printers on the market can keep up with that pace.

The number of failures that occur before a time out occurs varies with the contents of a BIOS variable. Each parallel port has a byte allocated at a memory range beginning at address 0040:0078H. These bytes specify the number of unsuccessful attempts allowed.

BIOS time out counter for parallel ports	
Address	Meaning
0040:0078	Time out counter: first parallel port
0040:0079	Time out counter: second parallel port
0040:007A	Time out counter: third parallel port

Instead of referring to a given period of time, the values contained in these variables refer to the number of failed attempts that are allowed before BIOS reports a time out error. The program code of the ROM-BIOS continually prompts the parallel port within a program loop. Since this loop consists of only a few assembly language instructions running in cycles of a few microseconds, the time out value from each BIOS variable acts as a factor used in the loop's counter, instead of as the loop counter itself. This factor is multiplied by the constant 262,140 (4 * 65535). The value 20, which the BIOS enters in all three memory locations after the system boots, corresponds to more than five million attempts.

If you use a loop counter instead of a time unit, the period of time that can elapse before a time out occurs depends on the processing speed of the computer. This means that the time span varies with the system's CPU and clock speed. That's why the loop counter must be increased on faster systems, because there isn't a connection between the printer speed and the CPU speed. If you don't make this adjustment, you'll discover, after purchasing a 486, that the system will suddenly send a time out error message during printing.

The BIOS manufacturers usually make this adjustment by using a larger constant instead of a larger default value. For example, if your new computer is twice as fast as a normal AT, instead of 4*65535, you might multiply 8 by 65535.

This is done because applications also access the three BIOS variables to change the time out rate for one of the ports. This is possible because these variables are accessible to any program as part of RAM. This gives the programmer the option of setting a higher time out rate for situations in which the printer would otherwise send a time out error. However, increasing the time out rate wouldn't work on a faster system, unless a large enough constant factor is also chosen.

Other printer status flags

Other bits provide more information about the printer's status. Bit 3 shows a transfer error (a data error in the line), while bit 4 indicates whether the printer is currently online or offline. This bit is the equivalent of the online button found on printers, with an LED indicating its status.

Bit 5 indicates whether the printer has any paper. Bit 6 confirms the printer's receipt of the last character. To determine whether a printer is connected to a particular port, simply prompt for this bit. If it contains a value of 1, then a printer exists.

Bit 7 represents the BUSY signal, which is used by the printer to indicate that it's busy and cannot accept any characters. This bit is also important to the time out error. This signal instructs the ROM-BIOS to repeat the output loop because a character cannot be sent to the printer. This is negative logic: if this bit is set to 0, the printer is busy, and if it is set to 1, the printer is not busy.

Different states of the printer can also result in changes to a series of bits in the status byte. For example, if the printer is ready to print and is online, bits 7 and 4 are set. If you switch the printer offline, not only are bits 7 and 4 cleared, but bit 3 is also set, which signals a transfer error.

Checking printer status

You may be wondering how you can use this status byte in programs. First, the status byte can prompt for the various states that correspond to the single bits before or after transferring a character. This means that you can determine whether the printer is out of paper, switched offline, or connected to the parallel port.

The status byte can also be used to check for printer access. If bit 1 (time out error), 3 (transfer error), or 5 (out of paper) is set, or bit 4 (printer online) or 7 (printer busy) is cleared, you cannot send characters to the printer. The following pseudocode demonstrates how this is done:

```
pstatus = PrinterStatus;
if ( ( (pstatus and 29h) <> 0 ) or
     ( (pstatus and 80h) = 0  ) or
     ( (pstatus and 10h) = 0  ) ) then
  PrinterOK = FALSE
else
  PrinterOK = TRUE;
```

Now let's return to the three BIOS printer interrupt functions.

Function 00H: Write character

Function 00H writes a character to the printer. Place the function number (00H) in the AH register and the ASCII code of the desired character in the AL register. After the function call, the AH register receives the status byte.

Function 01H: Initialize parallel port

Function 01H initializes the parallel port and printer. Always execute this function before sending data to the printer. Place the function number (01H) in the AH register. After the function call, the AH register receives the status byte.

Function 02H: Get status byte

Function 02H reads the status byte. With this function, a printing job and the initialization of the parallel port aren't involved. After the function call, the AH register receives the status byte.

7.1.1 Calling the BIOS Functions

Each of these functions can be called from a high level language program in the same way you would call any interrupt. Some C compilers support these functions through their runtime libraries. The following table provides an overview of the corresponding routines with Borland and Microsoft compilers.

C Compiler Support for Printer Functions	
Compiler	Function
Turbo C	
Borland C	
Borland C++	biosprint
Microsoft C	
QuickC	bios_printer

Although QuickBASIC and Turbo Pascal also have printer support, this support uses DOS output functions instead of BIOS functions. If an output error occurs, the DOS functions call critical error interrupt 24H instead of returning an error code to the program. However, this error can be intercepted (e.g., by Turbo Pascal).

QuickBASIC contains the LPRINT statement for transmitting printed output. Turbo Pascal uses Write and WriteLn for the same purpose, provided that the programmer opens a file variable, directs this variable toward the printer, and specifies the printer before calling Writeln or Write. The PRINTER.TPU unit included with Turbo Pascal performs this task for you (refer to your Turbo Pascal documentation for more information).

7.1.2 Redirecting the BIOS Printer Interrupt

TSR programs redirect the BIOS printer interrupt to their own routines to suit the needs of these TSRs. This allowed the development of print spoolers (programs that intercept characters sent by the original BIOS functions and store these characters in a buffer for later printing).

Demonstration program

The following assembly language program listed will help users whose printers uses a different character set than their PCs. For example, if you attempt to print a program listing or file containing PC linedraw characters on some older model Epson printers, the printout may look different than you expected. If the data on the screen looks as follows:

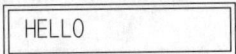

an older Epson printout may look like the following:

```
IMMMMMMMMMMMMMMMMMMMM;
: HELLO            :
HMMMMMMMMMMMMMMMMMMMM(
```

The PRCVT.ASM program converts some linedraw characters to ASCII equivalents. This enables you to see how the printout will look on printers that have IBM mode:

```
/--------------------\
| HELLO              |
\--------------------/
```

PRCVT converts these characters before transferring them to the printer by deflecting the BIOS printer interrupt to its own routine, which is called whenever the BIOS printer interrupt is called. This eliminates the need for a definition of the conversion tables provided by many word processing programs.

Automatic character conversion

The new interrupt handler, which is the focus of the PRCVT.ASM TSR program, first checks whether function 00H should be called. This is the only function to be changed. If another function is called, the call is passed to the old printer interrupt.

If a character should be output, the program checks a table called CODETAB to determine whether it contains this character. This table, which you can see at the beginning of the program listing of PRCVT.ASM, consists of 2-byte entries, with the first byte (the low byte) containing the new code of a character that will be converted, while the subsequent byte reflects the character's old code. The table is closed by a byte with the value 0.

This new function 00H checks the second byte of a table entry to determine whether it's identical to the character to be printed. If the character isn't found in the table, then it's passed, unchanged, to the old printer interrupt for output. If it's detected in the table, it's replaced by the first byte of the table entry and then passed on for output.

The rest of the program is structurally related to other TSR programs documented in this book. PRCVT was created as a COM program and doesn't require any parameters when called from the command line. After being called, it first checks whether it has been installed. If it hasn't been installed, it installs itself; otherwise it removes the installed copy from memory.

This program can be used for both BIOS and DOS printed output.

Assembler listing: PRCVT.ASM

```
;*************************************************************         ;*    Assembly     : MASM PRCVT;                              *;
;*                                                          *;         ;*                   LINK PRCVT;                              *;
;*                  P R C V T                               *;         ;*                   EXE2BIN PRCVT PRCVT.COM  or             *;
;*--------------------------------------------------------- *;         ;*                                                          *;
;* Task      :  Points the BIOS printer interrupt to its own *;        ;*                   TASM PRCVT                               *;
;*             routine and makes it possible for example    *;         ;*                   TLINK PRCVT /T                           *;
;*             to convert IBM-ASCII to EPSON.               *;         ;*--------------------------------------------------------- *;
;*             The program is de-installed on the           *;         ;* Call      :  PRCVT                                        *;
;*             second call and removed from memory.         *;         ;*************************************************************;
;*--------------------------------------------------------- *;
;* Author    :  Michael Tischer                             *;         ;== Actual program starts here ===========================
;* Developed on  : 08/02/87                                 *;
;* Last update   : 02/14/92                                 *;         code     segment para 'CODE'     ;Definition of the CODE segment
;*--------------------------------------------------------- *;
                                                                                org 100h
```

```
          assume cs:code, ds:code, es:code, ss:code

start:    jmp prcvtini           ;The first executable command

;== Data (remain in memory) ========================================

olderint  equ this dword         ;Old interrupt vector 17H
intoldofs dw (?)                 ;Offset address Interrupt vector 17H
intoldseg dw (?)                 ;Segment address Interrupt vector 17H

          ;-- The following table contains the new --------------------
          ;-- code followed by the old code --------------------------

codetab   db   64, 21            ; Paragraph --- > '@'
          db   47,201            ; 'π' ----------> '/'
          db   124,186           ; '||' ----------> '|'
          db   92,200            ; 'L' ----------> '\'
          db   45,205            ; '=' ----------> '-'
          db   92,187            ; 'π' ----------> '\'
          db   47,188            ; 'J' ----------> '/'
          db   43,206            ; '#' ----------> '+'
          db   0                 ;End of the table

;== this is the new printer interrupt (remains in memory) =============

newpri    proc far

          jmp  short newpri_1

          db "CW"                ;Identification of the program

newpri_1: or   ah,ah             ;Print character (function O)?
          jne  aint              ;No --> Call old interrupt

          pushf                  ;All registers changed in the
          push bx                ;program must be stored
          push si
          push ds

          push cs                ;Save CS on the stack
          pop  ds                ;Get DS from stack

          ;-- Does code have to be converted ? -----------------------

          cld                    ;Increment on string instructions
          mov  si,offset codetab ;Code table address
          mov  bl,al             ;Store code in BL

testcode: lodsw                  ;Load old (AH) and new code (AL)
          or   al,al             ;Reached end of table?
          je   notfound          ;Yes --> Code not found
          cmp  ah,bl             ;Is it the code for conversion?
          jne  testcode          ;No --> Continue to search table
          jmp  short nreset       ;It was a code for conversion

notfound: mov  al,bl             ;Move old code to AL again
nreset:   xor  ah,ah             ;Set function number O again
          pop  ds                ;Restore registers
          pop  si
          pop  bx
          popf

aint:     jmp cs:[olderint]      ;Go to old printer routine
```

```
newpri    endp

instend   equ this byte          ;Everything must remain resident
                                 ;up to this memory location

;== Data (can be overwritten by DOS) ================================

installm  db 13,10,"PRCVT (c) 1987,92 by Michael Tischer",13,10,13,10
          db "PRCVT installed. Call PRCVT again to de-
install.",13,10,"$"

removeit  db 13,10,"PRCVT de-installed.",13,10,"$"

;== Program (can be overwritten by DOS) ==============================

;-- Start and initialization routine --------------------------------

prcvtini  label near

          mov  ax,3517h          ;Get contents of interrupt vector 17H
          int  21h               ;Call DOS interrupt
          cmp  word ptr es:[bx+2],"WC" ;Test if PRCVT exists
          jne  install           ;Not installed --> INSTALL

          ;-- PRCVT was de-installed --------------------------------

          mov  dx,es:intoldofs   ;Offset address of interrupt 17H
          mov  ax,es:intoldseg   ;Segment address of interrupt 17H
          mov  ds,ax             ; to DS
          mov  ax,2517h          ;Redirect interrupt control
          int  21h               ;Vector 17H to old routine

          mov  bx,es
          mov  es,es:[2Ch]

          mov  ah,49h            ;Release storage of old PRCVT
          int  21h               ;Call DOS interrupt

          mov  es,bx
          mov  ah,49h
          int  21h
          mov  ah,49h
          int  21h

          push cs                ;Store CS on stack
          pop  ds                ;Restore DS

          mov  dx,offset removeit ;Message: Program removed
          mov  ah,9              ;Write function number for string
          int  21h               ;Call DOS interrupt

          mov  ax,4C00h          ;End program
          int  21h               ;Call DOS interrupt to end

          ;-- install PRCVT ------------------------------------------

install   label near

          mov  ax,3517h          ;Get contents of interrupt vector 17H
          int  21h               ;Call DOS interrupt
          mov  intoldseg,es      ;Save segment and offset addresses
          mov  intoldofs,bx      ;of interrupt vector 17H
```

```
mov  dx,offset newpri   ;Offset address new interrupt routine        mov  cl,4          ;paragraphs available
mov  ax,2517h           ;Redirect contents of interrupt             shr  dx,cl         ;to the program
int  21h                ;vector 17H to user routine                 inc  dx
                                                                     mov  ax,3100h      ;End program with end code 0 (0.0)
mov  dx,offset installm ;Message: Program installed                 int  21h           ;but remain resident
mov  ah,9               ;Function number: Display string
int  21h                ;Call DOS interrupt              ;== End =============================================================

;-- Only the PSP, the new interrupt routine and the ---------       code ends          ;End of CODE segment
;-- data pertaining to it must remain resident.  ----------         end  start
mov  dx,offset instend  ;Calculate the number of 16-byte
```

7.2   Direct Programming and the Parallel Port

If the receiver can keep up with the sender, the BIOS functions for parallel port character output work efficiently. Communicating with a printer is the safest method, but linking two computers through their parallel ports is more complicated. This often requires data transfer rates that extend beyond the capabilities of the BIOS functions. A special type of cable with different pin assignments (called a parallel transfer cable) is needed to connect two computers. The BIOS functions cannot be used with this type of cable because they assume that the normal assignments are being used for each line in the cable.

7.2.1 The I/O Ports

Up to three parallel ports can easily be installed in your computer. The I/O address space reserves three ranges for parallel interfaces:

Port	Interface
3BCH – 3BFH	Parallel interface on MDA card
378H – 37FH	Parallel interface 1
278H – 27FH	Parallel interface 2

The port addresses in the previous table are listed in the sequence in which BIOS examines them on startup, instead of in numerical order. From this table, BIOS determines which port addresses are LPT1, LPT2 ,and LPT3.

The BIOS begins by checking the block at address 3BCH—3BFH. This is part of a large address block that extends from 3B0H to 3BFH, and is reserved for a Monochrome Display Adapter (MDA) or Hercules Graphics Card. During the 1980s most PCs were delivered with this type of video card. In addition to the video logic, these cards included a parallel port.

If the BIOS finds a video card with a parallel port, the BIOS addresses that parallel port as LPT1. The next parallel port found will then be LPT2. If the video card doesn't have a parallel port, then the first parallel port located will be identified as LPT1.

The other two address blocks listed in the table are for additional parallel ports. These ports may exist on two different cards, or on a single I/O card.

Regardless of how the hardware for the parallel port is realized, the BIOS checks for the existence of parallel ports according to the previous table. Suppose that only one parallel port is installed, but it's using the address block reserved for the second. This port will still be recognized by the BIOS as LPT1.

Assigning LPT1, LPT2, and LPT3

The BIOS assigns the names LPT1, LPT2, and LPT3 to the parallel ports by entering their base addresses as variables in the BIOS variable segment. A four-word array starting at offset address 0008H of this segment retains the port addresses of the parallel ports:

Address	Contents
0040:0008H	Base address of LPT1
0040:000AH	Base address of LPT2
0040:000CH	Base address of LPT3
0040:000EH	Base address of LPT4

The variable segment can accommodate four parallel ports, even though the BIOS will only look for three parallel ports when you start your system. The BIOS functions will also let you work with a fourth parallel port if you enter its base address by hand at offset address 000EH in the BIOS variables segment. The BIOS then addresses it as interface 3.

The LPT terminology originates from DOS rather than BIOS. LPT1 represents interface number 0, LPT2 represents interface number 1, etc (DOS doesn't recognize LPT4).

If you want to change interface numbers (e.g., have DOS send output intended for LPT2 to LPT1), you must change the port addresses in these three BIOS variables. The pseudocode for this example would look similar to the following:

```
DummyWord = MEM[ 0040H: 0008H ]
MEM[ 0040H: 0008H ] = MEM[ 0040H: 000AH ]
MEM[ 0040H: 000AH ] = DummyWord
```

7.2.2 The Port Registers

Regardless of their locations in the addressable memory, all parallel ports use the same register interface, which consists of three ports. These ports occupy the first three port addresses of the card (e.g., 378H, 379H and 37AH) for the first parallel port.

The following tables show the meanings of each bit in the port registers. When you compare the assignments of each bit in the tables to the structure of a parallel cable (see Section 7.2.4), you'll see that they mainly coincide. A direct connection exists between the bits of the port registers and the lines in a parallel cable. When a bit in one of the registers is set to 1, then an electrical signal is immediately sent over the corresponding line. If the bit value is set to 0, then the current in the line returns to "low" status. The current in the line will always reflect the status of the corresponding register bit as it is manipulated by the software.

Some of the lines in the cable use negative logic. These lines have names preceded by minus signs. The condition associated with this type of line will be executed if the corresponding bit has a value of 0. For example, the ERROR line indicates a problem with printer output only if the corresponding bit is 0. As long as this bit remains set to 1, no error will be indicated.

Data lines

The eight bits of the first parallel port register use positive logic. This register stores the eight data bits that will be carried along data lines D0 to D7 and transferred to the receiver. Remember that this register was intended to be only an output register on a parallel port. It wasn't designed to receive data.

Remember that printers don't send data back to their hosts, and this type of port was never intended to be used for connecting two computers. This will cause some problems when you're developing a communications program because you must deal with communication between two computers as sender and receiver (more on this later).

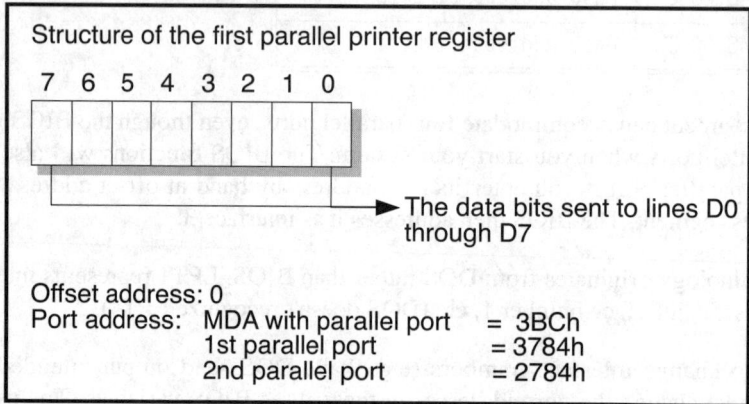

Printer status

The second register is responsible for the current printer status. It is read-only and cannot be written. This register reflects the condition of the status lines coming from the printer. The following illustration names the pins from the host's point of view.

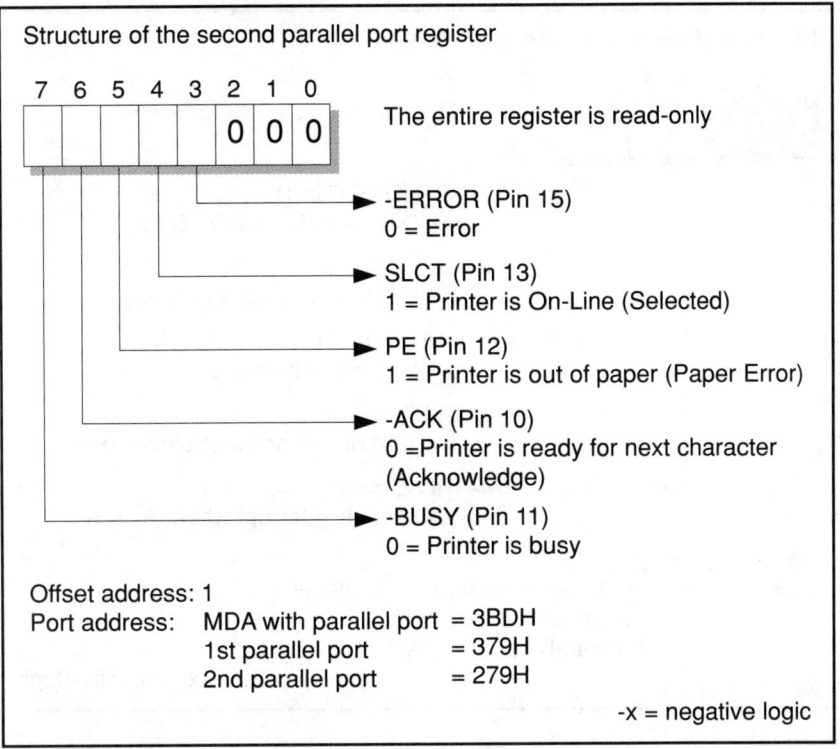

Structure of the second parallel port register

7 6 5 4 3 2 1 0

0 0 0

The entire register is read-only

-ERROR (Pin 15)
0 = Error

SLCT (Pin 13)
1 = Printer is On-Line (Selected)

PE (Pin 12)
1 = Printer is out of paper (Paper Error)

-ACK (Pin 10)
0 = Printer is ready for next character
(Acknowledge)

-BUSY (Pin 11)
0 = Printer is busy

Offset address: 1
Port address: MDA with parallel port = 3BDH
               1st parallel port   = 379H
               2nd parallel port   = 279H

-x = negative logic

Printer control

The third register controls the printer and its hardware, and plays an important role in transferring characters. Except for bit 4, all bits are connected to corresponding pins of the parallel port.

A bit hidden in this register can execute a hardware interrupt as soon as the ACK signal switches to low, which indicates that the printer has received the last character. You can usually determine which interrupt will be executed by setting some DIP switches on the port. You can choose between IRQ 7 and 5, which are associated with interrupts 0FH and 0DH. Unlike serial ports, this option is rarely used with parallel ports because these ports work on the polling principle instead of the interrupt principle. This also applies to the BIOS, which doesn't use this interrupt vector.

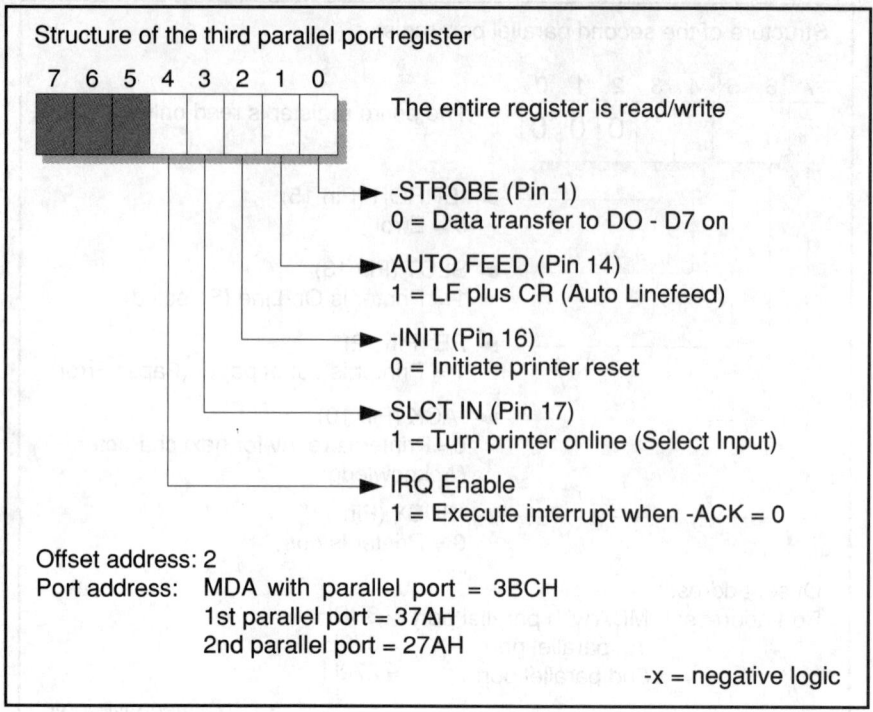

Structure of the third parallel port register

7 6 5 4 3 2 1 0

The entire register is read/write

-STROBE (Pin 1)
0 = Data transfer to DO - D7 on

AUTO FEED (Pin 14)
1 = LF plus CR (Auto Linefeed)

-INIT (Pin 16)
0 = Initiate printer reset

SLCT IN (Pin 17)
1 = Turn printer online (Select Input)

IRQ Enable
1 = Execute interrupt when -ACK = 0

Offset address: 2
Port address: MDA with parallel port = 3BCH
       1st parallel port = 37AH
       2nd parallel port = 27AH

-x = negative logic

7.2.3 Communication Between Printer and Host

The assignment of each pin in the port and the meanings of the corresponding register bits become apparent when you take a "behind the scenes" look at communication between host and printer. First, the byte sent out by the host passes to the first parallel port register and is transmitted through data lines D0 through D7. This signal immediately arrives at the printer but more information is needed before this first byte can be processed. Since there is always some sort of signal coming in on data lines D0 through D7, the printer doesn't know whether this is the first character to print or simply a stray byte from the last transmission.

The -STROBE line

The -STROBE line is important for keeping track of data. When the host sets this bit to 0 (and thus setting the current in the corresponding line to low), the printer knows that a character is coming over the data lines. The host must then disable the -STROBE signal quickly; otherwise the printer may read the character twice. The printer hardware needs only a microsecond to read the character from the data lines.

The BUSY line

Since a microsecond isn't a very long time, the printer would never be able to keep up with this kind of data transfer rate, even if it stored the characters in an internal buffer. The BUSY line pauses the communication long enough to process the character it has just received. A BUSY signal is generally sent immediately after a -STROBE signal.

The software or ROM BIOS must then wait until the printer removes the BUSY signal before it can send the next character. The BUSY line is the only pin in the parallel port that inverts the signal when it's received. In order for the host to receive 0, the printer must send a value of 1 over the BUSY line.

The -ACKnowledge line

The printer must also send an -ACK signal of 0 on the -ACKnowledge line. Because of the negative logic of this line, the host will receive this as a value of 1, which indicates that the printer received the character that was sent.

The durations of all signals needed to transmit one character add up to about 10 microseconds. Theoretically, this would produce a data transfer rate of 100,000 characters per second. However, in reality, processor overhead adds a lot of extra time. Real transfer rates are actually about 1/100th of this (1000 characters per second), even if the printer has its own buffer for storing characters as they are received.

The printer responds

Although communication between a host and a printer is mostly unilateral, the printer does offer feedback to the host. The printer uses three pins to send information back to the host: -ERROR, SLCT, and PE. All three of these pins have their corresponding bits in the first parallel port register.

SLCT represents "Select". This corresponds to the ONLINE switch found on the front of your printer. If you turn the printer offline, the printer will signal the host using the SLCT line.

PE represents "Paper Error". This allows the printer to tell the host that it's out of paper or that the paper feed is jammed. This type of error is separated from normal data transfer errors, which are transmitted through the ERROR line. This is done because paper errors can be immediately corrected by the user but data transfer errors are more serious. Data transfer errors are usually caused by cable failures or electrical disturbances.

Host control

Obviously, the host has some control signals that it uses to command the printer. These signals are -AUTO FEED, -INIT, and -SLCT IN. The bits that receive these signals are found in the third parallel port register, where the values can be read or manipulated by software.

-AUTO FEED tells the printer to add a linefeed to every CR (carriage return) character (ASCII code 13) it receives as long as this signal is set to high (1). This line is included because all printers don't react the same way when they receive a CR (carriage return) character. Many printers simply return to the start of the current line without adding the linefeed, which moves the print head down to the next line. So, the LF (linefeed) character must be added separately.

The host can use the -SLCT IN line to turn the printer OFFLINE by sending a signal of 1. Normally, this line will be set to low so that the printer stays online.

The host can use the -INIT line to reset the printer. To execute a reset, set the corresponding bit briefly to 0, and then immediately back to 1. If you don't set the value back to 1, the printer will reset itself repeatedly.

7.2.4 The Cable

The entire transfer of data between host and printer will only work if the correct pins on the two ports are connected by a proper cable. Which signals are found at which pins and the way in which the pins are connected is standardized. The Centronics standard describes both the pin assignments at each port and the lines in the cable.

The following table shows how the pins of the host and printer ports are connected. There is also a figure that shows the structure of a parallel cable along with the ground line.

Computer pin	Printer pin	Signal name	Meaning
1 → 1		-STROBE	Indicates data transfer
2 → 2		D0	Data line - bit 0
3 → 2		D1	Data line - bit 1
4 → 2		D2	Data line - bit 2 2
5 → 2		D3	Data line - bit 3
6 → 2		D4	Data line - bit 4
7 → 2		D5	Data line - bit 5
8 → 2		D6	Data line - bit 6
9 → 2		D7	Data line - bit 7
10 ← 10		-ACK	Last character received
11 ← 11		-BUSY	Printer busy
12 ← 12		PE	Printer has no paper
13 ← 13		SLCT	Printer is online
14 → 14		-AUTO FEED	Automatic CR after LF
15 ← 32		-ERROR	Data transfer error
16 → 31		-INIT	Reset printer
17 → 36		SLCT IN	Turn printer online
18-25 ← 19-30		GND	Ground

Cable connections between parallel port and printer

A do-it-yourself parallel transfer cable

If you want to "misuse" your parallel port for transferring data between two computers, a normal parallel cable won't work. One problem is that the parallel ports on both computers have identical female connectors. So, one end of the parallel cable won't plug into a second computer.

Another problem is that normal parallel communications travel in only one direction. One computer can use data lines D0 to D7 to send data, but it cannot receive data over these same lines and the other computer cannot send data over them.

Usually data transfer between two computers requires a bidirectional connection. For example, the receiver will return a checksum of the data it received, so the sender will know whether the data was received without error.

The status lines used by a printer to return status information to the computer can provide a solution. These are the -ERROR, SCLT, PE, -ACK, and BUSY lines, which are associated with

564

the second parallel port register. These lines are connected to data lines D0 to D4. This means that the receiver reads output from the sender through the status lines previously listed. Conversely, data lines D0 to D4 from the receiver are connected to the status lines of the sender, which enables two-way communication.

So, basically we're simply crossing data lines D0 - D4 with the -ERROR, SLCT, PE, -ACK, and -BUSY status lines. So, the following rule applies to both sender and receiver: Any data sent out via the first five bits of the first parallel port register will be received by bits 3 to 7 in the second register of the other communication partner. It doesn't matter which end of the cable is connected to the sender and which end is connected to the receiver.

The following illustration shows which pins to connect at each end of the cable to make a parallel transfer cable.

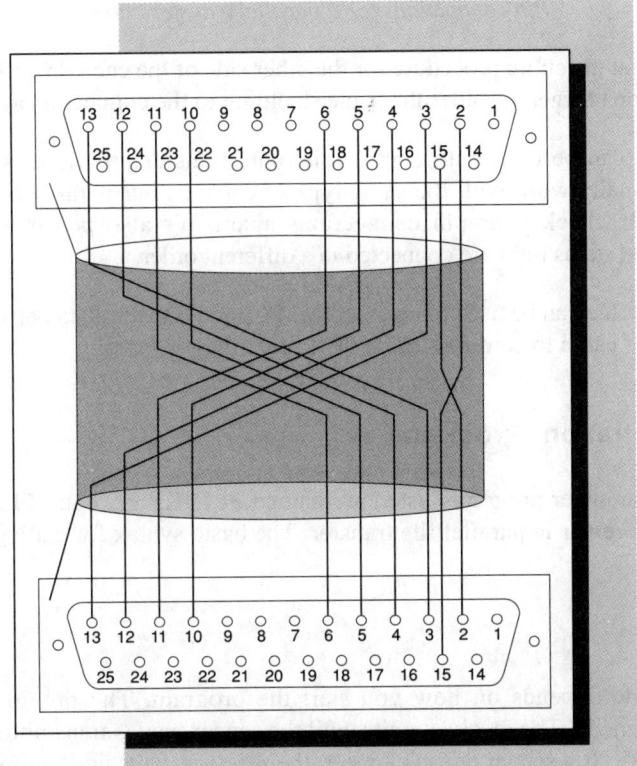

Pins to connect when you want to make a parallel transfer cable

This type of cable is very difficult to find commercially unless you own a LapLink® or similar cable. If you want to make your own, you need the following information:

You'll need two male DB-25 connectors and a shielded single-pole cable less than 10 feet in length. Parallel cables longer than this cause data transfer problems.

As the following table shows, you must connect pins 2 to 6 on one connector with pins 15 and 13 to 10 (leave pin 14 free) on the other. Solder any five lines from the cable to pins 2 to 6 on the first connector. Then connect the other end of each wire to the proper pin on the other connector. Be sure to follow the proper order. For example, D0 must be connected with -ERROR, not SLCT or BUSY.

Pin	Pin	Pin	Pin
2	15	15	2
3	13	13	3
4	12	12	4
5	10	11	6
6	11	10	5

Pin connections for a parallel transfer cable

Now you must repeat the entire procedure for the other side of the cable in order to properly cross the connections. Don't forget to solder the cable shielding to the connectors as a ground.

This type of cable can be used with commercial data transfer programs, such as LapLink®. These programs usually work with the same type of cable as our parallel transfer cable. If the cable doesn't work, check your pin connections again. It's also possible that the program assumes the data and status lines are connected in a different order.

A parallel transfer cable can be used to connect two PCs and transfer data between them. You can also use this type of cable to control a slave PC from a master PC.

7.2.5 Demonstration Programs

The following file transfer programs listed are named PLINKP.PAS and PLINKC.C. Both can act as a sender or receiver in parallel file transfer. The basic syntax for calling either program is as follows:

```
PLINKP
PLINKC
```

The operating mode depends on how you start the program. The previous syntax sets the program in receive mode. The receiver waits until the sender begins transmitting or until the user presses <Esc> to exit. If a sender doesn't appear, the receiver waits until a time out error occurs, then exits.

The following examples start the program in sender mode, and try to send FILENAME.EXE to the receiving computer:

```
PLINKP FILENAME.EXE
PLINKC FILENAME.EXE
```

The sender waits until it senses a receiver. If a receiver exists, file transfer begins. If it doesn't, the sender waits until it recognizes a receiver or until the user presses <Esc> to exit. If a receiver still doesn't appear, the sender waits until a time out error occurs, then exits. You can also use wildcards to specify entire groups of files for transfer. The following examples start the program in sender mode, and try to send all EXE files to the receiving computer:

```
PLINKP *.EXE
PLINKC *.EXE
```

The two optional switches /P and /T can also be entered when you start the program. The /P switch specifies the parallel port through which you want information sent other than the default (LPT1). A number between 1 and 4 must follow the /P. The following examples start the program in receive mode and configure LPT3 as the parallel port for receiving data:

```
PLINKP /P3
PLINKC /P3
```

The /T switch specifies the number of time out intervals. A single time out is 10 seconds; you can enter any group of 10-second intervals. Enter a number after the /T switch. The program multiplies this by 10. The following examples start the program in sender mode, request a 30-second time out, and attempt to send all TXT files:

```
PLINKP /T3 *.TXT
PLINKC /T3 *.TXT
```

You can get help by entering the PLINKC or PLINKP name and the /? parameter. Enter the following to see the command syntax:

```
PLINKP /?
PLINKC /?
```

The program lists the switches for interface and time out intervals.

Since these programs are coded, we omitted some features, such as checking for existing files. If you try to transfer a file to a receiver containing a file of the same name, the programs overwrite the existing filename, then time out. Check your receiver before sending files, or add your own code to check for files.

Transferring data over the parallel transfer cable

With a parallel transfer cable like the one we described, you can simultaneously send five bits through data lines D0 to D4. You can transmit data in both directions simultaneously because the connections are crossed. However, some kind of communications protocol is needed so that data can be transferred systematically. We need something similar to the -STROBE line to keep track of the data transfer pace. One of our five data lines must be used for this purpose.

The BUSY bit seems to be best suited for this job. The two outer bits (-ERROR and BUSY) are actually the only possibilities because the four data bits must be next to one another. Of these two, BUSY will be a better -STROBE line because it has no real application of its own for data transfer. Also, this bit is automatically inverted by the hardware. If you used this bit for data, it would have to be inverted after the transfer, which would be time-consuming.

The inversion doesn't affect a -STROBE bit. Actually, it's important for the communications protocol. A 0 at one end of the cable must come out as a 1 at the other end. We'll discuss this in more detail later.

Communications protocol refers to the two demo programs described in this section. Although there can be numerous communications protocols, in this instance we're being quite specific. The protocol used here works on two levels, the byte level and the data block level. Each of these levels is handled separately. The data block level is on top of the byte level. The byte level is hardware–oriented, but the block level works with the software.

Data transfer at byte level

First let's discuss the byte level from the sender's point of view. The first thing we must consider is that an entire byte cannot be sent at once. A byte consists of eight bits and we can only send four bits in one direction at one time. So, each byte is divided into two halves called *nibbles*, which are sent one after the other.

First, the low nibble of the byte is written to bits 0 to 3 of the first parallel port register. From here it is sent out through data lines D0 to D3. The bit for data line D4 is set to 0 so that the receiver will receive a value of 1 at its BUSY pin. This will tell the receiver that the low nibble of the next byte is ready to be read. This means that the receiver simply waits and reads the status line until the BUSY bit contains a value of 1.

The BUSY bit is then no longer useful, so the receiver proceeds by reading the nibble from the corresponding bits of the second port register. The contents of these four bits are stored in a variable and sent back to the sender through the data lines. The bit for data line D4 is set to 0, so that a value of 1 is received back on the other end. This indicates that the returned nibble can be read and saved.

When both nibbles have been returned in this way, the sender can determine whether the byte was properly transferred. The communication is therefore verified at the byte level. However, this isn't the usual procedure. Since it takes too much time to check each byte individually, this type of verification is normally performed only at the block level. In our case, this argument doesn't apply, since the BUSY line must be used to send a -STROBE signal back to the sender with each nibble anyway. It doesn't take any more time to send the entire nibble back.

The transmission of the second nibble is basically the same, except that the value of the status bit is changed to 1. So, the receiver will receive a value of 0 at the BUSY pin. The receiver has been waiting for this as the signal to read the high nibble. The nibble is then returned to the sender and the sender's BUSY bit is reset to 0. The two nibbles can then be combined to form the complete byte, and the transfer is complete from the receiver's point of view.

The sender combines the two nibbles sent back by the receiver and checks the complete byte for data transfer errors. The program's send routine alerts its caller of any errors so that the appropriate action can be taken and the data block can be re-sent if necessary. Just about any data transfer error can be detected in this way, except for some unusual type of cable interference.

As we saw with normal communication to a printer, successful communication between two computers requires the proper switching of the -STROBE signal over the BUSY line. Remember that because of the way the lines in the cable are crossed, we're dealing with two separate BUSY lines. The same applies to both sender and receiver: For output, the BUSY bit is data line D4. The signal is received, however, at the BUSY status line on the other side.

Sender and receiver both use the data lines D0 - D4 for sending information, and each has its own separate -STROBE line. The following illustration should demonstrate this.

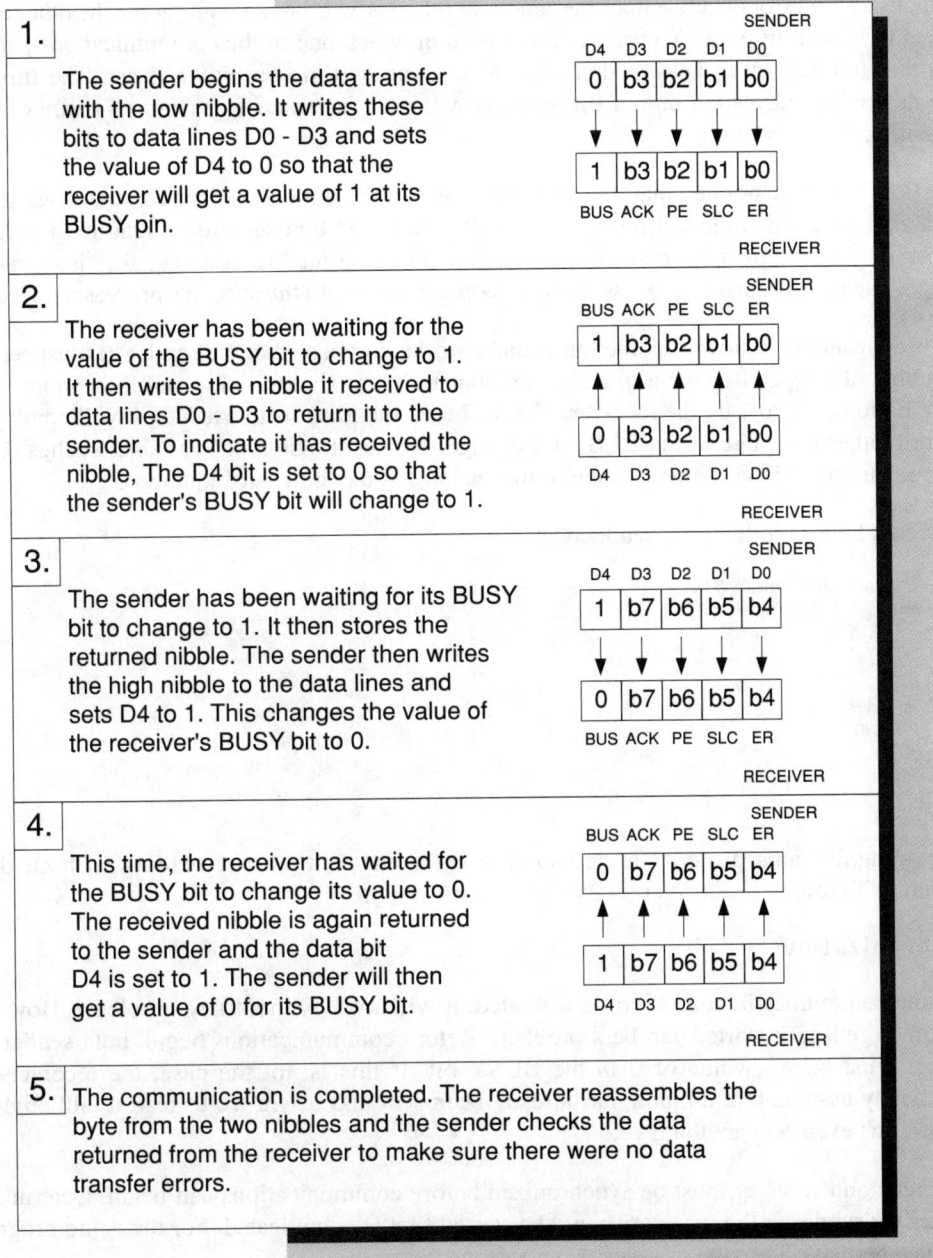

1. The sender begins the data transfer with the low nibble. It writes these bits to data lines D0 - D3 and sets the value of D4 to 0 so that the receiver will get a value of 1 at its BUSY pin.

2. The receiver has been waiting for the value of the BUSY bit to change to 1. It then writes the nibble it received to data lines D0 - D3 to return it to the sender. To indicate it has received the nibble, The D4 bit is set to 0 so that the sender's BUSY bit will change to 1.

3. The sender has been waiting for its BUSY bit to change to 1. It then stores the returned nibble. The sender then writes the high nibble to the data lines and sets D4 to 1. This changes the value of the receiver's BUSY bit to 0.

4. This time, the receiver has waited for the BUSY bit to change its value to 0. The received nibble is again returned to the sender and the data bit D4 is set to 1. The sender will then get a value of 0 for its BUSY bit.

5. The communication is completed. The receiver reassembles the byte from the two nibbles and the sender checks the data returned from the receiver to make sure there were no data transfer errors.

The communications protocol at the hardware oriented byte level

Time out problems

Communications protocols usually function without error as long as the electrical current isn't interrupted. If an error occurs, either the sender or receiver will be left waiting for the other end to respond to its last message. To prevent a situation in which one of the communications partners is waiting forever for an answer that may never come, a time out value is set. The time out value determines how long one of the systems will wait for an answer from its partner before terminating the connection.

In Section 7.1 we mentioned that the BIOS also uses a time out counter for communicating with the parallel port. The time out interval is usually measured by executing a read loop a certain number of times. For a program that must run on different PC systems, this isn't easy to manage. The time needed to process the read loop can vary with the system's processor speed.

Here is an example of how the time out counter works. Suppose that the sender has just sent the low nibble of a byte. It sets the time out counter to its maximum value and then waits for its BUSY bit to be set to 1 by the receiver. The read loop then begins to execute. It will continue to run until either the value of the BUSY bit changes to 1 or the time out variable reaches 0. The time out variable will continue to count down as long as its value isn't equal to 0.

This would look as follows in pseudocode:

```
TimeOutCount = MAXVALUE
WHILE ( BUSY-Bit = 0 ) AND ( TimeOutCount > 0 ) DO
  BEGIN
  END

IF TimeOutCount = 0 THEN
  error
ELSE
  o.k.
END
```

The communications protocol is activated along with the time out reading in both demo programs with routines called SendAByte and ReceiveAByte.

Synchronization

Once the communications protocol is activated, it will work without any problems. However, sometimes getting it started can be a problem. Before communications begin, both sender and receiver must have a value of 0 in the BUSY bit. If this is not the case, the receiver will immediately assume that a nibble has already been sent and it will try to read it, although the sender hasn't even sent anything yet.

The sender and receiver must be synchronized before communications can begin. Determining whether the sender or the receiver should be started first is complicated. For the demo programs presented here, we'll use the receiver as our starting point.

For initialization, the receiver waits for the sender to set its BUSY bit to 0. It then sets the sender's BUSY bit to 0. The synchronization is complete when the BUSY bits on both sides are set to 0. In the demo programs, this is done within the PortInit routine.

A time out limit is also used in the initialization procedure. It works according to the principle previously described. In addition, the programs enable the user to quit at any time by pressing the <Esc> key. Otherwise, you may have to wait several minutes for the time-out interval to be reached.

Stopping the program

Both programs include a keyboard interrupt handler that is activated by pressing the <Esc> key. Just as with the timer interrupt handler, the program also uses a variable to communicate with the keyboard interrupt handler. In this case, it's a variable of type BOOL, which is set to TRUE when the <Esc> key is pressed.

We can avoid having to read this variable separately in the read loop by coupling it with the time out variable. This is done by setting both the escape variable to TRUE and the time out variable to 0 when the <Esc> key is pressed.

The program will then simply respond as though the time out interval has been reached. A quick check of the escape variable will then allow you to determine the cause of the interrupt.

Block level protocol

The block level is above the byte level. As the name suggests, the block level is used for transferring entire data blocks from sender to receiver. This is strictly a software protocol. It's independent of the hardware because it relies on the send and receive routines from the byte level. In our demo programs, these are the SendABlock and ReceiveABlock routines.

A block always contains the following information: a token that precedes the block and describes its contents, the length of the block, and the block itself. The token is used so that the receiver can immediately recognize what is being sent without having to read the data block.

According to this convention, the SendABlock routine expects to be passed the token, the number of bytes in the block, and a pointer to the data block itself. Both the token and the number of bytes are handled as a sort of header and kept separate from the actual data block. The receiver must first correctly receive the header before the first byte of the data block will be sent. Imagine what would happen if the sender wanted to send a 120 byte data block but the receiver was expecting a block of 200 bytes. The receiver would count the next 80 bytes as part of the first data block, and the communication would be hopelessly tangled.

Remember that, at the byte level, the receiver is sending every byte it receives back to the sender. So, the block level protocol will immediately know whether the header was properly transferred. Unfortunately, this doesn't let the receiver know whether it received the header correctly. The sender therefore notifies the receiver by sending a standard character. So, the receiver doesn't have to assume that there weren't errors in the header.

As feedback, the sender will send an ACK (Acknowledge) character if the transfer was successful, or a NAK (Non-Acknowledge) character if there was an error. The ACK character isn't related to the port pin of the same name; it simply fulfills the same function. The ACK and NAK characters are represented by the codes 00H and FFH in the demo programs, but you can use any codes. These characters also play a part in the communications protocol, since they are also checked at the byte level for successful transfer.

When the receiver has received the header and the subsequent ACK character without errors, the sender can begin to transfer the actual data block. If there was a problem, the sender repeats the transfer of the header. The receiver will know that the header is being sent again because it would have received a NAK character from the previous attempt. Once the receiver has the header and the ACK character, it can concentrate on receiving the data block. As long as you use very different bit patterns for these two characters, it's unlikely that an ACK character could become a NAK character because of a data transfer error.

If it continues to encounter errors, the sender won't keep trying to send the header forever. The constant MAXTRY is set to tell the sender how many errors to count before aborting the attempt to send the current data block. The ACK and NAK characters are also used to confirm receipt of the data block. The feedback character is sent to the receiver only after the entire data block has been sent.

With this method, every type of communication error can be detected. This protocol eliminates the need for checksums, which is a common way of checking for data transfer errors in other communications software.

Reading <Esc> status

Once the data block is transferred, a final byte is sent to complete the process. But this byte is sent from the receiver to the sender. This also gives the receiver the ability to communicate an ESCAPE signal to the sender. However, this isn't really necessary because the receiver could simply exit the communications software with ESCAPE and then let the sender wait for a time out error.

Since this isn't the best solution, the protocol has the sender wait for an "escape byte" from the receiver after the data block has been completely transferred. If the sender receives a value of TRUE, it exits the program with an appropriate message. Otherwise, the sender continues with normal program execution.

Communicating this type of message must be allowed in both directions, since the sender could also decide to terminate the communication at any time. The procedure for this is different than with the receiver. When it starts, the SendABlock routine determines whether the <Esc> key has been pressed. If it has, it sends a special escape token instead of the actual data block header. This special escape token is known to the receiver. When the receiver recognizes this token, it considers it as a signal to exit the program.

By building this escape mechanism into the block protocol, we can avoid having to make a permanent escape query at a higher level. Both of the demo programs also deal with a file level above the block level. The file level uses the block level protocol to transfer entire files piece by piece. We won't go into detail here about the file level, since the program listings at the end of this section are well documented.

Remember that the routines at the byte and block level can be used to transfer any data between sender and receiver. Also, both the sender and receiver are able to abort the communication at any point. These routines could serve as the basis for your own data transfer programs, which can compete with commercial packages such as LapLink®. They may not be quite as fast, however, because this would require all of the byte level routines to be written completely in assembly language.

The higher levels

If an error, such as a time out error at the byte level or the receipt of an escape token at the block level, occurs, this error should be communicated to the highest level as quickly as possible. The various levels (byte, block, and file) in these demo programs use procedures and functions to communicate with each other. Each time a routine ends with an error, it returns to the routine that called it, working its way back to the top level by level.

Modern C compilers support the setjmp() and longjmp() functions in these instances. These functions allow jumps across several program levels. The setjmp() function sets the location in the program code that will be the destination of the jump. If an error occurs, you can change program control to this location by using the longjmp() function. For more information about these functions, refer to your C compiler documentation.

Unfortunately, Turbo Pascal doesn't have similar functions. But you can implement these commands yourself. (Refer to *Turbo Pascal System Programming*, which is also available from Abacus. Both of the routines used in PLINKP.PAS are from this book.)

Pascal listing: PLINKP.PAS

```
{***************************************************************}
{                    P L I N K P . P A S                        }
{---------------------------------------------------------------}
{   Task       : Transfers files over the parallel interface.   }
{---------------------------------------------------------------}
{   Author     : Michael Tischer                                }
{   Developed on : 09/27/91                                     }
{   Last update  : 01/30/92                                     }
{***************************************************************}

{$M 65520, 0, 655360 }

uses dos, crt;                          { Add DOS and CRT units }

{== Constants ================================================}

const ONESEC      = 18;                      { One second }
      TENSEC      = 182;                      { Ten seconds }
      TO_DEFAULT  = TENSEC;          { Time out default value }

      MAXBLOCK    = 4096;            { 4K maximum block size }

{-- Constants for transfer protocol ---------------------------}

      ACK      = $00;                        { Acknowledge }
      NAK      = $FF;                    { Non-Acknowledge }
      MAX_TRY  = 5;          { Maximum number of tries }

{-- Tokens for communication between sender and receiver -------}

      TOK_DATSTART = 0;            { Start of file data }
      TOK_DATNEXT  = 1;          { Next file data block }
      TOK_DATEND   = 2;        { End file data transfer }
      TOK_ENDIT    = 3;                    { End program }
      TOK_ESCAPE   = 4;    { <Esc> pressed on remote computer }

{-- Codes for LongJump call -----------------------------------}

      LJ_OKSENDER = 1;        { All data sent successfully }
      LJ_OKRECD   = 2;    { All data received successfully }
      LJ_TIMEOUT  = 3;            { Time out: No response }
      LJ_ESCAPE   = 4;    { <Esc> pressed on local computer }
      LJ_REMESCAPE = 5;  { <Esc> pressed on remote computer }
      LJ_DATA     = 6;          { Communication error }
      LJ_NOLINK   = 7;                        { No link }
      LJ_NOPAR    = 8;                    { No interface }
      LJ_PARA     = 9;        { Invalid call parameters }

{== Type definitions =========================================}

type BHEADER = record                { Block transfer header }
                 case boolean of
                   true  : ( Token : byte;
                             Len   : word );
                   false : ( HArr  : array[ 0..2 ] of byte );
               end;

     JMPBUF  = record                { Information needed for }
                 BP,                 { the return is stored here }
                 SP,
                 CS,    { Do not change the order of these elements! }
                 IP  : word;
               end;

     DBlock = array[ 1..MAXBLOCK ] of byte;        { Data block }

{== Global variables =========================================}

var InpPort     : word;                  { Input port address }
    OutPort     : word;
    Escape      : boolean;              { <Esc> not pressed }
    Timeout     : word;          { Selected time out value }
    TO_Count    : word;              { Counter for time out }
    ReturnToEnd : JMPBUF;        { Return address for end }
    BlockBuf    : DBLOCK;        { Buffer for passing a block }
    FiVar       : file;    { File variable for file being processed }

{== Declaration of assembler functions =======================}

{$L plinkpa.obj }                    { Link assembler module }
```

```
function getb : byte; external;

procedure putb( TpVar : byte ); external;

procedure intr_install(escape_flag, timeout_count : pointer); external;

procedure intr_remove; external;

procedure EscapeDirect( Disconnect : boolean ); external;


{*****************************************************************}
{ SetJmp : Determines when a call to LongJmp should follow.      }
{---------------------------------------------------------------}
{ Input    : JB : A data structure of type JumpBuf, needed for passing }
{                 information after the return                   }
{ Output   : NOJMP on return from this function; any other value on }
{                  return from a call to the LongJmp procedure   }
{*****************************************************************}

{$F+}                          { Setjmp and Longjmp must be coded as FAR }

function SetJmp( var JB : JMPBUF ) : integer;

type WordP = ^word;                          { Pointer to a word }

begin
  JB.BP := WordP( ptr( SSeg, Sptr+2 ) )^;
  JB.IP := WordP( ptr( SSeg, Sptr+4 ) )^;
  JB.CS := WordP( ptr( SSeg, Sptr+6 ) )^;

  { SP must point to the position for the new BP register contents }
  { after the LongJmp, as well as the stack's return address       }

  JB.SP := Sptr + 12 - 6 - 6;

  SetJmp := -1;                    { Shows that this is no LongJmp call }
end;


{*****************************************************************}
{ LongJmp : A procedure dependent GOTO that continues program   }
{           execution in the program line called by SetJmp.     }
{---------------------------------------------------------------}
{ Input    : JB      : Jump buffer which redirects program execution }
{                      through SetJmp                           }
{            RetCode : Function result which indicates SetJmp target }
{*****************************************************************}

procedure LongJmp( JB : JMPBUF; RetCode : integer );

type WordP = ^word;                          { Pointer to a word }

begin
  WordP( ptr( SSeg, JB.SP   ) )^ := JB.BP;
  WordP( ptr( SSeg, JB.SP+2 ) )^ := JB.IP;
  WordP( ptr( SSeg, JB.Sp+4 ) )^ := JB.CS;

  {-- Load return code into the AX register and emulate --------------}
  {-- SetJmp's function result                          --------------}

  inline( $8b / $46 / $06 );                   { mov ax,[bp+6] }

  inline( $8b / $ae / $fa / $ff );             { mov bp,[bp-6] }

  { mov   sp,bp    ;This command invokes the compiler }
  { pop   bp       ;automatically and restores the   }
  { ret   6        ;stack                            }
end;
```

```
{$F-}

{*****************************************************************}
{ GetPortAdr: Initializes a parallel interface's port addresses in }
{             the global variables INPPORT and OUTPORT.         }
{ Input      : LPTNUM = Parallel interface number (1-4)         }
{ Output     : TRUE if interface is valid                       }
{ Global vars. : InpPort/W, OutPort/W                           }
{ Info       : The base addresses of up to 4 parallel interfaces }
{              lie in the four memory words starting at 0040:0008. }
{*****************************************************************}

function GetPortAdr( LptNum : integer ) : boolean;

begin
  {-- Read port addresses from BIOS variable segment ----------------}
  OutPort := MemW[ $0040: 6 + LptNum * 2 ];
  if ( OutPort <> 0 ) then                { Interface available? }
    begin                                            { Yes }
      InpPort := OutPort + 1;             { Input register address }
      GetPortAdr := TRUE;                        { End error-free }
    end
  else
    GetPortAdr := FALSE;              { Error: Interface not available }
end;


{*****************************************************************}
{ Port_Init  : Initializes the registers needed for transfer.   }
{ Input      : SENDER = TRUE if sender, FALSE if receiver       }
{ Output     : TRUE if register initializes successfully        }
{ Global vars. : InpPort/R, OutPort/R                           }
{ Info       : The asymmetry (send 00010000, wait for 00000000) }
{              occurs because of signal inversion. Normally the }
{              input and output registers contain the desired   }
{              values, but initialization is needed after an    }
{              aborted transfer, or when restarting.            }
{*****************************************************************}

function Port_Init( Sender : boolean ) : boolean;

begin
  EscapeDirect( TRUE );             { Release thru Escape time out }
  if ( Sender ) then                        { Device = Sender? }
    begin
      TO_Count := Timeout * 5;          { Start time out counter }
      PutB( $10 );                          { Send: 00010000b }
      while ( ( GetB <> $00 ) and ( TO_Count > 0 ) ) do  { Wait for 0 }
        ;
    end
  else                                       { Device = Receiver }
    begin
      TO_Count := Timeout * 5;          { Start time out counter }
      while ( ( GetB <> $00 ) and ( TO_Count > 0 ) ) do  { Wait for 0 }
        ;
      PutB( $10 );                          { Send: 00010000b }
    end;
  EscapeDirect( FALSE );          { No time out released on Escape }
  Port_Init := ( TO_Count > 0 );          { End initialization }
end;


{*****************************************************************}
{ SendAByte : Sends a byte to the remote computer in two parts, }
{             then checks the result.                          }
{ Input     : B2Send = Byte to be sent                         }
```

```
{ Output       : Transfer successful? (0 = error, -1 = 0.K.)     }
{ Global vars. : Timeout/R, InpPort/R, OutPort/R (in macros)     }
{****************************************************************}


function SendAByte( B2Send : byte ) : boolean;


var RcvdB : byte;                               { Received byte }


begin
  {-- Send lower nibble -----------------------------------------}

  TO_Count := Timeout;              { Initialize time out counter }
  PutB( B2Send and $0F );                  { Sending, clear BUSY }
  while ( ( ( GetB and 128 ) = 0 ) and ( TO_Count > 0 ) ) do
    ;
  if ( TO_Count = 0 ) then                       { Time out error? }
    longjmp( ReturnToEnd, LJ_TIMEOUT );          { Cancel transfer }

  RcvdB := ( GetB shr 3 ) and $0F;            { Bits 3-6 in 0-3 }


  {-- Send upper nibble -----------------------------------------}

  TO_Count := Timeout;              { Initialize time out counter }
  PutB( ( B2Send shr 4 ) or $10 );           { Sending, set BUSY }
  while ( ( ( GetB and 128 ) <> 0 ) and ( TO_Count > 0 ) ) do
    ;
  if ( TO_Count = 0 ) then                       { Time out error? }
    longjmp( ReturnToEnd, LJ_TIMEOUT );          { Cancel transfer }

  RcvdB := RcvdB or ( ( GetB shl 1 ) and $F0 );  { Bits 3-6 in 4-7 }
  SendAByte := ( B2Send = RcvdB );           { Byte sent correctly? }
end;


{****************************************************************}
{ ReceiveAByte : Receives a two part byte from remote computer, and }
{                sends returned parts for testing.                }
{ Input        : None                                             }
{ Output       : Received byte                                    }
{ Global vars. : Timeout/R, InpPort/R, Outport/R (in macros)      }
{****************************************************************}


function ReceiveAByte : byte;


var LoNib,
    HiNib : byte;                           { Received nibbles }


begin
  {-- Receive and re-send lowest nibble --------------------------}

  TO_Count := Timeout;              { Initialize time out counter }
  while ( ( ( GetB and 128 ) = 0 ) and ( TO_Count > 0 ) ) do
    ;
  if ( TO_Count = 0 ) then                       { Time out error? }
    longjmp( ReturnToEnd, LJ_TIMEOUT );          { Cancel transfer }

  LoNib := ( GetB shr 3 ) and $0F;            { Bits 3-6 in 0-3 }
  PutB( LoNib );                                       { Re-send }

  {-- Receive and re-send highest nibble ------------------------}

  TO_Count := Timeout;              { Initialize time out counter }
  while ( ( ( GetB and 128 ) <> 0 ) and ( TO_Count > 0 ) ) do
    ;
```

```
  if ( TO_Count = 0 ) then                       { Time out error? }
    longjmp( ReturnToEnd, LJ_TIMEOUT );          { Cancel transfer }

  HiNib := ( GetB shl 1 ) and $F0;            { Bits 3-6 in 4-7 }
  PutB( ( HiNib shr 4 ) or $10 );         { Re-sending, set BUSY }

  ReceiveAByte := ( LoNib or HiNib );         { Received byte }
end;


{****************************************************************}
{ SendABlock: Sends a data block                                 }
{ Input   :  TOKEN  = Token for receiver                         }
{            TRANUM = Number of bytes to be transferred          }
{            DPTR   = Pointer to buffer containing data          }
{ Output  :  None, jumps immediately to an error handler if      }
{            an error occurs.                                     }
{****************************************************************}


procedure SendABlock( Token  : byte;
                      TraNum : word;
                      Dptr   : pointer );


var header    : BHEADER;   { Header for placing tokens and numbers }
    RcvrEscape : byte;             { <Esc> pressed on remote? }
    ok        : boolean;                         { Error flag }
    i         : word;                          { Loop counter }
    try       : word;           { Remaining number of tries }
    DbPtr     : ^DBlock;          { Pointer to data block }


begin
  if ( Escape ) then          { <Esc> pressed on local computer? }
    begin
      Token := TOK_ESCAPE;            { Yes --> Send Escape token }
      TraNum := 0;
    end;

  {-- Send header first -----------------------------------------}

  header.Token := Token;                        { Create header }
  header.Len := TraNum;

  try := MAX_TRY;
  repeat                          { Make MAX_TRY attempts at access }
    ok := TRUE;                   { Send on error-free transfer }
    for i := 0 to 2 do
      ok := ok and SendAByte( Header.HArr[ i ] );   { Send a byte }
    if ( ok ) then
      ok := ok and SendAByte( ACK )            { Send confirmation }
    else
      ok := ok and SendAByte( NAK );           { Send confirmation }
    if ( not ok ) then                             { Error? }
      dec( try );                         { Yes --> Try it again }
  until ( ( ok ) or ( try = 0 ) );

  if ( try = 0 ) then        { Could the header be sent successfully? }
    longjmp( ReturnToEnd, LJ_DATA );       { No --> Cancel transfer }

  if ( Token = TOK_ESCAPE ) then       { Was an Escape message sent? }
    longjmp( ReturnToEnd, LJ_ESCAPE );   { Yes --> Cancel transfer }

  {-- Send the data block itself --------------------------------}

  if ( TraNum > 0 ) then                          { Length > 0? }
```

```
  begin
    DbPtr := DPTR;
    try := MAX_TRY;
    repeat
      ok := TRUE;                           { Send on error-free transfer }
      for i := 1 to TraNum do
        ok := ok and SendAByte( DbPtr^[ i ] );
      if ( ok ) then
        ok := ok and SendAByte( ACK )       { Send confirmation }
      else
        ok := ok and SendAByte( NAK );       { Send confirmation }
      if ( not ok ) then                              { Error? }
        dec( try );                          { Yes --> Try again }
    until ( ( ok ) or ( try = 0 ) );
    if ( try = 0 ) then      { Could data block be sent successfully? }
      longjmp( ReturnToEnd, LJ_DATA );       { No --> Cancel transfer }
  end;


{-- Read ESCAPE byte from receiver ---------------------------------}

  try := MAX_TRY;
  repeat
    RcvrEscape := ReceiveAByte;             { Read remote Escape }
    dec( try );
  until ( ( RcvrEscape = byte( true ) ) or
          ( RcvrEscape = byte( false ) ) );

  if ( try = 0 ) then           { Was the Escape status received? }
    longjmp( ReturnToEnd, LJ_DATA );        { No --> Cancel transfer }

  if ( RcvrEscape = byte( true ) ) then  { <Esc> from remote computer? }
    longjmp( ReturnToEnd, LJ_REMESCAPE );   { Yes --> Cancel transfer }
end;


{*******************************************************************}
{ ReceiveABlock: Receives a data block.                           }
{ Input    : TOKEN  = Pointer to variable containing tokens        }
{            LEN    = Pointer to variable containing length        }
{            DPTR   = Pointer to buffer containing data            }
{ Output   : None, jumps immediately to an error handler if        }
{            an error occurs.                                      }
{ Info     : Buffer must be allocated using MAXBLOCK, since block   }
{            length cannot usually be anticipated.                 }
{*******************************************************************}

procedure ReceiveABlock( var Token : byte;
                         var Len   : word;
                             Dptr  : pointer );

var header       : BHEADER;  { Header for storing tokens and numbers }
    ok           : boolean;              { Error flag }
    i            : word;                 { Loop counter }
    try          : word;      { Remaining number of tries }
    EscapeStatus : boolean;
    ByteBuffer   : byte;
    DbPtr        : ^DBlock;             { Pointer to data block }

begin
  {-- Receive header first -------------------------------------}

  try := MAX_TRY;
  repeat
    for i:= 0 to 2 do
      Header.HArr[ i ] := ReceiveAByte;
```

```
    ByteBuffer := ReceiveAByte;
    if ( ByteBuffer <> ACK ) then  { All bytes received successfully? }
      dec( try );                     { Yes --> No need to try again }
  until ( ( try = 0 ) or ( ByteBuffer = ACK ) );

  if ( try = 0 ) then         { Header received successfully? }
    longjmp( ReturnToEnd, LJ_DATA );      { No --> Cancel transfer }

  Token := Header.Token;
  Len := Header.Len;
  if ( Token = TOK_ESCAPE ) then           { Sender Escape? }
    longjmp( ReturnToEnd, LJ_REMESCAPE );  { Yes --> Cancel transfer }

{-- Header was O.K., now receive the data block itself -------------}

  if ( Len > 0 ) then                       { No data block? }
    begin                                            { No }
      DbPtr := Dptr;
      try := MAX_TRY;

      repeat              { Receive data block byte for byte }
        for i := 1 to len do
          DbPtr^[ i ] := ReceiveAByte;

        ByteBuffer := ReceiveAByte;
        if ( ByteBuffer <> ACK ) then { Bytes received successfully? }
          dec( try );                   { Yes --> No need to try again }
      until ( ( try = 0 ) or ( ByteBuffer = ACK ) );

      if ( try = 0 ) then         { Block received successfully? }
        longjmp( ReturnToEnd, LJ_DATA );   { No --> Cancel transfer }
    end;

{-- Send current Escape status to the remote computer ---------------}

  EscapeStatus := Escape;                      { Note status }

  try := MAX_TRY;
  repeat
    dec( try );
  until ( SendAByte( byte( EscapeStatus ) ) or ( try = 0 ) );

  if ( try = 0 ) then            { Could Escape status be sent? }
    longjmp( ReturnToEnd, LJ_DATA );        { No --> Cancel transfer }

  if ( EscapeStatus ) then         { <Esc> pressed on this computer? }
    longjmp( ReturnToEnd, LJ_ESCAPE );      { Yes --> Cancel transfer }
end;

{*******************************************************************}
{ SendAFile : Sends a file.                                       }
{ Input    : NAME = Filename                                       }
{ Output   : None                                                 }
{*******************************************************************}

procedure SendAFile( Name : string );

var Status  : word;                            { Send status }
    WdsRead : word;                   { Number of bytes read }
    BytSent : longint;                { Number of bytes sent }
begin
  write( copy( Name + '            ', 1, 13 ) );
```

```
assign( FiVar, Name );
reset( FiVar, 1 );
SendABlock( TOK_DATSTART, length( Name ) + 1, @Name ); { Send names }

{-- Transfer file contents -----------------------------------------}

BytSent := 0;
repeat
  blockread( FiVar, BlockBuf, MAXBLOCK, WdsRead );    { Read block }
  if ( WdsRead > 0 ) then              { End of block not reached? }
    begin {                                                  { No }
      SendABlock( TOK_DATNEXT, WdsRead, @BlockBuf );   { Send block }
      inc( BytSent, WdsRead );
      write( #13, copy( Name + '              ', 1, 13 ),
             '(', BytSent, ')' );
    end;
until ( WdsRead = 0 );
writeln;

SendABlock( TOK_DATEND, 0, NIL );                   { End transfer }

close( FiVar );                                       { Close file }
end;

{*******************************************************************}
{ ReceiveAFile: Receives a file.                                   }
{ Input        : None                                              }
{ Output       : The last token received                          }
{*******************************************************************}

function ReceiveAFile : word;

var Status     : word;                             { Send status }
    LastBlkSize : word;                      { Size of last block }
    BytSent    : longint;
    Token      : byte;                        { Token received }
    Len        : word;                   { Block length received }
    i          : word;                         { Loop counter }
    Name       : string[ 13 ];                   { Filename }

begin
  ReceiveABlock( Token, Len, @BlockBuf );
  if ( Token = TOK_DATSTART ) then
    begin
      for i := 0 to BlockBuf[ 1 ] do
        Name[ i ] := chr( BlockBuf[ i + 1 ] );
      assign( FiVar, Name );
      rewrite( FiVar, 1 );
      write( copy( Name + '              ', 1, 13 ) );

      {-- Receive file contents -------------------------------------}

      BytSent := 0;
      repeat
        ReceiveABlock( Token, Len, @BlockBuf );   { Receive block }
        if ( Token = TOK_DATNEXT ) then        { Next data block? }
          begin                                           { Yes }
            blockwrite( FiVar, BlockBuf, Len );     { Write block }
            inc( BytSent, Len );
            write( #13, copy( Name + '              ', 1, 13 ),
                   '(', BytSent, ')' );
          end;
      until ( TOKEN <> TOK_DATNEXT );
      close( FiVar );                             { Close file }
```

```
      writeln;
    end;
  ReceiveAFile := Token;                       { Return error status }
end;

{*******************************************************************}
{             M A I N   P R O G R A M                              }
{*******************************************************************}

const ScnMesg : array[ 0..8 ] of string =
         ( 'DONE: All files sent successfully.',
           'DONE: All files received successfully.',
           'ERROR: Time out, remote system not responding.',
           'DONE: <Esc> key pressed.',
           'DONE: <Esc> key pressed on remote computer.',
           'ERROR: Check hardware (cable, interface, jacks).',
           'ERROR: No contact with remote computer.',
           'ERROR: Interface you requested not found.',
           'ERROR: Invalid or unknown parameters.' );

var SRec     : SearchRec;       { Structure for directory search }
    Sender   : boolean;      { Transfer mode (Send, Receive) }
    sjStatus : integer;                    { Longjump code }
    LptNum,                            { Interface number }
    i,                                   { Loop counter }
    DirFound : byte;              { For directory search }
    dummy    : integer;
    argv     : array[ 1..10 ] of string;        { Parameter }

begin
  write( #13#10'Parallel Interface File Transfer Program' );
  writeln( '   (c) 1992 by Michael Tischer' );
  write( '=================================================' );
  writeln( '============================' );

  Escape := false;
  Timeout := TO_DEFAULT;

  if ( paramstr( 1 ) = '/?' ) then          { Display syntax only? }
    begin                                              { Yes }
      writeln( 'Syntax: plinkp [/Pn] [/Tnn] [filename]' );
      writeln( '                   |          |' );
      writeln( '            Interface   Time out ' );
      halt( 0 );
    end;

  sjStatus := setjmp( ReturnToEnd );       { Return address to end }
  if ( sjStatus > 0 ) then                   { Longjump called? }
    begin                                              { Yes }
      Intr_remove;                    { Disable interrupt handler }
      writeln( #13#10#13#10, ScnMesg[ sjStatus - 1 ] );
      halt( 0 );
    end;

  Intr_Install( @Escape, @TO_Count );       { Interrupt handler init }

{-- Set default values and interpret command line --------------------}

Sender := FALSE;                            { Default is Receiver }
LptNum := 1;                                   { Default is LPT1 }

for i := 1 to paramcount do
  begin
```

```
      argv[ i ] := paramstr( i );                    { Note parameters }
      if ( argv[ i, 1 ] = '/' ) then                 { Parameter }
        begin
          case ( upcase( argv[ i, 2 ] ) ) of
            'T' : begin
                    delete( argv[ i ], 1, 2 );
                    val( argv[ i ], Timeout, dummy );
                    Timeout := ( Timeout * TENSEC ) div 10;
                    if ( Timeout = 0 ) then
                      longjmp( ReturnToEnd, LJ_PARA );      { Invalid }
                  end;
            'P' : begin
                    LptNum := ord( argv[ i, 3 ] ) - 48;     { Interface }
                    if ( ( LptNum = 0 ) or ( LptNum > 4 ) ) then
                      longjmp( ReturnToEnd, LJ_PARA );      { Invalid }
                  end;
          else longjmp( ReturnToEnd, LJ_PARA ); { Unknown parameters }
          end;
          argv[ i ] := '';                     { Clear argument }
        end
      else                         { No parameters, must be a filename }
        Sender := TRUE;                             { Sender }
  end;

{-- Start transfer ------------------------------------------------}

  if ( not GetPortAdr( LptNum ) ) then     { Does the interface exist? }
    longjmp( ReturnToEnd, LJ_NOPAR );              { No --> Error }

  if ( not Port_Init( Sender ) ) then            { Create link }
    longjmp( ReturnToEnd, LJ_NOLINK );      { Impossible, error }

  if ( Sender ) then                              { Sender? }
    begin
      writeln( 'Sending over LPT', LptNum, #13#10 );

      {-- Transfer all data --------------------------------------}

      for i := 1 to paramcount do          { Execute command line }
        begin
          if ( argv[ i ] <> '' ) then            { Filename? }
            begin                                  { Yes }
              findfirst( argv[ i ], AnyFile, SRec);
              while ( DosError = 0 ) do          { While found }
                begin
                  if ( SRec.Attr <> Directory ) then
                    SendAFile( SRec.Name );        { Transfer file }
                  findnext( SRec );
                end;
            end;
        end;
      SendABlock( TOK_ENDIT, 0 , NIL );       { All files sent? }
      longjmp( ReturnToEnd, LJ_OKSENDER );
    end
  else                                          { No --> Receiver }
    begin
      writeln( 'Receiving over LPT', LptNum, #13#10 );
      while ( ReceiveAFile <> TOK_ENDIT ) do    { Receive data    }
        ;                                       { until END token }
      longjmp( ReturnToEnd, LJ_OKRECD );
    end;
end.
```

Assembler listing: PLINKPA.ASM

```
;************************************************************************
;*                                                                     *;
;*                      P L I N K P A . A S M                          *;
;*---------------------------------------------------------------------*;
;*   Task        : Assembly language module for PLINKP program.        *;
;*                 This module contains an interrupt handler,          *;
;*                 as well as routines for fast port access.           *;
;*---------------------------------------------------------------------*;
;*   Author      : Michael Tischer                                     *;
;*   Developed on : 10/10/91                                           *;
;*   Last update  : 01/30/92                                           *;
;*---------------------------------------------------------------------*;
;*   Assembly     : TASM PLINKPA                                       *;
;*                  ... Link to PLINKP                                  *;
;************************************************************************

;== Constants ========================================================

KB_PORT   = 60h              ;Keyboard port
INT_CTR   = 20h              ;Interrupt controller port
EOI       = 20h              ;End of Interrupt instruction
ESCAPE    = 1                ;Scan code for Escape

;== Data =============================================================

DATA    segment word public          ;Turbo data segment

extrn      InpPort           ;Input port as Turbo variable
extrn      OutPort           ;Output port as Turbo variable

DATA    ends                         ;End data segment

;== Program ==========================================================

CODE      segment byte public    ;Turbo CODE segment

          assume cs:CODE, ds:DATA, es:nothing, ss:nothing

;-- Public declarations of internal functions ------------------------

public     intr_install          ;Allows call from Turbo program
public     intr_remove
public     escapedirect
public     getb
public     putb

;-- Variables for interrupt handler ----------------------------------
;-- (accessible from code segment only) ------------------------------

key_ptr   dd 0               ;Pointer to variable for ESCAPE
tout_ptr  dd 0               ;Pointer to time out counter
escdirect db 0               ;No time out occurs on escape

;-- The following variables refer to the old interrupt handler    --
;-- addresses, which are replaced by the new interrupt handler     --

int9_ptr   equ this dword    ;Old interrupt vector 9H
int9_ofs   dw 0              ;Offset address of old handler
int9_seg   dw 0              ;Segment address of old handler

int1C_ptr  equ this dword    ;Old interrupt vector 1CH
int1C_ofs  dw 0              ;Offset address of old handler
int1C_seg  dw 0              ;Segment address of old handler
```

```
;-----------------------------------------------------------------
;-- GETB : Reads a byte from the input port
;-- Call from Turbo: getb : BYTE;

getb      proc near

          mov    dx,InpPort      ;Move port address to DX
          in     al,dx           ;Read from port
          and    al,0F8h         ;Mask bits 0-2

          ret                    ;Return - result of function in AL

getb      endp

;-----------------------------------------------------------------
;-- PUTB : Writes a byte to the output port
;-- Call from Turbo: putb( TpVar : BYTE );

putb      proc near

TpVar     equ byte ptr [bp+4]    ;Variable passed from Turbo

          push   bp              ;Enable access to arguments
          mov    bp,sp

          mov    al, TpVar        ;Move TpVar to al
          mov    dx, OutPort      ;Pass OutPort to DX
          out    dx, al           ;Pass value to port

          pop    bp              ;Restore BP register
          ret    2               ;Release stack and return

putb      endp

;-----------------------------------------------------------------
;-- INTR_INSTALL: Installs the interrupt handler         ---
;-- Call from Turbo: intr_install( escape_flag, timeout_count : ptr );

intr_install   proc near

sframe0   struc                  ;Access structure on the stack
bp0       dw ?                   ;Sets BP
ret_adr0  dw ?                   ;Return address
toptr     dd ?                   ;FAR pointer to the time out counter
escptr    dd ?                   ;FAR pointer to the ESCAPE flag
sframe0   ends                   ;End of structure

frame     equ [ bp - bp0 ]

          push   bp              ;Push BP onto the stack
          mov    bp,sp           ;Move SP to BP
          push   es              ;Push ES onto the stack

          ;-- Get arguments from stack and process them --------------

          les    si,frame.escptr  ;Load pointer to ESCAPE flag
          mov    word ptr key_ptr,si   ;and place in the CODE segment
          mov    word ptr key_ptr+2,es ;variables

          les    si,frame.toptr   ;Load pointer to time out
          mov    word ptr tout_ptr,si   ;counter and place in the CODE
          mov    word ptr tout_ptr+2,es ;segment variables
```

```
;-- Get addresses of the replacement interrupt handler -----

          mov    ax,3509h        ;Get interrupt vector 9H
          int    21h             ;Call DOS interrupt
          mov    int9_ofs,bx     ;Place handler addresses
          mov    int9_seg,es     ;in corresponding variables

          mov    ax,351Ch        ;Get interrupt vector 1CH
          int    21h             ;Call DOS interrupt
          mov    int1C_ofs,bx    ;Place handler addresses
          mov    int1C_seg,es    ;in corresponding variables

          ;-- Install new interrupt handler ------------------------

          push   ds              ;Mark data segment
          mov    ax,cs           ;Place DS on CS
          mov    ds,ax

          mov    ax,2509h        ;Func. no.: Set interrupt 9H
          mov    dx,offset int09 ;DS:DX receives the handler address
          int    21h             ;Call DOS interrupt

          mov    ax,251Ch        ;Func. no.: Set interrupt 1CH
          mov    dx,offset int1C ;DS:DX receives the handler address
          int    21h             ;Call DOS interrupt

          pop    ds              ;Pop DS from stack
          pop    es
          pop    bp              ;Pop BP from stack
          ret    8               ;Return to caller

intr_install endp

;-----------------------------------------------------------------
;-- INTR_REMOVE: Disables the interrupt handler
;-- Call from Turbo: intr_remove;

intr_remove proc near

          cli                    ;Disable interrupts
          push   ds              ;Push DS onto stack

          mov    ax,2509h        ;Func. no.: Set INT 9H handler
          mov    ds,int9_seg     ;Segment address of old handler
          mov    dx,int9_ofs     ;Offset address of old handler
          int    21h             ;Re-install old handler

          mov    ax,251Ch        ;Func. no.: Set INT 1CH handler
          mov    ds,int1C_seg    ;Segment address of old handler
          mov    dx,int1C_ofs    ;Offset address of old handler
          int    21h             ;Re-install old handler

          pop    ds              ;Pop DS from stack
          sti                    ;Re-enable interrupts

          ret                    ;Return to caller

intr_remove endp                 ;End of procedure

;-----------------------------------------------------------------
;-- Escapedirect: Determines whether a time out should occur on -------
;--          an escape
;-- Call from Turbo: procedure Escapedirect( Disconnect : boolean );
```

579

```
Escapedirect proc near

sframe1      struc               ;Access structure on the stack
bp1          dw ?                ;Set BP
ret_adr1     dw ?                ;Return address
escflag      dw ?                ;TRUE or FALSE
sframe1      ends                ;End of structure

frame        equ [ bp - bp1 ]

             push bp             ;Push BP onto the stack
             mov  bp,sp          ;Transfer SP to BP

             mov  al,byte ptr frame.escflag ;Load flag and
             mov  escdirect,al            ;place in CS variable

             pop  bp
             ret  2              ;Return to caller, pop
                                 ;arguments from stack

Escapedirect endp

;------------------------------------------------------------------
;-- New interrupt handler follows ---------------------------------
;------------------------------------------------------------------

             assume CS:CODE, DS:nothing, ES:nothing, SS:nothing

;-- New interrupt 9H handler ---------------------------------------

int09        proc far

             push ax             ;Push AX onto stack
             in   al,KB_PORT     ;Get scan code from keyboard port

             cmp  al,128         ;Release code?
             jae  i9_end         ;Yes --> Don't test first

             cmp  al,ESCAPE      ;No --> Is it ESCAPE?
             jne  i9_end         ;No --> No, revert to old handler

             ;-- User presses <Esc> -------------------------------

             push ds             ;Push DS and SI onto stack
             push si
             lds  si,key_ptr     ;Load pointer to ESCAPE
             mov  word ptr [si],1 ;Set ESCAPE flag to 1
             cmp  escdirect,0    ;Clear time out flag?
             je   i9_1           ;No ---> I9_1

             lds  si,tout_ptr    ;Yes --> Load time out flag counter
             mov  word ptr [si],0 ;Set counter to 0

i9_1:        pop  si             ;Restore DS and SI
             pop  ds

             mov  al,EOI         ;Display end of interrupt
             out  INT_CTR,al

             pop  ax             ;Pop AX from stack
             iret                ;Return to interrupted program

i9_end:      pop  ax             ;Pop AX from stack
             jmp  cs:[int9_ptr]  ;Jump to old handler
```

```
int09        endp

;-- New interrupt 1CH handler --------------------------------------

int1C        proc far

             push ds             ;Push DS and SI onto stack
             push si
             lds  si,tout_ptr    ;Load pointer to time out counter
             cmp  word ptr [si],0 ;Counter already set to 0?
             je   no_decr        ;Yes --> No more decrementing

             dec  word ptr [si]  ;No --> Decrement

no_decr:     pop  si             ;Pop DS and SI from stack
             pop  ds

             jmp  cs:[int1C_ptr] ;Revert to old interrupt handler

int1C        endp

;------------------------------------------------------------------

CODE         ends               ;End of CODE segment
             end                ;End of program
```

C listing: PLINKC.C

```
/*********************************************************/
/*                    P L I N K C . C                    */
/*-------------------------------------------------------*/
/*  Task      : Transfers files over the parallel interface. */
/*-------------------------------------------------------*/
/*  Author    : Michael Tischer                          */
/*  Developed on : 09/27/91                              */
/*  Last update  : 01/31/92                              */
/*-------------------------------------------------------*/
/*  Memory model : SMALL                                 */
/*********************************************************/

/*== Add include files ================================*/

#include <stdlib.h>
#include <stdio.h>
#include <conio.h>
#include <dos.h>
#include <setjmp.h>
#include <string.h>
#ifdef __TURBOC__                        /* Turbo C compiler? */
  #include <dir.h>              /* Include directory functions */
  #include <ctype.h>                     /* for toupper() */
#endif

/*== Type definitions =================================*/

typedef unsigned char BYTE;              /* Define a byte */
typedef unsigned int WORD;               /* Create a WORD */
typedef struct {                         /* Block transfer header */
          BYTE       Token;
          unsigned int Len;
          } BHEADER;

/*== Assembler module functions =======================*/

extern void IntrInstall( int far * escape_flag,
                         WORD far * timeout_count );
extern void IntrRemove( void );
extern void EscapeDirect( int disconnect );

/*== Constants ========================================*/

#define ONESEC     18                    /* One second */
#define TENSEC     182                   /* Ten seconds */
#define TO_DEFAULT TENSEC                /* Time out default value */

#define TRUE       ( 0 == 0 )
#define FALSE      ( 0 == 1 )
#define MAXBLOCK   4096                  /* 4K maximum block size */

/*-- Constants for transfer protocol -----------------*/

#define ACK        0x00                  /* Acknowledge */
#define NAK        0xFF                  /* Non-Acknowledge */
#define MAX_TRY    5                     /* Maximum number of tries */

/*-- Tokens for communication between sender and receiver -----------*/

#define TOK_DATSTART 0                   /* Start of file data */
#define TOK_DATNEXT  1                   /* Next file data block */
#define TOK_DATEND   2                   /* End file data transfer */
#define TOK_ENDIT    3                   /* End program */
#define TOK_ESCAPE   4                   /* <Esc> pressed on remote computer */

/*-- Codes for LongJump call --------------------------------------*/

#define LJ_OKSENDER  1                   /* All data sent successfully */
#define LJ_OKRECD    2                   /* All data received successfully */
#define LJ_TIMEOUT   3                   /* Time out: No response */
#define LJ_ESCAPE    4                   /* <Esc> pressed on local computer */
#define LJ_REMESCAPE 5                   /* <Esc> pressed on remote computer */
#define LJ_DATA      6                   /* Communication error */
#define LJ_NOLINK    7                   /* No link */
#define LJ_NOPAR     8                   /* No interface */
#define LJ_PARA      9                   /* Invalid call parameters */

/*== Macros ===========================================*/

/*-- The lower three bits of the input register are not allocated ---*/
/*-- and can be set to 1 or 0 by the computer, so they are masked ---*/
/*-- by GetB().                                                   ---*/

#ifdef __TURBOC__                        /* Turbo C compiler? */
  #define GetB()                 ( inportb( InPort ) & 0xF8 )
  #define PutB( Was )            outportb( OutPort, Was )
  #define DIRSTRUCT              struct ffblk
  #define FINDFIRST( path, buf, attr ) findfirst( path, buf, attr )
  #define FINDNEXT( buf )        findnext( buf )
  #define DFILENAME              ff_name
#else                                    /* No --> Microsoft C */
  #define GetB()                 ( inp( InPort ) & 0xF8 )
  #define PutB( Was )            outp( OutPort, Was )
  #define DIRSTRUCT              struct      find_t
  #define FINDFIRST( path, buf, attr ) _dos_findfirst(path, attr, buf)
  #define FINDNEXT( buf )        _dos_findnext( buf )
  #define DFILENAME              name
#endif

#ifdef MK_FP                  /* Macro MK_FP already defined? */
  #undef MK_FP                /* Yes --> Undefine macro */
#endif

#define MK_FP(seg,ofs) ((void far *) ((unsigned long) (seg)<<16|(ofs)))

/*== Global variables =================================*/

int    InPort;                           /* Input port address */
int    OutPort;                          /* Output port address */
int    Escape = 0;                       /* <Esc> not pressed */
WORD   Timeout = TO_DEFAULT;             /* Selected time out value */
WORD   TO_Count;                         /* Counter for time out */
jmp_buf ReturnToEnd;                     /* Return address for end */
BYTE   *BlockBuf;                        /* Buffer for passing a block */
FILE   *FiVar = NULL;        /* File variable for file being processed */

/*********************************************************/
/* GetPortAdr: Initializes a parallel interface's port addresses in */
/*             the global variables INPPORT and OUTPORT.  */
/* Input     : LPTNUM = Parallel interface number (1-4)  */
/* Output    : TRUE if interface is valid                */
/* Global vars. : InPort/W, OutPort/W                    */
/* Info      : The base addresses of up to 4 parallel interfaces */
/*             lie in the four memory words starting at  */
/*             0040:0008H.                                */
/*********************************************************/
```

```c
int GetPortAdr( int LptNum )
{                                     /* Read port addresses from BIOS variable segment */
OutPort = *( WORD far * ) MK_FP( 0x0040, 6 + LptNum * 2 );
if ( OutPort != 0 )                   /* Interface available? */
  {                                                      /* Yes */
  InpPort = OutPort + 1;              /* Input register address */
  return TRUE;                               /* End error-free */
  }
else
  return FALSE;                /* Error: Interface not available */
}


/*********************************************************/
/* Port_Init   : Initializes the registers needed for transfer.  */
/* Input       : SENDER = TRUE if sender, FALSE if receiver      */
/* Output      : TRUE if register initializes successfully       */
/* Global vars.: InpPort/R, OutPort/R                            */
/* Info        : The asymmetry (send 00010000, wait for 00000000) */
/*               occurs because of signal inversion. Normally the */
/*               input and output registers contain the desired   */
/*               values, but initialization is needed after an    */
/*               aborted transfer, or when restarting.            */
/*********************************************************/

int Port_Init( int Sender )
{
EscapeDirect( TRUE );           /* Release through Escape time out */
if ( Sender )                        /* Device = Sender? */
  {
  TO_Count = Timeout * 5;            /* Start time out counter */
  PutB( 0x10 );                         /* Send: 00010000b */
  while ( ( GetB() != 0x00 ) && TO_Count )  /* Wait for 00000000b */
    ;
  }
else                                  /* Device = Receiver? */
  {
  TO_Count = Timeout * 5;            /* Start time out counter */
  while ( ( GetB() != 0x00 ) && TO_Count )   /* Wait for 00000000b */
    ;
  PutB( 0x10 );                          /* Send: 00010000b */
  }
EscapeDirect( FALSE );          /* No time out released on Escape */
return ( TO_Count != 0 );             /* End initialization */
}


/*********************************************************/
/* SendAByte   : Sends a byte to the remote computer in two parts, */
/*               then checks the result.                 */
/* Input       : B2Send = Byte to be sent                */
/* Output      : Transfer successful? (0 = error, -1 = O.K.)  */
/* Global vars.: Timeout/R, InpPort/R, OutPort/R (in macros)  */
/*********************************************************/

int SendAByte( BYTE B2Send )
{
BYTE RcvdB;                              /* Received byte */

/*-- Send lower nibble ------------------------------------*/

TO_Count = Timeout;               /* Initialize time out counter */
PutB( B2Send & 0x0F );                /* Sending, clear BUSY */
while ( ( ( GetB() & 128 ) == 0 ) && TO_Count )  /* Wait for message */
  ;
```

```c
if ( TO_Count == 0 )                       /* Time out error? */
  longjmp( ReturnToEnd, LJ_TIMEOUT );       /* Cancel transfer */

RcvdB = ( GetB() >> 3 ) & 0x0F;              /* Bits 3-6 in 0-3 */

/*-- Send upper nibble ------------------------------------*/

TO_Count = Timeout;               /* Initialize time out counter */
PutB( ( B2Send >> 4 ) | 0x10 );          /* Sending, set BUSY */
while ( ( ( GetB() & 128 ) != 0 ) && TO_Count )  /* Wait for message */
  ;

if ( TO_Count == 0 )                       /* Time out error? */
  longjmp( ReturnToEnd, LJ_TIMEOUT );       /* Cancel transfer */

RcvdB = RcvdB | ( ( GetB() << 1 ) & 0xF0 );   /* Bits 3-6 in 4-7 */
return ( B2Send == RcvdB );            /* Byte sent correctly? */
}


/*********************************************************/
/* ReceiveAByte : Receives a two part byte from remote computer, and */
/*                sends returned parts for testing.      */
/* Input        : None                                   */
/* Output       : Received byte                          */
/* Global vars. : Timeout/R, InpPort/R, OutPort/R (in macros)  */
/*********************************************************/

BYTE ReceiveAByte( void )
{
BYTE LoNib, HiNib;                       /* Received nibbles */

/*-- Receive and re-send lowest nibble --------------------*/

TO_Count = Timeout;               /* Initialize time out counter */
while ( ( ( GetB() & 128 ) == 0 ) && TO_Count )  /* Wait until BUSY 1 */
  ;

if ( TO_Count == 0 )                       /* Time out error? */
  longjmp( ReturnToEnd, LJ_TIMEOUT );       /* Cancel transfer */

LoNib = ( GetB() >> 3 ) & 0x0F;              /* Bits 3-6 in 0-3 */
PutB( LoNib );                              /* Re-send */

/*-- Receive and re-send highest nibble -------------------*/

TO_Count = Timeout;               /* Initialize time out counter */
while ( ( ( GetB() & 128 ) != 0 ) && TO_Count )  /* Wait until BUSY 0 */
  ;

if ( TO_Count == 0 )                       /* Time out error? */
  longjmp( ReturnToEnd, LJ_TIMEOUT );       /* Cancel transfer */

HiNib = ( GetB() << 1 ) & 0xF0;              /* Bits 3-6 in 4-7 */
PutB( ( HiNib >> 4 ) | 0x10 );        /* Re-sending, set BUSY */

return( LoNib | HiNib );                 /* Received byte */
}


/*********************************************************/
/* SendABlock: Sends a data block.                       */
/* Input     : TOKEN = Token for receiver                */
/*             TRANUM = Number of bytes to be transferred */
/*             DPTR  = Pointer to buffer containing data  */
/* Output    : None, jumps immediately to an error handler if  */
```

```
/*            an error occurs.                        */
/****************************************************************************/

void SendABlock( BYTE Token, int TraNum, void *DPtr )
{
  BHEADER header;              /* Header for placing tokens and numbers */
  BYTE    *bptr,               /* Pointer to current byte to be sent */
          RcvrEscape;          /* <Esc> pressed on remote? */
  int     ok,                  /* Error flag */
          i,                   /* Loop counter */
          try;                 /* Remaining number of tries */

  if ( Escape )               /* <Esc> pressed on local computer? */
  {
    Token = TOK_ESCAPE;                  /* Yes --> Send Escape token */
    TraNum = 0;
  }

  /*-- Send header first -----------------------------------------*/

  header.Token = Token;                    /* Create header */
  header.Len = TraNum;

  for ( try = MAX_TRY; try; --try )  /* Make MAX_TRY access attempts */
  {
    ok = TRUE;      /* Send on error-free transfer */
    for ( bptr = (BYTE *) &header, i = sizeof( header ); i; --i )
      ok = ok & SendAByte( *bptr++ );         /* Send a byte */

    ok = ok & SendAByte( (BYTE) (ok ? ACK : NAK) );  /* Confirmation */
    if ( ok )                 /* Everything transfer successfully? */
      break;                  /* Yes --> No need to try again */
  }

  if ( try == 0 )           /* Could the header be sent successfully? */
    longjmp( ReturnToEnd, LJ_DATA );      /* No --> Cancel transfer */

  if ( Token == TOK_ESCAPE )       /* Was an Escape message sent? */
    longjmp( ReturnToEnd, LJ_ESCAPE );    /* Yes --> Cancel transfer */

  /*-- Send the data block itself ------------------------------*/

  if ( TraNum )                           /* Length > 0? */
  {
    for ( try = MAX_TRY; try; -- try )     /* Make MAX_TRY attempts */
    {
      ok = TRUE;                  /* Send on error-free transfer */
      for ( bptr = (BYTE *) DPtr, i = TraNum; i; --i )
        ok = ok & SendAByte( *bptr++ );  /* Send byte and read status */

      ok = ok & SendAByte( (BYTE) (ok ? ACK : NAK) ); /* Confirmation */
      if ( ok )               /* Everything transfer successfully? */
        break;                /* Yes --> No need to try again */
    }
    if ( try == 0 )        /* Could data block be sent successfully? */
      longjmp( ReturnToEnd, LJ_DATA );    /* No --> Cancel transfer */
  }

  /*-- Read Escape byte from receiver --------------------------*/

  for ( try = MAX_TRY; try; -- try )          /* Enable tries */
  {
    RcvrEscape = ReceiveAByte();       /* Read remove Escape status */
    if ( RcvrEscape == (BYTE) TRUE || RcvrEscape == (BYTE) FALSE )
```

```
      break;                   /* Receive Escape status */
  }
  if ( try == 0 )            /* Was the Escape status received? */
    longjmp( ReturnToEnd, LJ_DATA );       /* No --> Cancel transfer */

  if ( RcvrEscape )            /* <Esc> from remote computer? */
    longjmp( ReturnToEnd, LJ_REMESCAPE ); /* Yes --> Cancel transfer */
}

/****************************************************************************/
/* ReceiveABlock: Receives a data block.                                    */
/* Input    : TOKEN  = Pointer to variable containing tokens                */
/*            LEN    = Pointer to variable containing length                */
/*            DPTR   = Pointer to buffer containing data                     */
/* Output   : None, jumps immediately to an error handler if               */
/*            an error occurs.                                              */
/* Info     : Buffer must be allocated using MAXBLOCK, since block          */
/*            length cannot usually be anticipated.                         */
/****************************************************************************/

void ReceiveABlock( BYTE *Token, int *Len, void *DPtr )
{
  BHEADER header;             /* Header for storing tokens and numbers */
  BYTE    *bptr;              /* Floating pointer for receive buffer */
  int     ok,                 /* Error flag */
          i,                  /* Loop counter */
          try,                /* Remaining number of tries */
          EscapeStatus;       /* For storing current Escape status */

  /*-- Receive header first -----------------------------------*/

  for ( try = MAX_TRY; try; -- try )  /* Make MAX_TRY access attempts */
  {
    for ( bptr = (BYTE *) &header, i = sizeof(header); i; --i )
      *bptr++ = ReceiveAByte( );

    if ( ReceiveAByte() == ACK );  /* All bytes received successfully? */
      break;                      /* Yes --> No need to try again */
  }

  if ( try == 0 )                  /* Header received successfully? */
    longjmp( ReturnToEnd, LJ_DATA );      /* No --> Cancel transfer */

  if ( ( *Token = header.Token ) == TOK_ESCAPE )   /* Sender Escape? */
    longjmp( ReturnToEnd, LJ_REMESCAPE );  /* Yes --> Cancel transfer */

  /*-- Header was O.K., now receive the data block itself ------------*/

  if ( ( *Len = header.Len ) != 0 )            /* No data block? */
  {                                            /* No */
    for ( try = MAX_TRY; try; -- try )/* Make MAX_TRY access attempts */
    {
      for ( bptr = (BYTE *) DPtr, i = header.Len; i; --i )
        *bptr++ = ReceiveAByte( );

      if ( ReceiveAByte() == ACK );   /* Bytes received successfully? */
        break;                        /* Yes --> No need to try again */
    }

    if ( try == 0 )                  /* Block received successfully? */
      longjmp( ReturnToEnd, LJ_DATA );    /* No --> Cancel transfer */
  }

  /*-- Send current Escape status to the remote computer -------------*/
```

```
EscapeStatus = Escape;                        /* Note status */
for ( try = MAX_TRY; try; -- try )      /* Enable access attempts */
{
  if ( SendAByte( (BYTE) (EscapeStatus != 0) ) )       /* Sent? */
  break;                          /* Yes --> No need to try again */
}

if ( try == 0 )                 /* Could Escape status be sent? */
  longjmp( ReturnToEnd, LJ_DATA );      /* No --> Cancel transfer */

if ( EscapeStatus )        /* <Esc> pressed on this computer? */
  longjmp( ReturnToEnd, LJ_ESCAPE );    /* Yes --> Cancel transfer */
}

/*****************************************************************/
/* SendAFile : Sends a file.                                    */
/* Input     : NAME = Pointer to buffer containing filenames    */
/* Output    : None                                             */
/*****************************************************************/

void SendAFile( char *Name )
{
int       Status;                         /* Send status */
WORD      WdsRead;                   /* Number of bytes read */
unsigned long BytSent;              /* Number of bytes sent */

printf( "%-13s", Name );
FiVar = fopen( Name, "rb" );              /* Open file */
SendABlock( TOK_DATSTART, strlen(Name)+1, Name ); /* Send filename */

/*-- Transfer file contents --------------------------------------*/
BytSent = 0;
do
{
  WdsRead = fread( BlockBuf, 1, MAXBLOCK, FiVar );   /* Read block */
  if ( WdsRead > 0 )                  /* End of block not reached? */
  {                                                  /* No */
    SendABlock( TOK_DATNEXT, WdsRead, BlockBuf );   /* Send block */
    BytSent += WdsRead;
    printf( "\r%-13s (%ld)", Name, BytSent );
  }
}
while ( WdsRead > 0 );
printf( "\n" );

SendABlock( TOK_DATEND, 0, NULL );              /* End transfer */

fclose( FiVar );                                /* Close file */
FiVar = NULL;                                   /* File is closed */
}

/*****************************************************************/
/* ReceiveAFile: Receives a file.                               */
/* Input     : None                                             */
/* Output    : The last token received                          */
/*****************************************************************/

int ReceiveAFile( void )
{
int       Status;                         /* Send status */
WORD      LastBlkSize;               /* Size of last block */
unsigned long BytSent;
BYTE      Token;                      /* Token received */
```

```
int       Len;                      /* Block length received */
char      Name[13];                         /* Filename */

ReceiveABlock( &Token, &Len, BlockBuf );
if ( Token == TOK_DATSTART )
{
  strcpy( Name, BlockBuf );
  FiVar = fopen( Name, "wb" );          /* Open (create) file */
  printf( "%-13s", Name );

  /*-- Receive file contents -------------------------------------*/

  BytSent = 0;
  do
  {
    ReceiveABlock( &Token, &Len, BlockBuf );    /* Receive block */
    if ( Token == TOK_DATNEXT )             /* Next data block? */
    {                                                /* Yes */
      fwrite( BlockBuf, 1, Len, FiVar );           /* Write block */
      BytSent += Len;
      printf( "\r%-13s (%ld)", Name, BytSent );
    }
  }
  while ( Token == TOK_DATNEXT );
  fclose( FiVar );                              /* Close file */
  FiVar = NULL;                                 /* File is closed */
  printf( "\n" );
}
return Token;                            /* Return error status */
}

/*****************************************************************/
/*                M A I N   P R O G R A M                       */
/*****************************************************************/

void main( int argc, char *argv[] )
{
DIRSTRUCT SRec;                 /* Structure for directory search */
BYTE      Sender;              /* Transfer mode (Send, Receive) */
int       sjStatus,                    /* Longjump code */
          LptNum,                    /* Interface number */
          i,                         /* Loop counter */
          DirFound;                /* For directory search */

static char *ScnMesg[ 9 ] =
{ "DONE: All files sent successfully.",
  "DONE: All files received successfully.",
  "ERROR: Time out, remote system not responding.",
  "DONE: <Esc> key pressed.",
  "DONE: <Esc> key pressed on remote computer.",
  "ERROR: Hardware problem (check cable and interface).",
  "ERROR: No contact with remote computer.",
  "ERROR: Interface you requested not found.",
  "ERROR: Invalid or unknown parameters." };

printf( "\n\nParallel Interface File Transfer Program   " );
printf( "(c) 1992 by Michael Tischer\n" );
printf( "=======================================================" );
printf( "===========================\n\n" );

if ( strcmp( argv[ 1 ], "/?" ) == 0 )     /* Display syntax only? */
{                                                  /* Yes */
  printf( "Syntax: plinkc [/Pn] [/Tnn] [filename]\n" );
  printf( "               |      |\n");
```

```
 printf( "          Interface   Time out ");
 exit ( 0 );
}


sjStatus = setjmp( ReturnToEnd );         /* Return address to end */
if ( sjStatus )                            /* Longjmp called? */
 {                                           /* Yes */
  IntrRemove( );                          /* Disable interrupt handler */
  if ( FiVar )                           /* Any files still open? */
    fclose( FiVar );
  free( BlockBuf );            /* Release allocated buffer memory */
  printf( "\n\n%s\n", ScnMesg[ sjStatus - 1 ] );
  exit( 0 );
 }


BlockBuf = malloc( MAXBLOCK );             /* Generate data buffer */
IntrInstall( &Escape, &TO_Count );         /* Interrupt handler init */

/*-- Set default values and interpret command line -----------------*/

Sender = FALSE;                            /* Default is Receiver */
LptNum = 1;                                /* Default is LPT1 */

for ( i = 1; i < argc; i++ )
 {
  if ( argv[i][0] == '/' )                          /* Parameter */
   {
    switch ( toupper( argv[i][1] ) )
     {
      case 'T' : Timeout = (atol( &argv[i][2] ) * TENSEC) / 10;
                 if ( Timeout == 0 )
                     longjmp( ReturnToEnd, LJ_PARA );      /* Invalid */
                 break;
      case 'P' : LptNum = argv[i][2] - 48;          /* Interface */
                 if ( LptNum == 0  ||  LptNum > 4 )
                     longjmp( ReturnToEnd, LJ_PARA );      /* Invalid */
                 break;
      default  : longjmp( ReturnToEnd, LJ_PARA ); /* Unknown params */
                 break;
     }
    argv[i][0] = '\0';                            /* Clear argument */
   }
  else                           /* No parameters, must be a filename */
    Sender = TRUE;                                  /* Sender */
 }

/*-- Start transfer --------------------------------------------*/

if ( GetPortAdr(LptNum) == FALSE )     /* Does the interface exist? */
 longjmp( ReturnToEnd, LJ_NOPAR );                 /* No --> Error */

if ( Port_Init( Sender ) == FALSE )            /* Create link */
 longjmp( ReturnToEnd, LJ_NOLINK );        /* Impossible, error */

if ( Sender )                                     /* Sender? */
 {
  printf( "Sending over LPT%d:\n\n", LptNum );

  /*-- Transfer all data -------------------------------------*/

  for ( i = 1; i < argc; i++ )          /* Execute command line */
   {
    if ( argv[i][0] != '\0' )                    /* Filename? */
     {                                             /* Yes */
      DirFound = FINDFIRST( argv[i], &SRec, 0 );
      while ( !DirFound )
       {
        if ( SRec.DFILENAME[0] != '.' )
          SendAFile( SRec.DFILENAME );        /* Transfer file */
        DirFound = FINDNEXT( &SRec );
       }
     }
   }
  SendABlock( TOK_ENDIT, 0 , NULL );           /* All files sent? */
  longjmp( ReturnToEnd, LJ_OKSENDER );
 }
else                                          /* No --> Receiver */
 {
  printf( "Receiving over LPT%d:\n\n", LptNum );
  while ( ReceiveAFile() != TOK_ENDIT )      /* Receive data until */
    ;                                         /* ENDIT token      */
  longjmp( ReturnToEnd, LJ_OKRECD );
 }
}
```

Listing: **PLINKCA.ASM**

```
;****************************************************************;
;*                  P L I N K C A . A S M                      *;
;*------------------------------------------------------------*;
;*    Task     : Assembly language module for PLINKC program. *;
;*               This module contains an interrupt handle,    *;
;*               as well as routines for fast port access.    *;
;*------------------------------------------------------------*;
;*    Author   : Michael Tischer                              *;
;*    Developed on  : 10/10/91                                *;
;*    Last update   : 01/31/92                                *;
;*------------------------------------------------------------*;
;*    Memory model   : SMALL                                  *;
;*------------------------------------------------------------*;
;*    Assembly   : MASM PLINKCA;  or TASM PLINKCA             *;
;*               ... Link to PLINKC                           *;
;****************************************************************;


IGROUP  group _text              ;Program segment
DGROUP  group _bss,  _data       ;Data segment
        assume CS:IGROUP, DS:DGROUP, ES:DGROUP, SS:DGROUP

_BSS    segment word public 'BSS' ;This segment contains all un-
_BSS    ends                      ;initialized static variables

_DATA   segment word public 'DATA' ;This segment contains all
                                   ;initialized global and static
                                   ;variables

_DATA   ends

;== Constants ===============================================

KB_PORT   = 60h                  ;Keyboard port
INT_CTR   = 20h                  ;Interrupt controller port
EOI       = 20h                  ;End of Interrupt instruction
ESCAPE    = 1                    ;Scan code for ESCAPE

;== Program ================================================

_TEXT  segment byte public 'CODE' ;Code segment

;-- Public declarations of internal functions -----------------

public    _IntrInstall           ;Enables calls from C programs
public    _IntrRemove
public    _EscapeDirect

;-- Interrupt handler variables -------------------------------
;-- (accessible from code segment only) -----------------------

key_ptr   dd 0                   ;Pointer to variable for ESCAPE
tout_ptr  dd 0                   ;Pointer to time out counter
escdirect db 0                   ;No time out occurs on ESCAPE

;-- The following variables refer to the old interrupt handler --
;-- addresses, which are replaced by the new interrupt handler --

int9_ptr  equ this dword         ;Old interrupt vector 9H
int9_ofs  dw 0                   ;Offset address of old handler
int9_seg  dw 0                   ;Segment address of old handler

int1C_ptr equ this dword         ;Old interrupt vector 1CH
```

```
int1C_ofs  dw 0                  ;Offset address of old handler
int1C_seg  dw 0                  ;Segment address of old handler

;------------------------------------------------------------
;-- IntrInstall : Installs the interrupt handler         ---
;-- Call from C: void IntrInstall( int far * escape_flag,
;--                      word far * timeout_count );

_IntrInstall  proc near

sframe0    struc                 ;Access structure on the stack
bp0        dw ?                  ;Sets BP
ret_adr0   dw ?                  ;Return address
escptr     dd ?                  ;FAR pointer to the ESCAPE flag
toptr      dd ?                  ;FAR pointer to the time out counter
sframe0    ends                  ;End of structure

frame      equ [ bp - bp0 ]

           push bp               ;Push BP onto the stack
           mov  bp,sp            ;Move SP to BP

           push si

;-- Get arguments from stack and process them --------------

           les  si,frame.escptr  ;Load pointer to ESCAPE flag
           mov  word ptr key_ptr,si   ;and place in the code segment
           mov  word ptr key_ptr+2,es ;variables

           les  si,frame.toptr   ;Load pointer to time out
           mov  word ptr tout_ptr,si  ;counter and place in the code
           mov  word ptr tout_ptr+2,es ;segment variables

;-- Get addresses of the replacement interrupt handler -----

           mov  ax,3509h         ;Get interrupt vector 9H
           int  21h              ;Call DOS interrupt
           mov  int9_ofs,bx      ;Place handler addresses
           mov  int9_seg,es      ;in corresponding variables

           mov  ax,351Ch         ;Get interrupt vector 1CH
           int  21h              ;Call DOS interrupt
           mov  int1C_ofs,bx     ;Place handler addresses
           mov  int1C_seg,es     ;in corresponding variables

;-- Install new interrupt handler ---------------------------

           push ds               ;Mark data segment
           mov  ax,cs            ;Place DS on CS
           mov  ds,ax

           mov  ax,2509h         ;Func. no.: Set interrupt 9H
           mov  dx,offset int09  ;DS:DX receives the handler address
           int  21h              ;Call DOS interrupt

           mov  ax,251Ch         ;Func. no.: Set interrupt 1CH
           mov  dx,offset int1C  ;DS:DX receives the handler address
           int  21h              ;Call DOS interrupt

           pop  ds               ;Pop DS from stack

           pop  si
           pop  bp
```

586

```
        ret                    ;Return to caller


_IntrInstall  endp


;-------------------------------------------------------------------
;-- IntrRemove : Disables the interrupt handler
;-- Call from C: void IntrRemove( void );


_IntrRemove  proc near

        cli                    ;Disable interrupts
        push ds                ;Push DS onto stack

        mov  ax,2509h          ;Func. no.: Set INT 9H handler
        mov  ds,int9_seg       ;Segment address of old handler
        mov  dx,int9_ofs       ;Offset address of old handler
        int  21h               ;Re-install old handler

        mov  ax,251Ch          ;Func. no.: Set INT 1CH handler
        mov  ds,int1C_seg      ;Segment address of old handler
        mov  dx,int1C_ofs      ;Offset address of old handler
        int  21h               ;Re-install old handler

        pop  ds                ;Pop DS from stack
        sti                    ;Re-enable interrupts

        ret                    ;Return to caller

_IntrRemove  endp             ;End of procedure


;-------------------------------------------------------------------
;-- EscapeDirect: Determines whether a time out should occur on -------
;--           an escape
;-- Call from C: void EscapeDirect( int Disconnect );


_EscapeDirect proc near

sframe1     struc             ;Access structure on the stack
bp1         dw ?              ;Sets BP
ret_adr1    dw ?              ;Return address
escflag     dw ?              ;TRUE or FALSE
sframe1     ends              ;End of structure

frame       equ [ bp - bp1 ]

        push bp                ;Push BP onto the stack
        mov  bp,sp             ;Move SP to BP

        mov  al,byte ptr frame.escflag ;Load flag and
        mov  escdirect,al              ;place in CS variable

        pop  bp
        ret                    ;Return to caller

_EscapeDirect endp


;-------------------------------------------------------------------
;-- New interrupt handler follows -------------------------------------
;-------------------------------------------------------------------


        assume CS:IGROUP, DS:nothing, ES:nothing, SS:nothing


;-- New interrupt 9H handler -----------------------------------------
```

```
int09   proc far

        push ax                ;Push AX onto stack
        in   al,KB_PORT        ;Get scan code from keyboard port

        cmp  al,128            ;Release code?
        jae  i9_end            ;Yes --> Don't test first

        cmp  al,ESCAPE         ;No --> Is it ESCAPE?
        jne  i9_end            ;No --> Revert to old handler

        ;-- User presses <Esc> -----------------------------------

        push ds                ;Push DS and SI onto stack
        push si
        lds  si,key_ptr        ;Load pointer to ESCAPE
        mov  word ptr [si],1   ;Set ESCAPE flag to 1
        cmp  escdirect,0       ;Clear time out flag?
        je   i9_1              ;No --> I9_1

        lds  si,tout_ptr       ;Yes --> Load time out flag counter
        mov  word ptr [si],0   ;Set counter to 0
i9_1:   pop  si                ;Restore DS and SI
        pop  ds

        mov  al,EOI            ;Display end of interrupt
        out  INT_CTR,al

        pop  ax                ;Pop AX from stack
        iret                   ;Return to interrupted program

i9_end: pop  ax                ;Pop AX from stack
        jmp  cs:[int9_ptr]     ;Jump to old handler

int09   endp

;-- New interrupt 1CH handler ----------------------------------------

int1C   proc far

        push ds                ;Push DS and SI onto stack
        push si
        lds  si,tout_ptr       ;Load pointer to time out counter
        cmp  word ptr [si],0   ;Counter already set to 0?
        je   no_decr           ;Yes --> No more decrementing

        dec  word ptr [si]     ;No --> Decrement

no_decr: pop  si               ;Pop DS and SI from stack
        pop  ds

        jmp  cs:[int1C_ptr]    ;Revert to old interrupt handler

int1C   endp

;-------------------------------------------------------------------

_text   ends                  ;End of code segment
        end                   ;End of program
```

587

Chapter 8

Accessing the Serial Port from the BIOS

Computers around the world communicate with each other and exchange data. Usually these computers use normal telephone lines for this communication. Although transferring data with phone lines is slow, it enables users to communicate from almost anywhere on the planet. Data is transferred serially (i.e., one bit at a time), while the sender and receiver maintain similar *transfer protocols* (parameters for data transfer).

Serial card

Since basic PC configurations aren't equipped for this type of data transmission, data transfer is only possible when the user adds an *asynchronous communication port* (IBM's catch phrase for an *RS-232 card* or *serial interface card*).

This type of card enables data transfer between two computers directly through a cable or through phone lines. Both the sender and receiver need a *modem* to communicate using phone lines. Modems convert computer signals into acoustical signals that can then be transmitted over telephone lines.

In addition to hardware, data communication requires software that controls the RS-232 card. BIOS offers this software in four functions called by interrupt 14H. Before discussing these functions in detail, let's examine data transfer protocol.

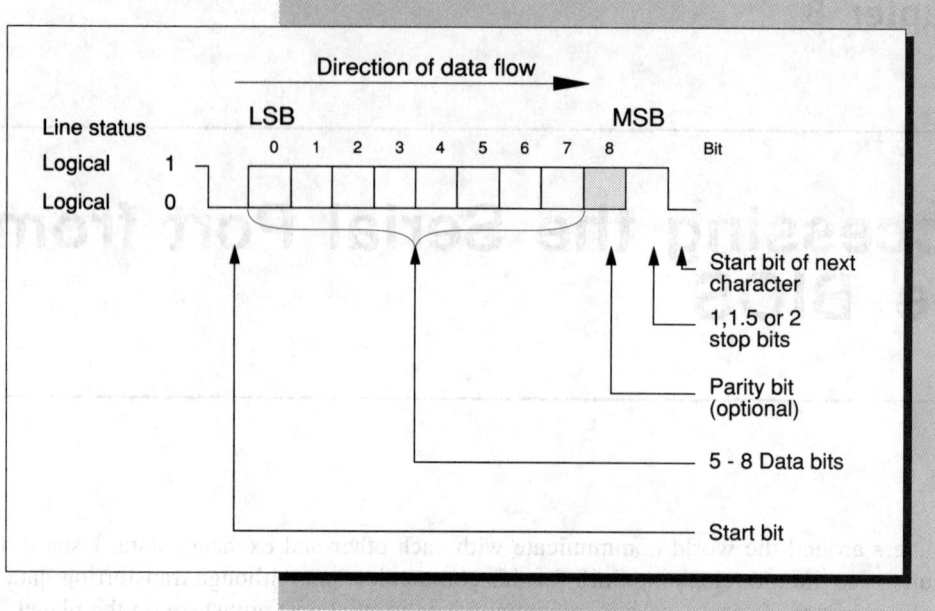

Asynchronous transmission protocol

Word length

As the previous figure shows, only the two line states, 0 and 1 (also called high and low), are important. The line remains high if data transmission doesn't occur. If the line's state changes to low, the receiver knows that data is being transmitted. Between 5 and 8 bits transfer over the line, depending on the *word length*. Unfortunately the BIOS functions only support a word length of 7 or 8 bits. If the line is low during data transmission, the bit to be sent is 0. High signals a set bit. The least significant bit is transferred first, and the most significant bit of the character to be transmitted is transferred last.

Parity

The character can be followed by a *parity bit*, which permits error detection during data transmission. Parity can be even or odd. For even parity, the parity bit augments the data word to be transmitted, so that an even number of bits results. For example, if the data word to be transmitted contains three bits set to 1, the parity bit becomes 1 so that the number of 1 bits increments to four, making an even number. If the data word contained an even number of 1 bits, the parity bit would be zero. For odd parity, the parity bit is set so that the total number of 1 bits is odd.

Stop bits

The *stop bits* signal the end of the data transmission. Data transmission protocol permits 1, 1.5, and 2 stop bits. Some users are confused by the option of working with 1.5 stop bits, since some believe that you can't divide a bit. The explanation for this paradox comes from the data transmission protocol.

Baud rate

Old standards dictate that data transfers at a rate of 300 *baud* (about 300 bits per second), and one stop bit. The signal for a 1 bit and the signal for a 0 bit are both *events*. When transmitted in an analog environment, binary bits, such as phone lines, cannot be identical to baud rates. Since stop bits always have the value 1, the line would be high for 1/300 second. If, instead, you keep the line high for 1/200 second, 1.5 bits are transmitted. The line remains high until a new character transfers and sets the line transmitting the start bit to low.

Some interfaces work with negative logic. In these instances, the conditions for 0 and 1 in the previous illustration must be reversed. However, this doesn't change the basic principle of serial transmission.

Protocol settings

Data transmission only works if the sender and receiver both match various protocol parameters. First the *baud rate* (the number of bits transmitted per second) must be set. The standard baud rates for data exchange over voice telephone lines are 300, 1200, and 2400 baud. These baud rates depend on the capabilities of the modem being used. For a dedicated (data only) telephone line or for direct data transmission through a cable, speeds up to 9600 baud are possible. Up to 80 bytes per second or 4800 bytes per minute can be transmitted at 9600 baud.

The *word length* depends on the data being transmitted. If the data consists of normal ASCII characters, a 7-bit word is sufficient since the ASCII character set has only 128 characters. If the data encompasses the complete PC set of 256 characters, 8-bit words are more useful.

Next, you must determine whether a *parity check* is necessary and whether even or odd parity should be used. In most cases, parity checking is recommended, since phone lines don't always transmit all data correctly. The parity selected isn't important as long as both sender and receiver select the same parity.

The number of *stop bits* must be defined. One stop bit transmits successive characters faster than a setting of two stop bits. However, two stop bits increase the reliability of transmission.

Sample protocol

The following illustration shows a sample transmission of an "A" character with a protocol of 8 data bits, odd parity, and one stop bit. Positive logic and a 300 baud transmission rate are assumed. Since the ASCII code of the "A" character is 65 (01000001(b)) and therefore contains only two 1 bits, the parity bit changes to 1 so that the number of 1 bits is set to an odd number.

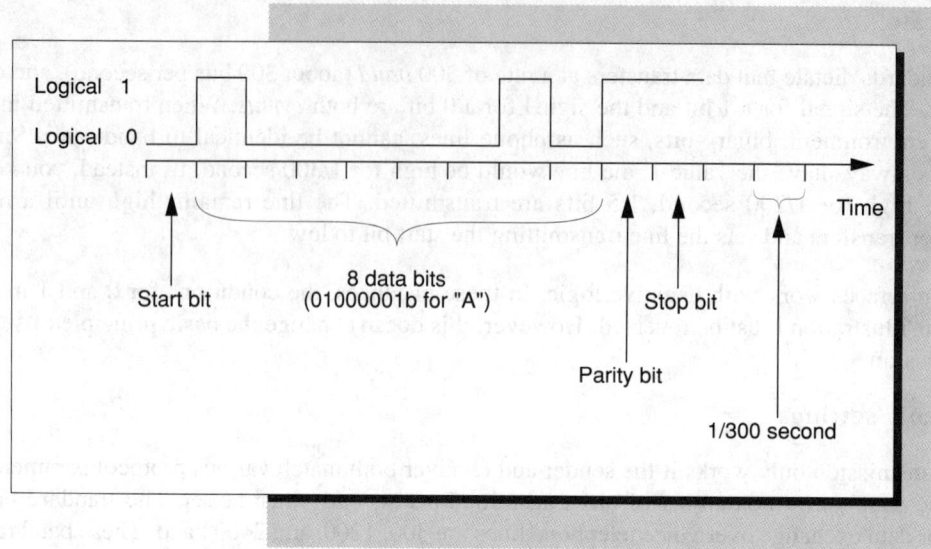

Transmitting A character: 8-bit word length, 1 stop bit, odd parity, and 300 baud

UART

The brain of an RS-232 card is the UART (Universal Asynchronous Receiver Transmitter). You should be familiar with the design and capabilities of this processor so that you can properly adapt programs to the error messages returned by the different BIOS functions.

Transfer registers

A character transmitted on a data line first passes to a register designated as a *transfer holding register*. The character remains there until processing on the character preceding it ends. Then the character moves to the *transfer shift register* from where the UART transmits the character bit by bit over the data line. Depending on the configuration, parity and stop bits implement the stream of data. When the BIOS function passes the status of the data lines to the AH register, bits 5 and 6 indicate whether these two registers are empty.

Receiver registers

The *receiver shift register* accepts received data, then transmits the data to the *receiver data register*, where the UART removes the parity and stop bits. If a previously received character is still in the data register, bit 1 of the line status is set to 1 to avoid overwriting. Bit 0 indicates that a character was received. If, while processing the character, the UART discovers that a parity error occurred during the transmission, it sets bit 2 of the line status. If a breakdown occurs in the agreed-upon protocol (number of parity and stop bits), bit 3 is set. The UART always sets bit 4 if the data line remains in low (0) status longer than required for the transmission of a character. Bit 7 signals a *time out* error. This occurs when the communication between the RS-232 card and the modem isn't working properly.

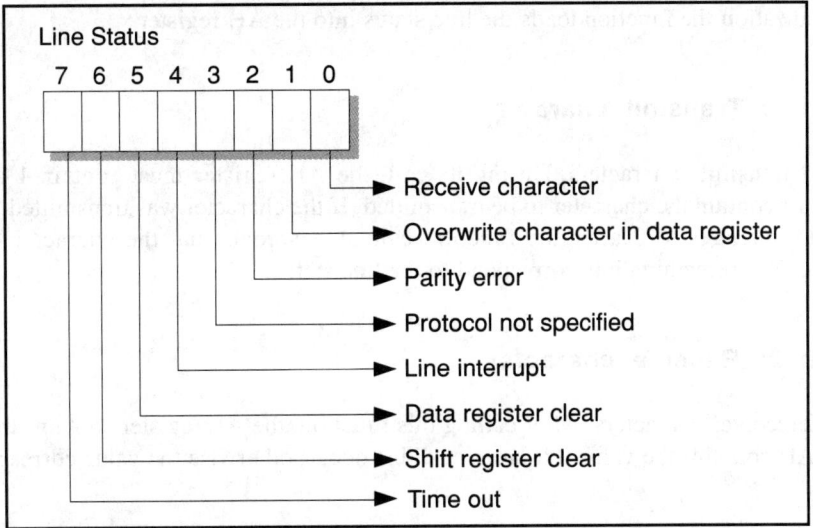

Function 0: Passing protocol

Before data can be transmitted or received, the UART must be informed of the number of stop bits, etc. Function 0 of interrupt 14H does this. The function number (0) enters the AH register, and the protocol passes to the AL register. The bits of the AL register indicate the various parameters:

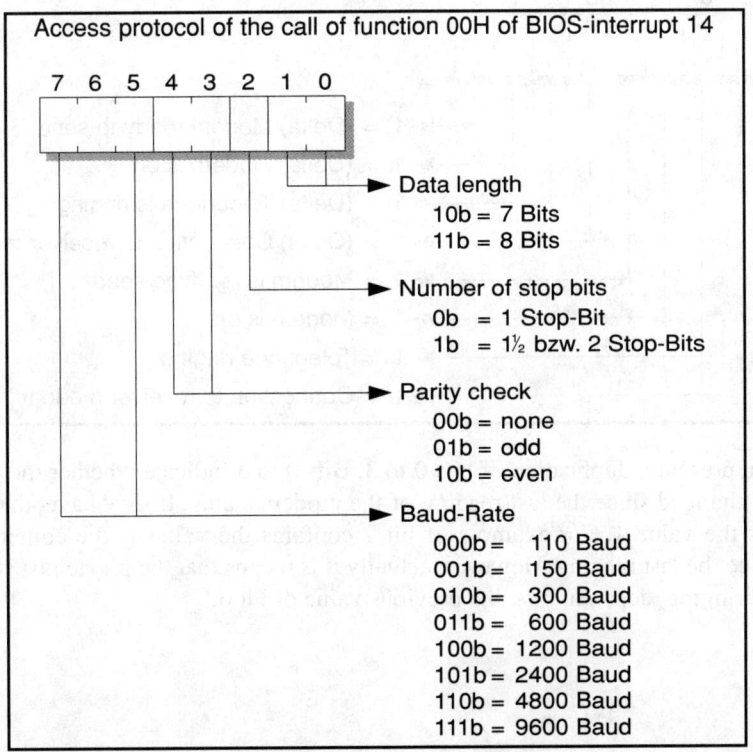

After initialization the function loads the line status into the AH register.

Function 1: Transmit character

Function 1 transmits characters. During its call, the AH register must contain 1 and the AL register must contain the character to be transmitted. If the character was transmitted, bit 7 of the AH register changes to 0 after the function call. A 1 signals that the character couldn't be transmitted. The remaining bits correspond to the line status.

Function 2: Receive character

Function 2 receives characters. After calling this function, the AL register contains the character received. AH contains the value 0 if an error didn't occur; otherwise the value corresponds to the line status.

Function 3: Line/modem status

Function 3 senses and returns the modem status and line status. It returns the line status in the AH register and the modem status in the AL register:

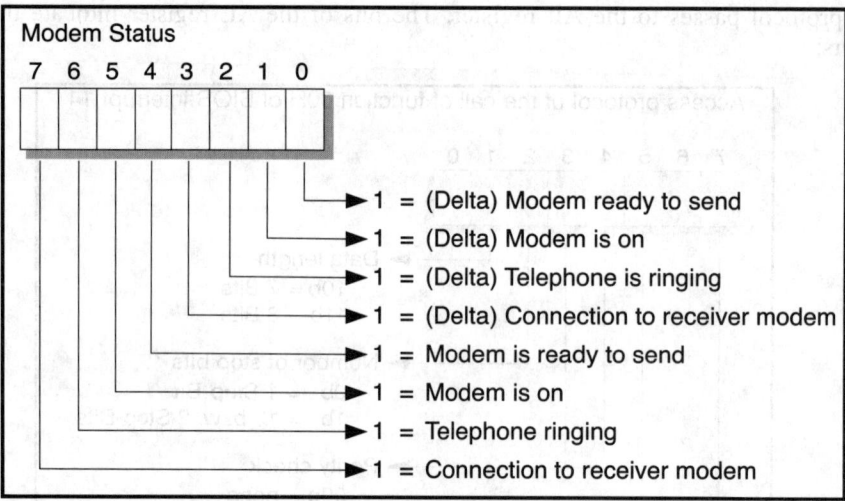

Bits 4 to 7 represent a duplication of bits 0 to 3. Bits 0 to 3 indicate whether the contents of bits 4 to 7 have changed since the last reading of the modem status. If they have, the corresponding bit contains the value 1. For example, if bit 2 contains the value 1, the contents of bit 6 has changed since the last reading. However, actually this means that the phone just started to ring or has stopped ringing, depending on the previous value of bit 6.

Chapter 9

Mouse Programming

A few years ago, using a mouse for PC applications was considered a luxury. Today most PCs have mice connected to them. One reason for the mouse's popularity is the development of new and more powerful video standards such as EGA, VGA, and Super VGA. These video cards helped advance graphical user interfaces, such as Microsoft Windows®. These interfaces are almost unusable without a mouse.

Applications and operating systems benefit from mouse support. Ventura Publisher® and Microsoft Works® both use the mouse extensively. Also, DOS Version 4.0 accepts mouse as well as keyboard input.

A software interface acts as the connection between a program and the mouse. Although Microsoft Corporation designed this interface for its own mice, other mouse manufacturers accept this interface as a standard. The interface was made available to the industry as a minimum standard to retain compatibility with the Microsoft mouse.

This function interface is usually installed either through a device driver that is loaded during system boot or through a terminate and stay resident (TSR) program, such as MOUSE.COM, that's included with the Microsoft mouse package.

9.1 Mouse Functions

Mouse functions can be accessed in the same way as DOS and BIOS functions (refer to Chapters 6 and 7 for more information on the techniques used for addressing DOS and BIOS functions). The individual functions can be called through interrupt 33H. The identification number of the function must be passed to the AX register. The other processor registers are used in various combinations to pass information to a function.

Although 53 different functions can be called in this way, most applications use only a few of these functions. Before we examine each function, let's look at the concepts behind the mouse interface. This will help you understand how the individual functions work. In our discussion, we deliberately concentrated on text oriented mouse control. Pixel oriented applications should use a graphical interface, such as the Windows API, because this interface provides friendlier functions for mouse input than the programming interface found in this chapter.

In the following table we've listed the functions found on mouse drivers up to and including Version 8.0. You'll find more than enough functions needed for mouse control in a text oriented application.

Fct.	Task	Ver.
00H*	Reset mouse driver	01
01H*	Display mouse cursor	01
02H*	Hide mouse cursor	01
03H*	Get cursor position/button status	01
04H*	Move mouse cursor	01
05H*	Determine number of times mouse button was activated	01
06H*	Determine number of times mouse button was released	01
07H*	Set horizontal range of movement	01
08H*	Set vertical range of movement	01
09H	Set mouse cursor (graphic mode)	01
0AH*	Set mouse cursor (text mode)	01
0BH*	Determine movement values	01
0CH*	Set event handler	01
0DH	Enable light pen emulation	01
0EH	Disable light pen emulation	01
0FH	Set cursor speed	01
10H*	Exclusion area	01
11H	Undocumented	01
12H	Undocumented	01
13H*	Set maximum for mouse speed doubling	01
14H	Exchange event handlers	01
15H	Determine mouse status buffer size	01
16H*	Store mouse status	01
17H*	Restore mouse status	01
18H*	Install alternate event handler	01
19H	Determine address of alternate event handler	01
1AH	Set mouse sensitivity	01
1BH	Determine mouse sensitivity	01
1CH	Set mouse hardware interrupt rate	01
1DH*	Set display page	01
1EH*	Determine display page	01
1FH	Disable mouse driver	01
20H	Enable mouse driver	01
21H	Reset mouse driver	01
22H	Set language for messages	01
23H	Get language number	01
24H	Determine mouse type	01
25H	Get general driver information	06
26H	Get maximum virtual coordinates	06
27H*	Get masks and mickey counts	7A
28H	Set video mode	07
29H	Count video modes	07

Fct.	Task	Ver.
2AH	Get cursor hotspot	7B
2BH	Set acceleration curves	07
2CH	Read acceleration curves	07
2DH	Set/get active acceleration curves	07
2EH	Undocumented	01
2FH	Mouse hardware reset	7B
30H	Set/get ballpoint information	7C
31H	Get minimum/maximum virtual coordinates	7D
32H	Get active advanced functions	7D
33H	Get switch settings	7D
34H	Get MOUSE.INI location	08

Legend:
* = Commonly used function (detailed in this chapter)
01 = Version 1.0 and up   7B = Version 7.02 and up
06 = Version 6.26 and up   7C = Version 7.04 and up
07 = Version 7.0 and up   7D = Version 7.05 and up
7A = Version 7.01 and up   08 = Version 8.0 and up

About mouse buttons

Unlike the keyboard, which has many keys and keyboard codes for each key, a PC mouse usually has two or even three mouse buttons. These buttons enable the user to select data in an application program.

The mouse buttons are also used to move the mouse cursor on the screen. The actual position of the mouse cursor on the screen is important. The mouse driver software always interprets the cursor's location on the screen relative to a virtual graphic screen. This virtual screen's resolution depends on the video mode and video card currently being used.

Since this virtual graphic display screen is also used within the text modes to determine the mouse's position and forms the basis for communication with the mouse interface, a conversion occurs between the graphic coordinates and the mouse cursor's line/column position. Since every column or line corresponds to eight pixels, the graphic coordinates must be either be divided by eight or shifted three places to the left in binary mode, which mathematically produces the same result. However, the processor performs the shifting much faster than it can perform the actual division.

About the mouse cursor

The mouse cursor shows the mouse's relative location on the screen. The cursor's shape can vary depending on the application and it can even change its appearance within an application. Word processors often display the mouse cursor as a block, similar to the text cursor. In text mode, the application can only determine the starting and ending line of the cursor. The cursor's size depends on the current character matrix and video mode. The options for creating a software cursor are more complicated because two 16-bit values, called the *screen mask* and *cursor mask*, determine the cursor's appearance.

The mouse driver must determine the appearance of the cursor each time the cursor's position on the screen changes. The cursor mask and screen mask values are linked with the two bytes that describe the character code and the character color within video RAM. This linkage occurs in two steps. First the character code and the attribute byte are combined with screen mask through a binary AND. The result of this connection is then combined with the cursor mask through an exclusive OR. The result then appears on the screen.

This type of combination provides numerous options for changing the cursor's appearance. Four of the most common cursor options are:

- Pointer appears as one specific character in one specific color.

- Pointer appears as one specific character, but the color changes when the cursor overlaps a character (e.g., inverse video).

- Pointer appears as one specific character, but the character color changes when the cursor overlaps a character.

- Pointer appears as one specific character, but character color changes to a variant of the character color when the cursor overlaps a character.

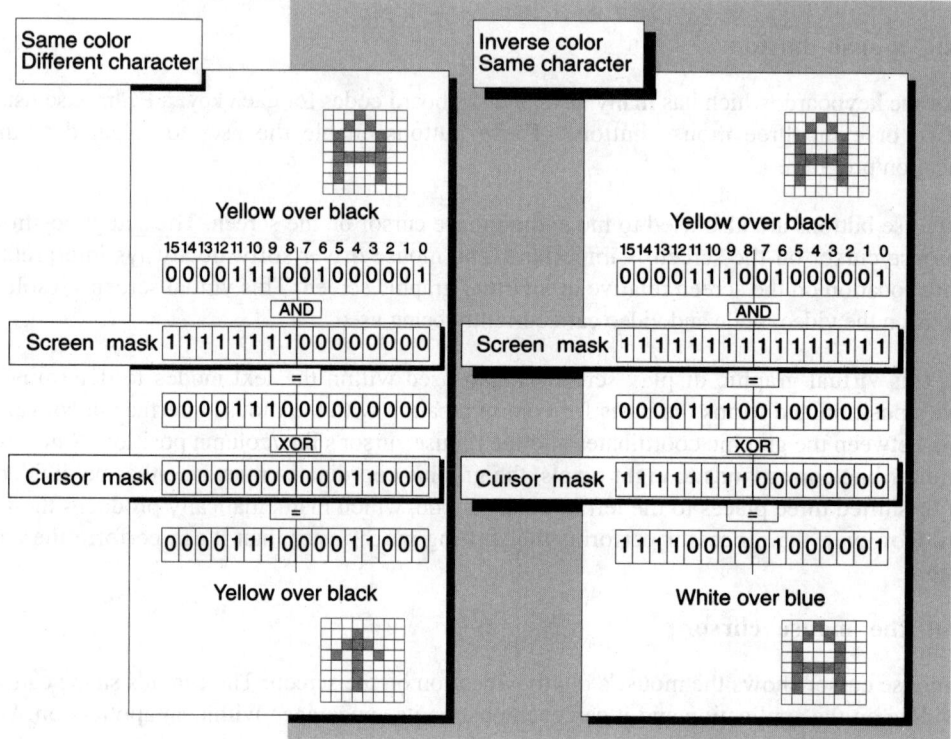

Formation of mouse cursor by combination of current character, cursor and screen mask

The standard measurement unit in the mouse interface is the *mickey*, which is named after Mickey Mouse®. Originally one mickey equaled 1/200". This measurement applies to older systems, which have a resolution of 200 pixels per inch. Newer mice and video cards have mickey measurements of 400 mickeys per inch. Although the mouse driver compensates for additional pixel information, we'll use this as the measurement standard in this chapter.

Function 00H: **Reset mouse driver**

A program should call the function 00H before calling any of the mouse functions. This function resets the mouse driver. It can also determine whether a mouse and mouse driver exist by examining the content of the AX register after the function call. If the AX register contains the value 0000H after the function call, a mouse driver wasn't installed. Even if a mouse is connected, the mouse driver no longer exists. If a mouse driver and mouse exist, function 00H returns the value FFFFH in the AX register. The BX register contains the number of buttons on the mouse. As we mentioned earlier, PC mice usually have two mouse buttons, although some mice have three buttons. Since very few applications need or use three buttons, usually you'll only need two buttons.

Function 00H resets the numerous mouse parameters to their default values. The mouse cursor moves to the center of the screen. The cursor mask and screen mask are defined so that the cursor appears as an inverse video rectangle. Video page 0 is selected as the default page on which the cursor appears. The cursor disappears from the screen immediately.

Function 01H: **Display mouse cursor**

Function 01H displays the cursor on the screen. Load the function number into the AX register; additional parameters aren't needed. Since the mouse driver follows the movement of the mouse even when the mouse cursor has been disabled, the mouse cursor may not reappear at the position where it was when it disappeared.

Function 02H: **Remove mouse cursor**

Function 02H removes the mouse cursor from the screen. Load the function number into the AX register; additional parameters aren't needed. The calls between functions 01H and 02H must be performed in the proper sequence in order to be effective. For example, calling function 02H twice in succession means that you must also call function 01H twice in succession to return the cursor to the screen.

Functions 01H and 02H aren't used very often. Usually, you simply must call function 00H and function 01H at the beginning of a program and call function 02H at the end of the program. These functions are frequently used when the application program writes characters directly into video RAM, bypassing the slow DOS and BIOS display routines. Avoid writing characters over the mouse cursor; otherwise the following will occur:

1)   The mouse cursor disappears if overwritten by another character.

2)   The mouse driver produces the wrong character on the screen when the user moves the mouse cursor. Before the cursor appears at a certain position on the screen, it records the character that occupied this position until now. This character is restored to the old position as soon as the cursor moves to another position on the screen. During a direct write access to video RAM, the driver doesn't record that a new character was output at the position of the cursor. So, the old (and incorrect) character is displayed on the screen while the cursor is moved.

To prevent this from happening, remove the cursor before character output and return the old character to the screen. The new character will be stored when the cursor is restored to the screen. However, don't do this for every character output because it slows the system down and negates the advantages of direct access to video RAM. We recommend removing the cursor once from the screen before extensive output, such as construction of a screen window. After the operation, the cursor can be restored on the screen.

Even though the DOS and BIOS character output functions write their output directly to video RAM, you shouldn't worry about programming the cursor when working with these functions. During installation, the mouse driver moved interrupt vector 10H, which handles BIOS and DOS screen output, to its own routine. So, the driver can then display or disable the cursor as needed.

Function 04H: Move mouse cursor

With function 04H you can move the mouse cursor to a specific location on the screen without moving the mouse. Pass the function number to the AX register, the new horizontal coordinate (column) to the CX register, and the new vertical coordinate (line) to the DX register. Remember that these coordinates, like all other functions, must be relative to the virtual screen. Text coordinates must be multiplied by eight (or shifted left three binary places) before they can be passed to function 04H. The coordinates must be located inside a screen area designated as the mouse's range of movement.

Function 00H sets the complete range of the mouse's movement to the entire screen area. Functions 07H and 08H limit this range to a smaller area.

Function 07H & 08H: Set range of movement

Function 07H specifies the horizontal range of movement. Pass the function number to the AX register, the minimum X-coordinate to the CX register, and the maximum X-coordinate to the DX register.

Function 08H specifies the vertical range of movement. Pass the function number to the AX register, the minimum Y-coordinate to the CX register and the maximum Y-coordinate to the DX register.

After calling these functions, the mouse driver automatically moves the cursor within the range, unless it's already within the indicated borders. The user cannot move the cursor outside this range.

Function 10H: Exclusion area

Besides the area of movement allotted to the cursor, the mouse driver also provides an exclusion area. When the user moves the cursor into this section of the screen, the mouse cursor becomes invisible. The mouse cursor becomes visible again as soon as the user moves the cursor away from the exclusion area. This area is undefined after the call of function 00H. It can be defined at any time by calling function 10H, but the mouse driver can control only one exclusion area at a time. The coordinates of the exclusion area are passed to function 10H in the CX:DX and SI:DI register pairs. These register pairs specify the upper-left corner and lower-right corner respectively. CX and SI accept the X-coordinate, and DX and DI accept the Y-coordinate.

The exclusion area and function 02H perform special tasks during direct access to video RAM. Although function 02H removes the cursor from the screen, this can occur in conjunction with function 10H only if the cursor is already within the exclusion area, or if the user moves the cursor within the exclusion area. This makes function 10H useful when creating large display areas (e.g., a window). This allows the cursor to remain on the screen as long as it isn't within this exclusion area.

The exclusion area can be removed by calling function 01H or function 00H. Function 01H makes the cursor visible automatically if it's already within the exclusion area.

Function 1DH: Set display page

Function 1DH sets the display page on which the cursor appears. This function is needed only if the program switches a display page other than the current one to the foreground through direct video card programming. Pass the number of the display page to the BX register. When BIOS interrupt 10H activates a display page, this function can be omitted because the mouse driver will automatically adapt to the change.

Function 0FH: Set cursor speed

Two parameters determine the speed at which the mouse cursor moves on the screen. These parameters specify the relationship between the distance of a cursor movement and the pixels traversed in the virtual mouse display screen. Function 0FH allows the user to set these parameters for horizontal and vertical movement. The parameters are passed in the CX and DX registers (horizontal and vertical, respectively). These numbers indicate the number of mickeys, which correspond to eight pixels in the virtual mouse display screen. These pixels correspond to one line or column in the text mode display screen.

The default values after calling function 00H are 8 horizontal mickeys and 16 vertical mickeys. In text mode, the cursor moves one column after the cursor is moved 8 mickeys horizontally. A jump to the next line occurs only after the cursor is moved 16 mickeys vertically.

Usually these settings can be used as default values because they work with all resolutions in text mode. This function also enables you to make the cursor movement faster or slower.

Function 0AH: Set cursor shape

Function 0AH determines the appearance of the cursor in text mode. The cursor mask and screen mask previously mentioned are determining factors of the cursor's appearance in text mode. Pass 0AH to the AX register and the value determining the cursor's shape to the BX register.

Software-specific cursor

If the BX register contains the value 0, the mouse driver selects the cursor as specified by the software. The screen mask number must be loaded into the CX register and the cursor mask number must be loaded into the DX register. These numbers indicate the addresses from which the mouse driver can access cursor shape parameters.

Hardware-specific cursor

If the BX register contains the value 1, the mouse driver selects the cursor as specified by the hardware. The starting line of the hardware cursor must be loaded into the CX register, and the ending line must be loaded into the DX register.

Video mode and cursor size

Remember that the allowable values for the starting line and ending line depend on the video mode currently in use:

- • The monochrome display adapter accepts values from 0 to 13.
- • The color graphics adapter accepts only values from 0 to 7.
- • EGA and VGA cards accept values from 0 to 7. The EGA/VGA BIOS automatically adapts the number selected to the size of the character matrix currently in use.

The functions we've discussed set the various parameters that control the mouse driver. The mouse driver also supports a group of functions that read the mouse's position as well as the status of the mouse buttons. These functions can be divided into two categories for reading external devices, such as the mouse, keyboard, printer, or disk drives. These categories are the *polling method* and the *interrupt method*. The mouse driver supports both of these methods.

Polling method

The polling method constantly reads a device within a loop. This loop terminates only when the desired event occurs. Since the execution of this loop requires the full capabilities of the CPU, usually there isn't enough time left to perform other tasks.

Interrupt method

The interrupt method has an advantage over the polling method because it allows the CPU to execute other tasks until the desired event occurs. Once this happens, the mouse driver calls an interrupt routine that reacts to the event and executes further instructions.

Function 03H: Get cursor position/button status

The polling method provides four functions that operate in conjunction with the mouse interface. These functions can be accessed through function 03H, which returns the current cursor position and mouse button status. Function 03H passes the horizontal cursor position to the CX register and the vertical cursor position to the DX register. Since these coordinates also refer to the virtual mouse screen, they must be converted to the text screen's coordinate system by dividing the components by eight, or by shifting the bits three binary places to the right.

The following table shows how the mouse button status is returned to the BX register. Only the three lowest bits represent the status of one of the two or three mouse buttons. The bit for the corresponding mouse button contains the value 1 when the user presses that mouse button during the function call.

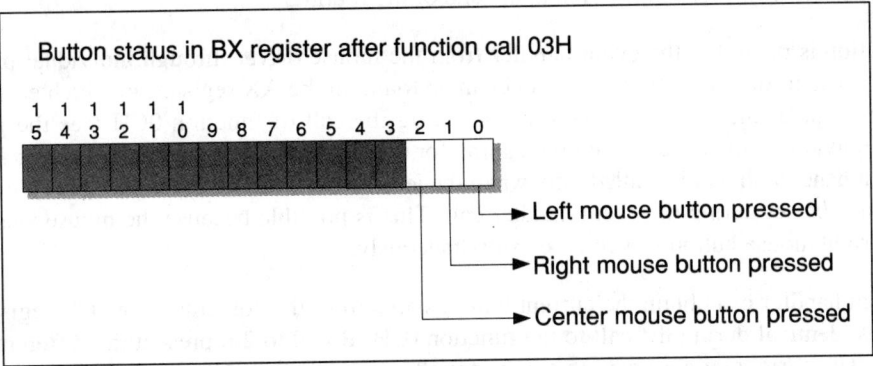

Function 0CH: **Set event handler**

Function 0CH sets the address of a mouse *event handler* (interrupt routine). The function number must be passed to the AX register. The segment and offset address of the event handler must be passed to the ES:DX register pair. The event mask must be passed to the CX register. The individual bits of this flag determine the conditions under which the event handler should be called. The following table shows the CX register coding:

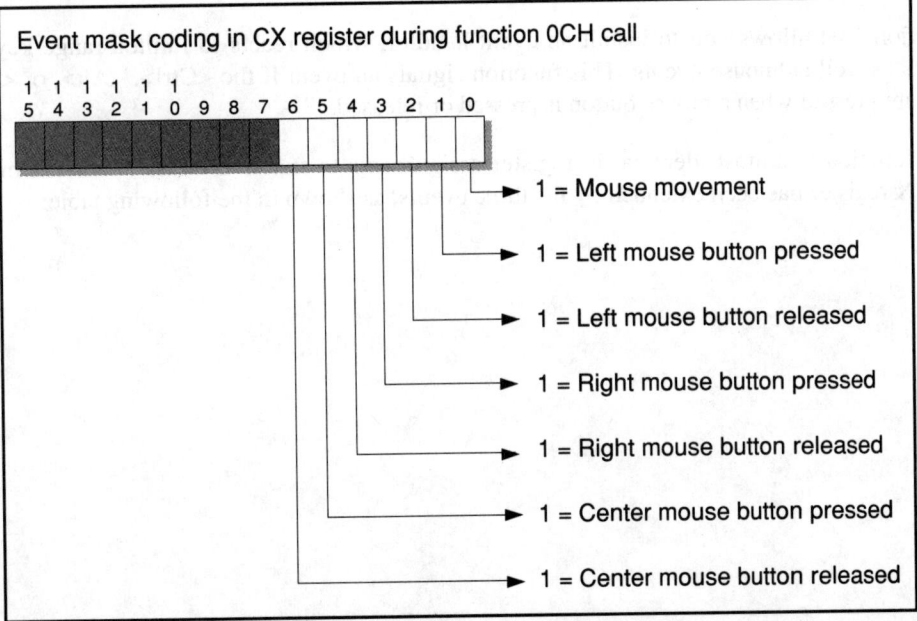

After executing the function, the mouse driver calls the event handler as soon as at least one of the specified events occurs. The call is made using the FAR call instead of the INT instruction.

This difference is important to remember when developing an event handler, because the handler must be ended with a FAR RET instruction instead of an IRET instruction. Similar to an interrupt routine, none of the various processor registers can be changed when they're returned to the caller. For this reason, the registers must be stored on the stack immediately after the call and the register contents must be restored at the end of the routine.

Information is passed to the event handler from the mouse driver through individual processor registers. The information about the event can be found in the AX register, in which each bit has the same significance as in the event mask during the call of function 0CH (see the previous table). Individual bits, which have no meaning for the event handler, may be set. For example, if the event handler should be called only when the left mouse button is activated (bit 1), bits 0 and 4 may also be set during the event handler call. This is possible because the mouse was moved and the right mouse button was released simultaneously.

The event handler can obtain the current button status from the contents of the CX register. The coding is identical during the call to the function 03H. Bits 0 to 2 represent the different mouse buttons. The current cursor position can be found in the CX and DX registers, which represent the horizontal and vertical positions. The position can only be set after conversion to the text screen's coordinate system.

During the development of an event handler, the DS register should point to the data segment of the mouse driver during the handler call, instead of the interrupted program. If the event handler accesses its own data segment, it must first load its address into the DS register.

Function 18H: Install alternate event handler

Function 18H allows you to install an event handler, which reacts to limited-range keyboard events as well as mouse events. This function signals an event if the <Ctrl>, <Alt>, or <Shift> keys are pressed when a mouse button is pressed or released.

This function is almost identical in register assignments to function 0CH. The event mask in the CX register has been extended by the three events, as shown in the following table:

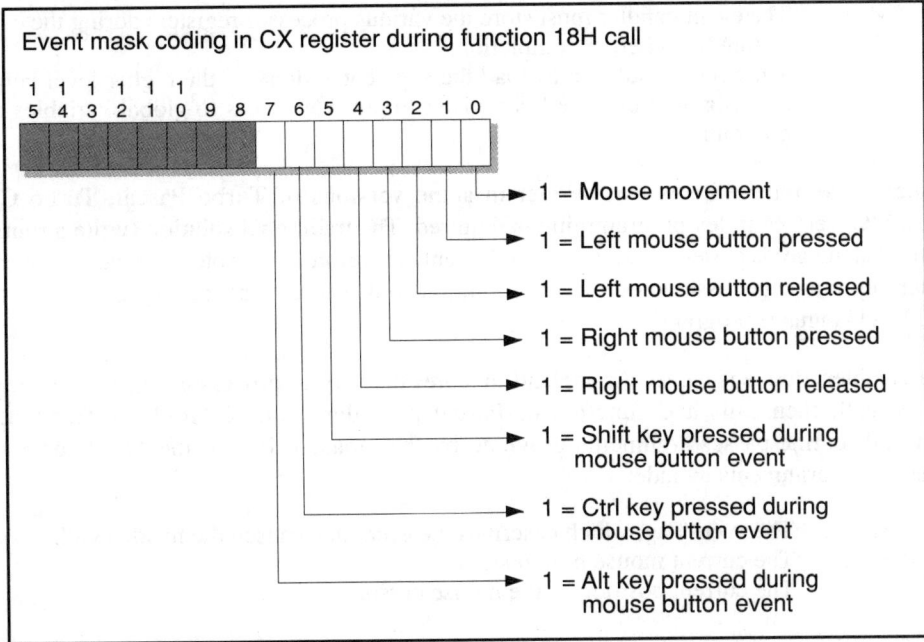

Event mask coding in CX register during function 18H call

```
1 1 1 1 1
5 4 3 2 1 0 9 8 7 6 5 4 3 2 1 0
```

1 = Mouse movement

1 = Left mouse button pressed

1 = Left mouse button released

1 = Right mouse button pressed

1 = Right mouse button released

1 = Shift key pressed during mouse button event

1 = Ctrl key pressed during mouse button event

1 = Alt key pressed during mouse button event

Even during the call of such an alternative event handler, little changes in comparison with the event handlers that were installed by calling function 0CH. Only the content of the AX register must be interpreted differently, since its construction corresponds to the event mask previously shown.

Up to three alternative event handlers can be installed by calling function 18H. During the function 0CH call, the event handler indicated replaces the previously installed handler. Three different event handlers can be installed by calling function 18H three times. This is only valid if the three event handlers are equipped with different event masks. If an event mask passes to function 18H, which is already equipped with a handler, the new handler replaces the existing handler.

9.2 Demonstration Programs

This section contains programs in C and Turbo Pascal that demonstrate mouse access functions. These programs show the techniques for developing and installing an event handler, which is the most complicated part of mouse reading. Both programs include functions or procedures that call various mouse functions. These routines require little programming; they load the processor registers with the necessary values, then call interrupt 33H. Since the event handler needs the most programming, we'll discuss this in detail.

Installing an event handler in a higher level language program is difficult because it must meet certain requirements, which usually cannot be controlled by a programmer. The requirements are as follows:

- The event handler must be a FAR procedure, and must be terminated with a FAR RET instruction.

- The event handler must store the various processor registers during the call and restore them before completion.
- The event handler must load the segment address of the higher level language data segment into the DS register to provide access to global variables of the program.

Although these requirements can be met in some versions of Turbo Pascal, Turbo C, and Microsoft C, very complex programming is required. The traditional solution (write a routine in assembly language) is easier and faster to implement. Therefore, we wrote the event handler itself in assembly language, assembled the program, and linked the resulting object module to the higher level language program.

This assembler routine is named AssmHand. It stores the various processor registers on the stack after the call, then calls a C function or Pascal procedure named MouEventHandler. The AssmHand routine passes arguments provided by the mouse driver to the MouEventHandler routine. These arguments include:

- The event flag, which describes the event that caused the handler call.
- The current mouse button status.
- The current position of the mouse cursor.

This information is converted from virtual graphic screen coordinates into text screen coordinates (25 lines x 80 columns).

The stack handles parameter passing. The C version of AssmHand must pass the arguments onto the stack in the reverse order of their declaration. After loading the DS register and calling the higher level language routine, these arguments must be taken from the stack again by incrementing the stack cursor by the memory requirements of the arguments (8 bytes). This is only required for the C version of the routine. The Turbo Pascal version performs this task on its own.

After calling this routine, the AssmHand routine returns the processor registers to the stack and passes control to the caller using a FAR RET instruction.

The AssmHand instructions execute very quickly, but the handler itself may require more execution time than expected. This introduces the problem of recursion, since an event in connection with the mouse may recur during the handler execution. The AssmHand driver then must be recalled before the previous call is terminated.

To avoid this situation and the complications that can occur, AssmHand maintains a variable named active in its code segment. During execution this variable contains the value 1. Before setting this variable, the program tests if active already contains the value 1. This indicates that the last call wasn't completed yet. If this situation occurs, the handler execution terminates immediately, thus avoiding recursion.

Even if this method avoids recursion problems, remember that it can produce its own problems. The suppression of the higher level language handler doesn't notice the event, because the handler wasn't called by the mouse driver. Although we offer the recursion trap as an option, we recommend that you program the higher level language handler as efficiently as possible to avoid using processor time. This will keep call suppression to a minimum.

The AssmHand handler

AssmHand must first be installed through function 0CH, using the MouISetEventHandler procedure/function. MouISetEventHandler is called by the MouInit procedure/function, which initializes the mouse module. This should be called by any application program as the first procedure/function of this module. The number of lines and columns of the display screen must be passed to it as arguments, to determine the size of an internal buffer needed for the various procedure/functions within the module.

This buffer can divide the screen into individual mouse ranges, each equipped with its own code, cursor mask, and screen mask. These mouse ranges are very important in mouse access. They permit the definition of objects such as sliders, command buttons, or menu items. As soon as the user moves the cursor to an object and presses a mouse button, the object executes a particular step in the program.

MouDefRange defines these ranges. The registration of these ranges occurs through the procedure/function MouDefRange, which must receive a cursor to a vector or array, and the number of elements stored there. These elements of the type RANGE describe a screen area and the cursor or screen mask assigned to the cursor as soon as it reaches this area. An area can comprise a single character or the entire screen. The user can define the array with individual area descriptors. The area code depends on the position of the descriptor within the array, and is provided automatically by the procedure/function MouDefRange. The first area has the value 0, the second the value 1, etc. The screen areas not covered by an area descriptor are assigned the code NO_RANGE.

During the creation of this array, especially during the definition of the cursor and screen mask in the PtrMask array, the C implementation provides helpful macros and constants. The Pascal program has functions and constants available for this purpose. The creation of a variable of the type PTRVIEW, stored in the PtrMask field within an area descriptor, is handled by the macro or function MouPtrMask. The cursor and screen mask for the character must be passed to MouPtrMask to define the cursor's appearance on the screen.

If PtrSameChar is indicated, the cursor appears as the character that it covers. If another cursor is desired, the cursor can be defined with PtrDifChar. When the call occurs, enter the ASCII code of the desired character for PtrDifChar.

As a second parameter, MouPtrMask receives the cursor's color from the cursor mask and screen mask. Many options for color are possible:

- PtrSameCol ensures that the cursor assumes the color of the character currently overlapped by the cursor.
- PtrSameColB creates a cursor that assumes the color of the character currently overlapped. However, bit 7 of the attribute byte is set to 1 so that the character either blinks or appears with a high-intensity background color.
- PtrInvCol makes the cursor appear in the inverse color of the character currently overlapped by the cursor.
- PtrDifCol displays the cursor on the screen in the color indicated by the code following PtrDifCol.

In addition to the different mouse areas specified through MouDefRange, a cursor can be assigned to the remaining screen, which is the area carrying the code NO_RANGE. A program can use MouSetDefaultPtr to obtain the cursor and screen mask of the cursor as a parameter of type PTRVIEW. The constants and macros or functions previously described can be used to create this parameter.

Changing the mouse cursor

The MouEventHandler changes the cursor and screen mask for each area. Since it's called for every mouse event (including mouse movement), it can determine the mouse area where the cursor is currently located. To make this happen as fast as possible, it tests if the mouse area contains the position of the cursor.

MouEventHandler uses the internal region buffer that was created by MouInit during the call. It reflects exactly the video RAM structure, and contains one byte for every screen position. Each byte contains the code of the area to which the screen position was assigned. The event handler can use the current position of the cursor as an index to this area buffer. A single memory access is enough to determine the mouse area in which the cursor is located. The area code found is stored in the global variable MouRng, and is used as an index to the array of the mouse descriptor from which it determines the cursor and screen mask for this area.

The higher level language event handler has another assignment that may be even more important. It controls the variable MouEvent, in which the current mouse events are stored. This task cannot be performed by simply copying the mouse events that were passed through AssmHand from the mouse driver. This only shows the current event, but no preceding events. If the user presses and holds the left mouse button, then presses the right mouse button, this results in two event handler calls. This signals each case of an active mouse button. The preceding call (the active left mouse button) is no longer recognized by the call, since it reports only the current event (the depressed right mouse button).

The event handler must isolate the various events that are reflected in the EvFlags variable, and accept only new events in the MouEvent variable. This variable reflects the current status of the mouse buttons, and the cursor's current movement or position. MouEvent can handle the most important mouse sensing tasks, waiting for the occurrence of a certain event (usually a pressed mouse button).

MouEventWait waits for the occurrence of an event, which was specified by the bitmask that was passed earlier. This bitmask can be defined through the logical OR function with the following constants:

EV_MOU_MOVE	Mouse movement
EV_LEFT_PRESS	Left mouse button pressed
EV_LEFT_REL	Left mouse button released
EV_RIGHT_PRESS	Right mouse button pressed
EV_RIGHT_REL	Right mouse button released

The procedure/function can be instructed to wait for one or more of these events to occur. The AND or OR correspond to the logical comparisons of the same names. Which events occur can be sensed through the results of a bitmask in which the individual bits represent the various events, and through which the constants previously described can be sensed.

Pascal listing: MOUSEP.PAS

```
{*****************************************************************}
{*                   M O U S E P . P A S                       *}
{*-------------------------------------------------------------*}
{*   Task       : Demonstrates the different functions available*}
{*               in mouse programming.                         *}
{*-------------------------------------------------------------*}
{*   Author     : Michael Tischer                             *}
{*   Developed on : 04/21/89                                   *}
{*   Last update : 01/10/92                          •        *}
{*****************************************************************}

uses Dos;                              { Add DOS unit }

{$L mousepa}                           { Link assembler module }
                                       { Adjust path to your system needs }
{== Declaration of external functions ===========================}

{$F+}                                  { FAR function }
procedure AssmHand; external ;         { Assembler event handler }
{$F-}                                  { FAR functions no longer accessible }

{== Constants ===================================================}

const

{-- Event codes --------------------------------------------------}

   EV_MOU_MOVE   = 1;                  { Mouse movement }
   EV_LEFT_PRESS = 2;                  { Left mouse button pressed }
   EV_LEFT_REL   = 4;                  { Left mouse button released }
   EV_RIGHT_PRESS = 8;                 { Right mouse button pressed }
   EV_RIGHT_REL  = 16;                 { Right mouse button released }
   EV_MOU_ALL    = 31;                 { All mouse events }

   LBITS         = 6;                  { EV_LEFT_PRESS or EV_LEFT_REL }
   RBITS         = 24;                 { EV_RIGHT_PRESS or EV_RIGHT_REL }

   NO_RANGE      = 255;                { Mouse cursor not in xy range }

   PtrSameChar   = $00ff;             { Same character }
   PtrSameCol    = $00ff;             { Same color }
   PtrInvCol     = $7777;             { Inverse color }
   PtrSameColB   = $807f;             { Same color, blinking }
   PtrInvColB    = $F777;             { Inverse color, blinking }

   EAND          = 0;                  { Event comparisons for MouEventWait }
   EVOR          = 1;

   CRLF          = #13#10;             { CR/LF }

{== Type declarations ===========================================}

type FNCTPTR  = longint;               { Address of a FAR function }
     PTRVIEW  = longint;               { Mask for mouse cursor }
     RANGE    = record                 { Describes a mouse range }
                  x1,                  { Upper left and lower }
                  y1,                  { right coordinates for }
                  x2,                  { the specified range }
                  y2   : byte;
                  PtrMask : PTRVIEW;    { Mask for mouse cursor }
                end;
     RNGARRAY = array [0..100] of RANGE;
```

```
     RNGPTR  = ^RNGARRAY;
     PTRREC  = record                  { Allows access to any }
                 Ofs : word;           { mouse cursor record }
                 Seg : word;           { existing }
               end;
     PTRVREC = record                  { Allows access to }
                 ScreenMask : word;    { PTRVIEW }
                 CursorMask : word;
               end;
     RNGBUF  = array [0..10000] of byte; { Range buffer }
     BBPTR   = ^RNGBUF;                 { Pointer to a range buffer }

{== Global variables ============================================}

var NumRanges,                         { Number of ranges }
    TLine,                             { Number of text lines }
    TCol      : byte;                  { Number of text columns }
    MouAvail  : boolean;               { TRUE if mouse is available }
    OldPtr,                            { Old mouse cursor appearances }
    StdPtr    : PTRVIEW;               { Mask for default mouse cursor }
    BufPtr    : BBPTR;                 { Pointer to range recognition buffer }
    ActRngPtr : RNGPTR;                { Pointer to current range vector }
    BLen      : integer;               { Range buffer length in bytes }
    ExitOld   : pointer;               { Pointer to old exit procedure }

{-- Variables which are loaded into mouse handler on every call ------}

    MouRng,                            { Current mouse range }
    MouCol,                            { Mouse column (text screen) }
    MouRow    : byte;                  { Mouse line (text screen) }
    MouEvent  : integer;               { Event mask }

{-- Variables which load with any occurrence of expected events ------}

    EvRng,                             { Range in which the mouse can be found }
    EvCol,                             { Mouse column }
    EvRow : byte;                      { Mouse line }

{*****************************************************************}
{* MouPtrMask: Executes cursor mask and screen mask from a bitmap *}
{*             containing character and color.                 *}
{*-------------------------------------------------------------*}
{* Input  : Chars = Bitmask of character as found in cursor mask *}
{*                  and screen mask                            *}
{*          Color = Bitmask of character color as found in     *}
{*                  cursor mask and screen mask                *}
{* Output : Cursor mask and screen mask as a value of typ PtrView *}
{* Info:   The constants PtrSameChar, PtrSameCol, PtrSameColB,  *}
{*         PtrInvCol, PtrInvColB, and the results of the PtrDifChar*}
{*         and PtrDifCol functions also control character & color *}
{*****************************************************************}

function MouPtrMask( Chars, Color : word ) : PTRVIEW;

var Mask : PTRVIEW;    { For creating cursor mask and screen mask }

begin
  PTRVREC( Mask ).ScreenMask := ( ( Color and $ff ) shl 8 ) +
                                ( Chars and $ff );
  PTRVREC( Mask ).CursorMask := ( Color and $ff00 ) + ( Chars shr 8 );
  MouPtrMask := Mask;                  { Return mask to caller }
end;

{*****************************************************************}
```

```
{*  PtrDifChar: Defines character structure of cursor and screen    *}
{*              masks in conjunction with character.                 *}
{**----------------------------------------------------------------**}
{*  Input  : ASCII code of the character on which cursor is based    *}
{*  Output : Cursor and screen masks for this cursor                 *}
{*  Info:    Function result should be computed with the help of the *}
{*           MouPtrMask function                                     *}
{*******************************************************************}

function PtrDifChar( Chars : byte ) : word;

begin
  PtrDifChar := Chars shl 8;
end;


{*******************************************************************}
{*  PtrDifCol: Creates the character segment of the cursor and screen*}
{*             masks in conjunction with the mouse cursor color.     *}
{**----------------------------------------------------------------**}
{*  Input  : Character color on which the mouse cursor will be based *}
{*  Output : cursor and screen masks for this color                  *}
{*  Info:    The function's result should be computed with the help  *}
{*           of the MouPtrMask function                              *}
{*******************************************************************}

function PtrDifCol( Color : byte ) : word;

begin
  PtrDifCol := Color shl 8;
end;


{*******************************************************************}
{*  MouDefinePtr: Assigns the mouse driver the cursor mask and       *}
{*                screen mask, from which the driver can create the  *}
{*                mouse cursor.                                       *}
{**----------------------------------------------------------------**}
{*  Input  : Mask = The cursor and screen mask as a parameter of     *}
{*                  type PTRVIEW                                      *}
{*  Info:    - The mask parameter should be created with the help of *}
{*             the MouPtrMask function                               *}
{*           - Most significant 16 bits represent the screen mask,   *}
{*             least significant 16 bits represent cursor mask       *}
{*******************************************************************}

procedure MouDefinePtr( Mask : PTRVIEW );

var Regs : Registers;         { Processor registers for interrupt call }

begin
  if OldPtr <> Mask then              { Mask change since last call? }
    begin                                              { Yes }
      Regs.AX := $000a;        { Funct. no.: Set text cursor type }
      Regs.BX := 0;               { Create software cursor }
      Regs.CX := PTRVREC( Mask ).ScreenMask;   { Low word is AND mask }
      Regs.DX := PTRVREC( Mask ).CursorMask; { High word is XOR mask }
      Intr( $33, Regs);                  { Call mouse driver }
      OldPtr := Mask;                 { Reserve new bitmask }
    end;
end;


{*******************************************************************}
{*  MouEventHandler: Called by the assembler routine AssmHand as soon*}
{*                   as a mouse event occurs.                        *}
{**----------------------------------------------------------------**}
```

```
{*  Input  : EvFlags  = The event mask                               *}
{*           ButState = Current mouse button status                  *}
{*           X, Y     = Current coordinates of the mouse cursor on   *}
{*                      the text screen                              *}
{*******************************************************************}

procedure MouEventHandler( EvFlags, ButState, x, y : integer );

var NewRng : byte;                        { Number of new range }

begin

  MouEvent := MouEvent and not(1);              { Bit 0 excluded }
  MouEvent := MouEvent or ( EvFlags and 1 );     { Bit 0 copied }

  if ( EvFlags and LBITS ) <> 0 then{ Lft button released or pressed? }
    begin                                              { Yes }
      MouEvent := MouEvent and not( LBITS ); { Remove previous status }
      MouEvent := MouEvent or ( EvFlags and LBITS );   { Add status }
    end;
  if ( EvFlags and RBITS ) <> 0 then{ Rgt button released or pressed? }
    begin                                              { Yes }
      MouEvent := MouEvent and not( RBITS ); { Remove previous status }
      MouEvent := MouEvent or ( EvFlags and RBITS );   { Add status }
    end;

  MouCol := x;                 { Convert columns to text columns }
  MouRow := y;                   { Convert lines to text lines }

  {-- Determine range in which the mouse should be found and    ----}
  {-- determine whether range has changes since the previous call ----}
  {-- of the handler. If so, the cursor image must be redefined.  ----}

  NewRng := BufPtr^[ MouRow * TCol + MouCol ];        { Get range }
  if NewRng <> MouRng then                        { New range? }
    begin                                              { Yes }
      if NewRng = NO_RANGE then          { Outside of a range? }
        MouDefinePtr( StdPtr )         { Yes --> Default cursor }
      else                            { No --> Range recognized }
        MouDefinePtr( ActRngPtr^[ NewRng ].PtrMask );
    end;
  MouRng := NewRng;         { Reserve range number in global variable }
end;


{*******************************************************************}
{*  MouIBufFill: Store the code for a mouse range within the         *}
{*               modular range memory.                               *}
{**----------------------------------------------------------------**}
{*  Input  : x1, y1 = Upper left corner of the mouse range           *}
{*           x2, y2 = Lower right corner of the mouse range          *}
{*           Code   = Range code                                     *}
{*******************************************************************}

procedure MouIBufFill( x1, y1, x2, y2, Code : byte );

var Index   : integer;                       { Points to array }
    Column,                                   { Loop counter }
    Line    : byte;

begin
  for Line:=y1 to y2 do                 { Count individual lines }
    begin
      Index := Line  * TCol + x1;           { First line index }
      for Column:=x1 to x2 do  { Go through the columns in this line }
```

```
        begin
          BufPtr^[ Index ] := Code;              { Save code }
          inc( Index );                  { Set index to next array }
        end;
    end;
end;


{*******************************************************************}
{*  MouDefRange:   Allows the registration of different screen    *}
{*                 ranges, which the mouse recognizes as different *}
{*                 ranges. The mouse cursor's appearance changes   *}
{*                 when it senses each range.                      *}
{**-------------------------------------------------------------**}
{*  Input  : Number = Number of screen ranges                     *}
{*           BPtr   = Pointer to the array in which the individual *}
{*                    ranges are written as a structure of type    *}
{*                    RANGE                                        *}
{*  Info:   - The free areas of the screen are assigned the code   *}
{*             NO_RANGE                                            *}
{*           - When the mouse cursor enters one of the ranges,     *}
{*             the mouse range calls the event handler             *}
{*******************************************************************}

procedure MouDefRange( Number : byte; BPtr : RNGPTR );

var ActRng,                              { Number of the current range }
    Range : byte;                        { Loop counter }

begin
  ActRngPtr := BPtr;                     { Reserve pointer to vector }
  NumRanges := Number;                   { and number of ranges }
  FillChar( BufPtr^, BLen, NO_RANGE );   { All elements=NO_RANGE }
  for Range:=0 to Number-1 do            { Check out different ranges }
    with BPtr^[ Range ] do
      MouIBufFill( x1, y1, x2, y2, Range );

  {-- Redefine mouse cursor ---------------------------------------}
  ActRng := BufPtr^[ MouRow * TCol + MouCol ];   { Get range }
  if ActRng = NO_RANGE then                { Outside a range? }
    MouDefinePtr( StdPtr )                 { Yes --> Default cursor }
  else
    MouDefinePtr( BPtr^[ ActRng ].PtrMask );  { No --> Range recognized }
end;


{*******************************************************************}
{*  MouEventWait: Waits for a specific mouse event.               *}
{**-------------------------------------------------------------**}
{*  Input  : TYP        = Type of comparison between different events*}
{*           WAIT_EVENT = Bitmask which specifies the awaited event *}
{*  Output : Bitmask of the occurring event                        *}
{*  Info:   - WAIT_EVENT can be used in conjunction with OR for    *}
{*             other constants like EV_MOU_MOVE, EV_LEFT_PRESS etc. *}
{*           - Comparison types can be given as AND or OR. If AND is*}
{*             selected, the function returns to the caller if all  *}
{*             anticipated events occur. OR returns the function to *}
{*             the caller if at least one of the events occurs.     *}
{*******************************************************************}

function MouEventWait( Typ : BYTE; WaitEvent : integer ) : integer;

var ActEvent : integer;
    Line,
    Column   : byte;
    CEnd     : boolean;
```

```
begin
  Column := MouCol;                    { Reserve current mouse position }
  Line := MouRow;
  CEnd := false;

  repeat
    {-- Wait for one of the events to occur ---------------------------}

    if Typ = EAND then                        { AND comparison? }
      repeat                        { Yes --> All events must occur }
        ActEvent := MouEvent;            { Get current event }
      until ActEvent = WaitEvent
    else                                    { OR comparison }
      repeat                        { At least one event must occur }
        ActEvent := MouEvent;            { Get current event }
      until ( ActEvent and WaitEvent ) <> 0;

    ActEvent := ActEvent and WaitEvent;      { Check event bits only }

    {-- While waiting for mouse movement, the event is accepted    -- }
    {-- only if the mouse cursor moves to another line and/or       -- }
    {-- column in the text screen                                   - }

    if ( ( (WaitEvent and EV_MOU_MOVE) <> 0 )  and
         ( Column = MouCol ) and ( Line = MouRow ) ) then
      begin           { Mouse moved, but still at the same screen position }
        ActEvent := ActEvent and not( EV_MOU_MOVE );   { Move bit out }
        CEnd := ( ActEvent <> 0);         { Still waiting for events? }
      end
    else                                      { Event occurs }
      CEnd := TRUE;
  until CEnd;

  EvCol := MouCol;                         { Determine current mouse }
  EvRow := MouRow;                         { position and range in }
  EvRng := MouRng;                         { global variables }

  MouEventWait := ActEvent;
end;


{*******************************************************************}
{*  MouISetEventHandler: Installs an event handler which is called *}
{*                       when a particular mouse event occurs.     *}
{**-------------------------------------------------------------**}
{*  Input  : EVENT = Bitmask which describes the event, called     *}
{*                   through an event handler                      *}
{*           FPTR  = Pointer to the event handler of type FNCTPTR  *}
{*  Info:   - EVENT can be used through OR comparisons in conjunc-  *}
{*             tion with constants like EV_MOU_MOVE, etc.          *}
{*           - The event handler must be a FAR procedure, and change*}
{*             none of the given processor registers              *}
{*******************************************************************}

procedure MouISetEventHandler( Event : integer; FPtr : FNCTPTR );

var Regs : Registers;       { Processor registers for interrupt call }

begin
  Regs.AX := $000C;                   { Funct. no.: Set Mouse Handler }
  Regs.CX := event;                          { Load event mask }
  Regs.DX := PTRREC( FPtr ).Ofs;       { Offset address of handler }
  Regs.ES := PTRREC( FPtr ).Seg;       { Segment address of handler }
  Intr( $33,  Regs );                        { Call mouse driver }
```

611

```
                                                   Regs.AX := $0002;              { Funct. no. for "Hide Mouse" }
 end;                                               Intr( $33, Regs);                      { Call mouse driver }
                                                  end;

 {***********************************************}
 {*  MouIGetX: Returns the text column in which the mouse cursor can  *}   {*******************************************************************}
 {*           be found                          *}   {*  MouSetMoveArea: Specify movement range for mouse cursor.       *}
 {**-------------------------------------------**}   {**-------------------------------------------------------------**}
 {*  Output : Mouse column converted to text screen  *}   {*  Input  :  x1, y1 = Coordinates of range's upper left corner   *}
 {***********************************************}   {*             x2, y2 = Coordinates of range's lower right corner  *}
                                                   {*  Info:    - The coordinates indicate the text screen coordinates, *}
 function MouIGetX : byte;                          {*             and not the virtual graphic screen used by the mouse *}
                                                   {*             driver                                              *}
 var Regs : Registers;       { Processor registers for interrupt call }   {*******************************************************************}

 begin                                             procedure MouSetMoveArea( x1, y1, x2, y2 : byte );
   Regs.AX := $0003;              { Funct. no.: Get mouse position }
   Intr( $33, Regs );                  { Call mouse driver }   var Regs : Registers;              { Processor regs for interrupt call }
   MouIGetX := Regs.CX shr 3;   { Convert column and return new value }
 end;                                              begin
                                                    Regs.AX := $0008;        { Funct. no. for "Set vertical limits" }
                                                    Regs.CX := integer( y1 ) shl 3;        { Conversion to virtual  }
 {***********************************************}   Regs.DX := integer( y2 ) shl 3;        { mouse screen          }
 {*  MouIGetY: Returns the text line in which the mouse cursor can  *}   Intr( $33, Regs );                      { Call mouse driver    }
 {*           be found.                         *}   Regs.AX := $0007;       { Funct. no. for "Set horizontal limits" }
 {**-------------------------------------------**}   Regs.CX := integer( x1 ) shl 3;        { Conversion to virtual  }
 {*  Output : Mouse line converted to text screen  *}   Regs.DX := integer( x2 ) shl 3;        { mouse screen          }
 {***********************************************}   Intr( $33, Regs );                      { Call mouse driver    }
                                                  end;
 function MouIGetY : byte;

 var Regs : Registers;       { Processor registers for interrupt call }   {*******************************************************************}
                                                   {*  MouSetSpeed: Configures movement speed of mouse cursor         *}
 begin                                             {**-------------------------------------------------------------**}
   Regs.AX := $0003;              { Funct. no.: Get mouse position }   {*  Input  : XSpeed = Speed in X-direction                        *}
   Intr( $33, Regs );                  { Call mouse driver }   {*          YSpeed = Speed in Y-direction                         *}
   MouIGetY := Regs.DX shr 3;   { Convert line and return new value }   {*  Info:    - Parameters are measured in units of                *}
 end;                                              {*             mickeys (8 per pixel)                              *}
                                                   {*******************************************************************}

 {***********************************************}   procedure MouSetSpeed( XSpeed, YSpeed : integer );
 {*  MouShowMouse: Show mouse cursor on the screen.  *}
 {**-------------------------------------------**}   var Regs : Registers;              { Processor regs for interrupt call }
 {*  Info: Calls between MouShowMouse and MouHideMouse must be evenly  *}
 {*        balanced                             *}   begin
 {***********************************************}   Regs.AX := $000f;     { Funct. no. for "Set mickeys to pixel ratio" }
                                                    Regs.CX := XSpeed;
 procedure MouShowMouse;                            Regs.DX := YSpeed;
                                                    Intr( $33, Regs);                      { Call mouse driver }
 var Regs : Registers;       { Processor regs for interrupt call }   end;

 begin
   Regs.AX := $0001;              { Funct. no. for "Show Mouse" }   {*******************************************************************}
   Intr( $33, Regs );                  { Call mouse driver }   {*  MouMovePtr: Moves mouse cursor to a specific position on the   *}
 end;                                              {*            screen                                              *}
                                                   {**-------------------------------------------------------------**}
                                                   {*  Input  : COL = New screen column for mouse cursor             *}
 {***********************************************}   {*          ROW = New screen line for mouse cursor                *}
 {*  MouHideMouse: Hide mouse cursor from the screen  *}   {*  Info:    - The coordinates indicate the text screen, and not the *}
 {**-------------------------------------------**}   {*             virtual graphic screen used by the mouse driver     *}
 {*  Info: Calls between MouShowMouse and MouHideMouse must be evenly  *}   {*******************************************************************}
 {*        balanced                             *}
 {***********************************************}   procedure MouMovePtr( Col, Row : byte );

 procedure MouHideMouse;

 var Regs : Registers;       { Processor regs for interrupt call }   var Regs   : Registers;            { Processor regs for interrupt call }
                                                    NewRng : byte;                 { Range into which the mouse is moved }
 begin
```

612

```
begin
  Regs.AX := $0004;        { Funct. no. for "Set mouse cursor position" }
  MouCol := col;                          { Store coordinates in }
  MouRow := row;                          { global variables }
  Regs.CX := integer( col ) shl 3;   { Convert coordinates and store }
  Regs.DX := integer( row ) shl 3;        { in global variables }
  Intr( $33, Regs );                      { Call mouse driver }

  NewRng := BufPtr^[ Row * TCol + Col ];             { Get range }
  if NewRng <> MouRng then                           { New range? }
    begin                                                  { YES }
      if NewRng = NO_RANGE then              { Outside of a range? }
        MouDefinePtr( StdPtr )              { YES, default cursor }
      else
        MouDefinePtr( ActRngPtr^[ NewRng ].PtrMask );  { NO, range recognized }
    end;
  MouRng := NewRng;            { Place range number in global variable }
end;


{*************************************************************}
{* MouSetDefaultPtr: Defines default cursor appearance for screen  *}
{*                   ranges not assigned as special ranges         *}
{**---------------------------------------------------------------**}
{* Input : default = Cursor and screen mask for mouse cursor       *}
{* Info:  - The parameters should be created with the help of the  *}
{*          MouPtrMask function                                    *}
{*************************************************************}

procedure MouSetDefaultPtr( default : PTRVIEW );

begin
  StdPtr := default;        { Reserve bitmask in global variable }

  {-- If the cursor isn't currently in a range, convert to default ---}

  if MouRng = NO_RANGE then                         { No range? }
    MouDefinePtr( default );                               { NO }
end;


{*************************************************************}
{* MouEnd: End the mouse module functions and procedures    *}
{**-------------------------------------------------------**}
{* Info: - This procedure doesn't have to be called direct from the*}
{*          application, since the MouInit function defines this    *}
{*          as the exit procedure                                   *}
{*************************************************************}

{$F+}              { must be FAR to allow call as exit procedure }

procedure  MouEnd;

var Regs : Registers;        { Processor regs for interrupt call }

begin
  MouHideMouse;                        { Hide mouse from screen }
  Regs.AX := 0;                        { Reset mouse driver }
  Intr( $33, Regs);                    { Call mouse driver }

  FreeMem( BufPtr, BLen );             { Release allocated memory }

  ExitProc := ExitOld;              { Restore old exit procedure }
end;

{$F-}                                 { No more FAR procedures }
```

```
{*************************************************************}
{* MouInit: Initializes mouse functions and procedures as well as *}
{*          variables                                             *}
{**-------------------------------------------------------------**}
{* Input  : Columns = Number of screen columns                    *}
{*          Lines  = Number of screen lines                       *}
{* Output : TRUE if a mouse driver is installed, else FALSE       *}
{* Info:   - This function must be the first called from an       *}
{*           application program, before other procedures and     *}
{*           functions can be called                              *}
{*************************************************************}

function MouInit( Columns, Lines : byte ) : boolean;

var Regs : Registers;        { Processor regs for interrupt call }

begin
  TLine := Lines;                      { Store number of lines and }
  TCol  := Columns;                    { columns in global variables }

  ExitOld := ExitProc;          { Set address of exit procedure }
  ExitProc := @MouEnd;          { Define MouEnd as exit procedure }

  {-- Allocate and fill mouse range ----------------------------------}

  BLen := TLine * TCol;           { Number of characters in screen }
  GetMem( BufPtr, BLen );         { Allocate internal range buffer }
  MouIBufFill( 0, 0, TCol-1, TLine-1, NO_RANGE );

  Regs.AX := 0;                        { Initialize mouse driver }
  Intr( $33, Regs );                   { Call mouse driver }
  MouInit := ( Regs.AX <> 0 );         { Mouse driver installed? }

  MouSetMoveArea( 0, 0, TCol-1, TLine-1 );          { Set move area }

  MouCol   := MouIGetX;           { Load current mouse position }
  MouRow   := MouIGetY;           { into global variables }
  MouRng   := NO_RANGE;           { cursor in no set range }
  MouEvent := EV_LEFT_REL or EV_RIGHT_REL;  { No mouse button pressed }
  StdPtr   := MouPtrMask( PTRSAMECHAR, PTRINVCOL );   { Std. cursor }
  OldPtr   := PTRVIEW( 0 );

  {-- Install assembler event handler "AssmHand" ---------------------}
  MouISetEventHandler( EV_MOU_ALL, FNCTPTR(@AssmHand) );

end;
```

```
{*************************************************************
*              M A I N   P R O G R A M                      *
*************************************************************}

const Ranges : array[0..4] of RANGE =           { The mouse range }
  (
    ( x1:  0; y1:  0; x2: 79; y2:  0 ),          { Top line          }
    ( x1:  0; y1:  1; x2:  0; y2: 23 ),          { Left column       }
    ( x1:  0; y1: 24; x2: 78; y2: 24 ),          { Bottom line       }
    ( x1: 79; y1:  1; x2: 79; y2: 23 ),          { Right column      }
    ( x1: 79; y1: 24; x2: 79; y2: 24 )           { Lower right corner }
  );

var Dummy : integer;                  { Get result from MouEventWait }

begin
```

613

```
{-- Configure mouse cursor for the different mouse ranges ----------}
Ranges[ 0 ].PtrMask := MouPtrMask( PtrDifChar($18), PtrInvCol);
Ranges[ 1 ].PtrMask := MouPtrMask( PtrDifChar($1b), PtrInvCol);
Ranges[ 2 ].PtrMask := MouPtrMask( PtrDifChar($19), PtrInvCol);
Ranges[ 3 ].PtrMask := MouPtrMask( PtrDifChar($1a), PtrInvCol);
Ranges[ 4 ].PtrMask := MouPtrMask( PtrDifChar($58), PtrDifCol($40));

writeln(#13#10,'MOUSEP - (c) 1989 by MICHAEL TISCHER'#13#10);
if MouInit( 80, 25 ) then            { Initialize mouse module }
  begin                      { OK, there's an installed mouse driver }
   writeln('Move the mouse cursor around the screen. As you move
',CRLF,
                'it around the edge of the screen, you will see the
mouse',CRLF,
                'cursor change its appearance. The cursor shape changes
',CRLF,
                'as you move the mouse from edge to edge.      ',CRLF,CRLF,
                'To end this program, move the mouse cursor to the
',CRLF,
                'lower right corner of the screen, and press both the
',CRLF,
                'left and right mouse buttons at the same time.       ');

   MouSetDefaultPtr( MouPtrMask( PtrDifChar( $DB ), PtrDifCol( 3 ) ) );
   MouDefRange( 5, @Ranges );               { Range definition }
   MouShowMouse;                  { Display mouse cursor on the screen }

   {-- Wait until the user presses both the left and right mouse -----
   }
   {-- buttons simultaneously while the cursor is in range 4      -----}

   repeat                              { Read loop }
    Dummy := MouEventWait( EAND, EV_LEFT_PRESS or EV_RIGHT_PRESS );
    until EvRng = 4;
   end
  else          { No mouse installed OR no mouse driver installed }
   writeln('Sorry, no mouse driver currently installed.');
end.
```

Assembler listing: MOUSEPA.ASM

```
;****************************************************************
;*                     M O U S E P A                          *;
;*------------------------------------------------------------*;
;*  Task       : Create mouse called event handler for use with *;
;*               a Turbo Pascal program.                      *;
;*------------------------------------------------------------*;
;*  Author     : MICHAEL TISCHER                              *;
;*  Developed on : 04/24/1989                                 *;
;*  Last update  : 04/24/1989                                 *;
;*------------------------------------------------------------*;
;*  assembly    : MASM /MX MOUSEPA;   or                      *;
;*               TASM -MX MOUSEPA                             *;
;*               ... add to MOUSEP program code               *;
;****************************************************************

;== Data segment ============================================

DATA    segment word public
DATA    ends                    ;note--no variables in this program

;== Program ================================================

CODE    segment byte public     ;Program segment

        assume CS:CODE           ;CS points to the code segment whose
                                 ;contents are unknown to DS, SS & ES

public    AssmHand               ;Allows the TP program to read
                                 ;the address of the assembler handlers

extrn    MouEventHandler : near  ;TP event handler to be called

active   db  0                   ;points to whether a call can occur

;------------------------------------------------------------
;-- AssmHand: The event handler which first calls the mouse driver, then
;--          calls the TP MouEventHandler procedure
;--          Direct call from TP not allowed

AssmHand   proc far

           ;-- First save all processor registers on stack ---

           cmp  active,0         ;Call done yet?
           jne  ende             ;NO --> Don't exit call

           mov  active,1         ;No more calls, please

           push ax
           push bx
           push cx
           push dx
           push di
           push si
           push bp
           push es
           push ds

           ;-- Push arguments for TP function call onto stack -------
           ;-- Call:
           ;--   MouEventHandler (EvFlags, ButStatus, x , y : integer );
```

```
        push ax                ;Push event flags onto stack
        push bx                ;Push mouse button status onto stack

        mov  di,cx             ;Move horizontal ordinate onto DI
        mov  cl,3              ;Counter for coordinate number

        shr  di,cl             ;Divide DI (horizontal ord.) by 8 and
        push di                ;push onto stack

        shr  dx,cl             ;Divide DX (vertical ord.) by 8 and
        push dx                ;push onto stack

        mov  ax,DATA           ;Segment address of data segment AX
        mov  ds,ax             ;Move data from AX to DS register

        call MouEventHandler   ;Call TP procedure

        ;-- Get reserved registers from stack ----------------------

        pop  ds
        pop  es
        pop  bp
        pop  si
        pop  di
        pop  dx
        pop  cx
        pop  bx
        pop  ax

        mov  active,0          ;Re-enable call

ende:   ret                    ;Return to mouse driver

AssmHand endp

;-----------------------------------------------------------------------

CODE    ends                   ;End of code segment
        end                    ;End of program
```

C listing: MOUSEC.C

```
/***********************************************************************/
/*                        M O U S E C . C                            */
/*-------------------------------------------------------------------*/
/*   Task          : Demonstrates mouse access from the C language   */
/*-------------------------------------------------------------------*/
/*   Author        : MICHAEL TISCHER                                 */
/*   Developed on  : 04/20/1989                                      */
/*   Last update   : 06/14/1989                                      */
/*-------------------------------------------------------------------*/
/*   Microsoft C                                                     */
/*   Creation      : CL /AS MOUSEC.C MOUSECA.OBJ                     */
/*   Call          : MOUSEC                                          */
/*-------------------------------------------------------------------*/
/*   Turbo C (integrated system)                                    */
/*   Creation      : Create a project file containing the following:*/
/*                   MOUSEC                                          */
/*                   MOUSECA.OBJ                                     */
/*                   Make sure that memory model is set to small.    */
/*                   If you didn't assemble the MOUSECA.ASM file     */
/*                   using the /MX option in MASM, make sure that    */
/*                   Case-Sensitive Link on Linker options is OFF.   */
/*                   Disable stack checking before compilation.      */
/*                   >>NOTE: One warning will occur (about the       */
/*                   ButState in the MouEventHandler function).      */
/*                   The program will run. Do  N O T  remove         */
/*                   the ButState declaration - the AssmHand routine*/
/*                   needs it<<                                      */
/*   Call          : MOUSEC                                          */
/***********************************************************************/

/*== Add include files ===============================================*/

#include <dos.h>
#include <stdlib.h>

extern void far AssmHand( void );        /* External declaration    */
                                         /* of assembler handler    */
/*== Typedefs ========================================================*/

typedef unsigned char BYTE;                      /* Create a byte */
typedef unsigned long PTRVIEW;            /* Mouse pointer mask */
typedef struct {                          /* Describe a mouse range */
                BYTE x1,                  /* Upper left coordinates of the */
                     y1,                  /* specified range        */
                     x2,                  /* Lower right corner of the */
                     y2;                  /* specified range        */
                PTRVIEW ptr_mask;         /* Mouse pointer mask */
               } RANGE;
typedef void (far * MOUHAPTR)( void );    /* Pointer to event handler */

/*== Constants =======================================================*/

#define TRUE  ( 1 == 1 )
#define FALSE ( 1 == 0 )

/*-- Event codes ----------------------------------------------------*/

#define EV_MOU_MOVE     1                        /* Move mouse */
#define EV_LEFT_PRESS   2               /* Left mouse button pressed */
#define EV_LEFT_REL     4               /* Left mouse button released */
#define EV_RIGHT_PRESS  8               /* Right mouse button pressed */
#define EV_RIGHT_REL   16               /* Right mouse button released */
```

615

```
#define EV_MOU_ALL      31                    /* all mouse events */

#define NO_RANGE 255                          /* mouse pointer not in range xy */

/*-- Macros -------------------------------------------------------*/

#define MouGetCol()     (ev_col)     /* Return mouse position & */
#define MouGetRow()     (ev_row)     /* range the moment the */
#define MouGetRange()   (ev_rng)     /* event occurs */
#define MouAvail()      ( mavail )   /* Available mouse = TRUE */
#define MouGetCurCol()  ( moucol )   /* Returns current mouse */
#define MouGetCurRow()  ( mourow )   /* position and current */
#define MouGetCurRng()  ( mourng )   /* mouse range        */
#define MouIsLeftPress() ( mouevent & EV_LEFT_PRESS )
#define MouIsLeftRel()   ( mouevent & EV_LEFT_REL )
#define MouIsRightPress() ( mouevent & EV_RIGHT_PRESS )
#define MouIsRightRel()  ( mouevent & EV_RIGHT_REL )
#define MouSetMoveAreaAll() MouSetMoveArea( 0, 0, tcol-1, tline-1 );

#define ELVEC(x) ( sizeof(x) / sizeof(x[0]) ) /* No. of elements in X */

/*-- Bitmask creation macros defining mouse pointer's appearance. ---*/
/*-- Syntax for calling MouPtrMask (sample):               ---*/
/*--    MouPtrMask( PTRDIFCHAR( 'x' ), PTRINVCOL )          ---*/
/*-- When the pointer is represented as a lowercase x, the inverse ---*/
/*-- character color takes effect.                         ---*/

#define MouPtrMask( z, f )\
  ( ((( PTRVIEW) f) >> 8 << 24) + ((( PTRVIEW) z) >> 8 << 16) +\
    (((f) & 255) << 8) + ((z) & 255) )

#define PTRSAMECHAR    ( 0x00ff )   /* Same character        */
#define PTRDIFCHAR(z)  ( (z) << 8 ) /* Other characters      */
#define PTRSAMECOL     ( 0x00ff )   /* Same color            */
#define PTRINVCOL      ( 0x7777 )   /* Inverse color         */
#define PTRSAMECOLB    ( 0x807f )   /* Same color (blinking) */
#define PTRINVCOLB     ( 0xF777 )   /* Inverse color (blinking) */
#define PTRDIFCOL(f)   ( (f) << 8 ) /* Other color           */
#define PTRDIFCOLB(f)  (((f)|0x80) << 8) /* Other color (blinking) */

#define EAND  0                     /* Event comparisons for MouEventWait() */
#define EVOR  1

#define MOUINT(rin, rout) int86(0x33, &rin, &rout)
#define MOUINTX(rin, rout, sr) int86x(0x33, &rin, &rout, &sr)

/*-- Macros for converting mouse coordinates between virtual mouse  */
/*-- screen and text screen                            ----*/

#define XTOCOL(x) ( (x) >> 3 )                     /* X v 8 */
#define YTOROW(y) ( (y) >> 3 )                     /* Row v 8 */
#define COLTOX(c) ( (c) << 3 )                     /* C x 8 */
#define ROWTOY(r) ( (r) << 3 )                     /* Row x 8 */

/*== global variables =============================================*/

BYTE tline,                        /* No. of text lines */
    tcol,                          /* No. of text columns */
    mavail = FALSE;                /* TRUE when mouse is available */

/*-- Mask for standard mouse pointer --------------------------------*/

PTRVIEW stdptr = MouPtrMask( PTRSAMECHAR, PTRINVCOL );
```

```
BYTE  * bbuf,                      /* Ptr to range recognition buffer */
        num_range = 0;             /* No range defined until now */

RANGE * cur_range;                 /* Pointer to current range vector */
int     blen;                      /* Length of BBUF in bytes */

/*-- Variables which load every time the mouse handler is called -----*/

BYTE mourng = NO_RANGE,            /* Current mouse range */
    moucol,                        /* Mouse column (text screen) */
    mourow;                        /* Mouse row (text screen) */
int  mouevent = EV_LEFT_REL + EV_RIGHT_REL;     /* Event mask */

/*-- Variables which load every time an event anticipated by the  ---*/
/*-- mouse handler occurs                                   ---*/

BYTE ev_rng,                  /* Range in which the mouse can be found */
    ev_col,                        /* Mouse column */
    ev_row;                        /* Mouse row */

/**********************************************************************
* Function       : M o u D e f i n e P t r            *
**------------------------------------------------------------------**
* Task           : Defines the cursor mask and screen mask which  *
*                  determines the mouse pointer's appearance      *
* Input parameters : MASK = Both bitmasks, made into a 32-bit value *
*                    of type UNSIGNED LONG                         *
* Return value   : None                                           *
* Info           : Most significant 16 bits of MASK = screen mask *
*                  least significant 16 bits of mask = cursor mask *
**********************************************************************/

#pragma check_stack(off)           /* No stack checking here */

void MouDefinePtr( PTRVIEW mask )
{
    static PTRVIEW oldercursor = (PTRVIEW) 0;   /* Last value for MASK */
    union REGS regs;                 /* Processor regs for interrupt call */

    if ( oldercursor != mask )       /* Changes since last call? */
    {                                            /* YES */
        regs.x.ax = 0x000a;        /* Funct. no. for "Set text pointer type" */
        regs.x.bx = 0;             /* Create software pointer */
        regs.x.cx = mask;          /* Low word is AND-mask */
        regs.x.dx = mask >> 16;    /* High word is XOR-mask */
        MOUINT(regs, regs);        /* Call mouse driver */
        oldercursor = mask;        /* Note old bitmask */
    }
}

/**********************************************************************
* Function       : M o u E v e n t H a n d l e r      *
**------------------------------------------------------------------**
* Task           : Calls AssmHand routine from mouse driver, when *
*                  a mouse related event occurs.                  *
* Input parameters : EvFlags  = Event's event mask                *
*                    ButState = Mouse button status               *
*                    X, Y     = Current pointer position, converted *
*                               into text screen coordinates       *
* Return value   : None                                           *
* Info           : - This function is only operational through a  *
*                    mouse driver call, and shouldn't be called   *
*                    from another function.                       *
**********************************************************************/
```

```
void MouEventHandler( int EvFlags, int ButState, int x, int y )
{
#define LBITS ( EV_LEFT_PRESS | EV_LEFT_REL )
#define RBITS ( EV_RIGHT_PRESS | EV_RIGHT_REL )

unsigned newrng;                             /* New range number */

mouevent &= ~1;                              /* Clear bit 0 */
mouevent |= ( EvFlags & 1 );                 /* Copy EvFlags to bit 0 */

if ( EvFlags & LBITS )   /* Left mouse button pressed or released? */
  {                                                    /* YES */
  mouevent &= ~LBITS;                /* Clear previous status */
  mouevent |= ( EvFlags & LBITS );          /* Add new status */
  }

if ( EvFlags & RBITS )   /* Right mouse button pressed or released? */
  {                                      /* YES, Clear and set bits */
  mouevent &= ~RBITS;                /* Clear previous status */
  mouevent |= ( EvFlags & RBITS );          /* Add new status */
  }

moucol = x;               /* Convert columns into text columns */
mourow = y;               /* Convert rows into text rows */

/*-- Check range in which mouse is currently located, and compare --*/
/*-- to range since last call. If a change occurs, the pointer's ---*/
/*-- appearance will have to be changed.                      ---*/

newrng = *(bbuf + mourow * tcol + moucol);        /* Get range */
if ( newrng != mourng )                            /* New range? */
  MouDefinePtr((newrng==NO_RANGE) ? stdptr :
                           (cur_range+newrng)->ptr_mask);
mourng = newrng;           /* Place range number in global variables */
}

#pragma check_stack              /* Re-enable stack checking and old */
#pragma check_stack              /* status                          */

/******************************************************************
* Function        : M o u I B u f F i l l                         *
**---------------------------------------------------------------**
* Task            : Stores a specific screen range code within    *
*                   screen memory affecting the module            *
* Input parameters : x1, y1 = Upper left corner of the screen     *
*                    x2, y2 = Lower right corner of the screen     *
*                    CODE   = Range code                          *
* Return value    : None                                          *
* Info            : This functions should only be called from within *
*                   this module.                                  *
******************************************************************/

static void MouIBufFill( BYTE x1, BYTE y1,
                         BYTE x2, BYTE y2, BYTE code )
{
register BYTE * lptr;         /* Floating pointer to range mem. */
BYTE i, j;                             /* Loop counter */

lptr = bbuf + y1 * tcol + x1;       /* Pointer to first line */

/*-- Go through individual lines ------------------------------*/
for (j=x2 - x1 + 1 ; y1 <= y2; ++y1, lptr+=tcol )
  memset( lptr, code, j );                     /* Set code */
```

```
}

/******************************************************************
* Function        : M o u D e f R a n g e                         *
**---------------------------------------------------------------**
* Task            : Allows the definition of different screen ranges *
*                   which configure a different code for the mouse *
*                   pointer, depending on the pointer's location. *
* Input parameters : - NUMBER = Number of screen ranges           *
*                    - PTR    = Pointer to screen description vector *
*                             (type RANGE)                        *
* Return value    : None                                          *
* Info            : - Free screen ranges receive the code NO_RANGE. *
*                   - When entering the specified screen range, the *
*                     mouse handler automatically changes the mouse *
*                     pointer's appearance to correspond with that *
*                     range.                                       *
*                   - Since the specified pointer is stored, but the *
*                     specified vector isn't copied to a separate  *
*                     buffer, the contents of the vector should not *
*                     be changed on the next call of this function. *
******************************************************************/

void MouDefRange( BYTE number, RANGE * ptr )
{
register BYTE i,                           /* Loop counter */
              range;                       /* Mouse range */

cur_range = ptr;                   /* Reserve pointer to vector */
num_range = number;                /* and number of ranges      */
memset( bbuf, NO_RANGE, blen );
for (i=0 ; i<number ; ++ptr )
  MouIBufFill( ptr->x1, ptr->y1, ptr->x2, ptr->y2, i++);

/*-- Redefine mouse pointer -----------------------------------*/

range = *(bbuf + mourow * tcol + moucol);    /* Current mouse range */
MouDefinePtr( ( range == NO_RANGE ) ? stdptr
             : (cur_range+range)->ptr_mask );
}

/******************************************************************
* Function        : M o u E v e n t W a i t                       *
**---------------------------------------------------------------**
* Task            : Waits for a specific event from the keyboard. *
* Input parameters : TYP       = Establishes comparison between   *
*                              different events.                  *
*                    WAIT_EVENT = Bitmask which specifies wait event. *
* Return value    : Bitmask which describes this or another event. *
* Info            : - WAIT_EVENT can be used with other constants *
*                     such as EV_MOU_MOVE or EV_LEFT_PRESS when used *
*                     in conjunction with EVOR.                   *
*                   - EAND & EVOR are allowable types. EAND has the *
*                     ability to return to the caller once ALL events*
*                     have occurred; EVOR returns to the caller when *
*                     at least one event occurs.                  *
******************************************************************/

int MouEventWait( BYTE typ, int wait_event )
{
int cur_event;                         /* Current event mask */
register BYTE column = moucol,         /* Last mouse position */
              line = mourow;
BYTE ende = FALSE;                /* TRUE if an event occurs */
```

617

```
  while ( !ende )                    /* Repeat until event occurs */
  {
    /*-- Wait until one of the events occurs --------------------------*/

    if ( typ == EAND )               /* EAND: All events must occur */
      while ( (cur_event = mouevent) != wait_event)
        ;
    else                             /* EVOR: At least one event must occur */
      while ( ( (cur_event = mouevent) & wait_event) == 0)
        ;

    cur_event &= wait_event;         /* Check event bits only */

    /*-- When moving the mouse, the event is only accepted if the   --*/
    /*-- pointer moves to another row or column on the text screen  --*/

    if ((wait_event & EV_MOU_MOVE) && column==moucol && line==mourow)
    {                                /* Mouse moves, but in same screen position */
      cur_event &= (~EV_MOU_MOVE);   /* Examine move bit */
      ende = (cur_event != 0);       /* Are events pending? */
    }
    else                             /* Event occurred */
      ende = TRUE;
  }
  ev_col = moucol;                   /* Set current mouse position */
  ev_row = mourow;                   /* and mouse range; place in */
  ev_rng = mourng;                   /* global variables          */
  return( cur_event );               /* Return event mask */
}

/**********************************************************************
* Function      : M o u I S e t E v e n t H a n d l e r              *
**------------------------------------------------------------------**
* Task          : Installs an event handler which handles events    *
*                 called from the mouse driver.                     *
* Input parameters : EVENT = Bitmask which specifies the event which *
*                 calls the event handler.                          *
*                 PTR   = Pointer to the mouse handler              *
* Return value  : None                                              *
* Info          : - EVENT can be used in conjunction with the EVOR  *
*                 comparison on constants such as EV_MOU_MOVE,      *
*                 EV_LEFT_PRESS                                     *
**********************************************************************/

static void MouISetEventHandler( unsigned event, MOUHAPTR ptr )
{
  union REGS regs;                   /* Processor regs for interrupt call */
  struct SREGS sregs;                /* Segment register for interrupt call */

  regs.x.ax = 0x000C;                /* Funct. no. for "Set Mouse Handler" */
  regs.x.cx = event;                 /* Load event mask */
  regs.x.dx = FP_OFF( ptr );         /* Offset address of handler */
  sregs.es = FP_SEG( ptr );          /* Segment address of handler */
  MOUINTX( regs, regs, sregs );      /* Call mouse driver */
}

/**********************************************************************
* Function      : M o u I G e t X                                   *
**------------------------------------------------------------------**
* Task          : Determines text column in which pointer lies.     *
* Input parameters : None                                           *
* Return value  : Mouse pointer column, relative to text screen     *
**********************************************************************/
```

```
static BYTE MouIGetX( void )
{
  union REGS regs;                   /* Processor regs for interrupt call */

  regs.x.ax = 0x0003;                /* Funct. no. for "Get mouse position" */
  MOUINT( regs, regs );              /* Call mouse driver */
  return XTOCOL( regs.x.cx );        /* Convert and return column */
}

/**********************************************************************
* Function      : M o u I G e t Y                                   *
**------------------------------------------------------------------**
* Task          : Determines text row in which pointer lies.        *
* Input parameters : None                                           *
* Return value  : Mouse pointer row, relative to the text screen    *
**********************************************************************/

static BYTE MouIGetY( void )
{
  union REGS regs;                   /* Processor regs for interrupt call */

  regs.x.ax= 0x0003;                 /* Funct. no. for "Get mouse position" */
  MOUINT(regs, regs);                /* Call mouse driver */
  return YTOROW(regs.x.dx);          /* Convert and return row */
}

/**********************************************************************
* Function      : M o u S h o w M o u s e                           *
**------------------------------------------------------------------**
* Task          : Display mouse pointer on the screen.              *
* Input parameters : None                                           *
* Return value  : None                                              *
* Info          : Calls of MouHidemMouse() and MouShowMouse() must  *
*                 be kept balanced.                                 *
**********************************************************************/

void MouShowMouse( void )
{
  union REGS regs;                   /* Processor regs for interrupt call */

  regs.x.ax = 0x0001;                /* Funct. no. for "Show Mouse" */
  MOUINT(regs, regs);                /* Call mouse driver */
}

/**********************************************************************
* Function      : M o u H i d e M o u s e                           *
**------------------------------------------------------------------**
* Task          : Hide mouse pointer from screen.                   *
* Input parameters : None                                           *
* Return value  : None                                              *
* Info          : Calls of MouHidemMouse() and MouShowMouse() must  *
*                 be kept balanced.                                 *
**********************************************************************/

void MouHideMouse( void )
{
  union REGS regs;                   /* Processor regs for interrupt call */

  regs.x.ax = 0x0002;                /* Funct. no. for "Hide Mouse" */
  MOUINT(regs, regs);                /* Call mouse driver */
}

/**********************************************************************
```

```
* Function       : M o u S e t M o v e A r e a           *
**-------------------------------------------------------**
* Task           : Defines a screen range within which the mouse *
*                  pointer may be moved.                  *
* Input parameters : x1, y1 = Coordinates of upper left corner  *
*                    x2, y2 = Coordinates of lower right corner *
* Return value    : None                                  *
* Info            : - Both parameters apply to text screen, NOT the *
*                    mouse driver's virtual graphic screen    - *
*********************************************************/

void MouSetMoveArea( BYTE x1, BYTE y1, BYTE x2, BYTE y2 )
{
  union REGS regs;              /* Processor regs for interrupt call */

  regs.x.ax = 0x0008;          /* Funct. no. for "Set vertical Limits" */
  regs.x.cx = ROWTOY( y1 );            /* Conversion to virtual */
  regs.x.dx = ROWTOY( y2 );            /* mouse screen          */
  MOUINT(regs, regs);                  /* Call mouse driver     */
  regs.x.ax = 0x0007;          /* Funct. no. for "Set horizontal Limits" */
  regs.x.cx = COLTOX( x1 );            /* Conversion to virtual */
  regs.x.dx = COLTOX( x2 );            /* mouse screen          */
  MOUINT(regs, regs);                  /* Call mouse driver     */
}


/*******************************************************
* Function       : M o u S e t S p e e d               *
**-------------------------------------------------------**
* Task           : Determines the difference between mouse movement *
*                  speed and the resulting pointer speed on the *
*                  screen.                                *
* Input parameters : - XSPEED = Horizontal speed          *
*                    - YSPEED = Vertical speed            *
* Return value    : None                                  *
* Info            : - Both parameters are based on mickeys *
*                    (mickey / 8 pixel).                  *
*********************************************************/

void MouSetSpeed( int xspeed, int yspeed )
{
  union REGS regs;              /* Processor regs for interrupt call */

  regs.x.ax = 0x000f;   /* Funct. no. for "Set mickeys to pixel ratio" */
  regs.x.cx = xspeed;
  regs.x.dx = yspeed;
  MOUINT(regs, regs);                  /* Call mouse driver */
}


/*******************************************************
* Function       : M o u M o v e P t r                 *
**-------------------------------------------------------**
* Task           : Moves the mouse pointer to a specific position *
*                  on the screen.                         *
* Input parameters : - COL = new screen column            *
*                    - ROW = new screen row               *
* Return value    : None                                  *
* Info            : - Both parameters apply to the text screen, NOT *
*                    to the mouse driver's virtual graphic screen *
*********************************************************/

void MouMovePtr( int col, int row )
{
  union REGS regs;              /* Processor regs for interrupt call */
  unsigned newrng;             /* Range in which the mouse can move */
```

```
  regs.x.ax = 0x0004;    /* Funct. no. for "Set mouse pointer position" */
  regs.x.cx = COLTOX( moucol = col ); /* Convert coordinates and store */
  regs.x.dx = ROWTOY( mourow = row ); /* in global variables       */
  MOUINT(regs, regs);                  /* Call mouse driver */

  newrng = *(bbuf + mourow * tcol + moucol);        /* Get range */
  if ( newrng != mourng )                      /* New range? */
    MouDefinePtr((newrng==NO_RANGE) ? stdptr :
                                (cur_range+newrng)->ptr_mask);
  mourng = newrng;           /* Place range number in global variables */
}


/*******************************************************
* Function       : M o u S e t D e f a u l t P t r     *
**-------------------------------------------------------**
* Task           : Defines mouse pointer for screen ranges without *
*                  the help of MouDefRange.              *
* Input parameters : STANDARD = Bitmask for standard mouse pointer *
* Return value    : None                                  *
*********************************************************/

void MouSetDefaultPtr( PTRVIEW standard )
{
  stdptr = standard;             /* Place bitmask in global variables */

  /*-- If mouse is currently in no range, go direct to conversion   ---*/
  /*-- to new pointer appearance                                    ---*/

  if ( MouGetRange() == NO_RANGE )             /* Not in any range? */
    MouDefinePtr( standard );                  /* NO */
}


/*******************************************************
* Function       : M o u E n d                         *
**-------------------------------------------------------**
* Task           : Ends mouseC module functions.         *
* Input parameters : None                                 *
* Return value    : None                                  *
* Info            : Function is called automatically when program *
*                  ends, as long as MouInstall is called first. *
*********************************************************/

void MouEnd( void )
{
  union REGS regs;              /* Processor regs for interrupt call */

  MouHideMouse();              /* Hide mouse pointer from screen */
  regs.x.ax = 0;                           /* Reset mouse driver */
  MOUINT(regs, regs);                      /* Call mouse driver */

  free( bbuf );                    /* Release allocated memory */
}


/*******************************************************
* Function       : M o u I n i t                       *
**-------------------------------------------------------**
* Task           : Initializes variables and mousec module *
* Input parameters : Columns, = Text screen resolution     *
*                    Lines                                *
* Return value    : TRUE if a mouse is installed, else FALSE *
* Info            : This function must be called as the first one in *
*                  the module.                            *
*********************************************************/
```

619

```
BYTE MouInit( BYTE columns, BYTE lines )
{
  union REGS regs;                    /* Processor regs for interrupt call */

  tline = lines;                      /* Store no. of lines and cols   */
  tcol  = columns;                    /* in global variables           */

  atexit( MouEnd );                   /* Call MouEnd at end of program */

  /*-- Allocate and fill mouse range buffer ---------------------------*/

  bbuf = (BYTE *) malloc( blen = tline * tcol );
  MouIButFill( 0, 0, tcol-1, tline-1, NO_RANGE );

  regs.x.ax = 0;                           /* Initialize mouse driver */
  MOUINT(regs, regs);                      /* Call mouse driver */
  if ( regs.x.ax != 0xffff )               /* Mouse driver installed? */
    return FALSE;                                /* NO */

  MouSetMoveAreaAll();                     /* Set range of movement */

  moucol = MouIGetX();                      /* Load current mouse pos. */
  mourow = MouIGetY();                      /* into global variables   */

  /*-- Install assembler event handler "AssmHand" ---------------------*/
  MouISetEventHandler( EV_MOU_ALL, (MOUHAPTR) AssmHand );

  return mavail = TRUE;                    /* Mouse is installed */
}

/**********************************************************************
*                M A I N     P R O G R A M                           *
**********************************************************************/

int main( void )
{
  static RANGE ranges[] =                    /* Mouse ranges */
  {
    {  0,  0, 79,  0, MouPtrMask( PTRDIFCHAR(0x18), PTRINVCOL) },
    {  0,  1,  0, 23, MouPtrMask( PTRDIFCHAR(0x1b), PTRINVCOL) },
    {  0, 24, 78, 24, MouPtrMask( PTRDIFCHAR(0x19), PTRINVCOL) },
    { 79,  1, 79, 23, MouPtrMask( PTRDIFCHAR(0x1a), PTRINVCOL) },
    { 79, 24, 79, 24, MouPtrMask( PTRDIFCHAR('X'),  PTRDIFCOLB(0x40) ) },
  };

  printf("\nMOUSEC - (c) 1989 by MICHAEL TISCHER\n\n");
  if ( MouInit( 80, 25 ) )                 /* Initialize mouse module */
  {                          /* OK, there is an installed mouse driver */
    printf("Move the mouse pointer around on the screen. When you move\n"\
           "the mouse  pointer  to  the  border  of  the  screen, the\n"\
           "mouse pointer changes in appearance,  depending  upon its\n"\
           "Current position.\n\n"\
           "Move  the mouse pointer  to the lower right corner  of the\n"\
           "screen,  and press both  the left  and right mouse buttons\n"\
           "to end this demo program.\n" );

    MouSetDefaultPtr( MouPtrMask( PTRDIFCHAR( '[' ), PTRDIFCOL( 3 ) ) );
    MouDefRange( ELVEC( ranges ), ranges );    /* Range definition */
```

```
    MouShowMouse();          /* Display mouse pointer on the screen */

    /*-- Wait until the user presses the left and right mouse     --*/
    /*-- buttons simultaneously, AND the mouse pointer lies in    --*/
    /*-- range 4                                                  --*/

    do                                              /* Read loop */
      MouEventWait( EAND, EV_LEFT_PRESS | EV_RIGHT_PRESS );
    while ( MouGetRange() != 4 );

    return 0;                              /* Return OK code to DOS */
  }
  else                       /* No mouse OR mouse driver installed */
  {
    printf("Sorry, no mouse driver installed.\n");
    return 1;                              /* Return error code to DOS */
  }
}
```

Assembler listing: MOUSECA.ASM

```
;*********************************************************************;
;*                        M O U S E C A                            *;
;*-----------------------------------------------------------------*;
;*    Task        : Mouse driver event handler intended for        *;
;*                  linking to a C program compiled as a SMALL     *;
;*                  memory model.                                  *;
;*-----------------------------------------------------------------*;
;*    Author      : MICHAEL TISCHER                                *;
;*    Developed on : 04/20/1989                                    *;
;*    Last update  : 06/14/1989                                    *;
;*-----------------------------------------------------------------*;
;*    assembly     : MASM /MX MOUSECA;                             *;
;*                   ... link to program MOUSEC                    *;
;*********************************************************************;

;== Segment declarations for the C program ===========================

IGROUP group _text              ;Inclusion for program segment
DGROUP group const,_bss, _data  ;Inclusion for data segment
       assume CS:IGROUP, DS:DGROUP, ES:DGROUP, SS:DGROUP

CONST  segment word public 'CONST';This segment includes all read-only
CONST  ends                      ;constants

_BSS   segment word public 'BSS' ;This segment includes all un-
_BSS   ends                      ;initialized static variables

_DATA  segment word public 'DATA' ;This segment includes all initialized
                                  ;global and static variables
_DATA  ends

;== Program =========================================================

_TEXT  segment byte public 'CODE' ;Program segment

public     _AssmHand             ;Gives the C program the ability to
                                 ;access assembler handler addresses

extrn      _MouEventHandler : near ;Event handler to be called

active    db  0                  ;Indicates whether a call is under
                                 ;execution


;--------------------------------------------------------------------
;-- _AssmHand : The event handler called by the mouse driver, then
;--           called by the MouEventHandler() function
;-- Call from C: not allowed!

_AssmHand    proc far

           ;-- Place all processor registers on the stack ---

           cmp  active,0     ;Call still not finished?
           jne  ende         ;NO --> Do not exit call

           mov  active,1         ;No more calls

           push ax
           push bx
           push cx
           push dx
           push di
           push si
           push bp
           push es
           push ds

           ;-- Place all arguments for calling C_FCT on the stack ---
           ;-- Call: MouEventHandler( int EvFlags, int ButStatus,
           ;--                  int x,      int y );

           mov  di,cx           ;Place horizontal coordinate in DI
           mov  cl,3            ;Counter for coordinate number
           shr  dx,cl           ;Divide DX (vertical coord.) by 8
           push dx              ;and place on the stack

           shr  di,cl           ;Divide DI (horizontal coord.) by 8
           push di              ;and place on the stack

           push bx              ;Push mouse button status onto stack
           push ax              ;Push event flag onto stack

           mov  ax,DGROUP       ;Move segment address of DGROUP to AX
           mov  ds,ax           ;Move AX to DS register

           call _MouEventHandler ;C function call

           add  sp,8            ;Get arguments from stack

           ;-- Pop register contents off of stack ---------

           pop  ds
           pop  es
           pop  bp
           pop  si
           pop  di
           pop  dx
           pop  cx
           pop  bx
           pop  ax

           mov  active,0        ;Re-enable call
ende:      ret                  ;Return to mouse driver

_AssmHand    endp

;--------------------------------------------------------------------

_text    ends                  ;End of code segment
         end                   ;End of program
```

9.3 Mouse — PC Communication

Let's briefly look at how the physical movements and button accesses of the mouse are translated into information the computer understands.

The method of data transfer depends on the manufacturer of the mouse, and the way the mouse interfaces with the computer. A serial mouse operates differently from a bus mouse. Since the serial mouse is more common than the bus mouse, we'll discuss only the serial mouse.

The mouse driver determines whether a mouse is connected during its initialization. For a Microsoft mouse, the mouse driver sets the serial port's DTR (DTR = Data Transfer Ready) line to 1. The mouse recognizes this signal and sends the ASCII code for the letter M over the data line. The driver doesn't wait very long for this return message. This is why a Microsoft-compatible mouse may not always work with the Microsoft mouse driver. Even though the mouse is set up to transfer data according to the Microsoft protocol, the driver may not recognize the mouse if the "M" isn't sent promptly.

Once successful handshaking has been established, the mouse uses the interrupt method to transfer its information to the driver. The mouse executes a hardware interrupt at the serial port as soon as it needs to inform the driver about a movement or button status change. The interrupts used are 0CH (COM1) or 0DH (COM2).

The mouse driver diverts the interrupts to a routine of its own so that it can read mouse data directly from the serial port. The data transfer for a Microsoft mouse uses the following parameters: 1200 baud, 7 data bits, no parity bit. Each mouse message consists of three bytes that indicate the mouse button status and the relative movement of the mouse since the last data transmission. The distance for mouse movements is measured in mickeys. Depending on the video card and mouse resolution, one mickey can be either be 1/200 or 1/400 of an inch.

As the following figure shows, only 7 bits are available to describe mouse movement along the X and Y axes. This allows us to cover distances between -128 and +127 mickeys. At the very latest, the new mouse position must be sent when the mouse moves outside this range. Generally, a new message will be sent much sooner than this.

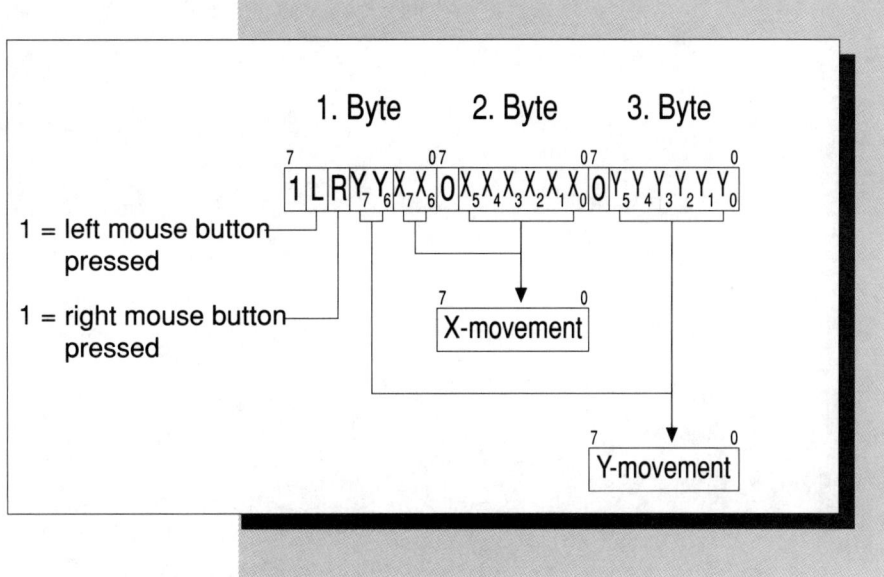

Data transfer format—Microsoft serial mouse

As the previous illustration shows, the Microsoft format is limited to two mouse buttons. The highest bit is reserved for synchronization with the mouse driver. This prevents the mouse driver from getting the second or third byte of the message first when the hardware interrupt fails and the first one or two bytes are lost. The high bit in the first byte is always set to 1 and the high bits of the other two bytes are always set to 0.

Other mouse manufacturers that use three buttons use a different communication format (e.g., eight data bits instead of seven). This extra bit allows transmission of the third mouse button's status. The other principles of communication are basically the same; the mouse is still connected to a serial port and the serial port interrupts communicate with the driver.

Chapter 10

Joysticks

Because of the recent improvements in video cards and joysticks, PC versions of many video games have become popular. In this chapter you'll learn how joysticks are connected to the PC, how to "read" the joystick from your own programs, and how the BIOS can help you adapt programs for joysticks.

Three demonstration programs at the end of this chapter demonstrate how joystick reading works in BASIC, Pascal, and C.

Connecting joysticks

The PC's hardware usually isn't configured to accept joysticks. An additional expansion card provides the hardware needed to implement joystick control. This card, called a *game control adapter* or simply a *game card*, is usually a half-size expansion card that plugs into one of the PC's expansion slots. Although these cards usually contain two connectors for two joysticks, usually you'll need only one.

The PC uses analog joysticks. This means that you can't simply use the joysticks from your old game machine or home computer and plug them into the PC; those joysticks are digital. The analog joystick handles a variety of information that isn't sensed by the digital joysticks, such as intensity. However, you'll see that this feature can sometimes be a disadvantage.

PC joysticks are equipped with two buttons that can be read independently of one another, and can be utilized to fit the software application. A few PC joysticks even have special purpose buttons (e.g., for rapid fire).

10.1 Reading Joysticks from BIOS

You don't need software drivers to monitor the joysticks because both the hardware and software interfaces were defined in the early stages of PC design. Hardware ports 200H to 20FH are reserved for a game card. The BIOS refers to the default values provided by these ports.

Two functions are available for software interfacing. These functions (sub-functions 00H and 01H) can be accessed from interrupt 15H, function 84H. They execute a joystick check using the polling method, which takes the current joystick position and joystick button status directly from the hardware ports.

However, the joysticks can be monitored only with the polling method because a special hardware interrupt, which executes when the user moves the joystick or presses a button, is assigned to the joystick cards. So, a program equipped for joystick access continually depends on sub-functions 00H and 01H for joystick movement.

Determining the joystick position

The joystick position can be determined by placing 84H in the AH register and 01H in the DX register, which calls function 84H, sub-function 01H. If the carry flag contains 0 after calling interrupt 15H, the BIOS supports the function (i.e., a game port exists), and joystick position data can be found in the AX, BX, CX, and DX registers.

The first joystick's position is conveyed by the contents of the AX and BX registers (indicating X-position and Y-position, respectively). The second joystick's position is indicated by the contents of the CX and DX registers (again, indicating X-position and Y-position).

The contents of these registers also indicate whether a joystick is connected to the port. If a stick is connected, the corresponding registers return values other than 0. So, if you find the CX and DX registers contain 0 after executing the function, a second joystick is connected. This rule also applies to the first joystick: If the AX and BX registers return 0, there isn't a first joystick.

Values other than 0 represent the joystick's position along the corresponding axis. However, there isn't a standard for these values. The values depend on the *potentiometers* (variable resistors, similar to the volume knob on a radio or television) contained in the joystick, which convert the joystick's position into a voltage. Different joysticks from different manufacturers and even different joystick models made by the same manufacturer return different voltages.

Many joystick oriented programs begin by prompting the user to move the joystick to the upper-right and the lower-left corners of the screen. This helps determine the range of movement offered by the potentiometers. Our in-house joysticks offer a range from 10 to 120 in the X-position, and from 9 to 102 in the Y-position. However, other joysticks may produce different values. It's important to remember that X-position values ascend from left to right, and that the Y-position values ascend from top to bottom (not from bottom to top).

Though it would be easy to assume that the joystick movement could be transformed into a linear coordinate system after simply determining its value range, this isn't true. The potentiometers in most joysticks operate exponentially rather than linearly.

Exponential operation means that the center position of the joystick doesn't correspond to the median value of the value range. The demonstration programs at the end of this chapter will demonstrate this as you run them and test your joystick.

To avoid the problems that result from the exponential measurements of the potentiometers, many programs avoid implementing joystick coordinates in a linear coordinate system. For example, a game such as PacMan® needs to recognize only four directions for game object movement (up, down, left, and right).

This type of application checks the joystick's position at the beginning of the program (i.e., the center position). From there, the application needs to compare only the center position with the current joystick values to determine the direction of movement. However, you cannot determine the intensity of the movement by using this method.

Reading the joystick buttons

In addition to the joystick position, the two joystick buttons are important to program operation.

The joystick position can be determined by placing 84H in the AH register and 00H in the DX register, thus calling function 84H, sub-function 00H. If the carry flag contains 0 after calling interrupt 15H, the BIOS supports the function (i.e., a game port exists), and the bits of the AL register indicate the status of the four available buttons on a set of two joysticks. The button being pressed sets the corresponding bit to a value of 1.

If the joystick buttons are arranged one above the other, the top button will be considered the first, and the lower button will be considered the second. When the joystick buttons are arranged side by side, the left one is considered the first, and the right one the second.

The following are the values of the AL register:

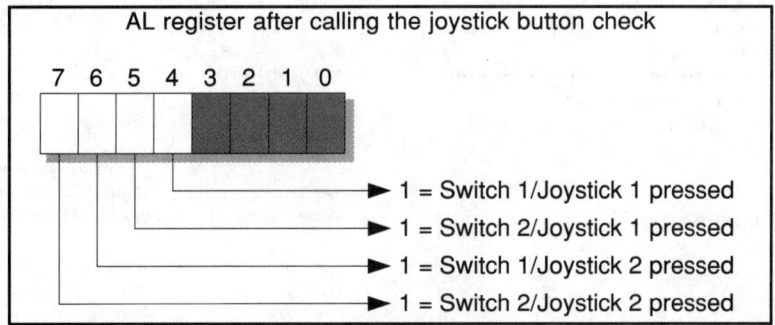

When working with this function, remember that it doesn't have a buffer function. So, it displays only the current joystick button status. If the user briefly presses a button when a joystick button check isn't being performed, the program won't sense the input and won't react to the user's action. So, if your program intends to use these buttons, it's especially important to permanently monitor the joystick button statuses in your programs using sub-function 00H.

10.2 Demonstration Programs

The three demonstration programs in BASIC, Pascal, and C read joystick position and button status using the GetJoyPos and GetJoyButton functions. Within the main program, these functions are used to first determine the joystick's minimum and maximum positions.

The program prompts the user to press the joystick up and right, and press a joystick button while the stick is in this position. This informs the program which joystick is being used (if two joysticks exist).

The program then prompts the user to press the joystick down and left, and press a joystick button while the stick is in this position. The program converts this range into the 80 columns and 25 rows of the text screen, and the current joystick position is calculated and indicated by an uppercase X. The resistance values yielded by the potentiometers are displayed in the upper-left corner of the screen, so that the user can see how the joystick operates.

The program ends when the user presses both joystick buttons simultaneously.

BASIC listing: JOYSTB.BAS

```
'***************************************************
'*                  J O Y S T B                  *'
'*-----------------------------------------------*'
'*  Task       : Demonstrates joystick reading through BIOS.  *'
'*  Author     : Michael Tischer                 *'
'*  Developed on : 02/25/91                       *'
'*  Last update  : 02/04/92                       *'
'***************************************************

DECLARE SUB GetJoyButton (j1b1%, j1b2%, j2b1%, j2b2%)
DECLARE SUB GetJoyPos (js1 AS ANY, js2 AS ANY)

REM $INCLUDE: 'g:qb.bi'

'-- Variable and type declarations -----------------

TYPE JSPOS 'Describes joystick position
  x AS INTEGER
  y AS INTEGER
END TYPE

DIM jsp(1 TO 2) AS JSPOS           'Current joystick position
DIM maxx AS INTEGER, maxy AS INTEGER   'Maximum joystick position
DIM minx AS INTEGER, miny AS INTEGER   'Minimum joystick position
DIM xold AS INTEGER, yold AS INTEGER    'Last joystick position
DIM curstick AS INTEGER            'Active joystick (1 or 2)
DIM xfactor AS SINGLE, yfactor AS SINGLE   'Coordinate factors
DIM j1but(1 TO 2) AS INTEGER       'Button 1 of joysticks 1 and 2
DIM j2but(1 TO 2) AS INTEGER       'Button 2 of joysticks 1 and 2

'-- Get maximum joystick positioning -----------------

CLS
PRINT "JOYSTICK POSITION TEST"
PRINT : PRINT "Push the joystick to the upper right, "
PRINT "then press one of the two buttons."

DO                                 'Wait for a joystick button
```

```
  CALL GetJoyButton(j1but(1), j2but(1), j1but(2), j2but(2))
LOOP WHILE (j1but(1) OR j2but(1) OR j1but(2) OR j2but(2)) = 0

IF j1but(1) OR j2but(1) <> 0 THEN        'Which joystick was that?
  curstick = 1
ELSE
  curstick = 2
END IF

CALL GetJoyPos(jsp(1), jsp(2))                    'Read position
maxx = jsp(curstick).x                  'Set as maximum position
miny = jsp(curstick).y

DO                                 'Wait for release of a joystick button
  CALL GetJoyButton(j1but(1), j2but(1), j1but(2), j2but(2))
LOOP UNTIL (j1but(curstick) = 0) AND (j2but(curstick) = 0)

'-- Get minimum joystick positioning -----------------

PRINT : PRINT
PRINT "Push the joystick to the lower left, "
PRINT "then press one of the two buttons."

DO                                 'Wait for a joystick button
  CALL GetJoyButton(j1but(1), j2but(1), j1but(2), j2but(2))
LOOP WHILE (j1but(curstick) = 0) AND (j2but(curstick) = 0)

CALL GetJoyPos(jsp(1), jsp(2))                    'Read position
minx = jsp(curstick).x                  'Set as minimum position
maxy = jsp(curstick).y

factorx = 80 / (maxx - minx + 1)        'Compute coordinate factor
factory = 23 / (maxy - miny + 1)        'using X-axis and Y-axis

'-- Read joystick, display position until -----------------
'-- the user presses both joystick buttons -----------------

CLS
LOCATE 2, 44
PRINT "JOYSTB  - (c) 1992 by Michael Tischer";
```

628

```
LOCATE 25, 1
PRINT "Press both joystick buttons to end the program"

xold = 1                                          'Set old position
yold = 1

DO
   '-- Read and display position -----------------------------------
   CALL GetJoyPos(jsp(1), jsp(2))
   LOCATE 1, 1
   PRINT "("; jsp(curstick).x; "/"; jsp(curstick).y; ")  ";

   '-- Compute new X-position of the joystick ----------------------
   x% = factorx * (jsp(curstick).x - minx% + 1)
   IF x% < 1 THEN x% = 1
   IF x% > 80 THEN x% = 80

   '-- Compute new Y-position of the joystick ----------------------
   y% = factory * (jsp(curstick).y - miny% + 1)
   IF y% < 1 THEN y% = 1
   IF y% > 23 THEN y% = 23

   '-- Display new position if position changes --------------------
   IF (x% <> xold) OR (y% <> yold) THEN
      LOCATE yold + 1, xold                    'Mask at old X-position
      PRINT " ";
      LOCATE y% + 1, x%                        'and display at new X-position
      PRINT "X";
      xold = x%                                'Make new position old position
      yold = y%
   END IF

CALL GetJoyButton(j1but(1), j2but(1), j1but(2), j2but(2))
LOOP UNTIL (j1but(curstick) = 1) AND (j2but(curstick) = 1)

CLS

'*****************************************************************'
'* GetJoyButton: Returns joystick button status.               *'
'*-------------------------------------------------------------*'
'* Input  : J1B1% = 1 if button 1 (stick 1) depressed, otherwise 0  *'
'*          J1B2% = 1 if button 2 (stick 1) depressed, otherwise 0  *'
'*          J2B1% = 1 if button 1 (stick 2) depressed, otherwise 0  *'
'*          J2B2% = 1 if button 2 (stick 2) depressed, otherwise 0  *'
'*****************************************************************'

SUB GetJoyButton (j1b1%, j1b2%, j2b1%, j2b2%)
   DIM regs AS RegType               'Dimension array for registers

   regs.ax = &H8400          'Call BIOS interrupt 15H, function 84H,
   regs.dx = &H0             'sub-function 00H
   CALL INTERRUPT(&H15, regs, regs)
   j1b1% = (regs.ax AND 16) \ 16 XOR 1          'Bit 4 of AX = J1B1
   j1b2% = (regs.ax AND 32) \ 32 XOR 1          'Bit 5 of AX = J1B2
   j2b1% = (regs.ax AND 64) \ 64 XOR 1          'Bit 6 of AX = J2B1
   j2b2% = (regs.ax AND 128) \ 128 XOR 1        'Bit 7 of AX = J2B2
END SUB

'*****************************************************************'
'* GetJoyPos : Gets positions of both joysticks.               *'
'*-------------------------------------------------------------*'
'* Input  : JS1 = Structure of type JSPOS for storing position of  *'
'*                joystick 1                                     *'
'*          JS2 = Structure of type JSPOS for storing position of  *'
```

```
'*                joystick 2                                    *'
'*****************************************************************'

SUB GetJoyPos (js1 AS JSPOS, js2 AS JSPOS)
   DIM regs AS RegType   'Dimension array for registers

   regs.ax = &H8400              'Call BIOS interrupt 15H, function 84H,
   regs.dx = &H1                 'sub-function 01H
   CALL INTERRUPT(&H15, regs, regs)
   js1.x = regs.ax                  'Store joystick position registers
   js1.y = regs.bx                  'in respective variables
   js2.x = regs.cx
   js2.y = regs.dx
END SUB
```

AX
not AH!

Pascal listing: JOYSTP.PAS

```
{***************************************************************}
{                      J O Y S T P                            }
{-------------------------------------------------------------}
{  Task        : Demonstrates joystick reading through BIOS.  }
{-------------------------------------------------------------}
{  Author      : Michael Tischer                              }
{  Developed on : 02/25/91                                    }
{  Last update  : 02/05/92                                    }
{***************************************************************}

program JOYSTP;

uses DOS, CRT;

{== Type declarations ========================================}

type JSPOS = record { Describes joystick position }
               x,
               y : integer;
             end;

{== Constants ================================================}

const CRLF = #13#10;

{== Global variables =========================================}

var jsp      : array [1..2] of JSPOS;  { Current joystick position }
    maxx, maxy,                        { Maximum joystick position }
    minx, miny,                        { Minimum joystick position }
    x, y,                              { Current screen position }
    xold, yold : integer;             { Last joystick position }
    curstick   : byte;                { Active joystick }
    j1but,                            { Button 1 of joysticks 1 and 2 }
    j2but    : array[1..2] of byte;   { Button 2 of joysticks 1 and 2 }
    xfactor,                          { Coordinate factors for X and Y }
    yfactor  : real;

{***************************************************************}
{* GetJoyButton:  Returns joystick button status.            *}
{*-----------------------------------------------------------*}
{* Input: J1B1 = 1 if button 1 (stick 1) depressed, otherwise 0 *}
{*        J1B2 = 1 if button 2 (stick 1) depressed, otherwise 0 *}
{*        J2B1 = 1 if button 1 (stick 2) depressed, otherwise 0 *}
{*        J2B2 = 1 if button 2 (stick 2) depressed, otherwise 0 *}
{***************************************************************}

procedure GetJoyButton( var j1b1, j1b2, j2b1, j2b2 : byte );

var Regs : Registers;     { Processor registers for interrupt call }

begin
  Regs.ah := $84;                          { Function 84H }
  Regs.dx := 0;                            { Sub-function 00H }
  intr( $15, Regs );                       { Call interrupt 15H }
  j1b1 := (( Regs.al and  16 ) shr 4) xor 1;  { Bit 4 of AL = J1B1 }
  j1b2 := (( Regs.al and  32 ) shr 5) xor 1;  { Bit 5 of AL = J1B2 }
  j2b1 := (( regs.al and  64 ) shr 6) xor 1;  { Bit 6 of AL = J2B1 }
  j2b2 := (( regs.al and 128 ) shr 7) xor 1;  { Bit 7 of AL = J2B2 }
end;

{***************************************************************}
```

```
{* GetJoyPos : Gets positions of both joysticks.             *}
{*-----------------------------------------------------------*}
{* Input    : JS1 = Joystick structure for joystick 1        *}
{*            JS2 = Joystick structure for joystick 2         *}
{***************************************************************}

procedure GetJoyPos( var Js1, Js2 : JSPOS );

var Regs : Registers;       { Processor registers for interrupt call }

begin
  Regs.ah := $84;                          { Function 84H }
  Regs.dx := 1;                            { Sub-function 01h }
  intr( $15, Regs );                       { Call interrupt 15H }
  Js1.x := Regs.ax;                        { X-position: Joystick 1 }
  Js1.y := Regs.bx;                        { Y-position: Joystick 1 }
  Js2.x := Regs.cx;                        { X-position: Joystick 2 }
  Js2.y := Regs.dx;                        { Y-position: Joystick 2 }
end;

{***************************************************************}
{*                    MAIN PROGRAM                           *}
{***************************************************************}

begin
{-- Get maximum joystick positioning --------------------------------}

ClrScr;
writeln( 'JOYSTICK POSITION TEST');
writeln( 'Push the joystick to the upper right, ' +
         CRLF + 'then press one of the two buttons, ');

repeat                              { Wait for a joystick button }
  GetJoyButton( j1but[1], j2but[1], j1but[2], j2but[2] );
until ( ( j1but[1] or j2but[1] or j1but[2] or j2but[2] ) > 0 );

if ( j1but[1] or j2but[1] ) <> 0 then   { Which joystick was that? }
  curstick := 1
else
  curstick := 2;

GetJoyPos( jsp[1], jsp[2] );                    { Read position }
maxx := jsp[curstick].x;                        { Set position }
miny := jsp[curstick].y;

repeat                       { Wait for release of a joystick button }
  GetJoyButton( j1but[1], j2but[1], j1but[2], j2but[2] );
until ( ( j1but[curstick] or j2but[curstick] ) = 0 );

{-- Get minimum joystick positioning --------------------------------}

writeln( CRLF + CRLF + 'Push the joystick to the lower left, ' +
         CRLF + 'then press one of the two buttons, ');
repeat                              { Wait for a joystick button }
  GetJoyButton( j1but[1], j2but[1], j1but[2], j2but[2] );
until ( ( j1but[curstick] or j2but[curstick] ) <> 0 );

GetJoyPos( jsp[1], jsp[2] );                    { Read position }
minx := jsp[curstick].x;                        { Set position }
maxy := jsp[curstick].y;

xfactor := 80.0 / ( maxx - minx + 1 );  { Compute coordinate factor }
yfactor := 23.0 / ( maxy - miny + 1 );  { using X-axis and Y-axis }
```

```
{-- Read joystick, display position until  -------------------------}
{-- the user presses both joystick buttons -----------------------}

ClrScr;
GotoXY( 40, 1 );
write( 'JOYSTP - (c) 1991, 92 by Michael Tischer' );
GotoXY( 1, 25 );
write( 'Press both joystick buttons to end the program');

xold := 0;                              { Set old position }
yold := 0;


repeat
  GetJoyPos( jsp[1], jsp[2] );                { Read position }

  {-- Compute new X-position of the joystick ------------------------}

  x := round(xfactor * ( jsp[curstick].x - minx + 1 ));
  if ( x < 0 ) then
    x := 0;
  if ( x > 79 ) then
    x := 79;

  {-- Compute new Y-position of the joystick ------------------------}

  y := round(yfactor * ( jsp[curstick].y - miny + 1 ));
  if ( y < 0 ) then
    y := 0;
  if ( y > 22 ) then
    y := 22;

  {-- Display new position if position changes ----------------------}

  if ( x <> xold ) or ( y <> yold ) then
    begin
      GotoXY( xold+1, yold+2 );
      write( ' ' );
      GotoXY( x+1, y+2 );
      write( 'X' );
      xold := x;
      yold := y;
    end;


  GotoXY( 1, 1 );
  write( '(', jsp[curstick].x:3, '/', jsp[curstick].y:3, ')' );
  GetJoyButton( j1but[1], j2but[1], j1but[2], j2but[2] );
until ( j1but[curstick] = 1 ) and ( j2but[curstick] = 1 );
ClrScr;
GotoXY( 1, 1 );
writeln( 'End program.' );
end.
```

C listing: JOYSTC.C

```c
/********************************************************************/
/*                      J O Y S T C                             */
/*------------------------------------------------------------------*/
/*    Task        : Demonstrates joystick reading through BIOS. */
/*------------------------------------------------------------------*/
/*    Author      : Michael Tischer                            */
/*    Developed on : 02/25/91                                  */
/*    Last update  : 02/06/92                                  */
/*------------------------------------------------------------------*/
/*    (MICROSOFT C)                                            */
/*    Compilation  : CL /AS JOYSTC.C                           */
/*    Call         : JOYSTC                                    */
/*------------------------------------------------------------------*/
/*    (BORLAND TURBO C)                                        */
/*    Compilation  : Use COMPILE/MAKE command                  */
/********************************************************************/

/*== Add include files ============================================*/

#include <dos.h>
#include <stdio.h>
#include <stdarg.h>

/*== Type declarations ============================================*/

typedef unsigned char BYTE;
typedef struct {                 /* Describes joystick position */
               int x;
               int y;
               } JSPOS;

/********************************************************************
* ClrScr: Clears the screen.                                      *
**----------------------------------------------------------------**
* Input : DCOLR  = Character attribute                            *
* Output: None                                                    *
********************************************************************/

void ClrScr( BYTE dcolr )
{
 union REGS regs;                /* Processor regs. for interrupt call */

 /*-- Clear screen using BIOS scroll function ----------------------*/

 regs.h.ah = 6;                       /* Function number: Scroll down */
 regs.h.al = 0;                       /* Scroll 0 lines (clear screen) */
 regs.h.bh = dcolr;                            /* Character color */
 regs.x.cx = 0;                       /* Upper-left corner of window */
 regs.x.dx = ( 24 << 8 ) + 79;        /* Lower-right corner of window */
 int86(0x10, &regs, &regs);           /* Call BIOS video interrupt */

 /*-- Place cursor in upper-left corner using BIOS -----------------*/

 regs.h.ah = 2;                       /* Function number:  Set cursor */
 regs.h.bh = 0;                            /* Access screen page 0 */
 regs.x.dx = 0;                       /* Upper-left corner of screen */
 int86(0x10, &regs, &regs);           /* Call BIOS video interrupt */
}


/********************************************************************
* printfat : Displays a formatted string anywhere on the screen.  *
**----------------------------------------------------------------**
```

```
*   Input : COLUMN = Column                                              *
*           SCROW  = Row                                                 *
*           STRING = Pointer to string                                   *
*           ...    = Arguments similar to PRINTF()                       *
*   Output: None                                                         *
*   Info  : This function should only be called if the system running    *
*           this program contains an EGA card or a VGA card.             *
**********************************************************************/

void printfat( BYTE column, BYTE scrow, char * string, ... )
{
 va_list parameter;               /* Parameter list for VA_... macros */
 union REGS regs;                 /* Processor regs. for interrupt call */

 /*-- Place cursor using BIOS -----------------------------------*/

 regs.h.ah = 2;                   /* Function number:  Set cursor */
 regs.h.bh = 0;                   /* Access screen page 0 */
 regs.h.dh = scrow;               /* Set row */
 regs.h.dl = column;              /* Set column */
 int86(0x10, &regs, &regs);       /* Call BIOS video interrupt */

 /*-- Display string --------------------------------------------*/

 va_start( parameter, string );
 vprintf( string, parameter );
}


/**********************************************************
*  Function      : G E T J O Y B U T T O N               *
**------------------------------------------------------**
*  Task : Returns joystick button status.                *
*  Input : J1B1 = 1 if button 1 (stick 1) depressed, otherwise 0   *
*          J1B2 = 1 if button 2 (stick 1) depressed, otherwise 0   *
*          J2B1 = 1 if button 1 (stick 2) depressed, otherwise 0   *
*          J2B2 = 1 if button 2 (stick 2) depressed, otherwise 0   *
*  Output: None                                          *
**********************************************************************/

void GetJoyButton( BYTE *j1b1, BYTE *j1b2, BYTE *j2b1, BYTE *j2b2 )
{
 union REGS regs;                 /* Get processor registers */

 regs.h.ah = 0x84;                /* Function 84H */
 regs.x.dx = 0;                   /* Sub-function 00H */
 int86( 0x15, &regs, &regs );     /* Call interrupt 15H */
 *j1b1 = (( regs.h.al &  16 ) >> 4) ^ 1;   /* Bit 4 of AL = J1B1 */
 *j1b2 = (( regs.h.al &  32 ) >> 5) ^ 1;   /* Bit 5 of AL = J1B2 */
 *j2b1 = (( regs.h.al &  64 ) >> 6) ^ 1;   /* Bit 6 of AL = J2B1 */
 *j2b2 = (( regs.h.al & 128 ) >> 7) ^ 1;   /* Bit 7 of AL = J2B2 */
}

/**********************************************************
*  Function      : G E T J O Y P O S                     *
**------------------------------------------------------**
*  Task : Gets positions of both joysticks.              *
*  Input : JS1PTR = Pointer to joystick structure for first joystick  *
*          JS2PTR = Pointer to joystick structure for second joystick *
*  Output: None                                          *
**********************************************************************/

void GetJoyPos( JSPOS *Js1Ptr, JSPOS *Js2Ptr )
{
 union REGS regs;                 /* Get processor registers */
```

```
 regs.h.ah = 0x84;                /* Function 84H */
 regs.x.dx = 1;                   /* Sub-function 01H */
 int86( 0x15, &regs, &regs );     /* Call interrupt 15H */
 Js1Ptr->x = regs.x.ax;           /* X-position: Joystick 1 */
 Js1Ptr->y = regs.x.bx;           /* Y-position: Joystick 1 */
 Js2Ptr->x = regs.x.cx;           /* X-position: Joystick 2 */
 Js2Ptr->y = regs.x.dx;           /* Y-position: Joystick 2 */
}


/**********************************************************************/
/**                    MAIN PROGRAM                                **/
/**********************************************************************/

void main()
{
 JSPOS jsp[2];                    /* Current joystick position */
 int   maxx, maxy,                /* Maximum joystick position */
       minx, miny,                /* Minimum joystick position */
       x, y,                      /* Current screen position */
       xold, yold;                /* Last screen position */
 BYTE  curstick,                  /* Active joystick */
       j1but[2],                  /* Button 1 of joysticks 1 and 2 */
       j2but[2];                  /* Button 2 of joysticks 1 and 2 */
 float xfactor, yfactor;          /* Coordinate factors X and Y */

 /*-- Get maximum joystick positioning ---------------------------*/

 ClrScr( 0x07 );
 printf( "JOYSTICK POSITION TEST\n\n");
 printf( "Push the joystick to the upper right,\n" \
         "then press one of the two buttons.\n" );

 do                               /* Wait for a joystick button */
  GetJoyButton( &j1but[0], &j2but[0], &j1but[1], &j2but[1] );
 while ( ( j1but[0] | j2but[0] | j1but[1] | j2but[1] ) == 0 );

 curstick = ( j1but[0] | j2but[0] ) ? 0 : 1;   /* Select joystick */

 GetJoyPos( &jsp[0], &jsp[1] );   /* Read position */
 maxx = jsp[curstick].x;          /* Set position */
 miny = jsp[curstick].y;

 do                               /* Wait for release of a joystick button */
  GetJoyButton( &j1but[0], &j2but[0], &j1but[1], &j2but[1] );
 while ( ( j1but[curstick] | j2but[curstick] ) != 0 );

 /*-- Get minimum joystick positioning ---------------------------*/

 printf( "\n\nPush the joystick to the lower left,\n"\
         "then press one of the two buttons.\n" );

 do                               /* Wait for a joystick button */
  GetJoyButton( &j1but[0], &j2but[0], &j1but[1], &j2but[1] );
 while ( ( j1but[curstick] | j2but[curstick] ) == 0 );

 GetJoyPos( &jsp[0], &jsp[1] );   /* Read position */
 minx = jsp[curstick].x;          /* Set position */
 maxy = jsp[curstick].y;

 do                               /* Wait for release of a joystick button */
  GetJoyButton( &j1but[0], &j2but[0], &j1but[1], &j2but[1] );
 while ( ( j1but[curstick] | j2but[curstick] ) != 0 );
```

```
xfactor = 80.0 / ( maxx - minx + 1 );   /* Compute coordinate factor */
yfactor = 23.0 / ( maxy - miny + 1 );   /* using X-axis and Y-axis   */

/*-- Read joystick, display position until  ------------------------*/
/*-- the user presses both joystick buttons ------------------------*/

ClrScr( 0x07 );
printfat( 43, 0, "JOYSTC - (c) 1992 by Michael Tischer" );
printfat( 0, 24 , "Press both joystick buttons to end the program" );

xold = yold = 0;                              /* Set old position */
do
 {
  GetJoyPos( &jsp[0], &jsp[1] );              /* Read position */

  /*-- Compute new X-position of the joystick ----------------------*/

  x = (int) ( xfactor * (float) ( jsp[curstick].x - minx + 1 ) );
  if ( x < 0 )
    x = 0;
  if ( x > 79 )
    x = 79;

  /*-- Compute new X-position of the joystick ----------------------*/

  y = (int) ( yfactor * (float) ( jsp[curstick].y - miny + 1 ) );
  if ( y < 0 )
    y = 0;
  if ( y > 22 )
    y = 22;

  /*-- Display new position if position changes --------------------*/

  if ( x != xold || y != yold )
   {
    printfat( (BYTE) xold, (BYTE) (yold+1), " " );
    printfat( (BYTE) x, (BYTE) (y+1), "X" );
    xold = x;
    yold = y;
   }

  printfat( 0, 0, "(%3d,%3d)", jsp[curstick].x, jsp[curstick].y );
  GetJoyButton( &j1but[0], &j2but[0], &j1but[1], &j2but[1] );
 }
while ( j1but[curstick] == 0  && j2but[curstick] == 0 );
ClrScr( 0x07 );
printf( "End program.\n");
```

Chapter 11

Accessing and Programming the AT Realtime Clock

DOS uses the date and the time to timestamp files and to provide programs with the current date and time. Many BIOS functions are available to pass this information. Almost all ATs and higher end machines include battery operated realtime clocks. These clocks continue to run when the PC is switched off.

11.1 Reading the Date and Time from BIOS

BIOS interrupt 1AH addresses the various ROM-BIOS time functions. Although the PC and the PC/XT had only two of these functions, the AT and higher end models have eight functions that control the realtime clock (RTC). The AT realtime clock keeps time differently than the older PCs and PC/XTs, which used a software interrupt to perform this task. Before we discuss the BIOS time and date functions, let's look at the earlier method of time control in PC clocks.

Time measurement using timer interrupt 08H

The PC's timer chip (an Intel 8254 or a compatible chip) receives 1,193,180 signals per second from the heart of the system, which is an oscillating quartz crystal. After 65,536 of these signals, or about 18.2 times (18.20648193) a second, the chip calls interrupt 08H. The interrupt controller passes the call to the CPU. Interrupt 08H is called separately from the CPU frequency and takes its frequency from the vibrating quartz crystal.

After 18.2 occurrences, BIOS sends interrupt 08H to the ROM-BIOS. This increments a time counter. The current time can easily be calculated in seconds by reading this counter and dividing its value by 18.2. This value can then be converted into hours, minutes, and seconds.

Interrupt 08H also switches off the disk drive motors after a specific period of inactivity. This is done in conjunction with the BIOS interrupt 13H, through which a disk drive can be accessed. Since starting a disk drive motor is time-consuming, the motor remains on after receiving a BIOS disk function so that it won't have to be restarted for the next disk operation.

After the interrupt interface has completed its tasks, it calls interrupt 1CH. Usually this interrupt carries an IRET instruction, which immediately returns program execution to the time interrupt interface. However, a program may define its own interface to use the cyclical time signal. This is useful for permanently displaying the current time on the screen, which is demonstrated by a TSR program in Chapter 32.

Timer interrupt 08H is the only way to measure time in PCs and PC/XTs. The AT and higher end computers contain realtime clocks with battery backup, which continue measure the time without a timer interrupt. The AT ROM-BIOS still manages the timer interrupt, however, to maintain downward software compatibility to the PC and PC/XT systems.

Function 00H: Get clock

Function number 00H obtains the current clock time. You can call this function by passing the number 00H to the AH register. The function loads the time into the CX and DX registers. These two registers combine to form a 32-bit counter value (CX contains the most significant 16 bits, while DX contains the least significant 16 bits). The BIOS timer increments this value by 1 each time interrupt 8H is called (18.2 times per second). The total value is the result of multiplying the contents of CX register by 65,536 and adding the contents of the DX register. Dividing this value by 18.2 returns the number of seconds elapsed, which can then be converted into minutes and hours.

The AT interprets time differently than the PC and XT. The PC/XT BIOS sets this counter to 0 during the system booting process. The value returned is the time passed since the computer was switched on (not the actual time). To obtain the time, the current time must be converted to the value corresponding to the counter, then passed to the BIOS (more on this later). The AT doesn't require this time value conversion because BIOS reads the actual time from the realtime clock during the system boot. It converts this time into a suitable timer value and then saves it. Reading the counter with the help of function 0 on the AT provides the current time.

Besides this counter, a value in the AL register indicates whether 24 hours have passed since the last reading. If the AL register contains a value other than 0, 24 hours have passed. This value doesn't indicate how many 24-hour periods have elapsed since the last reading.

If the conversion of time values into clock time is too complicated, function 2CH of DOS interrupt 21H can be used. This function simply reads and converts the current time using function 0 of interrupt 1AH. (See Chapter 18 of this book for more information about function 2CH of DOS interrupt 1AH.)

Function 01H: Set clock

Function number 01H sets the current clock time. You can call this function by loading the number 1 into the AH register, the most significant 16 bits of the counter into the CX register, and the least significant 16 bits into the DX register. These two registers combine to form a 32-bit time value. If the conversion of the current time into a timer value is too complicated, function 2DH of DOS interrupt 21H can be used instead (see Chapter 22 of this book for more information about function 2DH of DOS interrupt 21H.)

Functions for accessing the realtime clock

The following six functions are available only on the AT and higher end models. Although realtime clocks are also available for the PC and the PC/XT, they usually aren't supported by the computer's ROM-BIOS. So, unless the manufacturer also supplies a TSR program that implements the corresponding AT BIOS functions, calling these functions won't return any results on PCs and PC/XTs. When developing a program that accesses AT clock functions, test the model identification byte in F000:FFFE to ensure that the system is an AT or higher end machine (see Chapter 3 for more information about the model identification byte).

All six functions use BCD format for time and date indications. In this format, two characters are coded per byte; the higher number is coded in the higher nibble and the lower number in the lower nibble. All six functions use the carry flag following a return from the function call. If the carry flag is set, this indicates that the realtime clock is malfunctioning (e.g., from a dead battery). The called function couldn't be executed properly.

Function 02H: Get current time

Function 02H reads the realtime clock time. You can call the function by loading the function number (2) into the AH register. The current time is returned with the hour in the CH register, minutes in the CL register, and the seconds in the DH register.

Function 03H: Set current time

Function 03H sets the time on the realtime clock. You can call this function by loading the function number (3) into the AH register, the hour into the CH register, minutes into the CL register, and seconds into the DH register. The DL register indicates whether the "daylight savings time" option should be used. A 1 in the DL register selects daylight savings time, while 0 maintains standard time.

Functions 04H and 05H read and set the date stored in the realtime clock. Both functions use the century, year, month, and day as arguments. The day of the week (also administered by the realtime clock) doesn't apply to these functions. If you want to read the day of the week, you must directly access the realtime clock.

Function 04H: Get current date

Function 04H gets the current date from the realtime clock. You can call this function by loading the function number (4) into the AH register. The CH register contains the first two numbers of the year (the century). The CL register contains the last two numbers of the year (e.g., 88). The month is returned in the DH register and the day of the month in the DL register.

Function 05H: Set current date

Function 05H sets the current date in the realtime clock. You can call this function by loading the function number (5) into the AH register, either 19 decimal or 20 decimal into the CH register, the last two numbers of the year into the CL register (e.g., 89 decimal), the month into the DH register, and the day of the month into the DL register.

Function 06H: Set alarm time

Function 06H allows the user to set an alarm. Since only the hour, minute, and second can be indicated, the alarm time applies only to the current day. When the clock reaches the alarm time, the realtime clock calls a BIOS routine that in turn calls interrupt 4AH. A user routine can be installed under this interrupt to simulate the sound of an alarm clock. (You can program the routine to make other sounds.)

During the system initialization interrupt 4AH moves to a routine that contains only the IRET assembly language instruction. The IRET instruction forces the CPU to terminate the interrupt so that arriving at alarm time doesn't result in any action visible to the user. You can call this function by loading the function number (6) into the AH register, the alarm hour into the CH register, the alarm minute into the CL register, and the alarm second into the DH register.

Function 07H: Reset alarm time

Only one alarm time can be set. If this function is called while another alarm time is set or hasn't been reached yet, the carry flag is set after the function call. A new alarm time doesn't replace the old alarm time; the old time must be deleted first. You can call this function by loading the function number (7) into the AH register; no other parameters are required. This call clears the last alarm time so that a new alarm time can be programmed.

To call this function, place its function number in the AH register; no further arguments are required. This function call will then delete the current alarm time so that a new alarm time may be set, if desired.

11.2 Reading and Setting the Realtime Clock

The AT and higher end models each have a battery operated realtime clock on the main circuit board. This clock is part of the Motorola MC-146818 processor, which contains 64 bytes of battery backup RAM. This RAM accepts clock data and system configuration data. It can be accessed through port addresses 70H to 7FH. However, the user needs only ports 70H and 71H.

Realtime clock registers

As the following table shows, the clock has sixteen important memory registers:

Realtime clock registers	
Reg.	Meaning
00H	Current second
01H	Alarm second
02H	Current minute
03H	Alarm minute
04H	Current hour
05H	Alarm hour
06H	Day of the week
07H	Number of day
08H	Month
09H	Year
0AH	Clock status register A
0BH	Clock status register B
0CH	Clock status register C
0DH	Clock status register D
32H	Century (19 or 20)

Each time field (second, minute, hour) has a similar alarm field. With these alarm fields, a programmer can set the clock to trigger an interrupt at a particular time of the current day (more on this later).

Weekday

The day of the week provides the number of the current weekday. The value 1 represents Sunday, the value 2 represents Monday, 3 for Tuesday, etc.

Year

The year is counted relative to the century (the system assumes 1900). The value 87 in this field represents the year 1987.

The four status registers enable the user to program the clock.

Accessing the individual registers of the realtime clock

Since the registers are a part of the 64-byte RAM, you can access them like any other memory location. First load the number of the memory location to be accessed into the AL register. Then pass this value to port 70H using the OUT instruction. Since direct value output to a port is impossible, register AX is used for the output. The chip recognizes that an access to one of its memory locations occurred. Then either an OUT instruction writes to port 71H or an IN instruction reads the memory contents from port 71H.

The following instructions read or write a memory location in the realtime clock:

READ:

```
mov   al,Memory_location
out   70h,al
in    al,71h
```

WRITE:

```
mov   al,Memory_location
out   70h,al
mov   al,New_contents
out   71h,al
```

Status register A

The four status registers are of particular interest to us because these registers are used for programming the clock. The following is a description of status register A:

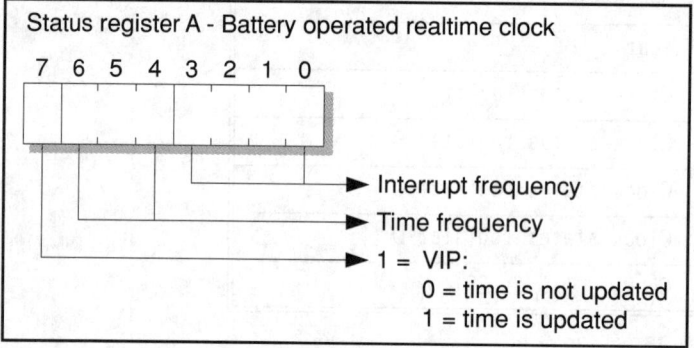

```
Status register A - Battery operated realtime clock

  7  6  5  4  3  2  1  0

                        ──► Interrupt frequency
                  ──► Time frequency
            ──► 1 = VIP:
                 0 = time is not updated
                 1 = time is updated
```

The ROM-BIOS set the two lower fields of these registers during the system boot. The interrupt frequency field has a default value of 0110(b). This value results in an interrupt frequency of 1024 interrupts per second (i.e., an interrupt every 976,562 microseconds).

The contents of the time frequency field is 010(b). This field triggers a time frequency of 32,768 kiloHertz.

Bit 7 of the status register is used with these two fields. This bit indicates whether a second has just elapsed and increments the time fields (seconds, minutes, hours). If a second hasn't elapsed, this bit contains a 1. With this bit, you can read the individual time fields only when the time isn't being updated. Otherwise, a minute could pass and the second counter reset to 0 before the minute counter could be incremented. This could cause a time jump from 13:59:59 to 13:59:00, then the correct display of 14:00:01 one second later.

Status register B

Several clock parameters can be programmed through status register B:

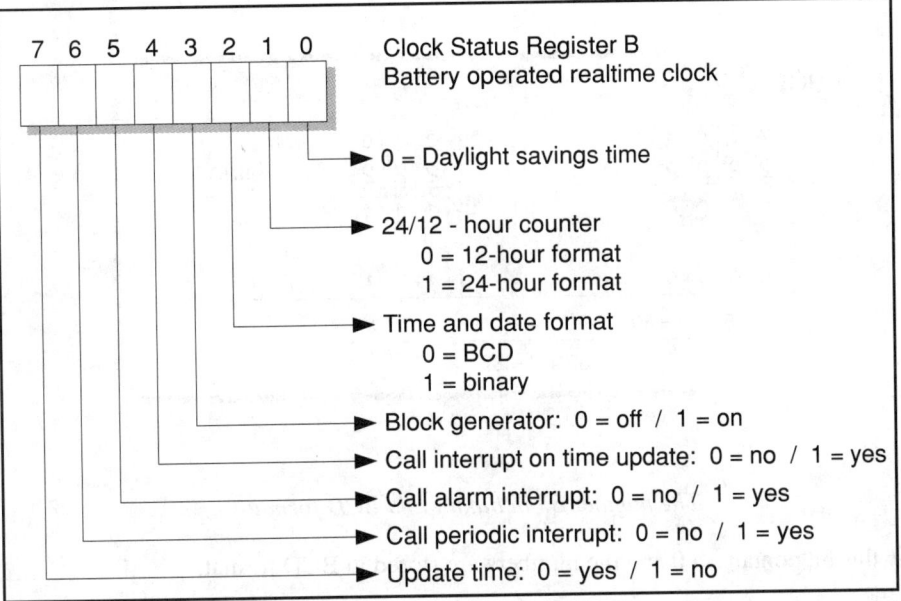

Some clock settings can be programmed through status register B. Bit 0 of status register B controls daylight savings time status. When this bit is set to 1, it indicates that daylight savings time is in effect. A value of 0 (the default value for this bit) indicates that standard time is in effect.

Bit 1 determines whether the clock should operate in 12-hour or 24-hour mode. In 12-hour mode, the clock switches to 1 o'clock after every 12 hours (midnight and noon). The 24-hour mode switches to 1 o'clock after 24 hours. This mode is active when you boot the system.

Bit 2 defines the format in which the time and date fields are stored. If this bit contains a 1, the various dates are stored in binary notation. The year (19)87 is coded as 01010111(b) in BCD format, which is switched on by the value 0 in bit 2. Two numbers are stored in every byte. The higher half is stored in the most significant four bits and the lower half is stored in the least significant four bits.

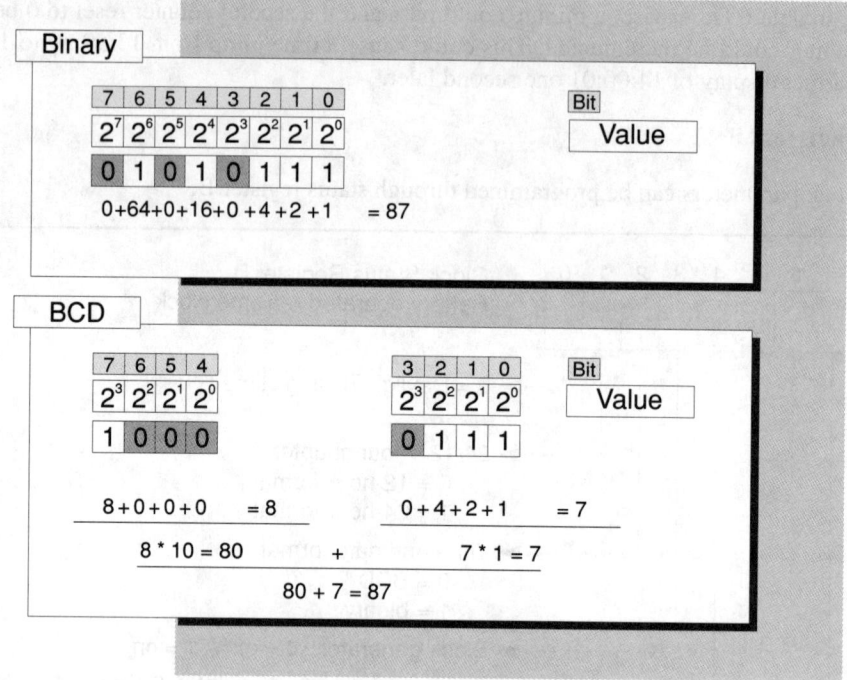

The number 87 in binary and BCD format

Usually this bit contains a 0 and the numbers are stored in BCD format.

Note: BIOS assumes BCD representation when performing the date function with interrupt 1AH. Programs that call these functions and obtain the information in binary format instead of the expected BCD may crash. The same applies to the 12-hour/24-hour time measurement, although a change to the 12-hour cycle wouldn't result in as serious consequences as the change in the date.

Bit 4 determines whether an interrupt should be called after the time (and date) update. This bit must contain a 1 if an interrupt should be called. The system suppresses this interrupt by setting this bit to 0 during the booting process.

Bit 5 can trigger an alarm. The clock reads the alarm time from locations 1, 3, and 5 (seconds, minutes, and hours) of clock RAM. When the alarm time is reached, an interrupt executes when bit 5 is set to 1. The system suppresses this interrupt when it sets bit 5 to 0 during the booting process.

Bit 6 controls periodic interrupt calls when it is set to 1. The frequency of the interrupt calls depends on the interrupt frequency coded into bits 0-3 of status register A. Since the default value on bootup is a frequency of 1,024 kiloHertz, the interrupt triggers every 967,562 microseconds. Since bit 6 is set to 0 at the system start, an application program must set it to 1 before periodic interrupt calls can execute.

Bit 7 controls the periodic updating of the time and date, once every second. This bit is set to 0 when you boot the system so that the time constantly increments. Before entering a new date and time in the various memory locations, this bit should be set to 1 first to prevent the clock from changing the time immediately. Once you've entered all the necessary data, this bit can be reset and the time can continue updating.

RTC interrupt 70H

While discussing the bits in status register B, we've repeatedly referred to interrupt 70H. The realtime clock calls this interrupt under certain conditions. Even though there are several reasons for the clock to call an interrupt (alarm time, periodic interrupts, etc.), interrupt 70H is consistently called. This interrupt contains a BIOS routine that controls the two time functions in interrupt 15H, among other things.

Status register C

The routine uses status register C of the clock to determine the reason for the call. Only bits 4, 5, and 6 of this register are important to us at the moment. These bits correspond to the bits in status register B. For example, when you trigger the alarm interrupt (which can only occur if bit 5 in status register B was set), then bit 5 in status register C is also set to indicate that the alarm time has been reached.

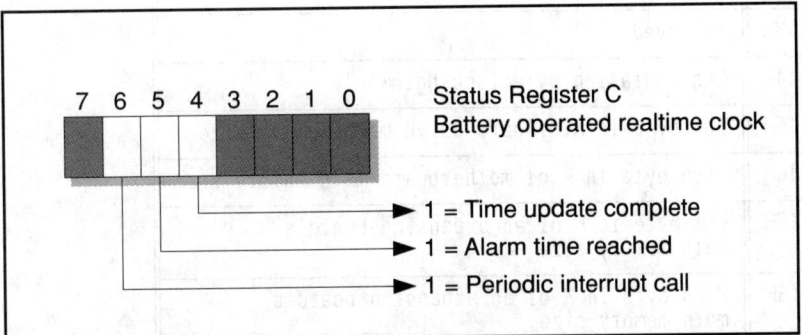

The first task of the routine that intercepts interrupt 70H is to read status register C. This routine then determines the reason for the interrupt call and reacts accordingly.

Status register D

Bit 7 is the only important bit in status register D. This bit indicates the status of the battery that maintains the data storage even when the PC's power supply is switched off. If this bit has the value 0, you should replace the battery because the present battery is dead or almost dead.

Some configuration data follows status register D.

11.3 Configuration Data and Battery Operated RAM

Besides the date and time information, the 64 battery backed memory registers also contain configuration data. Of the memory locations of various BIOS manufacturers, only those that are designated as unreserved contain the same information. Since all the other locations are used at the discretion of BIOS and hardware designers, these locations shouldn't be overwritten by a program.

Battery backed RAM registers	
Addr.	Content
0EH	Diagnostic byte (see below)
0FH	Status at system power–down
10H	Write to disk (see below)
11H	Hard drive 1 type
12H	Hard drive 2 type
13H	reserved
14H	Configuration byte (see below)
15H	Low byte in K of hard drive main memory size
16H	High byte in K of motherboard main memory size
17H	Low byte in K of an expansion board's main memory size
18H	High byte in K of an expansion board's main memory size
19H– 2DH	reserved reserved
2EH	Checksum high byte (memory locations 10H – 2DH)
2FH	Checksum low byte (memory locations 10H – 2DH)
30H	Low byte in K of expansion memory size
31H	High byte in K of expansion memory size
32H	First two century digits in BCD notation
33H– 3FH	reserved

Diagnostic byte (0EH)

The diagnostic byte documents various errors that may occur during the Power-On Self Test (POST).

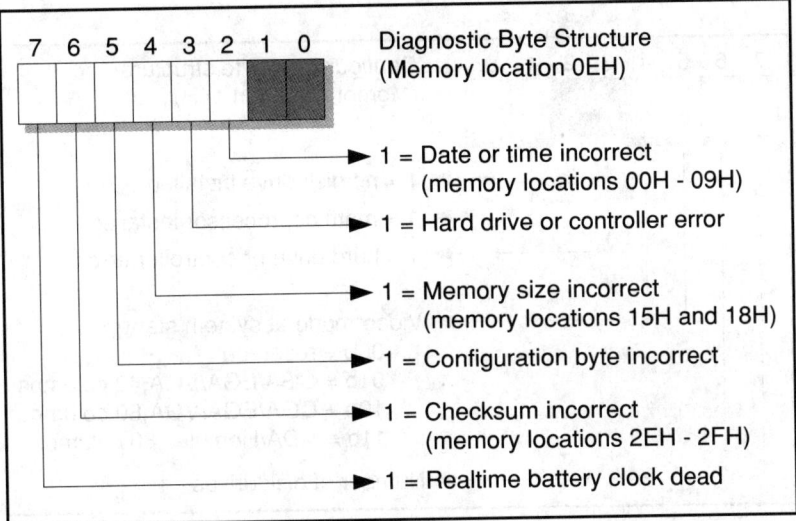

Disk description (10H)

Memory address 10H of the battery backed RAM contains information identifying the first and the second disk drive formats (5.25" or 3.5") and their capacities.

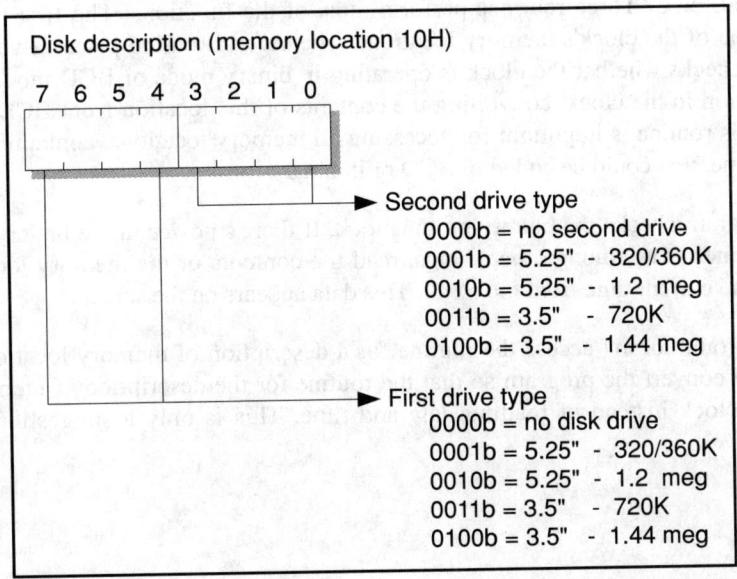

Configuration byte (14H)

Memory address 14H of the battery backed RAM contains configuration data that specifies the number of disk drives, the video mode at system startup, and the availability of a math coprocessor.

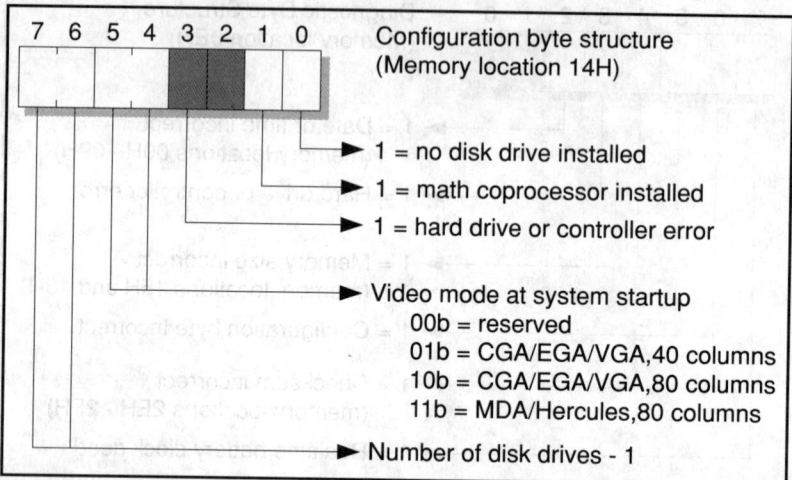

11.4 Demonstration Programs

The three programs listed below demonstrate how you can access the realtime clock from BASIC, Pascal, or C. Three routines perform most of the functions. The first routine reads a value from one of the clock's memory locations. The second routine places a value there. The third routine checks whether the clock is operating in binary mode or BCD mode, then reads a memory location in the clock, converting the contents of this location from BCD into binary if necessary. This routine is important for accessing all memory locations, containing information on date and time, that could be coded in BCD or in binary format.

The main program checks the battery on the clock. If there's power in the battery, the program calls two routines that, among other things, read the contents of the memory locations for the current date and current time from the clock. This data appears on the screen.

The main program doesn't access the routine for a description of memory locations. However, you can easily convert the program so that the routine for the description of memory locations writes to the clock instead of reading date and time. This is only a suggestion; feel free to experiment.

BASIC listing: RTCB.BAS

```
'************************************************************************
'*                         R T C B                                    *
'*--------------------------------------------------------------------*
'*  Task        : Makes different routines available for reading      *
'*                and writing realtime clock data.                    *
'*  Author      : Michael Tischer                                     *
'*  Developed on : 07/24/87                                           *
'*  Last update  : 03/03/92                                           *
'************************************************************************

DECLARE FUNCTION RTCRead% (Address%)
DECLARE FUNCTION RTCDT% (Address%)

CLS                                             'Clear screen
PRINT "RTCB (c) 1987, 92 by Michael Tischer": PRINT
PRINT "Information from the battery operated realtime clock"
PRINT "====================================================="
PRINT

IF (RTCRead(&HE) AND 128) = 128 THEN        'Bit 7 = 0 --> Battery O.K.
  PRINT "      WARNING! Clock battery is low"
ELSE
  PRINT "- The clock is running in";
  PRINT (RTCRead(&HB) AND 2) * 6 + 12; "hour mode"

  PRINT "- the time: ";
  PRINT USING "##:"; RTCDT(&H4);
  PRINT USING "##:"; RTCDT(&H2);
  PRINT USING "##"; RTCDT(&H0)

  PRINT "- the date: ";
  PRINT USING "##"; RTCDT(&H8);
  PRINT "-";
  PRINT USING "##"; RTCDT(&H7);
  PRINT "-";
  PRINT USING "####"; RTCDT(&H9) + 1900
  PRINT

END IF

'************************************************************************
'*  RTCDT: Reads the contents of a date or time memory location, and  *
'*         converts the contents to decimal.                          *
'*--------------------------------------------------------------------*
'*  Input : ADDRESS% = The memory address (0-63)                      *
'*  Output: The contents of this address in decimal notation          *
'************************************************************************

FUNCTION RTCDT% (Address%)

  Ret% = RTCRead(Address%)         'Read contents of the memory address
  IF (RTCRead(&HB) AND 2) <> 0 THEN               'Test for BCD mode
    RTCDT% = (Ret% AND 15) + INT(Ret% / 16) * 10  'Convert BCD to DEC
  ELSE
    RTCDT% = Ret%
  END IF

END FUNCTION

'************************************************************************
'*  RTCRead: Reads the contents of a memory location on the RTC.      *
'*--------------------------------------------------------------------*
```

```
'*  Input : ADDRESS% = The memory address (0-63)                      *
'*  Output : The contents of this address, or -1 if this address      *
'*           contains an invalid number                               *
'************************************************************************

FUNCTION RTCRead% (Address%)

  IF (Address% < 0) OR (Address% > 63) THEN
    RTCRead% = -1
  ELSE
    OUT &H70, Address%      'Memory location in the RTC address register
    RTCRead% = INP(&H71)    'Read contents of the RTC data register
  END IF

END FUNCTION

'************************************************************************
'*  RTCWrite: Writes a memory location to the RTC.                    *
'*--------------------------------------------------------------------*
'*  Input : ADDRESS%  = The memory address (0-63)                     *
'*          CONTENTS% = New contents of this memory location          *
'************************************************************************

SUB RTCWrite (Address%, Contents%)

  OUT &H70, Address%       'Memory location in the RTC address register
  OUT &H71, Contents%      'Write new contents to the RTC data register

END SUB
```

Pascal listing: RTCP.PAS

```
{*****************************************************************}
{*                        R T C P                              *}
{*-------------------------------------------------------------*}
{*  Task        : Provides two functions for accessing the     *}
{*                battery operated realtime clock.             *}
{*-------------------------------------------------------------*}
{*  Author      : Michael Tischer                              *}
{*  Developed on : 07/10/87                                    *}
{*  Last update  : 02/27/92                                    *}
{*****************************************************************}

program RTCP;

Uses Crt;                                    { Add CRT unit }

const RTCAdrPort = $70;                      { RTC address register }
      RTCDtaPort = $71;                      { RTC data register }

      SECONDS      = $00;  { Addresses for some RTC memory locations }
      MINUTE       = $02;
      ANHOUR       = $04;
      DAY          = $07;
      MONTH        = $08;
      YEAR         = $09;
      STATUSA      = $0A;
      STATUSB      = $0B;
      STATUSC      = $0C;
      STATUSD      = $0D;
      DIAGNOSE     = $0E;
      HUNDREDYEAR  = $32;

{*****************************************************************}
{* RTCRead: Reads one of the RTC memory locations.             *}
{* Input   : ADDRESS = Memory location in RTC                  *}
{* Output  : Contents of the memory location                  *}
{* Info    : If the address lies outside the valid range (0-63), *}
{*           the value -1 is returned.                        *}
{*****************************************************************}

function RTCRead(Address : integer) : integer;

begin
 if (Address < 0) or (Address > 63)        { Is the address O.K.? }
   then RTCRead := -1                       { No! }
   else
   begin
    Port[RTCAdrPort] := Address;            { Pass RTC address }
    RTCRead := Port[RTCDtaPort]             { Read address contents }
   end
end;

{*****************************************************************}
{* RTCDT: Reads a BCD date or time memory location from the RTC, and *}
{*        converts the value to a binary value.               *}
{* Input   : ADDRESS = Address of memory location in the RTC   *}
{* Output  : Contents of this memory location in binary notation *}
{* Info    : If the address lies outside the valid range (0-63), *}
{*           the value -1 is returned.                        *}
{*****************************************************************}

function RTCDT(Address : integer) : integer;
```

```
var Wert : integer;                          { For storing a value }

begin
 if (RTCRead(STATUSB) and 2 = 0)             { BCD or binary mode? }
   then RTCDT := RTCRead(Address)            { Binary }
   else                                      { BCD }
   begin
    Wert := RTCRead(Address);       { Get contents of memory location }
    RTCDT := (Wert shr 4) * 10 + Wert and 15  { Convert to binary }
   end
end;

{*****************************************************************}
{* RTCWrite: Writes a value to the RTC memory location.        *}
{* Input   : ADDRESS = Address of memory location in the RTC   *}
{*           CONTENT = New value for this memory location      *}
{* Output  : None                                             *}
{* Info    : This address should range from 0 to 63           *}
{*****************************************************************}

procedure RTCWrite(Address : integer;   { Address of memory location }
                   Content : byte);           { New contents }

begin
 Port[RTCAdrPort] := Address;                { Pass RTC address }
 Port[RTCDtaPort] := Content                 { Write new value }
end;

{*****************************************************************}
{*                      MAIN PROGRAM                           *}
{*****************************************************************}

begin
 ClrScr;                                     { Clear screen }
 writeln('RTCP (c) 1987, 92 by Michael Tischer'#13#10);
 writeln('Information from the battery operated realtime clock');
 writeln('======================================================'#13#10);
 if RTCRead(Diagnose) and 128 = 0 then       { Is the battery O.K.? }
   begin                                     { Yes --> Battery O.K. }
    writeln('- The clock is in ', (RTCRead(STATUSB) and 2)*6+12,
            ' hour mode');
    writeln('- The time : ', RTCDT(ANHOUR), ':', RTCDT(MINUTE):2,
            ':', RTCDT(SECONDS):2);
    write('- The date : ');
    writeln(RTCDT(MONTH), '-', RTCDT(DAY), '-',
            RTCDT(HUNDREDYEAR), RTCDT(YEAR));
   end
 else                                        { Dead battery }
   write('    Attention! Clock battery is dead')
end.
```

C listing: RTCC.C

```
/*****************************************************/
/*                       R T C C                     */
/*---------------------------------------------------*/
/*   Task        : Provides two functions for accessing the  */
/*                 battery operated realtime clock.          */
/*---------------------------------------------------*/
/*   Author      : Michael Tischer               */
/*   Developed on : 07/10/87                      */
/*   Last update  : 03/03/92                      */
/*****************************************************/
/*   (MICROSOFT C)                                */
/*   Compilation  : CL /AS RTCC.C                  */
/*   Call         : RTCC                           */
/*---------------------------------------------------*/
/*   (BORLAND TURBO C)                            */
/*   Compilation  : Use the RUN command (no project file needed) */
/*****************************************************/

/*== Include files ===================================*/

#include <dos.h>
#include <conio.h>
#include <stdio.h>

/*== Type declarations ===============================*/

typedef unsigned char BYTE;

/*== Constants =======================================*/

#define RTCAdrPort    0x70      /*  RTC address register */
#define RTCDtaPort    0x71      /*  RTC data register */

#define SECONDS       0x00      /*  Addresses for some */
#define MINUTE        0x02      /*  RTC memory locations */
#define ANHOUR        0x04
#define DAY           0x07
#define MONTH         0x08
#define YEAR          0x09
#define STATUSA       0x0A
#define STATUSB       0x0B
#define STATUSC       0x0C
#define STATUSD       0x0D
#define DIAGNOSE      0x0E
#define HUNDREDYEAR   0x32

/*****************************************************/
/* RTCRead : Reads one of the RTC memory locations.  */
/* Input   : ADDRESS = Memory location in RTC        */
/* Output  : Contents of the memory location         */
/* Info    : If the address lies outside the valid range (0-63), */
/*           the value -1 is returned.               */
/*****************************************************/

BYTE RTCRead(BYTE ADDRESS)
{
  outp(RTCAdrPort, ADDRESS);         /* Send address in RTC */
  return(inp(RTCDtaPort));           /* Get contents of RTC */
}

/*****************************************************/
/* RTCDT   : Reads a BCD date or time memory location from the RTC, */
/*           and converts the value to a binary value. */
/* Input   : ADDRESS = Address of memory location in the RTC */
/* Output  : Contents of this memory location in binary notation */
/* Info    : If the address lies outside the valid range (0-63), */
/*           the value -1 is returned.               */
/*****************************************************/

BYTE RTCDt(BYTE ADDRESS)

{
  if (RTCRead(STATUSB) & 2)                /* BCD or binary mode? */
   return((RTCRead(ADDRESS) >> 4) * 10 + (RTCRead(ADDRESS) & 15));
  else return(RTCRead(ADDRESS));           /* Binary */
}

/*****************************************************/
/* RTCWrite: Writes a value to the RTC memory location. */
/* Input   : ADDRESS = Address of memory location in the RTC */
/*           CONTENT = New value for this memory location */
/* Output  : None                                    */
/* Info    : This address should range from 0 to 63  */
/*****************************************************/

void RTCWrite(BYTE ADDRESS, BYTE Size)

{
  outp(RTCAdrPort, ADDRESS);        /* Send RTC address */
  outp(RTCDtaPort, Size);           /* Write new value */
}

/*****************************************************/
/**                  MAIN PROGRAM                   **/
/*****************************************************/

void main()

{

  printf("\nRTCC (c) 1987, 1992 by Michael Tischer\n\n");
  printf("Information from the battery operated realtime clock\n");
  printf("===========================================\n\n");
  if (!(RTCRead(DIAGNOSE) & 128))        /* Is the clock O.K.? */
   {                                     /* O.K. */
    printf("- The clock is in %d hour mode\n",
       (RTCRead(STATUSB) & 2)*6+12);
    printf("- The time: %2d:%02d:%02d\n",
       RTCDt(ANHOUR), RTCDt(MINUTE), RTCDt(SECONDS));
    printf("- The date: ");
    printf("%02d-%02d-%d%d\n", RTCDt(MONTH), RTCDt(DAY),
      RTCDt(HUNDREDYEAR), RTCDt(YEAR));
   }
  else printf("   Attention! The clock battery is dead.\n");
}
```

Chapter 12

Memory Expansion

When the IBM PC was being developed in 1980, its capabilities were quite advanced at the time. This was also true of its main memory size. The maximum size of 640K seemed so large in the early 1980s that no one could imagine what a user would do with so much memory. Thus, the first PCs were equipped with 64K, then 128K, and later 256K of memory. Today memory requirements continue to increase. The minimum amount of RAM for PCs has grown to 640K.

As we enter the age of 80486 microprocessors, graphical user interfaces, and multitasking operating systems, 640K just isn't enough memory to fully utilize the PC's capabilities. But we've reached a boundary that cannot be crossed by simply adding more memory chips to the computer. This boundary is the 1 megabyte limit, set by the 8086 microprocessor's addressing capabilities.

Another important factor affecting memory is compatibility. To maintain program compatibility in machines ranging from the simplest XT to a fully loaded 486, the processors must be compatible and the memory layouts of each machine must meet certain standards. In this chapter we'll examine ways to access alternate forms of memory.

The following illustration shows the basic memory configuration of the PC:

As the illustration on the next page shows, only the first 640K can be used for RAM storage. Any memory beyond that point is reserved for video RAM, hardware enhancements, and the BIOS.

Memory can easily be enlarged beyond the one megabyte limit. Today most 386 computers have 2 megabytes or more of RAM, but this memory cannot be addressed under DOS. Because DOS operates in real mode, memory beyond the 1 megabyte limit cannot be accessed.

There are many solutions for this RAM crisis. Memory needs can be handled by expanded memory and extended memory. These forms of memory can increase memory capacity by many megabytes, if the software can utilize this capacity.

Before we continue, let's clear up the confusion between expanded memory and extended memory. Since the two terms sound very similar, it's easy to forget which memory performs which task.

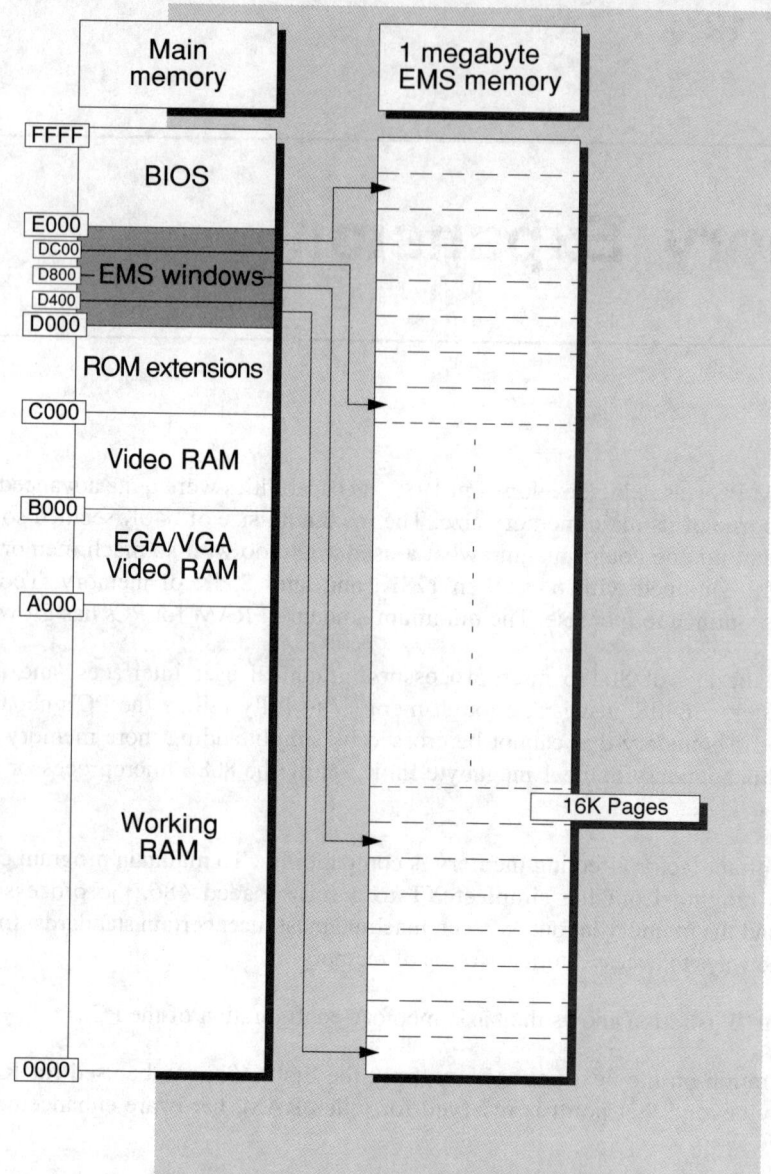

Accessing EMS memory of the LIM standard with the help of "windows"

Expanded memory

Expanded memory is the additional memory you'll find in PC/XT computers. Because of the 8088 processor, these computers are limited to 640K of working RAM. With expanded memory, RAM beyond the 640K boundary can be used. Remember that expanded memory *expands* RAM beyond 640K.

Extended memory

Extended memory is the additional memory found on 80286 and higher end computers. This memory *extends* beyond the 1 megabyte boundary.

Let's take a closer look at each memory type.

12.1 Expanded Memory

A PC or a PC/XT machine is limited to 640K of conventional memory. 80286 based computers are limited to 16 megabytes of RAM. However, those 16 megabytes are only available when the PC is running in Protected mode (see Chapter 33 for more information), which makes the memory inaccessible to DOS programs.

Several years ago some leading PC firms worked together to devise a way to add more memory, which could also be accessed under DOS, to PCs, XTs, and ATs. These companies were Lotus (the developers of Lotus 1-2-3), Intel (manufacturer of PC processors), and Microsoft (developers of MS-DOS and OS/2). They developed the LIM standard; "LIM" represents the first letters of the company names.

This standard allows up to 8 megabytes to be added to a PC on an expansion card. Only 64K of this 8 megabytes is visible in the 1 megabyte address range of the 8088 processor, in a window called the page frame. Memory installed in this manner is called *expanded memory*. This memory shouldn't be confused with the extended memory that goes beyond 1 megabyte on an AT. The entire system is referred to as the Expanded Memory System, or EMS.

The LIM standard used the reliable trick of *bank switching* for memory access. Bank switching creates a small memory window, through which a portion of expanded memory can be accessed beyond the address space of the computer. The total addressable memory capacity may extend over several megabytes. The software works with the hardware, moving this window to permit access to the portion of memory currently needed. The remaining memory stays invisible to the program.

Opening the memory window

At least 64K in the 1 megabyte address space of the PC is unused by conventional memory, BIOS, video RAM, or other system expansions. The EMS developers decided to use this as a window into expanded memory. Usually this window lies at segment address D000H, but EMS hardware allows this window to be relocated.

Since this window is under the 1 megabyte memory limit, it can be accessed with normal assembly language instructions, similar to video RAM access. Both read and write accesses are possible. We'll look at specific examples of these accesses later in this chapter.

Page frame division

The page frame is further divided into 16K pages. This allows the programmer to access four completely different pages in EMS memory.

The EMS card's registers allow the programmer to set which pages of the EMS memory will be visible in the page frame. The address lines on the EMS card are programmed so that the EMS pages are mapped into the page frame and appear in the 8088's address space. This process is the bank switching we mentioned earlier in this chapter.

Besides the hardware, the EMS also includes a software interface, which handles EMS register programming and other memory management tasks. This software interface, called the EMM (Expanded Memory Manager), provides a standard interface that you can use to access EMS cards from different manufacturers. This also applies to the extended EMS standard (EEMS) developed by AST Research, Quadram, and Ashton-Tate, which surpasses the LIM standard.

The best known examples of EEMS are 386-To-The-Max (Qualitas), QEMM-386 (Quarterdeck), and Microsoft Windows. Windows' 386 enhanced mode makes its applications available in expanded memory, where Windows stores extended memory.

The above products are based on a special 80386 operating mode, called the *virtual 8086 mode*. This mode lets you move memory from above the 1 megabyte barrier into conventional memory, and give this memory the look and feel of a normal page frame. Compared to a conventional hardware implementation, this immediately provides several advantages:

- Without EMS emulation, this memory is accessible as extended memory.
- Because hardware addressing or I/O addressing isn't required, EMS access and switching between pages occurs very quickly.
- Lower cost (EMS cards usually cost more than software emulation).
- One more expansion slot is free than there would be with true EMS memory.

This EMS emulation is possible with the 80386 microprocessor and its successors; it's also possible on 80286 machines but speed is decreased.

Many Asian AT manufacturers offer the option of using extended memory as expanded memory by using the NEAT (New Enhanced AT) chips available from Chips & Technologies Corporation. These chips allow hardware to view extended memory as expanded memory, without installing a special enhancement card.

The software interface between the EMM and a program resembles many other software interfaces found in the PC environment.

12.1.1 History of the LIM standard

While most programs appear on the market with a starting version number of 1.0, EMS Version 1.0 never existed; actually it never left the laboratory. When Intel and Lotus presented their proposal for an EMS standard in the spring of 1985, Version 3.0 already existed. Microsoft joined the other two firms shortly after this release because they could use a capability of this type for their own products.

Version 3.2 was released in the fall of 1985, and the EMS standard became the LIM standard. A few weeks later, a group of firms comprising AST, Quadram, and Ashton-Tate presented their own EMS standard, called the Enhanced Expanded Memory Specification (EEMS). This standard was based on EMS Version 3.2, but offered few advantages over EMS other than the ability to use page frames larger than 64K. EMS 4.0 now supports such capabilities, and EEMS is part of computing's past.

EMS 3.2 became a big success and received support from many well-known manufacturers. Lotus promoted the sale of EMS memory cards because EMS enabled Lotus 1-2-3 to handle very large spreadsheets. TSR (Terminate and Stay Resident) programs, RAM disks, and other utilities also used expanded memory. Microsoft eventually provided EMS support beginning with MS-DOS Version 4.0.

EMS Version 4.0

With its 14 functions, EMS Version 3.2 satisfied all the needs of software developers. EMS Version 4.0, released in the fall of 1987, had 58 functions available for enhanced hardware support. This release included the following features:

- Memory support for 32 megabytes instead of 8 megabytes.
- Ability to generate EMS windows at any location in addressable memory.
- Any size EMS windows, instead of the 64K required by earlier versions.
- EMS pages that can be protected from a system crash or an accidental reset, which increased the value of EMS based RAM disks.

Version 4.0 makes greater demands on the EMS hardware than earlier versions. This may be why Version 4.0 hasn't become very popular and Version 3.2 remains the standard for EMS programming.

12.1.2   EMS Version 3.2

The Expanded Memory Manager (EMM) enables the programmer to access EMS memory. We mentioned the major changes between Versions 3.2 and 4.0 earlier in this chapter. However, you'll probably use only a few Version 3.2 functions in EMS programming.

We'll concentrate on EMS Version 3.2 in this book because this version is considered the standard for expanded memory. If you want more information about Version 4.0, EMS Version 4.0's functions are documented in the Appendices of this book.

The EMM

Similar to DOS interrupt 21H, which provides a standard interface to the operating system functions, EMM functions can be called through interrupt 67H. Before a program tries to use EMS memory and the corresponding EMM, it should first check to ensure that an EMS is installed. If it doesn't do this and there is no EMM, the results of a call to interrupt 67H are completely unpredictable. The call simply may not work or the system may crash.

To prevent this from happening, a program that uses the EMS must first check to ensure that EMS exists. This can easily be done when you consider that the EMM is bound into the system as a normal device driver when the computer is booted. So, it naturally has a driver header that precedes it in memory and defines its structure for DOS. The name of the driver is found at address 10 in the driver header. The LIM standard requires that this name be EMMXXXX0.

The example programs at the end of this chapter test for this name by first determining the segment address of the interrupt handler for interrupt 67H. If the EMM is installed, the segment address points to the segment into which the EMMXXXX0 device driver was loaded. Since the driver header is at offset address 0, relative to the start of this segment, we simply compare the memory locations starting at 10 with the name EMMXXXX0 to determine whether the EMS memory and the corresponding EMM are installed.

Once this is verified, this memory can be accessed in three steps:

1.)   Just as conventional memory must be allocated with a DOS function, a program must first allocate a certain number of EMS pages for itself from the EMM. The number of pages to be allocated depends on both the memory requirements of the program and how much EMS memory is available.

2.)   If the desired number of pages were successfully allocated, the specified pages must first be loaded into one of the four pages of the page frame so that data can be written into them or read from them. This results in a mapping between one of the allocated pages and one of the four physical pages within the page frame.

3.)   When the program ends or it's finished using EMS, the allocated pages should be released again. If this isn't done, the allocated pages will still be owned by the program (even after it ends) and cannot be given to other programs.

As with DOS interrupt 21H, the function number of an EMM call must be loaded into the AH register before the interrupt call. After the function call this register contains the error status of the function. The value 0 signals that the function was executed successfully, while values greater than or equal to 80H indicate an error.

About errors

In the Appendices you'll find the error codes, which are listed in the error descriptions. However, you should be aware of one particular error. If the value 84H is in the AH register after a call to EMM interrupt 67H, this indicates that an invalid function number was passed in the AH register.

The following functions are needed for a transient program to access the EMS memory:

Function	Task
40H	Get EMM status
41H	Get segment address of page frame
42H	Get number of pages
43H	Allocate EMS pages
44H	Set mapping
45H	Release EMS pages

To ensure that the EMS hardware and the EMM operate properly, check the EMM status before allocating EMS memory. This is done with function 40H, which only requires the function number in the AH register. If it returns the value 0 in the AH register, then everything is OK and you can start working with the EMS memory.

Limits to EMS allocation

The number of allocatable EMS pages is limited by the number of free pages. So, you should ensure that the memory requirements of the program don't exceed the available memory. Here we can use function 42H, which returns the number of free EMS pages. This function requires only the function number and returns the number of unallocated pages in the BX register. It also returns the total number of installed EMS pages in the DX register.

If enough EMS memory exists for our program, or if the memory requirements are adapted to the available memory, then we can allocate the memory. The number of pages to be allocated must be passed to function 43H in the BX register. If the requested number of pages is successfully allocated (AH register contains 0 after the function call), the caller will find a handle to the allocated pages in the BX register. This handle, which must be used to access the allocated pages, identifies the caller to the EMM. The caller must save this handle. If the handle is lost, the allocated pages cannot be accessed and can no longer be released. A program can call this function several times to allocate multiple logical page blocks.

Once we have the page handle we can start accessing the pages. The handle is passed to the appropriate functions in the DX register. This also applies to function 44H, which maps a logical page to one of the four physical pages of the page frame. The number of the logical page is passed in the BX register and the physical page number in the AL register. Note that both specifications start at zero. So, if you've allocated 15 pages, then the numbers of the logical pages run from zero to 14.

Once the appropriate page is in the page frame, it can be accessed like normal memory. The offset address of the start-of-page is calculated from the physical page number, but the corresponding segment address must be determined with an EMM function. Since this address doesn't change while working with the EMS memory, you can read it once at the beginning of the program and then save it in a variable. Function 41H returns the segment address of the page frame in the BX register.

When you're finished using the EMS, you must return the allocated pages to the EMM. Simply pass the page handle to function 45H.

In addition to these six functions, which a normal program can use to access EMS memory, the following functions can also be useful under certain circumstances:

Function	Task
46H	Get EMM version number
47H	Save current mapping
48H	Reset saved mapping
49H	Get number of EMM handles
4AH	Get the number of pages allocated to a handle
4BH	Get all handles and numbers of allocated pages

Version numbers

Reading the EMM version number is important because the LIM standard has changed slightly since it was introduced. Some functions are no longer supported and new functions have been added. The functions presented here are from Version 3.2, which has been replaced by Version 4.0. Version 3.2 represents a good compromise not only because it's widely used, but also because it's completely compatible with Version 4.0. If you don't want to support earlier or later EMS versions in your program, you should check the version number at the start of the program. The version number will be returned in the AL register after a call to function 46H. It's encoded as a BCD number.

Functions 47H and 48H are important for TSR programs that want to use the EMS memory. When a TSR program interrupts a transient program and places itself in the foreground, it must consider that the interrupted program may have been using EMS memory and had created a certain mapping. Since this mapping shouldn't be changed when returning to the interrupted program, it must be saved when the TSR is activated and then restored when the TSR exits. Function 08H saves the current EMM mapping and function 09H resets the saved status. The handle of the function must be passed to both functions. In this case, it's the handle of the TSR program instead of the handle of the interrupted program.

Since the last three functions are only important to the memory manager, we won't discuss them here. More information can be found in the Appendices of this book.

Demonstration programs

The following pages contain two programs (one written in Pascal and one in C) that demonstrate how to use EMS memory. There isn't an assembly language program because, theoretically, calls to the EMM functions simply involve loading variables and constants into registers and calling the EMM interrupt 67H. By using the information in the Appendices, you should be able to write an assembly language program that uses the EMS. There isn't a BASIC program because EMS memory is intended to be used with complex and memory-intensive applications for which BASIC isn't suited.

Since the two programs are almost identical, we'll discuss only the basic program structure. The programs provide several functions and procedures that can be used to access the various EMM functions. Both programs also contain a function called EMS_INST (or EmsInst), which determines whether an EMM is installed.

In Pascal we encounter a problem because a pointer must be loaded with an address consisting of separate segment and offset addresses. Since this isn't possible in Pascal, there is an INLINE procedure, called MK_FP, that (like the C macro of the same name) combines a segment and an offset address into a (FAR) pointer. Since this is a FAR pointer, the page frame isn't in the program's data segment. So, it cannot be addressed by the DS register. This isn't a problem in Turbo Pascal because the code is generated to work with FAR data pointers. In C, we must ensure that the program is compiled in a memory model that uses FAR pointers for data. This occurs in compact, large, and huge models.

The main program firsts tests to determine whether EMM is present. Then it uses various functions to obtain status information about EMS memory, which it displays on the screen. Next, a page is allocated and mapped to the first page (page 0) of the page frame. The current contents of video RAM are copied into this page and the video RAM is then erased.

After the copy procedure, a message is displayed for the user and the program waits for a key to be pressed. Then it copies the old screen contents back to video RAM from page 0 of the page frame and the program ends.

This program shows that the contents of a page in the page frame can be treated like ordinary data. After you've created a pointer to the corresponding page, you can manipulate the data on this page, including complex objects like structures and arrays, like any other data. It's important to ensure that your objects fit on one page or that you don't forget to change pages or load a new page into the page frame to access larger objects.

C listing: EMMC.C

```
/***************************************************************/
/*                        E M M C                             */
/*-----------------------------------------------------------*/
/*   Description   : a collection of function for using EMS    */
/*                   memory (Expanded Memory).                 */
/*-----------------------------------------------------------*/
/*   Author        : MICHAEL TISCHER                           */
/*   developed on  : 08/30/1988                                */
/*   last update   : 02/19/1992                                */
/*-----------------------------------------------------------*/
/*   Memory model  : one with FAR pointer to the file, also    */
/*                   Compact, Large or Huge                    */
/***************************************************************/

/*== Include files ==========================================*/

#include <stdio.h>
#include <stdlib.h>
#include <string.h>
#include <conio.h>
#include <dos.h>

/*== Typedefs ===============================================*/

typedef unsigned char BYTE;          /* build ourselves a byte */
typedef unsigned int WORD;
typedef BYTE BOOL;                   /*like BOOLEAN in Pascal */

/*== Macros =================================================*/

/*-- MK_FP creates a FAR pointer out of segment and offset addresses-*/
/*-- to on objetc                          -------*/

#ifdef MK_FP                         /* is MK_FP defined yet */
 #undef MK_FP
#endif
#define MK_FP(seg, ofs) ((void far *) ((unsigned long) (seg)<<16|(ofs)))

/*-- PAGE_ADR returns a pointer to the physical page X within the ----*/
/*-- page frame of the EMS memory.                        ----*/

#define PAGE_ADR(x) ((void *) MK_FP(ems_frame_seg() + ((x) << 10), 0))

/*== Constants ==============================================*/

#define TRUE  1                      /* constants for working with BOOL */
#define FALSE 0

#define EMS_INT 0x67      /* Interrupt number for access tothe EMM*/
```

```
#define EMS_ERR -1                          /* returned on error */

/*== global Variables =======================================*/

BYTE emm_ec;                /* the EMM error codes are placed here */

/*************************************************************
*  Function      : E M S _ I N S T                          *
**---------------------------------------------------------**
*  Description   : Determines if EMS memory and the associated *
*                  EMS driver (EMM) are installed.          *
*  Input Parameter : none                                   *
*  Return value  : TRUE, when EMS memory is installed, else  *
*                  FALSE.                                    *
*************************************************************/

BOOL ems_inst()
 {
  static char emm_name[] = { 'E', 'M', 'M', 'X', 'X', 'X', 'X', '0' };
  union REGS regs;        /* Processor register for interrupt call  */
  struct SREGS sregs;     /* Segment register for the interrupt call */

  /*-- construct pointer to name in the header of a switch driver-----*/

  regs.x.ax = 0x3567;         /* ftn nr.: get interrupt vector 0x67 */
  intdosx(&regs, &regs, &sregs);          /* call DOS-Interrupt 0x21 */
  return !memcmp( MK_FP(sregs.es, 10), emm_name, sizeof emm_name );
 }

/*************************************************************
*  Function      : E M S _ N U M _ P A G E                  *
**---------------------------------------------------------**
*  Output        : Determines the total number of EMS pages. *
*  Input parameter : none                                   *
*  Return value  : EMS_ERR on error, else the number of     *
*                  EMS pages.                               *
*************************************************************/

int ems_num_page()
 {
  union REGS regs;       /* Processor register for the interrup call */

  regs.h.ah = 0x42;                    /* Fnt.nr.: get number of pages */
  int86(EMS_INT, &regs, &regs);                        /* Call EMM */
  if ((int) (emm_ec = regs.h.ah))             /* did an error occur? */
   return(EMS_ERR);                         /* YES, display error */
  else                                          /* no error */
   return( regs.x.dx );               /* return total number of pages */
 }

/*************************************************************
```

```
* Function        : E M S _ F R E E _ P A G E          *
**-----------------------------------------------------**
* Description     : Returns the number of free EMS pages.  *
* Input parameter : none                                *
* Return value    : EMS_ERR on error, else the number of free EMS *
*                   pages.                              *
********************************************************/

int ems_free_page()
{
  union REGS regs;        /* Processor register for the interrupt call */

  regs.h.ah = 0x42;                /* Ftn.nr.: get number of pages */
  int86(EMS_INT, &regs, &regs);                    /* Call EMM */
  if ((int) (emm_ec = regs.h.ah))          /* did an error occur? */
    return(EMS_ERR);                     /* Yes, display error */
  else                                        /* no error */
    return( regs.x.bx );          /* return number of free pages */
}


/********************************************************
* Function        : E M S _ F R A M E _ S E G          *
**-----------------------------------------------------**
* Description     : Determine the Segment address of the EMS page *
*                   frames.                             *
* Input parameter : none                                *
* Return value    : EMS_ERR on error, else the segment address of *
*                   the Page frames.                    *
********************************************************/

WORD ems_frame_seg()
{
  union REGS regs;        /* Processor register for the interrupt call */

  regs.h.ah = 0x41;        /* Fnt.nr.: get segment addr page frame */
  int86(EMS_INT, &regs, &regs);                   /* Call EMM */
  if ((int) (emm_ec = regs.h.ah))          /*did an error occur? */
    return(EMS_ERR);                     /* Yes, display error */
  else                                        /* no error */
    return( regs.x.bx );            /* return segment address */
}


/********************************************************
* Function        : E M S _ A L L O C                  *
**-----------------------------------------------------**
* Description     : Allocates the specified number of pages and *
*                   returns a handle for accessing these pages. *
* Input paramater : PAGES : the number of pages tobe allocated *
*                   (each 16 Kbyte)                     *
* Return value    : EMS_ERR on error, else the EMS handle *
********************************************************/

int ems_alloc(int pages)
{
  union REGS regs;        /* Processor register for the interrupt call */

  regs.h.ah = 0x43;                /* Fnt.nr.: Pages allocated */
  regs.x.bx = pages;        /* set number of pages to be allocated */
  int86(EMS_INT, &regs, &regs);                    /* Call EMM */
  if ((int) (emm_ec = regs.h.ah))          /* did an error occur? */
    return(EMS_ERR);                     /* Yes, display error */
  else                                        /* no error */
    return( regs.x.dx );              /* return EMS handle */
}
```

```
/********************************************************
* Function        : E M S _ M A P                      *
**-----------------------------------------------------**
* Description     : Maps one of the allocated pages specified *
*                   by the given handle onto a physical page in the *
*                   page frame.                         *
* Input parameter : HANDLE: the handle returned by EMS_ALLOC *
*                   LOGP  : the logical page (0 to n-1)  *
*                   PHYSP : the physical page (0 to 3)   *
* Return value    : FALSE on error , else TRUE.         *
********************************************************/

BOOL ems_map(int handle, int logp, BYTE physp)
{
  union REGS regs;        /* Processor register for the interrupt call */

  regs.h.ah = 0x44;                /* Fnt.nr.: set mapping */
  regs.h.al = physp;               /* set physical page */
  regs.x.bx = logp;                /* set logical page */
  regs.x.dx = handle;              /* set EMS handle */
  int86(EMS_INT, &regs, &regs);               /* call EMM */
  return (!(emm_ec = regs.h.ah));
}


/********************************************************
* Function        : E M S _ F R E E                    *
**-----------------------------------------------------**
* Description     : Releases the memory specified by the handle *
* Input patameter : HANDLE: the handle returned by EMS_ALLOC. *
* Return value    : FALSE on error, else TRUE.          *
********************************************************/

BOOL ems_free(int handle)
{
  union REGS regs;        /* Processor register for the interrupt call */

  regs.h.ah = 0x45;                /* Fnt.nr.: release pages */
  regs.x.dx = handle;              /* set EM handle */
  int86(EMS_INT, &regs, &regs);               /* call EMM */
  return (!(emm_ec = regs.h.ah));     /* if AH contains 0, all is o.k. */
}


/********************************************************
* Function        : E M S _ V E R S I O N              *
**-----------------------------------------------------**
* Description     : Determines the EMM version number   *
* Input parameter : none                                *
* Return value    : EMS_ERR on error, else the EMM version number. *
* Info            : In th eversion number, 10 stands for 1.0, 11 for *
*                   1.1, 34 for 3.4 etc.                *
********************************************************/

BYTE ems_version()
{
  union REGS regs;        /* Processor register for the interrupt call */

  regs.h.ah = 0x46;                /* Fnt.nr.: get EMM version number*/
  int86(EMS_INT, &regs, &regs);                    /* call EMM */
  if ((int) (emm_ec = regs.h.ah))          /* did an error occur? */
    return(EMS_ERR);                     /* Yes, display error */
  else           /* no error, calculate version numberfrom BCD number */
    return( (regs.h.al & 15) + (regs.h.al >> 4) * 10);
}
```

```
/*********************************************************
 * Function      : E M S _ S A V E _ M A P              *
 **-----------------------------------------------------**
 * Description   : Saves the mapping between the logical and *
 *                 physical pages.                      *
 * Input parameter : HANDLE: the handle returned by EMS_ALLOC. *
 * Return value   : FALSE on error, else TRUE.          *
 *********************************************************/

BOOL ems_save_map(int handle)
  {
  union REGS regs;        /* Processor register for the interrupt call */

  regs.h.ah = 0x47;                    /* Fnt.nr.: save mapping */
  regs.x.dx = handle;                     /* set EMS handle */
  int86(EMS_INT, &regs, &regs);                /* call EMM */
  return (!(emm_ec = regs.h.ah));/* if AH contains 0 everything is OK */
  }


/*********************************************************
 * Function      : E M S _ R E S T O R E _ M A P        *
 **-----------------------------------------------------**
 * Description   : Restores a mapping between logical and physical *
 *                 pages saved with EMS_SAVE_MAP.       *
 * Input parameters : HANDLE: the handle returned by EMS_ALLOC. *
 * Return value   : FALSE on error, else TRUE.          *
 *********************************************************/

BOOL ems_restore_map(int handle)
  {
  union REGS regs;        /* Processor register for the interrupt call */

  regs.h.ah = 0x48;                 /* Fnt.nr.: restore mapping */
  regs.x.dx = handle;                     /* set EMS handle */
  int86(EMS_INT, &regs, &regs);                /* call EMM */
  return (!(emm_ec = regs.h.ah));      /* if AH contains 0, all is OK. */
  }


/*********************************************************
 * Function      : P R I N T _ E R R                    *
 **-----------------------------------------------------**
 * Description   : Prints and EMS error message on the screen and *
 *                 ends the program.                    *
 * Input parameter : none                               *
 * Return value   : none                                *
 * Info          : This function may onlybe called if an error *
 *                 occurred on a prior call to the EMM. *
 *********************************************************/

void print_err()
  {
  static char nid[] = "unidentifiable";
  static char *err_vec[] =
    { "Error in the EMS driver (EMM destroyed)",        /* 0x80 */
      "Error in the EMS hardware",                      /* 0x81 */
      nid,                                              /* 0x82 */
      "Illegal EMM handle",                             /* 0x83 */
      "EMS function called does not exist",             /* 0x84 */
      "No more EMS handle available",                   /* 0x85 */
      "Error while saving or restoring the mapping",    /* 0x86 */
      "More pages requested than physically present",   /* 0x87 */
      "More pages requested than are still free",       /* 0x88 */
      "Zero page requested",                            /* 0x89 */
      "Logicalpage does not belong to handle",          /* 0x8A */
      "Illegal physical page number",                   /* 0x8B */
      "Mapping storag eis full",                        /* 0x8C */
      "The mapping has already been saved",             /* 0x8D */
      "Restored mapping without saving first"
    };

  printf("\nERROR! Error in access to EMS memory\n");
  printf("       ... %s\n", (emm_ec<0x80 || emm_ec>0x8E) ?
                            nid : err_vec[emm_ec-0x80]);

  exit( 1 );                      /* End program with error code */
  }


/*********************************************************
 * Function      : V R _ A D R                          *
 **-----------------------------------------------------**
 * Description   : Returns a pointer to video RAM.       *
 * Input parameter : none                               *
 * Return value   : VOID pointer to the video RAM.      *
 *********************************************************/

void *vr_adr()
  {
  union REGS regs;        /* Processor register for the interrupt call */

  regs.h.ah = 0x0f;                    /* Fnt.nr.: get video mode */
  int86(0x10, &regs, &regs);           /* call BIOS Video Interrupt */
  return ( MK_FP((regs.h.al==7) ? 0xb000 : 0xb800, 0) );
  }


/*********************************************************/
/**                  MAIN PROGRAM                      **/
/*********************************************************/

void main()
  {
  int numpage,                       /* number of EMS pages */
      handle,                /* handle to acces the EMS memory */
      i;                             /* loop counter */
  WORD pageseg ;             /* segment address of the page frame */
  BYTE emmver;                       /* EMM version number */

  printf("EMMC  - (c) 1988, 92 by MICHAEL TISCHER\n\n");
  if ( ems_inst() )                  /* is EMS memory installed? */
    {                                       /* Yes */
    /*-- output information about the EMS memory -----------------*/

    if ( (int) (emmver = ems_version()) == EMS_ERR) /* get version num */
      print_err();     /* error: output error message and end program */
    else                                    /* no error */
      printf("EMM-Version number       : %d.%d\n",
              emmver/10, emmver%10);

    if ( (numpage = ems_num_page()) == EMS_ERR)  /* get number pages */
      print_err();     /* Error: output error messag eand end program */
    printf("Number of EMS pages       : %d (%d KByte)\n",
            numpage, numpage << 4);

    if ( (numpage = ems_free_page()) == EMS_ERR)
      print_err();     /* Error: output erro messag eand end program */
    printf("...      free             : %d (%d KByte)\n",
            numpage, numpage << 4);

    if ( (int) (pageseg = ems_frame_seg()) == EMS_ERR)
```

661

```
   print_err();    /* Error: output erro message and end program */
   printf("Segment address of the page frame: %X\n", pageseg);

   printf("\nNow a page will be allocated from the EMS memory and\n");
   printf("the screen contents will be copied from video RAM\n");
   printf("to this page.\n");
   printf("                    ... press ay key\n");
   getch();                                     /* wait for a key */

   /*-- allocate a page and map it to he first logical page in   ---*/
   /*-- page frame.                                              ---*/

   if ( (handle = ems_alloc(1)) == EMS_ERR)
    print_err();   /* Error: output error message and end program */
   if ( !ems_map(handle, 0, 0) )                 /* set mapping */
   print_err();    /* Error: output error message and end program */

   /*-- copy 4000 bytes from the video rRAM to the EMS memory -------*/

   memcpy(PAGE_ADR(0), vr_adr(), 4000);

   for (i=0; i<24; ++i)                         /* clear the screen */
    printf("\n");

   printf("The old screen contents will now be cleared and will\n");
   printf("be lost. But since it was stored in the EMS memory, they\n");
   printf("can be copied from there back into the video RAM\n");
   printf("                    ...press any key\n");
   getch();                                     /* wait for a key */

   /*-- copy contents of the video RAM from the EMS memory ----------*/
   /*-- and release the allocated EMS memory again.           ----*/

   memcpy(vr_adr(), PAGE_ADR(0), 4000);         /* copy V-RAM back */
   if ( !ems_free(handle) )                     /* free memory */
    print_err();   /* Error: output error message and end program */
   printf("END");
  }
else                             /* the EMS driver was not detected */
 printf("No EMS memory installed\n");
}
```

Pascal listing: EMMP.PAS

```pascal
{*********************************************************************}
{*                      E M M P                                    *}
{*-----------------------------------------------------------------*}
{*   Description     : Implement certain function to demonstrate   *}
{*                     access to EMS meory using EMM.              *}
{*-----------------------------------------------------------------*}
{*   Author          : MICHAEL TISCHER                             *}
{*   Developed on    : 08/30/1988                                  *}
{*   Lats update on  : 02/19/1992                                  *}
{*-----------------------------------------------------------------*}
{*   Changes         : 02/19/92 : MK_FP replaced through PTR       *}
{*********************************************************************}

program EMMP;

Uses Dos, CRT;                           { Add DOS and CRT units }

type  ByteBuf = array[0..1000] of byte;  { One memory range as bytes }
      CharBuf = array[0..1000] of char;  { one memory range as Char }
      BytePtr = ^ByteBuf;                { Pointer to byte range }
      CharPtr = ^CharBuf;                { Pointer to character range }

const EMS_INT   = $67;          { Interrupt # for access to EMM }
      EMS_ERR   = -1;                { Error if this occurs }
      W_EMS_ERR = $FFFF;            { error code in WORD form }
      EmmName   : array[0..7] of char = 'EMMXXXX0';   { Name of EMM }

var   EmmEC,                     { Allocation of EMM erro codes. }
      i        : byte;                     { loop counter }
      Handle,                   { handle for acces to EMS memory }
      EmmVer   : integer;                { Version number of EMM }
      NumPage,                  { Number oo the EMS pages }
      PageSeg  : word;           { Segment address of page frame }
      KeyPress : char;

{*********************************************************************}
{* EmsInst : Determine the existance of EMS and correspondign EMM   *}
{* Input   : none                                                   *}
{* Output  : TRUE,when EMS memory is available, else FALSE          *}
{*********************************************************************}

function EmsInst : boolean;

type  EmmName  = array [1..8] of char;  { Name the EMM in driver header }
      EmmNaPtr = ^EmmName;          { Pointer ot name in driver header }

const Name : EmmName = 'EMMXXXX0';              { Name of EMS driver }

var   Regs : Registers;        { Processor register for interrupt call }

begin
  Regs.ax := $35 shl 8 + EMS_INT;        { over interrupt vector $67 }
  msdos( Regs );                              {Get DOS-Function 35h }

  EmsInst := (EmmNaPtr(Ptr(Regs.ES,10))^ = Name); {Driver name compare }
end;

{*********************************************************************}
{* EmsNumPage: Determine the total of EMS pages.                   *}
{* Input   : none                                                  *}
{* Output  : EMS_ERR if error occurs, otherwise number of EMS pages. *}
{*********************************************************************}
```

```
function EmsNumPage : integer;

var Regs : Registers;      { Processor register for the interrupt call }

begin
  Regs.ah := $42;          { Fnt.nr.: Determine number of pages }
  Intr(EMS_INT, Regs);                             { call EMM }
  if (Regs.ah <>0 ) then                    { did an error occur? }
    begin                                            { Yes }
      EmmEC := Regs.ah;                       { get error code }
      EmsNumPage := EMS_ERR;                    { display error }
    end
  else                                           { no error }
    EmsNumPage := Regs.dx;         { Return total number of pages }
end;


{*********************************************************************}
{* EmsFreePage: Determines the number of free EMS pages.           *}
{* Input   : none                                                  *}
{* Output  : EMS_ERR if error occurs, otherwise the number of un-  *}
{*           used EMS pages.                                        *}
{*********************************************************************}

function EmsFreePage : integer;

var Regs : Registers;      { Processor register for the interrupt call }

begin
  Regs.ah := $42;          { Fnt.nr.: Determine no. of pages }
  Intr(EMS_INT, Regs);                            { call EMM }
  if (Regs.ah <>0 ) then                    { did an error occur? }
    begin                                            { Yes }
      EmmEC := Regs.ah;                       { get error code }
      EmsFreePage := EMS_ERR;                   { display error }
    end
  else                                           { no error }
    EmsFreePage := Regs.bx;       { Return number of free pages }
end;


{*********************************************************************}
{* EmsFrameSeg: Determines the segment addres of the page frame.   *}
{* Input   : none                        4                         *}
{* Output  : EMS_ERR if error occurs, else the segment address.    *}
{*********************************************************************}

function EmsFrameSeg : word;

var Regs : Registers;      { Processor register for the interrupt call }

begin
  Regs.ah := $41;          { Fnt.nr.: get Segment adr. page frame }
  Intr(EMS_INT, Regs);                            { call EMM }
  if (Regs.ah <>0 ) then                    { did an error occur? }
    begin                                            { Yes }
      EmmEC := Regs.ah;                       { get error code }
      EmsFrameSeg := W_EMS_ERR;                 { display error }
    end
  else                                           { no error }
    EmsFrameSeg := Regs.bx;  { return segment addresse of page franme }
end;


{*********************************************************************}
{* EmsAlloc: Allocate the specified number of pages and returns a  *}
```

```
{*             handle for access to these pages.                   *}
{* Input   : PAGES: the number of allocated pages.              *  }
{* Output  : EMS_ERR returns the error, else the handle.           *}
{*********************************************************************}

function EmsAlloc( Pages : integer ) : integer;

var Regs : Registers;      { Processor register for the interrupt call }

begin
  Regs.ah := $43;                    { Fnt.nr.: Pages allocated }
  Regs.bx := Pages;           { set number of allocate pages }
  Intr(EMS_INT, Regs);                            { call EMM }
  if (Regs.ah <>0 ) then                    { did an error occur? }
    begin                                            { Yes }
      EmmEC := Regs.ah;                       { get error code }
      EmsAlloc := EMS_ERR;                     { display error }
    end
  else                                           { no error }
    EmsAlloc := Regs.dx;                      { Handle returned }
end;


{*********************************************************************}
{* EmsMap : Creates an allocated logical page from a physical page *}
{*          in the page frame.                                     *}
{* Input  : HANDLE: Handle recieved from EmsAlloc.                 *}
{*          LOGP : Logical page about to be created                *}
{*          PHYSP : The physical page in the page frame.           *}
{* Output : FALSE if error ,else TRUE.                             *}
{*********************************************************************}

function EmsMap(Handle, LogP : integer; PhysP : byte) : boolean;

var Regs : Registers;      { Processor register for the interrupt call }

begin
  Regs.ah := $44;                       { Fnt.nr.: set mapping }
  Regs.al := PhysP;                      { set physical page }
  Regs.bx := LogP;                       { set logical page }
  Regs.dx := Handle;                      { set EMS handle }
  Intr(EMS_INT, Regs);                            { call EMM }
  EmmEC := Regs.ah;                        { get error code }
  EmsMap := (Regs.ah = 0)          { TRUE returned, when no error }
end;


{*********************************************************************}
{* EmsFree : Frees memory when given with an allocated handle.     *}
{* Input   : HANDLE: Handle received by EmsAlloc.                  *}
{* Output  : FALSE on error, else TRUE.                            *}
{*********************************************************************}

function EmsFree(Handle : integer) : boolean;

var Regs : Registers;      { Processor register for the interrupt call }

begin
  Regs.ah := $45;                      { Fnt.nr.: Release pages }
  Regs.dx := handle;                      { set EMS handle }
  Intr(EMS_INT, Regs);                            { call EMM }
  EmmEC := Regs.ah;                        { get error code }
  EmsFree := (Regs.ah = 0)         { TRUE returned, when no error }
end;


{*********************************************************************}
```

663

```
{* EmsVersion: Determines the version number of EMM.        *}
{* Input   : none                                           *}
{* Output  : EMS_ERR on error, otherwise the version number. 6  *}
{*          ( 11 for 1.1, 40 for 4.0 etc.)                  *}
{***********************************************************}

function EmsVersion : integer;

var Regs : Registers;        { Processor register for the interrupt call }

begin
  Regs.ah := $46;                   { Fnt.nr.: Determine EMM version }
  Intr(EMS_INT, Regs);                         { call EMM }
  if (Regs.ah <>0 ) then            { did an error occur? }
    begin                                       { Yes }
      EmmEC := Regs.ah;                    { get error code }
      EmsVersion := EMS_ERR;              { display error }
    end
  else          { no error, computer version number from BCD number }
    EmsVersion := (Regs.al and 15) + (Regs.al shr 4) * 10;
end;


{***********************************************************}
{* EmsSaveMap: Saves display between logical and physical pages of the*}
{*             given handle.                                *}
{* Input   : HANDLE: Handle assigned by EmsAlloc.           *}
{* Output  : FALSE on error, else TRUE.                     *}
{***********************************************************}

function EmsSaveMap( Handle : integer ) : boolean;

var Regs : Registers;        { Processor register for the interrupt call }

begin
  Regs.ah := $47;                     { Fnt.nr.: Save mapping }
  Regs.dx := handle;                    { set EMS handle }
  Intr(EMS_INT, Regs);                    { call EMM }
  EmmEC := Regs.ah;                     { get erro code }
  EmsSaveMap := (Regs.ah = 0)      { TRUE returned, when no error }
end;


{***********************************************************}
{* EmsRestoreMap: Returns display between logical and physical pages, *}
{*               from the page saved by EmsSaveMap          *}
{* Input   : HANDLE: Handle assigned by EmsAlloc            *}
{* Output  : FALSE if an error occurs, otherwise TRUE       *}
{***********************************************************}

function EmsRestoreMap( Handle : integer ) : boolean;

var Regs : Registers;        { Processor register for the interrupt call }

begin
  Regs.ah := $48;                     { Fnt.nr.: Restore mapping }
  Regs.dx := handle;                    { set EMS handle }
  Intr(EMS_INT, Regs);                    { call EMM }
  EmmEC := Regs.ah;                     { mark erro code }
  EmsRestoreMap := (Regs.ah = 0)     { TRUE returned when no error }
end;


{***********************************************************}
{* PrintErr: Displays an error message and ends the program *}
{* Input   : none                                          *}
{* Output  : none                                          *}
```

```
{* Info   : This function is called only if an error occurs during a *}
{*          function call within this module               *}
{***********************************************************}

procedure PrintErr;

begin
  writeln('ATTENTION! Error during EMS memory access');
  write('    ... ');
  if ((EmmEC<$80) or (EmmEc>$8E) or (EmmEc=$82)) then
    writeln('Unidentifiable error')
  else
    case EmmEC of
      $80 : writeln('EMS driver error (EMM trouble)');
      $81 : writeln('EMS hardware error');
      $83 : writeln('Illegal EMM handle');
      $84 : writeln('Called EMS function does not exist');
      $85 : writeln('No more free EMS handles available');
      $86 : writeln('Error while saving or restoring mapping ');
      $87 : writeln('More pages requested than are actually ',
                    'available');
      $88 : writeln('More pages requested than are free');
      $89 : writeln('No pages requested');
      $8A : writeln('Logical page does not belong to handle');
      $8B : writeln('Illegal physical page number');
      $8C : writeln('Mapping memory range is full');
      $8D : writeln('Map save has already been done');
      $8E : writeln('Mapping must be saved before it can',
                    'be restored');
    end;
  Halt;                                       { Program end }
end;


{***********************************************************}
{* VrAdr: Returns a pointer to video RAM                   *}
{* Input   : none                                          *}
{* Output  : Pointer to video RAM                          *}
{***********************************************************}

function VrAdr : BytePtr;

var Regs : Registers;        { Processor register for the interrupt call }

begin
  Regs.ah := $0f;                 { Fnt.nr.: Determine video mode }
  Intr($10, Regs);                   { call BIOS-Video-Interrupt }
  if (Regs.al = 7) then              { monochrome video card? }
    VrAdr := ptr($B000, 0)       { Yes, Video-RAM at B000:0000 }
  else                          { Color-, EGA- or VGA-card }
    VrAdr := ptr($B800, 0);         { Video-RAM at B800:0000 }
end;


{***********************************************************}
{* PageAdr: Returns address of a physical page in page frame *}
{* Input   : PAGE: Physical page number (0-3)              *}
{* Output  : Pointer to the physical page                  *}
{***********************************************************}

function PageAdr( Page : integer ) : BytePtr;

begin
  PageAdr := Ptr( EmsFrameSeg + (Page shl 10), 0 );
end;
```

```
{*******************************************************************}
{**                          MAIN PRORAM                         **}
{*******************************************************************}

begin
  ClrScr;                                        { clear screen }
  writeln('EMMP  -  (c) 1988, 92 by MICHAEL TISCHER',#13#10);
  if EmsInst then                         { is EMS memory installed? }
    begin                                                    { Yes }
      {*--Display informationen about the EMS memory  --------------*}

      EmmVer := EmsVersion;          { Determine EMM version number }
      if EmmVer = EMS_ERR then              { did an error occur? }
        PrintErr;        { Yes, display error message and end program }
      writeln('EMM-Version number          : ',EmmVer div 10, '.',
              EmmVer mod 10);

      NumPage := EmsNumPage;           { Determine total no. pages }
      if NumPage = EMS_ERR then              { did an error occur? }
        PrintErr;         { Yes, display erro rmessage and end program }
      writeln('Number of EMS pages         : ', NumPage, ' (',
              NumPage shl 4, ' KByte)');

      NumPage := EmsFreePage;      { Determine number of free pages}
      if NumPage = EMS_ERR then              { did an error occur? }
        PrintErr;        { Yes, display erro messag eand end program }
      writeln('... free                    : ', NumPage, ' (',
              NumPage shl 4, ' KByte)');

      PageSeg := EmsFrameSeg;      { Segment addresse of page frame }
      if PageSeg = W_EMS_ERR then            { did an error occur? }
        PrintErr;       { Yes, displat erro rmessage and end program }
      writeln('Segment address of page frame: ', PAgeSeg);

      writeln;
      writeln('Now a page from EMS memory can be allocated,  and the');
      writeln('screen contents can be copied from video RAM into this');
      writeln('page.');
```

```
  writeln('                              ... Please press a key');
  Keypress := ReadKey;                          { Wait for a keypress }

  {*-- Page is allocated, and the data is passed to the first-----*}
  {*-- logical page in the page frame                        -----*}

  Handle := EmsAlloc( 1 );                       { Allocate one page }
  if Handle = EMS_ERR then                    { did an error occur? }
    PrintErr;        { Yes, display error message and end program }
  if not(EmsMap(Handle, 0, 0)) then                 { Set mapping }
    PrintErr;                  { Error: display error and end program }

  {*-- Copy 4000 Bytes from Video-RAM to EMS memory----------- -*}

  Move(VrAdr^, PageAdr(0)^, 4000);

  ClrScr;                                           { Clear screen }
  while KeyPressed do                      { Read keyboard buffer }
    Keypress := ReadKey;
  writeln('Old screen contents are cleared.  However, the  data ');
  writeln('from the screen is in EMS, and can be re-copied onto ');
  writeln('the screen.                                        ');
  writeln('                              ... Please press a key');
  Keypress := ReadKey;                          { Wait for a keypress }

  {*-- Copy contents of video RAM from EMS memory and release   --*}
  {*-- the allocated EMS memory                                 --*}

  Move(PageAdr(0)^, VrAdr^, 4000);          { Copy over Video RAM }
  if not(EmsFree(Handle)) then                    { Release memory }
    PrintErr;    { Error: display message and end program }
  GotoXY(1, 15);
  writeln('END')
  end
else                                      { the EMD driver not availabele }
  writeln('No EMS memory installed.');
end.
```

12.2 Extended Memory

Although EMS access must be performed in portions, placing the PC in protected mode allows access to all of extended memory. In real mode, the extended memory isn't used because the processor cannot address memory beyond the 1 megabyte limit. This explains why 8088 and 8086 based systems cannot use extended memory. These microprocessors recognize only real mode and cannot switch to protected mode.

Changing a single bit in the processor's flag register enables protected mode. Once this is done, a program can access up to 16 megabytes of extended memory, but crashes immediately. This occurs because of the mechanism through which the 80286 and its successors address memory in protected mode. This is completely different from memory access in real mode.

When in protected mode, the processor operates through segment descriptors instead of segment addresses. These segment descriptors point to local and global segment descriptor lists. However, DOS cannot handle this access because it's limited to real mode.

The proper descriptor lists must be created and initialized before you can switch to protected mode. To do this, you must be familiar with assembly language programming and understand how the processor operates in protected mode.

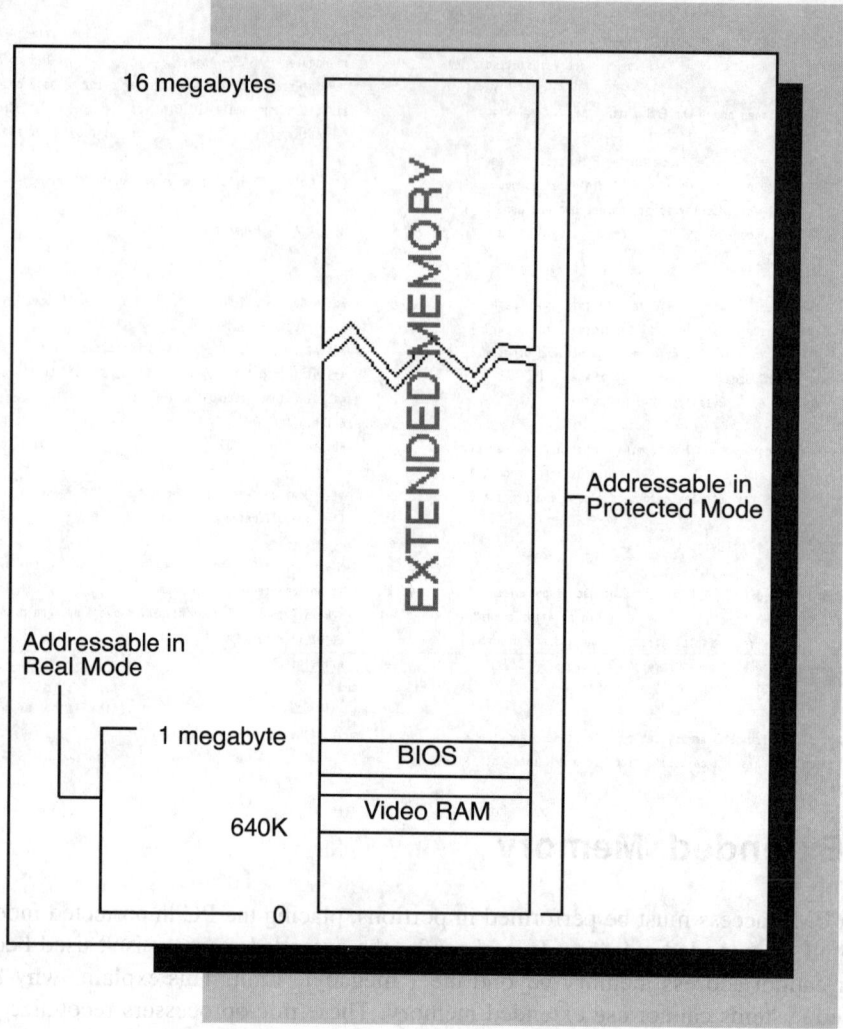

Extended memory address space of a PC

Some BIOS functions and the XMS drivers provide help for extended memory access. The XMS drivers are able to handle extended memory better than the BIOS functions. The drivers can ensure that extended memory is shared instead of limiting all extended memory to a single program.

The fight for access rights to extended memory is a significant problem, which we'll discuss later in this chapter. This problem is especially noticeable if you access extended memory directly. The lowest 64K of extended memory is accessible from real mode (more on this later).

In the following sections, we'll discuss access using BIOS functions, the High Memory Area (HMA), and XMS functions.

12.2.1   Extended Memory Access from BIOS

Extended memory can be accessed only if it exists. Normally this applies to all computers that have 1 megabyte of RAM because usually only 640K or 512K in the area below the 1 megabyte limit are used. The rest is located immediately above this limit and is therefore available as extended memory.

Function 88H of BIOS interrupt 15H returns the extended memory size. Interrupt 15H was originally intended for the cassette recorder interface (the cassette recorder was the original mass storage device used on the PC). When disk drives replaced the cassette recorder for mass storage, the cassette recorder functions were no longer used.

Interrupt 15H is used for extended memory and joystick reading. (See Chapter 10 for more information on joysticks.) Place function 88H in the AH register. The result, which is placed in the AX register, indicates the extended memory size in kilobytes.

Now that we know extended memory exists on the system, how can we access it? Function 87H moves blocks of memory within the total memory space. This means that blocks of memory can be moved from the area below the 1 megabyte limit to the area above the 1 megabyte limit and vice versa. However, the function shouldn't be used for the latter, since its call is complicated and has other disadvantages. To access memory beyond the 1 megabyte barrier, the processor must be switched to protected mode. Function 87H requires very comprehensive information, since the 80286 processor is more difficult to program in protected mode than in real mode (8086 emulation under DOS). At the end of this section you'll find a program that demonstrates how to use function 87H.

The function number 87H first must be passed to the AH register, then the number of the words to be moved (only words only, not bytes) must be passed to the CX register. A maximum value of 8000H corresponds to a maximum value of 64K.

Global Descriptor Table

The ES:SI register pair receive the address of the GDT (Global Descriptor Table), which must be installed in the user program. The GDT describes the individual memory segments of the 80x86 in protected mode. The segments in protected mode are exempt from the limitations made in real mode. While segments can only start at memory locations divisible by 16 in real mode, protected mode segments may start at any memory location. Also, protected mode segments may be any size from 1 byte to 64K.

Another protected mode innovation is the access code defined for every segment. This code indicates whether the segment described is a data segment or a code segment (only code segments can be executed). The access code also contains information on access priority, and whether access is even permitted. Each segment descriptor consists of 8 bytes. During its call, function 87H expects that six segment descriptors have been prepared in the GDT (i.e., memory space reserved for them). The figure below illustrates which segment descriptors are involved, as well as the construction of a segment descriptor.

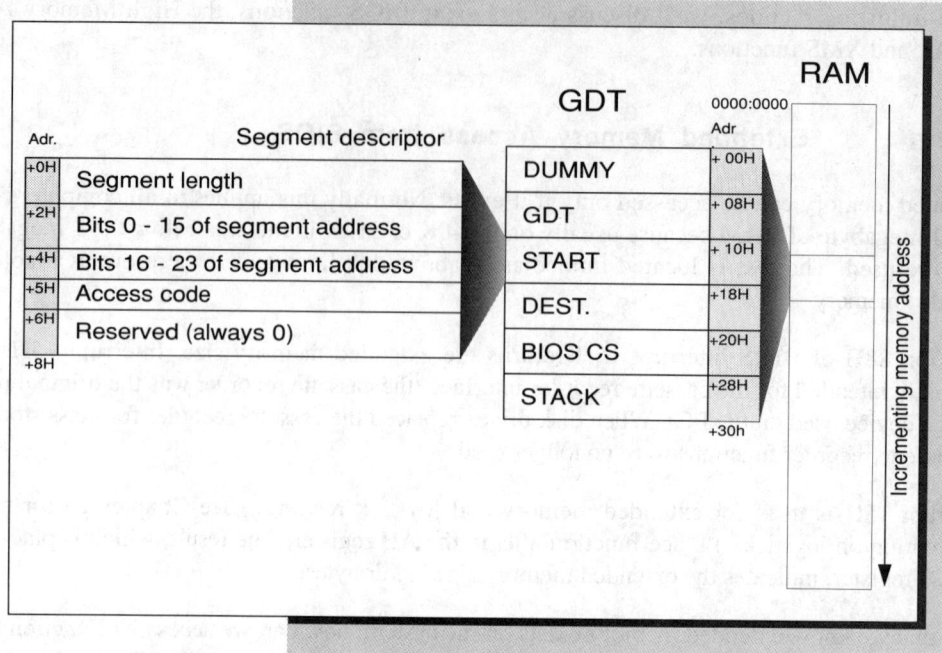

Segment descriptor structure as seen by function 87H

Since the BIOS functions fill out the other descriptors, we're only concerned with the segment descriptors designated as "start" and "destination". The start descriptor describes the segment, from which the data are taken. The destination descriptor describes the segment into which the data are copied.

The length of both segments can be 0FFFFH (64K decimal), even if fewer bytes (or words) copy over in the process. If a lower value is indicated, the number of bytes (number of words multiplied by 2) to be copied cannot exceed this amount. Otherwise, the processor notices an access across a segment boundary during copying, which triggers an error.

The address of the two memory areas must be converted to a (physical) 24-bit address. The lower 16 bits of this address enter the second field of the segment descriptor and the upper 8 bits enter the third field. Access code 92H can be used, which informs the processor that the described segment is a data segment with the highest priority, that the segment exists in memory, and that the segment can be written. The last field of the descriptor maintains compatibility with the 80386 processor; this field should always contain the value 0.

Although the address of the user program's buffer remains fixed, the address beyond the 1 megabyte boundary, to which data should be copied, can be freely selected (subject to RAM availability). The following table shows the addresses of the various 1K blocks beyond the 1 megabyte border as 24-bit addresses:

```
  0K  = 100000H              124K = 11F000H
  1K  = 100400H              125K = 11F400H
  2K  = 100800H              126K = 11F800H
  3K  = 100C00H              127K = 11FC00H
  4K  = 101000H              128K = 120000H
  5K  = 101400H              129K = 120400H
  6K  = 100800H              130K = 120800H
  7K  = 100C00H              131K = 120C00H
  8K  = 102000H              132K = 121000H
  9K  = 102400H              133K = 121400H

              . . . . . . . . .
              . . . . . . . . .
              . . . . . . . . .

 60K  = 10F000H              252K = 13F000H
 61K  = 10F400H              253K = 13F400H
 62K  = 10F800H              254K = 13F800H
 63K  = 10FC00H              255K = 13FC00H
 64K  = 110000H              256K = 140000H
 65K  = 110400H              257K = 140400H
 66K  = 110800H              258K = 140800H
 67K  = 110C00H              259K = 140C00H
 68K  = 111000H              260K = 141000H
 69K  = 111400H              261K = 141400H
```

After the function call, the carry flag indicates the success of the function call. If the carry flag is set, an error occurred. The value in the AH register indicates the cause of the error:

Error Number	Cause of Error
AH = 0	No error (carry flag reset)
AH = 1	RAM parity error
AH = 2	GDT defective at function call
AH = 3	Protected mode could not be properly initialized

A disadvantage of this function is that, while the processor is in protected mode, all interrupts must be suppressed. While in protected mode, BIOS interrupts (e.g., timer or keyboard) can be called, but these routines were designed to be used in real mode only. So, these interrupts may not work properly in protected mode.

This disadvantage is evident when you call the timer. Since its interrupts are suppressed, protected mode doesn't keep track of the time. So time remains frozen for a moment. If programs frequently call function 87H, the clock may slow down by 20 or 30 seconds per day. However, since the clock can be reset to the proper time with software, most of these disadvantages can be avoided.

The execution speed of this function (slow) is more important than interrupt suppression. This is especially true for ATs, which are equipped with an 80286 processor. Although ATs can easily be switched to protected mode, switching back to real mode is more difficult. Since an instruction that smoothly switches the system back to real mode doesn't exist, a processor reset must be used.

An 80286 reset can only be triggered through the keyboard controller. A six millisecond delay occurs between the time the controller receives the reset instruction and the time the controller responds to the instruction. Those six milliseconds can be an eternity in a 10 MHz, 12 MHz, or 16 MHz computer. Unfortunately, this still isn't the solution. Although the processor does change to real mode after the reset, the system begins program execution with the boot code from BIOS.

To prevent this reboot process, a memory location in the BIOS RAM receives a code before triggering the reset. This code informs BIOS of the purpose of the reset. BIOS then returns to the caller of function 87H. However, this process requires a lot of computer time.

PS/2 systems handle this shift more smoothly, even if the systems are equipped with 80286 processors. The PS/2 includes special circuitry that makes a smooth transition from protected mode to real mode.

The 80386 and 80486 machines switch between modes easily, proving that Intel Corporation made the appropriate improvements to their processors.

Demonstration programs

The following programs in Pascal and C copy data between buffers in extended memory.

Pascal listing: EXTP.PAS

```
{***************************************************
*                 E X T P . P A S                  *
**------------------------------------------------**
* Demmonstration of accessing the Extended-Memory using the BIOS- *
* Functions of Interrupts 15h taking into consideration any RAN disks.*
**------------------------------------------------**
* Author       : MICHAEL TISCHER                   *
* Developed on  : 05/18/1889                       *
* last update on : 02/19/1992                      *
***************************************************}

program ExtP;

uses Dos;

{-- globale variables------------------------------}

var RdLen    : integer;          { Size of the RAM disk in KB }
    ExtAvail : boolean;          { Extended Memory available? }
    ExtStart : longint;  { Start address of EXT-Memory as linear Adr. }
    ExtLen   : integer;          { size of extended Memory in KByte }

{***************************************************
* ExtAdrConv : convert a pointer into a 32-Bit large linear addrerss *
*              in the form of a LONGINTS return value *
*------------------------------------------------**
* Input   : Adr = of the convertedpointer          *
* Output  : the converted address                  *
***************************************************}

function ExtAdrConv ( Adr : pointer ) : longint;

type PTRREC = record
              Ofs : word;        { for accessing the }
              Seg : word;        { contents of any   }
              end;               { pointer you wish  }
```

```
begin
   ExtAdrConv := longint( PTRREC( Adr ).seg ) shl 4 + PTRREC( Adr ).ofs;
end;

{***************************************************
* ExtCopy : copy data between any buffers within the *
*           16-MB address range of the 80286/386/486. *
**------------------------------------------------**
* Input  : Start  = address of start buffers as 32-Bit linear Adr. *
*          Target = address of targe buffer as 32-Bit linear Adr. *
*          Len    = Number of bytes to be copied   *
* Info   : - The number of bytes to be copied must be an even number. *
*          - This procedure is only intended for use *
*            within this unit                      *
***************************************************}

procedure ExtCopy( Start, Target : longint; Len : word );

{-- Data structure for accesiing the extended RAM -----------------}

type SDES = record                  { Segment descriptor }
            Length  : word;       { Length of segment in bytes   }
            AdrLo   : word;       { Bit 0 to 15 of Segment adr.  }
            AdrHi   : byte;       { Bit 16 to 23 of Segment adr. }
            Attribut : byte;      { Segment attribute            }
            Res     : word;       { reserved for 80386           }
            end;

    GDT = record                      { Global Descriptor Table }
          Dummy : SDES;
          GDTS  : SDES;
          Start : SDES;               { copy from ... }
          Target : SDES;              { ... to        }
          Code  : SDES;
          Stack : SDES;
          end;

    LI = record                   { This accesses the contenst of the }
         LoWord : word;         { LongInts of the linear 32-Bit- }
```

```
              HiByte : byte;      { addresses                        }
              dummy  : byte;
            end;

var GTab : GDT;                              { Global Descriptor Table }
    Regs : Registers;                { Processor regs. for interrupt call }
    Adr  : longint;                     { for conversion of the address }

begin
   FillChar( GTab, SizeOf( GTab ), 0 );            { all fields to 0 }

   {-- Create segment descriptor of start segments ------------------}

   GTab.Start.AdrLo    := LI( Start ).LoWord;
   GTab.Start.AdrHi    := LI( Start ).HiByte;
   GTab.Start.Attribut := $92;
   GTab.Start.Length   := Len;

   {-- Creat segmentd escriptor of target segments -------------------}

   GTab.Target.AdrLo    := LI( Target ).LoWord;
   GTab.Target.AdrHi    := LI( Target ).HiByte;
   GTab.Target.Attribut := $92;
   GTab.Target.Length   := Len;

   {-- Copy memory range with help from function $87 the cassette- -----}
   {-- interrupts $15                                          -------}

   Regs.AH := $87;          { Function number for 'Memory copying' }
   Regs.ES := seg( GTab );                    { address of  GDT }
   Regs.SI := ofs( GTab );                    { to ES:SI        }
   Regs.CX := Len shr 1;          { Number of copied words to CX }
   intr( $15, Regs );                         { call function }
   if ( Regs.AH <> 0 ) then                    { Error? }
     begin                        { Yes AH contains erro rcode }
       writeln('Error accessing extended RAM (', Regs.AH, ')!');
       RunError;           { Abort program with Run-Time-Error }
     end;
end;

{*****************************************************************
* ExtRead : read the specified number of bytes fro extended     *
*           memory into main memory.                            *
**-----------------------------------------------------------**
* Input : ExtAdr = Source address in extended-RAM (linear address) *
*         BuPtr  = Pointer to the Target buffer in main memory  *
*         Len    = Number of bytes to bve copied                *
*****************************************************************}

procedure ExtRead( ExtAdr : longint;  BuPtr : pointer;  Len : word );;

begin
   ExtCopy( ExtAdr, ExtAdrConv( BuPtr ), len );
end;

{*****************************************************************
* ExtWrite : write the specified number of bytes from main      *
*            memory into extended memory.                       *
**-----------------------------------------------------------**
* Input : BuPtr = Pointer to source bufferinmain memory         *
*         ExtAdr = Target address in extended RAM (linear address) *
*         Len    = Number of bytes ot be copied                 *
*****************************************************************}
```

```
procedure ExtWrite( BuPtr : pointer;  ExtAdr : longint;  Len : word );

begin
   ExtCopy( ExtAdrConv( BuPtr ), ExtAdr, len );
end;

{*****************************************************************
* ExtGetInfo : Determine the start address of the extended RAM and *
*              its size considering any RAM disks that may be present *
**-----------------------------------------------------------**
* Input   : none                                                *
* Ausgabe : none                                                *
* Globals : ExtAvail/W, ExtStart/W, ExtLen/W                    *
*****************************************************************}

procedure ExtGetInfo;

type NAME_TYP    = array [1..5] of char;
type BOOT_SECTOR = record              { Boot-Sector of RAM disk }
          dummy1  : array [1..3] of byte;
          Name    : NAME_TYP;
          dummy2  : array [1..3] of byte;
          BpS     : word;
          dummy3  : array [1..6] of byte;
          Sectors : word;
          dummy4  : byte;            { fill to even length }
        end;

const VdiskName : NAME_TYP = 'VDISK';

var BootSec : BOOT_SECTOR;          { takes the supposed Boot Sector }
    Lastlp  : boolean;                      { mark loop end }
    Regs    : Registers;      { Processor regs. for interrupt call }

begin
   {-- Determine size of extended memory and whether is is available ---}

   Regs.ah := $88;    { Function nr.: "Determine size of Extended-RAM" }
   intr( $15, Regs );                 { call cassette interrupt }
   if ( Regs.AX = 0 ) then
     begin                            { no extended RAM available }
       ExtAvail := FALSE;
       ExtLen   := 0;
       ExtStart := 0;
       exit;                             { return to caller }
     end;

   ExtAvail := TRUE;                   { extended Memory available }
   ExtLen   := Regs.AX;        { extended RAM existing, mark size }

   {-- search for RAM disks of Typ VDISK ----------------------------}

   ExtStart := $100000;                      { start at1 MB }
   Lastlp := FALSE;                       { start for RAM-Disk }
   repeat                                 { loop start }
     ExtRead( ExtStart, @BootSec, SizeOf( BootSec ) );
     with BootSec do
       if Name = VdiskName then         { is boot sector a RAM disk? }
         inc( ExtStart, longint( Sectors ) * BpS ) {Yes, beyond RAM disk}
       else
         Lastlp := TRUE;                { no RAM disk is found }
   until Lastlp;

   {-- Calculate size of RAMdisk from free extended RAM ------------}
```

671

```
      dec( ExtLen, integer( (ExtStart - longint($100000)) shr 10 ) );
  end;

{*********************************************************************
 *  CheckExt : Examine the consistency of the free extended RAM     *
 *********************************************************************}

procedure CheckExt;

var AdrTest   : longint;                  { Address o fht etest blocks }
    i, j      : integer;                  { loop counter }
    WriteBuf,                             { Test block }
    ReadBuf   : array [1..1024] of byte;
    Ferror    : boolean;                  { Pointer to memory error }

begin
  Randomize;                           { initialize random number generator }
  AdrTest := ExtStart;
  for i := 1 to ExtLen do              { check memory in 1 KB-Blocks }
    begin
      for j := 1 to 1024 do           { Fill block withrandom value }
        WriteBuf[ j ] := Random( 255 );

      write(#13, AdrTest ); { output address of the checked KB-blocks. }

      {-- Write the buffer and then read the buffer -------------------}

      ExtWrite( @WriteBuf, AdrTest, 1024 );
      ExtRead( AdrTest, @ReadBuf, 1024 );

      {-- Determine idenity of WriteBuf and ReadBuf -----------------}

      for j := 1 to 1024 do
        if WriteBuf[j] <> ReadBuf[j] then { Buffer contenst identical? }
          begin                           { No, Error! }
            writeln( ' Error! Memory part ',
                   AdrTest + longint(j-1) );
            Ferror := TRUE;
          end;

      inc( AdrTest, longint( 1024 ) ); { AdrTest of next KB-Block     }
    end;                               { set                          }
  writeln;
  if not( Ferror ) then                { did an erro roccur? }
    writeln( 'All o.k.!' );            { No }
end;

{*********************************************************************
 *  M A I N   P R O G R A M                                         *
 *********************************************************************}

begin
  writeln( #13#10'EXTDEMO - (c) 1989 by Michael Tischer'#13#10);
  ExtGetInfo;      { Determine availability and size of extended memory }
  if ExtAvail then             { is extended RAM available? }
    begin                                              { Yes }
      RdLen := integer( (ExtStart - longint( $100000 ) ) shr 10 );
      if ( RdLen = 0 ) then            { are RAM disks installe? }
        begin                                          { no }
          writeln( 'There are no RAM disks installed. ');
          writeln( 'The free extended RAM begins with the ',
                 '1 MB memory boundary. ');
        end
      else                            { Yse RAM disks present }
        begin
          writeln( 'One or more RAM disks have reserved ', RdLen,
                 ' KB of extended RAM.');
          writeln( 'The free extended RAM begins ', RdLen,
                 ' KB after ther 1 MB n\memory boundry.');
        end;
      writeln( 'The size of the free extended RAM is ',
             ExtLen, ' KB.');
      writeln( #13#10'The extended RAM has also been checked for',
             ' consistency...'#13#10);
      CheckExt;
    end
  else
    writeln( 'There is no extended RAM installed in this computer!');
end.
```

C listing: EXTC.C

```
/********************************************************************
*                        E X T C . C                               *
**----------------------------------------------------------------**
* Demonstration of accessing extended memory with the BIOS-        *
* Function of Interrupt 15h taking into consideration RAM disks.   *
**----------------------------------------------------------------**
* Author        : MICHAEL TISCHER                                  *
* Developed on   : 05/18/1989                                      *
* Lastest update on: 02/19/1992                                    *
**----------------------------------------------------------------**
* memory model  : SMALL                                            *
**----------------------------------------------------------------**
* Microsoft C   : The warning "Segment lost in conversation"       *
*                 can't be avoided.                                *
********************************************************************/

/*-- Include-files------------------------------------------------*/

#include <stdio.h>
#include <stdlib.h>
#include <conio.h>
#include <string.h>
#include <dos.h>

/*== Typedefs ===================================================*/

typedef unsigned char BYTE;             /* we build it in one byte */
typedef unsigned int WORD;
typedef BYTE BOOL;                          /* BOOLEAN in Pascal */

#define TRUE  ( 0 == 0 )
#define FALSE ( 0 == 1 )

/*-- Macros -----------------------------------------------------*/

#ifndef __TURBOC__
  #define random(x) rand()
  #define randomize() srand(1)
#endif

/*-- globale variables ------------------------------------------*/

int  RdLen;                         /* size of the RAM-Disks in KB */
BOOL ExtAvail;                      /* extended Memory available? */
long ExtStart;/* Start addresse of the extended memory as linear Adr. */
int  ExtLen;                    /* size of the extended memory in KByte */

/********************************************************************
* ExtAdrConv : convert a single FAR-Pointer in one 32-Bit large    *
*              linear address in the form of one return word       *
**----------------------------------------------------------------**
* Input   : Adr = to the converted pointer                         *
* Output  : the converted address                                 *
********************************************************************/

long ExtAdrConv( void far *Adr )
{
 return (((long) Adr >> 16) << 4) + (unsigned int) Adr;
}

/********************************************************************
* ExtCopy : copy data between any two buffers within               *
```

```
*             the 16-MB size address range of th 80286/386/486.    *
**----------------------------------------------------------------**
* Input  : Start = address of start buffer as 32-Bit linear Adr.   *
*          Target = address of target buffer as 32-Bit linear Adr. *
*          Len   = Number of bytes ot copy                         *
* Output : none                                                    *
* Info   : - The number of bytes to be copied must be an even number. *
********************************************************************/

void ExtCopy( long Start, long Target, WORD Len )
{
 /*-- Data structure for accessing the extended RAM ---------------*/

 typedef struct {                          /* Segment descriptor */
          WORD Length,        /* Lenght of the segments in byte*/
               AdrLo,         /* Bit  0 to 15 of the Segment adr. */
          BYTE AdrHi,         /* Bit 16 to 23 of the Segment adr. */
               Attribut;      /* Segment attribute              */
          WORD Res;           /* reserved for 80386             */
        } SDES;

 typedef struct {                          /* Global Descriptor Table */
          SDES Dummy,
               GDTS ,
               Start,                       /* copy from ... */
               Target ,                     /* ... to        */
               Code ,
               Stack;
        } GDT;

#define LOWORD(x) ((unsigned int) (x))
#define HIBYTE(x) (*((BYTE *)&x+2))

 GDT      GTab;                         /* Global Descriptor Table */
 union REGS   Regs;            /* Define Processor regs. Interrupt */
 struct SREGS SRegs;                          /* Segment register */
 long     Adr;                /* the conversion of the address */

 memset( &GTab, 0, sizeof GTab );             /* all fields to 0 */

 /*-- Create segment descriptor start segments ---------------------*/

 GTab.Start.AdrLo    = LOWORD(Start);
 GTab.Start.AdrHi    = HIBYTE(Start);
 GTab.Start.Attribut = 0x92;
 GTab.Start.Length   = Len;

  /*-- Create segment descriptor of the second segments -------------*/

 GTab.Target.AdrLo    = LOWORD(Target);
 GTab.Target.AdrHi    = HIBYTE(Target);
 GTab.Target.Attribut = 0x92;
 GTab.Target.Length   = Len;

 /*-- Copy memory scope with help of Function 0x87 the cassette------*/
 /*-- Interrupts 0x15                                       -----*/

 Regs.h.ah = 0x87;              /* Function number for 'Memory copy' */
 SRegs.es = (long) (void far *) &GTab >> 16;   /* address of the GDT */
 Regs.x.si = (int) &GTab;                          /* to ES:SI */
 Regs.x.cx = Len >> 1;            /* Number of copied words to CX */
 int86x( 0x15, &Regs, &Regs, &SRegs );            /* Call function */
 if ( Regs.h.ah )                                    /* error? */
   {                             /* Yes, the display error code */
```

673

```
   printf( "\nError in access time to extended-Ram (%d)\n", Regs.h.ah);
   exit( 1 );                          /* End program with error code */
   }
}


/********************************************************************
 * ExtRead : Read a  definite number of bytes from the extended    *
 *           Memory in the main memory.                            *
 **--------------------------------------------------------------**
 * Input   : ExtAdr = Source address in extended-RAM (linear address) *
 *           BuPtr = Pointer to the Target buffer in main memory   *
 *           Len   = Number of bytes ot copy                       *
 * Output  : none                                                  *
 ********************************************************************/

void ExtRead( long  ExtAdr,  void far *BuPtr, WORD Len )
{
  ExtCopy( ExtAdr, ExtAdrConv( BuPtr ), Len );
}


/********************************************************************
 * ExtWrite : Write a specified number of bytes from main memory   *
 *            to  extended Memory.                                 *
 **--------------------------------------------------------------**
 * Input   : BuPtr = Pointer to the source buffer in  main memory  *
 *           ExtAdr = Target address in extended-RAM (linear address) *
 *           Len    = Number of bytes ot copy                      *
 * Output  : none                                                  *
 ********************************************************************/

void ExtWrite( void far *BuPtr, long ExtAdr, WORD Len)
{
  ExtCopy( ExtAdrConv( BuPtr ), ExtAdr, Len );
}


/********************************************************************
 * ExtGetInfo : Determine the start address of extended RAM and its *
 *              size considering that there may be  RAM disks of   *
 *              Type VDISK                                          *
 **--------------------------------------------------------------**
 * Input   : none                                                  *
 * Output  : none                                                  *
 * Globals : ExtAvail/W, ExtStart/W, ExtLen/W                      *
 ********************************************************************/

void ExtGetInfo( void )
{
  typedef struct {                        /* Boot sector of RAM disk */
               BYTE  dummy1[3];
               char  Name[5];
               BYTE  dummy2[3];
               WORD  BpS;
               BYTE  dummy3[6];
               WORD  Sectors;
               BYTE  dummy4;
               } BOOT_SECTOR;

  static char VDiskName[5] = { 'V', 'D', 'I', 'S', 'K' };

  BOOT_SECTOR BootSec;          /* takes alleged Boot Sector       */
  union REGS Regs;              /* Processor regs. for interrupt call */

  /*-- Determine the size of extended Memory and whether        -*/
  /*-- extended memory is available                             -*/
```

```
  Regs.h.ah = 0x88; /* Function nr.: "determine size of extended-RAM"*/
  int86( 0x15, &Regs, &Regs );            /* call cassette interrupt */
  if ( Regs.x.ax == 0 )
    {                                      /* no extended RAM present */
     ExtAvail = FALSE;
     ExtLen  = ExtStart = 0;
     return;                               /* return to caller */
    }

  ExtAvail = TRUE;                        /* extended Memory available */
  ExtLen  = Regs.x.ax;                    /* extended RAM present, mark size */

  /*-- Search RAM-Disks for Typ V6DISK -----------------------------*/

  ExtStart = 0x1000001;                   /* start at 1 MB */
  while ( TRUE )                          /* check looop */
    {
     ExtRead( ExtStart, &BootSec, sizeof BootSec );
     if ( memcmp( BootSec.Name, VDiskName,
       sizeof VDiskName ) == 0 )         /* is Boot sector a RAM disk? */
        ExtStart += (long) BootSec.Sectors * BootSec.BpS;   /* Yes */
     else
        break;                            /* loop end */
    }

  /*-- Subtract the size of the RAM disks from free extended RAM---*/

  ExtLen -= (int) ((ExtStart - 0x1000001) >> 10);
}


/********************************************************************
 * CheckExt : examine the consistency of free extended RAM         *
 **--------------------------------------------------------------**
 * Input   : none                                                  *
 * Output  : none                                                  *
 ********************************************************************/

void CheckExt( void )
{
  long  AdrTest;                          /* address of the test blocks */
  int   i, j;                             /* loop counter */
  BYTE  WriteBuf[1024],                   /* test block */
        ReadBuf[1024];
  BOOL  Ferror = FALSE;                   /* pointer to memory error */

  randomize();                            /* initialize random number generator*/
  AdrTest = ExtStart;
  for ( i = 1; i <= ExtLen; ++i, AdrTest += 1024 )
    {                                      /* run through memory in 1 KB-Blocks */
     for ( j = 0; j < 1024; )            /* Fill block with random number */
       WriteBuf[ j++ ] = random( 255 );

     printf("\r%ld", AdrTest );          /* address of the examined KB-Blocks */

     /*-- Write buffer WriteBuf, then return to ReadBuf to read      */

     ExtWrite( WriteBuf, AdrTest, 1024 );
     ExtRead( AdrTest, ReadBuf, 1024 );

     /*-- determine identity from WriteBuf and ReadBuf --------------*/

     for ( j = 0; j < 1024; ++j )        /* Fill block with random value */
       if ( WriteBuf[j] != ReadBuf[j] )  /* Buffer contenst identical? */
```

```
            {                              /* No, Error! */
              printf( "\n  Error! Memory location %ld\n", AdrTest + j - 1);
              Ferror = TRUE;
            }
          }                        /* set                    */
        printf( "\n\n" );
        if ( !Ferror )                     /* did an error occur? */
          printf( "All o.k.!\n" );                         /* No */
      }


/****************************************************************
*  M A I N   P R O G R A M                                      *
****************************************************************/

void main( void )
{
  printf ("EXTC - (c) 1989, 92 by Michael Tischer\n\n");
  ExtGetInfo();  /*Determine availability and size of extended Memory */
```

```
      if ( ExtAvail )                       /* is extended RAM available? */
      {                                                          /*Yes */
        RdLen = (int) ( (ExtStart - 0x1000001 ) >> 10 );
        if ( RdLen == 0 )                      /* is RAM disks installed? */
          printf( "No RAM disks installled.\nThe free boundry.\n" );
        else                                 /* Yes, RAM-Disks present */
          printf( "One or more RAM disks have reserved %d KB of extended " \
                  "RAM.\nThe free extended RAM begins at %d KB beyond the "\
                  "1 MB memory boundry.\n", RdLen, RdLen);
        printf( "The size of the free extended RAM is %d KB\n", ExtLen);
        printf( "\nThe extended RAM has also been examined for " \
                " consistency...\n\n" );
        CheckExt();
      }
      else
        printf( "There is no extended RAM installed in this computer!\n" );
    }
```

12.2.2   Conflicts in Extended Memory

Theoretically, extended memory should be shared by programs. However, some cache programs or other utilities may want to use all existing extended memory. This can cause memory overwriting by other programs and system crashes.

This problem is caused by a lack of control. A program that can help other programs coexist in extended memory is needed. The BIOS causes this problem. BIOS function 88H informs every program that all of extended memory is available. The BIOS cannot allocate single memory blocks.

The XMS standard provides some solutions to this problem (more on this later). This standard, which was developed in 1988, is based on the XMS standard. Two different procedures help avoid collisions in extended memory, but don't always succeed.

The first and most powerful method (the INT 15 method) redirects the interrupt vector of interrupt 15H so that it points to its own handler instead of the original interrupt handler in ROM BIOS.

The new interrupt 15H handler should concentrate on controlling function 88, which checks the size of extended memory. The handler redirects the interrupt call to the original handler as soon as the function number confirms that another function should be called.

If function 88H is called, the caller receives the amount of extended memory currently available (not the current size of extended memory). Function 88H subtracts the amount of extended memory being used from the total extended memory size. This ensures that the caller uses only the available extended memory.

Because the caller must also assume that the extended memory starts at the 1 megabyte border, the previously installed program must protect itself from the caller. The existing program is located at the end of extended memory instead of at the 1 megabyte limit. The caller views the starting location of the installed program as the end of extended memory.

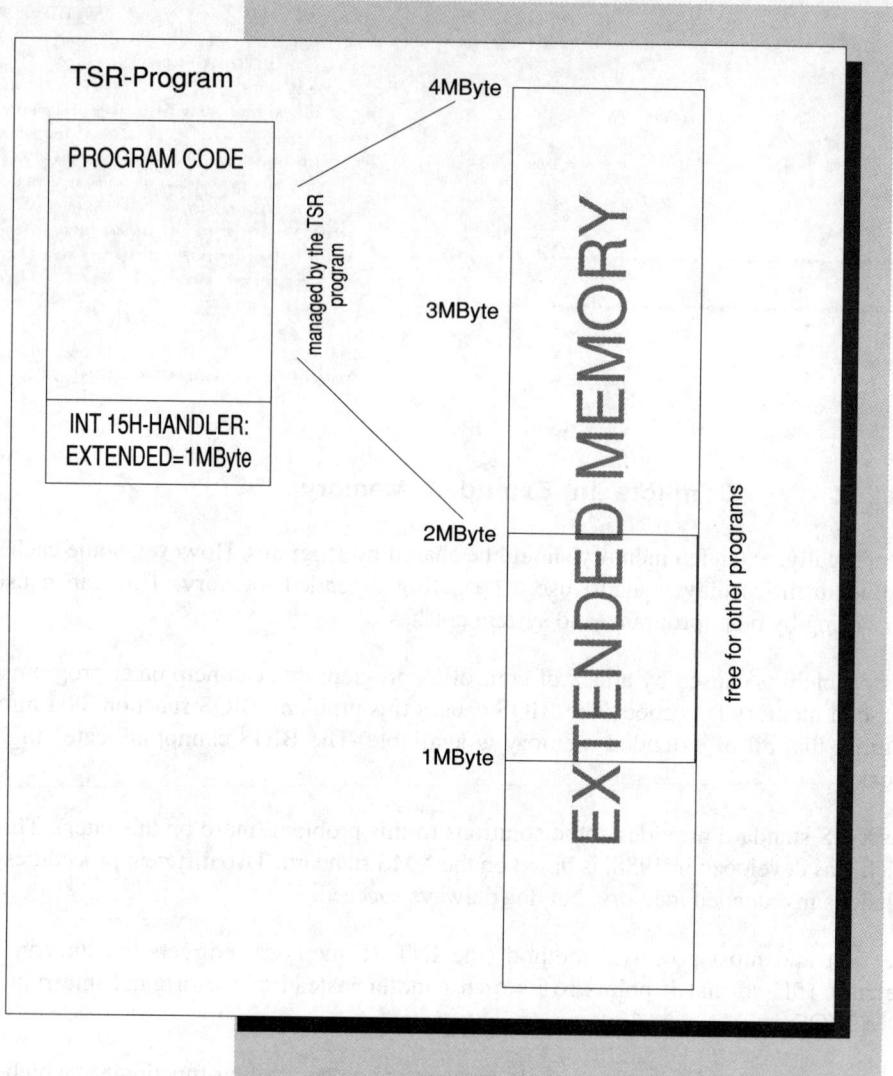

Extended memory access by redirecting interrupt 15H

The second method of extended memory control is frequently used by developers and tends to create new problems in programming.

This VDISK method was first used in the VDISK device driver. VDISK is a RAM disk that can use extended memory for file storage. You'll find VDISK available on MS/PC-DOS starting with Version 3.0. VDISK stores its data starting at the 1 megabyte border, instead of isolating itself from other programs.

VDISK won't overwrite memory reserved using the INT 15 method. However, programs called after VDISK will overwrite VDISK unless the subsequent programs can use the area at the end of extended memory. This is only possible through extensive testing, which are based on a knowledge of memory design under DOS.

The VDISK file header has a structure that's peculiar to all mass memory devices operating under DOS. This header contains status information and a small data structure, which can be designated as a BIOS Parameter Block (see Chapter 6 for more information about BPBs). This block lets you calculate the size of a storage medium and the length of the RAM disk currently in extended memory.

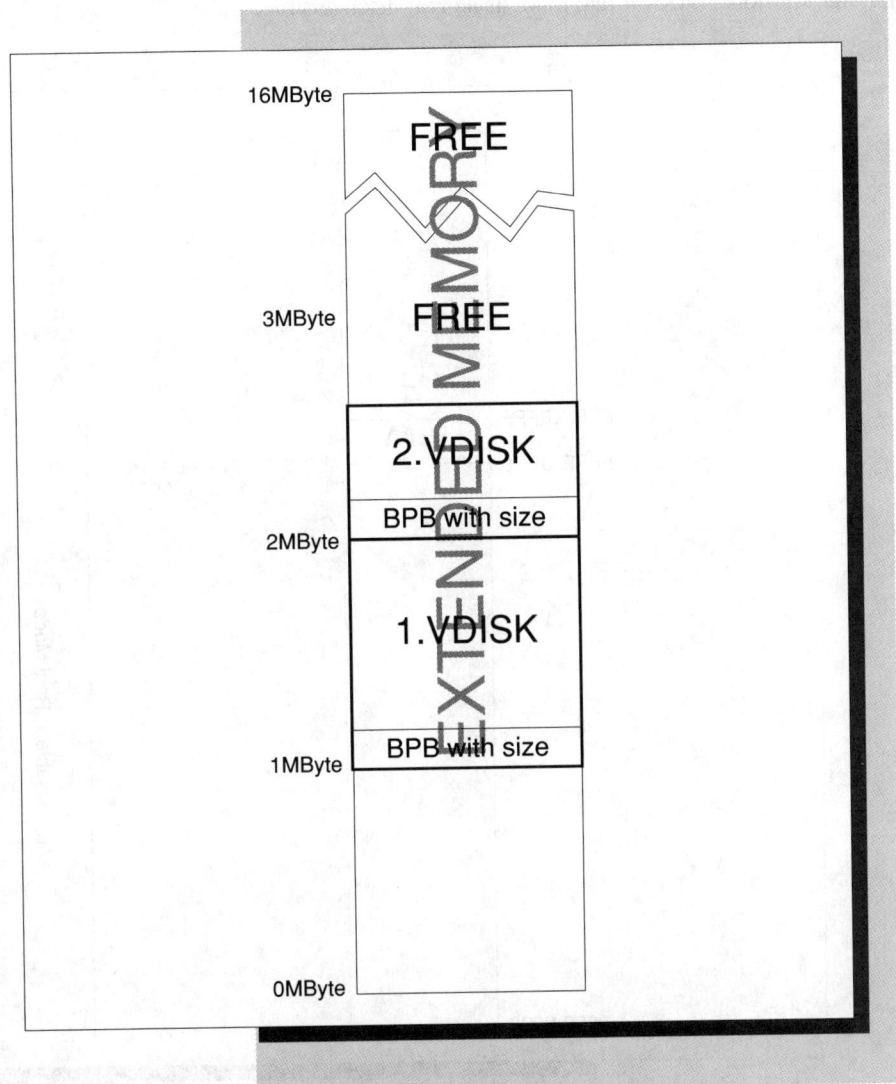

Extended memory structure with RAM disks of type VDISK

Multiple RAM disks complicate the search for available extended memory. We recommend that you always use an XMS driver for extended memory access, because this search doesn't work for every available type of RAM disk (more on this later).

12.2.3   Direct HMA Access from Real Mode

The High Memory Area (HMA) is the first 64K of extended memory. The HMA is the only portion of extended memory that can be accessed (indirectly) from real mode without switching to protected mode. Although various sources credit either Microsoft or Intel with developing the HMA, the additional 64K for real mode is a great discovery.

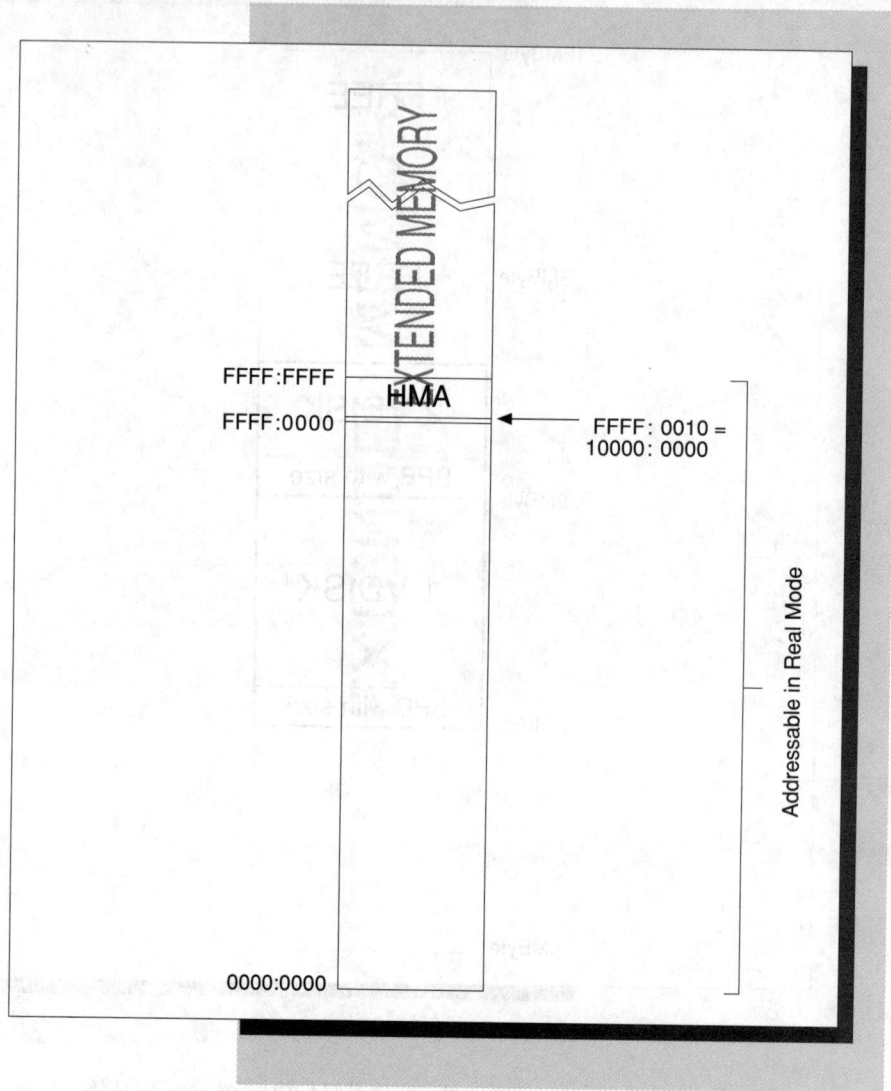

Crossing the 1 megabyte barrier in real mode thru segment FFFFH

How can we access memory locations that actually lie outside the address space of the microprocessor?

The answer lies in the way 80x86 processors form physical addresses, in real mode, from a segment address and offset address. Remember that the segment address is multiplied by 16, then the segment and offset addresses are added. If the last segment in the address space of the PC (segment FFFFH) is the segment address, this places offset address 000FH in the physical addresses beyond the 1 megabyte limit. This places you in extended memory in real mode, and you can still access the conventional RAM below the limit.

Since the HMA starts with offset 00010H instead of offset 0000H, you'll find the HMA is smaller than 64K (65,520 bytes). This memory is more than enough to store data and short TSR programs.

Steps required for HMA access

A program that accesses the HMA should first ensure that HMA access is possible. If an 80x86 processor is located, we can continue because this indicates that the A20 address line and extended memory exist.

Next, calling BIOS function 88H of interrupt 15H determines how much extended memory exists. HMA access is possible only if a minimum of 64K is available in extended memory.

Address line must be disabled from interfacing with the keyboard controller, and BIOS must enable address line A20 before HMA access can occur. This address line is usually disabled because some programs rely on address overflow at the 1 megabyte limit. This wraparound at address FFFF:0010 usually returns you to the start of conventional memory (address 0000:0000).

Address overflow with address line A20 disabled

Enabling address line A20 affects the keyboard controller as well as the switch from protected mode. On a system reset, the A20 switch occurs through the keyboard controller's output port. Bit 1 of this port must be set to 1 to make the A20 address line transparent, and set to 0 if a memory overflow occurs at the 1 megabyte limit. This bit cannot be easily accessed; the keyboard must receive the instruction to disable access to the output port. Also, the controller requires specific parameters in communication. Refer to Chapter 6 for detailed information on how this communication works.

A normal PC with an ISA (Industry Standard Architecture) bus uses the keyboard output port for controlling the status of address line A20. With PS/2 systems and computers upgraded to an 80386 using the Intel InBoard, this line must released using other methods.

A test should confirm the condition of the A20 address line. This is important because if this line isn't free, access to HMA cannot occur. With a small trick this can be determined, without a doubt, because a blocked line indicates an identical memory area through the address overflow at the 1 megabyte limit, such as the memory areas starting at FFFF:0010 and 0000:0000. By comparing the first bytes (e.g., the first 256) in this area, equality can be determined between the two, which proves that A20 is disabled.

Three routines are needed in order to work with the HMA:

- A routine to determine the existence of at least 64K of extended memory.
- A routine to switch address line A20.
- A routine to test address line A20 through memory comparison.

Demonstration programs

The demonstration programs listed below contain all three routines for HMA access. These programs, written in Pascal and C, provide a foundation on which you can build other HMA programs. Since all future HMA access should occur through the XMS driver (see Section 12.2.4), these demonstration programs don't test for VDISK compatible RAM disks. If this test doesn't exist, HMA access could overwrite the contents of the RAM disk. So, before starting one of these programs, ensure that a RAM disk doesn't exist in external memory. If a VDISK device or cache program exists, remove them, then run the demonstration program.

Both programs are based on the three routines mentioned above. We call these routines HMAAvail, Gate20, and IsA20On. These programs couldn't be developed in high level languages. So, we wrote them in assembly language and prepared them as INLINE commands (for the Pascal implementation) and as an assembly language module named HMACA.ASM (for the C implementation).

Both programs try to access HMA. If HMA cannot be accessed, the programs display an error message. A pointer of type FAR points to the beginning of the HMA. The Pascal implementation automatically creates FAR pointers, while the C implementation declares a FAR pointer.

If this pointer contains the address FFFF:0010, the HMA is accessible. Both programs perform a simple memory test, in which they fill the HMA with a constant value, then read this memory. Errors (if any) are then documented by the programs. It's unlikely errors will appear because any RAM failure would've been detected by the BIOS during bootup.

After this test, the program disables the A20 address line and suppresses HMA access. This must occur because other programs need the 1 megabyte limit for determining memory overflow.

Remember the following rules for HMA access. First, avoid passing pointers that indicate DOS and compiler runtime library routines that refer to the HMA themselves. If you do this, these routines may normalize the pointer.

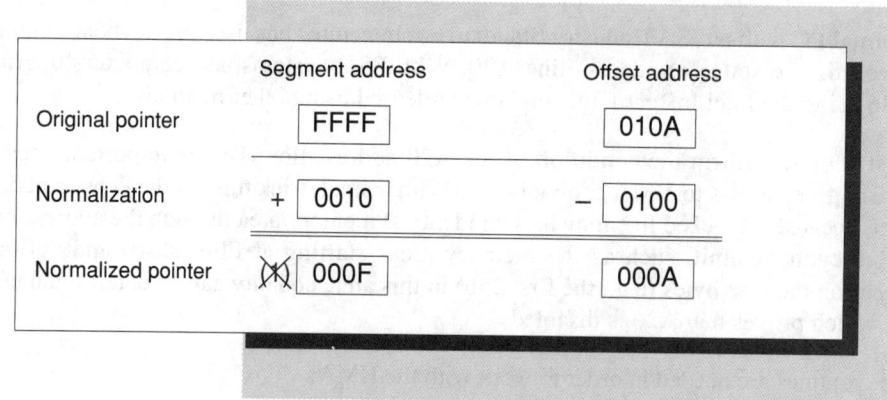

	Segment address	Offset address
Original pointer	FFFF	010A
Normalization	+ 0010	− 0100
Normalized pointer	⊠ 000F	000A

Normalization of HMA pointers

Normalization changes the segment of a pointer so that the offset becomes less than 16, but the original memory location is still accessed as before. This results in an overflow of the segment address, which is then set to 0000H. You should avoid the normalization process.

Also, diskette and hard disk operations shouldn't directly access HMA. The software often may cause problems in the DMA controller. This occurs because the DMA controller doesn't know how to properly handle addresses above the 1 megabyte limit.

If you follow these rules, you shouldn't have any problems with direct HMA access. Remember that these demonstration programs are simple examples. Section 12.2.4 describes the XMS driver and how HMA is used in commercial programs.

Pascal listing: HMAP.PAS

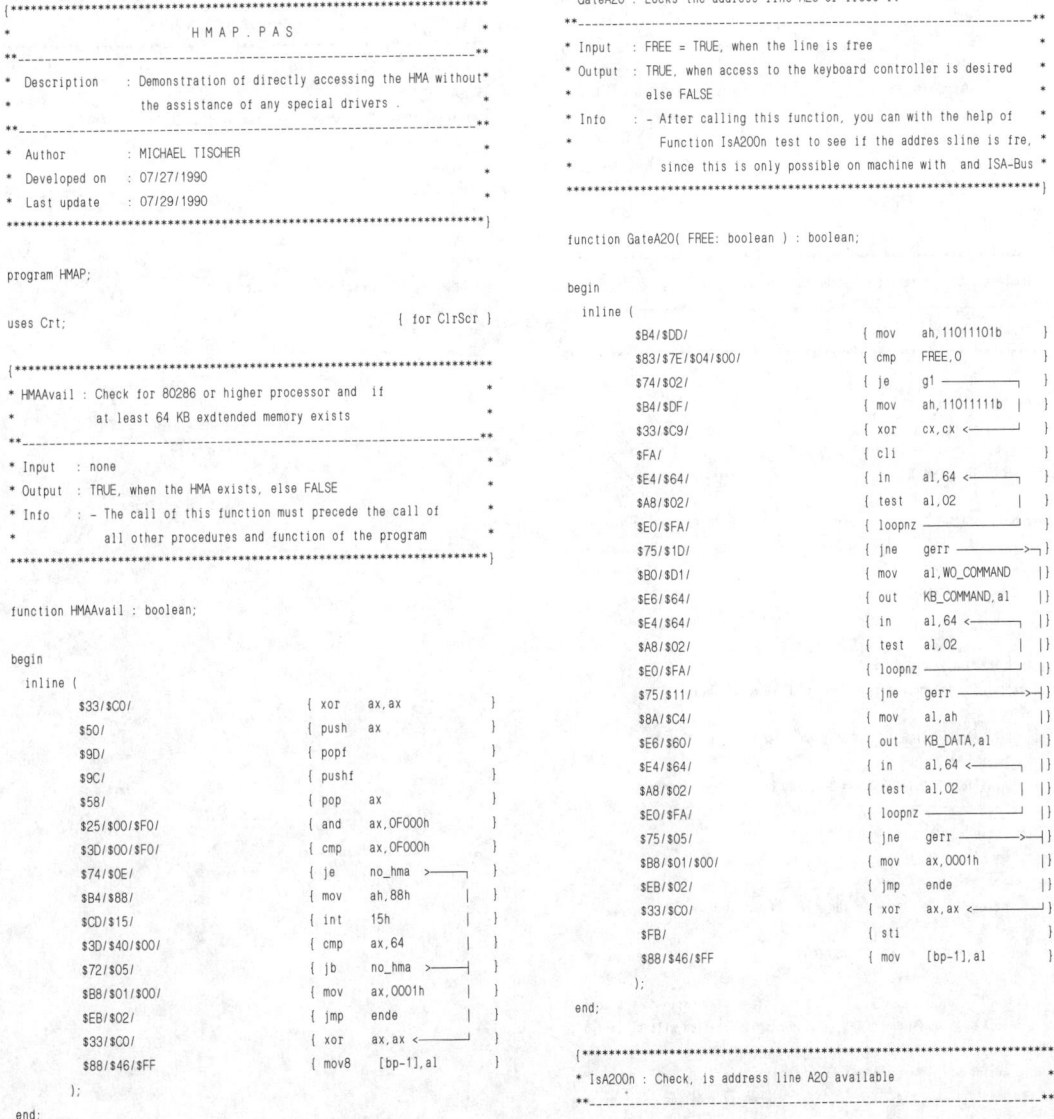

```
{***************************************************************
*                                                             *
*                    H M A P . P A S                          *
**-----------------------------------------------------------**
*                                                             *
*  Description    : Demonstration of directly accessing the HMA without*
*                   the assistance of any special drivers .   *
**-----------------------------------------------------------**
*                                                             *
*  Author         : MICHAEL TISCHER                           *
*  Developed on   : 07/27/1990                                *
*  Last update    : 07/29/1990                                *
***************************************************************}

program HMAP;

uses Crt;                                { for ClrScr }

{***************************************************************
*  HMAAvail : Check for 80286 or higher processor and  if     *
*             at least 64 KB exdtended memory exists          *
**-----------------------------------------------------------**
*  Input   : none                                             *
*  Output  : TRUE, when the HMA exists, else FALSE            *
*  Info    : - The call of this function must precede the call of *
*              all other procedures and function of the program *
***************************************************************}

function HMAAvail : boolean;

begin
  inline (
         $33/$C0/              { xor    ax,ax          }
         $50/                  { push   ax             }
         $9D/                  { popf                  }
         $9C/                  { pushf                 }
         $58/                  { pop    ax             }
         $25/$00/$F0/          { and    ax,0F000h      }
         $3D/$00/$F0/          { cmp    ax,0F000h      }
         $74/$0E/              { je     no_hma  >----- }
         $B4/$88/              { mov    ah,88h      |  }
         $CD/$15/              { int    15h         |  }
         $3D/$40/$00/          { cmp    ax,64       |  }
         $72/$05/              { jb     no_hma >--- |  }
         $B8/$01/$00/          { mov    ax,0001h  | |  }
         $EB/$02/              { jmp    ende      | |  }
         $33/$C0/              { xor    ax,ax <---- |  }
         $88/$46/$FF           { mov8   [bp-1],al      }
         );
end;
```

```
{***************************************************************
*  GateA20 : Locks the address line A20 or frees it           *
**-----------------------------------------------------------**
*  Input   : FREE = TRUE, when the line is free               *
*  Output  : TRUE, when access to the keyboard controller is desired *
*            else FALSE                                       *
*  Info    : - After calling this function, you can with the help of *
*              Function IsA200n test to see if the addres sline is fre, *
*              since this is only possible on machine with  and ISA-Bus *
***************************************************************}

function GateA20( FREE: boolean ) : boolean;

begin
  inline (
         $B4/$DD/              { mov    ah,11011101b  }
         $83/$7E/$04/$00/      { cmp    FREE,0         }
         $74/$02/              { je     g1 ---------   }
         $B4/$DF/              { mov    ah,11011111b | }
         $33/$C9/              { xor    cx,cx <------  }
         $FA/                  { cli                   }
         $E4/$64/              { in     al,64 <------  }
         $A8/$02/              { test   al,02       |  }
         $E0/$FA/              { loopnz --------------  }
         $75/$1D/              { jne    gerr ------->-| }
         $B0/$D1/              { mov    al,WO_COMMAND |}
         $E6/$64/              { out    KB_COMMAND,al |}
         $E4/$64/              { in     al,64 <------ |}
         $A8/$02/              { test   al,02       | |}
         $E0/$FA/              { loopnz ------------  |}
         $75/$11/              { jne    gerr ------->-|}
         $8A/$C4/              { mov    al,ah         |}
         $E6/$60/              { out    KB_DATA,al    |}
         $E4/$64/              { in     al,64 <------ |}
         $A8/$02/              { test   al,02       | |}
         $E0/$FA/              { loopnz ------------  |}
         $75/$05/              { jne    gerr ------->-|}
         $B8/$01/$00/          { mov    ax,0001h      |}
         $EB/$02/              { jmp    ende          |}
         $33/$C0/              { xor    ax,ax <------- |}
         $FB/                  { sti                   }
         $88/$46/$FF           { mov    [bp-1],al      }
         );
end;
```

```
{***************************************************************
*  IsA200n : Check, is address line A20 available             *
**-----------------------------------------------------------**
```

```
* Input   : none                                                      *
* Output  : TRUE, when the line is free, else FALSE                    *
**********************************************************************}

function IsA200n : boolean;

begin
  inline (
        $1E/                         { push    ds        }
        $06/                         { push    es        }
        $33/$F6/                     { xor     si,si     }
        $8E/$DE/                     { mov     ds,si     }
        $BF/$10/$00/                 { mov     di,0010   }
        $B8/$FF/$FF/                 { mov     ax,FFFF   }
        $8E/$C0/                     { mov     es,ax     }
        $B9/$40/$00/                 { mov     cx,64     }
        $FC/                         { cld               }
        $F3/$A7/                     { repe    cmpsw     }
        $07/                         { pop     es        }
        $1F/                         { pop     ds        }
        $E3/$05/                     { jcxz    a20off ─┐ }
        $B8/$01/$00/                 { mov     ax,0001h │}
        $EB/$02/                     { jmp     ende     │}
        $33/$C0/                     { xor     ax,ax <──┘}
        $88/$46/$FF                  { mov     [bp-1],al }
        );
end;


{*********************************************************************
* HMATest : Demonstration of accessing the HMA.                      *
**------------------------------------------------------------------**
* Input   : none                                                     *
*********************************************************************}

procedure HMATest;

type HMAR    = array [1..65520] of BYTE;        { the HMA-Array }
     HMARPTR = ^HMAR;                    { Pointer to the HMA-Array }

var hmap : HMARPTR;                      { Pointer of the HMA }
    i,                                   { loop counter }
    err  : word;                { Number of error of HMA access }
    dummy : boolean;

begin
  if ( IsA200n ) then
   writeln( 'The address line A20 is already switched on!' )
  else
    if ( GateA20( TRUE ) = FALSE ) or ( IsA200n = FALSE ) then
      begin
        writeln( 'Note! Address line A20 can not be switched' +
            'on.' );
        exit;
      end
    else
      writeln( 'The access to the H HMA is switched on.' );

  hmap := HMARPTR(Ptr( $FFFF, $0010 ));          { Pointer to HMA }

  err := 0;                     { we start with no n errors }
  for i := 1 to 65520 do        { each memory location will be tested }
    begin
      write( #13, 'Memory location: ', i );
      hmap^[i] := i mod 256;             { Memory location description }
```

```
      if ( hmap^[i] <> i mod 256 ) then      { and return selection }
        begin                                { Error! }
          writeln( ' ERROR!' );
          inc( err );
        end;
    end;

  writeln( #13 );
  if ( err = 0 ) then                   { Output the test results }
    writeln( 'HMA ok, no defective memory locations.' )
  else
    writeln( 'NOTE! ', err, ' Defective memory location in ' +
             'the HMA found! ' );

  dummy := GateA20( FALSE );                  { Address line release }
end;

{*********************************************************************
*                    M A I N   P R O G R A M                         *
*********************************************************************}

begin
  writeln( 'HMAP  -  HMA-Demo program by MICHAEL TISCHER'#10 );
  if HMAAvail then
    begin
      HMATest;                                  { HMA test }
      writeln;
    end
  else
    writeln( 'No access to HMA possible.' );
end.
```

C listing: HMAC.C

```
/*********************************************************************
*                          H M A C . C                             *
**-----------------------------------------------------------------**
* Description   : Demonstration of direct access to the HMA without *
*                 the assistance of any special drivers.            *
**-----------------------------------------------------------------**
* Author        : MICHAEL TISCHER                                   *
* Developed on   : 07/27/1990                                       *
* Last update on : 07/29/1990                                       *
**-----------------------------------------------------------------**
* (MICROSOFT C)                                                     *
* Creation      : CL /AS /Zp hmac.c hmaca                           *
* Call          : hmac                                              *
*                                                                   *
* (BORLAND TURBO C)                                                 *
* Creation      : create a project file with the following contents *
*                 hmac.c                                            *
*                 hmaca.obj                                         *
*********************************************************************/

/*-- Include files ------------------------------------------------*/

#include <dos.h>                        /* for interrupt call */

#ifdef __TURBOC__
  #include <alloc.h>
#else
  #include <malloc.h>
#endif

/*-- Constants ----------------------------------------------------*/

#define TRUE  ( 0 == 0 )
#define FALSE ( 0 == 1 )

/*-- Macros -------------------------------------------------------*/

#ifndef MK_FP
  #define MK_FP(seg,ofs) \
    ((void far *) (((unsigned long)(seg) << 16) | (unsigned)(ofs)))
#endif

#define Hi(x) (*((BYTE *) &x+1))        /* Hi-Byte one ints */
#define Lo(x) (*((BYTE *) &x))          /* Lo-Byte one ints */

/*-- Type declarations --------------------------------------------*/

typedef unsigned char BYTE;
typedef BYTE BOOL;
typedef unsigned WORD;

/*-- extern declarations ------------------------------------------*/

extern BOOL HMAAvail( void ); /* HMA available? */
extern BOOL GateA20( BOOL free ); /* A20 locked/free */
extern BOOL IsA20on( void ); /* A20 available? */

/*********************************************************************
* HMATest : Demonstration of accessing the HMA                     *
**-----------------------------------------------------------------**
* Input   : none                                                   *
```

```
*********************************************************************/

void HMATest( void )

{
BYTE far * hmap;                        /* Pointer to the HMA */
WORD i,                                 /* loop counter */
     err;                      /* Number of the errr for HMA access */

if ( IsA20on() )
 printf( "The address line A20 is  already switched on!\n" );
else
 if ( GateA20( TRUE ) == FALSE  || IsA20on() == FALSE )
  {
   printf( "Note! The address line A20 can not be " \
        "be made available." );
   return;
  }
 else
   printf( "The access to the HMA is switched on.\n" );

hmap = MK_FP( 0xFFFF, 0x0010 );         /* Pointer to HMA */
err = 0;                                /* start will no errors */
for ( i = 1; i < 65520; ++i, ++hmap )
 {                                      /* test the memory locations */
  printf( "\rMemory location: %u", i );
  *hmap = i % 256;                /* memory location description */
  if ( *hmap != i % 256 )          /* and return selection */
   {                                    /* ERROR! */
    printf( " ERROR!\n" );
    ++err;
   }
 }

printf( "\n" );
if ( err == 0 )                    /* Output test results */
 printf( "HMA ok, no defective memory locations.\n" );
else
 printf( "ATTENTION: %d defective memory locations in the HMA " \
      "discovered!\n", err );
GateA20( FALSE ); /* Address line switched off */
}

/*********************************************************************
*                      M A I N   P R O G R A M                     *
*********************************************************************/

void main( void )
{
 int i; /* loop counter */

 for ( i = 1; i < 25; ++i )                    /* clear screen */
  printf ( "\n" );

 printf("HMAC  -  HMA Demo program by MICHAEL TISCHER\n\n" );
 if ( HMAAvail() )
  {
   HMATest();                                   /* HMA test */
   printf( "\n" );
  }
 else
  printf( "No access to HMA possible.\n" );
}
```

Assembler listing: HMACA.ASM

```
;**************************************************************;
;*                    H M A C A . A S M                     *;
;*----------------------------------------------------------*;
;*  Task       : Provides extended memory routines for HMAC.C,*;
;*               as well as control for address line A20.    *;
;*----------------------------------------------------------*;
;*  Author     : Michael Tischer                            *;
;*  Developed on : 07/28/90                                 *;
;*  Last update  : 03/04/92                                 *;
;*----------------------------------------------------------*;
;*  Assembly   : MASM HAMCA;   or   TASM HMACA;             *;
;*               Link to HMAC.C                             *;
;**************************************************************;


;== Constants ================================================

KB_COMMAND equ 64h          ;Keyboard command port
KB_STATUS  equ 64h          ;is also status port
KB_DATA    equ 60h          ;Keyboard data port
IB_FREE    equ 2            ;Mask for testing free input buffer
WO_COMMAND equ 0D1h         ;Writes to output port

GATE_ON    equ 11011111b    ;A20 line free
GATE_OFF   equ 11011101b    ;A20 line busy

;== Segment declarations for C program ========================

IGROUP group _text              ;Program segment
DGROUP group const,_bss,_data   ;Data segment
       assume CS:IGROUP, DS:DGROUP, ES:DGROUP, SS:DGROUP


CONST  segment word public 'CONST';Readable constants
CONST  ends

_BSS   segment word public 'BSS'  ;Un-initialized static variables
_BSS   ends

_DATA  segment word public 'DATA' ;Initialized static and global vars.

_DATA  ends

;== Program =================================================

_TEXT  segment byte public 'CODE' ;Program

public    _HMAAvail
public    _GateA20
public    _IsA200n

;-----------------------------------------------------------
;-- HMAAvail : Determines whether an HMA is available
;-- Call from C: BOOL HMAAvail( void )
;-- Return val. : TRUE if HMA is available, otherwise FALSE

_HMAAvail  proc near

        ;-- Test for AT or 386 -----------------------------

        xor   ax,ax         ;Check for the existence of
        push  ax            ;8088 or 8086 processor
        popf
```

```
        pushf
        pop   ax
        and   ax,0F000h
        cmp   ax,0F000h
        je    nonhma        ;Normal PC ---> nonhma

        ;-- AT or 386, but does it have extended memory? -----------

        mov   ah,88h        ;Read extended memeory size using
        int   15h           ;BIOS
        cmp   ax,64         ;> 64K of extended memory?
        jb    nonhma        ;No --> No HMA

        mov   ax,0FFFFh     ;Yes --> HMA ready
        ret                 ;Return TRUE

nonhma: xor   ax,ax         ;Return 0 FALSE
        ret                 ;Return to caller

_HMAAvail endp

;-----------------------------------------------------------
;-- GateA20 : Enables or disables A20 line
;-- Call from C: BOOL GateA20( BOOL free )
;-- Return val. : TRUE if operation successful, otherwise FALSE

_GateA20  proc near

        ;-- Structure for easy access to parameters ---------------

sframe    struc                 ;Structure for stack access
bp0       dw ?                  ;Gets BP
ret_adr   dw ?                  ;Return address to caller
frei      dw ?                  ;Enable or disable line
sframe    ends                  ;End structure

frame     equ [ bp - bp0 ]      ;Addresses structure elements

        ;-- Macro for reading KB controller status -----------------

kbc_ready macro                 ;Keyboard controller ready?
          local  notready

notready: in    al,KB_STATUS   ;Read status port
          test  al,IB_FREE     ;Input buffer free?
          loopne notready       ;No, and CX still not null -->

          endm

        ;-- Procedure code begins here -----------------------------

        push  bp            ;Push BP onto stack
        mov   bp,sp         ;Move SP to BP

        mov   ah,11011101b  ;Free line
        cmp   frame.frei,0  ;Line freed?
        je    g1            ;Yes --> Code is O.K.

        mov   ah,11011111b  ;No --> Load Line free code

g1:     xor   cx,cx         ;Time out counter
        cli                 ;Disable interrupts
        kbc_ready           ;Wait for keyboard controller
        jne   gerr          ;Time out? Yes --> GERR
```

```
          mov   al,WO_COMMAND   ;Send code for output port access        extptr   dd 0FFFF0010h       ;Pointer to extended memory
          out   KB_COMMAND,al   ; to command port
                                                                  _IsA200n  proc near
          kbc_ready             ;Wait for keyboard controller
          jne   gerr            ;Time out? Yes --> GERR                   push  ds
                                                                         push  es
          mov   al,ah           ;Send command to
          out   KB_DATA,al      ;data port                               lds   si,cs:ramptr   ;Line shows identical memory locations
                                                                         les   di,cs:extptr   ;on both lines
          kbc_ready             ;Wait for keyboard controller
          sti                   ;Enable interrupts                       mov   cx,64          ;Compare 128 bytes
          jne   gerr            ;Time out? Yes --> GERR                   cld                  ;Increment on string inst.
                                                                         repe  cmpsw          ;Compare ranges
          mov   ax,0FFFFh       ;No time out, O.K.
          pop   bp              ;Pop BP from stack                       pop   es             ;Pop registers
          ret                                                            pop   ds
                                                                         jcxz  a20off         ;CX = 0 --> Ranges identical
gerr:     xor   ax,ax           ;No toggle possible
          pop   bp              ;Pop BP from stack                       mov   ax,0FFFFh      ;Range unequal --> A20 active
          ret                                                            ret

_GateA20  endp                                                   a20off:  xor   ax,ax         ;Range equal --> A20 disabled
                                                                         ret

;-------------------------------------------------------------   _IsA200n  endp
;-- IsA200n : Determines whether A20 is free
;-- Call from C: BOOL IsA20( void )                              ;-------------------------------------------------------------
;-- Return val. : TRUE if line is free, otherwise FALSE
                                                                 _text    ends               ;End code segment
ramptr    dd 000000000h         ;Pointer to conventional RAM            end                  ;End program
```

12.2.4   The XMS Standard

The EMS standard contains a standard software interface, but extended memory existed for years without a software standard. This prompted many software manufacturers to develop their own versions. In 1988, Microsoft, Intel, Lotus, and AST Research developed the Extended Memory Specification (XMS).

The XMS standard defines a software interface that allows multiple programs to access extended memory and other memory areas simultaneously. The following types of memory accesses are supported:

- The HMA, which includes the first 64K of extended memory and extends from 1024K to 1088K.
- Four Extended Memory Blocks (EMB), which appear in extended memory starting at 1088K (thus avoiding conflict with the HMA).
- Upper Memory Blocks (UMB), which lie in conventional RAM between 640K and 1024K.

HIMEM.SYS from Microsoft Corporation is probably the most widely known XMS driver. This driver has been included with recent versions of MS-DOS and Windows. The system calls HIMEM.SYS during bootup, through the CONFIG.SYS file.

In addition to MS-DOS and Windows, you can find XMS drivers in some memory management programs designed for 80386 and 80486 computers. The XMS interface usually supports the LIM standard as well as extended memory.

Some examples of XMS systems are Qualitas' 386-To-The-Max, Quarterdeck's QEMM-386, and Microsoft's EMM386.EXE, which is packaged with MS-DOS 5.0. These utilities can designate extended memory as Upper Memory Blocks in the range between 640K and 1024K (provided this range isn't allocated to video RAM, hardware enhancements, or ROM BIOS). The UMBs offer the developer RAM that can be addressed as if the UMBs are conventional RAM.

Few 80286 based systems without this driver can access Upper Memory Blocks, and not all XMS drivers will support 80286 systems. Exceptions to this rule use the NEAT chips from Chips & Technologies. A SETUP program lets the user configure memory, including UMBs.

Before you can access XMS functions, you must determine whether an XMS driver is available. Interrupt 2FH is accessed by the XMS driver, similar to SHARE, APPEND, and PRINT in DOS. Call interrupt 2FH with function code 4300H in the AX register. If an XMS driver exists in the system, this function returns the value 80H to the AL register. Any other value indicates that an XMS driver isn't available and that XMS functions cannot be accessed.

XMS functions are called by a FAR CALL instruction, instead of an actual interrupt. Consequently, the XMS handler's address is needed for the call. This XMS handler is sometimes called the Extended Memory Manager (XMM). Interrupt 2FH releases this address only if an XMS driver is actually installed, and if the first call of this interrupt returned the value 80H in the AL register.

Call interrupt 2FH and place the value 4310H in the AX register. The function returns the XMM's segment register to the ES register, and the XMM's offset register to the BX register. All XMS routines are accessible through this address.

Function	Task
00H	Determine XMS version number
01H	Allocate High Memory Area (HMA)
02H	Free High Memory Area (HMA)
03H	Globally enable address line A20
04H	Globally disable address line A20
05H	Locally enable address line A20
06H	Locally disable address line A20
07H	Query status of address line A20
08H	Query free extended memory
09H	Allocate Extended Memory Block (EMB)
0AH	Free allocated Extended Memory Block (EMB)
0BH	Move Extended Memory Block (EMB)
0CH	Lock Extended Memory Block (EMB)
0DH	Unlock Extended Memory Block (EMB)
0EH	Get EMB handle information
0FH	Resize Extended Memory Block (EMB)
10H	Allocate Upper Memory Block (UMB)
11H	Free allocated Upper Memory Block (UMB)

As the previous table shows, 18 different XMS functions currently exist, of which the last three aren't available to all XMS drivers.

Pass the XMS function number in the AH register to call the function. Other information may be placed in the other processor registers, but this differs among functions.

Almost all functions return a status code in the AX register. This status code provides information about the success of the operation. The value 0001H indicates successful execution, while 0000H indicates an error. If an error occurs, the BL register contains the error code, which provides details about the error. See the Appendices of this book for error codes and their meanings.

Next you should check the version number of the XMS driver by using function 00H. This function places the XMS version number in the AX register and the internal revision number in the BX register. The internal revision number indicates minor changes among drivers and is less important than the version number. Both items are returned as BCD numbers; the higher level byte accepts the version number preceding the decimal point and the lower byte accepts the internal revision number (the numbers following the decimal point). For example, 0200H represents Version number 2.0. XMS Version 2.0 is the lowest version you should own. If you have a Version 1 XMS, you should replace it.

Drivers with version numbers of 2.0 are most common, although some Version 3.0 XMS systems exist. We don't know the differences between the two versions, except that Version 3.0 was intended for 80386 memory management.

If you want to use the extended memory in your program as EMBs, use function 08H to determine the size of extended memory. This function returns the total amount of free extended memory (in kilobytes) in the DX register, and the size of the largest free EMB (in kilobytes) in the AX register. Use these values with caution; the HMA (64K in length) is included in calculating both values, but EMB allocation begins after the first HMA.

For example, suppose that you have a 4 megabyte system of which 3 of the 4 megabytes are available as extended memory and no memory has been assigned yet. Calling function 08H returns the number 3072 to both the AX register and the DX register for 3 megabytes. Then the XMM would be able to provide 3 megabytes of extended memory if you later called function 09H, as long as the memory is allocated after the HMA. The last 64K of this area exceed the end of extended memory, so that 64K isn't physically available. Always subtract 64K from the value returned by function 08H. This deduction lets the size of the HMA govern the calculation.

Once you've determined the size of the largest available EMB, function 09H lets you request a corresponding amount of extended memory. Place the function number (09H) in the AH register, and the size of the desired block (in kilobytes) in the DX register. The DX register returns the handle needed for addition access to this EMB, unless an error occurred during memory allocation.

Check the AX register for error codes. A memory block allocation may fail, even if enough extended memory is available. The handles returned in the DX register may cause this failure. Since the XMM has only a limited number of these handles available, you may find that free extended memory exists, but all handles have already been assigned to many small EMBs. To prevent this condition, request large EMBs and try to subdivide them internally into various memory areas that are used for different purposes.

We've mentioned the XMM handles several times. You may be wondering why the XMM uses handles, instead of immediately returning the address of the allocated area. The XMM's memory management system was designed to avoid fragmentation of extended memory. This means that the XMM will move the various EMBs back and forth in memory, creating a large memory range from smaller EMBs. This large EMB can then be passed to a program that calls function 09H. Another large area can be created from several small and released EMBs. This area can then be passed, as a whole, to a caller of function 09H. The addresses of the already allocated EMBs also change, so the XMM assigns logical handles instead of a physical address.

This handle must be stored safely, since it's required for all future access to an EMB. If the EMB is released, enlarged, or at least partially copied into conventional memory, this handle is required by the XMM to identify an EMB.

Releasing EMBs

It's very easy to release an EMB in order to make it accessible to other programs. This release doesn't occur automatically at the end of a program because TSR programs can also use EMBs for their own purposes. Function 0AH releases allocated EMBs before terminating a program. If you don't pass this function, the program will continue to access the EMBs until you reset the computer. Place the function number (0AH) in the AH register and the EMB handle's number in the DX register.

Copying EMBs

Since data can be stored in extended memory but not manipulated, complete or partial EMBs must frequently be copied from extended memory into conventional memory, or from conventional memory to extended memory. Function 0BH performs this task. Place the function number (0BH) to the AH register, and a pointer to the extended move structure to the DS:SI register pair. This structure contains all the information needed about the source and target areas, as well as the number of bytes to be copied.

Conveying the handle and offset address information of the two areas must be handled differently, depending on whether the area is in extended memory or conventional memory. If you want to address an EMB, you must then indicate the handle that was returned by function 09H when allocating the EMB. The offset address represents the offset relative to the beginning of the block. However, if you want to address an area in conventional memory, the value 0 must be passed as the handle, and the segment and offset addresses of the beginning of the block must be passed as the offset. Remember that the block's address must be passed in the order OFFSET:SEGMENT.

The execution speed of this copy process is slow, especially on 80286 based machines. There's no way to avoid the long and involved switching back from protected mode.

The XMS standard has four additional EMB functions that are rarely used. You'll find information about these functions in the Appendices of this book.

HMA access

XMM also provides access to the HMA. This minimizes memory conflicts between programs and offers hardware independent control of the A20 address line. This is important because not all PC systems control this line through a bit in the keyboard controller's output port, as we described in the previous section.

Unlike extended memory, HMA access cannot be parceled out to several programs because of its size. If a program requests access rights to the HMA using function 01H, it's an all-or-nothing situation. The program either receives complete access to the HMA, or no access at all. The latter occurs mainly when the HMA was already assigned, or when the size of the required HMA memory is less than the /HMAMIN parameter (an option available when the driver is initially called). This should prevent a TSR program (which may be only a few kilobytes in length) from receiving exclusive access rights to the HMA, while another program is denied access.

For normal purposes, pass FFFFH to the DX register as the amount of HMA memory needed when calling function 02H. For TSR programs, pass the exact number of bytes needed for the TSR to the DX register.

The contents of the AX register indicate whether the access rights were granted. The value 0001H indicates the release of the HMA, while the value 0000H indicates unsuccessful execution.

The A20 address line must be switched before direct access to HMA can occur. The XMM provides a total of four different functions for enabling and disabling this line. Pass the function number to the AH register for calling.

The four functions enable and disable the A20 address line both locally and globally. This distinction is important; global functions always act on the A20 address line, but the local functions rely on an internal counter. This ensures that A20 access occurs only when the calls are balanced (enable/disable). After two consecutive calls of the local enable function (function 05H), the line switches off only if two local disable calls (function 06H) follow.

Displaying and hiding the mouse cursor involves a similar process (see Chapter 9 for more information). Except on rare occasions, you'll use the global functions in HMA access.

Before ending program execution, remember to disable the A20 address using function 04H, and to release the HMA proper using function 04H. If you don't perform these two functions, programs called later will either crash (because a segment overflow was expected at the 1 megabyte limit) or will be denied access to the HMA.

Upper Memory Blocks

Upper Memory Blocks (UMBs) are within the processor's address space, which makes them directly accessible to a program. Unfortunately, RAM seldom exists in the range from 640K to 1 megabyte, unless you have an 80386 computer, in which programs are stored in upper RAM through software.

If the system for which you're developing software has UMBs available, or you just want to keep this memory option open, the XMS standard supports two functions for access to upper memory. MS-DOS Version 5.0 and up support UMB access, although this support merely acts as moderator between a program and the XMS driver (see Chapter 23 for more information).

Unlike the HMA, Upper Memory Blocks provide true memory management, which permits several programs to reside in upper memory. Segment addresses of the allocated blocks are used instead of handles. These segment addresses act as references for identifying a UMB for the XMM.

Allocating UMBs

Function 10H allocates a UMB when possible. Place the function number (10H) in the AH register, and the size of the block you want allocated (in paragraphs [= 16 bytes]) in the DX register. If enough memory isn't available, the DX register returns the size (in paragraphs) of the largest available UMB.

Releasing UMBs

The XMM lets you release a UMB as well as allocate one. Function 11H performs the release. Pass the function number (11H) to the AH register and the segment address of the addressed UMB to the DX register.

Demonstration programs

The following programs present some aspects of the XMS standard. Since these programs contain all the necessary XMS calls, you can adapt these routines to your own needs. Because XMM access is difficult in high level languages, both the Pascal and C implementations include some assembly language programming. C and Pascal libraries include compiler routines for calling almost any interrupt functions, but they don't include provisions for calling and passing register contents to normal subroutines. The C implementation uses an assembly language program (XMSCA.ASM) and the Pascal implementation directly stores the assembly language as INLINE commands.

This routine is similar to commands for calling interrupts. A structure is passed to call an XMM function. This structure contains the required processor register contents. After the function call the structure receives the return values.

The main program checks for the availability of the XMM driver. If this driver exists, two additional procedures check the viability of the HMA and extended memory.

Pascal listing: XMSP.PAS

```
{*********************************************************
*                                                       *
*                   X M S P . P A S                     *
*                                                       *
**-----------------------------------------------------**
*                                                       *
* Task      : Demonstrates access to extended memory and *
*             high memory area using XMS functions, as   *
*             implemented by the HIMEM.SYS device driver,*
*             for example.                               *
*                                                       *
**-----------------------------------------------------**
*                                                       *
* Author    : MICHAEL TISCHER                           *
* Developed on  : 07/27/90                              *
* Last update   : 07/29/90                              *
*                                                       *
*********************************************************}

program XMSP;

uses Crt, Dos;          { For interrupt call and keyboard access }

const ERR_NOERR          = $00;             { No error }
      ERR_NOTIMPLEMENTED = $80;   { Specified function not known }
      ERR_VDISKFOUND     = $81;      { VDISK-RAMDISK detected }
      ERR_A20            = $82;          { Error at handler A20 }
      ERR_GENERAL        = $8E;          { General driver error }
      ERR_UNRECOVERABLE  = $8F;            { Unrecoverable error }
```

```
      ERR_HMANOTEXIST    = $90;             { HMA does not exist }
      ERR_HMAINUSE       = $91;            { HMA already in use }
      ERR_HMAMINSIZE     = $92;        { Not enough space in HMA }
      ERR_HMANOTALLOCED  = $93;            { HMA not allocated }
      ERR_A20STILLON     = $94;            { Handler A20 still on }
      ERR_OUTOMEMORY     = $A0;         { Out of extended memory }
      ERR_OUTOHANDLES    = $A1;           { All XMS handles in use }
      ERR_INVALIDHANDLE  = $A2;                 { Invalid handle }
      ERR_SHINVALID      = $A3;          { Source handle invalid }
      ERR_SOINVALID      = $A4;          { Source offset invalid }
      ERR_DHINVALID      = $A5;     { Destination handle invalid }
      ERR_DOINVALID      = $A6;     { Destination offset invalid }
      ERR_LENINVALID     = $A7;  { Invalid length for move function }
      ERR_OVERLAP        = $A8;           { Illegal overlapping }
      ERR_PARITY         = $A9;                { Parity error }
      ERR_EMBUNLOCKED    = $AA;              { UMB is unlocked }
      ERR_EMBLOCKED      = $AB;           { UMB is still locked }
      ERR_LOCKOVERFLOW   = $AC;    { Overflow of UMB lock counter }
      ERR_LOCKFAIL       = $AD;          { UMB cannot be locked }
      ERR_UMBSIZETOOBIG  = $B0;          { Smaller UMB available }
      ERR_NOUMBS         = $B1;           { No more UMB available }
      ERR_INVALIDUMB     = $B2;       { Invalid UMB segment address }

type XMSRegs = record                 { Information for XMS call }
                 AX,                   { Only registers AX, BX, DX and SI }
```

```
                BX,              { required, depending on called    }
                DX,              { function along with a segment    }
                SI,              { address                          }
                Segment : word
              end;

{-- Global variables -----------------------------------------------}

var XMSPtr : pointer;  { Pointer to the extended memory manager (XMM) }
    XMSErr : BYTE;                   { Error code of the last operation }

{******************************************************************
 * XMSInit : Initializes the routines for calling the XMS functions  *
 **----------------------------------------------------------------**
 * Input   : None                                                    *
 * Output  : TRUE, if an XMS driver was discovered, otherwise FALSE  *
 * Info    : - The call of this function must precede calls of all   *
 *             all other procedures and functions from this program. *
 ******************************************************************}

function XMSInit : boolean;

var Regs : Registers;              { Registers for interrupt call }
    xr : XMSRegs;

begin
  Regs.AX := $4300;        { Determine availability of XMS manager }
  intr( $2F, Regs );
  if ( Regs.AL = $80 ) then                    { XMS manager found? }
    begin                                                    { Yes }
      Regs.AX := $4310;            { Determine entry point of XMM }
      intr( $2F, Regs );
      XMSPtr := ptr( Regs.ES, Regs.BX );{ Store address in glob. var. }
      XMSErr := ERR_NOERR;              { Still no error found }
      XMSInit := true;       { Handler found, module initialized }
    end
  else                             { No XMS handler installed }
    XMSInit := false;
end;

{******************************************************************
 * XMSCall : General routine for calling an XMS function             *
 **----------------------------------------------------------------**
 * Input   : FctNo = Number of XMS function to be called             *
 *           XRegs = Structure with registers for function call      *
 * Info    : - Before calling this procedure, only those registers   *
 *             can be loaded that are actually required for calling   *
 *             the specified function.                               *
 *           - After the XMS function call, the contents of the      *
 *             various processor registers are copied to the         *
 *             corresponding components of the passed structure.     *
 *           - Before calling this procedure for the first time, the *
 *             XMSInit must be called successfully.                  *
 ******************************************************************}

procedure XMSCall( FktNr : byte; var XRegs : XMSRegs );

begin
  inline ( $8C / $D9 /              { mov    cx,ds      }
           $51 /                    { push   cx         }
           $C5 / $BE / $04 / $00 /  { lds    di,[bp+0004] }
           $8A / $66 / $08 /        { mov    ah,[bp+0008] }
           $8B / $9D / $02 / $00 /  { mov    bx,[di+0002] }
           $8B / $95 / $04 / $00 /  { mov    dx,[di+0004] }
           $8B / $B5 / $06 / $00 /  { mov    si,[di+0006] }
           $8E / $5D / $08 /        { mov    ds,[di+08] }
           $8E / $C1 /              { mov    es,cx      }
           $26 / $FF / $1E / XMSPtr / { call  es:[XMSPTr] }
           $8C / $D9 /              { mov    cx,ds      }
           $C5 / $7E / $04 /        { lds    di,[bp+04] }
           $89 / $05 /              { mov    [di],ax    }
           $89 / $5D / $02 /        { mov    [di+02],bx }
           $89 / $55 / $04 /        { mov    [di+04],dx }
           $89 / $75 / $06 /        { mov    [di+06],si }
           $89 / $4D / $08 /        { mov    [di+08],cx }
           $1F                      { pop    ds         }
         );

{-- Test for error code --------------------------------------------}

  if ( XRegs.AX = 0 ) and ( XRegs.BX >= 128 ) then
    begin
      XMSErr := Lo(XRegs.BX)            { Error, store error code }
      {
              .

              .

              .

          Another error handling routine could follow here

              .

              .

              .
      }
    end
  else
    XMSErr := ERR_NOERR;                    { No error, all ok }
end;

{******************************************************************
 * XMSQueryVer: Returns the XMS version number and other status      *
 *              information                                          *
 **----------------------------------------------------------------**
 * Input   : VerNr = Gets the version number after the function call *
 *                   (Format: 235 = 2.35)                            *
 *           RevNr = Gets the revision number after the function call*
 * Output  : TRUE, if HMA is available, otherwise FALSE              *
 ******************************************************************}

function XMSQueryVer( var VerNr, RevNr : integer ): boolean;

var XR : XMSRegs;              { Registers for communication with XMS }

begin
  XmsCall( 0, XR );
  VerNr := Hi(XR.AX)*100 + ( Lo(XR.AX) shr 4 ) * 10 +
           ( Lo(XR.AX) and 15 );
  RevNr := Hi(XR.BX)*100 + ( Lo(XR.BX) shr 4 ) * 10 +
           ( Lo(XR.BX) and 15 );
  XMSQueryVer := ( XR.DX = 1 );
end;

{******************************************************************
 * XMSGetHMA : Returns right to access the HMA to the caller.        *
 **----------------------------------------------------------------**
 * Input   : LenB = Number of bytes to be allocated                  *
 * Info    : TSR programs should only request the memory size that   *
 *             they actually require, while applications should specify *
 *             the value $FFFF.                                      *
 * Output  : TRUE, if the HMA could be made available,               *
```

691

```
*          otherwise FALSE;                              *
*********************************************************************}

function XMSGetHMA( LenB : word ) : boolean;

var Xr : XMSRegs;           { Registers for communication with XMS }

begin
  XR.DX := LenB;                        { Pass length in DX register }
  XmsCall( 1, Xr );                       { Call XMS function #1 }
  XMSGetHMA := ( XMSErr = ERR_NOERR );
end;


{*******************************************************************
* XMSReleaseHMA : Releases the HMA, making it possible to pass     *
*                 to other programs.                               *
**---------------------------------------------------------------**
* Input   : None                                                  *
* Info    : - Call this procedure before ending a program if the  *
*             HMA was allocated beforehand through a call for      *
*             XMSGetHMA, because otherwise the HMA cannot be passed *
*             to any programs called afterwards.                  *
*           - Calling this procedure causes the data stored in HAM *
*             to be lost.                                          *
*******************************************************************}

procedure XMSReleaseHMA;

var Xr : XMSRegs;        { Call registers for communication with XMS }

begin
  XmsCall( 2, Xr );                       { Call XMS function #2 }
end;


{*******************************************************************
* XMSA200nGlobal: Switches on the A20 handler, making direct access *
*                 to the HMA possible.                            *
**---------------------------------------------------------------**
* None    : None                                                  *
* Info    : - For many computers, switching on the A20 handler is a *
*             relatively time-consuming process. Only call this   *
*             procedure when it is absolutely necessary.          *
*******************************************************************}

procedure XMSA200nGlobal;

var Xr : XMSRegs;           { Registers for communication with XMS }

begin
  XmsCall( 3, Xr );                       { Call XMS function #3 }
end;


{*******************************************************************
* XMSA200ffGlobal: A counterpart to the XMSA200nGlobal procedure,  *
*                  this procedure switches the A20 handler back off, *
*                  so that direct access to the HMA is no longer  *
*                  possible.                                       *
**---------------------------------------------------------------**
* Input   : None                                                  *
* Info    : - Always call this procedure before ending a program, *
*             in case the A20 handler was switched on before via a *
*             a call for XMSA200nGlobal.                          *
*******************************************************************}
```

```
procedure XMSA200ffGlobal;

var Xr : XMSRegs;           { Registers for communication with XMS }

begin
  XmsCall( 4, Xr );                       { Call XMS function #4 }
end;


{*******************************************************************
* XMSA200nLocal: See XMSA200nGlobal                               *
**---------------------------------------------------------------**
* Input   : None                                                  *
* Info    : - This local procedure differs from the global procedure *
*             in that it only switches on the A20 handler if it   *
*             hasn't already been called.                         *
*******************************************************************}

procedure XMSA200nLocal;

var Xr : XMSRegs;           { Registers for communication with XMS }

begin
  XmsCall( 5, Xr );                       { Call XMS function #5 }
end;


{*******************************************************************
* XMSA200ffLocal : See XMSA290ffGlobal                            *
**---------------------------------------------------------------**
* Input   : None                                                  *
* Info    : - This local procedure only differs from the global   *
*             procedure in that the A20 handler is only switched  *
*             off if hasn't already happened through a previous   *
*             call.                                                *
*******************************************************************}

procedure XMSA200ffLocal;

var Xr : XMSRegs;           { Registers for communication with XMS }

begin
  XmsCall( 6, Xr );                       { Call XMS function #6 }
end;


{*******************************************************************
* XMSIsA200n : Returns the status of the A20 handler              *
**---------------------------------------------------------------**
* Input   : None                                                  *
* Output  : TRUE, if A20 handler is on, otherwise FALSE.          *
*           FALSE.                                                *
*******************************************************************}

function XMSIsA200n : boolean;

var Xr : XMSRegs;           { Registers for communication with XMS }

begin
  XmsCall( 7, Xr );                       { Call XMS function #7 }
  XMSIsA200n := ( Xr.AX = 1 );        { AX = 1 ---> Handler is free }
end;


{*******************************************************************
* XMSQueryFree : Returns the size of free extended memory and the *
*                largest free block                              *
**---------------------------------------------------------------**
```

```
*  Input   : TotFree: Gets the total size of free extended memory.   *
*            MaxBl : Gets the size of the largest free block.        *
*  Info    : - Both specifications in kilobytes.                     *
*            - The size of the HMA is not included in the count,     *
*              even if it hasn't yet been assigned to a program.     *
********************************************************************}

procedure XMSQueryFree( var TotFree, MaxBl : integer );

var Xr : XMSRegs;          { Registers for communication with XMS }

begin
  XmsCall( 8, Xr );                   { Call XMS function #8 }
  TotFree := Xr.AX;                    { Total size in AX }
  MaxBl := Xr.DX;                      { Free memory in DX }
end;


{*****************************************************************
* XMSGetMem : Allocates an extended memory block (EMB)          *
**-----------------------------------------------------------**
*  Input   : LenKB : Size of requested block in kilobytes       *
*  Output  : Handle for further access to block or 0, if no block *
*            can be allocated. The appropriate error code would   *
*            also be in the global variable, XMSErr.              *
********************************************************************}

function XMSGetMem( LenKb : integer ) : integer;

var Xr : XMSRegs;          { Registers for communication with XMS }

begin
  Xr.DX := LenKB;                     { Length passed in DX register }
  XmsCall( 9, Xr );                   { Call XMS function #9 }
  XMSGetMem := Xr.DX                  { Return handle }
end;


{*****************************************************************
* XMSFreeMem : Releases previously allocated extended memory block *
*              (EMB).                                             *
**-----------------------------------------------------------**
*  Input   : Handle : Handle for access to the block returned when *
*            XMSGetMem was called.                                *
*  Info    : - The contents of the EMB are irretrievably lost and  *
*              the handle becomes invalid when you call this procedure.*
*            - Before ending a program, use this procedure to release *
*              all allocated memory areas, so that they can be      *
*              allocated for the next program to be called.         *
********************************************************************}

procedure XMSFreeMem( Handle : integer );

var Xr : XMSRegs;          { Registers for communication with XMS }

begin
  Xr.DX := Handle;                    { Handle passed in DX register }
  XmsCall( 10, Xr );                  { Call XMS function #10 }
end;


{*****************************************************************
* XMSCopy : Copies memory areas between extended memory and      *
*           conventional memory or within the two memory groups. *
**-----------------------------------------------------------**
*  Input   : FrmHandle : Handle of memory area to be copied.     *
*            FrmOffset : Offset in block being copied.           *
```

```
*            ToHandle  : Handle of memory area to which memory is *
*                        being copied.                           *
*            ToOffset  : Offset in the target block.             *
*            LenW      : Number of words to be copied.           *
*  Info    : - To include normal memory in the operation, 0 must be *
*              specified as the handle and the segment and offset  *
*              address must be specified as the offset in the usual *
*              form (offset before segment).                       *
********************************************************************}

procedure XMSCopy( FrmHandle : integer; FrmOffset : longint;
                   ToHandle  : integer; ToOffset  : longint;
                   LenW      : longint );

type EMMS = record            { An extended memory move structure }
       LenB    : longint;     { Number of bytes to be moved }
       SHandle : integer;                    { Source handle }
       SOffset : longint;                    { Source offset }
       DHandle : integer;               { Destination handle }
       DOffset : longint;               { Destination offset }
     end;

var Xr : XMSRegs;          { Registers for communication with XMS }
    Mi : EMMS;                                { Gets EEMS }

begin
  with Mi do                          { Prepare EMMS first }
    begin
      LenB := 2 * LenW;
      SHandle := FrmHandle;
      SOffset := FrmOffset;
      DHandle := ToHandle;
      DOffset := ToOffset
    end;

  Xr.Si      := Ofs( Mi );            { Offset address of EMMS }
  Xr.Segment := Seg(Mi);             { Segment address of EMMS }
  XmsCall( 11, Xr );                  { Call XMS function #11 }
end;


{*****************************************************************
* XMSLock : Locks an extended memory block from being moved by the *
*           XMM, returning its absolute address at the same time.  *
**-----------------------------------------------------------**
*  Input   : Handle : Handle of memory area returned during a prev- *
*                     ious call by XMSGetMem.                       *
*  Output  : The linear address of the block of memory.            *
********************************************************************}

function XMSLock( Handle : integer ) : longint;

var Xr : XMSRegs;          { Registers for communication with XMS }

begin
  Xr.DX := Handle;                              { Handle of EMB }
  XmsCall( 12, Xr );                  { Call XMS function #12 }
  XMSLock := longint(Xr.DX) shl 16 + Xr.BX;  { Compute 32 bit address }
end;


{*****************************************************************
* XMSUnlock : Releases a locked extended memory block again.     *
**-----------------------------------------------------------**
*  Input   : Handle : Handle of memory area returned during a prev- *
*                     ious call by XMSGetMem.                       *
```

```
*******************************************************************}

procedure XMSUnLock( Handle : integer );

var Xr : XMSRegs;              { Registers for communication with XMS }

begin
  Xr.DX := Handle;                              { Handle of EMB }
  XmsCall( 13, Xr );                      { Call XMS function #13 }
end;


{*****************************************************************
* XMSQueryInfo : Gets various information about an extended memory   *
*                block that has been allocated.                     *
**-----------------------------------------------------------------**
* Input   : Handle : Handle of memory area                          *
*           Lock   : Variable, in which the lock counter is entered *
*           LenKB  : Variable, in which the length of the block is  *
*                    entered in kilobytes                           *
*           FreeH  : Number of free handles                         *
* Info   : You cannot use this procedure to find out the start      *
*          address of a memory block, use the XMSLock function      *
*          instead.                                                 *
*****************************************************************}

procedure XMSQueryInfo( Handle   : integer; var Lock, LenKB : integer;
                        var FreeH : integer );

var Xr : XMSRegs;              { Registers for communication with XMS }

begin
  Xr.DX := Handle;                              { Handle of EMB }
  XmsCall( 14, Xr );                      { Call XMS function #14 }
  Lock  := Hi( Xr.BX );                     { Evaluate register }
  FreeH := Lo( Xr.BX );
  LenKB := Xr.DX;
end;


{*****************************************************************
* XMSRealloc : Enlarges or shrinks an extended memory block prev-   *
*              iously allocated by XMSGetMem                        *
**-----------------------------------------------------------------**
* Input   : Handle   : Handle of memory area                       *
*           NewLenKB : New length of memory area in kilobytes      *
* Output  : TRUE, if the block was resized, otherwise FALSE        *
* Info    : The specified block cannot be locked!                  *
*****************************************************************}

function XMSRealloc( Handle, NewLenKB : integer ) : boolean;

var Xr : XMSRegs;              { Registers for communication with XMS }

begin
  Xr.DX := Handle;                              { Handle of EMB }
  Xr.BX := NewLenKB;              { New length in the BX register }
  XmsCall( 15, Xr );                      { Call XMS function #15 }
  XMSRealloc := ( XMSErr = ERR_NOERR );
end;


{*****************************************************************
* XMSGetUMB : Allocates an upper memory block (UMB).               *
**-----------------------------------------------------------------**
* Input   : LenPara : Size of area to be allocated in paragraphs   *
*                     of 16 bytes each                             *
```

```
*           Seg     : Variable that gets the segment address of    *
*                     the allocated UMB in successful cases        *
*           MaxPara : Variable that specifies the length of the    *
*                     largest available UMB in unsuccessful cases  *
* Output  : TRUE, if a UMB could be allocated, otherwise FALSE     *
* Info    : Warning! This function is not supported by all XMS     *
*           drivers and is extremely hardware-dependent.           *
*****************************************************************}

function XMSGetUMB( LenPara        : integer;
                    var Seg, MaxPara : word ) : boolean;

var Xr : XMSRegs;              { Registers for communication with XMS }

begin
  Xr.DX := LenPara;                        { Desired length to }
  XmsCall( 16, Xr );                      { Call XMS function #16 }
  Seg := Xr.BX;                         { Return segment address }
  MaxPara := Xr.DX;                     { Length of largest UMB }
  XMSGetUMB := ( XMSErr = ERR_NOERR );
end;


{*****************************************************************
* XMSFreeUMB : Releases UMB previously allocated by XMSGetUMB.     *
**-----------------------------------------------------------------**
* Input   : Seg : Segment address of UMB being released           *
* Info    : Warning! This function is not supported by all XMS    *
*           drivers and is extremely hardware-dependent.          *
*****************************************************************}

procedure XMSFreeUMB( var Seg : word );

var Xr : XMSRegs;              { Registers for communication wit XMS }

begin
  Xr.DX := Seg;                   { Segment address of UMB to DX }
  XmsCall( 17, Xr );                      { Call XMS function #17 }
end;


{---------------------------------------------------------------}
{-- Test and Demo procedures                                 --}
{---------------------------------------------------------------}


{*****************************************************************
* HMATest : Tests the availability of HMA and demonstrates its use. *
**-----------------------------------------------------------------**
* Input   : None                                                  *
*****************************************************************}

procedure HMATest;

type HMAR = array [1..65520] of BYTE;              { HMA array }
     HMARPTR = ^HMAR;                      { Pointer to HMA array }

var ch   : char;                            { For reading keys }
    A20  : boolean;               { Current status of A20 handler }
    hmap : HMARPTR;                          { Pointer to HMA }
    i,                                       { Loop counter }
    err  : word;                  { Number of errors in HMA access }

begin
  write( 'HMA Test  -  Please press a key to start the test...' );
  ch := ReadKey;
  writeln( #10 );
```

```
{-- Allocate HMA and test each memory location ---------------------}

if ( XMSGetHMA( $FFFF ) ) then                    { HMA acquired? }
  begin                                           { Yes }
    A20 := XMSIsA200n;                 { Determine handler status }
    If ( A20 = FALSE ) then                    { Is A20 handler on? }
      XMSA200nGlobal;                      { No, switch it on now }

    hmap := HMARPTR(Ptr( $FFFF, $0010 ));         { Pointer to HMA }

    err := 0;                          { No errors up until now }
    for i := 1 to 65520 do        { Test each single memory location }
      begin
        write( #13, 'Memory location: ', i );
        hmap^[i] := i mod 256;             { Write memory location }
        if ( hmap^[i] <> i mod 256 ) then    { And read out again }
          begin                                   { Error! }
            writeln( ' ERROR!' );
            inc( err );
          end;
      end;

    XMSReleaseHMA;                                { Release HMA }
    If ( A20 = FALSE ) then                { Was A20 handler on? }
      XMSA200ffGlobal;                     { No, switch it off }

    writeln( #13 );
    if ( err = 0 ) then                   { Evaluate results of test }
      writeln( 'HMA O.K., no defective memory location.' )
    else
      writeln( 'ATTENTION: ', err, ' defective memory locations ' +
               'detected in HMA! ' );
  end
else
  writeln( 'ATTENTION: No access to HMA possible.' );
end;

{*********************************************************************
* EMBTest : Tests extended memory and demonstrates the calls of     *
*           different XMS functions                                 *
**----------------------------------------------------------------**
* Input  : None                                                    *
*********************************************************************}

procedure EMBTest;

type BAR = array [1..1024] of BYTE;          { Byte array with 1K }
     BARPTR = ^BAR;                          { Pointer to byte array }

var ch    : char;                            { for reading keys }
    Adr    : longint;                        { Start address of EMB }
    barp   : BARPTR;                         { Pointer to 1K buffer }
    i, j,                                    { Loop counter }
    err,                     { Number of errors in HMA access }
    Handle,                      { Handle for access to EMB }
    TotFree,               { Size of total free extended memory }
    MaxBl  : integer;                        { Largest free block }

begin
  write( 'EMB Test  -  Please press a key to start the test...' );
  ch := ReadKey;
  writeln( #10 );
```

```
  XMSQueryFree( TotFree, MaxBl );  { Determine size of extended memory }
  writeln( 'Total size of free extended memory (incl. HMA): ',
           TotFree, ' KB' );
  writeln( '                        Largest free block: ',
           MaxBl, ' KB' );

  TotFree := TotFree - 64;      { Calculate actual size without HMA }
  if ( MaxBl >= TotFree ) then         { Can the value be right? }
    MaxBl := MaxBl - 64;                              { No }

  if ( MaxBl <> 0 ) then              { Still enough memory free? }
    begin                                            { Yes }
      Handle := XMSGetMem( MaxBl );
      writeln( MaxBl, ' KB allocated.' );
      writeln( 'Handle      = ', Handle );
      Adr := XMSLock( Handle );              { Determine address }
      XMSUnlock( Handle );                       { Unlock again }
      writeln( 'Start address = ', Adr, ' (', Adr div 1024, 'K)' );

      GetMem( barp, 1024 );        { Buffer to Turbo heap allocated }
      err := 0;                           { No errors up to now }

      {-- Execute allocated EMB KB for KB and test -------------------}

      for  i := 0 to MaxBl-1 do
        begin
          write( #13, 'KB test: ', i+1 );
          FillChar( barp^, 1024, i mod 255 );
          XMSCopy( 0, longint(barp), Handle, longint(i)*1024, 512 );
          FillChar( barp^, 1024, 255 );
          XMSCopy( Handle, longint(i)*1024, 0, longint(barp), 512 );

          {-- Compare copied buffer with expected result ------------}

          j := 1;
          while ( j <= 1024 ) do
            if ( barp^[j] <> i mod 255 ) then
              begin                                   { Error! }
                writeln( ' ERROR!' );
                inc( err );
                j := 1025;
              end
            else                  { No error, next memory location }
              inc( j );
        end;

      writeln( #13 );
      if ( err = 0 ) then            { Evaluate results of test }
        writeln( 'EMB ok, none of the tested 1K blocks ' +
                 'were defective.' )
      else
        writeln( 'ATTENTION! ', err, ' defective 1K blocks detected' +
                 ' in EMB' );

      FreeMem( barp, 1024 );                { Release buffer again }
      XMSFreeMem( Handle );                 { Release EMB again }
    end;
end;

{*********************************************************************
*                    M A I N   P R O G R A M                        *
*********************************************************************}

var VerNr,
```

```
  RevNr : integer;

begin
 ClrScr;
 writeln( 'XMSP - XMS-Demo program by MICHAEL TISCHER' );
 writeln;
 if XMSInit then
  begin
   if XMSQueryVer( VerNr, RevNr ) then
    writeln( 'Access to HMA possible.' )
   else
    writeln( 'No access to HMA.' );
   writeln( 'XMS version number: ', VerNr div 100,
            '.', VerNr mod 100 );
   writeln( 'Revision number   : ', RevNr div 100,
            '.', RevNr mod 100 );
   writeln;
   HMATest;                                { Test HMA }
   writeln;
   EMBTest;                       { Test extended memory }
  end
 else
  writeln( 'No XMS driver installed!');
end.
```

C listing: XMSC.C

```
/********************************************************************
*                         X M S C . C                             *
**--------------------------------------------------------------**
* Task       : Demonstrates accessing extended memory and the     *
*              high memory area using XMS functions, as           *
*              implemented through the HIMEM.SYS device driver,    *
*              for example.                                        *
*                                                                 *
*                                                                 *
*              All device drivers must be loaded into             *
*              conventional memory prior to running this test.     *
*                                                                 *
**--------------------------------------------------------------**
* Author     : Michael Tischer                                    *
* Developed on : 07/27/90                                         *
* Last update  : 03/05/92                                         *
**--------------------------------------------------------------**
* (MICROSOFT C)                                                   *
* Compilation  : CL /AS /Zp /c xmsc.c                             *
*                LINK xmsc xmsca;                                 *
* Call         : xmsc                                             *
**--------------------------------------------------------------**
* (BORLAND TURBO C)                                               *
* Compilation  : Create a project file using the following:       *
*                   xmsc.c                                        *
*                   xmsca.obj                                     *
********************************************************************/

/*-- Link include files ---------------------------------------*/

#include <dos.h>                         /* for interrupt calls */

#ifdef __TURBOC__
  #include <alloc.h>
#else
  #include <malloc.h>
#endif

/*-- Constants ------------------------------------------------*/

#define ERR_NOERR          0x00                   /* No error */
#define ERR_NOTIMPLEMENTED 0x80   /* Specified function not known */
#define ERR_VDISKFOUND     0x81      /* VDISK-RAMDISK detected */
#define ERR_A20            0x82        /* Error on A20 handler */
#define ERR_GENERAL        0x8E        /* General driver error */
#define ERR_UNRECOVERABLE  0x8F         /* Unrecoverable error */
#define ERR_HMANOTEXIST    0x90         /* HMA does not exist */
#define ERR_HMAINUSE       0x91        /* HMA already in use */
#define ERR_HMAMINSIZE     0x92   /* Not enough space in HMA */
#define ERR_HMANOTALLOCED  0x93         /* HMA not allocated */
#define ERR_A20STILLON     0x94     /* A20 handler still on */
#define ERR_OUTOMEMORY     0xA0   /* Out of extended memory */
#define ERR_OUTOHANDLES    0xA1     /* All XMS handles in use */
#define ERR_INVALIDHANDLE  0xA2            /* Invalid handle */
#define ERR_SHINVALID      0xA3      /* Source handle invalid */
#define ERR_SOINVALID      0xA4      /* Source offset invalid */
#define ERR_DHINVALID      0xA5   /* Destination handle invalid */
#define ERR_DOINVALID      0xA6   /* Destination offset invalid */
#define ERR_LENINVALID     0xA7 /* Invalid length for move function */
#define ERR_OVERLAP        0xA8       /* Illegal overlapping */
#define ERR_PARITY         0xA9              /* Parity error */
#define ERR_EMBUNLOCKED    0xAA         /* UMB is unlocked */
#define ERR_EMBLOCKED      0xAB         /* UMB is still locked */
```

```
#define ERR_LOCKOVERFLOW    0xAC          /* UMB lock overflow */
#define ERR_LOCKFAIL        0xAD          /* UMB cannot be locked */
#define ERR_UMBSIZETOOBIG   0xB0          /* Smaller UMB available */
#define ERR_NOUMBS          0xB1          /* No more UMB available */
#define ERR_INVALIDUMB      0xB2     /* UMB segment address is invalid */

#define TRUE  ( 0 == 0 )
#define FALSE ( 0 == 1 )


/*-- Macros -------------------------------------------------*/

#ifndef MK_FP
  #define MK_FP(seg,ofs) \
              ((void far *) (((unsigned long)(seg) << 16) |
(unsigned)(ofs)))
#endif


#define Hi(x) (*((BYTE *) &x+1))          /* High byte of an int */
#define Lo(x) (*((BYTE *) &x))            /* Low byte of an int */


/*-- Type declarations ------------------------------------*/

typedef unsigned char BYTE;
typedef BYTE BOOL;
typedef unsigned WORD;

typedef struct                   /* Information for XMS call */
        {
          WORD AX,            /* Only registers AX, BX, DX and SI */
               BX,            /* depending on the called function, */
               DX,            /* along with a segment address */
               SI,
               Segment;
        } XMSRegs;

typedef struct                  /* An extended memory move structure */
        {
          long LenB;           /* Number of bytes to be moved */
          int  SHandle;                      /* Source handle */
          long SOffset;                      /* Source offset */
          int  DHandle;                    /* Destination handle */
          long DOffset;                    /* Destination offset */
        } EMMS;

/*-- External declarations ----------------------------------*/

extern void XMSCall( BYTE FktNr, XMSRegs *Xr );

/*-- Global variables -------------------------------------*/

void far * XMSPtr;   /* Pointer to the extended memory manager (XMM) */
BYTE XMSErr;             /* Error code of the last operation */

/****************************************************************
* XMSInit : Initializes the routines for calling the XMS functions *
**------------------------------------------------------------**
* Input   : None                                              *
* Output  : TRUE, if an XMS drive has been detected, otherwise FALSE *
* Info    : - The call for this function must precede the calls for *
*             all other procedures and functions from this program. *
****************************************************************/

BOOL XMSInit( void )
{
```

```
union REGS Regs;          /* Processor registers for interrupt call */
struct SREGS SRegs;                   /* Segment registers */
XMSRegs Xr;                        /* Registers for XMS call */

Regs.x.ax = 0x4300;       /* Determine availability of XMS manager */
int86( 0x2F, &Regs, &Regs );            /* Call DOS dispatcher */

if ( Regs.h.al == 0x80 )               /* XMS manager found? */
 {                                              /* Yes */
  Regs.x.ax = 0x4310;            /* Determine entry point of XMM */
  int86x( 0x2F, &Regs, &Regs, &SRegs );
  XMSPtr = MK_FP( SRegs.es, Regs.x.bx ); /* Store addr.in global var */
  XMSErr = ERR_NOERR;                     /* Still no error */
  return TRUE;               /* Handler found, module initialized */
 }
else                             /* No XMS-Handler installed */
 return FALSE;
}


/****************************************************************
* XMSQueryVer: Supplies the XMS version number and other status *
*              information                                     *
**------------------------------------------------------------**
* Input   : VerNo = Gets the version number after the functino call *
*                   (Format: 235 == 2.35)                     *
*           RevNo = Gets the revision number after the function call *
* Output  : TRUE, if an HMA is available, otherwise FALSE     *
****************************************************************/

BOOL XMSQueryVer( int * VerNr, int * RevNr )
{
  XMSRegs Xr;                        /* Registers for XMS call */

  XMSCall( 0, &Xr );                     /* Call XMS function #0 */
  *VerNr = Hi(Xr.AX)*100 + ( Lo(Xr.AX) >> 4 ) * 10 +
           ( Lo(Xr.AX) & 15 );
  *RevNr = Hi(Xr.BX)*100 + ( Lo(Xr.BX) >> 4 ) * 10 +
           ( Lo(Xr.BX) & 15 );
  return ( Xr.DX == 1 );
}


/****************************************************************
* XMSGetHMA : Gets the user access to the HMA.                *
**------------------------------------------------------------**
* Input   : LenB = Number of bytes to be allocated            *
* Info    : TSR programs should only request the memory size that is *
*           truly required, while applications specify the value *
*           0xFFFF.                                           *
* Output  : TRUE, if the HMA was made available, otherwise FALSE; *
****************************************************************/

BOOL XMSGetHMA( WORD LenB )
{
  XMSRegs Xr;                        /* Registers for XMS call */

  Xr.DX = LenB;                    /* Pass length in register DX */
  XMSCall( 1, &Xr );                   /* Call XMS function #1 */
  return XMSErr == ERR_NOERR;
}


/****************************************************************
* XMSReleaseHMA : Releases the HMA, making it possible to pass it on *
*                 to other programs.                          *
**------------------------------------------------------------**
```

```
*  None    : None                                           *
*  Info    : - Call this procedure before ending a program when the    *
*              HMA has been accessed beforehand by calling XMSGetHMA,   *
*              since otherwise, the HMA cannot be used by programs      *
*              called later.                                           *
*            - This procedure causes the data stored in the HMA to be  *
*              lost.                                                    *
************************************************************/

void XMSReleaseHMA( void )
{
  XMSRegs Xr;                            /* Registers for XMS call */

  XMSCall( 2, &Xr );                     /* Call XMS function #2 */
}


/************************************************************
* XMSA200nGlobal: Switches on A20 handler, making direct access *
*                 to the HMA possible.                     *
**--------------------------------------------------------**
*  None    : None                                           *
*  Info    : - On many computers, switching on the A20 handler is a     *
*              relatively time-consuming process. Call this procedure   *
*              only when necessary.                                     *
************************************************************/

void XMSA200nGlobal( void )
{
  XMSRegs Xr;                            /* Registers for XMS call */

  XMSCall( 3, &Xr );                     /* Call XMS function #3 */
}


/************************************************************
* XMSA200ffGlobal: As a counterpart to the XMSA200nGlobal procedure, *
*                  this process switches A20 back off, so that direct *
*                  access to the HMA is no longer possible.  *
**--------------------------------------------------------**
*  Input   : None                                           *
*  Info    : - Always call this procedure before ending a program,     *
*              in case A20 was switched on via a call for              *
*              XMSA200nGlobal.                                         *
************************************************************/

void XMSA200ffGlobal( void )
{
  XMSRegs Xr;                            /* Registers for XMS call */

  XMSCall( 4, &Xr );                     /* Call XMS function #4 */
}


/************************************************************
* XMSA200nLocal: See XMSA200nGlobal                         *
**--------------------------------------------------------**
*  Input   : None                                           *
*  Info    : - This local procedure differs from the global procedure  *
*              in that A20 is only switched on if hasn't been called   *
*              previously.                                             *
************************************************************/

void XMSA200nLocal( void )
{
  XMSRegs Xr;                            /* Registers for XMS call */
```

```
  XMSCall( 5, &Xr );                     /* Call XMS function #5 */
}


/************************************************************
* XMSA200ffLocal : See XMSA290ffGlobal                      *
**--------------------------------------------------------**
*  Input   : None                                           *
*  Info    : - This local procedure differs from the global procedure  *
*              in that A20 is only switched off if this hasn't already *
*              taken place via a previous call.                        *
************************************************************/

void XMSA200ffLocal( void )
{
  XMSRegs Xr;                            /* Registers for XMS call */

  XMSCall( 6, &Xr );                     /* Call XMS function #6 */
}


/************************************************************
* XMSIsA200n : Returns the status of the A20 handler        *
**--------------------------------------------------------**
*  Input   : None                                           *
*  Output  : TRUE, if A20 handler is switched on, otherwise FALSE   *
************************************************************/

BOOL XMSIsA200n( void )
{
  XMSRegs Xr;                            /* Registers for XMS call */

  XMSCall( 7, &Xr );                     /* Call XMS function #7 */
  return ( Xr.AX == 1 );                 /* AX == 1 ---> Handler is free */
}


/************************************************************
* XMSQueryFree : Returns the size of free extended memory and the  *
*                largest free block                         *
**--------------------------------------------------------**
*  Input   : TotFree: Gets the total size of free EM.       *
*            MaxBl  : Gets the size of the largest free block. *
*  Info    : - Both specifications in kilobytes             *
*            - The size of the HMA is not included in the count,       *
*              even if it hasn't yet been assigned to a program.       *
************************************************************/

void XMSQueryFree( int * TotFree, int * MaxBl )
{
  XMSRegs Xr;                            /* Registers for XMS call */

  XMSCall( 8, &Xr );                     /* Call XMS function #8 */
  *TotFree = Xr.AX;                      /* Total size in AX */
  *MaxBl   = Xr.DX;                      /* Free memory in DX */
}


/************************************************************
* XMSGetMem : Allocates an extended memory block (EMB)      *
**--------------------------------------------------------**
*  Input   : LenKB : Size of requested block in KB          *
*  Output  : Handle for further access to the block or 0, if no block *
*            could be allocated. The appropriate error code would     *
*            also be in the global variable, XMSErr.                  *
************************************************************/

int XMSGetMem( int LenKb )
```

```
{
    XMSRegs Xr;                          /* Registers for XMS call */

    Xr.DX = LenKb;                       /* Length passed in DX register */
    XMSCall( 9, &Xr );                   /* Call XMS function #9 */
    return Xr.DX;                        /* Return handle */
}


/*************************************************************************
* XMSFreeMem : Frees an extended memory block (EMB) that was prev-       *
*              iously allocated.                                         *
**---------------------------------------------------------------------**
* Input   : Handle : Handle for accessing the block returned when       *
*                    XMSGetMem was called.                              *
* Info     : - The contents of the EMB are irretrievably lost when      *
*              this procedure is called, and the handle is also invalid *
*            - Before ending a program, use this procedure to release   *
*              all allocated areas so the next program can allocate      *
*              them.                                                     *
*************************************************************************/

void XMSFreeMem( int Handle )
{
    XMSRegs Xr;                          /* Registers for XMS call */

    Xr.DX = Handle;                      /* Handle passed in DX register */
    XMSCall( 10, &Xr );                  /* Call XMS function #10 */
}


/*************************************************************************
* XMSCopy : Copies memory areas between extended memory and             *
*           conventional memory or within the two memory groups.        *
**---------------------------------------------------------------------**
* Input   : FrmHandle : Handle of memory area to be copied.             *
*           FrmOffset : Offset in block being copied                    *
*           ToHandle  : Handle of memory area to which memory is        *
*                       being copied.                                   *
*           ToOffset  : Offset in the target block.                     *
*           LenW      : Number of words to be copied.                   *
* Info     : - To include normal memory in the operation, O must be     *
*              specified as the handle and the segment and offset       *
*              address must be specified as the offset in the usual     *
*              form (offset before segment).                            *
*************************************************************************/

void XMSCopy( int FrmHandle, long FrmOffset, int ToHandle,
              long ToOffset, int LenW )

{
    XMSRegs Xr;                          /* Registers for XMS call */
    EMMS Mi;                             /* Gets EEMS */
    void far * MiPtr;

    Mi.LenB = 2 * LenW;                  /* Prepare EMMS first */
    Mi.SHandle = FrmHandle;
    Mi.SOffset = FrmOffset;
    Mi.DHandle = ToHandle;
    Mi.DOffset = ToOffset;

    MiPtr = &Mi;                         /* Far pointer to the structure */
    Xr.SI = FP_OFF( MiPtr );             /* Offset address of EMMS */
    Xr.Segment = FP_SEG( MiPtr );        /* Segment address of EMMS */
    XMSCall( 11, &Xr );                  /* Call XMS function #11 */
}
```

```
/*************************************************************************
* XMSLock : Locks an extended memory block from being moved by the      *
*           XMM, returning its absolute address at the same time.       *
**---------------------------------------------------------------------**
* Input   : Handle : Handle of memory area returned during a prev-      *
*                    ious call by XMSGetMem.                            *
* Output  : The linear address of the block of memory.                  *
*************************************************************************/

long XMSLock( int Handle )
{
    XMSRegs Xr;                          /* Registers for XMS call */

    Xr.DX = Handle;                      /* Handle of EMB */
    XMSCall( 12, &Xr );                  /* Call XMS function #12 */
    return ((long) Xr.DX << 16) + Xr.BX; /* Compute 32 bit address */
}


/*************************************************************************
* XMSUnlock : Releases a locked extended memory block again.            *
**---------------------------------------------------------------------**
* Input   : Handle : Handle of memory area returned during a prev-      *
*                    ious call by XMSGetMem.                            *
*************************************************************************/

void XMSUnlock( int Handle )
{
    XMSRegs Xr;                          /* Registers for XMS call */

    Xr.DX = Handle;                      /* Handle of EMB */
    XMSCall( 13, &Xr );                  /* Call XMS function #13 */
}


/*************************************************************************
* XMSQueryInfo : Gets various information about an extended memory       *
*                that has been allocated.                               *
**---------------------------------------------------------------------**
* Input   : Handle : Handle of memory area                              *
*           Lock   : Variable, in which the lock counter is entered     *
*           LenKB  : Variable, in which the length of the block is      *
*                    entered in kilobytes                               *
*           FreeH  : Variable, in which the number of free handles      *
*                    is entered                                         *
* Info     : You cannot use this procedure to find out the start        *
*            address of a memory block, use the XMSLock function        *
*            instead.                                                    *
*************************************************************************/

void XMSQueryInfo( int Handle, int * Lock, int * LenKB, int * FreeH )

{
    XMSRegs Xr;                          /* Registers for XMS call */

    Xr.DX = Handle;                      /* Handle of EMB */
    XMSCall( 14, &Xr );                  /* Call XMS function #14 */
    *Lock  = Hi( Xr.BX );                /* Evaluate register */
    *FreeH = Lo( Xr.BX );
    *LenKB = Xr.DX;
}


/*************************************************************************
* XMSRealloc : Enlarges or shrinks an extended memory block prev-       *
*              iously allocated by XMSGetMem                            *
```

```
**-------------------------------------------------------------**
* Input  : Handle   : Handle of memory area                     *
*          NewLenKB : New length of memory in kilobytes         *
* Output : TRUE, if the block was resized, otherwise FALSE      *
* Info   : The specified block cannot be locked!                *
*****************************************************************/

BOOL XMSRealloc( int Handle, int NewLenKB )
{
   XMSRegs Xr;                          /* Registers for XMS call */

   Xr.DX = Handle;                      /* Handle of EMB */
   Xr.BX = NewLenKB;                    /* New length in the BX register */
   XMSCall( 15, &Xr );                  /* Call XMS function #15 */
   return ( XMSErr == ERR_NOERR );
}


/****************************************************************
* XMSGetUMB : Allocates an upper memory block (UMB).            *
**-------------------------------------------------------------**
* Input  : LenPara : Size of area to be allocated in paragraphs *
*                     of 16 bytes each                          *
*          Seg     : Variable that gets the segment address of  *
*                     the allocated UMB in successful cases     *
*          MaxPara : Variable that specifies the length of the  *
*                     largest available UMB in unsuccessful cases*
* Output : TRUE, if a UBM could be allocated, otherwise FALSE   *
* Info   : Warning! This function is not supported by all XMS   *
*                   drivers and is extremely hardware-dependent. *
*****************************************************************/

BOOL XMSGetUMB( int LenPara, WORD * Seg, WORD * MaxPara )
{
   XMSRegs Xr;                          /* Registers for XMS call */

   Xr.DX = LenPara;                     /* Desired length to DX */
   XMSCall( 16, &Xr );                  /* Call XMS function #16 */
   *Seg = Xr.BX;                        /* Return segment address */
   *MaxPara = Xr.DX;                    /* Length of largest UMB */
   return ( XMSErr == ERR_NOERR );
}


/****************************************************************
* XMSFreeUMB : Releases UMB previously allocated by XMSGetUMB   *
**-------------------------------------------------------------**
* Input  : Seg : Segment address of UMB being released         *
* Info   : Warning! This function is not supported by all XMS   *
*                   drivers and is extremely hardware-dependent. *
*****************************************************************/

void XMSFreeUMB( WORD Seg )
{
   XMSRegs Xr;                          /* Registers for XMS call */

   Xr.DX = Seg;                         /* Segment address of UMB to DX */
   XMSCall( 17, &Xr );                  /* Call XMS function #17 */
}

/*------------------------------------------------------------*/
/*-- Test and Demo procedures                              --*/
/*------------------------------------------------------------*/

/****************************************************************
```

```
* HMATest : Tests the availability of HMA and demonstrates its use *
**-------------------------------------------------------------**
* Input  : None                                                *
*****************************************************************/

void HMATest( void )

{
   BOOL A20;                            /* Current status of A20 handler */
   BYTE far * hmap;                     /* Pointer to HMA */
   WORD i,                              /* Loop counter */
        err;                            /* Number of errors in HMA access */

   printf( "HMA-Test  -  Please press a key to start the test..." );
   getch();
   printf ("\n\n" );

   /*-- Allocate HMA and test each memory location --------------------*/

   if ( XMSGetHMA(0xFFFF) )             /* HMA acquired? */
   {                                    /* Yes */
      if ( ( A20 = XMSIsA20On() ) == FALSE )/* Determine handler status */
         XMSA20OnGlobal();              /* Switch it on now */

      hmap = MK_FP( 0xFFFF, 0x0010 );   /* Pointer to HMA */
      err = 0;                          /* No errors up until now */
      for ( i = 1; i < 65520; ++i, ++hmap )
      {                                 /* Test each single memory location */
         printf( "\r Testing Memory Location: %u", i );
         *hmap = i % 256;               /* Write memory location */
         if ( *hmap != i % 256 )        /* And read out again */
         {                              /* Error! */
            printf( " ERROR!\n" );
            ++err;
         }
      }

      XMSReleaseHMA();                  /* Release HMA */
      if ( A20 == FALSE )               /* Was A20 handler on? */
         XMSA20OffGlobal();             /* No, switch it off */

      printf( "\n" );
      if ( err == 0 )                   /* Evaluate results of test */
         printf( "HMA ok, no defective memory location.\n" );
      else
         printf( "ATTENTION! %d defective memory locations detected " \
                 "in HMA!\n", err );
   }
   else
      printf( "ATTENTION! No access to HMA possible.\n" );
}


/****************************************************************
* EMBTest : Tests extended memory and demonstrates the calls of *
*           different XMS functions                            *
**-------------------------------------------------------------**
* Input  : None                                                *
*****************************************************************/

void EMBTest( void )

{
   long Adr;
   BYTE * barp;                         /* Pointer to 1K buffer */
```

```
int  i, j,                            /* Loop counter */
     err,                       /* Number of errors in HMA access */
     Handle,                       /* Handle for access to EMB */
     TotFree,                 /* Size of total free extended memory */
     MaxBl;                         /* Largest free block */

printf( "EMB Test  -  Please press a key to start the test..." );
getch();
printf( "\n" );

XMSQueryFree( &TotFree, &MaxBl ); /* Determine size of extended mem */
printf( "Total size of free extended memory (incl. HMA): %d KB\n",
         TotFree );
printf( "                     Largest free block: %d KB\n",
         MaxBl );

TotFree -= 64;               /* Calculate actual size without HMA */
if ( MaxBl >= TotFree )              /* Can the value be right? */
  MaxBl -= 64;                                    /* No */

if ( MaxBl > 0 )                    /* Still enough memory free? */
  {                                               /* Yes */
   Handle = XMSGetMem( MaxBl );
   printf( "%d KB allocated.\n", MaxBl );
   printf( "Handle     = %d\n", Handle );
   Adr = XMSLock( Handle );             /* Determine address */
   XMSUnlock( Handle );                    /* Unlock again */
   printf( "Start address = %ld (%d KB)\n", Adr, Adr >> 10 );

   barp = malloc( 1024 );           /* Buffer to heap allocated */
   err = 0;                          /* No errors up to now */

   /*-- Execute allocated EMB KB for KB and test --------------------*/

   for  ( i = 0; i < MaxBl; ++i )
    {
     printf( "\rKB Test: %d", i+1 );
     memset( barp, i % 255, 1024 );
     XMSCopy( 0, (long) ((void far *) barp),
              Handle, (long) i*1024, 512 );
     memset( barp, 255, 1024 );
     XMSCopy( Handle, (long) i*1024, 0,
              (long) ((void far *) barp), 512 );

     /*-- Compare copied buffer with expected result ----------------*/

     for ( j = 0; j < 1024; ++j )
      if ( *(barp+j) != i % 255 )
       {                                          /* Error! */
        printf( " ERROR!\n" );
        ++err;
        break;
       }
    }

   printf( "\n" );
   if ( err == 0 )                  /* Evaluate results of test */
    printf( "EMB ok, none of the tested 1K blocks were " \
            "defective.\n");
   else
    printf( "ATTENTION! %d defective 1K blocks detected in EMB\n",
             err );

   free( barp );                    /* Release buffer again */
```

```
   XMSFreeMem( Handle );                    /* Release EMB again */
  }
}

/********************************************************************
*                    M A I N   P R O G R A M                      *
********************************************************************/

void main( void )
{
 int VerNr,                               /* Version number */
     RevNr,                               /* Revision number */
     i;                                   /* Loop counter */

 for ( i = 1; i < 25; ++i )               /* Clear screen */
  printf ( "\n" );

 printf("XMSC  -  XMS Demo program by Michael Tischer\n\n" );
 if ( XMSInit() )
  {
   if ( XMSQueryVer( &VerNr, &RevNr ) )
    printf( "Access to HMA possible.\n" );
   else
    printf( "No access to HMA.\n" );
   printf( "XMS version number: %d.%d\n", VerNr / 100, VerNr % 100 );
   printf( "Revision number   : %d.%d\n\n", RevNr / 100, RevNr % 100 );
   HMATest();                               /* Test HMA */
   printf( "\n" );
   EMBTest();                       /* Test extended Memory */
  }
 else
  printf( "No XMS driver installed!\n" );
}
```

Assembler listing: XMSCA.ASM

```
;*******************************************************************;
;*                     X M S C A . A S M                          *;
;*---------------------------------------------------------------*;
;*   Task       : Assembly routine for linking to the C program  *;
;*                XMSC.C. Makes a routine for calling the XMS     *;
;*                driver available.                               *;
;*                Implementation here for the SMALL memory        *;
;*                model.                                          *;
;*---------------------------------------------------------------*;
;*   Author     : MICHAEL TISCHER                                 *;
;*   Developed on : 07/27/90                                      *;
;*   Last update : 07/27/90                                       *;
;*---------------------------------------------------------------*;
;*   Assembly   : MASM XMSCA;   or    TASM XMSCA;                *;
;*               ... then link with compiled C program XMSC.C    *;
;*******************************************************************;


;== Segment declarations for the C program =========================

IGROUP group _text                  ;Program segment
DGROUP group const,_bss, _data     ;Data segment
       assume CS:IGROUP, DS:DGROUP, ES:DGROUP, SS:DGROUP

CONST  segment word public 'CONST';This segment handles all
CONST  ends                        ;readable constants

_BSS   segment word public 'BSS'  ;This segment handles all uninitial-
_BSS   ends                        ;ized static variables

_DATA  segment word public 'DATA' ;This segment handles all initialized
                                   ;global and static variables
extrn _XMSPtr : dword              ;Reference to the XMS pointer

_DATA ends

;== Program ========================================================

_TEXT  segment byte public 'CODE' ;Program segment

public    _XMSCall


;-------------------------------------------------------------------
;-- XMSCall : General routine for calling an XMS function
;-- Call of C : void XMSCall( BYTE FktNr, XMSRegs *Xr )    with
;--            typedef struct { WORD AX, BX, DX, SI, Segment } XMSRegs;
;-- Return value: None
;-- Info      : - Before calling this procedure, load only those registers
;--               necessary for calling the specified function.
;--             - After the XMS function call, the contents of the various
;--               processor registers are copied to the corresponding
;--               components of the passed structre.
;--             - Before this procedure is called for the first time, the
;--               XMSInit must have been called successfully.

_XMSCall  proc near

sframe    struc               ;Structure for stack access
bp0       dw ?                ;Gets BP
ret_adr   dw ?                ;Return address to caller
fktnr     dw ?                ;Number of XMS function
xrptr     dw ?                ;Pointer to register structure
sframe    ends                ;End of structure

frame     equ [ bp - bp0 ]    ;Address structure elements

          push  bp            ;Prepare for parameter addressing
          mov   bp,sp         ;through BP register

          push  si            ;Push SI and DI onto stack
          push  di

          mov   cx,ds         ;Store DS in CX
          push  cx            ;and push onto stack
          mov   di,frame.xrptr ;Load function number
          mov   ah,byte ptr frame.fktnr ;Load pointer to structure
          mov   bx,[di+2]     ;Load register from components
          mov   dx,[di+4]     ;of structure
          mov   si,[di+6]
          mov   ds,[di+8]
          mov   es,cx         ;Load ES with DS
          call  es:[_XMSPtr]  ;Call XMS handler
          mov   cx,ds         ;Store DS in CX
          pop   ds            ;Get old DS from stack
          mov   di,frame.xrptr ;Load pointer to structure
          mov   [di],ax       ;Enter registers in the
          mov   [di+02],bx    ;components of the structure
          mov   [di+04],dx    ;
          mov   [di+06],si
          mov   [di+08],cx

          pop   di            ;Get SI and DI from stack
          pop   si

          pop   bp            ;Get BP from stack
          ret                 ;Return to C program

_XMSCall  endp

;-------------------------------------------------------------------

_text     ends                ;End of code segment
          end                 ;End of program
```

Chapter 13

Sound on the PC

Every PC has a built-in speaker that beeps when certain errors occur or when the keyboard buffer is full. The speaker can also generate other sounds. This chapter demonstrates sound generation through software.

How the PC generates sound

Tones occur when the cone of a speaker *oscillates* (moves back and forth). A single oscillation creates a click instead of a musical sound. If a group of oscillations occur in rapid succession, a tone is produced. The *pitch* (the note value) of a tone depends on the number of *cycles* (oscillations) that occur per second. The pitch of a tone in cycles per second is measured in Hertz. For example, if the speaker oscillates at a rate of 440 times per second, it generates a tone with a frequency of 440 Hertz. Certain pitches have specific note names assigned to them, such as A440 (the note that sounds at 440 Hertz). The following table shows the pitches and frequencies of tones generated by the PC. This range covers 8 octaves (almost the range of a full piano keyboard):

Octave 0		Octave 1		Octave 2		Octave 3	
C	16.35	C	32.70	C	65.41	C	130.81
C#	17.32	C#	34.65	C#	69.30	C#	138.59
D	18.35	D	36.71	D	73.42	D	146.83
D#	19.45	D#	38.89	D#	77.78	D#	155.56
E	20.60	E	41.20	E	82.41	E	164.81
F	21.83	F	43.65	F	87.31	F	174.61
F#	23.12	F#	46.25	F#	92.50	F#	185.00
G	24.50	G	49.00	G	98.00	G	196.00
G#	25.96	G#	51.91	G#	103.83	G#	207.65
A	27.50	A	55.00	A	110.00	A	220.00
A#	29.14	A#	58.27	A#	116.54	A#	233.08
B	30.87	B	61.74	B	123.47	B	246.94

Octave 0		Octave 1		Octave 2		Octave 3	
C	261.63	C	523.25	C	1046.50	C	2093.00
C#	277.18	C#	554.37	C#	1108.74	C#	2217.46
D	293.66	D	587.33	D	1174.66	D	2349.32
D#	311.13	D#	622.25	D#	1244.51	D#	2489.02
E	329.63	E	659.26	E	1328.51	E	2637.02
F	349.23	F	698.46	F	1396.91	F	2793.83
F#	369.99	F#	739.99	F#	1479.98	F#	2959.96
G	392.00	G	783.99	G	1567.98	G	3135.96
G#	415.30	G#	830.61	G#	1661.22	G#	3322.44
A	440.00	A	880.00	A	1760.00	A	3520.00
A#	466.16	A#	923.33	A#	1864.66	A#	3729.31
B	493.88	B	987.77	B	1975.53	B	3951.07

The speaker in the PC can generate frequencies from 1 Hertz up to more than 1,000,000 Hertz. However, most human ears are only capable of hearing frequencies between 20 and 20,000 Hertz. Also, PC speakers don't reproduce music very well because they play some tones louder than others. Since the speaker has no volume control, this effect cannot be changed.

A sound program should oscillate the speaker according to the frequency of the tones desired. The following is a rough outline of a possible sound generation program:

- Execute the instruction to move the cone forward, then undo the instruction (i.e., move the cone back to its original position). Repeat these steps in a loop so that it occurs as many times per second as required by the frequency of the tone being generated.

The previous procedure has several disadvantages:

- The execution speed of individual instructions depends on the processing speed of the computer.

- This program must be adjusted to the processing speed of individual computers.

- The tone becomes distorted when the tone production loop ends.

8253 timer

Every PC uses one particular chip for tone generation: The 8253 programmable timer, which actually maintains control of the internal clock. The 8253 can perform both timing and sound because of its ability to enable a certain action at a certain point in time. It senses timing from oscillations it receives from the PC's 8284 oscillator, which generates 1,193,180 impulses per second. The 8253 can then be instructed how many of these impulses it should wait before triggering a certain action. In the case of tone generation, this action consists of sending an impulse to the speaker. Before executing this action, the chip must be programmed for the particular frequency it should generate. The frequency must be converted from cycles per second into the number of oscillations coming from the oscillator. This is done with the help of the following formula:

```
counter = 1,193,180 / frequency
```

The result of this formula, the variable counter, is passed to the chip. As the formula demonstrates, the result for a high frequency is relatively low, and the result for a low frequency is relatively high. This makes sense because it tells the 8253 chip how many of the 1,193,180 cycles per second it must wait until it can send another signal to the speaker. The lower the value, the more often it sends a signal to move the speaker cone back and forth, which produces a higher tone.

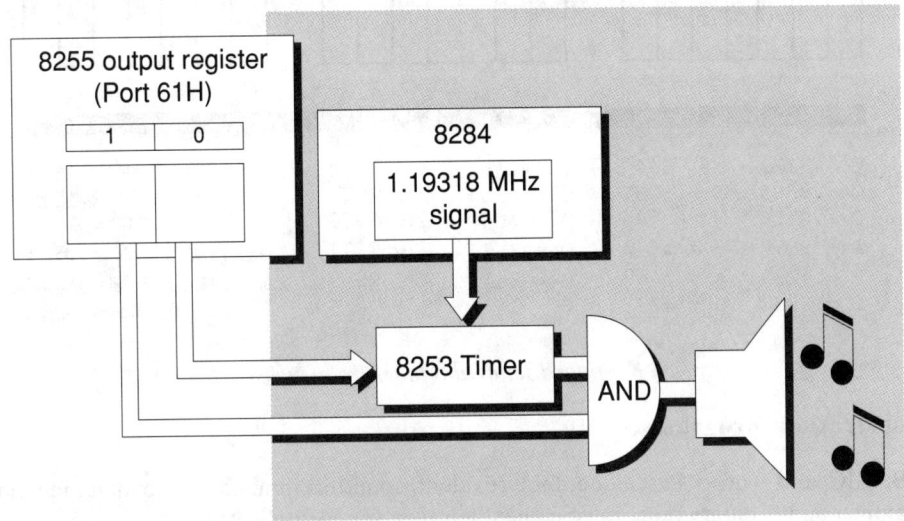

Creation of a tone on the PC

Ports and PC sound

Communication between the CPU and the 8253 occurs through ports. First the value 182 is sent to port 43H. This instructs the 8253 that it should start generating a signal as soon as the interval between individual signals has been passed. This interval is the value that was calculated with the previous formula. Since the 8253 stores this value internally as a 16-bit number (a value between 0 and 65,535), it limits the range of tones generated to frequencies between 18 and 1,193,180 Hertz. This number must be transmitted to port 42H. Since this is an 8-bit port, the 16 bits of this number cannot be transmitted simultaneously. First the least significant eight bits are transmitted, then the most significant eight bits are transmitted.

Now the second step occurs: The 8253 signal is sent to the speaker. The speaker access occurs through port 61H, which is connected to a programmable peripheral chip. The two lowest bits of this port must be set to 1 to transmit the 8253 signal to the speaker. Since the remaining six bits are used for other purposes, they cannot be changed. For this reason, the contents of port 61H must be read, the lowest two bits must be set to 1 (an OR combination with 3), and the resulting value must be returned to port 61H. A tone sounds, which ends only when the bits that were just set to 1 are reset again to 0.

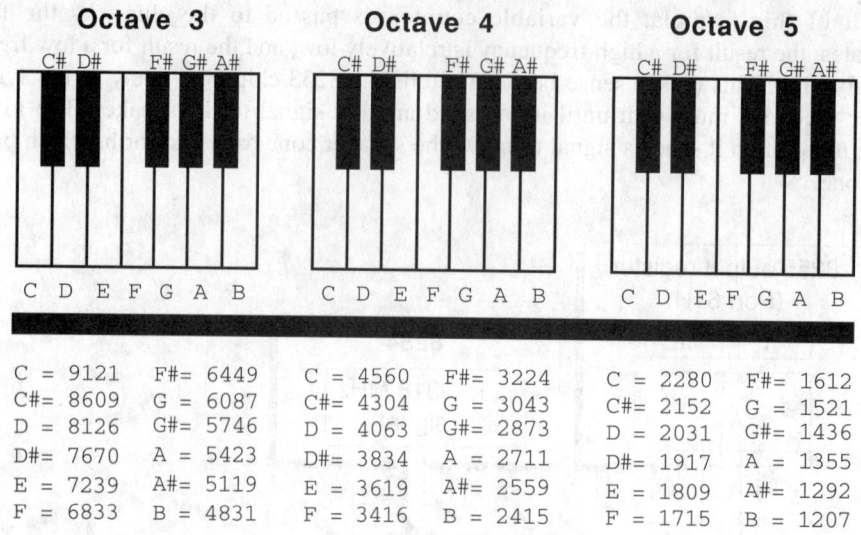

Keyboard setup and timer frequencies

Demonstration programs

GW-BASIC and Turbo Pascal contain resident sound commands. The machine language programmer and C programmer must create their own sound applications.

This chapter contains demonstration programs for both of these languages. These programs can be added to your own C or assembly language programs.

How they work

Both programs produce tones for specific time periods. This is done with the help of the timer interrupt 1CH, which is called by the timer interrupt 8H 18.2 times per second. When the tone generation routine executes, it receives the frequency of the tone and the tone's *duration* (length). The duration is measured in 18ths of a second, so the value 18 corresponds to a second and the value 9 corresponds to a half-second. This value is stored in a variable.

Immediately before activating the tone output, the interrupt routine of interrupt 1CH turns to a user-defined routine. This routine, called 18.2 times per second, decrements the tone duration in the variable during every call. When it reaches the value, the tone duration ends and the tone must be switched off. The routine allocates a variable to notify the actual sound routine of this end. The sound routine recognizes this immediately because it has been in a constant wait loop since switching on the tone. This loop simply monitors the contents of this variable. After recognizing the end of the tone, it stops the sound output and returns the timer interrupt to its old routine.

The sound routine requires the number assigned to this tone rather than the frequency itself. This number is related to the table containing the frequencies of octaves 3 to 5. The value 0 represents C of the third octave, 1 represents C-sharp, 2 represents D, 3 represents D-sharp, etc.

Both the C program and assembly language program demonstrate the sound routine by playing a scale over the course of two octaves, with each note sounding for a half a second. The machine language demo program and the sound routine are stored in one file. The C versions of these programs are split into two source code files. The C demo program contains the sound function call only, and the machine language program, which creates the sound, must be linked to the demonstration program.

Assembler listing: SOUNDA.ASM

```
;**************************************************************;
;*                    S O U N D A                          *;
;*----------------------------------------------------------*;
;*  Task     : Plays a scale between octaves 3 and 5 of the *;
;*             PC's musical range. This routine can be used *;
;*             for other applications                       *;
;*----------------------------------------------------------*;
;*  Author   : MICHAEL TISCHER                              *;
;*  Developed on : 08/06/1987                               *;
;*  Last update  : 05/26/89                                 *;
;*----------------------------------------------------------*;
;*  Assembly  : MASM SOUNDA;                                *;
;*              LINK SOUNDA;                                 *;
;*              EXE2BIN SOUNDA SOUNDA.COM                    *;
;*----------------------------------------------------------*;
;*  Call from DOS : SOUNDA                                  *;
;**************************************************************;

code    segment para 'CODE'    ;Definition of CODE segments

        org 100h               ;Starts at address 100H
                               ;directly following PSP

        assume cs:code, ds:code, es:code, ss:code

;== Program =================================================

sound   proc near

        ;-- Display message ---------------------------------

        mov ah,9               ;Function number for displaying string
        mov dx,offset initm    ;String's offset address
        int 21h                ;Call DOS interrupt 21H

        ;-- Play scale --------------------------------------

        xor bl,bl              ;Start at C of octave 3
        mov dl,9               ;for duration of 1/2 second
nextune: call play_tune        ;Play note
        inc bl                 ;Next note
        cmp bl,36              ;All notes in this octave played?
        jne nextune            ;NO --> Play next note

        ;-- Display end message -----------------------------

        mov ah,9               ;Function number for string display
        mov dx,offset endmes   ;String's offset address
        int 21h                ;Call DOS interrupt 21H

        mov ax,4C00h           ;Program ends when call to a DOS
        int 21h                ;function results in an error code
                               ;of 0
```

```
sound   endp

;== Main program data =======================================

initm   db 13,10,"SOUND (c) 1987 by Michael Tischer",13,10,13,10
        db "Your PC should now be playing a chromatic scale in the"
        db "3rd and 5th      ",13,10,"octaves of its range, if   "
        db "your PC speaker works.",13,10,"$"

endmes  db 13,10,"End",13,10,"$"

;-- PLAY_TUNE: Play a note ----------------------------------
;-- Input  : BL = Note number (relative to C of the 3rd octave)
;--          DL = Duration of note in 1/18 second increments
;-- Output : none
;-- Register : AX, CX, ES and FLAGS are changed
;-- Info   : Immediately after the tones, control returns to the
;--          calling routine

play_tune proc near

        push dx                ;Push DX and BX onto the stack
        push bx

        ;-- Adapt timer interrupt to user program -----------
        push dx                ;Push DX and BX onto stack
        push bx
        mov ax,351ch           ;Get address of time interrupt
        int 21h                ;Call DOS interrupt
        mov old_time,bx        ;Offset address of old interrupt
        mov old_time+2,es      ;and note segment address

        mov dx,offset sound_ti ;Offset address of new timer routine
        mov ax,251ch           ;Set new timer routine
        int 21h                ;Call DOS interrupt
        pop bx                 ;Pop BX and DX off of stack
        pop dx

        mov al,182             ;Prepare to play note
        out 43h,al             ;Send value to time command register
        xor bh,bh              ;BH for addressing note table  = 0
        shl bx,1               ;Double note number (fr. word table)
        mov ax,[note+bx]       ;Get tone value
        out 42h,al             ;LO-byte on timer counter register
        mov al,ah              ;Transfer HI-byte to AL
        out 42h,al             ;and to timer counter register
        in al,61h              ;Read speaker control bit
        or al,11b              ;Lowest two bits enable speaker
        mov s_ende,1           ;Note still has to be played
        mov s_counter,dl       ;Play note for duration
        out 61h,al             ;Disable speaker

play:   cmp s_ende,0           ;Note finished?
        jne play               ;(N) --> Wait
```

707

```
            in    al,61h          ;Read speaker control bit
            and   al,11111100b     ;Clear lowest two bits
            out   61h,al          ;Disable speaker

            ;-- Reactivate old timer interrupt --------------------------

            mov   cx,ds           ;Note DS
            mov   ax,251ch         ;Set function no. for intrrpt vector
            lds   dx,dword ptr old_time ;Load old address into DS:DX
            int   21h             ;Call DOS interrupt
            mov   ds,cx           ;Return DS

            pop   bx              ;Pop BX and DX off of stack
            pop   dx
            ret                   ;Return to calling program

play_tune endp

;-- new timer interrupt -----------------------------------------------

sound_ti  proc far              ;Call 18 times per second

            dec   cs:s_counter     ;Decrement counter
            jne   st_ende          ;If still >0, end
```

```
            mov   cs:s_ende,0     ;Signal note end
st_ende:    jmp   dword ptr cs:[old_time] ;Goto old timer interrupt

sound_ti  endp

;== Variable set needed by the routines ===================================

old_time  dw  (?),(?)                 ;Address of old timer interrupt
s_counter db  (?)                     ;counter for note duration in 1/18
                                      ; second increments
s_ende    db  (?)                     ;Displays whether note already played
note      dw  9121,8609,8126,7670 ;Note values for octave 3
          dw  7239,6833,6449,6087
          dw  5746,5423,5119,4831
          dw  4560,4304,4063,3834 ;Note values for octave 4
          dw  3619,3416,3224,3043
          dw  2873,2711,2559,2415
          dw  2280,2152,2031,1917 ;Note values for octave 5
          dw  1809,1715,1612,1521
          dw  1436,1355,1292,1207

;== End =================================================================

code      ends                   ;End of CODE segment
          end   sound            ;End of the Assembler-Program
```

C listing: SOUNDC.C

Here's the C program to call the sound function and the assembly language listing of the C sound function.

```
/*********************************************************/
/*                  S O U N D C                        */
/*-----------------------------------------------------*/
/*  Task       : Plays a scale between octaves 3 and 5 of the  */
/*               PC musical range, using an assembler function */
/*-----------------------------------------------------*/
/*  Author     : MICHAEL TISCHER                       */
/*  Developed on : 08/15/1987                          */
/*  Last update  : 05/26/1989                          */
/*-----------------------------------------------------*/
/*  (MICROSOFT C)                                      */
/*  Creation   : CL /AS SOUNDC.C                       */
/*               LINK SOUNDC SOUNDCA;                  */
/*  Call       : SOUNDC                                */
/*-----------------------------------------------------*/
/*  (BORLAND TURBO C)                                  */
/*  Creation   : Create a project file listing the following: */
/*               soundc                                */
/*               soundca.obj                           */
/*  Options    : Before compiling and linking, select the */
/*               Options menu and Linker option. Under the */
/*               Linker options menu, make sure that the */
/*               Case sensitive link option is set to Off */
/*********************************************************/

/*== Function declaration from the assembler module ==================*/

extern void Sound();        /* Add the external assembler routine  */

/*********************************************************/
/**                 MAIN  PROGRAM                     **/
```

```
/*********************************************************/

void main()

{
  int Note;

  printf("\nSOUND (c) 1987 by Michael Tischer\n\n");
  printf("Your PC should now be playing a musical scale in the 3rd & ");
  printf(" 5th octaves of\nits range. If you aren't hearing the notes");
  printf(" your PC's speaker may be damaged.\n\n");

  for (Note = 0; Note < 35; Sound(Note++, 9)) /* Play a note once each */
    ;                                         /* 1/2 second           */
  printf("End\n");
}
```

Assembler listing: SOUNDCA.ASM

```
;*********************************************************;
;*                  S O U N D C A                       *;
;*-----------------------------------------------------*;
;*  Task        : Creates a function suitable for inclusion in  *;
;*                C codes, which enables C to play notes in the *;
;*                3rd, 4th and 5th PC musical octave     *;
;*-----------------------------------------------------*;
;*  Author      : MICHAEL TISCHER                        *;
;*  Developed on : 08/15/1987                            *;
;*  Last update  : 05/26/1989                            *;
;*-----------------------------------------------------*;
;*  assembly    : MASM SOUNDCA;                          *;
;*********************************************************;

IGROUP group _text              ;Merging of program segment
DGROUP group const,_bss, _data  ;Merging of data segment
      assume CS:IGROUP, DS:DGROUP, ES:DGROUP, SS:DGROUP

      public _Sound             ;Make function public (accessible to
                                ;other programs)

CONST segment word public 'CONST';This segment denotes all read-only
CONST ends                      ;constants

_BSS  segment word public 'BSS' ;This segment denotes all static, non-
_BSS  ends                      ;initialized variables

_DATA segment word public 'DATA' ;This segment contains all initialized
                                ;global and static variables

old_time dw (?),(?)             ;Address of old timer interrupt
s_counter db (?)                ;Counts duration of notes in
                                ;1/18 second increments

s_endit   db (?)                ;Indicates whether note already played
tones  dw 9121,8609,8126,7670   ;Note values for octave 3
       dw 7239,6833,6449,6087
       dw 5746,5423,5119,4831
       dw 4560,4304,4063,3834   ;Note values for octave 4
       dw 3619,3416,3224,3043
       dw 2873,2711,2559,2415
       dw 2280,2152,2031,1917   ;Note values for octave 5
       dw 1809,1715,1612,1521
       dw 1436,1355,1292,1207

_DATA ends

;== Program ===========================================

_TEXT segment byte public 'CODE' ;Program msegment

;-- SOUND: Plays a note -------------------------------
;-- Call from C : Sound((int) Note, (int) Duration);
;-- Output     : none
;-- Info       : Note is the number of the note relative to 3rd octave
;--               C
;--               Duration=duration of the note in 1/18-sec. increments

_Sound   proc near

         push bp                 ;Push BP onto stack
         mov  bp,sp              ;Transfer SP to BP
```

```
;-- Modify timer interrupt for user application ----------
         mov  word ptr cs:setds+1,ds ;Store DS for new timer interrupt
         mov  ax,351ch           ;Get timer interrupt's address
         int  21h                ;Call DOS interrupt
         mov  old_time,bx        ;Note offset address and segment
         mov  old_time+2,es      ;address of old interrupt
         mov  word ptr cs:stjump+1,bx ;Save for new timer interrupt
         mov  word ptr cs:stjump+3,es ;
         mov  bx,ds              ;Place DS in BX
         push cs                 ;Push CS onto stack
         pop  ds                 ;and pop off DS
         mov  dx,offset sound_ti ;Offset address of new timer routine
         mov  ax,251ch           ;Set new timer routine
         int  21h                ;Call DOS interrupt
         mov  ds,bx              ;Restore DS

         mov  al,182             ;Get ready to generate tone
         out  43h,al             ;Send value to timer command register

         mov  bx,[bp+4]          ;Get note
         xor  bh,bh              ;BH for addressing of note table = 0
         shl  bx,1               ;Divide note number (for word table)
         mov  ax,[tones+bx]      ;Get note value
         out  42h,al             ;Pass low byte to timer counter
register
         mov  al,ah              ;Pass high byte to AL
         out  42h,al             ;and to timer counter register
         in   al,61h             ;Read speaker control bit
         or   al,11b             ;Two lowest bits activate speaker
         mov  s_endit,1          ;Still have to play note
         mov  dl,[bp+6]          ;Get note duration
         mov  s_counter,dl       ;and store it
         out  61h,al             ;Turn on speaker

play:    cmp  s_endit,0          ;Note ended?
         jne  play               ;NO --> wait

         in   al,61h             ;Read speaker control bit
         and  al,11111100b       ;Clear two lowest bits to
         out  61h,al             ;disable speaker

         ;-- re-activate original timer interrupt ----------------
         mov  cx,ds              ;Note DS
         mov  ax,251ch           ;Set function no. for interrupt vector
         lds  dx,dword ptr old_time ;Load old address into DS:DX
         int  21h                ;Call DOS interrupt
         mov  ds,cx              ;Return DS

         mov  sp,bp              ;Restore stack pointer
         pop  bp                 ;Pop BP off of stack
         ret                     ;Return to calling program

_Sound   endp

;-- new timer interrupt -------------------------------------

sound_ti proc far               ;Call this 18 times per second

         push ax                 ;Push AX and DS onto stack
         push ds
setds:   mov  ax,0000h           ;Transfer C to DS
         mov  ds,ax
         dec  s_counter          ;Decrememt time counter
```

```
          jne  st_endit         ;If still unequal to 0 then end
          mov  s_endit,0        ;Signal end of note duration
st_endit: pop  ds               ;Pop value off of DS (reset to old
value)
          pop  ax               ;Get AX from stack again

stjump:   db   0EAh,0,0,0,0     ;FAR-JUMP to old timer interrupt

sound_ti  endp

;== Ende ==============================================================

_text     ends                  ;End of program segment
          end                   ;End of assembler source
```

Chapter 14

System Configuration and Processor Types

Knowing the configuration of a computer is often important. Frequently, a program must know the number of serial ports, the size of the RAM memory, or whether there is a math coprocessor.

In this chapter we'll show you how to determine various configuration data with the help of two ROM-BIOS interrupts. You'll also learn how to determine the processor type and coprocessor type of a PC.

14.1 Determining the Configuration using the BIOS

The ROM-BIOS has two interrupts for reading configuration information: interrupt 11H and interrupt 12H. Each interrupt contains one function. With these interrupts you can obtain information about the hardware environment of a PC and determine the size of the RAM memory.

Unfortunately, even after using these interrupts, many of your questions will still be unanswered, as the following two sections will demonstrate.

14.1.1   Reading the Hardware Environment

Call BIOS interrupt 11H to obtain information about the hardware environment of a computer, the number of serial and parallel ports, disk drives, and the DMA controller.

Unlike many other BIOS interrupts, the contents of the processor register are unimportant at the time this interrupt is called because a function number or any other argument isn't necessary. This interrupt consists of only a single function, which returns the desired information about the configuration in the AX register.

As the following figure shows, after the function call, the contents of the AX register represent a bit field, whose fields provide information about various components of the hardware. However, this information is limited. Since this interrupt was introduced with the first PC and its original BIOS, it reflects the modest hardware environment that is typical of the early PCs.

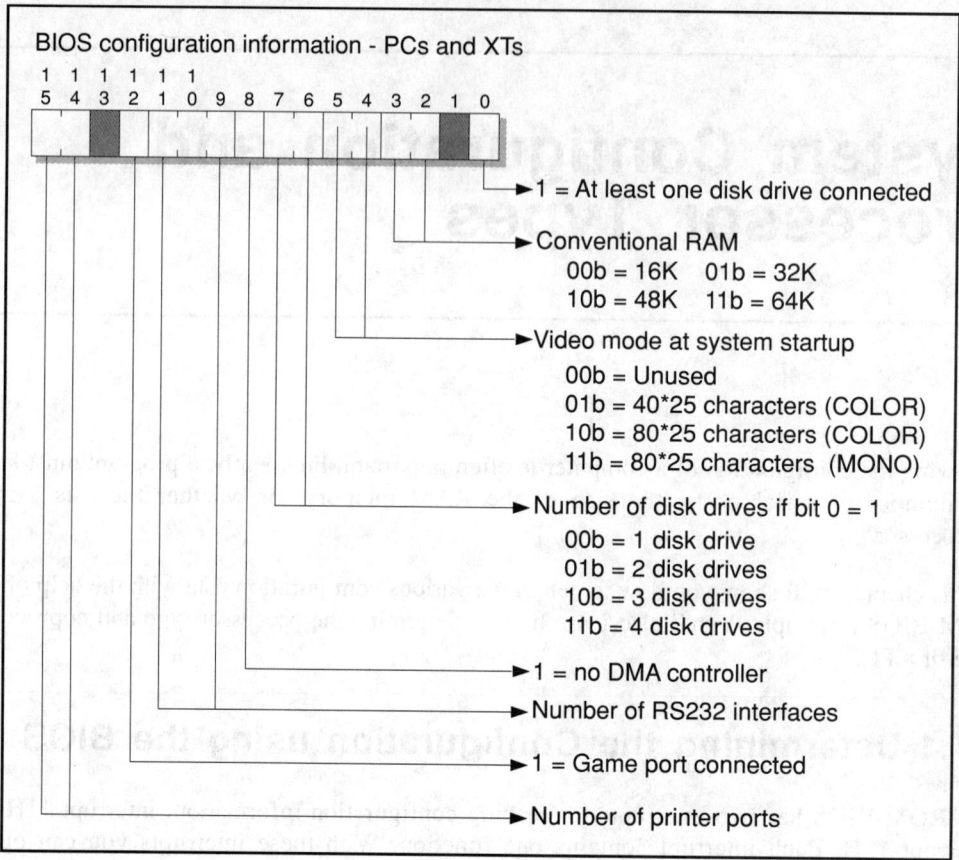

BIOS configuration information - PCs and XTs

1 = At least one disk drive connected

Conventional RAM
00b = 16K   01b = 32K
10b = 48K   11b = 64K

Video mode at system startup

00b = Unused
01b = 40*25 characters (COLOR)
10b = 80*25 characters (COLOR)
11b = 80*25 characters (MONO)

Number of disk drives if bit 0 = 1

00b = 1 disk drive
01b = 2 disk drives
10b = 3 disk drives
11b = 4 disk drives

1 = no DMA controller

Number of RS232 interfaces

1 = Game port connected

Number of printer ports

Although the bit assignment above applies to both PCs and XTs, it differs from the structure of the configuration word returned by the AT and its descendants. When the AT was introduced, this interrupt was revised to use the advancements in hardware technology and the improved PC equipment.

However, this interrupt doesn't provide important information, such as the processor type, the kind of keyboard, and the presence of a mouse or EMS memory. So, if you want to determine whether a mouse is present or what kind of video card is installed, refer to the appropriate chapters in this book.

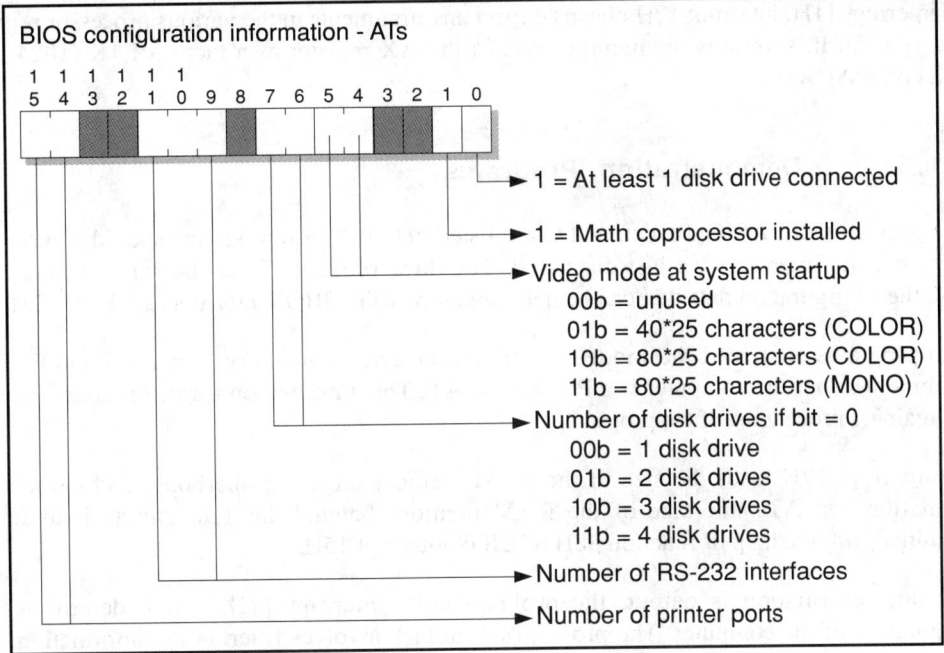

BIOS configuration information - ATs

1 = At least 1 disk drive connected

1 = Math coprocessor installed

Video mode at system startup
00b = unused
01b = 40*25 characters (COLOR)
10b = 80*25 characters (COLOR)
11b = 80*25 characters (MONO)

Number of disk drives if bit = 0
00b = 1 disk drive
01b = 2 disk drives
10b = 3 disk drives
11b = 4 disk drives

Number of RS-232 interfaces

Number of printer ports

Don't use this function to prompt for the current video mode because it only specifies the video mode that was switched on when the system was running. You should use function 0FH of interrupt 10H, which returns the number of the current video mode.

At the end of this chapter, we'll present a sample program that demonstrates how to use this interrupt.

14.1.2   Determining RAM Configuration using the BIOS

Interrupt 11H, which hasn't changed since 1981, provides only the size of the RAM memory on the motherboard. However, calling interrupt 12H provides the size of the entire RAM memory. When the system boots up, the size of the RAM on the motherboard and any existing memory expansion boards are added up and saved. On PCs and XTs, this information is taken from the settings of the single DIP switches on each memory board, while on ATs the information is read from one of the 64 memory locations of the battery operated clock.

However, this method only determines the size of the RAM memory below the 1 megabyte boundary. This is sufficient for PCs and XTs because the address space of their processors is limited to 1 megabyte. So, they cannot have any additional RAM memory.

ATs and their descendants, however, don't fit into this category; they have processors capable of managing up to 16 megabytes of memory. On these computers you can install additional memory, which interrupt 12H cannot detect. So you should use function 88H of BIOS interrupt 15H instead. This function reads the size of the memory above the 1 megabyte boundary.

Like interrupt 11H, interrupt 12H doesn't expect any arguments in the various processor registers when you call it. It returns the memory size in the AX register as a factor of 1K (1024 bytes instead of 1000 bytes).

14.1.3   Demonstration Programs

Three programs in BASIC, Pascal, and C are listed below. These programs should demonstrate how to use the interrupts we just discussed. The three programs have the same structure and output the configuration data that can be determined by using BIOS interrupts 11H and 12H.

These programs first read the model identification byte in memory location F000:FFFE to determine whether the computer is a PC, XT, or AT. This information forms the foundation for the remaining procedures of the program.

Then interrupt 12H reads the size of the RAM memory on the motherboard and outputs this information. On ATs, the size of the RAM memory beyond the 1 megabyte boundary is determined with the help of function 88H of BIOS interrupt 15H.

After this information is output, the program calls interrupt 11H, which determines the configuration of the computer. The program's final task involves filtering the information from the various bit fields.

To keep the program as short as possible, we only used bits that are identical in both the configuration word of the PC/XT and the AT. For example, on ATs, the information about whether the computer has a mathematical coprocessor isn't used. This information isn't always reliable and the programs from Section 14.2 are much better at determining it.

BASIC listing: CONFIGB.BAS

```
'*********************************************************
'*                      CONFIGB                         *
'*-----------------------------------------------------*
'* Task      : Displays the configuration of the PC.    *
'*             QuickBASIC and the QB.LIB must be loaded using *
'*             QB /L QB                                  *
'*             before loading and running this file.     *
'*-----------------------------------------------------*
'* Author    : Michael Tischer                          *
'* Developed on : 06/10/1991                            *
'* Last update  : 01/07/1992                            *
'*********************************************************

DECLARE SUB PrintConfig ()
DECLARE FUNCTION GetWord& (Register AS INTEGER)

'$INCLUDE: 'QB.BI'              'Contains register declarations

CONST TRUE = -1                           ' Define
CONST FALSE = NOT TRUE                     'constants

CALL PrintConfig               'Display configuration
END

'*********************************************************
'* GetWord : Converts an integer number (2 bytes plus leading *
```

```
'*           character) into a long integer, which can be modified by *
'*           bit operations to perform math functions(\, MOD).  *
'* Input   : See below                                  *
'* Output  : See below                                  *
'*********************************************************

FUNCTION GetWord& (Register AS INTEGER)

IF Register <= 0 THEN                           'BIT 16 set?
  GetWord = 65536 + Register   'Return pos. equivalent of a neg. number
ELSE                                           'BIT 16 not set?
  GetWord = Register                'Integer number is positive
END IF
END FUNCTION

'*********************************************************
'* PrintConfig : Displays PC configuration              *
'* Input       : None                                   *
'* Output      : None                                   *
'* Info        : Configuration varies with the type of PC *
'*********************************************************

SUB PrintConfig

DIM AT AS INTEGER                               'Is PC an AT?
DIM Word AS LONG                               'Get a word
DIM Register AS RegType         'Processor registers for interrupt call

CLS                                            'Clear screen
DEF SEG = &HF000         'Segment address of model identification byte
```

714

```
IF PEEK(&HFFFE) = &HFC THEN               'Determine PC type
    AT = TRUE                             'It is an AT
ELSE                                      'It is not an AT
    AT = FALSE
END IF
PRINT "CONFIGB  -  (c) 1987, 1991 by Michael Tischer": PRINT
PRINT "Your PC Configuration "
PRINT "----------------------------------------------------------"
PRINT "PC type            : ";
SELECT CASE PEEK(&HFFFE)                  'Read PC type and display
    CASE &HFF                            '&HFF is a PC
        PRINT "PC"
    CASE &HFE                            '&HFE is an XT
        PRINT "XT"
    CASE &HFC                            '&HFC is an AT
        PRINT "AT or higher"
END SELECT
CALL INTERRUPT(&H12, Register, Register)  'RAM from BIOS interrupt
PRINT "Conventional RAM  :"; Register.ax; "K"
IF AT THEN                               'If the PC is an AT
    Register.ax = &H8800       'Read function number for extended memory
    CALL INTERRUPT(&H15, Register, Register)'Call BIOS cassette interrupt
    PRINT "Additional RAM     :"; Register.ax; "K over 1 megabyte"
END IF
CALL INTERRUPT(&H11, Register, Register)  'Call BIOS configuration
PRINT "Default video mode : ";           'configuration interrupt
SELECT CASE (Register.ax MOD 256) AND 48   'Get video mode
    CASE 0
        PRINT "Undefined"
    CASE 16
        PRINT "40x25 character color card"
    CASE 32
        PRINT "80x25 character color card"
    CASE 48
        PRINT "80x25 character mono card"
END SELECT
Word = GetWord(Register.ax)                'Convert integer to word
PRINT "Disk drives       :"; (((Word MOD 256) \ 64) AND 3) + 1
PRINT "Serial   interfaces :"; ((Word \ 256) \ 2) AND 3
PRINT "Parallel interfaces :"; (Word \ 256) \ 64
END SUB
```

Pascal listing: CONFIGP.PAS

```pascal
{***********************************************************************}
{*                       C O N F I G P                              *}
{*-------------------------------------------------------------------*}
{*    Task       : Displays the configuration of the PC.            *}
{*-------------------------------------------------------------------*}
{*    Author     : Michael Tischer                                  *}
{*    Developed on : 07/07/87                                       *}
{*    Last update  : 01/29/92                                       *}
{***********************************************************************}
program CONFIGP;
Uses Crt, Dos;                          { Add CRT and DOS units }
{***********************************************************************}
{* PrintConfig: Displays PC configuration.                           *}
{* Input   : None                                                    *}
{* Output  : None                                                    *}
{* Info    : Configuration varies with the type of PC.               *}
{***********************************************************************}
procedure PrintConfig;
var AT  : boolean;                      { Is PC an AT? }
    Regs : Registers;     { Processor registers for interrupt call }

begin
ClrScr;                                 { Clear screen }
if Mem[$F000:$FFFE] = $FC then AT := true        { Test for AT, }
                     else AT := false;     { PC or XT    }
writeln('CONFIGP  -  (c) 1987, 1992 by Michael Tischer');
writeln;
writeln('Your PC Configuration ');
writeln('---------------------------------------------------');
write('PC Type          : ');
case Mem[$F000:$FFFE] of             { Read PC type and display }
  $FF : writeln('PC');                      { $FF (FFH) is a PC }
  $FE : writeln('XT');                      { $FE (FEH) is an XT }
  else writeln('AT or higher')              { $FC (FCH) is an AT }
end;

Intr($12, Regs);                        { RAM from BIOS interrupt }
writeln('Conventional RAM   = ',Regs.ax,' K');
if AT then                              { Is the PC an AT? }
  begin                                        { Yes }
    Regs.ah := $88;       { Read function number for extended memory }
    Intr($15, Regs );                  { Call BIOS cassette interrupt }
    writeln('Additional RAM     : ',Regs.ax,' K over 1 megabyte');
  end;
Intr($11, Regs);                { Call BIOS configuration interrupt }
write('Default video mode  : ');
case Regs.al and 48 of                       { Get video mode }
  0 : writeln('Undefined');
 16 : writeln('40x25 character color card');
 32 : writeln('80x25 character color card');
 48 : writeln('80x25 character mono card')
end;
writeln('Disk drives        : ', succ(Regs.al shr 6 and 3));
writeln('Serial interfaces   : ', Regs.ah shr 1 and 3);
writeln('Parallel interfaces : ', Regs.ah shr 6)
end;
{***********************************************************************}
{*                      MAIN PROGRAM                                *}
{***********************************************************************}
begin
PrintConfig;                            { Display configuration }
end.
```

715

C listing: CONFIGC.C

```
/*********************************************************************/
/*                      C O N F I G C                             */
/*-----------------------------------------------------------------*/
/*   Task         : Displays the configuration of the PC.          */
/*-----------------------------------------------------------------*/
/*   Author       : Michael Tischer                                */
/*   Developed on  : 08/13/87                                      */
/*   Last update   : 01/28/92                                      */
/*-----------------------------------------------------------------*/
/*   Memory model  : SMALL                                         */
/*********************************************************************/

/*== Add include files ============================================*/

#include <dos.h>
#include <stdio.h>

/*== Type definitions =============================================*/

typedef unsigned char BYTE;                    /* Create a byte */

/*== Macros =======================================================*/

#ifdef MK_FP
  #undef MK_FP
#endif

#ifdef peekb
  #undef peekb
#endif

#define MK_FP(seg, ofs) ((void far *) ((unsigned long) (seg)<<16|(ofs)))
#define peekb(seg, ofs) *((BYTE far *) MK_FP(seg, ofs))

/*== Constants ====================================================*/

#define TRUE  ( 0 == 0 )                   /* Constants make reading */
#define FALSE ( 0 == 1 )                   /* program code easier    */

/*********************************************************************/
/* CLS: Clears current screen and places cursor in upper-left corner.*/
/*   Input  : None                                                 */
/*   Output : None                                                 */
/*********************************************************************/

void Cls( void )
{
  union REGS Register;       /* Register variables for interrupt call */

  Register.h.ah = 6;               /* Function number for scroll up */
  Register.h.al = 0;                              /* 0 = Clear */
  Register.h.bh = 7;               /* White text on black background */
  Register.x.cx = 0;               /* Upper-left corner of screen */
  Register.h.dh = 24;              /* Bottom-right screen */
  Register.h.dl = 79;              /* coordinates */
  int86(0x10, &Register, &Register);    /* Call BIOS video interrupt */

  Register.h.ah = 2;       /* Function number for Set cursor position */
  Register.h.bh = 0;                       /* Screen page 0 */
  Register.x.dx = 0;               /* Upper-left screen coordinates */
  int86(0x10, &Register, &Register);    /* Call BIOS video interrupt */
}
```

```
/*********************************************************************/
/* PRINTCONFIG: Displays PC configuration.                         */
/*   Input   : None                                                */
/*   Output  : None                                                */
/*   Info    : Configuration varies with the type of PC            */
/*********************************************************************/

void PrintConfig( void )
{
  union REGS Register;       /* Register variables for interrupt call */
  BYTE AT;                                      /* AT or higher? */

  Cls();                                        /* Clear screen */
  AT = (peekb(0xF000, 0xFFFE) == 0xFC);
  printf("CONFIGC  -  (c) 1987, 92 by Michael Tischer\n\n");
  printf("Your PC Configuration \n");
  printf("-----------------------------------------------------------\n");
  printf("PC type           : ");

  switch( peekb(0xF000, 0xFFFE) )        /* Read PC type and display */
  {
    case 0xFF : printf("PC\n");              /* 0xFF (FFH) is a PC */
                break;
    case 0xFE : printf("XT\n");              /* 0xFE (FEH) is an XT */
                break;
    default   : printf("AT or higher\n");    /* 0xFC (FCH) is an AT */
                break;
  }
  printf("Conventional RAM     : ");
  int86(0x12, &Register, &Register);         /* RAM from BIOS interrupt */
  printf("%d K\n",Register.x.ax);               /* Display RAM */
  if ( AT )                                   /* Is the PC an AT? */
  {                                           /* Yes */
    Register.h.ah = 0x88;  /* Read function number for extended memory */
    int86(0x15, &Register, &Register);        /* Get RAM size */
    printf("Additional RAM     : %d K over 1 megabyte\n",
Register.x.ax);
  }
  int86(0x11, &Register, &Register);         /* Call BIOS configuration */
  printf("Default video mode   : ");         /* interrupt */
  switch(Register.x.ax & 48)
  {
    case  0 : printf("Undefined\n");
              break;
    case 16 : printf("40x25 character color card\n");
              break;
    case 32 : printf("80x25 character color card\n");
              break;
    case 48 : printf("80x25 character mono card\n");
              break;
  }
  printf("Disk drives          : %d\n", (Register.x.ax >> 6 & 3) + 1);
  printf("Serial interfaces    : %d\n", Register.x.ax >> 9 & 0x03);
  printf("Parallel interfaces  : %d\n\n", Register.x.ax >> 14);
}

/*********************************************************************/
/**                    MAIN PROGRAM                              **/
/*********************************************************************/

void main()
{
  PrintConfig();                             /* Display configuration */
}
```

14.2 Determining Processor and Coprocessor

Today there are numerous programs available that provide information about the configuration or layout of a PC. Besides the size of the RAM memory, the installed version of DOS, etc., you'll also learn which processor the computer uses and which coprocessor assists this processor.

This information can be very important, for example, when developing programs in high level languages because code generation can be adapted to a particular processor. Both the Microsoft C compilers and their Borland counterparts allow special code generation for the 8088, the 80286, or the 80386. This enables you to fully use the processor's capabilities and the command set. Generally this noticeably increases the performance of programs that work with large data sets.

One way you can use this capability is by compiling each of the processor types separately. Also, you can develop a program, which is used as a loader for the actual program, that prompts for the processor type after starting. Then it executes the particular program (of the three programs) that was compiled for the relevant processor. You can also do this with the numerical coprocessor.

However, now we must decide how to determine the installed processor. Unlike other configuration data, this cannot be determined by calling a BIOS or DOS function. Also, since there isn't a corresponding machine language command, which causes the processor to reveal its identity, you must use a complicated procedure that, according to statements of the hardware manufacturers, shouldn't even work.

This procedure involves a test that's based on how certain machine language commands are executed. Although the processors from the 8086 to the 80486 are software compatible, small changes were made in the logic of some commands during the development of this processor series. Since these changes are noticeable only in rare situations, a program developed for the 8088 will also run on all other processors of the Intel 80xxx series. So if you intentionally put the processor in this type of situation, you can establish the identity of the processor as a result of its behavior.

Since these differences are only noticeable on the machine language level, you can write such a test program only in machine language or assembly language. At the end of this chapter, this type of test routine is presented in the form of two assembly modules for linking to Pascal and C programs. We'll discuss how they operate and the differences between the individual processors in the following sections.

14.2.1   Determining the Processor Type

The test routine for determining the installed processor consists of several tests that can be used to differentiate the individual processor types. A test will run only if the preceding test fails.

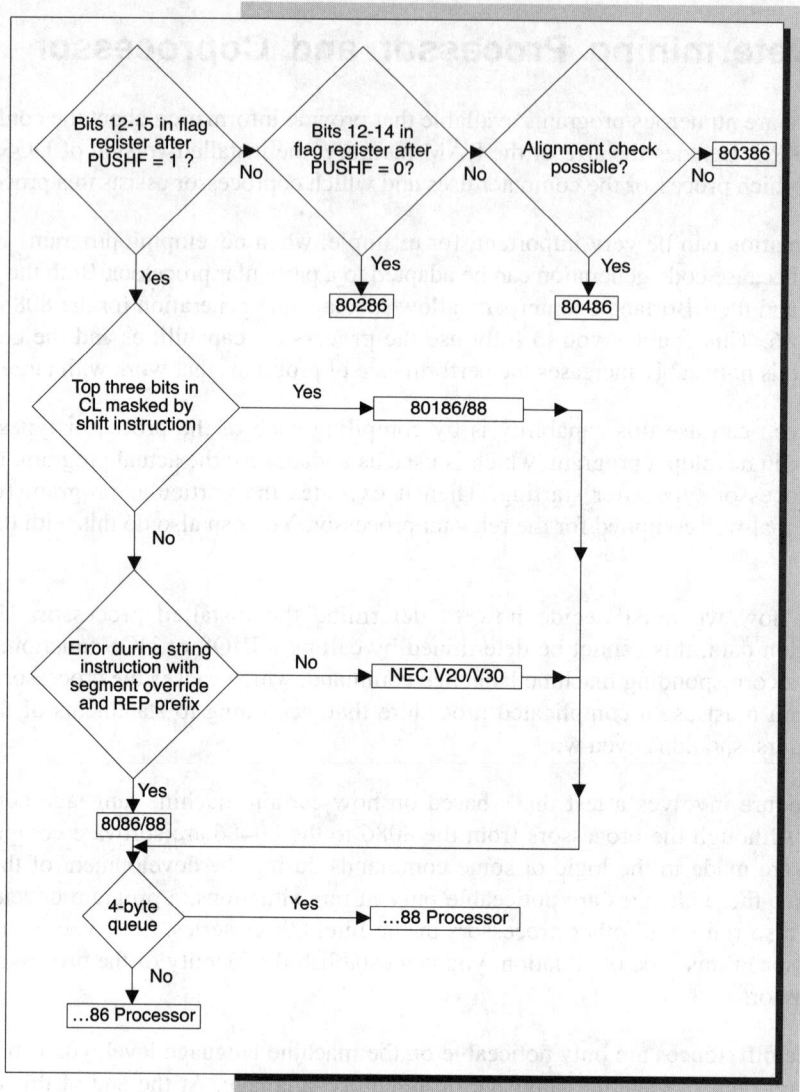

Determining the processor type

Varying layout of the flag register

The first test is based on the varying layout of the flag register on the different processors. Although the meaning of bits 0 to 11 are identical for all processors, bits 12 through 15 don't have a meaning until the 80286 (through the introduction of Protected Mode). The commands PUSHF (place contents of flag register on stack) and POPF (retrieve contents of flag register from stack) take this circumstance into account. These commands always set bits 12 to 15 of the flag register to 1 on all Intel processors up to the 80188. Beginning with the 80286, the processors behave differently.

The first test uses this by placing the value 0 on the stack and then using the POPF command to fetch it back to the flag register. Since there isn't a command for reading the contents of bits 12

718

through 15 in the flag register, the PUSHF command immediately places the flag register on the stack. However, this only happens so the POP AX command in the AX register can send for the flag register. It's easy to test the layout of bits 12 to 15 in the AX register. If all four bits are set, it cannot be a 80286 or any of its descendants, and the routine continues with the next test.

If all four bits aren't set, then the list of possible processors is limited to the 80286 and its descendants. Since the 80286 processes the POPF command differently than the 80386/80486, it's easy to distinguish the 80286 from its descendants. The entire procedure is repeated again, with the value 7000H, instead of 0, being placed on the stack. When the POPF command loads the flag register, it causes bits 12 to 14 to be set to 1.

However, if these bits no longer contain the value 1 when retrieving the flag register from the stack, the processor must be an 80286, which automatically sets these three bits to 0, unlike its successors. If this test indicates that the processor is an 80286, the test routine ends.

Distinguishing the 80386 and 80486

If the processor isn't an 80286, you must determine whether it's an 80386 or an 80486. Again, you can use the flag register to do this because the 80486 has a new flag in the extended flag register EFlags. This flag, which is called "Alignment Check", is located at bit position 15. When this flag is set, the processor checks all memory accesses with the specified offset address. If the address isn't a multiple of four, the processor releases a special interrupt, called an Exception.

If the Alignment Check is operating, this will be the fate of the subsequent machine language command, for example, because it reads out the contents of memory location 102. Since 102 isn't a multiple of four, it isn't aligned. This also applies to memory location 77, which is addressed in the following command:

```
mov  al,[102]
shl  word ptr [77],3
```

Both of these commands would execute an alignment exception, which causes an exception handler to be executed the same way as an interrupt. The operating system usually intercepts this exception handler to acknowledge the misalignment. Depending on the user's judgment, the program can either abort or continue executing the command.

Access to memory on the 80486 is especially fast when the data to be processed is located at an offset address that's divisible by four. So, if an offset address isn't divisible by four, memory access on the 80486 takes a long time. To prevent this from happening, an operating system can enable the alignment check so it's aware of programs that access data which are misaligned during execution.

The operating system considers the release of the exception as an opportunity to send a warning message to the developer. In this way, the alignment check can help optimize programs for the 80486.

The results of the alignment check make it easy to distinguish between the 80386 and the 80486. Since the 80386 isn't familiar with the Alignment flag, it doesn't change its contents. So, you should first read and save the previous contents of the EFlags to reset the alignment bit.

Then read the EFLags register again to check whether the contents of this flag have actually changed. If the contents have changed, you know that you're working with an 80486.

However, remember to set the Alignment flag back to its original value when you're finished. Since the EFlags register can be loaded and manipulated only from the stack, there are some other dangers. The following machine language commands demonstrate this process, which loads the EFlags register into the EAX register. This first command "pushes" the contents onto the stack so they can be "popped" into the AX register.

```
pushfd
pop eax
```

Although it isn't evident by looking at the two commands, memory is accessed twice because this is where the stack is located. If the alignment bit is already set when this command is executed, an exception is triggered if the stack pointer SP doesn't refer to an address that's divisible by four. However, this can easily be avoided by placing the following machine language command before the previous commands:

```
and esp,0FFFCh
```

This command simply sets the two bottom bits in the ESP register to 0, rounding off the stack pointer to the next address that's divisible by four. This type of processor test is usually executed within a subroutine. So, you should record the current contents of the stack pointer beforehand so that you can restore them later. Otherwise, at the end of the procedure, the stack pointer won't point to the return address of the caller, which was placed there when the subroutine was called. As a result, the program crashes.

Reading the SX versions

Although this test differentiates between 80386s and 80486s, it doesn't enable you to distinguish between the DX and SX versions of these processors. Also, no software programs distinguish between the 80386SX and the 80386DX.

However, it's possible to distinguish between the 80486SX and the 80486DX, even if only indirectly. The SX version of this processor doesn't have the mathematical coprocessor 80387, which is integrated in the DX version. Once you determine that you have an 80486 processor, you can easily determine whether the corresponding floating point commands are available. To do this, use a coprocessor test, which allows you to indicate the installed version of the processor.

However, just because floating point commands are supported doesn't mean that an 80486DX is present. It could also be an 80486SX that has a mathematical coprocessor. You can assume that you have an 80486SX only when you encounter an 80486 that doesn't support numerical operations of the floating point processor.

Distinguishing between 8086/8088 and 80186/80188

If the processor failed the first test, then the processor must be one of the four ancestors of the 80286. The following test determines whether the processor is an 80188 or 80186.

When these processors were introduced, the operation of the various shift commands (e.g., SHL and SHR) were changed to work in connection with the CL register as a shift counter. In the previous processors, the contents of the CL register specified the number of shifters in a range between 0 and 255. However, in the new processors the top three bits of the CL register are deleted before the shift, which limits the maximum number of shift operations. This makes sense because after 16 shifts of a word (17 if shifting by the carry flag), all bit positions contain the value 0. Additional shifting wastes valuable processor time, but no longer changes the value of the word.

The test considers this behavior by using the SHR command to shift the 0FFH value in the AL register by 21H positions to the right. If the processor is an 80188 or newer, it will first mask the upper 3 bits in the shift counter and then leave only a single shift of the 21H shifts.

```
   021H (00100001b)    Number of shifts
 & 01FH (000111111b)   Mask the upper 3 bits
 -----------------------------------------------------------
   001H (00000001b)    Actual number of shifts
```

Unlike its predecessors, which actually shift the value FFH 21H times to the right, returning the value 0, the 80188 and 80186 return the value 7FH as a result. By examining the AL register after the shift, it's easy to determine whether the processor is an 80186 or 80188 (AL doesn't equal 0) or neither (AL equals 0).

Differentiating between 8086/8088 and NEC V20/V30

If the processor didn't pass this test either, it must be an 8088, an 8086, or a clone from NEC. These clones, which are labeled V20 or V30, are the most common clones of the two Intel processors. They have the same command set as the Intel processors they're modeled after, but have a higher processing speed due to optimizations in the inner logic.

Along with these improvements, a small error, which occurred in some of the 8088 and 8086 processors, was eliminated in these processors. This error occurs if a hardware interrupt is triggered during the execution of a string command (e.g., LODS) in connection with the REP(eat) prefix and a segment override. After the interrupt ends, the command doesn't resume execution on some 8088 and 8086 processors. This is indicated by the fact that the CX register, which functions as a cycle counter for this command, doesn't contain the value 0, as expected, after execution of the command.

The test program first loads the value 0FFFFH into the CX register and then executes the subsequent string command, with the REP prefix and segment override, 65,535 times. This process is time-consuming even for a fast processor. So, during one of the 65,535 executions of this command, a hardware interrupt will be triggered. In the case of the 8088 and 8086, the command isn't resumed and the remaining "loop runs" aren't executed. The test program uses the CX register to check this after the command is executed.

Reading the width of the data bus

The last test is for processors that are predecessors to the 80386. In this test, you determine whether the processor has an 8 bit or a 16 bit data bus. In other words, you're finally going to discover whether the identified processor is an 8088 or 8086, a V20 or V30, or an 80186 or

80188. Although you cannot use machine language commands to determine the width of the data bus, the length of the prefetch queue within the processor is related to this size.

The prefetch queue, which is located inside the processor, is responsible for loading the machine code of the subsequent commands into the processor while the current command is being executed. This can significantly increase the execution speed of the processor because the mechanism for filling the prefetch queue works parallel to the actual execution of the command. This allows the processor to access the next command immediately after one command ends. The processor doesn't have to worry about the address bus and data bus for loading the command.

As long as it doesn't use *self-modified code*, a program usually doesn't see the prefetch queue being filled. This refers to changes to the program code that were made by the program (e.g., by overwriting one machine language command in the code segment with another one from the program code). However, this isn't an unusual technique.

Problems occur with this method when commands, whose machine codes have already been loaded into the prefetch queue, are changed. This occurs when the command to be modified is very close to the command that's modifying it. For example, in the following code excerpt, an INC-CX command is replaced by an NOP command. The INC command is still executed because the two commands are so close to each other that the modified INC command was already in the prefetch queue at the time of its execution.

```
        mov byte ptr cs:queue,Code NOP
    queue: inc dx
```

This procedure simplifies testing the length of the prefetch queue. With this information, you can also determine the width of the data bus. This is possible because processors with a 16 bit data bus have a 6 byte prefetch queue, while processors with an 8 bit data bus have 4 byte prefetch queues.

Test the length of the prefetch queue by using the STOSB (store string byte) string command to modify 3 bytes in the code segment. These three bytes appear immediately after the STOSB command. In this test, the bytes must be placed so they are already located within the queue on a processor with a 6 byte queue. This must be done so the processor doesn't notice this change to the program code. However, on a processor with a 4 byte queue, these commands are still outside the queue. So the changed commands are loaded and executed in their modified form the next time the queue is "filled up".

The program takes advantage of this because the INC DX command is among the modified commands. This command increments the contents of the DX register. Since this register receives the code of the determined processor within the test routine, it causes a switch to the next processor type. However, this happens only if this command is actually executed and if it's a processor with a 6 byte queue.

Since this always increases the processor code by 1 on xx86 processors, the processor codes within the test routine are chosen so the code for the corresponding xx88 processor is always followed by the code for the matching xx86 processor. For example, if processor code 4, for the 80188, is loaded into the DX register before the beginning of this test, then the processor code within this test is incremented by 1. The result is processor code 5, in the DX register, which is interpreted as a code for the 80186 by the test program.

722

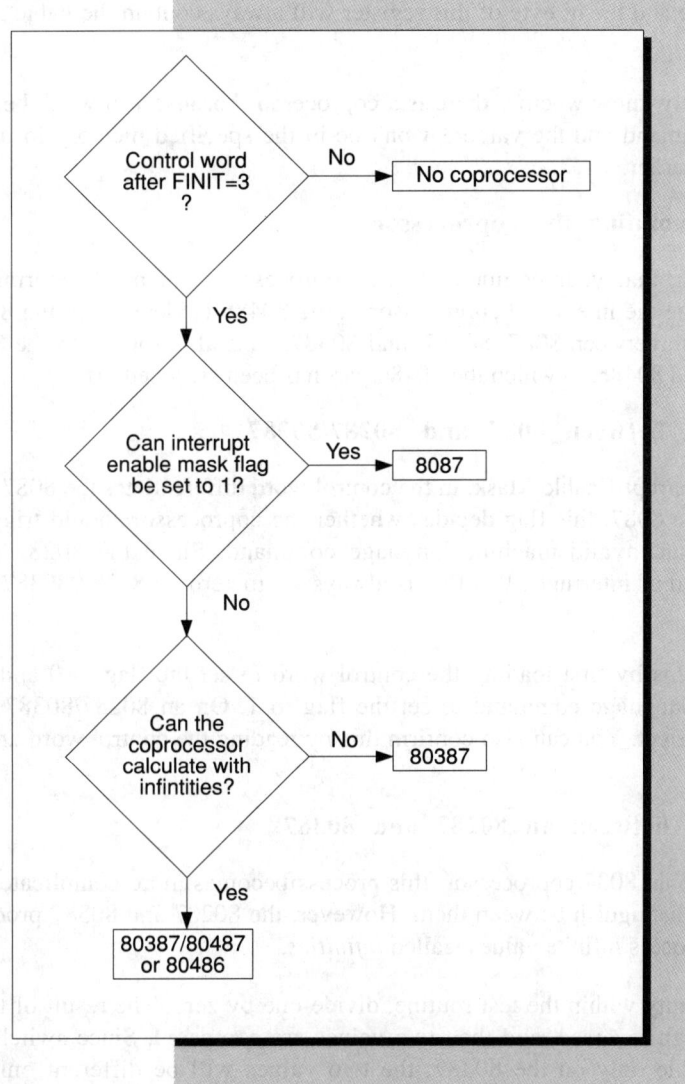

Determining the presence of a coprocessor

14.2.2   Coprocessor Test

The installed coprocessor is also important even though less than three percent of all computers have them. However, often just knowing that a mathematical coprocessor isn't installed is valuable information.

You can easily check whether a mathematical coprocessor is installed by using the machine language command FSTCW. Before using this command, reset the coprocessor with the FINIT machine language command. FSTCW deposits the control word of the coprocessor into a specified variable and the hi byte of this register will always contain the value 3 after you reset the coprocessor.

You'll immediately know whether there is a coprocessor because you won't be able to execute the FSTCW command and the value 3 won't be in the specified memory location unless you saved this value earlier.

Tests for determining the coprocessor

After discovering that your computer has a coprocessor, you must determine the type of coprocessor. Since the integrated coprocessor in the 80486 is identical to the 80387, you must simply distinguish between 8087, 80287, and 80387. This also applies to the 80487, which is simply a disguised 80486, in which the 80486 part has been switched off.

Differentiating between 8087 and 80287/80387

A flag, called Interrupt-Enable-Mask, in the control word differentiates the 8087 from the 80287 and 80387. In the 8087, this flag decides whether the coprocessor should trigger an interrupt upon receiving an invalid machine language command. Since the 80287 and 80387 use exceptions instead of interrupts, this flag is always set to zero on 80287/80387s and cannot be set to 1.

You can check this by first loading the control word to set the flag to 0 and then using the FDISI machine language command to set the flag to 1. On an 80287/80387, this command won't have any effect. You can also confirm this by reading the control word and checking this flag.

Differentiating between an 80287 and 80387

If you don't have an 8087 coprocessor, this process becomes more complicated because flags can't be used to distinguish between them. However, the 80287 and 80387 processors differ in their ability to process infinite values, called *infinities*.

To create an infinity within the test routine, divide one by zero. The result of this operation is duplicated, its sign reversed, and then two values are compared. Since switching the sign of infinity is possible only on the 80387, the two values will be different only on an 80387 coprocessor. Verify this by using the appropriate commands and then establish the identity of the coprocessor.

14.2.3   Demonstration Programs

You can see how this theory actually works by reading the processor and its helper in two assembler modules, which were designed for linking to Pascal and C programs. These modules are called PROCPA.ASM and PROCCA.ASM; both of them contain two routines named GETPROC and GETCO. These routines represent functions that return a numeric value which characterizes the type of processor (GETPROC) or the type of coprocessor (GETCO).

The high level language programs PROCP.PAS and PROCC.C clearly illustrate this by using the return values of these functions as indexes in string arrays. The names of the various Intel processors and coprocessors are stored in these string arrays.

Accessing the 32 bit register

When you examine the assembler modules, which are identical, you'll notice the numerous DB commands in the GETPROC function. These commands represent the machine codes of the various commands used to distinguish between 80386 and 80486. This is where machine language commands of the 80386 and 80486, which rely on the extended 32 bit register of these processors (EAX, EBX etc.), are used. However, these commands can be used only if the assembler is informed, by the pseudo command .386, that these commands are allowed.

Unfortunately this has an unpleasant side effect. The assembler gives the attribute "32-Bit" to the code segment and records this in the object file. The linker, which links the assembler module with the high level language model, doesn't approve of this because the various segments are no longer compatible. To avoid this conflict, the commands are specified directly in machine code so the assembler doesn't recognize them as enhanced 386 commands.

Listing: PROCP.PAS

```
{*******************************************************************}
{*                        P R O C P                              *}
{*---------------------------------------------------------------*}
{*    Task       : Examines the processor type in the PC and     *}
{*                 tells the user the processor type             *}
{*---------------------------------------------------------------*}
{*    Author     : MICHAEL TISCHER                               *}
{*    Developed on : 08/16/1988                                  *}
{*    Last update : 01/14/1992                                   *}
{*******************************************************************}

program PROCP;

{-- Declaration of assembler routines -----------------------------}

{$L procpa}                      { Link assembler module }

function GetProz : integer; external;
function GetCo   : integer; external;

{-- Types and global variables -----------------------------------}

type  ProName = string[20];      { Array of processor names }

const ProcName : array [0..8] of ProName =
                      ( 'INTEL 8088',        { Code 0 }
                        'INTEL 8086',        { Code 1 }
                        'NEC V20',           { Code 2 }
                        'NEC V30',           { Code 3 }
                        'INTEL 80188',       { Code 4 }
                        'INTEL 80186',       { Code 5 }
                        'INTEL 80286',       { Code 6 }
                        'INTEL 80386',       { Code 7 }
                        'INTEL 80486');      { Code 8 }
      CoName : array[0..3] of ProName =
                       ('No coprocessor',    { Code 0 }
                        '8087',              { Code 1 }
                        '80287',             { Code 2 }
                        '80387/80487');      { Code 3 }

{*******************************************************************}
{**                      MAIN PROGRAM                           **}
{*******************************************************************}

begin
  writeln('PROCP  - (c) 1988 by MICHAEL TISCHER');
  writeln;
  writeln('Processor       : ', ProcName[GetProz]);
  writeln('Coprocessor     : ', CoName [ GetCo ] );
  writeln;
end.
```

Listing: PROCPA.ASM

```
;**********************************************************
;*                    P R O C P A                        *;
;*------------------------------------------------------*;
;* Task        : Determines the type of processor installed in *;
;*               a PC.                                   *;
;*------------------------------------------------------*;
;* Author      : Michael Tischer                         *;
;* Developed on : 08/22/88                               *;
;* Last update : 01/14/92                                *;
;*------------------------------------------------------*;
;* assembly    : MASM PROCPA;    or TASM PROCPA          *;
;*               Use $L compiler directive to link to Pascal *;
;*               programs                                *;
;**********************************************************


;== Constants ============================================

p_80486   equ   8          ;Codes for different types of
p_80386   equ   7          ;processors
p_80286   equ   6
p_80186   equ   5
p_80188   equ   4
p_v30     equ   3
p_v20     equ   2
p_8086    equ   1
p_8088    equ   0


co_80387  equ   3          ;Math coprocessor codes
co_80287  equ   2
co_8087   equ   1
co_none   equ   0

NOP_CODE  equ   90h        ;Code for NOP assembler instruction
DEC_DX_C  equ   4Ah        ;Code for DEC DX

;== Data segment =========================================

DATA      segment word public

cpz       dw    ?          ;For coprocessor test

DATA      ends

;== Program ==============================================

code      segment byte public   ;Definition of CODE segment

          assume cs:code, ds:data

public    getproz            ;Function for accessing
public    getco              ;other programs

;-- GETPROZ: Describes processor type on board the PC -----------
;-- Call from Pascal: function getproz : integer;      -----------
;-- Output: Processor type number (see constants)      -----------

getproz   proc near

          pushf               ;Get contents of flag registers

          ;== Determine whether model is 80286 or lower ==============
```

```
          xor   ax,ax            ;Set AX to 0
          push  ax               ;and push onto stack
          popf                   ;Pop into flag register from stack
          pushf                  ;Return to stack
          pop   ax               ;And pop back into AX
          and   ax,0f000h        ;Avoid clearing the 4 bits
          cmp   ax,0f000h        ;Are bits 12-15 all equal to 1?
          je    not_286_386      ;YES->Not an 80386 or an 80286

;-- Test whether to handle it as an 80406, 80386 or 80286 ---

          mov   dl,p_80286       ;This narrows it down to one of
          mov   ax,07000h        ;the two processors
          push  ax               ;Push value 7000(h) onto the stack
          popf                   ;Pop off as flag register
          pushf                  ;and push it back onto the stack
          pop   ax               ;Pop off and return to AX register
          and   ax,07000h        ;Avoid masking bits 12-14
          je    pende            ;Are bits 12-14 all equal to 0?
                                 ;YES->Handle it as an 80286

          inc   dl               ;NO->Handle it as an 80386 or 80486

;-- The following tests for 80386/80486 status through ------
;-- the EFlags register at bit position 18 (found on  ------
;-- 80486 chips only).                                ------

          cli                    ;No interrupts right now

          db 066h,08Bh,0DCh      ;mov   ebx,esp      Mark current SP
          db 066h,083h,0E4h,0FCh ;and   esp,0FFFCh   Round to DWORD
          db 066h,09Ch           ;pushfd             Put Flag reg. on
          db 066h,058h           ;pop   eax          stack from AX,
          db 066h,08Bh,0C8h      ;mov   ecx,eax      mark in CX
          db 066h,035h,000h,0h,4h,0h ;xor eax,1 shl 18  Shift alignment
          db 066h,050h           ;push  eax          bit, pass it
          db 066h,09Dh           ;popfd              to flag register
          db 066h,09Ch           ;pushfd             Get flag from
          db 066h,058h           ;pop   eax          stack, AX
          db 066h,051h           ;push  ecx          Old flag data
          db 066h,09Dh           ;popfd              Restore
          db 066h,033h,0C1h      ;xor   eax,ecx      Test AL bit
          db 066h,0C1h,0E8h,012h ;xor   eax,12h      AL bit to bit 0
          db 066h,083h,0E0h,001h ;and   eax,1h       Mask all others
          db 066h,08Bh,0E3h      ;mov   esp,ebx      Restore SP

          sti                    ;Allow interrupts again
          add   dl,al            ;If AL = 1 then 486
          jmp   pende            ;End of test

;-- Test for 80186 or 80188 --------------------------------

not_286_386 label near

          mov   dl,p_80188       ;Load code for 80188
          mov   al,0ffh          ;Set all bits in AL register to 1
          mov   cl,021h          ;Number of shift operations after CL
          shr   al,cl            ;Shift AL CL times to the right
          jne   t88_86           ;If AL is unequal to 0 it must be
                                 ;handled as an 80188 or 80186

;-- Test for NEC V20 or V30 --------------------------------
```

```
        mov    dl,p_v20          ;Load code for NEC V20
        sti                      ;Interrupts should be enabled starting
        mov    si,0              ;with the first byte in ES
        mov    cx,0ffffh         ;Read a complete segment
        rep lods byte ptr es:[si]    ;REP w/ segment override only
                                 ;works with NEC V20 and V30 processors
        or     cx,cx             ;Has complete segment been read?
        je     t88_86            ;YES-> V20 or V30

        mov    dl,p_8088         ;NO-> Must be an 8088 or 8086

        ;-- Test for 8088 or 8086/V20 or V30 -----------------------
        ;-- Use queue to test for chip         ----------------------

t88_86  label near

        push cs                  ;Push CS onto stack
        pop  es                  ;Pop off to ES
        std                      ;Using string inst. count backwards
        mov  di,offset q2_end    ;Set DI to end of queue
        mov  al,0fbh             ;Instruction code for "STI"
        mov  cx,3                ;Execute string instruction 3 times
        cli                      ;Suppress interrupts
        rep stosb                ;Overwrite INC DX instruction
        cld                      ;Using string inst. count backwards
        nop                      ;Fill queue with dummy instruction
        nop
        nop

        inc  dx                  ;Increment processor code
        nop
q2_end: sti                      ;Re-enable interrupts

        ;------------------------------------------------------------

pende   label near               ;End testing

        popf                     ;Pop flag register from stack
        xor  dh,dh               ;Processor code high byte = 0
        mov  ax,dx               ;Processor code is return value of

        ret                      ;Return to caller

getproz endp                     ;End procedure

;-- GETCO Returns the type of coprocessor (if applicable) ------------
;-- Call from Pascal: function getco : integer;          ------------
;-- Output: Number of the coprocessor type (see constants) ------------

getco   proc near

        mov  dx,co_none          ;First assume no coproc. exists

        mov  byte ptr cs:wait1,NOP_CODE ;Replace 8087 WAIT with
        mov  byte ptr cs:wait2,NOP_CODE ;NOP

wait1:  finit                    ;Coproc. initialization
        mov  byte ptr cpz+1,0    ;High byte control word to 0
wait2:  fstcw cpz                ;Store control word
        cmp  byte ptr cpz+1,3    ;High-byte control word = 3?
        jne  gcende              ;No --> No coprocessor

        ;-- Coprocessor exists: Test for 8087 -----------------------

        inc  dx
        and  cpz,0FF7Fh          ;Mask interrupt enable mask flag
        fldcw cpz                ;Pass to control word
        fdisi                    ;Set IEM flag
        fstcw cpz                ;Reload control word
        test cpz,80h             ;IEM flag set?
        jne  gcende              ;Yes --> 8087, end test

        ;-- Coprocessor exists: Test for 80287/80387 ----------------

        inc  dx
        finit                    ;Coproc. initialization
        fld1                     ;Number 1 to Cop stack
        fldz                     ;Number 0 to Cop stack
        fdiv                     ;Reload control word
        fld  st                  ;IEM flag set?
        fchs                     ;Yes --> 8087, end test
        fcompp                   ;Pop return address off of stack
        fstsw cpz                ;Take first 9 bytes from there
        mov  ah,byte ptr cpz+1   ;Return to the testing routine
        sahf                     ;
        je   gcende              ;Zero flag = 1: 80287

        inc  dx                  ;No 80287? Must be 80387 or coproc.
                                 ;integrated in 80486

gcende: mov  ax,dx               ;AX gets result
        ret                      ;Return to caller

getco   endp

;== End ==========================================================

code    ends                     ;End of code segment
        end                      ;End program
```

Listing: PROCC.C

```
/*********************************************************************/
/*                          P R O C C                              */
/*-----------------------------------------------------------------*/
/*    Task        : Determines the processor type in a PC          */
/*-----------------------------------------------------------------*/
/*    Author      : MICHAEL TISCHER                                */
/*    Developed on : 08/14/88                                      */
/*    Last update  : 10/14/91                                      */
/*-----------------------------------------------------------------*/
/*    (MICROSOFT C)                                                */
/*    Compilation  : CL /AS /c PROCC.C                             */
/*                   LINK PROZC PROCCA                             */
/*    Call         : PROCC                                         */
/*-----------------------------------------------------------------*/
/*    (BORLAND TURBO C)                                            */
/*    Compilation  : Create a project file containing these lines: */
/*                   PROCC                                         */
/*                   PROCCA.OBJ                                    */
/*********************************************************************/

#include <stdio.h>

extern int getproz( void );    /* For linking the assembler routine */
extern int getco( void );

/*********************************************************************/
/**                     MAIN PROGRAM                              **/
/*********************************************************************/

void main()

{
static char * prozname[] = {   /* Vector with pointers to the names */
                    "Intel 8088",           /* Code 0 */
                    "Intel 8086",           /* Code 1 */
                    "NEC V20",              /* Code 2 */
                    "NEC V30",              /* Code 3 */
                    "Intel 80188",          /* Code 4 */
                    "Intel 80186",          /* Code 5 */
                    "Intel 80286",          /* Code 6 */
                    "Intel 80386",          /* Code 7 */
                    "Intel 80486"           /* Code 8 */
                    };

static char *coname[] = {       /* Vector with pointers to the names */
                    "No coprocessor",       /* Code 0 */
                    "8087",                 /* Code 1 */
                    "80287",                /* Code 2 */
                    "80387/80487"           /* Code 3 */
                    };

printf("▓▓▓▓▓▓ PROCC (c) 1988, 91 by Michael Tischer ███\n\n");
printf("Processor   : %s\n", prozname[ getproz() ] );
printf("Coprocessor : %s\n\n", coname[ getco() ] );
}
```

Listing: PROCCA.ASM

```
;*********************************************************************;
;*                        P R O C C A . A S M                      *;
;*-----------------------------------------------------------------*;
;*    Task        : Makes two functions available for linking to   *;
;*                  C programs. These functions help determine     *;
;*                  the processor type and the type of coprocess-  *;
;*                  or.                                            *;
;*-----------------------------------------------------------------*;
;*    Author      : MICHAEL TISCHER                                *;
;*    Developed on : 08/15/88                                      *;
;*    Last update  : 10/17/91                                      *;
;*-----------------------------------------------------------------*;
;*    Assembly     : MASM PROCCA;  or   TASM PROCCA                *;
;*                   ... then link with a C program               *;
;*********************************************************************;

IGROUP group _text                  ;Program segment
DGROUP group _bss, _data            ;Data segment
       assume CS:IGROUP, DS:DGROUP, ES:DGROUP, SS:DGROUP

_BSS    segment word public 'BSS'   ;This segment handles all uninitial-
_BSS    ends                        ;ized static variables

_DATA   segment word public 'DATA'  ;This segment handles all initialized
                                    ;global and static variables
_DATA   ends
;== Constants =======================================================

p_80486   equ   8                   ;Codes for different processor types
p_80386   equ   7
p_80286   equ   6
p_80186   equ   5
p_80188   equ   4
p_v30     equ   3
p_v20     equ   2
p_8086    equ   1
p_8088    equ   0

co_80387  equ   3                   ;Codes for the coprocessors
co_80287  equ   2
co_8087   equ   1
co_kein   equ   0

NOP_CODE  equ   90h                 ;Code for machine language command NOP
DEC_DX_C  equ   4Ah                 ;Code of DEC DX

;== Global variables ================================================

_DATA   segment word public 'DATA'

cpz       dw    0                   ;For coprocessor test

_DATA   ends

;== Program =========================================================

_TEXT   segment byte public 'CODE'  ;Program segment

public  _getproz                    ;Function made available for other
public  _getco                      ;programs

;-- GETPROC: Determines the type of processor a PC is equipped with ---
```

```
;-- Call from C : int getproz( void );
;-- Output      : The processor type number (see constants above)

_getproz proc near

        pushf                   ;Secure flag register contents
        push di

        ;== Determine whether model came before or after 80286 ======

        xor  ax,ax              ;Set AX to 0
        push ax                 ; and push onto stack
        popf                    ;Pop flag register off of stack
        pushf                   ;Push back onto stack
        pop  ax                 ; and pop off of AX
        and  ax,0f000h          ;Do not clear the upper four bits
        cmp  ax,0f000h          ;Are bits 12 - 15 all equal to 1?
        je   kleiner_286        ;YES --> Not 80386 or 80286

        ;-- Test for determining whether 80486, 80386 or 80286 ------

        mov  dl,p_80286         ;In any case, it's one of the
        mov  ax,07000h          ; three processors
        push ax                 ;Push 07000h onto stack
        popf                    ;Pop flag register off
        pushf                   ; and push back onto the stack
        pop  ax                 ;Pop into AX register
        and  ax,07000h          ;Mask everything except bits 12-14
        je   pende              ;Are bits 12 - 14 all equal to 0?
                                ;YES --> It's an 80286

        inc  dl                 ;No --> it's either an 80386 or an
                                ;80486. First set to 386

        ;-- The following test to differentiate between 80386 and ---
        ;-- 80486 is based on an extension of the EFlag register on
        ;-- the 80486 in bit position 18.
        ;-- The 80386 doesn't have this flag, which is why you
        ;-- cannot use software to change its contents.

        cli                     ;No interrupts now

db 066h,08Bh,0DCh       ;mov   ebx,esp        store current SP
db 066h,083h,0E4h,0FCh  ;and   esp,0FFFCh     round off DWORD
db 066h,09Ch            ;pushfd               Store flag register
db 066h,058h            ;pop   eax            from stack to AX
db 066h,08Bh,0C8h       ;mov   ecx,eax        and CX
db 066h,035h,000h,0h,4h,0h ;xor eax,1 shl 18  XOR alignment bit
db 066h,050h            ;push  eax            and put in flag
db 066h,09Dh            ;popfd                register
db 066h,09Ch            ;pushfd               Push flag onto stack
db 066h,058h            ;pop   eax            and pop AX off
db 066h,051h            ;push  ecx            Return old flag
db 066h,09Dh            ;popfd                contents
db 066h,033h,0C1h       ;xor   eax,ecx        Test AL bit
db 066h,0C1h,0E8h,012h  ;shr   eax,18         Shift AL bit to bit 0
db 066h,083h,0E0h,001h  ;and   eax,1h         Mask all others
db 066h,08Bh,0E3h       ;mov   esp,ebx        Restore SP.

        sti                     ;Allow interrupts again
        add  dl,al              ;AL is 1, if 486
        jmp  pende              ;Test is ended

        ;== Test for 80186 or 80188 ========================

kleiner_286 label near

        mov  dl,p_80188         ;Load code for 80188
        mov  al,0ffh            ;Set all bits in AL register to 1
        mov  cl,021h            ;Move number of shift operations to CL
        shr  al,cl              ;AL CL shift to the right
        jne  t88_86             ;If AL <> 0, it must be either an
                                ;80188 or 80186

        ;== Test for NEC V20 or V30 ============================

        mov  dl,p_v20           ;Load code for NEC V20
        sti                     ;Enable interrupts
        push si                 ;Mark contents of SI register
        mov  si,0               ;Starting with first byte in ES, read
        mov  cx,0ffffh          ;a complete segment
        rep  lods byte ptr es:[si] ;REP with a segment override
                                ;(works only with NEC V20, V30)
        pop  si                 ;Pop SI off of stack
        or   cx,cx              ;Has entire segment been read?
        je   t88_86             ;YES --> V20 or V30

        mov  dl,p_8088          ;NO --> Must be 8088 or 8086

        ;== Test for 88/86 or V20/V30 ==========================
        ;-- Run test with help of queue (as above), however, this is
        ;-- a smaller queue

t88_86   label near

        push cs                 ;Push CS onto stack
        pop  es                 ; and pop ES off
        std                     ;Increment on string instructions
        mov  di,offset q2_end   ;Set DI at end of queue
        mov  al,0fbh            ;Instruction code for "STI"
        mov  cx,3               ;Execute string instruction 3 times
        cli                     ;Suppress interrupts
        rep  stosb              ;Overwrite INC DX instruction
        cld                     ;Increment on string instructions
        nop                     ;Fill queue with dummy instructions
        nop
        nop

        inc  dx                 ;Increment processor code
        nop
q2_end:  sti                    ;Re-enable interrupts

        ;---------------------------------------------------------

pende    label near             ;End testing

        pop  di                 ;Pop DI off of stack
        popf                    ;Pop flag register off of stack
        xor  dh,dh              ;Set high byte of proc. code to 0
        mov  ax,dx              ;Proc. code = return value of funct.

        ret                     ;Return to caller

_getproz endp                   ;End of procedure

;-- GETCO: Determines the kind of coprocessor, if available ----------
;-- Call from C : int getco( void );
```

```
;-- Output      : The number of the coprocessor type (see constants)

_getco   proc near

         mov    dx,co_kein           ;First assume there is no CP

         mov    byte ptr cs:wait1,NOP_CODE    ;WAIT-instruction on 8087
         mov    byte ptr cs:wait2,NOP_CODE    ;Replace by NOP

wait1:   finit                       ;Initialize Cop
         mov    byte ptr cpz+1,0  ;Move high byte control word to 0
wait2:   fstcw cpz                   ;Store control word
         cmp    byte ptr cpz+1,3  ;High byte control word = 3?
         jne    gcende              ;No ---> No coprocessor

         ;-- Coprocessor exists. Test for 8087 -----------------------

         inc    dx
         and    cpz,0FF7Fh   ;Mask interrupt enable mask flag
         fldcw cpz                   ;Load in the control word
         fdisi                       ;Set IEM flag
         fstcw cpz                   ;Store control word
         test   cpz,80h              ;IEM flag set?
         jne    gcende              ;YES ---> 8087, end test

         ;-- Test for 80287/80387 ------------------------------------

         inc    dx
         finit                       ;Initialize cop
         fld1                        ;Number 1 to cop stack
         fldz                        ;Number 0 to cop stack
         fdiv                        ;Divide 1 by 0, erg to ST
         fld    st                   ;Move ST onto stack
         fchs                        ;Reverse sign in ST
         fcompp                      ;Compare and pop ST and ST(1)
         fstsw cpz                   ;Store result from status word
         mov    ah,byte ptr cpz+1 ;in memory and move AX register
         sahf                        ;to flag register
         je     gcende              ;Zero-Flag = 1 : 80287

         inc    dx            ;Not 80287, must be 80387 or inte-
                              ;grated coprocessor on 80486

gcende:  mov    ax,dx          ;Move function result to AX
         ret                   ;Return to caller

_getco   endp

;== Ende =============================================================

_text    ends          ;End of program segment
         end           ;End of assembler source
```

Chapter 15

A Brief History of DOS

In this chapter we'll discuss the PC's operating system, which the PC loads from a floppy diskette or hard drive. This system is usually referred to as PC-DOS, MS-DOS, or simply DOS.

What is DOS?

Most users are familiar with only the user interface of DOS, which is used to run programs, format disks, etc. In the following sections, however, you'll view DOS from a different perspective.

Beneath the surface of DOS, many processes occur. DOS uses numerous routines (called *functions*) to accomplish its tasks. These functions are available to the user as well as to DOS. We'll discuss how these functions can be used in practical applications.

This chapter includes background information on the development of DOS, highlighting its origins in the CP/M operating system. You'll learn the differences between transient and resident commands, COM and EXE files, and DOS file access.

We'll also examine the data structures that act as the connecting link between the different DOS functions. These data structures make mass storage devices, such as floppy disks and hard drives, possible.

Finally, this chapter discusses each DOS function in detail and includes a brief look at DOS Version 5.0.

15.1 DOS Development

Let's begin our examination of DOS programming by studying DOS's history. DOS is an operating system that has been used for many years. Today, because of its long existence and compatibility requirements, DOS often contains more data than it actually needs.

For example, it's been almost ten years since DOS Version 2.0 was released. This version included FCB functions for performing file access. However, these functions are now considered obsolete by many developers, but DOS continues to support FCB functions, which occupy valuable space in the DOS kernel.

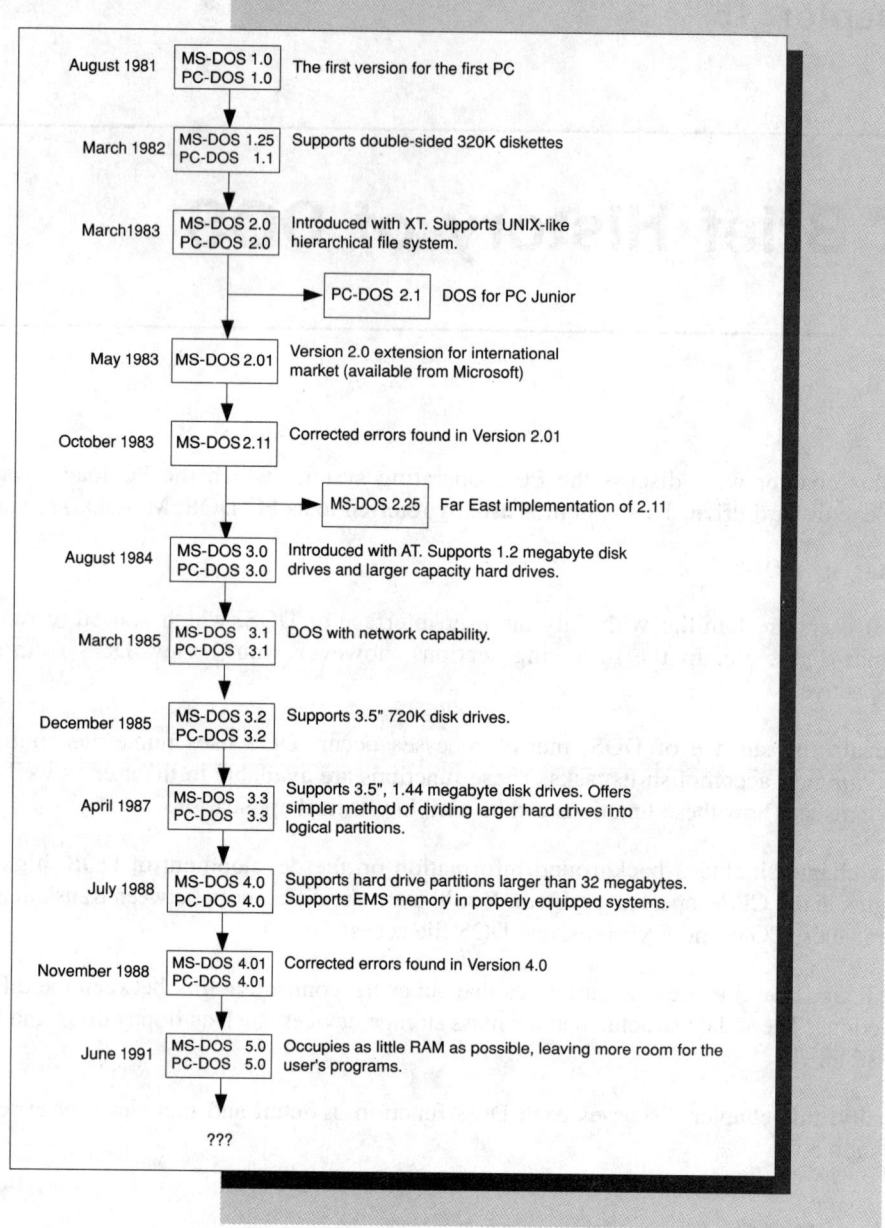

A visual history of DOS

DOS's story begins in the 1970s when Intel designed the 8086 microprocessor, which is the first generation of 16-bit microprocessors. In 1980, most microcomputers were 8-bit systems and the Intel 8080 and Zilog Z-80 processors were the microprocessors driving most micro systems. The PC was only a vision in the minds of developers, and the only microcomputer operating system available was CP/M 80, which was marketed by Digital Research Corporation.

Digital Research announced an operating system called CP/M-86 under development for the 8086. As of April 1980, the CP/M-86 operating system hadn't been released.

A programmer named Tim Paterson began developing a new operating system for the 8086. This operating system, originally called QDOS (Quick and Dirty Operating System) and later called 86-DOS, was the basis for MS-DOS.

In 1980 a lot of software was available for CP/M-80 systems. The development of new software for an 8086 operating system would have required enormous expenses and effort. Paterson's goal was to allow easy conversion of existing software from CP/M-80 to the new operating system. He tried to include the functions and the most important data structures of the CP/M-80 operating system, while removing the weak points of CP/M-80. The finished product was an operating system that occupied 400 lines of assembler code, and, when assembled, required only 6K of memory. Programs developed for CP/M-80 could be converted to the 8086 easily. The new system was named 86-DOS.

Meanwhile, IBM was developing a 16-bit microcomputer. A company named Microsoft, known at the time for its BASIC interpreter for 8-bit systems, offered to develop an operating system for this microcomputer. IBM sent a prototype of the new computer to Microsoft, who bought the rights to Paterson's operating system and made some enhancements to 86-DOS. Even though Paterson participated in the project, the strict security provisions of IBM prevented him from seeing the machine for which he had developed an operating system. Despite this, the development work was completed in August 1981.

Version 1.0

The new operating system was released for the IBM PC under the name MS-DOS Version 1.0 (by Microsoft) and PC-DOS Version 1.0 (by IBM). Compared to current versions, MS-DOS 1.0 was a minimal system. It had only one root directory, in which the user kept all files. This version represented a compromise for Microsoft. They had relied heavily on CP/M-80 and needed to transfer existing programs quickly and easily. For instance, the filename structure (eight-character filename, three-character extension) was identical with CP/M-80. Also, the designation of the disk drives and the internal structure were very similar to the successful 8-bit operating system. MS-DOS Version 1.0 supported one or two disk drives (the IBM PC didn't support hard drives at the time) capable of single-sided, 160K disk format.

During this time, improvements were made to the hardware. These improvements included more RAM and faster disk drives. Microsoft decided to make DOS more hardware independent by removing the association between physical file length and logical file length.

In CP/M-80, every disk was divided into 128-byte units that could be accessed only as a whole. This is why you couldn't access individual bytes on the disk, which created a programming problem that shouldn't have existed anyway. DOS solved this problem by making logical and physical data length independent of one another. Also, functions were implemented to permit reading or writing of more than one data set of a file on a disk. By treating the input and output devices like files, hardware independence was achieved. These input and output devices were assigned their own names:

CON   (Keyboard and display [CONsole])
PRN   (Printer)

AUX   (Serial interface [AUXiliary])

If, instead of a filename, you used one of these three names, the computer addressed the corresponding device instead of the disk drive. This also permitted redirecting input and output from the keyboard or screen to a file or other device.

Up until this point, DOS supported only program files that loaded and executed from a fixed location in memory. Since this wasn't practical, MS-DOS Version 1.0 introduced a new program file type. This new file type had a file extension of .EXE instead of .COM. An .EXE file could be stored and executed from almost any memory location.

Two changes were made to the *command processor*, which is the part of the operating system that accepts commands from the user and controls the execution of these commands. The first change was to store the command processor in a separate file named COMMAND.COM. This allowed programmers to develop a customized command processor and link it to the system.

The second change was to divide the command processor into a *resident* and a *transient* portion. This approach was taken because early PC systems contained only a small amount of memory. The resident portion was written to be as small as possible. Many DOS commands were stored on disk and loaded and run only when required (hence the name transient). Examples of transient commands are DISKCOPY and FORMAT.

A major innovation that enabled MS-DOS Version 1.0 to surpass CP/M-80 was the introduction of the *FAT* (File Allocation Table) on disk. Every entry in this table corresponds to a data area of 512 bytes (called a *sector*) on the disk. The FAT indicates whether the sector is allocated to a file or is still available.

The FAT has special significance in connection with the directory entry that exists for every file type. Besides the filename and other information, it also indicates the number of an entry in the FAT, which corresponds with the first sector of a file on the disk. This FAT entry points to another FAT entry, which indicates the next sector that was allocated to the file. The other FAT entries on a disk perform the same task.

Two additional features, which simplify working with the PC, were also developed:

The introduction of *batch processing* enabled the user to place several DOS commands into one file. When you "run" this file (which has a file extension of .BAT), DOS executes the individual commands from this file as if you had entered the commands from the keyboard. This saves the user time because he/she doesn't have to enter frequently used groups of commands repeatedly.

The *current date and time* follow every filename. DOS includes this data to help the user determine the last time a file was modified.

In 1982, when IBM introduced a new PC, which used both sides of a disk for data storage, Microsoft released DOS Version 1.25 (called Version 1.1 by IBM) to support double-sided disk formatting.

Version 2.0

In March of 1983, IBM announced a new personal computer, called the PC XT. In addition to the floppy disk drive, this computer also had a *hard drive* (also called a *fixed disk*). The enormous capacity of this hard drive (10 megabytes) allowed the user to store several hundred files on one unit. However, this capacity also created some problems for the operating system. The main problem was that DOS could only handle one directory for each storage unit. It would be almost impossible for the hard drive user to maintain hundreds of files in a single directory. Microsoft had two ways to solve this problem: They could either borrow an idea from the CP/M-80 operating system, or borrow an idea from the UNIX operating system.

CP/M divided a hard drive into user areas, representing several individual disk drives that share the total storage on the hard drive. Each user area had one directory.

UNIX uses a *hierarchical file system*, in which each storage unit has a root directory. The root directory can contain both subdirectories and files, and each of these subdirectories can have subdirectories within them. This creates a directory tree whose trunk is the root directory and whose branches are represented by the individual subdirectories.

Microsoft chose the hierarchical file system, which has become a popular component of DOS. This was another step away from CP/M-80 and toward an efficient 16-bit operating system. When the hierarchical file system was introduced, the way DOS controlled files had to be changed. Before this time, file access was conducted through a *file control block* or FCB. This file control block had been introduced for compatibility with CP/M-80. The FCB contained important information about the name, size, and location of a file on disk. This CP/M wouldn't allow access to a file in another directory.

The DOS developers standardized file access through DOS functions. The access to a file occurs exclusively through the *file handles*. A handle is a numerical value passed to the program as soon as it opens a file through a DOS function. Although the FCBs weren't eliminated, programmers never encountered them because DOS took over the control block manipulation.

An important innovation was the introduction of *installable device drivers*. By using these drivers, a programmer could easily include different devices in DOS, such as an exotic hard drive, a mouse, or a tape drive. Version 2.0 introduced the display device driver ANSI.SYS, which gave the programmer flexibility in cursor positioning and color selection through DOS functions.

Background processing represented the first step toward multitasking. This allowed a program (e.g., PRINT.COM) to run unnoticed in the background, taking processor time only as needed, while another program ran in the foreground.

Version 2.0 added the option of formatting the individual tracks of a disk with nine sectors instead of eight. This increased the storage capacity of a single-sided disk from 160K to 180K, and the capacity of a double-sided disk from 320K to 360K.

Additions to Version 2.0

Just as Version 1.25 corrected bugs in Version 1.0, three Microsoft sub versions and one IBM custom version of 2.0 appeared on the market in the same year.

Version 2.01 supported international character sets, including the Kanji alphabet. Shortly after the release of Version 2.01, Version 2.11 appeared, correcting other small errors. This final version was the standard DOS until Version 3.0 was released.

IBM requested a DOS designed specifically for the IBM PCjr. This computer was IBM's attempt to succeed in the home computer market, which was dominated by Commodore and Atari in the early to mid 1980s. DOS Version 2.1, like the PCjr, quickly disappeared from the market. This marked the last time IBM and Microsoft didn't have similar DOS versions. Besides small differences between third party manufacturers (e.g., the inclusion or omission of EXE2BIN.EXE), the version numbers for the two companies are equivalent.

In 1985, after the release of Version 3.0, Version 2 was upgraded for the final time. Version 2.25 was designed specifically for users in the Far East, and supports foreign character sets, such as Kanji.

Version 3.0 and its descendants

Version 3.0, like Version 2.0, was developed for a new PC, called the IBM PC AT. This PC, which was released in August of 1984, supported a 20 megabyte hard drive, as well as the high-density 1.2 megabyte floppy disk drive. Many changes occurred in DOS's internal routines. Although these changes contribute to faster execution of certain operations, they are invisible to the programmer.

Within six months, Version 3.1 was released. This was the first time network support was available. Some new functions were added to implement networking.

Version 3.2 was released in 1985. This version of DOS supported 3.5" floppy diskettes with 720K capacity. This version was the standard for DOS implementations until the release of DOS Version 3.3 in April 1987.

In addition to being the most comprehensive DOS, Version 3.3 supported devices included on the IBM PS/2 systems and the 3.5" high-density floppy diskette format (1.44 megabytes). This version featured improved foreign language support, using code pages.

Version 3.3 also offered improved hard drive support by using partitioning. The user could split a hard drive into primary and secondary partitions, just as single disk drives can be divided into physical and logical drives. Extra driver software wasn't needed for this partitioning.

Most of the changes separating Version 3.0 from Version 2.0 are internal. These changes produce faster program execution, but are otherwise invisible to the user.

Version 4.0

DOS Version 4.0 appeared on the market in August 1988. Earlier, Microsoft released a new multiprocessing operating system called OS/2. Before OS/2, multiprocessing wasn't possible with MS-DOS.

The differences between DOS 4.0 and earlier versions of DOS were obvious. The line-oriented command line interpreter used by DOS Versions 3.3 and earlier was replaced with the DOS Shell (a graphical user interface). Also, user-defined menus were offered and applications, files, and directories could easily be selected with both the mouse and keyboard.

The changes that couldn't be seen were even more important. For instance, the operating system was adapted to the new hardware standards currently available on the market. However, as the operating system became more powerful, it also became more complex and required more memory. For example, earlier versions of DOS were limited to 640K of RAM and a 32 megabyte hard drive. However, DOS 4.0 handled the Expanded Memory System (EMS) following the LIM standard, normal RAM capacity up to 8 megabytes, and hard drives up to 2 gigabytes (2048 megabytes) capacity.

Unfortunately, DOS Version 4.0 was released before it could be completely tested. So, many users experienced unprovoked system crashes and loss of data. Microsoft released an improved update (Version 4.01) in November 1988, but most users simply returned to Version 3.3 and waited for a thoroughly-tested release.

Version 5.0

Microsoft initiated a vast beta test program before the release of DOS Version 5.0. Over 7,000 users and software developers worldwide installed, ran, and contributed feedback about DOS Version 5.0. The final version was released in June 1991.

Version 5.0 includes efficient RAM use, which leaves more user RAM for applications and TSR programs. Since device drivers and TSR programs can now be placed above the 640K barrier, this frees up even more user RAM.

Ten years later: a look back at DOS

In review, DOS Version 2.0 laid the groundwork for all subsequent releases of DOS. However, the most revolutionary improvements are yet to come, and may lie in graphical user interfaces, such as Windows and OS/2.

DR DOS

Since 1981, Digital Research has released alternative operating systems and graphical user interfaces. They released GEM, a graphic interface, which was quickly overshadowed by Microsoft Windows.

With DR DOS, Digital Research has captured part of the PC market. DR DOS's greatest feature is its compatibility with Microsoft products. Virtually everything we say about DOS in this book also applies to MS-/PC-DOS and DR DOS.

Chapter 16

Internal Structure of DOS

In this chapter we'll discuss the internal structure of DOS and the booting process. Since these two items occur in everyday DOS programming, the programmer should understand what happens behind the scenes.

16.1 Components of DOS

Several major components comprise DOS, each with a certain task within the system. The three most important components are the DOS-BIOS, the DOS kernel, and the command processor. Each appear in a separate file.

DOS-BIOS

DOS-BIOS is stored in a system file that appears under various names (IBMBIO.COM, IBMIO.SYS or IO.SYS). This file has the file attributes Hidden and Sys, which indicates that this system file doesn't appear when the DIR command is entered. The DOS-BIOS contains the device drivers for the following units:

```
CON      (Keyboard and Display)
PRN      (Printer)
AUX      (Serial Interface)
CLOCK    (Clock)
Disk drives and/or hard disks which have the
drive specifiers A, B and C
```

If DOS wants to communicate with one of these, it accesses a device driver contained in this module, which in turn uses the routines of ROM-BIOS. The DOS-BIOS (i.e., the connection between individual device drivers and other hardware dependent routines) are the most hardware dependent components of the operating system and vary from one computer to another.

Don't confuse the device drivers in this module with the installable device drivers. The DOS-BIOS device drivers cannot be changed by the user.

DOS kernel

The DOS kernel in the IBMDOS.COM or MSDOS.SYS file is usually invisible to the user. It contains file access routine handles, character input and output, and more; it immediately follows the file IBMIO.SYS or IO.SYS. Both sets of files are assigned the SYSTEM, HIDDEN, and READ-ONLY file attributes. These attributes indicate that these files directly affect the system. So you can't view them or delete them by normal means.

These files contain the various DOS-API functions, which are called using interrupt 21H. The routines operate independent of the hardware and use the device drivers of DOS-BIOS for keyboard, screen, and disk access. The module can be used by different PCs without being limited to one machine. User programs can access these functions in the same way as the ROM-BIOS functions; every function can be called with a software interrupt. The processor registers pass the function number and the parameters.

Command processor

Unlike the two modules previously described, the command processor is contained in the file named COMMAND.COM. It displays the "A>" or "C>" prompt on the screen, accepts user input, and controls input execution. Many users incorrectly think that the command processor is actually the operating system. Actually it's only a special program that executes under DOS control.

The command processor, also called a shell in programmer's terminology, actually consists of three modules: A resident portion, a transient portion, and the initialization routine.

The resident portion (the part that's always in the computer's memory) contains various routines called critical error handlers. These allow the computer to react to different events, such as pressing the <Ctrl><C> or <Ctrl><Break> keys or errors during communication with external devices (e.g., disk drives and printers). The latter causes the message:

```
Abort, Retry, Ignore
or
Abort, Retry, Fail
```

The transient portion contains code for displaying the (A>) prompt, reading user input from the keyboard, and executing the input. The name of this module is derived from the fact that the RAM memory where it's located is unprotected and can be overwritten under certain circumstances. When a program ends, control returns to the resident portion of the command processor. It executes a checksum program to determine whether the transient portion was overwritten by the application program. If it was, the resident portion reloads the transient portion.

The initialization portion loads during the booting process and initializes DOS. This part of the command processor will be examined in detail in the next chapter. When its job ends, it's no longer needed and the RAM memory it occupies can be overwritten by another program. The commands accepted by the transient portion of the command processor can be divided into three groups: internal commands, external commands and batch files.

Internal commands lie in the resident portion of the command processor. COPY, RENAME, and DIR are internal commands.

External commands must be loaded into memory from a diskette or hard disk as needed. FORMAT and CHKDSK are external commands.

After execution the command processor releases the memory used by these programs. This memory can then be used for other purposes.

Batch files

A batch file is a text file containing a series of DOS commands. When a batch file is started, a special interpreter in the transient portion of the command processor executes the batch file commands. Execution of batch file commands is the same as if the user entered them from the keyboard. An important batch file is the AUTOEXEC.BAT file, which executes immediately after DOS is first loaded.

Like all commands of a batch file, these commands are checked for internal commands, external commands, or calls to other batch files. If the first is true, the command executes immediately, since the code is already in memory (in the transient part of the command processor). If it's an external command or another batch file, the system searches the current directory for the command. If such a file doesn't exist in this directory, all directories specified in the PATH command are searched in sequence. During the search, only files with the .COM, .EXE, or .BAT extensions are examined.

Since the command processor cannot search for all three extensions simultaneously, it first searches for files with .COM extensions, then for .EXE files, and finally for .BAT files. If the search is unsuccessful, the screen displays an error message and the system waits for new input.

16.2 Booting DOS

The interaction between the DOS-BIOS, the kernel, and the command processor is most obvious when a program is in memory. However, the process of booting the system also calls these modules.

Searching for boot files

When a PC is switched on, the program contained in ROM begins executing. This ROM program is sometimes called the ROM-BIOS, POST (power on self test), resident diagnostics, or bootstrap ROM. It performs several tests on the hardware and memory and then starts to load the DOS.

First the PC checks for a disk in the floppy disk drive. If a disk exists in the floppy disk drive, the PC checks the disk for the boot sector. If a disk isn't in the drive, the PC searches for a hard disk from which to boot DOS. If a hard disk doesn't exist, the PC displays an error message asking the user to insert a system disk.

The first sector on a bootable floppy disk or hard disk is called the boot sector. The program in the boot sector is read into memory and executes. First it checks for the presence of two files: IBMBIO.COM (sometimes called IO.SYS) and IBMDOS.COM (sometimes called MSDOS.SYS). A bootable floppy disk or hard disk must contain these two files or an error message is displayed. Next these program files are loaded into memory.

The program file IBMBIO.COM consists of two modules. The first contains the basic device drivers-keyboard, display, and disk. The second contains the initialization sequence for DOS.

When the IBMBIO.COM program executes, it continues to initialize the system by moving the DOS kernal (loaded in the IBMDOS.COM program file) to the last available memory location.

The DOS kernal builds several important tables and data areas, and performs initialization procedures for individual device drivers that were loaded with the IBMBIO.COM program file.

Next, DOS searches the boot disk for a file named CONFIG.SYS. If this file is found, the commands contained in the file are executed. These commands add device drivers to DOS, allocate disk buffers and file control blocks for DOS, and initialize the standard input and output devices.

Finally, the command processor COMMAND.COM (or other shell specified in the CONFIG.SYS file) is loaded and control is passed to it. The booting process ends and the initialization routines remain as "garbage" data in memory until overwritten by another program.

Chapter 17

COM and EXE Programs

Besides batch files, DOS also recognizes program files that have the file extensions .COM and .EXE. These extensions indicate that these files have different properties and that they are executable. These program types differ from others because of the way their program code is stored and the maximum program sizes that are allowed.

The differences between these program types aren't important to a programmer working in high level languages. The programmer only needs to know that the program runs; the file format doesn't matter. Also, development packages, such as Turbo Pascal and QuickBASIC, create only EXE files. Some C compilers can produce COM programs using the TINY memory model, in which the combination of program code, data segment, and stack occupies 64K of RAM or less.

The only advantage COM programs have over EXE programs is their slightly smaller program size, which is often only a few hundred bytes.

The programmer working in a high level language doesn't have to worry about the formats and peculiarities of COM and EXE programs because the compiler handles this. However, this information is important to the programmer that's developing software in assembly language.

In this chapter we'll describe the structure and functions of these two program types.

17.1 Differences Between COM and EXE Programs

The COM program is basically a relic from the CP/M era, when RAM was minimal and programs weren't larger than 64K. In DOS, a COM program cannot be larger than 64K. An EXE program can be as large as the memory capacity available to DOS or even larger. (Instead of being loaded into memory, portions of the EXE program may be reserved for later use.)

In a COM program, the program code, data, and stack are stored in one 64K partition. All of the segment registers are set at the start of the program and remain fixed for the duration of the program execution. They point to the start of the 64K memory segment. However, the contents of the ES register may be changed because that register doesn't directly affect program execution.

Except for the ES registers, these values must also be stored during program execution. Program code in this segment can be addressed through the CS register, the data can be addressed through the DS register, and the stack can be addressed through the SS register. However, there are exceptions to the rule. For example, if you call a DOS function, which expects another segment address in the DS register, the DS register may be loaded with another value before the function call. Neither DOS nor the processor will object to this. After execution, the DS register must be reloaded with the COM program's segment address to make the global variables of the program or other data accessible.

Unlike COM files, a direct sequence doesn't exist for EXE file segments. Code, data, and the stack are stored in different segments according to size; they could be distributed over several segments. This distribution applies to larger, commercial programs (e.g., Microsoft Word), which contain program code consisting of several hundred kilobytes. So, during the execution of an EXE program, the various segment registers point to individual code, data, or stack segments instead of a general memory segment.

Regardless of the program type, DOS creates a data structure in memory called the Program Segment Prefix (PSP) before the program starts. (We'll discuss this in more detail later.) This data structure contains 256 bytes. It immediately precedes the program in memory, as shown in the following illustration:

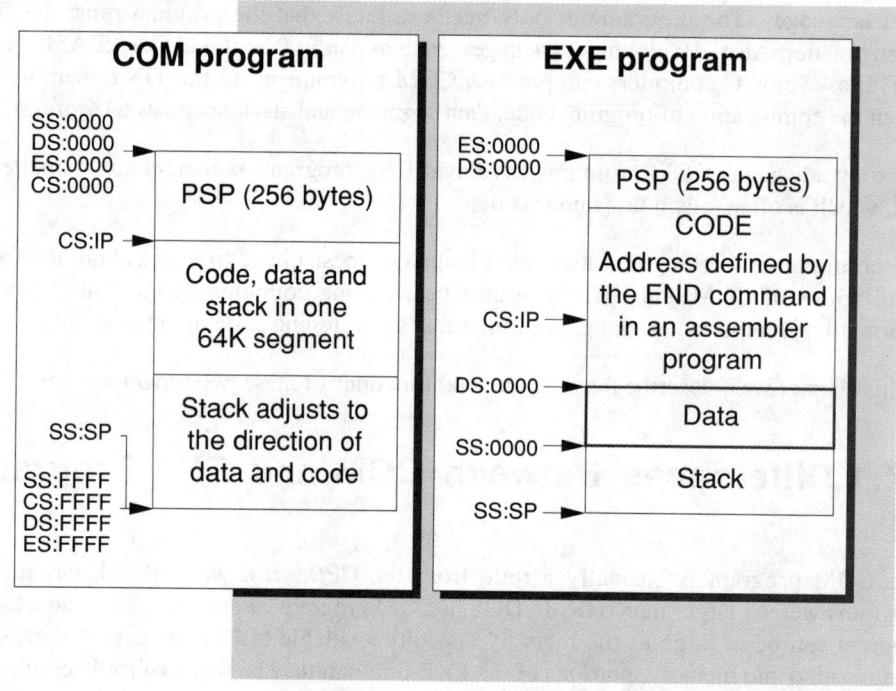

A comparison of COM and EXE programs in memory

17.2 COM Programs

COM program files are stored on disk as an image copy of memory. Because of this, no further processing is needed during loading. So, COM programs load and start execution faster than EXE programs. Also, COM programs are usually more compact than EXE programs because other information, besides the program code and the initialized variables, are also stored there.

Although these items may have been important in the past, they are no longer significant. Programs have become so large that two or three hundred additional bytes no longer make that much difference in an EXE file. Also, computers have become so fast that the speed advantage to loading a COM program has been reduced to a few milliseconds. Only a few dedicated assembly language programmers still use COM format when a program must be as compact as possible.

Microsoft and COM programs

Microsoft's COM program support is steadily decreasing. The Microsoft Assembler MASM assembles files as EXE programs. To convert these programs to COM programs, you need EXE2BIN, which is an important utility packaged with older versions of MS-DOS. MS-DOS 4.0 didn't contain EXE2BIN. The version check in all DOS programs ensured that copies of EXE2BIN, which were taken from older versions of MS-DOS, would not function under MS-DOS 4.0 or 4.01.

So, programmers who wanted to continue using EXE2BIN were forced to alter DOS's version check in order to make EXE2BIN compatible with MS-DOS.

Unlike the LINK program included with the Microsoft Assembler MASM, the Turbo Assembler from Borland International can create both EXE and COM programs.

When MS-DOS Version 5.0 was released, Microsoft again packaged EXE2BIN with DOS.

Registers during start of program

A COM program loads immediately following the PSP. Execution then begins at the first memory location following the PSP at offset 100H. For this reason, a COM program must begin with an executable instruction, even if it's only a jump instruction to the actual start of the program.

COM program memory limits

As we mentioned earlier, a COM program can be only 64K (65,536 bytes). The PSP (256 bytes) and at least 1 word (2 bytes) for the stack must also be reserved. Even though the length of the COM program can never exceed 64K, DOS reserves the entire available RAM for a program. So, DOS cannot allocate additional memory and the COM program cannot call another program using the EXEC function. You can bypass this limitation by releasing the unused memory for other uses with a DOS function.

When control is given to the COM program, all segment registers point to the beginning of the PSP. Because of this, the beginning of the COM program (relative to the beginning of the PSP) is always at address 100H. The stack pointer points to the end of the 64K memory segment containing the COM program (usually FFFEH). During every subroutine call within the COM program, the stack is adjusted by 2 bytes in the direction towards the end of the program. The programmer is responsible for preventing the stack from growing and overwriting the program, which would cause a crash.

There are several ways to end a COM program and return control to DOS or the calling program:

If the program runs under DOS Version 1.0, it can be terminated by calling interrupt 21H function 0 or by calling interrupt 20H. It can also be terminated by using the RET (RETurn) assembler instruction. When this instruction executes, the program continues at the address at the top of the stack. Since the EXEC function stored the value 0 at this location before turning control over to the COM program, program execution continues at location CS:0 (the start of the PSP). Remember that this location contains the call for interrupt 20H, which terminates the program.

Since the odds of a DOS Version 1.0 user are quite low, use DOS function 4CH. Microsoft recommends this function for terminating programs for all subsequent versions of DOS. The terminating program can pass a numeric return code to the calling program. For example, a value of 0 may indicate that the program executed successfully, while a non-zero value indicates an error occurred during execution.

Developing COM programs in assembly language

Now we'll discuss the details the assembly language programmer must handle when developing a COM program. If you're a high level programmer, you may want to skip this section because you don't have to worry about these details. The compiler or interpreter handles them for you.

Earlier in this chapter we mentioned that COM programs are stored on a diskette or hard drive as a direct image of the machine code. Also, instead of being placed at a fixed address by DOS, COM programs can be placed at any memory location divisible by 16. This placement means that COM programs cannot contain FAR calls or specific segment addresses. Only NEAR calls, which contain offset addresses but no segment address, are allowed. Because of this, commands always refer to the current segment in the CS, DS, ES, or SS registers instead of to a certain segment address.

COM programs cannot contain assembly language instructions, such as LDS or LES. The assembler and linker accept these instructions, but EXE2BIN will refuse to make the assembled EXE file into a COM file. This also applies to TLINK, the Turbo Linker.

You may load constants. For example, you can load the segment address of video RAM into a segment register. This is possible because a reference isn't made to the segments of the program, whose position is uncertain, until the actual start of the program.

Assembly language instructions such as the following aren't allowed because the MOV instruction reads the segment address of the program:

```
MOV  AX,SEG PROGRAM
MOV  DS,AX
```

The following instructions are allowed because a constant segment address is used for reference:

746

```
MOV  AX,0B000h
MOV  DS,AX
```

While the developer of a COM program is more limited in this instance than the developer of an EXE program, less work is required for the stack. Before the program is started, the stack is automatically placed at the end of the 64K COM segment by loading the SS register with the COM segment's address, and loading the SP register with the value 0FFFEH.

Before calling a COM program, DOS reserves all available memory for the program even though it normally uses only one 64K segment and indicates this by setting memory location 2 in the PSP. Usually the program terminates and the memory is made available to DOS again.

In some circumstances you may want to write a program that will remain resident after execution. However, DOS believes that there isn't any memory available. This prevents other programs from loading and executing.

In other circumstances you may want to execute another program from this COM program using the EXEC function. Again, since DOS thinks that memory is unavailable, it won't allow the new program to run.

Both of these problems can be avoided by freeing up the unused memory.

There are two ways to do this. Release only the memory outside of the 64K COM segment or release memory outside of the 64K COM segment and any unused memory within the 64K COM segment. Although this creates more memory for other programs, it relocates the stack outside the protected COM segment memory. So, the stack can be overwritten by other programs. Because of this, the stack must be relocated to the end of the code segment before releasing the memory. Also, the size of the stack must be limited (usually 512 bytes is sufficient).

The following sample program demonstrates how to develop a COM program. A small (init) routine relocates the stack to the end of the code segment after the start of the program and releases all remaining memory. Even when this program loads another program, it remains resident. This routine can be useful to applications and can be part of any COM program.

You can assemble this program with either MASM or TASM.

Assembler listing: TESTCOM.ASM

```
;*********************************************************;        ;*                    TASM:   tasm testcom              *;
;*              T E S T C O M . A S M                    *;        ;*                           tlink /t testcom            *;
;*-----------------------------------------------------*;        ;*********************************************************;
;*  Task       : Simple COM program: can be assembled using   *;
;*               either Turbo Assembler (TASM) or Microsoft's *;   com      segment para 'CODE'    ;Definition of COM segment
;*               Macro Assembler (MASM)                       *;            ;(freely selectable name)
;*-----------------------------------------------------*;
;*  Author     : MICHAEL TISCHER                         *;   org 100h                  ;Code begins at address 100H
;*  Developed on : 06/07/1987                            *;                             ;immediately following the PSP
;*  Last update : 12/20/1991                             *;
;*-----------------------------------------------------*;   assume cs:com, ds:com, es:com, ss:com
;*  Assembly   : MASM:  masm testcom;                    *;                             ;All segments point to the
;*                      link testcom;                    *;                             ;COM segment
;*                      exe2bin testcom.exe testcom.com  *;   start:   jmp  init         ;Program starts here
;*                                                       *;                             ;Jump to initialization
```

747

```
;== Data ==========================================================

        ;-- Data, buffer and variables ----------
        ;-- can be stored here        ----------

        ;...
        ;...
        ;...

;== Program =======================================================

prog    proc near              ;This procedure is the actual
                               ;main program and is executed
                               ;after initialization

        ;-- Main program code   ------
        ;-- can be inserted here ------

        ;...
        ;...
        ;...

        ;--- Call DOS function 4CH to end program ---------

        mov  ax,4C00h       ;Load function number 4CH, error code O
        int  21h            ;DOS interrupt call

        ;--- DOS interrupt 21H ends program, so no --
        ;--- more program cannot be added here     --

prog    endp               ;End program
;-- Other procedures ----------------------------------------
;-- Provisions for subroutines

a_proc  proc near

        ;...
        ;...
        ;...
        ret

a_proc  endp
```

```
b_proc  proc near

        ;...
        ;...
        ;...
        ret

b_proc  endp

;-- Initialization -------------------------------------------
;-- ENDE releases all memory and releases the stack

init:   mov  ah,4Ah            ;Function number - 'change memory
size'
        mov  bx,offset ende    ;Length of program in memory
        add  bx,15             ;Round off to next paragraph
        mov  cl,4              ;Compute offset in
        shr  bx,cl             ; paragraphs
        inc  bx
        int  21h               ;Call DOS interrupt 21H

        mov  sp,offset ende    ;Remove stack
        jmp  prog              ;Return to main program

init_ende label near

;== Stack =========================================================

        dw (256-((init_ende-init) shr 1)) dup (?)

                              ;The stack comprises 256 words and
                              ;includes the INIT routine code
                              ;(INIT code no longer needed after
                              ;initial routine call)

ende    equ this byte         ;End of allocated memory (no
                              ;code after this)

;== End ===========================================================

com     ends                  ;End of COM segment
        end start             ;End assembler programs - call
                              ;START to re-execute
```

You must assemble the source program using an assembler. Let's look at creating the program using the Microsoft assembler. First you assemble the code using MASM:

```
masm testcom;
```

After assembling the program, use the LINK program to create an EXE file:

```
link testcom;
```

When you execute LINK, the following message appears:

```
Warning: no stack segment
```

This message tells you what you already know: The program doesn't contain a stack segment, so it may not function correctly as an EXE file. Simply disregard this message.

If no other warnings or errors were indicated, you must convert the file to a COM file. The EXE2BIN program mentioned earlier performs this conversion using the following syntax:

```
exe2bin testcom.exe testcom.com
```

Now there may be two files named TESTCOM on the disk. Delete the one named TESTCOM.EXE; you want the TESTCOM.COM file. If all steps were performed correctly, the TESTCOM.COM program can be executed from DOS by simply typing "TESTCOM".

The following command set is required:

```
masm testcom;
link testcom;
exe2bin testcom.exe testcom.com
```

Borland's Turbo Assembler (TASM) and the TLINK linker perform the same task as MASM, LINK, and EXE2BIN, but in a slightly different manner. Assemble the TESTCOM.ASM file using TASM as follows:

```
tasm testcom
```

Use the following syntax for linking (this directly links the code to COM form):

```
tlink /t testcom
```

17.3 EXE Programs

EXE programs have an advantage over COM programs because they aren't limited to a maximum length of 64K for code, data, and stack. However, these files are more complicated. This means that in addition to the program itself, other information must be stored in an EXE file.

Future versions of DOS may enable EXE programs to adapt to innovations, such as multitasking, because it's easier for DOS to estimate memory requirements for EXE programs than for COM programs.

EXE vs. COM

EXE programs contain separate segments for code, data, and stack that can be organized in any sequence. Unlike a COM program, an EXE program loads into memory from disk, undergoes processing by the EXEC function and then finally begins execution. This is necessary because of the limitations already described for COM programs.

Instead of being limited to loading at a fixed memory location, EXE programs can load at any desired location in memory that's a multiple of 16. Since an EXE program can have several segments, FAR machine language instructions must be used. For example, a main program can be in one segment and call a subroutine in another segment. The segment address must be provided for this FAR instruction in addition to the offset for the routine to be called. The problem is that the segment address may be different for every execution of the program. Consulting the CS register doesn't help because only the segment address of the current code segment, instead of the one to which the jump will be made, is stored there.

749

COM files avoid this problem because the program size is limited to 64K. So, FAR commands are unnecessary. EXE programs solve this problem in a more complex way. The LINK program places a data structure at the beginning of every EXE file that contains (in addition to other things) the addresses of all segments. It contains the addresses of all memory locations in which the segment address of a certain segment is stored during program execution. More specifically, these addresses indicate the addresses of the segment references within instructions. The assembly language code for a FAR jump consists of the following five bytes: the instruction code (one byte), the segment address (one word), and the offset address (one word). The words refer to the location of the jump.

If the EXEC function loads the EXE program, it knows the addresses where the various segments should be loaded. So, it can enter these values into the memory locations at the beginning of the EXE file. Because of this, more time elapses between the initial program call and when the program actually begins execution than for a COM program. The EXE program also occupies more memory than a COM program. The following illustration shows the structure of the header for an EXE file:

EXE file header		
Address	Contents	Type
00H	EXE program identifier (5A4DH)	1 word
02H	file length MOD 512	1 word
04H	file length DIV 512	1 word
06H	Number of segment addresses for passing	1 word
08H	Header size in paragraphs	1 word
0AH	Minimum number of paragraphs needed	1 word
0CH	Maximum number of paragraphs needed	1 word
0EH	Stack segment displacement	1 word
10H	SP register contents when program starts	1 word
12H	Checksum based on EXE file header	1 word
14H	IP register contents when program starts	1 word
16H	Start of code segment in EXE file	1 word
18H	Relocation table address in EXE file	1 word
1AH	Overlay number	1 word
1CH	Buffer memory	??
??H	Address of passing segment addresses (relocation table)	??
??H	Program code, data and stack segment	??

After the segment references within the EXE program have been resolved to the current addresses, the EXEC function sets the DS and the ES segment register to the beginning of the PSP, which also precedes all EXE programs in memory. Because of this, the EXE program can access the information contained in the PSP, such as the address of the environment block and the parameters contained in the command line (command tail). The stack address and the contents of the stack pointer are stored in the EXE file header and accessed from there. This also applies to the code segment address containing the first instructions of the program and the program counter. After the values have been assigned, the program execution begins.

To ensure compatibility with future DOS versions, an EXE program should terminate by calling interrupt 21H function 4CH.

RAM allocation

Obviously, memory must be available for the EXE program. The EXE loader determines the total program size based on the size of the individual segments of the EXE program. Then it can allocate this amount of memory and some additional memory immediately following the EXE program. The first two fields of the EXE program file header contain the minimum and maximum size of memory required in *paragraphs* (1-6 bytes).

First, the EXE loader tries to reserve the maximum number of paragraphs. If this isn't possible, the loader tries to reserve the remaining memory, which cannot be smaller than the minimum number of paragraphs. These fields are determined by the compiler or assembler, instead of the linker. The minimum is 0 and the maximum allowed is FFFFH. In most instances, this last number is unrealistic (it adds up to 1 megabyte) but reserves the entire memory for the EXE program.

Now we encounter the same problems as in COM programs. EXE files make poor resident programs, but an EXE program may need to call another program during execution. This is only possible if you first release the additional reserved memory. The following program contains a routine that reduces the reserved memory to a minimum.

The program uses separate code, data, and stack segments. You can use this program as a model for other EXE programs.

Assembler listing:TESTEXE.ASM

```
;*****************************************************;
;*                                                  *;
;*               T E S T E X E . A S M              *;
;*                                                  *;
;*--------------------------------------------------*;
;*  Task       : Simple EXE program: can be assembled using  *;
;*               either Turbo Assembler (TASM) or Microsoft's *;
;*               Macro Assembler (MASM)             *;
;*--------------------------------------------------*;
;*  Author     : MICHAEL TISCHER                    *;
;*  Developed on : 06/07/1987                       *;
;*  Last update : 12/24/1991                        *;
;*--------------------------------------------------*;
;*  Assembly   : MASM:   masm testexe;              *;
;*                       link testexe;              *;
;*                                                  *;
;*               TASM:   tasm testexe               *;
;*                       tlink testexe              *;
;*****************************************************;

;== Stack ==============================================================

stackseg  segment para STACK 'STACK'     ;Definition of stack segment

          dw 256 dup (?)                 ;The stack comprises 256 words

stackseg  ends                           ;End of stack segment

;== Data ===============================================================

data      segment para 'DATA'            ;Definition of data segment

          ;-- All data, buffers and variables can be stored here -------

          ;...

          ;....

          ;....
```

751

```
data      ends                      ;End of data segment

;== Code ===========================================================

code      segment para 'CODE'       ;Definition of CODE segment

          assume cs:code, ds:data, ss:stackseg

                                     ;CS defines the code segment, DS
                                     ;DS the data segment and SS the stack
                                     ;segment. ES can be accessed freely

prog      proc far                  ;This procedure is the main routine,
                                     ;and is accessed right after the start
                                     ;of the program

          ;-- CS and SS are already initialized. DS must be initialized
          ;-- manually, because it pints to the PSP (like ES)

          mov   ax,data             ;Load segment address of data segment
          mov   ds,ax               ;into the DS register

          call  setfree             ;Release memory not needed

          ;-- Place additional main program code here ------------------

          ;...

          ;...

          ;...

          ;--- End program here using DOS function 4Ch ----------------

          mov   ax,4C00h            ;Load function number and error code
00
          int   21h                 ;DOS call

          ;--- Program execution stops here because of DOS call --------

prog      endp                      ;End of PROG procedure

;-- Subroutines ----------------------------------------------------
;-- This is the area provided for subroutines within the program -------

a_proc    proc near

          ;...
          ;...
```

```
          ;...
          ret

a_proc    endp

b_proc    proc near

          ;...

          ;...
          ret

b_proc    endp

;-- SETFREE: Release unused memory --------------------------------
;-- Input    : ES = Address of PSP
;-- Output   : none
;-- Registers: AX, BX, CL and FLAGS are affected
;-- Info     : Since the stack segment is always the last segment in an
;              EXE file, ES:0000 points to the beginning of the program
;              in memory, and SS:SP points to the end. This allows easy
;              calculation of the program's length.

setfree   proc near

          mov   bx,ss               ;Compute distance between
          mov   ax,es               ;PSP and stack
          sub   bx,ax

          mov   ax,sp               ;Compute stack length
          add   ax,15               ;in paragraphs
          mov   cl,4
          shr   ax,cl               ;Stack length

          add   bx,ax               ;Add two values of current length

          mov   ah,4ah              ;Reserve this memory only
          int   21h                 ;DOS call

          ret                       ;Return to caller

setfree   endp

;== End ============================================================

code      ends                      ;End of CODE segment
          end  prog                 ;Begin execution with PROG procedure
```

To create an EXE program, assemble it like a normal program with an assembler. Then link it with the LINK program. If the program doesn't contain errors, the LINK program creates an EXE file.

The following steps are used to prepare an EXE program from the assembly language source, named TESTEXE.ASM, using the MASM assembler:

```
masm testexe;
link testexe;
```

If you're using the Turbo Assembler TASM, the steps would be as follows:

```
tasm testexe
tlink testexe
```

If all these steps were executed correctly, the program TESTEXE.EXE can be started from the DOS level by typing "TESTEXE".

17.4 The PSP

We'll end this chapter by discussing the Program Segment Prefix (PSP), which DOS places in front of every EXE or COM program in memory. The PSP is a remnant of the CP/M era. It contains data DOS needs to manage the program to be executed. The PSP also stores information that's important to programmers, especially parameters supplied by the user when the program is called from the system prompt. While high level language compilers automatically read these parameters at the beginning of the program and write them to predefined global variables, the assembly language programmer must evaluate this information him/herself.

The following illustration shows the structure and fields of the PSP, many of which remain undocumented (or "reserved") by Microsoft. Most of these fields have been decoded, even though they are useless for practical programming.

Address	Contents	Type
\multicolumn{3}{c}{Structure of the PSP}		
00H	Interrupt 20H call	2 bytes
02H	Segment address of memory allocated for program	1 word
04H	Reserved	1 byte
05H	Interrupt 21H call	5 bytes
0AH	Copy of interrupt vector 23H	2 words
0EH	Copy of interrupt vector 23H	2 words
12H	Copy of interrupt vector 24H	2 words
16H	Reserved	22 bytes
2CH	Segment address of environment block	1 word
2EH	Reserved	46 bytes
5CH	FCB 1	16 bytes
6CH	FCB 2	16 bytes
80H	Number of characters in command line	1 byte
81H	Command line (CR-LF)	127 bytes

The PSP itself is always 256 bytes long and contains important information for DOS and the program to be executed.

Memory location 00H of the PSP contains a DOS function call to terminate a program. This function releases program memory and returns control to the command processor or the calling program. Memory location 05H of the PSP contains a DOS function call to interrupt 21H. Neither of these are used by DOS; they are remnants from the CP/M system.

Memory location 02H of the PSP contains the segment address to the end of the program. Memory location 0AH contains the previous contents of the program termination interrupt vector. Memory location 0EH contains the previous contents of the <Ctrl><C> or <Ctrl><Break> interrupt vector. Memory location 12H contains the previous contents of the critical error interrupt vector. For each of these memory locations, the program changes one of the corresponding vectors during execution; DOS can use the original vector if it detects an error.

Location 2CH contains the segment address of the environment block. The environment block contains information such as the current search path and the directory in which the COMMAND.COM command processor is located on disk.

Memory locations 5CH through 6CH contain a *file control block*. DOS doesn't use the FCB often because it doesn't support hierarchical files (paths) and is also a remnant from CP/M.

The string of parameters that are entered on the command line, following the program name is called the *command tail*. The command tail is copied to the *parameter buffer* in the PSP beginning at memory location 81H and its length is stored at memory location 80H. Any redirection parameters are eliminated from the command tail as it's copied to the parameter buffer. The program can examine the parameters in the parameter buffer to direct its execution.

The parameter buffer is also used by DOS as a disk transfer area (DTA) for transmitting data between the disk drive and memory. Most DOS programs do not use the DTA contained in the PSP because it's another remnant from CP/M.

Chapter 18

Character Input and Output from DOS

DOS input and output functions can address the keyboard, screen, printer, and serial interface. These functions can be divided into two types: those carried over from the CP/M operating system and those borrowed from the UNIX operating system. While the two types of functions can be intermingled, to maintain consistency, we recommend using one type of function throughout a program.

The UNIX type functions use a *handle* as an identifier to a device. Because of recent DOS trends to move closer to UNIX, you may want to give the handle functions precedence.

18.1 Handle Functions

The handle functions perform file access as well as character input to or output from a device. DOS recognizes the difference by examining the name assigned by the handle. If the handle is a device name, it addresses the device; otherwise it assumes that file access should occur. The device names are as follows:

Device	Purpose
CON	Keyboard and screen
AUX	Serial Interface
PRN	Printer
NUL	Imaginary device (nothing happens on access)

Output and input go to and from the AUX, PRN, and NUL devices. For the device CON, output is sent to the screen and input is read from the keyboard.

When DOS passes control to a program, five handles are available for access to individual devices. These handles have values from 0 to 4 and represent the following devices:

Handle	Purpose
0	Standard input (CON)
1	Standard output (CON)
2	Standard output for error messages (CON)
3	Standard serial interface (AUX)
4	Standard printer (PRN)

The following is a short example that demonstrates how to use this table.

Display error message

If a program wants to accept input from the user, this is indicated by the handle function 0 during the call because the standard input device is addressed. Handle 0 normally represents the keyboard, permitting input from the user to the program. Since the user can redirect standard input, you can redirect input to originate from a file instead of the keyboard. This redirection remains hidden from the program.

Before we discuss these devices, you should be familiar with some functions used to access any device.

Function 40H of interrupt 21H sends data to a device. The function number (40H) is passed in the AH register and the handle is passed in the BX register. For example, to display an error message, the value 2 indicates the handle for displaying the error message (this device cannot be redirected, so handle 2 always addresses the console). The number of characters to be in the error message is passed in the CX register. The characters that constitute the message are stored sequentially in memory, whose segment address is stored in the DS register and offset address in the DX register.

Following the call to the function, the carry flag signals any error. If there's no error, the carry flag is reset and the AX register contains the number of characters that were displayed. If the AX register contains the value 0, then there was no more space available on the storage medium for the message. If the carry flag is set, the error message wasn't sent and an error code is indicated in the AX register. An error code of 5 indicates that the device wasn't available. An error code of 6 indicates that the handle wasn't opened.

Function 3FH of interrupt 21H reads character data from a device and is very similar to the previous function. Both functions have identical register usage. The function number is passed in the AX register and the handle in the BX register. The number of characters read is passed in the CX register and the memory address of the characters transferred are passed in the DS:DX register pair.

Following the call to the function, the carry flag also signals any error. Again, any error code is passed in the AX register. Error codes 5 and 6 have the same meaning as in function 40H. If the carry flag is reset, then the function executed successfully. The AX register then contains the number of characters read into the buffer. A value of 0 in the AX register indicates that the data to be read should have come from a file but this file doesn't contain any more data.

As we already mentioned, it's possible to redirect the input or output when accessing DOS. For example, a program that normally expects input from the keyboard can be made to accept the input from a file. So, to avoid having input or output redirected, you can open a new handle to a specific device. This handle ensures that the transfer of data to or from the desired device takes place instead of to or from a redirected device.

Use function 3DH of interrupt 21H to open such a device.

The function number 3DH is passed in the AH register. The AL register contains 0 to enable reading from the device, 1 to enable writing to the device, and 2 for both reading and writing to the device. The name of the device is placed in memory whose address is passed in the DS:DX register pair. So that the DOS can properly identify the device name, the names must be specified in uppercase characters. The last character of the string must be an end character (ASCII value 0).

Following the function calls, the status is indicated by the carry flag. A reset flag means that the device was opened successfully and the handle number is passed back in the AX register. A set flag indicates an error and the AX register contains any error code.

The handle is closed using function 3EH of interrupt 21H. The function number is passed in the AH register and the handle number is passed in the BX register. The carry flag again indicates the status of the function call. A set carry flag indicates an error.

You can also close the predefined handles 0 through 4 using this function. But if you close handle 0 (the standard input device) you'll no longer be able to accept input from the keyboard.

Now let's examine the special characteristics of each device.

Keyboard

The keyboard can perform only read operations. The results of the read operations depend on the mode in which the device was addressed. Here DOS differentiates between *raw* and *cooked*. In the *cooked mode* DOS checks every character sent to or received from a device to determine whether it's a special control character. If DOS finds a special control character, it performs a certain action in response to the character. In *raw mode*, the individual characters are passed through unchecked and unmanipulated. DOS normally operates the device in cooked mode for character input and output. However, you can switch to raw mode within a program (see below).

The best way to illustrate the difference between cooked and raw mode is with an example of reading the keyboard. Suppose that 30 characters are read from the keyboard in cooked mode. As you enter the characters, DOS allows you to edit the input using several control keys. For example, <Ctrl><C> and <Ctrl><Break> abort the input. <Ctrl><S> temporarily halts the program until another key is pressed. <Ctrl><P> directs subsequent data from the screen to the printer (until <Ctrl><P> is pressed again). <Backspace> removes the last character from the DOS buffer. If the <Enter> key is pressed, the first 30 characters (or all characters input up to now if there are less than 30) are copied from the DOS buffer into the input buffer of the program without the control characters.

In raw mode all characters entered (including control characters) are passed to the calling program without requiring the user to press the <Enter> key. After exactly 30 characters, control passes to the calling program, even if you pressed the <Enter> key as the second character of the input.

Screen

To display characters on the screen, handle 1 is usually addressed as the standard output device. Since this device can be redirected, output through this handle can pass to devices other than the screen. However, you cannot redirect the standard error output device (handle 2). So, error messages that pass through this handle always appear on the screen. This handle is recommended only for character display on the screen.

The screen is normally addressed in cooked mode; every character displayed on the screen is tested for the <Ctrl><C> or the <Ctrl><Break> control characters. Since this test slows down the screen output, changing to raw mode occasionally decreases program execution time.

Printer

Unlike the keyboard and screen, printer output cannot be redirected (at least not from the user level). An exception to this rule is redirecting output from a parallel printer to a serial printer. Characters ready to print can be sent to a buffer before they are sent to the printer. Handle 4 is used to address the standard printer. There are three standard printer devices LPT1, LPT2, and LPT3. Device PRN is synonymous with LPT1. When this handle is opened, the device name is specified as one of the three: LPT1, LPT2, or LPT3.

Serial interface

Much of the information that applies to the printer also applies to the serial interface. For example, serial input and output cannot be redirected to another device (e.g., from a serial printer to a parallel printer). The programmer can use the predefined handle 3 for serial access, through which you can address the standard serial interface (AUX).

Handle 3 is used to address the standard serial device. The two are named COM1 and COM2. A PC can have multiple serial interfaces. Only the first two (COM1 and COM2) are supported by DOS. Since the system doesn't know exactly which interface to access during AUX device access, you should open a new handle for access to the specific device.

Errors during read operations in DOS mode are returned to the serial interface in cooked mode. The number returned to the AX register won't match the number of characters actually read. We recommend that you operate the serial interface in raw mode, even if this mode ignores control characters, such as <Ctrl><C> and EOF (end-of-file).

18.2 Traditional DOS Functions

The DOS functions for input and output aren't based on the handle oriented functions. If you use these functions you won't need to specify a handle, since each function pertains to a specific device.

The various input and output devices and the way in which these functions work with them are listed later.

Keyboard

There are seven DOS functions for addressing the keyboard but they differ in many ways. For example, these functions respond differently to the <Ctrl> <Break> key. While some functions echo the characters on the screen, others don't.

You can use DOS functions 01H, 06H, 07H, and 08H to read a single keyboard character. The function number is passed in the AH register. Following the call, the character is returned in the AL register.

For DOS function 01H, DOS waits for a keypress if the keyboard buffer is empty. When this happens, the character is echoed on the screen. If the keyboard buffer isn't empty, a new character is fetched and returned to the calling program. DOS function 06H can be used for both character input and output. To input a character, a value of FFH is loaded into the DL register. Instead of waiting for a character to be input, this function immediately returns to the calling program. If the zero flag is set, a character wasn't read. If the zero flag is reset, a character was read and returned in the AL register. The character isn't echoed on the screen.

DOS functions 07H and 08H are used to read the keyboard similar to function 1. Both either fetch a character from the keyboard buffer or wait for a character to be entered at the keyboard. Neither echo the character to the screen. They differ because function 08H responds to <Ctrl><C> but function 07H doesn't.

By using function 0BH, a program can determine whether one or more characters are in the keyboard buffer before calling any functions that read characters. After calling this function, the AL register contains 0 if the keyboard buffer is empty, and FFH if the keyboard buffer isn't empty.

DOS function 0CH is used to clear the keyboard buffer. After the buffer is cleared, the function, whose number was passed to function 0CH in the AL register, is automatically called.

DOS function 0AH is used to read a string of characters. Again, this function number is passed in the AH register. In addition, the memory address of a buffer for the character string is passed in the DS:DX register pair. This buffer is used to hold the character string. The first byte of the buffer indicates the maximum number of characters that may be contained in the buffer.

When this function is called, DOS reads up to the maximum number of characters and stores them in the buffer starting at the third byte. It reads until either the maximum number of characters is entered or the <Enter> key is pressed. The actual number of characters is stored in the second byte of the buffer. Extended key codes, which occupy two bytes each in the buffer, may be entered. The first byte of the pair (ASCII value 0) signifies that an extended key code follows. This means, for example, that for a maximum buffer size of 10 bytes, only five extended characters may be entered.

The following table illustrates how the various functions respond to <Ctrl><C> or <Ctrl><Break>, and provides a quick overview of the individual functions for character input.

Function	Task	<Ctrl><C>	Echo
01H	Character input	yes	yes
06H	Direct character input	no	no
07H	Character input	no	no
08H	Character input	yes	no
0AH	Character string input	yes	no
0BH	Read input status	yes	no
0CH	Reset input buffer then input	varies	varies

Screen output

There are three DOS functions for character output.

DOS function 02H outputs a single character to the screen or standard output device. This character is passed to the DL register.

DOS function 06H, which is multipurpose, is also used to output a single character. The character is passed in the DL register. You can see that the character, whose value is 255, cannot be output because this indicates that the function must perform an input operation. Output using this function is faster than using function 02H because it doesn't test for the <Ctrl><C> or <Ctrl><Break> keys.

DOS function 09H is used for string output. Again, the function number is passed in the AH register. The address of the string is passed in the DS:DX register pair. The last character of the string is a dollar sign. Also, the following control codes are recognized:

Code	Character	Operation
07	Bell	Sounds a beep
08	Backspace	Erases preceding character and moves cursor left by one character
10	Linefeed	Moves cursor one line down (LF)
13	Carriage return	Moves cursor to the beginning of the current line (CR)

As with function 02H, this function also checks for <Ctrl><C> or <Ctrl><Break>.

Printer

DOS function 05H is used to output a single character to the printer. If the printer is busy, this function waits until it's ready before returning control to the calling program. During this time, it will respond to the <Ctrl><C> and <Ctrl><Break> keys.

The function number is passed in the AH register. The character to output is passed in the DL register. The status of the printer isn't returned. Most programmers use the BIOS function instead of the DOS function for printer output because they can specify the exact printer device and determine the printer status using the BIOS version. Refer to Section 7.1 for more detailed information.

Serial interface

There are two DOS functions for communicating using a serial interface; one is used for input and one for output. Both functions respond to <Ctrl><C> and <Ctrl><Break>, but they don't return the status of the serial interface or recognize transmission errors.

DOS function 03H is used to input data from the serial interface. The character is returned in the AL register. Since the data isn't buffered, it can overrun the interface if the interface receives data faster than this function can handle it.

DOS function 04H is used to output data over the serial interface. The character to output is passed in the DL register. If the serial interface isn't ready to accept the data, this function waits until the serial interface is free.

Again, most programmers prefer to use the BIOS equivalent functions (see Chapter 3) to perform serial data transmission because of their complete data handling capabilities.

18.3 Toggling Between Raw and Cooked Modes

Earlier we mentioned that it's possible to switch a device from cooked mode to raw mode and then back again. The Pascal and C programs that follow demonstrate how to do this. They use the IOCTL functions, which permit access to the DOS device drivers (see Chapter 25 for details on this routine). These routines act as interfaces between the DOS input/output functions and the hardware. The IOCTL functions in these programs tell the CON device driver (responsible for the keyboard and the display) whether it should operate in the cooked mode or in the raw mode.

To demonstrate how differently characters respond in the two modes, the programs switch the CON driver into raw mode first. Then this driver displays a sample string several times. Unlike cooked mode, pressing <Ctrl><C> or <Ctrl><S> in raw mode has no effect on stopping program execution or text display.

After the program finishes displaying the sample string, the driver switches to the cooked mode. The sample string is displayed again several times. When you press <Ctrl><C>, the program stops (Turbo Pascal version). For the C version, you can press <Ctrl><C> to stop the program or press <Ctrl><S> to pause or continue the display.

Switching between the raw and the cooked mode doesn't occur directly through a function. First the *device attribute* of the driver is determined. This attribute contains certain information that identifies the driver and describes its method of operation. One bit in this word indicates whether the driver operates in raw or cooked mode. The programs set or reset this bit, depending on the mode you want running the driver.

Pascal listing: RAWCOOK.PAS

```
{*************************************************}
{*                   R A W C O O K                *}
{*-----------------------------------------------*}
{*  Task        :   provide two functions to switch      *}
{*                  a character device driver to the RAW- *}
{*                  or the COOKED mode                    *}
{*-----------------------------------------------*}
{*  Author      : MICHAEL TISCHER                 *}
{*  developed   : 08/16/87                        *}
{*  last Update : 05/11/89                        *}
{*************************************************}

program RAWCOOKP;

Uses Crt, Dos;                              { CRT and DOS units }

const STANDARDIN = 0;    { handle 0 is connected with Standard input }
      STANDARDOUT = 1;   { handle 1 is connected with Standard output }

var Keys : char;                    { only needed for Demo program }

{*************************************************}
{* GETMODE: read attribute of device driver in          *}
{* Input  : the handle passed must be connected to device addressed *}
{* Output : the device attribute                        *}
{*************************************************}

function GetMode(Handle : integer) : integer;

var Regs : Registers;          { register-Variable for Interrupt call }

begin
  Regs.ah := $44;              { Function number for IOCTL: Get Mode }
  Regs.bx := Handle;
  MsDos( Regs );               { Call DOS-Interrupt 21H }
  GetMode := Regs.dx           { Pass device attribute }
end;

{*************************************************}
{* SETRAW : Change a character driver into RAW-Mode     *}
{* Input  : the handle passed must be connected with    *}
{*          addressed device                            *}
{* Output : none                                        *}
{*************************************************}

procedure SetRaw(Handle : integer);

var Regs : Registers;          { register-Variable for Interrupt call }

begin
  Regs.ax := $4401;            { Function number for IOCTL: Set Mode }
  Regs.bx := Handle;
  Regs.dx := GetMode(Handle) and 255 or 32;  { new device attribute }
  MsDos( Regs );               { Call DOS-Interrupt 21H }
end;

{*************************************************}
{* SETCOOKED : Change a character driver into the COOKED-Mode *}
{* Input    : the handle passed must be connected with the   *}
{*            device addressed                               *}
{* Output   : none                                           *}
{*************************************************}

procedure SetCooked(Handle : integer);
```

```
var Regs : Registers;          { register-Variable for Interrupt call }

begin
  Regs.ax := $4401;            { Function number for IOCTL: Set Mode }
  Regs.bx := Handle;
  Regs.dx := GetMode(Handle) and 223;  { new device attribute }
  MsDos( Regs );               { Call DOS-Interrupt 21H }
end;

{*************************************************}
{* TESTOUTPUT : Output a Test-String 1000 times on the Standard *}
{*              output device                           *}
{* Input    : none                                      *}
{* Output   : none                                      *}
{*************************************************}

procedure TestOutput;

var Regs : Registers;          { register-Variable for Interrupt call }
    LoopCnt : integer;                    { Loop variable }
    Test    : string[9];         { The Test-String for output }

begin
  Test := 'Test.... ';
  Regs.bx := STANDARDOUT;      { output on the Standard output device }
  Regs.cx := 9;                        { Number of characters }
  Regs.ds := Seg(Test);               { Segment address of the text }
  Regs.dx := Ofs(Test)+1;             { Offset address of the text }
  for LoopCnt := 1 to 1000 do
  begin
    Regs.ah := $40;            { Write function number for handle }
    MsDos( Regs );             { Call DOS-Interrupt 21H }
  end;
  writeln;
end;

{*************************************************}
{*                   MAIN PROGRAM                *}
{*************************************************}

begin
  ClrScr;                              { Clear screen }
  writeln('RAWCOOK (c) 1987 by Michael Tischer'#13#10);
  writeln('The Console driver is now in RAW-Mode. Control keys such as
<Ctrl><C>');
  writeln('are not recognized during output. Press a key to display a
text on'#13#10);
  writeln('the screen, and try stopping the display by pressing
<Ctrl><C>');
  Keys := ReadKey;                     { wait for key }
  SetRaw(STANDARDIN);           { Console driver in RAW mode }
  TestOutput;                   { Output Test-String 1000 times }
  ClrScr;                              { Clear Screen }
  while KeyPressed do
    Keys := ReadKey;            { Empty keyboard buffer }
  writeln('The Console driver is now in COOKED mode. Control keys such
as');
  writeln('<CTRL><C> are recognized during output');
  writeln('Press a key to start, then press <Ctrl><C> to stop the
display');
  Keys := ReadKey;                     { Wait for key }
  SetCooked(STANDARDIN);
  TestOutput;                   { Output Test-String 1000 times }
end.
```

C listing: RAWCOOK.C

```
/***********************************************************/
/*                    R A W C O O K                     */
/*-------------------------------------------------------*/
/*   Task      : provides two functions for             */
/*               switching a character device driver into the RAW */
/*               or into the COOKED mode                */
/*-------------------------------------------------------*/
/*   Author    : MICHAEL TISCHER                        */
/*   developed on : 08/16/87                            */
/*   last Update  : 04/08/89                            */
/*-------------------------------------------------------*/
/*   (MICROSOFT C)                                      */
/*   Creation   : MSC RAWCOOKC;                         */
/*               LINK RAWCOOKC;                         */
/*   Call       : RAWCOOKC                              */
/*-------------------------------------------------------*/
/*   (BORLAND TURBO C)                                  */
/*   Creation   : through command RUN in the menu       */
/***********************************************************/

#include <dos.h>                  /* include Header files */
#include <stdio.h>
#include <conio.h>

#define STANDARDIN 0    /* handle 0 is the Standard input device */
#define STANDARDOUT 1   /* handle 1 is the Standard output device */

/***********************************************************/
/* GETMODE: read the attribute of a device driver         */
/* Input : the handle must be connected with the addressed device */
/* Output : the device attribute                          */
/***********************************************************/

int GetMode(Handle)
int Handle;                    /* points to the character driver */

{
 union REGS Register;       /* register-Variable for Interrupt call */

 Register.x.ax = 0x4400;    /* Function number for IOCTL: Get Mode */
 Register.x.bx = Handle;
 intdos(&Register, &Register);      /* Call DOS-Interrupt 21H */
 return(Register.x.dx);             /* Pass device attribute */
}

/***********************************************************/
/* SETRAW : Change a character driver into RAW mode        */
/* Input : the handle passed must be connected with the addressed */
/*         device                                          */
/* Output : none                                           */
/***********************************************************/

int SetRaw(Handle)
int Handle;                    /* points to the character driver */

{
 union REGS Register;       /* register-Variable for Interrupt call */

 Register.x.ax = 0x4401;    /* Function number for IOCTL: Set Mode */
 Register.x.bx = Handle;
 Register.x.dx = GetMode(Handle) & 255 | 32; /* new device attribute */
 intdos(&Register, &Register);      /* Call DOS-Interrupt 21H */
}
```

```
}

/***********************************************************/
/* SETCOOKED: Changes a character driver into the COOKED mode */
/* Input   : the handle passed must be connected with the device */
/*           addressed                                     */
/* Output  : none                                          */
/***********************************************************/

int SetCooked(Handle)
int Handle;                    /* points to the character driver */

{
 union REGS Register;       /* register-Variable for Interrupt call */

 Register.x.ax = 0x4401;    /* Function number for IOCTL: Set Mode */
 Register.x.bx = Handle;
 Register.x.dx = GetMode(Handle) & 223;   /* new device attribute */
 intdos(&Register, &Register);      /* Call DOS-Interrupt 21H */
}

/***********************************************************/
/* TESTOUTPUT: outputs a Test-String 1000 times on the Standard */
/*             output device                               */
/* Input   : none                                          */
/* Output  : none                                          */
/***********************************************************/

void TestOutput()

{
 int i;                                /* Loop Variable */
 static char Test[] = "Test.... ";     /* the text for output */

 printf("\n");
 for (i = 0; i < 1000; i++)            /* output 1000 times */
  fputs(Test, stdout);      /* Output String on the Standard output. */
 printf("\n");
}

/***********************************************************/
/**                   MAIN PROGRAM                      **/
/***********************************************************/

void main()

{
 printf("\nRAWCOOK (c) 1987 by Michael Tischer\n\n");

 printf("The Console Driver (Keyboard, Display) is now in ");
 printf("RAW Mode.\nDuring the following output control characters,\n");
 printf("such as <CTRL-S> will not be recognized.\n");
 printf("Try it.\n\n");
 printf("Please press a key to start...");
 getch();                              /* wait for key */
 SetRaw(STANDARDIN);          /* Console driver into RAW mode */
 TestOutput();
 while (kbhit())       /* in the meantime remove key codes from */
  getch();                           /* keyboard buffer */
 printf("\nThe console driver is now in COOKED mode. ");
 printf("Control keys such as\n<CTRL-S> are recognized during ");
 printf("output and answered accordingly!\n");
 printf("Please press a key to start ...");
 getch();                              /* wait for key */
 SetCooked(STANDARDIN);       /* Console driver in the COOKED mode */
 TestOutput();
```

18.4 DOS Filters

Filters are programs, routines, or utilities that accept input and modify the data for output. Filters also perform these tasks on the operating system level. Characters are passed to these filters as input. Then the filters modify the characters and send them as output. This manipulation takes many forms. Filters can sort data, replace certain data with other data, encode data, or decode data.

DOS has three basic filters available:

> FIND   Searches input for a specified set of characters.
>
> SORT   Arranges text or data in order.
>
> MORE Formats text display.

These filters perform simple redirection of standard input/output. They read characters from the standard input device, manipulate the characters as needed, then display them on the standard output device. Under DOS, the standard input device is the keyboard and the standard output device is the monitor. DOS Versions 2.0 and higher allow the user to redirect the standard input/output to files. So, depending on the standard input device selected, a filter can read characters from the keyboard or from a file. This is possible by using a filter along with one of the DOS handle functions for reading and writing. DOS provides five handles:

0	Standard input	CON (Keyboard)
1	Standard output	CON (Screen)
2	Standard error output	CON (Screen)
3	Standard serial interface	AUX
4	Standard printer	PRN

If the user calls a program from the DOS level, the "<" character redirects input and the ">" character redirects output. In the following example, the input comes from the file IN.TXT instead of the keyboard. The output is written to the file OUT.TXT instead of the screen:

```
sort <in.txt >out.txt
```

SORT

After the user enters the previous command, DOS recognizes that a program named SORT should be called. Then it encounters the expression <IN.TXT, which redirects the standard input. This occurs by assigning the handle 0 (standard input, which formerly pointed to the keyboard) to the file IN.TXT. The expression >OUT.TXT resets handle 1 to the OUT.TXT file instead of the screen. The affected handle is first closed, and then the redirected file is opened.

Once the command processor finishes with the command line, it calls the SORT program by using the EXEC function (DOS function 4BH). Since the program called with the EXEC function has all the handles of the calling program available, the SORT program can input/output characters to handles 0 and 1. Where the characters originate isn't important to the program.

After the SORT program completes its work, it returns control to the command processor. The command processor resets the redirection and waits for further input from the user.

Pipes

The filter principle, as supported by DOS, becomes especially powerful through pipes. This is similar to a pipeline used for transporting oil or gas. DOS pipes have a similar function; they carry characters from one program to another and allow various programs to be connected to each other.

When this happens, characters output from one program to the standard output device can be read by another program from the standard input device. As in the redirection of the standard input/output, the two programs don't notice the pipelines. The difference between the two procedures is that under redirection of the standard input/output devices, data can be redirected to only one device or file, while the use of pipes allows data transfer to another program.

Combined filters

Pipes allow users to connect multiple filters. The pipe character | is inserted between the programs to be connected. For example, suppose that a text file named DEMO.TXT is sorted and then displayed on the screen in page format. Even though this task appears to be very complicated at first, it can be performed easily using the DOS filters SORT and MORE. SORT sorts the file and MORE displays the file on the screen in page format.

How can you tell the command processor to perform these tasks? First SORT is used. This filter is told to sort the file DEMO.TXT. The redirection of standard input can be used, as illustrated at the beginning of the chapter:

```
SORT <DEMO.TXT
```

After the user enters this command, SORT sorts the file DEMO.TXT and then displays the file on the screen. This display would be much easier to read in page format. Formatted output can be implemented by redirecting the output from SORT to a file (e.g., TEMP.TXT) and displaying this file using the MORE command. The following sequence of commands do this:

```
SORT <DEMO.TXT >TEMP.TXT
MORE <TEMP.TXT
```

You can use a pipe to connect the SORT filter and the MORE filter, which saves typing time. The following command line sends the output from SORT directly to MORE and immediately displays the sorted file in page format:

```
SORT <DEMO.TXT | MORE
```

Any number of filters can be connected using pipes. DOS always executes these pipelined filters from left to right. It sends the output from the first program as input to the second program, the

765

second program's output as input to the third program, etc. The last program can again force the redirection of the output with the > character so that the final result of the whole program or filter chain travels to a file or other device instead of the screen.

Note: DOS cannot send data from one filter directly to another because it would have to execute both filters simultaneously. However, the current version of DOS doesn't have multiprocessing capabilities. Instead, the following method is used. The input calls the first filter and redirects its output to a pipe file. After the first filter ends its processing, it calls the second filter but redirects its input to the pipe file to read in the output from the first filter. This principle applies to all filters. The pipe file is stored in the current working directory.

18.5 A Filter Demonstration Program

"Dump" is a computer term that refers to a way to display the contents of a file in ASCII characters and/or hexadecimal numbers. The following DUMP programs perform this task as a filter. As the contents are displayed in ASCII format, DUMP differentiates between normal ASCII characters (letters, numbers, etc.) and control characters, such as a carriage return, linefeed, etc. These control characters are displayed in mnemonic form (e.g., <CR> for carriage return and <LF> for linefeed). Although this DUMP filter has a fairly simple structure, it can be very useful for quickly examining a file's contents.

The structure of the DUMP program is typical for a filter. Since DUMP displays a maximum of nine ASCII characters and/or hexadecimal codes per line, it asks for nine characters by using the read function from the standard input device. If enough characters aren't available, it reads the available characters. DUMP places these characters in a buffer, then converts the characters into ASCII characters and hex codes. This buffer will accept a complete line of 78 characters. When the buffer processing is complete, the filter uses the handle to write to the standard output device. This process is repeated until no more characters can be read from the standard input device.

The following programs are written in Pascal, C, and assembly language. Remember that there isn't a BASIC version because, as an interpreted language, it isn't suitable for developing a filter that can be called from the DOS level. A BASIC compiler is needed for this task.

Pascal listing: DUMPP.PAS

```
{****************************************************}
{*                    D U M P P                    *}
{*------------------------------------------------*}
{*  Task      : A filter, which reads in characters from the  *}
{*              standard input device and outputs them as     *}
{*              hex and ASCII dump on the standard output device *}
{*------------------------------------------------*}
{*  Author    : MICHAEL TISCHER                    *}
{*  Developed on : 08/08/87                        *}
{*  Last update  : 01/14/92                        *}
{*------------------------------------------------*}
{*  Info      : This program can only be called from the  *}
{*              DOS level after compiling to an EXE file   *}
{*              with TURBO                          *}
{****************************************************}
```

```
program DUMPP;

Uses Dos;                          { Add DOS unit }

{$V-}                              { Suppress length test on strings }

const NUL = 0;                     { ASCII code for NULL character }
      BEL = 7;                     { ASCII code for BELL }
      BS  = 8;                     { ASCII code for Backspace }
      TAB = 9;                     { ASCII code for Tab }
      LF  = 10;                    { ASCII code for Linefeed }
      CR  = 13;                    { ASCII code for Carriage Return }
      EOF = 26;                    { ASCII code for End of File }
      ESC = 27;                    { ASCII code for Escape }

type SZText = string[3];     { passes the name of a special character }
```

```
    DumpBf = array[1..80] of char;          { accepts the output Dump }


{*************************************************************************}
{* SZ     : Writes the name of a control character into a buffer       *}
{* Input  : See below                                                  *}
{* Output : None                                                       *}
{* Info   : After the call of this procedure the pointer               *}
{*          which was passed, points behind the last character of      *}
{*          the control character name in the dump buffer              *}
{*************************************************************************}

procedure SZ(var Buffer  : DumpBf;          { Text entered here }
                 Text     : SZText;         { Text to be entered }
                 var Pointer : integer);    { Addr. of text in buffer }

var Counter : integer;                              { Loop counter }

begin
  Buffer[Pointer] := '<';                   { Starts control character }
  for Counter := 1 to length(Text) do       { Transfer text to buffer }
    Buffer[Pointer + Counter] := Text[Counter];
  Buffer[Pointer + Counter + 1] := '>';     { Terminates control char }
  Pointer := Pointer + Counter + 2;         { Pointer to next character }
end;


{*************************************************************************}
{* DODUMP : Reads characters in and dumps them to screen              *}
{* Input  : None                                                       *}
{* Output : None                                                       *}
{*************************************************************************}

procedure DoDump;

var Regs     : Registers;     { Register variable for interrupt call }
    NineBytes: array[1..9] of char; { Accepts the characters read in }
    DumpBuf  : DumpBf;                 { Accepts a line for dumping }
    HexChr,
    Counter,
    NextA    : integer;       { Pointer in buffer for ASCII code }
    Endc     : boolean;              { Another byte read in? }

begin
  Endc := false;                                     { Not the end }
  repeat
    Regs.ah := $3F;              { Function number for reading handle }
    Regs.bx := 0;               { Standard input device is handle 0 }
    Regs.cx := 9;                         { Read in 9 characters }
    Regs.ds := seg(NineBytes);    { Segment address of the buffer }
    Regs.dx := ofs(NineBytes);    { Offset address of the buffer }
    MsDos( Regs );                     { Call DOS interrupt 21H }
    if (Regs.ax = 0) then Endc := true;      { No character read? }
    if not(Endc) then
    begin                                                  { No }
      for Counter := 1 to 30          { Fill buffer with spaces }
      do DumpBuf [Counter] := ' ';
      DumpBuf[31] := #219;     { Place separator between hex and ASCII }
      NextA := 32;             { ASCII characters follow separator }
      for Counter := 1 to Regs.ax do   { Start processing characters }
      begin                                           { Read in }
        HexChr := ord(NineBytes[Counter]) shr 4 + 48;  { Hex top 4 bits }
        if (HexChr > 57) then HexChr := HexChr + 7;    { Convert char }
        DumpBuf[Counter * 3 - 2] := chr(HexChr);    { Store in buffer }
        HexChr := ord(NineBytes[Counter]) and 15 + 48;
                                                { Hex bottom 4 bits }
        if (HexChr > 57) then HexChr := HexChr + 7;    { Convert number }
        DumpBuf[Counter * 3 - 1] := chr(HexChr);    { Store in buffer }
        case ord(NineBytes[Counter]) of          { Test ASCII code }
          NUL : SZ(DumpBuf, 'NUL', NextA);          { NULL          }
          BEL : SZ(DumpBuf, 'BEL', NextA);          { BELL          }
          BS  : SZ(DumpBuf, 'BS' , NextA);          { Backspace     }
          TAB : SZ(DumpBuf, 'TAB', NextA);          { Tab           }
          LF  : SZ(DumpBuf, 'LF' , NextA);          { Linefeed      }
          CR  : SZ(DumpBuf, 'CR' , NextA);          { Carriage Return }
          EOF : SZ(DumpBuf, 'EOF', NextA);          { End of File   }
          ESC : SZ(DumpBuf, 'ESC', NextA);          { Escape        }
        else
          begin
            DumpBuf[NextA] := NineBytes[Counter];   { Store ASCII char. }
            NextA := succ(NextA)          { Set pointer to next character }
          end
      end;
    end;
    DumpBuf[NextA] := #219;                      { Set end character }
    DumpBuf[NextA+1] := chr(CR);        { Carriage return followed }
    DumpBuf[NextA+2] := chr(LF);        { by linefeed to buffer end }
    Regs.ah := $40;            { Function number for writing handle }
    Regs.bx := 1;             { Standard output device is handle 1 }
    Regs.cx := NextA+2;                   { Number of characters }
    Regs.ds := seg(DumpBuf);       { Segment address of the buffer }
    Regs.dx := ofs(DumpBuf);       { Offset address of the buffer }
    MsDos( Regs );                        { Call DOS interrupt 21H }
  end;
  until Endc;        { Repeat until no more characters are available }
end;


{*************************************************************************}
{*                        MAIN PROGRAM                                 *}
{*************************************************************************}

begin
  DoDump;                                             { Output dump }
end.
```

C listing: DUMPC.C

```
/*******************************************************************/
/*                        D U M P C                            */
/*-----------------------------------------------------------------*/
/*   Task       : A filter, which reads in characters from the     */
/*                standard input device and outputs them as a      */
/*                hex and ASCII dump on the standard output device */
/*-----------------------------------------------------------------*/
/*   Author     : MICHAEL TISCHER                                  */
/*   Developed on : 08/14/87                                       */
/*   Last update  : 01/14/92                                       */
/*******************************************************************/

#include <stdio.h>                      /* Include header files */
#include <dos.h>

/*== Type definitions ============================================*/
typedef unsigned char BYTE;                /* Handle as a byte */

/*== Constants ===================================================*/
#define NUL   0              /* ASCII code for NULL character */
#define BEL   7              /* ASCII code for Bell          */
#define BS    8              /* ASCII code for Backspace     */
#define TAB   9              /* ASCII code for Tab           */
#define LF    10             /* ASCII code for Linefeed      */
#define CR    13             /* ASCII code for Carriage Return */
#define ESC   27             /* ASCII code for Escape        */

/*== Macros ======================================================*/
#define tohex(c) ( ((c)<10) ? ((c) | 48) : ((c) + 'A' - 10) )

/*******************************************************************/
/* GETSTDIN: Reads a certain number of characters from the standard */
/*           input device and places them in a buffer             */
/* Input  : BUFFER  = Pointer to buffer receiving characters      */
/*          MAXCHAR = Maximum number of characters read at a time  */
/* Output : Number of characters read                             */
/*******************************************************************/

int GetStdIn(char *Buffer, int MaxChar)
{
 union REGS Register;        /* Register variable for interrupt call */
 struct SREGS Segment;             /* Accepts the segment register */

 segread(&Segment);          /* Read contents of segment register */
 Register.h.ah = 0x3F;                   /* Function number */
 Register.x.bx = 0;           /* Standard input device is handle 0 */
 Register.x.cx = MaxChar;          /* Number of bytes to be read */
 Register.x.dx = (unsigned int) Buffer;  /* Offset address of buffer */
 intdosx(&Register, &Register, &Segment);    /* Call Interrupt 21H */
 return(Register.x.ax);         /* Number of bytes read to caller */
}

/*******************************************************************/
/* STRAP  : Attach character to string                           */
/* Input  : STRING    = Pointer to string to be appended         */
/*          TEXTPOINTER = Pointer to string with additional text  */
/* Output : Pointer behind the last added character              */
/*******************************************************************/

char *Strap(char *String, char *Textpointer)
{
 while (*Textpointer)         /* Repeat until '\0' detected */
  *String++ = *Textpointer++;         /* Transmit character */
 return(String);            /* Pass pointer to calling function */
}
```

```
/*******************************************************************/
/* DODUMP : Reads the characters in and outputs them as dump     */
/* Input  : None                                                 */
/* Output : None                                                 */
/*******************************************************************/

void DoDump( void )
{
 char NineBytes[9],                 /* Accepts the characters read */
      DumpBuf[80],                    /* Accepts a line of DUMP */
      *NextAscii;    /* Points to next ASCII character in the buffer */
 BYTE i,                                 /* Loop counter */
      Readbytes;                        /* Number of bytes read */

 DumpBuf[30] = 219;          /* Set separator between hex and ASCII */
 while((Readbytes = GetStdIn(NineBytes, 9)) != 0)
                             /* as long as characters are available */
 {
  for (i = 0; i < 30; DumpBuf[i++] = ' ');
                                /* Fill buffer with spaces */
  NextAscii = &DumpBuf[31];      /* ASCII characters start here */
  for (i = 0; i < Readbytes; i++)
                                /* Process all characters read */
  {
   DumpBuf[i*3] = tohex((BYTE) NineBytes[i] >> 4);
                                /* Convert code to hex */
   DumpBuf[i*3+1] = tohex((BYTE) NineBytes[i] & 15);
   switch (NineBytes[i])              /* Read ASCII code */
   {
    case NUL : NextAscii = Strap(NextAscii, "<NUL>");
           break;
    case BEL : NextAscii = Strap(NextAscii, "<BEL>");
           break;
    case BS  : NextAscii = Strap(NextAscii, "<BS>");
           break;
    case TAB : NextAscii = Strap(NextAscii, "<TAB>");
           break;
    case LF  : NextAscii = Strap(NextAscii, "<LF>");
           break;
    case CR  : NextAscii = Strap(NextAscii, "<CR>");
           break;
    case ESC : NextAscii = Strap(NextAscii, "<ESC>");
           break;
    case EOF : NextAscii = Strap(NextAscii, "<EOF>");
           break;
    default  : *NextAscii++ = NineBytes[i];
   }
  }
  *NextAscii = 219;       /* End character for ASCII representation */
  *(NextAscii+1) = '\r';      /* Carriage Return to end of buffer */
  *(NextAscii+2) = '\0';          /* NULL converted to LF on output */
  puts(DumpBuf);        /* Write string to standard output device */
 }
}

/*******************************************************************/
/**                      MAIN PROGRAM                          **/
/*******************************************************************/

void main()
{
 DoDump();                         /* Character input/output */
}
```

Assembler listing: DUMPA.ASM

```
;***************************************************************;
;*                       D U M P A                           *;
;*-----------------------------------------------------------*;
;*   Task : Filter which reads characters from the standard input  *;
;*          device and outputs these characters as Hex and ASCII   *;
;*          dumps on the standard output device.                   *;
;*-----------------------------------------------------------*;
;*   Author          : Michael Tischer                       *;
;*   Developed on     : 08/01/87                             *;
;*   Last update      : 12/24/91                             *;
;*-----------------------------------------------------------*;
;*   Assembly         : MASM DUMPA;                          *;
;*                      LINK DUMPA;                          *;
;*                      EXE2BIN DUMPA DUMPA.COM              *;
;*                      - or -                               *;
;*                      TASM DUMPA                           *;
;*                      TLINK /T DUMPA                       *;
;*-----------------------------------------------------------*;
;*   Call            : DUMPA [<Input] [>Output]              *;
;***************************************************************;


;== Constants =============================================

      NUL    equ 0            ;ASCII code for NUL character
      BEL    equ 7            ;ASCII code for Bell
      BS     equ 8            ;ASCII code for Backspace
      TAB    equ 9            ;ASCII code for Tab
      LF     equ 10           ;ASCII code for Linefeed
      CR     equ 13           ;ASCII code for Carriage Return
      EOF    equ 26           ;ASCII code for End of File
      ESCAPE equ 27           ;ASCII code for Escape

;== Program starts here ===========================

code     segment para 'CODE'     ;Definition of CODE segment

         org 100h

         assume cs:code, ds:code, es:code, ss:code

;-- Start routine -----------------------------------------

dump     label near

         ;-- Read 9 bytes from standard input device ----------------

         xor  bx,bx            ;Standard input has the handle 0
         mov  cx,9             ;Read 9 characters
         mov  dx,offset ninebyte ;Buffer address
         mov  ah,3Fh           ;Function code for handle reading
         int  21h              ;Call DOS function
         or   ax,ax            ;Characters read?
         jne  dodump           ;Yes --> Process line
         jmp  dumpend          ;No --> DUMPEND

dodump:  mov  dx,ax            ;Record number of characters read

         ;-- Fill output buffer with spaces ------------------------

         mov  cx,15            ;15 words (30 bytes)
         mov  ax,2020h         ;ASCII code of " " to AH and AL
         mov  di,offset dumpbuf ;Output buffer address
```

```
         cld                  ;Increment on string commands
         rep stosw            ;Fill buffer with spaces

;-- Construct output buffer -------------------------------

         mov  cx,dx            ;Get number of characters read in
         mov  di,offset dumpbuf+31 ;Position ASCII codes in buffer
         mov  bx,offset ninebyte ;Pointer to input buffer
         mov  si,offset dumpbuf ;Position for hex codes in buffer

bytein:  mov  ah,[bx]          ;Read byte
         push si               ;Store SI on stack
         mov  si,offset sotab  ;Address of special character table
         mov  dx,offset sotext-6 ;Address of special character text
sotest:  add  dx,6             ;Next entry in special text
         lodsb                 ;Load code from special char table
         cmp  al,255           ;Reached end of table?
         je   noso             ;Yes --> No special character
         cmp  ah,al            ;Do codes match?
         jne  sotest           ;No --> Test next table element

;-- Code was a special character --------------------------

         push cx               ;Store counter
         mov  si,dx            ;Copy DX to SI
         lodsb                 ;Read number of char control codes
         mov  cl,al            ;Transfer number of characters to CL
         rep  movsb            ;Copy designation into buffer
         pop  cx               ;Get counter
         pop  si               ;Return SI from stack
         mov  al,ah            ;Copy character to AL
         jmp  short hex        ;Calculate hex code

noso:    pop  si               ;Return SI from stack
         mov  al,ah            ;Copy character to AL
         stosb                 ;Store in buffer

hex:     mov  al,ah            ;Character code to AL
         and  ah,1111b         ;Mask upper 4 bits in AH
         shr  al,1             ;Shift AL right 4 bits
         shr  al,1
         shr  al,1
         shr  al,1
         or   ax,3030h         ;Convert AH and AL into ASCII codes
         cmp  al,"9"           ;Is AL a letter ?
         jbe  nobal            ;No --> No correction
         add  al,"A"-"1"-9     ;Correct AL
nobal:   cmp  ah,"9"           ;Is AH a letter ?
         jbe  hexout           ;No --> No correction
         add  ah,"A"-"1"-9     ;Correct AH
hexout:  mov  [si],ax          ;Store hex code in buffer
         add  si,3             ;Point to next position

         inc  bx               ;Set pointer to next byte
         loop bytein           ;Process next byte

         mov  al,219           ;Set separator
         stosb

         mov  ax,LF shl 8 + CR ;CR and LF terminate buffer
         stosw                 ;Write in buffer

;-- Send dump to the standard output device ---------------
```

769

```
          mov  bx,1              ;Standard output is handle 1
          mov  cx,di             ;Determine number of characters
          sub  cx,offset dumpbuf ; to be transmitted
          mov  dx,offset dumpbuf ;Buffer address
          mov  ah,40h            ;Function code for handle
          int  21h               ;Call DOS function
          jmp  dump              ;Read in next 9 bytes

dumpend   label near

          mov  ax,4C00h          ;Function number for ending program
          int  21h               ;End program with end code

;== Data ========================================================

ninebyte  db 9 dup (?)           ;The 9 bytes read in
dumpbuf   db 30 dup (?), 219     ;the output buffer
          db 49 dup (?)

sotab     db NUL,BEL,BS,TAB      ;Control character table
          db LF,CR,EOF,ESCAPE
          db 255

sotext    equ this byte          ;Text of special characters
          db 5,"<NUL>"           ;Null
          db 5,"<BEL>"           ;Bell
          db 4,"<BS> "           ;Backspace
          db 5,"<TAB>"           ;Tab
          db 4,"<LF> "           ;Linefeed
          db 4,"<CR> "           ;Carriage Return
          db 5,"<EOF>"           ;End of File
          db 5,"<ESC>"           ;Escape

;== End =========================================================

code      ends                   ;End of CODE segment
          end  dump
```

Chapter 19

File Management in DOS

The DOS file management functions are among the most basic available to the programmer. However, programmers using high level languages seldom access these DOS functions directly because the languages often have their own methods of file management. This chapter describes how the file functions are organized and how you can use them from higher level languages.

19.1 Two Sides of DOS

The term "file management functions" refers to the functions used to manage files, such as creating, deleting, opening, closing, reading from, and writing to files. Operating systems such as DOS provide the programmer with functions for file management. For example, DOS provides functions that return special file information or rename a file.

One peculiarity of DOS is that these functions exist in two forms because of the combined CP/M & UNIX compatibility. For every UNIX compatible file function, there is also a CP/M compatible file function. Versions 2.0 and up of DOS borrowed ideas from this UNIX compatibility.

FCB functions

The CP/M compatible functions are designated as FCB functions because they are based on a data structure called the FCB (File Control Block). DOS uses this data structure for storing information during file manipulation. The user must reserve space for the FCB within this program. The FCB permits access to the FCB functions which open, close, read from, and write to files.

Since the FCB functions were developed for compatibility with CP/M's functions, and since CP/M doesn't have a hierarchical file system, FCB functions don't support paths. As a result, FCB functions can only access files that are in the current directory.

The handle function concept

DOS Versions 2.0 and up support handle functions, which were first used in the UNIX environment. However, the UNIX compatible handle functions don't have the problems resulting from FCB functions. As the name suggests, a handle is used to identify the file to be accessed. DOS stores information about each open file in an area that is separate from the program.

No file structure differences

Remember that the differences between these function groups are related to how these files are created, instead of their actual structures. Files created and edited using FCB functions can cause problems if subsequently accessed by handle functions and vice versa.

The most important fact to remember is to keep the two groups of functions separate when developing high level language programs. In the following sections, we'll take a closer look at each group of functions.

19.2 Handle Functions

It's easier for the programmer to access a file using the handle functions than using the FCB functions. With handle functions a programmer doesn't have to use a data structure for file access like the FCB functions do. Similar to the functions of the UNIX operating system, file access is performed using a filename. The filename is passed as an ASCII string when the file is opened or first created. This must be performed before the first write or read operation to the file. In addition to the filename, it may contain a device designator, a pathname, and a file extension. The ASCII string ends with the end character (ASCII code 0). After the file is opened, a numeric value called the handle is returned. Any further operations to this file are performed using this 16-bit handle. For a subsequent read or write operation, the handle, instead of the filename, is passed to the appropriate function.

For each open file, DOS saves certain information pertaining to that file. If the FCB functions are used, DOS saves the information in the FCB table within the program's memory block. When the handle functions are used, the information is stored in an area outside of the program's memory block in a table that is maintained by DOS. The number of open files is therefore limited by the amount of available table space. The amount of table space set aside by DOS is specified by the FILES parameter of the CONFIG.SYS file:

```
FILES = X
```

In DOS Version 3.0, this maximum is 255. If you change the maximum number of files in the CONFIG.SYS file, the change will not become effective until the next time DOS is booted.

```
FILES
```

While the FILES parameter specifies the maximum number of open files for the entire operating system, DOS limits the number of open files to 20 per program. Since five handles are assigned to standard devices, such as the keyboard, monitor, and line printer, only 15 handles are available for the program. For example, if a program opens three files, DOS assigns three available handles and reduces the number of additional available handles by three. If this program calls another program, the three files opened by the original program remain open. If the new program opens additional files, the remaining number of handles available is reduced even further.

Variable access length

Another difference from FCB functions lies in read and write functions. While FCB functions work with records of constant lengths, handle functions specify how many bytes should be read or written. This makes dynamic access to consecutive data records possible.

In addition to the standard read and write functions, there is also a file positioning function. This lets you specify an exact location within the file for the next data access. Knowing both a record number and the length of each data record allows you to specify the position to access a particular data record:

```
position = record_number * record_length
```

This function isn't used during sequential file access because DOS sets the file pointer during the opening or creation of a file to the first byte within the file. Each subsequent read or write operation moves the file pointer, by the number of bytes read, towards the end of the file so the next file access starts where the previous one ended.

The following table summarizes the handle functions. For a more detailed description of these functions, see Appendix D, which documents the DOS API functions.

Function	Operation
3CH	Create file
3DH	Open file
3EH	Close file
42H	Move file pointer/determine file size
43H	Read/Write file attribute
56H	Rename file
57H/00H	Read/Write modifications & date/time of file
57H/01H	Read/Write modifications & date/time of file
5AH	Create temporary file
5BH	Create new file
5CH/00H	Protect file range against access (Version 3.0 and up)
5CH/01H	Release protected file range (Version 3.0 and up)
6CH	Extended OPEN function (Version 4.0 and up)

Here are a few general rules to follow when using these functions:

Functions that expect a filename or the address of a filename as an argument (e.g., Create File and Open File) expect the segment address of the name in the DS register and the offset address in the DX register. If the function successfully returns a handle, it's returned in the AX register.

Functions that expect a handle as an argument expect to find it in the DX register. After the call, the carry flag indicates whether an error occurred during execution. If an error occurs, the carry flag is set and the error code is returned in the AX register.

Function 59H of DOS interrupt 21H returns very detailed information about errors that occur during disk operations. This function is available only in DOS Versions 3.0 and higher.

19.3 FCB Functions

As we discussed earlier, DOS uses an FCB data structure for managing a file. The programmer can use this data structure to obtain information about a file or change information about a file. So, we'll examine the structure of an FCB before discussing the individual FCB functions.

The FCB is a 37-byte data structure that can be subdivided into different data fields. The following figure illustrates these fields:

FCB 37-byte data structure		
Address	Contents	Type
+00H	Device name	1 byte
+01H	Filename	8 bytes
+09H	File mode	3 bytes
+0CH	Current block number	1 word
+0EH	Data record size	1 word
+10H	File size	2 words
+14H	Modification date	1 word
+16H	Modification time	1 word
+18H	Reserved	1 word
+20H	Current data record number	1 byte
+21H	Data record number for random access	2 words

Notice that the name of the file is found beginning at offsets 01H through 0BH of the FCB. The byte at offset 0 is the device indicator, 0 is the current drive, 1 drive A, 2 drive B, etc.

The filename that begins at offset 1 is an ASCII string. It may not contain a pathname since it's limited to 8 characters. For this reason, the FCB functions can access only files in the current directory. Filenames shorter than eight characters are padded with spaces (ASCII code 32). The file extension, if any, occupies the next three bytes of the FCB.

At offset 0CH of the FCB is the current number of the block for sequential file access. The two bytes at offset 0EH are the record size. The four bytes at offset 10H are the length of the file.

The date and time of the last modifications to the file are stored beginning at offset 14H of the FCB in encoded form.

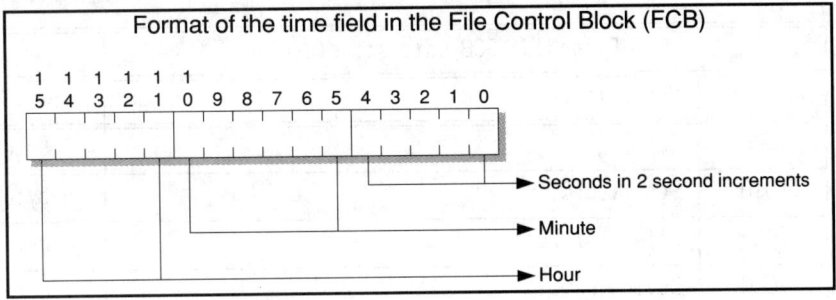

Format of the time field in the File Control Block (FCB)

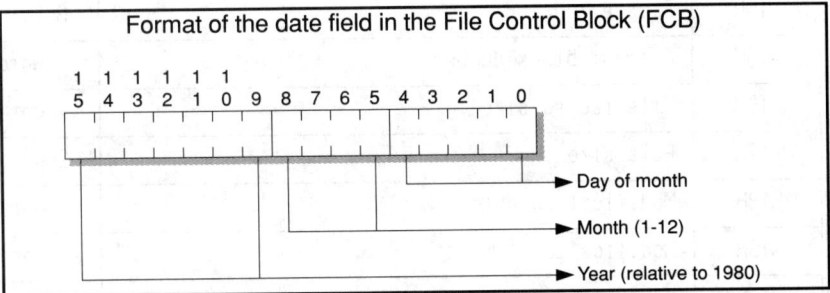

Format of the date field in the File Control Block (FCB)

An eight-byte data area follows and is reserved for DOS (no user modifications allowed). The use of this area varies from one version of DOS to another.

Following this reserved data area is the current record number which is used with the current block number to simulate CP/M operations.

Random files

The last data field of the FCB is used for a type of access in which the data within the file may be retrieved or written in a non-sequential order. This field is four bytes long. If a record is equal to or larger than 64 bytes, only the first three bytes are used for indicating the current record number. All four bytes of this field are used for records smaller than 64 bytes.

Extended FCB

Besides a standard FCB, DOS also supports the extended FCB. Unlike normal FCBs, extended FCBs access files with special attributes, such as hidden files or system files. They also permit access to volume names and subdirectories (this doesn't mean that you can access files in other directories besides the current directory).

An extended FCB is similar to a standard FCB, but it's seven bytes larger. These seven bytes are located at the beginning of the data structure. So, all subsequent fields are displaced by seven bytes.

Extended FCB data structure		
Address	Contents	Type
+OOH	FF	1 byte
+01H	Reserved(O)	5 bytes
+06H	File attribute	1 byte
+07H	Device name	1 byte
+08H	Filename	8 bytes
+10H	File extension	3 bytes
+13H	Current block number	1 word
+15H	File record size	1 word
+17H	File size	2 words
+1BH	Modification date	1 word
+1DH	Modification time	1 word
+1FH	Reserved	8 bytes
+27H	Current data record number	1 byte
+28H	Data record number	2 words

The first byte of an extended FCB always contains the value 255 and identifies this as an extended FCB. Since this address contains the device number in a normal FCB and therefore cannot contain the value 255, DOS can tell the difference between a normal and an extended FCB. The next five bytes are reserved exclusively for use by DOS. They shouldn't be changed. The seventh byte is a file attribute byte. Refer to Section 6.1.2 for the details of the file attribute byte.

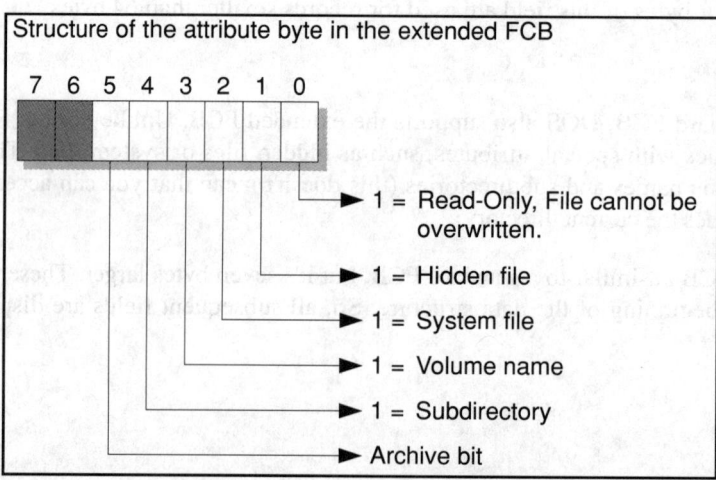

Now that you're familiar with the FCB structures, the next section focuses on using FCBs for accessing files.

FCB and file access

Before accessing a file, an FCB must be built in the program's memory area. The area can be reserved within the data segment of the program or by allocating additional memory using another DOS function (see Appendix D).

Although it's possible to write the data directly into the FCB, it is better to use one of the appropriate DOS functions to do this.

For example, to set the filename in the FCB you can use DOS function 29H. The function number is passed in the AH register. The address of the FCB is passed in the ES:DI register pair. The address of the filename is passed in the DS:SI register pair. The filename is an ASCII string terminated by the end character (ASCII code 0). The AL register contains flags for converting the filename and are discussed in more detail in Appendix C.

Open FCB

After the FCB is properly formatted, the file can be opened or created using a DOS function. When this happens, DOS stores information about that file, such as the file size, date and time of file creation, etc., in the FCB. At this point the FCB is considered opened.

By default, the record length is set to 128 bytes when the FCB is opened. To override this record length, store the desired record length at offset 0EH of the FCB after it's opened. Otherwise, the default length will be used.

DTA

For record lengths greater than 128 bytes, the record buffer, also known as the DTA or Disk Transfer Area, must be moved to accommodate the longer record size. Usually DOS builds the DTA in the PSP (Program Segment Prefix). Accessing the file using the default DTA for a record length greater than 128 bytes would overwrite some of the other fields in the PSP.

The most convenient way to select a new DTA is to reserve the space in the program's data segment. To change the address of the DTA, use DOS function 1AH. The address of the new DTA is passed in the DS:DX register pair. Since DOS assumes that you've set aside an area large enough to accommodate your largest record length, you don't have to specify the new length.

File access

For sequential file access, processing begins at the first record in the file. DOS maintains a record pointer in the FCB to keep track of the current record within the file. Each time the file is accessed, DOS advances the pointer so the second, third, fourth, etc. record is processed sequentially.

For random file access, the records can be processed in any order. The position of each record relative to the beginning of the file determines its record number. This record number is then passed to DOS to access a specific record. The last field of the FCB is used to specify the record number to DOS.

It's also possible to change from sequential access mode to random access mode and vice versa, since processing depends on a specific DOS function to access the file. There are actually two sets of independent functions, one for sequential access and one for random functions.

The following is a list of all of the FCB functions of DOS interrupt 21H. A more detailed description of the functions is found in Appendix D.

FCB functions of DOS interrupt 21H	
Function	Task
0FH	Open file
10H	Close file
13H	Delete file
14H	Sequential read
15H	Sequential write
16H	Create file
17H	Rename file
1AH	Set DTA address
21H	Random Read (of record)
22H	Random Write (of record)
23H	Determine file size
24H	Set record number for random access
27H	Random read (one or more records)
28H	Random write (one or more records)
29H	Enter filename into FCB

The following are some basic rules about these functions:

Using the FCB functions, you can access several files, each with their own unique FCB. To tell DOS which file should be accessed, pass the address of the file's FCB in the DS:DX register pair.

Most of the functions return an error code in the AL register or the value zero if the function was successfully completed. For functions that open, close, create, or delete a file, a code of 255 is returned if an error occurs. The other functions return specific error codes. More detailed information about these errors can be determined by calling DOS function 59H but this is available only in DOS Versions 3.0 or later.

Handles vs. FCBs

Now we'll briefly discuss the advantages and disadvantages of the individual functions. If you want to convert a program from the CP/M or UNIX operating systems into DOS, the choice will be easy. However, if you want to develop a new program under DOS, the following explanations should help you determine which set of functions to use.

Handles

There are two main advantages to using handle functions. The first is the ability to access a file in any subdirectory of the disk. The second is that the handle functions aren't limited to the number of FCBs that can be stored in a program's memory space.

There are also several additional considerations. You can access the name of a disk drive only by using an FCB. When the FCB is opened, you can easily determine its file size and the date of the last modification. The handle functions automatically provide an area large enough to accommodate the records in the file.

As you can see, there are arguments for and against using either the FCB functions or the handle functions. For future versions of DOS, the handle functions will become more important and the importance of the FCB functions will diminish. This is reason enough to use the handle functions for your new program development.

Chapter 20

Accessing DOS Directories

Two groups of DOS functions are used to work with directories. The first group is used to manipulate the subdirectories and the second group is used to search for files on the mass storage devices.

DOS Version 2.0 introduced subdirectories. A mass storage device could be logically divided into smaller subdirectories, which could also be divided. This organization creates a directory tree.

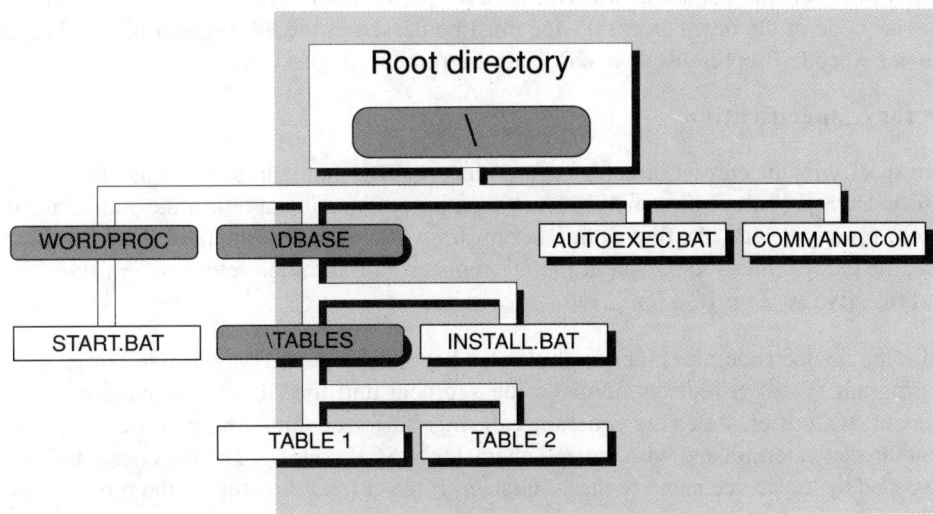

Directory tree

In this directory tree, the names and numbers of subdirectories are dynamic. So, there must be a way to add, change, and delete entries on the tree. Other functions must be available to set the current directory so a complete pathname isn't required for all file accesses.

At the user level, the MD, RD, and CD commands can be used to make a directory, remove a directory, and change a current directory. Internally, these commands are performed with functions 39H, 3A, and 3BH of DOS interrupt 21H.

All three functions use identical calling conventions.

781

The function number is passed in the AH register. The address of the path is passed in the DS:DX register pair. The path is a string and may be a complete path designation, including a preceding drive letter followed by a colon (a device name) and terminated by ASCII code 0. If the device name is omitted, the current device is the default.

Following execution, the carry flag indicates the return code. If the carry flag is reset (0), then execution was successful. If the carry flag is set, then an error occurred and the error code is passed back in the AX register.

Function 39H creates or makes a new directory (Make Directory). The name for the new directory is specified as the last element in the path. An error will be returned by the functions if one or more of the directories specified in the path doesn't exist, if the new directory name already exists, or if the maximum number of files in the root directory is exceeded.

Function 3AH deletes or removes a directory (Remove Directory). An error will be returned by the function if the target directory isn't empty or the specified directory doesn't exist in the current path.

Function 3BH changes the current directory (Change Directory). An error is returned if the directories named in the path don't actually exist.

Function 0EH sets the default disk drive. Besides the function number in the AH register, only the device code of the new current device must be passed in the DL register. Code 0 represents the device A, code 1 represents device B, code 2 represents device C, etc.

Directory specification

Before specifying the current directory using function 3BH, sometimes you must find the current directory. DOS provides function 47H for this purpose. Since it can return the path of the current directory for any device, the device number must be passed to the function. If this is the current device, the value 0 must be passed in the DL register. For all other devices, the value 1 must be passed for drive A, 2 for B, 3 for C, etc.

Besides the device code, the function must also have the address of a 64-byte buffer within the user program. The DS register contains the segment and the SI register contains the offset address of this buffer. After the function call, this buffer contains the path designation of the current directory, terminated with the end character (ASCII code 0). The path designation cannot be preceded by the device name or the \ character. If the current directory is the root directory, the buffer contains only the end character. If a device code unknown to DOS was passed during the function call, the carry flag is set and the AX register contains the error code 0FH.

Let's consider the functions for searching for one or more files in the current directory on the current device. Again you can see the connection between handle and FCB functions. Two function groups are used to search for files. The group of FCB functions limit the search to files in the current directory of a certain device, while handle functions allow you to search for files in any directories of any devices. The term "handle" functions isn't really appropriate for these functions because they aren't addressed with a handle. This designation originated with the introduction of subdirectories (and therefore the handle functions) in DOS Version 2.0. Version 1.0 offered only the FCB functions.

How the search function works

Although the handle and FCB functions have different capabilities, they are very similar. Both of them access functions called FindFirst and FindNext. FindFirst is called only once for each file because it initiates the search. This function expects the caller to pass the file's name and attribute (more on this later).

The search name can be conveyed as a filename with a path (e.g., C:\DOS\LETTER.DOC) or without a path (e.g., LETTER.TXT). Wildcard characters (* and ?) can be used to search for patterns instead of specific files. Similar to the DIR command used in DOS, FindFirst and FindNext can display all the files in a directory using these wildcards.

Regardless of the search name, FindFirst returns only the first filename found (if it exists in the indicated directory). This filename corresponds to the name or name pattern. All additional files can be found through subsequent calls of FindNext; with each call of this function, the next filename that fits the search pattern is returned.

Function	Assignment
11H	FindFirst (FCB)
12H	FindNext (FCB)
4EH	FindFirst (Handle)
4FH	FindNext (Handle)

The file attribute's role

The functions previously listed interact with the standard file attributes as assigned under DOS (see the following illustration for more information). The bits in the attribute byte specify different attributes. For example, when bit 4 is set, the directory entry is viewed as a subdirectory rather than a file. When bit 2 is set, this indicates that the file is hidden, and won't be visible when you call the DIR command from DOS.

After finding an entry, the attribute byte can be read for set attributes. Both FindFirst functions expect to receive a search attribute, which identifies the files to be found. These attributes don't include the read-only attribute or the archive bit. If the search attribute contains 0, all normal files are displayed whether their read-only and archive bits are set.

Directory entries that describe hidden files, system files, volume names, and subdirectories are treated differently. These are excluded from the file search if the corresponding bit in the search attribute isn't set. For example, if you set bit 4 in the search attribute, all subdirectories are returned as the result.

Attribute byte in file search		
Bit	Attribute	Meaning if set
00H	Read-only	File is read-only
01H	Hidden	File is hidden (invisible to DIR)
02H	System	File is part of operating system
03H	Volume label	Entry is volume label and not a file
04H	Subdirectory	Entry is a subdirectory and not a file
05H	Archive	Entry is a subdirectory and not a file
06H	Reserved	Reserved for later implementation
07H	Reserved	Reserved for later implementation

This method cannot exclude all normal files from the search in order to search exclusively for hidden files or subdirectories. However, you can evaluate the file attributes of the files that were found and only use the files that have the desired attribute flag set.

20.1 Searching for Files using FCB Functions

This method of searching for files uses functions 11H and 12H. By using these functions, you can search for files with a fixed name or an extension. Function 11H finds the first file in the current directory. Function 12H finds any additional files. The FCBs are important because they mediate between the calling program and the two functions. Let's see how we can search for files in a directory:

First the program must reserve space for two FCBs. This is done either by reserving memory in the data area of the program or by requesting memory from DOS using function 48H. The programmer can use either normal or extended FCBs, which are capable of searching for files with special attributes (system or hidden), volume names, and subdirectories. The filename for which the search will be made is specified in one of the FCBs. DOS places the name of the file(s) that it finds in the other FCB. The two FCBs are identified by their names Search FCB and Found FCB.

The address of the Found FCB must be passed to DOS using function 1AH. When this function call occurs, the Found FCB becomes the new data transmission area (DTA). This area is important for these two functions as well as all other functions that transfer data between computer and disks. For this reason, function 2FH should determine the address of the current DTA before activating the new DTA. When the file search ends, the DTA can be restored to its original status using function 1AH.

After the DTA is set to the Found FCB, place the name of the file you're looking for into the Search FCB. For a more general search, you can use the wildcards * and ?. You can transfer the filename directly or transfer it using function 29H. If you want to search through all files, use the filename *.*. If an extended FCB is used, you may insert an additional value into the attribute field of the Search FCB to limit the search to files with only certain attributes (see the preceding pages of this chapter for more information on the various attributes).

This concludes the preliminary work. The file search can begin with the current directory. For this purpose, function 11H is called with the function number in the AH register, the segment address of the Search FCB in DS, and the offset address in the DX register. If the system finds a file with the indicated name, the AL register contains the value 0 after the function call. If the filename wasn't found, the AL register contains a value of 255. The found filename and its attributes (if extended FCBs are used) can be read from the Found FCB. For additional searches, function 12H (not function 11H) is called. Function 12H's register contents during call and return are similar to function 11H. If it returns the value 255 in the AL register during one of the calls, the search has ended.

Demonstration programs

The assembly language program FF.ASM demonstrates FCB file searching by using FCB functions 11H and 12H. The assembled program is a COM program instead of an EXE program. FF represents FileFind because the program searches for a certain file, or a group of files, in all the directories of a drive. It shows that the FCB functions can be used for a file search in various directories by specifying the search directory as the current directory before the search begins.

Call FF by using the following syntax:

```
ff [dr:]filename [+|-|=date]
```

Let's look at these parameters:

[dr:]	This represents the optional drive specifier. FF defaults to the current drive.
filename	This represents the filename or pattern you want to find. This parameter can include wildcards. If you type FF.ASM as the filename, FF will search for only the file FF.ASM. If you type *.ASM, FF searches for all files with ASM extensions, in all directories of the current drive.
+date	Lists files created or last modified after the specified date.
[-date]	Lists files created or last modified before the specified date.
[=date]	Lists files created or last modified on the specified date.

The following command finds all TXT files created after January 10, 1991:

```
ff *.txt +1-10-1991
```

Assembler listing: FF.ASM

```
;****************************************************************
;*                 F F . A S M    ( FileFind )                 *;
;*------------------------------------------------------------*;
;*  Task        : Searches the specified drive for files.      *;
;*------------------------------------------------------------*;
;*  Author      : Michael Tischer                              *;
;*  Developed on : 09/12/90                                    *;
;*  Last update  : 01/20/92                                    *;
;*------------------------------------------------------------*;
;*  Assembly    : MASM FF;                                     *;
;*               LINK FF;                                      *;
;*               EXE2BIN FF FF.COM          or                 *;
;*                                                             *;
;*               TASM FF                                       *;
;*               TLINK FF /T                                   *;
;*------------------------------------------------------------*;
;*  Call        : FF [dr:]filename [+ | - | =date]             *;
;****************************************************************

;== Constants =================================================

CMD_OFS       equ   81h         ;Start system prompt in PSP
CR            equ   13          ;Carriage return
LF            equ   10          ;Linefeed
DELIMITER     equ   "-"         ;Date component delimiter

              ;-- DOS functions ------------------------------

GET_DR_NO     equ   19h         ;Get current drive number
WRT_CHAR      equ   02h         ;Display character on STDOUT
SEARCH_FIRST  equ   4Eh         ;Search first file
SEARCH_NEXT   equ   4Fh         ;Search next file
SET_DTA       equ   1Ah         ;Set new DTA range
PRINT_STR     equ   09h         ;Display string ended with $

ATTR_DIR      equ   10h         ;Search subdirectory
ATTR_NRM      equ   00h         ;Search for normal files

DATCOMP_NO    equ   0           ;No date comparison
DATCOMP_LS    equ   1           ;Files before date
DATCOMP_EQ    equ   2           ;Files on date
DATCOMP_GR    equ   3           ;Files after date

;== Structures ================================================

PSP           struc             ;Base PSP structure on
              intcall dw (?)     ;interrupt call 20H
              endadd  dw (?)     ;End address
                      db (?)     ;Reserved
              farcall db 5 dup (?) ;FAR call to interrupt 21h
              int22h  dd (?)     ;Copy of interrupt 22H
              int23h  dd (?)     ;Copy of interrupt 23H
              int24h  dd (?)     ;Copy of interrupt 24H
                      db 22 dup (?) ;Reserved
              envseg  dw (?)     ;Segment address of environment
                      db 46 dup (?) ;Reserved

              ;-- First FCB starts here ----------------------

              drvcode1 db (?)        ;Drive number
              fi_name1 db 8 dup (?)  ;Filename
              fi_ext1  db 3 dup (?)  ;File extension
```

```
              blockno1 dw (?)        ;Current block number
              fi_len1  dd (?)        ;File lengths
              datmod1  dw (?)        ;Date of last modification
              timemod1 dw (?)        ;Time of last modification
                       dw 4 dup (?)  ;Reserved
              currec1  db (?)        ;Current record number
              setfree1 dd (?)        ;Record number for free access

              ;-- Second FCB starts here ---------------------

              drvcode2 db (?)        ;Drive number
              fi_name2 db 8 dup (?)  ;Filename
              fi_ext2  db 3 dup (?)  ;File extension
              blockno2 dw (?)        ;Current block number
              fi_len2  dd (?)        ;File lengths
              datmod2  dw (?)        ;Date of last modification
              timemod2 dw (?)        ;Time of last modification
                       dw 4 dup (?)  ;Reserved
              currec2  db (?)        ;Current record number
              setfree2 dd (?)        ;Record number for free access

                       db 128 dup (?) ;Command line
PSP           ends

;------------------------------------------------------------

DTA           struc             ;DTA structure for file search
                      db 21 dup (?) ;Reserved
              attr    db (?)     ;Found file's attributes
              timemod dw (?)     ;Time of last modification
              datemod dw (?)     ;Date of last modification
              fi_len  dd (?)     ;File length
              fi_n    db 13 dup (?) ;Filename
DTA           ends

;------------------------------------------------------------

DATES         struc             ;Get date information
              month   db (?)     ;Month (1-12)
              day     db (?)     ;Day of the month (1-31)
              year    dw (?)     ;Year, including century
DATES         ends

;== Code segment definition and start =========================

code          segment para 'CODE'  ;Definition of code segment

              org 100h          ;Start after PSP

              assume cs:code, ds:code, es:code, ss:code

start:        jmp startff       ;Jump to program start

;== Data ======================================================

datcomp       db  DATCOMP_NO     ;Default = no date search
sdate         DATES < 0, 0, 0>   ;Get date from system prompt
tdate         DATES < 0, 0, 0>   ;Get date of file for comparison

dir_name      db  64, ":\"       ;Name of current directory
firstdir      db  79 dup (0)     ;in search
srchname      db  "*.*", 0       ;Directory to be searched
              db  9 dup (0)
```

```
wcname      db    "*.*", 0          ;Subdirectory wildcard
found       dw    0                 ;Number of files found

mes         db    CR, LF, "FF:   0  file(s) found."
crlf        db    CR, LF, "$"

date_buff   db    "ddddd-dd-dddd ",0 ;Buffer for date conversion
datbend     equ   this byte          ;into ASCII characters

errmes      db    "FF  -  (c) 1991, 92 by MICHAEL TISCHER", 13,10,10
            db    "Syntax: FF [dr:]Filename [+Date | -Date | =Date]",13,10
            db    "$"

;== Start of program =================================================

startff:    ;-- Get arguments from system prompt -----------------------

            cld                     ;Decrement on string instructions
            mov   di,offset srchname
            mov   si,CMD_OFS        ;SI at beginning of command line

arg1:       ;-- Get next drive specifier ---------------------------------

            lodsb                   ;Get character from system prompt
            cmp   al,CR             ;End of command reached?
            je    arg6              ;Yes --> End process
            cmp   al," "            ;No --> Are there spaces?
            jbe   arg1              ;No --> Tabs, continue

            ;-- Character found ------------------------------------------

            cmp   ds:[0].drvcode1,0 ;Is there a drive specifier?
            je    arg2              ;No --> Otherwise it's already in FCB
            lodsb                   ;Load colon
            lodsb                   ;Load next character
            cmp   al," "            ;<= SPACE?
            jbe   arg3              ;Yes --> End processing

arg2:       ;-- Place filenames in srchname buffer ----------------------

            stosb                   ;Place characters in search name
            lodsb                   ;Load next character
            cmp   al," "            ;<= SPACE?
            ja    arg2              ;No --> Character - continue loading

arg3:       ;-- End filename processing ---------------------------------

            cmp   al,CR             ;End of line found?
            je    arg6

            ;-- Check and process date expression -----------------------

arg4:       lodsb                   ;Load next character
            cmp   al," "            ;SPACE and TAB are valid
            je    arg4
            cmp   al,9
            je    arg4
            cmp   al,CR             ;End of line found?
            je    arg6

            cmp   al,"="            ;Same date?
            jne   arg4a             ;No --> Continue check
            mov   al,DATCOMP_EQ     ;Date comparison flag
            jmp   short arg5
```

```
arg4a:      cmp   al,"-"            ;Before date ...
            jne   arg4b             ;No --> Continue check
            mov   al,DATCOMP_LS     ;Date comparison flag
            jmp   short arg5

arg4b:      cmp   al,"+"            ;After date...
            jne   argerr            ;No --> Syntax error in command line
            mov   al,DATCOMP_GR     ;Date comparison flag

arg5:       mov   datcomp,al        ;Set date comparison flag
            mov   di,offset sdate   ;Pointer to date structure
            call  getdat            ;Get date from command syntax
            jc    argerr            ;Syntax error --> End program

arg6:       ;-- Finish processing command, everything is O.K. ----------

            mov   al,ds:[0].drvcode1 ;Get current drive number
            or    al,al             ;Does one already exist?
            jne   arg7              ;Yes --> Don't use current

            ;-- No drive specifier stated, use current -----------------

            mov   ah,GET_DR_NO      ;Get current drive number
            int   21h               ;(0=A)
            inc   al                ;Increment drive number (1 = A)

arg7:       add   dir_name,al       ;Convert specifier to ASCII
            mov   dx,offset startdta ;First DTA address
            mov   bx,offset firstdir ;Append directory name
            call  go                ;Begin search

            mov   ax,found          ;Load number of files found
            or    ax,ax             ;Files found?
            je    arg8              ;No --> display unchanged string
            mov   si,offset mes+6   ;Pointer to buffer
            call  toint

arg8:       mov   ah,09h            ;Display message
            mov   dx,offset mes
            int   21h

            mov   ax,4C00h          ;End program using
            int   21h               ;function 4CH

argerr:     ;-- Error occurred while reading command line --------------

            mov   ah,09h            ;Display error string
            mov   dx,offset errmes
            int   21h

            mov   ax,4C01h          ;Display error code, end program
            int   21h

;-- GO: Controls search for specified files ----------------------------
;-- Input    : BX = Pointer to search string, including
;--                 directory and filenames
;--            DX = Offset of previous DTA
;-- Output   : None
;-- Registers : AX, SI, CX and FLAGS are affected

go          proc  near

            push  dx                ;Set pointer to current DTA
```

```
          mov    si,offset srchname  ;Copy name of file to be
          call   strcopy             ;searched to buffer

          mov    cx,ATTR_NRM         ;Search for normal files only
          call   startsearch         ;Begin search
          jc     go2                 ;None found --> Search directories

          call   printname           ;File found

go1:      ;-- Execute search for all other files ---------------------

          call   nextfile            ;Search next file
          jc     go2                 ;No more files found
          call   printname           ;File found
          jmp    short go1           ;

go2:      ;-- Search current directory again, after ------------------
          ;-- searching subdirectories              ------------------

          pop    dx                  ;Release pointer to DTA
          push   dx                  ;Restore pointer to DTA
          mov    si,offset wcname;Add *.* to directory name
          call   strcopy

          mov    cx,ATTR_DIR         ;Now search subdirectories
          call   startsearch         ;Search first subdirectory
          jc     go_end              ;None found --> End routine

          mov    si,dx               ;Found, but it's a directory
          test   [si].attr,ATTR_DIR
          jne    go4                 ;Yes --> Process

go3:      ;-- No directory, continue search -------------------------

          call   nextfile            ;Search next file
          jc     go_end              ;None found --> End routine
          mov    si,dx               ;Found, but it's a directory
          test   [si].attr,ATTR_DIR
          je     go3                 ;Jump if zero

go4:      ;-- Subdirectory found ------------------------------------

          cmp    [si].fi_n,"."       ;"." or ".."
          je     go3                 ;Yes --> No processing

          push   di                  ;Push DX and
          push   bx                  ;DX onto stack
          mov    si,dx               ;Set SI to filenames in DTA in
          add    si,offset fi_n      ;which directory names are set
          mov    di,bx               ;Set DI to previous directory names

go5:      ;-- Add directory names to previous names ------------------

          lodsb                      ;Load character from directory name
          stosb                      ;and append to previous names
          or     al,al               ;Last byte found?
          jne    go5                 ;No --> Continue

          mov    bx,di               ;Set new end of buffer in BX
          stosb                      ;Write another NULL byte
          mov    byte ptr [bx-1],"\" ;Precede with a backslash
          call   go                  ;ReCursive call
```

```
          pop    bx                  ;Pop BX and
          pop    di                  ;DI from stack
          mov    byte ptr [bx],0 ;Append last directory names
                                     ;from previous calls

          mov    ah,SET_DTA          ;Reset DTA to old
          int    21h                 ;address in DX

          jmp    short go3

go_end:   pop    dx                  ;Release pointer to old DTA
          ret                        ;Return to caller

go        endp

;-- STARTSEARCH: Start search for new file ------------------------
;-- Input   : CX = Attribute of file to be searched for
;--           DX = Offset of previous DTA
;-- Output  : DX = New DTA address
;--           Carry flag=0: O.K.
;--           Carry flag=1: No file found
;-- Registers : AX, DX, BP and FLAGS are affected
;-- Info    : The dir_name buffer specifies the search filename

startsearch proc   near

          push   cx                  ;Push CX onto stack

          ;-- Set new DTA after current DTA --------------------------

          add    dx,2ch              ;One DTA = 42 bytes
          mov    ah,SET_DTA          ;Set new DTA
          int    21h

          ;-- Search for first filename listed in dir_name buffer ----

          mov    bp,dx               ;Store DX
          mov    ah,SEARCH_FIRST     ;Search first file
          mov    dx,offset dir_name ;DS:DX = Pointer to filename
          int    21h

          mov    dx,bp               ;Reset DX
          pop    cx                  ;Pop CX from stack
          ret                        ;Return to caller

startsearch        endp

;-- NEXTFILE: Search for next file --------------------------------
;-- Input   : None
;-- Output  : Carry flag=0: O.K.
;--           Carry flag=1: No file found
;-- Registers : AY and FLAGS are affected

nextfile  proc   near

          mov    bp,dx
          mov    ah,SEARCH_NEXT      ;Search for next file
          mov    dx,offset dir_name ;Path in dir_name buffer
          int    21h
          mov    dx,bp
          ret                        ;Return to caller

nextfile  endp
```

```
;-- STRCOPY: Copies an ASCII string ended with a NULL byte ------------
;-- Input    : SI = Source string offset
;--            BX = Target string offset
;--            DS = Source string segment
;--            ES = Target string segment
;-- Output   : None
;-- Registers : AL, DI, SI and FLAGS are affected

strcopy    proc    near

           mov     di,bx           ;Set DI to target string

sc1:       ;-- Copy loop -----------------------------------------

           lodsb                   ;Load character from source string
           stosb                   ;Store in target string
           or      al,al           ;Last character found?
           jne     sc1             ;No --> Continue

           ret                     ;Return to caller

strcopy    endp

;-- PRINTNAME: Display found filenames --------------------------------
;-- Input    : DX = Pointer to current DTA with names
;--            BX = Target string offset
;--            DS = Source string segment
;--            ES = Target string segment
;-- Output   : None
;-- Registers : AL, DI, SI and FLAGS are affected
;-- Info     : The filename will only be displayed if it is not
;--            handled as a subdirectory, and if the file matches the
;--            date parameter specified (if any)

printname  proc    near

           mov     bp,dx           ;Store pointer to DTA in BP
           cmp     [bp].fi_n,"."   ;"." or ".."
           je      prnend          ;Yes --> No output

           ;-- Execute date comparison if requested -------------------

           cmp     datcomp,DATCOMP_NO ;Date check?
           je      pn1             ;No --> Display names

           mov     ax,[bp].datemod ;Yes --> Get date and format
           mov     si,offset tdate
           call    unpackdate

           mov     di,offset sdate ;Compare date with command
           call    cmpdat          ;parameters
           cmp     al,datcomp      ;Do files match parameter?
           jne     prnend          ;No --> Do not display

           call    printdat        ;Date O.K., display

           ;-- Display first directory names --------------------------

pn1:       mov     dx,offset dir_name ;Pointer to directory names
           xor     al,al           ;Get last character of directory
           xchg    al,[bx]         ;and reset to 0
           mov     di,ax           ;Place character in DI
           call    printasciic     ;Display directory names
```

```
           xchg    ax,di           ;Place old value in AX
           mov     [bx],al         ;Return old character to its place

           ;-- Add filenames -----------------------------------------

           mov     dx,bp           ;Restore pointer to DTA
           add     dx,offset fi_n  ;Address filenames in DTA
           call    printasciic     ;and display these names

           mov     ah,PRINT_STR    ;Send linefeed (get linefeed
           mov     dx,offset crlf  ;from DOS)
           int     21h

           inc     found           ;Another file found
           mov     dx,bp           ;Release old DX again
prnend:    ret                     ;Return to caller

printname  endp

;-- PRINTASCIIC: Displays an ASCII string ended with a ------------
;--              NULL byte, on the standard output device -------------
;-- Input    : DX = Pointer to start of string
;--            DS = String segment
;-- Output   : None
;-- Registers : AX, DX, SI and FLAGS are affected

printasciic proc    near

           mov     si,dx           ;Get string from DX
           mov     ah,WRT_CHAR     ;Function number for character output
           lodsb                   ;Load first character

pa1:       ;-- Output loop -----------------------------------------

           mov     dl,al           ;Get DOS function character
           int     21h             ;from DL and display

           lodsb                   ;Load next character
           or      al,al           ;End of string found?
           jne     pa1             ;No --> Display character

           ret                     ;Return to caller

printasciic endp

;-- TOINT: Converts a binary number into ASCII and ------------------
;--        places this number in the caller's buffer ------------------
;-- Input    : DS:SI = Address for start of buffer
;--            AX    = Binary number to be converted
;-- Output   : DS:SI = Address of first number
;-- Registers : AX, SI and FLAGS are affected
;-- Info     : - Buffer must have a minimum of five characters free
;--            - Number will be right-justified in the buffer

toint      proc near

           push dx                 ;Place changed registers
           push bx                 ;on the stack

           ;-- Fill buffer with spaces -------------------------------

           mov word ptr [si],   32 shl 8 + 32
           mov word ptr [si+2], 32 shl 8 + 32
```

```
              mov   byte ptr [si+4], 32

              ;-- Divide number by 10, convert least significant portion --
              ;-- into ASCII and store this information in the buffer    --

              add   si,5              ;Set SI to end of buffer
              mov   bx,10             ;Always divide by 10

ti1:          dec   si               ;Set SI to previous character
              xor   dx,dx            ;Dividend is DX:AX
              div   bx               ;Divide DX:AX by 10
              or    dl,'0'           ;Convert DL to ASCII format
              mov   [si],dl          ;Place in buffer
              or    ax,ax            ;Is there a remainder?
              jne   ti1              ;Yes --> Next number

              pop   bx               ;Restore registers
              pop   dx

              ret                    ;Return to caller

toint  endp

;-- GETINT: Reads a positive decimal number from the command ----------
;--         line and converts this number into binary format ----------
;-- Input   : SI = Pointer to next character to be read
;--                in command line buffer
;-- Output  : Carry flag=0: Number O.K.
;--                AX = Number
;--           Carry flag=1: Error
;--                SI = Pointer following the last character read
;-- Registers : AX, CX, SI and FLAGS are affected

getint  proc near

              push  bx               ;Set changed registers
              push  dx
              push  di

              mov   di,10            ;Factor is always 10
              xor   bx,bx            ;BX gets binary number
              mov   ah,bh            ;High byte of AH is always 0

              ;-- Start processing from the beginning of the number -------

gi1:          lodsb                  ;Load next character
              cmp   al,'0'           ;Test for a number
              jb    gi2
              cmp   al,'9'
              jbe   gi5              ;Number found --> GI5
gi2:          cmp   al,' '           ;No number --> SPACEs and
              je    gi1              ;TABs allowed only
              cmp   al,9
              je    gi1

              ;-- Read number digit by digit, and convert to binary -------

gi4:          lodsb                  ;Load next character
              cmp   al,'0'           ;Is it a number?
              jb    gi7              ;No --> Process next character
              cmp   al,'9'
              ja    gi7              ;No --> Process next character

              ;-- Yes, digit is a number ----------------------------------
```

```
gi5:          xchg  ax,bx            ;Get char from BX and number from AX
              mul   di               ;Multiply AX by 10
              or    dx,dx            ;Product greater than 65536?
              jne   gierr            ;Yes --> Number too large
              and   bl,0Fh           ;Logical AND of lowest 4 bits
              add   ax,bx            ;Add to number
              xchg  ax,bx            ;Exchange AX and BX
              jmp   gi4              ;Read next character

gi6:          clc                    ;Read correct number
              mov   ax,bx            ;Move number to AX
              jmp   short giend      ;Return to caller

gi7:          dec   si               ;One character too many read,
              jmp   gi6              ;but the number is O.K.

gierr:        stc                    ;Display error

giend:        pop   di               ;Restore altered
              pop   dx               ;registers
              pop   bx
              ret                    ;Return to caller

getint  endp

;-- GETDAT: Reads date from the command line in "MM-DD-YY" format, ----
;--         converts the date into binary and places the result in ----
;--         the specified structure                              ----
;-- Input   : SI = Pointer to next character to be
;--                read in command line buffer
;--           DI = Pointer to the data structure into which
;--                the converted date should be placed
;-- Output  : Carry flag=0: Number O.K.
;--           Carry flag=1: Error
;--           SI = Pointer following the last character read
;-- Registers : AX, CX, SI and FLAGS are affected

getdat  proc near

              ;-- Process month -------------------------------------------

              call  getint           ;Get month
              jc    gderr            ;Error? ---> Abort routine

              or    ax,ax            ;Month O.K., but is it valid?
              je    gderr            ;No NULLs allowed --> Error
              cmp   ax,12            ;12 is the maximum
              ja    gderr            ;AX > 12? --> Error

              mov   [di].month,al    ;Month O.K., store and continue

              lodsb                  ;Hyphen delimiter should follow
              cmp   al,DELIMITER
              jne   gderr            ;No hyphen --> Error

              ;-- Month O.K., now process day -----------------------------

              call  getint           ;Get day
              jc    gderr            ;Error? --> Abort routine

              or    ax,ax            ;Day O.K., but is it valid?
              je    gderr            ;No NULLs allowed --> Error
              cmp   ax,31            ;31 is the maximum
```

```
              ja      gderr           ;AX > 31? --> Error

              mov     [di].day,al     ;Day O.K., store and continue

              lodsb                   ;Hyphen delimiter should follow
              cmp     al,DELIMITER
              jne     gderr           ;No hyphen --> Error


        ;-- Day O.K., now process year -----------------------------

              call    getint          ;Get year
              jc      gderr           ;Error? ---> Abort routine

              cmp     ax,100          ;Year include 19 prefix (e.g., 1999?)
              ja      gd1             ;Yes --> Continue

              add     ax,1900         ;No --> Add 1900

gd1:          cmp     ax,1980         ;1980 is earliest allowable year
              jb      gderr           ;AX < 1980? --> Error

              mov     [di].year,ax    ;Year O.K., so everything's O.K.
              clc
              ret

gderr:        stc                     ;Date could not be processed
              ret                     ;Return to caller

getdat        endp

;-- UNPACKDATE: Unpacks a date stored in DOS format, and places -------
;--             the unpacked date in a structure of type DATES -------
;-- Input    : AX = The date in DOS format to be unpacked
;--            SI = Pointer to the date block into which the
;--                 information should be stored
;-- Output   : None
;-- Registers : AX, CX and FLAGS are affected

unpackdate proc near

              push    bx              ;Push BX onto stack

              mov     bx,ax           ;Get entire date from BX
              mov     cl,5            ;Shift five bits to the right
              shr     bx,cl
              and     bl,15           ;AND upper four bits
              mov     [si].month,bl   ;Store month

              mov     bl,al           ;Get low byte of the date in BX
              and     bl,31           ;AND upper three bits
              mov     [si].day,bl     ;Store day of month

              shr     ah,1            ;Shift high byte one place to right
              mov     al,ah           ;Place year (rel. 1980) in low byte
              xor     ah,ah           ;Set high byte to 0
              add     ax,1980         ;Generate absolute year
              mov     [si].year,ax    ;Add to structure

              pop     bx              ;Restore BX (pop from stack)
              ret                     ;Return to caller

unpackdate endp

;-- CMPDAT: Compares two date parameters --------------------------------
```

```
;-- Input    : SI = Pointer to first date block
;--            DI = Pointer to second date block
;-- Output   : None
;-- Registers : AX and FLAGS are affected

cmpdat    proc near

        ;-- Compare year numbers -----------------------------------

              mov     ax,[si].year    ;Load year 1, then
              cmp     ax,[di].year    ;compare with year 2
              jb      datels          ;Date 1 < Date 2 --> DATELS
              ja      dategr          ;Date 1 > Date 2 --> DATEGR

        ;-- Year numbers are identical, now compare days ------------

              mov     al,[si].day     ;Load day 1, then
              cmp     al,[di].day     ;compare with day 2
              jb      datels          ;Date 1 < Date 2 --> DATELS
              ja      dategr          ;Date 1 > Date 2 --> DATEGR

        ;-- Year numbers are identical, now compare months ----------

              mov     al,[si].month   ;Load month 1, then
              cmp     al,[di].month   ;compare with month 2
              jb      datels          ;Date 1 < Date 2 --> DATELS
              ja      dategr          ;Date 1 > Date 2 --> DATEGR

              mov     al,DATCOMP_EQ   ;Both dates are identical
              ret                     ;Return to caller

datels:       mov     al,DATCOMP_LS   ;Date 1 < Date 2
              ret                     ;Return to caller

dategr:       mov     al,DATCOMP_GR   ;Date 1 > Date 2
              ret                     ;Return to caller

cmpdat    endp

;-- PRINTDAT: Displays date as a date structure on the screen ---------
;-- Input    : SI = Pointer to date structure
;-- Output   : None
;-- Registers : AX, DX, SI and FLAGS are affected

printdat proc    near

              push    si              ;Push SI, BX and DX onto the stack
              push    bx
              push    dx

              mov     bx,si           ;Set BX to the date structure
              mov     si,offset datbend-8;Allocate SI for year
              mov     ax,[bx].year    ;Get year and
              call    toint           ;convert to ASCII
              mov     byte ptr [si-1],DELIMITER ;Hyphen preceding year

              sub     si,6            ;Allocate space for day
              mov     al,[bx].day     ;Pass day to AX
              xor     ah,ah
              call    toint           ;and convert to ASCII

              cmp     [bx].day,10     ;First digit preceded by SPACE?
              jae     pd1             ;Yes --> Process without changes
```

```
        dec  si                    ;No --> Make SI first digit          pd3:    pop  dx                ;Pop DX, BX and SI from stack
        mov  byte ptr [si],"0"    ;and add NULL                                pop  bx
pd1:    mov  byte ptr [si-1],DELIMITER ;Hyphen preceding day                   pop  si
        sub  si,6                  ;Allocate SI space for month
        mov  al,[bx].month         ;Pass month to AX                           ret
        xor  ah,ah
        call toint                 ;and convert to ASCII                printdat endp
        cmp  [bx].month,10         ;Any NULLs?                          ;-- DTAs for recursive calls should be specified here
        jae  pd2                   ;No --> Continue                     startdta   equ this byte

        dec  si                                                         ;== End =========================================================
        mov  byte ptr [si],"0"

pd2:    mov  dx,si                 ;Start at DX                         code    ends                   ;End of CODE segment
        call printasciic           ;Display ASCII string                       end  start
```

20.2 Searching for Files using Handle Functions

Working with handle functions is easier than working with the FCB functions. Two of these functions are used to search for the first file (the 4EH function) and subsequent files (the 4FH function). Both functions return the information to the DTA. For this reason, the DTA should be moved into an area accessible to the current program before calling either of these functions. This area must have at least 43 bytes available. As mentioned in connection with the FCB functions, the DTA should be restored to its original address after the search ends.

During the call of the 4EH function, the function number is passed in the AH register, the attribute in the CX register, and the address of the file to be found in the DS:DX register pair. The filename is a series of ASCII characters followed by an end character (ASCII code 0). In addition to a device name, you may also add a complete path designation and the wildcard characters * and ?.

If a path isn't specified, DOS assumes that the search should be performed in the current directory of the indicated device. If a device isn't specified, the search continues on the current device. After the function call, the carry flag indicates whether a file was found. If the file couldn't be found, the carry flag is set and the AX register contains an error code. An error code of 2H is returned if the indicated path does not exist. If a file couldn't be found, an error code of 12H is returned. If the carry flag is reset, the DTA contains the information about the file that was found. It has the following structure:

DTA structure		
Address	Contents	Type
00H	Reserved for DOS	21 bytes
15H	Attribute of file found	1 byte
16H	Time of last modification	1 word
18H	Date of last modification	1 word
1AH	Low word of file size	1 word
1EH	High word of file size	12 bytes

Function 4FH performs any subsequent searches. The function number is passed in the AH register; additional parameters aren't necessary. The carry flag indicates whether the current directory contains any additional files that may apply to the search.

Demonstration programs

Two Pascal programs, two C language programs, and one BASIC program are listed. These dual implementations demonstrate how you can indirectly call DOS functions 4EH and 4FH. Many languages, such as Turbo Pascal, Microsoft C, and Turbo C, include FindFirst and FindNext functions in their libraries. These functions eliminate the need for direct calls to functions 4EH and 4 FH and also provide some other help for the programmer. (We'll discuss this in more detail later.)

QuickBasic contains only a rudimentary FILES command but not a library. The FILES command can display only the current directory's contents, without making this information available to the program. Direct calls to functions 4EH and 4FH are unavoidable in BASIC.

Program logic

All five programs are constructed according to the same basic framework. First the main program reads the command to determine which filenames should be displayed. If the program name was entered without parameters, the program defaults to the "*.*" wildcards. If the user entered a parameter after the program name, the program uses that as the pattern for file display. Entering more than one parameter ends the program and displays an error message.

The program passes the name of the file to be displayed and the attribute of the files to be displayed to the DIR function (or procedure). All the attributes are set to include volume name, subdirectories, system files, and hidden files. Although the attribute byte cannot be changed by the user, this byte setting can be altered from within the program code.

In the three programs, which directly communicate with functions 4EH and 4FH, the SetDTA procedure/function sets the DTA to a local data structure. SetDTA calls DOS function 1AH to move the DTA to the indicated address.

The data structure intended for the DTA exists in all three programs as type DirStruct. This structure represents a record in which the various fields are found by functions 4EH and 4FH.

After DTA's initialization, the DIR procedure/function calls the ScreenDesign procedure/function. This routine creates a window on the screen, in which the directory will be displayed.

FindFirst begins the search, after which a loop continuously calls FindNext until no other files are found. The PrintData procedure/function displays these files on the screen. This procedure/function expects DirStruct as an argument, specifying where DOS stored information about the file. This information is decoded and displayed on the screen.

The following is the BASIC version of this directory lister program:

BASIC listing: DIRB.BAS

```
'*****************************************************
'*                    D I R B                        *
'----------------------------------------------------
'* Task      : Displays all files in any directory, including  *
'*             subdirectories and volume label names.         *
'*             QuickBASIC and the QB.LIB must be loaded using  *
'*             QB /L QB                                        *
'*             before loading and running this file.           *
'----------------------------------------------------
'* Author     : Michael Tischer                      *
'* Developed on : 07/08/1987                         *
'* Last update  : 01/07/1992                         *
'*****************************************************

DECLARE FUNCTION MakeWord! (INum AS INTEGER)
DECLARE FUNCTION Dat$ (IVal AS INTEGER)
DECLARE SUB SetDTA (Segment AS LONG, Offset AS LONG)
DECLARE SUB ScreenDesign ()
DECLARE FUNCTION Month$ (Mon AS INTEGER)
DECLARE FUNCTION FindNext% ()
DECLARE FUNCTION FindFirst% (DFilename AS STRING, Attr AS INTEGER)
DECLARE SUB PrintData (DirBuf AS ANY)
DECLARE SUB Dir (DPath AS STRING, Attr AS INTEGER)

'$INCLUDE: 'QB.BI'                    'Include file for interrupt call

'-- Directory entry structure, returned in DOS functions 4EH and 4FH --

TYPE DirStruct
  Reserved AS STRING * 21
  Attrib AS STRING * 1
  Time AS INTEGER
  Date AS INTEGER
  Size AS LONG
  DatName AS STRING * 13
END TYPE

'-- Constants ----

CONST TRUE = -1                       'Declare truth
CONST FALSE = NOT TRUE

CONST FCARRY = 1                      'Carry flag
CONST FENTS = 14                      'Number of entries visible at a time
CONST OWINTOP = (20 - FENTS) \ 2      'Top row of output window

CONST FAReadOnly = &H1                'File attributes
CONST FAHidden = &H2
CONST FASysFile = &H4
CONST FAVolumeID = &H8
CONST FADirectory = &H10
CONST FAArchive = &H20
CONST FAAnyFile = &H3F

'-- Main program ------

IF COMMAND$ = "" THEN                 'No filename provided?
  CALL Dir("*.*", FAAnyFile)          'No --> Display all files in current dir.
ELSE
  CALL Dir(COMMAND$, FAAnyFile)       'Yes --> Display specified files
END IF

'*****************************************************
'* Dat$    : Converts a value to string for date and time display  *
'* Input   : Value to be converted                  *
'* Output  : Value converted to a string            *
'* Info    : STR$ or PRINT USING inserts no trailing zeros  *
'*****************************************************

FUNCTION Dat$ (IVal AS INTEGER)

DIM SStorage AS STRING                'Store temporary data

SStorage = LTRIM$(STR$(IVal))
WHILE LEN(SStorage) < 2               'Temp. data < 2 digits
  SStorage = "0" + SStorage
WEND
Dat$ = SStorage
END FUNCTION

'*****************************************************
'* Dir     : Controls directory reading and output  *
'* Input   : None                                    *
'* Output  : None                                    *
'*****************************************************

SUB Dir (DPath AS STRING, Attr AS INTEGER)

DIM NumOfEntries AS INTEGER           'Total number of entries found
DIM NumInScrn AS INTEGER              'Number of entries in screen
DIM DirBuf AS DirStruct               'Get file information

CALL SetDTA(VARSEG(DirBuf), VARPTR(DirBuf))   'DirBuf is new DTA
CLS                                           'Clear screen
CALL ScreenDesign                     'Create window for directory output

NumInScrn = -1                        'Still no entries displayed in window
NumOfEntries = 0                      'Still no entries found
IF FindFirst(DPath, Attr) THEN        'Find first entry (same attributes)
  DO                                  'Display all entries
    NumOfEntries = NumOfEntries + 1   'Another entry found
    NumInScrn = NumInScrn + 1         'Another entry displayed
    IF NumInScrn = FENTS THEN         'Window full?
      '-- Yes --> Wait for keypress, then display next window's worth
      VIEW PRINT (OWINTOP + 5 + FENTS) TO (OWINTOP + 6 + FENTS)
      PRINT "          Please press a key  "
      SLEEP                           'Wait for keypress
      VIEW PRINT (OWINTOP + 4) TO (OWINTOP + 3 + FENTS)
      NumInScrn = 0                   'Display new entries in window
    END IF
    CALL PrintData(DirBuf)            'Display entry data
  LOOP UNTIL NOT FindNext             'Next entry
END IF
VIEW PRINT (OWINTOP + 5 + FENTS) TO (OWINTOP + 6 + FENTS)
CLS
SELECT CASE NumOfEntries
CASE 0
  PRINT "File not found"
CASE 1
  PRINT " One file found"
CASE ELSE
  PRINT STR$(NumOfEntries); " files found"
END SELECT
VIEW PRINT 1 TO 25
END SUB

'*****************************************************
'* FindFirst : Finds the first directory entry      *
'* Input     : Filename and file attribute          *
```

```
'* Output    : TRUE if the entry is found, otherwise FALSE      *
'* Info      : Entry is placed in the DirBuf variable           *
'*****************************************************************
FUNCTION FindFirst% (DFilename AS STRING, Attr AS INTEGER)
DIM FBuff AS STRING * 65            'Buffer for filename (as text)
DIM Regs AS RegTypeX                        'Processor registers

FBuff = DFilename                           'Transfer filename
FBuff = FBuff + CHR$(0)         'Terminate filename with a null
Regs.ax = &H4E00           'AH = Function number: Search for first
Regs.cx = Attr                          'Search for attribute
Regs.ds = VARSEG(FBuff)          'Segment address of filename
Regs.dx = VARPTR(FBuff)          'Offset address of filename
CALL INTERRUPTX(&H21, Regs, Regs)          'Call DOS interrupt
IF (Regs.flags AND FCARRY) = 0 THEN         'Test carry flag
  FindFirst = TRUE                           'Unset = file found
ELSE
  FindFirst = FALSE                          'Set = file not found
END IF
END FUNCTION


'*****************************************************************
'* FindNext : Finds the next directory entry                    *
'* Input    : None                                              *
'* Output   : TRUE if the entry is found, otherwise FALSE        *
'* Info     : This function should execute after GetFirst. The entry  *
'*            is placed in the DirBuf variable.                  *
'*****************************************************************

FUNCTION FindNext%

DIM Regs AS RegType       'Processor registers for interrupt call

Regs.ax = &H4F00           'AH = 4F: Function number: Search for next
CALL INTERRUPT(&H21, Regs, Regs)          'Call DOS interrupt
IF (Regs.flags AND FCARRY) = 0 THEN         'Test carry flag
  FindNext = TRUE                            'Unset = file found
ELSE
  FindNext = FALSE                           'Set = file not found
END IF
END FUNCTION


'*****************************************************************
'* Makeword : Converts an integer to a long number, which permits  *
'*            BASIC to perform bit shift operations on a negative  *
'*            number using integer division.                     *
'* Input    : The integer number                                *
'* Output   : Corresponding long number                         *
'*****************************************************************
FUNCTION MakeWord! (INum AS INTEGER)

IF INum < 0 THEN
  MakeWord = 65536! + INum
ELSE
  MakeWord = INum
END IF
END FUNCTION


'*****************************************************************
'* Month   : Displays the month as a string (Jan, Feb, etc.).   *
'* Input   : Number of the month                                *
'* Output  : Month name as a string                             *
'*****************************************************************
FUNCTION Month$ (Mon AS INTEGER)
```

```
SELECT CASE Mon
  CASE 1
    Month$ = "Jan"
  CASE 2
    Month$ = "Feb"
  CASE 3
    Month$ = "Mar"
  CASE 4
    Month$ = "Apr"
  CASE 5
    Month$ = "May"
  CASE 6
    Month$ = "Jun"
  CASE 7
    Month$ = "Jul"
  CASE 8
    Month$ = "Aug"
  CASE 9
    Month$ = "Sep"
  CASE 10
    Month$ = "Oct"
  CASE 11
    Month$ = "Nov"
  CASE 12
    Month$ = "Dec"
END SELECT
END FUNCTION


'*****************************************************************
'* PrintData : Display information about a file entry           *
'* Input     : DirBufType with file information                 *
'* Output    : None                                             *
'* Info      : Information for this SUB is taken from the        *
'*             DirBuf variable                                   *
'*****************************************************************
SUB PrintData (DirBuf AS DirStruct)

DIM LCounter AS INTEGER                              'Loop counter

PRINT                                 'Display new line in table
LOCATE OWINTOP + FENTS + 3, 15   'Cursor at last line of output window
PRINT "|| ";
LCounter = 1
WHILE MID$(DirBuf.DatName, LCounter, 1) <> CHR$(0)  'Repeat until null
  PRINT MID$(DirBuf.DatName, LCounter, 1);   'Display name character
  LCounter = LCounter + 1                     'Next character
WEND

'-- Compute and display file length -----------------------------------
LOCATE OWINTOP + FENTS + 3, 30                      'Position cursor
PRINT USING "| ###### "; DirBuf.Size;

'-- Display date and time ----------------------------------------------
LOCATE OWINTOP + FENTS + 3, 40
PRINT "| "; Month$((MakeWord(DirBuf.Date) \ 32) AND 15);  'Show month
PRINT " "; Dat$(MakeWord(DirBuf.Date) AND 31);           'Show day
PRINT USING " ####"; (MakeWord(DirBuf.Date) \ 512) + 1980;  'Show year
LOCATE OWINTOP + FENTS + 3, 53
PRINT " | "; Dat$(MakeWord(DirBuf.Time) \ 2048); ":";    'Show hour
PRINT Dat$((MakeWord(DirBuf.Time) \ 32) AND 63);         'Show minutes

'-- Display file attributes --------------------------------------------
```

```
LOCATE OWINTOP + FENTS + 3, 63
PRINT "|";
LCounter = 1
WHILE (LCounter < 32)
  IF (ASC(DirBuf.Attrib) AND LCounter) <> 0 THEN          'Read-only?
    PRINT "X";
  ELSE
    PRINT " ";
  END IF
  LCounter = LCounter * 2
WEND
PRINT "||";                                    'Right margin of window

END SUB


'*******************************************************************
'* ScreenDesign    : Prepares screen for directory display        *
'* Input           : None                                         *
'* Output          : None                                         *
'*******************************************************************
SUB ScreenDesign
CONST LR = "          "         'Move left margin over to the right
DIM LCounter AS INTEGER                              'Loop counter

CLS                                                 'Clear screen
```

```
VIEW PRINT (OWINTOP + 1) TO (OWINTOP + 5 + FENTS)
PRINT LR + "┌─────────────────────────────────────────────────┐"
PRINT LR + "|| Filename | Size   | Date      | Time  |RHSVD||"
PRINT LR + "||─────────┼────────┼───────────┼───────┼──────||"
FOR LCounter = 1 TO FENTS
  PRINT LR + "||         |        |           |       |      ||"
NEXT
PRINT LR + "└─────────────────────────────────────────────────┘"
VIEW PRINT (OWINTOP + 4) TO (OWINTOP + 3 + FENTS)
END SUB


'*******************************************************************
'* SetDTA   : Set DTA address                                     *
'* Input    : Segment and offset address of DTA buffer            *
'* Output   : None                                                *
'*******************************************************************
SUB SetDTA (Segment AS LONG, Offset AS LONG)

DIM Regs AS RegTypeX                             'Processor registers

Regs.ax = &H1A00             'AH = 1AH: Function number: Set DTA
Regs.ds = Segment            'Segment address of DS register
Regs.dx = Offset             'Offset address of DX register
CALL INTERRUPTX(&H21, Regs, Regs)               'Call DOS interrupt
END SUB
```

Direct calls to functions 4EH and 4FH in Pascal and C

The following Pascal and C programs perform direct calls to functions 4EH and 4FH. Predefined FINDFIRST and FINDNEXT procedures/functions aren't used.

Turbo Pascal includes a statement that easily defines any part of the screen as a window. The C language must use functions of BIOS interrupt 10H to scroll the directory window up, one line at a time. The C program contains a function called PRINT. This function is similar to PRINTF() except that PRINT accepts the string's position on the screen and the color of the output. This display information can then be written directly to video RAM.

Pascal listing: DIRP1.PAS

```
{*****************************************************}
{*                 D I R P 1 . P A S                *}
{*-------------------------------------------------*}
{*  Task        : Displays all files in any directory on the   *}
{*                screen, including subdirectories and volume   *}
{*                label names. File handling is performed by a  *}
{*                direct call to DOS functions 4EH and 4FH.     *}
{*                See also DIRP2.PAS.                           *}
{*-------------------------------------------------*}
{*  Author      : Michael Tischer                  *}
{*  Developed on : 07/08/88                        *}
{*  Last update : 01/22/92                         *}
{*****************************************************}
program DIRP1;

Uses Crt, Dos;                    { Add CRT and DOS units }

{-- Type declarations --------------------------------------}

type DirBufTyp = record   { Data structures of functions 4EH and 4FH }
              Reserved  : array [1..21] of char;
```

```
              Attr      : byte;
              Time      : integer;
              Date      : integer;
              Size      : longint;
              Name      : array [1..13] of char
            end;

     MonVec    = array[1..12] of string[3];  { Array with month names }

{-- Constants ---------------------------------------------}

const FA_ReadOnly = $01;                       { File attributes }
      FAHidden    = $02;
      FA_SysFile  = $04;
      FA_VolumeID = $08;
      FA_Directory = $10;
      FA_Archive  = $20;
      FA_AnyFile  = $3F;

      FENTS = 14;              { Number of visible entries at a time }
      Months : MonVec = ( 'Jan', 'Feb', 'Mar', 'Apr', 'May', 'Jun',
                          'Jul', 'Aug', 'Sep', 'Oct', 'Nov', 'Dec');
{*****************************************************************}
```

```
{* FindFirst: Finds first directory entry.                  *}
{* Input   : None                                           *}
{* Output  : TRUE or FALSE, depending on whether entry is found  *}
{*******************************************************************}
function FindFirst(SFileName : string;      { File to be searched for }
                   Attribute : integer) : boolean; { Srch. attribute }

var Regs : Registers;          { Processor registers for interrupt call }

begin
  SFileName := SFileName + #0;           { Filename ended with null }
  Regs.ah := $4E;              { Function number: Search for first }
  Regs.cx := Attribute;              { Attribute to be sought }
  Regs.ds := Seg(SFileName);         { Segment addresses of filenames }
  Regs.dx := succ(Ofs(SFileName));   { Offset addresses of filenames }
  MsDos( Regs );                     { Call DOS interrupt 21H }
  FindFirst := ( (Regs.flags and 1) = 0 )    { Test carry flag }
end;


{*******************************************************************}
{* FindNext: Finds the next directory entry.                  *}
{* Input   : None                                             *}
{* Output  : TRUE if the entry is found, otherwise FALSE      *}
{* Info    : This function should be called after the FindFirst *}
{*           function is successfully called.                 *}
{*******************************************************************}
function FindNext : boolean;

var Regs : Registers;          { Processor registers for interrupt call }

begin
  Regs.ah := $4F;              { Function number: Search for next }
  MsDos( Regs );                     { Call DOS interrupt 21H }
  FindNext := ( (Regs.flags and 1) = 0 )     { Test carry flag }
end;


{*******************************************************************}
{* SetDTA: Sets the DTA address.                              *}
{* Input   : SEGMENT = Segment address of the new DTA         *}
{*           OFFSET  = Offset address of the new DTA          *}
{* Output  : None                                             *}
{*******************************************************************}
procedure SetDTA(Segment,              { New segment address of DTA }
                 Offset  : integer);   { New Offset address of DTA }

var Regs : Registers;          { Processor registers for interrupt call }

begin
  Regs.ah := $1A;              { Function number: Set DTA }
  Regs.ds := Segment;          { Segment address in DS register }
  Regs.dx := Offset;           { Offset address in DX register }
  MsDos( Regs );                     { Call DOS interrupt 21H }
end;


{*******************************************************************}
{* PRINTDATA: Displays entry information.                     *}
{* Input   : DIRBUF = Data structure with file information    *}
{* Output  : None                                             *}
{*******************************************************************}
procedure PrintData( DirBuf : DirBufTyp );

var Counter : byte;

begin
```

```
  writeln;                              { Scroll up by one line }

  Counter := 1;      { Start with the first character of the name }
  while (DirBuf.Name[Counter]<>#0) do         { Repeat until NULL }
  begin
    write(DirBuf.Name[Counter]);         { Display name character }
    Counter := succ(Counter)             { Process next character }
  end;

  GotoXY(13, FENTS);
  write('|', DirBuf.Size:7);
  GotoXY(21, FENTS);
  write('|', (Months[DirBuf.Date shr 5 and 15]),' '); { Display month }
  write (DirBuf.Date and 31:2,' ');                 { Display day }
  write(DirBuf.Date shr 9 + 1980:5);                { Display year }
  GotoXY(34, FENTS);
  write('| ', DirBuf.Time shr 11:2, ':');           { Display hour }
  write(DirBuf.Time shr 5 and 63:3);              { Display minutes }

  GotoXY(44, FENTS);
  write('|');                  { Separator preceding each field }
  Counter := 1;                { Attribute display counter }
  while ( Counter < 32 ) do
    begin
      if (DirBuf.Attr and Counter) <> 0 then write('X')
                                       else write(' ');
      Counter := Counter shl 1;
    end;
  write('||');                        { Right border of window }
end;


{*******************************************************************}
{* ScreenDesign    : Prepares screen for directory display.   *}
{* Input   : None                                             *}
{* Output  : None                                             *}
{*******************************************************************}
procedure ScreenDesign;

var Counter : integer;                            { Loop counter }

begin
  ClrScr;                                       { Clear screen }
  Window(14,(20-FENTS) shr 1+1,64,(20-FENTS) shr 1 +5+FENTS);
  GotoXY(1,1);                { Cursor in upper-left corner of window }

  write('┌─────────────────────────────────────┐');
  write('|| Filename | Size |   Date   |  Time  |RHSVD||');
  write('||─────────┼──────┼──────────┼────────┼─────||');

  for Counter := 1 to FENTS do
    write('||         |      |          |        |     ||');
  write('└─────────────────────────────────────┘');

  Window(15,(20-FENTS) shr 1+4,66,(20-FENTS) shr 1 +3+FENTS);
  GotoXY(1, FENTS);          { Cursor in upper-left corner of window }
end;


{*******************************************************************}
{* Dir: Controls directory reading and output.               *}
{* Input   : SPath     = Search path with file pattern       *}
{*           ATTRIBUTE = Search attribute                     *}
{* Output  : None                                             *}
{*******************************************************************}
procedure Dir( SPath : string; Attr : byte );
```

```pascal
var NumOfEntries,                      { Total number of entries found }
    NumInScrn    : integer;            { Number of entries per screen }
    WtKey        : char;               { Wait for a keypress }
    DirBuf       : DirBufTyp;          { Indicates a directory entry }


begin
  SetDTA(Seg(DirBuf), Ofs(DirBuf));            { DirBuf is the new DTA }
  clrscr;                                      { Clear screen }
  ScreenDesign;                 { Prepare screen for directory output }

  NumInScrn := -1;                     { No more entries to display }
  NumOfEntries := 0;                   { No more entries found }
  if FindFirst( SPath, Attr ) then     { Search for first entry }
    repeat
      NumOfEntries := succ(NumOfEntries);    { One more entry found }
      NumInScrn := succ(NumInScrn);    { One more entry in window }
      if NumInScrn = FENTS then             { Is the window full? }
        begin                                          { Yes }
          Window( 14, (20-FENTS) shr 1 + 5+ FENTS,
                  66 ,(20-FENTS) shr 1 + 6+ FENTS );
          GotoXY(1, 1);      { Move cursor to bottom line of window }
          TextBackground( LightGray );       { White background }
          TextColor( Black );                { Black text }
          write('          Please press a key              ');
          WtKey := ReadKey;                  { Read a key }
          GotoXY(1, 1);      { Cursor in upper-left corner of window }
          TextBackground( Black );           { Black background }
          TextColor( LightGray );            { White text }
          write('                                          ');
          Window(15,(20-FENTS) shr 1+4,65,(20-FENTS) shr 1 +3+FENTS);
          GotoXY(1, FENTS);       { Return cursor to old position }
          NumInScrn := 0;                    { Start counting at 0 }
        end;
      PrintData( DirBuf );                   { Display entry data }
    until not(FindNext);               { Are there any more entries? }

  Window(14,(20-FENTS) shr 1 +5+FENTS,65,(20-FENTS) shr 1 +6+FENTS);
  GotoXY(1, 1);              { Cursor in upper-left corner of window }
  TextBackground( LightGray );           { White background }
  TextColor( Black );                    { Black text }
  write('                                          ');

  GotoXY(2, 1);
  case NumOfEntries of
    0 : write('No files found');
    1 : write('One file found');
    else write(NumOfEntries,' files found')
  end;

  Window(1, 1, 80, 25);                  { Make entire screen a window }
end;


{***************************************************************}
{**                   MAIN PROGRAM                           **}
{***************************************************************}

begin
  case ParamCount of                     { Count parameters }
    0 : Dir( '*.*', FA_AnyFile );    { All files in current directory }
    1 : Dir( ParamStr(1), FA_AnyFile ); { Display specific directory }
    else writeln('Invalid number of parameters');
  end;
end.
```

C listing: DIRC1.C

```c
/***************************************************************/
/*                                                             */
/*                      D I R C 1                             */
/*-------------------------------------------------------------*/
/*  Task         : Displays all files in any directory on the  */
/*                 screen, including subdirectories and volume */
/*                 label names. File handling is performed by a*/
/*                 direct call to DOS functions 4EH and 4FH.   */
/*                 See also DIRC2.C                            */
/*-------------------------------------------------------------*/
/*  Author       : Michael Tischer                             */
/*  Developed on : 08/15/87                                    */
/*  Last update  : 01/22/92                                    */
/*-------------------------------------------------------------*/
/*  Memory model : SMALL                                       */
/***************************************************************/

/*== Add include files ========================================*/

#include <dos.h>
#include <stdio.h>
#include <string.h>
#include <stdarg.h>
#include <stdio.h>
#include <conio.h>


/*== Type definitions =========================================*/

typedef unsigned char BYTE;                   /* Create a byte */
typedef struct {          /* DIR structure for functions 4EH and 4FH */
                BYTE         Reserved[21];
                BYTE         Attribute;
                unsigned int Time;
                unsigned int Date;
                unsigned long Size;
                char         Name[13];
               } DIRSTRUCT;


/*== Constants ================================================*/

/*-- Attributes for file search -------------------------------*/

#define ATTR_RDONLY 0x01                       /* Read-only    */
#define ATTR_HIDDEN 0x02                       /* Hidden       */
#define ATTR_SYSTEM 0x04                       /* System       */
#define ATTR_LABEL  0x08                       /* Volume name  */
#define ATTR_DIREC  0x10                       /* Directory    */
#define ATTR_ARCH   0x20                       /* Archived     */
#define ATTR_ALL    0x3F                       /* All file types */

#define TRUE  ( 0 == 0 )                /* Constants make reading */
#define FALSE ( 0 == 1 )                /* program code easier */

#define FENTS 14          /* Number of visible entries at a time */
#define OT    (20-FENTS >> 1)           /* Top row of output window */
#define NOF   0x07           /* White text on black background */
#define INV   0x70    /* Black text on white background (inverse) */

/*== Macros ===================================================*/

#ifdef MK_FP                    /* Macro MK_FP already defined? */
  #undef MK_FP                          /* Yes --> Undefine macro */
#endif
```

```c
#define MK_FP(seg,ofs) ((void far *) ((unsigned long) (seg)<<16|(ofs)))

/********************************************************************/
/* PRINT : Similar to PRINTF, writes the string directly to         */
/*         video RAM.                                               */
/* Input  : COLUMN = Display column                                 */
/*          SCROW  = Display row                                    */
/*          DCOLR  = Display color                                  */
/*          STRING = Pointer to PRINTF string                       */
/*          ...    = other arguments                               */
/* Output : None                                                    */
/********************************************************************/

void Print( int Column, int ScRow, BYTE DColr, char * String, ...)
{
 struct vr {                        /* 2 bytes to a screen position */
          BYTE DisChar,             /* ASCII code */
               Attribute;           /* Corresponding attribute */
          } far * lptr;             /* Floating pointer to video RAM access */
 va_list parameter;                 /* Parameter list for VA_... macros */
 char Output [255],                 /* Buffer for formatted string */
      *aptr = Output ;              /* For string execution */
 static unsigned int vioseg = 0;
 union REGS Register;        /* Register variables for interrupt call */

 if ( vioseg == 0 )                 /* First call? */
  {                                 /* Yes --> Get segment address of video RAM */
   Register.h.ah = 0xOF;
   int86(0x10, &Register, &Register);
   vioseg = ( Register.h.al == 7 ? 0xb000 : 0xb800 );
  }

 va_start( parameter, String );     /* Convert parameter */
 vsprintf( Output , String, parameter );   /* Format */
 lptr = (struct vr far *)
        MK_FP( vioseg, ( ScRow * 80 + Column ) << 1 );

 for ( ; *aptr ; )                  /* Run string */
  {
   lptr->DisChar = *aptr++;         /* Character in video RAM */
   lptr++->Attribute = DColr;       /* Set character attribute */
  }
}

/********************************************************************/
/* SCROLLUP: Moves a screen range up by one or more rows, or clears */
/*           rows.                                                  */
/* Input  : NUMROW    = Number of rows to be scrolled               */
/*          DCOLR     = Color/attribute for blank lines             */
/*          COLUMNUL  = Upper-left screen corner (column)           */
/*          SCROWUL   = Upper-left screen corner (row)              */
/*          COLUMNLR  = Lower-right screen corner (column)          */
/*          SCROWLR   = Lower-right screen corner (row)             */
/* Output : None                                                    */
/* Info   : If NumRow contains 0, the screen range fills with       */
/*          blank spaces.                                           */
/********************************************************************/

void ScrollUp( BYTE NumRow, BYTE DColr, BYTE ColumnUL,
               BYTE ScRowUL, BYTE ColumnLR, BYTE ScRowLR)
{
 union REGS Register;        /* Register variables for interrupt call */

 Register.h.ah = 6;                 /* Function number */
 Register.h.al = NumRow;            /* Number of rows */
 Register.h.bh = DColr;             /* Color of blank lines */
 Register.h.ch = ScRowUL;           /* Coordinates for */
 Register.h.cl = ColumnUL;          /* scrolling or clearing. */
 Register.h.dh = ScRowLR;           /* Specify screen window */
 Register.h.dl = ColumnLR;
 int86(0x10, &Register, &Register);        /* Call interrupt 10H */
}

/********************************************************************/
/* SETPOS: Specifies a cursor position in the current screen page.  */
/* Input  : COLUMN = New cursor column                              */
/*          SCROW  = New cursor row                                 */
/* Output : None                                                    */
/********************************************************************/

void SetPos( BYTE Column, BYTE ScRow)
{
 union REGS Register;       /* Register variables for interrupt call */

 Register.h.ah = 2;                 /* Function number */
 Register.h.bh = 0;                 /* Screen page */
 Register.h.dh = ScRow;             /* Screen row */
 Register.h.dl = Column;            /* Screen column */
 int86(0x10, &Register, &Register);        /* Call interrupt 10H */
}

/********************************************************************/
/* CLS: Clears current screen page and places cursor in upper-left  */
/*      corner.                                                     */
/* Input  : None                                                    */
/* Output : None                                                    */
/********************************************************************/

void Cls( void )
{
 ScrollUp(0, NOF, 0, 0, 79, 24);           /* Clear screen */
 SetPos(0, 0);                             /* Place cursor */
}

/********************************************************************/
/* SCREENDESIGN     : Prepares screen for directory display.        */
/* Input  : None                                                    */
/* Output : None                                                    */
/********************************************************************/

void ScreenDesign( void )
{
 BYTE i;                                   /* Loop counter */

 Cls();                                    /* Clear screen */
 Print( 14, OT, NOF,
        "╔══════════════════════════════════════════╗");
 Print( 14, OT+1, NOF,
        "║ Filename | Size |   Date   | Time |RHSVD║");
 Print( 14, OT+2, NOF,
        "╠═══════════╪══════╪══════════╪══════╪═════╣");
 for (i = OT+3; i < OT+3+FENTS; i++)
  Print( 14, i, NOF,
         "║           │      │          │      ║");
 Print( 14, OT+FENTS+3, NOF,
        "╚══════════════════════════════════════════╝");
```

```c
}

/*************************************************************************/
/* PRINTDATA: Displays entry information.                              */
/* Input   : P2ENTRY = Pointer to a DirStruct with file information    */
/*           SCROW   = Screen row of entry                             */
/* Output  : None                                                      */
/*************************************************************************/

void PrintData(DIRSTRUCT *P2Entry, BYTE ScRow)
{
  BYTE i, j;                           /* Loop counter */
  static char *Month[] =       /* Vector with pointers to month name */
                     {
                       "Jan", "Feb", "Mar", "Apr", "May", "Jun",
                       "Jul", "Aug", "Sep", "Oct", "Nov", "Dec"
                     };

  /*-- Display miscellaneous file information ------------------------*/

  Print( 15, ScRow, NOF, "%s", P2Entry->Name);

  Print( 28, ScRow, NOF, "%7lu", P2Entry->Size);
  Print( 36, ScRow, NOF, "%s %2d %4d", Month[(P2Entry->Date >> 5 & 15) -
1],
         P2Entry->Date & 31,
         (P2Entry->Date >> 9) + 1980);
  Print( 51, ScRow, NOF, "%02d:%02d", P2Entry->Time >> 11,
                          P2Entry->Time >> 5 & 63 );

  for (i = j = 1; i <= 16; i <<= 1, ++j)  /* Display file attributes */
    Print( 58+j, ScRow, NOF, "%c", (P2Entry->Attribute & i) ? 'X' : ' ' );
}

/*************************************************************************/
/* FINDFIRST: Finds first directory entry.                             */
/* Input   : SPATH     = Pointer to search path with file mask         */
/*           ATTRIBUTE = Search attribute                              */
/* Output  : TRUE if the entry is found, otherwise FALSE               */
/* Info    : Entry is placed in the DirBuf variable                    */
/*************************************************************************/

BYTE findfirst( char *SPath, BYTE Attribute )
{
  union REGS Register;        /* Registers variable for interrupt call */
  struct SREGS Segmente;               /* Get the segment register */

  segread(&Segmente);         /* Read contents of the segment register */
  Register.h.ah = 0x4E;         /* Function number: Search for first */
  Register.x.cx = Attribute;         /* Attribute to be searched for */
  Register.x.dx = (unsigned int) SPath;    /* Offset address of path */
  intdosx(&Register, &Register, &Segmente); /* Call DOS interrupt 21H */
  return( !Register.x.cflag );      /* Carry flag=0: One file found */
}

/*************************************************************************/
/* FINDNEXT: Finds the next directory entry.                           */
/* Input   : None                                                      */
/* Output  : TRUE if the entry is found, otherwise FALSE               */
/* Info    : Entry is placed in the DTA.                               */
/*************************************************************************/

BYTE findnext( void )
{
```

```c
  union REGS Register;        /* Register variables for interrupt call */

  Register.h.ah = 0x4F;          /* Function number: Search for next */
  intdos(&Register, &Register);             /* Call DOS interrupt 21H */
  return( !Register.x.cflag );      /* Carry flag=0: One file found */
}

/*************************************************************************/
/* SETDTA: Places the DTA in a variable in the data segment.           */
/* Input   : OFFSET = DTA offset within the data segment               */
/* Output  : None                                                      */
/*************************************************************************/

void SetDTA( unsigned int Offset )
{
  union REGS Register;        /* Register variables for interrupt call */
  struct SREGS Segmente;               /* Get the segment register */

  segread(&Segmente);         /* Read contents of the segment register */
  Register.h.ah = 0x1A;                /* Function number: Set DTA */
  Register.x.dx = Offset;         /* Offset address in DX register */
  intdosx(&Register, &Register, &Segmente); /* Call DOS interrupt 21H */
}

/*************************************************************************/
/* DIR: Controls directory reading and output.                        */
/* Input   : SPath     = Pointer to search path with file pattern      */
/*           Attribute = Search attribute                              */
/* Output  : None                                                      */
/*************************************************************************/

void Dir(char *SPath, BYTE Attribute )
{
  int     NumOfEntries,             /* Total number of entries found */
          NumInScrn;                /* Number of entries per screen */
  DIRSTRUCT P2Entry;                /* Pointer to a directory entry */

  SetDTA( (unsigned int) &P2Entry );    /* This entry is the new DTA */
  ScreenDesign();              /* Prepare screen for directory display */

  NumInScrn = NumOfEntries = 0;       /* No more entries to display */
                                      /* No more entries found */
  if (findfirst(SPath, Attribute))      /* Search for first entry */
  {                                     /* One file found */
    do           /* Display file and use GetNext() to find next one */
    {
      PrintData(&P2Entry, OT+FENTS+2);         /* Display entries */
      if (++NumInScrn == FENTS )          /* Is the window full? */
      {
        NumInScrn = 0;                     /* Fill the window */
        Print(14, OT+4+FENTS, INV,
              "               Please press a key               ");
        getch();                            /* Wait for a key */
        Print(14, OT+4+FENTS, NOF,
              "                                                ");
      }
      ScrollUp(1, NOF, 15, OT+3, 63, OT+2+FENTS);
      Print(15, OT+2+FENTS, NOF,
            "          |         |         |         | ");
      ++NumOfEntries;
    }
    while ( findnext() );    /* End loop when no more files are found */
  }
}
```

```
SetPos(14, OT+4+FENTS);
switch (NumOfEntries)
{
  case 0 : printf("No files found");
           break;
  case 1 : printf("One file found");
           break;
  default : printf("%d files found", NumOfEntries);
           break;
  }
}

/**************************************************************/
/**                    MAIN PROGRAM                        **/
```

```
/***************************************************************************/

void main( int NumRow, char *Argumente[] )
{
  switch ( NumRow )                                  /* React to parameters */
  {                                                  /* as necessary        */
    case 1 : Dir("*.*", ATTR_ALL );      /* Display all files in */
             break;                       /* current directory    */
    case 2 : Dir( Argumente[1], ATTR_ALL );  /* Display all files in */
             break;                           /* specified directory  */
    default : printf("Invalid number of parameters\n");
  }
}
```

Using the predefined functions/procedures in Pascal and C

The DIRP2.PAS and DIRC2.C programs use the predefined FindFirst and FindNext functions from Turbo Pascal or the various C compilers supported by this book. This simplifies directory display because DTA positioning is bypassed.

Both programs use the 4EH and 4FH DOS functions, as well as a special data structure for storing file information. Turbo Pascal's SearchRec structure is defined in the DOS unit, along with FindFirst and FindNext. The DOS unit also defines various constants, which can be set with flags for controlling file attributes.

Unfortunately, the SearchRec structure combines the time and date fields into a long integer, which requires a little trick to divide the individual data elements. The DIRP2.PAS program demonstrates how this is done. Also, notice that FindFirst and FindNext in the Pascal version are procedures rather than functions. So, the program must check the DosError global variable after the function call to ensure that the file was found. After calling functions 4EH and 4FH, Turbo Pascal stores the contents of the AX register in DosError. If this variable contains 0, the file was found.

Pascal listing: DIRP2.PAS

```
{**************************************************************}
{*                       D I R P 2                          *}
{*----------------------------------------------------------*}
{*    Task         : Displays all files in any directory on the *}
{*                   screen, including subdirectories and volume *}
{*                   label names. File handling is performed by a *}
{*                   call to the FindFirst and FindNext functions *}
{*                   found in the Turbo Pascal DOS unit.     *}
{*                   See also DIRP1.PAS.                     *}
{*----------------------------------------------------------*}
{*    Author       : Michael Tischer                        *}
{*    Developed on : 07/08/88                               *}
{*    Last update  : 01/23/92                               *}
{**************************************************************}

program DIRP2;

Uses Crt, Dos;                          { Add CRT and DOS units }

{-- Type declarations -------------------------------------}

type MonVec   = array[1..12] of string[3]; { Array with month names }
```

```
{-- Constants ----------------------------------------------------}

const FENTS = 14;               { Number of visible entries at a time }
      Months : MonVec = ( 'Jan', 'Feb', 'Mar', 'Apr', 'May', 'Jun',
                          'Jul', 'Aug', 'Sep', 'Oct', 'Nov', 'Dec');


{***************************************************************}
{* PRINTDATA: Displays entry information.                     *}
{* Input   : DIRBUF = Data structure with file information    *}
{* Output  : None                                             *}
{***************************************************************}

procedure PrintData( DirBuf : SearchRec );

var Counter : byte;
    Date,                       { For splitting the TIME field in SearchRec }
    Time   : word;

type longrec = record     { For splitting a LONG record into two words }
                 LoWord,
                 HiWord : word
               end;
```

```pascal
begin
  writeln;                          { Scroll up by one line }

  write( DirBuf.Name );             { Name already converted by Pascal }

  GotoXY(13, FENTS);
  write('|', DirBuf.Size:7);

  Date := longrec(DirBuf.Time).HiWord; { Date and time from SearchRec }
  Time := longrec(DirBuf.Time).LoWord;

  GotoXY(21, FENTS);
  write('|',(Months[Date shr 5 and 15]),' ');   { Display month }
  write(Date and 31:2,' ');         { Display day }
  write(Date shr 9 + 1980:5);       { Display year }
  GotoXY(34, FENTS);
  write('|', Time shr 11:2, ':');   { Display hour }
  write(Time shr 5 and 63:3);       { Display minutes }
  GotoXY(44, FENTS);
  write('|');                       { Separator preceding each field }
  Counter := 1;                     { Attribute display counter }
  while ( Counter < 32 ) do
    begin
      if (DirBuf.Attr and Counter) <> 0 then write('X')
                                    else write(' ');
      Counter := Counter shl 1;
    end;
  write('||');                      { Right border of window }
end;


{***********************************************************}
{* ScreenDesign : Prepares screen for directory display.   *}
{* Input  : None                                           *}
{* Output : None                                           *}
{***********************************************************}
procedure ScreenDesign;

var Counter : integer;              { Loop counter }

begin
  ClrScr;                           { Clear screen }
  Window(14,(20-FENTS) shr 1+1,64,(20-FENTS) shr 1 +5+FENTS);
  GotoXY(1,1);                      { Cursor in upper-left corner of window }

  write('╒════════════════════════════════════╕');
  write('|| Filename | Size |  Date  |  Time  |RHSVD||');
  write('||─────────┼──────┼────────┼────────┼───────||');

  for Counter := 1 to FENTS do
    write('||        |      |        |        |     ||');
  write('╘════════════════════════════════════╛');

  Window(15,(20-FENTS) shr 1+4,66,(20-FENTS) shr 1 +3+FENTS);
  GotoXY(1, FENTS);                 { Cursor in upper-left corner of window }
end;


{***********************************************************}
{* Dir: Controls directory reading and output.             *}
{* Input  : SPATH     = Search path with file pattern      *}
{*          ATTRIBUTE = Search attribute                    *}
{* Output : None                                           *}
{***********************************************************}
procedure Dir( SPath : string; Attr : byte );


var NumOfEntries,                   { Total number of entries found }
    NumInScrn  : integer;           { Number of entries per screen }
    WKey       : char;              { Wait for a keypress }
    DirBuf     : SearchRec;         { Indicates a directory entry }

begin
  clrscr;                           { Clear screen }
  ScreenDesign;                     { Prepare screen for directory output }

  NumInScrn := -1;                  { No more entries to display }
  NumOfEntries := 0;                { No more entries found }
  FindFirst( SPath, Attr, DirBuf ); { Search for first entry }
  if DOSError = 0 then
    repeat
      NumOfEntries := succ(NumOfEntries);   { One more entry found }
      NumInScrn := succ(NumInScrn);         { One more entry in window }
      if NumInScrn = FENTS then             { Is the window full? }
        begin                               { Yes }
          Window(14, (20-FENTS) shr 1 + 5 + FENTS,
                 66, (20-FENTS) shr 1 + 6+ FENTS);
          GotoXY(1, 1);           { Move cursor to bottom line of window }
          TextBackground( LightGray );        { White background }
          TextColor( Black );                 { Black text }
          write('        Please press a key        ');
          WKey := ReadKey;                    { Read a key }
          GotoXY(1, 1);           { Cursor in upper-left corner of window }
          TextBackground( Black );            { Black background }
          TextColor( LightGray );             { White text }
          write('                              ');
          Window(15,(20-FENTS) shr 1+4,65,(20-FENTS) shr 1 +3+FENTS);
          GotoXY(1, FENTS);       { Return cursor to old position }
          NumInScrn := 0;         { Start counting at 0 }
        end;
      PrintData( DirBuf );        { Display entry data }
      FindNext( DirBuf );         { Search for next file until }
    until DOSError <> 0;          { no more files remain }

  Window(14,(20-FENTS) shr 1 +5+FENTS,65,(20-FENTS) shr 1 +6+FENTS);
  GotoXY(1, 1);                   { Cursor in upper-left corner of window }
  TextBackground( LightGray );              { White background }
  TextColor( Black );                       { Black text }
  write('                          ');

  GotoXY(2, 1);
  case NumOfEntries of
    0 : write('No files found');
    1 : write('One file found');
    else write(NumOfEntries,' files found')
  end;

  Window(1, 1, 80, 25);           { Make entire screen a window }
end;


{***********************************************************}
{**                 MAIN PROGRAM                          **}
{***********************************************************}
begin
  case ParamCount of              { Count parameters }
    0 : Dir( '*.*', AnyFile );    { All files in current directory }
    1 : Dir( ParamStr(1), AnyFile ); { Display specified directory }
    else writeln('Invalid number of parameters');
  end;
end.
```

The C program DIRC2.C encounters some problems because of differences between the Microsoft and Borland compiler libraries—especially those relating to DOS API interfaces. API is not yet enforced by ANSI standards, so compiler manufacturers can set their own standards for API. Thus, FindFirst and FindNext retain different names in the two different C compiler families, and operate using different data structures with different field names.

The DIRC2.C program can be compiled and linked by both compilers. Macros include the device-dependent commands needed by the respective compilers.

C listing: DIRC2.C

```c
/********************************************************************/
/*                          D I R C 2                            */
/*------------------------------------------------------------------*/
/*  Task       : Displays all files in any directory on the       */
/*               screen, including subdirectories and volume       */
/*               label names. File handling is performed by       */
/*               predefined C functions.                          */
/*               See also DIR1C.C.                                */
/*------------------------------------------------------------------*/
/*  Author     : Michael Tischer                                  */
/*  Developed on : 10/15/91                                       */
/*  Last update  : 01/23/91                                       */
/*------------------------------------------------------------------*/
/*  Memory model : SMALL                                          */
/********************************************************************/

/*== Add include files =============================================*/

#include <dos.h>
#include <stdio.h>
#include <string.h>
#include <stdarg.h>
#include <stdio.h>
#include <conio.h>

#ifdef __TURBOC__                          /* Turbo C compiler? */
 #include <dir.h>                      /* Then add directory include */
#endif

/*== Type definitions ==============================================*/

typedef unsigned char BYTE;                   /* Create a byte */

/*== Constants =====================================================*/

#define TRUE    ( 0 == 0 )            /* Constants make reading */
#define FALSE   ( 0 == 1 )            /* program code easier    */

#define FENTS 14          /* Number of visible entries at a time */
#define OT    (20-FENTS >> 1)       /* Top row of output window */
#define NOF   0x07        /* White text on black background */
#define INV   0x70        /* Black text on white background (inverse) */

#define FA_ALL 0x3F                      /* All file types */

/*== Macros ========================================================*/

#ifdef MK_FP              /* Macro MK_FP already defined? */
 #undef MK_FP             /* Yes --> Undefine macro */
```

```c
#endif

#define MK_FP(seg,ofs) ((void far *) ((unsigned long) (seg)<<16|(ofs)))

/*-- Compiler-specific constants and macros for file searching ------*/
/*-- (for Microsoft C and Borland compilers)             -----*/

#ifdef __TURBOC__                          /* Turbo C compiler? */
 #define DIRSTRUCT                   struct ffblk
 #define FINDFIRST( path, buf, attr ) findfirst( path, buf, attr )
 #define FINDNEXT( buf )             findnext( buf )
 #define NAME                        ff_name
 #define ATTRIBUTE                   ff_attrib
 #define TIME                        ff_ftime
 #define DATE                        ff_fdate
 #define SIZE                        ff_fsize
#else                                      /* No --> Microsoft C */
 #define DIRSTRUCT                   struct find_t
 #define FINDFIRST( path, buf, attr ) _dos_findfirst(path, attr, buf)
 #define FINDNEXT( buf )             _dos_findnext( buf )
 #define NAME                        name
 #define ATTRIBUTE                   attrib
 #define TIME                        wr_time
 #define DATE                        wr_date
 #define SIZE                        size
#endif

/********************************************************************/
/* PRINT : Similar to PRINTF, writes the string directly to       */
/*         video RAM.                                             */
/* Input : COLUMN = Display column                                */
/*         SCROW  = Display row                                   */
/*         DCOLR  = Display color                                 */
/*         STRING = Pointer to PRINTF string                      */
/*         ...    = other arguments                              */
/* Output : None                                                 */
/********************************************************************/

void Print( int Column, int ScRow, BYTE DColr, char * String, ...)
{
 struct vr {                          /* 2 bytes to a screen position */
           BYTE DisChar,                    /* ASCII code */
                Attribute;             /* Corresponding attribute */
          } far * lptr;       /* Floating pointer to video RAM access */
 va_list parameter;                  /* Parameter list for VA_... macros */
 char Output[255],                   /* Buffer for formatted string */
      *aptr = Output;                  /* For string execution */
 static unsigned int vioseg = 0;
 union REGS Register;       /* Register variables for interrupt call */

 if ( vioseg == 0 )                            /* First call? */
```

```
      {                       /* Yes --> Get segment address of video RAM */
       Register.h.ah = 0x0F;
       int86(0x10, &Register, &Register);
       vioseg = ( Register.h.al == 7 ? 0xb000 : 0xb800 );
      }

    va_start( parameter, String );           /* Convert parameter */
    vsprintf( Output, String, parameter );           /* Format */
    lptr = (struct vr far *)
          MK_FP( vioseg, ( ScRow * 80 + Column ) << 1 );

    for ( ; *aptr ; )                        /* Run string */
    {
      lptr->DisChar = *aptr++;               /* Character in video RAM */
      lptr++->Attribute = DColr;             /* Set character attribute */
    }
   }


/****************************************************************/
/* SCROLLUP: Moves a screen range up by one or more rows, or clears */
/*           rows.                                              */
/* Input    : NUMROW     = Number of rows to be scrolled       */
/*            DCOLR      = Color/attribute for blank lines      */
/*            COLUMNUL = Upper-left screen corner (column)      */
/*            SCROWUL  = Upper-left screen corner (row)         */
/*            COLUMNLR = Lower-right screen corner (column)     */
/*            SCROWLR  = Lower-right screen corner (row)        */
/* Output   : None                                             */
/* Info     : If NumRow contains 0, the screen range fills with */
/*            blank spaces.                                     */
/****************************************************************/

void ScrollUp( BYTE NumRow, BYTE DColr, BYTE ColumnOL,
               BYTE ScRowOL, BYTE ColumnUR, BYTE ScRowUR)
{
  union REGS Register;        /* Register variables for interrupt call */

  Register.h.ah = 6;                       /* Function number */
  Register.h.al = NumRow;                  /* Number of rows */
  Register.h.bh = DColr;             /* Color or blank lines) */
  Register.h.ch = ScRowOL;           /* Coordinates for */
  Register.h.cl = ColumnOL;          /* scrolling or clearing */
  Register.h.dh = ScRowUR;           /* Specify screen window */
  Register.h.dl = ColumnUR;
  int86(0x10, &Register, &Register);       /* Call interrupt 10H */
}


/****************************************************************/
/* SETPOS: Specifies a cursor position in the current screen page. */
/* Input    : COLUMN = New cursor column                       */
/*            SCROW  = New cursor row                          */
/* Output   : None                                             */
/****************************************************************/

void SetPos( BYTE Column, BYTE ScRow)
{
  union REGS Register;        /* Register variables for interrupt call */

  Register.h.ah = 2;                       /* Function number */
  Register.h.bh = 0;                       /* Screen page */
  Register.h.dh = ScRow;                   /* Screen row */
  Register.h.dl = Column;                  /* Screen column */
  int86(0x10, &Register, &Register);       /* Call interrupt 10H */
}
```

```
/****************************************************************/
/* CLS: Clears current screen page and places cursor in upper-left */
/*      corner.                                                 */
/* Input    : None                                             */
/* Output   : None                                             */
/****************************************************************/

void Cls( void )

{
  ScrollUp(0, NOF, 0, 0, 79, 24);          /* Clear screen */
  SetPos(0, 0);                            /* Place cursor */
}


/****************************************************************/
/* SCREENDESIGN    : Prepares screen for directory display.    */
/* Input    : None                                             */
/* Output   : None                                             */
/****************************************************************/

void ScreenDesign( void )
{
  BYTE i;                                  /* Loop counter */

  Cls();                                   /* Clear screen */
  Print( 14, OT, NOF,
        "┌──────────────────────────────────────┐");
  Print( 14, OT+1, NOF,
        "│ Filename │ Size │   Date   │  Time  |RHSVD│");
  Print( 14, OT+2, NOF,
        "├──────────┼──────┼──────────┼────────┼──────┤");
  for (i = OT+3; i < OT+3+FENTS; i++)
    Print( 14, i, NOF,
        "│          │      │          │        │      │");
  Print( 14, OT+FENTS+3, NOF,
        "└──────────────────────────────────────┘");

}


/****************************************************************/
/* PRINTDATA: Displays entry information.                      */
/* Input    : P2ENTRY = Pointer to a DirStruct with file information */
/*            SCROW   = Screen row of entry                    */
/* Output   : None                                             */
/****************************************************************/

void PrintData(DIRSTRUCT *P2Entry, BYTE ScRow)
{
  BYTE i, j;                               /* Loop counter */
  static char *Month[] =        /* Vector with pointers to month name */
              {
                "Jan", "Feb", "Mar", "Apr", "May", "Jun",
                "Jul", "Aug", "Sep", "Oct", "Nov", "Dec"
              };

/*-- Display miscellaneous file information ------------------------*/

Print(15, ScRow, NOF, "%s", P2Entry->NAME);

Print( 28, ScRow, NOF, "%7lu", P2Entry->SIZE);
Print( 36, ScRow, NOF, "%s %2d %4d", Month[(P2Entry->DATE >> 5 & 15) -
1],
       P2Entry->DATE & 31,
       (P2Entry->DATE >> 9) + 1980);
```

```
     Print(51, ScRow, NOF, "%02d:%02d", P2Entry->TIME >> 11,
                                  P2Entry->TIME >> 5 & 63 );

     for (i = j = 1; i <= 16; i <<= 1, ++j)    /* Display file attributes */
      Print( 58+j, ScRow, NOF, "%c", (P2Entry->ATTRIBUTE & i) ? 'X' : ' ' );
     }


/***********************************************************************/
/* DIR: Controls directory reading and output.                      */
/* Input   : SPath    = Pointer to search path with file pattern    */
/*           Attribute = Search attribute                           */
/* Output  : None                                                   */
/***********************************************************************/

void Dir( char *SPath, BYTE Attribute )
{
  int      NumOfEntries,          /* Total number of entries found */
           NumInScrn;             /* Number of entries per screen */
  DIRSTRUCT P2Entry;              /* Pointer to a directory entry */

  ScreenDesign();          /* Prepare screen for directory display */

  NumInScrn = NumOfEntries = 0;        /* No more entries to display */
                                       /* No more entries found */
  if ( !FINDFIRST(SPath, &P2Entry, Attribute) )  /* Search: 1st entry */
   {                                    /* One file found */
     do             /* Display file and use GetNext() to find next one */
      {
        PrintData(&P2Entry, OT+FENTS+2);       /* Display entries */
        if (++NumInScrn == FENTS )         /* Is the window full? */
         {
           NumInScrn = 0;                 /* Fill the window */
           Print(14, OT+4+FENTS, INV,
             "             Please press a key            ");
           getch();                      /* Wait for a key */
           Print(14, OT+4+FENTS, NOF,
             "                                           ");
         }
        ScrollUp(1, NOF, 15, OT+3, 63, OT+2+FENTS);
        Print(15, OT+2+FENTS, NOF,
          "         |      |        |       |   ");
        ++NumOfEntries;
      }
     while ( !FINDNEXT( &P2Entry ) );        /* End loop when no */
   }                                         /* more files exist */

  SetPos(14, OT+4+FENTS);
  switch (NumOfEntries)
   {
     case 0  : printf("No files found");
               break;
     case 1  : printf("One file found");
               break;
     default : printf("%d files found", NumOfEntries);
               break;
   }
}


/***********************************************************************/
/**                      MAIN PROGRAM                              **/
/***********************************************************************/

void main( int NumRow, char *Argumente[] )
{
```

```
  switch ( NumRow )                     /* React to parameters */
   {                                    /* as necessary        */
     case 1 : Dir("*.*", FA_ALL );      /* Display all files in */
              break;                     /* current directory    */
     case 2 : Dir( Argumente[1], FA_ALL ); /* Display all files in */
              break;                     /* specified directory  */
     default : printf("Invalid number of parameters\n");
   }
}
```

Chapter 21

Date and Time

The AT realtime clock provides the date and time for BIOS routines and files. Four DOS functions, which have been available since the release of Version 1.0 of DOS, can be used to access time and date.

```
┌──────────────────────────────────┐
│ DOS date and time functions      │
├──────────┬───────────────────────┤
│ Function │ Task                  │
├──────────┼───────────────────────┤
│   2AH    │ Read date             │
│   2BH    │ Set date              │
│   2CH    │ Read time             │
│   2DH    │ Set time              │
└──────────┴───────────────────────┘
```

DOS and the AT realtime clock

In DOS Versions 3.2 and lower, these four functions passed information to and from DOS environmental variables. However, in DOS Versions 3.3 and higher, these functions passed the same information to and from the battery operated realtime clock. The time and date information is still available, even if the user switches off the computer. The time and date are passed using the BIOS functions described in Chapter 11.

This is also possible in older versions of DOS. However, the system must contain a built-in clock driver because DOS will communicate only with an onboard device driver named $CLOCK.

Getting and setting the date

Functions 2AH and 2BH control the current date.

Function 2AH: Get date

Placing function number 2AH in the AH register returns the current date information in the following processor registers:

```
┌─────────────────────────────────────┐
│ Output registers: Function 2AH      │
│  ┌──────┬──────────────────────────┐│
│  │ Reg. │ Contents                 ││
│  ├──────┼──────────────────────────┤│
│  │ AL   │ Day of week*             ││
│  │ CX   │ Year                     ││
│  │ DH   │ Month                    ││
│  │ DL   │ Day                      ││
│  └──────┴──────────────────────────┘│
│  *0=Sunday, 1=Monday, etc.          │
└─────────────────────────────────────┘
```

Function 2BH: Set date

Function 2BH places date information in the same registers used by function 2AH. This is useful for changing a creation or modification date in a file.

```
┌─────────────────────────────────────┐
│ Input registers: Function 2BH       │
│  ┌──────┬──────────────────────────┐│
│  │ Reg. │ Contents                 ││
│  ├──────┼──────────────────────────┤│
│  │ AH   │ 2BH                      ││
│  │ CX   │ Year                     ││
│  │ DH   │ Month                    ││
│  │ DL   │ Day                      ││
│  └──────┴──────────────────────────┘│
└─────────────────────────────────────┘
```

The previous table shows that function 2BH requires the actual date (but not the day of the week). This is the only information DOS needs.

Remember that when working with this function, the earliest date allowed by the system is January 1, 1980 (01-01-1980). If an error occurs, check the AL register. If this register contains a value of 0, the data supplied in the other registers is valid. If the AL register contains a value of 255, the data couldn't be read.

Getting and setting the time

Functions 2CH and 2DH are similar to functions 2AH and 2BH, except that 2CH and 2DH handle time access.

Function 2CH: Get time

Function 2CH reads the current time in the form shown in the following table. Place function number 2CH of DOS interrupt 21H in the AH register to read the following registers:

```
┌─────────────────────────────────────┐
│ Output registers: Function 2CH       │
│ ┌─────┬─────────────────────────────┐│
│ │Reg. │ Contents                    ││
│ ├─────┼─────────────────────────────┤│
│ │ CH  │ Hour                        ││
│ │ CL  │ Minute                      ││
│ │ DH  │ Second                      ││
│ │ DL  │ Hundredths of a second      ││
│ └─────┴─────────────────────────────┘│
└─────────────────────────────────────┘
```

Function 2DH: Set time

Function 2DH sets the time. The AL register indicates whether the time is valid (e.g., a 36:48 setting generates a value of 255, which is an error).

```
┌─────────────────────────────────────┐
│ Input registers: Function 2DH        │
│ ┌─────┬─────────────────────────────┐│
│ │Reg. │ Contents                    ││
│ ├─────┼─────────────────────────────┤│
│ │ AH  │ 2DH                         ││
│ │ CH  │ Hour                        ││
│ │ CL  │ Minute                      ││
│ │ DH  │ Second                      ││
│ │ DL  │ Hundredths of a second      ││
│ └─────┴─────────────────────────────┘│
└─────────────────────────────────────┘
```

BIOS or DOS?

You can use either BIOS or DOS to access time and date. Both methods have their advantages, and both methods are available on any given PC system. Which functions you access depends on your preferences.

Chapter 22

RAM Management

One of the basic tasks an operating system must perform is managing the RAM (Random Access Memory). This is where all the various system components (device drivers, TSR programs, applications, etc.) come together. Since each of these components needs some of the memory, DOS must ensure that they work together. This prevents the components from overwriting each other and a single component from manipulating all the memory.

In this chapter we'll discuss the DOS memory management functions and how they work together to keep your RAM organized.

22.1 DOS RAM Management

The RAM management capabilities of DOS are based on the principle of using a DOS function to allocate a memory block of a pre-determined size. This memory block remains allocated to the program that requested it until it's freed by another DOS function. Then the block can be used by other programs.

DOS has four different functions for RAM management:

DOS functions for RAM management	
Function	Purpose
48H	Allocate memory
49H	Free memory
4AH	Change size of a memory block
58H	Read/set memory management model

The functions for allocating and freeing RAM are used by application programs, but they are also used by DOS itself in the form of EXEC loaders. When a program must be loaded and started, the EXEC loader reserves the RAM block, in which it will later load the program.

The amount of memory allocated depends on the type of program to be loaded. COM programs will reserve the entire RAM. The amount of memory required for an EXEC program is taken from the header of the EXE file. The EXEC loader can load the file only if a large enough block of RAM is available. If enough RAM cannot be found, the EXEC loader stops and displays the following error message:

```
Insufficient memory
```

Besides the EXEC loader, the application program itself can request memory from DOS. During execution, many programs will need more memory than they were given when they were initially loaded. This happens because they aren't able to determine the values of all variables or the sizes of all buffers at the time they are loaded. This information is usually determined by user input while the program is running.

Memory allocation with function 48H

If you're programming in a high level language, you don't have to worry about dynamic memory allocation. This is handled by the heap. However, assembler programmers must go to DOS when they need to allocate memory. This is done with function 48H. This function call requires the function number in the AH register and the size of the desired memory block in the BX register.

The size of the block is given in the number of paragraphs instead of the number of bytes. Since a paragraph consists of 16 bytes, allocated memory blocks will always be in multiples of 16 bytes. The smallest possible memory block that can be allocated is 16 bytes (BX = 1) and the largest is 1 Meg (BX = FFFFh).

However, requesting an entire megabyte from DOS isn't realistic because the processor doesn't even have that much RAM available in real mode. Actually, you cannot obtain 640K, 512K, or even 400K from DOS because a large portion of RAM is used by the DOS programs and the DOS device drivers. TSR programs, which remain resident in memory (i.e, they don't free the memory allocated to them when they are started) also occupy a lot of memory.

Since DOS cannot always fulfill the requests it receives with function 48H, you must check the carry flag after the function call. If this flag is set, then the requested amount of RAM wasn't available. The BX register will then contain a value that corresponds to the actual amount of remaining RAM. This value is also given in paragraphs, so you must multiply it by 16 to obtain the number of bytes.

If the program can be run with this amount of memory, then function 48H is called again with this value in the BX register. All of the RAM that's still available will then be allocated to the program.

After this function call, the program will discover that the carry flag isn't set. This means that the AX register will contain the segment address of the memory block that DOS has reserved. This block is now completely under the control of the application for which it was allocated.

The application must always remember the size of the block. Depending on the amount of memory allocated, you may or may not be able to use the entire segment at the address returned by function 48H. For example, if you asked for only one paragraph, you'll have a memory block such as AX:0000 through AX:000F. This corresponds to only the first 16 bytes of the segment. If you asked for more paragraphs, the memory block will be correspondingly larger. It will always start at the segment address returned by the function and at offset address 0000H.

812

What happens if you request 4096 paragraphs? This corresponds to 64K, which would be the entire memory segment from AX:0000 through AX:FFFF. If you ask for more than 4096 paragraphs, the memory block will extend into the next segment.

In all cases, the application that now owns the memory block can address only the portion of the segment that belongs to it. Anything outside of this block may belong to another program or be allocated to another in the future. If two applications try to use the same part of the RAM, the system will usually crash.

Determining the amount of available RAM

Because of the way it works, function 48H can also be used to check the current amount of free RAM. This is the only DOS function that performs this task.

To force DOS to return the amount of free memory, we'll make a request that it can't possibly fulfill. We'll pass the value 0FFFFH in the BX register, thereby requesting a 1 megabyte memory block. Although it's impossible for DOS to allocate a block of this size, the function result in the BX register indicates the number of free paragraphs. From this value, we can easily calculate the number of free bytes remaining.

Releasing memory with function 49H

Once an allocated memory block is no longer needed, it must be released with function 49H. Before a program ends, all of the memory allocated with function 48H must be released. Otherwise, the operating system will think that this memory is allocated to an application and other programs won't be able to use it. This can significantly reduce the amount of available memory and you may not be able to load the other programs you want to run. Only rebooting the computer can free this memory.

This function call requires the function number in the AH register and the segment address of the memory block to be freed in the ES register. This corresponds to the value that was returned to the AX register when the block was allocated with function 48H.

If the memory block was successfully released, function 49H returns with a cleared carry flag. DOS again has control of the memory block, which can be allocated to another application. If the function returns with the carry flag set, then the memory block couldn't be released because of an error. Various errors can cause this condition. The error code that describes what occurred is returned to the AX register.

An error code of 9 indicates that an incorrect segment address was given. This means that at the given address, a memory block allocated by this program wasn't found. It's possible that the program did own a memory block at this address, but that it has already been freed with a previous call to function 49H. In this instance, you should determine whether you've inadvertently tried to free the same block twice.

Error code 7 indicates that a problem occurred within DOS's internal memory manager. The cause of this problem is usually a program that has tried to operate outside of its reserved memory blocks. If you encounter this error code, you should end your program and recommend a soft reboot to the user.

Changing the size of memory blocks

The third memory management function is 4AH. This function changes the size of a previously allocated memory block. You can choose to make the block larger or smaller. However, you may not be able to increase the size of the block if there isn't enough memory.

To call function 4AH, pass the function number to the AH register and the segment address, of the memory block to change, to the ES register. The new size of the memory block is passed to the BX register. This value must be given in paragraphs. The contents of the registers after the function call will be the same as with function.48H. If the function fails due to lack of memory, it returns the maximum block size in the BX register. This is only important when increasing the size of a block. You should always be able to make a block smaller.

22.2 Where Does Memory Come From?

In DOS versions up to 5.0, the memory that DOS allocates via function 48H always originates from the Transient Program Area (TPA). This refers to a region of memory that extends from the end of the resident DOS kernel at the beginning of the RAM all the way to the 640K limit. If a system has less than 640K, the TPA ends there. However, these systems are very rare today.

The RAM usually ends at the 640K limit. Beyond this limit is the memory reserved for video RAM, the ROM-BIOS and ROM expansions. The page frame of an EMS card is also stored in this memory region. Systems equipped with 1 Meg or more are usually configured with 640K of RAM below the 640K limit and the rest of the memory starts at the 1 Meg limit.

More memory with Upper Memory Blocks (UMBs)

Memory above the 1 Meg limit and memory between 640K and 1 Meg, cannot be directly addressed by DOS in real mode unless you're using DOS Version 5.0. This DOS version supports the use of *Upper Memory Blocks* (UMBs). UMBs can be located anywhere above the 640K limit. The region from 640K to 1 Meg usually isn't completely occupied by the video RAM, the ROM-BIOS, or other expansions. So, DOS 5.0 can use and allocate the unused regions as normal blocks of RAM.

Memory in the region between 640K and 1 Meg is extremely valuable to DOS programs, because it can be addressed in real mode. With DOS 5.0, a program cannot tell the difference between memory above and below 640K. As long as the memory doesn't extend beyond the 1 Meg limit, it's considered the same. Add UMB memory to your system with:

- The proper software configuration, such as a NEAT chip set, which creates RAM in the UMB region out of extended memory.

- A special UMB card that's equipped with its own RAM, which is then added to the UMB region of the system's addressable memory.

- Memory management programs that move extended memory to the UBM region, such as EMM386.EXE, 386Max, or QUEMM.

The last option is becoming more popular since DOS 5.0 was introduced because this version includes the device driver for EMM386.EXE.

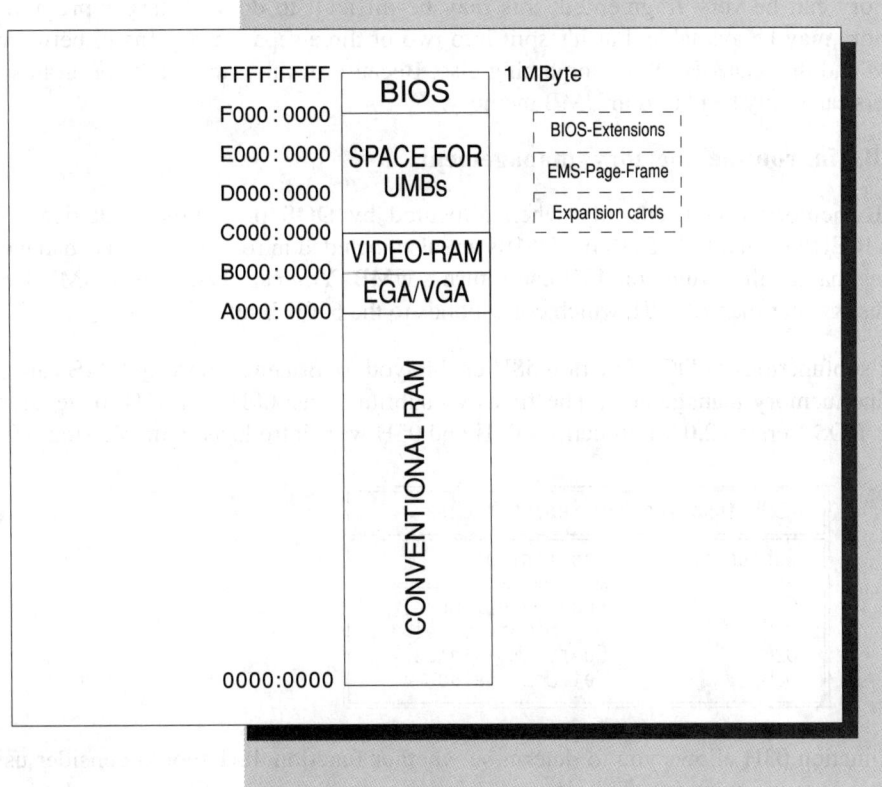

Upper memory blocks in the addressable memory of the PC

The amount of memory available for UMBs depends on how much memory is occupied by video RAM, expansion cards, and the ROM-BIOS. Many systems will have up to 260K available, while others may have less than 64K. Unlike RAM below 640K, this memory is often fragmented. So UMBs must make room wherever they can in the "holes" between 640K and 1 Meg.

Before DOS programs can use UMBs, either the command:

```
DOS=HIGH,UMB        or:        DOS=LOW,UMB
```

must be executed in the CONFIG.SYS file. After finding one of these commands, DOS looks for an XMS driver. DOS doesn't actually prepare the memory where the UMBs will be located. Instead, a device driver, such as EMM386.EXE (see above), performs this task. This is useful because different UMB cards have different ways of setting up the UMB memory. So, DOS can leave the setup to the driver that relates to the specific hardware.

These drivers must adhere to the XMS standard. This standard defines how DOS allocates UMBs. So, DOS has control over all RAM allocation from the time the system is started.

Special DOS commands, such as DEVICEHIGH and LOADHIGH, are used to load device drivers or DOS programs into a UMB, as long as an appropriate one can be found. Since the UMB memory can be very fragmented, this may be difficult to do with larger programs. Enough memory may be available, but it's split into two or three separate regions in between the video RAM and the ROM-BIOS or something else. Because of this, small TSR programs and device drivers can easily be placed in UMB memory.

UMBs in routine memory management

UMB memory isn't used only when allocated by DOS programs or device drivers with DEVICEHIGH and LOADHIGH. UMBs are also included in routine memory management. This means that a call to function 48H can return a UMB. You can recognize a UMB by a segment address greater than A000H, which corresponds to the 640K limit.

Four subfunctions of DOS function 58H enable you to influence the way UMBs are included in routine memory management. The first two subfunctions, 00H and 01H, have been available since DOS Version 2.0. Subfunctions 02H and 03H were introduced with Version 5.0.

DOS function 58H Subfunctions	
Subfunction	Description
00H	Read memory model
01H	Set memory model
02H	Query UMB status
03H	Set UMB status

Subfunction 03H allows you to determine whether function 48H should consider using UMBs when allocating memory. This is useful for programs that must allocate a lot of additional memory after they're called.

Subfunction 03 is called with the function number 5803H in the AX register and either 0 or 1 in the BX register. A value of 1 indicates that UMBs will be included in memory allocation; 0 indicates that all memory will be allocated below the 640K limit.

Before making this function call, you should check the status of the UMB memory so that you can restore it to its original condition after your program ends. Subfunction 02 will do this for you. This subfunction call only needs the function number 5802H in the AX register. After this function call, the AL register will contain a value of either 0 or 1. These values have the same meaning they have with subfunction 03H.

Remember that these two subfunctions are only supported under DOS Versions 5.0 and higher, and that the DOS UMB command must be run in the CONFIG.SYS file in order for them to work properly.

After calling either of these subfunctions, you should check the contents of the carry flag. If the carry flag is set, then one of the two conditions previously described hasn't been met and UMBs cannot be supported.

If you want to use UMBs in your program, you should try to work with small memory blocks. You probably won't find a contiguous memory block of several hundred K in the UMB region.

Instead, there will be numerous small blocks. So, you should request five 10K blocks instead of one 50K block, as long as your program algorithm will allow it.

Memory allocation models

Beginning with Version 2.0, DOS has allowed the use of various memory allocation models. The desired model is selected with subfunction 01H of function 58H. A memory allocation model refers to the way in which DOS searches for a free memory block. Three codes represent the three possibilities:

Code	Model
00H	Search low to high
01H	Search for the best fit
02H	Search high to low

Codes 00H and 02H are self-explanatory. These codes allow you to tell DOS to start the search for a memory block of the desired size starting either at the beginning or the end of the RAM. If the first free memory block that's found is at least the requested size, it's allocated.

"Search for the best fit" means that DOS will check the entire RAM for a free memory block that's either exactly the size requested or just a little larger. The idea behind this option is that the RAM may be fragmented (e.g., if a TSR program frees some memory before it becomes resident). This leaves holes, or "fragments" in the RAM. These fragments are usually very small.

If a program needs a small memory block, you can use this option to search for a memory fragment instead of simply using a small part of the first free memory block DOS finds.

Subfunction 01 is used to set the memory allocation model. One of three codes previously listed must be passed in the BL register. In addition to the codes, bit 7 of the BL register is also important in DOS Versions 5.0 and up. This bit can be set or cleared regardless of the code that's used. The status of this bit determines whether the search for the next memory block should begin with the UMBs or in the TPA. To begin with the UMBs, this bit must be set to 1. This is only useful when you've already included UMBs with the proper call to subfunction 03H.

You can query the memory allocation model with subfunction 00H. The result of this function is returned to the AL register. With DOS 5.0 and up, remember to check the value of bit 7.

22.3 Viewing Memory Allocation

In this section, we'll discuss a program that enables you to display a graphic representation of RAM allocation on screen. The Pascal and C versions of this program are called MEMDEMOP.PAS and MEMDEMOC.C. Both perform the same task and are almost identical internally.

Both of these programs allow you to allocate, free, and change the size of memory blocks using DOS functions 48H, 49H, and 4AH. The location and size of the memory blocks are displayed on screen. Since the screen is too small for the entire TPA and all UMBs, the program is limited to monitoring two specific regions: a 160K region of the TPA and a 40K region from the UMBs.

The program limits itself to these regions by first allocating them as two consecutive blocks at the start of the program. Then the rest of the memory is allocated in 1K blocks so that no free 1K blocks remain. We'll explain why 1K is used as the block size shortly.

In the next step, the two large memory blocks are freed again. This means that these two regions now contain the only memory that isn't allocated. So, all memory will now be allocated from these regions, as long as 1K or more is requested. The program ensures that all requests for memory are in multiples of 1K.

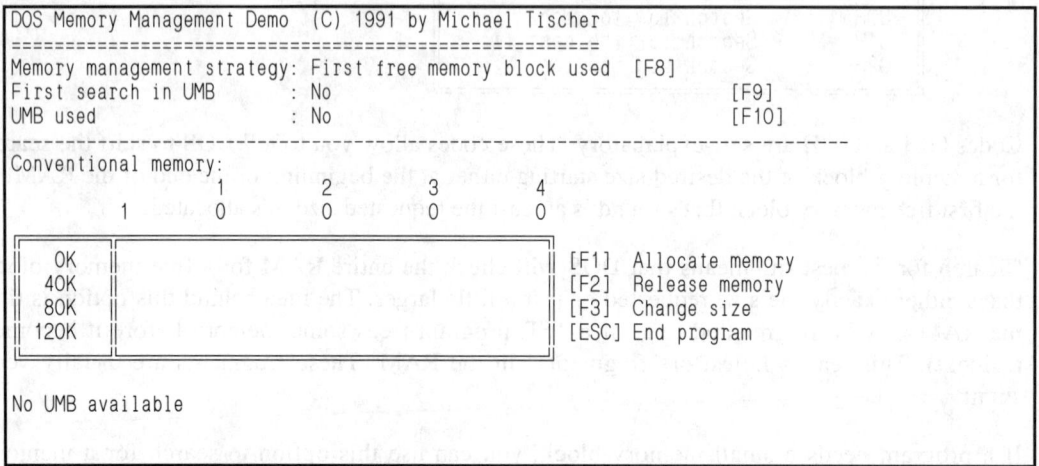

Allocating and freeing memory with the programs MEMDEMOP.PAS and MEMDEMOC.C

The F1 and F3 function keys can be used to allocate and free memory, as shown in the previous figure. When you press one of these keys, the program will then ask you with which block you want to work. Blocks are labeled within the program as A through Z (with no distinction between upper and lowercase). So, you can choose from a total of 26 blocks.

Enter the desired letter and press <Return>. Remember that the program will accept only those letters that haven't already been used when allocating a memory block. Only the letter of a memory block currently in use will be accepted if you want to free a memory block or change its size.

When you allocate a memory block or change the size of an existing memory block, you'll also be asked to enter the desired size in K. Enter a number and then press <Return>.

After one of these operations, the program will redraw the screen to reflect the changes that you've made. The memory occupied by an allocated block is identified with the letter that was assigned to the block. Memory that hasn't been allocated appears empty. Each character represents 1K from the TPA or UMB region. This explains the values used for the scale.

The UMB window will appear on screen only if a 40K UMB was allocated at the start of the program. If this window isn't present, either UMBs aren't supported on the system or a 40K block wasn't available.

Memory allocation is interesting to watch when you experiment with the F1, F2, and F3 function keys. These keys control the way in which memory will be allocated and whether or not UMBs will be included. They act as toggle switches to switch the various modes on and off.

After switching the modes around, you can see how the next allocated memory block is placed either at the beginning or the end of the available memory in the TPA or UMB region.

To end the program, press the <Escape> key. This also frees all memory allocated by the program.

Listing: **MEMDEMOP.PAS**

```pascal
{************************************************************}
{*                M E M D E M O P . P A S                  *}
{*--------------------------------------------------------*}
{*  Task       : Demonstrates DOS memory management.      *}
{*--------------------------------------------------------*}
{*  Author     : Michael Tischer                          *}
{*  Developed on : 10/08/91                               *}
{*  Last update  : 01/29/92                               *}
{************************************************************}
{$M 8096, 0, 10240 }

program MEMDEMOP;

uses crt,                        { Add CRT and DOS units }
     dos;

{== Constants ============================================}

const {-- Function numbers for interrupt 21H ------------}

      GET_MEM       = $48;                     { Reserve RAM }
      FREE_MEM      = $49;                     { Release RAM }
      CHANGE_MEM    = $4A;        { Change size of a memory range }
      GET_STRATEGY  = $5800;     { Get memory division strategy }
      SET_STRATEGY  = $5801;     { Set memory division strategy }
      GET_UMB       = $5802;                     { Get UMB }
      SET_UMB       = $5803;                     { Set UMB }

      {-- Search strategies for SET_STRATEGY ------------}

      SRCHS_BELOW = $00;        { Use the first free memory block }
      SRCHS_BEST  = $01;         { Use the best free memory block }
      SRCHS_ABOVE = $02;         { Use the last free memory block }
      SFIRST_UMB  = $80;            { Search for first in UMB }
                                    { (combined with SEARCH_...) }

      {-- Constants for SetUMB --------------------------}

      UMB_OUT = $00;                           { Ignore UMB }
      UMB_INC = $01;          { Include UMB in memory allocation }

      {-- Constants for Demo ----------------------------}

      TEST_EN     = 10240-1;  { 10239 paragraph test environment }
      TEST_EN_UMB    = 2560-1;  { 2559 paragraph UMB test environment }
      TEST_EN_KB     = 160;           { Test environment is 160K }
      TEST_EN_UMB_KB = 40;        { Test environment UMB is 40K }
      BLOCKAMT       = 26;   { Number of addresses for result display }

      {-- Key codes for control -------------------------------}

      ESC = #27;                       { Press <Esc> to cancel }
      F1  = #59;                            { Function key F1 }
      F2  = #60;                            { Function key F2 }
      F3  = #61;                            { Function key F3 }
      F8  = #66;                            { Function key F8 }
      F9  = #67;                            { Function key F9 }
      F10 = #68;                            { Function key F10 }

{== Type declarations ====================================}

type  BlockType = record       { Manage an allocated memory block }
                    SegAddr,                   { Segment address }
                    MBlSize : word;        { Memory block size in K }
                  end;

{== Typed constants ======================================}

const YesNo     : array[ false..true ] of string =
                    ( 'No ', 'Yes' );
      SText     : array[ SRCHS_BELOW..SRCHS_ABOVE ] of string =
                    ( 'First free memory block used',
                      'Best free memory block used ',
                      'Last free memory block used ' );
      ColArray  : array[ 0..1 ] of byte = ( $07, $70 );
      Keybd_Text : array[ 0..3 ] of string =
                    ( ' [F1]  Allocate memory',
                      ' [F2]  Release memory',
                      ' [F3]  Change size',
                      ' [ESC] End program' );

{== Global variables =====================================}

var Regs      : Registers;       { Registers for interrupt call }
    MAddrArray : array[ 0..1000 ] of word;    { Array for memory }
    Num_Addrs : word;              { Number of addresses }
    ConvSeg   : word;    { Address of test block in conventional RAM }
    UMBSeg    : word;            { Address of test block in UMB }
    BlocArray : array[ 0..BLOCKAMT - 1 ] of BlockType;  { Memory }

{************************************************************}
```

```
{ DOS_GetMem : Reserves memory.                                    }
{ Input      : Desired memory size in paragraphs                   }
{ Output     : Segment address of the allocated memory block,      }
{              number of paragraphs allocated or                   }
{              maximum number of available paragraphs              }
{*****************************************************************}

procedure DOS_GetMem(    Ps  : word;
                     var Adr : word;
                     var Res : word );

begin
  with Regs do
    begin
      ah := GET_MEM;                          { Function number }
      bx := Ps;                  { Number of paragraphs to be reserved }
      msdos( Regs );                          { Interrupt call }
      if ( flags and fcarry = 0 ) then        { Call successful? }
        begin
          Adr := regs.ax;       { Yes --> Return address and size }
          Res := Ps;
        end
      else                                    { No --> Error }
        begin
          Adr := 0;                           { No memory reserved }
          Res := bx;                          { Maximum available size }
        end;
    end;
end;


{*****************************************************************}
{ DOS_FreeMem: Releases reserved memory.                           }
{ Input       : Memory segment address                            }
{ Output      : None                                              }
{*****************************************************************}


procedure DOS_FreeMem( Adr : word );

begin
  with Regs do
    begin
      ah := FREE_MEM;                         { Function number }
      es := Adr;                 { Address of memory to be released }
      msdos( Regs );                          { Interrupt call }
    end;
end;


{*****************************************************************}
{ DOS_ChangeMem : Changes reserved memory size.                    }
{ Input         : Old segment address,                            }
{                 new (desired) segment address in paragraphs     }
{ Output        : Segment address of the allocated memory block,  }
{                 number of paragraphs allocated or               }
{                 maximum number of available paragraphs          }
{*****************************************************************}


procedure DOS_ChangeMem(    Ps  : word;
                        var Adr : word;
                        var Res : word );
begin
  with Regs do
    begin
      ah := CHANGE_MEM;                       { Function number }
      bx := Ps;                  { Number of paragraphs to be reserved }
```

```
      es := Adr;      { Segment address of memory block to be changed }
      msdos( Regs );                          { Interrupt call }
      if ( flags and fcarry = 0 ) then        { Call successful? }
        Res := Ps                             { Yes --> New memory size }
      else                                    { No --> Error }
        Res := bx;              { Maximum available memory size }
      end;
end;


{*****************************************************************}
{ Read_Strategy : Reads the DOS memory management strategy.        }
{ Input         : None                                            }
{ Output        : Memory management strategy                       }
{*****************************************************************}

function Read_Strategy : integer;

begin
  with Regs do
    begin
      ax := GET_STRATEGY;                     { Set function number }
      msdos( Regs );                          { Interrupt call }
      Read_Strategy := ax;                    { Display strategy }
    end;
end;


{*****************************************************************}
{ ReadUMB     : Reads UMB status.                                 }
{ Input       : None                                             }
{ Output      : UMB ignored during memory management             }
{ Info        : First available in DOS Version 5.0.              }
{*****************************************************************}

function ReadUMB : integer;

begin
  with Regs do
    begin
      ax := GET_UMB;                          { Set function number }
      msdos( Regs );                          { Interrupt call }
      ReadUMB := al;                          { Display status }
    end;
end;


{*****************************************************************}
{ SetDosStrategy: Sets DOS memory management strategy.             }
{ Input        : New strategy                                     }
{ Output       : None                                            }
{*****************************************************************}

procedure SetDosStrategy( Strategy : integer );

begin
  with Regs do
    begin
      ax := SET_STRATEGY;                     { Set function number }
      bx := Strategy;
      msdos( Regs );                          { Interrupt call }
    end;
end;


{*****************************************************************}
{ SetUMB      : Sets the UMB status.                              }
{ Input       : New UMB status                                   }
```

```
{ Output       : None                                    }
{ Info         : First available in DOS Version 5.0.     }
{***********************************************************}

procedure SetUMB( UMB : integer );

begin
  with Regs do
    begin
      ax := SET_UMB;                    { Set function number }
      bx := UMB;
      msdos( Regs );                    { Interrupt call }
    end;
end;


{***********************************************************}
{ Allocate_Memory: Creates a test environment for the memory test. }
{ Input        : None                                     }
{ Output       : None                                     }
{***********************************************************}

procedure Allocate_Memory;

var SegAdr    : word;         { Segment address of allocated memory }
    Des_Mem   : word;         { Desired memory size }
    MB1Size   : word;         { Size of allocated memory range }

begin
  {-- 1. Allocate test block -----------------------------}

  SetUMB( UMB_OUT );             { Test block in conventional memory }
  DOS_GetMem( TEST_EN, ConvSeg, MB1Size );      { Get test block }
  if ( ConvSeg = 0 ) then                       { Error? }
    exit;                      { No test block found, end procedure }

  SetUMB( UMB_INC );                      { Test block in UMB }
  SetDosStrategy( SRCHS_ABOVE or SFIRST_UMB );
  DOS_GetMem( TEST_EN_UMB, UMBSeg, MB1Size );
  if ( UMBSeg <> 0 ) and ( UMBSeg < $A000 ) then { No UMB available? }
    begin
      DOS_FreeMem( UMBSeg );              { Release memory }
      UMBSeg := 0;                        { No UMBs }
    end;

  {-- 2. Allocate remaining conventional/ UMB memory in 1K blocks ----}

  Des_Mem := 63;                  { First try allocating 15 paragraphs }
  Num_Addrs := 0;            { Set number of allocated 1K blocks to 0 }
  repeat
    DOS_GetMem( Des_Mem, SegAdr, MB1Size );      { Call for memory }
    if ( SegAdr <> 0 ) then                { Memory received? }
      begin
        MAddrArray[ Num_Addrs ] := SegAdr;        { Note address }
        inc( Num_Addrs );
      end;
  until ( SegAdr = 0 );            { Allocate all memory }

  {-- 3. Release test block -------------------------------}

  if ( ConvSeg > 0 ) then          { Could memory be allocated? }
    begin                                         { Yes }
      DOS_FreeMem( ConvSeg );
      dec( ConvSeg );                     { MCB is also free }
    end;
```

```
  if ( UMBSeg > 0 ) then               { Could UMB be allocated? }
    begin                                         { Yes }
      DOS_FreeMem( UMBSeg );
      dec( UMBSeg );                     { MCB is also free }
    end;
end;


{***********************************************************}
{ ReleaseThisMemory: Releases reserved memory.            }
{ Input        : None                                     }
{ Output       : None                                     }
{ Global variables: MAddrArray/R                          }
{***********************************************************}

procedure ReleaseThisMemory;

var i : word;                                 { Loop counter }

begin
  if ( Num_Addrs > 0 ) then           { Was memory allocated? }
    for i := 0 to Num_Addrs - 1 do  { Yes --> Release block by block }
      DOS_FreeMem( MAddrArray[ i ] );
end;


{***********************************************************}
{ DisplayMemLayout : Displays memory layout.              }
{ Input        : W_Borders = TRUE if the border should also }
{                            be displayed                 }
{ Output       : None                                     }
{***********************************************************}

procedure DisplayMemLayout( W_Borders : boolean );

var SArray     : array[ 0..TEST_EN_KB - 1 ] of char;
    SArray_UMB : array[ 0..TEST_EN_UMB_KB - 1 ] of char;
    i, j       : word;                        { Loop counter }
    Position   : word;                        { Help variable }
    Sdummy     : string;
    LastChar_M : char;       { Memory for last character displayed }
    CurColor   : byte;                 { Current output color }

begin
  fillchar( SArray[ 0 ], TEST_EN_KB, #32 );{ Initialize display array }
  fillchar( SArray_UMB[ 0 ], TEST_EN_UMB_KB, #32 );

  {-- Fill memory table ----------------------------------}

  for i := 0 to BLOCKAMT - 1 do
    begin
      if ( BlocArray[ i ].SegAddr > $A000 ) then       { UMB? }
        begin
          Position := ( BlocArray[ i ].SegAddr - UMBSeg ) div 64;
          for j := 0 to BlocArray[ i ].MB1Size div 64 do
            SArray_UMB[ Position + j ] := chr( i + 65 );
        end
      else if ( BlocArray[ i ].SegAddr > 0 ) then
        begin
          Position := ( BlocArray[ i ].SegAddr - ConvSeg ) div 64;
          for j := 0 to BlocArray[ i ].MB1Size div 64 do
            SArray[ Position + j ] := chr( i + 65 );
        end;
    end;

  {-- Draw border around memory table --------------------}
```

```
    if ( W_Borders ) then
      begin
        writeln( 'Conventional memory:' );
        writeln( '              1        2        3        4 ' );
        writeln( '              1        0        0        0 ' );
        writeln( '┌──────────────────────────────────────────┐' );
        for i := 0 to 3 do
          begin
            str( i * 40 : 3, Sdummy );
            writeln( '║ ' + Sdummy +
                        'K    ║                              ║',
                      Keybd_Text[ i ] );
          end;
        writeln( '└──────────┴───────────────────────────────┘' );
        if ( UMBSeg > 0 ) then
          begin
            writeln(#13#10'UMB:' );
            writeln('              1        2        3        4 ');
            writeln('              1        0        0        0 ');
            writeln('┌──────────────────────────────────────────┐');
            writeln('║    OK    ║                              ║');
            writeln('└──────────┴───────────────────────────────┘');
          end
        else
          writeln( #13#10, 'No UMB available' );
      end;

{-- Display table for conventional memory ------------------------}

    LastChar_M := #0;                     { Last character displayed }
    CurColor := 0;                        { Last display color }
    for i := 0 to 3 do
      for j := 0 to 39 do
        begin
          if ( LastChar_M <> SArray[ i * 40 + j ] ) then{ Color change? }
            begin
              CurColor := ( CurColor + 1 ) mod 2;  { New color number }
              textcolor( ColArray[ CurColor ] shr 4 );
              textbackground( ColArray[ CurColor ] and $0F );
              LastChar_M := SArray[ i * 40 + j ];  { Chars. to compare }
            end;
          gotoxy( j + 11, i + 11 );          { Display character }
          write( SArray[ i * 40 + j ] );
        end;

{-- Display table for UMB -----------------------------------}

    if ( UMBSeg > 0 ) then
      begin
        for j := 0 to 39 do
          begin
            if ( LastChar_M <> SArray_UMB[ j ] ) then   { Color change? }
              begin
                CurColor := ( CurColor + 1 ) mod 2;  { New color number }
                textcolor( ColArray[ CurColor ] shr 4 );
                textbackground( ColArray[ CurColor ] and $0F );
                LastChar_M := SArray_UMB[ j ];   { Chars. to compare }
              end;
            gotoxy( j + 11, 21 );
            write( SArray_UMB[ j ] );
          end;
      end;
    textcolor( $07 );
```

```
        textbackground( $00 );
    end;

{*******************************************************************}
{ Demo       : Demonstrates memory management.                      }
{ Input      : Included UMB, first UMB to search,                   }
{              memory division strategy                             }
{ Output     : None                                                 }
{ Info       : First available in DOS Version 5.0.                  }
{*******************************************************************}

procedure Demo( Inc_UMB   : boolean;
                UMB_first  : boolean;
                Strategy   : integer );


var i      : integer;                    { Loop counter }
    IKeys  : char;                       { Input keys }
    ResPtr : char;        { Pointer to the desired reservation (A-Z) }
    Des_Mem : word;                      { Size of reservation }
    MB1Size : word;
    sdummy  : string;

begin
  {-- Initialize address array ------------------------------}

  for i := 0 to BLOCKAMT - 1 do          { No more allocated blocks }
    with BlocArray[ i ] do
      begin
        SegAddr := 0;            { Segment address of memory block }
        MB1Size := 0;                    { Size of memory block }
      end;

  gotoxy( 1, 7 );
  DisplayMemLayout( TRUE );              { Display memory table }

  {-- Demonstration loop ------------------------------------}

  repeat
    {-- Specify selected memory management strategy ------------------}

    if ( Inc_UMB ) then                            { UMB used? }
      SetUMB( UMB_INC )
    else
      SetUMB( UMB_OUT );

    if ( UMB_first ) then
      SetDosStrategy( Strategy or SFIRST_UMB )
    else
      SetDosStrategy( Strategy );

    {-- Display current concept ------------------------------}

    gotoxy( 1, 3 );
    writeln( 'Memory management strategy: ', SText[ Strategy ],
             ' [F8] ' );
    writeln( 'First search in UMB      : ', YesNo[ UMB_first ],
             '                      [F9]' );
    writeln( 'UMB used                 : ', YesNo[ Inc_UMB ],
             '                      [F10]' );
    writeln( '--------------------------------------------------',
             '----------------------------' );

    {-- Entry and processing ----------------------------------}
```

```
repeat until keypressed;                       { Wait for a key }          i := -1;                    { No more valid blocks given }
IKeys := readkey;                              { Read key }               repeat
if ( ( IKeys = #0 ) and ( keypressed ) ) then  { Function key }             gotoxy( 1, 23 );
  IKeys := readkey;                            { Get 2nd key code }         write( 'Which block do you want changed [ A-Z ]: ' );
                                                                           readln( ResPtr );
case IKeys of                                                              ResPtr := upcase( ResPtr );
  F1 :                                   { Allocate memory block }          if ( ResPtr >= 'A' ) and ( ResPtr <= 'Z' ) then
    begin                                                                     if ( BlocArray[ ord( ResPtr ) - 65 ].SegAddr <> 0 ) then
      i := -1;           { No more valid memory blocks given }                   i := ord( ResPtr ) - 65;
      repeat                                                               until ( i <> - 1 );
        gotoxy( 1, 23 );                                                   write( 'How many K do you want reserved: ' );
        write( 'Reserve which block [ A-Z ]: ' );                          readln( Des_Mem );
        readln( ResPtr );                                                  Des_Mem := Des_Mem * 64 - 1;     { Convert to paragraphs }
        ResPtr := upcase( ResPtr );                                        DOS_ChangeMem( Des_Mem, BlocArray[ i ].SegAddr, MB1Size );
        if ( ResPtr >= 'A' ) and ( ResPtr <= 'Z' ) then                    if ( MB1Size <> Des_Mem ) then              { Error? }
          if ( BlocArray[ ord( ResPtr ) - 65 ].SegAddr = 0 ) then            begin
            i := ord( ResPtr ) - 65;                                            str( ( MB1Size + 1 ) div 64, sdummy );
      until ( i <> - 1 );                                                       write( 'Only ' + sdummy + 'K free' );
      write( 'How many K do you want reserved: ' );                            repeat until keypressed;
      readln( Des_Mem );                                                       while keypressed do
      Des_Mem := Des_Mem * 64 - 1;       { Convert to paragraphs }               IKeys := readkey;
      DOS_GetMem( Des_Mem, BlocArray[ i ].SegAddr,                              IKeys := #0;
              BlocArray[ i ].MB1Size );                                       end
      if ( BlocArray[ i ].MB1Size <> Des_Mem ) then   { Error? }            else
        begin                                                                 BlocArray[ i ].MB1Size := MB1Size;      { Set new size }
          str( ( BlocArray[ i ].MB1Size + 1 ) div 64, sdummy );            gotoxy( 1, 23 );
          write( 'Only ' + sdummy + 'K free' );                            writeln( '                                        ' );
          repeat until keypressed;                                         writeln( '                                        ' );
          while keypressed do                                              write( '                                        ' );
            IKeys := readkey;                                              gotoxy( 1, 7 );
          IKeys := #0;                                                     DisplayMemLayout( FALSE );       { Display memory table }
        end;                                                             end;
      gotoxy( 1, 23 );
      writeln( '                                        ' );          F8 :
      writeln( '                                        ' );            Strategy := ( Strategy + 1 ) mod 3;       { Change strategy }
      write( '                                        ' );
      gotoxy( 1, 7 );                                                   F9 :                               { Toggle: UMB first }
      DisplayMemLayout( FALSE );          { Display memory table }       UMB_first := not UMB_first;
    end;
                                                                       F10:                                { Toggle: Add UMB }
  F2 :                                   { Release memory block }         Inc_UMB := not Inc_UMB;
    begin
      i := -1;                   { No more valid blocks given }        end;
      repeat                                                          until ( IKeys = ESC );
        gotoxy( 1, 23 );                                            end;
        write( 'Release which block [ A-Z ]: ' );
        readln( ResPtr );                                          {***************************************************************}
        ResPtr := upcase( ResPtr );                                {                 M A I N   P R O G R A M                     }
        if ( ResPtr >= 'A' ) and ( ResPtr <= 'Z' ) then            {***************************************************************}
          if ( BlocArray[ ord( ResPtr ) - 65 ].SegAddr <> 0 ) then
            i := ord( ResPtr ) - 65;                               var StartStrategy    : integer;   { Memory division on startup }
      until ( i <> - 1 );                                              StartUMB        : integer;       { UMB layout on startup }
      DOS_FreeMem( BlocArray[ i ].SegAddr );                          Cur_UMB_inc     : boolean;          { UMB used (yes/no) }
      BlocArray[ i ].SegAddr := 0;                                    Cur_UMB_first   : boolean;       { Search first in UMB }
      BlocArray[ i ].MB1Size := 0;                                    Cur_Strategy    : integer;    { Current search strategy }
      gotoxy( 1, 23 );
      writeln( '                                        ' );       begin
      gotoxy( 1, 7 );                                                clrscr;
      DisplayMemLayout( FALSE );          { Display memory table }    writeln( 'DOS Memory Management Demo ',
    end;                                                                   ' (C) 1991 by Michael Tischer' );
                                                                     writeln( '=========================',
  F3 :                                   { Change one block's size }       '========================='#13#10 );
    begin                                                            writeln( '                    Processing memory layout now....' );

                                                                   {-- Store DOS values when program starts ----------------------}
```

```
StartStrategy := Read_Strategy;          { Memory layout strategy }
StartUMB := ReadUMB;                           { UMB inclusion }
Allocate_Memory;                         { Create test environment }
SetDosStrategy( StartStrategy );           { Restore old strategy }
SetUMB( StartUMB );

if ( ConvSeg = 0 ) then          { Allocate conventional memory? }
  begin                    { No --> End program with error message }
    clrscr;
    writeln('MEMDEMOP: Not enough memory!');
    exit;                                        { End program }
  end;

{-- Starting values for memory management --------------------------}

Cur_UMB_inc := ( StartUMB = UMB_INC );
Cur_UMB_first := ( ( StartStrategy and SFIRST_UMB ) = SFIRST_UMB );
Cur_Strategy := StartStrategy and ( $FF xor SFIRST_UMB );

{-- Demonstration of memory division ------------------------------}

clrscr;
writeln( 'DOS Memory Management Demo ',
         ' (C) 1991 by Michael Tischer' );
writeln( '===========================',
         '===========================' );
Demo( Cur_UMB_inc, Cur_UMB_first, Cur_Strategy );

{-- Restore old DOS values ----------------------------------------}

ReleaseThisMemory;                      { Release reserved memory }
SetDosStrategy( StartStrategy );
SetUMB( StartUMB );
clrscr;
end.
```

Listing: MEMDEMOC.C

```c
/***********************************************************************/
/*                      M E M D E M O C . C                          */
/*-------------------------------------------------------------------*/
/*    Task        : Demonstrates DOS memory management.              */
/*-------------------------------------------------------------------*/
/*    Memory model : SMALL                                           */
/*-------------------------------------------------------------------*/
/*    Author      : Michael Tischer                                  */
/*    Developed on : 10/08/91                                        */
/*    Last update  : 01/30/92                                        */
/***********************************************************************/

/*== Add include files ===============================================*/

#include <dos.h>
#include <conio.h>
#include <stdio.h>
#include <stdarg.h>
#include <string.h>
#include <ctype.h>
#include <stdlib.h>

/*== Constants =======================================================*/

#define TRUE   ( 0 == 0 )
#define FALSE  ( 0 == 1 )

/*-- Function numbers for interrupt 0x21 ----------------------------*/

#define GET_MEM       0x48                         /* Reserve RAM */
#define FREE_MEM      0x49                         /* Release RAM */
#define CHANGE_MEM    0x4A          /* Change size of a memory range */
#define GET_STRATEGY 0x5800          /* Get memory division strategy */
#define SET_STRATEGY 0x5801          /* Set memory division strategy */
#define GET_UMB       0x5802                         /* Get UMB */
#define SET_UMB       0x5803                         /* Set UMB */

/*-- Search strategies for SET_STRATEGY -----------------------------*/

#define SRCHS_BELOW  0x00          /* Use the first free memory block */
#define SRCHS_BEST   0x01              /* Use the best memory block */
#define SRCHS_ABOVE  0x02          /* Use the last free memory block */
#define SFIRST_UMB   0x80              /* Search for first in UMB    */
                                       /* (combined with SEARCH_...) */

/*-- Constants for SetUMB -------------------------------------------*/

#define UMB_OUT       0x00                         /* Ignore UMB */
#define UMB_INC       0x01          /* Include UMB in memory allocation */

/*-- Constants for Demo ---------------------------------------------*/

#define TEST_EN      (10240-1) /* 10239 paragraph test environment */
#define TEST_EN_UMB  (2560-1)/* 2559 paragraph UMB test environment */
#define TEST_EN_K     160                /* Test environment is 160K */
#define TEST_EN_UMB_K 40                 /* Test environment is 40K */
#define BLOCKAMT      26  /* Number of addresses for result display */

/*-- Key codes for control ------------------------------------------*/

#define ESC  27                         /* Press <Esc> to cancel */
#define F1   59                         /* Function key F1  */
```

```
#define F2    60                        /* Function key F2  */
#define F3    61                        /* Function key F3  */
#define F8    66                        /* Function key F8  */
#define F9    67                        /* Function key F9  */
#define F10   68                        /* Function key F10 */


/*== Type declarations ======================================*/

typedef struct { unsigned int SegAddr,        /* Segment address */
                              MBlSize;
                } BlockType;              /* Memory size */


typedef unsigned char BYTE;


/*== Macros =================================================*/

#ifdef MK_FP                          /* Macro MK_FP already defined? */
  #undef MK_FP                        /* Yes --> Undefine macro */
#endif

#define MK_FP(seg,ofs) ((void far *) ((unsigned long) (seg)<<16|(ofs)))

/*== Typed constants ========================================*/

char *YesNo[]    = { "No  ", "Yes " };
char *SText[]    = { "First free memory block used",
                     "Best free memory block used ",
                     "Last free memory block used " };
BYTE ColArray[]  = { 0x07, 0x70 };
char *Keybd_Text[] = { " [F1] Allocate memory",
                       " [F2] Release memory",
                       " [F3] Change size",
                       " [ESC] End program" };


/*== Global variables =======================================*/

union REGS   regs;              /* Registers for interrupt call */
struct SREGS sregs;      /* Segment registers for extended interrupt */
unsigned int MAddrArray[ 1000 ];         /* Array for memory */
unsigned int Num_Addrs;              /* Number of addresses */
unsigned int ConvSeg;    /* Address of test block in conventional RAM */
unsigned int UMBSeg;         /* Address of test block in UMB */
BlockType    BlocArray[ BLOCKAMT ];           /* Memory */

/*== Screen routines for Microsoft C ========================*/

#ifndef __TURBOC__                        /* Microsoft C? */

  #define textcolor( Color )
  #define textbackground( Color )

  /***********************************************************/
  /* Gotoxy     : Places the cursor.                        */
  /* Input      : Cursor coordinates                        */
  /* Output     : None                                      */
  /***********************************************************/

  void gotoxy( int x, int y )
  {
    regs.h.ah = 0x02;        /* Function number for interrupt call */
    regs.h.bh = 0;                        /* Color */
    regs.h.dh = y - 1;
    regs.h.dl = x - 1;
    int86( 0x10, &regs, &regs );           /* Interrupt call */
```

```
  }

  /***********************************************************/
  /* clrscr     : Clears the screen.                        */
  /* Input      : See below                                 */
  /* Output     : None                                      */
  /***********************************************************/

  void clrscr( void )
  {
    regs.h.ah = 0x07;            /* Function number for interrupt call */
    regs.h.al = 0x00;
    regs.h.ch = 0;
    regs.h.cl = 0;
    regs.h.dh = 24;
    regs.h.dl = 79;
    int86( 0x10, &regs, &regs );           /* Interrupt call */
    gotoxy( 1, 1 );                        /* Set cursor */
  }

#endif

/***********************************************************/
/* PRINT : Similar to PRINTF, writes the string directly to */
/*         video RAM.                                       */
/* Input   : COLUMN = Display column                        */
/*           SCROW = Display row                            */
/*           DCOLR = Display color                          */
/*           STRING = Pointer to PRINTF string              */
/*           ...   = other arguments                        */
/* Output  : None                                           */
/***********************************************************/

void Print( int Column, int ScRow, BYTE DColr, char * String, ...)
{
  struct vr {                      /* 2 bytes to a screen position */
            BYTE DisChar,                     /* ASCII code */
                 Attribute;          /* Corresponding attribute */
            } far * lptr;     /* Floating pointer to video RAM access */
  va_list parameter;              /* Parameter list for VA_... macros */
  char Output[255];                 /* Buffer for formatted string */
       *aptr = Output;              /* For string execution */
  static unsigned int vioseg = 0;
  union REGS Register;         /* Register variables for interrupt call */

  if ( vioseg == 0 )                        /* First call? */
  {                      /* Yes --> Get segment address of video RAM */
    Register.h.ah = 0x0F;
    int86(0x10, &Register, &Register);
    vioseg = ( Register.h.al == 7 ? 0xb000 : 0xb800 );
  }

  va_start( parameter, String );            /* Convert parameter */
  vsprintf( Output, String, parameter );         /* Format */
  lptr = (struct vr far *)
         MK_FP( vioseg, ( (ScRow-1) * 80 + (Column-1) ) << 1 );

  for ( ; *aptr ; )                         /* Run string */
  {
    lptr->DisChar = *aptr++;          /* Character in video RAM */
    lptr++->Attribute = DColr;        /* Set character attribute */
    ++Column;
  }
  gotoxy( Column, ScRow );           /* Place cursor after output */
```

```
                                          }

/*******************************************************/          /***************************************************************/
/* DOS_GetMem : Reserves memory.              */          /* ReadStrategy  : Reads the DOS memory management strategy.   */
/* Input    : Desired memory size in paragraphs.       */          /* Input        : None                                        */
/* Output   : Segment address of the allocated memory block,  */   /* Output       : Memory management strategy                  */
/*            number of paragraphs allocated or        */          /***************************************************************/
/*            maximum number of available paragraphs   */
/*******************************************************/          int ReadStrategy( void )
                                                                  {
void DOS_GetMem( unsigned int Ps,                                   regs.x.ax = GET_STRATEGY;              /* Set function number */
                 unsigned int *Adr,                                 intdos( &regs, &regs );
                 unsigned int *Res )                                return regs.x.ax;                         /* Display strategy */
{                                                                 }
 regs.h.ah = GET_MEM;                   /* Function number */
 regs.x.bx = Ps;           /* Number of paragraphs to be reserved */
 intdos( &regs, &regs );                  /* Interrupt call */     /***************************************************************/
 if ( !regs.x.cflag )                     /* Call successful? */    /* ReadUMB       : Reads UMB status.                          */
 {                                                                  /* Input        : None                                        */
  *Adr = regs.x.ax;           /* Yes --> Return address and size */ /* Output       : UMB ignored during memory management        */
  *Res = Ps;                                                        /* Info         : First available in DOS Version 5.0.         */
 }                                                                  /***************************************************************/
 else                                     /* No --> Error */
 {                                                                 int ReadUMB( void )
  *Adr = 0;                           /* No memory reserved */     {
  *Res = regs.x.bx;              /* Maximum available size */       regs.x.ax = GET_UMB;                   /* Set function number */
 }                                                                  intdos( &regs, &regs );                   /* Interrupt call */
}                                                                   return regs.h.al;                         /* Display status */
                                                                  }

/*******************************************************/
/* DOS_FreeMem: Releases reserved memory.             */          /***************************************************************/
/* Input      : Memory segment address                */          /* SetDosStrategy: Sets DOS memory management strategy.        */
/* Output     : None                                   */          /* Input        : New strategy                                */
/*******************************************************/          /* Output       : None                                        */
                                                                  /***************************************************************/
void DOS_FreeMem( unsigned int Adr )
{                                                                 void SetDosStrategy( unsigned int Strategy )
 regs.h.ah = FREE_MEM;                   /* Function number */     {
 sregs.es = Adr;            /* Address of memory to be released */  regs.x.ax = SET_STRATEGY;              /* Set function number */
 intdosx( &regs, &regs, &sregs );         /* Interrupt call */     regs.x.bx = Strategy;
}                                                                   intdos( &regs, &regs );
                                                                  }

/*******************************************************/
/* DOS_ChangeMem : Changes reserved memory size.      */          /***************************************************************/
/* Input    : Old segment address, new size in paragraphs */      /* SetUMB        : Sets the UMB status.                       */
/* Output   : Segment address of the allocated memory block,  */   /* Input        : New UMB status                              */
/*            number of paragraphs allocated or        */          /* Output       : None                                        */
/*            maximum number of available paragraphs   */          /* Info         : First available in DOS Version 5.0.         */
/*******************************************************/          /***************************************************************/

void DOS_ChangeMem( unsigned int Ps,                              void SetUMB( unsigned int UMB )
                    unsigned int *Adr,                            {
                    unsigned int *Res )                            regs.x.ax = SET_UMB;                   /* Set function number */
{                                                                  regs.x.bx = UMB;
 regs.h.ah = CHANGE_MEM;                  /* Function number */     intdos( &regs, &regs );
 regs.x.bx = Ps;           /* Number of paragraphs to be reserved */ }
 sregs.es = *Adr;   /* Segment address of memory block to be changed */
 intdosx( &regs, &regs, &sregs );         /* Interrupt call */     /***************************************************************/
 if ( !regs.x.cflag )                     /* Call successful? */    /* Allocate_Memory  : Creates a test environment for memory test.  */
  *Res = Ps;                            /* Yes --> New memory size */ /* Input        : None                                        */
 else                                     /* No --> Error */        /* Output       : None                                        */
  *Res = regs.x.bx;          /* Maximum available memory size */    /***************************************************************/
}
                                                                  void Allocate_Memory( void )
                                                                  {
                                                                   unsigned int SegAdr;       /* Segment address of allocated memory */
                                                                   unsigned int Des_Mem;                 /* Desired memory size */
```

```
    unsigned int MB1Size;              /* Size of allocated memory range */

    /*-- 1. Allocate test block -----------------------------------------*/

    SetUMB( UMB_OUT );
    DOS_GetMem( TEST_EN, &ConvSeg, &MB1Size );      /* Get test block */
    if ( ConvSeg == 0 )                             /* Error? */
      return;                                       /* Yes --> Return to caller */

    SetUMB( UMB_INC );
    SetDosStrategy( SRCHS_ABOVE | SFIRST_UMB );
    DOS_GetMem( TEST_EN_UMB, &UMBSeg, &MB1Size );
    if ( UMBSeg != 0  && UMBSeg < 0xA000 )          /* No UMB available? */
    {
      DOS_FreeMem( UMBSeg );                         /* Release memory */
      UMBSeg = 0;                                    /* No UMBs */
    }

    /*-- 2. Allocate remaining conventional/ UMB memory in 1K blocks ---*/

    Des_Mem = 63;                      /* First try allocating 15 paragraphs */
    Num_Addrs = 0;
    do
    {
      DOS_GetMem( Des_Mem, &SegAdr, &MB1Size );     /* Call for memory */
      if ( SegAdr != 0 )                            /* Memory received? */
        MAddrArray[ Num_Addrs++ ] = SegAdr;         /* Yes --> Note address */
    }
    while ( SegAdr != 0 );                          /* Allocate all memory */

    /*-- 3. Release test blocks -----------------------------------------*/

    if ( ConvSeg > 0 )
      DOS_FreeMem( ConvSeg-- );                      /* MCB is also free */
    if ( UMBSeg > 0 )
      DOS_FreeMem( UMBSeg-- );                       /* MCB is also free */
}

/*********************************************************************/
/* ReleaseThisMemory: Releases reserved memory.                    */
/* Input            : None                                          */
/* Output           : None                                          */
/* Global variables : MAddrArray/R                                  */
/*********************************************************************/

void ReleaseThisMemory( void )

{
    unsigned int i;                                 /* Loop counter */

    if ( Num_Addrs > 0 )                /* Release individual 1K blocks */
      for ( i = 0; i < Num_Addrs; i++ )
        DOS_FreeMem( MAddrArray[ i ] );
}

/*********************************************************************/
/* DisplayMemLayout : Displays memory layout.                      */
/* Input            : W_Borders = TRUE if the border should also   */
/*                    be displayed                                 */
/* Output           : None                                          */
/*********************************************************************/

void DisplayMemLayout( BYTE W_Borders )
{
```

```
    char       SArray[ TEST_EN_K ];
    char       SArray_UMB[ TEST_EN_UMB_K ];
    unsigned int i, j;                              /* Loop counter */
    unsigned int Position;                          /* Help variable */
    char       Sdummy[ 20 ];
    char       LastChar_M;      /* Memory for last character displayed */
    int        CurColor;                            /* Current output color */

    memset( SArray, 32, TEST_EN_K );        /* Initialize display array */
    memset( SArray_UMB, 32, TEST_EN_UMB_K );

    /*-- Fill memory table ---------------------------------------------*/

    for ( i = 0; i < BLOCKAMT; i++ )
    {
      if ( BlocArray[ i ].SegAddr > 0xA000 )            /* UMB? */
      {
        Position = ( BlocArray[ i ].SegAddr - UMBSeg ) / 64;
        for ( j = 0; j <= BlocArray[ i ].MB1Size / 64; j++ )
          SArray_UMB[ Position + j ] = i + 65;
      }
      else if ( BlocArray[ i ].SegAddr > 0 )
      {
        Position = ( BlocArray[ i ].SegAddr - ConvSeg ) / 64;
        for ( j = 0; j <= BlocArray[ i ].MB1Size / 64; j++ )
          SArray[ Position + j ] = i + 65;
      }
    }

    /*-- Draw border around memory table -------------------------------*/

    if ( W_Borders )
    {
      Print( 1, 7, 0x07, "Conventional memory:" );
      Print( 1, 8, 0x07,
             "                    1         2         3         4" );
      Print( 1, 9, 0x07,
             "          1         0         0         0         0" );
      Print( 1, 10, 0x07,
             "╔═══════════════════════════════════════════════════╗" );
      for ( i = 0; i < 4; i++ )
        Print( 1, 11 + i, 0x07, "║ %3i %s%s", i * 40,
               "K ║                                              ║",
               Keybd_Text[ i ] );
      Print( 1, 15, 0x07,
             "╚═══════════════════════════════════════════════════╝" );

      if ( UMBSeg > 0 )
      {
        Print( 1, 17, 0x07, "UMB:" );
        Print( 1, 18, 0x07,
               "                    1         2         3         4" );
        Print( 1, 19, 0x07,
               "          1         0         0         0         0" );
        Print( 1, 20, 0x07,
               "╔═══════════════════════════════════════════════════╗" );
        Print( 1, 21, 0x07,
               "║   0 KB ║                                          ║" );
        Print( 1, 22, 0x07,
               "╚════════╩══════════════════════════════════════════╝" );
      }
      else
        Print( 1, 17, 0x07, "No UMB available" );
    }
```

```
/*-- Display table for conventional memory ------------------------*/

LastChar_M = 0;                            /* Last character displayed */
CurColor = 1;                              /* Last display color */
for ( i = 0; i < 4; i++ )
 for ( j = 0; j < 40; j++ )
 {
   if ( LastChar_M != SArray[ i * 40 + j ] )      /* Color change? */
   {
     CurColor = ( CurColor + 1 ) % 2;            /* New color number */
     LastChar_M = SArray[ i * 40 + j ];          /* Chars. to compare */
   }
   Print( j + 11, i + 11, ColArray[ CurColor ],
          "%c", SArray[ i * 40 + j ] );
 }


/*-- Display table for UMB ------------------------------------*/

if ( UMBSeg > 0 )
{
 for ( j = 0; j < 40; j++ )
 {
   if ( LastChar_M != SArray_UMB[ j ] )          /* Color change? */
   {
     CurColor = ( CurColor + 1 ) % 2;            /* New color number */
     LastChar_M = SArray_UMB[ j ];               /* Chars. to compare */
   }
   Print( j + 11, 21, ColArray[ CurColor ],
          "%c", SArray_UMB[ j ] );
 }
}
}


/***********************************************************************/
/* Demo     : Demonstrates memory management.                  */
/* Input    : Included UMB, first UMB to search,               */
/*              memory division strategy                       */
/* Output   : None                                             */
/***********************************************************************/

void Demo( int Inc_UMB,
           int UMB_first,
           int Strategy )
{
int      i;                          /* Loop counter */
int      IKeys;                      /* Input keys */
char     ResPtr[ 5 ];    /* Pointer to desired reservation (A-Z) */
unsigned int Des_Mem;                /* Size of reservation */
unsigned int MBlSize;
char     *sdummy[ 20 ];

/*-- Initialize address array ------------------------------*/

for ( i = 0; i < BLOCKAMT; i++ )     /* Initialize all blocks */
{
 BlocArray[ i ].SegAddr = 0;     /* Segment address of memory block */
 BlocArray[ i ].MBlSize = 0;         /* Size of memory block */
}

DisplayMemLayout( TRUE );            /* Display memory table */

/*-- Demonstration loop -----------------------------------*/

do
{
/*-- Specify selected memory management strategy -----------------*/

if ( Inc_UMB )                       /* UMB used? */
SetUMB( UMB_INC );
else
SetUMB( UMB_OUT );

if ( UMB_first )
SetDosStrategy( Strategy | SFIRST_UMB );
else
SetDosStrategy( Strategy );

/*-- Display current strategy ------------------------------------*/

Print( 1, 3, 0x07,
        "Memory management strategy: %s  [F8]",
        SText[ Strategy ] );
Print( 1, 4, 0x07,
        "First search in UMB      : %s        %s",
        YesNo[ UMB_first ], "                   [F9]" );
Print( 1, 5, 0x07,
        "UMB used                 : %s        %s",
        YesNo[ Inc_UMB ], "                   [F10]" );
Print( 1, 6, 0x07, "----------------------------------------" );
Print( 40, 6, 0x07,"----------------------------------------" );

/*-- Entry and processing --------------------------------------*/

while ( ! kbhit() );                 /* Wait for a key */
IKeys = getch();                     /* Read key */
if ( ( IKeys == 0 ) && ( kbhit() ) ) /* Function key */
 IKeys = getch();                    /* Get 2nd key code */

switch( IKeys )
{
 case F1 :                           /* Allocate memory block */
  i = -1;                  /* No more valid memory blocks given */
  do                                 /* Enter up to valid block */
  {
    Print( 1, 23, 0x07, "Reserve which block [ A-Z ]: " );
    scanf( "%s", ResPtr );
    ResPtr[0] = toupper( ResPtr[ 0 ] );
    if (( ResPtr[0] >= 'A' ) && ( ResPtr[0] <= 'Z' ))
     if ( BlocArray[ (int) ResPtr[0] - 65 ].SegAddr == 0 )
      i = (int) ResPtr[0] - 65;
  }
  while ( i == -1 );
  Print( 1, 24, 0x07,
        "How many K do you want reserved: " );
  scanf( "%i", &Des_Mem );
  Des_Mem = Des_Mem * 64 - 1;        /* Convert to paragraphs */
  DOS_GetMem( Des_Mem, &BlocArray[ i ].SegAddr,
              &BlocArray[ i ].MBlSize );
  if ( BlocArray[ i ].MBlSize != Des_Mem )        /* Error? */
  {
    Print( 1, 25, 0x07, "Only %4dK free",
                  ( BlocArray[ i ].MBlSize + 1 ) / 64 );
    while ( !kbhit() )
      ;
    while ( kbhit() )
     IKeys = getch();
    IKeys = 0;
```

```
    }                                                                   case F9 :                            /* Toggle: UMB first */
  Print(1, 23, 0x07, "                              ");                   UMB_first = ! UMB_first;
  Print(1, 24, 0x07, "                              ");                   break;
  Print(1, 25, 0x07, "                              ");
  DisplayMemLayout( FALSE );       /* Display memory table */            case F10:                            /* Toggle: Add UMB */
  break;                                                                  Inc_UMB = ! Inc_UMB;
                                                                          break;
  case F2 :                        /* Release memory block */          }
    i = -1;                        /* No more valid blocks given */    }
    do                             /* Enter up to valid block */       while ( IKeys != ESC );
    {                                                                  }
      Print( 1, 23, 0x07, "Release which block [ A-Z ]: " ),
      scanf( "%s", ResPtr );
      ResPtr[0] = toupper( ResPtr[ 0 ] );                              /***********************************************************************/
      if (( ResPtr[0] >= 'A' ) && ( ResPtr[0] <= 'Z' ))               /*                  M A I N   P R O G R A M                      */
        if ( BlocArray[ (int) ResPtr[0] - 65 ].SegAddr != 0 )          /***********************************************************************/
          i = (int) ResPtr[0] - 65;
    }                                                                  void main( void )
    while ( i == -1 );                                                 {
    DOS_FreeMem( BlocArray[ i ].SegAddr );                              int StartStrategy;              /* Memory division on startup */
    BlocArray[ i ].SegAddr = 0;                                         int StartUMB;                   /* UMB layout on startup */
    BlocArray[ i ].MBlSize = 0;                                         int Cur_UMB_INC;                /* UMB used (yes/no) */
    Print(1, 23, 0x07, "                              ");               int Cur_UMB_first;             /* Search first in UMB */
    DisplayMemLayout( FALSE );       /* Display memory table */         int Cur_Strategy;              /* Current search strategy */
    break;
                                                                       /*-- Screen layout -----------------------------------------------*/
  case F3 :                        /* Change one block's size */
    i = -1;                        /* No more valid blocks given */     clrscr();
    do                             /* Enter up to valid block */        Print( 1, 1, 0x07,
    {                                                                          "DOS Memory Management Demo " );
      Print( 1, 23, 0x07, "Which block do you want changed [ A-Z ]: "   Print( 51, 1, 0x07,
);                                                                             " (C) 1991 by Michael Tischer" );
      scanf( "%s", ResPtr );                                            Print( 1, 2, 0x07, "======================================" );
      ResPtr[0] = toupper( ResPtr[ 0 ] );                               Print( 40, 2, 0x07, "======================================" );
      if (( ResPtr[0] >= 'A' ) && ( ResPtr[0] <= 'Z' ))                 Print( 25, 5, 0x07, "Processing memory layout now...." );
        if ( BlocArray[ (int) ResPtr[0] - 65 ].SegAddr != 0 )
          i = (int) ResPtr[0] - 65;
    }                                                                  /*-- Store DOS values when program starts ------------------------*/
    while ( i == -1 );
    Print( 1, 24, 0x07, "How many K do you want reserved: " );          StartStrategy = ReadStrategy();       /* Memory layout strategy */
    scanf( "%i", &Des_Mem );                                            StartUMB = ReadUMB();                 /* UMB inclusion */
    Des_Mem = Des_Mem * 64 - 1;      /* Convert to paragraphs */        Allocate_Memory();                    /* Create test envrionment */
    DOS_ChangeMem( Des_Mem, &BlocArray[ i ].SegAddr, &MBlSize );        SetDosStrategy( StartStrategy );      /* Restore old strategy */
    if ( MBlSize != Des_Mem )                  /* Error? */             SetUMB( StartUMB );
    {
      Print( 1, 23, 0x07, "Only %4iK free",                             if ( ConvSeg == 0 )              /* Allocate conventional memory? */
                          ( MBlSize + 1 ) /  64 );                      {                                /* No --> End program with error message */
      while ( !kbhit() );                                                 clrscr();
      while ( kbhit() )                                                   printf( "MEMDEMOC: Not enough memory!\n" );
        IKeys = getch();                                                  exit(1);
      IKeys = 0;                                                        }
    }
    else                                                               /*-- Starting values for memory management ------------------------*/
      BlocArray[ i ].MBlSize = MBlSize;       /* Set new size */
    Print(1, 23, 0x07,"                              ");                Cur_UMB_INC = ( StartUMB == UMB_INC );
    Print(1, 24, 0x07,"                              ");                Cur_UMB_first = ( ( StartStrategy & SFIRST_UMB ) == SFIRST_UMB );
    Print(1, 25, 0x07,"                              ");                Cur_Strategy = ( StartStrategy & ( 0xFF ^ SFIRST_UMB ) );
    DisplayMemLayout( FALSE );       /* Display memory table */
    break;                                                             /*-- Demonstration of memory division ----------------------------*/

  case F8 :                        /* Change strategy */               clrscr();
    Strategy = ( Strategy + 1 ) % 3;                                    Print( 1, 1, 0x07,
    break;                                                                     "DOS Memory Management Demo " );
                                                                       Print( 51, 1, 0x07,
                                                                              " (C) 1991 by Michael Tischer" );
                                                                       Print( 1, 2, 0x07, "======================================" );
```

```
Print( 40, 2, 0x07, "=====================================" );     ReleaseThisMemory();        /* Release reserved memory */
Demo( Cur_UMB_INC, Cur_UMB_first, Cur_Strategy );                   SetDosStrategy( StartStrategy );
                                                                    SetUMB( StartUMB );
/*-- Restore old DOS values ------------------------------------*/  clrscr();
                                                                    }
```

22.4 Behind the Scenes of Memory Management

You probably noticed the acronym "MCB" in the listings for the programs at the end of the previous section. This is an abbreviation for Memory Control Block. MCBs are important to the way DOS manages memory.

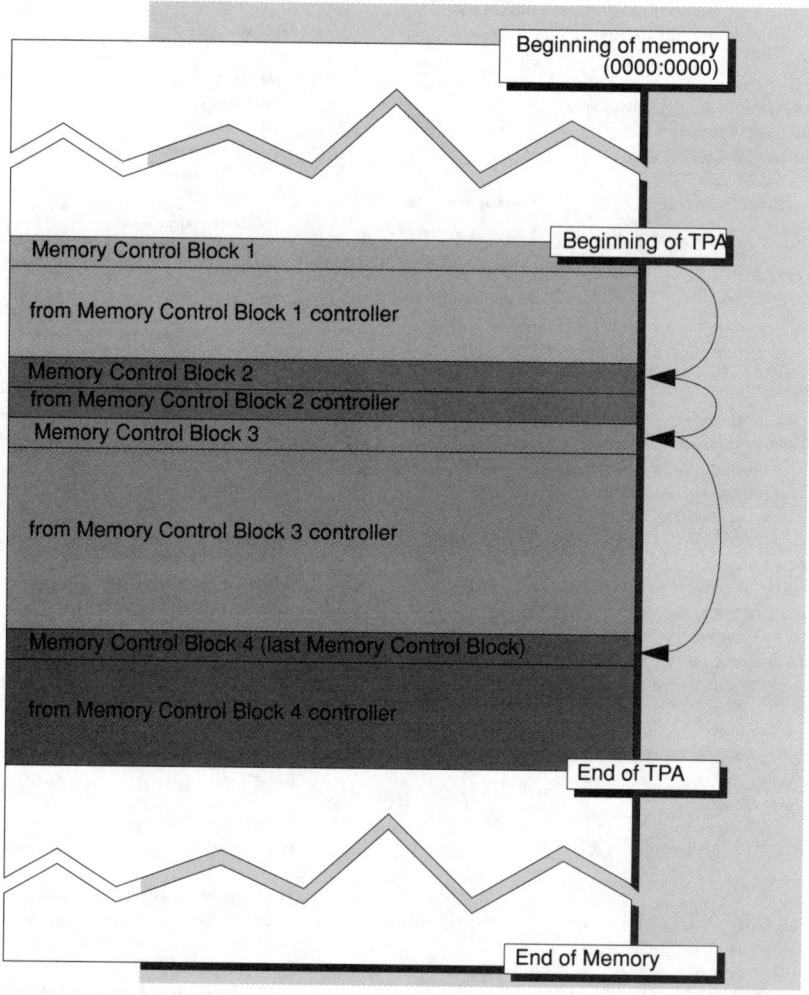

Managing allocated memory with Memory Control Blocks (MCBs)

In order to manage memory blocks allocated with DOS function 48H, a Memory Control Block (MCB) is created for each allocated block. An MCB consists of 16 bytes. It always starts at an offset address that is divisible by 16 and it precedes the memory block it describes. The DOS memory management functions always work with the segment address of the allocated block, so the segment address of the corresponding MCB can be easily obtained by subtracting 1 from the segment address of the allocated block.

Addr.	Contents	Type
	Structure of a Memory Control Blocks (MCB) in RAM	
+00h	ID ("Z" = last MCB, "M" = more to follow)	1 BYTE
+01h	Segment address of the corresponding PSP	1 WORD
+03h	Number of paragraphs in the allocated block	1 WORD
+05h	not used	11 BYTE
+10h	The allocated memory block	x PARAG.
	Length: 16 + the size of the allocated block	

The MCB contains three fields, as seen in the previous figure. Mark Zbikowski, one of the developers of MS-DOS, has immortalized himself by using his initials in the first field. If this field contains the letter "M", then additional MCBs follow this one. If it contains "Z", then this is the last MCB in memory.

The second field contains the segment address of the PSP for the corresponding program. This field is only significant if the allocated memory block is for the environment of a program. In this instance, this field establishes a link by pointing to the PSP. Before a program is loaded, the EXEC function allocates a separate memory block for the environment block of the program.

If the memory block is a PSP, then the second field of the MCB usually points directly to the memory block itself.

The third field is more important when evaluating the MCB. This field gives the size of the memory block in paragraphs. Since the next MCB follows directly after this memory block, this number represents the distance to the next MCB minus 1. In this way, each MCB indirectly points to the next one, which generates a linked list of all MCBs.

Accessing the MCB chain

You must know the address of the first MCB to access the entire MCB chain. DOS stores this address in an internal structure called the DOS Information Block (DIB). This structure usually isn't accessible to application programs. However, you can access it with the undocumented function 52H. This function returns a pointer to the DIB in the ES:BX register pair.

Curiously, this address points to the second field of the DIB instead of the first. However, the first field contains the address of the first MCB, which is what we're looking for. The pointer to the first MCB consists of an offset and segment address that occupies four bytes. So, we'll be able to find the desired information at the address ES:[BX-4].

This formula must be used carefully. You cannot simply subtract 4 from the contents of the BX register and end up with the desired address in all cases. This works only if the offset address in the BX register is greater than or equal to 4. If it's smaller, a negative number is the result. As the following example shows, negative numbers aren't used in memory addressing:

If the BX register returns a value of 0 as the offset address of the DIB, then subtracting 4 will result in the value 0FFFCH. In an arithmetic operation, this is correctly interpreted as -4, but as a memory address it points to 0FFFCH, which is at the end of the segment instead of before the given address. The desired information isn't located there.

The solution is to simply decrement the segment address by 1. This reduces the combined segment and offset address by 16. If you now add 12 to the offset address, this results in the original address minus 4, which takes us to the first field of the DIB and the address of the first MCB.

Demonstration program

- The number of the MCB
- The MCB's address in memory
- Address of the block managed by the MCB
- Contents of the ID field ("M" or "Z")
- Address of the corresponding PSP (regardless of whether it exists)
- Size of the corresponding memory block in paragraphs and bytes

Until DOS Version 3.0, the environment block contained only the previous information. Starting with Version 3.0, the name of the program, to which the environment block belongs, was added after the last environment string. The complete path is given along with the program name.

The null byte after the last environment string and the start of the name string are separated by a word. Only if this word contains the value 0001H will the following program name and path be valid. The program name string also ends with a null byte.

An example of program output

To help interpreting the output of this program, we ran the C version on a computer and received the following results. Each MCB is explained after the output.

```
MCBC (c) 1988, 91 by Michael Tischer

MCB number     = 1
MCB address    = 09C8:0000
Memory address= 09C9:0000
ID             = M
PSP address    = 0008:0000
Size           = 1554 paragraphs ( 24864 Byte )
Contents       = Unidentifiable as program or data

DUMP | 0123456789ABCDEF     00 01 02 03 04 05 06 07 08 09 0A 0B 0C 0D 0E 0F
-----+--------------------------------------------------------------------
0000 | n p  é! , $CLOCK      6E 01 70 00 08 80 21 00 2C 00 24 43 4C 4F 43 4B
0010 |    é                  20 06 03 80 02 1F 1D 1F 1E 1F 1E 1F 1F 1E 1F 1E
0020 | .æ  .ö  ╥PSQR         1F 2E 89 1E 11 00 2E 8C 06 13 00 CB 50 53 51 52
0030 | WVU ú╜ -> &Å]         57 56 55 1E 06 9C FC 0E 1F C4 3E 11 00 26 8A 5D
0040 | é├ t!é├ tJ ╨u ☻       02 80 FB 04 74 21 80 FB 08 74 4A 0A DB 75 03 E9
══════════════════════════════════ Please press a key ══
```

```
MCB number     = 2
MCB address    = 0FDB:0000
Memory address= 0FDC:0000
ID             = M
PSP address    = 0FDC:0000
Size           = 231 paragraphs ( 3696 Byte )
Contents       = PSP (with program following)
```
================================== Please press a key ===

```
MCB number     = 3
MCB address    = 10C3:0000
Memory address= 10C4:0000
ID             = M
PSP address    = 0000:0000
Size           = 3 paragraphs ( 48 Byte )
Contents       = Unidentifiable as program or data
```

```
DUMP | 0123456789ABCDEF      00 01 02 03 04 05 06 07 08 09 0A 0B 0C 0D 0E 0F
-----+-------------------------------------------------------------------------
0000 |       ╥    ╜╜╜╜╜╜     00 01 00 00 00 00 00 CB 00 00 00 FF FF FF FF FF
0010 | ╜╜╜╜╜╜╜╜╜╜╜╜╜╜╜╜C     FF FF FF FF FF FF FF FF FF FF FF FF FF FF FF 43
0020 | :\AUTOEXEC.BAT        3A 5C 41 55 54 4F 45 58 45 43 2E 42 41 54 00 00
0030 | M█                    4D DC 0F 0A 00 00 00 00 00 00 00 00 00 00 00 00
0040 | COMSPEC=C:\COMMA      43 4F 4D 53 50 45 43 3D 43 3A 5C 43 4F 4D 4D 41
```
============================ Please press a key ===

```
MCB number     = 4
MCB address    = 10C7:0000
Memory address= 10C8:0000
ID             = M
PSP address    = 0FDC:0000
Size           = 10 paragraphs ( 160 Byte )
Contents       = Environment
Program name   = Unknown
Environment string
         COMSPEC=C:\COMMAND.COM
         PATH=C:\;C:\DOS;C:\BATCHES;E:\;D:\MSC\BIN
         INCLUDE=d:\msc\include
         LIB=d:\msc\lib
         TMP=d:\msc\tmp
         PROMPT=[$p]
```
============================ Please press a key ===

```
MCB number     = 5
MCB address    = 10D2:0000
Memory address= 10D3:0000
ID             = M
PSP address    = 10DD:0000
Size           = 9 paragraphs ( 144 Byte )
Contents       = Environment
Program name   = C:\DOS\KEYB.COM
Environment string
         COMSPEC=C:\COMMAND.COM
         PATH=C:\;C:\DOS;C:\BATCHES;E:\;D:\MSC\BIN
         INCLUDE=d:\msc\include
         LIB=d:\msc\lib
         TMP=d:\msc\tmp
```
============================ Please press a key ===

```
MCB number     = 6
MCB address    = 10DC:0000
Memory address= 10DD:0000
ID             = M
PSP address    = 10DD:0000
Size           = 341 paragraphs ( 5456 Byte )
Contents       = PSP (with program following)
```
============================ Please press a key ===

```
MCB number     = 7
```

```
           MCB address    = 1232:0000
           Memory address= 1233:0000
           ID            = M
           PSP address    = 123D:0000
           Size          = 9 paragraphs ( 144 Byte )
           Contents      = Environment
           Program name  = C:\DOS\CED.COM
           Environment string
                   COMSPEC=C:\COMMAND.COM
                   PATH=C:\;C:\DOS;C:\BATCHES;E:\;D:\MSC\BIN
                   INCLUDE=d:\msc\include
                   LIB=d:\msc\lib
                   TMP=d:\msc\tmp
```
=== Please press a key ===
```
           MCB number     = 8
           MCB address    = 123C:0000
           Memory address= 123D:0000
           ID            = M
           PSP address    = 123D:0000
           Size          = 1030 paragraphs ( 16480 Byte )
           Contents      = PSP (with program following)
```
=== Please press a key ===
```
           MCB number     = 9
           MCB address    = 1643:0000
           Memory address= 1644:0000
           ID            = M
           PSP address    = 164E:0000
           Size          = 9 paragraphs ( 144 Byte )
           Contents      = Environment
           Program name  = C:\DOS\CACHE-AT.COM
           Environment string
                   COMSPEC=C:\COMMAND.COM
                   PATH=C:\;C:\DOS;C:\BATCHES;E:\;D:\MSC\BIN
                   INCLUDE=d:\msc\include
                   LIB=d:\msc\lib
                   TMP=d:\msc\tmp
```
=== Please press a key ===
```
           MCB number     = 10
           MCB address    = 164D:0000
           Memory address= 164E:0000
           ID            = M
           PSP address    = 164E:0000
           Size          = 1922 paragraphs ( 30752 Byte )
           Contents      = PSP (with program following)
```
=== Please press a key ===
```
           MCB number     = 11
           MCB address    = 1DD0:0000
           Memory address= 1DD1:0000
           ID            = M
           PSP address    = 1DDC:0000
           Size          = 10 paragraphs ( 160 Byte )
           Contents      = Environment
           Program name  = C:\DOS\KEYBUF.COM
           Environment string
                   COMSPEC=C:\COMMAND.COM
                   PATH=C:\;C:\DOS;C:\BATCHES;E:\;D:\MSC\BIN
                   INCLUDE=d:\msc\include
                   LIB=d:\msc\lib
                   TMP=d:\msc\tmp
                   PROMPT=[$p]
```
=== Please press a key ===
```
           MCB number     = 12
           MCB address    = 1DDB:0000
           Memory address= 1DDC:0000
```

```
ID               = M
PSP address      = 1DDC:0000
Size             = 27 paragraphs ( 432 Byte )
Contents         = Unidentifiable as program or data


DUMP | 0123456789ABCDEF        00 01 02 03 04 05 06 07 08 09 0A 0B 0C 0D 0E 0F
-----+--------------------------------------------------------------------------
0000 |  M M M M M M M          00 4D 00 4D 00 4D 00 4D 00 4D 00 4D 00 4D 00 4D
0010 |  M M M M M M M          00 4D 00 4D 00 4D 00 4D 00 4D 00 4D 00 4D 00 4D
0020 |  + 1  K K K K K K        2B 1B 31 02 00 4B 00 4B 00 4B 00 4B 00 4B 00 4B
0030 |  K K K K K K K          00 4B 00 4B 00 4B 00 4B 00 4B 00 4B 00 4B 00 4B
0040 |  K K K K K K K          00 4B 00 4B 00 4B 00 4B 00 4B 00 4B 00 4B 00 4B
                                                    === Please press a key ===
MCB number       = 13
MCB address      = 1DF7:0000
Memory address= 1DF8:0000
ID               = M
PSP address      = 0FDC:0000
Size             = 4 paragraphs ( 64 Byte )
Contents         = PSP (with program following)
                                                    === Please press a key ===
MCB number       = 14
MCB address      = 1DFC:0000
Memory address= 1DFD:0000
ID               = M
PSP address      = 1E08:0000
Size             = 10 paragraphs ( 160 Byte )
Contents         = Environment
Program name     = D:\PCI\C\TC.EXE
Environment string
         COMSPEC=C:\COMMAND.COM
         PATH=C:\;C:\DOS;C:\BATCHES;E:\;D:\MSC\BIN
         INCLUDE=d:\msc\include
         LIB=d:\msc\lib
         TMP=d:\msc\tmp
         PROMPT=[$p]
                                                    === Please press a key ===
MCB number       = 15
MCB address      = 1E07:0000
Memory address= 1E08:0000
ID               = M
PSP address      = 1E08:0000
Size             = 16200 paragraphs ( 259200 Byte )
Contents         = PSP (with program following)
                                                    === Please press a key ===
MCB number       = 16
MCB address      = 5D50:0000
Memory address= 5D51:0000
ID               = M
PSP address      = 5D5C:0000
Size             = 10 paragraphs ( 160 Byte )
Contents         = Environment
Program name     = C:\TC\OBEX\MCBC.EXE
Environment string
         COMSPEC=C:\COMMAND.COM
         PATH=C:\;C:\DOS;C:\BATCHES;E:\;D:\MSC\BIN
         INCLUDE=d:\msc\include
         LIB=d:\msc\lib
         TMP=d:\msc\tmp
         PROMPT=[$p]
                                                    === Please press a key ===
MCB number       = 17
MCB address      = 5D5B:0000
Memory address= 5D5C:0000
```

```
ID              = M
PSP address     = 5D5C:0000
Size            = 4512 paragraphs ( 72192 Byte )
Contents        = PSP (with program following)
================================================= Please press a key ===
MCB number      = 18
MCB address     = 6EFC:0000
Memory address  = 6EFD:0000
ID              = Z
PSP address     = 0000:0000
Size            = 12547 paragraphs ( 200752 Byte )
Contents        = Unidentifiable as program or data

DUMP | 0123456789ABCDEF      00 01 02 03 04 05 06 07 08 09 0A 0B 0C 0D 0E 0F
-----+---------------------------------------------------------------------
0000 | H   6   % E     L     48 00 00 00 36 00 08 00 25 00 88 08 00 00 A8 00
0010 | (   v   ⊔⊔ᴚ     '     28 04 1E 00 76 00 17 00 FF FF 96 08 00 00 27 0C
0020 | H   Q   ⊔⊔ᴚ â   .     48 1F 00 00 51 00 1E 00 FF FF 96 08 90 01 2E 05
0030 | HB  6   % ᴚ █   B     48 42 00 00 36 00 08 00 25 00 96 08 EC 01 42 00
0040 | ( ⌐| v  ⊔⊔ᴓ     E     28 0D E3 00 76 00 17 00 FF FF A4 08 00 00 45 0C
================================================= Please press a key ===
```

Dump from MCBC.EXE

1   Although the program couldn't identify the first MCB (so the given PSP address isn't significant), the memory dump provides information about its contents. The first line of the ASCII dump contains the word "$CLOCK", which is the name of the DOS device driver for the internal clock.

Ap you might expect, this does look like a device driver. The first 18 bytes corresponds to the exact structure of a device driver header. However, this cannot be a permanently installed device driver from DOS because these are installed below the TPA (Transient Program Area) and don't require memory to be allocated for them.

So, this must be a driver that's installed with the DEVICE command from within the CONFIG.SYS file. The first device driver installed in our CONFIG.SYS file is "AT-UHR.SYS". This device uses the name "$CLOCK" as its device name.

This driver requires only a few kilobytes, but the allocated memory block is much larger than this. So, there must be more program code or data after this driver. By examining the five lines of the dump, we can see that all drivers that were installed with the DEVICE command can be found here. This means that the first memory is already allocated by DOS during the boot procedure. It's given to all device drivers in the order in which they are named in the CONFIG.SYS file.

2   This memory block apparently contains a program. Since it's not preceded by an environment block that would provide the name of the program, we don't know which program this is. But from its location in the MCB chain and in RAM, we know that it was installed as a resident program shortly after the system was booted.

3   The contents of this memory block don't provide much information. Either it was allocated by a program for storing data at a later time, or it was simply left over after a memory block was freed.

4   This is obviously an environment block, but the corresponding program name is missing. 0FDC:0000 is given as the PSP address, which corresponds to the memory block managed by MCB 2. Since MCB 2 is a PSP and MCB 4 is an environment block, we can be almost certain that these two blocks represent a program and its environment. Since the environment block doesn't have a program name associated with it, we can also conclude that this program wasn't started from the DOS command line or by a command in a BATCH file.

MCB 2 seems to represent the resident portion of the command processor COMMAND.COM, with the environment managed by MCB 4. This is confirmed by examining the program code in MCB 2 with a debugger.

5   This is the environment block for the program KEYB.COM, which enables us to work with the German keyboard. This program is started within our AUTOEXEC.BAT file using the command KEYB.GR. This is a resident program that remains in memory after it's installed.

6   The environment for KEYB.COM is in MCB 5, and the actual program is in MCB 6 (the PSP, meaning the program code and data). We know this because the PSP address given in MCB 5 points to the memory block managed by MCB 6.

7, 8   These two blocks represent the environment and PSP for the CED.COM program, which is also started from within AUTOEXEC.BAT. This is also a memory resident program.

9, 10   Same as MCBs 7 and 8, except it's for the program CACHE-AT.COM.

11, 12   These blocks are for the program KEYBUF.COM (see Chapter 16). The environment block is clearly present, but the other block cannot be readily identified as the PSP. This is because this program uses (or rather misuses) a keyboard buffer as its PSP. So, the interrupt call at the start of the PSP is overwritten. This command identifies the PSP; without it the block cannot be identified as a block.

13   The program indicates that this block is occupied by a PSP. However, it must be only the beginning of a PSP, since this memory block is only 64 bytes and a PSP needs 256 bytes. This block was probably occupied by a PSP that wasn't completely overwritten after it was freed. So some of it still remains in memory.

14, 15   The program for outputting MCB contents was written in C, so we were in the Turbo C environment when we ran it. MCBs 14 and 15 therefore contain the environment and program code for Turbo C.

16, 17   To create this MCB memory dump, we compiled, linked, and executed the program MCBC within Turbo C. Executing this program also creates another process that starts Turbo C with the help of the EXEC loader. So, the block managed by MCBs 16 and 17 were allocated by the EXEC loader to run the program. After the program ends, they will be freed again.

18   The last memory block contains all the remaining memory that wasn't allocated at the time. This is about 200K of memory.

The following demonstration programs are written in BASIC, Pascal, and C versions. They can be used to generate MCB dumps like the one previously described. The three versions are very similar to one another. The BASIC version is slightly different because BASIC cannot use FAR pointers to query the memory. Instead, the PEEK and DEF SEG commands must be used (see Chapter 2 for more information).

Listing: MCBP.PAS

```
{*****************************************************}
{*                 M C B P . P A S                   *}
{*---------------------------------------------------*}
{*  Task       : Displays any memory block allocated by DOS.  *}
{*---------------------------------------------------*}
{*  Author     : Michael Tischer                     *}
{*  Developed on : 08/22/88                          *}
{*  Last update : 01/29/92                           *}
{*****************************************************}

program MCBP;

uses DOS, CRT;                        { Add DOS and CRT units }

type BytePtr = ^byte;                 { Pointer to a byte }
     MemRnge = array[0..1000] of byte;  { A range somewhere in RAM }
     RngPtr  = ^MemRnge;              { Pointer to a range }
     MCB     = record                 { A Memory Control Block }
                 IdCode  : char;      { "M" = block follows, "Z" = end }
                 PSP     : word;  { Segment address of appropriate PSP }
                 Spacing : word;      { Number of paragraphs - 1 }
               end;
     MCBPtr  = ^MCB;                   { Pointer to an MCB }
     MCBPtr2 = ^MCBPtr;                { Pointer to an MCBPtr }
     HexStr  = string[4];             { Stores a 4-digit hex string }

var CvHStr : HexStr;     { Stores the hex string after conversion }

{****************************************************************}
{* HexString: Converts a number into a hexadecimal string.     *}
{* Input    : - HexVal = Value to be converted                 *}
{* Output   : The converted hex string                         *}
{****************************************************************}

function HexString( HexVal : word ) : HexStr;

var counter,                          { Loop counter }
    Nibble  : byte;                   { Lower nibble of word }
begin
  CvHStr := 'xxxx';                   { Generate a string }
  for counter:=4 downto 1 do      { Get the 4 numbers in the string }
    begin
      Nibble := HexVal and $000f;     { Get the upper 4 bits only }
      if ( Nibble > 9 ) then          { Convert to a character? }
        CvHStr[ counter ] := chr(Nibble - 10 + ord('A'))   { Yes }
      else
        CvHStr[ counter ] := chr(Nibble + ord('0'));   { No --> Convert to number }
      HexVal := HexVal shr 4;   { HexVal 4 bit positions to the right }
    end;
  HexString := CvHStr;                { Pass the resulting string }
```

```
end;

{*****************************************************}
{* FirstMCB: Returns a pointer to the first MCB.     *}
{* Input   : None                                    *}
{* Output  : Pointer to the first MCB                *}
{*****************************************************}

function FirstMCB : MCBPtr;

var Regs : Registers;              { Store the processor registers }

begin
  Regs.ah := $52;        { Func. no.: Get DOS info block's address }
  MsDos( Regs );                   { Call DOS interrupt 21H }

  {*-- ES:(BX-4) points to the first MCB, create pointer ------------*}

  FirstMCB := MCBPtr2( ptr( Regs.ES-1, Regs.BX+12 ) )^;
end;

{*****************************************************}
{* Dump    : Display a memory range as hex and ASCII dumps.  *}
{* Input   : - DPtr = Pointer to the memory range to be dumped  *}
{*           - NumL = Number of 16-byte lines to be dumped  *}
{* Output  : None                                    *}
{*****************************************************}

procedure Dump( DPtr : RngPtr; NumL : byte);

type HBStr = string[2];                 { Get 2-digit hex number }

var Offset,                          { Offset in memory range }
    Z       : integer;              { Loop counter }
    HexStr  : HBStr;        { Create a hex string for hex dump }

procedure HexByte( HByte : byte );

begin
  HexStr[1] := chr( (HByte shr 4) + ord('0') );   { First digit }
  if HexStr[1] > '9' then               { Convert to character? }
    HexStr[1] := chr( ord(HexStr[1]) + 7 );   { Yes }
  HexStr[2] := chr( (HByte and 15) + ord('0') );   { Second digit }
  if HexStr[2] > '9' then               { Convert to character? }
    HexStr[2] := chr( ord(HexStr[2]) + 7 );   { Yes }
end;

begin
  HexStr := 'zz';                       { Generate hex string }
  writeln;
  write('DUMP | 0123456789ABCDEF      00 01 02 03 04 05 06 07 08');
  writeln('  09 0A 0B 0C 0D 0E 0F');
```

```
write('-----+-------------------------------------------
writeln('-----------------------');
Offset := 0;                      { Start with first byte in the range }
while NumL>0 do                            { Execute loop NumL times }
  begin
    write(HexString(Offset), ' | ');
    for Z:=0 to 15 do                            { Process 15 bytes }
      if (Dptr^[Offset+Z] >= 32) then   { Valid ASCII characters? }
        write( chr(Dptr^[Offset+Z]) )          { Yes --> Display }
      else                                                 { No }
        write(' ');            { Display a space instead of a character }
    write('       ');               { Place cursor at hex section }
    for Z:=0 to 15 do                            { Process 15 bytes }
      begin
        HexByte( Dptr^[Offset+Z] );          { Convert byte to hex }
        write(HexStr, ' ');                  { Display hex string }
      end;
    writeln;
    Offset := Offset + 16;            { Set offset at the next line }
    Dec( NumL );         { Decrement the number of remaining lines }
  end;
  writeln;
end;


{*****************************************************************}
{* TraceMCB: Display list of MCBs.                              *}
{* Input   : None                                               *}
{* Output  : None                                               *}
{*****************************************************************}

procedure TraceMCB;

const ComSpec : array[0..7] of char = 'COMSPEC=';

var CurMCB  : MCBPtr;
    EndIt   : boolean;
    PdKey   : char;
    NrMCB,                        { Number of MCBs to be checked }
    Z       : integer;                        { Loop counter }
    MemPtr  : RngPtr;

begin
  EndIt := false;
  NrMCB := 1;                        { Assign the first MCB the number 1 }
  CurMCB := FirstMCB;                { Get pointer to the first MCB }
  repeat                            { Add to group of MCBs }
    if CurMCB^.IdCode = 'Z' then           { Last MCB reached? }
      EndIt := true;                                       { Yes }
    writeln('MCB number    = ', NrMCB);
    writeln('MCB address   = ', HexString(seg(CurMCB^)), ':',
                                HexString(ofs(CurMCB^)) );
    writeln('Memory address = ', HexString(succ(seg(CurMCB^))), ':',
                                 HexString(ofs(CurMCB^)) );
    writeln('ID            = ', CurMCB^.IdCode);
    writeln('PSP address   = ', HexString(CurMCB^.PSP), ':0000');
    writeln('Size          = ', CurMCB^.Spacing, ' paragraphs ',
            '( ', longint(CurMCB^.Spacing) shl 4, ' bytes )');
    write('Contents      = ');

    {*-- Handle MCB as an environment? ------------------------------*}

    Z := 0;                        { Start comparison with first byte }
    MemPtr := RngPtr(ptr(Seg(CurMCB^)+1, 0));      { Pointer in RAM }
    while ( (Z<=7) and (ord(ComSpec[Z]) = MemPtr^[Z]) ) do
```

```
    Inc(Z);                        { Set Z at the next character }
    if Z>7 then                              { String found? }
      begin                         { Yes --> Handle as an environment }
        writeln('Environment');
        MemPtr := RngPtr(ptr(Seg(CurMCB^)+1, 0));
        if Lo(DosVersion) >= 3 then    { DOS Version 3.0 or higher? }
          begin                        { Yes --> List program name }
            write('Program name   = ');
            Z := 0;                        { Start with the first byte }
            while not( (MemPtr^[Z]=0) and (MemPtr^[Z+1]=0) ) do
              Inc( Z );                    { Search for null string }
            if ( MemPtr^[Z+2]=1 ) and ( MemPtr^[Z+3]=0 ) then
              begin                          { Program name found }
                Z := Z + 4; { Place Z at first character of prg. name }
                repeat                        { Show program names }
                  write( chr(MemPtr^[Z]) );     { Display character }
                  Inc( Z );                  { Process next character }
                until ( MemPtr^[Z]=0 );      { until end of string }
                writeln;
              end
            else                        { No program name found }
              writeln('Unknown');
          end;

    {*-- Display environment string -----------------------------*}

        writeln(#13,#10, 'Environment string');
        Z := 0;                    { Start with first byte in allocated range }
        while MemPtr^[Z]<>0 do          { Repeat until null string }
          begin
            write('        ');
            repeat                          { Display string }
              write( chr(MemPtr^[Z]) );       { Display a character }
              Inc( Z );                  { Process next character }
            until MemPtr^[Z]=0;          { until end of string }
            Inc( Z );                  { Set to start of next string }
            writeln;                          { End line }
          end
      end
    else                              { No environment }
      begin

    {*-- Handle it as a PSP? ---------------------------------------*}
    {*-- (If INT 20 (Code=$CD $20) starts the code) -------------*}

        MemPtr := RngPtr(ptr(seg(CurMCB^)+1, 0));      { Set pointer }
        if ( (MemPtr^[0]=$CD) and (MemPtr^[1]=$20) ) then
          begin                              { Handled as a PSP }
            writeln('PSP (with program following)');
          end
        else                    { INT 20H could not be implemented }
          begin
            writeln('Unidentifiable as program or data');
            Dump( MemPtr, 5);            { Dump the first 5x16 bytes }
          end;
      end;

    write('=======================================');
    writeln('========= Please press a key ===');
    if ( not EndIt ) then
      begin                        { Set pointer to the next MCB }
        CurMCB := MCBPtr(ptr(seg(CurMCB^) + CurMCB^.Spacing + 1, 0));
        Inc(NrMCB);                { Increment the number of MCBs }
```

```
    PdKey := ReadKey;
   end;
  until { EndIt }          { Repeat until the last MCB is processed }
end;

{*****************************************************************}
{**                    MAIN PROGRAM                           **}
{*****************************************************************}

begin
 ClrScr;                                        { Clear screen }
 writeln( 'MCBP  -  (c) 1988, 92 by Michael Tischer' );
 writeln;
 writeln;
 TraceMCB;                                   { Display MCB group }
end.
```

Listing: MCBC.C

```
/**************************************************************/
/*                    M C B C . C                           */
/*----------------------------------------------------------*/
/*    Task         : Displays any memory block allocated by DOS. */
/*----------------------------------------------------------*/
/*    Author       : Michael Tischer                        */
/*    Developed on : 08/23.88                               */
/*    Last update  : 01/29/92                               */
/*----------------------------------------------------------*/
/*    Memory model : SMALL                                  */
/*    Info         : When compiling with Microsoft C, use   */
/*                   CL /AS /Zp MCBC.C                       */
/**************************************************************/

/*== Add include files =====================================*/

#include <dos.h>
#include <stdlib.h>

/*== Type definitions ======================================*/

typedef unsigned char BYTE;                    /* Create a byte */
typedef unsigned int WORD;
typedef BYTE BOOLEAN;
typedef BYTE far *FB;                        /* FAR pointer to a byte */

/*== Constants =============================================*/

#define TRUE  ( 0 == 0 )      /* Needed when working with BOOLEANs */
#define FALSE ( 1 == 0 )

/*== Structures and unions =================================*/

struct MCB {                        /* Describes an MCB in memory */
             BYTE id_code;          /* 'M' = block follows, 'Z' = end */
             WORD psp;              /* Segment address of appropriate PSP */
             WORD spacing;           /* Number of reserved paragraphs */
           };

typedef struct MCB far *MCBPtr;            /* FAR pointer to an MCB */

/*== Macros ================================================*/

#ifdef MK_FP                          /* Is MK_FP already defined? */
  #undef MK_FP
#endif

#define MK_FP(seg, ofs) ((void far *) ((unsigned long) (seg)<<16|(ofs)))

/**************************************************************
* Function       : F I R S T _ M C B                        *
**----------------------------------------------------------**
* Task           : Returns a pointer to the first MCB.      *
* Input          : None                                     *
* Output         : Pointer to the first MCB                 *
**************************************************************/

MCBPtr first_mcb( void )
{
 union REGS   regs;                /* Store the processor registers */
 struct SREGS sregs;                  /* Store the segment register */
```

```
regs.h.ah = 0x52;          /* Func. no.: Get DOS info block's address */
intdosx( &regs, &regs, &sregs );          /* Call DOS interrupt 21H */

/*-- ES:(BX-4) points to the first MCB, create pointer -------------*/

return( *((MCBPtr far *) MK_FP( sregs.es-1, regs.x.bx+12 )) );
}

/**************************************************************
* Function        : D U M P                                 *
**--------------------------------------------------------**
* Task            : Display a memory range as hex and ASCII dumps.  *
* Input           : DPTR : Pointer to the memory range to be dumped *
*                   NUML : Number of 16-byte lines to be dumped     *
* Output          : None                                           *
**************************************************************/

void dump( FB dptr, BYTE numl)
{
FB    lptr;               /* Floating pointer for dump line display */
WORD offset;                 /* Offset address relative to dptr */
BYTE  i;                            /* Loop counter */

printf("\nDUMP | 0123456789ABCDEF        00 01 02 03 04 05 06 07 08");
printf(" 09 0A 0B 0C 0D 0E 0F\n");

printf("----+------------------------------------");
printf("--------------------\n");

for (offset=0;  numl-- ; offset += 16, dptr += 16)
  {                                /* Execute loop numl times */
   printf("%04x | ", offset);
   for (lptr=dptr, i=16; i-- ; ++lptr) /* Display character as ASCII */
    printf("%c", (*lptr<32) ? ' ' : *lptr);
   printf("      ");
   for (lptr=dptr, i=16; i-- ; )      /* Display character as hex */
    printf("%02X ", *lptr++);
   printf("\n");                        /* Move to next line */
  }
}


/**************************************************************
* Function        : T R A C E _ M C B                       *
**--------------------------------------------------------**
* Task            : Displays list of MCBs.                  *
* Input           : None                                    *
* Output          : None                                    *
**************************************************************/

void trace_mcb( void )
{
static char fenv[] = {           /* First environment string */
                 'C', 'O', 'M', 'S', 'P', 'E', 'C', '='
                    };

MCBPtr  cur_mcb;                  /* Pointer to the first current MCB */
BOOLEAN endit;                    /* TRUE when the last MCB is found */
BYTE    nr_mcb,                  /* Number of MCBs currently processed */
        i;                             /* Loop variable */
FB      lptr;                     /* Floating pointer to environment */

endit = FALSE;                       /* Continue looping */
nr_mcb = 1;                     /* Assign the first MCB the number 1 */
cur_mcb = first_mcb();               /* Get pointer to the first MCB */
```

```
do                                  /* Process individual MCBs */
{
  if ( cur_mcb->id_code == 'Z' )         /* Last MCB reached? */
   endit = TRUE;                            /* Yes */
  printf("MCB number       = %d\n", nr_mcb++);
  printf("MCB address      = %Fp\n", cur_mcb);
  printf("Memory address   = %Np:0000\n", FP_SEG(cur_mcb)+1);
  printf("ID               = %c\n", cur_mcb->id_code);
  printf("PSP address      = %Fp\n", (FB) MK_FP(cur_mcb->psp, 0) );
  printf("Size             = %u paragraphs ( %lu bytes )\n",
       cur_mcb->spacing, (unsigned long) cur_mcb->spacing << 4);
  printf("Contents         = ");

/*-- Handle MCB as an environment? -------------------------------*/

for (i=0, lptr=(FB)cur_mcb+16;  /* Compare 1st ENV string w/ FENV */
     ( i<sizeof fenv ) && ( *(lptr++) == fenv[i++] ) ; )
   ;
if ( i == sizeof fenv )                    /* String found? */
  {                             /* Yes --> Handle as an environment */
   printf("Environment\n");
   if ( _osmajor >= 3 )              /* DOS Version 3.0 or higher? */
    {                              /* Yes --> List program name */
     printf("Program name    = ");
     for ( ; !(*(lptr++)==0 && *lptr==0) ; )
      ;                            /* Search for last ENV string */
     if ( *(int far *)(lptr + 1) == 1 )
      {                              /* Program name found */
       for ( lptr += 3; *lptr ; )      /* Show program names */
        printf( "%c", *(lptr++) );      /* Display character */
      }
     else                             /* No program name found */
      printf("Unknown");
     printf("\n");                       /* Move to next line */
    }

/*-- Display environment string -----------------------------*/

   printf("Environment string\n");
   for (lptr=(FB) cur_mcb +16; *lptr ; ++lptr)
    {                                      /* Display string */
     printf("          ");
     for ( ; *lptr ; )      /* Display until null character occurs */
      printf( "%c", *(lptr++) );       /* Display as a character */
     printf("\n");                        /* Move to next line */
    }
  }
 else                                     /* No environment */
  {

/*- Handle it as a PSP? -------------------------------------*/
/*-- (If INT 20 (Code=0xCD 0x20) starts the code) ------------*/

   if (*((unsigned far *) MK_FP( cur_mcb->psp, 0 )) == 0x20cd)
    printf("PSP (with program following)\n");              /* Yes */
   else                        /* INT 20H could not be implemented */
    {
     printf("Unidentifiable as program or data\n");
     dump( (FB) cur_mcb + 16, 5);     /* Dump the dirst 5x16 bytes */
    }
  }

printf("=================================");
printf("============ Please press a key ===\n");
```

```
if ( !endit )                              /* Any more MCBs? */
  {                                /* Yes --> Set pointer to the next MCB */
  cur_mcb = (MCBPtr)
              MK_FP( FP_SEG(cur_mcb) + cur_mcb->spacing + 1, 0 );
  getch();                              /* Wait for a keypress */
  }
}
while ( !endit );       /* Repeat until the last MCB is processed */
}


/***************************************************************************/
/**                     MAIN PROGRAM                              **/
/***************************************************************************/

void main( void )
{
printf("\nMCBC (c) 1988, 92 by Michael Tischer\n\n");
trace_mcb();                              /* Display MCB group */
}
```

Listing: MCBB.BAS

```
'*************************************************************************
'*                          M C B B . B A S                            *
'*---------------------------------------------------------------------
'*   Task        : Displays any memory block allocated by DOS.          *
'*                 QuickBASIC and the QB.LIB must be loaded using       *
'*                 QB /L QB                                             *
'*                 before loading and running this file.                *
'*---------------------------------------------------------------------
'*   Author      : Michael Tischer                                      *
'*   Developed on : 05/16/91                                            *
'*   Last update : 01/10/92                                             *
'*************************************************************************
DECLARE SUB TraceMCB ()
DECLARE SUB FirstMCB (Adr AS ANY)
DECLARE SUB Dump (Adr AS ANY, Nmb%)
DECLARE FUNCTION HexByte$ (HByte%)
DECLARE FUNCTION GetDosVer% ()
DECLARE FUNCTION GetWord& (SegAdr AS LONG, OfsAdr AS LONG)
DECLARE FUNCTION HexString$ (HexVal&)


   '$INCLUDE: 'qb.bi'                              'Include QB file


CONST TRUE = -1                              'Define truth
CONST FALSE = NOT TRUE


TYPE AdrType                              'Pointer to an address
  OfsAdr AS LONG                              'Offset address
  SegAdr AS LONG                              'Segment address
END TYPE
CLS                                          'Clear screen
PRINT "MCBB  -  (c) 1988, 91 by Michael Tischer": PRINT : PRINT
CALL TraceMCB                              'Display MCB group
END


'*************************************************************************
'* DUMP    : Display a memory range as hex and ASCII dumps.            *
'* Input   : SegAdr = Segment address of memory range to be dumped     *
'*           Nmb    = Number of lines to be dumped (in 16 byte units)  *
'* Output  : None                                                      *
'*************************************************************************
SUB Dump (SegAdr AS LONG, Nmb AS INTEGER)

DIM HexStr AS STRING * 2                   'Get 2-digit hex number
DIM Offset AS LONG                         'Offset in memory range

HexStr = "zz"                              'Create hex string
PRINT
PRINT "DUMP | 0123456789ABCDEF      00 01 02 03 ";
PRINT "04 05 06 07 08 09 0A 0B 0C 0D 0E 0F"
PRINT "----+------------------------------------";
PRINT "--------------------------------"
Offset = 0                                 'Start with the first byte
DEF SEG = SegAdr                           'Define the segment address
WHILE Nmb > 0                              'Execute loop Nmb times
  PRINT HexString$(Offset); " | ";
  FOR z = 0 TO 15                          'Process every 16 bytes
    IF PEEK(Offset + z) >= 32 THEN         'Valid ASCII characters?
      PRINT CHR$(PEEK(Offset + z));             'Yes --> Display
    ELSE
      PRINT " ";                           'No --> Display spaces
    END IF
  NEXT
```

```
PRINT "     ";                        'Set cursor to hex portion
FOR z = 0 TO 15                       'Process every 16 characters
  PRINT HexByte$(PEEK(Offset + z)); " ";  'Display byte as hex string
NEXT
PRINT                                          'New line
Offset = Offset + 16                  'Set offset in the next line
Nmb = Nmb - 1                         'Decrement number of lines
WEND
PRINT
END SUB


'****************************************************************
'*  FirstMCB : Returns a pointer to the first MCB.             *
'*  Input    : None                                           *
'*  Output   : Pointer to first MCB in the MCBAdr variable    *
'****************************************************************
SUB FirstMCB (MCBAdr AS AdrType)

DIM Register AS RegTypeX        'Processor registers for interrupt call

Register.ax = &H52 * 256        'Func. No: Get DOS info block's address
CALL INTERRUPTX(&H21, Register, Register)       'Call DOS interrupt
'-- (ES:BX - &H4) = ES-1:12 returns pointer address to first MCB ------
DEF SEG = Register.es - 1               'Define segment address
MCBAdr.OfsAdr = PEEK(Register.bx + 13) * 256& + PEEK(Register.bx + 12)
MCBAdr.SegAdr = PEEK(Register.bx + 15) * 256& + PEEK(Register.bx + 14)
END SUB


'****************************************************************
'*  GetDosVer : Determines version of DOS in use.             *
'*  Input    : None                                           *
'*  Output   : DOS version number (30 = DOS 3.0, 33 = DOS 3.3, etc.) *
'****************************************************************
FUNCTION GetDosVer%

DIM Register AS RegType         'Processor registers for interrupt call

Register.ax = &H30 * 256                'AH = Funct. No: Get DOS version
CALL INTERRUPT(&H21, Register, Register)        'Call DOS interrupt 21H
GetDosVer = INT(Register.ax \ 256) + (Register.ax MOD 256) * 10
END FUNCTION


'****************************************************************
'*  Getword : Reads a word from a memory address as a long number. *
'*  Input    : SegAdr = Segment address of the word           *
'*             OfsAdr = Offset address of the word            *
'*  Output   : Contents of the word as a long number          *
'****************************************************************
FUNCTION GetWord& (SegAdr AS LONG, OfsAdr AS LONG)

DEF SEG = SegAdr                        'Set segment address
GetWord& = PEEK(OfsAdr + 1) * 256& + PEEK(OfsAdr)  'Read memory location
END FUNCTION


'****************************************************************
'*  Hexbyte : Converts a byte into a hexadecimal string.      *
'*  Input    : Hbyte = the byte                               *
'*  Output   : A string                                       *
'*  Info    : This replaces the HEX$ function, which doesn't  *
'*             consistently return two-digit hexadecimal numbers. *
'****************************************************************
FUNCTION HexByte$ (HByte AS INTEGER)

DIM HexSt AS STRING * 2                  'Get hex string
```

```
MID$(HexSt, 1, 1) = HEX$(HByte \ 16)                   'First digit
MID$(HexSt, 2, 1) = HEX$(HByte MOD 16)                 'Second digit
HexByte$ = HexSt                        'Return resulting string
END FUNCTION


'****************************************************************
'*  HexString : Converts a number into a hexadecimal string.   *
'*  Input    : Value to be converted                          *
'*  Output   : Resulting hex string                           *
'*  Info    : This replaces the HEX$ function, which doesn't   *
'*             consistently return two-digit hexadecimal numbers. *
'****************************************************************
FUNCTION HexString$ (HexValVar AS LONG)

DIM Nibble AS INTEGER                   'Lowest nibble of the word
DIM HexVal AS LONG                      ' Argument must be stored
                                        'with reference parameters
DIM HStr AS STRING * 4                  'The hex string to be converted

HexVal = HexValVar      'Store the argument of the word to be converted
HStr = "xxxx"                                   'Create string
FOR counter = 0 TO 3                            'Change four digits
  Nibble = HexVal AND &HF                       'Get upper four bits
  MID$(HStr, 4 - counter, 1) = HEX$(Nibble)   'Convert nibble into hex
  HexVal = HexVal \ 16   'Shift hex number right by four bit positions
NEXT
HexString$ = HStr                       'Pass resulting string
END FUNCTION


'****************************************************************
'*  TraceMCB : Display list of MCBs.                          *
'*  Input    : None                                           *
'*  Output   : None                                           *
'****************************************************************
SUB TraceMCB

CONST kom = "COMSPEC="          'Declare "COMSPEC=" as a constant

DIM CurMCB  AS AdrType                          'Pointer to MCB
DIM ID      AS STRING * 1       '"M" = block follows, "Z" = End
DIM PSP     AS LONG             'Segment address of corresponding PSP
DIM Spacing AS LONG                     'Number of paragraphs - 1
DIM MemPtr  AS LONG                             'Pointer in memory
DIM NrMCB   AS INTEGER                  'Number of MCBs available
DIM z       AS INTEGER                          'Loop counter
DIM EndIt   AS INTEGER                          'Cancel condition
DIM CurOfs  AS LONG

DosVer = GetDosVer                      'Get DOS version
NrMCB = 1                               'Start with first MCB
EndIt = FALSE
CALL FirstMCB(CurMCB)                   'Get pointer to first MCB
DO
  CurOfs = CurMCB.OfsAdr                        'Load offset address
  DEF SEG = CurMCB.SegAdr        'Define segment address for Peek()
  ID = CHR$(PEEK(CurOfs))                       'Read first MCB
  PSP = GetWord&(CurMCB.SegAdr, CurOfs + &H1)
  Spacing = GetWord&(CurMCB.SegAdr, CurOfs + &H3)

  IF ID = "Z" THEN                      'Last MCB read?
    EndIt = TRUE                'End loop - end retrieving new MCBs
  END IF
  PRINT "MCB number    ="; NrMCB
```

```
PRINT "MCB address     = "; HexString$(CurMCB.SegAdr); ":";
PRINT HexString$(CurOfs)
PRINT "Memory address = "; HexString$(CurMCB.SegAdr + 1); ":";
PRINT HexString$(CurOfs)
PRINT "ID              = "; ID
PRINT "PSP address     = "; HexString$(PSP); ":0000"
PRINT "Size            = "; HexString$(Spacing); " paragraphs ( ";
PRINT Spacing * 16; " bytes )"
PRINT "Contents        = ";

'---- Handle MCB as an environment? --------------------------------
z = 0                                   'Start comparison with first byte
MemPtr = CurMCB.SegAdr + 1                        'Pointer in RAM
DEF SEG = MemPtr                        'Set segment address for Peek()
WHILE (z <= 7) AND MID$(kom, z + 1, 1) = CHR$(PEEK(CurMCB.OfsAdr + z))
  z = z + 1                                          'next character
WEND
IF z > 7 THEN                           'COMSPEC = String found
  PRINT "Environment "
  IF DosVer > 30 THEN                   'DOS Version 3.0 or higher?
    PRINT "Program name   = ";          'Yes --> List program name
    z = 0                               'Start with first byte
    DO
      z = z + 1                         'Search for null string
    LOOP UNTIL PEEK(CurOfs + z) = 0 AND PEEK(CurOfs + z + 1) = 0
    IF PEEK(CurOfs + z + 2) = 1 AND PEEK(CurOfs + z + 3) = 0 THEN
      '--- Program name found ------------------------------------
      z = z + 4      'Place z at first character of the program name
      DO                                'Show program names
        PRINT CHR$(PEEK(CurOfs + z));       'Display character
        z = z + 1                           'Next character
      LOOP UNTIL PEEK(CurOfs + z) = 0       'until end of string
      PRINT
    ELSE                                'No program name found
      PRINT "Unknown"
    END IF
  END IF

'---- Display environment string ------------------------------------

  PRINT "Environment string:"
  z = 0                    'Start with first byte in allocated range
  WHILE PEEK(CurOfs + z) <> 0           'Repeat until null string
    PRINT "      ";                         'Indent line
    DO                                      'Display string
      PRINT CHR$(PEEK(CurOfs + z));         'Display character
      z = z + 1                             'Next character
    LOOP UNTIL PEEK(CurOfs + z) = 0     'Loop until end of string
    z = z + 1                           'Set to start of next string
    PRINT                               'End line
  WEND
ELSE
'---- Handle it as a PSP (if INT 20H  ------------------------------
'---- (code &HCD &H20) starts the code) ----------------------------

  MemPtr = CurMCB.SegAdr + 1                   'Set pointer in RAM
  IF PEEK(CurOfs) = &HCD AND PEEK(CurOfs + 1) = &H20 THEN
    PRINT "PSP (with program following)"       'Handled as a PSP
  ELSE                             'INT 20H could not be implemented
    PRINT "Unidentifiable as a program"
    CALL Dump(MemPtr, 5)                  'Dump the first 5*16 bytes
  END IF
END IF
```

```
PRINT "▬▬▬▬▬▬▬▬▬▬▬▬ Press any key to continue ▬▬▬▬▬";
PRINT "▬▬▬▬▬▬▬▬▬▬"
DO                                          'Wait for a key
a$ = INKEY$
LOOP UNTIL a$ <> ""
  IF NOT EndIt THEN                     'Still MCBs to be read?
    CurMCB.SegAdr = CurMCB.SegAdr + Spacing + 1    'Pointer to next MCB
    NrMCB = NrMCB + 1
  END IF
LOOP UNTIL EndIt                  'Loop until there are no more MCBs
END SUB
```

844

Chapter 23

The EXEC Function

We've briefly mentioned the EXEC function when discussing the command processor. In this chapter we'll closely examine the EXEC function and describe how it operates.

Parent/child

The EXEC function is one of the many DOS functions that can be called with interrupt 21H (function 4BH). This function allows a *parent program* (main program) to call a *child program* (secondary program). The child program is loaded from a mass storage device into memory and then executes. If this child program doesn't become resident, the memory occupied by the child is released following program execution. The child program can also call another program that works with the parent program. This creates a type of program chaining that's limited only by the amount of available RAM.

One example of the EXEC function is the command processor. Using the EXEC function, the command processor executes user-specified programs and becomes the parent program. Some programs (such as Microsoft Word®) permit the user to execute DOS commands from the main program using this function.

The parent program can pass parameters to the child program in the command line and can also pass parameters using the environment block. This program can also transfer information to the child program within the PSP. Since, like all executable programs, a PSP precedes the child program, information can be entered into the two FCBs within this PSP and made accessible to the child program.

Child program

When control is transferred to the child program, this program can access all the files and devices previously opened by the parent program (or one of the parent programs) with a handle function. This allows the child program to read information from a file or write information to a file whose handle is known (the child program doesn't need to know the filename). This is only possible if the handle was passed by the parent program in one of the three methods we described or if the child program refers to one of the five handles, which are always open. These file accesses affect the file pointer. Since values aren't reset, these file accesses become "visible" to the parent program when control returns to the parent program.

After the child program executes, control returns to the parent program and execution continues. To pass information (e.g., an error that occurred during the execution of the child program), the child program can pass a numeric value at the end of its execution. This can be done using DOS function 4CH, which terminates a program and returns a code to the parent program.

The communication between the parent and child programs works only if both programs agree on this return value. After control returns to the parent program, it can determine the code using function 4DH of interrupt 21H. To use function 4DH, only the function number is passed in the AH register. The code passed by the child program is returned to the calling (parent) program in the AL register.

Ending the child program

The contents of the AH register indicate how the child program terminated. The value 0 indicates a normal termination, while the value 1 indicates that the child program terminated when the user pressed <Control><C> or <Control><Break>. If an error during access to a mass storage device forced the child program to terminate, a code of 2 is passed in the AH register. The value 3 indicates that the child program terminated from a call to function 31H, or interrupt 27H; the child program then becomes resident in memory.

As we mentioned earlier, the EXEC function can load the child program only if sufficient memory is available. While DOS can estimate the memory needed for EXE programs fairly accurately, it cannot do the same for COM programs. For COM programs, DOS reserves all unused memory. Because of this, a COM program cannot call another program with the EXEC function because DOS doesn't reserve any extra memory. This also applies to many EXE programs. If a call to a child program is necessary, the required memory space must be released from the calling program before the EXEC function is called (refer to Sections 6.4.1 and 6.4.2 for explanations on how to do this).

EXEC

If the EXEC function is called, the various parameters are loaded into the registers before calling interrupt 21H. Function number 4BH is passed in the AH register. A value of 0 or 3 is passed in the AL register. A value of 0 indicates that the EXEC function will load and execute the program, while a value of 3 indicates that the program is loaded as an overlay (without executing it). The address of the name of the program to be loaded or executed is passed in the DS:DX register pair and the address of the *parameter block* is passed in the ES:BX register pair.

The program name is specified as an ASCII string and ends with a null character (ASCII code 0). This name can include the device name and a complete path description. Its last element is the program name that, besides the name itself, must have either the .COM or .EXE extension. If the device name or path designation are omitted, the system searches for the program in the current directory of the current device. Since the EXEC function cannot execute a batch file directly, the program name that's passed cannot contain the .BAT extension.

Batch child

If a batch file must be executed, first the COMMAND.COM (command processor) file must be invoked. To indicate that a batch file should be executed, the parameter /c, followed by the name of the appropriate batch file, is added to the command line. Calling the command processor with the /c parameter also enables you to call any other program and even internal DOS commands, such as DIR.

Besides directly calling a program, it's also possible to specify program names without file extensions during a command processor call. The command processor searches for an EXE file, then a COM file, and finally a BAT file. If none of these files exist in the current directory, it searches all directories specified in the PATH command. This procedure isn't used during a direct program call without the addition of the command processor.

The directory that contains the command processor should be specified. If it isn't specified, it will be loaded from the path indicated by the COMSPEC environment string of the SET command.

Parameter blocks

Parameters can be passed to the command processor in the parameter block following the program name. These are the same parameters that are entered from the keyboard when the program is called. Later we'll see how these parameters affect the EXEC function. However, first we must discuss the parameter block's structure when the AL register contains the value 0. This block's address is passed to the EXEC function in the register pair ES:BX.

1	0- 1	Segment address: Environment block
2	2- 3	Offset address: Command parameter
3	4- 5	Segment address: Command parameter
4	6- 7	Offset address: First FCB
5	8- 9	Segment address: First FCB
6	10-11	Offset address: Second FCB
7	12-13	Segment address: Second FCB

Field 1 indicates the segment address of the child program's environment block. This block doesn't require an offset address because it always starts at a location divisible by 16. So, its offset address is always 0.

Environment block

The command processor and other programs obtain information from the environment block. This is a series of ASCII character strings. This information can include paths for file searches. Each string has the following syntax, which ends in a null character (ASCII code 0):

```
Name = Parameter
```

The individual strings follow each other sequentially (i.e., the null character of one string is immediately followed by the first character of the next string). Environment blocks can have a maximum length of 32K.

The user can change the environment block by using the DOS SET and PATH commands. Programs that remain resident after execution are unaffected by any changes made to the environment block through these two DOS commands.

If the parent program wants to pass information to the child program using the environment block, it can either construct a new environment block or add the appropriate information to its own environment block. In the first instance, the segment address of the new environment block is specified in the first field of the parameter block. If the child program should have access to the environment block of the parent program, specify a value of 0 in this field. Before turning over control to the child program, the EXEC function stores the segment address of the environment block in the memory location at address 2CH of the child program's PSP.

If the child program must use a new environment block, it should contain at least 3 strings that are usually part of the environment block of the parent program and are important to the command processor:

```
COMSPEC = Parameter
PATH = Parameter
PROMPT = Parameter
```

If a child program modifies its environment block, the parent program's environment block remains unchanged after the child program completes its execution.

Fields 2 and 3 indicate the command parameters' address that is passed to the PSP of the program starting at address 80H. These fields must have the same structure in memory as expected by DOS in the PSP. The first byte indicates the number of command characters minus 1. This is followed by the command characters as normal ASCII codes. The command parameters terminate with a carriage return (ASCII code 13), which isn't included in the character count. For compatibility with COMMAND.COM, the first character in the string should be a space.

To call a batch program (called DO.BAT) using the command processor, the following command parameters must be specified as a string in memory:

```
DB 10, " /C DO.BAT", 13
```

The EXEC function copies the command parameters into the PSP of the program to be executed. It also removes all the parameters that would redirect the input or output, because a redirection of the standard input/output can only be performed by the parent program. The child program can still use input/output redirection if the standard input/output handles have been redirected by the parent program. (See Chapter 18 for more information and an example of this process.)

Fields 6, 7, 10, and 11 indicate two FCBs installed in the PSP at address 5CH or 6CH. If this isn't required, specify -1 (FFFFH) in these two fields. However, if this is needed for program execution, enter the first two command parameters in the two FCBs with DOS function 29H. Before passing control to the child program, the EXEC function copies these two FCBs into the PSP of the child program.

Even though all the registers and the parameter block now have the required values, the EXEC function cannot be called yet. Since this function destroys the contents of all registers up to the CS and IP registers during execution, the contents of all the registers must be placed on the stack before this function is activated. Then the contents of the SS and SP registers must be stored

848

within the code segment. Only then can interrupt 21H function 4BH be called to activate the EXEC function. After the EXEC function ends, the carry flag indicates whether the function executed normally. Before program execution can continue, the value of the SS and SP registers must be restored from the code segment. Then the contents of the other register can be restored again from the stack.

The EXEC function performs a different task when a value of 3 appears in the AL register. In this case, it loads a COM program or an EXE program into memory without executing. After the target program is loaded, control immediately returns to the calling program. Unlike subfunction 0, the program loads to a memory address indicated by the calling program instead of loading to any non-specific location. Since parameters aren't passed to the loaded program, the parameter block has a different structure during the call of subfunction 3 than during the call of subfunction 0:

Field	Byte	Purpose
1	0- 1	Segment address where overlay is located
2	2- 3	Relocation factor

Before the function is called, the segment address to which the program should be loaded is specified in the first field of the parameter block. If the calling program doesn't have enough memory available for loading the external program, it should request additional memory with one of the DOS memory management functions. The loaded program loads directly to the segment address indicated with the offset address 0 because a PSP doesn't precede the program.

Relocation

The *relocation factor* adjusts the segment address of the called program. Since this factor applies only to EXE programs (COM programs cannot have specific segment assignments), the relocation factor for COM programs should always equal 0. The relocation factor for EXE programs should indicate the segment address where the program will be loaded to conform to the program's segment assignments.

After the program is loaded, its routines are ready to be accessed. The routines of the loaded program should always be treated as subroutines (i.e., called with the machine language CALL instruction). It must always be a FAR type instruction even though the loaded program may be located immediately after the calling program, but it can never have the same segment address.

The offset address for CALL is always 100H for a COM program because execution always starts immediately after the PSP at address 100H. However, this creates a problem. Subfunction 3 prevents the PSP from loading. So, the code segment of the COM program starts at address 0, instead of at the offset address 100H (relative to the load segment). Since all jump instructions and accesses to data within the COM program are relative to address 100H instead of address 0, you cannot execute a FAR CALL instruction with the address of the load segment as the segment address, and address 0 as the offset address. The segment address for the FAR CALL must indicate the address of the load segment minus 10H and the address 100H as the offset address.

If the COM program specifically acts as an overlay for another program, entry addresses other than address 100H are possible. In this case, only the offset address for the FAR CALL instruction changes. The segment address must remain 10H smaller than the address of the load segment.

EXEC and memory

The problem is different for EXE programs. If these programs are loaded for execution using subfunction 0, the EXEC function sets the code segment and the instruction pointer to the instruction that was declared as the first instruction in the assembler source. However, this address is unknown to the program that loaded the EXE program as an overlay. This problem can easily be solved by placing the first executable instruction in the EXE program at the beginning of the EXE program. This makes its offset address 0. The EXE program source must not be in the normal sequence with the stack first. In this case, the code segment must be the first segment in the source to ensure that it begins the EXE program.

The FAR CALL uses the address of the load segment as the segment address, and address 0 as the offset address.

Demonstration program

While BASIC, Pascal, and C have commands or procedures to call a program from another program, assembly language routines must use DOS function 4BH. The following is an example program that should help you understand this function.

The framework of the EXE program listed in Chapter 17 acts as the basis for this program. The EXEPRG procedure performs the actual work. This procedure calls the new program using function 4BH. Two strings, which contain the name of the program to be called and the necessary parameters, are passed to it. Both strings end with the null character (ASCII code 0). All the variables EXEPRG needs for execution are located in the code segment.

The advantage of this method is that, in order to use this routine, the lines from the code segment must be copied into only one of the application programs. After calling EXEPRG, the carry flag signals whether an error occurred. If true (carry flag=1), the AX register contains the error code as returned by the EXEC function of DOS. If the called program executed correctly, the carry flag is reset (0) and the termination code of the called program, as returned by DOS function 4DH, is returned by the AX register.

Within this program, EXEPRG displays the current directory using the command processor. The command processor defaults to the current directory of the current device.

Assembler listing: EXEC.ASM

```
;*****************************************************************;
;                         E X E C                              *;
;*-------------------------------------------------------------*;
;*   Task       :   Calls a program using the DOS EXEC function. *;
;*                  This demonstration program displays the      *;
;*                  current device's directory contents.         *;
;*-------------------------------------------------------------*;
;*   Author     :   Michael Tischer                            *;
;*   Developed on :  08/01/87                                   *;
;*   Last update :   01/06/92                                   *;
;*-------------------------------------------------------------*;
;*   Assembly    :  MASM EXEC;                                  *;
;*                  LINK EXEC;                                  *;
;*                      or                                     *;
;*                  TASM EXEC                                   *;
;*                  TLINK EXEC                                  *;
;*-------------------------------------------------------------*;
;*   Call        :  EXEC                                       *;
;*****************************************************************;

;== data ========================================================

data      segment para 'DATA'    ;Definition of data segment

prgname   db "\command.com",0    ;Name of the program to be called
prgpara   db "/c dir",0          ;Parameters passed to program

          ;-- Messages used by this program --------------------

startmes  db " EXEC  -  (c) 1987,92 by Michael Tischer "
          db 13,10,"$"
mesok     db "OK",13,10,"$"
mesnotf   db "Error: COMMAND.COM not found",13,10,"$"
meselse   db "Error: DOS error code = "
mescode   db "    ",13,10,"$"

data      ends                   ;end of data segment

;== code ========================================================

code      segment para 'CODE'    ;Definition of CODE segment

          assume cs:code, ds:data, ss:stackseg

exec      proc far

          mov  ax,data           ;Load data segment's segment address
          mov  ds,ax             ;into the DS register

          mov  ah,09h            ;Display startup message
          mov  dx,offset startmes
          int 21h

          call setfree           ;release unused memory

          mov  dx,offset prgname ;Offset address of program name
          mov  si,offset prgpara ;Offset address of command line
          call exeprg            ;Call program

          mov  dx,offset mesok   ;Display if execution is error free
          jnc  ex_mes            ;No error --> Display message
```

```
          mov  dx,offset mesnotf ;Program may not be available
          cmp  al,2              ;Is this the case?
          je   ex_mes            ;Yes --> Display message

          xor  ah,ah             ;High byte of error code
          mov  si,offset mescode+2;Error code in ASCII
          call toint

          mov  dx,offset meselse
ex_mes:   mov  ah,09h            ;Display string in DOS
          int 21h

          mov  ax,4C00h          ;End program with DOS function call
          int 21h               ;on return of error code 0
exec      endp

;-- SETFREE: Releases unused memory -----------------------------
;-- Input   : ES = address of PSP
;-- Output  : none
;-- Registers : AX, BX, CL and FLAGS are affected
;-- Info    : Since the stack segment is always the last segment in
;             an EXE file, ES:0000 points to the beginning and SS:SP
;             to the end of the program in memory. Through this the
;             program's length can be calculated

setfree   proc near

          mov  bx,ss             ;Subtract the segment addresses from
          mov  ax,es             ;each other (result = the number of
          sub  bx,ax             ;paragraphs from PSP to the beginning
                                 ;of stack)
          mov  ax,sp             ;Since the stack pointer is at the
          mov  cl,4              ;end of the stack segment, its
          shr  ax,cl             ;contents indicate the stack length
          add  bx,ax             ;Add to current length
          inc  bx                ;Add another paragraph to be safe

          mov  ah,4ah            ;Pass new length to DOS
          int 21h

          ret                    ;Return to caller

setfree   endp

;-- EXEPRG: calls another program -------------------------------
;-- Input   : DS:DX = Address of the program name
;--                   DS:SI = Address of the command line
;-- Output  : Carry flag = 1: Error (AX = error code)
;-- Registers : AX and FLAGS are affected
;-- Info    : Program name and command line must be ASCII strings
;--                   terminated with ASCII code 0

exeprg    proc near

          ;Send command line to its own buffer and count characters ----

          push bx                ;Store all registers which are
          push cx                ;destroyed by the call to the
          push dx                ;DOS EXEC function
          push di
          push si
          push bp
          push ds
          push es
```

```
          mov  di,offset comline+1 ;Addresses of chars in command line
          push cs                  ;CS to stack
          pop  es                  ;Back as ES
          xor  bl,bl               ;Set character count to 0
copypara: lodsb                    ;Read a character
          or   al,al               ;Is it a null code (end)?
          je   copyend             ;Yes --> End copy process
          stosb                    ;Store in new buffer
          inc  bl                  ;Increment character count
          cmp  bl,126              ;Maximum reached?
          jne  copypara            ;No --> Continue

copyend:  mov  cs:comline,bl       ;Store number of characters
          mov  byte ptr es:[di],13 ;Finish command line

          mov  cs:merkss,ss        ;SS and SP must be stored in
          mov  cs:merksp,sp        ;variables in code segment

          mov  bx,offset parblock  ;ES:BX points to parameter block
          mov  ax,4B00h            ;Function number for EXEC function
          int  21h                 ;Call DOS function

          cli                      ;Momentarily set stack segment and
          mov  ss,cs:merkss        ;stack pointer interrupts to their
          mov  sp,cs:merksp        ;original values
          sti                      ;Re-enable interrupt

          pop  es                  ;Get all registers from stack again
          pop  ds
          pop  bp
          pop  si
          pop  di
          pop  dx
          pop  cx
          pop  bx

          jc   exeend              ;Errors? Yes --> End
          mov  ah,4dh              ;No errors, find end code of the
          int  21h                 ;program which was executed

exeend:   ret                      ;back to caller

          ;-- Variables of this routine only addressable through CS ----

merkss    dw (?)                   ;Accepts SS during program call
merksp    dw (?)                   ;Accepts SP during program call
parblock  equ this word            ;Parameter block for EXEC function
          dw 0                     ;Environment block
          dw offset comline        ;Offset and segment address of
          dw seg code              ;modified command line
          dd 0                     ;No data in PSP #1
          dd 0                     ;No data in PSP #2

comline   db 128 dup (?)           ;Accepts modified command line

exeprg    endp

;-- TOINT: Converts a binary number into an ASCII number and places ---
;--        this number in the caller's buffer right-justified
;-- Input   : DS:DI = Pointer to the position at which the least
;--                   significant number should be located
;--           AX    = Binary number to be converted
;-- Output  : DS:SI = Pointer to the most significant number
```

```
;-- Registers : AX, BX, DX, SI and FLAGS are affected
;-- Info      : - Buffer requires a minimum of five characters
;--              - Number is right-justified in the buffer

toint   proc near

        ;-- A loop divides the number by 10, converts the least
        ;-- significant place into ASCII format and places the
        ;-- result in the buffer

        mov  bx,10              ;Divisor is always 10
        jmp  short ti2

ti1:    dec  si                ;SI to next character

ti2:    xor  dx,dx             ;Dividend is DX:AX
        div  bx                ;Divide DX:AX by 10
        or   dl,'0'            ;Convert DL to ASCII format
        mov  [si],dl           ;Place in buffer
        or   ax,ax             ;Is there a remainder?
        jne  ti1               ;Yes --> Next digit

        ret                    ;Return to caller

toint   endp

;== stack =============================================================

        ;--- Stack segment is placed here at the end of the file,
        ;--- to ensure configuration after data and code segments
        ;--- are placed in memory

stackseg segment para stack 'STACK' ;Definition of stack segment

        dw 256 dup (?)         ;Stack is comprised of 256 words

stackseg ends                  ;End stack segment

;== End ===============================================================

code    ends                   ;End CODE segment
        end  exec              ;To re-execute start with EXEC
```

Chapter 24

<Ctrl><Break> and Critical Error Interrupts

In DOS, there are two ways to stop a program during execution. This occurs when the user presses <Ctrl><Break> (<Ctrl><C>) or when a *critical error* occurs during access to an external device (i.e., printer, hard disk, disk drive, etc.). Although the key combination that's used depends on the PC configuration, we'll use <Ctrl><Break> in this section.

<Ctrl><Break>

Pressing <Ctrl><Break> to stop a program during execution can have serious consequences. After the user presses this key combination, DOS abruptly takes control from the program without allowing the program to perform any necessary "housekeeping". For example, files aren't closed properly, diverted interrupt vectors aren't reset, and allocated memory isn't released. This can result in data loss and/or a system crash.

To prevent this from happening, DOS calls interrupt 23H, which is also known as the <Ctrl><Break> interrupt. When a program is started, this interrupt points to a routine that causes the program to end. However, a program is able to select a routine of its own, which enables the program to maintain control of what occurs when the user presses <Ctrl><Break>.

However, the interrupt routine doesn't execute immediately. Instead, the break flag determines when this routine occurs. This flag can be set at the DOS prompt using the BREAK (ON/OFF) command from DOS, or with the help of DOS function 33H, subfunction 1. If the break flag is on, every time a function of DOS interrupt 21H is called, the keyboard buffer will be checked to see if either <Ctrl><Break> or <Ctrl><C> has been pressed. If the break flag is off, this check will be performed only when calling the DOS functions that access the standard input and output devices.

If this test finds the appropriate key combination, the processor registers are loaded with the values contained in the DOS function to be executed. Interrupt 23H is called only after this occurs.

If a program directs this interrupt to a routine of its own, several things may occur. For example, the program could display a window on the screen that asks whether the user wants to end the program. The program can also decide for itself whether the program should end.

Maintenance

If the program chooses to stop execution, some type of clean-up routine should be performed. This type of routine closes all open files, resets any changed interrupt pointers, and releases any allocated memory. After this, function 4CH can end the program without returning control to the interrupt 23H caller.

The IRET assembly language instruction must return control to DOS if <Ctrl><Break> should be ignored. The program must then ensure that all processor registers contain the same values they had when interrupt 23H was invoked. Otherwise, the DOS function that was originally called cannot be performed without an error.

We'll demonstrate both of these methods in an example at the end of this section.

Critical error interrupt

Unlike the <Ctrl><Break> interrupt, the critical error interrupt call usually isn't a reaction to something the user does intentionally. Instead, it's usually a reaction to an error that occurs when accessing an external device, such as a printer, disk drive, or hard disk. Although the user can correct the error in many cases (e.g., the printer isn't switched on), other errors can be caused by hardware failures that require repairs (e.g., read error while accessing the hard disk).

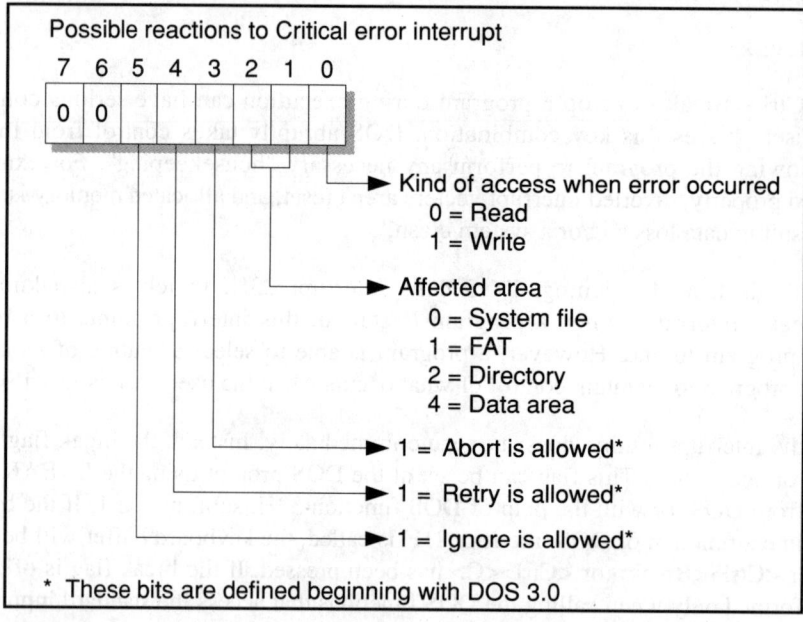

To make allowances for the various kinds of errors, the critical error interrupt (interrupt 24H) usually points to a DOS routine that displays the following or a similar message on the screen and waits for input from the user:

```
(A)bort (R)etry (I)gnore (F)ail
```

This clears the currently executing program from the screen. Similar to <Ctrl><Break>, this interrupt ends the program abruptly. So, the files aren't properly closed, allocated memory isn't released, etc.

Installing an interrupt handler in a program to replace the DOS handler can help. DOS uses a processor register to pass this handler various information when it's called. This helps the interrupt handler locate the source of the error. Bit 7 in the AH register indicates either a floppy or hard disk access error (bit 7 off) or some other error (bit 7 on). The other bits give information about the reaction to possible error codes.

Also, the BP:SI register pair points to the head of the device driver that was being called when the error appeared. A detailed error code is contained in the lower 8 bits of the DI register and the contents of the upper 8 bits are undefined. This returns the following error codes:

```
┌─────────────────────────────────────────────────────────┐
│ Error codes passed to the critical error handler        │
├──────┬──────────────────────────────────────────────────┤
│ Code │ Meaning                                          │
├──────┼──────────────────────────────────────────────────┤
│ 00h  │ Disk is write protected                          │
│ 01h  │ Access to an unknown device                      │
│ 02h  │ Drive not ready                                  │
│ 03h  │ Unknown command                                  │
│ 04h  │ CRC error                                        │
│ 05h  │ Wrong data length                                │
│ 06h  │ Seek error                                       │
│ 07h  │ Unknown device type                              │
│ 08h  │ Sector not found                                 │
│ 09h  │ Printer out of paper                             │
│ 0Ah  │ Write error                                      │
│ 0Bh  │ Read error                                       │
│ 0Ch  │ General error                                    │
└──────┴──────────────────────────────────────────────────┘
```

When called, the critical error handler can respond by opening a window on the screen that asks the user to decide to ignore the error, retry the access, or abort the program. The last option can only instruct the interrupt to call DOS functions 01H to 0CH. This means that the program ends abruptly, similar to pressing <Ctrl><Break>.

Although calling other DOS functions within the handler doesn't cause errors itself, the return to DOS causes a system crash. These handlers also aren't allowed to end a program by using DOS function 4CH. Instead, the handler must return to its caller with the help of the IRET command. With that, DOS expects a code in the AL register that will show it how to react to the error. It interprets the contents of the AL register as follows:

```
┌─────────────────────────────────────────────────────────┐
│ Output codes of a critical error handler                │
├──────┬──────────────────────────────────────────────────┤
│ Code │ Meaning                                          │
├──────┼──────────────────────────────────────────────────┤
│ 00h  │ Ignore error                                     │
│ 01h  │ Retry operation                                  │
│ 02h  │ End program with interrupt 23H                   │
│ 03h  │ End function called with error (DOS 3.0 and up)  │
└──────┴──────────────────────────────────────────────────┘
```

The last output code in the previous list represents the most sensible reaction to an error that can't be fixed by repeating the operation (e.g., when the printer must be switched on). The receipt of this code invokes the normal ending of the function call, in which the error occurred. The function then sets the carry flag to signal the error. While this makes a "critical" error and a "normal" error indistinguishable to the program, it's possible to distinguish them by setting a flag within the critical error handler.

Assembler listing: CEBHAND.ASM

```
;A°***************************************************************;
;*                      C E B H A N D                           *;
;*-------------------------------------------------------------*;
;*   Task       : Forms the basic structure of an assembler     *;
;*                program, in which the DOS Ctrl-Break and       *;
;*                Critical Error interrupt are captured.         *;
;*-------------------------------------------------------------*;
;*   Author     : Michael Tischer                               *;
;*   Developed on : 09/05/88                                    *;
;*   Last update : 01/24/92                                     *;
;*-------------------------------------------------------------*;
;*   Assembly   : MASM CEBHAND;                                 *;
;*                LINK CEBHAND;                                 *;
;*                            or                                *;
;*                TASM CEBHAND                                  *;
;*                TLINK CEBHAND                                 *;
;*-------------------------------------------------------------*;
;*   call       : CEBHAND                                       *;
;*                (Please leave the disk drive open so that a   *;
;*                Critical Error occurs.)                       *;
;***************************************************************;

;== Constants =============================================

;== Stack =================================================

stackseg  segment para stack 'STACK' ;Define stack segment
          dw 256 dup (?)          ;The stack is 256 words
stackseg  ends                    ;End of stack segment

;== Data ==================================================

data      segment para 'DATA'     ;Define data segment

cr_err    db 0                    ;Becomes 1 if a critical error occurs
                                  ;during access to a peripheral device
                                  ;(floppy, hard disk, or printer)
cr_typ    db 0                    ;Error number of the critical error

cr_mes    db "Critical error! (A)bort or (R)etry: $"
next_line db 13,10,"$"
end_mes   db "Program ended normally.$"
brk_mes   db "Program aborted.$"

dat_nam   db "A:TEST.DAT",0       ;Name of the test file

data      ends                    ;End of data segment

;== Code ==================================================

code      segment para 'CODE'     ;Define CODE segment
          assume cs:code, ds:data, ss:stackseg
```

```
start    proc far

;-- Install both interrupt handlers ------------------------

         push cs                  ;Push CS on the stack
         pop  ds                  ; and return as DS
         mov  ax,2523h            ;Funct.no.: Set Ctrl-Break handler
         mov  dx,offset cbreak    ;DS:DX now contains handler address
         int  21h                 ;Call DOS interrupt

         mov  al,24h              ;Set interrupt 24H
         mov  dx,offset cerror    ;DS:DX contains new handler address
         int  21h                 ;Call DOS interrupt

         mov  ax,data             ;Move data segment's segment address
         mov  ds,ax               ; to the DS register

;-- You can add your program here --------------------------
         ;
         ;

;-- For a demonstration, try to open a file ----------------
;-- on the opened disk drive            --------------

dat_open: mov ah,3dh              ;Function number: Open file
         mov  al,0                ;File mode: Read-only
         mov  dx,offset dat_nam   ;DS:DX = address of the filename
         int  21h                 ;Call DOS interrupt 21H
         jnc  exit                ;No error? No --> Jump to exit
         cmp  cr_err,0            ;Critical error?
         je   exit                ;No --> Jump to exit
         call crit_err            ;A critical error occurred
         jmp  dat_open            ;CRIT_ERR returns only if the
                                  ;operation should be retried
                                  ;(IGNORE is not possible)

;-- The handler must not be re-installed before the ---------
;-- end of the program, since this is done by DOS  ---------

exit:    mov  ah,9                ;Function number: Pass string
         mov  dx,offset end_mes   ;DS:DX = address of the message
         int  21h                 ;Call DOS interrupt
         mov  ax,4C00h            ;Funct. no.: End program (ERRCODE=0)
         int  21h                 ;Call DOS interrupt 21H
                                  ;and end the program
start    endp

;-- CRIT_ERR: Called within the program after discovery of a ---------
;--           critical error                                ---------

crit_err proc near

;-- Display message and ask for user input -----------------

ask:     mov  ah,9                ;Function number: Display string
```

```
        mov   dx,offset cr_mes    ;DS:DX = address of the message
        int   21h                ;Call DOS interrupt
        mov   ah,1               ;Function number: Input character
        int   21h                ;Call DOS interrupt
        push  ax                 ;Note the input
        mov   ah,9               ;Function number: Display string
        mov   dx,offset next_line;DS:DX = address of the message
        int   21h                ;Call DOS interrupt


        ;-- Interpret the user's input -----------------------------


        pop   ax                 ;Retrieve the input
        cmp   al,"A"             ;Abort?
        je    end_up             ;Go to "end_up" procedure
        cmp   al,"a"             ;Abort?
        je    end_up             ;Go to "end_up" procedure
        cmp   al,"r"             ;Retry?
        je    crend              ;Go to end of procedure
        cmp   al,"R"             ;Retry?
        jne   ask                ;No --> Ask again

crend:  ret                      ;Return to caller

crit_err endp

;-- END_UP: Executes a "clean" ending --------------------------------

end_up  proc near
        ;-- All opened files can be closed and the system      ----
        ;-- memory allocated by the program can be freed here  ----
                                 ;
                                 ;
                                 ;
        mov   ah,9               ;Function number: Display string
        mov   dx,offset brk_mes  ;DS:DX = address of the message
        int   21h                ;Call DOS interrupt
        mov   ax,4C00h           ;End the program normally with the
        int   21h                ;4CH function


end_up  endp

;-- CBREAK: The new Ctrl-Break handler --------------------------------

cbreak  proc far

        ;-- All registers altered within this routine (excluding ----
        ;-- the Flag register) have to be secured on the stack   ----

        push  ds
        mov   ax,data            ;Move the segment address of the
        mov   ds,ax              ;data segment in the DS-Register

        ;-- For example, you can open a window here in which the ----
        ;-- user is asked if he really wants to end the program  ----
                                 ;
                                 ;
                                 ;
        jmp   go_on              ;Don't end program

        ;-- If the user decides to end the program, a routine with --
        ;-- which the program can be ended can be started here    --

        jmp   end_up             ;Prepare to end program
```

```
        ;-- The program should not be aborted, continue normal  -----
        ;-- execution                                           -----

go_on:  pop   ds                 ;Restore saved register
        iret                     ;Back to DOS, where the interrupted
                                 ;function continues

cbreak  endp

;-- CERROR: the new Critical Error handler ----------------------------

cerror  proc far
        ;-- Each of the registers (SS, SP, DX, ES, DX, CX und BX)  --
        ;-- altered within this routine must be saved on the stack --

        sti                      ;Enable interrupts
        push  ds

        mov   ax,data            ;Load data segment's segment address
        mov   ds,ax              ; in the DS register

        mov   cr_err,1           ;Point to critical error
        mov   ax,di              ;Move error number to AX
        mov   cr_typ,al          ;Note error number
        mov   al,3               ;End function call with error

        pop   ds                 ;Pop DS from stack
        iret

cerror  endp

;---------------------------------------------------------------------
code    ends                     ;End of CODE segment
        end   start              ;Start program execution with
                                 ; the START procedure
```

857

Chapter 25

Device Drivers

The device driver is one of the most fascinating, and most complicated, aspects of system programming. DOS uses device drivers to access external devices. Device drivers are short programs that provide support to a wide variety of devices, ranging from keyboards to CD-ROM drives. However, they are difficult to use because they can be programmed only in assembly language.

In this chapter, we'll show you how device drivers are structured under DOS. You'll also learn how to develop your own drivers. We've included source code for several functional drivers, which can also serve as the basis for your own, more complicated drivers.

25.1 Device Drivers under DOS

A device driver is the part of the operating system that's responsible for controlling and communicating with the hardware. It represents the lowest level of an operating system, and permits all other levels to work independently of the hardware. This is useful when adapting an operating system to various computers because the device drivers can be changed instead of the entire operating system.

In earlier operating systems, device drivers resided in the operating system code. This meant that changing or upgrading these routines to match new hardware was difficult, if not impossible. DOS Version 2.0 introduced a flexible concept of device drivers. This flexibility makes it possible for the user to adapt even the most exotic hard drives and EMS expansion cards to DOS.

A device driver consists of status information, which tells DOS what kind of driver it is, and several software routines known as driver functions. These routines are responsible for tasks required by DOS in order to access the device that the driver serves. For example, a hard drive device driver must contain functions for handling read, write, and verify operations on sectors of the disk.

Custom drivers

Since communication between DOS and a device driver is based on relatively simple function calls and data structures, the assembly language programmer can develop a device driver to adapt any device to DOS. Unfortunately, device drivers cannot be programmed in a higher level language, as we mentioned earlier.

The rules for developing a COM program also apply when developing the code for a driver. Direct segment access isn't allowed. The difference is that a device driver starts at offset address 0H, instead of 100H. The end of this section explains the assembly language implementation in detail.

Device drivers are installed by DOS during the boot process. They cannot be activated from the command line like normal EXE or COM programs. The drivers present in the DOS kernel are installed automatically during the boot process. These drivers are named $CLOCK, CON, AUX, and PRN. In addition to these, drivers for the diskette drives and the hard disk will also be installed, if available.

Name	Driver for
NUL	Null (imaginary) device
$CLOCK	Clock
CON	Console (keyboard and screen)
AUX	Serial port
PRN	Parallel port (printer)

The drivers are arranged sequentially in memory and connected to each other. If the user wants to install another driver, DOS must be informed using the CONFIG.SYS file. This text file contains the information that DOS needs for configuring the system. Contents of the CONFIG.SYS file are read and evaluated during the boot process after linking the standard drivers. If DOS finds the DEVICE= command, the driver described in that line is installed, based on the optional path.

ANSI.SYS

The following command sequence includes the ANSI.SYS driver, which is supplied with DOS. This driver makes enhanced character output and keyboard functions available:

```
DEVICE=ANSI.SYS
```

The new driver is added to the chain immediately after the NUL device driver (the first driver in the chain). The ANSI.SYS driver replaces the default CON driver. To ensure that all function calls for monitor or keyboard communication operate through ANSI.SYS, the ANSI.SYS driver is placed first in the device group, and the CON driver is moved farther down the chain of devices. Since the operating system moves from link to link during the search, it finds the new CON driver (ANSI.SYS) first and uses it. So, the system ignores the old CON driver, as shown in the following illustration:

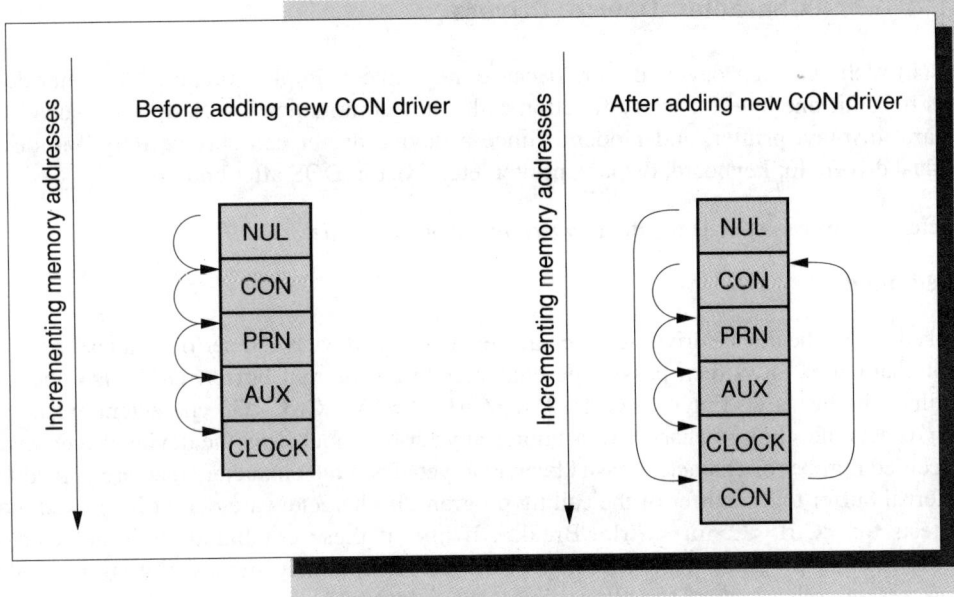

The driver chain

ASSIGN

Not all drivers can be replaced with new ones. The NUL driver is always the first driver in the chain. If you add a new NUL driver, the system ignores this driver and continues accessing the original NUL driver. This also applies to the drivers for floppy disk drives and hard drives. This occurs because disk drives have drive specifiers instead of names such as CON (e.g., A:). A new disk drive can be added to the system, but since DOS may assign it the name D:, it may not be addressed by all programs that want to access device A:.

This problem can be avoided by redirecting all device accesses using DOS's ASSIGN command. You can make the ASSIGN command part of the AUTOEXEC.BAT file. It executes after adding drivers and executing the CONFIG.SYS file. To redirect all accesses from drive A: (the first disk drive) to device D: (in this case, a new driver for a new disk drive), the AUTOEXEC.BAT file must contain the following command sequence:

```
ASSIGN A=D
```

The drivers for mass storage devices and the drivers, such as PRN, are handled differently. DOS has two kinds of device drivers:

- Character device drivers

- Block device drivers

25.1.1 Character Device Drivers

Let's start with character device drivers because they have a simple structure. Character device drivers transmit one byte for every function call. They communicate with devices, such as the keyboard, display, printer, and modem. Since a device driver can service only one device, individual drivers for keyboard, display, printer, etc., exist in DOS after booting.

Character devices can operate in either *cooked mode* or *raw mode*.

Cooked mode

In cooked mode, the device driver reads characters from the device and performs a test for certain control characters. DOS then passes the character to an internal buffer. DOS also checks to determine whether any <Enter>, <Ctrl><P>, <Ctrl><S>, or <Ctrl><C> characters exist. If the system detects the <Enter> character, it ignores any further input from the device driver, even if the specified number of characters hasn't been read yet. Then the characters read are copied from the internal buffer to the buffer of the calling program. If characters are output in cooked mode, DOS tests for <Ctrl><C> or <Ctrl><Break>. If one of these combinations is detected, the currently running program stops. Pressing <Ctrl><S> temporarily stops the program until the user presses any other key. <Ctrl><P> redirects the output from the screen to the printer (PRN). Pressing <Ctrl><P> a second time redirects the output from the printer back to the screen.

Raw mode

In raw mode, the device driver reads all characters without testing. If a program wants to read in 10 characters, it reads exactly 10 characters, even if the user presses the <Enter> key as the second character of the string. Raw mode transmits the characters directly to the calling program's buffer, instead of using an internal DOS buffer. During character output, raw mode doesn't test for <Ctrl><C> or <Ctrl><Break>.

DOS function 44H of interrupt 21H defines the mode of the character device driver (see the end of this section for a detailed description of this interrupt).

25.1.2 Block Device Drivers

Block device drivers usually communicate with mass storage devices, such as hard drives. Therefore, they simultaneously transmit a number of characters designated as a *block*. In some cases, a single call to a function transmits several blocks of data. The block sizes can differ depending on the mass storage device, and within one particular mass storage device.

When DOS wants to access a storage medium with a block driver, DOS passes the number of the sector being addressed. The driver must then convert the logical sector number (counted starting from 0) to a physical address consisting of head, cylinder, and sector numbers. The device driver selects the method used for converting logical sector numbers into physical sector addresses. It's only important that a unique, one-to-one relationship is maintained between logical and physical sectors. This means that a given logical sector uniquely identifies one and only one physical sector.

Unlike character device drivers, block device drivers can manage more than one device at a time. A single hard disk driver can work with two or more hard disks at once, for example. A block driver can also divide a mass storage device into several volumes, which is often done with hard disks.

Identifying devices managed by a driver

The drives managed by a block driver don't have device names or filenames. Instead, they use identifying letters such as A, B, or C. The device letters are assigned by DOS and aren't selected by the driver. The letters DOS assigns are determined by the location of the block driver within the list of drivers. The first drive managed by a block driver receives the letter A, the second B, and then C, etc.

Each of these devices must have a file allocation table (FAT) and a root directory. Block device drivers don't distinguish between cooked and raw modes. They always read and write the exact number of blocks unless an error is detected.

If a device driver supports several logical drives, these are assigned consecutive letters. For example, if a hard disk driver implements three logical drives and the first letter available is C, then the other two drives are assigned the letters D and E. The next block driver then begins with the letter F.

25.1.3   Device Driver Access

There are several ways to access a device driver. Character device drivers are accessed using the normal FCB or handle functions by simply indicating the name of a driver (e.g., CON: instead of a filename). A block device driver is accessed using the normal DOS functions (file, directory, etc.) by using the drive designator assigned by DOS during the boot process.

Functions 1H through CH of interrupt 21H invoke read and write operations in a device driver. There are also two other options for accessing device drivers, which we'll discuss shortly.

This can no longer be considered direct access, since various DOS functions are used to communicate between the driver and the device.

There are two other ways to communicate with device drivers. DOS function 44H, which is known as the IOCTL function (I/O control), is important to this communication. This function has many subfunctions, which we'll discuss in more detail later in this chapter.

25.2 Structure of a Device Driver

Even though the two types of device drivers differ in some important ways, they have similar structures. Each has a device header, a strategy routine, and an interrupt routine (a different kind of interrupt from the ones we've discussed so far).

Device header

The device header appears at the beginning of each device driver and contains information that DOS needs for implementing the driver.

Device driver header		
Address	Contents	Type
OOH	Offset address of next driver	1 word
02H	Segment address of next driver	1 word
04H	Device attribute	1 word
06H	Offset address of strategy routine	1 word
08H	Offset address of interrupt routine	1 word
OAH	Driver name (character driver) or number of devices (block driver)	8 bytes

The first field creates a link to the next device driver in the list. Once a driver is loaded, DOS enters the address of the next driver in this field. The programmer must initialize this field with the value -1 so that DOS will recognize the structure as a device driver.

Device attributes

The second field is a bit field that's used to describe the device driver. Bit 15 of this field tells DOS whether this is a block or a character driver. A value of 0 represents a block driver, and 1 represents a character driver. The interpretation of all other bits in this field depends on the setting of bit 15. The following is the entire structure of this bit field:

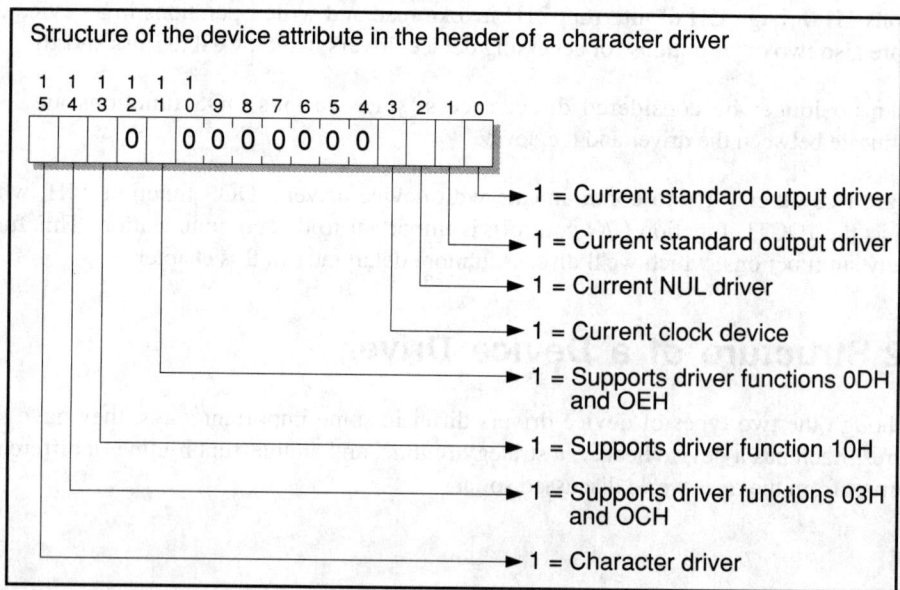

In the case of a character driver, bits 0 through 3 identify the driver (see the previous illustration). They indicate whether the new driver, instead of the CON driver, should be used for input and output, or whether it should replace the NUL driver or the clock driver. If none of these bits are set, then the new driver doesn't replace any of the standard drivers.

The other bits indicate whether the driver supports various driver functions. To understand this, you must also know that DOS recognizes 15 different driver functions, all of which aren't automatically available to a driver. The optional functions 03H, 0CH, 0DH, 0EH, and 10H must be explicitly requested by setting the corresponding bits. Some of these functions are available beginning only with DOS Version 3.1, and some aren't available until Version 5.0. You must be using the corresponding DOS version in order for the attribute bits to be properly recognized. We'll provide descriptions of these DOS driver functions later in this chapter.

Remember that the values of these bits are valid only if bit 15 contains the value 1b, which indicates a character driver. These bits will have different meanings if it's a block driver.

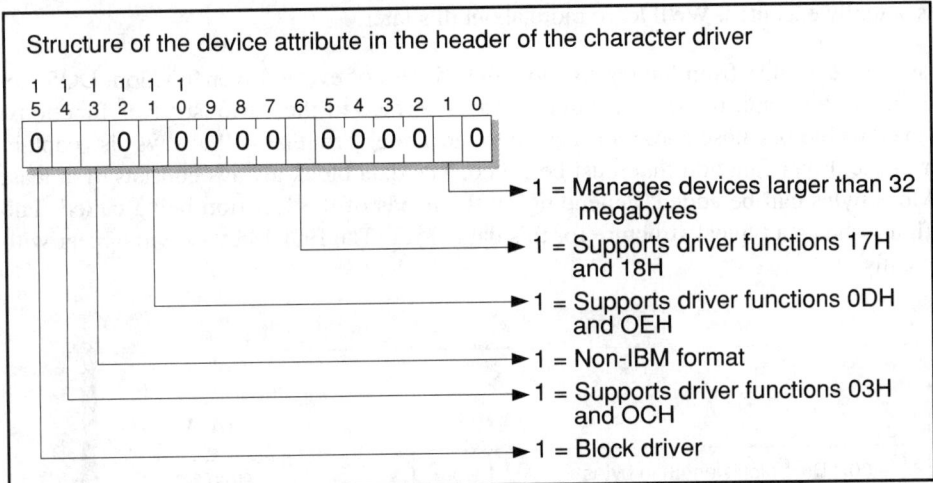

In addition to the bits that indicate which driver functions are supported, bit 1 is very important to block drivers. The feature indicated by this bit is supported in DOS Versions 4.0 and higher. If this bit is set, then the block driver is capable of supporting devices and partitions larger than 32 megabytes, which was made possible with the enlarged cluster size available starting with DOS 4.0.

With the 32 megabyte limit exceeded, the driver can no longer represent all the addressable sectors as 16-bit integers. This would allow for only 65,536 sectors, which, with a standard sector size of 512 bytes, corresponds to exactly 32 megabytes. Device drivers with attribute bit 1 set expect sector numbers to be passed in another format so that the sectors beyond the 32 megabyte limit can also be addressed. We'll provide more information about this when we discuss the driver functions.

Structure of the fields in the device driver header

Two fields that contain the offset addresses of the so-called strategy and interrupt routines follow the attributes field. DOS uses these routines to communicate with the driver. Only the offset addresses of these routines are required because device drivers, like COM programs, are limited to one segment. So, the explicit segment address isn't needed.

In the case of a character driver, the last field of the driver header contains the name of the device driver. If the name is less than the eight characters allowed in this field, the rest of the field must be filled with empty spaces (ASCII code 32). If the driver is a block driver, then this field contains the number of logical devices that the driver supports. The other 7 bytes of this field should then be filled with the value 0.

Strategy and interrupt routines

DOS calls the strategy routine to initialize the driver before any function of the driver is called. An address is passed to this routine in the ES:BX register pair. This address points to a data structure that contains information about the operation to be performed and the corresponding data. The strategy routine doesn't execute these operations itself; it simply stores the address of the data block and gives control back to DOS. Then the driver interrupt routine is called and the operation is actually executed. We'll learn more about this later.

This mechanism frees DOS from having to know the address of every driver function. DOS can simply use the strategy and interrupt routines as an interface to the various driver functions. Therefore, the data block whose address is passed to the strategy routine will always also contain the number of the driver function that must be called. The data block always consists of at least 13 bytes. More bytes can be added, depending on the needs of the function being called. The following figure shows a typical structure for this data block. The first 13 bytes will appear with all function calls.

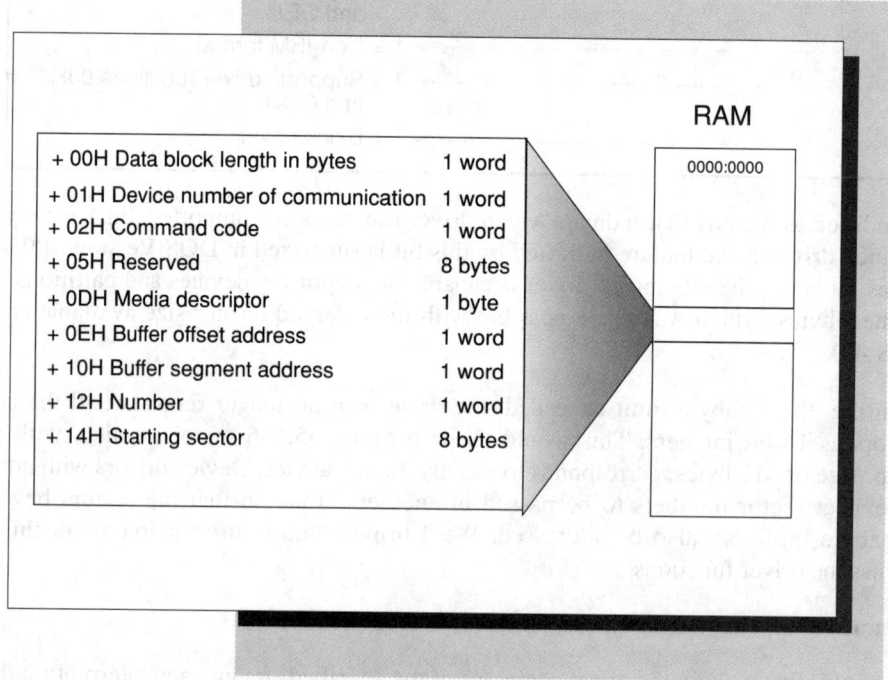

Structure of the request header

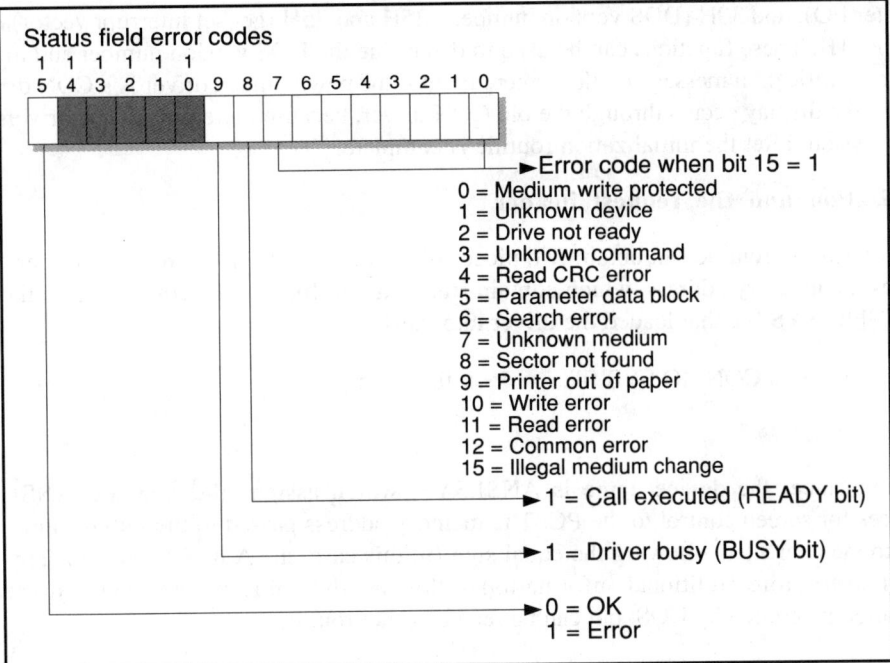

25.3 Device Driver Functions

Under DOS Version 2.0, any installable device driver must support 13 functions, numbered from 00H to 0CH, even if their only action consists of setting the DONE flag in the status word. DOS Versions 3.0, 4.0, and 5.0 include additional functions that can be supported, but aren't required. Some of these functions concern one of the two driver types, while others apply to both driver types (e.g., initialization). Unused functions must at least set the DONE flag of the status word. Let's look at the various functions in detail according to their function numbers.

Request header

Every function described here receives its arguments from the request header (whose address is passed by DOS to the strategy routine) and stores its "results" in the request header. Therefore, the offset address to the arguments, relative to the beginning of the request header, is passed to the specified function. These arguments are later transferred to variables. Besides this offset address, a flag indicates whether this information consists of a byte, word, or *PTR*. The PTR data type represents a pointer to a buffer and consists of two adjacent words. The first word is the offset address of the buffer. The second word is the segment address of the buffer.

Function 00H: **Driver Initialization**

During the system boot procedure, DOS calls this function to initialize the device driver. This function can involve hardware initialization, setting various internal variables to their default values, or the redirection of interrupts. Since the entire operating system hasn't been completely initialized at this point, the initialization routine can only call functions 01H through 0CH (character I/O), and 30H (DOS version number), 25H and 35H (get/set interrupt vector) of DOS interrupt 21H. These functions can be used to determine the DOS version number and to display a driver identification message on the screen. Even if the newly linked driver is a CON driver, the output to the display occurs through the old CON driver, because there are no new drivers linked into the system after the initialization routine is complete.

Initialization and the request header

The initialization routine can obtain two pieces of information from the request header. First, it provides the memory address, which contains the text that follows the equal sign on the line in the CONFIG.SYS file that loaded the driver into the system.

A typical line in a CONFIG.SYS file can look like this:

```
DEVICE=ANSI.SYS
```

In this instance, the device name is ANSI.SYS, which assigns the standard ANSI escape sequences for screen control to the PC. The memory address passed to the initialization routine points to the character following the equal sign (in this case, the A of ANSI.SYS). This makes it possible to store additional information following the name of the device driver. This information is ignored by DOS, but can be read by other routines.

Logical device designation

The second item is only available under DOS Version 3.0 and higher, and only if the driver is a block device driver. This is the letter designation of the first logical device of the driver. The value 0 represents A, 1 represents B, 2 represents C, etc.

The initialization routine must return four parameters to the calling DOS function. The first parameter is the status of the function (i.e., the indication of whether the function has executed properly). For a block device driver, the number of logical devices supported must also be passed. This information could also be obtained from the device driver's header, but is ignored by DOS.

The next parameter the device driver must pass to DOS is the highest memory address that it occupies or uses. This lets DOS know where the next device driver can be installed.

You should remember that, starting with DOS Version 5.0, drivers no longer have "unlimited" memory available to them. This DOS version allows you to load drivers into Upper Memory Blocks. Generally, there is less memory available there than in the TPA below the 640K limit. In Version 5.0, the "upper limit" address of the driver is loaded in the field where DOS normally would find the end address of the driver. The upper limit is the address in memory beyond which the driver may no longer allocate memory for itself. If this isn't sufficient for the driver, then it shouldn't even attempt to be installed.

BPB

If the driver is a block device driver, the last argument passed must be the address of an array that contains an entry for every logical device. This array contains the addresses of BIOS parameter blocks (BPBs). The address is passed as two words; the first word contains the offset, and the second word contains the segment address of the array. The first two words within this table are the address for the first logical device supported. The next two words indicate the address for the second logical device, etc. The BPB is a data block containing information that describes a logical device. If all or some of the logical devices have the same format, all entries in the BPB address table can point to a single BPB.

Notice that the last part of the BIOS parameter block, which is known as the expanded BPB, is only required for block drivers that support partitions larger than 32 megabytes. This is only possible with DOS 4.0 or higher. To indicate that you want to manage partitions larger than 32 megabytes, set bit 1 in the driver attribute bit field. The total number of sectors and the number of reserved sectors in the normal BPB must be set to 0 and the corresponding fields in the expanded BPB must be loaded. These are 32 bit fields that can handle values greater than 65,535 (which is the limit for these fields in the normal BPB).

+ 00H	Bytes per sector	(1 word)
+ 02H	Sectors per cluster	(1 byte)
+ 03H	Reserved sectors (including boot sectors)	(1 word)
+ 05H	Number of FATs	(1 byte)
+ 06H	Maximum number of entries in root directory	(1 word)
+ 08H	Total number of sectors	(1 word)
+ 0AH	Media descriptor	(1 byte)
+ 0BH	Number of sectors per FAT	(1 word)

BIOS Parameter Block design

F8H	=	hard disk
F9H	=	5.25" diskette, double-sided, 15 sectors per track
FCH	=	5.25" diskette, single-sided, 9 sectors per track
FDH	=	5.25" diskette, double-sided, 9 sectors per track
FEH	=	5.25" diskette, single-sided, 8 sectors per track
FFH	=	5.25" diskette, double-sided, 8 sectors per track

Media descriptor byte

Starting with DOS Version 4.0, the function can also return an error flag to offset address 17H of the data block. If DOS finds a value other than 0 at this location after the function call, the message "CONFIG.SYS error in line xx" is displayed.

Input parameters:

Offset 2 (byte)	Function number (0H)
Offset 18 (ptr)	Address of character that follows the equal sign after the DEVICE command in the CONFIG.SYS file
Offset 22 (byte)	Device number of the first device supported by the driver (0=A, 1=B...) (applies to block device drivers from DOS Version 3.0 and higher only)

Returned parameters:

Offset 3 (word)	Status word
Offset 13 (byte)	Number of devices supported (block devices only)
Offset 14 (ptr)	Address of first available memory location following the driver
Offset 18 (ptr)	Address of array containing BPB addresses (block devices only)

Function 01H: Media Check

This function is used only with a block device driver. A character device driver should simply set the DONE flag of the status word and exit. This function is used by DOS to determine whether the media (diskette) has changed. It's frequently used when examining a disk directory. If the disk medium wasn't changed since the last access, DOS still has this information in memory; otherwise DOS must reread the information from the media that delays the execution of the current task.

In some instances, as with floppy diskettes, the answer to the question is fairly complicated. Therefore, DOS permits function 1 to answer not only with "yes" and "no", but also with "don't know." The answer always affects further DOS activity.

If the media is unchanged, access to the media can occur immediately. If the media was changed, however, DOS closes all internal buffers related to the current logical device. This causes the loss of all data that should have been transmitted to the media. Then it calls function 2 of the current device driver, and loads the FAT and the root directory.

If the media check function answers with "don't know," the additional steps taken by DOS depend on the status of the internal buffers related to the current logical device. If these internal buffers are empty, DOS assumes that the media was changed and acts as if function 1 answered "yes." If the buffers contain data that should have been transmitted to the media, DOS assumes that the media is intact and writes the data. If the media was indeed changed, the data written to a changed media may damage the new diskette's file structure.

Since subsequent processing depends on the response from the media check function, the driver should handle the response carefully. Before enabling the mechanism used by the function to respond, the function examines the parameters passed to it. If the driver supports several logical devices, the first parameter is the number of devices. Next is a media descriptor code. This code contains information about the type of media last used in the current logical device. Only devices that can handle several different formats can use this task (e.g., AT disk drives that can use both 360K and 1.2 megabyte diskette formats).

If the media check function determines that the medium in a device is non-removable (e.g., a fixed disk), it can always respond "not changed". If, however, the device media can be changed (e.g., a disk), the correct response can only be determined with complex procedures. If these procedures aren't used, the response should be "don't know".

The following are the three procedures that provide fairly accurate results.

Since a device with changeable media has an opening and closing mechanism, the function should check to determine whether the media was removed. However, it cannot determine whether the removed media is identical to the newly inserted medium.

If the media has a name, the function should read this name to determine whether the media was changed. This procedure only makes sense if every media has a unique name.

The disk drive procedure used by DOS is based on the fact that changing medium is time-consuming. DOS assumes that a user needs about two seconds to remove a diskette from a drive and insert a new diskette in the same drive. If two consecutive diskette accesses occur less than two seconds apart, DOS assumes that the diskette wasn't changed.

A byte in the data block is used to indicate changes. The value -1 (FFH) means "changed", 0 means "don't know", and 1 means "not changed".

If the media was changed, the device driver indicates this (bit 11 in the device attribute = 1); the address of a buffer must be passed to DOS Version 3 and higher, which contains the volume name of the previous media. This name must be stored there as an ASCII string and terminated with an end character (ASCII code 0).

Input parameters:

Offset 1 (byte)	Device number
Offset 2 (byte)	Function number (1)
Offset 13 (byte)	Media descriptor byte

Returned parameters:

Offset 3 (word)	Status word
Offset 14 (byte)	Was media changed? FFH = yes, 00H = don't know, 01H = no
Offset 15 (ptr)	Address of buffer containing the previous volume name (only if device indicates a media change)

Function 02H:

**Build BIOS Parameter
Block (BPB)**

This function is used only by block device drivers. A character device driver should just set the DONE flag of the status word and exit. DOS calls this function when the media check function determines that the media was changed. This function returns a pointer to a new BPB for the media.

As you can see by the layout of the calling parameters, the device number media descriptor and a pointer to a buffer are passed to this function by DOS. If the device is a standard format (bit 13 of the device attribute =0), then the buffer contains the first sector of the FAT.

Starting with DOS Version 3.0, this function also reads and writes volume label names, because a call to function 01H must occur any time a device experiences a change of medium (bit 11 of the device attribute = 1).

Input parameters:

Offset 1 (byte)	Device number
Offset 2 (byte)	Function number (2)
Offset 13 (byte)	Media descriptor byte
Offset 14 (ptr)	Address of a buffer containing the FAT (see above)

Returned parameters:

Offset 3 (word)	Status word
Offset 18 (ptr)	Address of the BPB of addressed device

Function 03H: I/O Control Read

This function allows direct communication between a device driver and an application. This allows device drivers to implement additional logic not accessible from normal driver functions. It can only be called through function 44H of interrupt 21H if the IOCTL bit (bit 14), in the device attribute word in the device driver header, is set. Different parameters are passed to the function from a FAR pointer, depending on whether the driver is a character or a block device driver.

A character device driver is passed the number of characters to be transferred and the address of a buffer for the transfer of the data.

A block device driver is passed the device number, the media descriptor byte, the address of the buffer to be used for the data transfer, the pointer to the first sector to be read, and the number of sectors to be read.

Input parameters:

Offset 1 (byte)	Device number (block devices only)
Offset 2 (byte)	Function number (3)
Offset 13 (byte)	Media descriptor byte (block devices only)
Offset 14 (ptr)	Address of buffer into which data should be transmitted
Offset 18 (word)	Number of sectors to be read (block device) or
	Number of characters to be read (character device)
Offset 20 (word)	First sector to be read (block devices only)

Returned parameters:

Offset 3 (word)	Status word
Offset 18 (word)	Number of sectors read (block device) or
	Number of characters read (character device)

Function 04H: Read

This function reads data from the device to a buffer specified in the calling parameter. If an error occurs while reading the data, the error status must be set. Also, the function must report the number of sectors or bytes that were successfully read. Simply reporting an error isn't sufficient.

Block drivers have different methods of passing the sector number. The methods used depends on whether the driver is a 16-bit or a 32-bit driver. For 16-bit drivers, the sector number is stored in the data block as a word starting at offset address 14H. For 32-bit drivers, it is a dword starting at offset address 1AH. A 32-bit driver refers to a driver that can handle devices and partitions larger than 32 megabytes. This is indicated by setting bit 1 in the driver attribute bit field. In addition to this, the sector number at offset address 14H is set to FFFFH for 32-bit drivers in order to indicate the use of the 32-bit sector number at 1AH.

Input parameters:

Offset 1 (byte)	Device number (block device only)
Offset 2 (byte)	Function number (4)
Offset 13 (byte)	Media descriptor byte (block device only)
Offset 14 (ptr)	Address of buffer to which data should be read
Offset 18 (word)	Number of sectors to be read (block device) or
	Number of characters to be read (character device)
Offset 20 (word)	First sector to be read (block device only)

Returned parameters:

Offset 3 (word)	Status word
Offset 18 (word)	Number of sectors read (block device) or
	Number of characters read (character device)
Offset 22 (ptr)	Pointer to volume ID on return of error 0FH (Version 3.0 and higher)

Function 05H: Non-destructive Read

This function is used by a character device driver to test for unread characters in the input buffer. A block device should set the DONE flag of the status word and exit.

DOS tests for additional characters using this function. If more characters exist, the busy bit must be cleared (set to 0) and the next character passed to DOS. The character that is passed remains in the buffer so that a subsequent call to a read function will return this same character. If additional characters don't exist, the busy bit must be set (set to 1).

Input parameters:

Offset 2 (byte)	Function number (5)

Returned parameters:

Offset 3 (word)	Status word
Offset 13 (byte)	The character read

Function 06H: Input Status

This function is used to determine whether a character is waiting to be read from the input buffer of a character device. A block device driver should set the DONE flag of the status word and exit.

If a character is waiting to be read from the input buffer, the busy bit is cleared (set to 0). If a character isn't in the input buffer, the busy bit is set (set to 1).

When a character is waiting to be read, the Input Status function (06H) resets the status word busy bit to 0 and returns the character to DOS. The character isn't removed from the buffer and is therefore non-destructive. This function is equivalent to reading one character ahead.

Input parameters:

Offset 2 (byte)	Function number (6)

Returned parameters:

Offset 3 (word)   Status word: 0 = Characters already in buffer; 1 = Read request to physical device

Function 07H: **Flush Input Buffers**

This function clears the internal input buffers of a character device driver. Any characters read but not yet passed to DOS are lost when this function is used. A block device driver should set the DONE flag of the status word and exit.

Input parameters:

Offset 2 (byte)   Function number (7)

Returned parameters:

Offset 3 (word)   Status word

Function 08H: **Write**

This function transfers characters from a buffer to the current device. If an error occurs during transmission, the status word is used to indicate this error. Both block and character devices use this function.

The parameters used for this function depend on whether the driver is for a character or block device. Both pass a buffer address, from which a certain number of characters should be transferred. A character device driver is passed the number of bytes to be transferred in addition to this information.

A block driver is passed the number of sectors to transfer (not the number of characters), the number of the device to be addressed, its media descriptor, and the address of the first sector on the medium.

If an error occurs writing the data, the error status must be set. Also, the function must report the number of sectors or bytes written successfully. Simply reporting an error isn't sufficient.

Input parameters:

Offset 1 (byte)   Device number (block drivers only)
Offset 2 (byte)   Function number (8)
Offset 13 (byte)   Media descriptor of device addressed (block device only)
Offset 14 (ptr)   Address of the buffer containing data
Offset 18 (word)   Number of sectors to be written (block device) or
Number of characters to be written (character device)
Offset 20 (word)   First sector to be written (block device only)

Returned parameters:

Offset 3 (word)   Status word
Offset 18 (word)   Number of sectors written (block device) or
Number of characters written (character device)
Offset 22 (ptr)   Pointer to volume ID on return of error 0FH (Version 3.0 up)

Function 09H: **Write with Verify**

This function is similar to function 08H, except that the characters written are reread and verified.

Some devices, especially character devices, such as a monitor or a printer, don't require verification because either no errors occur during transmission (monitor) or the data cannot be verified (printer).

Input parameters:

Offset 1 (byte)	Device number (block drivers only)
Offset 2 (byte)	Function number (09H)
Offset 13 (byte)	Media descriptor of device addressed (block device only)
Offset 14 (ptr)	Address of the buffer containing data
Offset 18 (word)	Number of sectors to be written (block device) or
	Number of characters to be written (character device)
Offset 20 (word)	First sector to be written (block device only)

Returned parameters:

Offset 3 (word)	Status word
Offset 18 (word)	Number of sectors written (block device)
	Number of characters written (character device)
Offset 22 (ptr)	Pointer to volume ID on return of error 0FH (Version 3.0 up)

Function 0AH: **Output Status**

This function indicates whether the last write operation to a character device is completed. A block device should set the DONE flag in the status word and exit.

If the last write operation is complete, then the busy bit of the status word is cleared; otherwise the busy bit is set to 1.

Input parameters:

Offset 2 (byte)	Function number (0AH)

Returned parameters:

Offset 3 (word)	Status word: BUSY bit = 1 if the last character output hasn't been completed

Function 0BH: **Flush Output Buffers**

This function completely clears the output buffer even if it contains characters waiting for output. A block device should set the DONE flag on the status word and exit.

Input parameters:

Offset 2 (byte)	Function number (0BH)

Returned parameters:

Offset 3 (word)	Status word

Function 0CH: I/O Control Write

This function passes control information from the application program to the character or block device driver. It can only be called through function 44H of interrupt 21H, if the IOCTL bit in the device attribute word in the device driver header is set. Different parameters are passed to the function, depending on whether the driver is a character or a block device driver.

A character device driver is passed the number of characters to be written and the address of the buffer from which these characters are transferred.

A block device driver is passed the device number (in case the driver services logical devices), the media descriptor byte, the address of the buffer from which the data is to be written, the number of the first sector to be written, and the number of sectors to be written.

A character device driver returns the number of bytes written. A block device driver returns the number of sectors written.

Input parameters:
Offset 1 (byte)	Device number (block device only)
Offset 2 (byte)	Function number (0CH)
Offset 13 (byte)	Media descriptor of addressed device (block device only)
Offset 14 (ptr)	Address of buffer from which data should be read
Offset 18 (word)	Number of sectors to be written (block device) or Number of characters to be written (character device)
Offset 20 (word)	First sector to be written (block device only)

Returned parameters:
Offset 3 (word)	Status word
Offset 18 (word)	Number of sectors written (block device) or Number of characters written (character device)

The following four functions are supported by DOS Version 3.0 and higher.

Function 0DH: Open

This function can be used only if the OCR (Open/Close/RM) bit in the device attribute word in the device driver header is set. Its task differs, depending on whether it's a character or block driver.

A block driver uses this function every time a file is opened. This function determines how many open files exist on this device. Use this command carefully, since programs that access FCB function calls usually don't close open files. This problem can be avoided by assuming, during every media change, that no files remain open. For devices with non-changeable media (e.g., a hard drive), even this procedure may not help.

Within a character driver, this function can send an initialization string to the device before transmitting the data. This is helpful when used to communicate with the printer. The initialization string shouldn't be included in the driver, but can be called, for example, with the IOCTL function of interrupt 21H, which calls function 0CH of a driver to transmit it from an application program to the driver. The function can also be useful because it can prevent two processes (in a network or in multiprocessing) from both accessing the same device.

This function isn't called for the devices CON, PRN, and AUX because these functions are always open.

Input parameters:

Offset 1 (byte)	Device number (block device only)
Offset 2 (byte)	Function number (0DH)

Returned parameters:

Offset 3 (word)	Status word

Function 0EH: Device Close

This function is the opposite of function 0DH. This function can only be addressed if the OCR bit in the device attribute word of the device driver header is set. Its task differs, depending on whether it's a character or block driver.

A block driver calls it after closing a file. This can be used to decrement a count of open files. Once all files on a device are closed, the driver should flush the buffers on removable media devices, because it's likely that the user is about to remove the media.

A character driver can use this function to send some closing control information to a device after completing output. For a printer, this could be a formfeed. As in function 0DH, the string could be transmitted from an application using the IOCTL function.

Input parameters:

Offset 1 (byte)	Device number (block device only)
Offset 2 (byte)	Function number (0EH)

Returned parameters:

Offset 3 (word)	Status word

Function 0FH: Removable Media

This function indicates whether the media in a block device can be changed. This function is used only if the OCR bit in the device attribute word of the device driver is set. A character device driver should set the DONE flag in the status word and exit.

If the media can be removed, the busy bit is cleared; otherwise it is set to 1.

Input parameters:

Offset 1 (byte)	Device number (block device only)
Offset 2 (byte)	Function number (0FH)

Returned parameters:

Offset 3 (word)	Status word: If the media can be removed, the busy bit must contain the value 0

Function 10H: **Output Until Busy**

This function transfers data from a buffer to an output device until the device is busy (i.e., can no longer accept more characters). Since this function is supported by character devices, a block device driver should set the DONE flag on the status word and exit.

This function works particularly well with print spoolers, through which files can be sent to a printer as a background activity while a program executes in the foreground. It's possible that not all the characters in the transfer request will be sent to a device during this function call. This usually isn't an error; it could be the result of the device becoming busy. The function is passed the number of characters to be transmitted as well as the buffer address. If, during transmission, the output device indicates that it can no longer accept additional characters, it indicates the number of characters successfully transferred and returns control to the device driver.

Input parameters:

Offset 2 (byte)	Function number (10H)
Offset 14 (ptr)	Address of buffer from which data should be read
Offset 18 (word)	Number of characters to be read

Returned parameters:

Offset 3 (word)	Status word
Offset 18 (word)	Number of characters written

The following functions are supported by DOS Version 4.0 and higher.

Function 17H: **Get Logical Device**

This optional function can only be used with block drivers. If a block driver contains this function, bit 6 of the device attribute bit field must be set so that DOS will know it's available. This function is only useful in conjunction with the DOS device driver DRIVER.SYS, which enables a diskette drive to use two different formats. This function is used to tell the caller which of the two formats is currently in use.

The device code isn't required as a parameter for this function. By definition, only one driver with a switchable disk drive is allowed within a system.

Input parameters:

Offset 0 (byte)	Number of bytes requested
Offset 1 (byte)	Device number (block devices only)
Offset 2 (byte)	Function number (17H)

Returned parameters:

Offset 3 (word)	Status word

Function 18H: **Set Logical Device**

This function is the opposite of function 17H. DOS uses it to tell the device driver that the diskette drive it manages has another drive letter that can be addressed with a different diskette format.

Input parameters:

Offset 0 (byte)	Number of bytes requested
Offset 1 (byte)	Device number (block devices)
Offset 2 (byte)	Function number (18H)

Returned parameters:

Offset 3 (word)	Status word

25.4 Clock Drivers

The *clock driver* is a character device driver whose only function is to pass the date and time from DOS to an application. The clock driver can also have a different name (such as $CLOCK). This is possible because DOS identifies it by the fact that bit 2 in the device attribute word of the device driver header is set to 1, instead of by name. Bit 15 must also be set since the clock driver is a character device driver. Functions 2AH to 2DH of DOS interrupt 21H read the date and time and call the driver. A clock driver must support only functions 4, 8, and 0 (initialization). During the call of function 4 (reading), the date and time pass from the driver to DOS. DOS can set a new date and time with function 8. Both functions have the time and date passed in a buffer that is 6 bytes long.

+ 00H	Number of days since Jan.1,1980	(1 word)	RAM
+ 02H	Minutes	(1 byte)	0000:0000
+ 03H	Hour	(1 byte)	
+ 04H	Hundredths of seconds	(1 byte)	
+ 05H	Seconds	(1 byte)	

Passing date and time to a clock driver

The date format is unusual. Instead of passing the month, day, and year separately, DOS passes the number of days elapsed since January 1, 1980 as a 16-bit number. A fairly complex formula converts this number into normal date format, taking leap years into account. The clock driver normally uses function 0 and 1 of the BIOS interrupt 1AH to read and set the time.

Clocks on AT models

AT and AT-compatible computers have a battery powered realtime clock. Functions 0 and 1 of interrupt 1AH use a software controlled time counter instead of the battery powered realtime clock. When the computer is rebooted, the date and time previously set with driver function 8 is cleared. You can use the clock driver to access the realtime clock using functions 2 and 5 of interrupt 1AH instead of function 0 and 1.

25.5 Device Driver Calls from DOS

Now that you're familiar with the functions of the different device drivers, you can develop your own personal device driver. The following steps are performed before and after calling a device driver function.

A chain of events begins when a DOS function, which handles input and output, is called using interrupt 21H. Calling one of these functions can, in turn, call a series of other functions and corresponding read and write operations.

Open

One example of this is when the Open function 3DH is called to open a file in a subdirectory. Before it can be opened, DOS must find the file. This may require a search of a set of directories instead of simply reading in the FAT. During each access of interrupt 21H, DOS determines which of the available device drivers should be used to read or write characters. When this happens, DOS sets aside an area in memory to store the information required by the device driver.

For files, DOS must convert the number of records to be processed into logical sector numbers. DOS then calls the strategy routine of the device driver, to which it passes the address of the newly created data block (request header). Then the interrupt routine of the driver, which stores all registers, is called. It isolates the function code of the requested function from the data block and starts to process the function.

If the addressed driver is a character device driver, the function only has to send the characters to the hardware or request the characters to be read.

Block devices

For a block device (e.g., a mass storage device such as a floppy or hard disk), the logical sector number must be converted into a physical address before a read or write access. The logical sector number is divided into a head, track, and physical sector number.

After the read or write operation ends, the driver function must place a result code in the status field of the request header to be returned to the calling DOS function. Next, the contents of all registers are restored and control is returned to the calling DOS function, which, depending on the result of the driver function, sets or resets the carry flag and places any error code into the AX register. The interrupt function then returns control to the routine that called interrupt 21H.

25.6 Direct Device Driver Access: IOCTL

Now we'll discuss IOCTL in detail, because it offers an alternate method of communicating with the device driver. You can only use these functions if the IOCTL bit (bit 14) of the device attribute is set.

The IOCTL function itself is one of many functions addressable from DOS interrupt 21H. Its function number is 44H. Three groups of subfunctions are accessible:

- Device configuration

- Data transmission

- Driver status

The number of the desired subfunction is passed to the IOCTL function in the AL register. After the function call, the carry flag indicates whether the function executed correctly. A set carry flag indicates that an error occurred and the error code is located in the AX register.

Character device driver status

The number of the desired subfunction is passed to the IOCTL function in the AL register. After the function call, the carry flag indicates whether the function executed correctly. A set carry flag indicates that an error occurred and the error code is located in the AX register.

Subfunctions 06H and 07H can determine the status of a character device driver. Subfunction 6 can determine if the device is able to receive data. Subfunction 7 can determine if the device can send data. The handle of this device is passed in the BX register.

If the device is ready, both functions 06H and 07H return the value FFH in the AL register.

Subfunction 02H reads control data from the character device driver. The handle is passed in the BX register and the number of bytes to be read is passed in the CX register. Also, the DS:DX register pair contain the address of the buffer into which the data will be read. If the carry flag is clear, then the function was successful and the AX register contains the number of characters read. If the carry flag is set, then there was an error and the AX register contains the error code.

Subfunction 03H writes control information from a buffer to the character device driver. Again, the handle is passed in the BX register, the number of bytes to be written in the CX register, and the address of the buffer in the DS:DX register pair. The return codes are the same as for subfunction 02H. These two subfunctions are used to pass information between the application program and the device driver.

Block device driver status

Subfunctions 04H and 05H have the same task as subfunctions 2 and 3. However, they are used for block devices instead of character devices. Instead of passing the handle in register BX, you pass the drive code (0=A, 1=B, etc.) in the BL register.

Subfunction 0 is used to obtain device information for a specified handle. The subfunction number is passed in the AL register and the handle in the BX register. The function returns the device information word in the DX register.

For block devices:

bits 8-15	=	Reserved
bit 7	=	0 if a block device
bit 6	=	0 if file has been written
		1 if file has not been written
bits 0-5	=	Drive code (0=A, B=1, etc.)

For character devices:

bit 15	=	Reserved
bit 14	=	1 if device supports IOCTL subfunctions
		0 if device does not support IOCTL subfunctions
bits 8-13	=	reserved
bit 7	=	If a character device
bit 6	=	0 if end of file for input device
bit 5	=	0 if cooked mode
		1 if raw mode
bit 4	=	Reserved
bit 3	=	1 if clock device
bit 2	=	1 if NUL device
bit 1	=	1 if standard output device
bit 0	=	1 if standard input device

Cooked and raw modes

Subfunction 01H is used to set device information for a specified handle. This subfunction is often used to set the standard input device from cooked mode to raw mode or back.

Two final interrupts are sometimes used by block device drivers. These two interrupts, 25H and 26H, are used to read from and write to the disk drive. You can use these interrupts, for example, to process disks that were formatted using a "foreign" operating system.

The device number is passed in the AL register, the number of sectors to be transferred is passed in the CX register, the starting sector number to be transferred is passed in the DX register, and the buffer is passed in the DS:BX register pair. The carry flag is clear if no errors occurred. If the carry flag is set, then the error code is returned in the AX register.

Starting with DOS 4.0, the operation of these two interrupts had to be changed because the 16-bit sector number in the DX register can only be used to address 65,535 sectors, which does not allow access beyond the 32 megabyte limit. Starting with DOS 4.0, these interrupts are passed a pointer to a data block in the DS:BX register pair. This allows access to larger volumes and partitions.

Also, the value -1 (FFFFH) must be passed in the CX register. This informs DOS that the new parameters are being used and that it shouldn't search for parameters according to the old scheme. The old scheme can still be used for volumes larger than 32 megabytes as long as only sectors below the 32 megabyte limit are addressed.

25.7 Tips on Developing Device Drivers

When you're developing a device driver, problems occur when you test the new driver. First, a device driver must load into a memory location assigned to it by DOS, at an address unknown to the programmer. Also, a newly developed CON driver can't be tested using the DEBUG program, because DEBUG uses this driver for character input and output.

After you write the actual driver, you should write a short test program that calls the individual functions in the same way as DOS, but without having the driver installed as part of DOS. By doing this, everything executes under user control, and the entire process can be corrected with a debugger. Remember that a new device driver (especially a block device driver) should be linked into the system only after it's been tested completely and proven to be error-free.

> **Note:** When working with a hard disk, prepare a floppy system diskette before test booting the system from the hard disk with the new driver installed for the first time. If a small bug should exist in the new driver, and the initialization routine hangs up, the booting process will not end and DOS will be out of control. In such a case, the only remedy is to reset the system and boot with a DOS diskette in the floppy disk drive. Once DOS loads, you can then access the hard disk and remove the new driver.

25.8 Driver Examples

This section contains a sample device driver for each of the three types of device drivers. This sample demonstrates the information you've read so far. You'll see listings for an alternative console driver, a 160K RAM disk, and a driver for a battery operated AT clock.

All these drivers must follow the same rules set for a COM program. They must comprise a single segment containing program code and driver data. No direct segment references can exist. Unlike a COM program, the device driver must begin at offset 0H (not 100H), because a PSP cannot exist in memory.

The first program is a character driver that corresponds exactly to the format of a normal console driver. The second program is a block device driver, which creates a 160K RAM disk. The final program is a DOS clock driver to support an AT computer realtime clock.

Listing CONDRV.ASM

```
;******************************************************;
;*                   C O N D R V                     *;
;*--------------------------------------------------*;
;*  Task      : This program represents a normal Console *;
;*              Driver (Keyboard and Display Monitor). It should *;
;*              serve as a framework for a driver in the form of *;
;*              an ANSI.SYS driver.                  *;
;*--------------------------------------------------*;
;*  Author     : MICHAEL TISCHER                     *;
;*  Developed on : 08/04/87                          *;
;*  Last update  : 01/07/92                          *;
;*--------------------------------------------------*;
;*  Assembly    : MASM CONDRV;                       *;
;*               LINK CONDRV;                        *;
;*               EXE2BIN CONDRV CONDRV.SYS           *;
;*                            or                     *;
;*               TASM CONDRV                         *;
;*               LINK CONDRV;                        *;
;*               EXE2BIN CONDRV CONDRV.SYS           *;
;*--------------------------------------------------*;
;*  Call       : Copy into root directory, copy the command *;
;*               DEVICE=CONDRV.SYS into the file CONFIG.SYS *;
;*               and then boot the system.           *;
```

```
;******************************************************;

code      segment

          assume cs:code,ds:code

          org 0                    ;Program has no PSP therefore start
                                   ;at offset address 0

;== Constants =========================================

cmd_fld  equ 2                    ;Offset command field in data block
status   equ 3                    ;Offset status field in data block
end_adr  equ 14                   ;Offset driver end addr. in data block
num_db   equ 18                   ;Offset number in data block
b_adr    equ 14                   ;Offset buffer address in data block

KEY_SZ   equ 20                   ;Size of keyboard buffer
num_cmd  equ 16                   ;Subfunctions 0-16 are supported

;== Data ==============================================

;-- Device driver header ------------------------------

          dw -1,-1                 ;Link to next driver
```

```
            dw 1010100000000011b    ;Driver attribute
            dw offset strat         ;Pointer to strategy routine
            dw offset intr          ;Pointer to interrupt routine
            db "CONDRV  "           ;New console driver

;-- Jump table for functions -------------------------------------

fct_tab dw offset init          ;Function  0: Initialization
        dw offset dummy         ;Function  1: Media check
        dw offset dummy         ;Function  2: Create BPB
        dw offset no_sup        ;Function  3: I/O control read
        dw offset read          ;Function  4: Read
        dw offset read_b        ;Function  5: Non-destructive read
        dw offset dummy         ;Function  6: Input status
        dw offset del_in_b      ;Function  7: Delete input buffer
        dw offset write         ;Function  8: Write
        dw offset write         ;Function  9: Write & verify
        dw offset dummy         ;Function 10: Output status
        dw offset dummy         ;Function 11: Delete output buffer
        dw offset no_sup        ;Function 12: I/O control write
        dw offset dummy         ;Function 13: Open (Ver. 3.0 and up)
        dw offset dummy         ;Function 14: Close
        dw offset dummy         ;Function 15: Changeable medium
        dw offset write         ;Function 16: Output until busy

db_ptr  dw (?),(?)              ;Address of data block passed

key_a   dw 0                    ;Pointer to next character in KEY_SZ
key_e   dw 0                    ;Pointer to last character in KEY_SZ
key_bu  db KEY_SZ dup (?)       ;Internal keyboard buffer

;== Driver routines and functions ======================================

strat   proc far                ;Strategy routine

        mov cs:db_ptr,bx        ;Store address of data block in the
        mov cs:db_ptr+2,es      ;Variable DB_PTR

        ret                     ;Return to caller

strat   endp

;----------------------------------------------------------------------

intr    proc far                ;Interrupt routine

        push ax                 ;Push registers onto the stack
        push bx
        push cx
        push dx
        push di
        push si
        push bp
        push ds
        push es
        pushf                   ;Push flag register onto the stack

        push cs                 ;Set data segment register
        pop  ds                 ;Code and data are identical

        les  di,dword ptr db_ptr;Address of data block to ES:DI
        mov  bl,es:[di+cmd_fld]  ;Get command code
        cmp  bl,num_cmd          ;is command code permitted?
        jle  bc_ok               ;YES --> bc_ok
```

```
        mov ax,8003h            ;Code for "Unknown command"
        jmp short intr_end      ;Return to caller

;-- Command code was O.K. --> Execute command ----------------

bc_ok:  shl bl,1                ;Calculate pointer in jump table
        xor bh,bh               ;Clear BH
        call [fct_tab+bx]       ;Call function
        les  di,dword ptr db_ptr;Data block address to ES:DI

;-- End execution of the function -----------------------------

intr_end label near

        or  ax,0100h            ;Set ready bit
        mov es:[di+status],ax   ;Store everything in the status field

        popf                    ;Restore flag register
        pop es                  ;Restore other registers
        pop ds
        pop bp
        pop si
        pop di
        pop dx
        pop cx
        pop bx
        pop ax

        ret                     ;Return to caller

intr    endp

;----------------------------------------------------------------------

dummy   proc near               ;This routine does nothing

        xor ax,ax               ;Clear busy bit
        ret                     ;Return to caller

dummy   endp

;----------------------------------------------------------------------

no_sup  proc near               ;This routine called for all functions
                                ;which should really not be called
        mov ax,8003h            ;Error: Command not recognized
        ret                     ;Return to caller

no_sup  endp

;----------------------------------------------------------------------

store_c proc near               ;Stores a character in the internal
                                ;keyboard buffer
                                ;Input: AL = Character
                                ;       BX = Character position

        mov [bx+key_bu],al      ;Store character in internal buffer
        inc bl                  ;Increment pointer to end
        cmp bl,KEY_SZ           ;End of buffer reached?
        jne store_e             ;NO --> STORE_E

        xor bl,bl               ;New end is the beginning of buffer
```

```
store_e: ret                   ;Return to caller              mov  ax,0100h          ;Set busy bit (no character)
                                                               ret                    ;Return to caller
store_c  endp

                                                          read_b  endp

;------------------------------------------------------   ;------------------------------------------------------

read    proc near              ;Read a certain number of characters   del_in_b proc near        ;Clear input buffer
                               ;from the keyboard to a buffer
                                                               mov  ah,1              ;Still characters in the buffer?
        mov  cx,es:[di+num_db]  ;Read number of characters         int  16h               ;Call BIOS keyboard interrupt
        jcxz read_e            ;Test for equality to 0             je   del_e             ;No character in the buffer --> END
        les  di,es:[di+b_adr]  ;Address of character buffer to ES:DI
        cld                    ;Increment on STOSB                 xor  ah,ah             ;Remove character from buffer
        mov  si,key_a          ;Pointer to next character in KEY_SZ  int  16h               ;Call BIOS keyboard interrupt
        mov  bx,key_e          ;Pointer to last character in KEY_SZ  jmp  short del_in_b    ;Test for additional characters

read_1: cmp  si,bx             ;Other characters in keyboard buffer?  del_e:  xor  ax,ax           ;Everything O.K.
        jne  read_3            ;Yes --> READ_3                        ret                    ;Return to caller

read_2: xor  ah,ah             ;Function number for reading is 0    del_in_b endp
        int  16h               ;Call BIOS keyboard interrupt
        call store_c           ;Store characters in internal buffer  ;------------------------------------------------------
        cmp  al,0              ;Test if extended code
        jne  read_3            ;No --> READ_3                      write proc near            ;Write a specified number of
                                                                                              ;characters on the display screen
        mov  al,ah             ;Extended code is in AH
        call store_c           ;Store                                mov  cx,es:[di+num_db]  ;Number of characters read
read_3: mov  al,[si+key_bu]    ;Read character from keyboard buffer   jcxz write_e           ;Test for equality to 0
        stosb                  ;Transmit to buffer of calling funct.  lds  si,es:[di+b_adr]  ;Address of character buffer to DS:SI
        inc  si                ;Increment pointer to next character   cld                    ;Increment on LODSB
        cmp  si,KEY_SZ         ;End of buffer reached?
        jne  read_4            ;No --> READ_4                         mov  ah,3              ;Read current display page
                                                                      int  16h               ;Call BIOS video interrupt
        xor  si,si             ;Next character is the first character
                               ;in the keyboard buffer                mov  ah,14             ;Function number for BIOS interrupt

read_4: loop read_1            ;Repeat until all characters read    write_1:  lodsb            ;Read character to be output to AL
        mov  key_a,si          ;Store position of the next character    int  10h               ;Call BIOS video interrupt
                               ;in the keyboard buffer                   loop write_1           ;Repeat until all characters output

        mov  byte ptr key_e,bl ;Store position of the last character  write_e:  xor  ax,ax        ;Everything O.K.
                               ;in the keyboard buffer                   ret                    ;Return to caller

read_e: xor  ax,ax             ;Everything O.K.                     write endp
        ret                    ;Return to caller
                                                          ;------------------------------------------------------
read    endp
                                                          init    proc near            ;Initialization routine
;------------------------------------------------------
                                                               mov  word ptr es:[di+end_adr],offset init  ;Set end address of
read_b  proc near              ;Read the next character from the     mov  es:[di+end_adr+2],cs           ;the driver
                               ;keyboard but leave in the buffer
                                                               xor  ax,ax             ;Everything O.K.
        mov  ah,1              ;Function number for BIOS interrupt   ret                    ;Return to caller
        int  16h               ;Call BIOS keyboard interrupt
        je   read_p1          ;No character present --> READ_P1   init    endp

        mov  es:[di+13],al     ;Store character in data block     ;======================================================
        xor  ax,ax             ;Everything O.K.
        ret                    ;Return to caller                 code    ends
                                                                  end
read_p1 label near
```

The header of this driver describes a character device driver that handles both the standard input device (keyboard) and the standard output device (monitor). After linking it into the system, setting the two bits in the device attribute calls this driver on all function calls previously handled by the CON driver. Like any other driver, this driver has a strategy routine and an interrupt routine. The strategy routine stores the address of the data block in the variable DB_PTR.

The interrupt routine saves the contents of all registers that will be changed by it on the stack and obtains the routine number to be called from the data block. It then checks whether CONDRV supports this function. If it doesn't, it jumps directly to the end of the interrupt routine and sets the proper error code in the status field of the request header that was passed to the routine. Then it restores the registers that were saved on the stack and returns control to the calling DOS function.

For any of the functions that are supported by the device driver, the offset address of a routine to handle a particular function is determined from the table labeled FCT_TAB. Notice that the routines named DUMMY and NO_SUP appear several times. DUMMY is for all functions that apply only to block device drives and, therefore, aren't used in this driver. The DUMMY routine clears the AX register and sets the BUSY bit in the status word. The NO_SUP routine handles any functions that cannot be used since the drive attribute for CONDRV doesn't support these functions.

The STORE_C routine can be accessed from the lower level routines in this driver. Its purpose is to store a character in the internal keyboard buffer of the driver. The driver really shouldn't have this buffer available since BIOS (whose functions are used by the driver to read characters from the keyboard) also has this type of buffer. The problem is that the BIOS always returns two characters when pressing a key with extended codes (cursor keys, function keys, etc.). If the higher level functions of DOS only ask for one character at a time from CONDRV, the second character shouldn't be lost. Instead, it should be stored in a buffer and delivered to DOS by the read function on the next call. This is STORE_C's task.

Reading characters

The next routine is the READ function. It obtains the number of characters to be read from the request header passed by DOS. If it is 0, the routine is terminated immediately. If it isn't 0, then a loop, which executes once for every character read, starts. It first tests for characters still stored in the internal keyboard buffer. If characters are found, a character is passed to the buffer of the calling function. If an additional character exists in the keyboard buffer, function 0 of the BIOS keyboard interrupt 16H inputs a character from the keyboard. This character is also passed to the internal keyboard buffer. If it's an extended keycode, it's divided into two characters. The next step removes a character from the internal keyboard buffer and passes the character to the buffer of the calling function. The process repeats until all characters requested have been passed to DOS. Then the routine ends.

The higher level DOS functions also call the function named READ_P. It tests whether a character was entered from the keyboard. If not, it sets the BUSY bit in the status field of the request header passed by DOS, and returns to the calling function. If a character was entered without having been read, the driver reads this character and passes it to the calling DOS function in the request header, and resets the busy bit. The character remains in the keyboard buffer, and on a subsequent call of the read function, it's again passed to DOS. To test the availability of a character, the READ_P function uses function 1 of the BIOS keyboard interrupt 16H.

The function DEL_IN_B is also called by the higher level DOS functions. DEL_IN_B deletes the contents of the keyboard buffer. It removes characters from the buffer using function 0 of the BIOS keyboard interrupt until function 1 indicates that no more characters are available. This ends the function and it returns to the calling function after the BUSY bit is reset.

Writing characters

WRITE takes the number of characters from a buffer passed by DOS and displays the characters on the screen. This routine uses function 0EH of the BIOS video interrupt. Once all characters have been displayed, it sets the BUSY bit in the status field and ends the function. This function also executes when the higher level DOS functions call the Write and Verify functions.

Initialization

The last function, which is the initialization routine, is called first by DOS. Since CONDRV doesn't initialize variables and hardware, the routine simply enters the driver's ending address into the passed request header. The routine returns its own starting address since it will never be called again, and is the end of the chain of drivers.

In its current form, the driver isn't very useful because it uses only those functions already available to the CON driver of DOS. It would be more practical if an enhanced driver, such as ANSI.SYS, was developed. An enhanced driver provides more control over the screen design. For example, it's possible that such a driver would have complete windowing capability, which could be accessed from any program, in any programming language.

The following block device driver creates a 160K RAM disk:

Listing RAMDISK.ASM

```
;*******************************************************;
;*                  R A M D I S K                     *;
;*---------------------------------------------------*;
;* Task      : This program is a driver for a 160K RAM disk. *;
;*---------------------------------------------------*;
;* Author    : MICHAEL TISCHER                        *;
;* Developed on : 08/04/87                            *;
;* Last update  : 01/07/92                            *;
;*---------------------------------------------------*;
;* Assembly  : MASM RAMDISK;                          *;
;*             LINK RAMDISK;                           *;
;*             EXE2BIN RAMDISK RAMDISK.SYS             *;
;*                            or                       *;
;*             TASM RAMDISK                            *;
;*             LINK RAMDISK;                           *;
;*             EXE2BIN RAMDISK RAMDISK.SYS             *;
;*---------------------------------------------------*;
;* Call      : Copy into root directory, add the command *;
;*             DEVICE=RAMDISK.SYS to the CONFIG.SYS file and *;
;*             reboot the system.                      *;
;*******************************************************;

code    segment
```

```
        assume cs:code,ds:code,es:code,ss:code

        org 0                   ;Program has no PSP so begin
                                ;at offset address 0

;== Constants ===============================================

cmd_fld   equ 2                 ;Offset command field in data block
status    equ 3                 ;Offset status field in data block
num_dev   equ 13                ;Offset number of supported devices
changed   equ 14                ;Offset medium changed?
end_adr   equ 14                ;Offset driver end addr. in data block
b_adr     equ 14                ;Offset buffer address in data block
num_cmd   equ 16                ;Functions 0-16 are supported
num_db    equ 18                ;Offset number in data block
bpb_adr   equ 18                ;Offset Address of BPB of the media
sector    equ 20                ;Offset first sector number
dev_des   equ 22                ;Offset device description of RAM disk

;== Data ===============================================


frst_b  equ this byte           ;First byte of the driver

;-- Device driver header -----------------------------------
```

```
        dw  -1,-1              ;Link to next driver          intr  proc far              ;Interrupt routine
        dw  0100100000000000b  ;Driver attribute
        dw  offset strat       ;Pointer to strategy routine        push ax               ;Push registers onto the stack
        dw  offset intr        ;Pointer to interrupt routine       push bx
        db  1                  ;Device supported                   push cx
        db  7 dup (0)          ;These bytes give the name          push dx
                                                                   push di
;-- Jump table for individual functions ------------------         push si
                                                                   push bp
fct_tab dw offset init         ;Function  0: Initialization        push ds
        dw offset med_test     ;Function  1: Media test            push es
        dw offset get_bpb      ;Function  2: Created BPB           pushf                  ;Push the flag register onto the stack
        dw offset read         ;Function  3: Direct read
        dw offset read         ;Function  4: Read                  push cs                ;Set data segment register
        dw offset dummy        ;Function  5: Read, remain in buffer pop  ds                ;(Code and data are identical)
        dw offset dummy        ;Function  6: Input status
        dw offset dummy        ;Function  7: Erase input buffer    les  di,dword ptr db_ptr;Address of data block to ES:DI
        dw offset write        ;Function  8: Write                 mov  bl,es:[di+cmd_fld] ;Get command code
        dw offset write        ;Function  9: Write & verify        cmp  bl,num_cmd         ;Is command code permitted?
        dw offset dummy        ;Function 10: Output status         jle  bc_ok             ;Yes --> BC_OK
        dw offset dummy        ;Function 11: Clear output buffer
        dw offset write        ;Function 12: Direct write          mov  ax,8003h          ;Code for "Unknown command"
        dw offset dummy        ;Function 13: Open (Ver. 3.0 and up) jmp  short intr_end    ;Return to caller
        dw offset dummy        ;Function 14: Close
        dw offset no_rem       ;Function 15: Changeable medium?  ;-- Command code was O.K. --> Execute command ------------
        dw offset write        ;Function 16: Output until busy
                                                               bc_ok:  shl  bl,1             ;Calculate pointer in jump table
db_ptr  dw (?),(?)             ;Pass data block address             xor  bh,bh             ;Clear BH
rd_seg  dw (?)                 ;RD_SEG:0000 = start of RAM disk     call [fct_tab+bx]      ;Call function

bpb_ptr dw offset bpb,(?)      ;Accept BPB address              ;-- End execution of function ------------------

boot_sek db 3 dup (0)          ;Jump to the boot routine is     intr_end label near
                               ;normally stored here                push cs                ;Set data segment register
        db "MITI 1.0"          ;Name of creator & version number    pop  ds                ;(Code and data are identical)
bpb     dw 512                 ;512 bytes per sector
        db 1                   ;1 sector per cluster                les  di,dword ptr db_ptr;Address of the data block to ES:DI
        dw 1                   ;1 reserved sector (boot sector)     or   ax,0100h          ;Set ready bit
        db 1                   ;1 File Allocation Table (FAT)       mov  es:[di+status],ax ;Store everything in the status field
        dw 64                  ;64 entry maximum in root directory
        dw 320                 ;320 sectors total = 160 K           popf                   ;Restore flag register
        db 0FEh                ;Media descriptor (1 side, 40 tracks pop  es                ;Restore other registers
                               ;of 8 sectors each)                  pop  ds
        dw 1                   ;FAT occupies one sector             pop  bp
                                                                   pop  si
                                                                   pop  di
        ;-- Boot routine omitted (systems cannot --------------    pop  dx
        ;-- be booted from a RAM disk)                             pop  cx
                                                                   pop  bx
vol_name db "RAMDISK   "       ;The actual volume name             pop  ax
        db 8                   ;Attribute, defines volume name
                                                                   ret                    ;Return to caller
;== Driver routines and functions ======================
                                                               intr  endp
strat   proc far               ;Strategy routine
                                                               ;------------------------------------------------------
        mov  cs:db_ptr,bx      ;Store data block address
        mov  cs:db_ptr+2,es    ;in the DB_PTR variable         init  proc near            ;Initialization routine

        ret                    ;Return to caller                  ;-- the following code is overwritten -------------
                                                                  ;-- after the RAM disk is installed
strat   endp
                                                                  ;-- Determine device designation of the RAM disk -------
;------------------------------------------------------
```

```
        mov  ah,30h          ;Check DOS Version with function 30(h)
        int  21h             ;of DOS interrupt 21(h)
        cmp  al,3            ;is it Version 3 or higher?
        jb   prinm           ;Yes --> PRINM

        mov  al,es:[di+dev_des] ;Get device designation
        add  al,"A"          ;Convert to letters
        mov  im_ger,al       ;Store in installation message

prinm:  mov  dx,offset initm ;Address of installation message
        mov  ah,9            ;Output function number for string
        int  21h             ;Call DOS interrupt

;-- Calculate address of first byte following the RAM disk ---
;-- and set as the driver's end address

        mov  word ptr es:[di+end_adr],offset ramdisk+8000h
        mov  ax,cs           ;RAM disk size =
        add  ax,2000h        ;32K + (2 * 64K) = 160K
        mov  es:[di+end_adr+2],ax
        mov  byte ptr es:[di+num_dev],1    ;1 device supported
        mov  word ptr es:[di+bpb_adr],offset bpb_ptr ;BPB pointer
        mov  es:[di+bpb_adr+2],ds          ;address

        mov  ax,cs           ;Segment address: start of RAM disk
        mov  bpb_ptr+2,ds    ;Segment address: BPB in BPB pointer
        mov  dx,offset ramdisk ;Calculate to offset address 0
        mov  cl,4            ;Divide offset address by 16 and
        shr  dx,cl          ;convert into segment address
        add  ax,dx          ;Add the two segment addresses
        mov  rd_seg,ax      ;and store

;-- Create boot sector -----------------------------------

        mov  es,ax           ;Transfer segment address to ES
        xor  di,di           ;Boot sector begins at
                             ;byte 1 of the RAM disk
        mov  si,offset boot_sek ;Boot sector's address in memory
        mov  cx,15           ;Only the first 15 words are used
        rep  movsw           ;Copy boot sector into RAM disk

;-- Create FAT -------------------------------------------

        mov  di,512          ;FAT begins at byte 512 of the RAM disk
        mov  al,0FEh         ;Write media descriptor into the first
        stosb                ;byte of the FAT
        mov  ax,0FFFFH       ;Store code for bytes 2 and 3 of FAT
        stosw                ;in FAT
        mov  cx,236          ;Remaining 236 words occupied by FAT
        inc  ax              ;Set AX to 0
        rep  stosw           ;Set all FAT entries to unoccupied

;-- Create root directory with volume name -------------------

        mov  di,1024         ;Root directory starts in sector 3
        mov  si,offset vol_name ;Volume name address in memory
        mov  cx,6            ;Volume name is 6 words long
        rep  movsw           ;Copy volume name into RAM disk

        mov  cx,1017         ;Fill the rest of the directories in
        xor  ax,ax           ;sectors 2, 3, 4 and 5 with zeros
        rep  stosw
```

```
        xor  ax,ax           ;Everything O.K.
        ret                  ;Return to caller

init    endp

;-----------------------------------------------------------------

dummy   proc near           ;This routine does nothing

        xor  ax,ax           ;Clear busy bit
        ret                  ;Return to caller

dummy   endp

;-----------------------------------------------------------------

med_test proc near          ;RAM disk medium cannot be changed

        mov  byte ptr es:[di+changed],1
        xor  ax,ax           ;Clear busy bit
        ret                  ;Return to caller

med_test endp

;-----------------------------------------------------------------

get_bpb  proc near          ;Pass address of BPB to DOS

        mov  word ptr es:[di+bpb_adr],offset bpb
        mov  word ptr es:[di+bpb_adr+2],ds

        xor  ax,ax           ;Clear busy bit
        ret                  ;Return to caller

get_bpb  endp

;-----------------------------------------------------------------

no_rem   proc near          ;RAM disk medium cannot be changed
        mov  ax,20           ;Set busy bit
        ret                  ;Return to caller

no_rem   endp

;-----------------------------------------------------------------

write proc near

        xor  bp,bp           ;Send DOS --> RAM disk
        jmp  short move      ;Copy data

write endp

;-----------------------------------------------------------------

read    proc near

        mov  bp,1            ;Send RAM disk --> DOS

read    endp

;-- MOVE: Move a certain number of sectors between RAM disk and DOS
;-- Input    : BP = 0 : Transmit from DOS to RAM disk (Write)
;--              BP = 1 : Transmit from RAM disk to DOS (Read)
```

```
;-- Output    : none                                              mov  ds,ax              ;Reverse ES and DS
;-- Registers : AX, BX, CX, DX, SI, DI, ES, DS and FLAGS are affected   xchg si,di              ;Reverse SI and DI
;-- Info      : Information required (number, first sector)       move_3: rep movsw          ;Copy data into DOS buffer
;--             is taken from the data block passed by DOS           or  bp,bp              ;Read?
                                                                    jne  move_1             ;No --> Maybe other sectors to copy
                                                                    mov  ax,es              ;Store ES in AX
move    proc near                                                   push ds                 ;Store DS on the stack
                                                                    pop  es                 ;Read ES
        mov  bx,es:[di+num_db]  ;Number of sectors read            mov  ds,ax              ;Reverse ES and DS
        mov  dx,es:[di+Sector]  ;Number of first sector            xchg si,di              ;Reverse SI and DI
        les  di,es:[di+b_adr]   ;Address of buffer to ES:DI        jmp  short move_1       ;Additional sectors to copy

move_1: or   bx,bx         ;More sectors to read?               move_e: xor  ax,ax          ;Everything O.K.
        je   move_e        ;No more sectors --> END                 ret                    ;Return to caller
        mov  ax,dx         ;Sector number to AX
        mov  cl,5          ;Calculate number of paragraphs      move    endp
        shl  ax,cl         ;Multiply segment units by 32,
        add  ax,cs:rd_seg  ;add to segment start of RAM disk    ;-- RAM disk starts here -----------------------------------------
        mov  ds,ax         ;Transmit to DS
        xor  si,si         ;Offset address is 0                     if ($-frst_b) mod 16      ;Must start on a memory address
        mov  ax,bx         ;Number of sectors to be read to AX       org ($-frst_b) + 16 - (($-frst_b) mod 16) ; divisible by 16
        cmp  ax,128        ;More than 128 sectors to read?          endif
        jbe  move_2        ;No --> Read all sectors              ramdisk equ this byte
        mov  ax,128        ;Yes --> Read 128 sectors (64K)
move_2: sub  bx,ax         ;Subtract number of sectors read      initm   db "**** 160K RAMDISK DEVICE "
        add  dx,ax         ;Add to sectors to be read next       im_ger  db "?"
        mov  ch,al         ;Number sect. to be read * 256 words          db ": installed (c) 1987 by MICHAEL TISCHER8",13,10,10
        xor  cl,cl         ;Set word counter low byte to 0
        or   bp,bp         ;Should more be read?                 ;----------------------------------------------------------------
        jne  move_3        ;No --> MOVE_3
        mov  ax,es         ;Store ES in AX
        push ds            ;Store DS on the stack               code    ends
        pop  es            ;Read ES                                      end
```

This driver is similar to the CONDRV driver. The biggest difference between the two lies in the functions that each supports.

Note: The initialization routine INIT is more comprehensive than the CONDRV initialization routine, and remains in memory after the end of execution even though it's no longer needed. We'll explain why this occurs in the section on the "INIT routine".

First, this routine finds the DOS version number using function 30H. If the version number is equal to or greater than 3, the request header passed by DOS contains the device designation of the RAM disk. The system reads the designation, changes it to a character and places the character into the installation message. DOS function 09H is used to display this message on the screen.

Next, the program computes the ending address of the RAM disk. Since the actual data area of the RAM disk starts immediately after the last routine of this driver, 160K is added to the program's ending address. Also, the address of a variable (BPB_PTR) containing the address of the BIOS parameter block is passed to DOS. This variable describes the RAM disk's format. In this case, it tells DOS that the RAM disk uses 512 bytes per sector. Each cluster consists of one sector and only one reserved sector (the boot sector) exists. In addition, only one FAT exists. Additional information indicates that a maximum of 64 entries can be made in the root directory and that the RAM disk has 320 sectors available (160K of memory). The FAT occupies a single sector, and the media descriptor byte FEH designates a diskette with one side and 40 tracks of 8 sectors each.

These parameters are then placed into the request header of DOS and the segment address of the data area of the RAM disk is calculated. (This information is needed by the driver itself instead of by DOS.)

The INIT routine

The RAM disk must now be formatted to create a boot sector, FAT, and a root directory. Since these data structures are in the first sectors of the RAM disk, a normal INIT routine (which releases its memory to DOS), would overwrite itself with these data structures and would crash the system. This is why the initialization routine isn't at the end of the last routine of the driver, which would place it at the beginning of the RAM disk's data area.

The boot sector occupies the entire first sector of the RAM disk. However, only the first 15 words are copied into it because this is all DOS needs. The name "boot sector" is actually a misnomer here, because it's impossible to boot a system from a RAM disk.

The second sector of the RAM disk contains the FAT. The first two entries are the media descriptor byte and 0 in the subsequent entries. These zeros indicate unoccupied clusters (an empty RAM disk).

The last data structure is the root directory. It contains only the volume name.

Remaining routines

This concludes the work of the initialization routine and returns the system to the calling function. The remaining driver routines are explained in the order in which they appear.

The DUMMY routine performs the same task as the routine of the same name in the CONDRV driver.

The MED_TEST routine is found only in block device drivers. This routine informs DOS whether the medium was changed.

The next routine, GET_BPB, simply passes the addresses of the variables, which contain the address of the BPB of the RAM disk, to DOS, as the initialization routine had already done.

NO_REM allows DOS to sense whether the medium (the RAM disk) can be changed. You cannot change a RAM disk, so the program sets the BUSY bit in the status field.

The two most important functions of the driver perform read and write operations. As in CONDRV, the program calls Write and Verify instead of the normal Write function, since a data error cannot occur during RAM access. The routine itself does very little; it loads the value 0 into the BP register and jumps to the MOVE routine. The READ routine performs in a similar way, except that it loads a 1 into the BP register.

MOVE itself is an elementary routine for moving data. The BP register signals whether data is to move from the RAM disk to DOS or in the opposite direction. The routine receives all other data (the DOS buffer's address, the number of the sectors to be transferred, and the first sector to be transferred) from the data block passed by DOS. See the comments in the MOVE routine for details of the procedure.

Changes

Obviously, this RAM disk can be enhanced. If you have enough unused memory, you can extend the size of the RAM disk to 360K. AT owners could make the RAM disk resident beyond the 1 megabyte boundary. In this case, the data transfer between DOS and the RAM disk would use function 87H of interrupt 15H.

The clock driver

This final sample driver directly accesses the battery powered clock of an AT computer. It's useful because when the DOS commands DATE and TIME are used, the date and time are passed directly to the battery powered realtime clock. Reading the date and time reads the information directly from the memory locations of the realtime clock.

Listing ATCLK.ASM

```
;*****************************************************;
;*                                                   *;
;*                     A T C L K                     *;
;*---------------------------------------------------*;
;*  Task          : This program is a clock driver which can be  *;
;*                   used by DOS for functions which access date *;
;*                   and time from the battery powered AT clock. *;
;*---------------------------------------------------*;
;*  Author        : MICHAEL TISCHER                  *;
;*  Developed on  : 08/04/87                         *;
;*  Last update   : 01/07/92                         *;
;*---------------------------------------------------*;
;*  Assembly      : MASM ATCLK;                      *;
;*                   LINK ATCLK;                     *;
;*                   EXE2BIN ATCLK ATCLK.SYS         *;
;*                   or                              *;
;*                   TASM ATCLK                      *;
;*                   LINK ATCLK;                     *;
;*                   EXE2BIN ATCLK ATCLK.SYS         *;
;*---------------------------------------------------*;
;*  Call          : Copy into root directory, add the command    *;
;*                   DEVICE=ATCLK.SYS to the CONFIG.SYS file      *;
;*                   and then boot system.           *;
;*****************************************************;

code       segment

           assume cs:code,ds:code,es:code,ss:code

           org 0                 ;Program has no PSP, therefore
                                 ;it begins at offset address 0

;== Constants =============================================

cmd_fld    equ 2                 ;Offset command field in data block
status     equ 3                 ;Offset status field in data block
end_adr    equ 14                ;Offset driver end addr. in data block
num_db     equ 18                ;Offset number in data block
b_adr      equ 14                ;Offset buffer address in data block

;== Data =================================================

;-- Header of device driver --------------------------------

           dw -1,-1              ;Connection to next driver
           dw 1000000000001000b  ;Driver attribute
           dw offset strat       ;Pointer to strategy routine
           dw offset intr        ;Pointer to interrupt routine
           db "$CLOCK "          ;New clock driver

db_ptr     dw (?),(?)            ;Address of data block passed

mon_tab    db 31                 ;Table with number of days in
february   db 28                 ;the months
           db 31,30,31,30,31,31,30,31,30,31

;== Driver routines and functions ==========================

strat      proc far             ;Strategy routine

           mov cs:db_ptr,bx      ;Record address of the data block in
           mov cs:db_ptr+2,es    ;the variable DB_PTR

           ret                   ;Back to caller

strat      endp

;-----------------------------------------------------------

intr       proc far             ;Interrupt routine

           push ax               ;Store registers on the stack
           push bx
           push cx
           push dx
           push di
           push si
           push bp
           push ds
           push es
           pushf                 ;Store the flag register

           cld                   ;Increment for string commands

           push cs               ;Set data segment register
           pop ds                ;Code is identical with data here

           les di,dword ptr db_ptr ;Address of data block to ES:DI
           mov bl,es:[di+cmd_fld]  ;Get command code
           cmp bl,4              ;Should time/date be read?
           je ck_read            ;YES --> CK_READ
           cmp bl,8              ;Should time/date be written?
           je ck_write           ;YES --> CK_WRITE
```

```
        or    bl,bl       ;Should driver be initialized?
        jne   unk_fkt     ;NO --> UNK_FKT (Unknown function)

        jmp   init        ;Initialize driver

unk_fkt: mov  ax,8003h    ;Code for "unknown command"

        ;-- Execution completed ------------------------------------

intr_end label near
        or    ax,0100h    ;Set finished bit
        mov   es:[di+status],ax ;Store everything in status field

        popf              ;Restore flag register
        pop   es          ;Restore other registers
        pop   ds
        pop   bp
        pop   si
        pop   di
        pop   dx
        pop   cx
        pop   bx
        pop   ax

        ret               ;Back to caller

intr    endp

;-------------------------------------------------------------------

ck_read label near        ;Read time/date from the clock

        mov   byte ptr es:[di+num_db],6 ;6 bytes are passed
        les   di,es:[di+b_adr]  ;ES:DI points to the DOS buffer

        mov   ah,4        ;Read function number for date
        int   1Ah         ;Call BIOS time interrupt
        call  date_ofs    ;Change date after offset to 1-1-1980
        stosw             ;Store in buffer

        mov   ah,2        ;Read function number for time
        int   1Ah         ;Call BIOS time interrupt
        mov   bl,ch       ;Store hour in BL
        call  bcd_bin     ;convert minutes
        stosb             ;Store in buffer
        mov   cl,bl       ;Hour to CL
        call  bcd_bin     ;Convert hour
        stosb             ;Store in buffer
        xor   al,al       ;Hundredth of a second is 0
        stosb             ;Store in buffer
        mov   cl,dh       ;Seconds to CL
        call  bcd_bin     ;Convert seconds
        stosb             ;Store in buffer

        xor   ax,ax       ;Everything O.K.
        jmp   short intr_end  ;Back to caller

;-------------------------------------------------------------------

ck_write label near       ;Write time/date into clock

        mov   byte ptr es:[di+num_db],6 ;6 bytes are read
        les   di,es:[di+b_adr]  ;ES:DI points to the DOS buffer
```

```
        mov   ax,es:[di]  ;Get number of days since 1-1-1980
        push  ax          ;Store number
        call  ofs_date    ;Convert into a date
        mov   ch,19h      ;Year begins with 19..
        mov   ah,5        ;Set function number for date
        int   1AH         ;Call BIOS time interrupt

        mov   al,es:[di+2] ;Get minute from buffer
        call  bin_bcd     ;Convert to BCD
        mov   cl,al       ;Bring to CL
        mov   al,es:[di+5] ;Get seconds from buffer
        call  bin_bcd     ;Convert to BCD
        mov   dh,al       ;Bring to DH
        mov   al,es:[di+3] ;Get hours from buffer
        call  bin_bcd     ;Convert to BCD
        mov   ch,al       ;Bring to CH
        xor   dl,dl       ;No summer time
        mov   ah,3        ;Set function number for time
        int   1AH         ;Call BIOS time interrupt

        ;-- Calculate day of the week --------------------------
        xor   dx,dx       ;High word for division
        pop   ax          ;Get number of days from stack
        or    ax,ax       ;Is number 0?
        je    nodiv       ;Yes --> Bypass division
        xor   dx,dx       ;High word for division
        mov   cx,7        ;Week has seven days
        div   cx          ;Divide AX by 7
nodiv:  add   dl,3        ;1-1-80 was a Tuesday (Day 3)
        cmp   dl,8        ;Is it a Sunday or Monday?
        jb    nosomo      ;NO --> No correction necessary
        sub   dl,cl       ;Correct value
nosomo: mov   al,6        ;Location 6 in RTC is day of week
        out   70h,al      ;Address to RTC address register
        mov   al,dl       ;Day of the week to AL
        out   71h,al      ;Day of the week to RTC data register

        xor   ax,ax       ;Everything O.K.
        jmp   intr_end    ;Back to caller


;-- OFS_DATE: Convert number of days since 1-1-1980 into date --------
;-- Input   : AX = Number of days since 1-1-1980
;-- Output  : CL = Year, DH = Month and DL = Day
;-- Registers : AX, BX, CX, DX, SI and FLAGS are affected
;-- Info     : MON_TAB array converts offsets

ofs_date proc near

        mov   cl,80       ;Year 1980
        mov   dh,01       ;January
ly:     mov   bx,365      ;Number of days in a normal year
        test  cl,3        ;Is year a leap year?
        jne   ly1         ;NO --> LY1
        inc   bl          ;Leap year has one day more
ly1:    cmp   ax,bx       ;Another year passed?
        jb    mo          ;NO --> Calculate months
        inc   cl          ;YES --> Increment year
        sub   ax,bx       ;Deduct number of days in this year
        jmp   short ly    ;Calculate next year

mo:     mov   bl,28       ;Days in February in a normal year
        test  cl,11b      ;Is the year a leap year?
        jne   nolp2       ;NO --> NOLP2
```

```
        inc   bl              ;In leap year February has 29 days
nolp2:  mov   february,bl      ;Store number of days in February

        mov   si,offset mon_tab ;Address of months table
        xor   bh,bh            ;Every month has less than 256 days
mo1:    mov   bl,[si]          ;Get number of days in month
        cmp   ax,bx            ;Another month passed?
        jb    day              ;NO --> Calculate day
        sub   ax,bx            ;YES --> Deduct day of the month
        inc   dh               ;Increment month
        inc   si               ;SI to next month in the table
        jmp   short mo1        ;Calculate next month

day:    inc   al               ;The remainder + 1 is the day
        call  bin_bcd          ;Convert day to BCD
        mov   dl,al            ;Transmit to DL
        mov   al,dh            ;Transmit month to AL
        call  bin_bcd          ;Convert to BCD
        mov   dh,al            ;Move to DH
        mov   al,cl            ;Move year to AL
        call  bin_bcd          ;Convert to BCD
        mov   cl,al            ;Move to CL

        ret                    ;Back to caller

ofs_date endp

;-- BIN_BCD: Convert binary number to BCD ----------------------------
;-- Input    : AL = Binary value
;-- Output   : AL = corresponding BCD value
;-- Registers : AX, CX and FLAGS are affected

bin_bcd  proc near

        xor   ah,ah            ;Prepare 16 bit division
        mov   ch,10            ;Work in decimal system
        div   ch               ;Divide AX by 10
        shl   al,1             ;Shift quotient left 4 places
        shl   al,1
        shl   al,1
        shl   al,1
        or    al,ah            ;OR remainder
        ret                    ;Back to caller

bin_bcd  endp

;-- DATE_OFS: Convert Date in number of days since 1-1-1980 -----------
;-- Input    : CL = Year, DH = Month and DL = Day
;-- Output   : AX = Number of days since 1-1-1980
;-- Registers : AX, BX, CX, DX, SI and FLAGS are affected
;-- Info     : MON_TAB array converts date

date_ofs proc near
        call  bcd_bin          ;Convert year to binary
        mov   bl,al            ;Transmit to BL
        mov   cl,dh            ;Transmit month to CL
        call  bcd_bin          ;Convert Month to binary
        mov   dh,al            ;and transmit again to DH
        mov   cl,dl            ;Transmit day to CL
        call  bcd_bin          ;Convert day to binary
        mov   dl,al            ;and transmit again to DL

        xor   ax,ax            ;0 days
        mov   ch,bl            ;Store year
```

```
        dec   bl               ;Decrement one year
year:   cmp   bl,80            ;Counted back to year 1980 ?
        jb    month            ;YES --> convert month
        test  bl,11b           ;Is year a leap year ?
        jne   nolpyr           ;NO --> NOLPYR
        inc   ax               ;A leap year has one more day
nolpyr: add   ax,365           ;Add days of year
        dec   bl               ;Back one year
        jmp   short year       ;Process next year

month:  mov   bl,28            ;Days in February in a normal year
        test  ch,11b           ;Is current year a leap year?
        jne   nolpyr1          ;NO --> NOLPYR1
        inc   bl               ;February has 29 days during leap year
nolpyr1: mov  february,bl      ;Store in month table
        xor   ch,ch            ;Every month has less than 256 days
        mov   bx,offset mon_tab ;Address of month table
month1: dec   dh               ;Decrement number of months
        je    add_day          ;All month calculated --> ADD_DAY
        mov   cl,[bx]          ;Get number of days in month
        add   ax,cx            ;Add to total days
        inc   bx               ;BX to next month in the table
        jmp   short month1     ;Calculate next month

add_day: add  ax,dx            ;Add current day
        dec   ax               ;Deduct one day (1-1-80 = 0)
        ret                    ;Back to caller

date_ofs endp

;-- BCD_BIN: Convert BCD to binary number ----------------------------
;-- Input    : CL = BCD value
;-- Output   : AL = corresponding binary value
;-- Registers : AX, CX and FLAGS are affected

bcd_bin  proc near             ;Convert BCD value in CL to binary
                               ;Return in AL

        mov   al,cl            ;Transmit value to AL
        shr   al,1             ;Shift 4 places right
        shr   al,1
        shr   al,1
        shr   al,1
        xor   ah,ah            ;Set AH to 0
        mov   ch,10            ;Process in decimal system
        mul   ch               ;Multiply AX by 10
        mov   ch,cl            ;Transmit CL to CH
        and   ch,1111b         ;Set high nibble in CH to 0
        add   al,ch            ;Add AL and CH
        ret                    ;Back to caller

bcd_bin  endp

;--------------------------------------------------------------------

init    proc near              ;Initialization routine

        ;-- The following code can be overwritten --------------------
        ;-- by DOS after installing the clock       --------------------

        mov   word ptr es:[di+end_adr],offset init ;Set end address
        mov   es:[di+end_adr+2],cs                 ;of the driver

        mov   ah,9            ;Display installation message
```

```
     mov  dx,offset initm   ;Address of the text                      init    endp
     int  21h               ;Call DOS interrupt

     xor  ax,ax             ;Everything O.K.                     ;------------------------------------------------------------
     jmp  intr_end          ;Back to caller
                                                                  code    ends
initm  db 13,10,"**** ATCLK driver installed. (c) 1992 by"         end
       db " MICHAEL TISCHER",13,10,"$"
```

The basic structure of this driver differs from the other drivers because it calls the individual functions directly, instead of through a table of their addresses. Since it only supports functions 00H, 04H, and 08H, this driver can test the function numbers directly passed by DOS. If any other function occurs, it signals an error. Besides the INIT routine, which sets only the ending address of the driver like CONDRV, the driver also contains the Read Time and Date and Write Time and Date functions.

Time routine

The TIME routine is fairly simple. For reading the clock, the routine reads the time from the memory locations of the clock, converts the time from BCD to binary format, and then passes the time to the DOS buffer. For setting the time, the reverse occurs: The routine reads the time from the DOS buffer, converts the code from binary to BCD format, and writes the BCD code into the memory locations of the clock.

DOS uses the same format for indicating time as the clock: Hour, minute, and seconds, each comprise one byte.

Date routine

The DATE routine is more complicated. While the clock stores day, month, and year as one byte each, DOS encodes the date according to the number of days since January 1, 1980. This number must be converted into a date in the form of day, month, and year as DOS writes the time and date. The opposite occurs when you call the Read function; the clock date must be converted into the number of days. Let's discuss how this is done.

The conversion routine begins with the year 1980. January 1, 1980 (called NUMDAYS from this point on) is equal to the value 0. The routine tests whether this year is less than the current year. If it is, the routine adds the number of days in this year to NUMDAYS, adding a day to compensate for each leap year. Then it increments the year and tests again for a smaller number than the current year. This loop repeats until it reaches the current year. The routine then computes the number of days in the current year's month of February, and enters this month into a table that contains the number of days for each month.

In the next step, for every month less than the current month, the routine adds the number of days in this month to NUMDAYS. Once it reaches the current month, only the current days of the month are added to NUMDAYS. The end result is transferred to the DOS buffer and the routine terminates.

Converting to date format

Reverse this process to convert NUMDAYS into a date. The routine begins with the year 1980 and tests whether the number of days in this year is less than or equal to NUMDAYS. If this is the case, the year is incremented and the number of days in this year is subtracted from NUMDAYS. This loop is repeated until the number of days in a year is larger than NUMDAYS. The routine then computes the number of days in the current year's month of February, and enters this month into the table of the months.

January starts another loop, which tests whether the number of days in the current month is less than or equal to NUMDAYS. If this is the case, the month increments and the routine subtracts the number of days from NUMDAYS. If the number of days in a month is larger than NUMDAYS, the loop ends. NUMDAYS must only be incremented enough to give the day of the month and complete the date.

The routine then converts the date to BCD format and enters the date in the memory locations of the clock.

25.9 EXE Programs as Device Drivers

Over the past few years, more device drivers have been developed as EXE files. This means that you can either install the driver from a DEVICE = command in your CONFIG.SYS file, or you could install it directly from the DOS system prompt or a batch file. Even DOS has started to use this kind of device driver. The EMM386.EXE driver available in DOS Version 5.0 is an example of this type of device driver.

These programs aren't true device drivers. Actually they are TSR programs that function as device drivers. Like other driver programs, they can be installed with the CONFIG.SYS file when the system boots, so they don't have to compete for memory with other TSR programs.

These TSR drivers are character device drivers, which means that DOS doesn't assign drive letters to them. Their names are selected so that they won't be confused with other files (e.g., EMMXXX0 for EMS drivers). Also, since they aren't intended to replace normal device drivers, they can only use one driver function (function 00H for initialization). This function must be supported so that DOS can properly install the TSR program as a driver.

Since you can't determine whether one of the other driver functions might be called, such a function call should be indicated as an error from the status flag.

The following demonstration program, EXESYS.ASM, shows how this works. This program was written to be installed as a device driver, or called as a normal EXE file. DOS isn't restricted to the ".SYS" file extension for device drivers, even though most driver program files use it. DOS can load any EXE file as a device driver, as long as it consists of only one segment and starts at address 00H in this segment with the standard driver header.

This can be done easily by including the following instruction at the start of the segment:

```
org 0h
```

The driver header follows this instruction. When the driver is installed, DOS will then be able to obtain the offset addresses of the strategy and interrupt routines and call them as with any other driver.

896

To run the program from the DOS command line, it must also have an entry point just like any other EXE file. This is easily done by inserting the name of a special initialization procedure (as would be found in a normal EXE program) after the END instruction at the end of the assembly language listing.

This way, the program will also be able to determine whether it was started as a device driver from CONFIG.SYS or from the DOS system prompt. The initialization procedure will only be called if the program is started from the command line. DOS will call the strategy and interrupt routines if the program is started from CONFIG.SYS.

But once you've installed a TSR program as a driver, why would you want to recall it? Doing this allows you to pass information to the driver by using command line parameters. This can easily be done with the IOCTL functions (DOS function 44H).

The following demonstration program contains all the basics for developing a driver that can be installed from CONFIG.SYS or called from the system prompt. This particular driver simply displays a message that indicates which method was used to start it. You can easily modify this program to perform more complicated driver operations.

Assembler listing: EXESYS.ASM

```
;************************************************************;
;*                                                        *;
;*                  E X E S Y S . A S M                   *;
;*------------------------------------------------------- *;
;*  Task       : This driver can be called either from DOS *;
;*               as an executable file, or from CONFIG.SYS *;
;*               as a device driver.                      *;
;*------------------------------------------------------- *;
;*  Author     : MICHAEL TISCHER                          *;
;*  Developed on : 11/01/1991                             *;
;*  Last update  : 01/07/1991                             *;
;*------------------------------------------------------- *;
;*  Assembly   : MASM EXESYS;                             *;
;*               LINK EXESYS;                             *;
;*                          or                            *;
;*               TASM EXESYS                              *;
;*               TLINK EXESYS                             *;
;************************************************************;

code    segment

        assume cs:code,ds:code

        org 0                   ;The program has no PSP, so it
                                ;begins at offset address 0

;== Constants ================================================

cmd_fld  equ 2                  ;Command field offset in data block
status   equ 3                  ;Status field offset in data block
end_adr  equ 14                 ;Driver end address offset in data blk

;== Data =====================================================

;-- Device driver header ------------------------------------

        dw -1,-1                ;Link to next driver
        dw 1010000000000000b   ;Driver attribute
        dw offset strat         ;Pointer to strategy routine
        dw offset intr          ;Pointer to interrupt routine
        db "$$EXESYS"           ;Driver name

db_ptr  dw (?),(?)                   ;Address of specified data block


;=============================================================
;== EXE program routines =====================================
;=============================================================

exestart proc far

        push cs                 ;Set DS to CS
        pop  ds

        mov ah,09h              ;Display message
        mov dx,offset exemes
        int 21h

        mov ax,4C00h            ;End program as usual
        int 21h

exestart endp

exemes  db "EXESYS - (c) 1991 by Michael Tischer", 13,10,10
        db "Called as an EXE program!", 13, 10, "$"

;=============================================================
;== Driver routines and functions ============================
;=============================================================

strat   proc far                ;Strategy routine

        mov cs:db_ptr,bx        ;Set data block address in
        mov cs:db_ptr+2,es      ; the DB_PTR variable

        ret                     ;Return to caller

strat   endp
```

```
;-------------------------------------------------    pop  di
                                                      pop  dx
intr    proc far              ;Interrupt routine      pop  cx
                                                      pop  bx
        push ax               ;Place registers on stack  pop  ax
        push bx
        push cx                                       ret              ;Return to caller
        push dx
        push di               intr    endp
        push si
        push bp               ;-------------------------------------------------
        push ds               ;-- If called as a device driver,
        push es               ;-- memory is then released
        pushf                 ;Set flag register
                              init    proc near              ;Initialization routine
        push cs               ;Set data segment register (code
        pop  ds               ;and data are identical)       mov  word ptr es:[di+end_adr],offset init  ;Set end address
                                                             mov  es:[di+end_adr+2],cs              ;of driver
        les  di,dword ptr db_ptr;Data block address after ES:DI
        mov  ax,8003h         ;executed by error              mov  ah,09h           ;Display message
        cmp  byte ptr es:[di+cmd_fld],00h  ;Only INIT is permitted  mov  dx,offset ddmes
        jne  short intr_end   ;Error --> Return to caller     int  21h

        call init             ;Can only be function 00H       xor  ax,ax            ;Everything is O.K.
                                                             ret                   ;Return to caller
        ;-- End execution of the function ----------------------------
                              init    endp
intr_end label near
                              ;-- Data no longer needed after initialization -----------------------
        or   ax,0100h         ;Set ready bit
        mov  es:[di+status],ax ;Save entire contents in status field  ddmes  db "EXESYS - (c) 1991 by Michael Tischer", 13,10,10
                                                                      db "Called as a device driver!", 13, 10, "$"
        popf                  ;Pop flag register
        pop  es               ;Pop remaining registers     ;=================================================================
        pop  ds
        pop  bp               code    ends
        pop  si                       end exestart
```

25.10   CD-ROMs

After its introduction in the audio world, the compact disk was introduced to the PC market. A CD-ROM drive and a PC form an interesting combination. The compact disk medium itself is read-only, but 660 megabytes of data can be stored in the form of text, graphics, etc.

Many publications and references are currently available on CD-ROM, such as:

- Telephone directories

- Books in Print

- The Bible in various translations

- The English translation of Pravda

In addition, maps, photographic libraries, public domain program collections, and medical databases are available in CD-ROM format. New titles are being published daily in this growing market.

Why CD-ROM?

The CD-ROM has a clear advantage over the printed medium. Once captured and digitized, information can be processed by a computer in whatever form the user needs. The possibilities appear to be limitless, considering how easy it is to read and compare information.

Another important advantage of CD-ROM is how easily data can be accessed. The user simply loads the driver software, presses a key or two, and the information is displayed on the screen.

Currently, you can buy a PC-compatible CD-ROM player for $800 to $1,000. These players are available as either external or internal devices.

Interfacing

The PC's hardware can be easily interfaced to a CD-ROM player. However, the software may encounter some problems. This is understandable, since DOS was never intended to support these devices. In this section we'll show you how a CD-ROM drive, using the proper drivers and utility programs, can be accessed like a read-only floppy disk drive.

Earlier in the book we mentioned that the device drivers act as mediators between the disk operating system and the external devices, such as monitor, printer, disk drives, and hard disks. DOS differentiates between block device drivers and character device drivers. As a mass storage device capable of reading information in a block mode, a CD-ROM drive would normally be added to the rest of the system through a block driver. Here's where the problem begins: DOS makes a number of assumptions about block devices, but a CD-ROM drive cannot meet this criteria.

Memory limitations

In versions of DOS up to and including Version 3.3, the biggest obstacle to interfacing with a block driver was the 32 megabyte limit imposed on every volume designated as a block device. The second biggest obstacle is the lack of a file allocation table (FAT) on a CD-ROM. Instead of the FAT, the CD-ROM contains a form of data table into which the starting addresses of the various subdirectories and files are recorded. However, DOS still requires a FAT that it can read during driver initialization.

A character driver works better for implementing a CD-ROM driver, because DOS doesn't make assumptions about the structure of the devices connected through character drivers. However, even character drivers have problems communicating with a CD-ROM drive, because they transmit characters one at a time instead of in groups of characters. Another disadvantage is the need for a name (e.g., CON) instead of a device designation. DOS must first see the CD-ROM driver as a character driver to DOS in order to prevent read accesses to a non-existent FAT. The CONFIG.SYS file supplies the name of the device during the system booting process.

Configuring the CD-ROM

The manufacturer usually includes CD-ROM driver software with the CD-ROM drive package. A driver of this type usually has a name such as SONY.SYS or HITACHI.SYS, depending on the manufacturer.

The CONFIG.SYS sequence that installs this driver can look something like this:

```
DEVICE=HITACHI.SYS /D:CDR1
```

The device driver selects the name CDR1 as the name of the CD-ROM drive.

After executing the initialization routine from DOS, the CD-ROM is treated as a block driver that has been enhanced with a few special functions supporting CD-ROMs. However, DOS still views the CD-ROM player as a character driver: DOS cannot view the CD-ROM's directory, nor can it directly access the files on the CD-ROM.

Driver software extensions

To overcome this obstacle, many CD-ROM players include a TSR (Terminate and Stay Resident) program, named MSCDEX (Microsoft CD-ROM Extension), in addition to the device driver software. This program must be called from within the AUTOEXEC.BAT file. The name of the CD driver can be passed to the program from the DOS prompt, as shown in the following example:

```
MSCDEX /D:CDR1
```

MSCDEX first opens this driver through the DOS OPEN function and provides it with a device designation. DOS assumes that MSCDEX is a device on a remote network, as supported by DOS in Version 3.1.

MSCDEX brings us closer to the solution, since DOS handles network devices as files containing more than 32 megabytes. These devices are accessed through redirection, rather than direct access from DOS. The resident portion of MSCDEX interfaces to the redirector, and intercepts all calls to the redirector. If MSCDEX receives a call addressed to the CD-ROM drive, it adapts each instruction to a call applicable to the CD-ROM driver. This makes a perfect connection between DOS and the CD-ROM drive, while still allowing access to subdirectories and files at any time.

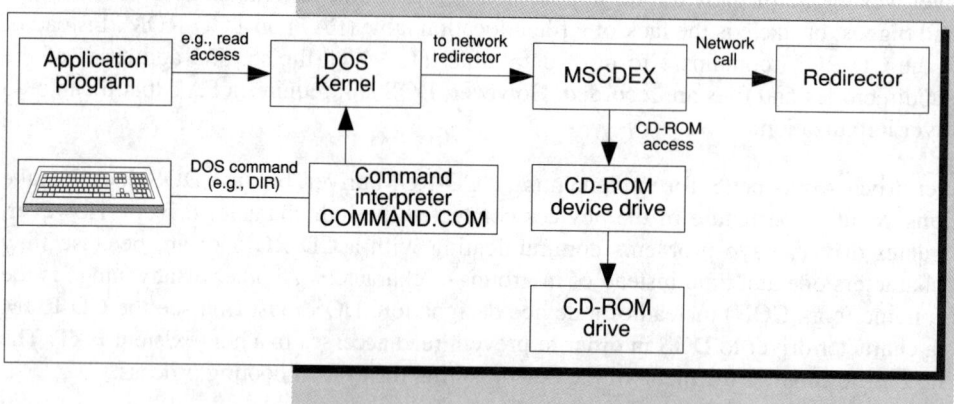

CD-ROM access through MSCDEX and its device driver

Chapter 26

The DOS File System

The user doesn't see many of the tasks that DOS performs. This is why some users underestimate the complexity of DOS. For example, DOS requires many data structures for handling a mass storage device, although this is not always realized by the user. The file system must perform many steps before executing even small tasks, such as copying files or searching for a file on the hard drive.

Disk drives recognize tracks, sectors, and read/write heads instead of files and subdirectories. Therefore, DOS's file system addresses all available mass storage devices at both physical and logical levels. A file system of this type consists of a series of data structures, which describe the capacity and contents of a disk drive. In this chapter we'll discuss how the DOS file system is designed and how it works.

26.1 Basic Structure of the File System

The *volume* is the basis of the DOS file system. From the user's viewpoint, DOS addresses mass storage devices as volumes. Each individual volume is assigned a letter. Floppy disk drives are identified by the letters A and B, while the letters C or D usually identify a hard drive. Although a hard drive can be divided into multiple volumes, a floppy disk drive can consist of only one volume.

DOS Versions 3.3 and lower limited volume size to a maximum of 32 megabytes. Therefore, any hard drives with capacities over 32 megabytes were divided into multiple volumes. In this chapter we explain how DOS Version 4.0 broke the 32 megabyte barrier.

Every DOS volume has its own structure, regardless of whether it's intended for diskettes or hard media. The size of the storage media isn't relevant to the structure because it only affects the number of individual data structures required to manage the volume.

Volume label names

Although not required, each volume can be assigned a *volume label name* when created. The DIR command lists volume label names when they're available. Each volume has its own root directory, which can contain multiple subdirectories and files. These subdirectories and files can be maintained and manipulated by using one or more of the interrupt 21H functions.

Sectors

DOS subdivides each volume into a series of *sectors* organized sequentially. Each sector contains a specific number of bytes (usually 512) and is assigned a consecutive logical sector number, beginning with sector 0. A 10 megabyte volume contains 20,480 sectors, consisting of logical sectors 0 to 20,479. DOS cannot control the physical arrangement of the sectors. This is controlled by the device driver, which mediates between the volume and DOS. The device driver's distribution of logical sectors (organized or not) is unimportant. It's only important that the device driver clearly differentiates between logical and physical sectors.

Since DOS API function calls with interrupt 21H are directed to files instead of individual sectors, DOS converts these file accesses into sector accesses. To do this, DOS uses the volume's directory structure and a data structure known as the FAT (File Allocation Table).

The following illustration shows the basic structure of a mass storage device:

```
┌─────────────────────────────────────────────────────────────────┐
│              Mass storage device structure                       │
├──────────────┬──────────────────────────────────────────────────┤
│          0   │ Manufacturer's name, device driver, boot routine  │
│              ├──────────────────────────────────────────────────┤
│              │ First file allocation table (FAT)                 │
│   Sector     ├──────────────────────────────────────────────────┤
│              │ One or more copies of FAT                         │
│   Number     ├──────────────────────────────────────────────────┤
│              │ Root directory with volume label names            │
│          V   ├──────────────────────────────────────────────────┤
│              │ Data register for files and subdirectories        │
└──────────────┴──────────────────────────────────────────────────┘
```

As we previously mentioned, every volume is divided into areas containing the various DOS data structures and individual files. The FORMAT command creates these data structures when you format a disk. Since the size of the individual areas can differ depending on the type of mass storage device (and the manufacturer), every volume contains a *boot sector*.

26.2 The Boot Sector

The boot sector contains all the information required to access the different areas and data structures. DOS creates this sector during disk formatting. Boot sectors always have the same structure and are always located in sector 0 so that DOS can find and interpret it properly.

The following illustration shows the layout of the boot sector:

Boot sector layout		
Address	Contents	Type
00H	Jump to boot routine (E9xxx or EBxx90)	3 bytes
03H	Manufacturer's name and version number	8 bytes
0BH	Bytes per sector	1 word
0DH	Sectors per cluster	1 byte
0EH	Number of reserved sectors	1 word
10H	Number of FATs	1 byte
11H	Number of entries in root directory	1 word
13H	Number of sectors in volume	1 word
15H	Media descriptor	1 byte
16H	Number of sectors per FAT	1 word
18H	Sectors per track	1 word
1AH	Number of read/write heads	1 word
1CH	Number of hidden sectors	1 word
1EH–1FFH	BOOT ROUTINE	

The term "boot sector" is used because DOS "boots" (i.e., starts) from this sector. Since DOS usually isn't stored in permanent PC memory (ROM), it's loaded and started from disk. After you switch on the computer, the BIOS takes over system initialization. It loads physical sector 0 (not logical sector 0) of the floppy disk or hard drive into memory. Since device drivers aren't in memory, the BIOS checks physical sector 0 for information. It then loads the boot information from that sector. Once it completes its work, the BIOS starts execution at address 0.

The boot sector always contains an assembly language JUMP instruction at address 00H. Execution of the boot sector's program code begins at this address. After execution, the program continues at a location further into the boot sector. This instruction can be either a normal jump instruction or a "short jump." The field for this jump instruction is 3 bytes long, but a "short jump" only requires 2 bytes. Therefore, a NOP (No Operation) instruction always follows the "short jump" to fill in the extra byte. As its name suggests, this NOP instruction doesn't do anything.

A series of fields, which contain certain information about the organization of the media, follow. The first field is 8 bytes long and contains the manufacturer's name, where the medium was formatted, as well as the DOS version number that performed the formatting. The field may also contain the name of a software manufacturer (e.g., if a program such as PCTools® formatted the volume).

The next fields contain the physical format of the media (i.e., the number of bytes per sector, the number of sectors per track, etc.) and the size of the DOS data structures stored on the medium.

The physical device information is needed when using the interrupt 13H BIOS functions. These fields are called the BIOS parameter block (BPB). DOS uses this information for various tasks.

Note: Some sources of undocumented DOS structures state that the BPB is a parameter table, which can be accessed by using Get Service Data, instead of part of the boot sector. These sources imply that the boot sector information is only part of the BPB.

Three additional fields, providing other volume information to the device driver, follow the BPB. However, these fields aren't used directly by DOS.

Bootstrap

Next is the *bootstrap* routine, to which the jump instruction branches at the beginning of this boot sector. This routine handles the loading and starting of DOS through the individual system components (see Chapter 3).

Several reserved sectors may follow the boot sector. These sectors can contain additional bootstrap code. The numbers of these sectors are recorded in the BPB in the field starting at offset address 0EH. This field terminates the boot sector; a 1 in this field indicates that additional reserved sectors don't follow the boot sector. This applies to most PCs, because no versions of DOS have required a bootstrap loader that cannot fit into the first boot sector.

26.3 The File Allocation Table (FAT)

DOS must know which sectors of the volume are still available before it can add new files or enlarge existing files. This information is contained in a data structure called the FAT (File Allocation Table), located immediately next to the media's reserved area. Each entry in the FAT corresponds to a certain number of logically contiguous sectors called *clusters*, on the media. Location 0DH of the boot sector specifies the number of sectors per cluster as part of the BIOS Parameter Block. Only powers of 2 (1, 2, 4, 8, etc.) are acceptable values. On an XT hard drive, this location contains the value 8 (8 consecutive sectors form a cluster). AT, 386, and 486 hard drives have only 4 sectors per cluster.

As the following table shows, the number of sectors comprising a cluster depends on the storage medium:

Sectors per cluster	
Device	Sectors per cluster
Single sided disk drive	1
Double sided disk drive	2
AT hard drive	4
XT hard drive	8

Despite the values in the previous table, a formatting utility, such as FORMAT, isn't limited to these cluster values. This applies particularly to volumes containing more than 32 megabytes. DOS Versions 4.0 and higher accommodate larger volumes by adding clusters. A volume larger than 32 megabytes quickly exceeds the 65,536 limit for clusters. So, the capacity of the file system can be extended at will, without changing the current structure, by including more sectors per cluster.

The following table shows the clustering used by DOS Version 4.0 for volumes larger than 32 megabytes and up to 2 gigabytes.

Volume and Cluster sizes of DOS 4.0					
Volume size (megabytes)	128	256	8K	16K	32K
Cluster size	2K	4K	8K	16K	32K
Sectors per cluster	4	8	16	32	64

This clustering allocates more memory to the last cluster of a file. This cluster is filled only when its size represents a multiple of the cluster size.

File fragmentation

The idea of joining several sectors into a cluster is based on the logic used by DOS to write files to a medium. Instead of selecting adjoining sectors for file storage, DOS fragments (disassembles) the file so that the various pieces can fit into the available sectors.

The following explains the reasons why DOS fragments the file. Users are constantly creating and deleting files. If you start with an empty volume, new files and their respective clusters are stored in sequence. However, when you delete a file, a gap may develop between two sectors. DOS doesn't adjust the clusters on a volume because this process requires too much time. This is especially true for larger volumes. So, DOS places new files in the gaps created when the older files were deleted. If the entire file could be stored in one of these gaps, it could be kept in one contiguous unit. However, this usually doesn't happen. As a result, DOS divides files and fits them into available gaps.

This process slows file access because the read/write head must be repositioned after almost every read function. To avoid an excessive disassembly of the file, DOS gathers several sequential sectors on the media into a cluster. This ensures that at least the sectors of a cluster contain a portion of a file. If DOS didn't use clusters, a file of 24 sectors could be stored in numerous sectors, which would require the read/write head to be positioned a maximum of 24 times to read the entire file. The cluster principle saves a lot of time, since a file comprised of 4 sectors per cluster is stored in 6 clusters and the read/write head must be repositioned only 6 times.

However, there is a problem with this process. Since a file is assigned at least one cluster, some storage space is wasted. Consider the AUTOEXEC.BAT file, which is usually no longer than 150 bytes. Normally, this file could be stored on a single sector (and still waste almost 400 bytes). However, AUTOEXEC.BAT occupies a cluster of 2048 bytes on an AT, which wastes more than 1.5K of hard disk space.

Disk optimizing programs such as the BeckerTools Disk Optimizer solve this problem by re-organizing the medium and storing all the files in consecutive clusters.

The FAT layout

Now let's return to the file allocation table. The size of individual entries in the FAT under DOS Versions 1.0 and 2.0 is 12 bits. For DOS Versions 3.0 and up, the size of an entry in the FAT depends on the number of clusters. If a volume has more than 4,096 clusters, then each FAT entry is 16 bits; otherwise each FAT entry is 12 bits.

A 12-bit FAT permits control of 4,096 clusters, which corresponds to 4 sectors per cluster, providing a total of 8 megabytes. Although this amount could be expanded by adding more sectors to a cluster, such an expansion isn't recommended. Therefore, you'll find only 16-bit FATs on newer hard drives of 20 megabytes and up, thus allowing the 65,536 maximum of addressable clusters.

The number of bits per FAT entry must be determined before file access. The information in the BIOS parameter block is used for this purpose. The total number of sectors in the volume can be found starting at location 13H. Divide this number by the number of sectors per cluster to obtain the number of clusters in the volume.

The first two entries of the FAT are reserved and aren't related to the cluster assignment. Depending on the sizes of the individual entries, 24 bits (3 bytes) or 32 bits (4 bytes) can be available. The first byte contains the media descriptor, while the value 255 fills in the other bytes. The media descriptor, which is also stored in address 15H of the BPB, indicates the device that the media uses (e.g., a diskette).

The following codes are possible:

Media descriptor codes		
Code	Device	Description
F0H	3.5" disk drive	2 sides, 80 tracks, 18 sectors per track
F8H	Hard disk	Varies
F9H	5.25" disk drive 3.5" disk drive	2 sides, 80 tracks, 15 sectors per track 2 sides, 80 tracks, 9 sectors per track
FAH	5.25" disk drive 3.5" disk drive	1 side, 80 tracks, 8 sectors per track 1 side, 80 tracks, 8 sectors per track
FBH	5.25" disk drive 3.5" disk drive	2 sides, 80 tracks, 8 sectors per track 2 sides, 80 tracks, 8 sectors per track
FCH	5.25" disk drive	1 side, 40 tracks, 9 sectors per track
FDH	5.25" disk drive	2 sides, 40 tracks, 9 sectors per track
FEH	5.25" disk drive	1 side, 40 tracks, 8 sectors per track
FFH	5.25" disk drive	2 sides, 40 tracks, 8 sectors per track

Perhaps you're wondering why the individual entries of the FAT are 12 or 16 bits wide if all they do is show whether a cluster is occupied. This could have been done with one bit; the bit could contain 1 when the cluster is occupied and 0 if the cluster is available.

The entries in the FAT help mark the available clusters and identify the individual clusters containing a specific file. The directory entry of a file tells DOS which cluster holds the first sectors of a file. The number of this cluster corresponds to the number of the FAT entry belonging to it. In this entry is the number of the cluster containing the next sector of file data. This search continues until the last cluster of a file has been reached.

However, the cluster numbers refer to the beginning of the data structure rather than the beginning of the volume (more on this later). For example, assume that the beginning of a file resides in the fourth cluster of the volume. You must read the fourth entry of the FAT to obtain the number of the next cluster containing the file, remembering that a FAT entry can be either 12-bit or 16-bit. This fourth entry contains the number of the next file cluster.

As the following illustration shows, a chain, in which the individual clusters assigned to a file can be located in the proper sequence, is formed. The logical number of each sector can be derived from the cluster number. DOS must send this logical number to the device driver before these sectors can be read or written by DOS. DOS device drivers operate at sector level rather than cluster level. To convert clusters to logical sectors, multiply the cluster number by the number of sectors per cluster.

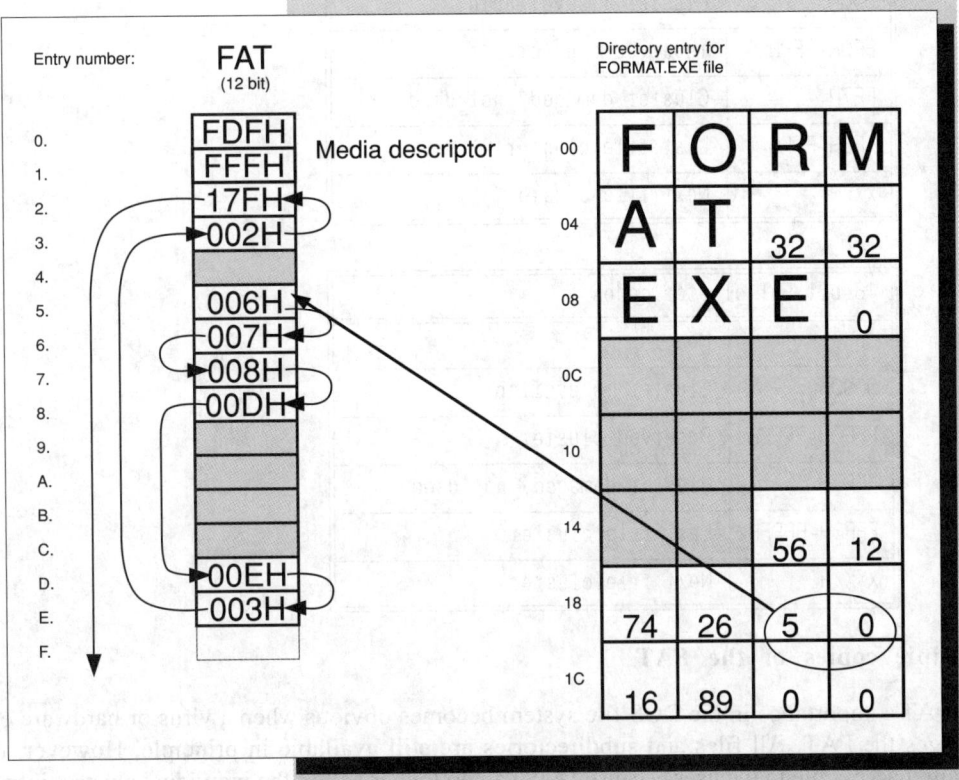

FAT entry and file clusters

The FAT entry corresponding to the last cluster of a file must contain a special code that tells DOS that the file ends here. A cluster number indicates this code, which is either greater than

FF8H (12-bit) or greater than FFF8H (16-bit). However, the following tables show the meanings of the various FAT entries. For example, cluster numbers FF0H—FF6H (12-bit) or FFF0H—FFF6H (16-bit) indicate a reserved cluster (i.e., the root directory of a volume). The root directory has a fixed position and size, and the cluster can be independent rather than chained to the FAT.

Cluster codes FF7H (12-bit) and FFF7H (16-bit) also have special significance. These codes identify clusters whose sectors contain errors, ensuring that DOS doesn't write data to these bad clusters.

Cluster code 0H indicates unoccupied clusters, as well as the first cluster of the volume. Like the first cluster, code 0H represents no sectors, because it contains the volume's medium type. As you'll see later in this book, this is why the cluster number must be reduced by two when converting cluster numbers into sector numbers.

12-bit FAT cluster codes	
Code	Meaning
000H	Cluster is available
FF0H–FF6H	reserved cluster
FF7H	Cluster damaged, not used
FF8H–FFFH	Last file cluster
xxxH	Next file cluster

16-bit FAT cluster codes	
Code	Meaning
0000H	Cluster is available
FFF0H–FFF6H	Reserved cluster
FFF7H	Cluster damaged, not used
FFF8H–FFFFH	Last file cluster
XXXXH	Next file cluster

Multiple copies of the FAT

The FAT's importance in the DOS file system becomes obvious when a virus or hardware error damages the FAT. All files and subdirectories are still available in principle. However, they remain inaccessible to the user because DOS can no longer gather the individual clusters into one unit.

DOS is designed so that several identical copies of the FAT can be kept on a volume. The boot sector's offset address 10H contains the number of FATs. If DOS finds a medium of this type, it automatically updates all copies of the FAT and records this update in offset 10H while creating

908

or deleting files. So, if one FAT is damaged, it can be replaced with another, which minimizes data loss.

The DOS CHKDSK command tests the various FATs to see if they are identical. If the primary FAT is damaged, CHKDSK replaces the damaged primary FAT with another FAT.

26.4 The Root Directory

Now let's look at the structure of a directory.

The root directory of a volume immediately follows the last copy of the FAT. This root directory (like all subdirectories) consists of 32-byte entries, in which information about individual files, subdirectories, and volume label names can be stored. The maximum number of entries in the root directory, and therefore its size, is stored in the BPB starting at address 11H. The FORMAT command specifies both the size number and the BPB. Before considering individual fields of this data structure, here's an overview of a directory entry:

Directory entry layout		
Address	Contents	Type
00H	Filename (blanks padded with spaces)	8 bytes
08H	File extension (blanks padded with spaces)	3 bytes
0BH	File attribute	1 byte
0CH	Reserved	10 bytes
16H	Time of last change	1 word
18H	Date of last change	1 word
1AH	First cluster of file	1 word
1CH	File size	2 words

The first eight bytes usually contain the name of the current file. If the filename is shorter than eight characters, DOS fills the remaining characters with spaces (ASCII code 32). If the directory entry doesn't contain information about a file, but the file is used in another way, the first byte of the filename (therefore the first byte of the directory entry) is identified by a special code:

The first byte of the directory entry	
Code	Meaning
00H	Last directory entry
05H	First character of filename has ASCII code E5H
2EH	File applies to current directory
E5H	File deleted

The second field contains the three character filename extension. If the extension is less than three characters long, DOS fills in the extra characters with blank spaces (ASCII code 32). The period between filename and extension is displayed by the DOS command DIR but isn't kept in the directory; DIR displays this character so that the names are easier to read.

The one-byte attribute field is next. As shown in the following figure, the individual bits of this field define certain attributes. The various attributes can be combined so that a file (as in the IBMBIOS.COM file) can have the attributes READ_ONLY, SYSTEM, and HIDDEN.

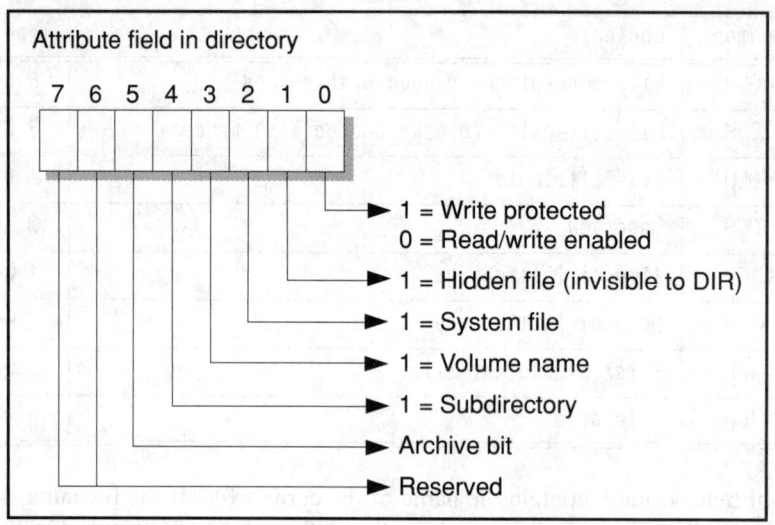

A reserved field follows the attribute field. DOS uses this field for internal operations, and some sources claim that Novell NetWare uses this bit for sharing data.

While the significance of bits 0 to 4 is easy to see, the significance of bit 5 needs additional explanation. The name *archive bit* comes from its use in making backup copies. Every time a file is created or modified, this bit is set to 1. If a program is used to backup this file, (for example the DOS BACKUP command), the archive bit is reset to 0. The next time the BACKUP command is used, it can determine, from the archive bit, whether this file has been modified since the last backup. If it still contains the value 0, the file doesn't have to be backed up again. If the archive bit contains a 1, the file was modified and should be backed up again.

The attributes volume label name and subdirectory will be discussed in more detail later.

910

A reserved field, which DOS requires for internal operations, follows the attribute field.

The time and date fields indicate when the file was last created or modified. Both are stored as words (2 bytes), but have special and different formats.

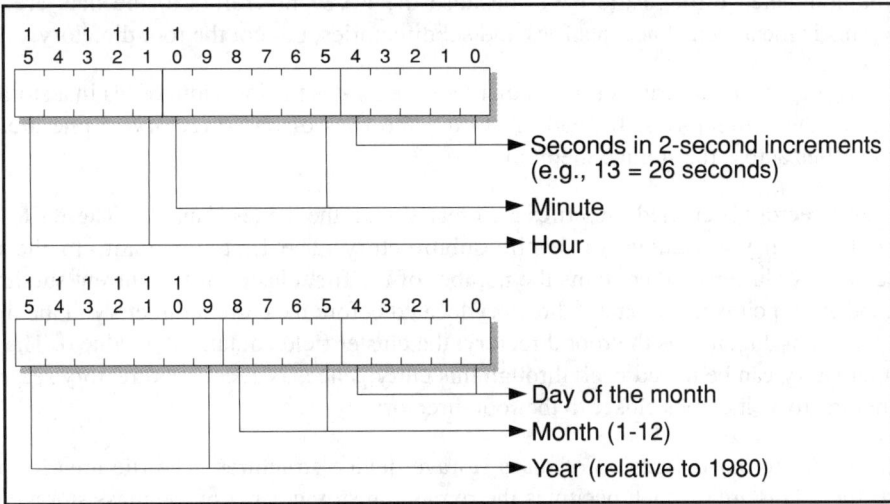

Time and date field formats in directory entry

The next field shows the number of the cluster that contains the first data of the file. It also shows the number of the FAT containing the number of the next cluster assigned to the file. This field forms the beginning of a chain through which all the clusters assigned to a file can be retrieved.

The file size in bytes is stored in two words with the lower word stored first. Using a small formula and the two words, the file size can be calculated as follows:

```
File size = word1 + word2 * 65,536
```

26.5 Subdirectories

Both subdirectories and volume label names deserve special consideration. The volume label name can exist only in the root directory. It's indicated by bit 3 of the current directory entry's attribute field. The filename in a volume entry acts as the volume label name. Use the DOS commands DIR, VOL, and TREE to display the volume label name.

If bit 4 of the current directory's attribute field is set, then this entry is for a subdirectory. If bit 1 in this field is also set, the subdirectory can be addressed. However, this subdirectory isn't displayed when you execute the DIR command. For these entries, the filename and extension field contain the subdirectory name; the date and time field contain the time of its creation. The file length field is always 0. The field that usually indicates the first cluster of the file now indicates the cluster that contains the directory entries of this subdirectory. They have the same 32-byte structure as the entries in the root directory.

As in a normal file, the entry in the FAT corresponding to the subdirectory cluster points to the next cluster of the subdirectory. This is true as long as one cluster is enough for the directory of the subdirectory. This doesn't apply to the root directory, which extends through several sectors or clusters that follow each other logically. Also, the individual clusters of the root directory cannot be connected through the FAT, because the FAT only refers to the data area of the volume. This is the area that accepts files and subdirectories, but not the root directory.

The process previously described reveals that DOS separates the individual files in a storage unit according to their directories. Instead of storing the files of one directory in one area, DOS scatters the files across the storage medium.

When a subdirectory is created, two files are created with the names '.' and '..'. These files can be erased only when you remove the entire subdirectory. The first file points to the current subdirectory. Its cluster field contains the number of the first cluster of the current subdirectory. The second entry points to the parent directory located before the current directory in the directory tree. If the parent directory is the root directory, the cluster field contains the value 0. The path to the root directory can be traced back through this entry, since, as every subdirectory searches for its parent directory, it comes closer to the root directory.

Now let's return to our discussion of mass storage device structures. The file area follows the root directory. This area, which occupies the remaining storage area of the mass storage device, accepts the individual files and various subdirectories. There is an entry in the FAT corresponding to every cluster in this area. If a file is enlarged, DOS reserves a cluster that is still available to store the additional data of the file. The FAT entry of the last cluster, which previously indicated the end of the file, is changed to point to the new cluster. This in turn contains the new end character.

Both DOS Versions 1.0 and 2.0 search for unused clusters from the beginning. In DOS Versions 3.0 and higher, a more complicated search procedure is used to try to select an unused cluster near the other clusters comprising the file. This reduces the access time to the file. Conversely, when reducing file size or deleting a file, the FAT is updated to indicate that the unused clusters are again available. They can be used again when a new file is created or expanded.

Let's begin at the point where DOS finds the first cluster or a file, and the FAT entry for the next cluster in the first cluster. We need to calculate the sector from this cluster.

1.) Subtract 2 from the cluster number. The first two FAT entries contain the media descriptor, so FAT entry 2 is the actual zero cluster on the volume.

2.) Multiply the cluster by the number of sectors per cluster. BIOS obtains this information from the BIOS Parameter Block loaded from the boot sector. The result relates to the first sector of the volume, instead of the first sector of the data range (which is the result we want). You can compute the logical sector where the data range starts, also using information from the BIOS Parameter Block.

3.) The boot sector, the FAT and its duplicates, and the root directory precede the volume's data range. The lengths of these ranges must be calculated and added together. Read the number of sectors reserved from offset address 0EH of the boot sector. Read the number of FAT sectors from offset address 16H of the boot sector, and multiply the number of FAT sectors by the number of FATs (found in address 10H), then add the total to the number of reserved sectors.

4.)   DOS also requires the number of sectors occupied by the root directory. This number is stored in the word beginning at offset 11H in the boot sector. Multiply this value by 32 (bytes per entry), and divide the result by 512 (bytes per sector). Add the result to the boot sector and FAT lengths to obtain the number of the first sector in the data range.

DOS performs this calculation only when booting, or when a medium has been changed (e.g, every time you change diskettes in a floppy disk drive).

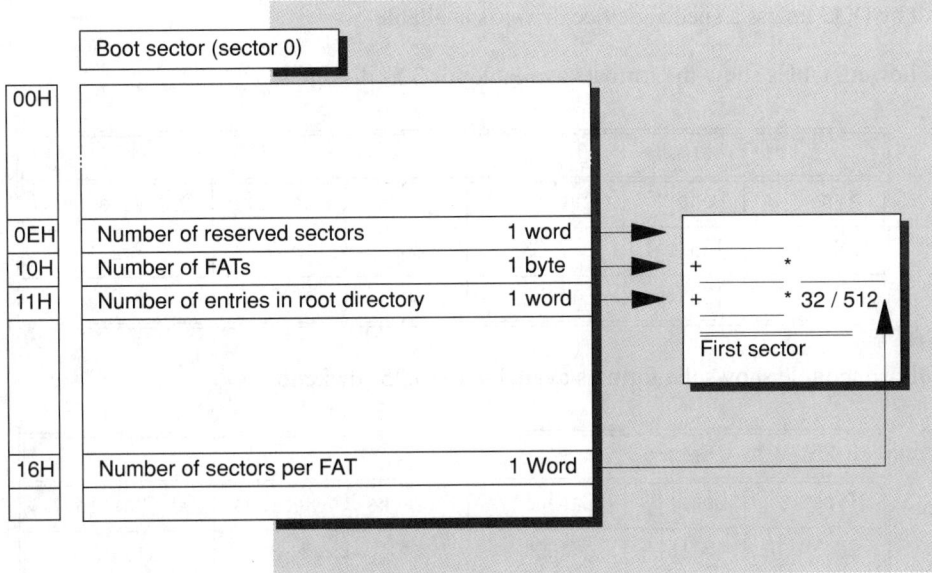

Calculating the first sector of the data range

By adding the number of the first sector in the data range to the first sector number of the addressed file, you receive the logical sector number. DOS can then pass this logical sector number to the device driver for file access.

When DOS requires access to both the first cluster and subsequent clusters of the file, it must read those subsequent clusters from the FAT. These calculations vary depending on the widths of the FAT entries. Reading the next adjacent cluster is easy to do with a 16-bit FAT. Simply multiply the cluster number by 2 to find the next cluster. The result represents the offset address relative to the beginning of the FAT in memory, where the next cluster can be found.

If DOS is dealing with a 12-bit FAT, multiply the cluster number by 1.5. The whole number part of the product becomes the offset in the FAT. The word at this memory address is read. If the product is a whole number, the word read must be combined with a logical AND to 0FFFFH to obtain the number of the next cluster. If the product isn't a whole number, the AND is omitted and the word is shifted by 4 bits to the right (divided by 16).

DOS usually doesn't have to load the FAT into memory, because it permanently stores a copy of this data structure in memory to save execution time.

Now DOS knows the next cluster of the file. If you're using a 12-bit FAT, the next cluster lies in the range from FF8H to FFFH. If you're using a 16-bit FAT, the next cluster lies in the range from FFF8H to FFFFH. This process repeats until DOS finds the end of the file.

26.6 Diskette Formats

Diskettes require formats that specify the exact qualities of a volume. Non-DOS diskettes cannot be read by DOS unless a special device driver is available.

The following tables show the formats available for 3.5" diskettes:

3.5" disk formats					
Type	Density	Capacity	Tracks	Sectors	DOS Version
2S DD	135 tpi	720K	80	9	3.2
2S HD	135 tpi	144Mb	80	18	3.3

The following table shows the formats available for 5.25" diskettes:

5.25" disk formats					
Type	Density	Capacity	Tracks	Sectors	DOS Version
SS SD	40 tpi	160K	40	8	1.0
SS SD	40 tpi	100K	40	9	2.0
DS SD	40 tpi	320K	40	8	1.1
DS SD	40 tpi	360K	40	9	2.0
DS HD	96 tpi	1.2 Mb	80	15	3.0

Chapter 27

The Multiplexer

Several DOS commands operate as TSR programs. This means that they become memory resident when called and remain in the background until needed. These include the PRINT, ASSIGN, SHARE, APPEND, DOSKEY, etc. commands. So these programs can be accessed once they've become memory resident; they use interrupt 2FH. This interrupt is called the *multiplexer*. In this chapter, we'll explain how this works and which programs use the multiplexer.

27.1 How the Multiplexer Operates

Interrupt 2FH is known as the multiplexer because it acts as a communications interface for all TSR programs instead of only one DOS program. After installing a TSR program in memory with an initial function call, it's often necessary to set specific parameters for the TSR or remove the TSR program from memory using DOS commands. These commands then use the multiplexer interrupt to address the memory resident TSR program.

However, it's also possible for application programs to use these calls to modify various resident DOS programs or determine whether they are currently active. For example, a network program requiring SHARE can determine whether this DOS program was loaded. If SHARE wasn't loaded, its startup is aborted and an error message is displayed.

TSR programs must ensure that more than one program can use interrupt 2FH simultaneously. This is done in the following way:

Before a program uses the multiplexer (or MUX), it must assign itself an eight bit identification number. This number is known as the MUX code. The MUX codes 00H to BFH are reserved for various DOS programs, and 0CH to FFH are reserved for application programs.

When this type of TSR program is loaded, it must install an interrupt handler for the multiplexer interrupt, in addition to the other interrupt handlers it may need. So, the program must redirect the interrupt 2FH to its own routine, which replaces the previous interrupt handler. When a program activates the multiplexer interrupt, the program's interrupt handler is executed.

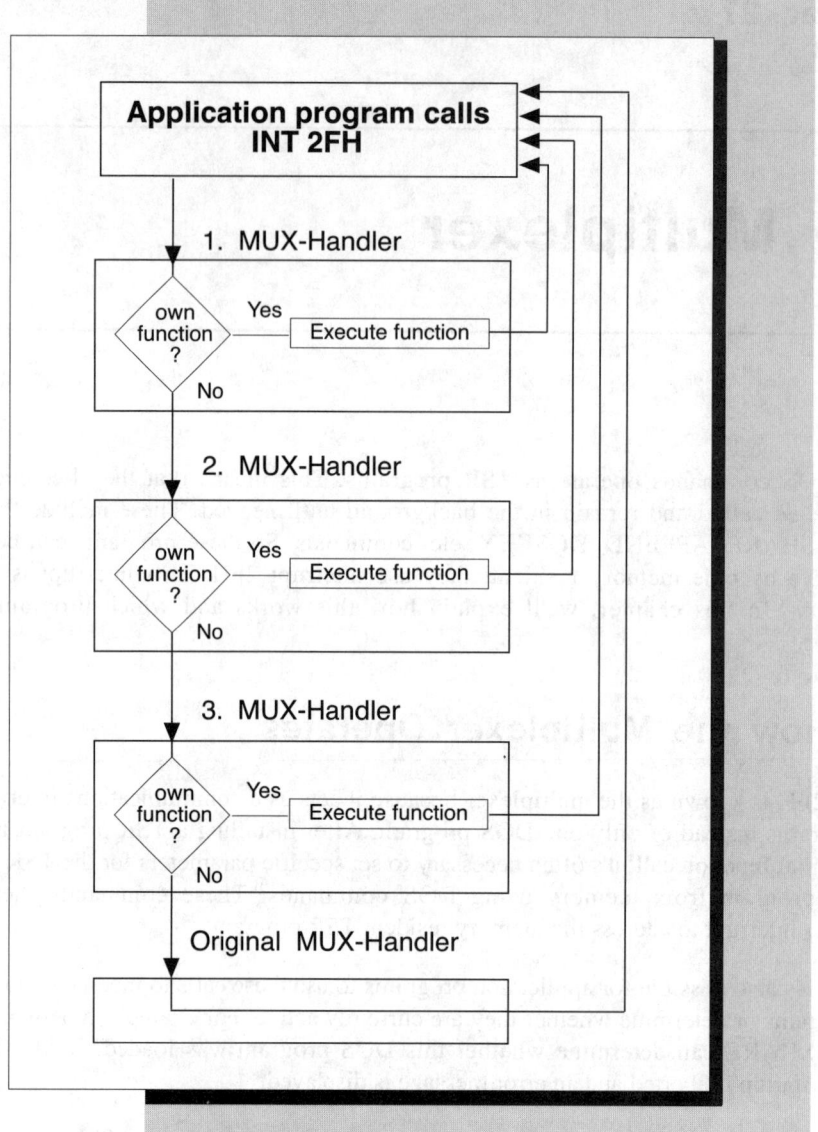

The chain of MUX handlers

First this interrupt handler must determine whether its own program or one of the other programs, which is tied to the multiplexer, is being addressed. It examines the AH register, which should contain the MUX code of the program that's being addressed.

If it finds its own MUX code in this register, the interrupt handler simply reads the remaining processor registers that are important, executes its function, and returns to the caller program with an IRET machine language command.

However, if the MUX code refers to a different TSR program, the interrupt handler cannot terminate its call and return. Instead, it must call the previous interrupt handler that it displaced upon its installation in the multiplexer. This means that a TSR program must note the address of the interrupt handler currently installed in the multiplexer before it can install its own handler.

Since each multiplexer interrupt handler checks the MUX code in this way, and calls the previous handler if the code isn't its own, the chain of interrupt handlers is passed until one of the handlers recognizes the code as its own. This handler then executes the appropriate function, instead of calling its predecessor. At the end of this chain is the first handler that was installed by BIOS when the system was booted. This handler is preceded only by the IRET machine language instruction.

Competition between multiplex handlers

This system works until two multiplex handlers use the same MUX code. When this happens, the more recent handler along this chain will identify the code as its own, and call the specified function. The "older" handler cannot be accessed.

This problem won't occur in DOS programs because Microsoft ensures that none of these programs use the same MUX code. However, if you develop your own TSR programs, it's possible that you'll use a code that's already in use by another program. However, there is a way to determine this at the start of your program.

Normally, each TSR program is stopped to run a function for the installation check. This function should be executed if, at the multiplexer call, the AH register contains the MUX code of the particular program and the value 00H is found in the AL register. If one of the installed handlers recognizes its own code, it must place a value that doesn't equal 00H (generally FFH) in the AL register.

However, if none of the resident handlers recognize the code as their own, it will be passed along the chain of interrupt handlers until it reaches the first handler that was installed. This handler consists of only an IRET instruction. If this is the case, the AL register will be returned unchanged. So, if the AL register still contains 0 after this check, then the specified MUX code isn't being used by an installed handler.

In Chapter 32 we'll demonstrate how the multiplexer interrupt is used with TSR programs.

27.2 How DOS Programs Use the Multiplexer

In this section we'll discuss how the multiplexer is used by various DOS programs and which functions these programs provide. For application programs, many people believe that only the PRINT command, which enables you to print text in the background, is useful. However, you'll see that this isn't really true.

DOS commands which work with the multiplexer

The following table shows the DOS commands which work with the multiplexer:

DOS commands which work with the multiplexer	
MUX code	DOS command
01H	PRINT
06H	ASSIGN
10H	SHARE
1AH	ANSI.SYS
43H	HIMEM
48H	DOSKEY
4AH	DBLSPACE.BIN
4DH	KEYB
B0H	GRAFTABL
B7H	APPEND

The functions of these individual DOS commands are listed and briefly explained below. You'll find detailed descriptions of their input and output parameters in Appendix E.

PRINT   MUX code 01H

The first DOS command to use the multiplexer was PRINT. The PRINT command uses this function to address its memory resident portion, to add files to the print queue list, to delete files from this list, or to delete the list entirely.

Applications can also use this function when they need to execute lengthy printing operations and don't want to monopolize the computer until the print operations are completed. Printers are normally slower than programs, which is why this function was introduced.

To use PRINT, an application must "print" the desired output to a file and then add this file to the print queue. This can easily be done by using the PRINT function.

Function	Description
00H	Installation check
01H	Add file to queue
02H	Delete file from wait list
03H	Delete entire wait list
04H	Interrupt output and check status
05H	Resume output
06H	Check for printer

ASSIGN   MUX code 06H
SHARE   MUX code 10H
ANSI.SYS   MUX code 1AH
GRAFTABL   MUX code B0H

These commands support only function 00H, which is used for the installation check. If this function call returns the value FFH in register AL, that particular program has been installed. Refer to the previous table for the MUX code of each of these programs.

HIMEM.SYS   MUX code 43H

The device driver HIMEM.SYS, which is responsible for managing memory according to the XMS standard, provides two multiplexer functions. The first function, 00H, supports the installation check. It returns the value 80H when HIMEM.SYS is installed. However, unlike other corresponding functions, it returns the value FFH. The second function represents the access point to this device driver, through which the various XMS functions are accessed. In this instance, however, the multiplexer simply enables access to HIMEM.SYS.

```
Function      Description

00H           Installation check
10H           Obtain access to XMS function calls
```

For more information about these functions and HIMEM.SYS, refer to Chapter 12.

DOSKEY (Version 5.0 and later)   MUX code 48H

Since DOS Version 5.0, the memory resident program DOSKEY has permitted the storing and recalling of DOS command line entries, as well as the implementation of macros.

DOSKEY makes these functions available to applications, instead of only at the DOS command line. This is possible through multiplex functions. The MUX code of DOSKEY is 48H, and its two function numbers are 00H and 01H. As with other DOS commands, function 00H is used to check whether DOSKEY is installed. This function performs the usual installation check.

The second function can be used by an application program to ask DOSKEY to receive a command line from the user, in the same way as on the DOS command line. By using the cursor up and down keys, the user can move through previous DOS command line entries. New command lines entered with this function are also added to the list of entries stored by DOSKEY.

DBLSPACE.BIN   MUX code 4AH

DoubleSpace, the DOS 6 on-line hard drive compressor, offers ten functions to disk utilities through the multiplexer interrupt. Unlike other MUX interfaces, 11H must always be given as the function number in register AL, with the subfunction number placed in register BX.

```
Function          Description

00H               Return version information
01H               Scan drive map
02H               Switch drive ID
05H               Link compressed drive
06H               Deactivate DoubleSpace drive
07H               Establish storage space
08H               Return information about CVF file fragmentation
09H               Scan for maximum number of compressed drives
```

See Chapter 35 for more information about DoubleSpace.

KEYB   MUX code ADH

The KEYB.COM keyboard device driver supplies a total of four multiplex functions. They can be used to check the current KEYB version number, the current code page, and the current country flag.

Function	Description
80H	Return version number
81H	Determine current code page
82H	Set country flag
83H	Return country flag

APPEND   MUX code B7H

Of the MUX codes used by the various DOS commands, the code used by APPEND carries the highest value. Although the function number sequence is slightly unconventional, these multiplex functions supply an application with all the functions offered to the user at the DOS command line.

Function	Description
00H	Installation check
02H	Check compatibility to DOS Version 5.0
04H	Return directory list
06H	Check operating mode
07H	Set operating mode
11H	Establish conversion to complete filename

Chapter 28

Network Programming

Over the last several years, networks have become an important part of using PCs. Networks were first used in large corporations, then in medium-sized companies, and now even in small private businesses. Most network systems can be purchased for several hundred dollars. As cheaper network cards become available, the cost of network systems will continue to decrease.

Because networks have become more popular, the demand for programs that support networking is steadily increasing. In this chapter will present the basics of network programming. Although we can't discuss network programming in detail in this book, you should have enough information to create your first network programs.

28.1 Basics of Network Programming

Networks can be used for various purposes. Usually they connect individual PCs, called *workstations*, to a more powerful server. The *server* is usually a fast PC, equipped with a large amount of memory and disk capacity. The server allows these workstations to utilize its resources and perform various tasks. One of the most common tasks is file sharing, which allows files, which are stored and managed by the server, to be accessed by individual workstations.

File sharing is usually performed with database files. Since these files are essential to a business' operation, they must be accessed by several employees. A good example of this is a mail order inventory. With a network, several employees, working on separate workstations, can directly access the inventory, which is stored in a central database.

Generally, the file server is also used to store programs that can be called from individual workstations. This saves disk space on the workstation and minimizes installation work. Obviously it's requires less work and time to install a program once on the file server, than to install it on every workstation.

For example, Windows requires that certain files must be present on individual workstations, even if the main program has been installed on the file server. While the main Windows programs (WIN.COM, PROGMAN.EXE, PAINTBRUSH.EXE, etc.) can be located on the file server, each workstation needs its own WIN.INI and SYSTEM.INI files so that each workstation can define its own environment.

However, even these files can be placed on the server by defining a private directory for each workstation or user. In this area, the private files of a given workstation can be stored without being modified by another workstation. A network operating system, which is the heart of any network system, manages these operations.

Besides making its storage media accessible to other workstations, the network file server can act as a print or communications server, giving workstations access to a printer, a modem, or even another network. These capabilities can significantly reduce equipment expenses, since they allow one printer to be used by many workstations.

Since the appearance of OS/2, SQL servers have become more popular. These servers operate under OS/2, which allows the network stations to access SQL (Structured Query Language) databases. SQL is a program-based language for accessing relational databases.

The SQL server not only manages the SQL databases, but also processes the queries directed to this database by individual workstations. For example, if a workstation queries a customer database for all addresses containing a zip code of 10000, the SQL server is responsible for screening and returning the appropriate records. This type of operation is often referred to as a *remote procedure call*, because the workstation is calling a procedure that's actually located in the SQL server.

The network operating system

Novell is the largest supplier of network operating systems. They offer a series of different NetWare versions. However, several other network operating system manufacturers, such as IBM, 3Com, an Banyan Vines, also produce both NetWare-compatible and independent systems.

A network operating system always consists of a server program, which manages the file server, and a workstation program, which manages each workstation and allows it to address the server. This software is usually supplied in the form of a device driver or a TSR program. Workstations must be able to use DOS as usual and must access the file server like a normal floppy diskette or hard drive. Because of this, the software is embedded deeply into DOS, which enables it to control how DOS manages files.

The network software intercepts all file operations and passes only local operations, which access the workstation's own disk space, to DOS. For example, if the server in a certain network is identified by the device letter "S", the network software would intercept "S:LETTER.TXT" and address this call to the server. So, files that are located on the server can be addressed from a workstation in the same way as local DOS files.

However, this doesn't mean that a workstation user automatically has access to all the information stored on the server hard disk. Since this information could total 1 gigabyte in size, this could be an enormous amount of information. Instead, a network administrator defines which directories and files can be accessed by a user or workstation. These access rights are often tied to passwords that must be entered with a workstations user's login.

Since many users can access the server simultaneously, the server is rarely operated under DOS, which would be too slow to process numerous simultaneous access requests. So, Novell NetWare supplies its own operating system. For instance, this is a system that runs in protected mode on the server and that doesn't need or work with DOS in any way. The server hard disk is managed by a special Novell file system, instead of under DOS. Even if the server could be booted on a DOS diskette, the hard disk still couldn't be accessed because DOS is unable to recognize the foreign disk format.

However, you don't need this information for network programming under DOS, unless you plan on developing tools for Novell NetWare, which is a completely different process.

This also applies to network hardware, which you also won't be dealing with internally, regardless of whether you're using a Token-Ring network, an Ethernet, or an Arc-Net. The function interfaces that facilitate access to the server and communication between workstations are more important.

Function interfaces

Three function interfaces have established themselves as standards for the PC. These are rudimentary DOS functions that were introduced with DOS Version 3.0. They allow numerous workstations to access server files. These functions are supported by all popular network operating systems.

The IPX/SPX interface has been widely used because of Novell's large market share. This interface refers to the numerous functions that are available to a program running on a Novell NetWare workstation. These functions permit communication between workstations, which is vital for such things as E-mail or the remote operation of workstations.

NetBIOS, which was developed by IBM with its PC-LAN network operating system, works similarly. This interface is so widely used that Novell even offers a NetBIOS emulator for its Netware. This emulator transforms NetBIOS function calls into IPX/SPX functions. This is possible because both function interfaces were designed with the same operating principles. So, programs that have been written for NetBIOS can also run on Novell Netware systems. This is why we recommend NetBIOS for network programming, if you want to tackle such a task.

Peer to peer networking

Peer to peer networking has become very popular. With this type of networking, workstations can also act as servers. This technique is particularly suited for smaller operations, because purchasing a large and powerful server may be too expensive. In peer to peer networking, each workstation is equipped with a DOS supplement that allows the workstations to be accessed using standard DOS commands and file operations. Programs such as NetWare Lite by Novell and LANStatic by Microware use this technique.

28.2 Network Programming under DOS

The two main DOS elements in network programming are DOS API functions and the SHARE program, which was introduced with DOS Version 3.0. This program implements the two DOS API functions, and, with their help, ensures that different programs don't interfere with one another while accessing files simultaneously. Often one program will run on several workstations simultaneously and store its files on the server, so that these files can be accessed by the individual workstations simultaneously.

To illustrate this, we'll use an example of a large health club. Several employees use individual workstations to manage the reservations for courts and equipment. These workstations are connected to a server via a network, where a central file contains all the court reservations for the coming days and weeks. The workstations use a single program, which manages court reservations and rentals. As we'll see below, the simultaneous actions of these employees create several problems for the network. First, however, let's take another look at the SHARE program.

Checking for SHARE

Because SHARE is needed in order to work with DOS networking functions, any network program you write should determine whether SHARE is present at program startup. Remember that SHARE is completely integrated in DOS Versions 4.0, 5.0, and higher, so you can omit this check if you're absolutely certain that your program won't be running on earlier versions of DOS.

The SHARE test consists of only an interrupt call. Simply call the multiplexer function 1000H, since this is where the resident portion of SHARE is located. If this function call returns the value FFH in the AL register, you know that SHARE has been installed. You'll learn more about the multiplexer in Chapter 27.

Record locking

The most important aspect of simultaneous file access by more than one workstation is *record locking*. To explain this concept, let's return to our example of the health club. The employees take court reservations from members over the phone. On their workstations, the employees check the availability of the courts for a particular date and time. This information is provided by a data file. Since the data file's records are only read, problems don't occur.

However, when one of these records must be changed, conflicts can occur. For example, this happens when one of the employees makes a reservation for a particular court. Since this reservation isn't recorded in the data file, this court still appears as available. So, it's possible that another employee will also make a reservation for the same court at the same time and date for another member. If the software isn't fast enough to display the previous record change before the second employee makes his or her reservation, the first reservation will be overwritten by the second.

Record locking is designed to prevent these type of situation. Under this principle, a program must first take possession of a record and lock it before the record can be changed in any way. Once this is done, another workstation cannot modify the record.

In our example, this would work as follows: when the first employee finds the record for the available court, he or she presses a special function key that informs the program that this court should be reserved. The program then locks the record, so that the necessary changes can be made to the record. Once this has occurred, the other employees cannot access the record from their workstations as long as it remains locked.

The program responds to this access attempt by displaying a message, which indicates that this court is currently being reserved. However, the first member may cancel his/her reservation immediately after placing it. So, the workstation that's requesting access to the record shouldn't give up immediately. Instead, it should repeatedly try to access the record until it becomes available or until a certain time limit is reached.

Once the record becomes available, the second employee can determine whether the court has already been reserved by another member or whether it's still available. However, this works only if the record is unlocked as quickly as possible after the change has been made.

The following guidelines apply to the shared use of files and records by one or more programs on numerous workstations:

- Records must be locked before they are modified, so that other programs or workstations cannot access them during that time.

- Records must be released immediately after they are modified, so that they are available to other programs or workstations.

SHARE, in conjunction with the network operating system, ensures that locked records cannot be accessed from other sources by displaying an error message when these function calls occur.

Although this process may sound complicated, it's actually very simple. Records can be locked with a single DOS function, 5CH. This function requires the correct file handle and the offset address and length of the segment to be locked. Since files are often larger than 64K, these parameters are considered 32 bit values and are therefore shared by two processor registers. The upper 16 bits of the start offset are written to the CX register and the lower 16 bits to the DX register. The segment length is handled in the same way, by registers SI and DI.

So, although you're not dealing directly with records, locking them isn't very complicated. At a given record length, you can easily use the record number to calculate the correct start offset, and the segment length is already specified.

```
Register          Description

AH                5Ch
AL                Mode: 00 = Lock, 01 = Unlock
BX                File handle
CX:DX             Start offset in the source file as 32 Bit value
SI:DI             Segment (record) length as 32 Bit value
BU:               Parameters for function call 5Ch
```

Since this function can also be used to unlock files, the AL register is used to indicate which operation the function should perform, either locking or unlocking the specified segment. It's also possible to lock more than one file segment with this function because many operations require more than one record to be locked at one time. This is necessary so that other programs cannot access these records.

However, before a file or file segment can be locked, the file first must be opened. This is the only place you can obtain the handle that the function needs to read from the BX register.

File sharing

In addition to record locking, SHARE enables DOS to implement file locking, which prevents other programs and workstations from accessing a specific file. This option is activated by the DOS function 3DH, which is also used to open files in non-network situations. The only difference in network programming is that more information must be provided for this function in the AL register.

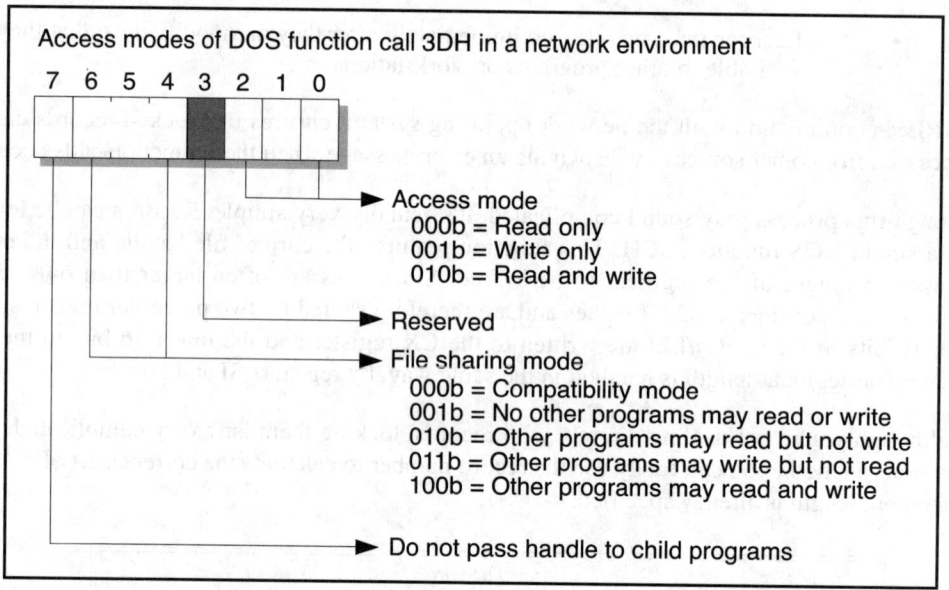

```
       Parameters for function call 3Dh

   Register          Description

   AH        3DH
   AL        Access mode (see below)
   DS:DX     Pointer to file name
```

```
Access modes of DOS function call 3DH in a network environment

   7 6 5 4 3 2 1 0

                    ──▶ Access mode
                          000b = Read only
                          001b = Write only
                          010b = Read and write

                    ──▶ Reserved

                    ──▶ File sharing mode
                          000b = Compatibility mode
                          001b = No other programs may read or write
                          010b = Other programs may read but not write
                          011b = Other programs may write but not read
                          100b = Other programs may read and write

                    ──▶ Do not pass handle to child programs
```

As the above diagram shows, bits 4 through 6 define the operations other programs are allowed to perform on the specified file in a network setting. So, you can determine whether other programs can, for example, read, but not write to your file, or whether access should be completely denied while your program is using the file.

In this context, the lower three bits, which usually aren't significant in DOS programming, are important. These bits declare which operations a program will perform with a file upon opening it. A program using a READ file access mode when requesting access to an already open file, will be granted access to this file if the first program has released the file for READ operations through its file sharing mode.

So, in a network environment you shouldn't declare a READ and WRITE access mode if you only intend to read information from the file. Otherwise, you may be denied access to the file by a program that has already opened the file and denied WRITE access to other programs.

If a file access request with a given access mode doesn't succeed, function 3DH will return error code 5 (access denied). This error code is also used by the functions for reading and writing files when they are denied access to a file.

You've probably noticed the "compatibility mode" among the file sharing modes listed in the diagram above. This mode serves the same purpose as mode 001b; it doesn't allow other programs to read from and write to the specified file. However, instead of calling the normal error code 5 (access denied), the compatibility code calls the DOS critical error handler when another program attempts to access the locked file. When such an error occurs, DOS displays the following message on the screen:

```
Illegal SHARE operation while reading drive C
(A)bort, (R)etry, (F)ail
```

You shouldn't use this file sharing mode when other programs shouldn't access the locked file. Instead, use file sharing mode 001b.

An example of network programming

To demonstrate how to use DOS in network programming, we've developed two programs that utilize its file and record locking capabilities. You'll find the Pascal and C versions of these programs at the end of this chapter. A network isn't needed in order to use these programs; Windows 3.0 is sufficient. If you call SHARE prior to starting Windows 3.0, open several DOS boxes within Windows, and then start programs from these boxes, you can simulate any number of workstations.

You don't have to do this for the file locking programs (FLOCK.PAS and FLOCK.C) because these open a file twice from within the same program. This is the same as trying to open the file from a different program.

First look at the two modules NETFILEP.PAS and NETFILEC.C, which provide the essential file access procedures for the two sample programs. Both of the programs use the same functions (or procedures) and constants. The difference between the two lies in the way the file, that should be accessed, is passed to these two programs. A list of available functions and procedures is listed below:

```
┌─────────────────────────────────────────────────────────┐
│        Procedures and functions provided by modules      │
│        NETFILEP.PAS and NETFILEC.C.                      │
│  ┌───────────────────────────────────────────────────┐   │
│  │ Name              Description                       │   │
│  │ ShareInst         Checks whether SHARE is installed │   │
│  │ NetErrorMsg       Returns an error message text     │   │
│  │ NetRewrite        Creates a file                    │   │
│  │ NetReset          Opens a specific file             │   │
│  │ NetClose          Closes a file                     │   │
│  │ NetLock           Locks records                     │   │
│  │ NetUnLock         Unlocks locked records            │   │
│  │ Is_NetWriteOk     Checks whether file may be written to │
│  │ Is_NetReadOk      Checks whether file may be read from  │
│  │ Is_NetOpen        Checks whether file is open       │   │
│  │ NetWrite          Writes to file                    │   │
│  │ NetRead           Reads from file                   │   │
│  │ NetSeek           Sets data pointer                 │   │
│  └───────────────────────────────────────────────────┘   │
└─────────────────────────────────────────────────────────┘
```

Although the Pascal version has been programmed as a UNIT, you can integrate the C version into a program using #INCLUDE. So, compiling the module and defining a make or project file isn't necessary.

Similar to the Pascal commands ASSIGN, READ, and WRITE, the functions and procedures of the Pascal version accept a normal, standardized file variable. However, in a network environment, these commands cannot be used for accessing this type of a file, because they execute as soon as a file isn't open to read or write access. Because of this, special procedures for reading from and writing to files have been defined in the NETFILEP unit. However, using Turbo Pascal file variables is still useful because they provide the procedures with, for example, the length of individual records within the file. The file handle and access mode, which are otherwise entered by the REWRITE Pascal procedure, are also stored here.

In the C version, the file is represented by the following data structure, which should be passed, in the form of a variable, to the various functions in the NETFILEC.C module:

```
typedef struct { unsigned int Handle,    /* File handle */
                              RecS,       /* Record size */
                              Mode;       /* Access mode */
               } NFILE;
```

Listing: **NETFILEP.PAS**

```
{*****************************************************}
{*                  N E T F I L E                    *}
{*---------------------------------------------------*}
{* Task        : Implements network supporting file functions. *}
{*---------------------------------------------------*}
{* Author      : Michael Tischer                     *}
{* Developed on : 09/07/91                           *}
{* Last update  : 01/29/92                           *}
{*****************************************************}

unit NetFile;

interface

uses Crt, Dos;                    { Add CRT and DOS units }
```

```
const {-- Types of file access available ----------------------------}

      fm_r   = 0;                              { Read-only }
      fm_w   = 1;                              { Write-only }
      fm_rw  = 2;           { Read and write in normal Pascal mode }

      {-- Types of file protection ------------------------------}

      sm_comp = $00;         { Compatibility mode, no file protection }
      sm_rw   = $10;           { Read and write prohibited by others }
      sm_r    = $20;   { Read by others permitted, writing prohibited }
      sm_w    = $30;      { Reading and writing by others permitted }
      sm_no   = $40;      { All permitted, protected by record lock }

      {-- Possible errors during procedure calls ----------------------}

      NE_OK         = $00;                          { No error }
      NE_FileNotFound = $02;              { Error: File not found }
```

```
    NE_PathNotFound   = $03;              { Error: Path not found }
    NE_TooManyFiles   = $04;         { Error: Too many open files }
    NE_AccessDenied   = $05;        { Error: Access to file denied }
    NE_InvalidHandle  = $06;          { Error: Invalid file handle }
    NE_AccessCode     = $07;          { Error: Illegal access code }
    NE_Share          = $20;          { Violation of Share rights }
    NE_Lock           = $21;    { Error while (un)locking a record }
    NE_ShareBuffer    = $24;             { Share buffer overflow }

var NetError : integer;          { Error number from DOS interrupt }

function ShareInst : boolean;                    { Share installed? }

function NetErrorMsg( Number : word ) : string;       { Error message }

procedure NetReset(   FName  : string;              { Open file }
                      AMode  : integer;
                      RecS   : word;
                  var DFile );

procedure NetRewrite(  FName  : string;           { Open new file }
                       AMode  : integer;
                       RecS   : word;
                   var DFile );

procedure NetClose( var DFile );                     { Close file }

function NetLock( var DFile;                     { Lock file range }
                  RecNo  : longint;
                  RngNum : longint ) : boolean;

function NetUnlock( var DFile;                { Unlock file range }
                    RecNo  : longint;
                    RngNum : longint ) : boolean;

function Is_NetOpen( var DFile ) : boolean;        { Is file open? }

function Is_NetWriteOk( var DFile ) : boolean;  { Writing to file O.K. }

function Is_NetReadOk( var DFile ) : boolean;  { Reading from file O.K. }

{-- The Read, Write and Seek procedures only work with files set in  -}
{-- input-output mode. The following procedures must be used if       -}
{-- files must be opened in other modes.                              -}

procedure NetWrite( var DFile;                    { Write to a file }
                    var FData );

procedure NetRead( var DFile;                    { Read from a file }
                   var FData );

procedure NetSeek( var DFile;              { Position file pointer }
                   RecNo : longint );

implementation

const {-- Function numbers for DOS calls ----------------------------}

    FCT_OPEN    = $3D;      { Function: Open file with handle }
    FCT_CLOSE   = $3E;      { Function: Close file with handle }
    FCT_CREATE  = $3C;      { Function: Create file with handle }
    FCT_WRITE   = $40;      { Function: Write to file }
    FCT_READ    = $3F;      { Function: Read from file }
    FCT_LSEEK   = $42;      { Function: Set file pointer }
```

```
    FCT_REC_LOCK = $5C;         { Function: Record locking }

    {-- Function & interrupt numbers for other interrupt calls -----}

    MULTIPLEX   = $2F;                  { Multiplex interrupt }
    FCT_SHARE   = $1000;           { Install text for Share }

    {-- Turbo Pascal file identifiers ----------------------------}

    fmClosed    = $D7B0;                    { File closed }
    fmInput     = $D7B1;           { File opened for reading }
    fmOutput    = $D7B2;           { File opened for writing }
    fmInOut     = $D7B3;   { File opened for reading and writing }
```

```
{*******************************************************************}
{* ShareInst  : Installs test for Share.                          *}
{* Input      : None                                              *}
{* Output     : TRUE if Share is installed                        *}
{* Global var. : NetError/W (error status after call)             *}
{*******************************************************************}

function ShareInst : boolean;

var regs    : registers;   { Processor registers for interrupt call }

begin
  regs.ax := FCT_SHARE;             { Test for installed Share }
  intr( MULTIPLEX, regs );          { Call multiplex interrupt }
  ShareInst := ( regs.al = $FF );          { Return result }
  NetError := NE_OK;                         { No error }
end;

{*******************************************************************}
{* NetErrorMsg : Error message text.                              *}
{* Input       : Error number                                     *}
{* Output      : Meaning                                          *}
{*******************************************************************}

function NetErrorMsg( Number : word ) : string;

var Sdummy : string;

begin
  case Number of
    NE_OK            : NetErrorMsg := 'No error';
    NE_FileNotFound  : NetErrorMsg := 'File not found';
    NE_PathNotFound  : NetErrorMsg := 'Path not found';
    NE_TooManyFiles  : NetErrorMsg := 'Too many files open';
    NE_AccessDenied  : NetErrorMsg := 'File access denied';
    NE_InvalidHandle : NetErrorMsg := 'Invalid file handle';
    NE_AccessCode    : NetErrorMsg := 'Illegal access code';
    NE_Share         : NetErrorMsg := 'Violation of Share rights';
    NE_Lock          : NetErrorMsg := 'Error during record lock';
    NE_ShareBuffer   : NetErrorMsg := 'Share buffer overflow';
    else               begin
                         str( Number, Sdummy );
                         NetErrorMsg := 'DOS error: ' + Sdummy;
                       end;
  end;
end;

{*******************************************************************}
{* NetCreate  : Creates a file.                                   *}
{* Input      : Filename, opening mode, record size               *}
```

```
(* Output       : Opened file                                    *)
(* Global var. : NetError/W (error status after call)            *)
(*****************************************************************)


procedure NetRewrite(    FName : string;
                         AMode : integer;
                         RecS  : word;
                     var DFile );

var regs   : registers;    { Processor registers for interrupt call }
    FName2 : string;                   { Filename for local access }

begin
  FName2 := FName + #0;              { Copy and prepare filename }
  with regs do
    begin
      ds := seg( FName2[ 1 ] );             { Assign filename }
      dx := ofs( FName2[ 1 ] );
      ah := FCT_CREATE;          { Function number: Open file }
      cx := 0 ;                         { File attribute }
      msdos( regs );                      { Interrupt call }
      if ( ( flags and fcarry ) = 0 ) then    { Open successful? }
        begin
          bx := ax;                  { Handle in register BX }
          ah := FCT_CLOSE;        { Function number: Close file }
          msdos( regs );
          if ( ( flags and fcarry ) = 0 ) then   { Close successful? }
            NetReset( FName, AMode, Recs, DFile )       { Open file }
          else
            NetError := ax;              { Note error number }
        end
      else
        NetError := ax;                  { Note error number }
    end;
end;


(*****************************************************************)
(* NetReset    : Opens a specific file.                         *)
(* Input       : Filename, open mode, record size              *)
(* Output      : Opened file                                    *)
(* Global var. : NetError/W (error status after call)          *)
(*****************************************************************)


procedure NetReset(    FName : string;
                       AMode : integer;
                       RecS  : word;
                   var DFile );

var regs : registers;       { Processor registers for interrupt call }

begin
  FName := FName + #0;            { Filename must end with #0 }
  with regs do
    begin
      ds := seg( FName[ 1 ] );             { Assign filename }
      dx := ofs( FName[ 1 ] );
      ah := FCT_OPEN;            { Function number: Open file }
      al := AMode;       { Status byte for access mode and locking }
      msdos( regs );                      { Interrupt call }
      if ( ( flags and fcarry ) = 0 ) then    { Open successful? }
        begin
          NetError := NE_OK;                { No error }
          with filerec( DFile ) do
            begin
```

```
              move( FName[ 1 ], filerec( DFile ).Name,    { Assign }
                    length( FName ) );              { filename }
              Handle := ax;                      { File handle }
              RecSize := RecS;            { Specify record size }
              case ( AMode and $0F ) of   { Specify Pascal file mode }
                fm_r  : Mode := fmInput;
                fm_w  : Mode := fmOutput;
                fm_rw : Mode := fmInOut;
              end;
            end;
        end
      else
        begin
          NetError := ax;              { Note error number }
          filerec( DFile ).Mode := fmClosed;     { File not opened }
        end;
    end;
end;


(*****************************************************************)
(* NetClose : Closes a file.                                    *)
(* Input    : File handle                                       *)
(* Output   : None                                              *)
(*****************************************************************)


procedure NetClose( var DFile );

var regs : registers;       { Processor registers for interrupt call }

begin
  if ( Filerec( DFile ).Mode <> fmClosed ) then        { File open? }
    begin
      with regs do
        begin
          ah := FCT_CLOSE;         { Function number: Close file }
          bx := FileRec( DFile ).Handle;           { File handle }
          msdos( regs );                      { Interrupt call }
        end;
      FileRec( DFile ).Mode := fmClosed;          { Close file }
      NetError := NE_OK;                        { No error }
    end
  else
    NetError := NE_InvalidHandle;              { File not open }
end;


(*****************************************************************)
(* Locking    : Locks or unlocks a file range.                  *)
(* Input      : File handle, operation, offset for start of file, *)
(*              length of range to be (un)locked                *)
(* Output     : TRUE if successful                              *)
(* Global var.: NetError/W (error status after call)           *)
(* Info       : Call NetLock and NetUnlock for internal access only.*)
(*****************************************************************)


function Locking( Handle    : word;
                  Operation : byte;
                  Offset    : longint;
                  WrdLen    : longint ) : boolean;

var regs : registers;       { Processor registers for interrupt call }

begin
  with regs do
    begin
```

```
    ah := FCT_REC_LOCK;         { Function number for interrupt call }
    al := Operation;                      { 0 = Lock, 1 = Unlock }
    bx := Handle;                               { File handle }
    cx := offset shr 16;                     { High word offset }
    dx := offset and $FFFF;                   { Low word offset }
    si := WrdLen shr 16;                     { High word length }
    di := WrdLen and $FFFF;                   { Low word length }
    msdos( regs );                             { Interrupt call }
    if ( ( flags and fcarry ) = 0 ) then    { Locking successful? }
      begin
        Locking := true;                          { No error }
        NetError := NE_OK;
      end
    else
      begin
        Locking := false;
        NetError := ax;                       { Note error number }
      end;
  end;
end;
```

```
{****************************************************************}
{* NetLock     : Locks records.                                *}
{* Input       : File, record number, number of records to be locked *}
{* Output      : TRUE if successful                            *}
{* Global var. : NetError/W (error status after call)          *}
{****************************************************************}

function NetLock( var DFile;
                  RecNo  : longint;
                  RngNum : longint ) : boolean;

begin
  NetLock := Locking( filerec( DFile ).Handle, 0,
                      filerec( DFile ).Recsize * RecNo,
                      filerec( DFile ).Recsize * RngNum );
end;
```

```
{****************************************************************}
{* NetUnLock   : Unlocks locked records.                       *}
{* Input       : File, record number, number of records to be locked *}
{* Output      : TRUE if successful                            *}
{* Global var. : NetError/W (error status after call)          *}
{****************************************************************}

function NetUnlock( var DFile;
                    RecNo  : longint;
                    RngNum : longint ) : boolean;
begin
  NetUnLock := Locking( filerec( DFile).Handle, 1,
                        filerec( DFile ).Recsize * RecNo,
                        filerec( DFile ).Recsize * RngNum );
end;
```

```
{****************************************************************}
{* Is_NetWriteOk : Enables file output.                        *}
{* Input         : File                                        *}
{* Output        : TRUE if output is enabled                   *}
{****************************************************************}

function Is_NetWriteOk( var DFile ) : boolean;

begin
  with Filerec( DFile ) do
```

```
    Is_NetWriteOk := ( Mode = fmOutput ) or ( Mode = fmInOut );
end;
```

```
{****************************************************************}
{* Is_NetReadOk : Enables file input.                          *}
{* Input        : File                                         *}
{* Output       : TRUE if output is enabled                    *}
{****************************************************************}

function Is_NetReadOk( var DFile ) : boolean;

begin
  with Filerec( DFile ) do
    Is_NetReadOk := ( Mode = fmInput ) or ( Mode = fmInOut );
end;
```

```
{****************************************************************}
{* Is_NetOpen  : Opens file.                                   *}
{* Input       : File                                          *}
{* Output      : TRUE if file is open                          *}
{****************************************************************}

function Is_NetOpen( var DFile ) : boolean;

begin
  with Filerec( DFile ) do
    Is_Netopen := ( Mode = fmInput ) or ( Mode = fmOutput ) or
                  ( Mode = fmInOut );
end;
```

```
{****************************************************************}
{* NetWrite    : Writes to file.                               *}
{* Input       : File, data                                    *}
{* Output      : None                                          *}
{* Info        : Output is only possible in Pascal procedures when *}
{*               files have been opened in input-output mode.  *}
{*               Attention: No type checking performed here.   *}
{****************************************************************}

procedure NetWrite( var DFile;
                    var FData );

var regs : registers;      { Processor registers for interrupt call }

begin
  with regs do
    begin
      ds := seg( FData );                       { Data address }
      dx := ofs( FData );
      ah := FCT_WRITE;             { Function number: Write file }
      bx := filerec( DFile ).Handle;             { File handle }
      cx := filerec( DFile ).Recsize;        { Number of bytes }
      msdos( regs );                             { Interrupt call }
      if ( ( flags and fcarry ) = 0 ) then    { Write successful? }
        NetError := NE_OK                         { No error }
      else
        NetError := ax;                       { Note error number }
    end;
end;
```

```
{****************************************************************}
{* NetRead     : Reads from file.                              *}
{* Input       : File, variable for accessing data             *}
{* Output      : Data                                          *}
```

```
{* Info       : Output is only possible in Pascal procedures when  *}
{*               files have been opened in input-output mode.       *}
{*               Attention: No type checking performed here.        *}
{*********************************************************************}

procedure NetRead( var DFile;
                   var FData );

var regs : registers;      { Processor registers for interrupt call }

begin
  with regs do
    begin
      ds := seg( FData );                        { Data address }
      dx := ofs( FData );
      ah := FCT_READ;                  { Function number: Read file }
      bx := filerec( DFile ).Handle;             { File handle }
      cx := filerec( DFile ).Recsize;       { Number of bytes }
      msdos( regs );                            { Interrupt call }
      if ( ( flags and fcarry ) = 0 ) then  { Write successful? }
        NetError := NE_OK                          { No error }
      else
        NetError := ax;                   { Note error number }
    end;
end;


{*********************************************************************}
{* NetSeek   : Sets file pointer.                                   *}
{* Input     : File, record number                                  *}
{* Output    : None                                                 *}
{* Info      : Output is only possible in Pascal procedures when    *}
{*              files have been opened in input-output mode.         *}
{*********************************************************************}

procedure NetSeek( var DFile;
                   RecNo : longint );

var regs : registers;      { Processor registers for interrupt call }

begin
  with regs do
    begin
      ah := FCT_LSEEK;        { Function number: Set file pointer }
      al := 0;                { Absolute position for start of file }
      bx := filerec( DFile ).Handle;             { File handle }
      RecNo := RecNo * filerec( DFile ).Recsize;  { Offset in bytes }
      cx := RecNo shr 16;                 { High word offset }
      dx := recNo and $FFFF;               { Low word offset }
      msdos( regs );                            { Interrupt call }
      if ( ( flags and fcarry ) = 0 ) then  { Write successful? }
        NetError := NE_OK                          { No error }
      else
        NetError := ax;                   { Note error number }
    end;
end;


begin
end.
```

Listing: NETFILEC.C

```c
/*********************************************************************/
/*                    N E T F I L E C . C                          */
/*-----------------------------------------------------------------*/
/*   Task         : Implements network supporting file functions.   */
/*-----------------------------------------------------------------*/
/*   Memory model : SMALL                                           */
/*-----------------------------------------------------------------*/
/*   Author       : Michael Tischer                                 */
/*   developed on : 02/10/1992                                      */
/*   last Update  : 02/13/1991                                      */
/*-----------------------------------------------------------------*/
/*   Microsoft C  : The "Segment lost in conversation" warning,     */
/*                  cannot be avoided.                              */
/*********************************************************************/

#include <dos.h>
#include <string.h>
#include <stdlib.h>

/*== Macros =======================================================*/

#ifdef FP_OFF
  #undef FP_OFF
  #undef FP_SEG
#endif

#define FP_OFF(fp)     ((unsigned)(fp))
#define FP_SEG(fp)     ((unsigned)((unsigned long)(fp) >> 16))

/*== Constants ====================================================*/

/*-- Wahrheitswerte -----------------------------------------------*/

#define TRUE  ( 1 == 1 )
#define FALSE ( 0 == 1 )

/*-- Types of file access -----------------------------------------*/

#define FM_R       0                              /* read only */
#define FM_W       1                             /* write only */
#define FM_RW      2                         /* read and write */

/*-- Types of file protection -------------------------------------*/

#define SM_COMP 0x00    /* compatibility mode, no file protection */
#define SM_RW   0x10        /* read and write prohibited by others */
#define SM_R    0x20 /* read by others permitted, writting prohibited */
#define SM_W    0x30    /* reading and writing by other permitted */
#define SM_NO   0x40   /* all permitted, protected by Record Lock */

/*-- Possible errors during procedure calls -----------------------*/

#define NE_OK            0x00                     /* no error */
#define NE_FileNotFound  0x02           /* error: file not found */
#define NE_PathNotFound  0x03           /* error: Path not found */
#define NE_TooManyFiles  0x04      /* error: to many open files */
#define NE_AccessDenied  0x05     /* error: access to file denied */
#define NE_InvalidHandle 0x06       /* error: invalid file handle */
#define NE_AccessCode    0x07       /* error: illegal access code */
#define NE_Share         0x20       /* violation of share error */
#define NE_Lock          0x21   /* error: (Un)locking of a record */
#define NE_ShareBuffer   0x24           /* Share buffer overflow */
```

```
/*-- Function numbers for DOS calls ----------------------------------*/

#define FCT_OPEN      0x3D    /* Function: open file with handle     */
#define FCT_CLOSE     0x3E    /* Function: close file with handle    */
#define FCT_CREATE    0x3C    /* Function: create file with handle   */
#define FCT_WRITE     0x40    /* Function: write to file             */
#define FCT_READ      0x3F    /* Function: read from file            */
#define FCT_LSEEK     0x42    /* Function: set file pointer          */
#define FCT_REC_LOCK  0x5C    /* Function: Record Locking            */

/*-- Function and interrupt numbers for other interrupt calls --------*/

#define MULTIPLEX     0x2F                  /* Multiplex Interrupt */
#define FCT_SHARE     0x1000      /* Test if share is installed */

/*-- File indentifiers (Werte analog Turbo-Pascal) ---------------*/

#define FMCLOSED      0xD7B0                   /* file closed */
#define FMINPUT       0xD7B1         /* file opened for reading */
#define FMOUTPUT      0xD7B2         /* file opened for writing */
#define FMINOUT       0xD7B3  /* file opened for reading and writing */

/*== Type declarations ===============================================*/

typedef struct { unsigned int Handle, RecS, Mode; } NFILE;

/*== Global Variables ================================================*/

int       NetError;         /* error number from DOS Interrupt */
union REGS regs;          /* processor registers for interrupt call */
struct SREGS sregs;        /* segment register for Interrupt call */

/*********************************************************************/
/* ShareInst  : Test if Share has been installed                   */
/* Input      : none                                               */
/* Ouput      : TRUE if Share is installed                         */
/* Globale Var.: NetError/W (error status from call)               */
/*********************************************************************/

int ShareInst( void )
{
  regs.x.ax = FCT_SHARE;           /* test if Share is installed  */
  int86( MULTIPLEX, &regs, &regs );    /* multiplex Interrupt call */
  NetError = NE_OK;                          /* no error */
  return ( regs.h.al == 0xFF );              /* return result */
}

/*********************************************************************/
/* NetErrorMsg : Error message text                                */
/* Input      : s.u.                                               */
/* Output     : s.u.                                               */
/*********************************************************************/

void NetErrorMsg( int  Number,              /* error number */
                  char *Text )              /* error text */
{
  char Sdummy[ 5 ];                         /* error number */

  switch ( Number )
  {
    case NE_OK          : strcpy( Text, "No error          " );
                   break;
    case NE_FileNotFound : strcpy( Text, "File not found          " );
```

```
                 break;
    case NE_PathNotFound : strcpy( Text, "Path not found        " );
                 break;
    case NE_TooManyFiles : strcpy( Text, "Too many open files   " );
                 break;
    case NE_AccessDenied : strcpy( Text, "File access denied    " );
                 break;
    case NE_InvalidHandle: strcpy( Text, "Invalid file handle   " );
                 break;
    case NE_AccessCode   : strcpy( Text, "Illegal access code   " );
                 break;
    case NE_Share        : strcpy( Text, "Violation of Share rights " );
                 break;
    case NE_Lock         : strcpy( Text, "Error during record lock  " );
                 break;
    case NE_ShareBuffer  : strcpy( Text, "Share buffer overflow " );
                 break;
    default       : {
                      itoa( Number, Sdummy, 2 );
                      strcpy( Text, "DOS Error:        " );
                      strcat( Text, Sdummy );
                    }
  }
}

/*********************************************************************/
/* NetReset    : opens a specific file                             */
/* Input       : s.u.                                              */
/* Output      : s.u                                               */
/* Globale Var.: NetError/W (error status from call)               */
/*********************************************************************/

void NetReset( char far   *DName,           /* file name */
               unsigned int AMode,          /* access mode */
               unsigned int RecS,           /* record size */
               NFILE        *TFile )        /* pointer to file */
{
  regs.x.dx = FP_OFF( DName );                /* assign filename */
  regs.h.ah = FCT_OPEN;              /* function number: Open file */
  regs.h.al = AMode;     /* status byte for access mode and locking */
  sregs.ds  = FP_SEG( DName );
  intdosx( &regs, &regs, &sregs );              /* call interrupt */
  if ( !regs.x.cflag )                      /* open successful? */
  {
    TFile->Handle = regs.x.ax;            /* specify file handle */
    TFile->RecS = RecS;                   /* specify record size */
    switch ( AMode & 0x0F )                 /* set access mode */
    {
      case FM_R  : TFile->Mode = FMINPUT;
                 break;
      case FM_W  : TFile->Mode = FMOUTPUT;
                 break;
      case FM_RW : TFile->Mode = FMINOUT;
                 break;
    }
    NetError = NE_OK;                           /* no error */
  }
  else
    NetError = regs.x.ax;                 /* note error number */
}

/*********************************************************************/
/* NetRewrite : Creates a file                                     */
/* Input      : s.u.                                               */
```

```
/* Output    : s.u                                      */
/* Globale Var.: NetError/W (error status from call)    */
/*******************************************************/


    void NetRewrite( char far  *DName,              /* filename */
                     unsigned int AMode,            /* access mode */
                     unsigned int RecS,             /* Record size */
                     NFILE       *TFile )           /* pointer to file */
    {
      regs.x.dx = FP_OFF( DName );         /* Adresse des Dateinmamens */
      regs.h.ah = FCT_CREATE;              /* function number: Open file */
      regs.x.cx = 0 ;                      /* file attribute */
      sregs.ds  = FP_SEG( DName );
      intdosx( &regs, &regs, &sregs );     /* call interrupt */
      if ( !regs.x.cflag )                 /* open successful? */
      {
        regs.x.bx = regs.x.ax;             /* Handle in Register BX */
        regs.h.ah = FCT_CLOSE;             /* Function number close file */
        intdos( &regs, &regs );
        if ( !regs.x.cflag )               /* close successful? */
          NetReset( DName, AMode, RecS, TFile );   /* open file */
        else
          NetError = regs.x.ax;            /* note error number */
      }
      else
        NetError = regs.x.ax;              /* note error number */
    }


/*******************************************************/
/* NetClose  : close a file                            */
/* Input     : s.u.                                    */
/* Output    : none                                    */
/*******************************************************/

    void NetClose( NFILE *TFile )
    {
      if ( TFile->Mode != FMCLOSED )           /* file open? */
      {
        regs.x.bx = TFile->Handle;             /* file handle */
        regs.h.ah = FCT_CLOSE;                 /* function number: Close file */
        intdos( &regs, &regs );
        if ( !regs.x.cflag )                   /* file closed? */
        {
          TFile->Handle = 0;                   /* reset handle */
          TFile->Mode = FMCLOSED;              /* close file */
          NetError = NE_OK;                    /* no error */
        }
        else
          NetError = regs.x.ax;
      }
      else
        NetError = NE_InvalidHandle;           /* file not open */
    }


/*******************************************************/
/* Locking   : Locks or unlocks a file range.          */
/* Input     : s.u                                     */
/* Output    : TRUE is successful                      */
/* Globale Var.: NetError/W (error status from call)    */
/* Info      : Call NetLock and NetUnlock for internal access only */
/*******************************************************/


    int Locking( int       Handle,              /* file handle */
                 int       Operation,           /* Oper. Lock, Unlock */
```

```
                 unsigned long Offset,   /* Offset zum Dateianfang in Bytes */
                 unsigned long WrdLen )  /* L_nge des Bereiches in Bytes */
    {
      regs.h.ah = FCT_REC_LOCK;        /* function number for interrupt call */
      regs.h.al = Operation;           /* 0 = Lock, 1 = Unlock */
      regs.x.bx = Handle;              /* file handle */
      regs.x.cx = Offset >> 16;        /* Hi Word Offset */
      regs.x.dx = Offset & 0xFFFF;     /* Lo Word Offset */
      regs.x.si = WrdLen >> 16;        /* Hi Word Length */
      regs.x.di = WrdLen & 0xFFFF;     /* Lo Word Lenght */
      intdos( &regs, &regs );          /* call Interrupt */
      if ( ! regs.x.cflag )            /* locking successful? */
      {
        NetError = NE_OK;
        return TRUE;                               /* no error */
      }
      else
      {
        NetError = regs.x.ax;          /* note error number */
        return FALSE;                             /* error */
      }
    }


/*******************************************************/
/* NetUnLock  : Unlocks locked records.                */
/* Input     : s.u.                                    */
/* Output    : TRUE if successful                      */
/* Globale Var.: NetError/W (error status from call)    */
/*******************************************************/

    int NetUnLock( NFILE    *TFile,                    /* file */
                   unsigned long RecNo,            /* Record Number */
                   unsigned long RngNum )          /* number of Records */
    {
      return Locking( TFile->Handle, 1, TFile->RecS * RecNo,
                      TFile->RecS * RngNum );
    }


/*******************************************************/
/* NetLock    : Locks records.                         */
/* Input     : s.u.                                    */
/* Output    : TRUE if successful                      */
/* Globale Var.: NetError/W (error status from call)    */
/*******************************************************/

    int NetLock( NFILE       *TFile,                   /* file */
                 unsigned long RecNo,              /* record number */
                 unsigned long RngNum )            /* number of Records */
    {
      return Locking( TFile->Handle, 0, TFile->RecS * RecNo,
                      TFile->RecS * RngNum );
    }


/*******************************************************/
/* Is_NetReadOk  : Enables file input.                 */
/* Input     : s.u                                     */
/* Output    : TRUE if output is enabled               */
/*******************************************************/

    int Is_NetReadOk( NFILE *TFile )
    {
      return ( ( TFile->Mode == FMINPUT ) ||
               ( TFile->Mode == FMINOUT ) );
    }
```

```
                                                               }
/*******************************************************/
/* Is_NetOpen   : Checks the status of a file        */      /*******************************************************************/
/* Input        : s.u                                */      /* NetRead    : Reads from a file.                      */
/* Output       : TRUE if file is open               */      /* Input      : s.u.                                    */
/*******************************************************/      /* Output     : none                                    */
                                                               /*******************************************************************/
int Is_NetOpen( NFILE *TFile )
{                                                              void NetRead( NFILE    *TFile,                   /* file */
 return ( ( TFile->Mode == FMOUTPUT ) ||                                      void far *DatPnt )         /* pointer to data */
          ( TFile->Mode == FMINPUT ) ||                       {
          ( TFile->Mode == FMINOUT ) );                        regs.x.dx = FP_OFF( DatPnt );             /* data address */
}                                                              regs.h.ah = FCT_READ;          /* function number: read file */
                                                               regs.x.bx = TFile->Handle;                  /* TFilehandle */
                                                               regs.x.cx = TFile->RecS;               /* number of Bytes */
/*******************************************************/      sregs.ds  = FP_SEG( DatPnt );
/* Is_NetWriteOk : Is a write to TFile allowed?      */       intdosx( &regs, &regs, &sregs );
/* Input        : s.u                                */       if ( !regs.x.cflag )
/* Output       : TRUE is output enabled             */        NetError = NE_OK;                         /* no error */
/*******************************************************/      else
                                                               NetError = regs.x.ax;             /* note error number */
int Is_NetWriteOk( NFILE *TFile )                             }
{
 return ( ( TFile->Mode == FMOUTPUT ) ||
          ( TFile->Mode == FMINOUT ) );                       /*******************************************************************/
}                                                             /* NetSeek    : Sets file pointer.                      */
                                                               /* Input      : s.u                                     */
                                                               /* Output     : none                                    */
/*******************************************************/      /*******************************************************************/
/* NetWrite    : Writes to a file.                   */
/* Input        : s.u.                               */       void NetSeek( NFILE         *TFile,              /* file */
/* Output       : none                               */                     unsigned long RecNo )        /* Record number */
/*******************************************************/      {
                                                               regs.h.ah = FCT_LSEEK;    /* function number: set file pointer */
void NetWrite( NFILE    *TFile,                 /* file */     regs.h.al = 0;         /* absolute position for start of file */
               void far *DatPnt )       /* Pointer to data */  regs.x.bx = TFile->Handle;                  /* file handle */
{                                                              RecNo = RecNo * TFile->RecS;             /* offset in Bytes */
 regs.x.dx = FP_OFF( DatPnt );            /* data address */   regs.x.cx = RecNo >> 16;                  /* hi Word Offset */
 regs.h.ah = FCT_WRITE;        /* function number: Write file */ regs.x.dx = RecNo & 0xFFFF;             /* lo Word Offset */
 regs.x.bx = TFile->Handle;               /* file handle */    intdos( &regs, &regs );
 regs.x.cx = TFile->RecS;               /* number of Bytes */  if ( !regs.x.cflag )
 sregs.ds  = FP_SEG( DatPnt );                                  NetError = NE_OK;                         /* no error */
 intdosx( &regs, &regs, &sregs );                             else
 if ( !regs.x.cflag )                                           NetError = regs.x.ax;             /* note error number */
  NetError = NE_OK;                         /* no error */     }
 else
  NetError = regs.x.ax;             /* note error number */
```

The FLOCKP.PAS and FLOCKC.C programs illustrate how files are locked. First they ask the user for the access and file sharing modes for the two files that should be opened. However, the program actually opens only one file, named either FLOCKC.DAT or FLOCKP.DAT, depending on the program used. This file is then opened by two OPEN statements, so that it can be addressed simultaneously over two handles. This simulates a network environment in which two programs are accessing the file simultaneously.

```
Demonstration of DOS File Locking Function    (C)1992 Michael Tischer
=====================================================================

Available access types:         Available lock types:
  1: Read-only                    1: Compatibility mode (no locking)
  2: Write-only                   2: Prohibit other file accesses generally
  3: Read and Write               3: Read access enabled only
                                  4: Write access enabled only
                                  5: All enabled (record locking)

File A: Name = flockc.dat  Access type = 1  Lock mode = 3
File B: Name = flockc.dat  Access type = 2  Lock mode = 4

Opening file A:  Status 0 = No error
Opening file B:  Status 5 = File access denied

Writing to file A: File not open for writing
Writing to file B: File not open for writing

Reading file A: Record "0" read
reading file B: File not open for reading
```

The program FLOCKP.PAS

Upon opening these two handles, the DOS error messages are displayed on the screen. These handles are also used to execute write and read operations, the status of which is also displayed on the screen. After the handles have been opened, the text "AAAA" is written to the first handle, and the text "BBBB" is written to the second handle.

The file content is read through both handles in the next program step, and is then displayed on the screen. If the write access over the second handle was successful, the text "BBBB" will be displayed through both handles. This means that the first text has been overwritten, assuming that the first write attempt actually was successful. If both write access attempts failed, the file will be empty and two empty strings will appear on your screen. The last program step finally closes both handles.

These two programs are helpful because they can be used to test all different combinations of access and file sharing modes. However, some of them don't make sense and may lead to rather strange results. However, these results are similar to what sometimes occurs in a network environment.

Listing: FLOCKP.PAS

```pascal
{***************************************************}
{*               F I L E L O C K                  *}
{*-----------------------------------------------*}
{* Task       : Opens files in network using file locking *}
{*              functions.                        *}
{*-----------------------------------------------*}
{* Author     : Michael Tischer                   *}
{* Developed on : 09/14/91                        *}
{* Last update : 01/29/92                         *}
{***************************************************}

program filelock;

uses Crt, Dos,                    { Add CRT and DOS units }
     Netfile;                     { Add network unit }

const TFileName = 'Filelock.dat';    { Filename for test file }

type  Test = array[ 1..4 ] of char;   { Data type for test }

var AxsTypeA,                      { File access modes }
    AxsTypeB,
    LockMdA,                      { File lock modes }
    LockMdB  : byte;

{***************************************************}
{* FiMode   : Create file mode from access type and locking. *}
{* Input    : Access type, file lock mode          *}
{* Output   : File mode                            *}
{***************************************************}
```

936

```pascal
function FiMode( AxsType, LockMd : byte ) : byte;

var res : byte;                          { Help in calculating results }

begin
  case AxsType of
    1 : res := fm_r;                              { Read-only }
    2 : res := fm_w;                              { Write-only }
    3 : res := fm_rw;                      { Read and write }
  end;
  case LockMd of
    1 : res := res or sm_comp;                   { No locking }
    2 : res := res or sm_rw;               { All prohibited }
    3 : res := res or sm_r;           { Read-only enabled }
    4 : res := res or sm_w;          { Write-only enabled }
    5 : res := res or sm_no;                     { No locking }
  end;
  FiMode := Res;
end;


{**********************************************************************}
{* DFileTest   : Demonstrates access conflicts or file locks with   *}
{*               and without file locking.                          *}
{* Input       : Access type and lock modes for both concurrent files*}
{* Output      : None                                               *}
{**********************************************************************}
procedure DFileTest( AxsTypeA, LockMdA, AxsTypeB, LockMdB : byte );

const TestAOut : Test = 'AAAA';          { Test data records }
      TestBOut : Test = 'BBBB';

var TestAInp,                            { Data records for read test }
    TestBInp  : Test;
    TFileA,                              { Test files for normal access }
    TFileB    : file of Test;

begin
  window( 1, 11, 80, 25 );
  clrscr;
  writeln( 'File A: Name = ', TFileName, ', Access type = ',
           AxsTypeA, ',  Lock mode = ', LockMdA );
  writeln( 'File B: Name = ', TFileName, ', Access type = ',
           AxsTypeB, ',  Lock mode = ', LockMdB );

  {-- Open files ----------------------------------------------}
  write( #13#10'Opening file A:  ' );
  NetReset( TFileName, FiMode( AxsTypeA, LockMdA ),
            sizeof( Test ), TFileA );
  if ( NetError = NE_FileNotFound ) then
    NetRewrite( TFileName, FiMode( AxsTypeA, LockMdA ),
                sizeof( test ), TFileA );
  Writeln( 'Status ', NetError : 2, ' = ', NetErrorMsg( NetError ) );

  write( 'Opening file B:  ' );
  NetReset( TFileName, FiMode( AxsTypeB, LockMdB ),
            sizeof( Test ), TFileB );
  Writeln( 'Status ', NetError : 2, ' = ', NetErrorMsg( NetError ) );

  {-- Write files -------------------------------------------}
  write( #13#10'Writing to file A:' );
  if ( Is_NetWriteOk( TFileA ) ) then            { Write enabled? }
    begin                                    { Yes --> Write it }
      Netwrite( TFileA, TestAOut );
      writeln( ' Record "', TestAOut, '" written ' );
```

```pascal
    end
  else                                          { No --> Error }
    writeln( ' File not open for writing' );

  write( 'Writing to file B:' );
  if ( Is_NetWriteOk( TFileB ) ) then            { Write enabled? }
    begin                                    { Yes --> Write it }
      Netwrite( TFileB, TestBOut );
      writeln( ' Record "', TestBOut, '" written ' );
    end
  else                                          { No --> Error }
    writeln( ' File not open for writing' );

  {-- File pointers for both files moved to beginning ---------------}

  if Is_NetOpen( TFileA ) then                   { File open? }
    NetSeek( TFileA, 0 );                    { Yes --> Continue }
  if Is_NetOpen( TFileB ) then                   { File open? }
    NetSeek( TFileB, 0 );                    { Yes --> Continue }

  {-- Read files --------------------------------------------}

  write( #13#10'Reading file A:' );
  if ( Is_NetReadOk( TFileA ) ) then             { Read enabled? }
    begin                                    { Yes --> Read it }
      Netread( TFileA, TestAInp );
      writeln( ' Record "', TestAInp, '" read ' );
    end
  else                                          { No --> Error }
    writeln( ' File not open for reading' );

  write( 'Reading file B:' );                    { Read enabled? }
  if ( Is_NetReadOk( TFileB ) ) then             { Yes --> Read it }
    begin
      Netread( TFileB, TestBInp );
      writeln( ' Record "', TestBInp, '" read ' );
    end
  else                                          { No --> Error }
    writeln( ' File not open for reading' );

  {-- Close file --------------------------------------------}

  NetClose( TFileA );
  NetClose( TFileB );
end;

{**********************************************************************}
{*                    M A I N   P R O G R A M                       *}
{**********************************************************************}
begin
  clrscr;
  writeln( 'Demonstration of DOS File Locking Functions       ',
           '(C) 1992 by Michael Tischer' );
  writeln( '==================================================',
           '==========================' );

  if ( ShareInst ) then                { Share program installed? }
    begin
      {-- Select file mode --------------------------------------}

      writeln( #13#10'Available access types:         ',
               'Available lock types:' );
      writeln( ' 1: Read-only                   ',
               ' 1: Compatibility mode (no locking)   ' );
```

```
      writeln( ' 2: Write-only                    ',
               ' 2: Prohibit other file accesses generally' );
      writeln( ' 3: Read and write               ',
               ' 3: Read access enabled only' );
      writeln( '                                 ',
               ' 4: Write access enabled only' );
      writeln( '                                 ',
               ' 5: All enabled (record locking)          ' );

      Write( #13#10'Access type: Test file A: ' );
      read( AxsTypeA );
      Write( 'Lock mode: Test file A: ' );
      read( LockMdA );
      Write( 'Access type: Test file B: ' );
      read( AxsTypeB );
      Write( 'Lock mode: Test file B: ' );
      read( LockMdB );

      DFileTest( AxsTypeA, LockMdA, AxsTypeB, LockMdB );
   end
 else
   writeln( #13#10'Please install SHARE before running this program.' );
 end.
```

Listing: FLOCKC.C

```c
/********************************************************************/
/*                      F L O C K C . C                         */
/*------------------------------------------------------------------*/
/*    Task       : Demonstration of the file locking functions on*/
/*                 a network. Uses the module NETFILEC.         */
/*------------------------------------------------------------------*/
/*    Memory model : SMALL                                      */
/*------------------------------------------------------------------*/
/*    Author     : Michael Tischer                              */
/*    developed on : 02/10/1992                                 */
/*    last Update  : 02/13/1992                                 */
/********************************************************************/

#include <stdio.h>
#include "netfilec.c"                     /* include network routine*/

/*== Constants ====================================================*/

#define TFileName "flockc.dat"            /* filename for test file*/

/*== Type definitions =============================================*/

typedef char Test[ 5 ];                   /* Test for file*/
typedef unsigned char BYTE;

/*== display routines for Microsoft C ============================*/

#ifndef __TURBOC__                        /* Microsoft C?*/

#define clrscr() clearwindow( 1, 1, 80, 25 )

/********************************************************************/
/* Gotoxy      : position the Cursor                            */
/* Input       : coordinates of the Cursor                      */
/* Output      : none                                           */
/********************************************************************/

void gotoxy( int x, int y )
{
  regs.h.ah = 0x02;        /* Function number for the Interrupt call*/
  regs.h.bh = 0;                            /* screen page*/
  regs.h.dh = y - 1;
  regs.h.dl = x - 1;
  int86( 0x10, &regs, &regs );             /* Call Interrupt*/
}
#endif

/********************************************************************/
/* clearwindow  : clear a portion of the screen                 */
/* Input        : s.u.                                          */
/* Ouput        : none                                          */
/********************************************************************/

void clearwindow( int x1, int y1, int x2, int y2 )
{
  regs.h.ah = 0x07;        /* Function number for the Interrupt call*/
  regs.h.al = 0x00;
  regs.h.bh = 0x07;
  regs.h.ch = y1 - 1;
  regs.h.cl = x1 - 1;
  regs.h.dh = y2 - 1;
  regs.h.dl = x2 - 1;
```

```
  int86( 0x10, &regs, &regs );                    /* Call Interrupt*/
  gotoxy( x1, y1 );                               /* position cursor*/
}


/**********************************************************************/
/* FiMode    : Create file mode from access type and locking        */
/* Input     : s.u.                                                  */
/* Output    : file mode                                            */
/**********************************************************************/

int FiMode( int AxsType,                /* access type of the file*/
            int LockMd )                /* locking mode of the file*/
{
  static BYTE AxsType_Ary[ 3 ] = { FM_R, FM_W, FM_RW };
  static BYTE LockMd_Ary[ 5 ] = { SM_COMP, SM_RW, SM_R,
                                  SM_W, SM_NO };

  return AxsType_Ary[ AxsType-1 ] | LockMd_Ary[ LockMd-1 ];
}


/**********************************************************************/
/* DFileTest  : Demonstrates access conflicts or file locks with    */
/*              and without file locking.                           */
/* Input      : s.u.                                                 */
/* Output     : none                                                */
/**********************************************************************/

void DFileTest( int AxsTypeA,           /* access type - file A*/
                int LockMdA,            /* lock mode - file A*/
                int AxsTypeB,           /* access type - file B*/
                int LockMdB )           /* lock mode - file B*/
{
  Test  TestAOut = "AAAA\0";            /* Test data records*/
  Test  TestBOut = "BBBB\0";

  Test  TestAInp;
  Test  TestBInp;                       /* Data records for read test*/
  NFILE TFileA;                         /* Test files for normal access*/
  NFILE TFileB;
  char  SDummy[ 50 ];                   /* Status of the network function*/

  clearwindow( 1, 11, 80, 25 );
  printf( "File A: Name = %s Access type = %2i Lock mode = %2i\n",
          TFileName, AxsTypeA, LockMdA );
  printf( "File B: Name = %s Access type = %2i Lock mode = %2i\n\n",
          TFileName, AxsTypeB, LockMdB );

  /*-- Open files --------------------------------------------*/

  printf( "Opening file A:  " );
  NetReset( TFileName, FiMode( AxsTypeA, LockMdA ),
            sizeof( Test ), &TFileA );
  if ( NetError == NE_FileNotFound )
    NetRewrite( TFileName, FiMode( AxsTypeA, LockMdA ),
                sizeof( Test ), &TFileA );
  NetErrorMsg( NetError, SDummy );
  printf( "Status %2u = %s\n", NetError, SDummy );

  printf( "Opening file B:  " );
  NetReset( TFileName, FiMode( AxsTypeB, LockMdB ),
            sizeof( Test ), &TFileB );
  NetErrorMsg( NetError, SDummy );
  printf( "Status %2u = %s\n\n", NetError, SDummy );
```

```
  /*-- Write files -----------------------------------------------*/

  printf( "Writing to file A:" );
  if ( Is_NetWriteOk( &TFileA ) )                 /* write enabled?*/
  {
    NetWrite( &TFileA, TestAOut );
    printf( " Record '%s' written\n", TestAOut );
  }
  else
    printf( " File not open for writing\n" );

  printf( "Writing to file B:" );
  if ( Is_NetWriteOk( &TFileB ) )                 /* write enabled?*/
  {
    NetWrite( &TFileB, TestBOut );
    printf( " Record '%s' written\n\n", TestBOut );
  }
  else
    printf( " File not open for writing\n\n" );

  /*-- File pointers for both file moved to beginning ----------------*/

  if ( Is_NetOpen( &TFileA ) )                     /* file open?*/
    NetSeek( &TFileA, 0L );
  if ( Is_NetOpen( &TFileB ) )                     /* file open?*/
    NetSeek( &TFileB, 0L );

  /*-- Read files ------------------------------------------------*/

  printf( "Reading file A:" );
  if ( Is_NetReadOk( &TFileA ) )                  /* read enabled?*/
  {
    NetRead( &TFileA, TestAInp );
    printf( " Record '%s' read\n", TestAInp );
  }
  else
    printf( " File not open for reading\n" );

  printf( "Reading file B:" );
  if ( Is_NetReadOk( &TFileB ) )                  /* read enabled?*/
  {
    NetRead( &TFileB, TestBInp );
    printf( " Record '%s' read\n\n", TestBInp );
  }
  else
    printf( " File not open for reading\n\n" );

  /*-- Close files -----------------------------------------------*/

  NetClose( &TFileA );
  NetClose( &TFileB );
}

/**********************************************************************/
/*                    M A I N   P R O G R A M                       */
/**********************************************************************/

void main( void )
{
  int AxsTypeA;                                   /* file access modes*/
  int AxsTypeB;
  int LockMdA;                                    /* file lock modes*/
  int LockMdB;
```

939

```
clrscr();                                              printf( " 4: Write access enabled only  \n" );
gotoxy( 1, 1 );                                        printf( "                               " );
printf( "Demonstration of DOS File Locking Functions       " \    printf( " 5: All enabled (record locking)\n" );
        "(C) 1992 by Michael Tischer\n" );
printf( "=================================================" \    printf( "\nAccess type Test file A: " );
        "==========================\n\n" );             scanf( "%i", &AxsTypeA );
                                                       printf( "Lock Mode Test file A: " );
if ( ShareInst() )                    /* SHARE installed?*/    scanf( "%i", &LockMdA );
{                                                      printf( "Access type Test file B: " );
/*-- Select file mode --------------------------------------*/    scanf( "%i", &AxsTypeB );
                                                       printf( "Lock mode Test file B: " );
  printf( "Available access types:       Available lock types:\n" );    scanf( "%i", &LockMdB );
  printf( " 1: Read-only                 " ),
  printf( " 1: Compatibility mode (no locking)\n" );   DFileTest( AxsTypeA, LockMdA, AxsTypeB, LockMdB );
  printf( " 2: Write-only                " );        }
  printf( " 2: Prohibit other file accesses generally\n" );    else
  printf( " 3: Read and Write            " );          printf( "\nPlease install SHARE before running this program.\n" );
  printf( " 3: Read access enabled only  \n" );      }
  printf( "                              " );
```

Unlike the two FLOCK programs, the RELOCK programs (RELOCKP.PAS and RELOCKC.C) must either run on two network computers or within two separate DOS boxes under Windows. These programs lock specified records of the RELOCKP.DAT (Pascal version) or RELOCKC.DAT (C version) file. This file is created at the beginning of the program and is equipped with a total of 10 records, each containing 160 bytes. These records are assigned specific ASCII codes. The first record receives the ASCII code of the capital letter A, the second record the capital letter B, and the third the capital letter C, etc.

```
┌──────────────────────────────────────────────────────────────┐
│ Demonstration of DOS File Locking Functions  (C)1992 Michael Tischer │
│ ==============================================================   │
│                                                                │
│ Available functions                        Status:             │
│    1: Position file pointer                   0  Unlocked      │
│    2: Lock record                             1  Unlocked      │
│    3: Read record                             2  Unlocked      │
│    4: Edit data record                        3  Unlocked      │
│    5: Write record                            4  Unlocked      │
│    6: Unlock record                           5  Locked        │
│    7: Exit                                    6  Locked        │
│                                               7  Unlocked      │
│ Select:                                       8  Locked        │
│                                               9  Unlocked      │
│                                                                │
│ Current Record :   0                                           │
│ Status         :   Unlocked                                    │
│ Network Status :   0 = No error                                │
│                                                                │
│ Current Data Record:                                           │
└──────────────────────────────────────────────────────────────┘
```

The program RECLOCK.PAS

Both programs allow you to access different records, to read from and write to them, and, most importantly, to lock them. Currently locked records are indicated at the right side of the screen.

It may be interesting to lock several records from within the first program and then attempt to access these from the second program. DOS won't permit this access and will return error code 5, which displays an error message on your screen.

Listing: **RECLOCKP.PAS**

```
{*************************************************************}
{*                    R E C L O C K                         *}
{*---------------------------------------------------------*}
{*   Task       : Demonstrates the DOS record locking functions. *}
{*---------------------------------------------------------*}
{*   Author     : Michael Tischer                          *}
{*   Developed on : 09/19/91                               *}
{*   Last update : 01/29/92                                *}
{*************************************************************}

program reclock;

uses Crt, Dos,                        { Add CRT and DOS units }
     NetFileP;                        { Add NetFileP unit }

const TFileName = 'Rec.dat';          { Filename for test file }

type  Test     = array[ 1..160 ] of char;  { Data type for test }
      TestFile = file of Test;

var DFile : TestFile;                 { Test file }

{*************************************************************}
{* CreateATRec : Creates a test data record.               *}
{* Input       : Characters for the record                 *}
{* Output      : Test data record                          *}
{*************************************************************}

procedure CreateATRec(     ReChars : char;
                       var DRec    : test );

var i : word;                         { Loop counter }

begin
  for i := 1 to 160 do
    DRec[ i ] := ReChars;
end;

{*************************************************************}
{* OpenNetFile : Open available network file. If one does not exist, *}
{*               create a new one and fill this new file with *}
{*               test data records.                        *}
{* Input       : File                                      *}
{* Output      : File                                      *}
{*************************************************************}

function OpenNetFile( var DFile : testfile ) : boolean;

var i      : word;                    { Loop counter }
    TestDRec : Test;                  { Needed for creating the test file }

begin
  {-- Open file for input & output in deny none mode -----------------}

  NetReset( TFileName, fm_rw or sm_no, sizeof( Test ), DFile );
  if ( NetError = NE_FileNotFound ) then    { File not found? }
    begin

      {-- Create file and fill with test data records ----------------}

      NetRewrite( TFileName, fm_rw or sm_no, sizeof( Test ), DFile );
      if ( NetError = 0 ) then        { No errors during creation? }
```

```
      begin
        if NetLock( DFile, 0, 26 ) then      { Store 26 records }
          begin
            NetSeek( DFile, 0 );       { Pointer to start of file }
            for i := 1 to 26 do
              begin
                CreateATRec( chr( ord( 'Z' ) + 1 - i ), TestDRec );
                NetWrite( DFile, TestDRec );   { Write test data }
              end;
            OpenNetFile := NetUnlock( DFile, 0, 26 );
          end
        else
          OpenNetFile := false;        { Error when locking }
      end
    else
      OpenNetFile := false;            { Error while creating the file }
  end
  else
    OpenNetFile := ( NetError = 0 );   { No errors while opening? }
end;

{*************************************************************}
{* NetEdits   : Demonstrates network functions.            *}
{* Input      : File                                       *}
{* Output     : File                                       *}
{*************************************************************}

procedure NetEdits( var DFile : TestFile );

var CurRecord : longint;              { Current record number }
    CurDRec   : Test;                 { Current data record }
    Action    : byte;                 { Desired action }
    Status    : boolean;              { Record locked? }
    ReChars   : char;

begin
  {-- Display menu -----------------------------------------}

  writeln( #13#10'Available functions' );
  writeln( '  1: Position file pointer' );
  writeln( '  2: Lock record' );
  writeln( '  3: Read record' );
  writeln( '  4: Edit data record' );
  writeln( '  5: Write record' );
  writeln( '  6: Unlock record' );
  writeln( '  7: Exit' );

  CurRecord := 0;                     { Current data record }
  Status := false;                    { Record not locked }
  CreateATRec( #32, CurDRec );        { Create empty data record }

  repeat
    {-- Display information -----------------------------------}

    gotoxy( 1, 16 );                  { Display file pointer position }
    writeln( 'Current Record: ', CurRecord : 4 );
    write( 'Status        : ' );
    if Status then
      writeln( 'Locked  ' )
    else
      writeln( 'Unlocked' );
    Writeln( 'Network Status : ', NetError : 4, ' = ',
      copy( NetErrorMsg( NetError ) + '                ', 1, 30 ) );
    gotoxy( 1, 21 );                  { Display test record }
```

941

```
writeln( 'Current Data Record:' );
writeln( CurDRec );

NetSeek( DFile, CurRecord );              { Position file pointer }

gotoxy( 1, 13 );
write( 'Select:                    ' );
gotoxy( 10, 13 );
readln( Action );
case Action of
  1 : begin
        gotoxy( 1, 13 );
        write( 'New data record number: ' );
        readln( CurRecord );
        Status := false;                 { Record not locked }
        CreateATRec( #32, CurDRec )
      end;
  2 : Status := Status or NetLock( DFile, CurRecord, 1 );
  3 : NetRead( DFile, CurDRec );         { Read data record }
  4 : begin
        gotoxy( 1, 13 );
        write( 'New character: ' );
        readln( ReChars );
        CreateATRec( ReChars, CurDRec );
      end;
  5 : NetWrite( DFile, CurDRec );        { Write data record }
  6 : Status := Status and not NetUnlock( DFile, CurRecord, 1 );
  end;
until ( Action = 7 );
end;

{*********************************************************************}
{*            M A I N   P R O G R A M                              *}
{*********************************************************************}

begin
  clrscr;
  writeln( 'Demonstration of DOS File Locking Functions ',
           '(C) 1991 by Michael Tischer ' + paramstr( 1 ) );
  writeln( '====================================================',
           '=========================' );

  if ( ShareInst ) then                  { Share program installed? }
    begin
      if OpenNetFile( DFile ) then       { File open or created? }
        begin
          NetEdits( DFile );    { Demonstration of network functions }
          NetClose( DFile );             { Close file }
        end
      else
        writeln( #13#10'Error while opening network file ' +
                 'Error number: ', NetError );
      ClrScr;
    end
  else
    writeln( #13#10'Please install SHARE before running this program.' );
end.
```

Listing: RECLOCKC.C

```c
/*********************************************************************/
/*                    R E C L O C K C . C                          */
/*-----------------------------------------------------------------*/
/*    Task        : Demonstrates the DOS record locking functions.*/
/*-----------------------------------------------------------------*/
/*    Memory model : SMALL                                         */
/*-----------------------------------------------------------------*/
/*    Author      : Michael Tischer                                */
/*    developed on : 02/10/1992                                    */
/*    last Update : 02/13/1991                                     */
/*********************************************************************/

#include "netfilec.c"              /* include network routine*/
#include <stdio.h>

/*== Constants ====================================================*/

#define TFILENAME "reclockc.dat"        /* file name for test file*/
#define NumOfRecs   10                  /* number of records*/

/*== Type definitions =============================================*/

typedef char Test[ 160 ];              /* Data type for Test*/
typedef char TestString[ 161 ];    /* Data type for screen output*/

#ifndef __TURBOC__                         /* Microsoft C?*/

  #define clrscr() clearwindow( 1, 1, 80, 25 )

/*********************************************************************/
/* Gotoxy      : Positions the Cursor                             */
/* Input       : coordinates of the Cursor                        */
/* Output      : none                                             */
/*********************************************************************/

  void gotoxy( int x, int y )

  {
    regs.h.ah = 0x02;        /* function number for Interrupt call*/
    regs.h.bh = 0;                                    /* color*/
    regs.h.dh = y - 1;
    regs.h.dl = x - 1;
    int86( 0x10, &regs, &regs );              /* call Interrupt*/
  }
#endif

/*********************************************************************/
/* clearwindow  : Clear a portion of the screen.                  */
/* Input        : s.u.                                            */
/* Output       : none                                            */
/*********************************************************************/

void clearwindow( int x1, int y1, int x2, int y2 )
{
  regs.h.ah = 0x07;        /* function number for the interrupt call*/
  regs.h.al = 0x00;
  regs.h.bh = 0x07;
  regs.h.ch = y1 - 1;
  regs.h.cl = x1 - 1;
  regs.h.dh = y2 - 1;
  regs.h.dl = x2 - 1;
  int86( 0x10, &regs, &regs );                  /* call interrupt*/
```

```
   gotoxy( x1, y1 );                          /* position cursor*/
}


/*****************************************************************/
/* OpenNetFile : Open available network file. If one does not exist,*/
/*                create a new one and fill this new file with     */
/*                test data records.                               */
/* Input       : s.u.                                              */
/* Output      : file                                              */
/*****************************************************************/

int OpenNetFile( NFILE *DFile )                   /* Network file*/
{
   int  i;                                        /* loop counter*/
   Test TestDRec;                  /* needed for creating the test file*/

/*-- Open file for input and output in Deny None mode ---------------*/

   NetReset( TFILENAME, FM_RW | SM_NO, sizeof( Test ), DFile );
   if ( NetError == NE_FileNotFound )            /* file not found?*/
   {
/*-- Create file and fill with test data records --------------------*/

      NetRewrite( TFILENAME, FM_RW | SM_NO, sizeof( Test ), DFile );
      if ( NetError == NE_OK )          /* no errors during creation?*/
      {
         if ( NetLock( DFile, 0L, (long) NumOfRecs ) )
         {
            NetSeek( DFile, 0L );      /* pointer to beginning of the file*/
            for ( i = 0; i < NumOfRecs; i++ )
            {
               memset( TestDRec, 'A' + i, 160 );
               NetWrite( DFile, TestDRec );        /* write test file*/
            }
            return NetUnLock( DFile, 0L, (long) NumOfRecs );
         }
         else
            return FALSE;                     /* error when locking*/
      }
      else
         return FALSE;              /* error while creating the file*/
   }
   else
      return ( NetError == 0 );         /* no errors while opeining?*/
}


/*****************************************************************/
/* NetEdits   : Demonstrates network functions                   */
/* Input      : s.u                                              */
/* Output     : File                                            */
/*****************************************************************/

void NetEdits( NFILE *TestFile )                 /* network file*/
{
   unsigned long CurRecord;          /* current Record number*/
   TestString    CurDRec;            /* current data record*/
   int           Action;             /* desired action*/
   int           Status;             /* Record locked?*/
   char          TChar[ 10 ];
   char          SDummy[ 50 ];       /* Network status*/
   int           LStatus[ NumOfRecs ];
   int           i;                  /* loop counter*/

/*-- Display menu ----------------------------------------------*/
```

```
   printf( "Available functions\n" );
   printf( "  1: Position file pointer\n" );
   printf( "  2: Lock record\n" );
   printf( "  3: Read Record\n" );
   printf( "  4: Edit data record\n" );
   printf( "  5: Write record\n" );
   printf( "  6: Unlock record\n" );
   printf( "  7: Exit\n" );

/*-- Initialize data record ------------------------------------*/

   gotoxy( 58, 4 );
   printf( "Status:" );
   for ( i = 0; i < NumOfRecs; ++i )
   {
      LStatus[i] = FALSE;
      gotoxy( 60, i+5 );
      printf( "%2d   Unlocked", i );
   }

   CurRecord = 0;                          /* current data record*/
   Status = FALSE;                         /* Record not locked*/
   memset( CurDRec, 32, 160 );       /* create empty data record*/

   do
   {
/*-- Display information ---------------------------------------*/

      gotoxy( 1, 16 );             /* display file pointer position*/
      printf( "Current Record: %4li\n", CurRecord );
      printf( "Status         : %s\n",
              LStatus[CurRecord] ? "Locked  " : "Unlocked" );
      NetErrorMsg( NetError, SDummy );
      printf( "Network Status : %4i = %s", NetError, SDummy );
      gotoxy( 1, 21 );                   /* display test record*/
      printf( "Current Data Record:\n" );
      CurDRec[ 160 ] = 0;
      printf( "%s", CurDRec );

      NetSeek( TestFile, CurRecord );      /* Position file pointer*/
      gotoxy( 1, 13 );
      printf( "Select:                      " );
      gotoxy( 10, 13 );
      scanf( "%i", &Action );
      switch( Action )
      {
         case 1 : gotoxy( 1, 13 );
                  printf( "New data record number: " );
                  do
                  {
                     gotoxy( 25, 13 );
                     printf( "              " );
                     gotoxy( 25, 13 );
                     scanf( "%li", &CurRecord );
                  }
                  while (!( CurRecord >= 0 && CurRecord < NumOfRecs ));
                  break;

         case 2 : Status = NetLock( TestFile, CurRecord, 1L );
                  if ( Status )
                  {
                     LStatus[ CurRecord ] = TRUE;
                     gotoxy( 60, (int) CurRecord +5 );
```

943

```
                    printf( "%2d   Locked   ", CurRecord );
                 }
              break;

       case 3 : NetRead( TestFile, CurDRec );        /* read data record*/
                break;

       case 4 : gotoxy( 1, 13 );
                printf( "New character: " );
                scanf( "%s", TChar );
                memset( CurDRec, TChar[ 0 ], 160 );
                break;

       case 5 : NetWrite( TestFile, CurDRec );     /* write data record*/
                break;

       case 6 : Status = NetUnLock( TestFile, CurRecord, 1L );
                if ( Status )
                 {
                  LStatus[ CurRecord ] = FALSE;
                  gotoxy( 60, (int) CurRecord+5 );
                  printf( "%2d   UnLocked   ", CurRecord);
                 }
                break;
    }

  }
  while ( Action != 7 );
}


/**********************************************************************/
/*                  M A I N   P R O G R A M                 */
/**********************************************************************/

void main( )

{
NFILE DFile;                                      /* Test file*/

clrscr();
printf( "Demonstration of DOS File Locking Funcitons" \
        "   (C)1992 by Michael Tischer\n" );
printf( "=================================================" \
        "============================\n\n" );

if ( ShareInst() )                    /* Share program installed?*/
 {
  if ( OpenNetFile( &DFile ) )          /* file open or created?*/
   {
    NetEdits( &DFile );        /* Demonstration of network functions*/
    NetClose( &DFile );                             /* close file*/
    clrscr( );
   }
  else
   printf( "\nError %i while opening network file", NetError );
 }
else
 printf( "\nPlease install SHARE before running this program" );
}
```

Chapter 29

DOS and Windows

Today anyone who produces DOS applications must expect that these applications will eventually be executed through Windows. Although Windows successfully simulates the DOS environment, there are certain things that DOS programs cannot do under Windows. So, if you're not careful, particularly with disk utilities, Windows may crash. TSR programs that access the DOS core deeply in order to shield themselves from other TSR programs will also cause problems.

In this chapter we'll discuss how a DOS application can detect the presence of Windows.

29.1 Sensing Windows

There isn't a single DOS function that indicates whether Windows is active, which version is active, and in which mode Windows is running. Multiple, unrelated functions must be called to provide this information.

The multiplex interrupt (interrupt 2FH) plays an important role in checking for Windows. Many resident DOS applications and utilities, such as SHARE and PRINT, use this interrupt to make their services available to other applications. Windows also assigns a few functions to this interrupt.

As the following flowchart shows, we begin by calling multiplex function 1600H, which is provided by Windows to specify the Windows operating mode. If another function wasn't linked to this function number in the multiplex interrupt, then the register settings will remain unchanged by the function call, and the AL register will remain set to 00H. This means that Windows 3.x is inactive. However, other tests must be performed to determine whether a different version of Windows is active.

If the AL register contains either 01H or FFH after the function call, Windows 2.x is active. Although the exact version is still unknown, this value indicates a running version of Windows.

If the AL register contains 80H, Windows 3.x is active in a mode other than enhanced mode.

If the AL register contains values other than 00H, 01H, 80H, or FFH, Windows 3.x (or even 4.x) is running in enhanced mode. The AL register value represents the major version number of the current Windows system, while the AH register value represents the minor version number.

Additional tests are needed to gather more information if the function call returned 00H or 80H. To determine whether Windows 3.x is active, use function 4680H, which links Windows 3.x to the multiplex interrupt. If this function returns the value 80H in the AL register, the function isn't even implemented and you can assume that no version of Windows is active.

The following flowchart illustrates how the Windows check should be performed:

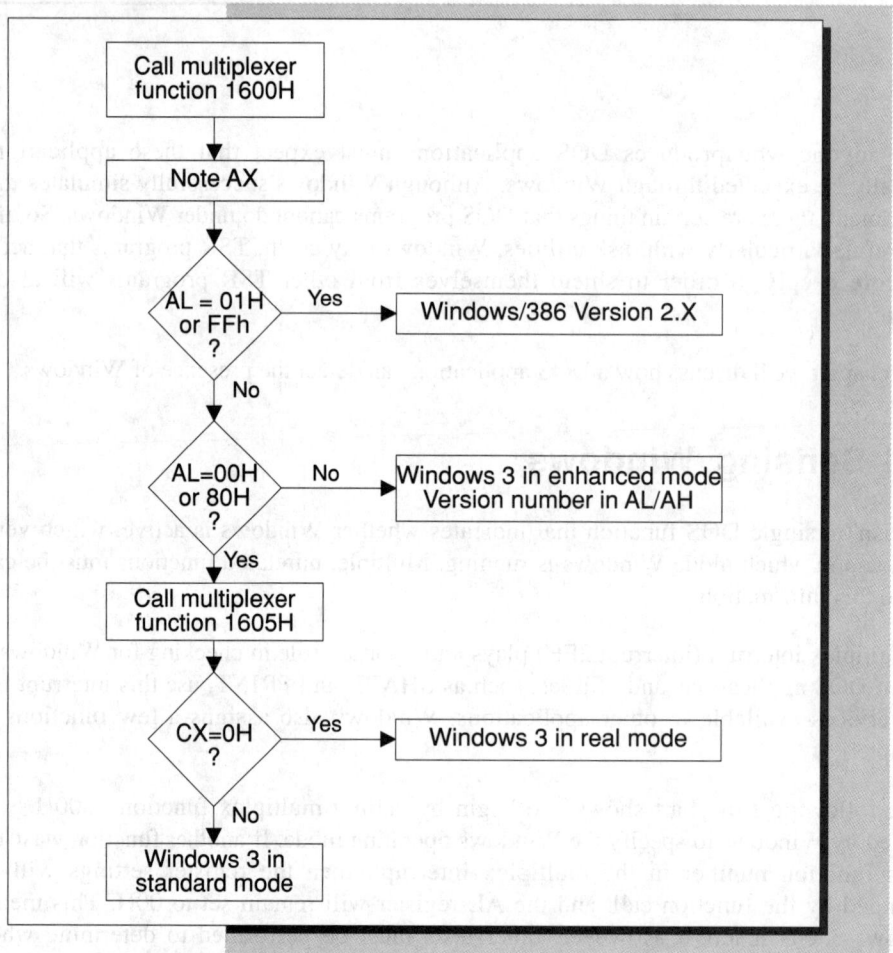

Algorithm for checking the Windows version and the operating mode

However, if you receive the value 00H, Windows 3 will be active. From there, all you need to do is determine the Windows operating mode. It can be running in either the standard or the real mode.

Function 1605H will help us determine the operating mode. This function switches Windows to standard mode from its current operating mode. If Windows is already in standard mode when function 1605H is called, this function will fail, placing 00H in the CX register to indicate this failure.

Function 1606H switches Windows from standard mode into real mode. If Windows is already in real mode when function 1606H is called, this function will fail, placing 00H in the CX register to indicate this failure.

Either function indicates the Windows 3.x operating mode, thus completing the test.

29.2 Demonstration Programs

The following contains programs in BASIC, C, and Pascal that implement the algorithm previously described. Each program contains a routine called WINDOWS, which returns constants named NO_WIN, WIN_386_X, WIN_REAL, WIN_STANDARD, or WIN_ENHANCED, depending on Windows status when the program is run. The programs will even tell you the exact version number if Windows 3.x is running in enhanced mode. For this, the function requires two integer variables (or in the case of the C implementation, the addresses of these variables) for storing the Windows version number.

BASIC listing: WINDAB.BAS

```
'***********************************************************
'*                   W I N D A B . B A S                *
'_____
'* Task          : Determines whether Windows is active, and if so, *
'*                 the operating mode.                   *
'*                 QuickBASIC and the QB.LIB must be loaded using *
'*                 QB /L QB                              *
'*                 before loading and running this file. *
'_____
'* Author        : Michael Tischer                       *
'* Developed on  : 08/22/91                              *
'* Last update   : 01/10/92                              *
'***********************************************************

DECLARE FUNCTION Windows% (MVersion AS INTEGER, SVersion AS INTEGER)

'$INCLUDE: 'Qb.bi'                   'Include file for interrupt calls

CONST MULTIPLEX = &H2F              'Interrupt number of multiplex interrupt
CONST NOWIN = &H0                             'Windows not active
CONST WIN386X = &H1                   'Windows/386 V2.x running
CONST WINREAL = &H81                  'Windows running in real mode
CONST WINSTANDARD = &H82             'Windows running in standard mode
CONST WINENHANCED = &H83             'Windows running in extended mode

DIM WindowsActive AS INTEGER                  'Windows mode
DIM MVer AS INTEGER                   'Main version of Windows
DIM SVer AS INTEGER                   'Alternate version of Windows

PRINT " WINDAB  -  (c) 1991 by Michael Tischer "
PRINT                                         'Blank line
WindowsActive = Windows(MVer, SVer)   'Get Windows version and mode
SELECT CASE WindowsActive
  CASE NOWIN
    PRINT "Windows not active "
  CASE WIN2X
    PRINT "Windows /386 V 2.x active "
  CASE WINREAL
    PRINT "Windows active in real mode "
  CASE WINSTANDARD
    PRINT "Windows active in standard mode "
  CASE WINENHANCED
    PRINT "Windows V"; LTRIM$(STR$(MVer)); ".";
    PRINT LTRIM$(STR$(SVer)); " active in extended mode"
END SELECT

'***********************************************************
'* Windows : Determines whether Windows is active        *
'* Input   : MVERSION = Integer variable of main version number *
'*           SVERSION = Integer variable of sub version number *
'* Output  : Windows status, from constants NOWIN, WIN386X, WINREAL, *
'*           WINSTANDARD or WINENHANCED                  *
'* Info    : Version number can only be passed and returned when *
'*           Windows 3.x is operating in enhanced mode   *
'***********************************************************
FUNCTION Windows% (MVersion AS INTEGER, SVersion AS INTEGER)

DIM Regs AS RegTypeX               'Processor registers for interrupt call
DIM VBf AS INTEGER                            'Version buffer

MVersion = 0                              'Initialize version numbers
SVersion = 0

Regs.ax = &H1600      'Function number: Install test for extended mode
CALL INTERRUPTX(MULTIPLEX, Regs, Regs)
VBf = Regs.ax                                 'Set regs.AX

SELECT CASE VBf MOD 256                        'Compute low byte

'---- Windows /386 running -------------------------------------
```

```
       CASE &H1, &HFF                        'Windows /386 running
         MVersion = 2                        'Main version
         SVersion = 0                        'Sub version unknown
         Windows = WIN386X


'---- Windows not running, running in real mode or standard mode ------

       CASE &H0, &H80
         Regs.ax = &H4680                    'Identify real or standard mode
         CALL INTERRUPTX(MULTIPLEX, Regs, Regs)
         IF (Regs.ax MOD 256) = &H80 THEN    'Is Windows running?
           Windows = NOWIN                                'No
         ELSE                   'Windows running in real or standard mode
           Regs.ax = &H1605                  'Emulate installation of DOS Extender
           Regs.bx = &H0
           Regs.si = &H0
           Regs.cx = &H0
           Regs.es = &H0
           Regs.ds = &H0
           Regs.dx = &H1
           CALL INTERRUPTX(MULTIPLEX, Regs, Regs)
           IF Regs.cx = &H0 THEN             'Windows in real mode?
             Windows = WINREAL                            'Yes
           ELSE               'No --> Windows runs in standard mode
             Windows = WINSTANDARD
           END IF
         END IF


'---- Windows in extended mode, AX contains version number -----------

       CASE ELSE
         MVersion = VBf AND &HF              'Low byte is main version
         SVersion = VBf \ 256                'High byte is sub version
         Windows = WINENHANCED
       END SELECT

       END FUNCTION
```

Pascal listing: WINDAP.PAS

```
{******************************************************************}
{                      W I N D A P . P A S                         }
{-----------------------------------------------------------------}
{   Task        : Determines whether windows is active, and if so, }
{                 the operating mode.                              }
{-----------------------------------------------------------------}
{   Author      : Michael Tischer                                 }
{   Developed on : 08/22/91                                       }
{   Last update  : 01/13/92                                       }
{******************************************************************}
uses Dos;                                    { Use DOS unit }

const MULTIPLEX = $2F;       { Interrupt number of multiplex interrupt }
      NO_WIN    = $00;                    { Windows not active }
      W_386_X   = $01;               { Windows/386 V2.X running }
      W_REAL    = $81;           { Windows running in real mode }
      W_STANDARD = $82;      { Windows running in standard mode }
      W_ENHANCED = $83;      { Windows running in extended mode }


{******************************************************************}
{ WINDOWS : Determines whether Windows is active                   }
{ Input   : MVERSION = Integer variable of main version number     }
{           SVERSION = Integer variable of sub version number      }
{ Output  : Windows status, from constants NO_WIN, W_386_X, W_REAL, }
{           W_STANDARD or W_ENHANCED                               }
{ Info    : Version number can only be passed and returned when    }
{           Windows 3.x is operating in enhanced mode             }
{******************************************************************}
function windows( var MVersion, SVersion : integer ) : integer;

var regs : registers;        { Processor registers for interrupt call }
    Erg  : integer;

{-- This function replaces intr( $2F, Regs ) with Regs.ax = $1600 ----}
{-- (installation test for extended mode), as the Pascal function ----}
{-- returns false values                                          ----}


function int2fcall : integer;


begin
  inline( $b8 / $00 / $16 /       { mov   ax,1600h     }
          $cd / $2f /             { int   2Fh          }
          $89 / $46 / $FE );      { mov   [bp-2], ax   }
  { This inline inserts the "mov ax, [bp-2]" instruction, which      }
  { places the local function variable in the return register       }
end;


begin
  MVersion := 0;                             { Initialize version numbers }
  SVersion := 0;

  {-- Windows x.y in extended mode -------------------------------------}

  erg := int2fcall; { Installation test for extended mode }

  case ( lo(Erg) ) of
    $01,
    $FF:  begin
            MVersion := 2;                           { main version }
            SVersion := 0;                     { sub version unknown }
            Windows := W_386_X;
          end;
```

```
            $00,
            $80:  begin
                       regs.ax := $4680;  { Identify real mode or standard mode }
                       intr( MULTIPLEX, regs );
                       if ( regs.al = $80 ) then
                          Windows := NO_WIN              { Windows not running }
                       else
                          begin
                             {-- Windows in real more or standard mode ------------}

                             regs.ax := $1605; { Emulate installation of DOS extdr }
                             regs.bx := $0000;
                             regs.si := $0000;
                             regs.cx := $0000;
                             regs.es := $0000;
                             regs.ds := $0000;
                             regs.dx := $0001;
                             intr( MULTIPLEX, regs );
                             if ( regs.cx = $0000 ) then
                                begin
                                   {-- Windows in real mode -------------------------}

                                   regs.ax := $1606;
                                   intr( MULTIPLEX, regs );
                                   Windows := W_REAL;
                                end
                             else
                                Windows := W_STANDARD;
                          end;
                    end;

            {-- Windows in extended mode, AX contains version number ---------}

            else
               begin
                  MVersion := lo(Erg);                 { Display Windows version }
                  SVersion := hi(Erg);
                  Windows := W_ENHANCED;              { Windows in extended mode }
               end;
          end;
end;

{*******************************************************************}
{              M A I N   P R O G R A M                             }
{*******************************************************************}

var WindowsActive,                        { Windows mode }
    MVer,                                 { Main version of Windows }
    SVer        : integer;                { Sub version of Windows }

begin
  writeln( ' WINDAP  -  (c) 1991 by Michael Tischer ' );
  writeln;
  WindowsActive := windows( MVer, SVer );
  case ( WindowsActive ) of
    NO_WIN:     writeln( 'Windows not active ' );
    W_REAL:     writeln( 'Windows in real mode ' );
    W_STANDARD: writeln( 'Windows active in standard mode' );
    W_386_X:    writeln( 'Windows/386 V 2.x active' );
    W_ENHANCED: writeln( 'Windows V ', Mver, '.', SVer,
                         ' active im extended mode' );
  end;
  halt( WindowsActive );
end.
```

C listing: WINDAC.C

```c
/*******************************************************************/
/*                     W I N D A C . C                          */
/*-----------------------------------------------------------------*/
/*  Task        : Determines whether Windows is active, and if so, */
/*                the operating mode.                              */
/*-----------------------------------------------------------------*/
/*  Author      : Michael Tischer                                 */
/*  Developed on : 08/22/91                                       */
/*  Last update  : 01/13/92                                       */
/*-----------------------------------------------------------------*/
/*  Memory model : SMALL                                          */
/*******************************************************************/

/*== Add include files ===========================================*/

#include <dos.h>
#include <stdio.h>

/*== Constants ===================================================*/

#define MULTIPLEX    0x2F /* Interrupt number of multiplex interrupt */

#define NO_WIN       0x00                        /* Windows not active */
#define W_386_X      0x01              /* Windows/386 V2.x running */
#define W_REAL       0x81             /* Windows running im real mode */
#define W_STANDARD   0x82        /* Windows running im standard mode */
#define W_ENHANCED   0x83        /* Windows running im extended mode */

/*******************************************************************/
/* WINDOWS : Determines whether Windows is active                */
/* Input   : MVERSION = Pointer to INT variable to which the main */
/*                      version number should be passed          */
/*           SVERSION = Pointer to INT variable to which the sub  */
/*                      version number should be passed          */
/* Output  : Windows status, from constants NO_WIN, W_386_X,     */
/*           W_STANDARD, W_STANDARD or W_ENHANCED                */
/* Info    : Version number can only be passed and returned when  */
/*           Windows 3.x is operating in enhanced mode           */
/*******************************************************************/

int windows( int *MVersion, int *SVersion )
{
  union REGS  regs;           /* Registers for interrupt call */
  struct SREGS sregs;         /* Segment register for interrupt call */

  *MVersion = 0;                        /* Initialize version number */
  *SVersion = 0;

  /*-- Windows x.y in extended mode ------------------------------*/

  regs.x.ax = 0x1600;                   /* Installation check for Windows */
  segread( &sregs );                    /* Read segment register */
  int86x( MULTIPLEX, &regs, &regs, &sregs );

  switch ( regs.h.al )
  {
  case 0x01:
  case 0xFF: *MVersion = 2;                        /* Main version */
             *SVersion = 0;                    /* Sub version unknown */
             return W_386_X;               /* Windows/386 Version 2.x */

  case 0x00:
```

```
case 0x80:  regs.x.ax = 0x4680;     /* Real mode and standard mode */
            int86x( MULTIPLEX, &regs, &regs, &sregs );
            if ( regs.h.al == 0x80 )
            return NO_WIN;                  /* Windows not running */
            else
            {
            /*-- Windows in real mode or standard mode -----------*/

            regs.x.ax = 0x1605;        /* Emulate initialization */
            regs.x.bx = regs.x.si = regs.x.cx =
                        sregs.es = sregs.ds = 0x0000;
            regs.x.dx = 0x0001;
            int86x( MULTIPLEX, &regs, &regs, &sregs );
            if ( regs.x.cx == 0x0000 )
            {
             /*-- Windows in real mode --------------------------*/

             regs.x.ax = 0x1606;
             int86x( MULTIPLEX, &regs, &regs, &sregs );
             return W_REAL;
             }
            else
             return W_STANDARD;
            }

 /*-- Windows in extended mode, AX contains version number ---------*/

 default: *MVersion = regs.h.al;      /* Display Windows version */
          *SVersion = regs.h.ah;
          return W_ENHANCED;          /* Windows in extended mode */
 }
}


/**********************************************************************/
/*                   M A I N   P R O G R A M                         */
/**********************************************************************/

int main( void )
{
 int WindowsActive,                     /* Windows mode */
     MVer,                              /* Main version of Windows */
     SVer;                              /* Sub version of Windows */

 printf(" WINDAC  -  (c) 1991 by Michael Tischer \n\n" );
 WindowsActive = windows( &MVer, &SVer );
 switch ( WindowsActive )
 {
  case NO_WIN:      printf( "Windows not active\n" );
                    break;
  case W_REAL:      printf( "Windows active in real mode\n" );
                    break;
  case W_STANDARD:  printf( "Windows active in standard mode\n" );
                    break;
  case W_386_X:     printf( "Windows/386 V 2.x active" );
                    break;
  case W_ENHANCED:  printf( "Windows V %d.%d active in %s\n",
                            MVer, SVer, "extended mode" );
                    break;
 }
 return( WindowsActive );
}
```

950

Chapter 30

Maintaining Compatibility

In this book we discuss three ways to access PC hardware. You can either access available DOS or BIOS functions or develop new functions and routines for direct hardware control. Although this doesn't provide any advantages in mass storage device and keyboard access, special routines for screen display are often much faster and more efficient than BIOS and DOS routines that perform the same task.

We recommend using DOS functions for compatibility. To develop programs that run without problems on virtually any DOS computer, you must follow some rules for DOS function calls. To develop programs, under the current DOS versions, that should execute without problems under future versions of DOS, follow these suggestions:

- Use only DOS functions for screen and hardware access. Don't use BIOS or other hardware dependent functions.

- Display error messages on the standard error device (handle 2).

- Use Version 2 UNIX-compatible handle functions for file access. This ensures compatibility with future versions of DOS. If you must use old FCB functions for file or directory access (e.g., for special attributes), be sure no FCBs, which are already open, are opened and no FCBs, which are already closed, are closed.

- Check the DOS version number at the beginning of the program and end the program with an error message if it cannot execute under this version.

- Store as many constants as needed for program execution (e.g., the paths of programs and files to be loaded) within the environment block. Access these values from the environment block within the program.

- Release all memory not required by the program using the DOS functions. (This is especially important when working with COM programs.)

- If you need additional memory, request it using the proper DOS functions.

- Use the available DOS functions for interrupt vectors; don't directly access interrupt vectors. To change the contents of various interrupt vectors within a program, first save the old contents and restore them before the end of the program.

- Call one of the DOS functions (31H or 4CH) before the end of the program to pass a value to the calling program to signal whether the program was executed correctly. Avoid using the other functions for ending a program (interrupt 20H and function 0 of interrupt 21H).

- Use function 59H of interrupt 21H (available in DOS Versions 3.0 and higher) to localize error sources.

The following is an overview of the older DOS functions you should avoid and their replacements:

Old		New	
00H	End program	4CH	End Process
0FH	Open file	3DH	Open Handle
10H	Close file	3EH	Close handle
11H	Find first entry	4EH	Find first entry
12H	Find next entry	4FH	Find next entry
13H	Erase file	41H	Erase directory entry
14H	Sequential read	3FH	Read (through handle)
15H	Sequential write	40H	Write (through handle)
16H	Created file	3CH 5AH 5BH	Created handle or Created temporary file or Created new file
17H	Rename file	56H	Rename directory entry
21H	Random access read	3FH	Read (through handle)
22H	Random access write	40H	Write (through handle)
23H	Sense file size	42H	Move file pointer
24H	Set data set number	42H	Move file pointer
26H	Create new PSP	4BH	Load and execute from file
27H	Random access read	3FH	Read (through handle)
28H	Random access write	40H	Write (through handle)

If you follow all these suggestions, your programs will execute on other computers and under future DOS versions with little or no modifications.

Chapter 31

Undocumented DOS Structures

Many reference books discuss undocumented information about DOS. Occasionally, we've found some DOS structures still undocumented, such as several DOS variables that contain extremely important information. In this chapter, we'll discuss some of these undocumented structures.

31.1 Documented and Undocumented Structures

DOS manages the operating storage media (RAM and mass storage) and programs that use multiple data structures. Some of these structures are thoroughly documented and have already been described in this book. These structures include:

- Program Segment Prefix (PSP), which precedes every program in memory

- File Control Blocks (FCBs), which control file access

- Memory Control Blocks (MCBs), which control RAM

- Structures in the header of a device driver

- Environment blocks, which contain information strings about every program in memory

- The many structures that DOS keeps in mass storage (boot sector, File Allocation Table [FAT], root directory, etc.)

There are also several undocumented structures. Until recently, only a few people knew of these structures because most technical manuals about DOS didn't describe them. The authors of many of these manuals believed that these structures weren't needed for programming, and that their coding would change in future versions of DOS. Actually, certain kinds of programming do depend on these structures and some applications couldn't be created without them.

Floppy disk and hard disk management utilities extensively use these undocumented structures. For example, if you examine Norton Utilities® with a debugging application, you'd see how much this program accesses these structures.

A minor change in these undocumented structures occurred between DOS Version 3.3 and Version 4.0, but this is the first change since the introduction of DOS Version 2.0 in 1983. So, you probably won't find altered coding in the undocumented structures of subsequent DOS versions.

Knowing about these structures can be very useful when you're programming certain applications.

31.2 The DOS Info Block (DIB)

The DOS Info Block (DIB) is the key to accessing the most important DOS structures. This block contains pointers to several DOS structures and to other information. The DIB is useful to a program only if its address in memory is known. This address isn't in a fixed memory location, and cannot be obtained with any of the documented functions of DOS interrupt 21H. However, the undocumented function 52H can help locate this address. Calling function 52H returns the address of the DOS Info Block to the ES:BX register pair.

Unlike other DOS functions that retrieve pointers to a structure or data area, the contents of the ES:BX register pair point to the second, instead of the first, field within the DIB after the function call.

DIB structure

The first field in the DIB contains a pointer to the Memory Control Block (MCB) of the first allocated memory area. In Section 6.9 (Memory Allocation from DOS) you'll find detailed information about this structure.

```
┌─────────────────────────────────────────────────────────────────────┐
│ DOS Info Block (DIB) structure                                        │
├───────┬─────────────────────────────────────────────────┬───────────┤
│ Addr. │ Contents                                         │ Type      │
├───────┼─────────────────────────────────────────────────┼───────────┤
│ -04H  │ Pointer to MCB                                   │ 1 ptr     │
│ ES:BX │ Pointer to first Drive Parameter Block (DPB)     │ 1 ptr     │
│ +04H  │ Pointer to last DOS buffer                       │ 1 ptr     │
│ +08H  │ Pointer to clock driver (CLOCK)                  │ 1 ptr     │
│ +0CH  │ Pointer to console driver (CON)                  │ 1 ptr     │
│ +10H  │ Maximum sector length (based on connected drives)│ 1 word    │
│ +12H  │ Pointer to first DOS buffer                      │ 1 ptr     │
│ +16H  │ Pointer to path table                            │ 1 ptr     │
│ +1AH  │ Pointer to System File Table (SFT)               │ 1 ptr     │
├───────┴─────────────────────────────────────────────────┴───────────┤
│ Length: 1EH (30) bytes                                                │
└─────────────────────────────────────────────────────────────────────┘
```

Drive Parameter Block

The pointer in the second field of the DIB provides access to information that cannot be accessed in any other way. It points to the first Drive Parameter Block (DPB), which is a structure that DOS creates for all mass storage devices (floppy diskettes, hard disks, tape drives, etc.).

```
┌─────────────────────────────────────────────────────────────────────────┐
│ Drive Parameter Block (DPB) structure                                     │
├────────┬──────────────────────────────────────────────────┬─────────────┤
│ Addr.  │ Contents                                         │ Type         │
├────────┼──────────────────────────────────────────────────┼─────────────┤
│ +00H   │ Drive number or character (0 = A, 1 = B, etc.)   │ 1 byte      │
│ +01H   │ Sub-unit of device driver for drive              │ 1 byte      │
│ +02H   │ Bytes per sector                                 │ 1 word      │
│ +04H   │ Interleave factor                                │ 1 byte      │
│ +05H   │ Sectors per cluster                              │ 1 byte      │
│ +06H   │ Reserved sectors (for boot sector)               │ 1 word      │
│ +08H   │ Number of File Allocation Tables (FATs)          │ 1 byte      │
│ +09H   │ Number of entries in root directory              │ 1 word      │
│ +0BH   │ First occupied sector                            │ 1 word      │
│ +0DH   │ Last occupied cluster                            │ 1 word      │
│ +0FH   │ Sectors per FAT                                  │ 1 byte      │
│ +10H   │ First data sector                                │ 1 word      │
│ +12H   │ Pointer to header (corresponding device driver)  │ 1 ptr       │
│ +16H   │ Media descriptor                                 │ 1 byte      │
│ +17H   │ Used flag (0FFH = Device not yet enabled)        │ 1 byte      │
│ +18H   │ Pointer to next DPB (xxxx:FFFF = last DPB)       │ 1 ptr       │
├────────┴──────────────────────────────────────────────────┴─────────────┤
│ Length: 1CH (28) bytes                                                    │
└─────────────────────────────────────────────────────────────────────────┘
```

The first field of the DPB indicates the device to which the block belongs. 0 represents drive A, 1 represents B, 2 represents C, etc. The second field specifies the number of the subunit. To understand the meaning of this field, remember that access to the individual devices occurs through the device driver. DOS doesn't perform direct access to a disk drive or hard disk. So, DOS doesn't have to deal with the physical characteristics of a mass storage device. Instead, DOS calls a device driver, which acts as mediator between DOS and hardware.

Obviously, not every device has a separate device driver, since one device driver can support many devices. For example, the device driver built into DOS manages the floppy disk drives and the first available hard disk. Since DOS configures a DPB for each device, a hard disk system automatically has 3 DPBs available. (A DPB is always configured for floppy disk drive B, even if only one floppy disk drive is actually available.) Each device receives a number between 0 and the total number of devices minus 1, to help each driver identify the devices it manages. This is the number found in the subunit field.

The next field lists the number of bytes per sector. Under DOS, this is usually 512. After this is the *interleave factor*, which provides the number of logical sectors displaced by physical sectors when the medium is formatted. This value can be 1 for floppy disk drives, 6 for the XT hard disk, and 3 for the AT hard disk. For floppy disk drives, this field can also have the value FEH if the disk in the drive hasn't been accessed. The value FEH indicates that the interleave factor is currently unknown.

Several other fields are related to these two fields. We mentioned these fields when we discussed managing mass storage devices through DOS (see Section 6.13). Among other things, these fields describe the status and the size of the structures DOS created to manage mass storage devices. A pointer to the header of the device driver is located within these fields. DOS uses this pointer when accessing the device. Additional information can be obtained with this pointer since, for example, the driver attribute is listed in the header of the device driver.

Following this field is the media descriptor to which the Used flag is connected. As long as the device hasn't been accessed, this flag contains the value 0FFH. After the first access, it changes to 0 and remains unchanged until a system reset.

The DPB ends with a pointer that establishes communication with the next DPB. Since every DPB defines its end with such a pointer, a kind of chain is created, through which all DPBs can be reached. To signal the end of the chain, the offset address of this pointer in the last DPB contains the value 0FFFFH.

DPB access

When a program needs the information within the DPB, there are many ways to find the address of the desired DPB. One method is to follow the chain previously described by first determining the address of the DIB. This gives you the pointer to the first DPB, from which you can follow the chain until you reach the desired DPB.

However, there's a better method, which isn't as susceptible to changes within the DIB. This method involves two undocumented DOS functions, 1FH and 32H functions. Although these functions have been included in DOS since Version 2.0, they weren't documented by Microsoft. When called, both return a pointer to a DPB to the DS:BX register pair. While function 1FH always delivers a pointer to the DPB of the current disk drive, the address delivered by function 32H refers to the device whose number is passed to the function in the DL register at the time it's called (0 represents the current drive, 1 is drive A, 2 drive B etc.). Function 32H is much more flexible than function 1FH.

Using 1FH and 32H to access the various DPBs is also useful because it forces DOS to retrieve other information, such as the interleave factor and the media descriptor byte, which is determined for the disk drive only after the first access. If you get to the DPB through the pointer in the DIB block, the various fields may not have been initialized, and could contain the wrong values.

The DOS buffer

Besides the pointer to the first DPB, the DIB also contains the pointer to the first DOS buffer at address 12H. These DOS buffers store individual sectors, so that the sectors don't have to be repeatedly loaded from disk. The DOS buffers are most effective when they're used to store disk sectors that are frequently needed by the currently running program. Besides the FAT, these sectors include the root directory and its subdirectories. The number of buffers can be defined by the user in the CONFIG.SYS file. If this number exceeds those needed for the FAT, root directory, and subdirectories, normal sectors can also be temporarily stored here. This is done so that if they are called again in the near future, they can be taken directly from the buffer.

The individual sectors are linked together. This enables DOS to quickly check each buffer for the desired sector with each read operation.

```
┌─────────────────────────────────────────────────────────────────────┐
│ DOS buffer structure                                                  │
│  ┌───────┬──────────────────────────────────────────┬──────────────┐ │
│  │ Addr. │ Contents                                 │ Type         │ │
│  ├───────┼──────────────────────────────────────────┼──────────────┤ │
│  │ +00H  │ Pointer to next DOS buffer               │   1 byte     │ │
│  │ +04H  │ Drive number (0 = A, 1 = B, etc.)        │   1 byte     │ │
│  │ +05H  │ Flags                                    │   1 byte     │ │
│  │ +06H  │ Sector number                            │   1 word     │ │
│  │ +08H  │ Reserved                                 │   2 bytes    │ │
│  │ +0AH  │ Contents of buffered sector              │ 512 bytes    │ │
│  └───────┴──────────────────────────────────────────┴──────────────┘ │
│  Length: 210H (528) bytes                                             │
└─────────────────────────────────────────────────────────────────────┘
```

As with DPBs, this occurs with the help of a pointer that appears at the start of every buffer. Also, the last buffer is reached when the offset address of the pointer contains the value 0FFFFH. After the field linking one buffer to the next is the number of the drive where the buffered sector originates. The value is 0 for drive A, 1 for B, 2 for C, etc. Besides the drive number, the identification of a sector requires a sector number. This is located beginning at position 06H in the DOS buffer. The last field in the buffer header stores a pointer to the corresponding DPB, so that DOS can obtain information about the device that loaded the buffered sector. Although this is the last field in the header of the DOS buffer, the buffered sector doesn't end immediately after this field. There are two more bytes which follow. The reason for this is that the DOS code is written in machine language. So, when working with memory blocks, it's most efficient to have the buffered sector begin with an address that is divisible by 16.

The path table

The header of the DOS buffer isn't the last place we encounter the DPB. It appears again in the path table, which starts at address 16H in the DIB. This table contains the current path for each drive as well as a pointer to its DPB.

```
       0  1  2  3  4  5  6  7  8  9  A  B  C  D  E  F
0000: 41 3A 5C 43 41 43 48 45-00 00 00 00 00 00 00 00   A:\CACHE........
0010: 00 00 00 00 00 00 00 00-00 00 00 00 00 00 00 00   ................
0020: 00 00 00 00 00 00 00 00-00 00 00 00 00 00 00 00   ................
0030: 00 00 00 00 00 00 00 00-00 00 00 00 00 00 00 00   ................
0040: 00 00 00 00 40 20 74 80-02 27 03 FF FF FF FF 02   ....@ t..'......
0050: 00 42 3A 5C 00 00 00 00-00 00 00 00 00 00 00 00   .B:\............
0060: 00 00 00 00 00 00 00 00-00 00 00 00 00 00 00 00   ................
0070: 00 00 00 00 00 00 00 00-00 00 00 00 00 00 00 00   ................
0080: 00 00 00 00 00 00 00 00-00 00 00 00 00 00 00 00   ................
0090: 00 00 00 00 00 40 40 74-80 02 00 00 FF FF FF FF   .....@@t........
00A0: 02 00 43 3A 5C 54 43 5C-42 41 55 53 5C 41 53 4D   ..C:\TC\BAUS\ASM
00B0: 5C 48 45 52 43 4D 4F 4E-4F 00 00 00 00 00 00 00   \HERCMONO.......
00C0: 00 00 00 00 00 00 00 00-00 00 00 00 00 00 00 00   ................
00D0: 00 00 00 00 00 00 00 00-00 00 00 00 00 00 00 00   ................
00E0: 00 00 00 00 00 00 40 60-74 80 02 65 05 FF FF FF   ......@`t..e....
00F0: FF 02 00 44 3A 5C 4D 53-43 5C 42 49 4E 00 00 00   ...D:\MSC\BIN...
0100: 00 00 00 00 00 00 00 00-00 00 00 00 00 00 00 00   ................
0110: 00 00 00 00 00 00 00 00-00 00 00 00 00 00 00 00   ................
0120: 00 00 00 00 00 00 00 00-00 00 00 00 00 00 00 00   ................
0130: 00 00 00 00 00 00 00 40-00 00 80 0D 17 00 FF FF   .......@........
0140: FF FF 02 00
```

Memory dump of the path table contents

As long as the LASTDRIVE command is in the system's configuration file, the table will have entries for drives A through the one specified by LASTDRIVE. If this command is missing, however, the table will have entries only for each device supported by the installed device driver. If you change the entries in this table, you can divert one drive to another. The JOIN and SUBST DOS commands also utilize this by manipulating the path table entry of the drive to be diverted.

Chapter 32

Terminate and Stay Resident Programs

Since it was introduced, DOS has been criticized for its inability to handle multitasking (running more than one program simultaneously). Even though OS/2 is capable of multitasking, it runs only on ATs or 80386-based computers. But TSR (Terminate and Stay Resident) programs can provide DOS machines with some of the advantages of multitasking. This type of program moves into the "background" once it's started, and becomes active when the user presses a particular key combination. The SideKick® program produced by Borland International made TSR programs very popular.

Running a TSR program isn't true multitasking because only one program is actually running at any given time. However, by pressing a key, the user can immediately access useful tools, such as a calculator, calendar, or note pad. In addition to these applications, macro generators, screen layout utilities, and text editors are also available in TSR form.

Many TSR programs can even interact with the programs they interrupt and transfer data between the TSR and the interrupted program. An example is a TSR appointment book that inserts a page from its calendar in a file that's loaded into a currently running word processor.

Although many different applications can be implemented with TSR programs, these programs share two characteristics:

- They operate in basically the same way

- They are based on similar programming concepts

In this chapter, we'll examine these two items and present simple implementations of TSR programs.

Before we begin, we must remind you that this involves very complex programming. So, in order to understand this material, you must know how things operate within the system. This especially applies to TSR programs, because, by their definition, they practically ignore the single-task nature of DOS, in which one program has access to all of the system resources (RAM, screen, disk, etc.).

A TSR program must contend with many other elements of the system, such as the BIOS, DOS, the interrupted program, and even other TSR programs. Managing this is a difficult task, and can only be accomplished using assembly language. Of the available PC languages, only assembly language offers the ability to work at the lowest system level, the interrupt level. However, although it has this capability, assembly language is as flexible as high level languages for writing TSR applications, such as calculators or note pads. Because of this, we'll list two assembly language programs in this chapter. These programs will allow you to "convert" Turbo Pascal, Turbo C, and Microsoft C programs into TSR programs.

32.1 Activating a TSR Program

Let's begin by discussing how a TSR program is activated. To place our TSR program in the foreground immediately after we press a certain key combination (called the *hotkey*), we must install some sort of activation mechanism that's tied to the keyboard. We can use interrupts 09H and 16H, which are two system keyboard calls. Interrupt 16H is the BIOS keyboard interrupt, which programs use to read characters and keyboard status. If we use this interrupt, then our TSR program can only be activated when the main program is using interrupt 16H for keyboard input.

So, instead we should use interrupt 09H, which is called by the processor whenever a key is pressed or released. We can redirect this interrupt to our own routine, which can check to see whether the TSR program should be activated. Before it does this, the routine should call the old interrupt 09H handler. There are two reasons for this. The first reason is related to the task of interrupt 09H, which informs the system that the keyboard needs the system's attention in order to transfer information about a key event. So, interrupt 09H usually points to a routine, within the ROM BIOS, that accepts and evaluates information from the keyboard. Specifically, it receives the code from the keyboard, converts it to an ASCII code, and then places this code in the BIOS's keyboard buffer. Since our TSR program neither wants nor is able to handle this job, we must call the original routine; otherwise keyboard input will be impossible.

The second reason has to do with the fact that other TSR programs may have been installed before ours. These routines would have redirected interrupt 09H to their own routines. Since our program is in front of these programs in the interrupt handler chain, their interrupt routines won't be called automatically if we don't call the old interrupt handler. So, we wouldn't be able to activate these TSR programs. Remember that when a TSR program is called using a redirected interrupt routine, it should always call the old interrupt handler before or after its own interrupt processing.

The call cannot be made with the INT assembly language instruction, because this would simply recall our own interrupt handler. Usually this leads to an infinite loop, a stack overflow, and, eventually, a system crash. To avoid this, we must save the address of the old interrupt handler when the TSR program is installed. We can then call the old interrupt handler with this stored address by using a FAR CALL instruction. To simulate calling this handler through the INT instruction, we must first place the contents of the flag register on the stack with the PUSHF instruction before the CALL.

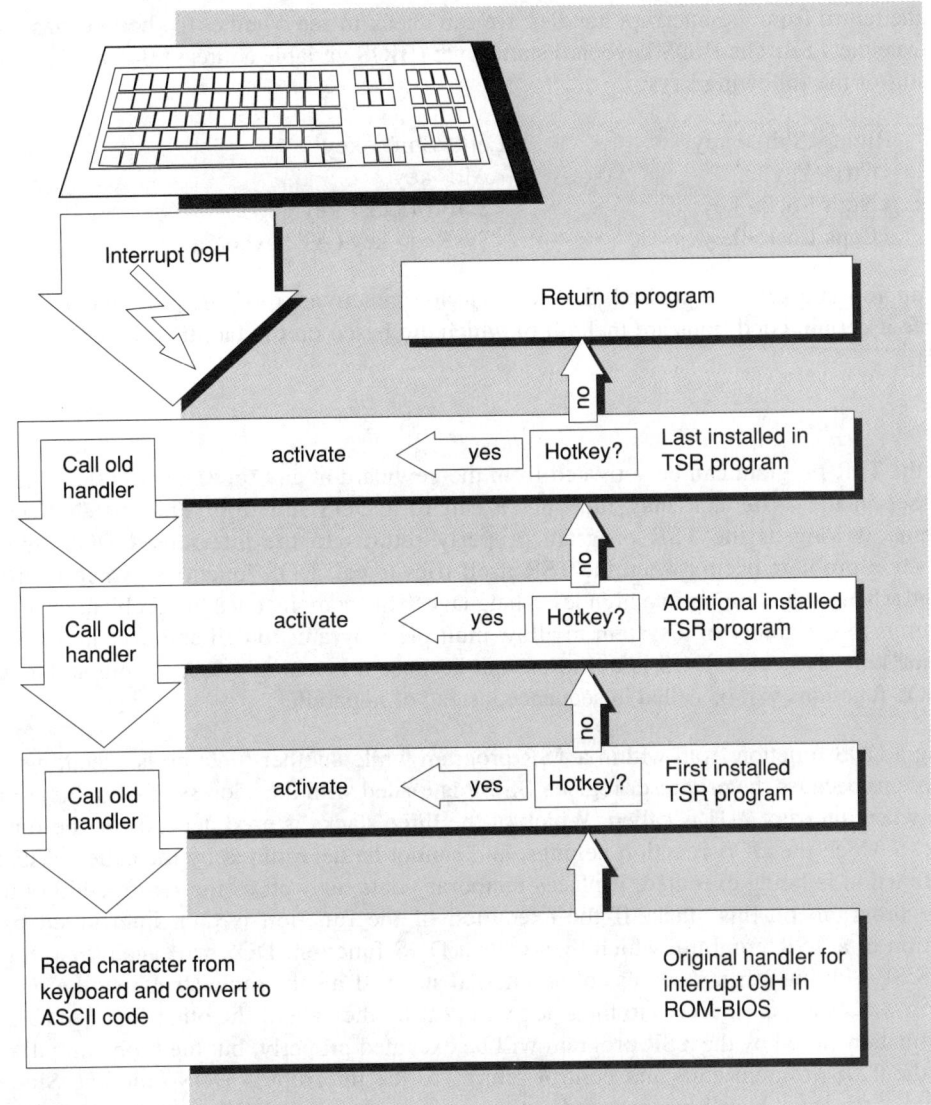

Reading keys for TSR programs using interrupt 09H

Following the interrupt handler call, the contents of port 60H are read. This port contains the scan code of the key most recently pressed (see Chapter 5 for more information on scan codes). The previous interrupt handler, which is called later, also reads the contents of this port to determine the scan code. When the new interrupt handler reads this port, the port's content remains unchanged, so that when the old handler reads its contents later, the same value will be returned. This value remains constant until a new key is pressed.

From the contents of keyboard port 60H, the new TSR interrupt handler can determine whether the user has pressed its designated hotkey. However, this value will correspond to only part of the hotkey, since hotkeys are generally used as key combinations, often combining a letter or number with one or more *modifier keys* (<Shift>, <Ctrl>, <Alt>, etc.).

After the return from the interrupt handler, we can check to see whether the hotkey was pressed to activate the TSR. The BIOS keyboard status byte (BIOS variable address 0040:0017) indicates the status of the following keys:

- Right <Shift> key
- <Ctrl> key
- <Num Lock> key
- <Caps Lock> key

- Left <Shift> key
- <Alt> key
- <Scroll Lock> key
- <SysReq> key (AT keyboard only)

If the appropriate keys are pressed, the user is trying to activate the TSR program. This is only possible if certain conditions are met, all of which are based on the fact that the DOS is not re-entrant.

DOS

Since the TSR program can be activated from the keyboard at any time, regardless of the other processes in the system, it may interrupt a call to a DOS function. This may not lead to problems as long as the TSR program properly returns to the interrupted DOS function. However, a problem occurs when the TSR itself tries to call DOS functions, which is difficult to avoid when programming in a high level language. This demonstrates the problem of re-entry. This refers to the ability of a system to allow multiple programs to call and execute its code at the same time. However, DOS is not re-entrant because it is a single-task system and assumes that DOS functions will be called in sequence, instead of in parallel.

Calling a DOS function from within a TSR program while another function is executing, leads to problems because the processor register SS:SP is loaded with the address of one of three DOS stacks when interrupt 21H is called. Which of the three stacks is used depends on the function group, to which the DOS function belongs, and cannot be determined by the caller. While the DOS function is being executed, it places temporary data, as well as the return address to the calling program, on this stack. If the execution of the function is then interrupted by the activation of a TSR program, which then calls a DOS function, DOS will again load register pair SS:SP with the starting address of an internal stack. If it's the same stack that the interrupt function was using, each access to the stack will destroy the data of the other function call. The DOS function called by the TSR program will be executed properly, but the problem will occur when the TSR program ends and control returns to the interrupted DOS function. Since the contents of the stack have been changed in the meantime by other DOS calls, the DOS function will probably crash the system.

Bypassing re-entry

There are two ways to avoid these re-entry problems. You can either avoid calling DOS functions or allow the TSR program to be activated only if DOS functions aren't being executed. Since we've already ruled out the first option, we must use the second. DOS helps us by providing the INDOS flag, which is normally used only inside DOS but which is very useful to us as well. This flag is a counter that counts the nesting depth of DOS calls. If it contains the value 0, no DOS functions are currently being executed. The value 1 indicates the current execution of a DOS function. Under certain conditions, this counter can also contain larger values, such as when one DOS function calls another DOS function, which is allowed only in special cases.

Since there isn't a DOS function that can read the value of this flag, we must read the contents directly from memory. Since the address doesn't change after the system is booted, we can obtain the address when the TSR is installed and save it in a variable. DOS function 34H returns the address of the INDOS flag in register pair ES:BX.

This flag is read in the interrupt handler for interrupt 09H since it checks to see whether the hotkey was pressed, and allows the TSR program to be activated only if the INDOS flag contains the value 0. However, this doesn't completely solve our problem. It coordinates the activation of the TSR program with DOS function calls of the transient program being executed in the foreground, but it doesn't allow the TSR program to be called from the DOS user interface. Since the DOS command processor (COMMAND.COM) uses some DOS functions for printing the prompt and accepting input from the user, the INDOS flag always contains the value 1. In this instance, we can interrupt the executing DOS function, but we must ensure that the INDOS flag contains the value 1, because a DOS function can be called from transient program or from the DOS command processor.

However, there is also a solution to this problem. It involves the fact that the DOS is in a kind of a wait state when it's waiting for input from the user in the command processor. To avoid wasting any valuable processor time, it periodically calls interrupt 28H, which is responsible for short term activation of background processes, such as the print spooler (DOS PRINT command) and other tasks. If this interrupt is called, it's relatively safe to interrupt DOS and call the TSR program.

To use this procedure, a new handler for interrupt 28H is installed when the TSR program is installed. First it calls the old handler for this interrupt and then checks to see whether the hotkey has been pressed. If this has occurred, the TSR program can be activated, even if the INDOS flag isn't 0.

We still must add another restriction. The TSR program cannot even be activated with the handler for interrupt 09H if time-critical actions are being performed in the system.

Time-critical actions

These are actions which, for various reasons, cannot be interrupted because they must complete execution in a relatively short time. In the PC, this includes accesses to the floppy and hard disk, which at the lowest levels are controlled by BIOS interrupt 13H. If an access to these devices isn't completed by a certain time, the system can be seriously disrupted. A dramatic example of this is if the TSR program performs an access to these devices before another access, which is initiated by the interrupted program, has finished. Even if this doesn't crash the system, it will lead to data loss.

We can avoid this by installing a new interrupt handler for BIOS interrupt 13H. When this handler is called, it sets an internal flag that shows that the BIOS disk interrupt is currently active. Then it calls the old interrupt handler, which performs the access to the floppy or hard disk. When it returns to the TSR handler, the flag is cleared, signaling the end of BIOS disk activity.

To prevent this interrupt handler from being interrupted, the other TSR interrupt handlers monitor this flag and will activate the TSR program only if the flag indicates that the BIOS disk interrupt isn't active.

Delayed activation

Depending on the current DOS or BIOS operations, occasionally a TSR program may be unable to move into the foreground. Because of this, most TSR programs also install an interrupt handler for timer interrupt 08H. This interrupt handler can delay the start of the TSR. If the hotkey is recognized and the TSR program is unable to execute at that moment, a special flag is set within the keyboard interrupt handler.

This flag is then checked by the new timer interrupt handler, which is called 18.2 times a second if the current application hasn't changed the timer frequency. If the handler discovers that the TSR program is waiting to be activated, and if DOS and BIOS have completed their operations, then the TSR program can be activated.

However, a time limit should be set for this delay. Otherwise, if the hotkey is pressed, and if DOS is currently executing a lengthy operation, the TSR program may only be activated after several seconds. If the length of this delay isn't limited, the user won't know whether the TSR program hasn't recognize the hotkey, or whether it's still waiting for an opportunity to start.

So, the flag that facilitates the delayed start of a TSR program also acts as a timekeeper. Its value decrements each time the timer interrupt is activated. When this value reaches 0, the interrupt handler stops trying to activate the TSR program. If the keyboard interrupt handler initializes this flag with a value of 6, for instance, then the maximum delay for the start of the TSR program consists of 6 timer interrupts, or about one third of a second. If the program cannot be activated within this time frame, the hotkey call has no effect.

Recursion

Since the hotkey can still be pressed after the TSR program has been activated, we must prevent the TSR program from being reactivated before it's finished. We can simply add another flag, which is checked before the TSR is activated. The TSR program sets this flag when it begins and clears it again just before it ends. If an interrupt handler determines that this flag is set, it will simply ignore the hotkey.

Once all these conditions have been met, we can activate the TSR program.

Context switch

The process of activating a TSR program is called a *context switch*. The program context or environment is the only information needed for operating the program. This includes such things as the contents of the processor registers, important operating system information, and the memory occupied by the program. We don't have to worry about the program memory in our context switch, however, since our TSR program is already marked as resident, which means that the operating system won't give the memory it occupies to other programs.

The processor registers, especially the segment registers, must be loaded with the values that the TSR program expects. These are saved in internal variables when the TSR program is installed. Since the contents of these and other registers will be changed by the TSR program, the contents of the registers must be saved because they belong to the context of the interrupted program and must be restored when it starts again.

This also applies to context dependent operating system information, which, for DOS, includes only the PSP (Program Segment Prefix) of the program and the DTA (Disk Transfer Area). The addresses of both structures must be determined and saved when the TSR program is installed so that they can be reset when context is changed to the TSR program. Also, remember to save the addresses of the PSP and DTA of the interrupted program before the context change to the TSR program. There are DOS functions for setting and reading the address of the DTA (DOS functions 1AH and 2FH), but there are no corresponding documented functions for the PSP. DOS Version 3.0 includes function 62H, which returns the address of the current PSP, but has no function for setting the address. Undocumented functions for doing both exist in DOS 2.0: function 50H (set PSP address) and 51H (get PSP address). Both of these are used in our TSR demonstration program.

The TSR code must perform one final task. When the TSR program is activated using interrupt 28H, an active DOS function is interrupted. This function's stack shouldn't be disturbed. Generally we should take the top 64 words from the current stack and place them on the stack of the TSR program. This completes the context change to the TSR program, which means that the TSR program can now be started.

At the moment, the TSR program can be viewed as a completely normal program which can call arbitrary DOS and BIOS functions. The only competitor left in the system is the foreground program. The TSR must ensure that it leaves both the foreground program and its screen undisturbed.

Saving the screen context

The tasks were exclusively handled in assembly language. However, the C or Pascal program comprising the TSR program itself can save the screen context. This screen context includes the current video mode, the cursor position, and the screen's contents. The contents of the color registers and other registers on the video card must also be saved, if any of these values are changed by the TSR program.

As we described in Chapter 4, the video mode can easily be determined with function 00H of BIOS video interrupt 16H. If the screen is in text mode (modes 0, 1, 2, 3, and 7), the TSR program must save the first 4000 bytes of video RAM. The video BIOS can be used for this or you can access the video RAM directly (see Chapter 4).

Saving the video mode becomes very complicated if a graphics mode is active, since the video RAM for EGA and VGA cards can be as large as 256K in some modes. If the TSR program interrupted a transient program, it may be impossible to allocate a large enough buffer to handle both programs.

This is why many TSR programs won't activate themselves from within graphics mode, and can only be used in text mode. Since PCs mostly use text mode, this isn't a major problem. Microsoft Windows®, which operates only in graphics mode, is an exception. Since this program usually supports some mechanism for parallel execution of calculators, note pads, etc., TSR programs aren't very useful under Windows.

32.2 TSR Programs in Pascal and C

You must understand the information we just presented in order to completely comprehend the assembler modules TSRPA.PAS (for Pascal programs) and TSRCA.ASM (for C programs). Since both modules are based on the same basic principles and the differences between these programs are limited to the different conventions found in Pascal and C, we'll discuss only their structure.

Both assembly modules can install the TSR program upon the first program call from the DOS command line, and can reinstall the program upon a second call. They also offer a TSR program, being called from the DOS command line, the option of communicating with a memory-resident copy of the same program. This makes it possible, for example, to specify a new hotkey for the installed version, without having to remove the program from memory and then reinstall it. Other parameters can also be changed in this way, since any desired Pascal or C routine can be called within the memory-resident TSR program, as you'll see below.

32.2.1   Assembly Language Modules

To support the mentioned functions, the assembly module offers the high level language program seven procedures, which are listed in the chart below.

Name	Description
TsrInit	Transforms the program into a TSR program, installs the interrupt handler, ends the program, and installs it in memory.
TsrIsInst	Determines whether a copy of the program is already resident in memory.
TsrCanUninst	Determines whether the resident copy of the program may be uninstalled.
TsrUnInst	Removes a memory-resident copy of the program from memory.
TsrSetPtr	Sets a pointer to the address of the procedure that is to be called within the memory-resident copy of the program.
TsrCall	Calls the procedure identified by TsrSetPtr.
TsrSetHotkey	Sets the program's hotkey.

Checking the installation status

The high level language program must first call the TsrIsInst procedure to determine whether a copy of the program is already installed in memory as a TSR program. To do this, the procedure uses the DOS multiplex interrupt 2FH (MUX). This is possible because an interrupt handler for interrupt 2FH is also installed when a TSR program is loaded into memory.

This interrupt only responds to a very specific function, whose function number is determined when TsrIsInst is called. If it's called with another function number, the TSR program simply passes the call to the previous interrupt handler. The new MUX interrupt handler supports two functions as subfunctions of the specified function number, with the subfunction numbers AAh and BBh. The first subfunction is used to locate a resident version of the TSR program.

As is commonly the case with MUX functions, the function and subfunction numbers in registers AH and AL are simply swapped when the subfunction is called. However, if the TSR program isn't installed, this swap doesn't occur, because none of the previous MUX handlers recognize the function. The contents of the AX register are therefore returned unchanged.

In calling this MUX function, TsrIsInst can easily determine whether the program has already been installed. If this is the case, TsrIsInst also calls the second TSR program's second MUX function, which returns the resident program's segment address. This value is then stored in a variable within the TSR program. Like all other variables of the assembly module, this variable is stored in the module's code segment. This ensures that the variables can also be addressed within the interrupt handler, even if the program's data segment cannot be accessed.

You now have enough information to understand how the two assembly language interfaces operate. The two programs are based on the principles we've outlined here; the differences between them reflect the different syntaxes of compiled C and Pascal programs. First we'll concentrate on the similarities between the two programs.

Both programs assume that the TSR program was installed by the first call from the DOS level and will be reinstalled on each new call. It's important to remember one general rule: a TSR program can be reinstalled only if no other TSR programs have been installed in the meantime. The LIFO (Last In, First Out) principle applies here, so the only way a TSR program can be reinstalled is if it was the last one to be installed, and if the corresponding interrupt vectors point to its interrupt handlers. If another TSR program was installed after it, the interrupt vectors point to its handlers.

To support this mechanism, the assembly language interface offers the high-level program three routines to install and later reinstall the TSR program. To decide whether the program should be installed or reinstalled, the first function should be called to determine whether the TSR program is already installed. This routine is passed an identification string, which will play an important role later when the program is installed. The routine looks for this ID string within the handler for interrupt 09H. If it finds the string, the TSR program is already installed and can be reinstalled.

If the ID string isn't found, the TSR program hasn't been installed, or another TSR program redirected the interrupt 09H vector in the meantime. The TSR program can then be installed with the help of the installation routine. This routine must receive the ID string used to detect whether the program has already been installed, the address of the high level routine that will be called when the TSR program is activated, and the hotkey value. The hotkey value is the bit pattern, in the BIOS keyboard flag, that will activate the TSR program and can be defined within the high level language program with the help of predefined constants.

The initialization routine first saves the addresses of the interrupt handlers for interrupts 09H, 13H and 28H. Then the data for the context of the high level program are read and saved in variables within the code segment, so that they are available for the interrupt handler and for activation of the TSR program. In the next step, the new interrupt handlers for interrupts 09H, 13H, and 28H are installed. Finally, the number of paragraphs after the end of the program, which are to remain resident, must be calculated. Here the C and Pascal modules differ from each other. Information about this calculation can be found in the individual descriptions of the modules.

The actual installation is now complete and the program is terminated as resident. Notice that the installation routine doesn't return to the high level language program, so all initialization, such as memory allocation or variable initialization, must be performed before the call to this routine.

If the installation test function of the assembly language module determines that the program is already installed, it can be reinstalled with the help of another function. This function is passed the address of a routine in the high level language program, which will perform a "cleanup" of the program. This process includes releasing allocated memory and other tasks. If no such routine is to be called, the assembly language routine must be passed the value -1. Since the "cleanup" function is in the TSR program, instead of in the program that is performing the reinstallation, a context switch is necessary. Unlike activation of the TSR program and the corresponding interruption of the foreground program, this is from the program that is performing the reinstallation to the already installed TSR program. The reinstallation returns the redirected interrupt handlers to their old routines and releases the memory allocated by the TSR program.

In addition to these three functions, which are called from the high level language program, the assembler module contains some routines that may not be called by high level language programs. These include the interrupt handlers for interrupts 09H, 13H, and 28H as well as a routine that accomplishes the context switch to and from the TSR program.

Installation and setting the hotkey

The TSR program is usually installed after TsrIsInst has determined that a copy of the program hasn't been installed yet. The installation consists of two steps; the first step determines the program's hotkey using TsrSetHotkey. The program is then loaded into memory as a TSR program by the TsrInit function, and is, temporarily, terminated.

First, let's discuss TsrSetHotkey: The arguments used by this function are the two parameters that determine the hotkey. These are the bit mask for the modifier keys, and the scan code of the accompanying letter or number key. Both parameters can be constructed using constants presented at the beginning of the two programs in Pascal and C.

For the modifier keys, these parameters carry the names LSHIFT (left SHIFT key), RSHIFT (right SHIFT key), ALT, CTRL, etc. When the hotkey key combination must use more than one of these keys simultaneously, such as Ctrl+Alt with another key, they can be linked with a binary OR operator. This binary OR has the same effect for the user as the logical AND.

The constants for the keyboard scan codes all begin with the prefix SC_, which is then followed by the letter, number, or name of that key (for instance, SC_5, SC_X, or SC_SPACE). These constants can easily be found in both the Pascal and C program, since they are grouped into a large block. If your TSR program must be activated by a combination of only modifier keys, so that no letter or number key must be pressed, you can use the SC_NOKEY constant.

Once the hotkey has been defined, TsrInit is called and transforms the program into a memory-resident TSR program. TsrInit also expects two arguments: the offset address of the actual TSR procedure and a value indicating the program's memory requirement. Since this parameter is handled differently in the Pascal and C assembly interfaces, we'll discus it in more detail later.

For now, simply remember that the first parameter for TsrInit, which specifies the TSR procedure offset address, also determines the high level language procedure that is called when the TSR program is activated. This procedure embodies the actual purpose of the TSR program and is capable of utilizing all functions provided by the particular high level language that's used. It can even access files, read directories, and perform any other operation involving DOS functions. Once this procedure has been completed, the TSR program will again move to the background and clear the way for the previously interrupted program.

TsrInit's first task is to determine the addresses of interrupt handlers 08H, 09H, 13H, 28H, and 2Fh, and to store these addresses. Then the data required by the applicable high level language program are determined. These are also stored in variables within the code segment, so that they'll be available to the interrupt handler as well as for activating the TSR program. Next, the new interrupt handlers for interrupts 08H, 09H, 13H, 28H, and 2FH are installed. The function number that was specified at the previous TsrIsInst call is assigned as the function number for MUX interrupt 2FH.

Before the program can be installed in memory by the DOS function 31H, the amount of memory or the number of paragraphs that the program will need in order to remain resident after execution must be calculated. The Pascal and C versions perform this task differently. Below, we'll explain how the two programs perform this task.

This step completes the installation, and the program is terminated, but remains resident. Remember that once TsrInit has been called, the procedure doesn't return to the high level language program. Because of this, all tasks, such as memory allocation or the initialization of variables, must be completed before this procedure is called.

The high level language programs

The following programs in C and Pascal demonstrate the assembly language routines. First they determine whether the program is installed. On a new installation, a TSR routine is installed. You can activate the TSR by pressing both <Shift> keys. It stores the screen contents, then displays a message and asks the user to press a key. After this is done, the old screen contents are copied back and the execution of the interrupted program continues.

On a reinstallation, the assembly language reinstallation program calls a cleanup function in the TSR program. It prints the number of activations of the TSR program, which is set to zero when the TSR program is installed and incremented on each activation. This makes it clear that the cleanup function is actually executed in the installed TSR program and not in the program that performs the reinstallation.

Removing TSR programs from memory

TSR programs are usually installed upon the first program call, and removed at the next call. So, if TsrIsInst determines, at the start of a program, that another copy is already resident, the resident copy must be removed.

For this, the TsrCanUninst function must be called. This function determines whether the program can be removed from memory because occasionally this won't be possible. This is the case when another TSR program has been installed since the original installation, because the second program also redirects the interrupt vectors of the timer, the keyboard, and other devices.

This program, like other TSR programs, located the address of the first program's interrupt handler when it was first installed, and accesses these through its own handler. However, since the preceding handlers belong to the TSR program that must be uninstalled, these must also be removed. Since it isn't possible to inform the second program about removing these handlers, this action will inevitably result in a system crash.

Because of this, TsrCanUninst checks whether all redirected interrupts still point to the interrupt handler of the first copy of the TSR program, and responds with a corresponding TRUE or FALSE. Only when this function returns TRUE can the program call TsrUninst to remove the resident copy from memory.

For the uninstallation of a TSR program, the old interrupt handlers for interrupts 08H, 09H, 13H, 28H, and 2FH are restored. The memory occupied by the program is then released, so that DOS can make it available to other programs. The program leaves no traces in memory.

Calling procedures in a resident TSR program

The possibility of utilizing procedures within the resident copy of the TSR program must be used when another copy is reinstalled. This is because even the high level language portion of a TSR program must frequently use operating resources (memory, interrupt vectors, files) that must be returned to the operating system once the program is removed from memory.

Since the segment address of the resident copy can easily be determined through the MUX handler, and since the offset address of the corresponding procedure is the same as that of the program that was just executed, it's possible to construct a FAR pointer identifying the procedure of the resident program that will be executed. The only prerequisite for this operation is that the routine to be called is of the type VAR, and that can also be arranged.

However, there's a problem with this procedure. By calling this procedure directly, the context isn't switched to the resident copy of the program. So, the data segment of the new running program, and its PSP and DTA, remain active. This means that the procedure being called couldn't access its variables stored in its data segment, because these belong to the copy of the program that was just called.

Therefore, a mediator must be used when calling a procedure within the resident copy so that the context can be switched to that copy of the TSR program. The same mediator would switch the context back to the program being executed once the procedure has been completed.

This type of mediating procedure would only require the offset address of the procedure within the resident program that must be called. Although this works, it doesn't provide a way to pass arguments to the resident procedure and return arguments from this procedure.

To make the transmission of such arguments possible, another method of calling procedures within the resident program was selected. This method utilizes two procedures within the assembly interface: TsrSetPtr and TsrCall.

Of these two procedures, TsrSetPtr is called first. This procedure determines the address of the resident procedure that must be called and stores it in a variable of the assembly module. Then TsrCall is activated, which switches the context and uses the recorded address to call the desired resident procedure.

Again, the parameters that must be passed to and from the resident routine present an obstacle, because TsrCall must be declared within the high level language module. After all, the number and types of parameters required depends on the particular procedure that is being called. However, as you'll learn in the description of the Pascal and C programs, this problem can also be solved.

32.2.2   The Interrupt Handler

The interrupt handlers of the assembly interface operate according to the principles illustrated above. The most prominent of these handlers is the keyboard interrupt handler, which serves interrupt 09H. The coordination between this particular handler and the interrupt handlers for interrupts 08h (timer), 13h (BIOS disk), and 28h (DOS idle) is managed by three flags in the code segment of the assembly interface: in_bios, tsraktiv, and tsrnow.

Flags

The tsractive flag indicates whether the TSR program is currently active. It carries either the value 0 or 1. The same applies to inbios, which is incremented upon accessing handler INT 13H and is decreased upon leaving the handler. Since inbios, like all other flags, is initialized at 0, it carries the value 1 during an INT 13H call and then returns to 0. However, when another function of interrupt 13H calls the interrupt recursively, this flag is further incremented, increasing its value. However, it's important that the flag carry the value 0 when no BIOS disk function is currently being executed. This indicates that at least this path is clear for the TSR program start.

The third flag, tsrnow, is set within the keyboard interrupt handler when the hotkey code has been detected and the TSR program currently cannot be activated, because of the reasons explained above. This flag is then checked by the timer and DOS idle interrupt handlers, to determine whether the TSR program is waiting to be executed.

The timer interrupt handler decreases the value of tsrnow with each call, so that it will eventually reach 0 and the attempt to activate the program will be discontinued (since the user believes that the program will never start).

Now let's discuss the code for the different interrupt handlers because it illustrates several interesting details of interrupt handler programming. We're particularly interested in the two handlers for timer interrupt 08H and keyboard interrupt 09H. Since the interrupt handlers of the assembly interfaces in both Pascal and C are identical, the discussion applies to both of these modules.

The timer interrupt handler

The following excerpt from the code of the assembly module contains the new interrupt handler for timer interrupt 08H.

The first command already checks the tsrnow flag. Interestingly, the command doesn't include a segment override (i.e., cmp cs:tsrnow,0), because this variable is found within the code segment. However, this override doesn't have to be included in the source code, because the assembler automatically includes it when the code is assembled into machine language. Also, an ASSUME command was used to indicate that only segment register CS is pointing to the code segment, and that the contents of the DS register, as well as all other segment registers, are unknown.

```
assume cs:code, ds:nothing, es:nothing, ss:nothing
```

So, all interrupt handlers can access the different variables and flags of the assembly interface without having to explicitly specify a segment override. All of these have been stored in the code segment, so the data segment of the corresponding high level language program doesn't have to be continually loaded.

Now let's return to the timer interrupt. If the handler discovers, from the comparison of the tsrnow flag with 0, that the TSR program isn't waiting to be activated (tsrnow = 0), it immediately jumps to label i8_end. There, the previous interrupt handler of the timer interrupt is called by the command:

```
jmp [int8_ptr]
```

Int8_ptr isn't a label, but rather a variable, in which the address of the previous interrupt handler was recorded at the installation of the TSR program using TsrInit. Since int8_ptr is a DWORD variable, the assembler knows that a FAR-JMP, instead of a NEAR-JMP, must be executed. After all, the previous handler is located in a different code segment than the currently active interrupt handler (belonging to the TSR program) and can be reached only in this way.

The IRET command found at the end of the old interrupt handler returns the execution to the program that was suspended by the call of the TIMER interrupt handler. So, the jump to the old handler ends the execution of the new handler from within the assembly interface.

```
;-- New interrupt 08h handler (timer) ----------------------------

int08       proc var

            cmp  tsrnow,0           ;is TSR to be activated?
            je   i8_end             ;no, continue to new handler

            dec  tsrnow             ;yes, decrease incrementation flag

            ;-- TSR is to be activate, but is this possible? --------

            cmp  in_bios, 0         ;is BIOS disk interrupt currently active?
            jne  i8_end             ;YES--> cannot activate

            call dosaktiv           ;may DOS be interrupted?
            je   i8_tsr             ;yes, call TSR

i8_end:     jmp  [int8_ptr]         ;jump to old handler

            ;-- activate TSR -------------------------------------

i8_tsr:     mov  tsrnow,0           ;TSR is no longer waiting to activate
            mov  tsraktiv,1         ;TSR will activate shortly
            pushf                   ;simulate call of old handler using
            call [int8_ptr]         ; INT 8h command
            call start_tsr          ;start TSR program
            iret                    ;return to interrupted program

int08       endp
```

However, what happens when tsrnow isn't equal to 0, which indicates that the TSR program is waiting to be activated? The value of this flag will then be decreased, so that possibly even at the next call of the TIMER interrupt handle the flag's value will have reached 0. At that point, the attempts to start the TSR program are discontinued so that the program isn't activated after a several second delay.

Before that, however, the TSR program must be activated so that the next step consists of testing whether this is possible. For this, the in_bios flag is first read. If this flag contains a value other than 0, then the timer interrupt has just interrupted a ROM BIOS disk operation in progress. In this case, the TSR program isn't activated and the execution jumps back to the old timer interrupt. If the flag's value is indeed 0, the INDOS flag is checked to test whether a DOS function has been interrupted during its execution.

For this check, the assembly procedure is called. This procedure simply reads the address of INDOS from a variable within the assembly module and then compares the value at this address (the INDOS flag) with 0. If this test indicates that DOS cannot be interrupted at this time (when INDOS > 1), execution returns to the old interrupt handler and the TSR program isn't activated.

If this test is passed as well, nothing can stop the TSR program from being activated. Before the actual start, however, the old interrupt handler of the timer interrupt must be executed. This handler plays an important role in time keeping and disk access. This handler also contains a machine language command that is very important to all interrupt handlers that are linked with hardware interrupts, specifically the following command:

```
out 20h,20h
```

This command informs the interrupt controller that the interrupt's execution has been completed. The interrupt controller won't trigger hardware interrupts until this command is executed. This would not only mean that all further timer calls would drop out, so that the PC's internal clock would freeze, but also that the PC could receive no further keyboard input, since the keyboard interrupt 09H would be blocked.

The address stored in the variable int8_ptr is used to call the old interrupt handler. However, here a CALL command is used, so that the CPU returns to the TSR program's new handler upon encountering the IRET command.

In order for this to occur, the contents of the flag register must be pushed onto the stack, using PUSHF, before CALL is executed. Usually CALL places only the return address on the stack, instead of the flag register, as is the case with an interrupt call. As a result of this, IRET would read part of its supposed return address from the flag register, and obtain the return address from the stack, which contains completely different information than was stored there earlier. This mixup results in a system crash.

Although the TSR program is started only after the old interrupt handler has been called, the tsrnow and tsractive flags are set to 0 and 1, respectively, before this point. Basically this indicates that the TSR program is already active, and is therefore no longer waiting to be started. This is justified because the old handler informs the interrupt controller that the execution of the interrupt has been completed (see above). This enables further interrupts to be processed while the timer interrupt handler is being executed. For example, a keyboard interrupt should be executed if the user pressed another key in the meantime.

If this keyboard input happened to be the program's hotkey, the TSR program would be activated again by the keyboard interrupt handler if tsractive wasn't already set to 1. This results in another unacceptable situation: the execution of the new timer interrupt handler could begin only after the TSR program has been terminated again, which means that the program would start again immediately afterwards.

However, since the proper flags have been set before the old handler is called, the other interrupt handlers are unable to call the TSR program at that time. This ensures that the problem we explained above doesn't occur.

Finally, start_tsr is called to activate the TSR program. This is an assembly procedure within the assembly module, which first secures the context of the current program that is being interrupted, sets the context of the TSR program, and then calls the TSR procedure that was specified in combination with TsrInit. After the TSR program has been completed, the context of the interrupted program is restored, and the procedure is ended.

Only then does the program execution return to the new timer interrupt handler, which finally returns to the interrupted program via IRET. Interestingly enough, the new timer handler is called repeatedly during execution of the TSR program, even though its own execution basically hasn't been completed yet. However, this remains without consequence, providing the address of the original, interrupted program is still located on the stack upon the return from start_tsr. Also, to the system, the execution of the new timer interrupt was completed the moment the "out 20h,20h" was executed.

The keyboard interrupt handler

Much of what has been said about the timer interrupt handler also applies to the keyboard interrupt handler, serving interrupt 09H. Here, the AX register contents are first saved to the stack, since this register will be changed within the handler. Remember that once it's completed its execution, an interrupt handler cannot leave any of the processor registers changed. This didn't cause problems for the timer interrupt handler because it didn't change any registers. However, this must be considered for the keyboard interrupt handler.

In the next step, the contents of port 60H are read. The keyboard controller will store the scan code of the key, which the user pressed, in this port. The new keyboard handler must examine this scan code in order to identify the hotkey.

First, however, this new keyboard handler checks whether the TSR program is already active. If it is, all further tests can be skipped. The contents of the AX register are then pulled off the stack, and from label i9_end, the execution jumps directly to the old keyboard interrupt handler.

The same steps are taken when tsractive is 0 and tsrnow carries a value unequal to 0. This indicates that the hotkey has already been detected and that the TSR program is waiting for an opportunity to activate. So why detect the hotkey a second time?

This happens when the TSR program is neither active, nor waiting to be activated. Therefore, the hotkey scan code is first read from the variable sc_code. If the value contained in this variable is 128, a real hotkey hasn't been defined, and only the status of the modifier keys must be checked. In this case, the execution jumps to label i9_ks.

```
;-- New interrupt 09h handler (keyboard) ------------------------

int09      proc var

           push ax
           in   al,60h              ;read keyboard port

           cmp  tsraktiv,0          ;is the TSR program already active?
           jne  i9_end              ;YES: call old handler, then return

           cmp  tsrnow,0            ;is the TSR waiting for activation?
           jne  i9_end              ;YES: call old handler, then return

           ;-- test for hotkey ----------------------------------

           cmp  sc_code,128         ;is a scan code defined?
           je   i9_ks               ;No, check modifier {{?}} keys

           cmp  al,128              ;if yes, is it the release code?
           jae  i9_end              ;yes, but it is not the hotkey

           cmp  sc_code,al          ;make code, compare with key
           jne  i9_end              ;not correct, do not activate

i9_ks:     ;-- check modifier  key status      -----------------

           push ds
           mov  ax,040h             ;pull DS to the variable segment
           mov  ds,ax               ;of ROM-BIOS
           mov  ax,word ptr ds:[17h] ;get BIOS keyboard flag
           and  ax,key_mask         ;screen out non-hotkey bits
           cmp  ax,key_mask         ;are only hotkey bits remaining?
           pop  ds
           jne  i9_end              ;hotkey detected? NO --> return

           cmp  in_bios, 0          ;BIOS disk interrupt currently active?
           jne  i9_e1               ;YES --> cannot activate

           call dosaktiv            ;may DOS be interrupted?
           je   i9_tsr              ;yes, start TSR

i9_e1:     mov  tsrnow,TIME_OUT     ;TSR waiting to be activated

i9_end:    pop  ax                  ;get AX back
           jmp  [int9_ptr]          ;jump to old handler

i9_tsr:    mov  tsraktiv,1          ;TSR active (in a second)
           mov  tsrnow,0            ;no delayed start wanted
           pushf
           call [int9_ptr]          ;call old handler
           pop  ax                  ;get AX back
           call start_tsr           ;start TSR programs
           iret                     ;return to interrupted program

int09      endp
```

If a hotkey has been defined (sc_code not equal to 128), the scan code of the key that's been pressed is read from port 60H. If this code is larger than 128, it's identified as a release code, which indicates that a key has been released, instead of pressed. Since the pressing, instead of the releasing, of a key must start the TSR program, the key code isn't analyzed further. The execution then immediately jumps to the old handler.

Assuming that a key has been pressed, it's code is then compared with the value stored in sc_code. If these values don't match, the key is identified as not being the hotkey, and the execution jumps to the old keyboard interrupt handler. However, if the hotkey code matches the specified value, the status of the modifier keys must be checked.

With this, we've returned to label i9_ks, which was mentioned above. Here, the current modifier key status is read from the BIOS variable at address 0040h:0017h and compared with the value stored in key_mask. If the two values don't match, execution returns to the old keyboard interrupt handler, which then takes over the task of processing the keyboard input.

If this comparison determines that the specified keys have been pressed, the TSR program must be activated. Before this can occur, you must check whether a BIOS disk interrupt or DOS API function is currently being executed. If any such function is currently active, the program isn't activated and execution returns to the old keyboard handler. However, before this jump, the tsrnow flag is set to the value specified by the TIME_OUT constant. This delay value gives the TSR program a chance to be activated during one of the next timer interrupt calls.

In the code listing provided, TIME_OUT is assigned the value 9, which corresponds to half of a second, since the timer interrupt is called 18.2 times each second. However, you may replace this value with one of your own values if you want to increase or decrease the maximum delay time in which the TSR program can be started after pressing the hotkey.

If DOS or BIOS functions aren't preventing the activation of the TSR program, it's necessary, as was the case with the timer handler, to call the old keyboard interrupt handler. Here again, the tsractive and tsrnow flags are initialized with appropriate values so that no other interrupt handler will be able to activate the TSR program during this time. This then occurs automatically within the keyboard interrupt handler once the old handler is called.

32.2.3   The Pascal and C Programs

Now we'll discuss the high level language programs, TSRP.PAS and TSRC.C, which demonstrate the use and function of the two assembly modules. Their structure is almost identical; they have several differences, which we'll discuss below. First, let's concentrate on the common characteristics of these two programs.

Upon program start, the ParamGetHotKey function evaluates any parameters entered on the command line. It accepts all parameters preceded by the prefix "/t" as hotkeys. This prefix may be followed either by the name of a modifier key (LSHIFT, RSHIFT, ALT, CTRL, etc.) or the scan code number of a particular key. This number must be entered as a decimal value.

To specify <LEFT SHIFT> and <SPACE> as the hotkey key combination, the following two parameters must be entered:

```
/tlshift /t57
```

If <ALT> must be included in this hotkey, the following parameters would be required:

```
/tlshift /talt /t57
```

The order in which these parameters are entered isn't important.

ParamGetHotkey then stores the specified modifier key status and scan code in the two variables Keymask and ScCode, which are passed to the function for this purpose.

If, an error is discovered when the command line entry is evaluated, the program execution is stopped and a corresponding error message is displayed. If the parameters were entered correctly, the TsrIsInst function then checks whether the program has already been installed. Here, the function number through which the program's MUX handler can later be reached is also determined. Although the constant I2F_CODE specifies the function C4H for this, you can select another function. You must do this if you develop more than one TSR program using these assembly interfaces; otherwise these TSR programs would use the same MUX function and therefore conflict with one another.

However, you must be careful when selecting other MUX function numbers, since some of these may coincide with the function numbers of existing programs. However, you shouldn't use values smaller than C0H. Refer to Chapter 27 for more information about the DOS multiplexer.

If TsrIsInst indicates that the program hasn't been installed yet, the values of KeyMasc and ScCode are checked to determine whether /t parameters were entered from the command line. If these parameters weren't entered, the variables will contain default values. In this case, the TsrSetHotkey assembly procedure will define Alt + H as the hotkey key combination. If /t parameters have been entered, then TsrSetHotkey sets this specified hotkey combination.

At this point, the only remaining procedure to be executed is TsrInit, which transforms the program into a TSR program. The high level language procedure TSR is thereby specified as the TSR procedure. We'll discuss this in more detail later.

If TsrIsInst indicates that the program has already been installed, then the following action depends on the original user input. If a hotkey was specified at the program call, TsrSetHotkey will install the specified key combination as the updated hotkey in the resident program, then the program is ended without performing a new installation. However, if a hotkey wasn't specified, TsrCanUninst is first used to check whether the resident copy may be deactivated. If it can, TsrUninst is called to remove the resident copy from memory.

Before the TSR program is uninstalled, however, a high level language routine named endFCT (in C) or EndTPrc (in Pascal) is called. This routine frees the program's internal resources and displays a message indicating the number of times the TSR program was activated.

This number is defined by the global variable ATimes, which is incremented each time the TSR program is activated. This is done in the program's TSR procedure named Tsr. Before the TSR program is removed, then, the keyboard buffer is emptied to remove the hotkey, the screen of the previously interrupted program is saved, and a message asking the user to press any key is displayed. As soon as the user has done this, the screen of the interrupted program is restored, and the TSR program procedure ends. Then the execution of the previous program resumes.

The C implementation

Since TSR programs should use as little memory as possible, the assembly language interface was developed to be linked with the smallest C memory model (the small model). In both

Microsoft and Turbo C compilers, the program code and data are placed in two separate segments, each of which cannot be larger than 64K. The data includes global and static data as well as the stack and the heap. As the following figures show, Turbo C and Microsoft C use different memory organization, despite their similarities. In Turbo C the stack is placed behind the heap and moves from the end of the data segment to the end of the heap and in Microsoft C the stack is between the global data and the heap.

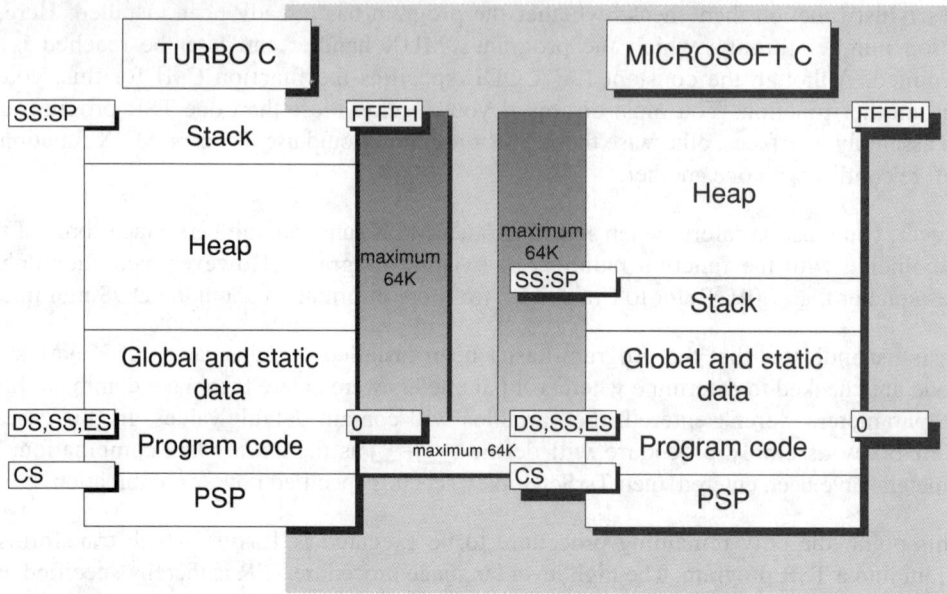

Structure of a small model program (Turbo C/Microsoft C)

If this organization doesn't affect the assembly language interface, we could allocate the entire 64K of the data segment resident in memory in addition to the program code. However, since this would waste a lot of memory and TSR programs should use as little memory as possible, only the part of the data segment that is actually needed should be marked as resident by the assembly language module.

The size of this memory area depends on the size of the data (or objects) that will be allocated on the heap by the functions calloc() and malloc(). You must guess this size and pass it to the initialization routine so that the end of the required memory in the data segment can be calculated.

This mechanism allows you to use the heap functions normally within the TSR program. Unfortunately, this applies only to the Turbo C compiler. Microsoft C uses an allocation algorithm that assumes that all of the memory to the end of the data segment is available. So, allocating heap storage should be avoided within a TSR program compiled with Microsoft C. You should allocate the buffers and variables required when the TSR program is initialized or place the required objects in global variables. The example C program allocates the two buffers it needs in the main() function and then places the addresses of the buffers in global variables.

There is something else you should be aware of when using Turbo C. Since the stack grows from the end of the 64K data segment to the heap, it finds itself outside the program when parts of the data segment are released again, and in an area of memory that DOS may give to other programs. To avoid problems with this, the assembly language module places the stack immediately after the heap, giving it 512 bytes of space. This should be sufficient for most applications, but may lead to problems if you use large objects (such as arrays) as local variables or pass them to other functions via the stack. In this case, you should enlarge the stack by setting the constant TC_STACK in the assembly language module to a larger value.

Because of this differentiated use of the stack, TsrInit must be informed whether the program has been developed using a Microsoft or a Borland compiler. However, since this is managed from within the C program with constants that are defined through conditional preprocessor instructions, you don't need to worry about this operation.

Such functions are also utilized by GetHeapEnd, which is called from the assembly module by TsrInit. It supplies the assembly module with a FAR pointer to the end of the occupied heap. With Borland compilers, this information can be gathered through the library function SBRK, which is also the case in MSC up to Version 6.0 and in QuickC up toVersion 2.5. However, in current versions, this function is no longer supported. So, the library function _heapwalk must be used to search the stack for the last occupied heap block.

The way in which the C version of the program calls functions within the resident copy of the program is also interesting. As we mentioned in the description of the assembly module, the assembler procedure TsrSetPtr must first be called. This procedure receives the address of the procedure that must be executed and stores it. The stored address is later accessed by TsrCall when this function is called.

In the C version of the assembly module, TsrSetPtr then directly returns a pointer to TsrCall. The advantage of this is that the desired function can be called directly using the result of TsrSetPtr. However, this requires a CAST operation to secure the compiler's cooperation. Let's take a closer look at this operation.

At the start of the C module, two types of function pointers, OAFP and SHKFP, are defined. Of these two, OAFP points to all function types that don't require arguments, and therefore also don't return function results. SHKFP, however, has been tailored specifically to meet then requirements of the TsrSetHotkey assembler procedure.

```
typedef void (*OAFP)(void);
typedef void (*SHKFP)( WORD Keymask, BYTE ScCode );
```

The following expression is used to call TsrSetHotkey using TsrSetPtr:

```
(*(SHKFP) TsrSetPtr(TsrSetHotkey))( Keymask, ScCode );
```

This expression first calls TsrSetPts, in which the address of TsrSetHotkey is passed, as one of its arguments, in the form of a FAR pointer. Actually, this operation requires only a NEAR pointer, since the segment address of the resident copy must later be used as the segment address anyway. However, the various functions that are called in this way must be FAR so that they can be called out of other code segments. To avoid the compiler error message following the otherwise impending transformation of a FAR pointer to a NEAR pointer, TsrSetPtr receives the FAR address of the desired function and processes only its offset address.

TsrSetPtr then returns the address of TsrCall as a NEAR pointer. However, in casting the pointer, the expression from above determines that this pointer is of type SHKFP. Only through this technique can the desired parameters be entered so that the compiler will copy them to the stack without any interjections. TsrCall is finally called by referencing the pointer cast in this way.

Therefore, when TsrCall is executed, it finds the arguments, which are actually intended for the function that will be called, located on the stack. These arguments must be copied to the stack of the resident copy of the TSR program, since we must switch to this stack before this function can be called. This is because most C compilers generate code under the assumption that the segment register DS point to the same memory segment as register SS. If the stack wasn't switched, this assumption wouldn't be true, and the function couldn't be executed properly.

Therefore, if you want to use the same technique for calling functions in a resident copy of your TSR program, you'll need to follow these two steps:

1.) Define a function pointer type that emulates a function with arguments that are also required by the actual function you want to call.

2.) Pass the address of this function to TsrSetPts, cast the function result in a previously defined pointer, and call the function using the required arguments.

C listing: TSRC.C

```
/*********************************************************************/
/*                           T S R C                             */
/*-----------------------------------------------------------------*/
/*   Task          : Creates a TSR program with the help of an     */
/*                   assembly language module.                     */
/*-----------------------------------------------------------------*/
/*   Author        : Michael Tischer                               */
/*   Developed on  : 08/15/88                                      */
/*   Last update   : 02/04/92                                      */
/*-----------------------------------------------------------------*/
/*   Memory model  : SMALL                                         */
/*   Compilation   : (Microsoft C)                                 */
/*                   CL /AS /c /WO tsrc.c                           */
/*                   LINK tsrc tsrca;                               */
/*-----------------------------------------------------------------*/
/*   Call          : TSRC [/tkeycode|/tnumber...]                  */
/*********************************************************************/

/*== Add include files ===========================================*/

#include <stdlib.h>
#include <stdio.h>
#include <dos.h>
#include <conio.h>
#include <string.h>
#include <bios.h>

/*== Type definitions =============================================*/

typedef unsigned char BYTE;              /* Create a byte */
typedef unsigned int WORD;
typedef BYTE BOOL;                       /* Like BOOLEAN in Pascal */
typedef union vel far * VP;       /* VP is a FAR pointer to video RAM */
```

```
typedef void (*OAFP)(void);  /* Pointer to function without arguments */
typedef void (*SHKFP)( WORD KeyMask, BYTE ScCode );  /* TsrSetHotkey */

/*== Macros =======================================================*/

#ifndef MK_FP                            /* MK_FP no defined yet? */
#define MK_FP(seg, ofs) ((void far *) ((unsigned long) (seg)<<16|(ofs)))
#endif
#define VOFS(x,y) ( 80 * ( y ) + ( x ) )
#define VPOS(x,y) (VP) ( vptr + VOFS( x, y ) )

/*== Structures and unions ========================================*/

struct velb {                 /* Describes a screen position as 2 bytes */
             BYTE thechar,                       /* ASCII code */
                  attribute;            /* Corresponding attribute */
             };

struct velw {                 /* Describes a screen position as 1 word */
             WORD content;       /* Get ASCII character and attribute */
             };

union vel {                            /* Describes a screen position */
           struct velb h;
           struct velw x;
           };

/*== Add functions from the assembler module ======================*/

extern void TsrInit( BOOL tc, void (*fct)(void), unsigned heap );
extern BOOL TsrIsInst( BYTE i2F_fctnr );
extern void TsrUnInst( void );
extern OAFP TsrSetPtr( void far *fct );
extern BOOL TsrCanUnInst( void );
extern void TsrCall( void );
extern void far TsrSetHotkey( WORD keymask, BYTE sccode );
```

```c
/*== Constants and macros =========================================*/

#ifdef __TURBOC__                        /* Compiling with Turbo C? */
  #include <alloc.h>
  #define TC TRUE                                          /* Yes */
  #define KeyAvail() ( bioskey(1) != 0 )
  #define GetKey() bioskey(0)
#else                              /* Compiling with Microsoft C */
  #include <malloc.h>
  #define TC FALSE
  #define KeyAvail() ( _bios_keybrd( _KEYBRD_READY ) != 0 )
  #define GetKey() _bios_keybrd( _KEYBRD_READ )
#endif


/*-- Scan codes of different keys ------------------------------------*/

#define SC_ESC          0x01
#define SC_1            0x02
#define SC_2            0x03
#define SC_3            0x04
#define SC_4            0x05
#define SC_5            0x06
#define SC_6            0x07
#define SC_7            0x08
#define SC_8            0x09
#define SC_9            0x0A
#define SC_0            0x0B
#define SC_HYPHEN       0x0C
#define SC_EQUALS       0x0D
#define SC_BACKSPACE    0x0E
#define SC_TAB          0x0F
#define SC_Q            0x10
#define SC_W            0x11
#define SC_E            0x12
#define SC_R            0x13
#define SC_T            0x14
#define SC_Y            0x15
#define SC_U            0x16
#define SC_I            0x17
#define SC_O            0x18
#define SC_P            0x19
#define SC_LBRACKET     0x1A
#define SC_RBRACKET     0x1B
#define SC_ENTER        0x1C
#define SC_CONTROL      0x1D
#define SC_A            0x1E
#define SC_S            0x1F
#define SC_D            0x20
#define SC_F            0x21
#define SC_G            0x22
#define SC_H            0x23
#define SC_J            0x24
#define SC_K            0x25
#define SC_L            0x26
#define SC_SEMICOLON    0x27
#define SC_APOSTROPHE   0x28
#define SC_GRAVE        0x29
#define SC_SHIFT_LEFT   0x2A
#define SC_BACKSLASH    0x2B
#define SC_Z            0x2C
#define SC_X            0x2D
#define SC_C            0x2E
#define SC_V            0x2F
#define SC_B            0x30
#define SC_N            0x31
#define SC_M            0x32
#define SC_COMMA        0x33
#define SC_PERIOD       0x34
#define SC_SLASH        0x35
#define SC_SHIFT_RIGHT  0x36
#define SC_ASTERISK     0x37
#define SC_ALT          0x38
#define SC_SPACE        0x39
#define SC_CAPS         0x3A
#define SC_F1           0x3B
#define SC_F2           0x3C
#define SC_F3           0x3D
#define SC_F4           0x3E
#define SC_F5           0x3F
#define SC_F6           0x40
#define SC_F7           0x41
#define SC_F8           0x42
#define SC_F9           0x43
#define SC_F10          0x44
#define SC_NUM_LOCK     0x45
#define SC_SCROLL_LOCK  0x46
#define SC_CURSOR_HOME  0x47
#define SC_CURSOR_UP    0x48
#define SC_CURSOR_PG_UP 0x49
#define SC_NUM_MINUS    0x4A
#define SC_CURSOR_LEFT  0x4B
#define SC_NUM_5        0x4C
#define SC_CURSOR_RIGHT 0x4D
#define SC_NUM_PLUS     0x4E
#define SC_CURSOR_END   0x4F
#define SC_CURSOR_DOWN  0x50
#define SC_CURSOR_PG_DOWN 0x51
#define SC_INSERT       0x52
#define SC_DELETE       0x53
#define SC_SYS_REQUEST  0x54
#define SC_F11          0x57
#define SC_F12          0x58
#define SC_NOKEY        0x80                 /* No more keys */


/*-- Bit masks for the different toggle keys ------------------------*/

#define RSHIFT     1                            /* Right SHIFT key */
#define LSHIFT     2                             /* Left SHIFT key */
#define CTRL       4                                  /* CTRL key */
#define ALT        8                                   /* ALT key */
#define SYSREQ     1024        /* SYS-REQ key (AT keyboard only) */
#define BREAK      4096                             /* BREAK key */
#define NUM        8192                         /* NUM LOCK key */
#define CAPS       16384                       /* CAPS LOCK key */
#define INSERT     32768                         /* INSERT key */

#define I2F_CODE   0xC4             /* Function number INT 2F */
#define I2F_FCT_0  0xAA        /* Code for INT 2F, function 0 */
#define I2F_FCT_1  0xBB        /* Code for INT 2F, function 1 */

#define NOF        0x07                        /* Normal color */
#define INV        0x70                       /* Inverse color */
#define HNOF       0x0f                 /* Bright normal color */
#define HINV       0xf0                /* Bright inverse color */

#define HEAP_FREE 1024            /* Allocate 1K of heap space */
```

981

```
#define TRUE  ( 0 == 0 )          /* Constants used with BOOL */
#define FALSE ( 0 == 1 )

/*== Global variables =======================================*/

VP vptr;              /* Pointer to the first character in video RAM */
unsigned atimes = 0;             /* Number of TSR activations */
union vel * scrbuf;              /* Pointer to a screen buffer */
char * blnkspace;               /* Pointer to a blank line */

/*****************************************************************
* Function       : D I S P _ I N I T                           *
**-------------------------------------------------------------**
* Task           : Passes the base address to video RAM.       *
* Input parameters : None                                      *
* Return values  : None                                        *
*****************************************************************/

void disp_init(void)
  {
  union REGS regs;        /* Processor registers for interrupt call */

  regs.h.ah = 15;                /* Function number: Get video mode */
  int86(0x10, &regs, &regs);            /* Call BIOS video interrupt */

  /*-- Compute base address of video RAM ----------------------*/

  vptr = (VP) MK_FP((regs.h.al == 7) ? 0xb000 : 0xb800, 0);
  }

/*****************************************************************
* Function       : D I S P _ P R I N T                         *
**-------------------------------------------------------------**
* Task           : Displays a string on the screen.           *
* Input parameters : - COLUMN  = Display column                *
*                    - SCROW   = Display row                   *
*                    - DCOLR   = Character attribute           *
*                    - STRING  = Pointer to a string           *
* Return values  : None                                        *
*****************************************************************/

void disp_print(BYTE column, BYTE scrow, BYTE dcolr, char * string)
  {
  register VP lptr;      /* Floating pointer for video RAM access */

  lptr = VPOS(column, scrow);       /* Set pointer in video RAM */
  for ( ; *string ; ++lptr)                  /* Execute string */
    {
    lptr->h.thechar = *(string++);  /* Write characters to video RAM */
    lptr->h.attribute = dcolr;       /* Set character attribute */
    }
  }

/*****************************************************************
* Function       : S A V E _ S C R E N                         *
**-------------------------------------------------------------**
* Task           : Saves the screen contents to a buffer.     *
* Input parameters : - SPTR   = Pointer to the buffer in which the *
*                               screen contents will be saved. *
* Return values  : None                                        *
* Info           : The buffer must be large enough to          *
*                  store the screen contents.                  *
*****************************************************************/
```

```
void save_screen( union vel * sptr )
  {
  register VP lptr;       /* Floating pointer for video RAM access */
  unsigned i;                              /* Loop counter */
  lptr = VPOS(0, 0);                 /* Set pointer in video RAM */

  for (i=0; i<2000; i++)         /* Execute the 2000 screen positions */
    (sptr++)->x.content = (lptr++)->x.content; /* Store char. & attb. */
  }

/*****************************************************************
* Function       : R E S T O R E _ S C R E E N                 *
**-------------------------------------------------------------**
* Task           : Copies the contents of a buffer to video RAM. *
* Input parameters : - SPTR  = Pointer to the buffer whose contents *
*                             are to be copied to video RAM     *
* Return values  : None                                        *
*****************************************************************/

void restore_screen( union vel * sptr )
  {
  register VP lptr;       /* Floating pointer for video RAM access */
  unsigned i;                              /* Loop counter */
  lptr = VPOS(0, 0);                 /* Set pointer in video RAM */

  for (i=0; i<2000; i++)         /* Execute the 2000 screen positions */
    (lptr++)->x.content = (sptr++)->x.content;  /* Return ch. & attb. */
  }

/*****************************************************************
* Function       : E N D F C T                                 *
**-------------------------------------------------------------**
* Task           : Called when the TSR program is uninstalled. *
* Input parameters : None                                      *
* Return values  : None                                        *
* Info           : This procedure must be FAR, so that it can be *
*                  called by the installed copy of the TSR.    *
*****************************************************************/

void far endFCT( void )
  {
  /*-- Release the allocated buffers --------------------------*/

  free( blnkspace );                /* Release allocated buffer */
  free( (void *) scrbuf );          /* Release allocated buffer */

  printf("The TSR was called %u times.\n", atimes);
  }

/*****************************************************************
* Function       : T S R                                       *
**-------------------------------------------------------------**
* Task           : Called by the assembler module after the hotkey *
*                  is pressed.                                 *
* Input parameters : None                                      *
* Return values  : None                                        *
*****************************************************************/

void tsr( void )
  {
  BYTE i;                                    /* Loop counter */

  ++atimes;                             /* Increment call counter */
```

```
while ( KeyAvail() )                    /* Clear keyboard buffer */
 GetKey();


disp_init();                           /* Get video RAM address */
save_screen( scrbuf );          /* Store current screen contents */
for (i=0; i<25; i++)                  /* Execute 25 screen rows */
 disp_print(0, i, INV, blnkspace);              /* Clear row */
disp_print(34, 11, INV, "My first TSR.");
disp_print(29, 13, INV, "Please press a key ...");
GetKey();                                    /* Wait for a key */
restore_screen( scrbuf );       /* Restore old screen contents */
}


/************************************************************/
/* GetHeapEnd: Gets the current end of heap, adapting to compilers. */
/* Input   : None                                          */
/* Output  : Pointer to the first byte after the end of heap */
/************************************************************/


void far *GetHeapEnd( void )
{
#ifdef __TURBOC__                               /* Turbo C? */
 return (void far *) sbrk(0);

#else                                        /* No --> MSC */
 struct _heapinfo hi;      /* Structure with heap entry information */
 unsigned heapstatus;             /* Status of _heapwalk() */
 void far *lastblk;          /* Pointer to last block allocated */

 hi._pentry = NULL;                /* Start at start of heap */

 /*-- Execute heap up to last block -----------------------*/

 while( (heapstatus = _heapwalk( &hi )) != _HEAPEND )
  if ( hi._useflag == _USEDENTRY )           /* Block used? */
   lastblk = (void far *) ((BYTE far *) hi._pentry + hi._size + 1);

 return lastblk;
#endif
}


/************************************************************/
/* ParamGetHotKey: Checks command line parameters for the hotkey  */
/*                 switch (/T) and implements these keys.         */
/* Input   : ARGC,  = Switch parameters, similar to main()        */
/*           ARGV                                                 */
/*           KEYMASK = Pointer to variable for storing the key mask */
/*           SCCODE = Pointer to variable for storing the scan code */
/* Output  : TRUE if the hotkeys are supported, otherwise FALSE   */
/* Info    : - Parameters not beginning with /T are ignored as    */
/*             parameters, but may be handled as other routines.  */
/*           - If no key exists for /T, SC_NOKEY is placed in the */
/*             appropriate variable.                              */
/************************************************************/


BOOL ParamGetHotKey(int argc, char *argv[], WORD *KeyMask, BYTE *ScCode)


{
 struct ToggleKey {
                    char Name[7];
                    WORD WVal;
                   };

 static struct ToggleKey TogKeys[9] =
                 { { "LSHIFT", LSHIFT },
```

```
                   { "RSHIFT" ,RSHIFT },
                   { "CTRL"   ,CTRL   },
                   { "ALT"    ,ALT    },
                   { "SYSREQ" ,SYSREQ },
                   { "BREAK"  ,BREAK  },
                   { "NUM"    ,NUM    },
                   { "CAPS"   ,CAPS   },
                   { "INSERT" ,INSERT }
                 };

 int i , j,                              /* Loop counter */
     code;                      /* Scan code conversion */
     char arg[80];                       /* Argument access */

 *KeyMask = 0;
 *ScCode = SC_NOKEY;

 for ( i = 1; i < argc; ++i )          /* Execute command line */
 {
  strcpy( arg, argv[i] );                 /* Get argument */
  strupr( arg );
  if ( arg[0] == '/' && arg[1] == 'T' )
  {                                     /* /T argument found */
   code = atoi( &arg[2] );         /* Convert code to binary */
   if ( code )                         /* Conversion O.K.? */
   {                                            /* Yes */
    if ( code < 128 )                    /* Valid code? */
     *ScCode = code;                     /* Yes --> Store */
    else
     return FALSE;                       /* Invalid code */
   }
   else       /* If not a number, must be the name of a toggle key */
   {
    for ( j = 0; j < 9; ++ j )     /* Search toggle key array */
     if ( !strcmp( TogKeys[j].Name, &arg[2] )) /* Compare string */
      break;                       /* Match --> End FOR loop */

    if ( j < 9 )                          /* Name found? */
     *KeyMask = *KeyMask | TogKeys[j].WVal;  /* Yes --> Flag */
    else
     return FALSE;           /* No --> Neither number nor toggle key */
   }
  }
 }
 return TRUE;                        /* If the function made it */
}                                      /* here, parameter is O.K. */


/************************************************************/
/**                  MAIN PROGRAM                        **/
/************************************************************/


void main( int argc, char *argv[] )
{
 WORD KeyMask;                      /* Get bit mask for toggle keys */
 BYTE ScCode;                       /* Get scan codes of hotkeys */

 printf("TSRC  - (c) 1988, 92 by Michael Tischer\n");
 if (!ParamGetHotKey( argc, argv, &KeyMask, &ScCode ))
 {                             /* Error in command line parameters */
  printf( "Illegal command line parameters\n" );
  exit(1);
 }

 /*-- Command line parameters were O.K. ----------------------*/
```

983

```
if ( !TsrIsInst( I2F_CODE ))          /* Program already installed? */
  {                                              /* No */
  atimes = 0;                      /* Program hasn't been enabled yet */
  printf( "TSR now installed. \n" );
  if ( KeyMask == 0  &&  ScCode == SC_NOKEY )    /* No parameters? */
    {                                   /* No --> Default is ALT-H */
    TsrSetHotkey( ALT, SC_H );
    printf( "Press <ALT> + H to enable\n" );
    }
  else                               /* Install user-defined hotkeys */
    TsrSetHotkey( KeyMask, ScCode );

  /*-- Allocate buffer for screen management -----------------------*/

  scrbuf = (union vel *) malloc(80 * 25 * sizeof(union vel));
  blnkspace = (char *) malloc( 80 + 1 );           /* Allocate buffer */
  *(blnkspace + 80 ) = '\0';                 /* End buffer with NULL */
  memset(blnkspace, ' ', 80);             /* Fill buffer with spaces */

  TsrInit( TC, tsr, HEAP_FREE );                  /* Install program */
  }
else                                      /* Program already installed */
  {                                              /* Yes */
  if ( KeyMask == 0  &&  ScCode == SC_NOKEY )    /* No parameters? */
    {                                   /* No --> Try uninstalling */
    if ( TsrCanUnInst() )
      {
      (*(OAFP) TsrSetPtr(endFCT))();
      TsrUnInst();
      printf( "Program now uninstalled.\n" );
      }
    else
      printf( "Program cannot be uninstalled.\n" );
    }
  else                                   /* Implement new hotkey */
    {
    printf( "New hotkey implemented\n" );
    (*(SHKFP) TsrSetPtr(TsrSetHotkey))( KeyMask, ScCode );
    }
  }
}
```

Assembler listing: TSRCA.ASM

```
;*********************************************************************;
;*                    T S R C A                                     *;
;*-----------------------------------------------------------------*;
;*   Task       : Assembler module for a C program demonstrating*;
;*                TSR access through hotkeys.                     *;
;*-----------------------------------------------------------------*;
;*   Author     : Michael Tischer                                *;
;*   Developed on : 08/10/88                                     *;
;*   Last update  : 02/18/92                                     *;
;*-----------------------------------------------------------------*;
;*   Assembly    : MASM -mx TSRCA;   or   TASM /mx TSRCA;         *;
;*                 ... link with C program                        *;
;*********************************************************************;

IGROUP group _text                ;Include program segment
DGROUP group _bss,  _data          ;Include data segment
       assume CS:IGROUP, DS:DGROUP, ES:DGROUP, SS:DGROUP


_BSS   segment word public 'BSS'  ;Include all un-initialized
_BSS   ends                        ;static variables

_DATA  segment word public 'DATA' ;Include all initialized
                                   ;global and static variables

extrn  __psp : word               ;Segment address of C program PSP

_DATA  ends

;== Constants ===============================================

TC_STACK  equ 512                 ;Turbo C stack
ARG_WORDS equ 32                  ;Stack words copied by TsrCall

I2F_FCT_0 equ 0AAh                ;Code for INT 2FH, function 0
I2F_FCT_1 equ 0BBh                ;Code for INT 2FH, function 1
TIME_OUT  equ 9                   ;Time out for activation in ticks

;== Program =================================================

_TEXT  segment byte public 'CODE' ;Program segment

;-- Reference to external (C) functions -----------------------

extrn  _GetHeapEnd:near           ;Returns ending address of heap

;-- Public declarations of internal functions -----------------

public  _TsrInit                  ;Enable calls within C program
public  _TsrIsInst
public  _TsrUnInst
public  _TsrCanUnInst
public  _TsrCall
public  _TsrSetHotkey
public  _TsrSetPtr

;-- Interrupt handler variables -------------------------------
;-- (accessible to code segment only) -------------------------

call_ptr equ this dword
call_ofs dw 0                     ;Offset address for TSRCall
call_seg dw 0                     ;Segment address not initialized yet
```

```
ret_ax    dw 0              ;Store function result
ret_dx    dw 0              ;from TsrCall

;-- Variables needed for activating the C program ---------------------

c_ss      dw 0              ;C stack segment
c_sp      dw 0              ;C stack pointer
c_ds      dw 0              ;C data segment
c_es      dw 0              ;C extra segment

c_dta_ofs dw 0              ;DTA address of C program
c_dta_seg dw 0

c_psp     dw 0              ;PSP segment address of C program
break_adr dw 0              ;Break address of heap
fct_adr   dw 0              ;Address of C TSR function

;-- Variables, used for testing hotkeys --------------------------------

key_mask  dw 3              ;Hotkey mask for BIOS keyboard flag
                           ;Default: Alt + H
sc_code   db 128            ;Hotkey scan code
                           ;Default: No key
i2F_code  db 0              ;Function number for INT 2FH

;-- Variables for TSR activation ---------------------------------------

tsrnow    db 0              ;Is TSR waiting for activation?
tsractive db 0             ;Is TSR already active?
in_bios   db 0              ;Display BIOS disk activity

daptr     equ this dword    ;Pointer to the DOS Indos flag
daptr_ofs dw 0              ;Offset address
daptr_seg dw 0              ;Segment address

;-- The following variables store the old interrupt handler     ---
;-- addresses, which are replaced by the new interrupt handler  ---

int8_ptr  equ this dword    ;Old interrupt vector 8H
int8_ofs  dw 0              ;Offset address of the old handler
int8_seg  dw 0              ;Segment address of the old handler

int9_ptr  equ this dword    ;Old interrupt vector 9H
int9_ofs  dw 0              ;Offset address of the old handler
int9_seg  dw 0              ;Segment address of the old handler

int13_ptr equ this dword    ;Old interrupt vector 13H
int13_ofs dw 0              ;Offset address of the old handler
int13_seg dw 0              ;Segment address of the old handler

int28_ptr equ this dword    ;Old interrupt vector 28H
int28_ofs dw 0              ;Offset address of the old handler
int28_seg dw 0              ;Segment address of the old handler

int2F_ptr equ this dword    ;Old interrupt vector 2FH
int2F_ofs dw 0              ;Offset address of the old handler
int2F_seg dw 0              ;Segment address of the old handler

;-- Variables for storing information about the uninterrupt program ---

u_dta_ofs dw 0              ;DTA address of interrupted program
u_dta_seg dw 0

u_psp     dw 0              ;Segment address: Interrupted prg PSP
```

```
uprg_ss   dw 0              ;SS and SP of interrupted program
uprg_sp   dw 0

;-----------------------------------------------------------------------
;-- TSRINIT: Ends the C program and activates the new interrupt     -
;--         handler
;-- Call from C: void TsrInit(  bool TC,
;--                             void (fct *)(void),
;--                             unsigned heap_byte );


_TsrInit  proc   near

sframe0   struc            ;Access structure from stack
bp0       dw ?             ;Gets BP
ret_adr0  dw ?             ;Return address
tc0       dw ?             ;Compiler (1 = TURBO C, 0 = MSC )
fctptr0   dw ?             ;Pointer to C TSR function
heap0     dw ?             ;Heap bytes needed
sframe0   ends             ;End structure

frame     equ [ bp - bp0 ]

          push bp          ;Push BP onto stack
          mov  bp,sp       ;Move SP to BP

;-- Store C segment register -------------------------------

          mov  c_ss,ss     ;Store registers in their
          mov  c_sp,sp     ;corresponding variables
          mov  c_es,es
          mov  c_ds,ds

;-- Store specified parameters -----------------------------

          mov  ax,frame.fctptr0  ;Get pointer to TSR function
          mov  fct_adr,ax  ;and store it

;-- Get DTA address of C program ---------------------------

          mov  ah,2fh      ;Funct. no.: Get DTA address
          int  21h         ;Call DOS interrupt
          mov  c_dta_ofs,bx ;Store address in
          mov  c_dta_seg,es ;corresponding variables

;-- Get address of INDOS flag ------------------------------

          mov  ah,34h      ;Funct. no.: Get INDOS flag address
          int  21h         ;Call DOS interrupt
          mov  daptr_ofs,bx ;Store address in
          mov  daptr_seg,es ;corresponding variables

;-- Get addresses of interrupt handler to be changed -------

          mov  ax,3508h    ;Get interrupt vector 8H
          int  21h         ;Call DOS interrupt
          mov  int8_ofs,bx ;Store handler address in
          mov  int8_seg,es ;corresponding variables

          mov  ax,3509h    ;Get interrupt vector 9H
          int  21h         ;Call DOS interrupt
          mov  int9_ofs,bx ;Store handler address in
          mov  int9_seg,es ;corresponding variables
```

```
        mov  ax,3513h        ;Get interrupt vector 13H
        int  21h             ;Call DOS interrupt
        mov  int13_ofs,bx    ;Store handler address in
        mov  int13_seg,es    ;corresponding variables

        mov  ax,3528h        ;Get interrupt vector 28H
        int  21h             ;Call DOS interrupt
        mov  int28_ofs,bx    ;Store handler address in
        mov  int28_seg,es    ;corresponding variables

        mov  ax,352Fh        ;Get interrupt vector 2FH
        int  21h             ;Call DOS interrupt
        mov  int2F_ofs,bx    ;Store handler address in
        mov  int2F_seg,es    ;corresponding variables

;-- Install new interrupt handler -------------------------

        push ds              ;Store data segment
        mov  ax,cs           ;Move CS to AX and pass to DS
        mov  ds,ax

        mov  ax,2508h        ;Funct. no.: Set interrupt 8H
        mov  dx,offset int08 ;DS:DX contains the handler address
        int  21h             ;Call DOS interrupt

        mov  ax,2509h        ;Funct. no.: Set interrupt 9H
        mov  dx,offset int09 ;DS:DX contains the handler address
        int  21h             ;Call DOS interrupt

        mov  ax,2513h        ;Funct. no.: Set interrupt 13H
        mov  dx,offset int13 ;DS:DX contains the handler address
        int  21h             ;Call DOS interrupt

        mov  ax,2528h        ;Funct. no.: Set interrupt 28H
        mov  dx,offset int28 ;DS:DX contains the handler address
        int  21h             ;Call DOS interrupt

        mov  ax,252Fh        ;Funct. no.: Set interrupt 2FH
        mov  dx,offset int2F ;DS:DX contains the handler address
        int  21h             ;Call DOS interrupt

        pop  ds              ;Pop DS from stack

;-- Compute number of paragraphs --------------------------
;-- that must remain in memory    --------------------------

        call _GetHeapEnd     ;Call C function in TSR module
        add  ax,frame.heap0  ;Add necessary heap memory

;-- Since Turbo C locates the stack after the heap, then  --
;-- begins with the end of segment, the heap must be      --
;-- determined first.                                     --

        cmp  byte ptr frame.tc0,0  ;Turbo C used?
        je   msc2            ;No --> Microsoft C

        add  ax,TC_STACK-1   ;Compute new stack pointer for TC
        mov  c_sp,ax         ;and store it
        inc  ax              ;Set break address

;-- Compute the number of paragraphs ----------------------
;-- that must be resident in memory  ----------------------

msc2:   mov  dx,ax           ;Move break address to DX
```

```
        add  dx,15           ;Avoid loss through integer division
        mov  cl,4            ;Shift 4 times to the right and then
        shr  dx,cl           ;divide by 16
        mov  ax,ds           ;Move DS to AX
        mov  bx,__psp        ;Get PSP segment address
        mov  c_psp,bx        ;Store in a corresponding variable
        sub  ax,bx           ;Subtract DS from PSP
        add  dx,ax           ;and add to the number of paragraphs
        mov  ax,3100h        ;Funct. no.: End resident program
        int  21h             ;Call DOS interrupt and end program

_TsrInit endp


        assume CS:IGROUP, DS:nothing, ES:nothing, SS:nothing

;----------------------------------------------------------------
;-- TSRSETHOTKEY: Configures program hotkey
;-- Aufruf von C: void TsrSetHotkey( unsigned KeyMask,
;--                                  byte     ScanCode );
;-- Info        : This procedure is FAR, so that it can be called
;--               from an already installed TSR.
;--

_TsrSetHotkey proc far

sframe1    struc             ;Access structure from stack
bp1        dw ?              ;Gets BP
ret_adr1   dd ?              ;Return address
keymask1   dw ?              ;Mask for hotkey
sc_code1   dw ?              ;Scan code of hotkey
sframe1    ends              ;End structure

frame      equ [ bp - bp1 ]

           push bp           ;Push BP onto stack
           mov  bp,sp        ;Move SP to BP

           ;-- Save passed parameters -----------------------------

           mov  ax,frame.keymask1 ;Get and store
           mov  key_mask,ax       ;hotkey
           mov  al,byte ptr frame.sc_code1 ;Get and store
           mov  sc_code,al        ;hotkey's scan code

           pop  bp           ;Pop BP from stack
           ret               ;zurück

_TsrSetHotkey endp

;----------------------------------------------------------------
;-- TSRISINST: Determines whether program is already installed   ---
;-- Call from C : bool TsrIsInst( byte i2f_fctnr);
;-- Return value: TRUE if the program is already installed,
;--               otherwise FALSE

_TsrIsInst proc   near

sframe2    struc             ;Access structure from stack
bp2        dw ?              ;Gets BP
ret_adr2   dw ?              ;Return address
i2F_code2  dw ?              ;Funct. no. for INT 2FH
sframe2    ends              ;End structure

frame      equ [ bp - bp2 ]
```

```
            push bp                ;Push BP onto stack
            mov  bp,sp             ;Move SP to BP

            mov  ah,byte ptr frame.i2F_code2 ;Funct. no. for INT 2FH
            mov  i2F_code,ah              ;Store it
            mov  al,I2F_FCT_0            ;Sub-function
            mov  bx,ax                   ;Store both numbers
            int  2Fh
            xchg bh,bl             ;Exchange numbers
            cmp  ax,bx            ;Compare with result
            mov  ax,0            ;Not from installation
            jne  isi_end            ;Unequal --> Not installed

            ;-- Get segment address of already installed copy

            mov  ah,i2f_code      ;No --> Segment address of INT 2FH
            mov  al,I2F_FCT_1     ;Load sub-function 01H
            int  2Fh
            mov  call_seg,ax      ;and store in variables
            mov  ax,-1            ;if installed

isi_end:    pop  bp               ;Pop BP from stack
            ret                   ;Return to caller

_TsrIsInst endp                    ;End procedure

;-----------------------------------------------------------------
;-- TSRCANUNIST: Determines whether installed copy of TSR can be -----
;--               reinstalled or uninstalled.
;-- Call from C : bool TsrCanUnInst( void );
;-- Output     : TRUE if reinstallation possible, otherwise FALSE
;-- Info       : Program can only be reinstalled if none of the
;--               interrupt vectors for the program have been
;--               redirected to another program.

tsrlist     db   08h,09h,13h,28h,2Fh,00h ;List of redirected INTs
                                         ;00H indicates end
_TsrCanUninst proc  near

            push di               ;Store DI (if reg. varaible)
            mov  dx,call_seg      ;Load segment of installed copy
            mov  di,offset tsrlist-1 ;Move DI to list

tcu_1:      inc  di               ;Increment DI to next int number
            mov  al,cs:[di]       ;Move next int number to AL
            or   al,al            ;End of list reached?
            je   tcu_ok           ;Yes --> All vectors O.K.

            mov  ah,35h           ;Funct. no.: Get interrupt
            int  21h              ;Call DOS interrupt
            mov  cx,es            ;Compare ES to CX
            cmp  dx,cx            ;Still in same segment?
            je   tcu_1            ;Yes --> No reinstallation or
            ;                         uninstallation possible
            xor  ax,ax            ;No  --> No reinstallation or
            ;                         uninstallation possible
            pop  di               ;Pop DI from stack
            ret

tcu_ok:     mov  ax,-1
            pop  di               ;Pop DI from stack
            ret
```

```
_TsrCanUninst endp

;-----------------------------------------------------------------
;-- TSRUNINST: Reinstalls the TSR and releases the allocated memory. -
;-- Call from C : void TsrUnInst( void );
;-- Info       : TSRCANUNINST() must be called successfully before
;--              calling this routine

_TsrUninst    proc    near

            push ds
            mov  es,call_seg      ;Load segment of installed TSR

            ;-- Reinstall TSR program's interrupt handler --------------

            cli                   ;Disable interrupts
            mov  ax,2508h         ;Funct. no.: Set INT 8H handler
            mov  ds,es:int8_seg   ;Segment address of the old handler
            mov  dx,es:int8_ofs   ;Offset address of the old handler
            int  21h              ;Reinstall old handler

            mov  ax,2509h         ;Funct. no.: Set INT 9H handler
            mov  ds,es:int9_seg   ;Segment address of the old handler
            mov  dx,es:int9_ofs   ;Offset address of the old handler
            int  21h              ;Reinstall old handler

            mov  ax,2513h         ;Funct. no.: Set INT 13H handler
            mov  ds,es:int13_seg  ;Segment address of the old handler
            mov  dx,es:int13_ofs  ;Offset address of the old handler
            int  21h              ;Reinstall old handler

            mov  ax,2528h         ;Funct. no.: Set INT 28H handler
            mov  ds,es:int28_seg  ;Segment address of the old handler
            mov  dx,es:int28_ofs  ;Offset address of the old handler
            int  21h              ;Reinstall old handler

            mov  ax,252Fh         ;Funct. no.: Set INT 2FH handler
            mov  ds,es:int2F_seg  ;Segment address of the old handler
            mov  dx,es:int2F_ofs  ;Offset address of the old handler
            int  21h              ;Reinstall old handler

            sti                   ;Enable interrupts

            ;-- Release memory ----------------------------------------

            mov  es,es:c_psp      ;Store PSP segment address of TSR
            mov  cx,es            ;program in CX
            mov  es,es:[ 02ch ]   ;Store environment segment address
            mov  ah,49h           ;Funct. no.: Release allocated memory
            int  21h              ;Call DOS interrupt

            mov  es,cx            ;Get ES from CX
            mov  ah,49h           ;Funct. no.: Release allocated memory
            int  21h              ;Call DOS interrupt

            pop  ds               ;Pop DS from stack
            ret                   ;Return to caller

_TsrUninst endp                    ;End of procedure

;-----------------------------------------------------------------
;-- TSRSETPTR: Stores the address of the routine from which TSRCALL --
;--            should be called
;-- Call from C: void (*)(void) TsrSetPtr( void far * Fct );
```

```
_TsrSetPtr  proc    near

sframe3     struc               ;Access structure from stack
bp3         dw ?                ;Gets BP
ret_adr3    dw ?                ;Return address
fctptr3     dd ?                ;Pointer to routine to be called
sframe3     ends                ;End structure

frame       equ [ bp - bp3 ]

            push bp             ;Push BP onto stack
            mov  bp,sp          ;Move SP to BP

            mov  ax,word ptr frame.fctptr3  ;Move offset address to AX
            mov  call_ofs,ax                ;and store it

            mov  ax,offset _TsrCall;Return near pointer to TSRCall
            pop  bp             ;Pop BP from stack

            ret                 ;Return to caller

_TsrSetPtr endp                 ;End of procedure

;-----------------------------------------------------------------------
;-- TSRCALL: Calls a routine in the previously installed copy of ------
;--          the TSR program.
;-- Call from C: void TsrCall( void )
;-- Attention     : - The stack should not be altered in this
;--                    routine.

_TsrCall    proc near

            ;-- Execute context change to C program and call the -------
            ;-- appropriate procedure

            push di             ;Push DS,
            push si             ;SI and
            push ds             ;DI

            mov  ah,2fh         ;Funct. no.: Get DTA address
            int  21h            ;Call DOS interrupt
            mov  u_dta_ofs,bx   ;Store DTA address of
            mov  u_dta_seg,es   ;interrupted program

            mov  es,call_seg    ;Pass segment address
                                ;of installed TSR to ES
            mov  ah,50h         ;Funct. no.: Set PSP address
            mov  bx,es:c_psp    ;Get PSP segment address
            int  21h            ;Call DOS interrupt

            mov  ah,1ah         ;Funct. no.: Set DTA address
            mov  dx,es:c_dta_ofs ;Get offset address and
            mov  ds,es:c_dta_seg ;segment address of new DTA
            int  21h            ;Call DOS interrupt

            ;-- Copy arguments to stack of installed TSR program -------

            push ss             ;Set DS:SI to arguments on
            pop  ds             ;the current stack
            mov  si,sp
            add  si,8

            mov  cx,ARG_WORDS*2
```

```
            mov  di,es:c_sp     ;Install ES:DI on the stack
            sub  di,cx
            mov  es,es:c_ss
            rep movsb           ;Copy arguments

            ;-- Implement and call segment register in installed TSR ---

            mov  es,call_seg    ;Move installed TSR segment register
                                ;to ES

            cli                 ;Disable interrupts
            mov  uprg_ss,ss     ;Store current stack segment
            mov  uprg_sp,sp     ;and stack pointer

            mov  ss,es:c_ss     ;Activate stack for installed
            mov  sp,es:c_sp     ;copy of program
            sub  sp,ARG_WORDS*2 ;Subtract arguments
            sti                 ;Enable interrupts

            mov  ds,es:c_ds     ;Set segment register
            mov  es,es:c_es     ;for C program

            call [call_ptr]     ;Set function results given by
            mov  ret_ax,ax      ;TSRSETPTR
            mov  ret_dx,dx

            cli                 ;Disable interrupts
            mov  ss,uprg_ss     ;Move data from stack
            mov  sp,uprg_sp     ;umschalten
            sti                 ;Enable interrupts

            ;-- Context change returning to current program ------------

            mov  ah,1ah         ;Funct. no.: Set DTA address
            mov  dx,u_dta_ofs   ;Get DTA offset and segment address
            mov  ds,u_dta_seg   ;Load interrupted program
            int  21h            ;Call DOS interrupt

            mov  es,call_seg    ;Return ES
            pop  ds             ;and DS

            mov  ah,50h         ;Funct. no.: Set PSP address
            mov  bx,cs          ;Move CS to BX
            sub  bx,10h         ;Calculate segment address of PSP
            int  21h            ;Call DOS interrupt

            mov  ax,ret_ax      ;Return function result
            mov  dx,ret_dx

            pop  si             ;Pop registers
            pop  di
            ret                 ;Return to caller

_TsrCall    endp                ;End of procedure

;-----------------------------------------------------------------------
;-- DOSACTIVE: Determines whether DOS will be interrupted, by checking
;--            the INDOS flag.
;-- Input  : None
;-- Output : Zero flag = 1 : DOS may be interrupted

dosactive   proc near

            push ds             ;Push DS and BX onto stack
```

```
        push bx
        lds  bx,daptr      ;DS:BX point to the INDOS flag
        cmp  byte ptr [bx],0  ;DOS function active?
        pop  bx            ;Pop BX and DS from stack
        pop  ds

        ret                ;Return to caller

dosactive  endp

;------------------------------------------------------------------
;-- New interrupt handler follows ---------------------------------
;------------------------------------------------------------------

;-- New interrupt 08H handler (Timer) -----------------------------

int08   proc far

        cmp  tsrnow,0      ;Should TSR be activated?
        je   i8_end        ;No --> Return to old handler

        dec  tsrnow        ;Yes --> Decrement activation flag

        ;-- TSR should be activated, but is it possible? -----------

        cmp  in_bios, 0    ;BIOS disk interrupt already active?
        jne  i8_end        ;Yes --> No activation possible

        call dosactive     ;Should DOS be interrupted?
        je   i8_tsr        ;Yes --> Call TSR

i8_end: jmp  [int8_ptr]    ;Jump to old handler

        ;-- Activate TSR -------------------------------------------

i8_tsr: mov  tsrnow,0      ;TSR no longer waiting for activation
        mov  tsractive,1   ;TSR is active
        pushf              ;Call old handler, using
        call [int8_ptr]    ;INT 8H emulation
        call start_tsr     ;Start TSR program
        iret               ;Return to interrupted program

int08   endp

;-- New interrupt 09H handler (Keyboard) --------------------------

int09   proc far

        push ax
        in   al,60h        ;Read keyboard port

        cmp  tsractive,0   ;Is TSR program already active?
        jne  i9_end        ;Yes --> Call old handler then return

        cmp  tsrnow,0      ;TSR waiting for activation?
        jne  i9_end        ;Yes --> Call old handler then return

        ;-- Test for hotkey ----------------------------------------

        cmp  sc_code,128   ;Scan code?
        je   i9_ks         ;No --> Check for toggle keys

        cmp  al,128        ;Yes --> Is it a release code?
        jae  i9_end        ;Yes --> Not a hotkey
```

```
        cmp  sc_code,al    ;Make code, compare with key
        jne  i9_end        ;No match --> No activation

i9_ks:  ;-- Check status of toggle keys ----------------------------

        push ds
        mov  ax,040h       ;Move DS to ROM-BIOS
        mov  ds,ax         ;variable segment
        mov  ax,word ptr ds:[17h] ;Get BIOS keyboard flag
        and  ax,key_mask   ;Mask non-hotkey bits
        cmp  ax,key_mask   ;Any hotkey bits remaining?
        pop  ds
        jne  i9_end        ;Hotkey implemented? No --> Return

        cmp  in_bios, 0    ;BIOS disk interrupt active?
        jne  i9_e1         ;Yes --> No activation possible

        call dosactive     ;Should DOS be interrupted?
        je   i9_tsr        ;Yes --> Start TSR

i9_e1:  mov  tsrnow,TIME_OUT;TSR waits for activation

i9_end: pop  ax            ;Pop AX from stack
        jmp  [int9_ptr]    ;Hump to old handler

i9_tsr: mov  tsractive,1   ;TSR now active
        mov  tsrnow,0      ;No delayed start wanted
        pushf
        call [int9_ptr]    ;Call old handler
        pop  ax            ;Pop AX from stack
        call start_tsr     ;Start TSR program
        iret               ;Return to interrupted program

int09   endp

;-- New interrupt 13H handler (diskette/hard drive) ---------------

int13   proc far

        inc  in_bios       ;Increment BIOS disk flag
        pushf              ;Call old interrupt handler
        call [int13_ptr]   ;using INT 13H emulation
        dec  in_bios       ;Reset BIOS disk flag

        sti                ;Enable interrupts
        ret  2             ;Return to caller without popping
                           ;flag register from stack

int13   endp

;-- New interrupt 28H handler (DOS idle) --------------------------

int28   proc far

        cmp  tsrnow,0      ;Is TSR waiting for activation?
        je   i28_end       ;No --> Return to caller

        cmp  in_bios, 0    ;Yes --> But is disk int active?
        je   i28_tsr       ;Yes --> No activation

i28_end: jmp [int28_ptr]   ;Return to old handler

        ;-- Start TSR ----------------------------------------------
```

989

```
i28_tsr:   mov   tsrnow,0       ;TSR no longer waiting for activation
           mov   tsractive,1    ;TSR is (already) active
           pushf                ;Call old interrupt handler
           call  [int28_ptr]    ;using INT 28H emulation
           call  start_tsr      ;Start TSR program
           iret                 ;Return to caller

int28  endp

;-- New interrupt 2FH handler (Multiplexer) -----------------------

int2F  proc far

           cmp   ah,i2F_code    ;Call for this TSR?
           jne   i2F_end        ;No --> Return to old handler

           cmp   al,I2F_FCT_0   ;Yes --> Is this sub-function 00H?
           je    i2F_0          ;Yes --> Execute

           cmp   al,I2F_FCT_1   ;Or is it sub-function 01H?
           je    i2F_1          ;Yes --> Execute

           iret                 ;No --> Ignore call

i2F_end:   ;-- TSR not planned, send call on -----------------------

           jmp   [int2F_ptr]    ;Return to old handler

i2F_0:     ;-- Sub-function 00: Installation check ----------------

           xchg  ah,al          ;Exchange function and sub-funct. no.
           iret                 ;Return to caller

i2F_1:     ;-- Sub-function 01: Return segment address ------------

           mov   ax,cs          ;Move segment address to AX
           iret                 ;Return to caller

int2F  endp

;-- START_TSR: Activate TSR program ------------------------------

start_tsr  proc near

           ;-- Execute context change to C program --------------------

           cli                  ;Disable interrupts
           mov   uprg_ss,ss     ;Store current stack segment and
           mov   uprg_sp,sp     ;stack pointer

           mov   ss,c_ss        ;Activate C program's stack
           mov   sp,c_sp
           sti                  ;Enable interrupts

           push  ax             ;Store processor registers
           push  bx             ;for the C stack
           push  cx
           push  dx
           push  bp
           push  si
           push  di
           push  ds
           push  es
```

```
;-- Store 64 words from the DOS stack ----------------------

           mov   cx,64          ;Loop counter
           mov   ds,uprg_ss     ;DS:SI indicates end of DOS stack
           mov   si,uprg_sp

tsrs1:     push  word ptr [si]  ;Push word from DOS stack to C stack
           inc   si             ;and make SI the next stack
           inc   si             ;word
           loop  tsrs1          ;Process all 64 words

           mov   ah,51h         ;Funct. no.: Get PSP address
           int   21h            ;Call DOS interrupt
           mov   u_psp,bx       ;Store segment address of PSP

           mov   ah,2fh         ;Funct. no.: Get DTA address
           int   21h            ;Call DOS interrupt
           mov   u_dta_ofs,bx   ;Store DTA address of the
           mov   u_dta_seg,es   ;interrupted program

           mov   ah,50h         ;Funct. no.: Set PSP address
           mov   bx,c_psp       ;Get PSP segment addr. of C program
           int   21h            ;Call DOS interrupt

           mov   ah,1ah         ;Funct. no.: Set DTA address
           mov   dx,c_dta_ofs   ;Get offset address and
           mov   ds,c_dta_seg   ;segment address of new DTA
           int   21h            ;Call DOS interrupt

           mov   ds,c_ds        ;Set segment register for
           mov   es,c_es        ;C program

           call  [fct_adr]      ;Call start function

;-- Execute context change to interrupted program ----------

           mov   ah,1ah         ;Funct. no.: Set DTA address
           mov   dx,u_dta_ofs   ;Get DTA offset and segment address
           mov   ds,u_dta_seg   ;Load interrupted program
           int   21h            ;Call DOS interrupt

           mov   ah,50h         ;Funct. no.: Set PSP address
           mov   bx,u_psp       ;PSP segment address of int'd. prg.
           int   21h            ;Call DOS interrupt

;-- Restore DOS stack ---------------------------------------

           mov   cx,64          ;Loop counter
           mov   ds,uprg_ss     ;Load DS:SI with ending
           mov   si,uprg_sp     ;address of DOS stack
           add   si,128         ;Set SI to start of DOS stack
tsrs2:     dec   si             ;SI to previous stack word
           dec   si
           pop   word ptr [si]  ;Pop word from C stack to DOS
           loop  tsrs2          ;Process all 64 words

           pop   es             ;Pop stored registers from
           pop   ds             ;C stack
           pop   di
           pop   si
           pop   bp
           pop   dx
           pop   cx
           pop   bx
```

```
pop  ax                                              ret                     ;Return to caller

cli              ;Disable interrupts                 start_tsr endp
mov  ss,uprg_ss  ;Move stack pointer and stack segment
mov  sp,uprg_sp  ;of interrupted program             ;----------------------------------------------------

mov  tsractive,0 ;TSR no longer active               _text     ends          ;End of code segment
sti              ;Enable interrupts                             end           ;End of program
```

The Pascal implementation

Turbo Pascal offers only one memory model, unlike the various C compilers. The organization of this model is well suited to TSR programs.

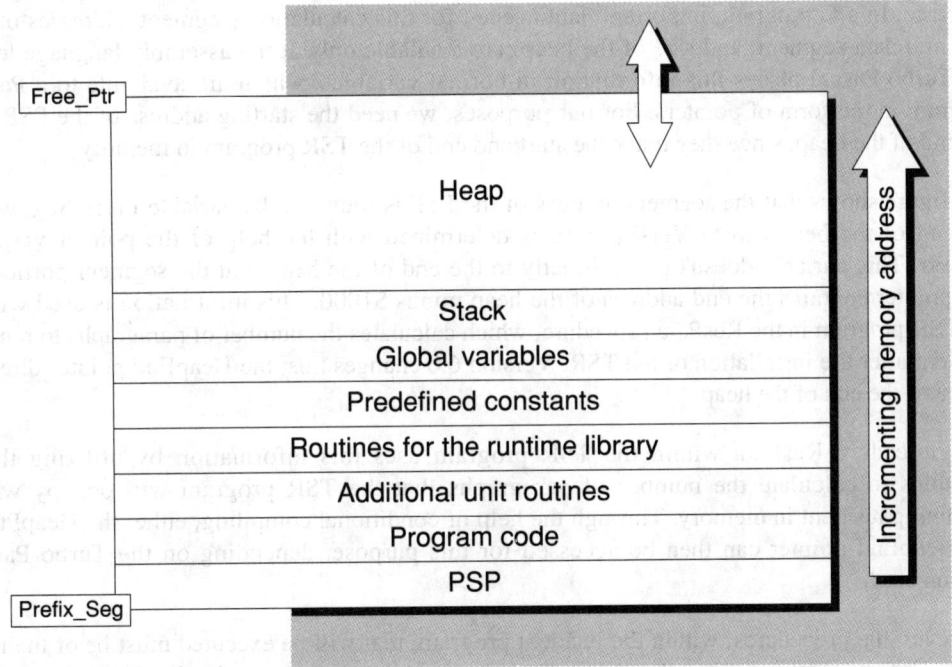

Memory layout of a Pascal program under Turbo Pascal 4.0

The figure above shows that the program code and the required routines from the various units and the runtime library follow the PSP. After these are the predefined constants, the global data, and the stack segment. While the size of these program components are set at compilation and cannot be changed after the program is loaded into memory, this doesn't apply to the size of the heap, which follows the stack segment. When new objects are created with the NEW command, the heap grows toward the end of memory.

Unlike C compilers, Turbo Pascal allow you to set the maximum size of the heap, as well as the stack size, with a compiler directive inside the source code. This is the $M directive, which must be passed the following parameters:

```
{$M stack size, minimum heap size, maximum heap size}
```

All specifications are in bytes, so the directive:

```
{$M 2048, 0, 5000}
```

results in a 2K stack and a maximum 5000 byte heap. If no such directive is found in a program, the heap isn't limited and it can grow to the end of main memory. This would have devastating results for a TSR program, because the entire memory must be reserved for the TSR program and there would be no memory left for additional programs. But with the $M directive placed at the beginning of the program, we can set the maximum size of the program in memory and the number of paragraphs that must remain resident after the program is terminated.

Turbo Pascal also allows the number of paragraphs to be reserved to be calculated from the Pascal program, which eliminates the complicated calculation in the assembly language interface. In a C program, important data needed for this calculation (segment addresses of the PSP and data segment, and size of the heap) are available only at the assembly language level, but Turbo Pascal places this information in normal variables, which are available to a Pascal program in the form of pointers. For our purposes, we need the starting address of the PSP and the end of the heap, since they mark the start and end of the TSR program in memory.

The figure shows that the segment address of the PSP is found in the variable PrefixSeg, while the end of the heap (up to Version 6.0) is determined with the help of the pointer variable FreePtr. This variable doesn't point directly to the end of the heap, but the segment portion of this pointer contains the end address of the heap minus $1000. This information is used within the TSR program in the ResPara procedure, which calculates the number of paragraphs to remain resident after the installation of the TSR. Version 6.0 changes this; the HeapEnd pointer directly indicates the end of the heap.

The procedure ResPara within the TSR program uses this information by utilizing these variables to calculate the number of paragraphs that the TSR program will occupy while remaining resident in memory. Through the help of conditional compiling, either the HeapPtr or the HeapEnd pointer can then be accessed for this purpose, depending on the Turbo Pascal version used.

However, the procedures, within the resident program, that will be executed must be of the type FAR. Unfortunately, calling these functions isn't as simple here as in the C version, since Turbo Pascal doesn't permit the casting of function pointers. Because of this, TsrSetPtr doesn't return a result upon its call, and the calls of TsrSetPtr and TsrCall cannot be combined.

However, in the Pascal version, it's also necessary to declare code pointers that depict the procedures and functions that will be called, and particularly their arguments. As you can see in the following listing of TSRP.PAS, these pointers are called WoAPrcK and SHKPrcK. WoAPrcK is a pointer to a procedure that doesn't require any arguments, while SHKPrc is specifically designed to serve the TsrSetHotkey procedure.

```
type WoAPrcK = procedure;                    { Procedure without arguments }
     SHKPrcK = procedure( KeyMask : word;               { TsrSetHotkey }
                          ScCode  : byte );
     PPtrT   = record         { Union for creating the procedure pointer }
                 case integer of
                   1 : ( WoAPrc : WoAPrcK );
                   2 : ( SHKPrc : SHKPrcK );
               end;
```

```
      const Call : PPtrT = ( WoAPrc : TsrCall );
```

These types are collected in a variant record that contains an entry for each of these types. Here these entries have been named WoAPrc for WoAPrcK and SHKPrc for SHKPrcK. A global variable named Call has been declared for calling the functions that are associated with these types. The WoAPrc component of this variable is initialized as a pointer to the TsrCall procedure.

This variable can then be used to call the desired procedure or function, providing its offset address is first passed to TsrSetPtr. This is illustrated by the following two program lines. At the TsrSetPtr function call, TsrSetHotkey is specified as the procedure that will be executed. TsrCall is then called together with the arguments for TsrSetHotkey.

```
      TsrSetPtr(ofs(TsrSetHotKey));
      Call.SHKPrc( Keymask, ScCode );
```

This approach works because, by employing the SHKPrc component of Call, the compiler assumes that such a procedure is actually being called. Actually, however, TsrCall is being executed. In respect to the stack, this function has it easier than its C counterpart.

The reason for this is that Turbo Pascal programs don't expect the data segment to correspond to the stack segment. So, the stack of the currently running program can remain active, even when a procedure or function within the resident copy of the program is being called.

Pascal listing: TSRP.PAS

```
{*****************************************************************}
{*                        T S R P                              *}
{*-------------------------------------------------------------*}
{*  Task       : Creates a TSR program with the help of an     *}
{*               assembly language module.                     *}
{*-------------------------------------------------------------*}
{*  Author     : Michael Tischer                               *}
{*  Developed on : 08/18/88                                    *}
{*  Last update  : 02/04/92                                    *}
{*****************************************************************}

program TSRP;

uses DOS, CRT;                      { Add DOS and CRT units }

{$M 2048, 0, 5120}   { Reserve 2K for the stack and 5K for the heap }
{$L tsrpa}                           { Link assembler module }

{-- Declare external functions in the assembler module --------------}

procedure TsrInit( PrcPtr  : word;  { Offset address: TSR procedure }
                   ResPara  : word   { Number of pars. to be reserved }
                 ) ; external ;             { ID string }
function TsrIsInst( i2F_fctno : byte ) : boolean ; external ;
procedure TsrUnInst; external;              { Uninstall TSR }
procedure TsrSetPtr( Offset : word ); external;
function TsrCanUnInst : boolean; external;

{$F+}                            { FAR procedures and functions }
procedure TsrCall ; external;
procedure TsrSetHotKey( KeyMask  : word;    { Hotkey (see CONST) }
```

```
                        ScCode   : byte        { Scan code }
                      ) ; external;
{$F-}

{-- Constants ------------------------------------------------------}

    {-- Scan codes for different keys ------------------------}

const SC_ESC      = $01;    SC_Z          = $2C;
      SC_1        = $02;    SC_X          = $2D;
      SC_2        = $03;    SC_C          = $2E;
      SC_3        = $04;    SC_V          = $2F;
      SC_4        = $05;    SC_B          = $30;
      SC_5        = $06;    SC_N          = $31;
      SC_6        = $07;    SC_M          = $32;
      SC_7        = $08;    SC_COMMA      = $33;
      SC_8        = $09;    SC_PERIOD     = $34;
      SC_9        = $0A;    SC_SLASH      = $35;
      SC_0        = $0B;    SC_SHIFT_RIGHT = $36;
      SC_HYPHEN   = $0C;    SC_ASTERISK   = $37;
      SC_EQUALS   = $0D;    SC_ALT        = $38;
      SC_BACKSPACE = $0E;   SC_SPACE      = $39;
      SC_TAB      = $0F;    SC_CAPS       = $3A;
      SC_Q        = $10;    SC_F1         = $3B;
      SC_W        = $11;    SC_F2         = $3C;
      SC_E        = $12;    SC_F3         = $3D;
      SC_R        = $13;    SC_F4         = $3E;
      SC_T        = $14;    SC_F5         = $3F;
      SC_Y        = $15;    SC_F6         = $40;
      SC_U        = $16;    SC_F7         = $41;
      SC_I        = $17;    SC_F8         = $42;
      SC_O        = $18;    SC_F9         = $43;
      SC_P        = $19;    SC_F10        = $44;
      SC_LBRACKET = $1A;    SC_NUM_LOCK   = $45;
```

```
SC_RBRACKET      = $1B;     SC_SCROLL_LOCK     = $46;
SC_ENTER         = $1C;     SC_CURSOR_HOME     = $47;
SC_CONTROL       = $1D;     SC_CURSOR_UP       = $48;
SC_A             = $1E;     SC_CURSOR_PG_UP    = $49;
SC_S             = $1F;     SC_NUM_MINUS       = $4A;
SC_D             = $20;     SC_CURSOR_LEFT     = $4B;
SC_F             = $21;     SC_NUM_5           = $4C;
SC_G             = $22;     SC_CURSOR_RIGHT    = $4D;
SC_H             = $23;     SC_NUM_PLUS        = $4E;
SC_J             = $24;     SC_CURSOR_END      = $4F;
SC_K             = $25;     SC_CURSOR_DOWN     = $50;
SC_L             = $26;     SC_CURSOR_PG_DOWN  = $51;
SC_SEMICOLON     = $27;     SC_INSERT          = $52;
SC_APOSTROPHE    = $28;     SC_DELETE          = $53;
SC_GRAVE         = $29;     SC_SYS_REQUEST     = $54;
SC_SHIFT_LEFT    = $2A;     SC_F11             = $57;
SC_BACKSLASH     = $2B;     SC_F12             = $58;
SC_NOKEY         = $80;              { No more keys }


    {-- Bit masks for the different toggle keys --------------------}

    LSHIFT  =     1;                        { Left SHIFT key }
    RSHIFT  =     2;                        { Right SHIFT key }
    CTRL    =     4;                        { CTRL key }
    ALT     =     8;                        { ALT key }
    SYSREQ  =  1024;            { SYS-REQ key (AT keyboard only) }
    BREAK   =  4096;                        { BREAK key }
    NUM     =  8192;                        { NUM LOCK key }
    CAPS    = 16384;                        { CAPS LOCK key }
    INSERT  = 32768;                        { INSERT key }


    I2F_CODE   = $C4;            { Function number INT 2F }
    I2F_FCT_0  = $AA;            { Code for INT 2F, function 0 }
    I2F_FCT_1  = $BB;            { Code for INT 2F, function 1 }

{-- Type declarations ------------------------------------------}

type VBuf = array[1..25, 1..80] of word;   { Describes the screen }
     VPtr = ^VBuf;                   { Pointer to a screen buffer }


     {-- Declaration of procedure and function types which copy  --}
     {-- procedures and functions in the already installed copy  --}
     {-- of the TSR.                                             --}

     WoAPrcK = procedure;              { Procedure without arguments }
     SHKPrcK = procedure( KeyMask : word;        { TsrSetHotkey }
                          ScCode : byte );
     PPtrT = record    { Union for creating the procedure pointer }
               case integer of
                 1 : ( WoAPrc : WoAPrcK );
                 2 : ( SHKPrc : SHKPrcK );
             end;

const Call : PPtrT = ( WoAPrc : TsrCall );

{-- Global variables -------------------------------------------}

var MBuf   : VBuf absolute $B000:0000;   { Monochrome video RAM }
    CBuf   : Vbuf absolute $B800:0000;       { Color video RAM }
    VioPtr : VPtr;                     { Pointer to the video RAM }
    ATimes : integer;               { Number of TSR activations }


{***************************************************************}
{* DispInit: Creates a pointer to video RAM.                  *}
```

```
{* Input   : None                                            *}
{* Output  : None                                            *}
{***************************************************************}

procedure DispInit;

var Regs: Registers;              { Store the processor registers }

begin
  Regs.ah := $0f;           { Funct. no. 15 = Read the video mode }
  Intr($10, Regs);             { Call the BIOS video interrupt }
  if Regs.al=7 then            { Monochrome video card? }
    VioPtr := @MBuf      { Yes --> Set pointer to monochrome video RAM }
  else                         { Handle it as EGA, VGA or CGA }
    VioPtr := @CBuf;       { Set pointer to color video RAM }
end;


{***************************************************************}
{* SaveScreen: Saves the screen contents to a buffer.        *}
{* Input   : SPTR : Pointer to the buffer in which the screen *}
{*                  contents will be saved.                  *}
{* Output  : None                                            *}
{***************************************************************}

procedure SaveScreen( SPtr : VPtr );

var scrow,                                      { Current row }
    column : byte;                           { Current column }

begin
  for scrow:=1 to 25 do             { Execute the 25 screen rows }
    for column:=1 to 80 do          { Execute the 80 screen columns }
      SPtr^[scrow, column] := VioPtr^[scrow, column];  { Store char. }
                                                       { & attribute }
end;


{***************************************************************}
{* RestoreScreen: Copies the contents of a buffer to video RAM. *}
{* Input   : BPTR : Pointer to the buffer whose contents are to be *}
{*                  copied to video RAM                      *}
{* Output  : None                                            *}
{***************************************************************}

procedure RestoreScreen( BPtr : VPtr );

var scrow,                                      { The current row }
    column : byte;                           { The current column }

begin
  for scrow:=1 to 25 do             { Execute the 25 screen rows }
    for column:=1 to 80 do          { Execute the 80 screen columns }
      VioPtr^[scrow, column] := BPtr^[scrow, column];  { Store char. }
                                                       { & attribute }
end;


{***************************************************************}
{* ResPara: Calculates the number of paragraphs which must be *}
{*          allocated for the program.                       *}
{* Input   : None                                            *}
{* Output  : The number of paragraphs to be reserved         *}
{***************************************************************}

function ResPara : word;
```

```
begin
  {-- Compute the number of bytes needed, using the proper method ----}

  {$ifdef VER50}                              { Turbo Ver. 5.0 }
    ResPara := Seg(FreePtr^)+$1000-PrefixSeg; { Number of paragraphs }
  {$endif}

  {$ifdef VER55}                              { Turbo Ver. 5.5 }
    ResPara := Seg(FreePtr^)+$1000-PrefixSeg; { Number of paragraphs }
  {$endif}

  {$ifdef VER60}                              { Turbo Ver. 6.0 }
    ResPara := Seg(HeapEnd^)-PrefixSeg;
  {$endif}
end;

{*********************************************************************}
{* ParamGetHotKey: Checks command line parameters for the hotkey    *}
{*                 switch (/T) and implements these keys.            *}
{* Input   : KEYMASK = Variable for storing the key mask            *}
{*           SCCODE  = Variable for storing the scan code           *}
{* Output  : TRUE if the hotkeys are supported, otherwise FALSE     *}
{* Info    : - Parameters not beginning with /T are ignored as      *}
{*             parameters, but may be handled as other routines      *}
{*           - If no parameter exists for /T, SC_NOKEY is placed in  *}
{*             the appropriate variable.                             *}
{*********************************************************************}

function ParamGetHotKey( var KeyMask : word;
                         var ScCode  : byte ) : boolean;

type ToggleKey = record
                   Name : string[6];
                   WVal : word;
                 end;

const TogKeys : array[ 1..9 ] of ToggleKey =
                  ( ( Name: 'LSHIFT'; WVal : LSHIFT ),
                    ( Name: 'RSHIFT'; WVal : RSHIFT ),
                    ( Name: 'CTRL';   WVal : CTRL   ),
                    ( Name: 'ALT';    WVal : ALT    ),
                    ( Name: 'SYSREQ'; WVal : SYSREQ ),
                    ( Name: 'BREAK';  WVal : BREAK  ),
                    ( Name: 'NUM';    WVal : NUM    ),
                    ( Name: 'CAPS';   WVal : CAPS   ),
                    ( Name: 'INSERT'; WVal : INSERT )
                  );

var i , j,                                  { Loop counter }
    code,                           { For scan code conversion }
    dummy : integer;                  { Error variable for VAL }
    arg   : string;                         { Argument access }

begin
  KeyMask := 0;
  ScCode := SC_NOKEY;

  for i := 1 to ParamCount do               { Execute command line }
    begin
      arg := ParamStr(i);                       { Get argument }
      for j := 1 to length(arg) do    { Convert string to upper case }
        arg[j] := upcase(arg[j]);
      if ( arg[1] = '/' ) and ( arg[2] = 'T' ) then
        begin                                 { /T argument found }
          delete( arg, 1, 2 );          { Remove '/T' from string }
          val( arg, code, dummy );      { Convert remainder to binary }
          if ( dummy = 0 ) then              { Conversion O.K.? }
            begin                                      { Yes }
              if ( code > 0 ) and ( code < 128 ) then  { Valid code? }
                ScCode := Code                       { Yes --> Store }
              else
                begin                            { Invalid code }
                  ParamGetHotKey := false;
                  exit;                    { End function with FALSE }
                end;
            end
          else     { If not a number, must be the name of a toggle key }
            begin
              j := 1;                  { Search toggle key array }
              while ( j < 10 ) and ( arg <> TogKeys[j].Name ) do
                j := j + 1;
              if ( j < 10 ) then                   { Name found? }
                KeyMask := KeyMask or TogKeys[j].WVal  { Yes --> Flag }
              else
                begin        { No --> Neither number nor toggle key }
                  ParamGetHotKey := false;
                  exit;                  { End function with FALSE }
                end;
            end;
        end;
    end;
  ParamGetHotKey := true;              { If everything checks out }
end;                                   { so far, parameters are O.K. }

{*********************************************************************}
{* EndTPrc: Called by the assembler module when the TSR program is  *}
{*          uninstalled.                                            *}
{* Input   : None                                                   *}
{* Output  : None                                                   *}
{* Info    : This procedure must be a FAR procedure to permit access *}
{*           from the installed copy of the TSR.                     *}
{*********************************************************************}

{$F+}

procedure EndTPrc;

begin
  TextBackground( Black );                      { Dark background }
  TextColor( LightGray );                          { Light text }
  writeln('The TSR was called ', ATimes, ' times.');
end;

{$F-}

{*********************************************************************}
{* Tsr: Called by the assembler module after the hotkey is pressed. *}
{* Input   : None                                                   *}
{* Output  : None                                                   *}
{* Info    : This procedure must be in the main program and may not  *}
{*           be turned into a FAR procedure by the $F+ compiler      *}
{*           directive.                                             *}
{*********************************************************************}

{$F-}                               { Don't make a FAR procedure }

procedure Tsr;
```

```
var BufPtr : VPtr;              { Stores pointer to the allocated blocks }
    Column,                          { The current screen column }
    ScRow  : byte;                    { The current screen row }
    PdKey  : char;

begin
  while KeyPressed do                  { Clear keyboard buffer }
    PdKey := ReadKey;
  inc( ATimes );                      { Increment call counter }
  DispInit;                         { Get video RAM address }
  GetMem(BufPtr, SizeOf(VBuf) );        { Allocate buffer }
  SaveScreen( BufPtr );              { Store screen contents }
  ScRow := WhereY;                 { Get current screen row }
  Column := WhereX;               { Get current screen column }
  TextBackground( LightGray );          { Light background }
  TextColor( Black );                    { Dark text }
  ClrScr;                            { Clear screen }
  GotoXY(34, 12);
  write('My first TSR.');
  GotoXY(29, 14);
  write('Please press a key ...');
  PdKey := ReadKey;                     { Wait for a key }
  RestoreScreen( BufPtr );        { Restore old screen contents }
  FreeMem( BufPtr, SizeOf(VBuf) );    { Release allocated buffer }
  GotoXY( Column, ScRow );   { Return cursor to original position }
end;


{*******************************************************************}
{**                    MAIN PROGRAM                        **}
{*******************************************************************}


var KeyMask : word;
    ScCode  : byte;

begin
  writeln('TSRP  -  (c) 1988, 92 by Michael Tischer');
  if not ParamGetHotKey( KeyMask, ScCode ) then
    begin                          { Error in command line parameters }
      writeln( 'Illegal command line parameters');
      exit;
    end;

  {-- Command line parameters were O.K. -----------------------------}

  if ( TsrIsInst( I2F_CODE ) = FALSE ) then      { Program already }
                                          { installed?       }
    begin                                 { No }
      ATimes := 0;                { Program hasn't been enabled yet }
      writeln( 'TSR now installed. ' );
      if ( KeyMask = 0 ) and ( ScCode = SC_NOKEY ) then { No params.? }
        begin                      { No --> Default is ALT-H }
          TsrSetHotkey( ALT, SC_H );
          writeln( 'Press <ALT> + H to enable');
        end
      else                         { Install user-defined hotkeys }
        TsrSetHotkey( KeyMask, ScCode );
      TsrInit( Ofs(Tsr), ResPara );          { Install program }
    end
  else                          { Program already installed }
    begin
      if ( KeyMask = 0 ) and ( ScCode = SC_NOKEY ) then { No params.? }
        begin                      { No --> Try uninstalling }
          if TsrCanUnInst then
            begin
              TsrSetPtr(ofs(EndTPrc));          { Call End procedure }
              Call.WoAPrc;                    { in installed copy }
              TsrUnInst;
              writeln( 'Program now uninstalled.');
            end
          else
            writeln( 'Program cannot be uninstalled.');
        end
      else                                { Implement new hotkey }
        begin
          writeln( 'New hotkey implemented' );
          TsrSetPtr(ofs(TsrSetHotKey));
          Call.SHKPrc( KeyMask, ScCode );
        end
    end;
end.
```

Assembler listing: TSRPA.ASM

```
;*****************************************************************;
;*                        T S R P A                            *;
;*-------------------------------------------------------------*;
;*   Task      : Assembler module for a Turbo Pascal program    *;
;*               demonstrating TSR access through hotkeys.      *;
;*-------------------------------------------------------------*;
;*   Author    : Michael Tischer                                *;
;*   Developed on : 08/12/88                                    *;
;*   Last update  : 02/04/92                                    *;
;*-------------------------------------------------------------*;
;*   Info      : This module must be linked to a program, not   *;
;*               added to a unit.                               *;
;*-------------------------------------------------------------*;
;*   Assembly  : MASM TSRPA;     or     TASM TSRPA              *;
;*               Then link with a Turbo Pascal program          *;
;*****************************************************************;


DATA    segment word public    ;Turbo data segment

DATA    ends                   ;End of data segments

;== Constants ================================================

I2F_FCT_0  equ 0AAh            ;Code for INT 2F, function 0
I2F_FCT_1  equ 0BBh            ;Code for INT 2F, function 1
TIME_OUT   equ 9              ;Time out for activation in ticks

;== Program =================================================

CODE    segment byte public    ;Turbo code segment

        assume cs:CODE, ds:DATA

;-- Public declarations of internal functions ---------------

public     tsrinit             ;Enable calls within Turbo program
public     tsrisinst
public     tsruninst
public     tsrcanuninst
public     tsrsetptr
public     tsrcall
public     tsrsethotkey

;-- Interrupt handler variables -----------------------------
;-- (accessible to code segment only) -----------------------

call_ptr   equ this dword
call_ofs   dw 0                ;Offset address for TSRCall
call_seg   dw 0                ;Segment address not initialized yet

ds_save    dw 0                ;Store DS during TSR call
rptr_save  equ this dword      ;FAR pointer for return from TSR call
rip_save   dw 0                ;Store return address
rcs_save   dw 0                ;from TSR call
ret_ax     dw 0                ;Store function result
ret_dx     dw 0                ;from TSR call

;-- Variables needed for activating the Turbo program -------------

t_ss       dw 0                ;Turbo stack segment
t_sp       dw 0                ;Turbo stack pointer
t_ds       dw 0                ;Turbo data segment
```

```
t_es       dw 0                ;Turbo extra segment

t_dta_ofs  dw 0                ;DTA address of  Turbo programs
t_dta_seg  dw 0

t_psp      dw 0                ;PSP segment address of Turbo prg.
prc_adr    dw 0                ;Address of Turbo TSR procedure

;-- Variables used for testing hotkeys ----------------------------

key_mask   dw 3                ;Hotkey mask for BIOS keyboard flag
                              ;Default: Alt + H
sc_code    db 128             ;Hotkey scan code
                              ;Default: No key
i2F_code   db 0               ;Function number for INT 2F

;-- Variables for TSR activation ----------------------------------

tsrnow     db 0               ;Is TSR waiting for activation?
tsractive  db 0               ;Is TSR already active?
in_bios    db 0               ;Display BIOS disk activity

daptr      equ this dword     ;Pointer to the DOS Indos flag
daptr_ofs  dw 0               ;Offset address
daptr_seg  dw 0               ;Segment address

;-- The following variables store the old interrupt handler      ---
;-- addresses, which are replace by the new interrupt handler    ---

int8_ptr   equ this dword     ;Old interrupt vector 8H
int8_ofs   dw 0               ;Offset address of the old handler
int8_seg   dw 0               ;Segment address of the old handler

int9_ptr   equ this dword     ;Old interrupt vector 9H
int9_ofs   dw 0               ;Offset address of the old handler
int9_seg   dw 0               ;Segment address of the old handler

int13_ptr  equ this dword     ;Old interrupt vector 13H
int13_ofs  dw 0               ;Offset address of the old handler
int13_seg  dw 0               ;Segment address of the old handler

int28_ptr  equ this dword     ;Old interrupt vector 28H
int28_ofs  dw 0               ;Offset address of the old handler
int28_seg  dw 0               ;Segment address of the old handler

int2F_ptr  equ this dword     ;Old interrupt vector 2FH
int2F_ofs  dw 0               ;Offset address of the old handler
int2F_seg  dw 0               ;Segment address of the old handler

;-- Variables for storing information about the interrupted program ---

u_dta_ofs  dw 0               ;DTA address of interrupted program
u_dta_seg  dw 0

u_psp      dw 0               ;Segment address: Interrupted prg PSP

uprg_ss    dw 0               ;SS and SP of interrupted program
uprg_sp    dw 0

;------------------------------------------------------------------
;-- TSRINIT: Ends the Turbo program and activates the new interrupt ---
;--          handler
;-- Call from Turbo: procdure TsrInit( PrcPtr  : word;
;--                                    ResPara : word );
```

```
tsrinit     proc    near

sframe0     struc                   ;Access structure from stack
bp0         dw ?                    ;Gets BP
ret_adr0    dw ?                    ;Return address
respara0    dw ?                    ;Number of paragraphs to be reserved
przptr0     dw ?                    ;Offset of Turbo TSR procedure
sframe0     ends                    ;End structure

frame       equ [ bp - bp0 ]

            push bp                 ;Push BP onto stack
            mov  bp,sp              ;Move SP to BP
            push es                 ;Push ES onto stack

            ;-- Store Turbo segment register --------------------------

            mov  t_ss,ss            ;Store registers in their
            mov  t_sp,sp            ;corresponding variables
            mov  t_es,es
            mov  t_ds,ds

            ;-- Get PSP for Turbo program -----------------------------

            mov  bx,cs              ;Move CS to BX
            sub  bx,10h             ;10H paragraphs = 256 bytes
            mov  t_psp,bx           ;Store segment address

            ;-- Store specified parameters ----------------------------

            mov  ax,frame.przptr0   ;Get pointer to TSR procedure
            mov  prc_adr,ax         ;and store it

            ;-- Get DTA address of Turbo program ----------------------

            mov  ah,2fh             ;Funct. no.: Get DTA address
            int  21h                ;Call DOS interrupt
            mov  t_dta_ofs,bx       ;Store address in
            mov  t_dta_seg,es       ;corresponding variables

            ;-- Get address of INDOS flag -----------------------------

            mov  ah,34h             ;Funct. no.: Get INDOS flag address
            int  21h                ;Call DOS interrupt
            mov  daptr_ofs,bx       ;Store address in
            mov  daptr_seg,es       ;corresponding variables

            ;-- Get addresses of interrupt handler to be changed ------

            mov  ax,3508h           ;Get interrupt vector 8H
            int  21h                ;Call DOS interrupt
            mov  int8_ofs,bx        ;Store handler address in
            mov  int8_seg,es        ;corresponding variables

            mov  ax,3509h           ;Get interrupt vector 9H
            int  21h                ;Call DOS interrupt
            mov  int9_ofs,bx        ;Store handler address in
            mov  int9_seg,es        ;corresponding variables

            mov  ax,3513h           ;Get interrupt vector 13H
            int  21h                ;Call DOS interrupt
            mov  int13_ofs,bx       ;Store handler address in
            mov  int13_seg,es       ;corresponding variables

            mov  ax,3528h           ;Get interrupt vector 28H
            int  21h                ;Call DOS interrupt
            mov  int28_ofs,bx       ;Store handler address in
            mov  int28_seg,es       ;corresponding variables

            mov  ax,352Fh           ;Get interrupt vector 2FH
            int  21h                ;Call DOS interrupt
            mov  int2F_ofs,bx       ;Store handler address in
            mov  int2F_seg,es       ;corresponding variables

            ;-- Install new interrupt handler -------------------------

            push ds                 ;Store data segment
            mov  ax,cs              ;Move CS to AX and pass to DS
            mov  ds,ax

            mov  ax,2508h           ;Funct. no.: Set interrupt 8H
            mov  dx,offset int08    ;DS:DX contains the handler address
            int  21h                ;Call DOS interrupt

            mov  ax,2509h           ;Funct. no.: Set interrupt 9H
            mov  dx,offset int09    ;DS:DX contains the handler address
            int  21h                ;Call DOS interrupt

            mov  ax,2513h           ;Funct. no.: Set interrupt 13H
            mov  dx,offset int13    ;DS:DX contains the handler address
            int  21h                ;Call DOS interrupt

            mov  ax,2528h           ;Funct. no.: Set interrupt 28H
            mov  dx,offset int28    ;DS:DX contains the handler address
            int  21h                ;Call DOS interrupt

            mov  ax,252Fh           ;Funct. no.: Set interrupt 2FH
            mov  dx,offset int2F    ;DS:DX contains the handler address
            int  21h                ;Call DOS interrupt

            pop  ds                 ;DS from stack

            ;-- End resident program ----------------------------------

            mov  ax,3100h           ;Funct. no.: End resident program
            mov  dx,frame.respara0  ;Get number of reserved paragraphs
            int  21h                ;Call DOS interrupt and end program

tsrinit endp

;------------------------------------------------------------------
;-- TSRSETHOTKEY: Configures program hotkey
;-- Call from Turbo: procdure TsrSetHotKey( KeyMask : word;
;--                                         ScanCode : byte );
;-- Info          : This procedure is FAR, so that it can be called
;--                  from an already installed TSR.
;--

tsrsethotkey proc far

sframe1     struc                   ;Access structure from stack
bp1         dw ?                    ;Gets BP
ret_adr1    dd ?                    ;Return address
sc_code1    dw ?                    ;Scan code of hotkey
keymask1    dw ?                    ;Mask for hotkey
sframe1     ends                    ;End structure
```

```
frame     equ [ bp - bp1 ]

          push bp                ;Push BP onto stack
          mov  bp,sp             ;Move SP to BP


          ;-- Save passed parameters --------------------------------

          mov  ax,frame.keymask1 ;Get and store
          mov  key_mask,ax       ;hotkey
          mov  al,byte ptr frame.sc_code1 ;Get and store
          mov  sc_code,al               ;hotkey's scan code


          pop  bp                ;Pop BP from stack
          ret  4                 ;Return

tsrsethotkey endp

;----------------------------------------------------------------------
;-- TSRISINST: Determines whether program is already installed    ----
;-- Call from Turbo: function TsrIsInst( i2f_fctno : byte ) : boolean;
;-- Return value: TRUE if the program is already installed,
;--               otherwise FALSE

tsrisinst proc    near

sframe2   struc                  ;Access structure from stack
bp2       dw ?                   ;Gets BP
ret_adr2  dw ?                   ;Return address
i2F_code2 dw ?                   ;Function number for INT 2F
sframe2   ends                   ;End structure


frame     equ [ bp - bp2 ]

          push bp                ;Push BP onto stack
          mov  bp,sp             ;Move SP to BP

          mov  ah,byte ptr frame.i2F_code2 ;Func. no. for INT 2F
          mov  i2F_code,ah             ;Store it
          mov  al,I2F_FCT_0            ;Sub-function
          mov  bx,ax                   ;Store both numbers
          int  2Fh
          xchg bh,bl                   ;Exchange numbers
          cmp  ax,bx                   ;Compare with result
          mov  ax,0                    ;Not from installation
          jne  isi_end                 ;Unequal --> Not installed

          ;-- Get segment address of already installed copy

          mov  ah,i2f_code       ;No --> Segment address of INT 2Fh
          mov  al,I2F_FCT_1      ;Load sub-function 01H
          int  2Fh
          mov  call_seg,ax       ;and store in variables
          mov  ax,-1             ;if installed

isi_end:  pop  bp                ;Pop BP from stack
          ret  2                 ;Return to caller

tsrisinst endp                   ;End procedure

;----------------------------------------------------------------------
;-- TSRCANUNIST: Determines whether installed copy of TSR can be  ----
;--              reinstalled or uninstalled.
;-- Call from Turbo : function TsrCanUnInst : boolean;
;-- Output          : TRUE if reinstallation possible, otherwise FALSE
```

```
;-- Info           : Program can only be reinstalled if none of the
;--                  interrupt vectors for the program have been
;--                  redirected to another program.

tsrlist   db 08h,09h,13h,28h,2Fh,00h ;List of redirected INTs
                            ;00H indicates end
tsrcanuninst  proc  near

          mov  dx,call_seg       ;Load segment of installed copy
          mov  di,offset tsrlist-1 ;Move DI to list

tcu_1:    inc  di                ;Increment DI to next int number
          mov  al,cs:[di]        ;Move next int number to AL
          or   al,al             ;End of list reached?
          je   tcu_ok            ;Yes --> All vectors O.K.

          mov  ah,35h            ;Funct. no.: Get interrupt
          int  21h               ;Call DOS interrupt
          mov  cx,es             ;Compare ES to CX
          cmp  dx,cx             ;Still in same segment?
          je   tcu_1             ;Yes --> No reinstallation or
                                 ;        uninstallation possible
          xor  ax,ax             ;No --> No reinstallation or
                                 ;        uninstallation possible
          ret

tcu_ok:   mov  ax,-1
          ret

tsrcanunist endp

;----------------------------------------------------------------------
;-- TSRUNINST: Reinstalls the TSR and releases the allocated memory. -
;-- Call from Turbo : procedure TsrUnInst;
;-- Info            : TSRCANUNIST() must be called successfully before
;--                   calling this routine

tsruninst proc near

          push ds
          mov  es,call_seg       ;Load segment of installed TSR

          ;-- Reinstall TSR program's interrupt handler --------------

          cli                    ;Disable interrupts
          mov  ax,2508h          ;Funct. no.: Set INT 8 handler
          mov  ds,es:int8_seg    ;Segment address of the old handler
          mov  dx,es:int8_ofs    ;Offset address of the old handler
          int  21h               ;Reinstall old handler

          mov  ax,2509h          ;Funct. no.: Set INT 9 handler
          mov  ds,es:int9_seg    ;Segment address of the old handler
          mov  dx,es:int9_ofs    ;Offset address of the old handler
          int  21h               ;Reinstall old handler

          mov  ax,2513h          ;Funct. no.: Set INT 13 handler
          mov  ds,es:int13_seg   ;Segment address of the old handler
          mov  dx,es:int13_ofs   ;Offset address of the old handler
          int  21h               ;Reinstall old handler

          mov  ax,2528h          ;Funct. no.: Set INT 28 handler
          mov  ds,es:int28_seg   ;Segment address of the old handler
          mov  dx,es:int28_ofs   ;Offset address of the old handler
          int  21h               ;Reinstall old handler
```

999

```
        mov   ax,252Fh           ;Funct. no.: Set INT 2F handler
        mov   ds,es:int2F_seg    ;Segment address of the old handler
        mov   dx,es:int2F_ofs    ;Offset address of the old handler
        int   21h                ;Reinstall old handler


;-- Release memory -------------------------------------

        sti                      ;Enable interrupts

        mov   es,es:t_psp         ;Store PSP segment address of TSR
        mov   cx,es               ;program in CX
        mov   es,es:[ 02ch ]      ;Store environment segment address
        mov   ah,49h              ;Funct. no.: Release allocated memory
        int   21h                ;Call DOS interrupt

        mov   es,cx               ;Get ES from CX
        mov   ah,49h              ;Funct. no.: Release allocated mem.
        int   21h                ;Call DOS interrupt

        pop   ds                 ;Pop DS from stack
        ret                      ;Return to caller

tsruninst endp                   ;End of procedure

;-------------------------------------------------------
;-- TSRSETPTR: Stores the address of the routine from which TSRCALL --
;--           should be called
;-- Call from Turbo: procedure TsrSetPtr( offset : word );
tsrsetptr proc    near

sframe3   struc                  ;Access structure from stack
bp3       dw ?                   ;Gets BP
ret_adr3  dw ?                   ;Return address
offset3   dw ?                   ;Offset of routine to be called
sframe3   ends                   ;End structure

frame     equ [ bp - bp3 ]

        push  bp                 ;Push BP onto stack
        mov   bp,sp              ;Move SP to BP

        mov   ax,frame.offset3   ;Move offset address to AX
        mov   call_ofs,ax        ;and store it

        pop   bp                 ;Pop BP from stack
        ret   2                  ;Return to caller

tsrsetptr endp                   ;End of procedure

;-------------------------------------------------------
;-- TSRCALL: Calls a routine in the previously installed copy of  ----
;--          the TSR program.
;-- Call from Turbo : procedure TsrCall;
;-- Attention     : - The stack should not be altered in this
;--                    routine.
;--                 - this procedure must be declared as FAR,
;--                   making it accessible as a procedure pointer.
tsrcall   proc far

        ;-- Execute context change to Turbo program and call the ---
        ;-- appropriate procedure
```

```
        pop   rip_save           ;Pop return address from stack and
        pop   rcs_save           ;store it
        mov   ds_save,ds         ;Store DS

        mov   ah,2fh             ;Funct. no.: Get DTA address
        int   21h                ;Call DOS interrupt
        mov   u_dta_ofs,bx       ;Store DTA address of
        mov   u_dta_seg,es       ;interrupted program

        mov   es,call_seg        ;Pass segment address
                                 ;of installed TSR to ES
        mov   ah,50h             ;Funct. no.:  Set PSP address
        mov   bx,es:t_psp        ;Get PSP segment address
        int   21h                ;Call DOS interrupt

        mov   ah,1ah             ;Funct. no.: Set DTA address
        mov   dx,es:t_dta_ofs    ;Get offset address of new DTA and
        mov   ds,es:t_dta_seg    ;segment address of new DTA
        int   21h                ;Call DOS interrupt

        mov   ds,es:t_ds         ;Set segment register for
        mov   es,es:t_es         ;Turbo program

        call  [call_ptr]         ;Call Turbo procedure
        mov   cs:ret_ax,ax       ;Store function result
        mov   cs:ret_dx,dx

;-- Context change returning to Turbo program --------------

        mov   ah,1ah             ;Funct. no.: Set DTA address
        mov   dx,u_dta_ofs       ;Get DTA offset and segment address
        mov   ds,u_dta_seg       ;Load interrupted program
        int   21h                ;Call DOS interrupt

        mov   es,call_seg        ;Return ES and
        mov   ds,ds_save         ;DS

        mov   ah,50h             ;Funct. no.:  Set PSP address
        mov   bx,cs              ;Move CS to BX
        sub   bx,10h             ;Calculate segment address of PSP
        int   21h                ;Call DOS interrupt

        mov   ax,cs:ret_ax       ;Return function result
        mov   dx,cs:ret_dx
        jmp   [rptr_save]        ;Return to caller

tsrcall   endp                   ;End of procedure

;-------------------------------------------------------
;-- DOSACTIVE: Determines whether DOS will be interrupted, by checking
;--            the INDOS flag.
;-- Input   : None
;-- Output  : Zero flag=1 : DOS may be interrupted

dosactiv  proc near

        push  ds                 ;Push DS and BX onto stack
        push  bx
        lds   bx,daptr           ;DS:BX point to the INDOS flag
        cmp   byte ptr [bx],0     ;DOS function active?
        pop   bx                 ;Pop BX and DS from stack
        pop   ds

        ret                      ;Return to caller
```

```
dosactive    endp


;--------------------------------------------------------------
;-- New interrupt handler follows -----------------------------
;--------------------------------------------------------------


;-- New interrupt 08H handler (Timer) -------------------------
int08    proc far

         cmp  tsrnow,0        ;Should TSR be activated?
         je   i8_end          ;No --> Return to old handler

         dec  tsrnow          ;Yes --> Decrement activation flag

         ;-- TSR should be activated, but is it possible? -----------

         cmp  in_bios, 0      ;BIOS disk interrupt already active?
         jne  i8_end          ;Yes --> No activation possible

         call dosactive       ;Should DOS be interrupted?
         je   i8_tsr          ;Yes --> Call TSR

i8_end:  jmp  [int8_ptr]      ;Jump to old handler

         ;-- Activate TSR -----------------------------------------

i8_tsr:  mov  tsrnow,0        ;TSR no longer waiting for activation
         mov  tsractive,1     ;TSR is active
         pushf                ;Call old handler, using
         call [int8_ptr]      ; INT 8H emulation
         call start_tsr       ;Start TSR program
         iret                 ;Return to interrupted program


int08    endp

;-- New interrupt 09H handler (Keyboard) ------------------------
int09    proc far

         push ax
         in   al,60h          ;Read keyboard port

         cmp  tsractive,0     ;Is TSR program already active?
         jne  i9_end          ;Yes --> Call old handler then return

         cmp  tsrnow,0        ;TSR waiting for activation?
         jne  i9_end          ;Yes --> Call old handler then return

         ;-- Test for hotkey -----------------------------------

         cmp  sc_code,128     ;Scan code?
         je   i9_ks           ;No --> Check for toggle keys

         cmp  al,128          ;Yes --> Is it a release code?
         jae  i9_end          ;Yes --> Not a hotkey

         cmp  sc_code,al      ;Make code, compare with key
         jne  i9_end          ;No match --> No activation

i9_ks:   ;-- Check status of toggle keys -----------------------
         push ds
         mov  ax,040h         ;Move DS to ROM-BIOS
         mov  ds,ax           ;variable segment
         mov  ax,word ptr ds:[17h] ;Get BIOS keyboard flag
```

```
         and  ax,key_mask     ;Mask non-hotkey bits
         cmp  ax,key_mask     ;Any hotkey bits remaining?
         pop  ds
         jne  i9_end          ;Hotkey implemented? No --> Return

         cmp  in_bios, 0      ;BIOS disk interrupt active?
         jne  i9_e1           ;Yes --> No activation possible

         call dosactive       ;Should DOS be interrupted?
         je   i9_tsr          ;Yes --> Start TSR

i9_e1:   mov  tsrnow,TIME_OUT;TSR waits for activation

i9_end:  pop  ax              ;Pop AX from stack
         jmp  [int9_ptr]      ;Jump to old handler

i9_tsr:  mov  tsractive,1     ;TSR now active
         mov  tsrnow,0        ;No delayed start wanted
         pushf
         call [int9_ptr]      ;Call old handler
         pop  ax              ;Pop AX from stack
         call start_tsr       ;Start TSR program
         iret                 ;Return to interrupted program


int09    endp

;-- New interrupt 13H handler (diskette/hard drive) ---------------

int13    proc far

         inc  in_bios         ;Increment BIOS disk flag
         pushf                ;Call old interrupt handler
         call [int13_ptr]     ;using INT 13H emulation
         dec  in_bios         ;Reset BIOS disk flag

         sti                  ;Enable interrupts
         ret  2               ;Return to caller without popping
                              ;flag register from stack
int13    endp

;-- New interrupt 28H handler (DOS idle) -------------------------
int28    proc far

         cmp  tsrnow,0        ;Is TSR waiting for activation?
         je   i28_end         ;No --> Return to caller

         cmp  in_bios, 0      ;Yes --> But is disk int active?
         je   i28_tsr         ;Yes --> No activation

i28_end: jmp  [int28_ptr]     ;Return to old handler

         ;-- Start TSR ---------------------------------------

i28_tsr: mov  tsrnow,0        ;TSR no longer waiting for activation
         mov  tsractive,1     ;TSR is (already) active
         pushf                ;Call old interrupt handler
         call [int28_ptr]     ;using INT 28H emulation
         call start_tsr       ;Start TSR program
         iret                 ;Return to caller


int28    endp

;-- New interrupt 2FH handler (Multiplexer) -------------------
int2F    proc far
```

```
            cmp   ah,i2F_code       ;Call for this TSR?
            jne   i2F_end           ;No --> Revert to old handler

            cmp   al,I2F_FCT_0      ;Yes --> Is this sub-function 00H?
            je    i2F_0             ;Yes --> Execute

            cmp   al,I2F_FCT_1      ;Or is it sub-function 01H?
            je    i2F_1             ;Yes --> Execute

            iret                    ;No --> Ignore call

i2F_end:    ;-- TSR not planned, send call on ----------------------------

            jmp   [int2F_ptr]       ;Revert to old handler

i2F_0:      ;-- Sub-function 00: Installation check --------------------
            xchg  ah,al             ;Exchange function and sub-funct. no.
            iret                    ;Return to caller

i2F_1:      ;-- Sub-function 01: Return segment address ----------------
            mov   ax,cs             ;Move segment address to AX
            iret                    ;Return to caller

int2F       endp

;-- START_TSR: Activate TSR program -------------------------------------
start_tsr   proc near

            ;-- Execute context change to Turbo program ----------------

            cli                     ;Disable interrupts
            mov   uprg_ss,ss        ;Store current stack segment and
            mov   uprg_sp,sp        ;stack pointer

            mov   ss,t_ss           ;Activate Turbo program's
            mov   sp,t_sp           ;stack
            sti                     ;Enable interrupts

            push  ax                ;Store processor registers
            push  bx                ;for the Turbo stack
            push  cx
            push  dx
            push  bp
            push  si
            push  di
            push  ds
            push  es

            ;-- Store 64 words from the DOS stack ----------------------

            mov   cx,64             ;Loop counter
            mov   ds,uprg_ss        ;DS:SI indicates end of DOS stack
            mov   si,uprg_sp
tsrs1:      push  word ptr [si]     ;Push word from DOS stack to TP stack
            inc   si                ;and make SI the next stack
            inc   si                ;word
            loop  tsrs1             ;Process all 64 words

            mov   ah,51h            ;Funct. no.:  Get PSP address
            int   21h               ;Call DOS interrupt
            mov   u_psp,bx          ;Store segment address of PSP
```

```
            mov   ah,2fh            ;Funct. no.: Get DTA address
            int   21h               ;Call DOS interrupt
            mov   u_dta_ofs,bx      ;Store DTA address of the
            mov   u_dta_seg,es      ;interrupted program

            mov   ah,50h            ;Funct. no.: Set PSP address
            mov   bx,t_psp          ;Get PSP segment addr. of Turbo prog.
            int   21h               ;Call DOS interrupt

            mov   ah,1ah            ;Funct. no.: Set DTA address
            mov   dx,t_dta_ofs      ;Get offset address and
            mov   ds,t_dta_seg      ;segment address of new DTA
            int   21h               ;Call DOS interrupt

            mov   ds,t_ds           ;Set segment register for
            mov   es,t_es           ;Turbo program

            call  [prc_adr]         ;Call start function

            ;-- Execute context change to interrupted program ----------

            mov   ah,1ah            ;Funct. no.: Set DTA address
            mov   dx,u_dta_ofs      ;Load DTA offset and segment addrs.
            mov   ds,u_dta_seg      ;for interrupted program
            int   21h               ;Call DOS interrupt

            mov   ah,50h            ;Funct. no.:  Set PSP address
            mov   bx,u_psp          ;PSP segment address: Interrupted prg
            int   21h               ;Call DOS interrupt

            ;-- Restore DOS stack --------------------------------------
            mov   cx,64             ;Loop counter
            mov   ds,uprg_ss        ;Load DS:SI with end
            mov   si,uprg_sp        ;address of DOS stack
            add   si,128            ;Set SI to start of DOS stack
tsrs2:      dec   si                ;SI to previous stack word
            dec   si
            pop   word ptr [si]     ;Pop word from Turbo stack to DOS
            loop  tsrs2             ;Process all 64 words

            pop   es                ;Pop stored registers from
            pop   ds                ;Turbo stack
            pop   di
            pop   si
            pop   bp
            pop   dx
            pop   cx
            pop   bx
            pop   ax

            cli                     ;Disable interrupts
            mov   ss,uprg_ss        ;Move stack pointer and stack segment
            mov   sp,uprg_sp        ;of interrupted program

            mov   tsractive,0       ;TSR no longer active
            sti                     ;Enable interrupts

            ret                     ;Return to caller

start_tsr   endp
;-------------------------------------------------------------------------
CODE        ends                    ;End of code segment
            end                     ;End of program
```

32.2.4   A Few Tips

In this chapter we've demonstrated how easily TSR programs can be developed, even in high level languages, by simply placing the core procedures in assembler modules and linking these with high level language modules. However, TSR programming is still a complicated task.

So, we recommend using several techniques that are suitable for TSR programs. First develop the program as a normal program that can be compiled from DOS, or an integrated development environment, and executed.

You should also try to reduce the number of changes needed to convert the program to a TSR program. To do this, you should also develop an initialization procedure, as well as the actual TSR procedure, which will be called when the hotkey is activated. However, unlike the final TSR program, these procedures should still be called from within the main program procedure (or function) so that their execution doesn't depend on the hotkey yet.

In this way, you can completely develop and test the program. Once you're satisfied with the results and have found all its bugs, you can convert it to a TSR program. Correcting all errors prior to this is particularly important, since it's almost impossible to detect errors once the conversion has occurred, even through the use of a debugger.

TSR The actual conversion into a TSR program is actually rather simple. You only need to integrate the assembly module with the program, and to call the appropriate functions from the assembler module. The two sample programs illustrate the logistics of this operation in detail, and all necessary function calls can be found within the main program.

Chapter 33

Protected Mode, DOS Extensions, DPMI/VCPI

Recently, 80286 Protected mode has been making headway into the world of DOS. However, DOS is a Real mode operating system. So, it cannot use Protected mode.

This is also true for the ROM-BIOS of a PC, which is also intended for Real mode operation. ROM-BIOS crashes when the first BIOS call is made after switching to Protected mode.

The 80386 and i486 demonstrate their true power in Protected mode. Many software developers have been searching for a back door to make Protected mode usable with DOS. This has resulted in the creation of EMS emulators, memory management programs, DOS extensions, and multitaskers. These utilities run DOS as a Protected mode operating system. In this chapter we'll explain how Protected mode works and how it can be distinguished from Real mode.

33.1 Protected Mode

Protected mode was introduced in 1982, when the 80286 microprocessor was introduced. It was originally developed for multitasking operating systems. However, since DOS is based on the older Real mode and would have to be completely rewritten in order to utilize Protected mode on Intel processors, it cannot use this mode.

Nearly ten years passed before Protected mode could actually be used. This occurred with the introduction of the 32-bit version of Windows and OS/2 Version 2.0. Previously, temporary solutions, such as the standard and enhanced modes used with Windows 3, were used.

33.1.1   Characteristics of Multitasking Operating Systems

To understand the various characteristics of Protected mode, we must study how these characteristics are applied. This involves the structure and requirements of multitasking operating systems and how they are related to the capabilities of the underlying processors. Protected mode was developed to interact with this type of operating system.

The most obvious characteristic of multitasking operating systems is their ability to run several programs or tasks simultaneously. Not only do different programs run simultaneously, but often separate executable files within these programs also run.

One example of this is a word processing program that formats a file and sends it to the printer while you continue entering text. These two tasks run concurrently within a single program. When executing programs concurrently in a multitasking environment, both tasks must be able to coexist in memory. Each task assumes that it's the only one controlling the computer. The tasks must operate in unison, while the operating system itself must be protected from the programs and their various tasks. This is why the name "Protected mode" was chosen.

Processor requirements for a multitasking environment

A multitasking environment must meet the following criteria:

     1.)   Mutual protection of tasks and the operating system from overwriting areas of memory.
     2.)   Support during task switching, particularly when restoring the executable state of a task.
     3.)   Privileged status for the operating system when executing specific assembly language instructions and operations.
     4.)   Support during the setup of virtual memory management.

We'll discuss how tasks and the memory areas are protected from each other later. However, remember that this is the first requirement imposed on an operating system.

Task switching support

The simultaneous execution of multiple programs in a multitasking environment is usually an illusion. Theoretically, true multitasking exists only when the hardware contains several processors, performing several tasks in parallel. Actually, usually only one processor is available at any given time. So, multitasking normally means that several tasks are sharing processor time, with each task using the processor for only a fraction of a second.

For example, suppose that a very slow system is running three tasks concurrently. The first task executes for a third of a second, then the second task executes for a third of a second, then the third task executes for a third of a second. Then the cycle repeats.

This is called *preemptive multitasking*, and follows the principle of *time slicing*. The time slicing process is based on an abrupt intrusion into task execution. After a specific period of time, the operating system simply stops executing the current task and continues with another task. This procedure must be transparent to the interrupted task. The task being interrupted cannot prepare for this interruption, because it can occur at any moment.

1006

The operating system is responsible for ensuring that program execution continues without interruption between tasks. System resources (i.e., memory, files being processed, and processor registers), must remain unchanged by the task switch. Maintaining system integrity following an interruption can be managed through software, although task switching speeds up if the processor manages this assignment.

Finally, the illusion of parallel execution occurs only when switching between tasks is repeated many times per second. However, this switching wastes a lot of processor time and doesn't help task execution. So, support for task switching is the second requirement imposed on a processor with a multitasking capability.

Operating system privileges

The third requirement is that the operating system must have certain privileges; priority must be given to certain assembly language instructions, while task execution remains on hold. These instructions include those involving task switching and those that influence the processor's operating mode.

Suppose that a task simply switched the processor from Protected mode to Real mode. This probably wouldn't result in a system crash, just as overwriting some areas of memory wouldn't cause a crash. However, data and other programs could be corrupted. The operating system is responsible for correcting these errors or, if a correction isn't possible, ending the offending program and removing it from memory. Other programs should remain undisturbed.

Virtual memory

The processor should help the operating system manage virtual memory. Memory requirements increase with the number and complexity of the programs being executed simultaneously. Often the memory requirements exceed the amount of physical memory that's available. The operating system should allow programs access to more memory than actually exists, by using virtual memory.

The memory areas that aren't needed by the current task can be moved to the hard drive until they are needed again. The processor supports the capacity to determine which memory is needed and which isn't.

Now let's see how these requirements are actually used. We'll look at Protected modes on the 80286, 80386, and i486. The latter two Protected modes are downwardly compatible with the 80286, but include significant improvements. You'll see how efficient and how complicated programming in this mode can be.

Unfortunately, all Intel processors work in Protected mode more slowly than in Real mode. In the following sections we'll explain why this occurs.

33.1.2   80286 Protected Mode

Anyone familiar with assembler programming in Real mode under DOS, but who hasn't worked in Protected mode, often asks how the differences between the two modes affect the processor. If the processor suddenly no longer recognizes such familiar instructions as JMP, PUSH, or MOV in Protected mode, you may be wondering whether the processor then recognizes new instructions. Some programmers also fear that since they are confronted with a different processor, programming concepts used in Real mode no longer apply.

However, this isn't true. Instructions used in Real mode are also used in Protected mode; only a few new instructions have been added. However, the assembly language programmer barely notices many of the instructions. These include memory addressing, such as loading of segment addresses in the segment register, and the creation and coding of FAR pointers within JMP instructions and subroutine calls.

80286 registers

The register complement of the 80286 was expanded from the 8086 instruction set, as shown in the following diagram. Although these new registers are also available to the programmer in Real mode, they have no meaning. Some of the registers, such as GDTR, LDTR, and IDTR, must be loaded before switching to Protected mode, because the system relies on these registers. We'll discuss the meaning of these registers below.

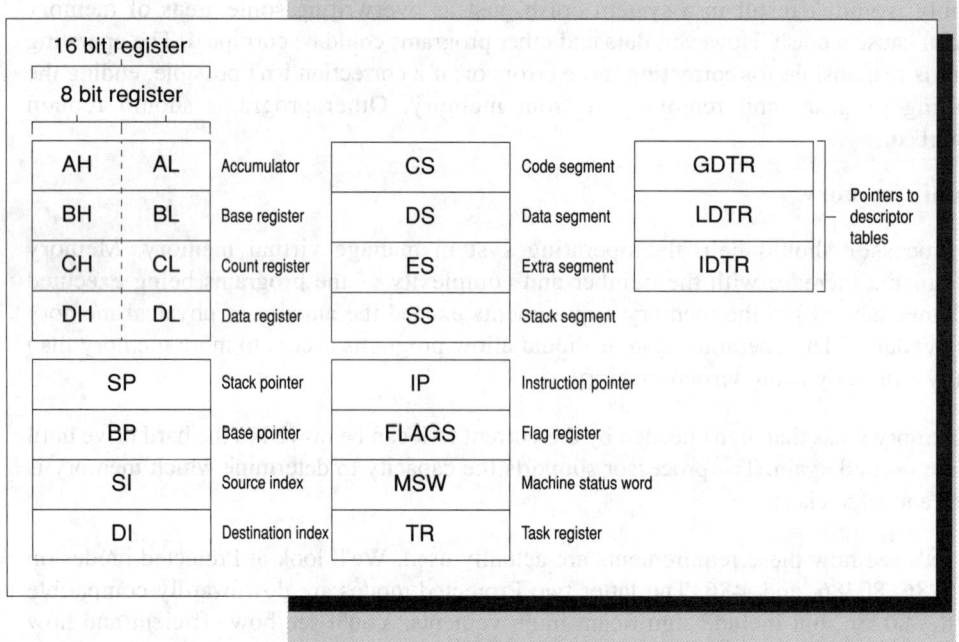

The 80286 registers in Protected mode

The Protected mode uses the flag register in almost the same way as Real mode. Existing flag positions remain unchanged, but Protected mode adds two new flags (IOPL and NT). Both flags are discussed in detail later in this section.

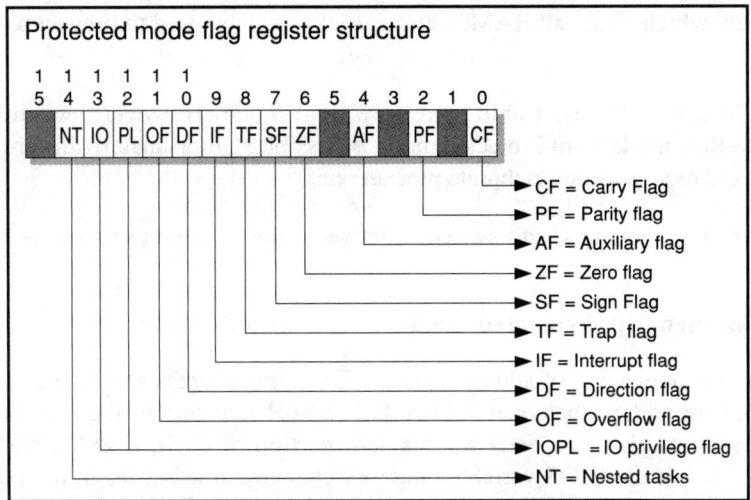

Switching to Protected mode

The machine status word (MSW) is a type of flag register because the individual bits describe the processor status. The 80286 processor uses only the lower four bits of the 16 available bits. Bits 1, 2, and 3 (MP, EM, and TS) support a math coprocessor and aren't important in the context of this chapter.

However, bit 0 (PE) is the key to the Protected mode. When the processor is initialized, this bit is set to 0, which places the processor in Real mode. If a program loads the value 1 into this bit, the processor returns to Protected mode.

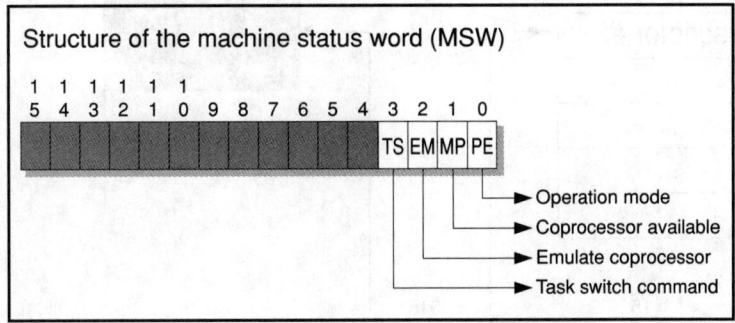

Unfortunately, resetting this bit doesn't automatically return the 80286 to Real mode. Eventually DOS programs, such as DOS extensions or EMS simulators, always reach a point where they must switch back to Real mode, when enables the user to continue working under DOS.

Complicated procedures are needed in order to do this because the 80286 doesn't have an instruction for resetting the PE bit in the machine status word. Usually the ROM-BIOS must be initialized, which clears all RAM. Various tricks must be used to prevent this from happening.

It's unknown why the 80286 isn't able to restore Real mode. However, switching the processor back to Real mode from Protected mode is possible. Unfortunately this process is time-consuming and requires some elaborate precautions.

The task register (TR) manages, and switches between, the various tasks (more on this later).

Memory management in Protected mode

Real mode offers one megabyte of address space. Within this address space, you can load any memory segment address between 0000H and FFFFH into one of the four segment registers. Now, suppose that you enter the resident portion of COMMAND.COM, then delete some variables in the BIOS variable range, or change a few entries in the interrupt vector table. The computer will promptly reset.

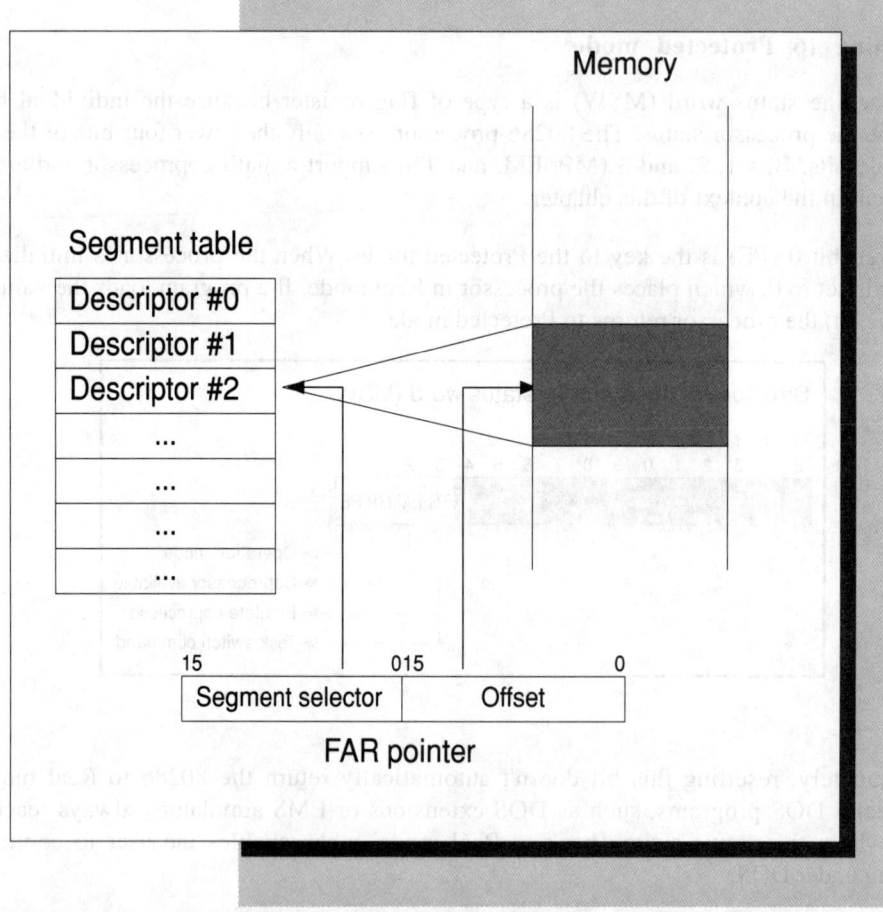

Memory access in Protected mode through segment selector and offset

If you do the same thing in Protected mode, or even load the wrong segment address, the computer reacts differently. Instead of a crash or reset, an *exception* occurs (more on this later). The operating system maintains control of program execution and the offending program ends.

This protection is possible because, even though Protected mode segment addresses contain 16 bits, additional segment addresses aren't created. Instead, segment selectors are used. This results in an index pointing to a segment table describing the various memory segments. This table is similar to a large array of segment descriptors that tells the processor the base address of the segment. The offset address, indicated by the FAR pointer, is added to this address to obtain the address of the memory location in question. Unlike the segment address in Real mode, this base address isn't multiplied. It's possible for memory segments in Protected mode to begin with the memory address desired, not merely at addresses divisible by 16.

The descriptor table in Protected mode provides a link between a virtual address (segment selector:offset) and a linear address (base address comprising the segment descriptor + offset). In the 80286, the linear address and physical address are identical (i.e., the actual memory location to which access is ultimately gained). The 80386 and 80486 addressing is coded to permit the physical address to be determined initially by this new transformation. We'll discuss this in greater detail later.

The above description doesn't show the structure of the segment descriptor within the descriptor table. There is more information stored here than just the starting address of the segment in question. The following chart shows the exact structure of a segment descriptor in Protected mode.

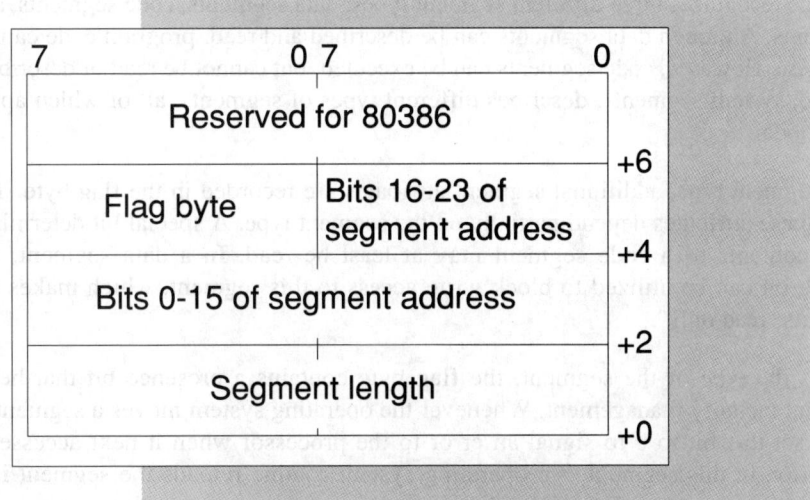

Structure of a segment descriptor

A segment descriptor consists of eight bytes distributed among various fields. The first byte is the segment length. Unlike Real mode, the Protected mode segments don't have to be exactly 64K. The first field in the segment descriptor specifies the length of the segment (between one byte and 64K).

The next three bytes yield the starting address of the segment in memory. The use of three bytes expands the *address width* from the 20 bits of Real mode to 24 bits. This also enlarges the physically addressable memory from 1 megabyte to 16 megabytes.

The fact that the location of a segment is coded in the segment descriptor instead of in the FAR pointers, which provides access to this segment, helps implement an efficient memory management system. The parallel execution of multiple programs is characterized by the continual allocation and release of memory ranges. This causes memory fragmentation. Constantly shifting these memory segments minimizes this fragmentation.

In Real mode, all references to such a segment within the appropriate program must be adjusted. However, in Protected mode, the segment must be displaced and the segment descriptor must be redirected to the new base address. Now it's possible to continue to use the original segment selector in the various references to the segment, even though the segment now resides at an entirely different location in memory.

Following the base address of the segment, within the segment descriptor, is the byte with the various flags that we'll discuss shortly. The last field contains a word reserved for the 80386 and its successors. This field always contains the value 0 for the 80286. This will also be discussed in more detail later in Section 33.1.3 (Mode Programming of the 80386 and i486).

Various segment types

Protected mode recognizes three different segment types: data segments, code segments, and system segments. Although data segments can be described and read, program code cannot be executed here. However, code segments can be executed, but cannot be read or described. The third type, system segments, describes different types of segments, all of which apply to Protected mode.

Besides the segment type, additional segment attributes are recorded in the flag byte. The meanings of these attributes depend partially on the segment type. A special bit determines whether the contents of a code segment may at least be read. In a data segment, the corresponding bit can be utilized to block write access to this segment, which makes the block's contents "read only".

Regardless of the type of the segment, the flag byte contains a presence bit that helps program virtual memory management. Whenever the operating system moves a segment to disk, it must set this bit to 0 to signal an error to the processor when it next accesses a memory location in this segment. An operating system routine reloads the segment into memory before program execution continues.

The access bit is also important. The processor sets this bit to 1 on each segment access. When virtual memory management must decide which segments should be removed from memory because additional room is needed, preference can be given to those segments not recently accessed (those with their access bits set to 0).

Privilege levels

The processor in Protected mode recognizes four different privilege levels for separate programs. These privilege levels specify the execution of various assembly language instructions, and govern access to memory segments. They are designated with numbers 0 through 3 (privilege level 0 is highest, 3 is lowest).

If you only had to distinguish between applications and the operating system, two privilege levels would obviously be sufficient. However, an operating system is usually divided into components that contain different privileges. The highest privileges (level 0) are used by the operating system kernel, which watches over memory management and task switching.

Privilege level 1 is granted to the various operating system services called by programs and operating system utilities. These include file management functions, routines for screen output, and printer control utilities.

Privilege level 2 is reserved for operating system extensions that rely on the system services of privilege level 1. In the OS/2 operating system, these include the SQL server and the LAN manager.

Privilege level 3 is for various programs that run under operating system control. Since these programs execute on a lower privilege level than the operating system, they can be controlled by the operating system (but not vice versa). Privilege level arrangement can be viewed as a series of concentric circles, as presented in the following illustration. The innermost circle, the heart of the system, is the kernel of the operating system. As they proceed outward from privilege 0, the privileges diminish as they approach program and user level.

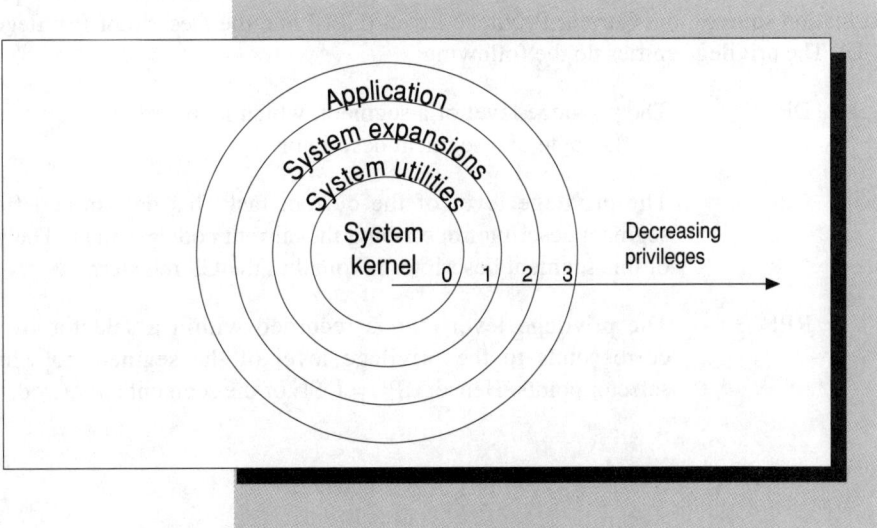

The four privilege levels in the 80286 and its successors

The various privilege levels are important for accessing memory in other segments and transferring program execution to other segments. A program must be prevented from accessing the memory segment of the operating system kernel, or from transferring executions to just any location within another segment without the actual specification of a destination point in a specific routine.

So, the processor compares the privilege levels before accessing memory and signals an error whenever a task tries to access a segment of higher priority. The segment selectors and the segment descriptors contain information on their respective privilege levels.

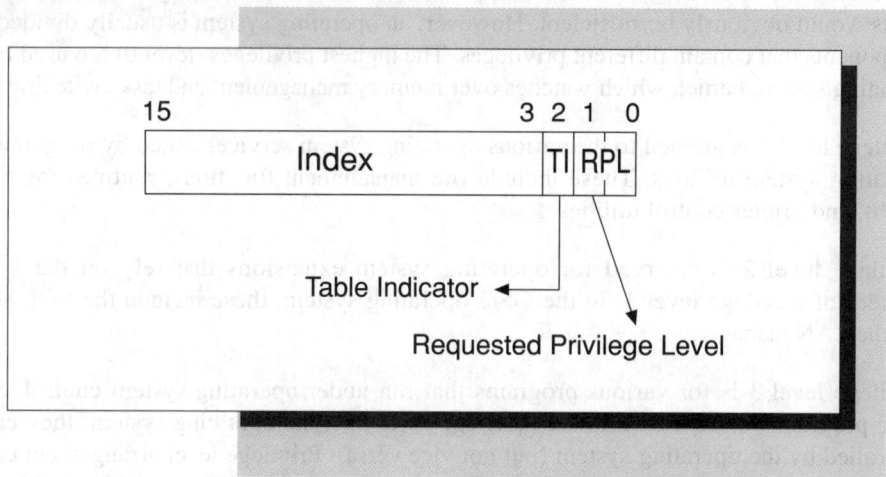

Segment selector structure in Protected Mode

As shown in the above chart, the Requested Privilege Level (RPL) is recorded in the low order two bits of each segment selector. The processor also uses two other privilege information sources, the Current Privilege Level (CPL) and the Descriptor Privilege Level (DPL). The privilege entries do the following:

DPL The privilege level of a segment, which is recorded in bits 5 and 6 in the flag byte of a segment descriptor.

CPL The privilege level of the current task. It's determined from the segment descriptor describing the current code segment. The selector of this segment descriptor is found in the CS register.

RPL The privilege level that is recorded within a selector. It always corresponds to the privilege level of the segment to which the selector points. Hence, RPL = DPL of the segment addressed.

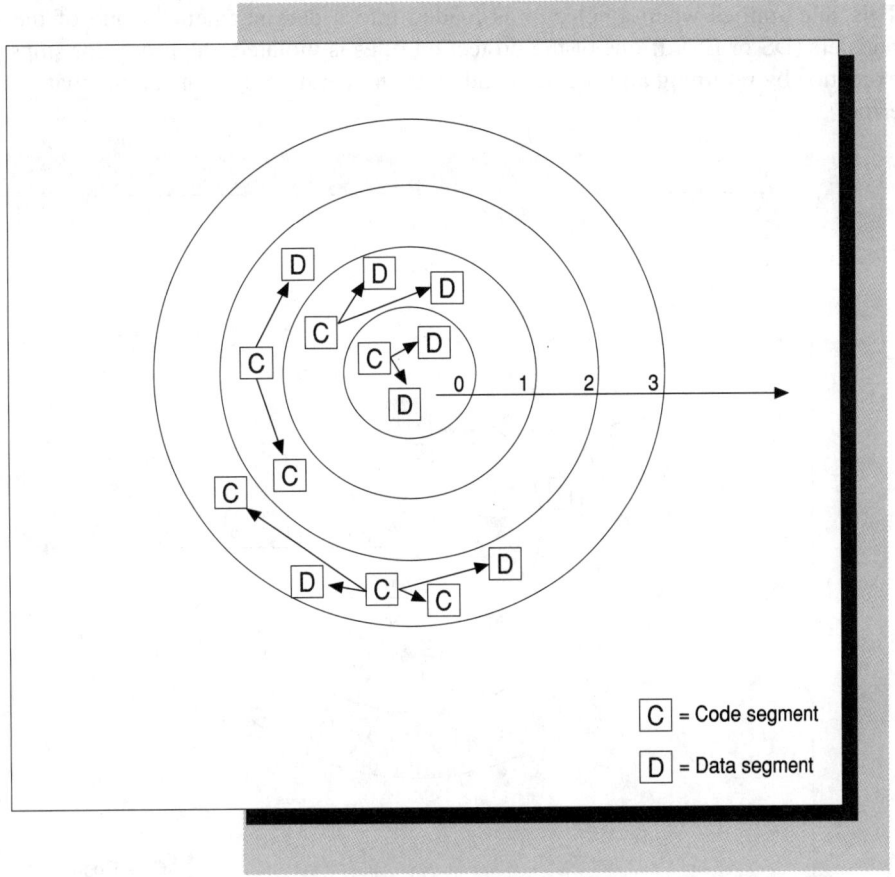

Permissible data and code access

Data and code accesses (jump instructions and subroutine calls) are permissible if:

CPL = DPL

In other words, the current code segment is on the same privilege level as the code or data segment addressed. If the two privilege levels happen to be different, other rules will apply, depending on the type of access that will be used by the processor as the basis for determining the validity of an access attempt.

Data access

For data access, this simple rule applies:

CPL <= DPL,

This means that a task cannot access a data segment on a higher level than itself. It's impossible for an application to access the data segments of the operating system, but the operating system can send data to the application in a buffer.

This rule applies when a selector is loaded into a data segment in one of the segment registers (DS or ES). If one of the protection rules is violated, the processor stops program execution by returning an exception and calls an operating system routine that handles this error.

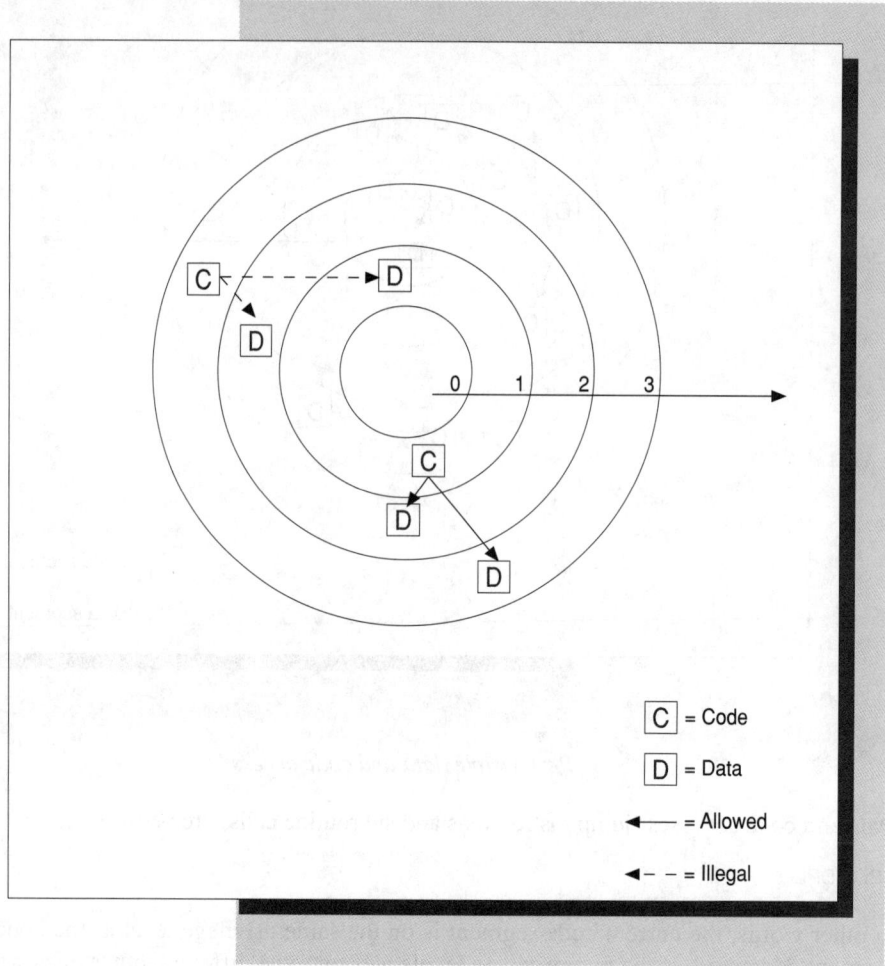

Permissible and impermissible data accesses in Protected mode

Code accesses and gates

The processor is even more restrictive with code accesses, which is the transfer of program execution by a JMP or CALL instruction. These are only permitted if the segment to which the jump is made is on the same privilege level as the caller. This prevents uncontrolled calls to code on another privilege level. You may be wondering how an application can invoke operating system services, which are on a higher privilege level, while it's on a lower privilege level.

The *gates* created especially for this purpose provides a solution to this problem. These are special segment descriptors (system descriptors) that occupy eight bytes like any other descriptor and are located in the descriptor table. But, unlike code and data segment descriptors, they don't define a memory segment. Instead, they define a point of entry into a routine whose code segment can be on a higher privilege level than that of the caller.

This segment is defined in the form of an entirely normal selector within the CALL gate descriptor, which must be an executable code segment. Not only the code segment in question is recorded here, but also the offset (i.e., the point of entry into the desired routine). This makes it impossible to jump to just any address within the code segment. Otherwise, it would be extremely easy to drop into the middle of a routine or an assembler instruction.

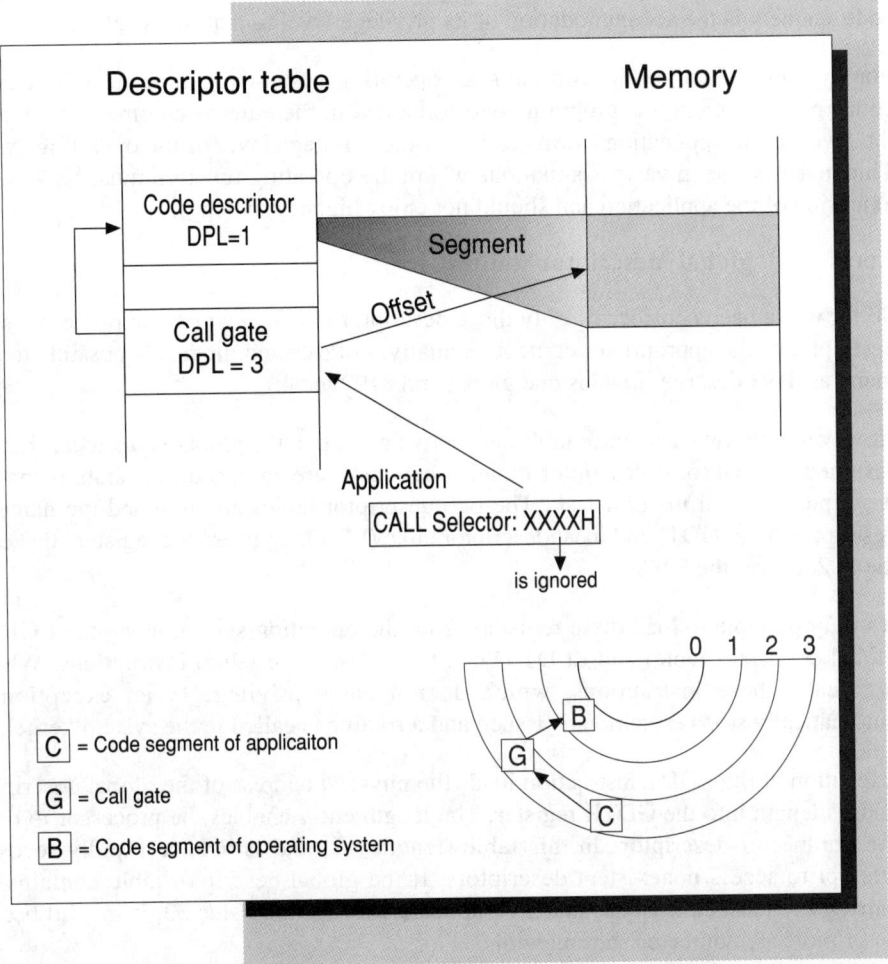

Use of a CALL gate to call an operating system routine

Because the offset address is recorded in the call gate, it loses its significance within the actual CALL instruction and is ignored. Only the selector for access to the call gate is used. However, you must still follow the privilege rules.

In this case, the CALL gate is treated like a data segment and can only be addressed if its DPL carries the same or a lower (numerically higher) level than the caller (CPL <= DPL). So, the operating system must position its CALL gates at level 3 if its use throughout all privilege levels is also to be permitted to applications.

An operating system provides CALL gates to each program so that they can call various system functions. The contents of these CALL gates (the address of the routine called) is unknown to the program, although its segment selector is supplied by the operating system. Another interesting feature is the *conforming segments*. In this case, we're concerned with normal coding segments, which are characterized as conforming segments by a special bit in the flag register of its segment descriptor. A characteristic feature of this code segment is the accommodation of its privilege level to that of its caller.

For example, if an application calls an operating system function, accommodated in a conforming segment, the program code contained in the latter is automatically executed at the level of the application (3) instead of at the privilege level of the operating system (0). This makes sense in various situations where the operating function must be viewed as an extension of the application and should not enjoy higher privileges.

Local and global descriptor tables

So far we've been considering only those descriptor tables in which the processor stores the descriptor of the appropriate segment. Actually, in Protected mode, it's possible to set up as many as 8193 descriptor tables:one global and 8192 local.

However, only two descriptor tables are active at a time: the global and a local. Each task is assigned its own local descriptor table. When tasks are switched, a change is made to the descriptor table of the new task. The two descriptor tables are assigned the names global descriptor table (GDT) and local descriptor table (LDT). They are the registers that expanded the 80286 over the 8086.

It's only possible to load these registers from the operating system using the LGDT (Load global descriptor table) and LLDT (Load local descriptor table) instructions. Whenever a task calls these instructions, which do not carry privilege 0, an exception, which automatically stops execution, is issued and a routine is called in the system kernel.

Execution of the LGDT instruction loads the physical address of the global descriptor table and its length into the GDTR register. The length entry enables the processor to determine the number of descriptors in this table (length / 8) and is able to rapidly recognize an attempt to access nonexistent descriptors. If the global descriptor table contains only 34 entries, each selector, whose index component exceeds the value 33, is invalid because the descriptors are numbered starting with 0.

Whether a selector addresses the global or the local descriptor table is determined by the TI bit. If it contains a 0, the global descriptor is referenced; a one refers to the local descriptor.

Usually an application will access its local descriptor table where the operating system stores the descriptors of all code and data segments of the task in question. However, the CALL gates for calling the operating system functions aren't located here. Storing information about the CALL gates, which can sometimes number into the hundreds, in each local description table would simply take up too much memory.

The global descriptor table contains not only the CALL gates of operating system functions, but also the code and data segment of the operating system, as well as various other system descriptors. Included among these are the descriptors of the memory segments containing the local descriptor tables. Unlike the GDTR register, which contains the physical address of the global descriptor table, the LDTR register contains only one selector that must point to an LDT descriptor in the LDT descriptor table. So, it's very easy to install a new local descriptor table when switching tasks. It's only necessary to load the LDTR register with the selector of the new local descriptor table.

Virtual address space size

When calculating the size of the virtual address space, it's necessary to multiply the maximum number of descriptors by the maximum segment size of 64K. To do this, first you must know the number of descriptors that can fit in the global descriptor table and in the various local descriptor tables. For both tables the size is 8192. There are two reasons for this.

First, local and global descriptor tables affect segments. In the 80286, segments cannot be larger than 64K. It's impossible to store more than 8192 descriptors in 64K because each descriptor occupies 8 bytes.

Also, you cannot address more than 8192 descriptors in the global or local descriptor table because the descriptor number within a selector is coded with only 13 bits. So, only numbers between 0 and 8192 can be accessed.

For example, suppose that the global descriptor table contains 8192 descriptors of local descriptor tables, each of them containing in turn 8192 descriptors of 64K code or data segments. The virtual memory capacity would be:

8192 * 8192 * 64K = 1 gigabyte

which can be addressed (theoretically) only by an efficient virtual memory management system.

Accessing a descriptor

Although the linkage between selectors and descriptors and between the global and local descriptor tables may be complicated, you'll rarely encounter it in application programming. Simply avoid conflict between the selectors.

Essentially, the values used by an application come directly or indirectly from the operating system. An application cannot directly access the local descriptor table or the global descriptor table. Also, it cannot expand this table with new descriptors, or alter existing descriptors. This is solely the task of the operating system kernel, running at privilege level 0. The various instructions needed to manipulate this table can be found at this privilege level.

The operating system also supplies the local descriptor table with the various segment descriptors it needs to receive program code and data when an application is being loaded. 64K segments aren't set up automatically. Only that amount of memory, which is actually required by the segment in question, is released. If the application, because of an application error, seeks access to data or program code beyond the segment end, execution of the program is immediately interrupted by an exception, and an operating system routine is called to handle the error.

Even with the establishment of the various segments and the associated descriptors, reference must be made to these segments within the program, as shown by the following sequence of instructions from an assembler program:

```
MOV AX, segment data
MOV DS, AX
```

In a C program, to transfer a FAR pointer of a function in code segment to a different function, the desired segment selector must be available. In this case, we're concerned with the selector of a code segment, instead of a data segment. The situation in both cases is the same.

In this respect, a multitasking operating system functions almost the same as DOS: The head of the EXE file contains the addresses of the instructions within the program code, or of the variables from the constant data segment within which the various program and data segments are referenced. This table allows the loading function of the operating system to write the selectors of the addressed segments directly into the program code or the variables in question. Operating system calls will probably be handled in the same way, except that a CALL gate selector is required.

Some operating system functions return selectors as function results, especially the functions from the memory management area. These functions can be treated as a component part of a FAR pointer, like normal segment addresses. You can avoid manipulating this presumed segment address, which is frequently required in DOS programming. Manipulating this presumed address could create a selector pointing to an entirely different, or even nonexistent, descriptor.

The RPL field is important to the interaction between the operating system and application selectors. The preceding section indicated that the privilege level of a task is always recorded in the RPL field of a selector by the task in possession of this selector (RPL = CPL).

It's possible to load any value into this field. However, when assigning selectors, the operating system will always enter the privilege level of the respective task into the RPL field of the selector transferred.

If such a selector is later transferred to an operating system function, permitting the latter to access a buffer, the high privilege level of the function shouldn't be used. Instead, this access should be executed at the privilege level of the caller, which prevents the latter from accessing data levels on all four privilege levels via the operating system function.

So, in these instances, the RPL field in the selector is set for the privilege check and points to the privilege level of the caller instead of to the privilege level of the operating system.

Shadow registers

When the various memory segments are addressed using selectors as pointers to segment descriptors (instead of their physical addresses), you can no longer address physical addresses in the segment register, as we demonstrated earlier. The processor must address the respective descriptor in the global or local descriptor table using a segment register selector, and from that determine the position and length of the segment in question. If the processor tried to do this in the case of each instruction, in whose execution one of the segment registers is involved, too much time would be wasted.

The data on the physical address of a segment and its length are loaded, when a segment register is loaded, into a *shadow register*. A shadow register exists for each segment register. Besides the visible 16-bit selector, each of the four segment register contains an additional invisible part that is 48 bits wide. This applies to the GDTR, LDTR, and IDTR registers, but these shadow registers manage different data.

Loading the shadow registers and the associated validity and privilege checks account for slower execution of all instructions affecting the content of the segment registers. For example, only two clock cycles are needed to execute the following instruction in Real mode:

MOV DS, AX

The same instruction line in Protected mode requires 18 clock cycles. This doesn't significantly affect execution speed when these instructions are rarely encountered within an application. However, this usually isn't the case, especially with high level language programs that are compiled using memory models with FAR pointers. For example, in C all memory models except SMALL and TINY use FAR pointers. The restriction of memory segments to 64K frequently makes any other procedure in Real mode impossible.

Aliasing

Data cannot be written into a code segment and the content of a data segment cannot be read by two tasks, whose code segments have different privileges. These are two of the many protection rules designed to ensure that a multitasking operating system runs smoothly.

However, there are other situations, in which these protection rules don't apply. For example, how can the operating system load the program code into an application segment, in which its contents may not be written? How can two tasks on different privilege levels gain access to the same data segment? In these situations, a mechanism known as *aliasing* circumvents the protection rules of the processor.

Although the processor controls access to a memory segment through its descriptor, it cannot prevent several descriptors from being entered in one or more different descriptor tables for the same memory range. So, it's possible that a memory range, which is already identified by a descriptor as a code segment, will be described partially or entirely as a data segment. The second descriptor is called an alias because it permits addressing a range in memory under another "name."

This makes it possible not only to load program code into a data segment, but to solve the problem of common memory usage. You can then set data segment descriptors in the task's LDT to duplicate the privilege level of the task. This duplicate then accesses the data segment using the descriptor.

Aliasing is useful whenever you must bypass the protection mechanisms of the processor. However, it can also cause numerous problems. So, the operating system uses aliases only in very special situations.

Hardware access

You can also restrict hardware access by using I/O ports. The INS and OUTS instructions (80286 extensions of the IN and OUT instructions) can be privileged.

The IOPL (I/O Privilege Level) bits in the flag register are responsible for this privileging. They indicate the privilege level a task must have before the task can execute the named assembler instructions. If both of these bits contain the value 1, only tasks on the 0 and 1 levels of privilege may execute this instruction. If they are executed from levels 2 or 3, the processor launches an exception, which activates an operating system routine.

This mechanism is only useful if the right to alter the contents of the IOPL bits isn't limited to the various applications. Conceding these rights could give applications the power to take over I/O execution themselves. Changing the flag register isn't difficult; simply push the desired contents onto the stack and execute the POPF instruction.

The 80286 developers made slight changes to the way the POPF instruction works. Although the POPF instruction can still be used at all privilege levels for setting the various flags in the flag register, this doesn't apply to the two IOPL bits. POPF changes the IOPL bits only when the calling task is executed on privilege level 0. This prevents normal applications from influencing the IOPL bits.

Task switching

The task register (TR) and the task state segments (TSS) support rapid task switching in Protected mode. These registers control memory ranges and comprise 44 bytes, which store the contents of all processor registers when a task is interrupted.

Also, a pointer to the task state segment of the previously active task is stored. This enables the processor to easily return to this task. As with all memory segments, each task state segment possesses a descriptor, which must be accommodated in the global descriptor table. However, this is a special system descriptor that points to the location and size of its segment like a normal descriptor.

This descriptor is referenced by the TR register, which contains the selector for the descriptor of the current task. In the case of a task switch, the contents of the processor registers can be stored immediately in its task state segment.

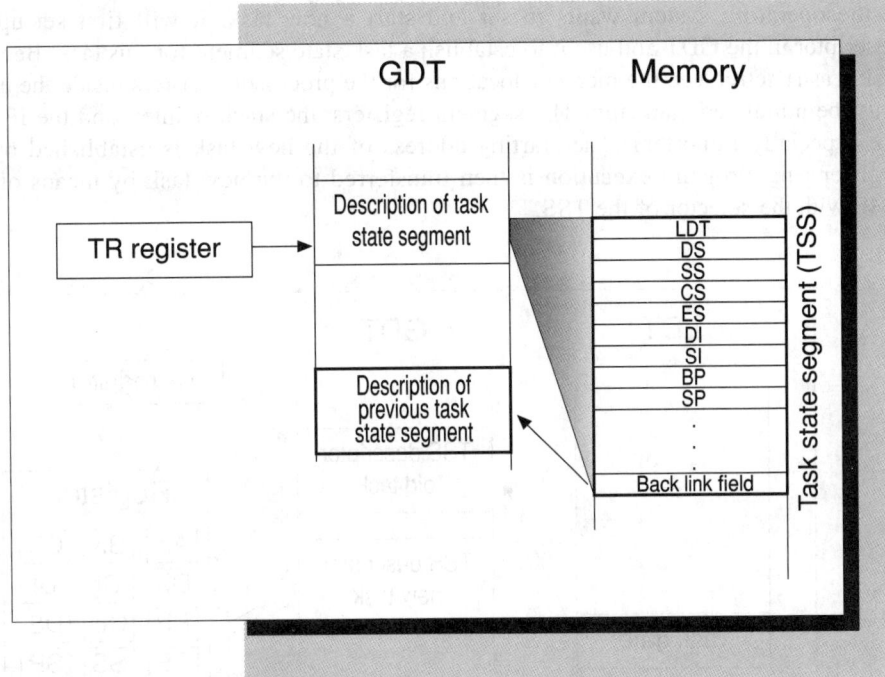

Linking the task register to a task state segment

A task switch can occur in several ways; usually a FAR JMP or FAR CALL instruction is used. In this type of instruction, an offset address must be indicated in addition to a selector. However, only the selector is important for the task switch, which is similar to a function call by using CALL gate. The offset address is essentially ignored.

This selector can be either the selector of a TSS descriptor from the GDT or the selector of a task gate. Similar to the CALL gate already described, such a gate serves as an intermediary and represents a system descriptor that can be accommodated either in the global or one of the local descriptor tables. The only significant data it contains is the selector of the TSS descriptor from the GDT, which identifies the new task.

Following the task gate route, the processor arrives at the required descriptor of the task state segment from the global descriptor table. The task change can be completed with its help; the former contents of the TR register are processed first (i.e., the pointer to the descriptor of the current task state segment).

This segment initially contains the current contents of the processor registers. The TR register is loaded with the TSS selector of the new task. In any case, the former content of the TR register is only stored briefly to permit it to be entered in the back link field of the new task state segment.

The processor contents stored here are loaded from the new task state segment. Because the CS and IP registers are also included among the secured registers, program execution continues at the exact location where the new task was interrupted.

If the operating system wants to set and start a new task, it will first set up a TSS descriptor in the GDT and use it to establish a task state segment for this task. Because the task wasn't active yet, the memory locations for the processor registers inside the new TSS must be initialized manually. The segment registers, the stack pointer, and the IP register are especially important. The starting address of the new task is established by CS:IP register pair. Program execution is then transferred to the new task by means of a FAR JMP with the selector of the TSS.

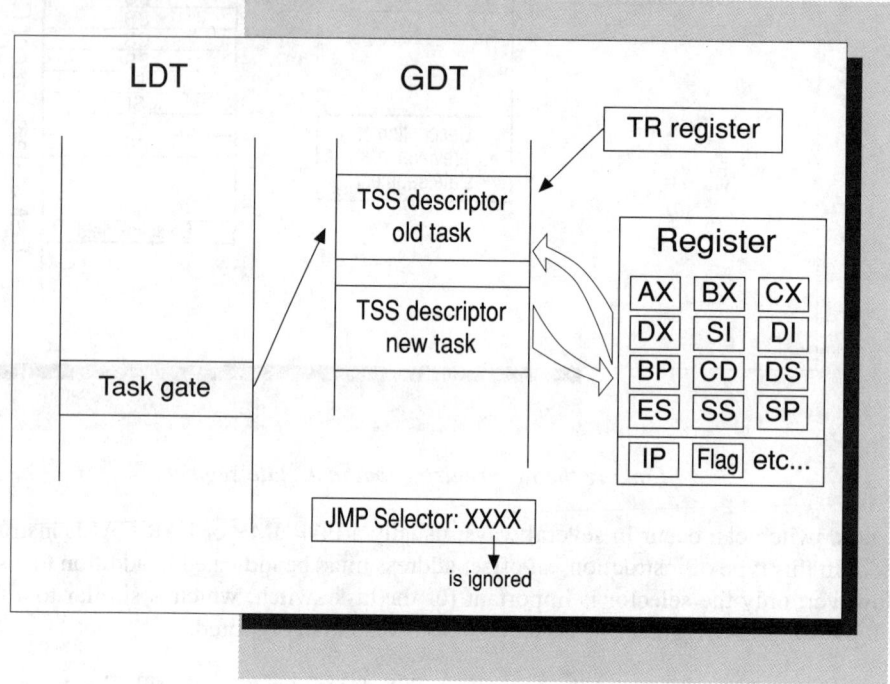

Task switching with a FAR JMP and task gate descriptor

Interrupts and exceptions

Interrupts are handled differently in Protected mode than in Real mode. The processor still recognizes 256 different interrupts, and still interacts between an interrupt and its interrupt handler, but the Real mode interrupt vector table no longer applies.

The solution is the interrupt descriptor table (IDT), which is structured like a global or local descriptor table. Its starting address is stored in physical memory, and its length in the IDTR processor register. Access to this register in Protected mode is reserved for the operating system kernel, and this access executes on privilege level 0.

Unlike Real mode, an application isn't able to influence interrupt execution. This is an important prerequisite for a stable multitasking system. Under DOS, many TSR problems are caused as a result of the free accessibility to the interrupt vector table.

If an interrupt is triggered over the INTR processor line by an external device, or as the result of an INT assembler instruction, the processor enters the interrupt vector as an index into the interrupt descriptor table and reads the corresponding descriptor. This can be either an interrupt or a trap gate, since their structures are very similar. Both contain a selector and an offset address.

The selector serves as the access key to a code segment descriptor in the global or local descriptor table. The processor notifies the code segment containing the interrupt handler for the triggered interrupt. The offset, however, serves as the point of entry into this code segment, thus representing the start address of the interrupt handler within this code segment.

The difference between an interrupt and a trap gate consists of the association with the interrupt flag in the interrupt register. In Real mode, further interrupts usually cannot be called immediately after calling one interrupt, because the processor automatically sets this flag to 0 until returning to the interrupted program.

The processor proceeds in much the same way with an interrupt call through an interrupt gate. However, if it encounters a trap gate, the interrupt flag in the flag register isn't deleted. This makes it possible to trigger additional interrupts even during execution of the interrupt handler.

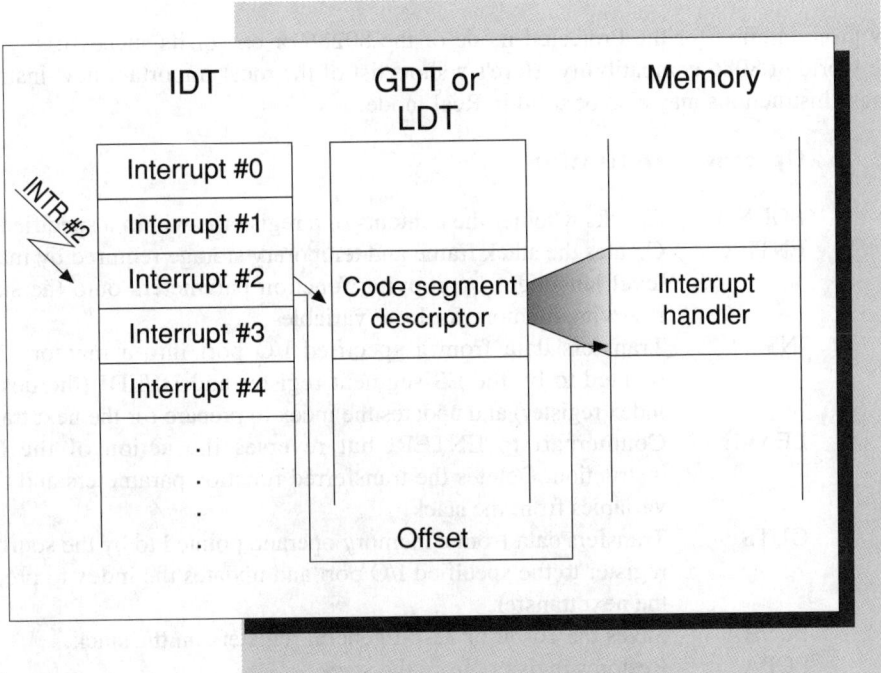

Using the interrupt descriptor table (IDT) to call an interrupt in Protected mode

Exceptions are essentially interrupts, except that they are directly called by the processor if an error occurs during the execution of an instruction. A reason for this could be infringement of privilege rights during access to memory segments or the specification of addresses following the end of the segment in question.

The processor recognizes interrupt requests from the interrupt controller, but only between the execution of two instructions. So, exceptions are triggered in the middle of the execution of a instruction. Once the error has been handled and removed by the exception handler of the operating system, the execution of the program must begin anew. The exceptions of the 80286 control occupy interrupts 0H through 10H. They are shown in the following table. Depending on the exception, the processor pushes data onto the stack before calling the exception handler, which more closely specifies the cause of the exception.

Exceptions in Protected Mode			
No.	Meaning	No.	Meaning
0	Division error	8	Double error
1	Single step	9	Coprocessor segment overflow
2	NMI (memory error)	10	Invalid Task Status Segment
3	Break point	11	Segment not available
4	Break caused by INTO	12	Stack error
5	Break caused by BOUND	13	Invalid segment access
6	Unknown command code	16	Coprocessor error
7	Coprocessor not available		

By programming for the Protected mode of the 80286 or one of its successors, you leave the world of 8086 compatibility. Here's a short list of the most important new instructions. These instructions may also be used in Real mode.

Op code	Definition
BOUND	Checks whether the contents of a register is within a specified range.
ENTER	Creates the stack frame and temporary storage required by many high level languages by copying function parameters onto the stack and reserving memory for local variables.
INS	Transfers data from a specified I/O port into a memory operand pointed to by the ES segment register and DI/EDI (the destination index register) and updates the index to prepare for the next transfer.
LEAVE	Counterpart to ENTER, but reverses the action of the ENTER instruction. Deletes the transferred function parameters and the local variables from the stack.
OUTS	Transfers data from a memory operand pointed to by the source index register to the specified I/O port and updates the index to prepare for the next transfer.
PUSHA	Saves the 16-bit or 32-bit general registers on the stack.
POPA	Restores registers from the stack.

The instructions from the following table aren't suitable for Protected mode programming because you must provide your own operating system services. All these instructions are privileged and may only be executed on privilege level 0. This makes them accessible in Real mode and are treated by the processor like a task with the privilege level 0.

Op code	Definition
ARPL	Checks and tests the privilege level of a code segment.
LAR	Loads the access rights byte of a descriptor.
LGDT	Loads the address and the length of the global descriptor table in the GDT register.
LIDT	Loads the address and the length of the interrupt descriptor into the IDT register.
LLDT	Loads the local descriptor table register.
LMSW	Loads the machine status word from the source operand.
LSL	Load segment limit.
LTR	Loads the task register (TR).
SGDT	Stores the contents of the GDT register.
SIDT	Stores the contents of the IDT register.
SLDT	Stores the contents of the LDT register.
SMSW	Stores the machine status word.
STR	Stores the contents of the task register TR.
VERR	Verifies a segment for reading.
VERW	Verifies a segment for writing.

33.1.3 Protected Mode on the 80386 and i486

Protected mode operation on the 80386 and i486 processors changes only slightly from that of the 80286. However, a few new concepts were included that shouldn't be used by a multitasking operating system. These include the paging of 4K memory blocks (vital to virtual memory management) and locking out individual I/O ports. These extensions are discussed in the following sections.

The Real mode changes are more important in these processors, especially the availability of 32-bit registers and the changes to the instruction set to accommodate the new register width. We'll start with an overview of the 80386 and i486's register complement, and how it affects Protected mode.

The 80386 and i486 registers

The introduction of the 80386 marked the start of the 32-bit processor age. This is evident in the processor's register structure, since most registers have a 32-bit width. The AX, BX, CX, DX, DI, SI, and BP registers are still six bits wide. However, these 16 bits form part of an expanded 32-bit register, representing the low word of the 32-bit register. These 32-bit registers are named EAX, EBX, ECX, etc. The E represents *extended*.

The 8-bit registers (AH, AL, BH, BL, etc.,) are still available, but the upper 16 bits of the E registers cannot be divided into two 8-bit registers. The number of available 8-bit registers remains unchanged, maintaining downward compatibility with the earlier 80xxx chips.

Instructions, such as MOV, SHL, ADD, etc., apply to 8-bit, 16-bit, and 32-bit registers alike. The 80386 and its successors use this to achieve higher speed, especially when processing dwords (long in C and LongInt in Pascal).

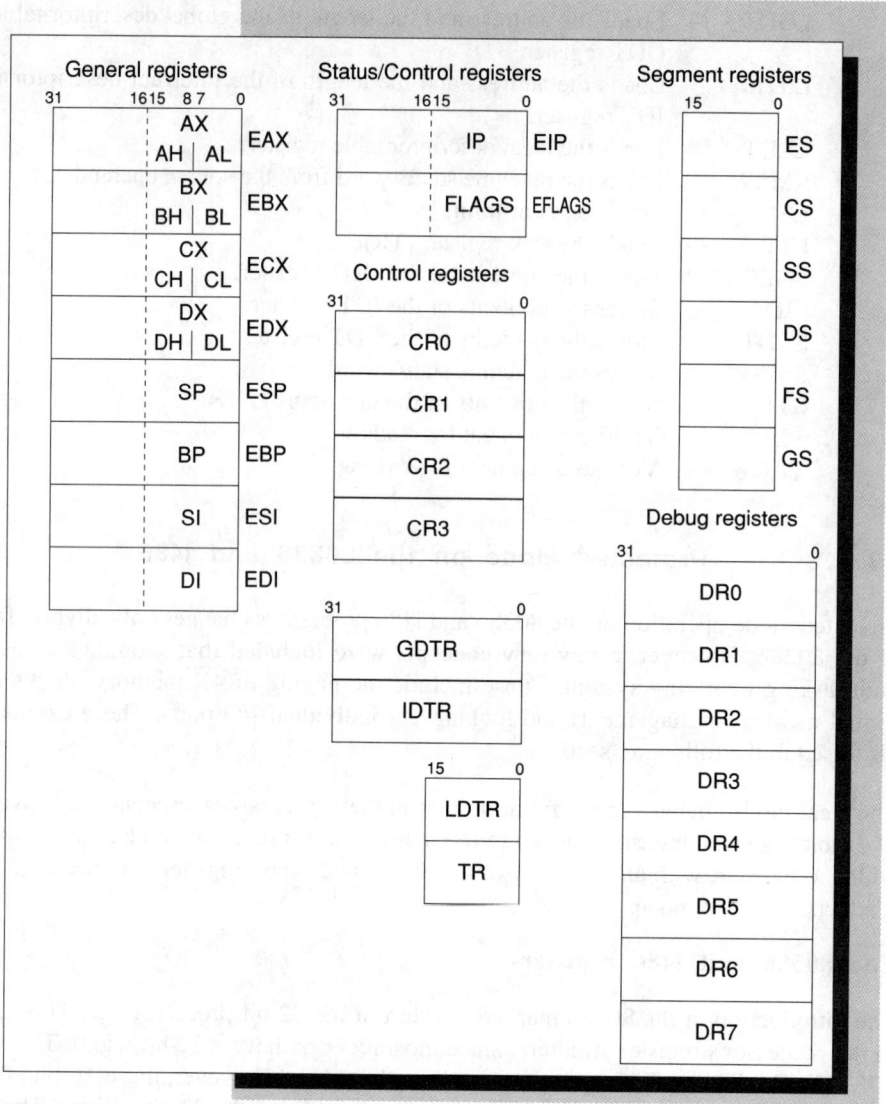

The register complement of the 80386 and i486 (no floating-point registers)

The chart above shows both wider registers than the 80286 and new registers. Notice the FS and GS registers. These two new segment registers can be used for memory access just like the ES register. As before, DS still acts as the default register for accessing data, and CS actsas the default register for program execution.

Like the 80286, the various segment registers in 80386 Real mode mirror the segment addresses of the segments addressed. While in Protected mode, they accept selectors for segment descriptor access from the local or global descriptor table.

The GDTR, LDTR, IDTR, and TR registers, which are used for memory management and task control, also remain the same. These registers can only access the operating system kernel on privilege level 0.

Four 32-bit control registers have been added: CR0, CR1, CR2, and CR3. These control registers are reserved for the operating system kernel (more on this later).

The 80386 includes eight debug registers called DR0 through DR7. These registers allow you to set four different break points that can be triggered at any point in a program (e.g., when execution reaches a specific instruction, when a read access occurs, or when a write access occurs). So, the 80386 presents software debugging options that were only possible with expensive hardware extensions.

Larger segments

The general registers (AX, BX, CX and DX) and the index registers (DI, SI, BP and SP) are all 32-bit registers in the 80386. The segment length was also expanded to 32 bits. This means a segment now has the capacity to hold up to 4 gigabytes (2^{32}), without changing the segment descriptor size from that of the 80286. The Intel developers had reserved a word at the end of the descriptor for the 80286 and its successors.

As you can see, so far the structure of the descriptor in the 80286 is identical to the more advanced 80386 and i486 processors. However, the seventh byte of the descriptor contains an extension of the flag register in the 80386 and i486. The lower four bits are used as bits 16 through 19 of the segment length. This produces a segment length of 20 bits and permits a segment to be expanded to only 1 megabyte, instead of 4 gigabytes, as we stated earlier.

At this point, the *granularity flag* is used. This flag occupies bit 7 of this second flag byte and specifies whether the segment length must be taken as a factor of one byte or 4K (2^{12}). In the latter case, the indicated segment length must be multiplied by 4K, which is equivalent to a shift of 12 bit positions to the left. This expands the segment length, however, to 32 bits, which results in the previously stated maximum length of 4 gigabytes.

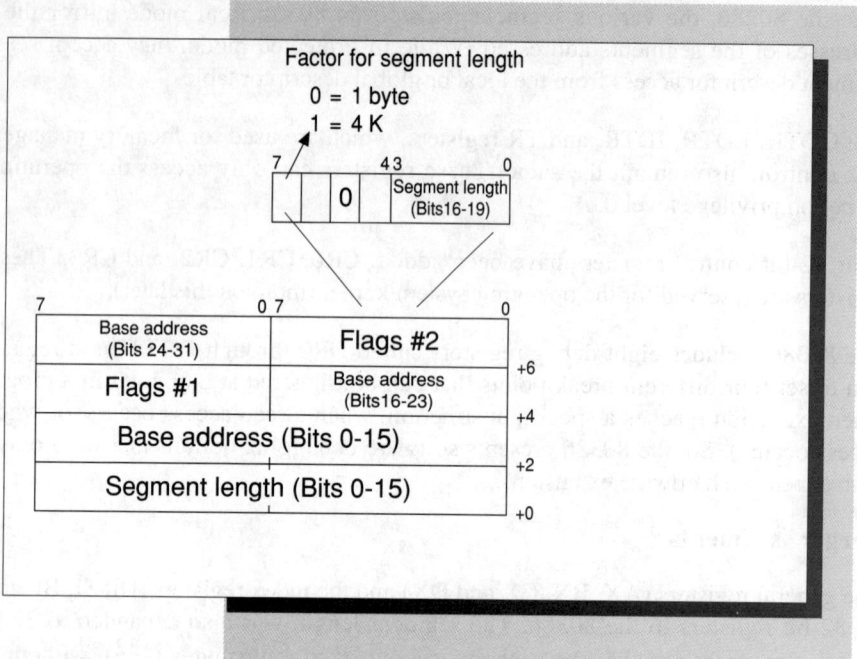

The 80386 and i486 segment descriptors

The segment's base address is expanded to 32 bits. Although the lower 24 bits are found in their traditional locations, bits 24 through 31 are located in the last byte of the descriptor. The 32-bit base addresses and length data extend the linear address space in the 80386 and i486 to 4 gigabytes, and the virtual address space to 64 terabytes (2^{46}).

The 512K memory chips (4 megabits) are becoming more affordable. Eight of these are usually combined into a single inline memory module (or SIMM) with a capacity of 4 megabytes. The 4 gigabyte goal is still off by the factor 2^{10} (1024). Assuming that a new generation of chips is developed every two years, we may not reach this level for another 20 years. This doesn't include trying to develop manufacturing standards. So, there's not much need to widen the address register to 64 bits.

By expanding the offset address to 24 bits, FAR pointers in 80386 and i486 Protected mode contain six bytes instead of four: two for the segment selector and four for the offset address.

Paging and virtual memory management

Virtual memory management can be implemented with the 80286, because each segment descriptor contains a flag indicating the presence of the segment in memory. If the processor encounters a missing segment during processing, it automatically triggers an exception. The operating system interprets the exception as a request to load the segment.

This is the best way to implement virtual memory management. The memory blocks to be moved in and out are always various lengths. They are always complete segments that (in the 80286) can have a length between 1 byte and 64K. However, only a portion of the

1030

segment may be needed, and this segment can be removed in the next instant when another task is executed. In each case, the entire segment must be unloaded, then reloaded. Also, the size of the unloading file (or *swap file*) steadily increases.

Now, imagine that you want the system to unload segment B. However, there's no space left in the swap file because of segment A, which was just reloaded into memory. Fragmentation also occurs in RAM because the various loaded and unloaded segments are different sizes. The virtual memory management continually compresses the memory segments. This occurs transparently, without interfering with the various programs (the segment descriptor changes, instead of the segment selector). This process is still time-consuming.

These problems are solved if the sizes of the blocks to be loaded and unloaded are kept constant, and this process is inserted after the segmentation process. This places it on a lower level and in makes it transparent. The 80386 and its successors implement a paging mechanism to solve this problem. The paging is based on a group of 4K memory blocks. When this mechanism is disabled, the linear addresses resulting from the dissolution of segment selectors and offset addresses represent physical addresses, just as in the 80286, and these addresses can actually be accessed by the processor.

Once paging is enabled, the *page table* models the linear addresses after physical addresses (i.e., the linear addresses are no longer identical to physical addresses). If we view this in executing a single memory access instruction, this slows the execution speed. However, if we think of this as part of a multitasking operating system, the mechanism is very efficient for implementing a virtual memory management system.

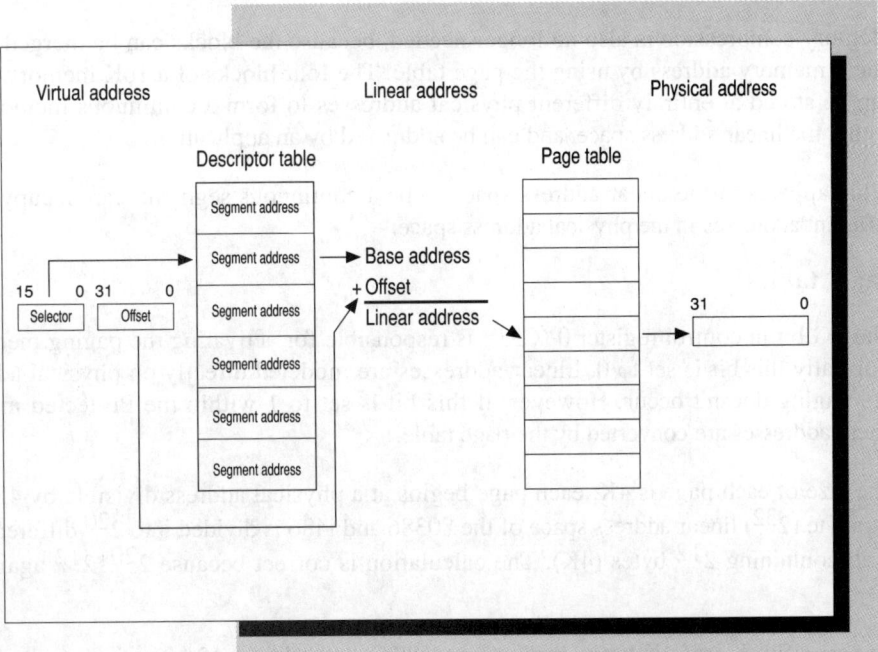

Physical address formation with paging enabled

Using constant memory blocks does more than simply manage the swap file. It also prevents the swap file from continually increasing. Memory can be allocated in 4K pages, instead of the entire 1 gigabyte segment.

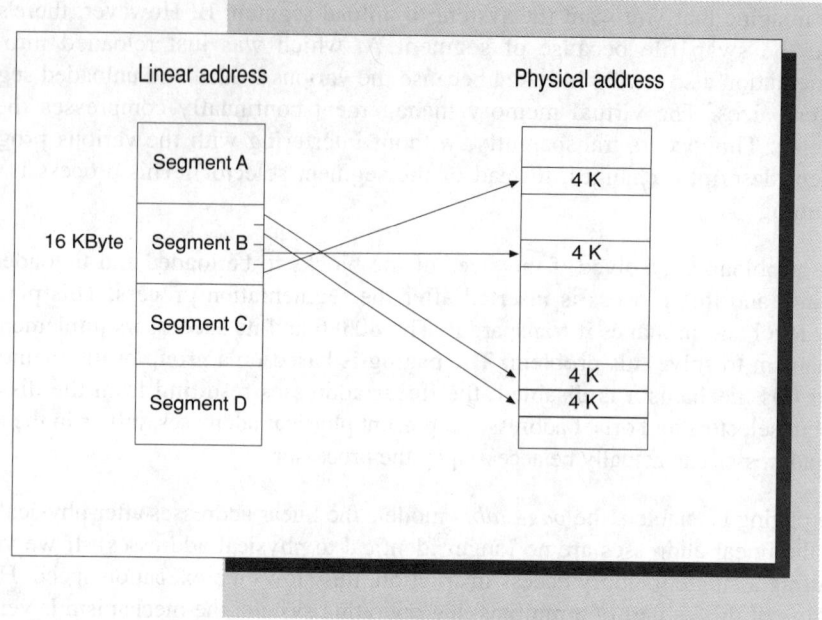

When a segment appears in the linear address space, different addresses can occur

Memory compression is also no longer needed, because the blocks can be merged into any linear memory address by using the page table. The four blocks of a 16K memory segment can be stored at entirely different physical addresses to form a continuous memory block within the linear address space, and can be addressed by an application.

What appears in the linear address space to be a continuous segment, can occupy entirely different addresses in the physical address space.

Page tables

The PG bit in control register 0 (CR0) is responsible for activating the paging mechanism. Normally this bit is set to 0. Linear addresses are modeled directly on physical addresses. So, paging doesn't occur. However, if this bit is set to 1 within the Protected mode, the linear addresses are converted by the page table.

The size of each page is 4K; each page begins at a physical address divisible by 4K. The 4 gigabyte (2^{32}) linear address space of the 80386 and i486 is divided into 2^{20} different pages, each containing 2^{12} bytes (4K). The calculation is correct because $2^{20}*2^{12}$ again yields 2^{32}.

The specification of 4K limits makes it possible for the lower 12 bits of a linear address to be incorporated directly into the physical address. They represent a type of offset in the respective page. The upper 20 bits of the linear address indicates the number of the page containing the memory location addressed. They are considered to be an index in the page table, from which the physical base index of the respective page can be taken.

The entries in the page table are respectively 32 bits wide. Only 20 bits are actually needed for the base address, which must begin at a physical memory location divisible by 4K. The lower 12 bits is 0 in each case. The lower 12 bits contain various flags for the virtual memory management system. For example, the flags indicate whether the page is currently present in memory or must first be loaded from the swap file.

Only the upper 20 bits from the page table entry are used to form the physical address. They are complemented by the 12 lower bits of the linear address, which are used unchanged.

Actually, the entire process is more complicated. The page table with its 2^{20} entries of four bytes each would otherwise use the entire four megabytes. This would mean throwing away several megabytes of valuable memory since only 1024 entries and 4K of memory are actually required for the page table with four megabytes of RAM installed.

An entry in the page table must be made available to the processor for each page in the linear address space. This considers instances, in which a false address is swapped into a segment descriptor, which results in the formation of a linear address, for which no entry was established in the page table. However, this can't be recognized by the processor. Unlike the global and local descriptor table, no length data is recorded for the page table.

The processor will read the presumed page table entry, although the corresponding memory location will contain an arbitrary data or code segment. The processor will then create one or more random physical addresses.

Dividing the page table

The page table is divided into two stages. The *page directory* handles several smaller page tables. As the following illustration shows, the upper 10 bits of the linear address constitute the index in the page directory, which consists of 1024 entries. Since each entry contains 32 bits, this table uses 4K of memory.

The individual entries are pointers to the addresses of the various page tables in the physical address space. This is where the processor first learns the address of a page. The entry number used in the respective page table for calculating the address is produced from bits 12 through 21 of the linear address, and is divided into two parts: a 10-bit index for the page directory and a 10-bit index for the page table in question. The page directory and each page table contains the addresses of 1024 pages and occupies 4K of memory.

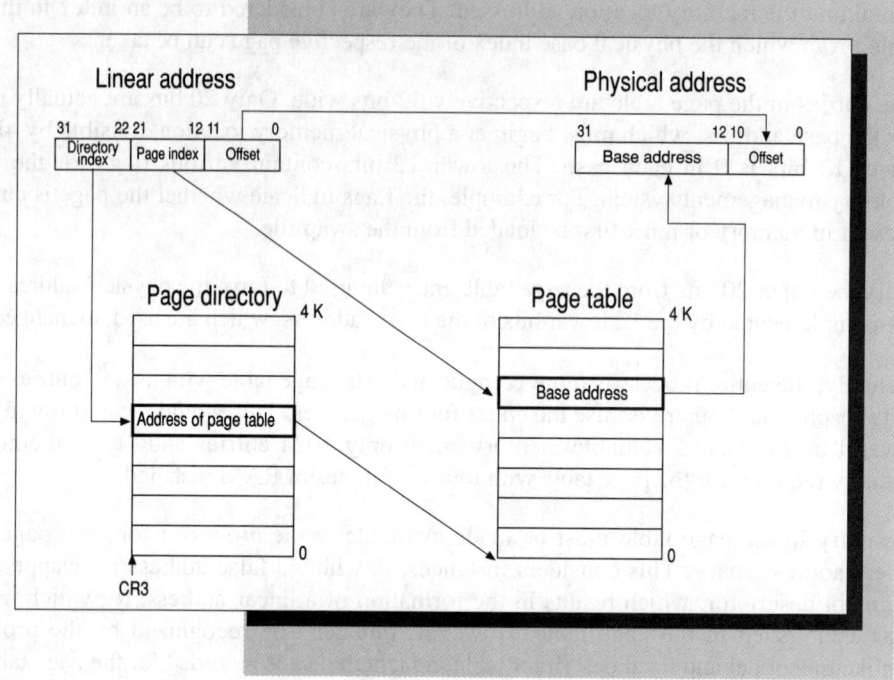

Converting a linear address using the page table structure

Because of the page table structure, each entry within the page directory occupies a four megabyte range within the linear address space. The advantage of this is that during initialization of the operating system only a page directory and a page table, to control the first four megabytes of memory, must be established. In the beginning more than four megabytes isn't required.

The operating system consistently divides this memory sequentially, instead of arbitrarily throughout the linear address space. The total assigned memory appears in the first four megabytes, controlled by the page table indicated by the first entry in the page directory. All other entries in the page directory can initially be marked invalid by setting special flags in the lower 20 bits. Setting these special flags instructs the processor to trigger exceptions (more on this later).

Once memory requirements exceed the four megabyte limit, the system must create a new page table, and store its address in the second entry of the page directory. For every four megabytes of memory, only 4K is needed in the page table, which is less than the four megabytes in a continuous page table for all the pages in the linear address space.

The page directory's address must be passed to the processor, along with the addresses of the page tables. The CR3 register contains the physical address of this data structure.

The CR2 register plays a subordinate role in the paging mechanism. When a paging error triggers an exception, the processor places the address to be converted in the CR2 register.

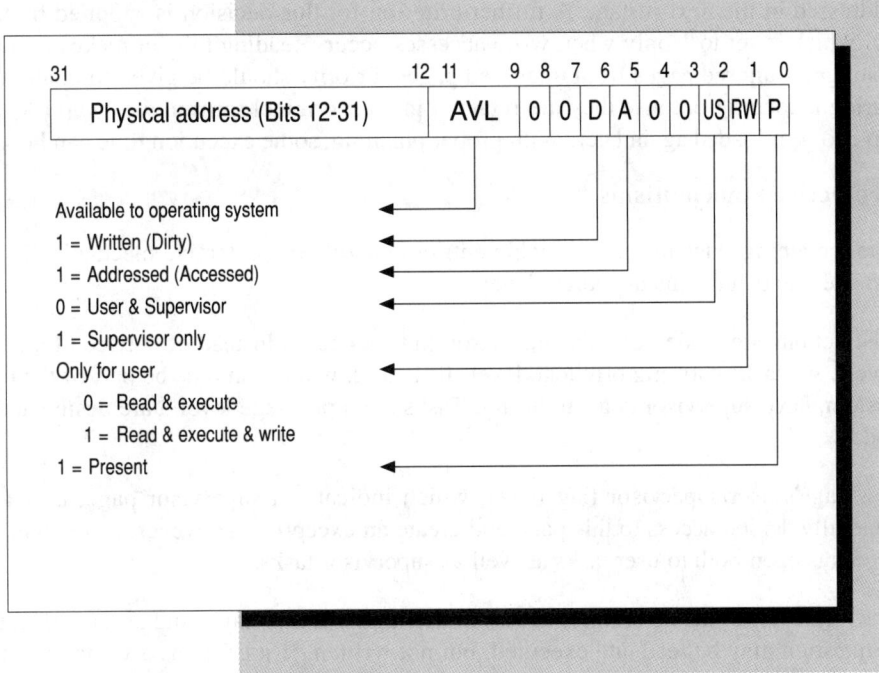

Structure of a page table entry

Page unloading strategies

The virtual memory management system performs its duties by using various flags in the lower 20 bits of the page table entries. The Present flag (bit zero of the page table entry) must be set to 0 by the operating system if a page was unloaded. The processor then triggers an exception when this page is accessed, enabling the operating system to take control of program execution and load the page. The Present flag must then be reset to 1, or the processor will again cause an exception on the next access.

The Dirty bit and the Accessed bit are also useful in virtual memory management. The Accessed bit is automatically set to 1 by the processor before accessing the page of a page table entry. This flag is even set to 1 if only one of the total of 1024 pages in a directory entry is addressed.

Because this flag is set only to 1 by the processor, and never to 0, the virtual memory management system can use it for marking addressed pages. It must set this bit to 0 after loading, or after establishing a page. The Accessed bit can then be used to test whether this page was already addressed.

This information is very helpful when space in physical memory is limited, which making it necessary to shift pages into the swap file. Then it's possible to give priority to recently addressed and immediately needed pages.

There are also reasons why the pages just addressed should be unloaded. Supporters of this theory argue that these pages were already in the queue, while the others are only to be addressed in the next instant. A further criterion for this decision is supplied by the Dirty bit, which is set to 1 only when write accesses occur. Reading this bit makes it possible to distinguish altered pages from unaltered pages. Priority should be given to unaltered pages during unloading because they are retained in their original form in the swap file, and will have to be reloaded again later. With proper planning, some execution time can be saved.

Protective mechanisms

The remaining flags in the page table entries constitute a protective mechanism, similar to the one found at the linear address level.

Distinctions are made between supervisor and user code, instead of between four privilege levels. All tasks carrying privilege levels 0, 1, or 2, which can thus be part of the operating system, have supervisor code authority. Tasks from privilege level 3 are designated as user codes.

If a page's user/supervisor flag is set, which indicates a supervisor page, user tasks are generally denied access to this page and create an exception. However, if this flag isn't set, access is open both to user tasks as well as supervisor tasks.

The Read/Write flag determines access to user tasks. If this flag contains a 0 value, the page in question may be read and executed, but not written. If it contains a value of 1, the page allows writing. Errors generate exceptions in this case also.

Converting a linear address into a physical address is time-consuming, particularly when loading page tables from memory. The 80386 and its successors have a built-in cache to store the page table entries that were just loaded. This cache is frequently called a *translation lookaside buffer* (TLB). In the 80386 and i486, this buffer stores the last 32 page table entries. Although only 120K are covered, Intel maintains that this cache is 98% effective.

Although this cache may be very helpful for the conversion rate, like all caches it has problems. These problems will most likely occur if a page table entry's contents change in memory, but the change isn't reflected in the cache.

In the 80386 and its successors, software must maintain the integrity of the translation lookaside buffers. The processor doesn't handle this task. However, the processor does provide a simple mechanism that can help the cache contents up to the point where they can be declared invalid, which allows the individual entries to be gradually reloaded into the cache. This consists of loading the CR3 register with the starting address of the page directory. Its starting address is changed, the cache is declared invalid, and the CR3 register is reloaded:

```
MOV AX,CR3
MOV CR3,AX
```

This keeps the translation lookaside buffer clear. However, the paging mechanism shouldn't be used globally for all tasks. Instead, it should only be switched on for individual tasks and suppressed for others. It's possible to set or delete the paging flag in the CR0 register or even load the CR3 directory with the start address of a page directory (or of several page directories) with each task switch.

Selective I/O port blocking

The 80386 and its successors have a slightly different approach than the 80286 for determining whether an I/O port may be addressed by a task.

Although only the IOPL flag in the flag register and the privilege level of the task in question count in the 80286, it's now possible to set up an I/O permission bitmap in the task state segment of a task. This bitmap is a large bit array with up to 2^{16} entries. Provisions are made for all 65536 possible ports to be tested as a group, to determine whether a basic access without reference to privilege level will be possible, or whether a test via the IOPL flag should occur. The value 0 indicates free access; 1 represents the IOPL test.

The starting offset within the task page segment isn't fixed, but can be selected by the operating system. It must be specified at offset address 66H in the task state segment, which, in the 80386, has grown to at least 102 bytes because of the expanded processor registers.

From this starting address and the length of the task state segment stored in the descriptor, the processor determines the size of the bit array. The ports, which are no longer covered by the bit array, are subject to the IOPL test.

If the offset address of the bit array is larger than or equal to the segment length, there won't be a bit array and the IOPL test is executed. If more room is left between the offset address and the segment length than the maximum length of 8K, all ports will be covered by the array. If none of these conditions are met, the interval between the end of the task state segment and the start of the bit array is calculated and this value is multiplied by 8 to determine the number of ports represented in it.

More flexible addressing modes

The types of addressing were also significantly expanded with the introduction of the 80386. All general registers are viewed as base and index registers, both in Real mode and Protected mode, instead of only certain combinations of the SI, DI, and BP registers. Also, it's possible to multiply an index register by a factor of 2, 4, or 8 to permit rapid access to word, dword, or qword arrays. A constant 8-bit or 32-bit offset can be added, as the following illustration shows:

The addressing modes of the 80386 and its successors

The 80386 and i486 processors include the ability to accommodate data and variables, according to their size in memory, to word, dword, or qword limits. Otherwise, access will last significantly longer because several read and write accesses are needed to compose the operands.

New instructions

As with the 80286, the 80386 was also extended by a few instructions or operation modes for instructions already familiar to programmers. These changes are for non-privileged instructions. System instructions on the 0 privilege level don't have any changes.

The following table provides an overview of the new options hidden in the 80386 instruction set:

BT,BTC,BTR,BTS

Instructions for testing and setting bits in registers and variables.

BSF,BSR   Instructions for scanning bits in registers and variables.

LSS,LFS,LGS

Loads one of the segment registers: SS, FS, or GS.

Jxx 32-bit

Conditional jump instruction (JC, JA, JBE, etc.) with 32-bit displacement.

MOVSX,MOVZX
> MOV instruction with automatic expansion of the prefix or setting the remainder register to 0.

MOV DRx,Reg
> Load one of the debug registers.

MOV Reg,DRx
> Load a register with one of the debug registers.

MOV CRx,Reg
> Load the control register.

MOV Reg,CRx
> Loads a registers with the control register.

SHRD,SHLD
> Shifts DWORDS left or right.

SETxx
> Loads one of the various 8-bit registers with an indicated value, if the condition of the instruction is met. Functions like a combination of CMP, Jxx, and MOV.

33.1.4   Virtual-86 Mode

Virtual-86 (V86) mode was created as a compromise between Real mode and Protected mode. Many EMS emulators (e.g., Microsoft Corporation's EMM386.SYS) and multitasking environments (e.g., DesqView/386) use V86.

When a system operates in V86 mode, the computer is running in Real mode, while retaining the background memory management, task management, and privilege rules found in Protected mode. When you run a program in V86 mode, it runs like an independent V86 task, while the Protected mode mechanisms remain hidden. The program sees only its one megabyte address space, which is addressed according to the standard rules of Real mode:

segment_address * 16 + offset_address

From the V86 task's point of view, we're concerned with ordinary segment addresses instead of selectors, as in Protected mode. A program can load any value into one of the segment registers without having to worry about an exception occurring.

The processor issues an exception for a V86 task if it uses one of the 80386's 32-bit address modes to generate an offset address outside the 64K segment limit. All the 80386 and i486 address types are available for a V86 task, including the use of 32-bit registers and offsets, with segments larger than 64K as the exception.

V86 mode is used for executing normal DOS programs that rarely access the expanded capabilities of the 80386 and its successors.

Only linear addresses exist in V86 mode because of the lack of selectors or descriptor tables. So, the one megabyte address space of a task is patterned after the first megabyte of physical RAM, as long as paging is disabled. If paging is enabled, it's possible for the address space of a V86 task to accommodate itself using the page directory and the necessary page table in any range in physical memory.

While a task is executed in V86 mode, it's possible for other tasks to be active not only in V86 mode. Protected mode is available both in the 80286 compatible 16-bit version, and in the 32-bit version of the 80386 and i486. These modes are generally used by a virtual control monitor, which controls the execution of the DOS program in V86 mode in the background, giving it the feel of a normal DOS machine. In the subsections on EMS emulators and multitaskers, we'll discuss how this occurs.

Protected mode also handles the interrupts and exceptions triggered by a V86 task. The processor switches to Protected mode and the interrupt or exception handlers are called using the associated gate in the interrupt descriptor table. The V86 task isn't responsible for the initialization of this table and preparing the interrupt and exception handlers. This is controlled by the virtual control monitor running the task.

Switching to V86 mode

There are several ways to switch from Protected mode to the V86 mode with the 80386 and its successors. The most common method is task switching through a task gate. The operating mode, in which the new task is executed, is controlled by the VM flag from the EFLAGS register, which is loaded from the task gate segment of the new task during the task change. If this flag is set, the program runs in V86 mode. If the flag isn't set, normal Protected mode is used.

Earlier we described how a new task can be "launched" by generating a task state segment, using an associated task gate and its call. In V86 mode, you can simply initialize the VM flag within the task state segment with a 1 to begin task execution in V86 mode.

V86 tasks always run on the lowest privilege level (3). All instructions with any sort of influence on the content of the interrupt or VM flags within the EFLAGS register (PUSHF, POPF, INIT, IRET, CLI and STI) are subject to the IOPL test and may be executed only if a value of 3 is in the IOPL flag. This prevents V86 tasks from acquiring the capacity to switch into Protected mode.

It's also possible to control changes in the interrupt flag. DOS programs have a tendency to delete this flag for a certain time interval in order to suppress INTR requests. This usually isn't a good practice for a virtual control monitor. During the time the INTR request is suppressed, interrupt requests for other tasks get backed up and cannot be processed quickly enough.

Exceptions are generally triggered from the IOPL for all attempts to access the EFLAGS register. Changes to the addressed flags are prevented.

Permanently calling these exception handlers slows down program execution. It's recommended that "safe" DOS programs be supplied with IOPL 3. In V86 mode, the instructions IN, OUT, INS, and OUTS aren't privileged, as they are in Protected mode.

Before executing such an instruction, the processor requests the I/O permission bitmap from the task state segment of the task in question to selectively block or release individual ports. Accessing a blocked port generates an exception and the virtual control monitor gains control of program execution. This gives it the ability to virtualize certain ports. We'll look at this process in more detail in the section on multitaskers.

As you can see, V86 mode supplies the means for executing DOS programs, even in multitasking operations. The following section explains how this is done.

33.2 Protected Mode Utilities

The V86 mode, which we described in the previous section, is mainly suitable for developing Protected mode DOS utilities. It's possible to develop a monitor program that runs in Protected mode, but controls one (or more) virtual machines in V86 mode. This provides DOS with an "assistant", which controls all the steps without being noticeable. The following two sections show what happens when V86 mode is combined with DOS.

33.2.1   EMS Emulators and Memory Management Programs

There are EMS (Expanded Memory Specification) simulators for systems ranging from the 8086 to the i486. These simulators are responsible for making expanded memory available according to the LIM (Lotus-Intel-Microsoft) specification. The various types of EMS emulators operate according to different principles, depending on the Intel processor for which they were designed.

The prerequisites for these utilities and their effectiveness have improved with each generation of processor. All of these utilities make the LIM specification available, but often the EMS memory is still inaccessible.

Using an EMS emulator is hardly worthwhile for 8086 processors because it utilizes the available EMS memory on a hard drive file and also unloads there. This process is too time-consuming. The EMS window, with its 64K, must be located in RAM below the 640K limit (conventional memory). This means that you'll lose valuable main memory. EMS emulators for the 8086 aren't very useful.

However, there's a difference when considering the 80286. Although it's possible to take the simulated EMS memory from the hard drive, you shouldn't do this. Instead, you should use the extended memory above the 1 megabyte limit. This memory area is available on almost any AT. The EMS emulator uses this as expanded memory by copying memory from extended memory into the EMS page frame with a special BIOS function.

In any case, you must locate the page frame below the 640K limit. When EMS memory is frequently used, you should install an EMS expansion card, even in 80286 computers. However, many ATs (especially those with the NEAT BIOS chip set) can configure extended memory as expanded memory.

The introduction of the 80386 finally permitted EMS emulators to achieve a significant breakthrough. Various performance characteristics of this processor were designed specifically for EMS emulators. The basis for making expanded memory available is the extended memory above the 1 megabyte limit. However, unlike the 80286, in this case, the memory doesn't have to be copied into a page frame.

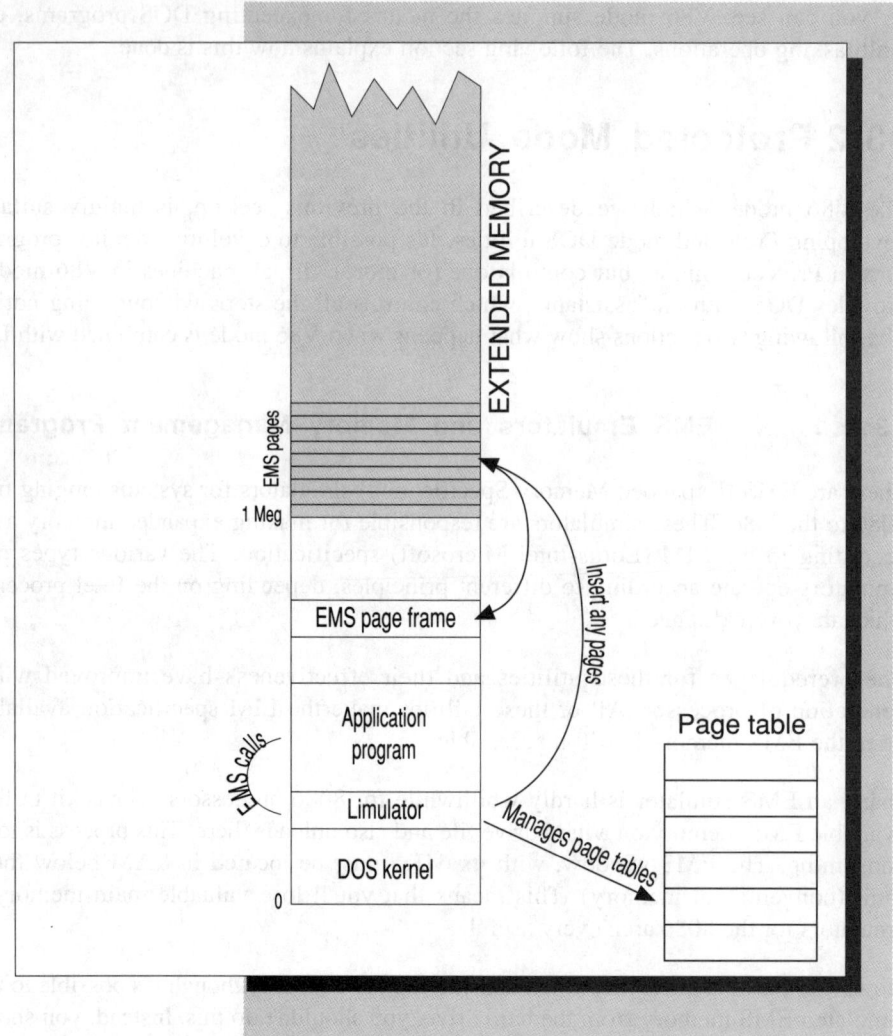

EMS emulator operation in the 80386 and its successors

The 80386 and its successors provide an efficient paging method. This method makes it easy to model extended memory in the EMS page frame and use the area between 640K and 1 megabyte, even when physical memory doesn't exist there. That's how efficient memory management programs like 386-To-The-Max, QEMM386, and EMM386 perform this task.

However, one small problem remains. In Real mode, from which DOS programs request and use EMS memory, you cannot use 80386 paging. You must use the V86 mode, which means that the EMS emulator must be switched into V86 mode at the very start, then continue in the background as the virtual control monitor. We'll discuss this in more detail in the section on multitaskers.

Memory management programs

Memory management programs, such as 386-To-The-Max or QEMM386, generally make access to extended memory available for EMS emulators and the XMS (eXtended Memory Specification) interface. They also provide an option for loading TSR programs, device drivers, and parts of DOS above the 640K limit, which creates more space in conventional RAM. These programs and drivers are loaded, using the page table, into memory ranges between the 640K and the 1 gigabyte limits, without actually being present there.

The main trick is to determine which parts of this memory range are unused by hardware or other software, rather than to program the page tables.

33.2.2   Multitaskers

Recently PCs have reached the performance levels of mainframe workstations. Because of this, many DOS users are demanding more advanced features, especially multitasking. Actually, many users are more concerned with being able to switch back and forth between programs, than with multitasking.

Programs that make task switching possible are available for all types of PCs. One of the most popular programs is DesqView from Quarterdeck. However, the Task Swapper available in the DOS 5.0 Shell has been giving DesqView some competition.

DesqView/386 and Windows 3 bring true multitasking to the DOS world. Both systems permit parallel execution of multiple DOS programs and can display output in separate screen windows.

These multitaskers, which are a type of operating system that's grafted onto DOS, can run other operating systems besides DOS.

Since this book is about system programming, we won't discuss these systems in detail. Instead, we'll examine a system programming problem called "hardware virtualizing". The V86 mode has been extremely important to the solution to this problem.

Virtualizing hardware presents the illusion of an independent PC to any program executed in a multitasking environment. DOS programs are inhospitable to other programs, writing directly to video RAM or programming the interrupt controller to reserve all available memory for themselves.

Hardware virtualization

The screen is one example of the basic problems that can occur in multitasking. Usually, each DOS program can assume that it can access the entire 80x25 text screen. However, multitasking provides a window smaller than the screen for each program. The multitasker places the output from each program into a buffer and displays a part of the buffer in the window assigned to the respective program.

To display all program output, the multitasker shifts the window contents. This displays other parts of the virtual screen. The virtual screen may also be expanded to use the entire physical screen, similar to Windows.

Intercepting video RAM access

Now that we know what happens from the user's perspective, let's see what goes on behind the scenes and how the multitasker handles the output from different programs.

Problems shouldn't occur as long as the program sends output to the screen using ROM-BIOS video functions. The multitasker simply redirects the ROM-BIOS video interrupt to its own function. The multitasker's function stores the characters in the virtual screen (the internal buffer mentioned above), instead of writing the characters directly to the screen. The multitasker then passes the characters to the respective program window.

The functions in the multitasker handler intercept DOS video functions and high level language commands, such as PRINT, printf(), and WriteLn(), as well as ROM-BIOS functions.

Suppose that the program doesn't support any of these options, and directly accesses video RAM (like most DOS based applications). Systems based on the 8086/8088 or 80286 processors can't be used because they don't provide an option for direct memory access. However, the V86 mode's paging mechanism allows you to control the memory access in 80386 and higher processors.

You may remember from the section on the 80386's paging mechanism that the linear address space is modeled on the physical address space using the page table. This page table is vital to the multitasker. All DOS applications must be given the illusion that they're operating in the first megabyte of memory, regardless of their physical locations in memory.

The paging mechanism also contributes to virtual screen management. The Present bit is part of this virtual management. This bit is part of the flag saved with each entry in one of the page tables.

If the Present bit is unset during page access, the processor assumes that the page currently doesn't exist in memory. An exception, which passes program control to the operating system, occurs. After program control is redirected, the page loads. The exception call occurs regardless of whether virtual memory is implemented.

A multitasker takes advantage of the exception by marking the pages, which correspond to video RAM, as not present. Each video RAM access calls the exception routine of the multitasker, which stores the video RAM access. The multitasker then places the byte (or word) to be displayed in the appropriate program's virtual screen for later display.

Actually, this procedure saves us from having to redirect the video BIOS function. The video RAM directly receives the data, which inadvertently calls the multitasker's exception handler. Since this requires a lot of microprocessor time, a multitasker usually reroutes video BIOS for its own use. By using the procedure we just explained, we can protect both video RAM and other memory ranges from access. This also applies to individual memory locations and entire 4K pages.

Since the offset address of the access is always transmitted to the exception handler of the multitasker, it's even possible to protect ranges smaller than 4K. If the exception handler determines that the memory location lies outside the range to be protected, it sets the Present bit to 1, executes the memory access, and changes the Present bit to 0.

I/O access interception

Hardware ports must also be handled if they're accessed simultaneously by DOS applications under multitasker control. Let's return to our screen output example. Think of how a video card changes to graphics mode or selects another color palette. The multitasker notices such changes through the I/O permission bitmap in Protected mode (see Section 33.1.3 for more information). This bitmap is always active in V86 mode and offers the multitasker the option of protecting ports from program access.

If a program tries to control of one of these ports, an exception occurs, notifying the multitasker. Windows Enhanced mode uses this method when a DOS window in V86 mode calls the DMA controller during disk access. Paging doesn't help; the addresses are viewed as true physical addresses. So, Windows must intercept each access to this chip within the DOS window and convert the specified physical addresses into their real physical addresses before passing them to the DMA chip.

The V86 mode, the paging mechanism, and the I/O permission bitmap can solve many of the other problems facing multitaskers. However, the conflict that occurs in Protected mode between multitaskers and DOS extensions cannot be solved by any of them. If you start a program, which was developed using a DOS extension, from a multitasker, accessing the program in Protected mode isn't possible and accessing the program from V86 mode will run it on the lowest privilege level.

The DPMI and VCPI software intercepts provide a solution to this problem (more on these in Section 33.4).

33.3 DOS Extensions

Memory must accommodate data and program code in extended memory, but this memory area must be kept separate. This is a typical situation in Real mode under DOS. Software drivers, such as EMS or XMS, grant access to more memory for data. However, this usually involves compatibility problems that require program reconfiguration. For years, software developers have been demanding options that enable DOS programs to use extended memory just like conventional RAM.

DOS extensions make these options available. These are development tools that are available from various software developers and are designed to work with specific compilers.

Standard C compilers and other languages (e.g., Turbo Pascal) provide DOS extensions. In this section, we'll discuss DOS extensions and how they are used in the C language.

DOS extensions must be specially adapted to the compiler because they interact with the executable code generated by the compiler. DOS extensions attempt to permit DOS program execution in Protected mode on 80286, 80386, or i486 processors. A program running in Protected mode can access all of RAM, instead of only the 640K specified by DOS.

How a DOS extension works

A short definition of how a DOS extension works is: Run a program in Protected mode and revert to Real mode before making DOS or BIOS calls.

You can change code in an EXE file to run it in Protected mode, but this doesn't apply to DOS or ROM-BIOS. This presents some problems, as you'll soon see.

DOS extensions operate according to a fairly simple principle, but with a twist. DOS extensions include various tools that apply to the standard compiler (e.g., Microsoft C 5.1 or 6.0). First, a new starting address for the program is passed, followed by the program code of the DOS extension.

The DOS extension built into the program copies the program into extended memory without executing it. Next, while still in Real mode, a global descriptor table appears, containing code and data segment descriptions of the program. The data needed for this is obtained from the OBJ file, which was generated by the compiler when the program was created.

The sequence in which the various segment descriptors are entered was established during program creation. The various segment references from the data and code segment were already selector entries that couldn't be changed. Adjusting segment references, such as with a DOS loader, isn't necessary when loading a Real mode program. The segment addresses are already defined in the segment descriptors and can no longer be changed.

The program is almost ready to run, although it still needs an interrupt descriptor table and the interrupt handlers used for calling DOS and BIOS functions. Once these are installed, the program can execute in Protected mode.

The DOS extension switches the processor into the Protected mode and starts the program. While the program is active, the DOS extension runs in the background above various DOS and BIOS functions (more on this later).

If the program ends in the usual way (i.e., DOS function 4CH), the DOS extension regains control of program execution. It releases memory and reverts to Real mode, thus returning to DOS level. The user receives no indication that Protected mode is being used.

DOS extensions for the 80286, 80386, and i486

DOS extensions can be divided into two areas: DOS extensions for the 80286, and DOS extensions for the 80386 and i486. The second group uses the full capabilities of the 80386 processor and its successors, and achieves higher execution speeds than the 80286 could handle. In order to fully utilize the 80386/i486 extension, the source code of your program must be changed. However, an 80286 extension may not require source changes (more on this later).

33.3.1   The Demands of Protected Mode

A DOS program in Protected mode first confronts changes to memory management, which is characterized by selectors, segment descriptors, and descriptor tables. Segment addresses and constant 64K segments don't exist. The DOS extension solved most of this problem by accessing the compiler generated code before calling the program.

The DOS program encounters problems if it must execute DOS or BIOS calls, or trigger external device interrupts. None of these were designed to be executed in Protected mode. So, calling them would crash the system when loading the first segment address into one of the segment registers.

Many programmers insist that their programs don't contain DOS or BIOS calls because they are designed to run under the XYZ system. However, even if a program doesn't directly call DOS or BIOS functions, many indirect calls still exist. If you use high level language statements and functions for screen display, file management, or reading the keyboard, these statements and functions are still DOS or BIOS calls at their lowest levels.

Now, let's see what happens if a software interrupt or the keyboard calls a BIOS or DOS function (e.g., a hardware interrupt) during execution. The DOS extension assumes control of program execution because it placed its interrupt handler in the interrupt descriptor table before the program started. The DOS extension provides its own interrupts to replace the DOS interrupts (20H, 21H, 24H, etc.), the BIOS interrupts (10H, 11H, 12H, 13H, 14H, 15H, 16H, etc.), and the hardware interrupts (08H, 09H, 0AH, etc.).

The IRQ0 to IRQ7 interrupt sources usually trigger the same interrupts as the various Protected mode exceptions (interrupts 08H through 0FH). Most DOS extensions reprogram the interrupt controller to redirect hardware interrupts IRQ0 through IRQ7 to other interrupts. This keeps hardware interrupts and exceptions separate.

Let's return to the DOS extension's interrupt handlers as they are executed from Protected mode. These interrupt handlers are responsible for reverting to Real mode, calling the original interrupt handler from the interrupt vector table, then returning to Protected mode. The return to Protected mode indicates the end of the interrupt handler execution, after which the program can continue running. This momentary switch into Real mode remains completely transparent to the program itself.

Switching between Protected mode and Real mode is time-consuming. This is especially true with the 80286, which directly supports only the switch from Real mode into Protected mode (returning to Real mode takes some effort). A modern AT with a clock speed of 16 MHz makes about 2000 loops from Real mode to Protected mode and back in a single second. An 80386 with a clock speed of 20 MHz makes nearly 9000 loops. This occurs because of the clock speed and the ease with which the 80386 returns to Real mode from Protected mode.

Both these numbers seem small when compared to the hundreds of thousands of assembly language instructions executed by a processor every second. However, fewer calls to DOS, BIOS, and hardware interrupts occur than you might think, especially in programs that access large quantities of data rather than interact with the user. These data access programs are good candidates for DOS extensions, because the standard 640K of RAM just isn't sufficient. So, the time loss between Real and Protected mode is minimal.

Transferring buffer addresses

Switching from Protected mode to Real mode doesn't affect many interrupt functions, especially interrupt 21H and its DOS functions. These functions expect parameters in the various processor registers and also frequently store data in these registers. The DOS extension's interrupt handler could pass this information to the original DOS interrupt handler unchanged, following the transition to Real mode, but a system crash would result. A crash will most likely occur when a call is made to a DOS function, which expects a buffer address as a parameter. This also applies to many DOS functions.

Before the DOS function call, the program loads the buffer address into the register provided. However, when the DOS function is called, the function finds a selector instead of the segment address it expected to find. Remember that the selector and segment address don't correspond. The DOS function might access segment 104H, although what was actually intended was selector 104H (and any segment above the 1 megabyte limit).

The DOS extension converts the indicated Protected mode buffer references into segment references before calling the DOS function. However, a look at the associated global or local descriptor table reveals additional problems. The table provides a 24-bit or 32-bit base address, but no 16-bit segment address. The Protected mode address is rarely converted into a normal segment address, because the program and its buffers are beyond the 1 megabyte barrier, and beyond the reach of the Real mode functions of DOS.

Before the function call, the DOS extension must copy the transmitted buffer contents into its own temporary buffer, allocated below the 1 megabyte limit. This process must be repeated after the function call, in reverse order. If DOS changed the content of this buffer, these changes must be passed to the function caller. This means that the contents of the temporary buffer must be copied back to the original Protected mode buffer.

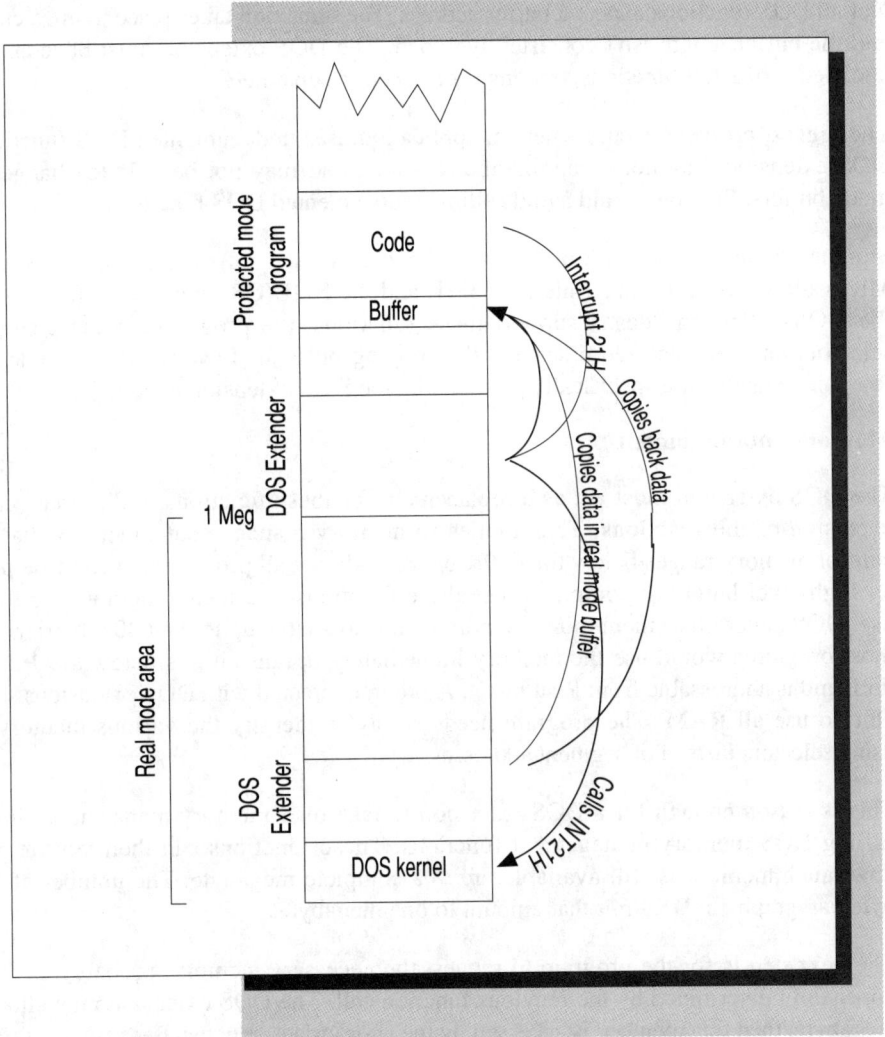

Buffer transfer on calling a DOS or BIOS function

Transferring the contents of buffers back and forth is time-consuming, especially when accessing files that contain large data blocks. However, this is actually where the recopying process barely matters because copying a buffer using a REPMOSW instruction takes less time than accessing an external storage medium.

As described, the DOS extension masks the various DOS functions and BIOS interrupts that can be called by an application. TSRs and other system extensions that alter functions have done this for years in DOS. Copying data back and forth between Real mode and Protected mode buffers involves a lot of work and also takes time, but this isn't the biggest problem confronting the developers of DOS extensions.

Not all DOS functions expect a buffer address. The transition takes place in different buffers and the buffer length isn't consistently coded. The DOS extension must have an intimate knowledge of DOS functions, treating each function separately.

The biggest problem occurs when an application uses undocumented DOS functions. The DOS extension may not recognize the registers, and may not be able to change to Real mode buffers. So, you should avoid calling undocumented DOS functions.

Similar problems arise with other, more frequently used software interfaces, such as the Microsoft Mouse Interface (interrupt 33H) and the NetBIOS functions (interrupt 5CH). If the DOS extension doesn't support these functions, the programmer must convert the selectors into segment addresses and the copying buffers. However, it's possible to use a few functions that are specifically provided by the DOS extension for this job.

Memory management

The DOS extension must act as a replacement for these functions, rather than simply an extension of the functions. This applies to memory management functions that usually control memory ranges below the 640K barrier. Almost all programs, even those produced by high level language compilers, use these functions to allocate memory for their own use. DOS never gives them more memory than is available up to the 640K barrier. If it did, most programs would use the memory immediately because it lies below the 1 megabyte limit and is addressable from Real mode. A program created with DOS extensions should be able to use all RAM. The program needs a way to identify the various memory ranges using selectors instead of segment addresses.

This is reason enough for a DOS extension to take over memory management instead of calling DOS memory management functions. These functions can then tell the program how much memory is still available, up to a complete megabyte. The number of free 16-byte paragraphs in BX limit that amount to one megabyte.

The next step is for the program to request the necessary memory, probably as far as the upper limit determined by the previous function call. The DOS extension may allocate one megabyte, then this memory is accessed by the appropriate selector. Because most programs make multiple memory requests for different purposes, this may make all physical memory available.

However, a problem occurs when you make memory ranges greater than 64K available. If the program code was written for an 80286 or one of its successors, it will work exclusively with 16-bit registers and, consequently, only 64K segments. When running through larger memory ranges, the program will occasionally be forced to increase the segment address to get past the first 64K of such a memory range. However, Protected mode prohibits segment address arithmetic, because new selectors, which point to entirely different memory ranges, are then created.

Making memory segments larger than 64K available in the 80286 creates problems for the DOS extension because a segment cannot accept more than 64K. Creating a larger memory block forces the DOS extension to access several segments and enter multiple segment descriptors in the global or local descriptor table. In turn, these descriptors require more selectors, which the DOS function doesn't return to its caller.

So that memory segments containing more than 64K can be allocated and accessed, in the case of the 80286, the interaction between a program and the DOS extension is read. This goes beyond the normal calling of a DOS function. We'll see how this actually works later in this section.

The absolute reference to specific segments also causes problems. Think of the interrupt vector table (segment 0000H), the BIOS variable range (segment 0040H), and the video RAM (segments A000H, B000H and B800H) that are addressed directly by many programs. The DOS extension can specify its own segment descriptors, with numbers identical to the corresponding segment addresses, although the video segments will cause some additional problems.

You must extend the global or local descriptor table, as needed, to B800 + 1 entries. This allows the video segment to be modeled by the descriptor with the number B800H. The descriptor table will exceed 360K, but most of the entries remain unused because no DOS extension needs B800H different segments for program execution.

DOS extensions form the cited segments using segment descriptors, which are appended to the original end of the descriptor table in question, and include an index with no relationship to the modeled memory segment. The DOS extension makes this selector available to its program functions. The memory segments can then be accessed easily.

33.3.2   DOS Extensions for the 80286

It's generally true that DOS extensions for 80386 and i486 result in more efficient programs than DOS extensions for the 80286. However, the 80286 extension simplifies porting programs.

In fact, porting with one of the best known of the 286 DOS extensions, DOS/16M from Rational Systems, is even restricted to recompilation under the Large memory model and subsequent attachment of the DOS extension. DOS/16M allows you to easily change a program for execution on a DOS machine that may have caused "insufficient memory" messages. After adding DOS/16M, the program can access more memory than before. This works as long as the developer follows the rules, especially in segment address interaction.

Creating a Protected mode program with DOS/16M

Program creation isn't very different for the compiler. The program is compiled in the Large memory mode to execute all data and code pointers as FAR pointers. So, data and code can exceed the 64K limit.

The OBJ file is initially still an ordinary Real mode program. The linking process combines the program, C libraries, and DOS extension object modules. These give the program a new starting routine and replace the various C compiler library routines with the extension's own routines. Memory is also allocated for the later attachment of the descriptor tables. The new starting routine ensures that program execution immediately terminates if the program is run on an 8086 system, or if insufficient extended memory exists. The resulting EXE file cannot run in Real Mode or protected mode. It must be sent through a conversion program named MAKEPM, which converts the EXE file into an EXP file.

MAKEPM configures the segment addresses to the physical location of the segments in memory.

Remember that a Protected mode program requires selectors instead of segment addresses. MAKEPM replaces the various segment addresses with selector numbers. The sequence of these selector numbers indicates which segment descriptors will be entered in the descriptor table when the program starts. After MAKEPM processing, the file won't start from DOS. It must be run through a special loader. This loader loads the segments from the EXE file, places them in memory and stores their locations in the global descriptor table.

Two programs are needed: the loader from the DOS extension and the EXP program. Most DOS extensions include utilities that incorporate the loader into the EXP file. The DOS/16M utility is named SLICE, and creates an ordinary EXE file that can be started from DOS.

Altered library functions

Creating a Protected mode program is an interesting task because a Real mode compiler, such as Microsoft C or Turbo C, acts as the point of departure. There is only a slight difference between Real mode and Protected mode assembly language, if you overlook the selectors. Selectors are the same size as segment addresses, are stored in the same way, are processed by the same instructions, follow the same limits, and can be generated by a "postprocessor" like MAKEPM without accessing the actual program code.

However, the compiler library functions are changed dramatically when they're linked to the program code. Although a few functions remain intact, most are changed to avoid conflicts with the Protected mode rules. Among these are functions that change the program code, which is usually done under DOS for interrupt functions such as int() and int86x(). Other examples are the functions that handle segment arithmetic.

The malloc() function also changes. This is important to remember when porting C programs. Malloc() controls memory allocation in the C language, which is performed dynamically using the heap. Unlike the old malloc() function, the version included in DOS extensions can relinquish all extended memory to a program. In doing so, mallo() returns the selector and offset address of the allocated memory range.

Since the malloc() function controls memory allocation, the DOS functions aren't used here.

Detecting pointer errors

Any program that extensively uses pointers will most likely encounter pointer errors. This is especially true for C programs; most crashes and errors in C code occur because of pointers that miss the intended memory object. If we assume that a single object was allocated using malloc(), such pointer errors can be easily detected from within Protected mode. The malloc() function specifies a new segment and a respective segment descriptor. This segment descriptor contains the size of the object as requested from the caller. If a pointer shoots past this segment, or accepts an invalid segment number, an exception occurs.

However, it's almost impossible to implement this procedure because the global descriptor table can accept only 8191 descriptors, many of which are also needed for other memory segments. Frequently using malloc() quickly fills the global descriptor table. It soon becomes impossible to allocate the remaining memory to the program. Although you could create a supplemental local descriptor table containing another 8192 segments, most DOS extensions rely exclusively on the global descriptor table.

Malloc() is forced to pack several memory ranges into a segment that increases with each call. Once the segment is full, or a requested memory block no longer fits, the next memory segment is established by appending a new descriptor to the global descriptor table. Different memory objects thereby share the same selector, even if their offset addresses are different. Problems occur only if a program wants to allocate more than 64K at the same time. The malloc() function in Real mode already allows this.

Despite the 64K limitation, it is fascinating how easily the data memory of an application can be expanded by changing the malloc() function. In the Real mode version, most C programs call malloc() until this function can allocate no more memory. Since Protected mode permits more memory, the process of allocating memory takes longer. This is the basis for the portability of normal C programs with an 80286 DOS extension.

It's still impossible to manage memory blocks larger than 64K, even though the DOS extensions offer special functions to handle this. For managing larger memory blocks, these functions simply create more sectors, one for each 64K segment. Obviously, it's impossible to run through such allocated memory ranges with normal pointer arithmetic. Instead, you must use special functions, which automatically switch to the previous or subsequent selector when a pointer approaches or overruns an offset part.

Additional options with the 80386

As we mentioned earlier, programs created for the 80386 with a DOS extension execute more rapidly than those converted into a Protected mode program using an 80286 DOS extension. Now we'll learn why this happens.

33.3.3   DOS Extensions for the 80386

DOS extensions for the 80386 let you develop faster and more efficient Protected mode applications than you could with a DOS extension designed for the 80286. There are several reasons for this, all of which involve the number 32. The 80386 is a 32-bit processor; this fact is important to high level language compilers:

- Segments can contain up to 4 gigabytes. This makes it possible to eliminate juggling multiple code and data segments.

- 32-bit integers can be accommodated in a single register and processed by a single instruction.

- String instructions for copying, traversing, and processing memory ranges can operate on a dword basis, resulting in higher execution speed.

The following are other reasons why the 80386's abilities are better than the 80286's abilities:

- The paging mechanism lets the DOS extension provide the Protected mode program with virtual memory management that's transparent to the program. There are no memory restrictions.

- The addressing possibilities are expanded. Each register can now be utilized as an index register and multiplied automatically by a factor of 2, 4, or 8. This accelerates array access and gives the compiler the option of retaining more local variables permanently in registers.

- The instruction set is expanded by the addition of efficient instructions for processing bit arrays. The compiler can use these instructions for processing bit fields and arrays for a dramatic increase in speed.

- Certain long distance jumps are also possible. Previously these could be made only by combining several instructions, which made the resulting program code larger and slower.

These options cannot be used with normal DOS compilers, which seldom support the 80286's expanded instruction set. Also, since pointer offsets are 32-bit instead of 16-bit, portability problems occur when using pointers.

The flat model

DOS compilers don't support the memory model used in most authentic 80386 compilers. This *flat model* is responsible for even greater increases in the execution speed of Protected mode programs.

This model represents programs that consist of only two parts: a code segment housing all the program code and a data segment containing all constants and variables. The TINY model in DOS is similar, although the size of both segments is restricted to 4K. The 80386 flat model's segments combined can be up to 4 gigabytes in length, which is more memory than most of us may ever need.

Since the flat model uses NEAR pointers, faster execution is guaranteed. An offset address is needed, but a segment selector isn't necessary. The data offset address is found in the DS register, and the program code is in the CS register.

The offset address occupies 32 bits. The flat model eliminates constant loading and reloading of the segment registers, as well as pointer arithmetic. So you can increment and decrement pointers just like normal numerical words (dwords) without having to worry about changes in the selector.

Version 2.0 of OS/2 uses the flat model. Speed was one reason for this choice. The other involved portability. DOS extensions for the 80386 are frequently utilized for porting large programs from UNIX (programs used for mathematical or statistical applications). In UNIX, however, memory segmentation is unknown and porting through a UNIX-compatible memory model is clearly simplified.

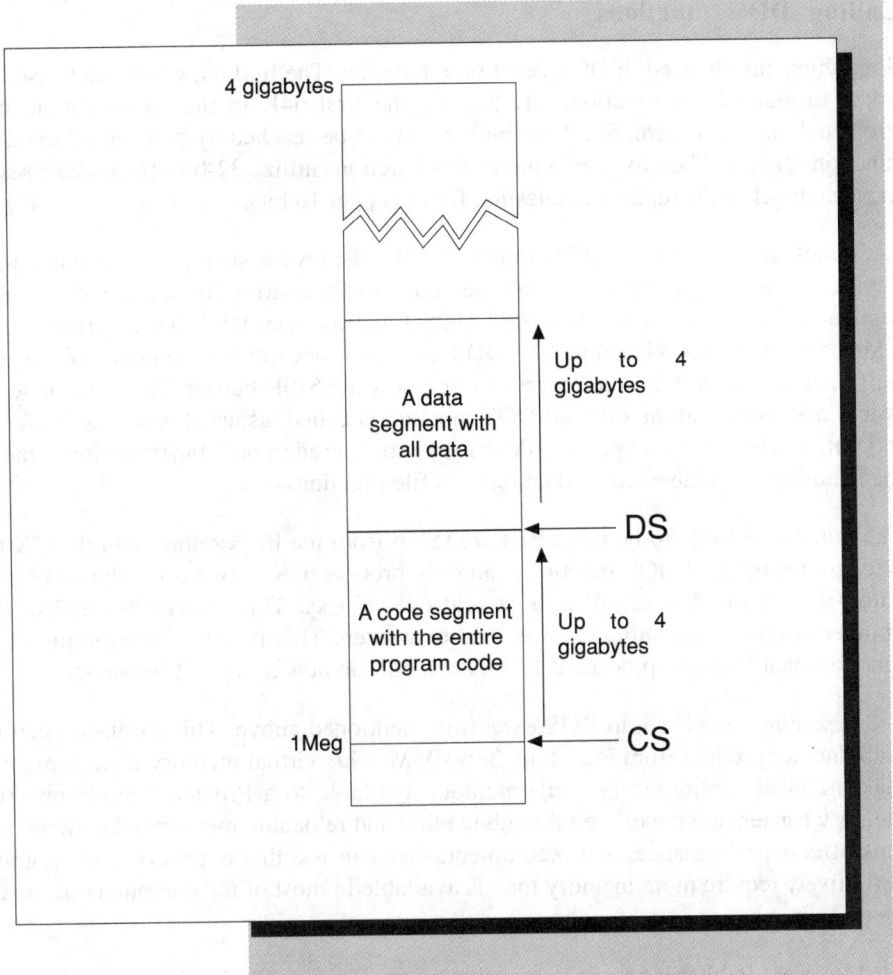

Flat model programs

The compiler itself was often carried over from the UNIX side by using a DOS extension. UNIX compilers frequently have features that overshadow their DOS counterparts. However, utilizes these features requires knowledge of the program, a lot of programming effort (resulting in large amounts of source code), and much compiler memory. The best known 386 compilers are the C386 compiler from MetaWare and the Watcom C/386 compiler by Watcom, Inc.

The best known DOS extension for the 80386 is the 386IDOS extension from Phar Lap. It works with both C386 and Watcom C/386. Its operation is barely different than the techniques described in conjunction with the DOS extensions for the 80286. DOS and BIOS calls in 80386 DOS extensions are frequently executed in V86 mode instead of in Real mode.

Calling DOS functions

Something has changed in DOS function emulation. The buffers, whose addresses must be given to many DOS functions, lie beyond the first 64K in the data segment of a 386 Protected mode program. So, these buffers cannot be reached by a 16-bit address, as DOS functions expect. Therefore, emulated DOS functions utilize 32-bit offset addresses and the expanded part of the register in question for the upper 16 bits.

Let's look at an example. DOS function 09H displays a string on the standard output device. To do this, it expects to find the address of the string to be entered in the DS:DX register pair. However, the emulated DOS function uses DS:EDX to process an offset address beyond the 64K limit. The DOS extension accepts the contents of the indicated buffer, but copies it into a temporary buffer below the 640K barrier. There the offset address is less than 64K, and the original DOS function is called, as usual, with the buffer address in DS:DX. The register expansion described here is used in both buffer address transfer and the handling of variable length data (e.g., in file functions).

The number of bytes to be processed are taken from the ECX rather than the CX register. Because the original DOS functions can only process 64K at one time, the DOS extension automatically divides its call into several 64K blocks. This repeats as needed, until the number of characters indicated was read or written. This is only one example of various functions that formerly processed 16-bit data, but can now accept 32-bit values.

Let's examine the Phar Lap DOS extension mentioned above. This extension can be used with another product from Phar Lap, 386|VMM. This virtual memory management system makes almost unlimited (virtual) memory available to a Protected mode program. All memory barriers are gone, even though loading and reloading memory takes some time and thus affects performance. We recommend that you use this extension for programs that definitively require more memory than is available in most of the computers of the targeted user group.

IBM Interleaf Publisher has also earned notoriety. This highly developed publishing system comes from UNIX. Before Phar Lap, it required a minimum of six megabytes of RAM; after Phar Lap it requires only two megabytes of RAM.

Utilizing a virtual memory management system should be an integral part of program development. For example, anyone allocating an eight megabyte array, which is constantly being accessed from one end to the other, should realize that this array is going to slow program execution.

DOS programmers must gradually learn how to work with 386 compilers because INT variables are now 32 bits wide instead of 16 bits. If you still want to work with 16-bit integers, you must use the SHORT type. Many functions (such as malloc()) were expanded.

33.4 DPMI and VCPI

The old saying, "Too many cooks spoil the soup," also applies to Protected mode. Resource conflicts in Protected mode are similar to the cooperation or dissension between cooks. Protected mode utilities fight between two resources: extended memory and the processor's Protected mode. Each utility thinks it has all of extended memory available, and each utility believes that it can select the processor's operating mode.

A central authority doesn't exist to assume control of these operations. So, we find ourselves back in the world of DOS, where concepts like extended memory and Protected mode are unknown. For this reason, the different cooks cannot prevent one another from acting. Nor can EMS emulators prevent the startup of programs developed with a DOS extension, or switch the processor into virtual 86 mode for multitasking.

The solution to this problem is important to system programmers, but not to the average user. From the user's viewpoint, he/she bought the 386 version of a program, and now must determine whether the program will work with the onboard memory management utility. The memory management utility is necessary because it keeps the RAM from filling with device drivers. However, the program refuses to work in multitasking operations.

Some progress has been made since the early days of Protected mode utilities. The participating software manufacturers defined software interfaces to ensure the peaceful coexistence of the various Protected mode utilities in the system. Two standards resulted: the somewhat older Virtual Control Programming Interface (VCPI), which is used in some DOS extensions and memory management programs, and the more recent DOS Protected Mode Interface (DPMI), which is used by Microsoft in Windows 3.

If we compare the two, DPMI easily wins. Although it's still too early to have found its niche in DOS extensions and other Protected mode utilities, DPMI seems more advanced than VCPI.

Discussing these interfaces in detail would exceed the scope of this book. So, in the following subsections we'll provide some general information about each interface and discuss the mechanisms used to keep DOS alive artificially.

33.4.1   VCPI

The VCPI interface was introduced in 1989 by a group of software firms under the leadership of Phar Lap (manufacturer of DOS extensions) and Quarterdeck (manufacturer of DESQView and QEMM). VCPI addresses the problems arising from the coexistence of DOS extensions, multitaskers, and memory management programs when these are run on an 80386 or i486 machine. The 80286 plays no role in this specification.

The problem begins with the installation of a memory management program supplying the PC with virtual EMS memory. To use the paging properties of the processor, the DOS engine is switched into V86 mode and restricted to privilege level 3.

If an application developed with a DOS extension is started on this plane from a multitasker, it won't be able to switch the processor into Protected mode or to install any sort of descriptor table. The processor's protective mechanisms perform this task.

VCPI offers these programs the option of switching into Protected mode, and offers peaceful coexistence in extended memory. Nearly all known memory management programs (QEMM, 386-To-The-Max, etc.,) support VCPI, just like the Phar Lap DOS extensions and the Quarterdeck DESQView/386 multitasking environment. DOS Version 5.0 also offers VCPI support, which gives the EMM386.SYS device driver the job of providing access to the upper memory blocks.

Programmers developing an application with a DOS extension, or designing software for use under DESQView, rarely encounter the VCPI interface. The DOS extension or the DESQView API handles this. This interface is only important to programs that want to use Protected mode but don't have access to these utilities.

Client and server

If you work with networks, the terms *client* and *server* may already be familiar to you. These terms have somewhat different meanings under VCPI.

Server designates the application made available by the VCPI functions for use by the various clients. Under VCPI, the server is always a memory management program (e.g., EMM386.EXE), because these programs are installed by the CONFIG.SYS file on booting the system, and are present even before the first call to a DOS extension or multitasking environment.

The installed VCPI uses DOS extensions and multitaskers as clients located through the memory management system. A DOS extension or multitasker could work just as well as a server, though memory management programs are only active from the time the computer is started until it is reset. The other Protected mode utilities don't immediately assume this. Also, whatever utility gets there first has first priority, which favors the memory management programs.

VCPI services

The VCPI server provides a total of 13 different services to its clients, covering the ranges in which conflicts between the various Protected mode utilities can occur:

- Three functions dedicated to VCPI initialization.

- Four functions for rudimentary extended memory management.

- Three functions for access to CR0 (the first control register) and the processor's debug registers.

- Two functions for driving the interrupt controller.

- One function for toggling between V86 mode and Protected mode.

These functions were implemented as an extension of the EMS memory manager. Each memory management program must also make the EMS function interface available for EMS support. The point of departure is Version 4.0 of the LIM standard. The various functions can be called from EMS interrupt 67H, all functions carrying the function number DEH.

The VCPI is specified by a function code in the AL register ranging from 00H to 0CH. The client receives the result of the function call in the AH register, which is common in most EMS functions. A value of 0 indicates O.K., and all other values indicate an error.

You can call interrupt 67H only from within Real mode or V86 mode. In Protected mode, the processor no longer uses the normal interrupt vector table, in which the pointer to the EMS handler is marked. Communication between the client and the server must be introduced in V86 mode by various function calls, which also give the client access to the server in Protected mode.

Initializing a client-server link

VCPI functions can only be used if a VCPI server is available. A potential client must first check for the presence of a VCPI server. This means that the client must determine whether an EMS driver is available at all (see Chapter 12).

Next, an EMS page must be called using the normal EMS functions. This is done because many EMS emulators leave the computer in Real mode when no EMS memory is requested. It's only possible to recognize many EMS emulators as VCPI servers after switching to V86 mode. The EMS page must remain allocated until the end of the program to prevent the EMS emulator from returning to Real mode and switching off its VCPI services.

Function 00H checks for EMS emulator support of the VCPI interface. Placing DE00H in the AX register returns 00H in the AH register if proper support is available, and 84H in the AH register if only the normal EMS interface is supported. The BX register receives the VCPI version, with the version number in BH and the subversion number in BL.

Function 01H receives the VCPI interface. This is a relatively complex function, and can be understood only against the background of memory management in Protected mode.

Using the page tables

The VCPI server and the client running in Protected mode don't have descriptor tables. They have complete control over the GDTR, LDTR, IDTR, and TR registers. This doesn't cause conflicts because the descriptor tables contain linear addresses instead of physical addresses. They first come into play through the page tables by using the EMS emulator. EMS emulator operation is based on the use of the paging mechanism.

The VCPI client must use the paging mechanism, and may not model linear addresses directly on physical addresses by switching it off.

There's a good reason for this. Although the VCPI server and client may use the same (linear) addresses in their linear address segment, this is impossible in the physical address space. Doing so would mean using common physical memory ranges, and mutually overwriting each other in memory. Dividing the physical address space means either using a single page table structure for server and client (and leaving the CR3 register constantly unchanged) or partially working with identical page tables.

This last option is handled by VCPI. The VCPI client must initiate its work with the interface by calling VCPI function 01H, which will fill its page table. This call must be made in Real mode, before switching into Protected mode. On calling the ES:DI register pair, the VCPI client must pass the physical address of a 4K range in memory, which it will use later as its first page table to the server, for modeling the first 4K of linear memory in physical memory.

The page directory, whose first entry to this page table must be denied, must be configured by the client before switching into Protected mode. The future page table is initialized by the server so that the first 256 entries, which model the first megabyte of the linear address space on the physical address space, produce a 1:1 ratio between linear and physical address space. This means that the client accesses the first megabyte of the physical address space using the first megabyte of its linear address space, the ROM-BIOS (which can access the video RAM), and conventional DOS memory.

This is how the VCPI server operates. It enables the use of this range for the exchange of data between client and server. However, the VCPI server can image further linear memory on physical memory with the aid of the indicated page table. VCPI function 01H returns the offset of the first entry in the page table in the DI register. From this address, the client can insert its own page table entries.

The length of the previously defined page table entries can be determined from the original offset address extracted from the value in the DI register. Because each entry takes up four bytes, the result of dividing the length by 4 is the number of pages already modeled, and the index of the next free page. Multiplying this index by 4K results in the first free address in the linear address space. This is important when allocating memory (more on this later).

Function 01H expects a pointer in the DS:SI register pair. Starting with this memory location, the server allocates three segment descriptors with a total size of 24 bytes, which the client must later add to its global descriptor table. It can copy the three descriptors for this purpose at any positions within its GDT, or reposition the GDT by the size of the memory range entered in DS:SI. It must also mark its position within the GDT and its index. This information will be used later as a selector to this first entry.

That describes the code segment by which the client is able to access the EMS functions of the server in Protected mode. However, here we're dealing with only one code segment instead of a CALL gate, so an offset address for the server call is needed. This is returned to the caller of function 01H, in the BX register.

Calling the server must be done using a FAR instruction referring to the selector of the server code segment. This indicates the value returned from the BX register as the offset address.

VCPI memory management

A VCPI client can usually assume that the VCPI server has taken control of all available memory for itself and is to remain free. This memory is probably reserved for a RAM disk, a cache program, or something similar.

Calling BIOS interrupt 15H or the XMS interface is ordinarily useless to extended memory. Memory can only be requested by the VCPI client in Protected mode using the VCPI server, if you overlook the small fragment which the program is able to gain control of by using DOS functions, while still in Real (V86) mode.

VCPI memory management is based on the 4K pages that the 80386 and its successors control by paging. Memory can be allocated and released in multiples of 4K. All four VCPI functions can be called in both V86 mode and Protected mode. This doesn't apply to all VCPI functions.

Function 02H determines the physical address of the highest page yielded by the VCPI server. Pass the value DE02H to the AX register. A value of 0H returned in the AH register indicates that the call was successful. The required information will then be found in the EDX register.

Use this information carefully. Many VCPI servers produce the address of that last possible page instead of the address of the last physically available page. The result can be that function 02H will always return the value FFF000H (last page before the 16 megabyte limit), and not 3FF000H, if the computer has four megabytes of RAM.

You should avoid using function 02H. Instead, call function 03H. This function returns the number of pages available in the EDX register. This page number total can then be requested using function 04H, but only under certain circumstances.

With each call, function 04H returns the physical address of the required page if the value in the AH register is 00H. Any other value points to an error in page allocation and proceeds with an undefined value in the EDX register.

The VCPI client must do two things to access this memory:

- It must establish a segment descriptor in its global or local memory descriptor table to address the allocated memory using a segment. The segment can contain more than 4K if several pages must be combined.

- It must make an entry in the memory table by which the 4K from the linear address space can be modeled on their physical address. Naturally, the linear address recorded in the segment descriptor will be important. It determines the position of the associated entry in the page table. Because a page table was already established for the first four megabytes (it must be returned by function 01H), a linear address within the first four megabytes should be chosen. Don't forget that the VCPI server, when calling function 01H, has already made some entries in the page table to image at least the first megabyte of the linear address space. The first free linear address and the index in the page table can be calculated, as we previously explained.

Function 05H frees pages if the VCPI client no longer needs them, but the client may no longer access them, even though this would seem to be possible through its page table. Besides the function number, the function expects the physical page address in the EDX register.

VCPI and EMS memory

Memory can also be requested by the VCPI client from the normal EMS functions by using a multiple of 16K. Access to these EMS pages occurs by focusing them in a page frame below the one megabyte barrier.

VCPI function 06H returns the physical address of a 4K page below the one megabyte barrier. You can also discover memory ranges not normally occupied by RAM, which can be used by the memory management program through the page table. DOS Version 5.0 also uses this *backfilling* process for accessing the upper memory blocks.

The number of the requested page is placed in the CX register after the call to function 06H. This is returned by dividing the linear address by 4096, which is the same as rotating this address 12 bits to the right. Calling the function returns the physical address of the memory page at this address in the EDX register.

If the content of the EDX register is identical to the returned CX value multiplied by 4096, no alien memory is being used at the address in question. The linear address of this 4K page is different from its physical address. You cannot request the entire one megabyte address space in this manner, especially for those ranges occupied by the ROM-BIOS or BIOS extensions. In these cases, the function 06H returns error code 8BH in the AH register. Otherwise, a value of 00H in the AH register indicates no error.

Accessing debug and status registers

It's possible to access, at least in V86 mode, the various debug registers because the privilege level 3 is active. VCPI functions 08H and 09H read from and write to the various debug registers from V86 mode. These registers aren't very useful to a normal program, but are extremely useful to Borland's Turbo Debugger, which also uses the VCPI interface.

These two functions process all eight debug registers. The register contents are passed to a buffer to which the ES:DI register points when calling the function. Because each debug register occupies 32 bits, this buffer must have room for 32 bits. DR0 is stored in the first dword of the buffer, DR1 in the second, etc. Function 08H copies the debug register contents into the buffer, while function 09H loads them from the buffer.

Function 07H, which returns the contents of the CR0 status register in the EBX register, appears as an anachronism. Although the current operating mode and the paging mechanism status can be determined through this register, it is also returned by the non privileged SMSW instruction which loads the content of this register into another processor register or a memory location.

Intercepting and setting interrupt vectors

Earlier in this chapter, we recommended reprogramming the first interrupt controller for V86 mode exceptions. If you don't reprogram, hardware interrupts IRQ0 through IRQ7 encounter many exceptions.

VCPI function 0AH returns the base interrupt of the first interrupt controller in the BX register, and the base interrupt of the second interrupt controller in the CX register. If the two controllers no longer contain their default values (08H and 70H), the VCPI server has already rerouted these interrupts. Further rerouting is then strictly forbidden.

If the interrupt controller hasn't already been changed, it is possible to reprogram the first and second interrupt controllers. Of course, access to the two controllers must be done after all interrupts have been switched off.

VCPI function 0BH notifies the VCPI server about the reprogramming. This function must be called by the client before the interrupt flag is reset. Like function 0AH, the base address of the first interrupt controller must be entered in the BX register and the second in the CX register.

Changing the operating mode

One of the most important services of the VCPI server is the controlled transition from V86 mode into Protected mode and back to V86 mode. VCPI function 0CH performs this task.

This function can be called from V86 mode using the normal EMS interrupt. In Protected mode, function 0CH is accessible only through the code segment and the offset address returned by the VCPI server on calling VCPI function 01H. When calling this function from V86 mode, the linear address of a data structure, whose structure is shown in the following table, is expected in the ESI register. The following values are loaded into the various system registers:

Data structure for switching from V86 mode to Protected mode after calling VCPI function 0CH		
Func.	Meaning	Type
00H	CR3 (Starting address of page directory)	dword
04H	Linear address of variables under dword one megabyte limit, containing the FAR pointer for the GDTR register	fword
08H	Linear address of variables under dword one megabyte limit, containing the FAR pointer for the IDTR register	
0CH	Selector for the LDTR register	word
0EH	Selector for the TR register	word
10H	Point of entry into the program code after switching into Protected mode with selector and 32 bit-offset address	fword

It's very important that this data structure be established beneath the one megabyte barrier. Only in this range are the address spaces of the VCPI server and its clients identical, as noted in connection with VCPI function 01H.

The CR3 function is loaded with the value provided in the first step after calling this function. The page tables of the VCPI server are no longer valid; the page tables of the client are used instead. The server can now read data only from the coincident ranges, from the range below one megabyte.

Next, the GDTR register is loaded. The global descriptor table is referenced and may be anywhere in the address space of the VCPI client. This table must have been previously initialized in V86 mode and it's assumed that the VCPI function was also previously called.

Now the LDT, IDTR, and TR registers are loaded and finally the switch to Protected mode is made. All interrupts are still blocked at this point and should remain so. Of the six segment registers, only the CS register is loaded with a valid selector at this time. It's time to set up the program's own stack and load the DS, ES, FS, and GS registers with valid selectors. Only then may the interrupt lines again be opened. If an interrupt does happen to occur before the segment register is loaded, invalid selectors will be loaded. The processor will trigger an exception. Returning to V86 mode is effected by function 0CH, but this time with entirely different register loading.

However, as the starting point, it's again necessary to obtain the code segment selector and the offset address returned by function 01H.

Before calling function 0CH, the VCPI client must establish a data structure in physical RAM below the one megabyte limit. The values which the VCPI server is to enter after switching into V86 mode are stored there. Using the entries for CS:EIP, the memory address is established for program execution in V86 mode. SS:ESP describe the new location of the stack.

Remember that the values for the various segment registers do not concern selectors, but base addresses (physical address divided by 16), as is normal in Real mode and V86 mode. Should the program in V86 mode not have been developed especially for the 80386 or its successors, any values can be specified for the FS and GS registers because they aren't important to program execution.

Although only one word is required for the various segment registers, two words are used in the data structure shown below. The respective segment address is entered in the first word, while the second word remains unused.

Data structure for switching from Protected mode to V86 mode after calling VCPI function 0CH		
Func.	Meaning	Type
00H	Reserved	dword
08H	EIP after switching into V86 mode	dword
0CH	CS after switching into V86 mode	dword
10H	Reserved for EFLAGS register	dword
14H	ESP after switching into V86 mode	dword
18H	SS after switching into V86 mode	dword
1CH	ES after switching into V86 mode	dword
20H	DS after switching into V86 mode	dword
24H	FS after switching into V86 mode	dword
28H	GS after switching into V86 mode	dword

In order for the VCPI server to access the above table after calling function 0CH, its linear address must be transferred to the SS:ESP register pair. It's also necessary for the client to load the DS register with a selector to a data segment descriptor which it has itself entered in its global or local descriptor table before calling the function. This descriptor must contain the base address 0 and have a size of one megabyte.

After switching into V86 mode, the content of the normal registers (EBX, ECX, etc.) is retained. Only the content of the EAX register has been changed and is undefined. The Protected mode registers GDTR, LDTR, etc. have again been loaded by the VCPI server with the addresses or the selectors of its descriptor tables; but that doesn't in any way affect a program in V86 mode.

33.4.2   DPMI

The DOS Protected Mode Interface (DPMI) wasn't originally created as a general standard for collaboration between multitaskers and other Protected mode utilities. Instead, it initially appeared during the development of Windows 3.0 as an in-house product used for enabling the execution of Windows applications in extended memory. For unknown reasons, Microsoft decided to publish and expand this interface. A DPMI committee met in early 1990. The members of this group include Microsoft, Borland, Intel, Eclipse, IBM, Lotus, Phar Lap, Quarterdeck, and Rational Systems. Since many of these companies are VCPI supporters, we can assume that the DOS extenders, multitaskers, and memory management programs of these manufacturers will also support both DPMI and VCPI in the future.

Differences from VCPI

Microsoft's marketing strength and the popularity of Windows are the principal driving forces behind this committee. The DPMI specification is superior to VCPI, in both concept and execution. DMPI is simply "cleaner" and more generic than VCPI.

DPMI covers the entire spectrum of services required by DOS programs in Protected mode for peaceful coexistence with other Protected mode programs. These include:

•   Managing descriptor tables of a protected mode program.

- Management and allocation of extended memory.

- Management of interrupts and exceptions.

- Communication with Real mode programs and interrupt handlers.

- Access to various processor registers.

- DMA virtualization.

These services show that DPMI clients must relinquish much of their Protected mode rights to the DPMI host. Unless the programs cooperate, this is impossible. The processor ensures that clients will use the services in this way.

Unlike the VCPI server, the DPMI host runs on a higher privilege level than its client, giving it control of all clients and their activities. The lack of such protection was one of Microsoft's greatest complaints against the VCPI interface.

Clients and hosts

DPMI uses the term *hosts* instead of servers. The two words mean basically the same thing, and the change was probably intended to separate DMPI from the old client-server model. Despite this name change, DPMI has a host (program) which makes the DPMI services available to clients. However, DPMI has only one host, which is Microsoft Windows. Windows 3.X supports DPMI Specification Version 0.9 (the version that the DPMI Committee released to the public). Version 1.0 was recently released, and has a few differences from Version 0.9 (more on this later).

16-bit or 32-bit DPMI

Unlike VCPI, DPMI was conceived for the 80286, even though Windows 3.0 doesn't support the 80286. Remember that DPMI becomes active in Windows enhanced mode, which is only available on 80386 or higher systems. As 80286 machines become less important, it isn't likely that an 80286 DPMI host will be released.

Because of the 80286 support, DPMI hosts exist in 16-bit and 32-bit versions. 16-bit hosts are designed for execution on 80286 computers, and support 64K memory segments. A 32-bit DPMI host works with 32-bit memory segments (up to four gigabytes) and the resulting flat model. So, a host of this type runs only on a computer with 80386/i486 processors.

The target group

Like VCPI, DPMI is aimed primarily at the developers of DOS extenders and memory management programs. They should take advantage of the services of this interface to enable their Protected mode programs to run without difficulty even under a multitasking environment like Windows 3. The first DOS extenders that use them are already available on the market. Such a DOS extender, or the program generated by it, must also be able to function as DPMI host. If the program is started namely from the DOS prompt, without another DPMI host having been activated first, it must make these services available itself.

Execution on a virtual machine

The DPMI host always runs its clients on a *virtual machine* (VM), such as the DOS screen under Windows. A VM can run more than one DPMI client. For example, the memory management program can use the DPMI host services in a Windows DOS screen, and a program using a DOS extender can also be started from the DOS screen. As part of a virtual machine, the various programs in Real mode thereby divide up an address space, emulating a one megabyte DOS machine plus HMA. Multitasking between the various clients within a VM is possible between the various VMs. Then Windows can run several DOS programs in various DOS screens simultaneously. This becomes possible using preemptive multitasking, where the DPMI host interrupts program execution in a VM after a time to continue running a program on the next VM.

This occurs automatically when a time slice ends, although it's possible for clients to support this procedure by reporting that they aren't busy, using the interrupt 2FH, function 1680H call. Once this happens, the DPMI host can pass execution on to the next VM, without the need to waste valuable processor time.

The biggest difference between Version 0.9 and Version 1.0 lies in management of the virtual machine. Under Version 0.9, all clients share a local descriptor table (LDT) and an interrupt descriptor table (IDT) within the VM. Clients can gain access to other memory segments (and perhaps other clients) by using the descriptors. The DPMI host cannot prevent this. However, this makes simultaneous execution of 16-bit and 32-bit clients impossible, because their respective segments cannot be merged into a single descriptor table.

DPMI Version 1.0 assigns each client its own LDT and IDT within a VM, which causes difficulties, especially in Windows. Many DOS Protected mode programs, which previously ran perfectly in Windows Protected mode from the DOS screen, are designed for the use of a common LDT with other programs, and require rewriting. Perhaps this why the Windows DPMI host continues to support only Version 0.9.

DPMI outputs and functions

The DPMI interface covers a series of output ranges. We'll provide a brief outline of these ranges, then list the most important data in more detail. We selected DPMI Version 0.9 as our standard.

Only 13 different functions process the local descriptor table of the client and the segment descriptors contained there. This is quite different from VCPI, where the processing of these descriptor tables remains in the hands of the client, thus leaving the system open to many types of problems. Remember, though, that some DPMI functions still leave a few openings with potential for mayhem.

Each task under DPMI can access its own local descriptor table, kept separate from global descriptor tables. Global descriptor tables are reserved exclusively for the DPMI host.

DPMI supports three different memory management function groups:

1.) The first group allocates and accesses conventional memory below the one megabyte barrier. As we explained in the section on DOS extenders, Protected mode programs require this memory when calling DOS functions that expect to find data in buffers.

2.) The second group handles extended memory. Memory blocks can be requested, freed, or altered.

3.) The third group handles virtual memory. The 80286's lack of a paging mechanism makes this group unavailable on 80286 machines. This group includes functions for page maintenance, such as locking a page to prevent removal from memory.

A fourth group calls Real mode routines and interrupt handlers from Protected mode. By calling DOS or BIOS functions, the DPMI host saves its client a lot of work. However, you can also call a Protected mode routine from a Protected mode interrupt handler using *callbacks*.

The DPMI specification also includes functions supporting the debug register in the 80386 and its successors, for requesting and setting Real mode or Protected mode interrupt handlers, for blocking hardware interrupt releases, and for initializing a client and switching into Protected mode.

Here's a summary of the various services offered to the DPMI client by the DPMI host.

Interrupt 2FH call in Real mode

```
1680H   Client unoccupied, pass on program execution
1686H   Query operating mode (also Protected mode)
1687H   Query DPMI availability status
```

Interrupt 31H call in Protected mode

```
LDT memory management

0000H   Allocate LDT segment descriptor
0001H   Release LDT segment descriptor
0002H   Image Real mode segment on segment descriptor
0003H   Query increment for selector
0004H   Block removal of segment
0005H   Permit segment removal
0006H   Query base address of segment
0007H   Establish segment base address
0008H   Establish segment length
0009H   Establish access rights/segment type
000AH   Create alias for a code segment
000BH   Query segment descriptor
000CH   Load segment descriptor
000DH   Request specific selector
```

Interrupt 31H call in Protected mode (continued)

DOS memory access	
0100H	Request DOS memory
0101H	Release DOS memory
0102H	Change size of a memory block

Interrupt and exception management	
0200H	Return address of a real mode interrupt handler
0201H	Set real mode interrupt handler
0202H	Query address of an exception handler
0203H	Install exception handler
0204H	Query address of a protected mode interrupt handler
0205H	Install protected mode interrupt handler
0900H	Block virtual interrupt flag
0901H	Release virtual interrupt flag
0902H	Query virtual interrupt flag

Calling real mode routines	
0300H	Simulate Real mode interrupt
0301H	Call Real mode routine
0302H	Call Real mode routine
0303H	Create callback
0304H	Return callback

Miscellaneous functions	
0400H	Query version number

Functions for accessing extended memory	
0500H	Request memory use data
0501H	Allocate memory in extended memory
0502H	Release memory block
0503H	Change size of memory block
0800H	Convert physical address into linear address

Functions for managing interrupts and exceptions	
0600H	Protect memory range from removal

Unlock memory region	
0602H	Unlock Real mode memory region
0603H	Relock Real mode memory region
0604H	Query page size
0702H	Privilege memory region during removal
0703H	Mark memory range as overwriteable

Support for the debug registers of the 80386 and successors	
0B00H	Define breakpoint
0B01H	Delete breakpoint
0B02H	Get breakpoint status
0B03H	Reset breakpoint status

Client initialization and switching into Protected mode

DPMI calls begin with querying the DPMI host. The services cannot be accessed until this query occurs. The query must occur in Real mode (after the potential client starts at the DOS level).

So you must use function 1678H, which the DPMI host clicks into the DOS multiplexer interrupt 2FH during initialization. If it returns a 0 value in the AX register following its call, a DPMI host is installed. Status data on the DPMI host is then found in the other processor registers. For example, bit 0 of the BX register indicates whether the DPMI host is 16-bit or 32-bit. If bit 0 = 0, the DPMI host is 32-bit.

However, the CL register indicates the processor type and the DX register indicates the version number of the DPMI host. The information in the SI register is also very important. SI conveys the memory block size in paragraphs required by the DPMI host for management tasks. The client must allocate this block size before the switch to Protected mode can occur.

The switch itself occurs through a routine whose address is returned in the ES:DI register pair once the multiplexer function is called. A jump must be made to this address using a FARCALL assembly language instruction. The segment address of the memory block made available to the DPMI host is placed in the ES register. If the DPMI routine called from ES:DI returns with the carry flag set, the program remains in Real mode because the switch to Protected mode failed for a reason not described in detail. But if the carry flag is unset, the program moves into Protected mode and can then call all DPMI services from interrupt 31H. Remember that most DPMI functions trigger an error during execution by setting the carry flag, but return no special error code beyond that. This, too, is a point of departure for future DPMI expansions.

Even after switching into protected mode, the program is still obviously below the 640K barrier. However it runs in an entirely normal manner, because the existing segment addresses in CS, DE, and SS were replaced by selectors. They point to memory segments of 64K each, whose segment descriptors were automatically established by the DPMI host. The selectors in DS and SS are identical, if the two segments were already coinciding in Real mode.

Aside from that, ES points to a segment descriptor describing the PSP of the program and records 100H bytes as the segment length. GS and FS, if present, are also loaded with the value 0.

After the successful switch into Protected mode, a DOS extender, for example, will attempt to load the program it created into extended memory from the hard drive, to run it there. However, to do this, it must first allocate extended memory from the DPMI host and enter (or cause the entry of) the associated segment descriptors in its local descriptor table (more on this later).

Calling DOS interrupt 21H, function 4CH from within Protected mode ends execution of the Protected mode program.

The DPMI host then switches back to Real mode automatically, removes the original Real mode program (the loader) from memory, and returns to the normal DOS prompt.

Managing the client's local descriptor table

Since it has 14 functions, the local descriptor table can be difficult to manage. You'll rarely use these functions because the memory management area of the DPMI simply divides extended memory into memory blocks, but doesn't specify segment descriptors for them. The client is responsible for this. Also, the client cannot access its descriptor table directly for reasons of privilege. Instead, the client must use the DMPI host functions.

Function 0000H lets the client request one or more segment descriptors in its local descriptor table. In this context, the word "request" means that the host establishes a desired number of data segment descriptors in the local descriptor table, each descriptor being first supplied with the starting address 0 and a corresponding length. Only additional DPMI calls allow the client to specify the desired starting address, segment length, and type, in case the client requires code segment descriptors instead of data. As the result, function 0000H returns a selector to the created segment descriptor. If several segment descriptors were requested, their numbers can be determined by addition of the value returned by function 0003H. Because of the complicated structure of selectors, you shouldn't assume, however, that it's always necessary to increment the returned selector by the value 1 to determine the following selectors one by one.

Before ending the program, all the selectors requested in this manner must be returned. Function 0001H performs this task for one sector.

If you want to address a memory segment beneath the one megabyte barrier while in protected mode, you'll need a segment descriptor and an associated selector. Passing the Real mode segment address to function 0002H produces a segment descriptor for a 64K data segment. This segment returns to this descriptor. A segment descriptor taken over by the client using function 0000H or 0002H can be modified with the help of functions 0007H, 0008H, and 0009H. These let you specify the starting address, the segment length, access rights, etc. Regarding the segment length and starting address, the client must ensure that memory segments that aren't allocated yet or allocated memory segments that are covered by several, overlapping segment descriptors aren't accessed. The functions named simply aren't responsible for tests of this sort. This is the back door we mentioned earlier.

These data can be read using the LSL (Load Segment Limit) and LAR (Load Access Rights) instructions, or function 0006H can return the base address of a segment.

Function 000BH can read a segment descriptor. Function 000CH loads a complete segment descriptor into a buffer. The DPMI ensures that the client isn't granted a priority higher than 3.

Function 000AH generates a corresponding data segment descriptor for a specific code segment. This descriptor contains the starting address and code segment length, returning a selector.

Extended memory allocation

Functions 0500H, 0501H, 0502H, and 0503H manage and allocate extended memory.

Function 0500H returns status data. This data includes free memory available and swap file size on a virtual memory management system.

Function 0501H allocates extended memory. After the function call, the BX:CX register pair contains the extent of the requested memory range available. Because the DPMI system is divided internally into 4K blocks due to virtual memory management (nearly always implemented in the case of a 32-bit host), we recommend that you request blocks in multiples of 4K. If the call was successful, the BX:CX register pair receives the linear address of the allocated memory block. The SI:DI register pair receives a handle required for further block processing by the various DPMI functions.

Once the client takes possession of the memory block by calling function 501H, the block is still inaccessible. First, the client lacks the associated segment descriptor mentioned earlier. Function 0000H must be called to allocate the block, then fill the block with the transmitted starting address and the known length.

The client now has the option of subdividing the required memory range into several contiguous segments. This is useful because DPMI doesn't have any kind of "garbage collection", which combines memory blocks that have become free to form larger units. A DPMI client should allocate all the memory required using function 501H.

Function 0502H returns a memory block from extended memory. The handle returned by this function identifies the memory block for the DPMI host (very important).

Function 0503H changes a previously allocated memory block. The block's size (not its contents) is changed by this function, which passes the memory block's handle and its new size. If the call was successful, the new starting address is returned along with a new handle (if needed). If the memory block was in fact moved, the client is then responsible for bringing the start into agreement with the segment or segments created for gaining access to the memory block.

DOS memory allocation

Functions 0100H, 0101H, and 0102H allocate and manage DOS memory. These functions are similar to standard DOS functions 48H, 49H, and 4AH. Unlike the extended memory functions, these functions create a segment for access to the memory block allocated immediately, making it unnecessary for the client to perform the same task.

Function 0100H requests the DOS memory. It requires the size, in paragraphs, of the desired range. If the call was successful, the function returns the selector to the allocated block's segment descriptor selector. Function 0101H releases the DOS block requested by function 0100H.

Function 0102H lets you change the size of a memory block. Pass the selector in the DX register, and the new memory block size (in paragraphs) in the BX register.

DOS memory blocks are needed by DOS extenders, in particular, when DOS function calls issue from Protected mode, which results in the transfer of data into buffers. This is frequently the case when accessing files.

Virtual memory management

Functions 0600H, 0601H, 0602H, 0603H, and 0604H manage virtual memory. These functions are implemented only with 32-bit hosts (the 80286 doesn't have page tables or virtual memory management). These functions lock and unlock memory ranges.

Function 0600H locks the specified memory range from removal. This prohibits the removal of interrupt handlers. Function 0601H unlocks locked memory ranges.

Functions 0602H and 0603H target RAM below the one megabyte barrier, which was allocated using function 0100H. Function 0602H unlocks pages for removal, and function 0603H locks pages.

As the last function in this group, function 0604H returns the size of a page to the caller.

Interrupt handling and calling Real mode routines

Interrupt handling, particularly the reaction to hardware interrupts, represents one of the greatest difficulties in the Real mode programming of DOS extenders and other Protected mode utilities. How should a program react if an interrupt, normally available in Real mode, occurs in Protected mode? VCPI leaves this question to the programmer, but DPMI offers various solutions. Before we discuss these functions, however, let's briefly look at the concepts behind them.

First, no problems exist in DPMI between the various exceptions and the hardware interrupts IRQ0 through IRQ7. The host reprograms the first interrupt controller in each case. The lower privilege level of the client keeps the client from doing the same thing.

The DPMI host also ensures that all hardware interrupts land in Protected mode, even if they occurred during program execution in Real mode or V86 mode.

The DPMI standard handler initially receives control over program execution, passing control to the first client that has recorded a handler for this interrupt through an appropriate DPMI function.

If it returns to the caller through an IRET assembly language instruction, this is completed during interrupt handling. The interrupt handlers of the other clients are no longer used. So, the existing handler should be queried with an appropriate DPMI function before installing a hardware interrupt handler, and called within its own interrupt routine.

When all interrupt handlers operate according to this scheme, the result is a sort of chain, with every interrupt handler getting its due time. Each DMPI client can protect itself against the release of hardware interrupts with certain functions. The DPMI host maintains a virtual interrupt flag for each client. This flag, which is stored in the Flag or EFlag register, ensures that no hardware interrupts can reach one client, while allowing passage to another client.

The situation changes with software interrupts triggered in Real mode. Only three of these interrupts reach protected mode, if the client makes corresponding handlers available: the BIOS timer interrupt (1CH), the <Ctrl><C> interrupt (23H), and the critical error interrupt (24H).

But software interrupts can also be triggered in Protected mode when, for example, a DOS extender enters an INT instruction in assembly language. If no DPMI client specified an interrupt handler for the respective interrupt, such a software interrupt results in a switch to Real mode, execution of the interrupt, and a subsequent switch back to Protected mode.

There's a problem with this switching. These functions generally receive data from the processor registers. There's no problem in the general registers, but the contents of the segment registers are destroyed during the shift into Real mode because they contain selectors instead of segment addresses. Because of this, DOS extenders break into the various software interrupts and convert the selectors in the segment registers into segment addresses while still in Protected mode, before passing the interrupt on to Real mode.

DPMI interrupt handling

Six different functions manage Real mode interrupt handlers, Protected mode interrupt handlers, and exception handlers. These functions, number 0200H through 0205H, install handlers, query handlers, and release handlers.

Also, the DPMI host uses function 0300H to simulate a Real mode interrupt from within Protected mode. The Protected mode software interrupt handlers intercept the various software interrupts (BIOS, DOS, etc.), check the indicated function number, and, on the basis of this data, convert the pointers returned in processor registers into Real mode format after previously copying the data addressed into a DOS buffer below the one megabyte barrier.

Functions 0301H and 0302H call Real mode routines residing below the one megabyte limit. Function 0301H ends with the VAR RET assembly language instruction, while function 0302H ends with the IRET instruction.

You can also simulate a Protected mode routine from within Real mode. For example, the mouse driver can allow a routine call when the mouse moves or button status changes. The routine must be performed in Real mode, but in certain cases, the mouse event should be readable from the context of a Protected mode program.

The DPMI host uses function 0303H for creating a callback. This callback is a short routine created independently in RAM by the DPMI host. When the callback is called, the desired Protected mode routine executes, if the switch to Protected mode has occurred.

Functions 0900H, 0901H, and 0902H manage the virtual interrupt flags, protecting your program from unauthorized hardware interrupts.

Access to debug registers

To permit each DPMI client to access the debug registers of the 80386 and its successors, the DPMI host centralizes register access in four different functions. Each client can install its own *breakpoints* (sometimes called *watchpoints*) whose addresses are loaded by the DPMI host into the processor's debug registers, as soon as the client reaches execution.

Function 0B00H defines a breakpoint. The function requires the parameters needed to configure the debug register: the linear address of the breakpoint, its size (bytes, word, or dword), and its type (read, write, or execute memory location). It then returns a breakpoint handle, as long as too many break points weren't installed or an invalid parameter wasn't indicated on calling the function.

Function 0B01H deletes a previously defined breakpoint. The function requires the handle of the defined breakpoint (function 0B00H returned this handle).

Function 0B02H queries the status of a breakpoint. This indicates whether the breakpoint was triggered. Function 0B03H resets breakpoint status, which permits execution of the next breakpoint.

Then you learn whether the break point was already triggered. The corresponding flag can then be reset with function 0B03H so that a new execution of the breakpoint can be detected.

Chapter 34

The Pentium Processor

With the Pentium processor, which was introduced by Intel in 1993, the technical possibilities of a PC have changed again. The Pentium features 100 MIPS (Million Instructions Per Second) at a clock speed of 66 MHz. This makes the Pentium almost twice as fast as a 486 DX2/66 in integer performance. The differences are even more significant in floating-point performance. Depending on the instruction mix, the Pentium beats its predecessor by three to seven times. Also, it's completely binary compatible with the 486, 386, 286, and even the 8086.

When asked about the performance of the Pentium, Intel has a very simple answer: 567. This measurement is a result of the ICOMP test developed by Intel for its own processors. This test, geared entirely to Intel's own processors, flows into the ICOMP index.

However, be careful when interpreting absolute data, such as the information returned by the ICOMP index. After all, selecting the processor test for such a benchmark is a subjective process, even if the manufacturers claim to be simulating real application conditions. Also remember that each manufacturer is eager to show its product in the best possible light. So, they may downplay the performance areas in which its chip suffers in comparison to the competition, or simply omit these performance areas.

On the whole, however, the direction in which this index is moving compared to the previous Intel processors might be correct, even though you can't assume that doubling processor performance from the 486 to the Pentium could be duplicated at the user and software levels. There are numerous hardware and software components between the CPU and the user. These components either benefit only partially from the processor's performance, or they don't benefit at all. For example, this applies to all expansion boards.

However, the Pentium has definitely advanced the PC world to previously unattainable dimensions. You're probably wondering what makes the Pentium so fast. Three components are responsible for the Pentium's speed: Superscalar integer execution unit, the first level processor cache, and the superscalar floating-point execution unit. We'll discuss these features in detail in this chapter.

First, let's review the most important facts about Intel's new "miracle chip":

- The Pentium is manufactured in 0.8-micron BiCMOS submicron technology. The traces or signal paths are only 0.8 millionths of a meter wide, or eight thousands of a millimeter wide.

- The chip has a total of 3.1 million transistors.

- The processor is completely binary compatible with its predecessors in relation to instruction set, register, addressing modes, and operating modes.

- The processor still works with 32-bit registers and 32-bit addressing, but can be connected to a 64-bit data bus, enabling faster communication with memory.

- A superscalar architecture based on two parallel integer pipelines. In ideal circumstances, this would allow simultaneous execution of 2 machine language instructions in one cycle.

- Two separate 8K data and code caches, in conjunction with the 64-bit bus interface (port), provide fast and continuous memory access.

- A special protocol called MESI (Modified, Exclusive, Shared, Invalid) ensures that a Pentium processor will work smoothly with other processors in a multiprocessor system.

- An improved floating-point unit executes commands significantly faster than the 486 and even provides the option of simultaneous execution of two instructions, although this happens on a limited scale.

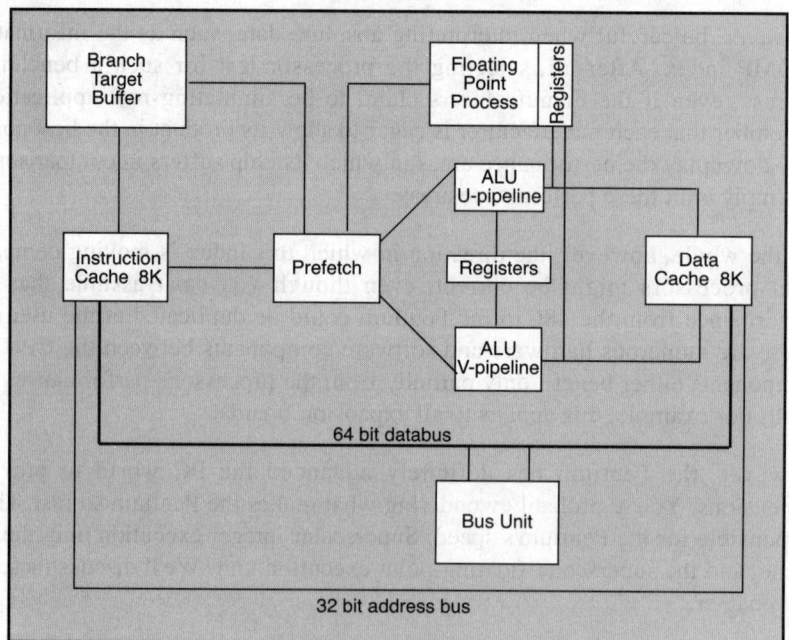

Block diagram of the Pentium processor

34.1 Program Execution

Program execution through the Pentium processor is based on a superscalar architecture with two parallel, five-stage integer pipelines that are connected with the processor cache and a branch target buffer (BTB).

Execution in the pipeline procedure

To understand this efficient, expensive mechanism of program execution, you must first know how a microprocessor executes programs and machine language instructions. Although this process appears as a monolithic block from the outside, in the interior of the processor it is divided into five stages. The i486 and Pentium both have five stages that each instruction undergoes during its execution in a set sequence. These stages are abbreviated to PF, D1, D2, EX, and WB.

The following table shows the five stages of instruction execution on the i486 and the Pentium:

PF	Prefetch
D1	Decode1
D2	Decode2
EX	Execute
WB	Writeback

The execution of an instruction begins in the PF stage, the "instruction prefetch". In this stage, the machine language instruction is fetched from memory to the processor for execution. Once the instruction reaches the processor, it enters D1 stage, the first phase of instruction decoding. In this phase, the objective is to evaluate (analyze) the instruction, thus determining what kind of action it is supposed to trigger. Depending on the type of instruction, the next job is to determine the operands of the instruction (e.g., for a displacement memory address). This is the task of the second stage of instruction decoding, called D2. In the next pipeline stage, called EX, the execution of the instruction takes place, along with the associated memory accesses. In the WB stage, execution of the instruction concludes, with the contents of the processor register and the internal status register being updated.

The processor requires one cycle per stage to run these stages, while stages D2 and EX can also require one extra cycle, depending on the type of instruction. This provides a minimum of five cycles. However, if you check the Intel manuals, you'll discover that many instructions are executed in significantly fewer cycles. Some instructions even require only one or two cycles. Now we must determine how this is possible, if all the stages of the pipeline are necessary.

The solution is found in a principle used in assembly line production. Instead of only one instruction, as many instructions as the pipeline has stages runs through the various stages of the pipeline. So the subsequent instruction isn't processed after the preceding instruction leaves the last stage of the pipeline. Instead, it is processed immediately after the first stage of the pipeline. This means that the different stages of the pipeline are busy at all times, always executing their function on a different instruction.

The instructions still require a minimum of five cycles to run through the complete pipeline, but because the pipeline finishes executing an instruction with each cycle, the instructions seem to require only one cycle for execution.

Superscalar pipelines

While the pipeline procedure of the 486 is already extremely fast, the Pentium multiplies this procedure by setting up a second, parallel pipeline. This is where the phrase "superscalar pipeline architecture" comes from. To keep the two pipelines separate, the first is called the "U pipeline" and the second one is called the "V pipeline."

With the help of these two pipelines, the Pentium should theoretically be able to execute two instructions simultaneously and, as a result, double the execution speed. However, in reality, this process isn't that easy. Frequently two sequential instructions can only be executed in sequence because they are dependent on each other. A simple example of this would be two machine language instructions, the first one describing a processor register on which the second instruction performs a read access. There are many other rules that make simultaneous execution of two sequential commands seem impossible. One such rule is the limitation of parallel execution to "simple" machine language instructions. Some examples of simple machine language instructions are MOV instructions, integer addition and subtraction, PUSH and POP instructions, and others. Only these instructions are actually "threaded" in the processor; all others are executed by Microcode, which is a type of processor operating system. It controls execution of complex machine language instructions through different execution units of the processor.

The second stage of the pipeline, D1, determines whether a parallel execution of both instructions is possible. In the PF stage, the current instruction to be executed and its successor are loaded into two parallel decoding units. This establishes the exact sequence. The current instruction goes to the decoding unit of the U pipeline and its successor goes to the decoding unit of the V pipeline.

If it is determined in D1 that simultaneous execution of the two instructions is possible, each of the two instructions then passes the various stages of its pipeline in parallel. If parallel execution is not possible, the instruction from the U pipeline goes to the next stage, while the instruction from the V pipeline is executed in the U pipeline as the instruction following the current instruction.

So the program code determines whether two instructions can be executed simultaneously, or whether they have to pass the various stages of the U pipeline in sequence. Optimizing compilers for the Pentium take this into consideration by organizing the machine code in such a way that the sequential machine language instructions permit simultaneous execution as often as possible.

Branch Target Buffer

The efficiency of the pipeline principle is based upon the constant provision of new instructions to the pipeline. Only when the various stages of the pipeline are permanently filled does it seem possible that the various instructions can be executed in one cycle. That is why two prefetch buffers are preset to the first stage of both pipelines. These prefetch buffers load the next instruction for the pipeline from memory or the processor-specific cache.

1080

However, even these aren't helpful when the processor has to execute a jump instruction. In this case, instead of continuing with the following instruction, program execution continues with an entirely different instruction. As a result, execution of the following instructions, which are already in the pipeline, must be canceled and the pipeline must be loaded with new instructions. It takes a few cycles before the first instruction leaves the pipeline after the jump instruction.

Pentium uses a Branch Target Buffer (BTB) to avoid the problem of jump instructions. This buffer is used in the D1 stage of instruction execution for all types of NEAR jump instructions (i.e., for conditional and unconditional jumps, as well as for procedure references). If the processor encounters such an instruction in the D1 stage, it uses the address of the instruction in memory to search the BTB for the instruction. Every time the processor executes one of these jump instructions, it stores both the instruction's address and the jump destination's address in the BTB. If the instruction is registered there because it has already been executed, the processor assumes that the jump should be executed again. Instead of loading the successor of the jump instruction into the pipeline, the processor loads the command to the target address.

However, if the jump instruction isn't registered in the BTB, the subsequent instruction is loaded in the pipeline. During the EX stage (at the latest), the processor will determine whether to execute the jump. If the processor predicted accurately with the address from the BTB, the instruction that follows the jump instruction will already be in the pipeline. So program execution can immediately continue. Even execution of a conditional jump will only take one cycle in this case.

However, if the processor's prediction is incorrect, this means that the wrong commands are in the pipeline. So the pipeline must be "flushed." This involves canceling the execution of the commands currently in the pipeline and completely reloading the pipeline. As a result, instead of only one cycle, at least three cycles are needed to execute the jump command.

34.2 The Cache

The Pentium processor has two separate 8K caches, one for data and one for program code. Both of these caches are two-way set-associative caches. Each path consists of 128 entries with a cache line size of 32 bytes. The data cache can be operated in Writethrough and in Copyback mode, and is capable of responding to two accesses from the U and V pipeline of the processor simultaneously. To guarantee this, each cache line of 32 bytes is divided into eight 4-byte blocks.

If you're a computer expert, the previous explanation reveals the most important information about the cache structure of the Pentium processor. However, the explanation is extremely confusing to average computer users. You've probably never encountered the terms "cache lines", "two-way associativity", and "Copyback mode." Therefore, in the following sections we'll discuss how a processor cache operates and discuss Pentium cache in detail. This information may not improve your programming skills. However, if you want to know what makes the Pentium so fast, you must understand the cache.

Also, since the on-chip cache was first used with the i486, we'll also briefly discuss the processor cache of the i486.

Processor cache, hard drive cache, font cache, and CD-ROM cache are different devices that use the term "cache." A cache accelerates access to specific data and information by holding a portion of the data in a reserved section of memory. This process provides faster access than the actual storage device. This means that, for example, a hard drive cache reserves sectors of a hard drive, which have already been read in RAM memory, to deliver the sectors directly from this memory to the caller for a new read request instead of getting the sectors from the hard drive. Because a hard drive is several hundred times slower in access time than RAM, you can use this method to save a great deal of time.

While hard drive, CD-ROM, and font caches use RAM memory as "high-speed memory", this doesn't apply to the processor cache. From the processor's view, it requires a cache because RAM doesn't supply data and program instructions fast enough for its purposes. This cache stores the memory locations that the processor addressed during the last memory accesses. As a result, the next time the processor needs to access these memory locations, it doesn't have to get them from RAM. Instead, the processor can take the memory locations directly from high-speed cache memory.

However, not all processor caches are the same. It makes a big difference whether you are dealing with a primary or secondary processor cache. These are sometimes also called "first level cache" and "second level cache."

Currently 128K or 256K caches always refer to secondary cache. This is the cache that is between the processor and RAM and usually consists of SRAM (a form of high-speed RAM). The main memory is equipped with lower-priced DRAM chips, which are three to four times slower in supplying data to the processor than SRAM chips. This is where the speed advantage of a secondary cache becomes important. For comparison, consider that while SRAM is able to produce response times between 20 and 25 nanoseconds (millionths of a second), most PCs use 70ns, 80ns, or 100ns DRAM chips as main memory.

While secondary cache memory is located outside the CPU, the primary cache refers to the memory located directly on the CPU. The CPU can read from primary cache memory just as fast as from its registers. This is why it would be best to place the entire cache memory of a system directory on the processor, or better still, all the RAM memory. However, considering the current status of processor technology, this is impossible.

There is also a third level cache, which refers to normal main memory (RAM). This serves cache memory for hard drives and other peripherals. The numbering sequence is intentional, because the higher the number, the farther the cache is from the processor. As the number increases, the cache memory speed decreases, as does the price for 1K of the cache memory.

Cache effectiveness

The quality and effectiveness of a cache is measured from the ratio of cache hits and cache misses. A cache hit occurs when the data requested by the processor is already in a cache. So, the processor doesn't have to access slower memory. A cache miss means that the data is not reserved in the cache, so first it must be loaded from memory into the cache, before it can be passed on to the processor. The greater the number of cache hits in comparison with cache misses, the more often the processor can be served from high-speed memory, ultimately causing it to work faster.

The ratio between cache hits and misses mainly depends on three factors: Organization of the cache, the type of program code being executed, and, obviously, the size of the cache. The third factor can be checked off quickly, because a growing cache size also increases the probability that the information, for which the processor is searching, is already in the cache.

For the second factor, the type of program code, the "locality" of this code is very important. First, remember that a process cache not only caches the data that a program reads from memory during its execution, but also the executed program code. Regardless of whether the processor reads a variable or the next machine language instruction, they both must be furnished from memory. Also, in both cases, the cache first checks whether the address has already "been there" once.

This is why self-contained program sections, especially loops, that fit in the cache can be executed so quickly. If the execution of programs mainly occurs in blocks that aren't bigger than the cache, the existence of the cache will increase the speed of program execution. However, if a program continually jumps back and forth between different program sections, the cache won't be as noticeable.

There are two other factors that are basic prerequisites for the efficient use of cache memory. These two factors fall into the category of "Cache Organization". The first factor is cache strategy, in relation to read and write accesses, while the second factor is cache architecture, i.e., the way cached information is stored in the cache.

Cache strategies

Writethrough and WriteBack caches are related to the read and write accesses of the CPU. Writethrough is the simpler type, because the cache is addressed only for read accesses of the CPU. The cache transfers write accesses directly to main memory (RAM). Before doing this, however, the cache checks whether the specified memory location is already stored in the cache as a result of a read access. If this is the case, the new value of the memory location must also be entered in the cache.

If this doesn't happen, the cache contents and the contents of conventional memory may be inconsistent, which is the worst thing that can happen to a cache. Because of this inconsistency, the next time you read access the cache, it will return the old contents of the memory location, while conventional memory already contains a completely different value.

Along with the pure Writethrough procedure, Intel 80486 processors and above support a slightly modified procedure called "buffered writethrough." To speed up write accesses to memory, the first-level cache of the processor is equipped with additional write buffers. The 486 has four of these buffers. When data must be written to memory, the cache first places the data in one of these write buffers. This lets the CPU continue working immediately, because this memory can be addressed very quickly, similar to cache memory. While the CPU works, the cache writes the contents of the write buffer to conventional memory on its own, as soon as the bus is free. As long as this buffer doesn't fill up because the CPU is attempting to write data to memory faster than the data can be transported from the write buffer, the CPU's write operations to conventional memory won't be affected.

The Writeback procedure competes with the Writethrough procedure. For read operations, a Writeback cache acts just like a Writethrough cache. However, the two caches handle write operations differently. If the information to be written to conventional memory is already in the cache, it is first updated only in the cache. The information doesn't go to memory until the cache is forced to remove the memory location from cache memory because it needs space for new entries as a result of a read access by the CPU. If a memory location is written over and over again, this saves you the trouble of relatively slow write accesses to conventional memory until the time the memory location has to leave the cache. To keep this from taking too long, a type of write buffer called a castoff buffer is installed. The data are first stored in this buffer and then transferred to conventional memory in parallel with the work of the CPU.

Cache architecture

Cache memory is usually organized into cache lines; each line can receive information from conventional memory that is cached during a read or write operation. The size of a cache line depends on the internal data capacity of the CPU or the capacity of its primary cache. On the 80386 the cache lines are 32-bit (one DWord = 4 bytes), on the 486 they are 128-bit (4 DWord = 16 bytes), and on the Pentium the cache lines are 256-bit (4 QWord = 32 bytes).

For a read access to memory, the entire cache line is always filled, even when the processor requested only a single byte. Modern processors support "burst mode", which dramatically speeds up access to byte sequences in memory. Usually the CPU must place the address on the bus before reading out the desired memory location. However, in a burst access, the data are read as a block. The CPU only has to place the address for the first byte on the bus; the memory automatically furnishes all subsequent memory locations upon request.

For example, the 486 usually requires 2 clock cycles to read a DWord from memory, so 4*2 clock cycles are necessary to fill a cache line. In burst mode, two cycles are required only for the first DWord; the three following words will be furnished in one cycle. That's why burst mode is also called a 2-1-1-1 burst; it takes only five cycles instead of the normal eight. The same procedure can also be used for write accesses.

Along with cached data, the cache must also store the memory addresses for the data. Each cache line is connected with a tag. This is where the cache stores the address of the data, as well as additional status information. (We'll talk about this information later in this chapter.) In secondary caches, the tags are not included with the cache lines. Instead, they are housed in separate memory components, which work even faster than the actual cache memory. In searching the cache for a memory location, the address not only has to be read out from the tag, but also must be compared with the address of the particular access by using a comparator. Naturally, this is time-consuming but is compensated for by speedier SRAM memory.

Along with cache lines and tags, a cache also always has a cache controller. A secondary cache usually has a microcontroller on the motherboard, while on a primary cache the controller is part of the processor. The controller controls communication with the CPU as well as the comings and goings of the cached information in the cache lines. It is the controller that translates the cache strategy into action and manages the pool of cache lines in accordance with a specific pattern.

Cache line organization

To determine the best possible cache line organization, first you must understand that the cached information cannot be saved in any cache line you choose. Otherwise, in a read access the cache controller would be forced to run through all the tags in search of the correct address and compare the addresses stored there with the CPU address. This process would take more time than loading the information directly from conventional memory.

For this reason, cache controllers always connect the addresses of the cached memory locations with the cache lines, in which the addresses are stored. In the simplest type of cache organization, called "direct mapping", each byte from conventional memory has only one cache line in which it can be stored.

The cache controller checks this cache line when the CPU performs a read access. If the address is not listed there, it isn't in the cache.

In a direct mapped cache, mapping between the address and the cache line, in which it is stored, takes place via the memory address. The address is broken down into various components. To describe this process, we'll use a 256K secondary cache for a 486 system as an example.

Direct mapped secondary cache for the 486

Secondary caches for the 486 work with a cache line size of 128 bits (16 bytes). So, a 256K cache provides 16,384 cache lines. The cache controller's task is to clearly map the CPU address to one of the 16,384 cache lines. Since 16,384 is 2 to the 14th power, the lower 14 bits of the CPU address determine the number of the cache line. However, instead of bits 0 to 13, these are bits 4 to 17. Bits 0 to 3 are needed to form the offset in the cache line; these four bits contain precisely the value between 0 and 15 that is needed for addressing the desired byte within the specific cache line.

Bits 0 to 3 make up the index in the cache line, and bits 4 to 17 are used as an index in the cache line pool. So bits 18 to 31 remain. Actually, these bits are supposed to be stored in the tag of a cache line. However, instead of the 14 bits, frequently only eight bits (bits 18 to 25) are stored there. This means that the cache can manage only the lower 64 Meg (2 to the power of 26) of RAM memory, since there usually aren't even enough sockets provided on the motherboard for this much memory.

While its simplicity makes this procedure appealing, it does have a big disadvantage. Because the 64 Meg of RAM are mapped only to 16,384 cache lines, 256 memory locations share the same cache line. These memory locations are always 256K apart. However, once an address is loaded into the cache, whose cache line is already loaded with another one of these 256 addresses, it forces the old address out of the cache.

Associative caches

To prevent memory addresses from excluding each other in advance, associative cache memory refines the direct mapping process. Instead of assigning a single cache line to each memory location, it assigns each memory location two, four, or even eight possible cache lines. These are also called twofold, fourfold, or eightfold associative caches. An example of such a cache is the primary, fourfold associative cache of the 486, which holds 8K.

An associative cache requires much more circuitry than a direct mapped cache. In searching for a memory location, the cache controller must read two, four, or eight tags (depending on associativity), rather than one tag. Then the controller uses a comparator to compare them with the specific CPU address (or part of it).

In addition, for a read access, the cache controller must choose which of the potential cache lines it will place the memory location(s) in, since it can be assumed that all imaginable cache lines are already occupied. Instead of randomly forcing one of the filled cache lines out of the cache, most cache controllers implement an LRU (Last Recently Used) algorithm. LRU means that the cache line which hasn't had a read hit for the longest time is removed from the cache. Next to the address in the tag, a couple of bits are also stored; the bits contain the sequence of the last accesses. On the whole, these measures significantly increase the effectiveness of an associative cache compared to a direct mapped cache.

Paging and interleaving

Paging or interleaving are other terms that are frequently used to describe the architecture of a cache. Both terms refer to the same concept, describing the distribution of the contents of various cache lines to different pages in memory. A page is a continuous block of memory; it's not the different cache lines that are divided, but their contents.

For example, the first level data cache of the Pentium is interleaved eightfold, meaning that eight DWords of a 256-bit cache line are also placed in eight separate pages. The first DWords from all cache lines are stored in the first page, the second DWords are stored in the second page, etc. This is done on the Pentium to enable simultaneous access to the cache from the U and V pipeline of the processor. As long as the U and V pipeline want to read different DWords from one of the cache lines, they access different pages so they can both be operated at the same time.

MESI protocol

The cache's greatest difficulties are caused by external memory accesses that bypass the processor and cache controller. What is written to memory during such accesses could destroy the consistency of the cache (i.e., the information stored in the cache would no longer match the actual contents of RAM). DMA controllers can cause such inconsistencies by bypassing the processor to write data to memory from an external device, such as a hard drive controller. However, bus masters on bus systems, such as EISA and MCA, can also destroy the consistency of a cache. In the bus mastering design, the CPU briefly passes bus control to the bus master. Usually the bus master is a component of an add-in board and it uses the control over the bus to shift data within RAM as quickly as possible, or to transfer data from its own memory to RAM.

To eliminate inconsistencies resulting from such accesses in advance, the cache controllers of secondary caches are linked to the system in such a way that they handle DMA transfers and bus master accesses. However, in multiprocessor systems, which will become more important in the era of the Pentium and Windows NT, this is not possible, because the CPUs are directly on the bus. Therefore, they cannot be connected to the bus from the cache controller.

Also, with multiprocessor systems, each processor has its own first level cache and consistency between these different caches (and RAM) must be preserved. INTEL solves this problem with the Pentium processor by using MESI protocol, which the Pentium supports for synchronization of caches in a multiprocessor system. MESI protocol has a feature called bus snooping, which is a procedure that helps a processor and other system components prompt for and manipulate the status of cached information in the caches of other processors.

We'll use the following example to illustrate this:

Two Pentium processors running in parallel cache a specific memory location simultaneously. One of the two processors modifies this memory location. Since the cache is operating in write-back mode, the memory location doesn't get updated in RAM until later. This makes the memory location in the cache of the second processor invalid, since it still has the old value. If the processor doesn't realize this, it will inevitably result in a conflict if the processor continues processing this memory location.

However, when the different processors communicate with each other by using MESI protocol, such inconsistencies are avoided. The acronym MESI stands for the four different states that a cache line of the processor cache can have, M, E, S and I. Each cache line has a tag containing the appropriate flags for identifying this state. The following is an explanation of each letter:

M - Modified	The cache line is only in this cache, but it has been modified and not yet written back to RAM. As a result, the contents in RAM no longer match the current contents of the memory location.
E - Exclusive	The cache line is exclusively in this one cache and hasn't been modified. The contents of RAM and the contents of the cache line still match.
S - Shared	The cache line may still be in other caches and hasn't been modified. A write access must take place in write-through mode (i.e, must be passed on directly to RAM). All other caches containing this cache line will recognize the change and automatically update the contents of their cache lines.
I - Invalid	The contents of the cache line are invalid; it is empty and free to receive new data.

First level cache of the Pentium

Now that we've discussed the principle and structure of first and second level caches, you may better understand the information presented at the beginning of this chapter. Now we'll discuss how a first level cache is implemented in the Pentium.

Actually the Pentium has two separate first level caches: one for data and one for code. Both caches are 8K and two-way associative. Each path contains 128 cache lines of 32 bytes each (2 paths * 128 cache lines * 32 bits = 8K).

Both caches can be prompted at the same time, while the data cache is capable of responding simultaneously to two requests from the U and V pipeline of the processors. To achieve this purpose, its cache lines are eight-fold interleave, permitting simultaneous access to each DWord in the cache. The tags in the data cache are even triple-ported, which means that they can be addressed by three sources at the same time. Two of these sources are the U pipeline and the V pipeline, while the third source is used for bus snooping when it is necessary to determine whether a specific address is in the cache.

You can switch each cache line in the data cache to Writethrough or Writeback mode using software or hardware. While operating the cache in Writeback mode makes sense from a performance standpoint, it can lead to problems with specific memory areas. For example, consider the video RAM on a graphics card. If this memory area is cached in Writeback mode, the cached information takes quite a while to get to video RAM, which, in turn, slows down composition of the screen.

Overall, the cache architecture in the Pentium is much more complicated than that of its predecessor, the 486. The double integer pipeline and the concept of using the Pentium in multiprocessing systems contribute to this factor. Nevertheless, the cache is an important driving force behind the outstanding performance of the Pentium.

34.3 Floating-point Unit

The floating-point unit of the Pentium is integrated on the chip, just like the 486. However, the performance of this unit has been significantly improved compared to its predecessor. The following table demonstrates this by showing a comparison of execution times for floating-point instructions on a 486 and on a Pentium. Intel claims that the execution of floating-point instructions on the Pentium is up to seven times faster than the 486, enabling the Pentium to compete with workstation processors.

The following table compares execution times for floating point instructions on a 486 and a Pentium:

Command	486	Pentium
FXCH	4	1
FLD	3	1
FST	3	2
FADD	10	3
FSUB	10	3
FMUL	16	3
FDIV	73	39

The FCXH command has a special position, since it is frequently used in floating-point programming. The reason for this has to do with the organization of the eight floating-point registers for all Intel processors and numerical coprocessors. These registers are handled like a stack; most floating-point instructions use the top of the stack as one of their arguments and also place their result there. As a result, a program must always take values to the top of the floating-point stack or move the values from there. Because the FXCH instruction handles this task, it is executed more frequently than all other floating-point instructions.

That is also why developers increased the speed of executing this instruction on the Pentium significantly over the 486's execution speed. The Pentium requires only one cycle, and sometimes doesn't even need any cycle at all. What makes this possible is the floating-point unit's ability to run the FXCH command parallel to another floating-point instruction. However, this is also the only case in which both floating-point pipelines can be occupied simultaneously with the execution of two floating-point instructions.

The superscalar, eight-stage floating-point pipeline forms the foundation for parallel execution of an FXCH instruction and any other floating-point instruction. Like an integer pipeline, the floating-point pipeline consists of two pipelines working in parallel. Actually, the floating-point pipeline shares its first five stages with the integer pipeline, but also requires three additional stages to complete execution of a floating-point instruction.

The following table shows the eight stages of the floating-point pipeline:

PF	Prefetch
D1	Decode1
D2	Decode2
EX	Execute
X1	Floating-point Execution Stage 1
X2	Floating-point Execution Stage 2
WF	Write File
ER	Error Report

The first three stages are identical to the execution of an integer command, because this is when the CPU finds out that it is dealing with a floating-point instruction. In the fourth pipeline stage (EX), in which the integer commands are executed, depending on the command, the floating-point unit first fetches the operands of the floating-point instruction from memory or a register and converts them into a special floating-point format, with which the floating-point operates internally. The actual execution of the instruction takes place in stages X1 and X2. In the WF stage, the result of the floating-point operation is then rounded off and transferred to the target register on the floating-point stack. Execution of the floating-point is completed in the ER stage, in which any errors that may have occurred in the operation are reported and the floating-point status register is updated.

34.4 Other Features

Along with its superscalar architecture, first level cache, and floating-point unit, the Pentium has several other features that distinguish it from its predecessors. They are:

- Paging in Protected and Virtual 86 mode is no longer limited to 4K pages, but can also operate with a page size of 2 Meg or 4 Meg. This should help reduce the management time necessary for paging in multitasking systems.

- The Pentium has a system management mode, as already implemented in special versions of the 486. It helps integrate a Pentium processor in programs designed to save power.

- The "Function Redundancy Check" allows parallel operation of two Pentium processors that check up on each other to ensure correct operation. This should spur the development of error-tolerant systems.

- Improvements in debugging support searching for complex errors and debugging with hardware add-ons.

- In Performance monitoring, the Pentium measures the progress of program execution.

Chapter 35

DOS 6

In 1993, Microsoft introduced the sixth version of DOS. Many users were surprised by how few of the promised features actually appeared in this version. For example, multitasking wasn't included. Instead, DoubleSpace and third-party memory support were added. In our opinion, DoubleSpace is the most important new feature of MS-DOS Version 6.

In this chapter, we'll discuss how DoubleSpace works and how it organizes information on a drive. We'll also discuss the DoubleSpace user interface. Then we'll explain the compression/decompression algorithms on which DoubleSpace is based, and show how you can use data compression and decompression capabilities in your own applications.

35.1 DoubleSpace

MS-DOS 6 includes an on-line disk compressor called DoubleSpace. Since similar products existed prior to DOS 6 (e.g., Stacker), DOS 6 provides for optimal integration of these components into the total system. Although the maximum performance is decreased by 10 percent, the hard drive capacity is almost doubled.

First we'll examine some basic concepts of disk compression, then we'll look at the internal workings of DoubleSpace. You'll learn how DoubleSpace manages the compressed data and what DoubleSpace has to offer.

35.1.1   Data compression

There's nothing mysterious about data compression. Compressing files and directories produces an (apparent) expansion of available hard drive space. All compression programs, such as LHARC, Stacker, and DoubleSpace, condense data according to one of the following algorithms:

- Run Length Encoding (RLE)

- Huffman Coding

- Lempel-Ziv Compression, also known as LZW (Lempel-Ziv-Welsh).

There are numerous variations of these algorithms. However, each is based on a specific principle of data compression. All three processes have advantages and disadvantages regarding the amount of compression that's possible and the system resources needed for compression and decompression. Obviously resource utilization also affects the speed of compression and decompression, which, in turn, affects file access performance. However, an on-line compressor such as DoubleSpace provides a balanced relationship between degree of compression and performance.

The following descriptions of the various compression techniques should help explain why the developers at Microsoft decided to use the Lempel-Ziv process.

Run Length Encoding

Run Length Encoding is the simplest form of data compression. When compressing a file containing sequences of identical bytes, only the first byte of each sequence is stored, followed by the number of repetitions. These two bytes must be preceded by an ESC character. During unpacking the ESC character indicates that a repetitive sequence was encoded in this particular location.

Since the Escape character can also occur as a "normal" character in the file, additional precautions must be taken to ensure that this character isn't later interpreted as the start of a repetitive sequence. This doesn't affect the basic mechanism of Run Length Encoding, however.

This type of data compression is especially suited to files containing numerous sequences of identical bytes, such as graphic files. Usually the greater the frequency of such sequences and the longer they are, the higher the degree of compression attained. The RLE process is relatively easy to implement, yet for large groups of differentiated files it yields the poorest results of all three algorithms. This is because it affects only constant byte sequences and leaves all other characters untouched.

Huffman coding

Huffman coding, named for the French mathematician Huffman, deviates from the commonly used standard in electronic data processing. Usually each character in a text or a file is represented by a constant number of bits (usually 8). However, with the Huffman method, the individual characters receive variable lengths.

The Huffman algorithm takes the file to be compressed and analyzes the frequencies with which various characters occur. Depending on these frequencies, the characters are then portrayed as bit sequences of varying lengths. The more frequently a character appears in the file, the shorter the bit sequence. As a result, some characters have bit lengths greater than eight. However, in the middle range of frequencies, lengths remain below eight, while the more frequently occurring characters are coded in far fewer than eight bits.

The actual process, once these bit sequences have been established and converted, is based on the creation of a binary tree, which contains the different characters and their frequencies. Since this is a relatively complicated procedure, we won't discuss it in detail here. The result of this process is that two bits are still needed for coding the most common characters, while longer bit sequences are needed for the less common characters. These sequences are usually longer than the original eight bits. However, a noticeable compression occurs relating to the common characters.

When comparing degrees of compression, the Huffman process is always superior to Run Length Encoding and in most cases superior to the LZ process. However, this depends on the contents of the file. The difference is smaller with the LZ process than with RLE. The Huffman process's disadvantage, as compared with the LZ process, lies in its complex conversions and the relative slowness of subsequent decompression. The file contents must be interpreted as bit sequences of varying lengths instead of as a group of 8-bit characters.

Lempel-Ziv process

Although the LZ process produces compression rates comparable to those of Huffman coding, it is much simpler and even has some similarities to Run Length Encoding. The focal point of this process is a search for repetitive sequences within a file. While Run Length Encoding looks only for sequences of the same byte, the LZ process checks the entire text.

For example, suppose the word "Miller" occurs in a file. The LZ algorithm searches for this word in the stored text. If it's found, a "match tag" is written into the file in place of the word. As a type of reverse-direction offset, the match tag indicates how many characters back one must go from the current location to the referenced character sequence, and how many characters should be taken from that point. In addition, the LZ process also incorporates Run Length Encoding for sequences of identical characters. The repeated character is written once to the file at its respective position and immediately after it's placed a match tag. Here the offset is 1 and the number equals the number of repetitions.

Of course this process is useful only if the match tag doesn't require more space than the text to which it refers. The version of the algorithm incorporated into DoubleSpace considers this and, depending on the type of file, achieves at least the following rates of compression:

File type	Compression ratio
Program files	1.4:1
Texts, spreadsheets, databases	2:1
Graphics and other highly redundant files	3:1 or more

In this way, with a balanced mix of files, DoubleSpace can virtually double available hard drive capacity.

CVFs

To optimize the available hard drive capacity, DoubleSpace uses a CVF (Compressed Volume File). Usually this file, whose fixed size is determined when DoubleSpace is installed, occupies the majority of the storage space. The CVF includes both compressed files and all data structures needed for file upkeep.

With DoubleSpace, you can have more than one CVF file within a system. Each of these files is treated as a separate drive with its own drive identifier (i.e., virtual drives) and can occupy up to 512 Meg on the (uncompressed) hard drive. So, after compression, up to 1 gigabyte or more of files can be stored.

The name "DBLSPACE.nnnh" is always assigned to this file; nnn is a sequential number. In converting an existing drive to a DoubleSpace drive, DoubleSpace always assigns the number "000" to the CVF file that is generated. Therefore, the file's name becomes "DBLSPACE.000."

When you start the system, this file isn't visible on drive C:. This occurs because what DOS states is drive C: is actually the contents of the CVF file; the original files from drive C: are stored as compressed files within the CVF file. However, the CVF file is accessible because the original drive C: now has drive identifier H:. When you look in the main directory of this drive, you'll see the file "DBLSPACE.000." You can also assign a device ID other than H:, as long you specifically define it during hard drive conversion.

While DoubleSpace sets up a slightly modified FAT system within the CVF file, the original drive (now H:) remains unchanged. Its structure and any files subsequently placed on it won't change. In particular, DoubleSpace leaves the DOS system files on the drive so the system can boot up as before from the hard drive. Actually, DoubleSpace is activated relatively late in the boot sequence. So, it isn't immediately available when the computer is switched on. The system first boots once using the normal FAT on drive C:. From the perspective of the C: drive, the CVF file looks like a completely normal file.

To display the contents of drive H:, use the DIR H: /A:HS command. The following files will appear:

```
        Volume in Drive H is HOST_FOR_C
        Volume Serial Number is 1AAB-734F
        Directory of H:\
IO       SYS      40,767  03-10-93    6:00a
MSDOS    SYS      38,186  03-10-93    6:00a
386SPART PAR  16,769,024  08-12-93    3:17p
DBLSPACE BIN      51,288  03-10-93    6:00a
DBLSPACE INI          91  06-30.93   10:37a
DBLSPACE 000 295,322,624  08-12-93    3:16p
        6 File(s)  312,221,980 bytes
                   111,099,904 bytes free
```

In addition to the DOS system files IO.SYS and MSDOS.SYS, and the CVF file DBLSPACE.000, three other files exist on this drive. One is the permanent Windows swap file (if installed), which for performance reasons should not be stored within a compressed drive. There are also two other DBLSPACE files which are needed for setting up the DoubleSpace drive at system startup (more on this later).

The following is a summary of the various DoubleSpace files:

Filename	Purpose
DBLSPACE.BIN	Enables access to compressed drives. This file is loaded while booting and executes even before DOS begins processing the CONFIG.SYS file.
DBLSPACE.EXE	Sets up and maintains DoubleSpace drives.
DBLSPACE.HLP	Help file for DBLSPACE.EXE.
DBLSPACE.INF	Stores the DoubleSpace configuration.

DBLSPACE.INI	DoubleSpace configuration file for Windows.
DBLSPACE.WIN	Used only during installation to record information about the current Windows system.
DBLSPACE.SYS	Device driver that determines the final location of the DBLSPACE.BIN program code and moves the code into upper memory when requested.
DBLSPACE.xxx	DoubleSpace CVF file containing a compressed drive.
DBLWIN.HLP	Help file for running DoubleSpace under Windows.

CVF file structure

To understand the structure of a CVF file, you must remember two requirements that existed when DoubleSpace was being developed and significantly influenced its development:

1. To utility programs, such as Norton's SpeedDisk and DirectorySort, a DoubleSpace drive must appear as a normal DOS drive.

2. The files stored on a DoubleSpace drive must always be compressed in blocks of fixed size, instead of compressed in their entirety.

The first requirement is related to compatibility, which is extremely important in DOS. So existing application programs and disk utilities can continue using DOS file access commands (especially interrupts 25H and 26H) to access DoubleSpace drives as well, the original FAT structure of such a drive must remain as close to intact as possible. Later you'll see that CVF files imitate the structure of a FAT volume, even though it's a slightly expanded and modified one.

Clustering compressed files

The second requirement is also clearly reflected in the CVF file structure. Based on the data compression techniques used in DoubleSpace, files shouldn't be compressed in their entirety. For example, to read in a record, a DOS program opens a file and positions the file pointer on the byte with offset 35,000. Under normal circumstances this operation, which eventually must be executed by the DOS file system, doesn't present a problem. As long as you don't have a virus-infected FAT, this byte will be found just where expected - 34,999 characters after the first byte in the file.

However, since the file exists in compressed form, DoubleSpace must first locate the byte within the framework of the compressed data. Because of the compression, the byte now located at the stated offset address may actually represent byte 48,000, 120,000, or any other byte in the system.

In this case, the only way to solve this problem is by completely decompressing the file, from the beginning of the file to the point at which 35,000 characters have been expanded. This process would be time-consuming. For this reason, DoubleSpace uses an alternate method of compressing files; it compresses in 8K blocks. For example, when accessing the byte with offset address 35,000 in the original (uncompressed) file, DoubleSpace can immediately find the block in which this byte is located. Although it must still decompress the entire block to reach the desired byte, all preceding blocks remain untouched.

This method of clustering of 8K blocks has both negative and positive effects on the quality of the compression. According to the LZW compression algorithm, references to already-encoded character strings are important.

One negative aspect is that the references must always refer to the current 8K block, and can no longer access the file contents in their entirety. During file compression, the statistical midpoint will therefore contain fewer repeating sequences, resulting in less data being compressed through references, and lowering the degree of compression. However, it would take too long to search through the entire file for the current byte to be written, each time a reference is being created. In addition, the entire file would have to be kept in memory, which certainly isn't feasible either.

Also, too much space would be needed for the references themselves. After all, they must also contain the offset address for the character strings to which they refer. Within a closed 8K block, this offset address requires a maximum of 13 bits. Depending on its size, an entire file may require 24 bits or even 32. In the end, clustering of a compressed file into blocks of 8K each is the only practical way of ensuring the fastest and most efficient compression and decompression possible.

Now we'll return to CVF file structure. The term "cluster" is also used in connection with a FAT drive. Here the drive sectors are managed as clusters (groups) of 2, 4, 8, etc., instead of individually. In fact, the compressed 8K blocks form the basis of a DoubleSpace drive. These are the clusters that are maintained by the drive's File Allocation Table.

Differences from a normal FAT drive

In the following sections, we'll describe the various data structures within a CVF file. As you'll see, most of this information also applies to a normal DOS drive: A BIOS Parameter Block at the beginning of the drive, the boot sector, the FAT, the main directory, etc. However, two new data structures, called BitFAT and MDFAT, are also included.

These data structures are needed because the compressed 8K file clusters aren't meant to be stored in identically-sized areas on the disk. Depending on the degree of compression, such a cluster will rarely require 16 sectors (8K), which is a complete cluster. This happens only if the data wasn't compressed at all or only very slightly. On average, perhaps eight 512-byte sectors will be needed (50% compression). However, in all cases the number will range from a minimum of one (maximum compression) to a maximum of 16 (no compression).

While an 8K cluster on a normal FAT drive is always given 16 sectors and, therefore, exactly 8K, a DoubleSpace drive must be flexible. Therefore, instead of the usual 16 sectors, an 8K cluster is allotted only as many sectors as it still requires after compression. It is precisely in this way that sectors are saved; the additional sectors make the drive appear larger than it actually is.

This is also the purpose of the two additional data structures; they reproduce, on the sector level, the cluster data from the normal FAT. Therefore, in the granularity of memory allocation, the sector is the most important unit (the cluster affects this granularity only superficially). In a certain sense, this undermines the concept of the cluster, although its existing structures are retained.

BitFAT

In this new scheme, the BitFAT acts as a type of free list, in which the still-free sectors within the CVF file are recorded. When a new 8K cluster must be written to the disk, DoubleSpace first looks here and searches for a corresponding number of free sectors. Usually it selects only adjacent sectors, so the cluster won't be scattered throughout the disk.

When allocating sectors, the corresponding entries in the BitFAT are marked as occupied. When they are later freed (by deleting the file belonging to them), they are designated as free.

MDFAT

Even though the FAT cannot record the sectors in which an 8K cluster is ultimately stored, the normal FAT structure had to be retained. This led to the introduction of the MDFAT. According to their original design, FAT entries point to the cluster, in which the next portion of the current file resides. This operation isn't changed by the MDFAT. However, the relationship between the number of a FAT entry and the number of the cluster, in which the data is stored, is now invalid. In a normal FAT, the sectors of the cluster belonging to FAT entry 43 are also stored in cluster 43.

So, instead of actually accessing the cluster, on a DoubleSpace drive first you must examine the 43rd entry of the MDFAT. It is only here that you can determine in which sectors cluster 43 is stored within the CVF file, and how many sectors are required for this. We'll discuss the construction of an MDFAT entry in more detail in the following sections.

Data structures in detail

Now that we've described the basic relationship between the various data structures in a CVF file, we'll discuss these structures in detail. You'll learn how the expanded BIOS Parameter Block and the MDFAT entries are constructed. As long as you're not planning to write programs that access these structures directly, these concepts should be easy to understand.

Data structure sequence

The following table shows the various data structures within a CVF file and their sizes. Note that the sizes of the different structures and their starting points, relative to the beginning of the CVF file, depend on the size of the CVF file itself. Therefore, their positions must be determined during program runtime by reading the corresponding data from the expanded BIOS Parameter Block at the beginning of the CVF file.

All data structures, except for the sectors in the sector heap, aren't compressed. Therefore, they can be read without any special precautions.

Data structure	Sector offset	Size in sectors	Description
MDBPB	0	1	Expanded BIOS Parameter Block (Microsoft DoubleSpace BIOS Parameter Block). This is a normal BIOS Parameter Block in the format used since MS-DOS 4.0, together with several additional "DoubleSpace fields". Specifically, this is where the size of the CVF file is recorded, which determines the starting points and the sizes of the data structures that follow.
BitFAT	1	*	Contains one bit for each sector in the sector heap, set to either 0 or 1 depending on whether or not the corresponding sector is currently being used. The size of this data structure adapts itself to that of the sector heap and thus also to the size of the CVF file. Its maximum size is 128K with a CVF file of 512 Meg.
Reserved	*	1	Free sector for use with a future version of DoubleSpace.
MDFAT	*	*	This table of 4-byte entries reproduces the FAT-entry clusters onto the sectors from the sector heap. Its size depends on the size of the CVF file, consisting of a maximum of 256K with a CVF file of 512 Meg.
Reserved	*	31	A reserved area of 31 sectors for a future version of DoubleSpace.
Boot sector	*	1	The boot sector of the CVF drive representing a copy of the host drive. It is not used for booting, but is returned upon performing a read access on Sector 0 of the DoubleSpace drive (the normal location of the boot sector).
FAT	*	*	The FAT for the DoubleSpace drive, whose structure corresponds to that of a normal DOS FAT. Its size also depends on the size of the CVF file.
Main directory	*	32	A normal DOS main directory with the usual 32-byte directory entries.
Reserved	*	2	Two additional sectors for later use by DoubleSpace.

Data structure	Sector offset	Size in sectors	Description
Sector heap	*	*	The sector storage location from which are obtained the sectors for storing the compressed clusters. It fills the rest of the CVF file until the end sectors are reached.
End sector	*	>=1*	Several sectors which close the CVF file.
* = Depends on the size of the CVF file and the length of the preceding data structures.			

Expanded BIOS Parameter Block (MDBPB)

With the expanded BIOS Parameter Block in MDBPB format (Microsoft DoubleSpace BIOS Parameter Block), DoubleSpace defines the structure of the CVF file. Therefore, all structures within the CVF file can be located.

Up to the byte with offset 22H, the MDBPB's structure is identical to the normal BPB that's been used since DOS Version 4.0. Various fields are added to this standard BPB. In DoubleSpace these fields contain information about the size and construction of the CVF file.

The MDBPB has the following structure:

Offset	Contents	Type
+00H	Branch instruction to boot-routine	3 bytes
+03H	Manufacturer and version number	8 bytes
+0BH	Bytes per sector	1 word
+0DH	Sectors per cluster	1 byte
+0EH	Number of reserved sectors	1 word
+10H	Number of File Allocation Tables (FAT)	1 byte
+11H	Number of entries in main directory (here always 512)	1 word
+13H	Number of sectors in volume	1 word
+15H	Media descriptor	1 byte
+16H	Number of sectors per FAT	1 word
+18H	Sectors per track	1 word
+1AH	Number of read/write heads	1 word
+1CH	Distance from the first sector in the volume to the first sector on the storage medium	1 word
+1EH	Total number of sectors in volume	1 dword

Offset	Contents	Type
DoubleSpace additions:		
+22H	First sector of the MDFAT	1 word
+24H	nlog2 of the number of bytes per sector	1 byte
+25H	Number of sectors preceding the DOS boot sector	1 word
+27H	First sector of main directory	1 word
+29H	First sector of sector heap	1 word
+2BH	Number of clusters (MDFAT entries) occupied by the DOS boot sector, the reserved area and the main directory	1 word
+2DH	Number of 2K pages in the BitFat	1 byte
+2EH	Reserved	1 word
+30H	nlog2 of the number of sectors per cluster	1 byte
+31H	Reserved	5 words
+3DH	FAT type (0 = 16-bit FAT, 1 = 12-bit FAT)	1 byte
+3EH	Maximum size of CVF file in megabytes (equals the size of the host drive)	1 word
+40H-1FFH	Boot routine (not needed here)	449 bytes
Length: 512 bytes		

Using an existing CVF file as an example, you can see that usually much more space is reserved for the BitFAT, the MDFAT, and the normal FAT than is actually needed. So, enlarging the CVF file is a quick and easy process. Instead of having to move the entire sector heap to the back, which involves re-shuffling almost the entire CVF file, you must make only a few changes to the appropriate MDBPB fields.

In creating these data structures during setup of a DoubleSpace drive, DoubleSpace doesn't adapt itself to the CVF file size chosen by the user. Instead, it adapts itself to the size of the host drive. This is the maximum size to which the user can later expand the CVF file.

BitFAT

DoubleSpace uses the BitFAT to keep track of the sectors from the sector heap. The BitFAT is organized as a large bit array whose bits correspond to the various sectors. A bit-value set to 1 means the corresponding sector is being used, while 0 means the sector is free. Each word from the BitFAT corresponds to 16 sectors; bit 15 represents the first sector within this group, bit 14 represents the second, etc.

Unlike the other data structures, which are permanent, the BitFAT is recreated by DoubleSpace each time you start the system. The MDFAT serves as the basis for this operation.

MDFAT

The MDFAT acts as a link between the FAT and the sector heap. To access the sectors of a FAT entry, the entry corresponding to this FAT entry must first be read from the MDFAT.

1100

Each MDFAT entry encompass 4 bytes and has the following structure:

```
Bits 0 - 21        Start sector
Bits 22 - 25       Size of compressed cluster
Bits 26 - 29       Size of uncompressed cluster
Bit 30             0 = Sector compressed
                   1 = Sector uncompressed
Bit 31             0 = MDFAT entry unused
                   1 = MDFAT entry used
Total 32 bits
```

The various bit groups within an MDFAT entry contain the following information:

Start sector

Number of the first sector from the sector heap, in which the compressed cluster is stored. Successive sectors contain the remaining bytes of the compressed cluster.

Size of compressed cluster

Provides the number of sectors that were required for compressed storage of the cluster. The minimum is one sector while the maximum is 16. The values 1 to 16 are represented by 0 to 15, so the number 0 represents one sector.

Size of uncompressed cluster

Records the uncompressed size of the cluster, which is normally 16. The only exception is the last cluster of a file when the file size is not a multiple of the cluster size of 16 sectors. Here also the values from 1 to 16 are represented by the numbers 0 to 15. Therefore, most of the time this field contains the number 15, representing 16 sectors.

Sector compressed/uncompressed

This flag shows whether the contents of the cluster were stored in compressed or uncompressed form. If, when compressing clusters, DoubleSpace doesn't save at least one sector, it forgoes the compression and stores the cluster as uncompressed.

MDFAT entry used/unused

Shows whether the MDFAT entry is currently being used. This bit is maintained for DOS Undelete programs, which, when restoring files, mark the FAT clusters as again being used.

Boot sector

The boot sector contains a 1:1 copy of the boot sector but doesn't actually boot the DoubleSpace drive. It's stored here only for compatibility reasons.

FAT

The File Allocation Table of a DoubleSpace drive acts just like a normal FAT that you would find on an uncompressed drive. However, unlike a normal drive, DoubleSpace maintains one FAT instead of two FATs. During read/write accesses by DOS programs, the second FAT is virtualized, so these programs don't notice the missing second FAT. Therefore, read accesses to the second FAT are rerouted to the first one while write accesses to the second FAT are ignored. Only write accesses to the first FAT are reflected in the FAT of a DoubleSpace drive.

Main directory

The structure of the main directory of a DoubleSpace drive is identical to that of an uncompressed drive. Here also the files and subdirectories stored in the main directory are represented by 32-byte entries. The main directory of a DoubleSpace drive contains space for 512 of these entries.

Sector heap

The sectors in the sector heap store the compressed files and subdirectories, which in this context are treated just like files. Sectors that contain compressed data always begin with a four-byte "tag", which describes how the data were compressed. For the standard DoubleSpace algorithm, the tag consists of the following bytes:

```
4DH 44H 00H 00H
```

Uncompressed sectors have no tag.

DoubleSpace and the boot process

So the user can address the compressed DoubleSpace drive in the same way as the original host drive, DoubleSpace is automatically started during the boot process. This occurs after loading and starting IO.SYS, which is one of the two core modules of DOS. At this point, all hardware tests have been executed, the active partition selected, and the boot sector contained therein loaded and started. In other words, DOS is on its way to taking control of the system.

Once IO.SYS is started, it begins by searching for the file DBLSPACE.BIN, which contains the program code for accessing compressed drives. If it finds the file in the main directory of the drive, it loads and executes the file. However, if the file is missing, IO.SYS follows its usual path of initializing the file system, completely oblivious to the possible existence of a DoubleSpace CVF file.

Once started, DBLSPACE.BIN first opens the initialization file DBLSPACE.INI, which lists the names of the CVF files on the drive and their future drive designations. DBLSPACE.BIN now mounts these CVF files (incorporates them as normal drives) into the DOS system. If DBLSPACE.BIN finds a CVF file with the number 000 (DBLSPACE.000), then this file's device ID is switched with that of the host drive, since DBLSPACE.000 always refers to the compressed contents of the host drive. The mounted drives from this moment on can be addressed, just like all other DOS drives, through their device IDs.

If DBLSPACE.BIN doesn't find a CVF file, it removes itself from memory and returns control to IO.SYS. This mechanism was included so you could also record on diskettes with the DBLSPACE.BIN file, without them actually being compressed.

After successfully mounting drives, the system continues as usual, processing the lines in the CONFIG.SYS file. Usually the kernel will arrive at the following line:

```
devicehigh=c:\dos\dblspace.sys /move
```

DoubleSpace inserts this line into CONFIG.SYS as part of its setup routine. Its function is to load DoubleSpace into upper memory (if available) so it no longer uses memory under 640K. The driver DBLSPACE.SYS's only purpose is to move the DoubleSpace kernel from DBLSPACE.BIN into Upper Memory. So, by itself DBLSPACE.SYS isn't involved in disk access via DoubleSpace.

This second "initialization" of DoubleSpace is necessary because, when DBLSPACE.BIN executes, no upper memory exists. Upper memory only appears after HIMEM.SYS (a file called from CONFIG.SYS) accesses upper memory.

Since DoubleSpace anticipates this shift, DBLSPACE.BIN is placed at the top of low memory, immediately below the 640K limit. This ensures that, when it's later removed, a gap isn't left in lower memory and valuable memory wasted.

If a call for DBLSPACE.SYS is included within the CONFIG.SYS file, upon completing the processing of this file, DOS automatically takes over the task of shifting the program code from DBLSPACE.BIN into lower RAM (instead of into upper memory).

DoubleSpace and applications

In relation to DOS commands, DoubleSpace is completely transparent to the user. Similar to other storage devices, a DoubleSpace drive can be addressed via its respective drive designation. From there, you can execute the commands.

DoubleSpace is equally transparent at the level of application programs, although you must consider different types of disk access. At the topmost level, application programs access files and directories using DOS interrupt 21H functions. At some point during the "processing chain" that initiates the call to these functions, DoubleSpace also becomes part of the file system. Using the mechanism described earlier, it finds its way to the appropriate sector from the CVF file sector heap, in which the desired bytes are stored or should be stored. The data are then either compressed or decompressed, depending on the type of access.

The next level involves DOS interrupts 25H and 26H, with whose help DOS programs can directly read and write to individual sectors of a volume. While most application programs avoid these functions, for many DOS utilities these interrupts are basic to their functioning. This especially applies to programs such as Norton's DirectorySort and defragmentation programs.

However, even to these programs, DoubleSpace provides the illusion of a normal DOS drive because it intercepts the two interrupts and converts the given sector numbers (via the MDFAT) to the sectors in which the respective information is actually stored or should be stored. Again, this also includes compression or decompression. The imitation goes so far that even DOS 5.0

defragmentation programs can be run under DOS 6 in combination with DoubleSpace. This occurs despite the fact that defragmentation is considered a very delicate operation.

In any case, there is not much to be gained from having such programs on a DoubleSpace drive, since they only re-combine the sectors of the file as they are defined in the FAT. They neglect to rearrange the various compressed cluster sectors in relation to their order in the sector heap. As children of the DOS 5 generation, these programs are completely unfamiliar with the sector heap. Therefore, on DoubleSpace drives we recommend installing the DEFRAG program included with DOS 6.2. This program takes the sector heap into consideration and restores order here as well.

DoubleSpace software interface

From the outside you can address DoubleSpace through a software interface, which depends mainly on an expansion of multiplexer interrupt 2FH. The eight functions address exclusively the requirements of disk utilities, and aren't intended for normal application programs. After all, DoubleSpace remains completely transparent to DOS programs, as long as they use the usual methods for accessing files, drives, and directories. Therefore, for normal application programs, a market doesn't exist for such a product.

The following is an overview of the eight multiplexer functions of DoubleSpace:

Function	Description
00H	Obtain version information
01H	Scan drive map
02H	Switch drive ID
05H	Link compressed drive
06H	Deactivate a DoubleSpace drive
07H	Establish storage space
08H	Obtain information about CVF file fragmentation
09H	Scan number of compressed drives

All these functions must be called with the value 4A11H in the AX register and the function number in the BX Register. The code 4A11H acts as an identifier for DoubleSpace within the framework of the multiplexer interrupt. In addition, all functions in the DL register await the device ID of the DoubleSpace drive currently to be addressed, where 0 stands for A:, 1 for B:, etc.

Function 0000H checks for the existence of DoubleSpace and obtains information about the drive designations used by DoubleSpace. This function call should precede all others, to ensure that DoubleSpace is resident in memory. It will also indicate whether DoubleSpace is in upper memory, or in conventional memory under 640K.

Function 0001H determines whether a particular drive is compressed and whether its drive identifier is genuine (i.e., not switched with the host drive). Function 0002H performs this drive identifier exchange, while function 0005H links drives. "Normal" DoubleSpace drives are linked automatically at system start, so this function is primarily designed for drivers governing

1104

interchangeable media. You can exchange any storage medium compressed by DoubleSpace and make it available to DoubleSpace in your system. In the opposite direction, Function 0006H provides a way for these programs to free a linked drive from DoubleSpace control, in which case it is no longer accessible under its previous device ID. It is not deleted however; its CVF file remains exactly as is.

Function 0007H determines the size of the sector heap within the CVF file and the maximum possible amount of compressed data. It doesn't indicate the maximum amount of data in uncompressed form, since this depends on the degree of compression, which you cannot predict for data that haven't been stored yet. This function also provides the number of sectors inside the sector heap.

Function 0008H offers some additional information of rather doubtful value, referring to CVF file fragmentation on the host drive. This function returns the same value as the MaxFileFragments setting in the DBLSPACE.INI configuration file. Similarly, Function 0009H is closely connected with another setting from this file. It returns the MaxRemovableDrives parameter setting. When DoubleSpace boots up, this function decides how many of a certain structure named DISK_UNIT DoubleSpace will create. One of these structures takes up 96 bytes and is required for the management of each active DoubleSpace drive.

In addition to the multiplexer functions, DoubleSpace offers two other functions, accessible from sub-function 04H of the DOS IOTCL function, rather than the multiplexer interrupt. The reason why these tasks are split up is simple. When you call functions through the multiplexer interrupt, DOS doesn't set the InDos flag, which enables reiterative calls to the function. In other words, while a multiplexer function is running, it can be called a second time by a TSR program or by another virtual DOS machine under Windows.

With the eight multiplexer functions, this potential for re-entry doesn't create a problem. However, this doesn't apply to the two IOCTL functions, since these relate to the internal caches that DoubleSpace maintains for temporary storage of cluster data and sectors from the MDFAT and BitFAT. Caches are always highly susceptible to re-entry problems.

In concrete terms, these two functions let you store the contents of the DoubleSpace caches onto disk, which is important if you want to exchange media or reset the system. For example, when a new drive is first installed, DoubleSpace can no longer write the contents of these caches onto the old one. That alone is bad enough, because data on the old drive can get lost. What's worse is that now the cache contents may be written to the new disk, which would guarantee even greater data losses from the new drive.

Therefore, any action, such as exchanging compressed media, must always be preceded by a call to one of the DoubleSpace IOCTL functions. The difference between them lies simply in that the second simultaneously declares the cache contents invalid, while the first keeps them valid.

A detailed listing of all DoubleSpace multiplexer functions can be found in Appendix E of this book. The two IOCTL functions are listed with the DOS API functions in Appendix D.

MRCI compression interface

DoubleSpace interacts closely with a software interface called MRCI (Microsoft Real-time Compression Interface). MRCI gives application programs, TSR programs, and device drivers access to an MRCI server, which compresses and decompresses data blocks.

An MRCI server loads into memory as a component of DoubleSpace during bootup. Although DoubleSpace itself uses MRCI for compressing and decompressing data blocks, other programs can also access it. For example, the DOS 6 backup program uses the MRCI server to store backup data in compressed form. It is also used by the Flash File System. The Flash File System from Microsoft is used in combination with flash-memory cards conforming to the PCMCIA standard, which serve as substitutes for hard disks.

Microsoft Real-time Compression Format

The data here are compressed according to a fixed format, called Microsoft Real-time Compression Format, or MRCF. Following this format guarantees that data compressed on one MRCI server can be decompressed on another MRCI server.

The MRCF format results in a "loss-free" compression, which means there are no differences between the compressed data and the subsequently decompressed data. Although this seems only natural, it's precisely what distinguishes this type of compression from other processes, such as JPEG or MPEG, which "calculate away" data to a certain extent, to achieve higher compression rates. Such a thing never occurs with MRCI servers.

Hardware servers

MRCI servers can be implemented in hardware as well as software. Until now the DoubleSpace MRCI server has existed only as a software implementation. However, there is nothing to stand in the way of third-party manufacturers also offering a hardware version. The biggest advantage of a hardware implementation would be an increase in speed, since dedicated compression/decompression hardware could accomplish this task much faster than the CPU running the corresponding software. Hardware enhancements of this type are assigned to a fast bus so they can receive and transmit the data as quickly as possible. Therefore, the first hardware servers will probably be designed for the VL bus or the PCI bus.

Another advantage of hardware servers is an improved compression rate. Because a hardware server works faster than a software server, it can run through the data more often and look for further redundancies. Microsoft estimates that this will result in a 15 percent higher compression rate.

Last but not least, dedicated compression hardware can also enhance multitasking systems, such as Windows/NT. The CPU first assigns a compression/decompression job to the MRCI hardware server and, in the meantime, busies itself with another task. This allows for more efficient use of the resource processor, and a kind of multiprocessing results.

MRCI clients

While Microsoft will reveal the secrets of its MRCI server only to selected hardware manufacturers, the development of MRCI clients is open to all. MRCI clients are application programs, TSRs, or device drivers that use MRCI servers to compress or decompress data. The

MRCI server can be used equally well by a terminal program compressing files to be transmitted, a program transmitting images over a network to various workstations, or a program compressing data for backup.

The remainder of this chapter is devoted to the software interface which the MRCI server makes available to MRCI clients.

An MRCI server makes five different tasks available to an MRCI client, as shown in the following list. The names listed here have only symbolic meanings, since access to the MRCI server occurs through a single point of entry, instead of through specialized functions. For this point of entry, a constant must be passed to register AX to access the desired function.

Name	Purpose
MRCQuery	Obtains information about an installed MRCI server
MRCCompress	Compresses data block with standard compression
MRCDecompress	Decompresses data block
MRCMaxCompress	Compresses data block to maximum
MRCIncrementalDecompress	Incrementally decompresses data block

Establishing contact by MRCI client

An MRCI client must always call MRCQuery first, since it is only through this function that it gains entry into the MRCI server, through which it can then call the other functions. MRCQuery is called using multiplexer interrupt 2FH, whereby 4A12H must be placed in register AX as an MUX code for the MRCI server. To prove that it is a legitimate MRCI client, the ASCII codes for the character combination "MR" must be placed in register CX, and those codes for "CI" must be placed in register DX. The server transposes these character combinations, so register CX receives "IC" and register DX receives "RM."

Although at first this procedure may seem rather strange, it guarantees that the MRCI client will be certain that it is dealing with an MRCI server. Any other program can engage the multiplexer interrupt under the code number 4A12H, yet none will answer the function call with precisely the same inversion of registers CH, CL, DH, and DL.

If this exchange didn't occur, then an MRCI server hasn't engaged the multiplexer interrupt. This means there is no MRCI software server in the system. However, this doesn't mean that a hardware server doesn't exist. This server enters the system through BIOS interrupt 1AH by using function B001H. Function B001H, newly developed by Microsoft, serves the same purpose as the multiplexer interrupt call, applying to registers CX and DX.

If this call is also unsuccessful, then an MRCI server doesn't exist in the system. However, if one of these two calls returns the desired combination in the register pair CX/DX, then the register pair ES:DI will contain the address of what is known as an MRCI info structure (see following table), which contains information about the MRCI server, its capabilities, and most importantly, the point of entry for calls to the various MRCI functions.

Offset	Meaning	Type
+00H	4-byte ASCII code with manufacturer name ("MSFT" for Microsoft)	4 bytes
+04H	Version number of MRCI server	1 word
	High byte contains main version number, low byte the sub-version number	
+06H	MRCI version upon which server is based High byte contains main version number, low byte the sub-version number	1 word
+08H	MRCI server entry point for calling MRCI functions	1 var ptr
+0CH	Flag for server capabilities (see below)	1 word
+0EH	Hardware flag for server capabilities implemented through hardware	1 word
+10H	Maximum data block size that server can compress	1 word
Length: 18 bytes		

The two flags returned within the structure are identical in their makeup. The first flag indicates which functions are available overall, while the second flag indicates which of these are implemented through hardware. If a bit is set in the first flag and not in the hardware flag, then the corresponding function is available through the software and not the hardware.

Total 16 bits	
Bit 0 = Standard compression (1)	Bit 1 = Standard decompression (2)
Bit 2 = Unused	Bit 3 = Maximum compression (8)
Bit 4 = Unused	Bit 5 = Incremental decompression (32)
Bits 6 - 15 = Unused	

While all MRCI servers support standard compression and decompression, this isn't true for maximum compression and incremental decompression. Maximum compression involves reducing the data even further than is possible with standard compression. However, doing this increases compression time. With incremental decompression, the idea is to decompress a compressed data block only up to a certain byte. This is useful when you need only a certain number of bytes instead of the entire data block. Instead of wasting time decompressing the entire block, with incremental decompression you can stop the unpacking of data at a certain byte and continue from that point later as desired. To determine whether each of these two functions is available, check the corresponding flags within the MRCI info structure.

One entry which you usually don't have to worry about is the maximum size of compressible data blocks. For MRCI servers, this always amounts to at least 8K, so for block sizes up to 8K checking the corresponding element within the data structure is unnecessary.

Calling the MRCI server functions

In the previous table, the various bits for the individual flags are purposely listed along with their order. Upon calling the MRCI server, these orders are the ones that must be given as a function code in register AX, as the entry point to the MRCI server. The MRCI server also looks in register CX for the value 0 or 1, depending on whether the client is a transient application program (0) or a resident system component (1), such as a TSR or device driver.

Furthermore, upon calling the MRCI server, it also awaits two FAR pointers in the register pairs ES:BX and DS:SI. ES:BX is for the pointer to the MRCI info block returned from the Query call, and DS:SI is for a pointer to an MRCI request block. Here the MRCI server obtains important information necessary for running the corresponding function (e.g., buffer addresses), where files to be compressed or decompressed are located. The following table gives the precise layout of this structure:

Offset	Contents	Type
+00H	FAR pointer to source buffer	1 var ptr
+04H	Length of source buffer in bytes	1 word
+06H	Reserved	1 word
+08H	FAR pointer to destination buffer	1 var ptr
+0CH	Length of destination buffer in bytes	1 word
+0EH	Block size for compressed data	1 word
+10H	Pointer for incremental decompression	1 var ptr
Length: 18 bytes		

The first four fields of the data structure describe the locations of the source and destination buffers in memory, as well as their length. During compression, data from the source buffer are compressed into the destination buffer (i.e., following a successful call to the function, the destination buffer contains a compressed version of the uncompressed data from the source buffer). The same happens with decompression, whereby the contents of the source buffer are decompressed into the destination buffer. The MRCI server requires that both buffers stay within their limits and, therefore, considers the given buffer sizes.

For the source buffer, the number of bytes to be compressed or decompressed is given during compression/decompression. The MRCI server uses this information to determine how much space is available in the destination buffer for the compressed or decompressed data. If there isn't enough space, the server function returns to the client with an error code. Therefore, there is no danger of overwriting the destination buffer. From the length of the destination buffer, you can also determine, following compression or decompression, the number of bytes in the compressed/decompressed data.

Offset 0EH (Block size for compressed data) applies only to data compression. This offset is designed to speed up the functioning of the MRCI server. Usually compressed data is stored in blocks of constant size. In DoubleSpace this is on the lowest level of the hard drive sector, which always contains 512 bytes. When compressing data, it's useless to carry the compression beyond 512 bytes, since you would still need the entire sector anyway. Even if you managed to squeeze the data into 300 or 200 bytes, as far as hard drive space is concerned it would make no difference. Therefore, the most practical method is stopping the compression at the 512-byte limit and saving the time that would otherwise have been used in continuing it.

Valid entries in this field are 1 to 32768. DoubleSpace sets the value to 512, but application programs can set it to 1 if they need a high degree of compression.

Server calls and Windows

The instruction code in AX, the type of application in CX, a pointer to the MRCI info block in ES:BX, and a pointer to the MRCI request block in DS:SI are needed to call an MRCI server function. However, first the program must enter a Windows Critical Section, for the case when the application is running in a virtual DOS machine under Windows in 386 Enhanced mode. Since true multitasking is being performed among these VMs, the MRCI server may be confronted with several function calls from different VMs simultaneously. The MRCI server can't handle this situation.

This problem is avoided by preceding the server call with entry into a Windows Critical Section. In a Critical Section of this type, only one VM or Windows application can exist at any given time. If another VM has already claimed this attribute, the call for entry into the Critical Section is held up until the other VM has left its Critical Section. The call for exiting a Critical Section is as important as the call for entering a Critical Section.

The entry code for a Critical Section and the subsequent exit code is precisely stipulated by Windows, and must be implemented in assembly language. The entry code is as follows:

Entry code		Exit code	
push	ax	push	ax
mov	ax,8001h	mov	ax,8101h
int	2ah	int	2ah
pop	ax	pop	ax

If Windows isn't active these calls go into oblivion, since no special handler exists for these calls after interrupt 2AH. The program will continue execution, instead of crashing the system. Although there is no entry into a Critical Section, once Windows is inactive this doesn't matter anyway. Before calling a server function, TSR programs and device drivers must take control of the InDos flag. This is necessary to prevent a re-entrance of DOS (see Chapter 32 of this book for information on TSR programming). Following a call to the MRCI server, a status value is returned in register AX. A value of 0 means the function was executed successfully, while all other values represent errors in accordance with the following table:

Code	Error	Code	Error
0	All OK	1	Incorrect function code
2	Server is busy	3	Destination buffer too small
4	Data cannot be compressed		

Appendix A

BIOS Interrupts and Functions

The various functions, which the ROM-BIOS makes available for the basic communication between a program and the hardware, can be accessed using interrupts 10H to 1AH. Besides functions for the access to the video-hardware, the keyboard, hard disks and diskette drives, this includes checking configuration data, as well as programming of the serial and parallel interface and the battery-buffered real-time clock.

Here is an overview of the various interrupts and their services. Please note, that the various functions of Interrupt 13H are explained twice, separated according to their use in relation to diskette and hard disk drives. Depending on the need for access to diskettes or hard disks, please consult the proper section.

Unless otherwise stated, the various functions are available on all types of PCs. An entire series of functions have only been available since the introduction of the XT models, others only since the introduction of the AT series. The numerous BIOS enhancements which companies such as Compaq added to the original ROM-BIOS were omitted here, since they did not establish themselves as a standard. This is also valid for the enhanced functions of the PS/2 systems of IBM, which are completely compatible with the functions presented here.

Interrupt 10H, Function 00H   **BIOS**
Video: Set video mode

Selects and initializes a video mode and clears the screen. This function is a fast method of clearing the screen while maintaining the current video mode.

Input: AH = 00H
                  AL = Video mode

	0:	40x25 text mode, monochrome	(color card)
	1:	40x25 text mode, color	(color card)
	2:	80x25 text mode, monochrome	(mono card)
	3:	80x25 text mode, color	(color card)
	4:	320x200 4-color graphics	(color card)
	5:	320x200 4-color graphics	(color card)
		(colors displayed in monochrome)	
	6:	640x200 2-color graphics	(color card)
	7:	Internal mode	(mono card)

Output: No output
Remarks: The colors for modes 4, 5 and 6 can be set with function 11.
                 The contents of the BX, CX, DX registers and the SS, CS and DS segment
                 registers are not affected by this function. The contents of all other registers
                 may change, especially the SI and DI registers.

Interrupt 10H, Function 01H   **BIOS**
Video: Define cursor type

Defines the starting and ending lines of the cursor. This cursor exists independently of the current
screen page.

Input: AH = 01H
                 CH = Starting line of the cursor
                 CL = Ending line of the cursor
Output: No output
Remarks: The values allowed for the cursor's starting and ending line depend on the
                 installed video card. The following values are permitted:
                     Monochrome display cards: 0–13
                     Color display cards: 0–7
                 BIOS defaults to the following values:
                     Monochrome display cards: 11–12
                     Color display cards: 6–7
                 You can use this function to set the cursor only within the permitted ranges.
                 Setting cursor lines outside these parameters may result in an invisible cursor
                 or system problems.
                 The contents of the BX, CX, DX registers and the segment registers SS, CS
                 and DS are not affected by this function. The contents of all the other registers
                 may change, especially the SI and DI registers.

Interrupt 10H, Function 02H   **BIOS**
Video: Position cursor

Repositions the cursor, which determines the screen position for character output by using one
of the BIOS functions.

Input: AH = 02H
                 BH = Screen page number
                 DH = Screen line
                 DL = Screen column
Output: No output
Remarks: The blinking cursor moves through this function when the addressed screen
                 page is the current screen page.
                 Values for the screen line parameter range from 0 to 24.
                 Values for the screen column parameter range from 0 to 79 (for an 80-column
                 display) or from 0 to 39 (for a 40-column display), depending on the selected
                 video mode.
                 You can make the cursor disappear by moving it to a nonexistent screen
                 position (e.g., column 0, line 25).
                 The number of the screen page parameter depends on how many screen pages
                 are available to the video card.

The contents of the BX, CX, DX registers and the SS, CS and DS segment registers are not affected by this function. The contents of all other registers may change, especially the SI and DI registers.

Interrupt 10H, Function 03H   **BIOS**
Video: Read cursor position

Senses the text cursor's position, starting line and ending line in a screen page.

Input:	AH = 03H
	BH = Screen page number
Output:	DH = Screen line in which the cursor is located
	DL = Screen column in which the cursor is located
	CH = Starting line of the blinking cursor
	CL = Ending line of the blinking cursor
Remarks:	The number of the screen page parameter depends on how many screen pages are available to the video card.

Line and column coordinates are related to the text coordinate system.

The contents of the BX register and the SS, CS and DS segment registers are not affected by this function. The contents of all the other registers may change, especially the SI and DI registers.

Interrupt 10H, Function 04H   **BIOS**
Video: Read lightpen position

Senses the position of the lightpen on the screen if applicable.

Input:	AH = 04H
Output:	AH = 0: Lightpen position unreadable
	AH = 1: Lightpen position readable
	DH = Screen line of the lightpen (text mode)
	DL = Screen column of the lightpen (text mode)
	CH = Screen line of the lightpen (graphic mode)
	BX = Screen column of the lightpen (graphic mode)
Remarks:	This function call must be repeated until 1 is returned in the AH register, because only then can coordinates be read from the other registers.

Coordinates indicated represent the current video mode's resolution.

Usually the coordinates of the light pen cannot be accurately sensed in the graphic mode. The Y-coordinate (line) is always a multiple of 2, so it isn't possible to determine whether the lightpen is in line 8 or 9. The X-coordinate (column) is always a multiple of 4 in 320x200 graphic mode and a multiple of 8 in the 640x200 bitmap mode.

The contents of the CL register and the SS, CS and DS segment registers are not affected by this function. The contents of all the other registers may change, especially the SI and DI registers.

Interrupt 10H, Function 05H   **BIOS**
Video: Select current screen page

Selects the current screen page (text mode only) which should be displayed.

Input:	AH = 05H
	AL = Screen page number
Output:	No output

Remarks: The number of the screen page depends on the number of screen pages available to the video card.

On switching to a new screen page, the screen cursor points to the position of the text cursor in this page.

Switching between various screen pages does not affect their contents (the individual characters).

You can write characters to an inactive screen page.

The contents of the BX, CX, DX registers and the SS, CS and DS segment registers are not affected by this function. The contents of the other registers, such as the SI and DI registers, may change.

Interrupt 10H, Function 06H
Video: Initialize window/scroll text upward

BIOS

Clears window or scrolls a portion of the current screen page up by one or more lines, depending on the input.

Input: AH = 06H
AL = Number of window lines to be scrolled upward (0=clear window)
CH = Screen line of the upper left corner of the window
CL = Screen column of the upper left corner of the window
DH = Screen line of the lower right corner of the window
DL = Screen column of the lower right corner of the window
BH = Color (attribute) for blank line(s)

Output: No output

Remarks: Initializing a window (placing a 0 in the AL register) fills the window with blank spaces (ASCII code 32).

The contents of the lines scrolled out of the window are lost and cannot be restored.

Function 0 of this interrupt is better for clearing the entire screen.

The contents of the BX, CX, DX registers and the SS, CS and DS segment registers are not affected by this function. The contents of all other registers may change, especially the SI and DI registers.

Interrupt 10H, Function 07H
Video: Initialize window/scroll text downward

BIOS

Clears window or scrolls a portion of the current screen page up by one or more lines, depending on the input.

Input: AH = 07H
AL = Number of window lines to be scrolled downward (0=clear window)
CH = Screen line of the upper left corner of the window
CL = Screen column of the upper left corner of the window
DH = Screen line of the lower right corner of the window
DL = Screen column of the lower right corner of the window
BH = Color (attribute) for blank line(s)

Output: No output

Remarks: This function only affects the current screen page.

Initializing a window (placing a 0 in the AL register) fills the window with blank spaces (ASCII code 32).

The contents of the lines scrolled out of the window are lost and cannot be restored.

Function 0 of this interrupt is better for clearing the entire screen.

The contents of the BX, CX, DX registers and the SS, CS and DS segment registers are not affected by this function. The contents of all other registers may change, especially the SI and DI registers.

Interrupt 10H, Function 08H

BIOS

Video: Read character/attribute

Reads the ASCII code of the character at the current cursor position and its color (attribute).

Input:	AH = 08H
	BH = Screen page number
Output:	AL = ASCII code of the character
	AH = Color (attribute)
Remarks:	The number of the screen page depends on the number of screen pages made available to the video card.

This function can also be called in graphic mode. The function compares the bit pattern of the character on the screen with the bit pattern of the character in character ROM of the video card and with the character patterns stored in a RAM table whose addresses appear in interrupt 1FH. If the character cannot be identified, the AL register contains the value 0 after the function call.

The contents of the BX, CX, DX registers and the SS, CS and DS segment registers are not affected by this function. The contents of the other registers may change, especially the SI and DI registers.

Interrupt 10H, Function 09H

BIOS

Video: Write character/attribute

Writes a character with a certain color (attribute) to the current cursor position in a predefined screen page.

Input:	AH = 09H
	BH = Screen page number
	CX = Number of times to write the character
	AL = ASCII code of the character
	BL = Attribute
Output:	No output
Remarks:	If the character should be displayed several times (the value of the CX register is greater than 1), all characters must fit into the current screen line in the graphic mode.

The control codes (e.g., bell, carriage return) appear as normal ASCII codes.

This function can display characters in graphic mode. The patterns of the characters, with the codes from 0 to 127, are determined by a table in ROM. The patterns of the characters with the codes from 128 to 255 are determined by a RAM table that was previously installed by the DOS GRAFTABL command.

In text mode, the contents of the BL register define the attribute byte of the character. In graphic mode this register determines the color of the character. The 640x200 bitmap mode only allows the values 0 and 1 for selecting colors from the color palette. The 320x200 bitmap mode only allows the values 0 to 3 for selecting colors from the color palette.

If the graphic mode is active during character output and bit 7 of the BL register is set, an exclusive OR is performed on the character pattern and the graphic pixels behind the character pattern.

After character output, the cursor remains in the same position as the character. The contents of the BX, CX, DX registers and the SS, CS and DS segment registers are not affected by this function. The contents of all other registers may change, especially the SI and DI registers.

Interrupt 10H, Function 0AH   **BIOS**
Video: Write character

Writes a character to the current cursor position in a predefined screen page by using the color of the character previously at this position.

Input:	AH = 0AH
	BH = Screen page number
	CX = Number of times to write the character
	AL = ASCII code of the character
Output:	No output
Remarks:	If the character should be displayed several times (the value of the CX register is greater than 1), all characters must fit into the current screen line in the graphic mode.

The control codes (e.g., bell, carriage return) appear as normal ASCII codes.

This function can display characters in graphic mode. The patterns of the characters with the codes from 0 to 127 are determined by a table in ROM and the patterns of the characters with the codes from 128 to 255 are determined by a RAM table previously installed by the GRAFTABL command.

In text mode, the contents of the BL register define the attribute byte of the character. In graphic mode this register determines the color of the character. The 640x200 bitmap mode only allows the values 0 and 1 for selecting colors from the color palette. The 320x200 bitmap mode only allows the values 0 to 3 for selecting colors from the color palette.

If the graphic mode is active during character output and bit 7 of the BL register is set, an exclusive OR is performed on the character pattern and the graphic pixels behind the character pattern.

The cursor remains in the same position after character output.

The contents of the BX, CX, DX registers and the SS, CS and DS segment registers are not affected by this function. The contents of all other registers may change, especially the SI and DI registers.

Interrupt 10H, Function 0BH, Subfunction 0   **BIOS**
Video: Select palette

Selects the border and background color for graphic or text mode.

Input:	AH = 0BH
	BH = 0
	BL = Border/background color
Output:	No output
Remarks:	In graphic mode, the color value passed defines the color of both the border and background. In text mode, the background color of each character is defined individually, so the passed color value only defines the color of the screen border.

Values for the color passed can range from 0 to 15.

The contents of the BX, CX, DX registers and the SS, CS and DS segment registers are not affected by this function. The contents of all other registers may change, especially the SI and DI registers.

Interrupt 10H, Function 0BH, Subfunction 1   **BIOS**
Video: Select color palette

Selects one of the two color palettes for the 320x200 bitmapped graphic mode.

Input:	AH = 0BH
	BH = 1
	BL = Color palette number
Output:	No output
Remarks:	Two color palettes are available. They have the numbers 0 and 1 and contain the following colors:

    Palette 0: Green, red, yellow

    Palette 1: Cyan, magenta, white

The contents of the BX, CX, DX registers and the SS, CS and DS segment registers are not affected by this function. The contents of all other registers may change, especially the SI and DI registers.

Interrupt 10H, Function 0CH   **BIOS**
Video: Write graphic pixel

Draws a color pixel at the specified coordinates in graphic mode.

Input:	AH = 0CH
	AL = Pixel color value (see below)
	BH = Graphics page
	CX = Screen column
	DX = Screen line
Output:	No output
Remarks:	The pixel value color parameter depends on the current graphic mode. 640x200 bitmapped mode only permits the values 0 and 1. In the 320x200 bitmapped mode, the values 0 to 3 are permitted, which generates a certain color according to the chosen color palette. 0 represents the selected background color; 1 represents the first color of the selected color palette; 2 represents the second color of the color palette, etc.

The contents of the BX, CX, DX registers and the SS, CS and DS segment registers are not affected by this function. The contents of all other registers may change, especially the SI and DI registers.

Interrupt 10H, Function 0DH   **BIOS**
Video: Read graphic pixel

Reads the color value of a pixel at the specified coordinates in the current graphic mode.

Input:	AH = 0DH
	DX = Screen line
	CX = Screen column
Output:	AL = Pixel color value
Remarks:	The pixel color value parameter depends on the current graphic mode. 640x200 bitmapped mode permits the values 0 and 1 only. In the 320x200 bitmapped

mode, the values 0 to 3 are permitted, which generates a certain color according to the color palette chosen. 0 represents the selected background color; 1 represents the first color of the selected color palette; 2 represents the second color of the color palette, etc.

The contents of the BX, CX, DX registers and the SS, CS and DS segment registers are not affected by this function. The contents of all other registers may change, especially the SI and DI registers.

Interrupt 10H, Function 0EH   **BIOS**
Video: Write character

Writes a character at the current cursor position in the current screen page. The new character uses the color of the character that was previously in this position on the screen.

Input:	AH = 0EH
	AL = ASCII code of the character
	BL = Foreground color of the character (graphic mode only)
Output:	No output
Remarks:	This function executes control codes (e.g., bell, carriage return) instead of reading them as ASCII codes. For example, the function sounds a beep instead of printing the bell character.

After this function displays a character, the cursor position increments so that the next character appears at the next position on the screen. If the function reaches the last display position, the display scrolls up one line and output continues in the first column of the last screen line.

The foreground color parameter depends on the current graphic mode. 640x200 bitmapped mode only permits the values 0 and 1. In the 320x200 bitmapped mode, the values 0 to 3 are permitted, which generates a certain color according to the chosen color palette. 0 represents the selected background color; 1 represents the first color of the selected color palette; 2 represents the second color of the color palette, etc.

The contents of the BX, CX, DX registers and the SS, CS and DS segment registers are not affected by this function. The contents of all other registers may change, especially the SI and DI registers.

Interrupt 10H, Function 0FH   **BIOS**
Video: Read display mode

Reads the number of the current video mode, the number of characters per line and the number of the current screen page.

Input:	AH = 0FH
Output:	AL = Video mode

0:	40x25 text mode, monochrome	(color card)
1:	40x25 text mode, color	(color card)
2:	80x25 text mode, monochrome	(mono card)
3:	80x25 text mode, color	(color card)
4:	320x200 4-color graphics	(color card)
5:	320x200 4-color graphics	(color card)
	(colors represented in monochrome)	
6:	640x200 2-color graphics	(color card)
7:	Internal mode	(mono card)

AH = Number of characters per line

BH = Current screen page number

Remarks: The contents of the BX, CX, DX registers and the SS, CS and DS segment registers are not affected by this function. The contents of all other registers may change, especially the SI and DI registers.

Interrupt 10H, Function 13H   **BIOS (AT only)**
Video: Write character string

Displays a character string on the screen, starting at a specified screen position on a specified screen page. The characters are taken from a buffer whose address passes to the function.

Input:
    AH = 13H
    AL = Output mode (0–3)
        0:   Attribute in BL, retain cursor position
        1:   Attribute in BL, update cursor position
        2:   Attribute in the buffer, retain cursor position
        3:   Attribute in the buffer, update cursor position
    BH = Screen page number
    BL = Attribute byte of the character (modes 0 and 1 only)
    BP = Offset address of the buffer
    CX = Number of characters to be displayed
    DH = display line
    DL = display column
    ES = segment address of the buffer

Output: No output

Remarks: Modes 1 and 3 set the cursor position following the last character of the character string. On the next call of a BIOS function for character output, the next string of characters appears following the original character string. This does not occur in the modes 0 and 2.

In modes 0 and 1, the buffer contains only the ASCII codes of the characters to be displayed. The BL register contains the color of the character string. However, in modes 2 and 3 each character has its own attribute byte when the character is stored in the buffer. The BL register doesn't have to be loaded in this mode. Even though the character string is twice as long in these modes as the number of the characters to be displayed, the CX register requires only the number of ASCII characters in the string and not the total length of the character string.

Control codes (e.g., bell) are interpreted as control codes only, and not as characters.

When the string reaches the last position on the screen, the display scrolls upward by one line and output continues in the first column of the last screen line.

The contents of the BX, CX, DX registers and the SS, CS and DS segment registers are not affected by this function. The contents of all other registers may change, especially the SI and DI registers.

Interrupt 11H   **BIOS**
Determine configuration

Reads the configuration of the system as recorded during the booting process.

Input: No input
Output: AX = Configuration

PC and XT: Bit 0:   1 if the system has one or more disk drives
Bit 1:   Unused
Bits 2-3:   RAM available on main circuit board
                     00: 16K
                     01: 32K
                     10: 48K
                     11: 64K
Bits 4-5:   Video mode after system boot
                     00: Unused
                     01: 40x25, color card
                     02: 80x25, color card
                     03: 80x25, mono card
Bits 6-7:   Number of disk drives in the system if bit 0 is equal to 1
                     00: 1 disk drive
                     01: 2 disk drives
                     10: 3 disk drives
                     11: 4 disk drives
Bit 8:   0 when a DMA chip is present
Bits 9-11:   Number of RS-232 cards connected
Bit 12:   1 when system has a joystick attached
Bit 13:   Unused
Bits 14-15:   Indicates the number of printers available
AT: Bit 0:   1 if the system has one or more disk drives
Bit 1:   1 when a math coprocessor exists in the system
Bit 2-3:   Unused
Bit 4-5:   Video mode during system boot
                     00: Unused
                     01: 40x25, color card
                     02: 80x25, color card
                     03: 80x25, mono card
Bits 6-7:   Number of disk drives in the system if bit 0 is equal to 1
                     00: 1 disk drive
                     01: 2 disk drives
                     10: 3 disk drives
                     11: 4 disk drives
Bit 8:   Unused
Bits 9-11:   Number of RS-232 cards connected
Bit 12-13:   Unused
Bits 14-15:   Indicates the number of printers available
Remarks: The type of PC must be known (PC, XT or AT) in order to properly interpret the meanings of the individual bits of the configuration word.

The memory size indicated in bits 2 and 3 of the PC/XT configuration word refers only to the main circuit board. Interrupt 12H lets you determine the total amount of available memory.

The video mode recorded in bits 4 and 5 is the mode that was activated when the system was switched on. To determine the current video mode use function 15 of interrupt 10H.

The contents of the AX register are affected by this function.

Interrupt 12H
Determine memory size

Input: No input
Output: AX = Memory size in kilobytes
Remarks: The PC and the XT can accept a maximum of 640K of RAM. The AT accepts up to 14 megabytes of RAM memory beyond the 1 megabyte limit. The memory size returned by this function ignores this extended memory. To determine the memory size beyond the 1 megabyte limit, use function 88H of interrupt 15H (available only on the AT).
The contents of the AX register are affected by this function.

Interrupt 13H, Function 00H
Diskette: Reset

Resets the disk controller and any connected disk drives. A reset should be executed after each disk operation during which an error occurred.

Input: AH = 00H
                  DL = 0 or 1
Output: Carry flag=0: Operation completed (AH=0)
                  Carry flag=1: Error (AH=error code)
Remarks: The value in the DL register is unnecessary since all the disk drives execute a reset. XT and AT models use this register to determine whether a reset should be performed on the disk drives or the hard disk.
The following error codes can occur:

01H:	Function number not permitted
02H:	Address not found
03H:	Write attempt on write protected disk
04H:	Sector not found
08H:	DMA overflow
09H:	Data transmission beyond segment border
10H:	Read error
20H:	Error in disk controller
40H:	Track not found
80H:	Time out error, unit not responding

The contents of the BX, CX, DX, SI, DI, PB registers and the segment registers are not affected by this function. The contents of all other registers may change.

Interrupt 13H, Function 01H
Diskette: Read status

Reads the status of the disk drive since the last disk operation.

Input: AH = 01H
                  DL = 0 or 1
Output: Carry flag=0: Operation completed (AH=0)
                  Carry flag=1: Error (AH=error code)
Remarks: The value in the DL register is unnecessary, since disk drives constantly return their status. XT and AT models use this register to determine whether the status of the hard disk should be checked.

The following error codes can occur:

01H:	Function number not permitted
02H:	Address not found
03H:	Write attempt on write protected disk
04H:	Sector not found
08H:	DMA overflow
09H:	Data transmission beyond segment border
10H:	Read error
20H:	Error in disk controller
40H:	Track not found
80H:	Time out error, unit not responding

The contents of the BX, CX, DX, SI, DI, PB registers and the segment registers are not affected by this function. The contents of all other registers may change.

The following error codes can occur:

01H:	Function number not permitted
02H:	Address not found
03H:	Write attempt on write protected disk
04H:	Sector not found
08H:	DMA overflow
09H:	Data transmission beyond segment border
10H:	Read error
20H:	Error in disk controller
40H:	Track not found
80H:	Time out error, unit not responding

The contents of the BX, CX, DX, SI, DI, PB registers and the segment registers are not affected by this function. The contents of all other registers may change.

Interrupt 13H, Function 02H
Diskette: Read disk   BIOS

Reads one or more disk sectors into a buffer.

Input:	AH = 02H
	AL = Number of sectors to be read
	BX = Offset address of buffer
	CH = Track number
	CL = Sector number
	DH = Disk side number (0 or 1)
	DL = Disk drive number
	ES = Buffer segment address
Output:	Carry flag=0: Operation completed (AH=0)
	Carry flag=1: Error (AH=error code)
Remarks:	The number of sectors to be read into the AL register is limited to sectors which logically follow each other on a track on one side of the disk.

The following error codes can occur:

01H:	Function number not permitted
02H:	Address not found
03H:	Write attempt on a write protected disk
04H:	Sector not found

08H:	DMA overflow	
09H:	Data transmission over segment border	
10H:	Read error	
20H:	Error in disk controller	
40H:	Track not found	
80H:	Time out error, drive not responding	

The contents of the BX, CX, DX, SI, DI, BP registers and the segment registers are not affected by this function. The contents of all the other registers may change.

Interrupt 13H, Function 03H   **BIOS**
Diskette: Write to disk

Writes one or more sectors to a disk. The data to be transmitted are taken from a buffer.

Input:	AH = 03H
	AL = Number of sectors to be written
	BX = Offset address of buffer
	CH = Track number
	CL = Sector number
	DH = Disk side number (0 or 1)
	DL = Disk drive number
	ES = Buffer segment address
Output:	Carry flag=0: Operation completed (AH=0)
	Carry flag=1: Error (AH=error code)
Remarks:	The number of sectors that can be written in the AL register is limited to sectors which logically follow each other on a track on one side of the disk. The following error codes can occur:

01H:	Function number not permitted	
02H:	Address not found	
03H:	Write attempt on a write protected disk	
04H:	Sector not found	
08H:	DMA overflow	
09H:	Data transmission over segment border	
10H:	Read error	
20H:	Error in disk controller	
40H:	Track not found	
80H:	Time out error, drive not responding	

The contents of the BX, CX, DX, SI, DI, BP registers and the segment registers are not affected by this function. The contents of all other registers may change.

Interrupt 13H, Function 04H   **BIOS**
Diskette: Verify disk sectors

Compares one or more sectors on disk with the data stored in a buffer. This can be used to verify that the data was properly saved to disk.

Input:	AH = 04H
	AL = Number of sectors to be verified
	BX = Offset address of buffer
	CH = Track number

CL = Sector number
DH = Disk side number (0 or 1)
DL = Disk drive number
ES = Buffer segment address

Output: Carry flag=0: Operation completed (AH=0)
              Carry flag=1: Error (AH=error code)

Remarks: The number of sectors to be verified in the AL register is limited to sectors which logically follow each other on a track on one side of the disk.
              The following error codes can occur:

01H:	Function number not permitted
02H:	Address not found
03H:	Write attempt on a write protected disk
04H:	Sector not found
08H:	DMA overflow
09H:	Data transmission over segment border
10H:	Read error
20H:	Error in disk controller
40H:	Track not found
80H:	Time out error, drive not responding

The contents of the BX, CX, DX, SI, DI, BP registers and the segment registers are not affected by this function. The contents of all other registers may change.

Interrupt 13H, Function 05H   BIOS
Diskette: Format track

Formats a complete track on one side of a disk. A buffer which contains information about the sectors to be formatted must be passed to the function.

Input: AH = 05H
              AL = Number of sectors to be formatted
              BX = Offset address of buffer
              CH = Track number
              DH = Disk side number (0 or 1)
              DL = Disk drive number
              ES = Buffer segment address

Output: Carry flag=0: Operation completed (AH=0)
              Carry flag=1: Error (AH=error code)

Remarks: The number of sectors to be formatted is limited to sectors which logically follow each other on a track on one side of the disk.
              The buffer passed in ES:BX contains an entry consisting of four consecutive bytes for every sector to be formatted.

1:	Track number
2:	Page number
3:	Logical sector number
4:	Number of bytes in this sector:

	0:	128 bytes
	1:	256 bytes
	2:	512 bytes (PC standard)
	3:	1,024 bytes

The logical sector number increments continuously, but may not be the same as the physical sector number.

The following error codes can occur:

01H:	Function number not permitted
02H:	Address not found
03H:	Write attempt on a write protected disk
04H:	Sector not found
08H:	DMA overflow
09H:	Data transmission over segment border
10H:	Read error
20H:	Error in disk controller
40H:	Track not found
80H:	Time out error, drive not responding

The contents of the BX, CX, DX, SI, DI, BP registers and the segment registers are not affected by this function. The contents of all the other registers may change.

Interrupt 13H, Function 15H
Diskette: Determine drive type

BIOS (AT only)

Senses disk change and drive type. The AT supports both the standard 320/360K drives and the 1.2 megabyte drives.

Input:　　　　AH = 15H
　　　　　　　DL = Disk drive number (0 or 1)
Output:　　　Carry flag=0: Operation completed (AH=unit type)
　　　　　　　　　AH=0: Device not present
　　　　　　　　　AH=1: Unit does not recognize disk change
　　　　　　　　　AH=2: Unit recognizes disk change
　　　　　　　　　AH=3: Hard disk (see remarks below)
　　　　　　　Carry flag=1: Error
Remarks:　　The AT has a controller which selectively controls 2 disk drives and a hard disk, or one disk drive and 2 hard disks. In the latter case, the first hard disk has the number 1 and can be accessed with this function.
　　　　　　　The contents of the BX, CX, DX, SI, DI, BP registers and the segment registers are not affected by this function. The contents of all other registers may change.

Interrupt 13H, Function 16H
Diskette: Media change

BIOS (AT only)

Senses a disk change. The AT supports both the standard 320/360K drives and the 1.2 megabyte drives. This function reads any disk change that may have occurred since the last disk access.

Input:　　　　AH = 16H
　　　　　　　DL = Disk drive number (0 or 1)
Output:　　　AH=0: No disk change
　　　　　　　AH=6: Disk changed since last disk access
Remarks:　　The contents of the BX, CX, DX, SI, DI, BP registers and the segment registers are not affected by this function. The contents of all other registers may change.

Interrupt 13H, Function 17H   **BIOS (AT only)**
Diskette: Determine disk format

Determines the format of a disk. The AT's 1.2 megabyte disk drive can read both 320/360K disks and 1.2 megabyte disks. While the BIOS can determine disk format during a read or write access, it first must be informed of the format. Function 23 must be called on the AT before you can call function 5 (format).

Input: AH = 17H
                  AL = Format
                      AL=1: 320/360K format on 320/360K drive
                      AL=2: 320/360K format on 1.2 megabyte drive
                      AL=3: 1.2 megabyte format on 1.2 megabyte drive
Output: Carry flag=0: Operation completed
                  Carry flag=1: Error
Remarks: The following error codes can occur:
                      01H: Function number not permitted
                      02H: Address not found
                      03H: Write attempt on a write protected disk
                      04H: Sector not found
                      08H: DMA overflow
                      09H: Data transmission over segment border
                      10H: Read error
                      20H: Error in disk controller
                      40H: Track not found
                      80H: Time out error, drive not responding
                  The contents of the BX, CX, DX, SI, DI, BP registers and the segment registers are not affected by this function. The contents of all other registers may change.

Interrupt 13H, Function 18H   **BIOS (AT and up)**
Diskette: Determine disk format

Determines the format of a disk. This function replaces function 17H for checking disk format in AT BIOS.

Input: AH = 18H
                  CH = Highest track number
                  CL = Highest sector number
                  DL = Drive number (0 or 1)
Output: Carry flag=0: Operation completed
                  Carry flag=1: Error
Remarks: This function should be called before calling function 05H (Format track) for the first time, to configure the BIOS to the proper format.
                  Error-Codes; see function 00H.

                  The contents of the BX, CX, DX, SI, DI, BP registers and the segment registers are not affected by this function. The contents of all other registers may change.

Interrupt 13H, Function 00H   **BIOS (XT and AT only)**
Hard disk: Reset

Resets the hard disk controller and any interfaced hard disk drives. A reset should be executed after every hard disk operation during which an error was reported.

Input:	AH = 00H
	DL = 80H or 81H
Output:	Carry flag=0: Operation completed (AH=0)
	Carry flag=1: Error (AH=error code)
Remarks:	The first hard disk drive is assigned the number 80H, the second is assigned the number 81H.

The value in the DL register is unnecessary since all the hard disk drives execute a reset. XT and AT models use this register to determine whether a reset should be performed on the disk drives or on the hard disk.

The following error codes can occur:

01H:	Addressed function or unit not available
02H:	Address not found
04H:	Sector not found
05H:	Error on controller reset
07H:	Error during controller initialization
09H:	DMA transmission error: Segment border exceeded
0AH:	Defective sector
10H:	Read error
11H:	Read error corrected by ECC
20H:	Controller defect
40H:	Search operation failed
80H:	Time out, unit not responding
AAH:	Unit not ready
CCH:	Write error

The contents of the BX, CX, DX, SI, DI, BP registers and the segment registers are not affected by this function. The contents of all other registers may change.

Interrupt 13H, Function 01H   **BIOS (XT and AT only)**
Hard disk: Read disk status

Reads the status of the hard disk since the last hard disk operation.

Input:	AH = 01H
	DL = 80H or 81H
Output:	Carry flag=0: Operation completed (AH=0)
	Carry flag=1: Error (AH=error code)
Remarks:	The first hard disk drive is assigned the number 80H, the second is assigned the number 81H.

The value in the DL register is unnecessary since the status is consistently returned for each disk drive. XT and AT models use this register to determine whether the status of the disk drives or hard disk should be checked.

The following error codes can occur:

01H:	Addressed function or unit not available
02H:	Address not found

1127

04H:	Sector not found
05H:	Error on controller reset
07H:	Error during controller initialization
09H:	DMA transmission error: Segment border exceeded
0AH:	Defective sector
10H:	Read error
11H:	Read error corrected by ECC
20H:	Controller defect
40H:	Search operation failed
80H:	Time out, unit not responding
AAH:	Unit not ready
CCH:	Write error

The contents of the BX, CX, DX, SI, DI, BP registers and the segment registers are not affected by this function. The contents of the other registers may change.

Interrupt 13H, Function 02H   BIOS (XT and AT only)
Hard disk: Read disk

Reads one or more hard disk sectors into a buffer.

Input:	AH = 02H
	AL = Number of sectors to be read (1-128)
	BX = Offset address of buffer
	CH = Cylinder number
	CL = Sector number
	DH = Read/write head number
	DL = Hard disk number (80H or 81H)
	ES = Buffer segment address
Output:	Carry flag=0: Operation completed (AH=0)
	Carry flag=1: Error (AH=error code)
Remarks:	The first hard disk drive is assigned the number 80H, the second is assigned the number 81H.

Since the eight bits of the CH register can address only 256 cylinders at a time, bits 6 and 7 of the CL register (sector number) form bits 8 and 9 of the cylinder number, which enables the addressing of up to 1,023 cylinders at a time.

If several sectors are being read and the system reaches the last sector of a cylinder, reading continues at the first sector of the next cylinder of the next read/write head. If the system reaches the last read/write head, reading continues on the first sector of the following cylinder on the first read/write head.

The following error codes can occur:

01H:	Addressed function or unit not available
02H:	Address not found
04H:	Sector not found
05H:	Error on controller reset
07H:	Error during controller initialization
09H:	DMA transmission error: Segment border exceeded
0AH:	Defective sector
10H:	Read error
11H:	Read error corrected by ECC

20H:	Controller defect
40H:	Search operation failed
80H:	Time out, unit not responding
AAH:	Unit not ready
CCH:	Write error

The contents of the BX, CX, DX, SI, DI, BP registers and the segment registers are not affected by this function. The contents of all other registers may change.

Interrupt 13H, Function 03H   **BIOS (XT and AT only)**
Hard disk: Write to disk

Writes one or more sectors to the hard disk. The data to be transmitted are taken from a buffer in the calling program.

Input:	AH = 03H
	AL = Number of sectors to be written (1-128)
	BX = Offset address of buffer
	CH = Cylinder number
	CL = Sector number
	DH = Read/write head number
	DL = Hard disk number (80H or 81H)
	ES = Buffer segment address
Output:	Carry flag=0: Operation completed (AH=0)
	Carry flag=1: Error (AH=error code)
Remarks:	The first hard disk drive is assigned the number 80H, the second is assigned the number 81H.

Since the eight bits of the CH register can address only 256 cylinders at a time, bits 6 and 7 of the CL register (sector number) form bits 8 and 9 of the cylinder number, enabling the addressing of up to 1,023 cylinders at a time.

If several sectors are being written and the system reaches the last sector of a cylinder, writing continues at the first sector of the next cylinder of the next read/write head. If the system reaches the last read/write head, writing continues on the first sector of the following cylinder on the first read/write head.

The following error codes can occur:

01H:	Addressed function or unit not available
02H:	Address not found
04H:	Sector not found
05H:	Error on controller reset
07H:	Error during controller initialization
09H:	DMA transmission error: Segment border exceeded
0AH:	Defective sector
10H:	Read error
11H:	Read error corrected by ECC
20H:	Controller defect
40H:	Search operation failed
80H:	Time out, unit not responding
AAH:	Unit not ready
CCH:	Write error

The contents of the BX, CX, DX, SI, DI, BP registers and the segment registers are not affected by this function. The contents of all other registers may change.

Interrupt 13H, Function 04H   **BIOS (XT and AT only)**
Hard disk: Verify disk sector

Verifies one or more sectors of a hard disk. Unlike the corresponding floppy disk function, the data on the hard disk are not compared with the data in memory. During data storage, four check bytes are stored for every sector; these check bytes verify the contents of a sector.

Input:	AH = 04H
	AL = Number of sectors to be verified (1-128)
	BX = Offset address of buffer
	CH = Cylinder number
	CL = Sector number
	DH = Read/write head number
	DL = Hard disk number (80H or 81H)
	ES = Buffer segment address
Output:	Carry flag=0: Operation completed (AH=0)
	Carry flag=1: Error (AH=error code)
Remarks:	The first hard disk drive is assigned the number 80H, the second is assigned the number 81H.

Since the eight bits of the CH register can only address 256 cylinders at a time, bits 6 and 7 of the CL register (sector number) form bits 8 and 9 of the cylinder number, which enables the addressing of up to 1,023 cylinders at a time.

If several sectors are being verified and the system reaches the last sector of a cylinder, verification continues at the first sector of the next cylinder of the next read/write head. If the system reaches the last read/write head, verification continues on the first sector of the following cylinder on the first read/write head.

The following error codes can occur:

01H:	Addressed function or unit not available
02H:	Address not found
04H:	Sector not found
05H:	Error on controller reset
07H:	Error during controller initialization
09H:	DMA transmission error: Segment border exceeded
0AH:	Defective sector
10H:	Read error
11H:	Read error corrected by ECC
20H:	Controller defect
40H:	Search operation failed
80H:	Time out, unit not responding
AAH:	Unit not ready
CCH:	Write error

The contents of the BX, CX, DX, SI, DI, BP registers and the segment registers are not affected by this function. The contents of all other registers may change.

Interrupt 13H, Function 05H   **BIOS (XT and AT only)**
Hard disk: Format cylinder

Formats a complete cylinder (17 sectors) of a hard disk. A buffer, which contains information about the sectors to be formatted, must be passed to the function.

Input:	AH = 05H
	AL = 17
	BX = Offset address of buffer
	CH = Cylinder number
	CL = 1
	DH = Read/write head number
	DL = Hard disk number (80H or 81H)
	ES = Buffer segment address
Output:	Carry flag=0: Operation completed (AH=0)
	Carry flag=1: Error (AH=error code)
Remarks:	The first hard disk drive is assigned the number 80H, the second is assigned the number 81H.

Since the eight bits of the CH register can only address 256 cylinders at a time, bits 6 and 7 of the CL register (sector number) form bits 8 and 9 of the cylinder number, which enables the addressing of up to 1,023 cylinders at a time.

Since a complete cylinder is always formatted, the first sector to be formatted in the CL register is always sector 1. For the same reason the number of sectors to be formatted in the AL register is always 17, since the average hard disk operates with 17 sectors per cylinder.

The buffer, whose address is passed in ES:BX, must always be at least 512 bytes long. Only the first 34 bytes of this buffer are used for formatting the 17 sectors of a cylinder. Two succeeding bytes contain information about the corresponding physical sector. Before the function call, the first byte isn't significant. After the function call the first byte indicates whether or not the sector could be formatted (00H) or (80H). The second byte returns the logical sector number of the physical sector and must be placed in the buffer by calling the program before the function call.

The following error codes can occur:

01H:	Addressed function or unit not available
02H:	Address not found
04H:	Sector not found
05H:	Error on controller reset
07H:	Error during controller initialization
09H:	DMA transmission error: Segment border exceeded
0AH:	Defective sector
10H:	Read error
11H:	Read error corrected by ECC
20H:	Controller defect
40H:	Search operation failed
80H:	Time out, unit not responding
AAH:	Unit not ready
CCH:	Write error

The contents of the BX, CX, DX, SI, DI, BP registers and the segment registers are not affected by this function. The contents of all other registers may change.

Interrupt 13H, Function 08H   **BIOS (XT and AT only)**
Hard disk: Check format

Conveys the formatting information found on the hard disk.

Input:	AH = 08H
	CH = Cylinder number
	CL = Sector number
	DH = Read/write head number (0=first head)
	DL = Hard disk number
Output:	Carry flag=0: Operation completed (AH=0)
	Carry flag=1: Error (AH=error code)
Remarks:	The first hard disk drive is assigned the number 80H, the second is assigned the number 81H.

Since the eight bits of the CH register can address only 256 cylinders at a time, bits 6 and 7 of the CL register (sector number) form bits 8 and 9 of the cylinder number, enabling the addressing of up to 1,023 cylinders at a time.

The total capacity of the hard disk unit in bytes can be calculated with the following formula:

Capacity = Heads * Cylinders * Sectors * 512

The following error codes can occur:

01H:	Addressed function or unit not available
02H:	Address not found
04H:	Sector not found
05H:	Error on controller reset
07H:	Error during controller initialization
09H:	DMA transmission error: Segment border exceeded
0AH:	Defective sector
10H:	Read error
11H:	Read error corrected by ECC
20H:	Controller defect
40H:	Search operation failed
80H:	Time out, unit not responding
AAH:	Unit not ready
CCH:	Write error

The contents of the BX, CX, DX, SI, DI, BP registers and the segment registers are not affected by this function. The contents of all other registers may change.

Interrupt 13H, Function 09H   **BIOS (XT and AT only)**
Hard disk: Adapt to foreign drives

Interfaces other hard disk drives for access through BIOS functions.

Input:	AH = 09H
	DL = Number of hard disk to be interfaced (80H or 81H)
Output:	Carry flag=0: Operation completed (AH=0)
	Carry flag=1: Error (AH=error code)

Remarks: The first hard disk drive is assigned the number 80H, the second is assigned the number 81H.

BIOS takes the information about the hard disk drive to be interfaced (number of units, read/write heads, etc.) from a table. The address of this table for the hard disk unit numbered 80H is stored in interrupt vector 41H, and the unit numbered 81H is stored in interrupt 46H.

The following error codes can occur:

01H:	Addressed function or unit not available
02H:	Address not found
04H:	Sector not found
05H:	Error on controller reset
07H:	Error during controller initialization
09H:	DMA transmission error: Segment border exceeded
0AH:	Defective sector
10H:	Read error
11H:	Read error corrected by ECC
20H:	Controller defect
40H:	Search operation failed
80H:	Time out, unit not responding
AAH:	Unit not ready
CCH:	Write error

The contents of the BX, CX, DX, SI, DI, BP registers and the segment registers are not affected by this function. The contents of all other registers may change.

Interrupt 13H, Function 0AH　　　　　　　　　**BIOS (XT and AT only)**
Hard disk: Extended read

Reads one or more sectors from the hard disk drive into a buffer. Besides the actual 512 bytes stored in the sector, the function also reads the four check bytes (ECC).

Input: AH = 0AH
AL = Number of sectors to be read (1–127)
BX = Offset address of buffer
CH = Cylinder number
CL = Sector number
DH = Read/write head number
DL = Hard disk number (80H or 81H)
ES = Buffer segment address

Output: Carry flag=0: Operation completed (AH=0)
Carry flag=1: Error (AH=error code)

Remarks: The first hard disk drive is assigned the number 80H, the second is assigned the number 81H.

Normally the controller computes the four check bytes. Here the buffer reads the information direct.

Since the eight bits of the CH register can only address 256 cylinders at a time, bits 6 and 7 of the CL register (sector number) form bits 8 and 9 of the cylinder number, enabling the addressing of up to 1,023 cylinders at a time.

If several sectors are being read and the system reaches the last sector of a cylinder, reading continues at the first sector of the next cylinder of the next read/write head. If the system reaches the last read/write head, reading continues on the first sector of the following cylinder on the first read/write head.

The following error codes can occur:

01H:	Addressed function or unit not available
02H:	Address not found
04H:	Sector not found
05H:	Error on controller reset
07H:	Error during controller initialization
09H:	DMA transmission error: Segment border exceeded
0AH:	Defective sector
10H:	Read error
11H:	Read error corrected by ECC
20H:	Controller defect
40H:	Search operation failed
80H:	Time out, unit not responding
AAH:	Unit not ready
CCH:	Write error

The contents of the BX, CX, DX, SI, DI, BP registers and the segment registers are not affected by this function. The contents of all other registers may change.

Interrupt 13H, Function 0BH   **BIOS (XT and AT only)**
Hard disk: Extended write

Writes one or more sectors to the hard disk drive. Besides the actual 512 bytes stored in a sector, four check bytes (ECC) stored at the end of every sector are transmitted from the buffer.

Input:	AH = 0BH
	AL = Number of sectors to be read (1–127)
	BX = Offset address of buffer
	CH = Cylinder number
	CL = Sector number
	DH = Read/write head number
	DL = Hard disk number (80H or 81H)
	ES = Buffer segment address
Output:	Carry flag=0: Operation completed (AH=0)
	Carry flag=1: Error (AH=error code)
Remarks:	The first hard disk drive is assigned the number 80H, the second is assigned the number 81H.

Normally the controller calculates the four check bytes. Here the system reads them direct from the buffer.

Since the eight bits of the CH register can only address 256 cylinders at a time, bits 6 and 7 of the CL register (sector number) form bits 8 and 9 of the cylinder number, enabling the addressing of up to 1,023 cylinders at a time.

If several sectors are being written and the system reaches the last sector of a cylinder, writing continues at the first sector of the next cylinder of the next read/write head. If the system reaches the last read/write head, writing continues on the first sector of the following cylinder on the first read/write head.

The following error codes can occur:

01H:	Addressed function or unit not available
02H:	Address not found
04H:	Sector not found
05H:	Error on controller reset

07H:	Error during controller initialization
09H:	DMA transmission error: Segment border exceeded
0AH:	Defective sector
10H:	Read error
11H:	Read error corrected by ECC
20H:	Controller defect
40H:	Search operation failed
80H:	Time out, unit not responding
AAH:	Unit not ready
CCH:	Write error

The contents of the BX, CX, DX, SI, DI, BP registers and the segment registers are not affected by this function. The contents of all other registers may change.

Interrupt 13H, Function 0CH   BIOS (XT and up)
Hard disk: Move read/write head

Positions a hard disk read/write head over a specific cylinder. This is useful for moving the head away from a cylinder containing data, as might be done when a computer must be transported.

Input:	AH = 0CH
	DL = Hard disk number (80H or 81H)
	DH = Read/write head number
	CH = Cylinder number
	CL = Sector number
Output:	Carry flag=0: Operation completed
	Carry flag=1: Error (AH=error code)
Remarks:	The first hard disk drive is assigned the number 80H, and the second the number 81H.

Since the 8 bits of the CH register can address only 256 cylinders, bits 6 and 7 of the sector number (CL register) form bits 8 and 9 of the cylinder number. This permits up to 1,023 cylinders to be addressed.

The read/write head is positioned automatically for these operations, so this function is not needed for normal operations.

The following error codes can occur:

01H:	Addressed function or unit not available
02H:	Address not found
04H:	Sector not found
05H:	Error on controller reset
07H:	Error during controller initialization
09H:	DMA transmission error: Segment border exceeded
0AH:	Defective sector
10H:	Read error
11H:	Read error corrected by ECC
20H:	Controller defect
40H:	Search operation failed
80H:	Time out, unit not responding
AAH:	Unit not ready
CCH:	Write error

The contents of the BX, CX, DX, SI, DI, BP registers and the segment registers are not affected by this function. The contents of all other registers may change.

Interrupt 13H, Function 0DH   **BIOS (XT and AT only)**
Hard disk: Reset

Resets the hard disk controller and any interfaced hard disk drives. A reset should be executed after every hard disk operation during which an error was reported.

Input:	AH = 0DH
	DL = Hard disk drive number (80H or 81H)
Output:	Carry flag=0: Operation completed (AH=0)
	Carry flag=1: Error (AH=error code)
Remarks:	The value in the DL register is unnecessary since all the hard disk drives execute a reset. XT and AT models use this register to determine whether a reset should be performed on the disk drives or on the hard disk.

This function is identical to function 0 listed above.

The first hard disk drive is assigned the number 80H, the second is assigned the number 81H.

The following error codes can occur:

01H:	Addressed function or unit not available
02H:	Address not found
04H:	Sector not found
05H:	Error on controller reset
07H:	Error during controller initialization
09H:	DMA transmission error: Segment border exceeded
0AH:	Defective sector
20H:	Controller defect
40H:	Search operation failed
80H:	Time out, unit not responding
AAH:	Unit not ready
CCH:	Write error

The contents of the BX, CX, DX, SI, DI, BP registers and the segment registers are not affected by this function. The contents of all other registers may change.

Interrupt 13H, Function 0EH   **BIOS (PS/2)**
Hard disk: Read from test buffer

Performs a data transmission test between controller and CPU in the PS/2.

Interrupt 13H, Function 0FH   **BIOS (PS/2)**
Hard disk: Write to test buffer

Performs a data transmission test between controller and CPU in the PS/2.

Interrupt 13H, Function 12H   **BIOS (PS/2)**
Hard disk: Controller RAM diagnostic

Performs an internal controller diagnostic in the PS/2.

Interrupt 13H, Function 13H **BIOS (PS/2)**
Hard disk: Drive diagnostic

Performs an internal drive/controller diagnostic in the PS/2.

Interrupt 13H, Function 10H **BIOS (XT and AT only)**
Hard disk: Drive ready?

Determines if the drive is ready (i.e., the last operation has been completed and the drive can perform the next task).

Input:	AH = 10H
	DL = Hard disk drive number (80H or 81H)
Output:	Carry flag=0: Drive ready (AH=0)
	Carry flag=1: Error (AH=error code)
Remarks:	The first hard disk drive is assigned the number 80H, the second is assigned the number 81H.

The following error codes can occur:

01H:	Addressed function or unit not available
02H:	Address not found
04H:	Sector not found
05H:	Error on controller reset
07H:	Error during controller initialization
09H:	DMA transmission error: Segment border exceeded
0AH:	Defective sector
10H:	Read error
11H:	Read error corrected by ECC
20H:	Controller defect
40H:	Search operation failed
80H:	Time out, unit not responding
AAH:	Unit not ready
CCH:	Write error

The contents of the BX, CX, DX, SI, DI, BP registers and the segment registers are not affected by this function. The contents of all other registers may change.

Interrupt 13H, Function 11H **BIOS (XT and AT only)**
Hard disk: Recalibrate drive

Recalibrates hard disk after an error occurs, especially after a read or write error.

Input:	AH = 11H
	DL = Hard disk drive number (80H or 81H)
Output:	Carry flag=0: Operation completed (AH=0)
	Carry flag=1: Error (AH=error code)
Remarks:	The first hard disk drive is assigned the number 80H, the second is assigned the number 81H.

The following error codes can occur:

01H:	Addressed function or unit not available
02H:	Address not found
04H:	Sector not found

05H:	Error on controller reset
07H:	Error during controller initialization
09H:	DMA transmission error: Segment border exceeded
0AH:	Defective sector
10H:	Read error
11H:	Read error corrected by ECC
20H:	Controller defect
40H:	Search operation failed
80H:	Time out, unit not responding
AAH:	Unit not ready
CCH:	Write error

The contents of the BX, CX, DX, SI, DI, BP registers and the segment registers are not affected by this function. The contents of all other registers may change.

Interrupt 13H, Function 14H   BIOS (XT and AT only)
Hard disk: Controller diagnostic

Initializes an internal diagnostic test of the hard disk controller.

Input:	AH = 14H
	DL = Hard disk drive number (80H or 81H)
Output:	Carry flag=0: Operation completed (AH=0)
	Carry flag=1: Error (AH=error code)
Remarks:	The first hard disk drive is assigned the number 80H, the second is assigned the number 81H.
	The following error codes can occur:

01H:	Addressed function or unit not available
02H:	Address not found
04H:	Sector not found
05H:	Error on controller reset
07H:	Error during controller initialization
09H:	DMA transmission error: Segment border exceeded
0AH:	Defective sector
10H:	Read error
11H:	Read error corrected by ECC
20H:	Controller defect
40H:	Search operation failed
80H:	Time out, unit not responding
AAH:	Unit not ready
CCH:	Write error

The contents of the BX, CX, DX, SI, DI, BP registers and the segment registers are not affected by this function. The contents of all other registers may change.

Interrupt 13H, Function 15H   BIOS (AT only)
Hard disk: Determine drive type

Determines whether or not the computer hardware assigned numbers 80H and 81H are hard disk drives. The AT contains a controller capable of controlling both hard disks and disk drives. This

1138

controller can manage either two disk drives and one hard disk, or one disk drive and two hard disks.

Input:	AH = 15H
	DL = Hard disk drive number (80H or 81H)
Output:	Carry flag=0: Operation completed (AH=drive type)

      0: Equipment not available
      1: Drive does not recognize disk change
      2: Drive recognizes disk change
      3: Hard disk unit

     Carry flag=1: Error (AH=error code)

Remarks: The first hard disk drive is assigned the number 80H, the second is assigned the number 81H.

     The contents of the BX, CX, DX, SI, DI, BP registers and the segment registers are not affected by this function. The contents of all other registers may change.

Interrupt 14H, Function 00H   BIOS
Serial port: Initialize

Initializes and configures a serial port. This configuration includes parameters for word length, baud rate, parity and stop bits.

Input:	AH = 00H
	DX = Number of serial port (0=first serial port, 1=second serial port)
	AL = Configuration parameters
Bits 0-1:	Word length

       10(b) = 7 bits
       11(b) = 8 bits

Bit 2:   Number of stop bits

       00(b) = 1 stop bit
       01(b) = 2 stop bits

Bits 3-4: Parity

       00(b) = none
       01(b) = odd
       11(b) = even

Bits 5-7: Baud rate

       000(b) = 110 baud
       001(b) = 150 baud
       010(b) = 300 baud
       011(b) = 600 baud
       100(b) = 1200 baud
       101(b) = 2400 baud
       110(b) = 4800 baud
       111(b) = 9600 baud

Output: AH = Serial port status

    Bit 0: Data ready
    Bit 1: Overrun error
    Bit 2: Parity error
    Bit 3: Framing error
    Bit 4: Break discovered
    Bit 5: Transmission hold register empty

Bit 6: Transmission shift register empty

Bit 7: Time out

AL = Modem status

Bit 0: Modem ready to send status change

Bit 1: Modem on status change

Bit 2: Telephone ringing status change

Bit 3: Connection to receiver status change

Bit 4: Modem ready to send

Bit 5: Modem on

Bit 6: Telephone ringing

Bit 7: Connection to receiver modem

Remarks: The contents of the BX, CX, DX, SI, DI, BP registers and the segment registers are not affected by this function. The contents of all the other registers may change.

Interrupt 14H, Function 01H   **BIOS**
Serial port: Send character

Sends a character to the serial port.

Input: AH = 01H

DX = Number of serial port (0=first serial port, 1=second serial port)

AL = Character code to be sent

Output: AH: Bit 7 = 0: Character transmitted

Bit 7 = 1: Error

Bit 0-6: Serial port status

Bit 0: Data ready

Bit 1: Overrun error

Bit 2: Parity error

Bit 3: Framing error

Bit 4: Break discovered

Bit 5: Transmission hold register empty

Bit 6: Transmission shift register empty

Remarks: The contents of the BX, CX, DX, SI, DI, BP registers and the segment registers are not affected by this function. The contents of all other registers may change.

Interrupt 14H, Function 02H   **BIOS**
Serial port: Read character

Receives a character from the serial port.

Input: AH = 02H

DX = Number of serial port (0=first serial port, 1=second serial port)

Output: AH: Bit 7 = 0: Character received:

AL = Character received

Bit 7 = 1: Error:

Bit 0-6: Serial port status:

Bit 0: Data ready

Bit 1: Overrun error

Bit 2: Parity error

Bit 3: Framing error

Bit 4: Break discovered

Bit 5: Transmission hold register empty

Bit 6: Transmission shift register empty

Remarks: This function should only be called if function 3 has determined that a character is ready for reception.

The contents of the BX, CX, DX, SI, DI, BP registers and the segment registers are not affected by this function. The contents of all other registers may change.

Interrupt 14H, Function 03H   BIOS
Serial port: Read status

Reads the status of the serial port.

Input: AH = 03H

DX = Number of the serial port (the first serial port has the number 0)

Output: AH = Serial port status

Bit 0:	Data ready
Bit 1:	Overrun error
Bit 2:	Parity error
Bit 3:	Framing error
Bit 4:	Break discovered
Bit 5:	Transmission hold register empty
Bit 6:	Transmission shift register empty

AL = Modem status:

Bit 0:	Modem ready to send status change
Bit 1:	Modem on status change
Bit 2:	Telephone ringing status change
Bit 3:	Connection to receiver status change
Bit 4:	Modem ready to send
Bit 5:	Modem on
Bit 6:	Telephone ringing
Bit 7:	Connection to receiver modem

Remarks: This function should always be called before calling function 2 (read character).

The contents of the BX, CX, DX, SI, DI, BP registers and the segment registers are not affected by this function. The contents of all other registers may change.

Interrupt 15H, Function 83H   BIOS (AT only)
Cassette interrupt: Set flag after time interval

Sets bit 7 of a flag to 1 after a certain amount of time in microseconds elapses.

Input: AH = 83H

ES = Segment address of the flag

BX = Offset address of the flag

CX = High word of elapsed time in microseconds

DX = Low word of elapsed time in microseconds

Output: No output

Remarks: A microsecond is a millionth of a second.

The contents of the BX, SI, DI, BP registers and the segment registers are not affected by this function. The contents of all other registers may change.

Interrupt 15H, Function 84H, Subfunction 0　　　　　**BIOS (AT only)**
Cassette interrupt: Read joystick switch settings

Reads the status of switches on joysticks interfaced to a PC, if game ports and joysticks are present.

Input:	AH = 84H
	DX = 0
Output:	Carry flag=1: No game port connected
	Carry flag=0: Game port present:
	AL = Switch settings:

　　　　　　　Bit 7=1: First joystick's first switch enabled
　　　　　　　Bit 6=1: First joystick's second switch enabled
　　　　　　　Bit 5=1: Second joystick's first switch enabled
　　　　　　　Bit 4=1: Second joystick's second switch enabled

Remarks:　　Subfunction 1 reads the joystick position(s).
　　　　　　The contents of the BX, CX, SI, DI, BP registers and the segment registers are not affected by this function. The contents of all other registers may change.

Interrupt 15H, Function 84H, Subfunction 1　　　　　**BIOS (AT only)**
Cassette interrupt: Read joystick position

Reads the positions of joysticks interfaced to a PC if game ports and joysticks are present.

Input:	AH = 84H
	DX = 1
Output:	Carry flag=1: No game port connected
	Carry flag=0: Game port present:

　　　　　　　AX = X-position of first joystick
　　　　　　　BX = Y-position of first joystick
　　　　　　　CX = X-position of second joystick
　　　　　　　DX = Y-position of second joystick

Remarks:　　Subfunction 0 reads the joystick switch status.
　　　　　　The contents of the SI, DI, BP registers and the segment registers are not affected by this function. The contents of all other registers may change.

Interrupt 15H, Function 85H　　　　　　　　　　　　**BIOS (AT only)**
Cassette interrupt: <Sys Req> key activated

Responds to pressure or release of the <Sys Req> key. The keyboard routine calls this function.

Input:	AH = 85H
	AL = 0: <Sys Req> key depressed
	AL = 1: <Sys Req> key released
Output:	No output
Remarks:	This function acts as an intermediary for application programs, so that the application program will respond appropriately when the user presses the <Sys Req> key.

Interrupt 15H, Function 86H　　　　　　　　　　　　**BIOS (AT only)**
Cassette interrupt: Wait

Returns control to the calling program after a certain amount of time has elapsed.

Input: AH = 86H
                CX = High word of pause time in microseconds
                DX = Low word of pause time in microseconds
Output: No output
Remarks: A microsecond is a millionth of a second.

The contents of the BX, SI, DI, BP registers and the segment registers are not affected by this function. The contents of all other registers may change.

Interrupt 15H, Function 87H   **BIOS (AT only)**
Cassette interrupt: Move memory areas

Moves areas of RAM from below the 1 megabyte limit to the range above the 1 megabyte limit, and from above the 1 megabyte limit to below the 1 megabyte limit.

Input: AH = 87H
                CX = Number of words to move
                ES = Segment address of global descriptor table
                SI = Offset address of global descriptor table
Output: Carry flag=0: No error
                Carry flag=1: Error:
                    AH=1:   RAM parity error
                    AH=2:   Incorrect GDT on function call
                    AH=3:   Protected mode could not be initialized
Remarks: Only words can be transferred; individual bytes cannot be transferred.
                Maximum amount of memory allowed in a transfer is 64K. The value in the CX register cannot exceed 8000H.
                All interrupts are disabled during the memory block move.
                The contents of the BX, CX, DX, SI, DI, BP registers and the segment registers are not affected by this function. The contents of all other registers may change.

Interrupt 15H, Function 88H   **BIOS (AT only)**
Cassette interrupt: Determine memory size beyond 1 megabyte

Determines the amount of memory installed beyond the 1 megabyte limit.

Input: AH = 88H
Output: AX = Memory size
Remarks: The value in the AX register represents memory in kilobytes (K).

Memory size below the 1 megabyte limit can be determined using interrupt 12H.
The contents of the BX, CX, DX, SI, DI, BP registers and the segment registers are not affected by this function. The contents of all other registers may change.

Interrupt 15H, Function 89H   **BIOS (AT only)**
Cassette interrupt: Switch to virtual mode

Switches the 80286 processor to virtual mode.

Input: AH = 89H
Output: No output

Remarks: This function should be called only if you know how virtual mode operates. Improper use of this function can easily lead to a system crash.

Interrupt 16H, Function 00H   **BIOS**
Keyboard: Read character

Reads a character from the keyboard buffer. If the buffer doesn't contain a character, the function waits until a character is entered. Then the character is read and removed from the keyboard buffer.

Input: AH = 00H
Output: AL = 0: Extended key code
AH = Extended key code
AL>1: Normal key activated
AL = ASCII code of key
AH = Scan code of key
Remarks: ASCII code definition occurs independent of the keyboard. Scan codes apply only to the type of keyboard attached to the PC.
The contents of the BX, CX, DX, SI, DI, BP registers and the segment registers are not affected by this function. The contents of all other registers may change.

Interrupt 16H, Function 01H   **BIOS**
Keyboard: Read keyboard for character

Reads the keyboard buffer for a character ready to be entered. If a character is available, the function passes the character to the calling function. The character remains in the keyboard buffer and can be re-read when a program calls either function 0 (see above) or function 1. The function returns to the calling program immediately after the call.

Input: AH = 01H
Output: Zero flag = 1: No character in the keyboard buffer
Zero flag = 0: Character available in keyboard buffer:
AL = 0: Extended key code
AH = Extended key code
AL>1: Normal key
AL = ASCII code of the key
AH = Scan code of the key
Remarks: ASCII code definition occurs independent of the keyboard. Scan codes only apply to the type of keyboard attached to the PC.
The contents of the CX, DX, SI, DI, BP registers and the segment registers are not affected by this function. The contents of all other registers may change.

Interrupt 16H, Function 02H   **BIOS**
Keyboard: Read

Reads and returns the status of certain control keys and various keyboard modes.

Input: AH = 02H
Output: AL = Keyboard status

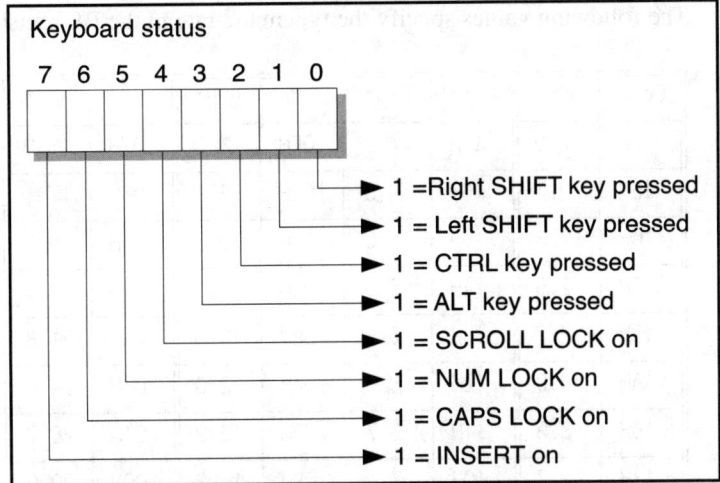

Keyboard status

7 6 5 4 3 2 1 0

1 = Right SHIFT key pressed
1 = Left SHIFT key pressed
1 = CTRL key pressed
1 = ALT key pressed
1 = SCROLL LOCK on
1 = NUM LOCK on
1 = CAPS LOCK on
1 = INSERT on

Remarks: The contents of the BX, CX, DX, SI, DI, BP registers and the segment registers are not affected by this function. The contents of all other registers may change.

Interrupt 16H, Function 03H   **BIOS (AT)**
Keyboard: Set typematic and delay rate

Sets typematic rate and delay rate for the keyboard.

Input: AH = 03H
              AL = 05H
              BH = Delay before typematic
              BL = Typematic (repetition) rate
Output: No output
Remarks: Not every BIOS supports this function.
              The following values specify the delay rate in the BH register:

Code	Delay rate
00H	1/4 second
01H	1/2 second
10H	1/4 second
11H	1 second

The following values specify the typematic rate in the BL register:

Code	RPS*	Code	RPS*	Code	RPS*	Code	RPS*
1FH	2.0	17H	4.0	0FH	8.0	07H	16.0
1EH	2.1	16H	4.3	0EH	8.6	06H	17.1
1DH	2.3	15H	4.6	0DH	9.2	05H	18.5
1CH	2.5	14H	5.0	0CH	10.0	04H	20.0
1BH	2.7	13H	5.5	0BH	10.9	03H	21.8
1AH	3.0	12H	6.0	0AH	12.0	02H	24.0
19H	3.3	11H	6.7	09H	13.3	01H	26.7
18H	3.7	10H	7.5	08H	15.0	00H	30.0
* Repetitions per second							

The contents of the BX, CX, DX, SI, DI, BP registers and the segment registers are not affected by this function. The contents of all other registers may change.

Interrupt 16H, Function 05H **BIOS (AT and up)**
Keyboard: Simulate keypress

Simulates a keypress by placing the specified key code at the end of the keyboard buffer.

Input:	AH = 05H
	CH = Scan code of key
	CL = ASCII code of key
Output:	AL = 00H: O.K.
	AL = 01H: Keyboard buffer full, error
Remarks:	Not every BIOS supports this function.

The contents of the BX, CX, DX, SI, DI, BP registers and the segment registers are not affected by this function. The contents of all other registers may change.

Interrupt 16H, Function 10H **BIOS (AT and up)**
Keyboard: Read key on extended keyboard

Reads the keyboard buffer. This function is similar to function 00H, except that function 10H is intended for extended keyboards with 101 or 102 keys (i.e., keyboards including the <F11> and <F12> keys).

Input:	AH = 10H
Output:	AH = Scan code of key
	AL = ASCII code of key
Remarks:	Not every BIOS supports this function.

The contents of the BX, CX, DX, SI, DI, BP registers and the segment registers are not affected by this function. The contents of all other registers may change.

Interrupt 16H, Function 11H   **BIOS (since AT)**
Keyboard: Read extended keyboard for character

Reads the keyboard buffer for a character ready to be entered. This function is similar to function 01H, except that function 11H is intended for extended keyboards with 101 or 102 keys (i.e., keyboards including the <F11> and <F12> keys).

Input: AH = 11H
Output: Zero flag=1: No character in the keyboard buffer
              Zero flag=0: Character available
              AL = 0: Extended key code
                  AH=Extended key code
              AL > 0: Normal key activated
                  AL=ASCII code of key
                  AH=Scan code of key
Remarks: Not every BIOS supports this function.
              The contents of the BX, CX, DX, SI, DI, BP registers and the segment registers are not affected by this function. The contents of all other registers may change.

Interrupt 17H, Function 00H   **BIOS**
Printer: Write character

Writes a character to one of the printers interfaced to the PC.

Input: AH = 00H
              AL = Character code to be printed
              DX = Printer number
Output: AH = Printer status:
                  Bit 0=1: Time out error
                  Bit 1: Unused
                  Bit 2: Unused
                  Bit 3=1: Transfer error
                  Bit 4=0: Printer offline
                  Bit 4=1: Printer online
                  Bit 5=1: Printer out of paper
                  Bit 6=1: Receive mode selected
                  Bit 7=0: Printer busy
Remarks: Parallel port LPT1 is assigned the number 0, parallel port LPT2 is assigned the number 1 and parallel port LPT3 is assigned the number 2.
              The contents of the BX, CX, DX, SI, DI, BP registers and the segment registers are not affected by this function. The contents of all other registers may change.

Interrupt 17H, Function 01H   **BIOS**
Printer: Initialize printer

Initializes the printer interfaced to the PC. This function should be executed before executing function 0 (see above).

Input:	AH = 01H
	DX = Printer number
Output:	AH = Printer status
Remarks:	Parallel port LPT1 is assigned the number 0, parallel port LPT2 is assigned the number 1 and parallel port LPT3 is assigned the number 2.
	The contents of the BX, CX, DX, SI, DI, BP registers and the segment registers are not affected by this function. The contents of all other registers may change.

Interrupt 17H, Function 02H   **BIOS**
Printer: Read printer status

Returns the status of the printer interfaced to the PC.

Input:	AH = 02H
	DX = Printer number
Output:	AH = Printer status
Remarks:	Parallel port LPT1 is assigned the number 0, parallel port LPT2 is assigned the number 1 and parallel port LPT3 is assigned the number 2.
	The contents of the BX, CX, DX, SI, DI, BP registers and the segment registers are not affected by this function. The contents of all other registers may change.

Interrupt 18H   **BIOS**
Call ROM BASIC

Accesses BASIC in ROM if a system disk cannot be found during the system bootstrap process.

Input:	No input
Output:	No output
Remarks:	Very few PCs or compatibles have built-in ROM BASIC (this is a throwback from the early days of the PC). If a PC doesn't have ROM BASIC, interrupt 18H returns the system to the calling program. However, if the PC does has ROM BASIC, interrupt 18H calls BASIC. In most cases, the only way to return to DOS is by warm-starting the computer (pressing the <Ctrl><Alt><Delete> keys) or turning the computer off and on again. Some versions of ROM BASIC allow an exit to DOS by entering the SYSTEM command from BASIC.

Interrupt 19H   **BIOS**
Boot process

Boots the computer.

Input:	No input
Output:	No output
Remarks:	Pressing the <Ctrl><Alt><Delete> keys invokes this interrupt from the keyboard.

Interrupt 1AH, Function 00H
Date and time: Read clock count

Reads the current clock count. The clock count increments 18.2 times per second. This calculates the time elapsed since the computer was switched on.

Input:	AH = 00H
Output:	CX = High word of the clock count
	DX = Low word of the clock count
	AL = 0: Less than 24 hours have elapsed since the last reading
	AL<>0: More than 24 hours have elapsed since the last reading
Remarks:	The AT, which has a battery powered realtime clock, sets the clock count to the current time when the computer boots. PCs (which don't have realtime clocks) set the counter to 0 during booting.
	The contents of the BX, CX, DX, SI, DI, BP registers and the segment registers are not affected by this function. The contents of all other registers may change.

Interrupt 1AH, Function 01H
Date and time: Set clock count

Sets the contents of the current clock count, which increments 18.2 times per second. This calculates the time elapsed since the computer was switched on and sets the current time through this function.

Input:	AH = 01H
	CX = High word of clock count
	DX = Low word of clock count
Output:	No output
Remarks:	The AT, which has a battery powered realtime clock, sets the clock count to the current time when the computer boots. PCs (which don't have realtime clocks) set the counter to 0 during booting. PC owners should use this function to set the current time.
	The contents of the AX, BX, CX, DX, SI, DI, BP registers and the segment registers are not affected by this function. The contents of all other registers may change.

Interrupt 1AH, Function 02H
Date and time: Read realtime clock

Reads the time from the realtime clock.

Input:	AH = 02H	
Output:	Carry flag = 0: O.K.:	
	CH =	Hours
	CL =	Minutes
	DH =	Seconds
	Carry flag = 1: Dead clock battery	
Remarks:	All time readings appear in BCD format.	
	The contents of the BX, SI, DI, BP registers and the segment registers are not affected by this function. The contents of all other registers may change.	

Interrupt 1AH, Function 03H   **BIOS (AT only)**
Date and time: Set realtime clock

Sets the time on the realtime clock.

Input: AH = 03H
                    CH = Hours
                    CL = Minutes
                    DH = Seconds
                    DL = 1: Daylight Saving Time
                    DL = 0: Standard Time
Output: No output
Remarks: All time settings must be in BCD format.
                    The contents of the BX, SI, DI, BP registers and the segment registers are not
                    affected by this function. The contents of all other registers may change.

Interrupt 1AH, Function 04H   **BIOS (AT only)**
Date and time: Read date from realtime clock

Reads the current date from the realtime clock.

Input: AH = 04H
Output: Carry flag = 0: O.K.:
                        CH =   Century (19 or 20)
                        CL =   Year
                        DH =   Month
                        DL =   Day
                    Carry flag = 1: Dead clock battery
Remarks: All date readings appear in BCD format.
                    The contents of the BX, SI, DI, BP registers and the segment registers are not
                    affected by this function. The contents of all other registers may change.

Interrupt 1AH, Function 05H   **BIOS (AT only)**
Date and time: Set date in realtime clock

Sets the current date in the realtime clock.

Input: AH = 05H
                    CH = Century (19 or 20)
                    CL = Year
                    DH = Month
                    DL = Day
Output: No output
Remarks: All date settings must be in BCD format.
                    The contents of the BX, CX, SI, DI, BP registers and the segment registers are
                    not affected by this function. The contents of all other registers may change.

Interrupt 1AH, Function 06H **BIOS (AT only)**
Date and time: Set alarm time

Sets alarm time for the current day. The alarm time triggers interrupt 4AH.

Input: AH = 06H
              CH = Hours
              CL = Minutes
              DH = Seconds
Output: Carry flag=0: O.K.
              Carry flag=1: Dead clock battery or programmed alarm time
Remarks: All alarm settings must be in BCD format.
              During booting, interrupt 4AH points to an IRET command. If this interrupt
              doesn't point to a particular routine responding to the alarm, nothing will
              happen once the alarm time is reached.
              Only one alarm time can be active at a time. If another alarm setting already
              exists, you must first delete it by using interrupt 26–1AH, function 7 (see
              below).
              The contents of the BX, CX, SI, DI, BP registers and the segment registers are
              not affected by this function. The contents of all other registers may change.

Interrupt 1AH, Function 07H **BIOS (AT only)**
Date and time: Reset alarm time

Clears an existing alarm setting created by using function 06H above.

Input: AH = 07H
Output: No output
Remarks: This function must be called when you want to change an alarm setting. Reset
              the alarm, then use function 06H to set the new alarm time.
              The contents of the BX, CX, SI, DI, BP registers and the segment registers are
              not affected by this function. The contents of all other registers may change.

Interrupt 1BH **BIOS/DOS**
Keyboard: <Break> key pressed

Records the occurrence of a <Ctrl><Break> key combination and triggers interrupt 1BH. During
the system boot, BIOS sets interrupt 1BH to an IRET command in order to prevent any reaction.

This routine sets a flag to indicate that the user has pressed <Ctrl><Break>. Following the
execution of one of the DOS functions, this flag is tested for character input or output. If the
system encounters <Ctrl><Break>, the current program stops. In addition, when a batch file is
in process, the program asks whether the batch file should be continued or terminated.

Pressing <Ctrl><C> doesn't activate the interrupt. This key combination forces DOS to end the
currently executing program. However, the DOS functions for character input/output search for
this key combination.

To prevent termination of an application program, this interrupt can also be pointed to a user
routine by pressing <Break> or <Ctrl><Break>.

Input: No input
Output: No output

Remarks: Before returning control to the calling program, this interrupt must restore all registers to their previous values.

Interrupt 1CH   **BIOS**
Periodic interrupt

The timer IC calls interrupt 8H approximately 18.2 times per second. After ending its task, it calls interrupt 1CH in order to allow an application program access to the signals from the timer IC. During booting, BIOS initializes the interrupt vector of interrupt 1CH so that it points to an IRET command, which prevents any response if the interrupt is called. For example, this interrupt can be pointed to a user routine to create a constant display clock on the screen.

Input: No input
Output: No output
Remarks: This interrupt must restore all registers to their previous values before returning control to the calling program.

Interrupt 1DH   **BIOS**
Video table

Sets a pointer to a table. The vector of this interrupt in the vector table, starting at address 0000:0074, stores the offset and segment address of this table. The table itself contains a collection of parameters used by BIOS for initializing a certain video mode. This involves the 16 memory locations on the video card, whose heart is a 6845 video processor. For this reason the table to which the vector points and which is part of the ROM-BIOS, consists of 16 consecutive bytes that indicate the contents of individual registers for a certain video mode. The first of these 16 bytes is copied into the first register of the 6845, the second byte into the second register, etc. The table in ROM contains a total of four 16-byte entries: 40x25 color mode, 80x25 color mode, 80x25 monochrome mode and one entry for the various color graphics modes.

Do not call this interrupt. If you do, the system will attempt to read the video table as executable code and will crash.

Input: No input
Output: No output

Interrupt 1EH   **BIOS/DOS**
Drive table

Sets a pointer to a table. The vector of this interrupt in the vector table starting at address 0000:0078 stores the offset and segment address of this table. The table itself contains a collection of parameters used by BIOS in disk drive access. BIOS has a table in ROM, but deviates the interrupt vector of interrupt 30 to its own table which allows faster disk access than the BIOS table.

Do not call this interrupt. If you do call it, the system will attempt to read the drive table as executable code and will crash.

Input: No input
Output: No output

Interrupt 1FH
Character table

BIOS/DOS

Sets a pointer to a table. The vector of this interrupt in the vector table, starting at address 0000:007C, stores the offset and segment address of this table. The table itself contains character patterns for the characters possessing ASCII codes 128 to 255. BIOS needs this table in order to display the graphic mode characters on the screen. These characters are displayed by placing the character patterns, which are stored in this table, on the screen as individual pixels.

Since the character patterns for codes 0 to 127 are already stored in a table in ROM-BIOS, this table contains only the character patterns for codes 128 to 255. The DOS GRAFTABL command loads a table for codes 127 to 255 into RAM and points the interrupt vector of interrupt 31 to this table. A user table can be added to display on the screen, in graphic mode, certain characters that are not part of the normal PC character set. The construction of the table requires that eight consecutive bytes define the appearance of the character. The first eight bytes of the table define the appearance of ASCII code 128, the next eight bytes define ASCII code 129, etc. Each set of eight bytes represent the eight lines which denote a character in graphic mode. The eight bits of each byte indicate the eight columns of pixels for each line.

Do not call this interrupt. If you do call it, the system will attempt to read the character table as executable code and will crash.

Input: No input
Output: No output

Appendix B

EGA/VGA-BIOS Functions

EGA and VGA cards enhance the BIOS Video-Interrupt 10H with numerous functions, which provide access to the extended capabilities of the cards. A description of these functions, which are called like the normal BIOS-functions of the Interrupt 10H, can be found in this chapter.

Interrupt 10H, Function 00H　　　　　　　　　　　　　　　　　　　　**EGA/VGA**
Screen: Set video mode

Sets and initializes the video mode.

Input:　　　　　　　AH = 00H
　　　　　　　　　　AL = EGA/VGA video mode
　　　　　　　　　　　　AL=0: 40x25-character text, 16 colors (EGA/VGA - color monitor)
　　　　　　　　　　　　AL=1: 40x25-character text, 16 colors (EGA/VGA - color monitor)
　　　　　　　　　　　　AL=2: 80x25-character text, 16 colors (EGA/VGA - color monitor)
　　　　　　　　　　　　AL=3: 80x25-character text, 16 colors (EGA/VGA - color monitor)
　　　　　　　　　　　　AL=4: 320x200 graphics, 4 colors (EGA/VGA - color monitor)
　　　　　　　　　　　　AL=5: 320x200 graphics, 4 colors (EGA/VGA - color monitor)
　　　　　　　　　　　　AL=6: 640x200 graphics, 2 colors (EGA/VGA - color monitor)
　　　　　　　　　　　　AL=7: 80x25-character text, mono (EGA/VGA - mono monitor)
　　　　　　　　　　　　AL=13: 320x200 graphics, 16 colors (EGA/VGA - color monitor)
　　　　　　　　　　　　AL=14: 640x200 graphics, 16 colors (EGA/VGA - color monitor)
　　　　　　　　　　　　AL=15: 640x350 graphics, mono (EGA/VGA - mono monitor)
　　　　　　　　　　　　AL=16: 640x350 graphics, 4 colors (64K EGA - high-res monitor)
　　　　　　　　　　　　　　　　640x350 graphics, 16 colors (128K EGA/VGA - high-res monitor)
　　　　　　　　　　　　AL=17: 640x480 graphics, 2 colors (VGA only)
　　　　　　　　　　　　AL=18: 640x480 graphics, 16 colors (VGA only)
　　　　　　　　　　　　AL=19: 320x200 graphics, 256 colors (VGA only)

Output:　　　　　　　No output
Remarks:　　　　　　Modes 0 and 1, 2 and 3, 4 and 5 differ in the output of the color signal that is suppressed in the first mode. This isn't possible on an EGA/VGA card so the modes are identical. If bit 7 of the AL register is set when this function is called, the contents of the video RAM will not be erased when the new mode is enabled. The task is to program the video controller and define a color

palette. The contents of registers BX, CX, DX, SI, DI, BP and the segment registers are not affected by this function.

Interrupt 10H, Function 01H   EGA/VGA
Screen: Define cursor appearance

Defines the starting and ending lines of the screen cursor. This function is independent of the display page being displayed.

Input:	AH = 01H
	CH = Starting line of the cursor
	CL = Ending line of the cursor
Output:	No output
Remarks:	Since the possible values depend on the size of the current video mode's character matrix, the values in the CH and CL registers always refer to an eight-line character matrix. The values should thus be between zero and seven. The EGA/VGA-BIOS adapts these values to the current size of its own character matrix.
	The contents of registers BX, CX, DX, SI, DI, BP and the segment registers are not affected by this function.

Interrupt 10H, Function 02H   EGA/VGA
Screen: Position cursor

Moves the cursor into position on the screen.

Input:	AH = 02H
	BH = Video page number
	DH = Screen line
	DL = Screen column
Output:	No output
Remarks:	The cursor moves only if the specified display page is the current page.
	The values for the screen line and column are based on the resolution of the current display mode.
	Assigning the DH and DL registers values for a non-existent screen position (e.g., column 0, line 255) makes the cursor disappear from the screen.
	The number of the display page is based on how many display pages the card has available.
	The contents of registers BX, CX, DX, SI, DI, BP and the segment registers are not affected by this function.

Interrupt 10H, Function 03H   EGA/VGA
Screen: Read cursor position

Reads the position of the text cursor on the screen and the starting and ending lines of the screen cursor.

Input:	AH = 03H
	BH = Video page number
Output:	DH = Screen line in which cursor is located
	DL = Screen column in which cursor is located
	CH = Starting line of screen cursor
	CL = Ending line of screen cursor

Remarks: The screen line and screen column parameters refer to the text coordinate system, even if a graphic mode is active.

The starting and ending lines of the cursor are returned correctly only in the text modes. They have no meanings in graphic modes.

The contents of registers BX, SI, DI, BP and the segment registers are not affected by this function.

Interrupt 10H, Function 04H   EGA
Read lightpen position

Reads the lightpen's position on the screen. This is only possible on EGA cards, since VGA cards do not support lightpens.

Input: AH = 04H
Output: AH = 0: Lightpen position cannot be read
                  AH = 1: Lightpen position read
                  DH = Screen row (text mode)
                  DL = Screen column (text mode)
                  CH = Screen row (graphic mode)
                  BX = Screen colum (graphic mode)
Remarks: This function call must be repeated until a 1 is returned in the AH register, since only then can the lightpen position be determined.

Graphic mode returns lightpen coordinates less accurately than in text mode. The Y-coordinate (row) is always a multiple of 2. For example, function 04H cannot differentiate between row 8 or row 9. In the 320x200 pixel graphic mode, the X-coordinate (column) is always a multiple of 4, and in the 640x200 pixel graphic mode the X-coordinate is a multiple of 8.

The contents of the CL register and the contents of the segment registers SS, CS and DS are not affected by this function. The content of all other registers may change, especially the SI and DI registers.

Interrupt 10H, Function 05H   EGA/VGA
Screen: Select current display page

Selects the current display page, and thereby the page which appears on the screen (text mode only).

Input: AH = 05H
                  AL = Display page number
Output: No output
Remarks: The number of available display pages depends on the amount of video RAM installed on the EGA/VGA card.

When a new page is selected the screen cursor will be moved to the position of the text cursor on this page.

Switching between different pages does not change the contents of these pages. The contents of registers BX, CX, DX, SI, DI, BP and the segment registers are not affected by this function.

Interrupt 10H, Function 06H
Screen: Scroll text lines up

Scrolls part of the current display page up by one or more lines.

Input:	AH = 06H
	AL = Number of lines to be scrolled up
	AL=0: Clear window
	CH = Screen line of upper left corner of window
	CL = Screen column of upper left corner of window
	DH = Screen line of lower right corner of window
	DL = Screen column of lower right corner of window
	BH = Color (attribute) for blank line(s)
Output:	No output
Remarks:	Normally the contents of the current display page are scrolled, but in the 320x200 four-color graphic mode this function only affects display page 0.

Clearing the screen window (number of lines = 0) is the same as filling it with spaces (ASCII code 32).

The contents of the lines scrolled out of the window are lost and cannot be recovered.

Use function 0 of this interrupt to clear the screen.

The interpretation of the attribute byte in the BL register depends on the current video mode. In text mode it is interpreted as any other attribute byte in video RAM. In 640x200 two-color mode this byte represents the color value for eight successive pixels. In 320x200 four-color mode this byte represents the color value of four successive pixels. In all other graphic modes it represents the color of all of the pixels in the cleared screen area.

The contents of registers BX, CX, DX, SI, DI, BP and the segment registers are not affected by this function.

Interrupt 10H, Function 07H
Screen: Scroll text lines down

Scrolls part of the current display page down one or more lines.

Input:	AH = 07H
	AL = Number of lines to be scrolled down
	AL=0: Clear window
	CH = Screen line of upper left corner of window
	CL = Screen column of upper left corner of window
	DH = Screen line of lower right corner of window
	DL = Screen column of lower right corner of window
	BH = Color (attribute) for blank line(s)
Output:	No output
Remarks:	Normally the contents of the current display page are scrolled, but in 320x200 four-color graphic mode this function only affects display page 0.

Clearing the screen window (number of lines = 0) is the same as filling it with spaces (ASCII code 32).

The contents of the lines scrolled out of the window are lost and cannot be recovered.

To clear the entire screen, use function 0 of this interrupt instead.

The interpretation of the attribute byte in the BL register depends on the current display mode. In the text mode it is interpreted like any other attribute byte in the video RAM. In the 640x200 two-color mode this byte represents the color value for eight successive pixels. In the 320x200 four-color mode it represents the color value of four successive pixels. In all other graphic modes it represents the color of all of the pixels in the cleared screen area.

The contents of registers BX, CX, DX, SI, DI, BP and the segment registers are not affected by this function.

Interrupt 10H, Function 08H   **EGA/VGA**
Screen: Read character/color

Reads and returns the ASCII code and color (attribute) of the character at the current cursor position.

Input: AH = 08H
                BH = Video page number
Output: AL = ASCII code of character
                AH = Color (attribute)
Remarks: This function can also be called in the graphic mode, whereby the bit pattern of the character on the screen will be compared with the bit patterns of the characters. If the character cannot be identified, the AL register will contain the value zero after the call.
                In the 320x200 four-color graphic mode this function only affects display page 0.
                The contents of registers BX, CX, DX, SI, DI, BP and the segment registers are not affected by this function.

Interrupt 10H, Function 09H   **EGA/VGA**
Screen: Write character/color

Writes character with the specified color at the current cursor position (in a specified display page).

Input: AH = 09H
                BH = Video page number
                CX = Repeat factor
                AL = ASCII code of character
                BL = Attribute
Output: No output
Remarks: If the graphic mode is active and the specified character is to be printed more than once (the value of the CX register is greater than 1), all of the characters must fit on the current screen line.
                In the 320x200 four-color graphic mode this function correctly works only on display page 0.
                Within a graphic mode the attribute in the BL register specifies the foreground color of the character, whereby the background color is zero. If bit seven is set, the character will be XORed with the bitmap at the output position.
                The controls codes for bell, carriage return, etc. are not recognized as control codes, and are displayed as normal ASCII characters.

This function can also be used to output characters in the graphic mode, in which case the character patterns are taken from one of the EGA character tables.

This function does not move the cursor to the next screen position.

The contents of registers BX, CX, DX, SI, DI, BP and the segment registers are not affected by this function.

Interrupt 10H, Function 0AH   **EGA/VGA**
Screen: Write character

Writes a character to the current screen position on the specified display page and the color of the old character at this position will be retained.

Input:	AH = 0AH
	AL = ASCII code of the character
	BH = Video page number
	BL = Foreground color of character for graphic modes
	CX = Repeat factor
Output:	No output
Remarks:	If the graphic mode is active and the specified character is to be printed more than once (the value of the CX register is greater than 1), all of the characters must fit on the current screen line.

The controls codes for bell, carriage return, etc. are not recognized as such and are displayed as normal ASCII characters.

This function can also be used to output characters in the graphic mode, in which case the character patterns are taken from one of the EGA character tables.

Within a graphic mode the attribute in the BL register specifies the foreground color of the character, whereby the background color is zero. If bit seven is set, the character will be XORed with the bitmap at the output position.

This function does not move the cursor to the next screen position.

The contents of registers BX, CX, DX, SI, DI, BP and the segment registers are not affected by this function.

Interrupt 10H, Function 0BH, Subfunction 0   **EGA/VGA**
Screen: Select border/background color

Selects the border and background color for the graphic or text mode.

Input:	AH = 0BH
	BH = 0
	BL = Border/background color
Output:	No output
Remarks:	This function should be called only when the EGA/VGA card is in the 320x200 or 640x200 graphic mode. Use function 10H for all other modes.

Bits zero to three of the BL register set the background and border color. Setting bit four will enable high-intensity colors.

The contents of registers BX, CX, DX, SI, DI, BP and the segment registers are not affected by this function.

Interrupt 10H, Function 0BH, Subfunction 1
Screen: Select color palette

EGA/VGA

Selects one of the two color palettes for the 320x200 graphic mode.

Input:	AH = 0BH
	BH = 1
	BL = Color palette number
Output:	No output
Remarks:	This function should be called only when the EGA/VGA card is in the 320x200 or 640x200 graphic mode. Use function 10H for all other modes.

The EGA/VGA-BIOS emulates the two CGA color palettes with the numbers 0 and 1. They contain the following colors:

> Palette 0: green, red, yellow
> Palette 1: cyan, magenta, white

The contents of registers BX, CX, DX, SI, DI, BP and the segment registers are not affected by this function.

Interrupt 10H, Function 0CH
Screen: Write pixel

EGA/VGA

Sets the color value of a screen pixel in the graphic mode.

Input:	AH = 0CH
	BH = Video page
	DX = Screen line
	CX = Screen column
	AL = Color value
Output:	No output
Remarks:	The color value depends on the colors available in the current display mode.

If bit seven of the AL register is set, the color value will be XORed with the previous color value of the pixel.

The display page is ignored in the 320x200 four-color graphic mode.

The contents of registers BX, CX, DX, SI, DI, BP and the segment registers are not affected by this function.

Interrupt 10H, Function 0DH
Screen: Read pixel

EGA/VGA

The color value of a pixel in the graphic mode is returned.

Input:	AH = 0DH
	BH = Video page
	DX = Screen line
	CX = Screen column
Output:	AL = Color value
Remarks:	The color value depends on the colors available in the current display mode.

The display page is ignored in the 320x200 four-color graphic mode.

The contents of registers BX, CX, DX, SI, DI, BP and the segment registers are not affected by this function.

Interrupt 10H, Function 0EH **EGA/VGA**
Screen: Write character

Writes a character to the current cursor position on the current display page. The color of the old character at this position will be retained.

Input: AH = 0EH
                AL = ASCII character code
                BL = Foreground color of character
Output: No output
Remarks: This function does not treat the various control codes like bell and carriage as normal characters, and implements them as the control characters they represent.

                After displaying a character with this function, the cursor position is incremented so that the next character will be printed at the following screen position. If the last screen position has been reached, the screen will be scrolled up one line and the output will continue in the first column of the last screen line.

                If bit seven of the BL register is set, the color value will be XORed with the previous color value of the pixels. The background color is zero.

                Characters can be displayed in the graphic mode with this function. The character patterns are taken from one of the EGA character tables.

                The contents of registers BX, CX, DX, SI, DI, BP and the segment registers are not affected by this function.

Interrupt 10H, Function 0FH **EGA/VGA**
Screen: Returns current display mode

Reads the number of the current display mode, the number of characters per line, and the number of the current display page.

Input: AH = 0FH
Output: AL = Video mode:
                AL=0: 40x25-character text, 16 colors (EGA/VGA - color monitor)
                AL=1: 40x25-character text, 16 colors (EGA/VGA - color monitor)
                AL=2: 80x25-character text, 16 colors (EGA/VGA - color monitor)
                AL=3: 80x25-character text, 16 colors (EGA/VGA - color monitor)
                AL=4: 320x200 graphics, 4 colors (EGA/VGA - color monitor)
                AL=5: 320x200 graphics, 4 colors (EGA/VGA - color monitor)
                AL=6: 640x200 graphics, 2 colors (EGA/VGA - color monitor)
                AL=7: 80x25-character text, mono (EGA/VGA - mono monitor)
                AL=13: 320x200 graphics, 16 colors (EGA/VGA - color monitor)
                AL=14: 640x200 graphics, 16 colors (EGA/VGA - color monitor)
                AL=15: 640x350 graphics, mono (EGA/VGA - mono monitor)
                AL=16: 640x350 graphics, 4 colors (64K EGA - high-res monitor)
                      640x350 graphics, 16 colors (128K EGA/VGA - high-res monitor)
                AL=17: 640x480 graphics, 2 colors (VGA only)
                AL=18: 640x480 graphics, 16 colors (VGA only)
                AL=19: 320x200 graphics, 256 colors (VGA only)
            AH = Number of characters per line

BH = Number of current display page

Remarks: The contents of registers BX, CX, DX, SI, DI, BP and the segment registers are not affected by this function.

Interrupt 10H, Function 10H, Subfunction 00H — EGA/VGA
Screen: Set palette registers

Sets the contents of a palette register in the attribute controller of the EGA/VGA card.

Input: AH = 10H
             AL = 00H
             BL = Color value
             BH = Register to be addressed
Output: No output
Remarks: Since the register number is not checked by the BIOS, you can also program the other registers in the attribute controller. These include the mode control register, overscan register and others.

The contents of registers BX, CX, DX, SI, DI, BP, and the segment registers are not affected by this function.

Interrupt 10H, Function 10H, Subfunction 01H — EGA/VGA
Screen: Set screen border color

Copies resulting value into the overscan register of the EGA attribute controller.

Input: AH = 10H
             AL = 01H
             BH = Border color
Output: No output
Remarks: The contents of registers BX, CX, DX, SI, DI, BP and the segment registers are not affected by this function.

Interrupt 10H, Function 10H, Subfunction 02H — EGA/VGA
Screen: Set all palette registers

Configures all 16 palette registers and the overscan register.

Input: AH = 10H
             AL = 02H
             ES = Segment address of color table
             DX = Offset address of color table
Output: No output
Remarks: The ES:BX register pair points to a 17-byte table. The first 16 bytes will be transferred to the 16 palette registers of the attribute controller and the 17th byte will be copied into the overscan register.

The contents of registers BX, CX, DX, SI, DI, BP and the segment registers are not affected by this function.

Interrupt 10H, Function 10H, Subfunction 03H   **EGA/VGA**
Screen: Set blinking attribute

Determines whether bit 7 in the attribute byte of a character in the text mode will enable character blinking, or display characters on a high-intensity background.

Input: AH = 10H
                    AL = 00H
                    BL = Blinking attribute
                        BL=0: high-intensity background
                        BL=1: blinking
Output: No output
Remarks: The contents of registers BX, CX, DX, SI, DI, BP and the segment registers
                    are not affected by this function.

Interrupt 10H, Function 10H, Subfunction 07H   **VGA**
Screen: Read out palette register

Reads the contents of one of the attribute controller's palette registers.

Input: AH = 10H
                    AL = 07H
                    BH = Number of palette register
Output: BL = Contents of addressed palette register
Remarks: Since the BIOS doesn't verify the number of the palette register read, this
                    function can read all the registers of the attribute controller.
                    The contents of registers BL, CX, DX, SI, DI, BP and all segment registers
                    are not affected by this function.

Interrupt 10H, Function 10H, Subfunction 08H   **VGA**
Screen: Read contents of overscan register

Returns the contents of the overscan register containing the screen's border color.

Input: AH = 10H
                    AL = 08H
Output: BH = Contents of the overscan register
Remarks: The contents of registers BL, CX, DX, SI, DI, BP and all segment registers
                    are not affected by this function.

Interrupt 10H, Function 10H, Subfunction 09H   **VGA**
Screen: Read contents of all palette registers and the overscan register

Copies the contents of the 16 palette registers and overscan register into a buffer.

Input: AH = 10H
                    AL = 09H
                    ES = Segment address of the buffer
                    DX = Offset address of the buffer
Output: No output
Remarks: The buffer must be a minimum of 17 bytes long to allow room for all the
                    palette registers (bytes 0-15) plus the overscan register (byte 16).
                    The contents of registers BL, CX, DX, SI, DI, BP and all segment registers
                    are not affected by this function.

Interrupt 10H, Function 10H, Subfunction 10H   **VGA**
Screen: Define a DAC color register

Allows the definition of one of the 256 available DAC color registers.

Input: AH = 10H
                BX = Number of the DAC color register (0-255)
                CH = Green value
                CL = Blue value
                DH = Red value
Output: No output
Remarks: Only bits 0 to 5 in the CH, CL and DH registers are of importance to this
                function. All other bits are ignored.
                The contents of registers BL, CX, DX, SI, DI, BP and all segment registers
                are not affected by this function.

Interrupt 10H, Function 10H, Subfunction 12H   **VGA**
Screen: Load multiple DAC color registers

Allows the definition of multiple DAC color registers.

Input: AH = 10H
                AL = 12H
                BX = Number of the first DAC color register (0-255)
                CX = Number of registers to be loaded
                ES = Segment address of the buffer
                DX = Offset address of the buffer
Output: No output
Remarks: The assigned buffer must be able to hold a group of three consecutive bytes for
                each DAC color register. The first byte contains the red value; the second byte
                contains the green value; and the third byte contains the blue value. These first
                three bytes correspond to the first DAC color register being accessed, the next
                three for the bytes to the next DAC color register.
                Only bits 0 to 5 in the CH, CL and DH registers are of importance to this
                function. All other bits are ignored.
                If the sum of BX and CX is greater than 255, the first DAC color register is
                reloaded after the last register is loaded.
                The contents of registers BL, CX, DX, SI, DI, BP and all segment registers
                are unchanged by this function.

Interrupt 10H, Function 10H, Subfunction 13H   **VGA**
Screen: Select color register or select a DAC register group

Manipulates bit 7 of the mode control registers.

Input: AH = 10H
                AL = 13H
                BL = 00H or 01H (see below)
                BH = see below
Output: No output
Remarks: This subfunction performs as two different subfunctions, depending on the
                value contained in the BL register. Subfunction 00H allows color selection,
                while subfunction 01H allows the selection of the active DAC register group.

Subfunction 00H copies bit 0 in the BH register into bit 7 of the mode control register, thus providing a method of color selection. If bit 0 in the BH register contains a value of 0, then the 256 DAC color registers are divided into four groups of 64 registers. Color selection involves bits 0-5 in the corresponding palette register, as well as bits 2-3 of the color select register. These eight bits act as the index for the DAC color register. If bit 0 in the BH register contains a 1, the DAC color registers are divided into 16 groups of 16 registers. Then color selection involves the lowest 4 bits of the palette register and the lowest 4 bits of the color select register, acting as the 8-bit index to the DAC color table.

Subfunction 01H loads the color select register, whose contents are specified by the active group of DAC color registers. The contents of the BH register are copied to the color select register.

The contents of registers BL, CX, DX, SI, DI, BP and all segment registers are not affected by this function.

Interrupt 10H, Function 10H, Subfunction 15H **VGA**
Screen: Read a DAC color register

Returns the contents of one of the 256 DAC color registers.

Input:	AH = 10H
	AL = 15H
	BX = Number of the DAC color registers
Output:	CH = Green value
	CL = Blue value
	DH = Red value
Remarks:	Only bits 0 to 5 in the CH, CL and DH registers are of importance to this function. All other bits are ignored.
	The contents of registers BX, DL, SI, DI, BP and all segment registers are not affected by this function.

Interrupt 10H, Function 10H, Subfunction 17H **VGA**
Screen: Load contents of multiple DAC color registers

Loads several DAC color registers at a time.

Input:	AH = 10H
	AL = 17H
	BX = Number of the first DAC color register to be loaded (0-255)
	CX = Number of registers to be loaded
	ES = Segment address of buffer
	DX = Offset address of buffer
Output:	No output
Remarks:	The contents of each DAC color register are represented within a buffer by three consecutive bytes. The red value is loaded into the first of these registers; the green value is loaded into the second of these registers; and the blue value is loaded into the third register. The first group of three bytes corresponds to the first DAC color register addressed, the second group to the next DAC color register, etc.
	Only bits 0 to 5 in the CH, CL and DH registers are of importance to this function. All other bits are ignored.

If the sum of BX and CX is greater than 255, the first DAC color register is reloaded after the last register is loaded (wrap-around occurs).

The contents of registers BX, CX, DX, SI, DI, BP and all segment registers are not affected by this function.

Interrupt 10H, Function 10H, Subfunction 18H   **VGA**
Screen: Load DAC mask register

Loads the specified value into the DAC mask register.

Input:	AH = 10H
	AL = 18H
	BL = Value of DAC mask register
Output:	No output
Remarks:	The contents of the DAC mask register play an important role in color selection. An AND instruction adds it to the index access to the DAC color table.
	The contents of registers BH, CX, DX, SI, DI, BP and all segment registers are not affected by this function.

Interrupt 10H, Function 10H, Subfunction 19H   **VGA**
Screen: Read out contents of the DAC mask register

Reads the current contents of the DAC mask register.

Input:	AH = 10H
	AL = 19H
Output:	BL = Contents of the DAC mask register
Remarks:	The contents of the DAC mask register play an important role in color selection. An AND instruction adds it to the index access to the DAC color table.
	The contents of registers BH, CX, DX, SI, DI, BP and all segment registers are not affected by this function.

Interrupt 10H, Function 10H, Subfunction 1AH   **VGA**
Screen: Returns method of color selection and color select register

Returns the method of color selection, contained in the contents of bit 7 of the mode control register. It also returns the contents of the color select register chosen by the active group of DAC color registers.

Input:	AH = 10H
	AL = 1AH
Output:	BL = Bit 7 of mode control register
	BH = Contents of color select registers
Remarks:	The contents of registers BX, CX, DX, SI, DI, BP and all segment registers are not affected by this function.

Interrupt 10H, Function 10H, Subfunction 1BH   **VGA**
Screen: Convert DAC color register into gray scales

Converts a specified range within a DAC color table into gray scales.

Input: AH = 10H
                AL = 1BH
                BX = Number of first DAC color register to be converted
                CX = Total number of DAC color registers to be converted
Output: No output
Remarks: Conversion into grays results from changes to the red, green and blue values,
                as well as the intensity of these values. The default factor for red is 0.3, the
                default factor for green is 0.59, and the default for blue 0.11.
                The contents of registers BX, CX, DX, SI, DI, BP and all segment registers
                are not affected by this function.

Interrupt 10H, Function 11H, Subfunction 00H   **EGA/VGA**
Screen: Load user-defined character set

Loads a user-defined character set from RAM into one of the two EGA character tables.

Input: AH = 11H
                AL = 00H
                BH = Lines per character (also bytes per character)
                BL = Character table (0 or 1)
                CX = Number of characters in table
                DX = ASCII code of first character in table
                ES = Segment address of character table in RAM
                BP = Offset address of character table in RAM
Output: No output
Remarks: A maximum of 512 characters can be loaded per character table.
                The loaded character set is not activated, nor are the CRTC registers
                programmed to the size of the characters. The changes will not be visible on
                the screen unless the character definitions are loaded into the active character
                table.
                The contents of registers BX, CX, DX, SI, DI, BP and the segment registers
                are not affected by this function.

Interrupt 10H, Function 11H, Subfunction 01H   **EGA/VGA**
Screen: Load 8x14 character set

Loads the entire 8x14-pixel character set from EGA/VGA ROM-BIOS into one of the two
character set tables.

Input: AH = 11H
                AL = 01H
                BL = Character table (0 or 1)
Output: No output
Remarks: The loaded character set is not activated, nor are the CRTC registers
                programmed to the size of the characters. The changes will not be visible on
                the screen unless the character definitions are loaded into the active character
                table.

1168

The contents of registers BX, CX, DX, SI, DI, BP and the segment registers are not affected by this function.

Interrupt 10H, Function 11H, Subfunction 02H   EGA/VGA
Screen: Load 8x8 character set

Loads the entire 8x8-pixel character set from EGA/VGA ROM-BIOS into one of the two character set tables.

Input:	AH = 11H
	AL = 02H
	BL = Character table (0 or 1)
Output:	No output
Remarks:	The loaded character set is not activated, nor are the CRTC registers programmed to the size of the characters. The changes will not be visible on the screen unless the character definitions are loaded into the active character table. The EGA card displays 43 lines on the screen, while the VGA card displays 50 lines.
	The contents of registers BX, CX, DX, SI, DI, BP and the segment registers are not affected by this function.

Interrupt 10H, Function 11H, Subfunction 03H   EGA/VGA
Screen: Activate character set

Activates one (or two) of the four 256-character character sets.

Input:	AH = 11H
	AL = 03H
	BL = Number of the character set to activate
Output:	No output
Remarks:	Bits zero and one of the BL register specify the number of the character set to be accessed when bit three of the attribute byte of the character is zero.
	Bits two and three of the BL register specify the number of the character set to be accessed when bit three of the attribute byte of the character is one.
	If the contents of bits zero and one are identical to the contents of bits two and three of the BL register, then bit three of the character attribute byte has no effect on the character displayed. Only 256 different characters can then be displayed on the screen.
	The contents of registers BX, CX, DX, SI, DI, BP and the segment registers are not affected by this function.

Interrupt 10H, Function 11H, Subfunction 04H   VGA
Screen: Load 8x16 character set

Loads the entire 8x16-pixel character set from the VGA-BIOS into one of the two character set tables.

Input:	AH = 11H
	AL = 04H
	BL = Corresponding character set table (0 or 1)
Output:	No output
Remarks:	The loaded character set is not activated, nor are the CRTC registers programmed to the size of the characters. The changes will not be visible on

the screen unless the character definitions are loaded into the active character table. The VGA card displays 25 text lines on the screen.

The contents of registers BX, CX, DX, SI, DI, BP and the segment registers are not affected by this function.

Interrupt 10H, Function 11H, Subfunction 10H   **EGA/VGA**
Screen: Load and activate user-defined character set

Loads a user-defined character set from RAM into one of the two EGA character tables and activates it by programming the CRTC registers.

Input:	AH = 11H
	AL = 10H
	BH = Lines per character (also bytes per character)
	BL = Character table (0 or 1)
	CX = Number of characters in table
	DX = ASCII code of first character in table
	ES = Segment address of character table in RAM
	BP = Offset address of character table in RAM
Output:	No output
Remarks:	A maximum of 512 characters can be loaded per character table.

The number of text lines displayed on the screen results from the height of the individual characters. It is calculated by dividing the number of screen lines (350) by the character height.

The starting and ending lines of the screen cursor are automatically adapted to the height of the new character matrix.

The contents of registers BX, CX, DX, SI, DI, BP and the segment registers are not affected by this function.

Interrupt 10H, Function 11H, Subfunction 11H   **EGA/VGA**
Screen: Load and activate 8x14 character set

Loads the entire 8x14-pixel character set from EGA/VGA ROM-BIOS into one of the two character set tables, and activates it by programming the CRTC registers.

Input:	AH = 10H
	AL = 11H
	BL = Character table (0 or 1)
Output:	No output
Remarks:	The function sets the EGA screen to display 25 lines of text, or sets the VGA screen to display 28 lines of text.

The starting and ending lines of the screen cursor are automatically adapted to the height of the new character matrix.

The contents of registers BX, CX, DX, SI, DI, BP and the segment registers are not affected by this function.

Interrupt 10H, Function 11H, Subfunction 12H   **EGA/VGA**
Screen: Load and activate 8x8 character set

Loads the entire 8x8-pixel character set from the ROM-BIOS of the EGA/VGA card into one of the two character set tables, and activates it by programming the CRTC registers.

Input:	AH = 10H
	AL = 12H
	BL = Character table (0 or 1)
Output:	No output
Remarks:	The function sets the screen to display 43 lines of text (EGA) or 50 lines of text (VGA).
	The starting and ending lines of the screen cursor are automatically adapted to the height of the new character matrix.
	The contents of registers BX, CX, DX, SI, DI, BP and the segment registers are not affected by this function.

Interrupt 10H, Function 11H, Subfunction 14H   VGA
Screen: Load 8x16 character set

Loads a complete 8x16 character set from the VGA card BIOS into one of the two character set tables, and activates it through CRTC register programming.

Input:	AH = 10H
	AL = 14H
	BL = Character table (0 or 1)
Output:	No output
Remarks:	When this function is called, the VGA card displays 25 lines of text on the screen.
	The starting and ending lines of the screen cursor automatically change to match the height of the new character matrix.
	The contents of registers BX, CX, DX, SI, DI, BP and all segment registers are not affected by this function.

Interrupt 10H, Function 11H, Subfunction 30H   EGA/VGA
Screen: Get information about the character generator

Returns various information about the current status of the character generator.

Input:	AH = 11H
	AL = 03H
	BH = Type of information desired
	BH=0: contents of interrupt vector 1FH
	BH=1: contents of interrupt vector 43H
	BH=2: address of the ROM 8x14 character table
	BH=3: address of the ROM 8x8 character table
	BH=4: address of the second half of the 8x8 character table
	BH=5: address of the alternative ROM 9x14 character table
	BH=6: Address of the alternative ROM 8x16 character table
	BH=7: Address of the alternative ROM 9x16 character table
Output:	CX = Height of current character matrix
	DL = Number of columns per line - 1
	ES = Segment address of the pointer
	BP = Offset address of the pointer
Remarks:	The contents of registers BX, CX, DX, SI, DI, BP and the segment registers CS, DS and SS are not affected by this function.

Interrupt 10H, Function 12H, Subfunction 10H   **EGA/VGA**
Screen: Determine EGA/VGA configuration

Reads the configuration of the EGA/VGA card.

Input: AH = 12H
                BL = 10H
Output: BH = Monitor connected
                     BH=0: color or high-resolution monitor
                     BH=1: monochrome monitor
                BL = EGA/VGA RAM capacity
                     BL=0: 64K
                     BL=1: 128K
                     BL=2: 192K
                     BL=3: 256K
Remarks: The contents of registers DX, SI, DI, BP and the segment registers are not
                affected by this function.

Interrupt 10H, Function 12H, Subfunction 20H   **EGA/VGA**
Screen: Activate alternate hardcopy routine

Installs an alternative hardcopy routine which prints as many lines as are displayed on the screen.
The hardcopy routine of the normal ROM-BIOS always prints 25 lines and is not suited for
creating a hardcopy of the EGA/VGA modes, which display more than 25 lines on the screen.

Input: AH = 12H
                BL = 20H
Output: No output
Remarks: The contents of registers BX, CX, DX, SI, DI, BP and the segment registers
                are not affected by this function.

Interrupt 10H, Function 12H, Subfunction 30H   **EGA/VGA**
Screen: Specify number of scan lines

Selects the number of scan lines on the screen.

Input: AH = 12H
                BL = 30H
                AL = Scan line status
                     AL=0: 200 scan lines (EGA and VGA)
                     AL=1: 350 scan lines (EGA and VGA)
                     AL=2: 400 scan lines (VGA only)
Output: No output
Remarks: The selected number of scan lines can only be displayed when the appropriate
                video card and monitor are in use. For example, a CGA monitor can only
                display 200 scan lines, even if the video card can operate in a higher
                resolution.
                The contents of registers BX, CX, DX, SI, DI and BP and all segment
                registers are not affected by this function.

Interrupt 10H, Function 12H, Subfunction 31H   **VGA**
Screen: Toggle palette registers loading

Toggles the automatic loading of palette registers in VGA-BIOS. The system either loads alternate display modes when function 00H is invoked, or loads default values.

Input: AH = 12H
                BL = 31H
                AL = Automatic palette register loading
                    AL=0: Yes
                    AL=1: No
Output: No output
Remarks: The contents of registers BX, CX, DX, SI, DI, BP and all segment registers are not affected by this function.

Interrupt 10H, Function 12H, Subfunction 32H   **EGA/VGA**
Screen: Enable/disable CPU access to video RAM

Enables or disables direct CPU access to video RAM and its different I/O ports.

Input: AH = 12H
                BL = 32H
                AL = Access status
                    AL=0: Access enabled
                    AL=1: Access denied
Output: No output
Remarks: The EGA BIOS doesn't recognize this function, but you can still suppress video card access directly using bit 1 of the output register (port address 3C2H).
                The contents of registers BX, CX, DX, SI, DI, BP and all segment registers are not affected by this function.

Interrupt 10H, Function 12H, Subfunction 33H   **VGA**
Screen: Enable/disable automatic gray scaling in DAC color registers

Toggles automatic gray scaling in VGA-BIOS. This is different from function 10H, subfunction 1BH, which enables selective gray scaling in DAC color registers.

Input: AH = 12H
                BL = 33H
                AL = DAC color register gray scaling
                    AL=0: On
                    AL=1: Off
Output: No output
                The contents of registers BX, CX, DX, SI, DI, BP and all segment registers are not affected by this function.

Interrupt 10H, Function 12H, Subfunction 34H   **VGA**
Screen: Enable/disable text cursor emulation

Toggles text cursor emulation mode. Calling function 01H (for defining the starting and ending lines of the cursor) doesn't compensate for character matrices in different resolutions. This function controls that change when in VGA mode.

Input:	AH = 12H
	BL = 34H
	AL = Cursor emulation mode
	AL=0: On
	AL=1: Off
Output:	No output
Remarks:	The contents of registers BX, CX, DX, SI, DI, BP and all segment registers are not affected by this function.

Interrupt 10H, Function 12H, Subfunction 36H   VGA
Screen: Suppress screen refresh

Temporarily suppresses screen refresh. Disabling refresh relieves video RAM of many system level tasks, especially those involving complex screen graphics.

Input:	AH = 12H
	BL = 36H
	AL = Screen refresh
	AL=0: On
	AL=1: Off
Output:	No output
Remarks:	The contents of registers BX, CX, DX, SI, DI, BP and all segment registers are not affected by this function.

Interrupt 10H, Function 13H   EGA/VGA
Screen: Display a string

Displays a string at a specified position on the screen, in a specific display page. The characters are taken from a buffer whose address is passed to the function.

Input:	AH = 13H
	AL = Output mode (0-3)
	AL=0: Attribute in BL, reserve cursor position
	AL=1: Attribute in BL, update cursor position
	AL=2: Attributes in buffer, reserve cursor position
	AL=3: Attributes in buffer, update cursor position
	BL = Attribute byte of characters (modes 0 and 1 only)
	CX = Number of characters to be printed
	DH = Screen line
	DL = Screen column
	BH = Video page
	ES = Segment address of the buffer
	BP = Offset address of the buffer
Output:	No output
Remarks:	In modes 1 and 3 the cursor position is placed after the last character of the string so that BIOS output will continue at the character after the string. This does not happen in modes 0 and 2.
	In modes 0 and 1 the buffer contains only the ASCII codes of the characters to be printed. The color of all of the characters in the string is specified by the BL register. In modes 2 and 3, each character in the buffer is followed by the corresponding attribute byte, so that each character has its own attribute. The BL register does not have to be loaded in these modes. Although the string

must be twice as long as the number of characters to be printed in these modes, the CX register contains just the number of ASCII characters to be printed, not the string buffer's length.

Control codes such as bell and carriage return are interpreted as control codes and not as normal ASCII codes. An error occurs when carriage return and linefeed are printed on a display page other than zero, however. These characters may be printed on display page 0, regardless of the display page specified in BH.

When the last screen position is reached the screen will move up one line and the output will continue with the first column of the last screen line.

When printing in the graphic mode the contents of the BL register determine the foreground color of the character (the background is zero). If bit seven of the BL register is set, the color value will be XORed with the old color value.

This function can also be used to print characters in the graphic mode, in which case the character patterns will be taken from one of the EGA/VGA character tables.

The contents of registers BX, CX, DX, SI, DI, BP and the segment registers are not affected by this function.

Interrupt 10H, Function 14H **Undocumented**	**EGA/VGA**
Interrupt 10H, Function 15H **Undocumented**	**EGA/VGA**
Interrupt 10H, Function 16H **Undocumented**	**EGA/VGA**
Interrupt 10H, Function 17H **Undocumented**	**EGA/VGA**
Interrupt 10H, Function 18H **Undocumented**	**EGA/VGA**
Interrupt 10H, Function 19H **Undocumented**	**EGA/VGA**
Interrupt 10H, Function 1AH **Screen: Determine video card type**	**VGA**

Determines the existence of the active video card.

Input:	AH = 1AH
	AL = 0
Output:	AL = 1AH
	BL = Device code for active video card
	BH = Device code for inactive video card

Remarks: If the value 1AH is not loaded into the AL register, then the video card in operation is not a VGA card (the 1AH indicates a VGA-BIOS). The function can return the following device codes:

FFH = Unknown video card
00H = No video card
01H = MDA with monochrome display
02H = CGA with CGA monitor
04H = EGA with EGA or multisync monitor
05H = EGA - monochrome display
07H = VGA - analog monochrome display
08H = VGA - analog color display (VGA, multisync)

The contents of registers CX, DX, SI, DI, BP and all segment registers are not affected by this function.

Interrupt 10H, Function 1BH   VGA
Get VGA-BIOS and video mode status

Gets information about the current VGA-BIOS and video card status.

Input: AH = 1BH
BX = 0
ES:DI = Pointer to a buffer
Output: AL = 1BH
Remarks: If the value 1BH is not loaded into the AL register, then the video card in operation is not a VGA card (the 1BH indicates a VGA-BIOS).

The buffer passed during the call of this function must have a minimum capacity of 64 bytes, because the VGA-BIOS stores a table there which contains information describing the current video mode.

The contents of registers BX, CX, DX, SI, DI and BP and all segment registers are not affected by this function.

```
┌─────────────────────────────────────────────────────────────────────────┐
│ Data block with mode dependent VGA-BIOS status information                │
├──────┬────────────────────────────────────────────────────────┬─────────┤
│ Off. │ Content                                                  │ Type    │
├──────┼────────────────────────────────────────────────────────┼─────────┤
│ 00H  │ Address of table containing static information           │ 1 ptr   │
│ 04H  │ Code number of current video mode                        │ 1 byte  │
│ 05H  │ Number of displayed screen or pixel columns              │ 1 word  │
│ 07H  │ Length of display page in video RAM                      │ 1 word  │
│ 09H  │ Starting address of current display page in video RAM    │ 1 word  │
│ 0BH  │ Cursor positions in maximum of eight display pages       │ 16 bytes│
│      │ in column/row order                                      │         │
│ 1BH  │ Ending row of cursor (pixel row)                         │ 1 byte  │
│ 1CH  │ Starting row of cursor (pixel row)                       │ 1 byte  │
│ 1DH  │ Number of current display page                           │ 1 byte  │
│ 1EH  │ Port address of the CRT controller address register      │ 1 word  │
│ 20H  │ Current contents of CRTC control registers at            │ 1 byte  │
│      │ port address 3B8H (MDA emulation) or 3D8H (VGA)          │         │
│ 21H  │ Current color selection register contents                │ 1 byte  │
│      │ at port address 3D9H                                     │         │
│ 22H  │ Number of screen rows displayed                          │ 1 byte  │
│ 23H  │ Height of characters in pixel rows                       │ 1 word  │
│ 25H  │ Code number of active video adapter                      │ 1 byte  │
│      │ (see function 1AH, subfunction 00H)                      │         │
│ 26H  │ Code number of inactive video adapter                    │ 1 byte  │
│      │ (see function 1AH, subfunction 00H)                      │         │
│ 27H  │ Number of displayable colors (0 = monochrome)            │ 1 word  │
│ 29H  │ Number of screen pages                                   │ 1 byte  │
│ 2AH  │ Number of displayed pixel rows                           │ 1 byte  │
│      │        0 = 200 pixel rows                                │         │
│      │        1 = 350 pixel rows                                │         │
│      │        2 = 400 pixel rows                                │         │
│      │        3 = 480 pixel rows                                │         │
│ 2BH  │ Number of character table used with characters whose     │ 1 byte  │
│      │ third bit of the attribute byte is 0                     │         │
│ 2CH  │ Number of character table used with characters whose     │ 1 byte  │
│      │ wthird bit of the attribute byte is 1                    │         │
│ 2DH  │ Miscellaneous information #1 (see below)                 │ 1 byte  │
│ 2EH  │ reserved                                                 │ 3 bytes │
│ 31H  │ Size of available video RAM                              │ 1 byte  │
│      │        0 =  64K                                          │         │
│      │        1 = 128K                                          │         │
│      │        2 = 192K                                          │         │
│      │        3 = 256K                                          │         │
│ 32H  │ reserved                                                 │ 14 bytes│
├──────┴────────────────────────────────────────────────────────┴─────────┤
│ 64 bytes                                                                  │
└─────────────────────────────────────────────────────────────────────────┘
```

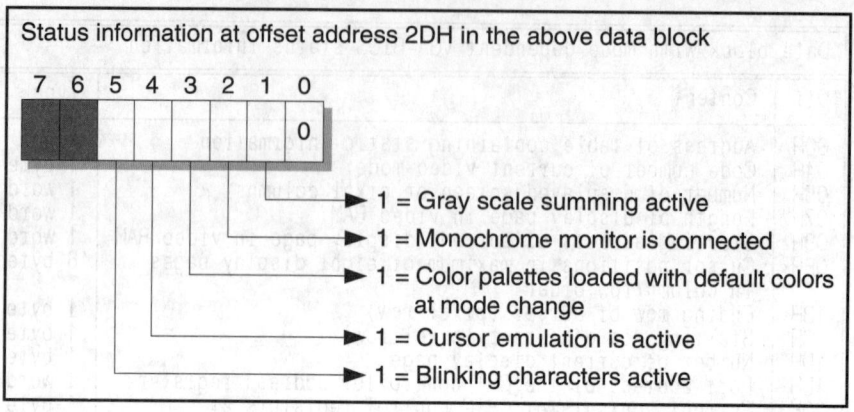

Status information at offset address 2DH in the above data block

1 = Gray scale summing active
1 = Monochrome monitor is connected
1 = Color palettes loaded with default colors at mode change
1 = Cursor emulation is active
1 = Blinking characters active

Data block with mode independent VGA-BIOS status information		
Off.	Content	Type
OOH	Address of table containing static information	1 ptr
OOH	Supported video modes (see below)	3 bytes
03H	reserved	4 bytes
07H	Number of pixel rows in text mode (see below)	1 byte
08H	Maximum number of character sets that can be displayed	1 byte
09H	Number of character sets loadable into video RAM	1 byte
OAH	VGA-BIOS capability information (see below)	1 byte
OBH	More VGA-BIOS capability information (see below)	1 byte
OCH	reserved	2 bytes
OEH	reserved	2 bytes
16 bytes		

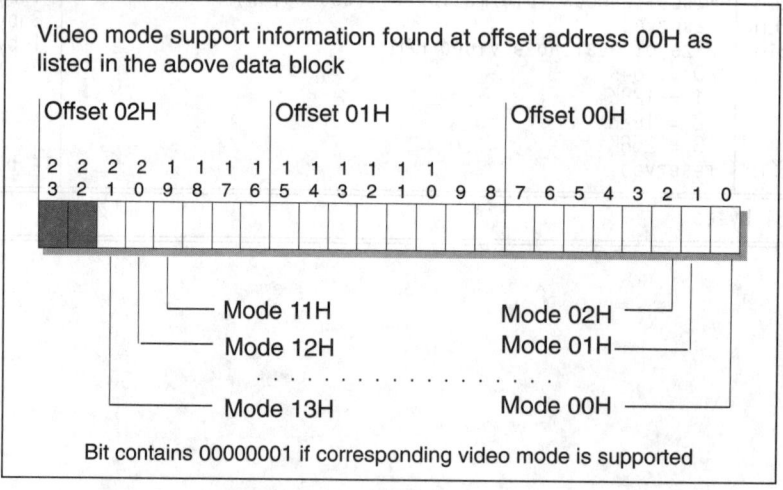

Video mode support information found at offset address 00H as listed in the above data block

Mode 11H
Mode 12H
Mode 13H

Mode 02H
Mode 01H
Mode 00H

Bit contains 00000001 if corresponding video mode is supported

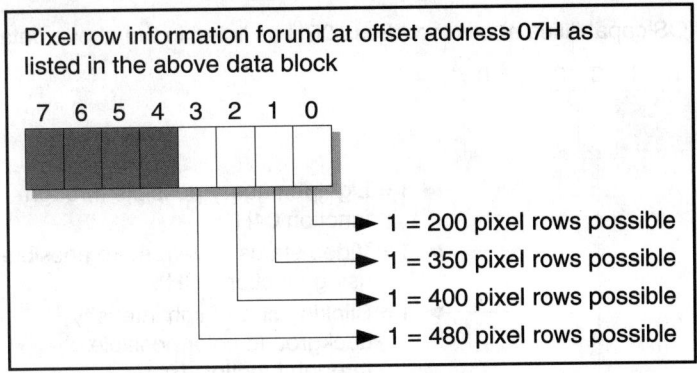

Pixel row information forund at offset address 07H as listed in the above data block

7 6 5 4 3 2 1 0

► 1 = 200 pixel rows possible
► 1 = 350 pixel rows possible
► 1 = 400 pixel rows possible
► 1 = 480 pixel rows possible

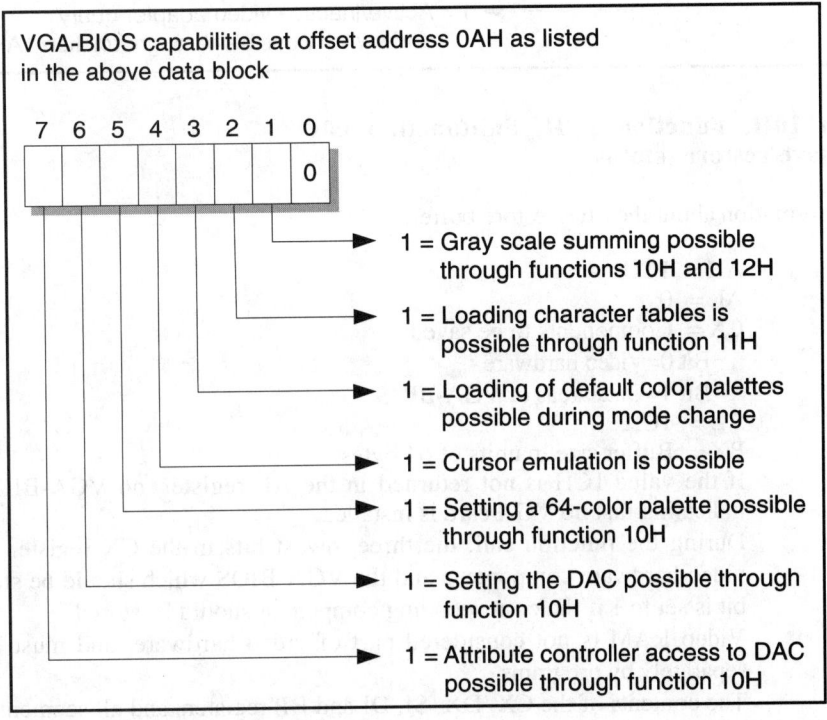

VGA-BIOS capabilities at offset address 0AH as listed in the above data block

7 6 5 4 3 2 1 0

► 1 = Gray scale summing possible through functions 10H and 12H
► 1 = Loading character tables is possible through function 11H
► 1 = Loading of default color palettes possible during mode change
► 1 = Cursor emulation is possible
► 1 = Setting a 64-color palette possible through function 10H
► 1 = Setting the DAC possible through function 10H
► 1 = Attribute controller access to DAC possible through function 10H

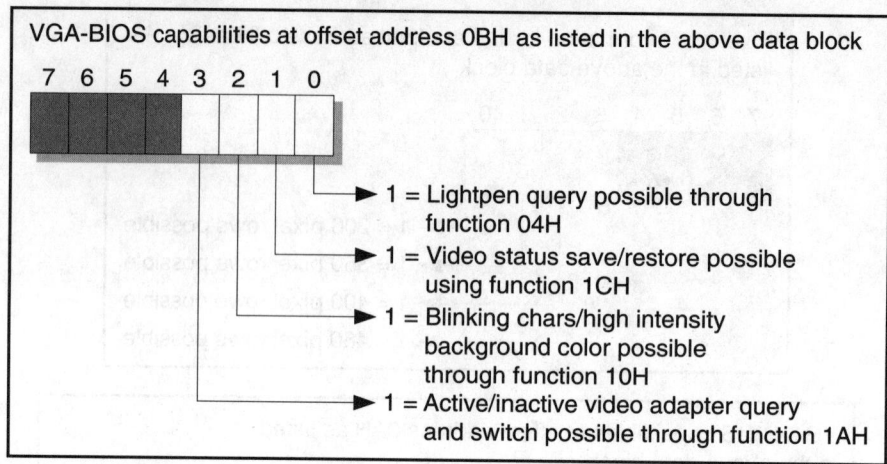

VGA-BIOS capabilities at offset address 0BH as listed in the above data block

► 1 = Lightpen query possible through function 04H
► 1 = Video status save/restore possible using function 1CH
► 1 = Blinking chars/high intensity background color possible through function 10H
► 1 = Active/inactive video adapter query and switch possible through function 1AH

Interrupt 10H, Function 1CH, Subfunction 00H   **VGA**
Return save/restore status

Returns information about the save/restore buffer.

Input:	AH = 1CH
	AL = 0
	CX = Components to be saved
	Bit 0=Video hardware
	Bit 1=Data areas of VGA-BIOS
Output:	AL = 1CH
	BX = Buffer size in units of 64 bytes
Remarks:	If the value 1CH is not returned in the AL register, no VGA-BIOS exists, indicating that no VGA card is installed.

During the function call, the three lowest bits in the CX register mark the video hardware components and the VGA-BIOS which should be stored. The bit is set to 1 if the corresponding component should be stored.

Video RAM is not considered part of video hardware, and must be stored separately by programs.

The contents of the CX, DX, SI, DI and BP registers and all segment registers are not affected by this function.

Interrupt 10H, Function 1CH, Subfunction 01H   **VGA**
Store video status

Stores video hardware/VGA-BIOS status received after calling subfunction 00H.

Input:	AH = 1CH
	AL = 1
	CX = Components to be stored
	Bit 0=Video hardware
	Bit 1=Data areas of VGA-BIOS
	ES:BX = Pointer to buffer in which information should be stored
Output:	AL = 1CH

Remarks: If the value 1CH is not returned in the AL register, no VGA-BIOS exists, indicating that no VGA card is installed.

Subfunction 00H must be used to determine the buffer size required before calling this function. Notice that the contents of the CX register remains unchanged between the two calls, During the function call, the three lowest bits in the CX register mark the video hardware components and the VGA-BIOS which should be stored. The bit is set to 1 if the corresponding component should be stored.

Video RAM is not considered part of video hardware, and must be stored separately by programs.

The contents of the BX, CX, DX, SI, DI and BP registers and all segment registers are not affected by this function.

10H, Function 1CH, Subfunction 02H   VGA
Restore video status

Restores video hardware/VGA-BIOS status stored by a preceding call to subfunction 01H.

Input: AH = 1CH
             AL = 2
             CX = Components to be restored
                 Bit 0=Video hardware
                 Bit 1=Data areas of VGA-BIOS
             ES:BX = Pointer to buffer in which information was previously stored
Output: AL = 1CH
Remarks: If the value 1CH is not returned in the AL register, no VGA-BIOS exists, indicating that no VGA card is installed.

This function call makes sense only following a call to subfunction 01H, where no more components can be restored than were stored previously. Before the function call note the content of the CX register.

The contents of the BX, CX, DX, SI, DI and BP registers and all segment registers are not affected by this function.

VESA Standard Functions

The VESA interface makes standardized functions available for access to Super VGA cards. This interface allows a program to connect with the various Super VGA cards, even though these cards are isolated from programs. The six different VESA standard functions are subfunctions of function 4FH, which links the VESA driver (or VESA compatible VGA BIOS) to BIOS interrupt 10H.

The following graphic modes are currently supported by the various VESA functions:

VESA BIOS Graphic Modes			
Code	Resolution	Colors	Memory
100H	640* 400	256	256 K
101H	640* 480	256	512 K
102H	800* 600	16	256 K
103H	800* 600	256	512 K
104H	1024* 768	16	512 K
105H	1024* 768	256	1 MEG
106H	1280*1024	16	1 MEG
107H	1280*1024	256	1.25 MEG
6AH	800* 600	16	256 K

Interrupt 10H, Function 4FH, Subfunction 00H   **VESA**
Get Super VGA card information

Reads the capabilities of the active Super VGA card, and determines which VESA functions are supported by that card

Input: AH = 4FH
                AL = 00H
                ES:DI = FAR pointer to the info buffer
Output: AL = 4FH: VESA functions are supported
                AH = 00H: VESA functions are supported

Remarks: The info buffer cited in the ES.DI registers must have 256 bytes of memory available. If the function executes correctly, it contains the following information after the call:

Structure of the Info Buffer		
Offset	Content	Type
00H	VESA signature ("VESA")	4 byte
04H	VESA version (higher level version number)	1 byte
05H	VESA version (lower level version number)	1 byte
06H	FAR pointer to ASCII string containing the name of card's manufacturer	1 dword
0AH	Flag, indicating capabilities of card (not used: Flag = 0000H)	1 dword
0EH	FAR pointer to list of code numbers indicating supported video modes	1 dword

The list with the code numbers of the supported video modes, which are passed in the last field of the buffer, consists of various words, which indicate the code of a video mode according to the table above. This list is terminated by a word containgin the value 0FFFFH. The length of the list varies from card to card.

Interrupt 10H, Function 4FH, Subfunction 01H   VESA
Query data for a VESA mode

This function returns information about a VESA mode, but does not switch it on.

Input: AH = 4FH
                AL = 01H
                CX = Code number of the desired VESA mode
                ES:DI = FAR pointer to info buffer

Output: AL = 4FH and
                AH = 00H : function was executed in an orderly manner

Remarks: This function should only be called, after the subfunction 00H was called successfully and therefore the existence of a VESA driver has been proven. Also only modes can be queried which appear in the mode list of function 00H.

The info-buffer, whose address is passed to the function, must offer 29 bytes of storage space. If the function returns successfully to the caller, it contains the following information:

```
┌─────────────────────────────────────────────────────────────────────┐
│  The Info-Buffer                                                      │
│  ┌──────┬──────────────────────────────────────────────┬──────────┐  │
│  │ Offs │ Content                                       │ Type     │  │
│  ├──────┼──────────────────────────────────────────────┼──────────┤  │
│  │ 00H  │ Mode-Flag, see below                          │ 1 WORD   │  │
│  │ 02H  │ Flags for the first access window, see below  │ 1 BYTE   │  │
│  │ 03H  │ Flags for the second access window, see below │ 1 BYTE   │  │
│  │ 04H  │ Granularity in KB, with which the two         │ 1 WORD   │  │
│  │      │            access windows can be moved        │          │  │
│  │ 06H  │ Size of the two access windows in KB          │ 1 WORD   │  │
│  │ 08H  │ Segment address of the first access window    │ 1 WORD   │  │
│  │ 0AH  │ Segment address of the second access window   │ 1 WORD   │  │
│  │ 0CH  │ FAR-pointer to the routine for setting of the │ 1 DWORD  │  │
│  │      │            visible area in the two access windows│        │  │
│  │ 10H  │ Number of bytes, occupied by the individual   │ 1 WORD   │  │
│  │      │            dot line in Video-RAM              │          │  │
│  ├──────┴──────────────────────────────────────────────┴──────────┤  │
│  │  Optional information, see mode-Flag                            │  │
│  ├──────┬──────────────────────────────────────────────┬──────────┤  │
│  │ 12H  │ X-resolution in dots/characters               │ 1 WORD   │  │
│  │ 14H  │ Y-resolution in dots/characters               │ 1 WORD   │  │
│  │ 16H  │ Width of the der character matrix in dots     │ 1 BYTE   │  │
│  │ 17H  │ Height of the character matrix in dots        │ 1 BYTE   │  │
│  │ 18H  │ Number of Bit-Planes                          │ 1 BYTE   │  │
│  │ 19H  │ Number of bits per screen dot                 │ 1 BYTE   │  │
│  │ 1AH  │ Number of storage blocks                      │ 1 BYTE   │  │
│  │ 1BH  │ Storage model                                 │ 1 BYTE   │  │
│  │ 1CH  │    Size of the storage blocks in KB           │ 1 BYTE   │  │
│  └──────┴──────────────────────────────────────────────┴──────────┘  │
└─────────────────────────────────────────────────────────────────────┘
```

The mode flag (offset 00H) tells if the optional fields in the info buffer of the VESA function were filled out and returns important information about the desired mode.

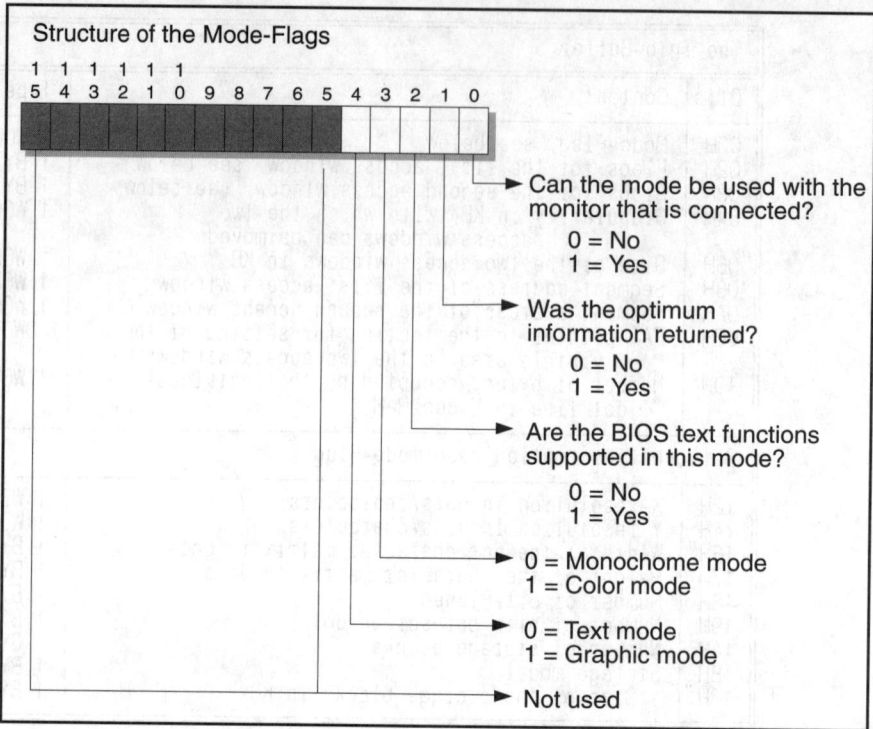

The two access windows (offset 02H and 03H) are described through the following bit fields:

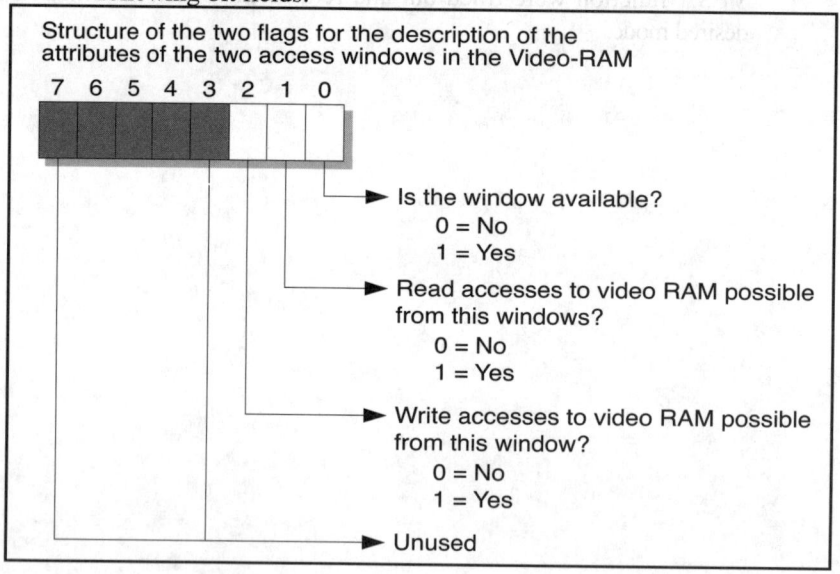

The storage model (offset 1BH) reflects the structure of the Video RAM in the desired video mode. The following codes are known.

```
┌─────────────────────────────────────────────────────────────┐
│ Valid Codes for the description of the storage model         │
├──────────┬──────────────────────────────────────────────────┤
│ Nr.      │ Task                                             │
├──────────┼──────────────────────────────────────────────────┤
│    00H   │ Text mode                                        │
│    01H   │ CGA-Format, i.e. 2 or 4 storage blocks           │
│    02H   │ Hercules-Format with 4 storage blocks            │
│    03H   │ Normal   EGA-/VGA format for 16 color graphic mode│
│    04H   │ Packed format with two dots with 4 bits per byte  │
│    05H   │ Normal EGA-/VGA format for 256 color graphic mode │
│ 06H-0FH  │ Reserved                                         │
│ 10H-FFH  │ Manufacturer specific code, not used until now    │
└──────────┴──────────────────────────────────────────────────┘
```

Interrupt 10H, Function 4FH, Subfunction 02H　　　　　　　　　**VESA**
Switch on VESA mode

With this function a VESA mode can be switched on.

Input:	AH = 4FH
	AL = 02H
	BX = Code number of the desired mode
Output:	AL = 4FH and
	AH = 00H: function was executed in an orderly manner
Remarks:	This function should only be called, after the subfunction 00H was called successfully and therefore the existence of a VESA driver has been proven. Also only modes can be queried which appear in the mode list of function 00H.
	Bit 15 in the code number of the video mode in the BX register, can be set when the Video RAM should not be erased during the initialization of the video mode.

Interrupt 10H, Function 4FH, Subfunction 03H　　　　　　　　　**VESA**
Query current mode

This function returns the code number of the current video mode and takes into consideration also the non VESA modes.

Input:	AH = 4FH
	AL = 03H
Output:	AL = 4FH and
	AH = 00H : was executed in an orderly manner in this case
	BX = Code-number of the current mode
Remarks:	This function should only be called, after the subfunction 00H was called successfully and therefore the existence of a VESA driver has been proven.

Interrupt 10H, Function 4FH, Subfunction 04H/00H   **VESA**
Determine the size of the safety buffer

For the call of the subfunction 04H/01H, which follows, this function can be used to determine the size of the required safety buffer.

Input: AH = 4FH
                AL = 04H
                DL = 00H
                CX = Components of the video-status to be stored
Output: AL = 4FH and
                AH = 00H : Function was executed in an orderly manner in this case
                BX = Number of consecutive 64 byte blocks which are required as safety buffer
Remarks: This function must be called before the subfunction 04H/01H to determine the size of the safety buffer which is made available to the subfunction 04H/01H.
                During the function call, the various bits in the CX register indicate, which components of the video-status should be stored. Only the low byte of the CX register is used, in which the following bits are of significance:

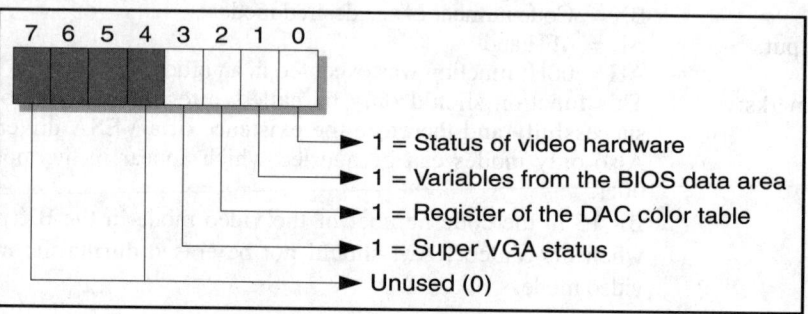

Interrupt 10H, Function 4FH, Subfunction 04H/01H   **VESA**
Store Video-Status of the Super VGA card

After a preceding call of the subfunction 04H/00H, the desired information about the various components of the video status are stored in a buffer of the caller by this function.

Input: AH = 4FH
                AL = 04H
                DL = 01H
                CX = Components of the video status to be stored
                ES:BX = FAR pointer to safety buffer
Output: AL = 4FH and
                AH = 00H: Function was executed in an orderly manner
Remarks: The buffer that was passed must have the size which was indicated through the BX register, during the preceding call of the subfunction 04H/00H.
                The various bits in the CX register indicate during the function call which components of the video status should be stored. See the subfunction 04H/00H.

Interrupt 10H, Function 4FH, Subfunction 04H/02H   **VESA**
Restore the video status of the Super VGA card

After the storage of the video-status with the help of the subfunction 04H/01H, this status can be restored again through the call of this function.

Input:	AH = 4FH
	AL = 04H
	DL = 01H
	CX = Components of the video-status to be restored
	ES:BX = FAR pointer to the segment address of the safety buffer
Output:	AL = 4FH and
	AH = 00H: Function was executed in an orderly manner
Remarks:	The buffer which was passed, must have been loaded previously with information about the video status, through a call of the subfunction 04H/01H.
	The various bits in the CX register indicate during the function call, which components of the video status should be restored. See the subfunction 04H/00H.

Interrupt 10H, Function 4FH, Subfunction 05H/00H   **VESA**
Determine access window in the video RAM

This function is used to include a certain part of the video RAM in one of the two VESA access windows and thereby make it addressable for a program.

Input:	AH = 4FH
	AL = 05H
	BH = 00H
	BL = Access window (0 or 1)
	DX = Start address
Output:	AL = 4FH and
	AH = 00H : Function was executed in an orderly manner
Remarks:	The start address in the DX-Register should be viewed in relation to the granularity of the window, which can be determined by the call of the subfunction 01H.
	The second access window can only be addressed with this function, if a preceding call of the subfunction 00H has indicated, that two access windows actually exist.

Interrupt 10H, Function 4FH, Subfunction 05H/01H   **VESA**
Query access window on the video RAM

With this function, the location of the access window in relation to the video RAM of the Super VGA card can be queried.

Input:	AH = 4FH
	AL = 05H
	BH = 01H
	BL = Access window (0 or 1)

Output: AL = 4FH and
           AH = 00H: Function was executed in an orderly manner
           DX = Starting address
Remarks: The start address in the DX register should be viewed in relation to the
           granularity of the window, which can be determined by the call of the
           subfunction 01H.

Appendix D

DOS API
Interrupts and Functions

More than 100 functions can be accessed using Interrupt 21h, which are made available to a program by DOS and therefore are designated as the Application-Program-Interface (DOS-API).

These functions are described in this chapter, including a whole series of functions whose significance were never officially publicized by Microsoft and are therefore designated as undocumented. The "undocumented" functions which are described here, have been already used in many thousands of commercial applications and Microsoft can't afford to leave them out of the API in a future DOS version. If you find no official function to help you in some application, you may use one of these undocumented functions.

Interrupt 20H	**DOS**
Terminate program	**(Version 1 and up)**

Restores the three interrupt vectors whose contents were stored in the PSP before the program call, terminates the currently running program and returns control to MS-DOS. If the program redirected the vectors to its own routine, these vectors cannot be overwritten by another program. However, the terminating program releases the RAM it had occupied. Before turning control over to the calling program, this memory releases and all data buffers clear.

Input:	CS = Segment address of the PSP
Output:	No output
Remarks:	COM programs automatically store the segment address of the PSP in the CS register. EXE programs require additional programming to load the segment address of the PSP into the CS register. Since the code and the PSP are stored in two separate segments, the address of the PSP must be loaded into the CS register. The code executes from another segment, which makes it impossible to call interrupt 32. To help overcome this problem, the value 0 and then the segment address of the PSP are pushed onto the stack. If a FAR RETURN command then executes, the program execution continues in the PSP segment at offset address 0. There a call for interrupt terminates the program.
	For the first version of DOS, this interrupt is the usual method for ending a program. To terminate a program in DOS Version 2 and up, functions 31H or 4CH of DOS interrupt 21 H should be called instead.

Interrupt 21H, Function 00H
Terminate program

DOS
(Version 1 and up)

Terminates execution of the currently running program and returns control to the calling program. Before this happens, the three interrupt vectors, whose contents had been stored in the PSP before the call of the program, are restored. If the program redirects these vectors to its own routine, they cannot be overwritten by another program. However, the terminating program does release the RAM it had occupied. Before turning control over to the calling program, the function releases this memory and clears all buffers.

Input: AH = 00H
                 CS = segment address of the PSP
Output: No output
Remarks: COM programs automatically store, in the CS register, the segment address of the PSP. Since the code and the PSP are stored in two separate segments, you cannot execute this function from an EXE program.

                 Instead of this function, use either function 31H or 4CH of interrupt 21H for terminating a program.

Interrupt 21H, Function 01H
Character input with echo

DOS
(Version 1 and up)

Reads a character from the standard input device and displays it on the standard output device. When the function is called but a character doesn't exist, the function waits until a character is available. Since standard input and output can be redirected, this function is able to read a character from an input device other than the keyboard and send it to an output device other than the screen. The characters that are read may originate from other devices or from a file. If the character comes from a file, the input doesn't redirect to the keyboard once it reaches the end of the file. So, the function continues to try to read data from the file after it passes the end.

Input: AH = 01H
Output: AL = Character read
Remarks: If extended key codes are read, the function passes code 0 to the AL register. The function must be called again to read the actual code.

                 If the function encounters a <Ctrl><C> character (ASCII code 3), it calls interrupt 23H.

                 The contents of the AH, BX, CX, DX, SI, DI, BP, CS, DS, SS, ES and the flag registers are not affected by this function.

Interrupt 21H, Function 02H
Character output

DOS
(Version 1 and up)

Displays a character on the standard output device. Since this device can be redirected, the character can be displayed on another output device or sent to a file. This function doesn't test whether or not the storage medium (disk or hard disk) is already full. Therefore, it will continue to try to write characters to this file.

Input: AH = 02H
                 DL = code of the character to be output
Output: No output

Remarks: Control codes such as backspace, carriage return and linefeed are executed when the function sends characters to the screen. If the output is redirected to a file, control codes are stored as normal ASCII codes.

            If the function encounters a <Ctrl><C> character (ASCII code 3), it calls interrupt 23H.

            The contents of the processor registers and the flag registers are not affected by this function.

Interrupt 21H, Function 03H   DOS
Read character auxiliary input   (Version 1 and up)

Reads a character from the serial port. Access defaults to the device with the designation COM1, unless a MODE command previously redirected serial access.

Input: AH = 03H
Output: AL = Character received
Remarks: Since the serial port has no internal buffer, it can receive characters faster than it can read them. The unread characters are then ignored.

            Before calling this function, communication parameters (baud rate, number of stop bits, etc.) must be set using the MODE command. Otherwise DOS defaults to 2400 baud, one stop bit, no parity and a word length of 8 bits.

            The BIOS functions called from interrupt 14H are a more efficient way to access the serial port. Since they also allow reading of the serial port status, these functions offer more flexibility than the DOS functions.

            If the function encounters a <Ctrl><C> character (ASCII code 3), it calls interrupt 23H.

            The contents of the AH, BX, CX, DX, SI, DI, BP, CS, DS, SS, ES and the flag registers are not affected by this function.

Interrupt 21H, Function 04H   DOS
Auxiliary output   (Version 1 and up)

Sends a character to the serial port. Unless a MODE command previously redirected serial access, access defaults to the device with the designation COM1.

Input: AH = 04H
            DL = Character set for output
Output: No output
Remarks: As soon as the receiving device sends a signal to the function indicating that it is ready to receive it, the function transmits the character. Control then returns to the calling program.

            Before calling this function, communication parameters (baud rate, number of stop bits, etc.) must be set using the MODE command. Otherwise DOS defaults to 2400 baud, one stop bit, no parity and a word length of 8 bits.

            The BIOS functions called from interrupt 14H are a more efficient way to access the serial port. Since they also allow reading of the serial port status, they offer more flexibility than the DOS functions.

            If the function encounters a <Ctrl><C> character (ASCII code 3), it calls interrupt 23H.

            The contents of the processor registers and the flag registers are not affected by this function.

Interrupt 21H, Function 05H   **DOS**
Character output to printer   **(Version 1 and up)**

Sends a character to the printer. Access defaults to the device with the designation LPT1 (identical to PRN), unless a MODE command previously redirected printer access.

Input: AH = 05H
                DL = Character code to be printed
Output: No output
Remarks: The function transmits the character only when the printer signals that it is
                ready to receive it. Then control returns to the calling program.
                If the function encounters a <Ctrl><C> character (ASCII code 3), it calls
                interrupt 23H.
                The BIOS functions called from interrupt 17H are more efficient for printer
                access. They offer more flexibility than the DOS printer functions for character
                output.
                The contents of the processor registers and the flag registers are not affected by
                this function.

Interrupt 21H, Function 06H   **DOS**
Direct console I/O   **(Version 1 and up)**

Reads characters from the standard input device and displays them on the standard output device. The read or written character isn't tested by the operating system (e.g., <Ctrl><C> has no effect on the program). Since standard input and output can be redirected, this function can read a character from an input device other than the keyboard and sends it to an output device other than the screen. The characters read may originate from other devices or from a file. When writing characters, this function doesn't test whether or not the storage medium (disk or hard disk) is already full. Also, the calling program cannot determine whether all the characters have been read from an input file.

During character input, the function doesn't wait until a character is available. Instead, the function returns control to the calling program.

Input: AH = 06H
                DL = 0–254: Send character code
                DL = 255: Read a character
Output: Character output: No output
                Character input: Zero flag=1: No character ready
                Zero flag=0: Character read is in the AL register
Remarks: If extended key codes are read, the function passes code 0 to the AL register.
                The function must be called again to read the actual code.

                ASCII code 255 (blank) cannot be displayed with this function because the
                function interprets ASCII code 255 as a command to input a character.
                The contents of the AH, BX, CX, DX, SI, DI, BP, CS, DS, SS and ES
                registers are not affected by this function.

Interrupt 21H, Function 07H   **DOS**
Unfiltered character input without echo   **(Version 1 and up)**

Reads a character from the standard input device without displaying the character on the standard output device. If a character doesn't exist when the function is called, the function waits until a character is available. The read character is not tested by the operating system (e.g., <Ctrl><C> has no effect on the program). Since standard input and output can be redirected, this function can read a character from an input device other than the keyboard. The characters that are read may originate from other devices or from a file. If the characters come from a file, the input doesn't redirect to the keyboard once it reaches the end of file. This causes the function to continue to try reading data from the file after it passes the end of file.

Input: AH = 07H
Output: AL = Character read
Remarks: If extended key codes are read, the function passes code 0 to the AL register. The function must be called again to read the actual code.
                     The contents of the AH, BX, CX, DX, SI, DI, BP, CS, DS, SS, ES and the flag registers are not affected by this function.

Interrupt 21H, Function 08H   **DOS**
Character input without echo   **(Version 1 and up)**

Reads a character from the standard input device without displaying the character on the standard output device. If no character exists when the function is called, the function waits until a character is available.

Since standard input can be redirected, this function can read a character from an input device other than the keyboard. The characters read may originate from other devices or from a file. If the characters come from a file, the input doesn't redirect to the keyboard on reaching the end of file, so the function continues to try reading data from the file after it passes the end of file.

Input: AH = 08H
Output: AL = Character read
Remarks: If extended key codes are read, the function passes code 0 to the AL register. The function must be called again to read the actual code.
                     If the function encounters a <Ctrl><C> character (ASCII code 3), it calls interrupt 23H.
                     The contents of the AH, BX, CX, DX, SI, DI, BP, CS, DS, SS, ES and the flag registers are not affected by this function.

Interrupt 21H, Function 09H   **DOS**
Output character string   **(Version 1 and up)**

Displays a character string on the standard output device. Since this device can be redirected, the character may be displayed on another output device or sent to a file. This function doesn't test whether or not the storage medium (disk or hard disk) is already full, and will continue to try to write the string to a file.

Input: AH = 09H
                     DS = String segment address
                     DX = String offset address
Output: No output

Remarks: The string must be stored in memory as a series of bytes which contain the ASCII codes of the characters to be output. A dollar sign character "$" (ASCII code 36) indicates, to DOS, the end of the string.

Control codes, such as backspace, carriage return and linefeed, are executed within the string.

The contents of the processor registers and the flag registers are not affected by this function.

Interrupt 21H, Function 0AH
Buffered input

DOS
(Version 1 and up)

Reads a number of characters from the standard input device and transmits the characters to a buffer. The input ends when the user presses the <Return> key. The ASCII code of this key (13) is then placed in the buffer as the last character of the string.

Since standard input can be redirected, this function can read a character from an input device other than the keyboard. The characters read may originate either from other devices or from a file. If the characters come from a file, the input doesn't redirect to the keyboard on reaching the end of file, so the function continues to try reading data from the file after it passes the end.

Input: AH = 0AH
DS = Buffer segment address
DX = Buffer offset address
Output: No output
Remarks: The first byte of the buffer accepts the maximum number of characters (including the carriage return which ends the input) which can be read into the buffer, starting at memory location 2. In order to inform the function of the maximum number of characters it may read, this information must be entered, by the calling program, into the buffer before the function call.

After completion of the input, DOS places the number of characters read (excluding the carriage return) in memory location 1.

The buffer must be the number of the characters to be read plus 2 bytes.

When the input reaches the second to last memory location in the buffer, the computer beeps if you attempt to enter any character other than the <Return> key (end of input).

Extended key codes occupy two bytes in the buffer. The first byte contains the code 0, and the second byte contains the extended key code.

If the function encounters a <Ctrl><C> character (ASCII code 3), it calls interrupt 23H.

The <Backspace> and cursor keys let you edit the input without storing these keys in the buffer.

The contents of the processor registers and the flag registers are not affected by this function.

Interrupt 21H, Function 0BH
Get input status

DOS
(Version 1 and up)

Determines whether a character is available for reading from the standard input device.

Input: AH = 0BH
Output: AL = 0: No character available

AL = 255: One or more characters available for reading
Remarks: If the function encounters a <Ctrl><C> character (ASCII code 3), it calls interrupt 23H.
The contents of the AH, BX, CX, DX, SI, DI, BP, CS, DS, SS, ES and the flag registers are not affected by this function.

Interrupt 21H, Function 0CH   DOS
Reset input buffer and then input   (Version 1 and up)

Clears the input buffer then calls one of the character input functions. Since all the character input functions get their characters from the standard input device and standard input may redirected, this function only operates when the keyboard is the standard input device. In this case the characters could be entered before the function call but not read by a function. These existing characters are erased to ensure that the function call only reads characters which were inputted after its call.

Input: AH = 0CH
            AL = Function to be called during call of function 10
            DS = Input buffer segment address
            DX = Input buffer offset address
Output: Functions 1, 6, 7 and 8: AL = Character to be read
            Function 10: No output
Remarks: Functions 1, 6, 7, 8 and 10 can be passed to the function as calling functions.
            The contents of the AH, BX, CX, DX, SI, DI, BP, CS, DS, SS, ES and the flag registers are not affected by this function.

Interrupt 21H, Function 0DH   DOS
Disk reset   (Version 1 and up)

Sends all data stored in an internal DOS buffer to a block driver device (e.g., disk drive, hard disk). The open files (handles or FCBs) remain open.

Input: AH = 0DH
Output: No output
Remarks: Despite this function call, all open files must be closed in an orderly manner. Otherwise the current directory entry of the file may not update properly, which prevents access to new file data.
            The contents of the processor registers and the flag registers are not affected by this function.

Interrupt 21H, Function 0EH   DOS
Select default disk drive   (Version 1 and up)

Defines the the current default disk drive. Its designation appears as a prompt on the screen when the command interpreter expects input from the user. The drive indicated here will be used for all file access in which no special device was specified.

Input: AH = 0EH
            DL = Drive number
Output: AL = Number of installed drives or volumes
Remarks: Drive A: has code number of 0, drive B: code number 1, etc.
            Even if the PC has only one disk drive and one hard disk, the number of volumes in the AL register can be greater than two because the hard disk can

be divided into multiple volumes. In addition, the PC can have one or more RAM disks as part of its configuration. For a PC with a single disk drive, you can only have two volumes because drive A: also simulates drive B:.

Unlike DOS Version 2, which permits 63 different device codes, DOS Version 3 permits 26 different devices (the letters A to Z). To keep compatibility between versions, limit your device access to a maximum of 26 devices.

BIOS interrupt 11H does a better job of reading the number of disk drives than this function.

The contents of the AH, BX, CX, DX, SI, DI, BP, CS, DS, SS, ES and the flag registers are not affected by this function.

Interrupt 21H, Function 0FH   **DOS**
Open file (FCB)   **(Version 1 and up)**

Opens a file if one is available. After this function call executes successfully, the file can be read or written.

Input:	AH = 0FH
	DS = FCB segment address of the file
	DX = FCB offset address of the file
Output:	AL = 0: File found and opened
	AL = 255: File not found
Remarks:	Both normal and extended FCBs can be used.

If the file was found, DOS enters, into the FCB, the file size, the date and the time of its creation or last modification.

DOS sets the record length at 128 bytes. This record length can be changed in the FCB before opening a file. If you need a longer record length, the DTA must be moved (the original DTA is only 128 bytes long).

If random file access is performed, the random record field in the FCB must be set after the file opens successfully.

The file pointer points to the first byte of the file after the file opens.

The contents of the AH, BX, CX, DX, SI, DI, BP, CS, DS, SS, ES and the flag registers are not affected by this function.

Interrupt 21H, Function 10H   **DOS**
Close file (FCB)   **(Version 1 and up)**

Writes all data currently in the DOS buffer to the file and closes the file. In addition, the directory entry changes to reflect the new file size and the date and time of the most recent modification to the file.

Input:	AH = 10H
	DS = FCB segment address of the file
	DX = FCB offset address of the file
Output:	AL = 0: File closed and directory entry revised
	AL = 255: File not found in directory
Remarks:	Only open files can be closed.

For disk files, the disk which was in the drive when the function call occurred must also be the disk that contains the file. Otherwise, the function call writes an incorrect FAT and an incorrect directory to the disk, which makes the data that is already on the disk useless.

The contents of the AH, BX, CX, DX, SI, DI, BP, CS, DS, SS, ES and the flag registers are not affected by this function.

Interrupt 21H, Function 11H   **DOS**
Search for first match (FCB)   **(Version 1 and up)**

Searches for the first occurrence in the disk directory of the filename indicated in the FCB.

Input:	AH = 11H
	DS = FCB segment address
	DX = FCB offset address
Output:	AL = 0: File found
	AL = 255: File not found
Remarks:	The FCB passed to the function contains the drive specifier and the filename for which the function should search.

The filename can contain the wildcard "?" to search for a group of files.

The search is made only in the current directory of the indicated device.

If the function searches for a normal file, a normal FCB can pass the information to the function. However, if you wish to search for a file with special attributes (volume name, subdirectories, hidden files, etc.), extended FCBs must be used.

If a file was found, the DTA contains an FCB of the same type as the FCBs. This FCB in the DTA contains the found filename. For this reason, the DTA must always be large enough to accept either a normal or an extended FCB.

The DTA can be switched to its own buffer using function 1AH, to ensure that it is large enough to accept the FCB.

The contents of the AH, BX, CX, DX, SI, DI, BP, CS, DS, SS, ES and the flag registers are not affected by this function.

Interrupt 21H, Function 12H   **DOS**
Search for next match (FCB)   **(Version 1 and up)**

Searches for additional occurrences in the disk directory of the filename indicated in the FCB, after the file was found by function 17 (see above).

Input:	AH = 12H
	DS = FCB segment address
	DX = FCB offset address
Output:	AL = 0: File found
	AL = 255: File not found (no other files available)
Remarks:	This function can only be called after calling function 11H.

The FCB passed to the function contains the drive specifier and the filename for which the function should search.

If another filename was found its name is recorded in the FCB at the beginning of the DTA.

The DTA can be switched with function 1AH to its own buffer to ensure that it is large enough to accept the FCB.

The contents of the AH, BX, CX, DX, SI, DI, BP, CS, DS, SS, ES and the flag registers are not affected by this function.

Interrupt 21H, Function 13H   **DOS**
Delete file (FCB)   **(Version 1 and up)**

Erases one or more files in the current directory of the specified device.

Input:	AH = 13H
	DS = FCB segment address
	DX = FCB offset address
Output:	AL = 0: file(s) erased
	AL = 255: No file(s) found, or file(s) assigned Read-Only attribute
Remarks:	The FCB passed to the function contains both the device on which the files to be erased are located and the name of the file.

The filename can contain the wildcard "?" to erase a group of files.

Only files in the current directory of the indicated device may be erased.

If the function is used to delete a normal file, a normal FCB can pass the information to the function. However, if you want to delete a file with special attributes (volume name, subdirectories, hidden files, etc.), extended FCBs must be used.

Volumes may be deleted with this function; subdirectories may not.

The contents of the AH, BX, CX, DX, SI, DI, BP, CS, DS, SS, ES and the flag registers are not affected by this function.

Interrupt 21H, Function 14H   **DOS**
Sequential read (FCB)   **(Version 1 and up)**

Reads the next sequential data block from a file.

Input:	AH = 14H
	DS = FCB segment address
	DX = FCB offset address
Output:	AL = 0: Block read
	AL = 1: End of file reached
	AL = 2: Segment wrap
	AL = 3: Partial record read
Remarks:	The function can only be called after the file was opened by the indicated FCB.

The DTA reads the block. If the DTA is not large enough, function 1AH must move the DTA into its own buffer.

The FCB records the size of the block and the corresponding number of bytes read.

Error 2 occurs when the DTA reaches the end of a segment and the block being read extends beyond the end of the segment.

Error 3 occurs when a partial block appears at the end of the file. The block is read in anyway and blank spaces bring the block up to the allocated block size.

After reading a block, the file pointer resets to the beginning of the next block so that the next function call automatically reads the next block.

The contents of the AH, BX, CX, DX, SI, DI, BP, CS, DS, SS, ES and the flag registers are not affected by this function.

Interrupt 21H, Function 15H   **DOS**
Sequential write (FCB)   **(Version 1 and up)**

Writes a sequential block to a file.

Input:	AH = 15H
	DS = FCB segment address
	DX = FCB offset address
Output:	AL = 0: Block written
	AL = 1: Medium (disk/hard disk) full
	AL = 2: Segment overflow
Remarks:	The function can only be called after the file was opened by the indicated FCB.

The DTA writes the block it contains to the file. If the DTA is not large enough to hold the file, function 1AH must be used to move the DTA into its own buffer.

The FCB records the size of the block and the corresponding number of bytes written.

Error 2 occurs if the DTA reaches the end of a segment and the block being written extends beyond the end of the segment.

After writing a block, the file pointer resets to the beginning of the next block, so that the next function call automatically writes the next block.

The contents of the AH, BX, CX, DX, SI, DI, BP, CS, DS, SS, ES and the flag registers are not affected by this function.

Interrupt 21H, Function 16H   DOS
Create or truncate file (FCB)   (Version 1 and up)

Creates a new file, or dumps the contents of an existing file (file size=0 bytes). This function call allows other functions to read or write to the open file.

Input:	AH = 16H
	DS = FCB segment address
	DX = FCB offset address
Output:	AL = 0: File created or cleared
	AL = 255: File could not be created (e.g., directory full)
Remarks:	The contents of an existing file called by this function are lost.

After calling this function, the file is already open; you don't need to open the file using function 0FH (see above).

If you open the file using an extended FCB, you can assign certain attributes to the file (e.g., volume name, hidden file, etc.).

You cannot create a subdirectory using this function.

After opening the file, the file pointer moves to the first byte of the file.

The contents of the AH, BX, CX, DX, SI, DI, BP, CS, DS, SS, ES and the flag registers are not affected by this function.

Interrupt 21H, Function 17H   DOS
Rename file (FCB)   (Version 1 and up)

Input:	AH = 17H
	DS = FCB segment address
	DX = FCB offset address
Output:	AL = 0: File(s) renamed
	AL = 255: No file found, or new filename matches old filename
Remarks:	The FCB here is a special FCB, based on a normal FCB. The first 12 bytes contain the drive specifier and the name of the file to be renamed. However, this type of FCB has the new drive specifier and the new filename stored

1201

starting at memory location 10H. The drive specifier must be identical for both filenames.

The name of the file to be renamed can contain the wildcard "?", which renames several files. If the new filename contains the wildcard "?", the places in the filename and extension where a question mark appears in this parameter remain unchanged.

The contents of the AH, BX, CX, DX, SI, DI, BP, CS, DS, SS, ES and the flag registers are not affected by this function.

Interrupt 21H, Function 18H   **DOS**
Reserved for internal use   **(Version 1.0 and up)**

Interrupt 21H, Function 19H   **DOS**
Get default disk drive   **(Version 1 and up)**

Returns the drive specifier of the default (current) disk drive.

Input:	AH = 19H
Output:	AL = Drive specifier
Remarks:	This function identifies drive A as code 0, drive B as code 1, etc.
	The contents of the AH, BX, CX, DX, SI, DI, BP, CS, DS, SS, ES and the flag registers are not affected by this function.

Interrupt 21H, Function 1AH   **DOS**
Set DTA address   **(Version 1 and up)**

Transfers the DTA (Disk Transfer Area) to another area of memory. The DTA acts as buffer memory for all FCB supported file accesses.

Input:	AH = 1AH
	DS = New DTA segment address
	DX = New DTA offset address
Output:	No output
Remarks:	This function must be called if the existing DTA has insufficient memory to handle the transmitted data.
	When the program starts, MS-DOS places the DTA at address 128 in the PSP. Since the program starts after address 255 of the PSP, it is 128 bytes long.
	DOS does not test the length of the DTA. Instead it assumes that the DTA is large enough to accept the transmitted data. If this is not the case, a DOS function can overwrite the excess data.
	DOS recognizes an error during various functions if the DTA is at the end of a segment and the data to be transmitted exceeds the end of the segment.
	The contents of the processor registers and the flag registers are not affected by this function.

Interrupt 21H, Function 1BH   **DOS**
Get allocation information for default drive   **(Version 1 and up)**

Returns information about the format of the default drive.

Input:	AH = 1BH
Output:	AL = Number of sectors per cluster

DS = Media descriptor segment address
BX = Media descriptor offset address
DX = Number of clusters

Remarks: The media descriptor can return the following codes:

F8H: Hard disk
F9H: Disk drive: double-sided, 15 sectors per track (AT only)
FCH: Disk drive: single-sided, 9 sectors per track
FDH: Disk drive: double-sided, 9 sectors per track
FEH: Disk drive: single-sided, 8 sectors per track
FFH: Disk drive: double-sided, 8 sectors per track

The contents of the AH, BX, CX, DX, SI, DI, BP, CS, DS, SS, ES and the flag registers are not affected by this function.

Interrupt 21H, Function 1CH   DOS
Get allocation information for specified drive   (Version 1 and up)

Returns information about the format of the specified drive.

Input: AH = 1CH
              DL = Drive specifier
Output: AL = Number of sectors per cluster
              DS = Media descriptor segment address
              BX = Media descriptor offset address
              DX = Number of clusters
Remarks: This function identifies drive A as code 0, drive B as code 1, etc.
              The media descriptor can return the following codes:

F8H: Hard disk
F9H: Disk drive: double-sided, 15 sectors per track (AT only)
FCH: Disk drive: single-sided, 9 sectors per track
FDH: Disk drive: double-sided, 9 sectors per track
FEH: Disk drive: single-sided, 8 sectors per track
FFH: Disk drive: double-sided, 8 sectors per track

The contents of the AH, BX, CX, DX, SI, DI, BP, CS, DS, SS, ES and the flag registers are not affected by this function.

Interrupt 21(h), Function 1DH   DOS
Reserved   (Version 1 and up)

Interrupt 21(h), Function 1EH   DOS
Reserved   (Version 1 and up)

Interrupt 21H, Function 1FH   DOS
Get DPB pointer to current drive   (Version 1 and up)

Gets the pointer to a DOS Parameter Block for the current disk drive.

Input: AH = 1FH
Output: AL = 000H: Operation successful
              AL = 0FFH: Error
              BX:DS = FAR pointer to DPB structure

1203

Remarks: If the device indicated is a diskette drive, DOS accesses the drive to fill the DPB with data about the drive and the format of the diskette. For hard disks this information is already stored in the memory and no hardware access is required.

An error during the function call can only occur if an invalid drive code was indicated. If this occurs, error code 15 is returned in the AL register.

The construction of the DOS Parameter Block varies between DOS versions.

The contents of the AH, CX, DX, SI, DI, BP, CS, SS and ES registers are not affected by this function.

Interrupt 21(h), Function 20H   DOS
Reserved   (Version 1 and up)

Interrupt 21H, Function 21H   DOS
Random read (FCB)   (Version 1 and up)

Reads a specified file record into the DTA.

Input: AH = 21H
             DS = FCB segment address
             DX = FCB offset address
Output: AL = 0: Record read
             AL = 1: End of file reached
             AL = 2: Segment overflow
             AL = 3: Partial record read
Remarks: The function can only be called after the file was opened by the indicated FCB.

The record whose address is stored in the FCB starting at location 21H is read.

The DTA reads the record. If the DTA is not large enough, function 1AH must be called to move the DTA into its own buffer.

The FCB records the size of the record and the corresponding number of bytes read.

During the function call, the file pointer moves to the beginning of the record being read so that a subsequent call of a sequential read (function 14H—see above) reads the same record sequentially.

The record number does not increment following the function call, so a new call of this function would read the same record.

Error 2 occurs when the DTA reaches the end of a segment and the record being read extends beyond the end of the segment.

Error 3 occurs when a partial record appears at the end of the file. The record is read in anyway and blank spaces bring the record up to the allocated record size.

The contents of the AH, BX, CX, DX, SI, DI, BP, CS, DS, SS, ES and the flag registers are not affected by this function.

Interrupt 21H, Function 22H   DOS
Random write (FCB)   (Version 1 and up)

Writes data from memory to the specified record in a file.

Input: AH = 22H
             DS = FCB segment address
             DX = FCB offset address
Output: AL = 0: record was written

1204

AL = 1: Medium (disk/hard disk) full

AL = 2: segment overflow

Remarks: The function can only be called after the file was opened by the indicated FCB.
The record whose address is stored in the FCB starting at location 21H is read.
The record is written from the DTA to the file. If the DTA is not large
enough, function 1AH must move the DTA into its own buffer.

The FCB records the size of the record and the number of bytes read.

During the function call, the file pointer moves to the beginning of the record
being read. This instructs subsequent calls of a sequential read (function 14H—
see above) to read the same record sequentially.

The record number does not increment following the function call, so a new
call of this function would read the same record.

Error 2 occurs when the DTA reaches the end of a segment and the record being
written extends beyond the end of the segment.

The contents of the AH, BX, CX, DX, SI, DI, BP, CS, DS, SS, ES and the
flag registers are not affected by this function.

Interrupt 21H, Function 23H   **DOS**
Get file size in records (FCB)   **(Version 1 and up)**

Determines the size of a file based on the number of records in that file.

Input: AH = 23H

DS = FCB segment address

DX = FCB offset address

Output: AL = 0: Number of records found starting at FCB address 21H

AL = 255: File not found

Remarks: The FCB passed contains the drive specifier as well as the name and extension
of the file to be examined.

Unlike the other FCB supported file accesses, the FCB requires the record size
before the application can call this function.

A record size of 1 returns the size of the file in bytes.

The contents of the AH, BX, CX, DX, SI, DI, BP, CS, DS, SS, ES and the
flag registers are not affected by this function.

Interrupt 21H, Function 24H   **DOS**
Set random record number   **(Version 1 and up)**

Sets the record number in the FCB to the current position of the file pointer. Random access
may begin at the point at which earlier sequential accesses left off.

Input: AH = 24H

DS = FCB segment address

DX = FCB offset address

Output: No output

Remarks: The function can only be called after the file was opened by the indicated FCB.
The contents of the processor registers and the flag registers are not affected by
this function.

Interrupt 21H, Function 25H   **DOS**
Set interrupt vector   **(Version 1 and up)**

Sets any interrupt vector to another routine.

Input: AH = 25H
                    AL = Interrupt number
                    DS = New interrupt routine segment address
                    DX = New interrupt routine offset address
Output: No output
Remarks: Before calling this function, the old contents of the interrupt vector to be
                    changed should be read and stored using function 35H. After the program
                    terminates, the old contents of the interrupt vector should be restored.
                    The contents of the processor registers and the flag registers are not affected by
                    this function.

Interrupt 21H, Function 26H   **DOS**
Create PSP   **(Version 1 and up)**

Copies the PSP (program segment prefix) of the executing program to a specified address in
memory.

Input: AH = 26H
                    DX = New PSP segment address
Output: No output
Remarks: The new PSP offset address is 0.
                    DOS Version 1 uses this function to execute other programs by creating a
                    PSP, loading the program after this PSP and executing it.
                    For DOS Version 2 up, use the EXEC function 4BH to load and execute
                    additional programs instead of this function.
                    The contents of the processor registers and the flag registers are not affected by
                    this function.

Interrupt 21H, Function 27H   **DOS**
Random block read (FCB)   **(Version 1 and up)**

Reads one or more sequentially stored records into memory.

Input: AH = 27H
                    CX = Number of records to be read
                    DS = FCB segment address
                    DX = FCB offset address
Output: AL = 0: Record read
                        CX=Number of records read
                    AL = 1: End of file reached
                    AL = 2: Segment overflow
                    AL = 3: Partial record read
Remarks: The function can only be called after the file was opened by the indicated FCB.
                    The starting record is the record whose address is stored in the FCB, starting at
                    location 21H.
                    The record data passes to the DTA. If the DTA is not large enough, function
                    1AH must move the DTA into its own buffer.

The FCB records the size of the record and the corresponding number of bytes read.

After the function call, the file pointer moves to the end of the last record that was read so that it points to the next record (following the last record read).

Error 2 occurs when the DTA reaches the end of a segment and the record being read extends beyond the end of the segment.

Error 3 occurs when a partial record appears at the end of the file. The record is read in anyway and blank spaces bring the record up to the allocated record size. The contents of the AH, BX, CX, DX, SI, DI, BP, CS, DS, SS, ES and the flag registers are not affected by this function.

Interrupt 21H, Function 28H	**DOS**
Random block write (FCB)	**(Version 1 and up)**

Writes one or more records in sequence to the specified file.

Input:	AH = 28H
	CX = Number of records to be written
	DS = FCB segment address
	DX = FCB offset address
Output:	AL = 0: Record written
	CX=Number of records written
	AL = 1: Medium (disk/hard disk) full
	AL = 2: Segment overflow
Remarks:	The function can only be called after the file was opened by the indicated FCB.

The starting record is the record whose address is stored in the FCB starting at location 21H.

The FCB records the size of the record and the corresponding number of bytes read.

The data is written from the DTA to the file. If the DTA is not large enough, function 1AH must move the DTA into its own buffer.

After the function call, the file pointer moves to the end of the last record written so that it points to the next record, which follows the last record written. The record number increments by the number of records written.

Error 2 occurs when the DTA reaches the end of a segment and the record being written extends beyond the end of the segment.

The contents of the AH, BX, CX, DX, SI, DI, BP, CS, DS, SS, ES and the flag registers are not affected by this function.

Interrupt 21H, Function 29H	**DOS**
Parse filename to FCB	**(Version 1 and up)**

Transfers an ASCII format filename into the proper fields of an FCB. The filename can include a drive specifier, filename and file extension.

Input:	AH = 29H
	DS = Segment address of filename in memory
	SI = Offset address of filename in memory
	ES = FCB segment address
	DI = FCB offset address
	AL = Transmission parameters:

Bit 1 = 1:   The drive specifier in the FCB changes only if the filename passed contains a drive specifier

0:   The drive specifier changes anyway. If the filename passed contains no drive specifier, the the FCB defaults to 0 (current drive)

Bit 2 = 1:   The filename in the FCB changes only if the filename parameter passed contains a filename

0:   The filename changes. If the filename passed does not contain a filename, the filename in the FCB fills with spaces (ASCII code 32)

Bit 3 = 1:   The file extension in FCB changes only if the filename passed contains an extension

0:   The file extension in the FCB changes. If the filename passed has no extension, the extension field is padded with spaces (ASCII code 32)

Bits 4–8:   Should contain the value 0

Output:	AL = 0: The filename passed contains no wildcards
	AL = 1: The filename passed contains wildcards
	AL = 255: Invalid drive specifier
	DS = Segment address of the first character after parsed filename
	SI = Offset address of the first character after parsed filename
	ES = FCB segment address
	DI = FCB offset address
Remarks:	The filename must end with an end character (ASCII code 0).

If the filename contains the wildcard "*", all corresponding fields in the FCB fill with the wildcard "?".

The contents of the AH, BX, CX, DX, SI, DI, BP, CS, DS, SS, ES and the flag registers are not affected by this function.

Interrupt 21H, Function 2AH
Get system date

DOS
(Version 1 and up)

Reads the current system date.

Input:	AH = 2AH
Output:	AL = Day of the week (0=Sunday, 1=Monday, etc.)
	CX = Year
	DH = Month
	DL = Day
Remarks:	DOS calls the clock driver to read the date.

The contents of the AH, BX, CX, DX, SI, DI, BP, CS, DS, SS, ES and the flag registers are not affected by this function.

Interrupt 21H, Function 2BH
Set system date

DOS
(Version 1 and up)

Sets the current system date as returned by function 2AH (see above).

Input:	AH = 2BH
	CX = Year
	DH = Month
	DL = Day

Output:	AL = 0: O.K.
	AL = 255: Date incorrect
Remarks:	The date passes to the clock driver.

If the PC does not have a realtime clock, the date remains in effect until the PC is switched off or rebooted.

If the date entry is incorrect, the PC retains the old date.

The contents of the AH, BX, CX, DX, SI, DI, BP, CS, DS, SS, ES and the flag registers are not affected by this function.

Interrupt 21H, Function 2CH
Get system time

DOS
(Version 1 and up)

Gets the current system time.

Input:	AH = 2CH
Output:	CH = Hours
	CL = Minutes
	DH = Seconds
	DL = Hundredths of a second
Remarks:	DOS calls the clock driver to read the time.

The contents of the AH, BX, CX, DX, SI, DI, BP, CS, DS, SS, ES and the flag registers are not affected by this function.

Interrupt 21H, Function 2DH
Set system time

DOS
(Version 1 and up)

Sets the current system time.

Input:	AH = 2DH
	CH = Hours
	CL = Minutes
	DH = Seconds
	DL = hundredths of a second
Output:	AL = 0: O.K.
	AL = 255: Incorrect time
Remarks:	The time passes to the clock driver.

If the PC does not have a realtime clock, the time remains in effect until the PC is switched off or rebooted.

If the time entry is incorrect, the PC retains the old time.

The contents of the AH, BX, CX, DX, SI, DI, BP, CS, DS, SS, ES and the flag registers are not affected by this function.

Interrupt 21H, Function 2EH
Set verify flag

DOS
(Version 1 and up)

Sets the verify flag. This flag determines whether data should be verified after a write operation to a block driver for proper transmission.

Input:	AH = 2EH
	DL = 0
	AL = 0: Don't verify data
	AL = 1: Verify data
Output:	No output

Remarks: This flag can be controlled at the user level with the VERIFY ON and VERIFY OFF commands.

The contents of the processor registers and the flag registers are not affected by this function.

Interrupt 21H, Function 2FH
Get DTA address
DOS
(Version 2 and up)

Returns the address of the DTA (Data Transmission Area), which serves as a data buffer for all FCB supported file accesses.

Input: AH = 2FH
Output: ES = DTA segment address
            BX = DTA offset address
Remarks: This function determines the address of the DTA, but not the DTA's size.

After the start of a program, the DTA starts at memory location 128 of the PSP and has a length of 128 bytes.

The contents of the AH, BX, CX, DX, SI, DI, BP, CS, DS, SS, ES and the flag registers are not affected by this function.

Interrupt 21H, Function 30H
Get MS-DOS version number
DOS
(Version 2 and up)

Returns the DOS version number.

Input: AH = 30H
Output: AL = Major version number (e.g., version 2.01=2)
            AH = Minor version number (e.g., version 3.01=01)
Remarks: The major (whole) version number represents the number preceding the decimal point. For example, the version number 3.3 returns the major version number 3.

The minor (fractional) version number represents the number following the decimal point. It is always given as two digits. For example, Version 2.1 returns the minor version number 10 (0AH).

If the AL register contains a value of 0, the program runs under DOS Version 1. DOS Version 1.0 cannot use this function.

The contents of the DX, SI, DI, BP, CS, DS, SS, ES and the flag registers are not affected by this function.

Interrupt 21H, Function 31H
Terminate and stay resident
DOS
(Version 2 and up)

Terminates the currently executing program and returns control to the calling program. The current program remains in memory for later recall.

Input: AH = 31H
            AL = Return code
            DX = Number of paragraphs to be reserved
Output: No output
Remarks: The return code in the AL register indicates whether or not the program called by it correctly executes. The calling program can read this number by calling function 77 (4DH). This value can be tested from within a batch file using the ERRORLEVEL and IF commands.

The number of 16-byte paragraphs to be reserved indicates how many bytes, beginning with the PSP, cannot be released for other uses.

Memory blocks reserved by function 48H are not affected by the value in the DX register because they can only be released by calling function 49H.

Interrupt 21H, Function 32H   **DOS**
Get DPB pointer for any drive   **(Version 1.0 and up)**

Gets the pointer to a DOS Parameter Block for any disk drive.

Input:	AH = 32H
	DL = Drive code (0=current, 1=A, 2=B, etc.)
Output:	Carry flag=1: Error
	Carry flag=0: O.K.
	DS:BX = FAR pointer to the DPB
Remarks:	If the device indicated is a diskette drive, DOS accesses the drive to fill the DPB with data about the drive and the format of the diskette. For hard disks this information is already stored in the memory and no hardware access is required.

An error during the function call can only occur if an invalid drive code was indicated. If this occurs, error code 15 is returned in the AL register.

The construction of the DOS Parameter Block varies between DOS versions.

The contents of the AH, CX, DX, SI, DI, BP, CS, SS and ES registers are not affected by this function.

Interrupt 21H, Function 33H, Subfunction 0   **DOS**
Get <Ctrl><Break> flag   **(Version 2 and up)**

Reads the <Ctrl><Break> flag. This determines whether DOS should test for active <Ctrl><C> or <Ctrl><Break> keys on each function call, or on character input/output calls. <Ctrl><C> and <Ctrl><Break> trigger interrupt 23H.

Input:	AH = 33H
	AL = 0
Output:	DL = 0: Test only during character input/output
	DL = 1: Test on every function call
Remarks:	Since the <Ctrl><Break> flag is not part of the environment block of a program, it affects all programs which call the DOS character functions that test for <Ctrl><C> or the <Break> key.

The contents of the AH, BX, CX, DX, SI, DI, BP, CS, DS, SS, ES and the flag registers are not affected by this function.

Interrupt 21H, Function 33H, Subfunction 1   **DOS**
Set <Ctrl><Break> flag   **(Version 2 and up)**

Sets and unsets the <Ctrl><Break> flag. This determines whether DOS should test for the activation of the <Ctrl><C> or <Ctrl><Break> keys on each DOS function call or character input/output calls. <Ctrl><C> and <Ctrl><Break> trigger interrupt 23H.

Input:	AH = 33H
	AL = 1
	DL = 0: Test only during character input/output
	DL = 1: Test on every function call

Output: No output
Remarks: Since the <Ctrl><Break> flag is not part of the environment block of a
                   program, it affects all programs which call the DOS character functions that
                   test for <Ctrl><C> or the <Break> key.
                   The contents of the processor registers and the flag registers are not affected by
                   this function.

Interrupt 21H, Function 34H   DOS
Get INDOS flag pointer   (Version 2.0 and up)

Returns the address of the INDOS flag. This is especially important for minimizing re-entry
problems in TSR programs.

Input: AH = 34H
Output: ES:BX = FAR pointer to the INDOS flag
Remarks: The INDOS flag is a byte, which counts the recursive calls made to interrupt
                   21H. It contains the value 0 as long as DOS is not active. This means that
                   DOS functions can be called from a TSR program. If this flag contains a value
                   larger than 0, DOS is presently active, where a value greater than 1 indicates a
                   corresponding number of recursive calls. If this occurs, DOS cannot be
                   interrupted with a function call from a TSR program, because in the worst case
                   a system crash occurs.
                   See Chapter 32 for more information on TSRs.
                   The contents of the CX, DX, SI, DI, BP, CS, SS and ES registers are not
                   affected by this function.

Interrupt 21H, Function 35H   DOS
Get interrupt vector   (Version 2 and up)

Returns the current contents of an interrupt vector and the address of the interrupt routine that
belongs to it.

Input: AH = 35H
                   AL = Interrupt number
Output: ES = Interrupt routine segment address
                   BX = Interrupt routine offset address
Remarks: To ensure compatibility with future versions of DOS, instead of reading the
                   vector's contents directly from the interrupt vector table, call this function for
                   reading an interrupt vector.
                   The contents of the AH, BX, CX, DX, SI, DI, BP, CS, DS, SS, ES and the
                   flag registers are not affected by this function.

Interrupt 21H, Function 36H   DOS
Get free disk space   (Version 2 and up)

Returns information about the device (the block driver) from which the available memory space
can be calculated.

Input: AH = 36H
                   DL = Device code
Output: AX = 65535: Device unavailable
                   AX< 65535: Number of sectors per cluster
                       BX =   Number of available clusters

CX = Number of bytes per sector
DX = Total number of clusters on the device

Remarks: This function identifies drive A as code 0, drive B as code 1, etc.

The remaining memory on the medium can be computed from the number of bytes per sector multiplied by the number of sectors per cluster, multiplied by the number of free clusters.

The contents of the SI, DI, BP, CS, DS, SS, ES and the flag registers are not affected by this function.

Interrupt 21H, Function 37H, Subfunction 00H — DOS
Get code for command line switch — (Version 2 and up)

Gets the command line switch character used in program calls.

Input: AH = 37H
AL = 00H
Output: DL = ASCII character code
Remarks: The default command line switch character is the division character (/). For this reason few programs check this code, and will not react to changes made to this code.

The contents of the BX, CX, DH, SI, DI, BP and segment registers are not affected by this function.

Interrupt 21H, Function 37H, Subfunction 01H — DOS
Set code for command line switch — (Version 2 and up)

Sets the command line switch character used in program calls.

Input: AH = 37H
AL = 01H
DL = ASCII character code
Output: Carry flag=0: Character accepted
Carry flag=1: Error
Remarks: The equal sign (=), slash (/) and hyphen (-) characters are valid command line switch characters.Other characters are invalid and are rejected.

Since few programs make use of the subfunction 00H of this function and instead always assume the (/) character as code for the command-line-switch, the call of subfunction 01H has effect on few programs. This includes in every case the various internal and external DOS programs which in this regard behave admirably.

The contents of the BX, CX, DX, SI, DI, BP and segment registers are not affected by this function.

Interrupt 21H, Function 38H — DOS
Get country — (Version 2 and up)

Determines country-specific parameters, which are set in the CONFIG.SYS file using the DOS COUNTRY command.

Input: AH = 38H
AL = 0
DS = Buffer segment address
DX = Buffer offset address

Output: No output
Remarks: Before the function call, function 30H should be used to determine the DOS
                  version. This can help the programmer compensate for differences between
                  DOS versions during the call and return of this function.

                  The buffer must have at least 32 bytes allocated for recording the various
                  country-specific parameters.

                  Following the function call, the individual bytes of this buffer contain the
                  following information:

    Bytes 0–1: Date format
      0=USA: Month-day-year
      1=Europe: day-month-year
      2=Japan: Year-month-day
    Byte 2: ASCII code of the currency symbol
    Byte 3: 0
    Byte 4: ASCII code of the thousand character (comma/period)
    Byte 5: 0
    Byte 6: ASCII code of decimal character (period/comma)
    Byte 7: 0
    Bytes 8–31: reserved

                  The contents of the processor registers and the flag registers are not affected by
                  this function.

Interrupt 21H, Function 38H, Subfunction 0   DOS
Get country   (Version 3 and up)

Gets the country-specific parameters that are currently set.

Input: AH = 38H
                  DS = Buffer segment address
                  DX = Buffer offset address
                  AL = 0: read current country parameters
                  AL = 1–254: Country code parameters to be read
                  AL = 255: Country code parameters to be read placed in the BX register
Output: Carry flag=0: O.K.
                  Carry flag=1: Invalid country code
Remarks: Before the function call, function 30H should be used to determine the DOS
                  version. This can help the programmer compensate for differences between
                  DOS versions during the call and return of this function.

                  The buffer must have at least 32 bytes allocated for recording the various
                  country specific parameters.

                  Following the function call, the individual bytes of this buffer contain the
                  following information:

    Bytes 0–1: Date format
      0=USA: Month-day-year
      1=Europe: Day-month-year
      2=Japan: Year-month-day
    Bytes 2–6: Currency indicator (string terminated by an end character)
    Byte 7: ASCII code of the thousand character (comma/period)
    Byte 8: 0
    Byte 9: ASCII code of decimal character (period/comma)
    Byte 10: 0

Byte 11: ASCII code of the date separation character

Byte 12: 0

Byte 13: ASCII code of the time separation character

Byte 14: 0

Byte 15: Currency format

bit 0=0: Currency symbol before the value

bit 0=1: Currency symbol after the value

bit 1=0: No spaces between value and currency symbol

bit 1=1: Space between value and currency symbol

Byte 16: Precision (number of decimal places)

Byte 17: Time format

bit 0=0: 12-hour clock

bit 0=1: 24-hour clock

Bytes 18-21: Address of character conversion routine (see below)

Bytes 22-33: reserved

Addresses 18 to 21 are the offset and segment addresses of a FAR procedure, which is used for accessing the country specific characters from the character set of the PC. The routine views the AL register's contents as the ASCII code of a lower case letter that should be converted to a capital letter. If a capital letter exists, it is retained in the AL register after the call. If the letter doesn't exist, the contents of the AL register remain unchanged. For example, the routine could be used to convert a lower case "a" into a capital "A".

The contents of the AH, BX, CX, DX, SI, DI, BP, CS, DS, SS, ES and the flag registers are not affected by this function.

Interrupt 21H, Function 38H, Subfunction 1
Set country

DOS
(Version 3 and up)

Sets the current country-specific parameters. These parameters can be read using function 38H, subfunction 0. Previous versions of DOS required country-specific settings from the CONFIG.SYS file using the COUNTRY command. This function allows the user to set and change these parameters after booting.

Input:	AH = 38H
	DX = 65535
	AL = 1–254: Number of the country
	AL > 254: Look in BX for country number
	BX = Number of the country (if AL > 254)
Output:	Carry flag=0: O.K.
	Carry flag=1: Invalid country code
Remarks:	Before the function call, function 30H should be used to determine that this command exists.
	This function only allows setting of the country code, for which DOS has preset parameters. These parameters cannot be changed from this function.
	The contents of the AH, BX, CX, DX, SI, DI, BP, CS, DS, SS and ES registers are not affected by this function.

Interrupt 21H, Function 39H
Create subdirectory

DOS
(Version 2 and up)

Creates a new subdirectory on the specified device.

Input:	AH = 39H
	DS = Subdirectory path segment address
	DX = Subdirectory path offset address
Output:	Carry flag=0: Subdirectory created
	Carry flag=1: Error (AX = error code)
	AX=3: Path not found
	AX=5: Access denied
Remarks:	The subdirectory path passed is an ASCII string which is terminated by an end character (ASCII code 0).

If the subdirectory path contains a drive specifier, the indicated device is accessed. Otherwise DOS creates the subdirectory on the current device.

An error can occur if any element of the path designation doesn't exist, a subdirectory already exists by that name, or the directory to be made is a subdirectory of the root directory and it is already filled.

The contents of the BX, CX, DX, SI, DI, BP, CS, DS, SS and ES registers are not affected by this function.

Interrupt 21H, Function 3AH   **DOS**
Delete subdirectory   **(Version 2 and up)**

Deletes a subdirectory from the specified drive.

Input:	AH = 3AH
	DS = Subdirectory path segment address
	DX = Subdirectory path offset address
Output:	Carry flag=0: Subdirectory deleted
	Carry flag=1: Error (AX = error code)
	AX=3: Path not found
	AX=5: Access denied
	AX=6: Directory to be deleted is the current directory
Remarks:	The subdirectory path passed is an ASCII string which is terminated by an end character (ASCII code 0).

If the subdirectory path contains a drive specifier, the indicated device is accessed. Otherwise DOS deletes the subdirectory from the current device.

An error can occur if any element of the path designation doesn't exist, the subdirectory is the current directory, or the directory to be deleted still contains files.

The contents of the BX, CX, DX, SI, DI, BP, CS, DS, SS and ES registers are not affected by this function.

Interrupt 21H, Function 3BH   **DOS**
Set current directory   **(Version 2 and up)**

Sets the current subdirectory for the device indicated.

Input:	AH = 3BH
	DS = Subdirectory path segment address
	DX = Subdirectory path offset address
Output:	Carry flag=0: Subdirectory set
	Carry flag=1: Error (AX = error code)
	AX=3: Path not found

Remarks: The subdirectory path passed is an ASCII string which is terminated by an end
              character (ASCII code 0).

              If the subdirectory path contains a drive specifier, the indicated device is
              accessed. Otherwise DOS deletes the subdirectory from the current device.

              An error can occur if any element of the path designation doesn't exist.

              The contents of the BX, CX, DX, SI, DI, BP, CS, DS, SS and ES registers
              are not affected by this function.

Interrupt 21H, Function 3CH   DOS
Create or truncate file (handle)   (Version 2 and up)

Creates a new file, or dumps the contents of an existing file (file size=0 bytes). This function
call allows other functions to read or write to the open file.

Input: AH = 3CH
              CX = File attribute
                  Bit 0=1: File is read only
                  Bit 1=1: Hidden file
                  Bit 2=1: System file
              DS = Filename segment address
              DX = Filename offset address
Output: Carry flag=0: O.K. (AX = file handle)
              Carry flag=1: Error (AX = error code)
                  AX=3: Path not found
                  AX=4: No available handle
                  AX=5: Access denied
Remarks: The various bits of the file attribute can be combined with each other.

              The filename must be available as an ASCII string terminated by an end
              character (ASCII code 0). The filename parameter can contain a driver specifier,
              path, filename and extension. No wildcards are allowed. If you omit the drive
              specifier or path, DOS accesses the current drive or current directory.

              An error can occur if any element of the path designation doesn't exist, if the
              file must be created in the root directory which is already full, or if a file with
              the same name already exists but cannot be cleared because it is write protected
              (bit 0 in the file attribute byte = 1).

              If the function call executed successfully, all other handle functions can be
              called with this handle once the file opens.

              The file pointer is set to the first byte of the file.

              The contents of the BX, CX, DX, SI, DI, BP, CS, DS, SS and ES registers
              are not affected by this function.

Interrupt 21H, Function 3DH   DOS
Open file (handle)   (Version 2 and up)

Opens an existing file for access by other functions.

Input: AH = 3DH
              AL = Access mode
              Bits 0–2: Read/write access
                  000(b)=File is read only
                  001(b)=File can only be written

010(b)=File can be read and written
Bit 3: 0(b)
Bits 4–6: File sharing mode
000(b)=Only current program can access the file (FCB mode)
001(b)=Only the current program can access the file
010(b)=Another program can read but not write the file
011(b)=Another program can write but not read the file
100(b)=Another program can read and write the file
Bit 7: Handle flag
0=Child program of the current program can access file handle
1=Current program can access file handle only
DS = Filename segment address
DX = Filename offset address

Output: Carry flag=0: O.K. (AX = file handle)
Carry flag=1: Error (AX = error code)
AX=1:Missing file sharing software
AX=2: File not found
AX=3: Path not found or file doesn't exist
AX=4: No handle available
AX=5: Access denied
AX=12: Access mode not permitted

Remarks: The filename must be available as an ASCII string terminated by an end character (ASCII code 0). The filename parameter can contain a driver specifier, path, filename and extension. No wildcards are allowed. If you omit the drive specifier or path, DOS accesses the current drive or current directory.

If the function call executes successfully, all other handle functions can be called with this handle once the file opens.

The file pointer is set to the first byte of the file.

DOS Version 2 uses only bits 0 to 2 of the access mode. All other bits, even under Version 3, should be 0 to ensure proper execution of the call.

DOS Version 3 uses the file sharing mode in bits 4 to 6 of the access mode only if the file is on a mass storage device which is part of a network. These three bits decide if and how the file, while it is open using the current call, may be accessed by other programs from other PCs on the network.

Error 12 can occur only under DOS Version 3 and only within a network when the file is already opened by another program and if no other program can gain access to that file.

The contents of the BX, CX, DX, SI, DI, BP, CS, DS, SS and ES registers are not affected by this function.

Interrupt 21H, Function 3EH   **DOS**
Close file (handle)   **(Version 2 and up)**

Writes any data in the DOS buffers to a currently open file, then closes the file. If changes occur to the file, the new file size and the last date and time of modification are added to the directory.

Input: AH = 3EH
BX = Handle to be closed
Output: Carry flag=0: O.K.
Carry flag=1: Error (AX = error code)

AX=6: Unauthorized handle or file not opened

Remarks: Do not accidentally call this function with the numbers of the previous handle (the numbers 0 to 4) because the standard input device or standard output device may close. This would leave you unable to enter characters from the keyboard or display characters on the screen.

The contents of the BX, CX, DX, SI, DI, BP, CS, DS, SS and ES registers are not affected by this function.

Interrupt 21H, Function 3FH
Read file or device (handle)

DOS
(Version 2 and up)

Reads a certain number of characters by using a handle from a previously opened file or device and passes the characters to a buffer. The read operation starts at the current file pointer position.

Input: AH = 3FH
              BX = File or device handle
              CX = Number of bytes to be read
              DS = Buffer segment address
              DX = Buffer offset address
Output: Carry flag=0: O.K. (AX = number of bytes read)
              Carry flag=1: Error (AX = error code)
                  AX=5: Access denied
                  AX=6: Illegal handle or file not open
Remarks: Characters can be read from a file or from a device (e.g., the standard input device [keyboard], which has the handle 0).

When the carry flag resets after the function call but the AX register has the value 0, this means that the file pointer has already reached the end of the file before the function call. So, no files could be read.

When the carry flag resets after the function call but the contents of the AX register are smaller than the contents of the CX register before the function call, this means that the desired number of bytes wasn't read because the end of the file was reached.

After the function call, the file pointer follows the last byte read.

The contents of the BX, CX, DX, SI, DI, BP, CS, DS, SS and ES registers are not affected by this function.

Interrupt 21H, Function 40H
Write to file or device (handle)

DOS
(Version 2 and up)

Writes a certain number of characters from a buffer to an open file or device by using a handle. The write operation begins at the file pointer's current position.

Input: AH = 40H
              BX = File or device handle
              CX = Number of bytes to be written
              DS = Buffer segment address
              DX = Buffer offset address
Output: Carry flag=0: O.K. (AX = number of bytes written)
              Carry flag=1: Error (AX = error code)
                  AX=5: Access denied
                  AX=6: Illegal handle or file not open

Remarks:

Characters can be written to a file or to a device (e.g., the standard output device [screen], which has the handle 1).

When the carry flag resets after the function call but the AX register has the value 0, this means that the file pointer has already reached the end of the file before the function call. Therefore no files could be written.

When the carry flag resets after the function call but the contents of the AX register are smaller than the contents of the CX register before the function call, this means that the desired number of bytes were not written because the end of file was reached.

After the function call, the file pointer follows the last byte written.

The contents of the BX, CX, DX, SI, DI, BP, CS, DS, SS and ES registers are not affected by this function.

Interrupt 21H, Function 41H   **DOS**
Delete file (handle)   **(Version 2 and up)**

Deletes the filename passed to the function. Through the call of this function, a file is erased and its name is passed to the function.

Input: AH = 41H
                DS = Filename segment address
                DX = Filename offset address
Output: Carry flag=0: O.K.
                Carry flag=1: Error (AX = error code)
                    AX=2: File not found
                    AX=5: Access denied
Remarks: The filename must be available as an ASCII string terminated by an end character (ASCII code 0). The filename parameter can contain a drive specifier, path, filename and extension. No wildcards are allowed. If you omit the drive specifier or path, DOS accesses the current drive or current directory.

An error occurs when any element of the path designation doesn't exist or when the file has the attribute Read Only and therefore can not be written to or deleted. This attribute can be changed by using function 43H.

You cannot delete subdirectories or volume names with this function.

The contents of the BX, CX, DX, SI, DI, BP, CS, DS, SS and ES registers are not affected by this function.

Interrupt 21H, Function 42H   **DOS**
Move file pointer (handle)   **(Version 2 and up)**

Moves the file pointer of a previously opened file by using its handle. This allows random access because the individual records don't have to be read in sequence. The new file pointer position is given as an offset from the current position, either from the beginning of the file or from the end of the file. The offset itself is indicated as a 32-bit number.

Input: AH = 42H
                AL = Offset code
                    AL=0: Offset is relative to the beginning of the file
                    AL=1: Offset is relative to the current position of the file pointer
                    AL=2: Offset is relative to the end of the file
                BX = Handle

Output:
CX = High word of the offset
DX = Low word of the offset
Carry flag=0: O.K.
    DX=High word of the file pointer
    AX=Low word of the file pointer
Carry flag=1: Error (AX = error code)
    AX=1: Illegal offset code
    AX=6: Illegal handle or File not open

Remarks:
If offset codes 1 and 2 are accessed, negative offsets may be used to move the file pointer backwards or to place the pointer at the beginning of the file. It's possible to set the file pointer before the end of the file, which causes an error during the next read or write access to the file.

The position of the file pointer passed after the function call is always relative to the beginning of the file. The offset code used during the function call is independent of this file pointer position.

Passing offset code 2 and offset 0 returns the size of the file. This action moves the file pointer to the last byte of the file and the pointer's position returns to the calling program after the function call.

The contents of the BX, CX, , SI, DI, BP, CS, DS, SS and ES registers are not affected by this function.

Interrupt 21H, Function 43H, Subfunction 0
Get file attributes

DOS
(Version 2 and up)

Determines file attributes.

Input:
AH = 43H
AL = 0
DS = Filename segment address
DX = Filename offset address

Output:
Carry flag = 0: O.K. (CX = file attribute)
    Bit 0=1: File can be read but not written
    Bit 1=1: File hidden (not displayed on DIR)
    Bit 2=1: File is a system file
    Bit 3=1: File is the volume name
    Bit 4=1: File is a subdirectory
    Bit 5=1: File was changed since the last date/time
Carry flag = 1: Error (AX = error code)
    AX=1: Unknown function code
    AX=2: File not found
    AX=3: Path not found

Remarks:
The filename must be available as an ASCII string terminated by an end character (ASCII code 0). The filename parameter can contain a driver specifier, path, filename and extension. No wildcards are allowed. If you omit the drive specifier or path, DOS accesses the current drive or current directory.

An error occurs when any element of the path designation or the file does not exist.

The contents of the BX, CX, , SI, DI, BP, CS, DS, SS and ES registers are not affected by this function.

Interrupt 21H, Function 43H, Subfunction 1   **DOS**
Set file attributes   **(Version 2 and up)**

Sets the file attributes.

Input: AH = 43H
                  AL = 1
                  CX = File attributes
                     Bit 0=1: File can be read but not written
                     Bit 1=1: File hidden (not displayed on DIR)
                     Bit 2=1: File is a system file
                     Bit 3=0
                     Bit 4=0
                     Bit 5=1: File was changed since the last date/time
                  DS = Filename segment address
                  DX = Filename offset address

Output: Carry flag=0: O.K.
                  Carry flag=1: Error (AX = error code)
                     AX=1: Unknown function code
                     AX=2: File not found
                     AX=3: Path not found
                     AX=5: Attribute cannot be changed

Remarks: The filename must be available as an ASCII string terminated by an end character (ASCII code 0). The filename parameter can contain a driver specifier, path, filename and extension. No wildcards are allowed. If you omit the drive specifier or path, DOS accesses the current drive or current directory.

                  An error occurs when any element of the path designation or the file does not exist.

                  Neither subdirectories nor volume names can be accessed with this function. For this reason bits 3 and 4 of the file attribute must be 0 during the function call. If you attempt to access a subdirectory or a volume name anyway, the function returns error code 5.

                  The contents of the BX, CX, DX, SI, DI, BP, CS, DS, SS and ES registers are not affected by this function.

Interrupt 21H, Function 44H, Subfunction 0   **DOS**
IOCTL: Get device information   **(Version 2 and up)**

Permits access of a character driver's device attribute.

Input: AH = 44H
                  AL = 0
                  BX = Handle

Output: Carry flag=0: O.K. (DX = device attribute)
                     Bit 14=1: Processes control characters through IOCTL
                     Bit 7=1: Character driver
                     Bit 5=0: Cooked mode operation
                     Bit 5=1: Raw mode operation
                     Bit 3=1: Clock driver operation
                     Bit 2=1: NUL driver operation
                     Bit 1=1: Console output driver (screen)

Bit 0=1: Console input driver (keyboard)

Carry flag=1: Error (AX = error code)

AX=1: Unknown function code

AX=6: Handle not opened or does not exist

Remarks: A handle is passed (not the name of the addressed character driver which must be connected with this driver). This can be one of the five pre-assigned handles (0 to 4). A handle could have been previously opened for a certain device with the help of the Open function (function 3DH), and then passed to the function. For example, since the standard input and output devices (handles 0 and 1) can be redirected, this method assures that the indicated device is accessed.

If bit 7 in the device attribute is unequal to 1, the driver addressed is not a character driver and the significance of the individual bits in the device attribute disagrees with those of the device driver.

The contents of the BX, CX, DX, SI, DI, BP, CS, DS, SS and ES registers are not affected by this function.

Interrupt 21H, Function 44H, Subfunction 1   DOS
IOCTL: Set device information   (Version 2 and up)

Sets the character device attributes.

Input: AH = 44H

AL = 1

BX = Handle

CX = Number of bytes written

DX = Device attributes

Bit 14=1: Processes control characters through IOCTL using subfunctions 2 and 3

Bit 7=1: Character driver

Bit 5=0: Cooked mode operation

Bit 5=1: Raw mode operation

Bit 3=1: Clock driver operation

Bit 2=1: NUL driver operation

Bit 1=1: Console output driver (screen)

Bit 0=1: Console input driver (keyboard)

Output: Carry flag=0: O.K.

Carry flag=1: Error (AX = Error code)

AX=1: Unknown function code

AX=6: handle not opened or handle does not exist

Remarks: A handle is passed but it is not the name of the addressed character device, which must be connected with this device. This can be one of the five pre-assigned handles (0 to 4). A handle could have previously been opened, with the Open function, for a certain device and then passed to the function. For example, since the standard input and output devices (handles 0 and 1) can be redirected, this method assures that the indicated device is accessed.

To change various device attribute bits with this function, use subfunction 0 to read the device attributes first. Then this subfunction can reset the device attribute bits in the device driver.

If bit 7 in the device attribute is unequal to 1, the driver addressed is not a character driver. The meanings of the individual bits in the device attribute disagree with those in the device driver.

This function is especially useful for switching between cooked mode and raw mode within a character driver (bit 5).

The contents of the BX, CX, DX, SI, DI, BP, CS, DS, SS and ES registers are not affected by this function.

Interrupt 21H, Function 44H, Subfunction 2   **DOS**
IOCTL: Read data from character device (Version 2 and up)   **(Version 2 and up)**

Reads data from a character device. This function defines the number of bytes of data to read from the buffer, which contains the data taken from the character device.

Input:	AH = 44H
	AL = 2
	BX = Handle
	CX = Number of bytes to be read
	DS = Buffer segment address
	DX = Buffer offset address
Output:	Carry flag=0: O.K. (AX = Number of bytes sent)
	Carry flag=1: Error (AX = Error code)
	AX=1: Unknown function code
	AX=6: Handle not opened or does not exist
Remarks:	A handle is passed, but it is not the name of the addressed character device which must be connected with this device. This can be one of the five pre-assigned handles (0 to 4). A handle could have previously been opened with the Open function (function number 3DH) for a certain device, then passed to the function. For example, since the standard input and output devices (handles 0 and 1) can be redirected, this method assures that the indicated device is accessed.

An error always occurs if the handle passed is connected with a block driver instead of a character driver.

The driver defines the data type and structure.

The contents of the BX, CX, DX, SI, DI, BP, CS, DS, SS and ES registers are not affected by this function.

Interrupt 21H, Function 44H, Subfunction 3   **DOS**
IOCTL: Send data to character device   **(Version 2 and up)**

Sends data from an application program directly to a character device. The calling function defines the number of bytes to be transferred from a buffer to the device.

Input:	AH = 44H
	AL = 3
	BX = Handle
	CX = Number of bytes to be transmitted
	DS = Buffer segment address
	DX = Buffer offset address
Output:	Carry flag=0: O.K.
	AX=Number of bytes sent
	Carry flag=1: Error (AX = Error code)
	AX=1: Unknown function code
	AX=6: Handle not opened or does not exist

Remarks: A handle is passed, but it is not the name of the addressed character device which must be connected with this device. This can be one of the five pre-assigned handles (0 to 4). A handle could have previously been opened with the Open function (function number 61) for a certain device, then passed to the function. For example, since the standard input and output devices (handles 0 and 1) can be redirected, this method assures that the indicated device is accessed.

An error always occurs if the handle passed is connected with a block driver instead of a character driver.

The driver defines the data type and structure.

The contents of the BX, CX, DX, SI, DI, BP, CS, DS, SS and ES registers are not affected by this function.

Interrupt 21H, Function 44H, Subfunction 4   DOS
IOCTL: Read data from block device   (Version 2 and up)

Reads data for an application directly from a block device. The calling function defines the number of bytes to be copied by the device into a buffer.

Input: AH = 44H
      AL = 4
      BX = Device designation
      CX = Number of bytes to be read
      DS = Buffer segment address
      DX = Buffer offset address

Output: Carry flag=0: O.K.
         AX = Number of bytes sent
      Carry flag=1: Error (AX = Error code)
         AX=1: Unknown function code
         AX=15: Unknown device

Remarks: Instead of defining the device driver, the device designation parameter defines the device from which data will be received. Code 0 represents device A:, 1 represents device B:, etc.

The driver defines the data type and structure.

The contents of the BX, CX, DX, SI, DI, BP, CS, DS, SS and ES registers are not affected by this function.

Interrupt 21H, Function 44H, Subfunction 4   DOS
IOCTL / DoubleSpace: Write internal caches   (Version 6 and up)

Instructs DoubleSpace to write the contents of its internal cache buffers for cluster data, BitFAT and MDFAT to disk.

Input: AH =   44H
      AL =   04H
      BX =   Device designation (0 = A)
      CX =   Number of bytes to be read
      DS:DX = FAR pointers to buffer (see below)

Output: Carry flag = 0: OK
      Carry flag = 1: Error

Remarks: In BX you can enter the device designation of any compressed drive.

The buffer referred to by DS:DX upon calling the function must contain the following:

Offset	Contents	Task	Type
+00H	'DM'	For identification of Microsoft DoubleSpace	1 word
+02H	'F'	For "Flush" instruction	1 byte
+03H	0	Receives error code following call	1 word
+05H	0, 0, 0, 0, 0	Five fill bytes	5 bytes
Length: 10 bytes			

Following the function call, the word at offset address 03H of the buffer contains the character combination "OK" if the function was carried out successfully.

Interrupt 21H, Function 44H, Subfunction 4   DOS
IOCTL/DoubleSpace: Write internal caches and invalidate   (Version 6 and up)

Instructs DoubleSpace to write the contents of its internal cache buffers for cluster data, BitFAT and MDFAT to disk, then declare the contents of these buffers invalid.

Input:	AH =	44H
	AL =	04H
	BX =	Device designation (0 = A)
	CX =	Number of bytes to be read
	DS:DX =	FAR pointer to buffer (see below)
Output:	Carry flag = 0: OK	
	Carry flag = 1: Error	
Remarks:	In BX you can enter the device designation of any compressed drive.	

The buffer referred to by DS:DX upon calling the function must contain the following:

Offset	Contents	Task	Type
+00H	'DM'	For identification of Microsoft DoubleSpace	1 word
+02H	'I'	For "Invalidate" instruction	1 byte
+03H	0	Receives error code following call	1 word
+05H	0, 0, 0, 0, 0	Five fill bytes	5 bytes
Length: 10 bytes			

Following the function call, the word at offset address 03H of the buffer contains the character combination "OK" if the function was carried out successfully.

Interrupt 21H, Function 44H, Subfunction 5   DOS
IOCTL: Send data to block device   (Version 2 and up)

Sends data from an application program directly to a character device. The calling function defines the number of bytes to be transferred from a buffer to the device.

Input:	AH = 44H	
	AL = 5	
	BX = Device designation	
	CX = Number of bytes to be sent	

	DS = Buffer segment address
	DX = Buffer offset address
Output:	Carry flag=0: O.K.
	AX=Number of bytes sent
	Carry flag=1: Error (AX = Error code)
	AX=1: Unknown function code
	AX=15: Unknown device
Remarks:	Instead of defining the device driver, the device designation parameter defines the device from which data will be received. Code 0 represents device A:, 1 represents device B:, etc.
	The driver defines the data type and structure.
	The contents of the BX, CX, DX, SI, DI, BP, CS, DS, SS and ES registers are not affected by this function.

Interrupt 21H, Function 44H, Subfunction 6 — DOS
IOCTL: Read input status — (Version 2 and up)

Determines whether a device driver can transmit data to an application program.

Input:	AH = 44H
	AL = 6
	BX = Handle
Output:	Carry flag=0: O.K. (AX = Input status)
	AX=0: Driver not ready
	AX=255: Driver ready
	Carry flag=1: Error (AX = Error code)
	AX=1: Unknown function code
	AX=5: Access denied
Remarks:	The handle passed can refer to either a character driver or a file.
	The contents of the BX, CX, DX, SI, DI, BP, CS, DS, SS and ES registers are not affected by this function.

Interrupt 21H, Function 44H, Subfunction 7 — DOS
IOCTL: Read output status — (Version 2 and up)

Determines whether a device driver can receive data from an application program.

Input:	AH = 44H
	AL = 7
	BX = Handle
Output:	Carry flag=0: O.K. (AX = Output status)
	AX=0: Driver not ready
	AX=255: Driver ready
	Carry flag=1: Error (AX = Error code)
	AX=1: Invalid function number
	AX=5: Access denied
Remarks:	The handle passed can refer to either a character driver or a file.
	If the handle refers to a file, the block device driver signals its readiness to receive data, even if the medium containing the file is full and no additional data can be appended to the end of the file.
	The contents of the BX, CX, DX, SI, DI, BP, CS, DS, SS and ES registers are not affected by this function.

Interrupt 21H, Function 44H, Subfunction 8   **DOS**
IOCTL: Test for changeable block device   **(Version 3 and up)**

Determines whether the block device medium (e.g., disk, hard disk, etc.) can be changed.

Input: AH = 44H
                       AL = 8
                       BL = Device designation
Output: Carry flag=0: O.K. (AX=status code)
                          AX=0: Medium changeable
                          AX=1: Medium unchangeable
                  Carry flag=1: Error (AX = Error code)
                          AX=1: Invalid function number
                          AX=15: Invalid drive number
Remarks: The device designation parameter defines the device being addressed instead of the device driver. Code 0 represents device A:, 1 represents device B:, etc.

                  The contents of the BX, CX, DX, SI, DI, BP, CS, DS, SS and ES registers are not affected by this function.

Interrupt 21H, Function 44H, Subfunction 9   **DOS**
IOCTL: Test for local or remote drive   **(Version 3.1 and up)**

Determines whether a drive (block device) is local (part of the PC making the inquiry) or remote (part of another PC in a network).

Input: AH = 44H
                       AL = 9
                       BL = Device designation
Output: Carry flag=0: O.K.
                          DX = device attribute
                          Bit 12=0: Local
                          Bit 12=1: Remote
                  Carry flag=1: Error (AX = Error code)
                          AX=1: Invalid function number
                          AX=15: Invalid drive specification
Remarks: You can access this subfunction only if networking software has previously been installed.

                  The contents of the BX, CX, DX, SI, DI, BP, CS, DS, SS and ES registers are not affected by this function.

Interrupt 21H, Function 44H, Subfunction 0AH   **DOS**
IOCTL: Test for local or remote handle   **(Version 3.1 and up)**

Determines whether a file associated with this handle is local (part of the PC making the inquiry) or remote (part of another PC in a network).

Input: AH = 44H
                       AL = 0AH
                       BX = Handle
Output: DX = IOCTL code
                          Bit 15 = 0: Local
                          Bit 15 = 1: Remote

Carry flag=1: Error (AX = Error code)
    AX=1: Invalid function number
    AX=6: Handle not opened or does not exist

Remarks: You can access this subfunction only if networking software has previously been installed.

The contents of the BX, CX, DX, SI, DI, BP, CS, DS, SS and ES registers are not affected by this function.

Interrupt 21H, Function 44H, Subfunction 0BH   DOS
IOCTL: Change retry count   (Version 3 and up)

Sets the variables that specify the number of attempts at file access. One PC within a network may try to access a file that is already being accessed by another PC. The PC attempting access repeats the file access procedure the number of times and the number of waiting periods defined by these variables.

Input:
    AH = 44H
    AL = 0BH
    BX = Number of attempts
    CX = Waiting time between attempts

Output:
    Carry flag=0: O.K.
    Carry flag=1: Error (AX = Error code)
        AX=1: Invalid function number

Remarks: You can only access this subfunction if networking software has previously been installed.

The contents of the BX, CX, DX, SI, DI, BP, CS, DS, SS and ES registers are not affected by this function.

Interrupt 21H, Function 44H, Subfunction 0CH   DOS
IOCTL character driver access   (Version 3.3 and up)

Permits character driver access to code pages. Since code pages are only supported by certain character drivers, these functions are available to these drivers only.

Input:
    AH = 44H
    AL = 0CH
    BX = Handle
    CH = Device designation
    CL = Device subfunction (see below)
    DS:DX = FAR pointer to buffer and other information

Output:
    Carry flag=0: O.K.
    Carry flag=1: Error (AX = Error code)

Remarks: The CH register specifies the device designation, using one of the following numbers:
    1 = Serial device (COM1, COM2, COM3 or COM4)
    2 = Display device (CON)
    5 = Parallel device (LPT1, LPT2 or LPT3)
    0 = None of the above

The following subfunctions can be addressed through the CL register:
    45H = Set iteration count for printer driver (DOS 3.3 and up)
    4AH = Select code page (DOS 3.3 and up)
    4CH = Start code page initialization (DOS 3.3 and up)
    4DH = End code page initialization (DOS 3.3 and up)

5FH = Set display mode (DOS 4.0 and up)
65H = Get iteration count for printer driver (DOS 3.3 and up)
6AH = Query current code page (DOS 3.3 and up)
6BH = Query code page initialization list (DOS 3.3 and up)
7FH = Get display mode (DOS 4.0 and up)

Calling this function requires the following steps:

- Call function 60H to query the current parameter. Verify and store the current parameter for later recall.
- Call function 40H to set the new parameter.
- Execute function 44H, subfunction 0CH.
- Call function 40H to restore the original parameter.

The contents of the BX, CX, DX, SI, DI, BP and the segment registers are not affected by this function.

Interrupt 21H, Function 44H, Subfunction 0DH   DOS
IOCTL block driver access   (Version 3.2 and up)

Permits block driver access to code pages. Since code pages are only supported by certain character drivers, these functions are available to these drivers only.

Input:	AH = 44H
	AL = 0DH
	BL = Device designation
	CH = 08H
	CL = Device subfunction (see below)
	DS:DX = FAR pointer to buffer and other information
Output:	Carry flag=0: O.K.
	Carry flag=1: Error (AX = Error code)
Remarks:	The device designation parameter defines the device being addressed instead of the device driver. Code 0 represents device A:, 1 represents B:, etc.

The following subfunctions can be addressed through the CL register:

40H = Set device parameters (DOS 3.2 and up)
41H = Write track on logical drive (DOS 3.2 and up)
42H = Format track on logical drive (DOS 3.2 and up)
46H = Set media ID (DOS 4.0 and up)
60H = Determine device parameters (DOS 3.2 and up)
61H = Read track on logical drive (DOS 3.2 and up)
62H = Verify track on logical drive (DOS 3.2 and up)
66H = Get media ID (DOS 3.2 and up)
68H = Sense media type (DOS 5.0 and up)

Calling this function requires the following steps:

- Call function 60H to query the current parameter. Verify and store the current parameter for later recall.
- Call function 40H to set the new parameter.
- Execute function 44H, subfunction 0DH.
- Call function 40H to restore the original parameter.

The contents of the BX, CX, DX, SI, DI, BP and the segment registers are not affected by this function.

Interrupt 21H, Function 44H, Subfunction 0EH   DOS
Get logical drive map   (Version 3.2 and up)

Determines whether multiple logical drives are assigned to one block device.

Input: AH = 44H
               AL = 0EH
               BL = Device code (0=current, 1=A, 2=B, etc.)
Output: Carry flag=0: O.K.
                       AL = 0 : Device is a logical device
                       AL =>1 : Number of logical device (1=A:, 2=B:, etc.)
               Carry flag=1: Error (AX = error code)
Remarks: This function is of interest mainly in relation to system with only one diskette
               drive, because this drive can be addressed as A and B. With the help of this
               function it can be determined if the drive was last addressed as either A or B. If
               the drive is addressed through this query, a DOS message for insertion of a
               diskette may be avoided during the access to the drive.
               The contents of the BX, CX, DX, SI, DI, BP and the segment registers are not
               affected by this function.

Interrupt 21H, Function 44H, Subfunction 0FH   **DOS**
Set logical drive map   **(Version 3.2 and up)**

With this function the logical drive designation can be determined, through which a device is
addressed during the next access.

Input: AH = 44H
               AL = 0FH
               BL = Device code (0=current, 1=A, 2=B, etc.)
Output: Carry-Flag=0: o.k., in this case
               AL = Device code, which the drive is addressed during the next access.
               Carry-Flag=1: Error, in this case AX = Error-Code
Remarks: This function is interesting mainly in relation to systems with only one
               diskette drive, because this drive can be addressed as either A or B. In this case,
               the diskette drive can be switched with the help of this function from A to B.
               Since the function works alternately, a subsequent call will switch a drive to A
               again.
               The contents of the BX, CX, DX, SI, DI, BP and the segment Registers are
               not affected by this function.

Interrupt 21H, Function 44H, Subfunction 10H   **DOS**
Query IOCTL handle   **Version 5.0 and up**

With this function the availability of an IOCTL-function, which is not available in version 3.2,
can be queried. This function is only available after version 5.0.

Input: AH = 44H
               AL = 10H
               BX = Handle, whose device should be considered during the call of the IOCTL
               function.
               CL = Number of the desired IOCTL function
Output: Carry-Flag=0: Function is available in relation to the indicated Handle
               Carry-Flag=1: Error, function not available in relation to the Handle
                       AX = 1 (Function not available)
Remarks: While the availability of a certain IOCTL function can be tested with the help
               of this function only in relation to the device which hides behind a Handle, the
               IOCTL function 11H makes a test in relation to a certain device possible.

The contents of the BX, CX, DX, SI, DI, BP and the segment registers are not affected by this function.

Interrupt 21H, Function 44H, Subfunction 11H   **DOS**
Query IOCTL device   **(Version 5.0 and up)**

After version 5.0, this function permits the query of the availability of this IOCTL function, before the call of an IOCTL function which was not included in the functions of version 3.2.

Input: AH = 44H
                    AL = 11H
                    BX = Device-Number (0=current, 1=A, 2=B, etc.)
                    CL = Number of the desired IOCTL function
Output: Carry-Flag=0: Function is available in relation to the indicated device
                    Carry-Flag=1: Error, function is not available in relation to the device
                        AX = 1 (Function not available)
Remarks: While the availability of a certain IOCTL function can be tested with the help of this function only in relation to the device which hides behind a Handle, the IOCTL function 10H makes a test possible in relation to a certain Handle and the device which is hidden behind it.
                    The contents of the BX, CX, DX, SI, DI, BP and the segment registers are not affected by this function.

Interrupt 21H, Function 45H   **DOS**
Duplicate handle   **(Version 2 and up)**

Creates a duplicate of the handle passed. This duplicate handle interfaces with the same file or device as the first handle. If the first handle refers to a file, the value of the first handler's file pointer joins with the file pointer of the duplicate handle.

Input: AH = 45H
                    BX = Handle
Output: Carry flag=0: O.K. (AX = New handle)
                    Carry flag=1: Error (AX = Error code)
                      AX=4: No additional handle available
                      AX=6: Handle not opened or does not exist
Remarks: Without having to close the file, this function updates a file directory entry after its modification. A file can be closed using function 62 (3EH).
                    If the file pointer of one of the two handles changes position due to the call of a read or write function, the other file pointer also changes automatically.
                    The contents of the BX, CX, DX, SI, DI, BP, CS, DS, SS and ES registers are not affected by this function.

Interrupt 21H, Function 46H   **DOS**
Force duplicate of handle   **(Version 2 and up)**

Refers a second file handle to the save device or file as the first file handle. The second handle's file pointer also contains the same value as the first handle's file pointer.

Input: AH = 46H
                    BX = First handle
                    CX = Second handle
Output: Carry flag=0: O.K.

Carry flag=1: Error (AX = Error code)

AX=4: No additional handle available

AX=6: Handle not opened or does not exist

Remarks: If the function call connects the second handle to an open file, the file closes before the forced duplication.

If the file pointer of one of the handles changes position due to the call of a read or write function, the other file pointer also changes automatically.

The contents of the BX, CX, DX, SI, DI, BP, CS, DS, SS and ES registers are not affected by this function.

Interrupt 21H, Function 47H   **DOS**
Get current directory   **(Version 2 and up)**

Gets an ASCII string listing the complete path designation of the current directory of the indicated device. This string passes to the specified buffer.

Input: AH = 47H

DL = Device designation

DS = Buffer segment address

SI = Buffer offset address

Output: Carry flag=0: O.K.

Carry flag=1: Error (AX=Error code)

AX=15: Invalid drive specification

Remarks: The device designation parameter defines the device being addressed instead of the device driver. Code 0 represents the current device, 1 represents device A:, etc.

The path description in the buffer terminates with an end character (ASCII code 0). This description has no drive specifier or \ character (root directory specifier). If the root directory is the current directory, the end character becomes the first character in the buffer.

The contents of the BX, CX, DX, SI, DI, BP, CS, DS, SS and ES registers are not affected by this function.

Interrupt 21H, Function 48H   **DOS**
Allocate memory   **(Version 2 and up)**

Reserves an area of memory for program use.

Input: AH = 48H

BX = Number of paragraphs to be reserved

Output: Carry flag=0: O.K.

AX=Memory area segment address)

Carry flag=1: Error (AX = Error code)

AX=7: Memory control block destroyed

AX=8: Insufficient memory

BX = Number of paragraphs available

Remarks: A paragraph consists of 16 bytes.

If memory allocation was successfully executed, the allocated range begins at address AX:0000.

This function always fails when executed from within a COM program because the PC assigns the total amount of free memory to a COM program when it executes.

The contents of the CX, DX, SI, DI, BP, CS, DS, SS and ES registers are not affected by this function.

Interrupt 21H, Function 49H   **DOS**
Release memory   **(Version 2 and up)**

Releases memory previously allocated by function 72 (49H—see above) for any purpose.

Input: AH = 49H
                                   ES = Memory area segment address
Output: Carry flag=0: O.K.
                                   Carry flag=1: Error (AX = Error code)
                                       AX=7: Memory control block destroyed
                                       AX=9: Incorrect memory area passed in ES
Remarks: Since DOS knows the size of the memory area to be released, no parameter exists for passing memory size.

If the wrong segment address appears in the ES register during the function call, memory assigned to another program can be released. This can lead to a system crash or other consequences.

The contents of the BX, CX, DX, SI, DI, BP, CS, DS, SS and ES registers are not affected by this function.

Interrupt 21H, Function 4AH   **DOS**
Modify memory allocation   **(Version 2 and up)**

Changes the size of a memory area previously reserved using function 72 (3FH—see above).

Input: AH = 4AH
                                     BX = New memory area size in paragraphs
                                   ES = Memory area segment address
Output: Carry flag=0: O.K.
                                   Carry flag=1: Error (AX = Error code)
                                       AX=7: Memory control block destroyed
                                       AX=8: Insufficient memory
                                 BX = Number of paragraphs available
Remarks: A paragraph has 16 bytes.

If the wrong segment address appears in the ES register during the function call, memory assigned to another program can be released. This can lead to a system crash or other consequences.

Since the PC assigns the total amount of free memory to a COM program when it executes, this function call always fails when executed from within a COM program.

COM programs should use this function to release all unnecessary memory since all RAM becomes part of a COM program. This is especially important before calling the EXEC function (function number 75 (4BH).

The contents of the CX, DX, SI, DI, BP, CS, DS, SS and ES registers are not affected by this function.

Interrupt 21H, Function 4BH, Subfunction 0   **DOS**
Execute program   **(Version 2 and up)**

Executes another program from within a program and continues execution of the original program after the called program finishes its run. The function requires the name of the program to be executed and the address of a parameter block, which contains information that is important to the function.

Input:	AH = 4BH
	AL = 0
	ES = Parameter block segment address
	BX = Parameter block offset address
	DS = Program name segment address
	DX = Program name offset address
Output:	Carry flag=0: O.K.
	Carry flag=1: Error (AX = Error code)
	AX=1: Invalid function number
	AX=2: Path or program not found
	AX=5: Access denied
	AX=8: Insufficient memory
	AX=10: Wrong environment block
	AX=11: Incorrect format

Remarks: The directory name passed is an ASCII string which is terminated by an end character (ASCII code 0). It can contain a path designation and drive specifier. No wildcards are allowed. If no drive specifier or path designation exists, the function accesses the current drive or directory.

Only EXE or COM programs can be executed. To execute a batch file, the command processor (COMMAND.COM) must be called using the /c parameter followed by the name of the batch file.

The parameter block must have the following format:

Bytes 0–1:   Environment block segment address
Bytes 2–3:   Command parameter offset address
Bytes 4–5:   Command parameter segment address
Bytes 6–7:   First FCB offset address
Bytes 8–9:   First FCB segment address
Bytes 10–11:   Second FCB offset address
Bytes 12–13:   Second FCB segment address

If the segment address of the environment block is a 0, the called program has the same environment block as the calling program.

The command parameters must be stored so that the parameter string begins with a byte representing the number of characters in the command line. Next follow the individual ASCII characters, which are terminated by a carriage return (ASCII code 13) (this carriage return is not counted as a character).

The first FCB passed is copied to the PSP of the called program starting at address 5CH. The second FCB passed is copied to the PSP of the called program starting at address 6CH. If the called program does not obtain information from the two FCBs, any desired value can be entered into the FCB fields at the parameter block.

After the call of this function, all registers are destroyed except the CS and IP registers. For later recall, save their contents before the function call.

The program called should have all the handles available to the calling program.

Interrupt 21H, Function 4BH, Subfunction 3   **DOS**
Execute overlay   **(Version 2 and up)**

Loads a second program into memory as an overlay without automatically executing the second program.

Input:	AH = 4BH
	AL = 3
	ES = Parameter block segment address
	BX = Parameter block offset address
	DS = Program name segment address
	DX = Program name offset address
Output:	Carry flag=0: O.K.
	Carry flag=1: Error (AX = Error code)
	AX=1: Invalid function number
	AX=2: Path or program not found
	AX=5: Access denied
	AX=8: Insufficient memory
	AX=10: Wrong environment block
	AX=11: Incorrect format
Remarks:	The directory name passed is an ASCII string which is terminated by an end character (ASCII code 0). It can contain a path designation and drive specifier. No wildcards are allowed. If no drive specifier or path designation exists, the function accesses the current drive or directory.

Only EXE or COM programs can be executed. To execute a batch file, the command processor (COMMAND.COM) must be called using the /c parameter followed by the name of the batch file.

The parameter block must have the following format:

Byte 0–1:	Segment address where the overlay will be stored (offset address=0)
Byte 2–3:	Relocation factor

The relocation factor requires the value 0 for COM programs. Use the segment address at which the program should load when accessing EXE programs.

The contents of the BX, CX, DX, SI, DI, BP, CS, DS, SS and ES registers are not affected by this function.

Interrupt 21H, Function 4BH, Subfunction 05H   **DOS**
Set EXECSTATE   **(Version 5.0 and up)**

Applications which load other programs or overlays without the DOS Exec function, must use this function after version 5.0 of DOS to avoid problems during loading of the programs and overlays.

Input:	AH = 4BH
	AL = 05H
	DS:DX = FAR-pointer to the Exec-State structure
Output:	Carry-Flag=0: o.k.
	Carry-Flag=1: Error, in this case
	AX = Error-Code

1: unknown function code

2: program not found

3: program not found

4: too many files opened

5: access denied

8: insufficient storage area

10: wrong Environment-Block

11: wrong format

Remarks: The call of this function must occur between the loading of the program or overlay and its execution. Between the call of this function and the start of the program or overlay, neither DOS- nor BIOS functions, nor any other software interrupts may be called.

In the ExecState structure, information about the overlay or program is stored. It consists of 18 Bytes and must have the following format.

■ Format of the ExecState structure		
Addr.	Content	Type
+00H	Reserved, must contain 0	1 WORD
+02H	1 = EXE-program 2 = Overlay	1 WORD
+04H	Pointer to an ASCIIZ string with the name of the program or overlay (Path not allowed in this string)	1 PTR
+08H	Segment address of the PSP of the program or overlay	1 WORD
+0AH	Jump location to the program or overlay	1 PTR
+0EH	Program- or overlay size including PSP	1 DWORD
■ Length: 12H (18 Bytes)		

Interrupt 21H, Function 4CH   **DOS**
Terminate with return code   **(Version 2 and up)**

Terminates a program and passes an end code for which function 77 (4DH-see below) searches. This function releases the memory previously occupied by the terminated program.

Input: AH = 4CH

AL = Return code

Output: No output

Remarks: This function may be used for program termination instead of the other functions listed earlier.

This function call restores the contents of the three interrupt vectors that were stored in the PSP when the program started execution.

Before passing control to the calling program, all handles opened by this program close, along with the corresponding files. This is not applicable to files accessed using FCBs.

1237

A batch file can test for the return code using the ERRORLEVEL and IF batch commands.

Interrupt 21H, Function 4DH   **DOS**
Get return code   **(Version 2 and up)**

Checks a program, called from another program by the EXEC function, for the return code passed by the called program when it terminates.

Input:	AH = 4DH
Output:	AH = Type of program termination
	AH=0: Normal end
	AH=1: End through <Ctrl><C> or <Break>
	AH=2: Device access error
	AH=3: Call of function 49 (31H)
	AL = Return code
Remarks:	This function reads the return code of the called program only once.
	The contents of the AX, BX, CX, DX, SI, DI, BP, CS, DS, SS, ES and flag registers are not affected by this function. The contents of all other registers may change.

Interrupt 21H, Function 4EH   **DOS**
Search for first match   **(Version 2 and up)**

Searches for the first occurrence of the filename listed. The file can have certain attributes, so a search can be made through subdirectories and volume names.

Input:	AH = 4EH
	CX = File attribute
	DS = Filename segment address
	DX = Filename offset address
Output:	Carry flag=0: O.K.
	Carry flag=1: Error (AX = Error code)
	AX=2: Path not found
	AX=18: No file with the attribute found
Remarks:	The directory name passed is an ASCII string which is terminated by an end character (ASCII code 0). It can contain a path designation and drive specifier. No wildcards are allowed. If no drive specifier or path designation exists, the function accesses the current drive or directory.
	The search defaults to normal files (attribute 0). Any set attribute bits extends the search to normal files and any other file types.
	If a matching file occurs, the first 43 bytes of the DTA contain the following information about this file:

        Bytes 0–20:   Reserved
        Byte 21:   File attribute
        Bytes 22–23:   Time of last modification to file
        Bytes 24–25:   Date of last modification to file
        Bytes 26–27:   Low word of file size
        Bytes 28–29:   High word of file size
        Bytes 30–42:   ASCII filename and extension terminated
                      by an end character (ASCII code 0)

This function may only be called to search for the first occurrence of a file. If you want to search for a group of files using wildcards, function 4FH (see below) must be called.

The contents of the BX, CX, DX, SI, DI, BP, CS, DS, SS and ES registers are not affected by this function.

Interrupt 21H, Function 4FH	**DOS**
Search for next match (handle)	**(Version 2 and up)**

Searches for subsequent occurrences of the filename listed after function 78 (above) executed successfully.

Input:	AH = 4FH
Output:	Carry flag=0: O.K.
	Carry flag=1: Error (AX=Error code)
	AX=18: No other files found with this attribute
Remarks:	If a matching file occurs, the first 43 bytes of the DTA contain the following information about this file:

Bytes 0–20:   Reserved
Byte 21:   File attribute
Bytes 22–23: Time of last modification to file
Bytes 24–25: Date of last modification to file
Bytes 26–27: Low word of file size
Bytes 28–29: High word of file size
Bytes 30–42: ASCII filename and extension terminated
                 by an end character (ASCII code 0)

This function can only be called if function 4EH has been called once and if the DTA remains unchanged.

The contents of the BX, CX, DX, SI, DI, BP, CS, DS, SS and ES registers are not affected by this function.

Interrupt 21H, Function 50H	**DOS**
Set active PSP	**(Version 2.0 and up)**

This function sets the current PSP, as opposed to the DOS. It is required for example in TSR programs to obtain data during file access from you PSP and not from the PSP of the current foreground program.

Input:	AH = 50H
	BX = Segment address of the PSP
Output:	Carry-Flag=0: o.k.
	Carry-Flag=1: Error, in this case
	AX = Error-code
Remarks:	DOS assumes that a PSP always starts at the Offset address 0000H in a segment. This should be noted during the call of this function.
	The contents of the BX, CX, DX, SI, DI, BP and the segment registers are not affected by this function.

Interrupt 21H, Function 51H **DOS**
Determine active PSP **(Version 2.0 and up)**

With this function the Segment address of the PSP of the current program can be determined. This is mostly used by TSR programs which note the address of the PSP of the foreground program, before setting their own PSP with the help of the function 50H.

Input: AH = 51H
Output: Carry-Flag=0: o.k. in this case
  BX = Segment address of the current PSP
  Carry-Flag=1: Error, in this case
  AX = Error-code
Remarks: The indicated PSP always begins at the Offset address 0000H relative to the indicated Segment address.
  Function 62H should be preferred to the call of this function, which is specifically designed for this purpose and in contrast to function 51H is documented openly. However, it is only available after version 3.0 of DOS, while the function 51H was already introduced with version 2.0.
  The contents of the BX, CX, DX, SI, DI, BP and the segment registers are not affected by this function.

Interrupt 21H, Function 52H **DOS**
Determine pointer to the DOS-Info-Block **(Version 2.0 and up)**

This function returns a pointer to the DOS-Info-Block (DIB). With this function much interesting information can be obtained, which otherwise would not be accessible to a program.

Input: AH = 52H
Output: Carry-Flag=0: o.k. in this case
  ES:BX =FAR-pointer to the DIB
  Carry-Flag=1: Error, in this case
  AX = Eror-code
Remarks: The structure of the DOS-Info-Block can be found in Chapter 6.
  The contents of the CX, DX, SI, DI, BP, CS, DS and SS registers are not affected by this function.

Interrupt 21H, Function 53H **DOS**
Convert BPB to DPB **(Version 2.0 and up)**

This undocumented function converts an available BIOS-Parameter-Block (BPB) to a Drive-Parameter-Block (DPB).

Input: AH = 53H
  DS:SI = FAR-pointer to the buffer with the BPB to be converted
  ES:BP = Pointer to the buffer, in which the Drive-Parameter-Block should be created (see below)

Output: Carry-Flag=0: o.k.
  Carry-Flag=1: Error, in this case
  AX = Error-code
Remarks: A description of the structure of the BIOS and the Drive-Parameter-Block, can be found in Chapter 6.

Interrupt 21H, Function 54H   **DOS**
Get verify flag   **(Version 2 and up)**

Gets the current status of the verify flag. This flag determines whether or not data transmitted to a medium (floppy disk or hard disk) should be verified after the transmission.

Input: AH = 54H
Output: AL = Verify flag
                        AL=0: Verify off
                        AL=1: Verify on
Remarks: Function 2EH (see above) controls the status of the verify flag.
                    The contents of the AH, BX, CX, DX, SI, DI, BP, CS, DS, SS, ES and flag registers are not affected by this function.

Interrupt 21H, Function 55H   **DOS**
Create new PSP   **(Version 2.0 and up)**

This function creates a new PSP by copying the indicated old PSP into the new one and then adding various new information into the new PSP. This new information is mainly the information which is dependent on the position of the PSP in storage and therefore can not be accepted unchanged from the old PSP into the new one.

Input: AH = 55H
                    DX = Segment address of the new PSP
                    CX = Segment address of the old PSP
Output: Carry-Flag=0: o.k.
                        Carry-Flag=1: Error
Remarks: This undocumented function was created to be able to create a PSP for a program before loading the program. In view of the function 4BH, it is not required any more, because function 4BH loads the program and also automatically creates a new PSP that includes the adjustment of the Segment address in the PSP and in the program that was loaded.
                    The contents of the BX, CX, DX, SI, DI, BP and the segment registers are not affected by this function.

Interrupt 21H, Function 56H   **DOS**
Rename file (handle)   **(Version 2 and up)**

Renames a file or moves the file to another directory of a block device. Moving is possible only within the different directories of one particular device (i.e., you can't move a file from a hard disk directory to a floppy disk directory).

Input: AH = 56H
                    DS = Old filename segment address
                    DX = Old filename offset address
                    ES = New filename segment address
                    DI = New filename offset address
Output: Carry flag=0: O.K.
                    Carry flag=1: Error (AX = Error code)
                        AX=2: File not found
                        AX=3: Path not found
                        AX=5: Access denied

AX=11: Not the same device

Remarks: The directory name passed is an ASCII string which is terminated by an end character (ASCII code 0). It can contain a path designation and drive specifier. No wildcards are allowed. If no drive specifier or path designation exists, the function accesses the current drive or directory.

An error occurs if you attempt to move the file to a filled root directory.

This function cannot access subdirectories or volume names.

The contents of the BX, CX, DX, SI, DI, BP, CS, DS, SS and ES registers are not affected by this function.

Interrupt 21H, Function 57H, Subfunction 0   **DOS**
Get file date and time   **(Version 2 and up)**

Gets the date and time of the creation or last modification of a file.

Input: AH = 57H
                AL = 0
                BX = Handle
Output: Carry flag=0: O.K.
                CX=Time
                DX=Date
                Carry flag=1: Error (AX = Error code)
                AX=1: Invalid function
                AX=6: Invalid handle
Remarks: In order for it to be accessed with a handle, the file must have been previously opened or created using one of the handle functions.

The time appears in the CX register in the following format:
                Bits 0–4:   Seconds in 2-second increments
                Bits 5–10:   Minutes
                Bits 11–15:   Hours
The date appears in the DX register in the following format:
                Bits 0–4:   Day of the month
                Bits 5–8:   Month
                Bit 9–15:   Year (relative to 1980)
The contents of the BX, CX, DX, SI, DI, BP, CS, DS, SS and ES registers are not affected by this function.

Interrupt 21H, Function 57H, Subfunction 1   **DOS**
Set file date and time   **(Version 2 and up)**

Stores the date and time of the creation or last modification of a file in the corresponding file and device.

Input: AH = 57H
                AL = 1
                BX = Handle
                CX = Time
                DX = Date
Output: Carry flag=0: O.K.
                Carry flag=1: Error (AX = Error code)
                AX=1: Invalid function
                AX=6: Invalid handle

Remarks: In order to be accessed with a handle, the file must have been previously opened or created using one of the handle functions.

The time appears in the CX register in the following format:

Bits 0–4:	Seconds in 2-second increments
Bits 5–10:	Minutes
Bits 11–15:	Hours

The date appears in the DX register in the following format:

Bits 0–4:	Day of the month
Bits 5–8:	Month
Bit 9–15:	Year (relative to 1980)

The contents of the BX, CX, DX, SI, DI, BP, CS, DS, SS and ES registers are not affected by this function.

Interrupt 21H, Function 58H, Subfunction 0 **DOS**
Get allocation strategy **(Version 3 and up)**

Determines the method currently in use by MS-DOS for allocating blocks of memory. If a program allocates memory using function 48H, different programs in memory may already have memory blocks assigned to them. Since these requested memory blocks vary in size, DOS has three methods of allocating memory to a program:

- First fit: DOS starts searching at the start of memory and allocates the first memory block it finds of the requested size.
- Best fit: DOS searches all available memory blocks and allocates the smallest suitable memory block it finds (the most efficient method).
- Last fit: DOS starts searching at the end of memory and allocates the first memory block it finds of the requested size.

Input: AH = 58H
AL = 0
Output: Carry flag=0: O.K.
AX=0: First fit (start from beginning of memory)
AX=1: Best fit (search for best-fitting memory block)
AX=2: Last fit (start from end of memory)
Carry flag=1: Error (AX = Error code)
AX=1: Invalid function number
Remarks: The allocation strategy applies to all programs.
The contents of the BX, CX, DX, SI, DI, BP, CS, DS, SS and ES registers are not affected by this function.

Interrupt 21H, Function 58H, Subfunction 1 **DOS**
Set allocation strategy **(Version 3 and up)**

Defines the method currently in use by MS-DOS for allocating blocks of memory. If a program allocates memory using function 48H, different programs in memory may already have memory blocks assigned to them. Since these requested memory blocks vary in size, DOS has three methods of allocating memory to a program:

- First fit: DOS starts searching at the start of memory and allocates the first memory block it finds of the requested size.
- Best fit: DOS searches all available memory blocks and allocates the smallest suitable memory block it finds (the most efficient method).

1243

- Last fit: DOS starts searching at the end of memory and allocates the first memory block it finds of the requested size.

Input: AH = 58H
              AL = 1
              BX = Allocation strategy
                   BX=0: First fit (start from beginning of memory)
                   BX=1: Best fit (search for best-fitting memory block)
                   BX=2: Last fit (start from end of memory)
Output: Carry flag=0: O.K.
              Carry flag=1: Error (AX = Error code)
                   AX=1: Invalid function number
Remarks: The allocation strategy applies to all programs.
              The contents of the BX, CX, DX, SI, DI, BP, CS, DS, SS and ES registers are not affected by this function.

Interrupt 21H, Function 58H, Subfunction 02H   DOS
Query the inclusion of the UMBs   (Version 5.0 and up)

Starting with the version 5.0, the Upper-Memory-Blocks (UMBs), which are located between 640 KB and the 1-MB border, can be included in the DOS storage administration. This function informs the caller, if the UMBs are participating at this time in the storage administration.

Input: AH = 58H
              AL = 02H
Output: Carry-Flag=0: o.k., in this case
                   AL = 0 : UMBs are not used
                   AL = 1 : UMBs are included in the storage administration
              Carry-Flag=1: Error, in this case
                   AX = 1: no UMB support, because the MS-DOS=UMB command was not
                           indicated
                   AX = 7: storage administration destroyed
Remarks: The error-code 7 is returned when DOS notices an inconsistency in its storage administration, which is usually caused by an erroneous access in a DOS program to this storage area.
              The contents of the BX, CX, DX, SI, DI, BP and the segment registers are not affected by this function.

Interrupt 21H, Function 58H, Subfunction 03H   DOS
Determine inclusion of the UMBs   (Version 5.0 and up)

Starting with the version 5.0, the Upper-Memory-Blocks (UMBs), which are located between 640 KB and the 1-MB border, can be included in the DOS storage administration. This function determines if the UMBs are participating at this time in the storage administration.

Input: AH = 58H
              AL = 03H
              BX = 0 : UMBs not participating
                   1 : UMBs are participating in the storage administration
Output: Carry-Flag=0: o.k.
              Carry-Flag=1: Error, in this case

AX = 1: no UMB support, because the MS-DOS=UMB command was not
indicated

AX = 7: storage administration destroyed

Remarks: The error-code 7 is returned when DOS notices an inconsistency in its storage administration, which is usually caused by an erroneous access in a DOS program to this storage area.

The contents of the BX, CX, DX, SI, DI, BP and the segment registers are not affected by this function.

Interrupt 21H, Function 59H
Get extended error information

DOS

(Version 3 and up)

Gets information about errors that occur during the call of one of the functions of either interrupt 21H or interrupt 24H. This information includes detailed information about the error, its origin and the action the user should take to alleviate the error.

Input: AH = 59H
BX = 0

Output: AX = Description of error
BH = Cause of error
BL = Recommended action
CH = Source of error

Remarks: The following codes describe the error:

Code	Error
0:	No error
1:	Invalid function number
2:	File not found
3:	Path not found
4:	Too many files open at once
5:	Access denied
6:	Invalid handle
7:	Memory control block destroyed
8:	Insufficient memory
9:	Invalid memory address
10:	Invalid environment
11:	Invalid format
12:	Invalid access code
13:	Invalid data
14:	Reserved
15:	Invalid drive
16:	Current directory cannot be removed
17:	Different device
18:	No additional files
19:	Medium write protected
20:	Unknown device
21:	Device not ready
22:	Unknown command
23:	CRC error
24:	Bad request structure length
25:	Seek error

26:     Unknown medium type
27:     Sector not found
28:     Printer out of paper
29:     Write error
30:     Read error
31:     General failure
32:     Sharing violation
33:     Lock violation
34:     Unauthorized disk change
35:     FCB not available
80:     File already exists
81:     Reserved
82:     Directory cannot be created
83:     Terminate after call of interrupt 24H

The following codes describe the cause of the error:

Code	Error
1:	No memory available on the medium
2:	Temporary access problem–may end soon
3:	Access unauthorized
4:	Internal error in system software
5:	Hardware error
6:	Software failure not caused by running application program
7:	Application program error
8:	File not found
9:	Invalid file format/type
10:	File locked
11:	Wrong medium in drive, bad disk or medium problem
12:	Other error

The following codes describe the action needed to fix the error:

Code	Error
1:	Repeat process several times, then ask user to abort/ignore
2:	Repeat process several times pausing each time, then ask user to abort/ignore
3:	Ask user for correct information (e.g., filename)
4:	Terminate program as completely as possible
5:	Terminate program NOW (no file closing, etc.)
6:	Ignore error
7:	Ask user to remove error source and repeat process

The following codes describe the source of the error:

Code	Error
1:	Unknown
2:	Block device (disk drive, hard disk, etc.)
3:	Network
4:	Serial device

5:      RAM

The contents of the CS, DS, SS and ES registers are not affected by this function. All other register contents are destroyed.

Interrupt 21H, Function 5AH   **DOS**
Create temporary file (handle)   **(Version 3 and up)**

Creates a temporary file in memory for storage during program execution. The filename doesn't matter because the access occurs through the assigned handle. Since this function allows several files open at the same time, DOS creates filenames from the current date and time. Every temporary file is ensured its own particular name because the function cannot be called more than once at a time.

Input: AH = 5AH
                CX = File attribute
                DS = Directory segment address
                DX = Directory offset address
Output: Carry flag=0: O.K.
                    AX=Handle
                    DS=Complete filename segment address
                    DX=Complete filename offset address
                Carry flag=1: Error (AX = Error code)
                    AX=3: Path not found
                    AX=5: Access denied
Remarks: The directory name passed is an ASCII string which is terminated by an end character (ASCII code 0). It can contain a path designation and drive specifier. No wildcards are allowed. If no drive specifier or path designation exists, the function accesses the current drive or directory.
                The bits of the file attribute have the following meanings:
                    Bit 0 = 1: Read only file
                    Bit 1 = 1: Hidden file
                    Bit 2 = 1: System file
                Temporary files are not automatically deleted after program execution. The file must be closed using function 3EH, then the temporary file must be deleted using function 41H.
                The contents of the BX, CX, DX, SI, DI, BP, CS, DS, SS and ES registers are not affected by this function.

Interrupt 21H, Function 5BH   **DOS**
Create new file (handle)   **(Version 3 and up)**

Creates a file in the specified directory based upon an ASCII file format. If no drive specifier or path is provided, the file opens in the default (current) directory.

Input: AH = 5BH
                CX = File attributes:
                    CX=00: Normal file
                    CX=01: Read-only file
                    CX=02: Hidden file
                    CX=04: System file

DS = ASCII file specification segment address
DX = ASCII file specification offset address
Output: Carry flag=0 (AX= file handle)
Carry flag=1 (AX = Error code)
AX=3: Path not found
AX=4: No handle available
AX=5: Access denied
AX=80 (50H): File already exists
Remarks: An error occurs when any element of the path designation doesn't exist, when the filename already exists in the specified directory, or when an attempt is made to create the file in an already full root directory.
The file defaults to the normal read/write attribute, which allows both read and write operations. This attribute can be changed by using function 43H.

Interrupt 21H, Function 5CH
Control record access

DOS
(Version 3 and up)

Locks or unlocks a particular section of a file. This function operates on multitasking and networking systems.

Input: AH = 5CH
AL = Function code
AL=00: Lock file section
AL=01: Unlock file section
BX = File handle
CX = High word of section offset
DX = Low word of section offset
SI = High word of section length
DI = Low word of section length
Output: Carry flag=0: Successful lock/unlock
Carry flag=1: Error (AX = Error code)
AX=1: Invalid function code
AX=6: Invalid handle
AX=33 (21H): All or part of section already locked
Remarks: This function can only be used on files already opened or created using functions 3CH, 3DH, 5AH or 5BH.
The corresponding call to unlock a file region must contain the identical file offset and file region length.

Interrupt 21H, Function 5CH, Subfunction 01H
Release of a blocked area in a file

DOS
(Version 3.0 and up)

With this function, areas in a file which had been blocked previously with the help of subfunction 00H, can be released again.

Input: AH = 5CH
AL = 01H
BX = Handle of the file
CX = Hi-word of the address of the first byte in the file, which should be released again
DX = Lo-Word, of the address of the first byte to be released
SI = Hi-Word of the number of bytes to be released

DI = Lo-Word of the number of bytes to be released

Output: Carry-Flag=0: o.k.
            Carry-Flag=1: Error, in this case AX = Error-Code
                1: Network software is not active
                6: invalid Handle
                33: the area indicated is not blocked

Remarks: This function can only be called after the SHARE-command or other network-software was previously called.
            The Start-offset of the region to be blocked and its length are indicated as positive LONGINTS, which consist of 2 words and therefore 4 bytes. They must agree exactly with the indications that were made during a preceding call of the subfunction 00H.
            The contents of the BX, CX, DX, SI, DI, BP and the segment registers are not affected by this function.

Interrupt 21H, Function 5DH   DOS
Reserved   (Version 1.0 and up)

Interrupt 21H, Function 5EH, Subfunction 0   DOS
Get machine name   (Version 3.1 and up)

Returns the address of an ASCII string which defines the local computer type within a network.

Input: AH = 5EH
            AL = 00
            DS = User buffer segment address
            DX = User buffer offset address
Output: Carry flag=0: Successful execution
                CH = 00: Name undefined
                CH > 00: Name defined
                CL = NETBIOS name number (when CH<>00)
                DS = Identifier segment address (when CH<>00)
                DX = Identifier offset address (when CH<>00)
            Carry flag=1: Error (AX = Error code)
                AX=1: Invalid function code
Remarks: The computer type is a 15-byte-long string terminated by an end character (ASCII code 0).

Interrupt 21H, Function 5EH, Subfunction 2   DOS
Set printer setup   (Version 3.1 and up)

Specifies a string which precedes all output to a particular printer used by a network. This string allows network users to assign their own individual printing parameters to the shared printer.

Input: AH = 5EH
            AL = 02
            BX = Redirection list index (see Remarks below)
            CX = Printer setup string length
            DS = Printer setup string segment address
            SI = Printer setup string offset address
Output: Carry flag=0: Successful execution
            Carry flag=1: Error (AX = Error code)

Remarks:
AX=1: Invalid function code
The contents of register BX (redirection list index) come from function 94 5EH, subfunction 2. Function 5EH, subfunction 3 (see below) can supply the current printer setup string.

Interrupt 21H, Function 5EH, Subfunction 3   DOS
Get printer setup   (Version 3.1 and up)

Gets the printer setup string assigned to a particular network printer by using function 5EH, subfunction 2 (see above).

Input:
AH = 5EH
AL = 03
BX = Redirection list index)
DS = Setup string receiving buffer segment address
SI = Setup string receiving buffer offset address

Output:
Carry flag=0: Successful execution
    CX=Printer setup string length
    ES=Segment address of buffer retaining setup string
    DI=Offset address of buffer retaining setup string
Carry flag=1: Error (AX = Error code)
    AX=1: Invalid function code

Remarks:
The contents of register BX (redirection list index) come from function 5EH, subfunction 2. Function 5EH, subfunction 3 can supply the current printer setup string.

Interrupt 21H, Function 5FH, Subfunction 2   DOS
Get redirection list entry   (Version 3.1 and up)

Gets the system redirection list. This list assigns local names to network printers, files or directories.

Input:
AH = 5FH
AL = 02
BX = Redirection list index (see Remarks below)
DS = Device name buffer segment address (16 bytes)
SI = Device name buffer offset address (16 bytes)
ES = Network name buffer segment address (128 bytes)
DI = Network name buffer offset address (128 bytes)

Output:
Carry flag=0: Successful execution
BH = Status flag
    BH=0: Valid device
    BH=1: Invalid device
BL = Device type
    BL=3: Printer
    BL=4: Drive
BP = Destroyed
CX = Parameter value in memory
DX = Destroyed
DS = ASCII format local device name segment address
SI = ASCII format local device name offset address
ES = ASCII format network name segment address
DI = ASCII format network name offset address

Carry flag=1: Error (AX = Error code)

AX=1: Invalid function code

AX=18: No more files available

Remarks: The contents of register CX come from function 5FH, subfunction 3 (see below).

Interrupt 21H, Function 5FH, Subfunction 3
Redirect device

DOS
(Version 3 and up)

Redirects device access in a network, assigning a network name to a local device.

Input: AH = 5FH

AL = 03

BL = Device type

     BL=3: Printer

     BL=4: Drive

CX = Parameter value in memory

DS = ASCII format local device name segment address

SI = ASCII format local device name offset address

ES = ASCII format network name and password segment address

DI = ASCII format network name and password offset address

Output: Carry flag=0: Successful execution

Carry flag=1: Error (AX = Error code)

     AX=1: Invalid function code; string format incorrect; device redirected

     AX=3: Path not found

     AX=5: Access denied

     AX=8: Insufficient memory

Remarks: The contents of register CX are taken from function 5FH, subfunction 3.

Device names can be drive specifiers (e.g., A:), printer names (i.e., LPT1, PRN, LPT2 or LPT3) or null strings. If you enter a null string and password as the device name, DOS tries to open access to the network using the password.

Interrupt 21H, Function 5FH, Subfunction 4
Cancel redirection

DOS
(Version 3 and up)

Disables the current redirection by removing local name assignments to network printers, files or directories.

Input: AH = 5FH

AL = 04

BX = Redirection list index (see Remarks below)

DS = ASCII format local device name segment address

SI = ASCII format local device name offset address

Output: Carry flag=0: Successful execution

Carry flag=1: Error (AX = Error code)

     AX=1: Invalid function code; device name not on network

     AX=15: Redirection halted

Remarks: Device names can be drive specifiers (e.g., A:), printer names (i.e., LPT1, PRN, LPT2 or LPT3) or strings beginning with double backslashes (i.e., \\). A string preceded by two backslashes terminates communications between the local computer and the network.

Interrupt 21H, Function 62H **DOS**
Get PSP address **(Version 3 and up)**

Gets the segment address of the PSP from the currently executing program.

Input: AH = 62H
Output: BX = PSP segment address
Remarks: The PSP starts at address BX:0000.
                The contents of the AX, CX, DX, SI, DI, BP, CS, DS, SS, ES registers and
                the flag registers are not affected by this function.

Interrupt 21H, Function 63H, Subfunction 0 **DOS**
Get lead byte table **(Version 2.25 only)**

Gets the address of the system table which defines the byte ranges for the PC's extended character sets.

Input: AH = 9963H
                AL = 00: Get address of system lead byte table
Output: DS = Table segment address
                SI = Table offset address
Remarks: This function is available only in DOS Version 2.25.

Interrupt 21H, Function 63H, Subfunction 1 **DOS**
Set or clear interim console flag **(Version 2.25 only)**

Clears the interim console flag.

Input: AH = 63H
                AL = 01: Clear or set interim console flag
                DL = Interim console flag setting
                    DL=01: Set interim console flag
                    DL=00: Clear interim console flag

Output: No output

Remarks: This function is available only in DOS Version 2.25.

Interrupt 21H, Function 63H, Subfunction 2 **DOS**
Get: interim console flag **(Version 2.25 only)**

Gets the interim console flag.

Input: AH = 63H
                AL = 02: Get interim console flag value
Output: DL = Flag value
Remarks: This function is available only in DOS Version 2.25.

Interrupt 21H, Function 64H
Reserved

DOS
(Version 3 and up)

Interrupt 21H, Function 65H
Get extended country information

DOS
(Version 3.3 and up)

Gets information about the specific country/code page.

Input: AH = 65H
AL = subfunction:
    AL = 1: Get international information
    AL = 2: Get uppercase pointer table
    AL = 4: Get pointer to uppercase pointer table (filename)
    AL = 6: Get pointer to collation table
BX = Code page:
BX = -1: active CON device
CX = Length of buffer allocated to receive information
DX = Country ID number
DX = -1: Default
ES:DI = Address of buffer allocated to receive information

Output: Carry flag=0: Successful execution
Carry flag=1: Error (AX = Error code)

Remarks: The information this function returns is an extended version of the information returned by int 21H, function 38H.

An error may occur if the country code in DX is invalid, or if the code page number is different from the country code, or if the buffer length specified in the CX register is less than five bytes. If the buffer is not long enough to receive all the information, the function accepts as much information as the buffer will accept. This buffer contains the following information after the call:

Byte 0: ID code for information
Bytes 1-2: Length of buffer
Bytes 3-4: Country ID
Bytes 5-6: Code page
Bytes 7-8: Date format
    0 = USA: Month-day-year
    1 = Europe: Day-month-year
    2 = Japan: Year-month-day
Bytes 9-13: Currency indicator
Bytes 14-15: ASCII code of the thousand character (comma/period)
Bytes 16-17: ASCII code of the decimal character (period/comma)
Bytes 18-19: ASCII code of the date separation character
Bytes 20-21: ASCII code of the time separation character
Byte 22: Currency format
    bit 0 = 0: Currency symbol before the value
    bit 0 = 1: Currency symbol after the value
    bit 1 = 0: No spaces between value and currency symbol
    bit 1 = 1: Space between value and currency symbol
Byte 23: Precision (number of decimal places)
Byte 24: Time format
    bit 0 = 0: 12-hour clock

bit 0 = 1: 24-hour clock
Bytes 25-28: Address of character conversion routine
Bytes 29-30: ASCII data separator
Bytes 31-40: Reserved

Interrupt 21H, Function 66H
Get or set code page
DOS
(Version 3.3. and up)

Gets or sets the current code page.

Input:	AH = 66H
	AL = subfunction:
	AL = 1: Get code page
	AL = 2: Select code page
	BX = Selected code page (if AL = 2)
Output:	Carry flag=0: Successful execution
	If AL =1 used for input:
	BX = active code page
	DX = default code page
	Carry flag=1: Error (AX = Error code)
Remarks:	If subfunction 2 is used, COUNTRY.SYS supplies the code page number.

The DEVICE... (CONFIG.SYS), NLSFUNC and MODE CP PREPARE commands (AUTOEXEC.BAT) must have already configured the system for code page switching before this function may be called.

Interrupt 21H, Function 67H
Set handle count
DOS
(Version 3.3 and up)

Sets the maximum number of accessible files and devices that may be currently opened using handles.

Input:	AH = 67H
	BX = Number of handles desired
Output:	Carry flag=0: Successful execution
	Carry flag=1: Error (AX = Error code)
Remarks:	The PSP's default table reserved for the process can control 20 handles.

An error occurs if the content of the BX register is greater than 20, or if insufficient memory exists to allocate a block for the extended table.

If the number in the BX register is greater than the number of entries assigned by the FILES entry in the CONFIG.SYS file, no error occurs. However, attempts at opening a file or device fail if all file entries are in use, even if file handles are still available.

Interrupt 21H, Function 68H
Commit file
DOS
(Version 3.3 and up)

Writes all DOS buffers associated to a specific handle to the specified device. If the handle points to a file, the file's contents, date and size are updated.

Input: AH = 68H
                BX = File handle
Output: Carry flag=0: Successful execution
                Carry flag=1: Error (AX = Error code)
Remarks: This function performs the same task as closing and reopening a file or
                duplicate handle, even without handles. If this function accesses a character
                device's handle, the carry flag returns 0 but nothing else happens.

                Multiprocessing and networking applciations maintain control of the file.

Interrupt 21H, Function 69H   **DOS**
Reserved   **(Version 1.0 and up)**

Interrupt 21H, Function 6AH   **DOS**
Reserved   **(Version 1.0 and up)**

Interrupt 21H, Function 6BH   **DOS**
Reserved   **(Version 1.0 and up)**

Interrupt 21H, Function 6CH   **DOS**
Extended Open function   **(Version 4.0 and up)**

Starting with version 4.0 of DOS there is the capability to create a file during the OPEN-call, or
to overwrite an already existing file. The function therefore enhances the capability of the normal
OPEN function 3DH.

Input: AH = 3DH
                AL = 0
                BX = access mode
                CX = file attribute
                DX = DOS reaction
                DS:SI = FAR-pointer to the buffer with the filename
Output: Carry-Flag=0: o.k., in this case AX = Handle of the file
                      CX = Status
                Carry-Flag=1: Error, in this case AX = Error-Code
                    1: File-Sharing software missing
                    2: file not found
                    3: Path not found or file does not exist
                    4: no more free Handles
                    5: access denied
                    12: this access mode not allowed
Remarks: The filename must be available as an ASCII string which is terminated with
                an end character (ASCII-Code 0). Besides a device designation it may contain a
                complete Path designation and a filename, but not a Wildcard. If the device
                designation or Path description is missing, access occurs to the current device
                or the current Directory.
The access mode is constructed as follows:
                Bit 0 - 2: Read/Write permission
                    000b   =   file can only be read
                    001b   =   file can only be written

    010b   =   file can be read and written

Bit 3: 0b

Bit 4 - 6: File-Sharing mode

    000b   =   only the current program may access the file (Compatibility mode)

    001b   =   only the current program may access the file

    010b   =   another program may read, but not write the file

    011b   =   another program may write, but not read the file

    100b   =   another program may read and write the file

Bit 7: Handle-Flag

    0   =   Also the child-program of the current program is allowed to access the Handle of this file.

    1   =   Only the current program can access the Handle of this file.

Bit 8 - 12: 0b

Bit 13: 0 = On a critical error call Interrupt 24h.

    1 =   On a critical error return the corresponding error code to AX, but do not call Interrupt 24h.

Bit 14   1 = For every write access to this file immediately change the Directory entry.

Bit 15: 0b

The file attribute in the CX-Register can be loaded before the function call with the following attributes:

    Bit 0 = 1:   file can only be read, but not written (Read-Only)

    Bit 1 = 1:   file is hidden (not displayed during DIR command)

    Bit 2 = 1:   file is a system-file

    Bit 5 = 1:   file has been changed since the last archiving

    Bit 6-15 : 0b

The reaction of the function is stored In the lower two nibbles of the DX-Register, if the file to be opened does not exist or does exist. Bits 0 to 3 represent the reaction if the file does not yet exist. The values mean:

    0000b = Terminate function with an error-code

    0001b = Create file

In bits 4 to 7 the reaction to an already existing file is recorded. The values have the following meaning:

    0000b = Terminate function with an error-code

    0001b = Open existing file

    0010b = Overwrite existing file and open

    The function 3DH can continued to be used to open a file also under DOS 4.0. If the function call was terminated in an orderly manner, all other Handle functions can be called through the passed Handle. In the CX register remains the function status which provides information about the action of the function as follows:

    0 = File opened

    1 = New file created and opened

    2 = Existing file overwritten and opened

The file pointer is set to the first byte of the file.

The File-Sharing mode in bits 4 to 6 of the access mode is also under DOS version 4 only interesting if the file is on a mass storage device which is part of a network. In this case, these 3 bits decide, if other programs in the network may access this file during the opening and the access rights of this program. If the value 0 is indicated for these bits, DOS treats this file in the Compatibility-Mode, in which the existence of a network in relation to this file is ignored and only the current program may access this file.

Error 12 can only occur under DOS version 3 and only in a network, if the file was already opened by another program and it was determined at that time that at this moment no other program may access it.

The contents of the BX, DX, SI, DI, BP and segment registers are not affected by this function.

Interrupt 22H	**DOS**
Terminate address	**(Version 1 and up)**

Contains the address of a routine which terminates a program. Control returns to the program that called for termination. You should never call this routine directly.

DOS stores the contents of this interrupt vector in the PSP of the program to be executed before passing control to the program. This prevents program changes to the vector, which could prevent DOS from calling the termination routine.

Interrupt 23H	**DOS**
<Ctrl><C> handler address	**(Version 1 and up)**

Contains the address of a routine which executes when the user presses <Ctrl><C> or <Ctrl><Break>. You should never directly call this routine.

DOS stores the contents of this interrupt vector in the PSP of the program to be executed before passing control to the program. This prevents program changes to the vector, which could prevent DOS from calling the termination routine.

Interrupt 24H	**DOS**
Critical error handler address	**(Version 1 and up)**

Represents a routine called during hardware access (e.g., disk drive) when a critical error occurs. You should never directly call this routine.

When an application routine is called during a critical error, bit 7 of the AH register indicates the type of failure (0 = disk/hard disk error, 1= other errors). A disk/hard disk error will only be reported after several attempted accesses. During the call, the DI register receives one of the following codes:

0:	Disk write protected
1:	Access on unknown device
2:	Drive not ready
3:	Invalid command
4:	CRC error
5:	Bad request structure length
6:	Seek error
7:	Unknown device type
8:	Sector not found
9:	Printer out of paper
10:	Write error
11:	Read error
12:	General failure

The error routine restores the SS, SP, DS, ES, BX, CX and DX registers to the same values that they contained during the call. During execution it can only access functions 1 to 0CH of interrupt 21H. It should be terminated by an IRET instruction and pass one of the following codes to the AL register:

0:	Ignore error
1:	Repeat the operation
2:	Terminate program using interrupt 23H
3:	Fail system call (Version 3 and up only)

If a program changes the content of this interrupt vector, the program can terminate without restoring the memory contents. Since RAM can be released and used by other programs, the critical error routine can be overwritten by another program in memory. When this occurs, a critical error could cause a system crash because a completely different code now exists at the location of the old error handler routine

Before passing control to the program, DOS stores the contents of this interrupt vector in the PSP of the program to be executed. This prevents program changes to the vector, which could prevent DOS from calling the termination routine. During program termination, the contents of the interrupt vector pass from the PSP to the vector; then the system calls the routine.

Interrupt 25H   **DOS**
Absolute disk read   **(Version 1 and up)**

Reads one or more consecutive sectors from a disk or hard disk.

Input:	AL = Drive specifier
	CX= Number of sectors to read
	DX= First sector to read
	DS= Buffer segment address
	BX= Buffer offset address
Output:	Carry flag=0: O.K.
	Carry flag=1: Error (AX = Error code)
	AX=1: Bad command
	AX=2: Bad address
	AX=4: Sector not found
	AX=8: DMA error
	AX=16: CRC error
	AX=32: Disk controller error
	AX=64: Seek error
	AX=128: Device does not respond
Remarks:	In the AL register 0 represents drive A:, 1 represents drive B:, etc.

All the sectors of the medium can be accessed. DOS itself uses this interrupt to read the root directory and the FAT of a medium. The data are read from the medium into the buffer of the calling program. After the function call, the contents of all registers, except the segment register, may change.

After the interrupt call, the stack pointer changes position because two bytes stored on the stack during the call are removed and not returned. These bytes represent the flag register, which can be read from the stack using the POPF instruction. The old value of the stack pointer can be set by adding 2 to its contents. If you omit the stack pointer correction, the stack could overflow. Because of this, you cannot call this interrupt from higher level languages. You must call it from assembly language.

The contents of the BX, CX, DX, SI, DI, BP, CS, DS, SS and ES registers are not affected by this function. The contents of all other registers may change.

Interrupt 26H	DOS
Absolute disk write	**(Version 1 and up)**

Writes one or more consecutive sectors to a disk or hard disk.

Input: AL = Device designation
                  CX = Number of sectors to be written
                  DX = First sector to be written
                  DS = Buffer segment address
                  BX = Buffer offset address

Output: Carry flag=0: O.K.
                  Carry flag=1: Error (AX = Error code)
                      AX=1: Bad command
                      AX=2: Bad address
                      AX=3: Medium write protected
                      AX=4: Sector not found
                      AX=8: DMA error
                      AX=16: CRC error
                      AX=32: Disk controller error
                      AX=64: Seek error
                      AX=128: Device does not respond

Remarks: In the drive specifier 0 represents drive A:, 1 represents drive B:, etc.

All the sectors of the medium can be accessed. DOS itself uses this interrupt to write the root directory and the FAT to a medium. The data are written from the buffer of the calling program to the medium. After the function call, the contents of all registers, except the segment register, may change.

After the interrupt call, the stack pointer changes position because two bytes stored on the stack during the call are removed and not returned. These bytes represent the flag register, which can be read from the stack using the POPF instruction. The old value of the stack pointer can be set by adding 2 to its contents. If you omit the stack pointer correction, the stack could overflow. Because of this, you cannot call this interrupt from higher level languages. You must call it from assembly language.

The contents of the BX, CX, DX, SI, DI, BP, CS, DS, SS and ES registers are not affected by this function. The contents of all other registers may change.

Interrupt 27H	DOS
Terminate and stay resident	**(Version 1 and up)**

Terminates the currently executing program and returns control to the program that called the current program. Unlike other functions used for program termination, the memory used by the current program keeps the program code for later recall.

Input:	CS = PSP segment address
	DX = Number of bytes + 1 to be reserved
Output:	No output
Remarks:	This function is only suitable for calling COM programs.
	The number of bytes to be reserved relates to the beginning of the PSP.
	The value in the DX register has no effect on memory blocks reserved by function 48H of interrupt 21H.
	An error occurs during the call of this interrupt if the value in the DX register ranges from FFF1H to FFFFH.
	This interrupt does not close open files.

Interrupt 2FH, Subfunction 0   **DOS**
Get print spool install status   **(Version 3 and up)**

Gets current installation status of the print spooler.

Input:	AH = 2FH
	AL = 0
Output:	Carry flag=0: Successful execution
	AL = 0: O.K. to install
	AL = 1: Don't install
	AL = 255: Already installed
	Carry flag=1: Error (AX = Error code)
	AX=1: Invalid function
	AX=2: File not found
	AX=3: Path not found
	AX=4: Too many files currently open
	AX=5: Access denied
	AX=8: Print queue full
	AX=9: Print spooler busy
	AX=12: Name too long
	AX=15: Invalid drive

Interrupt 2FH, Subfunction 1   **DOS**
Send file to print spooler   **(Version 3 and up)**

Passes a file to the print spooler.

Input:	AH = 2FH
	AL = 1
	DS = Print packet (see below) segment address
	DX = Print packet (see below) offset address
Output:	Carry flag=0: Successful execution
	Carry flag=1: Error (AX = Error code)
	AX=1: Invalid function
	AX=2: File not found
	AX=3: Path not found
	AX=4: Too many files currently open
	AX=5: Access denied
	AX=8: Print queue full
	AX=9: Print spooler busy
	AX=12: Name too long
	AX=15: Invalid drive

Remarks: The five-byte print packet contains print spooler information. The first byte indicates the DOS version (0=Versions 3.1 to 3.3); the remaining bytes indicate the segment and offset addresses of the file specification.

Interrupt 2FH, Subfunction 2   **DOS**
Remove file from print queue   **(Version 3 and up)**

Deletes a file from the print spooler queue.

Input: AH = 2FH
           AL = 2
           DS = ASCII-format file segment address
           DX = ASCII-format file offset address
Output: Carry flag=0: Successful execution
           Carry flag=1: Error (AX = Error code)
               AX=1: Invalid function
               AX=2: File not found
               AX=3: Path not found
               AX=4: Too many files currently open
               AX=5: Access denied
               AX=8: Print queue full
               AX=9: Print spooler busy
               AX=12: Name too long
               AX=15: Invalid drive
Remarks: This subfunction allows wildcards (? and *) in file specifications, allowing you to delete more than one file at a time from the print queue.

Interrupt 2FH, Subfunction 3   **DOS**
Cancel all files in print queue   **(Version 3 and up)**

Cancels all files waiting in the print spooler queue for printing.

Input: AH = 2FH
           AL = 3
Output: Carry flag=0: Successful execution
           Carry flag=1: Error (AX = Error code)
               AX=1: Invalid function
               AX=2: File not found
               AX=3: Path not found
               AX=4: Too many files currently open
               AX=5: Access denied
               AX=8: Print queue full
               AX=9: Print spooler busy
               AX=12: Name too long
               AX=15: Invalid drive

Interrupt 2FH, Subfunction 4   **DOS**
Hold print jobs for status check   **(Version 3 and up)**

Halts all print jobs while testing for spooler status.

Input: AH = 2FH
           AL = 4
Output: Carry flag=0: Successful execution

Carry flag=1: Error
DX = Number of errors
DS = Print queue segment address
SI = Print queue offset address

Remarks: The print queue segment and offset addresses point to a set of 64-byte filenames in the queue. Each entry contains an ASCII file specification.

The first filename in the queue is the file currently printing in the print spooler. The last filename in the queue has a zero in the first byte of the specification.

Appendix E

Multiplexer-Interrupt 2FH

Because interrupt 2FH represents an interface to various resident DOS programs and allows TSR programs to make their functions available to other programs, it is known as the multiplexer.

Interrupt 2FH, Code 01H, Function 00H   **MUX**
PRINT: Determine installation status

Programs can utilize this function to determine whether the memory resident portion of the PRINT DOS command has been loaded.

Input:	AH = 01H
	AL = 00H
Output:	AL = FFH: PRINT installed
Remarks:	If PRINT has been installed, this function will return the value FFH in the AL register. Only then can the other PRINT functions be called. This function call must therefore precede all other PRINT functions.

Interrupt 2FH, Code 01H, Function 01H   **MUX**
PRINT: Add file to wait list

This function allows a program to add a file to the end of the printer wait list, to be printed from the background via PRINT.

Input:	AH = 00H
	AL = 01H
	DS = Segment address of FAR pointer to file info data structure
	DX = Offset address of FAR pointer to file info data structure
Output:	Carry flag = 0 : o.k.
	Carry flag = 1: Error, in this case
	AX = error code (see remarks)
Remarks:	The data structure accessed through the pointer in DS:DX comprises 5 bytes and must adhere to the following structure:

Ofs   meaning   type
00H   always 0   1 Byte
01H   FAR pointer to ASCIIZ string with filename   1 FAR pointer
Wildcards are not permitted in the specified filename. However, drive and path may be designated.

If an error occurs, the one of the following error codes will be returned:

0001H	unknown function
0002H	file not found
0003H	path not found
0004H	too many files opened
0005H	file access denied
0008H	printer wait list is full
000FH	unknown device

This function should only be called after function 00H has indicated that the resident portion of PRINT has been installed.

Interrupt 2FH, Code 01H, Function 02H   **MUX**
PRINT: Delete file from wait list

This function can be used to remove one or more files from the printer wait list. If the file currently being printed is also specified, print output will be stopped.

Input:	AH = 01H
	AL = 02H
	DS = Segment address of pointer to filename as ASCIIZ string
	DX = Offset address of pointer to filename as ASCIIZ string
Output:	Carry flag = 0 : o.k.
	Carry flag = 1: Error, in this case
	AX = error code (see remarks)
Remarks:	Wildcards may be used in the specified filename so that several files can be removed from the wait list at one time.
	The only possible error code here is 0002H, "file not found", in the event that the specified file was not included in the printer wait list.
	This function should only be called when function 00H has indicated that the resident portion of PRINT has been installed.

Interrupt 2FH, Code 01H, Function 03H   **MUX**
PRINT: Delete wait list

This function deletes all files from the printer wait list, and any current print job is stopped immediately.

Input:	AH = 01H
	AL = 03H
Output:	none
Remarks:	This function should only be called when function 00H has indicated that the resident portion of PRINT has been installed.

Interrupt 2FH, Code 01H, Function 04H   **MUX**
PRINT: Stop printer output and get status

This function can be used to determine the current contents of the printer wait list and the number of previous output errors.

Input:	AH = 01H
	AL = 04H
Output:	DX = Error counter
	DS:SI = FAR pointer to wait list

Remarks:
Upon this function call the printer output is interrupted, and resumes after function 05H is called.

The pointer returned in DS:SI points to the buffer in which DOS retains the waiting list in a series of 64 byte entries. Each of these entries contains an ASCIIZ string with the name of the file which is to be printed. To identify the list's end, its last entry always begins with the NUL character (00).

The contents of this list may be read, but not modified.

This function should only be called when function 00H has indicated that the resident portion of PRINT has been installed.

Interrupt 2FH, Code 01H, Function 05H   MUX
PRINT: Continue print job

After a print job has been interrupted by function 04H, this function can be used to resume the print job.

Input: AH = 01H
                AL = 05H
Output: none
Remarks: This function call is only useful if function 04H has previously been executed.

Interrupt 2FH, Code 01H, Function 06H   MUX
PRINT: Locate printer

If the printer wait list contains one file, this function can be used to determine the printer to which the print job will be sent.

Input: AH = 01H
                AL = 06H
Output: Carry flag = 0 : Wait list is empty
                Carry flag = 1: Wait list is not empty, in this case
                    AX = 0008H
                    DS:SI = FAR pointer to the head of the printer driver
Remarks: The values returned by this function are confusing, since the information that's needed (the pointer to the head of the printer device driver) is returned only with a set carry flag and the error code 0008 (wait list full). If the wait list is not empty, the carry flag will be cleared. In this case the pointer to the head of the printer driver will be unavailable.

Interrupt 2FH, Code 06H, Function 00H   MUX
ASSIGN: Get installation status

This function allows a program to determine whether the resident portion of the DOS command ASSIGN has been loaded.

Input: AH = 06H
                AL = 00H
Output: AL = FFH: ASSIGN installed

Interrupt 2FH, Code 10H, Function 00H
SHARE: Get installation status

This function indicates whether the resident portion of the DOS command SHARE has been loaded.

Input:	AH = 10H
	AL = 00H
Output:	AL = FFH: SHARE installed

Interrupt 2FH, Code 1AH, Function 00H
ANSI.SYS: Determine installation status

This function indicates whether the device driver ANSI.SYS has been installed.

Input:	AH = 1AH
	AL = 00H
Output:	AL = FFH: ANSI.SYS installed

Interrupt 2FH, Code 43H, Function 00H
HIMEM.SYS: Get installation status

This function indicates whether the device driver HIMEM.SYS has been installed. This driver allows extended memory to be used in accordance with the XMS standard.

Input:	AH = 43H
	AL = 00H
Output:	AL = 80H: HIMEM.SYS installed
Remarks:	Please note that this function, in contrast to most other functions that perform installation checks, returns the value 80H when successful, instead of the value FFH.
	To maintain compatibility with HIMEM.SYS, this function call is also supported by other XMS memory managers.

Interrupt 2FH, Code 43H, Function 10H
HIMEM.SYS: Determine address for XMS function calls

Unlike other memory managers, HIMEM.SYS calls XMS functions through a FAR CALL procedure, instead of an interrupt. This function is used to determine the address of that procedure.

Input:	AH = 43H
	AL = 10H
Output:	ES:BX = FAR pointer for calling XMS functions
Remarks:	This function may only be called when a preceding call of function 00H has indicated that HIMEM.SYS has been installed.

Interrupt 2FH, Code 48H, Function 00H   **MUX**
DOSKEY: Get installation status

This function indicates whether the DOS program DOSKEY.COM has been loaded.

Input:	AH = 48H
	AL = 00H
Output:	AL = 00H: not installed
Remarks:	DOSKEY was introduced with DOS Version 5.0.
	Please note that, in contrast to other installation check functions, the only return value defined for this function is the value indicating that DOSKEY.COM has not been installed.

Interrupt 2FH, Code 48H, Function 10H   **MUX**
DOSKEY: Receive user input

A program can access the DOSKEY program to prompt and receive user input.

Input:	AH = 48H
	AL = 10H
	DS:DX = FAR pointer to data structure (see remarks)
Output:	none
Remarks:	The data structure referenced through the pointer in DS:DX encompasses 130 bytes and receives the user input. It must be structured according to the following pattern:

Ofs	meaning	type
00h	input buffer size, must be 128	1 Byte
01h	the number of character read minus 1	1 Byte
02h	the input buffer	128 Bytes

The number of bytes that have been read is entered into the data structure by DOSKEY. Therefore, unlike the length specification in the first byte, this field doesn't need to be initialized before DOSKEY is called.

Interrupt 2FH, Code 4A11H, Function 00H
DBLSPACE: Obtain version information

Enables a program to determine whether DoubleSpace is loaded and to obtain information about the DoubleSpace driver.

Input:	AX = 4A11H
	BX = 00H
Output:	AX = 00H: DoubleSpace installed
	BX = 444DH
	CL = First drive designation used by DoubleSpace (65 = A:)
	CH = Number of drive designations reserved for DoubleSpace
	DX = Internal DoubleSpace version number
Remarks:	If the function does not return 0 in register AX then DoubleSpace is not installed and the contents of the other return registers are undefined.
	The value in BX stands for the two ASCII characters "MD", i.e., Microsoft DoubleSpace.
	The two return values in CH and CL come from the FirstDrive and LastDrive settings in the DoubleSpace configuration file DBLSPACE.INI. Please note

that, contrary to normal conventions, CL receives the value 65 (the ASCII code for A) for drive A:, rather than 0.

The internal version number from register DX is utilized by DBLSPACE.BIN, IO.SYS, and DBLSPACE.EXE, in order to maintain consistency. If bit 15 of this number is set, it is due to omitting the /MOVE parameter when calling the DBLSPACE.SYS driver in the CONFIG.SYS file. In this case, DoubleSpace stays in memory under 640K instead of shifting into upper memory.

Interrupt 2FH, Code 4A11H, Function 01H
DBLSPACE: Scan drive map

Determines whether a drive actually has another drive hidden behind it, and whether a drive is compressed or not.

Input:	AX = 4A11H
	BX = 01H
	DL = Drive to be scanned (A: = 0)
Output:	AX = 00H: DoubleSpace installed
	BL = Bit 7 = 1 : Compressed drive
	= 0 : Uncompressed drive
	Bits 0 to 6 : Number of host drive
	BH = Number of CVF file (DBLSPACE.xxx), if drive is compressed
Remarks:	If the function does not return 0 in register AX then DoubleSpace is not installed, and the contents of the other return registers are undefined.

If Bit 7 in register BL is set following the function call, then the drive is compressed. In that case a new call to this function must be made, with the value returned from register BL (bits 0 to 6) as the device code in DL, to ascertain the host drive. If the value from DL is again returned in bits 0 to 6 of BL, then the drive is a "swapped" drive. The host drive in this case is the drive from the first call (the return value in BL). In the other case, the drive designation has not been swapped and is therefore genuine. Here the second function call has returned the number of the host drive in bits 0 to 6 of register BL.

A drive designation for an uncompressed drive is genuine if bit 7 of BL is not set following the function call, and bits 0 to 6 of BL contain the same device number as was given in DL when the function was called.

Interrupt 2FH, Code 4A11H, Function 02H
DBLSPACE: Swap drive designations

This function arranges the swapping of a DoubleSpace device designation with that of its host drive.

Input:	AX = 4A11H
	BX = 02H
	DL = Number of compressed drive whose drive designation is to be swapped (0 = A)
Output:	AX = 00H: Drive designations were successfully swapped
	101H: Invalid drive designation
	102H: Drive entered is not compressed
	103H: Drive designations already swapped
	All other values: DoubleSpace not installed

Remarks: This function is intended for internal DoubleSpace use only.

Interrupt 2FH, Code 4A11H, Function 03H
DBLSPACE: For internal use only

Interrupt 2FH, Code 4A11H, Function 04H
DBLSPACE: For internal use only

Interrupt 2FH, Code 4A11H, Function 05H
DBLSPACE: Mount compressed drive

Enables the mounting of a compressed drive into the system. The call is very complicated however, which is why Microsoft recommends a direct call to DBLSPACE.EXE using the DOS Exec function. The syntax here is as follows:

```
DBLSPACE.EXE /Mount=[CVFNumber] HostDrive: [/NEWDRIVE=NewDriveDesignation:]
```


Interrupt 2FH, Code 4A11H, Function 06H
DBLSPACE: Unmount a DoubleSpace drive

Unmounts an activated DoubleSpace drive, rendering it nonexistent from the user's perspective.

Input: AX = 4A11H
                BX = 06H
                DL = Drive to be deactivated (0 = A:)
Output: AX = 00H: Drive deactivated
                     102H: Drive entered is not compressed and cannot be deactivated
Remarks: If the function returns none of these values in Register AX, then DoubleSpace isn't installed.
                The compressed drive remains unchanged on the hard disk, yet DOS no longer recognizes its former device ID.

Interrupt 2FH, Code 4A11H, Function 0007H
DBLSPACE: Establish storage space

This function returns the total number of sectors in the sector heap of a compressed drive, as well as the number still free.

Input: AX =   4A11H
                BX =   07H
                DL =   Drive designation (0 = A:)
Output: AX =   00H: All OK
                DS:SI =   Refers to a Dword with the total number of sectors in the sector heap
                DS:SI+4 =   Refers to a Dword with the number of free sectors in the sector heap
Remarks: If the function does not return 0 in register AX then DoubleSpace is not installed and the contents of the other return registers are undefined.

Interrupt 2FH, Code 4A11H, Function 08H
DBLSPACE: Obtain information about CVF file fragmentation

Returns information regarding fragmentation of all CVF files on a particular host drive.

Input:	AX = 4A11H
	BX = 08H
	DL = Compressed drive (0 = A:)
Output:	AX = 00H: OK, in this case
	BX = Maximum value for fragmentation
	CX = Number of additional fragmentations permitted
	AX = 102H: Drive entered is not compressed and cannot be deactivated
Remarks:	If the function returns none of these values in Register AX then DoubleSpace is not installed and the contents of the other return registers are undefined.

Interrupt 2FH, Code 4A11H, Function 09H
DBLSPACE: Scan for maximum number of compressed drives

This function determines the number of DISK_UNIT structures which DOS needs for maintaining DoubleSpace drives, and which DoubleSpace creates in memory during the boot process for later definition of DoubleSpace drives.

Input:	AX = 4A11H
	BX = 09H
	DL = Device ID of any compressed drive (0 = A:)
Output:	AX = 0000H: OK, in this case
	CL = Number of DISK_UNIT structures allocated by DoubleSpace during bootup.
Remarks:	If the function does not return 0 in Register AX then DoubleSpace is not installed and the contents of the other return registers are undefined.
	Each DISK_UNIT structure takes up 96 bytes of memory. The number returned here is determined by the MaxRemovableDrives parameter from the DoubleSpace initialization file DBLSPACE.INI.

Interrupt 2FH, Code ADH, Function 80H   MUX
KEYB.COM: Return version number

This function returns the version number of the current DOS keyboard driver KEYB.COM.

Input:	AH = ADH
	AL = 80H
	BX = 0
Output:	BH = Main version number
	BL = Sub version number
Remarks:	If BH and BL are 00H after the function has been called, KEYB.COM is not installed.

Interrupt 2FH, Code ADH, Function 81H   MUX
KEYB.COM: Set active code page

This function is used to set the active code page.

Input:	AH = ADH
	AL = 81H
	BX = Code page number
Output:	Carry flag = 0 : o.k.
	Carry flag = 1: Error, in this case
	AX = 0001 "unknown code page"
Output:	none

Remarks: The following code pages are recognized by KEYB:

Code	Character set
437	USA
850	Multi-lingual (all European countries)
860	Portuguese
863	French Canadian
865	Scandinavian

Before calling this function, you should use function 80H to determine whether KEYB.COM is active.

You'll find more information on code pages in your DOS manual. In the framework of PC System Programming these do not come into play.

Interrupt 2FH, Code B0H, Function 00H   **MUX**
GRAFTABL: Get installation status

This function indicates whether the resident portion of the DOS command GRAFTABL has been loaded.

Input:	AH = B0H
	AL = 00H
Output:	AL = FFH: GRAFTABL loaded

Interrupt 2FH, Code B7H, Function 00H   **MUX**
APPEND: Get installation status

This function determines whether the resident portion of the DOS command APPEND has been loaded.

Input:	AH = B7H
	AL = 00H
Output:	AL = FFH: APPEND loaded

Interrupt 2FH, Code B7H, Function 02H   **MUX**
APPEND: Verify DOS 5 compatibility

Input:	AH = B7H
	AL = 02H
Output:	AX = FFFFH : DOS 5.0 compatible
Remarks	This function may only be called when function 00H has indicated that APPEND has been loaded.

Interrupt 2FH, Code B7H, Function 04H   **MUX**
APPEND: Get list of APPEND directories

This function returns the various directories that have been specified as the search path for files, using APPEND.

Input:	AH = B7H
	AL = 04H
Output:	ES:DI = FAR pointer to the buffer containing the APPEND directories.
Remarks	The buffer identified by the pointer in ES:DI, returned by the function, contains the various APPEND directories as ASCIIZ strings. As with the PATH command, the individual directories are separated by semicolons. The contents of this buffer must not be changed by the user.

1271

This function may be called only when function 00H has indicated that APPEND has been loaded.

Interrupt 2FH, Code B7H, Function 06H   **MUX**
APPEND: Determine operation mode

This function returns the operation mode specified in the DOS command line at the APPEND call, using the different function switches.

Input: AH = B7H
                AL = 06H
Output: BX = APPEND flag
Remarks: The individual bits of the returned flag represent the different operational modes. Bits that are not included in the following chart has no meaning and contain the value 0.

Bit	Description
0	1 = APPEND is active
12	1 = the APPEND directories will be included in the search only if a drive is specified with the file that is to be found, and if that drive specification corresponds to the drive declared in that particular APPEND string.
13	1 = the switch /PATH:ON is active
14	1 = the switch /E is active
15	1 = the switch /X:ON is active

This function may be called only when function 00H has indicated that APPEND has been loaded.

Interrupt 2FH, Code B7H, Function 07H
APPEND: Set operation mode

This function is the counterpart of function 06H and sets the different APPEND options.

Input: AH = B7H
                AL = 07H
                BX = APPEND flag
Output: none
Remarks: The bit values and their meaning for the append flag can be taken from the chart listed for function 06H.
                This function may be called only when function 00H has indicated that APPEND has been loaded.

Appendix F

EMM Functions

The EMS standard which was introduced by Lotus, Intel and Microsoft corporations. It defines the access to the memory expansion cards which operate on the "bank switching" principle which only accesses a small part of the whole memory expansion.

Most EMS cards in circulation support version 3.2 of this standard and therefore the EMS-functions, which were defined under version 3.0 and 3.2. Only a few memory cards support the EMS-specification 4.0 and the functions connected with it. This is not true for most of the commercial EMS emulators, which simulate the EMS memory with Extended Memory. They are usually similar to version 4.0.

Interrupt 67H, Function 40H   **LIM/EMS**
Expanded memory: Get status

Returns the error status of the EMM after calling any EMS functions.

Input:	AH = 40H
Output:	AH = EMM status
	AH=00H: O.K.
	AH=80H: Internal error, EMM possibly destroyed
	AH=81H: EMS hardware error
Remarks:	Do not call this function unless you know that EMS memory and a corresponding EMM are installed (see Chapter 12 for more information). This function should be the first EMM call a program makes, to ensure that the hardware and software are functioning properly.

Interrupt 67H, Function 41H   **LIM/EMS**
Expanded memory: Get segment address of the page frame

Determines the segment address of the page frame.

Input:	AH = 41H
Output:	AH = 0: O.K.
	BX = Page frame segment address
	AH > 0: Error
	AH=80H: Internal error, EMM possibly destroyed
	AH=81H: EMS hardware error

Remarks: Do not call this function unless you know that EMS memory and a corresponding EMM are installed (see Chapter 12 for more information). The addresses of the four physical pages can be calculated from this segment address, whereby the first page starts at address PAGE_FRAME:0000. The three other pages follow at 16K intervals.

Interrupt 67H, Function 42H   LIM/EMS
Expanded memory: Get number of EMS pages

Informs the calling program how many 16K EMS pages are installed, and how many EMS pages are still available or unallocated.

Input: AH = 42H
Output: AH = 0: O.K.
                BX = Number of free (unallocated) pages
                DX = Total number of EMS pages
                AH > 0: Error
                    AH=80H: Internal error, EMM possibly destroyed
                    AH=81H: EMS hardware error
Remarks: Do not call this function unless you know that EMS memory and a corresponding EMM are installed (see Chapter 12 for more information).
                The number of kilobytes of free EMS memory can be calculated by multiplying the number of free pages by 16.

Interrupt 67H, Function 43H   LIM/EMS
Expanded memory: Allocate EMS memory

Allocates a given number of 16K EMS pages for later access.

Input: AH = 43H
                BX = Number of logical (16K) pages to be allocated
Output: AH = 0: O.K.
                DX = Handle for accessing allocated memory
                AH > 9: Error
                    AH=80H: Internal error, EMM possibly destroyed
                    AH=81H: EMS hardware error
                    AH=85H: No more handles available
                    AH=87H: Not enough pages free
                    AH=88H: No pages were requested
Remarks: Do not call this function unless you know that EMS memory and a corresponding EMM are installed (see Chapter 12 for more information).
                The handle returned can be used for future access and for releasing the allocated memory. If this handle is "lost", the handle cannot be recovered, nor can memory be released or used by other programs.
                A call to this function may fail because there are not enough pages free or because the EMM has been called so often that no more handles are available.
                The handles normally have the numbers FF00H, FE01H, FD02H, FC03H, etc.

Interrupt 67H, Function 44H   **LIM/EMS**
Expanded memory: Set mapping

Places one of the pages previously allocated by function 43H in one of the four physical pages within the page frame.

Input: AH = 44H
                  AL = Physical page number (0 to 3)
                  BX = Logical page number
                  DX = Handle
Output: AH = Error status
                      AH=00H: O.K.
                      AH=80H: Internal error, EMM possibly destroyed
                      AH=81H: EMS hardware error
                      AH=83H: Invalid handle
                      AH=8AH: Invalid logical page
                      AH=8BH: Invalid physical page
Remarks: Do not call this function unless you know that EMS memory and a corresponding EMM are installed (see Chapter 12 for more information).
                  The handle used when calling this function must have been returned by a previous call to EMM function 43H.
                  The logical pages are numbered from 0 on, so that the value 0 must be passed to access the first logical page. The largest value allowed is the number of allocated pages minus one.
                  Before accessing the physical page, the segment address of the page frame must be determined with function 41H.

Interrupt 67H, Function 45H   **LIM/EMS**
Expanded memory: Release pages

Releases pages allocated with function 43H to the EMM. This makes these pages available to other applications.

Input: AH = 45H
                  DX = Handle
Output: AH = Error status:
                      AH=00H: O.K.
                      AH=80H: Internal error, EMM possibly destroyed
                      AH=81H: EMS hardware error
                      AH=83H: Invalid handle
                      AH=85H: Error while saving and restoring mapping
Remarks: Do not call this function unless you know that EMS memory and a corresponding EMM are installed (see Chapter 12 for more information).
                  The handle used when calling this function must have been returned by a previous call to EMM function 43H.
                  All of the pages allocated to this handle are released by this function. It is impossible to release individual pages.
                  After a successful call to this function the handle is no longer valid and cannot be used for accessing EMS memory.
                  If the function returns an error, you should repeat the call at least three times or the pages will remain allocated and will not be available for other programs.

Interrupt 67H, Function 46H   **LIM/EMS**
Expanded memory: Get EMM version

Determines the version number of the EMM (Expanded Memory Manager).

Input:	AH = 46H
Output:	AH = 0: O.K.
	AL = EMM version number
	AH > 0: Error
	AH=80H: Internal error, EMM possibly destroyed
	AH=81H: EMS hardware error
Remarks:	Do not call this function unless you know that EMS memory and a corresponding EMM are installed (see Chapter 12 for more information).
	The EMM version number is stored in the AL register as a BCD number, in which the upper four bits represent the version number preceding the decimal point and the lower four bits represent the version number following the decimal point. See also the demonstration programs in Chapter 12.

Interrupt 67H, Function 47H   **LIM/EMS**
Expanded memory: Save mapping

Saves current mapping between the four physical pages in the page frame and the associated logical pages.

Input:	AH = 47H
	DX = Handle
Output:	AH = Error status
	AH=00H: O.K.
	AH=80H: Internal error, EMM possibly destroyed
	AH=81H: EMS hardware error
	AH=83H: Invalid handle
	AH=8CH: Mapping memory full
	AH=8DH: Mapping for handle already stored, not restored using function 48H
Remarks:	Do not call this function unless you know that EMS memory and a corresponding EMM are installed (see Chapter 12 for more information).
	The handle used when calling this function must have been returned by a previous call to EMM function 43H.
	This function is intended for use within a TSR program or by the operating system in a multitasking environment, but can be used by any program.

Interrupt 67H, Function 48H   **LIM/EMS**
Expanded memory: Restore mapping

Restores mapping between the logical and physical pages saved by function 8H.

Input:	AH = 48H
	DX = handle
Output:	AH = Error status:
	AH=00H: O.K.
	AH=80H: Internal error, EMM possibly destroyed
	AH=81H: EMS hardware error

AH=83H: Invalid handle

AH=8EH: Mapping storage contains no entry for this handle

Remarks: Do not call this function unless you know that EMS memory and a corresponding EMM are installed (see Chapter 12 for more information).

The handle used when calling this function must have been returned by a previous call to EMM function 43H.

Calling this function fails whenever the mapping for this handle has not been saved with function 47H, or the mapping has already been restored by a previous call to function 48H.

This function is intended for use within a TSR program or by the operating system in a multitasking environment, but can be used by any program.

Interrupt 67H, Function 49H   LIM/EMS
Expanded memory: Undocumented

Interrupt 67H, Function 4AH   LIM/EMS
Expanded memory: Undocumented

Interrupt 67H, Function 4BH   LIM/EMS
Expanded memory: Get number of handles

Returns the number of memory blocks and the number of handles allocated by function 43H.

Input: AH = 4BH
Output: AH = 0: O.K.
            BX = Number of allocated handles
            AH > 0: Error
                AH=80H: Internal error, EMM possibly destroyed
                AH=81H: EMS hardware error
Remarks: Do not call this function unless you know that EMS memory and a corresponding EMM are installed (see Chapter 12 for more information).

            The number of allocated handles is not the same as the number of programs which are currently accessing the EMS memory. Each program can request an arbitrary number of EMS memory blocks/handles with function 4H.

Interrupt 67H, Function 4CH   LIM/EMS
Expanded memory: Get number of allocated pages

Returns the number of pages which have been allocated to the specified handle.

Input: AH = 4CH
            DX = Handle
Output: AH = 0: O.K.
            BX = Number of allocated pages
            AH > 0: Error
                AH=80H: Internal error, EMM possibly destroyed
                AH=81H: EMS hardware error
                AH=83H: Invalid handle
Remarks: Do not call this function unless you know that EMS memory and a corresponding EMM are installed (see Chapter 12 for more information).

            The number of allocated pages must range from 1 to 512.

Interrupt 67H, Function 4DH **LIM/EMS**
Expanded memory: Get all handles

Loads the numbers of all active handles and the number of pages allocated to each into an array.

Input: AH = 4DH
                  ES = Segment address of array
                  DI = Offset address of array
Output: AH = 0: O.K.
                  BX = Number of allocated logical pages
                  AH > 0: Error
                      AH=80H: Internal error, EMM possibly destroyed
                      AH=81H: EMS hardware error
Remarks: Do not call this function unless you know that EMS memory and a
                  corresponding EMM are installed (see Chapter 12 for more information).
                  If the function returns successfully, the memory area to which the ES:DI
                  register pair points will contain two words for each active handle. The first
                  word contains the handle itself and the second word contains the number of
                  pages allocated to the handle. The number of these entries is returned in the BX
                  register.
                  Since the EMM can manage a maximum of 256 handles, the array will never
                  occupy more than 1024 bytes (1K).

Interrupt 67H, Function 4EH, Subfunction 00H **LIM/EMS**
Expanded memory: Get page map **(Version 3.2 and up)**

Gets page map (a map of logical and physical EMS pages).

Input: AH = 4EH
                  AL = 00H
                  ES:DI = Pointer to empty array
Output: AH = 0: O.K.
                      ES:DI = Pointer to filled array
                  AH >0: Error
Remarks: Do not call this function unless you know that EMS memory and a
                  corresponding version of EMM are installed (see Chapter 12 for more
                  information).
                  This function requires no EMM handle (compare with function 48H).

Interrupt 67H, Function 4EH, Subfunction 01H **LIM/EMS**
Expanded memory: Set page map **(Version 3.2 and up)**

Sets the page map (a map of logical and physical EMS pages) to the status that existed before
calling subfunction 00H.

Input: AH = 4EH
                  AL = 01H
                  ES:DI = Pointer to page map array
Output: AH = 0: O.K.
                  AH >0: Error
Remarks: Do not call this function unless you know that EMS memory and a
                  corresponding version of EMM are installed (see Chapter 12 for more
                  information).

This function requires no EMM handle (compare with function 48H).

Interrupt 67H, Function 4EH, Subfunction 02H　　　　　**LIM/EMS**
Expanded memory: Swap page map　　　　　**(Version 3.2 and up)**

Swaps the current page map with the previously stored page map.

Input:	AH = 4EH
	AL = 02H
	DS:SI = Pointer to the array containing the page map to be restored
	ES:DI = Pointer to the array containing the current page map
Output:	AH = 0: O.K.
	AH >0: Error
Remarks:	Do not call this function unless you know that EMS memory and a corresponding version of EMM are installed (see Chapter 12 for more information).
	Before calling this function, the buffer containing the page map must have been previously lodaed using subfunction 00H or subfunction 02H.
	Subfunction 03H returns the size of the current page map array.
	This function requires no EMM handle (compare with functions 47H and 48H).

Interrupt 67H, Function 4EH, Subfunction 03H　　　　　**LIM/EMS**
Expanded memory: Get page map array size　　　　　**(Version 3.2 and up)**

Returns the amount of memory required for the page map.

Input:	AH = 4EH
	AL = 03H
Output:	AH = 0: OK
	AL=Page map array size in bytes
	AH >0: Error
Remarks:	Do not call this function unless you know that EMS memory and a corresponding version of EMM are installed (see Chapter 12 for more information).

Interrupt 67H, Function 4FH, Subfunction 00H　　　　　**LIM/EMS**
Expanded memory: Save partial page map　　　　　**(Version 4.0 and up)**

Saves part of a page map.

Input:	AH = 4FH
	AL = 00H
	DS:SI = Pointer to map list
	ES:DI = Pointer map state buffer
Output:	AH = 0: O.K.
	AH > 0: Error
Remarks:	Do not call this function unless you know that EMS memory and a corresponding version of EMM are installed (see Chapter 12 for more information).

The map list must contain the number of pages in its first word, followed by a word containing the segement address of these pages. The size of this map list is therefore:

```
2 + ( number_of_pages_to_be_stored * 2 ) bytes
```

Subfunction 02H of this function determines the buffer size needed for saving the selected entries from the page map.

Interrupt 67H, Function 4FH, Subfunction 01H   **LIM/EMS**
Expanded memory: Restore partial page map   **(Version 4.0 and up)**

Restores a page map previously saved using function 4FH, subfunction 00H.

Input:	AH = 4FH
	AL = 01H
	DS:SI = Pointer to the buffer with the stored page table
Output:	AH = 0: O.K.
	AH > 0: Error
Remarks:	Do not call this function unless you know that EMS memory and a corresponding version of EMM are installed (see Chapter 12 for more information).
	Before calling this function, the buffer must be saved using function 4FH, subfunction 00H.

Interrupt 67H, Function 4FH, Subfunction 02H   **LIM/EMS**
Expanded memory: Get partial page map size info   **(Version 4.0 and up)**

Determines the size of the buffer required for saving part of a page map.

Input:	AH = 4FH
	AL = 02H
	BX = Number of physical pages to be stored
Output:	AH = 0: O.K.
	AL=Array size in bytes
	AH > 0: Error
Remarks:	Do not call this function unless you know that EMS memory and a corresponding version of EMM are installed (see Chapter 12 for more information).

Interrupt 67H, Function 50H, Subfunction 00H   **LIM/EMS**
Expanded memory: Map multiple pages by number   **(Version 4.0 and up)**

Converts logical pages to physical pages, addressable through a numeric sequence.

Input:	AH = 50H
	AL = 00H
	CX = Number of logical pages
	DX = EMM handle by which pages are allocated
	DS:SI = Pointer to buffer containing conversion information
Output:	AH = 0: O.K.
	AH > 0: Error
Remarks:	Do not call this function unless you know that EMS memory and a corresponding version of EMM are installed (see Chapter 12 for more information).
	The buffer passed must contain two sequential words for every conversion. The first word specifies the logical page number, while the second word specifies the physical page number where the logical page will be reproduced.

If the logical page number is -1, the corresponding physical page is deleted and cannot be read or written.

Interrupt 67H, Function 50H, Subfunction 01H   LIM/EMS
Expanded memory: Map multiple pages by address   (Version 4.0 and up)

Converts logical pages to physical pages, addressable through segment addresses.

Input: AH = 50H
           AL = 01H
           CX = Number of logical pages
           DX = EMM handle by which pages are allocated
           DS:SI = Pointer to buffer containing conversion information

Output: AH = 0: O.K.
           AH > 0: Error

Remarks: Do not call this function unless you know that EMS memory and a corresponding version of EMM are installed (see Chapter 12 for more information).

The buffer passed must contain two sequential words for every conversion. The first word specifies the logical page number, while the second word specifies the physical page number where the logical page will be reproduced.

If the logical page number is -1, the corresponding physical page is deleted and cannot be read or written.

Function 58H, subfunction 00H lets you determine the segment addresses of the available physical pages.

Interrupt 67H, Function 51H   LIM/EMS
Expanded memory: Reallocate pages for handle   (Version 4.0 and up)

Reallocates larger or smaller numbers of logical pages. This number belongs to a handle allocated by function 43H.

Input: AH = 48H
           DX = EMM handle by which pages are allocated
           BX = New number of pages

Output: AH = 0: O.K.
           BX = Number of logical pages using this handle
           AH > 0: Error

Remarks: Do not call this function unless you know that EMS memory and a corresponding version of EMM are installed (see Chapter 12 for more information).

You can reduce the number of pages assigned easily. However, increasing the number of pages allocated depends on the amount of free EMS memory available.Check the AH register for errors after every call to this function.

If this function reduces the number of allocated pages, a corresponding number of pages at the upper end of the pages allocated up to now are cut, destroying the contents of those pages.

The handle remains valid after the call, even if the number of pages is reduced to zero.

Interrupt 67H, Function 52H, Subfunction 00H   **LIM/EMS**
Expanded memory: Get handle attribute   **(Version 4.0 and up)**

Indicates whether EMS pages assigned to a handle are volatile (will not survive in memory after a warm boot) or volatile (will survive a warm boot).

Input: AH = 52H
                AL = 00H
                DX = EMM page handle
Output: AH = 0: O.K.
                    AL=Page attribute
                        0 : Volatile pages
                        1 : Non-volatile pages
                AH > 0: Error
Remarks: Do not call this function unless you know that EMS memory and a corresponding version of EMM are installed (see Chapter 12 for more information).

Interrupt 67H, Function 52H, Subfunction 01H   **LIM/EMS**
Expanded memory: Set handle attribute   **(Version 4.0 and up)**

If an EMS-card has a capability to protect EMS-pages against a Warmstart of the computer, the corresponding attribute can be determined with the help of this function.

Input: AH = 52H
                AL = 01H
                BL = Page attribute
                    0 : Volatile pages
                    1 : Non-volatile pages
                DX = EMM page handle
Output: AH = 0: O.K.
                AH > 0: Error
Remarks: Do not call this function unless you know that EMS memory and a corresponding version of EMM are installed (see Chapter 12 for more information).
                Only a few EMS cards can protect EMS pages from overwriting during a warm boot, and no EMS emulators can perform this task. Before calling this function, select subfunction 02H to determine the availability of non-volatile EMS pages.

Interrupt 67H, Function 52H, Subfunction 02H   **LIM/EMS**
Expanded memory: Get attribute capability   **(Version 4.0 and up)**

Determines whether the EMS card can offer protection to EMS pages from a warm boot. This function dictates whether function 52H, subfunctions 00H and 01H can be used.

Input: AH = 52H
                AL = 02H
Output: AH = 0: O.K.
                AL = 0 : Non-volatile pages not supported
                AL = 1: Non-volatile pages supported
                AH > 0: Error

Remarks: Do not call this function unless you know that EMS memory and a corresponding version of EMM are installed (see Chapter 12 for more information).

Only a few EMS cards can protect EMS pages from overwriting during a warm boot, and no EMS emulators can perform this task. Call this function to determine the availability of non-volatile EMS pages.

Interrupt 67H, Function 53H, Subfunction 00H   LIM/EMS
Expanded memory: Get handle name   (Version 4.0 and up)

Stores a handle name in the caller's buffer.

Input: AH = 53H
          AL = 00H
          DX = EMM page handle
          ES:DI = Pointer to name buffer
Output: AH = 0: O.K.
          AH > 0: Error
Remarks: Do not call this function unless you know that EMS memory and a corresponding version of EMM are installed (see Chapter 12 for more information).

The name of a handle is always 8 characters in length. For this reason the buffer must have at least 8 bytes of storage capacity.

After function 43H allocates a handle, this new handle contains a 0 as its name. Before calling function 53H, subfunction 00H, call subfunction 01H to attach the name to a handle.

Interrupt 67H, Function 53H, Subfunction 01H   LIM/EMS
Expanded memory: Set handle name   (Version 4.0 and up)

Gives a name to a previously allocated handle for access.

Input: AH = 53H
          AL = 01H
          DX = EMM page handle
          ES:DI = Pointer to name buffer
Output: AH = 0: O.K.
          AH > 0: Error
Remarks: Do not call this function unless you know that EMS memory and a corresponding version of EMM are installed (see Chapter 12 for more information).

The name of a handle is always 8 characters in length. For this reason the buffer must have at least 8 bytes of storage capacity.

Interrupt 67H, Function 54H, Subfunction 00H   LIM/EMS
Expanded memory: Get all handle names   (Version 4.0 and up)

Returns all handle names to a buffer in the caller.

Input: AH = 54H
          AL = 00H
          ES:DI = Pointer to name buffer
Output: AH = 0: O.K.

AL = Number of active handles

ES:DI = Pointer to filled in name buffer

AH > 0: Error

Remarks: Do not call this function unless you know that EMS memory and a corresponding version of EMM are installed (see Chapter 12 for more information).

The buffer must offer 2,550 bytes of available memory (255 handles administered x 10 bytes for each handle entry). The first two bytes store the actual handle, and the remaining eight bytes contain the handle name.

Interrupt 67H, Function 54H, Subfunction 01H   **LIM/EMS**
Expanded memory: Search for handle name   **(Version 4.0 and up)**

Searches for the handle name supplied by the caller.

Input: AH = 54H

     AL = 01H

     DS:SI = Pointer to name buffer

Output: AH = 0: O.K.

     DX = EMM page handle

     AH > 0: Error

Remarks: Do not call this function unless you know that EMS memory and a corresponding version of EMM are installed (see Chapter 12 for more information).

Interrupt 67H, Function 54H, Subfunction 02H   **LIM/EMS**
Expanded memory: Get total handles   **(Version 4.0 and up)**

Returns total number of handles.

Input: AH = 54H

     AL = 02H

Output: AH = 0: O.K.

     BX = Number of handle

     AH > 0: Error

Remarks: Do not call this function unless you know that EMS memory and a corresponding version of EMM are installed (see Chapter 12 for more information).

Interrupt 67H, Function 55H, Subfunction 00H   **LIM/EMS**
Expanded memory: Map page by page number/jump   **(Version 4.0 and up)**

Maps the pages by page numbers, and jumps to one of the pages using a FAR jump.

Input: AH = 55H

     AL = 00H

     DX = EMM page handle

     DS:SI = Pointer to buffer

Output: AH = 0: O.K.

     AH > 0: Error

Remarks: Do not call this function unless you know that EMS memory and a corresponding version of EMM are installed (see Chapter 12 for more information). The buffer must have the following structure:

Addr.	Contents	Type
+00H	FAR pointer to the jump target	1 ptr
+05H	Number of pages to map before jump	1 byte
+06H	FAR pointer to map list	1 ptr
■ Length 9 bytes ████████		

The structure of the map list is identical to the structure of this list during the construction of function 50H, subfunction 00H. The logical page number and its corresponding physical page are retained.

Interrupt 67H, Function 55H, Subfunction 01H   **LIM/EMS**
Expanded memory: Map page by page segment/jump   **(Version 4.0 and up)**

Maps the pages by page segments, and jumps to one of the pages using a FAR jump.

Input:	AH = 55H
	AL = 01H
	DX = EMM page handle
	DS:SI = Pointer to buffer
Output:	AH = 0: O.K.
	AH > 0: Error
Remarks:	Do not call this function unless you know that EMS memory and a corresponding version of EMM are installed (see Chapter 12 for more information).

The buffer must have the following format:

Addr.	Contents	Type
+00H	FAR pointer to the jump target	1 ptr
+05H	Number of pages to map before jump	1 byte
+06H	FAR pointer to map list	1 ptr
■ Length 9 bytes ████████		

The format of the map list is identical to the format of this list during the execution of function 50H, subfunction 00H. The logical page number and its corresponding physical page are retained.

Interrupt 67H, Function 56H, Subfunction 00H   **LIM/EMS**
Expanded memory: Map page by page number/call   **(Version 4.0 and up)**

Maps pages by page numbers and calls a program through a FAR call. After this routine ends, a second page map occurs, and interrupt function control returns to the caller.

Input:	AH = 56H
	AL = 00H
	DX = EMM page handle
	DS:SI = Pointer to the buffer
Output:	AH = 0: O.K.
	AH > 0: Error
Remarks:	Do not call this function unless you know that EMS memory and a corresponding version of EMM are installed (see Chapter 12).
	The buffer must have the following format:

Addr.	Contents	Type
+00H	FAR pointer to the call's target	1 ptr
+05H	Number of pages to be mapped before call	1 byte
+06H	FAR pointer to list of pages to be mapped before call	1 ptr
+0AH	Number of pages to map before returning	1 byte
+0BH	FAR pointer to list of pages to be mapped before return	1 ptr

■ Length: 14 bytes

The format of the map list is identical to the format of this list during the execution of function 50H, subfunction 00H. The logical page number and its corresponding physical page are retained.

Call subfunction 02H to ensure that enough memory is available before calling this function.

Interrupt 67H, Function 56H, Subfunction 01H   **LIM/EMS**
Expanded memory: Map page by page segment/call   **(Version 4.0 and up)**

Maps pages by page segments and calls a program through a FAR call. After this routine ends, a second page map occurs, and interrupt function control returns to the caller.

Input:	AH = 56H
	AL = 01H
	DX = EMM page handle
	DS:SI = Pointer to the buffer
Output:	AH = 0: O.K.
	AH > 0: Error
Remarks:	Do not call this function unless you know that EMS memory and a corresponding version of EMM are installed (see Chapter 12 for more information).

The buffer must have the following format:

Addr.	Contents	Type
+00H	FAR pointer to the call's target	1 ptr
+05H	Number of pages to be mapped before call	1 byte
+06H	FAR pointer to list of pages to be mapped before call	1 ptr
+0AH	Number of pages to map before returning	1 byte
+0BH	FAR pointer to list of pages to be mapped before return	1 ptr

■ Length: 14 bytes

The format of the map list is identical to the format of this list during the execution of function 50H, subfunction 00H. The logical page number and its corresponding physical page are retained.

Call subfunction 02H to ensure that enough memory is available before calling this function.

Interrupt 67H, Function 56H, Subfunction 02H   **LIM/EMS**
Expanded memory: Get stack space for map page/call   **(Version 4.0 and up)**

Returns the memory space required by subfunctions 00H and 01H.

Input:	AH = 56H
	AL = 02H
Output:	AH = 0: O.K.
	BX = Space required
	AH > 0: Error
Remarks:	Do not call this function unless you know that EMS memory and a corresponding version of EMM are installed (see Chapter 12 for more information).

Interrupt 67H, Function 57H, Subfunction 00H   **LIM/EMS**
Expanded memory: Move memory region   **(Version 4.0 and up)**

Copies memory regions between expanded memory and conventional memory, or within either set of memory.

Input:	AH = 57H
	AL = 00H
	DS:SI = Pointer to buffer
Output:	AH = 0: O.K.
	AH > 0: Error
Remarks:	Do not call this function unless you know that EMS memory and a corresponding version of EMM are installed (see Chapter 12 for more information).
	The buffer must have the following format:

Addr.	Content	Type
+00H	Region length in bytes	1 dword
+04H	Source memory type (0 =conventional, 1 =EMS)	1 byte
+05H	Source memory handle (EMS only)	1 word
+07H	Source memory offset	1 word
+09H	Source memory segment address (conv. memory) or logical page number (EMS)	1 word
+0BH	Target memory type (0 =conventional, 1 =EMS)	1 byte
+0CH	Target memory handle (EMS only)	1 word
+0EH	Target memory offset	1 word
+10H	Target memory segment address (conv. memory) or logical page number (EMS)	1 word

■ Length: 18 bytes

Interrupt 67H, Function 57H, Subfunction 01H   **LIM/EMS**
Expanded memory: Exchange memory regions   **(Version 4.0 and up)**

This function operates similar to the subfunction 00H. It does not copy one storage area into another, but swaps the content of the indicated storage areas.

Input: AH = 57H
                   AL = 01H
                   DS:SI = Pointer to buffer
Output: AH = 0: O.K.
                   AH > 0: Error
Remarks: Do not call this function unless you know that EMS memory and a corresponding version of EMM are installed (see Chapter 12 for more information).
                   The buffer must have the following format:

Addr.	Content	Type
+00H	Region length in bytes	1 dword
+04H	Source memory type (0 = onventional, 1 =EMS)	1 byte
+05H	Source memory handle (EMS only)	1 word
+07H	Source memory offset	1 word
+09H	Source memory segment address (conv. memory) or logical page number (EMS)	1 word
+0BH	Target memory type (0 =conventional, 1 =EMS)	1 byte
+0CH	Target memory handle (EMS only)	1 word
+0EH	Target memory offset	1 word
+10H	Target memory segment address (conv. memory) or logical page number (EMS)	1 word

■ Length: 18 bytes

This function can swap up to 1 megabyte of memory.

If EMS pages are participating in this swap and the size specified exceeds the EMS page, other EMS pages will be used.

The source and destination regions may not overlap.

Interrupt 67H, Function 58H, Subfunction 00H **LIM/EMS**
Expanded memory: Get addresses of mappable pages **(Version 4.0 and up)**

Returns addresses of all physical EMS pages and related page numbers.

Input: AH = 58H
AL = 00H
ES:DI = Pointer to buffer

Output: AH = 0: O.K.
CX=Number of entries
ES:DI=Pointer to filled in buffer
AH > 0: Error

Remarks: Do not call this function unless you know that EMS memory and a corresponding version of EMM are installed (see Chapter 12 for more information).

Subfunction 01H helps determine the size of the buffer required.

EMM passes the desired information into the buffer in two word entries. The first word contains the segment address of an EMS page, while the second word indicates the page number that applies to the page.

Interrupt 67H, Function 58H, Subfunction 01H   **LIM/EMS**
Expanded memory: Get number of mappable pages   **(Version 4.0 and up)**

Determines the number of physical EMS pages, and calculates the size of the buffer required by subfunction 00H.

Input: AH = 58H
                 AL = 01H
Output: AH = 0: O.K.
                     CX=Number of pages
                 AH > 0: Error
Remarks: Do not call this function unless you know that EMS memory and a corresponding version of EMM are installed (see Chapter 12 for more information).
                 The size of the buffer required is the result of multiplying the number of pages (the contents of the CX register) by four.

Interrupt 67H, Function 59H, Subfunction 00H   **LIM/EMS**
Expanded memory: Get hardware configuration   **(Version 4.0 and up)**

Determines EMS hardware configuration. This function only applies to an operating system equipped with EMS.

Input: AH = 59H
                 AL = 00H
                 ES:DI = Pointer to buffer
Output: AH = 0: O.K.
                     AL=Page map size in bytes
                     ES:DI=Pointer to filled in buffer
                 AH > 0: Error
Remarks: Do not call this function unless you know that EMS memory and a corresponding version of EMM are installed (see Chapter 12 for more information).
                 The buffer must be a minimum size of 10 bytes. It contains the following information after the function call:

Addr.	Content	Type
+00H	Raw EMS page size in paragraphs	1 word
+02H	Alternate EMS register sets	1 word
+04H	Mapping context save area size in bytes	1 word
+06H	Number of assignable register sets	1 word
+08H	DMA operating mode (0 = DMA with alt register sets; 1 = One DMA register set)	1 word

■ Length: 10 bytes

Interrupt 67H, Function 59H, Subfunction 01H   **LIM/EMS**
Expanded memory: Get number of raw pages   **(Version 4.0 and up)**

Determines the total number of raw (non-standard EMS) pages, and indicates which of those
pages are available. A raw page has a size other than the default 16K.

Input: AH = 59H
                AL = 01H
Output: AH = 0: O.K.
                    DX=Total number of raw pages
                    BX=Number of raw pages not allocated
                AH > 0: Error
Remarks: Do not call this function unless you know that EMS memory and a
                corresponding version of EMM are installed (see Chapter 12 for more
                information).
                Not all EMS cards support raw pages. This may result in a value of zero
                returned in the DX register.

Interrupt 67H, Function 5AH, Subfunction 00H   **LIM/EMS**
Expanded memory: Allocate handle & standard pages   **(Version 4.0 and up)**

Allocates standard EMS pages. Unlike function 43H, this function can allocate zero pages
without error.

Input: AH = 5AH
                AL = 0H
                BX = Number of standard pages
Output: AH = 0: O.K.
                    DX=EMM page handle
                AH > 0: Error
Remarks: Do not call this function unless you know that EMS memory and a
                corresponding version of EMM are installed (see Chapter 12 for more
                information).

Interrupt 67H, Function 5AH, Subfunction 01H   **LIM/EMS**
Expanded memory: Allocate handle & raw pages   **(Version 4.0 and up)**

Allocates raw pages. A raw page has a size other than the default 16K.

Input: AH = 5AH
                AL = 01H
                BX = Number of pages to be allocated
Output: AH = 0: O.K.
                    DX=EMM page handle
                AH > 0: Error
Remarks: Do not call this function unless you know that EMS memory and a
                corresponding version of EMM are installed (see Chapter 12 for more
                information).
                Not all EMS cards support raw pages. Test the function status in the AH
                register.
                This function can also allocate zero pages.

Interrupt 67H, Function 5BH   **LIM/EMS**
Expanded memory: Alternate map and DMA services   **(Version 4.0 and up)**

Function 5BH contains nine subfunctions used exclusively in operating system development. None of these subfunctions are used in normal PC software development.

Interrupt 67H, Function 5CH   **LIM/EMS**
Expanded memory: Prepare EMM for warm boot   **(Version 4.0 and up)**

Prepares the Expanded Memory Manager for an imminent warm boot of the computer. This gives the EMM an opportunity to store internal data and prevent the loss of non-volatile pages when the warm boot occurs.

Input:	AH = 5CH
Output:	AH = 0: O.K.
	AH >0: Error
Remarks:	Do not call this function unless you know that EMS memory and a corresponding version of EMM are installed (see Chapter 12 for more information).
	See also function 52H for more information.

Interrupt 67H, Function 5DH   **LIM/EMS**
Expanded memory: EMM operating system services   **(Version 4.0 and up)**

Function 5BH contains three subfunctions used exclusively in operating system development. None of these subfunctions are used in normal PC software development.

Appendix G

XMS Functions

The XMS (eXtended Memory Specification) was created by Microsoft in cooperation with several other corporations, as a supplement to the EMS standard. This specification coordinates access to extended memory, the memory which lies beyond the 1 megabyte limit of conventional memory.

Interrupt 2FH must recognize an XMS driver, and the XMS handler's address must be specified, before calling any of these functions. XMS functions are called through a FAR CALL instruction, instead of the special interrupt used by other function interfaces. See Chapter 12 for more information.

Error codes are placed in the BL register. The following error codes can occur during XMS function calls:

80H: Function not implemented
81H: VDISK device driver was
    detected
82H: A20 error
8EH: General driver error
8FH: Unrecoverable driver error
90H: HMA does not exist
91H: HMA is already in use
92H: DX is less than /HMAMIN =
    parameter
93H: HMA is not allocated
94H: A20 line is still enabled
A0H: All extended memory is
    allocated
A1H: EMM handles are exhausted
A2H: Handle is invalid

A3H: Source handle is invalid
A4H: Source offset is invalid
A5H: Destination handle is invalid
A6H: Destination offset is invalid
A7H: Length is invalid
A8H: Overlap in move request is
    invalid
A9H: Parity error detected
AAH: Block not locked
ABH: Block locked
ACH: UMB count overflowed
ADH: Lock failed
B0H: Smaller UMB is available
B1H: No UMBs are available
B2H: UMB segment number is
    invalid

Function 00H   **XMS**
Determine XMS version number

Returns the XMS driver's version number and the driver's internal revision number.

Input: AH = 00H
Output: AX = XMS version number
                    BX = Internal revision number
                    DX = HMA status
                        0: No HMA
                        1: HMA available
Remarks: Interrupt 2FH must recognize an XMS driver, and the XMS driver jump
                    location must be specified, before calling this function.

Function 01H   **XMS**
Allocate High Memory Area (HMA)

Reserves all or part of the HMA for program use.

Input: AH = 01H
                    DX = Requested HMA space in bytes
                        FFFFH: Amount needed for application program
                        < FFFFH: Actual amount needed for operating system or driver
Output: AX = 0001H: Operation completed
                    AX = 0000H: Error
                    BL = Error code (see below)
Remarks: Interrupt 2FH must recognize an XMS driver, and the XMS driver jump
                    location must be specified, before calling this function.
                    Address line A20 must be freed using function 03H or function 05H, before
                    HMA access can occur.
                    This function can fail if a TSR doesn't request the entire HMA, and if the
                    amount of memory requested is less than the value passed by the /HMAMIN
                    parameter during driver installation. These factors give a TSR, which may
                    require only a few kilobytes, exclusive access rights to the HMA, while
                    prohibiting access by another program requiring more memory.
                    If the HMA should not remain in possession of the program beyond its
                    termination, it must be freed before the end of program execution by function
                    02H.

Function 02H   **XMS**
Free High Memory Area (HMA)

Releases the HMA previously allocated by function 01H.

Input: AH = 02H
Output: AX = 0001H: Operation completed
                    AX = 0000H: Error
                    BL = Error code (see below)
Remarks: Interrupt 2FH must recognize an XMS driver, and the XMS driver jump
                    location must be specified, before calling this function.
                    A previously allocated HMA remains allocated even after program execution
                    ends. This function must be called before the HMA can be allocated by other
                    subsequent program calls.

Calling function 02H destroys the HMA's current contents.

Function 03H   **XMS**
Globally enable address line A20

Globally enables address line A20, permitting direct HMA access when the processor is in real mode.

Input:	AH = 03H
Output:	AX = 0001H: Operation completed
	AX = 0000H: Error
	BL = Error code (see below)
Remarks:	Interrupt 2FH must recognize an XMS driver, and the XMS driver jump location must be specified, before calling this function.
	This function must be called before or after allocating the HMA. This ensures HMA access in real mode through segment address FFFFH.
	Function 04H should be used to disable address line A20 before program execution ends. This prevents a possible segment overflow in subsequent program calls.
	The process of enabling address line A20 can take much time. We recommend that you call function 03H only when necessary.

Function 04H   **XMS**
Globally disable address line A20

Globally disables address line A20, prohibiting direct HMA access when the processor is in real mode.

Input:	AH = 04H
Output:	AX = 0001H: Operation completed
	AX = 0000H: Error
	BL = Error code (see below)
Remarks:	Interrupt 2FH must recognize an XMS driver, and the XMS driver jump location must be specified, before calling this function.
	The process of disabling address line A20 can take much time. We recommend that you call function 04H only when necessary.

Function 05H   **XMS**
Locally enable address line A20

Locally enables address line A20. Calls to functions 05H and 06H are recorded internally with the help of a counter, which increments with every call to function 05H and decrements with every call to function 06H. This line can be enabled only if it is currently disabled.

Input:	AH = 05
Output:	AX = 0001H: Operation completed
	AX = 0000H: Error
	BL = Error code (see below)
Remarks:	This function must be called before or after allocating the HMA.
	Function 06H should be used to disable address line A20 before program execution ends. This prevents a possible segment overflow in subsequent program calls.
	The process of enabling address line A20 can take much time. We recommend that you call function 05H only when necessary.

Function 06H XMS
Locally disable address line A20

Locally disables address line A20, if line A20 was previously enabled by function 05H.

Input: AH = 06
Output: AX = 0001H: Operation completed
              AX = 0000H: Error
              BL = Error code (see below)
Remarks: Calls to functions 05H and 06H are recorded internally with the help of a counter, which increments with every call to function 05H and decrements with every call to function 06H. Only after reaching the value 0 is the address line actually disabled. Every call to function 06H must be preceded by a call to function 05H.
              Function 06H should be used to disable address line A20 before program execution ends. This prevents a possible segment overflow in subsequent program calls.
              The process of enabling address line A20 can take much time. We recommend that you call function 05H only when necessary.

Function 07H XMS
Query status of address line A20

Determines whether address line A20 has been enabled by functions 03H or 05H.

Input: AH = 07H
Output: AX = 0001H: Address line A20 enabled
              AX = 0000H: Address line A20 disabled
Remarks: Interrupt 2FH must recognize an XMS driver, and the XMS driver jump location must be specified, before calling this function.
              This query is hardware-controlled, and takes less time than the process of enabling or disabling address line A20.

Function 08H XMS
Query free extended memory

Returns the total amount of free extended memory, as well as the size of the largest free block of extended memory.

Input: AH = 08H
Output: AX = Size of the largest free block of extended memory in kilobytes
              DX = Total free extended memory in kilobytes
Remarks: Interrupt 2FH must recognize an XMS driver, and the XMS driver jump location must be specified, before calling this function.
              The HMA is excluded from this function, even if no HMA has been allocated. This results in a total 64K too large, because extended memory allocation always starts after the HMA. See Chapter 12 for more information.

Function 09H XMS
Allocate Extended Memory Block (EMB)

Allocates an EMB for program use.

Input: AH = 09H

1296

DX = Size of the requested block in kilobytes

Output: AX = 0001H: Operation completed

AX = 0000H: Error

BL = Error code (see below)

DX = Handle for additional EMB access, if additional access is possible

Remarks: Interrupt 2FH must recognize an XMS driver, and the XMS driver jump location must be specified, before calling this function.

The returned handle accesses the EMB during all subsequent calls, and must therefore be stored in the program. If the program loses the handle, the user can only free the EMB by resetting the computer.

The XMS can only honor an EMB allocation if a handle is free, and if a large enough memory block is available. Since the number of handles is limited (usually 32), large EMBs should be allocated to avoid calling the function too often, and to minimize handle calls.

The allocated EMB must be freed using 0AH before program execution ends, or the EMB will be lost for passing to subsequent applications.

Function 0AH   XMS
Free allocated Extended Memory Block (EMB)

Frees an Extended Memory Block (EMB) previously allocated using function 09H.

Input: AH = 0AH

DX = Handle

Output: AX = 0001H: Operation completed

AX = 0000H: Error

BL = Error code (see below)

Remarks: Interrupt 2FH must recognize an XMS driver, and the XMS driver jump location must be specified, before calling this function.

Calling function 0AH destroys the EMB's current contents and invalidates the handle.

Function 0BH   XMS
Move Extended Memory Block (EMB)

Transfers memory between conventional RAM and extended memory, or copies blocks within conventional RAM or extended memory.

Input: AH = 0BH

DS:SI = Pointer to the following structure which determines the memory area to be copied and its destination.

Output: AX = 0001H: Operation completed

AX = 0000H: Error

BL = Error code (see below)

Remarks: Interrupt 2FH must recognize an XMS driver, and the XMS driver jump location must be specified, before calling this function.

A handle value of 0 indicates access to conventional RAM. The segment and offset addresses specify the beginning of the memory block.

When addressing an EMB, the handle returned after allocating the EMB using function 09H must be indicated. The offset address then represents the offset relative to the start of the block.

The handles specified cannot be handles whose corresponding EMB was locked using function 0CH.

If the indicated blocks overlap, the source block must precede the destination block, or the function may fail.

The source block copies faster if both blocks begin at even numbered addresses in an AT, or if both blocks begin at addresses divisible by four in an 80386.

Addr.	Content	Type
	The Extended Memory Move Structure	
+00H	Block length in bytes (must be an even number)	1 DWORD
+04H	Handle of the source Block	1 WORD
+06H	Source block offset, where copying starts	1 DWORD
+0AH	Handle of the destination Block	1 WORD
+0CH	Destination block offset, where copying starts	1 DWORD
	Length: 16 bytes	

Function 0CH   **XMS**
Lock Extended Memory Block (EMB)

Locks an Extended Memory Block (EMB) to a specific memory location. The XMM moves EMBs to different locations after the release of an EMB, thus preventing memory gaps. Function 0CH ensures that the specified EMB remains in the same location in memory.

Input:	AH = 0CH
	DX = EMB handle
Output:	AX = 0001H: Operation completed
	AX = 0000H: Error
	BL = Error code (see below)
	DX:BX = Linear 32-bit address of the EMB in memory
Remarks:	Interrupt 2FH must recognize an XMS driver, and the XMS driver jump location must be specified, before calling this function.
	The function call returns the EMB's address. This address is valid until the EMB is freed.
	Release locked blocks as soon as possible using function 0DH. This minimizes any hindering of the XMM's tasks.
	Calls to functions 0CH and 0DH are recorded internally with the help of a counter, which increments with every call to function 0CH and decrements with every call to function 0DH. Only after reaching the value 0 can the corresponding EMB be unlocked.

Function 0DH   **XMS**
Unlock Extended Memory Block (EMB)

Unlocks an Extended Memory Block (EMB) previously locked using function 0DH. The XMM moves EMBs to different locations after the release of an EMB, thus preventing memory gaps. Function 0DH ensures that the specified EMB is also available to the XMM.

Input:	AH = 0DH

	DX = EMB handle
Output:	AX = 0001H: Operation completed
	AX = 0000H: Error
	BL = Error code (see below)
Remarks:	Interrupt 2FH must recognize an XMS driver, and the XMS driver jump location must be specified, before calling this function.

This function invalidates the EMB address returned during the call of function 0CH.

Calls to functions 0CH and 0DH are recorded internally with the help of a counter, which increments with every call to function 0CH and decrements with every call to function 0DH. Only after reaching the value 0 can the corresponding EMB be unlocked.

Function 0EH   XMS
Get EMB handle information

Provides information about an EMB. This includes the block size, its block counter and the number of handles free.

Input:	AH = 0EH
	DX = EMB handle
Output:	AX = 0001H: Operation completed
	BH = Block counter
	BL = Number of free EMB handles
	DX = EMB length in kilobytes
	DX = 0000H: Error
	BL = Error code (see below)
Remarks:	Interrupt 2FH must recognize an XMS driver, and the XMS driver jump location must be specified, before calling this function.

Calls to functions 0CH and 0DH are recorded internally with the help of a block counter, which increments with every call to function 0CH and decrements with every call to function 0DH. A value unequal to zero indicates the number of calls which must be made to 0DH before the EMB can be unlocked.

Function 0FH   XMS
Resize Extended Memory Block (EMB)

Allows the enlargement or reduction of the size of an EMB.

Input:	AH = 0FH
	BX = New size in kilobytes
	DX = EMB handle
Output:	AX = 0001H: Operation completed
	AX = 0000H: Error
	BL = Error code (see below)
Remarks:	Interrupt 2FH must recognize an XMS driver, and the XMS driver jump location must be specified, before calling this function.

The indicated EMB must not be locked.

If you reduce the size of the EMB, the contents of the upper end of the EMB are lost.

Function 10H   **XMS**
Allocate Upper Memory Block (UMB)

Allocates an upper memory block in the RAM existing between the 640K limit and the beginning of extended memory.

Input: AH = 10H
                DX = Size of the requested memory blocks in paragraphs
Output: AX = 0001H: Operation completed
                BX = Segment address of the UMB
                BX = 0000H: Error
                BL = Error code (see below)
                DX = Maximum size of an allocatable UMB in paragraphs
Remarks: Interrupt 2FH must recognize an XMS driver, and the XMS driver jump
                location must be specified, before calling this function.
                This function is extremely hardware dependent and not implemented in all
                XMS drivers. After its call the error status must be checked to ensure that a
                UMB actually was allocated.
                Direct UMB access is possible in real mode with the returned segment address.
                During this access, the offset address derived from the conversion of block
                length may not be exceeded.
                This function can also be used to determine the largest available UMB, by
                using an unrealistic value (for example FFFFH) for the size of the requested
                block. No UMB is allocated, but the function returns the length of the largest
                available UMB.

Function 11H   **XMS**
Free allocated Upper Memory Block (UMB)

Frees a UMB previously allocated using function 10H, making the UMB available to other programs.

Input: AH = 11H
                DX = UMB segment address
Output: AX = 0001H: Operation completed
                AX = 0000H: Error
                BL = Error code (see below)
Remarks: Interrupt 2FH must recognize an XMS driver, and the XMS driver jump
                location must be specified, before calling this function.
                After calling function 11H, the UMB's contents are lost. No memory access
                can be made through the block's segment address.
                All allocated UMBs should be released using this function before program
                execution ends. Otherwise, it may not be possible to pass the UMBs to
                subsequent programs.

Appendix H

Mouse Driver Functions

Microsoft has supported its mouse with a software-interface, in the form of the MOUSE.SYS device driver, or the MOUSE.COM program. This interface has been established and is imitated by all other mouse manufacturers. This insures full compatibility with the Microsoft mouse. The various functions of the mouse-interface are called through Interrupt 33h, where a 16 bit value is used as function number, which must be passed in the AX-Register.

Version 8.0 of the mouse driver supports 53 different functions, with function numbers from 0000h to 00034h. However, the functions 11h and 12h, as well as 002Eh are undocumented and therefore are only used inside the mouse driver.

The Microsoft mouse-driver has been subjected to many revisions and enhancements. Therefore numerous variants exist between the version 1.0 and 8.0. Versions with a version number smaller than 6.26 are rarely still in circulation, because they do not work with the latest video cards.

Unfortunately, Microsoft reveals the date of the introduction of the various mouse driver functions only since the function 25h, which was introduced with version 6.26. Many of preceding functions existed since version 1.0, but many were added during the course of development between version 1.0 and 6.26. Since more accurate information is lacking, it will be assumed in the framework of this reference, that these functions have been available since version 1.0. Even if this is not true in a particular case, you can assume that these functions are supported by all mouse-drivers which are in use.

Most mouse functions operate with the AX, BX, CX and DX, registers to pass information from the caller and to return function results. Only in exceptional cases are the ES, SI and DS registers used for the function call, usually when the address of buffers must be passed.

Basically only the content of the register changes for the return of the function results. The content of all other registers remains unchanged. For most functions, the AX-Register is used for the return of the function status, which in case of error indicates the failure of the operation.

Interrupt 33H, Function 00H   **Mouse**
Reset mouse driver

Resets (initializes) the mouse driver.

Input: AX = 00H
Output: AX = Mouse installation status
                        AX=FFFFH: Mouse driver installed
                        AX=0000H: Error, no mouse driver installed
                    BX = Number of mouse buttons
Remarks: The reset process executes the following tasks:
                    Moves the mouse cursor to the center of the screen and clears the cursor from
                    the screen. When enabled, the default cursor appears as an inverse video square.
                    The representation is always in display page 0, independent of the current
                    display mode. The entire screen area becomes the total range of mouse
                    movement.
                    Installs the event handler is installed by a program (default is disabled).
                    Installs light pen emulation (default is disabled).
                    Specifies mouse cursor's speed. Default relative speed is 8 mickeys per 8
                    horizontal pixels and 16 mickeys per 16 vertical pixels.
                    Specifies maximum mouse speed (default is 64 mickeys per second).

Interrupt 33H, Function 01H   **Mouse**
Display mouse cursor

Displays the mouse cursor on the screen. This cursor follows any movement the user makes
with the mouse device.

Input: AX = 01H
Output: No output
Remarks: This function increments an internal counter which determines whether the
                    mouse cursor should be displayed on the screen. When the mouse driver is
                    initialized using function 00H, this cursor contains the value -1 (i.e., the
                    mouse cursor does not appear). If this counter contains the value 0 after calling
                    function 01H, the mouse cursor appears on the screen.
                    The mouse driver follows the mouse movement even when the mouse cursor
                    is not displayed on the screen. After calling this function, the mouse cursor
                    may not appear at the same location as it was when the cursor was previously
                    removed by calling function 00H or function 02H.

Interrupt 33H, Function 02H   **Mouse**
Hide mouse cursor

Removes the mouse cursor from the screen.

Input: AX = 02H
Output: No output
Remarks: This function decrements an internal counter which determines whether the
                    mouse cursor should appear on the screen. If the counter contains the value 0,
                    the mouse cursor is displayed on the screen, while the value -1 removes the
                    mouse cursor from the screen.

The mouse driver follows the mouse movement even when the mouse cursor is not displayed on the screen.

After calling this function, the mouse cursor may not appear at the same location as it was when the cursor was previously removed by calling function 00H or function 02H.

Interrupt 33H, Function 03H   Mouse
Get cursor position/button status

Returns the current position of the mouse cursor and the current status of the mouse buttons.

Input:	AX = 03H
Output	BX = Mouse button status
	Bit 0=1: Left mouse button activated
	Bit 1=1: Right mouse button activated
	Bit 2=1: Center mouse button activated
	Bits 3-15: Unused
	CX = X coordinate (horizontal mouse position)
	DX = Y coordinate (vertical mouse position)
Remarks:	The coordinates returned in the CX and DX registers refer to the pixel positions in the virtual mouse display screen rather than physical positions on the actual display screen.
	If the mouse is equipped with only two mouse buttons, the information about the central mouse button does not have significance.

Interrupt 33H, Function 04H   Mouse
Move mouse cursor

Moves the active mouse cursor to a certain position on the screen.

Input:	AX = 04H
	CX = X coordinate (horizontal mouse position)
	DX = Y coordinate (vertical mouse position)
Output:	No output
Remarks:	The coordinates returned in the CX and DX registers refer to the pixel positions in the virtual mouse display screen rather than physical positions on the actual display screen.
	If the position indicated is outside the range of movement specified by functions 07H and 08H, the function adjusts coordinates so that the mouse cursor remains within this range of movement.
	The mouse cursor moves to the new position, even if the mouse is not currently visible. Once re-enabled, the mouse cursor appears at this new position.

Interrupt 33H, Function 05H   Mouse
Determine number of times mouse button was activated

Informs the calling program of how often a mouse button has been pressed since the last call of function 05H. Function 05H also informs the calling program of the cursor's location on the screen when the button was last activated.

Input:	AX = 05H

BX = Mouse button activated

    BX=0: Left mouse button

    BX=1: Right mouse button

    BX=2: Center mouse button

Output: BX = Status of all mouse buttons:

    Bit 0=1: Left mouse button activated

    Bit 1=1: Right mouse button activated

    Bit 2=1: Center mouse button activated

    Bits 3-15: Unused

    BX = Mouse buttons activated since last function call

    CX = Horizontal mouse position during the last activation

    DX = Vertical mouse position during the last activation

Remarks: The coordinates returned in the CX and DX registers refer to the pixel positions in the virtual mouse display screen rather than physical positions on the actual display screen. The activation counter for the mouse button addressed is reset to 0 when this function is called.

Interrupt 33H, Function 06H   Mouse
Determine number of times mouse button was released

Informs the calling program of how often a mouse button has been released since the last call of function 06H. Function 06H also informs the calling program of the cursor's location on the screen when the button was last activated.

Input: AX = 06H

    BX = mouse button addressed

        BX=0: Left mouse button

        BX=1: Right mouse button

        BX=2: Center mouse button

Output: BX = Status of all mouse buttons

    Bit 0=1: Left mouse button activated

    Bit 1=1: Right mouse button activated

    Bit 2=1: Center mouse button activated

    Bits 3-15: Unused

    BX = Mouse buttons activated since last function call

    CX = Horizontal mouse position during the last activation

    DX = Vertical mouse position during the last activation

Remarks: The coordinates returned in the CX and DX registers refer to the pixel positions in the virtual mouse display screen rather than physical positions on the actual display screen.

               The activation counter for the mouse button addressed is reset to 0 when this function is called.

Interrupt 33H, Function 07H   Mouse
Set horizontal range of movement

Defines the horizontal range of movement for the mouse cursor. Once set, the user cannot move the mouse cursor out of this range.

Input: AX = 07H

    CX = Minimal horizontal cursor position

    DX = Maximum horizontal cursor position

Output:	No output
Remarks:	The coordinates passed in the CX and DX registers refer to the pixel positions in the virtual mouse display screen rather than physical positions on the actual display screen.
	If the mouse cursor is outside of this range when function 07H is called, the mouse driver automatically moves the mouse cursor within the limits of the range of movement. If the value in the DX register is less than the value in the CX registers, the two parameters are exchanged.

Interrupt 33H, Function 08H   **Mouse**
Set vertical range of movement

Defines the vertical range of movement for the mouse cursor. Once set, the user cannot move the mouse cursor out of this range.

Input:	AX = 08H
	CX = Minimum vertical cursor position
	DX = Maximum vertical cursor position
Output:	No output
Remarks:	The coordinates passed in the CX and DX registers refer to the pixel positions in the virtual mouse display screen rather than physical positions on the actual display screen.
	If the mouse cursor is outside of this range when function 07H is called, the mouse driver automatically moves the mouse cursor within the limits of the range of movement.
	If the value in the DX register is less than the value in the CX registers, the two parameters are exchanged.

Interrupt 33H, Function 09H   **Mouse**
Set mouse cursor (graphic mode)

Defines the appearance of the mouse cursor in graphic mode, as well as the bitfield which compensates for the pixels around the mouse cursor.

Input:	AX = 09H
	BX = Cursor width starting at left border of bitfield
	CX = Cursor height starting at top border of bitfield
	ES = Segment address of bitfield
	DX = Offset address of bitfield
Output:	No output
Remarks:	The bitfield consists of 64 bytes, of which the first 32 are an AND comparison, and the remaining 32 are an OR combination. Both sets of bytes are based upon the current pixel pattern.

Interrupt 33H, Function 0AH   **Mouse**
Set mouse cursor (text mode)

Defines the bitmask which specifies the appearance of the mouse cursor in text mode.

Input:	AX = 0AH
	BX = Cursor type
	BX=0: Software cursor
	BX=1: Hardware cursor

CX = AND mask (software cursor) or starting line (hardware cursor)

DX = XOR mask (software cursor) or ending line (hardware cursor)

Output: No output

Remarks: If the software cursor is selected, the code of the character beneath the mouse cursor and its attribute byte are combined logically with the mask in the CX register through a binary AND, and then with the value in the DX register through an exclusive OR (XOR). The attribute byte is combined with the most significant byte (CH and DH). The character code is combined with the least significant byte (CL and DL).

The hardware cursor is the same shape as the normal text mode cursor. Monochrome mode values for the starting and ending lines range from 0 to 13. Color mode values for the starting and ending lines range from 0 to 7.

Interrupt 33H, Function 0BH   Mouse
Determine movement values

Determines the distance between the current mouse position and the mouse position during the last call of function 0BH.

Input: AX = 0BH

Output: CX = Horizontal distance from last point in mickeys

                 DX = Vertical distance from last point in mickeys

Remarks: These values must be interpreted as signed numbers. Positive values indicate movement toward the bottom or right border of the screen, while negative values indicate movement toward the top or left border of the screen.

These values are given in mickeys.(1 mickey=1/200 inch) rather than in pixels.

Interrupt 33H, Function 0CH   Mouse
Set event handler

Sets the address of an event handler called by the mouse driver when a particular mouse event occurs.

Input: AX = 0CH

                 CX = Events which trigger the call of the event handler (event mask)

                       Bit 0: Mouse movement

                       Bit 1: Left mouse button activated

                       Bit 2: Left mouse button released

                       Bit 3: Right mouse button activated

                       Bit 4: Right mouse button released

                       Bit 5: Center mouse button activated

                       Bit 6: Center mouse button released

                       Bits 7-15: Unused

                 ES = Segment address of handler

                 DX = Offset address of handler

Output: No output

Remarks: The event handler is called by the mouse driver through a FAR call assembler instruction, and therefore must be terminated with a FAR RET instruction. None of the various processor registers may be returned to the caller with a changed content.

The mouse driver passes the following information to the event handler through the processor registers during the call:

AX = event mask. The bits correspond to the various events as indicated in the CX register during the installation of the event handler. In addition, other bits can be set, since the value reflects the current status of the mouse driver, and is not limited to the selected events.

BX = mouse button status:
    Bit 0 = Left mouse button activated
    Bit 1 = Right mouse button activated
    Bit 2 = Center mouse button activated

CX = horizontal mouse position.

DX = vertical mouse position.

SI = length of last horizontal mouse movement.

DI = length of the last vertical mouse movement.

DS = data segment of the mouse driver.

The coordinates returned in the CX and DX registers refer to the pixel positions in the virtual mouse display screen rather than physical positions on the actual display screen.

The values in the SI and DI registers refer to mickeys (one mickey = 1/200 inch).

These mickey values must be interpreted as signed numbers. Positive values indicate movement toward the bottom or right border of the screen, while negative values indicate movement toward the top or left border of the screen.

Interrupt 33H, Function 0DH
Enable light pen emulation
Mouse

Enables emulation of the light pen, and simulates a light pen which if none is present.

Input:	AX = 0DH
Output:	No output
Remarks:	Light pen emulation only makes sense when used with an application which supports the light pen, or makes light pen reading routines available (e.g., the PEN command in PC-BASIC).

The light pen and mouse are closely related in programming: The position of the mouse cursor is directly related to the light pen's position on the screen, and pressing the left and right mouse button has the same result as pressing the button on the light pen.

Interrupt 33H, Function 0EH
Disable light pen emulation
Mouse

Disables the light pen emulation enabled by a previous call to function 0DH.

Input:	AX = 0EH
Output:	No output
Remarks:	Light pen emulation only makes sense when used with an application which supports the light pen, or makes light pen reading routines available (e.g., the PEN command in PC-BASIC).

The light pen and mouse are closely related in programming: The position of the mouse cursor is directly related to the light pen's position on the screen, and pressing the left and right mouse button has the same result as pressing the button on the light pen.

Interrupt 33H, Function 0FH   **Mouse**
Set cursor speed

Defines the relationship between mickeys and screen pixels. This specifies the sensitivity of the mouse and the speed at which the mouse cursor moves across the screen.

Input:	AX = 0FH
	CX = Number of horizontal mickeys
	DX = Number of vertical mickeys
Output:	No output
Remarks:	Values in the CX and DX registers can range from 1 to 32767.

The default setting is 8 horizontal mickeys and 16 vertical mickeys. This causes the mouse cursor to move twice as fast horizontally as it moves vertically.

Calling function 00H (Reset mouse driver) changes any previously set values to the default values.

Interrupt 33H, Function 10H   **Mouse**
Exclusion area

Designates any area of the screen as an exclusion area. The mouse cursor disappears if moved into the exclusion area.

Input:	AX = 10H
	CX = X-coordinate, upper left corner of exclusion area
	DX = Y-coordinate, upper left corner of exclusion area
	SI = X-coordinate, lower right corner of exclusion area
	DI = Y-coordinate, lower right corner of exclusion area
Output:	No output
Remarks:	The coordinates passed in the CX, DX, DI and SI registers refer to the pixel positions in the virtual mouse display screen rather than physical positions on the actual display screen.

Calling function 00H (Reset mouse driver) or function 01H (Display mouse cursor) deletes the exclusion area coordinates.

Interrupt 33H, Function 11H   **Mouse**
Undocumented   **(Version 1.0 and up)**

This undocumented function is used exclusively by the mouse driver, and cannot be called from a program.

Interrupt 33H, Function 12H   **Mouse**
Undocumented   **(Version 1.0 and up)**

This undocumented function is used exclusively by the mouse driver, and cannot be called from a program.

Interrupt 33H, Function 13H   **Mouse**
Set maximum for mouse speed doubling

Sets the maximum limit for doubling mouse speed. If the speed of the mouse movement exceeds a certain limit, the mouse driver doubles the mouse cursor speed by doubling the movement's relationship between points and mickeys.

Input: AX = 13H
                DX = Limit in mickeys per second
Output: No output
Remarks: 1 mickey=1/200 inches.
                To prevent doubling of the mouse speed, the limit can be set higher.
                Speeds in excess of 5,000 mickeys per second cannot be achieved by practical means.

Interrupt 33H, Function 14H   **Mouse**
Exchange event handlers

Installs a new event handler for certain mouse events, but also retains the address of the old event handler.

Input: AX = 14H
                CX = Events which should trigger event handler call
                Bit 0: Mouse movement
                Bit 1: Left mouse button activated
                Bit 2: Left mouse button released
                Bit 3: Right mouse button activated
                Bit 4: Right mouse button released
                Bit 5: Center mouse button activated
                Bit 6: Center mouse button released
                Bit 7-15: Unused

                ES = Segment address of new event handler
                DX = Offset address of new event handler
Output: CX = Event mask of the previously installed event handler
                ES = Segment address of previously installed event handler
                DX = Offset address of previously installed event handler
Remarks: The event handler is called by the mouse driver through a FAR call assembler instruction, and therefore must be terminated with a FAR RET instruction. None of the various processor registers may be returned to the caller with a changed content.
                The mouse driver passes the following information to the event handler through the processor registers during the call:
                AX = event mask. The bits correspond to the various events as indicated in the CX register during the installation of the event handler. In addition, other bits can be set, since the value reflects the current status of the mouse driver, and is not limited to the selected events.
                BX = mouse button status:
                        Bit 0 = Left mouse button activated
                        Bit 1 = Right mouse button activated
                        Bit 2 = Center mouse button activated
                CX = horizontal mouse position.

DX = vertical mouse position.

SI = length of last horizontal mouse movement.

DI = length of the last vertical mouse movement.

DS = data segment of the mouse driver.

The coordinates returned in the CX and DX registers refer to the pixel positions in the virtual mouse display screen rather than physical positions on the actual display screen.

The values in the SI and DI registers refer to mickeys (one mickey = 1/200 inch).

These mickey values must be interpreted as signed numbers. Positive values indicate movement toward the bottom or right border of the screen, while negative values indicate movement toward the top or left border of the screen.

Interrupt 33H, Function 15H   Mouse
Determine mouse status buffer size

Returns the size of the mouse status buffer, in which a program can store the complete status of the mouse driver.

Input: AX = 15H
Output: BX = Mouse status buffer size in bytes
Remarks: Function 16H (Store mouse status) stores the mouse status in the buffer.

Interrupt 33H, Function 16H   Mouse
Store mouse status

Stores mouse status information in a buffer.

Input: AX = 16H
                ES = Segment address of mouse status buffer
                DX = Offset address of mouse status buffer
Output: No output
Remarks: The caller is responsible for creating a buffer large enough to contain all the status information. Before calling this function, call function 15H (Determine mouse status buffer size) to determine the size of the mouse status buffer.

                This function works well when called before executing a program using the EXEC function. This allows the mouse status to be saved in memory, then restored from within the called program.

Interrupt 33H, Function 17H   Mouse
Restore mouse status

Reads all mouse parameters from a buffer stored by function 16H.

Input: AX = 17H
                ES = Segment address of mouse status buffer
                DX = Offset address of mouse status buffer
Output: No output

Interrupt 33H, Function 18H
Install alternate event handler

This function permits a program to install a limited range event handler. This handler can be called by the mouse driver when certain mouse events occur in conjunction with the keyboard.

Input:
    AX = 0018H
    CX = Events which should trigger the call of the event handler
        Bit 0: Mouse movement
        Bit 1: Left mouse button activated
        Bit 2: Left mouse button released
        Bit 3: Right mouse button activated
        Bit 4: Right mouse button released
        Bit 5: Shift key pressed during mouse button event
        Bit 6: Ctrl key pressed during mouse button event
        Bit 7: Alt key pressed during mouse button event
        Bits 8-15: Unused
    ES = Segment address of event handler
    DX = Offset address of event handler

Output:
    AX = Installation status
        AX=0018H: Event handler installed
        AX=FFFFH: Event handler could not be installed

Remarks:
At least one of bits 5 to 7 must be set in the event mask of the CX register to ensure that the event reacts to at least one of the control keys. If the programmer prefers not to read the Shift, Ctrl or Alt keys along with mouse buttons, use functions 0CH or 14H instead.

An error can occur if three alternate event handlers were previously installed, or if an event handler with the same event mask already exists.

Remarks:
The event handler is called by the mouse driver through a FAR call assembler instruction, and therefore must be terminated with a FAR RET instruction. None of the various processor registers may be returned to the caller with a changed content.

The mouse driver passes the following information to the event handler through the processor registers during the call:

    AX = event mask. The bits correspond to the various events as indicated in the CX register during the installation of the event handler. In addition, other bits can be set, since the value reflects the current status of the mouse driver, and is not limited to the selected events.

    BX = mouse button status:
        Bit 0 = Left mouse button activated
        Bit 1 = Right mouse button activated
        Bit 2 = Center mouse button activated

    CX = horizontal mouse position.
    DX = vertical mouse position.
    SI = length of last horizontal mouse movement.
    DI = length of the last vertical mouse movement.
    DS = data segment of the mouse driver.

The coordinates returned in the CX and DX registers refer to the pixel positions in the virtual mouse display screen rather than physical positions on the actual display screen.

The values in the SI and DI registers refer to mickeys (one mickey = 1/200 inch).

These mickey values must be interpreted as signed numbers. Positive values indicate movement toward the bottom or right border of the screen, while negative values indicate movement toward the top or left border of the screen.

Interrupt 33H, Function 19H   **Mouse**
Determine address of alternate event handler

Returns the address of an alternate event handler to the caller.

Input:	AX = 19H
	CX = Event handler event mask
Output:	CX = 00H: Error
	ES = Segment address of event handler
	DX = Offset address of event handler
Remarks:	See the description of function 18H above for additional information about the meanings of each bit in the event mask.

The function call fails if no alternate event handler with the indicated event mask was previously installed.

Interrupt 33H, Function 1AH   **Mouse**
Set mouse sensitivity

Defines the relationship between physical mouse movement and mouse cursor movement. Also defines the maximum for doubling mouse speed.

Input:	AX = 1AH
	BX = Number of horizontal mickeys
	CX = Number of vertical mickeys
	DX = Maximum limit for doubling the mouse speed
Output:	No output
Remarks:	Values in the CX and DX registers can range from 1 to 32767.

The default setting is 8 horizontal mickeys and 16 vertical mickeys. This causes the mouse cursor to move twice as fast horizontally as it moves vertically.

To prevent doubling of the mouse speed, the limit can be set higher.

Speeds in excess of 5,000 mickeys per second cannot be achieved by practical means.

Calling function 00H (Reset mouse driver) changes any previously set values to the default values.

Interrupt 33H, Function 1BH   **Mouse**
Determine mouse sensitivity

Returns the parameters previously set by calling function 1AH or functions 0FH and 13H.

Input:	AX = 1BH
Output:	BX = Number of horizontal mickeys
	CX = Number of vertical mickeys
	DX = Maximum limit for doubling the mouse speed

Interrupt 33H, Function 1CH
Set mouse hardware interrupt rate

Determines the frequency at which the mouse hardware reads the current mouse position and mouse button status.

Input:	AX = 1CH
	BX = Interrupt rate
	Bit 0: No interrupts
	Bit 1: 30 interrupts per second
	Bit 2: 50 interrupts per second
	Bit 3: 100 interrupts per second
	Bit 4: 200 interrupts per second
	Bits 5-15: Unused
Output:	No output
Remarks:	This function is only available for the Inport mouse.

If more than one bit is set in the BX register, only the least significant bit which is set counts.

The mouse's resolution increases with the number of interrupts. The increased number of mouse interrupts decreases the speed of the foreground program.

Interrupt 33H, Function 1DH
Set display page

Specifies the display page on which the mouse cursor appears.

Input:	AX = 1DH
	BX = Number of the display page
Output:	No output
Remarks:	Default value is display page 0.

Calling this function only makes sense if the application program works with several display pages, as available on CGA, EGA and VGA cards.

Interrupt 33H, Function 1EH
Determine display page

Determines the display page on which the mouse cursor appears.

Input:	AX = 1EH
Output:	BX = Number of the display page

Interrupt 33H, Function 1FH
Disable mouse driver

Deactivates the current mouse driver and returns the address of the previous interrupt handlers for interrupt 33H.

Input:	AX = 1FH
Output:	AX = Error status
	AX=FFFFH: Error
	AX=1FH: O.K.
	ES = Segment address of previous event handler
	BX = Offset address of previous event handler

Remarks: This call releases any previously installed and active mouse driver interrupt routines. The exception to this is the handler for interrupt 33H, but the caller can reload this interrupt vector with its original value since this address is returned in the ES:BX register pair.

Interrupt 33H, Function 20H
Enable mouse driver

Mouse

Activates a mouse driver previously deactivated by function 1FH.

Input: AX = 20H
Output: No output

Interrupt 33H, Function 21H
Reset mouse driver

Mouse

Resets the mouse driver, disables the mouse cursor and disables the currently installed event handler.

Input: AX = 21H
Output: AX = Error status
AX=FFFFH: Error
AX=0021H: O.K.
BX = Number of mouse buttons
Remarks: Unlike function 00H, this function does not perform a total mouse hardware reset.

Interrupt 33H, Function 22H
Set language for messages

Mouse

Specifies language for mouse messages.

Input: AX = 22H
BX = Language number
BX=0: English
BX=1: French
BX=2: Dutch
BX=3: German
BX=4: Swedish
BX=5: Finnish
BX=6: Spanish
BX=7: Portuguese
BX=8: Italian
Output: No output
Remarks: This function applies only to the mouse driver published for international use. Function 22H is not available on the domestic version of the mouse driver.

Interrupt 33H, Function 23H
Get language number

Mouse

Returns the number indicating the language under which the mouse driver is operating.

Input: AX = 23H
Output: BX = Language number

1314

BX=0: English

BX=1: French

BX=2: Dutch

BX=3: German

BX=4: Swedish

BX=5: Finnish

BX=6: Spanish

BX=7: Portuguese

BX=8: Italian

Remarks: This function applies only to the mouse driver published for international use. Function 23H is not available on the domestic version of the mouse driver.

Interrupt 33H, Function 24H   Mouse
Determine mouse type

Determines the type of mouse installed and the version number of the mouse driver.

Input: AX = 24H

Output: BH = Whole number of the version number

BL = Fraction of the version number

CH = Mouse type

CH=1: Bus mouse

CH=2: Serial mouse

CH=3: Inport mouse

CH=4: PS/2 mouse

CH=5: HP mouse

CL = IRQ number

CL=0: PS/2

CL=2, 3, 4, 5 or 7: IRQ number in the PC

Remarks: If the version number of the mouse driver is for example 6.24, the value 6 is returned in the BH register and the value 24 is returned in the BL register.

Interrupt 33H, Function 25H   Mouse
Get general driver information   (Version 6.26 and up)

Returns general information describing the mouse driver, such as the driver type and cursor type.

Input: AX = 25H

Output: AX = General information (see below)

BX = OS/2 status information

CX = OS/2 status information

DX = OS/2 status information

Remarks: The AX register receives the general information as a bit field. These bits have the following meanings:

Bit 15: Type of driver

0(b)=COM file

1(b)=Device driver accessed through CONFIG.SYS

Bit 12 and 13: Mouse cursor information

00(b)=Software text cursor

01(b)=Hardware text cursor

10(b), 11(b)=Graphic cursor

Bits 8 to 11 : Mouse hardware interrupt rate

The arguments returned in the BX, CX and DX registers apply only to mouse drivers in OS/2. They have no significance in DOS programming.

Interrupt 33H, Function 26H **Mouse**
Get maximum virtual coordinates **(Version 6.26 and up)**

Returns the maximum virtual mouse display coordinates, and indicates whether the mouse driver is active or inactive.

Input:	AX = 26H
Output:	BX = Mouse driver status
	BX=0: Inactive
	BX>0: Active
	CX = Maximum virtual X-coordinate
	DX = Maximum virtualY-coordinate
Remarks:	Functions 1FH and 20H control the mouse driver status, returned in the BX register after calling this function.
	The values returned in the CX and DX registers describe the size of the virtual mouse display screen, not the cursor positions specified in functions 07H and 08H.

Interrupt 33H, Function 27H **Mouse**
Get masks and mickey counts **(Version 7.01 and up)**

Reads screen and cursor masks. Also, this function returns information about mouse movement since the last reading.

Input:	AX = 27H
Output:	AX = AND mask (software cursor) or starting scan line (hardware cursor)
	BX = XOR mask (software cursor) or ending scan line (hardware cursor)
	CX = Length of horizontal movement in mickeys
	DX = Length of vertical movement in mickeys
Remarks:	The values returned vary with the type of cursor active during the function call. If the hardware cursor is active, the function receives the starting and ending scan lines of the cursor. If a software cursor is active, the function receives the current screen and cursor mask values.
	This function has been supported since Version 7.01 of the mouse driver. Version 7.02 was the first version to return the scan line information describing the hardware cursor.
	The movement values returned in the CX and DX registers are taken directly from the mouse hardware, and are not influenced by various software settings such as the threshold value for doubling mouse speed, or the acceleration curve.

Interrupt 33H, Function 28H **Mouse**
Set video mode **(Version 7.0 and up)**

Sets the video mode if the selected mode is supported by the active video card.

Input:	AX = 28H
	CX = Video mode number
	DX = Screen font size
Output:	CX = Function status

1316

Remarks: A list of the available video modes and their code numbers can be queried with function 29H.

The value zero is returned in the CX register if the video mode indicated is supported bu the active video-hardware and therefore could be set. Otherwise the code number from the AX register is returned.

The calling parameter in DX is only expected with a few video modes which operate with settable font sizes. In the higher level byte of DX the size of the font, together with the Y-axis and in the lower level byte the extent along the X-axis, must be coded.

Interrupt 33H, Function 29H
Count video modes

Mouse
(Version 7.0 and up)

Gets a numbered list of video modes supported by the active video card.

Input: AX = 29H
CX = Video mode
  CX=0: First video mode
  CX<>0: Next video mode
Output: BX = Segment of string
CX = Video mode number
DX = Offset of string
Remarks: Multiple calls of this function are required to generate a complete list of supported video modes. The value 0 must be passed in the CX parameter for the first call, with values unequal to 0 passed for any subsequent calls.

Each subsequent call describes a video mode. When the CX register returns 0, this indicates that all available video modes have been read.

Function 29H doesn't directly return the video mode's type (text or graphic), resolution or color capability. This information can usually be obtained from an ASCII string whose address is returned in the BX:DX register pair. If this ASCII string is available, and if the BX:DX registers contain values other than 0, the ASCII string ends with a dollar sign and a null byte.

Interrupt 33H, Function 2AH
Get cursor hotspot

Mouse
(Version 7.02 and up)

Returns information about the mouse type and cursor hotspot.

Input: AX = 2AH
Output: AX = Internal cursor flag
BX = Hotspot X-coordinate
CX = Hotspot Y-coordinate
DX = Type of mouse
Remarks: The internal cursor flag indicates whether the mouse cursor is visible or not. Functions 01H and 02H indirectly influence this flag. A value of 0 signals that the mouse cursor is currently invisible. Any other value indicates that the mouse cursor is currently visible.

The hotspot is the pixel in a graphic cursor mask whose position is returned when reading cursor position. Its distance from the upper-left corner of the bit mask is returned to the BX and CX registers as a signed integer. This integer can range from -128 to 127).

The DX register indicates the mouse type. This type code can be one of the following:

0 = No mouse
1 = Bus mouse
2 = Serial mouse
3 = InPort mouse
4 = PS/2 mouse
5 = Hewlett-Packard mouse

Interrupt 33H, Function 2BH   **Mouse**
Set acceleration curves   **(Version 7.0 and up)**

All four acceleration curves, which the mouse-driver administers internally, can be loaded with the help of this function and one can be selected as the current one.

Input: AX = 2BH
                         BX = Number of curve to activate
                         ES = Segment address of curve array
                         SI = Offset address of curve array
Output: AX = FFFFH: Error
                         AX = 0000H: O.K.
Remarks: This function changes the preset acceleration curves in the driver, by passing the value -1 as the number of the current acceleration curve. The passing of a buffer with the data of the acceleration curves is not required in this case.

                       The four acceleration curves are described through a data structure which is created by the caller in memory and must be passed using the ES:SI registers. See Chapter XXX for more information about this structure.

Interrupt 33H, Function 2CH   **Mouse**
Read acceleration curves   **(Version 7.0 and up)**

Reads the current acceleration curves.

Input: AX = 2CH
Output: AX = 00H: O.K.
                           BX=Number of the current acceleration curve (0 to 3)
                           ES=Segment address of curve array
                           SI=Offset address of curve array
                         AX = FFFH: Error
Remarks: The AX register should be read following every call of this function. The acceleration curves could only be read if the AX register contained a value of 0. The contents of the ES:SI register pair indicate the buffer containing the array describing the current acceleration curve. This data structure corresponds to the format used in function 2BH for setting an acceleration curve.

Interrupt 33H, Function 2DH   **Mouse**
Set/get active acceleration curves   **(Version 7.0 and up)**

Activates one of the four acceleration curves, and reads the current acceleration curve.

Input: AX = 2DH
                         BX = -1: Get current acceleration curve
                         BX = 1 - 4: Set current acceleration curve

Output: AX = 0: O.K.
                  BX=Number of current active acceleration curve
                  ES=Segment address of ASCII string describing acceleration curve
                  SI=Offset address of ASCII string describing acceleration curve
              AX=-2: Bad curve number

Remarks: If the value -1 is passed in the BX register as part of the function call, this
              function returns information describing the current acceleration curve in the
              BX, ES and SI registers. If a value from 1 to 4 is passed in the BX register,
              the corresponding acceleration curve becomes active. If this is the case, the BX
              register returns the current acceleration curve number.

              After setting the current acceleration curve, the ES:SI registers indicate the
              ASCII string containing acceleration curve data (see function 2BH). This string
              contains 16 bytes, and has no special end character (i.e., null byte or $). This
              string provides the symbolic name of the acceleration curve.

Interrupt 33H, Function 2EH   **Mouse**
Undocumented   **(Version 1.0 and up)**

This undocumented function is used exclusively by the mouse driver, and cannot be called from a
program.

Interrupt 33H, Function 2FH   **Mouse**
Mouse hardware reset   **(Version 7.02 and up)**

Resets the mouse hardware without affecting the software configuration (mouse cursor
appearance, threshold value, acceleration curve settings, etc.).

Input: AX = 2FH
Output: AX = FFFFH: O.K.
              AX = 0: Error
Remarks: This function is the hardware equivalent of function 21H, which resets the
              software parameters specified in the mouse driver.

Interrupt 33H, Function 30H   **Mouse**
Set/get ballpoint information   **(Version 7.04 and up)**

This function has been tailored specifically for the needs of the ballpoint mouse.

Input: AX = 30H
              BX = Angle of rotation
              CX = Command code
Output: AX = Function status
              BX = Angle of rotation
              CX = Active buttons
Remarks: After the function call, the function status in AX should be checked
              immediately, because the value -1 indicates that no Ballpoint-Mouse is
              installed. Any other value indicates however the existence of a Ballpoint-
              Mouse and reflects the status of the various mouse-buttons. The individual
              buttons are represented by the following bits in the AX register:
                  Bit 2 = Button 4
                  Bit 3 = Button 2
                  Bit 4 = Button 3

Bit 5 = Button 1

The remaining bits contain the value 0.

If the current angle of rotation and the active buttons are queried with this function, the CX register must be loaded with the value zero before the function call. An angle of rotation in BX is not required at this time.

As a function result, the angle of rotation is returned in the BX register. It is a value between 0 and 360 (degrees). The two active buttons can be read from the high byte of CX, while the inactive buttons are coded into the low byte of this register. In these two bytes are the following bits for the individual buttons:

Bit 2 = Button 4
Bit 3 = Button 2
Bit 4 = Button 3
Bit 5 = Button 1

the remaining bits contain the value 0.

If the mouse-driver should be informed with the help of this function of the current angle of rotation of the Ballpoint-Mouse and the two active buttons selected, the active and inactive buttons must be coded into the CX register. The coding is exactly as in the return for the active and inactive buttons after a query (see above). In addition, a value between 0 and 360 degrees is expected as the angle of rotation in BX.

Interrupt 33H, Function 31H   Mouse
Get minimum/maximum virtual coordinates   (Version 7.05 and up)

Returns current minimum and maximum coordinates of the virtual mouse display screen in the current video mode.

Input:	AX = 31H
Output:	AX = Minimum X-coordinate
	BX = Minimum Y-coordinate
	CX = Maximum X-coordinate
	DX = Maximum Y-coordinate
Remarks:	Functions 07H and 08H affect the size of the virtual mouse display screen.

Interrupt 33H, Function 32H   Mouse
Get active advanced Functions   (Version 7.05 and up)

Returns information describing advanced functions supported by the mouse driver, and not accessible from function 25H.

Input:	AX = 32H
Output:	AX = Supported functions
Remarks:	The function result in AX is a bit field, where each bit stands for a function. If it is set, the function is supported.
Remarks:	The AX register receives the function support as a bit field. These bits have the following meanings:
	Bit 15=Function 25H
	Bit 14=Function 26H
	Bit 13=Function 27H
	Bit 12=Function 28H
	Bit 11=Function 29H
	Bit 10=Function 2AH

Bit 9=Function 2BH
Bit 8=Function 2CH
Bit 7=Function 2DH
Bit 6=Function 2EH
Bit 5=Function 2FH
Bit 4=Function 30H
Bit 3=Function 31H
Bit 1=Function 32H
Bit 0=Function 33H

Interrupt 33H, Function 33H　　　　　　　　　　　　　　　　**Mouse**
Get switch settings　　　　　　　　　　　　　**(Version 7.05 and up)**

Returns all mouse parameters in the mouse driver that can be set through hardware or software.

Input:	AX = 33H
	CX = Buffer length
	ES = Segment address of buffer
	DX = Offset address of buffer
Output:	AX = 0
	CX = Number of bytes in buffer
	ES = Segment address of buffer
	DX = Offset address of buffer
Remarks:	The buffer has the following structure:

Offset	Content	Range
0	Mouse type (low nibble)	0-5
0	Mouse type (high nibble)	0-4
1	Language	0-10
2	Horizontal sensitivity	0-100
3	Vertical sensitivity	0-100
4	Double threshold	0-100
5	Ballistic curve	1-4
6	Interrupt rate	1-4
7	Cursor override mask	0-255
8	Laptop adjustment	0-255
9	Memory type	0-2
10	Super VGA support	0-1
11	Rotation angle	0-359
13	Primary button	1-4
14	Secondary button	1-4
15	Click lock enabled	0-1
16	Acceleration curve data	Bytes 16-339

Interrupt 33H, Function 34H　　　　　　　　　　　　　　　　**Mouse**
Get MOUSE.INI location　　　　　　　　　　　　**(Version 8.0 and up)**

Returns the exact path designation of the MOUSE.INI file as an ASCII string. This function applies only to Microsoft Windows.

Input:	AX = 34H
Output:	AX = 0
	ES = Segment address of buffer
	DX = Offset address of buffer

Remarks: The ASCII string is terminated by a null byte.

The path of MOUSE.INI is obtained from the MOUSE variable. If this variable was not defined, MOUSE.INI is assumed to be in the directory containing a mouse driver.

Appendix I

Hardware Interrupts

Interrupt 00H   **Hardware (CPU)**
Division by zero

The CPU calls this interrupt when it encounters a divisor of 0 during one of the two assembly language division instructions (DIV or IDIV). According to the rules of mathematics, dividing a number by 0 is illegal. During the booting process, this interrupt points to a routine that, when called, displays the "Division by Zero" error message (or a similar message) on the screen. The interrupt continues with the execution of the current program.

Interrupt 01H   **Hardware (CPU)**
Single step

The CPU calls this interrupt when the TRAP bit in the flag register of the CPU has been set to 1. Then the interrupt is called after the execution of each assembly language instruction. This allows the user to follow these instructions, determine the changes in register contents and determine which instructions are executed. To prevent the call of the interrupt after the execution of every instruction in the trap routine (which would create an endless loop and a stack overflow), the processor resets the TRAP bit upon entry to the trap routine. If the trap routine ends with the IRET instruction, it automatically resets the TRAP bit to its old value by restoring the complete flag register from the stack. Because of this, the execution of the next instruction calls interrupt 1 again. Once the programmer has obtained the necessary information about a program from single step mode, the TRAP mode (or TRAP bit) can be disabled.

Interrupt 02H   **Hardware (CPU)**
NMI

The hardware calls this interrupt when an error is discovered in the RAM chips. The system calls the non-maskable interrupt because this type of error impairs the capabilities of the system, and can lead to a crash. The NMI has the highest priority of all interrupts and therefore is executed faster than other interrupts. The NMI usually calls a BIOS routine which informs the user of a memory error, lists the number of defective memory chips and stops the system.

If the NMI detects an error, the math coprocessor included in some PCs can also trigger the NMI. Even though NMI usually cannot be suppressed, the PC allows an exception to this rule. Some PC/XT and AT models have a special port (port A0H on PCs and XTs, port 70H on ATs). If a 0 value is written to one of these ports, the NMI interrupt is disabled . If the ports return the value 80H, the NMI interrupt is enabled.

Interrupt 03H   **Hardware (CPU)**
Breakpoint

While the other interrupts can be called with a two-byte assembly language instruction (first byte CDH, second byte the number of the interrupt), interrupt 3 is called by the single-byte instruction CCH. This interrupt can be used to test programs when you want to execute the program up to a certain instruction, then stop and display the current register contents. Utilities designed for program testing like DEBUG implement this by placing calls for interrupt 3 where the break should occur. When the program is executed and the processor reaches the instruction, it calls interrupt 3. The program testing utility contains a routine which displays the register contents and other information.

Interrupt 04H   **Hardware (CPU)**
Overflow

This interrupt can be called by the INTO (INTerrupt on Overflow) conditional assembly language instruction. The call occurs when the overflow bit in the flag register is set during the execution of the INTO instruction. This can happen following math operations (e.g., multiplication with the MUL instruction) that produce a result which cannot be represented within a specified number of bits. This interrupt can also be called with the normal INT instruction, but this instruction isn't controlled by the status of the set overflow bit. Since it is seldom used, DOS points this interrupt to an IRET instruction.

Interrupt 05H   **BIOS**
Hardcopy

BIOS calls this interrupt when the user presses the <Prt Sc> key. The system then makes a hardcopy by sending the current screen contents to a printer. BIOS initializes the interrupt vector from the vector table and points to the BIOS hardcopy routine in ROM-BIOS. Assembly language and programs written in higher level languages can use this interrupt with the INT instruction to get a hardcopy during program execution.

Interrupt 08H   **Hardware (8259 interrupt controller)**
Timer

In the PC, the 8259 timer chip receives 1,193,180 signals per second from the heart of the system, which is an oscillating quartz crystal. After 65,536 of these signals (1 second), it triggers a call of interrupt 8, which the 8259 transmits to the CPU. Since the frequency of the call of this interrupt is independent of the system clock frequency, interrupt 8 works well for timekeeping. The PC also uses the interrupt for timekeeping. BIOS points the interrupt vector of this interrupt to its own routine, which is called 18.2 times per second. A time counter increments every second and disables the disk drive motor if disk access hasn't occurred within a certain time period.

Interrupt 09H   **Hardware (8259 interrupt controller)**
Keyboard

PC keyboards contain an independent processor. This Intel processor carries either the number 8048 (PC/XT) or 8042 (AT). This processor monitors the keyboard and registers whether a key was depressed or released. When either of these actions occur, this processor must inform the CPU so that the code of the activated key can be sent to the system and processed. The keyboard instructs the interrupt controller to call interrupt 9. This interrupt calls a BIOS routine that reads the character from the keyboard and places it into the keyboard buffer.

Appendix J

Introduction to Number Systems

Throughout this book we talked about numbers notated in the *binary* and *hexadecimal systems* instead of the normal decimal system. This Appendix presents a brief introduction to these number systems.

Decimal system

Before explaining the new number systems, you should know the basic concepts of the decimal system. The decimal number 1989 can also be written as 1*1000+9*100+8*10+9*1. This shows that if you number the digits from right to left, the first number represents a column of ones, the second number represents a column of tens, the third number represents a column of hundreds and the fourth number represents a column of thousands. The numbers increase from right to left in powers of 10.

The first digit of any number system has the value 1. The factor by which the value increases from one column to the next differs among the number systems. This factor corresponds to the numbers with which the number system works. The factor is 10 with the decimal system because ten different numbers are available for each digit (0 to 9).

This principle of powers for each column also applies to the binary and hexadecimal systems.

Binary system

Since a computer recognizes the numbers 0 and 1 on its lowest functional level, the binary system is essential to computing. The value of the numbers double from column to column because the binary system only uses powers of two for each column (i.e., the numbers 0 and 1 instead of the numbers 0 to 9).

Now let's count the binary places starting from right to left as we did in the decimal example described above. The first (right hand) position counts as one, the second as two, the third as four and the fourth as eight. The places then follow as 16, 32, 64, 128, etc.

For example, 11001 binary converts to 25 decimal, or the equation 1*16+1*8+0*4+0*2+1*1.

Hexadecimal system

Unlike the binary system, the hexadecimal system operates with more basic numbers than the decimal system. This system counts single digits from 0 to F. Since only the ten numbers of the decimal system are able to represent a number, the numbers from 10 to 15 in hexadecimal use the letters A to F in addition to the numbers 0 to 9. AH represents 10, BH for 11, CH for 12, DH for 13, EH for 14 and FH for 15.

By using 16 numbers or letters for each position, the value by which each position increments is 16.

The first position has the value 1, the second 16, the third 256 and the fourth 4,096.

For example, the hexadecimal number FB3H converts into 4,019 decimal, or 15*256+11*16+3*1.

Hex and binary

The hexadecimal system and the binary system are easily converted back and forth. For example, one four-digit binary number converts to a single-digit hexadecimal number. Because of this, the hexadecimal system is an important part of assembly language programming. It's much simpler to convey a byte (an eight-bit number) using two hexadecimal digits than it is for the developer to compute a 16-bit binary equivalent.

This book denotes all binary numbers by the letter b, and all hexadecimal numbers by the letter H.

The following illustrations should help explain number systems more clearly.

Places	5	4	3	2	1
Decimal:	10000	1000	100	10	1
Binary:	16	8	4	2	1
Hexadecimal:	65536	4096	256	16	1

Number positions in each number system

Comparing selected numbers

Decimal	Binary	Hexadecimal
0	0 (b)	0H
1	1 (b)	1H
2	10 (b)	2H
3	11 (b)	3H
4	100 (b)	4H
5	101 (b)	5H
6	110 (b)	6H
7	111 (b)	7H
8	1000 (b)	8H
9	1001 (b)	9H
10	1010 (b)	AH
11	1011 (b)	BH
12	1100 (b)	CH
128	10000000 (b)	80H
129	10000001 (b)	81H
256	100000000 (b)	100H
1024	10000000000 (b)	400H
4096	1000000000000 (b)	1000H
65535	1111111111111111 (b)	FFFFH

Comparing selected numbers in each number system

Program Listings

Appendix L

The Companion Diskette

The companion diskette for this book contains all the source codes and object listings of the programs documented in this book.

You'll find all these companion diskette codes in compressed form as self-extracting archive files using LHA (copyright © Haruyasu Yoshizaki).

The companion diskette contains the following files:

ASM.EXE:

Contains the PCINTERN\ASM directory and stand-alone ASM program source codes, ready for assembly with MASM or TASM.

BAS.EXE:

Contains the PCINTERN\BAS directory and BASIC program source codes, ready for running under QuickBASIC 4.5.

C_PRG.EXE:

Contains the PCINTERN\C_PRG directory, C source codes, supplementary assembly language modules and assembled OBJ files of these modules, for compiling and linking using Microsoft C or Borland Turbo C.

INSTALL.EXE:

Run this program to install the *PC Intern* files to your hard drive.

PAS.EXE:

Contains the PCINTERN\PAS directory, Pascal source codes, supplementary assembly language modules and assembled OBJ files of these modules, for compiling and linking using Borland Turbo Pascal 5.5 or 6.0, or a Turbo Pascal compatible compiler.

Installing the companion diskette

First, read the README.TXT file on the companion diskette. You can load the README.TXT into a word processor or text editor, or use the DOS TYPE command. Insert the companion diskette in a drive, change to that drive and type:

```
TYPE README.TXT (Enter)
```

The README.TXT file contains important information about this companion diskette.

Next, make sure that your hard drive has at least 2.5 megabytes of space available. The uncompressed companion diskette files take up just over 2,000,000 bytes of disk space.

Insert the companion diskette in a disk drive. Make sure your DOS prompt is set to your hard drive and enter whichever one applies to you:

```
A:INSTALL (Enter)
B:INSTALL (Enter)
```

The INSTALL program will ask you for the source drive specifier. Enter the drive specifier you entered to run INSTALL.

The INSTALL program will then ask you for the destination drive specifier. Enter the drive specifier indicating the hard drive to which you want the companion diskette data written.

INSTALL will then create the PCINTERN directory; add the ASM, BAS, C_PRG and PAS directories to the PCINTERN directory; then uncompress the companion diskette files to those directories.

Appendix M

Bibliography

Abrash, Michael	Power Graphics Programming (Que Books, 1989)
Angerneyer, John and K. Jaeger	MS-DOS Developer's Guide (The Waite Group, 1986)
Byres, T.J.	IBM PC/AT (McGraw-Hill, 1986)
Crawford, John H.	Programming the 80386 (Sybex, 1987)
DPMI Committee	DOS Protected Mode Interface (DPMI) Specification (Intel, 1991)
Duncan, Ray (ed.)	Extending DOS (Addison-Wesley, 1990)
Duncan, Ray	Advanced MS-DOS (Microsoft Press, 1986)
IBM Corporation	AT Technical Reference Manual (IBM, 1984)
IBM Corporation	PC Technical Reference Manual (IBM, 1980)
IBM Corporation	XT Technical Reference Manual (IBM, 1981)
Microsoft Corporation	Microsoft Mouse Programmer's Reference (Microsoft Press 1991)
Murray, Pappas	80386/80286 Assembly Language Programming (McGraw-Hill, 1986)
Nance, Barry	Network Programming in C (Que, 1990)
Norton, Peter	The New Peter Norton Programmer's Guide to the IBM PC and PS/2 (Microsoft Press, 1988)
Phoenix Technologies	System BIOS for IBM PC/XT/AT Computers and Compatibles (Addison-Wesley 1989)
Rosch, Winn L.	The Winn Rosch Hardware Bible (Brady, 1989)
Schulman, Andrew (ed.)	DOS Undocumented (Addison-Wesley, 1990)
Schwaderer, David W.	C Programmer's Guide to NetBIOS (Howard W. Sams, 1988)

Sutty, George	Advanced Programmer's Guide to Super VGAs (Brady 1990)
VCPI Committee	Virtual Control Program Interface (Phar Lap Software Inc., 1989)
Wilton, Richard	Programmer's Guide to PC and PS/2 Video Systems (Microsoft Press, 1987)
Young, Michael J.	Performace Programming under MS-DOS (Sybex, 1987)

ASCII Table

Dec	Hex	Char	Dec	Hex	Char	Dec	Hex	Char	Dec	Hex	Char
0	00		32	20		64	40	@	96	60	`
1	01	☺	33	21	!	65	41	A	97	61	a
2	02	☻	34	22	"	66	42	B	98	62	b
3	03	♥	35	23	#	67	43	C	99	63	c
4	04	♦	36	24	$	68	44	D	100	64	d
5	05	♣	37	25	%	69	45	E	101	65	e
6	06	♠	38	26	&	70	46	F	102	66	f
7	07	•	39	27	'	71	47	G	103	67	g
8	08	◘	40	28	(	72	48	H	104	68	h
9	09	o	41	29	)	73	49	I	105	69	i
10	0A	j	42	2A	*	74	4A	J	106	6A	j
11	0B	k	43	2B	+	75	4B	K	107	6B	k
12	0C	l	44	2C	,	76	4C	L	108	6C	l
13	0D	m	45	2D	-	77	4D	M	109	6D	m
14	0E	♪	46	2E	.	78	4E	N	110	6E	n
15	0F	☼	47	2F	/	79	4F	O	111	6F	o
16	10	►	48	30	0	80	50	P	112	70	p
17	11	◄	49	31	1	81	51	Q	113	71	q
18	12	↕	50	32	2	82	52	R	114	72	r
19	13	‼	51	33	3	83	53	S	115	73	s
20	14	¶	52	34	4	84	54	T	116	74	t
21	15	§	53	35	5	85	55	U	117	75	u
22	16	▬	54	36	6	86	56	V	118	76	v
23	17	↕	55	37	7	87	57	W	119	77	w
24	18	↑	56	38	8	88	58	X	120	78	x
25	19	↓	57	39	9	89	59	Y	121	79	y
26	1A	→	58	3A	:	90	5A	Z	122	7A	z
27	1B	←	59	3B	;	91	5B	[	123	7B	{
28	1C	∟	60	3C	<	92	5C	\	124	7C	|
29	1D	↔	61	3D	=	93	5D	]	125	7D	}
30	1E	O	62	3E	>	94	5E	^	126	7E	~
31	1F	P	63	3F	?	95	5F	_	127	7F	Δ

Dec	Hex	Char	Dec	Hex	Char	Dec	Hex	Char	Dec	Hex	Char
128	80	Ç	160	A0	á	192	C0	└	224	E0	α
129	81	ü	161	A1	í	193	C1	┴	225	E1	β
130	82	é	162	A2	ó	194	C2	┬	226	E2	Γ
131	83	â	163	A3	ú	195	C3	├	227	E3	π
132	84	ä	164	A4	ñ	196	C4	─	228	E4	Σ
133	85	à	165	A5	Ñ	197	C5	┼	229	E5	σ
134	86	å	166	A6	ª	198	C6	╞	230	E6	µ
135	87	ç	167	A7	º	199	C7	╟	231	E7	τ
136	88	ê	168	A8	¿	200	C8	╚	232	E8	Φ
137	89	ë	169	A9	⌐	201	C9	╔	233	E9	Θ
138	8A	è	170	AA	¬	202	CA	╩	234	EA	Ω
139	8B	ï	171	AB	½	203	CB	╦	235	EB	δ
140	8C	î	172	AC	¼	204	CC	╠	236	EC	∞
141	8D	ì	173	AD	¡	205	CD	═	237	ED	Ø
142	8E	Ä	174	AE	«	206	CE	╬	238	EE	∈
143	8F	Å	175	AF	»	207	CF	╧	239	EF	∩
144	90	É	176	B0	░	208	D0	╨	240	F0	≡
145	91	æ	177	B1	▒	209	D1	╤	241	F1	±
146	92	Æ	178	B2	▓	210	D2	╥	242	F2	≥
147	93	ô	179	B3	│	211	D3	╙	243	F3	≤
148	94	ö	180	B4	┤	212	D4	╘	244	F4	⌠
149	95	ò	181	B5	╡	213	D5	╒	245	F5	⌡
150	96	û	182	B6	╢	214	D6	╓	246	F6	÷
151	97	ù	183	B7	╖	215	D7	╫	247	F7	≈
152	98	ÿ	184	B8	╕	216	D8	╪	248	F8	°
153	99	Ö	185	B9	╣	217	D9	┘	249	F9	•
154	9A	Ü	186	BA	║	218	DA	┌	250	FA	·
155	9B	¢	187	BB	╗	219	DB	█	251	FB	√
156	9C	£	188	BC	╝	220	DC	▄	252	FC	ⁿ
157	9D	¥	189	BD	╜	221	DD	▌	253	FD	²
158	9E	₧	190	BE	╛	222	DE	▐	254	FE	■
159	9F	ƒ	191	BF	┐	223	DF	▀	255	FF	

Index

K

L

M

PC catalog

Order Toll Free 1-800-451-4319
Books and Software

 **To order direct call Toll Free 1-800-451-4319**

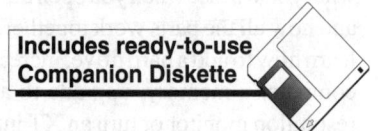

The Companion Diskette

PC Intern includes dozens of programs of interest to programmers of assembly language, BASIC, the C language, and Pascal. However, it would take the average user weeks to type in the listings (over two megabytes' worth).

The companion diskette included with this book saves you time because you don't have to type in the program listings presented in this book. The program listings include the source codes in QuickBASIC, Turbo Pascal, assembly language, and C (almost all the C source codes are compilable from Turbo C++ and Microsoft C 6.00). For those BASIC, Pascal, and C codes that require separate assembly language modules, the companion diskette has assembler source code and assembled object code for easy compilation.

The program files on this companion diskette demonstrate general interrupt calls, video card access, keyboard operation, disk drive access, parallel port control, mouse support, joystick support, extended and expanded memory, COM and EXE files, networking, sound, TSRs, and much more.

PLEASE NOTE: Microsoft QuickBASIC, the Microsoft Macro Assembler (MASM), Turbo C++, Microsoft C Version 6.00, and Turbo Pascal aren't included with this book and companion diskette package. We recommend that you call or write Microsoft Corporation and Borland International for information on purchasing these quality program development tools.

The companion diskette contains the following directories:

PCINTERN directory

- Contains the ASM directory, the BAS directory, the C_PRG directory and the PAS directory. The PCINTERN directory helps you keep organized.

ASM directory

- Contains all the stand alone assembly language programs described in this book, ready for assembly using the Microsoft Macro Assembler MASM. These programs include device drivers, a keyboard character dumper, a file finder, a macro key installer, a printer character converter, general examples of COM and EXE files, a sound program, and three video display programs.

BAS directory

- Contains all the BASIC programs described in this book. These programs, which can be run using Microsoft QuickBASIC 4.5, include a general interrupt demonstration, a PC configuration reader, a directory reader, a joystick support program, four keyboard support programs, a memory control block reader, a realtime clock reader, hard drive configuration reader, and a program that checks whether Microsoft Windows exists in memory. PLEASE NOTE: These programs will not run under QBasic, packaged with MS-DOS Version 5.0, BASICA, or GW-BASIC.

C_PRG

- Contains all C language programs, assembly language modules, and assembled object codes described in this book, ready for compiling with Microsoft C Version 6.00 or Borland's Turbo C++. Where applicable, special instructions for compiling are included at the beginning of each source code. These programs include a general interrupt demonstration, a PC configuration reader, a directory reader, a joystick support program, a mouse support program, four keyboard support programs, a memory control block reader, a realtime clock reader, hard drive configuration reader, a series of video programs for MDA, CGA, Hercules Graphics Card, EGA, VGA and Super VGA, sprite demonstrations, and a program for checking for the existence of Microsoft Windows in memory.

PAS directory

- Contains all Pascal programs, assembly language modules, and assembled object codes, ready for compiling with Turbo Pascal Version 6.0. These programs include a general interrupt demonstration, a PC configuration reader, a directory reader, a joystick support program, a mouse support program, four keyboard support programs, a memory control block reader, a realtime clock reader, hard drive configuration reader, a series of video programs for MDA, CGA, Hercules Graphics Card, EGA, VGA and Super VGA, sprite demonstrations, and a program for checking for the existence of Microsoft Windows in memory.

Installing the Companion Diskette

Use the INSTALL program on the companion diskette to install the companion diskette files on your hard drive. Simply insert the companion diskette in drive A: and type INSTALL at the A: prompt.

See Appendix L (The Companion Diskette) in **PC Intern** for more information on installing the companion diskette files on your hard drive.

Book/companion diskette packages:

- Save hours of typing in source listings from the book.
- Provide ready-to-compile program listings and multiple examples; help avoid printing and typing mistakes.
- This diskette contains the assembly language programs and modules, BASIC programs, C source codes, Pascal source codes, and assembled object codes described in the text, along with many examples to make you a well-read PC system programmer now.
  If you bought this book without the diskette, order your economical companion diskette today and save valuable time.

Abacus

5370 52nd Street SE • Grand Rapids MI 49512
Call 1-800-451-4319

PC Intern Companion Diskette

PCINTERN directory

This directory contains all the subdirectories holding source and object codes.

- The ASM directory contains all the stand alone assembly language programs described in this book.
- The BAS directory contains all the QuickBASIC programs described in this book (QuickBASIC 4.5 required).
- The C_PRG directory contains all the C language source codes and assembly language modules (Turbo C++ and Microsoft C Version 6.00 required).
- The PAS directory contains all the Pascal language source codes and assembly language modules (Turbo Pascal 6.0 or compatible implementation required).

Turn back: for information on Companion Diskette